Pronunciation

American English

This dictionary shows pronunciations used by speakers of the most common American English dialects. Sometimes more than one pronunciation is shown. For example, many Americans say the first vowel in *data* as /eɪ/, while many others say this vowel as /æ/. We show *data* as /ˈdeɪt̬ə, ˈdæt̬ə/. This means that both pronunciations are possible and are commonly used by educated speakers.
We have not, however, shown all American dialects and all possible pronunciations. For example, *news* is shown only as /nuz/ even though a few Americans might pronounce this word as /nyuz/. In words like *caught* and *dog* we show the vowel /ɔ/, but many speakers use the vowel /ɑ/ in place of /ɔ/, so that *caught* and *cot* are both said as /kɑt/.

Use of the Hyphen

When more than one pronunciation is given for a word, we usually show only the part of the pronunciation that is different from the first pronunciation, replacing the parts that are the same with a hyphen: **economics** /ˌɛkəˈnɑmɪks, ˌi-/. The hyphen is also used for showing the division between syllables when this might not be clear: **boyish** /ˈbɔɪ-ɪʃ/, **drawing** /ˈdrɔ-ɪŋ/, **clockwise** /ˈklɑk-waɪz/.

Symbols

The symbols used in this dictionary are based on the symbols of the International Phonetic Alphabet (IPA) with a few changes. The symbol /y/, which is closer to English spelling than the /j/ used in the IPA, is used for the first sound in *you* /yu/. Other changes are described in the paragraph **American English Sounds**.

Abbreviations

No pronunciations are shown for most abbreviations. This is either because they are not spoken (and are defined as "written abbreviations"), or because they are pronounced by saying the names of the letters, with main stress on the last letter and secondary stress on the first: **VCR** /ˌvi si ˈɑr/. Pronunciations have been shown where an abbreviation is spoken like an ordinary word: **RAM** /ræm/.

Words that are Forms of Main Words

A form of a main word that is a different part of speech may come at the end of the entry for that word. If the related word is pronounced by saying the main word and adding an ending (see list on page A43), no separate pronunciation is given. If the addition of the ending causes a change in the pronunciation of the main word, the pronunciation for the related word is given. For example: **impossible** /ɪmˈpɑsəbəl/, **impossibility** /ɪmˌpɑsəˈbɪlət̬i/. There are some pronuncation changes that we do not show at these entries, because they follow regular patterns: (1) When an *-ly* or *-er* ending is added to a main word ending in /-bəl/, /-kəl/, /-pəl/, /-gəl/, or /-dəl/, the /ə/ is usually omitted. For example, **practical** is shown as /ˈpræktɪkəl/. When *-ly* is added to it, it becomes **practically** /ˈpræktɪkli/. This difference is not shown. (2) When *-ly* or *-ity* is added to words ending in *-y* /i/, the /i/ becomes /ə/: **angry** /ˈæŋgri/ becomes **angrily** /ˈæŋgrəli/. This is not shown.

Stress

In English words of two or more syllables, at least one syllable is said with more force than the others. The sign [illegible] force. W[illegible] **percent** [illegible] on another syllable that is less strong than the main stress. We call this *secondary stress*, and the sign /ˌ/ is placed before such a syllable: **personality** /ˌpɚsəˈnæləṭi/, **personify** /pɚˈsɑnəˌfaɪ/. Secondary stress is not usually shown in the second syllable of a two-syllable word, unless it is necessary to show that the second syllable must not be shortened, as in **starlit** /ˈstɑrˌlɪt/ compared to **starlet** /ˈstɑrlɪt/.

Unstressed Vowels

/ə/ and /ɪ/
Many unstressed syllables in American English are pronounced with a very short unclear vowel. This vowel is shown as /ə/ or /ɪ/; however, there is very little difference between them in normal connected speech. For example, the word *affect* /əˈfɛkt/ and *effect* /ɪˈfɛkt/ usually sound the same. The word *rabbit* is shown as /ˈræbɪt/, but it may also be pronounced /ˈræbət/.

/ə/ and /ʌ/
These sounds are very similar. The symbol /ə/ is used in unstressed syllables, and /ʌ/, which is longer, is used in stressed and secondary stressed syllables. When people speak more quickly, secondary stressed syllables become unstressed so that /ʌ/ may be pronounced as /ə/. For example, *difficult* /ˈdɪfɪˌkʌlt/ and *coconut* /ˈkoʊkəˌnʌt/ may be pronounced as /ˈdɪfɪkəlt/ and /ˈkoʊkənət/. Only the pronunciation with /ʌ/ is shown.

Compound Words with a Space or Hyphen

Many compounds are written with either a space or a hyphen between the parts. When all parts of the compound appear in the dictionary as separate main words, the full pronunciation of the compound is not shown. Only its stress pattern is given. For example: **ˈbus stop**, **ˌtown ˈhall**. Sometimes a compound contains a main word with an ending. If the main word is in the dictionary, and the ending is a common one, only a stress pattern is shown. For example: **ˈwashing ˌmachine**. *Washing* is not a main word in the Dictionary, but *wash* is; so only a stress pattern is shown because *-ing* is a common ending. But if any part is not a main word, the full pronunciation is given: **helter-skelter** /ˌhɛltɚ ˈskɛltɚ/.

Stress Shift

Some words may have a shift in stress. The secondary stress becomes the main stress when the word comes before a noun. The mark /◂/ shows this. For example: **artificial** /ˌɑrt̬əˈfɪʃəl◂/, **artificial intelligence** /ˌɑrt̬əfɪʃəl ɪnˈtɛlədʒəns/.

Syllabic Consonants

The sounds /n/ and /l/ can be syllabic. That is, they can themselves form a syllable, especially when they are at the end of a word (and follow particular consonants, especially /t/ and /d/). For example, in **sudden** /ˈsʌdn/ the /n/ is syllabic; there is no vowel between the /d/ and the /n/, so no vowel is shown. In the middle of a word, a hyphen or stress mark after /n/ or /l/ shows that it is syllabic: **botanist** /ˈbɑtˀn-ɪst/ and **catalog** /ˈkæt̬lˌɔg/ are three-syllable words.

The sound *r* can be either a consonant, /r/, or a vowel, /ɚ/. When /ɚ/ is followed by an unstressed vowel, it may be pronounced as a sequence of two vowels, /ɚ/ plus the following vowel, or as /ə/ followed by a syllable beginning with /r/. For example, the word *coloring* may be pronounced as /ˈkʌlɚɪŋ/ instead of /ˈkʌlərɪŋ/. Only the pronunciation, /ˈkʌlərɪŋ/, is shown.

Short Forms Used in the Dictionary

Parts of Speech

Some parts of speech have short forms:

adj.	adjective	*prep.*	preposition
adv.	adverb	*pron.*	pronoun
n.	noun	*v.*	verb
phr. v.	phrasal verb		

Other Short Forms

etc.	et cetera (=and so on)
U.S.	United States
s/he	she or he
sb	somebody/someone
sth	something
sb/sth	someone or something

Grammar Patterns

Grammar patterns are shown in ***dark letters*** in the example sentences.

Grammar Codes Used in the Dictionary

Nouns – to learn more about the grammar of nouns, see the LEARNER'S HANDBOOK on pages A46–A47.

[C]
COUNTABLE nouns such as **chair** and **store** are the most common type of noun in English. Their plural is usually formed by adding *-s*, and they are used with a plural verb:
Most of the smaller stores in the area have closed down.

[U]
an UNCOUNTABLE noun, such as **happiness** and **furniture**. Uncountable nouns cannot be used with *a* or *an*. They do not have plural forms, and are used with a singular verb:
The new furniture is being delivered on Friday.

[C,U]
a noun that has both countable and uncountable uses, such as **wine**:
Our wines are specially chosen by our own buyer.
This is great wine – where did you buy it?

[singular]
a SINGULAR noun, such as **outcome**. Singular nouns can be used with *a*, *an*, or *the*, or without any determiner. They have no plural form, and they are used with a singular verb:
No one knew what the outcome of the discussion was.
We never dreamed there would be such a good outcome.

[plural]
a PLURAL noun, such as **pajamas**. Plural nouns do not have a singular form, and are used with a plural verb:
Your red pajamas are in the wash.

[C usually singular]
a noun such as **setting** that is countable, but is not used in the plural very often:
It was a lovely setting for a wedding.

[C usually plural]
a noun such as **resource** that is countable, and is usually used in the plural:
The country is rich in natural resources.

[singular, U]
a noun that has both singular and uncountable uses, such as **calm**:
The Smiths preferred the calm of the country.
Marta reacted with amazing calm.

Verbs – to learn more about the grammar of verbs, see the LEARNER'S HANDBOOK on page A48.

[I]
an INTRANSITIVE verb, such as **exist**. Intransitive verbs are not followed by objects:
Only five railroads from the old network still exist.

[T]
a TRANSITIVE verb, such as **take**. Transitive verbs are followed by objects:
Will you take my jacket to the dry cleaners for me?

[I,T]
a verb that has both intransitive and transitive uses, such as **decide**:
It's so hard to decide.
I can't decide what to wear.

[linking verb]
a verb such as **be**, **become**, **seem**, etc.:
Jared's father is a teacher.
Dana seems really sorry.

Adjectives

[only before noun]
an adjective, such as **amateur**, that is only used before a noun:
This picture was taken by her husband Larry, a gifted amateur phtographer.

[not before noun]
an adjective, such as **afraid**, that is never used before a noun:
Small children are often afraid of the dark.

Labels Used in the Dictionary

approving and disapproving
Words and phrases are labeled *approving* or *disapproving* if people use them in order to show that they like or dislike someone or something. For example, both **childlike** and **childish** describe behavior that is typical of a child, but **childlike** shows approval and **childish** shows disapproval.

formal
Formal words and phrases, such as **await** and **moreover**, are used only in formal speech and writing, for example in essays or official announcements, not in normal conversation.

humorous
Humorous words and phrases, such as **on the warpath**, are intended to be funny.

informal
Informal words and phrases, such as **grungy** and **long shot**, are used in normal conversation and informal letters or emails to friends. Do not use these words and phrases in essays.

literary
Literary words and phrases, such as **foe** and **inferno**, are used mostly in poetry and other types of literature. They are not usually suitable for essays

nonstandard
Nonstandard words and phrases do not follow the rules of grammar, but are still used a lot. For example, many people use **real** instead of **really**. Do not use nonstandard language in essays.

offensive
Offensive words and phrases are likely to make someone upset if you use them. People often use them when they intend to insult other people, but these can also be words and phrases that only particular people consider to be offensive.

old-fashioned
Old-fashioned words and phrases are ones that people still know, but that are not used very often in modern speech or writing.

slang
Slang words and phrases are used by a particular group of people, especially young people, but not by everyone. They are extremely informal and should not be used in essays.

spoken
Spoken words and phrases, such as **I mean** and **by the way**, are hardly ever used in writing. They are always informal, unless they have the label *spoken formal*. Do not use these words and phrases in essays.

taboo
Taboo words and phrases are extremely rude, offensive to everyone, and should be avoided.

technical
Technical words and phrases, such as **tautology** or **pro rata**, are used by experts in a particular subject, not by everyone.

trademark
A trademark is an official name for a product made by a particular company. It is always spelt with a capital letter.

written
Written words and phrases, such as **ablaze** or **exclaim**, are usually only used in written English.

Subject Labels

BIOLOGY the study of all living things

CHEMISTRY the study of gases, liquids, and solids, what they are composed of and how they react with each other

EARTH SCIENCES the study of the Earth, its weather systems, and the environment

ECONOMICS finance and business, and the ways in which money and goods are produced and used

ENG. LANG. ARTS languages, literature, art, sculpture, music and the performing arts

HISTORY significant events and institutions from the past

IT computers, data storage and processing, and communications

LAW institutions and principles relating to the legal system

MATH arithmetic, algebra, and geometry

PHYSICS the study of the universe, what it consists of, and the forces that affect it

POLITICS political institutions and activity

SCIENCE the aspects of science that go across the boundaries of biology, chemistry, and physics

SOCIAL SCIENCE the study of society and how particular social groups think and behave

Pearson Education Limited
Edinburgh Gate
Harlow
Essex CM20 2JE
England
and Associated Companies throughout the world

Visit our website at: www.longman.com/dictionaries

First edition published 1983
Second edition 1997
Third edition 2004
Fourth edition 2008

Paper 0132449803 9780132449809 6 7 DCR 11 10
Paper + CD-ROM 0132449773 9780132449779 4 DCR 11 10
Hardcover 0132449781 9780132449786 2 3 4 DCR 11 10 09
Hardcover + CD-ROM 013244979X 9780132449793 2 3 4 DCR 11 10 09

Library of Congress Cataloging-in-Publication Data
A catalog record for this book is available from the Library of Congress.

British Library Cataloguing-in-Publication Data
A catalog record for this book is available from the British Library.

Set in Nimrod by Letterpart, UK
Printed in the U.S.

Acknowledgments

Director
Michael Mayor

Senior Publisher
Laurence Delacroix

Managing Editor
Stephen Bullon

Lexicographers
Evadne Adrian-Vallance
Karen Cleveland-Marwick
Chris Fox
Elizabeth Manning
Michael Murphy
Martin Stark

Project Manager
Alan Savill

Production Manager
David Gilmour

Corpus and CD-ROM Development
Steve Crowdy

Computational Linguists and CD-ROM Project Management
Allan Ørsnes
Andrew Roberts

Production Editors
Michael Murphy
Paola Rocchetti

Project Administrator
Denise McKeough

Technical Support Manager
Trevor Satchell

Network Administrator
Kim Lee-Amies

Pronunciation Editor
Dinah Jackson

Language Notes
Stephen Handorf

Proofreaders
Lynda Carey
Isabel Griffiths
Ruth Hillmore
Ruth Noble
Carol Osbourne

Design
Mick Harris

Keyboarder
Pauline Savill

Administrative Assistance
Angela Wright

Artwork
Mark Duffin, Graham Humphries, Chris Paveley, Maltings Partnership, Oxford Designers and Illustrators

Photography credits
Hemera Technologies Inc "Copyright ©2004 (Pearson Education) and its licensors. All rights reserved"; Brand X Pictures; DK Picture Library; IMS Communications Ltd.; Corbis; Gareth Bowden; PhotoDisc; Dorling Kindersley; www.istockphoto.com

The publishers would like to thank **Averil Coxhead** for permission to highlight the Academic Wordlist (AWL, compiled in 2000) in the dictionary. Averil Coxhead is the author of AWL and a lecturer in English for Academic Purposes at Massey University, New Zealand. For further information on the AWL, go to Averil's Website at: http://language.massey.ac.nz/staff/awl

The Publishers would also like to thank:

- **Professor Jack du Bois** of the University of California at Santa Barbara, for the development of the Longman Corpus of Spoken American English. This unique corpus, developed especially for the *Longman Dictionary of American English*, consists of 5 million words of everyday conversation by US speakers of English. The corpus was designed to provide a representative sample of the US population, by age, sex, region, educational attainment, and ethnic origin. Volunteers were selected to wear a digital cassette recorder and record their conversations over a two-week period. The tapes were then transcribed and built into a computer system so that the lexicographic team could analyze exactly how native speakers use the language.
- the thousands of teachers and students from around the world who have contributed scripts for the Longman Learner's Corpus. This corpus consists of 12 million words of writing in English by learners, and helps lexicographers to analyze what students know and where they have difficulty.
- the Linguistic Data Consortium for texts included in the 80-million-word Longman Corpus of Written American English
- the many teachers and students who have taken part in the development of the new edition of the dictionary. This has included focus groups, questionnaires, student vocabulary notebooks (in which students kept a record of which words they looked up), classroom piloting of material, and written feedback on text by teachers.

Nancy Ackels, University of Washington Extension, Seattle; **Tom Adams**, University of Pennsylvania; **Monica Alvaraz**, California State University, Fullerton; **Isabella Anikst**, University of California, Los Angeles Extension; **Jan Barrett-Chow**, Northeastern University, Boston; **Catherine Berg**, Drexel University, Philadelphia; **Gretchen Bitterlin**, San Diego Community College; **Donna Brinton**, University of California, Los Angeles; **Arlene Bublick**, William Rainey Harper College, Palatine, Illinois; **Christine Bunn**, City College of San Francisco; **Dorothy Burak**, University of California, San Diego; **Randy Burger**, California State Polytechnic, Pomona; **Laura Cameron**, Intensive English Language Institute, Seattle; **Sarah Canady**, Bellevue Community College, Seattle; **Jane Cater**, Intensive English Language Institute, Seattle; **Rick Chapman**, California State University, Fullerton; **Martha Compton**, University of California, Irvine; **Jan Copeland**, Long Beach City College, Long Beach; **Patrick Cox**, Houston Community College; **Nick Crump**, Merritt College, Oakland; **Catherine Crystal**, Laney College, Oakland; **Kevin Curry**, Wichita State University; **Susan Davis**, EF International; **Chuck Delgado**, North Valley Occupational Center, Mission Hills, California; **Carolyn Dupaquier**, California State University, Fullerton; **Nancy Dyer**, Intensive English Language Institute, Seattle; **Julie Easton**, Adult Education Center, Santa Monica; **Gerry Eldred**, Long Beach City College, Long Beach; **Rita Esquivel**, Adult Education Center, Santa Monica; **Mary Fitzpatrick**, College of Marin, Novato; **Annette Fruehan**, Orange Coast College, California; **Caroline Gibbs**, College of Marin, Novato; **Janet Goodwin**, University of California, Los Angeles; **Lisa Hale**, St Giles College, London; **Jim Harris**, Rancho Santiago College, Santa Ana; **Tamara Hefter**, Truman College, Chicago; **Patti Heiser**, University of Washington Extension; **Julie Herrmann**, Intensive English Language Institute, Seattle; **Wayne Heuple**, Intensive English Language Institute, Seattle; **Kathi Holper**, William Rainey Harper College, Palatine, Illinois; **Barbara Howard**, Daley College, Chicago; **Kathryn Howard**; **Leann Howard**, San Diego Community College; **Stephannie Howard**, University of California, Los Angeles Extension; **Gail Hutchins**, East San Jose College; **Susan Jamieson**, Bellevue Community College; **Jeff Janulis**, Daley College, Chicago; **Linda Jensen**, University of California, Los Angeles; **Winston Joffrion**, Bellevue Community College, Seattle; **Deborah Jonas**, California State University, Long Beach; **Kathy Keesler**, Orange Coast College, California; **Barbara Logan**, Intensive English Language Institute, Seattle; **Walter Lowe**, Bellevue Community College, Seattle; **Lynne Lucas**, Daley College, Chicago; **Felicity MacDonald-Smith**, Eurocentre, Cambridge; **Robyn Mann**, William Rainey Harper College, Palatine, Illinois; **Anne McGinley**, San Diego State University; **Elaine McVey**, San Diego State University; **Amy Meepoe**; **Andy Muller**, Intensive English Language Institute, Seattle Pacific University; **Jill Neely**, Merritt College, Oakland; **Maura Newberry**; **Yvonne Nishio**, Evans Community Adult School, Los Angeles; **Roxanne Nuhaily**, University of California, San Diego; **Carla Nyssen**, California State University, Long Beach; **David Olshen**; **Jorge Perez**, Southwestern College, San Diego; **Ellen Pentkowski**, Truman College, Chicago; **Eileen Prince Lou**, Northeastern University, Boston; **Nancy Quinn**, Truman College, Chicago; **Ralph Radell**, Bunker Hill Community College, Boston; **Eva Ramirez**, Laney College, Oakland; **Alison Rice**, Hunter College; **Lenore Richmond**, California State University, Fullerton; **Jane Rinaldi**, California State Polytechnic, Pomona; **Bruce Rindler**, CELOP, University of Boston; **Shirley Roberts**, Long Beach City College, Long Beach; **William Robertson**, Northeastern University, Boston; **Bonnie Rose**, University of Denver; **Teresa Ross**, California State University, Long Beach; **Paul Safstrom**, South Seattle Community College; **Karen Santiago**, Beaver College, Philadelphia; **Irene Schoenberg**, Hunter College; **Esther Sunde**, South Seattle Community College, Seattle; **Barbara Swartz**, Northeastern University, Boston; **Priscilla Taylor**, California State University, Los Angeles; **Elizabeth Terplan**, College of Marin, Novato, California; **Bill Trimble**, Modesto Junior College; **Wendy Walsh**, College of Marin, Novato, California; **Colleen Weldele**, Palomar College, San Marcos, California; **Sabella Wells**, Intensive English Language Institute, Seattle; **Madeleine Youmans**, Long Beach City College, Long Beach; **Christine Zilkow**, California State University, Fullerton; **Janet Zinner**, Northeastern University, Boston; **Jean Zukowski-Faust**, Northern Arizona University.

Yuri Komuro, for assistance in compiling the results of teacher questionnaires and student word diaries.
Norma A. Register, Ph.D, for advice on coverage of socially sensitive language.

Table of Contents

LONGMAN

Dictionary of American English

4th EDITION

Key to the Dictionary

Words that are spelled the same but have different parts of speech have separate entries.

Definitions explain the meaning of the word in clear simple language, using the 2000-word Longman Defining Vocabulary whenever possible.

Subject labels before a definition show that this word has a specialized meaning in particular subject area.

The most common words in spoken and written English are shown in red letters. This shows you which are the most important words to know.

The meanings of each word are listed in order of frequency. The most common meaning is shown first.

Useful natural examples show how you can use the word.

Thesaurus boxes explain the differences between words with similar meanings, or between words related to a particular topic.

Synonyms (=words with the same meaning), antonyms (=words with the opposite meaning), and related words are shown after the definition.

Pronunciation is shown using the International Phonetic Alphabet

Usage notes help you avoid making common errors.

Dots show how words are divided into syllables.

Derived words are show at the end of an entry when the meaning is clear from the definition of the main form.

back·ward[1] /ˈbækwərd/ *also* **backwards** *adv.* **1** in the direction that is behind you (ANT) **forward**: *She took a step backwards.* **2** toward the beginning or the past: *Can you say the alphabet backward?*

backward[2] *adj.* **1** [only before noun] made toward the direction that is behind you (ANT) **forward**: *She left without a backward glance.* **2** developing slowly and less successfully than others: *a backward country*

bac·te·ri·um /bækˈtɪriəm/ *n.* (plural **bacteria** /-riə/) [C usually plural] BIOLOGY a very small living thing consisting of a single cell. Some bacteria cuase disease, but others are important in many natural processes. The plural form, "bacteria," is much more common than the singular form. [ORIGIN: 1800—1900 Modern Latin, Greek *bakterion* "stick, rod;" because of their shape]

bad[1] /bæd/ *adj.* (comparative **worse**, superlative **worst**) **1** not good or not nice (ANT) **good**: *I'm afraid I have some bad news for you.* | *a really bad smell*

THESAURUS

awful – very bad or unpleasant: *The weather was awful.*
terrible – extremely bad: *The hotel food was terrible.*
horrible – very bad or upsetting: *What a horrible thing to say!*
appalling/horrific (formal) – very bad and very shocking: *She suffered appalling injuries.* | *a horrific plane crash*
lousy (informal) – very bad in quality: *a lousy movie*
horrendous (formal) – very bad and very frightening or shocking: *a horrendous crash*
atrocious (formal) – extremely bad and often very severe: *Her driving is atrocious.* | *atrocious weather conditions*
abysmal (formal) – very bad, used especially to describe the standard of something: *The quality of care at the hospital was abysmal.* → GOOD[1], HORRIBLE

2 of a low quality or standard (ANT) **good**: *That was the worst pizza I ever ate.* | *Brian is really **bad at** sports.* **3** morally wrong or evil (ANT) **good**: *He plays one of the bad guys in the movie.*

bad·ly /ˈbædli/ *adv.* (comparative **worse**, superlative **worst**) **1** in a way that is not good (ANT) **well**: *a badly written book* | *She **did badly** on the exam.* ▸Don't say "I sing very bad." Say "I sing very badly."◂ **2** to a great or serious degree: *The refugees **badly need** food and clean water.* | *Our house was **badly damaged** during the storm.*

baf·fle /ˈbæfəl/ *v.* [T] if something baffles you, you cannot understand it: *Scientists were baffled by the results.* —**baffling** *adj.* —**baffled** *adj.*

THESAURUS **confused, bewildered, puzzled** → CONFUSED

ba·nal /bəˈnæl, bəˈnɑl, ˈbeɪnl/ *adj.* ordinary and not interesting → BORING: *a banal love song* [ORIGIN: 1800—1900 French, Old French *ban* "military service that everyone must do, something common"] —**banality** /bəˈnæləṭi/ *n.* [C,U]

beat[1] /bit/ *v.* (past tense **beat**, past participle **beaten** /ˈbitˀn/)
1 DEFEAT [T] to get more points, votes, etc. than other people in a game or competition: *New York beat Boston 4–1.* | *Stuart usually* ***beats me at*** *chess.* | *Has anyone ever* ***beaten the record*** *for home runs set by Babe Ruth?*

THESAURUS

defeat – to win a victory over someone: *I don't think anybody will be able to defeat Kennedy in a Senate election.*
trounce – to defeat someone completely: *The Bears trounced Nebraska 44–10.*
clobber/cream (informal) – to defeat someone easily: *We got creamed in the finals.*
vanquish (formal) – to defeat someone or something completely: *The allies vanquished the enemy.*
overcome – to fight and win against someone or something: *Union troops finally overcame rebel forces in the south.*

2 HIT SB [T] to hit someone many times with your hand, a stick, etc.: *He used to come home and beat us.* | *The woman had been* ***beaten to death.***
3 HIT STH [I,T] to hit against the surface of something continuously, or to make something do this: *waves* ***beating on/against*** *the shore*

SPOKEN PHRASES
8 [T] to be better or more enjoyable than something else: *It's not the greatest job, but* ***it beats*** *waitressing.* | ***You can't beat*** (=nothing is better than) *San Diego for good weather.*
9 (it) beats me used in order to say that you do not understand or know something: *"Where's Myrna?" "Beats me."*
10 beat it! an impolite way to tell someone to leave at once

beat down *phr. v.*
1 if the Sun beats down, it shines brightly and is hot
2 if the rain beats down, it rains very hard
beat sb ↔ **out** *phr. v.* (informal)
to defeat someone in a competition: *Lange* ***beat out*** *Foster* ***for*** *the award.*

ben·e·fi·cial /ˌbɛnəˈfɪʃəl/ (Ac) *adj.* good or useful: *The agreement will be* ***beneficial to*** *both groups.* | *Garlic has a* ***beneficial effect*** *in reducing harmful cholesterol.* [ORIGIN: 1400—1500 Latin *beneficium* "kindness, favor," from *bene* "well" + *facere* "to do"]

blonde[1], **blond** /blɑnd/ *adj.* **1** blonde hair is pale or yellow **2** someone who is blonde has pale or yellow hair

References to related words, pictures, and Thesaurus Boxes are shown after an arrow.

Information about irregular forms of verbs, nouns, and adjectives is shown at the beginning of the entry.

Parts of speech are shown in italics, then information about whether a word is countable, uncountable, transitive, intransitive, etc.

Signposts in long entries help you find the meaning you want quickly.

Grammar patterns and collocations (words that are typically used together) are shown in bold in examples.

Groups of phrases that are only used in spoken English are explained together, each with its own definition.

Idioms and fixed phrases are shown in dark type and have a definition which explains the whole phrase.

Phrasal verbs are listed in alphabetical order after the main verb.

Labels before the definition show if a word is typically used in informal, formal, written, etc. English.

The Ac label shows that a word is in the Academic Wordlist. These are important words which students need to understand, and be able to use in academic assignments.

Origin notes tell you when a word first entered the English language and the foreign language or languages it came from.

If a word can be spelled in different ways, both spellings are shown at the beginning of an entry.

Preface

The 4th edition of the ***Longman Dictionary of American English*** has been researched and revised to meet the real needs of learners of English. The up-dated text now includes thousands of words for **content areas** such as Science, Economics and Social Science, as well as **Word Origins** and updated **thesaurus boxes** that give extra help with vocabulary acquisition.

Real Language

All Longman dictionaries are based on the authentic language data in the **Longman Corpus Network**. This unique computerized language database now contains over 400 million words from all types of written texts, and from real conversations recorded across the US.

The Corpus tells us how frequently words and phrases are used, so there is no guesswork in deciding which ones students need to know most. The Corpus also shows which grammar patterns are the most important to illustrate, which important new words and idioms people use every day, and which words are frequently used together (*collocations*). We take our example sentences from the Corpus, and this makes the language come alive as never before.

Real Clarity

The definitions in Longman dictionaries are written using only the 2,000 most common English words – the **Longman American Defining Vocabulary**. Longman pioneered the use of a limited vocabulary as the best way to guarantee that definitions are clear and easy to understand. The meaning you want is easy to find. Words that have a large number of meanings have short, clear **signposts** to guide you to the right meaning quickly.

The comprehensive grammatical information is easy to understand and use. Important patterns are highlighted in the example sentences, so that you can see at a glance how to use a word in a sentence.

Real Help

The 4th edition of the ***Longman Dictionary of American English*** is the result of extensive research into learners needs and abilities. Thesaurus boxes explain thousands of synonyms and antonyms to help users expand their vocabulary, so that instead of using the same words all the time, such as the word angry, for example, they learn how to use related words such as *annoyed*, *irritated*, *furious*, etc. Additional Thesaurus boxes now also help learners expand their **academic** and **content vocabulary**.

The writers have also used their knowledge from years of teaching to analyze the **Longman Learner's Corpus**, which is a computerized collection of over 8 million words of writing in English by learners. By studying the errors students make in essays and exams, the writers were able to give clear, helpful usage information throughout the dictionary – in the definitions, example sentences, usage notes, and in the **new Learner's Handbook** – to help students avoid common errors.

Use the exercises in the **Workbook** to learn how to get the most from your dictionary. The grammar codes and labels are inside the front cover, and the IPA (International Phonetic Alphabet) pronunciation charts are inside the back cover, so they are always easy to find and use.

Whether you are writing an essay, sending an e-mail, or talking with friends, the ***Longman Dictionary of American English*** will help you choose the right words, understand them clearly, and use them correctly.

A, a /eɪ/ the first letter of the English alphabet

A /eɪ/ *n.* **1** [C] the best grade that a student can get in a class or on a test: ***I got an A** on my math test!* | *Rick was an **A student*** (=always received the best grades) *in high school.* **2** [C,U] ENG. LANG. ARTS the sixth note in the musical SCALE of C, or the musical KEY based on this note **3** [U] a common type of blood

a /ə; *strong* eɪ/ *also* **an** *indefinite article* **1** used before a noun to show that you are talking about a general type of thing, not a specific thing → THE: *Do you have a car?* | *I'll find you a pencil.* **2 a)** one: *a thousand dollars* | *a dozen eggs* **b)** used before some words that show how much of something there is: *a few weeks from now* | *a little water* | *a lot of people* **3** used before a noun that is one of many similar things, people, events, times, etc.: *I'd like to be a teacher.* | *This is a very good wine.* **4** every or each: *A square has 4 sides.* **5 once a week/$100 a day etc.** one time each week, $100 a day, etc. SYN **per** **6** used before two nouns that are frequently mentioned together: *a cup and saucer* | *a knife and fork* **7 a)** used before the -ing form of some verbs when they are used as nouns: *a loud screeching of brakes* **b)** used before some singular nouns that are actions: *Take a look at that!*

GRAMMAR

a, an
If the next word starts with a consonant sound, use **a:** *a cat* | *a white egg* | *a house* | *a CD*
If the next word starts with a vowel sound (the sounds shown by the letters a, e, i, o, or u), use **an:** *an apple* | *an old car*
If the next word begins with h, but the h is not pronounced, use **an:** *an hour* | *an honest man*
If the next word begins with u which is pronounced like "you," use **a:** *a union* | *a unique opportunity* → ANY[1]

AA *n.* **1 Alcoholics Anonymous** an organization for ALCOHOLICs who want to stop drinking alcohol **2 Associate of Arts** a college degree given after two years of study, usually at a COMMUNITY COLLEGE

AB *n.* [U] BIOLOGY a common type of blood

a·back /ə'bæk/ *adv.* **be taken aback** to be very surprised or shocked: *I was taken aback by her criticism.*

ab·a·cus /'æbəkəs/ *n.* [C] a tool used for counting and calculating, consisting of a frame with small balls that can be slid along on thick wires [ORIGIN: 1300—1400 Latin, Greek *abax* "flat piece of stone"]

a·ban·don /ə'bændən/ Ac *v.* [T] **1** to leave a person or thing, especially one that you are responsible for, and not go back: *How could she abandon her own child?* | *We had to abandon the car and walk the rest of the way.* **2** to stop doing or using something because of problems: *The policy had to be abandoned.* **3** to stop having a particular idea, belief, or opinion about something: *The U.N. seems to have abandoned all hope of finding a peaceful solution to the conflict.* [ORIGIN: 1300—1400 Old French *abandoner* "surrendering," from *a bandon* "into someone's power"] **—abandonment** *n.* [U]

a·ban·doned /ə'bændənd/ Ac *adj.* **1** an abandoned building, car, boat, etc. has been left by the people who owned or used it: *The mayor wants all the abandoned buildings in the downtown area to be demolished* (=knocked down). **2** an abandoned person or animal has been left completely alone by the person that was looking after him, her, or it: *He donates $20 a month to a home for abandoned children.*

a·base /ə'beɪs/ *v.* (formal) **abase yourself** to behave in a way that shows you accept that someone has complete power over you **—abasement** *n.* [U]

a·bashed /ə'bæʃt/ *adj.* embarrassed or ashamed: *an abashed grin*

a·bate /ə'beɪt/ *v.* [I] (formal) to become less strong → UNABATED: *Public anger does not appear to be abating.*

ab·bey /'æbi/ *n.* [C] a large church, with buildings next to it where MONKS and NUNS live [ORIGIN: 1200—1300 Old French *abaïe*, from Late Latin *abbas*, from Aramaic *abba* "father"]

ab·bre·vi·ate /ə'briviˌeɪt/ *v.* [T] (formal) to make a word, story, etc. shorter: *"Street" is often **abbreviated as** "St.".* [ORIGIN: 1400—1500 Late Latin, past participle of *abbreviare*, from Latin *brevis* "short"]

ab·bre·vi·a·tion /əˌbrivi'eɪʃən/ *n.* [C] the short form of a word used in writing. For example, Mr. is the abbreviation of Mister.

ABC *n.* **1 ABC's** [plural] the letters of the English alphabet as taught to children **2 American Broadcasting Company** one of the national companies that broadcasts television and radio programs in the U.S.

ab·di·cate /'æbdɪˌkeɪt/ *v.* **1** [I,T] to officially give up the position of being king or queen **2 abdicate (your) responsibility** (formal) to refuse to continue being responsible for something [ORIGIN: 1500—1600 Latin, past participle of *abdicare*, from *ab-* "away, off" + *dicare* "to say publicly"] **—abdication** /ˌæbdɪ'keɪʃən/ *n.* [C,U]

ab·do·men /'æbdəmən/ *n.* [C] BIOLOGY the front part of your body between your chest and the top of your legs, including your stomach **—abdominal** /æb'dɑmənəl, əb-/ *adj.*

ab·duct /əb'dʌkt, æb-/ *v.* [T] to take someone

A

away by force (SYN) **kidnap** [ORIGIN: 1600—1700 Latin, past participle of *abducere*, from *ab-* "away" + *ducere* "to lead"] —**abduction** /-'dʌkʃən/ *n.* [C,U]

a·ber·ra·tion /ˌæbə'reɪʃən/ *n.* [C,U] something that is completely different from what usually happens or from what someone usually does: *Duvall's lawyer claimed that the crime was an aberration in his client's otherwise blameless life.*

a·bet /ə'bɛt/ *v.* (**abetted, abetting**) [T] → **aid and abet** *at* AID²

ab·hor /əb'hɔr, æb-/ *v.* (**abhorred, abhorring**) [T] (formal) to hate something, especially because you think it is morally wrong: *I abhor discrimination of any kind.*

THESAURUS **hate, can't stand, detest, loathe, despise** → HATE¹

ab·hor·rent /əb'hɔrənt, -'hɑr-, æb-/ *adj.* (formal) behavior or beliefs that are abhorrent are unacceptable because they are morally wrong —**abhorrence** *n.* [U]

a·bide /ə'baɪd/ *v.* [T] **can't abide sb/sth** to hate someone or something very much: *I can't abide his stupid jokes.*

abide by sth *phr. v.* to obey a law, agreement, etc.: *If you're going to live here, you will abide by my rules.*

a·bid·ing /ə'baɪdɪŋ/ *adj.* (literary) continuing for a long time and not likely to change: *Our father had an* ***abiding love*** *for nature.*

a·bil·i·ty /ə'bɪləṭi/ *n.* (plural **abilities**) [C,U] the state of being able to do something, or your level of skill at doing something: *A manager must have the* ***ability to*** *communicate well.* | *a young girl with great* ***musical/athletic/acting etc. ability*** | *She worked* ***to the best of her ability*** (=as well as she could) *in school.* [ORIGIN: 1400—1500 Old French *habilité*, from Latin *habilis* "skillful"]

THESAURUS

power – the legal right or authority to do something: *Only the police have the power of arrest.*
capacity (formal) – someone's ability to do something, especially when he or she can do this a lot: *Children have a special capacity for learning language.*
capability (formal) – the ability of a machine, person, or organization to do something, especially something difficult: *Does the country have the capability to produce nuclear weapons?*
skill, talent, gift, aptitude → SKILL

ab·ject /'æbdʒɛkt, æb'dʒɛkt/ *adj.* **1 abject poverty/failure/terror/despair etc.** the state of being extremely poor, unsuccessful, frightened, unhappy, etc. **2 abject apology** an abject apology shows that you are ashamed of what you have done —**abjectly** *adv.*

ab·jure /æb'dʒʊr/ *v.* [T] (formal) to state publicly that you will give up a particular belief or way of behaving (SYN) **renounce** —**abjuration** /ˌæbdʒʊ'reɪʃən/ *n.* [U]

ab·la·tive /'æbləṭɪv/ *n.* [singular] ENG. LANG. ARTS a particular form of a noun in some languages, such as Latin or Finnish, which shows movement away or separation —**ablative** *adj.*

a·blaze /ə'bleɪz/ *adj.* (written) burning strongly with a lot of flames: *During the riot, a police car was* ***set ablaze.***

a·ble /'eɪbəl/ *adj.* **1 able to do sth a)** having the skill, strength, knowledge, etc. to do something: *I was just able to reach the handle.* **b)** in a situation in which it is possible for you to do something: *Will you be able to come tonight?* **2** smart or good at doing something: *an able student*

ab·ne·ga·tion /ˌæbnɪ'geɪʃən/ *n.* [U] (formal) the act of not allowing yourself to have or do something that you want

ab·nor·mal /æb'nɔrməl/ (Ac) *adj.* different from usual in a way that is strange, worrying, or dangerous (ANT) **normal**: *Scientists found abnormal levels of chemicals in the water.* | *Mike's parents began to worry about his increasingly* ***abnormal behavior.*** [ORIGIN: 1800—1900 *ab-* "away from, not" (from Latin *ab-* "away, off") + *normal*] —**abnormally** *adv.*: *an abnormally high heart rate* | *It has been an abnormally hot summer.* —**abnormality** /ˌæbnɔr'mæləṭi, -nɚ-/ *n.* [C,U]

a·board /ə'bɔrd/ *adv., prep.* on or onto a ship, airplane, or train: *The plane crashed, killing all 200 people aboard.* | *They were prevented from* ***going aboard.***

a·bode /ə'boʊd/ *n.* [C] (formal) the place where you live

THESAURUS **home, house, place, residence, dwelling** → HOME¹

a·bol·ish /ə'bɑlɪʃ/ *v.* [T] to officially end a law, system, etc.: *plans to abolish the death penalty* [ORIGIN: 1400—1500 Old French *abolir*, from Latin *abolere*]

ab·o·li·tion /ˌæbə'lɪʃən/ *n.* [U] **1** the official end of a law, system, etc., especially one that has existed for a long time: *He argued against the* ***abolition of*** *the death penalty.* **2** *also* **Abolition** HISTORY the official ending of the system and practice of owning, buying, and selling SLAVES in the U.S. during the 19th century

ab·o·li·tion·ist /ˌæbə'lɪʃənɪst/ *n.* [C] **1** SOCIAL SCIENCE someone who wants to end a system or law **2** HISTORY someone who took part in a series of actions intended to end the system and practice of owning, buying, or selling SLAVES in the U.S. during the 19th century

a·bom·i·na·ble /ə'bɑmənəbəl/ *adj.* extremely bad, or of very bad quality

ab·o·rig·i·nal /ˌæbə'rɪdʒənəl/ *adj.* **1 Aboriginal** relating to the Australian aborigines **2** EARTH

SCIENCES relating to the people or animals that have existed in a place from the earliest times

ab·o·rig·i·ne, Aborigine /ˌæbəˈrɪdʒəni/ *n.* [C] a member of the people who have lived in Australia from the earliest times [ORIGIN: 1500—1600 Latin *aborigines* (plural), from *ab origine* "from the beginning"]

a·bort /əˈbɔrt/ *v.* [T] **1** to stop an activity because it would be difficult or dangerous to continue: *An electrical fault caused the launch of the space shuttle to be aborted.* **2** to deliberately end a PREGNANCY when the baby is still too young to live

a·bor·tion /əˈbɔrʃən/ *n.* [C,U] the act of aborting a baby: *She decided to **have an abortion**.*

a·bor·tive /əˈbɔrt̬ɪv/ *adj.* an abortive action is not successful or not finished: *The Marines made an abortive attempt to seize the town.*

a·bound /əˈbaʊnd/ *v.* [I] (literary) to exist in large numbers: *Coffee shops **abound in** American small towns.*

a·bout¹ /əˈbaʊt/ *prep.* **1** relating to a particular subject: *a book about horses* | *We were talking about the stock market.* | *I'll tell you **all about*** (=everything about) *it later.* | *About that CD, I need it back by tomorrow.*

THESAURUS

on – if a book, lecture, conference, etc. is **on** a particular subject, it relates to it: *a seminar on résumé writing*
concerning/regarding (formal) – about or relating to something: *The police want to ask you some questions concerning the night of April 4th.*
with regard to (formal) – concerning a particular subject that you want to write or talk about: *What is U.S. policy with regard to foreign banks operating in the U.S.?*
re – used in business letters to introduce the subject that you are going to write about: *Re your letter of June 10...*

2 in the nature or character of a person or thing: ***There's something** weird **about** that guy.* **3 what about/how about** (spoken) **a)** used in order to make a suggestion: *How about coming to my house after we're done here?* **b)** used to ask a question concerning another person or thing involved in a situation: *What about Jack? Should we invite him?*

about² *adv.* **1** a little more or less than a number or amount SYN **approximately**: *I live about 10 miles from here.* | *We need to leave at about 7:30.*

THESAURUS

approximately – a little more or a little less than a number, amount, distance, or time: *A kilo is approximately 2 pounds.*
around – used when guessing a number, amount, time, etc., without being exact: *Around 50 people came to the meeting.*
roughly – a little more or a little less than a number, used when you are saying a number you know is not exact: *Roughly 7,000 vehicles a day cross the border.*
or so – used when you cannot be exact about a number, amount, or period of time: *Every month or so he drives up to visit his parents.*
in the region of – used when a number or amount will be a little more or a little less than the one mentioned: *It will cost in the region of $750 to fix it.*

2 almost: *Dinner's **just about** ready.*

about³ *adj.* **1 be about to do sth** if someone is about to do something, or if something is about to happen, s/he will do it or it will happen very soon: *I was about to step into the shower when the phone rang.* | *The parade is about to start.* **2 not be about to do sth** (informal) used to emphasize that you will not do something: *I'm not about to give him any more money!*

a·bove /əˈbʌv/ *adv., prep.* **1** in or to a higher position than something else ANT **below**: *Raise your arm above your head.* | *The sound came from the room above.* **2** more than a number, amount, or level ANT **below**: *Temperatures rose above freezing today.* | *Males aged 18 **and above** could be drafted.* **3** louder than other sounds: *He couldn't hear her voice above the noise.* **4** higher in rank, more powerful, or more important: *He never rose above the rank of corporal.* **5 above all** (formal) most importantly: *Above all, I would like to thank my parents.* **6 be above suspicion/criticism etc.** to be so honest or good that no one can doubt or criticize you **7** (formal) before, in the same piece of writing ANT **below**: *The graph above shows the growth in pollution levels.*

a·bove·board /əˈbʌvˌbɔrd/ *adj.* [not before noun] honest and legal: *The agreement seems to be aboveboard.*

a·bra·sion /əˈbreɪʒən/ *n.* **1** [C] an area on your skin that has been injured by rubbing against something hard: *She was treated for cuts and abrasions.* **2** [U] the process of rubbing a surface very hard so that it becomes damaged

a·bra·sive /əˈbreɪsɪv, -zɪv/ *adj.* **1** rude and annoying: *an abrasive personality* **2** having a rough surface that can be used to clean something or make it smooth —**abrasively** *adv.*

a·breast /əˈbrɛst/ *adv.* **1 keep abreast of sth** to make sure that you know the most recent facts about a subject: *We expect our sales staff to keep abreast of all the latest developments in computer technology.* **2** next to someone or something, usually in a line, and facing the same direction: *Patrol cars were lined up four abreast.*

a·bridged /əˈbrɪdʒd/ *adj.* ENG. LANG. ARTS an abridged form of a book, play, etc. has been made shorter ANT **unabridged**: *the **abridged version** of the dictionary*

a·broad /əˈbrɔd/ *adv.* in or to a foreign country: *He suggested that his son **go abroad** for a year.* | *There are more than a million Americans **living abroad**.*

A

ab·ro·gate /ˈæbrəˌgeɪt/ *v.* [T] (formal) to officially end a law, legal agreement, practice, etc.: *The Sioux chief was forced to sign a document that abrogated the treaty.* —**abrogation** /ˌæbrəˈgeɪʃən/ *n.* [C,U]

a·brupt /əˈbrʌpt/ *adj.* **1** sudden and unexpected: *An* ***abrupt change*** *in the weather forced many boats to pull out of the race.* **2** not polite or friendly, especially because you do not want to waste time: *She was very abrupt on the phone.* [ORIGIN: 1500—1600 Latin, past participle of *abrumpere*, from *ab-* "away, off" + *rumpere* "to break"] —**abruptly** *adv.*: *The train stopped abruptly.*

abs /æbz/ *n.* [plural] (informal) the muscles on your ABDOMEN (=stomach): *exercises that strengthen your abs*

ABS *n.* [U] **anti-lock braking system** a type of car BRAKE that makes the car easier to control when you have to stop very suddenly

ab·scess /ˈæbsɛs/ *n.* [C] BIOLOGY a swollen place on your body that is infected and contains a yellow liquid

ab·scond /əbˈskɑnd, æb-/ *v.* [I] (formal) to leave a place without permission, or to leave somewhere after stealing something

ab·sence /ˈæbsəns/ *n.* **1** [C,U] an occasion when you are not in a place where people expect you to be, or the time that you are away: *The vice president will handle things* ***in*** *my* ***absence****.* | *His frequent* ***absences from*** *work did not go unnoticed.* **2** [singular] the lack of something: *a complete* ***absence of*** *physical evidence*

ab·sent /ˈæbsənt/ *adj.* **1** not at work, school, a meeting, etc. because you are sick or decide not to go (ANT) **present**: *Ten children were* ***absent from*** *class today.* **2 absent look/smile/expression** a look, etc. that shows you are not thinking about what is happening [ORIGIN: 1300—1400 Old French, Latin, present participle of *abesse*, from *ab-* "away" + *esse* "to be"]

ab·sen·tee /ˌæbsənˈti/ *n.* [C] (formal) someone who is supposed to be in a place but is not there

ˌabsentee ˈballot *n.* [C] a process by which people can vote by mail before an election because they will be away during the election

ab·sen·tee·ism /ˌæbsənˈtiɪzəm/ *n.* [U] regular absence from work or school without a good reason

ab·sent·ly /ˈæbsəntˀli/ *adv.* in a way that shows you are not interested in or not thinking about what is happening: *He gazed absently out of the window.*

ˌabsent-ˈminded *adj.* often forgetting or not noticing things because you are thinking of something else —**absent-mindedly** *adv.*

ab·so·lute /ˈæbsəˌlut, ˌæbsəˈlut/ *adj.* **1** complete or total: *The king has* ***absolute power****.* | *I have absolute confidence in you.* **2** used to emphasize your opinion: *The show was an absolute disaster.* | *He's talking absolute nonsense.* **3** definite and not likely to change: *I can't give you any absolute promises.*

ab·so·lute·ly /ˌæbsəˈlutli, ˈæbsəˌlutli/ *adv.* **1** completely or totally: *Are you absolutely sure?* | *We had* ***absolutely nothing*** *in common.*

THESAURUS **completely, totally, entirely →** COMPLETELY

2 Absolutely (spoken) said when you agree completely with someone: *"Can I talk to you for a minute?" "Absolutely, come in."* **3 Absolutely not!** (spoken) said when you disagree completely with someone, or when you do not want someone to do something

ˌabsolute ˈmonarch *n.* [C] POLITICS a king or queen who rules a country and who is not limited by laws or a government controlling what s/he can do —**absolute monarchy** *n.* [C,U]

ˌabsolute ˈvalue *n.* [C] MATH the value of a number without considering if it is positive or negative, in other words, its distance from zero. For example, the absolute value of -3 is 3, and the absolute value of +3 is also 3.

ˌabsolute ˈzero *n.* [U] PHYSICS the lowest temperature that is possible. It is measured in the Kelvin scale, where it is 0°, and is equal to about -273° Celsius or -459° Fahrenheit.

ab·so·lu·tion /ˌæbsəˈluʃən/ *n.* [U] a process in the Christian religion by which someone is forgiven for the things that s/he has done wrong

ab·solve /əbˈzɑlv, -ˈsɑlv/ *v.* [T] (formal) to say publicly that someone should not be blamed for something, or to forgive him/her: *He cannot be* ***absolved of*** *all responsibility for the accident.*

ab·sorb /əbˈsɔrb, -ˈzɔrb/ *v.* [T] **1** if something absorbs liquid, heat, etc., it takes it in through its surface: *The towel absorbed most of the water.* **2 be absorbed in sth** to be interested in something so much that you do not pay attention to other things: *He's completely absorbed in his job.* **3** to learn, understand, and remember new information: *She's a good student who absorbs ideas quickly.* [ORIGIN: 1400—1500 French *absorber*, from Latin *absorbere*, from *ab-* "away" + *sorbere* "to suck up"]

ab·sorb·ent /əbˈsɔrbənt, -ˈzɔr-/ *adj.* something that is absorbent can take in liquid through its surface: *absorbent paper towel*

ab·sorb·ing /əbˈsɔrbɪŋ, -ˈzɔr-/ *adj.* so interesting that you do not notice or think about other things: *an absorbing article*

THESAURUS **interesting, enthralling, engrossing, compelling, gripping, riveting →** INTERESTING

ab·sorp·tion /əbˈsɔrpʃən, -ˈzɔrp-/ *n.* [U] **1** SCIENCE a process in which a material or object takes in liquid, gas, or heat: *This chapter describes the body's* ***absorption of*** *nutrients.* **2** a process in which a country or organization makes a smaller country, organization, or group of people become part of itself **3** the fact of being very interested in something

ab·stain /əb'steɪn/ *v.* [I] **1** to deliberately not vote for or against something: *Three members of the committee abstained.* **2** to not do something that you would normally enjoy doing: *For two weeks, I **abstained from** alcohol.* —**abstention** /əb'stɛnʃən/ *n.* [C,U]

ab·ste·mi·ous /æb'stimiəs/ *adj.* (formal) careful not to have too much food, drink, etc. —**abstemiously** *adv.*

ab·sti·nence /'æbstənəns/ *n.* [U] the practice of not doing something you enjoy, especially for health or religious reasons —**abstinent** *adj.*

ab·stract[1] /əb'strækt, æb-, 'æbstrækt/ (Ac) *adj.* **1** based on ideas rather than specific examples or real events: *He took the **abstract idea** of political reform and made it a reality.* | *Language and the capability for **abstract thought*** (=ability to think about ideas) *makes humans unique and separate from other animals.* **2** abstract art is made of shapes and patterns that do not look like real things or people → *see picture at* PAINTING —**abstraction** /əb'strækʃən/ *n.* [C,U]

ab·stract[2] /'æbstrækt/ (Ac) *n.* [C] ENG. LANG. ARTS a short written statement containing only the most important ideas in a speech, article, etc.: *People planning to give a talk must send in an abstract by July 1.*

ˌabstract 'noun *n.* [C] ENG. LANG. ARTS a noun that names a feeling, quality, or state rather than a thing, animal, or person. For example, "beauty," "hunger," and "happiness" are abstract nouns. → CONCRETE NOUN

ab·struse /əb'strus, æb-/ *adj.* (formal) difficult to understand, in a way that seems unnecessarily complicated: *the abstruse regulations on saving for pensions* —**abstrusely** *adv.* —**abstruseness** *n.* [U]

ab·surd /əb'sɚd, -'zɚd/ *adj.* completely unreasonable or silly: *an absurd situation* | *It's absurd to pay all that money for something you're only going to use once.* —**absurdly** *adv.* —**absurdity** *n.* [C,U]

a·bun·dance /ə'bʌndəns/ *n.* [singular, U] (formal) a large quantity of something: *The park has an **abundance of** wildlife.* | *Wild flowers grow **in abundance** on the hillsides.*

a·bun·dant /ə'bʌndənt/ *adj.* more than enough in quantity (SYN) **plentiful**: *an abundant supply of fresh fruit*

a·bun·dant·ly /ə'bʌndəntli/ *adv.* **1 abundantly clear** very easy to understand: *Kaplan **made it abundantly clear** that we weren't welcome.* **2** in large quantities: *Lavender will grow abundantly with little water.*

a·buse[1] /ə'byus/ *n.* **1** [U] cruel or violent treatment of someone: *There were several cases of **child abuse** at the home.* | *victims of **sexual abuse*** **2** [C,U] the use of something in a way it should not be used: *the government's **abuse of power*** | ***drug/alcohol abuse*** (=the practice of taking illegal drugs or drinking too much) **3** [U] cruel or offensive things someone says when s/he is angry: *People were **shouting abuse at** the soldiers.*

a·buse[2] /ə'byuz/ *v.* [T] **1** to do cruel or violent things to someone: *He used to get drunk and abuse his wife.* | *She was **sexually abused** as a child.* **2** to use something too much or in the wrong way: *He **abused** his **position** as mayor by giving jobs to his relatives.* | *She had been **abusing drugs/alcohol** since she was 12.* **3** to say cruel or unkind things to someone

a·bu·sive /ə'byusɪv/ *adj.* using cruel words or physical violence: *an abusive husband*

a·bys·mal /ə'bɪzməl/ *adj.* very bad: *the country's abysmal record on human rights* [ORIGIN: 1600—1700 *abysm* "abyss" (14—20 centuries), from Old French *abisme*, from Late Latin *abyssus*]

THESAURUS **bad, awful, terrible, horrible, appalling, horrendous, atrocious** → BAD[1]

a·byss /ə'bɪs/ *n.* [C] **1** (literary) a very dangerous or frightening situation: *The country might plunge into the **abyss of** economic ruin.* **2** a very deep hole or space that seems to have no bottom

AC **1** PHYSICS the abbreviation of ALTERNATING CURRENT **2** the abbreviation of AIR CONDITIONING

ac·a·de·mi·a /ˌækə'dimiə/ (Ac) *n.* [U] the activities and work done at universities and colleges, or the teachers and students involved in it: *Ph.D. students often look for jobs in academia.* [ORIGIN: 1900—2000 Modern Latin, Latin; ACADEMY]

ac·a·dem·ic[1] /ˌækə'dɛmɪk◂/ (Ac) *adj.* relating to education, especially in a college or university: *The academic year starts September 3rd.* | *Applicants for the job must show proof of their academic achievement.*

academic[2] *n.* [C] a teacher in a college or university: *The conference is attended by academics from many of the country's leading universities.*

a·cad·e·my /ə'kædəmi/ (Ac) *n.* (plural **academies**) [C] **1** a school or college that trains students in a special subject or skill: *a military academy* **2** an organization of people who want to encourage the progress of art, science, literature, etc.: *the American Academy of Arts and Sciences* [ORIGIN: 1500—1600 Latin *academia*, from Greek *Akademeia* the school in Athens at which the ancient Greek thinker Plato taught]

ac·cede /æk'sid, ɪk-/ *v.*

accede to sth *phr. v.* (formal) **1** to agree to a demand, proposal, etc., especially after first disagreeing with it: *The General acceded to a request for time to bury the dead.* **2** to achieve a position of power or authority: *He acceded to the papacy after the death of John Paul II.*

ac·cel·er·ate /ək'sɛləˌreɪt/ *v.* **1** [I] if a vehicle

A

or its driver accelerates, it moves faster ➔ DRIVE[1] **2** [I,T] to happen at a faster rate than usual, or to make something do this: *We tried to accelerate the process by heating the chemicals.* —**acceleration** /əkˌsɛləˈreɪʃən/ *n.* [U]

ac·cel·er·a·tor /əkˈsɛləˌreɪt̬ɚ/ *n.* [C] the part of a car that you press with your foot to make it go faster

ac·cent[1] /ˈæksɛnt/ *n.* **1** [C] a way of pronouncing words that someone has because of where s/he was born or lives: *a strong southern accent* | *a German/Korean, etc. accent* ➔ LANGUAGE **2** [C] the part of a word that you emphasize when you say it **3** [C] a mark, usually written above some letters, such as é or â, that shows how to pronounce that letter **4** [singular] the extra importance or emphasis given to something: *In this year's guide, there is an* ***accent on*** *restaurants that offer value for money.* [ORIGIN: 1500—1600 French, Latin *accentus*, from *ad-* "to" + *cantus* "song"]

ac·cent[2] /ˈæksɛnt, ækˈsɛnt/ *v.* [T] to emphasize a word in speech

ac·cen·tu·ate /əkˈsɛntʃuˌeɪt, æk-/ *v.* [T] to make something easier to notice: *Her scarf accentuated the blue of her eyes.*

THESAURUS **emphasize, stress, highlight, underline, underscore, exaggerate** ➔ EMPHASIZE

ac·cept /əkˈsɛpt/ *v.* **1** [I,T] to take something that someone offers you, or to agree to do something that someone asks you to do ANT **refuse**: *They offered him the job, and he accepted.* | *Mr. Ryan wouldn't* ***accept*** *any money* ***from*** *us.* | *They* ***accepted*** *our* ***invitation*** *to dinner.* | *She* ***accepted*** *his* ***offer*** *to repair the damage on her car.*

GRAMMAR

When someone asks you to do something, you **agree** to do it. Do not say "accept to do something": *The U.S. has agreed to provide aid.* You **accept** an invitation, a job, an offer, etc.: *Schroeder accepted a job offer to teach at Princeton University.*

2 [T] to admit that something bad or difficult is true, and continue with your normal life: *He's not going to change, and you just have to accept it.* | *I* ***accept that*** *we've made mistakes.* | *It took Ann months to accept her son's death.* **3** [T] to believe something, because someone has persuaded you to believe it: *The jury accepted his story.*

THESAURUS **believe, swallow, fall for sth, buy, give credence to sth** ➔ BELIEVE

4 [T] to let someone join an organization, university, etc. ANT **reject**: *I've been* ***accepted at/to*** *Harvard.* **5** [T] to let someone new become part of a group and to treat him/her in the same way as other members: *At first, the kids at school didn't accept him.* **6** [T] to let customers pay for something in a particular way SYN **take**: *We don't accept credit cards.* **7 accept responsibility/blame for sth** (formal) to admit that you are responsible for something bad that has happened: *Benson accepts full responsibility for his crimes.* [ORIGIN: 1300—1400 French *accepter*, from Latin *accipere* "to receive," from *ad-* "to" + *capere* "to take"]

ac·cept·a·ble /əkˈsɛptəbəl/ *adj.* **1** good enough for a particular purpose: *a deal that is* ***acceptable to*** *all sides* | *a cheap and acceptable substitute for rubber*

THESAURUS **satisfactory, good enough, reasonable, adequate** ➔ SATISFACTORY

2 acceptable behavior is considered morally or socially good enough: *Smoking used to be more* ***socially acceptable.*** | ***It is*** *now considered* ***acceptable for*** *mothers* ***to*** *work outside the home.* —**acceptability** /əkˌsɛptəˈbɪlət̬i/ *n.* [U]

ac·cept·ance /əkˈsɛptəns/ *n.* [U] **1** the act of agreeing that something is right or true: *the* ***acceptance of*** *Einstein's theory* **2** the act of agreeing to accept something that is offered to you: *a candidate's* ***acceptance of*** *illegal contributions* **3** the process of allowing someone to become part of a group: *the immigrants' gradual* ***acceptance into*** *the community* **4** the act of deciding that there is nothing you can do to change a bad situation **5 gain/find acceptance** to become popular: *Home computers first gained wide acceptance in the 1980s.*

ac·cess[1] /ˈæksɛs/ Ac *n.* [U] **1** the right to enter a place, use something, see someone, etc.: *Anyone with* ***access to*** *the Internet can visit our website.* | *Many people living in developing countries do not* ***have access to*** *clean drinking water.* **2** the way you enter a building or get to a place, or how easy this is: *The only* ***access to*** *the building is through the parking lot.* | *The law requires businesses to improve* ***access for*** *disabled customers.* ➔ **gain access** at GAIN[1] [ORIGIN: 1300—1400 Old French *acces* "arrival," from Latin *accessus* "approach"]

access[2] *v.* [T] to find information, especially on a computer: *You can even access the Internet from this cell phone.*

ac·ces·si·ble /əkˈsɛsəbəl/ Ac *adj.* **1** easy to reach or get into ANT **inaccessible**: *The park is not* ***accessible by*** *road.* **2** easy to obtain or use: *We want a low-cost health care system that is* ***accessible to*** *every citizen.* **3** easy to understand and enjoy: *We tried to make the play more accessible to a young audience by reducing it from its original three hours to ninety minutes.* | *I thought his last book was more accessible.* —**accessibility** /əkˌsɛsəˈbɪlət̬i/ *n.* [U]

ac·ces·so·ry /əkˈsɛsəri/ *n.* (plural **accessories**) [C] **1** something such as a belt, jewelry, etc. that you wear or carry because it is attractive: *a dress with matching accessories* **2** something that you can add to a machine, tool, car, etc. which is not necessary but is useful or attractive **3** LAW someone who helps a criminal

ac·ci·dent /'æksədənt, -ˌdɛnt/ *n.* [C] **1** a situation in which someone is hurt or something is damaged without anyone intending it to happen: *She didn't do it on purpose – **it was an accident**.* | *Her parents were killed in a **car/traffic/auto etc. accident**.* | *Ken **had** an **accident** on the way home from work.*

THESAURUS
crash/collision – an accident in which a vehicle hits something else
wreck – an accident in which a car or train is badly damaged
pile-up – an accident that involves several cars or trucks
disaster – something that happens which causes a lot of harm or suffering
catastrophe – a very serious disaster
mishap – a small accident that does not have a very serious effect

2 by accident in a way that is not intended or planned: *I discovered by accident that he'd lied to me.* [ORIGIN: 1300—1400 French, Latin *accidens* "additional quality, chance," from *accidere* "to happen," from *ad-* "to" + *cadere* "to fall"]

ac·ci·den·tal /ˌæksə'dɛntəl/ *adj.* happening without being planned or intended (ANT) **deliberate**: *He was killed in an accidental shooting.* **—accidentally** *adv.*: *I accidentally locked myself out of the house.*

'accident-ˌprone *adj.* someone who is accident-prone often has accidents

ac·claim¹ /ə'kleɪm/ *v.* [T] to praise someone or something publicly: *He was acclaimed as the best coach in football.*

acclaim² *n.* [U] strong praise for a person, idea, book, etc.: *Morrison's novels have won **critical acclaim**.*

ac·claimed /ə'kleɪmd/ *adj.* praised by a lot of people: *The film has been **highly/widely acclaimed** by critics.*

ac·cli·mate /'ækləˌmeɪt/ *also* **ac·cli·ma·tize** /ə'klaɪməˌtaɪz/ *v.* [I,T] to become used to the weather, way of living, etc. in a new place, or to make someone do this: *It takes the astronauts a day to **get acclimated to** conditions in space.* **—acclimatization** /əˌklaɪmət̬ə'zeɪʃən/ *n.* [U]

ac·co·lade /'ækəˌleɪd/ *n.* [C] praise and approval given to someone, or a prize given to someone for his/her work [ORIGIN: 1600—1700 French *accoler* "to embrace," from Vulgar Latin *accolare*, from Latin *collum* "neck"]

ac·com·mo·date /ə'kɑməˌdeɪt/ (Ac) *v.* **1** [T] to have enough space for a particular number of people or things: *The hall can accommodate 300 people.* **2** [T] to give someone a place to stay, live, or work: *The dorm was built in 1980 to accommodate new students.* **3** [I] to get used to a new situation, place, etc.: *It can take northerners a long time to **accommodate to** Florida's hot climate.* [ORIGIN: 1500—1600 Latin, past participle of *accommodare*, from *ad-* "to" + *commodare* "to make fit," from *commodus* "suitable"]

ac·com·mo·dat·ing /ə'kɑməˌdeɪt̬ɪŋ/ (Ac) *adj.* helpful and willing to do what someone else wants: *All the Japanese people I met seemed very polite and accommodating.*

ac·com·mo·da·tion /əˌkɑmə'deɪʃən/ (Ac) *n.* **1 accommodations** [plural] a place to live, stay, or work: *The cost of the trip includes meals and motel accommodations.* **2** [singular, U] (formal) a way of solving a problem between two people or groups so that both are satisfied: *The ruling party must **reach an accommodation** with one of the opposition parties or it will lose power.*

ac·com·pa·ni·ment /ə'kʌmpənimənt/ (Ac) *n.* **1** [C,U] ENG. LANG. ARTS music played while someone sings or plays another instrument: *He sang the national anthem, while another student provided piano accompaniment.* | *an orchestral accompaniment* **2** [C] (formal) something that is good to eat or drink with another food: *This wine makes a nice **accompaniment to** fish.* **3 to the accompaniment of something** while something else is happening, or while another sound can be heard: *The soldiers marched to the accompaniment of drums and whistles.*

ac·com·pa·nist /ə'kʌmpənɪst/ *n.* [C] ENG. LANG. ARTS someone who plays a musical instrument while another person sings or plays the main tune

ac·com·pa·ny /ə'kʌmpəni/ (Ac) *v.* (**accompanied, accompanies**) [T] **1** (formal) to go somewhere with someone: *Children under 12 must be **accompanied by** an adult.* | *She needed someone to **accompany** her **to** the doctor.* **2** to happen or exist at the same time: *Tonight, heavy rains will be accompanied by high winds.* **3** ENG. LANG. ARTS to play music while someone is playing or singing the main tune [ORIGIN: 1400—1500 Old French *acompaignier*, from *compaing* "companion"]

ac·com·plice /ə'kɑmplɪs/ *n.* [C] someone who helps a criminal do something wrong

ac·com·plish /ə'kɑmplɪʃ/ *v.* [T] to succeed in doing something: *We've accomplished our goal of raising $45,000.*

ac·com·plished /ə'kɑmplɪʃt/ *adj.* very skillful: *an accomplished musician*

THESAURUS skillful, expert, talented, gifted → SKILLFUL

ac·com·plish·ment /ə'kɑmplɪʃmənt/ *n.* **1** [U] the act of accomplishing something: *the **accomplishment of** policy goals* **2** [C] something you can do well: *Playing the piano is one of her many accomplishments.*

ac·cord¹ /ə'kɔrd/ *n.* **1 of sb's own accord** without being asked or forced to do something: *I didn't say anything. He left of his own accord.* **2** [C] (formal) an official agreement

A

between countries **3 in accord (with sth)** (formal) in agreement with someone or something: *These results are in accord with earlier research.*

accord² *v.* [T] (formal) to give someone or something special attention or a particular type of treatment: *the wealth and privilege* ***accorded to*** *those in power*

ac·cord·ance /ə'kɔrdns/ *n.* **in accordance with sth** according to a system or rule: *He placed pebbles on the grave, in accordance with Jewish tradition.*

ac·cord·ing·ly /ə'kɔrdɪŋli/ *adv.* **1** in a way that is appropriate for a particular situation, or based on what someone has done or said: *If you break the rules, you will be punished accordingly.* **2** (formal) as a result of something (SYN) **therefore**: *The law was ruled unconstitutional. Accordingly, Congress amended the bill in line with the court's ruling.*

THESAURUS **therefore, so, as a result/consequently/as a consequence, thus, hence** → THEREFORE

ac'cording to *prep.* **1** as shown by something or said by someone: *According to our records, you still have six of our books.* | *The president is still very popular, according to recent public opinion polls.* **2** in a way that is directly affected or determined by something: *You will be paid according to the amount of work you do.* | *Everything* ***went according to plan.***

ac·cor·di·on /ə'kɔrdiən/ *n.* [C] a musical instrument that is played by pulling the sides and pushing buttons to produce different notes

ac·cost /ə'kɔst, ə'kɑst/ *v.* [T] (formal) to go up to someone you do not know and speak to him/her in an impolite or threatening way: *I was accosted by a man asking for money.*

ac·count¹ /ə'kaʊnt/ *n.* **1** [C] a written or spoken description of an event or situation: *Can you* ***give us an account of*** *what happened?* | *a* ***detailed account*** *of the attack* | ***By/From all accounts*** (=according to what everyone says), *Frank was once a great player.* **2** [C] *also* **bank account** an arrangement with a bank that allows you to keep your money there and take money out when you need it: *I don't have much money in my account.* | *I'd like to* ***open an account****, please.* | ***checking account*** (=one that you can take money out of at any time) | ***savings account*** (=one in which you save money so that the amount increases)

TOPIC

You **open** an **account** at a **bank**.
You **pay**, **put**, or **deposit money into** your **account**.
You **take money out of** your **account** or **withdraw money from** your **account**.
You can do this at a bank, or you can use an **ATM** (=a machine that you use with a card). An ATM is also called a **cash machine**.
When there is money in your account, you **have a balance of** that amount of money, or you have that amount **in your account**.
When the amount of money in your account is less than zero, you are **overdrawn**.
Many banks have an **online banking** service, which allows you to check the balance in your account, make payments, etc. using a computer that is connected to the Internet.

THESAURUS

checking account – one that you use regularly for making payments, etc.
savings account – one where you leave money for longer periods of time, and which pays you a higher rate of interest than a checking account
joint account – one that is used by two people, usually a husband and wife
online account – one which allows you to check the balance in your account, make payments, etc. by using a computer that is connected to the Internet

3 take sth into account/take account of sth to consider particular facts when judging or deciding something: *The price does not take taxes into account.* **4** [C,U] an arrangement with a shop or company that allows you to buy goods and pay for them later: *buying a dishwasher* ***on account*** | *Please* ***settle your account*** (=pay all you owe) *as soon as possible.* | *I'd like to* ***charge*** *this* ***to*** *my* ***account*** (=pay using this arrangement). **5 accounts** [plural] ECONOMICS a record of the money that a company has received and spent: *The accounts for last year showed a profit of $2 million.* **6** [C] ECONOMICS a company or organization that regularly buys goods or a service from another company over a long period of time: *Our sales manager won five new accounts this year.* **7 not on my/his etc. account** (spoken) not for me or because of me: *Don't stay up late on my account.* **8 on no account** (formal) used in order to say that someone must not do something: *On no account should anyone go near the building.* [ORIGIN: 1300—1400 Old French *acompter*, from *compter* "to count"]

account² *v.*

account for sth *phr. v.* to be the reason for something, or to explain the reason for something: *How do you account for the $20 that's missing?*

ac·count·a·ble /ə'kaʊntəbəl/ *adj.* [not before noun] responsible for what you do, and willing to explain it: *If anything happens to Max, I'll* ***hold*** *you* ***accountable*** (=consider you responsible). —**accountability** /əˌkaʊntə'bɪləti/ *n.* [U]

ac·count·ant /ə'kaʊntənt, ə'kaʊnt˺nt/ *n.* [C] ECONOMICS someone whose job is to write or check financial records

ac·count·ing /ə'kaʊntɪŋ/ *n.* [U] ECONOMICS the job of being an accountant

ac·cred·it·ed /ə'krɛdɪtɪd/ *adj.* having official approval: *an accredited college* —**accreditation** /əˌkrɛdə'teɪʃən/ *n.* [U]

ac·cre·tion /ə'kriʃən/ *n.* **1** [C,U] (formal) a layer of a substance which slowly forms on something: *an **accretion of** minerals* **2** (formal) a gradual process by which new things are added and something gradually changes or gets bigger: *an **accretion of** knowledge*

ac·crue /ə'kru/ *v.* [I,T] to increase over a period of time: *tax benefits that **accrue to** investors*

ac·cu·mu·late /ə'kyumyə,leɪt/ (Ac) *v.* [I,T] to gradually increase in amount, or to make something do this: *Drifting snow began to accumulate at the entrance to the tunnel.* | *He accumulated a large fortune from investments in real estate.* —**accumulation** /ə,kyumyə'leɪʃən/ *n.* [C,U]: *the accumulation of greenhouse gases in the upper atmosphere*

ac·cu·ra·cy /'ækyərəsi/ (Ac) *n.* [U] the quality of being accurate: *The bombs can be aimed **with** amazing **accuracy**.*

ac·cu·rate /'ækyərɪt/ (Ac) *adj.* **1** correct in every detail (ANT) **inaccurate**: *The Hubble telescope provides scientists with accurate information about our solar system.* | *The book claims to be historically accurate.*

THESAURUS **right, correct, true** → RIGHT[1]

2 an accurate shot, throw, etc. succeeds in hitting the thing that it is aimed at [ORIGIN: 1500—1600 Latin, past participle of *accurare* "to take care of," from *ad* "toward" + *cura* "care"] —**accurately** *adv.*: *He estimated the cost of repairs pretty accurately.*

ac·cu·sa·tion /,ækyə'zeɪʃən/ *n.* [C] a statement saying that someone has done something wrong or illegal: *Serious **accusations** have been made **against** the Attorney General.* | *The boy's parents **face accusations** (=are accused) of neglect and abuse.*

THESAURUS

allegation (formal) – a statement that someone has done something illegal, which has not been proved: *He has denied the allegations of wrongdoing.*
charge – a statement that says what crime someone is accused of: *The charges against her were dismissed.*
indictment (Law) – an official written statement saying that someone has done something illegal and that there is enough evidence to have a trial in a court of law: *He is under indictment for credit card fraud.*
complaint (Law) – if you file a complaint, you make a formal statement saying that you think someone is guilty of a crime: *She filed a complaint against her employers, accusing them of discrimination.*

ac·cu·sa·tive /ə'kyuzət̬ɪv/ *n.* [C] ENG. LANG. ARTS a form of a noun that shows that the noun is the DIRECT OBJECT of a verb, in languages such as Latin or German → DATIVE

ac·cuse /ə'kyuz/ *v.* [T] to say that someone has done something wrong or illegal: *Norton was **accused of** murder.* | *Are you accusing me of cheating?* —**accuser** *n.* [C]

THESAURUS

allege – to say that something is true, though it has not been proved: *Ms. Ruiz alleges that she was harassed.*
charge – to state officially which crime someone may be guilty of: *He was charged with murder.*
indict (Law) – to officially charge someone with a crime and take him/her to a court of law: *He was indicted on charges of fraud.*

ac·cused /ə'kyuzd/ *n.* **the accused** LAW the person or people who are accused of a crime in a court of law

ac·cus·tomed /ə'kʌstəmd/ *adj.* (formal) **1 be accustomed to (doing) sth** to be used to something and accept it as normal: *Ed's eyes quickly **grew/became/got accustomed to** the dark.* **2** [only before noun] usual: *We sat at our accustomed table.* —**accustom** *v.* [T]

ace[1] /eɪs/ *n.* [C] **1** a PLAYING CARD with one mark on it, that has the highest or lowest value in a game: *the **ace of** spades* → *see picture at* PLAYING CARD **2** a SERVE (=first hit) in tennis or VOLLEYBALL that is so good that your opponent cannot hit it back **3** someone who is extremely skillful at doing something: *a World War II flying ace* | *the school's ace pitcher*

ace[2] *v.* [T] (spoken) to do very well on a test, a piece of written work, etc.: *Danny aced the spelling test.*

a·cer·bic /ə'sɚbɪk/ *adj.* criticizing someone or something in an intelligent but cruel way: *an acerbic wit*

a·cet·y·lene /ə'set̬l-ɪn, -in/ *n.* [U] CHEMISTRY a gas which burns with a bright flame and is used in equipment for cutting and joining pieces of metal

ache[1] /eɪk/ *n.* [C] a continuous pain: *I **have a headache/backache/toothache etc.*** [ORIGIN: Old English *acan*] —**achy** *adj.*: *My arm feels all achy.*

ache[2] *v.* [I] **1** to feel a continuous pain: *I ache all over.* → HURT[1] **2** to want to do or have something very much: *Jenny was **aching to** go home.*

a·chieve /ə'tʃiv/ (Ac) *v.* [T] to succeed in getting a good result or in doing something you want: *You will have to work a lot harder if you want to **achieve** your **goals**.* | *The company failed to achieve the results its major shareholders had expected.* —**achiever** *n.* [C]: *Many of our students are high achievers.* —**achievable** *adj.*

a·chieve·ment /ə'tʃivmənt/ (Ac) *n.* **1** [C] something good and impressive that you succeed in doing: *Winning the championship is quite an achievement.* | *He read about his son's achievements in the newspaper.* **2** [U] success in doing or getting what you worked for: *Juan received an award for his exceptional academic achievement.*

A

ac·id¹ /ˈæsɪd/ *n.* [C,U] a liquid chemical substance. Some types of acid can burn holes in things or damage your skin: *hydrochloric acid* [ORIGIN: 1600—1700 French *acide*, from Latin *acere* "to be sour"]

acid² *adj.* using humor in an unkind way or saying cruel things: *Everyone fears her acid tongue.*

a·cid·ic /əˈsɪdɪk/ *adj.* **1** having a very sour taste **2** containing acid —**acidity** /əˈsɪdət̬i/ *n.* [U]

ˌacid ˈrain *n.* [U] EARTH SCIENCES rain that can damage the environment because it contains acid from factory smoke, waste gases from cars and trucks, etc. ➔ ENVIRONMENT

ac·knowl·edge /əkˈnɑlɪdʒ/ (Ac) *v.* [T] **1** to accept or admit that something is true or official: *Angie* ***acknowledged (that)*** *she had made a mistake.* | *They are refusing to acknowledge the court's decision.* **2** to recognize how good or important someone or something is: *It is* ***acknowledged as*** *the finest restaurant in London.* | *He's widely* ***acknowledged to be*** *the best surgeon in his field.* **3** to let someone know that you have received something from him/her: *She never acknowledged my letter.* **4** to show someone that you have seen him/her or heard what s/he has said: *Jackson waved, acknowledging his fans.*

ac·knowl·edg·ment /əkˈnɑlɪdʒmənt/ (Ac) *n.* **1** [C,U] the act of admitting or accepting that something is true: *The public may consider Berry's silence to be an* ***acknowledgment of*** *his guilt.* **2** [C] a letter you write telling someone that you have received something s/he sent to you

ac·ne /ˈækni/ *n.* [U] a skin problem that causes spots to appear on the face and is common among young people

a·corn /ˈeɪkɔrn/ *n.* [C] the nut of an OAK tree ➔ *see picture at* PLANT¹

a·cous·tic /əˈkustɪk/ *adj.* **1** relating to sound and the way people hear things **2** an acoustic musical instrument is not electric: *an acoustic guitar* [ORIGIN: 1700—1800 Greek *akoustikos* "of hearing," from *akouein* "to hear"]

a·cous·tics /əˈkustɪks/ *n.* [plural] the way in which the shape and size of a room affect the quality of the sound you can hear in it

ac·quaint /əˈkweɪnt/ *v.* **acquaint yourself with sth** (formal) to deliberately find out about something: *We have already acquainted ourselves with the facts.*

ac·quaint·ance /əˈkweɪntˀns/ *n.* [C] someone you know, but not very well: *He's an old acquaintance of mine from school.*

ac·quaint·ed /əˈkweɪntɪd/ *adj.* if you are acquainted with someone, you know him/her, but not well: *Yes, I'm acquainted with Roger.* | *Why don't you two* ***get acquainted*** (=start to learn more about each other)*?*

ac·qui·esce /ˌækwiˈɛs/ *v.* [I] (formal) to agree to do what someone wants, or to allow something to happen, although you do not like it —**acquiescence** *n.* [U]

ac·quire /əˈkwaɪɚ/ (Ac) *v.* [T] **1** to buy a company or property: *The present owner, who acquired the property in 1995, is moving to Santa Monica.*

THESAURUS **buy, purchase, get** ➔ BUY¹

2 to develop or learn a skill, or become known for a particular quality: *She spent years completing her education and* ***acquiring*** *the necessary* ***skills*** *to become a surgeon.* | *He* ***acquired a reputation for*** *honesty.*

THESAURUS **learn, study, master** ➔ LEARN

3 an acquired taste something that you only begin to like after you have tried it a few times: *Whiskey is often an acquired taste.* [ORIGIN: 1400—1500 Old French *aquerre*, from Latin *acquirere*, from *ad-* "to" + *quaerere* "to look for, obtain"]

ac·qui·si·tion /ˌækwəˈzɪʃən/ (Ac) *n.* (formal) **1** [U] the act of getting something: *the* ***acquisition of*** *new companies* **2** [C] something that you have gotten: *a recent acquisition*

ac·quit /əˈkwɪt/ *v.* (**acquitted**, **acquitting**) [T] LAW to decide in a court of law that someone is not guilty of a crime: *Simmons was* ***acquitted of*** *murder.* [ORIGIN: 1200—1300 Old French *acquiter*, from *quite* "free of"]

ac·quit·tal /əˈkwɪt̬l/ *n.* [C,U] LAW an official statement in a court of law that someone is not guilty: *The trial ended with his acquittal.*

a·cre /ˈeɪkɚ/ *n.* [C] a unit for measuring an area of land, equal to 4,840 square yards or about 4,047 square meters

ac·rid /ˈækrɪd/ *adj.* having a very strong and bad smell that hurts your nose or throat: *a cloud of acrid smoke*

ac·ri·mo·ni·ous /ˌækrəˈmoʊniəs/ *adj.* (formal) an acrimonious meeting, argument, etc. involves a lot of anger and disagreement: *an acrimonious divorce*

ac·ri·mo·ny /ˈækrəˌmoʊni/ *n.* [U] (formal) very angry feelings between people, often strongly expressed

ac·ro·bat /ˈækrəˌbæt/ *n.* [C] someone who does difficult physical actions to entertain people, such as balancing on a high rope [ORIGIN: 1800—1900 French *acrobate*, from Greek *akrobatos* "walking on the ends of the toes"] —**acrobatic** /ˌækrəˈbæṭɪk/ *adj.*

ac·ro·bat·ics /ˌækrəˈbæṭɪks/ *n.* [plural] the skill or tricks of an acrobat

ac·ro·nym /ˈækrənɪm/ *n.* [C] ENG. LANG. ARTS a word that is made from the first letters of a group of words. For example, NATO is an acronym for the North Atlantic Treaty Organization. [ORIGIN: 1900—2000 *acr-* "beginning, end" (from Greek *akr-*) + *-onym* (as in *homonym*)]

a·cross /əˈkrɔs/ *adv., prep.* **1** from one side of something to the other side: *The road's too busy to walk across.* | *Vince stared across the canyon.* | *flying across the Atlantic* **2 10 feet/5 miles etc. across** used to show how wide something is: *At its widest point, the river is 2 miles across.* **3** on the opposite side of something: *Ben lives* ***across the street*** *from us.* | *Andi* ***sat across from*** *me.* | *The school is all the way* ***across town.*** **4** reaching or spreading from one side of an area to the other: *There was only one bridge across the bay.* | *a deep crack across the ceiling* **5 across the board** affecting everyone or everything: *Changes will have to be made across the board.*

a·cryl·ic /əˈkrɪlɪk/ *adj.* CHEMISTRY acrylic paints, cloth, etc. are made from a chemical substance rather than a natural substance

act[1] /ækt/ *v.* **1** [I] to do something: *We must act now in order to protect American jobs.* | *The jury decided that Walker had acted in self-defense.* | *We're* ***acting on*** *the advice of our lawyer* (=doing what s/he says). **2** [I] to behave in a particular way: *Nick's been acting strangely recently.* | *Pam's* ***acting like*** *a baby.* | *Gabe* ***acted as if*** *nothing was wrong.* **3** [I,T] to perform as a character in a play or movie: *I started acting in high school.* **4** [I] to produce a particular effect: *Salt* ***acts as*** *a preservative.*

act sth ↔ **out** *phr. v.* to show how an event happened by performing it like a play: *The children read the story and then acted it out.*

act up *phr. v.* to behave badly, or not work correctly: *The car's acting up again.*

act[2] *n.* **1** [C] something that you do: *a criminal act* | ***acts of*** *cruelty* | *Police caught the suspect* ***in the act of*** *making a bomb.*

> **USAGE**
>
> **Act** is always countable, and is used when you mean a particular type of action: *an act of kindness* | *acts of violence*
>
> **Action** can be countable or uncountable: *His actions were honorable.* | *We need to take immediate action.*

2 [C] *also* **Act** a law that has been officially accepted by the government: *the Civil Rights Act* **3** [C] *also* **Act** one of the main parts of a play, OPERA, etc.: *Hamlet kills the king in Act 5.* **4** [C] a short piece of entertainment on television or stage: *a* ***comedy act*** **5** [singular] behavior that is not sincere: *He doesn't care, Laura – it's* ***just an act.*** **6 get your act together** (informal) to start to do things in a more organized or effective way: *If Julie doesn't get her act together, she'll never graduate.* **7 get in on the act** (informal) to become involved in a successful activity that someone else has started

act·ing[1] /ˈæktɪŋ/ *adj.* **acting manager/director etc.** someone who replaces the manager, etc. for a short time

acting[2] *n.* [U] the job or skill of performing in plays or movies

ac·tion /ˈækʃən/ *n.* **1** [U] the process of doing something for a particular purpose: *He realized the need for immediate action.* | *We must* ***take action*** (=start doing something) *before it's too late.* | *The best* ***course of action*** (=way of dealing with the situation) *is to resign immediately.* | *His lawyers have threatened to take* ***legal action.*** **2** [C] something that you do: *The child could not be held responsible for his actions.* | *His* ***quick actions*** *probably saved my life.* **3 out of action** (informal) not working because of damage or injury: *My car's out of action.* | *Jim will be out of action for two weeks.* **4** [U] (informal) exciting things that are happening: *New York's* ***where the action is.*** | *an* ***action movie*** (=one with a lot of fast exciting scenes) **5 in action** doing a particular job or activity: *a chance to* ***see*** *ski jumpers* ***in action*** **6** [C,U] fighting in a war: *He was* ***killed in action.***

> **THESAURUS** war, fighting, combat, warfare
> → WAR

7 [U] the effect a substance has on something: *The rock is worn down by the* ***action of*** *the falling water.*

ˈaction ˌverb *n.* [C] ENG. LANG. ARTS a verb that describes an action rather than a state, for example "run" or "jump"

ac·ti·vate /ˈæktəˌveɪt/ *v.* [T] (formal) to make something start working: *This switch activates the alarm.* —**activation** /ˌæktəˈveɪʃən/ *n.* [U]

ac·tive[1] /ˈæktɪv/ *adj.* **1** always doing things, or moving around a lot (ANT) **inactive**: *Grandpa's very active for his age.* | *games for active youngsters* **2** involved in an organization or activity by doing things for it: *an* ***active member*** *of the American Civil Liberties Union* | *Mahke is* ***active in*** *the Republican Party.* **3** working or operating in the expected way: *The alarm is now active.* **4** EARTH SCIENCES an active VOLCANO is likely to explode and pour out fire and LAVA (=hot liquid rock) **5** ENG. LANG. ARTS an active verb or sentence has the person or thing doing the action as its SUBJECT. In "The boy kicked the ball," the verb "kick" is active. (ANT) **passive**

active[2] *n.* **the active (voice)** ENG. LANG. ARTS the active form of a verb → PASSIVE

A

A

ac·tive·ly /'æktɪvli/ *adv.* in a way that involves doing things or taking part in something: *My parents are **actively involved** with the church.*

ac·tiv·ist /'æktəvɪst/ *n.* [C] someone who works to achieve social or political change: *human rights activists* —**activism** *n.* [U]

ac·tiv·i·ty /æk'tɪvəṭi/ *n.* (plural **activities**) **1** [C usually plural] things that you do for pleasure: *after-school activities* | *She loves nature and **outdoor activities**.* **2** [C,U] things that you do because you want to achieve something: *an increase in terrorist activity* | *anti-government **political activity*** **3** [U] a situation in which a lot of things are happening or a lot of things are being done: *the noise and activity of the city*

ac·tor /'æktɚ/ *n.* [C] someone who performs in a play or movie: *a leading Hollywood actor* ➔ MOVIE

ac·tress /'æktrɪs/ *n.* [C] a woman who performs in a play or movie ➔ MOVIE

ac·tu·al /'æktʃuəl, 'ækʃuəl/ *adj.* real or exact: *Were those his actual words?* | *Well, the actual cost is a lot higher than they say.*

ac·tu·al·ly /'æktʃuəli, -tʃəli, 'ækʃuəli, -ʃəli/ *adv.* **1** used to emphasize that something is true, especially when it is a little surprising or unexpected: *They were never actually married.* | *What actually happened?* | *Actually, it was a lot of fun.* **2** used in order to give more information, give your opinion, etc.: *The watch actually belonged to my father.* | *Actually, I think I'll stay home tonight.*

a·cu·men /ə'kyumən, 'ækyəmən/ *n.* [U] the ability to think quickly and make good judgments: ***business acumen***

ac·u·punc·ture /'ækyə,pʌŋktʃɚ/ *n.* [U] a way of treating pain or illness by putting thin needles into parts of the body

a·cute /ə'kyut/ *adj.* **1** very serious or severe: ***acute pain*** | ***acute shortages** of food* **2** quick to notice and understand things: *an acute observation* | *an **acute mind*** **3** showing an ability to notice small differences in sound, taste, etc.: *acute hearing* **4** BIOLOGY an acute disease or illness quickly becomes dangerous ➔ CHRONIC: *acute tuberculosis* **5** ENG. LANG. ARTS an acute ACCENT (=a mark used to show how something is pronounced) is a small line written above a vowel. In the word "café," the letter "e" has an acute accent. [ORIGIN: 1300—1400 Latin, past participle of *acuere* "to sharpen," from *acus* "needle"]

a,cute 'angle *n.* [C] MATH an acute angle is less than 90° ➔ OBLIQUE ANGLE, OBTUSE ANGLE ➔ *see picture at* ANGLE[1]

a·cutely /ə'kyutli/ *adv.* feeling or noticing something very strongly: *We are **acutely aware** of the problem.*

a,cute 'triangle *n.* [C] MATH a TRIANGLE whose three angles are each less than 90°

ad /æd/ *n.* [C] (informal) an advertisement

A.D. **Anno Domini** used in order to show that a date is a particular number of years after the birth of Christ ➔ B.C.: *432 A.D.*

ad·age /'ædɪdʒ/ *n.* [C] ENG. LANG. ARTS a well-known phrase that says something wise about life

ad·a·mant /'ædəmənt/ *adj.* (formal) determined not to change your opinion, decision, etc. [ORIGIN: 800—900 Old French, Latin *adamas* "hardest metal, diamond," from Greek] —**adamantly** *adv.*: *The chairman has remained adamantly opposed to the project.*

Ad·am's ap·ple /'ædəmz ,æpəl/ *n.* [C] the lump at the front of a man's neck, that moves when he talks or swallows

Adam's apple

a·dapt /ə'dæpt/ (Ac) *v.* **1** [I,T] to change your behavior or ideas to fit a new situation: *The kids are having trouble **adapting to** their new school.* | *These plants are able to adapt themselves to desert conditions.* **2** [T] to change something so that it is appropriate for a new purpose: *The car has been **adapted to** take unleaded gas.* | *The house was **adapted for** wheelchair users.*

THESAURUS change, alter, adjust, modify ➔ CHANGE[1]

a·dapt·a·ble /ə'dæptəbəl/ (Ac) *adj.* able to change and be successful in new and different situations —**adaptability** /ə,dæptə'bɪləṭi/ *n.* [U]

ad·ap·ta·tion /,ædəp'teɪʃən, ,ædæp-/ (Ac) *n.* **1** [C] ENG. LANG. ARTS a play, movie, or television program that is based on a book **2** [U] the process of changing something so that it can be used in a different way or in different conditions

a·dapt·er /ə'dæptɚ/ *n.* [C] an object you use to connect two pieces of electrical equipment, or to connect more than one piece of equipment to the same power supply

add /æd/ *v.* [T] **1** to put something with something else, or with a group of other things: *Continue mixing, then add flour.* | *Do you want to **add** your name **to** the mailing list?* **2** MATH to put numbers or amounts together and then calculate the total: *If you add 5 and 3, you get 8.* | *The interest will be added to your savings every six months.* **3** to say something extra about what you have just said: *The judge **added that** this case was one of the worst she had ever tried.*

THESAURUS say, mention, state ➔ SAY[1]

4 add insult to injury to make a bad situation even worse for someone who has already been treated badly [ORIGIN: 1300—1400 Latin *addere*, from *ad-* "to" + *-dere* "to put"]

add on ↔ sth *phr. v.* to include or put on something extra: *Eating chocolate really adds on the calories.*

add to sth *phr. v.* to make a feeling or quality stronger and more noticeable: *The change of plans only added to our confusion.*

add up *phr. v.* **1 add** sth ↔ **up** to put numbers or amounts together and then calculate the total: *We're now adding up the latest figures.* **2 not add up** to not seem true or reasonable: *Her **story** (=explanation or account of what has happened) just **doesn't add up**.*

ad·den·dum /əˈdɛndəm/ *n.* (plural **addenda** /-də/) [C] ENG. LANG. ARTS something that is added to the end of a book, usually to give more information

ad·dict /ˈædɪkt/ *n.* [C] someone who is unable to stop taking drugs: *a heroin addict*

ad·dict·ed /əˈdɪktɪd/ *adj.* unable to stop taking a drug: *Marvin was **addicted to** sleeping pills.* —**addiction** /əˈdɪkʃən/ *n.* [C,U]: ***addiction to** alcohol* —**addictive** /əˈdɪktɪv/ *adj.*: *a highly addictive drug*

ad·di·tion /əˈdɪʃən/ *n.* **1 in addition** used in order to add another fact to what has already been mentioned: *We installed a new security system. In addition, extra guards were hired.* | ***In addition to** his job, Harvey also coaches Little League.*

THESAURUS

extra – if something is extra, it is not included in the price of something and you have to pay more for it: *Dinner costs $15, but drinks are extra.*
on top of – in addition to a lot of other things, or in addition to a large amount, when you do not think this is good: *On top of everything else, I have to work on Saturday.*
as well as – in addition to something or someone else: *She plays the piano as well as the violin.*

2 [U] MATH the process of adding together several numbers or amounts to get a total ➔ DIVISION, MULTIPLICATION, SUBTRACTION **3** [C] something that is added to something else: *The book will be a welcome **addition to** any travel reader's collection.*

THESAURUS

additive – a substance that is added to food to make it taste or look better or to keep it fresh: *food additives*
supplement – something that is added to something else to improve it: *vitamin supplements*

4 [C] an extra room that is added to a building

ad·di·tion·al /əˈdɪʃənəl/ *adj.* more than you already have, or more than was agreed or expected (SYN) **extra**: *We were charged an additional $50 in late fees.* | ***Additional information** is available on our website.*

THESAURUS **more, another, extra, further** ➔ MORE[2]

ad·di·tive /ˈædət̬ɪv/ *n.* [C usually plural] a substance that is added to food to make it taste or look better or to keep it fresh ➔ ADDITION

ad·dress[1] /əˈdrɛs, ˈædrɛs/ *n.* [C] **1** the details of where someone lives or works, including the number of a building, name of the street and town, etc.: *I forgot to give Damien my new address.* | *Write your **name and address** on a postcard.* | *Please notify us of any **change of address**.* **2** a series of letters or numbers used to send an email to someone, or to reach a page of information on the Internet: *Give me your **email address**.* ➔ INTERNET **3** /əˈdrɛs/ a formal speech: *the Gettysburg Address*

ad·dress[2] /əˈdrɛs/ *v.* [T] **1** to write a name and address on an envelope, package, etc.: *There's a letter here **addressed to** you.* **2** (formal) to speak directly to a person or a group: *A guest speaker then addressed the audience.* | *You should **address** your question **to** the chairman.* **3 address a problem/question/issue etc.** (formal) to start trying to solve a problem: *Special meetings address the concerns of new members.* **4** to use a particular name or title when speaking or writing to someone: *The President should be **addressed as** "Mr. President."*

a·dept /əˈdɛpt/ *adj.* good at doing something that needs care or skill: *He has become **adept at** cooking.* —**adeptly** *adv.*

THESAURUS **skillful, expert, accomplished, deft** ➔ SKILLFUL

ad·e·quate /ˈædəkwɪt/ (Au) *adj.* **1** enough in quantity or of a good enough quality for a particular purpose (ANT) **inadequate**: *We have not been given adequate information.* | *Her income is hardly **adequate to** pay the bills.*

THESAURUS **enough, sufficient** ➔ ENOUGH

2 fairly good, but not excellent: *an adequate performance* [ORIGIN: 1500—1600 Latin, past participle of *adaequare* "to make equal," from *ad-* "to" + *aequare* "to equal"]

THESAURUS **satisfactory, good enough, acceptable, passable, reasonable, respectable** ➔ SATISFACTORY

—**adequacy** *n.* [U] —**adequately** *adv.*

ad·here /ədˈhɪr/ *v.* [I] (formal) to stick firmly to something

adhere to sth *phr. v.* (formal) to continue to behave according to a particular rule, agreement, or belief: *Not all the states adhered to the treaty.*

ad·her·ence /ədˈhɪrəns/ *n.* [U] the act of behaving according to particular rules, ideas, or beliefs: *a strict **adherence to** religious beliefs*

ad·her·ent /ədˈhɪrənt/ *n.* [C] someone who agrees with and supports a particular idea, opinion, or political party

ad·he·sion /ədˈhiʒən/ *n.* **1** [U] the state of one thing sticking to another thing **2** [C,U] BIOLOGY a piece of body TISSUE (=flesh) that has grown around a small injury or damaged area and has joined it to other tissue, or the process of joining

A

two tissues together in this way **3** [U] PHYSICS a force that makes the atoms of different substances join tightly together when the substances touch each other

ad·he·sive /əd'hisɪv, -zɪv/ *n.* [C] a substance such as glue, that can stick things together —**adhesive** *adj.*: *adhesive tape*

ad hoc /ˌæd 'hɑk/ *adj., adv.* done when necessary, rather than planned or regular: *an ad hoc committee*

ad·ja·cent /ə'dʒeɪsənt/ (Ac) *adj.* (formal) next to something: *The library is **adjacent to** the main campus.* | *The warehouse is much bigger than the adjacent buildings.* [ORIGIN: 1400—1500 Latin, present participle of *adjacere* "to lie near," from *ad-* "to" + *jacere* "to lie"]

adˌjacent 'angles *n.* [plural] MATH two angles that are next to one another and share one side, formed when a straight line divides one angle into two parts

ad·jec·tive /'ædʒɪktɪv, 'ædʒətɪv/ *n.* [C] ENG. LANG. ARTS in grammar, a word that describes a noun or PRONOUN. In the sentence "I bought a new car," "new" is an adjective. [ORIGIN: 1300—1400 Old French *adjectif*, from Latin *adjectus*, past participle of *adjicere*, from *ad-* "to" + *jacere* "to throw"]

ad·join·ing /ə'dʒɔɪnɪŋ/ *adj.* next to something, and connected to it: *a bedroom with an adjoining bathroom* —**adjoin** *v.* [T]

ad·journ /ə'dʒɚn/ *v.* [I,T] to stop a meeting or a legal process for a short time or until a later date: *This court is **adjourned until** 2:30 p.m. tomorrow.* —**adjournment** *n.* [C,U]

ad·ju·di·cate /ə'dʒudɪˌkeɪt/ *v.* [I,T] (formal) to judge something such as a competition, or to make an official decision —**adjudication** /əˌdʒudɪ'keɪʃən/ *n.* [U]

ad·junct[1] /'ædʒʌŋkt/ *n.* [C] (formal) something that is added or joined to something else, but is not part of it.: *She took a course in computing as an **adjunct to** her degree studies.*

adjunct[2] *adj.* **adjunct professor/instructor** a professor or instructor who works PART-TIME at a college

ad·just /ə'dʒʌst/ (Ac) *v.* **1** [I] to gradually become familiar with a new situation: *When we moved to a new neighborhood, it took the children a long time to adjust.* | *It took a few seconds for her eyes to **adjust to** the darkness.* **2** [T] to change or move something slightly in order to improve it, make it more effective, etc.: *Adjust your seat and mirror before driving away.*

> THESAURUS change, alter, adapt, modify, revise, amend → CHANGE[1]

—**adjustable** *adj.*

ad·just·ment /ə'dʒʌstmənt/ (Ac) *n.* [C,U] **1** a small change made to a machine, system, or calculation: *We've **made some adjustments to** our original calculations.* | *a **slight/minor/fine adjustment*** (=a small change) **2** a change in the way you behave or think: *Moving to the city has been a difficult adjustment for us.*

ad-lib /ˌæd'lɪb/ *v.* (**ad-libbed**, **ad-libbing**) [I,T] to say something in a speech or a performance without preparing or planning it —**ad lib** *n.* [C]

ad·min·is·ter /əd'mɪnəstɚ/ *v.* [T] **1** to manage and organize the affairs of a company, government, etc. **2** to provide or organize something officially as part of your job: *The test was **administered to** all high school seniors.* **3** (formal) to give someone a medicine or drug: *Painkillers were **administered to** the boy.* [ORIGIN: 1300—1400 Old French *aministrer*, from Latin *administrare*, from *ad-* "to" + *ministrare* "to serve"]

ad·min·is·tra·tion /ədˌmɪnə'streɪʃən/ (Ac) *n.* **1** [C] the government of a country at a particular time: *He was Secretary of State during the Bush administration.* **2** [U] the activities that are involved in managing and organizing the affairs of a company, institution, etc.: *We're looking for someone with experience in administration.* **3 the administration** the people who manage a company, institution, etc.

ad·min·i·stra·tive /əd'mɪnəˌstreɪt̬ɪv/ (Ac) *adj.* relating to the work of managing a company or organization: *Our **administrative staff** will deal with all the paperwork for you.* | *The job is mainly administrative.*

adˌministrative as'sistant *n.* [C] someone who works in an office, typing letters, keeping records, answering telephone calls, arranging meetings, etc.

ad·min·is·tra·tor /əd'mɪnəˌstreɪt̬ɚ/ (Ac) *n.* [C] someone whose job is related to the management and organization of a company, institution, etc.: *A decision will be made next week by the hospital administrators.*

ad·mi·ra·ble /'ædmərəbəl/ *adj.* having many good qualities that you respect and admire: *an admirable achievement* —**admirably** *adv.*

ad·mi·ral /'ædmərəl/ *n.* [C] a very high rank in the navy, or an officer who has this rank [ORIGIN: 1200—1300 Old French *amiral*, from Medieval Latin *admirallus*, from Arabic *amir-al-* "commander of the"]

ad·mi·ra·tion /ˌædmə'reɪʃən/ *n.* [U] a feeling of approval and respect for something or someone: *She's always had great **admiration for** her father.*

ad·mire /əd'maɪɚ/ *v.* [T] **1** to approve of and respect someone or something: *I really **admire the way** she brings up those kids.* | *I **admired** her **for** having the courage to tell the truth.*

> THESAURUS
> **respect** – to admire someone because of his/her knowledge, skill, personal qualities, etc.: *He is respected by his colleagues.*
> **look up to sb** – to admire and respect someone who is older and more experienced than you: *The other kids looked up to him.*

A

idolize – to admire someone so much that you think s/he is perfect: *He's now competing with the players he idolized in high school.*
worship – to love and admire someone very much: *His son just worships him.*
revere (formal) – to respect and admire someone or something very much: *As a civil rights leader, Martin Luther King was revered for his courage and leadership.*
hold sb in high esteem (formal) – to respect and admire someone a lot: *Her colleagues held her in high esteem.*

2 to look at something and think how beautiful or impressive it is: *We stopped to admire the view.* [ORIGIN: 1500—1600 French *admirer*, from Latin *admirari*, from *ad-* "to" + *mirari* "to wonder"] —**admirer** *n.* [C] —**admiring** *adj.*: *She drew **admiring glances** from all the men* (=the men were looking at her with approval because she is attractive). —**admiringly** *adv.*

ad·mis·si·ble /əd'mɪsəbəl/ *adj.* LAW acceptable or allowed, especially in a court of law (ANT) **inadmissible**: *admissible evidence*

ad·mis·sion /əd'mɪʃən/ *n.* **1** [U] the price charged when you go to a movie, sports event, concert, etc.: *Admission is $6.50.* | *The museum has no **admission charge**.* **2** [C] a statement in which you admit that something is true or that you have done something wrong: *If he resigns, it will be an **admission of** guilt.* **3** [U] permission that is given to someone to enter a building or place, or to become a member of a school, club, etc.: *Tom has applied for **admission to** the university.* **4 admissions** [plural] the process of allowing people to enter a college, institution, hospital, etc., or the number of people who can enter

ad·mit /əd'mɪt/ *v.* (**admitted, admitting**) **1** [T] to accept or agree unwillingly that something is true or that someone else is right: *He was wrong, but he won't admit it.* | *You may not like her, but you have to **admit that** she is good at her job.* **2** [I,T] to say that you did something wrong or are guilty of a crime: *She finally **admitted to** the murder.* | *In court, he **admitted** his **guilt**.*

THESAURUS

confess – to admit that you have done something wrong or illegal: *Smith confessed to the shootings after his arrest.*
own up (informal) – to admit that you have done something wrong: *He finally owned up to the fact that he had lied to us.*
come clean (informal) – to finally tell the truth about something you have been hiding: *Do you think she'll ever come clean about her past?*

3 [T] to allow someone to enter a building or place, or to become a member of a school, club, etc.: *Only members will be **admitted to** the club for tonight's performance.*

ad·mit·tance /əd'mɪt˺ns/ *n.* [U] permission to enter a place: *Most journalists were unable to **gain admittance** backstage.*

ad·mit·ted·ly /əd'mɪt̬ɪdli/ *adv.* used when admitting that something is true: *Our net profit this year is, admittedly, much smaller than we had expected.*

ad·mon·ish /əd'mɑnɪʃ/ *v.* [T] (literary) to tell someone that s/he has done something wrong —**admonishment** *n.* [C,U]

THESAURUS **criticize, scold, rebuke, reprimand** → CRITICIZE

a·do·be /ə'doʊbi/ *n.* [U] a material made of clay and STRAW, used for building houses

a·do·les·cence /ˌædl'ɛsəns/ *n.* [U] the period of time, usually between the ages of 12 and 18, when a young person is developing into an adult

ad·o·les·cent[1] /ˌædl'ɛsənt/ *n.* [C] a young person who is developing into an adult

THESAURUS **child, kid, teenager, youngster, minor, juvenile** → CHILD

adolescent[2] *adj.* relating to or typical of a young person who is developing into an adult: *adolescent behavior*

a·dopt /ə'dɑpt/ *v.* **1** [I,T] to take someone else's child into your home and legally become his/her parent: *Melissa was adopted when she was two.* | *couples who are hoping to adopt* **2** [T] to begin to have or use an idea, plan, or way of doing something: *The city has adopted a new approach to fighting crime.* —**adopted** *adj.*: *our adopted son*

a·dop·tion /ə'dɑpʃən/ *n.* [U] **1** the act or process of adopting a child: *She decided to **put** the baby **up for adoption**.* **2** the act of deciding to use an idea, plan, or way of doing something: *the **adoption of** new technology*

a·dop·tive /ə'dɑptɪv/ *adj.* [only before noun] an adoptive parent is one who has adopted a child

a·dor·a·ble /ə'dɔrəbəl/ *adj.* very attractive and easy to like: *What an adorable little puppy!*

a·dore /ə'dɔr/ *v.* [T] **1** to love and admire someone very much: *Betty adores her grandchildren.*

THESAURUS **love, be crazy about sb, be devoted to sb, dote on sb** → LOVE[1]

2 (informal) to like something very much [ORIGIN: 1300—1400 French *adorer*, from Latin *adorare*, from *ad-* "to" + *orare* "to speak, pray"] —**adoring** *adj.*: *his adoring fans* —**adoration** /ˌædə'reɪʃən/ *n.* [U]

a·dorn /ə'dɔrn/ *v.* **be adorned with sth** (formal) to be decorated with something: *The church walls were adorned with religious paintings.* —**adornment** *n.* [C,U]

a·dren·a·line, adrenalin /ə'drɛnl-ɪn/ *n.* [U] BIOLOGY a chemical produced by your body that makes your heart beat faster and gives you extra strength when you are afraid, excited, or angry

a·drift /ə'drɪft/ *adj., adv.* a boat that is adrift is not tied to anything, and is moved around by the ocean or wind

A

a·droit /ə'drɔɪt/ *adj.* smart and skillful, especially in the way you use words and arguments: *an adroit negotiator* —**adroitly** *adv.*

ad·u·la·tion /ˌædʒə'leɪʃən/ *n.* [U] (formal) praise and admiration for someone, that is more than s/he really deserves

a·dult[1] /ə'dʌlt, 'ædʌlt/ (Ac) *n.* [C] a fully grown person or animal: *She's an adult – she can do what she pleases.* | *Children under 18 must be accompanied by an adult.* | *Admission is $8 for adults and $5 for children.* [ORIGIN: 1500—1600 Latin, past participle of *adolescere* "to grow up"]

adult[2] *adj.* [only before noun] **1** fully grown or developed: *an adult male frog* | *My son passed from one job to another throughout his* ***adult life*** (=the part of his life when he was an adult). **2** typical of an adult: *You need to deal with your problems in an adult way.* **3 adult movies/magazines/bookstores etc.** movies, magazines, etc. that show sexual acts, etc.

a·dul·ter·ate /ə'dʌltəˌreɪt/ *v.* [T] to make something less pure by adding a substance of a lower quality to it —**adulteration** /əˌdʌltə'reɪʃən/ *n.* [U]

a·dul·ter·y /ə'dʌltəri/ *n.* [U] sex between someone who is married and someone who is not that person's husband or wife: *men who* ***commit adultery*** —**adulterous** *adj.*

a·dult·hood /ə'dʌlthʊd/ (Ac) *n.* [U] the time when you are an adult ➔ CHILDHOOD: *By the time Mathew* ***reached adulthood****, he weighed over 250 pounds.*

ad·um·brate /'ædəmˌbreɪt, ə'dʌm-/ *v.* [T] (formal) to suggest or describe something in a way that is not complete

ad·vance[1] /əd'væns/ *n.* **1 in advance** before something happens or is expected to happen: *Reserve your ticket in advance by calling our telephone hotline.* **2** [C,U] a change, discovery, or invention that brings progress: *medical advances* | ***advances in*** *technology* **3** [C] a movement forward to a new position, especially by an army (ANT) **retreat**: *Napoleon's advance towards Moscow* **4** [C usually singular] money paid to someone before the usual time: *I asked for an* ***advance on*** *my salary.* **5 advances** [plural] efforts to start a sexual relationship with someone [ORIGIN: 1200—1300 Old French *avancier*, from Latin *abante* "before"]

advance[2] *v.* **1** [I] to move forward to a new position (ANT) **retreat**: *Troops* ***advanced on*** (=moved forward while attacking) *the rebel forces.* **2** [I,T] to develop or progress, or to make something develop or progress: *a job that will* ***advance*** *his* ***career*** **3** [T] to give someone money before s/he has earned it: *Will they advance you some money until you get your first paycheck?* —**advancement** *n.* [U]

advance[3] *adj.* **advance planning/warning/notice etc.** planning, etc. that is done before something else happens: *We had no advance warning of the hurricane.*

ad·vanced /əd'vænst/ *adj.* **1** using the most modern ideas, equipment, and methods: *advanced weapon systems*

THESAURUS

sophisticated – made or designed well, and often complicated: *sophisticated software*
modern – made or done using the most recent methods: *modern medicine*
high-tech – using the most modern machines and methods in industry, business, etc.: *high-tech weapons*
state-of-the-art – using the newest methods, materials, or knowledge: *state-of-the-art technology*
cutting-edge – using the newest design, or the most advanced way of doing something: *cutting-edge medical research*

2 studying or relating to a school subject at a difficult level: *an advanced student* | *advanced physics* **3** having reached a late point in time or development: *By this time, the disease was too far advanced to be treated.*

ad·van·tage /əd'væntɪdʒ/ *n.* **1** [C,U] something that helps you to be better or more successful than others (ANT) **disadvantage**: *Her computer skills gave her an* ***advantage over*** *the other applicants.* | *He turns every situation* ***to his advantage****.*

THESAURUS

benefit – a feature of something that has a good effect on people's lives: *Tourism has brought great benefits to the area.*
merit (formal) – a good feature that something has, which you consider when deciding whether it is the best choice: *The committee will meet to discuss the merits of the proposals.*
good point (especially spoken) – a good feature that something has: *The system has a lot of good points.*
the great/best/good thing about ... (spoken) – used when you want to talk about a good feature that something has: *The great thing about this phone is that it is so easy to use.*
the pros and cons – the advantages and disadvantages: *You need to weigh up* (=consider) *the pros and cons carefully before you start the treatment.* ➔ *see also* DISADVANTAGE

2 take advantage of sth to use a situation or thing to help you do or get something you want: *He* ***took advantage of*** *the* ***opportunity*** *given to him.* **3** [C] a good or useful quality that something has: *Good restaurants are one of the many* ***advantages of*** *living in a big city* **4 take advantage of sb** to treat someone unfairly or to control a particular situation in order to get what you want [ORIGIN: 1300—1400 Old French *avantage*, from *avant* "before," from Latin *abante*]

ad·van·ta·geous /ˌædvæn'teɪdʒəs, -vən-/ *adj.* helpful and likely to make you more successful (ANT) **disadvantageous**

ad·vec·tion /æd'vɛkʃən/ *n.* [U] **1** PHYSICS the HORIZONTAL movement of heat, cold, or HUMIDITY (=amount of water in the air) in the Earth's ATMOSPHERE, caused by wind **2** EARTH SCIENCES the HORIZONTAL movement of air or water

ad·vent /'ædvɛnt/ *n.* **the advent of sth** the time when something first begins to be widely used: *the advent of the computer*

ad·ven·ture /əd'vɛntʃɚ/ *n.* [C,U] an exciting experience in which dangerous or unusual things happen

ad·ven·tur·er /əd'vɛntʃərɚ/ *n.* [C] someone who enjoys traveling and doing exciting things

ad·ven·ture·some /əd'vɛntʃɚsəm/ *adj.* enjoying exciting and slightly dangerous activities

ad·ven·tur·ous /əd'vɛntʃərəs/ *adj.* **1** wanting to do new, exciting, or dangerous things: *adventurous travelers* **2** exciting and slightly dangerous: *an adventurous expedition up the Amazon*

ad·verb /'ædvɚb/ *n.* [C] ENG. LANG. ARTS in grammar, a word or a group of words that describes or adds to the meaning of a verb, an adjective, another adverb, or a sentence. For example, "slowly" in "He walked slowly" and "very" in "It was a very nice day" are adverbs. [ORIGIN: 1400—1500 French *adverbe*, from Latin *adverbium*, from *ad-* "to" + *verbum* "word"] **—adverbial** /əd'vɚbiəl/ *adj.*

ad·ver·sar·y /'ædvɚˌsɛri/ *n.* (plural **adversaries**) [C] (formal) a country or person you are fighting or competing against SYN **opponent**

ad·verse /əd'vɚs, æd-, 'ædvɚs/ *adj.* (formal) not good or favorable: *The recession will have an **adverse effect** on the building industry.* **—adversely** *adv.*

ad·ver·si·ty /əd'vɚsəṭi, æd-/ *n.* (plural **adversities**) [C,U] difficulties or problems that seem to be caused by bad luck: *We remained hopeful **in the face of adversity**.*

ad·ver·tise /'ædvɚˌtaɪz/ *v.* **1** [I,T] to tell the public about a product or service in order to persuade them to buy it: *The new perfume is being **advertised in** women's magazines.* | *companies who **advertise on** TV*

THESAURUS

promote – to advertise a product or event: *She's in Atlanta to promote her new book.*
market – to try to persuade someone to buy something by advertising it in a particular way: *The clothes are marketed to teenagers.*
publicize (formal) – to tell people about a new movie, book, event, etc.: *Reese has been giving interviews to publicize her new novel.*
hype – to try to make people think something is good or important by advertising or talking about it a lot on television, the radio, etc.: *The director is just using the controversy to hype his movie.*
plug – to advertise a book, movie, etc. by talking about it on a radio or television program: *Marc was on the show to plug his new play.*

2 [I] to make an announcement, for example in a newspaper, that a job is available, an event is going to happen, etc.: *They're **advertising for** an accountant.* [ORIGIN: 1400—1500 Early French *advertiss-*, stem of *advertir*, from Latin *advertere*, from *ad-* "to" + *vertere* "to turn"] **—advertiser** *n.* [C]

ad·ver·tise·ment /ˌædvɚ'taɪzmənt/ *n.* [C] a picture, set of words, or a short movie, that is intended to persuade people to buy a product or use a service, or that gives information about a job that is available, an event that is going to happen, etc. → COMMERCIAL: *an **advertisement for** laundry detergent*

THESAURUS

commercial – an advertisement on TV or radio
billboard – a very large sign at the side of a road or on a building, used as an advertisement
poster – an advertisement on a wall, often with a picture on it
want ads/classified ads – short advertisements in a newspaper, in which people offer things for sale
flier – a piece of paper with an advertisement on it, often given to you in the street
junk mail – unwanted letters that you receive in the mail, containing advertisements
spam – unwanted emails containing advertisements

ad·ver·tis·ing /'ædvɚˌtaɪzɪŋ/ *n.* [U] the business of advertising things on television, in newspapers, etc.

ad·vice /əd'vaɪs/ *n.* [U] an opinion you give someone about what s/he should do: *The book is full of **advice on/about** child care.* | *Can you **give** me some **advice** about buying a house?* | *If I were you, I'd **seek** (=get) some **legal/medical/financial advice**.* | *Did you **follow/take** your father's **advice**?* | *He offered them one **piece of advice**: Don't panic.* [ORIGIN: 1200—1300 Old French *avis* "opinion"]

THESAURUS

tip – a helpful piece of advice: *useful tips on healthy eating*
suggestion – an idea or plan that someone suggests: *He made a few suggestions about how I could improve my essay.*
recommendation – advice given to someone, especially about what to do: *Do you have any recommendations about hotels in the city?*
guidance – helpful advice about work, education, etc.: *His parents should provide more guidance.*
counseling – advice given by someone who is trained to help people with their personal problems or difficult decisions: *Each student receives career counseling.*
warning – a piece of advice that tells you that something bad or dangerous might happen, so that you can avoid or prevent it: *Cigarette packs must have health warnings printed on them.*

A

ad·vise /əd'vaɪz/ *v.* **1** [I,T] to tell someone what you think s/he should do: *Doctors **advised** her **to** have the operation.* | *We were **advised against** getting a cat because of Joey's allergies.*

THESAURUS

recommend – to advise someone to do something: *I recommend that you get some professional help.*
urge – to strongly advise someone to do something: *I urged Frida to reconsider her decision to drop out of school.*
suggest – to tell someone your ideas about what should be done: *Wilson suggested ways that students can improve their study habits.*
counsel (formal) – to talk to someone in order to help that person to deal with his/her problems, when it is your job to do this: *She counsels teenagers who have problems with drugs or alcohol.*

2 [T] (formal) to officially tell someone something: *You will be advised when the shipment arrives.*

ad·vis·er, advisor /əd'vaɪzɚ/ *n.* [C] someone whose job is to give advice about a particular subject: *a financial adviser*

ad·vi·so·ry /əd'vaɪzəri/ *adj.* having the purpose of giving advice: *an advisory committee*

ad·vo·cate¹ /'ædvə,keɪt/ (Ac) *v.* [T] to strongly support a particular way of doing things: *Extremists were openly advocating violence.* [ORIGIN: 1300—1400 Old French *avocat*, from Latin, past participle of *advocare* "to summon"] —**advocacy** /'ædvəkəsi/ *n.* [U]: *He is well-known for his advocacy of family values.*

ad·vo·cate² /'ædvəkət, -,keɪt/ (Ac) *n.* [C] someone who publicly supports someone or something: *She later became an **advocate for** prisoners' rights.*

aer·i·al /'ɛriəl/ *adj.* from the air, or happening in the air: *aerial photographs* | *aerial stunts*

ae·ro·bic /ə'roʊbɪk, ɛ-/ *adj.* **1** BIOLOGY relating to exercises that make your heart and lungs stronger **2** BIOLOGY needing oxygen in order to live → ANAEROBIC

ae·ro·bics /ə'roʊbɪks, ɛ-/ *n.* [U] a very active type of physical exercise done to music, usually in a class → EXERCISE²

aer·o·dy·nam·ics /,ɛroʊdaɪ'næmɪks/ *n.* [U] PHYSICS the scientific study of how objects move through the air —**aerodynamic** *adj.*

aer·o·sol /'ɛrə,sɔl, -,sɑl/ *n.* [C] a small metal container from which a liquid can be forced out using high pressure

aer·o·space /'ɛroʊ,speɪs/ *adj.* involving the designing and building of aircraft and space vehicles: *the aerospace industry*

aes·thet·ic, esthetic /ɛs'θɛt̬ɪk, ɪs-/ *adj.* relating to beauty and the study of beauty —**aesthetically** *adv.*: *The building's design is aesthetically pleasing.*

aes·thet·ics, esthetics /ɛs'θɛt̬ɪks, ɪs-/ *n.* [U] ENG. LANG. ARTS the study of beauty, especially beauty in art

a·far /ə'fɑr/ *adv.* **from afar** (literary) from a long distance away

AFC *n.* **American Football Conference** a group of teams that is part of the NFL

af·fa·ble /'æfəbəl/ *adj.* friendly and easy to talk to: *an affable guy* [ORIGIN: 1400—1500 French, Latin *affabilis*, from *affari*, from *ad-* "to" + *fari* "to speak"] —**affably** *adv.*

THESAURUS **sociable, outgoing, genial** → SOCIABLE
friendly, warm, cordial, amiable → FRIENDLY

af·fair /ə'fɛr/ *n.* [C] **1 affairs** [plural] **a)** public or political events and activities: *a **foreign affairs** correspondent for CNN* **b)** things connected with your personal life, your financial situation, etc.: *You need to get your financial affairs in order.* **2** an event or a set of related events, especially unpleasant ones: *the Watergate affair*

THESAURUS **event, occurrence, incident** → EVENT

3 a secret sexual relationship between two people, when at least one of them is married to someone else: *Ed is **having an affair with** his boss's wife.* → LOVE AFFAIR

af·fect /ə'fɛkt/ (Ac) *v.* [T] **1** to do something that produces a change in someone or something → INFLUENCE: *Thousands of homes were affected by the flooding* | *We feel that we do not have control over decisions which **affect** our daily **lives**.*

USAGE

Use the verb **affect** to talk about causing changes, and the noun **effect** to talk about the results of those changes: *Her illness was starting to affect her work.* | *The punishment seemed to have no effect.*
Effect can also be used as a verb to mean "to make something happen." This use is formal and not very common: *They have been unable to effect a permanent solution.*

2 to make someone feel strong emotions: *I was **deeply affected** by the news of Paul's death.* [ORIGIN: (1–2) 1300—1400 Latin, past participle of *afficere* "to influence," from *ad-* "to" + *facere* "to do"]

af·fec·ta·tion /,æfɛk'teɪʃən/ *n.* [C,U] an action or type of behavior that is not natural or sincere

af·fect·ed /ə'fɛktɪd/ (Ac) *adj.* not natural or sincere: *She seemed affected, and I wasn't sure what to make of her.*

af·fect·ing /ə'fɛktɪŋ/ (Ac) *adj.* (formal) producing strong emotions such as sadness, pity, etc.: *The movie is a genuinely affecting story of a child's search for his missing mother.*

af·fec·tion /ə'fɛkʃən/ *n.* [C,U] a feeling of gentle

A

love and caring: *Bart felt great **affection for** her.* | *He doesn't **show affection** easily.*

af·fec·tion·ate /ə'fɛkʃənɪt/ *adj.* showing that you like or love someone: *an affectionate child* | *an affectionate hug* —**affectionately** *adv.*

af·fi·da·vit /ˌæfə'deɪvɪt/ *n.* [C] LAW a written statement about something that you swear is true, used in a court of law [ORIGIN: 1500—1600 Medieval Latin "he or she has made a formal promise," from *affidare*]

af·fil·i·ate¹ /ə'fɪliˌeɪt/ *v.* **be affiliated with/to sth** if a group or organization is affiliated to a larger one, it is related to it or controlled by it: *a TV station affiliated to CBS* [ORIGIN: 1700—1800 Medieval Latin, past participle of *affiliare* "to take over as a son," from Latin *ad-* "to" + *filius* "son"] —**affiliation** /əˌfɪli'eɪʃən/ *n.* [C,U]: *What are Jean's political affiliations?*

af·fil·i·ate² /ə'fɪliɪt, -ˌeɪt/ *n.* [C] a small company or organization that is related to or controlled by a larger one

af·fin·i·ty /ə'fɪnəṭi/ *n.* (plural **affinities**) **1** [singular] the feeling you have when you like and understand someone or something: *The poet has a deep **affinity for** nature.* **2** [C,U] a close similarity or relationship between two things because of qualities or features that they both have [ORIGIN: 1300—1400 Old French *afinité*, from Latin *affinis* "sharing a border, related by marriage"]

af·firm /ə'fɚm/ *v.* [T] (formal) to state publicly that something is true: *The President affirmed his intention to reduce taxes.* —**affirmation** /ˌæfɚ'meɪʃən/ *n.* [C,U]

af·firm·a·tive /ə'fɚməṭɪv/ *adj.* (formal) a word, sign, etc. that is affirmative means "yes" (ANT) **negative** —**affirmative** *n.* [C]: *She answered in the affirmative.* —**affirmatively** *adv.*

afˌfirmative 'action *n.* [U] the practice of choosing people for jobs, education, etc. who have been treated unfairly because of their race, sex, etc.

af·fix /ə'fɪks/ *n.* [C] ENG. LANG. ARTS a group of letters added to the beginning or end of a word to change its meaning or use, such as "un-," "mis-," "-ness," or "-ly"

af·flict /ə'flɪkt/ *v.* [T usually passive] (formal) to make someone have a serious illness or experience serious problems: *a country **afflicted by** famine* | *people **afflicted with** AIDS* —**affliction** /ə'flɪkʃən/ *n.* [C,U]

af·flu·ent /'æfluənt/ *adj.* having a lot of money, nice houses, expensive things, etc. → RICH, WEALTHY: *an affluent suburb of Baltimore* [ORIGIN: 1400—1500 Old French, Latin, present participle of *affluere* "to flow in large quantities"] —**affluence** *n.* [U]

THESAURUS **rich, well-off, prosperous, well-to-do** → RICH

af·ford /ə'fɔrd/ *v.* [T] **1 can afford a)** to have enough money to buy or pay for something: *I can't **afford to** buy a new car.* | *Do you think we can afford a computer now?* **b)** to be able to do something without causing serious problems for yourself: *We can't **afford to** offend regular customers.* **c)** to have enough time to do something: *I really can't afford any more time away from work.* **2** (formal) to provide something or allow something to happen: *The walls afforded some protection from the wind.*

af·ford·a·ble /ə'fɔrdəbəl/ *adj.* not expensive: *affordable housing*

af·front /ə'frʌnt/ *n.* [C usually singular] a remark or action that offends or insults someone

a·float /ə'floʊt/ *adj.* [not before noun] **1** having enough money to operate or stay out of debt: *They're struggling to **stay afloat**.* **2** floating on water

a·fraid /ə'freɪd/ *adj.* [not before noun] **1** frightened because you think that you may get hurt or that something bad may happen (SYN) **scared**: *There's no need to be afraid.* | *Small children are often **afraid of** the dark.* | *Mary's **afraid to** walk home alone.*

THESAURUS **frightened, scared, terrified, petrified, fearful** → FRIGHTENED

2 very worried that something bad will happen: *A lot of people are **afraid of** losing their jobs.* | *He was **afraid (that)** the other kids would laugh at him.* **3 I'm afraid** (spoken) used in order to politely tell someone something that may annoy, upset, or disappoint him/her: ***I'm afraid (that)** this is a "no smoking" area.* | *"Are we late?" "**I'm afraid so** (=yes)."* | *"Are there any tickets left?" "**I'm afraid not** (=no)."* [ORIGIN: 1300—1400 Past participle of *affray* "to frighten" (14—19 centuries), from Old French *affreer*]

a·fresh /ə'frɛʃ/ *adv.* (formal) if you do something afresh, you do it again from the beginning: *We decided to move to Texas and **start afresh**.*

Af·ri·ca /'æfrɪkə/ *n.* one of the seven CONTINENTS, that includes land south of Europe and west of the Indian Ocean

Af·ri·can¹ /'æfrɪkən/ *adj.* relating to or coming from Africa

African² *n.* [C] someone from Africa

ˌAfrican A'merican *n.* [C] an American with dark skin, whose family originally came from the part of Africa south of the Sahara Desert —**African-American** *adj.*

af·ter¹ /'æftɚ/ *prep.* **1** when a particular time or event has happened: *I go swimming every day after work.* | *A **month/year after** the fire, the house was rebuilt.* **2** following someone or something else in a list or a piece of writing, or in order of importance: *Whose name is after mine on the list?* | *After baseball, tennis is my favorite sport.* **3 after 10 minutes/3 hours etc.** when a particular amount of time has passed: *After a while, the woman returned.* **4 day after day/year after year etc.**

continuing for a very long time: *Day after day, we waited, hoping she'd call.* **5** used when telling time to say how many minutes past the hour it is: *It's ten after five.* **6** because of something that happened earlier: *I'm not surprised he left her, after the way she treated him.* **7 after all a)** used in order to say that what you expected did not happen: *It didn't rain after all.* **b)** used in order to say that something should be remembered or considered because it helps to explain what you have just said: *Don't shout at him – he's only a baby, after all.* **8 one after the other** *also* **one after another** if a series of events, actions, etc. happen one after another, each one happens soon after the previous one: *Ever since we moved here, it's been one problem after another.* **9 be after sb** to be looking for someone and trying to catch him/her: *The FBI is after him for fraud.* **10 be after sth** (informal) to be trying to get something that belongs to someone else: *You're just after my money!* **11** in spite of: *After all the trouble I went to, Reese didn't even say thank you.* [ORIGIN: Old English *æfter*]

after² *conjunction* when a particular time has passed, or an event has happened: *Regan changed his name after he left Poland.* | *He discovered the jewel was fake* ***10 days/3 weeks after*** *he bought it.*

after³ *adv.* later than someone or something else: *Gina came on Monday, and I got here the day after.*

> **THESAURUS**
>
> **afterward** – after an event or time that has been mentioned: *He said afterward that it had been the scariest experience of his life.*
> **next** – immediately afterward: *What should we do next?*
> **later** – after the present time or a time you are talking about: *We can clean up later.*
> **subsequently** (formal) – after an event in the past: *Subsequently, the company filed for bankruptcy*

af·ter·ef·fect /ˈæftəəˌfɛkt/ *n.* [C usually plural] a bad effect that remains after something has ended

af·ter·life /ˈæftəˌlaɪf/ *n.* [singular] the life that some people believe you have after death

af·ter·math /ˈæftəˌmæθ/ *n.* [singular] the time after an important or bad event: *the danger of fire* ***in the aftermath of*** *the earthquake* [ORIGIN: 1600—1700 *aftermath* "grass that grows after earlier grass has been cut" (16—19 centuries), from *after* + *math* "mowing" (11—20 centuries)]

af·ter·noon /ˌæftəˈnun◂ / *n.* [C,U] the period of time between 12 p.m. and the evening → MORNING, EVENING: *a class on Friday afternoon* | *We should get there about 3* ***in the afternoon.*** | *Can you go swimming* ***this afternoon*** (=today in the afternoon)? —**afternoon** *adj.*: *an afternoon snack*

af·ter·shave /ˈæftəˌʃeɪv/ *n.* [C,U] a liquid with a pleasant smell that a man puts on his face after he SHAVES

af·ter·taste /ˈæftəˌteɪst/ *n.* [C usually singular] a taste that stays in your mouth after you eat or drink something: *The wine has a bitter aftertaste.*

af·ter·thought /ˈæftəˌθɔt/ *n.* [C usually singular] something that you mention or add later because you did not think of it before: *"Bring Claire too," he added* ***as an afterthought.***

af·ter·ward /ˈæftəwəd/ *also* **afterwards** *adv.* after an event or time that has been mentioned: *We met at college but didn't get married until* ***two years afterward.***

> **THESAURUS** after, later, subsequently → AFTER³

a·gain /əˈgɛn/ *adv.* **1** one more time: *Could you say that again? I couldn't hear you.* | *The cake burned, so we had to start* ***all over again*** (=from the beginning). **2** back to the same condition, situation, or place as before: *Thanks for coming! Please come again.* | *He's home again, after studying in Europe.* **3 again and again** repeating many times: *I've tried again and again to contact her.* **4 then again** (spoken) used in order to add a fact that is different from what you have just said, or makes it seem less likely to be true: *She says she's thirty,* ***but then again*** *she might be lying.*

a·gainst /əˈgɛnst/ *prep.* **1** opposed to or disagreeing with an idea, belief, etc.: *John was against the idea of selling the house.* | *You can't do that! It's* ***against the law*** (=illegal). **2** in a way that has a bad or unfair effect: *discrimination against racial minorities* **3** fighting or competing with someone or something: *He was injured in the game against the Cowboys.* **4** touching a surface: *The cat's fur felt soft against her face.* **5** in the opposite direction from something: *At least my drive to work is against the traffic.* **6 have sth against sb/sth** to dislike or disapprove of someone or something: *I have nothing against dogs, but I don't want one myself.*

age¹ /eɪdʒ/ *n.* **1** [C,U] the number of years that someone has lived or something has existed: *Patrick is* ***my age*** (=the same age as me). | *Jamie won his first tournament* ***at the age of*** *15.* | *Most kids start kindergarten* ***at age*** *5.* | *girls who become mothers* ***at an early age*** (=very young) | *Stop messing around and* ***act your age*** (=behave in a way that is suitable for how old you are)*!* | *Judy's very smart* ***for her age*** (=compared to others of the same age). **2** [C,U] a period in someone's life: *Who will look after you in old age?* | *women of childbearing age* **3** [U] the age when you are legally old enough to do something: ***voting/drinking/retirement age*** (=when you can legally vote, drink alcohol, etc.) | *You can't buy alcohol – you're* ***under age.*** **4** [C usually singular] a particular period of history: *the modern age* | *this* ***age of*** *new technology* **5 be/come of age** to be or become old enough to be considered a responsible adult **6** [U] the state of being old: *a letter that was brown with age* **7 ages** [plural] (informal) a long time: *I haven't been there* ***for ages.*** **8 age group/bracket** the people between two particular ages, considered as a group: *a book for children in the 8–12 age group*

age² *v.* [I,T] to become or look older, or to make someone look older: *Jim has really aged.* —**aging** *adj.*: *an aging movie star*

aged¹ /eɪdʒd/ *adj.* **aged 5/15/50 etc.** 5, 15, etc. years old: *a game for children aged 12 and over*

a·ged² /ˈeɪdʒɪd/ *adj.* **1** very old: *an aged man* **2 the aged** old people

age·less /ˈeɪdʒlɪs/ *adj.* never seeming old or old-fashioned: *an ageless song*

a·gen·cy /ˈeɪdʒənsi/ *n.* (plural **agencies**) [C] **1** a business that provides a particular service: *an employment agency*

THESAURUS **organization, institution, institute, association** → ORGANIZATION

2 an organization or department, especially within a government, that does a specific job: *the UN agency responsible for helping refugees*

a·gen·da /əˈdʒɛndə/ *n.* [C] **1** a list of the subjects to be discussed at a meeting: *Let's move on to item five **on the agenda**.* **2** a list of problems or subjects that a government, organization, etc. is planning to deal with: *Health care reforms are **high on the agenda*** (=very important). [ORIGIN: 1600—1700 Latin "things to be done," from *agere* "to drive, lead, act, move, do"]

a·gent /ˈeɪdʒənt/ *n.* [C] **1** a person or company that represents another person or company in business, in their legal problems, etc.: *a literary agent* **2** someone who works for a government or police department in order to get secret information about another country or an organization: *an FBI agent* [ORIGIN: 1400—1500 Medieval Latin, from the present participle of Latin *agere* "to drive, lead, act, move, do"] → REAL ESTATE AGENT, TRAVEL AGENT

ag·gran·dize·ment /əˈgrændɪzmənt, -daɪz-/ *n.* [U] (formal) the act of trying to increase your own or a country's power or importance, in a way that people disapprove of —**aggrandize** *v.* [T]

ag·gra·vate /ˈægrəˌveɪt/ *v.* [T] **1** to make a bad situation, illness, or injury worse: *The doctors say her condition is aggravated by stress.* **2** to annoy someone: *What really aggravates me is the way she won't listen.* —**aggravating** *adj.* —**aggravation** /ˌægrəˈveɪʃən/ *n.* [C,U]

ag·gre·gate /ˈægrɪgɪt/ (Ac) *adj* [only before noun] ECONOMICS being the total amount of something, especially money: *Aggregate production at the Detroit plant is being increased to handle the extra demand.* —**aggregate** *n* [singular, U]: *The twenty hotels in the chain have an aggregate of 1,952 rooms.*

ag·gres·sion /əˈgrɛʃən/ *n.* [U] angry or threatening behavior, especially in which you attack someone: *an **act of aggression*** [ORIGIN: 1600—1700 Latin *aggressio*, from *aggredi* "to attack"]

ag·gres·sive /əˈgrɛsɪv/ *adj.* **1** very determined to succeed: *aggressive sales tactics* **2** behaving in an angry or violent way toward someone: *aggressive behavior* —**aggressively** *adv.* —**aggressiveness** *n.* [U]

ag·gres·sor /əˈgrɛsɚ/ *n.* [C] a person or country that starts a fight or war

ag·grieved /əˈgrivd/ *adj.* angry or unhappy because you think you have been treated unfairly

a·ghast /əˈgæst/ *adj.* [not before noun] suddenly feeling or looking shocked

ag·ile /ˈædʒəl, ˈædʒaɪl/ *adj.* **1** able to move quickly and easily **2** someone who has an agile mind is able to think quickly and intelligently —**agility** /əˈdʒɪləṭi/ *n.* [U]

ag·i·tate /ˈædʒəˌteɪt/ *v.* [I] (formal) to protest in order to achieve social or political changes: *workers **agitating for** higher pay* —**agitator** *n.* [C]

ag·i·tat·ed /ˈædʒəˌteɪṭɪd/ *adj.* very anxious, nervous, or upset —**agitation** /ˌædʒəˈteɪʃən/ *n.* [U]

ag·nos·tic /ægˈnɑstɪk, əg-/ *n.* [C] someone who believes that it is impossible to know whether God exists or not [ORIGIN: 1800—1900 Greek *agnostos* "unknown, unknowable," from *a-* "not" + *gnostos* "known"] —**agnostic** *adj.* —**agnosticism** /ægˈnɑstəˌsɪzəm, əg-/ *n.* [U]

a·go /əˈgoʊ/ *adj.* used in order to show how far back in the past something happened: *Jeff left for work **10 minutes/2 hours ago**. | We went to Maine once, but it was **a long time ago**. | I had the tickets **a minute ago**! | Scott's dad called **a little while ago**.*

GRAMMAR

ago, for, since

Ago, **for**, and **since** are all used to talk about time.

Ago is used with the simple past tense to say how far back in the past something happened. It follows a length of time: *Her son left home two years ago.*

For is used with the present perfect or simple past tense to say how long a situation or event has lasted. It is followed by a length of time: *She has been living in the U.S. for over twenty years. | The meeting continued for five hours.*

Since is used with the present perfect tense to say when something started. It is followed by an exact day, date, or time: *He's lived here since 2005. | I've been waiting since 4 o'clock.*

a·gon·ize /ˈægəˌnaɪz/ *v.* [I] to think about a decision very carefully and with a lot of effort: *For a long time, she had **agonized about/over** what she should do.*

a·gon·iz·ing /ˈægəˌnaɪzɪŋ/ *adj.* extremely painful or difficult: *an agonizing decision* —**agonizingly** *adv.*

ag·o·ny /ˈægəni/ *n.* (plural **agonies**) [C,U] very severe pain or suffering: *The poor guy was **in agony**.*

a·grar·i·an /əˈgrɛriən/ *adj.* relating to farming or

A

farmers: *The country has a mainly agrarian economy.* [ORIGIN: 1600—1700 Latin *agrarius*, from *ager* "field"]

a·gree /ə'gri/ *v.* **1** [I,T] to have the same opinion as someone else (ANT) **disagree**: *I* ***agree with*** *Karen. It's much too expensive.* ▶Don't say "I am agree."◀ | *Most experts* ***agree that*** *global warming is a serious problem.* | *Mike and I certainly don't* ***agree on/about*** *everything.*

THESAURUS

concur (formal) – to agree: *Most modern historians would concur with this view.*
be of the same opinion/view (formal) – to agree with another person's opinion: *They were all of the same opinion.*
share sb's views/concerns – to agree with another person's opinion: *Her teachers shared her parents' concerns about her behavior.*
be unanimous – if a group of people are unanimous about something, they all agree about it: *The jury was unanimous.* | *a unanimous decision*

2 [I,T] to say yes to a suggestion, plan, etc. (ANT) **refuse**: *She* ***agreed to*** *stay home with Charles.* **3** [I,T] to make a decision with someone after discussing something: *We* ***agreed to*** *meet next week.* | *We're still trying to* ***agree on*** *a date for the wedding.* **4** [I] if two pieces of information agree, they say the same thing: *Your story doesn't* ***agree with*** *what the police have said.* [ORIGIN: 1300—1400 Old French *agréer*, from *gré* "will, pleasure," from Latin *gratus* "pleasing"]

agree with *phr. v.* **1 agree with sth** to think that something is the right thing to do: *I don't agree with the decision at all.* **2 not agree with sb** if something that you eat or drink does not agree with you, it makes you feel sick

a·gree·a·ble /ə'griəbəl/ *adj.* **1** acceptable and able to be agreed on: *a solution that's* ***agreeable to*** *both parties* **2** (old-fashioned) pleasant —**agreeably** *adv.*: *I was agreeably surprised.*

a·greed /ə'grid/ *adj.* **1** an agreed price, method, arrangement, etc. is one that people have discussed and accepted **2 be agreed** if people are agreed, they all agree about something: *Are we all* ***agreed on*** *the date for the meeting?*

a·gree·ment /ə'grimənt/ *n.* **1** [C] an arrangement or promise to do something, made by two or more people, organizations, etc.: *a trade agreement* | *Lawyers on both sides finally* ***reached an agreement.*** **2** [U] a situation in which two or more people have the same opinion as each other (ANT) **disagreement**: *All of us were* ***in agreement.***

agri,cultural revo'lution *n.* **1 the Agricultural Revolution** HISTORY a period a long time ago when people first began to grow crops and raise farm animals on farms **2** [C] HISTORY a period when there was great change in farming methods because, for example, chemicals were introduced to farming, or horses were replaced by machines

ag·ri·cul·ture /'ægrɪ,kʌltʃɚ/ *n.* [U] the science or practice of farming [ORIGIN: 1400—1500 French, Latin *agricultura*, from *ager* "field" + *cultura* "use of land for crops"] —**agricultural** /,ægrɪ'kʌltʃərəl/ *adj.*

ah /ɑ/ *interjection* used in order to show surprise, happiness, etc. or that you have just understood something: *Ah, yes, I see what you mean.*

a·ha /ɑ'hɑ/ *interjection* said when you suddenly understand or realize something: *Aha! So that's where you've been hiding!*

a·head /ə'hɛd/ *adv.* **1** in front of someone or something: *Do you see that red convertible* ***ahead of*** *us?* | *We could see the lights of Las Vegas* ***up ahead.*** **2** in or into the future: *We* ***have*** *a busy day* ***ahead*** *of us.* | *The* ***days/weeks/months ahead*** *are going to be difficult.* | *You need to* ***plan ahead*** (=plan for the future). **3** arriving, waiting, finishing, etc. before other people: *There were two people* ***ahead of*** *me at the doctor's.* **4** making more progress or more developed than other people or things: *Jane is* ***ahead of*** *the rest of her class.* | *You need to work hard if you want to* ***get ahead.*** **5 ahead of schedule/time** earlier than planned: *The building was completed ahead of schedule.* **6 go ahead a)** (spoken) used in order to tell someone s/he can do something: *Go ahead and help yourself to some punch.* **b)** used in order to say you are going to start doing something: *I'll go ahead and start the coffee.* **7** winning in a game or competition: *The 49ers finished two games ahead of the Cowboys.* | *He's* ***ahead by*** *17 points in the polls.*

aid[1] /eɪd/ (Ac) *n.* **1** [U] money, food, or services that an organization or government gives to help people ➔ FINANCIAL AID: *The UN is sending aid to the earthquake victims.* | *Countries in the region will receive extra military and economic aid from the U.S.* **2 with/without the aid of sth** using or not using something, such as a tool, to help you do something: *The star can only be seen with the aid of a telescope.* **3 come/go to sb's aid** (formal) to help someone: *Several people came to the man's aid after he collapsed on the sidewalk.* **4** [C,U] a thing that helps you do something: *The diet aids we tested contained mostly caffeine.*

aid[2] *v.* [T] **1** (formal) to help or give support to someone

THESAURUS **help, give sb a hand (with sth), lend a hand (with sth), assist, facilitate** ➔ HELP[1]

2 aid and abet LAW to help someone do something illegal

aide, aid /eɪd/ *n.* [C] someone whose job is to help someone in a more important position: *a nurse's aide*

AIDS /eɪdz/ *n.* [U] **Acquired Immune Deficiency Syndrome** a very serious disease that stops your body from defending itself against infection

ail·ing /'eɪlɪŋ/ *adj.* weak or sick: *the country's ailing economy* | *his ailing mother*

THESAURUS **sick, ill, not very well, infirm** → SICK

ail·ment /ˈeɪlmənt/ *n.* [C] an illness that is not very serious

aim¹ /eɪm/ *v.* **1** [I] to plan or intend to achieve something: *We **aim to** finish by Friday.* | *a program **aimed at** creating more jobs* **2 aim sth at sb** to do or say something that is intended for a particular person or group: *TV commercials aimed at children* **3** [I,T] to point a weapon at a person or thing you want to hit: *A gun was **aimed at** his head.*

aim² *n.* **1** [C] something that you are trying to achieve: *What is the **aim of** their research?* | *Our **main aim** is to provide good service.* | *I moved to California **with the aim of** finding a job.*

THESAURUS **goal, objective, target** → GOAL

2 take aim to point a weapon at someone or something: *He **took aim at** the target.* **3** [U] someone's ability to hit something by throwing or shooting something at it: *Mark's aim wasn't very good.*

aim·less /ˈeɪmlɪs/ *adj.* without a clear purpose or reason —**aimlessly** *adv.*: *We wandered aimlessly around the city.*

ain't /eɪnt/ *v.* (spoken, nonstandard) a short form of "am not," "is not," "are not," "has not," or "have not"

air¹ /ɛr/ *n.* **1** [U] the gases around the Earth, which we breathe: *There was a smell of burning **in the air**.* | *Let's go outside and get some **fresh air**.* | ***air pollution*** **2** [U] the space above the ground or around things: *David threw the ball up into the air.* **3 by air** traveling by or using an airplane: *Are you shipping that box by air or by land?* **4 air travel/safety etc.** travel, safety, etc. involving or relating to airplanes: *the worst air disaster in the state's history* **5 be in the air** if a feeling is in the air, a lot of people have it: *There was tension in the air.* **6** [singular] a quality that someone or something seems to have: *There was an **air of** mystery **about** her.* **7 be up in the air** (spoken) used to say that something has not been decided yet: *Our trip is still very much up in the air.* **8** [U] (spoken) AIR CONDITIONING **9 be on/off the air** to be broadcasting, or to stop broadcasting **10 airs** [plural] a way of behaving that shows someone thinks s/he is more important than s/he really is: *You shouldn't have to **put on airs** with your own friends.* [ORIGIN: (1–2) 1200—1300 Old French, Latin *aer*, from Greek]

air² *v.* **1** [T] to broadcast a program on television or radio: *Star Trek was first aired in 1966.* **2** [T] to express your opinions publicly: *You will all get a chance to **air your views**.* **3** [I,T] *also* **air out** to let fresh air into a room

air·bag /ˈɛrbæg/ *n.* [C] a bag in a car, that fills with air to protect people in an accident

ˈair ˌbladder *n.* [C] BIOLOGY an organ inside the body of most fish, that can fill with air and allows the fish to float in water (SYN) **swim bladder**

air·borne /ˈɛrbɔrn/ *adj.* flying or carried through the air

air·brush¹ /ˈɛrbrʌʃ/ *n.* [C] a piece of equipment that uses air to put paint onto a surface

airbrush² *v.* [T] to use an airbrush to make a picture or photograph look better

airbrush sb/sth ↔ **out** *phr. v.* to remove someone or something from a picture or photograph using an airbrush

ˈair conˌditioner *n.* [C] a machine that makes the air in a room, car, etc. stay cool

ˈair conˌditioning *n.* [U] a system of machines that makes the air in a room, building, etc. stay cool —**air conditioned** *adj.*

air·craft /ˈɛrkræft/ *n.* (plural **aircraft**) [C] an airplane or other vehicle that can fly

ˈaircraft ˌcarrier *n.* [C] a ship that airplanes can fly from and land on

air·fare /ˈɛrfɛr/ *n.* [U] the price of an airplane trip

air·field /ˈɛrfild/ *n.* [C] a place where military or small airplanes fly from

ˈair force *also* **Air Force** *n.* [C usually singular] the part of a country's military organization that uses airplanes to fight

air·i·ly /ˈɛrəli/ *adv.* (literary) in a way that shows you do not think something is important: *"I know all that," she said airily.*

air·less /ˈɛrlɪs/ *adj.* without fresh air

air·lift /ˈɛrlɪft/ *n.* [C] an occasion when people or things are taken to a place by airplane because it is too difficult or dangerous to get there by road —**airlift** *v.* [T]

air·line /ˈɛrlaɪn/ *n.* [C] a business that regularly flies passengers to different places by airplane

air·lin·er /ˈɛrˌlaɪnɚ/ *n.* [C] a large airplane for passengers

air·mail /ˈɛrmeɪl/ *n.* [U] letters, packages, etc. that are sent to another country by airplane, or the system of doing this —**airmail** *adj., adv.*

ˈair ˌmarshall *n.* [C] a SKY MARSHALL

air·plane /ˈɛrpleɪn/ *n.* [C] a vehicle that flies by using wings and one or more engines (SYN) **plane**

air·port /ˈɛrpɔrt/ *n.* [C] a place where airplanes take off and land, that has buildings for passengers to wait in

A

TOPIC

At the airport, you go into the **terminal**. You **check in** (=show your ticket, leave your bags, etc.) at the **check-in counter/desk**, usually one or two hours before your **flight** leaves. You go through **airport security**, where passengers and their bags are checked for weapons, etc. You wait in the **departure lounge** until your **flight number** is called. You go through the **departure gate** before **boarding** (=getting on) the plane. The airplane **takes off** from the **runway**. When the airplane **lands**, you get off. You then go to the **baggage claim** to get your suitcases. If you have traveled from another country, you show your **passport** as you go through **immigration**, and then you **go through customs**, where your bags may be checked before leaving the airport.
➔ PASSPORT, TRAVEL

air·space /ˈɛrspeɪs/ *n.* [U] the sky above a particular country, considered to be controlled by that country

ˈair strike *n.* [C] an attack on a place, in which military aircraft drop bombs on it

air·strip /ˈɛrstrɪp/ *n.* [C] a long narrow piece of land, that airplanes can fly from and land on

air·tight /ˈɛrˌtaɪt, ˌɛrˈtaɪt/ *adj.* **1** not allowing air to get in or out: *airtight containers* **2** planned or done carefully, so that there are no problems or mistakes: *Security at the airport is airtight.*

ˈair time *n.* [U] the amount of time that a radio or television station gives to a particular subject, advertisement, etc.

air·waves /ˈɛrweɪvz/ *n.* [plural] (informal) all the programs that are broadcast on radio and television

air·way /ˈɛrweɪ/ *n.* [C] BIOLOGY the passage in your throat that you breathe through

air·y /ˈɛri/ *adj.* an airy room, building, etc. has a lot of space and fresh air

aisle /aɪl/ *n.* [C] a long passage between rows of seats in a theater, airplane, church, etc.: *Frances **walked down the aisle** (=to get married) carrying a bouquet of flowers.* ➔ *see picture at* THEATER

a·jar /əˈdʒɑr/ *adj.* [not before noun] a door or window that is ajar is not completely closed

AK the written abbreviation of ALASKA

a.k.a. *adv.* **also known as** used when giving someone's real name together with the name s/he is known by: *John Phillips, a.k.a. The Mississippi Mauler*

a·kin /əˈkɪn/ *adj.* **akin to sth** (formal) similar to something: *His music is much more akin to jazz than rock.*

AL the written abbreviation of ALABAMA

à la carte /ˌɑləˈkɑrt, ˌælə-, ˌɑlɑ-/ *adj* food in a restaurant that is à la carte has its own separate price for each dish —**à la carte** *adv*

a·lac·ri·ty /əˈlækrət̬i/ *n.* [U] (formal) speed and eagerness: *He agreed **with alacrity**.*

à la mode /ˌɑləˈmoʊd, ˌælə-, ˌɑlɑ-/ *adj* served with ice cream

a·larm[1] /əˈlɑrm/ *n.* **1** [C] a piece of equipment that makes a noise to warn people of danger: *a **fire/burglar** alarm* | *He **set off the alarm*** (=made it start ringing). | *Someone's car **alarm** was **going off*** (=making a noise). **2** [C] (informal) an alarm clock: *I've **set the alarm** for six o'clock.* **3** [U] a feeling of fear because something bad might happen: *Calm down! There's no **cause for alarm**.* **4 raise/sound the alarm** to warn everyone about something bad or dangerous that is happening: *They first sounded the alarm about the problem of nuclear waste in 1955.* [ORIGIN: 1500—1600 French *alarme*, from Old Italian *all'arme* "to the weapon"]

alarm[2] *v.* [T] to make someone feel very worried or frightened: *The news about Tony alarmed me.* —**alarmed** *adj.*

aˈlarm clock *n.* [C] a clock that will make a noise at a particular time to wake you up ➔ *see picture at* CLOCK[1]

a·larm·ing /əˈlɑrmɪŋ/ *adj.* very frightening or worrying: *an alarming increase in violent crime*

a·larm·ist /əˈlɑrmɪst/ *adj.* making people feel worried about dangers that do not exist —**alarmist** *n.* [C]

a·las /əˈlæs/ *interjection* (literary) said in order to express sadness

al·be·it /ɔlˈbiɪt, æl-/ (Ac) *conjunction* (formal) although: *Many plants can grow at low temperatures, albeit slowly.*

al·bi·no /ælˈbaɪnoʊ/ *n.* (plural **albinos**) [C] a person or animal with a GENETIC condition that makes the skin and hair extremely pale or white [ORIGIN: 1700—1800 Portuguese, Spanish, from *albo* "white"]

al·bum /ˈælbəm/ *n.* [C] **1** a group of songs or pieces of music on a record, CD, or tape **2** a book in which you put photographs, stamps, etc. that you want to keep: *a photo album* [ORIGIN: 1600—1700 Latin "unused surface for writing on," from *albus* "white"]

al·co·hol /ˈælkəˌhɔl, -ˌhɑl/ *n.* **1** [U] drinks such as beer or wine that can make you drunk: *I don't drink alcohol anymore.* **2** [C,U] a chemical substance that can be used for cleaning medical or industrial equipment [ORIGIN: 1500—1600 Medieval Latin "fine powder, liquid made by a purifying process," from Old Spanish, from Arabic *al-kuhul* "the powdered antimony (=a type of metal)"]

al·co·hol·ic[1] /ˌælkəˈhɔlɪk◂, -ˈhɑ-/ *n.* [C] someone who cannot stop the habit of drinking too much alcohol

alcoholic[2] *adj.* containing alcohol, or relating to alcohol (ANT) **nonalcoholic**: *an alcoholic beverage*

al·co·hol·ism /ˈælkəhɔˌlɪzəm, -hɑ-/ *n.* [U] the medical condition of being an alcoholic

al·cove /'ælkoʊv/ *n.* [C] a small place in a wall of a room, that is built further back than the rest of the wall [ORIGIN: 1500—1600 French *alcôve*, from Spanish *alcoba*, from Arabic *al-qubbah* "the arch"]

al·der·man /'ɔldə·mən/ *n.* (plural **aldermen** /-mən/) [C] POLITICS a city or town government official who is elected

ale /eɪl/ *n.* [U] a type of beer

a·lert¹ /ə'lət/ *adj.* **1** always watching and ready to notice anything strange, unusual, dangerous, etc.: *Cyclists must always be* ***alert to*** *the dangers on a busy road.* **2** able to think quickly and clearly: *I didn't feel alert enough to do any more work.* [ORIGIN: 1500—1600 French *alerte*, from Italian *all'erta* "on the watch"]

alert² *v.* [T] to warn someone of a problem or of possible danger: *As soon as we suspected it was a bomb, we alerted the police.*

alert³ *n.* **1 be on the alert** to be ready to notice and deal with a problem: *Police are* ***on the alert for*** *trouble.* **2** [C] a warning to be ready for possible danger: *a flood alert*

al·fal·fa sprout /æl'fælfə spraʊt/ *n.* [C] a very small plant, eaten raw as a vegetable in SALADS

al·gae /'ældʒi/ *n.* [U] BIOLOGY a very simple plant without stems or leaves that lives in or near water [ORIGIN: 1500—1600 Latin *alga* "seaweed"]

al·gal bloom /ˌælgəl 'blum/ *n.* [U] BIOLOGY a sudden and great increase in the amount of algae growing on or near the surface of a body of fresh water, which uses up important supplies of oxygen in the water

al·ge·bra /'ældʒəbrə/ *n.* [U] MATH a type of mathematics that uses letters and signs to represent numbers and values [ORIGIN: 1500—1600 Medieval Latin, Arabic *al-jabr* "the reduction"] —**algebraic** /ˌældʒə'breɪ-ɪk/ *adj.*

al·go·rithm /'ælgəˌrɪðəm/ *n.* [C] IT a set of mathematical instructions that are done in a particular order

a·li·as¹ /'eɪliəs, 'eɪlyəs/ *prep.* used when giving a criminal's real name together with the name s/he uses: *the spy Margaret Zelle, alias Mata Hari* [ORIGIN: 1400—1500 Latin "otherwise"]

alias² *n.* [C] a false name, usually used by a criminal

al·i·bi /'æləbaɪ/ *n.* [C] LAW something that proves that someone was not where a crime happened and is therefore not guilty of the crime: *He* ***had*** *a perfect* ***alibi*** *and the police let him go.* [ORIGIN: 1600—1700 Latin "somewhere else"]

a·li·en¹ /'eɪliən, 'eɪlyən/ *adj.* **1** very different or strange: *The landscape was* ***alien to*** *me.* **2** relating to creatures from other worlds [ORIGIN: 1300—1400 Old French, Latin *alienus*, from *alius* "other"]

alien² *n.* [C] **1** someone who lives or works in a country but is not a citizen: ***illegal aliens*** *entering the country* **2** in stories, a creature that comes from another world

a·li·en·ate /'eɪliəˌneɪt, 'eɪlyə-/ *v.* [T] to make someone stop feeling friendly or stop feeling like s/he belongs in a group: *policies that will alienate some voters* —**alienation** /ˌeɪliə'neɪʃən, ˌeɪlyə-/ *n.* [U]

a·light¹ /ə'laɪt/ *adj.* **1** burning: *Several cars were* ***set alight*** *by rioters.* **2** someone whose face or eyes are alight is happy or excited

alight² *v.* [I] (formal) if a bird, insect, etc. alights on something, it stops flying in order to stand on it

a·lign /ə'laɪn/ *v.* [I,T] **1** to work together with another person or group because you have the same aims: *Five Democrats have* ***aligned*** *themselves* ***with*** *the Republicans on this issue.* **2** to arrange something so that it is in the same line as something else: *It looks like your wheels need aligning.* —**alignment** *n.* [C,U]

a·like¹ /ə'laɪk/ *adj.* almost exactly the same SYN **similar**: *She and her sister are very alike.*

THESAURUS **similar, like, identical, matching** → SIMILAR

alike² *adv.* **1** in a similar way, or in the same way: *The twins were dressed alike.* **2** in a way that includes both the people, groups, or things you have mentioned: *The rule was criticized by teachers and students alike.*

al·i·men·tary ca·nal /æləˌmɛntri kə'næl/ *n.* [C] BIOLOGY the tube in your body that takes food through your body from your mouth to your ANUS

al·i·mo·ny /'æləˌmoʊni/ *n.* [U] LAW money that someone has to pay regularly to his/her former wife or husband after a DIVORCE

a·live /ə'laɪv/ *adj.* **1** living and not dead: *Only one passenger was still alive.* | *the food you need to* ***stay alive*** | *He called his mother to tell her he was* ***alive and well.*** **2** continuing to exist: *Let's* ***keep*** *the traditions of the Inuit* ***alive.*** **3** full of activity or interest: *The streets* ***come alive*** *after ten o'clock.* | *Her eyes were* ***alive with*** *mischief.* [ORIGIN: Old English *on life* "in life"]

al·ka·li /'ælkəˌlaɪ/ *n.* [C,U] CHEMISTRY a substance that forms a chemical salt when combined with an acid [ORIGIN: 1300—1400 Medieval Latin, Arabic *al-qili* "the ashes (of a particular plant from which a type of alkali was obtained)"]

'alkali ˌmetal *n.* [C] CHEMISTRY any of the six soft white metal ELEMENTS that appear in group 1 of the PERIODIC TABLE. They are LITHIUM, SODIUM, POTASSIUM, RUBIDIUM, CESIUM, and FRANCIUM.

al·ka·line /'ælkəlɪn, -ˌlaɪn/ *adj.* CHEMISTRY containing an alkali

ˌalkaline 'earth ˌmetal *n.* [C] CHEMISTRY any of the six metal ELEMENTS that appear in group 2 of the PERIODIC TABLE. They are BERYLLIUM, MAGNESIUM, CALCIUM, STRONTIUM, BARIUM, and RADIUM.

A

ˌalkaline soˈlution *n.* [C] CHEMISTRY a liquid containing an alkali, which has a PH of more than 7 and will turn red LITMUS paper blue

all¹ /ɔl/ *determiner, pron.* **1** the whole of an amount, time, or thing: *Have you done all your homework?* | *We've spent it all.* | *I've been waiting* ***all day/week.*** | *Bill talks about work* ***all the time*** (=very often or too much). | *Professor Ito explained* ***all of*** *this.* **2** every one of a group of things or people: *Answer all twenty questions.* | *Have you told them all?* | *This is important to* ***all of*** *us.* | *She makes* ***almost all (of)*** *her own clothes.* **3** the only thing or things: *All I want is a cup of coffee.* **4 all kinds/sorts of sth** very many different types of things, people, or places: *The students are reading all kinds of books.* **5 for all...** in spite of a particular fact or situation: *For all his faults, he's a good father.* **6 at all** used in questions to mean "in any way": *Did the new drugs help her at all?* **7 not at all** not in any way: *The snow didn't affect us at all.* **8 in all** including every thing or person: *In all, there were 28 people there.* **9 all in all** considering everything: *All in all, it was a successful event.*

GRAMMAR

Use **all** with a singular verb when you are using an uncountable noun: *I've spent all my money.* Use **all** with a plural verb when you are using a plural noun form: *All my friends are coming to the party.* → EVERY

all² *adv.* **1** completely: *I walked all alone.* | *The judges were dressed all in black.* **2 all over a)** everywhere on a surface or in a place: *There was stuff all over the floor.* | *We looked* ***all over the place*** *for it.* **b)** finished: *Thank goodness it's all over; it was awful.* **3 all too** used in order to mean "very" when talking about a bad situation: *It's all too easy to blame parents for their children's problems.* **4** used in order to say that both sides have the same number of points in a game: *The score was 10–all at half time.* **5 all but** almost completely: *It was all but impossible to contact him.* **6 all along** from the beginning and all of the time after that: *I knew all along that I couldn't trust him.* **7 sb was all...** (spoken) used in order to report what someone said or did, when telling a story: *She was all, "Don't do it that way!"* **8 sb/sth is not all that** (spoken) used in order to say that someone or something is not very attractive or desirable: *Why him? He's not all that.* → **after all** *at* AFTER¹, **all of a sudden** *at* SUDDEN

Al·lah /ˈælə, ˈɑlə/ *n.* the Muslim name for God

ˌall-Aˈmerican *adj.* **1** typical of America or Americans: *an all-American girl* **2** belonging to a group of players who have been chosen as the best in their sport in college

ˌall-aˈround *adj.* good at doing many different things, especially in sports: *the best all-around player*

al·lay /əˈleɪ/ *v.* **allay sb's fears/concerns/worries etc.** to make someone feel less afraid, worried, etc.

al·le·ga·tion /ˌæləˈgeɪʃən/ *n.* [C] a statement that someone has done something illegal, which has not been proved: ***allegations of*** *child abuse*

THESAURUS **accusation, charge, complaint** → ACCUSATION

al·lege /əˈlɛdʒ/ *v.* [T] to say that something is true, though it has not been proved: *Three students* ***alleged that*** *they had been expelled unfairly.*

THESAURUS **accuse, charge** → ACCUSE

al·leged /əˈlɛdʒd/ *adj.* supposed to be true, but not proven: *the group's alleged connections with organized crime*

al·leg·ed·ly /əˈlɛdʒɪdli/ *adv.* used when reporting what other people say is true, although it has not been proved: *Felix allegedly offered him a bribe.*

al·le·giance /əˈlidʒəns/ *n.* [C,U] loyalty to or support for a leader, country, belief, etc.: *The class stood up and* ***pledged allegiance*** *to the flag of the United States of America.*

al·le·go·ry /ˈæləˌgɔri/ *n.* (plural **allegories**) [C,U] ENG. LANG. ARTS a story, poem, painting, etc. in which the events and characters represent good and bad qualities —**allegorical** /ˌæləˈgɔrɪkəl/ *adj.*

al·lele /əˈlil/ *also* **al·le·lo·morph** /əˈliləˌmɔrf/ *n.* [C] BIOLOGY one of a pair or series of GENEs that have a specific position on a CHROMOSOME and control which features an animal or plant gets from its parents

al·le·lu·ia /ˌæləˈluyə/ *interjection* HALLELUJAH

al·ler·gic /əˈlɚdʒɪk/ *adj.* **1** BIOLOGY having an allergy: *Jess is* ***allergic to*** *milk.* **2** BIOLOGY caused by an allergy: *an* ***allergic reaction*** *to the bee sting*

al·ler·gy /ˈælɚdʒi/ *n.* (plural **allergies**) [C] BIOLOGY a condition that makes you sick when you eat, touch, or breathe a particular thing: *He* ***has an allergy to*** *cats.*

al·le·vi·ate /əˈliviˌeɪt/ *v.* [T] to make something less bad or severe: *Aspirin should alleviate the pain.* | *The road was built to alleviate traffic problems.*

THESAURUS **reduce, relieve, ease, lessen** → REDUCE

al·ley /ˈæli/ *also* **al·ley·way** /ˈæliˌweɪ/ *n.* [C] a narrow street between buildings

al·li·ance /əˈlaɪəns/ *n.* [C] a close agreement or connection between people, countries, etc.: *the NATO alliance*

al·lied /əˈlaɪd, ˈælaɪd/ *adj.* joined or closely related, especially by a political or military agreement: *allied forces* | *The government was* ***allied with*** *oil companies.*

al·li·ga·tor /ˈæləˌgeɪtɚ/ *n.* [C] a large REPTILE (=type of animal) with a long body, a long mouth, and sharp teeth that lives in hot wet areas of the

U.S. and China [ORIGIN: 1500—1600 Spanish *el lagarto* "the lizard," from Latin *lacerta*]

ˌall-inˈclusive *adj.* including everything: *The firm will handle all your stock investments for an all-inclusive fee.*

al·lit·e·ra·tion /əˌlɪt̬əˈreɪʃən/ *n.* [U] ENG. LANG. ARTS the use of several words close together that begin with the same CONSONANT, for example "wet and windy weather", used in order to produce a special effect in writing or poetry [ORIGIN: 1600—1700 Latin *litera* "letter"]

ˌall-ˈnighter *n.* [C] (informal) an occasion when you spend the whole night studying or writing

al·lo·cate /ˈæləˌkeɪt/ (Ac) *v.* [T] to decide to use a particular amount of money, time, etc. for a particular purpose: *The state plans to increase the funding* (=money) ***allocated to*** *low-income housing.* [ORIGIN: 1600—1700 Medieval Latin, past participle of *allocare*, from Latin *ad-* "to" + *locare* "to place"] **—allocation** /ˌæləˈkeɪʃən/ *n.* [U]: *the allocation of educational resources*

al·lot /əˈlɑt/ *v.* (**allotted**, **allotting**) [T] to use a particular amount of time for something, or give a particular share of something to someone or something: *Each person was allotted four tickets.* | *Two hours were* ***allotted to*** *each interview.* → GIVE[1] **—allotment** *n.* [C,U]

al·lo·trope /ˈæləˌtroʊp/ *n.* [C] CHEMISTRY one of the several different physical forms or structures of the same ELEMENT (=simple chemical substance with only one type of atom). For example, coal and DIAMONDs are allotropes of CARBON.

al·low /əˈlaʊ/ *v.* **1** [T] to give someone permission to do something, have something, or go somewhere: *Smoking is not allowed.* | *Reporters were allowed access to the files.* | *Those over 18 are* ***allowed to*** *vote.* | *The cat's not* ***allowed in*** *the bedroom.*

THESAURUS

allow is used in both formal and informal English: *You're not allowed to use a calculator during the test.*
let is informal and is used a lot in spoken English: *Will your Mom let you come to the party?*
permit is formal and is mainly used in written English: *Smoking is not permitted in this building.*
authorize (formal) – to give official permission for something: *In the early 1900s, rangers were authorized to trap wolves in national forests.*
sanction (formal) – to officially accept or allow something: *The U.N. refused to sanction the use of force.*
condone (formal) – to accept or allow behavior that most people think is wrong: *I cannot condone the use of violence.*

2 [I,T] to make it possible for something to happen or for someone to do something: *The plan preserves the state's wild areas while allowing economic growth.* | *The waiting period* ***allows for*** *a background check.* **3** [T] to make sure you have enough time, money, etc. for a particular purpose: *Allow ten days for delivery.* | *I allow myself $75 a week for groceries.*

allow for sth *phr. v.* to consider the possible effects of something and make plans to deal with it: *Even allowing for delays, we should finish early.*

al·low·a·ble /əˈlaʊəbəl/ *adj.* acceptable according to particular rules: *the maximum allowable dosage of the drug*

al·low·ance /əˈlaʊəns/ *n.* **1** [C,U] money you are given regularly or for a special reason: *Do your kids get an allowance?* | *a travel allowance* **2** [C usually singular] an amount of something that is acceptable or safe: *a baggage allowance* | *the recommended daily allowance of vitamin C* **3 make allowances (for sb)** to consider something when dealing with someone's behavior

al·loy /ˈælɔɪ/ *n.* [C] CHEMISTRY a metal that is made by mixing two or more different metals or a metal and a substance that is not a metal: *The pipes are made of an alloy of copper and zinc.*

all ˈright *adj., adv.* (spoken) **1** acceptable, but not excellent: *"How was the movie?" "It was all right."* **2** not hurt, not upset, or not having problems: *Sue, are you all right?* | *The press conference* ***went all right*** (=happened without any problems). **3** used in order to say you agree with a plan, suggestion, etc.: *"Let's go." "All right."* **4 that's all right a)** used in order to reply when someone thanks you: *"Thanks for your help!" "That's all right."* **b)** used in order to tell someone you are not angry when s/he says s/he is sorry: *"Sorry I'm late!" "That's all right."* **5** used in order to say or ask whether something is convenient for you: *Would Thursday morning be all right?* **6** used in order to ask or give permission to do something: ***Is it all right if*** *I close the window?* | *It's* ***all right with*** *me.* **7** used in order to ask if someone has understood something: *Put the cards into three piles, all right?* **8 it's all right** used in order to make someone feel less afraid or worried: *It's all right, Mommy's here.* **9** used in order to get someone's attention, introduce a new subject, or end a conversation: *All right, quiet down now.* **10** used in order to say you are happy about something: *"I got the job!" "All right!"* **11 be doing all right** to be successful in your job or life

USAGE

All right is the usual way of spelling this phrase: *Are you all right?* | *The movie was all right.*
Alright is very informal, and most teachers think that it is not correct.

ˈall-time *adj.* **1 all-time high/low/best etc.** the highest, lowest, etc. level there has ever been: *The stock reached an all-time high last week.* **2 all-time record/classic etc.** the best thing of its type ever known: *the NHL's all-time leading goal scorer*

al·lude /əˈlud/ *v.*

allude to sb/sth *phr. v.* (formal) to talk about something in a way that is not direct

A

al·lure /ə'lʊr/ *n.* [singular, U] a pleasant or exciting quality that attracts people: *the* ***allure of*** *travel* —**alluring** *adj.*

al·lu·sion /ə'luʒən/ *n.* [C,U] (formal) something said or written that mentions a subject, person, etc. in a way that is not direct: *His poetry is full of* ***allusions to*** *the Bible.* —**allusive** /ə'lusɪv/ *adj.*

al·lu·vi·um /ə'luviəm/ *n.* [U] EARTH SCIENCES soil left by rivers, lakes, floods, etc.

al·ly[1] /ə'laɪ, 'ælaɪ/ *n.* (plural **allies**) [C] a person or country that helps another, especially in war: *the U.S. and its European allies* [ORIGIN: 1300—1400 Old French *alier*, from Latin *alligare*, from *ad-* "to" + *ligare* "to tie"]

ally[2] *v.* (**allied**, **allies**) **ally yourself to/with sb/sth** to join with other people or countries to help each other

al·ma ma·ter /ˌælmə 'mɑt̬ɚ, ˌɑl-/ *n.* [singular, U] (formal) **1** the school, college, or university where you used to study **2** the official song of a school, college, or university [ORIGIN: 1700—1800 a Latin phrase meaning "generous mother"]

al·ma·nac /'ɔlməˌnæk/ *n.* [C] **1** a book giving a list of the days of a year, times the Sun rises and sets, changes in the moon, etc. **2** a book giving information about a particular subject or activity: *the Almanac of American Politics*

al·might·y /ɔl'maɪt̬i/ *adj.* **1** having the power to do anything: *Almighty God* **2** very important or powerful: *the almighty dollar*

al·mond /'ɑmənd, 'æm-/ *n.* [C] a flat white nut with pale brown skin and a slightly sweet taste, or the tree on which these nuts grow

al·most /'ɔlmoʊst, ɔl'moʊst/ *adv.* nearly but not quite: *Are we almost there?* | *Supper's almost ready.* | *We've spent* ***almost all*** *the money.* | *They practice* ***almost every*** *day.*

a·loft /ə'lɔft/ *adv.* (literary) high up in the air

a·lo·ha /ə'loʊhɑ/ *interjection* used in order to say hello or goodbye in Hawaii

a·lone /ə'loʊn/ *adj., adv.* **1** without any other people: *She lives alone.* | *They had* ***left*** *their son* ***alone.*** | *I was* ***all alone*** *in a strange city.*

THESAURUS

on your own – without anyone helping you: *Finally, the baby started breathing on her own.*
(all) by yourself – without anyone helping you: *She raised four children by herself.*
single-handedly – done by one person, with no help from anyone else: *He almost single-handedly is responsible for the business's success.*
solo – done alone, without anyone else helping you: *Lindbergh's solo flight across the Atlantic Ocean*
independently – without other people's help or control: *The children are encouraged to work independently on the projects.*
unaided (formal) – without help: *She was no longer able to breathe unaided.*

2 used in order to emphasize that only one person can do something, that something belongs to only one person, etc.: *He alone can do the job.* → **leave sb alone** *at* LEAVE[1], **leave sth alone** *at* LEAVE[1], **let alone** *at* LET

a·long[1] /ə'lɔŋ/ *prep.* **1** from one place on something such as a line, road, or edge toward the other end of it: *We took a walk along the river.* | *She looked anxiously along the line of faces.* **2** in a line next to or on something: *a fence along the road* | *photographs arranged along the wall* **3** at a particular place on something, usually something long: *The house is somewhere along this road.* **4 along the way/line** during a process or experience, or during someone's life: *The company has had more successes than failures along the way.*

along[2] *adv.* **1** going forward: *I was driving along, listening to the radio.* **2 go/come/be along** to go to, come to, or be in the place where something is happening: *You're welcome to come along.* **3 take/bring sb/sth along** to take someone or something with you to a place: *Why don't you bring your guitar along?* **4 along with sb/sth** in addition to and at the same time as someone or something else: *Many heart patients now take aspirin, along with other drugs.* → **all along** *at* ALL[2], **get along** *at* GET, **come along** *at* COME

a·long·side /əˌlɔŋ'saɪd/ *adv., prep.* **1** close to and in line with the edge of something: *a boat tied up alongside the dock* **2** used in order to say that people or things do something or exist together: *The children were playing alongside each other.*

a·loof /ə'luf/ *adj., adv.* apart from other people and deliberately not doing things with them: *He* ***held himself*** *somewhat* ***aloof*** *from the others.*

a·loud /ə'laʊd/ *adv.* in a voice that you can hear: *Mama* ***read aloud*** *to us.* | *I was just* ***thinking aloud*** (=saying what I was thinking). | *The pain made him* ***cry aloud.***

al·pha·bet /'ælfəˌbɛt/ *n.* [C] ENG. LANG. ARTS a set of letters in a particular order, used in writing a language: *the Greek alphabet* [ORIGIN: 1500—1600 Late Latin *alphabetum*, from Greek, from *alpha* + *beta*]

al·pha·bet·i·cal /ˌælfə'bɛt̬ɪkəl/ *adj.* arranged according to the letters of the alphabet: *books* ***in alphabetical order*** —**alphabetically** *adv.*

'alpha ˌparticle *n.* [C] PHYSICS a PARTICLE (=a very small piece of matter) with a positive charge, that consists of two PROTONS and two NEUTRONS and is sent out by some RADIOACTIVE substances

al·pine /'ælpaɪn/ *adj.* EARTH SCIENCES being in or related to the Alps or other high mountains: *alpine flowers*

al·read·y /ɔl'rɛdi/ *adv.* **1** before a particular time: *By the time he arrived, the room was already crowded.* **2** before: *You already told me that.*

A

USAGE

Already is used in order to talk about something that has happened: *By the time we arrived, the concert had already started.*
All ready is used in order to say that someone is ready to do something, or that something is completely prepared: *We're all ready to go now.* | *Dinner is all ready.*

3 sooner than expected: *I've already forgotten her number.* | *Is he leaving already?* **4** (spoken) said in order to emphasize that you are annoyed: *Make up your mind already!*

al·so /'ɔlsoʊ/ *adv.* **1** in addition SYN **too**: *She speaks perfect English. She also speaks French and Spanish.* | *This question is* ***not only*** *about writing* ***but also*** *about reading.* **2** used in order to say that the same thing is true about another person or thing: *My father also died of a heart attack.*

USAGE

Also is more formal than **too**, and is used more often in writing than in speech: *Electric cars are cheap to run and they are also good for the environment.*
Too and **as well** are less formal and more often used in spoken English. They are used at the end of a sentence: *My sister wants to come too.* | *I like dance music, but I listen to other kinds of music as well.*
In negative sentences, use **either** rather than **also** or **too**. Do not say "Tom was also not hungry." or "Tom was not hungry too." Say "Tom was not hungry either."

GRAMMAR

Use **also** before a verb, unless the verb is "be": *He also plays tennis.* Use **also** after the verb "be": *His wife is also a doctor.*
If there are two or more verbs together, one of which is an auxiliary verb, **also** comes after the first one: *Patty can also speak Italian.*

al·tar /'ɔltɚ/ *n.* [C] a table or raised structure used in a religious ceremony

al·ter /'ɔltɚ/ Ac *v.* [I,T] to change, or to make someone or something change: *The design of the aircraft's wings had to be altered slightly.* | *The discovery of penicillin altered the course of medical history.* [ORIGIN: 1300—1400 French *altérer*, from Medieval Latin *alterare*, from Latin *alter* "other"]

THESAURUS **change, adapt, adjust, modify, revise, amend, transform** → CHANGE¹

al·ter·a·tion /ˌɔltə'reɪʃən/ Ac *n.* [C] a change in something or someone, that him, her, or it slightly different: *We're planning to* ***make*** *a few* ***alterations to*** *the house.* | *The bacteria can cause* ***alterations in*** *the DNA.*

al·ter·ca·tion /ˌɔltɚ'keɪʃən/ *n.* [C] (formal) a noisy argument

al·ter e·go /ˌæltɚ 'igoʊ, ˌɔl-/ *n.* [C] a person or character in a book who represents part of someone's character, or who has similar opinions, attitudes, etc.: *Gissing used his fictional alter ego to attack Victorian morals.*

al·ter·nate¹ /'ɔltɚˌneɪt/ Ac *v.* [I,T] if two things alternate, or if you alternate them, they happen one after the other in a repeated pattern: *Periods of laziness* ***alternated with*** *periods of frantic activity.* | *I tend to* ***alternate between*** *eating too much and eating too little.* [ORIGIN: 1500—1600 Latin, past participle of *alternare* "to alternate," from *alternus* "alternate," from *alter* "other"] **—alternation** /ˌɔltɚ'neɪʃən/ *n.* [C,U]

al·ter·nate² /'ɔltɚnɪt/ Ac *adj.* **1** able to be used instead of something or someone else SYN **alternative**: *We had to take an alternate route to the airport.* **2** happening in a regular way, first one thing and then the other thing: *She visits her aunt on alternate Saturdays.*

ˌalternating 'current *n.* [U] PHYSICS (*abbreviation* **AC**) a flow of electricity that regularly changes direction very quickly, for example the current used in buildings for electrical equipment → DIRECT CURRENT

al·ter·na·tive¹ /ɔl'tɚnətɪv/ Ac *adj.* **1** an alternative plan, idea, etc. can be used instead of another one: *We decided to take an alternative way home.* **2** different from what is usual or accepted: *Alternative medicine may cure some things, but not diseases like cancer.* | *Before the oil runs out, we will have to find alternative sources of energy.* **—alternatively** *adv.*

alternative² *n.* [C] something you can choose to do or use instead of something else: *This costs less than the other alternative.* | *There was no* ***alternative to*** *the use of force.*

al·ter·na·tor /'ɔltɚˌneɪtɚ/ *n.* [C] PHYSICS a GENERATOR (=machine that produces electricity) that produces an ALTERNATING CURRENT, used in cars, trucks, etc.

al·though /ɔl'ðoʊ/ *conjunction* **1** in spite of the fact that SYN **though**: *Although the car's old, it runs well.*

THESAURUS

however – used when saying that something seems different or surprising after your previous statement: *March is usually really cold. This year, however, the weather was surprisingly mild.*
in spite of/despite – even though something happens or is true: *We enjoyed the day, in spite of all the problems with the car.* | *Despite the heat, he still refused to take off his jacket.*
nevertheless/nonetheless – in spite of what has just been mentioned: *A lot of people are coming to the meeting. Nevertheless, there should be enough seats for everyone.*

2 but: *No, I'll do it, although I appreciate your offer.*

A

al·ti·tude /ˈæltəˌtud/ *n.* [C,U] the height of something above sea level: *aircraft flying **at high/low altitude***

al·to /ˈæltoʊ/ *n.* (plural **altos**) [C,U] ENG. LANG. ARTS a female singer with a low voice, or the line of a piece of music that this person sings

al·to·geth·er /ˌɔltəˈgɛðɚ, ˈɔltəˌgɛðɚ/ *adv.* **1** completely – used in order to emphasize what you are saying: *He uses an altogether different method.* | *Smoking in public buildings is banned altogether.* **2** considering everything or the whole amount: *There were five people altogether.* | *It did rain a lot, but altogether it was a good trip.*

USAGE

Use **altogether** to talk about the total amount or number of something: *The vacation cost about $2,000 altogether.*
Use **all together** to say that things or people are together in a group: *Try to keep the puzzle pieces all together.*

al·tru·ism /ˈæltruˌɪzəm/ *n.* [U] the practice of caring about the needs of other people before dealing with your own needs —**altruist** *n.* [C] —**altruistic** /ˌæltruˈɪstɪk◂ / *adj.*

a·lu·mi·num /əˈlumənəm/ *n.* [U] CHEMISTRY a silver-white metal that is an ELEMENT, and that is light and easily bent

a·lum·ni /əˈlʌmnaɪ/ *n.* [plural] the former students of a school, college, or university ➔ STUDENT

al·ve·o·lus /ælˈviələs/ *n.* (plural **alveoli**) [C] BIOLOGY one of the very many small hollow spaces inside your lungs, through which oxygen enters and CARBON DIOXIDE leaves ➔ *see picture at* LUNG

al·ways /ˈɔlweɪz, -wiz, -wɪz/ *adv.* **1** at all times, or each time: *Always lock the doors.* | *We always want to improve our service.*

THESAURUS

permanently – at all times: *The door is permanently locked.*
all the time/the whole time – continuously and often: *The baby cries all the time.*
constantly – always or regularly: *You're constantly complaining about everything!*
continuously (formal) – without stopping or pausing: *The tower clock has been working continuously for 270 years.*
invariably (formal) – always, without ever changing: *The disease almost invariably ends in death.*

2 for a very long time: *He said that he'd always love her.* | *She always dreamed of going to Paris.*

THESAURUS

permanently – forever or for a very long time: *His eyesight may be permanently damaged.*
forever – for all time in the future: *I could stay here forever.*
for life – for the rest of your life: *Marriage is supposed to be for life.*
for good – used to say that a change is permanent: *I've given up smoking for good.*

3 happening often, especially in an annoying way: *The stupid car is always breaking down!* **4 as always** as is usual or expected: *Her singing, as always, was wonderful.* **5 you can/could always...** (spoken) said in order to make a polite suggestion: *You could always try calling her.* [ORIGIN: 1300—1400 Old English *ealne weg* "all the way"]

GRAMMAR

Use **always** before a verb, unless the verb is "be": *I always have my driver's license with me.*
Use **always** after the verb "be": *She's always very helpful.*
If there are two or more verbs together, **always** comes after the first one: *He had always dreamed of being a pilot.*

Alz·heim·er's Dis·ease /ˈɑltshaɪmɚz dɪˌziz, ˈɑltsaɪ-, ˈæl-/ *also* **Alzheimer's** *n.* [U] BIOLOGY a disease that gradually destroys parts of the brain, especially in older people, so that they forget things and lose their ability to take care of themselves

AM /ˌeɪ ˈɛm◂ / *n* [U] **amplitude modulation** a system of broadcasting radio programs, in which the strength of the radio waves changes ➔ FM

am /m, əm; *strong* æm/ *v.* the first person singular and present tense of the verb BE

a.m. /ˌeɪ ˈɛm/ used when talking about times that are between MIDNIGHT and NOON ➔ P.M.: *I start work at 9:00 a.m.* [ORIGIN: 1700—1800 Latin *ante meridiem* "before noon"]

a·mal·gam·ate /əˈmælgəˌmeɪt/ *v.* (formal) **1** [I,T] to join in order to form one larger organization **2** [T] to combine two or more things to make one thing —**amalgamation** /əˌmælgəˈmeɪʃən/ *n.* [C,U]

a·mass /əˈmæs/ *v.* [T] to gather together or collect money or information in large amounts: *He had amassed a fortune.*

am·a·teur[1] /ˈæmətʃɚ/ *adj.* [only before noun] doing something for enjoyment, but not for money: *an amateur musician* [ORIGIN: 1700—1800 French, Latin *amator* "lover," from *amare* "to love"]

amateur[2] *n.* [C] **1** someone who does something because s/he enjoys it, but not for money (ANT) **professional** **2** someone who does not have experience or skill in a particular activity: *There's nothing worse than watching a blurred video, shot by an amateur.* —**amateurish** /ˌæməˈtʃʊrɪʃ/ *adj.*

a·maze /əˈmeɪz/ *v.* [T] to surprise someone very much: *He made a shot that amazed everyone.* | *You **never cease to amaze me*** (=always surprise me).

a·mazed /əˈmeɪzd/ *adj.* very surprised: *We were **amazed at** how quickly the kids learned.* | *I'm **amazed (that)** you remember him.* | *Many people were **amazed to** learn that he had grown up poor.*

THESAURUS surprised, astonished, astounded, flabbergasted, stunned, dumbfounded ➔ SURPRISED

a·maze·ment /ə'meɪzmənt/ *n.* [U] a feeling of great surprise: *We watched* ***in/with amazement****.*

a·maz·ing /ə'meɪzɪŋ/ *adj.* making someone feel very surprised, often because something is very good or very unexpected: *an amazing coincidence* | ***It's amazing how*** *many things have gone wrong.* —**amazingly** *adv.*

THESAURUS surprising, astonishing, astounding, staggering, stunning ➔ SURPRISING

am·bas·sa·dor /æm'bæsədɚ, əm-/ *n.* [C] an important official who represents his/her country in another country: *the Mexican* ***ambassador to*** *Canada* [ORIGIN: 1300—1400 French *ambassadeur*, from Latin *ambactus* "vassal"] —**ambassadorial** /æmˌbæsə'dɔriəl/ *adj.*

am·bi·ance, **ambience** /'æmbiəns, 'ɑmbiɑns/ *n.* [U] the way a place makes you feel: *the restaurant's friendly ambiance*

am·bi·dex·trous /ˌæmbɪ'dɛkstrəs/ *adj.* able to use both hands with equal skill

am·bi·gu·i·ty /ˌæmbə'gyuəṭi/ *n.* (plural **ambiguities**) [C,U] the state of being unclear or confusing, or something that produces this effect: *the ambiguity of her words* | *The report contains significant ambiguities.*

am·big·u·ous /æm'bɪgyuəs/ (Ac) *adj.* something that is ambiguous is confusing or not clear because it can be understood in more than one way: *The message being given to young people is ambiguous and unclear.* | *an ambiguous question* [ORIGIN: 1500—1600 Latin *ambiguus*, from *ambigere* "to wander around," from *ambi-* "about" + *agere* "to drive"]

am·bi·tion /æm'bɪʃən/ *n.* **1** [C] a strong desire to do or achieve something: *Her* ***ambition*** *is* ***to*** *climb Mount Everest.* | *She seems determined to* ***achieve*** *all her* ***ambitions****.* **2** [U] the quality of being determined to succeed: *Saul* ***has*** *no* ***ambition*** *at all.*

am·bi·tious /æm'bɪʃəs/ *adj.* **1** needing a lot of skill and effort to achieve something: *an ambitious mission to Mars* **2** having a strong desire to be successful or powerful: *a young and ambitious man* —**ambitiously** *adv.*

am·biv·a·lent /æm'bɪvələnt/ *adj.* not sure whether you want or like something or not: *His wife was* ***ambivalent about*** *having a child.* [ORIGIN: 1900—2000 *ambi-* "both" + *-valent* "having a particular value"] —**ambivalence** *n.* [U]

am·ble /'æmbəl/ *v.* [I] to walk slowly in a relaxed way: *We* ***ambled along/down*** *the beach.*

THESAURUS walk, stroll ➔ WALK[1]

am·bu·lance /'æmbyələns/ *n.* [C] a special vehicle for taking sick or injured people to the hospital: *Somebody should* ***call an ambulance****.* [ORIGIN: 1800—1900 French "place near a battle, where wounds are treated," from *ambulant* "walking," from Latin *ambulare*]

am·bush[1] /'æmbʊʃ/ *n.* [C] a sudden attack on someone by people who have been hiding and waiting to attack: *Two soldiers were killed in an ambush.* [ORIGIN: 1300—1400 Old French *embuschier*, from *en* "in" + *busche* "wood"] ➔ ATTACK[1]

ambush[2] *v.* [T] to attack someone from a place where you have been hiding

a·me·lio·rate /ə'milyəˌreɪt/ *v.* [I,T] (formal) to make something better —**amelioration** /əˌmilyə'reɪʃən/ *n.* [U]

a·men /ˌeɪ'mɛn, ˌɑ-/ *interjection* said at the end of a prayer, to express agreement or the hope that it will be true [ORIGIN: 1000—1100 Late Latin, Greek, from Hebrew, "truth"]

a·me·na·ble /ə'minəbəl, ə'mɛ-/ *adj.* **1** willing to listen to or do something: *From what we see and read in the media, his views are not* ***amenable to*** *change.* **2** appropriate for a particular type of treatment: *jobs that are* ***amenable to*** *flexible scheduling* [ORIGIN: 1500—1600 Old French *amener* "to lead up," from *mener* "to lead"]

a·mend /ə'mɛnd/ (Ac) *v.* [T] to make small changes or improvements, especially in the words of a law: *The act was amended to protect wildlife.* [ORIGIN: 1200—1300 Old French *amender*, from Latin *emendare*, from *ex* "out" + *menda* "something wrong, fault"]

THESAURUS change, alter, adapt, adjust, modify, revise ➔ CHANGE[1]

a·mend·ment /ə'mɛndmənt/ (Ac) *n.* [C,U] a change, especially in the words of a law: *Congress proposed three* ***amendments to*** *the bill.*

a·mends /ə'mɛndz/ (Ac) *n.* **make amends** to do something that shows you are sorry for something: *I tried to make amends by paying for the new window.*

a·men·i·ty /ə'mɛnəṭi, ə'mi-/ *n.* (plural **amenities**) [C usually plural] something in a place that makes living there enjoyable and pleasant: *a housing development with a pool and other amenities*

A·mer·i·can[1] /ə'mɛrɪkən/ *n.* [C] someone from the U.S.

American[2] *adj.* relating to or coming from the U.S.: *American cars*

A·mer·i·ca·na /əˌmɛrə'kɑnə/ *n.* [U] objects, styles, stories, etc. that are typical of America

Aˌmerican 'dream *n.* **the American Dream** the belief that everyone in the U.S. has the opportunity to be successful if s/he works hard

Aˌmerican 'Indian *n.* [C] another name for a NATIVE AMERICAN

A

A·mer·i·can·ize /ə'mɛrɪkə,naɪz/ *v.* [T] to change something or someone to make him, her, or it more American: *After ten years here, we've become very Americanized.* —**Americanization** /ə,mɛrɪkənə'zeɪʃən/ *n.* [U]

A·mer·i·cas /ə'mɛrɪkəz/ *n.* **the Americas** [plural] North, Central, and South America considered together as a whole

a·mi·a·ble /'eɪmiəbəl/ *adj.* friendly and pleasant: *an amiable child* —**amiably** *adv.*

am·i·ca·ble /'æmɪkəbəl/ *adj.* feeling friendly and doing things without arguments: *an amicable divorce*

a·mid /ə'mɪd/ *also* **a·midst** /ə'mɪdst/ *prep.* (formal) among or in the middle of: *life amid the horrors of war* [ORIGIN: Old English *onmiddan* "in the middle"]

a·mi·no ac·id /ə,minoʊ 'æsɪd/ *n.* [C] CHEMISTRY one of the substances that combine to form PROTEINS [ORIGIN: 1800—1900 *amine* type of chemical compound, from *ammonia*]

a·miss /ə'mɪs/ *adj.* **be amiss** (formal) to be a problem or to be wrong: *She sensed something was amiss.*

am·mo /'æmoʊ/ *n.* [U] (informal) ammunition

am·mo·nia /ə'moʊnyə/ *n.* [U] CHEMISTRY a gas or liquid with a strong unpleasant smell, used in cleaning [ORIGIN: 1700—1800 Modern Latin, Latin *sal ammoniacus* "salt of Amon," from *Amon* ancient Egyptian god near one of whose temples the substance was obtained]

am·mu·ni·tion /,æmyə'nɪʃən/ *n.* [U] **1** things such as bullets, bombs, etc. that are fired from guns **2** information that can be used in order to criticize someone or win an argument against him/her: *The scandal has given his opponents plenty of ammunition.*

am·ne·sia /æm'niʒə/ *n.* [U] the medical condition of not being able to remember anything [ORIGIN: 1700—1800 Modern Latin, Greek, "forgetfulness"]

am·ne·si·ac /æm'nizi,æk, -'niʒi-/ *n.* [C] someone with amnesia

am·nes·ty /'æmnəsti/ *n.* (plural **amnesties**) [C,U] an official order forgiving criminals or freeing prisoners, especially people who have opposed the government [ORIGIN: 1500—1600 Greek *amnestia* "forgetfulness," from *mnasthai* "to remember"]

a·moe·ba /ə'mibə/ *n.* [C] BIOLOGY a very small creature that has only one cell

a·mok /ə'mʌk, ə'mɑk/ *adv.* **run amok** to behave or happen in an uncontrolled way [ORIGIN: 1500—1600 Malay]

a·mong /ə'mʌŋ/ *also* **a·mongst** /ə'mʌŋst/ *prep.* **1** in a particular group of people or things: *unemployment among men under 25 | The university is among the top ten in the nation. | Relax, you're* ***among friends****. | They were talking* ***amongst themselves*** (=a group of people were talking). **2** in the middle of, through, or between: *We walked among the huge redwood trees. | He stood among the huge piles of papers, frowning.* **3** used when mentioning one or two people or things from a larger group: *Swimming and diving are among the most popular Olympic events. | We discussed,* ***among other things****, ways to raise money.*

a·mor·al /eɪ'mɔrəl, -'mɑr-/ *adj.* not moral: *his amoral actions*

am·o·rous /'æmərəs/ *adj.* showing or relating to sexual love

a·mor·phous /ə'mɔrfəs/ *adj.* (formal) without a fixed form or shape, or without clear organization

a·mount¹ /ə'maʊnt/ *n.* [C] how much of something there is, or how much is needed: *a large* ***amount of*** *money | Please pay the full amount. | a huge amount of time | Add a small amount of water.*

USAGE

Amount is used with uncountable nouns: *a large amount of money*
Number is used with countable nouns: *a small number of problems*

amount² *v.*

amount to sth *phr. v.* **1** to add up to a total of a particular amount: *Jenny's debts amount to over $1,000.* **2** to mean something without saying it directly: *What he said amounted to an apology.* **3 not amount to something/anything/much** to not be important, valuable, or successful: *His father never thought he'd amount to much.*

amp /æmp/ *also* **am·pere** /'æmpɪr, -pɛr/ *n.* [C] PHYSICS a unit for measuring an electric current

am·phet·a·mine /æm'fɛṭə,min, -mɪn/ *n.* [C,U] a drug that gives people more energy and makes them feel excited

am·phib·i·an /æm'fɪbiən/ *n.* [C] BIOLOGY an animal such as a FROG, that can live on land and in water

am·phib·i·ous /æm'fɪbiəs/ *adj.* **1** an amphibious vehicle can travel on land and water **2** BIOLOGY an amphibious animal can live on land and in water [ORIGIN: 1600—1700 Greek *amphibios* "living a double life," from *amphi-* "round, on both sides, both" + *bios* "way of life"]

am·phi·the·a·ter /'æmfə,θiəṭɚ/ *n.* [C] a large structure with no roof, and rows of seats that curve partly around a central space, used for performances

am·ple /'æmpəl/ *adj.* **1** more than enough: *There will be ample opportunity to ask questions.*

THESAURUS **enough, plenty, sufficient** → ENOUGH

2 ample belly/bosom etc. a big stomach, etc., in a way that is attractive or pleasant —**amply** *adv.*

am·pli·fi·er /'æmplə,faɪɚ/ *n.* [C] a piece of electronic equipment that makes an electrical sound signal stronger, so that it is loud enough to hear ➔ *see picture at* ACOUSTIC

am·pli·fy /ˈæmpləˌfaɪ/ *v.* (**amplified**, **amplifies**) [T] **1** to make something louder or stronger: *an amplified guitar* **2** (formal) to explain something in more detail —**amplification** /ˌæmpləfəˈkeɪʃən/ *n.* [singular, U]

am·pli·tude /ˈæmpləˌtud/ *n.* [U] PHYSICS the distance between the middle and the top or bottom of a wave of energy such as a SOUND WAVE

am·pu·tate /ˈæmpyəˌteɪt/ *v.* [I,T] to cut off a part of someone's body for medical reasons: *Doctors had to amputate his left leg.* [ORIGIN: 1500—1600 Latin, past participle of *amputare*, from *amb-* "around" + *putare* "to cut"] —**amputation** /ˌæmpyəˈteɪʃən/ *n.* [C,U]

am·pu·tee /ˌæmpyəˈti/ *n.* [C] someone who has a part of his/her body cut off for medical reasons

amu PHYSICS the abbreviation of ATOMIC MASS UNIT

a·muck /əˈmʌk/ *adv.* another spelling of AMOK

a·muse /əˈmyuz/ *v.* [T] **1** to make someone laugh or smile: *The question seemed to amuse him.* **2** to make the time pass in an enjoyable way for someone: *the stories she tells to amuse her daughter* [ORIGIN: 1400—1500 Old French *amuser*, from *muse* "mouth of an animal"]

a·mused /əˈmyuzd/ *adj.* **1** thinking something is funny: *He looked amused by my embarrassment.* **2 keep sb amused** to entertain or interest someone for a long time: *games to keep the kids amused*

a·muse·ment /əˈmyuzmənt/ *n.* **1** [U] the feeling you have when you think something is funny: *She looked at him **with/in amusement**.* **2** [C,U] something you do to make the time pass in an enjoyable way: *What do you do **for amusement**?*

a'musement ˌpark *n.* [C] a large park where people can play games of skill, go on rides, and see performances

a·mus·ing /əˈmyuzɪŋ/ *adj.* funny and entertaining: *Luckily, Joe **found it amusing*** (=thought it was funny). | *a **highly/mildly/fairly amusing** movie*

THESAURUS funny, witty, humorous, comical ➔ FUNNY[1]

an /ən; *strong* æn/ *indefinite article* a – used when the following word begins with a vowel sound: *an orange* | *an X-ray* | *an hour*

an·a·bol·ic ster·oid /ˌænəbɑlɪk ˈstɛrɔɪd, ˈstɪr-/ *n.* [C] a drug that makes muscles grow quickly, sometimes used illegally by people in sports

a·nach·ro·nism /əˈnækrəˌnɪzəm/ *n.* [C] someone or something that is or seems to be in the wrong historical time: *Today, small farmers are almost an anachronism.* —**anachronistic** /əˌnækrəˈnɪstɪk/ *adj.*

an·ae·ro·bic /ˌænəˈroʊbɪk◂/ *adj.* BIOLOGY not needing oxygen in order to live ➔ AEROBIC

an·a·gram /ˈænəˌgræm/ *n.* [C] ENG. LANG. ARTS a word or phrase made by changing the order of the letters in another word or phrase: *"Silent" is an anagram of "listen."*

a·nal /ˈeɪnl/ *adj.* **1** relating to the ANUS **2** (disapproving) showing a lot of concern with small details: *Don't be so anal.*

an·al·ge·sic /ˌænlˈdʒizɪk◂/ *n.* [C] CHEMISTRY a drug that reduces pain

a·nal·o·gous /əˈnæləgəs/ (Ac) *adj.* (formal) similar to another situation or thing: *The system of roads across the country is **analogous to** the veins and arteries in the human body.*

THESAURUS similar, like, alike, comparable, akin to sth ➔ SIMILAR

a·nal·o·gy /əˈnælədʒi/ (Ac) *n.* (plural **analogies**) [C,U] ENG. LANG. ARTS something that seems similar in two situations, processes, etc.: *We can **draw/make an analogy between** the brain and a computer.* [ORIGIN: 1400—1500 Greek *analogia*, from *analogos*; from *ana-* "according to" + *logos* "reason, ratio"]

a·nal·y·sis /əˈnæləsɪs/ (Ac) *n.* (plural **analyses** /-siz/) **1** [C,U] the careful examination of something in order to understand it better or see what it consists of: ***Analysis of** the data shows that skin cancer is on the increase.* | *The blood sample was sent to the lab **for analysis**.* | *The company did a variety of economic analyses to identify the likely cost of each option.* **2** [U] a process in which a doctor helps someone to talk about his/her past experiences, relationships, etc. in order to help him/her with mental or emotional problems (SYN) **psychoanalysis**: *My sister has been in analysis for several years.* [ORIGIN: 1500—1600 Modern Latin, Greek, from *analyein* "to break up"]

an·a·lyst /ˈænl-ɪst/ (Ac) *n.* [C] **1** someone whose job is to analyze things: *Most **political analysts** believe that Congress will make amendments to the bill.* | *a computer systems analyst* **2** a doctor who helps people with mental or emotional problems by listening to them talk about their experiences, relationships, etc. (SYN) **psychoanalyst**

an·a·lyt·ic·al /ˌænlˈɪṭɪkəl/ (Ac) *also* **an·a·lyt·ic** /ˌænlˈɪṭɪk/ *adj.* using methods that help you examine things carefully: *The job requires someone with an analytical mind who can assess data quickly.* | *the detective's analytic skills*

an·al·yze /ˈænlˌaɪz/ (Ac) *v.* [T] **1** to examine or think about something carefully in order to understand it: *We gather the data so that we can analyze the evidence objectively.* | *The material was taken to a police laboratory to be analyzed.*

THESAURUS examine, inspect, scrutinize ➔ EXAMINE

2 to examine someone's mental or emotional problems using PSYCHOANALYSIS: *The therapists work* *with the patients to analyze their behavioral problems.*

A

an·a·pest /ˈænəˌpest/ *n.* [C] ENG. LANG. ARTS an arrangement of words or SYLLABLES in poetry, that consists of two short sounds that are not STRESSed (=emphasized), followed by one long sound that is stressed. The word "immature" and the phrase "by myself" also have this pattern.

an·ar·chy /ˈænɚki/ *n.* [U] **1** a situation in which no one obeys rules or laws: *Without the rule of law, we would live in a state of chaos and anarchy.* **2** a situation in which there is no government in a country [ORIGIN: 1500—1600 Medieval Latin *anarchia*, from Greek, from *anarchos* "having no ruler"] —**anarchist** *n.* [C] —**anarchic** /æˈnɑrkɪk/ *adj.*

a·nath·e·ma /əˈnæθəmə/ *n.* [singular, U] (formal) something that is completely the opposite of what you believe in: *The party's liberal ideas that are* ***anathema to*** *conservative voters.* [ORIGIN: 1500—1600 Late Latin, Greek, "thing given over to evil, curse," from *anatithenai* "to set up, dedicate"]

a·nat·o·my /əˈnæt̬əmi/ *n.* [U] BIOLOGY the scientific study of the structure of the body [ORIGIN: 1300—1400 Late Latin *anatomia* "cutting up a body," from Greek *anatome*, from *anatemnein* "to cut up"] —**anatomical** /ˌænəˈtɑmɪkəl/ *adj.*

an·ces·tor /ˈænˌsɛstɚ/ *n.* [C] a member of your family who lived in past times ➔ DESCENDANT: *the traditions of their ancestors* [ORIGIN: 1300—1400 Old French *ancestre*, from Latin *antecessor* "one who goes before"] —**ancestral** /ænˈsɛstrəl/ *adj.*

an·ces·try /ˈænˌsɛstri/ *n.* [U] the members of your family who lived in past times: *people* ***of*** *Spanish* ***ancestry***

an·chor¹ /ˈæŋkɚ/ *n.* [C] **1** someone who reads the news on television or radio and introduces news reports: *the local evening news anchor* **2** a heavy metal object that is lowered into the water to prevent a ship or boat from moving **3** someone or something that provides a feeling of support, strength, or safety: *He's the anchor for the team's defense.*

anchor² *v.* **1** [I,T] to lower the anchor on a ship or boat to keep it from moving: *Three tankers were anchored in the harbor.* **2** [T] to be the person who reads the news and introduces reports on television or radio: *Collins anchors the six o'clock news.* **3** [T] to fasten something firmly to something so that it cannot move: *The main rope* ***anchors*** *the tent* ***to*** *the ground.* **4** [T] to provide a feeling of support, safety, or help: *The strong bond between my parents helped to anchor the family during some difficult times.*

an·chor·man /ˈæŋkɚˌmæn/, **an·chor·wom·an** /ˈæŋkɚˌwʊmən/ *n.* (plural **anchormen** /-mɛn/, **anchorwomen** /-ˌwɪmɪn/) [C] someone who reads the news on TV and introduces news reports (SYN) **anchor**

an·cho·vy /ˈænˌtʃoʊvi, -tʃə-, ænˈtʃoʊvi/ *n.* (plural **anchovies**) [C,U] a very small ocean fish that tastes very salty [ORIGIN: 1500—1600 Spanish *anchova*]

an·cient /ˈeɪnʃənt/ *adj.* **1** happening or existing very far back in history: *ancient Rome* ➔ OLD **2** (humorous) very old: *an ancient truck piled with furniture*

and /n, ən, ənd; *strong* ænd/ *conjunction* **1** used in order to join two words or parts of sentences: *a peanut butter and jelly sandwich* | *They have two kids, a boy and a girl.* | *Martha cooks, and Tom does the dishes.* **2** used in order to say that one thing happens after another: *Grant knocked and went in.* **3** (spoken) used instead of "to" after "come," "go," "try," and some other verbs: *Try and finish your homework before dinner, okay?* | *We're going to go and play basketball.* **4** used when adding numbers: *Six and four make ten.* | *a hundred and thirty dollars* **5** used in order to say that one thing is caused by something else: *I missed supper and I'm starving!* **6** used between repeated words to emphasize what you are saying: *She spent more and more time alone.*

and·ro·gyn·ous /ænˈdrɑdʒənəs/ *adj.* **1** someone who is androgynous looks both female and male **2** BIOLOGY an androgynous plant or animal has both male and female parts

an·droid /ˈændrɔɪd/ *n.* [C] a ROBOT that looks completely human

an·ec·dot·al /ˌænɪkˈdoʊt̬l◂/ *adj.* consisting of short stories based on someone's personal experience: *There is* ***anecdotal evidence*** *that this can help asthma sufferers.*

an·ec·dote /ˈænɪkˌdoʊt/ *n.* [C] a short interesting story about a particular person or event [ORIGIN: 1700—1800 French, Latin *anekdota* "things not published," from *ekdidonai* "to publish"]

THESAURUS **story, tale, yarn** ➔ STORY

a·ne·mi·a /əˈnimiə/ *n.* [U] BIOLOGY a medical condition in which there are not enough red cells in your blood [ORIGIN: 1800—1900 Modern Latin, Greek *anaimia* "bloodlessness," from *haima* "blood"] —**anemic** *adj.*

an·es·the·sia /ˌænəsˈθiʒə/ *n.* [U] the use of anesthetics in medicine [ORIGIN: 1700—1800 Modern Latin, Greek *anaisthesia*, from *an* "without" + *aisthesis* "feeling"]

an·es·thet·ic /ˌænəsˈθɛt̬ɪk/ *n.* [C,U] a drug that stops feelings of pain, used during a medical operation: *an operation done under a* ***local/general anesthetic*** (=affecting part or all of your body)

a·nes·thet·ist /əˈnɛsθətɪst/ *n.* [C] someone whose job is to give an anesthetic to people in hospitals

a·nes·the·tize /əˈnɛsθəˌtaɪz/ *v.* [T] to make someone unable to feel pain or strong emotions

a·new /ə'nu/ *adv.* (literary) in a new or different way: *She started life anew in New York.*

an·gel /'eɪndʒəl/ *n.* [C] **1** a spirit who lives with God in heaven, usually represented as a person with wings and dressed in white **2** (spoken) someone who is very kind or helpful: *Oh, thanks! You're an angel!* [ORIGIN: Old English *engel*, from Late Latin *angelus*, from Greek *angelos* "bringer of messages, angel"] —**angelic** /æn'dʒɛlɪk/ *adj.*

an·ger[1] /'æŋgɚ/ *n.* [U] a strong feeling of wanting to hurt or criticize someone because s/he has done something bad to you or been unkind to you: *his feelings of anger and frustration* | *Paul shouted at him* ***in anger.*** | *his* ***anger at*** *his mother*

anger[2] *v.* [T] to make someone feel angry: *The court's decision angered environmentalists.*

an·gi·o·sperm /'ændʒiə,spɚm/ *n.* [C] BIOLOGY a plant that produces fruit that contains the plant's seeds

angles

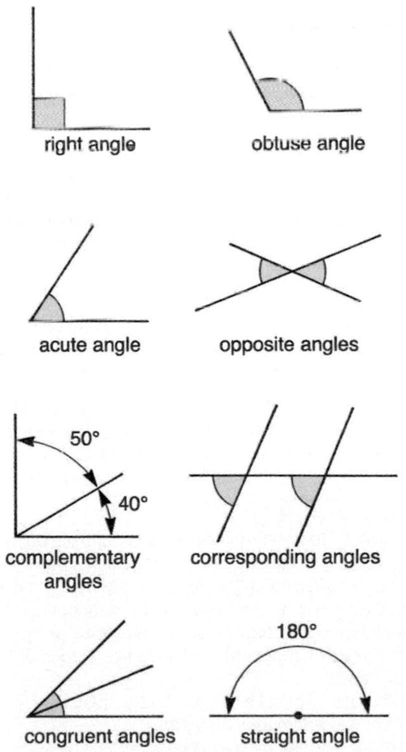

right angle

obtuse angle

acute angle

opposite angles

50°

40°

complementary angles

corresponding angles

180°

congruent angles

straight angle

an·gle[1] /'æŋgəl/ *n.* [C] **1** MATH the space between two lines or surfaces that meet or cross each other, measured in degrees → RIGHT ANGLE: *an angle of 90 degrees* | *a 45-degree angle* **2 at an angle** not upright or straight: *The case was leaning at an angle against the wall.* **3** a way of considering a problem or situation: *We need to* ***look at this from a new angle.***

angle[2] *v.* [T] to turn or move something so that it is not straight or upright: *a lamp angled to give the best light*

angle for sth *phr. v.* to try to get something without asking for it directly: *I think she's angling for an invitation.*

An·gli·can /'æŋglɪkən/ *adj.* relating to the official church of England or related churches, such as the Episcopal church —**Anglican** *n.* [C]

An·glo-Sax·on /,æŋgloʊ 'sæksən◂/ *n.* **1** [C] HISTORY a member of the group of people who lived in England from about 600 A.D. **2** [U] ENG. LANG. ARTS the language of the Anglo-Saxons **3** [C] a white person, especially someone whose family originally came from England —**Anglo-Saxon** *adj.*

an·go·ra /æŋ'gɔrə/ *n.* **1** [C] a type of goat, rabbit, or cat with very long soft hair or fur **2** [U] wool or thread made from the fur of an angora goat or rabbit

an·gry /'æŋgri/ *adj.* feeling or showing anger: *I'm so* ***angry with/at*** *her!* | *My parents were really* ***angry about*** *my grades.* | *Lerner* ***got angry*** *and started shouting.* [ORIGIN: 1200—1300 Old Norse *angr* "great sorrow"] —**angrily** *adv.*

THESAURUS

annoyed – a little angry: *I get annoyed with the kids.*
irritated – feeling annoyed and not patient with people or things: *I was getting irritated by all the noise.*
livid/furious – very angry: *My boss will be furious if I'm late again.*
mad (informal) – very angry: *Mom was mad at me for not cleaning up.*
indignant – angry because you feel you have been insulted or unfairly treated: *She was indignant that only her children had been punished, and not the others involved.*
irate (formal) – extremely angry: *a phone call from an irate customer*
outraged – feeling very angry or shocked: *Women were outraged at the way the court dealt with the sexual harassment case.*
resentful – feeling angry and upset about something you think is unfair: *Bethany felt resentful about her mother's interference.*
→ HAPPY, SAD

angst /'ɑŋst, 'æŋst/ *n.* [U] strong feelings of anxiety and sadness because you are worried about your life

an·guish /'æŋgwɪʃ/ *n.* [U] suffering caused by extreme pain or worry: *"No!" cried her mother* ***in anguish.*** —**anguished** *adj.*: *her anguished parents*

an·gu·lar /'æŋgyəlɚ/ *adj.* **1** having sharp corners: *an angular shape* **2** very thin, and without much flesh on your bones: *a tall, angular young man*

an·i·mal[1] /'ænəməl/ *n.* [C] **1** BIOLOGY a living

creature such as a cow or dog, that is not a bird, insect, fish, or person: *farm animals* | *wild animals* **2** BIOLOGY any living creature, including people: *Humans are highly intelligent animals.* **3** (informal) someone who behaves in a cruel, violent, or rude way: *He's an animal – stay out of his way.* [ORIGIN: 1300—1400 Latin *animalis* "having life," from *anima* "soul"] ➔ **party animal** *at* PARTY

animal² *adj.* **1** relating to or made from animals: *animal fats* **2 animal urges/instincts etc.** human feelings, desires, etc. that relate to sex, food, and other basic needs

An·i·ma·lia /ˌænɪˈmeɪlyə/ *n.* [U] BIOLOGY the KINGDOM that consists of all living creatures with more than one cell who obtain the food they need in order to live and grow by eating other living things ➔ PLANTAE

an·i·mate¹ /ˈænəˌmeɪt/ *v.* [T] to make something seem to have more life or energy: *Laughter animated his face.* [ORIGIN: 1300—1400 Latin, past participle of *animare* "to give life to," from *anima* "soul"]

an·i·mate² /ˈænəmɪt/ *adj.* (formal) living (ANT) **inanimate**

an·i·mat·ed /ˈænəˌmeɪt̬ɪd/ *adj.* **1** full of interest and energy: *an animated debate* **2** an animated CARTOON, movie, etc. is one in which pictures, clay models, etc. seem to move and talk —**animatedly** *adv.*

an·i·ma·tion /ˌænəˈmeɪʃən/ *n.* **1** [C,U] the process of making animated movies, television programs, or computer games, or the movie, program, or game itself **2** [U] energy and excitement: *They were talking with animation.*

an·i·mism /ˈænəˌmɪzəm/ *n.* [U] SOCIAL SCIENCE a religion in which all animals, plants, and objects in the world are believed to have spirits [ORIGIN: 1800—1900 From Latin *anima* "soul"] —**animist** *adj.* —**animist** *n.*

an·i·mos·i·ty /ˌænəˈmɑsət̬i/ *n.* (plural **animosities**) [C,U] (formal) strong dislike or hatred [ORIGIN: 1400—1500 Latin *animosus* "full of spirit"]

an·i·on /ˈænˌaɪən/ *n.* [C] PHYSICS an ION with a negative electrical charge, that is attracted to the part on a BATTERY that sends out a positive electrical charge

an·kle /ˈæŋkəl/ *n.* [C] the joint between your foot and your leg: *The skirt came down to her ankles.* ➔ *see picture on page A16*

an·nals /ˈænlz/ *n.* **in the annals of history/science etc.** in the whole history of a particular subject

an·nex¹ /əˈnɛks, ˈænɛks/ *v.* [T] to take control of a country or area next to your own, especially by using force —**annexation** /ˌænɪkˈseɪʃən, ˌænɛk-/ *n.* [C,U]

annex² *n.* [C] a separate building that has been added to a larger one

an·ni·hi·late /əˈnaɪəˌleɪt/ *v.* [T] to destroy something or defeat someone completely [ORIGIN: 1500—1600 Late Latin, past participle of *annihilare* "to reduce to nothing"] —**annihilation** /əˌnaɪəˈleɪʃən/ *n.* [U]

an·ni·ver·sa·ry /ˌænəˈvɚsəri/ *n.* (plural **anniversaries**) [C] a date on which something important or special happened in an earlier year ➔ BIRTHDAY: *Our **wedding anniversary** is in June.* | *A parade was held on the **anniversary of** the revolution.* [ORIGIN: 1200—1300 Latin *anniversarius* "returning each year," from *annus* "year" + *vertere* "to turn"]

an·no·tate /ˈænəˌteɪt/ *v.* [T usually passive] to add short notes to a book or piece of writing to explain parts of it: *The translation was annotated by W. H. Auden.* —**annotation** /ˌænəˈteɪʃən/ *n.* [C,U]

an·nounce /əˈnaʊns/ *v.* [T] **1** to officially and publicly tell people about something: *The company announced plans to build 300 homes.* | *The Senator **announced that** he was running for a fourth term.* **2** to say something in a loud or confident way, especially something other people will not like: *Randy suddenly **announced (that)** he was leaving.* [ORIGIN: 1400—1500 French *annoncer*, from Latin *annuntiare*, from *ad-* "to" + *nuntiare* "to report"]

an·nounce·ment /əˈnaʊnsmənt/ *n.* **1** [C] an official public statement: *School announcements are broadcast over the PA system.* | *Carter **made the announcement** on Wednesday.* | *the **announcement that** he had died* **2** [U] the act of telling people something publicly: *the announcement of the winners*

an·nounc·er /əˈnaʊnsɚ/ *n.* [C] someone who gives people news or tells them what is happening at an event, during a broadcast, etc.

an·noy /əˈnɔɪ/ *v.* [T] to make someone feel slightly angry about something (SYN) **irritate**: *His reaction annoyed her.* [ORIGIN: 1200—1300 Old French *enuier*, from Latin *inodiare*, from *odium* "hate"]

THESAURUS

irritate – to annoy someone by continually doing something or by continually happening: *His constant interruptions were starting to irritate me.*
get on sb's nerves (informal) – to annoy someone by continually doing something or by continually happening: *The noise was getting on my nerves.*
infuriate – to make someone very angry: *The referee's decision infuriated fans.*
bother – to annoy someone, especially by interrupting him/her when s/he is trying to do something: *Sorry to keep bothering you, but can I ask you one more thing?*
vex – to make someone feel annoyed or worried, and unable to stop thinking about something: *He was still feeling vexed by her previous remark.*
irk (formal) – to make someone feel annoyed: *The expression on his face irked her for some reason.*

an·noy·ance /ə'nɔɪəns/ *n.* **1** [U] the feeling of being slightly angry (SYN) **irritation**: *a look of annoyance* | ***To her annoyance**, he was late.* **2** [C] something that makes you slightly angry: *The constant noise was an annoyance.*

an·noyed /ə'nɔɪd/ *adj.* slightly angry ➔ IRRITATED: *I was **annoyed at** myself for telling him.* | *Joel is really **annoyed about** the mess.* | *My sister's **annoyed (that)** we didn't call.* | *Her father was **getting annoyed with** her.*

THESAURUS **angry, irritated, mad, indignant** ➔ ANGRY

an·noy·ing /ə'nɔɪ-ɪŋ/ *adj.* making you feel slightly angry (SYN) **irritating**: *an annoying habit* | ***It's annoying that** we didn't know about this before.* —**annoyingly** *adv.*

an·nu·al[1] /'ænyuəl/ (Ac) *adj.* **1** happening once a year: *The 98th annual conference of the NAACP was held in Detroit.*

THESAURUS **hourly, daily, weekly, monthly, yearly** ➔ REGULAR[1]

2 calculated over a period of one year: *My annual income before taxes is $68,200.* [ORIGIN: 1300—1400 Old French *annuel*, from Latin *annuus* "yearly" and *annalis* "yearly," both from *annus* "year"] —**annually** *adv.*: *The jazz festival is held annually in July.*

annual[2] *n.* [C] a plant that lives for one year or season

,annual per'centage rate *n.* [C] ECONOMICS APR

an·nu·i·ty /ə'nuəṭi/ *n.* (plural **annuities**) [C] ECONOMICS an amount of money that is paid each year to someone from an INVESTMENT

an·nul /ə'nʌl/ *v.* (**annulled**, **annulling**) [T] LAW to officially state that a marriage or legal agreement no longer exists: *Their marriage was annulled last year.* —**annulment** *n.* [C,U]

an·ode /'ænoʊd/ *n.* [C] PHYSICS the part of a BATTERY that collects ELECTRONS, often a wire or piece of metal with the sign (+) ➔ CATHODE

a·noint /ə'nɔɪnt/ *v.* [T] to put oil or water on someone's head or body during a religious ceremony —**anointment** *n.* [C,U]

a·nom·a·ly /ə'nɑməli/ *n.* (plural **anomalies**) [C,U] (formal) something that is very noticeable because it is so different from what is usual: *Women firefighters are still an anomaly in a largely male profession.*

a·non. /ə'nɑn/ the written abbreviation of ANONYMOUS

an·o·nym·i·ty /,ænə'nɪməṭi/ *n.* [U] the state of not having your name known

a·non·y·mous /ə'nɑnəməs/ *adj.* **1** not known by name: *an anonymous writer* | *an official who wished to **remain anonymous*** **2** done, made, or given by someone whose name is not known: *an anonymous letter* **3** without interesting features or qualities: *an anonymous black car* [ORIGIN: 1600—1700 Late Latin *anonymus*, from Greek, from *an-* "without" + *onyma* "name"] —**anonymously** *adv.*

A

a·no·rex·i·a /,ænə'rɛksiə/ *n.* [U] a mental illness that makes people, especially young women, stop eating [ORIGIN: 1500—1600 Modern Latin, Greek, from *an-* "without" + *orexis* "desire to eat"]

a·no·rex·ic /,ænə'rɛksɪk/ *adj.* having anorexia, or relating to anorexia —**anorexic** *n.* [C]

THESAURUS **thin, slim, slender, slight, skinny, lean, underweight, gaunt, emaciated, skeletal** ➔ THIN[1]

an·oth·er /ə'nʌðɚ/ *determiner, pron.* **1** one more person or thing of the same kind: *Do you want another beer?* | *I'll cancel that check and send you another.*

THESAURUS **more, extra, additional, further, supplemental, supplementary** ➔ MORE[2]

2 a different person or thing: *Is there another room we could use?* | *It is easy to send information from one place to another.* **3** something in addition to a particular amount, distance, period of time, etc.: *We'll wait another ten minutes.* ➔ **one after the other/one after another** at ONE[1], ONE ANOTHER

an·swer[1] /'ænsɚ/ *v.* [I,T] **1** to reply to something that someone has asked or written: *Why don't you answer me?* | *She thought for a minute before answering.* | *The witness refused to **answer the question**.* | *He **answered that** he did not know.*

THESAURUS
reply – to answer someone – used especially in written English: *"Are you coming?" "Yes," he replied.*
respond (formal) – to answer someone, especially in writing: *We would like to thank everyone who responded to our survey.*

2 to reply to a question in a test, competition, etc.: *Please answer questions 1–20.* **3 answer the telephone/door** to pick up the telephone when it rings, or go to the door when someone knocks or rings a bell **4** to react to something that someone else has done: *The army answered by firing into the crowd.*

answer (sb) **back** *phr. v.* to reply to someone in a rude way: *Don't answer back, young man!*

answer for sth *phr. v.* **1** to explain why you did something or why something happened, and be punished if necessary: *Voters should make politicians answer for the damage to the environment.* **2 have a lot to answer for** to be responsible for causing a lot of trouble

answer to sb *phr. v.* to be judged by someone or have to explain your actions to him/her, especially someone you work for: *As chairman of the company, Douglas is directly responsible for answering to shareholders.*

answer² *n.* **1** [C,U] a reply to what someone asks or writes: *the **answer to** my question* | *Can you **give** me **an answer** as soon as possible?* | *I **get** a different **answer** every time I ask him.* | ***In answer to** reporters' **questions**, Wallace said they were looking into the matter.* **2** [C] a reply to a question in a test, competition, etc.: *What was the **answer to** question 7?* **3** [C] something that you get as a result of thinking or calculating with numbers: *The answer is 255.* **4** [C] something that solves a problem: *There are no **easy/simple/right** answers.* | *the **answer to** the illegal immigration problem*

THESAURUS **solution, cure, remedy, panacea** ➔ SOLUTION

5 [singular, U] if you get an answer when you call someone, knock on his/her door, etc., s/he picks up the telephone or comes to the door: *I knocked, but there was **no answer**.*

an·swer·a·ble /'ænsərəbəl/ *adj.* **be answerable (to sb) for sth** to have to explain your actions to someone

'answering ma,chine *n.* [C] a machine that records your telephone calls when you cannot answer them ➔ PHONE¹

ant /ænt/ *n.* [C] a common small black or red insect that lives in groups

an·tac·id /,ænt'æsɪd/ *n.* [C] a drug that gets rid of the burning feeling in your stomach when you have eaten too much, drunk too much alcohol, etc.

an·tag·o·nism /æn'tægə,nɪzəm/ *n.* [U] strong opposition to or hatred of someone else: *Polucci's **antagonism toward** the press*

THESAURUS **opposition, objection, hostility, antipathy** ➔ OPPOSITION

an·tag·o·nist /æn'tægənɪst/ *n.* [C] your opponent in an argument, fight, etc.

an·tag·o·nis·tic /æn,tægə'nɪstɪk/ *adj.* showing opposition to or hatred of someone or something: *an antagonistic attitude* —**antagonistically** *adv.*

an·tag·o·nize /æn'tægə,naɪz/ *v.* [T] to make someone feel angry with you: *The White House has been careful not to antagonize its NATO allies.* [ORIGIN: 1600—1700 Greek *antagonizesthai*, from *anti-* + *agonizesthai* "to fight"]

Ant·arc·tic /ænt'ɑrktɪk, ænt'ɑrt̬ɪk/ *n.* **the Antarctic** the very cold, most southern part of the world —**antarctic** *adj.*

Ant·arc·tic·a /ænt'ɑrktɪkə, ænt'ɑrt̬ɪkə/ *n.* one of the seven CONTINENTS that is the most southern area of land on Earth

Ant,arctic 'Circle *n.* **the Antarctic Circle** an imaginary line around the world at a particular distance from the most southern point, which is the South Pole ➔ *see picture at* GLOBE

an·te¹ /'ænti/ *n.* **up/raise the ante** to increase your demands or try to get more things from a situation

ante² *v.*

ante up (sth) *phr. v.* to pay an amount of money in order to be able to do or be involved in something

ant·eat·er /'ænt̬it̬ə/ *n.* [C] an animal that has a very long nose and eats small insects

an·te·bel·lum /,ænt̬ɪ'bɛləm/ *adj.* existing before a war, especially the American Civil War: *an antebellum plantation*

an·te·ce·dent /,ænt̬ɪ'sidnt/ *n.* **1** [C] (formal) an event, organization, or thing that is similar to the one you have mentioned, but that existed earlier: *It was a highly unusual event, without any historical antecedents.* **2 sb's antecedents** [plural] (formal) the people in someone's family who lived a long time ago (SYN) **ancestors** **3** [C] ENG. LANG. ARTS a word, phrase, or sentence that is represented later by another word, for example a PRONOUN —**antecedent** *adj.*

an·te·di·lu·vi·an /,ænt̬ɪdə'luviən/ *adj.* (formal, humorous) very old-fashioned (SYN) **outdated**: *antediluvian attitudes about women*

an·te·lope /'ænt̬əl,oʊp/ *n.* [C] an animal that has long horns, can run very fast, and is very graceful

an·ten·na /æn'tɛnə/ *n.* [C] **1** a piece of equipment on a television, car, roof, etc. for receiving or sending radio or television signals **2** (plural **antennae** /-ni/) BIOLOGY one of two long thin parts on the head of insects or on some sea animals such as LOBSTERS, that they use to feel things ➔ *see picture on page A15* [ORIGIN: 1600—1700 Latin "pole holding up a sail"]

an·them /'ænθəm/ *n.* [C] **1** a formal or religious song **2** a song that a particular group of people consider to be very important to them: *The Rolling Stones' "Satisfaction" was an anthem for a generation.*

an·ther /'ænθə/ *n.* [C] BIOLOGY the part of a male flower that contains POLLEN ➔ *see picture at* FLOWER¹

ant·hill /'ænt,hɪl/ *n.* [C] a small pile of dirt on the ground over the place where ANTs live

an·thol·o·gy /æn'θɑlədʒi/ *n.* (plural **anthologies**) [C] ENG. LANG. ARTS a set of stories, poems, etc. by different people, collected together in one book: *an **anthology of** American literature* [ORIGIN: 1600—1700 Modern Latin *anthologia*, from Greek, "gathering flowers"]

an·thrax /'ænθræks/ *n.* [U] a serious disease that affects cattle and sheep, and that can affect people

an·thro·pol·o·gy /,ænθrə'pɑlədʒi/ *n.* [U] the scientific study of people, their societies, their beliefs, etc. [ORIGIN: Latin, Greek, from *anthropos* "human being" + *logia* "study"] —**anthropologist** *n.* [C] —**anthropological** /,ænθrəpə'lɑdʒɪkəl/ *adj.*

an·ti·air·craft /,ænti'ɛrkræft/ *adj.* able to be used against enemy aircraft: *antiaircraft missiles*

an·ti·bi·ot·ic /,ænt̬ɪbaɪ'ɑt̬ɪk, ,æntaɪ-/ *n.* [C usually plural] a drug that is used in order to kill

BACTERIA and cure infections —**antibiotic** *adj.*

an·ti·bod·y /ˈæntɪˌbɑdi/ *n.* (plural **antibodies**) [C] BIOLOGY a substance produced by your body to fight disease

an·tic·i·pate /ænˈtɪsəˌpeɪt/ (Ac) *v.* [T] **1** to expect that something will happen, and do something to prepare for it or prevent it: *The economy is growing faster than anticipated.* | *City officials are anticipating problems if the jury finds the officers not guilty.* | *We did not* ***anticipate that*** *the suspect would drive his car into the building.* **2** to think about something that is going to happen, especially something good: *Daniel was eagerly anticipating her arrival.*

an·tic·i·pa·tion /ænˌtɪsəˈpeɪʃən/ (Ac) *n.* [U] the act of expecting something to happen: *They cleaned the church* ***in anticipation of*** *the bishop's visit.*

an·ti·cli·max /ˌæntɪˈklaɪmæks/ *n.* [C,U] something that seems disappointing because it happens after something that was much better: *After all the advertising, the concert itself was kind of an anticlimax.* —**anticlimactic** /ˌæntɪklaɪˈmæktɪk/ *adj.*

an·tics /ˈæntɪks/ *n.* [plural] behavior that seems strange, funny, silly, or annoying: *We're all growing tired of his childish antics.*

an·ti·de·pres·sant /ˌæntɪdɪˈprɛsənt, ˌæntaɪ-/ *n.* [C,U] a drug used for treating DEPRESSION (=a mental illness that makes people very unhappy) —**antidepressant** *adj.*

an·ti·dote /ˈæntɪˌdoʊt/ *n.* [C] **1** a substance that stops the effects of a poison: *an* ***antidote to*** *the bite of a rattlesnake* **2** something that makes an unpleasant situation better: *Laughter is one of the best* ***antidotes to*** *stress.*

an·ti·freeze /ˈæntɪˌfriz/ *n.* [U] a substance that is put in the water in car engines to stop it from freezing

an·ti·his·ta·mine /ˌæntɪˈhɪstəˌmin, -mɪn/ *n.* [C,U] a drug that is used for treating an ALLERGY or COLD (=common illness) —**antihistamine** *adj.*

an·tip·a·thy /ænˈtɪpəθi/ *n.* [U] (formal) a feeling of strong dislike or opposition [ORIGIN: 1500—1600 Latin *antipathia*, from Greek *antipathes* "of opposite feelings"]

> THESAURUS **opposition, objection, antagonism, hostility** → OPPOSITION

an·ti·per·spi·rant /ˌæntɪˈpɚspərənt/ *n.* [U] a substance that you put under your arms to prevent you from SWEATing

an·ti·quat·ed /ˈæntɪˌkweɪt̬ɪd/ *adj.* old-fashioned and not appropriate for modern needs or conditions: *antiquated laws*

> THESAURUS **old-fashioned, outdated, out-of-date, outmoded, dated, obsolete** → OLD-FASHIONED

an·tique /ænˈtik/ *n.* [C] a piece of furniture, jewelry, etc. that is old and usually valuable → ANCIENT: *priceless antiques* [ORIGIN: 1400—1500 French, Latin *antiquus*, from *ante* "before"] —**antique** *adj.*: *an antique table*

> THESAURUS **old, ancient, vintage** → OLD

an·tiq·ui·ty /ænˈtɪkwət̬i/ *n.* (plural **antiquities**) **1** [U] ancient times: *a tradition that stretches back into antiquity* **2** [U] the state of being very old: *a building of great antiquity* **3** [C usually plural] a building or object made in ancient times: *a collection of Roman antiquities*

an·ti-Sem·i·tism /ˌæntiˈsɛməˌtɪzəm, ˌæntaɪ-/ *n.* [U] hatred of Jewish people —**anti-Semitic** /ˌæntisəˈmɪt̬ɪk, ˌæntaɪ-/ *adj.*

> THESAURUS **prejudice, racism, discrimination, intolerance, bigotry, sexism, homophobia** → PREJUDICE[1]

an·ti·sep·tic /ˌæntəˈsɛptɪk/ *n.* [C] a chemical substance that prevents a wound from becoming infected —**antiseptic** *adj.*: *antiseptic lotion*

an·ti·so·cial /ˌæntiˈsoʊʃəl, ˌæntaɪ-/ *adj.* **1** not liking to meet people and talk to them: *Peter's colleagues regarded him as antisocial.* **2** not caring if you cause problems for or injuries to other people: *His antisocial behavior prevents him forming lasting friendships.*

an·tith·e·sis /ænˈtɪθəsɪs/ *n.* [C] (formal) the exact opposite of something: *This chaotic, rigged election is the antithesis of democracy.*

an·ti·trust /ˌæntɪˈtrʌst, ˌæntaɪ-/ *adj.* preventing one company from unfairly controlling prices: *antitrust laws*

ant·ler /ˈæntˀlɚ/ *n.* [C] one of the two horns that look like tree branches on the head of animals such as DEER → *see picture on page A15*

an·to·nym /ˈæntəˌnɪm/ *n.* [C] ENG. LANG. ARTS a word that means the opposite of another word. For example, "war" is the antonym of "peace." (ANT) **synonym** [ORIGIN: 1800—1900 French *antonyme*, from Greek *anti-* "against" + *onyma* "name"]

a·nus /ˈeɪnəs/ *n.* [C] BIOLOGY the hole in your body through which solid waste leaves your BOWELS → *see picture at* ORGAN

an·vil /ˈænvɪl/ *n.* [C] a heavy iron block on which pieces of metal are shaped using a hammer

anx·i·e·ty /æŋˈzaɪət̬i/ *n.* [U] a strong feeling of worry about something: *a lifestyle that creates stress and anxiety* | *workers'* ***anxiety about*** *being fired*

anx·ious /ˈæŋkʃəs, ˈæŋʃəs/ *adj.* **1** very worried about something, or showing that you are worried: *June's* ***anxious about*** *the results of her blood test.* | *an anxious look*

> THESAURUS **worried, concerned, nervous, uneasy, stressed (out), tense, apprehensive** → WORRIED

2 feeling strongly that you want something to happen, especially in order to improve a bad situation: *The Moores are* ***anxious to*** *adopt a child.* | *Company directors were* ***anxious for*** *a meeting.*

an·y¹ /ˈɛni/ *quantifier, pron.* **1** some – used in negative statements and questions: *Is there any coffee left?* | *Do you want any?* | *I don't think that will make any difference.* | *Are* ***any of*** *your relatives coming for Christmas?* **2** used to say that it does not matter which person or thing you choose from a group, or that something is true of all people or things from that group: ***Any of*** *the restaurants in Chinatown would be fine.* | *There are bad things about any job.* → **in any case** *at* CASE¹, **at any rate** *at* RATE¹

USAGE

Do not say "Any country has its own special dishes." Say "Every country has its own special dishes."
Do not say "Any animals have ways of defending themselves from attack." Say "All animals have ways of defending themselves from attack."

GRAMMAR

any, a
Use **any** with uncountable nouns or plural noun forms: *Do you have any money?*
Use **a** with singular noun forms: *Do you have a car?* → A

any² *adv.* even a small amount or at all – used in negative statements or questions: *Are you feeling any better?* | *Sandra couldn't walk any farther.*

an·y·bod·y /ˈɛni,bɑdi, -,bʌdi, -bədi/ *pron.* (informal) ANYONE

an·y·how /ˈɛni,haʊ/ *adv.* (informal) ANYWAY

an·y·more, any more /,ɛniˈmɔr/ *adv.* **not anymore** used in order to say that something happened or was true before, but is not now: *Frank doesn't live here anymore.*

an·y·one /ˈɛni,wʌn, -wən/ *pron.* **1** any person or any people – used when it does not matter exactly who: *Anyone can learn to swim.* | *Why would anyone want to do that?* | *Have you told* ***anyone else****?* **2** a person or someone – used in questions and negative statements: *Is anyone home?* | *She'd just moved and didn't know anyone.*

an·y·place /ˈɛni,pleɪs/ *adv.* (informal) ANYWHERE

an·y·thing /ˈɛni,θɪŋ/ *pron.* **1** something or nothing – used in questions and negative statements: *Her dad didn't know anything about it.* | *Do you need* ***anything else*** *from the store?* **2** any thing, event, situation, etc., when it does not matter exactly which: *That cat will eat anything.* | *I was so worried it was hard to think about* ***anything else****.* **3 or anything** (spoken) said when there are several things or ideas that are possible: *Do you want a Coke or anything?* **4 anything like sb/sth** similar to someone or something: *Carrie doesn't look anything like her sister.* **5 anything but** used in order to emphasize that someone or something does not have a particular quality: *The book is anything but boring.* **6 anything goes** used in order to say that anything is acceptable: *Don't worry about what to wear – anything goes at Ben's parties.*

an·y·time /ˈɛni,taɪm/ *adv.* at any time: *Call me anytime.* | *Are you going to see him* ***anytime soon****?*

an·y·way /ˈɛni,weɪ/ *adv.* **1** in spite of something: *It was raining, but we went anyway.*

SPOKEN PHRASES

2 used in order to continue a story or change the subject of a conversation: *I think she's Lori's age, but anyway, she just had a baby.* | *Anyway, where do you want to go for lunch?* **3** used when you are ending a conversation: *Anyway, I guess I'd better go.* **4** used when you are saying something to support what you have just said: *We decided to sell it because nobody uses it anyway.* **5** used in order to add something that slightly changes what you have said: *Think about it a while – a few days, anyway.* **6** used in order to find out the real reason for something: *What were you doing at his house anyway?*

an·y·where /ˈɛni,wɛr/ *adv.* **1** in or to any place, when it does not matter exactly where: *Fly anywhere in the U.S. with this special offer.* | *I can't imagine living* ***anywhere else****.* **2** somewhere or nowhere – used in questions and negative statements: *I can't find my keys anywhere.* | *Are you going anywhere exciting?* **3 not anywhere near** not at all: *She doesn't consider her collection anywhere near complete.* **4 anywhere from one to ten** any age, number, amount, etc. between the two numbers: *He may get anywhere from 12 to 15% of the vote.* **5 not get anywhere** (spoken) to not be successful at something: *I'm trying to set up a meeting, but I don't seem to be getting anywhere.*

a·or·ta /eɪˈɔrt̬ə/ *n.* [C] BIOLOGY the largest ARTERY (=tube for carrying blood) in the body, that takes blood from the left side of the heart to all parts of the body except the lungs → *see picture at* HEART

a·part /əˈpɑrt/ *adv.* **1** separated by distance or time: *The two towns are 15 miles apart.* | *Our birthdays are only two days apart.* | *The baby's never been* ***apart from*** *his mother.* **2** separated into many pieces: *He had to* ***take*** *the camera* ***apart*** *to fix it.* | *The book just* ***came apart*** *in my hands.* → **fall apart** *at* FALL¹ **3 apart from a)** except for: *Apart from a couple of spelling mistakes, your paper looks fine.* **b)** in addition to: *What do you do for fun? Apart from volleyball, I mean.*

a·part·heid /əˈpɑrtaɪt, -teɪt, -taɪd/ *n.* [U] HISTORY a system in which the different races in a country are separated from each other [ORIGIN: 1900—2000 Afrikaans "separateness"]

a·part·ment /əˈpɑrt˺mənt/ *n.* [C] a place to live that consists of a set of rooms in a large building: *My apartment is really small.* | *She lives in a* ***studio/one-bedroom/two-bedroom apartment****.* → HOUSE¹

[ORIGIN: 1600—1700 French *appartement*, from Italian *appartamento*, from *appartare* "to put aside, separate"]

a'partment ˌbuilding *also* **a'partment ˌhouse** *n.* [C] a building that is divided into separate apartments

a'partment ˌcomplex *n.* [C] a group of apartment buildings built at the same time in the same area

ap·a·thet·ic /ˌæpəˈθɛt̬ɪk/ *adj.* not interested in something: *students who are apathetic about learning*

ap·a·thy /ˈæpəθi/ *n.* [U] the feeling of not being interested in something or not caring about life: *public apathy about the coming election*

1. gorilla 2. orangutan 3. chimpanzee

ape /eɪp/ *n.* [C] a large monkey without a tail or with a very short tail, such as a GORILLA

a·per·i·tif /əˌpɛrəˈtif, ɑ-/ *n.* [C] a small alcoholic drink that you have before a meal

ap·er·ture /ˈæpɚtʃɚ/ *n.* [C] a small opening, especially one that lets light into a camera

a·pex /ˈeɪpɛks/ *n.* [C] **1** the top or highest part of something: *the apex of the pyramid* **2** the most successful part of something: *the apex of her career*

aph·o·rism /ˈæfəˌrɪzəm/ *n.* [C] ENG. LANG. ARTS a short expression that says something true

a·pho·tic zone /eɪˈfoʊt̬ɪk ˌzoʊn/ *n.* **the aphotic zone** BIOLOGY the deep layer of an ocean where light from the Sun does not reach and PHOTOSYNTHESIS does not take place ➔ *see picture at* PHOTIC ZONE

aph·ro·di·si·ac /ˌæfrəˈdiziˌæk, -ˈdɪ-/ *n.* [C] a food or drug that makes someone feel sexual excitement [ORIGIN: 1700—1800 Greek *aphrodisiakos*, from *Aphrodite* the ancient Greek goddess of love] —**aphrodisiac** *adj.*

a·piece /əˈpis/ *adv.* each: *Oranges are 20¢ apiece* (=for each one). | *We gave $10 apiece for the gift* (=each of us gave $10).

a·plomb /əˈplɑm, əˈplʌm/ *n.* (formal) **with aplomb** in a confident or skillful way, especially in a difficult situation: *She answered all their questions with aplomb.*

a·po·ca·lypse /əˈpɑkəlɪps/ *n.* **1** [U] a dangerous situation that results in great destruction, death, or harm **2 the Apocalypse** the religious idea of the destruction and end of the world —**apocalyptic** /əˌpɑkəˈlɪptɪk/ *adj.*

a·poc·ry·phal /əˈpɑkrəfəl/ *adj.* an apocryphal story about a famous person or event is well known but probably not true

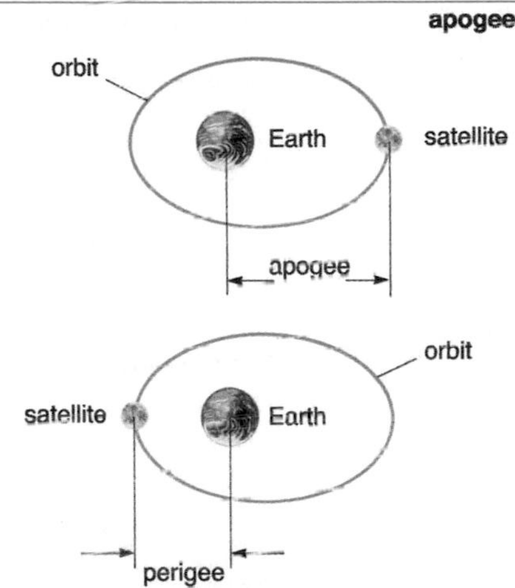

ap·o·gee /ˈæpədʒi/ *n.* [C] **1** (formal) the time or point when something is at its most successful: *Becoming a senator was the **apogee of** his political career.* **2** PHYSICS the furthest point away from the Earth that the Moon or a SATELLITE reaches as it travels in a curved path around the Earth [ORIGIN: 1500—1600 French *apogée*, from Modern Latin *apogaeum*, from Greek, from *apogaios* "far from the Earth"]

a·po·lit·i·cal /ˌeɪpəˈlɪt̬ɪkəl/ *adj.* not having any interest in or connection with politics

a·pol·o·get·ic /əˌpɑləˈdʒɛt̬ɪk/ *adj.* showing or saying that you are sorry about something: *Dave came in late, looking apologetic.* —**apologetically** *adv.*

a·pol·o·gize /əˈpɑləˌdʒaɪz/ *v.* [I] to say that you are sorry about something that you have done, said, etc.: *Harris **apologized for** being late.* | ***Apologize to** your sister now!*

a·pol·o·gy /əˈpɑlədʒi/ *n.* (plural **apologies**) [C] something that you say or write to show that you are sorry: *an **apology for** missing the meeting* | *The Senator **made** a formal **apology**.* | *Please **accept** our **apologies**.* | *I feel I **owe** you **an apology**.* [ORIGIN: 1500—1600 Late Latin *apologia* "written or spoken defense," from Greek, from *apo-* "away from, off" + *logos* "speech"]

ap·o·plec·tic /ˌæpəˈplɛktɪk◂/ *adj.* **1** so angry you cannot control yourself **2** relating to a STROKE —**apoplexy** /ˈæpəˌplɛksi/ *n.* [U]

A

a·pos·tle /ə'pɑsəl/ *n.* [C] **1** one of the 12 men chosen by Christ to teach his message **2** someone who believes strongly in a new idea and tries to persuade other people to believe it [ORIGIN: 900—1000 Late Latin *apostolus*, from Greek, "bringer of messages, apostle"] —**apostolic** /ˌæpə'stɑlɪk/ *adj.*

a·pos·tro·phe /ə'pɑstrəfi/ *n.* [C] **1** ENG. LANG. ARTS the mark (') used in writing to show that one or more letters or figures are missing, such as in don't (=do not) or '07 (=2007) **2** ENG. LANG. ARTS the same mark used before or after the letter "s" to show that something belongs or is related to someone or something, as in "Mandy's coat," or "the building's design" **3** ENG. LANG. ARTS the same sign used before "s" to show the plural of letters and numbers, as in "I got 4 A's and 2 B's on my report card."

ap·palled /ə'pɔld/ *adj.* very shocked and upset: *The boy's mother was **appalled at/by** the violence of the computer game.* —**appall** *v.* [T]

ap·pall·ing /ə'pɔlɪŋ/ *adj.* **1** shocking and terrible: *animals kept in appalling conditions* **2** (informal) very bad: *an appalling movie* —**appallingly** *adv.*

THESAURUS **bad, awful, terrible, horrible, horrific, lousy, horrendous, atrocious, abysmal** → BAD[1]

ap·pa·rat·us /ˌæpə'rætəs, -'reɪtəs/ *n.* (plural **apparatus** *or* **apparatuses**) **1** [C,U] a set of instruments, tools, machines, etc. used for a particular purpose: *an apparatus for breathing under water* **2** [C usually singular] the way in which a lot of people are organized to work together to do a job or control a country or company: *a large security apparatus*

ap·par·el /ə'pærəl/ *n.* [U] (formal) clothes: *men's apparel*

ap·par·ent /ə'pærənt, ə'pɛr-/ (Ac) *adj.* **1** easily seen or understood: ***It was apparent that** the enemy was stronger than they had believed.* | *Her embarrassment was **apparent to** everyone in the room.* | ***For no apparent reason*** (=without a clear reason), *he began to shout at her.*

THESAURUS **noticeable, clear, obvious, evident, conspicuous, manifest** → NOTICEABLE

2 seeming to be true or real, although it may not really be: *Students did well in the subject, despite their apparent lack of interest.* [ORIGIN: 1300—1400 Old French, Latin, present participle of *apparere* from *ad-* "to" + *parere* "to show yourself"]

ap·par·ent·ly /ə'pærəntˀli, ə'pɛr-/ (Ac) *adv.* **1** according to what you have heard is true, although you are not completely sure about it: *She apparently lied about her qualifications on the job application.* | *Apparently, the meeting went really well.* **2** according to the way something appears or someone looks, although it may not really be true: *The soldiers were lying in the road, apparently dead.*

ap·pa·ri·tion /ˌæpə'rɪʃən/ *n.* [C] a GHOST

ap·peal[1] /ə'pil/ *v.* **1** [I] to make an urgent public request for help, money, information, etc.: *The water company **appealed to** everyone **to** save water.* | *charities **appealing for** money* **2 appeal to sb** to seem attractive or interesting to someone: *The program should appeal to older viewers.* **3** [I,T] LAW to make a formal request to a higher court or to someone in authority to change a decision: *We plan to appeal the verdict.*

appeal[2] *n.* **1** [C] an urgent public request for money, information, etc.: *Kennedy **made** a dramatic **appeal** for peace.* | *an **appeal for** food and medical aid* **2** [U] the quality that makes you like or want something: *her glamor and **sex appeal*** (=sexual attractiveness) | *Their music **has** a broad **appeal.*** | *Romances have **appeal for** many readers.* **3** [C,U] LAW a request to a higher court or to someone in authority to change a decision: *an **appeal to** the Supreme Court* | *His conviction was overturned **on appeal**.*

ap·peal·ing /ə'pilɪŋ/ *adj.* attractive or interesting: *an appealing smile* | *These adventure stories are particularly **appealing to** young readers.* —**appealingly** *adv.*

ap·pear /ə'pɪr/ *v.* **1** [I] to begin to be seen: *Dark clouds began to appear in the sky.* | *A face appeared at the window.* **2** [linking verb] to seem: *The man **appeared to** be dead.* | *He tried hard to appear calm.* | *Light colors make a room appear bigger than it is.*

THESAURUS **seem, look, sound, come across as sth** → SEEM

3 [I] to take part in a movie, television program, play, etc.: *He'll be **appearing in** a new Broadway musical.* | *Davis **appeared on** Horn's breakthrough album.* **4** [I] to happen, exist, or become available for the first time: *Irving's novel is soon to **appear in** paperback.* **5** [I] to be present officially, especially in a court of law: *He failed to **appear in court**.* | *They were required to **appear before** a grand jury.* [ORIGIN: 1200—1300 Old French *aparoir*, from Latin *apparere*, from *ad-* "to" + *parere* "to show yourself"]

ap·pear·ance /ə'pɪrəns/ *n.* [C] **1** the way someone or something looks or seems to other people: *He cared little about his appearance.* | *The Christmas lights gave the house a festive appearance.* **2** an arrival by someone or something: *the sudden **appearance of** several reporters* **3** the point at which something begins to exist or starts being used: *The industry has changed with the **appearance of** new technology.* **4** a public performance in a film, play, concert, etc.: *his first appearance on stage* **5** the act of arriving at or attending an event: *his first **public appearance** since the election* | *I **put in an appearance** at the wedding but did not stay long.*

ap·pease /ə'piz/ *v.* [T] to make someone less angry, or stop him/her from attacking you by giving him/her what s/he wants: *A goat was killed to appease the spirits.*

ap·pease·ment /ə'pizmənt/ *n.* [C,U] HISTORY the act of trying to persuade people not to attack you, or to make them less angry by giving them what they want, especially in politics: *People who opposed the war were accused of appeasement.*

ap·pel·late /ə'pɛlɪt/ *adj.* LAW an appellate court, judge, etc. is able to change a decision that was made earlier in a court of law

ap·pend /ə'pɛnd/ (Ac) *v.* [T] (formal) to add something to a piece of writing: *The results of the survey are **appended to** this document.*

ap·pend·age /ə'pɛndɪdʒ/ *n.* [C] something that is added or attached to something larger or more important

ap·pen·di·ci·tis /ə,pɛndə'saɪtɪs/ *n.* [U] an illness in which your appendix swells and becomes painful

ap·pen·dix /ə'pɛndɪks/ (Ac) *n.* [C] **1** BIOLOGY a small organ in your body that has little or no use → *see picture at* ORGAN **2** (plural **appendixes** or **appendices** /-dɪsiz/) ENG. LANG. ARTS a part at the end of a book that contains additional information: *The test results are described in detail in the appendix.* [ORIGIN: 1500—1600 Latin from *appendere* "to hang something from"]

ap·pe·tite /'æpə,taɪt/ *n.* [C,U] **1** a desire for food: *I seem to have **lost** my **appetite** lately.* | *Don't eat that cake now – you'll **ruin/spoil** your **appetite**.* **2** a desire or liking for a particular activity: *his **appetite for** books*

ap·pe·tiz·er /'æpə,taɪzɚ/ *n.* [C] a small dish of food served at the beginning of a meal

ap·pe·tiz·ing /'æpə,taɪzɪŋ/ *adj.* food that is appetizing looks or smells very good

ap·plaud /ə'plɔd/ *v.* [T] **1** to hit your open hands together to show that you have enjoyed a play, concert, speaker, etc. (SYN) **clap**: *As Maria walked onto the stage, the **audience applauded**.* **2** (formal) to express strong approval of an idea, plan, etc.: *We applaud the company's efforts to improve safety.*

ap·plause /ə'plɔz/ *n.* [U] the sound of people hitting their hands together in order to show that they enjoy or approve of something: *There was a burst of applause as the band came on stage.* | *Let's give Rodney **a big round of applause**!*

ap·ple /'æpəl/ *n.* [C] a hard round red or green fruit that is white inside, or the tree this fruit grows on: *apple pie* [ORIGIN: Old English *æppel*] → *see picture on page 414*

'apple ,cider *n.* [C,U] CIDER

ap·ple·sauce /'æpəl,sɔs/ *n.* [U] a thick smooth food made from cooked apples

ap·plet /'æplət/ *n.* [C] IT a computer program that is part of a larger program, and which performs a particular job, such as finding documents on the Internet

ap·pli·ance /ə'plaɪəns/ *n.* [C] a piece of electrical equipment such as a REFRIGERATOR or a DISHWASHER, used in people's homes: *kitchen appliances*

THESAURUS **machine, device, gadget, mechanism, contraption** → MACHINE[1]

ap·pli·ca·ble /'æplɪkəbəl, ə'plɪkəbəl/ *adj.* affecting or relating to a particular person, group, or situation: *These tax laws are not **applicable to** foreigners.*

ap·pli·cant /'æplɪkənt/ *n.* [C] someone who has formally asked for a job, place at a college, etc., especially by writing a letter: *There were 30 **applicants for** the job.*

ap·pli·ca·tion /,æplɪ'keɪʃən/ *n.* **1** [C] a formal, usually written, request for a job, a place at a college, etc.: *an **application form*** | *a **job application*** | *The counselor will help students **fill out** college **applications**.* **2** [C] a piece of SOFTWARE: *multimedia applications* **3** [C,U] the use of a machine, idea, etc. for a practical purpose: *the **application of** fair housing laws* | *The research has many **practical applications**.* **4** [C,U] the act of putting something like paint, medicine, etc. onto a surface: *the **application of** fertilizer to the crops*

ap·pli·ca·tor /'æplɪ,keɪt̬ɚ/ *n.* [C] a special brush or tool used for putting paint, glue, medicine, etc. on something

ap·plied /ə'plaɪd/ *adj.* a subject such as applied mathematics or applied science is studied for a practical purpose

ap·ply /ə'plaɪ/ *v.* (**applied**, **applies**) **1** [I] to make a formal, especially written, request for a job, place at a college, permission to do something, etc.: *Fifteen people **applied for** the job.* | *He has **applied for** U.S. citizenship.* | *Anna **applied to** several colleges in California.* **2** [I,T] to have an effect on, involve, or concern a particular person, group, or situation: *The nutrition labeling requirements **apply to** most foods.* **3** [T] to use a method, idea, etc. in a particular situation, activity, or process: *Internships give students a chance to apply their skills in real situations.* **4** [T] to put something on a surface, or press on the surface of something: *Apply the lotion evenly.* | ***Apply pressure** to the wound.* **5** [T] **apply yourself (to sth)** to work very hard and very carefully, especially for a long time: *He never really applied himself in school.*

ap·point /ə'pɔɪnt/ *v.* [T] **1** to choose someone for a job, position, etc.: *Palmer was **appointed to** the Board of Trustees.* | *Dr. Gordon was **appointed as** the local representative.* **2** (formal) to arrange or decide a time or place for something to happen: *Judge Bailey appointed a new time for the trial.* | *They met at the appointed time.*

ap·point·ee /ə,pɔɪn'ti/ *n.* [C] someone who is chosen to do a particular job: *a Presidential appointee*

A

ap·point·ment /ə'pɔɪnt˺mənt/ *n.* **1** [C] a meeting that has been arranged for a particular time and place: *an **appointment with** a reporter* | *I'd like to **make an appointment** with Dr. Hanson.* | *Lisa **has an appointment** at two.* | *She called a client to **cancel an appointment**.* **2** [C,U] the act of choosing someone for a job, position, etc.: *the **appointment of** a new Supreme Court Justice* **3 by appointment** after arranging to meet at a particular time: *Dr. Sutton will only see you by appointment.*

ap'pointment ˌbook *n.* [C] a book you keep at work with a CALENDAR in it, in which you write meetings, events, and other things you plan to do

ap·por·tion /ə'pɔrʃən/ *v.* [T] (formal) to decide how something should be divided between various people

THESAURUS **separate, divide, split →** SEPARATE[2]

ap·po·si·tion /ˌæpə'zɪʃən/ *n.* [U] ENG. LANG. ARTS when two or more noun phrases are in apposition, they describe the same thing or person, but do not have a word such as "and" or "or" between them. For example, in the sentence "His brother, a musician, lived in New York," the two phrases "His brother" and "a musician" are in apposition.

ap·pos·i·tive /ə'pɑzət̬ɪv/ *n.* [C] ENG. LANG. ARTS a noun phrase that is used with another noun phrase, that gives information about the same person or thing

ap·prais·al /ə'preɪzəl/ *n.* [C,U] an official judgment about how valuable, effective, or successful someone or something is: *an **appraisal of** a watch* (=finding out how much it is worth) | *a performance appraisal* (=a judgment how well someone does his/her job)

ap·praise /ə'preɪz/ *v.* [T] to make an appraisal of someone or something: *The furniture was **appraised at** $14,000.* | *an appraising look*

THESAURUS **judge, evaluate, assess, gauge →** JUDGE[2]

ap·pre·cia·ble /ə'priʃəbəl/ (Ac) *adj.* large enough to be noticed, felt, or considered important: *There has been no appreciable change in the patient's condition.* —**appreciably** *adv.*: *Real estate values increased appreciably in the last year.*

ap·pre·ci·ate /ə'priʃiˌeɪt/ (Ac) *v.* **1** [T] to be grateful for something: *Mom really appreciated the flowers you sent.* | *Thanks for meeting with me. I **appreciate it**.* | ***I'd** really **appreciate it if** you'd turn the TV down.* **2** [T] to understand and enjoy the good qualities or value of something: *Dorm food made me appreciate Mom's home cooking.* **3** [T] to understand a difficult situation or problem: *I **appreciate that** many parents struggle to afford college fees.* | *You don't seem to **appreciate how** hard this is for us.* **4** [I] to gradually increase in value (ANT) **depreciate**: *The stock has appreciated steadily since the firm went public in 1996.* [ORIGIN: 1600—1700 Late Latin, past participle of *appretiare*, from Latin *ad-* "to" + *pretium* "price"]

ap·pre·ci·a·tion /əˌprɪʃi'eɪʃən, əˌpri-/ (Ac) *n.* [singular, U] **1** the feeling of being grateful for something: *I'd like to **show/express** my **appreciation** for everything you've done.* **2** an understanding of the importance or meaning of something: *The course helps children to develop an appreciation of poetry and literature.* | *I teach classes in music appreciation.* **3** the enjoyment you feel when you recognize the good qualities of something: *When Linda returned home, her **appreciation for** her family got deeper.* **4** ECONOMICS a rise in the value of something: *the **appreciation** of the dollar **against** the yen*

ap·pre·cia·tive /ə'priʃət̬ɪv/ *adj.* feeling or showing how much you enjoy, admire, or feel grateful for something or someone: *Appreciative laughter broke out in the room.* —**appreciatively** *adv.*

ap·pre·hend /ˌæprɪ'hɛnd/ *v.* [T] (formal) to find a criminal and take him/her to prison [ORIGIN: 1300—1400 Latin *apprehendere* "to take hold of," from *ad-* "to" + *prehendere* "to seize"]

THESAURUS **catch, capture, arrest →** CATCH[1]

ap·pre·hen·sion /ˌæprɪ'hɛnʃən/ *n.* [C,U] **1** anxiety or fear, especially about the future: *my sense of **apprehension about** flying* **2** (formal) the act of catching a criminal

ap·pre·hen·sive /ˌæprɪ'hɛnsɪv/ *adj.* worried or anxious, especially about the future: *She was **apprehensive about** the demands of the job.* —**apprehensively** *adv.*

THESAURUS **worried, anxious, concerned, nervous, uneasy, stressed (out), tense →** WORRIED

ap·pren·tice /ə'prɛntɪs/ *n.* [C] someone who works for an employer for an agreed amount of time, usually for low pay, in order to learn a particular skill

ap·pren·tice·ship /ə'prɛntɪˌʃɪp/ *n.* [C,U] the job of being an apprentice, or the time spent as one

ap·prise /ə'praɪz/ *v.* [T] (formal) to formally or officially tell someone about something: *Mrs. Bellamy has been **apprised of** the situation.*

ap·proach[1] /ə'proʊtʃ/ (Ac) *v.* **1** [I,T] to move closer to someone or something: *The officer approached him and asked to see his license.* | *She heard the sound of a car approaching.* **2** [T] to ask someone for something when you are not sure if s/he will do what you want: *She was **approached** by two schools **about** teaching jobs.* **3** [I,T] to almost be a particular time, age, amount, temperature, etc.: *By mid-afternoon, the temperature was* *approaching 100°.* | *Winter was **fast approaching.*** **4** [T] to begin to deal with something: *Different nations have approached the problem differently.* [ORIGIN: 1300—1400 Old French *aprochier*, from Late Latin *appropiare*, from Latin *ad-* "to" + *prope* "near"]

approach² (Ac) *n.* **1** [C] a way of doing something or dealing with a problem: *The school takes a practical **approach to** teaching science.*

THESAURUS **method, way, technique, strategy, procedure** → METHOD

2 [U] the act of coming closer in time or distance: *the **approach of** winter* **3** [C] if an airplane makes an approach, it starts the process of landing on the ground **4** [C] a road or path leading to a place: *a traffic jam at the **approach to** the bridge*

ap·proach·a·ble /ə'proʊtʃəbəl/ (Ac) *adj.* friendly and easy to talk to: *Dr. Grieg is very approachable.*

ap·pro·ba·tion /ˌæprə'beɪʃən/ *n.* [U] (formal) praise or approval

ap·pro·pri·ate¹ /ə'proʊpriɪt/ (Ac) *adj.* correct or good for a particular time, situation, or purpose (ANT) **inappropriate**: *The movie is **appropriate for** all ages.* | *books **appropriate to** elementary school children* | *There may come a time when **it is appropriate to** cut jobs.* | *an **appropriate time** to honor our veterans* **—appropriately** *adv.* **—appropriateness** *n.* [U]

THESAURUS

right – used to talk about something that is best or most appropriate for a particular situation or purpose: *Is she the right person for this position?*
suitable – used to talk about something that has the right qualities for a particular person or purpose: *a suitable school for the children*
suited – used to talk about someone who has the right qualities to do something: *He'd be well suited to the job.*
apt – used to talk about something, especially a word or description, that is exactly right for a particular situation or purpose: *She said it tasted like bubble gum, which seemed like an apt description.*
proper – used to talk about something that is correct or right for a particular situation: *You need the proper tools for the job.*

ap·pro·pri·ate² /ə'proʊpriˌeɪt/ (Ac) *v.* [T] (formal) **1** to use or take something that does not belong to you: *He is suspected of appropriating company funds.* **2** to keep something such as money separate, to be used for a particular purpose: *Congress **appropriated** $11.7 billion **for** anti-drug campaigns.*

apˌpropri'ations bill *n.* [C] POLITICS a bill which allows the government to spend money, if it is approved by the Senate and House of Representatives

ap·prov·al /ə'pruvəl/ *n.* [U] **1** official permission or acceptance: *The deal requires the **approval of** shareholders.* | *A two-thirds majority vote is required **for approval.*** | *The drug has **won** FDA **approval.*** | *The board never **gave** its **approval.*** **2** the belief that someone or something is good or doing something right: *a child trying to **win/earn** her father's **approval***

ap·prove /ə'pruv/ *v.* **1** [I] to believe that someone or something is good or acceptable (ANT) **disapprove**: *54% of voters **approve of** the president's performance.* | *Her parents did not **approve of** her marriage.* **2** [T] to officially agree to something: *The Senate is expected to approve the bill next week.*

THESAURUS

pass – to officially accept a law or proposal, especially by voting: *Many anti-smoking laws have been passed.*
ratify – to make a written agreement official by signing it: *Both sides are willing to ratify the treaty.*
sanction (formal) – to officially accept or allow something: *At that time, the government sanctioned slavery.*
endorse (formal) – to officially say that you support or approve of someone or something: *The principal endorsed the recommendations.*

—approving *adj.*: *an approving nod* **—approvingly** *adv.*

approx the written abbreviation of APPROXIMATELY

ap·prox·i·mate¹ /ə'prɑksəmɪt/ (Ac) *adj.* an approximate number, amount, or time is not exact: *The approximate cost will be around $50 per adult.* [ORIGIN: 1400—1500 Late Latin, past participle of *approximare* "to come near to," from Latin *ad-* "to" + *proximare* "to come near"] **—approximately** *adv.*: *The plane will land in approximately 20 minutes.*

ap·prox·i·mate² /ə'prɑksəˌmeɪt/ (Ac) *v.* [I, linking verb] (formal) to be similar to but not exactly the same as something else: *The animals' food approximates what they would eat in the wild.* | *The machine can only approximate the sound of a human voice.* **—approximation** /əˌprɑksə'meɪʃən/ *n.* [C,U]: *The growth chart shows a rough approximation of a child's ideal weight.*

APR /ˌeɪ pi 'ɑr/ *n.* [C] ECONOMICS **annual percentage rate** the rate of INTEREST that you must pay when you borrow money

ap·ri·cot /'eɪprɪˌkɑt, 'æ-/ *n.* [C] a small soft yellow-orange fruit with a single large seed

A·pril /'eɪprəl/ (*written abbreviation* **Apr.**) *n.* [C,U] the fourth month of the year, between March and May: *Sometimes it snows **in April.*** | *The twins were born **on April 15th.*** | *Mira will begin her training **next April.*** | *The president signed the treaty **last April.*** [ORIGIN: 1300—1400 Old French *avrill*, from Latin *Aprilis*]

A

ˌApril 'Fool's ˌDay *n.* April 1, a day for playing funny tricks on people

A

a·pron /'eɪprən/ *n.* [C] a piece of clothing you wear to protect your clothes when you cook

ap·ro·pos /ˌæprə'poʊ, 'æprəˌpoʊ/ *adv.* (formal) **apropos of sth** relating to something just mentioned: ***Apropos of nothing*** (=not relating to anything previously mentioned), *he suddenly asked me if I liked cats!*

apt /æpt/ *adj.* **1 apt to** likely to do something: *A sensitive child is apt to become overwhelmed in busy situations.* **2** exactly right for a particular situation or purpose: *an apt remark*

THESAURUS **appropriate, right, suitable, suited, proper** → APPROPRIATE[1]

3 able to learn or understand things quickly: *an apt pupil*

THESAURUS **intelligent, smart, bright, brilliant, clever, gifted** → INTELLIGENT

—**aptly** *adv.*

apt. the written abbreviation of APARTMENT

ap·ti·tude /'æptəˌtud/ *n.* [C,U] a natural ability or skill, especially in learning: *He never had much* ***aptitude for*** *business.*

THESAURUS **skill, talent, ability, knack, flair, gift** → SKILL

'aptitude ˌtest *n.* [C] a test used for finding out what someone's best skills are: *the Scholastic Aptitude Test*

a·quar·i·um /ə'kwɛriəm/ *n.* [C] **1** a clear glass or plastic container for fish or other water animals to live in **2** a building where people go to look at fish or other water animals

aquarium

A·quar·i·us /ə'kwɛriəs/ *n.* **1** [U] the eleventh sign of the ZODIAC, represented by a person pouring water **2** [C] someone born between January 20 and February 18

a·quat·ic /ə'kwæt̬ɪk, ə'kwɑt̬ɪk/ *adj.* living or happening in water: *aquatic plants | aquatic sports* [ORIGIN: 1400—1500 French *aquatique*, from Latin *aqua* "water"]

aq·ue·duct /'ækwəˌdʌkt/ *n.* [C] a structure like a bridge, for carrying water across a valley [ORIGIN: 1500—1600 Latin *aquaeductus*, from *aquae* "of water" + *ductus* "act of leading"]

ˌaqueous so'lution *n.* [C] CHEMISTRY a liquid mixture of water and at least one other substance

aq·ui·fer /'ækwəfɚ, 'ɑ-/ *n.* [C] EARTH SCIENCES a layer of stone or earth, under the surface of the ground, that contains water

AR the written abbreviation of ARKANSAS

Ar·a·bic nu·me·ral /ˌærəbɪk 'numərəl/ *n.* [C] MATH the sign 1, 2, 3, 4, 5, 6, 7, 8, 9, or 0, or a combination of these signs, used as a number → ROMAN NUMERAL

ar·a·ble /'ærəbəl/ *adj.* arable land is good for growing crops [ORIGIN: 1400—1500 Latin *arabilis*, from *arare* "to plow"]

a·rach·nid /ə'ræknɪd/ *n.* [C] BIOLOGY a small creature such as a SPIDER, that has eight legs and a body with two parts [ORIGIN: 1700—1800 Greek *arachne* "spider"]

ar·bi·ter /'ɑrbət̬ɚ/ *n.* [C] **1** a person or organization that settles an argument between two groups of people **2** an arbiter of style, fashion, taste, etc. influences society's opinions about what is fashionable

ar·bi·trar·y /'ɑrbəˌtrɛri/ (Ac) *adj.* decided or arranged without any reason or plan, often unfairly: *There are too many arbitrary rules and regulations.* [ORIGIN: 1400—1500 Latin *arbitrarius* "depending on the decision of a judge, uncertain," from *arbiter*] —**arbitrarily** /ˌɑrbə'trɛrəli/ *adv.*: *Z represents an arbitrarily chosen number.* —**arbitrariness** /'ɑrbəˌtrɛrinɪs/ *n.* [U]

ar·bi·trate /'ɑrbəˌtreɪt/ *v.* [I,T] to be a judge in an argument because both sides have asked for this —**arbitrator** *n.* [C]

ar·bi·tra·tion /ˌɑrbə'treɪʃən/ *n.* [U] the process in which someone tries to help two opposing sides settle an argument

ar·bo·re·al /ɑr'bɔriəl/ *adj.* BIOLOGY relating to trees, or living in trees

arc /ɑrk/ *n.* [C] MATH part of a circle or any curved line [ORIGIN: 1300—1400 Old French, Latin *arcus* "bow, arch, arc"] → *see picture at* CIRCLE[1]

ar·cade /ɑr'keɪd/ *n.* [C] **1** a special room or small building where people go to play VIDEO GAMES **2** a passage or side of a building that is covered with an ARCHed roof, and that often has small stores along it

ar·cane /ɑr'keɪn/ *adj.* (literary) secret and known or understood by only a few people: *the arcane rules of the Senate* [ORIGIN: 1500—1600 Latin *arcanus* "secret," from *arca* "box"]

arch[1] /ɑrtʃ/ *n.* (plural **arches**) [C] **1** a curved structure at the top of a door, window, bridge, etc., or something that has this curved shape **2** the curved middle part of the bottom of your foot —**arched** *adj.*: *an arched doorway*

arch

arch[2] *v.* [I,T] to make something form an arch, or be in the shape of an arch: *The cat arched her back and hissed.*

ar·chae·ol·o·gy, archeology /ˌɑrkiˈɑlədʒi/ *n.* [U] the study of ancient societies by examining what remains of their buildings, GRAVES, tools, etc. [ORIGIN: 1600—1700 French *archéologie*, from Late Latin *archaeologia* "history of ancient times," from Greek *archaios* "ancient" + *logia* "study"] **—archaeologist** *n.* [C] **—archaeological** /ˌɑrkiəˈlɑdʒɪkəl/ *adj.*

ar·cha·ic /ɑrˈkeɪ-ɪk/ *adj.* belonging to the past, or old-fashioned and no longer used

arch·bish·op /ˌɑrtʃˈbɪʃəp◂ / *n.* [C] a priest with a very high rank

ar·cher·y /ˈɑrtʃəri/ *n.* [U] the sport of shooting ARROWS from a BOW

ar·che·type /ˈɑrkɪˌtaɪp/ *n.* [C] **1** [usually singular] a perfect example of something, because it has all the most important qualities of things that belong to that type: *For a bedtime snack, milk and cookies are still the archetype.* **2** ENG. LANG. ARTS a character in a story, movie, etc. or a person who is very familiar to people and is considered a model for other characters **—archetypal** /ˌɑrkɪˈtaɪpəl◂ / *adj.*: *She grew up in an archetypal small Midwestern town.* **—archetypical** /ˌɑrkɪˈtɪpɪkəl◂ / *adj.*

ar·chi·pel·a·go /ˌɑrkəˈpɛləˌgoʊ/ *n.* (plural **archipelagos**) [C] EARTH SCIENCES a group of small islands [ORIGIN: 1600—1700 *Archipelago* "Aegean Sea" (16—19 centuries), from Italian, "main sea," from Greek *arhki* "chief" + *pelagos* "sea"]

ar·chi·tect /ˈɑrkəˌtɛkt/ *n.* [C] someone whose job is to design buildings [ORIGIN: 1500—1600 French *architecte*, from Latin, from Greek *architekton* "chief builder"]

ar·chi·tec·ture /ˈɑrkəˌtɛktʃɚ/ *n.* [U] **1** the style and design of a building or buildings: *medieval architecture* | *the architecture of Venice* **2** the art and practice of planning and designing buildings **—architectural** /ˌɑrkəˈtɛktʃərəl/ *adj.*

ar·chive /ˈɑrkaɪv/ *n.* [C usually plural] **1** a large number of records, reports, letters, etc. relating to the history of a country, organization, family, etc., or the place where these records are stored: *an **archive of** the writer's unpublished work* **2** copies of a computer's FILES that are stored on a DISK or in the computer's memory in a way that uses less space than usual, so that the computer can keep them for a long time

arch·way /ˈɑrtʃweɪ/ *n.* [C] a passage or entrance under an ARCH or arches

Arc·tic /ˈɑrktɪk, ˈɑrţɪk/ *n.* **the Arctic** the most northern part of the Earth, including parts of Alaska and Greenland, and the sea called the Arctic Ocean **—arctic** *adj.*

ˌArctic ˈCircle *n.* **the Arctic Circle** an imaginary line around the world at a particular distance from the most northern point, which is the North Pole ➔ *see picture at* GLOBE

ar·dent /ˈɑrdnt/ *adj.* having very strong feelings of admiration or determination about someone or something: *the team's ardent fans* [ORIGIN: 1300—1400 Old French, Latin, present participle of *ardere* "to burn"] **—ardently** *adv.*

THESAURUS **enthusiastic, eager, passionate, zealous, fanatical** ➔ ENTHUSIASTIC

ar·dor /ˈɑrdɚ/ *n.* [U] very strong feelings of admiration, excitement, or love: *He opposed the reforms with considerable ardor.*

ar·du·ous /ˈɑrdʒuəs/ *adj.* needing a lot of hard and continuous effort: *an arduous climb*

THESAURUS **difficult, hard, tough, challenging, demanding** ➔ DIFFICULT

are /ɚ; *strong* ɑr/ the present tense plural of the verb BE [ORIGIN: Old English *earun*]

ar·e·a /ˈɛriə/ (Ac) *n.* [C] **1** a particular part of a place, city, country, etc.: *Mom grew up **in** the Portland **area**.* | *people who live in **urban/rural areas*** (=in cities or the country) | *The police have searched the farm and **the surrounding area*** (=the area around a place).

THESAURUS

region – a large area of a country or the world: *the northwest region of Russia*
territory – land that is owned or controlled by a particular country: *Once you cross the river, you're in Canadian territory.*
zone – an area that is different in a particular way from the areas around it: *a no-parking zone*
district – a particular area of a city or the country: *San Francisco's Mission District*
neighborhood – an area of a town where people live: *a friendly neighborhood*
suburb – an area outside the center of a city, where people live: *a suburb of Boston*
slum – an area of a city that is in very bad condition, where many poor people live: *one of the city's worst slums*
ghetto – a very poor area of a city: *our urban ghettos*

2 a part of a house, office, park, etc. that is used for a particular purpose: *a large dining area* | *a no-smoking area* | *Each apartment has a storage area in the basement.* **3** a part of the surface of something such as land, water, or skin: *The fire spread over a wide area.* **4** MATH the amount of space that a flat surface or shape covers: *Use this formula to calculate the **area of** a circle.* | *The rate at which the ice melts depends on its surface area.* **5** a particular subject or type of activity: *Safety is a major **area of** concern.* | *experts in different **subject areas*** [ORIGIN: 1500—1600 Latin "piece of flat ground"]

ˈarea ˌcode *n.* [C] the three numbers before a telephone number, that you use when you telephone someone outside your local area in the U.S. and Canada

A

a·re·na /əˈrinə/ *n.* [C] **1** a building with a large flat central area surrounded by raised seats, used for sports or entertainment: *A new* ***sports arena*** *is under construction downtown.* **2 the political/public/national arena** all the people and activities relating to politics or public life: *More women are entering the political arena.*

aren't /ˈɑrənt/ *v.* **1** the short form of "are not": *They aren't here.* **2** the short form of "am not," used in questions: *I'm in big trouble, aren't I?*

ar·gon /ˈɑrgɑn/ *n.* [U] CHEMISTRY (*symbol* **Ar**) a type of gas that is an ELEMENT and that is found in the air. It does not react chemically with other gases or substances, and it is sometimes used in electric lights.

ar·gu·a·ble /ˈɑrgyuəbəl/ *adj.* if something is arguable, people can argue about it, because it is not certain

ar·gu·a·bly /ˈɑrgyuəbli/ *adv.* used when giving your opinion to say that there are good reasons why something might be true: *Wagner is arguably the best athlete in the school.*

ar·gue /ˈɑrgyu/ *v.* **1** [I] to disagree with someone, usually by talking or shouting in an angry way: *The kids are constantly arguing.* | *Two men at the bar were* ***arguing over/about*** politics. | *The catcher was* ***arguing with*** *the umpire.*

THESAURUS

have an argument: *They started arguing over money.* | *We've had serious arguments before but never split up.*
fight or **have a fight**: *My mom and dad were always fighting.* | *The neighbors had a huge fight.*
quarrel or **have a quarrel** – to have an angry argument: *Let's not quarrel about money.* | *She had a quarrel with her boyfriend.*
squabble/bicker – to argue about unimportant things: *The kids were bickering over what program to watch.*

2 [I,T] to clearly explain or prove why you think something is true or should be done: *Democrats* ***argued that*** *the cuts would hurt the poor.* | *Some experts* ***argue for/against*** *sex education in schools.* [ORIGIN: 1300—1400 Old French *arguer*, from Latin *arguere* "to make clear"]

ar·gu·ment /ˈɑrgyəmənt/ *n.* [C] **1** a disagreement, especially one in which people are angry and shout: *an* ***argument with*** *my husband* | *Jodie and I* ***had*** *a big* ***argument*** *last night.* | *Congressional* ***arguments about/over*** *the budget deficit* **2** a set of reasons you use to try to prove that something is right or wrong, true or false, etc.: *the* ***arguments for/against*** *becoming a vegetarian* | *the* ***argument that*** *the policy discriminates against women*

ar·gu·men·ta·tive /ˌɑrgyəˈmɛntət̬ɪv/ *adj.* someone who is argumentative often argues or likes arguing

a·ri·a /ˈɑriə/ *n.* [C] ENG. LANG. ARTS a song that is sung by only one person in an OPERA

ar·id /ˈærɪd/ *adj.* EARTH SCIENCES getting very little rain, and therefore very dry: *arid land* | *an arid climate*

Ar·ies /ˈɛriz/ *n.* **1** [U] the first sign of the ZODIAC, represented by a RAM **2** [C] someone born between March 21 and April 19

a·rise /əˈraɪz/ *v.* (past tense **arose** /əˈroʊz/, past participle **arisen** /əˈrɪzən/, present participle **arising**) [I] **1** to happen or appear: *the questions that arose during the discussion* | *the problems that* ***arise from*** *losing a job* **2** (literary) to get up

ar·is·toc·ra·cy /ˌærəˈstɑkrəsi/ *n.* (plural **aristocracies**) **1** [C usually singular] the people in the highest social class, who traditionally have a lot of land, money, and power **2** [U] POLITICS the system in which a country is governed by the people of the highest social class **3** [singular] HISTORY the group of rich and powerful men from a high social class who ruled the city states and controlled the government of ancient Greece [ORIGIN: 1400—1500 French *aristocratie*, from Late Latin, from Greek *aristokratia*, from *aristos* "best" + *-kratia* "-cracy"] —**aristocrat** /əˈrɪstəˌkræt/ *n.* [C] —**aristocratic** /əˌrɪstəˈkræt̬ɪk/ *adj.*

a·rith·me·tic /əˈrɪθmət̬ɪk/ *n.* [U] MATH the science of numbers involving adding, dividing, multiplying, etc. ➔ MATHEMATICS [ORIGIN: 1200—1300 Old French *arismetique*, from Latin, from Greek, from *arithmein* "to count"] —**arithmetic** /ˌærɪθˈmɛt̬ɪk◂/ *adj.*

ˌarithmetic ˈsequence *also* **ˌarithmetic proˈgression** *n.* [C] MATH a set of numbers in order of value, in which a particular number is added to each to produce the next number, for example 2, 4, 6, 8 ... ➔ GEOMETRIC SEQUENCE, NONLINEAR PROGRESSION

arm¹ /ɑrm/ *n.* [C] **1** one of the two long parts of your body between your shoulders and your hands: *He put his arm around her.* | *Marie touched her arm.* | *He had a tattoo on his* ***left/right arm.*** | *I had a pile of books* ***in my arms.*** | *She took him* ***by the arm*** (=holding his arm) *and pushed him out the door.* ➔ *see picture on page A16* **2 arms** [plural] weapons used for fighting wars ➔ ARMED: *sales of arms to the rebels* | ***nuclear arms*** | *the right to* ***bear arms*** (=keep weapons for protection) **3** the part of a chair, SOFA, etc. that you rest your arms on **4** a SLEEVE **5** a long part of an object, that moves like an arm: *the arm of the record player* **6** a particular part of a group: *the political arm of the terrorist organization* **7 be up in arms** (informal) to be very angry and ready to argue or fight: *Parents should be up in arms about the quality of the schools.* [ORIGIN: (1) Old English *earm*] [ORIGIN: (2) 1100—1200 Old French *armes* (plural), from Latin *arma*]

arm² *v.* [T] to give someone the weapons or information s/he needs ➔ ARMED: *The ship was* ***armed with*** *130 missiles.* | ***Armed with*** *a court order, Gilley moved the squatters off his land.*

ar·ma·dil·lo /ˌɑrməˈdɪloʊ/ *n.* (plural **armadillos**) [C] a small animal with a pointed nose and a hard shell that lives in hot dry parts of North and South America [ORIGIN: 1500—1600 Spanish *armado* "armed person"]

ar·ma·ments /'armәmәnts/ *n.* [plural] weapons and military equipment: *nuclear armaments*

arm·band /'armbænd/ *n.* [C] a band of material that you wear around your arm, for example to show that someone you love has died

arm·chair /'armtʃɛr/ *n.* [C] a chair with sides that you can rest your arms on → *see picture at* SEAT[1]

armed /armd/ *adj.* carrying one or more weapons: *an armed guard* | *a charge of* ***armed robbery*** (=stealing using guns) | *The fort was* ***heavily armed*** (=had a lot of weapons).

ˌarmed 'forces *n.* **the armed forces** [plural] a country's military organizations

arm·ful /'armfʊl/ *n.* [C] the amount of something that you can hold in one or both arms: *an* ***armful of*** *books*

ar·mi·stice /'arməstɪs/ *n.* [C] an agreement to stop fighting, usually for a specific period of time

ar·mor /'armɚ/ *n.* [U] **1** metal or leather clothing worn in past times by men and horses in battle: *a suit of armor* **2** a strong layer of metal that protects vehicles, ships, and aircraft

ar·mored /'armɚd/ *adj.* protected against bullets or other weapons by a strong layer of metal: *an armored car*

ar·mor·y /'arməri/ *n.* (plural **armories**) [C] a place where weapons are stored

arm·pit /'armˌpɪt/ *n.* [C] the hollow place under your arm where it joins your body

'arms conˌtrol *n.* [U] HISTORY the attempts by powerful countries to limit the number and types of war weapons that exist

'arms race *n.* **1** [C usually singular] POLITICS the competition between different countries to have a larger number of powerful weapons **2 the Arms Race** HISTORY the competition between the U.S. and the Soviet Union to produce and have the greatest number of powerful weapons, especially NUCLEAR weapons. The Arms Race began at the end of World War II and continued until the late 1980s.

ar·my /'armi/ *n.* (plural **armies**) [C] **1** *also* **Army** a military force that fights wars on land: *The two armies advanced across Europe.* | *Our son is* ***in the army***. | *He dropped out of school to* ***join the army***.

TOPIC

An army consists of **soldiers** or **troops**.
If you **join up** or **enlist**, you join the army.
If you are **drafted**, you are ordered to serve in the army by the government.
You can use **armed forces**, **the military**, or **the services** to talk in a general way about the Army, Navy, Marines, and Air Force.

2 a large group of people or animals involved in the same activity: *an* ***army of*** *ants* [ORIGIN: 1300—1400 Old French *armee*, from Medieval Latin *armata* "army, group of warships"]

a·ro·ma /ə'roʊmə/ *n.* [C] a strong pleasant smell: *the* ***aroma of*** *fresh coffee* —**aromatic** /ˌærə'mætɪk◂/ *adj.*: *aromatic oils*

THESAURUS **smell, scent, fragrance, perfume** → SMELL[2]

a·ro·ma·ther·a·py /əˌroʊmə'θɛrəpi/ *n.* [U] the use of pleasant-smelling oils to help you feel well —**aromatherapist** *n.* [C]

a·rose /ə'roʊz/ *v.* the past tense of ARISE

a·round /ə'raʊnd/ *adv., prep.* **1** surrounding something or someone: *We put a fence around the yard.* | *Mario put his arms around her.* **2** to or in many parts of a place: *Stan showed me around the office.* | *an international company with offices* ***all around*** (=in all parts of) *the world* **3** in or near a particular place: *Is there a bank around here?* **4** used when guessing a number, amount, time, etc., without being exact: *Dodger Stadium seats around 50,000 people.*

THESAURUS **about, approximately, roughly, or so, in the region of** → ABOUT[2]

5 in a circular movement: *Water pushes the wheel around.* | *Leaves were blowing* ***around and around*** (=in a continuous circular movement). **6** along the outside of a place, instead of through it: *We had to go around to the back of the house.* **7** toward or facing the opposite direction: *I'll turn the car around and pick you up at the door.* **8** present in the same place as you: *It was 11:30 at night, and nobody was around.* **9** existing: *That joke's been around for years.* **10 10 feet/3 inches etc. around** measuring a particular distance on the outside of a round object: *Redwood trees can measure 30 or 40 feet around.* → **around the clock** at CLOCK[1]

aˌround-the-'clock *adj.* [only before noun] continuing or happening all the time, both day and night: *a station where you can get around-the-clock news* —**around the clock** *adv.*

a·rouse /ə'raʊz/ *v.* [T] **1** to make someone have a particular feeling: *Her behavior aroused the suspicions of the police.* **2** to make someone feel sexually excited —**arousal** *n.* [U]

ar·raign /ə'reɪn/ *v.* [T] LAW to make someone come to court to hear what his/her crime is —**arraignment** *n.* [C,U]

ar·range /ə'reɪndʒ/ *v.* **1** [I,T] to make plans for something to happen: *Jeff will arrange our flights.* | *We've* ***arranged to*** *go to the cabin this weekend.* | *I've* ***arranged for*** *Mark* ***to*** *join us.* | *We still have to* ***arrange where*** *to meet.* **2** [T] to put a group of things or people in a particular order or position: *The file is arranged alphabetically.*

ar·range·ment /ə'reɪndʒmənt/ *n.* **1** [C usually plural] the things that you must organize for something to happen: *travel arrangements* | *We've been* ***making arrangements for*** *the wedding.*

2 [C,U] something that has been organized or agreed on: *We **have** a special **arrangement with** the bank.* | *I'm sure we can **come to some arrangement**.* | *Maxine canceled our **arrangement to** meet.* 3 [C,U] a group of things in a particular order or position, or the activity of arranging things in this way: *a flower arrangement* 4 [C,U] ENG. LANG. ARTS a piece of music that has been written or changed for a particular instrument ➔ MUSIC

ar·ray /ə'reɪ/ *n.* [C usually singular] **1** a group of people or things, especially one that is large or impressive: *a dazzling **array of** acting talent* **2** MATH a set of numbers or signs, or of computer memory units, arranged in lines across or down

ar·rears /ə'rɪrz/ *n.* [plural] **1 be in arrears** to owe someone money because your regular payment to him/her is late: *We're six weeks in arrears with the rent.* **2** money that is owed and should already have been paid: *The firm promised to pay all wage arrears promptly and in full.*

ar·rest¹ /ə'rɛst/ *v.* [T] **1** if the police arrest someone, the person is taken away because the police think s/he has done something illegal: *He was arrested and charged with murder.* | *The police **arrested** Eric **for** shoplifting.*

THESAURUS **catch, capture, apprehend ➔** CATCH¹

2 (formal) to stop something happening, or make it happen more slowly: *The drug is used to arrest the spread of the disease.* [ORIGIN: 1300—1400 Old French *arester* "to rest, arrest," from Latin *ad-* "to" + *restare* "to remain, rest"]

arrest² *n.* [C,U] the act of taking someone away and guarding him/her because s/he may have done something illegal: *The police expect to **make an arrest** soon.* | *Don't move, you're **under arrest**!*

ar·riv·al /ə'raɪvəl/ *n.* **1** [U] the act of arriving somewhere (ANT) departure: *Porter spoke to reporters shortly after his arrival.* | *The **arrival of** our flight was delayed.* | *Shortly after our **arrival in** Toronto, Lisa got sick.* **2 the arrival of sth** the time when a new idea, method, product, etc. is first used or discovered: *The arrival of the personal computer changed the way we work.* **3** [C] a person or thing that has arrived recently: ***Late arrivals** will not be admitted to the theater.*

ar·rive /ə'raɪv/ *v.* [I] **1** to get to a place: *Your letter arrived last week.* | *What time does the plane **arrive in** New York?* | *We **arrived at** Mom's two hours late.* | *We **arrived home** at ten o'clock.*

THESAURUS

get to – to reach a particular place: *What time will you get to Atlanta?*
reach – to arrive at a particular place: *The climbers reached the top of Mt. Everest.*
come – if someone comes, s/he arrives at the place where you are: *She came home yesterday.*
turn up also **show up** – to arrive somewhere, used especially when someone is waiting for you: *Lee turned up an hour late for the meeting.*
get in – to arrive at a particular time or in a particular place: *What time did your plane get in?*
come in – if an airplane, train, or ship comes in, it arrives in the place where you are: *I'll be there to pick you up when the train comes in.*
land – to arrive somewhere in an airplane, boat, etc.: *The first U.S. Marines landed in Vietnam in 1965.*

2 to happen: *At last the big day arrived!* **3 arrive at a conclusion/decision** to finally decide what to do about something **4** to begin to exist, or start being used: *Our toy sales have doubled since computer games arrived.* **5** to be born: *It was just past midnight when the baby arrived.* [ORIGIN: 1100—1200 Old French *ariver*, from Vulgar Latin *arripare* "to come to shore"]

GRAMMAR

arrive in, arrive at
Use **arrive in** with the name of a town, city, country, etc.: *What time do you arrive in New York?* | *When she first arrived in the U.S., she didn't speak any English.*
Use **arrive at** with a building such as an airport, a station, or a school: *They arrived at the airport half an hour early.* | *He was in a bad mood when he arrived at school.*

ar·ro·gant /'ærəgənt/ *adj.* behaving in a rude way because you think you are more important than other people: *an arrogant, selfish man* [ORIGIN: 1300—1400 Latin, present participle of *arrogare*, from Latin *ad-* "to" + *rogare* "to ask"] —**arrogance** *n.* [U]: *I couldn't believe her arrogance.* —**arrogantly** *adv.*

THESAURUS **proud, conceited, big-headed, vain, stuck-up, egotistical, haughty ➔** PROUD

ar·ro·gate /'ærə,geɪt/ *v.* **arrogate (to yourself) sth** (formal) to claim that you have a particular right, position, etc. without having the legal right to it

ar·row /'æroʊ/ *n.* [C] **1** a thin straight weapon with a point at one end, that you shoot from a BOW **2** a sign in the shape of an arrow, used in order to show the direction of something

ar·se·nal /'ɑrsənl/ *n.* [C] a large number of weapons, or the building where they are stored [ORIGIN: 1500—1600 Italian *arsenale*, from Arabic *dar sina'ah* "house where things are made"]

ar·se·nic /'ɑrsənɪk, 'ɑrsnɪk/ *n.* [U] a very strong poison

ar·son /'ɑrsən/ *n.* [U] the crime of deliberately burning a building —**arsonist** *n.* [C]

art /ɑrt/ *n.* **1** [U] ENG. LANG. ARTS the activity or skill of producing paintings, photographs, etc., or paintings, etc. that are produced using this skill: *Steve's studying art at college.* | *modern art* | *an art* *exhibition* | *Several famous* ***works of art*** *were stolen from the museum.*

THESAURUS

Types of art
painting – the art or skill of making a picture using paint
drawing – the art or skill of making a picture using a pen or pencil
photography – the art or skill of producing photographs
sculpture – the art or skill of making objects out of stone, wood, or clay
pottery – the activity of making pots, plates, etc. from clay
ceramics – the art or skill of making pots, plates, etc. from clay → ARTIST

2 the arts ENG. LANG. ARTS painting, music, literature, etc. all considered together: *government funding for the arts* **3 arts** [plural] ENG. LANG. ARTS subjects of study that are not considered scientific, such as history, languages, etc.: *a bachelor of arts degree* **4** [C,U] the skill involved in making or doing something: *the* ***art of*** *writing*

ar·ter·y /'ɑrt̬əri/ *n.* (plural **arteries**) [C] **1** BIOLOGY one of the tubes that carry blood from your heart to the rest of your body → VEIN **2** (formal) a main road, railroad line, or river

ar·thri·tis /ɑr'θraɪt̬ɪs/ *n.* [U] a disease that causes pain and swelling in the joints of your body [ORIGIN: 1500—1600 Latin, Greek, from *arthron* "joint"] **—arthritic** /ɑr'θrɪt̬ɪk/ *adj.*: *arthritic fingers*

ar·ti·choke /'ɑrt̬ɪ,tʃoʊk/ *n.* [C] a round green vegetable with thick pointed leaves and a firm base [ORIGIN: 1500—1600 Italian dialect *articiocco*, from Arabic *al-khurshuf* "the artichoke"]

ar·ti·cle /'ɑrt̬ɪkəl/ *n.* [C] **1** a piece of writing in a newspaper, magazine, etc.: *Did you read that* ***article on/about*** *the space shuttle?* | *magazine articles* → NEWSPAPER **2** a thing, especially one of a group of things: *an* ***article of*** *clothing*

THESAURUS **thing, object, something, item** → THING

3 ENG. LANG. ARTS in grammar, the word "the" (=the DEFINITE ARTICLE), or the word "a" or "an" (=the INDEFINITE ARTICLE), used before a noun to show whether the noun is a particular example of something or a general example of something **4** LAW a part of a legal document

ar·tic·u·late[1] /ɑr'tɪkyəlɪt/ *adj.* able to express your thoughts and feelings clearly (ANT) **inarticulate**: *a bright and articulate child* [ORIGIN: 1500—1600 Latin, past participle of *articulare* "to divide into joints, speak clearly," from *articulus* "joint, division"] **—articulately** *adv.*

ar·tic·u·late[2] /ɑr'tɪkjyə,leɪt/ *v.* [I,T] to put your thoughts or feelings into words: *It's hard to articulate what I'm feeling.* **—articulation** /ɑr,tɪkyə'leɪʃən/ *n.* [U]

ar·ti·fact /'ɑrt̬ɪ,fækt/ *n.* [C] an object such as a tool, weapon, etc. that was made in the past and is historically important: *Egyptian artifacts*

ar·ti·fi·cial /,ɑrt̬ə'fɪʃəl◂/ *adj.* **1** not real or natural, but made by people (ANT) **natural**: *artificial sweeteners* | *an artificial leg*

THESAURUS

synthetic – made from artificial substances, not natural ones: *synthetic fabrics*
fake – made to look or seem like something else in order to deceive people: *fake identity cards*
man-made – made by people, but similar to something natural: *a man-made lake*
simulated – not real, but made to look, sound, or feel real: *a simulated space journey*
imitation – not real, but made to look real: *imitation leather*
false – not real, but intended to seem real: *He was wearing a false mustache.*
virtual – made, done, seen, etc. on the Internet, rather than in the real world: *virtual reality*

2 (disapproving) not natural or sincere: *an artificial smile* [ORIGIN: 1300—1400 Old French *artificiel*, from Latin *artificium* from *artifex* "skilled worker"] **—artificially** *adv.*: *artificially colored*

,artificial in'telligence *n.* [U] IT the science of how to make computers do things that people can do, such as make decisions or see things

,artificial respi'ration *n.* [U] a way of making someone breathe again when s/he has stopped, by blowing air into his/her mouth

,artificial se'lection *n.* [U] BIOLOGY the process of breeding only those plants and animals that have useful qualities or features, in order to develop plants and animals with only these good qualities or features

ar·til·ler·y /ɑr'tɪləri/ *n.* [U] large heavy guns, usually on wheels

ar·ti·san /'ɑrt̬əzən, -sən/ *n.* [C] someone who does skilled work, making things by hand

art·ist /'ɑrt̬ɪst/ *n.* [C] **1** someone who produces art, especially paintings: *an exhibition of paintings by local artists*

THESAURUS

Types of artists
painter – someone who paints pictures
photographer – someone who takes photographs
sculptor – someone who makes sculptures
potter – someone who makes objects out of baked clay → ART

2 a professional performer such as a singer or dancer

ar·tis·tic /ɑr'tɪstɪk/ *adj.* **1** good at painting, drawing, etc.: *I never knew you were so artistic.* **2** relating to art or culture: *artistic freedom* **—artistically** *adv.*

art·ist·ry /'ɑrt̬əstri/ *n.* [U] skill in a particular artistic activity

A

A

art·sy /ˈɑrtsi/ *adj.* (informal) interested in art, or seeming to know a lot about art: *The movie has lots of artsy camera work.*

art·work /ˈɑrtˀwɚk/ *n.* **1** [U] pictures, photographs, etc. that are prepared for a book, magazine, etc. **2** [C,U] paintings and other pieces of art

as /əz; *strong* æz/ *adv., prep., conjunction* **1** used to compare people or things: *I can't run nearly* ***as*** *fast* ***as*** *I used to.* | *Tom works* ***just as*** *hard* ***as*** *the others.* | *Ask Carol to call me* ***as soon as possible*** (=very soon). **2** used to say what someone's job is or what purpose something has: *In the past, women were mainly employed as secretaries or teachers.* | *John used an old blanket as a tent.* **3** in a particular way or state: *Make sure you leave this room as you found it.* **4** while something is happening: *Be patient with your puppy as he adjusts to his new home.* | *The phone rang* ***just as*** *I was leaving.* **5** used when mentioning something that has been stated before: ***As you know****, I'm leaving at the end of this month.* | ***As I mentioned*** *in my letter, I plan to arrive on the 6th.* **6 as if/though** used when you are saying how someone or something seems: *She looked as if she had been crying.* **7 as for sb/sth** used when you are starting to talk about someone or something new that is related to what you were talking about before: *As for racism, much progress has been made, but there is still much to do.* **8 as of today/December 12th/next spring etc.** starting from a particular time: *The pay raise will come into effect as of January.* **9 as it is a)** already: *Keep quiet – we're in enough trouble as it is.* **b)** because of the situation that exists: *We were saving money to go to Hawaii, but as it is we can only afford a camping trip.* **10 as to** concerning: *The President asked for opinions as to the likelihood of war.* | *She offered no explanation as to why she'd left so suddenly.* **11** (formal) because: *James decided not to go out as he was still really tired.* ➔ **as long as** *at* LONG², **as a matter of fact** *at* MATTER¹, **as well (as sb/sth)** *at* WELL¹, **so as (not) to do sth** *at* SO¹, **such as** *at* SUCH

ASAP, **a.s.a.p.** *adv.* the abbreviation of "as soon as possible"

as·bes·tos /æsˈbɛstəs, æz-, əs-, əz-/ *n.* [U] a gray substance that does not burn easily and was used in some clothing and building material in the past [ORIGIN: 1600—1700 Latin, Greek from *asbestos* "that cannot be put out," from *sbennynai* "to put out a fire"]

as·cend /əˈsɛnd/ *v.* [I,T] (formal) **1** to move to a higher position (ANT) **descend**: *The plane ascended rapidly.* **2 in ascending order** arranged so that each thing in a group is bigger, more important, etc. than the one before

as·cen·dan·cy, **ascendency** /əˈsɛndənsi/ *n.* [U] (formal) a position of increasing power, influence, or control: *the* ***ascendancy of*** *conservative values in American life*

as·cent /əˈsɛnt, ˈæsɛnt/ *n.* **1** [C] the act of moving or climbing to a higher position (ANT) **descent**: *the first ascent of Everest* **2** [U] the process of becoming more important or successful: *Jerry's quick ascent into management surprised no one.* **3** [C] a path or road that goes gradually up (ANT) **descent**: *a* ***steep ascent***

as·cer·tain /ˌæsɚˈteɪn/ *v.* [T] (formal) to find out the truth about something: *The police have* ***ascertained that*** *the killer did not act alone.* [ORIGIN: 1500—1600 Old French *acertainer*, from *certain*]

as·cet·ic /əˈsɛt̬ɪk/ *adj.* living a simple life without any physical comforts or pleasures —**ascetic** *n.* [C] —**asceticism** /əˈsɛt̬əˌsɪzəm/ *n.* [U]

as·cribe /əˈskraɪb/ *v.*

ascribe sth **to** sb/sth *phr. v.* (formal) to say that something is caused by a particular person or thing: *Carter ascribed his problems to a lack of money.*

a·sex·u·al /eɪˈsɛkʃuəl/ *adj.* **1** not having sexual organs or not involving sexual activity **2** not interested in sex

aˌsexual reproˈduction *n.* [U] BIOLOGY a process by which some plants and some living creatures produce a new plant or creature without male and female sex cells joining together

ash /æʃ/ *n.* **1** [C,U] the soft gray powder that remains after something has been burned: *cigarette ash* ➔ *see picture at* VOLCANO **2 ashes** [plural] the ash that remains after the body of a dead person has been CREMATED (=burned) **3** [C,U] a tree that is common in Britain and North America, or the wood from this tree

a·shamed /əˈʃeɪmd/ *adj.* **1** feeling embarrassed or guilty about something: ***I felt ashamed of*** *the things I had said to him.* | *You should be* ***ashamed of yourself****, acting like that!* | *Fred was* ***ashamed to*** *admit his mistake.* | *We have* ***nothing to be ashamed of.***

> **THESAURUS** guilty, embarrassed, contrite
> ➔ GUILTY

2 be ashamed of sb feeling upset because someone's behavior embarrasses you: *Helen felt ashamed of her parents.*

ash·en /ˈæʃən/ *adj.* very pale because of shock or fear: *His face was ashen.*

a·shore /əˈʃɔr/ *adv.* onto or toward the shore of a lake, river, sea, or ocean: *The body* ***washed ashore*** *on a remote beach.* | *We* ***came ashore*** *at Long Beach.*

ash·tray /ˈæʃtreɪ/ *n.* [C] a small dish for used cigarettes and cigarette ASH

A·sia /ˈeɪʒə/ *n.* one of the seven CONTINENTS that includes land between the Ural Mountains and the Pacific Ocean

A·sian /ˈeɪʒən/ *n.* [C] someone who comes from Asia, or whose family came from Asia —**Asian** *adj.*

ˌAsian-Aˈmerican *n.* [C] an American whose family originally came from Asia —**Asian-American** *adj.*

a·side¹ /ə'saɪd/ *adv.* **1** to the side or away from you: *Jim stepped aside to let me pass.* | *He* ***took/pulled/called*** *Kate* ***aside*** *so they could talk privately.* **2 put/set sth aside a)** to keep or not use something so that you can use it later: *I try to* ***put aside*** *$30 a week* ***for*** *my vacation.* **b)** to leave something to be dealt with at another time: *We* ***put aside*** *our* ***differences*** *to fight a common enemy.* **3 aside from sb/sth a)** except for someone or something: *Aside from coal, copper is the state's largest natural resource.* **b)** in addition to: *Aside from providing maps of the downtown area, the book also contains a guide to the city's best restaurants.* (SYN) **apart from**

aside² *n.* [C] **1** a remark you make in a quiet voice so that only a few people can hear **2** ENG. LANG. ARTS words spoken by an actor to the people watching a play, that the other characters in the play do not hear

ask /æsk/ *v.* [I,T] **1** to make a request for someone to tell you something: *"What's your name?" she asked.* | *I asked him his phone number.* | *Can I* ***ask a question****?* | *He* ***asked how*** *this could have happened.* | ***Ask*** *Elaine* ***if*** *she knows what time it is.* | *Visitors often* ***ask about*** *the place.* | *You should* ***ask around*** (=ask a lot of people) *before deciding.*

THESAURUS

question/interrogate – if the police question or interrogate people, they ask them a lot of questions in order to get information: *The two men are being questioned by police about the robbery.*
inquire (formal) – to ask someone for information or facts about something: *I'm writing to inquire about the job you advertised.*
poll – to officially ask a lot of people about something, for example to find out their opinion: *58% of those polled supported the president.*

2 to make a request for help, advice, information, etc.: *If you need anything, just ask.* | ***Ask*** *Paula* ***to*** *mail the letters.* | *Some people don't like to* ***ask for*** *help.* | *I had to* ***ask*** *my parents* ***for*** *money.* | ***Ask*** *your dad* ***if*** *we can borrow his car.* | *Karen* ***asked to*** *see the doctor.*

THESAURUS

request – to ask for something officially: *I wrote to request information about the college.*
order – to ask for food or drinks in a restaurant: *He ordered a club sandwich.*
demand – to ask for something in a firm or angry way: *They're demanding immediate payment.*
beg – to ask for something that you want very much: *"Please can I have one?" she begged.* | *I begged her to stay.*
plead/implore – to ask for something important in an urgent way because you want it very much: *She pleaded with them not to hurt her daughter.*

3 to invite someone to go somewhere: *Jerry would like to* ***ask her out*** (=invite her to a movie, restaurant, etc. because he likes her). | *Why don't you* ***ask them over*** (=invite them to your house) *for dinner?* **4** to want a particular amount of money for something you are selling: *He's asking $2,000 for that old car!* **5 Don't ask me!** (spoken) said when you do not know the answer to a question: *"When will Vicky get home?" "Don't ask me!"* **6 If you ask me** used in order to emphasize your opinion: *If you ask me, he should be in jail.* **7 be asking for trouble/it** (informal) to be behaving in a way that will probably cause problems: *Eating lots of fatty food and not exercising is just asking for trouble.* [ORIGIN: Old English *ascian*]

a·skance /ə'skæns/ *adv.* **look askance (at sb/sth)** to look at someone or something in a way that shows you do not approve of him, her, or it

a·skew /ə'skyu/ *adv.* not straight or level: *His coat was wrinkled and his hat was askew.*

a·sleep /ə'slip/ *adj.* sleeping (ANT) **awake**: *Be quiet. The baby is asleep.* | *I* ***fell asleep*** (=started sleeping) *in front of the TV.* | ***fast/sound asleep*** (=sleeping very deeply)

as·par·a·gus /ə'spærəgəs/ *n.* [U] a long thin green vegetable

as·pect /'æspɛkt/ (Ac) *n.* [C] one part of a situation, plan, or subject that has many parts: *The committee discussed several* ***aspects of*** *the traffic problem.* | *The book deals with the social aspects of human behavior.* [ORIGIN: 1300—1400 Latin, past participle of *aspicere* "to look at," from *ad-* "to" + *specere* "to look"]

THESAURUS **characteristic, quality, feature**
→ CHARACTERISTIC¹

as·pen /'æspən/ *n.* [C] a tall thin straight tree that grows in the western U.S.

aspen

as·per·sion /ə'spɚʒən, -ʃən/ *n.* (formal) **cast aspersions on sb/sth** to criticize someone or something, or make an unfair judgment [ORIGIN: 1500—1600 Latin *aspersio* "throwing drops of water onto someone in a religious ceremony," from *aspergere*, from *ad-* "to" + *spargere* "to scatter"]

as·phalt /'æsˌfɔlt/ *n.* [U] a hard black substance used on the surface of roads

as·phyx·i·ate /ə'sfɪksiˌeɪt, æ-/ *v.* [I,T] (formal) to stop someone breathing (SYN) **suffocate** —**asphyxiation** /əˌsfɪksi'eɪʃən/ *n.* [U]

as·pi·ra·tion /ˌæspə'reɪʃən/ *n.* [C usually plural, U] a strong desire to have or achieve something: *a young man with* ***political aspirations***

as·pire /ə'spaɪɚ/ *v.* [I] to have a strong desire to

A

achieve something: *Milligan **aspires to be** Governor of the state.* [ORIGIN: 1300—1400 Old French *aspirer*, from Latin *aspirare* "to breathe on"] —**aspiring** *adj.*: *aspiring young actors*

as·pi·rin /'æsprɪn/ *n.* (plural **aspirins** *or* **aspirin**) [C,U] a drug that reduces pain and fever: *I **took** an **aspirin** and went to bed.* [ORIGIN: 1800—1900 German *acetylierte spirsäure* type of acid from which aspirin is obtained, from Modern Latin *spiraea* type of bush from which this acid is obtained]

ass /æs/ *n.* [C] (old-fashioned) a DONKEY

as·sail /ə'seɪl/ *v.* [T] **1** [usually passive] (literary) if a thought or feeling assails you, it worries or upsets you: *As soon as I'd finished the test, I was **assailed by doubts**.* **2** to criticize someone or something severely: *countries who are **assailed for** their human rights records* **3** (formal) to attack someone or something violently

as·sail·ant /ə'seɪlənt/ *n.* [C] (formal) someone who attacks someone else

as·sas·sin /ə'sæsən/ *n.* [C] someone who murders an important person

as·sas·si·nate /ə'sæsə,neɪt/ *v.* [T] to murder an important person: *a plot to assassinate the President* —**assassination** /ə,sæsə'neɪʃən/ *n.* [C,U]

THESAURUS **kill, murder, execute, put to death, slay** ➔ KILL[1]

as·sault[1] /ə'sɔlt/ *n.* [C,U] **1** (formal) the crime of attacking a person: *He served three years in prison for assault.* | *an increase in **sexual assaults*** | *He was charged with **assault on/against** a police officer.* **2** an attack by an army to take control of a place: *the assault on Iwo Jima*

assault[2] *v.* [T] to attack someone violently: *Two men assaulted him after he left the bar.*

as·sem·ble /ə'sɛmbəl/ (Ac) *v.* **1** [I,T] if you assemble people or things, or if people assemble, they are brought together in the same place: *A crowd had assembled in front of the White House.*

THESAURUS **meet, get together, gather, come together, congregate, convene** ➔ MEET[1]

2 [T] to put the different parts of something together: *You'll need to assemble the grill yourself.* [ORIGIN: 1200—1300 Old French *assembler*, from Latin *ad-* "to" + *simul* "together"]

THESAURUS **build, construct, put up, erect** ➔ BUILD[1]

➔ *see picture at* BUILD[1]

as·sem·bly /ə'sɛmbli/ (Ac) *n.* (plural **assemblies**) **1** [C] a group of people who are elected to make laws or decisions for a country, state, or organization: *the New York State Assembly* **2** [C,U] a meeting of a group of people for a particular purpose: *The mayor told an **assembly of** reporters that the fire was now under control.* | *The military government imposed strict controls on **freedom of assembly*** (=the right of people to gather as a group to discuss something). **3** [C,U] a meeting of all the teachers and students of a school **4** [U] the process of putting something together: *The fan comes with assembly directions.*

as'sembly ,line *n.* [C] a system for making things in a factory, in which the products move past a line of workers who each make or check one part

as·sem·bly·man /ə'sɛmblimən/ *n.* (plural **assemblymen** /-mən/) [C] a man who is a member of a state assembly

as·sem·bly·wom·an /ə'sɛmbli,wʊmən/ *n.* (plural **assemblywomen** /-,wɪmɪn/) [C] a woman who is a member of a state assembly

as·sent /ə'sɛnt/ *n.* [U] (formal) official agreement: *The court **gave its assent**.* —**assent** *v.* [I]

as·sert /ə'sɚt/ *v.* [T] **1** to state firmly that something is true: *Professor Ross **asserts that** American schools are not strict enough.* **2** to behave in a determined and confident way to make people respect you: *The president tried to assert his power over the military.* | *Don't be afraid to **assert yourself** in the interview.*

as·ser·tion /ə'sɚʃən/ *n.* [C,U] something that you say or write that you strongly believe: *He repeated his **assertion that** he was innocent.*

as·ser·tive /ə'sɚtɪv/ *adj.* behaving confidently so that people pay attention to what you say: *She needs to be more assertive.* —**assertively** *adv.* —**assertiveness** *n.* [U]

THESAURUS **confident, self-confident, self-assured, extrovert** ➔ CONFIDENT

as·sess /ə'sɛs/ (Ac) *v.* [T] **1** to make a judgment about a person or situation after thinking carefully about it: *Psychologists will assess the child's behavior.* | *The research aims to assess the impact of advertising on children* | *We're trying to **assess what** went wrong.*

THESAURUS **judge, evaluate, appraise, gauge** ➔ JUDGE[2]

2 to calculate the quality, amount, or value of something: *They **assessed** the house **at** $90,000.* [ORIGIN: 1400—1500 Old French *assesser*, from Latin, past participle of *assidere* "to sit beside, help in making judgments," from *ad-* "to" + *sedere* "to sit"] —**assessment** *n.* [C,U]: *The Federal Reserve Bank's assessment of the economy is gloomy.* | *a reading assessment test*

as·set /'æsɛt/ *n.* **1 assets** [plural] something, such as a building, machine, or money, which a company owns and uses to produce goods or services ➔ FINANCIAL ASSET: *a firm with $1.3 billion in assets* **2** [C usually singular] something or someone that helps you to succeed ➔ LIABILITY: *A sense of humor is a real asset.* | *You're an **asset to** the company, George.* [ORIGIN: 1800—1900 *assets* (singular) "enough money to pay debts," from Old French *assez* "enough"]

as·sid·u·ous /ə'sɪdʒuəs/ *adj.* (formal) very careful to make sure that something is done correctly or completely: *an assiduous examination of the paintings* —**assiduously** *adv.* —**assiduousness** *n.* [U]

as·sign /ə'saɪn/ (Ac) *v.* [T] **1** to give someone a job to do: *I've been assigned the task of looking after the new students.* | *Guards were* ***assigned to*** *the President.* **2** to give something to someone: *They assigned me a small room.* **3** to give a particular time, value, place, etc. to something: *To solve the equation, X and Y must be assigned a value.* [ORIGIN: 1300—1400 Old French *assigner*, from Latin *assignare*, from *ad-* "to" + *signare* "to mark"]

as·sign·ment /ə'saɪnmənt/ (Ac) *n.* **1** [C,U] a job or piece of work that is given to someone: *Have you all turned in your homework assignments?* | *The newspaper is sending her* ***on a*** *special* ***assignment to*** *Libya.* | *She was arrested while* ***on assignment*** *in Cambodia.*

> THESAURUS **essay, composition, paper →** ESSAY

2 [U] the act of giving people particular jobs to do: *The resources manager is responsible for the assignment of funds to each project.*

as·sim·i·late /ə'sɪmə,leɪt/ *v.* **1** [I,T] to accept someone completely as a member of a group, or to become an accepted member of a group: *Many ethnic groups have been* ***assimilated into*** *American society.* **2** [T] to learn and understand information: *We need someone who can assimilate new ideas quickly.* —**assimilation** /ə,sɪmə'leɪʃən/ *n.* [U]

as·sist /ə'sɪst/ (Ac) *v.* [I,T] (formal) to help someone do something: *Two nurses* ***assisted*** *Dr. Bernard* ***in*** *performing the operation.* [ORIGIN: 1400—1500 French *assister* "to be present, help," from Latin *assistere*, from *ad-* "to" + *sistere* "to cause to stand"]

> THESAURUS **help, give sb a hand (with sth), lend a hand (with sth), aid, facilitate, aid and abet →** HELP[1]

as·sist·ance /ə'sɪstəns/ (Ac) *n.* [U] help or support: *The company* ***provides*** *technical* ***assistance*** *for new computer users.* | *We offer* ***financial assistance*** *to students.* | *Can I* ***be of*** *any* ***assistance*** (=help you)? | *No one would* ***come to*** *her* ***assistance*** (=help her).

as·sist·ant /ə'sɪstənt/ (Ac) *n.* [C] **1** someone whose job is to help someone who has a higher rank: *an administrative assistant* **2 assistant manager/director/editor etc.** someone whose job is just below the position of manager, director, etc.

> THESAURUS **senior, chief, junior →** POSITION[1]

as·so·ci·ate[1] /ə'souʃi,eɪt, -si,eɪt/ *v.* **1** [T] if you associate two people or things, you see that they are connected in some way: *I always* ***associate*** *summer* ***with*** *travel.* **2 be associated with sb/sth a)** to be related to a particular subject, activity, group, etc.: *health problems associated with tobacco* **b)** *also* **associate yourself with sb/sth** to show support for someone or something: *I refuse to be friends with anyone who associates himself with racists.* **3 associate with sb** to spend time with someone: *I don't like the people she associates with.* [ORIGIN: 1300—1400 Latin, past participle of *associare*, from *ad-* "to" + *sociare* "to join"]

as·so·ci·ate[2] /ə'souʃiɪt, -siɪt/ *n.* [C] someone that you work or do business with: *a business associate*

As,sociate of 'Arts (*abbreviation* **A.A.**) *also* **As'sociate de,gree** *n.* [C] a degree given after two years of study at a COMMUNITY COLLEGE

as·so·ci·a·tion /ə,sousi'eɪʃən, -ʃi'eɪ-/ *n.* **1** [C] an organization for people who do the same kind of work or have the same interests: *the National Education Association*

> THESAURUS **organization, institution, institute, (political) party, club, society, union, agency →** ORGANIZATION

2 in association with sb/sth together with someone or something else: *Community groups are working in association with the schools.* **3** [C usually plural] a memory or feeling that is related to a particular place, event, etc.: *Los Angeles has happy associations for me.*

as,sociative 'property *n.* [C] MATH the quality of particular types of operations in mathematics, such as addition or MULTIPLICATION, by which the result is the same no matter what order the CALCULATIONS in PARENTHESES are done in, as long as the order of the series of numbers is not changed, as in $(3 + 5) + 2 = 3 + (5 + 2) = 10$

as·so·nance /'æsənəns/ *n.* [U] ENG. LANG. ARTS in poetry, the use of words that have similar vowel sounds, for example the words "born" and "warm"

as·sort·ed /ə'sɔrt̬ɪd/ *adj.* of various different types: *a box of assorted cookies*

as·sort·ment /ə'sɔrt˺mənt/ *n.* [C] a mixture of different types of the same thing: *an* ***assortment of*** *chocolates*

as·suage /ə'sweɪdʒ/ *v.* [T] (literary) to make a bad feeling less painful or severe (SYN) **relieve**: *What could possibly assuage his guilt?* [ORIGIN: 1200—1300 Old French *assouagier*, from Latin *ad-* "to" + *suavis* "sweet"]

as·sume /ə'sum/ (Ac) *v.* [T] **1** to think that something is true, although you have no proof: *Your light wasn't on, so I* ***assumed (that)*** *you were out.* | ***Assuming (that)*** *Dad agrees, when do you want to shop for cars?*

> THESAURUS
> **be under the impression that ...** – to wrongly believe that something is true: *They were under the impression that he was an FBI agent.*

A

presume – to think that something is true because it is likely, and you have no reason to doubt this: *The defendant is presumed innocent until proved guilty.*
take it for granted (that) – to be sure that something is true, without ever asking yourself whether you are right or not: *I never asked if he was single – I just took it for granted.*

2 (formal) to take control, power, or a particular position: *Stalin* ***assumed power/control*** *in 1941.* **3 assume an air/expression of sth** (formal) to pretend to feel something or be something you are not: *Andy assumed an air of innocence when the teacher walked by.* **4** to start having a particular quality or appearance: *Her family life assumed more importance after the accident.* **5** to be based on the idea that something else is correct: *The company's net earnings forecast assumes sales will grow at 7%.* [ORIGIN: 1500—1600 Latin *assumere*, from *ad-* "to" + *sumere* "to take"]

as·sumed /ə'sumd/ *adj.* **an assumed name/identity** a false name: *Davis applied for a loan* ***under an assumed name.***

as·sump·tion /ə'sʌmpʃən/ (Ac) *n.* **1** [C] something that you think is true, although you have no proof: *How can you* ***make an assumption*** *about her if you've never met her?* | *The budget is* ***based on the assumption*** *that the economy will grow at the same rate.* **2** [U] (formal) the act of starting to have control or power: *the general's assumption of power after the revolution*

as·sur·ance /ə'ʃʊrəns/ (Ac) *n.* **1** [C,U] a promise that something is true or will happen: *We need an* ***assurance that*** *you can pay off your loan.* | *The vaccine is untested and provides no assurance of immunity.* **2** [U] confidence in your own abilities or the truth of what you are saying: *Cindy answered their questions with quiet assurance.*

as·sure /ə'ʃʊr/ (Ac) *v.* [T] **1** to tell someone that something will definitely happen or is definitely true so that s/he is less worried: *The doctors* ***assured*** *me* ***(that)*** *her life was not in danger.* | *The concert won't be canceled,* ***I can assure you.*** | *The speech* ***assured*** *voters* ***of*** *the senator's continued commitment to health care.* **2** to make something certain to happen or be achieved: *The new contract means that the future of the company is assured.* [ORIGIN: 1300—1400 Old French *assurer*, from Medieval Latin *assecurare*, from Latin *ad-* "to" + *securus* "safe"]

as·sured /ə'ʃʊrd/ (Ac) *adj.* **1** showing confidence in your abilities: *Despite her assured manner, Amy felt nervous.* **2** certain to be achieved: *Victory was assured.*

as·sur·ed·ly /ə'ʃʊrɪdli/ (Ac) *adv.* (formal) definitely or certainly: *The governor is most assuredly in favor of the reforms.*

as·ta·tine /'æstə,tin, -tɪn/ *n.* [U] CHEMISTRY (*symbol* **At**) a RADIOACTIVE chemical ELEMENT belonging to the HALOGEN group

as·ter·isk /'æstərɪsk/ *n.* [C] a mark like a star (*), used especially to show something interesting or important [ORIGIN: 1300—1400 Late Latin *asteriscus*, from Greek, "little star"]

as·ter·oid /'æstə,rɔɪd/ *n.* [C] PHYSICS a large object made of rock, that moves around in space → SPACE[1] [ORIGIN: 1800—1900 Greek *asteroeides* "like a star," from *aster* "star"]

as·then·o·sphere /əs'θɛnə,sfɪr/ *n.* **the asthenosphere** EARTH SCIENCES a weak area of the Earth's MANTLE (=part of the Earth around the central core) consisting of several hundred kilometers of rock that can change its usual shape under pressure

asth·ma /'æzmə/ *n.* [U] an illness that makes it difficult to breathe [ORIGIN: 1300—1400 Medieval Latin *asma*, from Greek *asthma*, from *azein* "to breathe hard"] —**asthmatic** /æz'mæṭɪk/ *adj.*

as·ton·ish /ə'stɑnɪʃ/ *v.* [T] to surprise someone very much: *Einstein's work still astonishes physicists.* [ORIGIN: 1500—1600 *astone* "to astonish" (14—17 centuries) from Old French *estoner*, from Latin *tonare* "to thunder"]

as·ton·ished /ə'stɑnɪʃt/ *adj.* very surprised: *Parker seemed* ***astonished that*** *someone wanted to buy the house.* | *I was* ***astonished to*** *learn that she was only 22.*

THESAURUS **surprised, amazed, shocked, astounded, flabbergasted, stunned, dumbfounded, nonplussed, taken aback** → SURPRISED

as·ton·ish·ing /ə'stɑnɪʃɪŋ/ *adj.* very surprising: *astonishing news* —**astonishingly** *adv.*

THESAURUS **surprising, extraordinary, amazing, shocking, astounding, staggering, stunning** → SURPRISING

as·ton·ish·ment /ə'stɑnɪʃmənt/ *n.* [U] great surprise: ***To our astonishment,*** *Sue won the race.* | *Ken looked at her* ***in astonishment.***

as·tound /ə'staʊnd/ *v.* [T] to make someone feel very surprised: *My brother's decision astounded us all.*

as·tound·ed /ə'staʊndɪd/ *adj.* very surprised: *I was* ***astounded at*** *what I saw.*

THESAURUS **surprised, amazed, shocked, astonished, flabbergasted, stunned, dumbfounded, nonplussed, taken aback** → SURPRISED

as·tound·ing /ə'staʊndɪŋ/ *adj.* so surprising that it is difficult to believe: *the band's astounding success* —**astoundingly** *adv.*

THESAURUS **surprising, extraordinary, amazing, shocking, astonishing, staggering, stunning** → SURPRISING

a·stray /ə'streɪ/ *adv.* **1 go astray** (formal) to be lost: *One of the documents we sent them has gone* *astray.* **2 lead sb astray** to encourage someone to do bad or immoral things

a·stride /ə'straɪd/ *adv., prep.* having one leg on each side of something: *a young girl* ***sitting astride*** *a horse*

as·trin·gent /ə'strɪndʒənt/ *adj.* **1** criticizing someone very severely: *astringent remarks* **2** CHEMISTRY able to make your skin less oily or stop a wound from bleeding: *an astringent cream*

as·trol·o·gy /ə'strɑlədʒi/ *n.* [U] the study of the position and movements of stars and PLANETs and how they might affect people's lives [ORIGIN: 1300—1400 Old French *astrologie* "use of astronomy for human purposes"] **—astrologer** *n.* [C] **—astrological** /ˌæstrə'lɑdʒɪkəl/ *adj.*

as·tro·naut /'æstrəˌnɔt, -ˌnɑt/ *n.* [C] someone who travels in a spacecraft ➔ SPACE¹

as·tro·nom·i·cal /ˌæstrə'nɑmɪkəl/ *adj.* **1** extremely large in amount: *astronomical prices*

> THESAURUS **high, extortionate, exorbitant**
> ➔ EXPENSIVE

2 relating to the study of the stars and PLANETS

as·tron·o·my /ə'strɑnəmi/ *n.* [U] PHYSICS the scientific study of the stars and PLANETS **—astronomer** *n.* [C]

as·tute /ə'stut/ *adj.* quick to understand a situation and how to get an advantage from it: *an astute politician* **—astutely** *adv.*

a·sy·lum /ə'saɪləm/ *n.* **1** [U] protection that a government gives to someone who escapes from a country for political reasons: *He was granted* ***political asylum.*** **2** [C] (old-fashioned) a hospital for people with mental illness [ORIGIN: 1400—1500 Latin, Greek *asylon*, from *asylos* "not able to be seized"]

a·sym·met·ri·cal /ˌeɪsɪ'mɛtrɪkəl/ *also* **a·sym·met·ric** /ˌeɪsɪ'mɛtrɪk◂/ *adj.* having two sides that are different in size and shape (ANT) **symmetrical**

as·ymp·tote /'æsɪmˌtoʊt/ *n.* [C] MATH a straight line on a GRAPH, that a curved line continuously moves closer to but never touches

at /ət; *strong* æt/ *prep.* **1** used to say where someone or something is or where something happens: *Meet me at my house.* | *There was a long line at the bank.* | *I parked my car* ***at the end of*** *the road.* | *John's at work* (=in the place where he works). | *I'll see you at Jane's* (=Jane's house). **2** used to say when something happens: *The movie starts at 8:00.* | *Alison gets lonely at Christmas.* **3** used to say what event or activity someone is taking part in: *I'm sorry, Mr. Rivers is* ***at lunch*** (=eating lunch). **4** used to show who or what a particular action or feeling is directed toward: *Jake shot at the deer but missed.* | *Stop shouting at me!* | *Jenny, I'm surprised at you.* **5** used in order to show a price, rate, speed, level, age, etc.: *Gas is selling at over $3 a gallon.* | *I started school at age five.* **6** used in order to show what you are considering when making a judgment about someone's ability: *How's Brian doing at his new job?* | *Debbie is* ***good/bad at*** *math.* **7** in a particular state: *Many children are still at risk of disease.* | *The two nations are at war.* **8** the symbol @, used in email addresses [ORIGIN: Old English *æt*] ➔ **at all** *at* ALL¹, **at first** *at* FIRST³, **at least** *at* LEAST¹

ate /eɪt/ *v.* the past tense of EAT

a·the·ist /'eɪθiɪst/ *n.* [C] someone who does not believe in God ➔ AGNOSTIC **—atheism** *n.* [U]

ath·e·ro·scle·ro·sis /ˌæθəroʊsklə'roʊsɪs/ *n.* [U] BIOLOGY a medical condition in which substances containing a lot of fat form on the inside surface of the tubes that carry blood from your heart to the rest of your body, limiting or blocking the flow of blood

ath·lete /'æθlit/ *n.* [C] someone who is good at sports or who often plays sports: *a professional athlete* [ORIGIN: 1400—1500 Latin *athleta*, from Greek *athletes*, from *athlon* "prize, competition"]

ath·let·ic /æθ'lɛt̬ɪk/ *adj.* **1** physically strong and good at sports **2** relating to athletics: *the athletic department*

ath·let·ics /æθ'lɛt̬ɪks/ *n.* [U] sports in general

At·lan·tic O·cean /ətˀˌlænt̬ɪk 'oʊʃən/ *n.* **the Atlantic Ocean, the Atlantic** the large ocean between North and South America in the west, and Europe and Africa in the east

at·las /'ætˀləs/ *n.* [C] a book of maps: *a world atlas* [ORIGIN: 1500—1600 *Atlas* giant in an ancient Greek story who had to hold up the sky; because his name was used as the title of a 16th-century book of maps]

ATM *n.* [C] **Automated Teller Machine** a machine that you use with a card to get money from your bank account ➔ ACCOUNT¹

at·mos·phere /'ætˀməˌsfɪr/ *n.* **1** [singular, U] the feeling that an event, situation, or place gives you: *The atmosphere in the bar was casual.* | *The restaurant has a nice friendly atmosphere.* | *an* ***atmosphere of*** *suspicion* **2** [singular] PHYSICS the mixture of gases that surrounds the Earth or another PLANET **3** [singular] the air in a room: *a smoky atmosphere* [ORIGIN: 1600—1700 Modern Latin *atmosphaera*, from Greek *atmos* "liquid in the air, vapor" + Latin *sphaera* "sphere"] **—atmospheric** /ˌætˀmə'sfɪrɪk◂/ *adj.* *see picture on page 58*

ˌatmospheric 'pressure *n.* [U] PHYSICS the pressure caused by the weight of the gases in the Earth's atmosphere pressing down on the surface of the Earth

at·oll /'ætɔl, -tɑl/ *n.* [C] EARTH SCIENCES a CORAL ISLAND in the shape of a ring

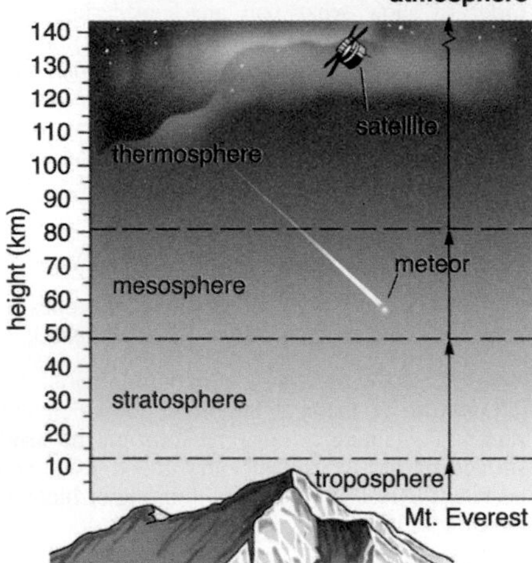

at·om /ˈæt̬əm/ *n.* [C] PHYSICS the smallest part of an ELEMENT that can exist alone [ORIGIN: 1500—1600 Latin *atomus*, from Greek, from *atomos* "that cannot be divided"]

atom
neutron
electron
proton

a·tom·ic /əˈtɑmɪk/ *adj.* PHYSICS relating to atoms and the energy produced by splitting them: *atomic energy*

aˌtomic ˈbomb *n.* [C] a very powerful bomb that splits atoms to cause an extremely large explosion

aˌtomic ˈmass *n.* [U] PHYSICS the weight of an atom, usually given in atomic mass units

aˌtomic ˈmass ˌnumber *n.* [C] PHYSICS the total number of PROTONS in the NUCLEUS (=central part) of an atom

aˌtomic ˈmass ˌunit *n.* [U] PHYSICS (*written abbreviation* **amu**) an amount used as a standard for representing the MASS (=weight) of an atom, based on the weight of a CARBON-12 atom

aˌtomic ˈnumber *n.* [C] PHYSICS an ATOMIC MASS NUMBER

a·to·nal /eɪˈtoʊnl/ *adj.* ENG. LANG. ARTS atonal music is not based on a particular KEY (=seven musical notes with a particular base note) —**atonally** *adv.* —**atonality** /ˌeɪtoʊˈnæləṭi/ *n.* [U]

a·tone /əˈtoʊn/ *v.* [I] (formal) to do something to show that you are sorry for doing something wrong: *Reilly would like to **atone for** his mistakes.* —**atonement** *n.* [U]

a·tri·um /ˈeɪtriəm/ *n.* (plural **atriums** *or* **atria** /-triə/) [C] **1** a large open hall, usually in the

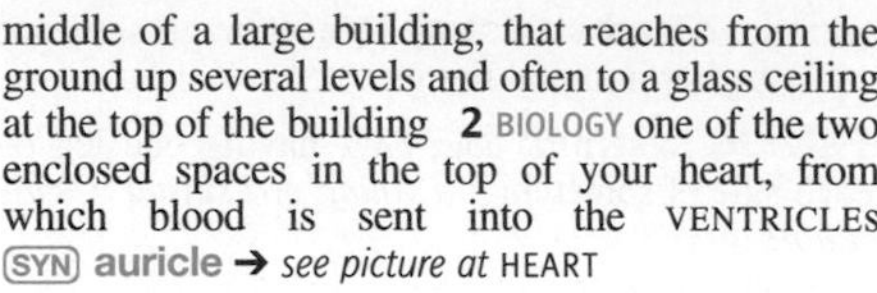
middle of a large building, that reaches from the ground up several levels and often to a glass ceiling at the top of the building **2** BIOLOGY one of the two enclosed spaces in the top of your heart, from which blood is sent into the VENTRICLES (SYN) **auricle** ➔ *see picture at* HEART

a·tro·cious /əˈtroʊʃəs/ *adj.* extremely bad: *atrocious weather* | *My spelling is atrocious.* —**atrociously** *adv.*

THESAURUS **bad, awful, terrible, horrible, appalling, horrific, lousy, horrendous, abysmal** ➔ BAD[1]

a·troc·i·ty /əˈtrɑsəṭi/ *n.* (plural **atrocities**) [C,U] very cruel or violent action: *the atrocities of war*

at·ro·phy /ˈætrəfi/ *v.* (**atrophied**, **atrophies**) [I,T] to become weak, or make something become weak, because of lack of use or lack of blood: *His muscles had atrophied after the surgery.*

at·tach /əˈtætʃ/ (Ac) *v.* [T] **1** to fasten or join one thing to another: *Please **attach** a photograph **to** your application.*

THESAURUS **fasten, secure, join, glue, tape, staple, clip, tie** ➔ FASTEN

2 be attached to sb/sth to like someone or something very much, especially because you have known him/her or had it for a long time: *As a doctor, I cannot get too attached to my patients.* **3** to connect a document or FILE to an email so that you can send them together: *I attach a copy of the spreadsheet with this email for your records.* **4 attach importance/blame etc. to sth** to believe that something is important, valuable, guilty, etc.: *They seem to attach more importance to money than to happiness.*

at·tach·ment /əˈtætʃmənt/ (Ac) *n.* **1** [C,U] a strong feeling of loyalty, love, or friendship: *a mother's deep **attachment to** her baby* **2** [C] a piece of equipment that you attach to a machine to make it do a particular job: *The vacuum cleaner has various attachments.* **3** [C] IT a FILE that you send with an email message: *I can't **open** the **attachment**.*

at·tack[1] /əˈtæk/ *n.* **1** [C,U] a violent action that is intended to hurt a person or damage a place: *There have been several **attacks on** foreigners recently.* | *a **terrorist attack*** | *a **bomb/knife/missile etc. attack*** | *The city is **under attack*** (=being attacked).

THESAURUS

military attack
invasion – an occasion when an army enters a country and takes control of it
raid – a short surprise military attack on a place
assault – an attack by an army to take control of a place
ambush – a sudden attack by people who have been waiting and hiding
counterattack – an attack that you make against someone who has attacked you

2 [C,U] strong criticism: *an **attack on** the government's welfare policy* | *The mayor is **under** heavy **attack for** his racist remarks.* 3 [C] a short period of time when you are sick, worried, afraid, etc.: *an **attack of** asthma* | ***panic attacks*** [ORIGIN: 1600—1700 French *attaquer*, from Old Italian *attaccare*, from *stacca* "sharp post"] → HEART ATTACK

attack² *v.* 1 [I,T] to try to hurt or kill someone: *Dan was attacked as he got into his car.* | *He was arrested for **attacking** his brother **with** a knife.* 2 [T] to criticize someone strongly: *Newspapers **attacked** the President **for** failing to cut taxes.*

THESAURUS criticize, lambast, knock, find fault with, be disparaging about sb/sth → CRITICIZE

3 [T] if a disease, insect, or substance attacks something, it damages it: *The virus attacks the body's immune system.*

at·tack·er /ə'tækə/ *n.* [C] someone who uses violence to hurt someone: *The police have been unable to identify her attacker.*

THESAURUS criminal, robber, mugger, murderer → CRIMINAL²

at·tain /ə'teɪn/ (Ac) *v.* [T] 1 to achieve something after trying for a long time: *More women are attaining high positions in business.* | *Sandra took every opportunity to **attain** her **goal**.* 2 to reach a particular level, age, size, etc.: *These fish can attain a length of eight feet and weigh over 300 pounds.* [ORIGIN: 1200—1300 Old French *ataindre*, from Latin *attingere*, from *ad-* "to" + *tangere* "to touch"] —**attainable** *adj.*: *The objectives must be reasonable and attainable.* —**attainment** *n.* [C,U]: *Educational attainment is the key to success.*

at·tempt¹ /ə'tɛmpt/ *v.* [T] to try to do something, especially something difficult: *The plane crashed while attempting an emergency landing.* | *He died when he **attempted to** rescue his wife.*

THESAURUS try, see if you can do sth, do your best, make an effort to do sth, endeavor → TRY¹

attempt² *n.* [C] 1 an act of trying to do something: *an **attempt to** be funny* | *Can't you **make an attempt to** be nice to your sister?* | *His early **attempts at** writing were a dismal failure.* | ***In an attempt to** save money, I offered to do the work myself.* 2 an act of trying to kill someone, especially someone important or famous, that fails: *an **assassination attempt** on the President*

at·tend /ə'tɛnd/ *v.* [I,T] 1 to be present at an event, such as a meeting, class, etc.: *More than 1,000 people attended the conference.* | *Please let us know if you are unable to attend.* 2 to go regularly to a school, church, etc.: *Neither of my parents attended college.*

attend to sb/sth *phr. v.* (formal) to give attention to someone or something: *I have some business to attend to.*

at·tend·ance /ə'tɛndəns/ *n.* [C,U] 1 the number of people who attend an event, such as a meeting, concert, etc.: *an average attendance of 4,000 fans per game* | *Be quiet while I **take attendance*** (=count how many students are in class today). 2 the act of regularly going to a meeting, class, etc.: *He continued his daily **attendance at** Mass.*

at·tend·ant /ə'tɛndənt/ *n.* [C] someone whose job is to take care of customers in a public place: *a parking lot attendant*

at·ten·tion /ə'tɛnʃən/ *n.* [U] 1 the state of carefully watching, listening, or thinking about someone or something: *Sorry, what did you say? I wasn't **paying attention**.* | *My **attention wasn't** really **on** the game.* | *He ended his sports career and **turned** his **attention to** politics.* | *This assignment requires your **full/undivided/complete attention**.* | ***May/Can I have your attention, please*** (=used when asking a group of people to listen carefully to you)? | *Most children have a short **attention span*** (=period of time that they are interested in watching, listening, etc. to something). | *Her boss admired her **attention to detail**.* 2 the interest that people show in someone or something: *Charlie tried to **get/attract/catch** our **attention**.* | *The governor's race has **drawn the attention of** the nation's media.* | *Rob loves being **the center of attention*** (=the person everyone notices). 3 special care or treatment: *The back yard really needs some attention – it's full of weeds.* | *Some of the children required urgent **medical attention**.* 4 **stand at/to attention** if soldiers stand to attention, they stand very straight, with their feet together

at·ten·tive /ə'tɛntɪv/ *adj.* listening or watching carefully: *an attentive audience* —**attentively** *adv.* —**attentiveness** *n.* [U]

at·test /ə'tɛst/ *v.* [I,T] to show or prove that something is true: *The crowd of people waiting outside his door **attests to** this young star's popularity.*

at·tic /'æṭɪk/ *n.* [C] a room at the top of a house, usually used for storing things: *I think the photos are **up in the attic**.* [ORIGIN: 1700—1800 French *attique* "of ancient Athens," from Latin *Atticus*; from the use of an ancient Greek style in designing structures around the top of buildings]

at·tire /ə'taɪə/ *n.* [U] (formal) clothes: *Reservations and **formal attire** are required.*

at·ti·tude /'æṭəˌtud/ (Ac) *n.* 1 [C,U] the opinions and feelings that you usually have about someone or something: *people with a **positive/negative attitude** to life* | *I don't like his **attitude toward** women.* | ***Attitudes about** smoking have changed immensely.*

THESAURUS opinion, view, point of view, position, stance, sentiment, conviction → OPINION

2 [C,U] the way that you behave toward someone or

A

in a particular situation: *Their whole attitude changed once they found out Ron was rich.* | *Cathy has a real* ***attitude problem*** (=she is not helpful or pleasant to be with). **3** [U] (informal) the confidence to do unusual and exciting things without caring what other people think: *a young singer* ***with attitude***

at·tor·ney /ə'tɚni/ *n.* (plural **attorneys**) [C] LAW a lawyer [ORIGIN: 1300—1400 Old French *atorné*, past participle of *atorner* "to give a particular job or position to"]

at,torney 'general *n.* [C] the chief lawyer in a state, or of the government in the U.S.

at·tract /ə'trækt/ *v.* [T] **1** to make someone like something or feel interested in it: *The story* ***attracted*** *a lot of* ***attention*** *from the media.* | *What* ***attracted*** *you* ***to*** *Atlanta?* **2** to make someone come to a place: *Disneyland attracts millions of tourists each year.* **3 be attracted to sb** to like someone in a sexual way: *I was immediately attracted to him.* **4** to make someone or something move toward another thing: *Flowers attract bees.*

at·trac·tion /ə'trækʃən/ *n.* **1** [C,U] a feeling of liking someone, especially in a sexual way: *I can't understand Beth's* ***attraction to*** *Stan.* **2** [C] something interesting or fun to see or do: *the attractions at the county fair* | *the city's top* ***tourist attraction*** (=place that many tourists visit)

at·trac·tive /ə'træktɪv/ *adj.* **1** pretty or nice to look at: *an attractive young woman* | *an attractive location for a wedding* | *Women seem to* ***find*** *him* ***attractive***.

THESAURUS

good-looking/nice-looking – used about anyone who is attractive
pretty – used about a girl or woman who is attractive
beautiful – used about a woman, girl, or baby who is extremely attractive
handsome – used about a man or boy who is attractive
gorgeous/stunning – used about anyone who is very attractive
cute – used about a baby or young child who is attractive
cute – used about someone you think is sexually attractive, especially someone young
hot (informal) – used about someone you think is sexually attractive

2 interesting or exciting: *an attractive salary/offer* | *Advertising campaigns make alcohol* ***attractive to*** *young people.*

at·tri·but·a·ble /ə'trɪbyəṭəbəl/ (Ac) *adj.* (formal) likely to have been caused by something: *The price increase is* ***attributable to*** *a rise in the cost of paper.*

at·trib·ute¹ /ə'trɪbyut/ (Ac) *v.*
attribute sth **to** sb/sth *phr. v.* **1** to believe or say that someone or something is responsible for causing something: *Many diseases can be attributed to stress.* **2** to say that most people believe that someone said, wrote, or painted, etc. something: *These paintings are generally attributed to Rembrandt.* [ORIGIN: 1300—1400 Latin, past participle of *attribuere*, from *ad-* "to" + *tribuere* "to give out to the tribes, pay"] **—attribution** /ˌætrə'byuʃən/ *n.* [U]

at·tri·bute² /'ætrəbyut/ (Ac) *n.* [C] a good or useful quality: *Kindness is just one of her many attributes.*

THESAURUS **characteristic, quality, trait, feature, property** → CHARACTERISTIC¹

at·trib·u·tive /ə'trɪbyəṭɪv/ *adj.* ENG. LANG. ARTS in grammar, an attributive adjective or noun comes before the noun or phrase it describes. In the sentence "I heard a funny story," the word "funny" is attributive.

at·tuned /ə'tund/ *adj.* **be/become attuned to sth** to be so familiar with someone or something that you know how to deal with him, her, or it: *It took me a while to become attuned to the strong southern accent.*

a·typ·i·cal /eɪ'tɪpɪkəl/ *adj.* not typical or usual

au·burn /'ɔbɚn/ *adj.* auburn hair is a red-brown color [ORIGIN: 1400—1500 Old French *auborne* "blond," from Medieval Latin *alburnus* "whitish"] **—auburn** *n.* [U]

auc·tion /'ɔkʃən/ *n.* [C] an event at which things are sold to the person who offers the most money [ORIGIN: 1500—1600 Latin *auctio* "increase," from *augere*; because the money offered increases] **—auction** *v.* [T]

auc·tion·eer /ˌɔkʃə'nɪr/ *n.* [C] someone who is in charge of an auction

au·da·cious /ɔ'deɪʃəs/ *adj.* brave and shocking: *audacious behavior* [ORIGIN: 1500—1600 French *audacieux*, from *audace* "audacity," from Latin *audax* "brave"] **—audaciously** *adv.*

au·dac·i·ty /ɔ'dæsəṭi/ *n.* [U] the quality of having enough courage to take risks or do things that are shocking or rude: *I can't believe he* ***had the audacity to*** *call your father at 3 a.m.*

au·di·ble /'ɔdəbəl/ *adj.* loud enough to be heard (ANT) **inaudible**: *Her voice was* ***barely audible***. | *an* ***audible sigh*** *of relief* **—audibly** *adv.*

au·di·ence /'ɔdiəns/ *n.* [C] **1** the people watching or listening to a performance: *an* ***audience of*** *300 people* | ***Members of the audience*** *were invited to ask questions.* → THEATER **2** the people who watch a particular television program, read a particular book or magazine, etc.: *The show attracts a regular* ***audience of*** *20 million viewers.* **3** a formal meeting with someone who is very important: *an* ***audience with*** *the Pope* [ORIGIN: 1300—1400 French, Latin *audientia* "hearing," from *audire* "to listen"]

au·di·o /'ɔdioʊ/ *adj.* relating to recording and broadcasting sound → VIDEO: *audio equipment*

[ORIGIN: 1900—2000 *audio-* "of hearing," from Latin *audire* "to listen"]

au·di·o·vis·u·al /ˌɔdioʊ'vɪʒuəl/ *adj.* using recorded pictures and sound: *an audiovisual presentation*

au·dit /'ɔdɪt/ *v.* [T] **1** ECONOMICS to officially examine a company's financial records in order to check that they are correct **2** to study a subject at college without getting a GRADE for it **—audit** *n.* [C] **—auditor** *n.* [C]

au·di·tion¹ /ɔ'dɪʃən/ *n.* [C] a short performance by an actor, singer, etc. to test whether s/he is good enough to perform in a play, concert, etc.: *The ballet company is* ***holding auditions for*** *"Swan Lake."*

audition² *v.* [I,T] to perform in an audition, or judge someone in an audition: *He plans to* ***audition for*** *a part in "Oklahoma!"*

au·di·to·ri·um /ˌɔdɪ'tɔriəm/ *n.* [C] a large building used for concerts or public meetings

aug·ment /ɔg'mɛnt/ *v.* [T] (formal) to increase the size or value of something

Au·gust /'ɔgəst/ (*written abbreviation* **Aug.**) *n.* [C,U] the eighth month of the year, between July and September: *The winner will be announced* ***on August 31st.*** | *They sold their house* ***in August.*** | ***Last August,*** *we traveled through Europe.* | *The changes will take effect* ***next August.*** [ORIGIN: 1000—1100 Latin *Augustus*, from *Augustus* Caesar (63 B.C. – 14 A.D.), Roman emperor]

aunt /ænt, ɑnt/ *n.* [C] the sister of your mother or father, or the wife of your UNCLE: *Aunt Jean* ➔ RELATIVE¹ [ORIGIN: 1200—1300 Old French *ante*, from Latin *amita*]

au pair /oʊ 'pɛr/ *n.* [C] a young person who stays with a family in a foreign country and looks after their children [ORIGIN: 1800—1900 French "on equal terms"]

au·ra /'ɔrə/ *n.* [C] a quality or feeling that seems to come from a person or place: *There's an* ***aura of*** *mystery around the castle.* [ORIGIN: 1700—1800 Latin "air, light wind," from Greek]

au·ral /'ɔrəl/ *adj.* related to the sense of hearing ➔ ORAL: *aural skills*

au·ri·cle /'ɔrɪkəl/ *n.* [C] BIOLOGY one of the two spaces inside the top of your heart, from which blood is sent into the VENTRICLES (SYN) **atrium**

aus·pic·es /'ɔspəsɪz, -ˌsiz/ *n.* **under the auspices of sb/sth** (formal) with the help and support of a person or organization: *The research was done under the auspices of Harvard Medical School.* [ORIGIN: 1700—1800 *auspice* "telling the future by watching the behavior of birds, good influence" (16—19 centuries), from Latin *auspicium*]

aus·pi·cious /ɔ'spɪʃəs/ *adj.* showing that something is likely to be successful (ANT) **inauspicious**: *an* ***auspicious start/beginning*** *to her career*

THESAURUS **lucky, fortunate, fortuitous, miraculous** ➔ LUCKY

aus·tere /ɔ'stɪr/ *adj.* **1** very strict and serious: *a cold, austere woman* **2** very plain and simple: *an austere style of painting* **3** without a lot of comfort or enjoyment: *They lived an austere life.*

aus·ter·i·ty /ɔ'stɛrəṭi/ *n.* [U] **1** ECONOMICS bad economic conditions in which people do not have enough money to spend: *the austerity of post-communist Eastern Europe* **2** the quality of being austere

Aus·tra·lia /ɑ'streɪliə/ *n.* one of the seven CONTINENTs that is also its own country

Aus·tra·li·an /ɑ'streɪliən/ *adj.* relating to Australia or its people

au·then·tic /ɔ'θɛntɪk/ *adj.* **1** done or made in a traditional way: *authentic Indian food* **2** proven to be made by a particular person (SYN) **genuine**: *an authentic Renoir painting* [ORIGIN: 1300—1400 Old French *autentique*, from Late Latin, from Greek *authentes* "person who did a particular thing"] **—authentically** *adv.* **—authenticity** /ˌɔθən'tɪsəṭi/ *n.* [U]: *Tests confirmed the book's authenticity.*

au·thor /'ɔθɚ/ (Ac) *n.* [C] **1** someone who writes a book, story, article, play, etc.: *Who is your favorite author?* | *Banville is the* ***author of*** *"The Book of Evidence."* **2** the person who starts a plan or idea: *Senator Norris was the principal author of the bill.* [ORIGIN: 1300—1400 Old North French *auctour*, from Latin *auctor* "maker, writer"]

au·thor·i·tar·i·an /əˌθɔrə'tɛriən, əˌθɑr-/ *adj.* forcing people to obey strict rules or laws and not allowing any freedom: *an authoritarian government* **—authoritarian** *n.* [C]: *Papa was a strict authoritarian.*

au·thor·i·ta·tive /ə'θɔrəˌteɪṭɪv, ə'θɑr-/ (Ac) *adj.* **1** an authoritative book, account, etc. is respected because the person who wrote it knows a lot about the subject: *an authoritative account of*

A

the country's history | *The figures in the report come from an authoritative source.* **2** behaving or speaking in a confident determined way that makes people respect and obey you: *The captain spoke to the passengers in a calm and authoritative voice.* —**authoritatively** *adv.*

au·thor·i·ty /ə'θɔrəṭi, ə'θɑr-/ (Ac) *n.* **1** [U] the power someone has because of his/her official position: *You have no* ***authority over*** *me!* | *Could I speak to someone* ***in authority*** (=who has a position of power), *please?* | *She has the* ***authority to*** *sign checks.* | *people* ***in positions of authority*** **2 the authorities** the people or organizations that are in charge of a particular place: *Please report any suspicious activities to the authorities immediately.* **3** [C] someone who is respected because of his/her knowledge about a subject: *Dr. Ballard is a leading* ***authority on*** *tropical diseases.* [ORIGIN: 1200—1300 Old French *auctorité*, from Latin *auctoritas* "opinion, decision, power"]

> THESAURUS expert, specialist, connoisseur, pundit → EXPERT

au·thor·ize /'ɔθə,raɪz/ *v.* [T] to give official permission for something: *Can you authorize my expenses?* | *No one* ***authorized*** *you* ***to*** *sign this.* —**authorization** /,ɔθərə'zeɪʃən/ *n.* [C,U]: *You'll need authorization from the Director to do that.*

> THESAURUS allow, let, permit, sanction, condone → ALLOW

au·tis·m /'ɔ,tɪzəm/ *n.* [U] a problem in the way the brain works that makes someone unable to communicate in a normal way, or to form normal relationships —**autistic** /ɔ'tɪstɪk/ *adj.*: *an autistic child*

au·to /'ɔṭoʊ/ *adj.* relating to cars: *auto parts*

au·to·bi·og·ra·phy /,ɔṭəbaɪ'ɑgrəfi/ *n.* (plural **autobiographies**) [C] ENG. LANG. ARTS a book that someone writes about his/her own life → BOOK[1] —**autobiographical** /,ɔṭəbaɪə'græfɪkəl/ *adj.*

au·toc·ra·cy /ɔ'tɑkrəsi/ *n.* (plural **autocracies**) [C,U] POLITICS a system of government in which one person or group has complete and unlimited power, or a country governed in this way

au·to·crat /'ɔṭə,kræt/ *n.* [C] **1** POLITICS a ruler who has complete and unlimited power to govern a country **2** someone, especially a person with a high rank in an organization, who makes decisions and gives orders to people without ever asking other people for their opinion

au·to·crat·ic /,ɔṭə'kræṭɪk/ *adj.* **1** POLITICS giving orders to people without considering their opinions: *an autocratic style of management* **2** POLITICS having unlimited power to govern a country: *an autocratic government*

au·to·graph /'ɔṭə,græf/ *n.* [C] a famous person's name, written in his/her own writing: *Can I have your autograph?* —**autograph** *v.* [T]: *a jacket autographed by all the players*

au·to·mat·ed /'ɔṭə,meɪṭɪd/ (Ac) *adj.* using computers and machines to do a job, rather than people: *The automated manufacturing system processes orders as they arrive.* —**automation** /,ɔṭə'meɪʃən/ *n.* [U]: *In this industry, the trend towards automation started in the 1950s.*

au·to·mat·ic[1] /,ɔṭə'mæṭɪk◂/ (Ac) *adj.* **1** an automatic machine is designed to operate by itself after you start it: *The automatic safety switch will stop the engine in an emergency.* **2** certain to happen: *We get an automatic pay increase every year.* **3** done without thinking: *At first, driving is hard, but then it just becomes automatic.* | *Fear is an automatic response to a threatening situation.* [ORIGIN: 1700—1800 Greek *automatos* "acting by itself"] —**automatically** *adv.*: *She automatically assumed that he was guilty.* | *The program runs automatically when the user logs on.*

automatic[2] *n.* [C] **1** a car with a system of GEARS that operate themselves **2** a gun that can shoot bullets continuously

au·to·mo·bile /,ɔṭəmə'bil, 'ɔṭəmə,bil/ *n.* [C] a car

au·to·mo·tive /,ɔṭə'moʊṭɪv/ *adj.* relating to cars: *the automotive industry*

au·ton·o·mous /ɔ'tɑnəməs/ *adj.* having the power to make your own decisions or rules: *an autonomous nation* —**autonomously** *adv.* —**autonomy** *n.* [U]: *political autonomy*

au,tonomous 'region *n.* [C] POLITICS a large area within a country, that has the official right to be independent and govern itself

au·top·sy /'ɔ,tɑpsi/ *n.* (plural **autopsies**) [C] an official examination of a dead body to discover the cause of death

au·to·some /'ɔṭə,soʊm/ *n.* [C] BIOLOGY any CHROMOSOME that does not influence whether a person or animal is male or female —**autosomal** *adj.*: *autosomal chromosomes*

au·to·troph /'ɔṭə,trɑf, -,troʊf/ *n.* [C] BIOLOGY a living thing that produces its own food from substances that do not contain living things, using the energy from the Sun or from a chemical process. Most plants and living creatures such as BACTERIA are autotrophs.

au·to·work·er /'ɔṭoʊ,wɚkɚ/ *n.* [C] someone whose job is to make cars

au·tumn /'ɔṭəm/ *n.* [C,U] FALL —**autumnal** /ɔ'tʌmnəl/ *adj.*

aux·il·ia·ry /ɔg'zɪləri, -'zɪlyəri/ *adj.* giving extra help or support: *auxiliary police* —**auxiliary** *n.* [C]

aux,iliary 'verb *n.* [C] ENG. LANG. ARTS a verb that is used with another verb to form questions, negative sentences, and tenses. In English, the auxiliary verbs are "be," "do," and "have."

a·vail[1] /ə'veɪl/ *n.* **to no avail** without success: *We searched everywhere to no avail.*

avail[2] *v.* **avail yourself of sth** (formal) to accept an offer, or use an opportunity: *Avail yourself of every chance to improve your English.*

a·vail·a·ble /ə'veɪləbəl/ (Ac) *adj.* **1** if something is available, you can have it, buy it, or use it: *The database in the library is* ***available to*** *anyone.* | *Several thousand seats are* ***available for*** *tonight's show.* | *films* ***available on*** *DVD* | *The book is* ***available in*** *the museum's bookstore.* | *Once it is approved by the FDA, the vaccine will become* ***readily/widely available*** (=easily available, or available from many places). **2** [not before noun] someone who is available is not busy and has enough time to talk to you: *I'm available after lunch.* | *The District Attorney is not* ***available for comment.*** —**availability** /əˌveɪlə'bɪləṭi/ *n.* [U]: *the easy availability of guns in the U.S.*

av·a·lanche /'ævəˌlæntʃ, -ˌlɑntʃ/ *n.* [C] **1** EARTH SCIENCES a large amount of snow, ice, and rocks that falls down the side of a mountain **2 an avalanche of sth** a very large number of things that happen or arrive at the same time: *The station received an avalanche of letters.* [ORIGIN: 1700—1800 French, French dialect *lavantse, avalantse*]

a·vant-garde /ˌævɑnt˺'gɑrd◂, ˌɑ-/ *adj.* avant-garde art, literature, or music is very modern and different from existing art, etc., often in a way that is strange or shocking

av·a·rice /'ævərɪs/ *n.* [U] (formal) an extreme desire for wealth (SYN) **greed** —**avaricious** /ˌævə'rɪʃəs/ *adj.*

av·a·tar /'ævəˌtɑr/ *n.* [C] IT a picture of a person, animal, or other character that represents you on a computer screen, for example when you are playing computer games on the Internet or when you are in a CHAT ROOM

Ave. the written abbreviation of AVENUE

a·venge /ə'vɛndʒ/ *v.* [T] (literary) to punish someone because s/he has harmed you, your family, or your friends: *plans to avenge his father's death* —**avenger** *n.* [C]

av·e·nue /'ævəˌnu/ *n.* [C] **1** *also* **Avenue** a street in a town or city: *Fifth Avenue* | *He lives on Melrose Avenue.*

THESAURUS **road, street, main street, lane, main road, the main drag, highway, freeway, expressway, toll road, turnpike** ➔ ROAD

2 a possible way of achieving something: *We* ***explored every avenue****, but couldn't find a solution.* [ORIGIN: 1600—1700 French *avenir* "to come up to," from Latin *advenire*]

av·erage¹ /'ævrɪdʒ/ *adj.* **1** [only before noun] the average amount is the amount you get when you add together several figures and divide this by the total number of figures: *the* ***average price*** *of a new home* | *The* ***average age*** *of teachers is rising steadily.* **2** [only before noun] having qualities that are typical of most people or things: *In an average week, I drive about 250 miles.* | *The average American has not even thought about next year's election.*

THESAURUS **normal, ordinary, standard, routine, conventional** ➔ NORMAL¹

3 not very good but not very bad: *an average book* [ORIGIN: 1700—1800 *average* "(fair sharing out of costs resulting from) damage to or loss of a ship or the goods it carries" (15—20 centuries), from French *avarie*, from Arabic *'awariyah* "damaged goods"]

average² *n.* **1** [C] MATH the amount that you get by adding several figures together and then dividing the result by the number of figures: *The* ***average of*** *3, 8, and 10 is 7.* **2 on average** based on a calculation of what usually happens: *On average, women live longer than men.* **3** [C,U] the usual level or amount: *an* ***above average/below average*** *student*

average³ *v.* [T] **1** to be a particular amount as an average: *The car averages about 20 miles per gallon.* **2** to calculate the average of an amount

average out *phr. v.* to result in a particular average amount: *Our weekly profits* ***average out at*** *about $750.*

a·verse /ə'vɚs/ *adj.* **not be averse to sth** to like to do something: *I don't drink much, but I'm not averse to the occasional glass of wine.*

a·ver·sion /ə'vɚʒən/ *n.* [singular, U] a strong dislike of something or someone: *Mary* ***has an aversion to*** *cats.*

a·vert /ə'vɚt/ *v.* [T] **1** to prevent something bad from happening: *The whole thing could've been averted if you'd listened to us.* **2 avert your eyes/gaze** to look away from something

a·vi·a·tion /ˌeɪvi'eɪʃən/ *n.* [U] the science or activity of flying or making aircraft [ORIGIN: 1800—1900 French, Latin *avis* "bird"]

a·vi·a·tor /'eɪviˌeɪṭɚ/ *n.* [C] (old-fashioned) a pilot

av·id /'ævɪd/ *adj.* [only before noun] doing something as much as possible: *an* ***avid reader*** | *an avid golfer*

av·o·ca·do /ˌævə'kɑdoʊ, ˌɑ-/ *n.* (plural **avocados**) [C,U] a firm green fruit with thick dark skin, used in GUACAMOLE [ORIGIN: 1600—1700 Spanish *aguacate* "avocado," from Nahuatl *ahuacatl* "testicle, avocado;" influenced by Spanish *avocado* "lawyer"] ➔ *see picture on page 414*

a·void /ə'vɔɪd/ *v.* [T] **1** to prevent something bad from happening: *Exercise will help you avoid heart disease.* | *He had to swerve to avoid being hit by the other car.* ▸Don't say "avoid to do something."◂ **2** to deliberately stay away from someone or something: *Paul's been avoiding me all day.* **3** to deliberately not do something: *To avoid paying tax, he moved to Canada.* —**avoidable** *adj.* —**avoidance** *n.* [U]

a·vow /ə'vaʊ/ *v.* [T] (formal) to say or admit something publicly

a·vowed /ə'vaʊd/ *adj.* said or admitted publicly: *an avowed atheist*

A

a·wait /ə'weɪt/ *v.* [T] (formal) **1** to wait for something: *Briggs is awaiting trial for murder.* **2** if a situation or event awaits someone, it is going to happen to him/her: *A terrible surprise awaited them.*

a·wake¹ /ə'weɪk/ *adj.* [not before noun] not sleeping: *Is she awake yet?* | *I couldn't **stay awake** during the movie.* | *I was **wide awake*** (=completely awake) *before dawn.* | *The baby **kept** us **awake*** (=stopped us from sleeping) *all night.*

awake² *v.* (past tense **awoke** /ə'woʊk/, past participle **awoken** /ə'woʊkən/) [I,T] (literary) **1** to wake up, or to wake someone up: *I **awoke to** the sound of rain pounding on the roof.* **2** to suddenly begin to feel an emotion, or to make someone do this

a·wak·en /ə'weɪkən/ *v.* [I,T] (formal) to wake up, or to make someone wake up: *He was awakened by the telephone.*

awaken sb/sth **to** sth *phr. v.* to make someone begin to realize something: *Churches are awakening to the needs of their older members.*

a·wak·en·ing /ə'weɪkənɪŋ/ *n.* [C,U] a situation when you suddenly realize that you understand or feel something: *a spiritual awakening*

a·ward¹ /ə'wɔrd/ *n.* [C] **1** a prize or money given to someone for something that s/he has achieved: *the **award for** best actor* | *an **award of** $10,000 to each victim* | *an experienced reporter who has **won** many **awards*** **2** an amount of money that is given to someone because of a judge's decision: *an **award for** injuries suffered*

award² *v.* [T] to officially give someone an award: *He was awarded the Nobel Prize.* | *A large sum of money was **awarded to** the survivors.*

> THESAURUS **give, present, grant** ➔ GIVE¹

a·ware /ə'wɛr/ (Ac) *adj.* [not before noun] **1** realizing that something is true, exists, or is happening (ANT) **unaware**: *Are you **aware of** the dangers of smoking?* | *Are you **aware (that)** your son has been skipping classes?* | *"Are there any more problems?" "**Not that I'm aware of.**"* | *Now that the school has been **made aware of** the situation, it will act.* **2 politically/socially/environmentally etc. aware** interested in politics, etc., and knowing a lot about it

a·ware·ness /ə'wɛrnɪs/ (Ac) *n.* [U] knowledge or understanding of a particular subject or situation: *The TV ads are meant to **raise** the public's **awareness of** environmental issues.* | *The possibility of getting drafted increased the students' **political awareness**.*

a·wash /ə'wɑʃ, ə'wɔʃ/ *adj.* **1 awash with/in sth** having too much of something: *TV is awash with talk shows.* **2** covered with water

a·way¹ /ə'weɪ/ *adv.* **1** moving further from a place, or staying far from a place: *Go away!* | *Diane drove away quickly.* | *Move **away from** the fire!* **2** in a different direction: *She looked away and began to cry.* **3 7 miles/40 feet/2 weeks etc. away** used to say how far it is to a place, thing, or time in the future: *a town about 50 miles **away from** Chicago* | *Christmas is only a month away.* **4** into a safe place: *Put all your toys away now, please.* **5** not at home, at work, or in school: *I'm sorry, Ms. Parker is away this week.* **6** used to say that something disappears or is removed: *He gave his money away to charity.* | *The music died away.* **7** used to say how close someone is to achieving something or experiencing something: *At one point, they were only two points **away from** victory.* **8** without stopping: *He's been working away on the patio all day.*

away² *adj.* **away team/game/match** a sports team that is playing at an opponent's field, or a game they are playing there (ANT) **home**

awe /ɔ/ *n.* [U] a feeling of great respect for someone or something: *We were **in awe of** our father.* —**awed** *adj.*: *an awed silence*

'awe-in,spiring *adj.* making you feel awe: *an awe-inspiring achievement*

> THESAURUS **impressive, imposing, dazzling, breathtaking, majestic, magnificent** ➔ IMPRESSIVE

awe·some /'ɔsəm/ *adj.* **1** very impressive, serious, or difficult: *an awesome responsibility* **2** (spoken) extremely good: *That concert was awesome!*

awe·struck /'ɔstrʌk/ *adj.* feeling great awe: *We gazed awestruck at the pyramids.*

aw·ful¹ /'ɔfəl/ *adj.* **1** very bad: *an awful movie* | *The weather was awful.* | *This soup tastes awful!*

> THESAURUS **bad, terrible, horrible, appalling, horrific, lousy, horrendous, atrocious, abysmal, disgusting, revolting, foul, dreadful** ➔ BAD¹, HORRIBLE

2 [only before noun] (spoken) used in order to emphasize how much, how good, how bad, etc. something is: *I have **an awful lot*** (=a very large amount) *of work to do.* **3 look/feel awful** to look or feel sick

awful² *adv.* (spoken, nonstandard) very: *She's awful cute.*

aw·fully /'ɔfli/ *adv.* (spoken) very: *Helen looks awfully tired.*

a·while /ə'waɪl/ *adv.* for a short time: *I stood at the bedroom door awhile, watching the boys sleeping.*

awk·ward /'ɔkwəd/ *adj.* **1** embarrassing: *This puts us in an **awkward position**.* | *For a few moments there was an **awkward silence**.* **2** moving or behaving in a way that does not seem relaxed or comfortable: *an awkward teenager*

> THESAURUS **clumsy, gawky, inelegant, klutzy** ➔ CLUMSY

3 not convenient: *They came at an awkward*

time. **4** difficult to use or handle: *The camera is awkward to use.*

THESAURUS **difficult, hard, tough, challenging, demanding, complicated, complex** → DIFFICULT

[ORIGIN: 1500—1600 *awk* "turned the wrong way" (15—17 centuries) (from Old Norse *öfugr*) + *-ward*] —**awkwardly** *adv.* —**awkwardness** *n.* [U]

awn·ing /ˈɔnɪŋ/ *n.* [C] a sheet of material outside a store, tent, etc., used for protection from the Sun or the rain

a·woke /əˈwoʊk/ *v.* the past tense of AWAKE

a·wok·en /əˈwoʊkən/ *v.* the past participle of AWAKE

AWOL /ˈeɪˌwɔl/ *adj.* **Absent Without Leave** absent from your military group without permission: *Private Ames has **gone AWOL**.*

a·wry /əˈraɪ/ *adj.* **go awry** to not happen in the way that was planned: *My carefully laid plans had already gone awry.*

ax[1], **axe** /æks/ *n.* [C] **1** a tool with a metal blade on a long handle, used for cutting wood **2 give sb/sth the ax** (informal) to dismiss someone from his/her job, or get rid of something: *The TV station gave Brown the ax.* **3 get the ax** (informal) to be dismissed from your job **4 have an ax to grind** to have a personal reason for doing something: *I have no political ax to grind.*

ax[2], **axe** *v.* [T] (informal) to get rid of a plan, a service, or someone's job: *Did you hear they're axing 500 jobs?*

ax·i·om /ˈæksiəm/ *n.* [C] (formal) a rule or principle that is considered by most people to be true

ax·i·o·mat·ic /ˌæksiəˈmæt̬ɪk/ *adj.* a principle that is axiomatic does not need to be proved because people can see that it is true

ax·is /ˈæksɪs/ *n.* (plural **axes** /ˈæksiz/) [C] **1** EARTH SCIENCES the imaginary line around which a large object, such as the Earth, turns → *see picture at* GLOBE **2** MATH a line at the side or bottom of a GRAPH, used for marking measurements **3** MATH a line drawn across the middle of a regular shape, that divides it into two equal parts

ˈAxis ˌPowers *n.* [plural] **the Axis Powers** HISTORY a group of countries, including Germany, Italy, and Japan, that united against the ALLIED POWERS (=Great Britain, the Soviet Union, the United States, and other countries) in World War II

ax·le /ˈæksəl/ *n.* [C] the bar that connects two wheels on a vehicle

ax·on /ˈækˌsɑn/ *n.* [C] BIOLOGY a long thin part of a nerve cell, along which short electrical signals containing messages travel away from the cell toward other cells

a·ya·tol·lah /ˌaɪyəˈtoʊlə, -ˈtɑ-/ *n.* [C] POLITICS an important Shiite Muslim religious and political leader, especially one living in Iran, who has special knowledge of Islamic law

aye /aɪ/ *adv.* (spoken, formal) used in order to say yes, especially when voting

AZ the written abbreviation of ARIZONA

Az·tec /ˈæztɛk/ *n.* HISTORY one of the tribes who lived in and controlled Mexico from the 14th century until the 16th century: *The Aztecs played a game that had elements of both soccer and basketball.* | *Aztec jewelry*

B

B, b /bi/ the second letter of the English alphabet

B /bi/ *n.* **1** [C] a grade that a teacher gives to a student's work to show that it is good but not excellent: *Greg **got a B** in Chemistry.* **2** [C,U] ENG. LANG. ARTS the seventh note in the musical SCALE of C, or the musical KEY based on this note **3** [U] a common type of blood

b. the written abbreviation of BORN: *A. Lincoln, b. 1809*

B.A. *n.* [C] **Bachelor of Arts** a university degree in a subject such as history or literature → B.S.: *He graduated from Stanford with a **B.A. in** English.*

baa /bɑ, bæ/ *v.* [I] to make the sound a sheep makes

bab·ble /ˈbæbəl/ *v.* [I,T] to talk a lot in a way that does not make sense: *I couldn't understand what he was babbling about.* —**babble** *n.* [U]

babe /beɪb/ *n.* [C] **1** (spoken, informal) an attractive young woman **2** (literary) a baby

ba·boon /bæˈbun/ *n.* [C] a large monkey that lives in Africa and south Asia [ORIGIN: 1400—1500 French *babouin*, from *baboue* "ugly face"]

ba·by /ˈbeɪbi/ *n.* (plural **babies**) [C] **1** a very young child: *A baby was crying upstairs.* | *Joyce **had a baby** (=gave birth to a baby) in September.* | *Pam **is expecting a baby** (=will have a baby).* | *a **baby boy/girl***

TOPIC

A baby that has just been born is called a **newborn**.
A very young baby who cannot walk or talk yet is called an **infant**.
A baby who has learned how to walk is called a **toddler**.
When babies **crawl**, they move around on their hands and knees. Babies usually crawl before they learn how to walk.
When you take a baby somewhere, you can push him/her there in a **baby carriage**, which is like a

bed on wheels. You can push an older baby along in a **stroller**, which is like a chair on wheels.
Babies sleep in a special bed with bars on it, called a **crib**.
If a baby is being fed milk from its mother's breast, the baby is **nursing**, or the mother is **breast-feeding** the baby. If a baby drinks milk from a bottle, s/he is being **bottle-fed**. When a baby is old enough to sit up and eat food, s/he sits in a **highchair**.

B

THESAURUS **child, kid, teenager, adolescent, youngster, minor, juvenile** → CHILD

2 a very young animal: *baby birds* **3** (spoken) someone, especially an older child, who is behaving in a stupid or silly way: *Don't be such a baby!* **4** (spoken) a way of speaking to someone you love: *Bye, baby. I'll be back by six.*

'baby boom *n.* [C] a time when a lot of babies are born in a particular country, used especially to talk about this period between 1946 and 1964

'baby ˌboomer *n.* [C] (informal) someone born between 1946 and 1964

'baby ˌcarriage *also* **'baby ˌbuggy** *n.* [C] a thing like a bed on wheels, used for pushing a baby around

ba·by·sit /ˈbeɪbiˌsɪt/ *v.* (past tense and past participle **babysat** /-ˌsæt/, present participle **babysitting**) [I,T] to take care of children while their parents are not at home —**babysitter** *n.* [C] —**babysitting** *n.* [U]

bach·e·lor /ˈbætʃələ, ˈbætʃlə/ *n.* [C] a man who has never been married

'bachelor ˌparty *n.* [C] a party given for a man before he gets married

'bachelor's deˌgree *n.* [C] a B.A.

back¹ /bæk/ *adv.* **1** where someone or something was before: ***Put** the milk **back** in the refrigerator.* | *Roger said he'd **be back*** (=return) *in an hour.* | *If the shirt doesn't fit, **take** it **back** to the store.* | *I was on my way **back home*** (=the place I come from or think of as my home). **2** into the condition that someone or something was in before: *I woke up at 5 a.m. and couldn't **get back to** sleep.* | *I never want to **go back to** being a waitress.* **3** in the direction that is behind you: *George glanced back to see if he was being followed.* **4** doing the same thing to someone that s/he has done to you: *Can you call me back later?* | *Sarah smiled, and the boy smiled back.* **5** away from someone or something: *Her hair was pulled back in a ponytail.* | *Stand **back from** the fire!* **6** in or toward an earlier time: *This all happened about three years back.* | *The building **dates back to** the 17th Century.* **7 back and forth** in one direction and then in the opposite direction several times: *He walked back and forth across the floor.*

back² *n.*
1 BODY [C] **a)** the part of your body between your neck and legs, opposite your stomach and chest: *My back was really aching.* | *The cat arched its back and hissed.* | *He lay **on** his **back**, staring at the sky.* | *Mrs. Ducin stood **with** her **back to** the camera.* **b)** the bone that goes from your neck to your BUTTOCKS: *He broke his back in a motorcycle accident.*
2 PART OF STH [C usually singular, U] the part of something that is furthest from the front (ANT) **front**: *a grocery list **on the back of** an envelope* | *The index is **at the back of** the book.* | *The pool's **in back of** the house.* | *Kids should always wear seat belts, even **in back*** (=in the seats behind the driver). | *Tom's working on the car **out back*** (=behind a building).
3 SEAT [C] the part of a seat that you lean against when you are sitting: *Jack leaned against the **back** of the chair.*
4 behind sb's back if you do something bad or unkind behind someone's back, you do it without him/her knowing: *I can't believe she said that about me behind my back!*
5 at/in the back of your mind a thought or feeling at the back of your mind is influencing you, even though you are not thinking about it: *There was always a slight fear in the back of his mind.*
6 get off my back (spoken) said when you want someone to stop annoying you or asking you to do something: *I'll do it in a minute. Just get off my back!*
7 be on sb's back (spoken) to keep telling someone to do something, in a way that annoys him/her: *The boss has been on my back about being late.*
8 have your back to/against the wall (informal) to be in a very difficult situation with no choice about what to do → **turn your back (on)** *at* TURN¹

back³ *v.* **1** [I,T] to move backward, or to make a vehicle move backward: *Teresa backed the car into the garage.* | *We slowly **backed away** from the snake.* **2** [T] to support someone or something, especially by using your money or power: *The bill is backed by several environmental groups.* **3** [T] to risk money on the team, person, horse, etc. that you think will win something: *Which team did you back in the Super Bowl?*

back down *phr. v.* to admit that you are wrong or that you have lost an argument or fight: *Neither side would back down.*

back off *phr. v.* **1** to move away from something: *Back off a little, you're driving too close.* **2** (spoken) said in order to tell someone to stop telling you what to do, or to stop criticizing you: *Back off! I don't need your advice.*

back onto sth *phr. v.* if a building backs onto a place, the back of the building faces it: *The house backs onto a busy road.*

back out *phr. v.* to decide not to do something you promised to do: *They **backed out of** the deal at the last minute.*

back up *phr. v.* **1 back** sb/sth ↔ **up** to support what someone is doing or saying, or show what s/he is saying is true: *He had evidence on video to back up his claim.* **2 back** (sth ↔) **up** to move backward, or to make a vehicle go backward: *Back* *up a little so they can get by.* **3 back** sth ↔ **up** IT to make a copy of information on a computer **4 be backed up** traffic that is backed up is moving very slowly

back⁴ *adj.* [only before noun] **1** at the back of something (ANT) **front**: *the back door* | *We sat in the back row of the theater.* **2 back street/road** a street that is away from the main streets **3 back rent/taxes/pay** money that someone owes from an earlier date

back·ache /'bækeɪk/ *n.* [C,U] a pain in your back

back·bit·ing /'bæk,baɪt̬ɪŋ/ *n.* [U] rude or cruel talk about someone who is not present

back·board /'bækbɔrd/ *n.* [C] the board behind the basket in the game of basketball

back·bone /'bækboʊn/ *n.* **1** [C] BIOLOGY SPINE → *see picture on page A16* **2 the backbone of sth** the most important part of something: *The cocoa industry is the backbone of Ghana's economy.* **3** [U] courage and determination: *Stuart doesn't have the backbone to be a good manager.*

back·break·ing /'bæk,breɪkɪŋ/ *adj.* backbreaking work is very difficult and tiring

back·date /'bæk,deɪt/ *v.* [T] to write an earlier date on a document or check than the date when it was really written

back·drop /'bækdrɑp/ *n.* [C] **1** the conditions in which something happens: *a love story **set against the backdrop of** war* **2** the painted cloth at the back of a stage

back·er /'bækɚ/ *n.* [C] someone who supports a plan, especially by providing money: *We're still trying to find **backers for** the new enterprise.*

back·fire /'bækfaɪɚ/ *v.* [I] **1** if a plan or action backfires, it has the opposite effect to the one you wanted **2** if a car backfires, it makes a sudden loud noise because the engine is not working correctly

back·gam·mon /'bæk,gæmən/ *n.* [U] a game for two players, using flat round pieces and DICE on a board

back·ground /'bækgraʊnd/ *n.* **1** [C] someone's education, family, and experience: *kids from very different **ethnic/religious/cultural backgrounds*** | *Steve **has a background in** computer engineering.* | *The position would suit someone **with a background in** real estate.* **2** [C usually singular] the area that is behind the main things that you are looking at, especially in a picture or photograph: *The background is slightly out of focus.* | *Palm trees swayed **in the background**.* → *see picture at* FOREGROUND **3 in the background** someone who keeps or stays in the background tries not to be noticed: *The president's wife preferred to stay in the background.* **4** [singular] sounds that are in the background are not the main ones that you can hear: *I could hear cars honking **in the background**.* | *soft lights and **background music*** **5** [singular, U] the general conditions in which something happens

,background radi'ation *n.* [U] PHYSICS a very low level of RADIATION that is present naturally in the air, water, soil, and objects such as buildings

back·hand /'bækhænd/ *n.* [C usually singular] a way of hitting the ball in tennis, etc. with the back of your hand turned toward the ball → FOREHAND

back·hand·ed /'bæk,hændɪd/ *adj.* **back-handed compliment** a statement that seems to express praise or admiration, but is actually insulting

back·ing /'bækɪŋ/ *n.* [U] *The agency has provided **financial backing** for the project.*

back·lash /'bæklæʃ/ *n.* [singular] a strong reaction from people against an idea or person: *a political **backlash against** immigrants*

back·log /'bæklɔg, -lɑg/ *n.* [C] work that still needs to be done and should have been done earlier: *a huge **backlog of** orders*

back·pack¹ /'bækpæk/ *n.* [C] a bag used to carry things on your back, especially when you go walking → *see picture at* BAG¹

backpack² *v.* [I] to go walking or traveling carrying a backpack —**backpacker** *n.* [C] —**backpacking** *n.* [U]

,back 'seat *n.* [C] **1** the seat behind where the driver sits in a car: *Holly and I were sitting **in the back seat**.* **2 back seat driver** someone who gives unwanted advice about how to drive to the driver of a car **3 take a back seat** to accept or be put in a less important position: *His career has taken a back seat while he raises his son.*

back·side /'bæksaɪd/ *n.* [C] (informal) the part of your body that you sit on

back·slash /'bækslæʃ/ *n.* [C] a line (\) used in writing to separate words, numbers, or letters

back·space /'bækspeɪs/ *n.* [singular] a button on a computer KEYBOARD or TYPEWRITER, that you press to move backward toward the beginning of the line

back·stab·bing /'bæk,stæbɪŋ/ *n.* [U] the act of secretly doing bad things to someone else, especially saying bad things about him/her, in order to gain an advantage for yourself —**backstabber** *n.* [C]

back·stage /,bæk'steɪdʒ/ *adv.* behind the stage in a theater

back·stroke /'bæk,stroʊk/ *n.* [singular] a style of swimming on your back → *see picture at* SWIM¹

,back-to-'back *adj., adv.* happening one after the other: *back-to-back wins*

back·track /'bæktræk/ *v.* [I] **1** to change something you have said so that it is not as strong as it was earlier: *Congress is **backtracking on** some of the welfare cuts imposed last year.* **2** to go back the way you have just come: *We had to backtrack about a mile.*

back·up /'bækʌp/ *n.* **1** [C] something that you can use to replace something that does not work or is lost: *Always have a backup plan.* | *a backup* *power supply* **2** [C] IT a copy of a computer document, program, etc., which is made in case the original becomes lost or damaged: ***Make a backup of*** *any work you do on the computer.* **3** [C,U] extra help or support that can be used if it is needed: *The officers decided to call for backup before entering the building.*

B

back·ward¹ /ˈbækwɚd/ *also* **backwards** *adv.* **1** in the direction that is behind you (ANT) **forward**: *She took a step backwards.* **2** toward the beginning or the past: *Can you say the alphabet backward?* **3** with the back part in front: *Your T-shirt is on backwards.* **4** toward a worse state (ANT) **forward**: *The new law is seen by some as a major step backward.*

backward² *adj.* **1** [only before noun] made toward the direction that is behind you (ANT) **forward**: *She left without a backward glance.* **2** developing slowly and less successfully than others: *a backward country*

back·wa·ter /ˈbækˌwɔt̬ɚ, -ˌwɑ-/ *n.* [C] a quiet town or place far away from cities, where not much happens

back·woods /ˈbækˌwʊdz/ *n.* [plural] an area in the forest, far from any towns —**backwoods** *adj.*: *a backwoods town*

back·yard, **back yard** /ˌbækˈyɑrd◂/ *n.* [C] the area of land behind a house

ba·con /ˈbeɪkən/ *n.* [U] meat from a pig, that has been put in salt and cut into thin pieces: *bacon and eggs* [ORIGIN: 1300—1400 Old French, from an ancient Germanic word meaning "back"]

bac·te·ri·al /bækˈtɪriəl/ *adj.* BIOLOGY relating to bacteria, or caused by bacteria: *If there is a* ***bacterial infection****, the skin will look red and be sore.* | *Cooking food thoroughly destroys* ***bacterial cells****.*

bac·te·ri·um /bækˈtɪriəm/ *n.* (plural **bacteria** /-riə/) [C usually plural] BIOLOGY a very small living thing consisting of a single cell. Some bacteria cuase disease, but others are important in many natural processes. The plural form, "bacteria," is much more common than the singular form. [ORIGIN: 1800—1900 Modern Latin, Greek *bakterion* "stick, rod;" because of their shape]

bad¹ /bæd/ *adj.* (comparative **worse**, superlative **worst**) **1** not good or not nice (ANT) **good**: *I'm afraid I have some bad news for you.* | *a really bad smell*

THESAURUS

awful – very bad or unpleasant: *The weather was awful.*
terrible – extremely bad: *The hotel food was terrible.*
horrible – very bad or upsetting: *What a horrible thing to say!*
appalling/horrific (formal) – very bad and very shocking: *She suffered appalling injuries.* | *a horrific plane crash*
lousy (informal) – very bad in quality: *a lousy movie*
horrendous (formal) – very bad and very frightening or shocking: *a horrendous crash*
atrocious (formal) – extremely bad and often very severe: *Her driving is atrocious.* | *atrocious weather conditions*
abysmal (formal) – very bad, used especially to describe the standard of something: *The quality of care at the hospital was abysmal.* → GOOD¹, HORRIBLE

2 of a low quality or standard (ANT) **good**: *That was the worst pizza I ever ate.* | *Brian is really* ***bad at*** *sports.* **3** morally wrong or evil (ANT) **good**: *He plays one of the bad guys in the movie.*

THESAURUS

evil/wicked – used to describe an evil person or his/her actions: *a fairy tale about a wicked witch* | *evil thoughts*
immoral/wrong – morally wrong, and not accepted by society: *It's wrong to steal.*
depraved – morally wrong and evil: *a depraved killer*
reprehensible (formal) – reprehensible behavior is very bad and deserves criticism: *His conduct was reprehensible.*

4 damaging or harmful (ANT) **good**: *Smoking is* ***bad for*** *your health.* | *Pollution in the lake is having a bad effect on fish stocks.* **5** serious or severe: *a bad cold* | *Traffic in this city is getting worse by the day.* **6 too bad** (spoken) said when you are sorry about something that has happened: *It's too bad she had to give up teaching.* **7 feel bad** to feel ashamed or sorry about something: ***I felt bad about*** *missing your birthday.* **8 a bad time** a time that is not suitable or convenient: *Is this a bad time to call?* **9** food that is bad is not safe to eat because it is not fresh: *The milk has* ***gone bad.*** **10** permanently injured or not working correctly: *a bad heart* | *a bad back* **11 not bad** (spoken) good or acceptable: *"How are you?" "Oh, not bad."* **12 bad language/words** swearing or rude words

bad² *adv.* (spoken, nonstandard) badly

bade /bæd, beɪd/ *v.* the past tense and past participle of BID

badge /bædʒ/ *n.* [C] a small piece of metal, plastic, etc. that you wear or carry to show people that you work for a particular organization: *a police officer's badge*

badg·er /ˈbædʒɚ/ *n.* [C] an animal with black and white fur, that lives under the ground

bad·lands /ˈbædˌlændz/ *n.* [plural] EARTH SCIENCES an area of rocks and hills where no crops can be grown

bad·ly /ˈbædli/ *adv.* (comparative **worse**, superlative **worst**) **1** in a way that is not good (ANT) **well**: *a badly written book* | *She* ***did badly*** *on the exam.* ▸Don't say "I sing very bad." Say "I sing very badly."◂ **2** to a great or serious degree: *The refugees* ***badly need*** *food and clean water.* | *Our house was* ***badly damaged*** *during the storm.*

bad·min·ton /ˈbædˌmɪntˀn, -ˌmɪntən/ *n.* [U] a game in which players hit a small object with feathers on it over a net [ORIGIN: 1800—1900 *Badminton* large house in Gloucestershire, England, where it was first played]

ˈbad-mouth *v.* [T] (informal) to criticize someone or something: *Divorced parents shouldn't bad-mouth each other in front of the kids.*

baf·fle /ˈbæfəl/ *v.* [T] if something baffles you, you cannot understand it: *Scientists were baffled by the results.* —**baffling** *adj.* —**baffled** *adj.*

THESAURUS **confused, bewildered, puzzled** ➔ CONFUSED

bags

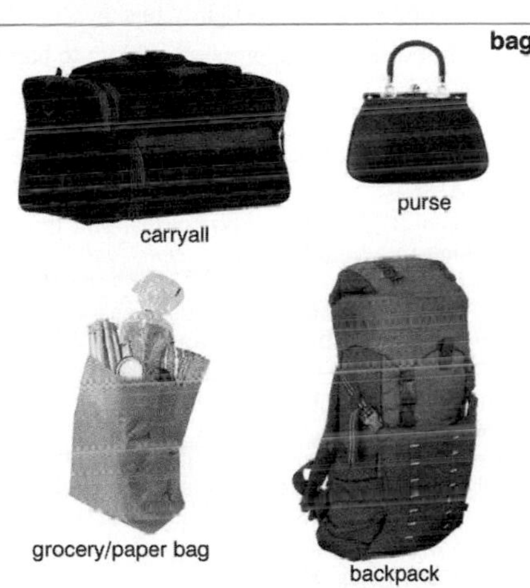

bag¹ /bæg/ *n.* [C] **1 a)** a container made of paper, plastic, cloth, etc., that opens at the top: *a paper bag* | *a shopping bag* **b)** a large bag that you use to carry your clothes, etc. when you are traveling: *She **packed** her **bags** and left.* **c)** a PURSE **2** the amount a bag can hold: *two **bags of** rice* **3 in the bag** certain to be won or to be a success: *We knew the game was in the bag.* **4 bags under your eyes** dark circles or loose skin under your eyes [ORIGIN: 1200—1300 Old Norse *baggi*]

bag² *v.* (**bagged**, **bagging**) [T] **1** to put things in a bag: *He got a job bagging groceries at the supermarket.* **2** (informal) to manage to get something that a lot of people want: *I'll get there early and bag some seats.*

ba·gel /ˈbeɪgəl/ *n.* [C] a type of bread that is shaped like a ring [ORIGIN: 1900—2000 Yiddish *beygel*, from Old High German *boug* "ring"]

bag·ful /ˈbægfʊl/ *n.* [C] the amount a bag can hold

bag·gage /ˈbægɪdʒ/ *n.* [U] **1** the bags that you carry with you when you are traveling (SYN) **luggage** **2** beliefs, opinions, and experiences from the past that influence the way a person behaves or thinks: *emotional baggage* [ORIGIN: 1400—1500 French *bagage*, from Old French *bague* "bundle"]

bag·gy /ˈbægi/ *adj.* baggy clothes are big and loose: *a baggy T-shirt*

ˈbag ˌlady *n.* [C] (informal) an impolite word for a woman who lives on the street and carries all her possessions with her

bag·pipes /ˈbægpaɪps/ *n.* [plural] a Scottish musical instrument which is played by blowing air into a bag and forcing it out through pipes

bail¹ /beɪl/ *n.* [U] LAW money left with a court of law so that someone can be let out of prison while waiting for his/her TRIAL ➔ SURETY: *Marshall's father **posted bail*** (=paid the bail) *for him.* | *Harrell was **released on bail*** (=let out of prison when bail was paid) *until his trial.* [ORIGIN: 1300—1400 Old French "keeping someone as a prisoner," from *baillier* "to deliver, keep as a prisoner," from Medieval Latin *bajulare* "to control"]

bail² *v.*

bail out *phr. v.* **1 bail** sb ↔ **out** to help someone get out of trouble, especially by giving him/her money: *Young people often expect their parents to bail them out.* **2 bail** sb ↔ **out** LAW to give money to a court of law so that someone can leave prison until his/her TRIAL: *Clarke's family paid $500 to bail him out.* **3** (informal) to escape from a situation that you no longer want to be involved in: *After ten years in the business, McArthur is bailing out.* **4 bail** sth ↔ **out** to remove water from the bottom of a boat

bai·liff /ˈbeɪlɪf/ *n.* [C] LAW an officer who watches prisoners and keeps order in a court of law

bail·out /ˈbeɪlaʊt/ *n.* [C] ECONOMICS a situation in which a person or organization gives money to help someone who needs it

bait¹ /beɪt/ *n.* [singular, U] **1** food used for attracting fish or animals so that you can catch them **2** something that is offered to someone to persuade him/her to do something: *Plenty of people **took the bait*** (=accepted what was offered) *and lost their life savings.*

bait² *v.* [T] **1** to put food on a hook to catch fish, or in a trap to catch animals **2** to deliberately try to make someone angry by criticizing him/her, using rude names, etc.: *He started baiting me, trying to get me to fight.*

bake /beɪk/ *v.* [I,T] to cook something such as bread or cakes in an OVEN: *I'm baking a cake.* | *baked potatoes* [ORIGIN: Old English *bacan*]

THESAURUS **cook, fry, roast, broil, grill, sauté, boil, steam, deep fry** ➔ COOK¹

bak·er /ˈbeɪkɚ/ *n.* [C] someone whose job is to bake bread, cakes, cookies, etc.

bak·er·y /ˈbeɪkəri/ *n.* (plural **bakeries**) [C] a place where bread, cakes, cookies, etc. are made or sold

ˈbake sale *n.* [C] an occasion when the members of a school group, church organization, etc. make cookies, cakes, etc. and sell them in order to make money for the organization

bal·ance[1] /'bæləns/ *n.* **1** [U] the ability to stand and walk steadily, without falling: *Billy fell when he **lost** his **balance*** (=was unable to stay steady). | *Tricia could not **keep** her **balance*** (=could not stay steady), *and slipped on the ice.* | *He hit me when I was still **off balance*** (=not standing steadily). **2** [singular, U] a state in which different or opposite qualities are given equal importance, or exist together in a way that is good: *Try to **keep a balance between** work and play.* | *The car's designers wanted to **strike a balance between** safety and style* (=make sure that two things have equal importance). | *We must not upset **the balance of** nature.* **3** [C] **a)** ECONOMICS the amount of money that you have in your bank account: *a **balance of** $1,247* **b)** ECONOMICS the amount of money that you owe for something: *The balance must be paid by the end of the month.* **4 on balance** used to tell someone your opinion after considering all the facts: *On balance, I'd say it was a fair decision.* **5 be/hang in the balance** to be in a situation where the result of something could be good or bad: *With the war still going on, thousands of lives hang in the balance.* [ORIGIN: 1200—1300 Old French, Vulgar Latin *bilancia*, from Late Latin *bilanx* "having two pans"]

balance[2] *v.* **1** [I,T] to be in a steady position, without falling, or to put something in this position: *They walked past, **balancing** heavy loads **on** their head.* | *He turned around, **balancing** awkwardly **on** one foot.* **2 balance the budget/books** ECONOMICS to make sure that you do not spend more money than you have **3** [T] to give the right amount of importance to two or more things: *A working mother has to **balance** her home life **with** a career.* | *The need for a new road must be **balanced against** the damage to the environment.* **4** [I,T] *also* **balance out** if two or more things balance, or if one balances the other, the effect of one equals the effect of the other: *Job losses in some departments were balanced by increases in others.*

bal·anced /'bælənst/ *adj.* **1** fair and sensible: *The government needs to take a balanced approach to the problem.*

THESAURUS **fair, just, reasonable, equitable, even-handed, impartial, unbiased** → FAIR[1]

2 including the right mixture of things: *a **balanced** **diet***

ˌbalanced e'quation *n.* [C] CHEMISTRY a chemical EQUATION which has the same number of atoms on each side of the equals sign. For example, $2H_20 = 2H_2 + 0_2$ is a balanced equation.

ˌbalance of 'power *n.* [singular] POLITICS a situation in which political or military strength is shared evenly between different political groups or different countries: *The legislation could change the balance of power between Congress and the President.*

'balance sheet *n.* [C] ECONOMICS a written statement of how much a business has earned and how much it has spent

bal·co·ny /'bælkəni/ *n.* (plural **balconies**) [C] **1** a structure that you can stand on that is built above ground level onto an outside wall of a building **2** the seats upstairs in a theater → THEATER

bald /bɔld/ *adj.* **1** having little or no hair on your head: *I'm **going bald**.* | *a **bald spot/patch*** (=a small area with no hair) **2** not having enough of what usually covers something: *bald tires*

'bald ˌeagle *n.* [C] a large North American wild bird with a white head and neck that is the national bird of the U.S. → *see picture at* EAGLE

bald·ing /'bɔldɪŋ/ *adj.* becoming bald: *a balding man in his mid-thirties*

bale /beɪl/ *n.* [C] a large amount of something such as paper or HAY that is tied tightly together

bale·ful /'beɪlfəl/ *adj.* expressing a desire to harm someone: *a baleful look*

balk /bɔk/ *v.* [I] to not want to do something: *Customers **balked at** paying $25 for a hamburger.* —**balky** *adj.*

ball /bɔl/ *n.* [C] **1** a round object that you throw, hit, or kick in a game or sport: *tennis balls* | *Troy **threw/kicked** the **ball** to Michael.* | *Try to **catch** the **ball**.* **2** something rolled into a round shape: *a **ball** of yarn* **3 on the ball** (informal) able to think or act quickly: *We need an assistant who's really on the ball.* **4 have a ball** (informal) to have a very good time **5** a ball thrown in baseball that the hitter does not try to hit because it is not within the correct area → STRIKE **6 set/start the ball rolling** to start something happening: *Just a small donation will start the ball rolling.* **7** a large formal occasion where people dance

THESAURUS **dance, prom, formal** → DANCE[2]

8 the ball of the foot the rounded part of the foot at the base of the toes [ORIGIN: (1) 1200—1300 Old Norse *böllr*] [ORIGIN: (7) 1600—1700 French *bal*, from *Old French baller* "to dance," from Late Latin *ballare*] → **play ball** *at* PLAY[1]

bal·lad /'bæləd/ *n.* [C] **1** a slow love song **2** ENG. LANG. ARTS a long song or poem that tells a story [ORIGIN: 1400—1500 Old French *balade*, from Old Provençal *balada* "dance, song sung while dancing," from Late Latin *ballare*]

bal·le·ri·na /ˌbælə'rinə/ *n.* [C] a woman who dances in ballets

bal·let /bæ'leɪ, 'bæleɪ/ *n.* **1** [C] ENG. LANG. ARTS a performance in which a story is told using dance and music, without any speaking: *the ballet "Swan Lake"* | *a **ballet dancer*** → THEATER **2** [U] this type of dancing **3** [C] a group of ballet dancers who work together: *the Bolshoi Ballet* [ORIGIN: 1600—1700 French, Italian *balletto*, from *ballo* "dance," from Late Latin *ballare*]

'ball game *n.* [C] **1** a game of baseball, basketball, or football **2 a whole new ball game/a different ball game** a situation that is very different from the one you were in before

bal·lis·tic /bəˈlɪstɪk/ *adj.* **go ballistic** (spoken) to suddenly become very angry

bal·lis·tics /bəˈlɪstɪks/ *n.* [U] PHYSICS the study of how objects move through the air when they are thrown or shot from a gun

bal·loon¹ /bəˈlun/ *n.* [C] **1** a small brightly colored rubber bag that can be filled with air: *Can you **blow up** these **balloons**?* **2** a HOT-AIR BALLOON

balloon² *v.* [I] to suddenly become much larger

bal·lot /ˈbælət/ *n.* **1** [C] a piece of paper that you use to vote **2** [C,U] a system of voting in secret, or an occasion when you vote in this way: *He won 54% of **the ballot*** (=the number of votes in an election). | *There were 17 propositions **on the ballot*** (=17 things to be voted on). [ORIGIN: 1500—1600 Italian *ballotta*, from *balla* "ball;" because small balls were used for voting]

ˈballot box *n.* [C] **1 the ballot box** the system of voting in an election: *The issue will be decided **at the ballot box**.* **2** a box that ballot papers are put in during the vote

ˈball park *n.* [C] **1** a field for playing baseball, with seats for people to watch the game **2 a ball park figure/estimate** a number or amount that is almost but not exactly correct

ball·point pen /ˌbɔlpɔɪnt ˈpɛn/ *n.* [C] a pen with a small ball at the end that rolls ink onto the paper

ball·room /ˈbɔlrum/ *n.* [C] a large room for formal dances

balm /bɑm/ *n.* [U] an oily liquid that you rub onto your skin to reduce pain

balm·y /ˈbɑmi/ *adj.* balmy weather or air is warm and pleasant: *a balmy summer night*

ba·lo·ney /bəˈlouni/ *n.* [U] **1** (informal) something that is silly or not true: *His explanation sounded like a bunch of baloney to me.* **2** another spelling of BOLOGNA

bam·boo /ˌbæmˈbu◂/ *n.* [C,U] a tall plant with hard hollow stems, often used for making furniture [ORIGIN: 1500—1600 Malay *bambu*]

bam·boo·zle /bæmˈbuzəl/ *v.* [T] (informal) to trick or confuse someone

ban¹ /bæn/ *n.* [C] an official order saying that people must not do something: *a global **ban on** nuclear testing* | *a movement to **lift** (=end) the **ban** on traveling to Cuba*

ban² *v.* (**banned**, **banning**) [T] to officially say that people must not do something or that something is not allowed: *The city council banned smoking in public areas in 1995.* | *The government **banned** Zhang **from** making films.*

THESAURUS forbid, not allow/permit/let, prohibit, bar, proscribe → FORBID

ba·nal /bəˈnæl, bəˈnɑl, ˈbeɪnl/ *adj.* ordinary and not interesting → BORING: *a banal love song* [ORIGIN: 1800—1900 French, Old French *ban* "military service that everyone must do, something common"] —**banality** /bəˈnæləṭi/ *n.* [C,U]

ba·nan·a /bəˈnænə/ *n.* [C] **1** a long curved yellow fruit → *see picture on page 414* **2 go bananas** (informal) to become very angry or excited: *The kids went bananas and tore open the boxes.* [ORIGIN: 1500—1600 Spanish, Portuguese, from Mande (a group of African languages)]

band¹ /bænd/ *n.* [C] **1** a group of musicians, especially a group that plays popular music: *a **rock/jazz/blues** band* | *Solem **played in a band** called "Great Buildings."* | *The **band** was **playing** old Beatles songs.* **2** a group of people who work together to achieve the same aims: *a small **band of** terrorists* **3** a narrow piece of something, with one end joined to the other to form a circle: *Her hair was pulled back with a **rubber band**.* **4** a narrow area of color or light that is different from the areas around it: *a fish with a black band along its back* [ORIGIN: (3–4) 1400—1500 French *bande* "flat strip, edge, side"]

THESAURUS line, stripe, streak → LINE¹

band² *v.*

band together *phr. v.* to work with other people in order to achieve something: *Neighbors banded together to fight for a health clinic*

ban·dage¹ /ˈbændɪdʒ/ *n.* [C] a long piece of cloth that you tie around a wound or injury

bandage² *v.* [T] to tie a bandage around a wound or injury

ˈBand-Aid *n.* [C] (trademark) a small piece of material that you stick over a small cut on your skin

ban·dan·na /bænˈdænə/ *n.* [C] a square piece of colored cloth that you can wear around your head or neck [ORIGIN: 1700—1800 Hindi *badhnu* "cloth tied and then colored," from *badhna* "to tie"]

ban·dit /ˈbændɪt/ *n.* [C] someone who robs people who are traveling [ORIGIN: 1500—1600 Italian *bandito*, from *bandire* "to banish"]

band·stand /ˈbændstænd/ *n.* [C] a structure in a park, used by a band playing music

band·wag·on /ˈbændˌwægən/ *n.* **jump/get/climb on the bandwagon** (disapproving) to start doing something because a lot of other people are doing it: *Many companies have jumped on the environmental bandwagon* (=started to give attention to the environment).

band·width /ˈbændˌwɪdθ/ *n.* [U] IT the amount of information that can be carried through a telephone wire or computer connection at one time

ban·dy /ˈbændi/ *v.* (**bandied**, **bandies**) **be bandied about/around** to be mentioned by a lot of people: *Her name was bandied about in connection with the recent scandal.*

bane /beɪn/ *n.* **be the bane of sth** to be the thing that causes trouble or makes people unhappy: *Locusts are **the bane of** farmers.*

bang¹ /bæŋ/ *v.* **1** [I,T] to make a loud noise, especially by hitting something against something hard: *Larren was **banging on** the wall with his fist.* | *The screen door banged shut behind him.*

THESAURUS **hit, punch, slap, beat, smack, whack, strike, knock, tap, pound, rap, hammer** ➔ HIT¹

2 [T] to hit a part of your body against something by accident: *I banged my knee on the corner of the bed.*

THESAURUS **hit, bump, strike** ➔ HIT¹

bang² *n.* [C] **1** a sudden loud noise such as an explosion or something hitting a hard surface: *There was a loud bang outside the kitchen door.* ➔ *see picture on page A20* **2** a painful blow to the body when you hit against something or something hits you: *a nasty **bang on** the head* **3 with a bang** in a way that is very exciting or noticeable: *He began his presidential campaign with a bang.* **4 bangs** [plural] hair that is cut straight across the front of your head, above your eyes ➔ *see picture on page 462*

bang³ *adv.* (informal) directly or exactly: *They've built a parking lot bang in the middle of town.*

bang⁴ *interjection* said in order to make the sound of a gun or bomb: *Bang! Bang! You're dead!*

ˌbanged-ˈup *adj.* (informal) damaged or injured: *a banged-up old car*

ban·ish /ˈbænɪʃ/ *v.* [T] to make someone leave a place as a punishment: *The king **banished** Roderigo **from** the court.*

ban·is·ter /ˈbænəstɚ/ *n.* [C] a row of wooden posts with a BAR along the top, that stops you from falling over the edge of the stairs

ban·jo /ˈbændʒoʊ/ *n.* (plural **banjos**) [C] a musical instrument like a GUITAR, with four or more strings, a circular body, and a long neck

bank¹ /bæŋk/ *n.* [C] **1** the company or place where you can keep your money or borrow money: *I went to the bank at noon to deposit my check.* | *a bank loan* | *We have very little money **in the bank**.* ➔ ACCOUNT¹ **2** land along the side of a river or lake: *the river bank* | *the **banks of** the Charles River*

THESAURUS **shore, coast, beach, seashore** ➔ SHORE¹

3 blood/sperm/organ etc. bank a place where human blood, etc. is stored until someone needs it **4** a large number of machines, etc. arranged close together in a row: *a **bank of** TV monitors* **5** a large pile of snow, sand, etc.: *a snow bank* **6 cloud/fog etc. bank** a mass of cloud, fog, mist, etc. [ORIGIN: (1, 3) 1400—1500 French *banque*, from Old Italian *banca* "long seat, bench"]

bank² *v.* **1** [T] to put or keep money in a bank: *She's managed to bank more than $300,000.* **2** [I] to use a particular bank: *Do you **bank with/at** First National?* **3** [I] if an airplane, MOTORCYCLE, etc. banks, it slopes to one side when it is turning **4** [I] to have steep sides like a hill: *The racetrack banks steeply in the third turn.*

bank on sb/sth *phr. v.* to depend on something happening or someone doing something: *We were banking on Jesse being here to help.*

bank·er /ˈbæŋkɚ/ *n.* [C] someone who has an important job in a bank

bank·ing /ˈbæŋkɪŋ/ *n.* [U] ECONOMICS the business of a bank

bank·rupt¹ /ˈbæŋkrʌpt/ *adj.* ECONOMICS unable to pay your debts: *Many small businesses **went bankrupt** during the recession.* [ORIGIN: 1500—1600 *bankrupt* "bankruptcy" (16—18 centuries), from French *banqueroute*, from Old Italian *bancarotta*, from *banca* "bank" + *rotta* "broken"]

bankrupt² *v.* [T] ECONOMICS to make someone become bankrupt: *The deal nearly bankrupted us.*

bank·rupt·cy /ˈbæŋkˌrʌptsi/ *n.* (plural **bankruptcies**) [C,U] ECONOMICS the state of being unable to pay your debts: *The company was forced to **declare bankruptcy**.*

ˈbank ˌteller *n.* [C] a TELLER

ban·ner¹ /ˈbænɚ/ *n.* [C] **1** a long piece of cloth with writing on it: *voters waving election banners* **2** a belief or principle: *Civil rights groups have achieved a lot **under the banner of** fair and equal treatment.*

banner² *adj.* excellent or successful: ***a banner year for** American soccer*

ban·quet /ˈbæŋkwɪt/ *n.* [C] a formal meal for many people

ban·ter /ˈbæntɚ/ *n.* [U] friendly conversation with a lot of jokes in it: *light-hearted banter* —**banter** *v.* [I]

bap·tism /ˈbæpˌtɪzəm/ *n.* [C,U] a religious ceremony in which a priest puts water on someone to make him/her a member of the Christian church —**baptismal** /bæpˈtɪzməl/ *adj.*

Bap·tist /ˈbæptɪst/ *adj.* relating to the Protestant church that believes baptism is only for people old enough to understand its meaning —**Baptist** *n.* [C]

bap·tize /ˈbæptaɪz, bæpˈtaɪz/ *v.* [T] to perform a baptism

bar¹ /bɑr/ *n.* [C] **1** a place where alcoholic drinks are sold and can be drunk: *a cocktail bar* **2** a COUNTER where alcoholic drinks are served: *O'Keefe and I stood **at the bar**.* | *He ordered a drink from the woman **behind the bar**.* **3** a long narrow piece of metal or wood: *iron bars* **4 a salad/coffee/sushi etc. bar** a place where a particular kind of food or drink is served **5** a small block of something: *a **bar of** soap* | *a candy bar* **6 bar to (doing) sth** something that prevents something else from happening: *His lack of a formal education was not a bar to his success.* **7 behind bars** (informal) in prison: *He spent the night behind bars.* **8 the Bar** *or* **the bar** LAW the profession of being a lawyer, or lawyers considered as a group [ORIGIN: 1100—1200 Old French *barre*] ➔ SALAD BAR, SNACK BAR

bar² *v.* (**barred**, **barring**) [T] **1** to officially prevent someone from doing something: *Photographers are* ***barred from*** *taking pictures inside the courtroom.*

THESAURUS forbid, not allow/permit/let, ban, prohibit, proscribe ➔ FORBID

2 to prevent people from going somewhere by placing something in their way: *She stood in the hall,* ***barring*** *my* ***way.*** **3** to put a piece of wood or metal across a door or window to prevent people from going in or out

bar·bar·i·an /bɑrˈbɛriən/ *n.* [C] someone who is rough, violent, and uneducated and does not respect art, education, etc.

bar·bar·ic /bɑrˈbærɪk, -ˈbɛrɪk/ *adj.* violent and cruel: *a barbaric act of terrorism* —**barbarism** /ˈbɑrbərɪzəm/ *n.* [U] —**barbarous** *adj.*

bar·be·cue¹ /ˈbɑrbɪˌkyu/ *n.* [C] **1** an occasion when you cook and eat food outdoors: *We're* ***having a barbecue*** *on Saturday.* **2** a metal frame for cooking food on outdoors [ORIGIN: 1600—1700 American Spanish *barbacoa*]

barbecue² *v.* [T] to cook food outdoors on a barbecue: *barbecued ribs*

barbed /bɑrbd/ *adj.* barbed humor or a barbed remark is unkind

ˌbarbed ˈwire *n.* [U] wire with short sharp points on it, usually used for making fences

bar·bell /ˈbɑrbɛl/ *n.* [C] a metal bar with weights at each end, which you lift to make you stronger ➔ *see picture at* DUMBBELL

bar·ber /ˈbɑrbɚ/ *n.* [C] a man whose job is to cut men's hair

bar·bi·tu·rate /bɑrˈbɪtʃərɪt/ *n.* [C,U] a drug that makes people calm and helps them to sleep

ˈbar chart *n.* [C] MATH a BAR GRAPH ➔ *see picture at* CHART¹

ˈbar code *n.* [C] a row of black lines on a product, that a computer can read to get information such as the price

bard /bɑrd/ *n.* [C] ENG. LANG. ARTS a poet

bare¹ /bɛr/ *adj.* **1** not covered by clothes: *children running around in bare feet* | *bare-chested/bare-legged etc.*

THESAURUS naked, nude, undressed, have nothing on, not have anything on ➔ NAKED

2 empty, or not covered by anything: *bare and treeless hills* | *Except for a few cans, the shelves were bare.*

THESAURUS empty, deserted, uninhabited, free, blank, vacant ➔ EMPTY¹

3 basic and with nothing extra: *The refugees took only the* ***bare necessities/essentials*** (=the most necessary things they owned). | *a report giving just the* ***bare facts*** **4 with your bare hands** without using a weapon or tool: *It is said that Daniel Boone killed a bear with his bare hands.* [ORIGIN: Old English *bær*]

bare² *v.* [T] **1** to let people see part of your body by removing something that is covering it: *The dog* ***bared*** *its* ***teeth*** *and growled.* **2 bare your soul** to tell your most secret feelings to someone

bare·back /ˈbɛrbæk/ *adj., adv.* on the back of a horse, without a SADDLE: *riding bareback*

ˌbare ˈbones *n.* **the bare bones** (informal) the most basic things, information, qualities, etc. that are needed: *He reduced his company to the bare bones.* —**bare-bones** *adj.*: *a bare-bones existence*

bare·foot /ˈbɛrfʊt/ *adj., adv.* not wearing any shoes or socks: *We walked barefoot in the sand.*

bare·ly /ˈbɛrli/ *adv.* **1** used in order to say that something only just happens, exists, etc.: *She was barely 18 when she had her first child.* | *I could barely stay awake.* **2** used in order to emphasize that something happens immediately after something else: *He'd barely sat down when she started asking questions.*

barf /bɑrf/ *v.* [I] (informal) to VOMIT —**barf** *n.* [U]

bar·gain¹ /ˈbɑrgən/ *n.* [C] **1** something bought for less than its usual price: *Check the advertisements for bargains.* | *At $8,500, this car is* ***a (real) bargain*** (=cheap). | *The stores were packed with* ***bargain hunters*** (=people looking for things that are cheap).

THESAURUS cheap, inexpensive, reasonable, a good/great deal, good/great/excellent value, competitive ➔ CHEAP¹

2 an agreement to do something in return for something else: *Management and unions have* ***struck a bargain*** *over wage increases.* | *The company* ***drove a hard bargain*** *in the negotiations* (=they made sure the agreement was favorable to them).

bargain² *v.* [I] to discuss the conditions of a sale, agreement, etc. in order to get a fair deal: *auto workers* ***bargaining with*** *management* | *teachers* ***bargained for*** *higher pay* | *union leaders* ***bargaining over*** *wages*

bargain for/on sth *phr. v.* to expect that something will happen: *I hadn't really bargained on things being so expensive there.* | ***I got more than I bargained for*** *in this job.*

ˈbargaining ˌchip *n.* [C] something that one person or group in a business deal or political agreement has that can be used in order to gain an advantage in the deal

barge[1] /bɑrdʒ/ *n.* [C] a boat with a flat bottom, used for carrying goods on a CANAL or river [ORIGIN: 1200—1300 Old French, Late Latin *barca*]

barge[2] *v.* [I] (informal) to walk somewhere so quickly or carelessly that you push people or hit things: *Dana **barged past** the guards at the door.* | *She **barged** her **way** through the crowds.*

barge in *also* **barge into** sth *phr. v.* to interrupt someone or go into a place when you were not invited: *The police just barged in.*

ˈbar graph *also* **ˈbar chart** *n.* [C] MATH a type of GRAPH with a series of boxes, in which the height of each box represents a particular amount

bar·i·tone /ˈbærəˌtoʊn/ *n.* [C,U] ENG. LANG. ARTS a male singing voice that is fairly low, but not the lowest, or a man with a voice like this ➔ BASS

bar·i·um /ˈbɛriəm, ˈbær-/ *n.* [U] CHEMISTRY (*symbol* **Ba**) a soft silver-white metal that is an ELEMENT

bark[1] /bɑrk/ *v.* **1** [I] to make the sound that a dog makes **2** [I,T] *also* **bark out** to say something in a loud angry voice: *Perry **barked at** his assistant.* **3 be barking up the wrong tree** (informal) to be doing something that will not get the result you want: *I realize now that I was barking up the wrong tree.* [ORIGIN: Old English *beorcan*]

bark[2] *n.* **1** [C] the sound a dog makes **2** [U] the outer covering of a tree ➔ *see picture at* PLANT[1]

bar·ley /ˈbɑrli/ *n.* [U] a grain used for making food and alcohol

barn /bɑrn/ *n.* [C] a large building on a farm, for storing crops or keeping animals in [ORIGIN: Old English *bereærn*, from *bere* "barley" + *ærn* "place"]

bar·na·cle /ˈbɑrnəkəl/ *n.* [C] a small sea animal with a hard shell, that sticks firmly to rocks, boats, etc. [ORIGIN: 1500—1600 *barnacle* type of goose (12—21 centuries), from Medieval Latin *bernaca*; from the former belief that the goose was born from a barnacle]

barn·yard /ˈbɑrnyɑrd/ *n.* [C] the area on a farm around a barn

ba·rom·e·ter /bəˈrɑmət̬ɚ/ *n.* [C] **1** an instrument for measuring changes in the air pressure and weather **2** something that shows any changes in a situation: *The election is seen as a **barometer of** the nation's mood.* [ORIGIN: 1600—1700 Greek *baros* "weight, pressure" + English *-meter*] —**barometric** /ˌbærəˈmɛtrɪk◂/ *adj.*

ba·roque /bəˈroʊk/ *adj.* ENG. LANG. ARTS relating to the very decorated style of art, music, buildings, etc. popular in Europe in the 17th century

bar·racks /ˈbærəks/ *n.* [plural] a group of buildings in which soldiers live [ORIGIN: 1600—1700 French *baraque* "small building," from Catalan *barraca*]

bar·rage /bəˈrɑʒ/ *n.* **1** [singular] a lot of complaints, questions, etc.: *a **barrage of** insults/abuse* **2** [C usually singular] the continuous shooting of guns

bar·rel[1] /ˈbærəl/ *n.* [C] **1** a large container with curved sides and a flat top and bottom: *a **barrel of** beer* **2** the part of a gun that the bullets are shot through **3 have sb over a barrel** (informal) to put someone in a situation where s/he is forced to do something: *I didn't really want to work overtime, but my boss had me over a barrel.* **4** a unit used for measuring oil, equal to about 42 gallons or 159 liters

barrel[2] *v.* [I] to move very fast, especially in an uncontrolled way: *We were **barreling down** the road at 90 miles an hour.*

bar·ren /ˈbærən/ *adj.* land that is barren cannot grow plants: *a barren desert*

bar·rette /bəˈrɛt/ *n.* [C] a small metal or plastic object used to keep a woman's hair in place

bar·ri·cade[1] /ˈbærəˌkeɪd/ *n.* [C] something that is put across a road, door, etc. to prevent people from going past: *Protesters were kept behind barricades.* [ORIGIN: 1500—1600 French *barrique* "barrel;" because early barricades were made from barrels]

barricade[2] *v.* [T] to use a barricade to prevent someone or something from going somewhere: *They **barricaded** themselves **in** and the police had to storm the building.*

bar·ri·er /ˈbæriɚ/ *n.* [C] **1** something that prevents people from doing something: *an attempt to reduce **trade barriers*** | *The **language barrier** prevents many people from working abroad.* | *A lack of education is a **barrier to** many good jobs.* **2** a type of fence that keeps people or things separate, or prevents people from entering a place: *The police put up barriers to hold back the crowds.* **3** a physical object that separates two areas, groups of people, etc.: *The mountains form a **natural barrier** between the two countries.*

bar·ring /ˈbɑrɪŋ/ *prep.* unless something happens: *Barring any last-minute problems, we should finish Friday.*

bar·ri·o /ˈbæriˌoʊ/ *n.* (plural **barrios**) [C] an area in a city where many poor Spanish-speaking people live [ORIGIN: 1800—1900 Spanish, Arabic *barri* "of the open country"]

bar·room /ˈbɑrˌrum/ *n.* [C] (informal) a BAR

bar·tend·er /ˈbɑrˌtɛndɚ/ *n.* [C] someone whose job is to make and serve drinks in a bar

bar·ter /ˈbɑrt̬ɚ/ *v.* [I,T] to exchange goods or services instead of money: *I had to **barter with** the locals for food.*

ba·salt /bəˈsɔlt, ˈbeɪsɔlt/ *n.* [U] EARTH SCIENCES a type of hard dark green or black rock that comes from a VOLCANO

base[1] /beɪs/ *v.* [T] to use somewhere as your main place of business: *a law firm **based in** Denver* | *Ohio-based/Miami-based etc.* [ORIGIN: 1300—

1400 Old French *bas*, from Medieval Latin *bassus* "short, low"]

base sth **on/upon** sth *phr. v.* to use something as the model from which you develop something else: *Discrimination based on race or sex is forbidden by law.* | *The movie was based on Amelia Earhart's life.*

base² *n.* [C]

1 LOWEST PART the lowest part or surface of something: *a black vase with a round base* | *Waves crashed against **the base of** the cliff.* | *the base of the skull*

2 MAIN PART all the people, companies, money, etc. that form the main part of something: *Roosevelt had a broad base of political support.* | *the city's **economic base*** (=things that produce jobs and money) | *Japan's **manufacturing base*** (=companies that make things)

3 PLACE the main place where someone works or stays, or from which work is done: *Microsoft's base is in Redmond.* | *The hotel is an ideal **base for** sightseeing.*

4 MILITARY a place where people in the army, navy, etc. live and work: *an army base*

5 IDEAS the most important part of something, from which new ideas develop: *Both French and Spanish come from a Latin base.*

6 off base (informal) completely wrong: *The estimate for painting the house seems **way off base**.*

7 cover/touch all the bases to prepare for or deal with a situation thoroughly: *The police have called in experts to make sure they've covered all the bases.*

8 SUBSTANCE/MIXTURE the main part of a substance, to which other things can be added: *paints with a water base*

9 BASEBALL one of the four places that a player must touch in order to score a point

10 SCIENCE CHEMISTRY a chemical substance that combines with an acid to form a salt

base·ball /ˈbeɪsbɔl/ *n.* **1** [U] a game in which two teams try to score points by hitting a ball and running around four bases → *see picture on page A17* **2** [C] the ball used in this game

base·ment /ˈbeɪsmənt/ *n.* [C] the room or rooms in a building that are below the level of the ground

bas·es /ˈbeɪsiz/ *n.* the plural of BASIS

bash¹ /bæʃ/ *v.* [I,T] **1** to hit someone or something hard, causing pain or damage: *He **bashed** his toe **on** the coffee table.* | *Police bashed down the door to get in.* **2** (informal) to criticize someone or something very strongly: *Hodge took every opportunity to bash the media.*

bash² *n.* [C] (informal) a party: *an anniversary bash*

bash·ful /ˈbæʃfəl/ *adj.* shy

THESAURUS **shy, timid, demure, self-conscious, reserved, introverted, retiring**
→ SHY¹

bash·ing /ˈbæʃɪŋ/ *n.* **gay-bashing/immigrant-bashing/media-bashing etc.** the act of physically attacking or strongly criticizing a particular group of people or businesses

ba·sic /ˈbeɪsɪk/ *adj.* **1** forming the main or most necessary part of something: *the **basic principles** of mathematics* | *a soldier's **basic training*** | *There are two basic problems here.*

THESAURUS

fundamental – relating to the most basic and important parts of something: *The fundamental problem is a lack of resources.*
essential – the essential parts, qualities, or features of something are the ones that are most important, typical, or easily noticed: *Religion is an essential part of their lives.*
elementary – relating to the most simple or basic parts of something: *the elementary human need for food*
central – more important than anything else: *Linda played a central role in the negotiations.*
underlying – relating to the reason or cause of something that is the most important or main one, but that is not easy to discover: *the underlying causes of her depression*

2 at the simplest or least developed level: *basic health care* | *The farm lacks even basic equipment.*
→ BASICS

ba·si·cally /ˈbeɪsɪkli/ *adv.* **1** (spoken) used to give a simple explanation of something: *Well, basically, the teacher said he'll need extra help with math.* **2** in the main or most important ways, without considering small details: *Norwegian and Danish are basically the same.* | *I believe that human beings are basically good.*

ba·sics /ˈbeɪsɪks/ *n.* [plural] **1 the basics** the most important facts or things that you need: *We were taught **the basics of** sailing.* **2 get/go back to basics** to return to teaching or doing the most important or the simplest part of something: *A lot of parents want schools to get back to basics.*

ba·sin /ˈbeɪsən/ *n.* [C] **1** EARTH SCIENCES a large area of land that is lower in the center than at the edges: *the Amazon basin* **2** a large bowl, especially one for water [ORIGIN: 1200—1300 Old French *bacin*, from Late Latin *bacchinon*]

ba·sis /ˈbeɪsɪs/ *n.* (plural **bases** /ˈbeɪsiz/) [C] **1 on a weekly/informal/freelance etc. basis** happening at a particular time or in a particular way: *Meetings are held on a monthly basis.* | *She still works, but on a part-time basis.* **2** the information or ideas from which something develops: *The video will provide a **basis for** class discussion.* | *In this remote part of the world, people's religious beliefs **form the basis of** their whole society.* **3 on the basis of sth** because of a particular fact or situation: *Employers may not discriminate on the basis of race or sex.*

bask /bæsk/ *v.* [I] **1** to enjoy sitting or lying somewhere warm: *a snake **basking in** the sun* **2** to enjoy the attention or approval you receive from someone: *She **basked in** her mother's praise.*

bas·ket /ˈbæskɪt/ *n.* [C] **1** a container made of thin pieces of dried plants, wire, etc., used for carrying or holding things: *a picnic basket* | *a **laundry basket*** (=for putting dirty clothes in) | *a **basket of** fruit* **2** the net in basketball: *Dean **scored/made a basket*** (=threw the ball into the basket) *with just under a minute to play.*

bas·ket·ball /ˈbæskɪtˌbɔl/ *n.* **1** [U] a game between two teams, in which each team tries to throw a ball through a net **2** [C] the ball used in this game

ˈbasket case *n.* [C] (informal) someone who you think is crazy

bass[1] /beɪs/ *n.* **1** [C] *also* **bass guitar** a GUITAR that plays low notes **2** [C,U] ENG. LANG. ARTS the lowest male singing voice, or a man with a voice like this **3** [U] the lower half of the whole range of musical notes **4** [C] a DOUBLE BASS

bass[2] /bæs/ *n.* [C,U] a fish that lives both in the ocean and in rivers, lakes, etc., or the meat from this fish

bas·si·net /ˌbæsɪˈnɛt/ *n.* [C] a small bed that looks like a basket, used for a very young baby

bas·soon /bəˈsun, bæ-/ *n.* [C] a very long wooden musical instrument with a low sound that you play by blowing into it → *see picture at* WOODWIND

bas·tard /ˈbæstɚd/ *n.* [C] (old-fashioned) someone whose parents were not married when s/he was born

baste /beɪst/ *v.* [T] to pour liquid fat over food that is cooking

bas·tion /ˈbæstʃən/ *n.* [C] a place, organization, etc. that protects old beliefs or ways of doing things: *the country's reputation as a **bastion of** free speech*

bat[1] /bæt/ *n.* [C] **1** a long wooden stick used for hitting the ball in baseball **2** a small animal like a mouse with wings that flies at night → *see picture at* NOCTURNAL **3 right off the bat** (informal) immediately: *He got into trouble right off the bat.* **4 be at bat** to be the person who is trying to hit the ball in baseball

bat[2] *v.* (**batted**, **batting**) [I,T] **1** to hit a ball with a bat: *Brent is **up to bat** next* (=he will try to hit the ball next). **2 bat your eyes/eyelashes** if a woman bats her eyes, she opens and closes them several times quickly in order to look attractive to men **3 not bat an eye/eyelash** (informal) without showing any emotion or guilty feelings: *He used to tell the worst lies without batting an eye.* **4 go to bat for sb** (informal) to help and support someone: *Andy really went to bat for me with my manager.* **5 bat a thousand** (informal) to be very successful

batch /bætʃ/ *n.* [C] a group of things or people that arrive or are dealt with at the same time: *She's just baked another **batch of** cookies*

bat·ed /ˈbeɪt̬ɪd/ *adj.* **with bated breath** in a very excited and anxious way: *I **waited** for her answer **with bated breath**.*

bath /bæθ/ *n.* (plural **baths** /bæðz, bæθs/) [C] **1** an act of washing your body in the water that you put in a bathtub: *You need to **take a bath** before you go to bed.* | *Dan, will you **give** the kids **a bath*** (=wash them) *tonight?* **2** a bathroom, used especially in advertising: *a three-bedroom, two-bath house* **3** water that you sit or lie in to wash yourself: *I love to sit and soak in a hot bath.* | *Lisa **ran a bath*** (=put water in a bathtub) *for herself.* [ORIGIN: Old English *bæth*]

bathe /beɪð/ *v.* **1** [I,T] to wash yourself or someone else in a bath: *Water was scarce, and we only bathed once a week.* | *He bathed the children and put them to bed.* **2** [T] to put water or another liquid on part of your body as a medical treatment **3 be bathed in light** if something is bathed in light, a lot of light is shining on it

bathing suit /ˈbeɪðɪŋ ˌsut/ *n.* [C] a piece of clothing you wear for swimming

ba·thos /ˈbeɪθɑs/ *n.* [U] ENG. LANG. ARTS in a book, a play, etc., a sudden change from a subject that is beautiful, moral, or serious to something that is ordinary, silly, or not important

bath·robe /ˈbæθroʊb/ *n.* [C] a loose piece of clothing like a coat, that you wear especially before or after taking a bath or SHOWER

bath·room /ˈbæθrum/ *n.* [C] **1** a room where there is a toilet and usually a bathtub or a SHOWER and sink

> THESAURUS **toilet, restroom, women's/ladies' room, men's room, lavatory, latrine, outhouse, privy** → TOILET

2 go to the bathroom to use the toilet: *Mommy, I have to go to the bathroom!*

bath·tub /ˈbæθtʌb/ *n.* [C] a long container in which you wash yourself

ba·ton /bəˈtɑn/ *n.* [C] **1** a short stick used by the leader of a group of musicians to direct the music **2** a metal stick that you spin and throw into the air **3** a stick that a police officer uses as a weapon **4** a stick passed from one runner to another in a race

bat·tal·ion /bəˈtælyən/ *n.* [C] a large group of soldiers

bat·ter[1] /ˈbæt̬ɚ/ *n.* **1** [C,U] a mixture of flour, eggs, milk, etc. used for making cakes, some types of bread, etc.: *pancake batter* **2** [C] the person who is trying to hit the ball in baseball

batter[2] *v.* [I,T] to hit someone or something very hard many times: *He was **battered to death**.* | *Waves were **battering against** the rocks.* —**battering** *n.* [C,U]

bat·tered /ˈbæt̬ɚd/ *adj.* **1** old and slightly damaged: *a battered old guitar* **2 battered woman/child** a woman who has been attacked by her husband, boyfriend, etc., or a child who has been attacked by a parent

bat·ter·y /ˈbæt̬əri/ *n.* (plural **batteries**) **1** [C] an object that provides electricity for something such as a radio or car: *a **dead battery*** (=one with no power) **2** [U] LAW the crime of beating someone **3** [C] a set of many things of the same type: *a **battery of** medical tests*

bat·tle¹ /ˈbæt̬l/ *n.* **1** [C,U] a fight between two armies or groups, especially during a war: *the Battle of Bunker Hill* | *Thousands of soldiers were killed **in battle*** (=during a war or battle). **2** [C] a situation in which people or groups compete or argue with each other: *the **battle for** control of Congress* | *a long and costly **legal battle*** **3** [C] an attempt to stop something happening or to achieve something difficult: *the **battle against** racial discrimination* | *a long **battle with** lung cancer* | *Gina **fought** a **losing battle** to hold back the tears.* [ORIGIN: 1200—1300 Old French *bataille*, from Late Latin *battalia* "fighting," from Latin *battuere* "to hit"]

THESAURUS **fight, campaign, drive, struggle, crusade** → FIGHT²

battle² *v.* [I,T] to try very hard to achieve something difficult: *My mother **battled** bravely **against** breast cancer.* | *Doctors **battled to** save his life.*

bat·tle·field /ˈbæt̬lˌfild/ *also* **bat·tle·ground** /ˈbæt̬lˌgraʊnd/ *n.* [C] **1** a place where a battle is being fought or has been fought **2** a subject that people disagree or argue a lot about: *This area of medical research has become an **ethical battlefield**.*

bat·tle·ship /ˈbæt̬lˌʃɪp/ *n.* [C] a very large ship used in wars

bawd·y /ˈbɔdi/ *adj.* bawdy songs, jokes, etc. are about sex

bawl /bɔl/ *v.* [I] (informal) to shout or cry loudly: *By the end of the movie, I was bawling.*

bawl sb ↔ **out** *phr. v.* (informal) to speak angrily to someone because s/he has done something wrong: *Mom bawled me out for not cleaning my room.*

bay /beɪ/ *n.* [C] **1** EARTH SCIENCES a place where the coast curves around the ocean: *Chesapeake Bay* → *see picture on page A24* **2 keep/hold sth/sb at bay** to prevent something dangerous or bad from happening, or someone from coming too close: *The dogs kept the intruder at bay.* **3** a small area used for a special purpose: *the plane's cargo bay* [ORIGIN: (1) 1300—1400 Old French *baie*, from Old Spanish *bahia*]

bay·o·net /ˈbeɪənɪt, -ˌnɛt, ˌbeɪəˈnɛt/ *n.* [C] a long knife attached to the end of a long gun [ORIGIN: 1600—1700 French *baïonnette*, from *Bayonne* city in southwest France where it was first made]

bay·ou /ˈbaɪu, ˈbaɪoʊ/ *n.* [C] EARTH SCIENCES a large area of water in the southeast U.S. that moves very slowly and has many water plants [ORIGIN: 1700—1800 Louisiana French, Choctaw *bayuk*]

ˌbay ˈwindow *n.* [C] a window that sticks out from the wall of a house, with glass on three sides

ba·zaar /bəˈzɑr/ *n.* [C] **1** an event at which a lot of people sell various things to collect money for an organization: *a church bazaar* **2** a market in Asian or Middle Eastern countries [ORIGIN: 1500—1600 Persian *bazar*]

B

BB gun /ˈbibi ˌgʌn/ *n.* [C] a gun that uses air pressure to shoot small metal balls

BBQ /ˈbɑrbɪˌkyu/ the abbreviation of BARBECUE

B.C. *adv.* **Before Christ** used after a date to show that it was before the birth of Christ (ANT) **A.D.**: *2600 B.C.*

be¹ /bi/ *auxiliary verb* (past tense **was, were**, past participle **been**) **1** used with a present participle to form the continuous tenses of verbs: *Jane was reading by the fire.* | *Don't talk to me while I'm* (=I am) *working.* **2** used with a PAST PARTICIPLE to form the PASSIVE: *Smoking is not permitted in public places, such as restaurants.* | *I was shown a copy of the contract.* **3** used in CONDITIONAL sentences to talk about an imagined situation: ***If** I **were** rich, I'd buy myself a Rolls Royce.* | *He could lose his job **if** he **were to** be charged with a crime.* **4 sb is to do sth** (formal) **a)** used in order to say what will happen: *I'll be* (=I will be) *leaving tomorrow.* **b)** used in order to say what must happen: *The children are to go to bed by 8:00.* **5 sb/sth is to be seen/found/heard etc.** (formal) used to say that someone or something can be seen, etc.: *The money was **nowhere to be found**.* → IS, AM, ARE, BEEN

be² *v.* [linking verb] **1** used in order to give or ask for information about someone or something, or to describe that person or thing in some way: *January is the first month of the year.* | *The concert was last night.* | *Julie wants to be a doctor.* | *Where are my shoes?* | *Is this your coat?* | *It's* (=it is) *going to be hot today.* | *I'm* (=I am) *cold.* **2 there is/are/were etc.** used in order to show that something exists or happens: *There were only eight people at choir practice.* | *There's* (=there is) *a hole in your jeans.* **3** to behave in a particular way: *Be careful.* | *He was just being silly.* **4** used to give your opinion about something: *"We won't be able to make it tomorrow night." "That's too bad."* | ***It's** strange **that** she hasn't phoned.* **5 be yourself** to behave in a natural way: *Don't worry about impressing them – just be yourself.* **6 not be yourself** to be behaving in a way that is unusual for you, especially because you are sick or upset: *She hasn't been herself lately.* → **let sb/sth be** *at* LET

beach /bitʃ/ *n.* [C] EARTH SCIENCES an area of sand or small stones at the edge of an ocean or a lake: *We spent the day **at the beach**.* | *children playing **on the beach*** | *a beach house* → *see picture on page A24*

THESAURUS **shore, coast, seashore, bank** → SHORE¹

ˈbeach ball *n.* [C] a large plastic ball that you fill with air and play with at the beach

B

bea·con /ˈbikən/ *n.* [C] a light or electronic signal used to guide boats, airplanes, etc.

bead /bid/ *n.* [C] **1** a small ball of plastic, wood, glass, etc. used for making jewelry **2** a small drop of liquid: *beads of sweat* [ORIGIN: Old English *bed, gebed* "prayer;" because people counted beads while saying their prayers]

bead·y /ˈbidi/ *adj.* beady eyes are small and shiny

bea·gle /ˈbigəl/ *n.* [C] a dog with large ears, short legs, and smooth fur, sometimes used in hunting

beak /bik/ *n.* [C] the hard pointed mouth of a bird [ORIGIN: 1200—1300 Old French *bec*, from Latin *beccus*] ➔ *see picture on page A15*

beak·er /ˈbikə/ *n.* [C] a glass cup with straight sides, used in a LABORATORY (=place where people do scientific tests)

beam¹ /bim/ *n.* [C] **1** a line of light or energy: *a* ***laser beam*** | *A* ***beam of light*** | *The* ***beam of*** *a flashlight was shining directly in my eyes.* **2** a long piece of wood or metal used in building houses, bridges, etc.

beam² *v.* **1** [I] to smile in a very happy way: *Uncle Willie* ***beamed at*** *us proudly.*

THESAURUS **smile, grin, smirk, simper ➔** SMILE

2 [I,T] to send out energy, light, radio, or television signals, etc.: *the first broadcast* ***beamed across*** *the Atlantic* | *The sun beamed through the clouds.*

bean /bin/ *n.* [C] **1** a seed or a case that seeds grow in, cooked as food: *green beans* | *baked beans* **2** a plant that produces beans **3 coffee/cocoa bean** a seed used in making coffee or COCOA, and food such as chocolate [ORIGIN: Old English]

bear¹ /bɛr/ *v.* (past tense **bore** /bɔr/, past participle **borne** /bɔrn/) [T]

1 BE RESPONSIBLE (formal) to be responsible for something: *In this case, you must* ***bear the blame/responsibility*** *yourself.* | *The federal government will* ***bear the cost*** *of the program.*

2 DEAL WITH STH to bravely accept or deal with a painful or difficult situation: *She didn't think she could bear the pain.* | *Make the water as hot as you* ***can bear.*** | *The pressure was* ***more than*** *he* ***could bear.***

3 can't bear sb/sth to dislike someone or something very much, or to feel unable to do something because it upsets you SYN **can't stand**: *I can't bear that woman.* | *He can't bear people watching him eat.* | *She can't* ***bear to*** *throw anything away.* | *I* ***couldn't bear the thought of*** *leaving the kids, even for one night.*

4 bear a resemblance/relation to sb/sth to be similar to or related to someone or something: *He* ***bears a striking resemblance to*** *his father* (=looks very like his father). | *The facts* ***bear little relation to*** (=are not similar to) *reality.*

5 bear (sth) in mind to consider a fact when you are deciding or judging something: ***Bear in mind*** *that this method might not work.*

6 HAVE FEELINGS (formal) to have bad feelings toward someone: *I don't* ***bear*** *a* ***grudge*** (=still feel angry about something).

7 bear fruit if a plan or decision bears fruit, it is successful: *The project may not begin to bear fruit for at least two years.*

8 WEIGHT to support the weight of something: *The ice wasn't thick enough to* ***bear*** *his* ***weight.***

9 sth doesn't bear thinking about used to say that something is very upsetting or shocking: *The long-term effects don't bear thinking about.*

10 MARK/NAME (formal) to have a particular name or appearance: *the company that* ***bore*** *her father's* ***name*** | *He bore the scars for the rest of his life.*

11 bear with me (spoken) used in order to politely ask someone to wait while you do something: *Bear with me for a minute while I check the files.*

12 bear right/left to turn toward the right or left: *Bear left where the road divides.*

13 BABY (formal) to give birth to a baby

14 CARRY (formal) to bring or carry something: *They came* ***bearing gifts.***

THESAURUS **carry, tote, lug, cart, haul, schlep, transport ➔** CARRY

➔ bring sth to bear (on) *at* BRING

bear down on sb/sth *phr. v.*
to move quickly toward someone or something in a threatening way: *We ran as the truck bore down on us.*

bear sb/sth **out** *phr. v.*
to show that something is true: *The study's findings were borne out by further research.*

bear up *phr. v.*
to succeed in being brave and determined during a difficult or upsetting time

bear² *n.* [C] a large strong animal with thick fur ➔ POLAR BEAR, TEDDY BEAR

bear·a·ble /ˈbɛrəbəl/ *adj.* a situation that is bearable is difficult but can be accepted or dealt with: *His friendship was the one thing that made life bearable.*

beard /bɪrd/ *n.* [C] the hair that grows on a man's chin [ORIGIN: Old English] —**bearded** *adj.* ➔ *see picture on page 462*

bear·er /ˈbɛrə/ *n.* [C] someone who brings or carries something: *the* ***bearer of bad news*** | *a flag bearer* ➔ PALLBEARER

bear·ing /ˈbɛrɪŋ/ *n.* **1 have a bearing on sth** to have some influence on or effect on something: *The new information* ***has no/some bearing on*** *the case.* **2 get your bearings** to find out where you are or what you should do **3 lose your bearings** to become confused about where you are **4** [singular, U] the way someone moves or stands: *an elderly man with a military bearing*

bear·ish /ˈbɛrɪʃ/ *adj.* ECONOMICS expecting the price of shares on a STOCK MARKET to fall ANT **bullish**

ˈbear ˌmarket *n.* [C] ECONOMICS a situation in

which the value of STOCKS is decreasing → BULL MARKET

beast /bist/ *n.* [C] **1** (literary) a wild animal **2** (old-fashioned) a cruel person

beat¹ /bit/ *v.* (past tense **beat**, past participle **beaten** /ˈbit˺n/)

1 DEFEAT [T] to get more points, votes, etc. than other people in a game or competition: *New York beat Boston 4–1.* | *Stuart usually* ***beats*** *me* ***at*** *chess.* | *Has anyone ever* ***beaten the record*** *for home runs set by Babe Ruth?*

THESAURUS

defeat – to win a victory over someone: *I don't think anybody will be able to defeat Kennedy in a Senate election.*
trounce – to defeat someone completely: *The Bears trounced Nebraska 44–10.*
clobber/cream (informal) – to defeat someone easily: *We got creamed in the finals.*
vanquish (formal) – to defeat someone or something completely: *The allies vanquished the enemy.*
overcome – to fight and win against someone or something: *Union troops finally overcame rebel forces in the south.*
conquer – to defeat someone, especially a country, and get control of land and people: *The Greeks conquered the Trojans.*

2 HIT SB [T] to hit someone many times with your hand, a stick, etc.: *He used to come home and beat us.* | *The woman had been* ***beaten to death***.

THESAURUS **hit, punch, slap, smack, whack, strike, knock, bang, tap, pound, rap, hammer** → HIT¹

3 HIT STH [I,T] to hit against the surface of something continuously, or to make something do this: *waves* ***beating on/against*** *the shore*

4 FOOD [I,T] to mix foods together quickly using a fork or a kitchen tool: *Beat the eggs and add them to the sugar mixture.* → *see picture on page A18*

THESAURUS **mix, combine, stir, blend** → MIX¹

5 SOUND [I,T] to make a regular sound or movement, or to make something do this: *She could feel her* ***heart beating***. | *I could hear* ***drums beating***.

6 beat around the bush to avoid talking about something embarrassing or upsetting: *Stop beating around the bush, and say it!*

7 AVOID [T] to do something early in order to avoid problems, because later everyone will be doing it: *We left at 5:00 to* ***beat the traffic***. | *Shop early and* ***beat the*** *Christmas* ***rush***!

SPOKEN PHRASES

8 [T] to be better or more enjoyable than something else: *It's not the greatest job, but* ***it beats*** *waitressing.* | ***You can't beat*** (=nothing is better than) *San Diego for good weather.*

9 (it) beats me used in order to say that you do not understand or know something: *"Where's Myrna?" "Beats me."*

10 beat it! an impolite way to tell someone to leave at once

[ORIGIN: Old English *beatan*] → **off the beaten track/path** *at* BEATEN

beat down *phr. v.*

1 if the Sun beats down, it shines brightly and is hot
2 if the rain beats down, it rains very hard

beat sb/sth ↔ **off** *phr. v.*
to hit someone who is attacking you until s/he goes away

beat sb ↔ **out** *phr. v.* (informal)
to defeat someone in a competition: *Lange* ***beat out*** *Foster* ***for*** *the award.*

beat sb **to** sth *phr. v.*
to get or do something before someone else: *I wanted the car, but someone* ***beat me to it***.

beat sb ↔ **up** *phr. v.*

1 to hit someone until s/he is badly hurt: *My boyfriend went crazy and beat me up.*

2 beat yourself up (informal) to blame yourself too much for something: *Don't beat yourself up over this!*

beat² *n.* **1** [C] one of a series of regular movements or sounds: *a heart rate of 80* ***beats per minute*** | *the* ***beat of*** *the drum* **2** [singular] the pattern of sounds in a piece of music **3** [singular] a subject or area of a city that someone is responsible for as his/her job: *journalists covering the political beat* | *a police officer* ***on the beat*** (=walking around the streets in a particular area)

beat³ *adj.* (informal) very tired: *You look beat!*

THESAURUS **tired, exhausted, worn out, weary, run-down, fatigued** → TIRED

beat·en /ˈbit˺n/ *adj.* **off the beaten track/path** far away from places that people usually visit: *a little hotel off the beaten track*

beat·er /ˈbiṭɚ/ *n.* [C] **1** a kitchen tool that is used for mixing foods together **2 wife/child beater** someone who hits his wife or his/her child

beat·ing /ˈbiṭɪŋ/ *n.* [C] **1** an act of hitting someone many times as a punishment or in a fight: *a severe beating* **2 take a beating** to lose very badly in a game or competition

ˈbeat-up *adj.* (informal) old and slightly damaged: *a beat-up old car*

beau·ti·cian /byuˈtɪʃən/ *n.* [C] (old-fashioned) a HAIRDRESSER

beau·ti·ful /ˈbyuṭəfəl/ *adj.* **1** extremely attractive to look at: *She was the most beautiful woman I've ever seen.* | *a beautiful baby* | *The views from the mountaintop were beautiful.*

THESAURUS **attractive, good-looking, nice-looking, pretty, handsome, gorgeous, stunning, cute, hot** → ATTRACTIVE

2 very good, or giving you great pleasure: *beautiful music* | *The weather was beautiful.*

beau·ty /ˈbyuṭi/ *n.* (plural **beauties**) **1** [U] a quality that people, places, or things have that makes them very attractive to look at: *a woman of* ***great beauty*** | *the* ***beauty of*** *Yosemite* **2** [U] a quality that something such as a poem, song, etc. has that gives you pleasure: *the* ***beauty of*** *Keats's poetry* **3** [C] (informal) something that is very good or impressive: *His new car's a beauty.* **4 the beauty of sth is...** used to explain why something is especially good: *The beauty of this exercise is that you can do it anywhere.* **5** [C] (old-fashioned) a woman who is very beautiful [ORIGIN: 1200—1300 Old French *biauté*, from Latin *bellus* "pretty"]

ˈbeauty saˌlon *also* **ˈbeauty ˌparlor** *n.* [C] a SALON

bea·ver /ˈbivɚ/ *n.* [C] a North American animal that has thick fur, a wide flat tail, and cuts down trees with its teeth ➔ *see picture at* RODENT

be·bop /ˈbibɑp/ *n.* [U] a style of JAZZ music

be·came /bɪˈkeɪm/ *v.* the past tense of BECOME

be·cause /bɪˈkɔz, -ˈkʌz/ *conjunction* used when you are giving the reason for something: *You can't go because you're too young.* | *We weren't able to have the picnic* ***because of*** *the rain.* | *They liked him* ***simply because*** *he could play basketball.* | *He moved to Florida* ***partly/largely/mainly because*** *he liked the weather.* [ORIGIN: 1300—1400 *by cause (that)*]

THESAURUS

due to – used when giving the reason why something happened: *The flight was delayed due to bad weather.*
since – used when giving the reason why someone decides to do something: *Since it was getting late, we decided to go back home.*
through – because of something: *They succeeded through a combination of hard work and determination.*
out of – because of a feeling: *I went there out of curiosity.*
thanks to – because of what someone has done, or because something exists: *Today, thanks to the Internet, you can find out information about almost anything.* | *We're late, thanks to you.*

➔ **just because ... (it) doesn't mean ...** *at* JUST[1]

beck·on /ˈbɛkən/ *v.* [I,T] to move your hand to show that you want someone to move toward you: *He beckoned her to join him.* | *He* ***beckoned to*** *her.*

be·come /bɪˈkʌm/ *v.* (past tense **became** /-ˈkeɪm/, past participle **become**) **1** [linking verb] to begin to be something, or to develop in a particular way: *The weather had become warmer.* | *In 1960, Kennedy became the first Catholic president.* | *It is becoming harder to find good housing for low-income families.* | *It became clear that she was lying.* | *She started to become anxious about her son.* ►Don't say "She started to be anxious about her son."◄ **2 become of sb/sth** to happen to someone or something: ***Whatever became of*** *Grandma's dishes?* | *No one knows* ***what will become of*** *him when his mother dies.*

USAGE

Become is used in both written and spoken English: *Their music has become very popular.* | *He quickly became very rich.*
Get and **go** are less formal than **become**, and are used more often in spoken English: *I'm getting tired.* | *Have you gone crazy?*
Become can be used in front of an adjective or a noun, but **get** and **go** are used only in front of an adjective: *She wants to become a lawyer.* | *People are becoming worried about the future of our planet.* | *It's getting dark.* | *Beethoven went deaf when he was 40 years old.*

be·com·ing /bɪˈkʌmɪŋ/ *adj.* (old-fashioned) a piece of clothing, HAIRSTYLE, etc. that is becoming makes you look attractive

bed[1] /bɛd/ *n.* **1** [C,U] a piece of furniture for sleeping on: *a* ***double bed*** (=a bed for two people) | *a* ***single bed*** (=a bed for one person) | *I was lying* ***in bed*** *reading.* | *She looked like she had just* ***gotten out of bed.*** | *What time do you usually* ***put*** *the kids* ***to bed****?* | *Jamie usually* ***goes to bed*** *around seven o'clock.* | *Sara, have you* ***made*** *your* ***bed*** *yet* (=pulled the sheets, etc. into place)*?* | *Come on, it's* ***time for bed*** (=time to go to sleep). **2 go to bed with sb** (informal) to have sex with someone **3** [C] the ground at the bottom of the ocean, a river, or a lake: *a river bed* **4** [C] an area of ground that has been prepared for plants to grow in: ***flower beds*** **5 a bed of sth** a layer of something that is a base for something else: *potato salad on a bed of lettuce* [ORIGIN: Old English *bedd*]

bed[2] *v.* (**bedded**, **bedding**)

bed down *phr. v.* to make yourself comfortable and sleep in a place where you do not usually sleep: *I'll just bed down on the sofa.*

ˌbed and ˈbreakfast *also* **B&B** *n.* [C] a house or a small hotel where you pay to sleep and have breakfast: *We plan to stay at a bed and breakfast while we're in England.*

THESAURUS **hotel, motel, inn, hostel, campground** → HOTEL

bed·clothes /ˈbɛdkloʊz, -kloʊðz/ *n.* [plural] BEDDING

bed·ding /ˈbɛdɪŋ/ *n.* [U] **1** the sheets, BLANKETS, etc. that you put on a bed **2** soft material that an animal sleeps on

bed·lam /ˈbɛdləm/ *n.* [U] a situation in which there is a lot of noise and you are not able to think clearly: *When the bomb exploded, there was bedlam.* [ORIGIN: 1600—1700 *bedlam* "mental hospital" (17—18 centuries), from *Bedlam* "Bethlehem" (10—17 centuries); from the Hospital of St. Mary of *Bethlehem*, former London mental hospital]

bed·pan /ˈbɛdpæn/ *n.* [C] a container used as a toilet by someone who is too sick or old to get out of bed

be·drag·gled /bɪˈdrægəld/ *adj.* looking dirty, wet, and messy: *bedraggled hair*

bed·rid·den /ˈbɛdˌrɪdn/ *adj.* not able to get out of bed because you are old or very sick

bed·room /ˈbɛdrum/ *n.* [C] a room for sleeping in: *a four-bedroom house* | *We use the **spare bedroom** as an office.*

bed·side /ˈbɛdsaɪd/ *n.* [C] the area around a bed: *His family has been **at his bedside*** (=stayed with him because he was very ill) *all night.* | *a bedside table*

bed·spread /ˈbɛdsprɛd/ *n.* [C] a large cover that goes on top of a bed

bed·time /ˈbɛdtaɪm/ *n.* [C,U] the time when you usually go to bed: *It's way past your bedtime!*

bee /bi/ *n.* [C] a yellow and black insect that flies, makes HONEY, and can sting you: *James was stung by a bee.* [ORIGIN: Old English *beo*]

beech /bitʃ/ *n.* [C,U] a large tree with smooth gray branches, or the hard wood of this tree

beef¹ /bif/ *n.* **1** [U] meat from a cow: *roast beef*

THESAURUS **meat, veal, pork, ham, bacon** → MEAT

2 [C] (informal) a complaint: *The guy **had a beef with** the manager and yelled at him for about 15 minutes.* [ORIGIN: 1100—1200 Old French *buef*, from Latin *bos* "ox"]

beef² *v.* [I] (informal) to complain: *They're always **beefing about** something.*

beef sth ↔ **up** *phr. v.* (informal) to improve something, especially to make it stronger or more interesting: *Security around the White House has been beefed up since the attack.*

beef·y /ˈbifi/ *adj.* a beefy man is big and strong

bee·hive /ˈbihaɪv/ *n.* [C] a HIVE

bee·line /ˈbilaɪn/ *n.* **make a beeline for sb/sth** (informal) to go quickly and directly toward someone or something: *The bear made a beeline for the woods.*

been /bɪn/ *v.* **1** the past participle of BE **2 have been to (do) sth** used in order to say that someone has gone to a place and come back: *Sandy has just been to Japan.* | *Have you been to see Katrina's new house?*

beep /bip/ *v.* **1** [I] if a machine beeps, it makes a short high sound: *The computer beeps when you push the wrong key.* **2** [I,T] if a horn beeps, or if you beep it, it makes a loud sound —**beep** *n.* [C]

beep·er /ˈbipɚ/ *n.* [C] a small machine that you carry with you that makes a sound to tell you to telephone someone (SYN) **pager**

beer /bɪr/ *n.* [C,U] an alcoholic drink made from grain, or a glass, can, or bottle of this drink: *a pitcher of beer* | *Would you like a beer?* → ROOT BEER

beet /bit/ *n.* [C] a dark red vegetable that is the root of a plant

bee·tle /ˈbitl/ *n.* [C] an insect with a hard round back [ORIGIN: Old English *bitula*, from *bitan*]

be·fall /bɪˈfɔl/ *v.* (past tense **befell** /-ˈfɛl/, past participle **befallen** /-ˈfɔlən/) [T] (formal) if something bad or dangerous befalls you, it happens to you: *We prayed that no harm should befall them.*

be·fit /bɪˈfɪt/ *v.* (**befitted, befitting**) [T] (formal) to be appropriate or seem right for someone: *a funeral befitting a national hero* —**befitting** *adj.*

be·fore¹ /bɪˈfɔr/ *prep.* **1** earlier than something or someone (ANT) **after**: *I usually shower before breakfast.* | *Denise got there before me.* | *He arrived **the day before yesterday*** (=two days ago). **2** ahead of someone or something else in a list or order (ANT) **after**: *There were ten people before us in line.* | *S **comes before** T in the alphabet.* **3** used to say that one thing or person is considered more important than another: *His wife and children **come before** his job.* | *companies who **put** profit **before** people* **4** if one place is before another as you go toward it, you will reach it first (ANT) **after**: *Turn right just before the stop light.* **5** if something is put before a person or group of people, they must consider it and make a decision about it: *The case is now before the Supreme Court.* **6** (formal) in front of: *The priest knelt before the altar.* [ORIGIN: Old English *beforan*, from *foran* "before"]

before² *adv.* at an earlier time: *They'd met before, at one of Sandra's parties.* | *Sales were up 14% from **the year/month/day etc. before*** (=the previous year, etc.).

THESAURUS

earlier – during the first part of a period of time, event, or process: *I saw Kim earlier today.*

previously – before now, or before a particular time: *Jim previously worked for Apple Bank.*

before³ *conjunction* **1** earlier than the time when something happens: *It will be several days before* *we know the results.* | *John wants to talk to you before you go.* **2** so that something bad does not happen: *You'd better lock your bike before it gets stolen.* **3 before you know it** (spoken) used in order to say that something will happen very soon: *We'd better get going – it'll be dark before you know it.*

B

be·fore·hand /bɪ'fɔrˌhænd/ *adv.* before something happens: *Never eat a piece of fruit without washing it beforehand.*

be·friend /bɪ'frɛnd/ *v.* [T] (formal) to become someone's friend, especially someone who needs your help: *An old woman befriended me and made me dinner.*

be·fud·dled /bɪ'fʌdld/ *adj.* completely confused

beg /bɛg/ *v.* (**begged**, **begging**) [I,T] **1** to ask for something in a way which shows you want it very much: *I **begged** him **to** stay, but he wouldn't.* | *a prisoner begging to be released* | *He **begged for** forgiveness.*

THESAURUS ask, request, order, demand, plead, implore → ASK

2 to ask someone for food, money, etc. because you are very poor: *children begging in the streets* | *homeless families **begging for** food* **3 I beg your pardon** (spoken) **a)** used in order to ask someone politely to repeat something: *"It's 7:00." "I beg your pardon?" "It's 7:00."* **b)** (formal) used in order to say you are sorry: *Oh, I beg your pardon – did I hurt you?* **c)** (formal) used in order to show that you strongly disagree: *"You never had to work hard in your life!" "I beg your pardon!"*

be·gan /bɪ'gæn/ *v.* the past tense of BEGIN

beg·gar /'bɛgɚ/ *n.* [C] **1** someone who lives by asking people for food and money **2 beggars can't be choosers** (spoken) used in order to say that when you have no money, no power to choose, etc., you have to accept whatever is available

be·gin /bɪ'gɪn/ *v.* (past tense **began** /-'gæn/, past participle **begun** /-'gʌn/, present participle **beginning**) **1** [I,T] to start doing something, or to start to happen or exist: *The meeting will **begin at** 10:00.* | *He began his career 30 years ago.* | *She began painting when she was a child.* | *I **began to** realize that he was lying.*

THESAURUS

start – to begin. **Start** is used more often in conversation than **begin**: *What time does the concert start?*
commence (formal) – to begin – used especially in official announcements: *The search for a new coach will commence immediately.*
set off – to leave a place in order to begin traveling: *We set off early in the morning, to avoid the traffic.*
break out – if a fire or a fight breaks out, it begins: *A fire broke out in one of the warehouses.*

2 [I] **a)** if you begin with something or begin by doing something, you do it first: *Let's **begin with** exercise 5.* | *May I **begin by** thanking you all for coming.* **b)** if a book, film, word, etc. begins with something, that is how it starts: *"Pharmacy" **begins with** a "p."* **3 to begin with a)** used in order to introduce the first or most important point: *To begin with, photography is not really an art form at all.* **b)** used in order to say what something was like before something else happened: *If his hands weren't dirty to begin with, they certainly are now.* **c)** in the first part of an activity or process: *The children helped me to begin with, but they soon got bored.* [ORIGIN: Old English *beginnan*]

be·gin·ner /bɪ'gɪnɚ/ *n.* [C] someone who has just started to do or learn something: *a class for beginners*

be·gin·ning /bɪ'gɪnɪŋ/ *n.* **1** [C usually singular] the start or first part of something: *the **beginning of** the book* | *Placement tests are given **at the beginning of** the year.* | *He didn't take me seriously **in the beginning**.* | *The whole trip was a disaster **from beginning to end**.* **2 beginnings** [plural] the early part or signs of something that later develop into something bigger or more important: *I think I **have the beginnings of** a cold.*

be·grudge /bɪ'grʌdʒ/ *v.* [T] to feel upset or JEALOUS about something: *Honestly, I don't begrudge him his success.*

be·guile /bɪ'gaɪl/ *v.* [T] to interest and attract someone: *She was beguiled by his smooth talk.* —**beguiling** *adj.*

be·gun /bɪ'gʌn/ *v.* the past participle of BEGIN

be·half /bɪ'hæf/ (Ac) *n.* **on behalf of sb/on sb's behalf** *also* **in behalf of somebody/in sb's behalf** instead of someone, or as someone's representative: *He agreed to speak on her behalf.* | *Lawyers have filed several suits on behalf of the victims.*

be·have /bɪ'heɪv/ *v.* **1** [I] to do or say things in a particular way: *Lions in a zoo do not **behave like** lions in the wild.* | *He began **behaving** differently **towards** me.* | *We were **behaving as if/though** nothing was wrong.* **2** [I,T] to be polite and not cause trouble (ANT) **misbehave**: *Will you boys please behave!* | *If you **behave yourself**, you can stay up late.* | *a **well-behaved** child*

be·hav·ior /bɪ'heɪvyɚ/ *n.* [U] **1** the things that a person or animal does, or the way in which they do them: *I'm not very pleased with your behavior.* | *criminal behavior* | *Reward your pet for **good behavior**.* | *We've noticed a change in his **behavior toward** the other children.*

THESAURUS

conduct (formal) – the way someone behaves: *The chairman has denied any improper conduct.*
manner – the way in which someone talks or behaves with other people: *They were teasing her in a friendly manner.*
demeanor (formal) – the way someone behaves, dresses, speaks, etc. that shows what his/her character is like: *her cheerful demeanor*

2 the things that a substance, material, etc. normally does: *the **behavior of** cancer cells*

be·head /bɪˈhɛd/ *v.* [T] to cut off someone's head as a punishment

be·held /bɪˈhɛld/ *v.* the past tense and past participle of BEHOLD

be·he·moth /bɪˈhiməθ/ *n.* [C] (literary) something that is very large

be·hind¹ /bɪˈhaɪnd/ *prep.* **1** at the back of something: *I was driving behind a truck on the freeway.* | *The liquor store is **right behind*** (=just behind) *the supermarket.* **2** not as successful or advanced as someone or something else: *The Lakers were four points behind the Celtics at half time.* | *Work on the new building is three months **behind schedule*** (=later than it should be). **3** supporting a person, idea, etc.: *Congress is behind the President on this issue.* **4** responsible for something, or causing something to happen: *The police believe a local gang is behind the killings.* **5 behind the times** old-fashioned [ORIGIN: Old English *behindan*, from *hindan* "from behind"]

behind² *adv.* **1** at or toward the back of something: *Several other runners followed **close behind.*** | *The car was bumped **from behind.*** **2** in the place where someone or something was before: *I got there and realized I'd **left** the tickets **behind.*** | *Barb **stayed behind** to wait for Tina.* **3 be/get behind** to be late or slow in doing something: *We are three months behind with the rent.*

behind³ *n.* [C] (informal) the part of your body that you sit on

be·hold /bɪˈhoʊld/ *v.* (past tense and past participle **beheld** /bɪˈhɛld/) [T] (literary) to see something —**beholder** *n.* [C]

> THESAURUS **see, notice, spot, glimpse/catch a glimpse of sth/sb, make sth out, catch sight of sb/sth, witness, observe** → SEE

beige /beɪʒ/ *n.* [U] a pale brown color —**beige** *adj.*

be·ing /ˈbiɪŋ/ *n.* **1** [C] a living thing or imaginary creature → HUMAN BEING: *stories about strange beings from outer space* **2 come into being** to begin to exist: *Their political system came into being in the early 1900s.*

be·lat·ed /bɪˈleɪt̬ɪd/ *adj.* happening or arriving late: *a belated birthday card* | *a belated effort to apologize*

> THESAURUS **late, overdue, delayed, tardy** → LATE¹

belch /bɛltʃ/ *v.* **1** [I] to let air from your stomach come out loudly through your mouth SYN **burp** **2** [T] to send out a large amount of smoke, flames, etc.: *factories belching blue smoke*

be·lea·guered /bɪˈligɚd/ *adj.* (formal) having a lot of problems: *the beleaguered tobacco industry*

be·lie /bɪˈlaɪ/ *v.* (**belied**, **belying**) [T] (formal) to give you a wrong idea about something: *With a quickness that belied her age, she ran across the road.*

be·lief /bəˈlif/ *n.* **1** [singular, U] the feeling that something is definitely true or definitely exists: *the medieval **belief that** the Sun went around the Earth* | *a strong **belief in** God* | ***Contrary to popular belief*** (=despite what most people believe), *eating carrots does not improve your eyesight.* **2** [singular] the feeling that someone or something is good and can be trusted: *a strong **belief in** the importance of education* **3** [C usually plural] an idea or set of ideas that you think are true: *religious beliefs*

> THESAURUS **faith, religion, creed** → FAITH

4 beyond belief used to emphasize that something is very bad, good, strange, etc.: *It seemed cruel beyond belief.*

be·liev·a·ble /bəˈlivəbəl/ *adj.* able to be believed because it seems possible, likely, or real: *There's not a single believable character in the book.*

be·lieve /bəˈliv/ *v.* **1** [T] to be sure that something is true or that someone is telling the truth: *Do you believe her?* | *You shouldn't believe everything you read.* | *Young children often **believe (that)** animals can understand them.* | *I **found** his excuse **hard to believe.*** ▶Don't say "...no one believed in him." Say "...no one believed him."◀

> THESAURUS
> **accept** – to believe what someone says is true or right: *His wife accepted his explanation for why he was late.*
> **take sb's word** – to believe that what someone says is true: *You don't have to take my word for it – go see for yourself.*
> **swallow** (informal) – to believe a story or explanation that is not actually true: *Did he really think we'd swallow that story?*
> **fall for sth** (informal) – to be tricked into believing something that is not true: *I can't believe she fell for that old excuse!*
> **buy** (informal) – to believe an explanation or reason for something: *I don't buy it. He'd never make that kind of mistake.*
> **give credence to sth** (formal) – to accept something as true: *The jurors gave credence to his testimony because of the details he remembered.*

2 [T] to think that something is true, although you are not completely sure: *I **believe (that)** she'll be back on Monday.* | ***It is believed that** the victim knew his killer.* | *Lane is **believed to be** about 60.*

> THESAURUS **think, suspect, consider, figure, guess** → THINK

3 [I] to have religious faith

SPOKEN PHRASES

4 [T] used in some phrases to show that you are surprised or shocked: ***I can't believe** you lied to me!* | ***Would you believe it**, he even remembered my* *birthday!* **5 believe it or not** said when something is true but surprising: *Believe it or not, we work hard around here.*

[ORIGIN: Old English *belefan*, from *lyfan, lefan* "to allow, believe"]

B

believe in sth *phr. v.* **1** to be sure that something or someone definitely exists: *Do you believe in ghosts?* **2** to think that someone or something is good, important, or right: *He believes in the democratic system.*

be·liev·er /bə'livɚ/ *n.* [C] **1** someone who believes that a particular idea or thing is very good: *I'm a* ***firm/great believer in*** *healthy eating.* **2** someone who believes in a particular religion

be·lit·tle /bɪ'lɪt̬l/ *v.* [T] (formal) to make someone or something seem small or unimportant: *I don't like the way he belittles his children.*

bell /bɛl/ *n.* [C] **1** a metal object that makes a ringing sound when you hit it or shake it: *church bells | The bell rang for school to start.* **2** a piece of electrical equipment that makes a ringing sound: *We ran out of the classroom as soon as the bell rang. | She walked up the path and* ***rang*** *the* ***door bell.*** [ORIGIN: Old English *belle*]

'bell ˌbottoms *n.* [plural] a pair of pants with legs that are wide at the bottom

bel·li·cose /'bɛləkous/ *adj.* (literary) always wanting to fight or argue SYN **aggressive**: *bellicose behavior*

bel·lig·er·ent /bə'lɪdʒərənt/ *adj.* wanting to fight or argue —**belligerence** *n.* [U]

bel·low /'bɛlou/ *v.* [I,T] to shout loudly in a deep voice: *Tony was bellowing orders from upstairs.*

THESAURUS **shout, call (out), scream, shriek, yell, cry out, raise your voice, cheer, holler** ➔ SHOUT[1]

'bell ˌpepper *n.* [C] a hollow red, green, yellow, or orange vegetable, often used to add flavor in cooking SYN **pepper**

bel·ly /'bɛli/ *n.* (plural **bellies**) [C] (informal) **1** your stomach, or the part of your body between your chest and the top of your legs **2 go belly up** (informal) to fail: *The store went belly up last year.*

'belly ˌbutton *n.* [C] (informal) the small hole or raised place in the middle of your stomach SYN **navel**

be·long /bɪ'lɔŋ/ *v.* [I] **1** to be in the right place or situation: *Please put the chair back where it belongs. | Books like that don't* ***belong in*** *the classroom.* **2** if you belong somewhere, you feel happy and comfortable there: *I'm going back to Colorado where I belong.*

belong to *phr. v.* **1 belong to sth** to be a member of a group or organization: *Mary and her husband belong to the yacht club.* **2 belong to sb** if something belongs to you, you own it: *Who does this umbrella belong to?*

be·long·ings /bɪ'lɔŋɪŋz/ *n.* [plural] the things that you own, especially things that you are carrying with you

THESAURUS **property, possessions, things, stuff, effects, valuables** ➔ PROPERTY

be·loved /bɪ'lʌvd, bɪ'lʌvɪd/ *adj.* (literary) loved very much: *his beloved wife Kelly* —**beloved** *n.* [singular]

be·low /bɪ'lou/ *adv., prep.* **1** in a lower place or position than someone or something else ANT **above**: *Jake lives in the apartment below. | Can you read the writing below the picture?* **2** less than a particular number or amount ANT **above**: *Sales for this year are below last year's. | It was 10 below outside* (=10 below zero in temperature). *| Tom's spelling is* ***well below*** *average* (=much worse than the normal standard). **3** on a later page, or lower on the same page ANT **above**: *For more information,* ***see below.*** **4** lower in rank ANT **above**: *There are people below him to handle that type of thing.*

belt[1] /bɛlt/ *n.* [C] **1** a band of leather or cloth that you wear around your waist ➔ *see picture at* CLOTHES **2** a circular band of material, such as rubber, that moves parts of a machine: *the car's fan belt* **3** a large area of land that has particular qualities: *America's farm belt* **4 have sth under your belt** to have already done something useful or important: *At 25, she already has two novels under her belt.* ➔ SEAT BELT

belt[2] *v.* [T] (informal) to hit someone or something hard

belt sth ↔ **out** *phr. v.* to sing a song loudly

belt·way /'bɛlt˺weɪ/ *n.* [C] **1** a road that goes around a city, keeping traffic away from the center **2 the Beltway** POLITICS the U.S. government in Washington, D.C., and the politicians, lawyers, LOBBYISTS, etc. who are involved in it; used in newspapers

be·mused /bɪ'myuzd/ *adj.* slightly confused: *a bemused expression*

bench[1] /bɛntʃ/ *n.* [C] **1** a long seat for two or more people, used especially outdoors: *a wooden bench* **2 the bench a)** LAW the job of a judge in a court of law: *He was appointed to the bench last year.* **b)** LAW the place where a judge sits in a court

bench[2] *v.* [T] to make a sports player stay out of a game for a period of time

bench·mark /'bɛntʃmark/ *n.* [C] something that is used for comparing and measuring other things: *The test results provide a* ***benchmark for*** *measuring student achievement.*

bend[1] /bɛnd/ *v.* (past tense and past participle **bent** /bɛnt/) [I,T] **1** to move a part of your body so that it is not straight, or so that you are not standing upright: *He* ***bent down/over*** *to tie his shoelace. | Bend your knees slightly.* ➔ *see picture at* BOW[1] **2** to push or press something so that it is no longer flat or straight: *First, the blacksmith heated the metal and then bent it into shape.* **3 bend over backwards** to try very hard to help someone: *The neighbors bent over backwards to help when we moved into the house.* **4 bend the rules** to allow someone to do something that is not normally allowed: *Can't we bend the rules just this one time?* [ORIGIN: Old English *bendan*]

bend² *n.* [C] a curve in something, especially a road or river: *a sharp bend in the road*

be·neath /bɪ'niθ/ *adv., prep.* (formal) **1** under or below something: *the warm sand beneath her feet* **2** if someone or something is beneath you, you think that he, she, or it is not good enough for you: *She seemed to think that talking to us was beneath her.* [ORIGIN: Old English *beneothan*, from *neothan* "below"]

ben·e·dic·tion /ˌbɛnə'dɪkʃən/ *n.* [C] a prayer that asks God to protect and help someone

ben·e·fac·tor /'bɛnəˌfæktɚ/ *n.* [C] (formal) someone who gives money or help to someone else

ben·e·fi·cial /ˌbɛnə'fɪʃəl/ (Ac) *adj.* good or useful: *The agreement will be* ***beneficial to*** *both groups.* | *Garlic has a* ***beneficial effect*** *in reducing harmful cholesterol.* [ORIGIN: 1400—1500 Latin *beneficium* "kindness, favor," from *bene* "well" + *facere* "to do"]

ben·e·fi·ci·ar·y /ˌbɛnə'fɪʃiˌɛri, -'fɪʃəri/ (Ac) *n.* (plural **beneficiaries**) [C] **1** someone who gets advantages from an action or change: *The rich were the main* ***beneficiaries of*** *the tax cut.* **2** LAW someone who gets money when someone dies: *The estate will be divided between relatives and other beneficiaries.*

ben·e·fit¹ /'bɛnəfɪt/ (Ac) *n.* **1** [C] the money or other advantages that you get from something such as insurance or the government, or as part of your job: *The company provides medical benefits.* | *Social Security benefits* **2** [C,U] an advantage, improvement, or help that you get from something: *What are the* ***benefits of*** *contact lenses?* | *The new credit cards will* ***be of*** *great* ***benefit to*** *our customers.* | *Marc translated what the minister said* ***for*** *my* ***benefit*** (=to help me). | *Consumers will* ***reap the benefits*** *if the value of the yen continues to fall because electrical goods will be cheaper.*

THESAURUS **advantage, merit, good point, the great thing about ..., the pros and cons** → ADVANTAGE

3 [C] a performance, concert, etc. that is done in order to make money for a CHARITY **4 give sb the benefit of the doubt** to believe or trust someone, even though it is possible that s/he is lying or is wrong: *His story was a little hard to believe, but I gave him the benefit of the doubt.* [ORIGIN: 1300—1400 Anglo-French *ben fet*, from Latin *bene factus* "well done"]

benefit² (Ac) *v.* (**benefitted** *or* **benefited**, **benefitting** *or* **benefiting**) [I,T] if you benefit from something or if it benefits you, it helps you: *These policy changes mainly benefit small companies.* | *Most of these children would* ***benefit from*** *an extra year at school.* | *Local employers* ***benefit by*** *having a trained workforce.*

be·nev·o·lent /bə'nɛvələnt/ *adj.* (formal) kind and generous [ORIGIN: 1400—1500 Latin *bene* "well" + *volens* (present participle of *velle* "to wish")] —**benevolence** *n.* [U]

be·nign /bɪ'naɪn/ *adj.* **1** (formal) kind and gentle **2** a benign TUMOR is not caused by CANCER (ANT) **malignant**

bent¹ /bɛnt/ *v.* the past tense and past participle of BEND

bent

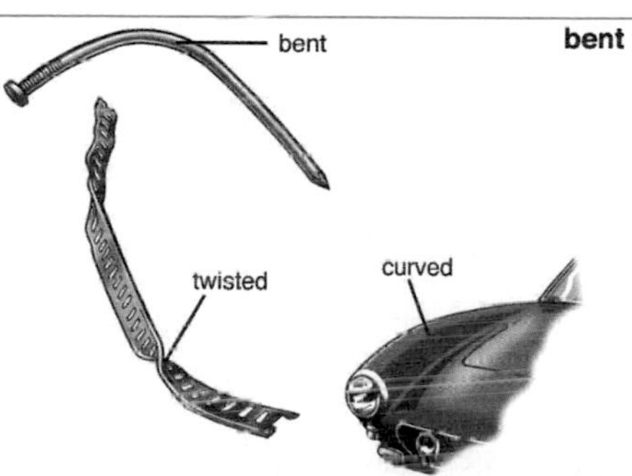

bent² *adj.* **1** curved and no longer flat or straight: *a bent nail*

THESAURUS

twisted – bent in many directions or turned many times: *a cable made of twisted strands of wire*
curved – bent in the shape of part of a circle, or having this shape: *curved wooden coat hangers*
warped – bent or twisted into the wrong shape: *The window frame was old and warped.*
crooked – not straight, but bending sharply in one or more places: *the crooked streets in the old part of the city*
wavy – having even curved shapes: *She had wavy black hair.*

2 be bent on (doing) sth to be determined to do something or have something: *Mendez was bent on getting a better job.*

bent³ *n.* [singular] a natural skill or ability: *Rebecca has an artistic bent.*

be·queath /bɪ'kwiθ, bɪ'kwið/ *v.* [T] LAW to arrange for someone to get something that belongs to you after your death

THESAURUS **give, donate, leave, present** → GIVE¹

be·quest /bɪ'kwɛst/ *n.* [C] LAW money or property that you bequeath to someone

be·rate /bə'reɪt/ *v.* [T] (formal) to speak angrily to someone because s/he has done something wrong: *Dunn berated Kelly in front of his staff.*

be·reaved /bəˈrivd/ *adj.* (formal) if someone is bereaved, someone s/he loves has died [ORIGIN: Old English *bereafian*, from *reafian* "to rob"] —**bereavement** *n.* [C,U]

be·reft /bəˈrɛft/ *adj.* (formal) completely without something: *The refugees returned to the camp, their eyes **bereft of** all hope.*

B

be·ret /bəˈreɪ/ *n.* [C] a soft round hat that is almost flat ➔ *see picture at* HAT

ber·ry /ˈbɛri/ *n.* (plural **berries**) [C] one of several types of small soft fruits with very small seeds

ber·serk /bɚˈsɚk, -ˈzɚk/ *adj.* **go berserk** (informal) to become very angry and violent in a crazy way [ORIGIN: 1800—1900 Old Norse *berserkr* "wild fighter," from *björn* "bear" + *serkr* "shirt"]

berth /bɚθ/ *n.* [C] **1** a place to sleep on a train or boat **2** a place near land where a ship can be kept

be·ryl·li·um /bəˈrɪliəm/ *n.* [U] CHEMISTRY (*symbol* **Be**) a light strong gray metal that is an ELEMENT, used especially as a building material or mixed with other metals to make ALLOYS

be·seech /bɪˈsitʃ/ *v.* (past tense and past participle **besought** /-ˈsɔt/ *or* **beseeched**) [T] (literary) to ask for something in an eager or anxious way

be·set /bɪˈsɛt/ *v.* (past tense and past participle **beset**, present participle **besetting**) [T] (formal) to make someone have a lot of trouble or problems: *The family was beset by financial difficulties.*

be·side /bɪˈsaɪd/ *prep.* **1** next to or very close to someone or something: *Gary sat down beside me.* | *a cabin beside the lake* **2** used in order to compare two people or things: *Pat looked big and clumsy beside her sister.* **3 be beside the point** to not be important compared to something else: *"I'm not hungry." "That's beside the point; you need to eat!"* **4 be beside yourself (with anger/fear/grief/joy etc.)** to feel a particular emotion very strongly: *Matt was beside himself with excitement.* [ORIGIN: Old English *be sidan* "at or to the side"]

be·sides /bɪˈsaɪdz/ *prep., adv.* **1** in addition to something or someone: *Besides going to college, she works 15 hours a week.* | *Who's going to be there besides David and me?* **2** (spoken) said when giving another reason: *I wanted to help her out. Besides, I needed the money.*

be·siege /bɪˈsidʒ/ *v.* **1 be besieged by people/worries/thoughts etc.** to be surrounded by a lot of people, or to be very worried, etc.: *a rock star besieged by fans* **2 be besieged with letters/questions/demands etc.** to receive a lot of letters, be asked a lot of questions, etc.: *The radio station was besieged with letters of complaint.* **3** [T] to surround a place with an army

be·sought /bɪˈsɔt/ *v.* the past tense and past participle of BESEECH

best¹ /bɛst/ *adj.* [the superlative of "good"] better than anyone or anything else: *the best player on the team* | *What's **the best way** to get to El Paso?* | ***The best thing** to do is to stop worrying.* | *my **best friend*** (=the one I know and like the most) [ORIGIN: Old English *betst*]

best² *adv.* [the superlative of "well"] **1** more than anyone else or anything else: *Helene knows him best.* | *Which song do you like best?* **2** in a way that is better than any other: *It works best if you warm it up first.* **3 as best you can** (spoken) as well as you can: *I'll deal with the problem as best I can.*

best³ *n.* **1 the best a)** someone or something that is better than any others: *Which motorcycle is the best?* **b)** the most successful situation or results you can achieve: *All parents want the best for their children.* **2 do/try your best** to try very hard to achieve something: *I did my best, but I still didn't pass.* **3 to the best of your knowledge/belief/ability etc.** used in order to say that something is as much as you know, believe, or are able to do: *I'm sure he'll do the work to the best of his ability.* **4 at best** used in order to emphasize that something is not very good, even when you consider it in the best possible way: *At best, sales have been good but not great.* **5 at your/its best** performing as well or as effectively as you are able to: *The movie shows Hollywood at its best.* **6 make the best of sth** to accept a bad situation and do what you can to make it better: *It's not going to be fun, but we'll have to make the best of it.* **7 be for the best** used in order to say that a particular event may seem bad now, but might have a good result later: *She's upset that they broke up, but it's probably for the best.*

bes·tial /ˈbɛstʃəl, ˈbis-/ *adj.* behaving like an animal, especially in a cruel way —**bestially** *adv.*

ˌbest ˈman *n.* [singular] a friend of a BRIDEGROOM (=man who is getting married), who helps him to get ready and stands next to him during the wedding ➔ WEDDING

be·stow /bɪˈstoʊ/ *v.* [T] (formal) to give someone something valuable or important

best·sell·er /ˌbɛstˈsɛlɚ/ *n.* [C] a new book that a lot of people have bought —**best-selling** *adj.* [only before noun]: *a best-selling novel*

THESAURUS blockbuster, hit, craze, fad, cult ➔ POPULAR

bet¹ /bɛt/ *v.* (past tense and past participle **bet**, present participle **betting**) **1** [I,T] to risk money on the result of a race, game, competition, or other future event ➔ GAMBLE: *She **bet** all her money **on** a horse that came in last.* | *I **bet** him $20 **that** he wouldn't do it.*

SPOKEN PHRASES

2 I/I'll bet a) said when you think something is true or likely to happen: *I bet they'll be late.* | *I'll bet that made her mad!* **b)** said in order to show that you agree with someone, or understand how s/he feels: *"I was furious." "I bet you were!"* **3 you bet a)** said in order to agree with someone, or to say that you are definitely going to do something: *"Would you like to come?" "You bet!"* **b)** used in order to reply to someone when s/he thanks you for something: *"Thanks for all your help, Bob." "You bet."*

bet² *n.* **1** [C] an agreement to risk money on the result of a race, game, competition, or other future event, or the money that you risk: *Higgins **had a bet on** the World Series. | I **lost/won the bet**. | a $10 bet* **2 your best bet** (spoken) said in order to give someone advice about the best thing to do: *Your best bet would be to take Highway 9.* **3 a good/safe bet** an action, situation, or thing that is likely to be successful or produce the results you want: *The earrings seemed like a good bet for a birthday present.*

be·ta par·ti·cle /ˈbeɪt̬ə ˌpɑrt̬ɪkəl/ *n.* [C] PHYSICS an ELECTRON given off by the NUCLEUS (=central part) of a RADIOACTIVE atom when it is breaking apart

beta ra·di·a·tion /ˌbeɪt̬ə reɪdiˈeɪʃən/ *n.* [U] PHYSICS a dangerous form of RADIATION that is produced when the NUCLEUS (=central part) of a RADIOACTIVE atom is breaking apart

bet·cha /ˈbɛtʃə/ a way of writing "bet you," used to show how people sound when they speak: *Betcha I can run faster than you.*

be·tray /bɪˈtreɪ/ *v.* [T] **1** to behave dishonestly toward someone who loves you or trusts you: *He felt that she had betrayed him.* **2** to be disloyal to your country, company, etc., for example by giving secret information to its enemies **3** to show feelings that you are trying to hide: *Keith's voice betrayed his nervousness.*

be·tray·al /bɪˈtreɪəl/ *n.* [C,U] the act of betraying your country, friends, or someone who trusts you

bet·ter¹ /ˈbɛt̬ɚ/ *adj.* **1** [the comparative of "good"] higher in quality, or more useful, appropriate, interesting, etc. than something or someone else (ANT) **worse**: *He's applying for a better job. | Your apartment is **better than** mine. | My sister's **better at** math than I am. | The Mexican place across the street has **much better** food. | Your English is **getting better*** (=improving). **2** [the comparative of "well"] less sick than you were, or no longer sick (ANT) **worse**: *He's much better today. | I hope your sore throat **gets better** soon. | Are you **feeling better**?*

THESAURUS **healthy, well, fine, in (good) shape, physically fit** → HEALTHY

3 it is better/it would be better used in order to give advice: *It's better to get a written agreement. | It would be **better if** you stayed here.* **4 have seen better days** (informal) to be in a bad condition: *The sofa had definitely seen better days.*

better² *adv.* [the comparative of "well"] **1** to a higher standard or degree: *He can speak French a lot **better than** I can. | She knows this town better than you do.* **2 better late than never** used in order to say that it is better for something to happen late rather than not happen at all **3 the sooner/bigger etc. the better** used in order to emphasize that something should happen as soon as possible, that it should be as big as possible, etc.: *He needs a wife, and the sooner the better.* **4 had better (do sth)** **a)** used in order to say that you or someone else should do something: *I think I'd better leave now.* **b)** said when threatening someone: *You'd better keep your mouth shut about this.* **5 do better** to perform better or reach a higher standard: *We **did better than** all the other schools.* → BETTER OFF

better³ *n.* **1 the better** the one that is the higher in quality, more appropriate, etc. when you are comparing two similar people or things: *It's hard to decide which one is the better.* **2 get the better of sb** **a)** if a feeling gets the better of you, you do not control it when you should: *His curiosity got the better of him and he opened the letter.* **b)** to defeat someone **3 for the better** in a way that improves the situation: *Smaller classes are definitely **a change for the better**.*

better⁴ *v.* [T] (formal) to achieve something that is higher in quality, amount, etc. than something else

ˌbetter ˈoff *adj.* **1** more successful, richer, or having more advantages than you did before: *The more prepared you are, the better off you'll be.* **2 sb is better off doing sth** (spoken) said when giving advice about what someone should do: *You're better off leaving before the traffic builds up.*

be·tween¹ /bɪˈtwin/ *prep.* **1** in or into the space or time that separates two things, people, events, etc.: *Jay was sitting between Kate and Lisa. | You know I don't want you to eat between meals.* → IN-BETWEEN **2** used in order to show a range of amounts, distances, times, etc.: *Why don't you come over between seven and eight? | The project will cost between 10 and 12 million dollars.* ▸ Don't say "between 10 to 12 million dollars." ◂ **3** used in order to show that something is divided or shared by two people, places, or things: *We had about two loads of laundry between us. | Linda and Dave split a milkshake between them.* **4** used in order to show a relationship between two people, things, events, etc.: *What's the difference between the two computers? | Trade relations between the countries have improved.* **5** used in order to show how two places are connected: *the highway between Fresno and Visalia* **6 between you and me** (spoken) said before you tell someone a secret or a private opinion: *Between you and me, I don't think she has a chance of getting that promotion.* [ORIGIN: Old English *betweonum*]

between² *adv.* in or into the space that separates two things, people, etc., or in or into the time that separates two events: *two yards with a fence between*

USAGE

Between and **among** are both used to talk about the position of someone or something. Use **between** when there is one other person or thing on each side of someone or something:

The store is between the bank and the post office. Use **among** when there are two or more people or things around someone or something: *I found the letter hidden among some old papers.*

→ IN-BETWEEN

B

bev·er·age /ˈbɛvrɪdʒ, ˈbɛvərɪdʒ/ *n.* [C] (formal) a drink: *alcoholic beverages* [ORIGIN: 1300—1400 Old French *bevrage*, from *beivre* "to drink," from Latin *bibere*]

bev·y /ˈbɛvi/ *n.* (plural **bevies**) [C] a large group of people: *a* ***bevy of*** *teenagers*

be·ware /bɪˈwɛr/ *v.* [I,T] used in order to warn someone to be careful: ***Beware of*** *the dog!* [ORIGIN: 1200—1300 *be* + *ware* "careful" (11—19 centuries) (from Old English *wær*)]

be·wil·dered /bɪˈwɪldəd/ *adj.* very confused and not sure what to do or think: *a bewildered expression* —**bewilderment** *n.* [U]

THESAURUS **confused, puzzled, baffled** → CONFUSED

be·wil·der·ing /bɪˈwɪldərɪŋ/ *adj.* making you feel very confused: *a bewildering number of choices*

be·witched /bɪˈwɪtʃt/ *adj.* so interested in or attracted by someone or something that you cannot think clearly —**bewitching** *adj.*

be·yond /bɪˈyɑnd/ *prep., adv.* **1** on or to the farther side of something: *There was a forest beyond the river.* | *a view from the mountains, with the plains beyond* **2** later than a particular time, date, etc.: *The ban has been extended beyond 2010.* | *planning for the year 2020 and beyond* **3** more than a particular amount, level, or limit: *The population has grown beyond estimated levels.* **4** outside the range or limits of someone or something: *an apple just beyond my reach* | *Chemistry was beyond my understanding.* **5 beyond belief/doubt/recognition etc.** used in order to say that you cannot believe something, doubt something, etc.: *In just six years, the town had changed beyond all recognition.* | *The car has been damaged beyond repair.* **6 it's beyond me why/what etc.** (spoken) said when you do not understand something: *It's beyond me why they ever got married at all.* **7** used in order to mean "except" in negative sentences: *Santa Fe doesn't have much industry beyond tourism.*

bi·as /ˈbaɪəs/ (Ac) *n.* [singular, U] an opinion about whether a person, group, or idea is good or bad, which influences how you deal with it: *Some employers have a* ***bias against*** *women.* | *When analyzing data, you must avoid having a* ***bias toward*** *any particular result.* [ORIGIN: 1500—1600 French *biais*, from Old Provençal] —**bias** *v.* [T]: *The wording of a test question may bias the answer.*

bi·ased /ˈbaɪəst/ (Ac) *adj.* unfairly preferring one person or group over another: *The referee was definitely biased.* | *biased news reporting*

bib /bɪb/ *n.* [C] a piece of cloth that you tie under a baby's chin to protect his/her clothes while s/he eats

bi·ble /ˈbaɪbəl/ *n.* [C] **1 the Bible** the holy book of the Christian religion **2** a copy of the Bible [ORIGIN: 1300—1400 Old French, Medieval Latin *biblia*, from Greek, plural of *biblion* "book"]

bib·li·cal, **Biblical** /ˈbɪblɪkəl/ *adj.* relating to the Bible

bib·li·o·graph·ic /ˌbɪbliəˈgræfɪk/ *adj.* ENG. LANG. ARTS concerning books or articles written about a particular subject: *Valuable bibliographic information can be found in the reading lists of reference books.*

bib·li·og·ra·phy /ˌbɪbliˈɑgrəfi/ *n.* (plural **bibliographies**) [C] ENG. LANG. ARTS a list of all the books and articles used in the preparation of another book, or a list of books and articles on a particular subject

bi·cen·ten·ni·al /ˌbaɪsɛnˈtɛniəl/ *n.* [C] the day or year exactly 200 years after an important event: *the **bicentennial of** the Declaration of Independence*

bi·cep /ˈbaɪsɛps/ *n.* [C usually plural] BIOLOGY the large muscle on the front of your upper arm

bick·er /ˈbɪkɚ/ *v.* [I] to argue about something that is not very important: *The kids were **bickering about/over** who would sleep in the top bunk.*

THESAURUS **argue, have an argument, fight, have a fight, quarrel, have a quarrel, squabble** → ARGUE

bi·con·di·tion·al /ˌbaɪkənˈdɪʃənəl/ *n.* [C] MATH a statement expressing two mathematical facts, one of which can be true only if the other one is true. It always contains the phrase "If and only if..." or the sign ↔. —**biconditional** *adj.*: *a biconditional proposition*

bi·cus·pid valve /baɪˈkʌspɪd ˌvælv/ *n* [C] BIOLOGY a small part on your heart between the left ATRIUM and the left VENTRICLE. It opens and closes to allow blood to flow from the atrium into the ventricle, and to prevent blood from flowing back into the atrium. → *see picture at* HEART

bi·cy·cle¹ /ˈbaɪsɪkəl/ *n.* [C] a vehicle with two wheels, that you ride by pushing the PEDALS with your feet (SYN) **bike**: *She usually **rides** her **bicycle** to work.* [ORIGIN: 1800—1900 French, from *bi-* "two" + Greek *kuklos* "wheel"]

bicycle² *v.* [I] to go somewhere by bicycle (SYN) **bike**

bid¹ /bɪd/ *n.* [C] **1** an offer to pay a particular price for something: *They put in a **bid for** the house.* **2** an offer to do work for someone at a particular price: *The company accepted the lowest **bid for** the project.* **3** an attempt to achieve or gain something: *the mayor's successful **bid for** the Senate* | *The prisoners made a desperate **bid to** escape.*

bid² *v.* (past tense and past participle **bid**, present participle **bidding**) **1** [I,T] to offer to pay a particular price for something: *Foreman **bid** $150,000 **for** an antique table.* | *The two men ended up **bidding against** each other at the auction.* **2** [I] to offer to do work for someone at a particular price: *Four companies were invited to **bid for** the contract.* —**bidder** *n.* [C]: *There are five bidders for the contract.*

bid³ *v.* (past tense **bade** /bæd, beɪd/ *or* **bid**, past participle **bid** *or* **bidden** /ˈbɪdn/, present participle **bidding**) (literary) **bid sb good morning/goodbye etc.** to say good morning, etc. to someone

bid·ding /ˈbɪdɪŋ/ *n.* [U] **1** the activity of offering to pay a particular price for something, or offering to do work **2 do sb's bidding** (literary) to do what someone tells you to do

bide /baɪd/ *v.* **bide your time** to wait until the right time to do something

bi·en·ni·al /baɪˈɛniəl/ *adj.* happening once every two years [ORIGIN: 1600—1700 Latin *biennium* "two-year period," from *bi-* "two" + *annus* "year"]

bi·fo·cals /ˈbaɪˌfoʊkəlz, baɪˈfoʊkəlz/ *n.* [plural] a pair of special glasses made so that you can look through the upper part to see things that are far away and through the lower part to see things that are close

big /bɪg/ *adj.* (comparative **bigger**, superlative **biggest**) **1** more than average size or amount (ANT) **small**: *a big house* | *Los Angeles is the biggest city in California.* | *That boy **gets bigger** every time I see him.*

THESAURUS

Big

large – big or bigger than usual in size or amount: *the largest city in America* | *People are now watching the program in large numbers.*
substantial – large in number or amount: *He earns a substantial amount of money.*
sizable – fairly large: *a sizable crowd*

Very Big

huge/enormous – extremely big: *He died owing a huge sum of money.* | *an enormous tree*
vast – extremely big or large: *The birds nest here in vast numbers.*
gigantic – extremely big or tall: *gigantic waves*
massive – very big, solid, and heavy: *a massive stone fireplace*
immense – extremely large or great: *We still have an immense amount of work to do.*
colossal – very large: *We have made a colossal mistake.*
prodigious (formal) – very large in a surprising or impressive way: *There is a prodigious amount of information available on the Internet.*
Big and **large** mean the same thing, but **large** is slightly more formal: *That's a big piece of cake!* | *It's the largest hotel in the city.*

Use **large**, not **big**, to describe amounts: *They have borrowed a large amount of money.*
Use **big**, not **large**, to describe something that is important: *a big opportunity | That's the big question.*

B

THESAURUS **fat, overweight, heavy, large, obese, chubby, plump, stout, corpulent, rotund** ➔ FAT[1]

2 important or serious: *a big decision | He has big plans for the house. | I'm having big problems with my PC.* **3** successful or popular: *The song was a big hit. | I knew I'd never* ***make it big*** (=become very successful) *as a professional golfer.* **4 big sister/big brother** (informal) your older sister or brother **5** [only before noun] (informal) doing something to a large degree: *I've never been a big baseball fan. | Both the girls are* ***big eaters*** (=they eat a lot). **6 big money/big bucks** a lot of money: *They are willing to pay big bucks to attract the best players.* **7 be big on sth** (spoken) to like something very much: *I'm not big on kids.*

big·a·my /ˈbɪgəmi/ *n.* [U] the crime of being married to two people at the same time —**bigamist** *n.* [C] —**bigamous** *adj.*

ˌBig ˈApple *n.* **the Big Apple** (informal) a name for New York City

ˌBig ˈBang *n.* **the Big Bang** PHYSICS a single very large explosion that many scientists believe started the universe, and from which pieces of MATTER are still traveling out into space

ˌbig ˈbrother *n.* [C] any person, organization, or system that seems to control people's lives and restrict their freedom

ˌbig ˈbusiness *n.* [U] ECONOMICS very large companies, considered as a group with a lot of influence

ˌbig ˈdeal *n.* [singular] (spoken) **1** said when you do not think something is as important as someone else thinks it is: *It's just a game. If you lose, big deal. |* ***It's no big deal****. Everybody forgets things sometimes.* **2** an important event or situation: *This audition is a big deal for Joey.* **3 make a big deal of/out of/about sth** to get too excited or upset about something, or make something seem more important than it is: *She's making a big deal out of nothing.*

ˌBig ˈDipper *n.* [C] a group of seven bright stars seen in the northern sky in the shape of a bowl with a long handle

big·gie /ˈbɪgi/ *n.* **no biggie** (spoken) said when something is not important, or when you are not upset or angry about something: *"Oh, I'm sorry." "That's okay, no biggie."*

ˈbig ˌgovernment *n.* [U] POLITICS government, when people think it is controlling their lives too much

big·head·ed /ˈbɪgˌhɛdɪd/ *adj.* someone who is bigheaded thinks s/he is better than other people

ˈbig-league *adj.* (informal) belonging or relating to the MAJOR LEAGUES

ˈbig mouth *n.* [C] (informal) someone who cannot be trusted to keep secrets

ˌbig ˈname *n.* [C] a famous person, especially an actor, musician, etc. —**big name** *adj.*

big·ot /ˈbɪgət/ *n.* [C] someone who is bigoted ➔ PREJUDICE[1]

big·ot·ed /ˈbɪgət̬ɪd/ *adj.* having strong opinions that most people think are unreasonable, especially about race, religion, or politics

big·ot·ry /ˈbɪgətri/ *n.* [U] bigoted behavior or beliefs: *religious bigotry*

THESAURUS **prejudice, racism, discrimination, intolerance, sexism, homophobia, anti-Semitism** ➔ PREJUDICE[1]

ˈbig shot *n.* [C] (informal) someone who is very important or powerful

ˌbig-ˈticket *adj.* very expensive: ***big-ticket items*** *such as houses and cars*

ˈbig time[1] *adv.* (spoken) a lot or very much: *He messed up big time.*

ˈbig time[2] *n.* **the big time** (informal) the position of being very famous or important: *The author has finally* ***hit the big time****.* —**big-time** *adj.* [only before noun]: *big-time drug dealers*

big·wig /ˈbɪgwɪg/ *n.* [C] (informal) an important person

bike[1] /baɪk/ *n.* [C] (informal) **1** a bicycle: *The kids were* ***riding*** *their* ***bikes****. | Do you want to* ***go for a bike ride****?* **2** a MOTORCYCLE

bike[2] *v.* [I] to ride a bicycle

bik·er /ˈbaɪkɚ/ *n.* [C] someone who rides a MOTORCYCLE

bi·ki·ni /bɪˈkini/ *n.* [C] a piece of clothing in two parts, that women wear for swimming [ORIGIN: 1900—2000 French *Bikini Atoll*, after a nuclear bomb test was held there in 1946]

bi·lat·er·al /baɪˈlæt̬ərəl/ *adj.* **bilateral agreement/treaty etc.** an agreement, etc. between two groups or countries: *bilateral Mideast peace talks* —**bilaterally** *adv.*

biˌlateral ˈsymmetry *n.* [U] BIOLOGY a quality that some animals, including humans, have, which means that they have two very similar sides. For example, humans have an arm and a leg on each side, an eye on each side, and so on.

bile /baɪl/ *n.* [U] BIOLOGY a liquid produced by the LIVER to help the body DIGEST food

bi·lin·gual /baɪˈlɪŋgwəl/ *adj.* **1** able to speak two languages: *Their children are completely bilingual.* **2** written or spoken in two languages: *a bilingual dictionary*

bilk /bɪlk/ *v.*

bilk sb **out of** sth *phr. v.* (informal) to trick someone, especially by taking his/her money (SYN) swindle

bill¹ /bɪl/ *n.* [C] **1** a written list showing how much you have to pay for services you have received, work that has been done, etc.: *I have to remember to* ***pay*** *the phone* ***bill*** *this week.* | *The* ***bill for*** *the repairs came to $600.*

THESAURUS

check – a bill that you are given in a restaurant: *Can I have the check, please?*
invoice – a document that shows how much you owe for goods, work, etc.: *Payment is due ten days after receipt of the invoice.*
tab – an amount of money that you owe for a meal or drinks you have had, but have not yet paid for: *I ordered a rum and Coke and had the bartender put it on my tab.*

2 a piece of paper money: *a ten-dollar bill*

THESAURUS **money, coin, penny, nickel, dime, quarter, cash, change, currency** → MONEY

3 a plan for a law, that is written down for a government to decide on: *The House of Representatives* ***passed*** *a new gun-control* ***bill*** (=made it a law). **4 fit/fill the bill** to be exactly what you need: *This car fits the bill perfectly.* **5** a program of entertainment at a theater, concert, etc., with details of who is performing, what is being shown, etc. **6** a wide or long beak on a bird such as a duck [ORIGIN: (1) 1300—1400 Medieval Latin *billa*, from Latin *bulla* "bubble, seal added to a document"] → **foot the bill** *at* FOOT²

bill² *v.* [T] **1** to send a bill to someone: *They've* ***billed*** *me* ***for*** *things I didn't order.* **2 bill sth as sth** to advertise or describe something in a particular way: *The boxing match was billed as "the fight of the century."*

bill·board /ˈbɪlbɔrd/ *n.* [C] a very large sign used for advertising, especially next to a road

THESAURUS **advertisement, commercial, poster, want ads/classified ads, flier, junk mail, spam** → ADVERTISEMENT

bill·fold /ˈbɪlfoʊld/ *n.* [C] a WALLET

bil·liards /ˈbɪlyɚdz/ *n.* [U] a game like POOL, in which the balls go into the holes in a special order [ORIGIN: 1500—1600 French *billard* "(stick used in) billiards," from *bille* "piece of wood, stick"]

bil·lion /ˈbɪlyən/ *number* (plural **billion** *or* **billions**) 1,000,000,000: *$7 billion* | ***Billions of*** *dollars have been invested.* —**billionth** *number*

ˌbill of ˈrights *n.* [singular] **1** POLITICS an official written list of the most important rights of the citizens of a country **2 the Bill of Rights** HISTORY the first ten AMENDMENTS to the U.S. Constitution, that state the basic rights of U.S. citizens

bil·low /ˈbɪloʊ/ *v.* [I] **1** if something made of cloth billows, it moves in the wind and fills with air: *Her long skirt billowed in the breeze.* **2** if a cloud or smoke billows, it rises in a round mass

bim·bo /ˈbɪmboʊ/ *n.* (plural **bimbos**) [C] (informal) an insulting word meaning an attractive but stupid woman [ORIGIN: 1900—2000 Italian "baby"]

bi·month·ly /baɪˈmʌnθli/ *adj., adv.* happening or being done every two months, or twice each month: *a bimonthly magazine*

bin /bɪn/ *n.* [C] a large container for storing things

bi·na·ry /ˈbaɪnəri/ *adj.* **the binary system** IT a system of counting, used in computers, in which only the numbers 0 and 1 are used

ˌbinary ˈcompound *n.* [C] CHEMISTRY a substance consisting of only two different types of atom

bind¹ /baɪnd/ *v.* (past tense and past participle **bound** /baʊnd/) **1** [T] to tie something firmly with string or rope: *His legs were bound with rope.* **2** [T] *also* **bind together** to form a strong relationship between two people, countries, etc.: *Religious belief binds this remote community together.* **3** [T] if you are bound by an agreement or promise, you must do what you agreed or promised to do: *Each country is bound by the treaty.* **4** [I,T] BIOLOGY to stick together in a mass, or to make small pieces of something stick together: *The hydrogen molecule* ***binds with*** *the oxygen molecule.* **5** [T] to fasten the pages of a book together and put them in a cover: *The book was printed and bound in Spain.*

bind² *n.* [C] an annoying or difficult situation: *I'm so mad at him for* ***putting*** *me* ***in*** *this* ***bind!***

bind·er /ˈbaɪndɚ/ *n.* [C] a cover for holding loose sheets of paper, magazines, etc. together

bind·ing¹ /ˈbaɪndɪŋ/ *adj.* a contract or agreement that is binding must be obeyed: *The contract isn't binding until you sign it.*

binding² *n.* **1** [C] the cover of a book **2** [U] material sewn along the edge of a piece of cloth for strength or decoration

binge /bɪndʒ/ *n.* [C] (informal) a short period of time when you do too much of something, especially drinking alcohol: *He* ***went on a*** *drinking* ***binge*** *last week.* —**binge** *v.* [I]: *Whenever she's depressed, she* ***binges on*** *chocolate.*

bin·go /ˈbɪŋgoʊ/ *n.* [U] a game played for money or prizes in which you win if a set of numbers chosen by chance are the same as one of the lines of numbers on your card

bin·oc·u·lars /bɪˈnɑkyəlɚz, baɪ-/ *n.* [plural] a pair of special glasses that you hold up and look through to see things that are far away [ORIGIN: 1800—1900 *binocular* "using both eyes" (18—21 centuries), from Latin *bini* "two by two" + *oculus* "eye"]

bi·no·mi·al /baɪˈnoʊmiəl/ *n.* [C] MATH a mathematical expression that has two parts connected by the sign + or the sign −, for example 3x + 4y or x − 7 —**binomial** *adj.*: *a binomial expression*

bi,nomial 'nomen,clature *n.* [singular,U] BIOLOGY a system of naming animals, plants, and other living things with a scientific word consisting of two separate parts. The first part of the word is the GENUS (=group of related animals, plants, etc., which do not breed), and the second part is the SPECIES (=group of animals, plants, etc. which breed and produce new animals, plants, etc.).

B

bi·o·chem·is·try /,baɪoʊ'kɛmɪstri/ *n.* [U] the scientific study of the chemistry of living things —**biochemist** *n.* [C] —**biochemical** /,baɪoʊ'kɛmɪkəl/ *adj.*: *a complex biochemical process*

bi·o·de·grad·a·ble /,baɪoʊdɪ'greɪdəbəl/ *adj.* BIOLOGY a material, product, etc. that is biodegradable is able to change or decay naturally so that it does not harm the environment: *Most plastic is not biodegradable.* ➔ ENVIRONMENT

bi·o·di·ver·sit·y /,baɪoʊdɪ'vɚsəṭi, -daɪ-/ *n.* [U] BIOLOGY the number and variety of different plants, animals, and other living things in a particular place: *The loss of biodiversity will weaken the ecosystem.* | *the biodiversity of the forest*

bi·o·fuel /'baɪoʊ,fyul, -,fyuəl/ *n.* [C,U] a substance produced from plants or other natural matter, that can be used as the FUEL for a car, truck, etc.

bi·og·ra·pher /baɪ'ɑgrəfɚ/ *n.* [C] ENG. LANG. ARTS someone who writes a biography of someone else

bi·og·ra·phy /baɪ'ɑgrəfi/ *n.* (plural **biographies**) [C] ENG. LANG. ARTS a book about a person's life: *a* ***biography of*** *Louis Armstrong* ➔ BOOK[1] [ORIGIN: 1600—1700 Late Greek *biographia*, from Greek *bios* "life" + *-graphia* "writing"]

bi·ol·o·gi·cal /,baɪə'lɑdʒɪkəl/ *adj.* **1** relating to the natural processes performed by living things: *a biological process* **2** [only before noun] relating to biology: *the biological sciences* **3 biological weapons/warfare/attack etc.** weapons, attacks, etc. that involve the use of living things, including BACTERIA, to harm people —**biologically** *adv.*

bi·ol·o·gy /baɪ'ɑlədʒi/ *n.* [U] the scientific study of living things [ORIGIN: 1800—1900 German *biologie*, from Greek *bios* "life" + *-logia* "study"] —**biologist** *n.* [C]

bi·o·mass /'baɪoʊ,mæs/ *n.* [U] **1** BIOLOGY the total number or weight of animals, plants, or other living things within a particular environment **2** BIOLOGY plant and animal matter, especially waste from farming, that can be used to provide power or energy: *biomass fuels*

bi·o·met·ric /,baɪə'mɛtrɪk◂/ *adj.* biometric equipment measures things such as a person's IRIS (=the colored part of the eye) or FINGERPRINTS, and can be used to check who someone is, for example when s/he shows a PASSPORT at an airport: ***Biometric technology****, including fingerprint and iris scanners, is being installed at all major airports.*

bi·op·sy /'baɪ,ɑpsi/ *n.* (plural **biopsies**) [C] BIOLOGY a medical test in which cells, TISSUE, etc. are removed from someone's body in order to find out more about a disease s/he may have

bi·o·tech·nol·o·gy /,baɪoʊtɛk'nɑlədʒi/ *n.* [U] BIOLOGY the use of living things such as cells and BACTERIA in science and industry to make drugs, chemicals, etc.

bi·par·ti·san /baɪ'pɑrṭəzən/ *adj.* POLITICS involving two political parties, especially parties with completely different opinions or beliefs: *The Senate is close to reaching a bipartisan agreement on the bill.*

birch /bɚtʃ/ *n.* [C,U] a tree with BARK like paper that comes off easily, or the wood of this tree

bird /bɚd/ *n.* [C] an animal with wings and feathers that lays eggs and can usually fly [ORIGIN: Old English *bridd*] ➔ **early bird** *at* EARLY[1], **kill two birds with one stone** *at* KILL[1]

'bird-brained *adj.* (informal) silly or stupid

bird·ie /'bɚdi/ *n.* [C] (informal) a small light object that you hit over the net in the game of BADMINTON

,bird of 'prey *n.* (plural **birds of prey**) [C] any bird that kills other birds and small animals for food

bird·seed /'bɚdsid/ *n.* [U] a mixture of seeds for feeding birds

,bird's eye 'view *n.* [singular] a view from a very high place: *a bird's eye view over the city*

birth /bɚθ/ *n.* **1 give birth** if a woman gives birth, she produces a baby from her body: *Jo* ***gave birth to*** *a baby girl at 6:20 a.m.* **2** [C,U] the time when a baby comes out of its mother's body: *The baby weighed 7 pounds* ***at birth****.* | *What is your* ***birth date*** (=the date on which you were born)*?* **3** [U] someone's family origin: *Her grandfather was French* ***by birth****.* **4 the birth of sth** the time when something begins to exist: *the birth of a nation* [ORIGIN: 1200—1300 Old Norse *byrth*]

'birth cer,tificate *n.* [C] an official document that shows when and where you were born

'birth con,trol *n.* [U] the practice of controlling the number of children you have, or the methods used SYN **contraception**

birth·day /'bɚθdeɪ/ *n.* [C] the date on which someone was born, usually celebrated each year: *When is your birthday?* | *It's my 18th birthday next week.* | *a* ***birthday present/card/party*** | ***Happy Birthday!*** (=said to someone on his/her birthday)

birth·mark /'bɚθmɑrk/ *n.* [C] a permanent mark on someone's skin that s/he has had since birth

birth·place /'bɚθpleɪs/ *n.* [C usually singular] the place where someone was born: *Cézanne's birthplace*

birth·rate /'bɚθreɪt/ *n.* [C] the average number of babies born during a particular period of time in a country or area

bis·cuit /'bɪskɪt/ *n.* [C] a type of bread that is baked in small round shapes

bi·sect /'baɪsɛkt, baɪ'sɛkt/ *v.* [T] MATH to divide

something, especially a line or angle, into two equal parts —**bisection** /ˈbaɪˌsɛkʃən, baɪˈsɛkʃən/ *n.* [U]

bi·sec·tor /ˈbaɪˌsɛktɚ/ *n.* [C] MATH a line that divides something into two equal parts: *a **perpendicular bisector*** (=line that crosses a line at 90 degrees and divides it into two equal parts) | *an **angular bisector*** (=line that divides an angle into two equal parts)

bi·sex·u·al /baɪˈsɛkʃuəl/ *adj.* sexually attracted to both men and women —**bisexual** *n.* [C] —**bisexuality** /ˌbaɪsɛkʃuˈæləṭi/ *n.* [U]

bish·op /ˈbɪʃəp/ *n.* [C] a Christian priest with a high rank who is in charge of the churches and priests in a large area [ORIGIN: Old English *biscеop*, from Late Latin *episcopus*, from Greek *episkopos* "person in charge, bishop"]

bi·son /ˈbaɪsən/ *n.* (plural **bison** *or* **bisons**) [C] a BUFFALO

bit[1] /bɪt/ *n.* [C]

1 SMALL PIECE a small piece of something: *The floor was covered with tiny **bits of** glass.* | *I tore the letter **to bits*** (=into small pieces) *and threw it away.*
2 COMPUTER IT the smallest unit of information that can be used by a computer ➔ BYTE
3 TOOL the sharp part of a tool for cutting or making holes: *a drill bit*
4 HORSE a piece of metal that is put in the mouth of a horse to control its movements [ORIGIN: (3) Old English *bita* "piece bitten off, small piece of food"]

bit[2] /bɪt/ *adv., pron* (informal) **1 a (little) bit** slightly, but not very: *I'm a little bit tired.* | *Enrollment is down a bit from last year.* **2 quite a bit** a fairly large amount: *He owes me quite a bit of money.* **3 a bit of sth** a small amount of a particular quality or thing: *We just need **a bit of luck**.* **4 a bit** a short amount of time: *We'll talk about the Civil War **in just a bit**.* **5 bit a bit** gradually: *I could see that she was learning, bit by bit.* **6 every bit as...** just as: *Ray was every bit as good-looking as his brother.*

bit[3] *v.* the past tense of BITE

bitch /bɪtʃ/ *n.* [C] a female dog

bite[1] /baɪt/ *v.* (past tense **bit** /bɪt/, past participle **bitten** /ˈbɪtˀn/, present participle **biting**) **1** [I,T] to cut or crush something with your teeth: *The dog bit him and made his hand bleed.* | *I had just **bitten into** the apple.* | *I wish I could stop **biting** my **nails*** (=biting the nails on my fingers). **2** [I,T] if an insect or snake bites you, it injures you by making a hole in your skin ➔ STING: *I think I've been bitten.* | *She was bitten by a rattlesnake.* **3 bite the bullet** to start dealing with a bad situation because you can no longer avoid it: *I finally bit the bullet and called her.* **4 bite sb's head off** (spoken) to speak to someone very angrily, especially when there is no good reason to do this: *I asked if she wanted help, and she bit my head off!* **5 bite your tongue** to not say what you really think, even though you want to **6 bite the dust** (informal) to die, fail, be defeated, or stop working **7 bite off more than you can chew** to try to do more than you are able to do **8** [I] to start having the effect that was intended, especially a bad effect: *The new tobacco taxes have begun to bite.* **9** [I] if a fish bites, it takes food from a hook [ORIGIN: Old English *bitan*]

bite[2] *n.* [C] **1** the act of cutting or crushing something with your teeth: *He **took a bite** of the cheese.* **2** a wound made when an animal or insect bites you ➔ STING: *I'm covered in mosquito bites!* **3 a bite (to eat)** (informal) a quick meal: *We can **grab a bite** at the airport before we go.*

ˈbite-size *also* **ˈbite-sized** *adj.* the right size to fit in your mouth easily: *bite-size pieces of chicken*

bit·ing /ˈbaɪṭɪŋ/ *adj.* **1** a biting wind feels very cold **2** biting criticism or remarks are very unkind

bit·map /ˈbɪtˌmæp/ (*written abbreviation* **BMP**) *n.* [C] IT a computer image that is stored or printed as an arrangement of BITs

bit·ten /ˈbɪtˀn/ *v.* the past participle of BITE

bit·ter /ˈbɪṭɚ/ *adj.* **1** angry and upset because you feel something bad or unfair has happened to you: *I **feel** very **bitter about** what happened.* | *a bitter old man* **2** [only before noun] making you feel very unhappy and upset: *a **bitter disappointment*** | *She knew **from bitter experience** that they wouldn't agree.* **3** a bitter argument, battle, etc. is one in which people oppose or criticize each other with strong feelings of hate or anger: *a bitter legal battle over custody of the children* **4** having a strong taste, like coffee without sugar **5** extremely cold: *a bitter wind* | *We had to walk home in **the bitter cold**.*

> THESAURUS **cold, cool, chilly, frosty, freezing (cold), icy (cold), frigid** ➔ COLD[1]

6 to/until the bitter end continuing until the end even though this is difficult: *We will **fight until the bitter end** to defend our land.* —**bitterness** *n.* [U]

bit·ter·ly /ˈbɪṭɚli/ *adv.* **1** with a lot of anger or sadness: *I was **bitterly disappointed**.* **2 bitterly cold** very cold

bit·ter·sweet /ˌbɪṭɚˈswit◂/ *adj.* feelings, memories, or experiences that are bittersweet are happy and sad at the same time: *a bittersweet goodbye*

bi·valve /ˈbaɪˌvælv/ *n.* [C] BIOLOGY any sea animal that has two shells that join together, for example an OYSTER

bi·week·ly /baɪˈwikli/ *adj., adv.* happening or being done every two weeks, or twice a week: *a biweekly meeting*

bi·zarre /bɪˈzɑr/ *adj.* very unusual and strange: *His increasingly bizarre behavior is starting to worry me.*

> THESAURUS **strange, funny, peculiar, curious, mysterious, odd, weird, eccentric** ➔ STRANGE[1]

blab /blæb/ *v.* (**blabbed, blabbing**) [I] (spoken) to talk too much about something, often something that should be secret: *This is not something you go **blabbing to** your friends about.*

blab·ber·mouth /ˈblæbɚˌmaʊθ/ *n.* [C] (spoken) someone who always talks too much and often says things that should be secret

B

black¹ /blæk/ *adj.* **1** having a color that is darker than every other color, like the sky at night: *a black dress* | *Outside, it was **pitch black*** (=completely dark). **2** *also* **Black** someone who is black has dark skin, and is from a family that was originally from Africa ➔ AFRICAN AMERICAN **3** black coffee does not have milk in it: *I take my coffee black.* **4** sad and without hope for the future: *a mood of black despair* **5 black humor/comedy** humor that makes jokes about serious subjects [ORIGIN: Old English *blæc*] —**blackness** *n.* [U]

black² *n.* **1** [U] the color of the sky at night: *She was wearing black* (=dressed in black clothing). **2** [C] *also* **Black** someone who has dark skin, and whose family originally came from Africa **3 be in the black** ECONOMICS to have money in your bank account (ANT) **be in the red**

black³ *v.*

black out *phr. v.* to suddenly become unconscious: *Sharon blacked out and fell to the floor.*

ˌblack and ˈblue *adj.* skin that is black and blue has BRUISES (=dark marks) on it as a result of being hit or injured: *Her leg was black and blue where she had fallen.*

ˌblack and ˈwhite *adj.* **1** showing pictures of images in black, white, and gray (ANT) **color**: *old black and white movies* **2 in black and white a)** written or printed: *The rules are there in black and white.* **b)** in a very simple way, as if there are clear differences between good and bad: *He tends to see the issues in black and white.*

ˈblack belt *n.* [C] a high rank in JUDO or KARATE, or someone who has this rank

black·ber·ry /ˈblækˌbɛri/ *n.* (plural **blackberries**) [C] a very sweet black or dark purple BERRY

black·bird /ˈblækbɚd/ *n.* [C] a common American and European bird, the male of which is completely black

black·board /ˈblækbɔrd/ *n.* [C] a board with a dark smooth surface, usually in a school, that you write on with CHALK

ˌblack ˈbox *n.* [C] a piece of equipment on an airplane, that records what happens on a flight and can be used to discover the cause of accidents

ˌblack eˈconomy *n.* **the black economy** ECONOMICS business activity that takes place secretly, especially in order to avoid tax

black·en /ˈblækən/ *v.* **1** [I,T] to become black, or to make something black: *Smoke had blackened the kitchen walls.* **2 blacken sb's name/character/reputation etc.** to say unpleasant things about someone so that other people will have a bad opinion of him/her

ˌblack ˈeye *n.* [C] if you have a black eye, you have a dark area around your eye because you have been hit

black·head /ˈblækhɛd/ *n.* [C] a small spot on someone's skin that has a black center

ˌblack ˈhole *n.* [C] PHYSICS an area in space where the force of GRAVITY is so strong that light and MATTER cannot escape. A black hole forms when a star stops existing. ➔ SPACE¹

black·jack /ˈblækdʒæk/ *n.* [U] a card game, usually played for money, in which you try to get as close to 21 points as possible

black·list /ˈblækˌlɪst/ *v.* [T] to put someone or something on a list of people or things that are considered bad or dangerous: *More than 200 people in the movie industry were blacklisted during the McCarthy era.* —**blacklist** *n.* [C]

ˌblack ˈmagic *n.* [U] magic that is believed to use the power of the Devil for evil purposes

> **THESAURUS** magic, witchcraft, sorcery, spell, curse, the occult, voodoo ➔ MAGIC¹

black·mail /ˈblækmeɪl/ *n.* [U] the practice of making someone do what you want by threatening to tell secrets about him/her [ORIGIN: 1500—1600 *black* + *mail* "payment" (11—20 centuries) (from Old Norse *mal* "speech, agreement")] —**blackmail** *v.* [T] —**blackmailer** *n.* [C]

ˌblack ˈmarket *n.* [C] ECONOMICS the system by which people illegally buy and sell foreign money, goods, etc. that are difficult to obtain: *These rare animals are being sold **on the black market**.* | *a **black market in** foreign currency*

black·out /ˈblækaʊt/ *n.* [C] **1** a period of darkness caused by a failure of the electricity supply: *Several neighborhoods in the San Francisco area experienced blackouts last night.* **2** if someone has a blackout, s/he becomes unconscious **3** *also* **news blackout** a situation in which particular pieces of news or information are not allowed to be reported

ˌblack ˈsheep *n.* [C usually singular] someone who is regarded by other members of his/her family as a failure or embarrassment: *My sister's **the black sheep of the family**.*

black·smith /ˈblæksmɪθ/ *n.* [C] someone who makes and repairs things made of iron

ˌblack-ˈtie *adj.* a party or social event that is black-tie is one at which you have to wear formal clothes

black·top /ˈblæktɑp/ *n.* [C,U] the thick black substance used for covering roads

blad·der /ˈblædɚ/ *n.* [C] BIOLOGY the part of your body that holds URINE until it is passed out of your body ➔ *see picture at* ORGAN

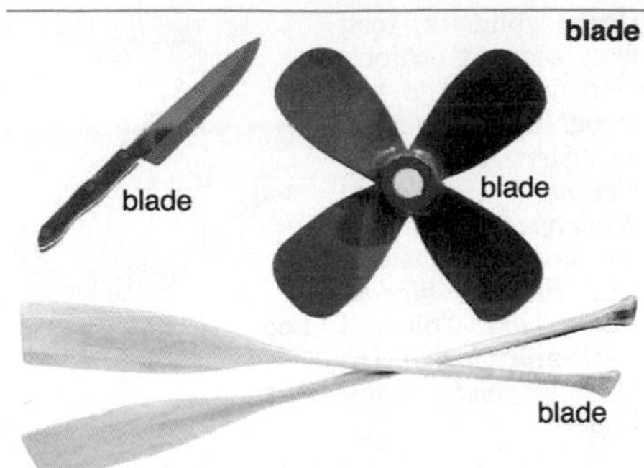

blade /bleɪd/ *n.* [C] **1** the flat cutting part of a knife, tool, or weapon: *The blade is sharp.* | *razor blades* **2** a leaf of grass or a similar plant **3** the flat wide part of an OAR, PROPELLER, etc. [ORIGIN: Old English *blæd*]

blah¹ /blɑ/ *adj.* (spoken) **1** not very interesting or exciting: *The color of the walls is kind of blah.* **2** slightly sick or unhappy: *I feel really blah today.*

blah² *n.* **blah, blah, blah** (spoken) said when you do not want to say or repeat something because it is boring: *Oh, you know Michelle; it's blah, blah, blah about her kids all the time.*

blame¹ /bleɪm/ *v.* [T] **1** to say or think that someone is responsible for something bad: *Don't blame me – it's not my fault.* | *Mom* ***blamed*** *herself* ***for*** *Keith's problems.* | *The accident was* ***blamed on*** *pilot error.* | *More than one person may be* ***to blame*** *for the fire.* **2 I don't blame you/them etc.** (spoken) said when you think it was right or reasonable for someone to do what s/he did: *I don't blame her for not letting her kids see that movie!*

blame² *n.* [U] responsibility for a mistake or for something bad: *Because she's the older child, she usually* ***gets the blame.*** | *You can't expect Terry to* ***take*** *all* ***the blame.*** | *Fans often* ***place/put/lay the blame on*** (=say that something is someone's fault, often when this is not true) *the coach when the team fails to win.*

blame·less /'bleɪmlɪs/ *adj.* not guilty of anything bad: *blameless behavior*

blanch /blæntʃ/ *v.* [I] (literary) to become pale because you are afraid or shocked

bland /blænd/ *adj.* **1** without any excitement, strong opinions, or special character: *bland TV shows* **2** bland food has very little taste: *bland cheese*

THESAURUS **sweet, tasty, sour, salty, hot, spicy** → TASTE¹

blan·dish·ments /'blændɪʃmənts/ *n.* [plural] (formal) nice things that you say in order to persuade or influence someone

blank¹ /blæŋk/ *adj.* **1** without any writing, print, or recorded sound: *a blank sheet of paper* | *Are there any blank tapes?*

THESAURUS **empty, bare, free, vacant** → EMPTY¹

2 go blank a) to be suddenly unable to remember something: *My mind went blank as I stood up to speak.* **b)** to stop showing any images, writing, etc.: *The screen suddenly went blank.* **3** showing no expression, understanding, or interest: *I said hello, and she gave me a blank look* [ORIGIN: 1200—1300 Old French *blanc* "white"]

blank² *n.* [C] **1** an empty space on a piece of paper, where you are supposed to write a word or letter: ***Fill in the blanks*** *on the application form.* **2** a CARTRIDGE (=container for a bullet in a gun) that has an explosive but no bullet: *The police were only firing blanks.* —**blankness** *n.* [U]

ˌblank 'check *n.* [singular] **1** a check that has been signed but has not had the amount written on it **2** (informal) the authority to do whatever you want, without any limits: *Congress gave President Johnson* ***a blank check*** *to wage war in Vietnam.*

blan·ket¹ /'blæŋkɪt/ *n.* **1** [C] a heavy cover that keeps you warm in bed **2** [singular] (literary) a thick covering of something: *a* ***blanket of snow*** *on the mountains* [ORIGIN: 1300—1400 *blanket* "white cloth" (13—15 centuries), from Old French *blankete*, from *blanc* "white"]

blanket² *adj.* **blanket statement/rule/ban etc.** a statement, rule, etc. that affects everyone or includes all possible cases: *The government imposed a blanket ban on the trade in ivory.*

blanket³ *v.* [T] to cover something with a thick layer: *The mountains were* ***blanketed in*** *snow.*

blank·ly /'blæŋkli/ *adv.* in a way that shows no expression, understanding, or interest: *He was staring blankly at the wall.*

ˌblank 'verse *n.* [U] ENG. LANG. ARTS poetry that has a particular RHYTHM, but does not RHYME: *Much of Shakespeare's plays are written in blank verse.*

blare /blɛr/ *v.* [I,T] to make a very loud unpleasant noise: *blaring horns* | *a radio* ***blaring out*** *music* —**blare** *n.* [singular]

bla·sé /blɑ'zeɪ/ *adj.* not worried or excited about things that most people think are important, impressive, etc.: *He's very blasé about money now that he's got that job.*

blas·phe·mous /'blæsfəməs/ *adj.* showing disrespect for God or people's religious beliefs: *The church has condemned the painting as blasphemous.* | *a blasphemous book*

blas·phe·my /'blæsfəmi/ *n.* [U] something you say or do that is insulting to God or to people's religious beliefs —**blaspheme** /blæs'fim, 'blæsfim/ *v.* [I,T]

blast¹ /blæst/ *n.* [C] **1** a sudden strong movement of wind or air: *a* ***blast of*** *icy air* **2** an explosion: *The blast was heard three miles away.* | *a bomb blast* **3 a blast** (spoken) an enjoyable and exciting experience: *We* ***had a blast*** *at Mitch's party.* **4 full blast** as strongly, loudly, or fast as possible: *She* *had the TV on full blast.* **5** a sudden very loud noise: *a trumpet blast*

blast² *v.* **1** [I,T] to break something into pieces using explosives: *They **blasted** a tunnel **through** the side of the mountain.* **2** [I,T] *also* **blast out** to produce a lot of loud noise, especially music: *Dance music blasted out from the stereo.* **3** [T] to attack a place or person with bombs or large guns: *Two gunmen **blasted** their way **into** the building.* **4** [T] to criticize something very strongly: *The President's remarks were quickly blasted by Democratic leaders.*

blast off *phr. v.* if a SPACECRAFT blasts off, it leaves the ground

'blast-off *n.* [U] the moment when a SPACECRAFT leaves the ground

blas·tu·la /'blæstʃələ/ *n.* [C] BIOLOGY an EMBRYO (=a person or animal that has not yet been born) in the early stage of its development, when it is a hollow ball of cells

bla·tant /'bleɪt˺nt/ *adj.* very noticeable and offensive: *blatant discrimination* —**blatantly** *adv.*

blaze¹ /bleɪz/ *v.* [I] to burn or shine very brightly and strongly: *a fire blazing in the fireplace*

blaze² *n.* [singular] **1** the strong bright flames of a fire: *Several firefighters were injured in the blaze.*

THESAURUS **fire, flames, inferno, bonfire, campfire** → FIRE¹

2 a very bright light or color: *a **blaze of** sunshine* **3 (in a) blaze of glory/publicity** receiving a lot of praise or public attention: *He launched the new magazine in a blaze of publicity.* [ORIGIN: (1, 2) Old English *blæse* "torch"]

blaz·er /'bleɪzɚ/ *n.* [C] a suit JACKET (=piece of clothing like a short coat) without matching pants: *a wool blazer* [ORIGIN: 1800—1900 *blaze*; from the originally bright colors of blazers]

blaz·ing /'bleɪzɪŋ/ *adj.* **1** extremely hot: *a blazing summer day* **2** burning strongly: *a **blazing fire*** **3** full of strong emotions, especially anger: *blazing eyes*

bleach¹ /blitʃ/ *n.* [U] a chemical used in order to make things white or to kill GERMS

bleach² *v.* [T] to make something white or lighter by using chemicals or the light of the Sun: *bleached hair*

bleach·ers /'blitʃɚz/ *n.* [plural] rows of seats where people sit to watch sports

bleak /blik/ *adj.* **1** without anything to make you feel happy or hopeful: *Without a job, the future can seem bleak.* **2** cold and unpleasant: *a bleak November day* [ORIGIN: 1300—1400 Old Norse *bleikr* "pale, white"] —**bleakness** *n.* [U]

blear·y /'blɪri/ *adj.* unable to see clearly because you are tired or have been crying: *Sam woke up looking **bleary-eyed**.* —**blearily** *adv.*

bleat /blit/ *v.* [I] to make the sound that a sheep or goat makes —**bleat** *n.* [C]

bleed /blid/ *v.* (past tense and past participle **bled** /blɛd/) [I] to lose blood, especially from an injury: *Your nose is bleeding.* | *He **bled to death** after being shot in the stomach.* [ORIGIN: Old English *bledan*, from *blod* "blood"] —**bleeding** *n.* [U]: *The bleeding had almost stopped.*

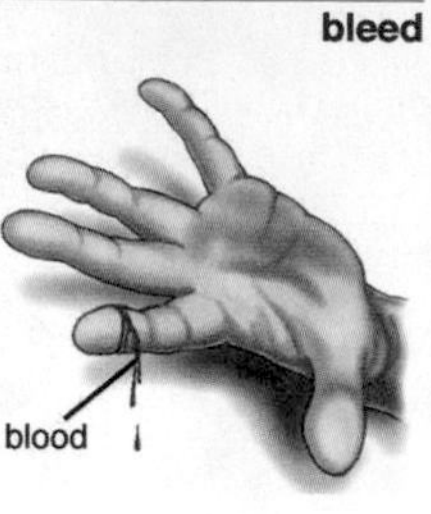

blem·ish /'blɛmɪʃ/ *n.* [C] a small mark that spoils the appearance of something or someone: *a small blemish on her cheek* [ORIGIN: 1300—1400 Old French *blemir* "to make pale, injure"] —**blemished** *adj.*

THESAURUS **bruise, scar, pimple, zit, wart, blister, freckle, mole** → MARK²

blend¹ /blɛnd/ *v.* [I,T] **1** to mix together soft or liquid substances to form a single smooth substance: ***Blend** the eggs **with** the sugar.* | *Stir in the sauce and **blend well**.*

THESAURUS **mix, combine, stir, beat** → MIX¹

2 to combine different things in a way that is attractive or effective: *a story that blends fact and fiction* **3** ENG. LANG. ARTS to combine parts of two words to make a new word: *The words "breakfast" and "lunch" were blended to produce "brunch."* **4** ENG. LANG. ARTS to combine two or more sounds together in a word [ORIGIN: 1300—1400 Old Norse *blanda*]

blend in *phr. v.* if something blends in with the things around it, it looks similar and you do not notice it: *curtains that **blend in with** the wallpaper*

blend² *n.* [C] **1** a mixture of two or more things: *the right **blend of** sunshine and soil for growing grapes*

THESAURUS **mixture, combination, compound, solution** → MIXTURE

2 ENG. LANG. ARTS a combination of parts of two words to make a new word: *"Smog" is a blend of "smoke" and "fog."* **3** ENG. LANG. ARTS a combination of two or more sounds within a word: *The word "broil" contains the consonant blend "br" and the vowel blend "oi."*

blend·er /'blɛndɚ/ *n.* [C] a small electric machine that you use to mix liquids together, or to make soft foods more liquid

bless /blɛs/ *v.* [T] **1 bless you** (spoken) said when someone SNEEZES **2** to ask God to protect someone or something: *May God bless you and keep you safe from harm.* **3** to make something holy: *The priest blessed the bread and wine.* **4 be blessed with sth** to have a special ability, good quality, etc.: *I'm blessed with good eyesight.* **5 bless him/her etc.** (spoken, old-fashioned) said in order to show that you like someone or are pleased by something s/he has done

bless·ed /ˈblɛsɪd/ *adj.* **1** [only before noun] enjoyable or desirable: *a moment of blessed silence* **2** (formal) holy and loved by God: *the Blessed Virgin Mary*

bless·ing /ˈblɛsɪŋ/ *n.* **1** [C] something good that improves your life and makes you happy: *The rain was a real blessing after all that heat.* **2** [U] someone's approval or encouragement for a plan, activity, etc.: *She left home **with her parents' blessing**.* **3 a mixed blessing** something that is both good and bad: *Living close to the office was a mixed blessing.* **4 a blessing in disguise** something that seems to be bad but that you later realize is good: *The lack of tourism on the island could be a blessing in disguise.* **5** [singular, U] protection and help from God, or the prayer in which you ask for this: *The priest gave the blessing.*

blew /blu/ *v.* the past tense of BLOW

blight /blaɪt/ *n.* [singular, U] something that damages or spoils something else, or the condition of being damaged or spoiled: *an area suffering from **urban blight*** (=severe problems that only a city has) —**blight** *v.* [T]

blight·ed /ˈblaɪṭɪd/ *adj.* damaged or spoiled: *the blighted downtown area*

blimp /blɪmp/ *n.* [C] an aircraft without wings that looks like a very large BALLOON

blind¹ /blaɪnd/ *adj.* **1** unable to see: *My grandmother is almost **totally blind**.* | *People with the disease often **go blind*** (=become blind). **2 the blind** people who cannot see: *special facilities for the blind* **3 blind faith/obedience/trust etc.** (disapproving) strong feelings that you have, without thinking about why you have them: *the army's blind obedience to the emperor* **4 be blind to sth** to completely fail to notice or realize something: *He was blind to the faults of his own children.* **5 turn a blind eye (to sth)** to ignore something that you know should not be happening: *Teachers were turning a blind eye to smoking in the school.* **6 blind corner/bend/curve** a corner, bend, etc. that you cannot see around when you are driving [ORIGIN: Old English] —**blindness** *n.* [U]

blind² *v.* [T] **1** to make someone unable to see, either permanently or for a short time: *The deer was blinded by our headlights.* **2** to make someone unable to notice or realize the truth about something: *Being in love **blinded** me **to** his faults.*

blind³ *n.* [C] a piece of cloth or other material that you can pull down to cover a window ➔ VENETIAN BLIND

ˌblind ˈdate *n.* [C] a DATE (=romantic meeting) arranged between a man and a woman who have not met each other before

blind·fold /ˈblaɪndfoʊld/ *n.* [C] a piece of cloth that you use to cover someone's eyes so that s/he cannot see —**blindfold** *v.* [T]

blind·ing /ˈblaɪndɪŋ/ *adj.* [usually before noun] **a blinding light/flash etc.** a very bright light that makes you unable to see for a short time

> THESAURUS **bright, strong, brilliant, dazzling, glaring** ➔ BRIGHT

blind·ly /ˈblaɪndli/ *adv.* **1** (disapproving) not thinking about something or trying to understand it: *Don't just blindly accept what you are told.* **2** not seeing or noticing what is around you: *She sat **staring blindly** out the window.*

blind·side /ˈblaɪndsaɪd/ *v.* [T] (informal) to hit the side of a car with your car in an accident

ˈblind spot *n.* [C] **1** something that you are unable or unwilling to understand: *He **has a blind spot** when it comes to his daughter's problems.* **2** the part of the road that you cannot see in front of you or in your mirrors when you are driving a car: *The other car was right **in my blind spot**.*

bling /blɪŋ/ *also* **bling ˈbling** *n.* [U] (informal) expensive things such as jewelry that are worn to be noticed

blink¹ /blɪŋk/ *v.* **1** [I,T] to close and open your eyes quickly: *He blinked as he stepped out into the sunlight.* **2** [I] if a light blinks, it goes on and off continuously: *The answering machine light was blinking.*

blink² *n.* **1 in the blink of an eye** very quickly: *With email, we can send messages across the globe in the blink of an eye.* **2 on the blink** (informal) not working correctly: *The radio's on the blink again.*

blink·ers /ˈblɪŋkɚz/ *n.* [plural] the small lights on a car that flash to show which direction you are turning

blip /blɪp/ *n.* [C] **1** a flashing light on the screen of a piece of electronic equipment **2** (informal) a sudden and temporary change from the way something normally happens: *This month's rise in prices could be just a blip.*

bliss /blɪs/ *n.* [U] perfect happiness —**blissful** *adj.* —**blissfully** *adv.* ➔ **ignorance is bliss** *at* IGNORANCE

blis·ter /ˈblɪstɚ/ *n.* [C] a painful swollen area on the skin containing a clear liquid, caused by a burn or by being rubbed too much: *New shoes always give me blisters.* —**blister** *v.* [I,T]

> THESAURUS **blemish, bruise, scar, pimple, zit, wart, freckle, mole** ➔ MARK²

blis·ter·ing /ˈblɪstərɪŋ/ *adj.* **1** extremely hot: *blistering summer days* **2 blistering attack/criticism etc.** very angry and disapproving remarks

blithe /blaɪð, blaɪθ/ *adj.* seeming not to care or worry about the effects of what you do: *the blithe* *assumption that he would always have a job* —**blithely** *adv.*: *They blithely ignored the danger.*

blitz /blɪts/ *n.* [C] **1** a situation when you use a lot of effort to achieve something, often in a short time: *an advertising blitz* **2** a sudden military attack, especially from the air —**blitz** *v.* [T]

B

bliz·zard /ˈblɪzɚd/ *n.* [C] EARTH SCIENCES a long heavy storm with a lot of wind and snow

THESAURUS **snow, snowflakes, sleet, slush, frost** → SNOW[1]

bloat·ed /ˈbloʊṭɪd/ *adj.* looking or feeling larger than usual because of being too full of water, food, gas, etc.: *I feel bloated after that meal.*

blob /blɑb/ *n.* [C] a small drop of a thick liquid: *a **blob of** paint*

bloc /blɑk/ *n.* [C] a large group of people or countries with the same political aims, working together: *the liberal bloc in Congress*

block[1] /blɑk/ *n.*
1 STREETS/AREA [C] **a)** the distance along a city street from where one street crosses it to the next: *We're just two blocks from the bus stop.* **b)** a square area of houses or buildings formed by four streets: *Let's walk around the block.* | *We were the first family **on our block** to get a swimming pool.*
2 SOLID MATERIAL [C] a solid piece of wood, stone, etc.: *a **block of** concrete* | *The baby was playing with wooden blocks.*

THESAURUS **piece, scrap, chunk, lump, fragment, crumb, slice, strip** → PIECE[1]

3 RELATED GROUP [C] a group of things of the same kind or an amount of something, considered as a single unit: *We were given a **block of** shares in the company.* | *Jason says he can get a **block of seats*** (=seats next to each other) *for the concert.*
4 a block of time a length of time that is not interrupted by anything: *Set aside a block of time to do your homework.*
5 UNABLE TO THINK [singular] the temporary loss of your normal ability to think, learn, write, etc.: *I can never remember his name – I must have a **mental block**.* | *After her first novel, she had **writer's block*** (=she could not write anything).
6 STOPPING MOVEMENT [C] something that makes it difficult to move or progress → ROADBLOCK: *The incident could be a **block to** the peace process.*
7 SPORTS [C] a movement in sports that stops an opponent going forward or moving the ball forward

block[2] *v.* [T] **1** to prevent people or things from moving through or along a space: *A fallen tree was blocking the road.* | *It looks like the sink is blocked.* | *I tried to get through, but there were too many people **blocking** my **way**.* | *blocked arteries* **2** to be in front of someone so that s/he cannot see something: *A tall man in front of me was **blocking** my **view**.* **3** to stop something happening, developing, or succeeding: *Why did the council block the plan?* **4** to stop a ball, a blow, etc. from getting to where your opponent wants it to go: *He also **blocked** 4 **shots** and scored 6 rebounds*

block sth ↔ **off** *phr. v.* to close a road or path so that people cannot use it: *The freeway exit has been blocked off.*

block sth ↔ **out** *phr. v.* **1** to stop light from reaching a place: *Heavy curtains blocked out the light.* **2** to stop yourself from thinking about or remembering something: *Carrie hears what she wants to hear and blocks out the rest.* **3** to decide that you will use a particular time only for a particular purpose: *I try to block out four hours a week for research.*

block·ade /blɑˈkeɪd/ *n.* [C] the action of surrounding an area with soldiers or ships, to stop people or supplies leaving or entering a place: *a naval blockade* —**blockade** *v.* [T]

block·age /ˈblɑkɪdʒ/ *n.* [C] something that is blocking a pipe, tube, etc.: *a blockage in the drain*

block·bust·er /ˈblɑkˌbʌstɚ/ *n.* [C] (informal) a book or movie that is very successful: *the latest Hollywood blockbuster*

THESAURUS **bestseller, hit, craze, fad, cult** → POPULAR

ˈblock ˌparty *n.* [C] a party that is held in the street for all the people living in the area

blog /blɑg/ *n.* [C] a website that is made up of information about a particular subject, in which the newest information is always at the top of the page → INTERNET —**blogger** *n.* [C]

blonde[1], blond /blɑnd/ *adj.* **1** blonde hair is pale or yellow **2** someone who is blonde has pale or yellow hair

blonde[2] *n.* [C] (informal) a woman who has pale or yellow hair: *a good-looking blonde*

blood /blʌd/ *n.* [U] **1** the red liquid that your heart pumps through your body: *She **lost** a lot of **blood** in the accident.* | *The Red Cross is asking people to **give/donate blood*** (=have blood taken from them for the medical treatment of other people). → *see picture at* BLEED **2 in cold blood** in a cruel and deliberate way: *He murdered the old man in cold blood.* **3** the family or group to which you belong from the time you are born: *There's French blood on his mother's side.* | *a **blood relative*** (=related by birth, not by marriage) **4 new blood** new members in a group or organization who bring new ideas and energy: *We need some new blood in the department.* **5 be/run in sb's blood** to be a strong and natural part of someone's character: *A love of politics was in his blood.* **6 bad blood** feelings of anger and hate between people: *There's been **bad blood between** them for years.* **7 -blooded** having a particular type of blood: *Fish are cold-blooded.* [ORIGIN: Old English *blod*]

ˌblood-and-ˈguts *adj.* (informal) full of action and violence: *a blood-and-guts horror movie*

'blood bank *n.* [C] a place where human blood is kept to be used in hospital treatment

blood·bath /'blʌdbæθ/ *n.* [singular] the violent killing of many people at the same time

blood·cur·dling /'blʌd,kɚdl-ɪŋ/ *adj.* extremely frightening: *a bloodcurdling scream*

blood·hound /'blʌdhaʊnd/ *n.* [C] a large dog with a very good sense of smell

blood·less /'blʌdlɪs/ *adj.* **1** without killing or violence: *a bloodless revolution* **2** extremely pale: *bloodless cheeks*

'blood ,pressure *n.* [U] BIOLOGY the force with which blood moves around your body: *a special diet for people with **high/low blood pressure***

blood·shed /'blʌdʃɛd/ *n.* [U] the killing of people in fighting or a war

blood·shot /'blʌdʃɑt/ *adj.* bloodshot eyes look slightly red

blood·stain /'blʌdsteɪn/ *n.* [C] a mark or spot of blood —**bloodstained** *adj.*

blood·stream /'blʌdstrim/ *n.* [singular] BIOLOGY blood as it flows around the body: *Drugs were found **in her bloodstream**.*

blood·thirst·y /'blʌd,θɚsti/ *adj.* eager to kill and wound, or enjoying killing and violence: *a cruel and bloodthirsty ruler who slaughtered men, women and children*

'blood type *n.* [C] BIOLOGY one of the groups into which human blood is divided, including A, B, AB, and O

'blood ,vessel *n.* [C] BIOLOGY one of the tubes through which blood flows in your body

blood·y /'blʌdi/ *adj.* **1** covered in blood, or losing blood: *a bloody nose* **2** with a lot of injuries or killing: *a bloody civil war*

bloom¹ /blum/ *n.* [C,U] a flower or flowers: *lovely yellow blooms* | *roses **in bloom*** (=with flowers completely open)

bloom² *v.* [I] **1** if a plant or flower blooms, its flowers appear or open **2** to look happy and healthy or successful: *Sheila bloomed like a woman in love.*

bloom·er /'blumɚ/ *n.* **late bloomer** (informal) someone who grows or becomes successful at a later age than most people

bloop·er /'blupɚ/ *n.* [C] (informal) an embarrassing mistake made in front of other people

blos·som¹ /'blɑsəm/ *n.* [C,U] a flower, or all the flowers on trees or bushes: *peach blossoms* → *see picture at* PLANT¹

blossom² *v.* [I] **1** if trees blossom, they produce flowers: *a blossoming plum tree* **2** to become happier, more beautiful, or successful: *By the end of the year she had **blossomed into** an excellent teacher.*

blot¹ /blɑt/ *v.* (**blotted**, **blotting**) [T] to dry a wet surface by pressing soft paper or cloth on it

blot sth ↔ **out** *phr. v.* **1** to cover or hide something completely: *Black clouds blotted out the sun.* **2** to forget something, often deliberately: *He tried to blot out the memory of that night.*

blot² *n.* [C] a mark or spot that spoils something or makes it dirty: *ink blots*

blotch /blɑtʃ/ *n.* [C] a pink or red mark on the skin, or a colored mark on something —**blotchy** *adj.*

'blotting ,paper *n.* [U] soft paper used for drying wet ink on a page

blouse /blaʊs/ *n.* [C] a shirt for a woman or girl: *a summer blouse*

blow¹ /bloʊ/ *v.* (past tense **blew** /blu/, past participle **blown** /bloʊn/)

1 WIND MOVING [I] if wind or air blows, it moves: *A cold wind was blowing from the east.*

2 WIND MOVING STH [I,T] to move in the wind, or to make something move somewhere in the wind: *Her hair was **blowing in** the breeze.* | *My ticket **blew away**.* | *Hundreds of trees were **blown down** in the storm.* | *The wind must have **blown** the door **shut/open**.*

3 USING YOUR MOUTH [I,T] to push air through your mouth: *Renée **blew on** her soup to cool it a little.* | *I hate people who blow smoke in your face.*

4 VIOLENCE [T] to damage or destroy something violently with an explosion or by shooting: *Part of his leg had been **blown off**.* | *A bomb like that would **blow** the building **to bits/pieces**.*

5 blow your nose to clear your nose by forcing air through it into a cloth or TISSUE (=piece of soft paper)

6 blow sth (up) out of (all) proportion to make something seem much more serious or important than it is: *The health risks had been blown out of proportion.*

7 MAKE A SOUND [I,T] to make a sound by pushing air into a whistle, horn, or musical instrument: *I could hear the train whistle blowing.*

8 ELECTRICITY STOPS [I,T] if an electrical FUSE blows, or a piece of electrical equipment blows a FUSE, the electricity suddenly stops working

9 blow the whistle (on sb) (informal) to tell the public or someone in authority about something wrong that is happening: *He blew the whistle on his colleagues.*

SPOKEN PHRASES

10 LOSE AN OPPORTUNITY [T] (informal) to lose a good opportunity, by making a mistake or being careless: *I **blew it** by talking too much in the interview.* | *We've **blown** our **chances** of getting that contract.*

11 LEAVE [T] (spoken) to leave a place quickly: *Let's **blow this joint*** (=leave this place).

12 SPEND MONEY [T] (informal) to spend a lot of money at one time in a careless way: *I blew all the money I won on a trip to Hawaii.*

13 sth blows your mind (informal) to make you

feel very surprised and excited about something: *Seeing her again really blew my mind.*

[ORIGIN: Old English *blawan*]

blow sb ↔ **away** *phr. v.* (spoken)
1 to completely surprise someone: *It just blows me away how friendly the islanders are.*
2 to kill someone by shooting him/her with a gun: *One move and I'll blow you away!*
3 to defeat someone completely, especially in a game: *The Lakers blew the competition away.*

blow in *phr. v.*
1 *also* **blow into sth** (informal) to arrive in a place, especially suddenly: *Guess who's just **blown into town**?*
2 if a storm or bad weather blows in, it arrives and begins to affect an area

blow sb/sth ↔ **off** *phr. v.* (spoken)
to treat someone or something as unimportant, for example by not meeting someone or not going to an event: *I blew off my 8 a.m. class again.* | *She blew us off and went out with Jim instead.*

blow sth ↔ **out** *phr. v.*
1 to blow air on a flame and make it stop burning: *Blow out all the candles.*
2 if a tire blows out, it bursts

blow over *phr. v.*
1 if an argument or a bad situation blows over, it does not seem important anymore or is forgotten: *Many people expected the scandal to blow over in a few days.*
2 if a storm blows over, it comes to an end

blow up *phr. v.*
1 blow (sth ↔) **up** to destroy something, or to be destroyed, by an explosion: *A car was blown up near the embassy.* | *Their plane blew up in mid-air.*
2 blow sth ↔ **up** to fill something with air or gas: *Come and help me blow up the balloons.*
3 to shout angrily at someone: *She **blew up at** me for no reason.*
4 blow sth ↔ **up** if you blow up a photograph, you make it larger: *I'd like to have this picture blown up.*

blow² *n.* [C] **1** something very sad and disappointing that happens to you: *Not getting the job was a **blow to** Kate's confidence.* | *The death of their father was **a terrible blow**.* **2** a hard hit with a hand, tool, or weapon: *The victim suffered several **blows to** the head.* **3** the act of blowing air out of your mouth: *One blow and the candles were out.* **4 come to blows** if two people come to blows, they start hitting each other: *They almost **came to blows over** the money.*

ˌblow-by-ˈblow *adj.* **a blow-by-blow account/description etc.** a description of an event, that gives all the details exactly as they happened

ˈblow dry *v.* (**blow-dried**, **blow-dries**) [T] to dry hair and give it shape by using a blow dryer

ˈblow ˌdryer *n.* [C] a small electric machine that you hold and use to blow hot air onto your hair in order to dry it

blown /bloʊn/ *v.* the past participle of BLOW

blow·out /ˈbloʊaʊt/ *n.* [C] (informal) **1** an occasion when a TIRE bursts suddenly as a vehicle is moving **2** a big expensive meal or a large party

blow·torch /ˈbloʊˌtɔrtʃ/ *n.* [C] a piece of equipment that produces a small very hot flame, used especially to remove paint

ˈblow-up *n.* [C] **1** a photograph, or part of a photograph, that has been made larger **2** (informal) a sudden loud argument

BLT *n.* [C] a SANDWICH that contains BACON, LETTUCE, and TOMATO

blub·ber¹ /ˈblʌbɚ/ *n.* [U] the fat of sea animals, especially WHALES

blubber² *v.* [I] (informal) to cry loudly, especially in a way that annoys people

blud·geon /ˈblʌdʒən/ *v.* [T] to hit someone many times with a heavy object: *He was **bludgeoned to death** with a hammer.*

blue¹ /blu/ *adj.* **1** having the same color as a clear sky during the day: *the blue lake water* | *a **dark/light** blue dress* **2** [not before noun] (informal) sad: *I've been **feeling** kind of **blue** lately.*

> THESAURUS **sad, unhappy, miserable, sorrowful, depressed, down, low, downhearted, melancholy, morose, gloomy, glum** → SAD

3 do sth till you're blue in the face (informal) to do something a lot but without achieving what you want: *You can argue till you're blue in the face, but I won't change my mind.* → **once in a blue moon** *at* ONCE¹

blue² *n.* **1** [C,U] the color of the sky on a clear day: *Carolyn's the one dressed in blue.* | *I like the rich greens and blues of the painting.* **2 blues** *also* **the blues** [plural] ENG. LANG. ARTS a slow and sad style of music that came from the African-American culture in the southern U.S.: *a blues singer* **3 out of the blue** (informal) suddenly and without warning: *The letter came completely out of the blue.* **4 have/get the blues** (informal) to feel sad

blue·bell /ˈblubɛl/ *n.* [C] a small plant with blue flowers that grows in the forest

blue·ber·ry /ˈbluˌbɛri/ *n.* (plural **blueberries**) [C] a small dark blue round BERRY: *blueberry muffins*

blue·bird /ˈbluˌbɚd/ *n.* [C] a small North American wild bird that sings and has a blue back and wings

ˌblue-ˈblooded *adj.* belonging to a royal or NOBLE family —**blue-blood** *n.* [U]

ˈblue book *n.* [C] **1** a book with a blue cover, that is used in colleges for writing answers to test questions **2** a book with a list of prices that you should expect to pay for any used car

ˌblue ˈcheese *n.* [C,U] a strong-tasting pale cheese with blue spots in it

ˈblue chip *adj.* **blue chip companies/shares etc.** companies or STOCKS that are very unlikely to lose money [ORIGIN: 1900—2000 *blue chip* "blue counter of high value used in gambling" (1900—2000)]

ˌblue-'collar *adj.* [only before noun] blue-collar workers do physical work, rather than working in offices ➔ WHITE-COLLAR

blue·grass /'blugræs/ *n.* [U] ENG. LANG. ARTS a type of COUNTRY MUSIC from the southern and western U.S., using string instruments such as the VIOLIN or BANJO

blue·jay /'bludʒeɪ/ *n.* [C] a common North American wild bird that has blue, black, and white feathers

'blue law *n.* [C] (informal) a law that controls activities that are considered immoral, such as drinking alcohol, working on Sundays, etc.

ˌblue 'movie *n.* [C] a movie that shows a lot of sexual activity

blue·print /'bluˌprɪnt/ *n.* [C] **1** a plan for achieving something: *a **blueprint for** health care reform* **2** a print of a plan for a building, machine, etc. on special blue paper

ˌblue 'ribbon *n.* [C] a small piece of blue material given to someone who wins a competition

'blue shift *n.* [U] PHYSICS a change in the light given off by an object in space such as a star, in which the light appears more blue as the object is moving toward the person looking at it ➔ RED SHIFT

Blue·tooth /'blutuθ/ *n.* [U] (trademark) IT a type of TECHNOLOGY that uses radio to allow electronic equipment such as a CELL PHONE and a computer to work together without a wire connecting them

bluff¹ /blʌf/ *v.* [I,T] to pretend that you are going to do something or that you know something, in order to get what you want: *I don't believe you – I think you're bluffing!*

bluff² *n.* **1** [C,U] an attempt to make someone believe that you are going to do something when you do not really intend to: *He threatened to resign, but I'm sure it's a bluff.* **2 call sb's bluff** to tell someone to do what s/he threatens because you believe s/he has no intention of doing it **3** [C] EARTH SCIENCES a very steep cliff or slope: *the bluffs near the river*

blun·der¹ /'blʌndɚ/ *n.* [C] a careless or stupid mistake: *a terrible political blunder*

blunder² *v.* [I] **1** to make a careless or stupid mistake: *Police admitted that they blundered when they let Wylie go.* **2** to move forward in an unsteady way, as if you cannot see well

blunt¹ /blʌnt/ *adj.* **1** speaking in an honest way even if it upsets people ➔ BLUNTLY: *Did you have to be so blunt?*

THESAURUS **honest, frank, candid, direct, upfront, straight, straightforward, forthright** ➔ HONEST

2 not sharp or pointed (ANT) **sharp**: *a blunt knife* ➔ *see picture at* SHARP¹ —**bluntness** *n.* [U]

blunt² *v.* [T] to make something less strong: *attempts to try to blunt the impact of anti-smoking laws*

blunt·ly /'blʌnt˺li/ *adv.* speaking in a direct honest way that sometimes upsets people: ***To put it bluntly**, you're failing the class.*

B

blur¹ /blɚ/ *n.* [singular] something that you cannot see clearly or cannot remember clearly: *a blur of horses running past* | *The days following the accident were **all a blur**.*

blur² *v.* (**blurred**, **blurring**) [I,T] **1** to become difficult to see, or to make something difficult to see, because the edges are not clear: *Tears blurred my vision.* | *The coastline was blurred by fog.* **2** to make the difference between two ideas, subjects, etc. less clear: *Computers have **blurred the distinction between** learning and play.* —**blurry** *adj.*: *blurry photos*

blurb /blɚb/ *n.* [C] a short description giving information about a book, new product, etc.

blurred /blɚd/ *adj.* **1** not clear in shape, or making it difficult to see shapes: *a blurred image* **2** difficult to understand or remember clearly: *blurred memories*

blurt /blɚt/ *also* **blurt out** *v.* [T] to say something suddenly and without thinking, usually because you are nervous or excited: *She blurted out the news before I could stop her.*

blush¹ /blʌʃ/ *v.* [I] to become red in the face, usually because you are embarrassed: *Carlos blushes every time he talks to her.* [ORIGIN: Old English *blyscan* "to become red," from *blysa* "flame"]

blush² *n.* **1** [C] the red color on your face that appears when you are embarrassed, confused, or ashamed **2** [U] *also* **blusher** cream or powder used for making your cheeks slightly red or pink

blus·ter¹ /'blʌstɚ/ *v.* [I] to talk loudly and behave as if what you are doing is extremely important

bluster² *n.* [U] noisy proud talk

blus·ter·y /'blʌstəri/ *adj.* blustery weather is very windy: *a blustery winter day*

Blvd. the written abbreviation of BOULEVARD

B-mov·ie /'bi ˌmuvi/ *n.* [C] a movie that is made cheaply and is of low quality

B.O., BO /bi 'oʊ/ *n.* [U] (spoken) **body odor** a bad smell from someone's body, caused by SWEAT

bo·a con·strict·or /'boʊə kənˌstrɪktɚ/ *n.* [C] a large snake that is not poisonous, but kills animals by crushing them

boar /bɔr/ *n.* [C] **1** a male pig **2** a wild pig

board¹ /bɔrd/ *n.*
1 FOR INFORMATION [C] a flat wide piece of wood, plastic, etc. where information is written or shown ➔ BLACKBOARD, BULLETIN BOARD: *The teacher wrote a list of words **on the board**. | Remember to check the board for dates and times.*
2 FOR PUTTING THINGS ON [C] a flat piece of wood, plastic, etc. that you use for a particular purpose: *a cutting board | Where's the chessboard?*
3 GROUP OF PEOPLE [C] a group of people in an organization who make the rules and important decisions: *the local **school board** | a board meeting | a **board of** directors*
4 FOR BUILDING [C] a long thin flat piece of wood used for making floors, walls, fences, etc.
5 on board on an airplane, ship, etc.: *There were over 1,000 passengers on board.*
6 take sth on board to accept a suggestion, idea, etc. and do something about it: *We'll try to take some of your points on board.*
7 across the board affecting everyone or everything: *Prices have been reduced across the board.*
8 MEALS [U] the meals that are provided for you when you pay to stay somewhere: ***Room and board** at the college is $4,000 per semester.*

board² *v.* [I,T] **1** to get on an airplane, ship, train, etc. in order to travel somewhere: *We invite our first-class passengers to board the plane now.* **2 be boarding** if an airplane or ship is boarding, passengers are getting on it: *Flight 503 for Toronto is now boarding.*
board sth ↔ **up** *phr. v.* to cover a window or door with wooden boards: *The house next door has been boarded up for months.*

board·er /ˈbɔrdɚ/ *n.* [C] someone who pays to live in another person's house with some or all of his/her meals provided

ˈboard game *n.* [C] any indoor game in which pieces are moved around a specially designed board made of thick CARDBOARD or wood

ˈboarding house *n.* [C] a private house where you pay to sleep and eat

ˈboarding pass *n.* [C] a card that you must show before you get on an airplane or a ship

ˈboarding school *n.* [C] a school where students live as well as study

board·room /ˈbɔrdrum/ *n.* [C] a room where the important people in a company have meetings

board·walk /ˈbɔrdwɔk/ *n.* [C] a raised path made of wood, usually built next to the ocean

boast¹ /boʊst/ *v.* **1** [I] to talk too much about your own abilities and achievements in a way that annoys other people (SYN) **brag**: *Scott was **boasting about** winning the game.* **2** [T] if a place boasts something good, the place has it: *The new athletic center boasts an Olympic-sized swimming pool.*

boast² *n.* [C] something you like telling people because you are very proud of it

boast·ful /ˈboʊstfəl/ *adj.* talking too much about your own abilities and achievements —**boastfully** *adv.*

boat /boʊt/ *n.* **1** [C] a vehicle that travels across water ➔ SHIP: *fishing boats | You can only get to the island **by boat**.* **2 be in the same boat (as sb)** to be in the same unpleasant situation as someone else: *We're all in the same boat, so stop complaining.* [ORIGIN: Old English *bat*] ➔ **miss the boat** *at* MISS¹, **rock the boat** *at* ROCK²

ˈboat ˌpeople *n.* [plural] people who escape from bad conditions in their country in small boats

bob¹ /bɑb/ *v.* (**bobbed**, **bobbing**) [I] to move up and down on water: *a boat **bobbing up and down** on the water*

bob² *n.* [C] a way of cutting straight hair so that it hangs to the level of your chin and is the same length all the way around your head ➔ *see picture on page 462*

bob·bin /ˈbɑbɪn/ *n.* [C] a small round object that you wind thread onto

bob·by pin /ˈbɑbi pɪn/ *n.* [C] a thin piece of metal that you use to hold your hair in place

bob·cat /ˈbɑbkæt/ *n.* [C] a North American wild cat that has no tail

bob·sled /ˈbɑbslɛd/ *n.* [C] a small vehicle with two long thin metal blades that is used for racing down a special ice track —**bobsled** *v.* [I]

bode /boʊd/ *v.* **bode well/ill** (literary) to be a good or bad sign for the future

bod·ice /ˈbɑdɪs/ *n.* [C] the part of a woman's dress above her waist

bod·i·ly¹ /ˈbɑdl-i/ *adj.* [only before noun] relating to the human body: ***bodily functions*** (=things your body does, especially going to the toilet) | *He did not suffer any **bodily harm**.*

bodily² *adv.* by moving all of your body or someone else's body: *She had to be carried bodily to bed.*

bod·y /ˈbɑdi/ *n.* (plural **bodies**)
1 PHYSICAL BODY [C] **a)** the physical structure of a person or animal: *a strong healthy body | Your*

body temperature is higher in the daytime than at night. → *see picture on page A16* **b)** the central part of a person or animal's body, not including the head, arms, legs or wings: *a creature with a short body and long legs* **c)** the body of a dead person: *The **body of** a girl had been found in the river.*
2 GROUP OF PEOPLE [C] a group of people who work together for a particular purpose: *the **governing body** of a university* | *the president of the **student body*** (=all the students in a school or college)
3 body of sth a) a large amount of information, knowledge, etc.: *He produced a body of work comparable with many of the jazz greats.* | *A growing **body of evidence** suggests that the girl committed suicide.* **b)** the main part of something: *The arguments are explained in **the body of the text**.*
4 HAIR [U] if your hair has body, it is thick and healthy
5 -bodied a) having a particular type of body: *thick-bodied men* **b)** having a particular amount of taste: *full-bodied red wine*
6 VEHICLE [C] the main structure of a vehicle, not including the engine, wheels, etc.: *The body of the airplane was not damaged.* [ORIGIN: Old English *bodig*]

'body ˌbuilding *n.* [U] an activity in which you do hard physical exercise in order to develop big muscles —**body builder** *n.* [C]

bodyguard

bod·y·guard /'badiˌgard/ *n.* [C] a person whose job is to protect an important person

'body ˌlanguage *n.* [U] movements that you make without thinking, that show what you are feeling or thinking: *I could tell from his body language that he was nervous.*

'body ˌodor *n.* [U] B.O.

bod·y·work /'badiˌwɚk/ *n.* [U] the frame of a vehicle, not including the engine, wheels, etc.

bog¹ /bag, bɔg/ *n.* [C,U] EARTH SCIENCES an area of wet muddy ground

bog² *v.* (**bogged**, **bogging**) **get/be bogged down (in sth)** to become too involved in thinking about or dealing with one particular thing, so that you are not able to make any progress: *Let's not get bogged down in minor details.*

bo·gey·man /'bugiˌmæn/ *n.* (plural **bogeymen** /-mən/) [C] **1** an evil spirit, especially in children's imagination or stories **2** someone who people think is evil or unpleasant

bog·gle /'bagəl/ *v.* **the mind boggles/sth boggles the mind** (informal) used in order to say that something is difficult to believe or very confusing: *The paperwork you have to fill out just boggles the mind.*

bo·gus /'bougəs/ *adj.* (informal) not true or real, although someone tries to make you think it is (SYN) **fake**: *a bogus insurance claim* [ORIGIN: 1800—1900 *bogus* "machine for making illegal money"]

bo·he·mi·an /bou'himiən/ *adj.* living in a very informal or relaxed way and not accepting society's rules or behavior: *a bohemian lifestyle* [ORIGIN: 1800—1900 *Bohemian* "of Bohemia, area and former country in the Czech Republic;" because of an association between Bohemia and traveling artists and gypsies] —**bohemian** *n.* [C]

boil¹ /bɔɪl/ *v.* [I,T] **1** if a liquid boils, or if you boil a liquid, it is hot enough for BUBBLES to rise to the surface and for the liquid to change to steam: *Drop the noodles into boiling salted water.* | *Water **boils at** 100 degrees Centigrade.* **2** to cook food in boiling water: *Boil the vegetables for 10 minutes.*

> THESAURUS cook, bake, fry, roast, broil, grill, sauté, steam, deep fry → COOK¹

3 to clean something using boiling water: *Boil the baby's bottles before using them.* [ORIGIN: 1200-1300 Old French *boillir*, from Latin *bullire*, from *bulla* "bubble"]

boil down to sth *phr. v.* if a long statement, argument, etc. boils down to a single statement, that statement is the main point or cause: *Think of the money you can make – that's what it all boils down to.*

boil over *phr. v.* **1** to boil and flow over the sides of a pan **2** if a situation or emotion boils over, people begin to get angry

boil² *n.* **1** [singular] the act or state of boiling: ***Bring** the soup **to a boil** and cook for 5 minutes.* | *Wait until the water **comes to a boil**.* **2** [C] a painful infected swelling under the skin

boil·er /'bɔɪlɚ/ *n.* [C] a container for boiling water, that provides heat and hot water in a house or steam in an engine

boil·ing /'bɔɪlɪŋ/ *also* **ˌboiling 'hot** *adj.* extremely hot: *It's **boiling hot** in here.*

'boiling point *n.* [C] the temperature at which a liquid boils

bois·ter·ous /'bɔɪstərəs, 'bɔɪstrəs/ *adj.* noisy and full of energy: *boisterous children*

bold /bould/ *adj.* **1** confident and willing to take risks: *Yamamoto's plan was bold and original.*

> THESAURUS brave, courageous, heroic, valiant, daring, fearless, intrepid → BRAVE¹

2 very clear and strong or bright: *wallpaper with bold stripes* **3 in bold (type/print/letters)**

B

printed in letters that are darker and thicker than ordinary printed letters: *All the headings are in bold.* [ORIGIN: Old English *beald*] —**boldly** *adv.* —**boldness** *n.* [U]

bo·lo·gna /bə'louni/ *n.* [C] a type of cooked meat often eaten in SANDWICHes

B

bol·ster /'boulstɚ/ *also* **bolster up** *v.* [T] to improve something by giving support and confidence: *She tried to bolster his confidence.*

bolt[1] /boult/ *n.* [C] **1** a piece of metal that you slide across a door or window to close or lock it ➔ *see picture at* LOCK[2] **2** a screw with a flat head and no point, used with a NUT for fastening two pieces of metal together **3 bolt of lightning** LIGHTNING that appears as a white line in the sky **4** a large long roll of cloth

bolt[2] *v.* **1** [I] to run away suddenly: *A gun fired, and the horse bolted.*

THESAURUS **run, sprint, dash, tear, race** ➔ RUN[1]

2 [I,T] to close or lock a door or window with a bolt: *Jason bolted the door and closed the curtains.* **3** [I,T] to fasten two things together using a bolt: *The bench is bolted to the sidewalk.*

bolt[3] *adv.* **sit/stand bolt upright** to sit or stand with your back very straight: *Suddenly, Dennis sat bolt upright in bed.*

bomb[1] /bɑm/ *n.* [C] **1** a weapon made of material that will explode: ***Bombs** were **dropped** on the city.* | *The **bomb went off/exploded** near the airport.* **2** (informal) a play, movie, etc. that is not successful **3 the bomb** the ATOMIC BOMB or any NUCLEAR WEAPON **4** a container in which insect poison, paint, etc. is kept under pressure: *a flea bomb* (=used for killing FLEAS) [ORIGIN: 1600—1700 French *bombe*, from Italian *bomba*]

bomb[2] *v.* **1** [T] to attack a place with bombs: *Terrorists threatened to bomb the building.* **2** [I,T] (spoken) to fail a test very badly: *I bombed my history test.* **3** [I] (informal) if a play, movie, or joke bombs, it is not successful

bom·bard /bɑm'bɑrd/ *v.* [T] **1** to attack a place for a long time with guns and bombs: *The town was bombarded from all sides.* **2** to ask a lot of questions or give a lot of information or criticism, so that it is difficult for someone to deal with: *Viewers **bombarded** the TV station **with** complaints.* —**bombardment** *n.* [C]

bom·bas·tic /bɑm'bæstɪk/ *adj.* (disapproving) bombastic language contains long words that sound important but have no real meaning

bomb·er /'bɑmɚ/ *n.* [C] **1** an airplane that carries and drops bombs **2** someone who puts a bomb somewhere: *a **suicide bomber*** (=someone who carries a bomb and allows himself/herself to be killed when the bomb explodes)

bomb·shell /'bɑmʃɛl/ *n.* [C] (informal) a shocking piece of news: *Last night, she **dropped the bombshell** and told him she wouldn't marry him.*

bo·na fide /'bounə ˌfaɪd, 'bɑnə-/ *adj.* real, true, and not pretending to be something else: *a bona fide job offer*

bo·nan·za /bə'nænzə, bou-/ *n.* [C] a lucky or successful situation in which people can make a lot of money: *The discovery could represent an amazing cash bonanza.* [ORIGIN: 1800—1900 Spanish "good weather," from Medieval Latin *bonacia*, changed from Latin *malacia* "calm at sea"]

bond[1] /bɑnd/ (Ac) *n.* **1** [C] a shared feeling or interest that unites people: *a strong **bond** of affection **between** the two women* | *Marilyn's **bond with** her mother was unusually strong.* **2** [C] ECONOMICS an official document promising that a government or company will pay back money that it has borrowed, often with INTEREST: *They invested in U.S. government bonds.* **3** [C,U] LAW money given to a court of law so that someone can be let out of prison while s/he waits for his/her TRIAL (SYN) **bail**: *His lawyers **posted** the $100,000 **bond**, and he was released.* **4** [C] CHEMISTRY a chemical force that holds atoms together in a MOLECULE: *the atom's ability to form chemical bonds with other atoms*

bond[2] *v.* **1** [I] to develop a special relationship with someone: *It takes a few months for new mothers to **bond with** their babies.* **2** [I,T] if two things bond to each other, they become firmly stuck together: *A special glue strongly **bonds** the insulation **to** panels on the space shuttle.*

bond·age /'bɑndɪdʒ/ *n.* [U] a situation in which people have no freedom ➔ SLAVERY

bond·ing /'bɑndɪŋ/ (Ac) *n.* [U] **1** a process by which a special close relationship develops between people: *the results of a four-year study into parent-infant bonding* **2 male/female bonding** (informal) the activity of doing things with other people of the same sex, so that you feel good about being a man or a woman **3** CHEMISTRY the joining together of two or more atoms: *The drug **chemically bonds** with cells in the body to stop the virus spreading.*

bone[1] /boun/ *n.* **1** [C] one of the hard parts that form the frame of a human or animal body: *She **broke** two **bones** in her arm.* | *the thigh bone* **2 make no bones about (doing) sth** to not feel nervous or ashamed about doing or saying something: *She makes no bones about her religious beliefs.* **3 be chilled/frozen to the bone** to be extremely cold **4 a bone of contention** something that causes arguments between people [ORIGIN: Old English *ban*]

bone[2] *v.* [T] to remove the bones from fish or meat

bone up on sth *phr. v.* (informal) to study something a lot for an examination: *I should bone up on grammar before the test.*

ˌbone 'dry *adj.* completely dry

'bone ˌmarrow *n.* [U] BIOLOGY the soft substance in the hollow center of bones: *a bone marrow transplant*

bon·fire /ˈbɑnˌfaɪɚ/ *n.* [C] a large outdoor fire [ORIGIN: 1500—1600 *bonfire* "fire made from bones" (14—17 centuries)]

THESAURUS fire, flames, blaze, inferno, campfire → FIRE[1]

bon·gos /ˈbɑŋgoʊz/ *also* **ˈbongo ˌdrums** *n.* [plural] a pair of small drums that you play with your hands

bon·kers /ˈbɑŋkɚz/ *adj.* [not before noun] (informal) slightly crazy: *I'd* ***go bonkers*** *if I had to stay at home with the kids all day.*

bon·net /ˈbɑnɪt/ *n.* [C] a hat that ties under the chin, worn by babies and by women in the past

bo·nus /ˈboʊnəs/ *n.* [C] **1** money added to someone's pay, especially as a reward for good work: *a Christmas bonus* | *a $2,000 bonus*

THESAURUS pay, income, salary, wages, earnings, remuneration → PAY[2]

2 something good that you did not expect in a situation: *The fact that our house is so close to the school is a bonus.* [ORIGIN: 1700—1800 Latin "good"]

bon·y /ˈboʊni/ *adj.* **1** very thin: *a bony hand* **2** full of bones: *bony fish*

boo[1] /bu/ *v.* [I,T] to shout "boo" to show that you do not like a person, performance, etc.

boo[2] *n.* (plural **boos**) [C] a noise made by people who do not like a person, performance, etc.

boo[3] *interjection* a word you shout suddenly to someone to try to frighten him/her as a joke

boob /bub/ *n.* [C] (slang) a woman's breast

ˈboo-boo *n.* [C] a silly mistake

ˈboob tube *n.* **the boob tube** (disapproving) television

ˈbooby prize *n.* [C] a prize given as a joke to the person who is last in a competition

ˈbooby trap *n.* [C] a hidden bomb that explodes when you touch something else that is connected to it —**booby-trapped** *adj.*

boog·ie man /ˈbʊgi ˌmæn/ *n.* [C] a BOGEYMAN

book[1] /bʊk/ *n.* [C] **1** ENG. LANG. ARTS a set of printed pages held together in a cover so that you can read them: *I'm* ***reading*** *a good* ***book***. | *a* ***book by*** *William Faulkner* | *a* ***book about*** *photography* | *She* ***wrote*** *a* ***book*** *of short stories which was published last year.*

THESAURUS

Types of books
nonfiction – books which describe real things or events
fiction – books which describe imaginary events
literature – fiction that people think is important
reference book – a book such as a dictionary or encyclopedia that you look at to find specific information
textbook – a book that is used in the classroom
hardcover/hardback – a book which has a hard stiff cover
paperback – a book which has a soft cover
novel – a book about imaginary events
science fiction – a book about imaginary events in the future or space travel
biography – a book about a real person's life, written by another person
autobiography – a book about someone's life, written by that person himself or herself

2 a set of sheets of paper held together in a cover so that you can write on them: *an* ***address book*** **3** a set of things such as stamps, tickets, etc. held together inside a paper cover: *a* ***book of*** *matches* **4** **books** [plural] ECONOMICS written records of the financial accounts of a business **5** **by the book** exactly according to rules or instructions: *They* ***do*** *everything* ***strictly by the book***. [ORIGIN: Old English *boc*] → **throw the book at sb** *at* THROW[1]

book[2] *v.* **1** [T] to arrange for someone such as a speaker or singer to perform on a particular date: *They have a speaker booked for next Tuesday.* **2** [I,T] to arrange to stay at a hotel, fly on an airplane, etc. at a particular time in the future: *I've* ***booked a room*** *for us at the Hilton.* | *The flight is* ***fully booked*** (=has no seats left). **3** [T] to put someone's name officially in police records, with the charge made against him/her: *Ramey was booked on suspicion of murder.*

book·case /ˈbʊk-keɪs/ *n.* [C] a piece of furniture with shelves to hold books

book·end /ˈbʊkɛnd/ *n.* [C] one of a pair of objects that you put at each end of a row of books to prevent them from falling

book·ie /ˈbʊki/ *n.* [C] (informal) someone whose job is to collect money that people BET on a race, sport, etc. and who pays them if they win

book·ing /ˈbʊkɪŋ/ *n.* [C] an arrangement in which a hotel, theater, etc. agrees to let you have a particular room, seat, etc. at a future time: *Cheaper prices are available on early bookings.*

book·keep·ing /ˈbʊkˌkipɪŋ/ *n.* [U] the job or activity of recording the financial accounts of an organization —**bookkeeper** *n.* [C]

book·let /ˈbʊklɪt/ *n.* [C] a very short book that contains information: *a booklet on AIDS*

book·mark /ˈbʊkmɑrk/ *n.* [C] **1** a piece of paper that you put in a book to show you the last page you have read **2** IT a way of saving the address of a page on the Internet so that you can find it easily

book·shelf /ˈbʊkʃɛlf/ *n.* (plural **bookshelves** /-ʃɛlvz/) [C] a shelf on a wall, or a piece of furniture with shelves, used for holding books

book·store /ˈbʊkstɔr/ *n.* [C] a store that sells books

book·worm /ˈbʊkwɚm/ *n.* [C] (informal, disapproving) someone who likes to read very much

B

boom¹ /bum/ *n.* [C] **1** ECONOMICS a sudden increase in business activity or the popularity of something (ANT) **slump**: *a boom in sales | the economic boom of the 1950s* **2** a loud deep sound that you can hear for several seconds after it begins: *the boom of guns in the distance*

boom² *v.* [I] **1** ECONOMICS if business or the economy is booming, it is very successful and growing quickly: *We're happy to report that business is booming this year.* **2** to make a loud deep sound —**booming** *adj.*: *a booming economy*

'boom box *n.* [C] (informal) a large radio and CD PLAYER, that you can carry with you

boo·mer·ang /'bumə,ræŋ/ *n.* [C] a curved stick that comes back to you when you throw it

'boom town *n.* [C] (informal) a city that suddenly becomes very successful because of new industry

boon /bun/ *n.* [C] something that is very useful and makes your life a lot easier: *The new sports complex will be a great* ***boon to*** *the city.*

boon·docks /'bundɑks/ *also* **boo·nies** /'buniz/ *n.* (informal) **the boondocks/boonies** [plural] a place that is a long way from any town

boor /bʊr/ *n.* [C] someone who behaves in an unacceptable way in social situations —**boorish** *adj.*

boost¹ /bust/ *n.* **1** [singular] something that helps someone be more successful and confident, or that helps something increase or improve: *Immigrants provide a* ***boost to*** *the U.S. economy. | a good publicity* ***boost for*** *his campaign | a* ***boost from*** *extra vitamins* **2 give sb a boost** to lift or push someone so s/he can get over or onto something high or tall

boost² *v.* [T] **1** to increase or improve something and make it more successful: *The new facility will help boost oil production. | The win* ***boosted*** *the team's* ***confidence.*** **2** to help someone get over or onto something high or tall by lifting or pushing him/her up

boost·er /'bustɚ/ *n.* [C] **1** a small quantity of a drug that increases the effect of one that was given before: *a measles booster shot* **2 confidence/morale/ego etc. booster** something that increases or improves someone's confidence, etc.: *Letters from home are a great* ***morale booster*** *for the soldiers.* **3** someone who gives a lot of support to a person, organization, or idea: *fund-raisers organized by the school's booster club* **4** a ROCKET that provides more power for a SPACECRAFT

boot¹ /but/ *n.* **1** [C] a type of shoe that covers your whole foot and the lower part of your leg: *hiking boots* → *see picture at* SHOE¹ **2 to boot** (spoken) used at the end of a list of remarks, to emphasize the last one: *Jack's tall, handsome, and rich to boot.* [ORIGIN: (1) 1300—1400 Old French *bote*]

boot² *v.* **1** [I,T] *also* **boot up** IT to make a computer ready to be used by putting in its instructions **2** [T] (informal) to force someone to leave a place, job, or organization: *Offenders are* ***booted out of/from*** *the dorms.*

'boot camp *n.* [C] a training camp for people who have joined the Army, Navy, or Marines

boot·ee /'buṭi/ *n.* [C] a sock that a baby wears instead of a shoe

booth /buθ/ *n.* [C] **1** a small, partly enclosed place where one person can do something privately: *a phone booth | a voting booth* **2** a partly enclosed place in a restaurant, with a table between two long seats **3** a place at a market or FAIR, where you can buy things, play games, or find information

boot·leg /'butˀlɛg/ *adj.* bootleg products are made and sold illegally —**bootlegging** *n.* [U] —**bootlegger** *n.* [C]

boot·straps /'butstræps/ *n.* **pull yourself up by your bootstraps** to get out of a difficult situation by your own effort

boo·ty /'buṭi/ *n.* [U] (literary) valuable things taken or won by the winners in a war, competition, etc.

booze¹ /buz/ *n.* [U] (informal) alcoholic drinks

booze² *v.* [I] (informal) to drink a lot of alcohol —**boozer** *n.* [C]

bop¹ /bɑp/ *v.* (**bopped**, **bopping**) [I] to hit someone gently

bop² *n.* **1** [C] a gentle hit **2** [U] BEBOP

bor·der¹ /'bɔrdɚ/ *n.* [C] **1** the official line that separates two countries, states, or areas: *the* ***border between*** *the U.S. and Mexico | The gang escaped* ***across the border.*** *| Mexico's* ***border with*** *Guatemala*

> THESAURUS **edge, boundary, perimeter, rim, margin** → EDGE¹

2 a band along the edge of something such as a picture or piece of material: *a skirt with a red border* [ORIGIN: 1300—1400 Old French *bordure*, from *border* "to border," from *bort* "border"]

border² *v.* [T] **1** to share a border with another country: *Spain borders Portugal.* **2** to form a line around the edge of something: *willow trees bordering the river*

border on sth *phr. v.* to be very close to reaching an extreme feeling or quality: *She stared at him with a fear bordering on terror.*

bor·der·line¹ /'bɔrdɚ,laɪn/ *adj.* very close to being unacceptable: *His grades are borderline.*

borderline² *n.* **1** [singular] the point at which one quality, condition, etc. ends and another begins: *The stories are on the borderline between romance and pornography.* **2** [C] a border between two countries

bore¹ /bɔr/ *v.* the past tense of BEAR

bore² *v.* **1** [T] to make someone feel bored

classes bored me. **2** [I,T] to make a deep round hole in a hard surface: *To build the tunnel, they had to* ***bore through*** *solid rock.*

> THESAURUS **pierce, make a hole in sth, prick, punch, puncture, drill** → PIERCE

3 [I] if someone's eyes bore into you or through you, s/he looks at you in a way that makes you feel nervous or afraid

bore[3] *n.* **1** [C] someone who talks too much about the same things: *Ralph is such a bore!* **2** [singular] something you have to do but do not like: *Ironing is a real bore.*

bored /bɔrd/ *adj.* tired and impatient because you do not think something is interesting, or because you have nothing to do: *I ignored him, hoping he'd* ***get bored*** *and leave.* | *I was* ***bored with*** *school.* | *I'm so bored!* ▸ Don't say "I'm so boring." ◂

bore·dom /ˈbɔrdəm/ *n.* [U] the feeling you have when you are bored

bor·ing /ˈbɔrɪŋ/ *adj.* not interesting in any way: *a boring book*

> THESAURUS
>
> **dull** – not interesting or exciting: *a dull lecture*
> **tedious** – boring, and continuing for a long time: *Removing the wallpaper was a long, tedious task.*
> **not (very/that/all that) interesting**: *The book wasn't all that interesting.*
> **humdrum** – boring, ordinary, and having very little variety: *a humdrum job*
> **monotonous** – boring and always the same: *Every song on the album is monotonous.*
> **insipid** (formal) – not interesting, exciting, or attractive: *the movie's insipid story* → INTERESTING

born /bɔrn/ *adj.* **1 be born** when a person or animal is born, it comes out of its mother's body or out of an egg: *We saw a lamb being born.* | *I was* ***born in*** *the South.* | *Lincoln was* ***born on*** *February 12.* **2 be born to do/be sth** to be very good at doing a particular job, activity, etc.: *Mantle was born to play baseball.* **3 born leader/teacher etc.** someone who has a natural ability to lead, teach, etc. **4** something that is born starts to exist: *Unions were* ***born out of*** (=started because of) *a need for better working conditions.* [ORIGIN: Old English *boren*, past participle of *beran*]

ˌborn-again ˈChristian *n.* [C] someone who has become an EVANGELICAL Christian after having an important religious experience

borne /bɔrn/ *v.* the past participle of BEAR

bor·ough /ˈbɚoʊ, ˈbʌroʊ/ *n.* [C] a town or part of a large city, that is responsible for managing its wn schools, hospitals, roads, etc. [ORIGIN: Old nglish *burg* "castle, town defended by a wall"]

·row /ˈbɑroʊ, ˈbɔroʊ/ *v.* [I,T] **1** to use some- that belongs to someone else and give it back n/her later → LEND: *Can I borrow your bike?* | *e* ***borrowed*** *money* ***from*** *his father to start a* s. | *They* ***borrowed heavily*** (=borrowed a lot of money) *to cover their losses.* **2** to take or copy ideas or words: *English has* ***borrowed*** *many words* ***from*** *French.* [ORIGIN: Old English *borgian*] —**borrower** *n.* [C]

bor·row·ing /ˈbɑroʊɪŋ, ˈbɔ-/ *n.* **1** [U] ECONOMICS the activity of borrowing money, or the total amount of money that is borrowed → LENDING: *When interest rates are low, borrowing is cheap.* | ***Government/public borrowing*** *has doubled in the last ten years.* | *Federal Reserve figures showed* ***consumer borrowing*** *is slowing down.* **2 borrowings** [plural] ECONOMICS the total amount of money that a person, company, or organization has borrowed, usually from a bank

bos·om /ˈbʊzəm/ *n.* **1** [C] (written) a woman's chest **2 bosom buddy** (informal) a very close friend

boss[1] /bɔs/ *n.* **1** [C] the person who employs you or who is in charge of your work: *The boss let us leave early today.*

> THESAURUS
>
> **manager** – the person in charge of a store, restaurant, or bank, or of a group of people who work for a company: *She wasn't satisfied with the service, and asked to speak to the manager.*
> **head/chief** – the person in charge of an organization: *the head of the FBI's New York office*
> **principal** – the person in charge of a school: *I had to go to the principal's office.*
> **president** – the person in charge of a business, bank, club, college, etc.: *the president of Brown University*
> **CEO** – the person who has the most authority in a large company: *Randall Stephenson became CEO of AT&T in 2007.*
> **supervisor** – someone who is in charge of a person or activity: *I reported the problem to my supervisor.*
> **foreman/forewoman** – the person in charge of a group of workers, for example in a factory: *The foreman told the workers to go back to their machines.*

2 [singular, U] the person who is the strongest in a relationship, who controls a situation, etc.: *You have to* ***let*** *the dog* ***know who's boss*** (=show that you are in control).

boss[2] *also* **boss around** *v.* [T] to tell people to do things, give them orders, etc., especially when you have no authority to do it: *She's always bossing her brother around.*

boss·y /ˈbɔsi/ *adj.* always telling other people what to do, in a way that is annoying: *her bossy older sister*

bot·a·ny /ˈbɑtˀn-i/ *n.* [U] BIOLOGY the scientific study of plants —**botanist** *n.* [C] —**botanical** /bəˈtænɪkəl/ *adj.*: *botanical gardens*

botch /bɑtʃ/ *also* **botch up** *v.* [T] (informal) to do something badly because you were careless or did not have the skill to do it well: *The police botched the investigation.*

both /boʊθ/ *quantifier, pron.* **1** used in order to talk about two people or things together: *They both have good jobs.* | *Hold it in both hands.* | ***Both of** my grandfathers are farmers.* **2 both ... and ...** used in order to emphasize that something is true of two people, things, situations, etc.: *Dan plays both football and basketball.* **3 have it both ways** (disapproving) used when someone wants the advantages from two situations that cannot exist together

GRAMMAR
both, both of
Do not say "The both men were caught." Say *Both men were caught, Both of the men were caught*, or *Both the men were caught.*

both·er[1] /ˈbɑðɚ/ *v.* **1** [T] to annoy someone, especially by interrupting what s/he is doing: *Don't bother your dad; he's working.*

THESAURUS **annoy, irritate, get on sb's nerves, infuriate, vex, irk** → ANNOY

2 [T] to make someone feel slightly worried, upset, or frightened: *Being in a crowd really bothers me.* | *It **bothered** her **that** he'd forgotten her birthday.* **3** [I,T] to make the effort to do something: *He hadn't bothered unpacking.* | *I'll never get the job, so **why bother** applying?* | *Only 58% of Americans even **bothered to** vote.* **4 sorry to bother you** (spoken) said in order to politely interrupt what someone is doing: *Sorry to bother you, but I have a question.* **5** [T] if a part of your body bothers you, it is slightly painful

bother[2] *n.* [U] someone or something that slightly annoys or upsets you: *"Thanks for your help." "That's okay; **it's no bother** (=used in order to say you were happy to help)."* —**bothersome** *adj.*

bot·tle[1] /ˈbɑt̬l/ *n.* [C] **1** a container with a narrow top, for keeping liquids in, usually made of glass or plastic: *a wine bottle* | *a baby's bottle* **2** the amount of liquid that a bottle contains: *We drank the entire bottle.* **3 hit the bottle** to start drinking a lot of alcohol regularly [ORIGIN: 1300—1400 Old French *bouteille*, from Late Latin *buttis* "wooden container for liquid"]

bottle[2] *v.* [T] to put a liquid into a bottle after you have made it: *wine bottled in California*
bottle sth ↔ **up** *phr. v.* to not allow yourself to show strong feelings or emotions: *He keeps his rage and frustration bottled up.*

bot·tled /ˈbɑt̬ld/ *adj.* **bottled water/beer etc.** water, beer, etc. that is sold in a bottle

bot·tle·neck /ˈbɑt̬lˌnɛk/ *n.* [C] **1** a place in a road where the traffic cannot pass easily, so that cars are delayed **2** a delay in part of a process that makes the whole process take longer: *Removing the bottleneck in the flow of materials has increased production significantly.*

bot·tom[1] /ˈbɑt̬əm/ *n.* [C] **1** the lowest part of something (ANT) **top**: *the **bottom of** the hill* | *The fruit **at the bottom of** the basket was spoiled.* **2** the flat surface on the lowest side of an object: *What's **on the bottom of** your shoe?* **3 the bottom** the lowest position in an organization or company, or on a list, etc. (ANT) **top**: *He started **at the bottom**, and now he manages the store.* | *Tony is **at the bottom of** the class in reading.* **4** (informal) a word meaning the part of your body that you sit on, used especially when talking to children **5** the ground under an ocean, river, etc., or the flat land in a valley: *The **bottom of** the river is rocky.* | *a ship **on/at the bottom of** the bay* **6** *also* **bottoms** the part of a set of clothes that you wear on the lower part of your body: *pajama bottoms* **7 get to the bottom of sth** (informal) to find the cause of a problem or situation: *We will get to the bottom of this and find out who was responsible.* [ORIGIN: Old English *botm*] → ROCK BOTTOM

bottom[2] *adj.* in the lowest place or position: *the bottom drawer*

bottom[3] *v.*
bottom out *phr. v.* if a situation, price, etc. bottoms out, it stops getting worse or lower, usually before it starts improving again: *The recession seems to have bottomed out.*

bot·tom·less /ˈbɑt̬əmlɪs/ *adj.* **1** extremely deep **2** seeming to have no end: *a bottomless supply of money*

ˌbottom ˈline *n.* **the bottom line a)** the main fact about a situation, or the most important thing to consider: ***The bottom line is** that we have to win this game.* **b)** ECONOMICS the profit or the amount of money that a business makes or loses

bot·u·lism /ˈbɑtʃəˌlɪzəm/ *n.* [U] BIOLOGY serious food poisoning caused by BACTERIA in preserved meat and vegetables

bough /baʊ/ *n.* [C] (literary) a main branch on a tree

bought /bɔt/ *v.* the past tense and past participle of BUY

boul·der /ˈboʊldɚ/ *n.* [C] a large stone or piece of rock

bou·le·vard /ˈbʊləvɑrd, ˈbu-/ *n.* [C] a wide road in a town or city

bounce[1] /baʊns/ *v.* **1** [I,T] if a ball or other object bounces, or you bounce it, it hits a surface and then immediately moves away from it: *The ball **bounced off** the rim.* | *In basketball, you have to bounce the ball while you run.* **2** [I] to move up and down, especially because you are walking or jumping on a surface that is made of rubber, has springs, etc.: *Stop **bouncing on** the bed!* → *see picture at* JUMP[1] **3** [I,T] ECONOMICS if a check bounces, or a bank bounces a check, the bank will not pay any money because there is not enoug money in the account of the person who wr it **4** [I] to walk quickly and with a lot of energy: *T kids came bouncing down the stairs.* **5** [I,T] IT email that you send bounces or is bounced returned to you and the other person do receive it **6 bounce ideas off sb** to ask s for his/her opinion about an idea, plan, etc you decide something [ORIGIN: 1500—1600 *bounce* "to hit" (13—19 centuries)]

bounce around (sth) *phr. v.* to move quickly from one place to another: *After college, I bounced around Europe for a year.* | *I bounced around between jobs quite a bit before ending up here.*

bounce back *phr. v.* to feel better quickly, or to become successful again after having a lot of problems: *Experts expect the economy to bounce back.*

bounce[2] *n.* **1** [C] an act of bouncing: *Catch the ball on the first bounce.* **2** [U] the ability to bounce

bounc·er /ˈbaʊnsɚ/ *n.* [C] someone whose job is to make people who behave badly leave a club, BAR, etc.

bounc·ing /ˈbaʊnsɪŋ/ *adj.* healthy and active – used especially about babies: *a bouncing baby boy*

bounc·y /ˈbaʊnsi/ *adj.* **1** able to bounce or be bounced easily: *a bouncy ball* **2** happy and full of energy

bound[1] /baʊnd/ *v.* the past tense and past participle of BIND

bound[2] *adj.* **1 be bound to do sth** to be certain to do something: *People are bound to spell your name wrong.* **2** having a legal or moral duty to do something: *The company is **bound by** law to provide safety equipment.* | *He felt **duty bound** to help his parents.* **3 fog-bound/wheelchair-bound/tradition-bound etc.** controlled or limited by something, so that you cannot do what you want: *a fog-bound airport* **4** intending to go in a particular direction or to a particular place: *a plane **bound for** Peru* | *homeward bound* **5 bound and determined** determined to do or achieve something, even if it is difficult: *Klein is bound and determined to win at least five races this year.*

bound[3] *v.* **1 be bounded by sth** if a place is bounded by something such as a wall, river, road, etc., it has the wall, etc. at its edge: *a valley bounded by high mountains* **2** [I] to move quickly and with a lot of energy: *George came **bounding down** the stairs.*

bound[4] *n.* **1 bounds** [plural] legal or social limits or rules: *His imagination **knows no bounds*** (=has no limits). | *The police acted **within/beyond the bounds of** the law* (=they acted legally or illegally). **2 out of bounds a)** if a subject is out of bounds, you are not allowed to talk about it: *Questions about his personal life will be out of bounds.* **b)** if a place is out of bounds, you are not allowed to go there **3 in bounds/out of bounds** inside or outside the legal playing area in some sports **4** [C] a long or high jump made with a lot of energy

bound·a·ry /ˈbaʊndəri, -dri/ *n.* (plural **boundaries**) [C] **1** the line that marks the edge of a surface, space, or area of land inside a country: *The Mississippi forms a natural **boundary between** Tennessee and Arkansas.*

THESAURUS edge, border, perimeter, rim, margin, hem, curb → EDGE[1]

2 the limit of what is acceptable or thought to be possible: *the **boundaries of** human knowledge*

bound·less /ˈbaʊndlɪs/ *adj.* without any limits or end: *boundless optimism*

boun·ty /ˈbaʊnti/ *n.* (plural **bounties**) **1** [C] money that is given as a reward for catching a criminal **2** [U] (literary) a generous amount of something, especially food —**bountiful** *adj.*: *a bountiful harvest*

bouquet

a bouquet of flowers

bou·quet /boʊˈkeɪ, bu-/ *n.* **1** [C] a group of flowers given to someone as a present or carried at a formal occasion **2** [C,U] the smell of a wine: *a rich bouquet* [ORIGIN: 1700—1800 French, Old North French *bosquet* "plants growing thickly together," from Old French *bosc* "forest"]

bour·bon /ˈbɚbən/ *n.* [U] a type of American WHISKEY made from corn [ORIGIN: 1800—1900 *Bourbon* county in Kentucky]

bour·geois /bʊrˈʒwɑ, ˈbʊrʒwɑ/ *adj.* (disapproving) too interested in having a lot of possessions and a high position in society [ORIGIN: 1500—1600 French "person who lives in a town," from Old French *borjois*, from *borc* "town"]

bour·geoi·sie /ˌbʊrʒwɑˈzi/ *n.* **the bourgeoisie** the MIDDLE CLASS

'bout /baʊt/ a short form of "about", used in writing to show how people sound when they speak

bout /baʊt/ *n.* [C] **1** a short period of time during which you do something a lot or suffer from a particular illness: *a drinking bout* | *a **bout of** the flu* **2** a BOXING or WRESTLING competition

bou·tique /buˈtik/ *n.* [C] a small store that sells very fashionable clothes or decorations

bo·vine /ˈboʊvaɪn/ *adj.* BIOLOGY relating to cows, or like a cow [ORIGIN: 1800—1900 Late Latin *bovinus*, from Latin *bos* "ox, cow"]

bow

bow[1] /baʊ/ *v.* [I,T] to bend your head or the top part of your body forward, as a sign of respect or as a way of thanking an AUDIENCE after you perform:

He bowed, then began to play. | *David* ***bowed*** *his* ***head*** *in prayer.*

bow down *phr. v.* to bend forward from your waist, especially when you are already kneeling, in order to pray: *Old women bowed down before the statue of Mary.*

B

bow out *phr. v.* to decide not to take part in something any longer: *Two more Republicans have* ***bowed out of*** *the race.*

bow to sb/sth *phr. v.* to finally agree to do something that other people want you to do, even though you do not want to: *Congress may bow to public pressure and reduce the gas tax.*

bow² /boʊ/ *n.* [C] **1** a knot of cloth or string with a curved part on each side: *a girl with a red bow in her hair* **2** a tool used for shooting ARROWs, made of a piece of wood held in a curve by a tight string **3** a long thin piece of wood with hair stretched tightly from one end to the other, used for playing an instrument such as a VIOLIN

bow³ /baʊ/ *n.* [C] **1** the act of bending the top part of your body forward, as a sign of respect or to thank an AUDIENCE: *The actors* ***took a bow*** (=bowed) *and the curtain came down.* **2** the front part of a ship

bow⁴ /boʊ/ *v.* [I] to bend or curve

bowd·ler·ize /ˈboʊdləˌraɪz, ˈbaʊ-/ *v.* [T] ENG. LANG. ARTS to remove the parts of a book, play, etc. that you think are offensive —**bowdlerized** *adj.*: *a bowdlerized version of the play* —**bowdlerization** /ˌboʊdlərəˈzeɪʃən, ˌbaʊ-/ *n.* [U]

bow·el /ˈbaʊəl/ *n.* [C usually plural] BIOLOGY the part of the body below the stomach, where food is made into solid waste material [ORIGIN: 1200—1300 Old French *boel*, from Medieval Latin *botellus*, from Latin *botulus* "sausage"]

bowl¹ /boʊl/ *n.* [C] **1** a wide round container that is open at the top, used for holding liquids, food, etc.: *Mix the eggs and butter in a large bowl.* | *a soup bowl* **2** *also* **bowlful** the amount that a bowl will hold: *a* ***bowlful of*** *rice* **3** a part of an object that is shaped like a bowl: *a toilet bowl* **4** *also* **Bowl** a special game played by two of the best football teams after the normal playing season: *the Rose Bowl* [ORIGIN: Old English *bolla*]

bowl² *v.* [I,T] to roll the ball in the game of bowling

bowl sb ↔ **over** *phr. v.* to surprise, please, or excite someone very much: *She was bowled over by her visit to the campus.*

bow-leg·ged /ˈboʊˌlɛgɪd, -ˌlɛgd/ *adj.* having legs that curve out at the knee

bowl·ing /ˈboʊlɪŋ/ *n.* [U] an indoor game in which you roll a heavy ball to try to knock down a group of objects shaped like bottles: *Let's* ***go bowling!***

ˈbowling ˌalley *n.* [C] a building where you can go bowling

bow tie /ˈboʊ taɪ/ *n.* [C] a short piece of cloth tied in the shape of a BOW, that a man wears around his neck

box¹ /bɑks/ *n.* [C] **1** a container for putting things in, especially one with four stiff straight sides: *a cardboard box* | *I put all her things* ***in a box.*** **2** the amount that a box can hold: *a* ***box of*** *candy* **3** an area of seats in a theater, sports STADIUM, etc. that is separate from where other people are sitting ➔ *see picture at* THEATER **4** the area in a court of law where the JURY sit **5** a small area on an official form for people to write information in: *Write your name in the box at the top.* **6** a P.O. BOX [ORIGIN: 900—1000 Latin *buxus*, from Greek *pyxis*, from *pyxos* type of tree, whose wood was used for making boxes]

box² *v.* **1** [I,T] to fight someone as a sport while wearing big leather GLOVES **2** [T] *also* **box up** to put things in a box or in boxes: *He boxed up his belongings and put his furniture in storage.*

box sb/sth ↔ **in** *phr. v.* to enclose someone or something in a small space where it is not possible to move freely: *A Honda was parked behind me, boxing me in.*

box·car /ˈbɑksˌkɑr/ *n.* [C] a railroad car with high sides and a roof, that is used for carrying goods

box·er /ˈbɑksɚ/ *n.* [C] **1** someone who boxes, especially as a job: *a heavyweight boxer* **2** a dog with short light brown hair and a flat nose

ˈboxer ˌshorts *n.* [plural] loose underwear for men ➔ *see picture at* CLOTHES

box·ing /ˈbɑksɪŋ/ *n.* [U] the sport of fighting while wearing big leather GLOVES

ˈbox ˌoffice *n.* [C] a place in a theater, concert hall, etc. where tickets are sold ➔ THEATER

ˈbox spring *n.* [C] a base containing metal springs, that you put under a MATTRESS to make a bed

boy¹ /bɔɪ/ *n.* [C] **1** a male child or young man: *a club for both boys and girls* | *Some* ***little boys*** (=young boys) *were playing with a ball.* | *One of the* ***big boys*** (=older boys) *was picking on Sam.*

THESAURUS man, guy, gentleman, fellow, youth, male ➔ MAN¹

2 someone's son, especially a young one: *How old is your* ***little boy?*** **3 paper/delivery etc. boy** a young man who does a particular job **4 city/local etc. boy** (informal) a man of any age from a particular place or social group **5 the boys** (informal) a group of men who are friends and often go out together: *playing cards with the boys* **6** (spoken) used when speaking to a male animal, such as a horse or a dog: *Good boy, Patches!*

boy² *also* **oh ˈboy** *interjection* said in order to emphasize a statement: *Boy, is he mad!*

boy·cott /ˈbɔɪkɑt/ *v.* [T] to refuse to buy some thing, use something, or take part in something as way of protesting: *We boycott all products tested animals.* [ORIGIN: 1800—1900 Charles *Boy* (1832-97), English official in Ireland refused to reduce rents, so the local p refused to do any business with him] —**boycott** *n.* [C]

THESAURUS protest, march, demonstrate, riot, hold/stage a sit-in, go on a hunger strike → PROTEST²

boy·friend /'bɔɪfrɛnd/ *n.* [C] a boy or man with whom you have a romantic relationship: *Have you met Leah's boyfriend?*

boy·hood /'bɔɪhʊd/ *n.* [U] (literary) the time in a man's life when he is very young

boy·ish /'bɔɪ-ɪʃ/ *adj.* looking or behaving like a boy: *his boyish laughter*

Boyle's law /'bɔɪlz ˌlɔ/ *n.* PHYSICS a scientific rule stating that the amount of space a gas fills at a particular temperature decreases (=goes down) as pressure increases and increases as pressure decreases

'Boy Scout *n.* **1 the Boy Scouts** an organization for boys, that teaches them practical skills and helps develop their character → GIRL SCOUTS **2** [C] a member of the Boy Scouts

bo·zo /'boʊzoʊ/ *n.* (plural **bozos**) [C] (informal) someone who you think is stupid or silly

bps, BPS /ˌbi pi 'ɛs/ IT **bits per second** a measurement of how fast a computer or MODEM can send or receive information

bra /brɑ/ *n.* [C] a piece of underwear that a woman wears to support her breasts → *see picture at* CLOTHES

brace¹ /breɪs/ *v.* [T] **1** to prepare for something unpleasant that is going to happen: *Hospitals are **bracing themselves for** a flu epidemic this winter.* **2** to prevent something from falling or moving by supporting it: *His feet were braced against the wall.*

brace² *n.* **1 braces** [plural] a connected set of wires that people, especially children, wear on their teeth to make them straight **2** [C] something used or worn in order to support something: *a neck brace*

brace·let /'breɪslɪt/ *n.* [C] a band or chain that you wear around your wrist or arm as a decoration → *see picture at* JEWELRY

brac·ing /'breɪsɪŋ/ *adj.* **1** bracing air or weather is cold and makes you feel very awake and healthy **2** making you feel excited and interested: *Meeting such a powerful man was a bracing experience.*

brack·et /'brækɪt/ *n.* [C] **1 income/tax/age etc. bracket** ECONOMICS an income, tax, etc. that is inside a particular range: *the highest tax bracket* **2** ENG. LANG. ARTS one of the pair of marks [ ] put around extra information: *All grammar information is given **in brackets**.* **3** a piece of metal, wood, or plastic put in or on a wall to support something such as a shelf

brack·ish /'brækɪʃ/ *adj.* brackish water is not [...] because it is slightly salty

brag /bræg/ *v.* (**bragged**, **bragging**) [I,T] (disapproving) to talk too proudly about what you have done, what you own, etc.: *Todd was **bragging about** his grades.*

brag·gart /'brægɚt/ *n.* [C] someone who brags

braid¹ /breɪd/ *n.* [C,U] a length of hair or a narrow band of material that has been separated into three parts and then woven together: *a girl with her hair **in braids*** → *see picture on page 462* —**braided** *adj.*

braid² *v.* [T] to twist together three pieces of hair or cloth to form one length

braille /breɪl/ *n.* [U] a form of printing that makes raised round marks on the paper, that blind people can read by touching [ORIGIN: 1800—1900 Louis *Braille*]

brain

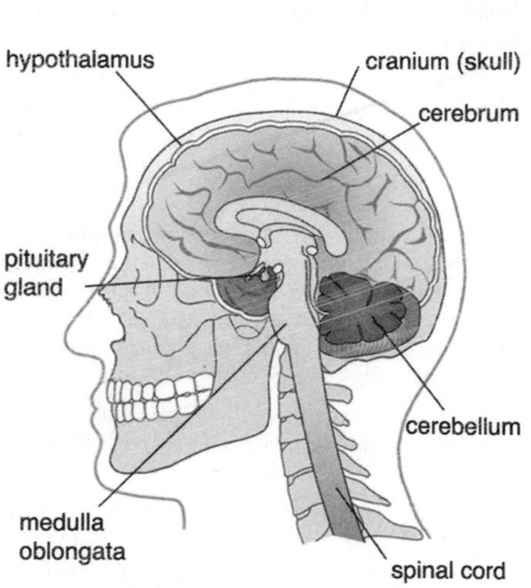

brain¹ /breɪn/ *n.* **1** [C,U] BIOLOGY the organ inside your head that controls how you think, feel, and move: *brain damage* | *the part of the brain that controls movement* **2** [C usually plural, U] the ability to think clearly and learn quickly: *The kid's definitely got brains.* **3** [C] (informal) someone who is very intelligent: *Some of the best brains in the country are here tonight.* **4 be the brains behind sth** to be the person who thought of and developed a particular plan, system, organization, etc. → NO-BRAINER, **pick sb's brain(s)** *at* PICK¹, **rack your brain(s)** *at* RACK²

brain² *v.* [T] (old-fashioned) to hit someone on the head very hard

brain·child /'breɪntʃaɪld/ *n.* [singular] (informal) an idea, organization, etc. that someone has thought of without any help from anyone else: *The project was the **brainchild of** photographer Rick Smolan.*

brain·less /'breɪnlɪs/ *adj.* (informal) silly and stupid: *a brainless movie*

brain·pow·er /'breɪnˌpaʊɚ/ *n.* [U] intelligence,

or the ability to think: *The space industry relies on scientific brainpower.*

'brain stem *n.* [C] BIOLOGY the lower part of your brain that connects your SPINAL CORD to your CEREBELLUM (=bottom part of the brain)

B

brain·storm¹ /'breɪnstɔrm/ *v.* [I,T] to think of many different ways of doing something, developing ideas, or solving a problem, especially in a group: *The students* ***brainstormed about*** *getting more people to participate.* —**brainstorming** *n.* [U]

brainstorm² *n.* [singular] (informal) a sudden intelligent idea

brain·wash /'breɪnwɑʃ, -wɔʃ/ *v.* [T] to make someone believe something that is not true, by using force, confusing him/her, or continuously repeating it over a long period of time: *Two former members of the Church claim they were brainwashed into joining.* —**brainwashing** *n.* [U]

brain·y /'breɪni/ *adj.* (informal) able to think clearly and learn quickly: *a brainy kid*

braise /breɪz/ *v.* [T] to cook meat or vegetables slowly in a small amount of liquid in a closed container

brake¹ /breɪk/ *n.* [C] **1** a piece of equipment that makes a vehicle go more slowly or stop: *Maria* ***hit the brakes/slammed on the brakes*** (=made the car stop quickly). **2 put the brakes on sth** to stop something that is happening: *efforts to put the brakes on rising prices*

brake² *v.* [I] to make a vehicle go more slowly or stop by using its brake: *Miguel braked suddenly.* ➔ DRIVE¹

bran /bræn/ *n.* [U] the crushed outer skin of wheat or a similar grain

branch¹ /bræntʃ/ *n.* [C] **1** part of a tree that grows out from the TRUNK (=main stem) and has leaves, fruit, or smaller branches growing from it ➔ see picture at PLANT¹ **2** a local business, store, etc. that is part of a larger business, etc.: *The bank has branches all over the country.* **3** one part of a large subject of study or knowledge: *a branch of medicine* **4** a part of a government or other organization that deals with one particular part of its work: *the executive branch of the U.S. government* **5** a smaller, less important part of a river, road, etc. that leads away from the larger, more important part of it: *a branch of the Mississippi River* **6** a group of members of a family who all have the same ANCESTORS [ORIGIN: 1200-1300 Old French *branche*, from Late Latin *branca* "animal's foot"]

branch² *also* **branch off** *v.* [I] to divide into two or more smaller, narrower, or less important parts: *Turn off where the road branches to the right.*

branch out *phr. v.* to do something new in addition to what you usually do: *The bookstore has* ***branched out into*** *renting movies.*

brand¹ /brænd/ *n.* [C] **1** a type of product made by a particular company: *different* ***brands of*** *soap*

THESAURUS type, kind, sort, category, make, model, variety ➔ TYPE¹

2 brand of humor/politics/religion etc. a particular type of humor, politics, etc.: *his conservative brand of politics* **3** a mark burned into an animal's skin that shows whom it belongs to [ORIGIN: Old English "torch, sword"]

brand² *v.* [T] **1** to burn a mark on an animal, in order to show whom it belongs to **2** to call someone a very bad type of person, often unfairly: *Republicans have been* ***branded as*** *anti-environmentalists.*

THESAURUS call, describe, characterize, label, portray ➔ CALL¹

brand·ing /'brændɪŋ/ *n.* [U] ECONOMICS a practice in which a company gives a product a name and uses it to make that name well known: *the global branding of Coca-Cola*

bran·dish /'brændɪʃ/ *v.* [T] to wave something around in a dangerous and threatening way: *He burst into the store brandishing a knife.* [ORIGIN: 1300-1400 Old French *brandir*, from *brant* "sword"]

'brand ,name *n.* [C] ECONOMICS the name a company gives to the goods it has produced: *names such as Jell-O and Coca-Cola*

,brand-'new *adj.* new and not used: *a brand-new car*

bran·dy /'brændi/ *n.* (plural **brandies**) strong alcoholic drink made from wine, or a glass of this drink [ORIGIN: 1600-1700 *brandewine* (1600-1700), from Dutch *brandewijn* "burnt wine, distilled wine"]

brash /bræʃ/ *adj.* (disapproving) behaving very confidently: *a brash young* [illegible]

brass /bræs/ *n.* **1** [U] a very hard metal that is a mixture of COPPER [illegible] **brass (section)** the people in [illegible] band who play musical instruments [illegible] TRUMPET or horn

bras·siere /brə'zɪr/ *n.* [C] [illegible]

,brass 'knuckles *n.* [plural] [illegible] worn over your KNUCKLES [illegible]

brass·y /'bræsi/ *adj.* [illegible] unpleasant **2** (disapproving) [illegible] talks loudly and beha[illegible] confidently

brat /bræt/ *n.* [C] [illegible] child: *Stop acting like* [illegible] **Army brat/military** [illegible] moves often [illegible] the Army, etc.

bra·va·do /brə[illegible] intended to [illegible] unnecessary

brave¹ /breɪ[illegible] difficult [illegible]

refused to do any business with him] —**boycott** *n.* [C]

THESAURUS **protest, march, demonstrate, riot, hold/stage a sit-in, go on a hunger strike** → PROTEST²

boy·friend /'bɔɪfrɛnd/ *n.* [C] a boy or man with whom you have a romantic relationship: *Have you met Leah's boyfriend?*

boy·hood /'bɔɪhʊd/ *n.* [U] (literary) the time in a man's life when he is very young

boy·ish /'bɔɪ-ɪʃ/ *adj.* looking or behaving like a boy: *his boyish laughter*

Boyle's law /'bɔɪlz ˌlɔ/ *n.* PHYSICS a scientific rule stating that the amount of space a gas fills at a particular temperature decreases (=goes down) as pressure increases and increases as pressure decreases

'Boy Scout *n.* **1 the Boy Scouts** an organization for boys, that teaches them practical skills and helps develop their character → GIRL SCOUTS **2** [C] a member of the Boy Scouts

bo·zo /'boʊzoʊ/ *n.* (plural **bozos**) [C] (informal) someone who you think is stupid or silly

bps, BPS /ˌbi pi 'ɛs/ IT **bits per second** a measurement of how fast a computer or MODEM can send or receive information

bra /brɑ/ *n.* [C] a piece of underwear that a woman wears to support her breasts → *see picture at* CLOTHES

brace¹ /breɪs/ *v.* [T] **1** to prepare for something unpleasant that is going to happen: *Hospitals are **bracing themselves for** a flu epidemic this winter.* **2** to prevent something from falling or moving by supporting it: *His feet were braced against the wall.*

brace² *n.* **1 braces** [plural] a connected set of wires that people, especially children, wear on their teeth to make them straight **2** [C] something used or worn in order to support something: *a neck brace*

brace·let /'breɪslɪt/ *n.* [C] a band or chain that you wear around your wrist or arm as a decoration → *see picture at* JEWELRY

brac·ing /'breɪsɪŋ/ *adj.* **1** bracing air or weather is cold and makes you feel very awake and healthy **2** making you feel excited and interested: *Meeting such a powerful man was a bracing experience.*

brack·et /'brækɪt/ *n.* [C] **1 income/tax/age etc. bracket** ECONOMICS an income, tax, etc. that is inside a particular range: *the highest tax bracket* **2** ENG. LANG. ARTS one of the pair of marks [ ] put around extra information: *All grammar information is given **in brackets**.* **3** a piece of metal, wood, or plastic put in or on a wall to support something such as a shelf

brack·ish /'brækɪʃ/ *adj.* brackish water is not pure because it is slightly salty

brag /bræg/ *v.* (**bragged, bragging**) [I,T] (disapproving) to talk too proudly about what you have done, what you own, etc.: *Todd was **bragging about** his grades.*

brag·gart /'brægɚt/ *n.* [C] someone who brags

braid¹ /breɪd/ *n.* [C,U] a length of hair or a narrow band of material that has been separated into three parts and then woven together: *a girl with her hair **in braids*** → *see picture on page 462* —**braided** *adj.*

braid² *v.* [T] to twist together three pieces of hair or cloth to form one length

braille /breɪl/ *n.* [U] a form of printing that makes raised round marks on the paper, that blind people can read by touching [ORIGIN: 1800—1900 Louis *Braille*]

brain

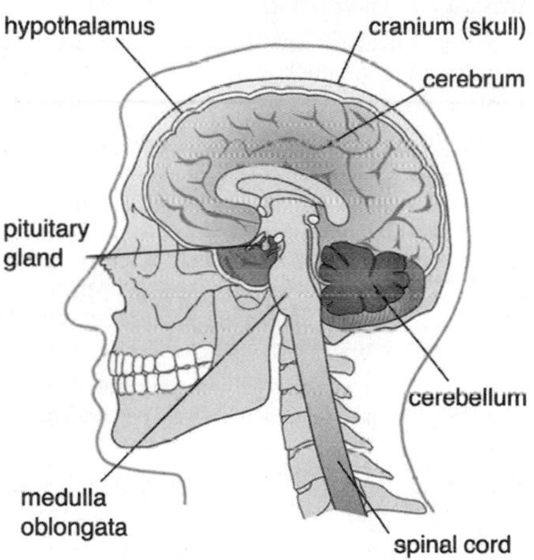

brain¹ /breɪn/ *n.* **1** [C,U] BIOLOGY the organ inside your head that controls how you think, feel, and move: *brain damage | the part of the brain that controls movement* **2** [C usually plural, U] the ability to think clearly and learn quickly: *The kid's definitely got brains.* **3** [C] (informal) someone who is very intelligent: *Some of the best brains in the country are here tonight.* **4 be the brains behind sth** to be the person who thought of and developed a particular plan, system, organization, etc. → NO-BRAINER, **pick sb's brain(s)** *at* PICK¹, **rack your brain(s)** *at* RACK²

brain² *v.* [T] (old-fashioned) to hit someone on the head very hard

brain·child /'breɪntʃaɪld/ *n.* [singular] (informal) an idea, organization, etc. that someone has thought of without any help from anyone else: *The project was the **brainchild of** photographer Rick Smolan.*

brain·less /'breɪnlɪs/ *adj.* (informal) silly and stupid: *a brainless movie*

brain·pow·er /'breɪnˌpaʊɚ/ *n.* [U] intelligence,

or the ability to think: *The space industry relies on scientific brainpower.*

'brain stem *n.* [C] BIOLOGY the lower part of your brain that connects your SPINAL CORD to your CEREBELLUM (=bottom part of the brain)

B

brain·storm¹ /ˈbreɪnstɔrm/ *v.* [I,T] to think of many different ways of doing something, developing ideas, or solving a problem, especially in a group: *The students **brainstormed about** getting more people to participate.* —**brainstorming** *n.* [U]

brainstorm² *n.* [singular] (informal) a sudden intelligent idea

brain·wash /ˈbreɪnwɑʃ, -wɔʃ/ *v.* [T] to make someone believe something that is not true, by using force, confusing him/her, or continuously repeating it over a long period of time: *Two former members of the Church claim they were brainwashed into joining.* —**brainwashing** *n.* [U]

brain·y /ˈbreɪni/ *adj.* (informal) able to think clearly and learn quickly: *a brainy kid*

braise /breɪz/ *v.* [T] to cook meat or vegetables slowly in a small amount of liquid in a closed container

brake¹ /breɪk/ *n.* [C] **1** a piece of equipment that makes a vehicle go more slowly or stop: *Maria **hit the brakes/slammed on the brakes*** (=made the car stop quickly). **2 put the brakes on sth** to stop something that is happening: *efforts to put the brakes on rising prices*

brake² *v.* [I] to make a vehicle go more slowly or stop by using its brake: *Miguel braked suddenly.* → DRIVE¹

bran /bræn/ *n.* [U] the crushed outer skin of wheat or a similar grain

branch¹ /bræntʃ/ *n.* [C] **1** part of a tree that grows out from the TRUNK (=main stem) and has leaves, fruit, or smaller branches growing from it → *see picture at* PLANT¹ **2** a local business, store, etc. that is part of a larger business, etc.: *The bank has branches all over the country.* **3** one part of a large subject of study or knowledge: *a branch of medicine* **4** a part of a government or other organization that deals with one particular part of its work: *the executive branch of the U.S. government* **5** a smaller, less important part of a river, road, etc. that leads away from the larger, more important part of it: *a branch of the Missouri River* **6** a group of members of a family who all have the same ANCESTORS [ORIGIN: 1200—1300 Old French *branche*, from Late Latin *branca* "animal's foot"]

branch² *also* **branch off** *v.* [I] to divide into two or more smaller, narrower, or less important parts: *Turn off where the road branches to the right.*

branch out *phr. v.* to do something new in addition to what you usually do: *The bookstore has **branched out into** renting movies.*

brand¹ /brænd/ *n.* [C] **1** a type of product made by a particular company: *different **brands of** soap*

THESAURUS type, kind, sort, category, make, model, variety → TYPE¹

2 brand of humor/politics/religion etc. a particular type of humor, politics, etc.: *his conservative brand of politics* **3** a mark burned into an animal's skin that shows whom it belongs to [ORIGIN: Old English "torch, sword"]

brand² *v.* [T] **1** to burn a mark on an animal, in order to show whom it belongs to **2** to call someone a very bad type of person, often unfairly: *Republicans have been **branded as** anti-environmentalists.*

THESAURUS call, describe, characterize, label, portray → CALL¹

brand·ing /ˈbrændɪŋ/ *n.* [U] ECONOMICS a practice in which a company gives a product a name and tries to make that name well known: *the global branding of Coca-Cola*

bran·dish /ˈbrændɪʃ/ *v.* [T] to wave something around in a dangerous and threatening way: *He burst into the store brandishing a knife.* [ORIGIN: 1300—1400 Old French *brandir*, from *brand* "sword"]

'brand ˌname *n.* [C] ECONOMICS the name a company gives to the goods it has produced: *brand names such as Jell-O and Coca-Cola*

ˌbrand-'new *adj.* new and not used: *a brand-new car*

bran·dy /ˈbrændi/ *n.* (plural **brandies**) [C,U] a strong alcoholic drink made from wine, or a glass of this drink [ORIGIN: 1600—1700 *brandywine* (1600—1700), from Dutch *brandewijn* "burnt wine, distilled wine"]

brash /bræʃ/ *adj.* (disapproving) behaving and talking very confidently: *a brash young man*

brass /bræs/ *n.* **1** [U] a very hard bright yellow metal that is a mixture of COPPER and ZINC **2 the brass (section)** the people in an ORCHESTRA or band who play musical instruments such as the TRUMPET or horn

bras·siere /brəˈzɪr/ *n.* [C] a BRA

ˌbrass 'knuckles *n.* [plural] a set of metal rings worn over your KNUCKLES, used as a weapon

brass·y /ˈbræsi/ *adj.* **1** sounding loud and unpleasant **2** (disapproving) a woman who is brassy talks loudly and behaves in a way that is too confident

brat /bræt/ *n.* [C] **1** (informal) a badly behaved child: *Stop acting like a **spoiled brat**.* **2 an Army/Air Force/military etc. brat** a child whose family moves often, because one or both parents work for the Army, etc.

bra·va·do /brəˈvɑdoʊ/ *n.* [U] behavior that is intended to show how brave you are, but is often unnecessary

brave¹ /breɪv/ *adj.* dealing with danger, pain, or difficult situations with courage (ANT) **cowardly**:

brave soldiers | *her brave fight against cancer* [ORIGIN: 1400—1500 French, Old Italian and Old Spanish *bravo* "brave, wild," from Latin *barbarus*] —**bravely** *adv.*

THESAURUS

courageous – someone who is courageous behaves very bravely: *an honest and courageous leader*
heroic – extremely brave or determined, and admired by many people: *the heroic work of the doctors*
valiant (formal) – very brave, especially in a difficult situation: *The firefighters made a valiant effort to rescue the people in the burning building.*
daring – willing to do dangerous things: *the daring young men who flew the first airplanes*
bold – confident and willing to take risks: *Rebecca was a bold woman, willing to say what she thought.*
fearless – not afraid of anything or anyone: *a fearless campaigner for human rights*
intrepid (formal) – willing to do dangerous things or go to dangerous places: *Lewis and Clark were the intrepid explorers who first crossed the country to the Pacific coast.*

brave² *v.* [T] to deal with a difficult, dangerous, or unpleasant situation: *15,000 people braved the hot sun to see Mandela.*

brave³ *n.* [C] a young fighting man from a Native American tribe

brav·er·y /ˈbreɪvəri/ *n.* [U] brave behavior (ANT) **cowardice**: *an act of great bravery*

THESAURUS **courage, guts, nerve, valor, mettle** ➔ COURAGE

bra·vo /ˈbrɑvoʊ, brɑˈvoʊ/ *interjection* said in order to show your approval when someone, especially a performer, has done well

brawl¹ /brɔl/ *n.* [C] a noisy fight, especially in a public place: *a drunken brawl*

THESAURUS **fight, free-for-all, scuffle, scrap** ➔ FIGHT²

brawl² *v.* [I] to fight in a noisy way, especially in a public place: *youths brawling in the street*

brawn /brɔn/ *n.* [U] physical strength: *She's the brain and he's the brawn behind the operation.* —**brawny** *adj.*: *brawny arms*

bray /breɪ/ *v.* [I] if a DONKEY brays, it makes a loud sound

bra·zen /ˈbreɪzən/ *adj.* showing that you do not feel ashamed about behavior that most people think is wrong or immoral: *a brazen lie* —**brazenly** *adv.*

breach /britʃ/ *n.* **1** [C,U] an act of breaking a law, rule, agreement, etc.: *You are **in breach of** your contract.* **2** [C] a serious disagreement between people, groups, or countries: *a **breach between** the allies over the issue of sanctions* **3** [C] a hole or broken place in a wall or a similar structure, especially one made during a military attack —**breach** *v.* [T]

bread /brɛd/ *n.* [U] **1** a common food made from flour, water, and YEAST: *We need **a loaf of bread**.* | ***a slice/piece of bread** with butter* | ***white/wheat/rye/French bread*** | *fresh-baked bread* **2 sb's bread and butter** (informal) the work that someone gets most of his/her income from: *Tourists are our bread and butter.* [ORIGIN: Old English]

bread·bas·ket /ˈbrɛdˌbæskɪt/ *n.* **1** [singular] (informal) the part of a country or other large area that provides most of the food: *The Midwest is **the breadbasket of** America.* **2** [C] a basket for holding or serving bread

bread·crumbs /ˈbrɛdkrʌmz/ *n.* [plural] very small pieces of bread used in cooking

bread·ed /ˈbrɛdɪd/ *adj.* covered in breadcrumbs, then cooked: *breaded veal*

breadth /brɛdθ, brɛtθ/ *n.* [U] **1** the distance from one side of something to the other, especially something very wide (SYN) **width**: *He could see the entire length and **breadth of** the canyon.* **2** a wide range or variety: *He had an enormous **breadth of** knowledge about the industry.* | *Older workers have a greater **breadth of** experience.*

bread·win·ner /ˈbrɛdˌwɪnɚ/ *n.* [C] the member of a family who earns the money to support the others

break¹ /breɪk/ *v.* (past tense **broke** /broʊk/, past participle **broken** /ˈbroʊkən/)
1 IN PIECES [I,T] if something breaks or someone breaks it, it separates into two or more pieces, especially because it has been hit or dropped: *Be careful or it'll break.* | ***I broke off** a handful of basil to put in the sauce.* | *They had to break the window to get into the house.*

THESAURUS

smash – used when a plate, glass, etc. breaks or is broken with a lot of force: *Angry crowds smashed windows downtown.*
shatter – used when a plate, glass, etc. breaks into a lot of small pieces: *The glass hit the floor, shattering everywhere.*

crack – used when a plate, glass, etc. is damaged so that there is a line between two parts of it: *One of the windows was cracked.*
tear – used about paper or cloth: *I tore the letter to pieces.*
snap – used about something that breaks into two pieces, making a loud noise: *The stick snapped in two.*
burst – used when a pipe with liquid inside it breaks: *Our pipes had burst in the freezing weather.*
pop – used when a bubble or balloon breaks: *The wind was so strong some of the balloons popped.*

2 BODY PART [T] if you break a part of your body, the bone splits into two or more pieces: *Sharon broke her leg skiing.*

THESAURUS **hurt, injure, wound, maim, bruise, sprain, twist, strain, pull, dislocate** → HURT[1]

3 END STH [I,T] to not continue, or to end something: *Annie finally broke the silence.* | *I don't smoke anymore, but it was hard to* ***break the habit.***
4 NOT WORK [I,T] if something such as a machine breaks, or you break it, it is damaged and does not work: *One of the kids poked something into the disk drive and broke it.* | *My camera broke.*
5 SURFACE/SKIN [T] to damage the surface of something so that it splits or has a hole in it: *Do not use this product if the seal has been broken.*
6 break free **a)** to escape from someone who is trying to hold you: *I broke free and ran.* **b)** to get out of a bad situation, or out of a situation that limits what you can do: *I desperately wanted to* ***break free from*** *my parents.*
7 RULES/LAWS [T] to disobey a law or rule: *Sometimes breaking the rules is the only way to get things done.*
8 PROMISE/AGREEMENT [T] to not do what you promised to do: *politicians who break their election promises*
9 break your neck (informal) to hurt yourself very badly: *Don't run; you'll slip and break your neck.*
10 break for lunch/coffee etc. to stop working in order to eat or drink something
11 break a record to do something faster or better than it has ever been done before: *After* ***breaking the world record,*** *she decided to retire from athletics.*
12 break sth to sb to tell someone about something bad that has happened: *Ellie called us to* ***break the news*** *personally.*
13 NEWS/EVENT [I] if news about an important event breaks, it becomes known by everyone after having been secret: *The next morning, the news broke that Monroe was dead.*
14 break even to neither make a profit nor lose money: *We broke even in our first year of business.*
15 break sb's heart to make someone very unhappy, by ending a relationship with him/her or doing something that upsets him/her
16 DAY [I] if day breaks, light begins to show in the sky as the Sun rises
17 VOICE [I] **a)** if a boy's voice breaks, it becomes lower as he gets older **b)** if someone's voice breaks, it does not sound smooth because s/he is feeling strong emotions
18 WAVE [I] if a wave breaks, it begins to look white on top because it is coming close to the shore [ORIGIN: Old English *brecan*] → **break the ice** *at* ICE[1]

break away *phr. v.*
1 to escape from someone who is holding you: *Nelson* ***broke away from*** *the policemen.*
2 to leave your family, a group, a political party, etc. and become separate from them: *The three Baltic States were the first to* ***break away from*** *the Soviet Union.*

break down *phr. v.*
1 if a large machine breaks down, it stops working: *A truck had broken down in the intersection.*
2 to fail or stop working in a successful way: *The talks broke down completely in June 2002.*
3 break sth ↔ **down** to change or remove something that prevents people from working together or having a good relationship: *attempts to break down prejudice*
4 break sth ↔ **down** to hit something, such as a door, so hard that it falls down
5 break (sth ↔) **down** CHEMISTRY if a substance breaks down, or something breaks it down, it changes as a result of a chemical process: *Bacteria break down the raw sewage.* | *The waste products* ***break down into*** *ammonia.*
6 to be unable to stop yourself from crying: *She broke down during the funeral.*
7 break sth ↔ **down** to separate something into smaller parts so that it is easier to do or understand: *Try to break the question down into two parts.*

break in *phr. v.*
1 to enter a building using force, in order to steal something
2 break sb/sth ↔ **in** to make a person or animal become used to the work he, she, or it has to do: *a training camp for breaking in new soldiers*
3 to interrupt someone when s/he is speaking: *She broke in, saying "You know that's not true!"*
4 break sth ↔ **in** to make new shoes or boots less stiff and more comfortable by wearing them

break into sth *phr. v.*
1 to enter a building or vehicle using force, in order to steal something: *They broke into the house through the back window.*
2 break into a run to suddenly begin running
3 to become involved in a new activity, especially a business activity: *companies trying to break into the East European markets*

break off *phr. v.*
1 break sth ↔ **off** to end a relationship, especially a political or romantic one: *Lisa and Mike have* ***broken off*** *their* ***engagement.***
2 break (sth ↔) **off** to suddenly stop talking: *She broke off, tears in her eyes.* | *Suddenly, they saw me and* ***broke off*** *their* ***conversation.***

break out *phr. v.*
1 if something bad such as a disease, fire, or war breaks out, it begins to happen: *Last night, a **fire broke out** in the 12th Street warehouse.*
2 to change the way you live or behave: *Rose was determined to **break out of** the cycle of poverty.*
3 to suddenly begin to have red spots on your skin, especially on your face: *Chocolate makes me break out.*
4 break out in a sweat to start SWEATing
5 to escape from prison
break through *phr. v.*
1 to manage to do something successfully: *His coach thinks he is ready to break through to the big leagues.*
2 break through (sth) if the Sun breaks through, you can see it through the clouds
break up *phr. v.*
1 break sth ↔ **up** to separate something into smaller parts: *The phone company was broken up to encourage competition.*
2 to end a marriage or romantic relationship, or to stop being together as a group: *Troy and I broke up last month.* | *The band broke up shortly after releasing their second album.*
3 break sth ↔ **up** to stop a fight or stop a group of people doing something: *The FBI broke up a crack ring.*
4 if a crowd or meeting breaks up, people start to leave
5 break (sth ↔) **up** to break into small pieces, or to break something into small pieces: *The plane hit the water and broke up.* | *We used shovels to break up the soil.*
break with sb/sth *phr. v.*
1 to leave a group or organization because you have had a disagreement with them: *Lewis broke with the Administration on this issue.*
2 break with tradition/the past etc. to do something in a completely new way

break[2] *n.*
1 A REST [C] a period of time when you stop working or doing something: *Matthews spoke for three hours without **taking a break**.* | *She took a two-year **break from** competitive running.* | *Harris is on his **lunch/coffee break**.* | *We needed a break, so we went up to the mountains.* | ***Spring break*** (=spring vacation from college) *is at the end of March.*

THESAURUS **vacation, holiday, leave, furlough, r & r, sabbatical** → VACATION

2 STH STOPS [C] a period of time when something stops for a while and then starts again: *There was a break of two years between his last book and this one.* | *a break in the conversation*
3 give sb a break (spoken) to stop annoying, criticizing, or being unkind to someone: *Give me a break! I can't do it that fast.*
4 A CHANCE [C] a chance to do something that allows you to become successful: *The band's **big break** came when they sang on a local TV show.*
5 END STH [singular] a time when you stop doing something, or end a relationship with someone: *a break in relations between the two countries* | *She finally **made the break** and left him.* | *In a **break with tradition**, the parade was canceled.*
6 A SPACE [C] a space or hole in something: *a **break in** the clouds*
7 TV/RADIO [C] a pause for advertisements during a television or radio program: *We'll return after this short **commercial break**.*
8 BROKEN PLACE [C] a place where something is broken: *a bad break in his leg*

break·a·ble /ˈbreɪkəbəl/ *adj.* made of material that breaks easily

break·age /ˈbreɪkɪdʒ/ *n.* [C] (formal) something that has been broken: *All breakages must be paid for.*

break·a·way /ˈbreɪkəˌweɪ/ *adj.* **breakaway republic/group/party etc.** a country, group, etc. that has been formed by people who left another country or group because of a disagreement: *He will try to negotiate a ceasefire between government troops and fighters from the breakaway republic.*

break·down /ˈbreɪkdaʊn/ *n.* **1** [C,U] the failure of a system or relationship: *a **breakdown in** the peace talks* | *the consequences of **family/marital/social etc. breakdown*** **2** [C] a NERVOUS BREAKDOWN **3** [C] a statement or list that separates something into parts: *a **breakdown of** how government agencies will be affected by the cuts* **4** [C] an occasion when a car or a piece of machinery stops working

break·er /ˈbreɪkɚ/ *n.* [C] a large wave with a white top, that rolls onto the shore

break·fast /ˈbrɛkfəst/ *n.* [C,U] the meal you have in the morning: *I **had** bacon and eggs **for breakfast**.* | *Make time to **eat breakfast**.* [ORIGIN: 1400—1500 *break* + *fast* "a period of time when you choose not to eat"]

ˈbreak-in *n.* [C] an act of entering a building illegally using force

ˈbreaking ˌpoint *n.* [U] the point at which someone or something is no longer able to work well or deal with problems: *Some of them are tired, almost **to the breaking point**.*

break·neck /ˈbreɪknɛk/ *adj.* extremely and often dangerously fast: *She drove home **at breakneck speed**.*

break·out[1] /ˈbreɪkaʊt/ *adj.* successful, and making someone or something famous or popular: *a breakout performance by Williamson*

breakout[2] *n.* [C] an escape from a prison

break·through /ˈbreɪkθru/ *n.* [C] an important new discovery in something you have been studying: *Scientists have **made an** important **breakthrough** in the treatment of heart disease.*

break·up /ˈbreɪkʌp/ *n.* [C,U] **1** the act of ending a marriage or other relationship **2** the separation of an organization, country, etc. into smaller parts: *the **breakup of** Yugoslavia*

B

B

breast /brɛst/ *n.* **1** [C] one of the two round raised parts on a woman's chest that produce milk when she has a baby **2** [C] the part of the body between the neck and the stomach: *He cradled his injured arm against his breast.* **3** [C,U] the front part of a bird's body, or the meat from this part: *turkey breast* → *see picture on page A15* [ORIGIN: Old English *breost*]

breast·bone /ˈbrɛstboʊn/ *n.* [C] BIOLOGY the long flat bone in the front of your chest, that is connected to the top seven pairs of RIBS

ˈbreast-feed *v.* (**breast-fed**) [I,T] if a woman breast-feeds, she feeds a baby with milk from her breasts

breast·stroke /ˈbrɛstˌstroʊk/ *n.* [U] a way of swimming in which you push your arms out from your chest and then bring them back in a circle to your sides, while on your stomach in the water → *see picture at* SWIM[1]

breath /brɛθ/ *n.* **1** [C,U] the air that goes in or comes out of your lungs when you breathe, or the action of breathing air into or out of your lungs: *Officers could smell alcohol on his breath.* | *The cat has* ***bad breath*** (=it smells bad). | ***Take a deep breath*** (=breathe in a lot of air once) *and relax.* | *I was hot and sweaty and* ***out of breath*** (=having difficulty breathing because I had just been exercising). | *One of the symptoms is* ***shortness of breath*** (=being unable to breathe easily). | *My heart was pounding and I was* ***gasping for breath*** (=trying hard to get enough air to breathe). **2 hold your breath a)** to breathe in and keep the air in your lungs: *I couldn't hold my breath anymore.* **b)** to wait anxiously to see what is going to happen: *Patrice held her breath, waiting for Dan's reply.* **3 catch your breath** to begin breathing normally again after you have been running or exercising: *I had to sit down to catch my breath.* **4 a breath of fresh air a)** a short time when you breathe air outside a building, after being inside: *I stepped outside for a breath of fresh air.* **b)** something that is different, exciting, and enjoyable: *These books bring a breath of fresh air into the classroom.* **5 under your breath** in a quiet voice: *"I hate you," he muttered under his breath.* **6 (don't) waste your breath** (spoken) used in order to tell someone that it is not worth saying something: *You're wasting your breath; he won't change his mind.* **7 don't hold your breath** used in order to say that something is not going to happen soon **8 take your breath away** to be extremely beautiful or exciting: *a view that will take your breath away* [ORIGIN: Old English *bræth*]

breath·a·ble /ˈbriðəbəl/ *adj.* **1** clothing that is breathable allows air to pass through it easily **2** able to be breathed: *The air was thin but breathable.*

Breath·a·lyz·er /ˈbrɛθəˌlaɪzɚ/ *n.* [C] (trademark) a piece of equipment used by the police to see if a car driver has drunk too much alcohol: *a* ***Breathalyzer test*** —**breathalyze** *v.* [T]

breathe /brið/ *v.* **1** [I,T] to take air into your lungs and send it out again: *the quality of the air we breathe* | *Relax and* ***breathe deeply*** (=take in a lot of air). | *He was sweating and* ***breathing hard*** (=breathing deeply and quickly).

THESAURUS

take a breath – to take air into your lungs: *Take deep breaths and try to relax.*
inhale (formal) – to breathe in air, smoke, or gas: *Try not to inhale the fumes from the glue.*
exhale (formal) – to breathe air, smoke, etc. out through your mouth and nose: *Take a deep breath, then exhale slowly.*

Ways of breathing
pant – to breathe quickly with short breaths, especially after exercising: *I ran to the station and arrived sweaty and panting.*
wheeze – to breathe with difficulty, making a noise in your throat and chest, usually because you are sick: *I woke up the next morning coughing and wheezing.*
be short of breath also **be out of breath** – to have difficulty breathing, often after physical activity such as running, or because of sickness: *Patients quickly become short of breath and unable to stand.*
gasp for breath – to breathe quickly and loudly, because you are having difficulty breathing either from exercising or because you are sick: *He was gasping for breath and his heart was pounding fiercely.*
gasp for air – to be unable to breathe because there is not enough air: *He came up from under the water, gasping for air.*

2 [I,T] to blow air, smoke, or smells out of your mouth: *Roy breathed on his hands to warm them.* **3 breathe a sigh of relief** to stop being worried about something: *We all breathed a sigh of relief as he climbed off the roof.* **4 breathe down sb's neck** (informal) to watch what someone is doing so carefully that it makes him/her feel nervous or annoyed: *I can't work with you breathing down my neck.* **5 not breathe a word** to not tell anyone about a secret [ORIGIN: 1200—1300 *breath*]

breathe (sth ↔) **in** *phr. v.* to take air into your lungs: *She breathed in deeply.* | *Wyatt breathed in the fresh sea air.*

breathe (sth ↔) **out** *phr. v.* to send air out from your lungs: *OK, now breathe out slowly.* | *He breathed out a sigh of relief.*

breath·er /ˈbriðɚ/ *n.* [C] (informal) a short period of rest from an activity: *OK, everybody,* ***take a breather.***

breath·ing /ˈbriðɪŋ/ *n.* [U] the process of breathing air in and out: *his deep, regular breathing*

breath·less /ˈbrɛθlɪs/ *adj.* having difficulty breathing in a normal way —**breathlessly** *adv.*

breath·tak·ing /ˈbrɛθˌteɪkɪŋ/ *adj.* extremely impressive, exciting, or surprising: *breathtaking scenery*

THESAURUS impressive, imposing, dazzling, awe-inspiring, majestic, magnificent → IMPRESSIVE

breath·y /ˈbrɛθi/ *adj.* if someone's voice is breathy, you can hear his/her breath when s/he speaks

breed¹ /brid/ *v.* (past tense and past participle **bred** /brɛd/) **1** [I] BIOLOGY if animals breed, they have babies **2** [T] BIOLOGY to keep animals or plants in order to produce babies, or to develop new animals or plants: *He breeds horses.* **3** [T] to cause a particular feeling or condition: *The crowded living conditions bred disease and crime.* [ORIGIN: Old English *bredan*]

breed² *n.* [C] **1** a type of animal, especially one that people have kept to breed: *Labradors and other breeds of dog* **2** a particular type of person or type of thing: *the first in a **new breed** of home computers*

breed·er /ˈbridɚ/ *n.* [C] someone who breeds animals or plants

breed·ing /ˈbridɪŋ/ *n.* [U] **1** BIOLOGY the act or process of animals producing babies: *the **breeding season*** **2** BIOLOGY the activity of keeping animals or plants in order to produce babies, or to develop new types **3** (old-fashioned) polite social behavior

ˈbreeding ˌground *n.* [C] a place or situation where something grows or develops: *The projects were a **breeding ground for** gangs.*

breeze¹ /briz/ *n.* [C] **1** a light gentle wind

THESAURUS wind, gust, gale, storm, hurricane, tornado, typhoon → WIND¹

2 be a breeze (spoken) to be very easy to do [ORIGIN: 1500—1600 French *brise*] → **shoot the breeze** at SHOOT¹

breeze² *v.* [I] (informal) to walk somewhere in a quick confident way: *She **breezed into** my office and sat down.*

breeze through sth *phr. v.* (informal) to finish a piece of work or pass a test very easily: *Sherry breezed through her final exams.*

breez·y /ˈbrizi/ *adj.* **1** confident and relaxed: *his breezy way of speaking* **2** breezy weather is when the wind blows in a fairly strong way

breth·ren /ˈbrɛðrən/ *n.* [plural] (old-fashioned, written) male members of an organization, especially a religious group

brev·i·ty /ˈbrɛvəṭi/ (Ac) *n.* [U] (formal) **1** the quality of expressing something in very few words: *The speech was praised for its brevity.* **2** the quality of continuing for only a short time: *the brevity of the meeting* [ORIGIN: 1400—1500 Latin *brevitas*, from *brevis* "short"]

brew¹ /bru/ *v.* **1** [I,T] if tea or coffee brews, or you brew it, you make it with boiling water and leave it to get a stronger taste **2** [I] if something unpleasant is brewing, it will happen soon: *There's a storm brewing.* **3** [T] to make beer

brew² *n.* [C,U] beer, or a can or glass of beer

brew·er /ˈbruɚ/ *n.* [C] a person or company that makes beer

brew·er·y /ˈbruəri/ *n.* (plural **breweries**) [C] a place where beer is made, or a company that makes beer

ˈbrew pub *n.* [C] a bar or restaurant that serves beer that is made locally, rather than by large companies

bribe¹ /braɪb/ *n.* [C] money or gifts that you use to persuade someone to do something, usually something dishonest: *a judge accused of **taking bribes*** | *The officials said that they had been **offered bribes** before an important game.* [ORIGIN: 1300—1400 Old French "bread given to a beggar"]

bribe² *v.* [T] to give someone a bribe: *Customs officials were **bribed to** let the trucks through.*

brib·er·y /ˈbraɪbəri/ *n.* [U] the act of giving or taking bribes

bric-a-brac /ˈbrɪk ə ˌbræk/ *n.* [U] small objects that are used for decoration in a house

brick /brɪk/ *n.* [C,U] a hard block of baked clay used for building walls, houses, etc. [ORIGIN: 1400—1500 French *brique*, from Middle Dutch *bricke*]

brick·lay·er /ˈbrɪkˌleɪɚ/ *n.* [C] someone whose job is to build things with bricks —**bricklaying** *n.* [U]

bri·dal /ˈbraɪdl/ *adj.* relating to a bride or a wedding: *a bridal gown*

bride /braɪd/ *n.* [C] a woman at the time she gets married or just after she is married: *You may kiss the bride.* → WEDDING [ORIGIN: Old English *bryd*]

bride·groom /ˈbraɪdgrum/ *n.* [C] a GROOM

brides·maid /ˈbraɪdzmeɪd/ *n.* [C] a woman who helps the bride and stands beside her during her wedding

bridge¹ /brɪdʒ/ *n.* **1** [C] a structure built over a river, road, etc. that allows people or vehicles to cross from one side to the other: *the Brooklyn Bridge* **2** [C] something that provides a connection between two ideas, subjects, groups, or situations: *His new book acts as a **bridge between** art and science.* **3 the bridge** the raised part of a ship from which it can be controlled **4** [U] a card game for four players, who play in pairs **5 the bridge of your nose** the upper part of your nose, between your eyes **6** [C] a piece of metal for keeping a false tooth in place [ORIGIN: (1) Old English *brycg*]

bridge² *v.* [T] **1** to reduce the difference between two things: *attempting to **bridge the gap between** rich and poor* **2** to build or form a bridge over something: *a log bridging the stream*

bri·dle¹ /ˈbraɪdl/ *n.* [C] a set of leather bands put on a horse's head and used to control its movements

bridle² *v.* **1** [T] to put a bridle on a horse **2** [I,T] to become angry or offended: *Amy* ***bridled at*** *the restrictions put on her.*

brief[1] /brif/ (Ac) *adj.* **1** continuing for a short time: *a brief period of silence*

THESAURUS short, quick, cursory, temporary, ephemeral → SHORT[1]

2 using only a few words and not describing things in detail: *I'll try to* ***be brief****.* | *a brief letter* | ***In brief****, the report found a direct relationship between a change in price and a change in demand.* [ORIGIN: 1200—1300 Old French, Latin *brevis*]

THESAURUS short, concise, succinct, curt → SHORT[1]

—**briefly** *adv.*: *He worked briefly for the state, promoting tourism.* | *The president spoke briefly to reporters.*

brief[2] (Ac) *n.* [C] **1** LAW a short statement giving facts about a law case: *a legal brief* | *The plaintiffs' attorneys* ***filed*** *a* ***brief*** *asking the judge to dismiss the evidence.* **2** a short report: *The brief should outline the current economic situation in Eastern Europe.* **3 briefs** [plural] men's or women's underwear worn on the lower part of the body

brief[3] (Ac) *v.* [T] to give someone all the information about a situation that s/he will need: *Senate staff were* ***briefed on*** *the new law.* —**briefing** *n.* [C,U]

brief·case /'brifkeɪs/ *n.* [C] a special flat bag used for carrying papers or documents → *see picture at* CASE[1]

bri·gade /brɪ'geɪd/ *n.* [C] **1** a large group of soldiers forming part of an army **2** a group of people who have similar qualities or beliefs: *the environmentalist brigade* [ORIGIN: 1600—1700 French, Italian *brigata*, from *brigare* "to fight"]

brig·a·dier gen·er·al, Brigadier General /ˌbrɪgədɪr 'dʒɛnərəl/ *n.* [C] an officer who has a high rank in the Army, Air Force, or Marines

bright /braɪt/ *adj.* **1** shining strongly, or with plenty of light: *a bright sunny day* | *bright lights*

THESAURUS

strong – a strong light is very bright: *Diana squinted in the strong sunlight.*
brilliant – a brilliant light is very bright and strong: *brilliant sunshine*
dazzling – a dazzling light is so bright that you cannot see for a short time after you look at it: *Under the Sun, the white of the snow is dazzling.*
glaring – a glaring light is too bright to look at: *When burned, the metal produces a glaring white light.*
blinding – a blinding light is very bright, and makes you unable to see for a short time: *There was a blinding flash, then the noise of an explosion.*

2 intelligent: *Vicky is a very bright child.* | *a bright idea*

THESAURUS intelligent, smart, brilliant, wise, clever, cunning, crafty, intellectual, gifted, apt → INTELLIGENT

3 bright colors are strong and easy to see: *a bright red sweater* **4** happy and full of energy: *a bright smile* **5** likely to be successful: *You have a* ***bright future*** *ahead of you.* **6 bright and early** (spoken) very early in the morning: *I'll be here bright and early to pick you up.* **7 the bright side** the good things about something that is bad in other ways: ***Look on the bright side*** *– at least you didn't lose your job.* [ORIGIN: Old English *beorht*] —**brightly** *adv.* —**brightness** *n.* [U]

bright·en /'braɪt¬n/ *also* **brighten up** *v.* **1** [I,T] to become brighter or lighter, or to make something do this: *The weather should brighten in the afternoon.* **2** [T] to make something more pleasant or attractive: *Flowers would brighten up this room.* **3** [I,T] to become happier, or to make someone else feel like this: *She brightened up when she saw us coming.*

brights /braɪts/ *n.* [plural] car HEADLIGHTS when they are on as brightly as possible

bril·liant /'brɪlyənt/ *adj.* **1** brilliant light or color is very bright and strong: *brilliant sunshine*

THESAURUS bright, strong, dazzling, glaring, blinding → BRIGHT

2 extremely intelligent: *a brilliant scientist* [ORIGIN: 1600—1700 French, present participle of *briller* "to shine," from Italian *brillare*]

THESAURUS intelligent, smart, bright, wise, clever, cunning, crafty, intellectual, gifted, apt → INTELLIGENT

—**brilliance** *n.* [U] —**brilliantly** *adv.*

brim[1] /brɪm/ *n.* [C] **1** the part of a hat that sticks out to protect you from sun and rain **2 the brim** the top of a container such as a glass: *The glass was* ***filled to the brim****.*

brim[2] *v.* (**brimmed**, **brimming**) [I] **1** to start to cry: *His eyes* ***brimmed with*** *tears.* **2 be brimming (over) with sth** to be full of a particular thing, quality, or emotion

brine /braɪn/ *n.* [U] water that contains a lot of salt —**briny** *adj.*

bring /brɪŋ/ *v.* (past tense and past participle **brought** /brɔt/) [T] **1** to take someone or something with you to a place or person: *I brought these pictures for you.* | *Will you bring me a glass of water?* | *Can I* ***bring*** *a friend* ***to*** *the party?* | *Dave* ***brought*** *a friend home* ***with*** *him.* | *She* ***brought*** *her daughter* ***along*** (=with her).

USAGE

bring – to take something or someone to the place where you are now, or the place where you are going: *Did you remember to bring your passport?* | *I have brought someone to see you.*
take – to move something from one place to another, or to help someone go from one place

to another: *Don't forget to take your umbrella.* | *I can take you to the airport.*
get – to go to another place and come back with something or someone: *I'll get my keys.*

2 to cause a particular type of result or reaction: *The article brought angry letters from readers.* | *The fishing industry brings lots of money into the area.* | *efforts to bring peace to the region* **3** to make someone or something come to a place: *The project has brought inner city children new opportunities.* | *"**What brings you here?**" "I need to talk to Mike."* **4** to move something in a particular direction: *Bring your arm up level with your shoulder.* | *He brought the axe down with a thud.* **5** to begin a legal case against someone: *Criminal charges were **brought against** 14 officials.* **6 bring the total/number/score etc. to sth** used in order to say what the new total, etc. is: *165 agents are being hired, bringing the total to 2,313.* **7 not bring yourself to do sth** to not be able to do something, especially because you know it will upset or harm someone: *Brenda couldn't bring herself to tell him that Helen was dead.* **8** to cause someone or something to reach a particular state or condition: *Bring the mixture to a full boil.* | *The demonstration was **brought to a** peaceful **conclusion/end**.* **9 bring sth to sb's attention** a phrase, used especially in formal writing, that means to tell someone something: *Thank you for bringing the problem to our attention.* **10 bring sth to bear (on)** to use something in order to get the result you want: *Pressure was brought to bear by women's rights groups, and the club began admitting women.*

bring sth ↔ **about** *phr. v.* to make something happen: *Lewis promised to bring about the needed changes.*

bring sb/sth **around** *phr. v.* **1** to change the subject of a conversation gradually to something new: *They keep **bringing the conversation/subject around** to their son.* **2** to make someone become conscious again

bring back *phr. v.* **1 bring** sth ↔ **back** to start using something again that had been used in the past: *Some states have brought back the death penalty.* **2 bring back** sth to make you remember something: *The smell of suntan lotion brought back memories of the summer.*

bring sb/sth ↔ **down** *phr. v.* **1** to reduce something to a lower level: *The changes have brought costs down.* **2** to make something fall or come down: *A missile brought the plane down.* **3 bring down a government/president etc.** to force a government, etc. to stop being in control of a country

bring sth ↔ **forth** *phr. v.* (formal) to make something happen, appear, or become available: *No evidence has been brought forth against Mr. Keele.*

bring sth ↔ **forward** *phr. v.* **1** to change an arrangement so that something happens sooner: *They had to bring the wedding forward because Lynn got a new job.* **2** to introduce or suggest a new plan or idea: *Many arguments were brought forward supporting the changes.*

bring sb/sth ↔ **in** *phr. v.* **1** to ask or persuade someone to become involved in a discussion, help with a problem, etc.: *The FBI were brought in to investigate.* **2** to earn or produce a particular amount of money: *The painting should bring in at least a million dollars.* **3 bring in a verdict** if a court or JURY brings in a verdict, it says whether someone is guilty or not

bring sth ↔ **off** *phr. v.* to succeed in doing something that is very difficult: *She'll get a promotion if she brings off the deal.*

bring sth ↔ **on** *phr. v.* to make something bad or unpleasant happen or begin: *Stress can bring on an asthma attack.*

bring sth ↔ **out** *phr. v.* **1** to make something become easier to notice, see, taste, etc.: *That shirt brings out the green in her eyes.* **2 bring out the best/worst in sb** to emphasize someone's best or worst qualities: *Becoming a father has brought out the best in Dan.* **3** to produce and begin to sell a new product, book, record, etc.: *The band is bringing out a new CD in September.*

bring sb ↔ **together** *phr. v.* if an event brings a group of people together, it makes them care about each other more: *Stuart's death really brought the family together.*

bring sb/sth ↔ **up** *phr. v.* **1** to start to talk about a particular subject or person: *The issue was brought up during the last election.* **2** to educate and care for a child until s/he is old enough to be independent: *She brought up three children by herself.* | *I was **brought up a Catholic/Muslim etc.*** (=taught to believe a particular religion). **3** to make something appear on a computer screen: *He brought up an airplane modeling website.*

brink /brɪŋk/ *n.* **the brink (of sth)** a situation in which you may soon begin a new or different situation: *Scientists say they're **on the brink of** a major discovery.*

brisk /brɪsk/ *adj.* **1** quick and full of energy: *a brisk walk* **2** trade or business that is brisk is very busy **3** weather that is brisk is cold and clear —**briskly** *adv.*

bris·tle[1] /ˈbrɪsəl/ *n.* [C,U] short stiff hair, wire, etc.: *a brush with short bristles*

bristle[2] *v.* [I] **1** to behave in a way that shows you are very angry or annoyed: *He **bristled at** my suggestion.* **2** if an animal's hair bristles, it stands up stiffly because the animal is afraid or angry

bristle with sth *phr. v.* to have a lot of something that sticks out: *Her hair bristled with curlers.*

bris·tly /ˈbrɪsəli, -sli/ *adj.* **1** bristly hair is short and stiff **2** having short stiff hairs on it: *The old man's face was all bristly with white whiskers.*

britch·es /ˈbrɪtʃɪz/ *n.* [plural] **1 too big for your britches** (informal) very confident, in a way that annoys other people **2** (old-fashioned) pants

Brit·ish[1] /ˈbrɪt̬ɪʃ/ *adj.* relating to or coming from Great Britain: *the British government*

British² *n.* **the British** [plural] the people of Great Britain

Brit·on /ˈbrɪtˀn/ *n.* [C] someone from Great Britain

brit·tle /ˈbrɪtl̬/ *adj.* **1** hard but easily broken: *The paper was old and brittle.* **2** a system, relationship, feeling, etc. that is brittle is easily damaged or destroyed: *a brittle friendship* **3** showing no kind feelings: *a brittle laugh* [ORIGIN: 1300—1400 Old English *gebryttan* "to break into pieces"]

bro /broʊ/ *n.* [C] (slang) **1** your brother **2** used by young men as a way of greeting a male friend

broach /broʊtʃ/ *v.* **broach the subject/question etc.** to mention a subject that may be embarrassing or cause an argument: *It's often difficult to broach the subject of sex.*

broad /brɔd/ *adj.* **1** very wide: *broad shoulders* | *He gave a broad smile.* | *The river is broad at this point.* **2** including many different kinds of things or people: *a movie that appeals to a* ***broad range*** *of people* | *The measure has broad support.* **3** concerning only the main ideas or parts of something: *a broad outline of the proposal* **4 in broad daylight** during the day when it is light: *He got stabbed in the street in broad daylight.* [ORIGIN: Old English *brad*]

broad·band /ˈbrɔdbænd/ *n.* [U] IT a system in which computers are connected to the Internet and can receive information at very high speed → INTERNET

broad·cast¹ /ˈbrɔdkæst/ *n.* [C] a program on the radio or television: *a news broadcast*

broadcast² *v.* (past tense and past participle **broadcast**) [I,T] to send out a radio or television program: *Channel 5 will broadcast the game at six o'clock.*

broad·cast·er /ˈbrɔdˌkæstɚ/ *n.* [C] **1** someone who speaks on radio and television programs → NEWSCASTER **2** a company that sends out television or radio programs

broad·cast·ing /ˈbrɔdˌkæstɪŋ/ *n.* [U] the business of making radio and television programs

broad·en /ˈbrɔdn/ *v.* **1** [T] to increase something such as your knowledge, experience, or number of activities: *The class will broaden your knowledge of wine.* | *Travel* ***broadens the mind*** (=helps you understand and accept other people's beliefs, customs, etc.). **2** [T] to make something affect or include more people or things: *This novel will broaden her appeal to younger readers.* **3** [I,T] *also* **broaden out** to make something wider, or to become wider: *The river broadens out here.*

broad·ly /ˈbrɔdli/ *adv.* **1** in a general way: *I know broadly what to expect.* **2 smile/grin broadly** to have a big smile on your face **3** including a range of people, things, subjects, etc.: *The policy is broadly supported.*

broad·mind·ed /ˌbrɔdˈmaɪndɪd◂/ *adj.* willing to respect opinions or behavior that are very different from your own

broad·sheet /ˈbrɔdʃit/ *n.* [C] a serious newspaper printed on large sheets of paper → NEWSPAPER

broad·side¹ /ˈbrɔdˌsaɪd/ *adv.* with the longest side facing you: *He hit the car broadside.*

broadside² *v.* [T] to crash into the side of another vehicle

Broad·way /ˈbrɔdweɪ/ *n.* a street in New York that is known as the center of American theater

bro·cade /broʊˈkeɪd/ *n.* [U] thick heavy cloth that has a pattern of gold and silver threads

broc·co·li /ˈbrɑkəli/ *n.* [U] a green vegetable with thick groups of small dark green parts that look like flowers [ORIGIN: 1600—1700 Italian, plural of *broccolo*, from *brocco* "small nail," from Latin *broccus*] → *see picture at* VEGETABLE

bro·chure /broʊˈʃʊr/ *n.* [C] a thin book that gives information or advertises something: *a travel brochure*

brogue /broʊg/ *n.* [C] **1** a strong leather shoe, especially one with a pattern in the leather **2** an ACCENT, especially an Irish or Scottish one

broil /brɔɪl/ *v.* [I,T] if you broil something, or if something broils, you cook it under or over direct heat: *broiled chicken* [ORIGIN: 1300—1400 Old French *bruler* "to burn"]

THESAURUS **cook, bake, fry, roast, grill, sauté, boil, steam, deep fry** → COOK¹

broil·er /ˈbrɔɪlɚ/ *n.* [C] a special area of a STOVE, used for cooking food under direct heat

broke¹ /broʊk/ *v.* the past tense of BREAK

broke² *adj.* (informal) **1** completely without money: *I'm* ***flat broke.***

THESAURUS **poor, needy, destitute, impoverished, impecunious, indigent, penurious, poverty-stricken** → POOR

2 go broke if a company or business goes broke, it can no longer operate because it has no money: *The record store went broke last year.* **3 go for broke** to take big risks trying to achieve something

bro·ken¹ /ˈbroʊkən/ *v.* the past participle of BREAK

broken² *adj.* **1** not working correctly: *a broken clock* | *How did the lawn mower* ***get broken?*** **2** cracked or in pieces because of being hit, dropped, etc.: *a broken leg* | *There was broken glass everywhere.* **3** not continuous: *a broken white line* | *broken sleep* **4** a broken relationship is one that has ended because the husband and wife have separated: *a broken marriage* | *children from* ***broken homes*** (=children whose parents are divorced) **5** extremely mentally or physically weak after suffering a lot: *a broken man* **6 broken agreement/promise etc.** a situation in which someone did not do what s/he promised to do **7 a broken heart** a feeling of extreme sadness because someone you love has died or left you **8 broken English/French etc.** if someone speaks broken English, French, etc., s/he speaks very slowly, with a lot of mistakes, because s/he does not know the language well

ˌbroken-ˈdown *adj.* broken, old, and needing a lot of repair: *a broken-down sofa*

ˌbroken-ˈhearted *adj.* very sad, especially because someone you love has died or left you

bro·ker¹ /ˈbroʊkɚ/ *n.* [C] ECONOMICS someone whose job is to buy and sell property, insurance, etc. for someone else: *a real-estate broker* ➔ STOCKBROKER

broker² *v.* [T] to arrange the details of a deal, plan, etc. so that everyone can agree to it: *an agreement brokered by the UN*

bro·ker·age /ˈbroʊkərɪdʒ/ *n.* [U] ECONOMICS the business of being a broker

bro·mine /ˈbroʊmin/ *n.* [U] CHEMISTRY (*symbol* **Br**) a dark red poisonous chemical liquid that changes easily into a gas, often used in photography or for making other chemicals change color. It is a chemical ELEMENT belonging to the HALOGEN group.

bronchi /ˈbrɑŋkaɪ/ *n.* the plural of BRONCHUS

ˈbronchial tube *n.* [C usually plural] BIOLOGY one of two tubes that take air into your lungs from your TRACHEA (SYN) **bronchus** ➔ *see picture at* ORGAN

bron·chi·ole /ˈbrɑŋkiˌoʊl/ *n* [C] BIOLOGY a narrow tube that carries air into the lung from the BRONCHIAL TUBES (=the main air passages leading to the lungs) ➔ *see picture at* LUNG

bron·chi·tis /brɑŋˈkaɪt̬ɪs/ *n.* [U] an illness that affects your breathing and makes you cough —**bronchitic** /brɑŋˈkɪt̬ɪk/ *adj.*

bron·chus /ˈbrɑŋkəs/ *n.* (plural **bronchi** /-kaɪ/) [C] BIOLOGY one of two tubes that take air into your lungs from your TRACHEA (SYN) **bronchial tube** ➔ *see picture at* LUNG

bron·co /ˈbrɑŋkoʊ/ *n.* (plural **broncos**) [C] a wild horse

bron·to·sau·rus /ˌbrɑntəˈsɔrəs/ *n.* [C] a large DINOSAUR with a very long neck and body

bronze¹ /brɑnz/ *n.* **1** [U] a hard metal that is a mixture of COPPER and TIN **2** [U] a dull red-brown color **3** [C] a work of art made of bronze: *a bronze by Henry Moore* [ORIGIN: 1700—1800 French, Italian *bronzo*]

bronze² *adj.* **1** made of bronze: *a bronze statue* **2** having the red-brown color of bronze

ˈBronze Age *n.* **the Bronze Age** HISTORY the period of time, between about 6,000 and 3,500 years ago, when bronze was used for making tools, weapons, etc. ➔ IRON AGE, STONE AGE

ˌbronze ˈmedal *n.* [C] a prize that is given to the person who finishes third in a race, competition, etc., usually made of bronze

brooch /broʊtʃ, brutʃ/ *n.* [C] a piece of jewelry that you fasten to your clothes

brood¹ /brud/ *v.* [I] to think for a long time about something that you are worried, angry, or sad about: *Louise was **brooding about/over** what had happened at work.*

brood² *n.* [C] **1** a family of young birds **2** (humorous) someone's children

brook /brʊk/ *n.* [C] a small stream

broom /brum, brʊm/ *n.* [C] a large brush with a long handle, used for sweeping floors

broom·stick /ˈbrumˌstɪk, ˈbrʊm-/ *n.* [C] the long thin handle of a broom. In stories, WITCHes fly on broomsticks.

broth /brɔθ/ *n.* [U] a soup made by cooking meat or vegetables in water and then removing them: *beef broth*

broth·el /ˈbrɑθəl, ˈbrɔ-, -ðəl/ *n.* [C] a house where men pay to have sex with PROSTITUTES

broth·er¹ /ˈbrʌðɚ/ *n.* [C] **1** a boy or man who has the same parents as you ➔ SISTER: *Isn't that your **big/little brother*** (=older or younger brother)? ➔ RELATIVE¹ **2** (spoken) a male friend – used especially by African Americans **3** a man who belongs to the same race, religion, organization, etc. as you **4** a MONK: *Brother Francis* [ORIGIN: Old English *brothor*]

brother² *interjection* **Oh brother!** said when you are annoyed or surprised

broth·er·hood /ˈbrʌðɚˌhʊd/ *n.* (old-fashioned) **1** [U] a feeling of friendship between people: *He called for his countrymen to unite in a spirit of brotherhood.* **2** [C] a men's organization formed for a particular purpose

ˈbrother-in-law *n.* [C] **1** the brother of your husband or wife **2** the husband of your sister

broth·er·ly /ˈbrʌðɚli/ *adj.* showing feelings of kindness, loyalty, etc. that you would expect a brother to show: *brotherly love*

brought /brɔt/ *v.* the past tense and past participle of BRING

brou·ha·ha /ˈbruhɑhɑ/ *n.* [U] (informal) unnecessary noise and activity (SYN) **commotion**

brow /braʊ/ *n.* [C] **1** a FOREHEAD **2** an EYEBROW

brow·beat /ˈbraʊbit/ *v.* (past tense **browbeat**, past participle **browbeaten** /-bitˀn/) [T] to make someone do something by continuously asking him/her to do it, especially in a threatening way

brown¹ /braʊn/ *adj.* having the same color as earth, wood, or coffee: *brown shoes* [ORIGIN: Old English *brun*] —**brown** *n.* [C,U]

brown² *v.* [I,T] to become brown, or to make food do this: *Brown the meat in hot oil.*

Brown·ie /ˈbraʊni/ *n.* **1 the Brownies** [plural] the part of the GIRL SCOUTS that is for younger girls **2** [C] a member of this organization

brown·ie /ˈbraʊni/ *n.* **1** [C] a thick flat piece of chocolate cake **2 get/earn brownie points** (informal) if you do something to get brownie points, you do it to get praise

'brown-nose *v.* [I,T] (informal, disapproving) to try to make someone in authority like you by being very nice to him/her —**brown-noser** *n.* [C]

brown·stone /'braʊnstoʊn/ *n.* **1** [U] a type of red-brown stone, often used for building in the eastern U.S. **2** [C] a house with a front made of this stone

browse /braʊz/ *v.* **1** [I] to look at the goods in a store without wanting to buy a particular thing: *"Can I help you?" "No thanks. I'm just browsing."* **2** [I] to look through the pages of a book, magazine, etc. without a particular purpose, reading only the most interesting parts: *I was* ***browsing through*** *the catalog, and I found this.* **3** [I,T] IT to search for information on a computer or on the Internet: *software for browsing the Internet*

brows·er /'braʊzɚ/ *n.* [C] IT a computer program that lets you find and use information on the INTERNET: *a Web browser*

bruise¹ /bruz/ *n.* [C] a mark on the skin of a person or piece of fruit, where it has been damaged by a hit or a fall: *She was covered in cuts and bruises.* [ORIGIN: Old English *brysan* "to press so as to break, bruise," later influenced by Old French *brisier*, *bruisier* "to break"]

> THESAURUS **blemish, scar, pimple, zit, wart, blister, freckle, mole** → MARK²
> **injury, wound, contusion, cut, laceration, scrape, sprain, bump, fracture** → INJURY

bruise² *v.* [I,T] to bruise a person or piece of fruit, or to get a bruise: *He fell and bruised his knee.* | *a bruised apple* —**bruising** *n.* [U]

> THESAURUS **hurt, injure, wound, maim, break, sprain, twist, strain, pull, dislocate** → HURT¹

brunch /brʌntʃ/ *n.* [C,U] a meal eaten in the late morning, as a combination of breakfast and LUNCH

bru·nette /bru'nɛt/ *n.* [C] a woman with dark brown hair

brunt /brʌnt/ *n.* **bear/take the brunt of sth** to have to deal with the worst part of something bad: *Women usually bear the brunt of caring for the sick.*

brushes

paintbrush

hairbrush

toothbrush

brush¹ /brʌʃ/ *n.* **1** [C] an object that you use for cleaning, painting, making your hair neat, etc., consisting of a handle with BRISTLEs or thin pieces of plastic attached to it → HAIRBRUSH, PAINTBRUSH, TOOTHBRUSH **2** [U] small bushes and trees covering an open area of land: *a brush fire* **3** [C] a short time when you are in an unpleasant situation or argument: *the boy's first* ***brush with the law*** (=when he was stopped by police) [ORIGIN: (1) 1300—1400 Early French *broisse*, from Old French *broce*]

brush² *v.* **1** [T] to use a brush to clean something or to make it look smooth and neat: *Go brush your teeth.* | *He hadn't brushed his hair.* **2** [T] to remove something with a brush or your hand: *She* ***brushed*** *the crumbs* ***off*** *her lap.* **3** [I,T] to touch someone or something lightly as you pass by: *Her hair* ***brushed against*** *my arm.*

> THESAURUS **touch, feel, handle, stroke, rub, scratch, pat, pet, tickle** → TOUCH¹

brush sb/sth ↔ **aside** *phr. v.* to refuse to listen to someone or consider someone's opinion: *He brushed her objections aside.*

brush sth ↔ **off** *phr. v.* to refuse to talk about something: *The President calmly brushed off their questions about his health.*

brush up (on) sth *phr. v.* to quickly practice and improve your skills or knowledge of a subject: *I have to brush up on my French before I go to Paris.*

'brush-off *n.* [singular] (informal) rude or unfriendly behavior that shows you are not interested in someone: *I thought she really liked me, but she* ***gave me the brush-off.***

brusque /brʌsk/ *adj.* using very few words, in a way that seems impolite: *a brusque manner* [ORIGIN: 1600—1700 French, Italian *brusco*, from Medieval Latin *bruscus* type of bush with sharp points]

brus·sels sprout /'brʌsəl ˌspraʊt/ *n.* [C] a small round green vegetable that has a slightly bitter taste [ORIGIN: 1600—1700 *Brussels*, where it was first grown] → *see picture at* VEGETABLE

bru·tal /'brut̬l/ *adj.* **1** very cruel and violent: *a brutal attack* **2** not sensitive to people's feelings: *the brutal truth* —**brutally** *adv.* —**brutality** /bru'tæləṱi/ *n.* [C,U]

bru·tal·ize /'brut̬lˌaɪz/ *v.* [T] to treat someone in a cruel and violent way

brute¹ /brut/ *n.* [C] **1** a man who is rough, cruel, and not sensitive **2** an animal, especially a large one

brute² *adj.* **brute force/strength** physical strength that is used rather than thought or intelligence

brut·ish /'brut̬ɪʃ/ *adj.* very cruel: *brutish behavior*

B.S. *n.* [C] **Bachelor of Science** a university degree in a science subject → B.A.

bub·ble¹ /'bʌbəl/ *n.* [C] a ball of air in a liquid or solid substance: *soap bubbles* | *the bubbles in a glass of soda*

bubble² *v.* [I] **1** to produce bubbles: *Heat the sauce until it starts to bubble.* **2** *also* **bubble over** to be full of a particular emotion, activity, etc.: *The kids were* ***bubbling over with*** *excitement.*

'bubble gum *n.* [U] a type of CHEWING GUM that you can blow into a bubble

bub·bly¹ /'bʌbli/ *adj.* **1** full of BUBBLES **2** happy and friendly: *a bubbly personality*

bubbly² *n.* [U] (informal) CHAMPAGNE

buck¹ /bʌk/ *n.* [C] **1** (spoken) a dollar: *Could you lend me 20 bucks?* **2 the buck stops here** *also* **the buck stops with sb** used to say that a particular person is responsible for something: *I'm paid to make the decisions; the buck stops here.* **3 pass the buck** to make someone else responsible for something that you should deal with: *It's a way for the politicians to* ***pass the buck*** *to voters.* **4** (plural **buck** *or* **bucks**) BIOLOGY the male of some animals, such as DEER, rabbits, etc.

buck² *v.* **1** [I] if a horse bucks, it kicks its back feet up in the air **2** [T] if a horse bucks someone off, it throws the person riding off its back by bucking **3** [T] (informal) to oppose something, or do the opposite of something: *Unemployment in the state* ***bucked the*** *national* ***trend*** *by falling for the last month.*

buck·et /'bʌkɪt/ *n.* [C] **1** an open container with a handle, used for carrying and holding things, especially liquids **2** the amount that a bucket will hold: *a* ***bucket of*** *water* [ORIGIN: 1200—1300 Anglo-French *buket*, from Old English *buc* "container for pouring liquid, belly"] ➔ **a drop in the bucket** *at* DROP², **kick the bucket** *at* KICK¹

buck·le¹ /'bʌkəl/ *v.* **1** [I,T] to fasten a buckle, or be fastened with a buckle: *The strap buckles at the side.* **2** [I] to do something that you do not want to do because of a difficult situation: *The senator accused supporters of the amendment of* ***buckling under pressure*** *from groups lobbying against the bill.* **3** [I] if your knees buckle, they become weak and bend **4** [I,T] to bend because of heat or pressure, or to make something do this [ORIGIN: 1300—1400 Old French *bocle* "buckle, raised part in the center of a shield," from *buccola* "strap for a helmet"]

buckle down *phr. v.* (informal) to start working seriously: *Sanders buckled down, and his grade-point average improved.*

buckle (sth ↔) **up** *phr. v.* to fasten your SEAT BELT in a car, aircraft, etc.

buckle² *n.* [C] a piece of metal used for fastening the two ends of a belt, or for fastening a shoe, bag, etc. ➔ *see picture at* WATCH²

,buck 'teeth *n.* [plural] teeth that stick forward out of your mouth —**buck-toothed** *adj.*

bud¹ /bʌd/ *n.* [C] **1** BIOLOGY a young flower or leaf that is still tightly rolled up ➔ *see picture at* PLANT¹ **2** (spoken) BUDDY ➔ **nip sth in the bud** *at* NIP¹

bud² *v.* (**budded**, **budding**) [I] BIOLOGY to produce buds

Bud·dha /'budə, 'bʊdə/ *n.* **the Buddha** the title given to Gautama Siddhartha, the man who taught the ideas on which Buddhism is based

Bud·dhism /'budɪzəm, 'bʊ-/ *n.* [U] a religion of east and central Asia, based on the teaching of Buddha —**Buddhist** *n.* [C] —**Buddhist** *adj.*

bud·ding¹ /'bʌdɪŋ/ *adj.* beginning to develop: *a budding poet*

budding² *n.* [U] **1** BIOLOGY the process by which a plant produces new BUDS **2** BIOLOGY a process by which YEAST produces more of itself, and some simple living creatures produce new creatures by separating to form two new parts **3** BIOLOGY a way of producing a new type of plant or tree, especially a fruit tree, that involves putting the BUD of one plant onto the stem of a different plant

bud·dy /'bʌdi/ *n.* (plural **buddies**) [C] **1** (informal) a friend: *We're good buddies.* **2** (spoken) used in order to speak to a man or boy: *Hey, buddy! Leave her alone!* | *Thanks, buddy!*

budge /bʌdʒ/ *v.* [I,T] **1** to move, or to make someone or something move: *I pulled the door, but it wouldn't budge.* | *Marshal refused to* ***budge from*** *his seat.* **2** to change your opinion, or to make someone change his/her opinion: *The Union wouldn't* ***budge from*** *their demands.*

budg·et¹ /'bʌdʒɪt/ *n.* [C] ECONOMICS a plan of how to spend the money that is available in a particular period in time, or the money itself: *a* ***budget of*** *$2 million for the project* | *the* ***budget for*** *the new library system* | ***Budget cuts*** (=a decrease in the amount of money spent) *have meant job losses.* | *He wants to* ***balance the budget*** (=make the money that is spent equal to the money coming in) *and cut taxes.* [ORIGIN: 1400—1500 Old French *bougette* "small leather bag," from Latin *bulga*; from the idea of bringing your spending plan out of its bag] —**budgetary** /'bʌdʒə,tɛri/ *adj.*: *budgetary limits*

budget² *v.* [I] ECONOMICS to carefully plan and control how much you will spend: *$150,000 has been* ***budgeted for*** *the after-school program.*

budget³ *adj.* [only before noun] very low in price: *a budget flight*

'budget ,deficit *n.* [C] ECONOMICS the amount by which the money a government spends is more than it receives in taxes or other income during a particular period

'budget ,surplus *also* **,surplus 'budget** *n.* [C] ECONOMICS money that a government still has available when it spends less than it receives in taxes or other income during a particular period

buff¹ /bʌf/ *n.* **1 movie/car/jazz etc. buff** someone who is interested in and knows a lot about movies, cars, etc. **2** [U] a pale yellow-brown color

buff² *v.* [T] to make a surface shine by polishing it with something soft

buff³ *adj.* (informal) having an attractive body

buf·fa·lo /ˈbʌfəˌloʊ/ *n.* (plural **buffaloes** *or* **buffalo**) [C] **1** a large animal like a cow, with a very large head and thick hair on its neck and shoulders SYN **bison** **2** an animal like a large black cow, with long curved horns that lives in Africa and Asia

B

buff·er /ˈbʌfɚ/ *n.* [C] **1** something that protects one thing from being affected by another thing: *The walls are a* ***buffer against*** *noise from the airport.* | *Use your commuting time as a* ***buffer between*** *work and home.* **2 buffer zone** an area between two armies, which is intended to separate them so that they do not fight **3** *also* **buffer state** POLITICS a smaller country between two larger countries, which makes war between the large countries less likely **4** IT a place in a computer's memory for storing information for a short time **5** *also* **buffer solution** CHEMISTRY a substance in a solution, that reduces effects on the PH (=the level of acid) when an acid or base is added to the solution

buf·fet¹ /bəˈfeɪ, bʊ-/ *n.* [C] a meal in which people serve themselves at a table and then sit down somewhere else to eat: *a breakfast buffet*

buf·fet² /ˈbʌfɪt/ *v.* [T] to make someone or something move by hitting him, her, or it again and again: *The small boats were buffeted by the wind and the rain.*

buf·foon /bəˈfun/ *n.* [C] someone who does silly things that make you laugh [ORIGIN: 1500—1600 French *boufon*, from Old Italian *buffone*] —**buffoonery** *n.* [U]

bug¹ /bʌg/ *n.* [C] **1** any small insect: *a little green bug* **2** (informal) a GERM (=very small creature) that causes an illness that is not very serious: *a stomach bug* **3** IT a small mistake in a computer program that stops it from working correctly

THESAURUS **defect, problem, flaw, fault, imperfection** → DEFECT¹

4 the travel/skiing/writing etc. bug (informal) a sudden strong interest in doing something, that usually only continues for a short time: *I'd been* ***bitten by the*** *travel* ***bug***. **5** a small piece of electronic equipment for listening secretly to other people's conversations

bug² *v.* (**bugged**, **bugging**) [T] **1** (informal) to annoy someone: *It bugs me that he doesn't listen.* **2** to use a bug in order to listen secretly to other people's conversations: *According to the FBI's report, the room had been bugged.*

bug·gy /ˈbʌgi/ *n.* (plural **buggies**) [C] a light carriage pulled by a horse

bu·gle /ˈbyugəl/ *n.* [C] a musical instrument like a TRUMPET, which is used in the army to call soldiers [ORIGIN: 1300—1400 *bugle horn* "instrument made from buffalo horn, bugle" (13—16 centuries), from *bugle* "buffalo"]

build¹ /bɪld/ *v.* (past tense and past participle **built** /bɪlt/) **1** [I,T] to make a structure such as a house, factory, ship, etc.: *the money to build a new bridge* | *More homes are being built near the lake.* | *houses* ***built of*** *bricks*

THESAURUS

construct – to build something large such as a building, bridge, etc.: *There are plans to construct a new library.*
put up – to build something such as a wall or building: *It took five years to put up the skyscraper.*
erect (formal) – to build something: *plans to erect a memorial at the site of the World Trade Center*
assemble – to put all the parts of something such as a machine or a piece of furniture together: *The bicycle is easy to assemble.*

2 [T] *also* **build up** to make something develop or form: *We're working to build a more peaceful world.* | *He'd been working 14-hour days to build up the business.* **3** [I,T] *also* **build up** to increase, or to make something increase: *The tension between them was building.* | *In diabetes, sugar builds up in the bloodstream and causes damage.* | *a confidence-building pre-game talk* [ORIGIN: Old English *byldan*]

build sth ↔ **into** sth *phr. v.* **1** to make something a permanent part of a system, agreement, etc.: *A completion date was built into the contract.* **2** to make something so that it is a permanent part of a structure, machine, etc.: *a cash machine built into the wall*

build on *phr. v.* **1 build on** sth to use your achievements in order to develop something further: *The soccer league hopes to build on the popularity of the game among young people.* **2 build** sth **on** sth to base something on an idea or thing: *a relationship built on loyalty and trust*

build up *phr. v.* **build up sb's hopes** to unfairly make someone think that s/he will get what s/he is hoping for: *Don't build her hopes up.*

build up to sth *phr. v.* to gradually prepare for something: *I had built up to swimming 50 lengths.*

build² *n.* [singular, U] the shape and size of someone's body: *She has black hair and a slim build.*

build·er /ˈbɪldɚ/ *n.* [C] **1** a person or company that builds buildings **2** someone or something that makes something develop or form: *The win was a real confidence-builder for the team.* | *her role as a bridge builder between the communities*

build·ing /ˈbɪldɪŋ/ *n.* **1** [C] a structure such as a house, church, or factory, that has a roof and walls: *Tall buildings lined the street.* ▸Don't say "high buildings."◂ **2** [U] the process or business of building things

ˈbuilding ˌblock *n.* **1** [C] a block of wood or plastic for young children to build things with **2 building blocks** [plural] the pieces or parts that make it possible for something big or important to exist: *Reading and writing are the building blocks of education.*

ˈbuilding code *n.* [C] one of a set of official rules about the standards that must be followed in the structure and safety of new buildings, or when changing the inside of an existing building

build·up /ˈbɪldʌp/ *n.* **1** [singular, U] a gradual increase: *a **buildup of** greenhouse gases in the atmosphere* **2** [C] the length of time spent preparing for an event: *the **buildup to** the war*

built¹ /bɪlt/ *v.* the past tense and past participle of BUILD

built² *adj.* used to describe someone's size or shape: *a man who is **built like** a tank*

ˌbuilt-ˈin *adj.* forming a part of something that cannot be separated from it: *a modern kitchen with built-in cabinets*

bulb /bʌlb/ *n.* [C] **1** the glass part of an electric light, that the light shines from: *a 40-watt bulb* **2** BIOLOGY a root shaped like a ball, that grows into a plant: *tulip bulbs* → *see picture at* PLANT¹

bul·bous /ˈbʌlbəs/ *adj.* fat and round: *a bulbous nose*

bulge¹ /bʌldʒ/ *n.* [C] **1** a curved place on the surface of something, caused by something under or inside it: *The gun made a bulge under his jacket.* **2** an increase in the amount or level of something: *the population bulge that happened after World War II*

bulge² *v.* [I] to stick out in a rounded shape: *bags **bulging with** shopping*

bu·li·mi·a /bəˈlimiə, bu-/ *n.* [U] a mental illness in which someone eats too much and then VOMITS because s/he is afraid of gaining weight [ORIGIN: 1800—1900 Modern Latin, Greek *boulimia* "great hunger," from *bous* "ox, cow" + *limos* "hunger"] —**bulimic** /bəˈlimɪk/ *adj.*

bulk /bʌlk/ (Ac) *n.* **1 the bulk (of sth)** the main or largest part of something: *The bulk of the work has already been done.* | *The bulk of the troops are stationed in the north of the country.* **2** [C,U] the large size of something or someone: *the elephant's huge bulk* | *Let dough rise in a warm place until it has doubled in bulk.* **3 in bulk** in large quantities: *Businesses buy paper in bulk.*

bulk·y /ˈbʌlki/ (Ac) *adj.* big and heavy: *a bulky package*

bull /bʊl/ *n.* **1** [C] a male cow, or the male of some other large animals, such as an ELEPHANT or WHALE **2** [U] (informal) something someone says that is stupid or not true: *That's bull. I never saw him before.* **3 take the bull by the horns** (informal) to bravely or confidently deal with a difficult, dangerous, or unpleasant problem [ORIGIN: (1) Old English *bula*]

bull·dog /ˈbʊldɔg/ *n.* [C] a dog with a large head, a flat nose, a short neck, and short thick legs

bull·doze /ˈbʊldoʊz/ *v.* [T] to move dirt and rocks, destroy buildings, etc. with a bulldozer

bull·doz·er /ˈbʊlˌdoʊzɚ/ *n.* [C] a powerful vehicle with a broad metal blade, used for moving dirt and rocks, destroying buildings, etc.

bul·let /ˈbʊlɪt/ *n.* [C] a small round piece of metal that is fired from a gun

bul·le·tin /ˈbʊlətˀn, ˈbʊlətɪn/ *n.* [C] **1** a short official news report or announcement that is made to tell people about something important: *a news bulletin* **2** a letter or printed statement that a group or organization produces to tell people its news [ORIGIN: 1700—1800 French, Italian *bullettino*, from *bulla* "official announcement by the Pope"]

ˈbulletin ˌboard *n.* [C] **1** a board on a wall, that you put information or pictures on **2** IT a place in a system of computers where you can read or leave messages

bull·fight /ˈbʊlfaɪt/ *n.* [C] a type of entertainment in some countries, in which a man fights and kills a BULL —**bullfighter** *n.* [C] —**bullfighting** *n.* [U]

bull·horn /ˈbʊlhɔrn/ *n.* [C] a piece of equipment that you hold up to your mouth when you talk, to make your voice louder

bul·lion /ˈbʊlyən/ *n.* [U] blocks of gold or silver

bull·ish /ˈbʊlɪʃ/ *adj.* ECONOMICS expecting the price of shares on a STOCK MARKET to rise (ANT) **bearish**

ˈbull ˌmarket *n.* [C] ECONOMICS a STOCK MARKET in which the prices of STOCKS are rising and prices are expected to continue rising (ANT) **bear market**

bull·pen /ˈbʊlpɛn/ *n.* [C] the area in a baseball field, in which PITCHERS practice throwing

ˈbull's-eye *n.* [C] the center of a TARGET that you try to hit when shooting

bul·ly /ˈbʊli/ *v.* (**bullied**, **bullies**) [T] to threaten to hurt someone or frighten him/her, especially someone weaker or smaller than you: *At camp, the bigger boys bullied him.* | *Don't let them **bully** you **into** working on Saturdays.* —**bully** *n.* [C]

bum¹ /bʌm/ *n.* [C] (informal) **1** (disapproving) a man who has no home or job, and who asks people

B

on the street for money **2** someone who is very lazy: *Get up, you lazy bum!* **3 beach/ski etc. bum** someone who spends all of his/her time on the beach, SKIing, etc.

bum² v. (**bummed**, **bumming**) [T] (slang) to ask someone if you can borrow or have something small: *He bummed a cigarette from her.*

bum around phr. v. (slang) **1** to spend time doing nothing, or in a very lazy way **2 bum around** sth to travel around, living very cheaply, without having any plans: *He spent a year bumming around Europe.*

bum³ adj. (informal) **1** bad and useless: *He got a bum deal.* **2** injured: *a bum leg*

bum·ble·bee /ˈbʌmbəlˌbi/ n. [C] a large hairy BEE

bum·bling /ˈbʌmblɪŋ/ adj. behaving in a careless way and making a lot of mistakes

bummed /bʌmd/ also **ˌbummed ˈout** adj. (spoken) feeling disappointed: *I'm really bummed that we can't go!*

bum·mer /ˈbʌmɚ/ n. [singular] (spoken) a situation that is disappointing: *You can't go? What **a bummer**.*

bump¹ /bʌmp/ v. **1** [I,T] to hit or knock against something, especially by accident: *It was so dark I **bumped into** a tree.* | *Don't bump your head!*

THESAURUS hit, collide, bang, strike → HIT¹

2 [I] to move up and down as you move forward in a vehicle: *We **bumped along** the dirt road.*

bump into sb phr. v. (informal) to meet someone you know when you were not expecting to: *Guess who I bumped into this morning?*

bump sb ↔ **off** phr. v. (informal) to kill someone

bump² n. [C] **1** an area of skin that is swollen because you have hit it on something: *a **bump on** his head*

THESAURUS injury, wound, bruise, contusion, cut, laceration, scrape, sprain, fracture → INJURY

2 a small raised area on a surface: *a **bump in** the road* **3** a movement in which one thing hits against another thing, or the sound that this makes: *The elevator stopped **with a bump**.*

bump·er¹ /ˈbʌmpɚ/ n. [C] **1** the part at the front and back of a car that protects it if it hits anything **2 bumper-to-bumper** bumper-to-bumper traffic is very close together and moving slowly

bumper² adj. very large: *a bumper crop*

ˈbumper ˌsticker n. [C] a small sign with a message on it on the bumper of a car

bump·y /ˈbʌmpi/ adj. **1** a bumpy surface has a lot of raised parts on it: *a bumpy road* **2** a bumpy trip by car or airplane is uncomfortable because of bad road or weather conditions

bun /bʌn/ n. [C] **1** a type of bread that is small and round: *a hamburger bun* **2** if a woman has her hair in a bun, she fastens her hair in a small round shape at the back of her head **3 buns** [plural] (informal) the two round parts of a person's bottom → BUTTOCKS

bumpy

bumpy smooth

bunch¹ /bʌntʃ/ n. [singular] a group or number of similar people or things, or a large amount of something: *The doctor asked me a **bunch of** questions.* | *a **bunch of grapes*** | *There are **a whole bunch of** little restaurants by the beach.* | *This beer is **the best of the bunch**.*

bunch² v. [I,T] **1** also **bunch together** to stay close together in a group, or to form a group: *The runners were bunched together.* **2** also **bunch up** to pull material together tightly in folds: *Her socks were bunched up around her ankles.*

bun·dle¹ /ˈbʌndl/ n. **1** [C] a group of things such as papers, clothes, or sticks that are fastened or tied together: *a **bundle of** newspapers* **2** [C] IT SOFTWARE that is included with the computer you buy **3** [singular] (informal) a lot of money: *That car must have **cost a bundle**.* **4 be a bundle of nerves/laughs etc.** (informal) to be very nervous, a lot of fun, etc.

bundle² v. **1** [I,T] also **bundle up** to make a bundle: *Dave bundled up the newspapers.* **2** [I,T] also **bundle up** to dress in a lot of warm clothes because it is cold: *Fans were **bundled up against** the cold.* **3** [T] to make someone move quickly into a particular place: *The police **bundled** him **into** a car.* **4** [T] IT to include computer software or other services when you sell a new computer

bun·ga·low /ˈbʌŋgəˌloʊ/ n. [C] a small house that usually has only one level → HOUSE¹ [ORIGIN: 1600—1700 Hindi *bangla* "(house) in the Bengal style"]

bun·gee jump·ing /ˈbʌndʒi ˌdʒʌmpɪŋ/ n. [U] a sport in which you jump off something very high while you are attached to a long length of special rope that stretches —**bungee jump** n. [C] —**bungee jumper** n. [C]

bun·gle /ˈbʌŋgəl/ v. [T] to do something badly: *They bungled the job completely.* —**bungler** n. [C] —**bungling** adj.

bun·ion /ˈbʌnyən/ n. [C] a painful sore on your big toe

bunk /bʌŋk/ n. **1** [C] a narrow bed that is attached to the wall, for example on a train or a ship **2** [C] one of the two beds that form bunk beds → *see picture at* BED[1] **3** [U] (informal) something that is not true or that does not mean anything

'bunk beds *n.* [plural] two beds that are attached together, one on top of the other

bun·ker /'bʌŋkɚ/ *n.* [C] a strongly built shelter for soldiers, usually under the ground

bun·ny /'bʌni/ *also* **'bunny ˌrabbit** *n.* [C] (plural **bunnies**) a rabbit – a word used especially by or to children

buoy[1] /'bui, bɔɪ/ *n.* [C] an object that floats on the water, used for showing boats which parts of the water are safe or dangerous

buoy[2] *also* **buoy up** *v.* [T] **1** to make someone feel happier, more confident, etc.: *The team was buoyed by their win against Stanford.* **2** ECONOMICS to keep profits, prices, etc. at a high level

buoy·ant /'bɔɪənt/ *adj.* **1** happy and confident: *a buoyant mood* **2** ECONOMICS buoyant prices, etc. tend not to fall **3** able to float —**buoyancy** *n.* [U] —**buoyantly** *adv.*

bur·den[1] /'bɚdn/ *n.* [C] (formal) **1** something that is difficult or worrying that you are responsible for: *I don't want to* ***be a burden on*** *my children when I'm old.* **2 the burden of proof** the duty to prove that something is true **3** (literary) something heavy that you have to carry [ORIGIN: Old English *byrthen*]

burden[2] *v.* [T] **1** to make someone worry or cause problems for him/her: *families* ***burdened with*** *debt* **2** to make someone carry something heavy

bu·reau /'byʊroʊ/ *n.* [C] **1** a government department or part of a government department: *the Federal Bureau of Investigation* **2** an office or organization that collects or provides information: *an employment bureau* **3** a CHEST OF DRAWERS [ORIGIN: 1600—1700 French "desk, cloth covering for desks," from Old French *burel* "woolen cloth"]

bu·reauc·ra·cy /byʊ'rɑkrəsi/ *n.* (plural **bureaucracies**) **1** [U] an official system that is annoying or confusing because it has a lot of rules, processes, etc.: *We need less bureaucracy in the school system.* **2** [C] a government organization that is divided into departments and operated by a large number of officials who are not elected, or a system in which this happens **3** [singular] the officials who are employed rather than elected to do the work of a government, business, etc.

bu·reau·crat /'byʊrəˌkræt/ *n.* [C] someone who works in a bureaucracy and follows official rules very carefully

bu·reau·crat·ic /ˌbyʊrə'kræt̬ɪk/ *adj.* involving a lot of complicated official rules and processes

bur·geon·ing /'bɚdʒənɪŋ/ *adj.* growing, increasing, or developing very quickly: *the city's burgeoning population*

burg·er /'bɚgɚ/ *n.* [C] (informal) a HAMBURGER: *a burger and fries*

bur·glar /'bɚglɚ/ *n.* [C] someone who goes into buildings, cars, etc. in order to steal things [ORIGIN: 1500—1600 Anglo-French *burgler*, from Medieval Latin *burgare* "to burgle," from Latin *burgus* "defended place"]

> THESAURUS **criminal, thief, robber, shoplifter, pickpocket, mugger** → CRIMINAL[2]

bur·glar·ize /'bɚgləˌraɪz/ *v.* [T] to go into a building, car, etc. and steal things from it

> THESAURUS **steal, rob, mug, shoplift, rip off sth, loot, plunder, pilfer** → STEAL[1]

bur·gla·ry /'bɚgləri/ *n.* (plural **burglaries**) [C,U] the crime of going into a building, car, etc. to steal things

> THESAURUS **crime, theft, robbery, shoplifting, mugging** → CRIME

bur·gun·dy /'bɚgəndi/ *n.* (plural **burgundies**) **1** [C,U] red or white wine from the Burgundy area of France **2** [U] a dark red color —**burgundy** *adj.*

bur·i·al /'bɛriəl/ *n.* [C,U] the act or ceremony of putting a dead body into a GRAVE

bur·lap /'bɚlæp/ *n.* [U] a type of thick rough cloth

bur·ly /'bɚli/ *adj.* a burly man is big and strong

burn[1] /bɚn/ *v.* (past tense and past participle **burned** *or* **burnt** /bɚnt/)

1 DESTROY/INJURE WITH FIRE [I,T] to damage something or hurt someone with fire, heat, or the Sun, or to be hurt or damaged in this way: *Ricky* ***burned*** *his hand* ***on*** *the stove.* | *Parts of the building are still burning.* | *I burned the toast.* | *You can still get burned at the beach even if it's cloudy.*

2 PRODUCE FLAMES [I] to produce heat and flames: *a fire burning in the fireplace*

3 get burned (spoken) **a)** to be emotionally hurt by someone or something: *I'm going to take things slowly because I don't want to get burned again.* **b)** to lose a lot of money, especially in a business deal

4 FUEL [I,T] if you burn a FUEL, or if it burns, it is used for producing power, heat, light, etc.: *Cars burn gasoline.*

5 FACE/CHEEKS [I] if your face or cheeks are burning, you feel hot because you are embarrassed or upset

6 FAT/ENERGY [T] if you burn fat or CALORIES, you use up energy stored in your body by being physically active: *a fat-burning exercise*

7 CD/DVD [T] IT if you burn a CD or DVD, you record information onto it using special computer equipment

8 LIGHT [I] (literary) if a light or lamp burns, it shines or produces light [ORIGIN: Old English *byrnan* "to burn" and *bærnan* "to cause to burn"] —**burned** *adj.* —**burnt** *adj.*

B

burn (sth ↔) **down** *phr. v.* if a building burns down or is burned down, it is destroyed by fire

burn sth ↔ **off** *phr. v.* **burn off energy/fat/calories** to use energy that is stored in your body by doing physical exercise

B

burn out *phr. v.*
1 burn (sth ↔) **out** if a fire burns out or burns itself out, it stops burning because there is no coal, wood, etc. left
2 burn (sth ↔) **out** if an engine or electric wire burns out or is burned out, it stops working because it has become too hot
3 be burned out if a building, car, etc. is burned out, the inside of it is destroyed by fire
4 burn (sb) **out** to work so hard over a period of time that you become very tired and do not want to continue: *After three years of 14-hour days, he was burned out.*

burn up *phr. v.*
1 burn sth ↔ **up** if something burns up or is burned up, it is completely destroyed by fire or great heat
2 burn sb **up** (informal) to make someone angry: *The way she treats him really burns me up.*

burn² *n.* [C] an injury or mark caused by fire or heat: *a burn on her arm*

burn·er /ˈbɚnɚ/ *n.* **1** [C] the part of a STOVE that produces heat or a flame **2 put sth on the back burner** (informal) to delay dealing with something until a later time

burn·ing /ˈbɚnɪŋ/ *adj.* **1** on fire: *The boys were rescued from the burning house.* **2** feeling very hot: *a burning fever* **3 burning ambition/need etc.** a very strong ambition, need etc. **4 burning question/issue** a very important or urgent question, etc. —**burning** *adv.*

bur·nish /ˈbɚnɪʃ/ *v.* [T] to polish metal until it shines —**burnished** *adj.*

burnt /bɚnt/ *v.* a past tense and past participle of BURN

burp /bɚp/ *v.* (informal) **1** [I] if you burp, gas comes up from your stomach through your mouth and makes a noise **2** [T] to help a baby get rid of stomach gas, especially by rubbing his/her back —**burp** *n.* [C]

bur·ri·to /bəˈriṭoʊ/ *n.* (plural **burritos**) [C] a Mexican food made from a TORTILLA folded around meat or beans

bur·ro /ˈbɚoʊ, ˈbʊroʊ/ *n.* (plural **burros**) [C] a small DONKEY

bur·row¹ /ˈbɚoʊ, ˈbʌroʊ/ *v.* [I] to make a hole or passage in the ground: *Gophers had* ***burrowed under*** *the wall.*

burrow² *n.* [C] a passage in the ground made by an animal such as a rabbit or a FOX for it to live in

burst¹ /bɚst/ *v.* (past tense and past participle **burst**) **1** [I,T] to break open or apart suddenly and violently, or to make something do this: *a game in which kids sit on balloons to try to burst them*

THESAURUS break, smash, shatter, crack, tear, snap, pop → BREAK¹

2 be bursting to be very full of something: *This town* ***is bursting with*** *tourists.* | *School classrooms* ***are bursting at the seams*** (=are too full of students). **3** [I] to move suddenly, quickly, and often violently: *She* ***burst through*** *the door of my room.* **4 be bursting with pride/confidence/energy etc.** to be very proud, confident, etc. [ORIGIN: Old English *berstan*]

burst in on sb/sth *phr. v.* to suddenly enter a room and interrupt someone or something, in a way that embarrasses you or other people: *I burst in on her mother in the bathroom.*

burst into sth *phr. v.* to suddenly start to do something: *Ellen* ***burst into tears*** (=began crying). | *The car hit a tree and* ***burst into flames*** (=began burning).

burst out *phr. v.* **1 burst out laughing/crying etc.** to suddenly start to laugh, cry, etc. **2** to suddenly say something in a strong way: *"I don't believe it!" she burst out angrily.*

burst² *n.* **a burst of sth** a short sudden period of increased activity, loud noise, or strong feeling: *a sudden* ***burst of*** *laughter* | *a* ***burst of*** *machine gun fire*

bur·y /ˈbɛri/ *v.* (**buried**, **buries**) [T] **1** to put a dead body into a GRAVE: *Aunt Betty was* ***buried in*** *Woodlawn Cemetery.* **2** to cover something with something else so that it cannot be seen: *a dog burying a bone* | *She* ***buried*** *her face* ***in*** *her hands.* | *His glasses were* ***buried under*** *a pile of papers.* **3** to ignore a feeling or memory and pretend that it does not exist **4 bury the hatchet/bury your differences** to end a disagreement about something and become friends again

bus¹ /bʌs/ *n.* (plural **buses**) [C] a large vehicle that people pay to travel on: *Are you going to drive or go* ***by bus****?* | *Five people* ***got on the bus****.* ▸Don't say "...get in the bus."◂ | *They* ***ride/take the bus*** *to school.* | *I* ***caught the bus*** *at 6th Street.* [ORIGIN: 1800—1900 *omnibus*] → *see picture at* TRANSPORTATION

bus² *v.* [T] **1** to take a group of people somewhere in a bus: *Many children are being* ***bused to*** *schools in other areas.* **2** to take away dirty dishes from the tables in a restaurant: *a job* ***busing tables***

bus·boy /ˈbʌsbɔɪ/ *n.* [C] a man whose job is to take away dirty dishes from the tables in a restaurant

bush /bʊʃ/ *n.* **1** [C] a plant with many thin branches growing up from the ground: *a rose bush* → *see picture on page A23* **2 the bush** EARTH SCIENCES wild country that has not been cleared in Australia or Africa → **beat around the bush** *at* BEAT¹

bushed /bʊʃt/ *adj.* (informal) very tired: *I'm bushed.*

bush·el /ˈbʊʃəl/ *n.* [C] a unit for measuring dry food, equal to 8 gallons, or 36.4 liters

bush·y /ˈbʊʃi/ *adj.* bushy hair or fur grows thickly: *a bushy tail*

bus·i·ly /ˈbɪzəli/ *adv.* in a busy way

busi·ness /ˈbɪznɪs/ *n.*

1 WORK DONE BY COMPANIES [U] the activity of buying or selling goods or services: *We **do** a lot of **business with** a company in Texas.* | *jobs in the **music/advertising/publishing business***

THESAURUS

commerce – the buying and selling of goods and services: *laws that regulate commerce between nations*
industry – the production of goods, especially in factories: *a decline in manufacturing industry*
trade – the business of buying and selling things, especially between countries: *restrictions on trade*
private enterprise – the economic system in which private businesses can compete, and the government does not control industry

2 A COMPANY [C] an organization that produces or sells goods or services: *a real-estate business* | *He **runs a** printing **business**.* | *the owner of a **small business***

THESAURUS **company, firm, corporation, subsidiary** → COMPANY

3 YOUR JOB [U] work that you do as part of your job: *Al's gone to Japan **on business**.* | *a **business trip***
4 AMOUNT OF WORK [U] the amount of work a company does, or the amount of money it makes: ***Business is good/bad/slow** during the winter.*
5 be in business to be operating as a company: *He's in business for himself* (=he owns a small company).
6 go into business/go out of business to begin or stop operating as a company: *Many small companies have recently gone out of business.*
7 big business a) large and powerful companies in general: *the Republican's links with big business* **b)** something that makes a lot of profit: *Toys are big business.*
8 PERSONAL LIFE [U] if something is not your business, you should not be involved in it or ask about it: *It's **none of your business** how much I earn.* | *Why don't you just **mind your own business*** (=used in order to tell someone rudely that you do not want his/her advice, help, etc.)!
9 SUBJECT/ACTIVITY [singular] a subject, event, or activity, especially one that you have a particular opinion of: *Rock climbing can be a risky business.*
10 get down to business to start dealing with an important subject
11 business as usual if a situation is business as usual, things are happening as they usually do, even though there is a reason why you might expect them not to happen normally: *The owners have changed, but it's business as usual for the popular restaurant.*
12 mean business (informal) to be determined to do something: *The border is being guarded by troops who mean business.*
13 have no business doing sth if someone has no business doing something, s/he should not do it: *He was drunk and had no business driving.* [ORIGIN: 1300—1400 *busy*] → BIG BUSINESS

ˈbusiness ˌcard *n.* [C] a card that shows your name, the name of your company, the company's address, etc.

busi·ness·like /ˈbɪznɪsˌlaɪk/ *adj.* effective and practical in the way you do things: *a businesslike attitude*

THESAURUS **organized, efficient, well-run** → ORGANIZED

busi·ness·man /ˈbɪznɪsˌmæn/, **busi·ness·wom·an** /ˈbɪznɪsˌwʊmən/ *n.* (plural **businessmen** /-ˌmɛn/, **businesswomen** /-ˌwɪmɪn/) [C] someone who works at a fairly high level in a company, or who owns a business

ˈbusiness ˌsuit *n.* [C] a suit that a man wears during the day at work

bus·ing /ˈbʌsɪŋ/ *n.* [U] a system in which students ride buses to schools that are far from where they live, so that a school has students of different races

ˈbus lane *n.* [C] a part of a wide street, that only buses can use

ˈbus ˌstation *n.* [C] a place where buses start and finish their trips

ˈbus stop *n.* [C] a place at the side of a road, marked with a sign, where buses stop for passengers

bust[1] /bʌst/ *v.* [T] (informal) **1** to break something: *I busted my watch.* **2 bust sb (for sth)** if the police bust someone, they catch someone who has done something illegal **3** to use too much money: *A new car would bust our budget.* **4 crime-busting/union-busting/budget-busting etc.** used with nouns to show that a situation is being ended or an activity is being stopped

bust[2] *n.* [C] **1** a woman's breasts, or the measurement around a woman's breasts and back: *a 34-inch bust* **2** (informal) a situation in which the police go into a place in order to catch people doing something illegal: *a drug bust* **3** ENG. LANG. ARTS a model of someone's head, shoulders, and upper chest: *a **bust of** Beethoven*

bust[3] *adj.* **go bust** a business that goes bust stops operating because it does not have enough money

bust·er /ˈbʌstɚ/ *n.* [C] **1** (informal) something that ends a situation, or that stops a particular activity: *The storm should be a drought-buster.* **2** (spoken) used when speaking to a man who is annoying you, or whom you do not respect

bus·tle[1] /ˈbʌsəl/ *n.* [singular] busy and usually noisy activity: *the **bustle of** the big city* —**bustling** *adj.*

bustle[2] *v.* [I] to move around quickly, looking very busy: *Linda **bustled around** the kitchen.*

B

bus·y¹ /ˈbɪzi/ *adj.* (comparative **busier**, superlative **busiest**) **1** a busy person is working hard and has a lot of things to do: *Hawkins is **busy with** a customer.* | *He's busy studying for his finals.* | *a busy mother* | *I found some paper and crayons to **keep** the kids **busy**.* **2** a busy time is full of work or other activities: *a very busy day* **3** a busy place is full of people or vehicles, or has a lot happening in it: *a busy airport* **4** a telephone that is busy is being used: *I keep getting a **busy signal**.* **5** (disapproving) a pattern or design that is busy is full of details

busy² *v.* (**busied**, **busies**) **busy yourself with sth** to do something in order to make time seem to go faster: *He busied himself with cleaning.*

bus·y·bod·y /ˈbɪzi,bɑdi, -,bʌdi/ *n.* (plural **busybodies**) [C] someone who is too interested in other people's private activities

but¹ /bət; *strong* bʌt/ *conjunction* **1** used in order to connect two statements or phrases, when the second statement adds something different or seems surprising after the first one: *It's an old car, but it's reliable.* | *an expensive but useful book* **2** used before you give the reason why something did not happen or is not true or possible: *I'd like to go, but I'm awfully busy.* **3** used in order to show surprise at what has just been said: *"I have to leave tomorrow." "But you only got here this morning!"* **4** except: *I had no choice but to leave.*

SPOKEN PHRASES

5 used in order to introduce a new subject: *That's why I've been so busy this week. But, how are you anyway?* **6 but then (again)...** used in order to show that what you have just said is not as surprising as it seems: *He doesn't have a strong accent, **but then** he has lived here for 35 years.* **7** used after phrases such as "Excuse me" and "I'm sorry": *I'm sorry, but you're not allowed to go in there.*

but² *prep.* except for: *Joe can come any day but Monday.* | *There's nobody here but me.*

butch·er¹ /ˈbʊtʃɚ/ *n.* [C] someone who owns or works in a store that sells meat [ORIGIN: 1200—1300 Old French *bouchier*, from *bouc* "male goat"]

butcher² *v.* [T] **1** to kill animals and prepare them to be used as meat **2** to kill people in a cruel way —**butchery** *n.* [U]

but·ler /ˈbʌtˀlɚ/ *n.* [C] the main male servant of a house

butt¹ /bʌt/ *n.* [C] **1** (informal) the part of your body that you sit on → BUTTOCKS **2** the end of a cigarette after most of it has been smoked **3** the end of the handle of a gun **4 be the butt of sth** to be the person or thing that other people often make jokes about

butt² *v.* [I,T] if a person or animal butts something or someone, it hits or pushes him, her, or it with its head

butt in *phr. v.* to become involved in someone else's private situation or conversation

butt out *phr. v.* (informal) used in order to tell someone to stop being involved in something private: *This has nothing to do with you, so just butt out!*

butte /byut/ *n.* [C] EARTH SCIENCES a large hill with steep sides and a flat top

but·ter¹ /ˈbʌt̬ɚ/ *n.* [U] a yellow food made from milk or cream, that you spread on bread or use in cooking [ORIGIN: Old English *butere*, from Latin *butyrum*, from Greek *boutyron*, from *bous* "cow" + *tyros* "cheese"] —**buttery** *adj.*

butter² *v.* [T] to spread butter on something

butter sb ↔ **up** *phr. v.* (informal) to say nice things to someone so that s/he will do what you want

but·ter·cup /ˈbʌt̬ɚ,kʌp/ *n.* [C] a small shiny yellow wild flower

but·ter·fin·gers /ˈbʌt̬ɚ,fɪŋgɚz/ *n.* [singular] (informal) someone who often drops things

butterfly

moth butterfly

but·ter·fly /ˈbʌt̬ɚ,flaɪ/ *n.* (plural **butterflies**) [C] **1** an insect with large and usually colored wings **2 have butterflies (in your stomach)** (informal) to feel very nervous

but·ter·milk /ˈbʌt̬ɚ,mɪlk/ *n.* [U] the liquid that remains after butter has been made, used for drinking or cooking

but·ter·scotch /ˈbʌt̬ɚ,skɑtʃ/ *n.* [C,U] a type of candy made from butter and sugar boiled together

but·tock /ˈbʌt̬ək/ *n.* [C usually plural] (formal) one of the soft parts of your body that you sit on

but·ton¹ /ˈbʌtˀn/ *n.* [C] **1** a small round flat object on your shirt, coat, etc. that you pass through a hole to fasten it: *He left the top **button undone**.* **2** a small object on a machine that you press to make it work: ***Push** the "play" **button**.* **3** a small metal or plastic pin with a message or picture on it [ORIGIN: 1300—1400 Old French *boton*, from *boter* "to push"]

button² *also* **button up** *v.* [I,T] to fasten something with buttons, or to be fastened with buttons: *Button up your coat.*

THESAURUS **fasten, secure, join, glue, tape, staple, clip, tie, zip (up)** → FASTEN

but·ton·hole /ˈbʌtˀn,hoʊl/ *n.* [C] a hole for a button to be put through to fasten a shirt, coat, etc.

but·tress¹ /ˈbʌtrɪs/ *v.* [T] (formal) to do something to support a system, idea, argument, etc.: *The evidence clearly buttresses the Treasury's argument.*

buttress² *n.* [C] a structure built to support a wall

bux·om /ˈbʌksəm/ *adj.* a woman who is buxom has large breasts

buy¹ /baɪ/ *v.* (past tense and past participle **bought** /bɔt/) **1** [I,T] to get something by paying money for it: *Let me buy you a drink.* | *It's best to* ***buy*** *plants* ***from*** *a good nursery.* | *The money will be used to* ***buy*** *equipment* ***for*** *the school.*

THESAURUS

purchase (formal) – to buy something: *Tickets for the performance can be purchased by phone.*
acquire (formal) – to buy a company or property: *They want to acquire valuable works of art as cheaply as possible.*
get – to buy or obtain something: *I never know what to get Dad for his birthday.*
procure (formal) – to buy or obtain something, especially something that is difficult to get: *The organization helps workers procure insurance at cheaper rates.*
snap sth up – to buy something immediately, especially because it is very cheap: *Real estate in the area is being snapped up by developers.*
pick sth up – to buy something: *Could you pick up some milk on your way home?*
stock up – to buy a lot of something that you intend to use later: *Before the blizzard, we stocked up on food.*

2 [T] (informal) to believe an explanation or reason for something: *"I'll tell the police it was an accident." "They'll never buy it."*

THESAURUS **believe, accept, take sb's word, swallow, fall for sth, give credence to sth** → BELIEVE

3 buy time (informal) to do something that will get you more time to finish something **4** [T] *also* **buy off** (informal) to pay money to someone in order to persuade him/her to do something dishonest SYN **bribe**: *They say the judge was bought.*

buy into sth *phr. v.* **1** to accept that an idea is right and allow it to influence you: *women who buy into the idea of having a "perfect body"* **2** ECONOMICS to buy part of a business or organization: *How much does it cost to buy into a hamburger franchise?*

buy sb/sth ↔ **out** *phr. v.* ECONOMICS to buy someone's share of a business or property that you previously owned together, so that you gain control

buy sth ↔ **up** *phr. v.* to quickly buy as much as you can of something: *Even small local papers have been bought up by the national newspaper chains.*

buy² *n.* **be a good/bad buy** to be worth or not worth the price you paid: *These shoes were a good buy.*

buy·er /ˈbaɪɚ/ *n.* [C] **1** someone who is buying or has bought something: *a first-time home buyer*

THESAURUS **customer, client, shopper, patron, consumer** → CUSTOMER

2 someone whose job is to choose and buy the goods that a store or company will sell

buy·out /ˈbaɪaʊt/ *n.* [C] ECONOMICS a situation in which someone gains control of a company by buying all of its STOCK: *a management buyout*

B

buzz¹ /bʌz/ *v.* **1** [I] to make a continuous noise like the sound of a BEE: *What's making that buzzing noise?* **2** [I] if a group of people or a place is buzzing, people are making a lot of noise because they are excited: *The room* ***buzzed with*** *excitement.* **3** [I,T] to call someone by pressing a buzzer: *Tina* ***buzzed for*** *her secretary.*

buzz off *phr. v.* (informal) used in order to tell someone to go away in an impolite way

buzz² *n.* **1** [C] a continuous noise like the sound of a BEE: *the buzz of traffic in the distance* → *see picture on page A20* **2** [singular] (informal) a strong feeling of excitement, pleasure, or success, especially one you get from alcohol or drugs

buz·zard /ˈbʌzɚd/ *n.* [C] a large wild bird that eats dead animals

buzz·er /ˈbʌzɚ/ *n.* [C] a small thing like a button, that makes a buzzing sound when you press it: ***Press the buzzer*** *if you know the answer.*

buzz·word /ˈbʌzˌwɚd/ *n.* [C] a word or phrase relating to a particular subject that is suddenly very popular

by¹ /baɪ/ *prep.* **1** used with PASSIVE forms of verbs to show who did something or what caused something: *a play by Shakespeare* | *a film made by Steven Spielberg* | *Her money is controlled by her family.* **2** near or beside: *He was standing by the window.* **3** past: *Two dogs ran by me.* **4** used in order to say what means or method someone uses to do something: *Send the letter by airmail.* | *Carolyn earns extra money by babysitting.* | *We went from New York to Philadelphia* ***by car/plane/train/bus.*** **5** no later than a particular time: *This report has to be done by 5:00.* **6 by mistake/accident** without intending to do something: *She locked the door by mistake.* **7** according to a particular way of doing things: *By law, cars cannot pass a school bus that has stopped.* **8** used in order to show which part of something someone holds: *I picked up the pot by the handle.* | *She grabbed him by the arm.* **9** used in order to show a distance, amount, or rate: *The room is 24 feet by 36 feet.* | *Are you paid by the hour?* **10 by the way** (spoken) used in order to begin talking about a subject that is not related to the one you were talking about: *Oh, by the way, Vicky called while you were out.* **11 (all) by yourself** completely alone: *They left the boy by himself for two days!* **12 day by day/little by little etc.** used in order to show that something happens gradually: *Little by little, he began to understand the language.*

by² *adv.* **1** past: *One or two cars went by.* | *Three hours went by before we heard any* *news.* **2 come/stop/go by** to visit or go to a place for a short time when you intend to go somewhere else afterward: *Come by* (=come to my house, office, etc.) *any time tomorrow.* | *I had to stop by the supermarket on the way home.* **3 by and large** used when talking generally about something: *By and large, the new arrangements are working well.*

bye /baɪ/ *also* **ˌbye-ˈbye** *interjection* (spoken) goodbye: *Bye, Sandy!*

C

ˈby-eˌlection *n.* [C] POLITICS a special election to replace a politician who has left the government or died

by·gone /ˈbaɪgɔn, -gɑn/ *adj.* **bygone days/age/era etc.** a period in the past

by·gones /ˈbaɪgɔnz, -gɑnz/ *n.* **let bygones be bygones** (informal) to forgive someone for something bad that s/he has done to you

by·law /ˈbaɪlɔ/ *n.* [C] a rule made by an organization

ˈby-line *n.* [C] a line at the beginning of a newspaper or magazine article that gives the writer's name

BYOB *adj.* **bring your own bottle** used in order to describe a party or event that you bring your own alcoholic drinks to

by·pass¹ /ˈbaɪpæs/ *n.* [C] **1** a medical operation that repairs the system of ARTERIES around the heart: *a triple heart bypass operation* **2** a road that goes around a town or other busy place rather than through it

bypass² *v.* [T] **1** to avoid a place by going around it: *If we bypass the town, we'll save time.* **2** to avoid obeying a rule, system, or someone in an official position: *He bypassed the complaints procedure and wrote straight to the chairman.*

by-product, by·prod·uct *n.* /ˈbaɪˌprɑdʌkt/ [C] **1** a substance that is produced during the process of making something else: *Sausages are made from a variety of meats and meat by-products.* **2** an unexpected result of an event or of something you do: *Job losses are a* ***by-product of*** *the economic slowdown.*

by·stand·er /ˈbaɪˌstændɚ/ *n.* [C] someone who watches what is happening without taking part: *Several* ***innocent bystanders*** *were killed.*

byte /baɪt/ *n.* [C] IT a unit for measuring the amount of information a computer can use, equal to 8 BITS

by·way /ˈbaɪˌweɪ/ *n.* [C] a small road or path that is not used very much

by·word /ˈbaɪˌwɚd/ *n.* [C] the name of someone or something that has become so well known for a particular quality that it represents that quality: *The housing projects have become a* ***byword for*** *poverty.*

C, c /si/ **1** the third letter of the English alphabet **2** the number 100 in the system of ROMAN NUMERALS

C¹ /si/ *n.* **1** [C] a grade given to a student's work to show that it is of average quality: *Terry* ***got a C*** *on the final exam.* **2** [C,U] ENG. LANG. ARTS the first note in the musical SCALE of C MAJOR, or the musical KEY based on this note

C² PHYSICS the written abbreviation of CELSIUS or CENTIGRADE

c. the written abbreviation of CIRCA

CA the written abbreviation of CALIFORNIA

cab /kæb/ *n.* [C] **1** a car with a driver who you pay to drive you somewhere (SYN) **taxi**: *We'll just* ***take a cab*** *home.*

COLLOCATIONS

call a cab – to telephone and ask a cab to come to where you are
call sb a cab – to telephone and ask for a cab for someone else
hail a cab – to stand outside and raise your arm so that a cab will stop for you

2 the part of a truck or train where the driver sits

cab·a·ret /ˌkæbəˈreɪ/ *n.* [C,U] entertainment such as music and dancing performed in a restaurant while customers eat and drink [ORIGIN: 1600—1700 French "drinking place, bar"]

cab·bage /ˈkæbɪdʒ/ *n.* [C,U] a large round vegetable with thick green or purple leaves that can be cooked or eaten raw [ORIGIN: 1400—1500 French *caboche* "head"] ➔ *see picture at* VEGETABLE

cab·bie, cabby /ˈkæbi/ *n.* [C] (informal) someone who drives a cab

cab·in /ˈkæbɪn/ *n.* [C] **1** a small house made of wood, usually in a forest or the mountains: *a log cabin* **2** a small room on a ship, in which you sleep **3** the area inside an airplane where the passengers sit ➔ *see picture at* AIRPLANE [ORIGIN: 1300—1400 Old French *cabane*, from Old Provençal *cabana* "small wooden building"]

ˈcabin crew *n.* [C] the people who take care of the passengers and serve meals on an airplane

cab·i·net /ˈkæbənɪt/ *n.* [C] **1** a piece of furniture with doors and shelves or drawers, used for storing or showing things: *a filing cabinet* | *the kitchen cabinets* **2** an important group of politicians who make decisions or advise the leader of a government: *cabinet members* [ORIGIN: 1500—1600 French "small room," from Old North French *cabine* "room for gambling"]

ca·ble¹ /ˈkeɪbəl/ *n.* **1** [C,U] a plastic or rubber tube containing wires that carry electronic signals, telephone messages, etc.: *an underground telephone cable* **2** [U] a system of broadcasting television by using cables, paid for by the person watching it: *I'll wait for the movie to come out* ***on cable****.* | *the growth of* ***cable television*** **3** [C,U] a thick strong metal rope used on ships, to support bridges, etc. **4** [C] a TELEGRAM

cable² *v.* [I,T] to send a TELEGRAM

cable car

'cable car *n.* [C] **1** a vehicle that is pulled along by a cable, used like a bus to take people from one place to another **2** a vehicle that hangs from a cable and takes people up a mountain

ca·boose /kə'bus/ *n.* [C] a small railroad car at the end of a train

cache /kæʃ/ *n.* [C] **1** a group of things that are hidden, or the place where they are hidden: *The soldiers found a* ***cache of*** *weapons in the forest.* **2** IT a special part of a computer's MEMORY that helps it work faster by storing information for a short time —**cache** *v.* [T]

ca·chet /kæ'ʃeɪ/ *n.* [U] a quality that is good or desirable: *It's a great college, but it lacks the cachet of Harvard.*

cack·le /'kækəl/ *v.* [I] **1** to make the loud noise a chicken makes **2** to laugh or talk in a loud rough voice

THESAURUS **laugh, giggle, chuckle, snicker, titter, guffaw** → LAUGH¹

—**cackle** *n.* [C]

ca·coph·o·ny /kæ'kɑfəni/ *n.* [singular] (formal) a mixture of loud sounds together that are not pleasant to listen to: *a* ***cacophony of*** *car horns* —**cacophonous** *adj.*

cac·tus /'kæktəs/ *n.* (plural **cacti** /'kæktaɪ/ *or* **cactuses**) [C] a desert plant with thick stems and sharp points *see picture on page A23*

cactus

ca·dav·er /kə'dævɚ/ *n.* [C] (formal) a dead human body

cad·dy /'kædi/ *n.* (plural **caddies**) [C] someone who carries the equipment for someone who is playing GOLF —**caddy** *v.* [I]

ca·dence /'keɪdns/ *n.* [C] **1** the way someone's voice rises and falls **2** ENG. LANG. ARTS a regular repeated pattern of sounds

ca·det /kə'dɛt/ *n.* [C] someone who is studying to become an officer in the military or the police

cad·mi·um /'kædmiəm/ *n.* [U] CHEMISTRY (*symbol* **Cd**) a type of metal that is an ELEMENT and that is used in BATTERIES

ca·dre /'kædri, 'kɑ-, -dreɪ/ *n.* [C] (formal) a small group of specially trained people in a profession, political party, or military force: *a cadre of highly trained scientists*

cae·sar·e·an /sɪ'zɛriən/ *n.* [C] another spelling of CESAREAN

ca·fe, café /kæ'feɪ, kə-/ *n.* [C] a small restaurant [ORIGIN: 1800—1900 French "coffee, café," from Turkish *kahve*]

caf·e·te·ri·a /ˌkæfə'tɪriə/ *n.* [C] a restaurant where people get their own food at a COUNTER and take it to a table themselves: *the school cafeteria* [ORIGIN: 1800—1900 American Spanish "coffee shop," from Spanish *café* "coffee"]

THESAURUS **restaurant, cafe/coffee shop, fast food restaurant, diner** → RESTAURANT

caf·feine /kæ'fin, 'kæfin/ *n.* [U] a chemical substance in coffee, tea, and some other drinks that makes people feel more active: *caffeine-free beverages*

cage¹ /keɪdʒ/ *n.* [C] a structure made of wires or bars in which birds or animals can be kept: *a hamster cage* [ORIGIN: 1100—1200 Old French, Latin *cavea* "hollow place, cage"]

cage² *v.* [T] to put an animal or bird in a cage

cag·ey /'keɪdʒi/ *adj.* (informal) not willing to talk about your plans or intentions: *The White House is being very* ***cagey about*** *the contents of the report.*

ca·hoots /kə'huts/ *n.* **be in cahoots (with sb)** (informal) to be working secretly with others, usually to do something that is not honest

cai·man /'keɪmən/ *n.* [C] a type of small CROCODILE that lives in tropical areas of North, Central, and South America

ca·jole /kə'dʒoʊl/ *v.* [T] to persuade someone to do something by praising him/her or making promises to him/her: *She* ***cajoled*** *him* ***into*** *helping.* [ORIGIN: 1600—1700 French *cajoler* "to make noises like a bird in a cage, cajole," from Old North French *gaiole* "birdcage"]

THESAURUS **persuade, talk sb into sth, get sb to do sth, encourage sb to do sth, influence, convince, coax, prevail on/upon sb** → PERSUADE

Ca·jun /'keɪdʒən/ *n.* [C] a member of a group of

people in southern Louisiana whose family originally came from the French-speaking part of Canada —**Cajun** *adj.*

cake[1] /keɪk/ *n.* **1** [C,U] a sweet food made by baking a mixture of flour, fat, sugar, and eggs: *chocolate cake* | *a* ***birthday cake*** | *Do you want a* ***piece of cake****?* **2** [C] a small piece of something, made into a flat shape: *a cake of soap* **3 salmon/rice/potato etc. cake** fish, rice, etc. that has been formed into a flat round shape and cooked **4 be a piece of cake** (informal) to be very easy: *We looked at the other team and thought, "piece of cake!"* **5 take the cake** (informal) to be worse than anything else you can imagine: *Of all the stupid things you've done, this takes the cake!* **6 have your cake and eat it too** (informal) to have all the advantages of something without any of the disadvantages [ORIGIN: 1100—1200 Old Norse *kaka*]

cake[2] *v.* **be caked in/with sth** to be covered with a thick layer of something: *Irene's boots were caked with mud.*

cal. *or* **Cal.** CHEMISTRY a written abbreviation of CALORIE

ca·lam·i·ty /kə'læməṭi/ *n.* (plural **calamities**) [C] a very bad unexpected event that causes a lot of damage or suffering: *If the crops fail again, it will be a calamity for the country.* —**calamitous** *adj.*

cal·ci·um /'kælsiəm/ *n.* [U] CHEMISTRY (*symbol* **Ca**) a silver-white metal that is an ELEMENT and that helps to form teeth, bones, and CHALK [ORIGIN: 1800—1900 Modern Latin, Latin *calx* "lime"]

cal·cu·late /'kælkyə,leɪt/ *v.* **1** [I,T] MATH to find out something or measure something using numbers: *These instruments calculate distances precisely.* | *Researchers* ***calculated that*** *the chances of having an accident rose 4.3%.* | *I'm trying to* ***calculate how*** *long it will take us to drive to Denver.*

THESAURUS

figure out – a less formal word for calculate: *Let's try to figure out how much this will cost.*
tally (up) – to calculate the total number of points won, things done, etc.: *Can you tally up the scores?*
add sth and sth – to put two or more numbers together to find the total: *Add 7 and 5 to make 12.*
subtract sth from sth also **take sth away from sth** – to reduce one number by another number: *If you subtract 12 from 15, you get 3.* | *8 take away 2 is 6.*
multiply – to add a number to itself a particular number of times: *4 multiplied by 10 is 40.*
divide – to calculate how many times one number contains another number: *10 divided by 2 equals 5.*
plus (spoken) – used between numbers to show that you are adding them together: *Two plus two equals four.*
minus (spoken) – used between numbers to show that you are taking one away from the other: *Six minus five is one.*
times (spoken) – used between numbers to show that you are multiplying them together: *Six times three is eighteen.*

2 be calculated to do sth to be intended to have a particular effect: *The ads are calculated to attract Hispanic buyers.* [ORIGIN: 1500—1600 Latin, past participle of *calculare*, from *calculus* "stone used in counting"]

cal·cu·lat·ed /'kælkyə,leɪṭɪd/ *adj.* **1 calculated risk/gamble** something you do after thinking carefully, although you know it may have bad results **2** deliberately and carefully planned to have a particular effect: *a calculated attempt to deceive the public*

cal·cu·lat·ing /'kælkyə,leɪṭɪŋ/ *adj.* (disapproving) someone who is calculating makes careful plans to get what s/he wants, without caring about how it affects other people

cal·cu·la·tion /,kælkyə'leɪʃən/ *n.* [C usually plural, U] MATH the act of adding, multiplying, or dividing numbers to find out an amount, price, etc.: *I* ***made*** *a few quick* ***calculations****.* | *an approximate* ***calculation of*** *the cost* | ***By*** *their* ***calculations****, the debt will be paid off in four years.*

cal·cu·la·tor /'kælkyə,leɪṭɚ/ *n.* [C] a small machine that can add, multiply, divide, etc. numbers

cal·cu·lus /'kælkyələs/ *n.* [U] MATH the part of mathematics that studies changing quantities, such as the speed of a falling stone or the slope of a curved line

cal·de·ra /kæl'dɛrə/ *n.* [C] EARTH SCIENCES a large deep hole in the top of a VOLCANO, formed by an ERUPTION (=explosion which sends smoke, fire, and rock into the sky)

cal·en·dar /'kæləndɚ/ *n.* [C] **1** a set of pages showing the days, weeks, and months of a year, that you usually hang on the wall **2** all the things that you plan to do in the following days, months, etc.: *My calendar is full this week.* **3** a system that divides and measures time in a particular way: *the Jewish calendar* **4 calendar year/month** a period of time that continues from the first day of the month or year until the last day of the month or year [ORIGIN: 1100—1200 Anglo-French *calender*, from Medieval Latin *kalendarium*, from Latin *kalendae* "first day of an ancient Roman month"]

calf /kæf/ *n.* (plural **calves** /kævz/) [C] **1** the part at the back of your leg between your knee and foot **2** the baby of a cow, or of some other large animals such as an ELEPHANT

cal·i·ber /'kæləbɚ/ *n.* [C] **1** the level of quality or ability that someone or something has achieved: *musicians* ***of*** *the highest* ***caliber*** **2** the width of a bullet or the inside part of a gun [ORIGIN: 1500—1600 French *calibre*, from Old Italian *calibro*, from Arabic *qalib* "block on which shoes are made"]

cal·i·brate /ˈkæləˌbreɪt/ *v.* [T] SCIENCE to mark an instrument or tool so you can use it for measuring —**calibration** /ˌkæləˈbreɪʃən/ *n.* [C,U]

cal·i·co /ˈkælɪˌkoʊ/ *n.* [U] a light cotton cloth with a small pattern on it

ca·liph /ˈkeɪlɪf, ˈkæ-/ *n.* [C] HISTORY a title of some MUSLIM rulers, especially in the past. A caliph's right to rule came from being related to the PROPHET Muhammad. [ORIGIN: 1300—1400 Old French *calife*, from Arabic *khalifah* "person who comes after;" because a caliph is regarded as a successor of Muhammad]

CALL /kɔl/ *n.* [U] IT **computer-assisted language learning** the use of computers to help people learn foreign languages

call¹ /kɔl/ *v.*

1 TELEPHONE [I,T] to telephone someone: *I called about six o'clock.* | *He said he'd call me tomorrow.*
2 DESCRIBE [I] to describe someone or something in a particular way, or to say that s/he has a particular quality: *News reports have called it the worst disaster of this century.* | *Are you calling me a liar?*

THESAURUS

describe – to say what someone or something is like by giving details: *The suspect has been described as a young white man.*
characterize – to describe the character of someone or something in a particular way: *Psychologists characterized her as mentally unstable.*
label – to use a particular word or phrase in order to describe someone: *He labeled their comments "ridiculous."*
brand – to call someone a very bad type of person, often unfairly: *His opponents branded him a racist.*
portray – to describe or show someone or something in a particular way: *a politician who portrayed himself as an opponent of big business*

3 ASK/ORDER [T] to ask or order someone or something to come to you: *Somebody call an ambulance!* | *I can hear Mom calling me.*
4 ARRANGE [T] to arrange for something to happen at a particular time: *A meeting was called for 3 p.m. Wednesday.*
5 SAY/SHOUT [I,T] to say or shout something so that someone can hear you: *"I'm coming!" Paula called.*

THESAURUS **shout, scream, shriek, yell, cry out, raise your voice, cheer, bellow, holler** → SHOUT¹

6 NAME [T] to give a person, animal, or thing a name: *What are you going to call the dog?* | *What **was** that movie **called** again* (=what was its name)?
7 READ NAMES [T] *also* **call out** to read names or numbers in a loud voice in order to get someone's attention: *When I call your name, go stand at the front.*
8 call the shots (informal) to be the person who decides what to do in a situation: *He's the boss, so he gets to call the shots.*
9 call it a day (spoken) said when you want to stop working, either because you are tired or because you have done enough: *Come on, guys, let's call it a day.* [ORIGIN: 1100—1200 Old Norse *kalla*]

call (sb) **back** *phr. v.*
to telephone someone again, or to telephone someone who tried to telephone you earlier: *Okay, I'll call back around three.* | *Can I call you back later?*

call for sth *phr. v.*

1 to ask publicly for something to be done: *Parents are calling for a return to basics in education.*

2 to need or deserve a particular type of behavior or treatment: *a situation that calls for immediate action*

3 to say that a particular type of weather is likely to happen: *The forecast calls for more rain.*

call in *phr. v.*

1 call sb ↔ **in** to ask or order someone to come and help you with a difficult situation: *The governor called in the National Guard to deal with the riots.*

2 to telephone the place where you work, especially to report something: *Jan **called in sick** this morning.*

3 to telephone a radio or television show to give your opinion or ask a question

call sb/sth ↔ **off** *phr. v.*

1 to decide that a planned event will not happen or will not continue: *The game had to be called off due to bad weather.*

2 to order a dog or person to stop attacking someone: *Call off your dog!*

call on sb *phr. v.*

1 to formally ask someone to do something: *The UN has called on both sides to observe the cease-fire.*

2 to visit someone for a short time: *a salesman calling on customers*

call out *phr. v.*

1 call (sth ↔) **out** to say something loudly: *"Phone for you," Rosie called out.*

2 call sb/sth ↔ **out** to ask or order someone to come and help you with a difficult situation: *The Army has been called out to help fight the fires.*

call up *phr. v.*

1 call (sb ↔) **up** to telephone someone: *Dave called me up to tell me about it.*

2 call sth ↔ **up** IT to make information appear on a computer screen

call² *n.* [C] **1** an action of talking to someone by telephone: *Were there any **phone calls** for me?* | *I **got a call** yesterday from Teresa.* | *Just **give me a call** from the airport.* | *I have to **make** a telephone* *call.* | *Why haven't you* ***returned*** *my* ***call*** (=telephoned me back)? | *a* ***local/long-distance call***

TOPIC

cell phone, switch it on, listen to messages, voice mail, text messages, text → CELL PHONE

2 be on call ready to go to work if you are needed: *Heart surgeons are on call 24 hours a day.* **3** a shout or cry: *a call for help* **4** the sound that a bird or animal makes **5** a request or demand for someone to do something: *There have been* ***calls for*** *him to resign.* **6 no call for sth/no call to do sth** (spoken) used in order to tell someone that his/her behavior is wrong or that something is unnecessary: *She had no call to talk to you like that.* **7** a decision made by the REFEREE in a sports game: *All the calls went against us.* **8** a message or announcement: *the last call for flight 134* **9** a short visit to someone

'call ˌcenter *n.* [C] an office where a lot of people are employed to deal with customers who telephone them with questions, orders for goods, etc.

call·er /'kɔlɚ/ *n.* [C] someone who is making a telephone call

'call girl *n.* [C] a PROSTITUTE

cal·lig·ra·phy /kə'lɪgrəfi/ *n.* [U] the art of writing using special pens or brushes, or the beautiful writing produced in this way [ORIGIN: 1600—1700 Greek *kalligraphia*, from *kallos* "beauty" + *-graphein* "to write"]

call·ing /'kɔlɪŋ/ *n.* [C] a strong desire or feeling of duty to do a particular type of work, especially work that helps other people: *She found her calling as a nurse.*

'call-in ˌshow *n.* [C] a radio or television program in which people telephone to give their opinions

cal·lous /'kæləs/ *adj.* unkind and not caring that other people are suffering —**callousness** *n.* [U] —**callously** *adv.*

cal·lus /'kæləs/ *n.* [C] an area of hard rough skin: *calluses on his feet* —**callused** *adj.*

ˌcall 'waiting *n.* [U] a telephone service that allows you to receive another call without ending the call you are already making

calm¹ /kɑm/ *also* **calm down** *v.* [I,T] to become quiet after you have been angry, excited, or upset, or to make someone become quiet: *Calm down and tell me what happened.* | *It took a while to calm the kids down.* [ORIGIN: 1300—1400 Old French *calme*, from Late Latin *cauma* "heat;" because everything is quiet and still in the heat of the middle part of the day]

calm² *adj.* **1** relaxed and not angry or upset: *Glen was calm and composed at the funeral.* | *Please, everyone, try to* ***keep/stay calm!***

THESAURUS

relaxed – calm and not worried or angry: *He seemed relaxed and confident.*
laid-back – relaxed and not seeming to worry about anything: *My dad's pretty laid-back, but my mother's always nagging.*
easygoing – not easily worried or annoyed: *She's pretty easygoing; you'll get along with her fine.*
mellow – friendly, relaxed, and calm: *Annie's family is pretty mellow, and they liked me.*
cool – calm, and not nervous or excited: *Try to stay cool during the interview.*
placid (formal) calm and peaceful and not easy to annoy or make excited: *She was a good-natured, placid woman.*
serene (formal) – very calm or peaceful: *the serene expression on her face*

2 if a situation or place is calm, there is not a lot of activity or trouble: *The streets are calm again after last week's riots.*

THESAURUS **quiet, tranquil, peaceful, sleepy, still** → QUIET¹

3 completely still, or not moving very much: *the calm water of the lake* → *see picture at* CHOPPY **4** not windy: *a calm day* —**calmly** *adv.*

calm³ *n.* **1** [singular, U] a time that is quiet and peaceful: *the calm of the evening* **2 the calm before the storm** a peaceful situation just before a big problem or argument

cal·o·rie /'kæləri/ *n.* [C] **1** a unit for measuring the amount of energy a particular food can produce: *An average potato has about 90 calories.* | *a* ***low-calorie*** *snack* **2 count calories** to try to control your weight by calculating the number of calories you eat **3** *also* **small calorie** CHEMISTRY (*written abbreviation* **cal.**) the amount of heat that is needed to raise the temperature of one gram of water by one degree Celsius, used as a unit for measuring energy **4** *also* **large calorie** CHEMISTRY (*written abbreviation* **Cal.**) the amount of heat that is needed to raise the temperature of one kilogram of water by one degree Celsius, used as a unit for measuring energy [ORIGIN: 1800—1900 French, Latin *calor* "heat"]

cal·um·ny /'kæləmni/ *n.* (plural **calumnies**) [C,U] (formal) an untrue and unfair statement about someone that is intended to give people a bad opinion of him/her, or the act of saying this (SYN) **slander**

calves /kævz/ *n.* the plural of CALF

ca·lyx /'keɪlɪks/ *n.* (plural **calyxes** *or* **calyces** /-lɪsiz/) [C] BIOLOGY the green outer part of a flower that protects it before it opens

ca·ma·ra·der·ie /kæm'rɑdəri, kɑm-/ *n.* [U] a feeling of friendship that the people in a group have, especially when they work together: *the camaraderie of firefighters*

cam·cord·er /'kæmˌkɔrdɚ/ *n.* [C] a type of camera that you can hold in one hand to record pictures and sound onto VIDEOTAPE

came /keɪm/ *v.* the past tense of COME

cam·el /'kæməl/ *n.* [C] a large animal with a long neck and one or two HUMPS (=large raised parts) on its back that lives in the desert and carries goods or people [ORIGIN: 900—1000 Latin *camelus*, from Greek *kamelos*]

cam·e·o /ˈkæmioʊ/ *n.* (plural **cameos**) [C] **1** ENG. LANG. ARTS a small part in a movie or play acted by a famous actor: *Brad Pitt made a **cameo appearance** in the show.* **2** a piece of jewelry with a raised shape, usually of a person's face, on a dark background: *a cameo brooch*

cam·er·a /ˈkæmrə, -ərə/ *n.* [C] a piece of equipment used for taking photographs, or for making movies or television programs [ORIGIN: 1700—1800 *camera obscura* "box with a hole through which an image is made to appear on the inside of the box" (18—21 centuries), from Modern Latin, "dark room"] → *see picture on page A19*

TOPIC

Before you can **take** any **pictures**, you need to **load film into** the **camera**.
Digital cameras do not need film because the pictures you take are stored in the camera until you **download** them onto a computer.
When you take pictures, you need to **focus**, so the people or things in your picture will be clear. If you are taking a picture indoors or at night, you might need to use a **flash**.
After you have taken pictures, you take the **film** to be **developed** and **printed**. The printed **photographs** are also called **prints**. When you get the prints, you also get the **negatives**, which you can use in the future to get more copies of your photographs.

cam·er·a·man /ˈkæmrəˌmæn, -mən/, **cam·er·a·wom·an** /ˈkæmrəˌwʊmən/ *n.* (plural **cameramen** /-ˌmɛn, -mən/, **camerawomen** /-ˌwɪmɪn/) [C] someone who operates a camera for a television or film company → PHOTOGRAPHER

ca·mi·sole /ˈkæmɪˌsoʊl/ *n.* [C] a light piece of clothing that women wear on the top half of their bodies under other clothes

cam·o·mile /ˈkæməˌmil, -ˌmaɪl/ *n.* [C,U] a plant with small white and yellow flowers, often used for making tea

cam·ou·flage /ˈkæməˌflɑʒ, -ˌflɑdʒ/ *n.* [C,U] the act of hiding something by making it look the same as the things around it, or the things you use to do this: *a soldier **in camouflage** | The Arctic fox's white fur is an excellent winter camouflage.* [ORIGIN: 1900—2000 French *camoufler* "to change the appearance of," from Italian *camuffare*] —**camouflage** *v.* [T]

camp¹ /kæmp/ *n.* [C,U] **1** a place where people stay in tents in the mountains, forest, etc. for a short time: *We got back to camp at sunset. | The **base camp*** (=main camp) *was 6,000 feet below the summit. | a **mining/logging camp*** (=one where people stay when they are doing those jobs) **2** a place where children go to do special activities during their vacation, often staying there for a week or more: *a **summer camp** for girls only* **3** a place where people are kept for a particular reason, when they do not want to be there: *a refugee camp* **4** a group of people who support the same ideas or principles, especially in politics: *The debate between the two camps is becoming heated.* [ORIGIN: 1500—1600 French, Latin *campus* "field"] → CONCENTRATION CAMP, DAY CAMP

camp² *v.* [I] to set up a tent or shelter in a place and stay there for a short time —**camping** *n.* [U]: *We **went camping** in Yellowstone Park.*

camp out *phr. v.* to sleep outdoors, usually in a tent: *The kids camped out in the backyard.*

cam·paign¹ /kæmˈpeɪn/ *n.* [C] a series of actions that are intended to achieve a particular result, especially in business, politics, or war: *a presidential campaign | a military campaign | a **campaign for/against** a constitutional amendment* [ORIGIN: 1600—1700 French *campagne*, from Italian *campagna* "level country, campaign," from Latin *campus*; because soldiers went out into the country for military exercises]

THESAURUS **fight, battle, drive, struggle, crusade** → FIGHT²

campaign² *v.* [I] to take part in a public series of actions to try to achieve a particular result, especially in business or politics: *a group **campaigning for/against** gun control*

camp·er /ˈkæmpɚ/ *n.* [C] **1** someone who is staying in a tent or shelter for a short time **2** a vehicle that has beds and cooking equipment so that you can stay in it while you are on vacation

Camp·fire /ˈkæmpfaɪɚ/ *n.* an organization for girls and boys that teaches them practical skills and helps develop their character

camp·ground /ˈkæmpgraʊnd/ *n.* [C] a place where people can camp in tents or CAMPERS

THESAURUS **hotel, motel, inn, bed and breakfast (b&b), hostel** → HOTEL

camp·site /ˈkæmpsaɪt/ *n.* [C] a place where you can camp: *a lakeside campsite*

cam·pus /ˈkæmpəs/ *n.* [C] the land or buildings of a college: *the campus bookstore | Many students live **on campus**.*

can¹ /kən; *strong* kæn/ *modal verb* **1** to be able to do something or know how to do something: *I can't* (=cannot) *swim! | Jean can speak French. | Even a small computer can store immense amounts of information.*

USAGE

Use **can** and **be able to** to say that someone has the ability to do something. **Be able to** is more

formal: *Can you speak Spanish?* | *He is able to see with his left eye.*
Use **could** to say that someone has the ability to do something, but does not do it: *He could be a much better player.*
Could is also the past form of **can**. Use **could** or a past form of **be able to** to say that someone had the ability to do something in the past: *She could ride a bike when she was three.* | *He was able to walk with a cane.*
C
Use **will be able to** to talk about future ability: *People will soon be able to travel to other planets.*

2 to be allowed to do something: *You can go home now.* | *In soccer, you can't touch the ball with your hands* (=it is against the rules). **3** (spoken) used in order to ask someone to do something or give you something, or when you offer or suggest something: *Can I have a cookie?* | *Can I give you a hand?* **4** used in order to show what is possible or likely: *It can't be Steve; he's in New York right now.* | *I still think the problem can be solved.* **5** used with the verbs "see," "hear," "feel," "smell," and "taste," and with verbs relating to thinking, to show that an action is happening: *Nancy can't understand why I'm so upset.* | *I can see Ralph coming now.* **6** used in order to show what often happens or how someone often behaves: *It can get pretty cold here at night.* **7** used in order to express surprise or anger: *You can't be serious!* | *How can you be so stupid!* **8** [in questions and negatives] used in order to say that you do not believe something is true or right: *This can't be the right road.* | *It can't be easy living with him.* **9** [in questions and negatives] used in order to say that someone should not or must not do something: *You can't expect him to change.* [ORIGIN: Old English *cunnan*] → COULD

can² /kæn/ *n.* [C] **1** a metal container in which food or liquid is kept without air, or the amount the can holds: *a soft drink can* | *Add two* ***cans of*** *kidney beans.* | *a large can of paint* **2 a (whole) can of worms** a complicated situation that causes a lot of problems when you start to deal with it [ORIGIN: Old English *canne*]

can³ /kæn/ *v.* (**canned**, **canning**) [T] **1** to preserve food by putting it in a closed container without air: *We canned the vegetables we'd grown.* **2** (spoken) to dismiss someone from his/her job → CANNED

Ca·na·di·an¹ /kəˈneɪdiən/ *adj.* relating to or coming from Canada

Canadian² *n.* [C] someone from Canada

ca·nal /kəˈnæl/ *n.* [C] a long passage dug into the ground and filled with water, either for boats to travel along, or to bring water from somewhere: *the Panama Canal* → *see picture at* RIVER

ca·nar·y /kəˈnɛri/ *n.* (plural **canaries**) [C] a small yellow bird that sings and is often kept as a pet [ORIGIN: 1500—1600 *Canary* Islands, islands in the Atlantic Ocean, where the bird comes from]

can·cel /ˈkænsəl/ *v.* [T] **1** to decide that something you have planned will not happen: *I had to cancel my trip.* **2** to end an agreement or arrangement, especially because you no longer want something: *We're canceling our subscription to the magazine.* [ORIGIN: 1300—1400 French *canceller* "to cross out," from Latin *cancellare* "to make like a frame of crossed bars"]

cancel sth ↔ **out** *phr. v.* to have an equal but opposite effect on something, so that a situation does not change: *The losses canceled out the profits made the previous year.*

can·cel·la·tion /ˌkænsəˈleɪʃən/ *n.* [C,U] **1** a decision that something you have planned will not happen: *The show's low ratings led to cancellation.* **2** a decision to end an agreement or arrangement: *the cancellation of an employment contract*

Can·cer /ˈkænsɚ/ *n.* **1** [U] the fourth sign of the ZODIAC, represented by a CRAB **2** [C] someone born between June 22 and July 22

cancer *n.* [C,U] a serious disease in which cells in one part of the body start to grow in a way that is not normal: *cases of* ***breast/lung/bowel etc. cancer*** | *She* ***has cancer***. | *He died of cancer at the age of 63.* [ORIGIN: 1600—1700 Latin "crab, cancer"] **—cancerous** *adj.*

can·did /ˈkændɪd/ *adj.* telling the truth, even when the truth may be unpleasant or embarrassing: *He was surprisingly* ***candid about*** *the difficulties the government is facing.* [ORIGIN: 1600—1700 French *candide*, from Latin *candidus* "bright, white"] **—candidly** *adv.*

THESAURUS **honest, frank, direct, upfront, straight, straightforward, blunt, forthright** → HONEST

can·di·da·cy /ˈkændədəsi/ *n.* (plural **candidacies**) [C,U] the fact of being a candidate, usually for a political position: *She announced her* ***candidacy for*** *the Senate.*

can·di·date /ˈkændəˌdeɪt, -dɪt/ *n.* [C] **1** someone who is competing in an election or who is being considered for a job: *a presidential candidate* | *Sara seems to be a likely* ***candidate for*** *the job.* **2** someone or something that may be chosen for something: *Which patients are good* ***candidates for*** *the new treatment?* | *The book is a strong* ***candidate to*** *win the award.* [ORIGIN: 1600—1700 Latin *candidatus*, from *candidatus* "dressed in white;" because someone trying to get elected in ancient Rome wore white clothes]

can·died /ˈkændid/ *adj.* cooked in or covered with sugar: *candied fruit*

can·dle /ˈkændl/ *n.* [C] a round stick of WAX with a piece of string through the middle, that you burn to produce light: *She sat down and* ***lit the candle***. [ORIGIN: 600—700 Latin *candela*, from *candere* "to shine"] → *see picture at* LIGHT¹

can·dle·stick /ˈkændlˌstɪk/ *n.* [C] a specially shaped metal or wooden object used for holding candles

can·dor /ˈkændɚ/ *n.* [U] the quality of being honest and telling the truth ➔ CANDID: *She spoke with candor about the affair.*

can·dy /ˈkændi/ *n.* (plural **candies**) **1** [C,U] a sweet food made of sugar or chocolate, or a piece of this: *a **box of candy** | I gave her a **piece of candy**.* **2 mind/brain/eye etc. candy** (informal) something that is entertaining or pleasant to look at, but that does not make you think [ORIGIN: 1200—1300 Old French *candi*, from Arabic *qandi* "covered with sugar"]

ˈcandy bar *n.* [C] a long narrow bar of candy, usually covered with chocolate

ˈcandy cane *n.* [C] a stick of hard sugar with a curved shape, colored red and white

cane /keɪn/ *n.* [C] a long thin stick, usually with a curved handle, used for helping you walk: *She **walks with a cane** because of her arthritis.* [ORIGIN: 1300—1400 Old French, Old Provençal *cana*, from Latin *canna*, from Greek *kanna*]

ca·nine /ˈkeɪnaɪn/ *adj.* BIOLOGY relating to dogs

can·is·ter /ˈkænəstɚ/ *n.* [C] a metal container with a lid, used for storing dry food or a gas: *a **flour/sugar/salt canister***

can·ker /ˈkæŋkɚ/ *n.* **1** [C,U] BIOLOGY an infected area on the wood of trees, or the disease that causes this **2** [C] *also* **canker sore** a painful sore inside your mouth

can·na·bis /ˈkænəbɪs/ *n.* [U] MARIJUANA

canned /kænd/ *adj.* **1** preserved without air in a container: *canned tomatoes* **2 canned music/laughter/applause** music, etc. that has been recorded and is used on television or radio programs

can·ner·y /ˈkænəri/ *n.* (plural **canneries**) [C] a factory where food is put into cans

can·ni·bal /ˈkænəbəl/ *n.* [C] someone who eats human flesh [ORIGIN: 1500—1600 Spanish *Canibal* "member of the Carib people of the West Indies, who were said to eat human flesh"] **—cannibalism** *n.* [U] **—cannibalistic** /ˌkænəbəˈlɪstɪk◂ / *adj.*

can·non /ˈkænən/ *n.* [C] a large gun, fixed to the ground or on wheels, used in past times

can·not /ˈkænɑt, kəˈnɑt, kæ-/ *modal verb* the negative form of CAN: *I cannot accept your offer.*

can·ny /ˈkæni/ *adj.* smart, careful, and showing that you understand a situation very well

ca·noe /kəˈnu/ *n.* [C] a long light narrow boat that is pointed at both ends, which you move using a PADDLE [ORIGIN: 1500—1600 French, Spanish *canoa*, from Arawakan (a group of South American languages)] **—canoe** *v.* [I] **—canoeing** *n.* [U]

can·on /ˈkænən/ *n.* [C] **1** (formal) a generally accepted rule or standard for behaving or thinking **2** ENG. LANG. ARTS the books, pieces of music, etc. that are recognized as being the most important: *the literary canon* **3** an established law of the Christian church

ˈcan ˌopener *n.* [C] a tool used for opening cans of food

can·o·py /ˈkænəpi/ *n.* (plural **canopies**) [C] **1** a cover attached above a bed or seat, used as a decoration or as a shelter **2** EARTH SCIENCES the top branches and leaves of the tallest trees in a forest, which completely cover large areas of the forest **—canopied** *adj.*

C

can't /kænt/ *modal verb* the short form of "cannot": *I can't go with you today.*

can·ta·loupe /ˈkænṭəlˌoʊp/ *n.* [C,U] a type of MELON with a hard skin and sweet orange flesh [ORIGIN: 1700—1800 *Cantelupo* former house of the Pope near Rome in Italy, where it was grown]

can·tan·ker·ous /kænˈtæŋkərəs/ *adj.* easily annoyed and complaining a lot: *a cantankerous old man*

can·teen /kænˈtin/ *n.* [C] **1** a small container for carrying water or other drinks **2** a store or place where people in the military can buy things or go to be entertained [ORIGIN: 1700—1800 French *cantine*, from Italian *cantina* "wine store"]

can·ter /ˈkænṭɚ/ *v.* [I,T] when a horse canters, it runs fast, but not as fast as possible **—canter** *n.* [C]

can·to /ˈkæntoʊ/ *n.* (plural **cantos**) [C] ENG. LANG. ARTS one of the parts into which a very long poem is divided ➔ STANZA

Can·to·nese /ˌkæntənˈiz◂ / *n.* [U] a language used in Hong Kong and parts of southern China

can·vas /ˈkænvəs/ *n.* **1** [U] a type of strong cloth that is used for making tents, sails, bags, etc.: *a canvas bag* **2** [C] ENG. LANG. ARTS a painting done with oil paints, or the piece of cloth that it is painted on [ORIGIN: 1300—1400 Old North French *canevas*, from Latin *cannabis* "hemp"]

can·vass /ˈkænvəs/ *v.* [I,T] **1** to try to persuade people to support a political party, politician, plan, etc. by going from place to place and talking to people: *Supporters were canvassing door to door.* **2** to ask people about something in order to get information: *Residents were canvassed about community needs.*

can·yon /ˈkænyən/ *n.* [C] EARTH SCIENCES a deep valley with very steep sides: *the Grand Canyon* [ORIGIN: 1800—1900 American Spanish *cañón*, from Spanish, "tube, pipe"]

cap[1] /kæp/ *n.* [C] **1 a)** a soft hat with a curved part sticking out at the front: *a baseball cap* **b)** a hat that fits closely over your head: *a shower cap* **2** something that covers and protects the end or top of an object: *a bottle cap | a pen cap*

THESAURUS **cover, lid, top, wrapper, wrapping** ➔ COVER[2]

3 ECONOMICS a limit on the amount of money that

someone can earn or spend: *a **cap on** campaign spending* [ORIGIN: 900—1000 Late Latin *cappa* "covering for the head, cloak"] → ICE CAP, KNEECAP

cap² *v.* (**capped**, **capping**) [T] **1** to be the last and usually best thing that happens in a game, situation, etc.: *Wilkes capped a perfect season by winning the 100-meter sprint.* **2** to cover the top of something: *the **snow-capped** peaks of the Rocky Mountains* | *a tower **capped with** a golden dome* **3** to cover a tooth with a special hard white substance: *Her front teeth had to be capped.* **4** ECONOMICS to limit the amount of something, especially money, that can be used or spent: *The law caps the amount of interest that credit card companies can charge.*

C

ca·pa·bil·i·ty /ˌkeɪpəˈbɪləṭi/ (Ac) *n.* (plural **capabilities**) [C] the ability of a machine, person, or organization to do something, especially something difficult: *The country has the **capability to** produce nuclear weapons.* | *the computer's graphics capability* | *The virus has the **capability of** attaching itself to a specific white blood cell.*

THESAURUS **ability, power, capacity** → ABILITY

ca·pa·ble /ˈkeɪpəbəl/ (Ac) *adj.* **1 capable of (doing) sth** having the power, skill, or other qualities that are needed to do something: *He is not **capable of** making these decisions by himself.* | *The machine is capable of very precise calculations.* **2** able to do things well: *Mary Beth is a capable lawyer.* | *The hospital's staff were all very capable.* [ORIGIN: 1500—1600 French, Late Latin *capabilis* "able to take things in," from Latin *capere* "to take"]

ca·pa·cious /kəˈpeɪʃəs/ *adj.* (formal) able to contain a lot: *a capacious handbag* —**capaciousness** *n.* [U]

ca·pac·i·tor /kəˈpæsəṭə/ *n.* [C] PHYSICS a piece of equipment that collects and stores electricity for a short time

ca·pac·i·ty /kəˈpæsəṭi/ (Ac) *n.* (plural **capacities**) **1** [singular, U] the amount that something can hold, produce, or carry: *The computer has a **capacity of** 400 megabytes.* | *The theater was **filled to capacity*** (=completely full). **2** [C,U] the ability to do or produce something: *a child's **capacity for** learning* | *The groups **have the capacity to** influence Congress.* | *The factory is not yet working **at full capacity**.*

THESAURUS **ability, power, capability** → ABILITY

3 [singular] someone's job, position, or duty: *She has traveled a lot **in** her **capacity as** a photojournalist.* [ORIGIN: 1400—1500 French *capacité*, from Latin *capacitas*]

cape /keɪp/ *n.* [C] **1** a long loose piece of clothing without SLEEVES that fastens around your neck and hangs from your shoulders: *The bishop was wearing a long red cape.* **2** EARTH SCIENCES a large piece of land surrounded on three sides by water: *Cape Cod*

ca·per¹ /ˈkeɪpə/ *n.* [C] **1** a small dark green part of a flower, that is used in cooking to give a sour taste to food **2** a planned activity, especially an illegal or dangerous one

caper² *v.* [I] to jump around and play in a happy excited way

cap·il·lar·y /ˈkæpəˌlɛri/ *n.* (plural **capillaries**) [C] BIOLOGY a very small narrow tube that carries blood around your body → ARTERY, VEIN

cap·i·tal¹ /ˈkæpəṭl/ *n.* **1** [C] the city where a country or state's main government is → CAPITOL: *The New York state capital is Albany.* | *What's the **capital of** Sweden?* **2** [singular, U] ECONOMICS money or property you use to start a business or to make more money: *Investors lent him the capital to start the business.* **3** [C] a letter of the alphabet written in its large form, for example at the beginning of someone's name: *Please write your name **in capitals**.* | *a capital "T"* **4** [C] a place that is important for a particular activity: *Hollywood is the **capital of** the movie industry.* [ORIGIN: 1100—1200 Latin *capitalis*, from *caput* "head"]

capital² *adj.* **1** ECONOMICS relating to money that you use to start a business, make more money, improve things, etc.: *We need greater capital investment to improve our schools.* **2 capital letter** a letter of the alphabet that is printed in its large form, for example at the beginning of someone's name **3 capital offense/crime** LAW a crime that may be punished by death

ˌcapital ˈgain *n.* [C] ECONOMICS the profit you make by selling something for more than it cost you to buy: *The sale of its overseas assets resulted in a capital gain of $10 million for the group.*

cap·i·tal·ism /ˈkæpəṭlˌɪzəm/ *n.* [U] ECONOMICS an economic and political system in which businesses belong mostly to private owners, not to the government → COMMUNISM, SOCIALISM

cap·i·tal·ist /ˈkæpəṭl-ɪst/ *adj.* ECONOMICS relating to a system or person who supports or takes part in capitalism —**capitalist** *n.* [C]

cap·i·tal·ize /ˈkæpəṭlˌaɪz/ *v.* [T] **1** to write a letter of the alphabet using a CAPITAL letter **2** ECONOMICS to supply a business with money so that it can operate **3** ECONOMICS to calculate the value of a business, based on the value of its SHARES —**capitalization** /ˌkæpəṭləˈzeɪʃən/ *n.* [U]

capitalize on sth *phr. v.* to use something in order to gain an advantage: *The company is trying to capitalize on the popularity of fruit-based drinks.*

ˌcapital ˈpunishment *n.* [U] the punishment of legally killing someone for a crime s/he has done

THESAURUS **punishment, sentence, penalty, fine, community service, corporal punishment** → PUNISHMENT

→ DEATH PENALTY

Cap·i·tol /ˈkæpəṭl/ *n.* **1 the Capitol** the building

in Washington, D.C. where the U.S. Congress meets **2** [C] the building in each U.S. state where the people who make laws for that state meet

ˌCapitol 'Hill *n.* POLITICS the place where the U.S. Congress meets, often used to refer to Congress itself: *The bill has wide support on Capitol Hill.*

ca·pit·u·late /kə'pɪtʃəˌleɪt/ *v.* [I] to stop fighting someone and accept his/her conditions or demands —**capitulation** /kəˌpɪtʃə'leɪʃən/ *n.* [C,U]

cap·puc·ci·no /ˌkæpə'tʃinoʊ, ˌkɑ-/ *n.* (plural **cappuccinos**) [C,U] a type of Italian coffee made with hot milk

ca·price /kə'pris/ *n.* [C,U] (literary) a sudden and unreasonable change in someone's opinion or behavior

ca·pri·cious /kə'priʃəs/ *adj.* (literary) likely to change very suddenly: *capricious spring weather*

Cap·ri·corn /'kæprɪˌkɔrn/ *n.* **1** [U] the tenth sign of the ZODIAC, represented by a goat **2** [C] someone born between December 22 and January 19

capsize

cap·size /'kæpsaɪz, kæp'saɪz/ *v.* [I,T] if a boat capsizes, or if you capsize it, it turns over in the water

cap·sule /'kæpsəl/ *n.* [C] **1** a very small object with medicine inside that you swallow whole

THESAURUS **medicine, pill, tablet, eye/ear drops, drug, medication** → MEDICINE

2 the part of a space vehicle in which people live and work

cap·tain¹ /'kæptən/ *n.* [C] **1** someone who is in charge of a ship or airplane **2** a fairly high rank in the Army, Air Force, Marines, police force, etc., or an officer who has this rank **3** someone who leads a team or group: *the* ***captain of*** *the football team* [ORIGIN: 1300—1400 French *capitain*, from Late Latin *capitaneus* "chief," from Latin *caput* "head"]

captain² *v.* [T] to be the captain of a team, ship, or airplane

cap·tion /'kæpʃən/ *n.* [C] words written above or below a picture that explain what the picture is about

cap·ti·vate /'kæptəˌveɪt/ *v.* [T] to attract and interest someone very much: *Alex was captivated by her beauty.* —**captivating** *adj.*: *a particularly captivating story*

cap·tive¹ /'kæptɪv/ *adj.* **1** kept in prison or in a place that you are not allowed to leave: *captive animals* | *His son had been* ***taken captive*** (=taken and kept as a prisoner). **2 captive audience** people who listen to or watch someone or something because they have to, not because they want to

captive² *n.* [C] someone who is kept as a prisoner, especially in a war SYN **hostage**

cap·tiv·i·ty /kæp'tɪvəṭi/ *n.* [U] the state of being kept as a prisoner or in a small space: *Many animals won't breed* ***in captivity.***

cap·tor /'kæptɚ/ *n.* [C] (formal) someone who is keeping another person as a prisoner

cap·ture¹ /'kæptʃɚ/ *v.* [T] **1** to catch someone in order to keep him/her as a prisoner: *40 French soldiers were captured.*

THESAURUS **catch, arrest, apprehend, corner, trap** → CATCH¹

2 to get control of a place that previously belonged to an enemy, during a war: *The town was captured by enemy troops.* **3 capture sb's imagination/attention etc.** to make someone feel very interested in something **4** to succeed in showing or describing something, using words or pictures: *The book really* ***captures the essence/spirit of*** *what the 1920s were like.* **5** to get something that you are competing with others for, especially in business or politics: *Mayor Agnos captured 30% of the vote.* **6** to catch an animal without killing it [ORIGIN: 1500—1600 French, Latin *captura*, from *captus*]

capture² *n.* [U] **1** the act of catching someone in order to keep him/her as a prisoner: *The two soldiers somehow managed to* ***avoid capture.*** **2** the act of getting control of something: *the* ***capture of*** *the village*

car /kɑr/ *n.* [C] **1** a vehicle with four wheels and an engine, used by a small number of people for traveling from one place to another: *Joe* ***got in the car*** *and buckled his seat belt.* | *She* ***got out of the car.*** | *You can't* ***park*** *your* ***car*** *here.* **2** one of the connected parts of a train: *I'll meet you in the* ***dining car.***

ca·rafe /kə'ræf/ *n.* [C] a glass bottle with a wide top, used for serving wine or water at meals

car·a·mel /'kærəməl, -ˌmɛl, 'kɑrməl/ *n.* [C,U] candy made of cooked sugar, butter, and milk [ORIGIN: 1700—1800 French, Spanish *caramelo*]

car·a·pace /'kærəˌpeɪs/ *n.* [C] BIOLOGY a hard shell on the outside of some animals such as a CRAB or TURTLE

car·at, karat /'kærət/ *n.* [C] a unit for measuring how pure gold is, or how heavy jewels are: *Pure gold is 24 carats.*

car·a·van /'kærəˌvæn/ *n.* [C] a group of people

with animals or vehicles, who travel together [ORIGIN: 1500—1600 Italian *caravana*, from Persian *karwan*]

car·bo·hy·drate /ˌkɑrboʊˈhaɪdreɪt, -drɪt, -bə-/ *n.* [C,U] CHEMISTRY a substance in foods such as rice, bread, and potatoes that provides your body with heat and energy

car·bon /ˈkɑrbən/ *n.* [U] CHEMISTRY a chemical that is an ELEMENT and that forms into DIAMONDS, and is in gas, coal, etc.

C

car·bon·at·ed /ˈkɑrbəˌneɪt̬ɪd/ *adj.* carbonated drinks have a lot of BUBBLES in them

ˌcarbon ˈcopy *n.* [C] someone or something that is very similar to another person or thing

ˌcarbon ˈcycle *n.* [C] EARTH SCIENCES a continuous series of related events in which carbon that exists in the air as carbon dioxide is taken in by plants, and is sent back out into the air again, either by plants or animals or as the result of burning substances such as oil or coal

ˌcarbon diˈoxide *n.* [U] CHEMISTRY the gas produced when people and animals breathe out

ˌcarbon ˈfootprint *n.* [C] EARTH SCIENCES a measure of the amount of harmful carbon dioxide that a person, company, industry, etc. produces when doing his, her, or its normal activities, such as driving a car, heating a building, or producing goods

ˌcarbon moˈnoxide *n.* [U] CHEMISTRY a poisonous gas produced when engines burn gasoline

ˈcarbon ˌpaper *n.* [C,U] special paper with a blue or black substance on one side, used especially in the past to make copies of documents written on a TYPEWRITER

car·bu·re·tor /ˈkɑrbəˌreɪt̬ɚ/ *n.* [C] the part of an engine that mixes the air and gasoline to provide power

car·cass /ˈkɑrkəs/ *n.* [C] the body of a dead animal

car·cin·o·gen /kɑrˈsɪnədʒən/ *n.* [C] BIOLOGY a substance that can cause CANCER —**carcinogenic** /ˌkɑrsɪnəˈdʒɛnɪk/ *adj.*

car·ci·no·ma /ˌkɑrsəˈnoʊmə/ *n.* [C] BIOLOGY a small growth on your skin or in your body caused by CANCER → TUMOR

card[1] /kɑrd/ *n.* [C] **1** a small piece of plastic or stiff paper that shows information about someone or something: *a library card* | *an employee ID card* | *Here's my* ***business card.*** **2** a small piece of plastic which you use to pay for goods or to get money → CREDIT CARD, DEBIT CARD: *I'll use my card.* **3** a piece of folded stiff paper, usually with a picture on the front, that you send to people on special occasions: *a* ***birthday card*** **4** one of a set of 52 small pieces of stiff paper with pictures or numbers on them that are used for playing games: *Let's* ***play cards*** (=play a game using cards). | *a* ***deck of cards*** **5** a POSTCARD **6 baseball/sports etc. card** a small piece of thick stiff paper with a picture on one side, that is part of a set which people collect **7** a small piece of thick stiff paper that information can be written or printed on → INDEX CARD: *a set of recipe cards* **8** the thing inside a computer that the CHIPs are attached to that allows the computer to do specific things: *a* ***sound card*** **9 be in the cards** to seem likely to happen: *The increase in price has been in the cards for a long time.* **10 play your cards right** (informal) to do the things that make you succeed in getting what you want **11 put/lay your cards on the table** (informal) to be completely honest about what your plans and intentions are [ORIGIN: 1400—1500 French *carte*, from Old Italian *carta* "sheet of paper," from Latin *charta*]

card[2] *v.* [T] to ask someone to show a card proving that s/he is old enough to be in a particular place or to buy alcohol or cigarettes: *I can't believe I still get carded.*

card·board /ˈkɑrdbɔrd/ *n.* [U] a thick material like stiff paper, used especially for making boxes

ˈcard ˌcatalog *n.* [C] a set of cards that contain information about something, especially books in a library, and that are arranged in a particular order

car·di·ac /ˈkɑrdiˌæk/ *adj.* [only before noun] BIOLOGY relating to the heart or to heart disease

ˌcardiac arˈrest *n.* [C] BIOLOGY a HEART ATTACK

car·di·gan /ˈkɑrdəgən/ *n.* [C] a SWEATER that is fastened at the front [ORIGIN: 1800—1900 Earl of *Cardigan* (1797-1868), British soldier]

car·di·nal[1] /ˈkɑrdn-əl, -nəl/ *adj.* [only before noun] very important or basic: *a* ***cardinal rule***

cardinal

cardinal[2] *n.* [C] **1** a priest of very high rank in the Roman Catholic Church **2** a common North American wild bird that is a bright red color

ˌcardinal ˈnumber *n.* [C] MATH any of the numbers 1, 2, 3, etc. that show the quantity of something → ORDINAL NUMBER

car·di·ol·o·gy /ˌkɑrdiˈɑlədʒi/ *n.* [U] the study or science of medical treatment of the heart

care[1] /kɛr/ *v.* **1** [I,T] to be concerned about or interested in someone or something: *He doesn't* ***care about*** *anybody but himself.* | *I don't* ***care what*** *you do.* **2** [I] to like or love someone: *He really* ***cared for*** *you.*

SPOKEN PHRASES

3 who cares? used in order to say that something does not worry or upset you because you think it is not important **4 I/he/they etc. couldn't care less** used in order to say that someone is not at all concerned about or interested in something: *I* *couldn't care less about the Super Bowl.* **5 what do I/you/they etc. care?** used in order to say that someone does not care at all about something: *What does he care? He'll get his money whatever happens.* **6 would you care to do sth?/would you care for sth?** (formal) used in order to ask someone if s/he wants to do something: *Would you care to meet us after the show?* | *Would you care for a drink?*

---

care for sb/sth *phr. v.* **1** to do things for someone who is old, sick, weak, etc. and not able to do things for himself/herself (SYN) **look after**: *Angie cared for her mother after her stroke.* **2 not care for sb/sth** to not like someone or something: *I don't care for his brother.*

care² *n.*

1 HELP [U] the process of doing things for someone because s/he is old, sick, weak, etc.: *Your father will need constant **medical care**.* | *They shared **the care of** their children.*

2 KEEPING STH IN GOOD CONDITION [U] the process of keeping something in good condition or working correctly: *skin care* | *With proper care, your washing machine should last years.*

3 take care of sb/sth a) to watch and help someone and be responsible for him/her: *Who's taking care of the baby?* **b)** to keep something in good condition or working correctly: *Karl will take care of the house while we're on vacation.* **c)** to do the work or make the arrangements that are necessary for something to happen: *I'll take care of making the reservations.* **d)** to pay for something: *Don't worry about the bill – it's taken care of.*

4 take care a) (spoken) used when saying goodbye to family or friends **b)** to be careful: *It's very icy, so take care driving home.*

5 CAREFULNESS [U] carefulness to avoid damage, mistakes, etc.: *You need to **put** more **care into** your work.* | ***Handle** the package **with care**.*

6 WORRY [C,U] something that causes problems and makes you anxious or sad: *Eddie **doesn't have a care in the world*** (=does not have any problems or worries).

7 in care of sb (*written abbreviation* **c/o**) used when sending letters to someone at someone else's address: *Send me the package in care of my cousin.*

ca·reen /kəˈrin/ *v.* [I] to move quickly forward in an uncontrolled way, making sudden sideways movements: *Morillo's truck **careened down** the hillside and burst into flames.*

ca·reer /kəˈrɪr/ *n.* [C] **1** a job or profession that you have been trained for and intend to do for a long time: *a **career in** law* | *She's considering making a **career change**.*

THESAURUS **job, work, employment, position, post, occupation, profession, vocation** → JOB

2 the period of time in your life that you spend working: *Will spent most of his career as a teacher.* **3 career soldier/teacher etc.** someone who intends to be a soldier, teacher, etc. for most of his/her life, not just for a particular period of time: *a career diplomat* [ORIGIN: 1500—1600 French *carrière*, from Old Provençal *carriera* "street," from Latin *carrus*]

care·free /ˈkɛrfri/ *adj.* without any problems or worries: *a carefree summer vacation*

care·ful /ˈkɛrfəl/ *adj.* **1** trying very hard not to make mistakes, damage something, or cause problems (ANT) **careless**: *a careful driver* | *Anna was **careful** not **to** upset Steven.* **2 (be) careful!** (spoken) used in order to tell someone to think about what s/he is doing so that something bad does not happen: *Be careful – there's broken glass on the sidewalk!* **3** paying a lot of attention to detail: *careful planning*

THESAURUS

methodical – done in a careful and well-organized way, or always doing things this way: *a methodical approach to the problem*
thorough – careful to do everything that you should and avoid mistakes: *The police conducted a thorough investigation of the affair.*
meticulous – very careful about details, and always trying to do things correctly: *She keeps meticulous records.*
systematic – organized carefully and done thoroughly: *We need a systematic way to measure employees' performance.*
painstaking – very careful and thorough: *Cleaning the paintings involves a lot of painstaking work.*
scrupulous (formal) – done very carefully so that every detail is correct: *The research shows scrupulous attention to detail.*
conscientious (formal) – careful to do everything that it is your job or duty to do: *a conscientious student*

—**carefully** *adv.*: *Please listen carefully.*

care·giv·er /ˈkɛrˌgɪvɚ/ *n.* [C] someone who takes care of a child or of someone who is old or sick

care·less /ˈkɛrlɪs/ *adj.* not paying enough attention to what you are doing, so that you make mistakes, damage things, cause problems, etc. (ANT) **careful**: *a careless mistake* | *It was very **careless of** you to leave your keys in the car.* —**carelessly** *adv.* —**carelessness** *n.* [U]

ˈcare ˌpackage *n.* [C] a package of food, candy, etc. that is sent to someone living away from home, especially a student at college

ca·ress /kəˈrɛs/ *v.* [T] to gently touch or kiss someone in a way that shows you love him/her —**caress** *n.* [C]

THESAURUS **touch, feel, handle, stroke, rub, scratch, pat, pet, tickle** → TOUCH¹

care·tak·er /ˈkɛrˌteɪkɚ/ *n.* [C] **1** someone whose job is to take care of a building or land when the person who owns it is not there **2** someone such as a nurse, who takes care of other people

car·go /ˈkɑrgoʊ/ *n.* (plural **cargoes**) [C,U] the goods that are being carried in a ship, airplane, truck, etc.: *The ship was carrying a* ***cargo of*** *oil.* [ORIGIN: 1600—1700 Spanish "load, charge," from *cargar* "to load," from Late Latin *carricare*]

Car·ib·be·an /ˌkærəˈbiən, kəˈrɪbiən/ *adj.* from or relating to the islands in the Caribbean Sea, such as the Bahamas and Jamaica —**Caribbean** *n.* [C]

C

ca·ri·bou /ˈkærəbu/ *n.* [C] a North American REINDEER

car·i·ca·ture /ˈkærəkətʃɚ, -ˌtʃʊr/ *n.* [C,U] ENG. LANG. ARTS a funny drawing or description of someone that makes him/her seem silly, or the activity doing this [ORIGIN: 1700—1800 French, Italian *caricatura*, from *caricare* "to load, make seem larger, worse, etc.," from Late Latin *carricare*] —**caricature** *v.* [T]

THESAURUS picture, sketch, painting, portrait, cartoon, illustration, image ➔ PICTURE[1]

car·ies /ˈkɛriz/ *n.* [U] BIOLOGY decay in one or more teeth

car·ing /ˈkɛrɪŋ/ *adj.* someone who is caring is kind to other people and tries to help them: *a warm and caring person*

THESAURUS kind, nice, considerate, thoughtful, warm-hearted, compassionate, sympathetic ➔ KIND[2]

car·jack·ing /ˈkɑrˌdʒækɪŋ/ *n.* [C,U] the crime of using a weapon to force the driver of a car to drive you somewhere or give you his/her car —**carjacker** *n.* [C]

car·nage /ˈkɑrnɪdʒ/ *n.* [U] (formal) the killing and wounding of a lot of people, especially in a war

car·nal /ˈkɑrnl/ *adj.* (formal) relating to sex: *carnal desires*

car·na·tion /kɑrˈneɪʃən/ *n.* [C] a white, pink, or red flower that smells nice

car·ni·val /ˈkɑrnəvəl/ *n.* **1** [C] a noisy outdoor event where you can ride on special machines and play games for prizes (SYN) **fair** **2** [C,U] a public event at which people play music, wear special clothes, and dance in the streets: *carnival time in Rio* [ORIGIN: 1500—1600 Italian *carnevale*, from *carne* "meat" + *levare* "to remove;" because after Carnival people stopped eating meat for a period]

car·ni·vore /ˈkɑrnəˌvɔr/ *n.* [C] BIOLOGY an animal that eats meat [ORIGIN: 1800—1900 Latin *carnivorus* "flesh-eating," from *caro* "flesh" + *-vorus* "eating"] —**carnivorous** /kɑrˈnɪvərəs/ *adj.*

car·ol /ˈkærəl/ *n.* [C] a CHRISTMAS CAROL

ca·rot·id ar·te·ry /kəˌrɑṭɪd ˈɑrṭəri/ *n.* [C] BIOLOGY one of the two ARTERIES in your neck that supply blood to your head

ca·rouse /kəˈraʊz/ *v.* [I] (literary) to drink a lot, be noisy, and have fun

car·ou·sel, carrousel /ˌkærəˈsɛl/ *n.* [C] **1** a machine with painted wooden horses on it that turns around, which people can ride on for fun **2** the circular moving belt that you collect your bags and suitcases from at an airport

carp[1] /kɑrp/ *n.* (plural **carp**) [C] a large fish that lives in lakes or rivers and can be eaten

carp[2] *v.* [I] to complain about something in an annoying way, or to criticize someone all the time

car·pel /ˈkɑrpəl/ *n.* [C] BIOLOGY the part of a flower where new seeds are formed

car·pen·ter /ˈkɑrpəntɚ/ *n.* [C] someone whose job is making and repairing wooden objects [ORIGIN: 1100—1200 Old North French *carpentier*, from Latin *carpentarius* "carriage-maker"]

car·pen·try /ˈkɑrpəntri/ *n.* [U] the art or work of a carpenter

car·pet[1] /ˈkɑrpɪt/ *n.* [C,U] a heavy woven material for covering all of a floor and stairs, or a piece of this material ➔ RUG: *a wine stain on the carpet | I'd like red carpet in the hall.* [ORIGIN: 1300—1400 Old French *carpite*, from Old Italian *carpita*, from *carpire* "to pull out"] ➔ *see picture at* RUG

carpet[2] *v.* [T] to cover something with a carpet

car·pet·ing /ˈkɑrpəṭɪŋ/ *n.* [U] carpets in general, or heavy woven material used for making carpets

ˈcar pool *n.* [C] a group of people who travel together to work, school, etc. in one car and share the costs —**carpool** *v.* [I]

car·port /ˈkɑrpɔrt/ *n.* [C] a shelter for a car, that has a roof and is often built against the side of a house ➔ GARAGE

car·riage /ˈkærɪdʒ/ *n.* [C] **1** a vehicle with wheels that is pulled by a horse, used in past times **2** a BABY CARRIAGE

car·ri·er /ˈkæriɚ/ *n.* [C] **1** a company that moves goods or passengers from one place to another, especially by airplane **2** BIOLOGY someone who passes a disease to other people without having it himself/herself **3** a telephone or insurance company: *a cell phone carrier*

car·rot /ˈkærət/ *n.* [C] a long orange vegetable that grows under the ground [ORIGIN: 1400—1500 French *carotte*, from Late Latin, from Greek *karoton*] ➔ *see picture at* VEGETABLE

carrousel *n* [C] another spelling of CAROUSEL

car·ry /ˈkæri/ *v.* (**carried**, **carries**)

1 LIFT AND TAKE [T] to hold something in your hands or arms, or on your back, as you take it somewhere: *Can you carry that suitcase for me? | Angela was* ***carrying*** *the baby* ***in*** *her arms.* ➔ *see picture on page A22*

THESAURUS

cart – to carry or take something large and heavy somewhere: *Workers carted away several tons of trash.*

haul – to carry or pull something heavy: *Contractors have begun hauling away the debris.*
transport (formal) – to move or carry goods, people, etc. from one place to another in a vehicle: *Helicopters are used to transport military equipment.*
bear (formal) – to bring or carry something: *They arrived bearing gifts.*
tote (informal) – to carry something: *guards toting machine guns*
lug (informal) – to pull or carry something that is very heavy: *We lugged our bags and chairs to the beach.*
schlep (informal) – to carry or pull something heavy: *He schlepped the luggage up the steps.*

2 VEHICLE/SHIP/PLANE [T] to take people or things from one place to another: *The bus was carrying 25 passengers.*
3 PIPE/ROAD/WIRE [T] if pipe, road, wire, etc. carries something such as liquid or electricity, the liquid etc. flows along, on, or in it: *Pipes* ***carry*** *the water* ***across*** *the desert.*
4 HAVE WITH YOU [T] to have something with you in your pocket, on your belt, in your bag, etc. as you move from place to place: *The security guard usually carries a gun.* | *I never carry much cash.*
5 STORE [T] if a store carries goods, it has a supply of them for sale: *I'm sorry, we don't carry that brand anymore.*
6 INFORMATION/NEWS ETC. [T] to contain a particular piece of information or news: *The morning paper* ***carried*** *a* ***story*** *about the demonstration in New York.*
7 HAVE A QUALITY [T] to have a particular quality: *The job* ***carries*** *certain* ***risks***. | *Lee's opinions usually* ***carry*** *a lot of* ***weight*** (=have influence) *with the boss.* | *Matthew's voice did not* ***carry*** *much* ***conviction*** (=he did not sound certain).
8 be/get carried away to be or become so excited that you are no longer in control of what you do or say
9 carry insurance/a guarantee etc. to have insurance, etc.: *All our products carry a 12-month guarantee.*
10 DISEASE [T] BIOLOGY to have a disease and pass it to others: *Many diseases are carried by insects.*
11 carry yourself to stand and move in a particular way: *It was obvious by the way they carried themselves that they were soldiers.*
12 CRIME/PUNISHMENT [T] if a crime carries a particular punishment, that is the usual punishment for the crime: *Murder carries a life sentence in this state.*
13 carry sth too far to do or say too much about something: *It was funny at first, but you've* ***carried*** *the joke too far.*
14 ELECTION [T] to win an election in a state or particular area: *Reagan carried California in 1980.*
15 SUPPORT [T] to support the weight of something else: *Those columns carry the whole roof.*
16 SOUND/SMELL [I] to be able to go as far as a particular place or a particular distance: *The sound of their laughter carried as far as the lake.*
17 carry a tune to sing the notes of a song correctly
18 MATHEMATICS [T] *also* **carry over** to move a total to the next row of figures for adding to other numbers [ORIGIN: 1300—1400 Old North French *carier* "to take in a vehicle," from *car* "vehicle," from Latin *carrus*]

carry sth ↔ **off** *phr. v.*
to do something difficult successfully: *No one believed he could carry the plan off.*

carry on *phr. v.*
1 to continue doing something: *Jane plans to carry on and finish writing the book.*
2 (spoken) to behave in a silly or excited way: *We won't get anything done if you two don't stop carrying on!*

carry sth ↔ **out** *phr. v.*
1 to do something that has to be organized and planned: *The police department will carry out a thorough investigation.*
2 to do something that you have said you will do: *The bombers have threatened to carry out more attacks.*

carry sth ↔ **over** *phr. v.*
to make an amount of something available to be used at a later time: *Can I carry over my vacation time to next year?*

carry sth ↔ **through** *phr. v.*
to complete or finish something successfully: *Once he starts a project, he always carries it through.*

'carry-on *adj.* a carry-on bag is one that you can take with you onto an airplane

car·ry·out /'kæri,aʊt/ *n.* [C] a TAKEOUT

'car seat *n.* [C] a special seat for babies or young children, that you attach to the seat of a car

car·sick /'kɑr,sɪk/ *adj.* feeling sick because of the movement of traveling in a car —**carsickness** *n.* [U]

cart¹ /kɑrt/ *n.* [C] **1** *also* **shopping cart** a large wire basket on wheels that you use when shopping in a SUPERMARKET **2** a vehicle with two or four wheels that is pulled by a horse, used for carrying heavy things **3** a small table on wheels, used for moving and serving food: *The waiter wheeled the dessert cart over to our table.*

cart² *v.* [I,T] to carry or take something large and heavy somewhere: *Workers* ***carted away*** *several tons of trash.*

THESAURUS **carry, haul, transport, bear, tote, lug, schlep** → CARRY

carte blanche /,kɑrt 'blɑnʃ/ *n.* [U] permission or freedom to do whatever you want: *He was* ***given carte blanche*** *to pick the team he wanted.*

car·tel /kɑr'tɛl/ *n.* [C] ECONOMICS a group of companies who all agree to charge a particular price for something they produce or sell, which limits competition in an unfair way: *The price of a barrel of oil is set by OPEC, the oil cartel.*

car·ti·lage /'kɑrtl-ɪdʒ/ *n.* [C,U] BIOLOGY a strong

substance that can bend and stretch, which is around the joints in your body

car·tog·ra·phy /kɑrˈtɑgrəfi/ *n.* [U] the skill or practice of making maps —**cartographer** *n.* [C]

car·ton /ˈkɑrt˺n/ *n.* [C] a box made of CARDBOARD, that contains food or a drink: *a milk carton* | *a **carton of** juice*

C

car·toon /kɑrˈtun/ *n.* [C] **1** a movie or television program made with characters that are drawn and not real: *a Bugs Bunny cartoon* → MOVIE **2** a funny drawing in a newspaper, usually about someone or something that is in the news [ORIGIN: 1500—1600 Italian *cartone* "pasteboard, cartoon," from *carta* "sheet of paper"]

THESAURUS **drawing, picture, sketch, comic strip, portrait, caricature, illustration, image** → DRAWING, PICTURE[1]

car·toon·ist /kɑrˈtunɪst/ *n.* [C] someone who draws cartoons

car·tridge /ˈkɑrtrɪdʒ/ *n.* [C] **1** a small piece of equipment that you put inside something to make it work: *The printer needs a new **ink cartridge**.* **2** a tube containing explosive material and a bullet for a gun

cart·wheel /ˈkɑrt˺wil/ *n.* [C] a movement in which you throw your body sideways onto your hands and bring your legs over your head —**cartwheel** *v.* [I]

carve /kɑrv/ *v.* **1** [T] to make an object by cutting it from a piece of wood or stone: *The statue was **carved from** a single block of marble.* **2** [T] to cut a pattern or letter on the surface of something: *Someone had **carved** their initials **on** the tree.* **3** [I,T] to cut a large piece of cooked meat into smaller pieces with a large knife: *Dad always carves the turkey.* → *see picture at* CUT[1]

THESAURUS **cut, chop (up), slice, dice, peel, shred, grate** → CUT[1]

carve sth ↔ **out** *phr. v.* **carve out a career/niche/reputation etc.** to become successful and be respected

carve sth ↔ **up** *phr. v.* (disapproving) to divide land, a company, etc. into smaller parts: *The country was carved up after the war.*

carv·ing /ˈkɑrvɪŋ/ *n.* **1** [C] an object that has been cut from wood, stone, etc. **2** [U] the activity of cutting objects from wood, stone, etc., or cutting patterns into wood, stone, etc.

ˈcar wash *n.* [C] a place where you can take your car to be washed with special equipment

cas·cade /kæˈskeɪd/ *n.* [C] **1** a small steep WATERFALL **2** (literary) something that seems to flow or hang down: *Her hair fell in a **cascade of** soft curls.* —**cascade** *v.* [I]

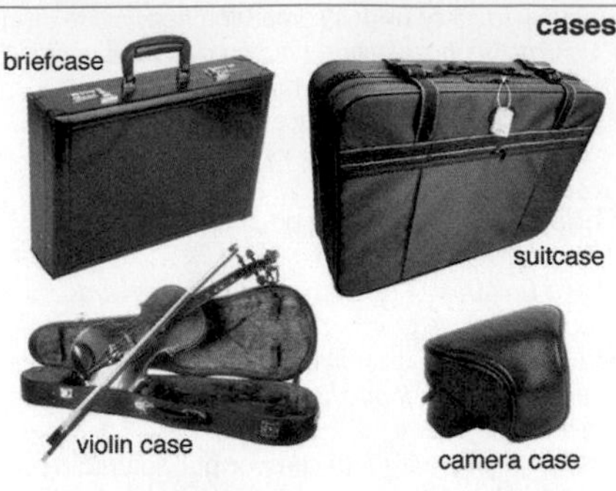

case[1] /keɪs/ *n.*

1 SITUATION/EXAMPLE [C] a particular situation, or an example of that situation (SYN) **example, instance**: ***In some cases**, snoring indicates a real medical problem.* | *Miller's actions were a clear **case of** sexual harassment.* | *We live far apart now, but that won't always **be the case**.* | *Many western cities are growing. Las Vegas is **a case in point*** (=a clear example).

2 (just) in case a) as a way of being prepared for something that might happen: *Take your umbrella in case it rains.* **b)** if: *In case my train is late, start the meeting without me.*

3 COURT [C] LAW a legal matter or question that must be decided in a court of law: *a **court case*** | *Watson is expected to **win/lose** the **case**.*

4 POLICE [C] a crime or set of events that the police are trying to find out the truth about: *Sturgis is investigating a murder case.*

5 ARGUMENT [C] all the facts or reasons that support one side of an argument: *The prosecution's **case against** him is very strong.* | *There is a good **case for** changing the rule.*

6 CONTAINER [C] a container for storing something: *a jewelry case* | *a **case of** wine*

7 in case of sth if or when something happens: *In case of fire, break the glass and push the alarm button.*

8 DISEASE/ILLNESS [C] an example of a disease or illness, or the person suffering from this disease or illness: *There have been ten **cases of** malaria in the village recently.*

9 in that case (spoken) used in order to say what you will do or what will happen in a particular situation: *"I'll be home late tonight." "Well, in that case, I won't cook dinner."*

10 in any case used in order to give the reason why you will do something, or to say that you are determined to do it: *Sure we'll take you home – we're going that way in any case.*

11 be on sb's case (spoken) to be criticizing someone a lot: *Dad's always on my case about something.*

12 get off my case (spoken) used in order to tell someone to stop criticizing you: *OK, OK, just get off my case, will you?*

13 GRAMMAR [C,U] ENG. LANG. ARTS the form of a word, usually a noun, or the way the form changes, showing its relationship to other words in a sentence [ORIGIN: (6) 1200—1300 Old North French *casse*, from Latin *capsa* "box, case"] → LOWERCASE, UPPERCASE

case² *v.* **1 be cased in sth** to be surrounded by a substance: *The reactor will be cased in metal.* **2 case the joint** (informal) to look around a place that you intend to steal from, in order to find out information

case·load /'keɪsloʊd/ *n.* [C] the number of people a doctor, SOCIAL WORKER, etc. has to deal with

'case ˌstudy *n.* [C] a detailed study of a particular person, group, or situation over a long period of time

case·work /'keɪswɚk/ *n.* [U] work done to help particular people or families with their social problems —**caseworker** *n.* [C]

cash¹ /kæʃ/ *n.* [U] **1** money in the form of coins and bills: *There's a small discount if you pay cash.* | *He had about $200 **in cash** in his wallet*

> THESAURUS **money, bill, coin, penny, nickel, dime, quarter, change, currency** → MONEY

2 (informal) money in any form: *I'm kind of short of cash at the moment.* | *The company had problems **raising cash** for the deal.* **3 cash on delivery** (*abbreviation* **C.O.D.**) used when the customer must pay the person who delivers goods to them

cash² *v.* **cash a check/money order etc.** to exchange a check for money: *Can I get this check cashed here?*

cash in *phr. v.* **1** to gain money or advantages from a situation: *He **cashed in on** his fame as a basketball player by advertising sportswear.* **2 cash** sth ↔ **in** to exchange something for its value in money: *We decided to cash in our insurance policy early.*

'cash cow *n.* [C] ECONOMICS a business or product you can always depend on to make a profit

'cash crop *n.* [C] ECONOMICS a crop that is grown to be sold rather than to be used by the people growing it

cash·ew /'kæʃu, kæ'ʃu/ *n.* [C] a small curved nut that you can eat, or the tropical American tree on which these nuts grow [ORIGIN: 1500—1600 Portuguese *cajú*, from Tupi *acajú*]

'cash flow *n.* [singular, U] ECONOMICS the movement of money into and out of a business or someone's bank account: *They're having **cash flow problems** and might be going out of business.*

cash·ier /kæ'ʃɪr/ *n.* [C] someone whose job is to receive and pay out money in a store

cash·less /'kæʃləs/ *adj.* done or working without using coins or paper money

'cash maˌchine *n.* [C] a machine from which you can get money by using a special plastic card (SYN) **ATM** → ACCOUNT¹

cash·mere /'kæʒmɪr, 'kæʃ-/ *n.* [U] a type of fine soft wool: *a cashmere sweater* [ORIGIN: 1600—1700 *Cashmere*, old spelling of *Kashmir* area on the border of India and Pakistan]

'cash ˌregister *n.* [C] a machine used in stores to keep money in and to show how much customers have to pay

cas·ing /'keɪsɪŋ/ *n.* [C] an outer layer of rubber, metal, etc. that covers and protects something, for example a wire

ca·si·no /kə'sinoʊ/ *n.* (plural **casinos**) [C] a place where people try to win money by playing games [ORIGIN: 1700—1800 Italian *casa* "house"]

cask /kæsk/ *n.* [C] a round wooden container used for holding alcohol, or the amount contained in this [ORIGIN: 1500—1600 French *casque* "helmet," from Spanish *casco* "broken piece of a pot, skull, helmet"]

cas·ket /'kæskɪt/ *n.* [C] a COFFIN

cas·se·role /'kæsəˌroʊl/ *n.* [C,U] food that is cooked slowly in liquid in a covered dish in the OVEN [ORIGIN: 1700—1800 French "cooking pan," from *casse* "big spoon, pan," from Greek *kyathos* "big spoon"]

cas·sette /kə'sɛt/ *n.* [C] a small flat plastic case containing tape, that can be used for playing or recording sound or pictures (SYN) **tape**: *an **audio/video cassette***

cast¹ /kæst/ *v.* (past tense and past participle **cast**) [T]

1 ACTORS to choose a particular actor for a part in a movie, play, etc.: *He was **cast as** the romantic leading man in many famous movies.*

2 cast doubt/suspicion on sth to make people feel less certain about something: *Recent information has cast doubt on the evidence.*

3 cast a vote to vote in an election: *I'd like to know more about the candidates before I cast my vote.*

4 cast a spell (on/over sb/sth) a) to make someone feel very strongly attracted to something and keep his/her attention completely: *Within minutes, Sinatra's voice had cast a spell on the audience.* **b)** to say magic words to make something happen

5 cast a shadow a) to make people feel less happy or hopeful about something: *Her father's illness **cast a shadow over** the wedding celebrations.* **b)** (literary) to make a shadow appear on something: *trees casting a shadow across the lawn*

6 cast light on/onto sth a) to explain or give new information about something: *His research has cast light on the origin of the universe.* **b)** (literary) to send light onto a surface

7 cast a look/glance (at sb/sth) (literary) to look at someone or something: *She cast an anxious glance at Guy.*

8 ART to make something by pouring metal or plastic into a specially shaped container: *a statue of Lincoln **cast in** bronze*

9 THROW to throw something somewhere: *fishermen casting their nets into the sea*

THESAURUS throw, toss, chuck, hurl, fling, pass, pitch, lob → THROW¹

cast sb/sth ↔ **aside** *phr. v.*
to get rid of something or someone: *It's time to cast aside the past and make a new start.*

cast off *phr. v.*
1 to untie the rope that keeps a boat on shore so that it can sail away
2 cast sb/sth ↔ **off** (literary) to get rid of something or someone

cast sb/sth ↔ **out** *phr. v.* (literary)
to force someone or something to go away

C

cast² *n.* [C] **1** all of the actors in a movie, play, etc.: *an **all-star cast*** (=all the actors are famous) **2** a hard cover for a part of your body, that supports a broken bone while it gets better: *a leg cast* **3** a MOLD (=specially shaped container) into which you pour metal or plastic in order to make an object of a particular shape

cast·a·way /ˈkæstəˌweɪ/ *n.* [C] someone who is alone on an island after his/her ship has sunk

caste /kæst/ *n.* [C,U] SOCIAL SCIENCE one of the social classes in India into which people are born, that cannot be changed

cast·er /ˈkæstɚ/ *n.* [C] a small wheel fixed to the bottom of a piece of furniture so it can be moved easily

ˈcaste ˌsystem *n.* [C] SOCIAL SCIENCE the Hindu system of social classes, which people are born into and cannot change

cas·ti·gate /ˈkæstəˌgeɪt/ *v.* [T] (formal) to criticize or punish someone in a severe way **—castigation** /ˌkæstəˈgeɪʃən/ *n.* [U]

cast·ing /ˈkæstɪŋ/ *n.* [U] the act of choosing actors for a movie, play, etc.: *a casting director*

ˌcast ˈiron *n.* [U] a type of iron that is very hard

ˌcast-ˈiron *adj.* **1** made of cast iron: *a cast-iron skillet* **2 cast-iron excuse/alibi/guarantee etc.** an excuse, etc. that is very certain and cannot fail

cas·tle /ˈkæsəl/ *n.* [C] a very large strong building built in past times to protect the people inside from attack [ORIGIN: 1000—1100 Old North French *castel*, from Latin *castellum* "building with a defensive wall"]

cast·offs /ˈkæstɔfs/ *n.* [plural] clothes or other things that someone does not want anymore and gives or throws away

cas·trate /ˈkæstreɪt/ *v.* [T] to remove the sexual organs of a male animal or a man **—castration** /kæˈstreɪʃən/ *n.* [C,U]

cas·u·al /ˈkæʒuəl, -ʒəl/ *adj.* **1** casual clothes are comfortable and not worn on formal occasions: *Many companies allow **casual dress** on Fridays.* | *the **casual look*** **2** relaxed and not worried about things: *The restaurant has a **casual atmosphere**.* | *Sport is talked about a lot in **casual conversation**.* | *His **casual attitude** toward work really irritates me.* **3** [only before noun] without any serious interest or attention: *Most **casual observers** won't notice anything different.* **4** knowing someone without wanting a close relationship with him/her: *a **casual acquaintance*** | *We had a **casual relationship** when we were at college.* **—casually** *adv.*: *He was casually dressed.*

cas·u·al·ty /ˈkæʒəlti, -ʒuəlti/ *n.* (plural **casualties**) [C] **1** someone who is hurt or killed in an accident or war: *The army suffered **heavy casualties*** (=a lot of people were hurt or killed). **2 be a casualty of sth** to suffer because of a particular event or situation: *The city library is the latest casualty of the cutbacks.*

cat /kæt/ *n.* [C] **1** a small animal that is often kept as a pet or is used for catching mice → *see picture at* PET¹ **2** a large wild animal, such as a lion, that is related to cats **3 let the cat out of the bag** (informal) to tell a secret without intending to [ORIGIN: Old English *catt*]

cat·a·clysm /ˈkætəˌklɪzəm/ *n.* [C] (literary) a sudden violent event or change, such as a big flood or EARTHQUAKE [ORIGIN: 1600—1700 French *cataclysme*, from Latin, from Greek, from *kataklyzein* "to flood," from *kata-* "down" + *klyzein* "to wash"] **—cataclysmic** /ˌkætəˈklɪzmɪk/ *adj.*

cat·a·log¹, **catalogue** /ˈkætlˌɔg, -ˌɑg/ *n.* [C] **1** a book with pictures and information about goods or services that you can buy: *a mail order catalog* **2** a list of the objects, paintings, books, etc. in a place such as a MUSEUM or library

catalog² *v.* [T] to make a complete list of something

cat·a·lyst /ˈkætl-ɪst/ *n.* [C] **1** something or someone that causes an important change or event to happen: *These events were the **catalyst for** the war.* **2** CHEMISTRY a substance that makes a chemical reaction happen more quickly without being changed itself **—catalytic** /ˌkætlˈɪtɪk◂/ *adj.* **—catalyze** /ˈkætlˌaɪz/ *v.* [T]

ˌcatalytic conˈverter *n.* [C] a piece of equipment that is attached to the EXHAUST of a car, which reduces the amount of poisonous gases the engine sends into the air

cat·a·ma·ran /ˈkætəməˌræn/ *n.* [C] a type of small boat with sails and two separate HULLS (=part that goes in the water)

cat·a·pult¹ /ˈkætəˌpʌlt, -ˌpʊlt/ *v.* [T] **1** to push or throw something very hard so that it moves through the air very quickly: *Two cars were catapulted into the air by the force of the blast.* **2 catapult sb to stardom/fame etc.** to suddenly make someone very famous or successful

catapult² *n.* [C] a large weapon used in former times to throw heavy stones, iron balls, etc.

cat·a·ract /ˈkætəˌrækt/ *n.* [C] BIOLOGY a medical

condition that affects the eye and makes you slowly lose your sight

ca·tas·tro·phe /kəˈtæstrəfi/ *n.* [C,U] a terrible event that causes a lot of destruction or suffering: *The oil spill will be an ecological catastrophe.* —**catastrophic** /ˌkæt̬əˈstrɑfɪk◂/ *adj.*: *catastrophic floods*

THESAURUS **accident, disaster, mishap** → ACCIDENT

catch¹ /kætʃ/ *v.* (past tense and past participle **caught** /kɔt/)

1 HOLD [I,T] to get hold of and stop something that is moving through the air (ANT) **drop**: *He **caught the ball** and started to run.* → *see picture on page A22*

2 FIND SB/STH [T] **a)** to stop a person or animal that is running away: *"You can't catch me!" she yelled over her shoulder.* **b)** to find a criminal and put him/her somewhere so that s/he cannot escape: *The police have caught the man suspected of the murder.* **c)** to get a fish or animal by using a trap, net, or hook: *Did you **catch** any **fish**?*

THESAURUS

capture – to catch someone in order to keep him/her as a prisoner: *A French soldier was captured in the battle.*

arrest – if the police arrest someone, the person is taken away because the police think s/he has done something illegal: *He was arrested and charged with murder.*

apprehend (formal) – if the police apprehend someone they think has done something illegal, they catch him/her: *The two men were later apprehended after robbing another store.*

corner – to move closer to a person or an animal so that he, she, or it cannot escape: *Once the dog was cornered, he began to growl.*

trap – to catch an animal in a trap: *These animals used to be trapped for their fur.*

3 SEE SB DOING STH [T] to see someone doing something wrong or illegal: *I caught him looking through my letters.* | *A store detective **caught** him **red-handed*** (=saw him stealing).

4 GET SICK [T] to get an illness: *Put your coat on or you'll **catch a cold**.*

5 catch a train/plane/bus to get on a train, etc. in order to travel somewhere: *I should be able to catch the 12:05 train.*

6 NOT BE TOO LATE [T] to not be too late to do something, talk to someone, etc. (ANT) **miss**: *If you hurry, you might catch her before she leaves.*

7 GET STUCK [I,T] to become stuck on or in something by mistake: *His shirt caught on the fence and tore.*

8 catch sb by surprise/catch sb off guard to do something or happen in an unexpected way, so that someone is not ready to deal with it

9 SEE/SMELL [T] to see or smell something for a moment: *I suddenly **caught sight of** Luisa in the crowd.* | *Yuck – did you **catch a whiff** of* (=did you smell) *his aftershave?*

10 catch sb's eye a) to attract someone's attention and make him/her look at something: *A photograph on his desk caught my eye.* **b)** to look at someone at the same moment that s/he is looking at you: *Every time she caught his eye, she would look away embarrassed.*

11 be caught in/without etc. sth to be in a situation that is difficult because you cannot easily get out of it, or because you do not have what you need: *We got caught in the storm.*

12 catch (on) fire to start burning, especially accidentally

13 catch your breath to begin breathing normally again after you have been running or exercising

14 catch sb's attention/interest/imagination to make someone feel interested in something: *a story that will catch children's imaginations*

15 STOP PROBLEM/DISEASE [T] to discover a problem, especially a disease, and stop it from developing: *It's a type of cancer that can be cured, if it is caught early.*

SPOKEN PHRASES

16 not catch sth to not hear or understand something clearly: *I'm sorry, I didn't catch your name.*

17 you won't catch me doing sth used in order to say you would never do something: *You won't catch me ironing his shirts.*

18 Catch you later! used in order to say goodbye

catch on *phr. v.*

1 to begin to understand something: *It may take time for some of the children to catch on.*

2 to become popular: *The idea never caught on in this country.*

catch up *phr. v.*

1 to reach a person or vehicle that was in front of you by going faster than him, her, or it: *I had to run to **catch up with** her.*

2 to reach the same standard or level as other people: *If you miss class, it can be difficult to catch up.*

3 be/get caught up in sth to be or become involved in something, especially without wanting to: *young people who get caught up in crime*

catch up on sth *phr. v.*

to do something that needs to be done that you have not had time to do in the past: *I need to catch up on some work.*

catch² *n.* **1** [C] the act of catching something that has been thrown or hit: *That was a great catch!* **2** [U] a game in which two or more people throw a ball to each other: *Let's play catch.* **3** [C] (informal) a hidden problem or difficulty: *The rent is so low there must be a catch.*

THESAURUS **disadvantage, drawback, downside, bad point** → DISADVANTAGE

4 [C] a hook for fastening something and holding it shut: *the catch on my necklace*

Catch-22 /ˌkætʃ twɛnti ˈtu/ *n.* [singular, U] a situation in which, whatever you do, you are prevented from achieving what you want: *You can't*

get a job without experience, and you can't get experience without a job. It's a Catch-22. [ORIGIN: 1900—2000 *Catch-22* book (1961) by Joseph Heller in which such situations are described]

catch·er /'kætʃɚ/ *n.* [C] the baseball player who SQUATS behind the BATTER in order to catch balls that are not hit

catch·ing /'kætʃɪŋ/ *adj.* [not before noun] (informal) a disease or illness that is catching spreads easily from one person to another

C

'catch phrase *n.* [C] a word or phrase that is easy to remember and is repeated by a political party, newspaper, etc.

catch·y /'kætʃi/ *adj.* a catchy tune or phrase is easy to remember: *There are some really catchy songs on the album.*

cat·e·chism /'kætə͵kɪzəm/ *n.* [C] a set of questions and answers about the Christian religion, that people learn before becoming members of the church

cat·e·gor·i·cal /͵kætə'gɔrɪkəl, -'gɑr-/ *adj.* clearly stating that something is true: *Weber's agent issued a* ***categorical denial*** *that the incident had ever happened.* —**categorically** *adv.*: *James categorically denied the charges.*

cat·e·go·rize /'kætəgə͵raɪz/ *v.* [T] to put people or things into groups according to what type, level, etc. they are: *We've* ***categorized*** *the wines* ***by*** *region.*

cat·e·go·ry /'kætə͵gɔri/ (Ac) *n.* (plural **categories**) [C] a group of people or things that are all of the same type: *There are several* ***categories of*** *patients.* | *Voters* ***fall into*** (=belong to) *one of three* ***categories***.

THESAURUS **type, kind, sort, brand, make, model, genre, variety, species** ➔ TYPE[1]

ca·ter /'keɪtɚ/ *v.* [I,T] to provide and serve food and drinks at a party, meeting, etc., usually as a business: *Who's catering your daughter's wedding?* —**caterer** *n.* [C]

cater to sb *phr. v.* to provide a particular group of people with something that they need or want: *newspapers that cater to business people*

ca·ter·ing /'keɪtərɪŋ/ *n.* [U] the job of providing and serving food and drinks at parties, meetings, etc.

cat·er·pil·lar /'kætɚ͵pɪlɚ, 'kætə-/ *n.* [C] a small creature with a long rounded body and many legs that develops into a BUTTERFLY or MOTH [ORIGIN: 1400—1500 Old North French *catepelose* "hairy cat, caterpillar"] ➔ *see picture on page A15*

cat·fish /'kæt˺fɪʃ/ *n.* [C,U] a common fish with long hairs around its mouth that lives mainly in rivers and lakes, or the meat from this fish

ca·thar·tic /kə'θɑrtɪk/ *adj.* (literary) helping you to deal with difficult emotions and get rid of them —**catharsis** /kə'θɑrsɪs/ *n.* [U]

ca·the·dral /kə'θidrəl/ *n.* [C] the main church in a particular area [ORIGIN: 1500—1600 *cathedral church* "cathedral" (13—21 centuries); from Old French *cathedral*; from Latin *cathedra* "chair, bishop's chair"]

cath·ode /'kæθoʊd/ *n.* [C] PHYSICS the negative ELECTRODE, marked (-), from which an electric current leaves a piece of equipment such as a BATTERY ➔ ANODE

Cath·o·lic /'kæθlɪk, -θəlɪk/ *adj.* relating to the part of the Christian religion whose leader is the Pope —**Catholic** *n.* [C] —**Catholicism** /kə'θɑlə͵sɪzəm/ *n.* [U]

catholic *adj.* (formal) including a great variety of things: *Susan has* ***catholic tastes*** *in music.* [ORIGIN: 1300—1400 French *catholique*, from Late Latin, from Greek *katholikos* "general, universal"]

cat·i·on /'kæt͵aɪən/ *n.* [C] PHYSICS an ION with a positive electrical charge that is attracted to the part on a BATTERY that sends out a negative electrical charge

cat·nap /'kæt˺næp/ *n.* [C] (informal) a short sleep during the day

cat·nip /'kæt˺nɪp/ *n.* [U] a type of grass with a pleasant smell that cats are attracted to

CAT scan /'kæt skæn/ *also* **CT scan** /si 'ti skæn/ *n.* [C] an image of the inside of someone's body produced by a special piece of hospital equipment called a SCANNER

cat·sup /'kɛtʃəp, 'kæ-/ *n.* [U] another spelling of KETCHUP

cat·tle /'kætl/ *n.* [plural] cows and BULLS kept on a farm

cat·ty /'kæti/ *adj.* (informal) deliberately unkind in what you say about someone —**cattiness** *n.* [U]

'catty-͵cornered *adv.* KITTY-CORNER

cat·walk /'kæt˺wɔk/ *n.* [C] **1** a long raised path that models walk on in a fashion show **2** a narrow structure high up in a building or above something such as a bridge, built for people to walk on while they are working

Cau·ca·sian /kɔ'keɪʒən/ *adj.* someone who is Caucasian belongs to the race that has pale skin —**Caucasian** *n.* [C]

cau·cus /'kɔkəs/ *n.* [C] POLITICS a group of people in a political party, who meet to discuss and decide on political plans

caught /kɔt/ *v.* the past tense and past participle of CATCH

caul·dron /'kɔldrən/ *n.* [C] a large round metal pot for boiling liquids over a fire

cau·li·flow·er /'kɔlɪ͵flaʊɚ, 'kɑ-/ *n.* [C,U] a white vegetable with short firm stems and thick groups of small round flower-like parts [ORIGIN: 1500—1600 Italian *cavolfiore*, from *cavolo* "cabbage" + *fiore* "flower"] ➔ *see picture at* VEGETABLE

cau·sa·tion /kɔˈzeɪʃən/ *n.* [U] MATH the relationship between two VARIABLES (=mathematical quantity that is not fixed), in which a change in one produces a change in the other

'cause /kəz/ *conjunction* (spoken) because

cause[1] /kɔz/ *n.* **1** [C] a person, event, or thing that makes something happen: *What was the* ***cause of*** *the accident.* **2** [C,U] a reason for doing something or having a particular feeling: *There is* ***no cause for concern/alarm.*** **3** [C] a principle or aim that a group of people support or fight for: *I don't mind giving money if it's* ***for a good cause.*** [ORIGIN: 1200—1300 Old French, Latin *causa*]

cause[2] *v.* [T] to make something happen, especially something bad: *Heavy traffic is causing long delays.* | *We still don't know what* ***caused*** *the computer* ***to*** *crash.*

THESAURUS

make – to cause a particular state or situation to happen: *I'm sorry, I didn't mean to make you cry.*
be responsible for sth – if you are responsible for something bad, it is your fault that it happened: *The jury found him responsible for the deaths of his wife and child.*
bring about sth – to make something happen: *Working together, the community brought about significant changes in the local area.*
result in sth – if an action or event results in something, it makes that thing happen: *The fire resulted in the deaths of two children.*
lead to sth – if one thing leads to something else, the first thing causes the second thing to happen or exist at a later time: *The information led to several arrests.*
trigger – if one event triggers another, it makes the second event happen: *The incident triggered a wave of violence.*
prompt (formal) – to make someone do something as a reaction to an event or situation: *The changes prompted several people to resign from the committee in protest.*
induce (formal) – to make someone decide to do something: *What induced you to spend so much money on a car?*

ˌcause and efˈfect *n.* [U] ENG. LANG. ARTS a way of organizing a piece of written work, in which you describe an event or a situation and explain the reasons why it happened and the effects that it has

caus·tic /ˈkɔstɪk/ *adj.* **1 caustic remark/comment etc.** something you say that is extremely unkind or full of criticism **2** CHEMISTRY a caustic substance can burn through things by chemical action

cau·tion[1] /ˈkɔʃən/ *n.* [U] **1** the quality of doing something carefully, not taking risks, and avoiding danger: *The animals should be handled* ***with caution.*** | *Travelers in the area should* ***use*** *extreme* ***caution.*** **2 word/note of caution** a warning to be careful: *A word of caution – be sure to make copies of all files.*

caution[2] *v.* [T] (formal) to warn someone that something might be dangerous or difficult: *The children were* ***cautioned against*** *talking to strangers.*

cau·tion·ar·y /ˈkɔʃəˌnɛri/ *adj.* giving a warning: *a* ***cautionary tale*** (=a story that is used to warn people)

cau·tious /ˈkɔʃəs/ *adj.* careful to avoid danger: *a cautious driver* | *He was* ***cautious about*** *making any predictions.* —**cautiously** *adv.*

cav·a·lier /ˌkævəˈlɪr/ *adj.* not caring or thinking enough about other people or how serious a situation might be: *drivers with a* ***cavalier attitude*** *toward road safety*

cav·al·ry /ˈkævəlri/ *n.* [U] soldiers who fight while riding on horses

cave[1] /keɪv/ *n.* [C] a large natural hole in the side of a cliff or under the ground [ORIGIN: 1200—1300 Old French, Latin *cava*, from *cavus* "hollow"]

cave[2] *v.*

cave in *phr. v.* **1** if the top or sides of something cave in, they fall down or inward: *The roof of the old house had caved in.* **2** to stop opposing something because you have been persuaded or threatened

cave·man /ˈkeɪvmæn/ *n.* (plural **cavemen** /-mɛn/) [C] someone who lived in a cave many thousands of years ago

cav·ern /ˈkævən/ *n.* [C] a large deep cave —**cavernous** *adj.*

cav·i·ar /ˈkæviˌɑr/ *n.* [U] fish eggs, eaten as a special expensive food

cav·i·ty /ˈkævət̬i/ *n.* (plural **cavities**) [C] **1** a hole in a tooth, made by decay: *The dentist told me that* ***I have a cavity.*** **2** a hole or space inside something solid

THESAURUS **hole, space, gap, leak, crack, opening** ➔ HOLE[1]

ca·vort /kəˈvɔrt/ *v.* [I] to jump or dance in an excited or sexual way

CB *n.* [C,U] **Citizens Band** a radio on which people can speak to each other over short distances

CBS *n.* **Columbia Broadcasting System** one of the national companies that broadcasts television and radio programs in the U.S.

cc **1** the abbreviation of CUBIC CENTIMETER: *a 2,000 cc engine* **2 carbon copy** used in business letters and emails to show that you are sending a copy to someone else

CD *n.* [C] **1 compact disc** a small circular piece of hard plastic on which music or computer information is recorded ➔ *see picture on page A19* **2** a CERTIFICATE OF DEPOSIT

CˈD ˌplayer *n.* [C] a piece of equipment used for playing music CDs

CD-ROM /ˌsi di ˈrɑm/ *n.* [C,U] IT **compact disc read-only memory** a CD on which a large amount of computer information is stored

CD-RW *n.* [C,U] IT **compact disc-rewritable** a type of CD that you can record music, images, or other information onto, using special equipment on your computer, and that can be recorded onto several times

cease /sis/ Ac *v.* [I,T] (formal) to stop doing something, or to make an activity stop happening: *By noon, the rain had ceased.* | *He never **ceases to amaze me*** (=I am always surprised by what he does). | *East Germany ceased to exist in 1990, shortly after the collapse of the Berlin Wall.* [ORIGIN: 1300—1400 Old French *cesser*, from Latin *cessare* "to stop," from *cedere* "to give up"]

cease·fire /ˌsisˈfaɪɚ, ˈsisfaɪɚ/ *n.* [C] an agreement for both sides in a war to stop fighting for a period of time

cease·less /ˈsislɪs/ Ac *adj.* (formal) continuing for a long time without stopping: *the ceaseless motion of the waves* —**ceaselessly** *adv.*

ce·dar /ˈsidɚ/ *n.* [C,U] a tall EVERGREEN tree with leaves shaped like needles, or the red sweet-smelling wood of this tree ➔ *see picture on page A23*

cede /sid/ *v.* [T] (formal) to give land, power, etc. to another country or person

ce·dil·la /sɪˈdɪlə/ *n.* [C] ENG. LANG. ARTS a mark under the letter "c" in French and some other languages, to show that it is an "s" sound instead of a "k" sound. The letter is written "ç."

ceil·ing /ˈsilɪŋ/ *n.* [C] **1** the inside surface of the top part of a room ➔ ROOF: *an apartment with **high ceilings*** **2** the largest number or amount of something that is officially allowed: *They have put a **ceiling of** $2 million **on** the project*

cel·e·brate /ˈsɛləˌbreɪt/ *v.* [I,T] to do something special because of a particular event or special occasion: *It's our anniversary, and we're going out to dinner to celebrate.* | *How do you want to celebrate your birthday?*

cel·e·brat·ed /ˈsɛləˌbreɪt̬ɪd/ *adj.* famous or talked about a lot: *Chicago is **celebrated for** its architecture.*

THESAURUS **famous, well-known, legendary, infamous, notorious, renowned, noted, distinguished, eminent** ➔ FAMOUS

cel·e·bra·tion /ˌsɛləˈbreɪʃən/ *n.* **1** [C] an occasion or party when you celebrate something: *New Year's celebrations* **2** [U] the act of celebrating

ce·leb·ri·ty /səˈlɛbrət̬i/ *n.* (plural **celebrities**) [C] a famous person, especially someone in the entertainment business: *Hollywood celebrities*

cel·er·y /ˈsɛləri/ *n.* [U] a vegetable with long firm pale green stems, often eaten raw [ORIGIN: 1600—1700 Italian dialect *seleri*, from Late Latin *selinon* "parsley," from Greek] ➔ *see picture at* VEGETABLE

ce·les·tial /səˈlɛstʃəl/ *adj.* relating to the sky or heaven

cel·i·bate /ˈsɛləbɪt/ *adj.* someone who is celibate does not have sex —**celibacy** /ˈsɛləbəsi/ *n.* [U]

cell

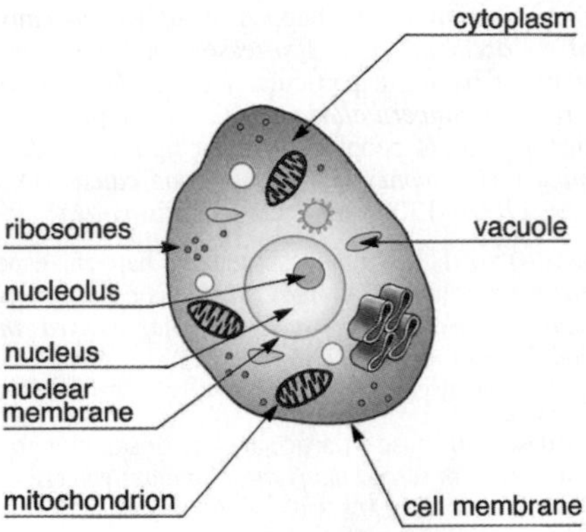

cell /sɛl/ *n.* [C] **1** BIOLOGY the smallest part of any living thing except a VIRUS: *red blood cells* **2** a small room where prisoners are kept: *a jail cell* **3** PHYSICS a piece of equipment that produces electricity from chemicals, heat, or light: *cars powered by **fuel cells*** **4** a small space that an insect or other small creature has made to live in or use ➔ *see picture at* HIVE [ORIGIN: 1100—1200 Old French *celle*, from Latin *cella* "small room"]

cel·lar /ˈsɛlɚ/ *n.* [C] a room under a house or other building, often used for storing things

ˈ**cell ˌbody** *n.* [C] BIOLOGY the main part of a nerve cell, which contains the NUCLEUS (=central part) and the parts that keep the cell alive

ˈ**cell ˌculture** *n.* [C] BIOLOGY a group of cells grown in a special chemical solution from a single original cell

ˈ**cell ˌcycle** *n.* [C] BIOLOGY a process in which a cell divides and forms two new cells

ˈ**cell diˌvision** *n.* [U] BIOLOGY the process by which a cell divides to form two new cells

cel·list /ˈtʃɛlɪst/ *n.* [C] someone who plays the cello

ˈ**cell ˌmembrane** *n.* [C,U] BIOLOGY a thin layer of material that covers a cell, through which substances pass in and out ➔ *see picture at* CELL

cel·lo /ˈtʃɛloʊ/ *n.* (plural **cellos**) [C] a large wooden musical instrument that you hold between your knees and play by pulling a BOW (=special stick) across the strings

Cel·lo·phane /ˈsɛləˌfeɪn/ *n.* [U] (trademark) a thin transparent material used for wrapping things

ˈ**cell phone** *also* ˈ**cellular ˌphone** *n.* [C] a telephone that you carry with you ➔ *see picture on page A19*

TOPIC

To use a cell phone, you first **switch it on**. Then you can either **call** someone or **listen to messages** that people have left you on your **voice mail**. You can also send or receive **text messages** (=written messages) or **text** someone (=send him/her a text message).

'cell respi,ration *also* **'cellular respi,ration** *n.* [U] BIOLOGY the process in which a cell changes sugar and other substances into the energy it needs, usually by using oxygen

'cell speciali,zation *n.* [U] BIOLOGY the fact that different cells in the body have different purposes and are involved in different activities

cel·lu·lar /'sɛlyələ/ *adj.* **1** relating to cellular phones: *a cellular network* **2** BIOLOGY relating to the cells in a plant or animal

'cellular ,phone *n.* [C] a CELL PHONE → *see picture on page A19*

cel·lu·lite /'sɛlyə,laɪt/ *n.* [U] fat just below someone's skin that makes it look uneven and unattractive

cel·lu·loid /'sɛlyə,lɔɪd/ *n.* [U] (trademark) a substance like plastic, used in the past to make film

cel·lu·lose /'sɛlyə,lous/ *n.* [U] BIOLOGY a substance that forms the walls of plant cells

,cell 'wall *n.* [C] BIOLOGY the stiff outer part of the cells of plants and BACTERIA, which helps to support the growing plants or bacteria

Cel·si·us /'sɛlsiəs, -ʃəs/ *n.* [U] PHYSICS (*written abbreviation* **C**) a temperature scale in which water freezes at 0° and boils at 100° (SYN) **Centigrade** → FAHRENHEIT [ORIGIN: 1800—1900 Anders *Celsius* (1701-44), Swedish scientist who invented the scale]

ce·ment¹ /sɪ'mɛnt/ *n.* [U] a gray powder used in building that is mixed with sand and water and allowed to dry and become hard [ORIGIN: 1300—1400 Old French *ciment*, from Latin *caementum* "small pieces of stone used in making mortar"]

cement² *v.* [T] **1** to make a relationship, position, etc. stronger: *China has cemented its trade connections with the U.S.* **2** to cover something with cement

cem·e·ter·y /'sɛmə,tɛri/ *n.* (plural **cemeteries**) [C] a place where dead people are buried [ORIGIN: 1300—1400 Old French *cimitere*, from Late Latin *coemeterium*, from Greek *koimeterion* "sleeping room, burying place"]

Ce·no·zo·ic /,sinə'zouɪk/ *n.* **the Cenozoic** EARTH SCIENCES the period of time in the Earth's history from when the DINOSAURS died out about 65 million years ago until the present day → MESOZOIC, PALEOZOIC, PRECAMBRIAN —**Cenozoic** *adj.*: *the Cenozoic era*

cen·sor¹ /'sɛnsə/ *v.* [T] to examine books, movies, etc. and remove anything that is offensive, politically dangerous, etc. —**censorship** *n.* [U]

censor² *n.* [C] someone whose job is to censor books, movies, etc.

cen·sure /'sɛnʃə/ *v.* [T] (formal) to officially criticize someone —**censure** *n.* [U]

cen·sus /'sɛnsəs/ *n.* (plural **censuses**) [C] an occasion when a government collects information about the number of people in a country, their ages, jobs, etc.: *When was the first U.S.* ***census taken****?*

cent /sɛnt/ *n.* [C] **1** a unit of money that is worth 1/100 of a dollar. Its sign is ¢. **2 put in/add/say your two cents' worth** (informal) to give your opinion about something, when no one has asked to hear it [ORIGIN: 1300—1400 Old French "hundred," from Latin *centum*]

C

cen·ten·ni·al /sɛn'tɛniəl/ *also* **cen·ten·a·ry** /sɛn'tɛnəri/ *n.* [C] the day or year exactly 100 years after an important event: *This year marked the* ***centennial of*** *the composer's death.*

cen·ter¹ /'sɛntə/ *n.* [C] **1** the middle part or point of something: *We moved the table to* ***the center of*** *the room.* | *an old hotel* ***in the center of*** *town* **2** a building used for a particular purpose: *a shopping center* | *the Kennedy Space Center* **3** a place where there is a lot of a particular type of business or activity: *a major banking center* | *Nashville is the* ***center of*** *the country music industry.* **4 be at the center of sth** to be the main cause of something bad, or have a very important part in it: *The senator* ***is at the center of a controversy*** *over political donations.* **5 be the center of attention** to be the person that everyone is giving attention to **6 the center** a political position which does not support extreme views **7** in basketball, the player who usually plays near the basket **8** in football, the player who starts the ball moving in each PLAY

center² *v.* [T] to move something to a position at the center of something else: *Is this painting centered?*

center on/around sth *phr. v.* if something centers on a particular thing, that is the most important thing in it or what it mainly concerns: *Their whole life centers around their children.* | *The discussion centered on gun control.*

'center field *n.* [singular] the area in baseball in the center of the OUTFIELD —**centerfielder** *n.* [C]

,center of 'gravity *n.* [singular] the point on an object at which it can balance

cen·ter·piece /'sɛntə,pis/ *n.* **1** [singular] the most important, attractive, or noticeable part of something: *the* ***centerpiece of*** *Canada's foreign policy* **2** [C] a decoration in the middle of a table, usually made of flowers

Cen·ti·grade /'sɛntə,greɪd/ *n.* [U] PHYSICS CELSIUS

cen·ti·me·ter /'sɛntə,mitə/ *n.* [C] (*written abbreviation* **cm**) a unit for measuring length, equal to 1/100 of a meter, or 0.39 inches

cen·ti·pede /'sɛntə,pid/ *n.* [C] a very small

creature with a long thin body and many legs [ORIGIN: 1600—1700 Latin *centipeda*, from *centi-* "hundred" + *pes* "foot"]

cen·tral /'sɛntrəl/ *adj.* **1** [only before noun] in the middle of an object or area: *Central Asia | the central part of the island* **2** [only before noun] having control over the rest of a system, organization, etc.: *The computers are linked to a central database.* **3** more important than anything else: *Owen **played a central role in** the negotiations. | The environment was **central to** his election campaign.*

THESAURUS basic, fundamental, essential, elementary, underlying → BASIC

4 a place that is central is near the center of a town: *I want a hotel that's central.* —**centrally** *adv.*

ˌcentral 'air conˌditioning *n.* [U] a system for making the air in a building cooler, in which cool air produced in one place is taken to the rest of the building by pipes

ˌcentral 'bank *n.* [C] ECONOMICS the official bank of a country, which is responsible for controlling the country's MONEY SUPPLY and controlling the country's banking system. A central bank can also lend money to the country's other banks.

ˌcentral 'heating *n.* [U] a system of heating buildings, in which heat is produced in one place and taken to the rest of the building by pipes

ˌCentral In'telligence ˌAgency *n.* the CIA

cen·tral·ize /'sɛntrəˌlaɪz/ *v.* [T] POLITICS to control a country, organization, or system from one place

ˌcentral 'nervous ˌsystem *n.* [C] BIOLOGY the main part of the NERVOUS SYSTEM, consisting of your brain and your SPINAL CORD

ˌcentral 'processing ˌunit *n.* [C] IT a CPU

cen·tri·fu·gal /sɛn'trɪfyəgəl, -'trɪfə-/ *adj.* PHYSICS moving away from the center (ANT) **centripetal**: *centrifugal movement*

cenˌtrifugal 'force *n* [C,U] PHYSICS a force that makes things move away from the center of something when they are moving or turning quickly around it [ORIGIN: 1700—1800 Modern Latin *centrifugus*, from *centr-* "center" + Latin *fugere* "to run away"]

cen·trip·e·tal /sɛn'trɪpət̬l/ *adj.* PHYSICS moving toward the center (ANT) **centrifugal**: *centripetal acceleration*

cenˌtripetal 'force *n.* [C,U] PHYSICS a force that makes things move toward the center of something when they are moving or turning quickly around it [ORIGIN: 1700—1800 Modern Latin *centripetus*, from *centr-* "center" + Latin *petere* "to go to, try to find"]

cen·tu·ry /'sɛntʃəri/ *n.* (plural **centuries**) [C] **1** one of the 100-year periods measured from before or after the year of Christ's birth: ***the 6th/11th/21st etc. century** | My grandparents moved west **at the turn of the century*** (=at the beginning of the century). **2** a period of 100 years

CEO *n.* [C] **Chief Executive Officer** the person with the most authority in a large company

ce·ram·ics /sə'ræmɪks/ *n.* [plural, U] ENG. LANG. ARTS pots, plates, etc. made from clay, or the art of making them —**ceramic** *adj.*

THESAURUS art, painting, drawing, photography, sculpture, pottery → ART

ce·re·al /'sɪriəl/ *n.* **1** [C,U] breakfast food made from grain and usually eaten with milk: *a **bowl of cereal*** **2** [C] a plant grown to produce grain for foods, such as wheat, rice, etc. [ORIGIN: 1800—1900 French *céréale*, from Latin *cerealis* "of Ceres," from *Ceres* ancient Roman goddess of grain and farming]

cer·e·bel·lum /ˌsɛrə'bɛləm/ *n.* (plural **cerebellums** *or* **cerebella** /-lə/) [C] BIOLOGY the bottom part of your brain that controls your muscles → *see picture at* BRAIN[1]

cerebra /sə'ribrə/ *n.* a plural form of CEREBRUM

ce·re·bral /sə'ribrəl, 'sɛrə-/ *adj.* BIOLOGY relating to the brain [ORIGIN: 1800—1900 French *cérébral*, from Latin *cerebrum* "brain"]

ceˌrebral 'cortex *n.* [C] BIOLOGY the outer layer of the front part of your brain, where you think and receive information from your eyes, ears, etc.

ceˌrebral 'palsy *n.* [U] BIOLOGY a medical condition that affects someone's ability to move or speak, caused by damage to the brain at birth

cer·e·brum /sə'ribrəm/ *n.* (plural **cerebra** /-brə/ *or* **cerebrums**) [C] BIOLOGY the front, larger part of the brain, where thoughts and decisions happen, and that also controls movements of the body → *see picture at* BRAIN[1]

cer·e·mo·ni·al /ˌsɛrə'mouniəl/ *adj.* used in a ceremony, or done as part of a ceremony: *Native American ceremonial pipes*

cer·e·mo·ny /'sɛrəˌmouni/ *n.* (plural **ceremonies**) **1** [C] a formal event that happens in public on special occasions: *a wedding ceremony | a graduation ceremony | The treaty was signed during a ceremony at the White House.* **2** [U] the formal actions and words always used on particular occasions: ***With great ceremony**, the Mayor opened the new concert hall.* [ORIGIN: 1300—1400 Old French *cerymonie*, from Latin *caerimonia*]

cer·tain /'sɚt˺n/ *adj.* **1** completely sure: *I'm not **certain (that)** he's telling me the truth. | She was **absolutely certain** he was the killer. | No one was **certain what** to expect. | Are you **certain about** that?*

THESAURUS sure, convinced, confident, satisfied, positive → SURE[1]

2 sure to happen or be true: ***It's** almost **certain that** the enemy will attack from the north. | **It seems certain** that the case will not end for months. | He's*

certain to** be offered the job.* | *The poison causes **certain death**.* **3** [only before noun] a certain thing, person, idea, etc. is a particular thing, person, etc. that you are not naming or describing exactly: *The plant grows in certain conditions.* | *There are certain things I just can't talk about with her.* **4 make certain (that) a)** to check that something is correct or true: *We need to make certain that it's going to fit first.* **b)** to do something in order to be sure something will happen: *Employers are required to make certain that all employees are treated fairly.* **5 a certain a)** some, but not a lot: *I had to spend **a certain amount of** time practicing, but it wasn't hard.* | *I agree with you **to a certain extent (=partly, but not completely). **b)** difficult to describe exactly: *The restaurant has a certain charm.* **6 for certain** without any doubt: *I can't **say for certain** when her plane will arrive.* [ORIGIN: 1200—1300 Old French, Vulgar Latin *certanus*, from Latin *certus* "decided, certain"]

cer·tain·ly /ˈsɚtˀnli/ *adv* without any doubt (SYN) **definitely**: *Diana certainly spends a lot of money on clothes.* | *His lawyers will **almost certainly** appeal.* | *"Can I borrow your notes?" "Certainly* (=yes, of course)."

cer·tain·ty /ˈsɚtˀnti/ *n.* (plural **certainties**) **1** [U] the state of being completely sure about something: *We cannot say **with** complete **certainty** whether your father will be all right.* **2** [C] something that is definitely true or will definitely happen: *Winning the championship is almost a certainty.*

cer·ti·fi·a·ble /ˌsɚţəˈfaɪəbəl/ *adj.* (informal) crazy

cer·tif·i·cate /sɚˈtɪfəkɪt/ *n.* [C] an official document that states the facts about something or someone: *a **birth/marriage/death certificate*** (=giving details of someone's birth, etc.) [ORIGIN: 1400—1500 French *certificat*, from Late Latin, past participle of *certificare*, from Latin *certus* "decided, certain"] → GIFT CERTIFICATE

cerˌtificate of deˈposit *n.* [C] ECONOMICS a bank account that you must leave a particular amount of money in for a particular amount of time in order to get INTEREST

cer·ti·fi·ca·tion /ˌsɚţəfəˈkeɪʃən/ *n.* [C,U] an official document that says that someone is allowed to do a certain job, that something is of good quality, etc., or the process of doing this

ˌcertified ˈcheck *n.* [C] ECONOMICS a check that you get from a bank for a particular amount of money that the bank promises to pay

ˌcertified ˈmail *n.* [U] a method of sending mail, in which a written record is kept of when it is sent and when it is received

ˌcertified ˌpublic acˈcountant *n.* [C] a CPA

cer·ti·fy /ˈsɚţəˌfaɪ/ *v.* (**certified**, **certifies**) [T] **1** to officially state that something is correct or true: *Two doctors **certified that** the patient was dead.* **2** to give someone an official document that states that s/he has completed a course of training: *He has been certified as a mechanic.* | *a certified nurse*

cer·vix /ˈsɚvɪks/ *n.* [C] BIOLOGY the narrow opening into a woman's UTERUS [ORIGIN: 1400—1500 Latin "neck"] —**cervical** /ˈsɚvɪkəl/ *adj.*

ce·sar·e·an /sɪˈzɛriən/ *also* **ceˌsarean ˈsection** *n.* [C] an operation in which a woman's body is cut open to take a baby out [ORIGIN: 1600—1700 Julius *Caesar* (100-44 B.C.), Roman soldier and political leader, who is said to have been born in this way]

ce·si·um /ˈsiziəm/ *n.* [U] CHEMISTRY (*symbol* **Cs**) a very soft silver-gold metal that is an ELEMENT

ces·sa·tion /sɛˈseɪʃən/ *n.* [C] (formal) a pause or stop: *the **cessation of** nuclear tests*

cess·pool /ˈsɛspul/ *n.* [C] a large hole or container under the ground for collecting waste water from a building

CFC *n.* [C] SCIENCE **chlorofluorocarbon** a gas used in AEROSOLS and REFRIGERATORS which causes damage to the OZONE LAYER

CGI *n.* [U] IT **computer-generated imagery** the use of computers to produce artificial images and sounds in movies and television programs → SPECIAL EFFECTS

chafe /tʃeɪf/ *v.* [I,T] if a part of your body chafes, or if something chafes it, your skin becomes sore because something is rubbing against it

cha·grin /ʃəˈgrɪn/ *n.* [U] (formal) a feeling of being disappointed and annoyed: ***To the surfers' chagrin**, the beach was closed.*

chain¹ /tʃeɪn/ *n.* **1** [C,U] a series of metal rings connected together: *a delicate gold chain* | *a **bicycle chain*** (=that makes the wheels turn) → *see picture at* BICYCLE¹ **2** [C] a group of stores, hotels, etc. that is owned by the same person or company: *a **chain of** restaurants* | *a hotel chain* **3 chain of events** a series of related events or actions: *the chain of events that caused World War I* **4** [C] a series of similar things in a line: *a mountain chain* | *a **chain of** islands* **5 in chains** prisoners in chains have heavy chains fastened around their legs or arms, to prevent them from escaping [ORIGIN: 1200—1300 Old French *chaeine*, from Latin *catena*]

chain² *v.* [T] to use a chain to fasten one thing or person to another: *a bicycle **chained to** a fence*

ˈchain ˌletter *n.* [C] a letter that is sent to several people, who send copies to more people

ˌchain of comˈmand *n.* [C] a system in an organization by which decisions are made and passed from people at the top of the organization to people lower down

ˌchain reˈaction *n.* [C] a series of related events or chemical changes that happen quickly, with each one causing the next

chain·saw /ˈtʃeɪnsɔ/ *n.* [C] a tool used for cutting wood, consisting of a circular chain with sharp edges, that is moved by a motor

'chain-smoke *v.* [I,T] to smoke cigarettes one after the other —**chain-smoker** *n.* [C]

'chain store *n.* [C] one of a group of stores owned by the same company

chair¹ /tʃɛr/ *n.* **1** [C] a piece of furniture for one person to sit on: *He sat in a chair next to the fireplace.* ➔ *see picture at* SEAT¹ **2** [C] someone who is in charge of a meeting, a committee, or a university department: *She was named* ***chair of*** *the Public Safety Committee.* **3 the chair** the position of being in charge of a meeting or committee [ORIGIN: 1200—1300 Old French *chaiere*, from Latin *cathedra*, from Greek, from *kata-* + *hedra* "seat"]

chair² *v.* [T] to be the person in charge of a meeting or committee

chair·man /'tʃɛrmən/ *n.* (plural **chairmen** /-mən/) [C] **1** someone, especially a man, who is in charge of a meeting or committee **2** someone, especially a man, who is in charge of a large company or organization

USAGE

Chairman can be used for both men and women, though some women prefer to be called a **chairwoman**. Many people prefer to use **chairperson**, especially if the sex of the person is not known.

—**chairmanship** *n.* [U]

chair·per·son /'tʃɛr,pɚsən/ *n.* (plural **chairpersons**) [C] someone who is in charge of a meeting or directs the work of a committee or organization

chair·wom·an /'tʃɛr,wʊmən/ *n.* (plural **chairwomen** /-,wɪmɪn/) [C] a woman who is a chairperson

chalet

cha·let /ʃæ'leɪ, 'ʃæleɪ/ *n.* [C] a wooden house, especially one in a mountain area

chalk¹ /tʃɔk/ *n.* **1** [U] EARTH SCIENCES soft white rock **2** [C,U] small sticks of this substance, used for writing or drawing: *a* ***piece of chalk*** [ORIGIN: Old English *cealc*, from Latin *calx*, from Greek *chalix* "small stone"]

chalk² *v.*

chalk sth ↔ **up** *phr. v.* (informal) to succeed in winning or getting something: *Boston chalked up another win over Detroit last night.*

chalk·board /'tʃɔkbɔrd/ *n.* [C] a BLACKBOARD

chalk·y /'tʃɔki/ *adj.* similar to chalk or containing chalk

chal·lenge¹ /'tʃæləndʒ/ (Ac) *n.* **1** [C,U] something that tests your skill or ability, especially in a way that is interesting: *the* ***challenge of*** *a new job* | *Together we can* ***meet*** (=deal with) *this* ***challenge.*** | *The firm* ***faces*** *several* ***challenges*** *if it is to improve sales.* | *The trial will* ***pose a*** (=be a) *difficult* ***challenge*** *for the defense.* | *Hopefully, the students are looking forward to the* ***intellectual challenge.*** **2** [C] the act of questioning whether something is right, fair, or legal: *If I make any decisions myself, my boss thinks it's a direct* ***challenge to*** *her authority.* **3** [C] an invitation from someone to try to beat him/her in a fight, game, argument, etc.: *The mayor has* ***accepted the challenge*** *for a debate.*

challenge² (Ac) *v.* [T] **1** to question whether something is right, fair, or legal: *They plan to* ***challenge the*** *court's* ***decision.*** **2** to invite someone to compete or fight against you: *They* ***challenged us to a game*** *of tennis.* **3** to test the skills or abilities of someone or something: *A good teacher challenges his or her students, often so that they achieve more than they think they can.* —**challenger** *n.* [C]

chal·lenged /'tʃæləndʒd/ (Ac) *adj.* **visually/mentally/physically challenged** an expression for describing someone who has difficulty doing things because s/he is blind, etc., used in order to be polite

chal·leng·ing /'tʃæləndʒɪŋ/ (Ac) *adj.* difficult in an interesting way: *a challenging new job*

THESAURUS **difficult, hard, tough, awkward, demanding, arduous, complicated, complex** ➔ DIFFICULT

cham·ber /'tʃeɪmbɚ/ *n.* **1** [C] a room used for a special purpose: *a gas/torture chamber* (=used for killing people by gas or for hurting them) | *the council chamber in the Town Hall* **2** [C] an enclosed space inside something, such as your body or a machine: *a gun with six chambers* | *the four chambers of the heart* **3** [C] POLITICS one of the two parts of a PARLIAMENT or LEGISLATURE (=institutions that have the power to make or change laws): *the* ***upper/lower*** *chamber of parliament* **4 chambers** [plural] the offices used by judges [ORIGIN: 1100—1200 Old French *chambre*, from Late Latin *camera*, from Latin, "curved roof," from Greek *kamara*]

cham·ber·maid /'tʃeɪmbɚ,meɪd/ *n.* [C] a woman whose job is to clean hotel BEDROOMS

'chamber ,music *n.* [U] CLASSICAL MUSIC performed by a small group of musicians

,Chamber of 'Commerce *n.* an organization of business people in a town or city, whose aim is to encourage business

cha·me·leon /kə'milyən, -liən/ *n.* [C] a small

LIZARD (=type of animal) that can make its skin the color of the things around it

cham·o·mile, **camomile** /ˈkæməˌmil, -ˌmaɪl/ *n.* [C,U] a plant with small white and yellow flowers, often used for making tea

champ /tʃæmp/ *n.* [C] (informal) a CHAMPION

cham·pagne /ʃæmˈpeɪn/ *n.* [U] a French white wine with a lot of BUBBLES, often drunk on special occasions [ORIGIN: 1600—1700 French *Champagne* area of northeastern France]

cham·pi·on¹ /ˈtʃæmpiən/ *n.* [C] **1** a person, team, etc. that has won a competition, especially in sports: *the* ***world*** *heavyweight boxing* ***champion*** | *the* ***defending/reigning*** *national soccer* ***champions*** (=the champions right now) **2 champion of sb/sth** someone who fights for and defends an aim or idea: *a champion of civil rights*

champion² *v.* [T] to publicly fight for and defend an aim or idea: *She consistently* ***championed the cause of*** *working mothers.*

cham·pi·on·ship /ˈtʃæmpiənˌʃɪp/ *n.* **1** [C] *also* **championships** [plural] a competition to find the best player or team in a particular sport: *the women's figure skating championships*

THESAURUS **competition, tournament, contest, playoff** → COMPETITION

2 [singular] the position or period of being a champion: *Can she win the championship again?*

chance¹ /tʃæns/ *n.* **1** [C] an opportunity to do something that you want to do: *Now I'll* ***have/get a chance to*** *find out what her boyfriend looks like.* | *If you'll just* ***give me a chance****, I'll tell you what happened.* | *You should* ***take the chance*** (=use the opportunity) *to travel while you're young.* | *He deserves a* ***second chance*** (=another chance). | *Friday is our* ***last chance*** *to see the show.* **2** [C,U] a possibility that something will happen: *What are Deirdre's* ***chances of*** *getting the job?* | *Davis* ***has no chance*** *of playing on Sunday.* | ***There's a chance (that)*** *she left her keys in the office.* | ***Chances are*** (=it is likely) *they're stuck in traffic.* **3 by any chance** (spoken) used in order to ask politely whether something is true or possible: *Are you Ms. Murphy's daughter, by any chance?* **4 fat chance/not a chance/no chance** (spoken) used in order to emphasize that you do not think something will happen: *"Do you think Mark would let me borrow his car?" "Not a chance!"* **5 take a chance** to do something that involves risk: *The team* ***took a chance on*** *a young coach with no experience.* | *I'm* ***not taking any chances****.* **6** [U] the way things happen without being planned or caused: *We met* ***by chance*** *at a friend's party.* | *He supervises every detail of the business and* ***leaves nothing to chance****.* → **stand a chance (of doing sth)** *at* STAND¹

chance² *v.* [T] (informal) to do something that involves a risk: *The bus might get me there on time, but I don't want to* ***chance it****.*

chance³ *adj.* not planned or expected: *a* ***chance encounter/meeting***

chan·cel·lor /ˈtʃænsələ/ *n.* [C] **1** the person in charge of some universities **2** POLITICS the leader of the government in some countries [ORIGIN: 1000—1100 Old French *chancelier*, from Late Latin *cancellarius* "doorkeeper, secretary"]

chanc·y /ˈtʃænsi/ *adj.* (informal) uncertain or involving risks: *The weather there can be chancy in the spring.*

C

chan·de·lier /ˌʃændəˈlɪr/ *n.* [C] a frame that holds lights or CANDLES, hangs from the ceiling, and is decorated with small pieces of glass

change¹ /tʃeɪndʒ/ *v.* **1** [I,T] to become different, or to make someone or something become different: *Ed changed after Ricky died.* | *There are plans to change the voting system.* | *In the fall, its leaves* ***change from*** *green* ***to*** *gold.* | *The rain on the roads had* ***changed to*** *ice during the night.*

THESAURUS

alter – to change something, or to make something change: *Can we alter the date of the meeting?*
adapt/adjust/modify – to change something slightly: *The group is pressuring Congress to modify the plan.* | *His doctor has adjusted the dosage of his medication.*
revise/amend – to change something because of new information or ideas: *The rules of volleyball were revised to give the game a faster pace.* | *The act was amended to protect wildlife.*
reform/reorganize/restructure – to change a system or organization: *plans to reform the welfare system* | *The company has been restructured from top to bottom.*
transform/revolutionize – to change something completely: *They've completely transformed the downtown area.* | *The discovery of penicillin revolutionized medicine.*
twist/distort/misrepresent – to deliberately change facts, information, someone's words, etc. in a way that is not completely true or correct: *He accused reporters of twisting his words.*

2 [I,T] to stop doing or using one thing, and start doing or using something else: *I'm thinking about changing jobs.* | *The company has* ***changed*** *its name* ***to*** *Cortlandt Capital.* | *I think we'd better* ***change the subject*** (=talk about something else). **3 change your mind** to change your decision or opinion about something: *I've* ***changed my mind about*** *selling the house.* **4** [I,T] to take off your clothes and put on different ones: *I went upstairs to change my shirt.* | *Go upstairs and* ***change into*** *your play clothes.* | *Eric went to* ***get changed****.* **5** [T] to put something new or different in place of something else: *We had to get out and change the tire.* | *She cleaned the room and* ***changed the sheets*** (=put clean sheets on the bed). | *Do you mind* ***changing the baby*** (=putting a clean DIAPER on the baby)? **6** [T] if you change money, you give it to someone and s/he gives it back to you in smaller amounts, or in money from a different country: ***Can you change a $10 bill?*** | *I want to* ***change*** *my dollars* ***into*** *pesos.* **7** [I,T] to get out of one train, bus, or aircraft and into another in order to continue your trip: *We had to change planes in Chicago.* **8 change hands** to become someone else's property: *The house has changed hands twice in the last ten years.* [ORIGIN: 1100—1200 Old French *changier*, from Latin *cambiare* "to exchange"]

C

change sth ↔ **around** *phr. v.* to move things into different positions: *The room looks bigger since we changed the furniture around.*

change over *phr. v.* to stop doing or using one thing and start doing or using something different: *We're* ***changing over to*** *the new software next month.*

change² *n.* **1** [C,U] the process or result of something or someone becoming different: *Many people find it hard to accept change.* | *a* ***change in*** *diet* | *a* ***change of*** *temperature* | *Grandpa's health has* ***taken a change for the worse*** (=become worse). **2** [C] an action or event that involves replacing one thing with another: *The car needs an oil change.* | *a* ***change of*** *leadership* | *the* ***change from*** *communism* ***to*** *democracy* **3** [singular] something that is interesting or enjoyable because it is different from what is usual: *Why don't we go out* ***for a change?*** | *I* ***need a change.*** **4** [U] **a)** the money you get back when you pay more money than something costs: *Here's your change, ma'am.* **b)** money in the form of coins: *I have about a dollar* ***in change.*** **c)** coins or paper money that add up to the same value as a larger unit of money: *Do you have* ***change for*** *a dollar?*

THESAURUS money, bill, coin, penny, nickel, dime, quarter, cash, currency → MONEY

5 change of clothes/underwear etc. another set of clothes that you can use if necessary: *Bring a change of clothes just in case.*

change·a·ble /ˈtʃeɪndʒəbəl/ *adj.* likely to change, or changing often: *Kids' tastes are very changeable.*

change·o·ver /ˈtʃeɪndʒˌoʊvɚ/ *n.* [C] a change from one activity or system to another: *the* ***changeover from*** *military* ***to*** *civilian rule*

chan·nel¹ /ˈtʃænl/ (Ac) *n.* [C] **1** a television station: *What's on channel 2?* | *Do you mind if I* ***change*** *the* ***channel?*** **2** [usually plural] a way of sending or obtaining information, ideas, etc.: *You'll have to* ***go through*** *official* ***channels*** *for help.* | *It is important that the U.S. opens* ***channels of communication*** *with the North Korean government.* **3** a long passage dug into the earth that water or other liquids flow along: *Farmers dug a series of channels to allow water from the river to flow across the land.* **4 a)** EARTH SCIENCES water that connects two larger areas of water: *the English Channel* **b)** EARTH SCIENCES the deepest part of a river, ocean, etc. that ships can sail through **5 channel surf** (informal) to change quickly from one television channel to another many times [ORIGIN: 1300—1400 Old French *chanel*, from Latin *canalis* "pipe, channel"]

channel² *v.* [T] to direct something toward a particular purpose, place, or situation: *Cody needs to* ***channel*** *his creativity* ***into*** *something useful.* | *Profits are* ***channeled to*** *conservation groups.*

chant¹ /tʃænt/ *v.* [I,T] **1** to repeat a word or phrase many times: *Crowds of protesters chanted "Give peace a chance!"* **2** to sing a religious song or prayer using only one or two notes

chant² *n.* [C] **1** words or phrases that are repeated many times: *The crowd responded with* ***chants of*** *"Resign! Resign!"* **2** a religious song or prayer that is sung using only one or two notes

Cha·nu·kah /ˈhɑnəkə/ *n.* another spelling of HANUKKAH

cha·os /ˈkeɪɑs/ *n.* [U] a situation in which everything is confused and nothing is happening in an organized way: *After the earthquake, the city was* ***in chaos.*** | *There was* ***total chaos*** *on the roads.* [ORIGIN: 1400—1500 Latin, Greek]

cha·ot·ic /keɪˈɑt̬ɪk/ *adj.* confused and without any order: *a chaotic scene at the site of the accident*

chap·ar·ral /ˌʃæpəˈræl/ *n.* [U] EARTH SCIENCES land on which many bushes and small trees, especially OAKs, grow closely together, in areas such as California where there are hot dry summers

chap·el /ˈtʃæpəl/ *n.* [C] a small church or a room where Christians have religious services [ORIGIN: 1100—1200 Old French *chapele*, from Medieval Latin *cappella*, from Late Latin *cappa* "cloak;" because the cloak of St. Martin of Tours was kept in such a building]

chap·e·rone¹ /ˈʃæpəˌroʊn/ *n.* [C] an older person who is responsible for young people on social occasions

chaperone² *v.* [T] to go somewhere with someone as a chaperone

chap·lain /ˈtʃæplɪn/ *n.* [C] a minister who works for the army, a hospital, a university, etc.

chapped /tʃæpt/ *adj.* chapped lips or hands are sore, dry, and cracked

chap·ter /ˈtʃæptɚ/ (Ac) *n.* [C] **1** one of the parts into which a book is divided: *Chapter 6* | *For homework, read the first two chapters of the book.* | *This detailed study contains chapters on each geographic region.* → PART¹ **2** a particular period in someone's life or in history: *a sad* ***chapter in*** *our country's history* | *one of the most shameful* ***chapters of*** *French history* **3** the local members of a large organization or club: *the local chapter of the Sierra Club* [ORIGIN: 1100—1200 Old French *chapitre*, from Late Latin *capitulum*, from Latin *caput* "head"]

char·ac·ter /ˈkærɪktɚ/ *n.* **1** [C,U] the qualities that make a person, place, or thing different from any other: *There's a very serious side to her* *character.* | *All these new buildings have really changed the* ***character of*** *this town.* | *He swore, which was completely* ***out of character*** (=not typical of the way he usually behaves). **2** [C] ENG. LANG. ARTS a person in a book, play, movie, etc.: *I don't like the* ***main character*** *in the book.* **3** [U] qualities that make someone or something special or interesting: *an old house with a lot of character* **4** [U] good qualities such as courage, loyalty, and honesty that people admire: *a woman of great moral character* **5** [C] a particular kind of person: *Dan's a strange character.* **6** [C] an unusual and humorous person: *Charlie's such a character!* **7** [C] a letter, mark, or sign used in writing, printing, or on a computer: *Chinese characters* [ORIGIN: 1300—1400 Old French *caractere*, from Latin *character* "mark, particular quality"]

char·ac·ter·is·tic[1] /ˌkærɪktəˈrɪstɪk/ *n.* [C] a special quality or feature that someone or something has, and that makes that person or thing different from others: *Each wine has particular characteristics.* | *the* ***characteristics of*** *a good manager*

THESAURUS

quality – something that someone has as part of his/her character, especially something good: *Tina has a lot of good qualities.*
trait – a particular quality in someone's character: *The personality test reveals traits such as shyness or risk-taking.*
attribute – a good or useful quality: *What attributes should a good manager possess?*
feature – an important, interesting, or typical part of something: *An important feature of Van Gogh's paintings is their bright color.*
property – a natural quality of something: *an herb with healing properties*
aspect – one part of a situation, activity, etc. that has many parts: *She enjoys most aspects of her job.*

characteristic[2] *adj.* typical of a particular thing or person: *The vase is* ***characteristic of*** *16th-century Chinese art.* | *Mark, with characteristic kindness, offered to help.* **—characteristically** *adv.*

char·ac·ter·ize /ˈkærɪktəˌraɪz/ *v.* [T] **1** to be typical of someone or something: *Alzheimer's disease is characterized by memory loss.* **2** to describe the character of someone or something in a particular way: *His book* ***characterizes*** *Eisenhower* ***as*** *a natural leader.*

THESAURUS **call, describe, label, brand, portray** → CALL[1]

—characterization /ˌkærɪktərəˈzeɪʃən/ *n.* [C,U]

cha·rade /ʃəˈreɪd/ *n.* **1** [C] a situation in which people pretend to think, feel, etc. something, although they clearly do not: *Their happy marriage is just a charade.* **2 charades** [U] a game in which one person uses actions and no words to show the meaning of a word or phrase, and other people have to guess what it is

char·coal /ˈtʃɑrkoʊl/ *n.* [U] a black substance made of burned wood, used as FUEL or for drawing

charge[1] /tʃɑrdʒ/ *n.*
1 MONEY [C,U] the amount of money you have to pay for something: *an admission* ***charge of*** *$5* | *There's a $70* ***charge for*** *every extra piece of luggage.* | *We deliver* ***free of charge*** (=at no cost).

THESAURUS **cost, expense, price, fee, fare, rent, rate** → COST[1]

2 CONTROL [U] the position of having control over or responsibility for something or someone: *Who* ***is in charge of*** *the department?* | *Diane* ***took charge of*** *the business when her husband died.*
3 CRIME [C] LAW a statement that says that someone has done something illegal or bad: *He's in court* ***on charges of*** *murder.* | *He denied* ***charges that*** *he used illegal drugs.* | *The* ***charge against*** *her was shoplifting.* | *They decided not to* ***bring/press charges*** (=to officially say that they think someone is guilty of a crime). | *The police agreed to* ***drop the charges*** (=decided to stop making charges) *against him.*

THESAURUS **accusation, allegation, indictment, complaint** → ACCUSATION

4 ELECTRICITY [U] PHYSICS electricity that is put into a piece of electrical equipment such as a BATTERY
5 ATTACK [C] an attack in which people or animals move forward quickly
6 ENERGY [U] PHYSICS the electrical energy contained in all MATTER (=the material that everything in the universe is made of), which exists in a positive and negative form [ORIGIN: 1100—1200 Old French *chargier*, from Late Latin *carricare*, from Latin *carrus*]

charge[2] *v.* **1 a)** [I,T] to ask for a particular amount of money for something you are selling: *How much do you* ***charge for*** *your eggs?* | *They* ***charged*** *me $2* ***for*** *a candy bar.* **b)** [T] to record the cost of something that someone buys or uses, so that s/he can pay for it later: ***Charge*** *the room* ***to*** *my account.* | *"Would you like to pay cash?" "No, I'll* ***charge it*** (=pay with a CREDIT CARD)." **2** [T] to state officially that someone might be guilty of a crime: *Ron's been* ***charged with*** *assault.*

THESAURUS **accuse, allege, indict** → ACCUSE

3 [I,T] if a BATTERY charges, or if you charge it, it takes in and stores electricity **4** [I,T] to move quickly forward, especially in a threatening way: *The bear charged toward her at full speed.*

THESAURUS **rush, race, dash, hurry, speed, hasten** → RUSH[1]

ˈcharge card *n.* [C] a CREDIT CARD that you can use in a particular store

char·i·ot /ˈtʃæriət/ *n.* [C] a vehicle with two wheels pulled by a horse, used in ancient times in battles and races

cha·ris·ma /kəˈrɪzmə/ *n.* [U] the natural ability to attract other people and make them admire you: *He **has** a lot of **charisma**.* [ORIGIN: 1600—1700 Greek "favor, gift," from *charizesthai* "to favor"] —**charismatic** /ˌkærɪzˈmæṭɪk◂ / *adj.*

C

char·i·ta·ble /ˈtʃærəṭəbəl/ *adj.* **1** relating to charities and their work: *The money went to a charitable group.* **2** kind, generous, and sympathetic —**charitably** *adv.*

char·i·ty /ˈtʃærəṭi/ *n.* (plural **charities**) **1** [C] an organization that gives money, goods, or help to people who need it: *Several charities sent aid to the flood victims.* | *a **charity event*** **2** [U] charity organizations in general: *He's donated over $200,000 **to charity**.* | *The auction raised more than $75,000 **for charity**.* **3** [U] money or gifts given to people who need help: *She's too proud to accept charity.* **4** [U] (formal) kindness or sympathy that you show toward other people [ORIGIN: 1100—1200 Old French *charité*, from Late Latin *caritas* "Christian love"]

char·la·tan /ˈʃɑrlətən/ *n.* [C] (disapproving) someone who pretends to have special skills or knowledge

charm¹ /tʃɑrm/ *n.* **1** [C,U] the special quality someone or something has that makes people like him, her, or it: *Lee's boyish charm* | *This town has a charm you couldn't find in a big city.* **2** [C] something you wear, have, etc. because you believe it brings you good luck: *a **lucky charm*** [ORIGIN: 1200—1300 Old French *charme*, from Latin *carmen* "song," from *canere* "to sing"]

charm² *v.* [T] to attract or please someone: *Grant has been charming audiences for years.* —**charmer** *n.* [C]

charmed /tʃɑrmd/ *adj.* **lead/live/have a charmed life** to be lucky all the time, especially by succeeding in avoiding danger, injury, etc.

charm·ing /ˈtʃɑrmɪŋ/ *adj.* very pleasing or attractive: *What a charming house!* —**charmingly** *adv.*

charred /tʃɑrd/ *adj.* something that is charred is so burned that it has become black

chart¹ /tʃɑrt/ (Ac) *n.* [C] **1** a drawing, set of numbers, GRAPH, etc. that shows information: *medical charts* | *The **chart shows** last year's sales.* | *Students should present the results of their experiment in the form of a chart.* **2 the charts** [plural] the official list of the most popular songs and records, produced each week: *Her new album went **to the top of the charts**.* **3** a map, especially of the ocean or stars: *navigation charts* [ORIGIN: 1500—1600 French *charte*, from Latin *charta* "piece of papyrus, document," from Greek *chartes*]

chart² *v.* [T] **1** to record information about something over a period of time: *Scientists have been charting temperature changes in the oceans.* | *a book that charts the history of the city* | *Each case of the disease was **charted on** a graph.* **2** to make a plan of what should be done in order to achieve something: *She needs to **chart a course** for her future.* **3** to make a map of an area: *The survey team began charting the hills and ravines in the area.*

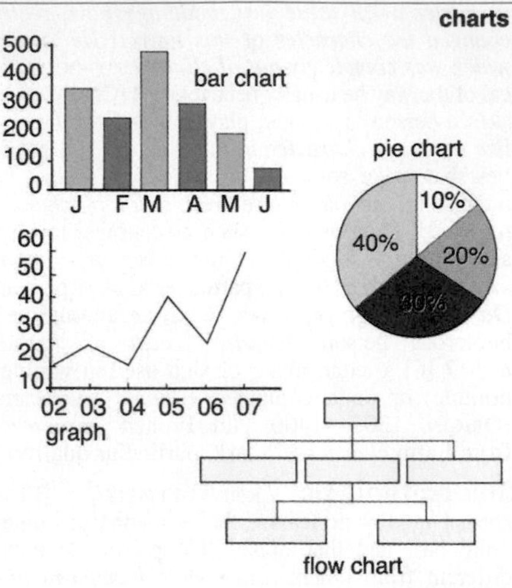

char·ter¹ /ˈtʃɑrṭɚ/ *n.* **1** [C] a written statement of the principles, duties, and purposes of an organization: *the UN charter* **2** [C,U] the practice of renting a boat, aircraft, etc. from a company, usually for a short time, or the boat, etc. that is used in this way: *a charter service* | *fishing boats **for charter***

charter² *v.* [T] to rent a boat, aircraft, etc. from a company: *We'll have to charter a bus.*

ˈcharter flight *n.* [C] an airplane trip that is arranged for a particular group or for a particular purpose

ˌcharter ˈmember *n.* [C] an original member of a club or organization

ˈcharter ˌschool *n.* [C] a school that is run by parents, companies, etc. rather than by the public school system, but which the state government provides money for

chase¹ /tʃeɪs/ *v.* **1** [I,T] to quickly follow someone or something in order to catch him, her, or it: *Cops **chased** the mugger **down** the street.* | *a cat **chasing after** a mouse*

THESAURUS follow, pursue, run after, tail, track, stalk → FOLLOW

2 [T] to make someone or something leave a place by running after them: *There was a raccoon in the yard, but the dog **chased** it **away**.* **3** [I,T] to try very hard to get something: *reporters **chasing after** a story*

chase² *n.* [C] an act of following someone or something quickly to catch him, her, or it: *a **car chase*** | *Police spotted the speeding car and **gave chase*** (=chased it).

chasm /ˈkæzəm/ *n.* **1** [singular] a big difference between ideas or groups of people: *the **chasm between** rich and poor* **2** [C] a very deep space between two areas of rock or ice

chas·sis /ˈtʃæsi, ˈʃæ-/ *n.* (plural **chassis** /-siz/) [C] the frame on which the body, engine, etc. of a vehicle are built

chaste /tʃeɪst/ *adj.* (old-fashioned) not having sex, or not showing sexual feelings

chas·ten /ˈtʃeɪsən/ *v.* [T] (formal) to make someone realize that his/her behavior is wrong

chas·tise /tʃæˈstaɪz, ˈtʃæstaɪz/ *v.* [T] (formal) to criticize or punish someone

chas·ti·ty /ˈtʃæstət̬i/ *n.* [U] the principle or state of not having sex with anyone except your husband or wife

chat¹ /tʃæt/ *v.* (**chatted**, **chatting**) [I] to talk in a friendly and informal way, especially about unimportant things: *We were **chatting about** the weather.*

chat² *n.* [C,U] a friendly informal conversation: *I **had a long chat with** Rick.*

cha·teau /ʃæˈtoʊ/ *n.* (plural **chateaux** /-ˈtoʊz/ *or* **chateaus**) [C] a castle or large country house in France

ˈchat room *n.* [C] a place on the Internet where you can have a conversation with people by writing messages to them and immediately receiving their reply → INTERNET

chat·ter /ˈtʃæt̬ɚ/ *v.* [I] **1** to talk a lot in a quick and friendly way about unimportant things **2** if your teeth chatter, they knock together because you are cold or afraid —**chatter** *n.* [U]

chat·ty /ˈtʃæt̬i/ *adj.* (informal) **1** liking to talk a lot in a friendly way **2** having a friendly informal style: *a chatty letter*

chauf·feur /ˈʃoʊfɚ, ʃoʊˈfɚ/ *n.* [C] someone whose job is to drive a car for someone else [ORIGIN: 1800—1900 French "person attending to the fire of a steam-driven vehicle, driver," from *chauffer* "to heat"] —**chauffeur** *v.* [T]: *I spent all day chauffeuring my kids everywhere.*

chau·vin·ist /ˈʃoʊvənɪst/ *n.* [C] (disapproving) **1** a man who thinks that men are better than women: *He's a **male chauvinist pig**.* **2** someone who believes that his/her country or race is better than any other —**chauvinism** *n.* [U] —**chauvinistic** /ˌʃoʊvəˈnɪstɪk◂/ *adj.*

cheap¹ /tʃip/ *adj.* **1** not expensive, or lower in price than you expected (ANT) **expensive**: *Back then, gas was really cheap.* | *I bought the cheapest computer I could find.* | *Their jeans are **dirt cheap*** (=very low in price)!

THESAURUS

If something is **inexpensive**, it is not expensive and is usually of good quality: *an inexpensive coat*
If something is **reasonable**, it is not too expensive and seems fair: *The restaurant serves good food at reasonable prices.*
If something is a **good/great/excellent deal** or **good/great/excellent value**, it is worth the price you pay for it: *At $3, it's a good deal.* | *The hotel offers great value for your money.*
If you think that something is worth more money than you paid for it, you can say that it is a **bargain**: *You can get some real bargains at the market.* | *bargain prices*
If a price or product is **competitive**, it is slightly cheaper than other similar things, but is still good quality: *goods for your home at competitive prices*
→ EXPENSIVE

2 (disapproving) low in price and quality: *cheap wine* **3** (disapproving) not liking to spend money: *He's so cheap we didn't even go out on my birthday.* **4 cheap shot** an unkind and unfair criticism [ORIGIN: 1500—1600 *good cheap* "at a good price, cheaply," from *cheap* "trade, price" (11—18 centuries), from Old English *ceap*] —**cheaply** *adv.* —**cheapness** *n.* [U]

cheap² *adv.* at a low price: *I was lucky to **get** it so **cheap**.* | *Cars like that **don't come cheap*** (=are expensive).

cheap·en /ˈtʃipən/ *v.* **1** [T] to make someone or something seem to have or deserve to have less respect: *As an actress, I'd be **cheapening myself by** doing TV commercials.* **2** [I,T] to become lower in price or value, or to make something do this: *The dollar's rise in value has cheapened imports.*

cheap·skate /ˈtʃipˌskeɪt/ *n.* [C] (informal, disapproving) someone who does not like spending money

cheat¹ /tʃit/ *v.* **1** [I] to behave in a dishonest way in order to win or get an advantage: *He always **cheats at** cards.* | *She was caught **cheating on** the history **test**.* **2** [T] to trick or deceive someone: *The salesman **cheated** me **out of** $100.* | *The band's 30-minute show left fans **feeling cheated*** (=feeling that they had been treated unfairly). —**cheating** *n.* [U]

cheat on sb *phr. v.* to be unfaithful to your husband, wife, or sexual partner by secretly having sex with someone else: *I think Dan's cheating on Debbie again.*

cheat² *also* **cheat·er** /ˈtʃit̬ɚ/ *n.* [C] someone who cheats

check¹ /tʃɛk/ *v.* **1** [I,T] to look at or test something carefully in order to be sure that it is correct, in good condition, safe, etc.: *"Did Barry lock the back door?" "I don't know — I'll check."* | *I need to check the mailbox; I'm expecting a letter.* | *It's a good idea to **check for** ticks after being out in the woods.* | *Make sure you **double-check*** (=check twice) *the spellings of these names.* **2** [I] to ask someone about something: ***Check with** Dave to see if you can leave early.* | *Can you **check whether** we're still having a meeting?* | *We'd better **check that** he received your message.* **3** [T] to leave your bags, coat, etc. in a special place where they can be kept safe or put on an airplane, bus, etc., or to take someone's bags in order to do this: *Can I check that bag for you, sir?* **4** [T] to suddenly stop yourself

C

from saying or doing something: *I had to check the urge to laugh out loud.* **5** [T] to stop something bad from getting worse: *The treatment checks the spread of the cancer.*

check in *phr. v.* to go to the desk at a hotel, airport, etc. to say that you have arrived: *Please check in at gate number 5.*

check sth ↔ **off** *phr. v.* to put a mark (✔) next to something on a list to show that you have dealt with it: *Check their names off the list as they arrive.*

C

check on sb/sth *phr. v.* to make sure that someone or something is all right or is doing what he, she, or it is supposed to be doing: *I have to go check on the roast.*

check out *phr. v.* **1 a) check** sth ↔ **out** to make sure that something is actually true, correct, or acceptable: *The police* ***checked out*** *his story* ***with*** *the other suspects.* | *"He said I could probably get a scholarship." "You should* ***check it out*** *—that would be great.'* **b)** if something checks out, it is proven to be true, correct, or acceptable: *If your references check out, you can start the job on Monday.* **2 check** sb/sth ↔ **out** (spoken) to look at someone or something because he, she, or it is interesting or attractive: *Hey, check out that car!* **3** to pay the bill and leave a hotel: *You must check out before 12 o'clock.* **4 check** sth ↔ **out** to borrow a book from a library: *You can only check out five books at a time.*

check sth ↔ **over** *phr. v.* **1** to look closely at something to make sure it is correct or acceptable: *Can you check over my paper for spelling mistakes?* **2** to examine someone to make sure s/he is healthy: *The doctor checked her over and couldn't find anything wrong.*

check up on sb/sth *phr. v.* to try to find out if someone is doing what s/he is supposed to be doing: *She was calling every ten minutes to check up on me.*

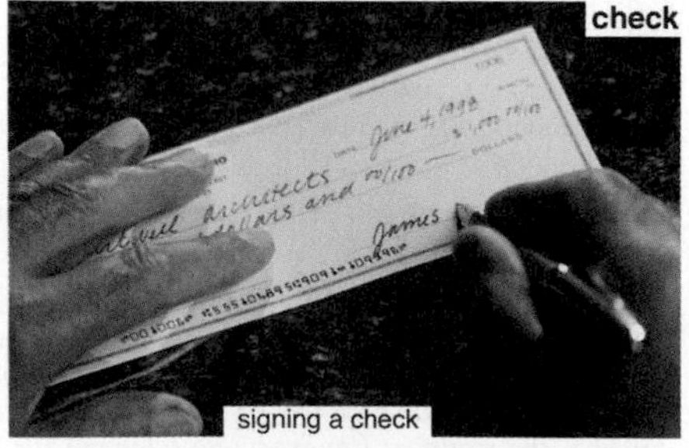
check
signing a check

check² *n.*

1 MONEY [C] one of a set of printed pieces of paper that you can sign and use to pay for things: *a* ***check for*** *$50* | *Can I* ***pay by check****?* | *I* ***wrote*** *her* ***a check*** *for $300.* | *Did you* ***cash the check*** (=get cash in exchange for the check)*?*

2 EXAMINATION [C] a careful look at or test of something, to see if it is safe, correct, in good condition, etc.: *a* ***security check*** | *The building inspector must first do a* ***safety check****.* | *I want a* ***check on*** *the quality of all goods leaving the factory.* | *I want you to* ***do/run a check on*** (=find out information about) *this blood sample.*

3 CONTROL [C usually singular] something that controls something else and stops it from increasing: *The policy should act as a* ***check on*** *inflation.* | *We've* ***kept/held*** *the disease* ***in check*** (=kept it under control) *for over a year now.*

4 BILL [C] a list you are given in a restaurant showing what you have eaten and how much you must pay: *Can I have the check, please?*

COLLOCATIONS

If you have eaten in a restaurant and are ready to pay, you **ask for the check**.
If someone who eats with other people pays for the whole meal, they **pick up the check**.
If people share the cost of the meal between them, they **split the check**. ➔ RESTAURANT

THESAURUS **bill, invoice, tab** ➔ BILL¹

5 MARK [C] a mark (✔) that you put next to an answer to show that it is correct, or next to something on a list to show that you have dealt with it

6 SQUARES [C] a pattern of squares on something: *a tablecloth with red and white checks*

7 checks and balances a system of rules in government that keeps any one person or group from having too much power or control

check·book /ˈtʃɛkbʊk/ *n.* [C] a book of checks

checked /tʃɛkt/ *adj.* having a regular pattern of different colored squares: *a checked skirt*

check·ered /ˈtʃɛkɚd/ *adj.* **1** marked with squares of two different colors: *a checkered flag* **2 checkered past/history etc.** periods of failure as well as success in someone's or something's past: *a cop with a checkered past*

check·ers /ˈtʃɛkɚz/ *n.* [U] a game for two players, using 12 flat round pieces each and a special board with 64 squares

ˈcheck-in *n.* **1** [U] the process of reporting your arrival at a hotel, airport, hospital, etc.: *Passengers should arrive early for check-in.* **2** [singular] a place where you report your arrival at an airport, hotel, etc.: *Be at the check-in counter at least two hours before your flight.* ➔ **check in** *at* CHECK¹

ˈchecking acˌcount *n.* [C] a bank account that you can take money out of at any time

THESAURUS **account, savings account, joint account, online account** ➔ ACCOUNT¹

check·list /ˈtʃɛkˌlɪst/ *n.* [C] a list of things you have to do for a particular job or activity

check·mate /ˈtʃɛkmeɪt/ *n.* [U] the position in a game of CHESS when the KING cannot escape and the game has ended

check·out coun·ter /ˈtʃɛk-aʊt ˌkaʊntɚ/ *also* **checkout** *n.* [C] the place in a SUPERMARKET where you pay for things

check·point /ˈtʃɛkpɔɪnt/ *n.* [C] a place, especially at a border between countries, where an official person stops people and vehicles to examine them

check·up, check-up /ˈtʃɛk-ʌp/ *n.* [C] an occasion when a doctor or DENTIST examines you to see if you are healthy: *Dentists recommend regular check-ups.*

ched·dar /ˈtʃɛdɚ/ *n.* [U] a firm smooth yellow or orange cheese

cheek /tʃik/ *n.* [C] the soft round part of your face below each of your eyes: *He kissed her lightly on the cheek.* ➔ *see picture on page A16* [ORIGIN: Old English *ceace*] ➔ *see picture on page A16*

cheek·bone /ˈtʃikboun/ *n.* [C] the bone just below your eye: *She had* ***high cheekbones*** *and green eyes.* ➔ *see picture on page A16*

cheep /tʃip/ *v.* [I] if a young bird cheeps, it makes a weak high noise —**cheep** *n* [C]

cheer[1] /tʃɪr/ *v.* [I,T] to shout approval, encouragement, etc.: *The audience cheered as the band began to play.*

THESAURUS **shout, call (out), scream, shriek, yell, cry out, raise your voice, bellow, holler** ➔ SHOUT[1]

cheer sb **on** *phr. v.* to encourage someone by cheering for him/her: *Hansen's family was there cheering him on.*

cheer up *phr v* **1 cheer** sb ↔ **up** to make someone feel happier: *I tried to cheer her up by taking her out to dinner.* **2** to become happier: *Cheer up, Connie!*

cheer[2] *n.* [C] a shout of approval and happiness: *The team was greeted with applause and cheers.*

cheer·ful /ˈtʃɪrfəl/ *adj.* **1** happy, or behaving in a way that shows you are happy: *a cheerful and easygoing guy* | *a* ***cheerful voice/smile*** **2** bright, pleasant, and making you feel happy: *a cheerful kitchen* —**cheerfully** *adv.* —**cheerfulness** *n.* [U]

cheer·lead·er /ˈtʃɪrˌlidɚ/ *n.* [C] a member of a team of young women who encourage a crowd to cheer at sports events

cheer·y /ˈtʃɪri/ *adj.* happy, or making you feel happy: *Sullivan was in a cheery mood.*

cheese /tʃiz/ *n.* [C,U] a solid food made from milk, that is usually white or yellow: *a* ***grilled cheese sandwich*** | *a* ***piece/slice/wedge of cheese*** | *I'd like a bagel with* ***cream cheese***. [ORIGIN: Old English *cese*]

cheese·burg·er /ˈtʃizˌbɚgɚ/ *n.* [C] a HAMBURGER cooked with a piece of cheese on top of the meat

cheese·cake /ˈtʃizkeɪk/ *n.* [C,U] a sweet cake made with soft white cheese

cheese·cloth /ˈtʃizklɔθ/ *n.* [U] a type of very thin cotton cloth, used especially for wrapping food

chees·y /ˈtʃizi/ *adj.* (informal) not sincere or of good quality: *a really cheesy movie* | *a cheesy grin*

chee·tah /ˈtʃiṭə/ *n.* [C] an African wild cat that has black spots and is able to run very fast

chef /ʃɛf/ *n.* [C] a skilled cook, especially the main cook in a restaurant [ORIGIN: 1800—1900 French *chef de cuisine* "head of the kitchen"]

chem·i·cal[1] /ˈkɛmɪkəl/ (Ac) *adj.* CHEMISTRY relating to substances used in chemistry, or involving the changes that happen when two substances combine: *Mixing the two substances causes a chemical reaction.* | *The minerals are grouped together by chemical composition.* | *chemical compounds* [ORIGIN: 1500—1600 Modern Latin *chimicus* "alchemist," from Medieval Latin *alchimicus*] —**chemically** *adv.*: *The Earth's crust is chemically distinct from the mantle.* | *The acid reacts chemically with oxygen.*

chemical[2] *n.* [C] CHEMISTRY a substance used in chemistry or produced by a chemical process: ***Toxic*** (=poisonous) ***chemicals*** *from the factory created some serious health problems.* | *Everything is grown organically without the use of chemicals.*

ˌchemical ˈbond *n.* [C] CHEMISTRY a force holding together the atoms in a chemical compound

ˌchemical ˈchange *n.* [C] CHEMISTRY a process by which the chemical structure of something changes, and the chemical parts combine with other chemicals or break apart into separate chemicals

ˌchemical eˈquation *n.* [C] CHEMISTRY a written record of what happens when two or more chemicals are mixed together, with letters and numbers representing chemical substances

ˌchemical equiˈlibrium *n.* [singular,U] CHEMISTRY a situation in which a chemical reaction and its opposite reaction are balanced or happen at the same rate and there is no change

ˌchemical ˈformula *n.* [C] CHEMISTRY a series of numbers and letters that represents the number and types of atoms in a chemical compound or chemical reaction

ˌchemical ˈproperty *n.* [C] CHEMISTRY the features or qualities of a substance that have an effect on the ways in which the chemical structure changes

ˌchemical reˈaction *n.* [C,U] CHEMISTRY a chemical change that happens when two or more substances are mixed together, or the process in which this happens

ˌchemical ˈsymbol *n.* [C] CHEMISTRY the letter or letters and numbers that represent the chemicals in a substance

chem·ist /ˈkɛmɪst/ *n.* [C] a scientist who does work related to chemistry

chem·is·try /ˈkɛməstri/ *n.* [U] **1** the science of studying substances and the way that they change or combine with each other **2** the way substances combine in a process, thing, person, etc.: *This drug causes changes to the body's chemistry.* **3** if there is chemistry between two people, they like each other or work well together

che·mo·ther·a·py /ˌkimoʊˈθɛrəpi/ *n.* [U] BIOLOGY the treatment of CANCER using special drugs

cher·ish /ˈtʃɛrɪʃ/ *v.* [T] **1** if you cherish something, it is very important to you: *He cherishes his privacy.* **2** to take care of someone or something you love very much

C

cher·ry /ˈtʃɛri/ *n.* (plural **cherries**) **1** [C] a small round soft red fruit with a large seed: *a bowl of cherries | cherry pie* → *see picture on page 414* **2** [C,U] a tree that produces cherries, or the wood of this tree [ORIGIN: 1300—1400 Old North French *cherise* (taken as plural), from Latin *cerasus* "cherry tree," from Greek *kerasos*]

cher·ub /ˈtʃɛrəb/ *n.* [C] an ANGEL shown in paintings as a small child with wings

chess /tʃɛs/ *n.* [U] a game for two players in which you must trap your opponent's KING in order to win: *Do you know how to* ***play chess****?* [ORIGIN: 1100—1200 Old French *esches*, plural of *escec*] → *see picture at* BOARD[1]

chest /tʃɛst/ *n.* [C] **1** the front part of your body between your neck and stomach: *a man with a hairy chest | chest pains* → *see picture on page A16* **2** a large strong box with a lid, that you use to keep things in: *a large wooden chest* **3 get sth off your chest** (informal) to tell someone about something that has worried or annoyed you for a long time [ORIGIN: Old English *cest*, from Latin *cista* "box, basket"]

chest·nut /ˈtʃɛsnʌt/ *n.* **1** [C] a smooth red-brown nut you can eat **2** [C,U] the tree on which these nuts grow, or the wood of this tree **3** [U] a dark red-brown color —**chestnut** *adj.*

ˌchest of ˈdrawers *n.* (plural **chests of drawers**) [C] a piece of furniture with drawers that clothes can be kept in

chew /tʃu/ *v.* [I,T] **1** to bite food several times before swallowing it: *The meat's so tough I can hardly chew it. | We gave the dog a bone to* ***chew on****.* **2** to bite something several times without eating it: *Students are not allowed to* ***chew gum*** *in the classroom.* [ORIGIN: Old English *ceowan*]

chew sb ↔ **out** *phr. v.* (informal) to speak angrily to someone who has done something wrong: *Mom chewed me out for coming home late.*

chew sth ↔ **over** *phr. v.* to think about something carefully for a period of time: *Let me chew it over for a few days, and then I'll let you have my answer.*

ˈchewing gum *n.* [U] GUM

chew·y /ˈtʃui/ *adj.* food that is chewy is not hard and dry, and needs to be chewed before you swallow it: *moist chewy brownies*

chic /ʃik/ *adj.* fashionable and showing good judgment about style: *a chic clothes store*

chi·can·er·y /ʃɪˈkeɪnəri/ *n.* [U] the use of complicated plans or tricks to deceive people: *He refused to stoop to such political chicanery.*

Chi·ca·no /tʃɪˈkɑnoʊ/ *n.* (plural **Chicanos**) [C] a U.S. citizen who was born in Mexico or whose family came from Mexico [ORIGIN: 1900—2000 Mexican Spanish, Spanish *mejicano* "Mexican man"]

chick /tʃɪk/ *n.* [C] **1** a baby bird, especially a baby chicken **2** (informal) a word meaning a young woman, that many women think is offensive

chick·a·dee /ˈtʃɪkəˌdi/ *n.* [C] a small North American wild bird with a black head

chick·en[1] /ˈtʃɪkən/ *n.* **1** [C] a farm bird that is kept for its meat and eggs → *see picture at* FARM[1] **2** [U] the meat from this bird: *fried chicken* **3** [C] (informal) someone who lacks courage: *Don't be such a chicken!* [ORIGIN: Old English *cicen* "young chicken"]

chicken[2] *adj.* (informal) not brave enough to do something: *Dave's too chicken to ask her out.*

chicken[3] *v.*

chicken out *phr. v.* (informal) to decide at the last moment not to do something because you are afraid: *I was going to ask for a raise but I chickened out.*

chicken pox, chick·en·pox /ˈtʃɪkənˌpɑks/ *n.* [U] BIOLOGY a disease that children often get that causes ITCHY spots on the skin and a fever

chide /tʃaɪd/ *v.* [I,T] (written) to speak in an angry way to someone who has done something wrong

chief[1] /tʃif/ *n.* [C] **1** the leader of a group or organization: *the* ***chief of*** *police*

> THESAURUS **boss, manager, head, principal, president, CEO, supervisor, foreman, forewoman** → BOSS[1]

2 the leader of a tribe: *Native American* ***tribal chiefs*** [ORIGIN: 1200—1300 Old French "head, chief," from Latin *caput* "head"]

chief[2] *adj.* [only before noun] **1** most important: *Safety is our* ***chief concern****.* **2** highest in rank: *the company's chief financial officer*

> THESAURUS **senior, high-ranking, top, junior, assistant** → POSITION[1]

ˌChief Exˈecutive *n.* **the Chief Executive Officer** POLITICS the President of the United States

ˌchief exˈecutive ˌofficer *n.* [C] a CEO

ˌchief ˈjustice *n.* [C] LAW the most important judge in a court of law, especially in the U.S. Supreme Court

chief·ly /ˈtʃifli/ *adv.* mainly: *The agency deals chiefly with recent immigrants.*

> THESAURUS **mainly, principally, largely, primarily** → MAINLY

ˌchief of ˈstaff *n.* (plural **chiefs of staff**) [C] an official of high rank, who advises the person in charge of an organization or government: *the White House chief of staff*

chief·tain /ˈtʃiftən/ *n.* [C] the leader of a tribe

chif·fon /ʃɪˈfɑn/ *n.* [U] a soft thin silk or NYLON material that you can see through: *a chiffon scarf*

chi·hua·hua /tʃɪˈwɑwə/ *n.* [C] a very small dog from Mexico with smooth short hair [ORIGIN: 1800—1900 *Chihuahua* city in Mexico]

child /tʃaɪld/ *n.* (plural **children** /ˈtʃɪldrən/) [C] **1** a young person who is not yet fully grown: *Admission is free for children under 8.* | *I was very happy **as a child*** (=when I was a child).

THESAURUS

Child is a word that you can use to talk about young children and teenagers. You do not normally use **child** to refer to babies.
Kid is an informal word for a child.
You are a **baby** when you are first born.
You are a **toddler** when you have just learned to walk.
You are a **teenager** between 13 and 19.
adolescent – a more formal word for a teenager: *Many adolescents fall prey to peer pressure.*
youngster – a young person, used especially in writing: *The after-school program is great for active youngsters.*
minor (formal) – someone who is not yet legally an adult: *It is illegal to sell alcohol to minors.*
juvenile (formal) – a young person who is not yet an adult, used especially when this person has committed a crime: *As a juvenile, he faces a maximum sentence of five years.* → BABY

2 a son or daughter: *How many **children** does Jane **have**?* | *Alex is an **only child*** (=he has no brothers or sisters). [ORIGIN: Old English *cild*]

child·bear·ing /ˈtʃaɪldˌbɛrɪŋ/ *n.* **1** [U] the process of being PREGNANT and then giving birth **2 childbearing age** the period of a woman's life during which she is able to have babies: *women **of childbearing age***

child·birth /ˈtʃaɪldbɚθ/ *n.* [U] the act of giving birth: *His wife had died **in childbirth**.*

child·care /ˈtʃaɪldkɛr/ *n.* [U] an arrangement in which someone takes care of children while their parents are at work

child·hood /ˈtʃaɪldhʊd/ *n.* [C,U] the time when you are a child: *Sara had a very happy childhood.* | *We've been friends **since childhood**.*

child·ish /ˈtʃaɪldɪʃ/ *adj.* **1** (disapproving) behaving in a silly way that makes you seem younger than you really are (SYN) **immature**: *At your age, don't you think playing on the swings is a little childish?* **2** relating to or typical of a child: *a childish game* —**childishly** *adv.*

child·less /ˈtʃaɪldlɪs/ *adj.* having no children: *childless couples*

child·like /ˈtʃaɪldlaɪk/ *adj.* (approving) having the good qualities of a child, such as natural or trusting behavior: *childlike innocence*

child·proof /ˈtʃaɪldpruf/ *adj.* designed to prevent a child from being hurt: *Most medicine bottles have a childproof cap.*

chil·dren /ˈtʃɪldrən/ *n.* the plural of CHILD

ˈchild supˌport *n.* [U] money that someone pays regularly to his/her former husband or wife in order to help support his/her children

chil·i /ˈtʃɪli/ *n.* (plural **chilies**) **1** [C,U] *also* **ˈchili ˌpepper** a small thin type of red or green pepper with a very hot taste **2** [U] a dish made with beans and usually meat cooked with chilies [ORIGIN: 1600—1700 Spanish *chile*, from Nahuatl *chilli*]

C

chill¹ /tʃɪl/ *v.* **1** [I,T] to make something or someone very cold: *This wine should be chilled before serving.* **2** [I] (informal) *also* **chill out** to relax instead of feeling angry or nervous: *Chill out, Dave – it doesn't matter.*

chill² *n.* **1** [singular] a feeling of coldness: *There was a slight **chill in the air**.* **2** [C] a slight feeling of fear: *His laugh **sent a chill down** her **spine*** (=made her feel very frightened). **3 chills** a feeling of being cold, caused by being sick

chill·ing /ˈtʃɪlɪŋ/ *adj.* making you feel frightened because something is cruel, violent, or dangerous: *a chilling report on child abuse*

chill·y /ˈtʃɪli/ *adj.* **1** cold enough to make you feel uncomfortable: *a chilly November morning* | *It's a little bit chilly in here.*

THESAURUS **cold, cool, frosty, freezing (cold), icy (cold), bitter (cold), frigid** → COLD¹

2 unfriendly: *The speech met with a **chilly reception**.*

chime¹ /tʃaɪm/ *n.* **1 chimes** [plural] a set of bells or other objects that produce musical sounds: ***wind chimes*** **2** [C] the ringing sound of a bell or clock

chime² *v.* [I,T] if a clock or bell chimes, it makes a ringing sound: *The clock chimed six.*

chime in *phr. v.* to say something in order to add your opinion to a conversation: *"The kids could go too," Maria chimed in.*

chim·ney /ˈtʃɪmni/ *n.* [C] a pipe inside a building for smoke from a fire to go out through the roof [ORIGIN: 1200—1300 Old French *cheminée*, from Latin *caminus* "fireplace," from Greek *kaminos*]

chimpanzee

chim·pan·zee /ˌtʃɪmpænˈzi/ *also* **chimp** /tʃɪmp/ *n.* [C] an African animal that is like a monkey without a tail

chin /tʃɪn/ *n.* [C] the front part of your face below your mouth: *She tied the scarf under her chin.* [ORIGIN: Old English *cinn*] ➔ *see picture on page A16*

chi·na /ˈtʃaɪnə/ *n.* [U] plates, cups, etc. that are made from white clay of good quality [ORIGIN: 1500—1600 Persian *chini* "Chinese;" because it was originally made in China]

C

Chi·na·town /ˈtʃaɪnəˌtaʊn/ *n.* an area in a city where there are Chinese restaurants and stores, and where a lot of Chinese people live

Chi·nese[1] /ˌtʃaɪˈniz◂/ *adj.* **1** relating to or coming from China **2** relating to a Chinese language

Chi·nese[2] /tʃaɪˈniz/ *n.* **1** [U] any of the languages that come from China, such as Mandarin or Cantonese **2 the Chinese** [plural] the people of China

chink /tʃɪŋk/ *n.* [C] a narrow crack or hole in something, that lets light or air through: *I could see light through a chink in the wall.*

chi·nos /ˈtʃinoʊz/ *n.* [plural] loose pants made from heavy cotton

chintz /tʃɪnts/ *n.* [U] smooth cotton cloth with brightly colored patterns on it: *chintz covers on the chairs*

chintz·y /ˈtʃɪntsi/ *adj.* (informal) **1** cheap and badly made: *a chintzy chest of drawers* **2** unwilling to give people things or spend money

ˈchin-up *n.* [C] an exercise in which you hang on a bar and pull yourself up until your chin is above the bar

chip[1] /tʃɪp/ *n.* [C]
1 FOOD a thin dry flat piece of potato or TORTILLA cooked in very hot oil and eaten cold: *chips and salsa* | *a bag of* ***potato chips***
2 COMPUTER IT a small piece of SILICON with electronic parts on it that is used in computers: *a* ***silicon chip***
3 PIECE a small piece of wood, stone, etc. that has broken off something: *Wood chips covered the floor of the workshop.*
4 MARK a small hole, crack, or mark on a plate, cup, etc. where a piece has broken off: *This plate has a* ***chip in*** *it.*
5 have a chip on your shoulder (informal) to have an angry attitude to life because you think you have been treated unfairly in the past: *He's always had a chip on his shoulder about not going to college.*
6 GAME a small flat colored piece of plastic, used in games to represent money: *a gambling chip*
7 be a chip off the old block (informal) to be like one of your parents in the way you look or behave
8 when the chips are down (spoken) in a serious or difficult situation: *When the chips are down, you only have yourself to depend on.* [ORIGIN: Old English *cipp*, *cyp* "small piece of wood," from Latin *cippus* "sharp post"] ➔ BARGAINING CHIP, BLUE CHIP

chip[2] *v.* (**chipped**, **chipping**) [I,T] **1** to break a small piece off something accidentally: *She fell and chipped a tooth.* **2** to remove something by breaking it off in small pieces: *She started chipping the ice off the windshield.* —**chipped** *adj.*: *chipped fingernail polish*

chip away at sth *phr. v.* to gradually make something weaker or less effective: *His comments were starting to chip away at my self-esteem.*

chip in *phr. v.* if each person in a group chips in, they each give a small amount of money so that they can buy something: *We all chipped in to buy Amy a graduation present.*

chip·munk /ˈtʃɪpmʌŋk/ *n.* [C] a small brown North American animal similar to a SQUIRREL, that has black and white lines on its fur ➔ *see picture at* RODENT

chip·per /ˈtʃɪpɚ/ *adj.* (informal) happy and healthy

chi·ro·prac·tor /ˈkaɪrəˌpræktɚ/ *n.* [C] someone who treats medical problems such as back pain by moving and pressing the muscles and bones [ORIGIN: 1800—1900 Latin *chiro-* "of the hand" (from Greek *cheiro-* + Greek *praktikos*, from *prassein* "to do"]

chirp /tʃɚp/ *v.* [I] if a bird or insect chirps, it makes short high sounds —**chirp** *n.* [C]

chis·el[1] /ˈtʃɪzəl/ *n.* [C] a metal tool with a sharp edge, used to cut wood or stone

chisel[2] *v.* [T] to use a chisel to cut wood or stone, especially into a particular shape

ˈchit-chat *n.* [U] (informal) informal conversation about unimportant things

chiv·al·rous /ˈʃɪvəlrəs/ *adj.* (formal) a man who is chivalrous behaves in a polite and honorable way to women —**chivalry** /ˈʃɪvəlri/ *n.* [U]

chive /tʃaɪv/ *n.* [C usually plural] a long thin green plant that looks and tastes like an onion and is used in cooking

chlo·ride /ˈklɔraɪd/ *n.* [C,U] CHEMISTRY a chemical COMPOUND that is a mixture of chlorine and another substance: *sodium chloride*

chlo·ri·nat·ed /ˈklɔrəˌneɪṭɪd/ *adj.* CHEMISTRY chlorinated water has had chlorine added to it in order to kill BACTERIA

chlo·rine /ˈklɔrin, klɔˈrin/ *n.* [U] CHEMISTRY (*symbol* **Cl**) a dark yellow-green gas, often used to keep swimming pools clean. It is a chemical ELEMENT belonging to the HALOGEN group. [ORIGIN: 1800—1900 Greek *chloros* "green"]

chlo·ro·fluo·ro·car·bon /ˌklɔrəˌflʊroʊˈkɑrbən/ *n.* [C] SCIENCE a CFC

chlo·ro·form /ˈklɔrəˌfɔrm/ *n.* [U] CHEMISTRY a liquid that makes you unconscious if you breathe it

chlo·ro·phyll /ˈklɔrəˌfɪl/ *n.* [U] BIOLOGY the green substance in plants [ORIGIN: 1800—1900 French *chlorophylle*, from Greek *chloros* "green" + *phyllon* "leaf"]

chlo·ro·plast /ˈklɔrəˌplæst/ *n.* [C] BIOLOGY one of several parts of plant cells that contain chlorophyll, that react with light from the Sun to produce the substance that the plant uses as food

chock-full /ˌtʃɑk ˈfʊl/ *adj.* [not before noun] (informal) completely full: *The bus was* ***chock-full of*** *people.*

choco·late /ˈtʃɑklɪt/ *n.* **1** [U] a sweet brown food that is eaten as candy or is used in cooking: *a chocolate bar | chocolate cake* **2** [C] a small candy that consists of something such as a nut or CARAMEL covered with chocolate: *a box of chocolates* [ORIGIN: 1600—1700 Spanish, Nahuatl *xocoatl*]

ˌchocolate ˈchip *n.* [C usually plural] a small piece of chocolate put in foods such as cookies and cakes

choice¹ /tʃɔɪs/ *n.* **1** [C,U] the right to choose or the chance to choose between two or more things: *a* ***choice between*** *three candidates. | You* ***have*** *a* ***choice*** *– you can take French or Spanish. | He* ***had no choice*** *but to move back into his parents' house. | We were* ***given*** *a* ***choice of*** *morning or afternoon flights. | You* ***get*** *a* ***choice of*** *soup or salad.* **2** [C] the act of choosing someone or something: *career choices | I think I* ***made*** *the right* ***choice.*** **3** [C usually singular] the range of people or things that you can choose from: *We had* ***little choice*** *in the matter. | The bookstore has a wide* ***choice of*** *magazines.* **4** [C usually singular] the person or thing that someone has chosen: *Carrot sticks are a* ***good choice*** *for a snack. | Her* ***first choice*** *of college was Stanford.* **5 the sth of your choice** the person or thing of your choice is the one you would most like to choose: *Many children are not able to go to the school of their choice.* **6 the sth of choice** the thing of choice is the one that people prefer to use: *It is the treatment of choice for this particular disease.* **7 by choice** if you do something by choice, you do it because you want to: *She lives alone by choice.* [ORIGIN: 1200—1300 Old French *chois*, from *choisir* "to choose"]

choice² *adj.* having a high quality or standard: *choice apples*

choir /kwaɪɚ/ *n.* [C] a group of people who sing together, especially in a church or school: *Amelia* ***sings in the choir.***

choke¹ /tʃoʊk/ *v.* **1** [I,T] to have difficulty breathing because something is in your throat or there is not enough air: *The fumes were choking me. | He* ***choked on*** *a piece of bread.* **2** [T] to put your hands around someone's throat and press on it so s/he cannot breathe: *He choked me so I couldn't talk or breathe.* **3** [I,T] to be almost unable to talk because of strong emotion: *Her voice was* ***choked with*** *rage.* **4** [T] to fill a space or passage so that things cannot move through it: *The roads were* ***choked with*** *traffic.* **5** [I] (spoken) to fail at doing something that you have prepared for because there is a lot of pressure on you

choke sth ↔ **back** *phr. v.* to control a strong feeling so that you do not show it: *Anna* ***choked back tears*** *as she tried to explain.*

choke up *phr. v.* **be/get choked up** to feel such strong emotions about something that you are almost crying

choke² *n.* [C] **1** the act of choking, or the sound someone makes when s/he is choking **2** a piece of equipment that controls the amount of air going into a car engine

chok·er /ˈtʃoʊkɚ/ *n.* [C] a piece of jewelry or narrow cloth that fits closely around your neck

chol·er·a /ˈkɑlərə/ *n.* [U] BIOLOGY a serious infectious disease that attacks the stomach and BOWELS [ORIGIN: 1300—1400 Old French *colère*, from Latin *cholera* "disease caused by bile," from Greek, from *chole* "bile;" because bile was thought to cause anger]

cho·les·ter·ol /kəˈlɛstəˌrɔl, -ˌroʊl/ *n.* [U] BIOLOGY a substance in your body which doctors think may cause heart disease: *She's had* ***high cholesterol*** *for many years.* [ORIGIN: 1800—1900 Greek *chole* "bile" + *stereos* "solid" + English *-ol* "chemical compound"]

choose /tʃuz/ *v.* (past tense **chose** /tʃoʊz/, past participle **chosen** /ˈtʃoʊzən/, present participle **choosing**) [I,T] **1** to decide which one of a number of things, possibilities, people, etc. that you want → CHOICE: *A panel of six judges will choose the winner. | They* ***chose*** *Roy* ***to be*** *the team captain. | You can* ***choose between*** *two types of fabric. | There are so many movies to* ***choose from.*** *| Why did they* ***choose*** *her* ***for*** *the job?*

THESAURUS

pick – to choose something or someone from a group of people or things: *Pick any number from one to ten.*
select (formal) – to choose something or someone by thinking carefully about which is the best, most appropriate, etc.: *The advisors help students select classes that meet graduation requirements.*
opt for sth – to choose one thing instead of another: *Many drivers opt for Japanese cars.*
decide on sth – to choose one thing from many possible choices: *Have you decided on a name for the baby?*

2 to decide to do something: *Donna* ***chose to*** *quit her job after she had the baby.* [ORIGIN: Old English *ceosan*]

THESAURUS **decide, make up your mind, resolve, determine** → DECIDE

choos·y /ˈtʃuzi/ *adj.* difficult to please: *Jean's very* ***choosy about*** *what she eats.*

chop¹ /tʃɑp/ *v.* (**chopped**, **chopping**) **1** [T] *also* **chop up** to cut something, especially food, into smaller pieces: *Can you chop up some onions for me? |* ***Chop*** *the tomatoes* ***into*** *fairly large* ***pieces.*** → *see picture at* CUT¹

THESAURUS **cut, slice, dice, peel, carve, shred, grate** → CUT¹

2 [I,T] to cut something by hitting it many times with a heavy sharp tool such as an AX: *She was outside chopping wood for the fire.*

chop sth ↔ **down** *phr. v.* to make a tree fall down by cutting it with a heavy sharp tool such as an AX: *A couple of the older trees will have to be chopped down.*

chop sth ↔ **off** *phr. v.* to remove something by cutting it with a sharp tool: *The branch had been chopped off.*

C

chop² *n.* [C] **1** a small flat piece of meat on a bone: *a pork chop* **2** a quick hard hit with the side of your hand or with a heavy sharp tool: *a karate chop*

chop·per /'tʃɑpɚ/ *n.* [C] (informal) a HELICOPTER

choppy

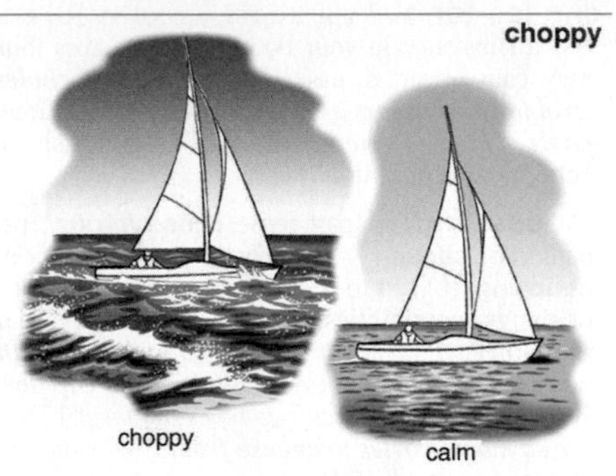

chop·py /'tʃɑpi/ *adj.* choppy water has many small waves

chop·sticks /'tʃɑpstɪks/ *n.* [plural] a pair of thin sticks used for eating food, especially by people in Asia

cho·ral /'kɔrəl/ *adj.* ENG. LANG. ARTS related to music that is sung by a large group of people ➔ CHORUS: *choral music*

chord /kɔrd/ *n.* [C] **1** ENG. LANG. ARTS a combination of two or more musical notes played at the same time **2 strike/touch a chord** to say or do something that people feel is true or familiar to them: *Many of her experiences will **strike a chord with** other young women.* **3** MATH a straight line joining two points on a curve ➔ *see picture at* CIRCLE¹

chore /tʃɔr/ *n.* [C] a job that you have to do, especially a boring one: *household chores*

cho·re·og·ra·phy /ˌkɔri'ɑgrəfi/ *n.* [U] the art of arranging how dancers should move during a performance [ORIGIN: 1700—1800 French *choréographie*, from Greek *choreia* "dance" + *-graphein* "to write"] —**choreographer** *n.* [C] —**choreograph** /'kɔriəˌgræf/ *v.* [T]

chor·tle /'tʃɔrṭl/ *v.* [I] (formal) to laugh because something is funny or pleases you —**chortle** *n.* [C]

cho·rus /'kɔrəs/ *n.* [C] **1** ENG. LANG. ARTS the part of a song that is repeated after each VERSE **2** a large group of people who sing together **3** a group of singers, dancers, or actors who perform together in a show but do not have the main parts **4 a chorus of thanks/disapproval/protest etc.** something expressed by a lot of people at the same time

chose /tʃoʊz/ *v.* the past tense of CHOOSE

chos·en /'tʃoʊzən/ *v.* the past participle of CHOOSE

chow¹ /tʃaʊ/ *n.* [U] (slang) food

chow² *v.*

chow down *phr. v.* (spoken) to eat, especially in a noisy way or in a way that shows you are very hungry

chow·der /'tʃaʊdɚ/ *n.* [U] a thick soup made with milk, vegetables, and usually fish: *clam chowder*

Christ /kraɪst/ *also* **Jesus Christ, Jesus** *n.* the man who Christians believe to be the son of God, and whose life and TEACHING Christianity is based on

chris·ten /'krɪsən/ *v.* [T] **1** to officially give a child its name at a Christian religious ceremony ➔ BAPTIZE: *She was christened Elizabeth Ann.* **2** to give something or someone a name

chris·ten·ing /'krɪsənɪŋ/ *n.* [C,U] a Christian ceremony in which a baby is officially given a name and becomes a member of a Christian church ➔ BAPTISM

Chris·tian /'krɪstʃən, 'krɪʃtʃən/ *adj.* relating to Christianity: *Christian ministers* | *Christian beliefs* [ORIGIN: 1200—1300 Latin *christianus*, from Greek, from *Christos* "Christ," from *chriein* "to pour holy oil on"] —**Christian** *n.* [C]

Chris·ti·an·i·ty /ˌkrɪstʃi'ænəṭi/ *n.* [U] the religion that is based on the life and teaching of Jesus Christ

ˌChristian 'Science *n.* [U] a religion whose members believe they can cure their own illnesses using their minds rather than with medical help —**Christian Scientist** *n.* [C]

Christ·mas /'krɪsməs/ *n.* **1** December 25, the day when Christians celebrate the birth of Jesus Christ: *Are you going home **for Christmas**?* | ***a Christmas present*** **2** the period of time just before and after this day: *We spent Christmas in Colorado.* [ORIGIN: Old English *Cristes mæsse* "Christ's MASS¹"]

ˌChristmas 'carol *n.* [C] a Christian song that people sing at Christmas

ˌChristmas 'Day *n.* December 25, the day when Christians celebrate the birth of Jesus Christ

ˌChristmas 'Eve *n.* December 24, the day before Christmas

'Christmas tree *n.* [C] a tree that people put inside their house and decorate for Christmas

chro·ma·tid /'kroʊmətɪd/ *n.* [C] BIOLOGY one of

the two parts that a chromosome divides into during the process in which two new cells are formed from an original cell

chro·ma·tin /'kroumətɪn/ *n.* [C] BIOLOGY a substance that chromosomes are formed from, that consists of DNA, RNA, and PROTEINS

chrome /kroum/ *also* **chro·mi·um** /'kroumiəm/ *n.* [U] a hard metal substance used for covering objects with a shiny protective surface: *the car's chrome hubcaps*

chro·mo·some /'krouməˌsoum, -ˌzoum/ *n.* [C] BIOLOGY a part of every living cell, that contains the GENEs that control the size, shape, etc. that a plant or animal has [ORIGIN: 1800—1900 Greek *chroma* "skin, color" + *soma* "body;" because chromosomes easily take up coloring substances]

chron·ic /'krɑnɪk/ *adj.* **1** a chronic disease or illness is one that continues for a long time and cannot be cured ➔ ACUTE: *chronic back pain* **2** a chronic problem is one that continues for a long time and cannot easily be solved: *California is trying to cope with chronic water shortages.* [ORIGIN: 1400—1500 French *chronique*, from Greek *chronikos* "of time"] —**chronically** *adv.*: *patients who are chronically ill*

chron·i·cle /'krɑnɪkəl/ *n.* [C] HISTORY a written record of historical events, arranged in the order in which they happened —**chronicle** *v.* [T]

chron·o·log·i·cal /ˌkrɑnl'ɑdʒɪkəl/ *adj.* arranged according to when something happened: *a list of World Series champions* ***in chronological order*** —**chronologically** *adv.*

chro·nol·o·gy /krə'nɑlədʒi/ *n.* (plural **chronologies**) [C] a list of events arranged according to when they happened: *a chronology of events in the Middle East*

chrys·a·lis /'krɪsəlɪs/ *n.* [C] BIOLOGY a MOTH or BUTTERFLY at the stage of development when it has a hard outer shell, before becoming a LARVA and then an adult ➔ COCOON ➔ *see picture on page A15*

chry·san·the·mum /krɪ'sænθəməm/ *n.* [C] a garden plant with large brightly colored flowers

chub·by /'tʃʌbi/ *adj.* slightly fat, used especially about children —**chubbiness** *n.* [U]

> THESAURUS **fat, overweight, big, heavy, large, obese, plump, stout, corpulent, rotund** ➔ FAT[1]

chuck /tʃʌk/ *v.* [T] (informal) **1** to throw something in a careless or relaxed way: *Chuck that magazine over here, would you?*

> THESAURUS **throw, toss, hurl, fling, cast, pass, pitch, lob** ➔ THROW[1]

2 *also* **chuck away/out** to throw something away: *Just go ahead and chuck out the old batteries.*

chuck·le /'tʃʌkəl/ *v.* [I,T] to laugh quietly: *Terry chuckled to himself as he read his book.* | *"You're wearing a wig," Mario chuckled.* —**chuckle** *n.* [C]

> THESAURUS **laugh, giggle, cackle, snicker, titter, guffaw** ➔ LAUGH[1]

chug /tʃʌg/ *v.* (**chugged**, **chugging**) **1** [I] if a car, boat, or train chugs somewhere, it moves there slowly, with the engine making a repeated low sound: *The little boat* ***chugged along*** *the river.* **2** [T] (informal) to drink all of something without stopping: *Chug that Coke and let's go.* —**chug** *n.* [C usually singular]

chum /tʃʌm/ *n.* [C] (old-fashioned) a good friend

chump /tʃʌmp/ *n.* (informal) **1** [C] someone who is silly or stupid, and who can be easily deceived **2** **chump change** (informal) a very small amount of money: *That sort of investment is mere chump change for a multi-billion dollar company.*

chunk /tʃʌŋk/ *n.* [C] **1** a large thick piece of something that does not have an even shape: *a* ***chunk of*** *cheese*

> THESAURUS **piece, scrap, lump, fragment, crumb, slice, strip, block** ➔ PIECE[1]

2 a large part or amount of something: *The rent takes a large* ***chunk out of*** *my monthly salary.*

chunk·y /'tʃʌŋki/ *adj.* **1** thick and heavy: *chunky jewelry* **2** someone who is chunky has a broad heavy body

church /tʃɚtʃ/ *n.* **1** [C] a building where Christians go to have religious services **2** [U] the religious services in a church: *Come over after church.* | *She* ***goes to church*** *every Sunday.* **3** [C] *also* **Church** one of the separate groups within the Christian religion: *the Catholic Church* [ORIGIN: Old English *cirice*, from Greek *kyriakos* "of the Lord"]

> THESAURUS
> **denomination** – a religious group that has slightly different beliefs from other groups who belong to the same religion: *Roman Catholicism is the largest religious denomination in the nation.*
> **sect** – a group of people who have their own set of beliefs or religious habits, especially a group that has separated from a larger group: *He joined a Buddhist sect.*
> **cult** – an extreme religious group that is not part of an established religion: *Members of the cult all committed suicide on the same day.*

> GRAMMAR
> Do not use "a" or "the" before **church** when you are talking about a religious ceremony: *How often do you* ***go to church****?*

churl·ish /'tʃɚlɪʃ/ *adj.* (formal) not polite or friendly

C

churn¹ /tʃɚn/ *n.* [C] a container in which milk is shaken until it forms butter

churn² *v.* **1** [I] if your stomach churns, you feel sick because you are frightened or nervous: *Thinking about the test **made my stomach churn**.* **2** [T] to make butter using a churn **3** [I,T] *also* **churn up** if water, mud, etc. churns, or if something churns it, it moves around violently

churn sth ↔ **out** *phr. v.* to produce large quantities of something quickly, especially without caring about quality: *She keeps churning out romance novels.*

C

chute /ʃut/ *n.* [C] **1** a long narrow structure that slopes down, so that things or people can slide down it from one place to another: *a mail chute* **2** (informal) a PARACHUTE

chutz·pah /ˈhʊtspə/ *n.* [U] (informal, approving) if someone has chutzpah, s/he has a lot of confidence and says rude or shocking things without feeling embarrassed [ORIGIN: 1800—1900 Yiddish, Late Hebrew *huspah*]

CIA *n.* **the CIA Central Intelligence Agency** the department of the U.S. government that collects secret information about other countries

ci·der /ˈsaɪdɚ/ *also* **ˈapple ˌcider** *n.* [C,U] a drink made from apples

ci·gar /sɪˈgɑr/ *n.* [C] a thick tube-shaped thing that people smoke, and which is made from tobacco leaves that have been rolled up

cig·a·rette /ˌsɪgəˈrɛt, ˈsɪgəˌrɛt/ *n.* [C] a thin tube-shaped thing that people smoke, that is made from finely cut tobacco leaves that have been rolled into a tube of paper: ***a pack of cigarettes*** [ORIGIN: 1800—1900 French *cigare* "cigar," from Spanish *cigarro*]

cil·i·um /ˈsɪliəm/ *n.* (plural **cilia** /-liə/) [C] BIOLOGY one of many hair-like structures that grow from the surface of some cells, that help move liquids past the cell or help the living thing move around

cinch¹ /sɪntʃ/ *n.* **be a cinch** (informal) **a)** to be almost certain to happen: *The Cubs are a cinch to win the National League East.* **b)** to be very easy to do: *The test was a cinch.* | *Good pie crust is a cinch to make.*

cinch² *v.* [T] to pull a belt, STRAP, etc. tightly around something

cin·der /ˈsɪndɚ/ *n.* [C] a very small piece of burned wood, coal, etc.

ˈcinder block *n.* [C] a large gray brick used to build houses, etc., made from CEMENT and cinders

cin·e·ma /ˈsɪnəmə/ *n.* **1** [U] the art or business of making movies: *an important director in Brazilian cinema* **2** [C] (old-fashioned) a MOVIE THEATER [ORIGIN: 1900—2000 *cinematograph* "movie camera, movie show" (19—20 centuries), from French *cinématographe*, from Greek *kinema* "movement" + French *-graphe* "recording instrument"]

cin·e·ma·tog·ra·phy /ˌsɪnəməˈtɑgrəfi/ *n.* [U] the skill or art of movie photography —**cinematographer** *n.* [C]

cin·na·mon /ˈsɪnəmən/ *n.* [U] a sweet-smelling brown SPICE used especially in baking cakes and cookies

ci·pher /ˈsaɪfɚ/ *n.* [C] a system of secret writing SYN **code**

cir·ca /ˈsɚkə/ *prep.* (*written abbreviation* **c.**) used before a date to show that it is not the exact date when something happened: *He was born circa 1100.*

cir·ca·di·an rhythm /sɚˌkeɪdiən ˈrɪðəm/ *n.* [C] BIOLOGY the regular pattern of changes that take place in your body during a 24-hour period

circle

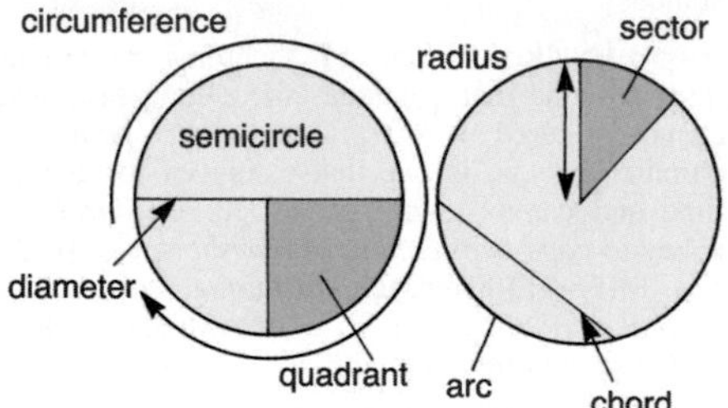

cir·cle¹ /ˈsɚkəl/ *n.* [C] **1** a round shape like the letter O: *Draw a circle around the right answer.* ➔ *see picture at* SHAPE¹

THESAURUS shape, square, semicircle, triangle, rectangle, oval, cylinder ➔ SHAPE¹

2 a group of people or things forming the shape of a circle: *The women sat **in a circle**.* **3** a group of people who know each other or have a common interest: *a large **circle of** friends* | *She is very well-known **in political/legal/medical etc. circles*** (=the group of people who work in a particular profession or industry). **4 come/go full circle** to end in the same situation in which you began, even though there have been changes during the time in between: *After the experiments of the 1960s, education has come full circle in its methods of teaching reading.* **5 go/run around in circles** to think or argue about something a lot without deciding anything or making any progress [ORIGIN: 1000—1100 Old French *cercle*, from Latin *circulus*]

circle² *v.* **1** [T] to draw a circle around something: *Circle the correct answer.* **2** [I,T] to move in a circle around something: *a plane circling an airport before landing.*

cir·cuit /ˈsɚkɪt/ *n.* **1 the talk show/golf/lecture etc. circuit** all the places that are usually visited by someone who is doing a particular activity: *Vesey returned to the nightclub circuit as a singer.* **2** [C] the complete circle that an electric current travels [ORIGIN: 1300—1400 Old French *circuite*, from Latin *circuitus*, past participle of *circumire, circuire* "to go around"]

'circuit board *n.* [C] PHYSICS a set of connections between points on a piece of electrical equipment, that uses a thin line of metal to CONDUCT (=carry) the electricity

'circuit ˌbreaker *n.* [C] PHYSICS a piece of equipment that stops an electric current if it becomes dangerous

'circuit ˌcourt *n.* [C] LAW a court of law in a U.S. state that meets in different places within the area it is responsible for

cir·cu·i·tous /sɚ'kyuəṭəs/ *adj.* (formal) going from one place to another in a way that is longer than the most direct way: *the river's circuitous course*

cir·cuit·ry /'sɚkətri/ *n.* [U] PHYSICS a system of electric circuits

cir·cu·lar¹ /'sɚkyəlɚ/ *adj.* **1** shaped like a circle: *a circular table*

THESAURUS round, oval, semicircular, triangular, rectangular, cylindrical ➤ SHAPE¹

2 moving around in a circle: *a circular hike around the lake* **3 circular argument/discussion/logic etc.** an argument, etc. that is not helpful because it always returns to the same statements or ideas that were expressed at the beginning —**circularity** /ˌsɚkyə'lærəṭi/ *n.* [U]

circular² *n.* [C] a printed advertisement or notice that is sent to a lot of people at the same time

cir·cu·late /'sɚkyəˌleɪt/ *v.* **1** [I,T] to move around within a system, or to make something do this: *Blood circulates around the body.* **2** [I] if information, facts, or ideas circulate, they become known by many people: ***Rumors are circulating** that the senator's health is getting worse.* **3** [T] to send or give information, facts, goods, etc. to a group of people: *I'll circulate the report at the meeting.* —**circulatory** /'sɚkyələˌtɔri/ *adj.*

cir·cu·la·tion /ˌsɚkyə'leɪʃən/ *n.* **1** [singular, U] BIOLOGY the movement of blood around your body: *I feel like these tight shoes are **cutting off** my **circulation**.* **2** [singular] the average number of copies of a newspaper, magazine, or book that are usually sold over a particular period of time: *The newspaper has a daily **circulation** of 400,000.* **3 in/out of circulation** if something is in circulation, it is being used by people in a society and passing from one person to another: *The government has reduced the number of $100 bills in circulation.* **4** [singular, U] the movement of liquid, air, etc. in a system: *Open a window and get some circulation in here.*

cir·cum·cise /'sɚkəmˌsaɪz/ *v.* [T] **1** to cut off the skin at the end of the PENIS (=male sex organ) **2** to cut off a woman's CLITORIS (=part of her sex organs) —**circumcision** /ˌsɚkəm'sɪʒən/ *n.* [C,U]

cir·cum·ference /sɚ'kʌmfrəns/ *n.* [C,U] MATH the distance around the outside of a circle or a round object: *the **circumference of** the Earth* | *The island is only nine miles **in circumference**.* [ORIGIN: 1300—1400 Old French, Latin *circumferentia*, from *circumferre* "to carry around," from *circum-* "around" + *ferre* "to carry"] ➔ *see picture at* CIRCLE¹

cir·cum·flex /'sɚkəmˌflɛks/ *n.* [C] ENG. LANG. ARTS a mark placed above a letter in some words in French, Portuguese, etc. to show its pronunciation, for example "â"

cir·cum·lo·cu·tion /ˌsɚkəmloʊ'kyuʃən/ *n.* [C,U] (formal) the practice of using too many words to express an idea instead of saying it directly, or a statement that does this —**circumlocutory** /ˌsɚkəm'lɑkyəˌtɔri/ *adj.*

cir·cum·nav·i·gate /ˌsɚkəm'nævəˌgeɪt/ *v.* [T] (formal) to sail, fly, or travel all the way around the Earth, an island, etc.: *the first successful attempt to **circumnavigate the globe*** —**circumnavigation** /ˌsɚkəmnævə'geɪʃən/ *n.* [C,U]

cir·cum·scribe /'sɚkəmˌskraɪb/ *v.* [T] **1** (formal) to limit power, rights, or abilities (SYN) **restrict** **2** MATH to draw a line around something: *a circle circumscribed by a square* ➔ INSCRIBE

cir·cum·scribed /'sɚkəmˌskraɪbd/ *adj.* MATH used to describe a shape that goes around and touches the outside points or edges of a square, a TRIANGLE, or other flat GEOMETRIC shape

cir·cum·spect /'sɚkəmˌspɛkt/ *adj.* (formal) thinking carefully about things before doing them (SYN) **cautious**: *In politics, you have to be circumspect about what you say in public.*

cir·cum·stance /'sɚkəmˌstæns/ (Ac) *n.* **1** [C usually plural] the facts or conditions that affect a situation, action, event, etc.: *You shouldn't judge him until you know the circumstances.* | *There are plenty of people **in similar circumstances**.* | *Prisoners can leave their cells only **under** certain **circumstances**.* **2 under the circumstances** *also* **given the circumstances** used in order to say that a particular situation makes an action, decision, etc. necessary, acceptable, or true when it would not normally be: *Under the circumstances, she did the best job she could.* **3 under no circumstances** used in order to emphasize that something must definitely not happen: *Under no circumstances are you to leave the house.* **4** [U] (formal) the combination of facts, events, and luck that influences your life, that you cannot control: *Circumstance played a large part in her getting the job.* **5 circumstances** [plural] (formal) the conditions in which you live, especially how much money you have: *The family's financial problems won't improve until their **economic circumstances** change.* [ORIGIN: 1100—1200 Old French, Latin *circumstantia*, from *circumstare* "to stand around"]

cir·cum·stan·tial /ˌsɚkəm'stænʃəl◂/ *adj.* based on something that appears to be true but is not proven: *The case against McCarthy is based largely on **circumstantial evidence**.*

cir·cum·vent /ˌsɚkəm'vɛnt, 'sɚkəmˌvɛnt/ *v.* [T] (formal) to avoid having to obey a rule or law, especially in a dishonest way: *The company has opened an office abroad in order to circumvent the tax laws.* —**circumvention** /ˌsɚkəm'vɛnʃən/ *n.* [U]

cir·cus /'sɚkəs/ *n.* [C] a group of performers and animals that travel to different places doing tricks and other kinds of entertainment: *circus acts* [ORIGIN: 1300—1400 Latin "circle, circus"]

C

cir·rho·sis /sɪ'roʊsɪs/ *n.* [U] BIOLOGY a serious disease of the LIVER, often caused by drinking too much alcohol [ORIGIN: 1800—1900 Modern Latin, Greek *kirrhos* "orange-colored;" from the appearance of the diseased liver]

cir·rus /'sɪrəs/ *n.* (plural **cirri** /'sɪraɪ/) [C,U] EARTH SCIENCES a type of cloud that is light and shaped like feathers, high in the sky → CUMULONIMBUS, CUMULUS, NIMBUS, STRATUS

cis·tern /'sɪstɚn/ *n.* [C] a large container that water is stored in

cit·a·del /'sɪṭədəl, -ˌdɛl/ *n.* [C] HISTORY a strong FORT built in past times as a place where people could go for safety if their city was attacked

ci·ta·tion /saɪ'teɪʃən/ (Ac) *n.* [C] **1** LAW an official order for someone to appear in court or pay a FINE for doing something illegal: *Turner was issued a traffic* ***citation for*** *reckless driving.* **2** an official statement publicly praising someone's actions or achievements: *a* ***citation for*** *bravery* **3** ENG. LANG. ARTS a line taken from a book, speech, etc. (SYN) **quotation**: *The speech contained a citation from "Hamlet."*

cite /saɪt/ (Ac) *v.* [T] **1** to mention something as an example or proof of something else: *The mayor* ***cited*** *the latest crime figures* ***as*** *proof of the need for more police.*

> THESAURUS **mention, refer to sth, note, raise, allude to sth, bring sth up** → MENTION[1]

2 LAW to order someone to appear before a court of law: *He has been* ***cited for*** *speeding.* **3** ENG. LANG. ARTS to give the exact words of something that has been written in order to support an opinion or prove an idea (SYN) **quote**: *Patrick cited parts of the First Amendment to support his argument on freedom of speech.*

cit·i·zen /'sɪṭəzən/ *n.* [C] **1** someone who lives in a particular town, state, or country: *The mayor urged citizens to begin preparing for a major storm.* **2** someone who has the legal right to live and work in a particular country: *a Brazilian citizen* **3 second class citizen** someone who is not as important as other people in a society and who is treated badly [ORIGIN: 1200—1300 Anglo-French *citezein*, from Old French *citeien*, from *cité*]

cit·i·zen·ship /'sɪṭəzənˌʃɪp/ *n.* [U] the legal right of belonging to a particular country: *She has applied for U.S. citizenship.*

cit·ric ac·id /ˌsɪtrɪk 'æsɪd/ *n.* [U] CHEMISTRY a weak acid that is in some fruits such as oranges and LEMONS

cit·rus /'sɪtrəs/ *also* **'citrus ˌfruit** *n.* [C] a fruit such as an orange or a LEMON

cit·y /'sɪṭi/ *n.* (plural **cities**) [C] **1** a large important town: *New York City* | *I've always lived in* ***big cities.*** **2** the people who live in a city: *The city has been living in fear since last week's earthquake.* [ORIGIN: 1100—1200 Old French *cité*, from Latin *civitas* "citizenship, state, city of Rome"]

ˌcity 'council *n.* [C] the group of elected officials who are responsible for making a city's laws

ˌcity 'hall *n.* [C,U] the local government of a city, or the building it uses as its offices

ˌcity-'state *n.* [C] HISTORY a city, especially in past times, that forms an independent country: *The city-state of Monaco is an interesting place to visit.*

civ·ic /'sɪvɪk/ *adj.* relating to a city or the people who live in it: *an important civic and business leader* | *It's your* ***civic duty*** *to vote.*

civ·ics /'sɪvɪks/ *n.* [U] a school subject dealing with the rights and duties of citizens and the way government works

civ·il /'sɪvəl/ (Ac) *adj.* **1** not related to military or religious organizations: *We were married in a civil ceremony, not in church.* **2** related to laws concerning the private affairs of citizens, such as laws about business or property, rather than laws concerning crime: *a civil lawsuit* | *a civil case* **3 civil unrest/disorder etc.** violence involving different groups within a country **4** polite but not very friendly: *Please try to be civil.* [ORIGIN: 1300—1400 Old French, Latin *civilis*, from *civis* "citizen"]

> THESAURUS **polite, well-behaved, courteous** → POLITE

—**civilly** *adv.*

ˌcivil diso'bedience *n.* [U] actions done by a large group of people in order to protest against the government, but without being violent

ˌcivil engi'neering *n.* [U] the planning, building, and repair of roads, bridges, large buildings, etc.

ci·vil·ian /sə'vɪlyən/ *n.* [C] anyone who is not a member of the military or the police: *Many innocent civilians were killed in the attack.* —**civilian** *adj.*

civ·i·li·za·tion /ˌsɪvələ'zeɪʃən/ *n.* **1** [C,U] a society that is well organized and developed: *modern American civilization* | *the ancient* ***civilizations of*** *Greece and Rome* **2** [U] all the societies in the world considered as a whole: *The book looks at the relationship between religion and civilization.*

civ·i·lize /'sɪvəˌlaɪz/ *v.* [T] (old-fashioned) to improve a society so that it is more organized and developed

civ·i·lized /'sɪvəˌlaɪzd/ *adj.* **1** a civilized society is one that has laws and CUSTOMS and a well-developed social system: *Care for the elderly is* *essential in a civilized society.* **2** behaving in a polite and sensible way: *Let's discuss this in a civilized way.*

ˌcivil ˈliberty *n.* (plural **civil liberties**) [C,U] SOCIAL SCIENCE the right of all citizens to be free to do whatever they want while obeying the law and respecting the rights of other people

ˌcivil ˈrights *n.* [plural] SOCIAL SCIENCE the legal rights that every person in a particular country has. In the U.S., these include the right to have the same treatment whatever your race or religion.

ˌcivil ˈrights ˌmovement *n.* **the civil rights movement** HISTORY the actions by black people in the U.S. during the 1950s and 1960s to gain equal rights and to end SEGREGATION (=when people of different races are kept apart)

ˌcivil ˈservant *n.* [C] someone who works in the civil service

ˌcivil ˈservice *n.* **the civil service** the government departments that deal with all the work of the government except the military

ˌcivil ˈwar *n.* **1** [C,U] a war in which opposing groups of people from the same country fight each other **2 the Civil War** HISTORY a war that was fought from 1861 to 1865 in the U.S. between the northern and southern states over whether it was right to own SLAVES

clack /klæk/ *v.* [I,T] to make a short hard sound: *the sound of high heels clacking across the courtyard* —**clack** *n.* [singular]

clad /klæd/ *adj.* (literary) wearing or covered in a particular thing: *The model was **clad in** silk and lace*

claim¹ /kleɪm/ *v.* **1** [T] to state that something is true even though it might not be: *The company **claims that** their products will help you lose weight.* | *George **claims to** remember exactly what Emily said that night.* **2** [I,T] to officially ask for money that you have a right to receive: *Your income must be less than a certain amount to claim food stamps.* **3** [T] to state that you have a right to something, or to take something that belongs to you: *Lost items can be claimed between 10 a.m. and 4 p.m.* **4** [T] (formal) if a war, accident, etc. claims lives, people die because of it: *Officials say the violence has claimed 21 lives.* [ORIGIN: 1300—1400 Old French *clamer*, from Latin *clamare* "to cry out, shout"]

claim² *n.* **1** [C] a statement that something is true even though it might not be: *Cardoza denied **claims that** he was involved in drug smuggling.* **2** [C,U] an act of officially saying that you have a right to receive or own something, or the state of having this right: *The contract proves he has no **claim on** the house.* | *Both groups believe they **have a claim to** the land.* **3** [C] an official request for money that you think you have a right to: *insurance claims* | *She is filing a **claim for** unpaid child support.* **4 claim to fame** the most important or interesting thing about a person or a place: *Her main claim to fame is the men she married.*

clair·voy·ant /klɛrˈvɔɪənt/ *n.* [C] someone who says s/he can see what will happen in the future —**clairvoyance** *n.* [U] —**clairvoyant** *adj.*

clam¹ /klæm/ *n.* [C,U] a small sea animal that has a shell and lives in sand and mud, or the meat from this animal → *see picture at* SHELLFISH

clam² *v.* (**clammed**, **clamming**)

clam up *phr. v.* (informal) to suddenly stop talking: *Lou always clams up if you ask him too many questions about his past.*

clam·ber /ˈklæmbɚ, ˈklæmɚ/ *v.* [I] to climb something that is difficult to climb, using your hands and feet: *Jenny and I **clambered up** the side of the hill.*

clam·my /ˈklæmi/ *adj.* wet, cold, and sticky in a way that is unpleasant: *clammy hands*

THESAURUS damp, humid, moist → DAMP

clam·or¹ /ˈklæmɚ/ *n.* [singular, U] **1** a complaint or a demand for something: *a public **clamor for** better schools* **2** a very loud continuous noise: *a **clamor of** voices in the next room* —**clamorous** *adj*

clamor² *v.* [I] to demand something loudly: *All the kids were **clamoring for** attention at once.* | *The children were **clamoring to** have their photo taken with Santa.*

clamp¹ /klæmp/ *v.* [T] **1** to hold something tightly so that it does not move: *He **clamped** his hand **over** her mouth.* **2** to fasten or hold two things together with a clamp: ***Clamp** the boards **together** until the glue dries.*

clamp down *phr. v.* to become very strict in order to stop people from doing something: *The police are **clamping down on** drunk drivers.*

clamp² *n.* [C] a tool used for fastening or holding things together tightly

clamp·down /ˈklæmpdaʊn/ *n.* [C] a sudden action by the government, police, etc. to stop a particular activity: *a **clampdown on** illegal immigration*

clan /klæn/ *n.* [C] (informal) a large family: *The whole clan will be coming over for Thanksgiving.*

clan·des·tine /klænˈdɛstɪn/ *adj.* secret: *a clandestine meeting*

THESAURUS secret, confidential, classified, sensitive, covert, undercover → SECRET¹

clang /klæŋ/ *v.* [I,T] to make a loud sound like metal being hit: *The gate clanged shut behind him.* —**clang** *n.* [C]

clank /klæŋk/ *v.* [I] to make a short loud sound like metal objects hitting each other: *clanking chains* —**clank** *n.* [C]

clap¹ /klæp/ *v.* (**clapped**, **clapping**) **1** [I,T] to hit your hands together loudly and continuously to show that you approve of something, or want to attract someone's attention: *The audience was clapping and cheering.* | *The coach **clapped** his **hands** and yelled, "OK, listen up!"* ➔ *see picture on page A21* **2 clap sb on the back/shoulder** to hit someone on the back or shoulder with your hand in a friendly way —**clapping** *n.* [U]

clap² *n.* [C] **1 a clap of thunder** a very loud sound made by THUNDER **2** the sound that you make when you hit your hands together

C

clap·board /'klæbərd, 'klæpbɔrd/ *n.* [C,U] a set of boards that cover the outside walls of a building, or one of these boards: *a clapboard house*

clar·i·fy /'klærəˌfaɪ/ (Ac) *v.* (**clarified, clarifies**) [I,T] to make something easier to understand by explaining it in more detail: *I need you to clarify a few points.* | *Could you **clarify what** you mean?* | *Reporters asked the Speaker of the House to clarify his statement.* —**clarification** /ˌklærəfə'keɪʃən/ *n.* [C,U]

THESAURUS **explain, tell, show, demonstrate, go through sth, elucidate** ➔ EXPLAIN

clar·i·net /ˌklærə'nɛt/ *n.* [C] a wooden musical instrument shaped like a long black tube that you play by blowing into it ➔ *see picture at* WOODWIND —**clarinetist** *n.* [C]

clar·i·ty /'klærət̬i/ (Ac) *n.* [U] the quality of speaking, writing, or thinking in a clear way: *the **clarity of** Irving's writing style* | *The novel's lack of clarity made it difficult to follow the plot.* [ORIGIN: 1600—1700 Latin *claritas*, from *clarus* "clear, bright"]

clash¹ /klæʃ/ *v.* **1** [I] to fight or argue with someone: *Soldiers **clashed with** rebels near the border.* **2** [I] if two colors or patterns clash, they do not look nice together: *That red tie **clashes with** your jacket.* **3** [I,T] to make a loud sound by hitting two metal objects together

clash² *n.* [C] **1** a fight or argument between two people, groups, or armies: *a **clash between** Democrats and Republicans in the Senate* | *a **culture/personality clash*** (=a situation in which different types or groups of people do not like each other) **2** a loud sound made by two metal objects hitting together: *the clash of the cymbals*

clasp

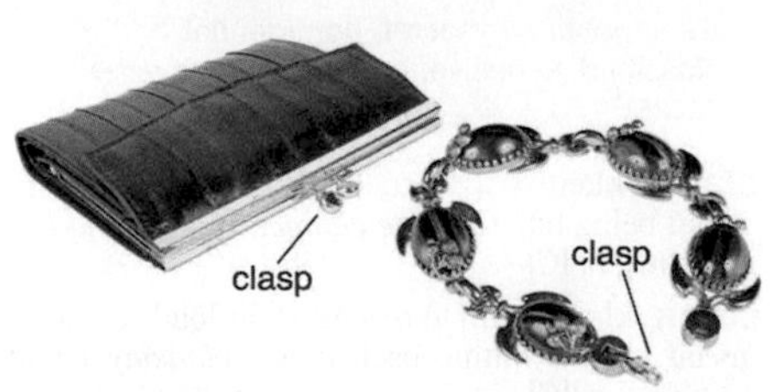

clasp¹ /klæsp/ *n.* **1** [C] a small metal object used for fastening a bag, belt, piece of jewelry, etc. **2** [singular] a tight firm hold (SYN) **grip**: *the firm clasp of her father's hand*

clasp² *v.* [T] to hold someone or something tightly: *Lie down with your **hands clasped** behind your head.*

THESAURUS **hold, grip, clutch, catch/take/keep/get (a) hold of sth, grasp, grab (hold of sth)/seize** ➔ HOLD¹

class¹ /klæs/ *n.*

1 GROUP OF STUDENTS [C] **a)** a group of students who are taught together: *a small class of ten people* **b)** a group of students who finish college or HIGH SCHOOL in the same year: *Our class had its 30th reunion this year.* | *Howard was a member of the **class of '05*** (=the group of students who finished in 2005).

2 TEACHING PERIOD [C,U] a period of time during which students are taught: *When's your next class?* | *Bob wasn't **in class** today.*

THESAURUS

lesson – a class, especially to learn practical skills such as music, swimming, or driving: *She takes dance lessons on Saturday mornings.*

course – a class in a particular subject: *a writing course*

period – one of the equal parts that a day is divided into in middle or high school, during which students study a particular subject: *What's your fourth period class?*

lecture – a talk about something, which is given to a large group of students at a college or university: *Professor Calder's lectures are always really good.*

seminar – a class, usually at a college or university, where a teacher and small group of students discuss a subject: *He's teaching a graduate seminar on Herman Melville.*

3 SUBJECT [C] a set of lessons in which you study a particular subject: *a **class in** computer design* | *She's **taking** a yoga **class**.* | *a **Spanish/math/science class***

4 IN SOCIETY a) [C] a group of people in a society that earn a similar amount of money, have similar types of jobs, etc. ➔ LOWER CLASS, MIDDLE CLASS, UPPER CLASS: *The middle class is feeling the pressure of lower wages and higher expenses.* **b)** [U] the system in which people are divided into such groups: *People were excluded from education based on class and race.*

5 QUALITY [C] a group into which people or things are divided according to how good they are: *We can't afford to travel **first class*** (=the most expensive way) *on the plane.* | *As a tennis player, she's **not in the same class** as* (=not as good as) *Williams.* | *The car is **in a class of its own*** (=very good quality).

6 STYLE/SKILL [U] a particular style, skill, or way of doing something that makes people admire you: *Margaret really **has class**.*

7 PLANTS/ANIMALS [C] BIOLOGY one of the groups into which scientists divide animals and plants. A class is larger than an ORDER but smaller than a PHYLUM. [ORIGIN: 1500—1600 French *classe*, from Latin *classis* "class of citizens, social class"]

class² *v.* [T] to decide that someone or something belongs in a particular group: *Heroin and cocaine are* ***classed as*** *hard drugs.*

ˌclass-ˈaction *adj.* LAW a class-action LAWSUIT is one that a group of people bring to a court of law for themselves and all other people with the same problem —**class action** *n.* [C,U]

clas·sic¹ /ˈklæsɪk/ (Ac) *adj.* [usually before noun] **1** a classic book, movie, etc. is considered to be very good and has been popular for a long time: *The Coca-Cola bottle is one of the classic designs of the last century.* | *Orson Welles directed the classic film "Citizen Kane."* ➔ OLD **2 a classic example/case etc.** a typical or very good example, etc.: *Forgetting to release the emergency brake is a classic mistake that many new drivers make.* **3** a classic style of dressing, art, etc. is attractive in a simple or traditional way: *a classic blue suit*

classic² *n.* [C] **1** a book, movie, etc. that is considered to be very good and has been popular for a long time: *"Moby Dick" is a classic of American literature.* | *literary classics* **2** something that is very good and one of the best examples of its kind: *The '65 Ford Mustang is a classic.* **3 classics** [plural] the study of the languages, literature, and history of ancient Greece and Rome

clas·si·cal /ˈklæsɪkəl/ (Ac) *adj.* **1** based on a traditional style or set of ideas: *classical ballet* **2** relating to classical music: *a classical pianist* **3** belonging to the language, literature, history, etc. of ancient Greece and Rome: *classical architecture* | *Challenging the gods is a common theme in classical literature.*

ˌclassical conˈditioning *n.* [U] BIOLOGY a learning process in which an animal makes a connection in its mind between something that makes it move or react and a reward or a punishment

ˌclassical ˈmusic *n.* [U] ENG. LANG. ARTS a type of music, originally from Europe, that includes OPERAS and symphonies (SYMPHONY), that is played mainly on instruments such as the VIOLIN and piano, and is considered to have serious artistic value

clas·si·cism /ˈklæsəˌsɪzəm/ *n.* [U] ENG. LANG. ARTS a style of art that is simple, regular, and does not show much emotion, based on the models of ancient Greece or Rome

clas·si·fi·ca·tion /ˌklæsəfəˈkeɪʃən/ *n.* [C,U] the process of putting people or things into groups according to their age, type, etc., or one of these groups: *the* ***classification of*** *chilis according to their strength* | *my job classification*

clas·si·fied /ˈklæsəˌfaɪd/ *adj.* classified information, documents, etc. are kept secret by the government or an organization

THESAURUS secret, confidential, sensitive, covert, undercover, clandestine ➔ SECRET¹

ˌclassified ˈad *n.* [C] a small advertisement that you put in a newspaper if you want to buy or sell something

clas·si·fy /ˈklæsəˌfaɪ/ *v.* (**classified**, **classifies**) [T] to put things into groups according to their age, type, etc.: *Whales are* ***classified as*** *mammals rather than fish.*

class·less /ˈklæslɪs/ *adj.* a classless society is one in which people are not divided into different social classes

class·mate /ˈklæsmeɪt/ *n.* [C] someone who is in the same class as you at school or college: *I'm younger than most of my classmates.*

class·room /ˈklæsrum/ *n.* [C] **1** a room in a school, where students are taught: *classroom materials* **2 in the classroom** in schools or classes in general: *the use of computers in the classroom*

class·work /ˈklæswɚk/ *n.* [U] work that students do in class, not at home ➔ HOMEWORK

class·y /ˈklæsi/ *adj.* (comparative **classier**, superlative **classiest**) (informal) expensive and fashionable: *a classy restaurant*

clat·ter /ˈklæt̬ɚ/ *v.* [I,T] if something clatters, it makes a loud noise when it hits something: *The pots clattered to the floor.* —**clatter** *n.* [singular, U]

clause /klɔz/ (Ac) *n.* [C] **1** a part of a written law or legal document: *A clause in the contract states when payment must be made.* **2** ENG. LANG. ARTS in grammar, a group of words that is part of a sentence ➔ PHRASE: *In the sentence "Can you tell me what time it is?" the main clause is "Can you tell me," and "what time it is" is a subordinate clause.* ➔ INDEPENDENT CLAUSE

claus·tro·pho·bi·a /ˌklɔstrəˈfoʊbiə/ *n.* [U] a strong fear of being in a small enclosed place or in a crowd of people [ORIGIN: 1800—1900 Modern Latin, Latin *claustrum* "bar keeping a door closed" + Modern Latin *phobia* "fear"] —**claustrophobic** /ˌklɔstrəˈfoʊbɪk/ *adj.*: *I began to feel a little claustrophobic in the elevator.*

clav·i·cle /ˈklævɪkəl/ *n.* [C] BIOLOGY a COLLARBONE

claw¹ /klɔ/ *n.* [C] a sharp curved nail on an animal, bird, or some insects: *lobster claws* [ORIGIN: Old English *clawu*] ➔ *see picture on page A15*

claw² *v.* [I,T] to tear or pull at something, using your fingers or claws: *The cat keeps* ***clawing at*** *the rug.*

clay /kleɪ/ *n.* [U] a type of heavy wet soil that is used to make pots or bricks: *a clay pot*

clean¹ /klin/ *adj.* **1 a)** not dirty or messy (ANT) **dirty** ➔ CLEANLINESS: *Are your hands clean?* | *clean sheets* | *I want you to* ***keep*** *this room* ***clean.*** | *a* ***squeaky clean*** *(=very clean) floor* **b)** not containing or producing anything harmful or dirty (ANT) **polluted**: *clean water/air* **2** not rude or offensive, or not about sex: *good clean fun* **3** honest or legal and showing that you have not broken any rules or laws: *I've had a* ***clean record*** (=no official record of having broken the law) *for five years now.* | *a clean driving record* **4** having a simple and attractive style or design: *a shape that emphasizes the furniture's* ***clean lines*** **5 come clean** (informal) to finally tell the truth about something you have been hiding: *Josh finally* ***came clean about*** *denting the car.* **6 a clean break** a complete and sudden separation from a person, organization, or situation: *She wanted to* ***make a clean break*** *with the past.* **7 a clean sweep** a very impressive victory in a competition, election, etc.: *It was looking like* ***a clean sweep for*** *the Democrats.* **8 a clean slate** a new situation in which there is no record of you ever breaking any rules or behaving badly, even if you have broken rules or behaved badly in the past: *He will start his school life here* ***with a clean slate.*** **9 a clean bill of health** a report saying that a person is healthy or that a machine or building is safe [ORIGIN: Old English *clæne*]

clean² *v.* [I,T] **1** to remove dirt from somewhere or something: *I need to clean the bathtub.* | *She's busy cleaning.* | *We've hired someone to clean our house.*

THESAURUS

do/wash the dishes – to wash plates and pans after a meal
scour – to wash dirty pots and pans with a rough cloth
do the housework – to clean the house
dust/polish – to clean furniture
vacuum – to clean carpets with a special machine
sweep (up) – to clean the dirt from the floor or ground using a broom (=brush with a long handle)
scrub – to clean something by rubbing it with a hard brush
mop – to clean the floor with water and a mop (=soft brush on a long handle)
do the laundry – to wash clothes
dry clean – to clean clothes with chemicals instead of water

2 to make something look neat by putting things in their correct places SYN **clear**: *Pam began to clean her desk.*

clean out *phr. v.* **1 clean** sth ↔ **out** to make the inside of a car, room, house, etc. clean, especially by removing things from it: *We cleaned out the garage last Sunday.* **2 clean** sb/sth ↔ **out** (informal) to steal everything from a place or from someone: *Two armed men cleaned out the computer store.* **3 clean** sb **out** if buying something cleans you out, it is so expensive you have no money left: *The new refrigerator really cleaned me out.*

clean up *phr. v.* **1 clean** sb/sth ↔ **up** to make something or someone clean and neat: *Clean up your room – it's a mess!* | *I need to go upstairs and get cleaned up.* **2 clean** sth ↔ **up** to remove crime, bad behavior, etc. from a place or organization: *The new chief promised to clean up the police department.* **3 clean up your act** (informal) to begin to behave in a responsible way: *You'll have to clean up your act if you want to impress Diane's parents.* —**cleaning** *n.* [U]: *A woman comes twice a week to* ***do the cleaning.***

clean³ *adv.* (informal) completely: *I'm sorry, I* ***clean forgot*** *your birthday.*

ˌclean-ˈcut *adj.* (approving) a man who is clean-cut is clean and neat in his appearance

clean·er /ˈklinɚ/ *n.* **1** [C] a machine or substance used to clean things: *a vacuum cleaner* **2** [C] someone whose job is to clean something: *a street cleaner* **3 the cleaners** [plural] a DRY CLEANERS **4 take sb to the cleaners** (informal) to get all of someone's money in a way that is not honest: *Juanita threatened to take her former husband to the cleaners.*

clean·li·ness /ˈklɛnlinɪs/ *n.* [U] the practice of keeping yourself or the things around you clean

clean·ly /ˈklinli/ *adv.* done quickly, smoothly, and neatly: *The doctor cut cleanly through the skin.*

cleanse /klɛnz/ *v.* [T] to make something completely clean: *Cleanse the wound with alcohol.*

cleans·er /ˈklɛnzɚ/ *n.* [C,U] **1** a substance used for cleaning your skin **2** a substance used for cleaning surfaces in a house, office, etc.

clean-shaven

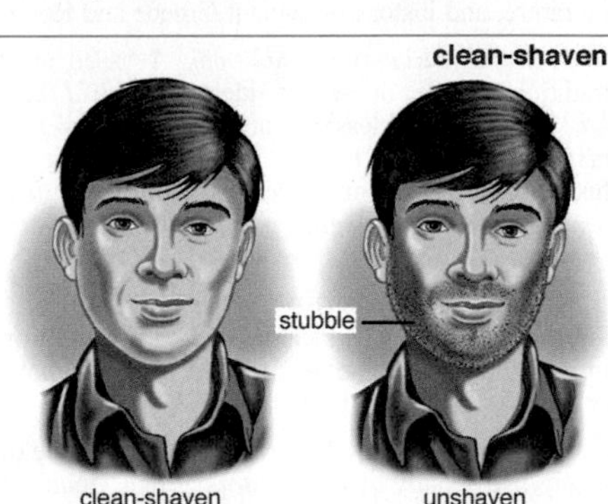

ˌclean-ˈshaven *adj.* a man who is clean-shaven does not have hair on his face

clean·up /ˈklinʌp/ *n.* [C usually singular] a process in which you clean something thoroughly: *The cleanup of the oil spill took months.* —**cleanup** *adj.*

clear¹ /klɪr/ *adj.*

1 SIMPLE/EASY easy to understand, hear, read, or see: *clear instructions* | *The law is quite* ***clear on*** *this issue.* | *Smith was very* ***clear about*** *the school's policies on the matter.* | *It is* ***clear to*** *me that the company will have to make further job cuts.* | *Have I* ***made myself clear****?* | *Hugh had* ***made it*** *perfectly* ***clear (that)*** *he wasn't interested.* | *We must send out a* ***clear message/signal*** *to voters.*

THESAURUS noticeable, obvious, striking, evident, apparent, conspicuous, unmistakable, manifest ➔ NOTICEABLE

2 CERTAIN impossible to doubt: *clear evidence* | *It's not* ***clear how*** *it happened.* | *It became* ***clear that*** *he would soon die.* | *a* ***clear case/example of*** *fraud* | *In this situation, there is no* ***clear winner****.*
3 SURE ABOUT STH [not before noun] feeling sure that you understand something (ANT) **confused**: *I'm not* ***clear about*** *what you want me to do.*
4 SEE THROUGH easy to see through: *clear glass bottles* | *a clear mountain lake*
5 WEATHER weather that is clear is bright with no rain or clouds: *a clear sky*
6 NOT BLOCKED not blocked, hidden, or covered by anything: *a clear view of the harbor* | *smooth clear skin*
7 a clear conscience the knowledge that you have done the right thing and should not feel guilty [ORIGIN: 1200—1300 Old French *cler*, from Latin *clarus* "clear, bright"]

clear[2] *v.*
1 MAKE NEAT [T] to make a place neat by removing things from it: *Snowplows quickly* ***cleared*** *the streets* ***of*** *snow.* | *They spent the morning* ***clearing*** *garbage* ***from*** *the front yard.* | *If you* ***clear the table*** (=take away the dishes, forks, etc.), *I'll make the coffee.* | *Can you* ***clear a space*** *for my books?*
2 REMOVE [T] to make people, cars, etc. leave a place: *Within minutes, police had cleared the area.* | *Trucks have just finished* ***clearing*** *the wreck* ***from*** *the road.*
3 LEGAL CHARGE [T] to prove that someone is not guilty of something: *The jury* ***cleared*** *Johnson* ***of*** *the murder charge.*
4 WEATHER [I] *also* **clear up** if the weather or sky clears, it becomes brighter
5 PERMISSION [T] to give or get official permission to do something: *Has the plane been* ***cleared for*** *landing?* | *I'll have to* ***clear*** *it* ***with*** *my boss first.*
6 CHECK [I,T] if a check that is made out to you clears, the money is paid into your bank account
7 clear your throat to cough a little so that you can speak clearly
8 clear the air to talk about a problem in order to solve a disagreement: *You need to meet with him and try to clear the air.*
9 GO OVER [T] to go over a fence, wall, etc. without touching it: *The plane barely cleared the fence as it came down.*
10 clear a debt/loan to get rid of a debt by paying what you owe

clear sth ↔ **away** *phr. v.*
to make a place look neat by removing things or putting them where they belong: *Clear all these toys away before you go to bed.*

clear sth ↔ **out** *phr. v.*
to make a place neat by removing things from it: *I need to clear out that closet.*

clear up *phr. v.*
1 clear sth ↔ **up** to explain or solve something, or make it clearer: *We need to clear up a few points before the meeting begins.*
2 if an infection clears up, it gets better

clear[3] *adv.* **1** away from someone or something: *Firemen pulled the driver* ***clear of*** *the wreckage.* **2 steer/stay/keep clear (of sb/sth)** to avoid someone or something because of possible danger or trouble: *She told us to stay clear of the construction site.* **3** all the way: *You can see* ***clear to*** *the Rockies today.*

clear[4] *n.* **in the clear a)** not having difficulties because of something: *The debt is being paid off, but we're not in the clear yet.* **b)** not guilty of something

clear·ance /ˈklɪrəns/ *n.* [C,U] **1** official permission to do something: *Kameny was denied a* ***security clearance****.* **2** the distance between two objects that is needed to stop them touching: *We need twelve feet of overhead clearance for the truck.*

ˈclearance sale *n.* [C] an occasion when goods in a shop are sold cheaply in order to get rid of them

ˈclear-cut *adj.* certain or definite: *a clear-cut decision*

ˌclear-ˈheaded *adj.* able to think clearly and sensibly

clear·ing /ˈklɪrɪŋ/ *n.* [C] a small area in a forest, where there are no trees

clear·ly /ˈklɪrli/ *adv.* **1** without any doubt: *Clearly, he felt he was to blame.* | *Leslie was clearly annoyed.* **2** in a way that is easy to see, understand, hear, etc.: *Slow down and speak clearly.* | *Prices were clearly marked.* **3** if you cannot think clearly, you are confused

cleat /klit/ *n.* **1** [C] one of a set of short pieces of rubber, metal, etc. attached to the bottom of a sports shoe **2 cleats** [plural] a pair of shoes with cleats attached to them

cleav·age /ˈklivɪdʒ/ *n.* [C,U] the space between a woman's breasts

cleave /kliv/ *v.* (past tense **cleaved**, **clove** /kloʊv/, **cleft** /klɛft/, past participle **cleaved**, **cloven** /ˈkloʊvən/, **cleft**) [I always + adv./prep.,T always + adv./prep.] (literary) to cut something into separate parts using a heavy tool: *The wooden door had been cleft in two.*

cleave to sb/sth *phr. v.* **1** (formal) to be faithful to an idea, belief, or person: *The Bible says that a man must leave his parents and cleave to his wife.* **2** (literary) to stick to someone or something, or to seem to surround him, her, or it: *The dirt still cleaved to the roots.*

clea·ver /ˈklivɚ/ *n.* [C] a knife with a large square blade: *a meat cleaver*

clef /klɛf/ *n.* [C] ENG. LANG. ARTS a sign used in written music to show the PITCH of the notes

cleft[1] /klɛft/ *n.* [C] a natural crack in the ground or in rocks

cleft[2] *adj.* partly split or divided: *a cleft chin*

C

C

cleft³ *v.* a past tense and past participle of CLEAVE

clem·en·cy /ˈklɛmənsi/ *n.* [U] (formal) the act of forgiving someone for a crime and making his/her punishment less severe: *His appeal for clemency has been denied.*

clench /klɛntʃ/ *v.* [T] to close your hands, mouth, etc. tightly: *He **clenched** his **fist** and pounded it into his palm.* | *He had a cigar **clenched between** his teeth.*

cler·gy /ˈklɚdʒi/ *n.* **the clergy** [plural] the official leaders of organized religions

cler·gy·man /ˈklɚdʒimən/, **cler·gy·wom·an** /ˈklɚdʒiˌwʊmən/ *n.* (plural **clergymen** /-mən/, **clergywomen** /-ˌwɪmɪn/) [C] a male or female member of the clergy

cler·ic /ˈklɛrɪk/ *n.* [C] a member of the clergy

cler·i·cal /ˈklɛrɪkəl/ *adj.* **1** relating to office work: *a clerical worker* **2** relating to the clergy

clerk /klɚk/ *n.* [C] **1** someone who deals with people arriving at a hotel: *Please return your keys to the desk clerk.* **2** someone whose job is to help people in a store **3** someone whose job is to keep records, accounts, etc. in an office [ORIGIN: 1000—1100 Old French *clerc* "man in a religious order, scholar, man who keeps records," from Late Latin *clericus*] ➔ SALES CLERK

clev·er /ˈklɛvɚ/ *adj.* **1** able to use your intelligence to do something, especially in a slightly dishonest way: *a lawyer's clever tricks* **2** able to learn things quickly: *a clever child*

> THESAURUS **intelligent, smart, bright, brilliant, wise, cunning, crafty, intellectual, gifted, apt** ➔ INTELLIGENT

3 showing ability, skill, or imagination: *a clever idea* —**cleverly** *adv.* —**cleverness** *n.* [U]

cli·ché /kliˈʃeɪ/ *n.* [C] ENG. LANG. ARTS an idea or phrase that has been used so much that it is no longer effective or no longer has any real meaning: *The movie avoids most of the usual clichés.*

click¹ /klɪk/ *v.* **1** [I,T] to make a short hard sound, or to make something produce this sound: *The door clicked shut.* | *He **clicked** his **heels*** (=hit the heels of his shoes together) *and jumped into the air.* **2** [I] (informal) to suddenly understand or realize something: *I was having a lot of trouble with algebra until one day **it just clicked**.* **3** [I] (informal) if two people click, they immediately like each other **4** [I,T] IT to press a button on a computer MOUSE to make the computer do something ➔ DOUBLE-CLICK: ***Click on** the icon at the bottom of the screen.* [ORIGIN: 1500—1600 From the sound]

click² *n.* [C] a short hard sound: *I heard a click, and the phone went dead.* ➔ *see picture on page A20*

cli·ent /ˈklaɪənt/ *n.* [C] someone who pays a person or organization for a service: *important clients* [ORIGIN: 1300—1400 Old French, Latin *cliens*]

> THESAURUS **customer, shopper, patron, consumer, buyer** ➔ CUSTOMER

cli·en·tele /ˌklaɪənˈtɛl, ˌkliɑn-/ *n.* [singular] the people who regularly go to a store, restaurant, etc.: *The Sports Cafe attracts a mostly male clientele.*

cliff /klɪf/ *n.* [C] EARTH SCIENCES a large area of rock with steep sides [ORIGIN: Old English *clif*] ➔ *see picture on page A24*

cliff·hang·er /ˈklɪfˌhæŋɚ/ *n.* [C] (informal) a situation in a story, that excites you because you do not know what will happen next

cli·mac·tic /klaɪˈmæktɪk/ *adj.* forming an exciting or important part at the end of a story or event: *the final climactic scene of the play*

cli·mate /ˈklaɪmɪt/ *n.* **1** [C] EARTH SCIENCES the typical weather conditions in an area: *a hot and humid climate* **2** [singular] the general feelings in a situation at a particular time: *in the current **climate** of uncertainty* | *a **climate of fear/violence/hostility etc.*** | *the **economic/political etc. climate*** [ORIGIN: 1300—1400 Old French *climat*, from Late Latin *clima*, from Greek *klima* "angle, latitude, climate;" because the weather depends on the angle of the Sun to the Earth] —**climatic** /klaɪˈmæt̬ɪk/ *adj.*

cli·max¹ /ˈklaɪmæks/ *n.* [C] the most important or exciting things that come near the end of a story or experience: *Winning the gold medal was the **climax of** his sports career.* | *The crisis **reached a climax** last week, when two senators resigned.* [ORIGIN: 1500—1600 Latin, Greek *klimax* "ladder," from *klinein* "to lean"]

climax² *v.* [I,T] to reach the most important or exciting part of something: *The tournament **climaxes with** the championship game on March 31.*

climb¹ /klaɪm/ *v.* **1** [I,T] to move toward the top of something: *kids climbing a tree* | *the first man to climb Mount Everest* | *We watched as the plane **climbed into** the sky.* | *I slowly climbed three flights of stairs.* ➔ *see picture on page A22* **2** [I] to move somewhere with difficulty, using your hands and feet: *Ford **climbed into** a waiting limousine.* **3** [I] to increase in number, amount, or level: *The temperature was climbing steadily.* **4** [I,T] to move to a better position in your social or professional life: *women trying to **climb the** corporate **ladder*** (=become more successful) **5 be climbing the walls** (spoken) to become extremely anxious, annoyed, or impatient: *When he hadn't gotten back by midnight, I was climbing the walls.* [ORIGIN: Old English *climban*]

climb² *n.* [C usually singular] **1** a process in which you move up toward a place while using a lot of effort: *a tough **climb to** the top* **2** an increase in value or amount: *a steady **climb in** house prices* **3** the process of improving your professional or social position: *a politician's **climb to** power*

climb·er /ˈklaɪmɚ/ *n.* [C] someone who climbs rocks, mountains, etc. as a sport ➔ SOCIAL CLIMBER

climb·ing /'klaɪmɪŋ/ *n.* [U] the sport of climbing mountains or rocks: *Let's **go climbing** this weekend.* → *see picture on page A17*

clinch /klɪntʃ/ *v.* [T] (informal) to manage to win or get something after trying hard: *I think I know how we can **clinch** this **deal**.*

clinch·er /'klɪntʃɚ/ *n.* [C] (informal) a fact or action that finally persuades someone to do something, or that ends an argument or competition: *The real clincher was her threat to sue the city.*

cling /klɪŋ/ *v.* (past tense and past participle **clung** /klʌŋ/) [I] **1** to hold onto someone or something tightly because you do not feel safe: *a climber **clinging onto** a rock* | *They **clung to** each other and cried.* **2** to stick to something: *The wet shirt **clung to** his body.*

cling to sth *phr. v.* to continue to believe or do something, even though it may no longer be true or useful: *He clung to the possibility that she would be cured.*

cling·y /'klɪŋi/ *adj.* **1** (disapproving) someone who is clingy is too dependent on another person: *a shy, clingy child* **2** clingy clothing or material sticks tightly to your body and shows its shape: *a clingy dress*

clin·ic /'klɪnɪk/ *n.* [C] **1** a place where medical treatment is given to people who do not need to stay in a hospital: *a dental clinic* **2** a group of doctors who share the same offices **3** a meeting during which a professional person gives advice or help to people: *a marriage clinic* [ORIGIN: 1800—1900 French *clinique*, from Greek *klinike* "medical practice by the bed"]

clin·i·cal /'klɪnɪkəl/ *adj.* **1** relating to treating or testing people who are sick: *The drug has undergone a number of **clinical trials/tests**.* **2** (disapproving) not influenced by personal feelings: *a cold clinical attitude* —**clinically** *adv.*

clin·i·cian /klɪ'nɪʃən/ *n.* [C] a doctor who examines and treats people who are sick rather than studying disease

clink /klɪŋk/ *v.* [I,T] if glass or metal objects clink, or if you clink them, they make a short ringing sound when they touch —**clink** *n.* [singular]

clip¹ /klɪp/ *n.* [C] **1** a small metal or plastic object for holding things together: *a paper clip* **2** a short part of a movie or television program that is shown by itself, especially as an advertisement: ***clips from** Pitt's new movie* **3 at a good/rapid/fast clip** quickly: *Witnesses say the car was moving at a rapid clip.*

clip² *v.* (**clipped**, **clipping**) **1** [I,T] to put a clip on things to hold them together: *She'd **clipped** her business card **to** the letter.*

> THESAURUS **fasten, attach, secure, join, glue, tape, staple, tie** → FASTEN

2 [T] to cut something out of a newspaper, magazine, etc.: *Tara showed him an ad she'd **clipped out of** the Sunday paper.* **3** [T] to cut small amounts from something to make it look neater: *He went out in the yard to clip the hedges.*

clip·board /'klɪpbɔrd/ *n.* [C] **1** a small flat board with a clip that holds paper onto it **2** IT part of a computer MEMORY that stores information when you cut, copy, or move it

'clip-on *adj.* attached to something using a clip: *clip-on earrings*

clip·pers /'klɪpɚz/ *n.* [plural] a tool for cutting small pieces off something: *nail clippers*

clip·ping /'klɪpɪŋ/ *n.* **1** [C] an article, picture, etc. that you cut out of a newspaper or magazine **2** [C usually plural] a small piece cut from something bigger: *grass clippings*

clique /klik, klɪk/ *n.* [C] (disapproving) a small group of people who do not want others to join their group: *The girls have their own little clique.* —**cliquish** *adj.*

clit·o·ris /'klɪt̬ərɪs/ *n.* [C] BIOLOGY a small part of a woman's outer sex organs where she can feel sexual pleasure

cloak¹ /kloʊk/ *n.* [C] a warm piece of clothing like a coat without sleeves [ORIGIN: 1200—1300 Old North French *cloque* "bell, cloak," from Medieval Latin *clocca* "bell;" because of its shape]

cloak² *v.* [T] (written) to deliberately cover or hide something: *The early stages of the negotiations were **cloaked in secrecy**.*

ˌcloak-and-'dagger *adj.* very secret and mysterious: *a cloak-and-dagger operation*

cloak·room /'kloʊk-rum/ *n.* [C] a small room where you can leave your coat, bag, etc.

clob·ber /'klɑbɚ/ *v.* [T] (informal) **1** to hit someone hard **2** to affect someone or something badly, especially by making him, her, or it lose money: *Their new business was clobbered by rising interest rates.* **3** to defeat someone easily: *Boston clobbered New York 11–1.*

> THESAURUS **beat, defeat, trounce, cream, vanquish, overcome** → BEAT¹

clock¹ /klɑk/ *n.* [C] **1** an instrument in a room or building that shows the time → WATCH: *What **time** does that **clock say**?* | *The **clock** had **stopped**.* | *The **clock struck** three* (=made three loud noises to show it was three o'clock). | *Mary **set** her **alarm clock** for 7:00 a.m.* (=adjusted it so that it would ring at 7:00 a.m.) | *The kitchen **clock is** five minutes **slow/fast*** (=shows a time that is five minutes less or more than the right time). **2 turn/set the clock back** (disapproving) to make a situation the same as it was in the past: *Women's groups warned that the law would turn the clock back fifty years.* **3 set the clock(s) back/ahead/forward** to change the time shown on the clock to one hour earlier or later, when the time officially changes **4 around the clock** all day and all night without stopping: *We've been **working around the clock** to get done on time.* **5 race/work against the clock** to work quickly in order to finish something because you do not have much time: *"The harvest is a race against the clock to beat the winter rains," Johnson says.* [ORIGIN: 1300—1400 Middle Dutch *clocke* "bell, clock," from Medieval Latin *clocca* "bell"] → O'CLOCK, **punch a clock** *at* PUNCH¹, **watch the clock** *at* WATCH¹

clock² *v.* [T] **1** to measure the speed at which someone or something is moving: *The police clocked her at 86 miles per hour.* **2** to travel a particular distance in a particular time: *She clocked her best time in the 200-meter sprint.*

clock in/out *phr. v.* to record on a special card the time when you begin or stop working: *I clocked in at 8:00 this morning.*

,clock 'radio *n.* [C] a clock that you can set so that it turns on a radio to wake you up

clock·wise /ˈklɑk-waɪz/ *adj., adv.* in the same direction in which the HANDS (=parts that point to the time) of a clock move ANT **counterclockwise**: *Turn the dial clockwise.*

clock·work /ˈklɑk-wɚk/ *n.* **like clockwork a)** (informal) happening in exactly the way you planned: *Fortunately, production has been **going like clockwork**.* **b)** happening at the same time and in the same way every time: *At 6:30 every evening, like clockwork, Ari would milk the cows.*

clod /klɑd/ *n.* [C] **1** a lump of mud or earth **2** (informal) someone who is not graceful and behaves in a stupid way

clog¹ /klɑg/ *v.* (**clogged**, **clogging**) [I,T] *also* **clog up** to block something, or to become blocked: *Potato peelings **clogged up** the drain.* | *freeways **clogged with** heavy traffic*

clog² *n.* [C] a shoe made of wood → *see picture at* SHOE¹

clone¹ /kloʊn/ *n.* [C] **1** BIOLOGY an exact copy of a plant or animal that scientists produce from one of its cells **2** IT a computer that is built as an exact copy of a more famous computer: *an IBM clone* [ORIGIN: 1900—2000 Greek *klon* "small branch"]

clone² *v.* [T] BIOLOGY to produce a plant or an animal that is a clone

close¹ /kloʊz/ *v.* [I,T] **1** to shut something, or to become shut SYN **shut** ANT **open**: *Rita walked over and closed the curtains.* | *The hinges creaked slightly as the door closed.* | ***Close** your **eyes** and go to sleep.*

> **USAGE**
>
> Do not use **open** and **close** to talk about things that use electricity or things that provide water or gas. Use **turn on/off** instead: *Can you turn off the lights?* | *I turned on the TV.*
>
> For things that use electricity, you can also use **switch on/off**: *Don't forget to switch off your computer.*

2 if a store or building closes, or if someone closes it, it stops being open to the public for a period of time: *What time does the mall close tonight?* | *Prentice Street has been **closed to** traffic.* **3** to end something, or to end: *Professor Schmidt **closed** his speech **with** a quote from Twain.* **4** to stop existing or operating, or to stop something from existing or operating: *Hundreds of lumber mills have **closed down** since World War II.* | *I've closed my bank account.* **5 close a deal/sale/contract** to successfully arrange a business deal, sale, etc. [ORIGIN: 1200—1300 Old French *clos*, past participle of *clore* "to close," from Latin *claudere*]

close in *phr. v.* to move closer in order to catch someone or something: *a tiger closing in for the kill*

close sth ↔ **off** *phr. v.* if a road or area is closed off, people cannot go into it

close² /kloʊs/ *adj.*

1 NEAR STH not far from someone or something: *The closest gas station is 20 miles away.* | *We live **close to** the school.* | *The victim was shot **at close range*** (=from a short distance).

2 NEAR IN TIME near to something in time: *By the time we left it was **close to** midnight.*

3 NEAR TO A NUMBER/AMOUNT near to a number: *Inflation is now **close to** 6%.*

4 LIKELY TO HAPPEN SOON if you are close to something, you are likely to experience it soon: *They haven't reached an agreement yet, but they're close.* | *Erickson was **close to tears** as he described the accident.* | *A few of the injured people were **close to death**.*

5 SIMILAR very similar to each other: *Do you have any shoes that are **closer** in color **to** this scarf?* | *A dirt road was **the closest thing to** a highway in the area.*

6 CAREFUL giving careful attention to details: ***Take a closer look** at the facts.* | *Scientists are **keeping a close watch/eye on** the volcano.* | *The jury **paid** very **close attention to** the evidence.*

7 LIKE/LOVE SB if people are close, they like or love each other very much: *Are you very **close to** your sister?* | *We were **close friends** in high school.*

8 AT WORK relating to a situation in which people work or talk well together: *The school encourages close partnerships between teachers and parents.* | *Our job required **close contact** with the general manager.*

9 COMPETITION a close competition or game is won or lost by only a few points: *Right now it's **too close to call*** (=no one can say who the winner will be).

10 ALMOST BAD (informal) used when you just manage to avoid something bad happening: ***That was close!** You almost hit that car!* | *I had a couple of **close calls**, but they weren't my fault.*

11 too close for comfort if something bad is too close for comfort, it is near you or happens near to you, making you feel nervous or afraid: *The terrible storm was too close for comfort.*

12 close relative a family member such as a parent, brother, or sister —**closeness** *n.* [U]

close³ /kloʊs/ *adv.* **1** very near: *The grocery store is **close by**.* | *You're planting your tomatoes too **close together**.* | *Dockery walked out of the* *room, with Shane following* ***close behind.*** | *The woman* ***held*** *her baby* ***close.***

THESAURUS near, not far (away), nearby, within walking distance (of sth) → NEAR¹

2 come close to (doing) sth to almost do something: *I was so angry I came close to hitting him.* | *Carey came very close to victory.* **3 close up/up close** from only a short distance away: *When I saw her close up, I realized she wasn't Jane.*

close⁴ /klouz/ *n.* [singular] the end of an activity or period of time: *The police* ***brought*** *the investigation* ***to a close.*** | *The summer was* ***drawing to a close.***

closed /klouzd/ *adj.* **1** not open (SYN) **shut**: *Make sure all the windows are closed.* **2** if a store or public building is closed, it is not open and people cannot go into it or use it (SYN) **shut**: *Sorry, the store's closed on Sundays.* **3** restricted to a particular group of people or things (ANT) **open**: *a closed meeting between the mayor and community leaders* **4** not willing to accept new ideas or influences (ANT) **open**: *Don't go with a* ***closed mind.*** **5 behind closed doors** privately, without involving other people: *The deal was made behind closed doors.*

ˌclosed ˌcircuit 'television *n.* [C,U] cameras which are used in public places in order to help prevent crime

ˌclosed 'circulatory ˌsystem *n.* [C] BIOLOGY a system in which blood flows around the body contained in blood VESSELS, without directly flowing over the surrounding TISSUES

close-knit /ˌklous 'nɪt◂ / *adj.* a close-knit family or group of people know each other well and help each other a lot

close·ly /'klousli/ *adv.* **1** very carefully: *The police were* ***watching*** *him* ***closely.*** | *a* ***closely guarded*** *secret* **2** if you work closely with someone, you work with and help him/her **3 closely related/linked/tied etc.** having a strong connection: *Diet and health are closely connected.* **4** in a way that is close to other things in time or space: *a flash of lightning,* ***followed closely*** *by thunder*

close-set /ˌklous 'sɛt◂ / *adj.* close-set eyes are very near to each other

clos·et¹ /'klɑzɪt/ *n.* [C] **1** an area that you keep clothes and other things in, built with a door behind the wall of a room: *Let me hang your coat up in the closet.* **2 come out of the closet** (informal) to say openly and publicly that you are HOMOSEXUAL after keeping it a secret

closet² *adj.* **closet liberal/homosexual etc.** someone who does not admit in public what s/he thinks or does in private

close-up /'klous ʌp/ *n.* [C] a photograph of someone or something that is taken from very near to him, her, or it: *a* ***close-up of*** *the children*

clo·sure /'klouʒɚ/ *n.* [C,U] **1** the act of permanently closing a building, factory, school, etc.: *Several military bases are* ***threatened with closure.*** **2** an occasion in which a bad situation has ended and you can finally stop thinking about it: *Funerals help give people a sense of closure.*

clot¹ /klɑt/ *n.* [C] a mass of blood or another liquid which has become almost solid: *a* ***blood clot*** *in his leg*

clot² *v.* (**clotted**, **clotting**) [I,T] if a liquid such as blood clots, or if something clots it, it becomes thicker and more solid

cloth /klɔθ/ *n.* **1** [U] material used for making things such as clothes → FABRIC: *These pants are made with the finest wool cloth.*

USAGE

Do not use **cloth** or **cloths** to mean "things that you wear." Use **clothes**: *He usually wears casual clothes.*

2 [C] a piece of cloth used for a particular purpose: *Cover the bowl with a damp cloth.* [ORIGIN: Old English *clath* "cloth, piece of clothing"]

clothe /klouð/ *v.* [T] to provide clothes for someone: *He could barely afford to feed and clothe his family.*

clothed /klouðd/ *adj.* (formal) dressed: *The kids were fast asleep, still* ***fully clothed.***

clothes /klouz, klouðz/ *n.* [plural] the things that people wear to cover their bodies or keep warm: *Go to your room and* ***put on*** *some clean* ***clothes.*** | *Pete* ***took*** *his* ***clothes off*** *and went to bed.* | *What sort of* ***clothes*** *was he* ***wearing?*** | *The kids ran upstairs to* ***change into*** *dry* ***clothes.*** → *see picture on page 182*

COLLOCATIONS

tight: *tight jeans*
loose/baggy: *a baggy T-shirt*
fashionable/stylish: *fashionable clothes*
casual – comfortable and informal: *a casual top*
formal – appropriate for an official or serious situation: *Everyone was dressed in formal wear.*
dressy – fairly formal and appropriate for wearing to work: *a pair of dressy pants* → CLOTH

TOPIC

You **look at clothes** in a store and then **try** them **on**. You want to be sure that they **fit** you (=are the right size for you), and also that they **look good on** you. At home, you **fold** them and put them in a drawer, or you **hang** them **up** in a **closet**. If clothes are **wrinkled** (=have lines in the material), you can **iron** them.

GRAMMAR

There is no singular form of **clothes**. You have to say **a piece of clothing**, **an article of clothing** *(formal)*, or **an item of clothing** *(formal)*: *They found a piece of clothing in the bushes.*

clothes·line /ˈklouzlaɪn/ *n.* [C] a rope that you hang clothes on so that they will dry

clothes·pin /ˈklouzpɪn/ *n.* [C] a small object that you use to fasten clothes to a clothesline

cloth·ing /ˈklouðɪŋ/ *n.* [U] clothes: *The refugees needed* ***food and clothing.*** | ***Protective clothing*** *should be worn in the lab.*

cloud[1] /klaud/ *n.* **1** [C,U] a white or gray mass in the sky, from which rain falls: *There wasn't a cloud in the sky.* | ***Storm/Dark clouds*** *moved overhead.* **2** [C] a mass of smoke, dust, or gas: *a* ***cloud of dust*** **3** [C] something that makes you feel worried or afraid: *Ryder resigned* ***under a cloud of*** *suspicion.* | *Marshall's injury* ***cast a cloud over*** *the rest of the game.* **4 on cloud nine** (informal) very happy: *When Caitlin was born, Adam was on cloud nine.* [ORIGIN: Old English *clud* "rock, hill;" because some clouds look like rocks]

cloud[2] *v.* **1** [T] to make something more difficult to understand or deal with: *These unnecessary details are only* ***clouding*** *the* ***issue.*** | *Don't allow personal feelings to* ***cloud*** *your* ***judgment.*** **2** [I,T] *also* **cloud up** to become difficult to see through, or to make this happen: *Steam clouded up the windows.*

cloud over *phr. v.* if the sky clouds over, it becomes darker and full of clouds

cloud·burst /ˈklaudbɚst/ *n.* [C] a sudden storm of rain

cloud·y /ˈklaudi/ *adj.* **1** dark and full of clouds: *a cloudy day* **2** cloudy liquids are not clear

clout /klaut/ *n.* [U] (informal) power or the ability to influence important people: *He has a lot of* ***political/economic/financial etc. clout*** *in this town.*

clove[1] /klouv/ *n.* [C] **1** a piece of GARLIC: *a* ***clove of garlic*** **2** a strong sweet spice with a pointed stem

clove[2] *v.* a past tense of CLEAVE

cloven /ˈklouvən/ *v.* a past participle of CLEAVE

clo·ver /ˈklouvɚ/ *n.* [C] a small plant with three round leaves on each stem

clown[1] /klaun/ *n.* [C] a performer who wears MAKEUP and funny clothes and tries to make people laugh, especially in a CIRCUS

clown[2] *v.* [I] to behave in a silly or funny way: *a couple of boys* ***clowning around***

cloy·ing /ˈklɔɪ-ɪŋ/ *adj.* **1** a cloying attitude or

clothes

quality annoys you because it is too nice and seems false: *a cloying poem about love* **2** cloying food or smells are too sweet and make you feel sick: *the cloying smell of cheap perfume*

club¹ /klʌb/ *n.* [C] **1** an organization for people who share an interest or who enjoy similar activities: *a **member of** the drama **club** | I just **joined a** health **club**. | He **belongs to** the chess **club**.*

> THESAURUS **organization, institution, institute, association, (political) party, society, union, agency** ➔ ORGANIZATION

2 a NIGHTCLUB **3** the building used by a club: *The restaurant is located next to the fitness club.* **4** a specially shaped stick for hitting the ball in golf (SYN) **golf club** **5 clubs** [plural] in card games, the cards with black symbols with three round parts: *the five of clubs* ➔ *see picture at* PLAYING CARD **6** a heavy stick used as a weapon

club² *v.* (**clubbed, clubbing**) [T] to hit someone with a club

club·house /ˈklʌbhaʊs/ *n.* [C] a building used by a club, especially a sports club

ˌclub ˈsandwich *n.* [C] a sandwich consisting of three pieces of bread with meat and cheese between them

ˌclub ˈsoda *n.* [C,U] water filled with BUBBLES that is often mixed with other drinks

cluck /klʌk/ *v.* [I] to make a noise like a HEN —**cluck** *n.* [C]

clue¹ /klu/ *n.* [C] **1** a piece of information or an object that helps to solve a crime or mystery: *The police are still **searching for clues**. | No one seems to **have a clue as to** the bomber's identity.* **2 not have a clue** (informal) to definitely not know or understand something: *I don't have a clue what you're talking about. | "Where's Jamie?" "I don't have a clue."* [ORIGIN: 1500—1600 *clew* "ball of string" (11—19 centuries), from Old English *cliewen*; from the use of a ball of string for finding the way out of a network of passages]

clue²

clue sb ↔ **in** *phr. v.* (informal) to give someone information about something: *He **clued** me **in on** how the washing machine works.*

clue·less /ˈklulɪs/ *adj.* (disapproving) having no understanding or knowledge of something: *Jason is clueless when it comes to women.*

clump¹ /klʌmp/ *n.* [C] a group of trees or plants growing together

clump² *v.* [I] to walk with slow noisy steps: *I could hear Grandpa **clumping around** in the basement.*

clum·sy /ˈklʌmzi/ *adj.* **1** moving in an awkward way and tending to knock things over: *She was clumsy and shy.*

> THESAURUS
> **awkward** – moving or behaving in a way that does not seem relaxed or comfortable: *an awkward hug*
> **gawky** – awkward in the way you move: *a gawky teenager*
> **inelegant** (formal) – not graceful or well done: *She was sprawled in an inelegant pose.*
> **klutzy** (informal) – often dropping things or falling easily: *I've always been a little klutzy.*

2 a clumsy object is large, heavy, and difficult to use **3** if you say or do something in a clumsy way, you do it in a careless way, without considering other people's feelings: *a clumsy attempt to apologize* —**clumsily** *adv.* —**clumsiness** *n.* [U]

C

clung /klʌŋ/ *v.* the past tense and past participle of CLING

clunk /klʌŋk/ *v.* [I,T] to make the loud sound of two heavy objects hitting each other —**clunk** *n.* [C]

clunk·er /ˈklʌŋkɚ/ *n.* [C] (informal) **1** an old car or other machine that does not work very well **2** something that is completely unsuccessful because people think it is bad or stupid

clus·ter¹ /ˈklʌstɚ/ *n.* [C] a group of things that are close together: *a **cluster of** grapes*

cluster² *v.* [I,T] to form a group of people or things: *The tulips were **clustered around** the fence.*

clutch¹ /klʌtʃ/ *v.* [T] to hold something tightly: *Jamie stood there, clutching her purse.*

> THESAURUS **hold, grip, catch/take/keep/get (a) hold of sth, grasp, clasp, grab (hold of sth)/seize** ➔ HOLD¹

➔ **be grasping/clutching at straws** *at* STRAW

clutch² *n.* **1** [C] the part of a car that you press with your foot to change GEARS **2 sb's clutches** if you are in someone's clutches, s/he controls you **3 in the clutch** (informal) in an important or difficult situation

clut·ter¹ /ˈklʌt̬ɚ/ *v.* [T] to make something messy by covering or filling it with things: *His desk is always **cluttered with** paper.*

clutter² *n.* [U] a lot of things scattered in a messy way

cm the written abbreviation of CENTIMETER

CNN *n.* **Cable News Network** an organization that broadcasts television news programs all over the world

CO the written abbreviation of COLORADO

Co. /koʊ/ **1** the written abbreviation of COMPANY: *E.F. Hutton & Co.* **2** the written abbreviation of COUNTY

c/o /ˌsi ˈoʊ◂ / the written abbreviation of **in care of**, used when you are sending a letter for someone to another person who will keep it for him/her: *Send the letter to me c/o Anne Miller, 8 Brown St., Peoria, IL*

C.O.D. *adv.* **cash on delivery** a system in which you pay for something when it is delivered: *Send the equipment C.O.D.*

coach¹ /koʊtʃ/ *n.* **1** [C] someone who trains a

person or team in a sport: *a basketball/football, etc. coach*

THESAURUS teacher, professor, lecturer, instructor → TEACHER

2 [U] the cheapest type of seats on an airplane or a train: *We **flew coach** to Seattle.* **3** [C] someone who gives private lessons in singing, acting, etc. [ORIGIN: 1500—1600 French *coche*, from German *kutsche*]

C

coach² *v.* [I,T] **1** to train a person or team in a sport: *He coaches our tennis team.* **2** to give someone private lessons in singing, acting, etc.

co·ag·u·late /koʊˈægyəˌleɪt/ *v.* [I,T] to change from a liquid into a thicker substance or a solid: *Blood had coagulated around the wound.* —**coagulation** /koʊˌægyəˈleɪʃən/ *n.* [U]

coal /koʊl/ *n.* **1** [U] EARTH SCIENCES a black mineral that is dug from the earth and is burned for heat: *a lump of coal | coal miners* **2 coals** [plural] pieces of coal that are burning [ORIGIN: Old English *col*] → CHARCOAL, **rake sb over the coals** *at* RAKE²

co·a·lesce /ˌkoʊəˈlɛs/ *v.* [I] (formal) to combine or grow together to form one single group

co·a·li·tion /ˌkoʊəˈlɪʃən/ *n.* [C] a union of separate political parties or people for a special purpose, usually for a short time: *a new **coalition government** in Japan | The two parties have decided to **form a coalition**.*

coarse /kɔrs/ *adj.* **1** rough and thick, not smooth or fine: *a coarse cloth* **2** rude and offensive: *coarse language* —**coarsely** *adv.* —**coarseness** *n.* [U]

coast¹ /koʊst/ *n.* [C] **1** EARTH SCIENCES the land next to the ocean: *the Pacific coast | the west **coast of** Mexico | an island **off the coast*** (=in the water near the land) *of California | a small beach house **on the coast***

THESAURUS shore, beach, seashore, bank → SHORE¹

2 the coast is clear (informal) if the coast is clear, it is safe for you to do something without being seen or caught: *Let's leave now while the coast is clear!* [ORIGIN: 1300—1400 Old French *coste*, from Latin *costa* "rib, side"] —**coastal** *adj.*

coast² *v.* [I] **1** to continue to move forward in a car without using the engine, or on a bicycle without turning the PEDALS **2** to succeed without using any effort: *Wilson **coasted to** victory in the election.*

coast·er /ˈkoʊstɚ/ *n.* [C] a small round object you put under a glass, bottle, etc. to protect a table

ˈcoast guard *n.* **the Coast Guard** the military organization whose job is to watch for ships in danger and prevent illegal activity in the ocean

coast·line /ˈkoʊstlaɪn/ *n.* [C,U] EARTH SCIENCES the land on the edge of the coast: *the California coastline* → *see picture on page A24*

coat¹ /koʊt/ *n.* [C] **1** a piece of clothing that you wear over other clothes to keep you warm when you go outside: ***Put** your **coat on**, it's cold outside! | He **took off** his **coat** and dropped it on the bed.* → *see picture at* CLOTHES **2** a jacket that you wear as part of a suit **3** a thin layer of something that covers a surface: *a **coat of** paint* **4** an animal's fur: *a dog with a black and brown coat* **5** a light piece of clothing that a doctor, etc. wears over other clothes: *a lab coat* [ORIGIN: 1300—1400 Old French *cote*]

coat² *v.* [T] to cover a surface with a layer of something: *The books were thickly **coated with** dust.*

ˈcoat ˌhanger *n.* [C] a HANGER

coax /koʊks/ *v.* [T] to persuade someone to do something by talking gently and kindly: *See if you can **coax** him **into** giving us a ride home. | Firefighters **coaxed** the man **down**.*

THESAURUS persuade, talk sb into sth, get sb to do sth, encourage sb to do sth, influence, convince, cajole, prevail on/upon sb → PERSUADE

cob /kɑb/ *n.* [C] the long hard middle part of the corn plant: *corn on the cob*

co·balt /ˈkoʊbɔlt/ *n.* [U] CHEMISTRY (*symbol* **Co**) a shiny silver-white metal that is a chemical ELEMENT

cob·bled /ˈkɑbəld/ *adj.* covered with round flat stones: *a cobbled street*

cob·bler /ˈkɑblɚ/ *n.* **1** [C,U] cooked fruit covered with a sweet bread-like mixture: *peach cobbler* **2** [C] (old-fashioned) someone who makes or repairs shoes

cob·ble·stone /ˈkɑbəlˌstoʊn/ *n.* [C] a small round stone set in the ground, especially in past times, to make a hard surface for a road

co·bra /ˈkoʊbrə/ *n.* [C] an African or Asian poisonous snake [ORIGIN: 1800—1900 Portuguese *cobra (de capello)* "snake with a hood," from Latin *colubra* "snake"]

cob·web /ˈkɑbwɛb/ *n.* [C] a very fine structure of sticky threads made by a SPIDER

Co·ca-Co·la /ˌkoʊkə ˈkoʊlə/ *n.* [C,U] (trademark) a sweet brown SOFT DRINK, or a glass of this drink (SYN) **Coke**

co·caine /koʊˈkeɪn, ˈkoʊkeɪn/ *n.* [U] an illegal drug, usually in the form of a white powder

coch·le·a /ˈkɑkliə/ *n.* (plural **cochleas** *or* **cochleae** /-li-i/) [C] BIOLOGY a part of the inner ear that is shaped like a SPIRAL, and that has small hair-like cells that help you to hear

cock¹ *v.* [T] **1** to raise or move part of your head or face: *Jeremy **cocked** his **head** to one side and smiled.* **2** to pull back the part of a gun that hits the back of a bullet, so that you are ready to shoot

cock² /kɑk/ *n.* [C] (old-fashioned) a ROOSTER

cock-a-doo·dle-doo /ˌkɑk ə ˌdudl ˈdu/ *n.* [C] the loud sound make by a ROOSTER

cock·eyed /ˈkɑkaɪd/ *adj.* (informal) **1** not sensible or practical: *a cockeyed idea* **2** not straight or level: *His hat was on cockeyed.*

cock·pit /ˈkɑkˌpɪt/ *n.* [C] the part of an airplane or racing car where the pilot or driver sits → *see picture at* AIRPLANE

cock·roach /ˈkɑk-roʊtʃ/ *n.* [C] a large insect that often lives where food is kept [ORIGIN: 1600—1700 Spanish *cucaracha*, from *cuca* "caterpillar"]

cock·tail /ˈkɑkteɪl/ *n.* [C] **1** an alcoholic drink made from a mixture of different drinks **2** a dish of small pieces of food, usually eaten at the start of a meal: *a shrimp cocktail* | *fruit cocktail*

ˈcocktail ˌlounge *n.* [C] a public room in a hotel, restaurant, etc., where people can buy alcoholic drinks

ˈcocktail ˌparty *n.* [C] a formal party where alcoholic drinks are served

cock·y /ˈkɑki/ *adj.* (informal) too confident, in a way which people do not like: *Howitt was young and cocky.* —**cockiness** *n.* [U]

co·coa /ˈkoʊkoʊ/ *n.* [U] **1** a dark brown powder that tastes like chocolate and is used in cooking **2** a hot chocolate drink: *a cup of cocoa*

co·co·nut /ˈkoʊkəˌnʌt/ *n.* [C,U] a very large brown nut which is white inside and has liquid in the middle [ORIGIN: 1600—1700 *coco* "coconut" (16—18 centuries) (from Portuguese, "grinning face;" because the bottom of a coconut, with its three spots, looks like a face) + *nut*] → *see picture on page 414*

co·coon /kəˈkun/ *n.* [C] **1** BIOLOGY a silk cover that some insects make to protect themselves while they are growing **2** a place or situation in which you feel comfortable and safe: *the comfortable **cocoon of** college life* —**cocoon** *v.* [T]

cod /kɑd/ *n.* (plural **cod**) [C,U] a large ocean fish that you can eat, or the meat from this fish

co·da /ˈkoʊdə/ *n.* [C] **1** ENG. LANG. ARTS an additional part at the end of a piece of music, that is considered separate from the main piece **2** ENG. LANG. ARTS a separate piece of writing at the end of a work of literature or a speech

code[1] /koʊd/ (Ac) *n.* **1** [C] a set of rules, laws, or principles that tells people how to behave: *the company's employee **code of conduct*** | *The school has a **dress code*** (=rules about what to wear). | *Their religious beliefs are the basis for their strong **moral code**.*

> THESAURUS rule, law, regulation, restriction, guidelines, statute, precept → RULE[1]

2 [C,U] a system of words, letters, or symbols used instead of ordinary writing to keep something secret: *Important reports were sent **in code**.* | *Agents spent years trying to **break/crack** the enemy's **code**.* **3** [C] a set of numbers, letters, or symbols that give you information about something: *Goods that you order must have a product code.* [ORIGIN: 1500—1600 French, Latin *codex* "main part of a tree, piece of wood for writing on, book"] → AREA CODE, BAR CODE, ZIP CODE

code[2] *v.* [T] to put a message into code —**coded** *adj.*: *He sent a coded message to CIA headquarters.*

cod·i·fy /ˈkɑdəˌfaɪ, ˈkoʊ-/ *v.* (**codified**, **codifies**) [T] LAW to arrange laws, principles, facts, etc. in a system: *The agreement must still be codified by federal legislation.* —**codification** /ˌkɑdəfəˈkeɪʃən, ˌkoʊ-/ *n* [C,U]

co·dom·i·nance /koʊˈdɑmənəns/ *n.* [U] BIOLOGY a situation in which both ALLELES (=pair of GENES) are present to an equal degree on a CHROMOSOME, and both have an equal influence on a person's or animal's physical appearance and the type of blood they have —**codominant** *adj.*

co-ed /koʊ ˈɛd/ *adj.* using a system in which students of both sexes study or live together: *co-ed dormitories*

co·ef·fi·cient /ˌkoʊəˈfɪʃənt/ *n.* [C] MATH the number that does not change in a mathematical expression that has a VARIABLE: *In 8x, the coefficient of x is 8.*

co·en·zyme /koʊˈɛnzaɪm/ *n.* [C] BIOLOGY a substance, often a VITAMIN or a mineral, that forms part of an ENZYME, and that must combine with a PROTEIN to make the enzyme work

co·erce /koʊˈɚs/ *v.* [T] (formal) to force someone to do something by threatening him/her: *The women were **coerced into** hiding the drugs.* —**coercion** /koʊˈɚʃən, -ʒən/ *n.* [U]: *torture and other extreme forms of coercion*

> THESAURUS force, make, compel, impel, pressure → FORCE[2]

co·ex·ist /ˌkoʊɪgˈzɪst/ *v.* [I] to exist together: *Can the two countries coexist after the war?* —**coexistence** *n.* [U]

cof·fee /ˈkɔfi, ˈkɑ-/ *n.* **1** [U] a hot dark brown drink that has a slightly bitter taste: *a **cup of coffee*** **2** [C] a cup of this drink: *Two **black coffees*** (=coffee with no milk added), *please.* **3** [U] whole coffee beans, crushed coffee beans, or a powder from which you make coffee: *a pound of coffee* | ***instant coffee*** (=powdered coffee) [ORIGIN: 1500—1600 Italian *caffè*, from Turkish *kahve*, from Arabic *qahwa*]

ˈcoffee cake *n.* [C,U] a sweet heavy cake, usually eaten along with coffee

ˈcoffee house *n.* [C] a small restaurant where people go to talk and drink coffee

ˈcoffee maˌchine *n.* [C] a machine that gives you a cup of coffee, tea, etc. when you put money in it

cof·fee·mak·er /ˈkɔfiˌmeɪkɚ, ˈkɑ-/ *n.* [C] an electric machine that makes a pot of coffee

'coffee shop *n.* [C] a small restaurant that serves cheap meals

'coffee ˌtable *n.* [C] a low table in a LIVING ROOM

cof·fers /'kɔfɚz, 'kɑ-/ *n.* [plural] the money that an organization has: *The tax would add an estimated $500,000 to the city's coffers.*

cof·fin /'kɔfɪn/ *n.* [C] the box in which a dead person is buried [ORIGIN: 1300—1400 Old French *cophin*, from Latin *cophinus* "basket"]

C

cog /kɑg/ *n.* [C] **1** a wheel in a machine, with small parts on its edge that fit together with the parts of another wheel as they turn **2 a cog in the machine/wheel** an unimportant worker in a large organization

co·gent /'koʊdʒənt/ *adj.* (formal) if a reason, argument, etc. is cogent, it seems reasonable and correct

co·gnac /'kɑnyæk, 'kɔn-, 'koʊn-/ *n.* [C,U] a type of BRANDY (=strong alcoholic drink) from France, or a glass of this drink

cog·ni·zant /'kɑgnəzənt/ *adj.* (formal) **cognizant of sth** having knowledge or information about something: *The social worker was* ***cognizant of the fact that*** *the boy's father was abusive.*

co·hab·it /ˌkoʊ'hæbɪt/ *v.* [I] (formal) to live as husband and wife, without being married —**cohabitation** /koʊˌhæbə'teɪʃən/ *n.* [U]

co·her·ence /koʊ'hɪrəns/ (Ac) *n.* [U] **1** ENG. LANG. ARTS the quality of having ideas or parts that relate to each other in a way that is clear, reasonable, and easy to understand, especially in a piece of writing: *Writing down your central idea will help give your arguments coherence.* **2** the quality that a group has when its members are connected or united because they share common aims, qualities, or beliefs

co·her·ent /koʊ'hɪrənt/ (Ac) *adj.* clear and easy to understand (ANT) **incoherent**: *He was slightly drunk, and not very coherent.* | *The article makes a coherent argument in favor of economic change.* | *Your manager should set coherent objectives.* —**coherently** *adv.*

co·he·sion /koʊ'hiʒən/ *n.* [U] **1** the ability to fit together or stay together well: *social cohesion* **2** ENG. LANG. ARTS the way in which different parts of sentences or different parts of larger pieces of writing are connected, based on grammar or meaning **3** PHYSICS a physical force that holds together MOLECULEs in a solid or liquid substance

coil¹ /kɔɪl/ *also* **coil up** *v.* [I,T] to wind or twist into a round shape, or to make something do this: *Dad coiled up the hose.* | *The snake coiled around the branch.*

coil² *n.* [C] a piece of wire or rope that has been wound into a circular shape

coil

a coil of rope

coin¹ /kɔɪn/ *n.* [C] **1** a round piece of money made of metal → BILL: *Uncle Henry collects foreign coins.*

THESAURUS **money, bill, penny, nickel, dime, quarter, cash, change, currency** → MONEY

2 toss/flip a coin to choose or decide something by throwing a coin into the air and guessing which side will show when it falls **3 the other side of the coin** a different fact or way of thinking about something [ORIGIN: 1300—1400 Old French "three-sided piece, corner," from Latin *cuneus* "wedge"]

coin² *v.* [T] to invent a new word or phrase that many people start to use: *Who coined the word "cyberpunk"?*

coin·age /'kɔɪnɪdʒ/ *n.* **1** [C] ENG. LANG. ARTS a word or phrase that has been recently invented **2** [U] ENG. LANG. ARTS the use or making of new words or phrases **3** [U] the system of money used in a country

co·in·cide /ˌkoʊɪn'saɪd/ (Ac) *v.* [I] to happen at the same time as something else: *Their wedding anniversary* ***coincides with*** *Thanksgiving.*

co·in·ci·dence /koʊ'ɪnsədəns/ (Ac) *n.* [C,U] a situation in which two things happen together by chance, in a surprising way: ***By coincidence****, my husband and my father went to the same high school.* | *It's* ***no coincidence that*** *veterans are more likely to smoke than other people.* | *By* ***sheer/pure coincidence****, he was seated next to his ex-wife.* —**coincidental** /koʊˌɪnsə'dɛntl/ *adj.*: *The link between the two events could be merely coincidental.* —**coincidentally** *adv.*

coke /koʊk/ *n.* **1 Coke** [C,U] (trademark) the drink COCA-COLA, or a bottle, can, or glass of this drink **2** [U] (informal) COCAINE

co·la /'koʊlə/ *n.* [C,U] a sweet brown SOFT DRINK, or a bottle, can, or glass of this drink

col·an·der /'kɑləndɚ, 'kʌ-/ *n.* [C] a metal or plastic bowl with a lot of small holes in the bottom and sides, used for separating liquid from food

cold¹ /koʊld/ *adj.* **1** having a low temperature: *a cold winter morning* | *It was* ***freezing cold*** (=very cold) *in the car.* | *Let's go inside – I'm cold.* | ***bitterly cold*** *weather* | *Your coffee's* ***getting cold*** (=becoming cold). → ICE-COLD

THESAURUS

cool – cold in a pleasant way, especially after it has been hot: *It's very hot during the day, but cooler at night.*
chilly – cold, but not very cold: *a chilly fall day*
frosty – very cold, with the ground covered in frost (=ice that is white and powdery): *a bright frosty morning*
freezing (cold) – extremely cold, so that water outside becomes ice: *It was freezing cold last night.*
icy (cold) – extremely cold: *an icy wind*

bitter (cold) – very cold in a way that feels very unpleasant: *The bitter wind seemed to go right through us.*
frigid (formal) – very cold: *I stepped out into the frigid darkness of a December night.* → HOT[1], WEATHER[1]

2 cold food has been cooked, but is not eaten while it is warm: *cold chicken* **3** without friendly feelings: *a polite but cold greeting*

THESAURUS **matter-of-fact, detached, impassive, dispassionate** → MATTER-OF-FACT

4 leave sb cold (informal) to not interest someone at all: *Ballet just leaves me cold.* **5 get/have cold feet** (informal) to suddenly feel that you are not brave enough to do something: *She was getting cold feet about getting married.* **6 cold snap** a sudden short period of very cold weather **7 give sb the cold shoulder** to deliberately ignore someone or be unfriendly to him/her **8 in cold blood** in a cruel and deliberate way: *They shot him in cold blood.* [ORIGIN: Old English *ceald, cald*] —**coldness** *n.* [U]

cold[2] *n.* **1** [C] a common illness that makes it difficult to breathe through your nose: *You sound like you **have a cold**. | Did you **catch a cold** (=get a cold)?* **2 the cold** a low temperature or cold weather: *Don't go out in the cold without your coat.*

cold[3] *adv.* **1** suddenly and completely: *In the middle of his speech, he stopped cold.* **2 out cold** (informal) unconscious, especially because of being hit on the head

ˌcold-ˈblooded *adj.* **1** cruel and showing no feelings: *a **cold-blooded killer*** **2** BIOLOGY a cold-blooded animal, such as a snake, has a body temperature that changes with the air or ground around it → WARM-BLOODED

ˈcold cuts *n.* [plural] thin pieces of different kinds of cooked meat eaten cold

ˌcold-ˈhearted *adj.* without sympathy or pity: *a cold-hearted man*

cold·ly /ˈkoʊldli/ *adv.* in an unfriendly way: *"I'm busy," said Sarah coldly.*

ˈcold sore *n.* [C] a painful spot on the inside or outside of your mouth that you sometimes get when you are sick

ˌcold ˈturkey *n.* **go cold turkey** (informal) to suddenly stop taking a drug that you are ADDICTED to, and to feel sick because of this: *The only way to quit smoking is to go cold turkey.*

ˌcold ˈwar *n.* [C] **1** POLITICS an unfriendly political relationship between two countries that do not actually fight with each other **2 the Cold War** HISTORY this type of relationship between the U.S. and the Soviet Union, after World War II

cole slaw /ˈkoʊl slɔ/ *n.* [U] a SALAD made with thinly cut raw CABBAGE and CARROTS

col·ic /ˈkɑlɪk/ *n.* [U] pain in the stomach that babies often get

col·lab·o·rate /kəˈlæbəˌreɪt/ *v.* [I] **1** to work together with another person or group in order to achieve or produce something: *The author and illustrator wanted to **collaborate on** a book for children.* **2** to help a country that your country is at war with: *He was accused of **collaborating with** the Nazis.* [ORIGIN: 1800—1900 Late Latin, past participle of *collaborare*, from Latin *com* "with" + *laborare* "to work"] —**collaborator** *n.* [C]

col·lab·o·ra·tion /kəˌlæbəˈreɪʃən/ *n.* [U] **1** the act of working with another person or group in order to achieve or produce something: *Our departments worked **in close collaboration** on the project. | The project has involved **collaboration with** the geography department.* **2** the act of helping an enemy during a war

C

col·lab·o·ra·tive /kəˈlæbrət̮ɪv/ *adj.* **collaborative project/effort/work etc.** a project, effort, etc. that involves two or more people working together to achieve something

col·lage /kəˈlɑʒ, koʊ-/ *n.* **1** [C] a picture made by sticking pictures, photographs, cloth, etc. onto a surface **2** [U] the art of making pictures in this way

col·lapse[1] /kəˈlæps/ (Ac) *v.* [I] **1** to fall down or inward suddenly: *Many buildings collapsed during the earthquake.* **2** to suddenly fall down or become unconscious because you are sick or very weak: *He looked like he was going to collapse.* **3** to fail suddenly and completely: *We sold the property just before the real estate market collapsed.* [ORIGIN: 1700—1800 Latin *collapsus*, past participle of *collabi*, from *com-* + *labi* "to fall, slide"]

collapse[2] *n.* **1** [singular, U] a sudden failure in the way something works, so that it cannot continue: ***the collapse of** communism in Eastern Europe | The industry faces **economic collapse**.* **2** [U] the act of falling down or inward: *Floods caused **the collapse of** the bridge.* **3** [singular, U] an occasion when someone falls down or becomes unconscious because of a sickness

col·laps·i·ble /kəˈlæpsəbəl/ (Ac) *adj.* something that is collapsible can be folded up into a smaller size: *collapsible chairs*

col·lar[1] /ˈkɑlɚ/ *n.* [C] **1** the part of a shirt, coat, dress, etc. that fits around your neck **2 open-collared/fur-collared etc.** having a particular type of collar: *a white-collared shirt* **3** a narrow band of leather or plastic put around the neck of a dog or cat [ORIGIN: 1300—1400 Old French *coler*, from Latin *collare*, from *collum* "neck"]

collar[2] *v.* [T] (informal) to catch and hold someone: *Two policemen collared the suspect near the scene.*

col·lar·bone /ˈkɑlɚˌboʊn/ *n.* [C] one of a pair of bones that go from the base of your neck to your shoulders → *see picture on page A16*

col·late /kəˈleɪt, kɑ-, ˈkoʊleɪt, ˈkɑ-/ *v.* [T] **1** to arrange things such as papers in the right order **2** to gather information together in order to examine it and compare it: *The system allows us to collate data from all over the country.*

col·lat·er·al /kəˈlæt̬ərəl/ *n.* [U] ECONOMICS property or other goods that you promise to give to someone if you cannot pay back a debt: *They* ***put up*** *their house* ***as collateral*** *in order to raise the money.*

col·league /ˈkɑlig/ (Ac) *n.* [C] someone you work with, especially in a profession: *The research was carried out by Dr. Francis and her colleagues at Johns Hopkins University in Baltimore.* [ORIGIN: 1500—1600 French *collègue*, from Latin *collega*, from *com* "with" + *legare* "to choose for a particular job"]

C

col·lect¹ /kəˈlɛkt/ *v.* **1** [T] to get things and bring them together: *I'll collect everyone's tests at the end of class.* **2** [T] to get and keep objects of the same type because you think they are attractive or interesting: *She collects stamps.*

THESAURUS **keep, store, save, reserve, file, hoard** ➔ KEEP¹

3 [I,T] to get money from people: *We're* ***collecting for*** *charity.* | *The landlord was at the door, trying to collect the rent.* **4** [I] to come or gather together: *Dust had collected in the corners of the room.* **5 collect yourself/collect your thoughts** to make yourself calmer and able to think more clearly: *I had a few minutes to collect my thoughts before the meeting began.* [ORIGIN: 1500—1600 Latin, past participle of *colligere*, from *com* "together" + *legere* "to gather"]

collect² *adj., adv.* **1 call sb collect** if you call someone collect, the person who gets the telephone call pays for it **2 collect call** a telephone call that is paid for by the person who gets it

col·lect·ed /kəˈlɛktɪd/ *adj.* **1 collected works/poems/stories etc.** all of the poems, stories, etc. of a particular writer included together in one book: *the collected works of Emily Dickinson* **2** in control of yourself and your thoughts, feelings, etc.: *Jason seemed* ***calm and collected.***

col·lect·i·ble /kəˈlɛktəbəl/ *n.* [C] an object that you keep as part of a group of similar things: *a store that sells antiques and collectibles*

collection

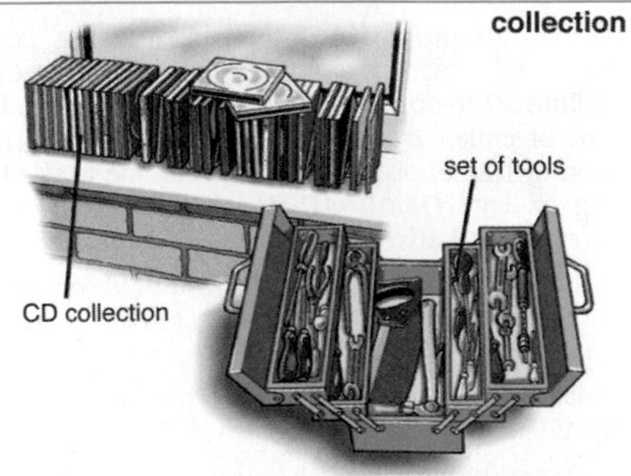

col·lec·tion /kəˈlɛkʃən/ *n.* **1** [C] a set of similar things that you keep or put together: *a coin collection* | *a* ***collection of*** *toy soldiers*

THESAURUS

set – a complete group of similar things that belong together or are related in some way: *a set of keys to the building*
batch – a group of things that are made or dealt with at the same time: *a fresh batch of pancakes*
anthology – a collection of stories, poems, or songs: *an anthology of poems for children*

2 [U] the act of bringing together things of the same type from different places: *different methods of data collection* **3** [C] several stories, poems, pieces of music, etc. that are put together: *a* ***collection of*** *fairy tales* **4** [C,U] the act of taking something away from a place: *Garbage collection is on Fridays.* **5** [C,U] the act of asking people for money: *tax collection* | *We're planning to* ***have a collection*** *for UNICEF*

col·lec·tive¹ /kəˈlɛktɪv/ *adj.* [only before noun] shared or done by all the members of a group together: *We had made a collective decision.* | *collective farms* —**collectively** *adv.*

collective² *n.* [C] a business or farm that is owned and operated by a group of workers who share the profits equally

col,lective 'bargaining *n.* [U] discussions between employers and unions about pay, working conditions, etc.

col,lective ,noun *n.* [C] ENG. LANG. ARTS a noun such as "family" or "committee," that is the name of a group of people or things ➔ COMMON NOUN, PROPER NOUN

col·lec·tor /kəˈlɛktɚ/ *n.* [C] **1** someone whose job is to collect taxes, tickets, debts, etc.: *a tax collector* **2** someone who collects things that are interesting or attractive: *a stamp collector*

col·lege /ˈkɑlɪdʒ/ *n.* **1** [C,U] a large school where you can study after high school ➔ UNIVERSITY: *My oldest son is* ***in college*** (=is a student at a college). | *I'm planning to* ***go to college.*** **2** [C] the part of a university that teaches a particular subject: *the College of Engineering* [ORIGIN: 1300—1400 Old French, Latin *collegium* "society"]

GRAMMAR

Do not use "a" or "the" before **college** when you are talking about the time when someone is studying there: *They met when they were in college.*

➔ UNIVERSITY

col·le·giate /kəˈlidʒət/ *adj.* relating to college or a college: *collegiate sports*

col·lide /kəˈlaɪd/ *v.* [I] to crash violently into something or someone: *His car* ***collided with*** *a bus.*

THESAURUS **hit, bump, bang, strike** ➔ HIT¹

col·lin·e·ar points /kə,lɪniɚ ˈpɔɪnts/ *n.* [plural] MATH two or more points that lie on the same straight line

col·li·sion /kəˈlɪʒən/ *n.* **1** [C,U] a violent crash in which one vehicle hits another: *a **midair collision*** (=one involving two planes)

THESAURUS **accident, crash, wreck, pile-up, disaster, catastrophe, mishap** → ACCIDENT

2 be on a collision course to be likely to have trouble because your aims are very different from someone else's: *The two nations are on a collision course that could lead to war.*

col·loid /ˈkɑlɔɪd/ *n.* [C] CHEMISTRY a mixture of substances in which small amounts of one substance are SUSPENDED (=floating) in the other substance

col·lo·qui·al /kəˈloʊkwiəl/ *adj.* colloquial language is the kind of language that is used in informal conversations: *colloquial expressions* —**colloquially** *adv.* —**colloquialism** *n.* [C]

col·lu·sion /kəˈluʒən/ *n.* [U] (formal) the act of agreeing secretly with someone else to do something dishonest or illegal —**collude** /kəˈlud/ *v.* [I]: *The companies colluded to keep prices high.*

co·logne /kəˈloʊn/ *n.* [U] a liquid with a pleasant smell, which you put on your skin

co·lon /ˈkoʊlən/ *n.* [C] **1** ENG. LANG. ARTS the mark (:) used in writing to introduce a list, examples, etc. **2** BIOLOGY the lower part of the INTESTINES, in which food is changed into waste matter → *see picture at* ORGAN

colo·nel /ˈkɚnl/ *n.* [C] a high rank in the Army, Air Force, or Marines, or an officer who has this rank

co·lo·ni·al /kəˈloʊniəl/ *adj.* **1** relating to the control of countries by a more powerful distant country: *the end of colonial rule in India* **2** *also* **Colonial** relating to the time when the U.S. was a colony of England: *a Colonial-style brick house*

co·lo·ni·al·ism /kəˈloʊniəˌlɪzəm/ *n.* [U] POLITICS the principle or practice in which a powerful country rules a weaker one and establishes its own trade and society there

col·o·nize /ˈkɑləˌnaɪz/ *v.* [I,T] to control a country or area and send your own people to live there: *Argentina was colonized by Spain.* —**colonist** *n.* [C] —**colonizer** *n.* [C] —**colonization** /ˌkɑlənəˈzeɪʃən/ *n.* [U]

col·o·ny /ˈkɑləni/ *n.* (plural **colonies**) [C] **1** a country or area that is ruled by a more powerful country, usually one that is far away: *Massachusetts was one of the original British colonies in America.* **2** a group of people with the same interests who live together: *an artists' colony* **3** a group of the same kind of animals living together [ORIGIN: 1300—1400 Old French *colonie*, from Latin *colonia*, from *colonus* "farmer, someone who develops a new place"]

col·or¹ /ˈkʌlɚ/ *n.* **1** [C] red, blue, yellow, etc.: *"What color is your new car?" "Blue."* ► Don't say "What color does your new car have?" ◄ | *the color of his eyes* | *I love wearing **bright colors**.* | *The leaves were pale green **in color**.* **2** [U] the quality of having colors: *Flowers can add color to a patio or backyard.* **3** [C,U] a substance such as paint or DYE, that makes something red, blue, etc.: *He mixed the colors with his paintbrush.* **4** [C,U] how dark or light someone's skin is, which shows which race s/he belongs to: *They are trying to bring together people of all colors and religions.* | *The awards will be given without discrimination based on color, religion, or sex.* **5 people/men/women etc. of color** people who are not white: *We need to get more women and people of color into elected office.* **6** [U] showing all the different colors such as red, green, and blue rather than just black and white (ANT) **black and white**: *The book includes 200 **color photographs/pictures**.* | *"The Wizard of Oz" was the first film shot **in color**.* **7** [U] if you have some color in your face, your face is pink or red, usually because you are healthy or embarrassed: *He felt the color rise to his face.*

color² *v.* **1** [T] to give color to something: *Do you color your hair?* **2** [I,T] to put color onto a drawing or picture, or to draw a picture using colored pencils or pens: *Give Grandma the picture you colored, Jenny.* **3 color sb's judgment/opinions/attitudes etc.** to influence the way that someone thinks about something, especially so that s/he becomes less fair or reasonable: *Personal feelings colored his judgment.*

col·or·blind /ˈkʌlɚˌblaɪnd/ *adj.* **1** not able to see the difference between particular colors **2** treating all races of people fairly: *In this court, justice is colorblind.*

ˌcolor-coˈordinated *adj.* clothes or decorations that are color-coordinated have colors that look good together

col·ored /ˈkʌlɚd/ *adj.* **1** having a color such as red, blue, yellow, etc. rather than being black, white, or plain: *brightly colored tropical birds* **2** (old-fashioned) a word used for describing a person who has dark or black skin, now considered offensive

col·or·fast /ˈkʌlɚˌfæst/ *adj.* colorfast clothing has a color that will not become lighter when you wash or wear it

col·or·ful /ˈkʌlɚfəl/ *adj.* **1** having a lot of bright colors: *a colorful stained-glass window* **2** interesting and full of variety: *a colorful career* —**colorfully** *adv.*

col·or·ing /ˈkʌlərɪŋ/ *n.* **1** [U] the color of something, especially someone's hair, skin, eyes, etc.: *Mandy had her mother's dark coloring.* **2** [C,U] a substance used for giving a particular color to something, especially food: *They had added yellow **food coloring** to the rice.*

ˈcoloring book *n.* [C] a book full of pictures that are drawn without color so that a child can color them in

col·or·less /ˈkʌlɚlɪs/ *adj.* **1** not having any

C

color: *a colorless gas* **2** not interesting or exciting

co·los·sal /kəˈlɑsəl/ *adj.* very large: *They've run up colossal debts.*

THESAURUS big, large, substantial, sizable, prodigious, huge, enormous, vast, gigantic, massive, immense → BIG

co·los·sus /kəˈlɑsəs/ *n.* [C usually singular] someone or something that is very large or very important

C

colt /koʊlt/ *n.* [C] a young male horse

col·umn /ˈkɑləm/ *n.* [C] **1** a tall solid round upright stone post used to support a building or as a decoration **2** an article by a particular writer that appears regularly in a newspaper or magazine: *an advice column* → NEWSPAPER **3** something with a long narrow shape: *a* ***column of*** *smoke* **4** one of two or more areas of print that go down the page of a newspaper or book and that are separated from each other by a narrow space: *Let's look at the second column of table 8.5.* **5** a long moving line of people, vehicles, etc.: *A* ***column of*** *soldiers marched through the streets.*

col·um·nist /ˈkɑləmnɪst, ˈkɑləmɪst/ *n.* [C] someone who regularly writes an article for a newspaper or magazine: *a sports columnist* → NEWSPAPER

com /kɑm/ IT **commercial organization** – used in Internet addresses

co·ma /ˈkoʊmə/ *n.* [C] a state in which someone is not conscious for a long time, usually after an accident or illness: *Ben was* ***in a coma*** *for six days.* [ORIGIN: 1600—1700 Modern Latin, Greek *koma* "deep sleep"]

co·ma·tose /ˈkoʊməˌtoʊs, ˈkɑ-/ *adj.* in a coma

comb¹ /koʊm/ *n.* [C] a flat piece of plastic or metal with a row of thin parts like teeth on one side that you use to make your hair neat → BRUSH

comb² *v.* [T] **1** to make your hair neat with a comb: *Go comb your hair.* **2** to search a place thoroughly: *Police* ***combed*** *the woods* ***for*** *the missing boy.*

com·bat¹ /ˈkɑmbæt/ *n.* [U] fighting during a war: *Her husband was killed* ***in combat.*** [ORIGIN: 1500—1600 French *combattre*, from Latin *com* "together" + *battuere* "to hit"] —**combat** *adj.*

THESAURUS war, warfare, fighting, conflict, action, hostilities → WAR

com·bat² /kəmˈbæt, ˈkɑmbæt/ *v.* [T] to try to stop something bad from happening or getting worse: *efforts to combat terrorism*

com·bat·ant /kəmˈbæt˺nt/ *n.* [C] someone who fights in a war

com·ba·tive /kəmˈbæt̬ɪv/ *adj.* ready to fight or argue: *Paul was in a combative mood.*

com·bi·na·tion /ˌkɑmbəˈneɪʃən/ *n.* **1** [C,U] two or more different things, substances, etc. that are used or put together: *A* ***combination of*** *factors led to the decision.* | *The medication should be taken* ***in combination with*** *vitamin C.*

THESAURUS mixture, blend, compound, solution → MIXTURE

2 [C] a series of numbers or letters you need to open a combination lock: *I forgot the combination on my lock.*

ˌcombiˈnation lock *n.* [C] a lock that is opened by using a special series of numbers or letters

com·bine¹ /kəmˈbaɪn/ *v.* **1** [I,T] to be joined together with another thing, or to join two or more things together: *The two chemicals* ***combine to*** *form a powerful explosive.* | *The heat,* ***combined with*** *the loud music, was beginning to make her feel sick.*

THESAURUS mix, stir, blend, beat → MIX¹

2 [T] to do two different activities at the same time: *It's hard to* ***combine*** *family life* ***with*** *a career.* [ORIGIN: 1400—1500 French *combiner*, from Late Latin *combinare*, from Latin *com* "together" + *bini* "two by two"]

com·bine² /ˈkɑmbaɪn/ *n.* [C] **1** *also* **combine harvester** a large machine used on a farm to cut a crop and separate the grain at the same time **2** a group of people, businesses, etc. that work together

com·bo /ˈkɑmboʊ/ *n.* (plural **combos**) [C] (informal) **1** a small group of musicians who play dance music: *a jazz combo* **2** a combination of things, especially food at a restaurant: *I'll have the fish combo and a Coke.*

com·bus·ti·ble /kəmˈbʌstəbəl/ *adj.* able to catch fire and burn easily: *Gasoline is* ***highly combustible.*** —**combustible** *n.* [C]

com·bus·tion /kəmˈbʌstʃən/ *n.* [U] the process of burning

comˈbustion reˌaction *n.* [C,U] CHEMISTRY a chemical change that happens when a substance reacts with oxygen to produce energy in the form of heat and light

come /kʌm/ *v.* (past tense **came** /keɪm/, past participle **come**) [I]

1 MOVE TOWARD SB/STH to move toward you or arrive at the place where you are → GO: ***Come here*** *right now!* | *A young woman* ***came into*** *the room.* | *There were no cars coming the opposite way.* | *What time will you be* ***coming home?***

THESAURUS arrive, get to, reach, turn up, show up, get in, come in, land → ARRIVE

2 GO WITH SB if someone comes with you, s/he goes to a place with you: *I asked Rosie if she'd like to* ***come with*** *us.* | *Do you want to* ***come along?***

3 TRAVEL TO A PLACE to travel to or reach a place: *He had* ***come a long way*** *to see us.* | *Will you be* ***coming by*** *bus?*

4 MAIL if a letter, etc. comes, it is delivered to you in the mail: *The phone bill hasn't come yet.*

5 HAPPEN if a time or event comes, it arrives or starts to happen: *Spring came early that year.*
6 LIST/COMPETITION ETC. to have a particular position in the order of something: *Jason **came first/last** in the 10 mile race.* | *P **comes before** Q in the alphabet.*
7 **come open/loose/undone etc.** to become open, loose, etc.: *The buttons had come undone.*
8 BE PRODUCED/SOLD to be produced or sold with particular features: *This shoe doesn't **come in** size 11.*
9 **come as a surprise/relief/shock etc. (to sb)** to make someone feel surprised, RELIEVED, etc.: *His decision to retire came as a surprise.*
10 **sb/sth has come a long way** to have made a lot of progress: *Computer technology has come a long way since the 1970s*
11 REACH A LENGTH/HEIGHT to reach a particular height or length: *The grass **came up to** our knees.*

THESAURUS reach, go → REACH[1]

12 **come naturally/easily (to sb)** to be easy for someone to do: *Acting came naturally to Rae.*
13 **in the years/days to come** in the future: *I think you might regret this decision in the years to come.*
14 **come of age** a) to reach the age, usually 18 or 21, when you are legally considered to be an adult b) to develop into a successful form, or to reach the time when this happens: *The sport has finally come of age.*
15 **come and go** to be allowed to go into and leave a place whenever you want

SPOKEN PHRASES
16 **how come?** used in order to ask someone why something happened or is true: *"She's moving to Alaska." "How come?"* | *So, how come we haven't met your boyfriend yet?*
17 **here comes sb** said when someone is about to arrive at the place where you are: *Here comes Karen now.*
18 **come to think of it** said when you have just realized or remembered something: *Come to think of it, Cooper did mention it to me.*
19 **take sth as it comes** to accept something as it happens, without trying to plan for it or change it: *I'm not going to worry about it. I'll just **take each day as it comes**.*
20 **have it coming** to deserve to be punished or to have something bad happen to you: *I don't feel sorry for Brad – he had it coming.*

[ORIGIN: Old English *cuman*]

come about *phr. v.*
to happen or develop: ***How did** this change **come about**?*

come across *phr. v.*
1 **come across sb/sth** to meet, find, or discover someone or something by chance: *I came across this photograph among some old newspapers.*
2 if someone comes across in a particular way, s/he seems to have certain qualities: *She **comes across as** a really happy person.*

come along *phr. v.*
1 to appear or arrive: *Jobs like this don't come along very often!*
2 to develop or improve: *Terry's work has really come along this year.*

come apart *phr. v.*
1 to split or separate easily into pieces: *The book just came apart in my hands.*
2 to begin to fail: *Their marriage was coming apart.*

come around *phr. v.*
1 to visit someone: *What's a good time to come around and drop off his present?*
2 if someone comes around, s/he decides to agree with you after disagreeing with you: *I know he'll come around.*
3 if a regular event comes around, it happens as usual: *I can't believe his birthday is coming around already.*

come at sb *phr. v.*
to move toward someone in a threatening way: *She came at him with a knife.*

come away *phr. v.*
to leave a place with a particular feeling or idea: *I came away with a good impression.*

come back *phr. v.*
1 to return from a place: *When is your sister coming back from Europe?*
2 **come back to sb** to be remembered, especially suddenly: *Then, everything Williams had said came back to me.*
3 to become fashionable or popular again: *The styles of the seventies are coming back.* → COME-BACK

come between sb/sth *phr. v.*
1 to cause trouble between two or more people: *Don't let money come between you and David.*
2 to prevent someone from giving enough attention to something: *She never let anything come between her and her work.*

come by *phr. v.*
1 **come by (sth)** to visit someone for a short time before going somewhere else: *I'll come by later to pick up Katrina.*
2 **come by sth** to get something that is difficult to get: *Good jobs are **hard to come by** right now.*

come down *phr. v.*
1 a) to become lower in price, level, etc.: *Wait until interest rates come down before you buy a house.* b) to offer or accept a lower price: *They refused to **come down on** the price.*
2 to fall to the ground: *A lot of trees came down in the storm.*
3 if someone comes down to a place, s/he travels south to the place where you are: *Why don't you come down for the weekend sometime?*

come down on sb/sth *phr. v.*
1 to punish someone severely: *The school **came down hard on** the students who were caught drinking.*
2 **come down on the side of sth** to decide to

support something or someone: *The court came down on the side of the boy's father.*

come down to sth *phr. v.*
if a difficult or confusing situation comes down to something, that is the single most important thing: *It all comes down to money in the end.*

come down with sth *phr. v.*
to get an illness: *I think I'm coming down with the flu.*

come forward *phr. v.*
to offer to help: *Several witnesses have come forward with information.*

come from sth *phr. v.*
1 to have been born in a particular place: ***"Where do you come from?"*** *"Texas."*
2 to have first existed, been made, or produced in a particular place, thing, or time: *A lot of medicines come from quite common plants.* | *The lines she read come from a Rilke poem.*
3 if a sound comes from a place, it begins there: *I heard a weird sound coming from the closet.*

come in *phr. v.*
1 to enter a room or house: *Come in and sit down.*
2 to arrive or be received: *Reports were coming in of an earthquake in Mexico.*
3 come in first/second etc. to finish first, second, etc. in a race or competition
4 to be involved in a plan, deal, etc.: *I need somebody to help, and that's **where** you **come in**.*
5 come in useful/handy to be useful: *Bring the rope – it might come in handy.*
6 when the TIDE comes in, it moves toward the land (ANT) **go out**

come in for sth *phr. v.*
come in for criticism/blame to be criticized or blamed: *After the riots, the police came in for a lot of criticism.*

come into sth *phr. v.*
1 to begin to be in a particular state or position: *As we turned the corner, the town **came into view**.* | *The new law **comes into effect** tomorrow.*
2 to be involved in something or to influence it: *Where do I come into all this?*
3 come into money to receive money because someone has died and given it to you

come of sth *phr. v.*
to result from something: *What good can come of getting so angry?*

come off *phr. v.*
1 come off sth to no longer be on something, connected to it, or fastened to it: *A button had come off my coat.*
2 to seem like you have a particular attitude or quality because of something you say or do: *She **came off as** a phony.*
3 to happen in a particular way: *The wedding came off as planned.*
4 come off it! (spoken) said when you think someone is being stupid or unreasonable

come on *phr. v.*
1 if a light or machine comes on, it starts working: *The lights suddenly came on in the theater.*
2 if a television or radio program comes on, it starts: *What time does the show come on?*
3 if an illness comes on, you start to have it: *I can feel a headache coming on.*
4 come on! (spoken) **a)** used in order to tell someone to hurry, or to come with you **b)** said in order to encourage someone to do something: *Come on! It's not that hard!* **c)** used in order to tell someone that you know that what s/he said was not true or right: *Oh, come on! Don't lie to me!*

come out *phr. v.*
1 to become known, especially after being hidden: *The truth will come out eventually.*
2 if something you say comes out in a particular way, you say it in that way, or it is understood by someone in that way: *When I try to explain, it **comes out all wrong**, and she gets mad.*
3 to say something publicly or directly: *Senator Peters has **come out against** abortion.* | *Why don't you just **come out and say** what you think?*
4 if a book, movie, etc. comes out, it is available for people to buy or see
5 if dirt or a mark comes out of cloth, it can be washed out
6 come out well/badly/ahead etc. to finish an action or process in a particular way: *I can never get cakes to come out right.*
7 if a photograph comes out, it looks the way it is supposed to: *Some of our wedding photos didn't come out.*
8 when the Sun, moon, or stars come out, they appear in the sky

come out with sth *phr. v.*
if a company comes out with a new product, it makes it available to be bought: *Ford has come out with a new sports truck.*

come over *phr. v.*
1 to visit someone at his/her house: *Do you want to come over on Friday night?*
2 to move to the country where you are now, especially from across an ocean: *Her dad came over from Italy in the 1960s.*
3 come over sb if a feeling comes over someone, s/he begins to feel it: *A wave of sleepiness came over her.*

come through *phr. v.*
1 come through sth to continue to live, exist, be strong, or succeed after a difficult or dangerous time (SYN) **survive**: *Bill came through the operation all right.*
2 to be made official, especially by having the correct documents officially approved: *She's still waiting for her visa to come through.*

come to *phr. v.*
1 come to do sth to begin to have a feeling or opinion: *She had come to think of New York as her home.*
2 come to sb if an idea or memory comes to you, you suddenly realize or remember it: *Later that afternoon, the answer came to him.*
3 come to $20/$3 etc. to add up to a total of $20, $3, etc.: *That comes to $24.67, ma'am.*
4 when it comes to sth relating to a particular

subject: *She's hopeless when it comes to money.*
5 to become conscious again after having been unconscious: *When I came to, I was lying on the grass.*
come under sth *phr. v.*
1 come under attack/fire/pressure etc. to be attacked, criticized, threatened, etc.: *The president has come under fire from Democrats in Congress.*
2 to be controlled or influenced by something such as a set of rules: *All doctors come under the same rules of professional conduct.*
come up *phr. v.*
1 if someone comes up to you, s/he comes close to you, especially in order to speak to you
2 if someone comes up to a place, s/he travels north to the place where you are: *Why don't you come up to Chicago for the weekend?*
3 to be mentioned or suggested: *The subject didn't come up at the meeting.*
4 be coming up to be happening soon: *Isn't your anniversary coming up?*
5 when the sun or moon comes up, it appears in the sky and starts to rise
6 if something, especially a problem, comes up, it suddenly happens: *Something's come up, so I won't be able to go with you Thursday.*
come up against sb/sth *phr. v.*
to have to deal with difficult people or problems: *He came up against fierce resistance.*
come upon sb/sth *phr. v.* (literary)
to find or discover something by chance
come up with sth *phr. v.*
1 to think of an idea, plan, reply, etc.: *They still haven't come up with a name for the baby.*
2 to be able to produce a particular amount of money: *I'll never be able to come up with $2,000.*

come·back /ˈkʌmbæk/ *n.* **1 make a comeback** to become popular or successful again: *Every few years, short skirts make a comeback.* **2** [C] a quick reply that is smart or funny: *I can never think of a good comeback when I need one.*

co·me·di·an /kəˈmidiən/ *n.* [C] someone whose job is to tell jokes and make people laugh (SYN) **comic**: *a stand-up comedian*

com·e·dy /ˈkɑmədi/ *n.* (plural **comedies**) **1** [C,U] a funny movie, play, television program, etc. that makes people laugh, or this type of entertainment: *a TV comedy* | *stand-up comedy* → MOVIE **2** [U] the quality in something, such as a book or movie, that makes you laugh (SYN) **humor** [ORIGIN: 1300—1400 French *comédie*, from Latin, from Greek *komoidia*, from *komos* "having fun, partying" + *aeidein* "to sing"]

ˈcome-on *n.* [C] (informal) something that someone does to try to make someone else sexually interested in him/her: *Rick seems to think every smile is a come-on.*

com·et /ˈkɑmɪt/ *n.* [C] PHYSICS an object in the sky like a very bright ball with a tail, that moves through SPACE (=the area beyond the Earth where the stars are) → SPACE[1] [ORIGIN: 1100—1200 Latin *cometa*, from Greek *kometes* "long-haired, comet;" because of its long tail]

come·up·pance /kʌmˈʌpəns/ *n.* [singular] (informal) a punishment or something bad that happens to you, that you deserve: *the story of a crook who finally **gets his comeuppance***

com·fort[1] /ˈkʌmfɚt/ *n.* **1** [U] a feeling of being physically relaxed and satisfied, so that nothing is hurting you, making you feel too hot or cold, etc. (ANT) **discomfort**: *the air-conditioned **comfort of** his car* | *We slept there **in comfort** until the dawn appeared.* **2** [U] if someone or something gives you comfort, he, she, or it makes you feel happier when you are upset or worried: *I **took comfort from** the fact that I had done my best.* | *She turned to her church **for comfort**.* **3 (be) a comfort to sb** to help someone feel happier or less worried: *Her children were a **great comfort** to her.* **4** [U] a way of living in which you have everything you need to be happy: *They had enough money to live **in comfort**.* **5 comforts** [plural] all the things that make your life easier and more comfortable: *The beach cabin has all **the comforts of home**.* [ORIGIN: 1100—1200 Old French *conforter*, from Late Latin *confortare* "to strengthen"] → **too close for comfort** *at* CLOSE[2]

comfort[2] *v.* [T] to make someone feel less worried or unhappy, for example by saying kind things to him/her —**comforting** *adj.* —**comfortingly** *adv.*

com·fort·a·ble /ˈkʌmftəbəl, ˈkʌmfɚṭəbəl/ *adj.* **1** something that is comfortable makes you feel physically relaxed: *Remember to wear comfortable shoes.* | *a **comfortable chair/bed/sofa*** **2** if you are comfortable, you feel physically relaxed: *Come in and **make yourself comfortable**.* **3** not worried about what someone will do or about what will happen: *I **feel** very **comfortable with** him.* **4** having enough money to live on without worrying: *We're not rich, but we are comfortable.* —**comfortably** *adv.*

com·fort·er /ˈkʌmfɚṭɚ/ *n.* [C] a thick cover for a bed → *see picture at* BED[1]

com·fy /ˈkʌmfi/ *adj.* (spoken) comfortable

com·ic[1] /ˈkɑmɪk/ *adj.* funny or amusing: *a comic actress* | *At least Marlene was there to give us **comic relief*** (=make us laugh in a serious situation).

comic[2] *n.* [C] **1** a COMEDIAN **2** a COMIC BOOK **3 the comics** [plural] the part of a newspaper that has COMIC STRIPS

com·i·cal /ˈkɑmɪkəl/ *adj.* funny, especially in a strange or unexpected way —**comically** *adv.*

THESAURUS **funny, hilarious, hysterical, witty, amusing, humorous** → FUNNY[1]

ˈcomic book *n.* [C] a magazine that tells a story using pictures that are drawn like comic strips

ˈcomic strip *n.* [C] a series of pictures that are drawn inside boxes and tell a story

com·ing¹ /ˈkʌmɪŋ/ *n.* **1 the coming of sb/sth** the time when something or someone arrives or begins: *With the coming of the railroad, the town changed considerably.* **2 comings and goings** the movements of people as they arrive and leave places

coming² *adj.* [only before noun] happening soon: *the coming winter*

com·ma /ˈkɑmə/ *n.* [C] ENG. LANG. ARTS the mark (,) used in writing to show a short pause [ORIGIN: 1500—1600 Latin "part of a sentence," from Greek *komma* "part, clause," from *koptein* "to cut"]

C

com·mand¹ /kəˈmænd/ *n.* **1** [U] the control of a group of people or a situation: *How many officers are **under** your **command**?* | *Who is **in command** here?* **2** [C] an order that must be obeyed: *Shoot when I **give the command**.* **3 command of sth** knowledge of something, especially a language, or the ability to use something: *Fukiko **has a good command of** English.* **4** [C] IT an instruction to a computer to do something

command² *v.* **1** [I,T] to tell someone officially to do something, especially if you are a military leader, king, etc.: *The captain **commanded** the crew **to** remain on the main deck.* **2** [T] to get attention, respect, etc. because you are important or popular: *He commands one of the highest fees in Hollywood.*

com·man·dant /ˈkɑmənˌdɑnt/ *n.* [C] the chief officer in charge of a military organization

com·man·deer /ˌkɑmənˈdɪr/ *v.* [T] to officially take someone's property for military use: *The hotel was commandeered for use as a war hospital.*

com·mand·er, Commander /kəˈmændɚ/ *n.* [C] **1** an officer in charge of a military organization or group **2** an officer who has a middle rank in the Navy

comˌmander in ˈchief *n.* [C] **1** someone of high rank who is in control of all the military organizations in a country or of a specific military activity **2 Commander in Chief** POLITICS a title for the U.S. president in his position as the official head of the military

com·mand·ing /kəˈmændɪŋ/ *adj.* [only before noun] **1** having authority or confidence that makes people respect and obey you: *his **commanding presence*** **2** being in a position from which you are likely to win a race or competition easily: *Stevens has a **commanding lead** in the polls.*

com·mand·ment /kəˈmændmənt/ *n.* [C] one of ten rules given by God in the Bible that tell people how they should behave

com·man·do /kəˈmændoʊ/ *n.* (plural **commandos**) [C] a soldier who is specially trained to make quick attacks into enemy areas

com·mem·o·rate /kəˈmɛməˌreɪt/ *v.* [T] to remember someone or something by a special action, ceremony, object, etc.: *The monument commemorates the soldiers who died during the Vietnam war.* [ORIGIN: 1600—1700 Latin, past participle of *commemorare*, from *memorare* "to remind of"] —**commemoration** /kəˌmɛməˈreɪʃən/ *n.* [U] —**commemorative** /kəˈmɛmərət̬ɪv/ *adj.*

com·mence /kəˈmɛns/ (Ac) *v.* [I,T] (formal) to begin: *Work on the building will commence soon.* | *The trial **commenced with** the testimony of the first witness.* [ORIGIN: 1300—1400 Old French *comencer*, from Vulgar Latin *cominitiare*, from Latin + *initiare* "to begin"]

THESAURUS **begin, start, break out** → BEGIN

com·mence·ment /kəˈmɛnsmənt/ (Ac) *n.* **1** [C,U] a ceremony at which college or HIGH SCHOOL students receive their DIPLOMAS (SYN) **graduation** **2** [U] (formal) the beginning of something: *The Olympic torch will be carried into the stadium prior to* (=before) *the **commencement of** the games.*

com·mend /kəˈmɛnd/ *v.* [T] (formal) to praise someone or something publicly or formally: *The three firefighters were **commended for** their bravery.*

THESAURUS **praise, congratulate, flatter, compliment sb/pay sb a compliment, extol** → PRAISE¹

com·mend·a·ble /kəˈmɛndəbəl/ *adj.* (formal) deserving praise: *Baldwin answered with commendable honesty.* —**commendably** *adv.*

com·men·da·tion /ˌkɑmənˈdeɪʃən/ *n.* [C] (formal) an honor or prize given to someone for being brave or successful

com·men·su·rate /kəˈmɛnsərɪt, -ʃərɪt/ *adj.* (formal) matching something else in size, quality, or length of time: *The salary is **commensurate with** experience* (=the salary for the job is higher if you have experience).

com·ment¹ /ˈkɑmɛnt/ (Ac) *n.* **1** [C,U] an opinion that you give about someone or something: *Does anyone have any questions or comments?* | *He **made** rude **comments about** her.* **2 no comment** (spoken) said when you do not want to answer a question, especially in public [ORIGIN: 1300—1400 Late Latin *commentum*, from Latin, "invention," from *comminisci* "to invent"]

comment² (Ac) *v.* [I,T] to give an opinion about someone or something: *The police have refused to **comment on** the case.* | *His teacher **commented that** his writing was poor.*

com·men·tar·y /ˈkɑmənˌtɛri/ (Ac) *n.* (plural **commentaries**) [C,U] **1** a spoken description of an event, given while the event is happening, especially on the television or radio: *the **commentary on** the World Series* **2** a book or article that explains or discusses something, or the explanation itself: *political commentary* **3 be a sad commentary on sth** to be a sign or example of how bad a situation is: *It's a sad commentary on our culture that we need constant entertainment.*

com·men·ta·tor /ˈkɑmənˌteɪt̬ɚ/ (Ac) *n.* [C] **1** someone on television or radio who describes an event as it is happening: *a **sports commentator*** **2** someone who knows a lot about a subject, and who writes about it or discusses it on the television or radio: *political commentators* [ORIGIN: 1300—1400 Latin *commentari* "to comment," from *comminisci* "to invent"]

com·merce /ˈkɑmɚs/ *n.* [U] the buying and selling of goods and services: ***interstate commerce*** (=among U.S. states) [ORIGIN: 1500—1600 French, Latin *commercium*, from *com-* + *merx* "things to be sold"]

THESAURUS business, industry, trade, private enterprise → BUSINESS

com·mer·cial¹ /kəˈmɚʃəl/ *adj.* **1** relating to business and the buying and selling of things: *commercial activity* **2** relating to making money or a profit: *The movie was **a commercial success/failure**.* —**commercially** *adv.*

commercial² *n.* [C] an advertisement on television or radio: *TV commercials*

THESAURUS advertisement, billboard, poster, want ads/classified ads, flier, junk mail, spam → ADVERTISEMENT

com·mer·cial·ism /kəˈmɚʃəˌlɪzəm/ *n.* [U] (disapproving) the practice of being more concerned with making money than with the quality of what you sell

com·mer·cial·ize /kəˈmɚʃəˌlaɪz/ *v.* [T] (disapproving) to be more concerned with making money from something than about its quality: *Christmas is getting more and more commercialized!* —**commercialization** /kəˌmɚʃələˈzeɪʃən/ *n.* [U]

com·mis·e·rate /kəˈmɪzəˌreɪt/ *v.* [I] (formal) to express your sympathy for someone who is unhappy: *He's able to talk to and **commiserate with** students in a sincere way.* —**commiseration** /kəˌmɪzəˈreɪʃən/ *n.* [U]

com·mis·sion¹ /kəˈmɪʃən/ (Ac) *n.* **1** [C] a group of people who have been given the official job of finding out about something or controlling something: *the U.N. Commission on Human Rights* **2** [C,U] an amount of money paid to someone for selling something: *Salespeople earn a 30% **commission on** each new car.* | *Some firms work **on commission** and others charge a fee.* **3** [C] a piece of work that someone, especially an artist or a musician, is asked to do: *a commission for a new sculpture* **4 out of commission a)** not working correctly, or not able to be used: *The toilets are out of commission.* **b)** (informal) sick or injured

commission² *v.* [T] to ask someone to do a piece of work for you: *He has been **commissioned to** design a bridge.*

com·mis·sion·er /kəˈmɪʃənɚ/ (Ac) *n.* [C] someone who is officially in charge of an organization: *a police commissioner*

com·mit /kəˈmɪt/ (Ac) *v.* (**committed**, **committing**) [T] **1** to do something wrong or illegal: *Police still don't know who **committed** the **crime**.* **2 commit suicide** to kill yourself deliberately **3 commit adultery** if a married person commits adultery, s/he has sex with someone who is not his/her husband or wife **4** to say that you will definitely do something: *Going to the interview doesn't **commit** you **to** anything.* | *I had **committed myself** and there was no turning back.*

THESAURUS promise, give sb your word, swear, take/swear an oath, vow, pledge, undertake to do sth, guarantee → PROMISE¹

5 to decide to use money, time, effort, etc. for a particular purpose: *A lot of money has been **committed to** the project.* [ORIGIN: 1300—1400 Latin *committere*, from *com-* "together" + *mittere* "to send, put"]

com·mit·ment /kəˈmɪtˀmənt/ (Ac) *n.* **1** [C] a promise to do something or behave in a particular way: *Volunteers must be able to **make a commitment** of four hours a week.* | *Our company has a **commitment to** customer service.* **2** [U] the hard work and loyalty that someone gives to an organization, activity, etc.: *You cannot question Sara's **commitment to** her work.* **3** [C] (formal) something that you have promised you will do or that you have to do: *He had other commitments and could not attend.* | *The company will have to raise ticket prices to meet its **financial commitments**.*

com·mit·ted /kəˈmɪt̬ɪd/ (Ac) *adj.* willing to work hard at something you believe is right or important: *Her parents are both committed liberals.* | *The group is **committed to** improving civil rights.*

com·mit·tee /kəˈmɪt̬i/ *n.* [C] a group of people chosen to do a particular job, make decisions, etc.: *I'm **on** the finance **committee**.*

com·mo·di·ous /kəˈmoʊdiəs/ *adj.* (formal) a house or room that is commodious is very big (SYN) **spacious** —**commodiously** *adv.*

com·mod·i·ty /kəˈmɑdət̬i/ (Ac) *n.* (plural **commodities**) [C] ECONOMICS a product that is bought and sold: *agricultural commodities* | *rising commodity prices*

com·mo·dore, **Commodore** /ˈkɑməˌdɔr/ *n.* [C] an officer who has a high rank in the Navy

com·mon¹ /ˈkɑmən/ *adj.* **1** something that is common is often seen or often happens (ANT) **rare**: *"Smith" is a common last name.* | *Heart disease is **common among** smokers.* | *It's **common for** new fathers **to** feel jealous of their babies.* ► Don't say "It is common that." ◄ **2** belonging to, or shared by two or more people or things: *We are all working towards a **common goal**.* | *a theme that is **common to** all her novels* **3 common ground** facts, opinions, and beliefs that a group of people can agree on, in a situation in which they are arguing about something: *Let's see if we can establish some common ground.* **4 the common good** what is best for everyone in a society: *They truly believed they were acting for the common good.* **5 common knowledge** something that everyone knows: ***It's common knowledge** that he's an alcoholic.* **6** ordinary and not special in any way: *The song is a tribute to **the common man*** (=ordinary people). [ORIGIN: 1200—1300 Old French *commun*, from Latin *communis*]

common² *n.* **1 have sth in common (with sb/sth)** to have the same interests, attitudes, etc. as someone else: *Terry and I **have a lot in common**.* **2 have sth in common (with sth)** if objects or ideas have something in common, they share the same features: *The two games **have much/little in common**.* **3** [C] a word meaning a public park, used mostly in names: *Boston Common*

C

ˌcommon ˈcold *n.* [C] a slight illness in which your throat hurts and it is difficult to breathe normally SYN **cold**

ˌcommon deˈnominator *n.* [C usually singular] MATH a number that can be divided exactly by all the DENOMINATORS (=bottom numbers) in a set of FRACTIONS

ˌcommon ˈfactor *n.* [C] MATH a number that divides exactly into each of a set of two or more other numbers. For example, 3 is a common factor of 6, 12, and 18.

ˈcommon-law *adj.* **common-law husband/wife** someone you have lived with for a long time as if s/he was your husband or wife

com·mon·ly /ˈkɑmənli/ *adv.* often or usually: *the most commonly used computer*

ˌcommon ˈnoun *n.* [C] ENG. LANG. ARTS a noun that is not the name of a particular person, place, or thing. For example, "book" and "sugar" are common nouns. ➔ COLLECTIVE NOUN, PROPER NOUN

com·mon·place /ˈkɑmənˌpleɪs/ *adj.* very common or not unusual: *Divorce has become commonplace.*

ˌcommon ˈsense *n.* [U] the ability to behave in a sensible way and make practical decisions: ***Use** your **common sense**.*

com·mon·wealth /ˈkɑmənˌwɛlθ/ *n.* [C] (formal) **1** POLITICS a group of countries that are related politically or economically, for example the group of countries that have a strong relationship with Great Britain **2** the official legal title of some U.S. states: *The Commonwealth of Virginia* **3** POLITICS the official legal title of some places, such as Puerto Rico, that are governed by the U.S. but are not states

com·mo·tion /kəˈmoʊʃən/ *n.* [singular, U] sudden noisy activity or arguing: *Everyone looked to see what was **causing the commotion**.*

com·mu·nal /kəˈmyunl/ *adj.* shared by a group of people: *a communal bathroom in the dorm*

com·mune¹ /ˈkɑmyun/ *n.* [C] SOCIAL SCIENCE a group of people who live and work together and share their possessions [ORIGIN: 1600—1700 French, Medieval Latin *communia*, from Latin *communis* "common"]

com·mune² /kəˈmyun/ *v.*

commune with sb/sth *phr. v.* (formal) **1** to communicate with a person, god, or animal, especially in a mysterious way **2 commune with nature** to spend time in the COUNTRYSIDE, enjoying it in a quiet peaceful way

com·mu·ni·ca·ble /kəˈmyunɪkəbəl/ Ac *adj.* a communicable disease is one that can be passed on to other people SYN **infectious**

com·mu·ni·cate /kəˈmyunəˌkeɪt/ Ac *v.* **1** [I] to exchange information or conversation with other people, using words, signs, writing, etc.: *We communicate mostly by email.* | *It's difficult to **communicate with** people if you don't speak their language.* **2** [I,T] to express your thoughts or feelings clearly, so that other people understand them: *A baby communicates its needs by crying.* [ORIGIN: 1500—1600 Latin, past participle of *communicare* "to give information, take part," from *communis* "common"]

com·mu·ni·ca·tion /kəˌmyunəˈkeɪʃən/ Ac *n.* **1** [U] the process of speaking, writing, etc. by which people exchange information or express their thoughts and feelings: ***Communication between** parents and teachers is vital.* | *We've stayed **in** constant **communication** with each other.* | *Radio was the pilot's only **means of communication**.* **2 communications a)** [plural] ways of sending and receiving information using computers, telephones, radios, etc.: *Modern communications enable people to work from home.* **b)** [U] the study of using radio, television, movies, etc. to communicate **3** [C] (formal) a letter, message, or telephone call: *I received a communication from my bank informing me of the charge.*

com·mu·ni·ca·tive /kəˈmyunəkətɪv, -ˌkeɪtɪv/ Ac *adj.* **1** willing or able to talk or give information: *My son isn't very communicative.* **2** relating to the ability to communicate: *The test evaluates students' communicative skills.*

Com·mun·ion /kəˈmyunyən/ *n.* also **Holy Communion** the Christian ceremony in which people eat bread and drink wine as signs of Christ's body and blood

com·mu·ni·qué /kəˈmyunəˌkeɪ, kəˌmyunəˈkeɪ/ *n.* [C] an official report or announcement

com·mu·nism /ˈkɑmyəˌnɪzəm/ *n.* [U] POLITICS a political system in which the government controls all the production of food and goods and there is no privately owned property

com·mu·nist /ˈkɑmyənɪst/ *n.* [C] POLITICS someone who is a member of a political party that supports communism, or who believes in communism —**communist** *adj.*: *the Communist Party*

com·mu·ni·ty /kəˈmyunəti/ Ac *n.* (plural **communities**) [C] **1** a group of people who live in the same town or area: *The library serves the whole* *community.* **2** a group of people who have the same interests, religion, race, etc.: *Miami has a large Cuban community.* | *politicians who have close ties to the business community* | *Most of the world's scientific community now accept the theory.* **3 sense of community** the feeling that you belong to a group in which people work together and help each other: *Teachers are working to build a sense of community in the school.* [ORIGIN: 1300—1400 Old French *comuneté*, from Latin *communitas*, from *communis* "common"]

com'munity ˌcollege *n.* [C] a college that people can go to, usually for two years, in order to learn a skill or to prepare to go to another college or university

comˌmunity 'service *n.* [U] work that someone does to help other people without being paid, especially as punishment for a crime → PUNISHMENT

com·mute¹ /kə'myut/ *v.* **1** [I] to travel regularly in order to get to work: *Jerry* ***commutes from*** *Scarsdale* ***to*** *New York every day.* **2** [T] LAW to change the punishment given to a criminal to one that is less severe: *Her sentence was* ***commuted*** *from death* ***to*** *life imprisonment.* [ORIGIN: 1400—1500 Latin *commutare* "to exchange, change"]

commute² *n.* [C usually singular] the trip made to work every day: *My morning commute takes 45 minutes.*

com·mut·er /kə'myuṭə/ *n.* [C] someone who travels a long distance to work every day

com·pact¹ /'kɑmpækt, kəm'pækt/ *adj.* small but arranged so that everything fits neatly into the available space: *a compact car* [ORIGIN: 1300—1400 Latin *compactus*, past participle of *compingere* "to put together"]

com·pact² /'kɑmpækt/ *n.* [C] **1** a small flat container with a mirror, containing powder for a woman's face **2** a small car **3** LAW an agreement between two or more people, countries, etc. with laws or rules that they must obey

com·pact³ /kəm'pækt/ *v.* [T] to press something together so that it becomes smaller or more solid —**compacted** *adj.*

THESAURUS **press, squash, crush, mash, grind, squeeze, compress** → PRESS¹

ˌcompact 'disc *n.* [C] a CD → *see picture on page A19*

com·pan·ion /kəm'pænyən/ *n.* [C] **1** someone you spend a lot of time with, especially a friend: *For ten years, he had been her* ***constant companion.*** | *my* ***traveling companions*** **2** one of a pair of things that go together or can be used together: *This book is a* ***companion to*** *Professor Farrer's first work.* [ORIGIN: 1200—1300 Old French *compagnon*, from Late Latin *companio*, from Latin *com-* "with" + *panis* "bread, food"]

com·pan·ion·a·ble /kəm'pænyənəbəl/ *adj.* pleasantly friendly: *They sat in a companionable silence.*

com·pan·ion·ship /kəm'pænyənˌʃɪp/ *n.* [U] the state of being with someone so that you have someone to talk to and do not feel lonely: *the need for companionship*

com·pa·ny /'kʌmpəni/ *n.* (plural **companies**) **1** [C] a business that makes or sells things or provides a service: *What company do you work for?* | ***insurance/software/phone companies***

THESAURUS

firm – a company that usually provides a service rather than producing goods: *a law firm*
business – a company that often employs only a small number of people: *She set up her own catering business.* | *small businesses*
corporation – a large company that often includes several smaller companies
subsidiary – a company that is owned by a larger company

2 [U] the state of being with someone so that s/he does not feel lonely: *Why don't you come with me? I could use the company.* | *Tim is* ***good company*** (=someone you enjoy being with). | *I'll stay here to* ***keep you company*** (=be with you so you are not alone). **3** [U] one or more guests, or someone who is coming to see you: *We're* ***having company*** *tonight, so I want you back home by five.* **4** [singular, U] the group of people that you are friends with or spend time with: *I don't like* ***the company*** *she* ***keeps.*** **5** [C] a group of actors, dancers, or singers who work together: *a ballet company* [ORIGIN: 1200—1300 Old French *compagnie*, from *compain* "companion," from Late Latin *companio*]

com·pa·ra·ble /'kɑmpərəbəl/ *adj.* (formal) similar to something else in size, number, quality, etc.: *Is the pay rate* ***comparable to*** *that of other companies?*

THESAURUS **similar, like, alike, akin to sth, analogous, identical, matching** → SIMILAR

com·par·a·tive¹ /kəm'pærəṭɪv/ *adj.* **1** showing what is different and similar between things of the same kind: *a* ***comparative study*** *of European languages* **2 comparative comfort/freedom/wealth etc.** comfort, freedom, etc. that is fairly good when measured or judged against something else, or against what the situation was before (SYN) **relative**: *After a lifetime of poverty, his last few years were spent in comparative comfort.*

comparative² *n.* **the comparative** ENG. LANG. ARTS in grammar, the form of an adjective or adverb that shows an increase in quality, quantity, degree, etc. For example, "better" is the comparative of "good."

com·par·a·tive·ly /kəm'pærəṭɪvli/ *adv.* as compared to something else or to a previous state: *The disease is comparatively rare.*

com·pare¹ /kəm'pɛr/ *v.* **1** [T] to examine or judge two or more things in order to show how they are similar to or different from each other: *We went* *to a few different stores to compare prices.* | ***Compared to*** *me, Al is tall.* | *The police* ***compared*** *the suspect's fingerprints* ***with*** *those found at the crime scene.*

THESAURUS

make a comparison – to compare two or more people, situations, etc.: *The article makes a comparison between Hemingway and Thoreau.*
draw a parallel – to say that people or things are similar in some aspects: *There are parallels that can be drawn between the two writers – they both grew up in the South.*
draw an analogy (formal) – to say that two things or situations are similar, even though they may seem very different: *Some people have drawn an analogy between poetry and mathematics.*
contrast – to compare two things, situations, etc., in order to show how they are different from each other: *In the novel, he contrasts the lives of two families living in New York.*
make/draw a distinction – to emphasize that two things are very different: *It is important to draw a distinction between people's fear of crime and the actual amount of crime that really happens.*

2 [I,T] to say that someone or something is similar to someone or something else: *Critics have* ***compared*** *him* ***to*** *Robert De Niro.* | *The oranges out here* ***don't compare with*** (=are not as good as) *the Florida ones.* **3 compare notes (with sb)** (informal) to talk with someone in order to find out if his/her experience is the same as yours [ORIGIN: 1400—1500 French *comparer*, from Latin *comparare*, from *compar* "like," from *com* "with" + *par* "equal"]

compare² *n.* **beyond/without compare** (literary) a quality that is beyond compare is the best of its kind: *beauty beyond compare*

com·par·i·son /kəm'pærəsən/ *n.* **1** [U] the process of comparing two people or things: ***In comparison with/to*** *his brother, he's really shy.* | *My last job was so boring that this one seems great* ***by comparison.*** **2** [C] a statement or examination of how similar or different two people or things are: *a* ***comparison of*** *crime figures in Chicago and Detroit* **3** [C] a statement that someone or something is like someone or something else: *The writer* ***draws comparisons between*** *the two presidents.* | *You can't* ***make*** *a* ***comparison between*** *American and Japanese schools – they're too different.* **4 there's no comparison** used when you think that someone or something is much better than someone or something else: ***There's*** *just* ***no comparison between*** *canned vegetables and fresh ones.*

com·part·ment /kəm'pɑrt˺mənt/ *n.* [C] a smaller enclosed space inside something larger: *the overhead compartment on a plane*

com·part·men·tal·ize /kəm,pɑrt˺'mɛntəl,aɪz/ *v.* [T] to divide things into separate groups

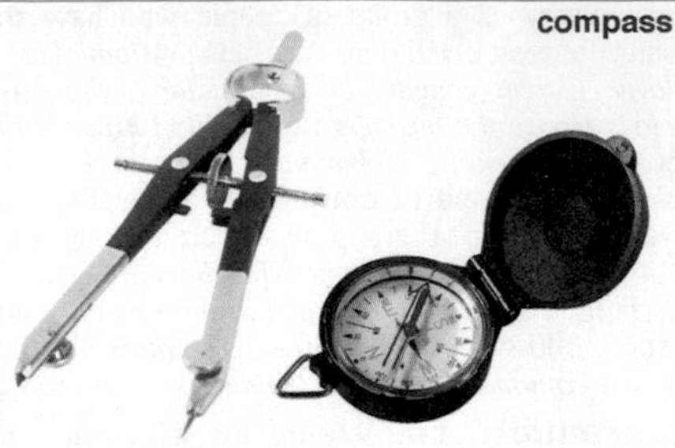

compass

com·pass /'kʌmpəs/ *n.* [C] **1** an instrument that shows the direction you are traveling in, with an ARROW that always points north **2** MATH an instrument with a sharp point, used for drawing circles or measuring distances on maps

com·pas·sion /kəm'pæʃən/ *n.* [U] sympathy for someone who is suffering: *her* ***compassion for*** *the poor* | *We should* ***have compassion*** *for others.* [ORIGIN: 1300—1400 Old French, Late Latin *compassio*, from *compati* "to feel sympathy"]

com·pas·sion·ate /kəm'pæʃənɪt/ *adj.* feeling sympathy for people who are suffering: *a compassionate man*

THESAURUS **kind, nice, considerate, thoughtful, caring, warm-hearted, sympathetic** → KIND²

com·pat·i·ble /kəm'pæṭəbəl/ (Ac) *adj.* **1** two people who are compatible are able to have a good relationship because they share interests, ideas, etc. **2** two things that are compatible are able to exist or be used together without problems: *Is the software* ***compatible with*** *your PC?* | *The two businesses have compatible aims, and they may eventually merge* (=join together to form one larger business). —**compatibility** /kəm,pæṭə'bɪləṭi/ *n.* [U]

com·pa·tri·ot /kəm'peɪtriət/ *n.* [C] someone who is from the same country as you: *I took an English class with several of my compatriots.*

com·pel /kəm'pɛl/ *v.* (**compelled**, **compelling**) [T] to force someone to do something: *He* ***felt compelled to*** *resign because of the scandal.*

THESAURUS **force, make, coerce, impel, pressure** → FORCE²

com·pel·ling /kəm'pɛlɪŋ/ *adj.* **1** very interesting or exciting: *a compelling story*

THESAURUS **interesting, fascinating, intriguing, absorbing, enthralling, engrossing, gripping, riveting** → INTERESTING

2 a compelling argument, reason, etc. seems very good or strong: *The jury was presented with* ***compelling evidence.***

com·pen·di·um /kəm'pɛndiəm/ *n.* [C] (formal) a book that contains a complete collection of facts, drawings, etc. on a particular subject: *a baseball compendium*

com·pen·sate /ˈkɑmpən,seɪt/ (Ac) *v.* **1** [I] to do something so that something bad has a smaller effect: *Her intelligence more than **compensates for** her lack of experience.* **2** [T] to pay someone money because s/he has suffered injury, loss, or damage: *The firm will **compensate** workers **for** their loss of earnings.* | *The fund was set up to compensate victims of the disaster.* [ORIGIN: 1600—1700 Latin, past participle of *compensare*, from *compendere* "to weigh together"] **—compensatory** /kəmˈpɛnsə,tɔri/ *adj.*: *The court awarded Ms. Jones $2 million in compensatory damages.*

com·pen·sa·tion /,kɑmpənˈseɪʃən/ (Ac) *n.* **1** [U] money that someone is given because s/he has suffered injury, loss, or damage: *The fishermen have demanded **compensation for** the damage.* | *The jury awarded Tyler $1 million **in compensation**.* **2** [C,U] something that makes a bad situation seem better: *One of the few compensations of losing my job was seeing more of my family.*

com·pete /kəmˈpit/ *v.* [I] to try to win or gain something, or try to be better or more successful than someone else: *How many runners will be **competing in** the race?* | *We just **can't compete with/against** big companies like theirs.* | *The stores are **competing for** customers.*

com·pe·tent /ˈkɑmpətənt/ *adj.* having enough skill or knowledge to do something to a satisfactory standard: *A competent mechanic should be able to fix the problem quickly.* [ORIGIN: 1300—1400 Old French, Latin, present participle of *competere* "to be suitable"] **—competence** *n.* [U] **—competently** *adv.*

com·pet·ing /kəmˈpitɪŋ/ *adj.* **1 competing interests/demands/claims etc.** two or more interests, claims, etc. that cannot both be right **2 competing products** products, etc. that are trying to be more successful than each other

com·pe·ti·tion /,kɑmpəˈtɪʃən/ *n.* **1** [singular, U] a situation in which people or organizations compete with each other: *The **competition between** the two sisters is obvious.* | ***Competition for** the job was intense.* | *Prices have gone down due to **competition among** the airlines.* **2** [singular, U] the people or groups that are competing against you, especially in business: *You'll have **no competition**.* | *Our aim is to be better than **the competition**.* **3** [C] an organized event in which people or teams compete against each other: *a dancing competition* | *He decided to **enter** the **competition**.* | *Who **won** the **competition**?*

THESAURUS

championship – a competition to find the best player or team in a particular sport: *the Iowa State Girls' Basketball Championships*
tournament – a competition in which many players or teams compete against each other until there is one winner: *a local volleyball tournament at Sunset Park*
contest – a competition in which a judge or group of judges decides the winner: *the school's essay contest*
playoff – a game or series of games played by the best teams or players in a sports competition, in order to decide the final winner: *The Yankees have often made the playoffs.* | *the divisional playoff game against San Francisco*

com·pet·i·tive /kəmˈpɛt̬ət̬ɪv/ *adj.* **1** determined to be more successful than other people or companies: *Steve's very competitive.* | *What can we do to maintain our **competitive edge** (=ability to be more successful)?* **2** relating to competition: *competitive sports* | *Advertising is a **highly competitive** industry.* **3** competitive prices or products are cheaper than others but still of good quality

THESAURUS **cheap, inexpensive, reasonable, a good/great deal, good/great value, a bargain** → CHEAP[1]

—competitiveness *n.* [U]

com·pet·i·tor /kəmˈpɛt̬ət̬ɚ/ *n.* [C] a person, team, company, etc. that is competing with another one: *Last year they sold twice as many computers as their **main competitor**.*

com·pi·la·tion /,kɑmpəˈleɪʃən/ (Ac) *n.* **1** [C] a book, list, record, etc. that consists of different pieces of information, music, etc.: *a **compilation of** love songs* **2** [U] the process of making a book, list, record, etc. from different pieces of information, music, etc.: *the **compilation of** the report*

com·pile /kəmˈpaɪl/ (Ac) *v.* [T] to make a book, list, record, etc. using different pieces of information, music, etc.: *The report is **compiled from** a survey of 5,000 households.* | *It took several months to compile the database.* [ORIGIN: 1300—1400 Old French *compiler*, from Latin *compilare* "to seize together, steal"]

com·pla·cen·cy /kəmˈpleɪsənsi/ *also* **com·pla·cence** /-ˈpleɪsəns/ *n.* [U] a feeling of satisfaction with a situation or with what you have achieved, so that you stop trying to improve or change things: *Successful companies avoid complacency and constantly strive to improve.*

com·pla·cent /kəmˈpleɪsənt/ *adj.* pleased with what you have achieved so that you stop trying to improve or change things: *We've been winning, but we're not going to get complacent.*

com·plain /kəmˈpleɪn/ *v.* [I,T] **1** to say that you are annoyed, not satisfied, or unhappy about something or someone: *Fred's always **complaining about** something.* | *My kids **complained that** they hardly ever saw me, because I was working too much.* | *She **complained to** the manager.* **2 I can't complain** (spoken) said when you think a situation is satisfactory even though there may be a few problems: *I still don't feel too great, but I can't complain.* [ORIGIN: 1300—1400 Old French *complaindre*, from Vulgar Latin *complangere*]

complain of sth *phr. v.* to say that you feel sick or have a pain in a part of your body: *He complained of stomach pains.*

com·plaint /kəm'pleɪnt/ *n.* **1** [C,U] a statement in which someone complains about something: *We've **received** a large number of **complaints** from customers.* | *There have been **complaints about** the quality of her work.* | ***complaints against** the police* **2** [C] LAW a formal statement saying that someone is guilty of a crime: *She has **filed** a formal **complaint** against her employer, alleging sexual harassment.*

C

THESAURUS accusation, allegation, charge, indictment → ACCUSATION

3 [C] something that you complain about: *My only complaint is the high prices they charge.* **4** [C] a sickness that affects a part of your body

com·ple·ment¹ /'kɑmpləmənt/ (Ac) *n.* [C] **1** someone or something that combines well with another thing, and brings out the good qualities in it: *The wine was the perfect **complement to** the meal.* **2** the number or quantity needed to make a group complete: *The school has its **full complement** of teachers.* **3** ENG. LANG. ARTS in grammar, a word or phrase that follows a verb and describes the subject of the verb. In the sentence "You look angry," "angry" is a complement. [ORIGIN: 1300—1400 Latin *complementum*, from *complere* "to fill up"]

com·ple·ment² /'kɑmplə,mɛnt/ (Ac) *v.* [T] to combine well with another thing, and bring out the good qualities in it: *Buy a hat and scarf that complements your coat.* —**complementary** /,kɑmplə'mɛntri◂, -'mɛntəri◂/ *adj.*: *a small team of people with complementary skills*

,complementary 'angles *n.* [plural] MATH two angles whose total is 90° → *see picture at* ANGLE¹

,complementary 'colors *n.* [plural] two colors that produce white or gray when they are mixed, for example red and green

com·plete¹ /kəm'plit/ *adj.* **1** something that is complete has all the parts it should have: *a complete set of china dishes* | *the **complete works** of Shakespeare* | *The list of guests is not complete.* **2** [only before noun] (informal) used in order to emphasize that a quality or situation is as great as it could possibly be: *I made a **complete fool** of myself.* | *The meeting was a **complete waste of time**.* | *The news came as a **complete surprise**.* **3** finished: *Our research is nearly complete.*

THESAURUS done, finished, over, through → DONE²

4 complete with sth having particular equipment or features: *The house **comes complete with** a swimming pool.* [ORIGIN: 1300—1400 Old French *complet*, from Latin, past participle of *complere* "to fill up"] —**completeness** *n.* [U]

complete² *v.* [T] **1** to finish doing or making something: *The book took five years to complete.* **2** to make something whole or perfect by adding what is missing: *I need one more stamp to complete my collection.* **3** to write the information that is needed on a form: *65 people completed the questionnaire.*

com·plete·ly /kəm'plit˺li/ *adv.* in every way or to the greatest degree possible: *I completely forgot about her birthday.*

THESAURUS

absolutely – used especially to emphasize something, or to show that you strongly agree with something: *I was absolutely exhausted.* | *He's absolutely right.*
totally – used especially to show that you are annoyed about something or strongly disagree with something: *She totally ignored me.* | *The price was totally ridiculous.*
entirely – used especially in negative sentences or after "almost": *I'm not entirely sure.* | *The class was almost entirely girls.*
wholly – used especially in negative sentences to mean "in every possible way": *Is the company wholly responsible for the damage?*
utterly (formal) – used to emphasize something, especially a negative quality: *The game seemed utterly pointless.*

com,pleting the 'square *n.* [U] MATH a method for changing the form of a QUADRATIC EQUATION so that it is easier to solve

com·ple·tion /kəm'pliʃən/ *n.* [U] the state of being finished, or the act of finishing something: *The construction is **nearing completion**.* | *the **completion of** the $80 million project*

com·plex¹ /kəm'plɛks, kɑm-, 'kɑmplɛks/ (Ac) *adj.* something that is complex has a lot of different parts and is difficult to understand or deal with: ***complex systems** of irrigation* | *a **complex issue*** | *The technology is **highly complex**.* [ORIGIN: 1600—1700 Latin *complexus*, past participle of *complecti* "to include (many different things)"] —**complexity** /kəm'plɛksəṭi/ *n.* [U]: *the increasing complexity of large construction projects*

THESAURUS complicated, elaborate, convoluted, intricate → COMPLICATED

com·plex² /'kɑmplɛks/ (Ac) *n.* [C] **1** a group of buildings or one large building used for a particular purpose: *a new shopping complex* **2** an emotional problem in which someone is too anxious about something or thinks too much about it: *Linda has a **complex about** her appearance.*

com,plex 'conjugate *also* **com,plex ,conjugate 'number** *n.* [C] MATH either of a pair of complex numbers that have the same REAL NUMBER parts but opposite IMAGINARY NUMBER parts. For example, a + bi is the complex conjugate of a – bi.

com,plex 'fraction *n.* [C] MATH a FRACTION (=number such as ½ or ⅛) in which either the number above the line or the number below the line is a fraction, or the numbers above and below the line are both fractions

com·plex·ion /kəm'plɛkʃən/ *n.* [C] the natural color and appearance of the skin on your face: *a young woman with a* ***pale/dark complexion***

com,plex 'number *n.* [C] MATH any number that can be written in the form a + bi, where a and b are REAL NUMBERS and i is the square root of −1 → IMAGINARY NUMBER

com,plex 'word *n.* [C] ENG. LANG. ARTS a word that contains more than one MORPHEME (=the smallest unit of meaning in a language). "Girls" is a complex word because it contains two morphemes, "girl" and "s."

com·pli·ance /kəm'plaɪəns/ *n.* [U] (formal) the act of obeying a rule or law: ***Compliance with*** *the law is expected of everyone.*

com·pli·ant /kəm'plaɪənt/ *adj.* willing to obey or agree to other people's wishes and demands

com·pli·cate /'kɑmplə,keɪt/ *v.* [T] to make a problem or situation more difficult (ANT) **simplify**: *There may be other factors, but let's not* ***complicate matters*** *right now.*

com·pli·cat·ed /'kɑmplə,keɪṭɪd/ *adj.* something that is complicated has a lot of different parts and is difficult to understand or deal with (ANT) **simple**: *The instructions are much too complicated.* | *an extremely complicated process*

THESAURUS

complex – difficult to understand because of having a lot of different parts that are all connected in different ways: *Scientists are still trying to understand the complex relationship between the genes that cause the disease.*
elaborate – having lots of parts or details and very carefully planned, but often more complicated than is necessary: *Josh and Maria have made elaborate plans for their wedding.*
convoluted – too complicated and difficult to understand – used especially about language, arguments, or a story: *He tends to use long convoluted sentences, which make the book difficult for the ordinary reader.*
intricate – very well designed, or made with a lot of small parts or details: *The rug has an intricate design.*

THESAURUS **difficult, hard, tough, awkward, challenging, demanding** → DIFFICULT

com·pli·ca·tion /,kɑmplə'keɪʃən/ *n.* **1** [C usually plural] a medical problem or illness that happens while someone is already sick: *There were no complications following surgery.* **2** [C,U] a problem or situation that makes something more difficult to understand or deal with: *The drop in student numbers added further complications.*

com·plic·i·ty /kəm'plɪsəṭi/ *n.* [U] **1** LAW the act of being involved in a crime with other people: *Fifteen men were arrested for* ***complicity in*** *the lynching.* **2** (formal) involvement in or knowledge of a situation that is morally wrong or dishonest: *None of these terrible events could have happened without the complicity of the state.* —**complicit** *adj.*

com·pli·ment¹ /'kɑmpləmənt/ *n.* **1** [C] something you say that shows you admire someone or something: *"You look great." "Thanks for the compliment."* | *I was trying to* ***pay*** *her a* ***compliment*** (=give her a compliment). | *I wasn't sure exactly what they meant, but I* ***took it as a compliment*** (=accepted what was said as a compliment rather than an insult). **2 with the compliments of sb/with sb's compliments** (formal) used by a person or company when he, she, or it sends or gives something to you: *Please accept these tickets with our compliments.*

com·pli·ment² /'kɑmplə,mɛnt/ *v.* [T] to say something nice to someone in order to praise him/her: *They* ***complimented*** *John* ***on*** *his excellent Spanish.*

com·pli·men·ta·ry /,kɑmplə'mɛntri, -'mɛntəri/ *adj.* **1** saying that you admire or respect someone or something: *He was very* ***complimentary about*** *your work.* **2** given free to someone: *complimentary tickets*

com·ply /kəm'plaɪ/ *v.* (**complied, complies**) [I] (formal) to do what you are asked to do or what a law or rule tells you to do: *Those who fail to* ***comply with*** *the law will be fined.*

THESAURUS **obey, do what sb says, do what you are told/do as you are told, follow sb's orders/instructions, observe** → OBEY

com·po·nent /kəm'poʊnənt/ (Ac) *n.* [C] one of several parts that make up a whole machine or system: *stereo components* | *Oxygen is a major component of the Earth's atmosphere.* [ORIGIN: 1500—1600 Latin, present participle of *componere* from *com-* "together" + *ponere* "to put"]

com·pose /kəm'poʊz/ *v.* **1 be composed of sth** to be formed from a number of substances, parts, or people: *Water is composed of hydrogen and oxygen.* **2** [T] to write a piece of music: *Schumann was better at composing music than playing it.* **3 compose yourself** to become calm after feeling angry, upset, or excited: *Lynn took a deep breath and tried to compose herself.* **4 compose a letter/poem/speech etc.** to write a letter, poem, etc., thinking very carefully about it as you write it

com·posed /kəm'poʊzd/ *adj.* calm, rather than upset or angry

com·pos·er /kəm'poʊzɚ/ *n.* [C] someone who writes music

com·pos·ite /kəm'pɑzɪt/ *adj.* made up of different parts or materials: *a composite drawing* —**composite** *n.* [C]

com·po·si·tion /ˌkɑmpəˈzɪʃən/ *n.* **1** [U] the way in which something is made up of different parts, things, or people: *the chemical* ***composition of*** *soil* **2 a)** [U] the art or process of writing music, a poem, or an ESSAY, etc. **b)** [C] a piece of music, or art, or a poem: *one of Beethoven's early compositions* **3** [U] the way in which the different parts of a painting or photograph are arranged **4** [C,U] a short piece of writing about a particular subject, that is done by a student

C

THESAURUS **essay, paper, assignment, thesis, dissertation** → ESSAY

com·post /ˈkɑmpoʊst/ *n.* [U] a mixture of decayed leaves, plants, etc. used for improving the quality of soil

com·po·sure /kəmˈpoʊʒɚ/ *n.* [singular, U] a calm feeling that you have when you feel confident about dealing with a situation: *She stopped crying and* ***regained*** *her* ***composure****.*

com·pound¹ /ˈkɑmpaʊnd/ (Ac) *n.* [C] **1** CHEMISTRY a chemical compound is a substance that consists of two or more different substances: *Organic compounds have been found in meteorites.* | *Sulfur dioxide is a compound of sulfur and oxygen.*

THESAURUS **mixture, combination, blend, solution** → MIXTURE

2 an area that contains a group of buildings and is surrounded by a fence or wall: *a prison compound* **3** *also* **compound word/noun/adjective/verb** ENG. LANG. ARTS two or more words that are used together as a noun, adjective, or verb. For example, the noun "ice cream" is a compound. [ORIGIN: 1500—1600 Old French *compondre*, from Latin *componere*, from *com* "together" + *ponere* "to put"]

com·pound² /kəmˈpaʊnd/ (Ac) *v.* [T] to make a difficult situation worse by adding more problems: *Our difficulties were* ***compounded by*** *other people's mistakes.*

ˌcompound ˈinterest *n.* [U] ECONOMICS INTEREST that is calculated both on the sum of money lent or borrowed and on the unpaid interest already earned or charged → SIMPLE INTEREST

ˌcompound ˈsentence *n.* [C] ENG. LANG. ARTS a sentence that consists of two or more CLAUSES, each of which can stand independently and which are often joined by a conjunction. For example, "The mountain was steep, but we eventually reached the top" is a compound sentence.

com·pre·hend /ˌkɑmprɪˈhɛnd/ *v.* [I,T] (formal) to understand something: *I did not* ***fully comprehend*** *what had happened.* [ORIGIN: 1300—1400 Latin *comprehendere* "to take hold of completely"]

com·pre·hen·si·ble /ˌkɑmprɪˈhɛnsəbəl/ *adj.* easy to understand (ANT) **incomprehensible**: *The book explains the process in language that is* ***comprehensible to*** *the average reader.*

com·pre·hen·sion /ˌkɑmprɪˈhɛnʃən/ *n.* [U] the ability to understand something, or knowledge about something: *The complexities of the situation are* ***beyond*** *my* ***comprehension*** (=impossible for me to understand). | *a test of* ***reading/listening comprehension*** (=a student's ability to understand written or spoken language)

com·pre·hen·sive /ˌkɑmprɪˈhɛnsɪv◂/ (Ac) *adj.* including everything that is necessary: *comprehensive health insurance* | *a comprehensive study of the city's public transportation system*

com·press /kəmˈprɛs/ *v.* **1** [I,T] to press something or make it smaller so that it takes up less space: *This program compresses computer files so they can be easily sent by email.*

THESAURUS **press, squash, crush, mash, grind, squeeze, compact** → PRESS¹

2 [T] to reduce the amount of time it takes for something to happen or be done —**compression** /kəmˈprɛʃən/ *n.* [U]

com·prise /kəmˈpraɪz/ (Ac) *v.* (formal) **1** [linking verb] to consist of particular parts: *The World Trade Organization comprises more than 100 nations.* | *The committee* ***is comprised of*** *eight members.*

USAGE

Comprise, **be composed of**, and **consist of** can each be used in order to talk about the parts that things are made of, or the things that something contains.

Comprise is the more formal word.

Each of the following sentences means the same thing, but the patterns are different: *The United States comprises 50 states.* | *The United States is composed of 50 states.* | *The United States consists of 50 states.*

2 [T] to form part of a larger group: *Women comprise over 75% of our staff.* [ORIGIN: 1400—1500 Old French, past participle of *comprendre*, from Latin *comprehendere* "to take hold of completely"]

com·pro·mise¹ /ˈkɑmprəˌmaɪz/ *n.* [C,U] an agreement that is achieved after everyone involved accepts less than what s/he wanted at first: *The President and Congress are attempting to* ***reach a compromise****.* | *Neither of them was willing to* ***make compromises****.* [ORIGIN: 1400—1500 French *compromis*, from Latin *compromissum* "joint promise," from *compromittere*]

compromise² *v.* **1** [I] to end an argument by making an agreement in which everyone involved accepts less than what s/he wanted at first: *The governor is not willing to* ***compromise on*** *the issue.* **2** [T] to risk harming or damaging something that is important: *The safety of employees had been compromised.*

com·pro·mis·ing /ˈkɑmprəˌmaɪzɪŋ/ *adj.* making it seem that someone has done something dishonest or wrong: *a compromising photograph*

comp time /ˈkɑmp ˌtaɪm/ *n.* [U] vacation time that you are given instead of money because you have worked more hours than you should have

com·pul·sion /kəmˈpʌlʃən/ *n.* **1** [C] a strong desire to do something that is wrong: *Drinking is a compulsion with her.* **2** [singular, U] the act of forcing or influencing someone to do something that s/he does not want to do: *You are **under** no **compulsion to** sign the agreement.*

com·pul·sive /kəmˈpʌlsɪv/ *adj.* **1** compulsive behavior is very difficult to stop or control: *compulsive eating* **2 compulsive liar/gambler etc.** someone who has a strong desire to lie, GAMBLE, etc. which s/he cannot control —**compulsively** *adv.*

com·pul·so·ry /kəmˈpʌlsəri/ *adj.* if something is compulsory, it must be done because of a rule or law ANT **voluntary**: *compulsory military service*

THESAURUS **necessary, essential, vital, mandatory, requisite** ➔ NECESSARY

com·punc·tion /kəmˈpʌŋkʃən/ *n.* **have/feel no compunction about (doing) sth** (formal) to not feel guilty or sorry about something although other people may think that it is wrong: *He seemed to feel no compunction about lying to us.*

com·pute /kəmˈpyut/ Ac *v.* [I,T] (formal) to calculate an answer, total, result, etc.: *The machine can compute the time it takes a sound wave to bounce back.* —**computation** /ˌkɑmpyəˈteɪʃən/ *n.* [C,U]: *He is below average in spelling and math computation.* | *The software is able to perform* (=do) *complex computations.*

com·put·er /kəmˈpyuṭɚ/ Ac *n.* [C] IT an electronic machine that stores information and uses programs to help you find, organize, or change the information ➔ LAPTOP, PC: *I can't get the program to work on my computer.* | *We do all our work **on computer**.* | *Our office has switched to a different **computer system**.* | *the latest **computer software***
➔ *see picture on page A19*

TOPIC

You **start up/boot up a computer** and **log in/on** in order to start using it.
People use computers to do a lot of different things, such as send and receive **emails**, look for information on **the Internet**, and work on **files** or other **documents**.
You need to **open a file** before you can work on it. When you have finished, you **save** your **work/file**, **close** the **document** or **file** that you were working on, and **shut down** the computer.
If your computer **crashes**, it suddenly stops working. You have to **reboot** or **restart** the computer to make it start working again.

com·put·er·ize /kəmˈpyuṭəˌraɪz/ *v.* [T] to use a computer to control the way something is done, to store information, etc.: *plans to computerize all our financial records* —**computerization** /kəmˌpyuṭərəˈzeɪʃən/ *n.* [U]

comˌputer ˈliterate *adj.* able to use a computer —**computer literacy** *n.* [U]

com·put·ing /kəmˈpyuṭɪŋ/ Ac *n.* [U] the use of computers as a job, in a business, etc.: *personal computing*

com·rade /ˈkɑmræd/ *n.* [C] (formal) a friend, especially someone who is in the same army as you, or who shares the same political aims as you [ORIGIN: 1500—1600 French *camarade*, from Old Spanish *camarada* "group of people sleeping in one room, friend"] —**comradeship** *n.* [U]

con[1] /kɑn/ *v.* (**conned**, **conning**) [T] (informal) to trick someone, either to take his/her money or to get him/her to do something: *That guy tried to **con** me **out of** $20.*

con[2] *n.* [C] **1** (informal) a trick to get someone's money or make someone do something: *The ads you see in the paper are just a con.* **2** (slang) a CONVICT ➔ **pros and cons** *at* PRO

ˈcon ˌartist *n.* [C] (informal) someone who tricks people in order to get money from them

con·cave /ˌkɑnˈkeɪv◂/ *adj.* PHYSICS curved inward like a bowl ANT **convex**: *a concave lens*

con·ceal /kənˈsil/ *v.* [T] (formal) to hide something carefully: *She tried to **conceal** her emotions **from** Ted.* | *He was carrying a **concealed weapon**.* [ORIGIN: 1200—1300 Old French *conceler*, from Latin *concelare*, from *com* "with" + *celare* "to hide"] —**concealment** *n.* [U]

THESAURUS **hide, cover/cover up, disguise, mask, secrete** ➔ HIDE[1]

con·cede /kənˈsid/ *v.* **1** [T] to admit that something is true although you do not want to: *She reluctantly **conceded that** I was right.* **2** [I,T] to admit that you are not going to win a game, argument, battle, etc.: *Hawkins **conceded defeat** in the election.*

THESAURUS **surrender, give in, yield, submit, admit/accept defeat** ➔ SURRENDER

3 [T] to let someone have something although you do not want to: *They have refused to **concede** any territory **to** the rebels.* [ORIGIN: 1400—1500 French *concéder*, from Latin *concedere*]

con·ceit /kənˈsit/ *n.* [U] an attitude that shows that you are too proud of what you can do, how you look, etc. [ORIGIN: 1600—1700 *conceit* "thought, opinion" (14—19 centuries), from *conceive*]

con·ceit·ed /kənˈsiṭɪd/ *adj.* (disapproving) behaving in a way that shows that you are too proud of what you can do, how you look, etc.: *I don't want to seem conceited, but I know I'll win.*

THESAURUS proud, big-headed, vain, arrogant, stuck-up, egotistical, haughty → PROUD

C

con·ceiv·a·ble /kən'sivəbəl/ (Ac) *adj.* able to be believed or imagined (ANT) **inconceivable**: ***It is conceivable that*** *the experts could be wrong.* | *Doctors looked at every conceivable cause of her illness.* —**conceivably** *adv.*

con·ceive /kən'siv/ (Ac) *v.* **1** [I,T] to imagine a situation or what something is like: *It is impossible to* ***conceive of*** *the size of the universe.* | *I can hardly* ***conceive what*** *it would be like to live in the Antarctic during winter.* | *At that time, the Native American people had heard about life in a city, but they could not conceive it.* **2** [T] to think of a new idea or plan: *It was Dr. Salk who conceived the idea of a polio vaccine.*

THESAURUS invent, create, think up, come up with sth, devise, make up, dream up → INVENT

3 [I,T] BIOLOGY to become PREGNANT → CONCEPTION: *Ben and Tracy are hoping to conceive a second child soon.* [ORIGIN: 1200—1300 Old French *conceivre*, from Latin *concipere* "to take in, conceive"]

con·cen·trate¹ /'kɑnsən,treɪt/ (Ac) *v.* **1** [I] to think very carefully about something you are doing: *With all this noise, it's hard to concentrate.* | *Children with attention deficit disorder find it difficult to* ***concentrate on*** *their work.* **2 be concentrated in/on/at etc. sth** to be present in large numbers or amounts in a particular place: *Most of the state's population is concentrated in the cities.*

concentrate on sth *phr. v.* to give most of your attention to one thing: *I want to concentrate on my career for a while before I have kids.* | *The authorities are concentrating their efforts on preventing the disease spreading.*

concentrate² *n.* [C,U] a substance or liquid that has been made stronger by removing most of the water from it: *orange juice concentrate*

con·cen·trat·ed /'kɑnsən,treɪt̬ɪd/ (Ac) *adj.* **1** showing a lot of determination or effort: *He made a concentrated effort to raise his grades.* **2** a substance that is concentrated has been made stronger by removing most of the water from it: *a concentrated detergent* | *Heating the substance produced a concentrated solution containing sodium and calcium chlorides.*

con·cen·tra·tion /,kɑnsən'treɪʃən/ (Ac) *n.* **1** [U] the act of thinking very carefully about something that you are doing: *The children got tired and* ***lost*** *their* ***concentration****.* **2** [U] a process in which you put a lot of attention, energy, etc. into a particular activity: *There was too much* ***concentration on*** *one type of industry.* **3** [C,U] a large amount of something in a particular place: *This concentration of industry has made the province one of the most polluted regions of China.* | *Workers were exposed to huge concentrations of asbestos.* **4** [C] CHEMISTRY the amount of a substance contained in a liquid: *Tests showed high* ***concentrations of*** *minerals in the water.*

,concen'tration ,camp *n.* [C] a prison where large numbers of people are kept in very bad conditions, usually during a war

concentric

concentric circles

con·cen·tric /kən'sɛntrɪk/ *adj.* MATH concentric circles are of different sizes and have the same center [ORIGIN: 1300—1400 Medieval Latin *concentricus*, from Latin *com-* "together" + *centrum* "center"]

con·cept /'kɑnsɛpt/ (Ac) *n.* [C] an idea of how something is, or how something should be done: *He strongly believed in the* ***concept of*** *universal human rights.* | *The discovery supports the* ***concept that*** *our solar system is not unique.* [ORIGIN: 1500—1600 Latin *conceptum*, from the past participle of *concipere* "to take in, conceive"]

THESAURUS idea, theory, hypothesis → IDEA

con·cep·tion /kən'sɛpʃən/ (Ac) *n.* **1** [C] a general idea about what something is like, or a way of understanding what something is like: *One common* ***conception of*** *democracy is that it means "government by the people."* **2** [U] BIOLOGY the process by which a woman or female animal becomes PREGNANT, or the time when this happens → CONCEIVE

con·cep·tu·al /kən'sɛptʃuəl/ (Ac) *adj.* (formal) relating to ideas, or based on them, and not yet real: *The plans are in the conceptual stage.* —**conceptually** *adv.*

con·cern¹ /kən'sɚn/ *n.* **1** [U] a feeling of worry about something important: *There is growing* ***concern about/over*** *ocean pollution.* | *There is* ***concern that*** *the war could continue for a long time.* | *The police officer said that there was* ***no cause for***

concern. **2** [C] something important that worries you or involves you: *The destruction of the rainforest is a* ***concern to*** *us all.* | *Our* ***main/primary/major concern*** *is safety.*

concern² *v.* [T] **1** to affect someone or involve him/her: *What we're planning doesn't concern you.* **2** to make someone feel worried or upset: *My daughter's problems at school concern me greatly.* **3** to be about something or someone: *Most of her books concern the problems of growing up.* **4 concern yourself (with sth)** to become involved in something that interests or worries you: *You don't need to concern yourself with this, Jan.*

con·cerned /kən'sɚnd/ *adj.* **1** [not before noun] involved in something or affected by it: *It was a shock for* ***all concerned*** (=everyone involved). | *Everyone* ***concerned with*** *the car industry will be interested.* **2** worried about something important: *We're* ***concerned about*** *the results of the test.* | *letters from concerned parents*

THESAURUS **worried, anxious, nervous, uneasy, stressed (out), tense, apprehensive** → WORRIED

3 believing that something is important: *They seem to be only* ***concerned with*** *making money.* **4 as far as sth is concerned** used in order to show which subject or thing you are talking about: *As far as money is concerned, the club is doing fairly well.* **5 as far as sb is concerned** used in order to show what someone's opinion on a subject is: *As far as I'm concerned, the whole idea is crazy.*

con·cern·ing /kən'sɚnɪŋ/ *prep.* (formal) about or relating to something: *We have questions concerning the report.*

THESAURUS **about, on, regarding, with regard to, re** → ABOUT¹

con·cert /'kɑnsɚt/ *n.* [C] **1** a performance given by musicians or singers: *a rock concert* | *We* ***went to a concert*** *last night.* **2 in concert a)** playing or singing at a concert **b)** (formal) done together with someone else: *Police are working* ***in concert with*** *local businesses.* [ORIGIN: 1500—1600 French, Italian *concerto*, from *concertare*, from Latin, "to fight, compete"]

con·cert·ed /kən'sɚt̬ɪd/ *adj.* **a concerted effort/action/attempt etc.** something that is done by people working together in a determined way: *Libraries have* ***made a concerted effort*** *to attract young people.*

con·cer·to /kən'tʃɛrt̬oʊ/ *n.* (plural **concertos**) [C] ENG. LANG. ARTS a piece of CLASSICAL MUSIC, usually for one instrument and an ORCHESTRA

con·ces·sion /kən'sɛʃən/ *n.* [C] **1** something that you do in order to end an argument: *Neither side is willing to* ***make concessions*** *on the issue of pay.* **2** a special right given to someone by the government, an employer, etc.: *tax concessions for married people* **3** the right to have a business in a particular place, especially in a place owned by someone else

con'cession ˌstand *n.* [C] a small business that sells food, drinks, and other things at sports events, theaters, etc.

con·cierge /kɔn'syɛrʒ/ *n.* [C] someone in a hotel whose job is to help guests with problems, give advice about local places to go, etc. [ORIGIN: 1500—1600 French, Latin *conservus* "fellow slave"]

con·cil·i·a·tion /kənˌsɪli'eɪʃən/ *n.* [U] (formal) the process of trying to end an argument between people

con·cil·i·a·to·ry /kən'sɪliəˌtɔri/ *adj.* (formal) intended to make someone stop being angry with you or with someone else: *a conciliatory remark*

con·cise /kən'saɪs/ *adj.* short and clear, without using too many words: *a concise answer* [ORIGIN: 1500—1600 Latin *concisus*, from the past participle of *concidere* "to cut up"] **—concisely** *adv.* **—conciseness** *n.* [U]

THESAURUS **short, brief, quick, succinct, curt** → SHORT¹

con·clude /kən'klud/ (Ac) *v.* **1** [T] to decide something after considering all the information you have: *Doctors have* ***concluded that*** *sunburn can lead to skin cancer.* | *There are a number of things that we can conclude from this experiment* **2** [T] (formal) to complete something that you have been doing: *The study was concluded last month.* **3** [I,T] to end a meeting, speech, event, etc. by doing or saying one final thing, or to end in this way: *The carnival* ***concluded with*** *a fireworks display.* **—concluding** *adj.*: *concluding remarks*

con·clu·sion /kən'kluʒən/ (Ac) *n.* [C] **1** something that you decide after considering all the information you have: *I've* ***come to the conclusion*** *that she's lying.* | *The appeal court* ***reached*** *the same* ***conclusion.*** | *It's hard to* ***draw*** *any* ***conclusions*** (=decide whether something is true) *without more data.* | *Megan, you're* ***jumping to conclusions*** (=deciding something is true without knowing all the facts). **2** the end or final part of something: *The* ***conclusion of*** *his essay was clear and concise.* **3 in conclusion** (formal) used in speech or a piece of writing to show that you are about to finish: *In conclusion, I want to thank everyone who came out today.* [ORIGIN: 1300—1400 French, Latin *conclusio*, from *concludere* "to shut up, end, decide"]

con·clu·sive /kən'klusɪv/ (Ac) *adj.* showing that something is definitely true: *There is no* ***conclusive evidence*** *connecting him with the crime.* **—conclusively** *adv.*: *The theory has not been proved conclusively.*

con·coct /kən'kɑkt/ *v.* [T] **1** to invent a false explanation or illegal plan: *She* ***concocted*** *a* ***story*** *about her mother being sick.* | *He* ***concocted*** *a* ***scheme*** *to rob the bank.* **2** to make something unusual by mixing different things together [ORIGIN: 1500—1600 Latin, past participle of *concoquere* "to cook together"] —**concoction** /kən'kɑkʃən/ *n.* [C]

con·com·i·tant¹ /kən'kɑmət̬ənt/ *adj.* [only before noun] (formal) existing or happening together, especially as a result of something: *members' concomitant rights and responsibilities* —**concomitantly** *adv.*

C

concomitant² *n.* [C] (formal) something that often or naturally happens with something else: *Deafness is a frequent* ***concomitant of*** *aging.*

con·cord /'kɑŋkɔrd/ *n.* [U] (formal) the state of having a friendly relationship, so that you agree on things and live in peace (SYN) **harmony** (ANT) **discord**: *Concord between the Democrats and Republicans is not easy.*

con·course /'kɑŋkɔrs/ *n.* [C] a large hall or open place in an airport, train station, etc. [ORIGIN: 1800—1900 *concourse* "coming together of people, crowd" (14—21 centuries), from French *concours*, from Latin *concursus*]

con·crete¹ /'kɑŋkrit/ *n.* [U] a substance used for building that is made by mixing sand, water, small stones, and CEMENT

con·crete² /kɑn'krit, 'kɑŋkrit/ *adj.* **1** made of concrete: *a concrete floor* → *see picture at* MATERIAL¹ **2** clearly based on facts, not on beliefs or guesses: *We need* ***concrete evidence*** *to prove that he did it.* —**concretely** *adv.*

ˌconcrete 'noun *n.* [C] ENG. LANG. ARTS a noun that names a physical thing, animal, or person you are able to hear, see, smell, touch, or taste. For example, "book" and "child" are concrete nouns. → ABSTRACT NOUN

con·cur /kən'kɚ/ *v.* (**concurred**, **concurring**) [I] (formal) to agree with someone or have the same opinion: *Dr. Hastings* ***concurs with*** *the decision of the medical board.* [ORIGIN: 1300—1400 Latin *concurrere*, from *com* "together" + *currere* "to run"] —**concurrence** /kən'kɚəns, -'kʌrəns/ *n.* [U]

> THESAURUS agree, be of the same opinion, share sb's views/concerns, be unanimous → AGREE

con·cur·rent /kən'kɚənt, -'kʌrənt/ (Ac) *adj.* (formal) **1** existing or happening at the same time: *His work is being displayed in three concurrent art exhibitions.* **2** (formal) in agreement: *concurrent opinions* —**concurrently** *adv.*

conˌcurrent 'lines *n.* [plural] MATH two or more lines that pass through the same single point

con·cus·sion /kən'kʌʃən/ *n.* [C,U] a small amount of damage to the brain that makes you become unconscious or feel sick, caused by hitting your head

con·demn /kən'dɛm/ *v.* [T] **1** to say very strongly that you do not approve of someone or something: *Politicians were quick to condemn the bombing.* **2** to give a severe punishment to someone who is guilty of a crime: *The murderer was* ***condemned to death.*** **3** to force someone to live in an unpleasant way or to suffer: *families who are* ***condemned to*** *a life of poverty* **4** to say officially that a building is not safe enough to be lived in or used [ORIGIN: 1300—1400 Old French *condemner*, from Latin *condemnare*]

con·dem·na·tion /ˌkɑndəm'neɪʃən/ *n.* [C,U] an expression of very strong disapproval: *international* ***condemnation of*** *the war*

con·den·sa·tion /ˌkɑndən'seɪʃən/ *n.* [U] small drops of water that appear when steam or hot air touches something that is cool, such as a window → EVAPORATION → *see picture at* WATER CYCLE

con·dense /kən'dɛns/ *v.* **1** [I,T] PHYSICS if gas or hot air condenses, it becomes a liquid as it becomes cooler **2** [T] to make a speech or piece of writing shorter by using fewer words to say the same thing **3** [T] to make a liquid thicker by removing some of the water from it: *condensed soup*

con·de·scend /ˌkɑndɪ'sɛnd/ *v.* [I] (disapproving) to behave as if you are better or more important than other people —**condescension** /ˌkɑndɪ'sɛnʃən/ *n.* [U]

con·de·scend·ing /ˌkɑndɪ'sɛndɪŋ◂/ *adj.* showing that you think you are better or more important than other people: *He gave us a condescending smile.*

con·di·ment /'kɑndəmənt/ *n.* [C] (formal) something such as KETCHUP or MUSTARD that you add to food when you are eating it in order to make it taste better [ORIGIN: 1400—1500 French, Latin *condimentum*, from *condire* "to pickle"]

con·di·tion¹ /kən'dɪʃən/ *n.* **1** [singular, U] the particular state that someone or something is in: *the miserable* ***condition of*** *the roads* | *The car is still* ***in*** *excellent* ***condition.*** | *He remained in a* ***critical condition*** (=very sick or very badly injured) *at Emory University Hospital.* **2 conditions** [plural] the situation or environment in which someone lives or something happens: *Poor* ***working/living conditions*** *are part of their daily lives.* | ***Under*** *these* ***conditions****, the plant will grow rapidly.* | *Schools closed early because of the bad* ***weather conditions.*** **3 be in no condition to do sth** to be too sick, drunk, or upset to be able to do something: *He is in no condition to drive.* **4** [C] an illness or health problem that affects you permanently or for a very long time: *She has a serious* ***heart condition.*** **5** [C] something that you must agree to or must happen before something else can happen: *The bank sets strict* ***conditions for*** *new loans.* | *Two employees agreed to speak* ***on condition that*** *they not be named.*

condition² *v.* [T] **1** SOCIAL SCIENCE to make a person or animal behave in a particular way by training him, her, or it over a period of time: *Pavlov* ***conditioned*** *the dogs* ***to*** *expect food at the sound of a bell.* **2** to put conditioner on your hair when you wash it

con·di·tion·al[1] /kən'dɪʃənəl/ *adj.* **1** if an offer, agreement, etc. is conditional, it will only be done if something else happens: *Our buying the house is* ***conditional on*** *our loan approval.* **2** ENG. LANG. ARTS a conditional sentence is one that usually begins with "if" or "unless," and states something that must be true or must happen before something else can be true or happen

conditional[2] *n.* **1 the conditional** ENG. LANG. ARTS in grammar, the form of the verb that expresses something that must be true or that happens before something else can be true or happens **2** [C] ENG. LANG. ARTS a conditional sentence or CLAUSE

con·di·tion·er /kən'dɪʃənɚ/ *n.* [C] a liquid that you put on your hair when you wash it in order to make it healthy and easy to comb

con·di·tion·ing /kən'dɪʃənɪŋ/ *n.* [U] SOCIAL SCIENCE the process by which people or animals learn to behave in a particular way: *social conditioning*

con·do /'kɑndoʊ/ *n.* (plural **condos**) [C] (informal) a CONDOMINIUM → HOUSE[1]

con·do·lence /kən'doʊləns/ *n.* [C usually plural, U] sympathy for someone when someone s/he loves has died: *Please* ***offer*** *my* ***condolences*** *to your mother.* [ORIGIN: 1600—1700 Late Latin *condolere* "to express sympathy," from Latin *com-* "with" + *dolere* "to feel pain"]

con·dom /'kɑndəm/ *n.* [C] a thin piece of rubber that a man wears over his PENIS during sex, to prevent a woman from becoming PREGNANT or to protect against disease

con·do·min·i·um /ˌkɑndə'mɪniəm/ *n.* [C] a building that consists of separate apartments, each of which is owned by the people living in it, or one of these apartments → HOUSE[1] [ORIGIN: 1700—1800 Modern Latin, Latin *com-* + *dominium* "area ruled"]

con·done /kən'doʊn/ *v.* [T] to accept or allow behavior that most people think is wrong: *I cannot condone the use of violence.* [ORIGIN: 1800—1900 Latin *condonare* "to forgive"]

THESAURUS **tolerate, accept, stand, put up with sth, live with sth** → TOLERATE
allow, let, permit, authorize, sanction → ALLOW

con·du·cive /kən'dusɪv/ *adj.* **be conducive to sth** (formal) to provide conditions that make it easier to do something: *The sunny climate is conducive to outdoor activities.*

con·duct[1] /kən'dʌkt/ (Ac) *v.* **1** [T] to do something in an organized way, especially in order to get information or prove facts: *The District Attorney's office is* ***conducting*** *the* ***investigation.*** | *I don't think it's right to* ***conduct experiments/tests*** *on animals.* **2** [I,T] to stand in front of a group of musicians or singers and direct their playing or singing: *the Boston Pops Orchestra,* ***conducted by*** *John Williams.* **3** [T] if something conducts electricity or heat, it allows the electricity or heat to travel along or through it: *Metal conducts electricity easily but plastic does not.* **4 conduct yourself** (formal) to behave in a particular way: *He conducted himself well in the job interview.* [ORIGIN: 1400—1500 Latin *conductus*, past participle of *conducere* "to lead or bring together"]

con·duct[2] /'kɑndʌkt, -dəkt/ (Ac) *n.* [U] (formal) **1** the way someone behaves: *standards of professional conduct*

THESAURUS **behavior, manner, demeanor** → BEHAVIOR

2 the way a business, activity, etc. is organized and done: *Democrats have been critical of the conduct of the hearings.*

con·duc·tion /kən'dʌkʃən/ *n.* [U] PHYSICS the process by which energy, in the form of heat, sound, or electricity, passes through a substance or object without movement in the substance or object, for example heat passing through metal

con·duc·tiv·i·ty /ˌkɑndʌk'tɪvət̬i/ *n.* [U] PHYSICS the degree to which something allows electricity or heat to travel along or through it

con·duc·tor /kən'dʌktɚ/ *n.* [C] **1** ENG. LANG. ARTS someone who conducts a group of musicians or singers **2** PHYSICS something that allows electricity or heat to travel along it or through it **3** someone who is in charge of a train or the workers on it

con·du·it /'kɑnduɪt/ *n.* [C] **1** a pipe or passage through which water, gas, electric wires, etc. pass **2** a connection that allows people to pass ideas, news, money, weapons, etc. from one place to another: *The Internet is a tremendous* ***conduit for*** *information.*

cone /koʊn/ *n.* [C] **1** a hollow or solid object with a round base and a point at the top: *an orange traffic cone* **2** a hard thin cookie, shaped like a cone, that you put ICE CREAM into → ICE CREAM CONE **3** BIOLOGY the hard brown fruit of a PINE or FIR tree → *see picture at* PLANT[1]

con·fec·tion /kən'fɛkʃən/ *n.* [C] (formal) **1** something sweet and decorated, such as candy or cake: *chocolate confections* **2** something that is complicated or has a lot of decoration, such as clothing or a building **3** something such as a movie or a song that is entertaining and not serious at all: *The movie is a pretty light-hearted confection.*

con·fed·er·a·cy /kən'fɛdərəsi/ *n.* (plural **confederacies**) **1 the Confederacy** HISTORY the southern states that fought against northern states in the American Civil War **2** [C] a confederation

con·fed·er·ate /kən'fɛdərɪt/ *n.* [C] HISTORY a soldier in the Confederacy —**confederate** *adj.*

con·fed·e·ra·tion /kənˌfɛdə'reɪʃən/ *n.* [C] a group of people, political parties, or organizations that have united in order to achieve an aim

con·fer /kən'fɚ/ (Ac) *v.* (**conferred, conferring**) **1** [I] to discuss something with other people so everyone can give his/her opinion: *You may want to **confer with** the other team members.* **2 confer a degree/honor etc. on sb** to officially give someone a degree, etc. [ORIGIN: 1400—1500 Latin *conferre* "to bring together"]

con·ference /'kɑnfrəns/ (Ac) *n.* [C,U] **1** a private meeting in which a few people discuss something: *We're **having** parent-teacher **conferences** at my kids' school this week.* | *The meeting will be held in the second floor **conference room**.* **2** a large formal meeting, often lasting for several days, at which members of an organization, profession, etc. discuss things related to their work: *a sales conference* | *The American Medical Association is sponsoring a **conference on** men's health.* | *Professor Roth is in London **attending** an international **conference**.*

THESAURUS **discussion, negotiations, debate, talks, dialogue** → DISCUSSION

3 a group of teams that play against each other in a LEAGUE

'conference ˌcall *n.* [C] a telephone conversation in which several people in different places can all talk to each other

'conference comˌmittee *n.* [C] POLITICS a temporary committee, consisting of members of the House of Representatives and the Senate, whose job is to reach an agreement on a bill that has been passed in two different forms by each house

con·fess /kən'fɛs/ *v.* [I,T] **1** to admit that you have done something wrong or illegal: *It didn't take long for her to confess.* | *He has **confessed to** the crime.*

THESAURUS **admit, own up, come clean** → ADMIT

2 to admit something that you feel embarrassed about: *I **confessed that** I hadn't understood.* **3** to tell a priest or God about the bad things you have done —**confessed** *adj.*

con·fes·sion /kən'fɛʃən/ *n.* **1** [C] a statement that you have done something wrong or illegal: *He **made a** full **confession** at the police station.* **2** [C,U] the act of telling a priest or God about the bad things you have done

con·fet·ti /kən'fɛt̬i/ *n.* [U] small pieces of colored paper thrown into the air at a wedding, party, etc. [ORIGIN: 1800—1900 Italian, plural of *confetto* "candy," from Latin *conficere*; because candy was thrown at Italian street celebrations]

confetti

con·fi·dant /'kɑnfəˌdɑnt/ *n.* [C] someone to whom you tell secrets or personal information

con·fi·dante /'kɑnfəˌdɑnt/ *n.* [C] a woman to whom you tell secrets or personal information

con·fide /kən'faɪd/ *v.* [T] to tell someone about personal things that you do not want other people to know: *He had **confided to** friends that he was unhappy.*

confide in sb *phr. v.* to tell someone about something that is very private or secret because you feel you can trust him/her: *I've never been able to confide in my sister.*

con·fi·dence /'kɑnfədəns/ *n.* **1** [U] the feeling that you can trust someone or something to be good or successful: *Public **confidence in** the economy is at an all-time low.* | *We **have** complete **confidence** in your ability to handle the situation.* | *Employees are **losing confidence** in the company.* **2** [U] belief in your ability to do things well: *I didn't **have** any **confidence in** myself.* | *Her **lack of confidence** showed.* | *Living in another country **gave** me more **confidence**.* **3 gain/win/earn sb's confidence** if you gain someone's confidence, s/he begins to trust you: *Gradually, the new manager began to win the employees' confidence.* **4** [U] the feeling that something is definite or true: *I **have confidence (that)** the dispute will be settled before long.* **5 in confidence** if you say something in confidence, you tell someone something and trust him/her not to tell anyone else **6** [C] a secret, or a piece of information that is private or personal

con·fi·dent /'kɑnfədənt/ *adj.* **1** sure that you have the ability to do things well or deal with situations successfully (ANT) **insecure**: *She **feels** very **confident about** her ability to do the work.* | *a **confident voice/smile/manner***

THESAURUS

self-confident – sure that you can do things well and that other people will like you: *He's much more self-confident since he started college.*
self-assured – confident about what you are doing, and dealing with people in a calm way: *The doctor spoke in a slow, self-assured voice.*
assertive – behaving in a confident way, so that you are able to get what you want: *Men tend to be more assertive than women.*

2 [not before noun] sure that something will happen in the way you want or expect: *I'm **confident (that)** he'll help us out.* | *He was **confident of** winning the election.*—**confidently** *adv.*

THESAURUS **sure, certain, convinced, satisfied, positive** → SURE[1]

con·fi·den·tial /ˌkɑnfə'dɛnʃəl◂/ *adj.* secret and not intended to be shown or told to other people: *confidential information* —**confidentially** *adv.* —**confidentiality** /ˌkɑnfədɛnʃi'ælət̬i/ *n.* [U]

THESAURUS **secret, classified, sensitive, covert, undercover, clandestine** → SECRET[1]

con·fig·u·ra·tion /kənˌfɪgyə'reɪʃən/ *n.* [C] the way in which parts of something are arranged or formed into a particular shape: *a star-shaped configuration*

con·fig·ure /kən'fɪgjɚ/ *v.* [T] IT to do things that allow something, especially computer equipment, to work with other equipment

con·fine /kən'faɪn/ (Ac) *v.* [T] **1** to stop something bad from spreading to another place: *The fire was **confined to** one building.* **2** if you are confined to a place, you have to stay in that place, especially because you are sick: *Rachel is **confined to bed**.* **3** to keep someone or something within the limits of a particular subject or activity: *Try to **confine yourself to** spending $120 a week.* | *We **confined** our research **to** young people.* **4** to keep someone in a place s/he cannot leave, such as a prison: *The prisoners are **confined to** their cells for most of the day.* [ORIGIN: 1500—1600 French *confiner*, from Latin *confinis*, from *confine* "border"]

con·fined /kən'faɪnd/ (Ac) *adj.* a confined space or area is very small: *It wasn't easy to sleep in such a confined space.*

con·fine·ment /kən'faɪnmənt/ *n.* [U] the act of forcing someone to stay in a room, prison, etc., or the state of being there → SOLITARY CONFINEMENT

con·fines /'kɑnfaɪnz/ (Ac) *n.* [plural] the walls, limits, or borders of something: *His son has only seen him **within the confines of** the prison.*

con·firm /kən'fɚm/ (Ac) *v.* [T] **1** to say or prove that something is definitely true: *Blood tests confirmed the diagnosis.* | *Further studies **confirmed that** fish oil can lower blood pressure.* | *The article **confirms what** many experts have been saying for years.* **2** to tell someone that a possible plan, arrangement, etc. is now definite: *Please confirm your reservations 72 hours in advance.* [ORIGIN: 1200—1300 Old French *confirmer*, from Latin *confirmare*]

con·fir·ma·tion /ˌkɑnfɚ'meɪʃən/ (Ac) *n.* [C,U] a statement or letter that says that something is definitely true, or the act of stating this: *We're waiting for **confirmation of** the report.* | *These figures provide **confirmation that** inflation is the lowest it has been for ten years.*

con·firmed /kən'fɚmd/ (Ac) *adj.* **1 a confirmed bachelor/alcoholic etc.** someone who seems unlikely to change the way of life s/he has chosen **2 confirmed case/sighting/report of sth** proved and therefore known to be true or real: *There have been two confirmed sightings of jaguars in Arizona this year.*

con·fis·cate /'kɑnfəˌskeɪt/ *v.* [T] to officially take something away from someone: *U.S. customs officers confiscated his passport.* —**confiscation** /ˌkɑnfə'skeɪʃən/ *n.* [C,U]

con·fla·gra·tion /ˌkɑnflə'greɪʃən/ *n.* [C] (formal) **1** a very large fire over a large area, that destroys a lot of buildings, forests, etc. **2** a violent situation or war: *the conflagration in the Middle East*

con·flict¹ /'kɑnˌflɪkt/ (Ac) *n.* **1** [C,U] angry disagreement between people, groups, countries, etc.: *a **conflict between** father and son* | ***conflicts over** land* | *The two groups have been **in conflict with** each other for years.* **2** [C,U] fighting or a war: ***Armed conflict** might be unavoidable.* | *The fighting continues despite efforts to **resolve** the **conflict**.*

THESAURUS war, warfare, fighting, combat, action, hostilities → WAR

3 [C,U] a situation in which you have to choose between opposing things: *a **conflict between** the demands of one's work and one's family* **4** [C] something that you have to do at the same time that someone wants you to do something else: *Sorry – I **have a conflict** Friday. Can we do it on Monday?* **5 conflict of interest(s)** a situation in which you cannot do your job fairly because you are personally affected by the decisions you make: *She sold her shares in the company to avoid any conflict of interest.* **6** ENG. LANG. ARTS a situation in a book, play, movie, etc. in which different characters or forces oppose each other in a way that causes or influences the action of the story: *The central conflict in the story is between the boy and his father.* [ORIGIN: 1400—1500 Latin *conflictus*, from the past participle of *confligere* "to strike together"]

con·flict² /kən'flɪkt/ (Ac) *v.* [I] if two ideas, beliefs, opinions, etc. conflict, they cannot both be true: *The new evidence **conflicts with** the findings from previous studies.* | *We have heard many **conflicting opinions** on the subject.*

con·flu·ence /'kɑnfluəns/ *n.* [singular] **1** the place where two or more rivers or roads meet and join: *the **confluence of** the Missouri and Yellowstone rivers* **2** a situation in which two or more things happen or exist at the same time: *It was a confluence of events that changed my life.* —**confluent** *adj.*

con·form /kən'fɔrm/ (Ac) *v.* [I] **1** to behave in the way that most people behave: *There's always pressure on kids to conform.* **2** to obey a law, rule, etc.: *Restaurants must **conform to** health and safety laws.* | *The proposed site of the new factory must **conform with** the zoning laws.* [ORIGIN: 1300—1400 Old French *conformer*, from Latin *conformare*, from *com-* "together" + *formare* "to form"] —**conformity** /kən'fɔrməṭi/ *n.* [U]

con·form·ist /kən'fɔrmɪst/ *n.* [C] someone who behaves or thinks like everyone else because s/he does not want to be different (ANT) **nonconformist**

con·found /kən'faʊnd/ *v.* [T] to confuse and surprise people by not being what they expected: *Her amazing recovery has confounded doctors.*

con·front /kən'frʌnt/ *v.* [T] **1** if you are confronted with a problem, difficulty, etc., it appears and needs to be dealt with: *It was the first time the* *team had been* ***confronted with*** *a stronger opponent, but they still played well.* **2** to try to make someone admit s/he has done something wrong, especially by showing him/her proof: *I'm afraid to* ***confront*** *her* ***about*** *her drinking.* **3** to deal with something difficult or bad in a brave and determined way: *Sooner or later you'll have to* ***confront*** *your* ***problems****.* **4** to stand in front of someone, as though you are going to attack him/her: *She was confronted by two men.*

C

con·fron·ta·tion /ˌkɑnfrənˈteɪʃən/ *n.* [C,U] an argument or fight: ***confrontations between*** *police and protesters*

con·fuse /kənˈfyuz/ *v.* [T] **1** to make someone feel that s/he is unable to think clearly or understand something: *His directions really confused me.* **2** to think wrongly that a person or thing is someone or something else: *It's easy to* ***confuse*** *Sue* ***with*** *her sister.* **3** to make something more complicated or difficult to understand: *His questions were just* ***confusing*** *the* ***issue****.*

con·fused /kənˈfyuzd/ *adj.* **1** unable to understand clearly what someone is saying or what is happening: *I'm totally confused.* | *I'm still* ***confused about*** *what happened.*

THESAURUS
bewildered – very confused and not sure what to do or think: *People are often bewildered by all the rules and regulations about taxes.*
puzzled – confused and unable to understand something: *He seemed puzzled by her question.*
baffled – very confused and completely unable to understand something: *The police are still baffled by the man's disappearance.*

2 complicated and difficult to understand: *confused feelings* [ORIGIN: 1300—1400 Old French *confus*, from Latin *confusus*, past participle of *confundere* "to pour together, confuse"]

con·fus·ing /kənˈfyuzɪŋ/ *adj.* difficult to understand: *The diagram is really confusing.*

con·fu·sion /kənˈfyuʒən/ *n.* **1** [U] a state of not understanding what is happening or what something means: *There's a lot of* ***confusion about/over*** *the new rules.* | *The changes in the schedule have* ***created confusion****.* **2** [U] a situation in which you wrongly think that a person or thing is someone or something else: *To* ***avoid confusion****, the teams wore different colors.* **3** [singular, U] a very confusing situation, usually with a lot of noise and action: *With all* ***the confusion****, nobody noticed the two boys leave.* | *The country is in a* ***state of confusion****.*

con·geal /kənˈdʒil/ *v.* [I] if a liquid such as blood congeals, it becomes thick or solid

con·ge·nial /kənˈdʒinyəl/ *adj.* (formal) pleasant in a way that makes you feel comfortable and relaxed: *a congenial atmosphere*

con·gen·i·tal /kənˈdʒɛnətl̩/ *adj.* **1** BIOLOGY a congenital medical condition or disease affects someone from the time s/he is born: *a congenital heart problem* **2** [only before noun] a congenital quality is one that has always been part of your character and is unlikely to change: *He's a* ***congenital liar****.*

con·gest·ed /kənˈdʒɛstɪd/ *adj.* **1** too full or blocked because of too many vehicles or people: *congested freeways* **2** a congested nose, chest, etc. is filled with thick liquid that does not flow easily —**congestion** /kənˈdʒɛstʃən/ *n.* [U]

con·glom·er·ate /kənˈglɑmərɪt/ *n.* [C] ECONOMICS a large company made up of many different smaller companies

con·glom·er·a·tion /kənˌglɑməˈreɪʃən/ *n.* [C] (formal) a group of many different things or people gathered together

con·grat·u·late /kənˈgrætʃəˌleɪt/ *v.* [T] to tell someone that you are happy because s/he has achieved something, or because something good has happened to him/her: *I want to* ***congratulate*** *you* ***on*** *a fine achievement.* [ORIGIN: 1500—1600 Latin, past participle of *congratulari* "to wish happiness"] —**congratulatory** /kənˈgrætʃələˌtɔri/ *adj.*

THESAURUS **praise, flatter, compliment sb/pay sb a compliment, commend** → PRAISE[1]

con·grat·u·la·tions /kənˌgrætʃəˈleɪʃənz/ *n.* [plural] used in order to congratulate someone: *You won? Congratulations!* | ***Congratulations on*** *your engagement!* | ***Congratulations to*** *all the winners.*

con·gre·gate /ˈkɑŋgrəˌgeɪt/ *v.* [I] to come together in a group: *A group of protesters had congregated outside.* [ORIGIN: 1400—1500 Latin, past participle of *congregare*, from *com* "together" + *grex* "crowd"]

THESAURUS **meet, get together, gather, assemble, come together, convene** → MEET[1]

con·gre·ga·tion /ˌkɑŋgrəˈgeɪʃən/ *n.* [C] a group of people gathered in a church for a religious service, or the people who usually go to a particular church

con·gress /ˈkɑŋgrɪs/ *n.* **1 Congress** POLITICS the group of people elected to make laws for the U.S., consisting of the Senate and the House of Representatives: *The bill has been approved by both houses of Congress.* | *an act of Congress* **2** [C] a formal meeting in which representatives of different groups, countries, etc. exchange information and make decisions [ORIGIN: 1400—1500 Latin *congressus* "meeting," from the past participle of *congredi* "to come together"] —**congressional** /kəŋˈgrɛʃənəl/ *adj.*

con·gress·man /ˈkɑŋgrɪsmən/ *n.* (plural **congressmen** /-mən/) [C] a man who is elected to be in Congress

THESAURUS **politician, president, congresswoman, senator, governor, mayor** → POLITICIAN

con·gress·wom·an /ˈkɑŋgrɪsˌwʊmən/ *n.* (plural **congresswomen** /-ˌwɪmɪn/) [C] a woman who is elected to be in Congress

THESAURUS politician, president, congressman, senator, governor, mayor ➔ POLITICIAN

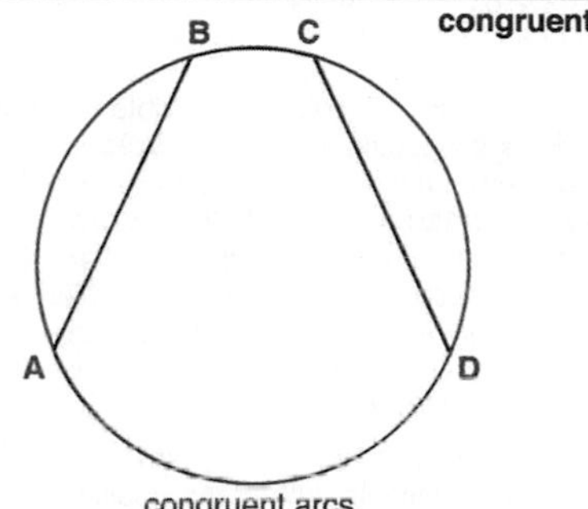

congruent arcs

con·gru·ent /kəŋˈgruənt, ˈkɑŋgruənt/ *adj.* **1** (formal) fitting together well, or suitable **2** MATH congruent shapes are the same size and shape as each other: *congruent circles* | *congruent polygons* **3** MATH congruent angles are angles that measure the same in degrees ➔ *see picture at* ANGLE[1] **4** MATH congruent numbers are two numbers whose difference can be divided exactly by a third number. For example, 8 and 23 are congruent when the third number is 5, because the difference (15) can be divided exactly by 5. **5** MATH congruent ARCs are parts of the outside of the same circle, or of two IDENTICAL circles that curve with the same degree **6** MATH congruent SEGMENTS are exactly the same length [ORIGIN: 1400—1500 Latin, present participle of *congruere* "to come together, agree"]

con·gru·ous /ˈkɑŋgruəs/ *adj.* (formal) appropriate for something because it is similar in some way —**congruity** *n.* [C,U]

con·i·cal /ˈkɑnɪkəl/ *adj.* shaped like a CONE, or relating to cones

ˌconic ˈsection *n.* [C] MATH a curved shape formed by a PLANE (=flat shape) crossing through a CONE. It can be a circle, an ELLIPSE, a HYPERBOLA, or a PARABOLA, depending on the angle at which the plane meets and goes through the cone.

con·i·fer /ˈkɑnəfɚ/ *n.* [C] BIOLOGY a tree that keeps its leaves in winter and has CONEs containing its seeds ➔ *see picture on page A23* —**coniferous** /kəˈnɪfərəs, koʊ-/ *adj.*

con·jec·ture /kənˈdʒɛktʃɚ/ *n.* [C,U] (formal) the act of forming ideas about something when you do not have enough information to base them on: *There has been some conjecture in the press about a possible merger.* —**conjecture** *v.* [I,T]

con·ju·gal /ˈkɑndʒəgəl/ *adj.* [only before noun] (formal) relating to marriage or married people

con·ju·gate[1] /ˈkɑndʒəˌgeɪt/ *v.* [T] ENG. LANG. ARTS to state the different forms that a verb can have —**conjugation** /ˌkɑndʒəˈgeɪʃən/ *n.* [C,U]

con·ju·gate[2] /ˈkɑndʒəgɪt/ *n.* [C] MATH a COMPLEX CONJUGATE

con·junc·tion /kənˈdʒʌŋkʃən/ *n.* [C] **1 in conjunction with sb/sth** working, happening, or being used with someone or something else: *The worksheets should be used in conjunction with the video.* **2** ENG. LANG. ARTS a word such as "but," "and," or "while" that connects parts of sentences, phrases, or CLAUSEs

con·jure /ˈkɑndʒɚ/ *v.* [I,T] to perform tricks in which you seem to make things appear, disappear, or change as if by magic —**conjurer, conjuror** *n.* [C]

conjure sth ↔ **up** *phr. v.* **1** make an image, idea, memory, etc. very clear and strong in someone's mind: *Smells can often conjure up memories.* **2** to make, get, or achieve something, as if by magic

con·man /ˈkɑnˌmæn/ *n.* (plural **conmen** /-ˌmɛn/) [C] (informal) someone who gets money or valuable things from people by tricking them

con·nect /kəˈnɛkt/ *v.* **1** [T] to join two or more things together (ANT) **disconnect**: ***Connect** the speakers **to** the stereo.* **2** [T] to realize or show that a fact, event, person, etc. is related to or involved in something: *There is little evidence to **connect** him **with** the crime.* **3** [T] to attach something to a supply of electricity, gas, or water, or to a computer or telephone network (ANT) **disconnect**: *Has the phone been connected yet?* | *Click here to **connect to** the Internet.* ➔ INTERNET **4** [I] if an airplane, train, etc. connects with another one, it arrives just before the other one leaves so you can change from one to the other: *a **connecting flight** to Omaha* **5** [I] (informal) if people connect, they feel that they like and understand each other: *I really felt I **connected with** Jim's parents.* [ORIGIN: 1400—1500 Latin *connectere*, from *com* "together" + *nectere* "to tie"]

con·nect·ed /kəˈnɛktɪd/ *adj.* **1** if two facts, events, people, etc. are connected, there is some kind of relationship between them: *symptoms **connected with** the disease*

THESAURUS related, linked, relevant, pertinent ➔ RELATED

2 joined to something else: *The computer is **connected to** a printer* **3 well-connected** having important or powerful friends or relatives: *a wealthy and well-connected lawyer*

con·nec·tion /kəˈnɛkʃən/ *n.* **1** [C,U] a relationship between things, people, ideas, etc.: *the **connection between** smoking and lung disease* | *Does this have any **connection with/to** our project?* **2** [C] a piece of wire or metal joining two parts of a machine together or to an electrical system: *There must be a **loose connection** – I'm not getting any power.* **3** [C,U] the process of joining together two or more things: *free Internet connection* **4** [C] an airplane, bus, or train that leaves at a time that allows passengers from an earlier airplane, bus, or train to use it to continue their trip: *I **missed** my **connection**.* **5 in connection with sth** concerning something: *Police are questioning a man in connection with the crime.* **6 connections** [plural] people you know who can help you, especially because they are in positions of power: *He has connections in high places.*

con'nective ˌtissue *n.* [U] BIOLOGY parts of the body such as fat or bone that support or join together organs and other body parts

C

con·nive /kə'naɪv/ *v.* [I] to plan something secretly, especially something that is wrong or illegal: *Together, they **connived to** deceive her.* [ORIGIN: 1600—1700 French *conniver*, from Latin *connivere* "to close the eyes, connive"] —**connivance** *n.* [C,U]

con·nois·seur /ˌkɑnə'sɚ, -'sʊr/ *n.* [C] someone who knows a lot about something such as art, food, or music: *a **connoisseur of** fine wines*

THESAURUS **expert, specialist, authority, pundit** → EXPERT

con·no·ta·tion /ˌkɑnə'teɪʃən/ *n.* [C] an idea or a feeling that a word makes you think of, in addition to its basic meaning: *The word "liberal" has **negative connotations** these days.* —**connote** /kə'noʊt/ *v.* [T]

con·no·ta·tive /'kɑnəˌteɪt̬ɪv/ *adj.* ENG. LANG. ARTS making you think of a quality or an idea that is more than the basic meaning of a word

con·quer /'kɑŋkɚ/ *v.* **1** [I,T] to get control of land or people by force: *Egypt was conquered by the Ottoman Empire in 1517.*

THESAURUS **beat, defeat, vanquish, overcome** → BEAT[1]

2 [T] to succeed in controlling a strong feeling or solving a serious problem that you have: *I didn't think I'd ever conquer my fear of heights.* —**conqueror** *n.* [C]

con·quest /'kɑŋkwɛst/ *n.* [singular, U] the act of getting control of land or people by force: *the Spanish **conquest of** Central America*

con·science /'kɑnʃəns/ *n.* [U] **1** the set of feelings that tell you whether what you are doing is morally right or wrong: *He had a **guilty conscience*** (=feeling of guilt). | *At least my **conscience** is **clear*** (=I know I have done nothing wrong).

THESAURUS **guilt, shame, remorse** → GUILT

2 on sb's conscience making you feel guilty: *I lied and it's always going to be on my conscience.* [ORIGIN: 1200—1300 Old French, Latin *conscientia*, from *conscire* "to be conscious (of being guilty)"]

con·sci·en·tious /ˌkɑnʃi'ɛnʃəs◂/ *adj.* careful to do everything that it is your job or duty to do: *a conscientious teacher*

THESAURUS **careful, methodical, thorough, meticulous, systematic, painstaking, scrupulous** → CAREFUL

ˌconscientious ob'jector *n.* [C] someone who refuses to fight in a war because of his/her moral beliefs

con·scious /'kɑnʃəs/ *adj.* **1** [not before noun] noticing or realizing something SYN **aware**: *I became **conscious of** the fact that someone was watching me.* **2** awake and able to understand what is happening ANT **unconscious**: *Owen was still conscious when they arrived at the hospital.* **3 conscious effort/decision/attempt etc.** a deliberate effort, decision, etc.: *Vivian had made a conscious effort to be friendly.* **4** thinking that something is very important: *fashion-conscious teenagers* | *She's very **conscious of** safety.* —**consciously** *adv.*

con·scious·ness /'kɑnʃəsnɪs/ *n.* [U] **1** the condition of being awake and understanding what is happening: *Charlie fell down the stairs and **lost consciousness**.* | *It was two weeks before he **regained consciousness**.* **2** someone's mind, thoughts, and ideas: *research into human consciousness* **3** the state of knowing that something exists or is true SYN **awareness**: *The march is intended to **raise** people's **consciousness** about women's health issues.*

cons·cript /kən'skrɪpt/ *v.* [T] (formal) to make someone join the army, navy, etc. —**conscription** /kən'skrɪpʃən/ *n.* [U]

con·se·crate /'kɑnsəˌkreɪt/ *v.* [T] to make something holy by performing a religious ceremony —**consecration** /ˌkɑnsə'kreɪʃən/ *n.* [U]

con·sec·u·tive /kən'sɛkyət̬ɪv/ *adj.* consecutive numbers or periods of time happen one after the other: *It rained for three consecutive days.* —**consecutively** *adv.*

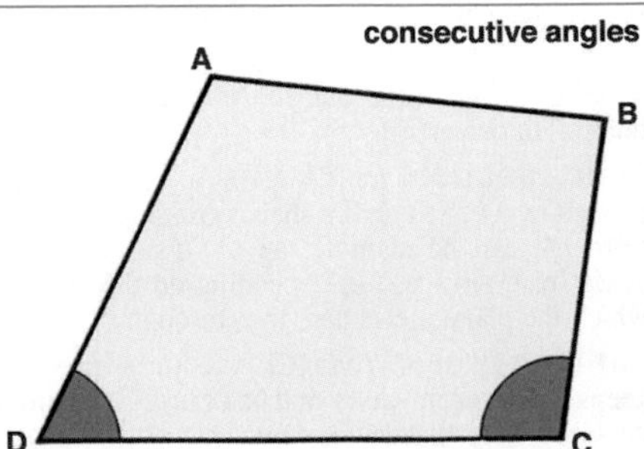

conˌsecutive 'angles *n.* [plural] MATH angles of a POLYGON (=flat shape with three or more sides) that share one of their sides with each other

con·sen·su·al /kən'sɛnʃuəl/ *adj.* giving your permission for something, or agreeing to something

con·sen·sus /kən'sɛnsəs/ Ac *n.* [singular, U] an opinion that everyone in a group agrees with or accepts: *We failed to **reach a consensus** on the issue.* | *The decisions are made **by consensus**.* | *There seems to be a lack of **consensus on/about** how to deal with the situation.* [ORIGIN: 1200—1300 Latin *consentire* "to feel together, agree"]

con·sent¹ /kən'sɛnt/ (Ac) *n.* [U] permission to do something: *parental consent* | *He took the car **without** my **consent**.*

consent² *v.* [I] (formal) to give your permission for something to happen: *Her father reluctantly **consented to** the marriage.* | *His boss asked him to work late, and he consented.*

con·se·quence /'kɑnsə,kwɛns, -kwəns/ (Ac) *n.* **1** [C] something that happens as a result of a particular action: *She never thinks about the **consequences of** her actions.* | *He broke the law, and now he must **face the consequences*** (=accept the bad results of his actions). | *He died **as a consequence of** injuries he received in the accident.* | *Increased taxes on fuel could have disastrous **consequences** for the airline industry.*

THESAURUS **result, aftereffects, side effect, outcome, upshot, repercussions** → RESULT¹

2 of little/no consequence (formal) not important: *a matter of little consequence*

con·se·quent /'kɑnsə,kwɛnt, -kwənt/ (Ac) *adj.* [only before noun] (formal) happening as a result of something: *racial prejudice and its consequent violence* [ORIGIN: 1400—1500 French, Latin, present participle of *consequi*, from *com* "with" + *sequi* "to follow"]

con·se·quent·ly /'kɑnsə,kwɛntli, -kwənt-/ (Ac) *adv.* as a result: *He didn't study and consequently failed the final exam.* | *The employees received very little training. Consequently, they made mistakes.*

con·ser·va·tion /,kɑnsə'veɪʃən/ *n.* [U] **1** the protection of natural things such as animals, plants, forests, etc.: *the **conservation of** wildlife* **2** the controlled use of a limited amount of water, gas, electricity, etc. to prevent the supply from being wasted —**conservationist** *n.* [C]

conser,vation of 'charge *n.* [U] PHYSICS a scientific principle that says that the total electric charge of a system remains the same in spite of any changes that happen inside the system

conser,vation of 'energy *n.* [U] PHYSICS a scientific principle that says that the total amount of energy in a system remains the same even though the type of energy may change

conser,vation of 'mass *n.* [U] PHYSICS a scientific principle that says that the total MASS of a system remains the same in spite of any changes that happen inside the system

conser,vation of mo'mentum *n.* [U] PHYSICS a scientific principle that says that the total MOMENTUM of a system remains the same in spite of any changes that happen inside the system

con·serv·a·tism /kən'sɚvə,tɪzəm/ *n.* [U] the belief that any changes to the way things are done must happen slowly and have very good reasons: *political conservatism*

con·serv·a·tive¹ /kən'sɚvət̬ɪv/ *adj.* **1** preferring to continue doing things the way they are being done or have been proven to work, rather than risking changes: *a very conservative attitude to education* **2** not very modern in style, taste, etc.: *a conservative business suit* **3** POLITICS supporting political ideas that include less involvement by the government in business and people's lives, for example by encouraging everyone to work and earn their own money, and having strong ideas about moral behavior (ANT) **liberal**: *a politically conservative family* **4 a conservative estimate** a guess that is deliberately lower than the real amount probably is —**conservatively** *adv.*

conservative² *n.* [C] POLITICS someone with conservative opinions or principles (ANT) **liberal**: *Conservatives in Congress want to reduce the agency's funds.*

con·serv·a·to·ry /kən'sɚvə,tɔri/ *n.* (plural **conservatories**) [C] **1** a school where students are trained in music or acting **2** a GREENHOUSE

con·serve /kən'sɚv/ *v.* [T] to prevent something from being wasted, damaged, or destroyed: *efforts to conserve water* | *Try and rest frequently to conserve your energy.* [ORIGIN: 1300—1400 Old French *conserver*, from Latin *conservare*, from *com* "together" + *servare* "to keep, guard"]

THESAURUS **protect, guard, safeguard, shield, give/offer/provide protection, shelter, preserve** → PROTECT

con·sid·er /kən'sɪdɚ/ *v.* **1** [I,T] to think about something very carefully, especially before making a decision: *I considered resigning.* | *He was considering whether to apply for the job.* | *You should **consider the possibility** of moving there permanently.* **2** [T] to think of someone or something in a particular way, or have a particular opinion: *Mrs. Greenwood was **considered to be** an excellent teacher.* | *We **consider it important** to get the Director's advice on this.* | *Greg should **consider** himself **lucky*** (=be glad) *he wasn't badly hurt.*

THESAURUS **think, believe, suspect, figure, guess** → THINK

3 [T] to think about someone or his/her feelings, and try to avoid upsetting him/her: *It's all right for you, but have you considered the children?* [ORIGIN: 1300—1400 Old French *considerer*, from Latin *considerare* "to look at the stars, look at closely, examine"]

con·sid·er·a·ble /kən'sɪdərəbəl/ (Ac) *adj.* large enough to be important or have an effect: *We spent a **considerable amount** of money on the interior of the house.* —**considerably** *adv.*: *It's considerably colder tonight.*

con·sid·er·ate /kən'sɪdərɪt/ *adj.* thinking and

caring about other people's feelings, wants, or needs (ANT) **inconsiderate**: *He was always kind and considerate.* —**considerately** *adv.*

THESAURUS **kind, nice, thoughtful, caring, warm-hearted, compassionate, sympathetic** → KIND²

con·sid·er·a·tion /kən,sɪdə'reɪʃən/ *n.* **1** [U] (formal) careful thought and attention: *Several plans are* ***under consideration.*** | *We will* ***give*** *careful* ***consideration*** *to your proposal.* **2** [C] a fact or detail that you think about when making a decision: *financial considerations* **3 take sth into consideration** to think about something when making a decision: *We'll take into consideration the fact that you were sick.* **4** [U] the quality of thinking and caring about other people's feelings, wants, or needs: *He* ***shows*** *no* ***consideration*** *for others.*

C

con·sid·ered /kən'sɪdəd/ *adj.* **1 considered opinion/judgment** an opinion based on careful thought **2 all things considered** after thinking about all the facts: *All things considered, I think the meeting went pretty well.*

con·sid·er·ing /kən'sɪdərɪŋ/ *prep., conjunction* used to say that you are thinking about a particular fact when giving your opinion: *She did very well* ***considering (that)*** *it was her first attempt.*

con·sign /kən'saɪn/ *v.* [T] (formal)
consign sb/sth **to** sth *phr. v.* **1** to cause someone or something to be in a bad situation: *a decision that consigned him to political obscurity* **2** to put something somewhere, especially in order to get rid of it

con·sign·ment /kən'saɪnmənt/ *n.* **1** [C] a quantity of goods that is sent to someone in order to be sold **2 on consignment** goods that are on consignment are being sold by a store owner for someone else, for a share of the profit

con·sist /kən'sɪst/ (Ac) *v.*
consist of sth *phr. v.* to be made of or contain particular things or people: *The top layer of earth* ***consists largely of*** *clay, gravel and sand.* | *The audience* ***consisted solely of*** *teenagers.* [ORIGIN: 1500—1600 Latin *consistere* "to stand still or firm, exist"]

con·sist·en·cy /kən'sɪstənsi/ (Ac) *n.* (plural **consistencies**) **1** [U] (approving) the quality of always being the same, or of always behaving in an expected way (ANT) **inconsistency**: *There's no* ***consistency in*** *the way they apply the rules.* **2** [C,U] how thick, smooth, etc. a substance is: *a dessert with a nice creamy consistency*

con·sist·ent /kən'sɪstənt/ (Ac) *adj.* **1** (approving) always happening in the same way, or having the same attitudes, quality, etc. (ANT) **inconsistent**: *I've tried to be* ***consistent in*** *applying the rules.* **2** containing facts, ideas, etc. that agree with other facts, etc.: *His story is not* ***consistent with*** *the facts.* [ORIGIN: 1500—1600 Latin, present participle of *consistere* "to stand still or firm, exist"] —**consistently** *adv.*: *consistently good grades*

con·so·la·tion /,kɑnsə'leɪʃən/ *n.* [C,U] something that makes you feel better when you are sad or disappointed: *If it's any* ***consolation to*** *you, I think that you're improving.*

,conso'lation prize *n.* [C] a prize that is given to someone who has not won a competition

con·sole¹ /kən'soʊl/ *v.* [T] to help someone who is sad or disappointed to feel better: *No one could console her when her dog died.* | *Danny* ***consoled himself with*** *the thought that he had done his best.*

con·sole² /'kɑnsoʊl/ *n.* [C] IT a flat board that contains the controls for a machine, piece of electrical equipment, computer, etc.: *a video game console* → *see picture on page A19*

con·sol·i·date /kən'sɑlə,deɪt/ *v.* [I,T] **1** to make something stronger or more successful: *The company has consolidated its position in the Japanese market.* **2** to combine things so that they are more effective or easier to manage: *a loan to consolidate debts* —**consolidation** /kən,sɑlə'deɪʃən/ *n.* [C,U]

con·so·nance /'kɑnsənəns/ *n.* [U] ENG. LANG. ARTS the action of repeating the same consonant sound or sounds, especially at the end of words, in a piece of writing or speech

con·so·nant /'kɑnsənənt/ *n.* [C] ENG. LANG. ARTS any letter of the English alphabet except a, e, i, o, and u → VOWEL [ORIGIN: 1300—1400 Old French, Latin, present participle of *consonare* "to sound together, agree"]

con·sort /kən'sɔrt/ *v.*
consort with sb *phr. v.* (formal) to spend time with someone who other people do not approve of

con·sor·ti·um /kən'sɔrʃiəm, -t̬iəm/ *n.* (plural **consortia** /-ʃiə, -t̬iə/ *or* **consortiums**) [C] a combination of several companies, organizations, etc. working together: *a* ***consortium of*** *banks*

con·spic·u·ous /kən'spɪkyuəs/ *adj.* very easy to notice (ANT) **inconspicuous**: *The notice must be displayed in a conspicuous place.* —**conspicuously** *adv.*

THESAURUS **noticeable, clear, obvious, striking, eye-catching, evident, apparent, unmistakable, manifest** → NOTICEABLE

con,spicuous con'sumption *n.* [U] (disapproving) the act of buying a lot of expensive things, so that other people will see how rich you are

con·spir·a·cy /kən'spɪrəsi/ *n.* (plural **conspiracies**) [C,U] a secret plan made by two or more people to do something illegal: *a* ***conspiracy to*** *distribute drugs*

THESAURUS **plan, plot, scheme, strategy** → PLAN¹

con·spir·a·tor /kən'spɪrət̬ə/ *n.* [C] someone who is involved in a secret plan to do something illegal —**conspiratorial** /kən,spɪrə'tɔriəl/ *adj.*

con·spire /kən'spaɪɚ/ *v.* [I] **1** to secretly plan with other people to do something bad or illegal: *The company was accused of **conspiring with** local stores to fix prices.* **2** (formal) if events conspire to make something happen, they happen at the same time and have a bad result

con·stant¹ /'kɑnstənt/ (Ac) *adj.* **1** happening regularly or all the time: *There was a **constant stream** of visitors to the house.* | *He's under constant pressure.* **2** staying at the same level for a long period of time: *driving at a constant speed* | *The experiment was carried out at a constant temperature.* —**constancy** *n.* [singular, U]

constant² (Ac) *n.* [C] **1** MATH a number or quantity that never changes **2** (formal) something that stays the same even though other things change

con·stant·ly /'kɑnstənt˺li/ (Ac) *adv.* always or regularly: *The English language is **constantly changing**.*

THESAURUS often, a lot, frequently, regularly, repeatedly, again and again/over and over (again) → OFTEN
always, permanently, all the time/the whole time, continuously, invariably → ALWAYS

con·stel·la·tion /ˌkɑnstə'leɪʃən/ *n.* [C] a group of stars that forms a particular pattern and has a name → SPACE¹

con·ster·na·tion /ˌkɑnstɚ'neɪʃən/ *n.* [U] a feeling of shock or worry

con·sti·pa·tion /ˌkɑnstə'peɪʃən/ *n.* [U] a condition in which someone is unable to get rid of solid waste from his/her body —**constipated** /'kɑnstəˌpeɪtɪd/ *adj.*

con·stit·u·en·cy /kən'stɪtʃuənsi/ (Ac) *n.* (plural **constituencies**) [C] POLITICS the people who live and vote in a particular area: *The governor plans to visit a rural constituency.*

con·stit·u·ent /kən'stɪtʃuənt/ (Ac) *n.* [C] **1** someone who votes in a particular area: *The congressman is committed to issues that are important to his constituents.* **2** one of the parts that combine to form something: *Sodium is one of the **constituents of** salt.* —**constituent** *adj.*

con·sti·tute /'kɑnstəˌtut/ (Ac) *v.* [linking verb] (formal) **1** if several parts constitute something, they form it together: *Alaska is the largest of the 50 states that constitute the U.S.A.* | *Nitrogen constitutes 78% of the Earth's atmosphere.* **2** to be considered to be something: *The rise in crime constitutes a threat to society.*

con·sti·tu·tion /ˌkɑnstə'tuʃən/ (Ac) *n.* **1** [C] *also* **Constitution** a set of laws and principles that a country or organization is governed by: *the Constitution of the United States* **2** [singular] your general health and your body's ability to fight disease and illness: *a boy with a **strong/weak constitution*** **3** [singular] (formal) the structure of something, or the way something is organized: *the constitution of the Earth's crust*

con·sti·tu·tion·al /ˌkɑnstə'tuʃənəl◂/ (Ac) *adj.* **1** officially allowed or restricted by the constitution of a country or organization: *The court ruled that the officers had violated the men's **constitutional rights**.* **2** relating to the constitution of a country or organization: *a constitutional reform*

ˌconstitutional 'monarchy *n.* **1** [U] POLITICS a political system in which a country is ruled by a king or queen whose powers are limited by law **2** [C] POLITICS a country that is ruled by a king or queen whose powers are limited by law

con·strain /kən'streɪn/ (Ac) *v.* [T] (formal) to limit someone's freedom to do what s/he wants to do: *Our research was **constrained by** a lack of funds.*

con·straint /kən'streɪnt/ (Ac) *n.* [C] something that restricts what you are doing: ***constraints on** government spending* | *We did the best we could, given the **time/budget constraints**.*

con·strict /kən'strɪkt/ *v.* [I,T] to become smaller, narrower, or tighter, or to make something do this: *Her throat constricted.* —**constriction** /kən'strɪkʃən/ *n.* [C,U]: *constriction of the arteries*

con·struct /kən'strʌkt/ (Ac) *v.* [T] **1** to build something large such as a building, bridge, etc.: *The Empire State Building was constructed in 1931.* | *The cabin is constructed from thick, heavy timbers.* → *see picture at* BUILD¹

THESAURUS build, put up, erect, assemble, make, produce, manufacture, create → BUILD¹, MAKE¹

2 ENG. LANG. ARTS to form something such as a sentence or argument by joining words, ideas, etc. together: *The younger students found it hard to construct a sentence in Spanish.* **3** MATH to draw a mathematical shape: *Construct a triangle with three equal angles.* [ORIGIN: 1400—1500 Latin, past participle of *construere*, from *com* "together" + *struere* "to build"]

con·struc·tion /kən'strʌkʃən/ (Ac) *n.* **1** [U] the process or method of building something large such as a house, road, etc.: *the **construction of** a new airport* | *The hotel is **under construction*** (=being built). | *a construction worker* **2** [C] ENG. LANG. ARTS the way in which words are put together in a sentence: *difficult **grammatical constructions***

con'struction ˌpaper *n.* [U] a thick colored paper that is used especially by children at school

con·struc·tive /kən'strʌktɪv/ (Ac) *adj.* useful and helpful, or likely to produce good results: ***constructive criticism** of students' essays* | *His suggestions were positive and constructive.*

con·strue /kən'stru/ *v.* [T] to understand something in a particular way (ANT) **misconstrue**: *It might be **construed as** a threat.*

con·sul /'kɑnsəl/ *n.* [C] an official who lives in a foreign city and whose job is to help citizens of his/her own country who also live or work there → AMBASSADOR —**consular** *adj.*

con·sul·ate /ˈkɑnsəlɪt/ *n.* [C] the official building where a consul lives and works → EMBASSY: *the Danish Consulate*

con·sult /kənˈsʌlt/ (Ac) *v.* [I,T] **1** to ask or look for advice, information, etc. from someone or something that should have the answers: *Consult your physician.* | *Don't do anything without* ***consulting with*** *your lawyer.* **2** to discuss something with someone so that you can make a decision together: *I'd better consult my wife first.* **3** to look for information in a book, list, map, etc.: *The police officer consulted his notes before answering Judge Eggar's question.*

C

con·sul·tan·cy /kənˈsʌltənsi/ (Ac) *n.* (plural **consultancies**) [C] a company that gives advice and training in a particular area of business to people in other companies

con·sult·ant /kənˈsʌltənt/ (Ac) *n.* [C] someone with a lot of experience in a particular area of business, whose job is to give advice about it: *a marketing consultant*

con·sul·ta·tion /ˌkɑnsəlˈteɪʃən/ (Ac) *n.* [C,U] **1** a discussion in which people who are affected by a decision can say what they think should be done: *The changes were made* ***in consultation with*** *community groups.* | *The interest rate rise follows close consultations with Treasury officials.* **2** a meeting in which you get advice from a professional, or the process of getting this advice: *a* ***consultation with*** *the school counselor*

con·sume /kənˈsum/ (Ac) *v.* [T] **1** to completely use time, energy, goods, etc.: *Smaller cars consume less fuel.* **2** to eat or drink something: *The boys seemed able to consume large quantities of food.* **3 be consumed with passion/guilt/rage etc.** to have a very strong feeling that you cannot ignore **4** (formal) if a fire consumes something, it completely destroys it [ORIGIN: 1300—1400 Old French *consumer*, from Latin *consumere*, from *com* "completely" + *sumere* "to take up, take"] → TIME-CONSUMING

con·sum·er /kənˈsumɚ/ (Ac) *n.* [C] someone who buys or uses goods and services: *Consumers will soon be paying higher airfares.* | *There are laws that protect* ***the consumer*** (=consumers in general) *from fraud.* | *advertisements for* ***consumer goods*** (=things that people buy for their own use, rather than things bought by businesses)

THESAURUS **customer, client, shopper, patron, buyer** → CUSTOMER

con·sum·er·ism /kənˈsuməˌrɪzəm/ *n.* [U] (disapproving) the belief that it is good to buy and use a lot of goods and services

con·sum·mate¹ /ˈkɑnsəmɪt/ *adj.* very skillful: *a consummate politician*

con·sum·mate² /ˈkɑnsəˌmeɪt/ *v.* [T] (formal) **1** to make a marriage or a relationship complete by having sex **2** to make something such as an agreement complete —**consummation** /ˌkɑnsəˈmeɪʃən/ *n.* [U]

con·sump·tion /kənˈsʌmpʃən/ (Ac) *n.* [U] **1** the amount of electricity, gas, etc. that is used: *the aircraft's fuel consumption* **2** (formal) the act of eating or drinking: *The consumption of alcohol is not permitted on these premises.*

con·tact¹ /ˈkɑntækt/ (Ac) *n.* **1** [C,U] communication with a person, organization, country, etc.: *Have you* ***kept/stayed in contact with*** *any of your school friends?* | *The soldiers* ***had*** *little* ***contact with*** *citizens of the country.* | *the establishment of diplomatic contacts* **2** [U] the state of touching or being close to someone or something: *What happens when different cultures* ***come in contact with*** *each other?* | *The disease spreads by sexual contact.* **3** [C] someone you know who may be able to help you or give you advice: *He* ***has a few contacts*** *in the movie industry.* **4** [C] a contact lens **5** [C] PHYSICS an electrical part that completes a CIRCUIT when it touches another part

contact² (Ac) *v.* [T] to telephone or write to someone: *I've been trying to contact you for the past three days!* ►Don't say "I've been trying to contact with you."◄

ˈcontact ˌlens *n.* [C] a small round piece of plastic you put on your eye to help you see clearly

contact lens

con·ta·gious /kənˈteɪdʒəs/ *adj.* **1** a disease that is contagious can be passed from person to person by touch or through the air **2** a person who is contagious has a disease like this **3** a feeling, attitude, action, etc. that is contagious is quickly felt or done by other people: *Jeannie's laughter was contagious.*

con·tain /kənˈteɪn/ *v.* [T] **1** to have something inside: *a wallet containing $50* **2** to be included in something or be part of something: *The report contained some shocking information.* | *products that contain nuts* **3** to control the emotions you feel: *Greg was so excited he could hardly* ***contain himself.*** [ORIGIN: 1200—1300 Old French *contenir*, from Latin *continere* "to hold together, hold in, contain"]

con·tain·er /kənˈteɪnɚ/ *n.* [C] something such as a box, a bowl, a bottle, etc. that can be filled with something: *an eight-gallon container*

con·tain·ment /kənˈteɪnmənt/ *n.* [U] POLITICS the act of controlling something, such as the cost of a plan or the power of an unfriendly country

con·tam·i·nate /kənˈtæməˌneɪt/ *v.* [T] **1** to spoil something by adding a dangerous or poisonous substance to it: *These areas of the ocean are* ***contaminated with/by*** *oil.* **2** to influence someone or something in a way that has a bad effect: *Lack of trust will contaminate your whole relationship.*

—contaminated *adj.* **—contamination** /kən,tæmə'neɪʃən/ *n.* [U]

contd. the written abbreviation of CONTINUED

con·tem·plate /'kɑntəm,pleɪt/ *v.* [T] to think seriously for a long time about something you intend to do, or something you want to understand: *The group is contemplating legal action.* [ORIGIN: 1500—1600 Latin, past participle of *contemplari*] **—contemplation** /,kɑntəm'pleɪʃən/ *n.* [U]

con·tem·pla·tive /kən'tɛmplət̬ɪv/ *adj.* spending a lot of time thinking seriously and quietly

con·tem·po·ra·ne·ous /kən,tɛmpə'reɪniəs/ *adj.* (formal) happening or existing in the same period of time SYN **contemporary**: *Built in the 13th century, the churches are* ***contemporaneous with*** *many of the great gothic cathedrals.* **—contemporaneously** *adv.* **—contemporaneity** /kəntɛmpərə'niət̬i, -'neɪət̬i/ *n.* [U]

con·tem·po·rar·y¹ /kən'tɛmpə,rɛri/ AC *adj.* **1** belonging to the present time SYN **modern**: *a museum of contemporary art* **2** happening or existing in the same period of time: *letters* ***contemporary with*** *his earliest compositions* [ORIGIN: 1600—1700 Medieval Latin *contemporarius*, from Latin *com-* "together" + *tempus* "time"]

contemporary² *n.* (plural **contemporaries**) [C] someone who lives in the same period of time as a particular person or event: *Mozart's contemporaries | Christopher Marlowe was a* ***contemporary of*** *Shakespeare.*

con·tempt /kən'tɛmpt/ *n.* [U] **1** a feeling that someone or something does not deserve any respect: *actions that show* ***contempt for*** *women* **2 contempt of court** not doing what a judge or court of law has told you to: *Cooper was fined $100 for contempt of court.* [ORIGIN: 1300—1400 Latin *contemptus*, from *contemnere* "to think of with contempt"]

con·tempt·i·ble /kən'tɛmptəbəl/ *adj.* not deserving any respect: *contemptible behavior* **—contemptibly** *adv.*

con·temp·tu·ous /kən'tɛmptʃuəs/ *adj.* showing that you believe someone or something does not deserve any respect: *young people who are contemptuous of authority*

con·tend /kən'tɛnd/ *v.* **1** [T] to argue or say that something is true: *Opponents* ***contend that*** *the changes will create even more problems.* **2** [I] to compete for something: *Twelve teams are* ***contending for*** *the title.*

contend with sth *phr. v.* to deal with a problem or difficult situation: *The police would then have less paperwork to contend with.*

con·tend·er /kən'tɛndɚ/ *n.* [C] someone who is involved in a competition: *She is a* ***contender for*** *the Democratic nomination for president.*

con·tent¹ /'kɑntɛnt/ *n.* **1 contents** [plural] **a)** the things that are in a box, bag, room, etc.: *Officers searched through the* ***contents of*** *the desk.* **b)** the words or ideas that are written in a book, letter, etc.: *The contents of the document are still unknown. | the* ***table of contents*** (=a list at the beginning of a book, that tells you what is in it) **2** [singular] the ideas, information, or opinions that are expressed in a speech, book, etc.: *First of all, concentrate on the content of your essay, not its appearance.* **3** [singular] the amount of a substance that something contains: *Peanut butter has a high fat content.*

con·tent² /kən'tɛnt/ *adj.* happy or satisfied, or willing to do or accept something: *She seemed* ***content to*** *sit and wait. | I'd say she's pretty* ***content with*** *her life.* **—contentment** *n.* [U]

THESAURUS **happy, glad, pleased, delighted, thrilled, overjoyed, ecstatic, jubilant, elated** → HAPPY

content³ *v.* **content yourself with sth** to do or have something that is not what you really want, but is still satisfactory: *Jack's driving, so he'll have to content himself with a soft drink.*

content⁴ *n.* **do sth to your heart's content** to do something as much as you want

con·tent·ed /kən'tɛntɪd/ *adj.* satisfied or happy ANT **discontented**: *a contented cat*

con·ten·tion /kən'tɛnʃən/ *n.* **1** [C] a belief or opinion that someone expresses: *It was the defense's* ***contention that*** *their client was wrongly arrested.* **2** [U] a situation in which people or groups are competing: *Oregon remains* ***in contention for*** *the playoffs.* **3** [U] arguments and disagreement between people: *City planning has been a* ***bone of contention*** (=subject that people argue about) *for a long time.*

con·ten·tious /kən'tɛnʃəs/ *adj.* likely to cause a lot of argument **—contentiously** *adv.*

con·test¹ /'kɑntɛst/ *n.* [C] **1** a competition, usually a small one: *a contest to see who can run the fastest | The deadline for* ***entering the contest*** *is May 1. | Who* ***won/lost the contest****?*

THESAURUS **competition, championship, tournament, playoff** → COMPETITION

2 a struggle to win control or power: *the 1960 presidential* ***contest between*** *Kennedy and Nixon* **3 no contest** (informal) if a victory is no contest, it is very easy to achieve: *In the end, it was no contest, with the Dolphins beating the Bengals 37–13.* **4 plead no contest** LAW to state that you will not give a defense in a court of law for something wrong you have done [ORIGIN: 1500—1600 French *contester*, from Latin *contestari* "to call a witness, bring a legal case"]

con·test² /kən'tɛst/ *v.* [T] **1** to say formally that you do not think something is right or fair: *We intend to contest the judge's decision.* **2** to compete for something: *a* ***hotly contested*** (=competed for very strongly) *election*

C

con·test·ant /kən'tɛstənt/ *n.* [C] someone who competes in a contest

con·text /'kɑntɛkst/ (Ac) *n.* [C] **1** the situation, events, or information that are related to something, and that help you to understand it: *The events have to be considered in their* ***historical/social/political context.*** | *Can students apply the skills learned in school* ***in*** *a different* ***context,*** *such as the workplace?* **2** the words and sentences that come before and after a word and that help you understand its meaning: *"Smart" can mean "intelligent" or "sarcastic," depending on the context.* **3 take sth out of context** to repeat a sentence or phrase without describing the situation in which it was said, so that its meaning seems different from what was intended: *Journalists had taken his comments completely out of context.* [ORIGIN: 1400—1500 Latin *contextus* "connection of words," from *contexere* "to weave together"]

'context ˌclue *n.* [C] ENG. LANG. ARTS information that helps you understand the meaning of a particular word or phrase, which you obtain from the surrounding words or from the situation or events, etc. being described

con·tig·u·ous /kən'tɪgyuəs/ *adj.* (formal) next to something, or sharing the same border: *the 48 contiguous States*

con·ti·nent /'kɑntənənt, 'kɑnt˺n-ənt/ *n.* [C] one of the main areas of land on the Earth: *the continent of Africa* [ORIGIN: 1500—1600 Latin *continens* "continuous area of land," from *continere*]

con·ti·nen·tal /ˌkɑntən'ɛntl◂ / *adj.* relating to a continent: *flights across the continental U.S.*

ˌcontinental 'breakfast *n.* [C] a breakfast consisting of coffee, juice, and a sweet ROLL (=type of bread)

ˌcontinental di'vide *n.* [C] EARTH SCIENCES a very large area of high ground on a CONTINENT, from each side of which river systems flow in opposite directions

ˌcontinental 'drift *n.* [U] EARTH SCIENCES the very slow movement of the CONTINENTS across the surface of the Earth

ˌcontinental 'shelf *n.* [C] EARTH SCIENCES the area of land on the edge of a CONTINENT that slopes down into the bottom of the ocean → *see picture at* PHOTIC ZONE

con·tin·gen·cy /kən'tɪndʒənsi/ *n.* (plural **contingencies**) [C] an event or situation that might happen and could cause problems: *a* ***contingency plan*** *to cope with any computer failures*

con·tin·gent¹ /kən'tɪndʒənt/ *adj.* (formal) dependent on something that may or may not happen in the future: *The purchase of the house is* ***contingent on/upon*** *a satisfactory inspection.*

contingent² *n.* [C] a group of people who have the same aims or are from the same area, and who are part of a larger group: *By late summer, a* ***contingent of*** *scientists had arrived.*

continua *n.* a plural of CONTINUUM

con·tin·u·al /kən'tɪnyuəl/ *adj.* repeated often, over a long period of time: *Their continual arguing really upset me.*

USAGE

Continual and **continuous** can be used in a very similar way: *a continual/continuous process*
Continual is also used when something happens many times, especially something annoying: *There were continual interruptions all day.*
Continuous is used in order to emphasize that there is no pause or break between things: *a continuous flow of water* | *a continuous line of trees*

—**continually** *adv.*

con·tin·u·a·tion /kənˌtɪnyu'eɪʃən/ *n.* **1** [U] the act or state of continuing for a long time without stopping: *the continuation of family traditions* **2** [C] something that follows after or is joined to something else and seems a part of it: *Community colleges offer students a continuation of their education.*

con·tin·ue /kən'tɪnyu/ *v.* **1** [I,T] to keep happening, existing, or doing something without stopping: *She will continue her work at UCSD.* | *The city's population will* ***continue to*** *grow.* | ***Continuing with*** *the peace process is very important.* **2** [I,T] to start doing something again after a pause: *Rescuers will continue the search tomorrow.* | *After a brief ceasefire, fighting continued.* **3** [I] to go further in the same direction: *Route 66* ***continues on*** *to Texas from here.* [ORIGIN: 1300—1400 French *continuer*, from Latin *continuare*, from *continuus*]

conˌtinuing edu'cation *n.* [U] classes for adults, often on subjects that relate to their jobs

con·ti·nu·i·ty /ˌkɑntə'nuəṭi/ *n.* [U] the state of continuing over a long period of time without being interrupted or changing: *Changing doctors can affect the* ***continuity of*** *your treatment.*

con·tin·u·ous¹ /kən'tɪnyuəs/ *adj.* **1** continuing to happen or exist without stopping or pausing: *The church has been in continuous use since 1732.* → see USAGE box at CONTINUAL **2** without any spaces or holes in it: *a continuous line of cars* —**continuously** *adv.*

continuous² *n.* **the continuous** ENG. LANG. ARTS in grammar, the form of a verb that shows that an action or activity is continuing to happen, and that is formed with "be" and the PRESENT PARTICIPLE. In the sentence "She is watching TV," "is watching" is in the continuous.

con·tin·u·um /kən'tɪnyuəm/ *n.* (plural **continuums** *or* **continua** /-nyuə/) [C] (formal) a series of related things, in which each thing is only slightly different from the one before or the one after, so that there are no clear dividing points: *Depression exists* ***on a continuum,*** *with mild sadness at one end to suicide at the other.*

con·tort /kən'tɔrt/ *v.* [I,T] to twist your face or

body so that it does not have its normal shape —**contortion** /kən'tɔrʃən/ *n.* [C,U]

con·tour /'kantʊr/ *n.* [C] the shape of the outer edges of something such as an area of land or someone's body

con·tra·band /'kantrəˌbænd/ *n.* [U] **1** goods that are brought into or taken out of a country illegally, especially to avoid paying tax **2** goods that are illegal to supply to either side in a war [ORIGIN: 1500—1600 Italian *contrabbando*, from Medieval Latin *contrabannum*, from *contra-* "against" + *bannum* "official order"] —**contraband** *adj.*

con·tra·cep·tion /ˌkantrə'sɛpʃən/ *n.* [U] the practice or methods of preventing a woman from becoming PREGNANT when she has sex (SYN) **birth control**

con·tra·cep·tive /ˌkantrə'sɛptɪv/ *n.* [C] a drug, object, or method used so that a woman does not become PREGNANT when she has sex —**contraceptive** *adj.*

con·tract¹ /'kantrækt/ (Ac) *n.* [C] **1** a legal written agreement between two people, companies, etc. that says what each will do: *Stacy* ***signed*** *a three-year* ***contract***. | *His firm has a* ***contract with*** *the Forest Service to supply firefighting equipment.* | *The shipyard won the* ***contract to*** *build seven ships.* **2** (informal) an agreement to kill someone for money [ORIGIN: 1500—1600 Latin *contractus*, past participle of *contrahere* "to pull together, make a contract, make smaller"]

con·tract² /kən'trækt/ (Ac) *v.* **1** [T] (formal) to get an illness (SYN) **catch**: *The disease is contracted from drinking contaminated water.* **2** [I] to become smaller (ANT) **expand**: *The economy is likely to contract over the coming year.*

con·tract³ /'kantrækt/ *v.* [I,T] to sign a contract to do something: *The city has* ***contracted with*** *a private company* ***to*** *remove garbage.*

contract sth ↔ **out** *phr. v.* to arrange to have a job done by a person or company outside your own organization: *The city has contracted its garbage collection out to an independent company.*

con·trac·tion /kən'trækʃən/ *n.* **1** [C] BIOLOGY a very strong and painful movement of a muscle in which it suddenly becomes tight, used especially about the muscles that become tight when a woman is going to give birth **2** [U] the process of becoming smaller or shorter **3** [C] ENG. LANG. ARTS a short form of a word or words, such as "don't" for "do not"

con·trac·tor /'kanˌtræktɚ, kən'træk-/ (Ac) *n.* [C] a person or company that does work or supplies material for other companies

con·trac·tu·al /kən'træktʃuəl/ *adj.* agreed in a contract: *contractual obligations*

con·tra·dict /ˌkantrə'dɪkt/ (Ac) *v.* **1** [T] if a statement, story, etc. contradicts another one, the facts in it are so different that both statements cannot be true: *The witnesses' reports contradicted each other.* | *Recent experiments seem to contradict the earlier results.* **2** [I,T] to say that what someone else has just said is wrong or not true: *You shouldn't contradict me in front of the kids.* **3 contradict yourself** to say something that is the opposite of what you have said before [ORIGIN: 1500—1600 Latin, past participle of *contradicere*, from *contra-* "against" + *dicere* "to say"] —**contradictory** /ˌkantrə'dɪktəri/ *adj.*

con·tra·dic·tion /ˌkantrə'dɪkʃən/ (Ac) *n.* **1** [C] a difference between two stories, facts, etc. that means they cannot both be true: *There were* ***contradictions between*** *the testimonies of the two men.* **2** [U] the act of saying that what someone has just said is wrong or not true **3 contradiction in terms** a combination of words that seem to be the opposite of each other, so that the phrase does not have a clear meaning

con·trap·tion /kən'træpʃən/ *n.* [C] (informal) a piece of equipment that looks strange

THESAURUS **machine, appliance, device, gadget, mechanism** → MACHINE¹

con·trar·y¹ /'kanˌtrɛri/ (Ac) *n.* (formal) **1 on the contrary** used in order to show that the opposite of what has just been said is actually true: *We didn't start the fire. On the contrary, we helped put it out.* **2 to the contrary** showing or saying the opposite: *In spite of rumors to the contrary, their marriage is fine.* [ORIGIN: 1300—1400 Latin, *contrarius* "opposed, opposite," from *contra-* "against"]

contrary² *adj.* **1** completely different or opposite: *This idea is* ***contrary to*** *Catholic teaching.* **2 contrary to popular belief** used in order to show that something is true even though people may think the opposite: *Contrary to popular belief, gorillas are shy and gentle.*

con·trar·y³ /kən'trɛri/ *adj.* deliberately doing or saying the opposite of what someone else wants: *an extremely contrary child*

con·trast¹ /'kantræst/ (Ac) *n.* **1** [C,U] a difference between two people, situations, ideas, etc. that are being compared: *the* ***contrast between*** *the rich and poor in America* | *Claire is tall and dark,* ***in contrast to*** *her mother, who is short and fair.* | *At that time, the life of West Berlin stood* ***in sharp/stark/marked contrast to*** *East Berlin.* **2** [U] the differences in color or in light and darkness on photographs, a television picture, etc. [ORIGIN: 1600—1700 French *contraster*, from Italian *contrastare* "to stand out against, fight against"]

con·trast² /kən'træst/ (Ac) *v.* **1** [T] to compare two people, ideas, objects, etc. to show how they are different from each other: *In another passage, Melville again* ***contrasts*** *the land* ***with*** *the sea.* | *Students should* ***compare and contrast*** *the motives of each character in the story.*

THESAURUS **compare, make a comparison, draw a parallel, draw an analogy, make/draw a distinction** → COMPARE¹

2 [I] if two things contrast, they are very different from each other: *His thick, bulky body* ***contrasted with*** *Len's tall lankiness.* —**contrasting** *adj.*: *Different cultures have contrasting interpretations of the story.*

con·tra·vene /ˌkɑntrəˈvin/ *v.* [T] (formal) to do something that is not allowed by a law or a rule [ORIGIN: 1500—1600 French *contrevenir*, from Late Latin *contravenire*, from Latin *contra-* "against" + *venire* "to come"] —**contravention** /ˌkɑntrəˈvɛnʃən/ *n.* [C,U]

C

THESAURUS disobey, break a rule/law, rebel, defy, flout, violate, infringe → DISOBEY

con·trib·ute /kənˈtrɪbyut, -yət/ (Ac) *v.* **1** [I,T] to give money, help, or ideas to something that other people are also giving to: *Large companies* ***contribute*** *money* ***to*** *both parties.* | *Other people had good ideas, but I felt I had nothing to contribute.* **2** [I] to help make something happen: *An electrical problem may have* ***contributed to*** *the crash.* **3** [I,T] to write something for a newspaper or magazine: *Several hundred people contributed articles, photographs, and cartoons.* —**contributor** *n.* [C] —**contributory** /kənˈtrɪbyəˌtɔri/ *adj.*

con·tri·bu·tion /ˌkɑntrəˈbyuʃən/ (Ac) *n.* [C] **1** something that is given or done to help something else be successful: *The Mayo Clinic has* ***made*** *important* ***contributions to*** *cancer research.* | *Einstein's* ***significant/important/valuable contributions to*** *physics* **2** an amount of money that is given to help pay for something: *Would you like to* ***make a contribution to*** *the Red Cross?* | *a* ***contribution of*** *$25* **3** a piece of writing that is printed in a newspaper or magazine

con·trite /kənˈtraɪt/ *adj.* feeling guilty and sorry for something bad that you have done: *a contrite apology* —**contrition** /kənˈtrɪʃən/ *n.* [U]

THESAURUS guilty, ashamed, embarrassed → GUILTY

con·trive /kənˈtraɪv/ *v.* [T] to manage to do something difficult or to invent something by being very smart or dishonest: *Schindler* ***contrived to*** *save more than 1,000 Polish Jews from the Nazis.*

con·trived /kənˈtraɪvd/ *adj.* seeming false and not natural: *The plot was contrived.*

con·trol[1] /kənˈtroʊl/ *n.* **1** [U] the power or ability to make someone or something do what you want: *They don't* ***have*** *any* ***control over*** *their son.* | *Newborn babies have little* ***control of/over*** *their movements.* | *The car went* ***out of control*** *and hit a tree.* | *The situation is now* ***under control.*** | *These events are* ***beyond our control*** (=not possible for us to control). **2** [U] the power to rule or govern a place, organization, or company: *Rioters* ***took control of*** *the prison.* | *The airport is now* ***under the control of*** *UN troops.* | *The government is no longer* ***in control*** *of the country.* **3** [C,U] an action, method, or law that limits the amount or growth of something: *an agreement on arms control* | *Firefighters* ***brought*** *the fire* ***under control*** (=stopped it from getting worse). **4** [U] the ability to remain calm even when you are angry or excited: *I just* ***lost control*** *and punched him!* **5** [C] something that you use to make a television, machine, vehicle, etc. work: *the volume control* | *the controls of the airplane* **6** [singular] *also* **control key** IT a button on a computer, that allows you to do particular things: *Press "control" and "S" to save the document.* —**controlled** *adj.*

control[2] *v.* (**controlled**, **controlling**) [T] **1** to make someone or something do what you want or work in a particular way: *If you can't control your dog, you should put it on a leash.* **2** to limit the amount or growth of something: *a chemical used to control weeds* **3** to rule or govern a place, organization, or company, or to have more power than someone else: *Rebels control all the roads into the capital.* **4** to make yourself behave calmly, even if you feel angry, excited, or upset: *I was furious, but I managed to* ***control myself.***

conˈtrol ˌfreak *n.* [C] (informal, disapproving) someone who is very concerned about controlling all the details in every situation s/he is involved in

conˌtrolled exˈperiment *n.* [C] SCIENCE a scientific test in which you change only one single condition of the test and do not change any of the other conditions that might affect the test

conˌtrolled ˈvariable *n.* [C] SCIENCE in a scientific EXPERIMENT (=test), one of the conditions that you do not change, so that its effect is always the same

con·trol·ler /kənˈtroʊlɚ/ *n.* [C] ECONOMICS someone whose job is to collect and pay money for a government or company department: *the state controller*

conˈtrol ˌtower *n.* [C] a building at an airport, from which people direct the movements of airplanes on the ground and in the air

con·tro·ver·sial /ˌkɑntrəˈvɚʃəl◂/ (Ac) *adj.* something that is controversial causes a lot of disagreement because many people have strong opinions about it: *the controversial subject of abortion* | *He is a* ***controversial figure*** (=person who does controversial things) *in the art world.* —**controversially** *adv.*

con·tro·ver·sy /ˈkɑntrəˌvɚsi/ (Ac) *n.* (plural **controversies**) [C,U] a serious disagreement among many people over a plan, decision, etc., over a long period of time: *There is* ***controversy over*** *the proposed development.* | *The controversy surrounding the theory continues to this day.* [ORIGIN: 1300—1400 Latin *controversia*, from *controversus* "disagreed about"]

con·tu·sion /kənˈtuʒən/ *n.* [C] (formal) a BRUISE —**contused** *adj.*

co·nun·drum /kəˈnʌndrəm/ *n.* [C] **1** something or someone that is confusing and difficult to understand: *a moral conundrum* **2** a trick question asked for fun (SYN) **riddle**

con·ur·ba·tion /ˌkɑnɚˈbeɪʃən/ *n.* [C] SOCIAL SCIENCE a group of towns that have grown and joined together to form an area where a lot of people live, often with a large city as its center

con·va·lesce /ˌkɑnvəˈlɛs/ *v.* [I] (formal) to spend time getting well after a serious illness SYN **recuperate** —**convalescence** *n.* [singular, U] —**convalescent** *n.* [C]

con·va·les·cent /ˌkɑnvəˈlɛsənt/ *adj.* **convalescent home/hospital etc.** a place where people stay when they need care from doctors and nurses but are not sick enough to be in a hospital

con·vec·tion /kənˈvɛkʃən/ *n.* [U] **1** PHYSICS the circular movement in a gas or liquid, caused by an outside force such as GRAVITY **2** PHYSICS the movement of heat through a liquid, caused by the action of MOLECULES → CONDUCTION [ORIGIN: 1800—1900 Late Latin *convectio*, from Latin *convehere*, from *con-* "together" + *vehere* "to carry"]

con·vene /kənˈvin/ Ac *v.* [I,T] (formal) if a group of people convenes, or if someone convenes them, they come together for a formal meeting: *A board was convened to judge the design competition.* | *The matter will be discussed when the Assembly convenes on November 4th.*

> THESAURUS **meet, get together, gather, assemble, come together, congregate** → MEET[1]

con·ven·ience /kənˈvinyəns/ *n.* **1** [U] the quality of being good or useful for a particular purpose, especially because it makes something easier ANT **inconvenience**: *Most people like the* ***convenience of*** *using a credit card.* **2** [U] what is easiest and best for someone ANT **inconvenience**: *The package can be delivered* ***at your convenience.*** **3** [C] something such as a service, piece of equipment, etc. that is useful because it saves you time or work: *modern conveniences such as washing machines*

conˈvenience ˌfood *n.* [C,U] food that is partly or completely prepared already

conˈvenience ˌstore *n.* [C] a store where you can buy food, newspapers, etc. and that is often open 24 hours each day

con·ven·ient /kənˈvinyənt/ *adj.* **1** useful to you because it makes something easier or saves you time ANT **inconvenient**: *Catalogs are a convenient way to shop.* | *What time would be* ***convenient for*** *you?* **2** near and easy to get to ANT **inconvenient**: *a restaurant in a convenient location* [ORIGIN: 1300—1400 Latin, present participle of *convenire* "to come together, be suitable"] —**conveniently** *adv.*

con·vent /ˈkɑnvɛnt, -vənt/ *n.* [C] a place where NUNS live and work [ORIGIN: 1200—1300 Old French *covent*, from Latin *conventus* "group of people who have come together," from *convenire*]

con·ven·tion /kənˈvɛnʃən/ Ac *n.* **1** [C] a large formal meeting of people who belong to the same profession, organization, etc., or who have the same interests: *the Democratic National Convention* | *a convention of science fiction fans* **2** [C,U] behavior and attitudes that most people in society think are normal and right: *He defied* ***social conventions*** *to follow his own path.*

> THESAURUS **habit, custom, tradition, practice** → HABIT

3 [C] a formal agreement between countries: *the Geneva convention on human rights*

con·ven·tion·al /kənˈvɛnʃənəl/ Ac *adj.* **1** used or existing for a long time, and considered usual: *Acupuncture is one alternative to conventional medicine.*

> THESAURUS **normal, ordinary, average, standard, routine, orthodox** → NORMAL[1]

2 always following the behavior and attitudes that most people in society think are normal and right, so that you seem boring: *The twins share a very conventional taste in clothing.* | *My family is extremely* ***conventional in*** *its attitude and morals.* **3 conventional wisdom** the opinion that most people consider to be normal and right **4** conventional weapons and wars do not use NUCLEAR explosives —**conventionally** *adv.*

con·verge /kənˈvɚdʒ/ *v.* [I] to move or come together from different directions to meet at the same point ANT **diverge**: *Thousands of fans* ***converged on*** *the stadium.* [ORIGIN: 1600—1700 Medieval Latin *convergere*, from Latin *con-* "together" + *vergere* "to bend, turn"] —**convergence** *n.* [C,U]

convergent /kənˈvɚdʒənt/ *adj.* coming together at a point: *convergent lines* → *see picture at* LINE[1]

conˌvergent evoˈlution *n.* [U] BIOLOGY the natural way that SPECIES of animals, plants, etc. living in different areas have developed similar physical features as they have EVOLVED (=changed gradually over a long period of time)

con·ver·sant /kənˈvɚsənt/ *adj.* (formal) having knowledge or experience of something: *Staff members are* ***conversant with*** *all the safety rules.*

con·ver·sa·tion /ˌkɑnvɚˈseɪʃən/ *n.* **1** [C,U] a talk between two or more people in which people ask questions, exchange news, etc.: *They* ***had a*** *pleasant* ***conversation*** *during dinner.* | *a short* ***conversation with*** *his mother* | *a* ***conversation about*** *the tensions between work and family life* | *The two women were deep* ***in conversation*** (=they were concentrating on their conversation). **2 make conversation** to talk to someone to be polite, not because you really want to: *"Nice weather we're having," he said, trying to make conversation.* [ORIGIN: 1300—1400 Old French, Latin *conversatio*, from *conversari* "to live with, be with"] —**conversational** *adj.* —**conversationally** *adv.*

con·verse[1] /kən'vɚs/ (Ac) *v.* [I] (formal) to have a conversation with someone: *She enjoyed the chance to* ***converse with*** *someone who spoke her language.* [ORIGIN: 1300—1400 Old French *converser*, from Latin *conversari* "to live with, be with"]

> THESAURUS **talk, have a conversation, chat (with/to sb)/have a chat, visit with sb, discuss, gossip, whisper** → TALK[1]

C

con·verse[2] /'kɑnvɚs/ (Ac) *n.* (formal) **1 the converse** the opposite of something: *Most people's income grew, but the converse was true in some cases.* **2** [singular, U] MATH a mathematical or LOGICAL statement in which the subject and the statement about the subject have been changed around. For example, the converse of "All X is Y" is "All Y is X". → INVERSE —**converse** /kən'vɚs, 'kɑnvɚs/ *adj.* —**conversely** *adv.*

con·ver·sion /kən'vɚʒən, -ʃən/ (Ac) *n.* [C,U] **1** the act or process of changing something from one form, system, or purpose to another: *Canada's* ***conversion to*** *the metric system* **2** a change in which someone accepts a completely new religion, belief, etc.: *his* ***conversion to*** *Islam*

con'version ˌfactor *n.* [C] MATH a fixed quantity that, when multiplied or divided by another number, changes one type of measurement into a different type of measurement, for example miles into kilometers

con·vert[1] /kən'vɚt/ (Ac) *v.* [I,T] **1** to change, or to make something change, from one form, system, or purpose to another: *We're going to* ***convert*** *the garage* ***into*** *a workshop.* | *Energy from the* ***converts to*** *heat.* **2** to change your opinions, beliefs, or habits, or to make someone do this: *She* ***converted to*** *Christianity.* [ORIGIN: 1200—1300 Old French *convertir*, from Latin *convertere* "to turn around, convert"]

con·vert[2] /'kɑnvɚt/ (Ac) *n.* [C] someone who has accepted a completely new religion, belief, etc.

con·vert·i·ble[1] /kən'vɚt̬əbəl/ (Ac) *adj.* **1** an object that is convertible can be folded or arranged in a different way, so that it can be used as something else: *a convertible couch* (=one that unfolds to become a bed) **2** ECONOMICS able to be exchanged for the money of another country, for STOCKS, etc.: *a convertible currency* | *This type of stock is convertible.*

convertible[2] *n.* [C] a car with a roof that you can fold back or remove

con·vex /ˌkɑn'vɛks◂, kən-/ *adj.* PHYSICS curved toward the outside like the surface of the eye (ANT) **concave**: *a convex lens*

con·vey /kən'veɪ/ *v.* [T] (formal) to communicate a message or information, with or without using words: *Please* ***convey*** *my thanks* ***to*** *her.* [ORIGIN: 1300—1400 Old French *conveier* "to go with someone to a place," from Vulgar Latin *conviare*]

con'veyor belt *n.* [C] a long continuous moving band of rubber or metal, used in a place such as a factory or airport to move things from one place to another

con·vict[1] /kən'vɪkt/ *v.* [T] LAW to prove or announce that someone is guilty of a crime after a TRIAL in a court of law (ANT) **acquit**: *Both men were* ***convicted of*** *fraud.*

con·vict[2] /'kɑnvɪkt/ *n.* [C] LAW someone who has been proved to be guilty of a crime and sent to prison

con·vic·tion /kən'vɪkʃən/ *n.* [C,U] **1** a very strong belief or opinion: *his religious convictions* | *He argued* ***with conviction*** *that the economy was growing.*

> THESAURUS **opinion, view, point of view, position, stance, attitude, sentiment** → OPINION

2 LAW an official announcement in a court of law that someone is guilty of a crime (ANT) **acquittal**: *his third* ***conviction for*** *theft*

con·vince /kən'vɪns/ (Ac) *v.* [T] **1** to make someone feel certain that something is true: *His lawyers* ***convinced*** *the jury* ***that*** *Booth was innocent.* **2** to persuade someone to do something: *I* ***convinced*** *him* ***to*** *stay.* [ORIGIN: 1500—1600 Latin *convincere* "to prove untrue, convict, prove"]

> THESAURUS **persuade, talk sb into sth, get sb to do sth, encourage sb to do sth, influence, coax, cajole, prevail on/upon sb** → PERSUADE

con·vinced /kən'vɪnst/ (Ac) *adj.* **be convinced** to feel certain that something is true: *I was* ***convinced (that)*** *we were doing the right thing.* | *Doctors are* ***convinced of*** *the medicine's effectiveness.*

> THESAURUS **sure, certain, confident, satisfied, positive** → SURE[1]

con·vinc·ing /kən'vɪnsɪŋ/ (Ac) *adj.* making you believe that something is true or right: *Their argument is not very convincing.* | *The most convincing evidence that light travels as a wave came from the experiments of James Maxwell.* —**convincingly** *adv.*

con·viv·i·al /kən'vɪviəl/ *adj.* (formal) friendly and

pleasant: *a convivial atmosphere* —**conviviality** /kənˌvɪvi'æləṭi/ *n.* [U]

THESAURUS sociable, outgoing, extroverted, gregarious, affable, genial → SOCIABLE

con·vo·lut·ed /'kɑnvəˌluṭɪd/ *adj.* (formal) complicated and difficult to understand: *a convoluted plot*

THESAURUS complicated, complex, elaborate, intricate → COMPLICATED

con·voy /'kɑnvɔɪ/ *n.* [C,U] a group of vehicles or ships traveling together

con·vul·sion /kən'vʌlʃən/ *n.* [C] **1** an occasion when someone cannot control the violent movements of his/her body because s/he is sick **2** [usually plural] a great change that affects a country: *the political convulsions in Eastern Europe*

coo /ku/ *v.* **1** [I] to make a sound like the low cry of a DOVE or a PIGEON **2** [I,T] to make soft loving noises: *a mother cooing to her baby*

cook[1] /kʊk/ *v.* **1** [I,T] to prepare food for eating by using heat: *Whoever gets home first* ***cooks dinner/supper***. | *Alice said she'd cook tonight.* | *Cook the pasta for 10–12 minutes.*

THESAURUS

bake – to cook food such as bread in the oven
fry – to cook food in oil on the top part of an oven
roast – to cook meat or vegetables in an oven
broil – to cook food by placing it near to strong heat from above
grill – to cook food over strong heat, especially over flames: *a grilled steak*
sauté – to fry vegetables for a short time in a small amount of oil
boil – to cook vegetables in very hot water on the top part of the oven
steam – to cook vegetables by placing them in a container over very hot water, so that the steam from the hot water cooks them
deep fry – to fry food in a pan containing a lot of hot oil

2 [I] to be prepared for eating by using heat: *How long does it take the stew to cook?* **3 be cooking (with gas)** (spoken) to be doing something very well, or in the correct way: *The band is really cooking tonight.* [ORIGIN: Old English *coc*, from Latin *coquus*, from *coquere* "to cook"]

cook sth ↔ **up** *phr. v.* **1** (informal) to invent an excuse, reason, plan, etc. that is slightly dishonest or will not work: *the plan that Larry and Jim had cooked up between them* **2** to prepare food, especially quickly: *She cooked up some beans and cornbread.*

cook[2] *n.* [C] someone who cooks and prepares food: *Kevin works as a cook.* | *My cousin's a* ***wonderful/good/terrible cook***.

cook·book /'kʊkbʊk/ *n.* [C] a book that tells you how to prepare and cook food

cooked /kʊkt/ *adj.* ready for eating and not raw: *cooked vegetables*

cook·ie /'kʊki/ *n.* [C] **1** a small flat sweet cake: *chocolate chip cookies* **2** IT information that a WEB SITE leaves on your computer so that the website will recognize you when you use it again [ORIGIN: 1700—1800 Dutch *koekje*, from *koek* "cake"]

'cookie ˌcutter[1] *n.* [C] an instrument that cuts cookies into special shapes before you bake them

C

cookie cutter[2] *adj.* [only before noun] almost exactly the same as other things of the same type, and not very interesting: *cookie cutter houses*

'cookie sheet *n.* [C] a flat metal pan that you bake food on

cook·ing[1] /'kʊkɪŋ/ *n.* [U] **1** the act of making food and cooking it: *I* ***do*** *most* ***of the cooking***. **2** food made in a particular way or by a particular person: *Italian cooking*

cooking[2] *adj.* used for cooking: *cooking oil* | *a cooking pot*

cool[1] /kul/ *adj.* **1** low in temperature but not cold: *a cool summer evening* | *a nice cool drink*

THESAURUS cold, chilly, frosty, freezing (cold), icy (cold), bitter (cold), frigid → COLD[1]

2 (spoken) said in order to show that you agree with something, that you understand it, or that it does not annoy you: *"Do you mind if I bring my sister?" "No,* ***that's cool***.*"* **3** (spoken, approving) fashionable, attractive, interesting, etc. in a way that people admire: *He's a really cool guy.* | *That's such a cool car.* **4** calm and not nervous or excited: ***Stay cool;*** *don't let him get to you.*

THESAURUS calm, relaxed, laid-back, easygoing, mellow, placid, serene → CALM[2]

5 unfriendly: *a cool welcome* [ORIGIN: Old English *col*] —**coolness** *n.* [U] —**coolly** /'kul-li/ *adv.*

cool[2] *v.* **1** [I,T] *also* **cool down** to make something slightly colder, or to become slightly colder: *Allow the cake to cool before cutting it.* **2** [I] feelings or relationships that cool become less strong or friendly: *Relations between the two countries have cooled considerably.* **3 cool it** (spoken) used in order to tell someone to stop being angry: *Jeez, Jim, just cool it, will you?*

cool down *phr. v.* **1** to become calm after being angry: *The long walk home helped me cool down.* **2** to do gentle physical exercises after doing more difficult exercises, so that you do not get injuries

cool off *phr. v.* **1** to return to a normal temperature after being hot: *They went for a swim to cool off.* **2** to become calm after being angry: *Give him some time to cool off first.*

cool[3] *n.* [U] **1 the cool** a temperature that is cool: *the cool of a spring morning* **2 keep your cool**

to stay calm in a difficult situation: *The players kept their cool and started scoring.* **3 lose your cool** to stop being calm in a difficult situation: *The waiter never lost his cool.*

cool·er /'kulɚ/ *n.* [C] a small box in which you can keep food or drinks cool

coop /kup/ *n.* [C] a cage for chickens

ˌcooped 'up *adj.* [not before noun] having to stay indoors or in a place that is too small for a long period of time: *I've been cooped up in this apartment all day.*

C

co·op·er·ate /koʊ'ɑpəˌreɪt/ (Ac) *v.* [I] **1** to work with someone else to achieve something that you both want: *The local police are* ***cooperating with*** *the FBI.* **2** to do what someone asks you to do: *Some of the kids refused to* ***cooperate with*** *him.* [ORIGIN: 1500—1600 Late Latin, past participle of *cooperari* "to work with"]

co·op·er·a·tion /koʊˌɑpə'reɪʃən/ (Ac) *n.* [U] **1** the act of working with someone else to achieve what you both want: *The sales team will be working* ***in cooperation with*** *other departments.* | *the* ***cooperation between*** *Congress and the White House* **2** willingness to work with other people, or to do what they ask you to do: *Thank you for your cooperation.*

co·op·era·tive¹ /koʊ'ɑprət̬ɪv/ (Ac) *adj.* **1** willing to help or willing to do what you ask: *a happy and cooperative child* **2** made, done, or owned by people working together: *a cooperative farm* —**cooperatively** *adv.*

cooperative² *n.* [C] a company, farm, etc. that is owned and operated by people working together: *They turned their business into a cooperative.*

co-opt /koʊ'ɑpt/ *v.* [T] (disapproving) to use something that was not originally yours to help you do something, or to persuade someone to help you: *He saw his best ideas co-opted by his rivals.*

co·or·di·nate¹ /koʊ'ɔrdn-ɪt/ (Ac) *n.* [C usually plural] MATH one of a set of numbers showing the exact position of a point on a line, map, or GRAPH, etc. [ORIGIN: 1600—1700 Late Latin, past participle of *coordinare*, from Latin "to arrange with"]

co·or·di·nate² /koʊ'ɔrdnˌeɪt/ (Ac) *v.* [T] to organize people or things so that they work together well: *The group is coordinating medical and food aid to the area.* | *Diplomatic efforts in London were coordinated with those in Washington.*

co·or·di·nat·ed /koʊ'ɔrdnˌeɪt̬ɪd/ *adj.* **1** able to control your body and make it move smoothly: *a well-coordinated young boy* **2** organized so that people or things work together well: *a coordinated effort to get the law changed*

coˌordinate of a 'point *n.* [C] MATH one of a set of numbers showing the exact position of a point on a line or PLANE (=completely flat surface)

co'ordinate ˌplane *n.* [C] MATH a PLANE (=completely flat surface) formed when two straight lines go across each other at right angles

coˌordinating con'junction *n.* [C] ENG. LANG. ARTS a word such as "and" or "but," which joins together two CLAUSEs of the same type

co·or·di·na·tion /koʊˌɔrdn'eɪʃən/ (Ac) *n.* [U] **1** the organization of people or things so that they work together well: *More* ***coordination between*** *departments is needed.* **2** the way that the parts of your body work together to do something: *Alcohol affects your coordination.*

co·or·di·na·tor /koʊ'ɔrdnˌeɪt̬ɚ/ (Ac) *n.* [C] someone who organizes the way people work together

coo·ties /'kut̬iz/ *n.* [plural] LICE (=small insects that live in your hair) – used by children as an insult when they do not want to play with or sit with another child: *Jenny* ***has cooties.***

cop /kɑp/ *n.* [C] (informal) a police officer [ORIGIN: 1800—1900 *copper* "police officer" (19—21 centuries), from *cop* "to arrest" (19—20 centuries)]

co·pay·ment /koʊ'peɪmənt/ *n.* [C] an amount that someone with medical insurance has to pay for using particular medical services, for example visits to the doctor

cope /koʊp/ *v.* [I] to succeed in dealing with a difficult problem or situation: *The country is trying to* ***cope with*** *high levels of unemployment.* | *children who have trouble* ***coping with*** *change*

> **THESAURUS** deal with sth, handle, tackle, attend to sth, take care of sth ➔ DEAL²

cop·i·er /'kɑpiɚ/ *n.* [C] a machine that quickly copies documents onto paper by photographing them

co·pi·lot /'koʊˌpaɪlət/ *n.* [C] a pilot who helps the main pilot fly an airplane

co·pi·ous /'koʊpiəs/ *adj.* produced in large amounts: *He took copious notes.* [ORIGIN: 1300—1400 Latin *copiosus*, from *copia* "large amounts," from *co-* + *ops* "wealth"] —**copiously** *adv.*

co·pla·nar /koʊ'pleɪnɚ/ *adj.* MATH coplanar lines or points all lie in the same PLANE (=completely flat surface)

'cop-out *n.* [C] (informal) something you do or say in order to avoid doing something: *Blaming kids' failing grades on TV is a cop-out.* —**cop out** *phr. v.*

cop·per /'kɑpɚ/ *n.* [U] an orange-brown metal that is an ELEMENT and is often used to make wire [ORIGIN: Old English *coper*, from Late Latin *cuprum*, from Latin *(aes) Cyprium* "metal of Cyprus, copper"] —**copper** *adj.*

cop·ter /'kɑptɚ/ *n.* [C] (informal) a HELICOPTER

cop·u·late /'kɑpyəˌleɪt/ *v.* [I] (formal) to have sex —**copulation** /ˌkɑpyə'leɪʃən/ *n.* [U]

cop·y¹ /'kɑpi/ *n.* (plural **copies**) **1** [C] something that is made to look exactly like something else: *Please* ***make*** *me a* ***copy*** *of the report.* | *a good* ***copy***

of Van Gogh's famous painting **2** [C] one of many books, magazines, etc. that are exactly the same: *a copy of Cornwell's new novel* **3** [U] something written to be printed, especially for an advertisement: *We need someone who can write good copy.* [ORIGIN: 1300—1400 Old French *copie*, from Latin *copia* "large amounts"]

copy² *v.* (**copied**, **copies**) **1** [T] to make a thing that is exactly like something else: *I copied a CD for him.* | *To copy a file, press "F3."*

THESAURUS
reproduce – to make a copy of something: *Printing presses allowed books to be reproduced cheaply.*
duplicate – to copy something exactly, in order to have more than one: *They duplicate the DVDs and then sell them illegally.*
replicate (formal) – to do or make something again, so that you make an exact copy: *How does DNA replicate itself?*
photocopy/Xerox (trademark) – to copy a piece of paper with writing or pictures on it, using a special machine
forge – to illegally copy something written or printed: *He forged my signature.* | *forged documents*
pirate – to illegally copy and sell a movie, book, CD, or DVD that was made by another company: *pirated DVDs*

2 [T] *also* **copy down** to write something down exactly as it was said or written: *She copied down the homework assignment.* **3** [T] to do something that someone else has done, or behave like someone else: *The system has been copied by other organizations, and has worked well.* **4** [I,T] to cheat by looking at someone else's work and writing what s/he has written as an answer: *Several students were punished for copying.* **5** [T] to copy writing, etc. from a computer document in order to put it in another place or document ➔ CUT, PASTE
copy sb ↔ **in** *phr. v.* to send someone a copy of an EMAIL message you are sending to someone else

cop·y·cat /ˈkɑpiˌkæt/ *n.* [C] (informal) **1** (disapproving) someone who copies other people's clothes, behavior, etc. – used especially by children **2 copycat crime/murder etc.** a crime, murder, etc. that is similar to a crime that someone else has done

cop·y·right /ˈkɑpiˌraɪt/ *n.* [C,U] the legal right to produce and sell a book, play, movie, or record

cor·al /ˈkɔrəl, ˈkɑrəl/ *n.* [U] a hard colored substance formed in warm ocean water from the bones of very small creatures

coral

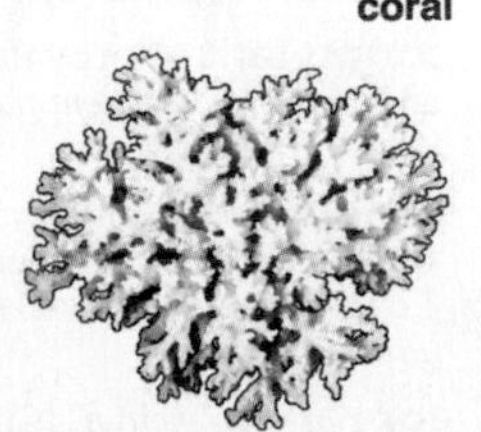

ˌcoral ˈisland *n.* [C] EARTH SCIENCES an island formed from coral covered in sand and other natural substances

ˌcoral ˈreef *n.* [C] EARTH SCIENCES a long hard structure formed of coral in warm ocean water that is not very deep

cord /kɔrd/ *n* [C,U] **1** a piece of wire covered with plastic, used especially for connecting electrical equipment to the supply of electricity: *an extension cord* | *a long phone cord* ➔ *see picture at* ACOUSTIC **2** a piece of thick string or thin rope **3 cords** [plural] CORDUROY pants [ORIGIN: 1200—1300 Old French *corde*, from Latin *chorda* "string," from Greek *chorde*]

cor·dial /ˈkɔrdʒəl/ *adj.* friendly and polite but formal: *a cordial greeting* [ORIGIN: 1300—1400 Medieval Latin *cordialis*, from Latin *cor* "heart"] **—cordially** *adv.* **—cordiality** /ˌkɔrdʒiˈæləṭi/ *n.* [U]

THESAURUS **friendly, warm, amiable, genial, affable, welcoming, hospitable** ➔ FRIENDLY

cord·less /ˈkɔrdlɪs/ *adj.* a piece of equipment that is cordless is not connected to its power supply by wires: *a cordless phone*

cor·don¹ /ˈkɔrdn/ *n.* [C] a line of police, soldiers, or vehicles that is put around an area to protect or enclose it

cordon² *v.*
cordon sth ↔ **off** *phr. v* to surround and protect an area with police officers, soldiers, or vehicles: *Police have cordoned off the building.*

cor·du·roy /ˈkɔrdəˌrɔɪ/ *n.* [U] thick strong cotton cloth with raised lines on one side: *a corduroy jacket*

core¹ /kɔr/ (Ac) *n.* [C] **1** the central or most important part of something: *The **core of** the proposal is a tax credit.* | *the company's core customers* | *The department has a small core of experienced staff.* **2** the hard central part of an apple or PEAR ➔ *see picture on page 414* **3** EARTH SCIENCES the central part of the Earth or any other PLANET ➔ *see picture at* GLOBE **4** PHYSICS the central part of a NUCLEAR REACTOR [ORIGIN: 1300—1400 Old French *coeur*, from Latin *cor* "heart"] ➔ HARDCORE

core² *v.* [T] to remove the hard center of a piece of fruit

cork¹ /kɔrk/ *n.* **1** [U] the light outer part of a particular type of tree, that is used for making things: *cork mats* **2** [C] a round piece of this material that is put into the top of a bottle to keep liquid inside

cork² *v.* [T] to close a bottle tightly by putting a cork in it

cork·screw /ˈkɔrkskru/ *n.* [C] a tool used for pulling corks out of bottles

corn /kɔrn/ *n.* [U] **1** a tall plant with yellow seeds that are cooked and eaten as a vegetable: *an **ear of corn*** (=the top part of a corn plant on which these yellow seeds grow) | *steak and **corn on the cob*** (=an ear of corn that is cooked and eaten) ➔ *see*

C

picture at VEGETABLE **2** a thick, hard, and painful area of skin on your foot [ORIGIN: Old English]

corn·bread /ˈkɔrnbrɛd/ *n.* [U] bread that is made from CORNMEAL

cor·ne·a /ˈkɔrniə/ *n.* [C] BIOLOGY the strong transparent covering on the outer surface of your eye [ORIGIN: 1300—1400 Medieval Latin, Latin, "horny," from *cornu* "horn;" because its structure is like horn] —**corneal** *adj.*

C

corned beef /ˌkɔrnd ˈbif◂ / *n.* [U] BEEF that has been preserved in salt water and SPICEs

cor·ner¹ /ˈkɔrnɚ/ *n.* [C] **1** the point at which two lines, surfaces, or edges meet: *a table* ***in the corner*** *of the room* | *Jess sat* ***on the corner*** *of the bed.* **2** the place where two roads, streets, or paths meet: *Meet me* ***on the corner*** *of 72nd and Central Park.* | *We went to a place* ***around the corner*** *for coffee.* | *Some kids were standing* ***at the corner.*** | *When you* ***turn the corner*** (=go around the corner), *you'll see a bookstore.* **3** a particular part of an area, especially one that is far away or quiet: *a pretty corner of the state* | *a sunny corner of the yard* **4** the sides of your mouth or eye **5 see sth out of the corner of your eye** to notice something without turning your head **6 be just around the corner** to be going to happen very soon: *Victory seemed to be just around the corner.* ➔ **cut corners** *at* CUT¹

corner² *v.* [T] **1** to move closer to a person or an animal so that he, she, or it cannot escape: *Gibbs cornered Cassetti after the meeting.*

> THESAURUS **catch, capture, trap** ➔ CATCH¹

2 corner the market to sell or produce all of a particular type of goods

cor·ner·stone /ˈkɔrnɚˌstoʊn/ *n.* [C] **1** a stone set at one of the bottom corners of a building, often as part of a special ceremony **2** something that is very important because everything else depends on it: *Free speech is* ***the cornerstone of*** *democracy.*

cor·net /kɔrˈnɛt/ *n.* [C] a small musical instrument like a TRUMPET

corn·flakes /ˈkɔrnfleɪks/ *n.* [plural] a type of breakfast food made from corn

corn·meal /ˈkɔrnmil/ *n.* [U] a rough type of flour made from crushed dried corn

corn·starch /ˈkɔrnstɑrtʃ/ *n.* [U] a fine white flour made from corn, used in cooking to make liquids thicker

ˈcorn ˌsyrup *n.* [U] a very sweet thick liquid made from corn, used in cooking

corn·y /ˈkɔrni/ *adj.* (informal) old, silly, and very familiar: *a corny song from the 1940s*

cor·ol·lar·y /ˈkɔrəˌlɛri, ˈkɑr-/ *n.* (plural **corollaries**) [C] **1** MATH a statement that is true as a direct result of a THEOREM (=a statement that can be proven by showing that it has been correctly developed from facts) **2** (formal) something that is the direct result of something else: *Increases in unemployment were the corollary of the government's economic policy.* [ORIGIN: 1300—1400 Latin *corollarium* "money paid for a circle of flowers, something additional," from *corolla* "circle of flowers"]

co·ro·na /kəˈroʊnə/ *n.* [C] PHYSICS the shining circle of light seen around the Sun when the Moon passes in front of it during an ECLIPSE

cor·o·na·ry¹ /ˈkɔrəˌnɛri/ *adj.* BIOLOGY relating to the heart: *coronary disease* [ORIGIN: 1600—1700 Latin *coronarius* "like a crown," from *corona* "crown," because the blood-tubes coming out of the top of the heart look like a crown]

coronary² *n.* (plural **coronaries**) [C] a HEART ATTACK

cor·o·na·tion /ˌkɔrəˈneɪʃən/ *n.* [C] a ceremony in which someone officially becomes a king or queen

cor·o·ner /ˈkɔrənɚ/ *n.* [C] an official whose job is to discover the cause of someone's death, if it is sudden or unexpected, by examining his/her body

cor·po·ral /ˈkɔrpərəl/ *n.* [C] a low rank in the Army or Marines, or an officer who has this rank

ˌcorporal ˈpunishment *n.* [U] punishment that involves hitting someone

> THESAURUS **punishment, sentence, penalty, fine, community service, capital punishment** ➔ PUNISHMENT

cor·po·rate /ˈkɔrpərɪt/ (Ac) *adj.* belonging to or relating to a corporation: *corporate headquarters* | *an increase in corporate profits* —**corporately** *adv.*

cor·po·ra·tion /ˌkɔrpəˈreɪʃən/ (Ac) *n.* [C] ECONOMICS a large company, or a group of companies acting together as a single organization: *the Chief Executive Officer of a* ***large/big/major corporation*** [ORIGIN: 1300—1400 Late Latin *corporatio*, from *corporare* "to combine together in one body," from *corpus* "body"]

> THESAURUS **company, firm, business, subsidiary** ➔ COMPANY

corps /kɔr/ *n.* [singular] **1** a trained group of people with special duties in the military: *the Naval Air Corps* **2** a group of people who do a particular job: *the press corps*

corpse /kɔrps/ *n.* [C] a dead body

cor·pu·lent /ˈkɔrpyələnt/ *adj.* (formal) very fat and large: *a corpulent man* —**corpulence** *n.* [U] ➔ FAT¹

cor·pus·cle /ˈkɔrˌpʌsəl/ *n.* [C] BIOLOGY a red or white blood cell in your body [ORIGIN: 1600—1700 Latin *corpusculum* "small body," from *corpus* "body"]

cor·ral¹ /kəˈræl/ *n.* [C] an enclosed area where cattle, horses, etc. are kept

corral² *v.* [T] to put animals into a corral

cor·rect¹ /kəˈrɛkt/ *adj.* **1** right or without any mistakes (ANT) **incorrect**: *the correct answers* | *"Your name is Ives?" "Yes, that's correct."*

THESAURUS **right, accurate, true** → RIGHT¹

2 right for a particular occasion or use: *the correct way to lift a heavy weight* [ORIGIN: 1300—1400 Latin, past participle of *corrigere*, from *com* "together" + *regere* "to lead straight"] —**correctly** *adv.* —**correctness** *n.* [U]

correct² *v.* [T] **1** to make something right or better: *Your eyesight can be corrected with glasses.* | *Paola corrected his pronunciation.* **2** if a teacher corrects a student's written work, s/he shows where the mistakes are and what the right answer is

cor·rec·tion /kəˈrɛkʃən/ *n.* [C] a change in something that makes it right or better: *Johnson* ***made*** *a few* ***corrections*** *to the article.*

cor·rec·tive /kəˈrɛktɪv/ *adj.* (formal) intended to make something right or better: *corrective lenses for the eyes*

cor·re·la·tion /ˌkɔrəˈleɪʃən, ˌkɑr-/ *n.* [C,U] **1** a relationship between two ideas, facts, etc., especially when one may be the cause of the other: *There's a strong* ***correlation between*** *poverty and poor health.* **2** MATH a relationship between two mathematical VARIABLES (=quantities that can represent any of several different values) —**correlate** /ˈkɔrəˌleɪt, ˈkɑr-/ *v.* [I,T]

corre'lation coef,ficient *n.* [C] MATH a number between +1 and -1, used to represent the relationship between quantities that increase or decrease in direct relation to one another

cor·re·spond /ˌkɔrəˈspɑnd, ˌkɑr-/ (Ac) *v.* [I] **1** if two things correspond, they are similar to each other or relate to each other: *The figures in columns A and B do not correspond.* | *The name on the envelope doesn't* ***correspond with*** *the one on the letter.* | *The test gives you a qualification that* ***corresponds to*** *a high school diploma.* **2** if two people correspond, they write letters to each other: *They've been corresponding for years.* [ORIGIN: 1500—1600 French *correspondre*, from Medieval Latin, from Latin *com-* "together" + *respondere* "to promise in return, answer"]

cor·re·spond·ence /ˌkɔrəˈspɑndəns, ˌkɑr-/ (Ac) *n.* [U] **1** letters that people send and receive: *Her secretary deals with her correspondence.* **2** the activity of writing letters: *His* ***correspondence with*** *Hemingway continued until his death.* **3** a relationship or connection between two things: *the correspondence between a letter and the sound it represents*

corre'spondence ,course *n.* [C] a course of lessons that you receive by mail and do at home

cor·re·spond·ent /ˌkɔrəˈspɑndənt, ˌkɑr-/ *n.* [C] **1** someone whose job is to report news from a distant area, or about a particular subject, for a newspaper or television: *the White House correspondent* → NEWSPAPER **2** someone who writes to another person regularly

cor·re·spond·ing /ˌkɔrəˈspɑndɪŋ◂, ˌkɑr-/ (Ac) *adj.* relating or similar to something: *She was given a promotion and a corresponding increase in salary.* | *As the price of the product fell, the corresponding demand rose.* —**correspondingly** *adv.*

,corresponding 'angles *n.* [plural] MATH a pair of angles formed when two parallel lines are crossed by another line. The corresponding angles are on the same side of the two parallel lines and on the same side of the single line crossing them. → *see picture at* ANGLE¹

C

cor·ri·dor /ˈkɔrədə˞, -ˌdɔr, ˈkɑr-/ *n.* [C] **1** a passage between two rows of rooms: *The bathroom is* ***down the corridor*** *to your right.* | *Please wait* ***in the corridor.*** **2** a narrow area of land between cities or countries, especially one used for traveling from one place to another: *the New York–Washington, D.C. corridor* [ORIGIN: 1500—1600 French, Old Italian *corridore*, from *correre* "to run"]

cor·rob·o·rate /kəˈrɑbəˌreɪt/ *v.* [T] (formal) to support an opinion or claim with new information or proof: *Several witnesses corroborated McDougal's story.* [ORIGIN: 1500—1600 Latin, past participle of *corroborare*, from *cor-* "together" + *robur* "strength"] —**corroboration** /kəˌrɑbəˈreɪʃən/ *n.* [U] —**corroborative** /kəˈrɑbərət̬ɪv/ *adj.*

cor·rode /kəˈroʊd/ *v.* [I,T] if metal corrodes, or if something corrodes it, it is slowly destroyed by water, chemicals, etc. [ORIGIN: 1300—1400 Latin *corrodere* "to eat away"]

cor·ro·sion /kəˈroʊʒən/ *n.* [U] the gradual process of being destroyed by the effects of water, chemicals, etc., or a substance such as RUST that is produced by this process

cor·ro·sive /kəˈroʊsɪv/ *adj.* **1** CHEMISTRY a corrosive substance such as an acid can destroy metal, plastic, etc. **2** gradually making something weaker, and possibly destroying it: *the corrosive effect of guilt on your relationships*

cor·ru·gat·ed /ˈkɔrəˌgeɪt̬ɪd, ˈkɑr-/ *adj.* formed in rows of folds that look like waves: *corrugated cardboard*

corrugated

corrugated cardboard

cor·rupt¹ /kəˈrʌpt/ *adj.* **1** dishonest and ready to do things that will give you an advantage: *a corrupt judge who took a bribe* **2** very bad morally: *a corrupt society* [ORIGIN: 1300—1400 Latin *corruptus*, past participle of *corrumpere*, from *rumpere* "to break"] —**corruptly** *adv.*

corrupt² *v.* [T] **1** to make someone dishonest or immoral: *Younger prisoners are being corrupted by the older, long-term offenders.* **2** to change or spoil something so that it is not as good: *a traditional culture corrupted by outside influences* **3** IT to change the information in a computer, so that the information is wrong and the computer does not work correctly: *The data had been corrupted.* —**corruptible** *adj.*

C

cor·rup·tion /kəˈrʌpʃən/ *n.* [U] **1** dishonest or immoral behavior: *corruption in city politics* **2** the act or process of making someone dishonest or immoral: *the corruption of today's youth by drugs*

cor·sage /kɔrˈsɑʒ/ *n.* [C] a small bunch of flowers that a woman wears on her dress for special occasions

cor·set /ˈkɔrsɪt/ *n.* [C] a type of underwear that fits very tightly, that women in past times wore in order to look thinner

cor·tege /kɔrˈtɛʒ/ *n.* [C] (formal) a line of people, cars, etc. that move slowly in a funeral

cor·tex /ˈkɔrtɛks/ (plural **cortices**) *n.* [C] BIOLOGY the outer layer of an organ in the body, especially the brain [ORIGIN: 1600—1700 Latin "bark (=outer covering of a tree)"]

co·sine /ˈkoʊsaɪn/ *n.* [C] MATH a number relating to an angle in a RIGHT TRIANGLE, that is calculated by dividing the length of the side next to the right angle by the length of the HYPOTENUSE (=side opposite the right angle) SYN **sine**

cos·met·ic /kɑzˈmɛṭɪk/ *adj.* **1** intended to make your skin or body more beautiful: *cosmetic surgery* **2** dealing only with the appearance of something: *cosmetic changes to the policy* —**cosmetically** *adv.*

cos·met·ics /kɑzˈmɛṭɪks/ *n.* [plural] cream, powder, etc. that you use to make your face and body more attractive ➔ MAKEUP

cos·mic /ˈkɑzmɪk/ *adj.* relating to space or the universe: *a cosmic explosion* —**cosmically** *adv.*

cos·mo·naut /ˈkɑzməˌnɔt/ *n.* [C] an ASTRONAUT from the former Soviet Union

cos·mo·pol·i·tan /ˌkɑzməˈpɑlətən, -lətˀn/ *adj.* (approving) **1** a cosmopolitan place has people from many different parts of the world: *a cosmopolitan city* **2** a cosmopolitan person, attitude, etc. shows a lot of experience of different people and places: *Her cosmopolitan view of the world was formed during her time in Paris, Tokyo, and New York.*

cos·mos /ˈkɑzmoʊs, -məs/ *n.* **the cosmos** the universe considered as a whole system [ORIGIN: 1200—1300 Greek "order, universe"]

cost¹ /kɔst/ *n.* **1** [C,U] the amount of money you must pay in order to buy, do, or produce something: *the* ***cost of*** *a college education* | *Will $100* ***cover the cost*** *of books* (=be enough to pay for them)*?* | *the* ***high cost*** *of car insurance* | *Legal services were provided at a* ***low cost.*** | *The software is available* ***at a cost of*** *$30.* | *Glasses were offered* ***at no extra cost.***

THESAURUS

expense – a very large amount of money that you spend on something: *the expense of buying a car*
price – the amount of money you must pay for something: *House prices keep going up.* | *the price of oil*
charge – the amount that you have to pay for a particular service or to use something: *There's no additional charge for the service.* | *telephone charges*
fee – the amount you have to pay to enter or join something, or that you pay to a lawyer, doctor, etc.: *There is no entrance fee to the museum.* | *The membership fee is $125 a year.* | *legal fees*
fare – the amount you have to pay to travel somewhere by bus, airplane, train, etc.: *the bus fare*
rent – the amount you have to pay to live in or use a place that you do not own: *My rent is $900 a month.*
rate – a charge or payment that is set according to a standard scale: *Most TV stations offer special rates to local advertisers.*

2 costs [plural] **a)** the money that you must regularly spend in order to run a business, your home, car, etc.: *the university's annual* ***operating costs*** | *high* ***labor costs*** | *We're trying to* ***cut/reduce/lower costs*** (=spend less money) *by driving a smaller car.* **b)** the money that you must pay to lawyers if you are involved in a legal case: *Burdell lost the case and was ordered to pay the defense's costs.* **3** [C,U] something that you must give or lose in order to get something else: *War is never worth its cost in human life.* | *He saved his family,* ***at the cost of*** *his own life.* | *He intends to hold on to power,* ***whatever the cost.*** **4 at all costs/at any cost** whatever happens, or whatever effort is needed: *We need to get that contract, at any cost.* **5 at cost** for the same price that you paid: *We had to sell the van at cost.*

cost² *v.* (past tense and past participle **cost**) **1** [linking verb] to have a particular price: *This dress cost $75.* | *How much did your watch cost?* | *The wedding ended up costing them $50,000.* | *It'll* ***cost*** *thousands of dollars* ***to*** *fix this place up.* | *I love these boots, but they* ***cost an arm and a leg/cost a fortune*** (=are extremely expensive). **2** [T] to make someone lose something important: *Your mistake cost us the deal.* **3** [T] (past tense and past participle **costed**) to calculate how much money is needed to pay for something: *The options are being costed and analyzed.*

co-star /ˈkoʊ stɑr/ *n.* [C] one of two or more famous actors who work together in a movie or play —**co-star** *v.* [I,T]: *He* ***co-starred with*** *De Niro* ***in*** *the movie "Heat."*

ˈcost-ˌcutting *n.* [U] the things that a company or

organization does in order to reduce its costs: *Cost-cutting efforts included the elimination of 4,000 jobs.*

ˈcost-efˌfective *adj.* producing the best profits or advantages at the lowest cost: *a cost-effective way to reduce pollution*

cost·ly /ˈkɔstli/ *adj.* **1** costing a lot of money: *costly repairs*

THESAURUS **expensive, high, pricey, overpriced, fancy, posh** → EXPENSIVE

2 causing a lot of problems: *The delay **proved costly**.*

ˌcost of ˈliving *n.* [singular] the amount of money you need to spend in order to buy the food, clothes, etc. that you need to live: *The cost of living is much higher in California than in Iowa.*

cos·tume /ˈkɑstum/ *n.* [C,U] **1** clothes worn to make you look like a particular type of person, animal, etc.: *a prize for the best **Halloween costume** | The actors put on their costumes and makeup.* **2** clothes that are typical of a particular country or time in the past: *We took a tour given by volunteers **in period costume*** (=the clothes of a period of history). [ORIGIN: 1700—1800 French, Italian, "custom, dress," from Latin *consuetudo*]

ˈcostume ˌjewelry *n.* [U] cheap jewelry that looks expensive

cot /kɑt/ *n.* [C] a light narrow bed that folds up [ORIGIN: 1600—1700 Hindi *khat* "hammock, bed"] → *see picture at* BED[1]

cot·tage /ˈkɑt̬ɪdʒ/ *n.* [C] a small house in the country, especially an old one → HOUSE[1] [ORIGIN: 1300—1400 Anglo-French *cotage*, from English *cot* "cottage," from Old English]

ˌcottage ˈcheese *n.* [U] a soft wet white cheese

ˌcottage ˈindustry *n.* [C] ECONOMICS a business that consists of people who produce things in their homes

cot·ton /ˈkɑtˀn/ *n.* [U] **1** cloth or thread made from the cotton plant: *a cotton shirt* **2** a plant with white hairs used for making cotton cloth and thread **3** a soft mass of cotton, used especially for cleaning your skin [ORIGIN: 1300—1400 Old French *coton*, from Arabic *qutn*]

ˈcotton ball *n.* [C] a small soft ball made from cotton, used for cleaning skin

ˈCotton Belt *n.* **the Cotton Belt** HISTORY an area of the Southeast U.S., especially South Carolina, Georgia, Alabama, and Mississippi, where cotton was the main crop in the past

ˈcotton ˌcandy *n.* [U] a type of sticky pink candy that looks like cotton

ˈcotton gin *n.* [C] a machine that separates the seeds of a cotton plant from the cotton

cot·ton·wood /ˈkɑtˀnˌwʊd/ *n.* [C] a North American tree with seeds that look like cotton

cot·y·le·don /ˌkɑt̬əˈlidn, ˌkɑt̬lˈidn/ *n.* [C] BIOLOGY the first leaf that grows from a seed → DICOTYLEDON, MONOCOTYLEDON

couch[1] /kaʊtʃ/ *n.* [C] a long comfortable piece of furniture on which you can sit or lie (SYN) **sofa**: *Tom offered to sleep on the couch.*

couch[2] *v.* **be couched in sth** (formal) to be expressed in a particular way: *His refusal was couched in polite terms.*

ˈcouch poˌtato *n.* [C] (informal) someone who spends a lot of time sitting and watching television

cou·gar /ˈkugɚ/ *n.* [C] a large brown wild cat from the mountains of western North and South America [ORIGIN: 1700—1800 French *couguar*, from Modern Latin *cuguacuarana*, from Tupi *suasuarana*, from *suasu* "deer" + *rana* "false"]

cougar

cough[1] /kɔf/ *v.* [I] if you cough, air suddenly comes out of your throat with a short loud sound, especially because you are sick: *He's been coughing and sneezing all day.* [ORIGIN: 1300—1400 From an unrecorded Old English *cohhian*]

cough up *phr. v.* **1 cough** sth ↔ **up** (informal) to give someone money, information, etc. when you do not really want to: *I'm trying to get my dad to cough up some money for a motorcycle.* **2 cough up** sth if you cough up a substance such as blood, it comes from your lungs or throat into your mouth when you cough: *We rushed her to the hospital when she started coughing up blood.*

cough[2] *n.* [C] **1** the action of coughing, or the sound made when you cough: *She gave a nervous cough before speaking.* **2** an illness that makes you cough a lot: *He **had a** terrible **cough**.*

ˈcough drop *n.* [C] a type of medicine like a piece of candy, that you suck to help you stop coughing

ˈcough ˌsyrup *n.* [U] a thick liquid medicine that you take to help you stop coughing

could /kəd; *strong* kʊd/ *modal verb* **1** used as the past tense of "can" to say what someone was able to do or was allowed to do in the past: *I looked everywhere, but I couldn't* (=could not) *find it. | I could hear children playing. | When I was young, you could buy a concert ticket for $5. | He said we could smoke if we wanted.* **2** used in order to say that something is possible or might happen: *Most accidents in the home could easily be prevented. | It could be weeks before they're finished.* **3 could have** used in order to say that something was possible in the past, but did not actually happen: *She could have been killed.* **4** (spoken) used in order to make a polite request: *Could I ask you a couple of questions? | Could you deposit this check at the bank for me?* **5** (spoken) said when you are annoyed about someone's behavior: *You could have told me you were going to be late!* | *How could you be so stupid!* **6** (spoken) used in order to emphasize how angry, happy, etc. you are by saying how you want to express your feelings: *I could have murdered Kerry for telling Jason that!* | *I'm so happy I could scream.* **7** (spoken) used in order to suggest doing something: *We could always stop and ask directions.* **8 I couldn't care less** (spoken) used in order to say that you are not interested at all in something: *I couldn't care less what the neighbors say.*

C

could·n't /ˈkʊdnt/ *modal verb* the short form of "could not": *We couldn't stop laughing.*

cou·lomb /ˈkulɑm/ *n.* [C] PHYSICS a unit for measuring electric current, equal to the amount produced by one AMP in one second

coun·cil /ˈkaʊnsəl/ *n.* [C] **1** a group of people who are elected as part of a town or city government: *Millard is running for city council.* | *council members* **2** a group of people who make decisions for a church, organization, etc., or who give advice: *the UN Security Council* [ORIGIN: 1100—1200 Old French *concile*, from Latin *concilium*, from *com* "together" + *calare* "to call"]

coun·cil·man /ˈkaʊnsəlmən/ *n.* (plural **councilmen** /-mən/) [C] a male councilor

ˈcouncil-ˌmanager ˌgovernment *n.* [C,U] POLITICS a system of local government in many U.S. towns or cities, in which people elect a council and a MAYOR, who then choose a manager who is paid to run the town or city

ˌcouncil of ˈgovernments *n.* (plural **councils of governments**) [C] POLITICS a group of government officials in the U.S. from the towns or cities in one area, who get together to make decisions that affect the whole area SYN **regional council**

coun·cil·or /ˈkaʊnsələ/ *n.* [C] a member of a council

coun·cil·wom·an /ˈkaʊnsəlˌwʊmən/ *n.* (plural **councilwomen** /-ˌwɪmɪn/) [C] a female councilor

coun·sel¹ /ˈkaʊnsəl/ *v.* [T] (formal) to advise or support someone who has problems: *Tyrone got a job counseling patients who have cancer.*

THESAURUS **advise, recommend, urge, suggest** → ADVISE

counsel² *n.* **1** [C] LAW a lawyer who speaks for someone in a court of law: *The counsel for the defense gave her opening statement.* **2** [U] (formal) advice

coun·sel·ing /ˈkaʊnsəlɪŋ/ *n.* [U] advice given by a counselor to people about their personal problems or difficult decisions: *family/career counseling*

coun·sel·or /ˈkaʊnsələ/ *n.* [C] **1** someone whose job is to help and support people with problems: *a* ***marriage counselor*** **2** someone who takes care of a group of children at a camp

count¹ /kaʊnt/ *v.* **1** [T] *also* **count up** to calculate the total number of things or people in a group: *The nurses counted the bottles of medicine as they put them away.* **2** [I] to say numbers in the correct order: *My daughter is learning to count in French.* | *He's only three, but he can* ***count to*** *ten.* **3** [I] to be allowed or accepted: *"I won!" "You cheated, so it doesn't count."* | *Your sculpture class* ***counts as*** *a Humanities credit.* **4** [T] to include someone or something in a total: *There are five in our family, counting me.* **5** [T] to think of something or someone in a particular way: *I* ***count*** *her* ***as*** *one of my best friends.* | *You should* ***count yourself lucky*** *that you weren't hurt.* **6** [I] to be important or valuable: *I felt my opinion didn't* ***count for*** *much.* **7 I/you can count sth on one hand** (spoken) used in order to emphasize how small the number of something is: *I can count on one hand the number of times he's come to visit me.* [ORIGIN: 1300—1400 Old French *conter*, from Latin *computare*]

count sth ↔ **down** *phr. v.* to count the number of days, minutes, etc. until a particular moment or event: *She's counting down the days until Nathan arrives.*

count sb **in** *phr. v.* (informal) to include someone or something in an activity: *If you're going dancing, count me in.*

count on sb/sth *phr. v.* **1** to depend on someone or something, especially in a difficult situation: *You can always count on him to help.* **2** to expect something to happen, or someone to do something: *We didn't count on this many people coming.*

count out *phr. v.* **1 count** sb **out** (informal) to not include someone or something in an activity: *If you're looking for a fight, count me out.* **2 count out** sth to put things down one by one as you count them: *He counted out ten $50 bills.*

count² *n.* [C] **1** the process of counting, or the total that you get when you count things: *The final count showed that Gary had won by 110 votes to 86.* | ***At last count*** (=the last and most recent time you counted), *46 students were interested in the trip.* **2** a measurement of how much of a substance is present in a place, area, etc.: *The* ***pollen count*** *is high today.* **3 keep count** to keep a record of the changing total of something over a period of time: *Are you* ***keeping count of*** *the people you've invited?* **4 lose count** to forget how many there are of something: *I've* ***lost count of*** *how many times she's been married.* **5** LAW one of the crimes that the police say someone has done: *He's guilty on two* ***counts of*** *robbery.*

count·a·ble /ˈkaʊntəbəl/ *adj.* ENG. LANG. ARTS a countable noun has both a singular and a plural form ANT **uncountable**

count·down /ˈkaʊnt˺daʊn/ *n.* [C] **1** the act of counting backward to zero before something happens, especially before a spacecraft is sent into the sky **2** the period before an important event happens, when it gets closer and closer: *the* ***countdown*** *to Christmas*

coun·te·nance¹ /ˈkaʊntənəns/ *n.* [C] (literary) your face or your expression

countenance² *v.* [T] (formal) to accept, support, or approve of something: *We cannot countenance violent behavior.*

coun·ter¹ /ˈkaʊntɚ/ *n.* [C] **1** a flat surface in the kitchen where you prepare food **2** the place where you pay or are served in a shop, bank, restaurant, etc.: *He started chatting with the woman* ***behind the counter***. **3 over the counter** over the counter medicines can be bought without a PRESCRIPTION from your doctor **4 under the counter** secretly and not legally: *She gets paid under the counter.*

counter² *v.* [I,T] **1** to do something in order to prevent something bad from happening or to reduce its bad effects: *Hospitals must offer better salaries to counter the shortage of nurses.* **2** to say something to show that what someone has just said is not true: *"I could ask you the same question," she countered.*

counter³ *adv.* (formal) in a way that is opposite to something: *Bradley has always done things in a way that* ***runs counter to*** *expectations.* —**counter** *adj.*

coun·ter·act /ˌkaʊntɚˈækt/ *v.* [T] to reduce or prevent the bad effect of something, by doing something that has the opposite effect: *a drug to counteract the poison*

coun·ter·ar·gu·ment /ˌkaʊntɚˌɑrgyəmənt/ *n* [C] ENG. LANG. ARTS a fact, opinion, set of reasons, etc. that shows that the ideas or reasons someone is using in an argument may be wrong or not good enough

coun·ter·at·tack /ˈkaʊntɚəˌtæk/ *n.* [C] an attack that you make against someone who has attacked you, in a sport, war, or argument —**counterattack** *v.* [I]

THESAURUS **attack, invasion, raid, ambush** → ATTACK¹

coun·ter·bal·ance /ˈkaʊntɚˌbæləns/ *v.* [T] to have an equal and opposite effect to something else: *Good sales in Europe have counterbalanced the weak sales in the U.S.* —**counterbalance** *n.* [C]

coun·ter·clock·wise /ˌkaʊntɚˈklɑk-waɪz/ *adj., adv.* in the opposite direction to the way the HANDS (=parts that point to the time) of a clock move (ANT) **clockwise**: *Turn the lid counterclockwise.*

coun·ter·cul·ture /ˈkaʊntɚˌkʌltʃɚ/ *n.* [C] SOCIAL SCIENCE the beliefs, behavior, and way of living of a group of people, especially young people, that are very different from the accepted beliefs, behavior, etc. of society

coun·ter·ex·am·ple /ˈkaʊntɚɪgˌzæmpəl/ *n.* [C] ENG. LANG. ARTS a fact proving that the opposite of an existing fact is true, which is used to question whether someone's argument is reasonable or correct.

coun·ter·feit /ˈkaʊntɚfɪt/ *adj.* made to look exactly like something else in order to deceive people: *counterfeit money* [ORIGIN: 1300—1400 Old French, past participle of *contrefaire* "to copy"] —**counterfeit** *v.* [T] —**counterfeiter** *n.* [C]

THESAURUS **fake, phony, forged** → FAKE²

coun·ter·part /ˈkaʊntɚˌpɑrt/ *n.* [C] a person or thing that has the same job or purpose as someone or something else in a different place: *a meeting between the U.S. president and his French counterpart*

coun·ter·pro·duc·tive /ˌkaʊntɚprəˈdʌktɪv/ *adj.* achieving the opposite result to the one you want: *Punishing children too harshly can be counterproductive.*

coun·ter·sign /ˈkaʊntɚˌsaɪn/ *v.* [T] to sign a paper that someone else has already signed: *My boss will countersign the check.*

count·less /ˈkaʊntˀlɪs/ *adj.* [only before noun] very many: *She spent countless hours making that clock.*

THESAURUS **many, a large number, a lot/lots, plenty, numerous, innumerable, a multitude of sb/sth, a plethora of sth, myriad** → MANY

coun·try¹ /ˈkʌntri/ *n.* (plural **countries**) **1** [C] an area of land that is controlled by its own government, president, king, etc.: *Bahrain became an independent country in 1971.* | *I've always wanted to live in a* ***foreign country***. | ***developing countries*** (=countries that are poor but are trying to increase trade and industry)

THESAURUS

nation – a country and its people, used especially when considering its political and economic structures: *the major industrialized nations*
state – a country and its people, used especially when considering its political and economic structures: *state-owned industries*
power – a country that is very strong and important: *Germany is a major industrial power in Europe.*
land (literary) – a country or place: *Lessing's memoirs describe her many journeys to foreign lands.*
realm (literary) – a country ruled over by a king or queen: *the richest man in the realm*

2 the country a) land that is away from towns and cities: *We went for a drive in the country.* **b)** all the people who live in a country: *The President has the support of over 50 per cent of the country.* **3** [U] a type of land: *farming country* **4** [U] COUNTRY MUSIC [ORIGIN: 1200—1300 Old French *contrée*, from Medieval Latin *contrata* "(land) which lies opposite," from Latin *contra*]

country² *adj.* in the area outside cities, or relating to this area: *clean country air | country roads*

ˈcountry ˌclub *n.* [C] a sports and social club, especially one for rich people

coun·try·man /ˈkʌntrimən/ *n.* (plural **country-men** /-mən/) [C] (old-fashioned) someone from your own country

ˈcountry ˌmusic *also* **ˌcountry and ˈwestern** *n.* [U] popular music in the style of music from the southern and western U.S.

C

coun·try·side /ˈkʌntriˌsaɪd/ *n.* [U] land that is outside cities and towns → COUNTRY: *the English countryside*

coun·ty /ˈkaʊnti/ *n.* (plural **counties**) [C] an area of land within a state or country that has its own local government: *Orange County in California* [ORIGIN: 1200—1300 Old French *conté* "area ruled by a count," from Medieval Latin *comitatus*, from Latin *comes*]

ˌcounty ˈfair *n.* [C] an event that happens each year in a particular county, with games and competitions for the best farm animals, for the best cooking, etc.

coup /ku/ *n.* [C] **1** *also* **coup d'état** /ˌku deɪˈtɑ/ an act in which citizens or the army suddenly take control of the government by force: *a military coup*

> THESAURUS **revolution, rebellion, revolt, uprising, insurrection, insurgency** → REVOLUTION

2 [usually singular] an impressive achievement: *Getting that job was quite a coup.*

cou·ple¹ /ˈkʌpəl/ (Ac) *n.* [C] **1 a couple** (informal) **a)** two things or people of the same kind: *He's got **a couple of** kids.* **b)** a few: *I need to make **a couple (of)** phone calls.* **2** two people who are married or have a romantic relationship: *the young couple next door | a **married couple** with children* [ORIGIN: 1200—1300 Old French *cople*, from Latin *copula* "something that joins"]

couple² *v.* [T] to join two things together: *The two sections of the plane's wing are coupled together using rivets.*

couple sth **with** sth *phr. v.* if one thing is coupled with another, the two things happen or exist together and produce a particular result: *Technology, coupled with better health care, means people live longer.*

cou·plet /ˈkʌplɪt/ *n.* [C] ENG. LANG. ARTS two lines of poetry that follow each other and are the same length

cou·pon /ˈkupɑn, ˈkyu-/ *n.* [C] **1** a small piece of paper that allows you to pay less money for something or get it free: *a coupon for fifty cents off a jar of coffee* **2** a printed form, used when you order something, enter a competition, etc. [ORIGIN: 1800—1900 French, Old French, "piece," from *couper* "to cut"]

cour·age /ˈkɚɪdʒ, ˈkʌr-/ *n.* [U] the quality of being brave when you are in danger, a difficult situation, etc.: *He didn't **have the courage to** face the media. | It must have **taken** a lot of **courage** for him to drive again after the accident.* [ORIGIN: 1200—1300 Old French *corage*, from *cuer* "heart," from Latin *cor*] —**courageous** /kəˈreɪdʒəs/ *adj.*: *a courageous decision* —**courageously** *adv.*

> THESAURUS
> **bravery** – brave behavior in a dangerous or frightening situation: *Troops on both sides fought with bravery.*
> **guts** (informal) – the courage and determination that you need to do something difficult, dangerous, or unpleasant: *He didn't even have the guts to tell me himself.*
> **nerve** (informal) – the ability to stay calm in a dangerous, difficult, or frightening situation: *It takes a lot of nerve to stand up and give a speech.*
> **valor** (formal) – great courage, especially in war: *He received the Congressional Medal of Honor for valor in battle.*
> **mettle** (literary) – courage and determination: *Walking the length of the Pacific Coast Trail will certainly test your mettle.*

cou·ri·er /ˈkʊriɚ, ˈkɚ-/ *n.* [C] someone whose job is to deliver documents and packages

course /kɔrs/ *n.*

1 of course a) used when what you or someone else has just said is not surprising: *The insurance has to be renewed every year, of course.* **b)** (spoken) used in order to say yes very strongly, or to give permission politely: *"Can I borrow your notes?" "Of course you can."* **c)** (spoken) said in order to emphasize that what you are saying is true or correct: *"You'll tell her?" "Of course!"*

2 of course not (spoken) used to say no strongly: *"Do you mind if I'm a little late?" "Of course not."*

3 SCHOOL [C] a class in a particular subject: *a computer course | a three-month **course in** English literature*

> THESAURUS **class, lesson, period, lecture, seminar** → CLASS¹

4 SPORTS [C] an area of land or water where races are held, or an area of land designed for playing golf: *a race course | a 9-hole golf course*

5 MEAL [C] one of the parts of a meal: *the **main course** | a four-course dinner*

6 ACTION [C] something you can do to deal with a situation: *The best **course of action** is to speak to her alone.*

7 DIRECTION [C,U] the planned direction taken by a boat or airplane to reach a place: *During the flight, we had to **change course**. | The ship was blown **off course*** (=in the wrong direction).

8 in/during/over the course of sth (formal) during a period of time or a process: *During the course of our conversation, I found out that he had worked in France.*

9 be on course (for sth/to do sth) to be likely to achieve something because you have already had

some success: *Hodson is on course to break the world record.*
10 WAY STH DEVELOPS [singular] the way that something changes or develops: *a major event that changed* ***the course of history*** | *The popularity of World Music has* ***run its course*** (=it is not as popular as it was before).
11 PLAN [singular, U] a general plan to achieve something, or the general way something is happening: *The President described how he would get the economy back* ***on course.***

court¹ /kɔrt/ *n.* **1** [C,U] LAW the people who make a legal judgment, for example about whether someone is guilty of a crime, or the place where these judgments are made: *A crowd of reporters had gathered outside the court.* | *Please tell* ***the court*** *where you were on the night of the 15th.* | *a* ***court of law*** | *He had to appear* ***in court*** *as a witness.* | *We decided to* ***take*** *them* ***to court*** (=make them be judged in a court) *to get our money back.* | *The case should* ***go to court*** (=start being judged in a court) *in August.* | *The insurance company* ***settled out of court*** (=they made an agreement without going to court). → LOWER COURT, SUPERIOR COURT

TOPIC

In court, the person who is said to have committed a crime is called the **defendant**. The defendant's lawyers, who are called **the defense**, try to prove that the defendant is **not guilty**. The **prosecution** tries to prove that the defendant is **guilty**. The **judge** and a **jury** listen to **testimony** and examine **evidence** in order to decide if the defendant is guilty or not guilty. Their decision is called the **verdict**.

2 [C] an area made for playing games such as tennis: *a volleyball court* **3 a)** [C,U] the place where a king or queen lives and works **b)** [singular] the king or queen, their family, and all the people who work for them or advise them: *Court officials denied the rumors.* [ORIGIN: 1200—1300 Old French, Latin *cohors* "enclosed place, people in an enclosure, unit of soldiers in the ancient Roman army"]

court² *v.* **1** [T] to try to please someone so that s/he will support you: *Politicians are courting voters before the election.* **2 court disaster/danger etc.** to do something that is likely to have very bad results: *To cut taxes now would be courting disaster.* **3** [I,T] (old-fashioned) to have a romantic relationship with someone, especially someone you are likely to marry

cour·te·ous /ˈkɚt̬iəs/ *adj.* (formal) polite and respectful: *a courteous reply* —**courteously** *adv.*

THESAURUS polite, well-behaved, civil → POLITE

cour·te·sy /ˈkɚt̬əsi/ *n.* (plural **courtesies**) **1** [U] polite behavior: *She didn't* ***have the courtesy*** *to apologize.* **2** [C] something you do or say to be polite: ***As a courtesy to*** *other diners, please switch off your cell phone.* **3 courtesy of sb** used in order to say in a grateful way who provided or did something for you: *We were put up in a fancy hotel, courtesy of the airline.*

court·house /ˈkɔrthaʊs/ *n.* [C] a building containing courts of law and government offices

ˌcourt-ˈmartial *n.* [C] a military court, or an occasion when a soldier is judged by a military court —**court-martial** *v.* [T]

court·room /ˈkɔrtˀrum/ *n.* [C] the room where a case is judged by a court of law

court·ship /ˈkɔrtˀʃɪp/ *n.* [C,U] (old-fashioned) the time when a man and a woman have a romantic relationship before getting married

court·yard /ˈkɔrtˀyɑrd/ *n.* [C] an open space surrounded by walls or buildings

cous·in /ˈkʌzən/ *n.* [C] a child of your aunt or uncle: *Bill and I are cousins.* → RELATIVE¹ [ORIGIN: 1200—1300 Old French *cosin*, from Latin *consobrinus*, from *com* + *sobrinus* "cousin on the mother's side"]

co·va·lent /koʊˈveɪlənt/ *adj.* [only before noun] CHEMISTRY relating to the force that joins and holds two or more different chemical substances together: *Adjacent atoms can share electrons through* ***covalent bonding.*** | *covalent molecules*

cove /koʊv/ *n.* [C] EARTH SCIENCES a small area on the coast, that is partly surrounded by land and is protected from the wind

cov·e·nant /ˈkʌvənənt/ *n.* [C] **1** a formal agreement between two or more people or groups **2** in the Bible, a promise made between God and the Israelites in which God promised to help them if they did not WORSHIP (=pray to) other gods [ORIGIN: 1200—1300 Old French *covenir* "to agree," from Latin *convenire* "to come together"]

cov·er¹ /ˈkʌvɚ/ *v.* [T]
1 PUT STH OVER STH *also* **cover up** to put something over the top of something else in order to hide, protect, or close it: *Cover the pan and simmer the beans for two hours.* | *We* ***covered*** *the sofa* ***with*** *a large blanket.* | *Dan covered his face with his hands.*
2 BE OVER STH to be on top of something or spread over something: *His bedroom walls are* ***covered with*** *posters.* | ***snow-covered*** *mountains*
3 INCLUDE to include or deal with something: *The class covers 20th-century American poetry.*
4 NEWS to report the details of an event for a newspaper or a television or radio program: *As a young reporter, he covered the war in Vietnam.*
5 PAY FOR STH to be enough money to pay for something: *The award should be enough to cover her college fees.* | *His family will* ***cover*** *the* ***cost*** *of the funeral.*
6 INSURANCE if your insurance covers you or your possessions, it promises to pay you money if you have an accident, something is stolen, etc.: *a policy that covers medical expenses*
7 DISTANCE to travel a particular distance: *We should cover another 50 miles before lunch.* | *A leopard can* ***cover*** *a lot of* ***ground*** *very quickly.*

C

8 cover your tracks to try to hide something you have done so that other people do not find out

9 GUN to aim a gun somewhere to protect someone from being attacked or to prevent someone from escaping: *We'll cover you while you run for it.* | *The police covered the back entrance.*

10 cover (all) the bases (informal) to make sure that you can deal with any situation or problem

cover for sb *phr. v.*

C

1 to do someone's work because s/he is sick or is somewhere else: *I'll be covering for Sandra next week.*

2 to prevent someone from getting into trouble by lying about where s/he is or what s/he is doing: *Can you cover for me? Just say I had an appointment.*

cover sth ↔ **up** *phr. v.*

to prevent people from discovering a mistake or an unfavorable fact: *A lot of people tried to cover up the Watergate affair.*

cover up for sb *phr. v.*

to protect someone by hiding unfavorable facts about him/her: *The mayor's friends tried to cover up for him.*

cover² *n.* **1** [C] something that protects something else by covering it: *a plastic cover*

THESAURUS

lid – a cover for a container
top/cap – the lid or cover for a container or a pen
wrapper – paper or plastic that is around something you buy

2 [C] the outer front or back part of a book, magazine, etc.: *The Pope was **on the cover** of Time magazine.* | *I **read** the book **from cover to cover*** (=all of it). **3** [U] protection from bad weather or attack: *The soldiers **ran for cover** when the shooting started.* | *We **took cover** under a tree.* **4 covers** [plural] sheets, BLANKETS, etc. that cover you in bed **5 a cover (for sth)** something a criminal uses to hide his/her activities or keep them secret: *The company is just a cover for the Mafia.* **6 under cover** pretending to be someone else in order to do something secretly: *Policemen **working under cover** arrested several drug dealers.*

cov·er·age /ˈkʌvrɪdʒ, -vərɪdʒ/ *n.* [U] **1** the amount of attention that is given to a particular subject or event on television, on the radio, or in newspapers, or the way in which the subject is reported: *excellent news coverage of the elections* | *Most of the **media/press coverage** has been negative.* **2** the protection your insurance gives you, for example paying you money if you are injured or something is stolen: *Millions of people have no formal health care coverage.*

cov·er·alls /ˈkʌvəˌɔlz/ *n.* [plural] a piece of clothing that you wear over all your clothes to protect them

ˈcover charge *n.* [C] money that you have to pay in a restaurant in addition to the cost of food and drinks, especially when there is a band or dancing

cov·er·ing /ˈkʌvrɪŋ, -vərɪŋ/ *n.* **1** [singular] something that covers something: *a light **covering** of snow* **2** [C] something that covers part of a wall or floor: *silk **wall coverings***

ˈcover ˌletter *n.* [C] a letter that you send with a document or package, which gives more information about it: *Never send a résumé without a cover letter.*

co·vert /ˈkoʊvət, ˈkʌ-, koʊˈvət/ *adj.* secret or hidden: *a covert operation* —**covertly** *adv.*

THESAURUS **secret, confidential, classified, sensitive, undercover, clandestine**
➔ SECRET¹

ˈcover-up *n.* [C] an attempt to prevent the public from discovering the truth about something: *CIA officials denied there had been a cover-up.*

cov·et /ˈkʌvɪt/ *v.* [T] (literary) to want something that someone else has: *The Michelin Awards are coveted by restaurants all over the world.* —**coveted** *adj.*

cow¹ /kaʊ/ *n.* [C] **1** a large female animal that is kept on farms and used to produce milk or meat ➔ BULL ➔ *see picture at* FARM¹ **2** the female of some large animals, such as the ELEPHANT or the WHALE [ORIGIN: Old English *cu*]

cow² *v.* [T] to frighten someone in order to make him/her do something: *The children were **cowed into** obedience.*

cow·ard /ˈkaʊəd/ *n.* [C] someone who is not brave at all —**cowardly** *adj.*: *a cowardly act*

cow·ard·ice /ˈkaʊədɪs/ *n.* [U] a lack of courage (ANT) **bravery**

cow·boy /ˈkaʊbɔɪ/ *n.* [C] a man whose job is to take care of cattle

cow·er /ˈkaʊə/ *v.* [I] to bend low and move back because you are afraid: *The hostages were cowering in a corner.*

cow·girl /ˈkaʊgəl/ *n.* [C] a woman whose job is to take care of cattle

co-work·er /ˈkoʊˌwəkə/ *n.* [C] someone who works with you

coy /kɔɪ/ *adj.* **1** pretending to be shy in order to attract people's interest: *a coy smile* **2** not wanting to tell people about something: *Bourne was coy about his plans.* [ORIGIN: 1300—1400 Old French *coi* "calm," from Latin *quietus* "quiet"] —**coyly** *adv.*

coy·o·te /kaɪˈoʊṭi, ˈkaɪ-oʊt/ *n.* [C] a small wild dog that lives in western North America and Mexico [ORIGIN: 1700—1800 Mexican Spanish, Nahuatl *coyotl*]

co·zy /ˈkoʊzi/ *adj.* small, comfortable, and warm: *a cozy cabin in the woods* —**cozily** *adv.* —**coziness** *n.* [U]

CPA *n.* [C] **Certified Public Accountant** an ACCOUNTANT who has passed all of his/her examinations

CPR *n.* [U] **cardiopulmonary resuscitation** a set of actions that you do to help someone who has stopped breathing or whose heart has stopped beating

CPU *n.* [C] IT **Central Processing Unit** the part of a computer that controls what it does

crab /kræb/ *n.* [C,U] a sea animal with a round flat shell and two large CLAWS on its front legs, or the meat from this animal

crab·by /ˈkræbi/ *adj.* easily annoyed or upset: *She's been crabby all day.*

crack[1] /kræk/ *v.*

1 BREAK [I,T] if you crack something, or if something cracks, it breaks so that it gets a line on its surface, and may then break into pieces: *I just cracked my favorite coffee mug.* | *The ice was starting to crack.* | *He cracked three eggs into a bowl.*

THESAURUS **break, smash, shatter, tear, snap, burst, pop** → BREAK[1]

2 NOISE OF BREAKING [I,T] to make a loud sudden noise like the sound of something breaking, or to make something do this: *A stick cracked under his foot.* | *He **cracked** his **knuckles**.*

3 HIT STH [T] to accidentally hit something very hard: *Carly tripped and **cracked** her head **on** the sidewalk.*

4 LOSE CONTROL [I] to lose control of your emotions and become unable to deal with a situation because there is too much pressure on you: *a spy who never **cracked under** questioning*

5 VOICE [I] if your voice cracks, it changes from one level to another suddenly, especially because of strong emotions

6 SOLVE [T] to solve a difficult problem or a CODE: *Detectives believe they've finally **cracked** the **case**.* | *It took them nearly two months to **crack** the **code**.*

7 crack a joke (informal) to tell a joke: *John keeps **cracking jokes about** my hair.*

8 not be all sth is cracked up to be (informal) not as good as people say it is: *The movie was OK, but it's not all it's cracked up to be.*

crack down *phr. v.*
to become more strict in dealing with a problem and punishing the people involved → CRACKDOWN: *Police are **cracking down on** drunk drivers.*

crack up *phr. v.* (informal)
1 crack (sb) **up** to laugh a lot at something, or to make someone laugh a lot: *I'll try to tell the story without cracking up.* | *Sue just cracks me up!*
2 to become mentally ill because you have too many problems or too much work

crack[2] *n.* [C] **1** a very narrow space between two things or two parts of something: *He could see them through a **crack in** the door.* | *Can you **open** the window **a crack**?*

THESAURUS **hole, space, gap, leak, opening, cavity** → HOLE[1]

2 a thin line on the surface of something when it is broken but has not actually come apart: *cracks on the wall* **3** a weakness or fault in an idea, system, or organization: *The **cracks in** their relationship were starting to show.* **4** (informal) an attempt to do something: *Okay, Dave, let's **take a crack** at fixing this bike.* **5** a sudden loud noise that sounds like a stick breaking: *There was a loud crack of thunder as the storm began.* **6** (informal) a cruel joke or remark: *Stop **making cracks about** my sister!* **7 at the crack of dawn** very early in the morning: *We were up at the crack of dawn.*

crack[3] *adj.* having a lot of experience and skill: *a **crack shot*** (=someone who is very good at shooting)

crack·down /ˈkrækdaʊn/ *n.* [C] an effort to stop bad or illegal behavior by being more strict: *a national **crackdown on** illegal immigrants*

cracked /krækt/ *adj.* something that is cracked has lines on the surface because it is damaged but not completely broken: *a cracked mirror*

crack·er /ˈkrækɚ/ *n.* [C] a type of hard dry bread that is thin and flat

crack·le /ˈkrækəl/ *v.* [I] to make a lot of short sharp noises: *a log fire crackling in the fireplace* —**crackle** *n.* [C] → *see picture on page A20*

crack·pot /ˈkrækpɑt/ *adj.* (informal) slightly crazy: *a crackpot idea*

cra·dle[1] /ˈkreɪdl/ *n.* [C] **1** a small bed for a baby, that can swing gently from side to side **2 the cradle of sth** the place where something important began: *Some say Athens was the cradle of democracy.*

cradle[2] *v.* [T] to hold someone or something gently in your arms: *Tony cradled the baby in his arms.*

craft[1] /kræft/ *n.* [C] **1** (plural **crafts**) a skilled activity in which you make something using your hands: *a craft such as knitting* **2** (plural **craft**) a boat, ship, or airplane [ORIGIN: Old English *cræft* "strength, skill"]

craft[2] *v.* [T] **1** to write a book, speech, etc. with great skill and care **2** to make something with your hands, using a special skill

crafts·man /ˈkræftsmən/ *n.* (plural **craftsmen** /-mən/) [C] someone who is very skilled at making things with his/her hands: *furniture made by the finest craftsmen* —**craftsmanship** *n.* [U]

craft·y /ˈkræfti/ *adj.* good at getting what you want by deceiving people —**craftily** *adv.*

THESAURUS **intelligent, smart, bright, brilliant, wise, clever, cunning** → INTELLIGENT

crag·gy /ˈkrægi/ *adj.* a craggy mountain or cliff is very steep and covered with large rocks

cram /kræm/ *v.* (**crammed**, **cramming**) **1** [T] to force a lot of people or things into a small space: *I managed to **cram** all my stuff **into** the closet.*

THESAURUS **shove, stick, thrust, jam** → SHOVE

2 be crammed with sth to be full of people or things: *The mall was crammed with shoppers.* **3** [I] to prepare yourself for a test by studying a lot of information very quickly: *Julia stayed up all night **cramming for** her math final.* —**crammed** *adj.*: *crammed sidewalks*

cramp /kræmp/ *n.* [C] **1** a severe pain that you get when a muscle becomes very tight: ***I have a cramp** in my wrist from writing all day.* **2 cramps** [plural] a severe pain in the stomach that women get when they MENSTRUATE

C

cramped /kræmpt/ *adj.* a cramped room or building does not have enough space for the people or things in it: *a cramped apartment*

THESAURUS small, little, tiny, minute, miniature, diminutive → SMALL

cran·ber·ry /ˈkrænˌbɛri/ *n.* (plural **cranberries**) [C] a small sour red berry: *cranberry sauce* [ORIGIN: 1600—1700 Low German *kraanbere*, from *kraan* "crane" + *bere* "berry;" because a part of the flower looks like a crane's beak]

crane[1] /kreɪn/ *n.* [C] **1** a tall machine with a long metal arm for lifting heavy things **2** a water bird with very long legs

crane[2] *v.* [I,T] to look around or over something by stretching or leaning: *All the kids **craned their necks** to see who Mrs. Miller was talking to.*

cra·ni·um /ˈkreɪniəm/ *n.* [C] BIOLOGY the part of your head that is made of bone and covers your brain (SYN) **skull** → *see picture at* BRAIN[1]

crank[1] /kræŋk/ *n.* [C] **1 crank (telephone) call/letter** (informal) a telephone call or letter that is intended to frighten, annoy, or upset someone **2** (informal) someone who easily becomes angry or annoyed **3** a handle that you turn in order to make a machine work

crank[2] *v.* (informal)

crank sth ↔ **out** *phr. v.* to produce a lot of something very quickly without caring about quality: *He cranks out two novels a year.*

crank sth ↔ **up** *phr. v.* to make the sound from a radio, etc. a lot louder: *Hey, Vince, crank up the stereo!*

crank·y /ˈkræŋki/ *adj.* very easily annoyed or made angry, especially because you are tired: *Steve woke up cranky this morning.*

craps /kræps/ *n.* [U] a game played for money, using two DICE

crash[1] /kræʃ/ *v.* **1** [I,T] to have an accident in which a car, airplane, etc. hits something: *The jet crashed shortly after takeoff.* | *We **crashed** straight **into** the car ahead of us.* **2** [I,T] to hit something hard, causing a lot of damage or making a loud noise: *A baseball **crashed into/through** our living room window.* | *the sound of waves **crashing against** the rocks* **3** [I,T] IT if a computer crashes, or if you crash it, it suddenly stops working: *Electrical problems caused our computers to crash.* **4** [I] (spoken) **a)** *also* **crash out** to go to bed, or to go to sleep very quickly because you are very tired: *I crashed out on the sofa, watching TV.* **b)** to stay at someone's house for the night: *You can crash at our place tonight.* **5** [I] ECONOMICS if a STOCK MARKET crashes, the value of STOCKS falls suddenly and by a large amount **6** [T] (informal) if you crash a party or event, you go to it although you have not been invited

crash[2] *n.* [C] **1** an accident in which a vehicle hits something else: *The driver was killed in the crash.* | *a **plane/car/bus etc. crash***

THESAURUS accident, collision, wreck, pile-up, disaster, catastrophe, mishap → ACCIDENT

2 a sudden loud noise made by something falling, breaking, etc.: *I heard a crash coming from the kitchen.* | *The tree fell over **with a crash**.* → *see picture on page A20* **3** IT an occasion when a computer suddenly stops working **4** ECONOMICS an occasion when the value of STOCKS on a STOCK MARKET falls suddenly and by a large amount: *a stock market crash*

THESAURUS recession, depression, slump, downturn → RECESSION

ˈcrash course *n.* [C] a short course in which you study a subject very quickly

ˈcrash ˌdiet *n.* [C] an attempt to make yourself thinner quickly by strictly limiting how much you eat

ˈcrash ˌhelmet *n.* [C] a hard hat worn by people who drive race cars, MOTORCYCLES, etc. to protect their heads

ˌcrash ˈlanding *n.* [C] an occasion when a pilot has to bring an airplane down to the ground in a more dangerous way than usual because the airplane has a problem: *He was forced to **make a crash landing** in the middle of the desert.*

crass /kræs/ *adj.* offensive and stupid: *a crass remark*

crate /kreɪt/ *n.* [C] a large box used for carrying fruit, bottles, etc.: *a crate of wine*

crater

cra·ter /ˈkreɪt̬ɚ/ *n.* [C] **1** a round hole in the ground made by something that has fallen on it or exploded on it: *a bomb crater* **2** the round open top of a VOLCANO [ORIGIN: 1600—1700 Latin "bowl for mixing things, crater," from Greek *krater*, from *kerannynai* "to mix"] ➔ *see picture at* VOLCANO

crave /kreɪv/ *v.* [T] to want something very much: *Most little kids crave attention.*

crav·ing /ˈkreɪvɪŋ/ *n.* [C] a very strong desire for something: *a **craving for** chocolate*

craw·fish /ˈkrɔˌfɪʃ/ *n.* (plural **crawfish**) [C] a CRAYFISH

crawl¹ /krɔl/ *v.* [I] **1** to move on your hands and knees or with your body close to the ground: *They had to **crawl through** a tunnel to escape.* | *The baby **crawled across** the floor.* ➔ *see picture on page A22* **2** if a vehicle crawls, it moves very slowly: *We got stuck behind a truck crawling along at 25 mph.* **3 be crawling with sth** to be completely covered with insects or people: *The food was crawling with ants.* **4** if an insect crawls somewhere, it moves there

crawl² *n.* **1** [singular] a very slow speed: *Traffic has slowed to a crawl.* **2 the crawl** a way of swimming in which you lie on your stomach and move one arm, and then the other, over your head ➔ *see picture at* SWIM¹

cray·fish /ˈkreɪˌfɪʃ/ *n.* (plural **crayfish**) [C,U] a small animal like a LOBSTER that lives in rivers and streams, or the meat from this animal [ORIGIN: 1300—1400 Old French *crevice*; influenced by *fish*]

cray·on /ˈkreɪɑn, -ən/ *n.* [C] a stick of colored WAX that children use to draw pictures [ORIGIN: 1600—1700 French *craie* "chalk"]

craze /kreɪz/ *n.* [C] a fashion, game, type of music, etc. that is very popular for a short time: *Shoes with wheels in the heel were the latest craze.*

THESAURUS **bestseller, blockbuster, hit, fad, cult** ➔ POPULAR

crazed /kreɪzd/ *adj.* a crazed person behaves in a wild and uncontrolled way, as if s/he is mentally ill: *a crazed gunman*

cra·zy /ˈkreɪzi/ *adj.* (comparative **crazier**, superlative **craziest**) (informal) **1** very strange or not sensible: *You must be crazy to drive in that snow!* | *Whose **crazy idea** was it to go hiking in November?* **2 be crazy about sb/sth** to like someone or something very much: *John's crazy about skiing.* **3** angry or annoyed SYN **mad**: *Shut up! You're **driving** me **crazy*** (=really annoying me)*!* | *Dad's going to **go crazy*** (=be very angry) *when he hears that I flunked math.* **4 like crazy** very much or very quickly: *These mosquito bites on my leg are itching like crazy.* **5** mentally ill: *Sometimes I think I'm **going crazy**.*

THESAURUS

mentally ill – having an illness of the mind that affects the way you behave: *Her father had been mentally ill.*
insane – permanently and seriously mentally ill: *A psychiatrist said that he was insane at the time of the crime.*
disturbed – not behaving in a normal way because of mental or emotional problems: *emotionally disturbed children*
nuts (informal) – crazy: *He looked at me like I was nuts.*
loony (informal) – crazy: *De Niro plays a loony baseball fan stalking his favorite player.*
demented – crazy or very strange: *his demented fantasies*
psychotic (formal) – relating to having a serious mental illness: *psychotic behavior*
unstable – if someone is unstable, his/her emotional state changes very suddenly: *Her mother was mentally unstable.*

—**crazily** *adv.* —**craziness** *n.* [U]

creak /krik/ *v.* [I] if something such as a door or wooden floor creaks, it makes a long high noise when it moves: *The door creaked shut behind him.* —**creak** *n.* [C] —**creaky** *adj.* ➔ *see picture on page A20*

cream¹ /krim/ *n.* **1** [U] a thick white liquid that comes from milk: *Do you take cream and sugar in your coffee?* **2** [U] a pale yellow-white color **3** [C,U] used in the names of foods containing cream or something similar to it: *banana cream pie* | *cream of mushroom soup* **4** [C,U] a thick smooth substance that you put on your skin to make it feel soft, treat a medical condition, etc.: *The doctor gave me a cream to put on my sunburn.* **5 the cream of the crop** the best people or things in a group: *These students represent the cream of the academic crop.* [ORIGIN: 1300—1400 Old French *craime, cresme*, from Latin *cramum*] —**cream** *adj.* —**creamy** *adj.*

cream² *v.* [T] **1** to mix foods together until they become a thick smooth mixture: *Next, cream the butter and sugar.* **2 cream sb** (informal) to hit someone very hard or easily defeat someone in a game, competition, etc.: *The Yankees creamed the Red Sox 11–1.*

THESAURUS **beat, defeat, trounce, clobber, vanquish, overcome** ➔ BEAT¹

ˈcream cheese *n.* [U] a type of soft white cheese

cream·er /ˈkrimɚ/ *n.* [U] a white substance you can use instead of milk or cream in coffee or tea

crease¹ /kris/ *n.* [C] **1** a line on a piece of cloth, paper, etc. where it has been folded, crushed, or IRONed: *She smoothed the creases from her skirt.* **2** a fold in someone's skin

crease² *v.* [I,T] to become marked with a line or lines, or to make a line appear on cloth, paper, etc. by folding or crushing it: *Try not to crease your jacket.* —**creased** *adj.*

cre·ate /kriˈeɪt/ (Ac) *v.* [T] **1** to make something new exist or happen: *Scientists believe the universe was created by a big explosion.* | *Why do you want to create problems for everyone?* | *The chemical reaction creates two new substances.*

THESAURUS make, produce, manufacture, build, construct, generate ➔ MAKE[1]

2 to invent or design something: *Janet created a wonderful chocolate dessert for the party.* [ORIGIN: 1300—1400 Latin, past participle of *creare*]

THESAURUS invent, think up, come up with sth, conceive, devise, make up sth, dream sth up ➔ INVENT

C

cre·a·tion /kri'eɪʃən/ (Ac) *n.* **1** [U] the act of creating something: *the **creation of** 300 new jobs* **2** [C] something that has been created: *the artist's latest creation* **3 the Creation** according to many religions, the time when God made the universe and everything in it

cre·a·tive /kri'eɪt̬ɪv/ (Ac) *adj.* **1** good at thinking of new ideas: *I try to surround myself with creative people.* **2** involving the use of imagination to produce new ideas or things: *a creative solution to our problems | the writer's creative process | He is full of creative ideas.* **—creatively** *adv.* **—creativity** *n.* [U]: *The company encourages creativity and innovation.*

cre·a·tor /kri'eɪt̬ɚ/ (Ac) *n.* **1** [C] someone who made or invented a particular thing: *Walt Disney, the creator of Mickey Mouse | The toy made enormous profits for its creators.* **2 the Creator** God

crea·ture /'kritʃɚ/ *n.* [C] **1** an animal, fish, or insect: *Native Americans believe that all **living creatures** should be respected.* **2** an imaginary animal or person, or one that is very strange and frightening: *creatures from outer space* **3 creature comforts** all the things that make life comfortable and enjoyable **4 a creature of habit** someone who always does things in the same way or at the same time

cre·dence /'kridns/ *n.* [U] (formal) the acceptance of something as true: *His ideas quickly **gained credence*** (=started to be believed) *among economists.*

cre·den·tials /krə'dɛnʃəlz/ *n.* [plural] **1** someone's education, achievements, experience, etc. that prove that s/he has the ability to do something: *a woman with **impressive credentials*** **2** a document that proves who you are: *May I see your credentials?*

cred·i·bil·i·ty /ˌkrɛdə'bɪlət̬i/ *n.* [U] the quality of deserving to be believed and trusted: *The scandal has ruined his credibility as a leader.*

cred·i·ble /'krɛdəbəl/ *adj.* deserving or able to be believed or trusted: *a credible witness* **—credibly** *adv.*

cred·it[1] /'krɛdɪt/ (Ac) *n.* **1** [U] an arrangement with a bank, store, etc., that allows you to buy something and pay for it later: *We bought a new stove **on credit**.* **2** [U] praise given to someone for doing something: *They never **give** Jesse any **credit for** all the extra work he does. | I can't **take** all **the credit**; Nicky helped a lot too. | The team **deserves credit** for playing hard until the end. | Much **to** Todd's **credit**, the dance was a great success.* **3 be a credit to sb/sth** to be so successful or good that the people around you can be proud of you: *Jo's a credit to her family.* **4 be in credit** to have money in your bank account **5** [C] a successfully completed part of a course at a university or college: *She needs 30 more credits to graduate.* **6 have sth to your credit** to have achieved something: *She already has two best-selling novels to her credit.* **7 the credits** [plural] a list of all the people involved in making a television program or movie [ORIGIN: 1500—1600 French *crédit*, from Italian, from Latin *creditum* "something given to someone to keep safe, loan"]

credit[2] *v.* [T] **1** to add money to a bank account (ANT) **debit**: *The check has been **credited to** your account. | For some reason, the bank has **credited** my account **with** an extra $237.* **2 be credited to sb/sth** if something is credited to someone or something, he, she, or it is said to have achieved it or be the reason for it: *The revolutionary new drug is widely credited to Arthur Kessler.* **3 credit sb with (doing) sth** to believe that someone has a good quality or has done something good: *I wouldn't have credited him with that much intelligence.*

cred·it·a·ble /'krɛdɪt̬əbəl/ *adj.* deserving praise or approval: *a creditable piece of scientific research*

'credit card *n.* [C] a small plastic card that you use to buy goods or services and pay for them later: *Can I **pay by credit card**?*

'credit ˌlimit *n.* [C] the amount of money that you are allowed to borrow or spend using your credit card

cred·i·tor /'krɛdət̬ɚ/ (Ac) *n.* [C] a person or organization that you owe money to ➔ DEBTOR

'credit ˌrating *n.* [C] ECONOMICS a judgment made by a bank or other company about how likely a person or a business is to pay their debts

cre·do /'kridoʊ/ *n.* (plural **credos**) [C] a short statement that expresses a belief or rule

cre·du·li·ty /krɪ'dulət̬i/ *n.* [U] (formal) willingness or ability to believe that something is true: *Her story **strained credulity*** (=was difficult to believe).

creed /krid/ *n.* [C] a set of beliefs or principles: *people of every creed, color, and nationality*

THESAURUS faith, religion, belief ➔ FAITH

creek /krik, krɪk/ *n.* [C] **1** a small narrow stream or river **2 be up the creek (without a paddle)** (spoken) to be in a difficult situation: *I'll really be up the creek if I don't pay my bills by Friday.*

creep[1] /krip/ *v.* (past tense and past participle **crept** /krɛpt/) [I] **1** to move very carefully and quietly so that no one will notice you: *She **crept down** the hall, trying not to wake up her mom.* **2** to move somewhere very slowly: *a tractor creeping along the road at 15 mph* **3** to gradually begin to appear: *Bitterness **crept into** his voice.* **4** to gradually increase: *The total number of people out of work **crept up** to five million.*

creep² *n.* [C] (informal) **1** someone who you dislike a lot: *Get lost, you little creep!* **2 give sb the creeps** to make you feel nervous and frightened: *That house gives me the creeps.*

creep·y /'kripi/ *adj.* making you feel nervous and slightly frightened: *a really creepy movie*

cre·mate /'krimeɪt, krɪ'meɪt/ *v.* [T] to burn the body of a dead person at a funeral ceremony —**cremation** /krɪ'meɪʃən/ *n.* [C,U]

cre·ma·to·ri·um /ˌkrimə'tɔriəm/ *n.* (plural **crematoriums** *or* **crematoria** /-riə/) [C] a building in which the bodies of dead people are cremated

cre·ole /'krioʊl/ *n.* **1** [C,U] ENG. LANG. ARTS a language that is a combination of a European language and one or more others **2 Creole** [C] **a)** someone whose family were originally from both Europe and Africa **b)** someone whose family were originally French SETTLERS in the southern U.S. [ORIGIN: 1700—1800 French *créole*, from Spanish, from Portuguese *crioulo* "black person born in Brazil, home-born slave," from *criar* "to breed"] —**creole** *adj.*

crepe, crêpe /kreɪp/ *n.* **1** [C] a very thin PANCAKE **2** [U] thin light cloth with very small folded lines on its surface, made from cotton, silk, wool, etc.

'crepe ˌpaper *n.* [U] thin brightly colored paper with small folded lines on its surface, used for making decorations

crept /krɛpt/ *v.* the past tense and past participle of CREEP

cre·scen·do /krə'ʃɛndoʊ/ *n.* (plural **crescendos**) [C] ENG. LANG. ARTS a gradual increase in the loudness of a piece of music until it becomes very loud

cres·cent /'krɛsənt/ *n.* [C] a curved shape that is wider in the middle and pointed on the ends: *a crescent moon* [ORIGIN: 1300—1400 Old French *creissant*, from *creistre* "to grow, increase," from Latin *crescere*] → *see picture at* SHAPE¹

crest /krɛst/ *n.* [C] **1** [usually singular] the top of a hill or wave: *It took us over an hour to reach the **crest of** the hill.* **2** a pointed group of feathers on top of a bird's head

crest·fall·en /'krɛstˌfɔlən/ *adj.* (formal) disappointed and sad: *Thomas was crestfallen when he heard the judge's decision.*

cre·vasse /krə'væs/ *n.* [C] EARTH SCIENCES a deep wide crack, especially in thick ice

crev·ice /'krɛvɪs/ *n.* [C] a narrow crack, especially in rock

crew /kru/ *n.* [C] **1** all the people that work together on a ship, airplane, etc.: *the **crew of** the space shuttle* **2** a group of people who work together on something: *the movie's cast and crew* [ORIGIN: 1500—1600 *crew* "additional soldiers, reinforcements" (15—16 centuries), from Old French *creue* "increase," from *creistre*]

'crew cut *n.* [C] a very short style of hair for men

crib /krɪb/ *n.* [C] a baby's bed with bars around the sides → *see picture at* BED¹

'crib death *n.* [C] the sudden and unexpected death of a healthy baby while s/he is asleep

'crib sheet *also* **'crib note** *n.* [C] (informal) something on which answers to questions are written, usually used in order to cheat on a test

crick /krɪk/ *n.* [C] a sudden stiff and painful feeling in a muscle in your neck or back

crick·et /'krɪkɪt/ *n.* **1** [C] a small brown insect that can jump, and makes a short loud noise by rubbing its wings together **2** [U] a game in which two teams try to get points by hitting a ball and running between two sets of sticks

crime /kraɪm/ *n.* **1** [U] illegal activities in general: *There's very little crime in this neighborhood.* | *Women are less likely to **commit crime**.* | *methods of **crime prevention*** | *The **crime rate** has gone down in the last few years.* | ***Violent crime** is up by 8%.*

THESAURUS

Crimes that involve stealing things
theft – the crime of stealing things: *car theft*
robbery – the crime of stealing money or valuable things from a bank, store, etc.: *armed robbery*
burglary – the crime of going into someone's home in order to steal money or valuable things
shoplifting – the crime of taking things from a store without paying for them

crimes that involve attacking people
assault – a crime in which someone is physically attacked
mugging – a crime in which someone is attacked and robbed in a public place
murder – a crime in which someone is deliberately killed → ATTACK¹, CRIMINAL², STEAL¹

2 [C] an illegal action that can be punished by law: *She **committed** a number of **crimes** in the area.* ▸Don't say "Do a crime."◂ | ***crimes against** the elderly* | *Rape is a very **serious crime**.* **3 it's a crime (to do sth)** (spoken) said when you think something is morally wrong: *It's a crime to throw away all that food.* [ORIGIN: 1200—1300 Latin *crimen* "judgment, accusation, crime"]

crim·i·nal¹ /'krɪmənəl/ *adj.* **1** relating to crime: *a **criminal record*** (=an official record of crimes someone has committed) | *street gangs involved in **criminal activity*** | *Drinking and driving is a **criminal offense*** (=a crime). **2** (informal) wrong but not illegal: *It's criminal to charge so much to go to a movie.* —**criminally** *adv.*

criminal² *n.* [C] someone who has done something wrong or illegal: *Police have described the man as a violent and dangerous criminal.*

THESAURUS

Types of criminals
offender (Law) – someone who is guilty of a crime
thief – someone who steals things
robber – someone who steals things, especially from stores or banks
burglar – someone who goes into buildings to steal things
shoplifter – someone who takes things from stores without paying for them
pickpocket – someone who steals things from people's pockets
attacker – someone who uses violence to hurt someone
mugger – someone who attacks and steals from another person in a public place
murderer – someone who deliberately kills another person → CRIME

C

crimp[1] /krɪmp/ *n.* **put a crimp in/on sth** to reduce or restrict something, so that it is difficult to do something else: *Falling wheat prices have put a crimp on farm incomes.*

crimp[2] *v.* [T] to restrict the development, use, or growth of something: *The lack of effective advertising has crimped sales.*

crim·son /ˈkrɪmzən/ *n.* [U] a dark slightly purple red color —**crimson** *adj.*

cringe /krɪndʒ/ *v.* [I] **1** to move away from someone or something because you are afraid: *a dog cringing in the corner* **2** to feel embarrassed by something: *Paul* ***cringed at the thought*** *of having to speak in public.* —**cringe** *n.* [C]

crin·kle /ˈkrɪŋkəl/ *also* **crinkle up** *v.* [I,T] to become covered with small folds, or to make something do this: *Mandy crinkled her nose in disgust.* —**crinkled** *adj.* —**crinkly** *adj.*

crip·ple[1] /ˈkrɪpəl/ *n.* [C] (old-fashioned) someone who has difficulty walking because his/her legs are damaged or injured. This word is considered to be offensive, and you should avoid using it. It is better to say that someone is DISABLED.

cripple[2] *v.* [T] **1** to injure someone so s/he can no longer walk: *He was crippled in a car accident.* **2** to make something very weak, or damage it: *The country's economy has been crippled by drought.* —**crippled** *adj.* —**crippling** *adj.*

cri·sis /ˈkraɪsɪs/ *n.* (plural **crises** /ˈkraɪsiz/) [C,U] a time when a situation is very bad or dangerous: *an* ***economic/budget/financial etc. crisis*** | *The president faces a* ***political crisis.*** | *In times of crisis, you find out who your real friends are.* | *The stock market is suffering from a crisis of confidence.*

crisp /krɪsp/ *adj.* **1** pleasantly dry, and hard enough to be broken easily: *He stepped carefully through the crisp, deep snow.* **2** food that is crisp is pleasantly hard or firm when you bite it: *a nice crisp salad* **3** paper or clothes that are crisp are fresh, clean, and new: *a crisp $20 bill* **4** weather that is crisp is cold and dry: *a crisp winter morning* [ORIGIN: 1500—1600 *crisp* "curly" (10—20 centuries), from Latin *crispus*] —**crisply** *adv.*

crisp·y /ˈkrɪspi/ *adj.* crispy food is pleasantly hard: *crispy bacon*

criss·cross /ˈkrɪskrɔs/ *v.* [I,T] **1** to travel many times from one side of an area to the other: *crisscrossing the country by plane* **2** to make a pattern of straight lines that cross over each other

cri·te·ri·on /kraɪˈtɪriən/ (Ac) *n.* (plural **criteria** /-riə/) [C usually plural] a fact or standard that you use to judge something or make a decision about something: *What are the main* ***criteria for*** *awarding the prize?* | *To qualify for funding, students must* ***meet*** *certain* ***criteria.***

crit·ic /ˈkrɪt̬ɪk/ *n.* [C] **1** someone whose job is to give his/her judgment about whether a movie, book, etc. is good or bad: *a literary critic for "The Times"* **2** someone who says that a person, organization, or idea is bad or wrong: *a* ***critic of*** *the tobacco industry* [ORIGIN: 1500—1600 Latin *criticus*, from Greek *kritikos*, from *krinein* "to judge, decide"]

crit·i·cal /ˈkrɪt̬ɪkəl/ *adj.* **1** if you are critical, you say that you think someone or something is bad or wrong: *Darren was* ***critical of*** *the plan.* | *a* ***highly critical*** *report* **2** very important: *Newspapers play a critical role in our society.* | *This next phase is* ***critical to*** *the project's success.* **3** very serious or dangerous: *The victim remains* ***in a critical condition*** (=seriously ill or injured). **4** [only before noun] making a careful judgment about whether someone or something is good or bad: *a* ***critical analysis*** *of the play* —**critically** *adv.*

ˌcritical ˈangle *n.* [C] PHYSICS the angle at which a beam of light needs to be traveling toward a surface in order for all of the light to be sent back from the surface

crit·i·cism /ˈkrɪt̬əˌsɪzəm/ *n.* [C,U] **1** remarks that show what you think is bad about someone or something (ANT) **praise**: *I don't think his* ***criticisms of*** *the project are justified.* | *The movie* ***drew criticism*** *from religious groups.* | *U.S. officials have come under* ***harsh/sharp/fierce etc. criticism*** *for their handling of the war.* | *Kate doesn't* ***take/accept criticism*** *well* (=accept that it may be true). | *We try to give students* ***constructive criticism*** (=helpful advice). **2** the activity of giving a professional judgment of a movie, play, book, etc., or the writing that expresses this judgment: *literary criticism*

crit·i·cize /ˈkrɪt̬əˌsaɪz/ *v.* [I,T] to say what faults you think someone or something has (ANT) **praise**: *Journalists* ***criticized*** *the White House* ***for*** *cutting the Social Security budget.* | *The government's policies have been* ***sharply/harshly/severely etc. criticized.*** | *a* ***widely criticized*** (=criticized by a lot of people) *ad campaign*

THESAURUS

To say that you do not think something is very good
attack – to strongly criticize someone or something: *Critics attacked the novel when it first came out.*

lambast (formal) – to strongly and publicly criticize someone or something: *Republicans lambasted the president's defense budget plan.*
knock – to criticize someone or something, especially unfairly: *I know a lot of people knock them, but I think they're a really good band.*
find fault with – to criticize things that are wrong with someone or something, especially small and unimportant things: *He's always finding fault with her driving.*
be disparaging about sb/sth – to say that you do not think what someone has done is very good or important: *She was somewhat disparaging about his work.*

To tell someone that he or she should not have done something
scold – to angrily criticize a child about something s/he has done: *My mother scolded me for being late.*
rebuke (formal) – to tell someone that s/he should not have done something: *The president publicly rebuked him and said his comments were unacceptable.*
admonish (formal) – to tell someone firmly that s/he should not have done something and that this must not happen again: *The witness was admonished for refusing to answer the question.*
reprimand – to tell someone officially that s/he has done something wrong: *He was reprimanded for being rude to the principal.*

cri·tique[1] /krɪ'tik/ *n.* [C] a piece of writing describing the good and bad qualities of a play, film, book, etc.: *a **critique of** John Updike's latest novel*

critique[2] *v.* [T] to judge whether someone or something is good or bad: *a group of artists meeting to critique each other's work*

crit·ter /'krɪt̬ɚ/ *n.* [C] (spoken) a creature, especially an animal

croak /kroʊk/ *v.* **1** [I] to make a deep low sound like the sound a FROG makes **2** [I,T] to speak in a low rough voice **3** [I] (slang) to die —**croak** *n.* [C]

cro·chet /kroʊ'ʃeɪ/ *v.* [I,T] to make clothes, hats, etc. from YARN, using a special needle with a hook at one end

croc·o·dile /'krɑkəˌdaɪl/ *n.* [C] a large REPTILE with a long body and a long mouth with sharp teeth that lives in rivers and lakes in hot countries [ORIGIN: 1200—1300 Old French *cocodrille*, from Latin *crocodilus*, from Greek, "lizard, crocodile," from *kroke* "small stone" + *drilos* "worm"]

cro·cus /'kroʊkəs/ *n.* [C] a small purple, yellow, or white flower that appears in spring

crois·sant /krwɑ'sɑnt/ *n.* [C] a curved piece of soft bread, usually eaten for breakfast → *see picture at* BREAD

cro·ny /'kroʊni/ *n.* (plural **cronies**) [C] (informal, disapproving) one of a group of friends who use their power or influence to help each other: *one of his **political cronies***

crook /krʊk/ *n.* [C] **1** (informal) a criminal or dishonest person: *a bunch of crooks* **2 the crook of your arm** the inside part of your arm, where it bends

crook·ed /'krʊkɪd/ *adj.* **1** not straight: *crooked teeth*

THESAURUS **bent, twisted, curved, warped, wavy** → BENT[2]

2 (informal) not honest: *a crooked cop*

croon /krun/ *v.* [I,T] to sing or speak softly about love —**crooner** *n.* [C]

crop[1] /krɑp/ *n.* [C] **1** a plant such as corn, wheat, etc. that farmers grow and sell: *Most of the land is used for **growing crops**.* **2** the amount of corn, wheat, etc. that is produced in a single season: *a **bumper crop** (=a very large amount) of barley* **3 a crop of sb/sth** (informal) a group of people, problems, etc. that arrive at the same time: *this year's crop of college freshmen*

crop[2] *v.* (**cropped, cropping**) [T] to make something shorter by cutting it: *Her hair was **closely cropped**.*

crop up *phr. v.* to suddenly happen or appear: *Several problems cropped up soon after we bought the car.*

cro·quet /kroʊ'keɪ/ *n.* [U] an outdoor game in which you hit heavy balls under curved wires using a wooden hammer

cross[1] /krɔs/ *v.* **1** [I,T] to go from one side of a road, river, place, etc. to the other: *Look both ways before **crossing the street**!* | *the first ship to cross the Pacific* | *Thousands of people **cross the border** from Mexico to the U.S. each year.* | *Thompson was the first runner to cross the finish line.* **2** [I,T] if two or more roads, lines, etc. cross, or if one crosses another, they go across each other: *There's a post office where Main Street crosses Elm.* **3** [T] if you cross your arms, legs, or ANKLEs, you put one on top of the other: *She sat down and crossed her legs.* **4 cross your mind** if something crosses your mind, you suddenly think about it: ***It** never **crossed** my **mind that** she might be sick.* **5** [T] to make someone angry by refusing to do what s/he wants: *I wouldn't cross her if I were you.* **6 cross the line** to go beyond the limits of appropriate behavior and begin acting in an unacceptable way: *The officers crossed the line when they began beating the suspect.* **7** [T] to mix two different types of animals or plants to produce young animals or plants: *Wolves can be **crossed with** domestic dogs.* **8 cross my heart (and hope to die)** (spoken) used to say that you promise that you will do something, or that what you are saying is true **9 cross your fingers** *also* **keep your fingers crossed** used to say that you hope something will happen: *People vote, cross their fingers, and hope for the best.* [ORIGIN: 900—1000 Old

Norse *kross*, from an unrecorded Old Irish *cross*, from Latin *crux*]

cross sth ↔ **off** *phr. v.* to draw a line through something on a list to show that you have dealt with it: *Cross off their names as they arrive.*

cross sth ↔ **out** *phr. v.* to draw a line through something that you have written because it is not correct: *The salesman crossed out $222 and wrote $225.*

C

cross² *n.* [C] **1** an upright wooden post with another post crossing it near the top. In the past, people were punished by being fastened to the post and left to die. People use "the cross" to mean the particular cross that Jesus Christ was left to die on, according to the Christian religion. **2** an object, sign, etc. in the shape of a cross, that is used to represent the Christian faith: *She wore a tiny gold cross around her neck.* **3** a mixture of two things: *His dog is a* ***cross between*** *a retriever and a collie.*

cross³ *adj.* (old-fashioned) annoyed and angry

cross·bow /ˈkrɔsboʊ/ *n.* [C] a weapon used in order to shoot ARROWS

cross·check /ˌkrɔsˈtʃɛk, ˈkrɔsttʃɛk/ *v.* [T] to make sure that something is correct by using a different method to check it again

ˌcross-ˈcountry *adj.* [only before noun] **1** across fields and not along roads: *cross-country running* | *cross-country skiers* **2** from one side of a country to the other side: *a cross-country flight*

ˌcross-ˈcultural *adj.* belonging to or involving two or more societies, countries, or cultures: *cross-cultural trade*

ˌcross-exˈamine *v.* [T] LAW to ask someone questions to discover whether s/he has been telling the truth, especially in a court of law —**ˌcross-examiˈnation** *n.* [C,U]

ˌcross-ˈeyed *adj.* having eyes that both look inward toward each other

cross·fire /ˈkrɔsfaɪɚ/ *n.* [U] **1** a situation in which you are badly affected by an argument, even though it does not involve you: *During a divorce, kids often get* ***caught in the crossfire.*** **2** bullets traveling toward each other from different directions: *A few reporters were* ***caught in the crossfire.***

cross·ing /ˈkrɔsɪŋ/ *n.* [C] **1** a marked place where you can safely cross a road, railroad, river, etc. **2** a place where two roads, lines, etc. cross **3** a trip across the ocean, a lake, a river, etc.

cross-leg·ged /ˈkrɔs ˌlɛgɪd, -lɛgd/ *adj., adv.* in a sitting position with your knees apart and one foot over the opposite leg: *We* ***sat cross-legged*** *on the floor*

cross·o·ver /ˈkrɔsˌoʊvɚ/ *n.* [C,U] a situation in which something or someone is popular or successful in different areas, or is liked by different types of people, for example when a popular song is liked by people who usually like only serious music: *The song became a crossover hit.*

ˌcross-ˈpurposes *n.* **at cross-purposes** if two people are at cross-purposes, they become confused because they think they are talking about the same thing, although they are not

ˌcross-ˈreference *n.* [C] a note in a book telling you to look on a different page for more information

cross·roads /ˈkrɔsroʊdz/ *n.* (plural **crossroads**) [C] **1** a place where two roads cross each other **2** a time when you have to make an important decision about your future: *Neale's career was* ***at a crossroads.***

ˌcross ˈsection, cross-section *n.* [C] **1** a group of people or things that is typical of a larger group: *a* ***cross-section of*** *the American public* **2** something that has been cut in half so that you can look at the inside, or a drawing of this: *a* ***cross section of*** *the brain*

ˈcross street *n.* [C] a large street that crosses another street: *The nearest cross street to our house is Victory Boulevard.*

ˌcross-ˈtrainer *n.* [C usually plural] a type of shoe that can be worn for playing different types of sports

ˌcross-ˈtraining *n.* [U] the activity of training for more than one sport at the same time

cross·walk /ˈkrɔswɔk/ *n.* [C] a marked place where people can cross a road safely ➔ CROSSING

cross·word puz·zle /ˈkrɔswɚd ˌpʌzəl/ *also* **crossword** *n.* [C] a word game in which you write the answers to CLUES (=questions) in a pattern of numbered boxes ➔ *see picture at* PUZZLE¹

crotch /krɑtʃ/ *n.* [C] the place where your legs join at the top, or the part of a piece of clothing that covers this

crotch·et·y /ˈkrɑtʃət̬i/ *adj.* (informal) easily annoyed or made angry: *a crotchety old man*

crouch /kraʊtʃ/ *also* **crouch down** *v.* [I] to lower your body close to the ground by bending your knees and back: *We crouched down behind the wall to hide.* ➔ *see picture on page A22*

crow¹ /kroʊ/ *n.* [C] **1** a large black bird that makes a loud sound **2 as the crow flies** used to describe the distance between two places when measured in a straight line: *My house is ten miles from here as the crow flies.*

crow² *v.* [I] **1** to make the loud sound of a ROOSTER **2** to talk very proudly about yourself or your achievements: *His supporters are still crowing about the court's decision.*

crow·bar /ˈkroʊbɑr/ *n.* [C] a strong iron bar with a curved end, used for forcing things open

crowd¹ /kraʊd/ *n.* **1** [C] a large group of people in one place: *a* ***crowd of*** *reporters* | *A* ***crowd gathered*** *to watch the parade.* | *Shop early and* ***avoid the crowds.*** | ***The crowd*** (=audience at an event) *roared for more.* **2** [singular] ordinary people: *He likes to* ***stand out from the crowd*** (=be different from ordinary people). **3** [singular] (informal) a group of people who know each other well: *I guess **the usual crowd** will be at the party.*

crowd² *v.* [I,T] if people crowd somewhere, they are there in large numbers: *People **crowded around** the scene of the accident.* | *The prisoners were all **crowded together** in a small cell.* | *Shoppers crowded the malls in the week before Christmas.*

crowd sb/sth ↔ **out** *phr. v.* to force someone or something to leave a place: *Big supermarkets have been crowding out small grocery stores for years.*

crowd·ed /ˈkraʊdɪd/ *adj.* very full of people or things: *a crowded room* | *The streets were **crowded with** tourists.*

crown¹ /kraʊn/ *n.* [C] **1** a circle made of gold and jewels that a king or queen wears on his/her head **2** an artificial top for a damaged tooth **3** the position you have if you have won a sports competition: *He lost the heavyweight boxing crown in 1972.* **4** the top part of a hat, head, or hill: *a hat with a high crown* [ORIGIN: 1100—1200 Old French *corone*, from Latin *corona* "circle of leaves put on someone's head, crown," from Greek *korone*]

crown² *v.* [T] **1** to put a crown on someone's head, so that s/he officially becomes king or queen: *He was crowned at the age of six.* **2** to make something complete or perfect by adding to it: *His career was crowned by the best actor award.*

crown·ing /ˈkraʊnɪŋ/ *adj.* [only before noun] better, more important, etc. than anything else: *Winning a fourth championship was her **crowning achievement**.*

cru·cial /ˈkruʃəl/ (Ac) *adj.* very important: *This election is **crucial to** Israel's future.* | *Sunday's game is **crucial for** the Giants.* | *Two witnesses **played a crucial role** in tracking down the killer.* | *The attack on Pearl Harbor was a crucial moment in American history.* [ORIGIN: 1700—1800 French "cross-shaped," from Latin *crux*] —**crucially** *adv.*

THESAURUS **important, of great/considerable importance, vital, essential, major, key, paramount, significant, salient** → IMPORTANT

cru·ci·ble /ˈkrusəbəl/ *n.* [C] **1** CHEMISTRY a container in which substances are heated to very high temperatures **2** a situation that is very difficult, but that often produces something new or good

cru·ci·fix /ˈkrusəˌfɪks/ *n.* [C] a cross with a figure of Christ on it

cru·ci·fix·ion /ˌkrusəˈfɪkʃən/ *n.* **1** [C,U] the act of killing someone by fastening him/her to a cross **2 the Crucifixion** the death of Christ in this way, or a picture or object that represents it

cru·ci·fy /ˈkrusəˌfaɪ/ *v.* (**crucified**, **crucifies**) [T] **1** to kill someone by fastening him/her to a cross **2** (informal) to criticize someone severely and cruelly: *If the newspapers find out, you'll be crucified.*

crud /krʌd/ *n.* [U] (informal) something that is bad or disgusting to look at, taste, smell, etc.: *I can't get this crud off my shoe.* —**cruddy** *adj.*

crude /krud/ *adj.* **1** offensive or rude, especially by referring to sex in an unacceptable way → VULGAR: *crude language* **2** in a natural or raw condition: *crude oil* **3** not developed to a high standard: *a crude shelter in the forest* —**crudely** *adv.*

cru·el /ˈkruəl/ *adj.* **1** deliberately hurting people or animals: *Children can be very **cruel to** each other.* | *Keeping animals in cages seems cruel.*

THESAURUS **mean, unkind, nasty, thoughtless, spiteful, abusive, vicious, malicious** → MEAN²

2 making someone suffer or feel unhappy: *Her father's death was **a cruel blow**.* | *Show business can be cruel.* [ORIGIN: 1200—1300 Old French, Latin *crudelis*, from *crudus* "raw, rough, cruel"] —**cruelly** *adv.*

cru·el·ty /ˈkruəlti/ *n.* (plural **cruelties**) [C,U] behavior or actions that are cruel: ***cruelty to** animals* | *the cruelties of war*

cruise¹ /kruz/ *v.* **1** [I] to move at a steady speed in a car, airplane, boat, etc.: *We cruised along at 65 miles per hour.* **2** [I,T] (informal) to drive a car without going to any particular place: *Kids were cruising up and down Main Street.* **3** [I,T] to sail somewhere for pleasure: *We will cruise the Caribbean.* **4** [I] to win something easily: *Blair **cruised to victory** by a little over two minutes.*

cruise² *n.* [C] a vacation on a large boat: *a Caribbean cruise*

cruis·er /ˈkruzɚ/ *n.* [C] **1** a large fast ship used by the navy **2** a police car **3** a boat used for pleasure

ˈcruise ship *n.* [C] a large ship with restaurants, bars, etc. that people travel on for a vacation

crumb /krʌm/ *n.* [C] **1** a very small piece of bread, cake, etc.

THESAURUS **piece, scrap, chunk, lump, fragment, slice, strip, block** → PIECE¹

2 a very small amount: *a few **crumbs of** information*

crum·ble /ˈkrʌmbəl/ *v.* **1** [I,T] to break into small pieces, or to make something do this: *an old stone wall, crumbling with age* | *Crumble the cheese on top.* **2** [I] to lose power, become weak, or fail: *the crumbling peace process*

crum·my /ˈkrʌmi/ *adj.* (spoken) bad or of bad quality: *a crummy movie*

crum·ple /ˈkrʌmpəl/ *v.* [I,T] to crush paper or cloth, or to be crushed in this way: *Dan tore the page out, crumpled it, and threw it in the wastepaper basket.* —**crumpled** *adj.*

crunch¹ /krʌntʃ/ *v.* **1** [I] to make a sound like

C

something being crushed: *Our feet* ***crunched on*** *the frozen snow.* **2** [I,T] to eat hard food in a way that makes a noise: *The dog was* ***crunching on*** *a bone.* —**crunchy** *adj.*

crunch² *n.* **1** [singular] a noise like the sound of something being crushed: *the* ***crunch of*** *footsteps on gravel* → *see picture on page A20* **2** [singular] a difficult situation caused by a lack of something, especially money or time: *the hospital's* ***budget crunch*** **3 the crunch** *also* **crunch time** the moment in a situation when you must make an important decision: *Crunch time is approaching for college applicants.*

C

cru·sade /kru'seɪd/ *n.* [C] a determined attempt to change something because you think you are morally right: *a* ***crusade for*** *better schools* —**crusade** *v.* [I]: *students crusading against nuclear weapons*

THESAURUS **fight, battle, campaign, drive, struggle** → FIGHT²

crush¹ /krʌʃ/ *v.* [T] **1** to press something so hard that it breaks or is damaged: *Crush two cloves of garlic.* | *a car crushed by falling rocks* | *Two workers were* ***crushed to death*** *when a building collapsed.* → *see picture on page A18*

crush

THESAURUS **press, squash, mash, grind, squeeze, compress, compact** → PRESS¹

2 to completely defeat someone or something, using severe methods: *The uprising was crushed by the military.* **3 crush sb's hopes/enthusiasm/confidence etc.** to make someone lose all hope, confidence, etc. [ORIGIN: 1300—1400 Old French *cruisir*]

crush² *n.* **1** [C] (informal) a strong feeling of love for someone that continues only for a short time: *Ben* ***has a crush on*** *his teacher.* **2** [singular] a crowd of people in a very small space

crush·ing /'krʌʃɪŋ/ *adj.* **1** very hard to deal with, and making you lose hope and confidence: *The army suffered a* ***crushing defeat.*** **2** a crushing remark, reply, etc. contains a very strong criticism

crust /krʌst/ *n.* [C,U] **1** the baked outside part of bread, a PIE, etc.: *bread rolls with a thick brown crust* **2** a hard covering on the surface of something: *The surface of the lake was covered by a thin crust of ice.* **3** EARTH SCIENCES the hard outer layer of a PLANET, moon, etc., made up mostly of rocks: *the Earth's crust* → *see picture at* GLOBE

crus·ta·cean /krʌ'steɪʃən/ *n.* [C] BIOLOGY an animal such as a LOBSTER or a CRAB that has a hard outer shell and several pairs of legs, and usually lives in water [ORIGIN: 1800—1900 Modern Latin *crustaceus*, from Latin *crusta* "crust, shell"] —**crustacean** *adj.*

crust·y /'krʌsti/ *adj.* having a hard crust: *crusty bread*

crutch /krʌtʃ/ *n.* [C] **1** [usually plural] one of a pair of sticks that you lean on to help you walk: *He was* ***on crutches*** *after breaking his leg.* **2** (disapproving) something that gives someone support or help, especially when this is not good for him/her: *Tom* ***uses*** *those pills* ***as a crutch.***

crux /krʌks/ *n.* **the crux** the most important part of a problem, question, argument, etc.: *The budget plan is* ***the crux of*** *the dispute between the White House and Congress*

cry¹ /kraɪ/ *v.* (**cried**, **cries**) **1** [I] to produce tears from your eyes, usually because you are unhappy or hurt: *What are you* ***crying about?*** | *Sydney* ***cried for*** *her mother.* | *a woman* ***crying over*** *the death of her son* | *Sad movies always* ***make me cry.***

THESAURUS

If someone **weeps**, s/he cries a lot because s/he feels very sad – a formal word.
If someone **sobs**, s/he cries a lot in a noisy way.
If someone **bawls**, s/he cries a lot in a noisy way – an informal word.
If someone **is in tears**, s/he is crying.
If someone **bursts into tears** or **dissolves into tears**, s/he suddenly starts crying.
If someone **breaks down**, s/he starts crying after having tried not to cry.

2 [I,T] to say something loudly: *"Stop!" she cried.* | *He* ***cried for help.*** | *The crowd cried his name.* **3 for crying out loud** (spoken) said when you feel annoyed with someone: *For crying out loud, will you shut up!* **4 cry over spilled milk** (informal) to waste time worrying about something that cannot be changed **5** [I] if an animal or bird cries, it makes a loud high sound **6 cry wolf** to often ask for help when you do not need it, so that people do not believe you when you really need help

cry out *phr. v.* **1** to make a loud sound of fear, shock, pain, etc.: *He* ***cried out in*** *pain.* **2 be crying out for sth** to need something urgently: *The health care system is crying out for reform.*

cry² *n.* (plural **cries**) [C] **1** a loud sound showing fear, pain, shock, etc.: *a baby's cry* | *a* ***cry of pain/joy/alarm etc.*** **2** a loud shout: *Miller heard a cry of "Stop, thief!"* **3** a sound made by a particular animal or bird: *the cries of seagulls* **4** a phrase used in order to unite people in support of a particular action or idea: *a war/battle cry* **5 a cry for help** something someone does that shows s/he is unhappy and needs help: *A suicide attempt is a cry for help.*

cry·ba·by /'kraɪˌbeɪbi/ *n.* (plural **crybabies**) [C] (informal, disapproving) someone who cries or complains too much

cry·ing /'kraɪ-ɪŋ/ *adj.* **1 a crying need for sth** a serious need for something: ***There's a crying need for*** *better housing.* **2 it's a crying shame** (spoken) used in order to say that something is very sad or upsetting: *It would be a crying shame if the school had to close down.*

crypt /krɪpt/ *n.* [C] a room under a church, used in past times for burying people

cryp·tic /ˈkrɪptɪk/ *adj.* having a meaning that is hard to understand: *a cryptic message* —**cryptically** *adv.*

crys·tal /ˈkrɪstəl/ *n.* **1** [U] high-quality clear glass: *crystal wine glasses* **2** [C,U] rock that is clear, or a piece of this **3** [C] a small evenly shaped object that forms naturally when a liquid becomes solid: *ice crystals* **4** [C] CHEMISTRY a solid substance that has atoms arranged in a regular repeated pattern: *copper sulfate crystals* [ORIGIN: 1000—1100 Old French *cristal*, from Latin *crystallum*, from Greek *krystallos* "ice, crystal"]

ˌcrystal ˈball *n.* [C] a glass ball that you look into, that some people believe can show the future

ˌcrystal ˈclear *adj.* **1** clearly stated and easy to understand: *I made it crystal clear that you weren't allowed to go!* **2** completely clean and clear: *The lake was crystal clear.*

crys·tal·lize /ˈkrɪstəˌlaɪz/ *v.* [I,T] **1** if a liquid crystallizes, it forms crystals **2** if an idea or plan crystallizes, it becomes clear in your mind: *The recent events really crystallized my opposition to war.*

c-sec·tion /ˈsi ˌsɛkʃən/ *n.* [C] a CESAREAN

CT the written abbreviation of CONNECTICUT

cub /kʌb/ *n.* [C] the baby of a lion, bear, etc.

cub·by hole /ˈkʌbi ˌhoʊl/ *n.* [C] a small space or room, used for storing things

cube¹ /kyub/ *n.* [C] **1** a solid square object with six equal sides: *a sugar cube* | *ice cubes* ➔ *see picture at* SHAPE¹ **2 the cube of sth** MATH the number you get when you multiply a number by itself twice: *The cube of 3 is 27.* [ORIGIN: 1500—1600 Latin *cubus*, from Greek *kybos* "cube, vertebra"]

cube² *v.* [T] **1** MATH to multiply a number by itself twice: *2 cubed is 8.* **2** to cut something into cubes

ˌcube ˈroot *n.* [C] MATH the cube root of a particular number is the number which, when multiplied by itself twice, equals that number. For example, the cube root of 64 is 4. ➔ SQUARE ROOT

cu·bic /ˈkyubɪk/ *adj.* **cubic inch/centimeter/yard etc.** MATH a measurement of space which is calculated by multiplying the length of something by its width and height

cu·bi·cle /ˈkyubɪkəl/ *n.* [C] a small partly enclosed part of a room: *office cubicles* [ORIGIN: 1400—1500 Latin *cubiculum*, from *cubare* "to lie"]

ˈCub Scouts *n.* [plural] the part of the BOY SCOUTS that is for younger boys

cuck·oo /ˈkuku/ *n.* (plural **cuckoos**) [C] a gray European bird that puts its eggs in other birds' nests and that has a call that sounds like its name [ORIGIN: 1200—1300 Old French *cucu*, from the sound it makes]

cu·cum·ber /ˈkyuˌkʌmbɚ/ *n.* [C] a long thin green vegetable, usually eaten raw [ORIGIN: 1300—1400 Old French *cocombre*, from Latin *cucumis*] ➔ *see picture at* VEGETABLE

cuddle

cud·dle /ˈkʌdl/ *v.* [I,T] to put your arms around someone or something as a sign of love: *Chris cuddled her new puppy.* —**cuddle** *n.* [C usually singular]

THESAURUS hug, embrace, hold, wrap your arms around sb ➔ HUG¹

cuddle up *phr. v.* to lie or sit very close to someone or something: *The children* ***cuddled up to*** *each other in the dark.*

cud·dly /ˈkʌdli/ *adj.* soft, warm, and nice to hold: *a cuddly stuffed animal*

cue /kyu/ *n.* [C] **1** an action or event that is a signal for something else to happen: *That was a* ***cue for*** *me to leave.* **2** a word or action that is a signal for someone to speak or act in a play, movie, etc.: *Tony stood by the stage, waiting for his cue.* **3 (right/as if) on cue** happening or done at exactly the right moment: *Then Bart walked in, right on cue.* **4 take a/your cue from sb** to copy what someone else does because s/he does it correctly **5** a long straight wooden stick used for hitting the ball in games such as POOL **6** a movement of the hand, body, or face that communicates meaning without words: *Cues such as smiling or lowering your eyes show that you are attracted to someone.*

cuff¹ /kʌf/ *n.* [C] **1** the end of a sleeve **2** a narrow piece of cloth turned up at the bottom of your pants **3 off-the-cuff** without previous thought or preparation: *an* ***off-the-cuff remark*** **4 cuffs** [plural] (informal) HANDCUFFS

cuff² *v.* [T] (informal) to put HANDCUFFS on someone

ˈcuff link *n.* [C] a small piece of jewelry that a man can use instead of a button to fasten the cuff of his shirt

cui·sine /kwɪˈzin/ *n.* [U] a particular style of cooking: *French cuisine*

cul-de-sac /ˌkʌl də ˈsæk, ˌkʊl-/ *n.* [C] a street with only one way in and out [ORIGIN: 1800—1900 a French word meaning "bottom of the bag"]

cul·i·nar·y /ˈkʌləˌnɛri, ˈkyu-/ *adj.* (formal) relating to cooking: *a culinary magazine*

cull /kʌl/ *v.* **1** [T] (formal) to collect information from different places: *data* ***culled from*** *various sources* **2** [I,T] to kill some of the animals in a group so that the size of the group does not increase too much —**cull** *n.* [C]

cul·mi·nate /ˈkʌlməˌneɪt/ *v.*

culminate in/with sth *phr. v.* to end with a particular event, especially a big or important one: *a series of arguments that culminated in divorce*

C

cul·mi·na·tion /ˌkʌlməˈneɪʃən/ *n.* **the culmination of sth** something important that happens after a period of development: *That discovery was the culmination of his life's work.*

cul·pa·ble /ˈkʌlpəbəl/ *adj.* (formal) deserving blame: *Both sides were equally culpable.* —**culpability** /ˌkʌlpəˈbɪləṭi/ *n.* [U]

cul·prit /ˈkʌlprɪt/ *n.* [C] **1** someone who has done something wrong: *Police are still looking for the culprit.* **2** the reason for a particular problem or difficulty: *High labor costs are* ***the main culprit*** *for the rise in prices.* [ORIGIN: 1600—1700 Anglo-French *cul* (from *culpable* "guilty") + *prit* "ready (to prove it)"]

cult¹ /kʌlt/ *n.* [C] **1** an extreme religious group that is not part of an established religion: *a* ***religious cult***

THESAURUS **church, denomination, sect**
➔ CHURCH

2 a fashionable or popular belief, idea, or attitude: *The whole movie industry is built on the* ***cult of*** *personality.*

cult² *adj.* [only before noun] a cult movie, person, group, etc. is one that is very popular but only among a particular group of people: *The band has developed a* ***cult following.*** ➔ POPULAR

cul·ti·vate /ˈkʌltəˌveɪt/ *v.* [T] **1** to prepare and use land for growing crops and plants **2** to work hard to develop a particular skill, quality, or attitude: *He's spent years cultivating a knowledge of art.* **3** to try to develop a friendship with someone who can help you: *She worked hard to cultivate friendships with local government leaders.* —**cultivation** /ˌkʌltəˈveɪʃən/ *n.* [U]

cul·ti·vat·ed /ˈkʌltəˌveɪṭɪd/ *adj.* **1** intelligent and knowing a lot about music, art, literature, etc.: *a cultivated gentleman* **2** cultivated land is used for growing crops or plants

cul·tur·al /ˈkʌltʃərəl/ (Ac) *adj.* **1** relating to a particular society and its way of life: *England has a rich* ***cultural heritage.*** | *cultural differences* **2** relating to art, literature, music, etc.: *a guide to* ***cultural events*** *in London* | *The museum is a welcome addition to the city's* ***cultural life.*** **3 cultural diffusion** SOCIAL SCIENCE the spread of ideas, CUSTOMS (=traditional ways of doing something), etc. between people from different cultures **4 cultural diversity** SOCIAL SCIENCE the fact that there are many clearly different cultures in a city, country, etc. **5 cultural institution** SOCIAL SCIENCE an important practice or CUSTOM (=traditional way of doing something) that has existed in a society or within a social group for a long time —**culturally** *adv.*: *Europe is a culturally diverse continent.*

cul·ture /ˈkʌltʃɚ/ (Ac) *n.* **1** [C,U] SOCIAL SCIENCE the art, beliefs, behavior, ideas, etc. of a particular society: *the culture of ancient Greece* | *I love working abroad and meeting people from different cultures.* | ***American/Western/Hispanic etc. culture*** ►Don't say "The American culture."◄ **2** [U] ENG. LANG. ARTS art, literature, music, etc.: *Boston is a good place for anyone who is interested in culture.* | ***popular culture*** (=the music, movies, etc. that are liked by a lot of people) **3** [C,U] BIOLOGY the process of growing BACTERIA for scientific use, or the bacteria or cells produced by this: *tissue cultures* [ORIGIN: 1200—1300 Old French, Latin *cultura*, from *cultus* "care, worship"]

cul·tured /ˈkʌltʃɚd/ (Ac) *adj.* intelligent, polite, and interested in art, music, etc.

ˈculture ˌshock *n.* [singular, U] a feeling of being confused or anxious when you visit a foreign country for the first time

cum·ber·some /ˈkʌmbɚsəm/ *adj.* **1** a cumbersome process is slow and difficult: *Getting a passport can be a cumbersome process.* **2** heavy and difficult to move or use: *cumbersome equipment*

cu·mu·la·tive /ˈkyumyələṭɪv, -ˌleɪ-/ *adj.* increasing gradually: *the* ***cumulative effect of*** *air pollution* —**cumulatively** *adv.*

cu·mu·lo·nim·bus /ˌkyumyəlouˈnɪmbəs/ *n.* (plural **cumulonimbuses** *or* **cumulonimbi** /-baɪ/) [C,U] EARTH SCIENCES a type of thick large cloud that often produces a RAINSTORM or a THUNDERSTORM ➔ CIRRUS, CUMULUS, NIMBUS, STRATUS

cu·mu·lus /ˈkyumyələs/ *n.* (plural **cumuli** /-laɪ/) [C,U] EARTH SCIENCES a thick white cloud with a flat bottom edge, which shows that the weather is good, but which can build up to form rain ➔ CIRRUS, CUMULONIMBUS, NIMBUS, STRATUS

cun·ning /ˈkʌnɪŋ/ *adj.* intelligent in a dishonest way: *a cunning criminal* | *a cunning plan* [ORIGIN: 1200—1300 Present participle of *cun* "to know," an early form of *can*] —**cunning** *n.* [U] —**cunningly** *adv.*

THESAURUS **intelligent, smart, bright, brilliant, wise, clever, crafty** ➔ INTELLIGENT
skillful, expert, accomplished, talented, gifted, adept, deft ➔ SKILLFUL

cup¹ /kʌp/ *n.* [C] **1** a small round container, usually with a handle, that you use to drink tea, coffee, etc., or the drink it contains ➔ SAUCER: *a cup and saucer* | *a* ***cup of*** *coffee* | *a* ***paper/plastic cup*** **2** a unit for measuring liquid or food in cooking, equal to eight FLUID OUNCES or 237 MILLILITERS: *Stir in a cup of flour.* **3** a specially shaped container that is given as a prize in a competition ➔ TROPHY [ORIGIN: Old English *cuppe*, from Late Latin *cuppa*, from Latin *cupa* "barrel"]

cup² *v.* (**cupped, cupping**) [T] to form your hands into the shape of a cup: *Greta* ***cupped*** *her hands* ***around*** *the mug.*

cup·board /ˈkʌbɚd/ *n.* [C] a piece of furniture with doors and shelves, used for storing clothes, plates, food, etc. [ORIGIN: 1500—1600 *cupboard* "shelf or table for cups" (14—18 centuries)]

cup·cake /ˈkʌpkeɪk/ *n.* [C] a small round cake

cu·pid·i·ty /kyuˈpɪdəṭi/ *n.* [U] (formal) very strong desire for something, especially money or property SYN greed

cur·a·ble /ˈkyʊrəbəl/ *adj.* able to be cured ANT incurable: *a curable disease*

cu·ra·tor /ˈkyʊˌreɪṭɚ, -rəṭɚ, kyʊˈreɪṭɚ/ *n.* [C] someone who is in charge of a MUSEUM

curb¹ /kɚb/ *n.* [C] the edge of a SIDEWALK, where it joins the road [ORIGIN: 1400—1500 French *courbe* "curve, curved piece of wood or metal," from Latin *curvus*]

THESAURUS edge, perimeter, rim, margin → EDGE¹

curb² *v.* [T] to control or limit something: *Doctors are trying to curb the spread of the disease.*

curd /kɚd/ *n.* [C,U] the thick substance that forms in milk when it becomes sour

cur·dle /ˈkɚdl/ *v.* [I,T] if a liquid curdles, it becomes unpleasantly thick: *Do not let the sauce boil or it will curdle.*

cure¹ /kyʊr/ *v.* [T] **1** to make an injury or illness better, so that the person who was sick is well → HEAL: *Many types of cancer can now be cured.* | *Penicillin will cure most infections.* **2** to solve a problem, or improve a bad situation: *No one can completely cure unemployment.* **3** to preserve food, leather, etc. by drying it, hanging it in smoke, or covering it with salt: *cured ham* [ORIGIN: 1200—1300 Old French, Latin *cura* "care"]

cure² *n.* [C] **1** a medicine or medical treatment that can cure an illness or disease: *a* ***cure for*** *cancer* **2** something that solves a problem: *There's no easy* ***cure for*** *poverty.*

THESAURUS solution, answer, remedy, panacea → SOLUTION

cur·few /ˈkɚfyu/ *n.* [C] a law that forces people to stay indoors after a particular time at night: *The government* ***imposed*** *a* ***curfew*** *from sunset to sunrise.* [ORIGIN: 1200—1300 Old French *covrefeu* "signal to put out fires, curfew," from *covrir* "to cover" + *feu* "fire"]

cu·ri·o /ˈkyʊriˌoʊ/ *n.* (plural **curios**) [C] a small object that is interesting because it is old, beautiful, or rare

cu·ri·os·i·ty /ˌkyʊriˈɑsəṭi/ *n.* [singular, U] the desire to know about something: *Children have a natural* ***curiosity about*** *the world around them.* | *Just* ***out of curiosity*** (=because of curiosity), *how old are you?* | *I just had to* ***satisfy*** *my* ***curiosity****, so I opened the box.*

cu·ri·ous /ˈkyʊriəs/ *adj.* **1** wanting to know or learn about something: *We were* ***curious about*** *what was going on next door.* | *I was* ***curious to*** *see how it worked.* **2** strange or unusual: *a curious noise* | ***It's curious that*** *she left without saying goodbye.* [ORIGIN: 1300—1400 Old French *curios*, from Latin *curiosus* "careful, wanting to know"]

THESAURUS strange, funny, peculiar, mysterious, odd, weird, bizarre, eccentric → STRANGE¹

—curiously *adv.*

curl¹ /kɚl/ *n.* [C] **1** a piece of hair that hangs in a curved shape: *a little girl with blonde curls* → see picture at HAIR **2** something that forms a curved shape: *a* ***curl of*** *smoke* **—curly** *adj.*

curl² *v.* [I,T] to form a curved shape, or to make something do this: *I don't know if I should curl my hair or leave it straight.* | *Thick smoke curled from the chimney.* | *The phone cord was* ***curled around*** *her hand.*

curl up *phr. v.* **1** to lie or sit comfortably with your arms and legs bent close to your body: *Pepe curled up on the couch to watch TV.* **2** if paper, leaves, etc. curl up, their edges become curved and point up

curl·er /ˈkɚlɚ/ *n.* [C usually plural] a small metal or plastic tube for making hair curl

ˈcurling ˌiron *n.* [C] a piece of electrical equipment that you heat and use to curl your hair

cur·rant /ˈkɚənt, ˈkʌr-/ *n.* [C] a small round red or black berry, usually dried [ORIGIN: 1500—1600 *raison of Coraunte* "raisin of Corinth" (14—17 centuries), from *Corinth* city and area in Greece]

cur·ren·cy /ˈkɚənsi, ˈkʌr-/ Ac *n.* (plural **currencies**) **1** [C,U] the type of money that a country uses: *Japanese currency* | ***foreign currency***

THESAURUS money, bill, coin, cash, change → MONEY

2 [U] the state of being accepted or used by a lot of people: *During the 1880s, Marxism began to* ***gain currency****.* [ORIGIN: 1600—1700 Medieval Latin *currentia* "flowing," from Latin *currere*]

cur·rent¹ /ˈkɚənt, ˈkʌr-/ *adj.* happening, existing, or being used now: *Sales for the current year are low.* | *the current edition of "Newsweek"* [ORIGIN: 1200—1300 Old French *curant*, present participle of *courre* "to run," from Latin *currere*]

THESAURUS present, existing, prevailing → PRESENT¹

current² *n.* [C] **1** a continuous movement of water or air in a particular direction: *We were swimming against a* ***strong current****.* **2** a flow of electricity through a wire: *an **electrical current***

ˌcurrent af'fairs *n.* [U] important political or social events that are happening now

cur·rent·ly /ˈkɚəntli, ˈkʌr-/ *adv.* at the present time: *She's currently studying in Japan.* | *These are the most effective drugs currently available.*

THESAURUS now, at the moment, for the moment, at present/at the present time, presently → NOW[1]

C

cur·ric·u·lum /kəˈrɪkyələm/ *n.* (plural **curricula** /-kyələ/ *or* **curriculums**) [C] all of the subjects that are taught at a school, college, etc. [ORIGIN: 1800—1900 Modern Latin, Latin, "running, course," from *currere*]

cur·ry /ˈkɚi, ˈkʌri/ *n.* (plural **curries**) [C,U] meat or vegetables cooked in a spicy sauce

curse¹ /kɚs/ *v.* **1** [I] to swear: *He **cursed at** the lawn mower when it didn't start.* **2** [T] to say or think bad things about someone or something because he, she, or it that has made you angry: *I **cursed** myself **for** not buying the car insurance sooner.* **3** [T] to ask God or a magical power to harm someone

curse² *n.* [C] **1** a swear word, or words, that you say when you are angry **2** magic words that bring someone bad luck: *It feels like someone has **put a curse on** my career.*

THESAURUS magic, witchcraft, sorcery, black magic, spell, the occult, voodoo → MAGIC[1]

3 something that causes trouble or harm: *Being a war hero has been both a blessing and a curse.*

cursed /kɚst/ *adj.* **be cursed with sth** to be affected by something bad: *All his life, he's been cursed with bad luck.*

cur·sor /ˈkɚsɚ/ *n.* [C] a shape on a computer screen that moves to show where you are writing

cur·so·ry /ˈkɚsəri/ *adj.* done quickly without much attention to detail: *After a **cursory glance/look** at the menu, Grant ordered coffee.*

THESAURUS short, brief, quick → SHORT[1]

curt /kɚt/ *adj.* using very few words, in a way that seems rude: *a curt response* —**curtly** *adv.*

THESAURUS short, brief, concise, succinct → SHORT[1]

cur·tail /kɚˈteɪl/ *v.* [T] (formal) to reduce or limit something: *new laws to curtail immigration* —**curtailment** *n.* [C,U]

cur·tain /ˈkɚtˀn/ *n.* [C] a piece of hanging cloth that can be pulled across to cover a window, divide a room, etc.: *a shower curtain* | *a new **pair of curtains*** | *Can you **close/draw/pull the curtains** for me?* [ORIGIN: 1200—1300 Old French *curtine*, from Late Latin *cortina*, from Latin *cohors* "enclosure, court"]

curt·sy, curtsey /ˈkɚtsi/ *v.* (**curtsied, curtsies**) [I] if a woman curtsies, she bends her knees with one foot in front of the other as a sign of respect for an important person [ORIGIN: 1500—1600 *courtesy*] —**curtsy** *n.* [C]

curve¹ /kɚv/ *n.* [C] **1** a line or shape that bends like part of a circle: *a sharp curve in the road* → *see picture at* BENT[2] **2** a method of giving GRADES based on how a student's work compares with other students' work: *The test will be graded **on a curve**.*

curve² *v.* [I,T] to bend or move in the shape of a curve, or to make something do this: *a golf ball curving through the air* —**curved** *adj.* —**curvy** *adj.*

cur·vi·lin·e·ar /ˌkɚvəˈlɪniɚ/ *adj.* MATH having a curved line: *a huge curvilinear arch*

cush·ion¹ /ˈkʊʃən/ *n.* [C] **1** a bag filled with soft material, that you put on a chair or the floor to make it more comfortable → PILLOW **2** something, especially money, that prevents you from being immediately affected by a bad situation: *Savings can act as a **cushion against** unemployment.* [ORIGIN: 1300—1400 Old French *coissin*, from Latin *coxa* "hip"]

cushion² *v.* [T] to reduce the effects of something bad: *The law will **cushion the blow** for homeowners by gradually phasing in the tax increases.*

cusp /kʌsp/ *n.* **on/at the cusp of sth** at the time when a situation is going to change, or something important is about to happen: *They were young people on the cusp of adulthood.*

cuss /kʌs/ *v.* [I] (informal) to use offensive language SYN **swear, curse**

cuss sb ↔ out *phr. v.* (informal) to swear and shout at someone because you are angry

cus·tard /ˈkʌstɚd/ *n.* [C,U] a soft baked mixture of milk, eggs, and sugar [ORIGIN: 1600—1700 *custard*, *crustade* type of pie (14—17 centuries)]

cus·to·di·an /kəˈstoʊdiən/ *n.* [C] someone who takes care of a public building or something valuable

cus·to·dy /ˈkʌstədi/ *n.* [U] **1** the legal right to take care of a child: *My ex-wife **has custody of** the kids.* | *The judge awarded us **joint custody*** (=both parents will have custody) *of the children.* **2 in custody** being kept in prison until going to court: *Two robbery suspects are being **held/kept in custody**.* [ORIGIN: 1400—1500 Latin *custodia* "guarding," from *custos* "person who guards"] —**custodial** /kəˈstoʊdiəl/ *adj.*

cus·tom /ˈkʌstəm/ *n.* **1** [C,U] something that people in a particular society do because it is traditional: *the **custom of** throwing rice at weddings* | ***It's the custom for** the bride's parents **to** pay for the wedding.* | *Chinese customs and culture*

THESAURUS habit, tradition, practice, convention ➔ HABIT

2 customs [plural] the place where your bags are checked for illegal goods when you go into a country: *It took forever to* ***go through customs.*** [ORIGIN: 1100—1200 Old French *custume*, from Latin *consuetudo*, from *consuescere* "to make someone used to something"]

cus·tom·ar·y /ˈkʌstəˌmɛri/ *adj.* usual or normal: ***It is customary for*** *a local band* ***to*** *lead the parade.* —**customarily** /ˌkʌstəˈmɛrəli/ *adv.*

ˈcustom-built *adj.* a custom-built car, machine, etc. is built specially for a particular person

cus·tom·er /ˈkʌstəmə/ *n.* [C] someone who buys things from a store or company: *Dow is one of our* ***biggest customers.*** | *Foster was a* ***regular customer*** *at Brennan's Restaurant.* | *efforts to improve* ***customer service***

THESAURUS

client – someone who pays for a service: *a business meeting with clients*
shopper – someone who goes to a store looking for things to buy: *streets full of Christmas shoppers*
patron (formal) – someone who uses a particular store, restaurant, company, etc.: *the patrons of the restaurant*
consumer – anyone who buys goods or uses services: *the rights of consumers*
buyer – someone who buys something very expensive, such as a car or a house: *first-time home buyers* ➔ STORE[1]

cus·tom·ize /ˈkʌstəˌmaɪz/ *v.* [T] to change something to make it more appropriate for a particular person or purpose: *a customized software package*

ˈcustom-made *adj.* a custom-made shirt, pair of shoes, etc. is made specially for a particular person

cut[1] /kʌt/ *v.* (past tense and past participle **cut**, present participle **cutting**)
1 USE KNIFE/SCISSORS [I,T] to divide something into two or more pieces using a knife or scissors: *Do you want me to cut the cake?* | *Abby, go* ***cut*** *Grandpa* ***a piece*** *of pie.* | ***Cut*** *the cheese* ***into*** *cubes.* | *He* ***cut*** *the tomato* ***in half/two.*** | ***Cut along*** *the dotted line.*

THESAURUS

chop (up) – to cut meat, vegetables, or wood into pieces
slice – to cut bread, meat, or vegetables into thin pieces
dice – to cut vegetables or meat into small square pieces
peel – to cut the outside part off an apple, potato, etc.
carve – to cut pieces from a large piece of meat
shred – to cut vegetables into small thin pieces
grate – to cut cheese, vegetables, etc. into small pieces using a grater

cut

2 MAKE SHORTER [T] to make something shorter using a knife, scissors, etc.: *We* ***cut the grass*** *once a week.* | *Did you* ***get*** *your* ***hair cut****?*

THESAURUS

saw – to cut wood, using a saw (=a tool with a row of sharp points)
chop down – to make a tree fall down by cutting it
mow – to cut grass using a special machine: *I need to mow the lawn.*
trim – to cut off a small amount of something to make it look neater, for example hair or a bush
snip – to cut something quickly, using scissors

3 REDUCE [T] to reduce the amount of something: *You need to cut the amount of fat in your diet.* | *The company had to close several factories to* ***cut costs.*** | *The number of soldiers had to be* ***cut in half.***

THESAURUS reduce, lower, decrease, slash, roll back ➔ REDUCE

4 INJURE [T] to injure yourself or someone else with a knife or something else that is sharp: *He* ***cut*** *his finger* ***on*** *a piece of broken glass.* | *She fell and* ***cut*** *her head* ***open.***
5 cut sb free/loose to cut something such as a

rope or metal in order to let someone escape: *Firemen were carefully cutting the driver free from the wreckage.*

6 MAKE A HOLE/MARK [T] to make a mark in the surface of something, open something, etc. using a sharp tool: *She used a saw to **cut** a **hole in** the ice.* | *Strange letters had been **cut into** the stone.*

7 GO A QUICK WAY [I] to go somewhere by a quicker and more direct way than usual: *We **cut through/across** our neighbor's yard.*

C

8 ON A COMPUTER [T] to remove writing, a picture, etc. from a computer document: ***Cut and paste** the picture into a new file* (=remove it and move it to another place).

9 REMOVE PARTS FROM A MOVIE, ETC. [T] to remove parts from a movie, book, speech, etc.: *The original version was cut by more than 30 minutes.*

10 cut corners to do something less well than you should, in order to save time, effort, or money: *Parents are worried that the city is cutting corners in education.*

11 cut class/school to deliberately not go to class or school

12 cut your losses to stop doing something that is failing so that you do not waste any more money, time, or effort: *He decided to cut his losses and sell the business.*

13 cut sth short to end something earlier than you had planned: *His career was cut short by a back injury.*

SPOKEN PHRASES

14 not cut it to not be good enough to do something: *Barry's just not cutting it as a journalist.*

15 cut it close to leave yourself just enough time or money to do something: *He cut it pretty close, but he made it to the airport all right.*

[ORIGIN: 1200—1300 From an unrecorded Old English *cytan*] → **cut/give sb some slack** *at* SLACK²

cut across sth *phr. v.*
if a problem or feeling cuts across different groups of people, they are all affected by it: *Basketball's popularity cuts across racial lines.*

cut sth ↔ **back** *phr. v.*
to reduce the amount, size, cost, etc. of something: *Education spending cannot be cut back any further.* | *The company is attempting to **cut back on** expenses.*

cut down *phr. v.*
1 to eat, drink, or use less of something, especially in order to improve your health: *I've always smoked, but I'm trying to cut down.* | *I'm trying to **cut down on** the fat in my diet.*
2 cut sth ↔ **down** to reduce the amount of something: *Email cuts down the amount of paper passed between staff.* | *By getting the design right, you can **cut down on** accidents.*
3 cut sth ↔ **down** to cut a tree so that the whole of it falls to the ground: *Beautiful old oaks had been cut down to build houses.*

cut in *phr. v.*
cut in front/cut in line to unfairly go in front of other people who are waiting to do something: *Some idiot cut in front of me on the freeway and almost caused an accident.*

cut off *phr. v.*
1 cut sth ↔ **off** to separate something by cutting it away from the main part: *Cut the top off a large ripe pineapple.* | *His finger was cut off in the accident.*
2 cut sth ↔ **off** to stop the supply of something: *They're going to cut off our electricity if you don't pay that bill.*
3 be/get cut off to be unable to finish talking to someone because something is wrong with the telephone connection
4 be cut off if a place is cut off, it is difficult or impossible to get to or leave: *The ski resort was cut off by a heavy snowfall.*
5 cut sb **off** to interrupt someone: *He cut her off in mid-sentence.*

cut out *phr. v.*
1 cut sth ↔ **out** to remove something by cutting it with a knife or scissors: *The children cut star shapes out of colored paper.*
2 cut it/that out! (spoken) used in order to tell someone to stop doing something that is annoying you: *Cut that out, you two, or you'll go to your rooms.*
3 not be cut out for sth/to be sth to not have the qualities that you need for a particular job or activity: *I decided I wasn't really cut out to be a teacher.*

cut sth ↔ **up** *phr. v.*
to cut something into smaller pieces: *Cut up two carrots and three potatoes.*

cut² *n.* [C] **1** a reduction in the size, number, or amount of something: ***a cut in** government spending* | ***tax/job/budget etc. cuts*** **2** a wound that you get if a sharp object cuts your skin: *Luckily, I only got a few cuts and bruises.*

> THESAURUS **injury, wound, bruise, contusion, laceration, scrape, sprain, bump, fracture** → INJURY

3 a hole or mark in a surface made by something sharp: *Make a **cut in** the paper.* **4** [usually singular] (informal) a HAIRCUT **5** [usually singular] a share of something: *Everyone's taking a **cut of** the profits.* **6** a piece of meat that is cut so you can cook it: *tender cuts of beef* **7 be a cut above sb/sth** to be better than someone or something else: *The Yankees are clearly **a cut above the rest** of baseball.*

ˌcut and ˈdried *adj.* a situation, decision, or result that is cut and dried cannot be changed

cut·back /ˈkʌtbæk/ *n.* [C] a reduction in something, especially to save money: *a number of **cutbacks in** funding for public libraries*

cute /kyut/ *adj.* **1** attractive: *What a cute little baby!* | *a cute skirt* | *Tim is so cute.*

> THESAURUS **attractive, good-looking, nice-looking, pretty, beautiful, handsome, gorgeous, stunning, hot** → ATTRACTIVE

2 smart in a way that can seem rude: *Ignore him; he's just trying to be cute.* —**cutely** *adv.* —**cuteness** *n.* [U]

cu·ti·cle /'kyuṭɪkəl/ *n.* [C] the hard thin skin at the bottom of your FINGERNAILS

cut·ler·y /'kʌt˺ləri/ *n.* [U] knives, forks, and spoons (SYN) **silverware**

cut·let /'kʌt˺lɪt/ *n.* [C] a small flat piece of meat: *veal cutlets*

cut·off /'kʌṭɔf/ *n.* **1** [C] a time or level at which something stops: *The **cutoff date** for applying was June 3rd.* **2 cutoffs** [plural] a pair of SHORTS that you make by cutting off the bottom part of a pair of pants

'cut-rate *also* **'cut-price** *adj.* cheaper than normal: *cut-rate insurance*

cut·ter /'kʌṭɚ/ *n.* [C] a tool that cuts things: *wire cutters | a cookie cutter*

cut·throat /'kʌt˺θroʊt/ *adj.* a cutthroat activity or business involves people competing with each other in an unpleasant way: *cutthroat competition*

cut·ting /'kʌṭɪŋ/ *adj.* unkind and intended to upset someone: *a cutting remark*

'cutting board *n.* [C] a piece of wood or plastic that you cut food on when you are cooking

ˌcutting 'edge *n.* **the cutting edge (of sth)** the newest design or the most advanced way of doing something: *artists **on the cutting edge of** computer animation* —**cutting-edge** *adj.*: *cutting-edge technology*

cy·a·nide /'saɪəˌnaɪd/ *n.* [U] a very strong poison

cy·ber·ca·fé /'saɪbɚkæˌfeɪ/ *n.* [C] a CAFE where you can use computers connected to the Internet

cy·ber·space /'saɪbɚˌspeɪs/ *n.* [U] the imaginary place that electronic messages go through when they travel from one computer to another

cy·cle¹ /'saɪkəl/ (Ac) *n.* [C] a number of related events that happen again and again in the same order: *the **cycle of** the seasons | the plant's **life cycle** | The company's poor profits were put down to a temporary downturn in the business cycle.* [ORIGIN: 1300—1400 French, Late Latin *cyclus*, from Greek *kyklos* "circle, wheel, cycle"]

cycle² *v.* [I] **1** to ride a bicycle (SYN) **bike**: ***I cycled** to the store.* **2** to go through a series of related events again and again in the same order: *Waste water is cycled through the machine and reused.* —**cyclist** *n.* [C]

cy·cli·cal /'saɪklɪkəl, 'sɪ-/ (Ac) *also* **cy·clic** /'saɪklɪk, 'sɪ-/ *adj.* happening again and again in a regular pattern: *the cyclical nature of fashion* —**cyclically** *adv.*

cy·cl·ing /'saɪkəlɪŋ/ *n.* [U] the sport or activity of riding a bicycle

cy·clone /'saɪkloʊn/ *n.* [C] a TORNADO

cyl·in·der /'sɪləndɚ/ *n.* [C] **1** a shape, object, or container with circular ends and long straight sides → *see picture at* SHAPE¹

THESAURUS **shape, square, circle, semicircle, triangle, rectangle, oval** → SHAPE¹

2 the part of an engine that is shaped like a tube, where the PISTON moves up and down: *a six-cylinder engine* [ORIGIN: 1500—1600 Latin *cylindrus*, from Greek, from *kylindein* "to roll"]

cy·lin·dri·cal /sə'lɪndrɪkəl/ *adj.* in the shape of a cylinder

THESAURUS **oval, circular, round, semicircular, triangular, rectangular** → SHAPE¹

cym·bal /'sɪmbəl/ *n.* [C] a thin round metal plate that you hit to make a musical sound

cyn·ic /'sɪnɪk/ *n.* [C] a cynical person [ORIGIN: 1500—1600 Latin *cynicus*, from Greek *kynikos* "like a dog"] —**cynicism** /'sɪnəˌsɪzəm/ *n.* [U]

cyn·i·cal /'sɪnɪkəl/ *adj.* unwilling to believe that people have good, honest, or sincere reasons for doing something: *Since her divorce she's become very **cynical about** men.* —**cynically** *adv.*

cy·pher /'saɪfɚ/ *n.* [C] another spelling of CIPHER

Cy·ril·lic /sə'rɪlɪk/ *adj.* ENG. LANG. ARTS relating to the alphabet used for Russian, Bulgarian, and other Slavonic languages: *Cyrillic writing*

cyst /sɪst/ *n.* [C] BIOLOGY a small LUMP containing liquid, that grows in your body or under your skin

cy·to·plasm /'saɪṭəˌplæzəm/ *n.* [U] BIOLOGY all the material in the cell of a living thing except the NUCLEUS (=central part)

cy·to·skel·e·ton /ˌsaɪṭoʊ'skɛlət˺n/ *n.* [C] BIOLOGY a system of very thin connected tubes in the cytoplasm of a cell, that gives the cell its shape and structure

czar /zɑr/ *n.* [C] **1** (informal) someone who is very powerful in a particular job or activity: *the President's drug czar* **2** HISTORY a male ruler of Russia before 1917 [ORIGIN: 1500—1600 Russian *tsar*, from Gothic *kaisar* "emperor," from Greek, from Latin *Caesar*, from Julius *Caesar*]

Dd

D, d /di/ **1** the fourth letter of the English alphabet **2** the number 500 in the system of ROMAN NUMERALS

D /di/ *n.* **1** [C] a grade that a teacher gives to a student's work to show that it is poor and just above the point of failing: *I got a D on the history test.* **2** [C,U] ENG. LANG. ARTS the second note in the musical SCALE of C, or the musical KEY based on this note

d. the written abbreviation of DIED: *d. 1937*

-'d /d/ the short form of "would" or "had": *Ask her if she'd like to go with us.* | *If only I'd known you were there!*

D.A. *n.* [C] LAW a DISTRICT ATTORNEY

dab¹ /dæb/ *n.* [C] a small amount of something: *a* ***dab of*** *butter*

dab² *v.* (**dabbed**, **dabbing**) **1** [I,T] to lightly touch something several times, usually with a cloth: *Emily* ***dabbed at*** *her eyes* ***with*** *a handkerchief.* **2** [T] to quickly put a small amount of a substance onto something: *She* ***dabbed*** *some suntan lotion* ***onto*** *her cheeks.*

D

dab·ble /ˈdæbəl/ *v.* [I] to do something or be involved in something in a way that is not very serious: *He* ***dabbles in*** *art.*

dachs·hund /ˈdɑkshʊnt, -hʊnd/ *n.* [C] a small dog with short legs and a long body

dac·tyl /ˈdæktəl/ *n.* [C] ENG. LANG. ARTS a RHYTHM in poetry in which a STRESSed word or SYLLABLE is followed by two words or syllables that are not stressed, as in the word "poetry"

dad /dæd/ *also* **dad·dy** /ˈdædi/ *n.* [C] (informal) father: *I'm having dinner with my mom and dad.* | *Dad, can I borrow $20?* → RELATIVE¹

daf·fo·dil /ˈdæfəˌdɪl/ *n.* [C] a tall yellow flower that appears in early spring

dag·ger /ˈdægɚ/ *n.* [C] a short pointed knife used as a weapon

dai·ly¹ /ˈdeɪli/ *adj.* **1** happening, done, or produced every day: *daily flights to Miami* | *a daily newspaper*

THESAURUS **regular, hourly, weekly, monthly, yearly, annual** → REGULAR¹

2 relating to a single day: *a daily rate of pay* **3 daily life** the ordinary things that you usually do

daily² *adv.* every day: *The zoo is open daily.*

dain·ty /ˈdeɪnti/ *adj.* small, pretty, and delicate: *dainty white gloves*

dai·qui·ri /ˈdaɪkəri, ˈdæk-/ *n.* [C] a sweet alcoholic drink made with RUM and fruit juice

dair·y¹ /ˈdɛri/ *n.* (plural **dairies**) [C] **1** a place on a farm, where milk is kept and butter and cheese are made **2** a company that sells milk and makes cheese, butter, etc.

dairy² *adj.* [only before noun] **1** made from milk: *dairy products* **2** relating to the production of milk: *a dairy farm*

dai·sy /ˈdeɪzi/ *n.* (plural **daisies**) [C] a white flower with a bright yellow center [ORIGIN: Old English *dægeseage* "day's eye"]

dal·ly /ˈdæli/ *v.* (**dallied**, **dallies**) [I] (old-fashioned) to move slowly or waste time: *children dallying on their way to school*

Dal·ma·tian, dalmatian /dælˈmeɪʃən/ *n.* [C] a dog with white fur and small black or brown spots

dam

dam¹ /dæm/ *n.* [C] a wall built across a river in order to stop the water and make a lake

dam² *v.* (**dammed**, **damming**) [T] to build a dam across a river

dam·age¹ /ˈdæmɪdʒ/ *n.* [U] **1** physical harm that is done to something, so that it is broken or injured: *Was there any* ***damage to*** *your car?* | *The earthquake* ***caused/did*** *serious* ***damage.*** | ***brain damage*** **2** a bad effect on someone or something: *The closure of the factory will cause severe* ***damage to*** *the local economy.* **3 damages** [plural] LAW money that a court orders someone to pay someone else for harming that person or his/her property: *The court ordered her to pay $2,000* ***in damages.*** [ORIGIN: 1200—1300 Old French *dam* "damage," from Latin *damnum* "damage, loss"]

damage² *v.* [T] **1** to physically harm someone or something: *The storm damaged the tobacco crop.* **2** to have a bad effect on someone or something: *She didn't want to do anything that would damage her reputation.* —**damaging** *adj.*

dame /deɪm/ *n.* [C] (old-fashioned) a woman

damn /dæmd/ *v.* **be damned** to be punished by God after your death by being sent to HELL

damn·ing /ˈdæmɪŋ/ *adj.* showing that someone has done something very bad or wrong: *damning evidence*

damp /dæmp/ *adj.* slightly wet, usually in a cold and unpleasant way: *The house was cold and damp.* | *a damp sponge* | *damp weather* —**dampness** *n.* [U]

THESAURUS

humid – used to say that the weather, especially hot weather, is slightly wet and makes you uncomfortable: *humid weather/climate* | *It's unbearably humid.*

moist – used to say that something, especially food, is slightly wet, especially in a way that seems nice: *The turkey was moist and tender.* | *moist cake*

clammy – wet, cold, and sticky in a way that is unpleasant: *My mother's hand felt clammy.*

damp·en /ˈdæmpən/ *v.* [T] **1** to make something slightly wet **2** to make something such as a feeling or activity less strong: *The rainy weather didn't* ***dampen*** *our* ***enthusiasm****.*

damp·er /ˈdæmpɚ/ *n.* **put a damper on sth** to stop something from being enjoyable: *The sad news put a damper on our celebrations.*

dam·sel /ˈdæmzəl/ *n.* **damsel in distress** (humorous) a young woman who needs help

dance[1] /dæns/ *v.* **1** [I] to move your body to match the style and speed of music: *Would you like to dance?* | *Jack* ***danced with*** *his wife.* | *The children* ***danced to*** *the radio.* **2 dance the waltz/tango etc.** to do a particular type of dance —**dancer** *n.* [C] —**dancing** *n.* [U]: *We* ***go dancing*** *every Friday night.*

dance[2] *n.* **1** [C] an act of dancing: *May I have this dance* (=will you dance with me)*?* **2** [C] a particular set of movements that you perform with music: *The only dance I know is the tango.* **3** [C] a social event or party where you dance: *a school dance*

THESAURUS

ball – a large formal occasion where people dance
prom – a formal dance party for high school students, usually held at the end of a school year
formal – a dance at which you have to wear formal clothes

4 [U] the art or activity of dancing: *dance lessons* | *modern dance*

dan·de·li·on /ˈdændəˌlaɪən/ *n.* [C] a small bright yellow wild flower [ORIGIN: 1400—1500 French *dent de lion* "lion's tooth" (because of the shape of the leaves)]

dan·druff /ˈdændrəf/ *n.* [U] small white pieces of dead skin from your head

dan·dy /ˈdændi/ *adj.* (humorous) very good: *This gadget makes a dandy present for a cook.*

dan·ger /ˈdeɪndʒɚ/ *n.* **1** [C,U] the possibility that someone or something will be harmed, or that something bad will happen: *Is there any* ***danger of*** *infection?* | *The UN wants to move civilians who are* ***in danger*** (=in a dangerous situation). | *Margie is* ***in danger of*** *losing her job.* | *There is a* ***danger that*** *museums will attempt to entertain rather than educate.*

THESAURUS

risk – the chance that something bad may happen: *Smoking greatly increases the risk of lung cancer.*
threat – the possibility that something bad will happen: *At that time, there seemed to be a constant threat of nuclear war.*
hazard – something that may be dangerous or cause accidents, problems, etc.: *Lighting fires in the park is a safety hazard.*
peril (formal) – danger of being harmed or killed: *They prayed for the sailors in peril on the sea.*

2 [C] something or someone that may harm you: *the* ***dangers of*** *scuba diving* | *He's a* ***danger to*** *the community.* [ORIGIN: 1200—1300 Old French *dangier*, from Vulgar Latin *dominiarium* "power to do harm"]

dan·ger·ous /ˈdeɪndʒərəs/ *adj.* **1** able or likely to harm you: *a dangerous criminal* | *Cigarette smoking is* ***dangerous to*** *your health.* | *It's* ***dangerous for*** *women* ***to*** *walk alone at night.* | *Even tiny amounts of the gas are* ***extremely/highly etc. dangerous****.* **2** likely to cause problems, or involving a lot of risk: *The company is in a dangerous financial position.* —**dangerously** *adv.*

dan·gle /ˈdæŋgəl/ *v.* [I,T] to hang or swing loosely, or to make something do this: *keys* ***dangling from*** *a chain*

da·nish /ˈdeɪnɪʃ/ *n.* [C] a small sweet type of cake, often with fruit inside

dank /dæŋk/ *adj.* wet and cold, in a way that does not feel nice

dap·per /ˈdæpɚ/ *adj.* a dapper man is neatly dressed

dare[1] /dɛr/ *v.* **1** [T] to try to persuade someone to do something dangerous: ***I dare*** *you* ***to*** *jump!* **2** [I] to be brave enough to do something, used especially in negative sentences: *Susan wouldn't dare tell the boss he was wrong.* **3 don't you dare** (spoken) said in order to warn someone not to do something because it makes you angry: *Don't you dare be late!* **4 how dare you/he etc.** (spoken) said when you are very upset about what someone has said or done: *How dare you lie to me!*

dare[2] *n.* [C] something dangerous that you have dared someone to do: *He swam across the river* ***on a dare****.*

dare·dev·il /ˈdɛrˌdɛvəl/ *n.* [C] someone who likes doing dangerous things —**daredevil** *adj.*

dar·ing[1] /ˈdɛrɪŋ/ *adj.* **1** involving danger, or willing to do dangerous things: *a daring escape*

THESAURUS **brave, courageous, heroic, valiant, bold, fearless, intrepid** → BRAVE[1]

2 new or unusual in a way that may shock some people: *a daring movie*

daring[2] *n.* [U] courage that makes you willing to take risks

dark[1] /dɑrk/ *adj.* **1** with very little or no light (ANT) **light**: *a dark room* | *Turn on the light; it's dark in here.* | *We'd better go home;* ***it's getting dark*** (=it is becoming night). | *Suddenly the room* ***went dark*** (=became dark). **2** closer to black than to white in color → LIGHT: *a dark blue tie* | *dark hair* **3** a dark person has black hair, brown skin, or brown eyes (ANT) **fair**: *a small dark woman* **4** threatening, mysterious, or frightening: *a dark side to his character* **5** unhappy or without hope: *the dark days of the war* [ORIGIN: Old English *deorc*]

dark[2] *n.* **1 the dark** a situation in which there is no light: *My son is afraid of the dark.* **2 after/before dark** at night or before night begins: *Don't go out after dark.* **3 in the dark** (informal) not knowing about something important because no one has told you about it: *Employees were **kept in the dark** about the possible layoffs.*

dark·en /ˈdɑrkən/ *v.* [I,T] to make something dark, or to become dark: *The sky darkened before the storm.* | *a darkened room*

ˌdark ˈhorse *n.* [C] someone who is not well known and who surprises people by winning a competition

dark·ly /ˈdɑrkli/ *adv.* in a sad, angry, or threatening way: *scientists speaking darkly about the future*

dark·ness /ˈdɑrknɪs/ *n.* [U] a place or time when there is no light: *The whole room was **in darkness**.* | *We made it home just as **darkness fell*** (=it became night).

D

dark·room /ˈdɑrkrum/ *n.* [C] a special room with a red light or no light, where film from a camera is made into photographs

dar·ling¹ /ˈdɑrlɪŋ/ *n.* [C] (spoken) used when speaking to someone you love: *Come here, darling.*

darling² *adj.* [only before noun] much loved: *my darling child*

darn¹ /dɑrn/ *v.* **1 darn it!** (spoken) said when you are annoyed about something: *Darn it! I broke my shoelace.* **2** [T] to repair a hole in clothes by sewing thread through it many times

darn² *also* **darned** *adj., adv.* (spoken) said in order to emphasize what you are saying: *a darned good movie* | *The darn fool got lost.*

darned /dɑrnd/ *adj.* **I'll be darned** (spoken) said when you are surprised about something: *You went to Rutgers too? Well, I'll be darned.*

dart¹ /dɑrt/ *n.* **1** [C] a small pointed object that is thrown in a game of darts or used as a weapon **2 darts** [U] a game in which you throw darts at a circular board: *A couple of men were **playing darts**.*

dart² *v.* [I] to move suddenly and quickly in a particular direction: *The dog **darted into** the street.*

dash¹ /dæʃ/ *v.* **1** [I] to go somewhere very quickly: *She **dashed into** the room just before the boss arrived.*

THESAURUS **run, sprint, tear, race, bolt** → RUN¹
rush, race, hurry, charge, speed, hasten → RUSH¹

2 dash sb's hopes to ruin someone's hopes completely: *Her hopes of running in the Olympics were dashed after the accident.* **3** [T] to make something hit violently against something else: *The ship was **dashed against** the rocks.*

dash off *phr. v.* **1 dash** sth ↔ **off** to write or draw something very quickly **2** to leave somewhere very quickly

dash² *n.* **1 make a dash for sth** to run very quickly toward something: *I made a dash for the house to get my umbrella.* **2** [singular] a small amount of a liquid: *a **dash of** lemon* **3** [C] ENG. LANG. ARTS a mark (–) used in writing to separate parts of a sentence **4** [C] dashboard

dash·board /ˈdæʃbɔrd/ *n.* [C] the board in front of the driver in a car, that has the controls on it [ORIGIN: 1800—1900 *dash* "to strike with small drops of liquid" (17—19 centuries) + *board* (because it was originally a board to stop mud getting into a vehicle)]

DAT /dæt/ *n.* [U] **digital audio tape** tape for recording music, sound, or information in DIGITAL form

da·ta /ˈdeɪt̬ə, ˈdæt̬ə/ (Ac) *n.* [U, plural] **1** information or facts: *He's **collecting data** for his report.* | *The team gathered **data on** voting patterns in each state.* **2** IT information stored and used on a computer: *This laptop can **store** as much **data** as many larger PCs.* [ORIGIN: 1600—1700 plural of *datum* "fact, piece of information" (17—21 centuries), from Latin, past participle of *dare* "to give"]

da·ta·base /ˈdeɪt̬əˌbeɪs/ *n.* [C] IT a large amount of data stored in a computer system

ˈdata ˌmining *n.* [U] IT the process of using a computer to find new patterns and relationships in large amounts of information kept on a computer

ˌdata ˈprocessing *n.* [U] IT the use of computers to store and organize information

date¹ /deɪt/ *n.* [C] **1** a particular day of the month or of the year, shown by a number: *"What's today's date?" "It's August 11th."* | *Have you **set a date** (=chosen a day) for the wedding?* | *She refused to give her **date of birth/birth date*** (=the day she was born). **2** an arrangement to meet someone, especially someone you like in a romantic way: *Mike's **going (out) on a date** on Friday.* | *I **have a date with** Andrea tomorrow night.* | *Let's **make a date*** (=arrange a time) *to see that new movie.* **3** someone you go on a date with: *My date's taking me out to dinner.* **4 to date** up to now: *This is the best research on the subject to date.* **5 at a later date** at some time in the future **6** a small sweet sticky brown fruit with a single long seed [ORIGIN: (1) 1200—1300 Old French, Greek *daktylos* "finger"] → OUT-OF-DATE, UP-TO-DATE

date² *v.* **1** [I,T] to have a romantic relationship with someone: *How long have you been dating Mona?* **2** [T] to write the date on something: *a letter dated May 1, 2007* **3** [T] to find out the age of something that is very old: *Scientists have not yet dated the human remains.*

date from sth *also* **date back to** sth *phr. v.* to have existed since a particular time: *Independence Hall dates from the 17th century.*

dat·ed /ˈdeɪt̬ɪd/ *adj.* no longer fashionable: *These shoes are really dated.*

THESAURUS **old-fashioned, outdated, out-of-date, outmoded, antiquated, obsolete** → OLD-FASHIONED

'date rape *n.* [C,U] a RAPE that happens during a date

da·tive /'deɪt̬ɪv/ *n.* [C] ENG. LANG. ARTS a form of a noun, in languages such as Latin and German, that shows that the noun is the INDIRECT OBJECT of a verb ➔ ACCUSATIVE

daub /dɔb/ *v.* [T] to put paint or a soft substance on a surface in a careless way [ORIGIN: 1300—1400 Old French *dauber*, from Latin *dealbare* "to make white, whitewash"]

daugh·ter /'dɔt̬ɚ/ *n.* [C] someone's female child ➔ SON: *the* ***daughter of*** *a local farmer* [ORIGIN: Old English *dohtor*]

'daughter-in-law *n.* (plural **daughters-in-law**) [C] the wife of your son

daunt·ed /'dɔntɪd/ *adj.* [not before noun] feeling afraid or worried: *Cooper is feeling* ***daunted by*** *his new responsibilities.*

daunt·ing /'dɔntɪŋ/ *adj.* frightening or worrying: *a daunting task*

daw·dle /'dɔdl/ *v.* [I] to take a long time to do something or go somewhere: *Stop dawdling; we'll be late.*

dawn¹ /dɔn/ *n.* [C,U] **1** the time of day when light first appears: *We talked until dawn.* | *I got up* ***at dawn*** *to milk the cows.* | *As* ***dawn broke*** (=it started to get light), *the fire was under control.* | *The boat left* ***at the crack of dawn*** (=very early in the morning). **2 the dawn of sth** the time when something began or first appeared: *the dawn of civilization* [ORIGIN: 1200—1300 *daw* "to dawn" (10—19 centuries), from Old English *dagian*; related to *day*]

dawn² *v.* [I] if a day or morning dawns, it begins: *The morning dawned cool and clear.*

dawn on sb *phr. v.* to realize something for the first time: ***It*** *suddenly* ***dawned on*** *me* ***that*** *he was right.*

day /deɪ/ *n.*

1 24 HOURS [C] a period of time equal to 24 hours ➔ DAILY: *I'll be back in ten days.* | *The letter arrived two days ago.* | *"What day is it today?" "Tuesday."* | *The* ***next/following day****, Hayes was fired.* | *I got a phone call from Eve* ***the other day*** (=a few days ago). | *We're leaving for Arizona* ***the day after tomorrow****.* | *I saw Margo* ***the day before yesterday****.* ▸Don't say "We're leaving for Arizona after tomorrow" or "I saw Margo before yesterday."◂

2 MORNING UNTIL NIGHT [C,U] the period of time between when it becomes light in the morning and when it becomes dark in the evening (ANT) **night**: *The days begin to get longer in the spring.* | *a beautiful summer day*

3 WHEN YOU ARE AWAKE [C usually singular] the time during the day when you are usually awake: *He started his day with a three-mile run.* | *It's been a* ***long day*** (=a day when you had to get up early and were busy all day). | *Jan's been studying* ***all day*** (=for the whole day).

4 WORK [C] the hours you work in a day: *I work an eight-hour day.* | *Did you have a* ***good day*** *at work?* | *I need a* ***day off*** (=a day when you do not have to work).

5 PAST [C] used in order to talk about a time in the past: ***One day*** (=on a day in the past), *the police came and took her away.* | *Things were different* ***in my day*** (=when I was young). | *I didn't like him* ***from day one*** (=from the beginning). | *Grandpa was telling stories about* ***the good old days*** (=a time in the past when things seemed better than now).

6 NOW [C] used in order to talk about the situation that exists now: *It's not safe to walk the streets* ***these days*** (=now). | ***To this day*** (=until and including now), *we haven't heard the whole story.*

7 FUTURE [C] used in order to talk about a time in the future: *We'll buy our dream home* ***one/some day*** (=at some time in the future). | ***One of these days*** (=some time soon), *he's going to end up in jail.* | *Kelly's expecting the baby* ***any day now*** (=very soon).

8 make sb's day (informal) to make someone very happy: *That card made my day.*

9 has had its day to no longer be popular or successful: *The old steam trains have had their day.*

10 those were the days (spoken) used in order to say that a time in the past was better than the present time

11 day after day/day in day out used in order to emphasize that something bad or boring continues to happen: *I drive the same route to work day in day out.*

12 from day to day/from one day to the next if a situation changes from day to day or from one day to the next, it changes often: *My job changes from day to day.*

13 day by day slowly and gradually: *She was getting stronger day by day.*

14 sb's days (literary) the time when someone is alive: *He began his days in a small town.*

15 be working days/be on days to work during the day at a job you sometimes have to do at night [ORIGIN: Old English *dæg*] ➔ DAILY¹, **call it a day** *at* CALL¹

> **GRAMMAR**
>
> Use **on** to talk about a particular day of the week: *The class is on Monday.*
> Use **this** to talk about a day that is during the week that we are in now: *Can we meet up this Thursday?*
> Use **next** to talk about a day in the week after this one: *See you next Saturday.*
> Use **last** to talk about a day in the week before this one: *She left last Friday.*

day·break /'deɪbreɪk/ *n.* [U] the time of day when light first appears (SYN) **dawn**: *We broke camp* ***at daybreak****.*

'day camp *n.* [C] a place where children go during the day to do activities, sports, art, etc. on their summer vacation from school

day·care /'deɪker/ *n.* [U] care of young children,

D

or of sick or old people, during the day: *a daycare center* | *My youngest boy is **in daycare**.*

day·dream /ˈdeɪdrim/ *v.* [I] to think about nice things so that you forget what you should be doing: *Joan sat at her desk, **daydreaming about** Tom.* —**daydream** *n.* [C] —**daydreamer** *n.* [C]

> THESAURUS **imagine, visualize, picture, fantasize, envision, envisage** → IMAGINE

Day-Glo /ˈdeɪ gloʊ/ *adj.* (trademark) having a very bright orange, green, yellow, or pink color

day·light /ˈdeɪlaɪt/ *n.* **1** [U] the light produced by the Sun during the day: *The market is crowded during **daylight hours**.* | *She was attacked **in broad daylight*** (=during the day when it is light). **2 scare/frighten the (living) daylights out of sb** (informal) to frighten someone a lot **3 beat the (living) daylights out of sb** (informal) to hit someone many times and hurt him/her badly

D

ˌdaylight ˈsaving time *also* **ˌdaylight ˈsavings** *n.* [U] the time in the spring when clocks are set one hour ahead of standard time

day·time /ˈdeɪtaɪm/ *n.* [U] the time between when it gets light in the morning and when it gets dark in the evening (ANT) **nighttime**: *I've never been here **in/during the daytime**.* | *daytime talk shows*

ˌday-to-ˈday *adj.* happening every day as a regular part of life: *our day-to-day routine at work*

daze /deɪz/ *n.* **in a daze** unable to think clearly

dazed /deɪzd/ *adj.* unable to think clearly, usually because you are shocked, have been hurt, etc.: *dazed victims of the bombing*

daz·zle /ˈdæzəl/ *v.* [T] **1** if a very bright light dazzles you, you are unable to see for a short time **2** to make someone admire someone or something a lot: *We were all dazzled by her charm.*

daz·zling /ˈdæzlɪŋ/ *adj.* **1** very impressive, exciting, or interesting: *a dazzling performance*

> THESAURUS **impressive, imposing, awe-inspiring, breathtaking, majestic, magnificent** → IMPRESSIVE

2 a dazzling light is so bright that you cannot see for a short time after you look at it

> THESAURUS **bright, strong, brilliant, glaring, blinding** → BRIGHT

DC PHYSICS the abbreviation of DIRECT CURRENT

D.C. *n.* **District of Columbia** the area containing the city of Washington, the capital of the U.S.

DDT *n.* [U] a chemical used in order to kill insects that harm crops, which is now illegal

DE the written abbreviation of DELAWARE

dea·con /ˈdikən/, **dea·con·ess** /ˈdikəˌnɛs/ *n.* [C] a religious official in some Christian churches

de·ac·ti·vate /diˈæktəˌveɪt/ *v.* [T] to SWITCH a piece of equipment off, or to stop it from working

dead¹ /dɛd/ *adj.*
1 NOT ALIVE no longer alive: *Her mom's been dead for two years.* | *I think that plant is dead.* | *She found a **dead body*** (=a dead person) *in the woods.*

> USAGE
> **Dead** is an adjective used to describe people or things that are no longer alive: *a dead fish*
> **Died** is the past tense and past participle of the verb "to die," used to talk about how and when someone died: *He died of a heart attack when he was only 58.*

> THESAURUS
> **lifeless** (literary) – dead or seeming to be dead: *dull, lifeless eyes*
> **late/deceased** (formal) – dead: *her late husband* | *their recently deceased grandmother*

2 NOT WORKING not working, especially because there is no power: *Is the **battery dead**?* | *The phones **went dead** during the storm.*
3 PLACE [not before noun] a place that is dead is boring because nothing interesting happens there: *The bar is usually dead until around 10:00.*
4 NOT USED no longer active or being used: *He says the peace plan is dead.* | *a dead language*
5 COMPLETE [only before noun] complete or exact: *For about five minutes, there was **dead silence**.* | *Hit the **dead center** of the nail so it doesn't bend.* | *The train came to a **dead stop**.*
6 TIRED [not before noun] (informal) very tired: *I think I'll go to bed early; I'm absolutely dead.*
7 PART OF BODY a part of your body that is dead has no feeling in it for a short time: *I'd been sitting so long my legs **went dead**.*
8 over my dead body (spoken) used when you are determined not to allow something to happen: *You'll marry him over my dead body!*
9 IN TROUBLE (spoken) *also* **dead meat** in serious trouble: *If anything happens to the car, you're dead!*
10 sb wouldn't be caught/seen dead in sth (spoken) used to say that someone would never wear particular clothes, go to particular places, or do particular things because s/he would feel embarrassed: *I wouldn't be caught dead in a dress like that!* [ORIGIN: Old English]

dead² *adv.* (informal) completely or exactly: *Paula **stopped dead** when she saw us.* | *I'm **dead tired**.* | *You can't miss it; it's **dead ahead**.*

dead³ *n.* **1 in the dead of winter/night** in the middle of winter or in the middle of the night **2 the dead** [plural] all the people who have died (ANT) **the living**

dead·beat /ˈdɛdbiːt/ *n.* [C] someone who does not pay his/her debts

dead·en /ˈdɛdn/ *v.* [T] to make a feeling or sound less strong: *a drug to deaden the pain*

ˌdead ˈend *n.* [C] **1** a street with no way out at one end **2** a situation from which no progress is possible

dead·line /ˈdɛdlaɪn/ *n.* [C] a time by which you must finish something: *The **deadline for** applications is May 27th.* | *Can you **meet the deadline**?*

dead·lock /ˈdɛdlɑk/ *n.* [C,U] a situation in which a disagreement cannot be settled: *The UN is attempting to **break the deadlock*** (=end it) *in the region.*

dead·ly /ˈdɛdli/ *adj.* very dangerous and likely to cause death: *a deadly virus*

dead·pan /ˈdɛdpæn/ *adj.* sounding and looking completely serious when you are not: *a deadpan sense of humor*

deaf /dɛf/ *adj.* **1** physically unable to hear, or unable to hear well → HEARING IMPAIRED: *I'm deaf in my right ear.* **2 the deaf** [plural] people who are deaf **3 be deaf to sth** unwilling to listen to something: *The guards were deaf to the prisoners' complaints.* **4 fall on deaf ears** if something you say falls on deaf ears, everyone ignores it [ORIGIN: Old English] —**deafness** *n.* [U]

deaf·en·ing /ˈdɛfənɪŋ/ *adj.* **1** noise or music that is deafening is very loud

THESAURUS **loud, noisy, rowdy, thunderous, ear-splitting, shrill, raucous, resounding, sonorous** → LOUD¹

2 deafening silence complete silence, used especially when this is uncomfortable or unusual —**deafen** *v.* [T]

deal¹ /dil/ *n.* **1** [C] an agreement or arrangement, especially in business or politics: *She has just signed a new book deal with a different publisher.* | *Diaz tried to **cut/make/strike a deal** with the government.* | *You can **get** some **good deals*** (=buy things at a good price) *at the new travel agency.* | *"I'll give you $100 for your TV." "OK, **it's a deal**."* **2 a great/good deal** a large quantity of something: *The new exhibit has gotten **a good deal of** attention.* | *He knows a great deal more* (=a lot more) *than I do about computers.* **3** [C usually singular] the way someone is treated in a situation: *This new law is **a fair deal** for the American taxpayer.* | *Women often get **a raw deal*** (=unfair treatment) *from their employers.* **4 what's the deal?** (spoken) used when you want to know what is happening in a situation: *So what's the deal? Why is he so mad?* **5** [singular] the process of giving out cards to players in a card game: *It's your deal.* → BIG DEAL

deal² *v.* (past tense and past participle **dealt** /dɛlt/) [I,T] **1** *also* **deal out** to give out playing cards to players in a game: *It's my **turn to deal**.* **2** to buy and sell illegal drugs: *He was arrested for dealing heroin.* **3 deal a blow (to sb/sth)** to harm someone or something: *The ban dealt a severe blow to local tourism.*

deal in sth *phr. v.* to buy and sell a particular product: *a business dealing in medical equipment*

deal with sb/sth *phr. v.* **1** to do what is necessary, especially in order to solve a problem: *Who's dealing with the new account?*

THESAURUS

handle – to deal with someone or something: *He's finding it hard to handle the pressure at work.*
tackle – to try to deal with a difficult problem: *There are still a number of problems which we need to tackle.*
cope – to succeed in dealing with a difficult problem or situation: *Exercise can help people cope with stress.*
attend to sb/sth – to give attention to someone or something: *I have some business to attend to.*
take care of sth – to do the work or make the arrangements that are necessary for something to happen: *I'll take care of making the reservations.*

2 to succeed in controlling your feelings and being patient in a difficult situation: *I can't deal with any more crying children today.* **3** to do business with someone: *We've been dealing with their company for ten years.* **4** to be about a particular subject: *a book dealing with 20th-century art*

deal·er /ˈdilɚ/ *n.* [C] **1** someone who buys and sells a particular product: *a car dealer* **2** someone who buys and sells illegal drugs **3** someone who gives out the playing cards in a game

deal·er·ship /ˈdilɚˌʃɪp/ *n.* [C] a business that sells a particular company's product, especially cars

deal·ing /ˈdilɪŋ/ *n.* **1** [U] the buying and selling of things: *penalties for drug dealing* **2 dealings** [plural] personal or business relations with someone: *Have you had any **dealings with** IBM?*

dealt /dɛlt/ *v.* the past tense and past participle of DEAL

dean /din/ *n.* [C] a university official with a high rank: *the dean of admissions* [ORIGIN: 1300—1400 Old French *deien*, from Late Latin *decanus* "person in charge of ten others"]

ˈdean's list *n.* [C] a list of the best students at a university

dear¹ /dɪr/ *interjection* said when you are surprised, annoyed, or upset: ***Oh dear!** I forgot to phone Jill.*

dear² *n.* [C] (spoken) used when speaking to someone you like or love: *How was your day, dear?*

dear³ *adj.* **1** used before a name at the beginning of a letter: *Dear Sue, ...* | *Dear Dr. Ward, ...* **2** much loved and very important to you: *She's a **dear friend**.*

dear·ly /ˈdɪrli/ *adv.* very much: *Sam **loved** her **dearly**.*

dearth /dɚθ/ *n.* [singular] (formal) a lack of something: *a **dearth of** original ideas*

death /dɛθ/ *n.* **1** [C,U] the end of a person's or animal's life (ANT) **birth**: *Maretti lived in Miami until his death.* | *Heart disease is the number one **cause of death** in the U.S.* | *The number of **deaths from** AIDS is increasing.* | *He choked **to death*** (=choked until he died) *on a fish bone.* | *The horse was so badly injured it had to be **put to death*** (=killed). **2 be bored/scared etc. to death**

(informal) to be very bored, afraid, etc. **3 the death of sth** the permanent end of something: *the death of Communism* → **be sick (and tired) of/be sick to death of** *at* SICK

death·bed /ˈdɛθbɛd/ *n.* **sb's deathbed** the point in time when someone is dying and will be dead very soon: *Marquez flew home to be with his mother, who was **on her deathbed**.*

death knell /ˈdeθ nɛl/ *n.* [singular] a sign that something will soon stop existing or stop being used: *The new bridge will be **the death knell for** the ferry crossing.*

ˈdeath ˌpenalty *n.* [singular] the legal punishment of being killed for a serious crime: *Gilmore was **given the death penalty** for murder.* → CAPITAL PUNISHMENT

ˌdeath ˈrow *n.* [U] the part of a prison where prisoners are kept before they are killed as a punishment: *a murderer **on death row***

ˈdeath toll *n.* [C usually singular] the total number of people who die in an accident, war, etc.

ˈdeath trap *n.* [C] (informal) a vehicle, building, etc. that is in such bad condition that it might injure or kill someone

de·ba·cle /deɪˈbɑkəl, -ˈbæ-/ *n.* [C] an event or situation that is a complete failure (SYN) **fiasco** [ORIGIN: 1800—1900 French *débâcle*, from *débâcler* "to remove a bar"]

de·base /dɪˈbeɪs/ *v.* [T] (formal) to make someone or something lose its value or people's respect —**debasement** *n.* [C,U]

de·bat·a·ble /dɪˈbeɪt̬əbəl/ (Ac) *adj.* an idea, fact, or decision that is debatable may be right but it could easily be wrong: *It is **debatable whether** alternative medical treatments actually work.*

de·bate¹ /dɪˈbeɪt/ (Ac) *n.* [C,U] **1** a discussion or argument on a subject in which people express different opinions: *a **debate about/over/on** equal pay* | *The drug has become the subject of a **heated/fierce/intense debate** within the medical profession.* **2** a formal discussion of a subject in which people express different opinions, and sometimes vote: *After much debate, the committee decided to raise the fees.* | *a **debate on/about** welfare reform* [ORIGIN: 1200—1300 Old French *debatre*, from *batre* "to hit"]

THESAURUS **discussion, negotiations, talks, conference, dialogue** → DISCUSSION

debate² *v.* **1** [I,T] to discuss a subject formally so that you can make a decision or solve a problem: *The Senate is debating the future of health care.* | *We were **debating which** person to hire.* | *The impact of the reforms has been **hotly debated** by economists.* **2** [T] to think about something carefully before making a decision: *I was **debating whether** to go to work.*

de·bauch /dɪˈbɔtʃ, -ˈbɑtʃ/ *v.* [T] (formal) to make someone behave in an immoral way, especially with alcohol, drugs, or sex —**debauched** *adj.*

de·bauch·e·ry /dɪˈbɔtʃəri/ *n.* [U] immoral behavior involving drugs, alcohol, sex, etc.

de·bil·i·tat·ing /dɪˈbɪləˌteɪt̬ɪŋ/ *adj.* a debilitating disease or condition makes your body or mind weak: *a debilitating illness* —**debility** /dɪˈbɪlət̬i/ *n.* [C,U]

deb·it¹ /ˈdɛbɪt/ *n.* [C] an amount of money that has been taken out of your bank account (ANT) **credit**

debit² *v.* [T] to take money out of a bank account (ANT) **credit**: *The payment has been **debited from** your account.*

ˈdebit card *n.* [C] a plastic card that you can use to buy goods or services. The money is taken directly from your bank account. → CREDIT CARD

deb·o·nair /ˌdɛbəˈnɛr/ *adj.* a man who is debonair is fashionable and confident [ORIGIN: 1200—1300 Old French *de bonne aire* "of good family or nature"]

de·brief /diˈbrif/ *v.* [T] to officially ask someone such as a soldier to give a report of a job that s/he has just done —**debriefing** *n.* [C,U]

de·bris /dɪˈbri/ *n.* [U] the pieces remaining from something that has been destroyed: *The street was full of debris after the explosion.*

debt /dɛt/ *n.* **1** [C,U] money that you owe to someone: *Al can finally **pay off** his **debts**.* | ***debts of** $25 million* | *a company **heavily in debt*** (=owing a lot of money) | *He lost his job and **fell/went/got into debt**.* **2** [singular] the degree to which you have been influenced by, or helped by, someone or something: *Our organization **owes a** great **debt of gratitude** to Martha Graham.* | *She **is** forever **in** his **debt*** (=thankful for something someone has done for her). [ORIGIN: 1200—1300 Old French *dette*, from Latin *debitum*, from *debere* "to owe"]

debt·or /ˈdɛt̬ɚ/ *n.* [C] someone who owes money

de·bug /diˈbʌg/ *v.* (**debugged**, **debugging**) [T] IT to take the mistakes out of a computer program

de·bunk /diˈbʌŋk/ *v.* [T] to show that an idea or belief is false

de·but /deɪˈbyu, ˈdeɪbyu/ *n.* [C] the first time that a performer or sports player performs in public: *her debut album* | *his Broadway debut* | *Foster **made** her **debut** in movies at a young age.* [ORIGIN: 1700—1800 French *début*, from *débuter* "to begin," from *but* "starting point"] —**debut** *v.* [I]

dec·ade /ˈdɛkeɪd/ (Ac) *n.* [C] a period of ten years: *The cost of health care has doubled in the last decade.* [ORIGIN: 1400—1500 French *décade*, from Greek *dekas*, from *deka* "ten"]

dec·a·dent /ˈdɛkədənt/ *adj.* having low moral standards and interested only in pleasure: *a decadent lifestyle* —**decadence** *n.* [U]

de·caf /ˈdikæf/ *n.* [U] decaffeinated coffee

de·caf·fein·at·ed /diˈkæfəˌneɪt̬ɪd/ *adj.* decaffeinated drinks have had the CAFFEINE removed: *decaffeinated coffee*

dec·a·gon /ˈdekəˌɡɑn/ *n.* [C] MATH a flat shape with ten straight sides and ten angles

THESAURUS **polygon, pentagon, hexagon, heptagon, octagon, dodecagon** → POLYGON

de·cal /ˈdikæl/ *n.* [C] a piece of paper with a pattern or picture on it that you stick onto a surface

de·cant·er /dɪˈkæntɚ/ *n.* [C] a container used for serving alcoholic drinks

de·cap·i·tate /dɪˈkæpəˌteɪt/ *v.* [T] to cut off someone's head: *a decapitated body* —**decapitation** /dɪˌkæpəˈteɪʃən/ *n.* [C,U]

dec·ath·lon /dɪˈkæθlɑn, -lən/ *n.* [singular] a sports competition consisting of ten running, jumping, and throwing events → HEPTATHLON, PENTATHLON

de·cay[1] /dɪˈkeɪ/ *v.* **1** [I,T] to be slowly destroyed by a natural chemical process, or to destroy something in this way: *The dead animal started to decay.* | *Sugar decays teeth.*

THESAURUS

rot – to decay by a gradual natural process, or to make something do this: *Old food was rotting on the table.*
decompose – to decay, or to make something decay: *a decomposed body*
putrefy (formal) – to decay and smell very bad: *The dead bodies had putrefied in the Sun.*

2 [I] if buildings decay, they are slowly destroyed because no one takes care of them: *the decaying downtown area* [ORIGIN: 1400—1500 Old North French *decaïr*, from Late Latin *decadere* "to fall, sink"]

decay[2] *n.* [U] the process, state, or result of decaying: ***tooth decay*** | *The building has **fallen into decay**.*

de'cay rate *n.* [C] PHYSICS the speed at which a RADIOACTIVE substance breaks apart and sends out ATOMIC PARTICLES or RADIATION

de·ceased /dɪˈsist/ *adj.* (formal) **1** dead: *Both my parents are deceased.*

THESAURUS **dead, lifeless, late** → DEAD[1]

2 the deceased someone who has recently died [ORIGIN: 1300—1400 *decease* "to die" (15—19 centuries), from French *décès* "death," from Latin *decedere* "to leave, die"]

de·ceit /dɪˈsit/ *n.* [U] behavior that is intended to make someone believe something that is not true: *lies and deceit* —**deceitful** *adj.*

de·ceive /dɪˈsiv/ *v.* [T] **1** to make someone believe something that is not true: *Owen tried to deceive the police.* | *Customers were **deceived into** paying more than they should have.*

THESAURUS **lie, make sth up, tell (sb) a lie, invent, mislead, perjure yourself/commit perjury, falsify** → LIE[2]

2 deceive yourself to pretend to yourself that something is not true because you do not want to accept the truth [ORIGIN: 1200—1300 Old French *deceivre*, from Latin *decipere*]

De·cem·ber /dɪˈsɛmbɚ/ (*written abbreviation* **Dec.**) *n.* [C,U] the twelfth month of the year, between November and January: *Franny's birthday is **on December 6th**.* | *We mailed the invitations **in December**.* | *Kevin was promoted **last December**.* | *We're going to Florida **next December**.* [ORIGIN: 1200—1300 Old French, Latin, name of the tenth Roman month, from *decem* "ten"]

de·cen·cy /ˈdisənsi/ *n.* [U] morally correct behavior: *At least **have the decency to** call if you'll be late.*

de·cent /ˈdisənt/ *adj.* **1** acceptable and good enough: *a decent living* | *a decent job* | *a decent education* **2** honest and good: *Dr. Green was a decent man.* **3** wearing enough clothes, so that you are not showing too much of your body: *Don't come in – I'm not decent.* —**decently** *adv.*

de·cen·tral·ize /diˈsɛntrəˌlaɪz/ *v.* [T] to change a government or organization so that decisions are made in local areas rather than in one place —**decentralization** /diˌsɛntrələˈzeɪʃən, ˌdisɛn-/ *n.* [U]

de·cep·tion /dɪˈsɛpʃən/ *n.* [C,U] the act of deliberately making someone believe something that is not true: *People were outraged when they learned of the deception.*

de·cep·tive /dɪˈsɛptɪv/ *adj.* **1** something that is deceptive seems very different from how it really is: *Clark has deceptive speed* (=moves faster than you think or expect). **2** deliberately intended to make someone believe something that is not true: *deceptive advertising* —**deceptively** *adv.*

dec·i·bel /ˈdɛsəˌbɛl, -bəl/ *n.* [C] PHYSICS a unit for measuring how loud a sound is [ORIGIN: 1900—2000 *deci-* + *bel* unit of sound power (20—21 centuries), from Alexander Graham *Bell* (1847-1922), U.S. inventor]

de·cide /dɪˈsaɪd/ *v.* **1** [I,T] to make a choice or judgment about something → DECISION: *I've **decided to** stay home.* | *Jane **decided against** going* (=decided not to go) *to Washington on vacation.* | *Ted **decided (that)** the car would cost too much.* | *I can't **decide whether/if** I want fish or chicken.*

THESAURUS

make up your mind – to decide something, especially after thinking about it for a long time: *Henry made up his mind to go to college in the spring.*
choose – to decide which of a number of things, possibilities, etc. you want: *I let the kids choose their own clothes.*
resolve – to make a definite decision to do something: *She had resolved to work hard and not disappoint her parents.*
determine (formal) – to officially decide what something shall be: *Details of the plan have yet to be determined.*

2 deciding factor a very strong reason for making a particular decision: *Zimmer's testimony was the deciding factor in the case.* **3** [T] to be the reason why something has a particular result: *One punch decided the fight.*

decide on sth *phr. v.* to choose one thing from many possible choices: *Have you decided on a name for the baby?*

de·cid·ed /dɪˈsaɪdɪd/ *adj.* [only before noun] definite and easy to notice: *The new color is a decided improvement.* —**decidedly** *adv.*

de·cid·u·ous /dɪˈsɪdʒuəs/ *adj.* deciduous trees lose their leaves in winter → EVERGREEN [ORIGIN: 1600—1700 Latin *deciduus*, from *decidere* "to fall off"]

D

dec·i·mal[1] /ˈdɛsəməl/ *adj.* a decimal system is based on the number ten [ORIGIN: 1600—1700 Modern Latin *decimalis*, from Latin *decem* "ten"]

decimal[2] *n.* [C] MATH a number less than one, that is shown by a mark (.) followed by the number of TENTHS, then the number of HUNDREDTHS, etc., for example 0.8 or 0.25

ˌdecimal ˈpoint *n.* [C] MATH the mark (.) in a decimal

dec·i·mate /ˈdɛsəˌmeɪt/ *v.* [T] to destroy a large part of something: *a nation decimated by war*

de·ci·pher /dɪˈsaɪfɚ/ *v.* [T] to find the meaning of something that is difficult to read or understand: *I can't decipher his handwriting.*

de·ci·sion /dɪˈsɪʒən/ *n.* **1** [C] a choice or judgment that you make: *We'll **make a decision** by Friday.* | *Gina's **decision to** go to college pleased her parents.* | *Do you expect to **reach a decision** soon?* | ***Decisions about** medical treatment should not be based on cost.* **2** [U] the ability to make choices or judgments quickly: *This job requires the ability to act with speed and decision.*

deˈcision-ˌmaking *n.* [U] the process of deciding on something —**decision-maker** *n.* [C]

de·ci·sive /dɪˈsaɪsɪv/ *adj.* **1** having an important effect on the result of something: *a decisive moment in his career* | *The U.N. **played a decisive role** in peace-making.* **2** good at making decisions quickly: *a decisive leader* **3** definite and clear: *a decisive advantage* —**decisively** *adv.*: *The President was criticized for failing to **act decisively**.*

deck[1] /dɛk/ *n.* [C] **1** a wooden floor built out from the back of a house, where you can sit outdoors **2** a set of playing cards: *a **deck of** cards* **3 a)** the flat top part of a ship, that you can walk on: *Let's go up **on deck**.* **b)** one of the levels on a ship, airplane, or bus: *the lower deck*

deck[2] *v.* [T] *also* **deck** sth ↔ **out** to decorate something with flowers, flags, etc.: *The street was **decked out with** flags for the big parade.*

deck sb ↔ **out** *phr. v.* to dress in fashionable clothes or to dress in a certain style of clothes for a special occasion: *On her eighty-fifth birthday, Amy **decked herself out** in a cowgirl outfit and rode in the parade.*

deck

dec·la·ra·tion /ˌdɛkləˈreɪʃən/ *n.* [C,U] an official or important statement about something: *a **declaration of** war*

de·clare /dɪˈklɛr/ *v.* [T] **1** to state officially and publicly that something is happening or that something is true: *The bridge has been declared unsafe.* | *Jones was declared the winner.* | *The U.S. **declared war on** England in 1812.* | *The doctor **declared that** she was dead.* **2** to say something in a clear firm way: *Parson **declared (that)** he would never go back there.* **3** to officially state the value of things that you have bought or own, or the amount of money you have earned, because you may have to pay taxes on them: *You must declare your full income.* [ORIGIN: 1300—1400 Latin *declarare*, from *clarare* "to make clear"]

de·clen·sion /dɪˈklɛnʃən/ *n.* [C] ENG. LANG. ARTS the set of forms that a noun, PRONOUN, or adjective can have depending on whether it is the SUBJECT, OBJECT, etc. of a sentence, in a language such as Latin or German

de·cline[1] /dɪˈklaɪn/ (Ac) *v.* **1** [I] to decrease in quality, quantity, or importance: *As his health has declined, so has his influence.* | *Car sales have declined.*

THESAURUS **decrease, go down, drop, fall, plummet, diminish, dwindle** → DECREASE[1]

2 [I,T] (formal) to say no to something, usually politely: *We asked them to come, but they **declined** our **invitation**.* | *The senator **declined to** make a statement.*

THESAURUS **reject, refuse, turn down, say no** → REJECT[1]

decline[2] *n.* [C usually singular, U] a decrease in the quality, quantity, or importance of something: *a **decline in** profits* | *During the last ten years, the construction industry has been **in decline**.* | *the **decline of** marriage in western society*

de·code /diˈkoʊd/ *v.* [T] to discover the meaning of a secret or complicated message

de·com·pose /ˌdikəmˈpoʊz/ *v.* [I,T] to decay, or to make something do this: *a partially decomposed* *body* —**decomposition** /ˌdikɑmpəˈzɪʃən/ *n.* [U]

THESAURUS decay, rot, putrefy → DECAY[1]

de·cor /ˈdeɪkɔr, deɪˈkɔr/ *n.* [C,U] the way that the inside of a building is decorated

dec·o·rate /ˈdɛkəˌreɪt/ *v.* [T] **1** to make something look more attractive by adding pretty things to it: *We **decorated** the Christmas tree **with** big red bows.* **2** to give someone an official sign of honor, such as a MEDAL: *soldiers **decorated for** bravery* [ORIGIN: 1500—1600 Latin *decoratus*, past participle of *decorare* "to decorate," from *decus* "honor, decoration"]

dec·o·ra·tion /ˌdɛkəˈreɪʃən/ *n.* **1** [C] something pretty that you add to something in order to make it look more attractive: *the Christmas decorations around the house* **2** [U] the style in which something is decorated **3** [C] an official sign of honor, such as a MEDAL, that is given to someone

dec·o·ra·tive /ˈdɛkərət̬ɪv/ *adj.* pretty and used as a decoration: *a decorative pot*

dec·o·rous /ˈdɛkərəs, dɪˈkɔrəs/ *adj.* (formal) having the correct appearance or behavior for a particular occasion —**decorously** *adv.*

de·cor·um /dɪˈkɔrəm/ *n.* [U] (formal) behavior that is respectful and correct for a formal or serious situation

de·coy /ˈdikɔɪ/ *n.* [C] a person or object that is used to trick a person or animal into going somewhere or doing something —**decoy** /dɪˈkɔɪ/ *v.* [T]

de·crease[1] /dɪˈkris, ˈdikris/ *v.* [I,T] to become less, or to make something do this (ANT) **increase**: *The company's profits decreased in 2007.* | *the need to decrease costs* | *By 1881, the population had **decreased to** 5.2 million.* [ORIGIN: 1300—1400 Anglo-French *decreistre*, from Latin *decrescere*, from *crescere* "to grow"]

THESAURUS

go down – to become lower or less in level, amount, size, quality, etc.: *The income of ordinary workers has been going down.*
drop – to decrease to a lower level or amount, or to make something do this: *Sales have dropped 15% this year.*
fall – to decrease to a lower level or amount: *Temperatures fell below zero last night.*
plummet – to suddenly and quickly become lower or less: *The show's ratings have plummeted.*
diminish – to become smaller or less important: *Union membership diminished from 30,000 at its height to just 20 today.*
decline – to decrease in quality, quantity, or importance: *The company's earnings declined 17% last year.*
dwindle – to gradually become fewer or smaller: *Their lead had dwindled to only two points.*

THESAURUS reduce, lower, cut, slash, roll back → REDUCE

de·crease[2] /ˈdikris, dɪˈkris/ *n.* [C,U] the process of reducing something, or the amount by which it is reduced (ANT) **increase**: *a **decrease in** sales*

de·cree /dɪˈkri/ *n.* [C] an official order or decision —**decree** *v.* [T]

de·crep·it /dɪˈkrɛpɪt/ *adj.* old and in bad condition [ORIGIN: 1400—1500 Latin *decrepitus*, from *crepare* "to make a high cracking sound"]

de·crim·i·nal·ize /diˈkrɪmənəˌlaɪz/ *v.* [T] to state officially that something is no longer illegal —**decriminalization** /diˌkrɪmɪnələˈzeɪʃən/ *n.* [U]

de·cry /dɪˈkraɪ/ *v.* (**decried**, **decries**) [T] (formal) to state publicly that you do not approve of something: *The candidate has decried the use of negative campaign ads.*

ded·i·cate /ˈdɛdəˌkeɪt/ *v.* [T] **1** to say that a book, movie, song, etc. has been written, made, or sung in honor of someone: *The book is **dedicated to** his mother.* **2 dedicate yourself/your life to (doing) sth** to give all your attention and effort to one thing: *I've **dedicated my life to** my work.* [ORIGIN: 1400—1500 Latin *dedicare*, from *dicare* "to say publicly"]

ded·i·cat·ed /ˈdɛdəˌkeɪt̬ɪd/ *adj.* working very hard at something because you think it is important: *a **dedicated** teacher*

ded·i·ca·tion /ˌdɛdəˈkeɪʃən/ *n.* **1** [U] hard work or effort that you put into a particular activity because you think it is important: *He shows great **dedication to** his work.* **2** [C] the act or ceremony of dedicating something to someone **3** [C] the words used in dedicating a book, movie, song, etc. to someone

de·duce /dɪˈdus/ (Ac) *v.* [T] (formal) to make a judgment based on the information that you have: *From his observations, Darwin **deduced that** animals adapt to their environment.* | *The time of death can be **deduced from** the temperature of the body.* [ORIGIN: 1400—1500 Latin *deducere* "to lead out," from *ducere* "to lead"]

de·duct /dɪˈdʌkt/ *v.* [T] to take away an amount from a total: *Taxes are **deducted from** your pay.*

de·duct·i·ble[1] /dɪˈdʌktəbəl/ *n.* [C] the part of a bill you must pay before the insurance company will pay the rest

deductible[2] *adj.* ECONOMICS an amount of money that is deductible can be taken away from the total money you must pay taxes on: *The money you give to a charity is **tax deductible**.*

de·duc·tion /dɪˈdʌkʃən/ (Ac) *n.* [C,U] **1** the process of taking away an amount from a total, or the amount that is taken away: *I earn about $2,000 a month, after deductions.* **2** the process of making a judgment about something, based on the information that you have: *a game that teaches logic and deduction*

deˌductive ˈreasoning *n.* [U] **1** the process of forming a scientific judgment about something, based on existing facts **2** MATH a process of proving a mathematical statement or solving a mathematical problem using an existing mathematical principle or facts that develop from one to the next in a reasonable or correct way

deed /did/ *n.* [C] **1** (literary) an action: *good deeds* **2** LAW an official paper that is a record of an agreement, especially one that says who owns property

deem /dim/ *v.* [T] (formal) to say that something has a particular quality (SYN) **consider**: *The judge deemed the question inappropriate.*

D

deep[1] /dip/ *adj.*
1 GO FAR DOWN going far down from the top or from the surface (ANT) **shallow** ➔ DEPTH: *The path was covered in deep snow.* | *The water's about **10 feet/6 inches etc. deep**.* ➔ *see picture at* SHALLOW
2 GO FAR IN going far in from the outside or from the front: *Terry had a deep cut in his forehead.* | *a shelf 3 feet long and 8 inches deep*
3 FEELING/BELIEF a deep feeling or belief is very strong and sincere: *deep feelings of hatred*
4 SOUND a deep sound is very low: *a deep voice*
5 COLOR a deep color is dark and strong (ANT) **light**, **pale**: *a plant with deep green leaves*
6 SERIOUS serious and often difficult to understand: *a deep conversation about the meaning of life*
7 deep sleep if someone is in a deep sleep, it is difficult to wake him/her
8 a deep breath a deep breath is one in which you breathe a lot of air in, especially because you are upset or nervous: *I **took a deep breath** and jumped into the water.*
9 be in deep trouble (informal) to be in serious trouble or in an extremely difficult situation: *Many smaller companies are in deep trouble.*
10 deep in thought/conversation etc. thinking so hard or talking so much that you do not notice anything else: *Martin sat at his desk, deep in thought.* [ORIGIN: Old English *deop*]

deep[2] *adv.* **1** far into something: *He stepped **deep into** the mud.* **2 deep down a)** if you feel or know something deep down, that is what you really feel or know even though you may not admit it: *Deep down, I knew she was right.* **b)** if someone is good, evil, etc. deep down, that is what s/he is really like even though s/he usually hides it: *He seems mean, but deep down he's really nice.* **3 two/three etc. deep** in two, three, etc. rows or layers

deep·en /ˈdipən/ *v.* [I,T] to make something deeper, or to become deeper

ˌdeep ˈfreeze *n.* [C] a FREEZER

ˈdeep fried *adj.* cooked in a lot of hot oil —**deep fry** *v.* [T]

deep·ly /ˈdipli/ *adv.* **1** extremely or very much: *Wood is a deeply religious man.* | *They knew Frank was deeply involved in criminal activities.* **2** a long way into something: *We started sinking even more deeply into the mud.* **3 breathe deeply** to take a large breath of air into your lungs and then let all the air out again

ˌdeep-ˈseated *also* **ˌdeep-ˈrooted** *adj.* a deep-seated feeling or idea is strong and very difficult to change

deer /dɪr/ *n.* (plural **deer**) [C] a large wild animal that lives in forests. The male has long horns that look like tree branches. [ORIGIN: Old English *deor* "animal"]

de·face /dɪˈfeɪs/ *v.* [T] (formal) to damage the appearance of something, especially by writing or making marks on it: *walls defaced by graffiti*

de fac·to /dɪ ˈfæktoʊ, di-/ *adj.* LAW actually existing or happening without being approved of legally or officially ➔ DE JURE: *Iverson is their de facto leader.*

def·a·ma·tion /ˌdɛfəˈmeɪʃən/ *n.* [U] LAW writing or saying something that makes people have a bad opinion of someone or something

de·fame /dɪˈfeɪm/ *v.* [T] (formal) to write or say something that makes people have a bad opinion of someone or something: *She sued him for defaming her character.* —**defamatory** /dɪˈfæməˌtɔri/ *adj.*

de·fault[1] /dɪˈfɔlt/ *v.* [I] to not do something that you are legally supposed to: *He **defaulted on** his loan payments.*

default[2] *n.* **1** [U] failure to do something that you are supposed to do: *We won the first game **by default*** (=because the other team failed to arrive). | *The loan is **in default*** (=it has not been paid back on time). **2** [C usually singular] IT the standard way in which things are arranged on a computer screen or in a program unless you change them

de·feat[1] /dɪˈfit/ *n.* **1** [C,U] failure to win or succeed: *Miami's first defeat* | *an **embarrassing defeat*** | *He'll never **admit defeat*** (=admit that he has failed). **2** [singular] victory over someone or something: *the **defeat of** the President's tax plan*

defeat[2] *v.* [T] **1** to win a victory over someone: *Davis easily defeated his opponent in the election.*

THESAURUS **beat, trounce, clobber, cream, vanquish, overcome, conquer** ➔ BEAT[1]

2 to make something fail: *The plan was defeated by a lack of money.*

def·e·cate /ˈdɛfəˌkeɪt/ *v.* [I] (formal) to get rid of waste matter from your BOWELS —**defecation** /ˌdɛfəˈkeɪʃən/ *n.* [U]

de·fect[1] /ˈdifɛkt, dɪˈfɛkt/ *n.* [C] a fault or a lack of something that makes something not perfect: *The cars are tested for defects before being sold.* | *a **birth defect*** (=a physical problem that a baby was born with) [ORIGIN: 1400—1500 Old French, Latin *defectus* "lack"]

THESAURUS

problem – a bad or difficult situation that needs to be dealt with: *There's a problem with the brakes.*

flaw – a mark or weakness that makes something not perfect: *a flaw in its construction*
bug – a defect in a computer program: *The program had some minor bugs.*
fault – something that is wrong with a machine, design, etc., which prevents it from working correctly: *a fault in the power unit*
imperfection (formal) – a mark or weakness that makes something not perfect: *The glasses are then inspected for any imperfections.*

de·fect² /dɪˈfɛkt/ *v.* [I] to leave your own country or a group and join or go to an opposing one: *a Cuban baseball player who **defected to** the United States* —**defector** *n.* [C] —**defection** /dɪˈfɛkʃən/ *n.* [C,U]

de·fec·tive /dɪˈfɛktɪv/ *adj.* not made correctly or not working correctly: *defective products*

de·fend /dɪˈfɛnd/ *v.* **1** [T] to protect someone or something from being attacked ➔ DEFENSE: *You should learn to **defend yourself**.* | *Soldiers **defended** the fort **from** attack* **2** [T] to use arguments to protect something or someone from criticism: *The mayor defended his plan to raise taxes.* | *He had to **defend himself against** their charges.* **3** [I,T] to try to prevent your opponents from getting points in a sports game **4** [T] to be a lawyer for someone who is said to be guilty of a crime [ORIGIN: 1200—1300 Old French *defendre*, from Latin *defendere*, from *fendere* "to hit"] —**defender** *n.* [C] —**defensible** /dɪˈfɛnsəbəl/ *adj.*

de·fend·ant /dɪˈfɛndənt/ *n.* [C] LAW the person in a court of law who has been ACCUSEd of doing something illegal ➔ PLAINTIFF

de·fense¹ /dɪˈfɛns/ *n.* **1** [U] the act of protecting someone or something from attack or criticism: *Senator Stevens spoke **in defense of** a bill to make handguns illegal.* **2** [U] the weapons, people, systems, etc. that a country uses to protect itself from attack: *the Department of Defense* | *Defense spending* (=money spent on weapons, etc.) *has increased.* **3** [C] something that is used for protection against something else: *Vitamin C is my **defense against** colds.* **4 a)** [C,U] LAW the things that are said in a court of law to prove that someone is not guilty of a crime: *His defense is that he didn't remember the incident.* **b) the defense** LAW the people in a court of law who are trying to show that someone is not guilty of a crime ➔ PROSECUTION: *Are the defense ready to call the first witness?*

de·fense² /ˈdifɛns/ *n.* [U] the players on a sports team whose job is to try to prevent the other team from scoring points ➔ OFFENSE

de·fense·less /dɪˈfɛnslɪs/ *adj.* unable to protect yourself from being hurt or criticized: *a defenseless old woman*

deˈfense ˌmechanism *n.* [C] **1** a process in your brain that makes you forget things that are painful to think about **2** a reaction in your body that protects you from an illness or danger

de·fen·sive¹ /dɪˈfɛnsɪv/ *adj.* **1** used or intended for protection against attack ➔ OFFENSIVE: *defensive weapons* **2** behaving in a way that shows you think someone is criticizing you even if s/he is not: *She **got** really **defensive** when I asked her why she was late.* **3** relating to stopping the other team from getting points in a game ➔ OFFENSIVE: *a defensive play* —**defensively** *adv.* —**defensiveness** *n.* [U]

defensive² *n.* **on the defensive** protecting yourself because someone is criticizing you: *Her boss's comment **put** her **on the defensive**.*

de·fer /dɪˈfɚ/ *v.* (**deferred**, **deferring**) [T] (formal) to delay something until a later date: *His military service was deferred until he finished college.*

THESAURUS **delay, postpone, put off, procrastinate** ➔ DELAY¹

defer to sb/sth *phr. v.* (formal) to accept someone's opinion or decision because you have respect for that person or because s/he has power over you: *I usually defer to my wife when it comes to shopping.*

def·er·ence /ˈdɛfərəns/ *n.* [U] (formal) polite behavior that shows that you respect someone and are willing to accept what s/he says or believes: ***In deference to** local custom, we covered our heads.* —**deferential** /ˌdɛfəˈrɛnʃəl◂/ *adj.* —**deferentially** *adv.*

de·fer·ment /dɪˈfɚmənt/ *n.* [C,U] an occasion when you delay doing something that you have been officially ordered to do, such as join the army or pay back a debt, or the act of officially allowing someone to delay doing something: *College students were given draft deferments.*

de·fi·ant /dɪˈfaɪənt/ *adj.* refusing to do what someone tells you to do because you do not respect him/her —**defiance** *n.* [U] —**defiantly** *adv.*

de·fi·cien·cy /dɪˈfɪʃənsi/ *n.* (plural **deficiencies**) [C,U] **1** a lack of something that is needed: *a vitamin deficiency* **2** a weakness or fault in something: *The computer system has serious deficiencies.*

de·fi·cient /dɪˈfɪʃənt/ *adj.* **1** not having or containing enough of something: *food **deficient in** iron* **2** not good enough

def·i·cit /ˈdɛfəsɪt/ *n.* **1** [C] the difference between the amount of something that you have and the higher amount that you need: *The Celtics had a 22-point deficit at halftime.* **2** [C,U] ECONOMICS the difference between the amount of money that a government spends and the amount that it takes in from taxes and other activities: *The objectives are to control the **budget deficit** and reduce inflation.* | *The balance of payments was **in deficit**.*

de·file /dɪˈfaɪl/ *v.* [T] (formal) to make something less pure, good, or holy: *graves defiled by Nazi symbols*

de·fine /dɪˈfaɪn/ (Ac) *v.* [T] **1** to explain the exact meaning of a particular word or idea ➔ DEFINITION: *Please define what you mean by "democracy."* | *A*

D

*lie is **defined as** saying something in order to deceive someone.* **2** to describe something correctly and show what qualities it has that make it different from other things: *Teachers need to give students rules that are **clearly defined**.* [ORIGIN: 1300—1400 Old French *definer*, from Latin *definire*, from *finire* "to limit, end"] **—definable** *adj.*

def·i·nite /ˈdɛfənɪt/ (Ac) *adj.* **1** certain and not likely to change: *I'll give you a **definite answer** by tomorrow.* | *Will the FBI be able to come to a definite conclusion about the cause of the explosion?* **2** clear and noticeable: *The team has shown definite improvement in the last few games.* [ORIGIN: 1500—1600 Latin *definitus*, past participle of *definire* "to limit, end"]

D

ˌdefinite ˈarticle *n.* [C] ENG. LANG. ARTS the word "the" in English, or a word in another language that is like "the" → ARTICLE

def·i·nite·ly /ˈdɛfənɪtli/ (Ac) *adv.* without any doubt: *That was definitely the best movie I've seen all year.* | *"Are you going to be there tomorrow?" "Definitely."* | *It's **definitely not** the right time to tell her.* | *After seeing the statistics, we can definitely say that pollution has increased.*

def·i·ni·tion /ˌdɛfəˈnɪʃən/ (Ac) *n.* **1** [C] a phrase or sentence that says exactly what a word, phrase, or idea means: *What's the **definition of** "defamation?"* | *a **dictionary definition*** **2** [U] the clear edges, shapes, or sound that something has: *The photograph **lacks definition**.* | *a high definition television* **3 by definition** if something has a particular quality by definition, it must have that quality because all things of that type have it: *A carcinogenic substance* (=one that can cause cancer) *is, by definition, hazardous to humans.*

de·fin·i·tive /dɪˈfɪnət̬ɪv/ (Ac) *adj.* [only before noun] **1** the definitive book, description, etc. is considered to be the best of its type and cannot be improved: ***the definitive** biography of Charlie Chaplin* **2** a definitive statement, answer, etc. cannot be doubted or changed: *The group has taken a definitive stand against pornography.* **—definitively** *adv.*

de·flate /dɪˈfleɪt, di-/ *v.* **1** [I,T] if a tire, ball, etc. deflates, or if you deflate it, it becomes smaller because the air or gas inside it comes out (ANT) **inflate** **2** [T] to make someone feel less important or confident **3** [T] ECONOMICS to change the economic rules or conditions in a country so that prices become lower or stop rising **—deflation** /dɪˈfleɪʃən/ *n.* [U]

de·flect /dɪˈflɛkt/ *v.* **1** [I,T] to hit something that is already moving and make it move in a different direction: *The ball was deflected into the crowd.* **2 deflect attention/criticism/anger etc.** to stop people from noticing something, criticizing it, etc.: *attempts to deflect attention away from his private life* **—deflection** /dɪˈflɛkʃən/ *n.* [C,U]

de·for·es·ta·tion /diˌfɔrəˈsteɪʃən/ *n.* [U] EARTH SCIENCES the cutting or burning down of all the trees in an area: *After years of deforestation, the area lost a lot of its natural wildlife.* → ENVIRONMENT

de·formed /dɪˈfɔrmd/ *adj.* something that is deformed has the wrong shape, especially because it has grown or developed wrongly: *a deformed foot* **—deform** *v.* [T] **—deformation** /ˌdifɔrˈmeɪʃən/ *n.* [C,U]

de·form·i·ty /dɪˈfɔrmət̬i/ *n.* (plural **deformities**) [C,U] a condition in which part of someone's body is not the normal shape

de·fraud /dɪˈfrɔd/ *v.* [T] to trick a person or organization in order to get money from him, her, or it: *He **defrauded** his clients **of** over $5 million.*

de·frost /dɪˈfrɔst/ *v.* **1** [I,T] if frozen food defrosts, or if you defrost it, it gets warmer until it is not frozen anymore **2** [I,T] if a FREEZER or REFRIGERATOR defrosts, or if you defrost it, it is turned off so that the ice inside it melts **3** [T] to remove ice from the windows of a car by blowing warm air onto them

deft /dɛft/ *adj.* quick and skillful: *a deft catch* **—deftly** *adv.*

> THESAURUS **skillful, expert, accomplished, talented, gifted, adept, cunning** → SKILLFUL

de·funct /dɪˈfʌŋkt/ *adj.* no longer existing or useful

de·fuse /diˈfyuz/ *v.* [T] **1** to remove or disconnect part of a bomb so that the bomb does not explode **2** to improve a difficult situation by making someone less angry: *Tim tried to **defuse** the **tension/situation**.*

de·fy /dɪˈfaɪ/ *v.* (**defied**, **defies**) [T] **1** to refuse to obey someone or something: *He defied his father's wishes and joined the army.*

> THESAURUS **disobey, break a rule/law, rebel, flout, violate, infringe, contravene** → DISOBEY

2 defy description/explanation/imagination etc. to be almost impossible to describe, explain, understand, etc.: *Her outfit defied description.*

de·gen·er·ate¹ /dɪˈdʒɛnəˌreɪt/ *v.* [I] to become worse: *The party **degenerated into** a drunken fight.* **—degeneration** /dɪˌdʒɛnəˈreɪʃən/ *n.* [U]

de·gen·e·rate² /dɪˌdʒɛnərɪt/ *adj.* **1** worse than before in quality **2** having very low moral standards **—degenerate** *n.* [C]

de·gen·er·a·tive /dɪˈdʒɛnərət̬ɪv/ *adj.* BIOLOGY a degenerative illness gradually gets worse and cannot be stopped

de·grade /dɪˈgreɪd, di-/ *v.* [T] **1** to treat someone without respect and make him/her lose respect for himself or herself: *Pornography degrades women.* **2** (formal) to make a situation or condition worse: *The proposed law could degrade safety standards.* **—degradation** /ˌdɛgrəˈdeɪʃən/ *n.* [U]

de·grad·ing /dɪ'greɪdɪŋ/ *adj.* showing no respect for someone, or making him/her feel very ashamed: *It was degrading to have to ask strangers for money.*

de·gree /dɪ'gri/ *n.* **1** [C] a unit for measuring temperature: *It got up to 86 degrees today.* **2** [C] a unit for measuring the size of an angle: *The plane was climbing at an angle of 20 degrees.* **3** [C,U] the level or amount of something: *students with different* ***degrees of*** *ability* | ***To what degree*** *is his smoking contributing to his health problems?* **4** [C] something that you get from a college or university, which officially shows that you have successfully completed a program of study: *a law degree* | *Ryan* ***has a degree in*** *chemistry.* | *You need a* ***college degree*** *for most of these jobs.* [ORIGIN: 1200—1300 Old French *degré*, from Latin *gradus* "step, grade"]

ˌdegree of a 'monomial // *n.* [C] MATH the number you get when you add together the EXPONENTS of the TERM in a MONOMIAL

ˌdegree of a 'polynomial // *n.* [C] MATH the number you get when you add together the EXPONENTS of the TERM that is multiplied by itself the most in a POLYNOMIAL

ˌdegree of a 'term *n.* [C] MATH the number you get when you add together the EXPONENTS of one of the TERMS in an EQUATION

de·hy·drat·ed /di'haɪˌdreɪtɪd/ *adj.* people or things that are dehydrated do not have enough water inside them: *dehydrated potatoes* | *Be careful you don't get dehydrated outside in this heat.* **—dehydration** /ˌdihaɪ'dreɪʃən/ *n.* [U]: *Several runners were suffering from dehydration.*

deign /deɪn/ *v.* **deign to do sth** (humorous) to agree to do something that you think you are too important to do: *She finally deigned to join us for lunch.*

de·i·ty /'diəṭi, 'deɪ-/ *n.* (plural **deities**) [C] a god or GODDESS

THESAURUS god, divinity, idol ➔ GOD

dé·jà vu /ˌdeɪʒɑ 'vu/ *n.* [U] the feeling that what is happening now has happened before in exactly the same way

de·ject·ed /dɪ'dʒɛktɪd/ *adj.* sad and disappointed: *The players looked dejected after the game.* **—dejectedly** *adv.* **—dejection** /dɪ'dʒɛkʃən/ *n.* [U]

de jure /di 'dʒʊreɪ/ *adj.* LAW true or right because of a law ➔ DE FACTO

de·lay[1] /dɪ'leɪ/ *v.* **1** [I,T] to wait until a later time to do something: *We cannot delay any longer.* | *We've decided to* ***delay*** *the trip* ***until*** *next month.*

THESAURUS

postpone – to change an event to a later time or date: *The meeting was postponed.*
put off – to delay something, or delay doing something, especially something that you do not want to do: *Regular checkups are important – don't put off visits to the dentist!*
procrastinate – to delay doing something that you ought to do: *A lot of people procrastinate when it comes to doing paperwork.*
defer (formal) – to delay something until a later date: *Tell the builder what the problem is, and defer payment until it is corrected.*

2 [T] to make someone or something late: *Our flight was delayed by bad weather.* **—delayed** *adj.*

delay[2] *n.* (plural **delays**) [C,U] a situation in which someone or something is made to wait, or the length of the waiting time: ***Delays of*** *two hours or more are common.* | *There are* ***severe delays*** *on Route 95.* | *The President urged Congress to pass the bill* ***without delay***.

D

de·lec·ta·ble /dɪ'lɛktəbəl/ *adj.* (formal) very good to taste or smell

del·e·gate[1] /'dɛləgɪt/ *n.* [C] someone who is chosen to speak, vote, and make decisions for a group: *Delegates from 50 colleges met to discuss the issue.* [ORIGIN: 1400—1500 Medieval Latin *delegatus*, from Latin *legare* "to send as a representative"]

del·e·gate[2] /'dɛləˌgeɪt/ *v.* [I,T] to give part of your work, or something you are responsible for doing, to someone who is in a lower position than you in your organization: *Smaller jobs should be* ***delegated to*** *your assistant.*

ˌdelegated 'powers *n.* [plural] POLITICS powers given to the U.S. government under the CONSTITUTION. They include the EXPRESSED POWERS, the IMPLIED POWERS, and the INHERENT POWERS.

del·e·ga·tion /ˌdɛlə'geɪʃən/ *n.* **1** [C] a group of people who represent a company, organization, etc.: *A UN delegation was sent to the peace talks.* **2** [U] the process of giving power to someone else and making that person responsible for some of your work: *the* ***delegation of*** *authority*

de·lete /dɪ'lit/ *v.* [T] **1** to remove a letter, word, etc. from a piece of writing **2** IT to remove a document, FILE, etc. stored on a computer: *The data has been* ***deleted from*** *the file.* [ORIGIN: 1400—1500 Latin *deletus*, past participle of *delere* "to destroy"] **—deletion** /dɪ'liʃən/ *n.* [C,U]

del·e·te·ri·ous /ˌdɛlə'tɪriəs/ *adj.* (formal) damaging or harmful: *the* ***deleterious effects*** *of smoking*

del·i /'dɛli/ *n.* [C] a small store that sells cheese, cooked meat, bread, etc.

de·lib·er·ate[1] /dɪ'lɪbrɪt, -bərɪt/ *adj.* **1** intended or planned: *I'm sure her story was a* ***deliberate attempt*** *to confuse us.* **2** deliberate speech, thought, or movement is slow and careful [ORIGIN: 1400—1500 Latin *deliberatus*, past participle of *deliberare* "to weigh in the mind," from *libra* "balance"]

de·lib·e·rate[2] /dɪ'lɪbəˌreɪt/ *v.* [I,T] to think about something very carefully: *The jury deliberated for three days before finding him guilty.*

de·lib·er·ate·ly /dɪˈlɪbrɪt˺li/ *adv.* done in a way that is intended: *Someone had set the fire deliberately.*

THESAURUS

on purpose (especially spoken) – deliberately, especially in order to annoy someone or get an advantage for yourself: *He told the teacher I'd pushed him on purpose.*
intentionally – deliberately, especially in order to have a particular result or effect: *Very few teenagers become pregnant intentionally.*
purposely – deliberately, in order to achieve a particular aim: *Some day-care centers are purposely built near senior centers, so that old and young people can interact.*

D

de·lib·er·a·tion /dɪˌlɪbəˈreɪʃən/ *n.* [C,U] careful thought or discussion about a problem: *The committee will finish its deliberations today.*

del·i·ca·cy /ˈdɛlɪkəsi/ *n.* (plural **delicacies**) **1** [C] something good to eat that is expensive or rare: *The red sea urchins, a delicacy in Japan, are caught off the coast of California.* **2** [U] a careful way of speaking or behaving so that you do not upset anyone: *We need to handle this business with great delicacy.* **3** [U] the quality of being easy to harm or damage: *the delicacy of the clock's machinery*

del·i·cate /ˈdɛlɪkɪt/ *adj.* **1** easily damaged or broken: *a delicate porcelain cup* **2** needing to be done very carefully in order to avoid causing problems: *delicate surgery* **3** a part of the body that is delicate is attractive, thin, and graceful: *long delicate fingers* —**delicately** *adv.*

del·i·ca·tes·sen /ˌdɛlɪkəˈtɛsən/ *n.* [C] a DELI

de·li·cious /dɪˈlɪʃəs/ *adj.* having a very enjoyable taste or smell: *a delicious meal* | *The soup* ***smelled/tasted delicious****.* [ORIGIN: 1200—1300 Old French, Latin *delicere* "to attract"]

THESAURUS **sweet, tasty, sour, salty, hot, spicy** ➔ TASTE[1]

de·light[1] /dɪˈlaɪt/ *n.* **1** [U] a feeling of great pleasure and satisfaction: *Krystal laughed* ***with delight****.* **2** [C] something that makes you feel very happy or satisfied: ***the delights of*** *traveling* [ORIGIN: 1200—1300 Old French *delit*, from Latin *delectare* "to please greatly"]

delight[2] *v.* [T] to give someone a feeling of great pleasure and satisfaction: *This movie classic will delight the whole family.*

delight in sth *phr. v.* to enjoy something very much, especially something that annoys someone else: *little boys who delight in scaring people*

de·light·ed /dɪˈlaɪt̬ɪd/ *adj.* very happy or pleased: *We were* ***delighted to*** *hear their good news.* | *They were* ***delighted with*** *the results of the recent election.*

THESAURUS **happy, glad, pleased, content, thrilled, overjoyed, ecstatic, jubilant, elated** ➔ HAPPY

de·light·ful /dɪˈlaɪt˺fəl/ *adj.* very nice, pleasant, and enjoyable: *a delightful story for younger children* —**delightfully** *adv.*

de·lin·e·ate /dɪˈlɪniˌeɪt/ *v.* [T] (formal) to make something very clear by describing it or drawing it in great detail

de·lin·quen·cy /dɪˈlɪŋkwənsi/ *n.* [U] illegal or socially unacceptable behavior, especially by young people: *the problem of* ***juvenile delinquency*** (=crime done by young people)

de·lin·quent /dɪˈlɪŋkwənt/ *adj.* **1** late in paying the money you owe: *delinquent loans* **2** behaving in a way that is illegal or that society does not approve of ➔ JUVENILE DELINQUENT —**delinquent** *n.* [C]

de·lir·i·ous /dɪˈlɪriəs/ *adj.* **1** confused, anxious, and excited because you are very sick **2** extremely happy and excited: *Her parents were* ***delirious with joy*** *to see her again.* —**delirium** /dəˈlɪriəm/ *n.* [C,U]

de·liv·er /dɪˈlɪvɚ/ *v.* **1** [I,T] to take a letter, package, goods, etc. to a particular place or person: *I delivered newspapers when I was a kid.* | *I'm having some furniture delivered to the apartment.* **2** [T] to make a speech to a lot of people: *Rev. Whitman delivered a powerful sermon.* **3** [I,T] to do the things that you have promised: *Voters are angry that politicians haven't* ***delivered on their promises****.* **4 deliver a baby** to give birth to a baby, or to help a woman give birth to a baby **5** [T] to get votes or support from a particular group of people: *We're expecting Rigby to deliver the blue-collar vote.* [ORIGIN: 1200—1300 Old French *delivrer*, from Latin *liberare* "to set free"]

de·liv·er·y /dɪˈlɪvəri/ *n.* (plural **deliveries**) **1** [C,U] the act of bringing something to someone or somewhere: *Pizza Mondo offers free delivery for any pizza over $10.* **2** [C] something that is delivered: *All deliveries should be taken to the rear entrance.* **3** [C] the process of a baby being born: *Mrs. Haims was rushed into the* ***delivery room*** (=hospital room where babies are born) *at 7:42.* **4** [singular, U] the way that someone speaks or performs in public: *I liked his jokes, but his delivery needs work.*

del·ta /ˈdɛltə/ *n.* [C] EARTH SCIENCES a low area of land where a river separates into many smaller rivers flowing toward an ocean: *the Mississippi Delta* | *an* ***inland delta*** (=a delta that is not near the ocean)

de·lude /dɪˈlud/ *v.* [T] to make someone believe something that is not true SYN **deceive**: *He's* ***deluding himself*** *if he thinks he can eat what he wants and lose weight.* —**deluded** *adj.*

del·uge[1] /ˈdɛlyudʒ/ *n.* [C] **1** a period of time when it rains continuously **2** a large amount of something such as letters, questions, etc. that someone gets at the same time [ORIGIN: 1400—1500 Old French, Latin *diluvium* "flood"]

deluge[2] *v.* [T] **1** to send a lot of letters, questions, etc. to someone at the same time: *The radio station*

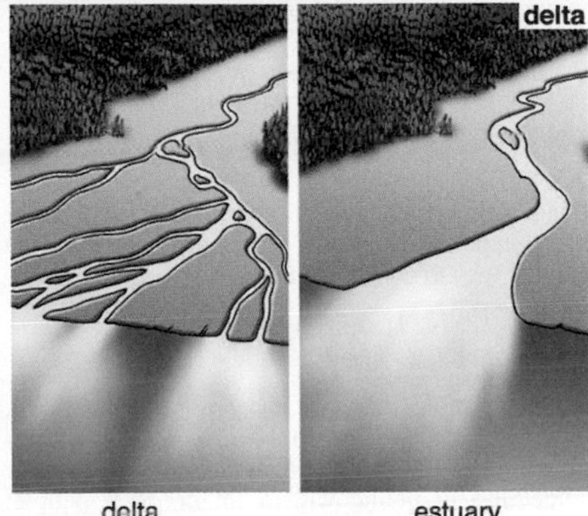

delta estuary

was **deluged with** complaints. **2** (literary) to completely cover something with water

de·lu·sion /dɪ'luʒən/ *n.* [C,U] a false belief about something: *Walter's still* ***under the delusion that*** (=wrongly believes that) *his wife loves him.*

de·luxe /dɪ'lʌks/ *adj.* of better quality and more expensive than other similar things: *a deluxe resort*

delve /dɛlv/ *v.*

delve into sth *phr. v.* to search for more information about someone or something: *Reporters are always delving into actors' personal lives.*

dem·a·gogue /'dɛmə,gɑg/ *n.* [C] (disapproving) a political leader who tries to make people feel strong emotions in order to influence their opinions [ORIGIN: 1600—1700 Greek *demagogos*, from *demos* "people" + *agogos* "leading"]

de·mand¹ /dɪ'mænd/ *n.* **1** [singular, U] the need or desire that people have for particular goods or services, and their willingness to buy them ➔ SUPPLY: ***Demand for*** *the new model is outstripping supply.* | *Nurses are* ***in*** *great* ***demand*** (=wanted by a lot of people) *these days.* | *The factory will have to increase production to* ***meet demand.*** **2** [C] a strong request that shows you believe you have the right to get what you ask for: *Union members will strike until the company agrees to their demands.* **3 demands** [plural] the difficult or annoying things that you need to do: *women dealing with* ***the demands of*** *family and career* | *The school* ***makes*** *heavy* ***demands on*** *its teachers.* [ORIGIN: 1300—1400 Old French *demander*, from Latin *mandare* "to order"]

demand² *v.* **1** [T] to ask strongly for something, especially because you think you have a right to do this: *The President demanded the release of the hostages.* | *Hughes* ***demanded that*** *he get his money back.*

THESAURUS **ask, request, order, beg, plead, implore** ➔ ASK

2 [I,T] to order someone to tell you something or do something: *"What are you doing here?" she demanded.* **3** [T] if something demands your time, skill, attention, etc., it makes you use a lot of your time, skill, etc.: *The baby demands most of her time.*

de·mand·ing /dɪ'mændɪŋ/ *adj.* **1** making you use a lot of your time, skill, attention, etc.: *a demanding job*

THESAURUS **difficult, hard, tough, awkward, challenging, arduous, complicated, complex** ➔ DIFFICULT

2 expecting a lot of attention, or expecting to have things exactly the way you want them, especially in a way that is not fair: *a demanding boss*

de·mar·ca·tion /,dimɑr'keɪʃən/ *n.* [U] the process of deciding on a border or dividing line between two areas, activities, etc.: *the lines of demarcation between national and state authority*

de·mean /dɪ'min/ *v.* [T] to behave in a way that shows disrespect for someone or something

de·mean·ing /dɪ'minɪŋ/ *adj.* not showing respect for someone and making him/her feel ashamed: *demeaning comments*

de·mean·or /dɪ'minɚ/ *n.* [singular, U] (formal) the way someone behaves, dresses, speaks, etc., that shows what his/her character is like

THESAURUS **behavior, conduct, manner** ➔ BEHAVIOR

de·ment·ed /dɪ'mɛntɪd/ *adj.* crazy or very strange [ORIGIN: 1600—1700 *dement* "to drive mad" (16—19 centuries), from Latin *mens* "mind"]

THESAURUS **crazy, mentally ill, insane, disturbed, nuts, loony, psychotic, unstable** ➔ CRAZY

de·mer·it /dɪ'mɛrɪt/ *n.* [C] a warning, or a written symbol, showing this warning that is given to a student or a soldier to tell him/her not to do something wrong again

de·mise /dɪ'maɪz/ *n.* [singular] (formal) **1** the end of something that used to exist: *the* ***demise of*** *the steel industry* **2** death [ORIGIN: 1400—1500 Anglo-French, Old French *demis* "sent away"]

dem·o /'dɛmoʊ/ *n.* (plural **demos**) [C] **1** (informal) a recording containing an example of someone's music: *a demo tape* **2** IT a computer program that shows what a new piece of software will be able to do when it is ready to be sold

de·moc·ra·cy /dɪ'mɑkrəsi/ *n.* (plural **democracies**) **1** [U] a system of government in which citizens in a country can vote to elect its leaders **2** [C] a country that allows its people to elect government officials [ORIGIN: 1500—1600 Old French *democratie*, from Greek *demokratia*, from *demos* "people" + *-kratia* "rule"]

THESAURUS **government, republic, monarchy, regime, dictatorship, totalitarian country/state etc., police state** ➔ GOVERNMENT

dem·o·crat /ˈdɛmə,kræt/ *n.* [C] **1 Democrat** POLITICS a member or supporter of the Democratic Party of the U.S. ➔ REPUBLICAN **2** POLITICS someone who believes in or works to achieve democracy

dem·o·crat·ic /,dɛməˈkræṭɪk/ *adj.* **1 Democratic** POLITICS relating to or supporting the Democratic Party of the U.S. ➔ REPUBLICAN: *the Democratic senator from Hawaii* **2** organized by a system in which everyone has the same right to vote, speak, etc.: *a democratic way of making decisions* **3** POLITICS based on a system in which a government is elected by the people of a country: *a democratic government*

D

Demo'cratic ,Party *n.* **the Democratic Party** one of the two main political parties of the U.S. ➔ REPUBLICAN PARTY

dem·o·graph·ics /,dɛməˈgræfɪks/ *n.* [plural] SOCIAL SCIENCE information about the people who live in a particular area, for example what they earn or how old they are: *The **demographics of** America's population have changed dramatically over the past century.* —**demographic** *adj: The under-25s buy more downloads than any other demographic group.*

de·mol·ish /dɪˈmɑlɪʃ/ *v.* [T] **1** to completely destroy a building or other structure: *Several houses were demolished to make space for a new park.* **2** to prove that an idea or opinion is completely wrong: *Each of his arguments was demolished by the defense lawyer.* [ORIGIN: 1500—1600 Old French *demolir*, from Latin *de* "down" + *moliri* "to build"] —**demolition** /,dɛməˈlɪʃən/ *n.* [C,U]

de·mon /ˈdimən/ *n.* [C] an evil spirit —**demonic** /dɪˈmɑnɪk/ *adj.*

dem·on·strate /ˈdɛmən,streɪt/ (Ac) *v.* **1** [T] to show a fact clearly: *The research demonstrates the need to treat cancer early.* | *His lawyer will try to **demonstrate that** Lee was out of town on the night of the murder.* | *The graph **demonstrates how** air travel has increased over the last fifty years.*

THESAURUS

show – to make it clear that something is true or exists by providing facts or information: *The case shows that women still face discrimination at work.*
indicate (formal) – if scientific facts, tests, official figures, etc. indicate something, they show that something exists or is likely to be true: *Research indicates that the drug may be linked to birth defects.*
suggest – to show that something is probably true, even though there is no proof: *There was nothing in the letter to suggest that he was thinking of suicide.*
prove – to show that something is definitely true: *Researchers have not been able to prove there is a link between living near a power line and getting cancer.*
establish (formal) – to find out facts that will prove that something is true: *Studies have established that good daycare does children no harm.*
substantiate (formal) – to prove the truth of something that someone has said: *The data substantiates this theory.*

2 [T] to show or describe how to use or do something: *Instructors should **demonstrate how** to use the equipment.* | *Our teacher demonstrated the correct way to construct an essay.*

THESAURUS explain, tell, show, go through sth, clarify ➔ EXPLAIN

3 [T] to show that you have a particular skill, quality, or ability: *The contest gave her a chance to demonstrate her ability.* **4** [I] to protest or support something in public with a lot of other people: *Thousands came to **demonstrate against** the war.* [ORIGIN: 1500—1600 Latin *demonstratus*, past participle of *demonstrare*, from *monstrare* "to show"]

THESAURUS protest, march, riot, hold/stage a sit-in, go on a hunger strike, boycott ➔ PROTEST²

dem·on·stra·tion /,dɛmənˈstreɪʃən/ (Ac) *n.* **1** [C] an event at which a lot of people meet to protest or support something in public: *Students **staged/held a demonstration against** gun violence.* **2** [C,U] the act of showing and explaining how to do something: *Pam **gave a demonstration** on how to use the new computer system.* | *Make sure you get a **demonstration of** the software before you buy it.* **3** [C] an action, fact, etc. that proves that someone or something has a particular quality, ability, emotion, etc.: *People gathered in a **demonstration of support** for the missing children.* | *The city's polluted air is a clear demonstration of the need for tougher environmental laws.*

de·mon·stra·tive /dɪˈmɑnstrəṭɪv/ (Ac) *adj.* willing to show how much you care about someone: *He loves me, but he's not very demonstrative.*

de,monstrative 'pronoun *n.* [C] ENG. LANG. ARTS a PRONOUN such as "that" or "this" that shows which person or thing is meant out of a group

dem·on·strat·or /ˈdɛmən,streɪṭə/ (Ac) *n.* [C] **1** someone who takes part in a public demonstration **2** someone who shows people how to do something or how something works

de·mor·al·ize /dɪˈmɔrə,laɪz, di-, -ˈmɑr-/ *v.* [T] to make someone lose his/her confidence or courage: *Too many changes can demoralize your employees.* —**demoralizing** *adj.*

de·mote /dɪˈmoʊt, di-/ *v.* [T] to make someone have a lower rank or less important position (ANT) **promote** —**demotion** /dɪˈmoʊʃən/ *n.* [C,U]

de·mot·ic /dɪˈmɑṭɪk/ *adj.* **1** ENG. LANG. ARTS used by or popular with most ordinary people: *a play written in the demotic language of Chicano gangs* **2 Demotic** HISTORY relating to an ancient form of Egyptian writing that was simple and could be used by ordinary people

de·mure /dɪˈmyʊr/ *adj.* a girl or woman who is demure is shy, quiet, and always behaves well

THESAURUS **shy, timid, bashful, self-conscious, reserved, introverted, retiring** → SHY[1]

den /dɛn/ *n.* [C] **1** a room in a house, where people relax, read, watch television, etc. **2** the home of some types of animals, such as lions and FOXes [ORIGIN: Old English *denn*]

den·drite /ˈdɛndraɪt/ *n.* [C] BIOLOGY a small part on the body of a nerve cell, that makes electrical signals come toward the cell from other cells

de·ni·al /dɪˈnaɪəl/ (Ac) *n.* **1** [C,U] a statement saying that something is not true → DENY: *Diaz made a public **denial of** the rumor.* **2** [U] a situation or condition in which you refuse to admit or believe that something bad exists or has happened: *I think Becky's **in denial** about her drinking problem.* **3** [C] (formal) the act of refusing to allow someone to have or do something → DENY: *the **denial of** basic human rights*

den·i·grate /ˈdɛnɪˌgreɪt/ *v.* [T] (formal) to do or say things to make someone or something seem less important or good [ORIGIN: 1400—1500 Latin *denigrare*, from *niger* "black"]

den·im /ˈdɛnəm/ *n.* [U] a type of strong cotton cloth used for making JEANS [ORIGIN: 1600—1700 French *(serge) de Nîmes* "(type of cloth) from Nîmes," French city where it was first made]

de·nom·i·na·tion /dɪˌnɑməˈneɪʃən/ *n.* [C] **1** a religious group that has slightly different beliefs from other groups who belong to the same religion

THESAURUS **church, sect, cult** → CHURCH

2 the value of a coin, paper money, or a stamp: *The robbers escaped with $12,000 **in small/large denominations**.*

de·nom·i·na·tor /dɪˈnɑməˌneɪtə/ *n.* [C] MATH the number below the line in a FRACTION → COMMON DENOMINATOR, LOWEST COMMON DENOMINATOR, NUMERATOR

de·no·ta·tion /ˌdinoʊˈteɪʃən/ (Ac) *n.* [C] ENG. LANG. ARTS the thing that is actually described by a word, rather than the feelings or ideas it suggests

de·not·a·tive /dɪˈnoʊt̬ət̬ɪv/ *adj.* ENG. LANG. ARTS representing or explaining something in a clear way using facts: *Denotative language is factual, whereas connotative language is emotional.*

de·note /dɪˈnoʊt/ (Ac) *v.* [T] (written) to represent or mean something: *Each X on the map denotes 500 people.* | *In this painting, the red sky denotes danger.*

de·nounce /dɪˈnaʊns/ *v.* [T] to say publicly that you disapprove of someone or something: *The bishop **denounced** the film **as** immoral.*

dense /dɛns/ *adj.* **1** made of or containing a lot of things or people that are very close together: *the city's dense population* | *the dense jungles of northern Vietnam* **2** difficult to see through or breathe in: *a dense fog* **3** (informal) stupid —**densely** *adv.*

den·si·ty /ˈdɛnsət̬i/ *n.* (plural **densities**) [C,U] **1** the degree to which an area is filled with things or people: *a high density* (=very crowded) *neighborhood* **2** PHYSICS the relationship between an object's weight and the amount of space it fills

dent[1] /dɛnt/ *n.* [C] **1** a mark made when you hit or press something so that its surface is bent: *a big **dent in** the car* **2** a reduction in the amount of something: *I haven't **made a dent in** the money I have to pay back on my loan.*

D

dent[2] *v.* [T] to hit or press something so that its surface is bent and marked: *Some idiot dented my car door.*

den·tal /ˈdɛntl/ *adj.* relating to your teeth: *dental care* [ORIGIN: 1500—1600 Latin *dentalis*, from *dens* "tooth"]

ˌdental ˈfloss *n.* [U] thin string that you use to clean between your teeth

den·tine /ˈdɛntin/ *n.* [U] BIOLOGY the type of bone that your teeth are made of

dentist

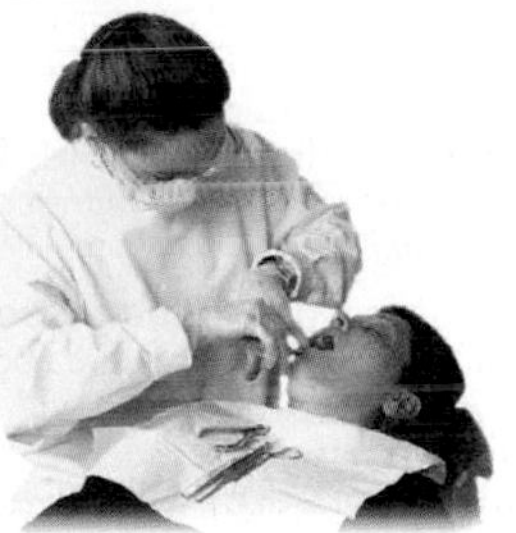

den·tist /ˈdɛntɪst/ *n.* [C] someone whose job is to treat people's teeth: *I **go to the dentist** twice a year.*

THESAURUS **doctor, physician, surgeon, specialist, psychiatrist, pediatrician** → DOCTOR[1]

den·tures /ˈdɛntʃəz/ *n.* [plural] artificial teeth worn to replace the natural ones that someone has lost (SYN) **false teeth**

de·nun·ci·a·tion /dɪˌnʌnsiˈeɪʃən/ *n.* [C,U] a public statement in which you criticize someone or something

de·ny /dɪˈnaɪ/ (Ac) *v.* (**denied**, **denies**) [T] **1** to say that something is not true → DENIAL: *Simmons **denied that** he had murdered his wife.* | *He has repeatedly denied the rumor.* **2** to refuse to allow someone to have or do something → DENIAL: *The judge denied a request to close down the school immediately.* [ORIGIN: 1200—1300 Old French *denier*, from Latin *negare* "to deny"]

de·o·dor·ant /diˈoʊdərənt/ *n.* [C,U] a substance that you put on the skin under your arms to stop you from smelling bad

de·ox·y·ri·bo·nu·cle·ic ac·id /di,ɑksi,raɪboʊnu,kliɪk 'æsɪd/ *n.* [U] BIOLOGY DNA

de·part /dɪ'pɑrt/ *v.* [I] (formal) to leave (ANT) **arrive**: *All passengers* ***departing for*** *New York on flight UA179 should go to Gate 7.* | *The train will* ***depart from*** *track 9.*

> THESAURUS **leave, go away, set off, drive off/away, take off, withdraw** → LEAVE[1]

depart from sth *phr. v.* (formal) to start to use new ideas or do something in an unusual or unexpected way: *Parker's approach departs from the usual classroom routine.*

D

de·part·ment /dɪ'pɑrt˺mənt/ *n.* [C] **1** any of the groups of people working together that form part of a large organization such as a college, government, or business: *a typical university music department* | *the Department of Energy* **2** an area in a large store, where particular types of product are sold: *the men's department* (=where clothes for men are sold)

de'partment ,store *n.* [C] a large store that sells many different products such as clothes, kitchen equipment, etc.

de·par·ture /dɪ'pɑrtʃɚ/ *n.* **1** [C,U] the action of leaving a place, especially to travel in an airplane, car, etc. (ANT) **arrival**: *Check in at the airport an hour before departure.* | *her* ***departure for*** *Japan* **2** [C] a change from what is usual or expected: *Their new designs represent a* ***departure from*** *their usual style.*

de·pend /dɪ'pɛnd/ *v.* **it/that depends** (spoken) used to say that you are not sure about something because you do not know what will happen: *"Are you coming to my house later?" "It depends. I might have to work."*

depend on/upon sb/sth *phr. v.* **1** to need the help or support of someone or something else: *Charles* ***depends on*** *money from his parents* ***to*** *pay his rent.* **2** to be directly affected by something else: *The amount you spend depends on where you live.* **3** to trust someone or something: *Sometimes I think you're the only person I can depend on.* [ORIGIN: 1400—1500 French *dépendre*, from Latin *pendere* "to hang"]

> THESAURUS
> **rely on/upon** – to trust or depend on someone or something: *I knew I could rely on David.*
> **trust** – to believe that someone is honest and will not do anything bad or wrong: *I wouldn't trust him if I were you.*
> **count on** – to depend on someone or something: *You can always count on me.*

de·pend·a·ble /dɪ'pɛndəbəl/ *adj.* someone or something that is dependable will always do what you need or expect him, her, or it to do: *a highly dependable employee* | *a dependable car*

de·pend·ent[1] /dɪ'pɛndənt/ *adj.* **1** needing someone or something else in order to exist, be successful, etc. (ANT) **independent**: *dependent children* | *Jan's mother was* ***dependent on*** *her* ***for*** *physical care.* **2 be dependent on/upon sth** to be directly affected by something else: *Your success is dependent on how hard you work.* —**dependence** *n.* [U]

dependent[2] *n.* [C] someone, especially a child, who depends on someone else for food, money, clothing, etc.

de,pendent 'clause *n.* [C] ENG. LANG. ARTS a CLAUSE that gives information related to the main clause in a sentence, but which cannot exist alone. For example, in the sentence, "I have hated milk since I was child," the clause "since I was a child" is a dependent clause. → INDEPENDENT CLAUSE

de,pendent 'variable *n.* [C] SCIENCE in a scientific EXPERIMENT (=test), a result that is likely to change depending on the different conditions used in the experiment (SYN) **responding variable**

de·pict /dɪ'pɪkt/ *v.* [T] to describe or show a character, situation, or event in writing or by using pictures: *the people depicted in the movie* | *The god is* ***depicted as*** *a bird with a human head.* [ORIGIN: 1400—1500 Latin *depictus*, past participle of *depingere*, from *pingere* "to paint"]

de·plete /dɪ'plit/ *v.* [T] (formal) to reduce the amount of something: *Many of our forests have been depleted by the paper industry.*

de·plor·a·ble /dɪ'plɔrəbəl/ *adj.* (formal) very bad, shocking, and deserving strong disapproval: *deplorable prison conditions*

de·plore /dɪ'plɔr/ *v.* [T] (formal) to severely criticize something that you disapprove of: *a statement deploring the use of chemical weapons* [ORIGIN: 1500—1600 French *déplorer*, from Latin *plorare* "to cry out"]

de·ploy /dɪ'plɔɪ/ *v.* [T] to move soldiers and military equipment to a place so that they can be used if necessary: *Nuclear missiles were being deployed in Europe.* [ORIGIN: 1400—1500 French *déployer*, from Latin *displicare* "to scatter"]

de·pop·u·la·tion /di,pɑpyə'leɪʃən/ *n.* [U] SOCIAL SCIENCE a large reduction in the number of people living in a particular area: *The movement of people into the cities led to the depopulation of rural areas.*

de·port /dɪ'pɔrt/ *v.* [T] to officially make a person from a foreign country return to the country they came from —**deportation** /,dipɔr'teɪʃən/ *n.* [C,U]

de·pos·it[1] /dɪ'pɑzɪt/ *n.* [C] **1** a part of the cost of something that you pay before paying the total amount later: *We* ***put down a deposit on*** *the house yesterday.* **2** an amount of money that is put into someone's bank account (ANT) **withdrawal**: *I'd like to* ***make a deposit*** *into my savings account.* **3** money that you pay when you rent something such as an apartment or car, which will be given back if you do not damage it **4** an amount or layer of a substance in a particular place: *oil deposits*

deposit² *v.* [T] **1** to put money into a bank account (ANT) **withdraw**: *I'd like to deposit this in my checking account.* **2** to put something down, especially in a particular place

de·pot /ˈdipoʊ/ *n.* [C] **1** a small train or bus station **2** a place where goods are stored

de·praved /dɪˈpreɪvd/ *adj.* morally unacceptable and evil: *a depraved murderer* [ORIGIN: 1500—1600 *deprave* "to make evil" (14—21 centuries), from French *dépraver*, from Latin *pravus* "bent, bad"]

THESAURUS **bad, evil, wicked, immoral, wrong, reprehensible** → BAD¹

de·prav·i·ty /dɪˈprævəṭi/ *n.* [U] the state of being evil or morally unacceptable: *sexual depravity*

dep·re·cate /ˈdɛprəˌkeɪt/ *v.* [T] (formal) to disapprove of or criticize something strongly: *The Senator deprecated the riots that had broken out after the court's decision.* —**deprecation** /ˌdɛprəˈkeɪʃən/ *n.* [U]

de·pre·ci·ate /dɪˈpriʃiˌeɪt/ *v.* [I] ECONOMICS to decrease in value or price (ANT) **appreciate**: *A new car depreciates as soon as it is driven.* —**depreciation** /dɪˌpriʃiˈeɪʃən/ *n.* [U]

de·press /dɪˈprɛs/ (Ac) *v.* [T] **1** to make someone feel very sad → DEPRESSION: *All this rain is depressing me.* **2** to reduce the amount or value of something → DEPRESSION: *The value of the peso fell, depressing the nation's economy.* [ORIGIN: 1300—1400 Old French *depresser*, from Latin *premere* "to press"]

de·pressed /dɪˈprɛst/ (Ac) *adj.* **1** very sad → DEPRESSION: *I started feeling **depressed about** my mother's illness.*

THESAURUS **sad, unhappy, miserable, sorrowful, down, low, blue, downhearted, melancholy, morose, gloomy, glum** → SAD

2 not having enough jobs or business activity to make an area, industry, etc. successful → DEPRESSION: *a depressed economy*

de·press·ing /dɪˈprɛsɪŋ/ (Ac) *adj.* making you feel sad: *a depressing movie*

de·pres·sion /dɪˈprɛʃən/ (Ac) *n.* **1** [C,U] **a)** a strong feeling of sadness and a loss of hope → DEPRESSED: *After her son died, she **went into** a long period of **depression**.* **b)** a medical condition that makes you feel extremely unhappy, so that you cannot live a normal life → DEPRESSED: *The patient is suffering from depression.* **2** [C,U] ECONOMICS a long period when businesses do not buy, sell, or produce very much, and many people do not have jobs: *the Great Depression of the 1930s*

THESAURUS **recession, slump, downturn, crash** → RECESSION

3 [C] an area of a surface that is lower than the other parts: *Water had collected in a shallow depression between the hills.*

de·prive /dɪˈpraɪv/ *v.*
deprive sb **of** sth *phr. v.* to take something that someone needs away from him/her: *The troops had been deprived of food and water.*

de·prived /dɪˈpraɪvd/ *adj.* not having the things that are considered to be necessary for a comfortable or happy life: *a deprived childhood*

THESAURUS **poor, needy, destitute, impoverished, impecunious, indigent, penurious, poverty-stricken, disadvantaged, underprivileged** → POOR

dept. the written abbreviation of DEPARTMENT

depth /dɛpθ/ *n.* **1** [C usually singular] **a)** the distance from the top of something to the bottom of it: *The water rose to a **depth of** 12 feet.* **b)** the distance from the front of an object to the back of it: *the **depth of** the shelves* → *see picture at* DIMENSION **2** [U] how strong an emotion is or how serious a situation is: *the depth of their friendship* **3 in depth** including all the details → IN-DEPTH: *In her new book, she analyzes the problem in depth.*

dep·u·ty /ˈdɛpyəṭi/ *n.* (plural **deputies**) [C] **1** someone who is directly below someone else in rank, and who is officially in charge when that person is not there: *the deputy director of the Foundation* **2** someone whose job is to help a SHERIFF [ORIGIN: 1400—1500 French *député*, from Latin *deputare* "to give a particular job to someone"]

de·rail /dɪˈreɪl, di-/ *v.* [I,T] to make a train go off the railroad tracks, or to go off the tracks

de·ranged /dɪˈreɪndʒd/ *adj.* behaving in a crazy or dangerous way: *a deranged criminal*

der·by /ˈdɚbi/ *n.* (plural **derbies**) [C] **1** a type of horse race: *the Kentucky Derby* **2** a stiff round hat for men, worn in past times

der·e·lict¹ /ˈdɛrəˌlɪkt/ *adj.* a building or piece of land that is derelict is in bad condition because no one has used it in a long time [ORIGIN: 1600—1700 Latin *derelictus*, past participle of *derelinquere* "to leave something you are responsible for"]

derelict² *n.* [C] (disapproving) someone who has no home or money, and is very dirty

de·ride /dɪˈraɪd/ *v.* [T] (formal) to say something that shows you have no respect for someone or something —**derision** /dɪˈrɪʒən/ *n.* [U]

de·ri·so·ry /dɪˈraɪsəri/ *adj.* a derisory amount of money is very small and is not worth considering seriously

der·i·va·tion /ˌdɛrəˈveɪʃən/ (Ac) *n.* [C,U] the act or process of coming from something else, such as when a new word develops from another word: *"Verse" is a derivation of the Latin word "versus."*

de·riv·a·tive¹ /dɪˈrɪvəṭɪv/ (Ac) *n.* [C] something that has developed or been produced from something else: *The drug is a **derivative of** Vitamin A.*

derivative² *adj.* (disapproving) copied or taken from something else: *I find his painting style very derivative.*

de·rive /dɪ'raɪv/ (Ac) *v.* **1** [T] to get something such as happiness, strength, or satisfaction from someone or something: *He* ***derives*** *pleasure* ***from*** *helping others.* **2** [I,T] to develop or come from something else: *The word "benefit" is* ***derived from*** *Latin.* **3** [T] CHEMISTRY to get a chemical substance from another substance: *A variety of compounds can be* ***derived from*** *the acid.* [ORIGIN: 1300—1400 French *dériver*, from Latin *derivare* "to draw out water," from *rivus* "stream"]

D

der·ma·tol·o·gy /ˌdɚmə'tɑlədʒi/ *n.* [U] the part of medical science that deals with the skin, its diseases, and their treatment —**dermatologist** *n.* [C]

der·mis /'dɚmɪs/ *n.* [U] BIOLOGY the layer of skin under the EPIDERMIS (=the outside layer of skin)

de·rog·a·to·ry /dɪ'rɑgəˌtɔri/ *adj.* insulting and disapproving: *He was constantly making* ***derogatory remarks*** *about women.*

der·rick /'dɛrɪk/ *n.* [C] the tall tower over an oil well, that holds the DRILL

de·scend /dɪ'sɛnd/ *v.* [I,T] (formal) to move from a higher level to a lower one (ANT) **ascend**: *She began to descend the stairs.* [ORIGIN: 1300—1400 Old French *descendre*, from Latin *de* "down" + *scandere* "to climb"]

descend from sb *phr. v.* **be descended from sb** to be related to someone who lived a long time ago: *My father's family is descended from the Pilgrims.*

descend on/upon sth *phr. v.* if a lot of people descend on a place, they arrive there at the same time: *A large troop of soldiers descended on the village.*

de·scend·ant /dɪ'sɛndənt/ *n.* [C] someone who is related to a person who lived a long time ago ➔ ANCESTOR: *She was a* ***direct descendant of*** *one of the Pilgrims on the Mayflower.*

de·scent /dɪ'sɛnt/ *n.* **1** [C,U] (formal) the process of going down (ANT) **ascent**: *The plane began its descent.* **2** [U] your family origins, especially in relation to the country where your family came from: *We're* ***of*** *Italian* ***descent.***

de·scribe /dɪ'skraɪb/ *v.* [T] to say what someone or something is like by giving details ➔ DESCRIPTION: *Can you describe the man who took your purse?* | *It's hard to* ***describe how*** *I feel.* | *One child* ***described*** *hiccups* ***as*** *'having jumping beans' inside her stomach.* [ORIGIN: 1400—1500 Latin *describere*, from *scribere* "to write"]

THESAURUS **call, characterize, label, brand, portray** ➔ CALL¹

de·scrip·tion /dɪ'skrɪpʃən/ *n.* [C,U] a piece of writing or speech that gives details about what someone or something is like ➔ DESCRIBE: *Kate* ***gave us a description of*** *her new house.* | *Police have a* ***detailed description*** *of the missing child.* | *You* ***fit the description of*** (=look like) *a man seen running from the scene.*

de·scrip·tive /dɪ'skrɪptɪv/ *adj.* giving a description of something in words or pictures

des·e·crate /'dɛsəˌkreɪt/ *v.* [T] to damage something holy or respected —**desecration** /ˌdɛsə'kreɪʃən/ *n.* [U]

de·seg·re·gate /di'sɛgrəˌgeɪt/ *v.* [T] to end a system in which people of different races are kept separate (ANT) **segregate**: *an attempt to desegregate the schools* —**desegregated** *adj.* —**desegregation** /diˌsɛgrə'geɪʃən/ *n.* [U]

desert

des·ert¹ /'dɛzɚt/ *n.* [C,U] EARTH SCIENCES a large area of land where it is always hot and dry, there are few plants, and there is often a lot of sand: *the Sahara desert*

de·sert² /dɪ'zɚt/ *v.* **1** [T] to leave someone alone and not help him/her anymore: *My boyfriend deserted me when I got pregnant.* **2** [I] to leave the military without permission **3** [T] to leave a place so that it is empty: *Everyone deserted the village and fled to the hills.* —**desertion** /dɪ'zɚʃən/ *n.* [C,U]

de·sert·ed /dɪ'zɚt̬ɪd/ *adj.* empty and quiet because the people who are usually there have left: *At night, the streets are deserted.*

THESAURUS **empty, bare, uninhabited, free, vacant** ➔ EMPTY¹

de·sert·er /dɪ'zɚt̬ɚ/ *n.* [C] a soldier who leaves the military without permission

de·sert·i·fi·ca·tion /dɪˌzɚt̬əfə'keɪʃən/ *n.* [U] EARTH SCIENCES a process in which land that is able to produce crops gradually becomes a desert: *Sub-Saharan Africa is constantly under threat of desertification.*

de·serve /dɪ'zɚv/ *v.* [T] if someone deserves something, s/he should get it because of the way s/he has behaved: *After all that work, you deserve a rest.* | *Migrant workers* ***deserve to*** *make more than $3 an hour.* | *People who go to jail for abusing children* ***get what they deserve*** (=receive the right punishment). —**deserved** *adj.*

des·ic·cat·ed /'dɛsɪˌkeɪt̬ɪd/ *adj.* (formal) completely dried: *desiccated coconut*

de·sign¹ /dɪ'zaɪn/ (Ac) *n.* **1** [U] the way that

something has been planned or made: *We're working to improve the **design of** the computer.* | *The two cars are similar **in design**.* **2** [C] a pattern used for decorating something: *curtains with a floral design*

THESAURUS pattern, markings, motif → PATTERN

3 [C] a drawing that shows how something will be made or what it will look like: *We're working on **designs for** a new office building downtown.* **4** [U] the art or process of making drawings or plans for something: *Vicky studied graphic design at college.* **5 have designs on sth** to want something and be planning a way to get it [ORIGIN: 1300—1400 *French désigner*, from Latin *designare*, from *signare* "to mark"]

design² (Ac) *v.* **1** [I,T] to make a drawing or plan of something that will be made or built: *Armani is designing some exciting new suits for fall.* **2** [T] to plan or develop something for a particular purpose: *an exercise **designed to** strengthen your legs* | *The animal's sharp claws are **designed for** attacking its prey.* | *The book is **designed as** a reference manual.*

des·ig·nate /ˈdɛzɪɡˌneɪt/ *v.* [T] to choose someone or something for a particular job or purpose: *$200 million was **designated for** new schools.* | *She has been **designated to** take over the position of treasurer.*

ˌdesignated ˈdriver *n.* [C] someone who does not drink alcohol at a party, bar, etc. so that s/he can drive his/her friends home

des·ig·na·tion /ˌdɛzɪɡˈneɪʃən/ *n.* **1** [U] the act of choosing someone or something for a particular purpose, or giving him, her, or it a particular description: *the **designation of** 100 acres around the lake as a protected area for wildlife* **2** [C] the description or title that someone or something is given: *Any beef with the designation "extra lean" must only have 5% of its weight in fat.*

de·sign·er /dɪˈzaɪnɚ/ (Ac) *n.* [C] someone whose job is to make plans or patterns for clothes, jewelry, etc.: ***designer sunglasses*** (=sunglasses from a well-known designer)

de·sir·a·ble /dɪˈzaɪrəbəl/ *adj.* (formal) **1** worth having or doing because it is useful, popular, or good: *a desirable job with a big law firm* **2** someone who is desirable is sexually attractive —**desirability** /dɪˌzaɪrəˈbɪləṭi/ *n.* [U]

de·sire¹ /dɪˈzaɪɚ/ *n.* [C] **1** a strong hope or wish: *the country's **desire for** peace* | *I have no **desire to** meet her.* **2** (formal) a strong wish to have sex with someone [ORIGIN: 1200—1300 Old French *desirer*, from Latin *desiderare*]

desire² *v.* [T] **1 sth leaves a lot to be desired** said when something is not as good as it should be: *This coffee leaves a lot to be desired.* **2** (formal) to want or hope for something very much (SYN) **want**: *Muller never **desired to** return to the United States.* **3** (formal) to want to have sex with someone

de·sist /dɪˈzɪst, dɪˈsɪst/ *v.* [I] (formal) to stop doing something

desk /dɛsk/ *n.* [C] **1** a piece of furniture like a table, that you sit at to write and work: *Marie was sitting **at her desk**.* **2** a place where you can get information at a hotel, airport, etc.: *Check in at the **front desk**.*

desk·top /ˈdɛsktɑp/ *n.* [C] **1** IT the main area on a computer screen where you find the ICONS that represent PROGRAMS **2** the top surface of a desk

ˌdesktop comˈputer *n.* [C] a computer that is designed to be used on a desk → LAPTOP

ˌdesktop ˈpublishing *n.* [U] the work of producing magazines, books, etc. with a desktop computer

D

des·o·late /ˈdɛsəlɪt/ *adj.* **1** a place that is desolate is empty and looks sad because there are no people there and not much activity: *a desolate stretch of highway* **2** feeling very sad and lonely [ORIGIN: 1300—1400 Latin *desolatus*, from *solus* "alone"] —**desolation** /ˌdɛsəˈleɪʃən/ *n.* [U]

de·spair¹ /dɪˈspɛr/ *n.* [U] a feeling that you have no hope at all: *Nancy's suicide left him **in deep despair**.* [ORIGIN: 1200—1300 Old French *desperer*, from Latin *desperare*, from *sperare* "to hope"]

despair² *v.* [I] (formal) to feel that there is no hope at all: *Margaret **despaired of** ever finding a husband.*

des·per·ate /ˈdɛsprɪt, -pərɪt/ *adj.* **1** willing to do anything to change a very bad situation, and not caring about danger: *I hadn't eaten for days and was **getting desperate**.* **2** needing or wanting something very much: *By then I was so broke I was **desperate for** a job.* | *After a week in the hospital he was **desperate to** go home.* **3** a desperate situation is very bad or serious: *a **desperate shortage** of food* —**desperately** *adv.*: *The doctors tried desperately to save her life.*

des·per·a·tion /ˌdɛspəˈreɪʃən/ *n.* [U] a strong feeling that you will do anything to change a very bad situation: *The drowning man grabbed at the life raft **in desperation**.*

de·spic·a·ble /dɪˈspɪkəbəl/ *adj.* extremely bad or cruel

de·spise /dɪˈspaɪz/ *v.* [T] (formal) to dislike someone or something very much: *He despised her from the moment they met.*

THESAURUS hate, can't stand, detest, loathe, abhor → HATE¹

de·spite /dɪˈspaɪt/ (Ac) *prep.* without being prevented or affected by something (SYN) **in spite of**: *Despite the doctors' efforts, the patient died.* | *The trade in ivory continues **despite the fact that** it is illegal.*

THESAURUS although, however, in spite of, nevertheless/nonetheless → ALTHOUGH

de·spond·ent /dɪ'spɑndənt/ *adj.* unhappy and without hope —**despondency** *n.* [U] —**despondently** *adv.*

des·pot /'dɛspət, -pɑt/ *n.* [C] someone, especially the ruler of a country, who uses power in a cruel and unfair way [ORIGIN: 1500—1600 Old French *despote*, from Greek *despotes* "lord"] —**despotic** /dɛ'spɑtɪk/ *adj.*

des·pot·ism /'dɛspə,tɪzəm/ *n.* [U] POLITICS rule by a despot

des·sert /dɪ'zɚt/ *n.* [C,U] sweet food served after the main part of a meal: *What's **for dessert**?* [ORIGIN: 1500—1600 French *desservir* "to clear the table," from *servir* "to serve"]

D

des·ti·na·tion /,dɛstə'neɪʃən/ *n.* [C] the place that someone or something is going to: *The Alamo is a popular **tourist destination** in Texas.* | *We have just enough gas to **reach** our **destination**.*

des·tined /'dɛstənd/ *adj.* seeming certain to happen or do something at some time in the future: *The album is **destined to** become a classic.*

des·ti·ny /'dɛstəni/ *n.* (plural **destinies**) [C,U] the things that will happen to someone in the future, or the power that controls this SYN **fate**: *a nation fighting to **control** its **destiny*** [ORIGIN: 1300—1400 Old French *destinee*, from Latin *destinare* "to fasten, fix"]

des·ti·tute /'dɛstə,tut/ *adj.* having no money, no place to live, no food, etc.: *The floods left thousands of people destitute.* —**destitution** /,dɛstə'tuʃən/ *n.* [U]

> THESAURUS **poor, needy, impoverished, broke, impecunious, indigent, penurious, poverty-stricken** → POOR

de·stroy /dɪ'strɔɪ/ *v.* [T] to damage something so badly that it cannot be used or no longer exists → DESTRUCTION: *Two houses were destroyed in the fire.* [ORIGIN: 1100—1200 Old French *destruire*, from Latin *destruere*, from *struere* "to build"]

de·stroy·er /dɪ'strɔɪɚ/ *n.* [C] **1** a small fast military ship with guns **2** someone or something that destroys things or people

de·struc·tion /dɪ'strʌkʃən/ *n.* [U] the act or process of destroying something or of being destroyed: *the **destruction of** the rain forests* —**destructive** /dɪ'strʌktɪv/ *adj.*

de,structive inter'ference *n.* [U] PHYSICS the combination of two WAVES of energy whose highest and lowest points are not the same, which results in a wave that is weaker than either of them

de·tach /dɪ'tætʃ/ *v.* [T] to remove something from something that it is attached to —**detachable** *adj.*

de·tached /dɪ'tætʃt/ *adj.* not reacting to something in an emotional way: *My father was always **emotionally detached from** the rest of us.* —**detachment** *n.* [U]

de·tail¹ /'diteɪl, dɪ'teɪl/ *n.* [C,U] a single fact or piece of information about something: *Dad planned our vacation **down to the smallest/last detail**.* | *The judge refused to discuss the case **in detail*** (=using lots of details). | *There's no need to **go into detail*** (=give a lot of details) *about the contract at this early stage.* [ORIGIN: 1600—1700 French *détail*, from Old French *detail* "piece cut off"]

detail² *v.* [T] to list things or give all the facts or information about something: *Wooley detailed the dangers of dieting.*

de·tailed /dɪ'teɪld, 'diteɪld/ *adj.* containing or using a lot of information or facts: *a detailed examination of the body*

de·tain /dɪ'teɪn/ *v.* [T] to officially stop someone from leaving a place: *Police detained two suspects for questioning.*

de·tect /dɪ'tɛkt/ (Ac) *v.* [T] to notice or discover something, especially something that is not easy to see, hear, etc.: *I detected the faint smell of perfume.* | *Cancer cells are often **difficult to detect**.* [ORIGIN: 1400—1500 Latin *detectus*, past participle of *detegere* "to uncover"] —**detectable** *adj.* —**detection** /dɪ'tɛkʃən/ *n.* [U]: *The search led to the detection of a second bomb.*

> THESAURUS **find, discover, trace, locate** → FIND¹

de·tec·tive /dɪ'tɛktɪv/ (Ac) *n.* [C] a police officer whose job is to discover information about crimes and catch criminals

de·tect·or /dɪ'tɛktɚ/ (Ac) *n.* [C] a machine or piece of equipment that finds or measures something: *Students must pass through **metal detectors** when entering the school.*

dé·tente /deɪ'tɑnt/ *n.* [C,U] POLITICS a time or situation in which two countries that are not friendly toward each other agree to behave in a more friendly way

de·ten·tion /dɪ'tɛnʃən/ *n.* **1** [U] the state of being kept in prison: *The suspect was held **in detention** for three days.* **2** [C,U] a punishment in which students who have behaved badly must stay at school for a short time after other students have left

de·ter /dɪ'tɚ/ *v.* (**deterred**, **deterring**) [T] to stop someone from doing something by making it difficult or threatening him/her with punishment: *The high cost of cigarettes has deterred many smokers.* | *The security camera was installed to **deter** people **from** stealing.* [ORIGIN: 1500—1600 Latin *deterrere*, from *terrere* "to frighten"]

de·ter·gent /dɪ'tɚdʒənt/ *n.* [C,U] a liquid or powder containing soap, used for washing clothes, dishes, etc. [ORIGIN: 1600—1700 French *détergent*, from Latin *tergere* "to clean by rubbing"]

de·te·ri·o·rate /dɪ'tɪriə,reɪt/ *v.* [I] to become worse: *Her health is deteriorating quickly.* [ORIGIN: 1500—1600 Late Latin *deteriorare*, from Latin *deterior* "worse"] —**deterioration** /dɪ,tɪriə'reɪʃən/ *n.* [U]

de·ter·mi·na·tion /dɪˌtɚməˈneɪʃən/ *n.* [U] the quality of trying to do something even when it is difficult: *Marco **shows** great **determination to** learn English.*

de·ter·mine /dɪˈtɚmɪn/ *v.* [T] **1** (formal) to find out the facts about something: *Using sonar, they determined exactly where the ship had sunk.* **2** to decide something, or to influence a decision about something: *The number of incoming students will determine the size of the classes.* [ORIGIN: 1300—1400 Old French *determiner*, from Latin *terminus* "edge, limit"]

THESAURUS **decide, make up your mind, choose, resolve** → DECIDE

de·ter·mined /dɪˈtɚmɪnd/ *adj.* having a strong desire to do something even when it is difficult: *a determined opponent* | *Beth was **determined to** make her marriage work.*

de·ter·min·er /dɪˈtɚmənɚ/ *n.* [C] ENG. LANG. ARTS in grammar, a word that is used before a noun in order to show which thing you mean. In the phrases "the car" and "some cars," "the" and "some" are determiners.

de·ter·rence /dɪˈtɚəns/ *n.* [U] **1** POLITICS a situation in which a country continues to have a strong army or powerful weapons in order to prevent a military attack from another country: *nuclear deterrence* **2** (formal) the act of stopping people from doing something bad: *Does the punishment provide adequate deterrence?*

de·ter·rent /dɪˈtɚənt/ *n.* [C] something that makes someone not want to do something: *Car alarms can be an effective **deterrent to** burglars.*

de·test /dɪˈtɛst/ *v.* [T] to hate someone or something very much: *I detest cigarettes.*

THESAURUS **hate, can't stand, loathe, despise, abhor** → HATE[1]

det·o·nate /ˈdɛt˺nˌeɪt, -t̬əˌneɪt/ *v.* [I,T] to explode, or to make something do this: *Nuclear bombs were detonated in tests in the desert.* [ORIGIN: 1700—1800 Latin *detonare*, from *tonare* "to thunder"] **—detonation** /ˌdɛt˺nˈeɪʃən/ *n.* [C,U]

det·o·na·tor /ˈdɛt˺nˌeɪt̬ɚ, -t̬əˌneɪt̬ɚ/ *n.* [C] a small object that is used to make a bomb explode

de·tour[1] /ˈditʊr/ *n.* [C] a way of going from one place to another that is longer than the usual way because you want to avoid traffic, go somewhere special, etc.: *We **made/took a detour** to avoid the street repairs.*

detour[2] *v.* [I,T] to make a detour

de·tox /ˈditɑks/ *n.* [U] (informal) a special treatment to help people stop drinking alcohol or taking drugs

de·tract /dɪˈtrækt/ *v.*
detract from sth *phr. v.* to make something seem less good than it really is: *The rain did not detract from our vacation.*

det·ri·ment /ˈdɛtrəmənt/ *n.* [U] (formal) harm or damage that is done to something: *He works long hours, **to the detriment of** his marriage.* **—detrimental** /ˌdɛtrəˈmɛntl/ *adj.*

de·val·ue /diˈvælyu/ *v.* **1** [I,T] ECONOMICS to reduce the value of a country's money, especially in relation to the value of another country's money **2** [T] to make someone or something seem less important or valuable **—devaluation** /diˌvælyuˈeɪʃən/ *n.* [C,U]

dev·as·tate /ˈdɛvəˌsteɪt/ *v.* [T] **1** to make someone feel extremely sad or shocked: *Mike was devastated by his parents' divorce.* **2** to damage something, or to destroy something completely: *Bombing raids devastated parts of London.* [ORIGIN: 1600—1700 Latin *devastare*, from *vastare* "to lay waste, destroy"] **—devastation** /ˌdɛvəˈsteɪʃən/ *n.* [U]

D

dev·as·tat·ing /ˈdɛvəˌsteɪt̬ɪŋ/ *adj.* **1** badly damaging or destroying something: *Heavy rains caused devastating floods in the region.* **2** making someone feel extremely sad or shocked: *the devastating news of her sister's death*

de·vel·op /dɪˈvɛləp/ *v.* **1** [I,T] to grow or change into something bigger or more advanced, or to make someone or something do this: *It's amazing that a tree can **develop from** a small seed.* | *Chicago **developed into** a big city in the late 1800s.* | *plans to develop the local economy* **2** [T] to work on a new idea or product to make it successful: *The mayor is developing a plan to fight crime.* **3** [T] to begin to have a quality or illness: *Her baby developed a fever during the night.* **4** [I] to begin to happen, exist, or be noticed: *Clouds are developing over the mountains.* **5** [T] to use land to build things that people need: *This area will be developed over the next five years.* **6** [T] to make pictures out of film from a camera

de·vel·oped /dɪˈvɛləpt/ *adj.* **1** larger, stronger, or more advanced: *a child with **fully developed** social skills* | ***well-developed** muscles* **2 developed countries/nations** rich countries that have many industries, comfortable living for most people, and usually elected governments

de·vel·op·er /dɪˈvɛləpɚ/ *n.* [C] someone who makes money by buying land and then building houses, factories, etc. on it

de·vel·op·ing /dɪˈvɛləpɪŋ/ *adj.* **1** growing or changing: *a developing child* **2 developing countries/nations** poor countries that are trying to increase their industry and trade and improve life for their people

de·vel·op·ment /dɪˈvɛləpmənt/ *n.* **1** [U] the process of becoming bigger, stronger, or more advanced: *A healthy diet can prevent the **development of** heart disease.* | ***economic/industrial development*** **2** [C] a new event that changes a situation: *Our reporter in Denver has the latest developments.* **3** [C] a change that makes a product, plan, idea, etc. better: *new **developments in** computer technology* **4** [U] the process of planning and building new streets, buildings, etc. on land: *100 acres ready for development* **5** [C] a group of new buildings that have all been planned and built together on the same piece of land: *a housing development*

de·vi·ant /'diviənt/ *also* **de·vi·ate** /'divi-ɪt/ *adj.* (formal) different, in a bad way, from what is normal: *deviant behavior* —**deviant** *n.* [C]

de·vi·ate /'diviˌeɪt/ (Ac) *v.* [I] (formal) to be or become different from what is normal or acceptable: *The daytime temperature rarely **deviates from** 70 degrees.* [ORIGIN: 1600—1700 Late Latin *deviatus*, from Latin *de* "away from" + *via* "way"]

D

de·vi·a·tion /ˌdivi'eɪʃən/ (Ac) *n.* [C,U] (formal) a noticeable difference from what is expected or normal: *Any **deviation from** procedures will not be tolerated.*

de·vice /dɪ'vaɪs/ (Ac) *n.* [C] **1** a machine or other small object that does a special job: *a **device for** sorting mail* | *The device records the level of oxygen in the water.*

THESAURUS **machine, appliance, gadget, mechanism, contraption** → MACHINE[1]

2 a way of achieving a particular purpose: *A contest could be a good device for raising money.*

dev·il /'dɛvəl/ *n.* **1 the Devil** the most powerful evil spirit in some religions, such as Christianity (SYN) **Satan** **2** [C] any evil spirit [ORIGIN: Old English *deofol*, from Greek *diabolos*]

dev·il·ish /'dɛvəlɪʃ/ *adj.* (old-fashioned) very bad, difficult, or evil —**devilishly** *adv.*

ˌdevil's 'advocate *n.* [C] someone who pretends to disagree with you in order to have a good discussion about something: *I've always enjoyed **playing devil's advocate**.*

de·vi·ous /'diviəs/ *adj.* using tricks or lies to get what you want: *a devious plan*

de·vise /dɪ'vaɪz/ *v.* [T] to plan or invent a way of doing something: *A teacher devised the game as a way of making math fun.* | *He finally **devised a way to** divide the money fairly.*

THESAURUS **invent, create, think up, come up with sth, conceive, make up, dream up** → INVENT

de·void /dɪ'vɔɪd/ *adj.* **be devoid of sth** to not have a particular quality at all: *The food is **completely devoid of** taste.*

de·vote /dɪ'voʊt/ (Ac) *v.* [T] **1 devote time/money/attention etc. to sb/sth** to give your time, money, etc. to someone or something: *She devotes much of her time to her family.* **2 devote yourself to sth** to do everything that you can to achieve something or help someone: *McCarthy devoted himself to ending the war.* **3** to use a particular area, period of time, or amount of space for a specific purpose: *This chapter is **devoted to** Lincoln's presidency.*

de·vot·ed /dɪ'voʊt̬ɪd/ (Ac) *adj.* giving someone or something a lot of love, concern, and attention: *a **devoted wife/father*** —**devotedly** *adv.*

THESAURUS **faithful, loyal, staunch, steadfast, true** → FAITHFUL

dev·o·tee /ˌdɛvə'ti, -'teɪ, -voʊ-/ *n.* [C] someone who enjoys or admires someone or something very much: ***devotees of** Italian wine*

de·vo·tion /dɪ'voʊʃən/ (Ac) *n.* [U] **1** a strong feeling of love that you show by paying a lot of attention to someone or something: *a father's **devotion to** his family* **2** the act of spending a lot of time and energy on something: *The actress is famous for her **devotion to** animal rights.* **3** strong religious feeling

de·vour /dɪ'vaʊə/ *v.* [T] **1** to eat something quickly because you are very hungry

THESAURUS **eat, gobble sth up, wolf sth down, nibble (on), pick at, ingest** → EAT

2 if you devour information, books, etc., you read a lot very quickly [ORIGIN: 1300—1400 Old French *devorer*, from Latin *vorare* "to swallow"]

de·vout /dɪ'vaʊt/ *adj.* having very strong beliefs, especially religious ones: *a devout Catholic* —**devoutly** *adv.*

THESAURUS **religious, pious, god-fearing, practicing, orthodox** → RELIGIOUS

dew /du/ *n.* [U] the small drops of water that form on outdoor surfaces during the night

dex·ter·i·ty /dɛk'stɛrət̬i/ *n.* [U] skill in using your hands to do things —**dexterous, dextrous** /'dɛkstrəs/ *adj.*

dex·trose /'dɛkstroʊs/ *n.* [U] CHEMISTRY a type of sugar that is found naturally in many sweet fruits, and that is also produced naturally in the body. It is sometimes also known as GLUCOSE. → SUCROSE, LACTOSE, FRUCTOSE

di·a·be·tes /ˌdaɪə'bit̬iz, -'bit̬ɪs/ *n.* [U] a disease in which there is too much sugar in the blood

di·a·bet·ic /ˌdaɪə'bɛt̬ɪk/ *n.* [C] someone who has diabetes —**diabetic** *adj.*

di·a·bol·i·cal /ˌdaɪə'bɑlɪkəl/ *adj.* very bad, evil, or cruel: *a diabolical killer* [ORIGIN: 1300—1400 French *diabolique*, from Greek *diabolos* "devil"]

di·ag·nose /ˌdaɪəg'noʊs, 'daɪəgˌnoʊs/ *v.* [T] to find out what illness a person has or what is wrong with something: *A technician diagnosed a bad pump in the engine.* | *He was **diagnosed with** hepatitis.*

di·ag·no·sis /ˌdaɪəg'noʊsɪs/ *n.* (plural **diagnoses** /-'noʊsiz/) [C,U] the result of diagnosing someone or something → PROGNOSIS: *The doctor* will **make a diagnosis** and recommend treatment. [ORIGIN: 1600—1700 Modern Latin, Greek, from *diagignoskein* "to know apart"] —**diagnostic** /ˌdaɪəgˈnɑstɪk/ *adj.*

di·ag·o·nal /daɪˈægənəl/ *adj.* **1** a diagonal line joins two opposite corners of a square shape **2** following a sloping angle: *diagonal parking spaces* —**diagonal** *n.* [C] —**diagonally** *adv.*

di·a·gram /ˈdaɪəˌgræm/ *n.* [C] a drawing that shows how something works, where something is, what something looks like, etc.: *a **diagram of** a car engine* [ORIGIN: 1600—1700 Greek *diagramma*, from *diagraphein* "to mark out with lines"]

di·al¹ /ˈdaɪəl/ *v.* [I,T] to press the buttons or turn the dial on a telephone in order to make a telephone call: *Dial 911 – there's been an accident.* | *I think I dialed the wrong number.* → PHONE¹

dial² *n* [C] **1** the round part of a clock, watch, machine, etc., that has numbers that show you the time or a measurement **2** the part of a piece of equipment, such as a radio or THERMOSTAT, that you turn in order to do something, such as find a different station or set the temperature **3** the wheel with holes for fingers on some telephones

di·a·lect /ˈdaɪəˌlɛkt/ *n.* [C,U] ENG. LANG. ARTS a form of a language that is spoken in one area which is different from the way it is spoken in other areas: *a dialect of Arabic* | *literature written **in** native **dialects*** [ORIGIN: 1500—1600 French *dialecte*, from Greek *dialektos* "conversation, dialect"]

THESAURUS **language, accent, tongue, vernacular, lingo, slang, jargon** → LANGUAGE

di·a·logue, **dialog** /ˈdaɪəˌlɔg, -ˌlɑg/ *n.* [C,U] **1** a conversation in a book, play, or movie → MONOLOGUE **2** a formal discussion between countries or groups in order to solve problems: *an opportunity for **dialogue between** the fighting countries* | *a **dialogue on** human rights* [ORIGIN: 1100—1200 Old French, Greek *dialogos*, from *dialegesthai* "to talk to someone"]

THESAURUS **discussion, negotiations, debate, talks, conference** → DISCUSSION

ˈdial tone *n.* [C] the sound you hear when you pick up a telephone, that lets you know that you can make a call

di·am·e·ter /daɪˈæmət̬ɚ/ *n.* [C,U] MATH a line or measurement from one side of a circle or SPHERE to the other, that passes through the center: *a wheel two feet **in diameter*** [ORIGIN: 1300—1400 Old French *diametre*, from Greek *diametros* "measure across"] → *see picture at* CIRCLE¹

di·a·met·ri·cally /ˌdaɪəˈmɛtrɪkli/ *adv.* **diametrically opposed/opposite** completely different or opposite: *We have diametrically opposed views on raising children.*

di·a·mond /ˈdaɪmənd, ˈdaɪə-/ *n.* **1** [C,U] a clear very hard valuable stone, used in jewelry and in industry: *a diamond ring* **2** [C] a shape with four straight sides of equal length that stands on one of its points **3** [C] a playing card with red diamond shapes on it → *see picture at* PLAYING CARD **4** [C] **a)** the area in a baseball field that is within the shape formed by the four BASES **b)** the whole playing field used in baseball [ORIGIN: 1200—1300 Old French *diamant* "hard metal, diamond," from Greek *adamas*]

di·a·per /ˈdaɪpɚ, ˈdaɪə-/ *n.* [C] a piece of material that is put between a baby's legs and fastened around its waist to hold liquid and solid waste: *I think we need to **change** the baby's **diaper*** (=put on a new one).

di·aph·a·nous /daɪˈæfənəs/ *adj.* (literary) diaphanous cloth is so fine and thin that you can almost see through it SYN **sheer**

di·a·phragm /ˈdaɪəˌfræm/ *n.* [C] **1** BIOLOGY the muscle between your lungs and your stomach that controls your breathing **2** a small round rubber object that a woman can put inside her VAGINA to stop her from getting PREGNANT [ORIGIN: 1300—1400 Late Latin *diaphragma*, from Greek *diaphrassein* "to make a fence across, block"] → *see picture at* LUNG

di·ar·rhe·a /ˌdaɪəˈriə/ *n.* [U] BIOLOGY an illness in which waste from the BOWELS is watery and comes out often

di·a·ry /ˈdaɪəri/ *n.* (plural **diaries**) [C] a book in which you write down important or interesting things that happen to you each day: *I **kept a diary*** (=wrote in it regularly) *when I was in high school.* [ORIGIN: 1500—1600 Latin *diarium*, from *dies* "day"]

THESAURUS **record, journal, ledger, log (book)** → RECORD¹

dice¹ /daɪs/ *n.* **1** the plural form of DIE: *Jeanie **rolled the dice**.* **2 no dice** (spoken) said when you refuse to do something: *I asked if I could borrow the car, but she said no dice.*

dice² *v.* [T] to cut food into small square pieces: *Dice the carrots.*

THESAURUS **cut, chop (up), slice, peel, carve, shred, grate** → CUT¹

→ *see picture at* CUT¹

dic·ey /ˈdaɪsi/ *adj.* (informal) risky and possibly dangerous: *a dicey situation*

di·cot·y·le·don /ˌdaɪkɑt̬əˈlidn/ *also* **di·cot** /ˈdaɪkɑt/ *n.* [C] BIOLOGY a type of plant that has seeds which produce two COTYLEDONS (=first

D

leaves) when it first starts to grow → MONOCOTYLEDON

dic·tate /ˈdɪkteɪt, dɪkˈteɪt/ *v.* **1** [I,T] to say words for someone else to write down: *She **dictated** a letter **to** her secretary.* **2** [I,T] to tell someone exactly what s/he must do: *You can't **dictate how** I should live my life!* **3** [T] to influence or control something: *Where I go on vacation will be dictated by the amount of money I've saved.* [ORIGIN: 1500—1600 Latin *dictare* "to say often, say firmly," from *dicere* "to say"]

dic·ta·tion /dɪkˈteɪʃən/ *n.* **1** [U] the act of saying words for someone to write down **2** [C] sentences that a teacher reads out to test your ability to hear and write the words correctly: *Dictations are the hardest part of learning French.*

D

dic·ta·tor /ˈdɪkteɪt̬ɚ/ *n.* [C] a leader of a country who controls everything, and who usually has gained power by force —**dictatorial** /ˌdɪktəˈtɔriəl/ *adj.*

dic·ta·tor·ship /dɪkˈteɪt̬ɚˌʃɪp, ˈdɪkteɪt̬ɚ-/ *n.* **1** [U] government by a dictator **2** [C] a country ruled by a dictator

THESAURUS **government, democracy, republic, monarchy, regime, totalitarian country/state etc., police state** → GOVERNMENT

dic·tion /ˈdɪkʃən/ *n.* [U] **1** the way in which someone pronounces words **2** ENG. LANG. ARTS the choice and use of words and phrases to express meaning, especially in literature or poetry

dic·tion·ar·y /ˈdɪkʃəˌnɛri/ *n.* (plural **dictionaries**) [C] a book that gives a list of words in alphabetical order, and explains their meanings in the same or another language: *a Spanish-English dictionary* [ORIGIN: 1500—1600 Medieval Latin *dictionarium*, from Late Latin *dictio* "word"]

did /dɪd/ *v.* the past tense of DO

di·dac·tic /daɪˈdæktɪk/ *adj.* (formal) speech or writing that is didactic is intended to teach people a lesson

did·n't /ˈdɪdnt/ *v.* the short form of "did not": *She didn't have enough money.*

die¹ /daɪ/ *v.* (past tense and past participle **died**, present participle **dying**) [I] **1** to stop living → DEAD, DEATH: *She was afraid her son would die.* | *Mrs. Chen **died of/from** (=because of) heart disease.* | *Mary **died** peacefully **in** her **sleep**.* **2** to disappear or stop existing: *The hope that her husband would return never died.* **3** (informal) if a machine or motor dies, it stops working: *I was going down a hill when my car died.*

SPOKEN PHRASES

4 be dying to do something to want to do something very much: *I'm dying to meet her brother.* **5 be to die for** if something is to die for, it is extremely good: *Max's chocolate cake is to die for!* **6 die laughing** to laugh a lot: *When Alex fell off the stage, I almost died laughing.* **7 I could have died** *also* **I almost died** said when you are very surprised or embarrassed: *I could've died when Ed said that!*

die away *phr. v.* if a sound dies away, it becomes weaker and then stops

die down *phr. v.* to become less strong or violent: *The wind finally died down this morning.*

die off *phr. v.* to die one at a time until none is left: *All the elm trees are dying off.*

die out *phr. v.* to disappear or stop existing completely: *The last bears in this area died out 100 years ago.*

die² *n.* (plural **dice** /daɪs/) [C] one of two or more small blocks of wood, plastic, etc. with a different number of spots on each side, used in games

die·hard, **die-hard** /ˈdaɪhɑrd/ *adj.* (informal) **1** opposing change and refusing to accept new ideas: *a diehard opponent of free speech* **2 diehard fan/communist/supporter etc.** someone who is very loyal to a team, political party, person, etc.: *a diehard Dodgers fan*

di·er·e·sis /daɪˈɛrəsɪs/ *n.* (plural **diereses** /-rəsiz/) [C] ENG. LANG. ARTS a sign that is put over the second of two vowels to show that it is pronounced separately from the first, for example in the word "naïve"

die·sel /ˈdizəl/ *also* **ˈdiesel ˌfuel** *n.* [U] a type of FUEL used instead of gas in a special type of engine [ORIGIN: 1800—1900 Rudolf *Diesel* (1858-1913), German engineer who invented the engine]

di·et¹ /ˈdaɪət/ *n.* **1** [C,U] the type of food that you eat each day: *Many kids don't get enough fruit in their diet.* | *The animals live on a **diet of** fruit and insects.* **2** [C] a plan to eat only particular kinds or amounts of food, especially because you want to get thinner or because you have a health problem: *a low-fat diet* | *No dessert for me – I'm **on a diet**.* [ORIGIN: 1200—1300 Old French *diete*, from Greek *diaita* "way of living, food to be eaten"]

diet² *v.* [I] to eat less or eat only particular foods in order to lose weight: *Jill's always dieting.*

dif·fer /ˈdɪfɚ/ *v.* [I] **1** to be different: *How does the movie **differ from** the book?* **2** (formal) to have different opinions: *The two groups **differ on/about/over** where to have the meeting.* [ORIGIN: 1300—1400 French *différer* "to delay, be different," from Latin *differre*]

dif·ference /ˈdɪfrəns/ *n.* **1** [C] a way in which two or more things or people are not like each other: *the **differences between** England and America* | *Can you **tell the difference** between the twins* (=recognize that they are different)? **2** [singular, U] the fact of not being the same as something else, or an amount by which one thing is not the same as another: *What's the **difference in** price?* | *There's an age **difference** of 4 years **between** the two children.* **3 make a difference/make all the difference** to have a good effect on a situation or person: *Swimming twice a week can **make a big***

difference in the way you feel. **4 make no difference** to be unimportant or to have no effect: *It **makes no difference to** me whether we win by one goal or ten.* **5 have your differences** to have disagreements with someone: *My sister and I have always had our differences.* **6 difference of opinion** a disagreement: *Perkins left his job because of a **difference of opinion with** his boss.*

dif·ferent /ˈdɪfrənt/ *adj.* **1** not like something or someone else, or not the same as before: *Did you get a haircut? You look different.* | *Anna is **different from** most kids at her school.* | *Writing for films is **different than** writing plays.* **2** separate: *The bookstore has a lot of different books about Kennedy.* **3** (spoken) unusual, often in a way that you do not like: *"How do you like my shirt?" "Well, it's different."*

GRAMMAR

different from, different than

You can use **different from** or **different than** to talk about two things that are not the same. However, most teachers prefer **different from**.

—**differently** *adv.*

dif·fer·en·ti·ate /ˌdɪfəˈrɛnʃiˌeɪt/ (Ac) *v.* **1** [I,T] to recognize or express the difference between things or people: *It was difficult for him to **differentiate between** light and dark.* **2** [T] to make one thing different from another: *We try to **differentiate** our products **from those of** the competitors.* —**differentiation** /ˌdɪfəˌrɛnʃiˈeɪʃən/ *n.* [U]

dif·fi·cult /ˈdɪfəˌkʌlt/ *adj.* **1** not easy to do or understand: *a difficult question* | *She **finds** math **difficult**.*

THESAURUS

hard – making you tired because you have to use a lot of physical or mental effort: *I've had a long hard day.* | *The midterms were harder than I expected.*
tough – very difficult to do or deal with: *They asked some tough questions at the interview.* | *a tough decision*
awkward – difficult to deal with or handle: *The big pieces of wood were awkward to handle.*
challenging – difficult in a way that is interesting and enjoyable: *The class is intended to be challenging for students.*
demanding – a demanding job needs a lot of time, effort, and skill: *Being a nurse is a demanding job.*
arduous (written) – long and tiring, and needing a lot of effort: *a long and arduous trip*
complicated/complex – difficult to understand because of having a lot of different parts: *The rules of the game are very complicated.* | *a complex issue*

2 involving a lot of problems and causing trouble: *This past year has been a very difficult time in my life.* | *The bus strike is **making life/things difficult for** commuters.* **3** someone who is difficult is never satisfied, friendly, or pleased

dif·fi·cul·ty /ˈdɪfɪˌkʌlti/ *n.* (plural **difficulties**) **1** [C usually plural, U] a problem, or something that causes trouble: *Peter's **having difficulty in** finding a job.* | *She walks **with great difficulty**.* | *Their business is **in financial difficulty**.* | *We **ran into difficulties*** (=had trouble) *buying the house.*

THESAURUS **problem, setback, snag, hitch, trouble, hassle** → PROBLEM

2 [U] the state of being hard to do or understand: *The books vary in **level of difficulty**.* [ORIGIN: 1300—1400 Latin *difficultas*, from *difficilis* "difficult," from *facilis* "easy"]

dif·fi·dent /ˈdɪfədənt/ *adj.* (formal) shy and not wanting to make people notice you or talk about you, because you lack confidence: *a diffident young man* —**diffidence** *n.* [U] —**diffidently** *adv.*

dif·frac·tion /dɪˈfrækʃən/ *n.* [U] PHYSICS the process or result of dividing sound or light waves into smaller waves, by sending them around something or through a small hole —**diffract** /dɪˈfrækt/ *v* [I,T]

dif·fuse¹ /dɪˈfyus/ *adj.* spread over a large area or in many places: *a large and diffuse organization*

dif·fuse² /dɪˈfyuz/ *v.* (formal) **1** [T] to make a bad feeling less strong: *Mara told jokes to diffuse the tension.* **2** [I,T] to make ideas, information, etc. available to many people: *The language was diffused throughout the Balkans and into central Europe.* **3** [I,T] to make heat, light, liquid, etc. spread through something, or to spread like this: *Smoke diffused into the living room and got into the carpet.*

dif·fu·sion /dɪˈfyuʒən/ *n.* [U] **1** the process of spreading over a large area **2** PHYSICS a process in which light spreads in many directions when it is REFLECTed from an uneven surface or moves through a material **3** PHYSICS a process in which substances become completely mixed because of movement of their PARTICLES

dig¹ /dɪg/ *v.* (past tense and past participle **dug** /dʌg/, present participle **digging**) **1** [I,T] to break up and move earth, stone, snow, etc. with a tool, your hands, or a machine: *The kids enjoyed digging in the sand.* | *She dug a hole and threw some seeds in it.* | *The company began **digging for** minerals many years ago.* **2** [I] to move many things such as papers, boxes, rocks, or clothing in order to find something: *She **dug through** her purse, looking for her keys.* **3 dig yourself (into) a hole** to do or say something that makes a problem or situation so bad that it is difficult to make it better: *The mayor dug himself into a hole when he promised 3,000 new jobs.* **4** [T] (spoken) to like something or someone: *You really dig her, don't you?*
dig in *phr. v.* (spoken) to start eating food that is in front of you: *Come on, everyone – dig in!*
dig (sth) **into** sth *phr. v.* to push hard into something, or to make something do this: *She dug her fingernails into my arm.*

D

dig sth ↔ **out** *phr. v.* **1** to get someone or something out of a place using a tool, your hands, or a machine: *We had to dig our car out after the blizzard.* **2** to find something that you have not seen for a long time, or that is not easy to find: *Mom dug out her wedding dress and showed it to us.*

dig sth ↔ **up** *phr. v.* **1** to remove something from under the ground with a tool, your hands, or a machine: *Police dug up the missing man's body from the yard.* **2** (informal) to find hidden or forgotten information by careful searching: *See what you can dig up on this guy Stark.*

D

dig² *n.* [C] **1** an unkind thing you say to annoy someone: *Greene's remark was meant to be a **dig at** his opponent.* **2** a small quick push that you give someone with your finger or elbow: *a dig in the ribs* **3** the process of digging in a place in order to find ancient objects to study

di·gest¹ /daɪ'dʒɛst, dɪ-/ *v.* [I,T] **1** if food digests, or if you digest it, it changes in the stomach into a form your body can use: *Some babies can't digest cow's milk.* **2** to understand something after thinking about it carefully: *He'll need some time to digest the news.*

di·gest² /'daɪdʒɛst/ *n.* [C] a short piece of writing that gives the most important facts from a book, report, etc.

di·ges·tion /daɪ'dʒɛstʃən, dɪ-/ *n.* [C,U] the process or ability to digest food **—digestive** *adj.*: *digestive problems*

dig·it /'dɪdʒɪt/ *n.* [C] **1** a written sign that represents any of the numbers from 0 to 9: *a seven-digit phone number* **2** (formal) a finger or toe [ORIGIN: 1300—1400 Latin *digitus* "finger, toe"]

dig·i·tal /'dɪdʒɪtl/ *adj.* **1** giving information in the form of numbers: *a digital clock* **2** IT using a system in which information is represented in the form of numbers: *a digital camera* **—digitally** *adv.*

dig·ni·fied /'dɪgnə,faɪd/ *adj.* calm, serious, and making people feel respect: *a dignified leader*

dig·ni·tar·y /'dɪgnə,tɛri/ *n.* (plural **dignitaries**) [C] someone who has an important official position: *foreign dignitaries*

dig·ni·ty /'dɪgnəṭi/ *n.* [U] **1** calm serious behavior, even in difficult situations, that makes people respect you: *a woman of compassion and dignity* | *She spoke **with** courage and **dignity**.* **2** the quality of being serious and formal: *Lawyers must respect the dignity of the court.* [ORIGIN: 1100—1200 Old French *dignité*, from Latin *dignitas* "worth"]

di·gress /daɪ'grɛs, dɪ-/ *v.* [I] (formal) to begin talking about something that is not related to the subject you were talking about **—digression** /daɪ'grɛʃən/ *n.* [C,U]

di·lap·i·dat·ed /də'læpə,deɪṭɪd/ *adj.* old, broken, and in very bad condition: *a dilapidated church* [ORIGIN: 1500—1600 Latin *dilapidare* "to scatter like stones, misuse, destroy," from *lapidare* "to throw stones"] **—dilapidation** /dɪ,læpə'deɪʃən/ *n.* [U]

di·late /daɪ'leɪt, 'daɪleɪt/ *v.* [I,T] to become wider or more open, or to cause something to do this: *Her eyes were dilated and her face was red.* **—dilation** /daɪ'leɪʃən/ *n.* [U]

dil·a·to·ry /'dɪlə,tɔri/ *adj.* (formal) slow and tending to delay decisions or actions

di·lem·ma /də'lɛmə/ *n.* [C] a situation in which you have to make a difficult choice between two or more actions: *We're **in a dilemma** about whether to move or not.* | *a **moral dilemma*** [ORIGIN: 1500—1600 Greek "double statement," from *lemma* "statement"]

dil·i·gent /'dɪlədʒənt/ *adj.* **1** someone who is diligent always works hard and carefully: *a diligent student* **2** done in a careful and thorough way: *diligent research* [ORIGIN: 1300—1400 French, Latin, present participle of *diligere* "to put high value on, love"] **—diligence** *n.* [U] **—diligently** *adv.*

dill /dɪl/ *n.* [U] a plant whose seeds and leaves are used in cooking

di·lute /dɪ'lut, daɪ-/ *v.* [T] to make a liquid weaker by adding water or another liquid: ***Dilute** the paint **with** oil.* [ORIGIN: 1500—1600 Latin *dilutus*, past participle of *diluere* "to wash away"] **—diluted** *adj.* **—dilution** /daɪ'luʃən, dɪ-/ *n.* [C,U]

di,lute so'lution *n.* [C] CHEMISTRY a liquid that contains a SOLUTE (=substance that has mixed with and become part of a liquid)

dim¹ /dɪm/ *adj.* (comparative **dimmer**, superlative **dimmest**) **1** not bright or easy to see well: *a dim hallway* | *The curtains were closed and the light was dim.* | *the dim outline of a building* **2 a dim recollection/awareness etc.** something that is difficult for someone to remember, understand, etc.: *She only has a dim memory of her parents.* **3 take a dim view of sth** to disapprove of something **—dimly** *adv.*

dim² *v.* (**dimmed**, **dimming**) [I,T] **1** if a light dims, or if you dim it, it becomes less bright: *Can you dim the lights?* **2** if a feeling or quality dims, or if something dims it, it grows weaker: *The painful memory began to dim.*

dime /daɪm/ *n.* [C] **1** a coin worth 10 cents (=1/10 of a dollar), used in the U.S. and Canada

> THESAURUS **money, bill, coin, penny, nickel, quarter** → MONEY

2 a dime a dozen (informal) very common and not valuable: *Jobs like his are a dime a dozen.* **3 stop/park/turn on a dime** to stop, park, etc. within a small area

dimension

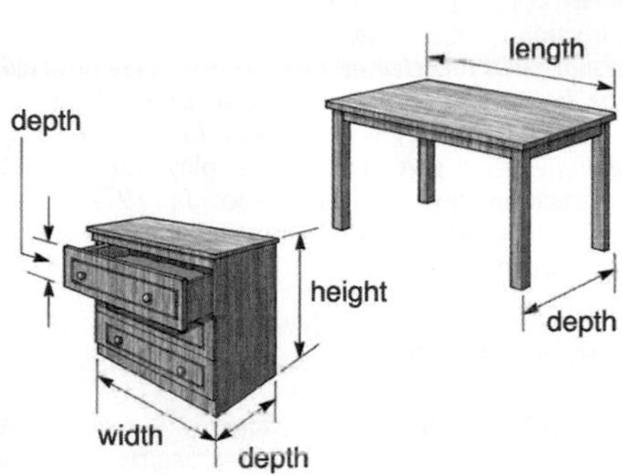

dine

di·men·sion /dɪ'mɛnʃən, daɪ-/ (Ac) *n.* [C] **1** a part of a situation that affects the way you think about it: *The baby added **a new dimension** to our life.* | *Because the boat sank in Cuban waters, there is a political dimension to the incident.* **2** a measurement of something in length, height, or width **3 dimensions** [plural] **a)** the measurement or size of something: *What are the **dimensions of** the room?* **b)** how great or serious a problem is: *The government needs to recognize the full **dimensions of** the problem.* [ORIGIN: 1300—1400 Old French, Latin *dimetiri* "to measure out"]

'dime store *n.* [C] a store that sells different types of cheap things, especially for the house

di·min·ish /dɪ'mɪnɪʃ/ (Ac) *v.* [I,T] to become smaller or less important, or to make something do this: *The show's audience has slowly diminished.* | *The tobacco companies tried to diminish the significance of the findings.* [ORIGIN: 1400—1500 *diminue* (14—16 centuries), from Old French *diminuer*, from Latin *minuere* "to make less"]

THESAURUS decrease, go down, drop, fall, plummet, decline, dwindle → DECREASE[1]

dim·i·nu·tion /ˌdɪmə'nuʃən/ (Ac) *n.* [C,U] (formal) a reduction in the size, number, or amount of something

di·min·u·tive /dɪ'mɪnyət̬ɪv/ *adj.* (formal) very small: *a diminutive man*

THESAURUS small, little, tiny, minute, miniature, minuscule, petite → SMALL

dim·ple /'dɪmpəl/ *n.* [C] a small hollow place on your cheek or chin, especially one that forms when you smile —**dimpled** *adj.*

din /dɪn/ *n.* [singular, U] (literary) a loud, continuous, and annoying noise

dine /daɪn/ *v.* [I] (formal) to eat dinner

dine on sth *phr. v.* (formal) to eat a particular type of food for dinner, especially expensive food: *We dined on shrimp and pasta.*

dine out *phr. v.* (formal) to eat in a restaurant

din·er /'daɪnɚ/ *n.* [C] **1** a small restaurant that serves cheap meals

THESAURUS restaurant, cafe/coffee shop, fast food restaurant, cafeteria → RESTAURANT

2 someone who is eating in a restaurant

ding-dong /'dɪŋ dɔŋ, -dɑŋ/ *n.* [U] the noise made by a bell

din·gy /'dɪndʒi/ *adj.* a dingy room, street, or place is dirty and in bad condition: *dingy offices*

'dining room *n.* [C] a room where you eat meals in a house

din·ner /'dɪnɚ/ *n.* **1** [C,U] the main meal of the day, usually eaten in the evening: *We had fish **for dinner**.* | *My aunt invited me for Thanksgiving dinner.* **2** [C] a formal occasion when an evening meal is eaten, often to celebrate something: *There was a dinner in honor of his retirement.* [ORIGIN: 1200—1300 Old French *diner*, from *diner* "to eat"]

din·ner·time /'dɪnɚˌtaɪm/ *n.* [U] the time when most people eat dinner, usually between 5 p.m. and 7 p.m.

di·no·saur /'daɪnəˌsɔr/ *n.* [C] a very large animal that lived millions of years ago and no longer exists [ORIGIN: 1800—1900 Greek *deinos* "terrible" + *sauros* "lizard"]

di·ode /'daɪoʊd/ *n.* [C] PHYSICS a piece of electrical equipment that makes an electrical current flow in one direction

dip[1] /dɪp/ *v.* (**dipped**, **dipping**) **1** [T] to put something into a liquid and quickly lift it out again: *Janet **dipped** her feet **into** the water.* | *strawberries **dipped in** chocolate* **2** [I] (informal) to go down or become lower: *The temperature could dip down to the 20s tonight.*

dip into sth *phr. v.* to use some of an amount of money that you have: *Medical bills forced her to dip into her savings.*

dip[2] *n.* **1** [C,U] a thick mixture that you can dip food into before you eat it: *a cheese dip* **2** [C] an occasion when the level or amount of something becomes lower: *a **dip in** prices* **3** [C] a place where the surface of something goes down suddenly, and then goes up again: *a dip in the road* **4** [C] (informal) a quick swim: *Is there time for a dip in the pool before lunch?*

diph·the·ri·a /dɪf'θɪriə, dɪp-/ *n.* [U] BIOLOGY a serious infectious throat disease that makes breathing difficult

diph·thong /'dɪfθɔŋ, 'dɪp-/ *n.* [C] ENG. LANG. ARTS a vowel sound made by pronouncing two vowels quickly one after the other. For example, the vowel sound in "my" is a diphthong [ORIGIN: 1400—1500 French, Late Latin *diphthongus* "two sounds," from Greek *phthongos* "voice, sound"]

D

dip·loid /'dɪplɔɪd/ *n.* [C] BIOLOGY a cell or ORGANISM that contains two complete sets of CHROMOSOMES, one from each parent —**diploid** *adj.*

di·plo·ma /dɪ'ploʊmə/ *n.* [C] an official paper showing that someone has successfully finished his/her HIGH SCHOOL or college education: *a high school diploma* [ORIGIN: 1600—1700 Latin "passport, diploma," from Greek, "folded paper"]

di·plo·ma·cy /dɪ'ploʊməsi/ *n.* [U] **1** the management of political relations between countries: *an expert at international diplomacy* **2** skill in dealing with people and difficult situations successfully: *I would have handled the situation with a little more diplomacy.*

dip·lo·mat /'dɪplə,mæt/ *n.* [C] someone who officially represents his/her government in a foreign country

dip·lo·mat·ic /,dɪplə'mæt̬ɪk◂/ *adj.* **1** relating to the work of diplomats: *Feingold plans to join the diplomatic service.* **2** good at dealing with people politely and skillfully without upsetting them: *She tried to be diplomatic, but I could tell she was upset.* —**diplomatically** *adv.*

dip·stick /'dɪpstɪk/ *n.* [C] a stick used for measuring the amount of liquid in a container, such as oil in a car's engine

dire /daɪɚ/ *adj.* **1** extremely serious or terrible: *Officials say the situation is not as dire as they first thought.* | *The country is* ***in dire need of*** *food aid.* **2 be in dire straits** to be in an extremely difficult or serious situation

di·rect¹ /də'rɛkt, daɪ-/ *adj.* **1** done without involving other people, actions, processes, etc. (ANT) **indirect**: *He has direct access to the president.* **2** going straight from one place to another, without stopping or changing direction: *What's the most direct route to the airport?* **3** saying exactly what you mean in an honest and clear way (ANT) **indirect**: *The senator avoided giving* ***direct answers*** *to reporters' questions.*

THESAURUS **honest, frank, candid, upfront, straight, straightforward, blunt, forthright** → HONEST

4 likely to change something immediately (ANT) **indirect**: *This job allows me to have a direct impact on people's lives.* **5** exact or total: *a direct translation from Spanish* —**directness** *n.* [U]

direct² *v.* [T] **1** to aim something in a particular direction or at a particular person, group, etc.: *My remark was* ***directed at*** *Tom, not you.* | *He* ***directed*** *the light* ***toward*** *the house.* **2** to be in charge of something: *Hanley was asked to direct the investigation.* **3** to give actors in a play, movie, etc. instructions about what to do: *In 1977, Scott directed his first movie.* **4** (formal) to tell someone the way to a place: *He directed me to the airport.*

THESAURUS **lead, guide, point, show, escort, usher** → LEAD[1]

direct³ *adv.* **1** without stopping or changing direction: *You can fly direct from Seattle to Nashville.* **2** without dealing with anyone else first: *You'll have to contact the manager direct.*

di,rect 'current *n.* [U] PHYSICS *abbrevation* **DC** a flow of electricity that moves in one direction only, for example the current produced by a BATTERY → ALTERNATING CURRENT

di,rect de'posit *n.* [U] a method of paying someone's salary directly into his/her bank account —**direct deposit** *v.* [T]

di·rec·tion /də'rɛkʃən, daɪ-/ *n.* **1** [C] the way someone or something is moving, facing, or aimed: *Brian drove off* ***in the direction of*** (=toward) *the party.* | *As she walked along the trail, she saw a large man coming* ***in the opposite direction.*** **2** [C] the general way in which someone or something changes or develops: *Suddenly the conversation changed direction.* **3 directions** [plural] instructions about how to go from one place to another, or about how to do something: *Could you* ***give*** *me* ***directions to*** *the airport?* | *Read the directions at the top of the page.* **4** [U] control, management, or helpful advice: *The company's been successful* ***under*** *Martini's* ***direction.*** **5** [U] a general purpose or aim: *Sometimes I feel that my life lacks direction.* **6 sense of direction** the ability to know which way to go in a place you do not know well **7** [U] the instructions given to actors and other people in a play, movie, etc.

di·rec·tive /də'rɛktɪv/ *n.* [C] an official order or instruction to do something

di·rect·ly /də'rɛktli, daɪ-/ *adv.* **1** with no other person, action, process, etc. involved: *McNealy will report directly to the new sales manager.* **2** exactly: *Lucas sat directly behind us.*

,direct 'object *n.* [C] ENG. LANG. ARTS in grammar, the person or thing that is affected by the action of the verb in a sentence. For example, in the sentence "Sheila closed the door," "door" is the direct object. → INDIRECT OBJECT

di·rec·tor /də'rɛktɚ, daɪ-/ *n.* [C] **1** someone who gives instructions to actors and other people in a movie or play → MOVIE **2** someone who controls or manages a company, organization, or activity: *Her new job is marketing director of Sun Life.*

di·rec·to·ry /də'rɛktəri, daɪ-/ *n.* (plural **directories**) [C] **1** a book or list of names, facts, events, etc., usually arranged in alphabetical order: *the telephone directory* **2** IT a place in a computer where FILES or programs are organized

di,rect 'speech *n.* [U] ENG. LANG. ARTS the style of writing used to report what someone says by giving the actual words that were spoken. The sentence "Julie said, 'I don't want to go.'" is an example of direct speech. ➔ REPORTED SPEECH

di,rect vari'ation *n.* [U] MATH a relationship between two VARIABLES (=mathematical quantities that can represent any of several different amounts), in which, if one variable increases or decreases, the other variable increases or decreases by the same amount or to the same degree. Direct variation can be shown by the expression y = kx, where k is a quantity that stays the same.

dirge /dɚdʒ/ *n.* [C] a slow sad song, especially one that is sung or played at a funeral

dirt /dɚt/ *n.* [U] **1** earth or soil: *a dirt road* **2** any substance, such as dust or mud, that makes things not clean ➔ DIRTY: *The floor was covered with dirt!* **3** (informal) information about someone's private life or activities that might give people a bad opinion about him/her [ORIGIN: 1200—1300 Old Norse *drit*]

,dirt 'cheap *adj., adv.* (informal) extremely cheap. *We bought this house when it was dirt cheap.*

dirt·y¹ /'dɚṭi/ *adj.* (comparative **dirtier**, superlative **dirtiest**) **1** not clean, or covered in dirt: *dirty dishes in the sink* | *How did your shoes get so dirty?*

THESAURUS

filthy – very dirty: *The carpet was filthy.*
dusty – covered with dust: *piles of dusty books*
muddy – covered in mud: *muddy hiking boots*
greasy – covered with a lot of oil or grease (=an oily substance): *greasy fingermarks on the table*
grimy – covered in thick black dirt: *a farmer's grimy hands*
soiled (formal) – made dirty, especially by waste from your body: *a soiled diaper*
polluted – used about air, land, or water that has been made dirty: *a polluted river*

2 relating to sex, in a way that is considered bad or immoral: *dirty jokes* | *students who use* ***dirty words*** *in class* **3** unfair or dishonest and intended to harm someone: *a dirty fighter* **4 do sb's dirty work** to do a bad or dishonest job for someone so that s/he does not have to do it himself/herself: *I told them to do their own dirty work.*

dirty² *v.* (**dirtied**, **dirties**) [T] to make something dirty

dis /dɪs/ *v.* (**dissed**, **disses**, **dissing**) [T] (informal) to make unfair and unkind remarks about someone

dis·a·bil·i·ty /ˌdɪsə'bɪləṭi/ *n.* (plural **disabilities**) [C,U] a physical or mental condition that makes it difficult for someone to do the things most people are able to do: *Her disability prevented her from getting a driver's license.* | *learning to live with disability*

dis·a·bled /dɪs'eɪbəld/ *adj.* **1** someone who is disabled cannot use a part of his/her body in a way that most people can: *a disabled worker* **2 the disabled** people who are disabled: *The bank has an entrance for the disabled.*

dis·ad·van·tage /ˌdɪsəd'væntɪdʒ/ *n.* **1** [C,U] something that may make someone less successful than other people ➔ ADVANTAGE: *Your main disadvantage is lack of experience.* | *I was* ***at a disadvantage*** *because I didn't speak Spanish.* **2** [C] something that is not good or causes problems: *The only* ***disadvantage of*** *the job is the traveling.*

THESAURUS

drawback – a disadvantage that makes something seem less attractive: *It's an excellent camera. The only drawback is the price.*
downside – the main disadvantage of something, which in other ways seems good: *I like the job, but the downside is that I have to get up at five to get to work.*
catch (spoken) – a hidden disadvantage: *It sounded like a great investment, but I knew there had to be a catch somewhere.*
bad point (especially spoken) – a bad feature of something: *Every area has its good and bad points.*

dis·ad·van·taged /ˌdɪsəd'væntɪdʒd/ *adj.* someone who is disadvantaged has social problems, such as a lack of money or education, that make it difficult for him/her to succeed: *a program for disadvantaged students*

THESAURUS **poor, needy, destitute, impoverished, underprivileged, deprived ➔** POOR

dis·ad·van·ta·geous /ˌdɪsædvæn'teɪdʒəs, -vən-/ *adj.* unfavorable and likely to cause you problems ANT **advantageous**

dis·af·fect·ed /ˌdɪsə'fɛktɪd◂/ *adj.* no longer loyal because you are not satisfied with your leader, ruler, etc.: *Candidates are trying to attract disaffected voters.* —**disaffection** /ˌdɪsə'fɛkʃən/ *n.* [U]

dis·a·gree /ˌdɪsə'gri/ *v.* [I] **1** to have or express a different opinion from someone else: *Roth doesn't like anybody who* ***disagrees with*** *him.* | *We* ***disagree about*** *the best way to solve the problem.* | *Doctors* ***disagree on*** *the best way to treat the disease.*

THESAURUS

be divided/split – if a group of people are divided or split about something, they have very different opinions about it: *The country was deeply divided about the war.*
opinions differ – if opinions differ about something, people have a range of different opinions about it: *Opinions differ among scientists about the causes of the disease.*
dispute – to say that you think that something is

not correct or not true: *Many people would dispute these claims.*
dissent – to say that you disagree with an opinion or decision that most other people agree with: *Only one of the nine judges dissented from the decision.*

2 if statements or reports about the same thing disagree, they are different from each other

disagree with sb *phr. v.* if food disagrees with you, it makes you feel sick

dis·a·gree·a·ble /ˌdɪsəˈgriəbəl/ *adj.* **1** not enjoyable or pleasant: *a disagreeable incident* **2** unfriendly and in a bad mood: *a disagreeable person*

D

dis·a·gree·ment /ˌdɪsəˈgrimənt/ *n.* **1** [C,U] a situation in which people express different opinions about something and sometimes argue: *We **had a disagreement with** our neighbors.* | *a **disagreement between** the two countries* | *There was a slight **disagreement over** who should pay the bill.* **2** [U] differences between two statements, reports, etc. that should be similar: *There was major **disagreement between** the witnesses' statements.*

dis·al·low /ˌdɪsəˈlaʊ/ *v.* [T] (formal) to officially refuse to allow something because a rule has been broken: *The touchdown was disallowed.*

dis·ap·pear /ˌdɪsəˈpɪr/ *v.* [I] **1** to become impossible to see anymore: *The scars will disappear in a year or two.* | *The cat had **disappeared under** the couch.* **2** to become impossible to find, or to be lost: *The plane mysteriously disappeared while flying over the Atlantic.* **3** to stop existing: *Many species of plants and animals disappear every year.* —**disappearance** *n.* [C,U]

dis·ap·point /ˌdɪsəˈpɔɪnt/ *v.* [T] to make someone unhappy because something s/he hoped for does not happen or is not as good as s/he expected: *I'm sorry to disappoint you, but the trip is canceled.*

dis·ap·point·ed /ˌdɪsəˈpɔɪntɪd/ *adj.* unhappy because something you hoped for did not happen, or because something or someone was not as good as you expected: *We're **disappointed (that)** the director is unable to attend.* | *She was **disappointed with** the election results.* | *I've been **disappointed in** his work.*

dis·ap·point·ing /ˌdɪsəˈpɔɪntɪŋ/ *adj.* not as good as you expected or hoped something would be: *disappointing sales* —**disappointingly** *adv.*

dis·ap·point·ment /ˌdɪsəˈpɔɪnt˺mənt/ *n.* **1** [U] a feeling of sadness because something is not as good as you expected or has not happened: *his **disappointment at** not being chosen for the job* | *Labor unions expressed their **disappointment with** the president's proposal.* | *She tried to **hide** her **disappointment**.* **2** [C] someone or something that is not as good as you hoped or expected: *Her new book was **a big/major/real disappointment**.* | *Kate feels like she's **a disappointment to** her family.*

dis·ap·prov·al /ˌdɪsəˈpruvəl/ *n.* [U] a feeling or opinion that someone is behaving badly or that something is bad: *public **disapproval of** the war* | *Marion shook her head **in disapproval**.*

dis·ap·prove /ˌdɪsəˈpruv/ *v.* [I] to think that something or someone is bad, wrong, etc.: *Her parents **disapproved of** her boyfriend.*

dis·arm /dɪsˈɑrm/ *v.* **1** [I] to reduce the size of your army, navy, etc. and the number of weapons: *Both sides must disarm before the peace talks.* **2** [T] to take away someone's weapons: *Benson disarmed the man as he tried to rob a liquor store.* **3** [T] to make someone less angry and more friendly: *She uses humor to disarm people.*

dis·ar·ma·ment /dɪsˈɑrməmənt/ *n.* [U] the reduction in numbers or size of a country's weapons, army, navy, etc.: *plans for **nuclear disarmament***

dis·arm·ing /dɪsˈɑrmɪŋ/ *adj.* making you feel less angry and more friendly or trusting: *a **disarming smile***

dis·ar·ray /ˌdɪsəˈreɪ/ *n.* [U] (formal) the state of being messy or not organized: *papers **in disarray** on the desk*

dis·as·so·ci·ate /ˌdɪsəˈsoʊʃiˌeɪt, -siˌeɪt/ *v.* [T] DISSOCIATE

dis·as·ter /dɪˈzæstɚ/ *n.* [C,U] **1** a sudden event such as an accident, flood, or storm that causes great harm or damage: *The 1889 flood was the most spectacular **natural disaster** the state had ever seen.* | ***Disaster struck** when one rider was hit by a car while cycling.* | *The town was **declared a disaster area** after the floods.*

THESAURUS **accident, catastrophe, mishap** → ACCIDENT

2 a complete failure: *The party was a total disaster.* [ORIGIN: 1500—1600 French *désastre*, from Italian *disastro*, from *dis* "not" + *astro* "star" (from the idea of luck coming from the stars)]

dis·as·trous /dɪˈzæstrəs/ *adj.* very bad, or ending in failure: *a disastrous marriage* —**disastrously** *adv.*

dis·a·vow /ˌdɪsəˈvaʊ/ *v.* [T] (formal) to say that you are not responsible for something, or that you do not know about it: *The President has disavowed any knowledge of the affair.* —**disavowal** *n.* [C,U]

dis·band /dɪsˈbænd/ *v.* [I,T] (formal) to stop existing as an organization, or to make something do this

dis·be·lief /ˌdɪsbəˈlif/ *n.* [U] a feeling that something is not true or does not exist: *Linder shook his head **in disbelief**.* —**disbelieving** *adj.*

disc /dɪsk/ *n.* [C] another spelling of DISK

dis·card /dɪˈskɑrd/ *v.* [T] to get rid of something: *discarding old clothes*

dis·cern /dɪˈsɚn, dɪˈzɚn/ *v.* [T] (formal) to see, notice, or understand something by looking at it or thinking about it carefully: *Walters couldn't discern* *any difference between the two plants.* —**discernible** *adj.* —**discernibly** *adv.*

dis·cern·ing /dɪ'sɚnɪŋ, -'zɚ-/ *adj.* able to make good judgments about people, styles, and things: *the discerning traveler's guide to the Southeast*

dis·charge[1] /dɪs'tʃɑrdʒ/ *v.* **1** [T] to officially allow someone to go or to send him/her away from a place: *Blanton was **discharged from** the hospital last night.* **2** [I,T] to send, pour, or let out a substance: *Chemicals were being **discharged into** a nearby river.* **3** [I,T] (formal) if you discharge a gun, or if it discharges, it shoots a bullet

dis·charge[2] /'dɪstʃɑrdʒ/ *n.* [U] **1** the official action of sending someone or something away, especially from a hospital or the military: *After his **discharge from** the army, he got married.* **2** a substance that comes out of something, especially a wound or part of your body

dis·ci·ple /dɪ'saɪpəl/ *n.* [C] **1** a follower of a religious teacher, especially one of the 12 original followers of Jesus Christ **2** a follower of any great leader or teacher: *a **disciple of** Gandhi* [ORIGIN: 800—900 Latin *discipulus* "pupil"]

dis·ci·pli·nar·i·an /ˌdɪsəplə'nɛriən/ *n.* [C] someone who believes that people should obey rules, and who makes them do this: *Sam's father is a **strict disciplinarian**.*

dis·ci·plin·a·ry /'dɪsəpləˌnɛri/ *adj.* relating to trying to make someone obey rules, or to the punishment of someone who has not obeyed rules: *disciplinary problems*

dis·ci·pline[1] /'dɪsəplɪn/ *n.* **1** [U] controlled behavior in which people obey rules and orders: *maintaining discipline in the classroom | military discipline | serious **discipline problems** in the police force* **2** [U] the ability to control your own behavior and way of working: *Writing requires discipline. | It takes a lot of **self-discipline** to work from home.* **3** [U] punishment for not obeying rules: *Employees who joined the strike face discipline.* **4** [C] (formal) an area of knowledge or teaching [ORIGIN: 1200—1300 Old French *descepline*, from Latin *disciplina* "teaching, learning"]

discipline[2] *v.* [T] **1** to punish someone: *The staff members were disciplined for their carelessness.* **2** to train someone to obey rules and control his/her own behavior: *Working in a bakery has **disciplined** Joe **to** get up early.*

dis·claim·er /dɪs'kleɪmɚ/ *n.* [C] (formal) a statement saying that you are not responsible for something or do not know about something, often used in advertising

dis·close /dɪs'kloʊz/ *v.* [T] to make something known publicly: *GM did not disclose details of the agreement.* [ORIGIN: 1400—1500 Old French *desclore*, from Medieval Latin *disclaudere* "to open"]

dis·clo·sure /dɪs'kloʊʒɚ/ *n.* [C,U] a secret that someone tells people, or the act of telling this secret: *the **disclosure of** state secrets*

dis·co /'dɪskoʊ/ *n.* (plural **discos**) **1** [U] a type of dance music with a strong repeating beat that was first popular in the 1970s **2** [C] a place where people dance to recorded popular music

dis·col·or /dɪs'kʌlɚ/ *v.* [I,T] to change color, or to make something change color, so that it looks unattractive: *His teeth were discolored from smoking.* —**discoloration** /dɪsˌkʌlə'reɪʃən/ *n.* [C,U]

dis·com·fit /dɪs'kʌmfɪt/ *v.* [T] (formal) to make someone feel uncomfortable, annoyed, or embarrassed SYN **unsettle**: *Her comment discomfited her husband.* —**discomfited** *adj.* —**discomfiting** *adj.* —**discomfiture** /dɪs'kʌmfətʃɚ/ *n.* [U]

dis·com·fort /dɪs'kʌmfɚt/ *n.* **1** [U] slight pain or a bad feeling: *We need to treat the disease without increasing the discomfort of the patient.* **2** [C] something that makes you uncomfortable: *the **discomforts of** long-distance travel* **3** [U] a feeling of embarrassment, shame, or worry: *She could sense his **discomfort at** having to speak in front of a large group.*

dis·con·cert·ing /ˌdɪskən'sɚtɪŋ/ *adj.* making you feel slightly embarrassed, confused, or worried: *It was disconcerting to be watched while I worked.* —**disconcert** *v.* [T] —**disconcerted** *adj.*

dis·con·nect /ˌdɪskə'nɛkt/ *v.* **1** [I,T] to separate something from the thing it is connected to, or to become separated: *Disconnect the cables before you move the computer.* **2** [T] to remove the supply of power to something such as a telephone line, building, or machine: *I tried to call, but the phone had been disconnected.* —**disconnection** /ˌdɪskə'nɛkʃən/ *n.* [C,U]

dis·con·tent /ˌdɪskən'tɛnt/ *n.* [U] a feeling of not being happy or satisfied —**discontented** *adj.*

dis·con·tin·ue /ˌdɪskən'tɪnyu/ *v.* [T] to stop doing or providing something: *Five bus routes will be discontinued.* —**discontinuation** /ˌdɪskənˌtɪnyu'eɪʃən/ *n.* [U]

dis·cord /'dɪskɔrd/ *n.* [U] (formal) disagreement between people: *marital discord*

dis·cor·dant /dɪs'kɔrdnt/ *adj.* **1** (literary) seeming strange, wrong, or inappropriate in relation to everything around it: *the discordant images in her pictures* **2** (formal) not in agreement: *The two experiments gave us discordant results.* **3** made up of musical notes that do not go together well: *discordant, jarring music*

dis·count[1] /'dɪskaʊnt/ *n.* [C] a reduction in the usual price of something: *He says he can get me a **discount on** a new computer. | a **discount of** 25% | I saved $20 with my **employee discount**. | a **discount store***

dis·count[2] /dɪs'kaʊnt/ *v.* [T] **1** to reduce the price of something: *Flights to Florida have been deeply discounted.* **2** to regard something as

D

unlikely to be true or important: *Scientists discounted his method of predicting earthquakes.*

dis·cour·age /dɪ'skɚɪdʒ, -'skʌr-/ *v.* [T] **1** to persuade someone not to do something, especially by making it seem difficult or bad (ANT) **encourage**: *Keith's mother tried to* ***discourage*** *him* ***from*** *joining the navy.* **2** to make someone less confident or less willing to do something (ANT) **encourage**: *His failure to find a job did not discourage him.* **3** to make something become less likely to happen (ANT) **encourage**: *Put the plant in a cold room to discourage growth.*

D

dis·cour·aged /dɪ'skɚɪdʒd, -'skʌr-/ *adj.* no longer having the confidence you need to continue doing something: *Children may* ***get discouraged*** *if they are criticized too often.*

dis·cour·age·ment /dɪ'skɚɪdʒmənt, -'skʌr-/ *n.* **1** [C,U] a feeling of being discouraged **2** [U] the act of trying to discourage someone from doing something

dis·cour·a·ging /dɪ'skɚɪdʒɪŋ, -'skʌr-/ *adj.* making you lose the confidence you need to continue doing something: *It was very discouraging to see my sister do it so easily.*

dis·course /'dɪskɔrs/ *n.* [U] serious conversation between people: *a chance for meaningful discourse between the two leaders*

dis·cour·te·ous /dɪs'kɚt̬iəs/ *adj.* (formal) not polite or respectful —**discourtesy** /dɪs'kɚt̬əsi/ *n.* [C,U]

dis·cov·er /dɪ'skʌvɚ/ *v.* [T] **1** to find something that was hidden or that people did not know about before: *The Vikings may have discovered America long before Columbus.*

THESAURUS **find, detect, trace, locate, track sb/sth down, turn sth up, unearth** → FIND[1]

2 to find out something that is a fact, or the answer to a question: *Doctors* ***discovered that*** *her left wrist was broken.* | *Did you ever* ***discover who*** *sent you the flowers?* [ORIGIN: 1300—1400 Old French *descovrir*, from Late Latin *discooperire* "to uncover"] —**discoverer** *n.* [C]

dis·cov·er·y /dɪ'skʌvri, -vəri/ *n.* (plural **discoveries**) **1** [C] a fact, thing, or answer to a question that someone discovers: *Einstein* ***made an*** *important scientific* ***discovery***. | *the* ***discovery that*** *bees can communicate with each other* **2** [U] the act of finding something that was hidden or not known before: *the* ***discovery of*** *gold in 1848*

dis·cred·it /dɪs'krɛdɪt/ *v.* [T] to make people stop trusting or having respect for someone or something: *The defense lawyer will try to discredit our witnesses.*

dis·creet /dɪ'skrit/ *adj.* careful about what you say or do, so that you do not upset or embarrass people: *Can you please* ***be discreet*** *about this?* —**discreetly** *adv.*

dis·crep·an·cy /dɪ'skrɛpənsi/ *n.* (plural **discrepancies**) [C,U] a difference between two amounts, details, etc. that should be the same: *There were* ***discrepancies in*** *the expense accounts.*

dis·crete /dɪ'skrit/ (Ac) *adj.* (formal) clearly separate (SYN) **distinct**: *The developing insect passes through several discrete stages.*

dis·cre·tion /dɪ'skrɛʃən/ (Ac) *n.* [U] **1** the ability to be careful about what you say or do in a particular situation, so that you do not upset or embarrass people: *This situation must be handled with discretion.* **2** the ability and right to decide what should be done in a particular situation: *Pay raises are* ***left to the discretion of*** *the manager.* | *Prisoners are released* ***at the discretion of*** *the parole board.* —**discretionary** *adj.*: *The president has the discretionary authority to send troops.*

dis·crim·i·nate /dɪ'skrɪmə,neɪt/ (Ac) *v.* **1** [I] to treat one person or group differently from another in an unfair way: *a law that* ***discriminates against*** *immigrants* | *Employers may not discriminate in favor of younger candidates.* **2** [I,T] to recognize a difference between things (SYN) **differentiate**: *You must learn to* ***discriminate between*** *facts and opinions.* | *The test is useful for* ***discriminating*** *those students who have reached a higher level* ***from*** *those at a lower level.* [ORIGIN: 1600—1700 Latin *discriminare* "to divide," from *discernere* "to separate"]

dis·crim·i·nat·ing /dɪ'skrɪmə,neɪt̬ɪŋ/ (Ac) *adj.* able to judge whether or not something is good quality: *customers with discriminating tastes*

dis·crim·i·na·tion /dɪ,skrɪmə'neɪʃən/ (Ac) *n.* [U] **1** the practice of treating one person or group of people differently from another in an unfair way: *The company has been accused of* ***racial/age/sex discrimination***. | *The law prohibits* ***discrimination against*** *handicapped persons.*

THESAURUS **prejudice, racism, intolerance, bigotry, sexism, homophobia, anti-Semitism** → PREJUDICE[1]

2 the ability to judge whether or not something is good quality

di·scur·sive /dɪ'skɚsɪv/ *adj.* discussing many different ideas, facts, etc. rather than keeping to a single subject: *a discursive letter* —**discursively** *adv.* —**discursiveness** *n.* [U]

dis·cus /'dɪskəs/ *n.* **1** [C] a heavy flat circular object that people throw as far as possible as a sport **2 the discus** the sport of throwing this object

dis·cuss /dɪ'skʌs/ *v.* [T] **1** to talk about something with someone in order to exchange ideas or decide something: *I wanted to* ***discuss*** *my plans* ***with*** *my father.* | *We need to* ***discuss how*** *to raise money for the project.*

THESAURUS **talk, have a conversation, chat (with/to sb)/have a chat, converse, visit with sb, gossip** → TALK[1]

2 to talk or write about a subject in detail: *The Roman Empire will be discussed in the next chapter.* [ORIGIN: 1300—1400 Latin *discussus*, past participle of *discutere* "to shake to pieces"]

dis·cus·sion /dɪˈskʌʃən/ *n.* [C,U] **1** the act of discussing something, or a conversation in which people discuss something: *We need to **have a discussion about** your behavior in class.* | *The proposal is still **under discussion*** (=being discussed).

THESAURUS

negotiations – official discussions between two groups who are trying to agree on something: *Contract negotiations are continuing between the union and the management.*
debate – a formal discussion of a subject, during which people express different opinions: *the debate between the presidential candidates*
talks – formal discussions between governments, organizations, etc.: *the recent talks on global warming*
conference – a large formal meeting at which members of an organization, profession, etc. discuss things related to their work: *an annual conference for software developers*
dialogue – a formal discussion between countries or groups in order to solve problems: *We want to encourage dialogue between the two nations.*

2 a piece of writing about a subject that considers different ideas or opinions about it: *The report includes a **discussion of** global warming.*

dis·dain /dɪsˈdeɪn/ *n.* [U] (formal) a lack of respect for someone or something because you think he, she, or it is not important or not good enough: *Mason's **disdain for** people without education* —**disdainful** *adj.*

dis·ease /dɪˈziz/ *n.* [C,U] an illness that affects a person, animal, or plant, with specific SYMPTOMS (=things wrong with your body which show that you have a particular illness): *My uncle has **heart disease.*** | *Tina **suffers from a** rare brain **disease.*** | ***infectious diseases** such as tuberculosis* [ORIGIN: 1300—1400 Old French *desaise*, from *des* "not, without" + *aise* "relaxed feeling, comfort"] —**diseased** *adj.*

THESAURUS

People often use **disease** and **illness** to mean the same thing, but it is a **disease** that actually makes you sick: *He suffers from heart disease.*
Illness is the state of being sick: *Janey missed a lot of school because of illness.*
Sickness is a particular type of illness: *radiation sickness* | *motion sickness*

dis·em·bark /ˌdɪsɪmˈbɑrk/ *v.* [I] to get off a vehicle such as a ship or airplane —**disembarkation** /ˌdɪsɛmbɑrˈkeɪʃən/ *n.* [U]

dis·em·bod·ied /ˌdɪsɪmˈbɑdid/ *adj.* a disembodied sound or voice comes from someone who cannot be seen

dis·en·chant·ed /ˌdɪsɪnˈtʃæntɪd/ *adj.* disappointed with someone or something, and no longer liking or believing in the value of that person or thing: *She was becoming **disenchanted with** her marriage.* —**disenchantment** *n.* [U]

dis·en·fran·chised /ˌdɪsɪnˈfræntʃaɪzd/ *adj.* (formal) not having any rights, especially the right to vote, and not feeling part of society —**disenfranchise** *v.* [T]

dis·en·gage /ˌdɪsɪnˈgeɪdʒ/ *v.* **1** [I,T] if you disengage parts of a machine, the machine stops operating because two parts are separated from each other: *Disengage the gears when you park the car.* **2** [I] to deliberately stop being involved with a group or activity: *Some politicians feel that America should **disengage from** the United Nations.* —**disengagement** *n.* [U]

dis·en·tan·gle /ˌdɪsɪnˈtæŋgəl/ *v.* [T] **1 disentangle yourself (from sth)** to escape from a difficult situation that you are involved in **2** to separate different ideas or pieces of information that have become confused together: *It's very difficult to disentangle fact from fiction in what she's saying.*

dis·fa·vor /dɪsˈfeɪvɚ/ *n.* [U] (formal) a feeling of dislike or disapproval

dis·fig·ure /dɪsˈfɪgyɚ/ *v.* [T] to spoil the appearance of someone or something: *His face was badly disfigured in the accident.* —**disfigurement** *n.* [C,U]

dis·grace[1] /dɪsˈgreɪs/ *n.* **1 sth is a disgrace** used in order to say that someone or something is very bad or unacceptable: *The public schools in the area are a disgrace.* | *He was a **disgrace to** the legal profession.* **2** [U] the loss of other people's respect because you have done something they strongly disapprove of: *Harry left the school **in disgrace.*** | *There's **no disgrace** in trying.*

disgrace[2] *v.* [T] to do something so bad that people lose respect for your family or for the group you belong to: *How could you disgrace us like that?*

dis·grace·ful /dɪsˈgreɪsfəl/ *adj.* very bad, embarrassing, or unacceptable: *Their behavior was absolutely disgraceful.*

dis·grun·tled /dɪsˈgrʌntəld/ *adj.* annoyed, disappointed, and not satisfied: *disgruntled employees*

dis·guise[1] /dɪsˈgaɪz/ *v.* [T] **1** to change your appearance or voice so that people cannot recognize you: *She **disguised** herself **as** a man.* **2** to hide a fact or feeling so that people will not notice it: *We can't **disguise the fact that** the business is losing money.* [ORIGIN: 1300—1400 Old French *desguiser*, from *guise* "appearance"]

THESAURUS **hide, conceal, cover/cover up, mask** → HIDE[1]

disguise[2] *n.* [C,U] something that you wear to change your appearance and hide who you really are, or the act of wearing this: *She went out **in disguise** to avoid reporters.*

dis·gust¹ /dɪsˈgʌst/ *n.* [U] a strong feeling of dislike and disapproval: *Everyone was looking at him **with disgust**. | He walked out of the meeting **in disgust**.*

disgust² *v.* [T] to make someone feel very annoyed or upset about something that is not acceptable —**disgusted** *adj.*: *We **felt disgusted** by the way we'd been treated.*

dis·gust·ing /dɪsˈgʌstɪŋ/ *adj.* **1** shocking and unacceptable: *The way he treats her is disgusting.* **2** extremely unpleasant and making you feel sick: *a disgusting smell*

D

THESAURUS **horrible, awful, revolting, foul, terrible, dreadful, horrendous** ➔ HORRIBLE

—**disgustingly** *adv.*

THESAURUS **hurt, injure, wound, maim, break, bruise, sprain, twist, strain, pull** ➔ HURT¹

dish¹ /dɪʃ/ *n.* [C] **1** a round container with low sides, used for holding food ➔ PLATE, BOWL: *a serving dish* **2 dishes** [plural] all the plates, cups, bowls, etc. that are used during a meal: *Who's going to **do/wash the dishes**?* **3** food cooked or prepared in a particular way: *a wonderful pasta dish | You can serve this soup as a **main dish*** (=the biggest part of a meal). [ORIGIN: Old English *disc*, from Latin *discus* "disk, plate"]

dish² *v.*

dish sth ↔ **out** *phr. v.* (informal) to give something to people: *He's always dishing out unwanted advice.*

dish sth ↔ **up** *phr. v.* (informal) to put food for a meal onto dishes, ready to be eaten

dis·heart·ened /dɪsˈhɑrt̚nd/ *adj.* disappointed because you no longer feel that you are able to do or achieve something —**dishearten** *v.* [T]

dis·heart·en·ing /dɪsˈhɑrt̚n-ɪŋ/ *adj.* making you lose hope and confidence: ***It** was **disheartening to** see that the changes we made didn't help.* —**dishearteningly** *adv.*

di·shev·eled /dɪˈʃɛvəld/ *adj.* very messy: *She looked tired and disheveled.*

dis·hon·est /dɪsˈɑnɪst/ *adj.* not honest: *a dishonest car salesman* —**dishonesty** *n.* [U] —**dishonestly** *adv.*

dis·hon·or /dɪsˈɑnɚ/ *n.* [U] (formal) a state in which people no longer respect you or approve of you because you have done something dishonest or immoral: *His behavior **brought dishonor on** the family.* —**dishonor** *v.* [T] —**dishonorable** *adj.*

ˈdish rack *n.* [C] an object that holds dishes while they dry

dish·tow·el /ˈdɪʃˌtaʊəl/ *n.* [C] a cloth used for drying dishes

dish·wash·er /ˈdɪʃˌwɑʃɚ/ *n.* [C] **1** a machine that washes dishes **2** someone whose job is to wash dirty dishes in a restaurant

ˈdishwashing ˌliquid *n.* [U] liquid soap used to wash dishes

dis·il·lu·sion /ˌdɪsəˈluʒən/ *v.* [T] to make someone realize that something s/he thought was true or good is not —**disillusionment** *n.* [U]

dis·il·lu·sioned /ˌdɪsəˈluʒənd/ *adj.* unhappy because you have lost your belief that someone or something is true or good: *I have become increasingly **disillusioned with** politics.*

dis·in·cen·tive /ˌdɪsɪnˈsɛntɪv/ *n.* [C] something that makes people less willing to do something (ANT) **incentive**: *Higher taxes may act as a **disincentive to** business.*

dis·in·fect /ˌdɪsɪnˈfɛkt/ *v.* [T] to clean something with a chemical that destroys BACTERIA

dis·in·fect·ant /ˌdɪsɪnˈfɛktənt/ *n.* [C,U] a chemical that destroys BACTERIA, used for cleaning something

dis·in·gen·u·ous /ˌdɪsɪnˈdʒɛnyuəs/ *adj.* (formal) not sincere and slightly dishonest: *It's disingenuous to talk of federal budget cuts when the level of government spending will actually rise.* —**disingenuously** *adv.*

dis·in·her·it /ˌdɪsɪnˈhɛrɪt/ *v.* [T] to prevent someone from receiving any of your money or property after your death

dis·in·te·grate /dɪsˈɪntəˌgreɪt/ *v.* [I] **1** to break up into small pieces: *They saw the space shuttle disintegrate in the sky.* **2** to become weaker and be gradually destroyed: *Their marriage was disintegrating.* —**disintegration** /dɪsˌɪntəˈgreɪʃən/ *n.* [U]

dis·in·terest·ed /dɪsˈɪntrɪstɪd, -ˈɪntəˌrɛstɪd/ *adj.* able to judge a situation fairly because you will not gain an advantage from it (SYN) **objective**: *a disinterested observer of the voting process*

USAGE

In spoken English, many people use **disinterested** to mean "not interested." However, many teachers think that this is not correct. If you want to say that someone is "not interested," use **uninterested**: *She seemed uninterested in politics.*

—**disinterest** *n.* [U]

dis·joint·ed /dɪsˈdʒɔɪntɪd/ *adj.* disjointed words or images are not easy to understand because they are not arranged in a clear order

disk /dɪsk/ *n.* [C] **1** a small flat piece of plastic or metal used for storing information in a computer ➔ COMPACT DISK, FLOPPY DISK, HARD DISK **2** something that is flat and round, or that looks this way **3** a flat piece of CARTILAGE (=a strong substance that stretches) between the bones of your back

ˈdisk drive *n.* [C] IT a piece of equipment in a

computer, that is used in order to get information from a disk or to store information on a disk

disk·ette /dɪ'skɛt/ *n.* [C] IT a FLOPPY DISK

'disk ,jockey *n.* [C] a DJ

dis·like¹ /dɪs'laɪk/ *v.* [T] to not like someone or something: *Many men dislike shopping.*

dislike² *n.* [C,U] a feeling of not liking someone or something: *She shared her mother's **dislike of** housework.*

dis·lo·cate /dɪs'loʊkeɪt, 'dɪsloʊ,keɪt/ *v.* [T] to make a bone move out of its normal position in a joint, usually in an accident: *I dislocated my shoulder playing football.* —**dislocation** /,dɪsloʊ'keɪʃən/ *n.* [C,U]

dis·lodge /dɪs'lɑdʒ/ *v.* [T] to force or knock something out of its position: *Lee dislodged a few stones as he climbed over the old wall.*

dis·loy·al /dɪs'lɔɪəl/ *adj.* doing or saying things that do not support your friends, your country, or the group you belong to: *He felt he had been **disloyal to** his friends.* —**disloyalty** /dɪs'lɔɪəlti/ *n.* [C,U]

dis·mal /'dɪzməl/ *adj.* making you feel unhappy and without hope: *dismal weather | the team's dismal record in the past month* [ORIGIN: 1300—1400 Anglo-French, Medieval Latin *dies mali* "evil days"] —**dismally** *adv.*

dis·man·tle /dɪs'mæntəl/ *v.* [I,T] **1** to take something apart so that it is in separate pieces: *I'll have to dismantle the engine.* **2** to gradually get rid of a system or organization: *plans to dismantle the existing tax laws*

dis·may¹ /dɪs'meɪ/ *n.* [U] a strong feeling of disappointment and worry: *He realized **to his dismay** that he had left the money behind.*

dismay² *v.* [T] to make someone feel worried, disappointed, or upset: *I was **dismayed to** see how thin she had become.*

dis·mem·ber /dɪs'mɛmbɚ/ *v.* [T] (formal) to cut or tear a body into pieces

dis·miss /dɪs'mɪs/ *v.* [T] **1** to refuse to consider someone's idea or opinion because you think it is not serious, true, or important: *He **dismissed** the idea **as** impossible.* **2** (formal) to make someone leave his/her job (SYN) **fire**: *The teacher was **dismissed for** incompetence.* **3** to send someone away, or allow him/her to go: *Class is dismissed.* **4** LAW if a court CASE is dismissed, a judge decides that it should not continue [ORIGIN: 1400—1500 Latin *dimissus*, past participle of *dimittere* "to send away"] —**dismissal** *n.* [C,U]

dis·mis·sive /dɪs'mɪsɪv/ *adj.* refusing to consider someone or something seriously: *Her doctor was **dismissive of** her concerns.*

dis·mount /dɪs'maʊnt/ *v.* [I] to get off a horse, bicycle, or MOTORCYCLE

dis·o·be·di·ent /,dɪsə'bidiənt/ *adj.* deliberately not doing what you are told to do by someone in authority such as your parents, teacher, employer, etc.: *a disobedient child* —**disobedience** *n.* [U]

dis·o·bey /,dɪsə'beɪ/ *v.* [I,T] to refuse to do what someone in authority tells you to do, or to refuse to obey a rule or law: *She would never disobey her parents.*

THESAURUS

break a rule/law – to disobey a rule or law: *What happens if you break the rules?*
rebel – to oppose or fight against someone who is in authority: *Hannah eventually rebelled against her mother's control.*
defy – to refuse to obey someone or something: *Several teenagers were caught defying the curfew.*
flout (formal) – to deliberately disobey a rule, law, or custom: *He seemed determined to flout his father's authority.*
violate – to disobey or do something against a law, rule, agreement, etc.: *Using the money in this way clearly violates the tax laws.*
infringe (formal) – to do something that is against the law or someone's legal rights: *A treaty cannot be valid if it infringes on the Constitution.*
contravene (formal) – to do something that is not allowed by a law or rule: *The building contravened New York's construction codes.*

dis·or·der /dɪs'ɔrdɚ/ *n.* **1** [U] a situation in which things or people are very messy or not organized **2** [C] a disease or illness that prevents part of your body from working correctly: *a mental disorder* **3** [U] a situation in which a lot of people behave in an uncontrolled, noisy, or violent way in public: *The nation is in a state of **civil disorder**.*

dis·or·der·ly /dɪs'ɔrdɚli/ *adj.* **1** messy: *clothes left in a disorderly heap* **2** behaving in a noisy or violent way in public: *He was arrested for **disorderly conduct**.*

dis·or·ga·nized /dɪs'ɔrgə,naɪzd/ *adj.* not arranged or planned very well: *The meeting was completely disorganized.* —**disorganization** /dɪs,ɔrgənə'zeɪʃən/ *n.* [U]

dis·o·ri·ent·ed /dɪs'ɔri,ɛntɪd/ *adj.* confused and not really able to understand what is happening around you, or where you are —**disorienting** *adj.* —**disorientation** /dɪs,ɔriən'teɪʃən/ *n.* [U]

dis·own /dɪs'oʊn/ *v.* [T] if your parents disown you, they decide that they no longer want to have any connection with you, usually because you have done something very bad

dis·par·age /dɪ'spærɪdʒ/ *v.* [T] (formal) to criticize someone or something in a way that shows you do not think he, she, or it is very good or important

dis·par·a·ging /dɪ'spærədʒɪŋ/ *adj.* showing that you think someone or something is not very good or important: *She **made** some **disparaging comments** about his work.*

dis·par·ate /'dɪspərɪt/ *adj.* (formal) very different from and not related to each other

dis·par·i·ty /dɪ'spærəṭi/ *n.* (plural **disparities**) [C,U] a difference between things, especially an unfair difference: *the **disparities between** rich and poor*

dis·pas·sion·ate /dɪs'pæʃənɪt/ *adj.* not easily influenced by personal feelings: *a dispassionate opinion* —**dispassionately** *adv.*

dis·patch¹ /dɪ'spætʃ/ *v.* [T] to send someone or something somewhere

dispatch² *n.* **1** [C] a message sent between government or military officials **2** [C] a report sent to a newspaper from one of its writers who is in another town or country **3** [singular] the act of sending people or things to a particular place: *the **dispatch of** troops to the area*

D

dis·pel /dɪ'spɛl/ *v.* (**dispelled**, **dispelling**) [T] (formal) to stop someone from believing or feeling something, especially because it is harmful or not correct: *Mark's calm words dispelled our fears.*

dis·pen·sa·ry /dɪ'spɛnsəri/ *n.* (plural **dispensaries**) [C] a place where medicines are prepared and given out

dis·pen·sa·tion /ˌdɪspən'seɪʃən, -pɛn-/ *n.* [C,U] special permission from someone in authority, especially a religious leader, to do something that is not usually allowed

dis·pense /dɪ'spɛns/ *v.* [T] (formal) **1** to give or provide something to people, especially as part of an official activity: *Volunteers helped dispense food and blankets.*

THESAURUS **give out, hand out/pass out, share, distribute** → GIVE¹

2 to officially provide medicine to people

dispense with sth *phr. v.* to not use or do something that people usually use or do because it is not necessary

dis·pens·er /dɪ'spɛnsɚ/ *n.* [C] a machine from which you can get things such as drinks or money when you press a button

dis·perse /dɪ'spɚs/ *v.* [I,T] to scatter in different directions, or to make something do this: *The police used tear gas to disperse the crowd.* —**dispersal** *n.* [U]

dis·per·sion /dɪs'pɚʒən/ *n.* [U] **1** the state of being spread over a wide area or between a wide group of people **2** MATH the way in which the DATA in a set is spread around a number that is usually the middle number in the set or the average of the set **3** PHYSICS the separation of white light into different bands of colored light, that happens when light passes through a PRISM or water

dis·pir·it·ed /dɪ'spɪrɪt̬ɪd/ *adj.* (literary) sad and without hope

dis·place /dɪs'pleɪs/ (Ac) *v.* [T] **1** to take the place of someone or something by becoming more important or useful (SYN) **replace**: *Coal has been displaced by natural gas as a major source of energy.* **2** to make a group of people leave the place where they normally live: *When the river flooded the area, nearly a million people were displaced.* **3** to force something out of its usual place or position: *When you get into a full bathtub, you displace water, which flows over the side.* —**displacement** *n.* [U]: *the **displacement of** native peoples from their land* —**displaced** *adj.*

dis·play¹ /dɪ'spleɪ/ (Ac) *n.* (plural **displays**) **1** [C,U] an arrangement of objects for people to look at: *a **display of** African masks | The pictures are **on display** in the lobby.* **2** [C] a public performance or something that is intended to entertain people: *a fireworks display* **3 a display of anger/affection etc.** an occasion when someone clearly shows a particular attitude, feeling, or quality **4** [C] the part of a piece of equipment that shows information, for example a computer screen: *A light flashed on the display.* [ORIGIN: 1500—1600 Anglo-French *despleier*, from Latin *displicare* "to unfold"]

display² (Ac) *v.* [T] **1** to put things in a place where people can see them easily: *a row of tables displaying pottery* **2** to clearly show a feeling or quality: *He displayed no emotion at the funeral.* **3** if a computer displays information, it shows it: *An error message was displayed.*

dis·pleased /dɪs'plizd/ *adj.* (formal) annoyed and not satisfied: *Many employees were **displeased with** the decision.* —**displease** *v.* [T] —**displeasure** /dɪs'plɛʒɚ/ *n.* [U]

dis·pos·a·ble /dɪ'spoʊzəbəl/ (Ac) *adj.* intended to be used once or for a short time and then thrown away: *disposable razors*

disˌposable 'income *n.* [C] the amount of money that you have available to spend each month after you have paid for rent, food, etc.

dis·pos·al /dɪ'spoʊzəl/ (Ac) *n.* **1** [U] the act of getting rid of something: *the safe **disposal of** radioactive waste* **2 at sb's disposal** available for someone to use: *He had a lot of cash at his disposal.* **3** [C] a GARBAGE DISPOSAL

dis·pose /dɪ'spoʊz/ (Ac) *v.*

dispose of sth *phr. v.* to get rid of something: *a facility that disposes of industrial waste* [ORIGIN: 1300—1400 French *disposer*, from Latin *disponere* "to arrange"]

dis·posed /dɪ'spoʊzd/ (Ac) *adj.* (formal) **1 be/feel disposed to do sth** to be willing to do something or behave in a particular way: *I don't feel disposed to interfere.* **2 well/favorably disposed to sb/sth** liking someone or something

dis·po·si·tion /ˌdɪspə'zɪʃən/ *n.* [C] (formal) the way someone tends to behave: *Jenny has such a sweet disposition.*

dis·pos·sess /ˌdɪspə'zɛs/ *v.* [T] (formal) to take property or land away from someone —**dispossession** /ˌdɪspə'zɛʃən/ *n.* [U]

dis·pro·por·tion·ate /ˌdɪsprə'pɔrʃənɪt/ (Ac) *adj.* too much or too little in relation to something else, used when comparing two things: *The project consumed a disproportionate amount of time.* —**disproportionately** *adv.*

dis·prove /dɪs'pruv/ *v.* [T] to show that something is definitely wrong or not true

dis·pute¹ /dɪ'spyut/ *n.* [C,U] **1** a serious argument or disagreement: *The two men got into a **dispute over** money.* | *He was involved in a legal **dispute with** his neighbor.* | *The facts of the case are still **in dispute*** (=being argued about). **2 be beyond dispute** if something is beyond dispute, everyone agrees that it is true or has really happened: *Mitchell's guilt is beyond dispute.* [ORIGIN: 1500—1600 Old French *desputer*, from Latin *disputare* "to discuss"]

dispute² *v.* [T] to say that something such as a fact or idea is not correct or true: *The facts of the book have never been disputed.*

THESAURUS disagree, be divided/split, dissent → DISAGREE

dis·qual·i·fy /dɪs'kwɑlə,faɪ/ *v.* (**disqualified, disqualifies**) [T] to stop someone from taking part in an activity or competition, usually because s/he has done something wrong: *Dennis was **disqualified from** the race.* —**disqualification** /dɪs,kwɑləfə'keɪʃən/ *n.* [C,U]

dis·re·gard¹ /,dɪsrɪ'gɑrd/ *v.* [T] to ignore something, or to not treat something as important or serious: *The judge told the jury to disregard that statement.*

disregard² *n.* [U] the act of ignoring something, especially something important or serious: *His actions show a total **disregard for** the law.*

dis·re·pair /,dɪsrɪ'pɛr/ *n* [U] buildings, roads, etc. that are in disrepair are in bad condition because they have not been cared for: *The old house had **fallen into disrepair**.*

dis·rep·u·ta·ble /dɪs'rɛpyət̬əbəl/ *adj.* not good or respected, and often thought to be involved in dishonest or illegal activities

dis·re·pute /,dɪsrə'pyut/ *n.* [U] (formal) a situation in which people no longer trust or respect a person or an idea: *His reputation has **fallen into disrepute**.*

dis·re·spect /,dɪsrɪ'spɛkt/ *n.* [U] lack of respect for someone or something: *his **disrespect for** the law* —**disrespectful** *adj.*

dis·rupt /dɪs'rʌpt/ *v.* [T] to prevent something from continuing in its usual way by causing problems: *The blizzard disrupted transportation into the city.* | *We cannot allow terrorists to **disrupt** our **lives**.* [ORIGIN: 1400—1500 Latin *disruptus*, from *rumpere* "to break"] —**disruption** /dɪs'rʌpʃən/ *n.* [C,U] —**disruptive** /dɪs'rʌptɪv/ *adj.*: *disruptive students*

dis·sat·is·fac·tion /dɪ,sæt̬ɪs'fækʃən, dɪs,sæ-/ *n.* [U] a feeling of not being satisfied because something is not as good as you had expected: *She expressed her **dissatisfaction with** the service.*

dis·sat·is·fied /dɪ'sæt̬ɪs,faɪd/ *adj.* not satisfied because something is not as good as you had expected: *Katie is **dissatisfied with** her job.*

dis·sect /dɪ'sɛkt, daɪ-/ *v.* [T] BIOLOGY to cut up the body of a person or animal in order to study it —**dissection** /dɪ'sɛkʃən/ *n.* [C,U]

dis·sem·ble /dɪ'sɛmbəl/ *v.* [I,T] (formal) to hide your true feelings, ideas, desires, etc., especially in order to deceive someone

dis·sem·i·nate /dɪ'sɛmə,neɪt/ *v.* [T] (formal) to spread information, ideas, etc. to as many people as possible: *The rumor has been widely disseminated on the Internet.* —**dissemination** /dɪ,sɛmə'neɪʃən/ *n.* [U]

dis·sent /dɪ'sɛnt/ *n.* [U] refusal to accept an opinion or decision that most people accept: *political dissent* —**dissent** *v.* [I]: *Two of the court's nine judges dissented from the majority decision.*

THESAURUS disagree, be divided/split, dispute → DISAGREE

D

dis·sent·er /dɪ'sɛntə/ *n.* [C] HISTORY a PROTESTANT in England during the 17th and 18th centuries who disagreed with the religious ideas and practices of the Church of England

dis·ser·ta·tion /,dɪsə'teɪʃən/ *n.* [C] a long piece of writing about a subject, that you write to get a PH.D.

THESAURUS essay, composition, paper, thesis → ESSAY

dis·serv·ice /dɪ'səvɪs, dɪs'sə-/ *n.* **do sb/sth a disservice** to do something that makes people have a bad opinion of someone or something, especially when this is unfair: *The players' actions have **done a** great **disservice to** the game.*

dis·si·dent /'dɪsədənt/ *n.* [C] POLITICS someone who publicly criticizes the government in his/her country, when doing this is a crime in that country [ORIGIN: 1500—1600 Latin *dissidere* "to sit apart, disagree," from *sedere* "to sit"] —**dissidence** *n.* [U] —**dissident** *adj.*

dis·sim·i·lar /dɪ,sɪmələ, dɪs'sɪ-/ (Ac) *adj.* not the same: *These fish are quite **dissimilar to** those found in the deep ocean.* | *The system of government here is not too **dissimilar from** the one in our own country.* —**dissimilarity** /dɪ,sɪmə'lærət̬i/ *n.* [C,U]

dis·si·pate /'dɪsə,peɪt/ *v.* [I,T] (formal) to gradually get weaker and then disappear completely, or to make something do this

dis·so·ci·ate /dɪ'souʃi,eɪt, -si,eɪt/ *also* **disassociate** *v.* [T] (formal) to do or say something to show that you do not agree with the views or actions of someone with whom you had a connection: *Mr. Garcia tried to **disassociate** himself **from** the chairman's remarks.* —**dissociation** /dɪ,sousi'eɪʃən, -,souʃi-/ *n.* [U]

dis·so·lute /'dɪsə,lut/ *adj.* (written) having an immoral way of life: *a dissolute life*

dis·so·lu·tion /,dɪsə'luʃən/ *n.* [U] (formal) the

act of officially ending a marriage, business arrangement, etc.

dissolve

dis·solve /dɪ'zɑlv/ *v.* **1** [I,T] if a solid dissolves, or if you dissolve it, it mixes with a liquid and becomes liquid itself: *Stir the mixture until the sugar dissolves.* | ***Dissolve*** *the tablets* ***in*** *warm water.* **2** [T] to officially end a marriage, business arrangement, etc.

THESAURUS **divorce, separate, split up/break up, annul** → DIVORCE[2]

3 dissolve into tears/laughter etc. to start crying or laughing a lot

dis·so·nance /'dɪsənəns/ *n.* **1** [C usually singular, U] (formal) a lack of agreement between ideas, opinions, or facts: *There is a* ***dissonance between*** *her school life and her home life.* **2** [C,U] ENG. LANG. ARTS the sound made by a group of musical notes that do not go together well (SYN) **discord** (ANT) **harmony**: *a choral piece full of dissonance and odd rhythms* —**dissonant** *adj.*

dis·suade /dɪ'sweɪd/ *v.* [T] (formal) to persuade someone not to do something: *efforts to* ***dissuade*** *teenagers* ***from*** *drinking*

dis·tance¹ /'dɪstəns/ *n.* **1** [C,U] the amount of space between two places or things: *What's the* ***distance from*** *Louisville* ***to*** *Memphis?* | *the* ***distance between*** *the moon and the sun* | *We had gone a* ***long/short distance.*** | *The subway is within* ***walking distance*** (=near enough to walk to) *of my house.* **2** [singular] a point or place that is far away, but close enough to be seen or heard: *The ruins look very impressive* ***from a distance.*** | *We could see the Sears Tower* ***in the distance.*** **3 keep your distance a)** to stay far away from someone or something: *The dogs looked fierce, so I kept my distance.* **b)** *also* **keep sb at a distance** to avoid becoming too friendly with someone: *He tends to keep his distance from employees.*

distance² *v.* **distance yourself (from sb/sth)** to say that you are not involved with someone or something: *The party is distancing itself from its violent past.*

dis·tant /'dɪstənt/ *adj.* **1** far away in space or time: *the sound of distant laughter* | *The building is a relic of* ***the distant past.*** **2** not friendly or not interested: *She seemed cold and distant.* **3** [only before noun] not closely related to you (ANT) **close**: *a distant cousin* —**distantly** *adv.*

dis·taste /dɪs'teɪst/ *n.* [singular, U] a feeling of dislike for someone or something that you think is annoying or offensive: *her* ***distaste for*** *modern art*

dis·taste·ful /dɪs'teɪstfəl/ *adj.* unpleasant or offensive

dis·tend·ed /dɪ'stɛndɪd/ *adj.* stretched larger than the normal size because of pressure from inside: *the distended bellies of famine victims* —**distend** *v.* [I,T] —**distention**, **distension** /dɪ'stɛnʃən/ *n.* [U]

dis·till /dɪ'stɪl/ *v.* [T] to make a liquid more pure by heating it until it becomes gas and then letting it cool: *distilled water* —**distillation** /ˌdɪstə'leɪʃən/ *n.* [C,U]

dis·till·er·y /dɪ'stɪləri/ *n.* (plural **distilleries**) [C] a factory where strong alcoholic drinks are produced by distilling

dis·tinct /dɪ'stɪŋkt/ (Ac) *adj.* **1** clearly different or separate: *African and Asian elephants are distinct species.* | *Many people think that the soul is* ***distinct from*** *the body.* **2 as distinct from sth** used in order to emphasize that you are talking about one thing and not another: *I am talking about childhood as distinct from adolescence.* **3** a distinct possibility, feeling, quality, etc. definitely exists and cannot be ignored: *There's a* ***distinct possibility*** *that we'll all lose our jobs.* | *I had the* ***distinct impression*** *that she didn't like me.* **4** clearly seen, heard, smelled, etc.: *the distinct smell of cigarette smoke* —**distinctly** *adv.*: *I distinctly remember his words.*

dis·tinc·tion /dɪ'stɪŋkʃən/ (Ac) *n.* **1** [C] a clear difference between things: *The law* ***makes/draws a distinction between*** *children and adults.* **2** [U] the quality of being very good, important, or special: *a poet of distinction* | *Neil Armstrong* ***had the distinction of*** *being the first man on the moon.*

dis·tinc·tive /dɪ'stɪŋktɪv/ (Ac) *adj.* different from other people or things and very easy to recognize: *The male birds have distinctive blue and yellow markings.* | *The flavor is slightly sharp and very distinctive.* —**distinctively** *adv.* —**distinctiveness** *n.* [U]

dis·tin·guish /dɪ'stɪŋgwɪʃ/ *v.* **1** [I,T] to recognize or understand the difference between things or people: *Young children often can't* ***distinguish between*** *TV programs and commercials.* **2** [T] to be the thing that makes someone or something different from other people or things: *The bright feathers* ***distinguish*** *the male peacock* ***from*** *the female.* **3** [T] to be able to see, hear, smell, etc. something, even if it is difficult: *It was too dark for me to distinguish anything clearly.* **4 distinguish yourself** to do something so well that people notice you, praise you, or remember you: *Eastwood distinguished himself as an actor before becoming a director.* [ORIGIN: 1500—1600 French *distinguer*, from Latin *distinguere* "to separate using a sharp pointed object"] —**distinguishable** *adj.*

dis·tin·guished /dɪ'stɪŋgwɪʃt/ *adj.* **1** successful and respected: *a distinguished scientist* | *his distinguished career*

THESAURUS **famous, well-known, legendary, celebrated, renowned, noted, eminent** → FAMOUS

2 looking important and successful

dis·tort /dɪ'stɔrt/ (Ac) *v.* [T] **1** to report something in a way that is not completely correct, so that the true meaning is changed (SYN) **twist, misrepresent**: *a reporter accused of distorting the facts* **2** to change the shape or sound of something so that it is strange or difficult to recognize: *Tall buildings can distort radio waves.* [ORIGIN: 1400—1500 Latin *distortus*, past participle of *distorquere* "to twist out of shape"] —**distorted** *adj.*

dis·tor·tion /dɪ'stɔrʃən/ *n.* [C,U] **1** a change in the appearance, sound, or shape of something so that it is strange or unclear **2** a report of something that is not completely true or correct **3** a change in a situation from the way it would naturally be **4** PHYSICS an image of something in which the PROPORTIONS are not correct because something is wrong with a LENS or mirror → *see picture at* REFLECTION

dis·tract /dɪ'strækt/ *v.* [T] to do something that takes someone's attention away from what s/he is doing: *Don't distract me while I'm driving!* | *The government is trying to* ***distract attention*** *from its failures.*

dis·tract·ed /dɪ'stræktɪd/ *adj.* anxious and not able to think clearly

dis·trac·tion /dɪ'strækʃən/ *n.* [C,U] something that takes your attention away from what you are doing: *I can't study at home – there are too many distractions.*

dis·traught /dɪ'strɔt/ *adj.* extremely anxious or upset: *Friends comforted his distraught mother.*

THESAURUS **upset, unsettled, troubled, disturbed, perturbed, distressed, traumatized** → UPSET[1]

dis·tress[1] /dɪ'strɛs/ *n.* [U] **1** a feeling of extreme worry and sadness: *Children suffer emotional distress when their parents divorce.* **2** a situation in which someone suffers because s/he does not have any money, food, etc.: *charities that help families* ***in distress*** **3 be in distress** if a ship, airplane, etc. is in distress, it is in danger of sinking or crashing —**distressed** *adj.*

distress[2] *v.* [T] to make someone feel very worried or upset: *We were distressed to learn of Thomas's death.*

dis·tress·ing /dɪ'strɛsɪŋ/ *adj.* making someone feel very worried or upset

dis·trib·ute /dɪ'strɪbyət/ (Ac) *v.* [T] **1** to give something such as food or medicine to each person in a large group: *The Red Cross is* ***distributing*** *food and clothing* ***to*** *the refugees.*

THESAURUS **give out, hand out/pass out, share, dispense** → GIVE[1]

2 to supply goods to stores and companies in a particular area so that they can be sold: *The movie is being distributed by Warner Bros.* [ORIGIN: 1400—1500 Latin *distribuere* "to give out," from *tribuere* "to give to a particular person"]

dis·tri·bu·tion /ˌdɪstrə'byuʃən/ (Ac) *n.* **1** [U] the act of giving something to each person in a large group: *the* ***distribution of*** *food to disaster victims* **2** [C,U] the way in which people or things are spread over an area: *The* ***distribution of*** *wealth has become more unequal.* **3** [U] the act of supplying goods to stores, companies, etc. in a particular area so that they can be sold: *the production and* ***distribution of*** *goods* **4** [C,U] MATH a set of numbers and how often they appear in a set of DATA, especially as shown on a GRAPH or table

dis·tri·bu·tor /dɪ'strɪbyət̬ɚ/ (Ac) *n.* [C] a company or person that supplies goods to stores or companies: *a beer distributor*

dis·trict /'dɪstrɪkt/ *n.* [C] a particular area of a city, country, etc., especially an area officially divided from others: *Ken works in the* ***financial district.*** | *Many* ***school districts*** *have cut music programs.*

THESAURUS **area, region, territory, zone, neighborhood, suburb, slum, ghetto** → AREA

ˌdistrict at'torney *n.* [C] LAW (*abbreviation* **D.A.**) a lawyer who works for the government in a particular district and who makes sure that possible criminals are examined in court

ˌdistrict 'court *n.* [C] LAW a U.S. court of law where people are judged in cases that involve national rather than state law

dis·trust /dɪs'trʌst/ *n.* [U] a feeling that you cannot trust someone: *He has a deep* ***distrust of*** *politicians.* —**distrust** *v.* [T] —**distrustful** *adj.*

dis·turb /dɪ'stɚb/ *v.* [T] **1** to annoy someone or interrupt what someone is doing by making a noise, asking a question, etc.: *Keep your voices low, so you don't disturb the others.* | ***Do Not Disturb*** (=a sign that you put on a door so that people will not interrupt you) **2** to make someone feel worried or upset: *Something about the situation disturbed him.* **3** (formal) to move something: *The detectives were careful not to disturb anything.* [ORIGIN: 1100—1200 Old French *destourber*, from Latin *turbare* "to put into disorder"]

dis·turb·ance /dɪ'stɚbəns/ *n.* **1** [C] a situation in which people fight or behave violently in public: *The police arrested three men for* ***causing/creating a disturbance*** *at the bar.* **2** [C,U] something that interrupts you so that you cannot continue what you are doing

dis·turbed /dɪ'stɚbd/ *adj.* **1** not behaving in a

D

normal way because of mental or emotional problems: *an **emotionally disturbed** child*

THESAURUS **crazy, mentally ill, insane, nuts, loony, demented, psychotic, unstable** → CRAZY

2 very worried or upset

THESAURUS **upset, unsettled, troubled, perturbed, distressed, distraught, traumatized** → UPSET[1]

dis·tur·bing /dɪˈstɚbɪŋ/ *adj.* worrying or upsetting: *a disturbing increase in crime*

D

di·syl·lab·ic /ˌdaɪsəˈlæbɪk◂/ *adj.* ENG. LANG. ARTS a disyllabic word has two SYLLABLES → MONOSYLLABIC, POLYSYLLABIC

ditch[1] /dɪtʃ/ *n.* [C] a long narrow hole in the ground for water to flow through, usually at the side of a field, road, etc.

ditch[2] *v.* [T] (informal) to get rid of something or stop using it because it is no longer useful to you: *The bank robbers ditched the stolen car as soon as they could.*

dith·er /ˈdɪðɚ/ *v.* [I] to be unable to make a decision: *He's been **dithering about** what to do.*

dit·to[1] /ˈdɪt̬oʊ/ *interjection* (informal) used in order to say that you have exactly the same opinion as someone else about something, or that something is also true for you: *"I hated P.E. when I was in school." "Ditto."* [ORIGIN: 1600—1700 Italian, past participle of *dire* "to say"]

dit·to[2] *n.* (plural **dittos**) *also* **ˈditto mark** [C] ENG. LANG. ARTS the mark (″) that you write beneath a word in a list so that you do not have to write the same word again

dit·ty /ˈdɪt̬i/ *n.* (plural **ditties**) [C] (humorous) a short simple song or poem

di·va /ˈdivə/ *n.* [C] a very successful and famous female singer

dive

dive[1] /daɪv/ *v.* (past tense **dived** *or* **dove** /doʊv/, past participle **dived**) [I] **1** to jump into the water with your head and arms going in first: *Harry **dived into** the swimming pool.*

THESAURUS

plunge – to move, fall, or be thrown or pushed suddenly forward or downward: *The car swerved and plunged off the cliff.*

submerge – to go or put something completely under the surface of the water: *The turtle submerged again.*

sink – to go down below the surface of water, mud, etc., or to make something do this: *The coin sank to the bottom of the pool.* → JUMP[1]

2 to swim under the water using special equipment to help you breathe **3** to travel straight down through the air or water: *The birds were **diving for** fish.* **4** to move or jump quickly: *They dove into the bushes to avoid the enemy.*

dive[2] *n.* [C] **1** a jump into water with your head and arms going in first **2** a sudden movement in a particular direction: *He **made a dive for** the ball.* **3** a sudden drop in the amount or value of something: *Share prices **took a dive**.* **4** a movement straight down through air or water: *The plane suddenly **went into a dive**.* **5** (informal) a place such as a BAR or a hotel that is cheap and dirty: *We ate at a dive out by the airport.*

div·er /ˈdaɪvɚ/ *n.* [C] **1** someone who swims under the water using special equipment to help him/her breathe: *a scuba diver* **2** someone who jumps into water with his/her head and arms first

di·verge /dəˈvɚdʒ, daɪ-/ *v.* [I] to be different, or to develop in a different way: *At this point, his version of events **diverges from** hers.* —**divergence** *n.* [C,U] —**divergent** *adj.*: *divergent views*

di·verse /dəˈvɚs, daɪ-/ (Ac) *adj.* very different from each other: *The U.S. is a **culturally diverse** nation.* | *diverse political opinions*

di·ver·si·fy /dəˈvɚsəˌfaɪ, daɪ-/ (Ac) *v.* (**diversified**, **diversifies**) [I,T] ECONOMICS if a company diversifies, it begins to make new types of products or to become involved in new types of business in addition to what it already does: *They started as a cosmetics company and then **diversified into** clothing.* | *The company needs to diversify its products.* —**diversification** /dəˌvɚsəfəˈkeɪʃən/ *n.* [U]

di·ver·sion /dəˈvɚʒən, daɪ-/ *n.* **1** [C,U] a change in the direction or purpose of something: *the illegal **diversion of** money from the project* **2** [C] something that takes your attention away from something else: *One man **creates a diversion** while the other steals your purse.* **3** [C] (formal) an activity that you do for pleasure or amusement: *Fishing is a pleasant diversion.*

THESAURUS **game, sport, recreation, hobby** → GAME[1]

di·ver·si·ty /dəˈvɚsət̬i, daɪ-/ (Ac) *n.* [singular, U] a range of different people or things (SYN) **variety**: *The school prides itself on its **ethnic diversity**.* | *Environmentalists claim that the biological diversity of the area is under threat.* | *a **diversity of** opinions*

di·vert /dəˈvɚt, daɪ-/ *v.* [T] **1** to change the direction in which something travels: *Traffic is being diverted to avoid the accident.* **2** to use something for a different purpose: *They plan to **divert** money **from** production **to** design.* **3 divert (sb's) attention from sth** to stop someone from paying attention to something: *The war will divert attention from the country's economic problems.* [ORIGIN: 1400–1500 Old French *divertir*, from Latin *divertere*, from *vertere* "to turn"]

di·vest /dɪˈvɛst, daɪ-/ *v.*

divest sb of sth *phr. v.* (formal) to take something away from someone

di·vide /dəˈvaɪd/ *v.* **1** [I,T] to separate something into two or more parts, groups, etc., or to become separated in this way: *The teacher **divided** the class **into** groups.* | *Brenda's trying to **divide** her time **between** work and school.*

THESAURUS separate, split, break up, segregate, partition, apportion → SEPARATE²

2 [T] to keep two areas separate from each other: *A river divides the north and south sides of the city.* | *A curtain **divided** his sleeping area **from** ours.* **3** [T] *also* **divide up** to separate something into two or more parts and share it among two or more people, groups, places, etc.: *The money will be **divided** equally **among** his children.* | *She **divides** her time **between** Atlanta and Houston.* **4** [I,T] MATH to calculate how many times one number is contained in a larger number: *15 **divided by** 3 is 5.* → CALCULATE **5** [T] to make people disagree and form groups with different opinions: *Experts are **divided over** the question.* [ORIGIN: 1300–1400 Latin *dividere*, from *videre* "to separate"]

div·i·dend /ˈdɪvəˌdɛnd, -dənd/ *n.* [C] ECONOMICS a part of a company's profit that is paid to people who have SHARES in the company

di·vid·er /dəˈvaɪdɚ/ *n.* **1** [C] something such as a wall that divides something else into two or more parts: *the center divider on a road* | *You could put a screen over there as a room divider.* **2 dividers** [plural] MATH an instrument used for measuring or marking lines or angles, that consists of two pointed pieces of metal joined together at the top

di·vine /dəˈvaɪn/ *adj.* having the qualities of God, or coming from God: *a divine plan* [ORIGIN: 1300–1400 Old French *divin*, from Latin *divus* "god"]

div·ing /ˈdaɪvɪŋ/ *n.* [U] **1** the sport of swimming under the water using breathing equipment **2** the activity of jumping into water with your head and arms first

ˈdiving board *n.* [C] a board above a SWIMMING POOL, from which you can jump into the water

di·vin·i·ty /dəˈvɪnət̬i/ *n.* (plural **divinities**) **1** [U] the study of God and religious beliefs (SYN) **theology** **2** [U] the quality of being like God **3** [C] a male or female god

THESAURUS god, deity, idol → GOD

di·vis·i·ble /dəˈvɪzəbəl/ *adj.* MATH able to be divided by another number: *15 is **divisible by** 3 and 5.*

di·vi·sion /dəˈvɪʒən/ *n.* **1** [C,U] the act of separating something into two or more parts or groups, or the way that these parts are separated: *the **division of** words **into** syllables* | *the **division of** the money **between** the government departments* **2** [C,U] a disagreement among members of a group: *There are **deep divisions** within the Republican party.* **3** [U] MATH the process of calculating how many times a small number is contained in a larger number → ADDITION, MULTIPLICATION, SUBTRACTION **4** [C] a group within a large company, army, organization, etc.: *the finance **division of** the company* **5** [C] a group of teams that a sports LEAGUE is divided into: *the NFC central division*

di·vi·sion·al /dəˈvɪʒənəl/ *adj.* [only before noun] relating to a sports division: *the **divisional playoffs*** (=games to decide who wins a division)

di·vi·sive /dəˈvaɪsɪv, -ˈvɪs-/ *adj.* causing a lot of disagreement among people: *a divisive issue*

di·vi·sor /dəˈvaɪzɚ/ *n.* [C] MATH the number by which another number is to be divided. In 9 ÷ 3, 3 is the divisor. → DIVIDEND

di·vorce¹ /dəˈvɔrs/ *n.* [C,U] LAW the legal ending of a marriage: *She wants to **get a divorce**.* | *Their marriage **ended in divorce**.* [ORIGIN: 1300–1400 French, Latin *divertere* "to divert, leave one's husband"]

divorce² *v.* **1** [I,T] LAW to legally end a marriage: *His parents divorced when he was six.* | *They decided to **get divorced**.* | *My father threatened to divorce her.*

THESAURUS

separate – to start to live apart from your husband or wife: *They separated six months ago.*
split up/break up – to end a marriage or a long romantic relationship: *When Andy was nine, his parents split up.* | *What would it do to the kids if he and Judy broke up?*
leave sb – to stop living with your husband, wife, or partner: *Her husband left her after 27 years of marriage.*
annul (Law) – to officially state that a marriage no longer exists: *The marriage was annulled after only six days.*
dissolve (Law) – to officially end a marriage: *She said she wanted a divorce, and the marriage was later dissolved.*

2 [T] (formal) to separate two ideas, values, organizations, etc.: *It is difficult to **divorce** religion **from** politics.* —**divorced** *adj.*: *a divorced woman*

di·vor·cee /dəˌvɔrˈsi, -ˈseɪ/ *n.* [C] a woman who is divorced

di·vulge /dəˈvʌldʒ, daɪ-/ *v.* [T] to give someone information, especially about something that was secret: *Doctors cannot divulge information about their patients.*

Dix·ie /ˈdɪksi/ *n.* HISTORY an informal name for the

southern states of the U.S. that fought against the North in the U.S. Civil War

diz·zy /ˈdɪzi/ *adj.* **1** having a feeling of not being able to balance yourself, especially after spinning around or because you feel sick: *She felt dizzy when she stood up.* **2** (informal) someone who is dizzy is silly or stupid [ORIGIN: Old English *dysig* "stupid"] —**dizziness** *n.* [U]

DJ /ˈdi dʒeɪ/ *n.* [C] **disk jockey** someone whose job is to play the music on the radio or in a club where you can dance

DNA *n.* [U] **deoxyribonucleic acid** BIOLOGY an acid found in the cells of living things, that carries GENETIC information

D

ˌDNA ˈsequence *n.* [C] BIOLOGY the order of the many pairs of MOLECULEs that DNA consists of, represented as a series of letters

do¹ /də; *strong* du/ *auxiliary verb* (past tense **did** /dɪd/, past participle **done** /dʌn/, third person singular **does** /dəz; *strong* dʌz/) **1** used with another verb to form questions or negatives: *Do you like pasta?* | *What time does Linda usually go to bed?* | *I don't think I'll be able to come.* **2** (spoken) used at the end of a sentence to make a question, or to ask someone to agree with it: *You know Tom, don't you?* | *She didn't understand, did she?* **3** used in order to emphasize the main verb: *He hasn't been here in a while, but he does come to visit us most weekends.* **4** used in order to avoid repeating another verb: *"Go clean up your room." "I already did!"* | *"Craig really likes Thai food." **"So do I."*** | *"I didn't like the movie." **"Neither did I.**'* | *Emilio speaks much better English than he did a year ago.* [ORIGIN: Old English *don*]

do² /du/ *v.* (past tense **did**, past participle **done**, third person singular **does**) **1** [T] to perform an action or activity: *Have you done your homework yet?* | *It's Jim's turn to **do the dishes/laundry**.* | *"What are you doing?" "Making cookies."* | *It's a pleasure **doing business** with you.* **2** [I] used in order to talk about how successful someone is: *How is Jayne doing in her new job?* | *He **did well/badly** at school.* **3** [T] to have a particular effect on something or someone: *The new car factory has **done a lot for*** (=had a good effect on) *the local economy.* | *Let's take a break. Come on, it will **do you good*** (=make you feel better). **4** [T] to have a particular job: ***What do you do for a living?*** | *She doesn't know what she wants to do.* **5 what is sb/sth doing?** used when you are surprised or annoyed that someone or something is in a particular place or doing a particular thing: *What is my jacket doing on the floor?* | *What are you doing with my purse?* **6 do your hair/nails/makeup etc.** to spend time making your hair, nails, etc. look good **7** [T] to travel at a particular speed, or to travel a particular distance: *He was doing over 90 miles per hour.* **8** [I,T] used in order to say that something is acceptable or enough: *The recipe calls for butter, but oil will do.* | *My old black shoes **will have to do**.* **9** [T] to provide a service or sell a product: *They do home deliveries.* **10 do lunch/a meeting/a movie etc.** (informal) to have LUNCH (=meal eaten in the middle of the day), have a meeting, see a movie, etc. with someone else: *Let's do lunch next week.* → **how are you?/how's it going?/how are you doing?** *at* HOW, **how do you do?** *at* HOW, **make do** *at* MAKE¹

do away with *phr. v.* (informal) **1 do away with** sth to get rid of something: *We should do away with those old customs.* **2 do away with** sb to kill someone

do sb **in** *phr. v.* (informal) **1** to make someone feel very tired: *That long walk did me in.* **2** to kill someone

do sth **over** *phr. v.* to do something again, especially because you did it wrong the first time: *If there are mistakes, the teacher makes you do it over.*

do with *phr. v.* **1 have/be to do with sth** to be related to or involved with something: *The book has to do with new theories in physics.* | *Jack's job is **something to do with** marketing* (=related to marketing, but you are not sure exactly how).

SPOKEN PHRASES

2 what has sb done with sth? used in order to ask where someone has put something: *What have you done with the scissors?* **3 I can/could do with sth** used in order to say that you need or want something: *I could do with some help.* **4 what sb does with himself/herself** the activities that someone does as a regular part of his/her life: *What is your dad doing with himself since he retired?*

→ **make do** *at* MAKE¹

do without sth *phr. v.* **1** to manage to continue living or doing something without having a particular thing: *It's almost impossible to do without a car in Los Angeles.* **2 I can/could do without sth** (spoken) used in order to say that something is annoying you or causing problems: *I could do without his stupid comments.*

do³ *n.* **dos and don'ts** things that you should or should not do in a particular situation: *I'm still learning all the dos and don'ts of the job.*

d.o.b. the written abbreviation of "date of birth"

do·ber·man pin·scher /ˌdoʊbəˑmən ˈpɪntʃəˑ/ *also* **doberman** *n.* [C] a large black and brown dog with very short hair, often used in order to guard property

dock

doc /dɑk/ *n.* [C] (spoken) a doctor

doc·ile /ˈdɑsəl/ *adj.* quiet and easy to control: *a docile animal*

dock¹ /dɑk/ *n.* [C] a place where goods are put onto or taken off ships [ORIGIN: 1300—1400 Middle Dutch *docke*]

dock² *v.* [I,T] **1** if a ship docks, it sails into a

dock **2 dock sb's pay** to take money from someone's pay, as a punishment: *If you come in late one more time, we'll have to dock your pay.*

dock·et /'dɑkɪt/ *n.* [C] LAW a list of legal cases that will take place in a particular court

doc·tor[1] /'dɑktɚ/ *n.* [C] **1** someone whose job is to treat people who are sick: *You really should* ***see a doctor*** *about that cough.* | *He very rarely* ***goes to the doctor****.* | *I have a* ***doctor's appointment*** *tomorrow.*

THESAURUS

physician (formal) – a doctor: *our family physician*
surgeon – a doctor who does operations in a hospital: *a brain surgeon*
specialist – a doctor who knows a lot about a particular area of medicine: *He's one of the world's leading heart specialists.*
psychiatrist – a doctor who treats mental illness
dentist – someone whose job is to take care of people's teeth
pediatrician – a doctor who treats children who are sick

2 someone who has the highest level of degree given by a university: *a Doctor of Philosophy* [ORIGIN: 1300—1400 Old French *doctour*, from Latin *doctor* "teacher"]

doctor[2] *v.* [T] to change something, especially in a way that is not honest: *The police may have doctored the evidence.*

doc·tor·ate /'dɑktərɪt/ *n.* [C] a university degree at the highest level

doc·trine /'dɑktrɪn/ *n.* [C,U] **1** a set of religious or political beliefs: *Catholic doctrine* **2** POLITICS a formal statement of a government's way of dealing with something, especially the way it deals with other countries [ORIGIN: 1300—1400 French, Latin *doctrina*, from *doctor* "teacher"] —**doctrinal** *adj.*

doc·u·ment[1] /'dɑkyəmənt/ (Ac) *n.* [C] **1** a piece of paper that has official information written on it: *a legal document* | *historical documents* **2** IT a piece of work that you write and keep on a computer: *Click on the document you want to open.* → COMPUTER [ORIGIN: 1400—1500 French, Late Latin *documentum*, from Latin *docere* "to teach"]

doc·u·ment[2] /'dɑkyə,mɛnt/ (Ac) *v.* [T] **1** to record information about something by writing about it, photographing it, etc.: *The program documents the daily life of a teenager.* **2** to support an opinion, statement, etc. with facts: *It is well documented that men die younger than women.*

doc·u·men·tary /,dɑkyə'mɛntri, -'mɛntəri/ *n.* (plural **documentaries**) [C] a movie or television program that gives facts and information on something: *He made a* ***documentary about*** *a farming community in Iowa.* → TELEVISION

doc·u·men·ta·tion /,dɑkyəmən'teɪʃən/ (Ac) *n.* [U] **1** official documents that are used in order to prove that something is true or correct **2** the process of recording information in writing, on film, etc.: *The accounting records contain careful documentation of all the company's costs.*

do·dec·a·gon /doʊ'dɛkə,gɑn/ *n.* [C] MATH a flat shape with 12 straight sides

THESAURUS **polygon, pentagon, hexagon, heptagon, octagon, decagon** → POLYGON

dodge /dɑdʒ/ *v.* **1** [I,T] to move quickly in order to avoid someone or something: *We had to* ***dodge the bullets****.* **2** [T] to avoid talking about something or doing something that you do not want to do: *The senator dodged the reporter's question.* —**dodge** *n.* [C]

D

doe /doʊ/ *n.* [C] a female DEER

does /dəz; strong dʌz/ *v.* the third person singular of the present tense of DO

does·n't /'dʌzənt/ *v.* the short form of "does not"

dog[1] /dɔg/ *n.* [C] a very common animal with four legs that is often kept as a pet or used for guarding buildings: *I could hear a* ***dog barking****.* | *I'm going out to* ***walk the dog****.* [ORIGIN: Old English *docga*]

dog[2] *v.* (**dogged**, **dogging**) [T] if a problem or bad luck dogs you, it causes trouble for a long time

'dog-eared *adj.* dog-eared books have been used so much that the corners of their pages are folded or torn

dog·ged /'dɔgɪd/ *adj.* determined to do something even though it is difficult: *a* ***dogged determination*** *to succeed* —**doggedly** *adv.*

dog·gone /,dɔ'gɔn◂/ also **dog'gone it** *interjection* (old-fashioned) said when you are annoyed: *Doggone it, I said leave that alone!* —**doggone** *adj.*: *It's a doggone shame.*

dog·gy, **doggie** /'dɔgi/ *n.* (plural **doggies**) [C] a dog – used by or when speaking to young children

'doggy bag *n.* [C] a small bag for taking home the food you did not eat from a meal at a restaurant

dog·house /'dɔghaʊs/ *n.* **1 be in the doghouse** (informal) to be in a situation in which someone is angry or annoyed with you **2** [C] a little building for a dog to sleep in

dog·ma /'dɔgmə, 'dɑgmə/ *n.* [C,U] an important belief or set of beliefs that people are supposed to accept as true without asking for any explanation: *church dogma*

dog·mat·ic /dɔg'mæṭɪk, dɑg-/ *adj.* someone who is dogmatic is completely certain about his/her beliefs and expects other people to accept them without arguing —**dogmatically** *adv.*

do-good·er /'du ,gʊdɚ/ *n.* [C] (informal) someone who does things to help other people, but who often gets involved when his/her help is not wanted or needed

'dog ˌpaddle *also* **'doggy ˌpaddle** *n.* [singular] (informal) a simple way of swimming that you do by moving your arms and legs like a swimming dog

dog·wood /'dɔgwʊd/ *n.* [C] an eastern North American tree or bush with flat white or pink flowers

do·ing /'duɪŋ/ *n.* **1 be sb's (own) doing** to be someone's fault: *His bad luck was all his own doing.* **2 take some doing** (informal) to be hard work: *Getting this old car to run is going to take some doing.*

dol·drums /'doʊldrəmz, 'dɑl-/ *n.* [plural] (informal) **1** a state in which something is not improving or developing: *The stock market has been* ***in the doldrums*** *for most of this year.* **2** a state in which you feel sad SYN **depression**

dole /doʊl/ *v.*

dole sth ↔ **out** *phr. v.* to give something such as money, food, advice, etc. in small amounts to a lot of people: *Vera was* ***doling out*** *candy* ***to*** *the kids.*

dole·ful /'doʊlfəl/ *adj.* very sad: *a doleful song*

doll /dɑl/ *n.* [C] a toy that looks like a small person or baby: *a small wooden doll* [ORIGIN: 1500—1600 The female name *Doll*, from *Dorothy*]

dol·lar /'dɑlɚ/ *n.* [C] **1** the standard of money used in the U.S., Canada, Australia, New Zealand, and other countries. Its sign is $ and it is worth 100 cents: *These pants cost $40.* | *That will be three dollars, please.* **2** a piece of paper money or a coin of this value: *dollar bills* **3 the dollar** ECONOMICS the value of U.S. money in relation to the money of other countries: *The peso has dropped almost 1%* ***against the dollar***. [ORIGIN: 1500—1600 Dutch *daler*, from German *joachimstaler*, from *Sankt Joachimsthal*, name of a Bavarian town where the coins were first made]

dol·lop /'dɑləp/ *n.* [C] a small amount of soft food, usually dropped from a spoon: *a* ***dollop of*** *whipped cream*

dol·phin /'dɑlfɪn, 'dɔl-/ *n.* [C] a very intelligent sea animal with a long gray pointed nose [ORIGIN: 1300—1400 Old French *dalfin*, from Greek *delphis*]

do·main /doʊ'meɪn, də-/ Ac *n.* [C] **1** (formal) a particular activity that is controlled by one person, group, organization, etc.: *In the past, politics was exclusively* ***a male domain***. | *This problem is* ***outside the domain of*** *medical science.* **2** BIOLOGY one of the groups into which scientists divide animals or plants, in which the animals or plants are closely related but cannot produce babies or more plants together **3** MATH all the possible values that can be used as INDEPENDENT VARIABLES in a mathematical FUNCTION

do'main ˌname *n.* [C] IT a part of an Internet WEBSITE's address that tells you the name of the website

dome

dome /doʊm/ *n.* [C] a round curved roof on a building or room [ORIGIN: 1600—1700 French *dôme* "dome, cathedral," from Latin *domus* "house"] —**domed** *adj.*

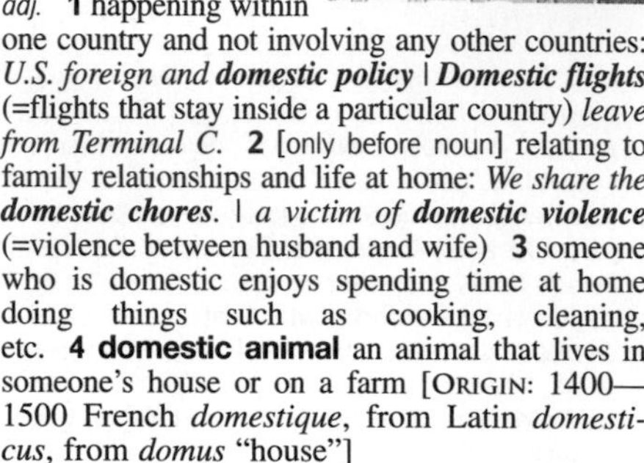

do·mes·tic /də'mɛstɪk/ Ac *adj.* **1** happening within one country and not involving any other countries: *U.S. foreign and* ***domestic policy*** | ***Domestic flights*** (=flights that stay inside a particular country) *leave from Terminal C.* **2** [only before noun] relating to family relationships and life at home: *We share the* ***domestic chores***. | *a victim of* ***domestic violence*** (=violence between husband and wife) **3** someone who is domestic enjoys spending time at home doing things such as cooking, cleaning, etc. **4 domestic animal** an animal that lives in someone's house or on a farm [ORIGIN: 1400—1500 French *domestique*, from Latin *domesticus*, from *domus* "house"]

do·mes·ti·cat·ed /də'mɛstɪˌkeɪt̬ɪd/ Ac *adj.* domesticated animals live with people as pets or on a farm —**domesticate** *v.* [T] —**domestication** /dəˌmɛstɪ'keɪʃən/ *n.* [U]

do·mes·tic·i·ty /ˌdoʊmɛ'stɪsət̬i/ *n.* [U] life at home with your family and the activities that relate to this

doˌmestic 'partner *n.* [C] someone who you live with and have a sexual relationship with, but who you are not married to

dom·i·nance /'dɑmənəns/ Ac *n.* [U] a situation in which someone is more powerful, more important, or more noticeable than other people or things: *the* ***dominance of*** *youth culture in the U.S.* | *A male lion must fight for dominance within the pride* (=group of lions).

dom·i·nant /'dɑmənənt/ Ac *adj.* **1** strongest, most important, or most noticeable: *America's* ***dominant role*** *in international business* | *The dominant male gorilla is the largest in the group.*

THESAURUS **powerful, influential, strong**
→ POWERFUL

2 controlling other people or things, or wanting to do this: *her husband's dominant behavior* **3** BIOLOGY a dominant GENE results in a physical feature even if it has been passed on from only one parent → RECESSIVE

dom·i·nate /'dɑməˌneɪt/ Ac *v.* [I,T] **1** to have power and control over someone or something: *Five large companies dominate the auto industry.* **2** to be the strongest, most important, or most noticeable feature of something: *The murder trial has been dominating the news this week.* [ORIGIN: 1600—1700 Latin *dominatus*, past participle of *dominari* "to rule"] —**domination** /ˌdɑmə'neɪʃən/ *n.* [U]

dom·i·neer·ing /ˌdɑməˈnɪrɪŋ/ *adj.* (disapproving) trying to control other people without considering how they feel or what they want: *his domineering father*

do·min·ion /dəˈmɪnyən/ *n.* **1** [U] (literary) the power or right to rule people **2** [C] *also* **Dominion** HISTORY one of the countries that was a member of the British Commonwealth in past times **3** [C] HISTORY a large area of land owned or controlled by one person or a government

dom·i·no /ˈdɑməˌnoʊ/ *n.* (plural **dominoes**) **1** [C] a small piece of wood, plastic, etc. with a different number of spots on each half of its top side, used in playing a game **2 dominoes** [U] the game that you play using dominoes **3 domino effect** a situation in which one event or action causes several other things to happen one after the other: *The weakness of the dollar had a domino effect, hurting stocks and bonds.*

do·nate /ˈdoʊneɪt, doʊˈneɪt/ *v.* **1** [I,T] to give something, especially money, to a person or organization that needs help: *Our school **donated** $500 **to** the Red Cross.*

THESAURUS give, leave, bequeath, present, grant → GIVE¹

2 donate blood/an organ/a kidney etc. to allow some of your blood or a part of your body to be used to help someone who is sick or injured

do·na·tion /doʊˈneɪʃən/ *n.* [C,U] something, especially money, that you give to help a person or organization: *Please **make a donation to** UNICEF.* [ORIGIN: 1400—1500 Latin *donare* "to give"]

done¹ /dʌn/ *v.* the past participle of DO

done² *adj.* **1** finished or completed: *The job's almost done. | Are you **done with** this magazine?*

THESAURUS

finished – done, and dealt with in the way you wanted: *She showed him the finished drawing.*
complete – finished, and having all the necessary parts: *The project is almost complete.*
over – if an event, activity, or period of time is over, it is finished: *The game was over by 10 o'clock.*
through – if you are through with something, you have finished using it or doing it: *Are you through with those scissors?*

2 cooked enough to be eaten: *I think the hamburgers are done.* **3 it's a done deal** (spoken) used in order to mean that an agreement has been made and it cannot be changed **4 be done in** (spoken) to be extremely tired: *I've got to sit down – I'm done in.*

done³ *interjection* used in order to accept a deal that someone offers you: *"How about I give you $25 for it?" "Done!"*

don·key /ˈdɑŋki, ˈdʌŋ-, ˈdɔŋ-/ *n.* [C] a gray or brown animal like a horse, but smaller and with longer ears

do·nor /ˈdoʊnɚ/ *n.* [C] **1** someone who gives something, especially money, to an organization in order to help people: *The art museum received $10,000 from an **anonymous donor**.* **2** someone who gives blood or a part of his/her body so that it can be used to help someone who is sick or injured: *an **organ donor***

don't /doʊnt/ *v.* the short form of "do not": *I don't know.*

do·nut /ˈdoʊnʌt/ *n.* [C] another spelling of DOUGHNUT

doo·dad /ˈdudæd/ *also* **doo·hick·ey** /ˈduˌhɪki/ *n.* [C] (informal) a small object whose name you have forgotten or do not know: *What's this doodad for?*

D

doo·dle /ˈdudl/ *v.* [I,T] to draw shapes or patterns without really thinking about what you are doing: *Stein was doodling on a napkin.* —**doodle** *n.* [C]

THESAURUS draw, sketch, scribble → DRAW¹

doom¹ /dum/ *n.* [U] **1** destruction, death, or failure that is certain to happen: *a sense of **impending doom*** (=a feeling that something bad will happen soon) **2 doom and gloom** a feeling that there is no hope for the future

doom² *v.* [T] to make someone or something certain to fail, be destroyed, or die: *The program was **doomed to failure** from the start.* —**doomed** *adj.*

Dooms·day /ˈdumzdeɪ/ *n.* JUDGMENT DAY

door /dɔr/ *n.* [C] **1** a large tall flat piece of wood, glass, etc. that you push or pull in order to go into a building, room, car, etc.: *Could someone please **open/close/shut the door**? | Don't forget to lock the **front/back/side door**. | She ran into her bedroom and **slammed the door*** (=shut it very hard). *| Did you hear someone **knock on/at the door**? | Marie, can you **get/answer the door*** (=open it after someone has knocked)? **2** the space made by an open door: *You just **go out/through** this **door** and turn right.* **3 next door** in the room, house, etc. next to where you are: *the people who live next door* **4 at the door** if someone is at the door, s/he is waiting for you to open it **5 two/three etc. doors down** a particular number of rooms, houses, etc. away from where you are: *Her office is just two doors down.* **6 (from) door to door a)** between one place and another: *If you drive, it should only take you 20 minutes door to door.* **b)** going to each house on a street to sell something, collect money, etc.: *We went door to door asking people to sponsor us in the race.* **7 show/see sb to the door** to walk with someone to the main door of a building [ORIGIN: Old English *duru* "door" and *dor* "gate"]

door·bell /ˈdɔrbɛl/ *n.* [C] a button by the door of a house, that you press to make a sound that lets the people inside know you are there

door·knob /ˈdɔrnɑb/ *n.* [C] a round handle that you turn to open a door

door·man /ˈdɔrmæn, -mən/ *n.* (plural **doormen** /-mɛn, -mən/) [C] a man who works at the door of a hotel or theater, helping people who are coming in or out

door·mat /ˈdɔrmæt/ *n.* [C] **1** a thick piece of material just outside a door for you to clean your shoes on **2** (informal) someone who lets other people treat him/her badly and never complains

door·step /ˈdɔrstɛp/ *n.* **1** [C] a step just outside a door to a building **2 on your doorstep** very near to where you live or are staying: *Wow! You have the beach right on your doorstep!*

D

door·way /ˈdɔrweɪ/ *n.* [C] the space where a door opens into a room or building: *Cindy stood **in the doorway**.*

dope¹ /doʊp/ *n.* (informal) **1** [U] an illegal drug, especially MARIJUANA **2** [C] a stupid person

dope² *also* **dope up** *v.* [T] (informal) **1** to give a drug to a person or animal in order to make him, her, or it unconscious **2** to give a drug to a person or animal in order to make him, her, or it perform better in a race —**doping** *n.* [U]

Dop·pler ef·fect /ˈdɑplɚ ɪˌfɛkt/ *n.* [singular] PHYSICS a change in how you hear a sound or see a light that is moving toward or away from you, so that a sound seems higher as it is moving closer to you, and a light seems more blue

dork /dɔrk/ *n.* [C] (informal) someone who you think is silly or stupid because s/he behaves strangely or wears strange clothes: *I look like such a dork in that picture.* —**dorky** *adj.*

dorm /dɔrm/ *n.* [C] (informal) a dormitory

dor·mant /ˈdɔrmənt/ *adj.* not active now, but able to be active at a later time: *a dormant volcano* —**dormancy** /ˈdɔrmənsi/ *n.* [U]

dor·mi·to·ry /ˈdɔrməˌtɔri/ *n.* (plural **dormitories**) [C] a large building at a college or university, where students live

dor·sal /ˈdɔrsəl/ *adj.* BIOLOGY on or relating to the back of a fish or animal: *a whale's dorsal fin* → *see picture on page A15*

dos·age /ˈdoʊsɪdʒ/ *n.* [C] the amount of medicine that you should take at any one time

dose /doʊs/ *n.* [C] **1** a measured amount of medicine: *She was injected with a **dose of** insulin.* **2** an amount of something that you experience at one time: *I can only handle Jason **in small doses*** (=for short amounts of time).

dos·si·er /ˈdɑsiˌeɪ, ˈdɔ-/ *n.* [C] a set of papers that include detailed information about someone or something: *The police keep **dossiers on** all their prisoners.*

dot¹ /dɑt/ *n.* **1** [C] a small round mark or spot: *a pattern of dots on the screen* **2 on the dot** (informal) exactly at a particular time: *He arrived at nine o'clock on the dot.*

dot² *v.* (**dotted**, **dotting**) [T] **1** to mark something by putting a dot on it or above it: *She never dots her "i's."* **2** to spread things out within an area: *We have over 20 stores **dotted around** the state.*

ˌdot-ˈcom, **dot.com**, **dot com** *adj.* [only before noun] (informal) relating to a person or company that sells a product or service on the Internet: *a dot-com company* —**dot-com** *n.* [C]

dote /doʊt/ *v.*

dote on sb *phr. v.* to love someone very much and to show this by your actions: *They dote on their grandson.* —**doting** *adj.*: *doting parents*

ˌdotted ˈline *n.* [C] **1** a series of printed dots that form a line **2 sign on the dotted line** to officially agree to something by signing a contract

dou·ble¹ /ˈdʌbəl/ *adj.* **1** having two parts that are similar or exactly the same: *a double sink* | *the **double doors** of the cathedral* **2** twice the usual amount, size, or number: *a double espresso* (=type of coffee) | *They have asked me to work **double shifts**.* **3** intended to be used by two people → SINGLE: *a **double bed*** → *see picture at* BED¹ **4** combining or involving two things of the same type: *a double major in English and French* | *Her husband was secretly **leading a double life*** (=had two separate and different lives, each one secret from the other). [ORIGIN: 1100—1200 Old French, Latin *duplus*, from *duo* "two" + *-plus* "multiplied by"]

double² *v.* [I,T] to become twice as large or twice as much, or to make something do this: *Our house has **doubled in value** since we bought it.* | *The mayor wants to double the number of police officers on the street.*

> THESAURUS **increase, go up, rise, grow, shoot up, multiply** → INCREASE¹

double as sb/sth *phr. v.* to have a second use, job, or purpose: *The sofa doubles as a bed.*

double back *phr. v.* to turn around and go back in the direction you just came from: *I doubled back and headed south.*

double up, **double over** *phr. v.* **be doubled up/over with pain/laughter etc.** to bend at the waist because you are in pain or laughing a lot: *Both the girls were doubled up with laughter.*

double³ *n.* **1** [C,U] something that is twice as big or twice as much as usual: *Scotch and water, please – make it a double.* **2 sb's double** someone who looks very similar to someone else: *She's her mother's double.* **3** [C] a room or bed for two people → SINGLE **4 on the double** (informal) very soon, or immediately: *I want that report here on the double!* **5 doubles** [plural] a tennis game played by two pairs of players

double⁴ *adv.* **see double** to have a problem with your eyes so that you see two things instead of one

double⁵ *determiner* twice as much or twice as many: *The car is worth **double the amount** we paid for it.*

double bass /ˌdʌbəl ˈbeɪs/ *n.* [C] a very large

wooden musical instrument, shaped like a VIOLIN, that you play while standing up

ˌdouble ˈboiler *n.* [C] a pot for cooking food, made of one pot resting on top of another pot that has hot water in it

ˌdouble-ˈbreasted *adj.* a double-breasted jacket or coat has two rows of buttons on the front

ˌdouble-ˈcheck *v.* [I,T] to check something again to find out if it is safe, ready, correct, etc.: *I think I turned off the oven, but let me go double-check.*

ˌdouble ˈchin *n.* [C] an additional fold of skin under someone's chin, that looks like a second chin

ˌdouble-ˈclick *v.* [I] IT to press a button on a computer MOUSE twice in order to make the computer do something: ***Double-click on** the Printer icon.* **—double click** *n.* [C]

ˌdouble-ˈcross *v.* [T] to cheat someone when you are involved in something dishonest together **—double cross** *n.* [C]

ˌdouble ˈdate *n.* [C] an occasion when two COUPLES meet to go to a movie, restaurant, etc. together

ˌdouble-ˈdigit *adj.* [only before noun] relating to the numbers 10 to 99: *double-digit unemployment rates*

ˌdouble ˈdigits *n.* [plural] the numbers from 10 to 99: *Three of the team's players scored **in double digits**.*

ˌdouble ˈduty *n.* **do double duty** to do more than one job or be used for more than one purpose at the same time: *The lids on the pots do double duty as plates when we're camping.*

ˌdouble ˈfigures *n.* [plural] DOUBLE DIGITS

ˌdouble-ˈheader *n.* [C] two baseball games that are played one after the other

ˌdouble ˈhelix *n.* [C] BIOLOGY a shape found in the structure of DNA, consisting of two parallel SPIRALs that twist around the same center

ˌdouble-ˈjointed *adj.* able to move the joints in your arms, fingers, etc. backward as well as forward

ˌdouble ˈnegative *n.* [C] ENG. LANG. ARTS two negative words used in one sentence when you should use only one in correct English grammar, for example in the sentence "I don't want nobody to help me!"

ˌdouble-ˈpark *v.* [I,T] to leave a car on the road beside another car that is already parked there: *I got a ticket for double-parking.*

ˌdouble ˈplay *n.* [C] in the game of baseball, the action of making two players who are running between the BASEs have to leave the field by throwing the ball quickly from one base to the other before each runner gets there

ˌdouble ˈstandard *n.* [C] a rule or principle that is unfair because it treats one group or type of people more severely than another in the same situation

ˌdouble ˈtake *n.* **do a double take** to suddenly look at someone or something again because you are surprised by what you originally saw or heard

ˈdouble-talk *n.* [U] (disapproving) speech that is complicated, and is intended to deceive or confuse people

ˌdouble ˈvision *n.* [U] a medical condition in which you see two of everything

ˌdouble ˈwhammy *n.* (plural **double whammies**) [C] (informal) two bad things that happen at the same time or one after the other

dou·bly /ˈdʌbli/ *adv.* **1** much more than usual: *Be doubly careful when driving in fog.* **2** in two ways or for two reasons: *You are doubly mistaken.*

D

doubt¹ /daʊt/ *n.* **1** [C,U] a feeling of not being certain whether something is true or possible: *I began to **have** serious **doubts about** his ability to do the job.* | ***There is no doubt that** one day a cure will be found.* | ***Without a doubt**, Kevin is the best player on the team.* **2 no doubt** used when emphasizing that you think something is probably true: *No doubt they'll win.* | *She was a top student, **no doubt about it**.* **3 be in doubt** if something is in doubt, it may not happen, continue, exist, or be true: *The future of the peace talks is in doubt.* **4 beyond doubt** if something is beyond doubt, it is completely certain: *The state must **prove beyond** reasonable **doubt** that he is guilty.*

doubt² *v.* [T] **1** to think that something may not be true or that it is unlikely: ***I doubt that** we will ever see her again.* | *He might come, but **I doubt it**.* **2** to not trust or believe in someone or something: *Nobody doubts his ability to stay calm in a crisis.*

GRAMMAR

doubt that, doubt if, doubt whether
When you use the verb **doubt** in a simple statement, it can be followed by "that," "if," or "whether": *I **doubt that** the car will be ready yet.* | *I **doubt if/whether** she can help.*
However, if the statement is negative, **doubt** can only be followed by "that": *I don't **doubt that** he's honest* (=I'm sure that he's honest).
When you use the noun **doubt** after "no" or "not," it is always followed by "that": *There is no **doubt that** she's guilty.*

doubt·ful /ˈdaʊt˺fəl/ *adj.* **1** probably not true or not likely to happen: *It's **doubtful that** voters will approve the bill.* **2** not certain about something: *I could see that he still looked doubtful.*

THESAURUS

dubious – if you are dubious about something, you do not think it is a good idea or that it is true: *At first, I was dubious about the idea of taking a vacation in Europe.*
unconvinced – not persuaded by someone's arguments: *Some people remain unconvinced about the threat of global warming.*
skeptical – not willing to believe that something is really true: *Scientists are skeptical about the benefits of the treatment.*

—doubtfully *adv.*

doubt·less /ˈdaʊt˺lɪs/ *adv.* used when saying that something is very likely to happen or be true: *Readers will doubtless be disappointed by her new novel.*

dough /doʊ/ *n.* [U] **1** a mixture of flour and water ready to be baked into bread, cookies, etc. **2** (informal) money

dough·nut /ˈdoʊnʌt/ *n.* [C] a small round cake that is usually shaped like a ring

dour /ˈdaʊɚ, dʊɚ/ *adj.* very severe and not smiling: *a dour expression*

douse /daʊs/ *v.* [T] **1** to stop a fire from burning by throwing water on it: *Firefighters quickly doused the blaze.* **2** to cover something in water or other liquid

D

dove¹ /dʌv/ *n.* [C] a type of small white bird often used as a sign of peace [ORIGIN: Old English *dufe*]

dove² /doʊv/ *v.* a past tense of DIVE

dow·dy /ˈdaʊdi/ *adj.* unattractive or unfashionable

down¹ /daʊn/ *adv.* **1** toward a lower place or position (ANT) **up**: *She looked down at the street from her window.* | *David bent down to tie his shoelace.* **2** into a sitting or lying position: *Come in and sit down.* | *trees blown down by the big storm* **3** in a lower place or position (ANT) **up**: *The cows are down in the valley.* | *The bathroom is down those stairs.* **4** toward or in the south (ANT) **up**: *Gail drove down to North Carolina to see her brother.* | *We moved down south when I was a baby.* **5** at or to a place that is further along a path, road, etc.: *Could you go down to the store and get some bread?* **6** decreasing in loudness, strength, heat, activity, etc. (ANT) **up**: *Can you turn the TV down a little?* | *House prices have come down in recent months.* **7 write/note/take etc. sth down** to write something on paper: *I'll write down the address for you.* **8** (informal) paid to someone immediately → DOWN PAYMENT: *The landlord wants a lot of money down.* **9** from an earlier time to a later time: *The story was **handed down** in the family from father to son.* | *traditions that have **come down to** us from Medieval times* → COME DOWN WITH

down² *adj.* [not before noun] **1** sad: *I've never seen Bret looking so down.*

> **THESAURUS** sad, unhappy, miserable, sorrowful, depressed, low, blue, downhearted, melancholy, morose, gloomy, glum → SAD

2 losing to an opponent by a certain number of points (ANT) **up**: *We were down by 6 points at half-time.* **3** IT a computer system that is down is not working (ANT) **up** **4** a level, number, or amount that is down is lower than before (ANT) **up**: *At lunchtime, the stock market was down 77 points.* **5** (spoken) used in order to say that a particular number of things have been finished, when there are more things left to do: *That's two down. Only two more to do.* **6 be down on sb/sth** (spoken) to have a bad opinion of someone or something: *Why is Jerome so down on work?*

down³ *prep.* **1** toward the ground or a lower point, or in a lower position: *The store is just down the hill.* **2** along or toward the far end of something: *We walked down the beach as the sun rose.* | *They live down the road from us.* **3 down the road/line** (informal) at some time in the future: *We'd like to have children sometime down the line.*

down⁴ *v.* [T] (informal) to drink something very quickly: *Matt downed his coffee and left for work.*

down⁵ *n.* **1** [U] thin soft feathers or hair: *a down pillow* **2** [C] one of the four chances that a football team has to move forward ten yards with the ball: ***first/second etc. down***

ˌdown-and-ˈout *adj.* (informal) having no luck or money: *a down-and-out actor*

down·cast /ˈdaʊnkæst/ *adj.* sad or upset because something bad has happened

down·er /ˈdaʊnɚ/ *n.* [singular] (spoken) someone or something that makes you feel unhappy: *The movie was a real downer.*

down·fall /ˈdaʊnfɔl/ *n.* [C] a sudden loss of money, power, social position, etc., or something that leads to this: *Greed will be his downfall.*

down·grade /ˈdaʊngreɪd/ *v.* [T] to state that something is not as good or as valuable as it was before: *Several analysts have downgraded the stock.*

down·heart·ed /ˌdaʊnˈhɑrt̬ɪd◂/ *adj.* **be downhearted** to feel sad about something

> **THESAURUS** sad, unhappy, miserable, sorrowful, depressed, down, low, blue, melancholy, morose, gloomy, glum → SAD

down·hill¹ /ˌdaʊnˈhɪl/ *adv.* **1** toward the bottom of a hill or toward lower land (ANT) **uphill**: *The truck's brakes failed, and it rolled downhill.* **2 go downhill** to become worse: *After he lost his job, things went downhill.*

down·hill² /ˈdaʊnhɪl/ *adj.* **1** on a slope that goes down to a lower point: *downhill skiing* **2 be (all) downhill** to become worse: *We got three runs in the first inning, but **it was all downhill from there**.*

download *n.* [C] IT something that you download from the Internet, for example software, a computer game, or a song: *I've got downloads of all their songs.*

down·load /ˈdaʊnloʊd/ *v.* [T] IT to move information or programs from a computer network to your computer: *The software can be downloaded from the Internet.*

ˌdown ˈpayment *n.* [C] the first payment you make on something expensive that you will pay for over a longer period: *a **down payment on** a car*

down·play /ˈdaʊnpleɪ/ *v.* [T] to make something seem less important than it really is: *Fred downplayed the seriousness of his illness.*

down·pour /ˈdaʊnpɔr/ *n.* [C usually singular] a lot of rain that falls in a short time

THESAURUS **rain, drizzle, shower, storm** → RAIN[1]

down·right /ˈdaʊnraɪt/ *adv.* (informal) thoroughly and completely: *You're just downright lazy.*

down·riv·er /ˌdaʊnˈrɪvɚ/ *adv.* in the direction that the water in a river is flowing ANT **upriver**

down·shift /ˈdaʊnʃɪft/ *v.* [I] **1** to put the engine of a vehicle into a lower GEAR in order to go slower **2** if someone downshifts, s/he chooses to work less so that s/he has more time to enjoy life

down·side /ˈdaʊnsaɪd/ *n.* [singular] a disadvantage to something: *The* ***downside of*** *the plan is the cost.*

THESAURUS **disadvantage, drawback, catch, bad point** → DISADVANTAGE

down·size /ˈdaʊnsaɪz/ *v.* [I,T] to reduce the number of people who work for a company in order to cut costs —**downsizing** *n.* [U]

ˈDown's ˌSyndrome *n.* [U] BIOLOGY a condition that someone is born with that stops him/her from developing normally both mentally and physically

down·stairs /ˌdaʊnˈstɛrz/ *adv.* **1** on or going toward a lower floor of a building, especially a house ANT **upstairs**: *He* ***went downstairs*** *to make coffee.* | ***Run downstairs*** *and answer the door.* **2 the downstairs** the rooms on the first floor of a house ANT **upstairs**: *Let's paint the downstairs blue.* —**downstairs** /ˈdaʊnstɛrz/ *adj.*: *the downstairs rooms*

down·state /ˌdaʊnˈsteɪt◂/ *adj., adv.* in or toward the southern part of a state ANT **upstate**: *He lives downstate, near the city.*

down·stream /ˌdaʊnˈstrim/ *adv.* in the direction that the water in a river or stream is flowing ANT **upstream**

down·time /ˈdaʊntaɪm/ *n.* [U] **1** IT the time when a computer is not working **2** (informal) time spent relaxing

ˌdown-to-ˈearth *adj.* practical and honest: *She's a friendly, down-to-earth person.*

down·town[1] /ˈdaʊntaʊn/ *n.* [U] the business center of a city or town: *efforts to revitalize the city's downtown*

down·town[2] /ˌdaʊnˈtaʊn◂/ *adv., adj.* to or in the business center of a city or town → UPTOWN: *Do you work downtown?* | *downtown Atlanta* | *I need to* ***go downtown*** *later.*

down·trod·den /ˈdaʊnˌtrɑdn/ *adj.* (literary) treated badly by people who have power over you

down·turn /ˈdaʊntɚn/ *n.* [C usually singular] a time during which business activity is reduced and conditions become worse: *a* ***downturn in*** *the economy*

THESAURUS **recession, depression, slump, crash** → RECESSION

down·ward[1] /ˈdaʊnwɚd/ *also* **downwards** *adv.* from a higher place or position to a lower one ANT **upward**: *The balloon drifted slowly downward.*

downward[2] *adj.* going or moving down to a lower level or place ANT **upward**: *Stock prices continued their downward trend.*

down·wind /ˌdaʊnˈwɪnd◂/ *adj., adv.* in the same direction that the wind is moving

down·y /ˈdaʊni/ *adj.* having thin soft feathers or hair: *the baby's downy head*

D

dow·ry /ˈdaʊri/ *n.* (plural **dowries**) [C] money or property that a woman gives to her husband when they marry in some societies

doze /doʊz/ *v.* [I] to sleep lightly for a short time
doze off *phr.v.* to fall asleep, especially when you did not intend to: *He dozed off watching TV.* [ORIGIN: 1600—1700 From a Scandinavian language; related to Old Norse *dúsa* "to sleep lightly"]

doz·en /ˈdʌzən/ *number* **1** a group of 12 things: ***a dozen eggs*** **2** (informal) a lot: *I've heard this story* ***dozens of*** *times.* [ORIGIN: 1200—1300 Old French *dozeine*, from *doze* "twelve"]

Dr. /ˈdɑktɚ/ the written abbreviation of DOCTOR

drab /dræb/ *adj.* not colorful or interesting: *a drab office building* [ORIGIN: 1500—1600 *drab* "(dull-colored) cloth" (16—18 centuries), from Old French *drap* "cloth"]

dra·co·ni·an /dræˈkoʊniən/ *adj.* (formal) very strict and severe: *draconian laws* [ORIGIN: 1800—1900 Greek *Drakon* "Draco," ancient Greek judge who had criminals killed for very small crimes]

THESAURUS **strict, tough, firm, rigorous, stern, rigid, stringent** → STRICT

draft[1] /dræft/ Ac *n.* [C] **1** a piece of writing, a drawing, or a plan that is not yet in its finished form: *the* ***rough draft*** *of his essay* | *I read the* ***first draft*** *and thought it was very good.* | *She still has to review the* ***final draft*** (=final form). **2 the draft** a system in which people must join the military, especially when there is a war **3** cold air that moves through a room and that you can feel: *Is the window closed all the way? I feel a draft in here.* **4 on draft** beer that is on draft is served from a large container, rather than from a bottle or can

draft[2] *v.* [T] **1** to write a plan, letter, report, etc. that you will need to change before it is finished: *The House plans to draft a bill on education.* **2** to order someone to fight for his/her country during a war: *Jim* ***was drafted into*** *the army.*

ˈdraft ˌdodger *n.* [C] someone who illegally

avoids joining the military, even though s/he has been ordered to join

drafts·man /ˈdræftsmən/ *n.* (plural **draftsmen** /-mən/) [C] someone whose job is to make detailed drawings of a building, machine, etc. that is being planned

draft·y /ˈdræfti/ *adj.* a drafty room is uncomfortable because cold air is blowing through it

drag¹ /dræg/ *v.* (**dragged**, **dragging**)
1 PULL STH [T] to pull something along the ground, often because it is too heavy to carry: *Ben **dragged** his sled **through** the snow.* → *see picture on page A22*

D

THESAURUS pull, tug, haul, tow, heave → PULL¹

2 PULL SB [T] to pull someone in a strong or violent way when s/he does not want to go with you: *He grabbed her arm and dragged her into the room.*
3 drag yourself up/over/along etc. (informal) to move somewhere when it is difficult: *I dragged myself out of bed to call the doctor.*
4 GO SOMEWHERE [T] (informal) to make someone go somewhere that s/he does not want to go: *Mom **dragged** us **to** a concert last night.*
5 drag yourself away (from) (informal) to stop doing something, although you do not want to: *Can you drag yourself away from the TV for 5 minutes?*
6 BORING [I] if time or an event drags, it is boring and seems to go very slowly: *The last hour of the play really dragged.*
7 COMPUTER [T] to move words, images, etc. on a computer screen by pulling them along with the MOUSE
8 TOUCHING GROUND [I] if something is dragging along the ground, part of it is touching the ground as you move: *Your coat is **dragging in** the mud.*
9 drag your feet (informal) to take too much time to do something because you do not want to do it: *The police are being accused of dragging their feet on this case.* [ORIGIN: 1300—1400 Old Norse *draga* or Old English *dragan*]

drag sb **into** sth *phr. v.*
to make someone get involved in a situation even though s/he does not want to: *I'm sorry to drag you into this mess.*

drag on *phr. v.*
to continue for too long: *The meeting dragged on all afternoon.*

drag sth ↔ **out** *phr. v.*
to make a situation or event last longer than necessary: *How long are you going to drag this discussion out?*

drag sth **out of** sb *phr. v.*
to force someone to tell you something when s/he had not intended to or was not supposed to do so

drag² *n.* **1 a drag** (informal) something or someone that is boring or annoying: *"I have to stay home tonight." "**What a drag.**"* **2 the main drag** (informal) the biggest or longest street that goes through a town, especially the middle of a town: *There are a lot of restaurants along the main drag.* **3** [C] the act of breathing in smoke from a cigarette: *Al **took a drag on** his cigarette.* **4 in drag** (informal) wearing clothes that are intended for people of the opposite sex, especially for fun or entertainment

drag·on /ˈdrægən/ *n.* [C] a large imaginary animal that has wings, a long tail, and can breathe out fire [ORIGIN: 1200—1300 Old French, Greek *drakon* "large snake"]

drag·on·fly /ˈdrægənˌflaɪ/ *n.* (plural **dragonflies**) [C] a flying insect with a long brightly colored body

ˈdrag race *n.* [C] a car race over a short distance

drain¹ /dreɪn/ *v.* **1 a)** [T] to make the water or liquid in something flow away: *The swimming pool is drained and cleaned every winter.* | *Brad **drained** all the oil **from** the engine.* **b)** [I] if something drains, the liquid in it or on it flows away: *Let the pasta drain well.* **c)** [I] if a liquid drains, it flows away: *The bath water slowly **drained away**.* **2** [T] to use up all of your energy, making you feel very tired: *Working with children all day really drains you.* **3** [I] if the color drains from your face, you suddenly become pale **4** [T] to drink all the liquid in a glass, cup, etc.: *Lori quickly drained her cup.*

drain² *n.* **1** [C] a pipe or hole that dirty water or other waste liquids flow into: *The drain in the sink is blocked.* **2 a drain on sth** something that uses a lot of something, such as time, money, or strength: *Doing a graduate degree has been a drain on Fran's savings.* **3 down the drain** (informal) wasted or having no result: *There's another $50 down the drain.*

drain·age /ˈdreɪnɪdʒ/ *n.* [U] the system or process by which water or waste liquids can flow away from a place

drained /dreɪnd/ *adj.* very tired: *I felt completely drained after they had all gone home.*

dra·ma /ˈdrɑmə, ˈdræmə/ (Ac) *n.* **1** [C,U] a play for the theater, television, radio, etc., usually a serious one, or plays in general **2** [U] the study of acting and plays: *drama school* **3** [C,U] an exciting and unusual situation or event: *a life full of drama* | *The photograph captures the drama of the moment.* [ORIGIN: 1500—1600 Late Latin, Greek, "action, theater plays," from *dran* "to do"]

dra·mat·ic /drəˈmæt̬ɪk/ (Ac) *adj.* **1** sudden and surprising: *His work has shown **dramatic improvement**.* | *a **dramatic change** in temperature* | *The changes were small, but their effect was dramatic.* **2** exciting and impressive: *a dramatic speech*

THESAURUS exciting, thrilling, gripping, exhilarating, electric → EXCITING

3 related to the theater or plays: *Miller's dramatic works* **4** showing your feelings in a way that makes other people notice you: *Don't be so dramatic.* | *Rosa raised her hands in a dramatic gesture of despair.* —**dramatically** *adv.*: *Output has increased dramatically.*

dra·mat·ics /drə'mæṭɪks/ *n.* [plural] behavior that is intended to get attention and is not sincere: *I'm really tired of your dramatics.*

dram·a·tist /'dræməṭɪst, 'drɑ-/ (Ac) *n.* [C] someone who writes plays, especially serious ones: *plays by contemporary dramatists*

dram·a·tize /'dræmə,taɪz, 'drɑ-/ (Ac) *v.* [T] **1** to make a book or event into a play, movie, television program, etc.: *a novel dramatized for TV* **2** to make an event seem more exciting than it really is: *Do you always have to dramatize everything?* —**dramatization** /,dræməṭə'zeɪʃən/ *n.* [C,U]

dram·a·turg /'dræmə,tɚdʒ, 'drɑ-/ *n.* [C] ENG. LANG. ARTS someone who works for a theater and helps theater directors and PLAYWRIGHTS, for example by developing new plays, employing actors, and doing RESEARCH

drank /dræŋk/ *v.* the past tense of DRINK

drape /dreɪp/ *v.* [T] to put cloth, clothing, etc. loosely over or around something: *Mina's scarf was* ***draped over*** *her shoulders.*

drap·er·y /'dreɪpəri/ *n.* (plural **draperies**) [C,U] cloth or clothing that is arranged in folds over something

drapes /dreɪps/ *n.* [plural] heavy curtains

dras·tic /'dræstɪk/ *adj.* extreme and sudden: *Don't make any* ***drastic changes*** *just yet.* —**drastically** *adv.*

draw[1] /drɔ/ *v.* (past tense **drew** /dru/, past participle **drawn** /drɔn/)

1 PICTURE [I,T] to make a picture of something with a pencil or a pen: *Could you draw me a map?* | *He drew an elephant on the paper.* | *She was* ***drawing a picture of*** *a tree.*

> **THESAURUS**
>
> **sketch** – to draw something quickly and without a lot of detail: *He sketched a rough street plan of Moscow.*
> **doodle** – to draw shapes or patterns without really thinking about what you are doing: *He was doodling on a sheet of paper.*
> **scribble** – to draw or write something quickly in a messy way: *She scribbled her name and phone number on the back of the card.*
> **trace** – to copy a picture by putting a piece of thin paper over it and drawing the lines that you can see through the paper: *The kids were tracing designs on the paper.*

2 draw (sb's) attention to sth to make someone notice something: *I'd like to draw your attention to the six exit doors in the plane.*
3 draw a conclusion to decide that something is true based on facts that you have: *Other people might easily draw a different conclusion.*
4 draw a distinction/comparison etc. to make someone understand that two things are different from or similar to each other: *It's important to* ***draw a distinction between*** *business and non-business expenses.*
5 PULL SB/STH [T] to move someone or something by pulling him, her, or it gently: *Grant* ***drew*** *me* ***aside*** *to tell me the news.*
6 MOVE [I] to move in a particular direction: *She drew away, but he pulled her close again.* | *A police car drew up behind me.*
7 ATTRACT/INTEREST [T] to attract or interest someone: *The movie* ***drew*** *large* ***crowds*** *on the first day.* | *What first* ***drew*** *you* ***to*** *him?*
8 GET A REACTION [T] to get a particular kind of reaction from someone: *His remarks drew an angry response from Democrats.* | *Her idea* ***drew praise/criticism*** *from the others.*
9 PLAYING CARD/TICKET [I,T] to choose a card, ticket, etc. by chance: *The winning lottery numbers will be drawn on Saturday.*
10 draw the line (at sth) to refuse to do something because you do not approve of it, although you are willing to do other things: *I don't mind helping you, but I draw the line at telling lies.*
11 draw a blank (informal) to be unable to think or remember something: *I drew a blank when I tried to remember the number.*
12 draw a gun/knife/sword etc. to take a weapon from its container or from your pocket: *He had drawn a knife and was pointing it at me.*
13 draw the curtains to open or close the curtains
14 draw to a close/an end (formal) to gradually stop or finish: *Our vacation in Acapulco was drawing to a close.*
15 draw comfort/strength etc. (from sb/sth) to get something such as comfort or strength from someone or something: *I drew a lot of comfort from her kind words.*
16 draw blood a) to take blood from someone at a hospital **b)** to make someone bleed: *The dog bit her so hard that it drew blood.*
17 draw near/close (literary) to move closer in time or space: *Summer vacation is drawing near.*
18 PULL A VEHICLE [T] to pull a vehicle using an animal: *a carriage drawn by six horses* [ORIGIN: Old English *dragan*]

draw back *phr. v.*
to move back from something: *The crowd drew back to let the police by.*

draw sb **into** sth *phr. v.*
to make someone become involved in something when s/he does not want to be: *Keith refused to be drawn into our argument.*

draw on sth *phr. v.*
to use your money, experiences, etc. to help you do something: *A good writer draws on his or her own experience.*

draw out *phr. v.*
1 draw sb ↔ **out** to make someone feel less nervous and more willing to talk: *She just needed someone to draw her out and take an interest in her.*
2 draw sth ↔ **out** to make an event last longer than usual

draw sth ↔ **up** *phr. v.*
to prepare a written document: *We drew up some guidelines for the new committee.*

D

draw² *n.* [C] **1** an occasion when someone or something is chosen by chance, especially the winning ticket in a LOTTERY **2** something or someone that a lot of people are willing to pay to see: *The Lakers are always a **big draw**.* **3** a game that ends with both teams or players having the same number of points (SYN) **tie**

draw·back /ˈdrɔbæk/ *n.* [C] something that might be a problem or disadvantage: *The main drawback to the job is that the hours wouldn't be regular.*

THESAURUS **disadvantage, downside, catch, bad point** → DISADVANTAGE

D

draw·bridge /ˈdrɔbrɪdʒ/ *n.* [C] a bridge that can be pulled up to let ships go under it

drawer /drɔr/ *n.* [C] a part of a piece of furniture that slides in and out and is used for keeping things in: *The pens are in the **bottom/top drawer** of my desk.* | *Put it in the **desk drawer**.*

draw·ing /ˈdrɔ-ɪŋ/ *n.* **1** [C] a picture you make with a pen or pencil: *She showed us a **drawing of** the house.*

THESAURUS

picture – a drawing, painting, or photograph: *On the refrigerator were pictures the kids had drawn.*
sketch – a drawing that you do quickly and without a lot of details: *Andrew did a quick sketch of the harbor.*
doodle – a picture or pattern that you draw without really thinking about what you are doing: *The paper was covered in doodles.*
comic strip – a series of pictures that are drawn inside boxes and tell a story: *The Doonesbury comic strip comments on political and social events.*
cartoon – a funny drawing in a newspaper, usually about someone or something that is in the news: *An editorial cartoon showed him as a baby throwing a tantrum.*

2 [U] the art or skill of making pictures with a pen or pencil: *I've never been good at drawing.*

THESAURUS **art, painting, photography, sculpture, pottery, ceramics** → ART

ˈdrawing board *n.* **(go) back to the drawing board** to start working on a new plan or idea after an idea you have tried has failed: *They rejected our proposal, so it's back to the drawing board.*

drawl /drɔl/ *n.* [singular] a way of speaking in which vowels are longer than usual: *a Southern drawl* —**drawl** *v.* [I,T]

drawn¹ /drɔn/ *v.* the past participle of DRAW

drawn² *adj.* someone who is drawn has a thin pale face because s/he is sick, tired, or worried

ˌdrawn-ˈout *adj.* seeming to continue for a very long time: *a **long drawn-out** process*

draw·string /ˈdrɔstrɪŋ/ *n.* [C] a string through the top of a bag, piece of clothing, etc. that you can pull tight or make loose

dread¹ /drɛd/ *v.* [T] to feel very worried about something that is going to happen or may happen: *I've got an interview tomorrow and I'm dreading it.*

dread² *n.* [singular, U] a strong fear of something that is going to happen or may happen: *The thought filled me **with dread**.*

dread·ful /ˈdrɛdfəl/ *adj.* very bad: *a dreadful movie* —**dreadfully** *adv.*

THESAURUS **horrible, disgusting, awful, revolting, foul, terrible, horrendous** → HORRIBLE

dread·locks /ˈdrɛdlɑks/ *n.* [plural] a way of arranging your hair in which it hangs in lots of thick pieces that look like rope

dream¹ /drim/ *n.* [C] **1** a series of thoughts, images, and experiences that come into your mind when you are asleep: *I **had a** funny **dream** last night.* | *a **bad dream*** (=a frightening or unpleasant dream) **2** something that you hope will happen: *Her dream was to become an opera singer.* **3 beyond your wildest dreams** better than anything you imagined or hoped for **4 a dream come true** something that you have wanted to happen for a long time: *Owning this boat is a dream come true.* [ORIGIN: Old English *dream* "noise, great happiness"]

dream² *v.* (past tense and past participle **dreamed** *or* **dreamt** /drɛmt/) **1** [I,T] to have a dream while you are asleep: *I often **dream that** I'm falling.* **2** [I,T] to think about something that you would like to happen: *She **dreamed of** becoming a pilot.* | *He **never dreamed that** he would make it to the finals* (=never thought that it would happen). | *I've been **dreaming about** this moment all my life.* **3 sb wouldn't dream of (doing) sth** (spoken) used in order to say that you would never do something: *I wouldn't dream of letting you walk home alone.* **4 dream on** (spoken) said when you think that what someone is hoping for will not happen: *You really believe we'll win? Dream on!*
dream sth ↔ **up** *phr. v.* to think of a plan or idea, especially an unusual one: *Who dreams up these TV commercials?*

THESAURUS **invent, create, think up, come up with sth, conceive, devise, make up** → INVENT

dream³ *adj.* **dream car/house/team etc.** the best car, house, etc. that you can imagine: *A Porsche is my dream car.*

dream·er /ˈdrimɚ/ *n.* [C] someone who has plans that are not practical

dream·y /ˈdrimi/ *adj.* **1** looking like you are thinking about something pleasant rather than what is happening around you: *a dreamy smile* **2** someone who is dreamy has a good imagination but is not very practical **3** pleasant, peaceful, and relaxing: *dreamy music* —**dreamily** *adv.*

drear·y /ˈdrɪri/ *adj.* dull and uninteresting: *a wet and dreary afternoon* —**drearily** *adv.* —**dreariness** *n.* [U]

dredge /drɛdʒ/ *v.* [I,T] to remove mud or sand from the bottom of a river, or to search the bottom of a river or lake for something

dredge sth ↔ **up** *phr. v.* (informal) to start talking about something bad or unpleasant that happened a long time ago: *Why do the papers have to dredge up that old story?*

dregs /drɛgz/ *n.* [plural] small solid pieces in a liquid such as wine or coffee that sink to the bottom of the cup, bottle, etc.

drench /drɛntʃ/ *v.* [T] to make something completely wet: *I forgot my umbrella and got drenched.*

dress¹ /drɛs/ *v.* **1** [I,T] to put clothes on someone or yourself: *Can you dress the kids while I make breakfast?* | *Hurry up and **get dressed**!* **2 be dressed** to be wearing clothes: *Are you dressed yet?* | *She **was dressed in** a simple black dress.* | *a **well-dressed** gentleman* **3** [I] to wear a particular type of clothes: *Dress warmly – it's cold out.* | *You can **dress casually** at our office.* **4 dress a wound/cut etc.** to clean and cover a wound in order to protect it

dress down *phr. v.* to wear clothes that are less formal than the ones you usually wear

dress up *phr. v.* **1** to wear clothes that are more formal than the ones you usually wear: *It's only a small party. You don't need to dress up.* **2** to wear special clothes for fun: *She **dressed up as** a witch for Halloween.*

dress² *n.* **1** [C] a piece of clothing worn by a woman or girl, that covers the top of her body and some or all of her legs: *a summer dress* | *She was **wearing a red dress**.* → *see picture at* CLOTHES **2** [U] clothes for men or women of a particular type or for a particular occasion: ***casual dress** in the workplace* | *He was wearing **evening dress*** (=formal clothes worn at important social events). **3 dress shirt/dress shoes** a shirt or shoes that you wear with formal clothes such as a suit

ˈdress code *n.* [C] a standard of what you should wear for a particular situation

dress·er /ˈdrɛsɚ/ *n.* [C] a piece of furniture with drawers for storing clothes, sometimes with a mirror on top

dress·ing /ˈdrɛsɪŋ/ *n.* **1** [C,U] a mixture of oil and other things that you pour over SALAD: *salad dressing* **2** [C,U] STUFFING **3** [C] a special piece of material used for covering and protecting a wound: *a clean dressing for the cut*

ˈdressing room *n.* [C] **1** a room or area in a store, where you can try on clothes **2** a room where an actor, performer, etc. gets ready before going on stage, appearing on television, etc.

ˈdress reˌhearsal *n.* [C] the last time actors practice a play, using all the clothes, objects, etc. that will be used in the real performance

dress·y /ˈdrɛsi/ *adj.* dressy clothes are appropriate for formal occasions

drew /dru/ *v.* the past tense of DRAW

drib·ble /ˈdrɪbəl/ *v.* **1** [I,T] to flow slowly in irregular drops, or to make a liquid flow in this way: *Blood was **dribbling from** his cut lip.* **2** [T] to move forward with a ball by BOUNCING or kicking it again and again —**dribble** *n.* [C]

dribs and drabs /ˌdrɪbz ən ˈdræbz/ *n.* **in dribs and drabs** in small amounts: *People arrived in dribs and drabs.*

dried¹ /draɪd/ *v.* the past tense and past participle of DRY

dried² *adj.* dried food or flowers have had all the water removed from them

drift¹ /drɪft/ *v.* [I] **1** to move very slowly on water or in the air: *Gray clouds were drifting over from the north.* **2** to move or go somewhere without any plan or purpose: *Julie drifted toward the window.* | *Her thoughts drifted away.* **3** to gradually change from being in one condition, situation, etc. into another: *During the ambulance ride, he drifted in and out of consciousness.* **4** snow or sand that drifts is blown into a large pile by the wind

drift apart *phr. v.* if people drift apart, they gradually stop having a relationship: *Over the years, my college friends and I have drifted apart.*

drift off *phr. v.* to gradually fall asleep: *After a while, I **drifted off to sleep**.*

drift² *n.* [C] **1** a large pile of snow, sand, etc. that has been blown by the wind: *snow drifts*

THESAURUS **pile, heap, mound, stack** → PILE¹

2 catch/get sb's drift to understand the general meaning of what someone says: *I don't speak much Spanish, but I got her drift.* **3** a gradual change or development in a situation, people's opinion, etc.: *a long downward drift in the birthrate* **4** a very slow movement: *continental drift*

drift·er /ˈdrɪftɚ/ *n.* [C] someone who is always moving to a different place or doing different jobs

drift·wood /ˈdrɪftwʊd/ *n.* [U] wood floating in the ocean or left on the shore

drill

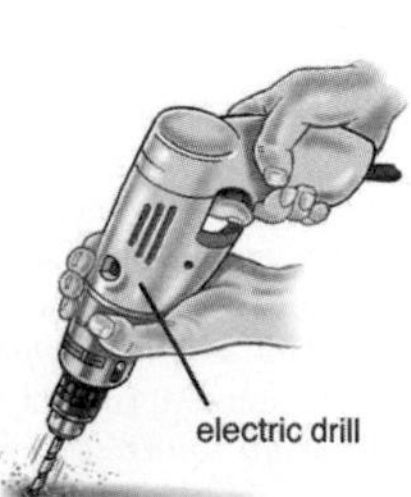

drill¹ /drɪl/ *n.* **1** [C] a tool or machine used for making holes in something hard: *an electric drill* | *a dentist's drill* **2** [C,U] a method of teaching something by making people repeat the same lesson, exercise, etc. many times: *a spelling drill* **3 fire/**

D

emergency etc. drill an occasion when you practice what you should do during a dangerous situation

drill² *v.* **1** [I,T] to make a hole with a drill: *Drill a hole for the screw in each corner.* | ***drilling for*** *oil*

THESAURUS pierce, make a hole in sth, prick, punch, puncture, bore ➔ PIERCE

2 [T] to teach people something by making them repeat the same exercise, lesson, etc. many times ➔ PRACTICE²

drill sth **into** sb *phr. v.* to tell something to someone many times, until s/he knows it very well: *Mom drilled it into us that we shouldn't talk to strangers.*

D

dri·ly /ˈdraɪli/ *adv.* another spelling of DRYLY

drink¹ /drɪŋk/ *n.* **1** [C,U] liquid that you can drink, or an amount of liquid that you drink: *Here,* ***have a drink*** *of water.* | *a* ***drink of*** *coffee* | *soft drinks* | *food and drink* **2** [C] an alcoholic drink: *How about a drink later?* [ORIGIN: Old English *drincan*]

drink² *v.* (past tense **drank** /dræŋk/, past participle **drunk** /drʌŋk/) **1** [I,T] to pour a liquid into your mouth and swallow it: *Let me get you* ***something to drink***. | *Charlie drinks way too much coffee.*

THESAURUS

sip/take a sip – to swallow only a small amount of a liquid
slurp (informal) – to drink something in a noisy way
gulp sth down also **down sth** (informal) – to drink all of something very quickly: *I downed my beer and left.*
knock sth back (informal) – to drink all of an alcoholic drink very quickly
swig (informal) also **take/have a swig** (informal) – to drink something quickly by taking large amounts into your mouth, especially from a bottle: *He ate a few peanuts and took a swig of his beer.*
guzzle (informal) – to drink a lot of something eagerly and quickly: *It was a hot day, and people were sitting on their porches guzzling lemonade.*
imbibe (formal, humorous) – to drink something, especially alcohol: *Throughout the evening, he had imbibed more and more wine.* ➔ EAT

2 [I] to drink alcohol, especially too much or too often: *I* ***don't drink***. | *His father began* ***drinking heavily*** (=a lot).

drink sth ↔ **in** *phr. v.* to listen, look at, feel, or smell something in order to enjoy it: *We spent the day drinking in the sights and sounds of Paris.*

drink to sth *phr. v.* to wish someone success, good health, etc. before having an alcoholic drink: *Let's all drink to their happiness!*

drink (sth ↔) **up** *phr. v.* to drink all of something: *Drink up your milk.* | *Come on, drink up!*

drink·er /ˈdrɪŋkɚ/ *n.* [C] someone who often drinks alcohol: *Greg's a* ***heavy drinker*** (=he drinks a lot).

ˈdrinking ˌfountain *n.* [C] a piece of equipment in a public place, that produces a stream of water for you to drink from

ˈdrinking ˌproblem *n.* [singular] someone who has a drinking problem drinks too much alcohol

drip¹ /drɪp/ *v.* (**dripped**, **dripping**) **1** [I,T] to produce small drops of liquid: *The faucet sounds like it's dripping.* | *His finger was dripping blood.* | *They were both* ***dripping with sweat***. **2** [I] to fall in drops: *Rain dripped off the trees.*

THESAURUS pour, flow, leak, ooze, gush, spurt, run, come out ➔ POUR

drip² *n.* **1** [C] one of the small drops of liquid that falls from something **2** [singular, U] the action or sound of a liquid falling in small drops: *the drip of rain from the roof* **3** [C] (informal) someone who is boring and annoying

drive¹ /draɪv/ *v.* (past tense **drove** /droʊv/, past participle **driven** /ˈdrɪvən/) **1** [I,T] to make a car, bus, etc. move and control where it goes: *teenagers learning to drive* | *He drives a red Porsche.*

TOPIC

When you get into a car, you **buckle/fasten your seatbelt**, then put the key in the **ignition** and turn it to **start the engine**.
You **release** the **parking/emergency brake**, and put the car in **drive**. You **check your mirrors** (=look into them) before driving onto the street. You press the **gas pedal** with your foot to make the car **accelerate** (=go faster).
When you turn right or left, you must **indicate/put on your turn signals**. When you want to slow down, you press the **brake (pedal)** with your foot. When you **park** your car, you put the car **in park** and **set/put on the parking brake**.

2 [I,T] to travel in a car or take someone somewhere by car: *We're* ***driving up/down*** *to Washington this weekend.* | *Would you mind* ***driving*** *me* ***to*** *the airport?* | *After the party, he* ***drove*** *her* ***home***. **3** [I,T] to make people, animals, or an activity move somewhere: *We were driven indoors by the rain.* | *Large grocery chains* ***drove out*** *the small family-owned stores.* **4** [T] to strongly influence someone to do something: *What drove him to suicide?* **5 drive sb crazy/nuts/insane etc.** *also* **drive sb up the wall** to make someone feel very annoyed and angry: *The kids are driving me crazy!* **6** [T] to hit something very hard: *Barry drove the ball into left field.* **7** [T] to provide the power for a vehicle or machine: *the motor that drives the propeller* [ORIGIN: Old English *drifan*]

drive sb ↔ **away** *phr. v.* to behave in a way that makes someone want to leave you: *If you keep on drinking, I guarantee you'll drive her away.*

drive sth ↔ **down** *phr. v.* to make prices, costs, etc. fall quickly

drive off *phr. v.* **1** if a driver or a car drives off, he, she, or it leaves **2 drive** sb/sth ↔ **off** to force someone or something to go away from you: *Police used tear gas to drive off the rioters.*

drive sth ↔ **up** *phr. v.* to make prices, costs, etc. increase

drive[2] *n.* **1** [C] a trip in a car: *Let's* ***go for a drive****.* | *It's a twenty-minute drive from the city.* **2** [C] a strong natural need or desire: *As men get older, their sex drive gradually declines.* **3** [C] a planned effort by an organization to achieve a particular result: *the senator's reelection drive* | *a drive to raise money for starving children*

THESAURUS **fight, battle, campaign, struggle, crusade** ➔ FIGHT[2]

4 [C] IT a piece of equipment in a computer that is used to get information from a DISK or to store information on it: *the C drive* **5** [C] an act of hitting a ball hard: *a line drive to right field* **6** [U] a determination to succeed: *He has considerable drive.* **7** [C] the power from an engine that makes the wheels of a car, bus, etc. turn: *a four-wheel drive pickup*

'drive-by *adj.* **drive-by shooting/killing** the act of shooting someone from a moving car

'drive-in[1] *n.* [C] a place where you can watch movies outdoors while sitting in your car

'drive-in[2] *adj.* **drive-in restaurant/movie** a restaurant, theater, etc. where you stay in your car to eat, watch the movie, etc.

driv·el /ˈdrɪvəl/ *n.* [U] something written or said that is silly or does not mean anything

driv·en /ˈdrɪvən/ *v.* the past participle of DRIVE

driv·er /ˈdraɪvə/ *n.* [C] **1** someone who drives: *a* ***truck/cab/bus driver*** | *Joyce is a* ***good/bad driver****.* **2** IT a piece of software that makes a computer work with another piece of equipment such as a PRINTER or a MOUSE

'driver's ˌlicense *n.* [C] an official card with your name, picture, etc. on it that says you are legally allowed to drive

'drive-through *adj.* a drive-through restaurant, bank, etc. can be used without getting out of your car

drive·way /ˈdraɪvweɪ/ *n.* [C] the road or area for cars between a house and the street: *Park your car* ***in the driveway****.*

driz·zle[1] /ˈdrɪzəl/ *n.* [singular, U] weather that is a combination of mist and light rain

THESAURUS **rain, shower, downpour, storm, hail, sleet** ➔ RAIN[1]

drizzle[2] *v.* **1 it drizzles** if it drizzles, mist and light rain come out of the sky: *It started to drizzle.* **2** [T] to pour a liquid over food in small drops or a thin stream

droll /droʊl/ *adj.* (old-fashioned) unusual and slightly funny

drone[1] /droʊn/ *v.* [I] to make a continuous low noise: *An airplane droned overhead.*

drone[2] *n.* **1** [singular] a continuous low noise: *the drone of the lawnmower* **2** [C] an aircraft that does not have a pilot, but is operated by radio

drool /drul/ *v.* [I] **1** to have SALIVA (=the liquid in your mouth) flow from your mouth: *The dog began to drool.* **2** to show in a silly way that you like or want someone or something a lot: *The thought of all that money made us drool.* —**drool** *n.* [U]

droop /drup/ *v.* [I] to hang or bend down: *Her shoulders drooped with tiredness.*

drop[1] /drɑp/ *v.* (**dropped**, **dropping**)
1 LET GO [T] to stop holding or carrying something, so that it falls: *One of the waiters tripped and dropped a tray full of food.* | *With this technology, planes are able to drop bombs accurately.* ➔ *see picture on page A22*
2 FALL [I] to fall: *The bottle rolled off the table and* ***dropped onto*** *the floor.* | *He* ***dropped into*** *his chair with a sigh.*
3 TAKE IN A CAR [T] *also* **drop off** to take someone or something to a place in a car, when you are going on to somewhere else: *I'll drop you at the corner, okay?* | *She drops the kids off at school on her way to work.*
4 DECREASE [I,T] to decrease to a lower level or amount, or to make something decrease: *Crime on the buses has dropped 25%.* | *The store has dropped its prices.*

THESAURUS **decrease, go down, fall, plummet, diminish, decline, dwindle** ➔ DECREASE[1]

5 STOP DOING STH [T] to stop doing something or stop planning to do something: *The charges against him have been dropped.* | *He expects me to just* ***drop everything*** (=stop everything I am doing) *and go with him.* | *I wasn't doing very well, so I dropped French* (=stopped studying French). | ***Drop it*** (=stop talking about it), *Ted, it's just a rumor.*
6 STOP INCLUDING [T] to decide not to include someone or something: *Morris has been* ***dropped from*** *the team.*
7 STOP A RELATIONSHIP [T] to stop having a relationship with someone, especially suddenly: *She found out he was seeing someone else, so she dropped him.*
8 drop dead a) to die suddenly **b)** (spoken) used when you are very angry with someone
9 drop the ball to stop doing something, when people expected you to continue doing it
10 work/run etc. until you drop (informal) to do something until you are extremely tired
11 drop sb a line (informal) to write to someone: *Drop us a line sometime.* [ORIGIN: Old English droppian]

drop by *also* **drop in** *phr. v.*
to visit someone when you have not arranged to come at a particular time: *Doris and Ed dropped by on Saturday.*

drop off *phr. v.*
1 to begin to sleep: *The baby dropped off to sleep in the car.*
2 to become less in level or amount: *The demand for leaded fuel dropped off in the late 1970s.*

D

drop out *phr. v.* to stop going to school or stop an activity before you have finished it: *teenagers* ***dropping out of*** *high school | The injury forced him to* ***drop out of*** *the race.*

drop[2] *n.* **1** [C] a very small amount of liquid that falls in a round shape: *big* ***drops of*** *rain | a tear drop* **2** [C] a small amount of a liquid: *Add a couple of* ***drops of*** *lemon juice.* **3** [singular] a distance from something down to the ground: *It's a twenty-five foot drop from this cliff.* **4** [singular] a decrease in the amount, level, or number of something: *a* ***steep/sharp drop*** *from 72% to 34% | a* ***drop in*** *temperature* **5 eye/ear/nose drops** medicine that you put in your eye, etc. one drop at a time **6 a drop in the bucket** an amount of something that is too small to have any effect **7 at the drop of a hat** immediately: *He could fall asleep at the drop of a hat.*

D

'drop-down ˌmenu *n.* [C] IT a list that appears on a computer screen, that shows you what you can choose to do. You press the button on the mouse on one of the choices to send an instruction to the computer.

drop·let /ˈdrɑplɪt/ *n.* [C] a very small drop of liquid

drop·out /ˈdrɑp-aʊt/ *n.* [C] someone who leaves school or college without finishing it

drop·per /ˈdrɑpɚ/ *n.* [C] a short glass tube with a hollow rubber part at one end, used for measuring liquid in drops

drop·pings /ˈdrɑpɪŋz/ *n.* [plural] solid waste from animals or birds

drought /draʊt/ *n.* [C] a long period of dry weather when there is not enough water: *a* ***severe drought***

drove[1] /droʊv/ *v.* the past tense of DRIVE

drove[2] *n.* [C] a large group of animals or people that move or are moved together: *Tourists* ***come in droves*** *to see the White House.*

drown /draʊn/ *v.* **1** [I,T] to die from being under water too long, or to kill someone in this way: *Many people drowned when the boat overturned. | Five people* ***drowned in*** *the flood. | She* ***drowned herself*** *in the river.* **2** [T] *also* **drown out** if a loud noise drowns out another sound, it prevents it from being heard: *The president's words were drowned out by cheers.* **3** [T] to completely cover something with liquid: *Dad always* ***drowns*** *his pancakes* ***in/with*** *maple syrup.* **4 drown your sorrows** to drink a lot of alcohol in order to forget your problems

drown·ing /ˈdraʊnɪŋ/ *n.* [C,U] death caused by staying under water for too long

drows·y /ˈdraʊzi/ *adj.* tired and almost asleep (SYN) **sleepy**: *The medicine can make you drowsy.* —**drowsiness** *n.* [U]

drudge /drʌdʒ/ *n.* [C] someone who does difficult boring work —**drudge** *v.* [I]

drudg·er·y /ˈdrʌdʒəri/ *n.* [U] difficult boring work

drug[1] /drʌg/ *n.* [C] **1** an illegal substance that people smoke, INJECT, etc. for pleasure: *Bill was accused of* ***taking/using drugs.*** *|* ***be on drugs*** (=be using drugs) **2** a medicine or a substance for making medicines: *a* ***drug*** *used* ***for*** *depression* [ORIGIN: 1300—1400 Old French *drogue*]

THESAURUS **medicine, pill, tablet, capsule, eye/ear drops, medication** → MEDICINE

drug[2] *v.* (**drugged, drugging**) [T] to give a person or animal a drug, especially to make him, her, or it feel tired or go to sleep, or to get rid of pain: *The kidnappers drugged him and bundled him into the car.*

drug·store /ˈdrʌgstɔr/ *n.* [C] a store where you can buy medicines, beauty products, etc. (SYN) **pharmacy**

drum[1] /drʌm/ *n.* [C] **1** a musical instrument made of skin stretched over a circular frame, which you play by hitting it with your hand or a stick: *a bass drum | Johnny* ***plays the drums*** *in a band.* **2** something that looks like a drum, especially part of a machine **3** a large round container for storing liquids such as oil, chemicals, etc.

drum[2] *v.* (**drummed, drumming**) **1** [I,T] to hit the surface of something again and again in a way that sounds like drums: *He* ***drummed*** *his* ***fingers*** *on the table. | rain drumming on the roof* **2** [I] to play a drum

drum sth **into** sb *phr. v.* to say something to someone so often that s/he cannot forget it: *Safety rules are drummed into the workers.*

drum sth ↔ **up** *phr. v.* to obtain help, money, etc. by asking a lot of people: *The group drummed up corporate sponsors for the event.*

drum·mer /ˈdrʌmɚ/ *n.* [C] someone who plays the drums

drum·stick /ˈdrʌmˌstɪk/ *n.* [C] **1** the leg of a chicken, TURKEY, etc. cooked as food **2** a stick that you use to hit a drum

drunk[1] /drʌŋk/ *adj.* unable to control your behavior, speech, etc. because you have drunk too much alcohol: *college students* ***getting drunk*** *at parties | He was too drunk to drive.*

drunk[2] the past participle of DRINK

drunk[3] *also* **drunk·ard** /ˈdrʌŋkɚd/ *n.* [C] (disapproving) someone who is drunk or often gets drunk

ˌdrunk 'driving *n.* [U] the illegal act of driving a car after having drunk too much alcohol

drunk·en /ˈdrʌŋkən/ *adj.* **1** drunk: *a drunken crowd* **2** resulting from or related to drinking too much alcohol: *drunken shouting* —**drunkenness** *n.* [U] —**drunkenly** *adv.*

dry[1] /draɪ/ *adj.* **1** having no water or other liquid inside or on the surface (ANT) **wet**: *I changed into dry clothes. | Store in a cool, dry place. | Is the paint dry yet?* **2** dry weather does not have much rain or

MOISTURE (ANT) **wet**: *The weather was hot and dry.* | *the beginning of the **dry season*** **3** if your mouth, throat, or skin is dry, it does not have enough of the natural liquid that is usually in it: *My skin has been so dry lately.* | *Ted's mouth was dry and his heart pounded.* **4 dry wine/champagne etc.** wine, etc. that is not sweet: *a glass of dry white wine* **5** someone with a dry WIT or humor, or who says things in a dry voice, says funny things in a serious way **6** boring and very serious: *a dry subject* [ORIGIN: Old English *dryge*]

dry² *v.* (**dried**, **dries**) [I,T] to become dry, or to make something dry: *It'll only take me a few minutes to dry my hair.* | *Mae hung the washing out to dry.*

dry (sth ↔) **off** *phr. v.* to become dry, or to make the surface of something dry: *We swam, then dried off in the sun.* | *She began to dry herself off.*

dry (sth ↔) **out** *phr. v.* to dry completely, or to dry something completely: *Keep the dough covered so that it doesn't dry out.*

dry up *phr. v.* **1 dry** (sth ↔) **up** a river, lake, or area of land that dries up has no more water in it: *Water holes and wells have dried up across the state.* **2** if a supply of something dries up, there is no more of it: *Companies get rid of employees when the work dries up.*

'dry clean *v.* [T] to clean clothes with chemicals instead of water

,dry 'cleaners *n.* [C] a place where you take clothes to be dry cleaned

dry·er /ˈdraɪɚ/ *n.* [C] a machine that dries things, especially clothes or hair

,dry 'ice *n.* [U] CARBON DIOXIDE in a solid state, often used for keeping food and other things cold

dry·ly /ˈdraɪli/ *adv.* speaking in a serious way, although you are actually joking

,dry 'run *n.* [C] an occasion when you practice for an important event

,dry 'wall *n.* [U] a type of board made of two large sheets of CARDBOARD with PLASTER between them, used to cover walls and ceilings **—'dry-wall** *v.* [I,T]

du·al /ˈduəl/ *adj.* having two of something, or two parts: *My wife has **dual nationality/citizenship** – American and Brazilian.*

dub /dʌb/ *v.* (**dubbed**, **dubbing**) [T] **1** to give someone or something a name that describes him, her, or it in some way: *The area was dubbed "Tornado Alley" because of its strong winds.* **2** to replace the original spoken language of a film, television show, etc. with a recording of a different language: *an Italian movie that's been **dubbed into** English*

du·bi·ous /ˈdubiəs/ *adj.* **1** not sure whether something is good, true, etc.: *Employees are **dubious about** the proposed changes.*

THESAURUS **doubtful, unconvinced, skeptical** → DOUBTFUL

2 not seeming honest, safe, valuable, etc.: *an idea based on dubious research* | *He had the **dubious distinction** of coming second in the spelling bee three years in a row.*

duch·ess /ˈdʌtʃɪs/ *n.* [C] a woman with the highest social rank below a PRINCESS, or the wife of a DUKE

duck¹ /dʌk/ *n.* **1** [C] a common water bird with short legs and a wide beak, that is used for its meat, eggs, and soft feathers **2** [U] the meat from this bird: *roast duck* [ORIGIN: Old English *duce*]

duck² *v.* **1** [I,T] to lower your body or head very quickly, or move away very quickly, especially to avoid being hit or seen: *She **ducked** her **head** to get through the doorway.* | *Tom **ducked into** an alley.* **2** [T] (informal) to avoid something that is difficult or unpleasant: *His campaign speech ducked all the major issues.*

duck·ling /ˈdʌklɪŋ/ *n.* [C] a young duck

duct /dʌkt/ *n.* [C] **1** a pipe or tube in a building, that liquid, air, electric CABLES, etc. go through **2** BIOLOGY a thin narrow tube inside your body, a plant, etc., that liquid, air, etc. goes through: *a tear duct*

dud /dʌd/ *n.* (informal) **1** [C] something that does not work or is useless: *This battery's a dud.* **2 duds** [plural] (humorous) clothes **—dud** *adj.*

dude /dud/ *n.* [C] (informal) a man: *Hey, dudes, how's it going?*

'dude ranch *n.* [C] a vacation place where you can ride horses and live like a COWBOY

due¹ /du/ *adj.* **1 be due** to be expected to happen or arrive at a particular time: *The flight from Chicago is **due at** 7:48 p.m.* | *Your final research paper is **due in** March.* | *What's the baby's **due date*** (=the day it is expected to be born)? | *My library books are **due back** tomorrow.* | *The book is **due out** in the spring.* | *The new museum is **due to** open next year.* | *I feel I'm **due for** a raise.* **2 due to** because of: *The program was canceled, due to lack of funds.* | *She was absent due to illness.* **3** needing to be paid: *The first installment of $250 is now due.* **4** deserved by someone or owed to someone: *He never got the recognition he was due.* | *Much of the credit **is due to** our backup team.* **5 in due course/time** at a more appropriate time in the future: *The committee will answer your complaints in due course.* **6 with (all) due respect** (spoken) used when you disagree with someone or criticize him/her in a polite way

due² *adv.* **due north/south/east/west** directly or exactly north, etc.

due³ *n.* **1 dues** [plural] the money that you pay to be a member of an organization: *union dues* **2 give sb his/her due** to admit that someone has good qualities, even though you are criticizing him/her: *To give him his due, he tries very hard.*

du·el /ˈduəl/ *n.* [C] **1** a situation in which two

people or groups are involved in a competition or disagreement: *The two runners will face a duel for the 100-meter record.* **2** a fight in past times between two people with guns or swords —**duel** *v.* [I]

ˌdue 'process *also* **due ˌprocess of 'law** *n.* [U] LAW the correct process that should be followed by law in order to protect someone's legal rights

du·et /du'ɛt/ *n.* [C] a piece of music written for two performers

duf·fel bag /'dʌfəl ˌbæg/ *n.* [C] a cloth bag with a round bottom and a string around the top to tie it closed

D

dug /dʌg/ *v.* the past tense and past participle of DIG

dug·out /'dʌgaʊt/ *n.* [C] a low shelter at the side of a baseball field, where players and team officials sit

duh /dʌ/ *interjection* (spoken) used in order to say that what someone else has just said is stupid

duke /duk/ *n.* [C] a man with the highest social rank below a PRINCE [ORIGIN: 1100—1200 Old French *duc*, from Latin *dux* "leader"]

dull¹ /dʌl/ *adj.* **1** not interesting or exciting: *a dull book*

THESAURUS **boring, tedious, not (very/that/all that) interesting, humdrum, monotonous, insipid** → BORING

2 a dull sound is not clear or loud: *I heard a dull thud from upstairs.* **3** a dull pain is not severe but does not stop: *a dull ache in my shoulder* **4** not bright or shiny: *dull brown walls* **5** not sharp SYN **blunt**: *a dull knife* → *see picture at* SHARP¹ [ORIGIN: Old English *dol*] —**dully** *adv.* —**dullness** *n.* [U]

dull² *v.* [T] to make something become less sharp, less clear, etc.: *a drug to dull the pain*

du·ly /'duli/ *adv.* (formal) at the correct time or in the correct way: *Your suggestion has been duly noted.*

dumb¹ /dʌm/ *adj.* **1** (informal) stupid: *a dumb movie | How could you be so dumb?* **2** (old-fashioned) unable to speak SYN **mute**

dumb² *v.*

dumb sth ↔ **down** *phr. v.* (informal) to make something such as news or information less detailed and present it in an attractive way, so that more people can understand it very easily: *Local news programs seem to have been dumbed down.*

dumb·bell /'dʌmbɛl/ *n.* [C] **1** two weights connected by a short piece of metal, that you lift for exercise **2** (informal) someone who is stupid

dumb·found·ed /'dʌmˌfaʊndɪd/ *adj.* so surprised that you cannot speak

THESAURUS **surprised, amazed, shocked, astonished, astounded, flabbergasted, stunned, nonplussed, taken aback** → SURPRISED

dum·my¹ /'dʌmi/ *n.* (plural **dummies**) [C] **1** (informal) someone who is stupid **2** a figure made to look like a person

dummy² *adj.* a dummy tool, weapon, etc. looks like a real one but does not work: *a dummy rifle*

dump¹ /dʌmp/ *v.* [T] **1** to drop or put something somewhere in a careless way, sometimes in order to get rid of it: *Illegal chemicals have been* ***dumped in*** *the river. | They* ***dumped*** *their bags* ***on*** *the floor and left.*

THESAURUS **shove, stick, thrust** → SHOVE

2 [informal] to suddenly end a relationship: *Tammy dumped her boyfriend.*

dump on *phr. v.* (informal) **1 dump on** sb to criticize someone or complain to someone: *Reporters have been dumping on the White House because of the war.* **2 dump** sth **on** sb to unfairly give someone an unwanted job, duty, or problem to deal with: *Don't just dump the extra work on me.*

dump² *n.* [C] **1** a place where unwanted waste is taken and left: *the town's* ***garbage dump*** *| a toxic waste dump* **2** a place where military supplies are stored, or the supplies themselves: *an ammunition dump* **3** (informal) a place that is unpleasant because it is dirty, ugly, or boring: *This place is such a dump.* **4 be down in the dumps** (informal) to feel very sad

Dump·ster /'dʌmpstɚ/ *n.* [C] (trademark) a large metal container used for holding waste

'dump truck *n.* [C] a vehicle with a large open container at the back that can pour sand, soil, etc. onto the ground

dump·y /'dʌmpi/ *adj.* (informal) short and fat: *a dumpy little man*

dunce /dʌns/ *n.* [C] (informal) someone who is slow at learning things

dune /dun/ *n.* [C] EARTH SCIENCES a hill made of sand near the ocean or in the desert → *see picture on page A24*

dung /dʌŋ/ *n.* [U] solid waste from animals, especially from large animals

dun·geon /'dʌndʒən/ *n.* [C] a prison under the ground, used in past times [ORIGIN: 1300—1400 Old French *donjon* "central part of a castle," from Latin *dominus* "lord"]

dunk /dʌŋk/ *v.* [T] **1** to quickly put something that you are eating into coffee, milk, etc., and take it out again **2** to push someone under water for a short time as a joke **3** to jump up toward the basket in a game of basketball and throw the ball down into it —**dunk** *n.* [C]

dun·no /də'noʊ/ **I dunno** a way of writing "I do not know," used to show how people sound when they speak

du·o /'duoʊ/ *n.* (plural **duos**) [C] two people who do something together, especially play music or sing

du·o·de·num /,duə'dinəm, du'ɑdn-əm/ *n.* [C] BIOLOGY the beginning part of your SMALL INTESTINE

dupe /dup/ *v.* [T] to trick or deceive someone: *People were* ***duped into*** *buying worthless insurance.* —**dupe** *n.* [C]

du·plex /'duplɛks/ *n.* [C] a type of house that is divided so that it has two separate homes in it → HOUSE¹

du·pli·cate¹ /'dupləkɪt/ *n.* [C] an exact copy of something that you can use in the same way: *a duplicate of the front door key* [ORIGIN: 1400—1500 Latin *duplicatus*, past participle of *duplicare* "to double"] —**duplicate** *adj.*: *a duplicate key*

du·pli·cate² /'duplə,keɪt/ *v.* [T] **1** to copy something exactly: *Duplicate the letter, just changing the addresses.*

> THESAURUS **copy, reproduce, replicate, photocopy, Xerox, forge, pirate** → COPY²

2 to have a situation in which something is done twice, in a way that is not necessary: *To avoid duplicating each other's work, each person should have a specific job to do.* —**duplication** /,duplə'keɪʃən/ *n.* [U]

du·plic·i·ty /du'plɪsəṭi/ *n.* [U] (formal) dishonest behavior that is intended to deceive someone

dur·a·ble /'dʊrəbəl/ *adj.* **1** staying in good condition for a long time: *durable materials* **2** (formal) continuing for a long time: *a durable peace* —**durability** /,dʊrə'bɪləṭi/ *n.* [U]

du·ra·tion /dʊ'reɪʃən/ (Ac) *n.* [U] (formal) the length of time that something continues: *Food was rationed* ***for the duration of*** *the war.*

du·ress /dʊ'rɛs/ *n.* (formal) **under duress** as a result of using illegal or unfair threats: *Her confession was made under duress.*

dur·ing /'dʊrɪŋ/ *prep.* **1** all through a particular period of time: *These animals sleep during the day.*

> USAGE
> **During** is followed by a particular period of time and is used to say when something happens: *During the summer, she worked as a lifeguard.* **For** is followed by words describing a length of time and is used to say how long something continues: *I lived in Chicago for two years.*

2 at some point in a period of time: *Henry died during the night.* [ORIGIN: 1300—1400 *dure* "to continue in existence" (13—19 centuries), from Old French *durer*, from Latin *durare*]

dusk /dʌsk/ *n.* [U] the time before it gets dark, when the sky is becoming less bright [ORIGIN: Old English *dox*]

D

dust¹ /dʌst/ *n.* [U] dry powder that consists of extremely small pieces of dirt, sand, etc.: *The truck drove off in a* ***cloud of dust***. | *The piano was covered* ***with/in dust***. [ORIGIN: Old English]

dust² *v.* **1** [I,T] to clean the dust from something: *I just dusted the living room.* | *He got to his feet and* ***dusted himself off***.

> THESAURUS **clean, do the housework, polish, vacuum, sweep (up), scrub, mop** → CLEAN²

2 [T] to cover something with a fine powder: *Lightly dust the cakes with sugar.*

dust sth ↔ **off** *phr. v.* to remove something such as dust or dirt from a surface, using a dry cloth or your hand

'dust ,jacket *n.* [C] a paper cover that fits over the hard cover of a book

dust·pan /'dʌstpæn/ *n.* [C] a flat container with a handle, that you use with a brush to remove dust and waste from the floor

dust·y /'dʌsti/ *adj.* covered or filled with dust: *a dusty room*

> THESAURUS **dirty, filthy, muddy, greasy, grimy, soiled, polluted** → DIRTY¹

Dutch¹ /dʌtʃ/ *adj.* **1** relating to or coming from the Netherlands **2** relating to the Dutch language

Dutch² *n.* **1** [U] the language used in the Netherlands **2 the Dutch** [plural] the people of the Netherlands

du·ti·ful /'duṭɪfəl/ *adj.* doing what you are expected to do and behaving in a loyal way: *a dutiful son* —**dutifully** *adv.*

du·ty /'duṭi/ *n.* (plural **duties**) **1** [C,U] something that you have to do because it is morally or legally right: ***It is our duty to*** *speak out against injustice.* | *Parents* ***have a duty to*** *protect their children.* | *jury duty* **2** [C,U] something that you have to do because it is part of your job: *Soldiers are expected to* ***do their duty***. | *Please* ***report for duty*** *tomorrow morning.* | *his duties at the airport* **3 be on/off duty** to be working or not working at a particular time: *Which nurse was on duty last night?* **4** [C] a tax you pay on something, especially on goods you bought in another country

ˌduty-ˈfree *adj.* duty-free goods can be brought into a country without paying tax on them —**duty-free** *adv.*

DVD *n.* [C] **digital versatile disc** *or* **digital video disc** a type of CD that can store large amounts of sound, VIDEO, and information ➔ *see picture on page A19*

COLLOCATIONS

get/rent a DVD
watch a DVD
fast forward a DVD – to press a button to go forward to a later part
pause a DVD – to stop the DVD for a short time

D

DVˈD ˌplayer *n.* [C] a piece of equipment for playing DVDs ➔ *see picture on page A19*

dwarf[1] /dwɔrf/ *n.* [C] **1** an imaginary creature that looks like a small man: *Snow White and the Seven Dwarfs* **2** a person, animal, or plant that does not grow to the normal height

dwarf[2] *v.* [T] to be so big that other things seem very small: *The church is dwarfed by the surrounding buildings.*

ˌdwarf ˈplanet *n.* [C] SCIENCE an object in space like a small PLANET that has a round shape and that goes around the Sun, but whose GRAVITY is not strong enough to attract all the small objects near it, so that the area around it is not clear. Pluto is a dwarf planet.

dweeb /dwib/ *n.* [C] (slang) a weak, slightly strange person who is not popular or fashionable

dwell /dwɛl/ *v.* (past tense and past participle **dwelled** *or* **dwelt** /dwɛlt/) [I] (literary) to live in a particular place

dwell on/upon sth *phr. v.* to think or talk for too long about something, especially something unpleasant: *Quit dwelling on the past.*

dwell·er /ˈdwɛlɚ/ *n.* **city/town/cave dweller etc.** a person or animal that lives in a city, town, etc.

dwell·ing /ˈdwɛlɪŋ/ *n.* [C] (formal) a house, apartment, etc. where people live

THESAURUS **home, house, place, residence, abode** ➔ HOME[1]

dwelt /dwɛlt/ *v.* a past tense and past participle of DWELL

dwin·dle /ˈdwɪndl/ *v.* [I] to gradually become fewer or smaller: *Their ten-point lead has* ***dwindled*** *now* ***to*** *only four points.* —**dwindling** *adj.*

THESAURUS **decrease, go down, drop, fall, plummet, diminish, decline** ➔ DECREASE[1]

dye[1] /daɪ/ *n.* [C,U] a substance you use to change the color of your hair, clothes, etc.

dye[2] *v.* [T] to give something a different color using a dye: *Brian dyed his hair green.*

ˌdyed-in-the-ˈwool *adj.* having strong beliefs or opinions that will never change: *a dyed-in-the-wool Republican*

dy·ing /ˈdaɪ-ɪŋ/ *v.* the present participle of DIE

dy·nam·ic /daɪˈnæmɪk/ (Ac) *adj.* **1** interesting, exciting, and full of energy and determination to succeed: *She is a dynamic young woman with a lot of ambition.*

THESAURUS **energetic, vigorous, full of energy, hyperactive, tireless, lively, vital** ➔ ENERGETIC

2 continuously moving or changing: *a dynamic process* **3** PHYSICS relating to a force or power that causes movement: *The dynamic pressure of the fluid is caused by its motion.* [ORIGIN: 1800—1900 French *dynamique*, from Greek *dynamikos* "powerful"]

dy·nam·ics /daɪˈnæmɪks/ (Ac) *n.* [U] **1** the way in which systems or people behave, react, and affect each other: *family dynamics* | *the* ***dynamics of*** *power in large businesses* **2** PHYSICS the science that studies the movement of objects and the forces related to movement

dy·na·mism /ˈdaɪnəˌmɪzəm/ *n.* [U] energy and determination to succeed

dy·na·mite[1] /ˈdaɪnəˌmaɪt/ *n.* [U] a powerful explosive

dynamite[2] *v.* [T] to damage or destroy something with dynamite

dy·na·mo /ˈdaɪnəˌmoʊ/ *n.* (plural **dynamos**) [C] **1** (informal) someone who has a lot of energy and is very excited about what s/he does **2** PHYSICS a machine that changes some other form of power into electricity

dy·nas·ty /ˈdaɪnəsti/ *n.* (plural **dynasties**) [C] a family of kings or other rulers who have ruled a country for a long time, or the period of time during which this family rules: *the Ming dynasty* [ORIGIN: 1300—1400 Late Latin *dynastia*, from Greek *dynastes* "lord"] —**dynastic** /daɪˈnæstɪk/ *adj.*

dys·en·ter·y /ˈdɪsənˌtɛri/ *n.* [U] BIOLOGY a serious disease of the BOWELS that makes someone pass much more waste than usual

dys·func·tion·al /dɪsˈfʌŋkʃənəl/ *adj.* not working normally or not showing normal social behavior: *a dysfunctional family*

dys·lex·i·a /dɪsˈlɛksiə/ *n.* [U] a condition that makes it difficult for someone to learn to read or write because s/he cannot recognize or understand written words —**dyslexic** /dɪsˈlɛksɪk/ *adj.*

E, e /i/ the fifth letter of the English alphabet

E[1] /i/ *n.* [C,U] **1** ENG. LANG. ARTS the third note in the musical SCALE of C, or the musical KEY based on this note **2** (slang) the illegal drug ECSTASY

E[2], E. the written abbreviation of EAST or EASTERN

each[1] /itʃ/ *determiner, pron.* **1** every one of two or more things or people, considered separately: *Each student will be given a book.* | *We watched as* ***each of*** *the children performed a dance.*

USAGE

Each, **every**, and **all** are all used to talk about every person or thing in a group.
When you are considering them separately, use **each** or **every** with a singular noun: *Each/Every room has a shower.*
When you are considering them together, use **all** with a plural noun: *You answered all the questions correctly.*

2 each and every used in order to emphasize that you are talking about every person or thing in a group: *This will affect each and every one of us.*

each[2] *adv.* for or to every one: *The tickets are $5 each.* | *You can have two cookies each.*

each 'other *pron.* used in order to show that each of two or more people does something to the other or others: *Susan and Robert kissed each other.* | *They played with each other all morning.* | *It's normal for people to ignore each other in an elevator.*

ea·ger /'igɚ/ *adj.* **1** having a strong desire to do something or a strong interest in something: *I've been* ***eager to*** *meet you.* | *a young woman* ***eager for*** *success* | *hundreds of eager fans*

THESAURUS **enthusiastic, passionate, ardent, zealous, fanatical** → ENTHUSIASTIC

2 eager to please willing to do what people want [ORIGIN: 1200—1300 Old French *aigre*, from Latin *acer* "sharp"] **—eagerly** *adv.* **—eagerness** *n.* [U]

ea·gle /'igəl/ *n.* [C] a large wild bird, with a beak like a hook, that eats small animals, birds, etc. [ORIGIN: 1300—1400 Old French *aigle*, from Latin *aquila*]

ear /ɪr/ *n.* **1** [C] one of the two parts of your body that you hear with: *She got her ears pierced.* | *Mark whispered something in her ear.* → *see picture on page A16* **2** [U] the ability to hear, recognize, or copy sounds, especially in music and languages: *Joel* ***has a good ear for*** *music.* **3** [C] the top part of plants, that produces grain: *an ear of corn* **4 go in one ear and out the other** (informal) to be heard and then forgotten immediately **5 be all ears** (informal) to be very interested in listening to someone: *Go ahead, I'm all ears.* **6 be up to your ears in sth** (informal) to be very busy with something: *I'm up to my ears in work.* **7 smile/grin from ear to ear** to smile in a very happy way [ORIGIN: (1) Old English *eare*] → **play it by ear** *at* PLAY[1], **play sth by ear** *at* PLAY[1], **wet behind the ears** *at* WET[1]

ear·drum /'ɪrdrʌm/ *n.* [C] a tight thin MEMBRANE (=layer like skin) over the inside of your ear that allows you to hear sound

ear·lobe /'ɪrloʊb/ *n.* [C] the soft piece of flesh at the bottom of your ear

ear·ly[1] /'ɚli/ *adj.* **1** in the first part of a period of time, event, or process (ANT) **late**: *She woke in the early morning.* | *a man in his early twenties* | *George Gershwin's early musical compositions* **2** before the usual or expected time (ANT) **late**: *The train was ten minutes early.* | *I was a few minutes* ***early for*** *my appointment.* **3** existing before other people, events, machines, etc. of the same kind (ANT) **late**: *early settlers in New England* **4 the early days** the time when something had just started to be done or to exist: *the early days of television* | *the early days of his presidency* **5 at an early age** when someone is very young: *He was orphaned at an early age.* **6 at the earliest** used in order to say that a particular time is the soonest that something can happen: *He'll arrive on Monday at the earliest.* **7 the early hours** the time between MIDNIGHT and morning **8 early bird** someone who gets up early or arrives early [ORIGIN: Old English *ærlice*, from *ær* "early, soon"]

early[2] *adv.* **1** before the usual, arranged, or expected time (ANT) **late**: *Arrive early if you want a good seat.* **2** near the beginning of a period of time, an event, a process, etc. (ANT) **late**: *These flowers were planted early in the spring.* | *I'll have to leave early.* **3 early on** near the beginning of an event, relationship, process, etc.: *I realized early on that it wasn't going to work.*

ear·mark /'ɪrmɑrk/ *v.* [T] to decide that something will be used for a particular purpose: *funds that are* ***earmarked for*** *highway repairs*

ear·muffs /'ɪrmʌfs/ *n.* [plural] two pieces of material attached to the ends of a band, that you wear to keep your ears warm

earn /ɚn/ *v.* [T] **1** to get money for the work you do: *Alan earns $40,000 a year.* | *I'd like to* ***earn*** *some extra* ***money.*** | *She* ***earns a living*** (=gets the money for the things she needs) *as a teacher.*

THESAURUS

make – to earn or get money: *Ashley makes a little money by babysitting.*
get – to receive money for doing work or selling something: *How much do you get an hour?*
be/get paid – to be given money for doing a job: *I get paid monthly.*
gross – to earn an amount as a total amount, before tax has been taken away: *The movie grossed 18 million dollars in its first weekend.*
net – to earn a particular amount of money after paying taxes: *She netted only $300 for a rug that took her 150 hours to weave.*

E

2 to make a profit from business, or from putting money in a bank, lending it, etc.: *The movie earned $7 million during the opening weekend.* | *I* ***earned*** *$5,000* ***from*** *my investments last year.* **3** to get something that you deserve or have worked for: *Amelia Earhart had earned the respect of the male pilots.* | *He earned a degree in history at Columbia.*

ear·nest¹ /ˈɚnɪst/ *adj.* serious and sincere —**earnestly** *adv.* —**earnestness** *n.* [U]

earnest² *n.* **1 in earnest** happening more seriously or with greater effort than before: *Training begins in earnest on Monday.* **2 be in earnest** to be serious about what you are saying: *Are you sure he was in earnest?*

earn·ings /ˈɚnɪŋz/ *n.* [plural] **1** the money that you earn by working

THESAURUS **pay, income, salary, wages, bonus, remuneration** → PAY²

2 the profit that a company makes

ear·phones /ˈɪrfoʊnz/ *n.* [plural] electrical equipment that you put over or into your ears to listen to a radio, CD player, etc.

ear·plug /ˈɪrplʌg/ *n.* [C usually plural] a small piece of rubber that you put into your ear to keep out noise or water

ear·ring /ˈɪrɪŋ/ *n.* [C usually plural] a piece of jewelry that you fasten to your ear → *see picture at* JEWELRY

ear·shot /ˈɪrʃɑt/ *n.* **within earshot/out of earshot** near enough or not near enough to hear what someone is saying

ˈear-ˌsplitting *adj.* very loud: *an ear-splitting scream*

THESAURUS **loud, noisy, rowdy, thunderous, deafening, shrill, raucous, resounding, sonorous** → LOUD¹

earth /ɚθ/ *n.* **1** *also* **(the) Earth** EARTH SCIENCES the PLANET that we live on, which is third from the Sun: *The Earth moves around the Sun.* | *the return to Earth after landing on the moon* | *Oil is found below the Earth's surface.* | *the most beautiful woman* ***on earth*** → *see picture at* SOLAR SYSTEM

THESAURUS

Earth – the planet we live on: *the origin of life on Earth.*
world – the planet we live on, considered as a place where there are people and countries, mountains and oceans, etc.: *It's one of the largest countries in the world.*
You can use **Earth** to mean "the world": *It's the highest mountain on Earth.* | *It's the highest mountain in the world.*
When you compare the Earth's surface to the ocean, use **land**: *After weeks at sea, the sailors saw land.*
When you compare the Earth's surface to the sky, use **Earth**: *The space shuttle returned to Earth safely.*

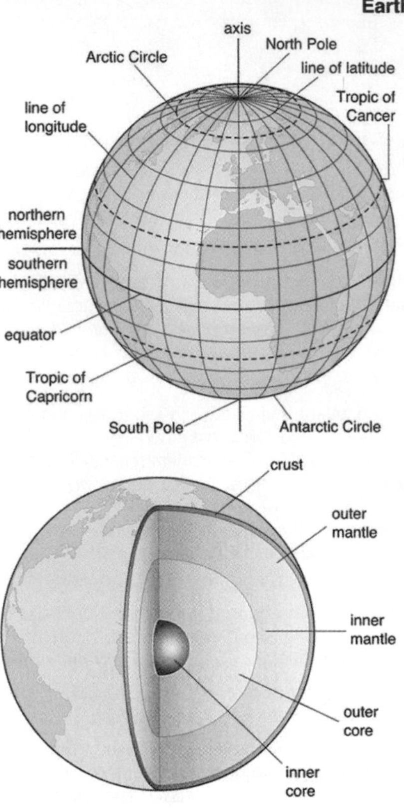

2 [U] the substance that plants, trees, etc. grow in (SYN) **dirt, soil**: *footprints in the wet earth*

THESAURUS **ground, floor, land, soil** → GROUND¹

3 what/why/how etc. on earth...? (spoken) said when you are asking a question when you are very surprised or annoyed: *What on earth did you do to your hair?* [ORIGIN: Old English *eorthe*] → DOWN-TO-EARTH

earth·ly /ˈɚθli/ *adj.* **1** (literary) relating to life on Earth rather than in heaven: *all my earthly possessions* **2 no earthly reason/use/chance etc.** no reason, use, etc. at all

earth·quake /ˈɚθkweɪk/ *n.* [C] EARTH SCIENCES a sudden shaking of the Earth's surface that often causes a lot of damage

ˌearth ˈscience *n.* [C] a science such as GEOLOGY or GEOGRAPHY, that involves studying the physical structure and development of the Earth

ˈearth-ˌshattering *also* **ˈearth-ˌshaking** *adj.* surprising or shocking and very important

earth·worm /ˈɚθwɚm/ *n.* [C] a WORM

earth·y /ˈɚθi/ *adj.* **1** talking about life, sex, and the human body in an honest and direct way: *an* *earthy sense of humor* **2** tasting, smelling, or looking like earth or soil: *mushrooms with an earthy flavor* —**earthiness** *n.* [U]

ease[1] /iz/ *n.* **1 with ease** if you do something with ease, it is very easy for you to do it: *They won with ease.* **2 at ease a)** feeling comfortable and confident: *She tried to make the new students **feel at ease**. | She felt completely **at ease with** Barry. | You always look **ill at ease** (=not relaxed) in a suit. | Miguel's smile **put her at ease**.* **b)** (spoken) used in order to tell soldiers to stand in a relaxed way with their feet apart **3 ease of use/access/repair etc.** the quality of being easy to use, etc.: *The software's ease of use is an important selling point.* **4** [U] the ability to feel or behave in a natural or relaxed way: *He had a natural ease, which made him very popular.*

ease[2] *v.* **1** [I,T] to make something less severe or difficult, or to become less severe or difficult: *He was given drugs to ease the pain. | Tensions in the region have eased slightly.*

THESAURUS **relieve, lessen, soothe, alleviate, palliate** → REDUCE

2 [T] to move something or someone slowly and carefully into another place: ***Ease** the patient **onto/out of** the bed.*

ease up *phr. v.* **1** *also* **ease off** if something, especially something that annoys you, eases off or eases up, it becomes less or gets better: *The rain is starting to ease up.* **2** to work less hard or do something less often than before: *In the last quarter of the game, some of the players seemed to be easing up.*

ea·sel /ˈizəl/ *n.* [C] a frame that you put a painting on while you paint it [ORIGIN: 1500—1600 Dutch *ezel* "donkey;" because an easel carries a painting as a donkey carries a person]

eas·i·ly /ˈizəli/ *adv.* **1** without difficulty: *They won easily. | The instructions can be easily understood.* **2** without doubt SYN **definitely**: *She is easily the most intelligent girl in the class.* **3** used in order to say that something is possible or very likely: *The first signs of the disease can easily be overlooked.*

east[1], **East** /ist/ *n.* [singular, U] **1** the direction from which the Sun rises: *Which way is east?* → *see picture at* NORTH[1] **2 the east** the eastern part of a country, state, etc.: *Rain will spread **to the east** later today. | the **east of** Texas* **3 the East a)** the part of the U.S. east of the Mississippi River, especially the states north of Washington, D.C.: *He was born in the East but now lives in California.* **b)** the countries in Asia, especially China, Japan, and Korea **c)** the countries in the eastern part of Europe, especially those that had Communist governments [ORIGIN: Old English]

USAGE

Use **north/south/east/west of sth** in order to describe where a place is in relation to another place: *Chicago is south of Milwaukee.*

Use **in the north/south/east/west of sth** in order to say which part of a place you are talking about: *The mountains are in the west of the country*

Use **northern, southern, eastern, western** with the name of a place: *She grew up in northern Ontario.*

Don't say "in the north of Ontario."

east[2] *adj.* **1** in, to, or facing east: *12 miles **east of** Portland | the east coast of the island* **2 east wind** a wind coming from the east

east[3] *adv.* **1** toward the east: *Go east on I-80 to Omaha. | The window faces east.* **2 back East** in or to the eastern part of the U.S.: *He went to college back East.*

east·bound /ˈistbaʊnd/ *adj.* traveling or leading toward the east: *eastbound traffic | the eastbound lanes of the freeway*

ˌEast ˈCoast *n.* **the East Coast** the part of the U.S. that is next to the Atlantic Ocean, especially the states north of Washington, D.C.

Eas·ter /ˈistɚ/ *n.* **1** a holiday on a Sunday in March or April when Christians celebrate the death of Christ and his return to life: *Easter Sunday* **2** the period of time just before and after this day: *We went skiing in Vermont **at Easter**.* [ORIGIN: from Old English *eastre*]

ˌEaster ˈBunny *n.* **the Easter Bunny** an imaginary rabbit that children believe brings colored eggs and chocolate at Easter

ˈEaster egg *n.* [C] an egg that has been colored and decorated

east·er·ly /ˈistɚli/ *adj.* **1** in or toward the east: *sailing in an easterly direction* **2** easterly winds come from the east

east·ern /ˈistɚn/ *adj.* **1** in or from the east part of an area, country, state, etc.: *eastern Oregon* **2 Eastern** in or from the countries in Asia, especially China, Japan, and Korea: *Eastern religions* **3** in or from the countries in the eastern part of Europe, especially those that used to have Communist governments → see USAGE box at EAST[1]

east·ern·er, Easterner /ˈistɚnɚ/ *n.* [C] someone who comes from the eastern part of a country or the eastern HEMISPHERE

ˌEastern ˈEurope *n.* the eastern part of Europe, including places such as Poland and part of Russia —**Eastern European** *adj.*

east·ern·most /ˈistɚnˌmoust/ *adj.* farthest east: *the easternmost part of the island*

east·ward /ˈistwɚd/ *adj., adv.* toward the east

eas·y[1] /ˈizi/ *adj.* **1** not difficult: *Making brownies is easy. | I want a book that's **easy to** read. | There must be an easier way to do this. | The programs are **easy for** teachers to use in the classroom. | Having some more people to help will definitely **make things** a lot **easier**.*

THESAURUS simple, straightforward, uncomplicated, facile ➔ SIMPLE

2 comfortable and not feeling worried or anxious: *I have a pretty easy life.* **3 easy way out** a way of doing something that ends a difficult situation, but that is not the best way **4 I'm easy** (spoken) used in order to show that you do not mind what choice is made: *"Do you want to go to the movies or stay in and watch a DVD?" "Oh, I'm easy."* **5 easy money** (informal) money that you do not have to work hard to get **6** (informal, disapproving) someone who is easy has a lot of sexual partners **7 eggs over easy** eggs cooked on a hot surface and turned over quickly before serving, so that the YOLKS (=yellow part) are not completely cooked [ORIGIN: 1100—1200 Old French *aisié*, from *aise* "comfort"]

E

easy² *adv.* **1 take it easy a)** to relax and not do very much: *The doctor told him to take it easy when he got home.* **b)** (spoken) used in order to tell someone to become less upset or angry **2 go easy on/with sth** (informal) to not use too much of something: *Go easy on the salt; it's not good for you.* **3 go easy on sb** (informal) to be more gentle and less strict or angry with someone: *Go easy on Peter – he's having a hard time at school.* **4 rest/sleep easy** to be able to relax because you are not worried or anxious: *I won't rest easy until I know she's safe.* **5 easier said than done** (spoken) used when it would be difficult to actually do what someone has suggested: *I should just tell her to go away, but that's easier said than done.* **6 easy does it** (spoken) used in order to tell someone to be careful, especially when s/he is moving something

'easy chair *n.* [C] a large comfortable chair

eas·y·go·ing /ˌizi'goʊɪŋ◂/ *adj.* not easily worried or annoyed: *Phil's pretty easygoing.*

THESAURUS calm, relaxed, laid-back, mellow, cool, placid, serene ➔ CALM²

ˌeasy 'listening *n.* [U] music that is relaxing to listen to

eat /it/ *v.* (past tense **ate** /eɪt/, past participle **eaten** /'it˺n/) **1** [I,T] to put food in your mouth and swallow it: *Paula ate a sandwich.* | *Jimmy chatted happily as he ate.* | *Do you and Kevin want* ***something to eat****?* | *Tom sat at the table,* ***eating breakfast/lunch/dinner****.* | *You need to exercise,* ***eat right*** (=eat healthy food)*, and get plenty of rest.* | *I haven't had a* ***bite to eat*** (=some food) *all day!*

THESAURUS
devour (formal), gobble up (informal), wolf down (informal) – to eat something very quickly: *He devoured the rest of the cake.* | *She wolfed down a hamburger.*
nibble (on) – to take small bites of something and eat only a little bit of it: *Sarah nibbled on a cookie and sipped her coffee.*
pick at – to eat only a little bit of your food because you are not hungry: *He only picked at his dinner.*
ingest (formal) – to eat or swallow something: *The drug produces an unpleasant reaction if the patient then ingests alcohol.*
be dieting/be on a diet – to eat less than normal in order to become thinner: *No cake for me, thanks – I'm on a diet.* ➔ DRINK²

2 [I] to have a meal: *What time do we eat?* | *We can't afford to eat at restaurants very often.* **3 eat your words** (informal) to admit that what you said was wrong **4** [T] *also* **eat up** (spoken) to use all of something until it is gone: *That car of mine just eats up money.* [ORIGIN: Old English *etan*]

eat sth ↔ **away, eat away at** sth *phr. v.* to gradually remove, reduce, or destroy something: *Rust had eaten away at the metal frame.*

eat into sth *phr. v.* **1** to gradually reduce the amount of time, money, etc. that is available: *Unexpected car expenses are really eating into our savings.* **2** to damage or destroy something: *Acid has eaten into the surface of the metal.*

eat out *phr. v.* to eat in a restaurant: *Do you eat out a lot?*

eat (sth ↔) **up** *phr. v.* (spoken) to eat all of something: *Come on, Kaylee, eat up!* | *I told her to eat up her breakfast.*

eat·er /'iṭɚ/ *n.* **big/light/fussy etc. eater** someone who eats a lot, not much, only particular things, etc.

eat·er·y /'iṭəri/ *n.* (plural **eateries**) [C] a restaurant, especially an informal one

'eating disˌorder *n.* [C] a medical condition in which you do not eat normal amounts of food or do not eat regularly ➔ ANOREXIA, BULIMIA

eaves /ivz/ *n.* [plural] the edges of a roof that stick out beyond the walls

eaves·drop /'ivzdrɑp/ *v.* (**eavesdropped**, **eavesdropping**) [I] to listen secretly to other people's conversations ➔ OVERHEAR: *Her sister had been* ***eavesdropping on*** *our conversations.* [ORIGIN: 1600—1700 *eavesdropper* "someone who stands close to a wall, where rainwater drops from the eaves, in order to listen secretly"] —**eavesdropper** *n.* [C]

ebb¹ /ɛb/ *n.* **1 ebb and flow** a situation or state in which something decreases and increases in a type of pattern: *the ebb and flow of his popularity* **2 be at a low ebb** to be in a bad state or condition: *By March 1933, the economy was at its lowest ebb.* **3** [singular, U] EARTH SCIENCES an ebb tide ➔ FLOOD

ebb² *v.* [I] **1** *also* **ebb away** (literary) to gradually decrease: *His courage slowly ebbed away.* **2** EARTH SCIENCES if the TIDE ebbs, it flows away from the shore

'ebb tide *n.* [C] EARTH SCIENCES the flow of the ocean away from the shore, when the TIDE goes out ➔ FLOOD TIDE

eb·o·ny /'ɛbəni/ *n.* **1** [C,U] a tree with dark hard wood, or the wood itself **2** [U] (literary) a black color —**ebony** *adj.*

e·bul·lient /ɪ'bʌlyənt, ɪ'bʊl-/ *adj.* (formal) very happy and excited: *an ebullient live performance* —**ebullience** *n.* [U]

e-busi·ness /'i ˌbɪznɪs/ *n.* [U] IT E-COMMERCE

ec·cen·tric¹ /ɪk'sɛntrɪk/ *adj.* behaving in a way that is unusual and different from most people: *an eccentric professor* [ORIGIN: 1500—1600 Late Latin *eccentricus*, from Greek *ekkentros* "out of the center"] —**eccentricity** /ˌɛksɛn'trɪsəṭi/ *n.* [C,U]

THESAURUS **strange, funny, peculiar, curious, mysterious, odd, weird, bizarre** → STRANGE¹

eccentric² *n.* [C] someone who behaves in a way that is different from what is usual or socially accepted

ec·cle·si·as·ti·cal /ɪˌklizi'æstɪkəl/ *adj.* relating to the Christian church

ech·e·lon /'ɛʃəˌlɑn/ *n.* [C] a rank or level of authority in an organization, business, etc., or the people at that level

ech·o¹ /'ɛkoʊ/ *v.* (past tense and past participle **echoed**) **1** [I] if a sound echoes, it is heard again because it was made near something such as a wall or a hill: *voices echoing around the cave* **2** [I] if a place echoes, it is full of a sound: *The theater **echoed with** laughter.* **3** [T] to repeat what someone else has said, an idea, or an opinion: *This man's words echo the feelings of soldiers throughout history.*

ech·o² /'ɛkoʊ/ *n.* (plural **echoes**) [C] **1** a sound that you hear again because it was made near something such as a wall or a hill **2** something that is very similar to something that has happened or been said before: *The play has **echoes of** Chekhov.*

e·clec·tic /ɪ'klɛktɪk/ *adj.* including a mixture of many different things or people

e·clipse¹ /ɪ'klɪps/ *n.* [C] PHYSICS an occasion when you cannot see the Sun because the Moon is between the Sun and the Earth, or when you cannot see the Moon because it is covered by the Earth's shadow: *an **eclipse of** the Moon* [ORIGIN: 1200—1300 Old French, Greek *ekleipsis*, from *ekleipein* "to leave out, fail"]

eclipse² *v.* [T] **1** to become more powerful, famous, important, etc. than someone or something else, so that he, she, or it is no longer noticed: *The state of the economy has eclipsed every other issue in this election year.* **2** PHYSICS to make the sun or moon disappear in an eclipse

e·co·log·i·cal /ˌikə'lɑdʒɪkəl, ˌɛ-/ *adj.* **1** EARTH SCIENCES relating to the way that plants, animals, and people are connected to each other and to their environment: *The oil spill caused ecological problems.* **2** relating to making or keeping the environment healthy: *an ecological study* —**ecologically** *adv.*

e·col·o·gy /ɪ'kɑlədʒi/ *n.* [singular, U] EARTH SCIENCES the way in which plants, animals, and people are connected to each other and to their environment, or the study of this [ORIGIN: 1800—1900 Greek *oikos* "house, living place" + *-logia* "study"] —**ecologist** *n.* [C]

e-com·merce /'i ˌkɑmɚs/ *also* **e-business** *n.* [U] IT the practice of buying and selling things using the Internet

ec·o·nom·ic /ˌɛkə'nɑmɪk◂, ˌi-/ (Ac) *adj.* ECONOMICS relating to business, industry, and managing money: ***Economic growth** has been slow.* | *the country's economic system* | *Economic conditions have changed.*

ec·o·nom·i·cal /ˌɛkə'nɑmɪkəl, ˌi-/ (Ac) *adj.* using time, money, products, etc. without wasting any: *an economical way to produce energy* | *Smaller goods are more economical to transport than large, heavy goods.*

ec·o·nom·i·cally /ˌɛkə'nɑmɪkli, ˌi-/ *adv.* **1** ECONOMICS in a way that is related to systems of money, trade, or business: *economically depressed areas of the country* | *Economically, our city has never been stronger.* **2** in a way that uses money, goods, time, etc. without wasting any → EFFICIENTLY: *We need to produce food as economically as possible.*

ec·o·nom·ics /ˌɛkə'nɑmɪks, ˌi-/ (Ac) *n.* [U] ECONOMICS the study of the way in which money, goods, and services are produced and used: *One law of economics says that competition drives down prices.* | *market economics*

ˌeconomic 'sanctions *n.* [plural] ECONOMICS official orders or laws that stop trade, communication, etc. with another country, as a way of forcing its leaders to make political changes

eˌconomies of 'scale *n.* [plural] ECONOMICS the decrease in the cost of each product a company makes, which happens as the total number of products they make increases

e·con·o·mist /ɪ'kɑnəmɪst/ (Ac) *n.* [C] ECONOMICS someone who studies economics

e·con·o·mize /ɪ'kɑnəˌmaɪz/ *v.* [I] to reduce the amount of money, time, goods, etc. that you use

e·con·o·my¹ /ɪ'kɑnəmi/ (Ac) *n.* (plural **economies**) **1** [C] ECONOMICS the way that money, businesses, and products are organized in a particular country, area, etc.: *the growing economies of southeast Asia* | *The project will add 600 jobs to the **local economy*** (=in a particular town or city). | *the **global/world economy*** **2** [U] the careful use of money, time, products, etc. so that nothing is wasted: *For reasons of economy, the oil is cleaned and reused.* [ORIGIN: 1400—1500 French, Greek *oikonomia*, from *oikonomos* "manager of a house"]

economy² *adj.* **economy size/package etc.** the biggest container that a product is sold in

e'conomy ˌclass *also* **economy** *n.* [U] the cheapest way to travel on an airplane

e·co·sys·tem /'ikoʊˌsɪstəm/ *n.* [C] BIOLOGY all the animals and plants in a particular area, and the way in which they are connected to each other and to their environment

e·co·tour·ism /ˌikoʊˈtʊrɪzəm/ *n.* [U] the business of organizing vacations to areas where people can see the beauty of nature in a way that will not hurt the environment

ec·sta·sy /ˈɛkstəsi/ *n.* **1** [C,U] a feeling of extreme happiness: *I laughed **in** pure **ecstasy**.* **2 Ecstasy** [U] an illegal drug that gives a feeling of happiness and energy [ORIGIN: 1300—1400 Old French, Greek *ekstasis*, from *existanai* "to make mad"]

ec·stat·ic /ɪkˈstæt̬ɪk, ɛk-/ *adj.* feeling extremely happy and excited: *Luke is **ecstatic about** being accepted at Harvard.*

THESAURUS **happy, glad, pleased, content, delighted, thrilled, overjoyed, jubilant, elated** → HAPPY

E

ec·to·therm /ˈɛktoʊˌθɚm/ *n.* [C] BIOLOGY an animal that depends on the Sun or the heat from its environment to raise and control the temperature of its body. All animals except birds and MAMMALS are ectotherms. → ENDOTHERM

ec·u·men·i·cal /ˌɛkyəˈmɛnɪkəl/ *adj.* bringing together different Christian churches, or supporting this

ec·ze·ma /ˈɛksəmə, ˈɛgzəmə, ɪgˈzimə/ *n.* [U] BIOLOGY a condition in which skin becomes dry and red, and begins to ITCH

ed. the written abbreviation of EDUCATION

ed·dy /ˈɛdi/ *n.* (plural **eddies**) [C] a circular movement of water, wind, dust, etc. —**eddy** *v.* [I]

edge[1] /ɛdʒ/ *n.* [C] **1** the part of something that is farthest from the center: *the **edge of** the table* | *Bill sat **on the edge** of the bed.* | *cars parked **at the edge** of the street*

THESAURUS

border – the official line that separates two countries, states, or areas: *the border between Mexico and the United States*
boundary – the line that marks the edge of a surface, space, or area of land inside a country: *The Mississippi River forms a natural boundary between Tennessee and Arkansas.*
perimeter – the border around an area of land, an area, or a shape: *the fence around the perimeter of the school*
rim – the outside edge of something, especially something circular such as a glass: *There was lipstick on the rim of the cup.*
margin – the empty space at the side of a printed page: *I wrote some notes in the margins.*
hem – the edge of a piece of cloth that is turned over and sewed down, especially the lower edge of a skirt, pair of pants, etc.: *The hem of her dress was coming down.*
curb – the edge of the sidewalk, next to the street: *If the curb is painted red, you may not park next to it.*

2 the area beside a steep slope: *the edge of a cliff* **3** the thin sharp part of a tool used for cutting **4** an advantage in a competition, game, or fight: *Good service **gives** our company **an edge**.* | *American companies **have an edge over/on** their competition in this technology.* **5 be on edge** to feel nervous because you are expecting something bad to happen: *Rudy was on edge all night.* **6** a quality in someone's voice that makes it sound angry or not sympathetic **7 on the edge of sth** close to the point at which something different, especially something bad, will happen: *The country's economy is on the edge of collapse.* **8 on the edge of your seat** excited and interested: *a thriller that will keep you on the edge of your seat* [ORIGIN: Old English *ecg*] → CUTTING EDGE

edge[2] *v.* **1** [I,T] to move slowly and gradually, or to make something do this: *Robert **edged toward** the door.* | *We edged closer, trying to see.* **2** [I,T] to develop or increase slowly and gradually, or to make something do this: *The price of gasoline is **edging up**.* **3** [T] to put something on the edge or border of something else: *a tablecloth **edged with** lace*

edge sb ↔ **out** *phr. v.* to beat someone in an election, competition, etc. by a small amount: *He edged out Sorenson by fewer than 200 votes.*

edge·wise /ˈɛdʒwaɪz/ *adv.* **1 not get a word in edgewise** to not be able to say something in a conversation because someone else is talking too much **2** with the edge or thinnest part forward: *Slide the table in edgewise.*

edg·y /ˈɛdʒi/ *adj.* nervous and easy to upset

ed·i·ble /ˈɛdəbəl/ *adj.* something that is edible is safe or acceptable to eat (ANT) **inedible** [ORIGIN: 1600—1700 Late Latin *edibilis*, from Latin *edere* "to eat"]

e·dict /ˈidɪkt/ *n.* [C] (formal) an official public order made by someone in a position of power

ed·i·fice /ˈɛdəfɪs/ *n.* [C] (formal) a large building [ORIGIN: 1300—1400 French, Latin *aedificium*, from *aedificare* "to build a house"]

ed·it /ˈɛdɪt/ (Ac) *v.* [T] to prepare a book, movie, article, etc. for printing or broadcasting by removing mistakes, deciding what to include, etc.: *The magazine is written, edited, and published by students.* | *Editing documents is much easier on a computer.*

e·di·tion /ɪˈdɪʃən/ (Ac) *n.* [C] **1** the form that a book is printed in: *the new edition of this dictionary* **2** the copies of a book, newspaper, etc. that are produced and printed at the same time: *They published a limited edition of 2,000 copies.* | *The **first edition** of the book was published in 1836.* [ORIGIN: 1400—1500 Latin *editus*, past participle of *edere* "to give out, produce"]

ed·i·tor /ˈɛdət̬ɚ/ (Ac) *n.* [C] **1** the person who decides what should be included in a newspaper, magazine, etc.: *the managing editor of the Miami Herald* | *Mr. Murray is a former newspaper editor.* → NEWSPAPER **2** ENG. LANG. ARTS someone who prepares a book, movie, etc. for printing or broadcasting by deciding what to include and checking for any mistakes **3** IT a computer program that allows you to write and make changes to saved information —**editorial** /ˌɛdəˈtɔriəl/ *adj.*

ed·i·to·ri·al /ˌɛdəˈtɔriəl/ (Ac) *n.* [C] a piece of writing in a newspaper that gives the opinion of the writer rather than reporting facts: *The New York Times published an* ***editorial on*** (=about) *gun control laws.*

ed·u·cate /ˈɛdʒəˌkeɪt/ *v.* [T] to teach someone, especially in a school or college: *Most Americans are* ***educated in*** *public schools.* | *He was* ***educated at*** *Harvard.* | *a program to* ***educate*** *teenagers* ***about*** *contraception* [ORIGIN: 1400—1500 Latin, past participle of *educare* "to bring up, educate"] —**educator** *n.* [C]

ed·u·cat·ed /ˈɛdʒəˌkeɪtɪd/ *adj.* **1** having knowledge as a result of studying or being taught: ***well-educated*** *women* **2 educated guess** a guess that is likely to be correct because you know something about the subject

ed·u·ca·tion /ˌɛdʒəˈkeɪʃən/ *n.* **1** [singular, U] the process of learning in a school or other program of study: *They wanted their children to* ***get a*** *good* ***education.*** | *parents saving for their kids'* ***college education*** **2** [U] the institutions and people involved with teaching: *careers in education* | *funding for schools and* ***higher education*** (=colleges)

ed·u·ca·tion·al /ˌɛdʒəˈkeɪʃənəl/ *adj.* **1** relating to teaching and learning: *educational systems* **2** teaching you something that you did not know: *educational television* | *The games are educational.* —**educationally** *adv.*

ed·u·tain·ment /ˌɛdʒuˈteɪnmənt/ *n.* [U] movies, television programs, or computer SOFTWARE that both educate and entertain children

eel /il/ *n.* [C] a long thin fish that looks like a snake

ee·rie /ˈɪri/ *adj.* strange and frightening: *an eerie light* —**eerily** *adv.*

ef·face /ɪˈfeɪs/ *v.* [T] **1** (formal) to destroy or remove something so that it cannot be seen or noticed: *textbooks that efface certain incidents in the past*

> THESAURUS **remove, erase, expunge** → REMOVE

2 efface yourself (literary) to behave in a way that makes other people not notice you → SELF-EFFACING

ef·fect¹ /ɪˈfɛkt/ *n.* **1** [C,U] the way in which an event, action, or person changes someone or something → AFFECT: *the* ***effects of*** *a long illness* | *Her parents' divorce* ***had*** *a big* ***effect on*** *her.* | *One* ***side effect*** (=additional effect) *of the drug is drowsiness.* | *What parents do has a* ***profound/lasting/major effect*** *on children's lives.*

> THESAURUS **result, consequences, aftereffects, side effect, outcome, upshot, repercussions** → RESULT¹

2 put sth into effect to make a plan or idea happen: *The policy was put into effect in 2006.* **3 come/go into effect** to start officially: *The new tax laws come into effect January 1st.* **4 be in effect** to be being used: *The ban is already in effect.* **5 take effect** to start to have results, or to start being used: *The drug should take effect in about ten minutes.* **6 in effect** used when you are describing what the real situation is, instead of what it seems to be: *In effect, I'll be earning less than last year.* **7 effects** [plural] (formal) the things that someone owns (SYN) **belongings** → SPECIAL EFFECTS

effect² *v.* [T] (formal) to make something happen

ef·fec·tive /ɪˈfɛktɪv/ *adj.* **1** producing the result that was wanted or intended (ANT) **ineffective**: *an effective medicine for headaches* | *an effective way to teach reading* | *Bicycle helmets are* ***effective in*** *preventing some types of injuries.* **2 be/become effective** to be in use, or to start to be in use officially: *These prices* ***are effective from*** *April 1.* —**effectiveness** *n.* [U]

ef·fec·tive·ly /ɪˈfɛktɪvli/ *adv.* **1** in a way that produces the result you wanted: *The game helps children practice their times tables effectively.* **2** used in order to describe the real facts of a situation (SYN) **actually**: *Many poor people effectively do not have any health care.*

ef·fem·i·nate /ɪˈfɛmənɪt/ *adj.* a man or boy who is effeminate behaves like a woman or girl

ef·fer·ves·cent /ˌɛfɚˈvɛsənt/ *adj.* **1** a liquid that is effervescent has BUBBLEs of gas rising in it **2** someone who is effervescent is very active and happy —**effervescence** *n.* [U]

ef·fi·ca·cious /ˌɛfəˈkeɪʃəs◂/ *adj.* (formal) producing the result that was intended (SYN) **effective** —**efficaciously** *adv.* —**efficacy** /ˈɛfɪkəsi/ *n.* [U]

ef·fi·cient /ɪˈfɪʃənt/ *adj.* working well, quickly, and without wasting time, energy, or effort (ANT) **inefficient**: *an efficient use of space* | *She's very efficient.* [ORIGIN: 1300—1400 Latin, present participle of *efficere* "to cause to happen"] —**efficiency** *n.* [U]: *The company needs to improve the efficiency of its factories.* —**efficiently** *adv.*

> THESAURUS **organized, well-run, businesslike** → ORGANIZED

ef·fi·gy /ˈɛfədʒi/ *n.* (plural **effigies**) [C] a model of someone, especially one that is burned as a protest

ef·flu·ent /ˈɛfluənt/ *n.* [C,U] (formal) liquid waste

ef·fort /ˈɛfɚt/ *n.* **1** [U] the physical or mental energy needed to do something: *Kenny* ***put*** *a lot of* ***effort into*** *his report.* | *It* ***takes*** *very little* ***effort*** *to watch TV.* | *This dish takes time to prepare, but it's* ***worth the effort.*** **2** [C,U] an attempt to do something, especially something difficult: *The area has been restored* ***in an effort to*** *attract tourists.* | *Ken* ***made a*** *conscious* ***effort*** (=deliberate effort) *to avoid the same mistakes.* | *a famine relief effort*

ef·fort·less /ˈɛfɚtˀlɪs/ *adj.* done in a skillful way that seems easy: *Brad's effortless skiing* —**effortlessly** *adv.*

ef·front·er·y /ɪˈfrʌntəri/ *n.* [U] (old-fashioned) behavior that you think someone should be ashamed of, although s/he does not seem to be ashamed: *He* ***had the effrontery to*** *challenge his teacher!*

ef·ful·gent /ɪˈfʊldʒənt/ *adj.* (literary) beautiful and bright

ef·fu·sive /ɪˈfyusɪv/ *adj.* showing strong excited feelings: *effusive greetings* —**effusively** *adv.*

EFL *n.* [U] **English as a Foreign Language** the methods used for teaching English to people whose first language is not English, and who do not live in an English-speaking country

E

e.g. /ˌi ˈdʒi/ a written abbreviation that means "for example": *the Gulf States, e.g. Texas, Louisiana, and Mississippi*

e·gal·i·tar·i·an /ɪˌgæləˈtɛriən/ *adj.* believing that everyone should have the same rights and opportunities —**egalitarianism** *n.* [U]

egg¹ /ɛg/ *n.* [C] **1** a round object with a hard surface, that contains a baby bird, insect, snake, etc.: *a turtle* ***laying eggs*** *in the sand* | *Some of the* ***eggs*** *were* ***hatching*** (=breaking open to allow the baby out). ➔ *see picture on page A15* **2** an egg, especially from a chicken, used as food: *fried eggs* | *Joe dipped his toast in his* ***egg yolk*** (=the yellow part). | *Whisk the* ***egg whites*** (=white part) *until stiff.* **3** BIOLOGY a cell produced inside a female, that can combine with a SPERM (=male cell) to make a baby animal or person [ORIGIN: 1300—1400 Old Norse]

egg² *v.*

egg sb ↔ **on** *phr. v.* to encourage someone to do something, especially something s/he does not want to do or should not do

egg·plant /ˈɛgplænt/ *n.* [C,U] a large shiny dark purple fruit that is cooked and eaten as a vegetable ➔ *see picture at* VEGETABLE

egg·shell /ˈɛgʃɛl/ *n.* [C,U] the hard outside part of a bird or REPTILE's egg

e·go /ˈigoʊ/ *n.* (plural **egos**) [C] **1** the opinion that you have about yourself: *a player with a* ***big ego*** (=he thinks he is very good) **2 ego trip** (informal, disapproving) something that someone does for himself/herself because it makes him/her feel good or important

e·go·tism /ˈigəˌtɪzəm/ *also* **e·go·ism** /ˈigoʊˌɪzəm/ *n.* [U] the belief that you are more interesting or important than other people —**egotist** *n.* [C] —**egotistical** /ˌigəˈtɪstɪkəl/ *adj.*

e·gre·gious /ɪˈgridʒəs/ *adj.* (formal) an egregious ERROR (=mistake), failure, etc. is extremely bad and noticeable —**egregiously** *adv.*

eight /eɪt/ *number* **1** 8 **2** eight o'clock: *Dinner will be at eight.* **3** eight years old: *My cousin is eight.* [ORIGIN: Old English *eahta*]

eight·een /ˌeɪˈtin◂/ *number* 18 —**eighteenth** *number*

eighth /eɪtθ/ *number* **1** 8th **2** 1/8

eight·y /ˈeɪṭi/ *number* **1** 80 **2 the eighties a)** the years between 1980 and 1989 **b)** the numbers between 80 and 89, especially when used in measuring temperature **3 be in your eighties** to be between 80 and 89 years old: *He's* ***in*** *his* ***early/mid/late eighties.*** —**eightieth** /ˈeɪṭiɪθ/ *number*

ei·ther¹ /ˈiðɚ, ˈaɪ-/ *conjunction* used in order to begin a list of possibilities separated by "or": *There's either coffee or tea to drink.* | *Either she leaves, or I do!*

either² *determiner, pron.* **1** one or the other of two people or things: *Do you know* ***either of*** *these two women?* | *There's chocolate or vanilla – you can have either.* **2** used in order to show that a negative statement is true about both of two things or people: *I've lived in New York and Chicago, but I don't like either city very much.* **3 either side/end/hand etc.** both sides, ends, etc.: *He was standing there with a policeman* ***on either side*** *of him.* **4 either way** used to show that both of two things are true, possible, or likely: *You can go by train or plane, but either way it's expensive.* | *The vote could* ***go either way*** (=both results are possible).

GRAMMAR

either, either of

Either is used with a singular noun form and a singular verb: *I can meet you on Wednesday or Thursday – either day is good for me.*

Either of is used with a plural noun form or pronoun. In formal speech and writing, use a singular verb: *Has either of them called yet?* In informal speech and writing, you can use a plural verb: *Have either of them called yet?*

either ... or, neither ... nor

When you use these phrases in formal speech or writing, use a singular verb if the second noun is singular: *If either Doris or Meg calls, please take a message.* | *Neither she nor her husband want to live there.*

If the second noun is plural, use a plural verb: *If either my sister or my parents come, please let them in.*

either³ *adv.* **1** used in negative sentences to mean "also": *"I can't swim." "I can't either."* **2 me either** (spoken, nonstandard) used in order to say that a negative statement is also true about you: *"I don't like broccoli." "Me either."*

e·jac·u·late /ɪˈdʒækyəˌleɪt/ *v.* [I,T] when a male ejaculates, SPERM comes out of his PENIS —**ejaculation** /ɪˌdʒækyəˈleɪʃən/ *n.* [C,U]

e·ject /ɪˈdʒɛkt/ *v.* **1** [T] to make something come out of a machine by pressing a button: *Press the red button to eject the DVD.* **2** [T] to push or throw out with force: *the lava and ash ejected by the volcano* **3** [T] to make someone leave a place: *Both players were ejected from the game.* **4** [I] to jump out of an airplane that is going to crash [ORIGIN: 1400—1500 Latin *ejectus*, past participle of *eicere* "to throw out"] —**ejection** /ɪˈdʒɛkʃən/ *n.* [C,U]

eke /ik/ *v.*

eke sth ↔ **out** *phr. v.* **1** to make something such as food or money last a long time by carefully using only small amounts of it **2 eke out a living/an existence** to get just enough food or money to live on

e·lab·o·rate¹ /ɪˈlæbrɪt/ *adj.* having a lot of small details or parts that are connected together in a complicated way: *elaborate plans for the wedding* | *an elaborate design* —**elaborately** *adv.*

THESAURUS complicated, complex, convoluted, intricate → COMPLICATED

e·lab·o·rate² /ɪˈlæbəˌreɪt/ *v.* [I] to give more details about something you have said or written: *The spokesman would not **elaborate on** the investigation.* —**elaboration** /ɪˌlæbəˈreɪʃən/ *n.* [U]

e·lapse /ɪˈlæps/ *v.* [I] (formal) if a period of time elapses, it passes

e·las·tic /ɪˈlæstɪk/ *adj.* **1** made of elastic: *an elastic waistband* **2** material that is elastic can stretch and then go back to its normal length or size: *The ligaments around her joints are more elastic than normal.* **3** ECONOMICS if demand for a particular product or service is elastic, any change in the price of the product leads to a greater change in the amount sold (ANT) **inelastic** —**elastic** *n.* [U]

e·las·tic·i·ty /iˌlæˈstɪsət̬i, ˌilæ-/ *n.* [U] **1** the ability of an object or material to return to its normal shape or size after it has been stretched or pressed **2 elasticity of demand** ECONOMICS the degree to which a change in the price of something has an effect on the amount of it that is sold

e·lat·ed /ɪˈleɪt̬ɪd/ *adj.* [not before noun] extremely happy and excited —**elation** /ɪˈleɪʃən/ *n.* [U]

THESAURUS happy, glad, pleased, content, delighted, thrilled, overjoyed, ecstatic, jubilant → HAPPY

el·bow¹ /ˈɛlboʊ/ *n.* [C] **1** the joint where your arm bends → *see picture on page A16* **2 elbow room** (informal) enough space, so that you can move easily **3 elbow grease** (informal) hard physical effort, especially when cleaning something [ORIGIN: Old English *elboga*]

elbow² *v.* [T] to push someone with your elbows, especially in order to move past him/her: *She **elbowed her way through** the crowd.*

THESAURUS push, roll, poke, shove, nudge → PUSH¹

el·der¹ /ˈɛldɚ/ *adj.* the elder of two people, especially brothers and sisters, is the one who was born first: *My elder sister is a nurse.*

USAGE

Use **elder** to talk about the members of a family: *Nick is my elder brother.*
Use **older** to compare the age of people or things: *My sister is two years older than I am.*

elder² *n.* **1** [C usually plural] someone who is older than you are: *Young people should have respect for their elders.* **2** [C] an older person who is important and respected: *the town elders*

el·der·ly /ˈɛldɚli/ *adj.* **1** old, used in order to be polite: *an elderly woman with white hair* **2 the elderly** people who are old

el·dest /ˈɛldɪst/ *adj.* the eldest of a group of people, especially brothers and sisters, is the one who was born first: *My eldest daughter is 17.*

e·lect¹ /ɪˈlɛkt/ *v.* [T] **1** to choose someone for an official position by voting: *She was first **elected to** Congress in 1988.* | *What are the chances that a Democrat will be **elected president/governor/mayor**?* **2 elect to do sth** (formal) to choose to do something: *Hanley elected to take early retirement.* [ORIGIN: 1400—1500 Latin *electus*, past participle of *eligere* "to choose"]

elect² *adj.* **president-elect/senator-elect etc.** the person who has been elected but has not officially started his/her job

e·lec·tion /ɪˈlɛkʃən/ *n.* [C] an occasion when you vote in order to choose someone for an official position: *The election results are still coming in.* | *She **won** the **election** by a large margin.* | *the **national/local elections** on Tuesday* | *More people voted **in** this **election** than in previous years.* —**electoral** /ɪˈlɛktərəl/ *adj.* → GENERAL ELECTION

e·lec·tive¹ /ɪˈlɛktɪv/ *n.* [C] a subject that a student chooses to study, that is not one of the classes s/he must take

elective² *adj.* **1** an elective office, position, etc. is one for which there is an election **2** elective medical treatment is treatment that you choose to have

Eˌlectoral ˈCollege *n.* **the Electoral College** POLITICS an official group of people who meet to elect the U.S. President and Vice President. Each state sends a particular number of members to the Electoral College, and these members vote for the CANDIDATES who won the most votes in their state.

e·lec·tor·ate /ɪˈlɛktərɪt/ *n.* [singular] all the people who are allowed to vote in an election

e·lec·tric /ɪˈlɛktrɪk/ *adj.* **1** needing electricity in order to work: *an electric oven* | *an electric guitar*

USAGE

Use **electric** before the names of things that need electricity in order to work: *electric lights* | *an electric toothbrush*
Use **electrical** to talk about things that use or

produce electricity, or to refer to someone who works with electricity: *electrical goods* | *an electrical engineer*

2 making people feel very excited: *The atmosphere at the concert was electric.* [ORIGIN: 1600—1700 Modern Latin *electricus*, from Latin *electrum* "amber;" because electricity was first made by rubbing amber]

THESAURUS **exciting, thrilling, gripping, dramatic, exhilarating** ➔ EXCITING

e·lec·tri·cal /ɪˈlɛktrɪkəl/ *adj.* relating to or using electricity: *Solar panels change sunlight into electrical power.* | *electrical goods* ➔ see USAGE box at ELECTRIC

eˌlectrical poˈtential *n.* [U] PHYSICS the energy that is likely to be produced by something that produces electricity (SYN) **voltage**

E

eˌlectric ˈchair *n.* **the electric chair** a chair in which criminals are killed using electricity

e·lec·tri·cian /ɪˌlɛkˈtrɪʃən, i-/ *n.* [C] someone whose job is to fit and repair electrical equipment

e·lec·tric·i·ty /ɪˌlɛkˈtrɪsət̬i, i-/ *n.* [U] **1** PHYSICS the power that is carried by wires and used in order to provide heat or light, to make machines work, etc.: *houses that lack electricity or running water* | *Wind power is used to* ***generate electricity*** (=make electricity). **2** a feeling of excitement

e·lec·tri·fy /ɪˈlɛktrəˌfaɪ/ *v.* (**electrified, electrifies**) [T] **1** to make people feel very excited or interested: *His speech electrified the Democratic Convention.* **2** to make electricity available in a particular area —**electrified** *adj.* —**electrifying** *adj.*

e·lec·tro·chem·i·cal /ɪˌlɛktroʊˈkɛmɪkəl/ *adj.* CHEMISTRY relating to chemical changes caused by electricity, and the production of electricity as the result of a chemical reaction

e·lec·tro·cute /ɪˈlɛktrəˌkyut/ *v.* [T] to kill someone by passing electricity through his/her body —**electrocution** /ɪˌlɛktrəˈkyuʃən/ *n.* [U]

e·lec·trode /ɪˈlɛktroʊd/ *n.* [C] PHYSICS the point at which electricity enters or leaves something such as a BATTERY [ORIGIN: 1800—1900 *electro-* + Greek *hodos* "way, path"]

e·lec·trol·y·sis /ɪˌlɛkˈtrɑləsɪs/ *n.* [U] the process of using electricity to remove hair from your face, legs, etc.

e·lec·tro·lyte /ɪˈlɛktrəˌlaɪt/ *n.* [C] CHEMISTRY a liquid or solid substance that allows electricity to pass through it

e·lec·tro·mag·net /ɪˌlɛktroʊˈmægnɪt, ɪˈlɛktroʊˌmægnɪt/ *n.* [C] PHYSICS a type of MAGNET that usually consists of a piece of wire wound around some metal. The metal becomes MAGNETIC when an electric current is passed through the wire. —**electromagnetic** /ɪˌlɛktroʊmægˈnet̬ɪk/ *adj.*

e·lec·tron /ɪˈlɛktrɑn/ *n.* [C] PHYSICS a very small piece of matter that moves around the NUCLEUS (=central part) of an atom ➔ *see picture at* ATOM

e·lec·tron·ic /ɪˌlɛkˈtrɑnɪk/ *adj.* **1** electronic equipment, such as computers or televisions, uses electricity that has passed through computer CHIPS, TRANSISTORS, etc. **2** using electronic equipment: *electronic banking* —**electronically** *adv.*

e·lec·tron·ics /ɪˌlɛkˈtrɑnɪks/ *n.* [U] the study or industry of making electronic equipment, such as computers or televisions

e·lec·tro·va·lent bond /ɪˌlɛktroʊveɪlənt ˈbɑnd/ *n.* [C] CHEMISTRY a chemical BOND that is the result of atoms gaining and losing an ELECTRON, so that a negative ION and a positive ion are formed (SYN) **ionic bond**

el·e·gant /ˈɛləgənt/ *adj.* very beautiful and graceful: *a tall elegant woman* [ORIGIN: 1400—1500 French, Latin *elegans* "specially chosen as being of good quality"] —**elegance** *n.* [U] —**elegantly** *adv.*

el·e·gy /ˈɛlədʒi/ *n.* (plural **elegies**) [C] ENG. LANG. ARTS a sad poem or song, especially about someone who has died

el·e·ment /ˈɛləmənt/ (Ac) *n.* **1** [C] one part of a plan, system, piece of writing, etc.: *the two main* ***elements of*** *the bill* | *a* ***key/major/basic element*** *of his campaign* | *The trial is a central* ***element in*** *the novel.* **2 an element of danger/truth/risk etc.** a small amount of danger, truth, risk, etc.: *The movie is a fantasy, but there is still an element of truth in it.* **3** [C] CHEMISTRY a simple chemical substance such as oxygen or gold, that is made of only one type of atom ➔ COMPOUND: *The periodic table is a list of all the chemical elements.* **4 be in your element** to be in a situation that you enjoy a lot because you are good at it: *Joe's in his element when he steps out onto the football field.* **5 be out of your element** to be in a situation that makes you uncomfortable or unhappy because you are not good at it: *I felt completely out of my element studying French.* **6 the elements** [plural] the weather, especially bad weather: *A tent provided shelter from the elements.* **7** [C] MATH a number that is a single part of a mathematical set or MATRIX [ORIGIN: 1300—1400 Old French, Latin *elementum*]

el·e·men·tal /ˌɛləˈmɛnt̬əl/ *adj.* an elemental feeling is simple, basic, and strong

el·e·men·ta·ry /ˌɛləˈmɛntri, -ˈmɛnt̬əri/ *adj.* **1** relating to the first and easiest part of a subject: *elementary piano exercises* **2** simple or basic: *the elementary human need for food*

THESAURUS **basic, fundamental, essential, central, underlying** ➔ BASIC

3 relating to an elementary school

eleˈmentary ˌschool *n.* [C] a school in the U.S. for the first six or eight years of a child's education (SYN) **grade school**

el·e·phant /ˈɛləfənt/ *n.* [C] a very large gray animal with two TUSKS (=long curved teeth), big ears, and a TRUNK (=a long nose) that it can use to pick things up [ORIGIN: 1200—1300 Old French *oliphant*, from Greek *elephas* "elephant, ivory"]

el·e·vate /ˈɛləˌveɪt/ *v.* [T] (formal) **1** to make someone more important, or to make something better: *Sloane was* ***elevated to*** *captain.* **2** to raise someone or something to a higher position or level: *This drug tends to elevate body temperature.*

el·e·va·tion /ˌɛləˈveɪʃən/ *n.* **1** [C] a height above the level of the ocean: *The city of Boulder is at an* ***elevation of*** *5,400 feet.* **2** [U] (formal) the act of moving someone to a more important rank or position: *the judge's* ***elevation to*** *the Supreme Court* **3** [C,U] (formal) an increase in the quantity or level of something: *Elevation of blood pressure can cause headaches.*

el·e·va·tor /ˈɛləˌveɪtɚ/ *n.* [C] a machine in a building, that takes people from one level to another: *I decided to* ***take the elevator.***

e·lev·en /ɪˈlɛvən/ *number* **1** 11 **2** 11 o'clock: *an appointment at eleven* **3** 11 years old: *My son is eleven.* [ORIGIN: Old English *endleofan*]

e·lev·enth /ɪˈlɛvənθ/ *number* **1** 11th **2** 1/11

elf /ɛlf/ *n.* (plural **elves** /ɛlvz/) [C] a small imaginary person with pointed ears —**elfin** /ˈɛlfɪn/ *adj.*

e·lic·it /ɪˈlɪsɪt/ *v.* [T] (formal) to get information, a reaction, etc. from someone when this is difficult: *Short questions are more likely to* ***elicit a response.***

el·i·gi·ble /ˈɛlədʒəbəl/ *adj.* **1** able or allowed to do something: *You are* ***eligible to*** *vote at the age of 18.* | *Are you* ***eligible for*** *a loan?* **2** an eligible man or woman would be good to marry because s/he is rich, attractive, etc.: *an* ***eligible bachelor*** —**eligibility** /ˌɛlədʒəˈbɪləṭi/ *n.* [U]

e·lim·i·nate /ɪˈlɪməˌneɪt/ (Ac) *v.* [T] **1** to get rid of something completely: *a plan to eliminate all nuclear weapons* | *The aim is to* ***eliminate*** *the disease* ***from*** *the entire world.* **2 be eliminated** to be defeated in a sports competition, so that you can no longer take part in it [ORIGIN: 1500—1600 Latin *eliminatus*, past participle of *eliminare* "to put out of doors"]

e·lim·i·na·tion /ɪˌlɪməˈneɪʃən/ (Ac) *n.* [U] **1** the removal or destruction of something: *the* ***elimination of*** *250 jobs* **2 process of elimination** a way of finding out the answer to something by getting rid of other answers that are not correct until only one is left: *Try to solve the problem by a process of elimination.*

e·lite[1] /eɪˈlit, ɪ-/ *n.* [C] a small group of people who are powerful or important because they have money, knowledge, special skills, etc.: *the country's ruling elite*

e·lite[2] *adj.* [only before noun] an elite group contains the best, most skilled, or most experienced members of a larger group: *The competition is only open to an elite group of athletes.*

e·lit·ist /eɪˈliṭɪst, ɪ-/ *adj.* (disapproving) an elitist system, government, etc. is one in which a small group of people have much more power than other people —**elitism** *n.* [U]

elk /ɛlk/ *n.* (plural **elk** *or* **elks**) [C] a large DEER with a lot of hair around its neck

el·lipse /ɪˈlɪps/ *n.* [C] MATH a curved shape that is similar to a circle, but has two sides that are longer and flatter. It is formed by a PLANE (=flat shape) crossing completely through a CONE at an angle, so that the sum of the distances from any point on the curve to two fixed points inside the ellipse is always the same. → CONIC SECTION

el·lip·sis /ɪˈlɪpsɪs/ *n.* (plural **ellipses** /-siz/) **1** [C] ENG. LANG. ARTS the sign (...) used in writing, to show that some words have deliberately been left out of a sentence **2** [C,U] ENG. LANG. ARTS an occasion when words are deliberately left out of a sentence, though the meaning can still be understood

el·lip·ti·cal /ɪˈlɪptɪkəl/ *also* **el·lip·tic** /ɪˈlɪptɪk/ *adj.* shaped like a circle but with slightly flat sides (SYN) **oval**: *the elliptical orbit of the planets*

elm /ɛlm/ *n.* [C,U] a large tall tree with broad leaves, or the wood of this tree

El Niño /ɛl ˈninyoʊ/ *n.* EARTH SCIENCES a process in which the water on the surface of the Pacific Ocean near the western coast of South America becomes warmer than usual. This happens every 4 to 12 years and often results in unusual weather conditions that can cause severe damage to countries that have coasts on the Pacific Ocean.

e·lon·gat·ed /ɪˈlɔŋˌgeɪṭɪd/ *adj.* long and thin: *elongated shadows* —**elongate** *v.* [I,T]

e·lope /ɪˈloʊp/ *v.* [I] to go away secretly with someone to get married —**elopement** *n.* [C,U]

el·o·quent /ˈɛləkwənt/ *adj.* able to express ideas, opinions, or feelings clearly, in a way that influences other people: *Brennan's eloquent response* [ORIGIN: 1300—1400 French, Latin, present participle of *eloqui* "to speak out"] —**eloquently** *adv.* —**eloquence** *n.* [U]

else /ɛls/ *adv.* **1** in addition – used after words beginning with "any-," "no-," "some-," and after question words: *Clayton needs someone else to help him.* | *There's nothing else we can do.* | *What else can I get you?* **2** different – used after words beginning with "any-," "no-," "some-," and after question words: *Is there anything else to eat?* | *She was wearing someone else's coat* (=not her own coat). | *Well, what else can I do?* **3 or else** used when saying that there will be a bad result if someone does not do something: *Hurry up, or else you'll be late for school!* **4 if nothing else** used in order to say that there is one good quality or feature of something, even if there are no others: *If nothing else, the report shows that better facilities are needed.*

else·where /ˈɛlswɛr/ *adv.* in or to another place: *Most of the city's residents were born elsewhere.*

e·lu·ci·date /ɪˈlusəˌdeɪt/ *v.* [I,T] (formal) to explain very clearly something that is difficult to understand

THESAURUS explain, tell, go through sth, clarify → EXPLAIN

e·lude /ɪ'lud/ *v.* [T] **1** to avoid being found or caught by someone, especially by tricking him/her: *Jones eluded the police for six weeks.* **2** if something that you want eludes you, you do not find it or achieve it: *Success has eluded him so far.* **3** if a fact, someone's name, etc. eludes you, you cannot remember it

e·lu·sive /ɪ'lusɪv/ *adj.* **1** difficult to find: *an elusive animal* **2** difficult to achieve or understand: *Success has been elusive.* | *the poem's elusive meaning*

elves /ɛlvz/ *n.* the plural of ELF

'em /əm/ *pron.* (spoken, nonstandard) them: *Tell the kids I'll pick 'em up after school.*

E

e·ma·ci·at·ed /ɪ'meɪʃiˌeɪt̬ɪd/ *adj.* extremely thin because of illness or lack of food

THESAURUS thin, slim, slender, slight, skinny, lean, underweight, gaunt, anorexic, skeletal → THIN[1]

email, e-mail /'i meɪl/ *n.* **1** [U] **electronic mail** a system that allows you to send and receive messages by computer: *What's your **email address**?* | *A confirmation of your order will be sent **by/via email**.* → INTERNET **2** [C,U] a message that is sent using this system: *I got an email from her yesterday.* | *I haven't **checked** my **email** yet.*

COLLOCATIONS

You can **read**, **write**, **send**, and **receive** an **email**.
If you **check** your **email**, you look on your computer to see if you have received any.
If you **reply to** an **email**, you write an email to someone who has sent one to you.
If you get a **reply**, you receive an email from someone you have written an email to.
If you **forward** an **email**, you send an email that you have received to another person.
If you **send an attachment**, you send someone a document which can be opened and read when s/he receives your **email message**.
If an email **bounces back**, it is sent back to the person who sent it, usually because the address is wrong. → INTERNET, COMPUTER

—**email, e-mail** *v.* [T]

em·a·nate /'ɛməˌneɪt/ *v.*

emanate from sth *phr. v.* to come from or out of something: *Wonderful smells were emanating from the kitchen.*

e·man·ci·pate /ɪ'mænsəˌpeɪt/ *v.* [T] POLITICS to make someone free from social, political, or legal rules that limit what s/he can do [ORIGIN: 1600—1700 Latin *emancipatus*, past participle of *emancipare*, from *mancipium* "ownership"] —**emancipated** *adj.* —**emancipation** /ɪˌmænsə'peɪʃən/ *n.* [U]

em·balm /ɪm'bɑm/ *v.* [T] to use chemicals to prevent a dead body from decaying

em·bank·ment /ɪm'bæŋkmənt/ *n.* [C] a wide wall of earth or stones built to stop water from flooding an area, or to support a road or railroad

em·bar·go¹ /ɪm'bɑrgoʊ/ *n.* (plural **embargoes**) [C] POLITICS an official order to stop trade with another country: *The UN **imposed an** arms **embargo on** the country.* [ORIGIN: 1500—1600 Spanish *embargar* "to stop, prevent, seize"]

embargo² *v.* (past tense and past participle **embargoed**) [T] POLITICS to officially stop particular goods from being traded with another country

em·bark /ɪm'bɑrk/ *v.* [I] to go onto a ship or airplane (ANT) **disembark** [ORIGIN: 1500—1600 French *embarquer*, from *barque* "ship"]

embark on/upon sth *phr. v.* to start something new, difficult, or exciting: *Terry then embarked on a new career as a teacher.*

em·bar·rass /ɪm'bærəs/ *v.* [T] to make someone feel embarrassed: *I didn't want to embarrass her in front of Paul.* [ORIGIN: 1600—1700 French *embarrasser*, from Spanish *embarazar*]

em·bar·rassed /ɪm'bærəst/ *adj.* ashamed, nervous, or uncomfortable, especially in front of other people: *I could see he **felt embarrassed**, so I changed the subject.* | *I was **embarrassed about** how messy my house was.* | *He was too **embarrassed to** talk about it.* | *an embarrassed silence*

em·bar·ras·sing /ɪm'bærəsɪŋ/ *adj.* making you feel embarrassed: *a lot of embarrassing questions*

em·bar·rass·ment /ɪm'bærəsmənt/ *n.* **1** [U] the feeling that you have when you are embarrassed: *Jody squirmed **with embarrassment**.* **2** [C] something that causes problems and makes someone look stupid: *The matter has been an **embarrassment to** the White House.*

em·bas·sy /'ɛmbəsi/ *n.* (plural **embassies**) [C] a group of officials who represent their country in a foreign country, or the building they work in: *the Peruvian Embassy*

em·bat·tled /ɪm'bæt̬ld/ *adj.* (formal) **1** surrounded by enemies, especially in a war: *the embattled city* **2** an embattled person, company, etc. has many problems or difficulties

em·bed /ɪm'bɛd/ *v.* (**embedded**, **embedding**) [T] **1** to put something firmly and deeply into something else: *a spider **embedded in** a glass paperweight* **2** if your ideas, feelings, or attitudes are embedded, you believe them very strongly: *The idea of freedom is **deeply embedded in** America's values.*

em·bel·lish /ɪm'bɛlɪʃ/ *v.* [T] **1** to make something more beautiful by adding decorations to it: *a crown **embellished with** jewels* **2** to make a story or statement more interesting by adding details to it that are not true: *Larry couldn't help embellishing his story.* —**embellishment** *n.* [C,U]

em·ber /'ɛmbɚ/ *n.* [C] a piece of wood or coal that stays red and very hot after a fire has stopped burning

em·bez·zle /ɪm'bɛzəl/ *v.* [I,T] LAW to steal money from the place where you work —**embezzlement** *n.* [U] —**embezzler** *n.* [C]

em·bit·tered /ɪm'bɪṭəd/ *adj.* angry, sad, or full of hate because of bad or unfair things that have happened to you —**embitter** *v.* [T]

em·bla·zoned /ɪm'bleɪzənd/ *adj.* showing a name, design, etc.: *a T-shirt* ***emblazoned with*** *the group's name*

em·blem /'ɛmbləm/ *n.* [C] a picture, shape, or object that represents a country, company, idea, etc.: *The national* ***emblem of*** *Canada is the maple leaf.*

em·bod·y /ɪm'bɑdi/ *v.* (**embodied**, **embodies**) [T] to be the best example of an idea or quality: *Mrs. Miller embodies everything I admire in a teacher.* —**embodiment** *n.* [U]

em·boss /ɪm'bɔs, ɪm'bɑs/ *v.* [T] to decorate the surface of metal, leather, paper, etc. with a raised pattern —**embossed** *adj.*: *embossed stationery*

em·brace /ɪm'breɪs/ *v.* [T] **1** to put your arms around someone and hold him/her in a caring way: *Rob reached out to embrace her.*

THESAURUS **hug, cuddle, hold, wrap your arms around sb** → HUG[1]

2 (formal) to eagerly accept ideas, opinions, religions, etc.: *young men who are embracing Islam* —**embrace** *n.* [C]

em·broi·der /ɪm'brɔɪdə/ *v.* **1** [I,T] to decorate cloth by sewing a picture or pattern on it with colored threads **2** [T] to add details that are not true to a story to make it more interesting or exciting —**embroidery** *n.* [U]

em·broil /ɪm'brɔɪl/ *v.* [T] to involve someone in a difficult situation: *Soon, the whole group was* ***embroiled in*** *a fierce argument.*

em·bry·o /'ɛmbri,oʊ/ *n.* (plural **embryos**) [C] BIOLOGY an animal or human that has not yet been born and has just begun to develop. In humans, an embryo becomes a FETUS after eight weeks of development.

em·bry·o·nic /,ɛmbri'ɑnɪk◂/ *adj.* not fully developed: *the country's embryonic nuclear weapons program*

em·cee /,ɛm'si/ *n.* [C] **master of ceremonies** someone who introduces the performers on a television program or at a social event —**emcee** *v.* [I,T]

e·mend /ɪ'mɛnd/ *v.* [T] (formal) to take the mistakes out of something that has been written → AMEND —**emendation** /ɪ,mɛn'deɪʃən, ,imɛn-/ *n.* [C,U]

em·er·ald /'ɛmərəld/ *n.* [C] a valuable bright green jewel

e·merge /ɪ'mədʒ/ (Ac) *v.* [I] **1** to appear after being hidden: *The sun* ***emerged from*** *behind the clouds.* **2** if facts emerge, they become known after being hidden or secret: *During the court case,* ***it emerged that*** *both men had previous convictions for robbery.* **3** to have a particular quality or position after experiencing a difficult situation: *She* ***emerged from*** *the divorce a stronger person.* [ORIGIN: 1500—1600 Latin *emergere*, from *e* "out of" + *mergere* "to dip, sink"] —**emergence** *n.* [U]: *the emergence of a rare political talent*

e·mer·gen·cy /ɪ'mədʒənsi/ *n.* (plural **emergencies**) [C] an unexpected and dangerous situation that you must deal with immediately: *Call an ambulance! This is an emergency!* [ORIGIN: 1600—1700 From the idea of something suddenly "emerging" or happening] —**emergency** *adj.*: *an emergency exit*

e'mergency ,room *n.* [C] the part of a hospital that immediately treats people who have been hurt in a serious accident

e·mer·gent /ɪ'mədʒənt/ (Ac) *adj.* beginning to develop and be noticeable: *the emergent nations of Eastern Europe and Africa*

e·mer·i·tus /ɪ'mɛrəṭəs/ *adj.* a PROFESSOR emeritus is no longer working but still has an official title

em·er·y board /'ɛməri bɔrd/ *n.* [C] a NAIL FILE made from thick card covered with a mineral powder

em·i·grant /'ɛməgrənt/ *n.* [C] someone who leaves his/her own country in order to live in another: *an* ***emigrant to*** *the United States* → IMMIGRANT

em·i·grate /'ɛmə,greɪt/ *v.* [I] to leave your own country in order to live in another: *Maria* ***emigrated from*** *Guatemala three years ago.* —**emigration** /,ɛmə'greɪʃən/ *n.* [C,U]

THESAURUS **immigrate, migrate** → IMMIGRATE

em·i·nent /'ɛmənənt/ *adj.* famous and admired by many people: *an eminent professor of medicine*

THESAURUS **famous, well-known, legendary, celebrated, renowned, noted, distinguished** → FAMOUS

,eminent do'main *n.* [U] LAW the right of the U.S. government to pay for and take someone's private land so it can be used for a public purpose

em·i·nent·ly /'ɛmənənt˺li/ *adv.* (formal) completely, and without any doubt: *He's eminently qualified to do the job.*

e·mir /ɛ'mɪr, ɪ-/ *n.* [C] a Muslim ruler, especially in Asia and parts of Africa

e·mir·ate /'ɛmərɪt/ *n.* [C] the country ruled by an emir

em·is·sar·y /'ɛmə,sɛri/ *n.* (plural **emissaries**) [C] someone who is sent with an official message, or who must do other official work: *an emissary from the Italian government*

e·mis·sion /ɪ'mɪʃən/ *n.* [C,U] the sending out of gas, heat, light, sound, etc., or the gas, etc. that is sent out: *an emissions test* (=a test to make sure the gases your car sends out are at the right level)

e·mit /ɪ'mɪt/ *v.* (**emitted**, **emitting**) [T] (formal) to send out gas, heat, light, sound, etc.: *The kettle emitted a shrill whistle.* [ORIGIN: 1600—1700 Latin *emittere*, from *mittere* "to send"]

Em·my /'ɛmi/ *n.* (plural **Emmies**) [C] a prize given every year to the best program, actor, etc. on U.S. television

e·mol·lient /ɪ'mɑlyənt/ *adj.* (formal) **1** making something, especially your skin, softer and smoother **2** making you feel calmer when you have been angry —**emollient** *n.* [C]

e·mote /ɪ'moʊt/ *v.* [I] to clearly show emotion, especially when you are acting: *Some of the poets just read their work, while others emoted.*

e·mo·tion /ɪ'moʊʃən/ *n.* [C,U] a strong human feeling such as love or hate: *David doesn't usually* ***show*** *his true* ***emotions****.* | *Her voice was* ***full of emotion****.* | *She trembled* ***with emotion****.* [ORIGIN: 1500—1600 French *émouvoir* "to cause to have strong feelings," from Latin *movere* "to move"]

E

e·mo·tion·al /ɪ'moʊʃənəl/ *adj.* **1** making people have strong feelings: *The end of the movie was really emotional.*

THESAURUS

moving – making you feel strong emotions, especially sadness or sympathy: *Kelly's book about her illness is deeply moving.*
touching – making you feel sympathy or sadness: *a touching tribute to the victims of the attack*
poignant – making you feel sad or full of pity: *poignant memories*
emotive (formal) – making people have strong feelings: *In his book, he expresses his ideas in highly emotive language.*
sentimental – showing emotions such as love, pity, and sadness too strongly: *a sentimental poem*
schmaltzy (informal) – showing strong emotions such as love and sadness in a way that seems silly: *a schmaltzy love song*

2 showing your emotions to other people, especially by crying: *Please don't* ***get all emotional****.* **3** relating to your feelings or how they are controlled: *the emotional development of children* | *Ann suffered from a number of* ***emotional problems****.* **4** influenced by what you feel rather than what you know: *an emotional response to the problem* —**emotionally** *adv.*: *Family members reacted emotionally to the verdict.*

e·mo·tive /ɪ'moʊtɪv/ *adj.* making people have strong feelings: *an emotive speech about the effects of war*

THESAURUS **emotional, moving, touching, poignant, sentimental, schmaltzy →** EMOTIONAL

em·pa·thy /'ɛmpəθi/ *n.* [U] the ability to understand someone else's feelings and problems [ORIGIN: 1900—2000 Greek *empatheia*, from *pathos* "suffering, feeling"] —**empathize** *v.* [I] → SYMPATHY

em·per·or /'ɛmpərər/ *n.* [C] the ruler of an EMPIRE [ORIGIN: 1100—1200 Old French *empereor*, from Latin *imperare* "to command"]

THESAURUS **king, queen, prince, princess, monarch, ruler, sovereign →** KING

em·pha·sis /'ɛmfəsɪs/ (Ac) *n.* (plural **emphases** /-fəsiz/) [C,U] special importance: *Jamieson's report* ***puts/places an emphasis on*** *the need for better working conditions.* [ORIGIN: 1500—1600 Latin, Greek, from *emphainein* "to show"]

em·pha·size /'ɛmfə,saɪz/ (Ac) *v.* [T] to show that an opinion, idea, quality, etc. is important: *My teacher emphasized the importance of grammar.* | *Scientists* ***emphasized that*** *more research needs to be done.* ►Don't say "emphasize on."◄

THESAURUS

stress – to emphasize a statement, fact, or idea: *Mother always stressed the importance of good manners.*
highlight – to make a problem, subject, etc. easy to notice so that people will pay attention to it: *Your résumé should highlight your skills and experience.*
underline – to show that something is important: *The tragic incident underlines the need for improved safety standards.*
accentuate – to make something easier to notice: *Let's try to accentuate the positive aspects of the report.*
underscore – to emphasize that something is important: *The president's speech repeatedly underscored the progress that has been made.*
exaggerate – to make something seem more important, better, larger, worse, etc. than it really is: *News reports exaggerated the severity of the disaster.*

em·phat·ic /ɪm'fætɪk/ (Ac) *adj.* done or said in a way that shows something is important or should be believed: *Dale's answer was an emphatic "No!"* | *The alarm bell gives a clear and emphatic warning that there is smoke in the building.* —**emphatically** *adv.*

em·phy·se·ma /,ɛmfə'zimə, -'si-/ *n.* [U] BIOLOGY a serious disease that affects the lungs, making it difficult to breathe [ORIGIN: 1600—1700 Modern Latin, Greek, from *emphysan* "to swell"]

em·pire /'ɛmpaɪər/ *n.* [C] **1** POLITICS a group of countries that are all controlled by one ruler or government: *the Roman Empire* **2** a group of organizations that are all controlled by one person or company: *a media empire*

em·pir·i·cal /ɪm'pɪrɪkəl, ɛm-/ (Ac) *adj.* based on practical experience or scientific tests rather than on ideas: *The theory is based on* ***empirical evidence****.* [ORIGIN: 1500—1600 *empiric* "person who puts trust only in practical experience" (16—21 centuries), from Latin *empiricus*]

em·pir·i·cism /ɪm'pɪrə,sɪzəm, ɛm-/ (Ac) *n.* [U] the belief that your ideas about the world should be based on experience or scientific tests —**empiricist** *n.* [C]

em·ploy /ɪm'plɔɪ/ *v.* [T] **1** to pay someone to work for you: *The factory employs over 2,000 people.* **2** to use a particular object, method, or skill in order to achieve something: *research methods employed by scientists* [ORIGIN: 1400—1500 French *emploier* "to use," from Latin *implicare*]

em·ploy·ee /ɪm'plɔɪ-i, ,ɪmplɔɪ'i, ,ɛm-/ *n.* [C] someone who is paid to work for a person, organization, or company: *a government employee* → WORK[1]

em·ploy·er /ɪm'plɔɪɚ/ *n.* [C] a person, company, or organization that employs people: *The shoe factory is the largest employer in this area.* → WORK[1]

em·ploy·ment /ɪm'plɔɪmənt/ *n.* [U] **1** work that you do to earn money: *Steve's still looking for employment.*

THESAURUS **job, work, position, post, occupation, profession, career, vocation** → JOB

2 the number of people who have jobs (ANT) **unemployment** **3** the act of paying someone to work for you: *the employment of minorities* **4** the use of an object, method, skill, etc. to achieve something: *the employment of weapons to gain control of the area*

em·po·ri·um /ɪm'pɔriəm/ *n.* [C] a word meaning a large store, used in the names of stores

em·pow·er /ɪm'paʊɚ/ *v.* [T] to give someone the confidence, power, or right to do something: *Our aim is to **empower** women **to** defend themselves.*

em·press /'ɛmprɪs/ *n.* [C] the female ruler of an EMPIRE, or the wife of an EMPEROR

emp·ty[1] /'ɛmpti/ *adj.* **1** having nothing inside: *Your glass is empty – would you like some more lemonade?* | *an empty box*

THESAURUS

bare – used about a room or area that has very little in it: *Apart from a bed, the room was bare.*
deserted – used about a place or building that is empty and quiet because no people are there: *a deserted beach* | *By now, the streets were deserted.*
uninhabited – used about a place that has no people living in it: *an uninhabited island*
free – used about a seat, space, or room that no one is using: *Is this seat free?*
blank – used about a computer screen, a page, a piece of paper, or a wall that has no writing or pictures on it: *He stared at the blank page, not sure what to write.*
vacant (formal) – used about rooms, seats, buildings, or areas of land that are empty and available for someone to use: *vacant motel rooms*

2 not filled with people, or not being used by anyone: *Is this seat empty?* | *an empty restaurant* **3** unhappy because nothing seems interesting, important, or worth doing: *After the divorce, my life felt empty.* **4 empty words/promises/gestures etc.** words, etc. that are not sincere and therefore have no meaning **5 on an empty stomach** without having eaten anything first: *You shouldn't go to school on an empty stomach.* **6 empty nest (syndrome)** a situation in which parents become sad because their children have grown up and left home [ORIGIN: Old English *æmettig*]

empty[2] *v.* (**emptied, empties**) **1** [T] *also* **empty out** to remove everything that is inside of something else: *I found your umbrella when I was emptying out the closet.* | *Troy, please empty the dishwasher.* **2** [T] to pour the things that are in a container into or onto something else: ***Empty** the contents of one pudding package **into** a large bowl.* **3** [I,T] to leave a place, vehicle, etc., or to make someone do this: *Judge Sinclair ordered the courtroom to be emptied.* **4** [I] to flow into a large area of water: *the place where Waddell Creek **empties into** the ocean*

,empty-'handed *adj.* without gaining or getting anything: *The thieves fled the building empty-handed.*

em·u·late /'ɛmyə,leɪt/ *v.* [T] (formal) to try to do something or behave in the same way as someone (SYN) **copy**: *Children emulate their parents' behavior*

e·mul·sion /ɪ'mʌlʃən/ *n.* [U] **1** CHEMISTRY a mixture of liquids, such as oil and water, that contains very small drops of one liquid floating in the other, instead of the liquids combining completely **2** the substance on the surface of photographic film or paper that makes it react to light

en·a·ble /ɪ'neɪbəl/ (Ac) *v.* [T] to make someone or something able to do something: *A new type of plastic has enabled us to make our products more cheaply.*

en·act /ɪ'nækt/ *v.* [T] LAW to make something a law: *The measure was enacted to prevent tax abuses.*

en·am·el /ɪ'næməl/ *n.* [U] **1** a substance like glass that is put on metal, clay, etc. for decoration or for protection **2** the hard smooth outer surface of your teeth

en·am·ored /ɪ'næmɚd/ *adj.* [not before noun] liking or loving someone or something very much: *Since the early 1960s, teenagers around the world have been **enamored of** American popular culture.* —**enamor** *v.* [T]

en·case /ɪn'keɪs/ *v.* [T] to cover or surround something completely: *art objects **encased in** a glass box*

en·chant·ed /ɪn'tʃæntɪd/ *adj.* something that is enchanted has been changed by magic so that it has special powers: *an enchanted forest*

en·chant·ing /ɪn'tʃæntɪŋ/ *adj.* very pleasant in a

way that makes you feel very interested, happy, or excited: *an enchanting movie about young love*

en·chi·la·da /ˌɛntʃəˈlɑdə/ *n.* [C] a Mexican food made from a corn TORTILLA rolled around meat or beans and covered with a hot-tasting liquid [ORIGIN: 1800—1900 American Spanish, past participle of *enchilar* "to put chili into"]

en·clave /ˈɛnkleɪv, ˈɑŋ-/ *n.* [C] a place or group of people that is surrounded by areas or groups of people that are different from it: *the Italian-American enclave in New York*

en·close /ɪnˈkloʊz/ *v.* [T] **1** to put something inside an envelope with a letter: *A copy of the article is enclosed.* **2** to surround an area, especially with a fence or wall: *A high wall enclosed the yard.* —**enclosed** *adj.*

E

en·clo·sure /ɪnˈkloʊʒɚ/ *n.* [C] **1** an area that is surrounded by something such as a fence or wall: *The animals are kept in a large enclosure.* **2** things such as documents, photographs, money, etc. that you send with a letter

en·com·pass /ɪnˈkʌmpəs/ *v.* [T] **1** to include a range of ideas, subjects, etc.: *Crosby's career encompassed radio, records, TV, and movies.* **2** to completely cover or surround an area: *a national park encompassing 400 square miles*

en·core /ˈɑŋkɔr/ *n.* [C] an additional piece of music a performer plays because the people listening want to hear more

en·coun·ter¹ /ɪnˈkaʊntɚ/ (Ac) *n.* [C] **1** an occasion when you meet or experience something: *It was my first **encounter with** blatant racism.* **2** an occasion when you meet someone without planning to: *an **encounter with** an old college friend* | *Her acting career began after a **chance encounter** (=one that happens by luck) with Orson Welles in Hamburg.* [ORIGIN: 1200—1300 Old French *encontrer*, from Late Latin *incontra* "toward"]

encounter² *v.* [T] **1** to experience something bad that you have to deal with: *She encountered a lot of difficulties trying to get her article published.* | *The president **encountered resistance** to his plans.* **2** (formal) to see or meet someone or something without planning to

en·cour·age /ɪnˈkɚɪdʒ, -ˈkʌr-/ *v.* [T] **1** to persuade someone to do something (ANT) **discourage**: *a program to **encourage** children **to** wear bicycle helmets* **2** to help someone become confident or brave enough to do something (ANT) **discourage**: *Cooder's father **encouraged** him **to** play the guitar.* **3** to make something more likely to happen (ANT) **discourage**: *a plant food that encourages growth* —**encouragement** *n.* [U]: *words of encouragement*

en·cour·ag·ing /ɪnˈkɚɪdʒɪŋ, -ˈkʌr-/ *adj.* giving you hope and confidence: *This is encouraging news.* —**encouragingly** *adv.*

en·croach /ɪnˈkroʊtʃ/ *v.* [I] **1** to gradually cover more and more land: *Housing developments are **encroaching on** the habitats of wild animals.* **2** to gradually take away more and more of someone's time, rights, etc.: *new laws that **encroach on** civil liberties*

en·crust·ed /ɪnˈkrʌstɪd/ *adj.* covered with something hard and sharp, such as jewels, ice, or dried mud

encrusted

en·cum·ber /ɪnˈkʌmbɚ/ *v.* [T] (formal) to make it more difficult for someone to do something, or for something to happen —**encumbrance** /ɪnˈkʌmbrəns/ *n.* [C]

en·cy·clo·pe·di·a /ɪnˌsaɪkləˈpidiə/ *n.* [C] a book, set of books, or CD that contains facts about many subjects or about one particular subject [ORIGIN: 1500—1600 Medieval Latin *encyclopaedia* "course of general education," from Greek *enkyklios paideia* "general education"]

end¹ /ɛnd/ *n.*

1 LAST PART [singular] the last part of a period of time, activity, book, movie, etc. (ANT) **beginning**: *There are study questions **at the end of** each chapter.* | *I'll know **by the end of** the week.*

2 FARTHEST POINT [C] the part of a place or long object that is furthest from its beginning or center: *the **ends of** his fingers* | *I went to the **end of** the line.* | *the **far end** of the room* | *The two teams pull at **opposite ends** of the rope.*

THESAURUS

point – the sharp end of something: *the point of a needle*

tip – the end of something, especially something pointed: *the tip of your nose*

3 OF A SITUATION [singular] a situation in which something is finished or no longer exists: *The conversation seemed to have **come to an end.*** | *the UN's latest plan to **put an end to** (=stop) the war* | *My month of freedom was **at an end.***

4 in the end after a lot of thinking or discussion (SYN) **finally**: *In the end, we decided to go to Florida.*

5 for days/weeks etc. on end for many days, weeks, etc. without stopping

6 at the end of the day (spoken) used in order to say what the most important point is: *At the end of the day, it's up to Jim to make the changes.*

7 make ends meet to have just enough money to buy what you need

8 it's not the end of the world (spoken) used in order to say that a problem is not too serious or bad

9 RESULT [C] (formal) the aim or purpose of something, or the result that you hope to achieve: *Learning can be both **an end in itself** (=a good goal), and a means to success.* | *We need to cut costs, and **to***

that end (=to achieve that result) *we have had to cut jobs.*
10 no end a lot: *He was enjoying himself no end.* | *The changes caused **no end of** trouble.*
11 PART OF AN ACTIVITY [singular] (informal) the part of a job, activity, or situation that involves a person or group: *She works in the sales end of things.*
12 SCALE [C usually singular] one of the two points that begin or end a scale or range: *a politician at the liberal **end of the** political **spectrum***
13 end to end with the end of something next to the end of something else: *cars parked end to end*
14 IN SPORTS [C] in football, one of two players who play on the outside of the TACKLES and try to catch the ball [ORIGIN: Old English *ende*] → DEAD END

end² *v.* [I,T] to stop or finish, or to make something do this (ANT) **begin**: *World War II ended in 1945.* | *Janet finally ended the relationship.* | *The concert **ended with** fireworks.*

THESAURUS

stop – to not continue, or to make someone or something not continue: *The shooting had stopped.*
finish – to stop when everything has been done, or to do the last part of something: *What time does your class finish?*
come to an end – to finally end, after continuing for a long time: *The war finally came to an end.*
be over – if something is over, it has ended: *The vacation was almost over.*

end in sth *phr. v.* to have a particular result or to finish in a particular way: *One in three marriages ends in divorce.*

end up *phr. v.* to be in a place, situation, or condition after a series of events, usually when you did not plan this: *I always end up paying the bill.*

en·dan·ger /ɪn'deɪndʒɚ/ *v.* [T] to put someone or something in a dangerous or harmful situation: *Smoking seriously endangers your health.* —**endangered** *adj.* —**endangerment** *n.* [U]

en,dangered 'species *n.* [C] a type of animal or plant that soon might not exist

en·dear /ɪn'dɪr/ *v.*

endear sb **to** sb *phr. v.* to make someone be liked by other people: *The proposals are meant to endear him to the voters.*

en·dear·ing /ɪn'dɪrɪŋ/ *adj.* making someone like or love you: *an endearing smile*

en·dear·ment /ɪn'dɪrmənt/ *n.* [C,U] something you say that shows your love for someone

en·deav·or¹ /ɪn'dɛvɚ/ *n.* [C,U] (formal) an attempt or effort to do something new or difficult: *an **endeavor to** create a lasting peace*

endeavor² *v.* [I] (formal) to try very hard to do something: *One must always **endeavor to** do one's best.*

THESAURUS try, attempt, see if you can do sth, do your best, make an effort to do sth → TRY¹

en·dem·ic /ɛn'dɛmɪk, ɪn-/ *adj.* regularly happening in a particular place or among a particular group of people: *Violent crime is now endemic in parts of the city.*

end·ing /'ɛndɪŋ/ *n.* **1** [C] the end of a story, movie, play, etc.: *a happy ending* **2** [U] the act of finishing or stopping a process: *the ending of travel restrictions*

en·dive /'ɛndaɪv/ *n.* [C,U] a vegetable with bitter-tasting leaves that are eaten raw in SALADS

end·less /'ɛndlɪs/ *adj.* continuing for a very long time, especially in a way that is annoying: *the endless hours of practice* | *The **possibilities** are **endless**.*

en·do·crine /'ɛndəkrɪn/ *adj.* [only before noun] BIOLOGY relating to HORMONES in your blood: *an endocrine gland*

en·dorse /ɪn'dɔrs/ *v* [T] **1** to officially say that you support or approve of someone or something: *Several South American countries have endorsed the idea.* | *The mayor has decided not to endorse a candidate in the presidential election this year.* **2** to sign your name on the back of a check —**endorsement** *n.* [C,U]

en·do·skel·e·ton /'ɛndoʊ,skɛlət‿n/ *n.* [C] BIOLOGY the structure made by all the bones inside living creatures that have a BACKBONE → EXOSKELETON

en·do·sperm /'ɛndə,spɚm/ *n.* [C] BIOLOGY the part of a seed that contains the supply of food for the growing seed

en·do·therm /'ɛndə,θɚm/ *n.* [C] BIOLOGY an animal that produces heat inside its body and is able to control the temperature of its body when the temperature of its environment changes. Birds and MAMMALS are endotherms. → ECTOTHERM

en·do·ther·mic /,ɛndə'θɚmɪk◂/ *adj.* BIOLOGY relating to or describing a chemical reaction in which heat is taken in from the surrounding area → EXOTHERMIC: *an endothermic process*

en·dow /ɪn'daʊ/ *v.* [T] **1** to give an endowment to a college, hospital, etc. **2 be endowed with talent/resources/rights etc.** (formal) to have or be given a good quality, feature, or ability [ORIGIN: 1300—1400 Anglo-French *endouer*, from Latin *dotare* "to give"]

en·dow·ment /ɪn'daʊmənt/ *n.* [C,U] a large amount of money or property that is given to a college, hospital, etc. so that it has an income

en·dur·ance /ɪn'dʊrəns/ *n.* [U] the ability to continue doing something difficult or painful over a long period of time: *Jogging will help increase your endurance.*

en·dure /ɪn'dʊr/ *v.* **1** [T] to suffer pain or deal with a very difficult situation for a long time:

People have endured months of fighting. **2** [I] to continue for a long time: *a marriage that has endured for fifty years*

en·dur·ing /ɪn'dʊrɪŋ/ *adj.* continuing to exist in spite of difficulties: *an enduring peace*

'end zone *n.* [C] the end of a football field where players take the ball in order to win points

en·e·my /'ɛnəmi/ *n.* (plural **enemies**) [C] **1** someone who hates you and wants to harm you or prevent you from being successful: *Judge Lonza has* ***made a lot of enemies*** *during her career.* **2** the person or group of people that you are fighting in a war: ***The enemy*** *had at least 50 large aircraft in good condition.* | *an attack on an* ***enemy submarine/ship/soldier etc.*** **3** something that people think is harmful or damaging: *This policy was declared an enemy of economic growth.* [ORIGIN: 1200—1300 Old French *enemi*, from Latin *inimicus*, from *amicus* "friend"]

E

en·er·get·ic /ˌɛnə'dʒɛt̬ɪk◂/ (Ac) *adj.* very active: *a cast of young and energetic actors* | *The governor fought an energetic campaign.* —**energetically** *adv.*

THESAURUS

vigorous – using a lot of energy and strength or determination: *a vigorous opponent of capital punishment*
full of energy – having a lot of energy: *Katie is fun and full of energy.*
dynamic – interesting, exciting, and full of energy and determination to succeed: *a dynamic new candidate*
hyperactive – too active, and not able to keep still or quiet for very long: *a hyperactive child*
tireless – working very hard in a determined way: *a tireless defender of human rights*
lively – very active and cheerful: *a lively group of kids*
vital – full of life and energy: *He was still young and vital when cancer struck.*

en·er·gize /'ɛnəˌdʒaɪz/ *v.* [T] to make someone feel more determined and full of energy

en·er·gy /'ɛnədʒi/ (Ac) *n.* (plural **energies**) [C,U] **1** the physical and mental strength that makes you able to do things: *Younger people generally* ***have*** *more* ***energy.*** | *She's usually* ***full of energy.*** | *She had* ***put*** *a good deal of time and* ***energy into*** *the project.* **2** power that is used to produce heat, make machines work, etc.: *atomic energy* | *electrical energy* | *the world's energy resources* **3** PHYSICS the ability of something to do work, move, or produce heat [ORIGIN: 1500—1600 Late Latin *energia*, from Greek *energeia* "activity"]

en·er·vat·ed /'ɛnəˌveɪt̬ɪd/ *adj.* (formal) feeling weak, tired, and without energy: *After the long journey, he felt enervated and barely able to speak.* —**enervate** *v.* [T] —**enervating** *adj.*

en·force /ɪn'fɔrs/ (Ac) *v.* [T] to make people obey a rule or law: *It's our responsibility to* ***enforce*** *the* ***law.*** | *The speed limit is* ***strictly enforced.*** —**enforcement** *n.* [U] —**enforceable** *adj.*

en·fran·chise /ɪn'frænˌtʃaɪz/ *v.* [T] POLITICS to give a group of people rights, especially the right to vote (ANT) **disenfranchise**

en·gage /ɪn'geɪdʒ/ *v.* [T] (formal) **1** to make someone remain interested in something: *a storyteller able to engage the children's imaginations* **2 engage sb in (a) conversation** to begin talking to someone **3** to employ someone

engage in sth *phr. v.* to be doing or become involved in an activity: *Only 10% of Americans engage in regular exercise.*

en·gaged /ɪn'geɪdʒd/ *adj.* two people who are engaged have agreed to marry each other: *Viv and Tyrell* ***got engaged*** *last month.* | *Sheri's* ***engaged to*** *a guy in the Army.* ►Don't say "engaged with someone."◄

en·gage·ment /ɪn'geɪdʒmənt/ *n.* **1** [C] an agreement to marry someone: *Charlene and I have* ***broken off*** *our* ***engagement*** (=decided to end it). | *an* ***engagement ring*** (=a ring that a man gives a woman to show that they are engaged) **2** [C] (formal) an arrangement to do something or meet someone: *Professor Campbell is in Fort Worth for a speaking engagement.* **3** [U] the process of being involved with someone or something: *a strategy of engagement and cooperation with China* **4** [C,U] fighting between people or armies: *military* ***rules of engagement*** (=rules that say when you should fight)

en·gag·ing /ɪn'geɪdʒɪŋ/ *adj.* attracting people's attention and interest: *an engaging personality*

en·gen·der /ɪn'dʒɛndə/ *v.* [T] (formal) to be the cause of something such as a situation, action, or emotion: *the excitement engendered by the Pope's visit*

en·gine /'ɛndʒɪn/ *n.* [C] **1** the part of a vehicle or machine that produces power to make it move: *the engine of a car* | *I waited with the* ***engine running*** (=with the engine on). **2** the vehicle at the front of a train, that pulls it along (SYN) **locomotive** [ORIGIN: 1300—1400 Old French *engin* "cleverness, machine," from Latin *ingenium* "abilities you are born with"]

en·gi·neer¹ /ˌɛndʒə'nɪr/ *n.* [C] **1** someone whose job is to design, build, and repair roads, bridges, machines, etc. **2** someone who controls the engines on a ship, airplane, or train

engineer² *v.* [T] **1** to arrange something, especially secretly: *He engineered a cover-up.* **2** to design, plan, and make something new: ***genetically engineered*** *corn* (=in which the GENEs have been changed)

en·gi·neer·ing /ˌɛndʒə'nɪrɪŋ/ *n.* [U] the profession or activity of designing, building, and repairing roads, bridges, machines, etc.

En·glish¹ /'ɪŋglɪʃ/ *n.* **1** [U] the language used in places such as the U.S., Canada, and Great Britain **2 the English** [plural] the people of England

English² *adj.* **1** relating to the English language **2** relating to or coming from England

en·grave /ɪn'greɪv/ *v.* [T] to cut words or pictures onto the surface of metal, wood, glass, etc. —**engraver** *n.* [C]

en·grav·ing /ɪn'greɪvɪŋ/ *n.* [C] a picture printed from an engraved piece of metal or wood

en·grossed /ɪn'groʊst/ *adj.* so interested in something that you do not notice anything else: *Kit was* ***engrossed in*** *a book.*

en·gross·ing /ɪn'groʊsɪŋ/ *adj.* so interesting that you do not notice anything else: *an engrossing story*

> THESAURUS **interesting, fascinating, intriguing, absorbing, enthralling, compelling, gripping, riveting** → INTERESTING

en·gulf /ɪn'gʌlf/ *v.* [T] **1** if a bad feeling engulfs you, you feel it very strongly: *Fear suddenly engulfed him.* **2** to completely surround or cover something: *a home* ***engulfed in*** *flames*

en·hance /ɪn'hæns/ (Ac) *v.* [T] to improve something: *Adding lemon juice will enhance the flavor.* —**enhancement** *n.* [C,U]

e·nig·ma /ɪ'nɪgmə/ *n.* [C] a person, thing, or event that is strange, mysterious, and difficult to understand [ORIGIN: 1500—1600 Latin *aenigma*, from Greek, from *ainos* "story"]

en·ig·mat·ic /ˌɛnɪg'mæt̬ɪk◂/ *adj.* mysterious, and difficult to understand or explain: *an enigmatic man* —**enigmatically** /-kli/ *adv.*

en·joy /ɪn'dʒɔɪ/ *v.* [T] **1** if you enjoy something, it gives you pleasure: *Did you enjoy the movie?* | *I really enjoy walking the dog.* ▶Don't say "I enjoy to walk the dog."◀

> THESAURUS
> **like** – to enjoy something, or think that it is nice or good: *Do you like Mexican food?*
> **love** – to like something very much, or enjoy doing something very much: *My daughter loves to read.*
> **have a good/great time** – to have experiences that you enjoy: *Did you have a good time at the party?*
> **have fun** – to enjoy doing something: *I had a lot of fun in class today.*
> **relish** (formal) – to enjoy something and be eager to do it: *He's the kind of guy who relishes a challenge.*

2 enjoy yourself to be happy and have fun in a particular situation: *I didn't think I'd like sailing, but I was starting to enjoy myself.* **3** to have a particular ability, advantage, or success: *The team has enjoyed some success this season.* [ORIGIN: 1300—1400 Old French *enjoir*, from Latin *gaudere* "to show great happiness"] —**enjoyment** *n.* [U]

en·joy·a·ble /ɪn'dʒɔɪəbəl/ *adj.* giving you pleasure: *an enjoyable afternoon*

> THESAURUS **nice, pleasant, great, fantastic, wonderful** → NICE

en·large /ɪn'lɑrdʒ/ *v.* [I,T] to become bigger, or to make something become bigger: *I'm going to get some of these pictures enlarged.* | *Enlarge your vocabulary by reading books.*

en·large·ment /ɪn'lɑrdʒmənt/ *n.* [C] a photograph that has been printed again in a larger size

en·light·en /ɪn'laɪt̚n/ *v.* [T] (formal) to explain something to someone —**enlightening** *adj.*: *an enlightening experience*

en·light·ened /ɪn'laɪt̚nd/ *adj.* having sensible modern attitudes and treating people fairly and kindly: *an enlightened company that treats its employees well*

en·light·en·ment /ɪn'laɪt̚nmənt/ *n.* [U] the process of understanding something clearly, or when you help someone do this

E

en·list /ɪn'lɪst/ *v.* **1** [T] to persuade someone to help you, support you, etc.: *Children who are doing well are* ***enlisted to help*** *children who are struggling.* **2** [I] to join the army, navy, etc.: *I've* ***enlisted in*** *the Marines.* —**enlistment** *n.* [C,U]

en·list·ed /ɪn'lɪstɪd/ *adj.* **enlisted man/woman/personnel etc.** someone in the army, navy, etc. whose rank is below that of an officer

en·liv·en /ɪn'laɪvən/ *v.* [T] to make something more interesting or exciting

en masse /ɑn 'mæs, -'mɑs, ɛn-/ *adv.* together as one group: *City councilors threatened to resign en masse.*

en·mi·ty /'ɛnmət̬i/ *n.* [U] feelings of hatred and anger

en·nui /ɑn'wi/ *n.* [U] (literary) a feeling of being tired and bored, especially as a result of having nothing to do

e·nor·mi·ty /ɪ'nɔrmət̬i/ (Ac) *n.* [singular, U] the fact of being very large or serious: *People were shocked by* ***the enormity of*** *the crime.*

e·nor·mous /ɪ'nɔrməs/ (Ac) *adj.* extremely large in size or amount: *You should see their house – it's enormous!* | *an enormous amount of work* [ORIGIN: 1500—1600 Latin *enormis* "out of the ordinary," from *norma* "rule"] —**enormously** *adv.*: *The brain makes enormously complex decisions very quickly.* | *House prices have grown enormously.*

> THESAURUS **big, large, substantial, sizable, prodigious, huge, vast, gigantic, massive, immense, colossal** → BIG

e·nough /ɪ'nʌf/ *adv., determiner, pron.* **1** as big, as many, as far, as much, etc. as necessary: *This bag isn't big* ***enough to*** *hold all my stuff.* | *He doesn't even earn* ***enough to*** *pay the rent.* | *Is he old* ***enough for*** *school?* | *Do we have* ***enough*** *food* ***for*** *everybody?* | *The coach thinks she's not trying hard* *enough.* | *Do you have enough money?* | *I think we've done enough.*

THESAURUS

plenty – a large amount that is enough or more than enough: *Try to eat plenty of fresh fruit and vegetables.*
ample – more than enough: *There will be ample opportunity to ask questions.*
sufficient – as much as you need for a particular purpose: *The court has to decide if there is sufficient evidence to prove that he is guilty.*
adequate – enough in quantity or good enough in quality for a particular purpose: *The workers did not receive adequate training.*

2 (spoken) used in order to say that you are tired or angry about a situation and want it to stop: *I **have had enough** of your lies!* | ***That's enough**, you two. Stop yelling!* | *Finally, my mother said **enough is enough** and kicked him out of the house.* **3** (spoken) said when a situation is already bad and you do not want it to get worse: *It's **bad enough** that you lied to me, without lying to Mother too.* | *I have **enough trouble/problems** – don't you go making it worse!* **4** not very, but in an acceptable way: *She's nice enough, but we don't have much in common.* **5 strangely/oddly/funnily enough** (spoken) used in order to say that a fact or something that happens is strange or surprising: *Funnily enough, I met him today after not having seen him for months.* → **sure enough** *at* SURE²

GRAMMAR

Use **enough** after adjectives or adverbs, or before nouns: *This apartment isn't big enough for three people.* | *There's enough food for everyone.*

E

en·rage /ɪn'reɪdʒ/ *v.* [T] to make someone very angry —**enraged** *adj.*

en·rich /ɪn'rɪtʃ/ *v.* [T] to improve the quality of something: *vitamin-enriched flour* —**enrichment** *n.* [U]

en·roll, enrol /ɪn'roʊl/ *v.* [I,T] to officially join a school, university, etc., or to arrange for someone else to do this: *the students **enrolled in** honors classes* | *Nathan **enrolled at** City College.*

en·roll·ment /ɪn'roʊlmənt/ *n.* [C,U] the number of students who are enrolled in a school or class, or the process of enrolling them: *Enrollment was high this year.*

en route /ɑn 'rut, ɛn-/ *adv.* on the way: *We stopped at my aunt's house **en route to** Grandma's.*

en·sconce /ɪn'skɑns/ *v.* [T] (formal) to put someone in a safe and comfortable place: *Martha was **ensconced in** the biggest chair.*

en·sem·ble /ɑn'sɑmbəl/ *n.* [C] a small group of musicians who play together regularly

en·shrine /ɪn'ʃraɪn/ *v.* [T] (formal) to put something in a special place so that people can see it and remember it: *civil rights **enshrined in** the Constitution*

en·sign /'ɛnsən/ *n.* [C] a low rank in the Navy, or an officer who has this rank

en·slave /ɪn'sleɪv/ *v.* [T] (formal) **1** if something enslaves you, it completely controls your life and your actions **2** to make someone a SLAVE

en·sue /ɪn'su/ *v.* [I] (formal) to happen after something, often as a result of it: *A heated discussion ensued.* —**ensuing** *adj.*

en·sure /ɪn'ʃʊr/ (Ac) *v.* [T] to do something to be certain of a particular result: *The troops will **ensure that** food aid goes where it is most needed.* | *Strict measures were taken to ensure the accuracy of the results.*

en·tail /ɪn'teɪl/ *v.* [T] to make something necessary, or have something as a necessary part: *Does your job entail much traveling?*

en·tan·gle /ɪn'tæŋgəl/ *v.* [T] **1 be/get entangled in/with** to be or become involved with someone or something bad: *fears that the U.S. will get **entangled in** another war* **2** to make something be twisted or caught in a rope, net, etc.: *a fish **entangled in** the net* —**entanglement** *n.* [C,U]

en·ter¹ /'ɛntɚ/ *v.* **1** [I,T] to go or come into a place: *A nurse entered.* | *Army tanks entered the capital.*

THESAURUS

go in – to move into a particular place: *Frank opened the door, and we went in.*
come in – to enter a room or house: *Come in and sit down.*
barge in – to interrupt someone or go into a place when you were not invited: *He just barged in.*
sneak in – to go somewhere quietly and secretly: *After the movie had already started, we snuck in.*
get in – to be allowed or able to enter a place: *You can't get in without ID.*
trespass – to go onto someone's land without permission: *The sign said "No Trespassing."*
intrude – to go into a place where you are not wanted: *Anyone intruding into the space sets off an alarm.*
penetrate (formal) – to enter something or pass through it, especially when this is difficult: *The soldiers penetrated deep into enemy territory.*

2 [T] to go inside something: *The virus enters the body through the lungs.* **3** [T] to start working in a particular profession, or studying at a particular university, school, etc.: *Both boys entered the Navy.* | *Many older students are now entering university.* **4** [T] to start to take part in an activity: *The U.S. entered the war in 1941.* | *More women began entering the workforce.* **5** [I,T] to take part in something such as a competition, or to arrange for someone else to do this: *The senator announced that he would not enter the presidential race.* | *The school **entered** three candidates **in** the spelling bee.* **6** [T] to put information into a computer by pressing the keys, or to write information on a form, document, etc.: *Enter your name in block* *capitals.* **7** [T] to begin a period of time: *The economy is entering a period of growth.* [ORIGIN: 1200—1300 Old French *entrer*, from Latin *intra* "inside"]

enter into sth *phr. v.* **1** to start doing something, discussing something, etc.: *Both sides must enter into negotiations.* **2** to be considered as a reason for something: *Money didn't enter into my decision to leave.* **3 enter into an agreement/contract etc.** (formal) to officially make an agreement

enter[2], Enter *n.* [singular] IT the key on a computer that you press to put information into a document, give an instruction, etc.: *Make a selection from the menu, then press "Enter."*

en·ter·prise /ˈɛntɚˌpraɪz/ *n.* **1** [C] a company, organization, or business: *The store is a family enterprise* (=owned by one family). **2** [U] ECONOMICS the activity of starting and running businesses: *private enterprise* **3** [C] a large and complicated plan or process that you work on with other people: *The show is a huge enterprise.* **4** [U] the ability to work hard and think of new ideas, especially in business: *his enterprise and creativity* → FREE ENTERPRISE

en·ter·pris·ing /ˈɛntɚˌpraɪzɪŋ/ *adj.* able and willing to do things that are new or difficult: *an enterprising law student*

en·ter·tain /ˌɛntɚˈteɪn/ *v.* **1** [I,T] to do something that interests and amuses people: *She **entertained** the children **with** stories and songs.* | *A museum should aim to entertain as well as educate.* **2** [I,T] to treat someone as a guest by providing food and drink for him/her: *Mike's entertaining clients tonight.* **3** [T] (formal) to consider or think about an idea, doubt, suggestion, etc.

en·ter·tain·er /ˌɛntɚˈteɪnɚ/ *n.* [C] someone whose job is to tell jokes, sing, etc.

en·ter·tain·ing /ˌɛntɚˈteɪnɪŋ/ *adj.* amusing and interesting: *an entertaining movie*

en·ter·tain·ment /ˌɛntɚˈteɪnmənt/ *n.* [U] things such as television, movies, etc. that amuse or interest people: *the entertainment industry* | *a bar with **live entertainment*** (=people who perform)

en·thrall /ɪnˈθrɔl/ *v.* [T] to completely hold someone's attention and interest —**enthralling** *adj.*

en·thuse /ɪnˈθuz/ *v.* [I] to talk about something with excitement and admiration

en·thu·si·asm /ɪnˈθuziˌæzəm/ *n.* [U] a strong feeling of interest and enjoyment: *He sang **with enthusiasm**.* | *a teacher who shared my **enthusiasm for** history* | *The new students were **full of enthusiasm*** (=very enthusiastic). [ORIGIN: 1500—1600 Greek *enthousiasmos*, from *entheos* "filled (by a god) with sudden strong abilities"] —**enthusiast** /ɪnˈθuziəst/ *n.* [C]

en·thu·si·as·tic /ɪnˌθuziˈæstɪk/ *adj.* showing a lot of interest and excitement about something: *a program that makes kids **enthusiastic about** learning* | *an enthusiastic crowd*

THESAURUS

eager – wanting very much to do, get, or see something soon: *They were eager to hear what he had to say.*
passionate – having very strong feelings about something: *She is passionate about her work.*
ardent – very enthusiastic and having very strong feelings of admiration or determination: *He became an ardent admirer of Matisse's paintings.*
zealous – extremely enthusiastic about something such as a political or religious idea: *Only his most zealous supporters would agree with this policy.*
fanatical – very enthusiastic, especially in a way that seems too extreme: *Her husband was fanatical about keeping the house clean.*

—**enthusiastically** *adv.*

en·tice /ɪnˈtaɪs/ *v.* [T] to persuade someone to do something by offering him/her something nice: *The tax break is meant to **entice** businesses **to** locate in the city.* —**enticing** *adj.* —**enticement** *n.* [C,U]

en·tire /ɪnˈtaɪɚ/ *adj.* whole or complete – used in order to emphasize what you are saying: *I've spent the entire day cooking.*

en·tire·ly /ɪnˈtaɪɚli/ *adv.* completely: *Things are entirely different now.*

THESAURUS **completely, absolutely, totally, wholly, utterly** → COMPLETELY

en·tire·ty /ɪnˈtaɪɚt̬i/ *n.* **in sth's entirety** including all of something: *The speech is published in its entirety.*

en·ti·tle /ɪnˈtaɪt̬l/ *v.* **1** [T] to give someone the right to have or do something: *Full-time employees are **entitled to** receive health insurance.* | *Membership **entitles** you **to** the full use of our fitness facilities.* **2 be entitled sth** if a book, play, etc. is entitled something, that is its name: *a book entitled "The Stone Diaries"*

en·ti·tle·ment /ɪnˈtaɪt̬lmənt/ *n.* [C,U] the official right to have or receive something, or the amount you receive: *an employee's **entitlement to** free medical care*

en'titlement ˌprogram *n.* [C] SOCIAL SCIENCE a government program or system that gives money or help to particular groups in society, for example old people or poor people

en·ti·ty /ˈɛntət̬i/ (Ac) *n.* (plural **entities**) [C] (formal) something that exists as a single and complete unit: *After the war, Germany was partitioned* (=divided) *into two **separate entities**.*

en·to·mol·o·gy /ˌɛntəˈmɑlədʒi/ *n.* [U] BIOLOGY the scientific study of insects —**entomologist** *n.* [C]

en·tou·rage /ˌɑntʊˈrɑʒ/ *n.* [C] a group of people who travel with an important person: *the President's entourage*

E

en·trails /ˈɛntreɪlz/ *n.* [plural] the inside parts of a person or animal, especially the BOWELS

en·trance¹ /ˈɛntrəns/ *n.* **1** [C] a door, gate, or other opening that you go through to enter a place (ANT) **exit**: *the main* ***entrance to*** *the school* | *the* ***back/front/side entrance*** *of the hotel* **2** [U] the right or opportunity to enter a place: *Entrance will be denied to those without tickets.* | *an* ***entrance fee*** *for the museum* | ***Entrance to*** *the park is free.* **3** [U] permission to become a member of or become involved in a profession, a university, etc.: *the requirements for college entrance* **4 make an entrance** to come into a place in a way that makes people notice you

en·trance² /ɪnˈtræns/ *v.* [T usually passive] to make someone feel very interested in and pleased with something: *We were entranced by the brilliant colors.* —**entranced** *adj.*: *his entranced listeners* —**entrancing** *adj.*: *entrancing stories*

en·trant /ˈɛntrənt/ *n.* [C] (formal) someone who enters a competition

en·trap /ɪnˈtræp/ *v.* (**entrapped**, **entrapping**) [T] (formal) to trick someone so that s/he is caught doing something illegal —**entrapment** *n.* [U]

en·treat /ɪnˈtrit/ *v.* [T] (formal) to ask someone, with a lot of emotion, to do something —**entreaty** *n.* [C,U]

en·trée /ˈɑntreɪ/ *n.* [C] the main dish of a meal

en·trenched /ɪnˈtrɛntʃt/ *adj.* strongly established and not likely to change: *entrenched attitudes*

en·tre·pre·neur /ˌɑntrəprəˈnɚ, -ˈnʊr/ *n.* [C] ECONOMICS someone who starts a company, arranges business deals, and takes risks in order to make a profit —**entrepreneurial** /ˌɑntrəprəˈnʊriəl/ *adj.*

en·tro·py /ˈɛntrəpi/ *n* [U] **1** PHYSICS a way of measuring or describing the tendency of energy in a MOLECULE to spread out, so that the energy in the molecules around it changes to the same level, if there is nothing to stop them doing so **2** a lack of order in a system, including the idea that the lack of order increases over a period of time

en·trust /ɪnˈtrʌst/ *v.* [T] to give someone something to be responsible for: *Bergen was* ***entrusted with*** *delivering the documents.*

en·try /ˈɛntri/ *n.* (plural **entries**) **1** [C,U] the act of going into a place, or the right or opportunity to enter a place (ANT) **exit**: *The papers granted him* ***entry into*** *the country.* | *There were no signs of* ***forced entry*** *into the house.* | *They were refused entry at the border.* **2** [U] the right or opportunity to become a member of a group or take part in something, or the fact of doing this: *the* ***entry of*** *new firms* ***into*** *the market* | *America's* ***entry into*** *the war* **3** [C] *also* **entryway** a door, gate, or passage that you pass through to go into a place **4** [C] something written or printed in a book, list, etc.: *a dictionary entry* **5** [U] the act of recording information on paper or in a computer: *data entry* **6** [C] a person or thing that takes part in a competition, race, etc.: *the winning entry* **7** [U] the act of entering a competition, race, etc.: *Entry is open to anyone over 18.*

en·twine /ɪnˈtwaɪn/ *v.* [T] **1 be entwined** if two things or people are entwined, they are closely connected with each other in a complicated way **2** to twist something around something else: *flowers* ***entwined in*** *her hair*

e·nu·mer·ate /ɪˈnuməˌreɪt/ *v.* [T] (formal) to name a list of things, one by one

eˌnumerated ˈpowers *n.* [plural] POLITICS another name for EXPRESSED POWERS

e·nun·ci·ate /ɪˈnʌnsiˌeɪt/ *v.* (formal) **1** [I,T] to pronounce words or sounds clearly **2** [T] to express ideas or principles clearly and firmly —**enunciation** /ɪˌnʌnsiˈeɪʃən/ *n.* [C,U]

en·vel·op /ɪnˈvɛləp/ *v.* [T] to cover something completely: *The building was* ***enveloped in*** *flames.* —**enveloping** *adj.*

en·ve·lope /ˈɛnvəˌloʊp, ˈɑn-/ *n.* [C] the paper cover in which you put a letter [ORIGIN: 1700—1800 French *enveloppe*, from Old French *voloper* "to wrap"]

en·vi·a·ble /ˈɛnviəbəl/ *adj.* an enviable quality, position, or possession is good and other people would like to have it: *an enviable position in the company* —**enviably** *adv.*

en·vi·ous /ˈɛnviəs/ *adj.* wishing that you had someone else's qualities or things (SYN) **jealous**: *Jackie was* ***envious of*** *Sylvia's success.* —**enviously** *adv.*

en·vi·ron·ment /ɪnˈvaɪrənmənt/ (Ac) *n.* **1 the environment** EARTH SCIENCES the land, water, and air in which people, animals, and plants live: *laws to protect the environment*

TOPIC

Things that are harmful to the environment

pollution – damage caused to air, water, soil, etc. by harmful chemicals and waste

the greenhouse effect – the warming of the air around the Earth as a result of the Sun's heat being trapped by pollution
global warming – an increase in world temperatures, caused by pollution in the air
acid rain – rain that contains acid chemicals from factory smoke and cars, etc.
deforestation – when all the trees in an area are cut down or destroyed

Describing things that are good for the environment
environmentally friendly/eco-friendly – products that are environmentally friendly or eco-friendly are not harmful to the environment
recycle – if materials such as glass or paper are recycled, they are put through a special process so that they can be used again
biodegradable – a material that is biodegradable can be destroyed by natural processes, in a way that does not harm the environment
organic – organic food or organic farming does not use chemicals that are harmful to the environment

2 [C,U] the situations, things, people, etc. that affect the way in which people live and work: *a pleasant work environment* **3** [C] EARTH SCIENCES the natural features of a place, for example its weather, the types of plants that grow there, etc.: *a forest environment* | *Human activity, such as farming, changes the natural environment.* **4** [C] BIOLOGY the physical, chemical, natural, etc. conditions that affect the way a living thing lives or develops: *The moths were able to adapt to their new environment.* [ORIGIN: 1600—1700 *environ* "to surround" (14—21 centuries), from Old French *environer*]

en·vi·ron·men·tal /ɪnˌvaɪrənˈmɛntl/ (Ac) *adj.* **1** relating to or affecting the air, land, or water on Earth: *environmental damage caused by oil spills* **2** concerning the people and things around you that affect your life, for example the place where you live: *Environmental factors, including poor diet and dirty water, were partly responsible for the rapid spread of the disease.* —**environmentally** *adv.*

en·vi·ron·men·tal·ist /ɪnˌvaɪrənˈmɛntl-ɪst/ (Ac) *n.* [C] someone who is concerned about protecting the environment

en·vi·rons /ɪnˈvaɪrənz, ɛn-/ *n.* [plural] (formal) the area surrounding a place

en·vi·sion /ɪnˈvɪʒən/ *also* **en·vis·age** /ɪnˈvɪzɪdʒ/ *v.* [T] to imagine something as a future possibility: *Eve had envisioned a career as a diplomat.*

THESAURUS **imagine, visualize, picture, fantasize, daydream** → IMAGINE

en·voy /ˈɛnvɔɪ, ˈɑn-/ *n.* [C] someone who is sent to another country as an official representative [ORIGIN: 1600—1700 French *envoyé*, past participle of *envoyer* "to send"]

en·vy¹ /ˈɛnvi/ *n.* [U] **1** the feeling of wanting to have the qualities or things that someone else has: *She watched the other girls* ***with envy***. **2 be the envy of sb** to be something that other people admire and want: *an education system that is the envy of the world* [ORIGIN: 1200—1300 Old French *envie*, from Latin *invidere* "to look at with bad feelings"]

envy² *v.* (**envied**, **envies**) [T] to wish you had the qualities or things that someone else has: *I really envy you and Meg; you seem so happy together.* | *I envied John his freedom.*

en·zyme /ˈɛnzaɪm/ *n.* [C] BIOLOGY a chemical substance that living cells produce in plants and animals, and that causes changes in other chemical substances [ORIGIN: 1800—1900 German *enzym*, from Greek *zyme* "substance that makes a flour-and-water mixture swell"]

e·on /ˈiɑn/ *n.* [C] an extremely long period of time

ep·au·let /ˌɛpəˈlɛt, ˈɛpəˌlɛt/ *n.* [C] a shoulder decoration on a military uniform

e·phem·er·al /ɪˈfɛmərəl/ *adj.* existing only for a short time [ORIGIN: 1500—1600 Greek *ephemeros* "lasting a day," from *hemera* "day"]

THESAURUS **short, brief, quick, temporary** → SHORT¹

ep·ic¹ /ˈɛpɪk/ *adj.* **1** full of brave action and excitement: *an epic journey* **2** very big, long, or impressive: *an epic movie*

epic² *n.* [C] **1** a book or movie that tells a long story **2** ENG. LANG. ARTS a long poem about what gods or important people did in past times: *Homer's epic "The Odyssey"*

ep·i·cen·ter /ˈɛpəˌsɛntɚ/ *n.* [C] EARTH SCIENCES the place on the Earth's surface that is above the point where an EARTHQUAKE begins

ep·i·dem·ic /ˌɛpəˈdɛmɪk/ *n.* [C] **1** a large number of cases of a particular infectious disease happening at the same time: *a typhoid epidemic* **2** something bad that develops and spreads quickly: *an epidemic of crime* [ORIGIN: 1600—1700 French *épidémique*, from Greek *epidemos* "visiting"] —**epidemic** *adj.*

ep·i·der·mal cell /ˌɛpədɚməl ˈsɛl/ *n.* [C] BIOLOGY any cell that is part of the epidermis of an animal or plant

ep·i·der·mis /ˌɛpəˈdɚmɪs/ *n.* [C,U] **1** BIOLOGY the outer layer of skin on a person or animal, formed by a layer of cells **2** BIOLOGY the outside surface of a plant, formed by a layer of cells

ep·i·glot·tis /ˌɛpəˈglɑtɪs/ *n.* [C] BIOLOGY the thin piece of flesh at the back of your throat, that covers part of your throat when you swallow

ep·i·gram /ˈɛpəˌgræm/ *n.* [C] ENG. LANG. ARTS a short amusing poem or saying that expresses a wise idea

ep·i·lep·sy /ˈɛpəˌlɛpsi/ *n.* [U] a medical condition in the brain that can make someone become unconscious or unable to control his/her movements for a short time

ep·i·lep·tic /ˌɛpəˈlɛptɪk◂ / *n.* [C] someone who has epilepsy —**epileptic** *adj.*

ep·i·logue /ˈɛpəˌlɔg, -ˌlɑg/ *n.* [C] ENG. LANG. ARTS a speech or piece of writing added to the end of a book, movie, or play, which usually gives information about what happened after the main action

e·piph·a·ny /ɪˈpɪfəni/ *n.* **1** (plural **epiphanies**) [C] a moment of sudden very strong emotions, when someone suddenly understands something important **2 Epiphany** a Christian holy day on January 6, that celebrates the visit of the Three Wise Men to the baby Jesus Christ

E·pis·co·pal /ɪˈpɪskəpəl/ *adj.* relating to the Protestant church in America that developed from the Church of England —**Episcopalian** /ɪˌpɪskəˈpeɪliən/ *n.* [C], *adj.*

E

ep·i·sode /ˈɛpəˌsoʊd/ *n.* [C] **1** a television or radio program that is one of a series of programs that tell a story: *It's my favorite episode of "Lost."* **2** an event, or a short time that is different from the time around it: *several episodes of depression* —**episodic** /ˌɛpəˈsɑdɪk/ *adj.*

e·pis·tle /ɪˈpɪsəl/ *n.* [C] **1** (formal) a long and important letter **2 Epistle** one of the letters written by the first Christians, which are in the New Testament of the Bible [ORIGIN: 1100—1200 Old French, Greek *epistole* "message, letter," from *epistellein* "to send to"]

e·pis·to·lar·y /ɪˈpɪstəˌlɛri/ *adj.* ENG. LANG. ARTS an epistolary book is written in the form of a series of letters

ep·i·taph /ˈɛpəˌtæf/ *n.* [C] a statement about a dead person, on the stone over his/her grave

ep·i·the·li·al tis·sue /ˌɛpəθiliəl ˈtɪʃu/ *n.* [U] BIOLOGY a material made up of cells that are very close together, which forms a thin protective layer on the inner surfaces of the body and around organs

ep·i·thet /ˈɛpəˌθɛt/ *n.* [C] ENG. LANG. ARTS an adjective or short phrase used for describing someone

e·pit·o·me /ɪˈpɪt̬əmi/ *n.* **the epitome of sth** the perfect example of something: *Hitler is considered the epitome of evil.*

e·pit·o·mize /ɪˈpɪt̬əˌmaɪz/ *v.* [T] to be the perfect or most typical example of something: *Chicago's busy liveliness seemed to epitomize the U.S.*

ep·och /ˈɛpək/ *n.* [C] a period in history during which important events or developments happened

e·qual¹ /ˈikwəl/ *adj.* **1** the same in size, value, amount, etc.: *Divide the dough into three equal parts.* | *Both candidates received an* ***equal number*** *of votes.* | *Population growth is* ***equal to*** *2% a year.* | *two areas* ***of equal*** *size* **2** having the same rights, chances, etc. as everyone else: *The Constitution says that all people are created equal.* | *equal partners in the business* | *equal rights for women* | *an equal opportunity employer* **3 be equal to the task/challenge etc.** to have the ability to deal with something successfully **4 on (an) equal footing** *also* **on equal terms** with neither side having any advantages over the other [ORIGIN: 1300—1400 Latin *aequalis*, from *aequus* "level, equal"]

equal² *v.* (**equaled** *or* **equalled**, **equaling** *or* **equalling**) **1** [linking verb] to be the same as something else in size, number, amount, etc.: *Four plus four equals eight.* **2** [T] to be as good as something or someone else: *He has equalled the Olympic record!*

equal³ *n.* [C] someone who is as important, intelligent, etc. as you are, or who has the same rights and opportunities as you do: *My boss treats her employees as equals.* | *Rembrandt was an artist* ***without equal*** (=no one was as good as he).

e·qual·i·ty /ɪˈkwɑlət̬i/ *n.* [U] the state of having the same conditions, opportunities, and rights as everyone else (ANT) **inequality**: *Women haven't achieved equality in the workforce.* | ***equality of*** *opportunity* | *the struggle for* ***racial equality***

e·qual·ize /ˈikwəˌlaɪz/ *v.* [T] to make two or more things equal in size, value, etc.: *The funds given to all schools should be equalized.*

e·qual·ly /ˈikwəli/ *adv.* **1** to the same degree or limit: *The candidates are equally qualified for the job.* **2** in parts that are the same size: *We'll divide the work equally.*

ˌequal proˈtection *n.* [U] LAW the principle that the government must treat all people and groups of people in a fair and equal way, as promised in the Equal Protection Clause of the Fourteenth Amendment of the U.S. Constitution

ˈequal sign *n.* [C] MATH the sign (=), used in mathematics to show that two amounts or numbers are the same

e·qua·nim·i·ty /ˌikwəˈnɪmət̬i, ˌɛk-/ *n.* [U] (formal) calmness in a difficult situation

e·quate /ɪˈkweɪt/ (Ac) *v.* [T] (formal) to consider that one thing is the same as something else: *Don't* ***equate*** *criticism* ***with*** *blame.* [ORIGIN: 1400—1500 Latin, from *aequare* "to make equal"]

e·qua·tion /ɪˈkweɪʒən/ (Ac) *n.* [C] MATH a statement in mathematics showing that two quantities are equal, for example 2 x 3 + 4 = 10: *Solve the first ten equations for homework.* [ORIGIN: 1400—1500 Latin, past participle of *aequare* "to make equal," from *aequus* "equal"]

e·qua·tor /ɪˈkweɪt̬ɚ/ *n.* **the equator** an imaginary circle around the Earth, that divides it equally into its northern and southern halves —**equatorial** /ˌɛkwəˈtɔriəl◂ / *adj.* → *see picture at* GLOBE

e·ques·tri·an /ɪˈkwɛstriən/ *adj.* relating to horse riding [ORIGIN: 1600—1700 Latin *equester* "of a horse-rider," from *equus* "horse"]

e·qui·an·gu·lar /ˌikwiˈæŋgyəlɚ, ˌɛk-/ *adj.* MATH an equiangular TRIANGLE or another shape has angles that are the same size and sides that are the same length: *A square is an equiangular polygon.*

e·qui·lat·er·al tri·an·gle /ˌikwəˌlæt̮ərəl ˈtraɪˌæŋgəl/ *n.* [C] MATH a TRIANGLE whose three sides are the same length → *see picture at* TRIANGLE

e·qui·lib·ri·um /ˌikwəˈlɪbriəm/ *n.* [U] **1** a balance between opposing forces, influences, etc.: *The supply and the demand for money must be kept **in equilibrium**.* **2** a calm emotional state **3** CHEMISTRY a state of balance between the substances in a chemical solution after a chemical reaction

e·qui·nox /ˈikwəˌnɑks, ˈɛ-/ *n.* [C] one of the two times each year when day and night are equal in length everywhere

e·quip /ɪˈkwɪp/ (Ac) *v.* (**equipped**, **equipping**) [T] **1** to provide a person, group, building, etc. with the things that are needed for a particular purpose: *The new school will be **equipped with** the latest computers.* **2** to prepare someone for a particular purpose: *The program **equips** youngsters **with** technical skills.* | *a problem we weren't **equipped to** handle* [ORIGIN: 1500—1600 French *équiper*] —**equipped** *adj.*

e·quip·ment /ɪˈkwɪpmənt/ (Ac) *n.* [U] the tools, machines, etc. that you need for a particular activity: *camera equipment* | *new **pieces of equipment** for the chemistry lab*

GRAMMAR

Equipment does not have a plural form. You can say **some equipment**, **any equipment**, or **pieces of equipment**. *We need to buy some extra equipment.*

eq·ui·ta·ble /ˈɛkwət̮əbəl/ *adj.* (formal) fair and equal to everyone involved: *an equitable solution*

THESAURUS **fair, just, reasonable, balanced, even-handed, impartial, unbiased** → FAIR[1]

eq·ui·ty /ˈɛkwət̮i/ *n.* [U] **1** (formal) a situation in which everyone is fairly treated **2** ECONOMICS the value of something you own, such as a house or SHARES, after you have taken away the amount of money you still owe on it

e·quiv·a·lent[1] /ɪˈkwɪvələnt/ (Ac) *adj.* equal in value, purpose, rank, etc. to something or someone else: *The atomic bomb has power **equivalent to** 10,000 tons of dynamite.* [ORIGIN: 1400—1500 French, Late Latin, from *aequivalere* "to have equal power"]

equivalent[2] *n.* [C] something that has the same value, size, etc. as something else: *Some French words have no equivalents in English.* | *He had drunk the **equivalent of** two bottles of wine.*

eˌquivalent eˈquations *n.* [plural] MATH two or more EQUATIONS that have the same set of solutions

e·quiv·o·cal /ɪˈkwɪvəkəl/ *adj.* **1** deliberately not clear or definite in meaning: *an equivocal answer* **2** difficult to understand or explain: *The results of the test were equivocal.*

ER *n.* [C] an EMERGENCY ROOM

e·ra /ˈɪrə, ˈɛrə/ *n.* [C] **1** a long period of time that begins with a particular date or event: *the colonial era* **2** EARTH SCIENCES one of the three long periods of time that the history of the Earth is divided into, starting 550 million years ago [ORIGIN: 1600—1700 Late Latin *aera* "number for calculating from," from Latin, "counters," plural of *aes* "copper, money"]

e·rad·i·cate /ɪˈrædəˌkeɪt/ *v.* [T] to completely destroy something: *Smallpox has been eradicated.* [ORIGIN: 1400—1500 Latin, past participle of *eradicare* "to pull out by the root," from *radix* "root"] —**eradication** /ɪˌrædəˈkeɪʃən/ *n.* [U]

e·rase /ɪˈreɪs/ *v.* [T] **1** to completely remove written or recorded information so that it cannot be seen or heard: *I erased the answer.* | *The information had been erased from the hard drive.*

THESAURUS **remove, rub off, efface, expunge** → REMOVE

2 to get rid of something so that it is gone completely: *I could not erase the memories from that time.* [ORIGIN: 1500—1600 Latin, past participle of *eradere*, from *radere* "to rub roughly, scrape"]

e·ras·er /ɪˈreɪsɚ/ *n.* [C] **1** a piece of rubber used for erasing pencil marks from paper **2** an object used for cleaning marks from a BLACKBOARD

e·rect[1] /ɪˈrɛkt/ *adj.* in a straight upright position: *He stood erect.*

erect[2] *v.* [T] **1** (formal) to build something: *Officials plan to erect a monument in Lindbergh's honor.*

THESAURUS **build, construct, put up, assemble** → BUILD[1]

2 to put something in an upright position: *The tents for the fair were erected overnight.*

e·rec·tion /ɪˈrɛkʃən/ *n.* **1** [C] the swelling of a man's PENIS during sexual excitement **2** [U] the act of building something: *the erection of a new church*

e·rode /ɪˈroʊd/ (Ac) *v.* **1** [I,T] to destroy something gradually by the action of wind, rain, or acid, or to be destroyed in this way: *The cliffs had been eroded by the ocean.* **2** [T] to gradually reduce someone's power, authority, etc.: *The government was accused of eroding civil rights.*

e·ro·sion /ɪˈroʊʒən/ (Ac) *n.* [U] **1** EARTH SCIENCES the process by which rock or soil is gradually washed away by wind, rain, or water: *soil erosion* → *see picture on page 340* **2** the process of gradually making something weaker: *the **erosion of** society's values*

e·rot·ic /ɪˈrɑt̮ɪk/ *adj.* relating to sexual love and desire: *erotic pictures* —**erotically** *adv.* —**eroticism** /ɪˈrɑt̮əˌsɪzəm/ *n.* [U]

err /ɛr, ɚ/ *v.* [I] **1 err on the side of caution/mercy etc.** to be very careful, very kind, etc.

E

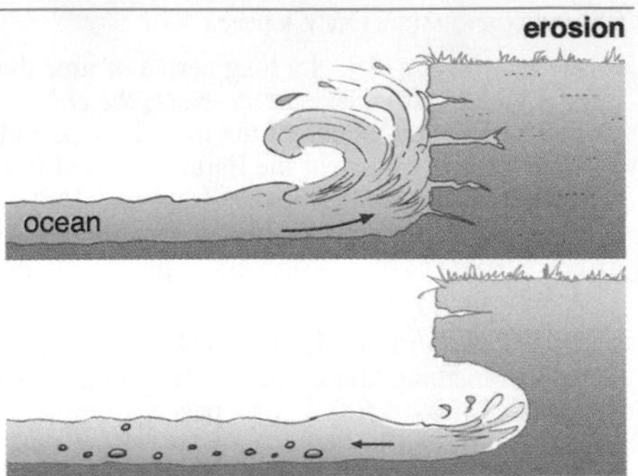

rather than risk making mistakes **2** (formal) to make a mistake

E

er·rand /ˈɛrənd/ *n.* [C] a short trip that you make to take a message or buy something: *I **have** some **errands** to do downtown.* | *Could you **run an errand** for Grandma?*

er·rant /ˈɛrənt/ *adj.* (formal) **1** behaving badly: *an errant husband* **2** going in the wrong direction: *A member of the other team caught the errant pass.*

er·rat·ic /ɪˈrætɪk/ *adj.* changing often or moving in an irregular way, without any reason: *erratic behavior* —**erratically** *adv.*

er·ro·ne·ous /ɪˈroʊniəs/ (Ac) *adj.* (formal) not correct: *erroneous statements* | *The information we were given was erroneous.* [ORIGIN: 1300—1400 Latin *erroneus*, from *errare* "to wander"] —**erroneously** *adv.*

THESAURUS **wrong, incorrect, inaccurate, misleading, false, fallacious** → WRONG[1]

er·ror /ˈɛrɚ/ (Ac) *n.* [C,U] a mistake: *They had **made** several **errors**.* | *an accident caused by **human error*** (=by a person rather than a machine) | *The company admitted it **was in error*** (=had made a mistake). | *Kovitz apologized yesterday for his **error in/of judgment*** (=a decision that was a mistake). [ORIGIN: 1200—1300 Old French *errour*, from Latin *error*, from *errare*]

er·u·dite /ˈɛryəˌdaɪt, ˈɛrə-/ *adj.* (formal) showing a lot of knowledge —**erudition** /ˌɛryəˈdɪʃən/ *n.* [U]

e·rupt /ɪˈrʌpt/ *v.* [I] **1** to happen suddenly: *A bloody civil war erupted in Iran.* **2** EARTH SCIENCES if a VOLCANO erupts, it sends out smoke, fire, and rock into the sky **3** if a place erupts, the people there suddenly become very angry or excited: *The crowd erupted into applause.* [ORIGIN: 1600—1700 Latin, past participle of *erumpere* "to burst out"] —**eruption** /ɪˈrʌpʃən/ *n.* [C,U]: *a volcanic eruption*

es·ca·late /ˈɛskəˌleɪt/ *v.* **1** [I,T] if violence or a war escalates, or if someone escalates it, it becomes much worse: *Fighting has escalated in several areas.* | *a dispute which has **escalated into** violence* **2** [I] to become higher or increase: *Housing prices escalated recently.* —**escalation** /ˌɛskəˈleɪʃən/ *n.* [C,U]

es·ca·la·tor /ˈɛskəˌleɪtɚ/ *n.* [C] a set of stairs that move and carry people from one level of a building to another

es·ca·pade /ˈɛskəˌpeɪd/ *n.* [C] an exciting adventure or series of events that may be dangerous

es·cape[1] /ɪˈskeɪp/ *v.* **1** [I,T] to succeed in going away from a place where you do not want to be, or from a dangerous situation: *He **escaped from** a maximum security prison.* | *The girl climbed through a window to escape the fire.*

THESAURUS

get away – to escape from someone who is chasing you: *In the dream, a man with a knife is chasing me, and I can't get away.*
flee – to leave somewhere very quickly in order to escape from danger: *The refugees were forced to flee their country.*
get out – to escape from a place: *Is the window locked? Maybe we can get out that way.*
break out – to escape from prison: *Several inmates have broken out of the state penitentiary.*
break free/break away – to escape from someone who is trying to hold you: *She broke free and started running.*
abscond (formal) – to leave a place without permission or after stealing something: *Two employees allegedly absconded with the money.*

2 [I,T] to avoid something bad: *The two boys managed to escape punishment.* | *The driver narrowly escaped death.* | *She escaped with minor **injuries*** (=she avoided being seriously hurt). **3** [I] if gas, liquid, light, etc. escapes from somewhere, it comes out **4 escape sb's notice/attention** to not notice something —**escaped** *adj.*: *escaped prisoners*

escape[2] *n.* **1** [C,U] the act of escaping: *There was no chance of escape.* | *He crouched down, ready to **make** his **escape**.* | *Passengers talked about their **escape from** the wreckage.* **2** [U] a way to forget about an unpleasant situation: *Books are a good form of escape.*

es·cap·ism /ɪˈskeɪpˌɪzəm/ *n.* [U] a way of forgetting about an unpleasant situation and thinking of pleasant things: *the escapism that the movies provide for us* —**escapist** *adj.*

es·chew /ɛsˈtʃu/ *v.* [T] (formal) to deliberately avoid doing, using, or having something

es·cort[1] /ɪˈskɔrt, ˈɛskɔrt/ *v.* [T] **1** to go somewhere with someone, especially in order to protect him/her: *Armed guards escorted the prisoners.* | *I escorted her to the door.*

THESAURUS **lead, guide, show, usher** → LEAD[1]

2 to go with someone of the opposite sex to a social event: *The princess was escorted by her cousin.*

es·cort[2] /ˈɛskɔrt/ *n.* [C] the person or people who

escort someone: *The governor arrived at the Convention Center with a **police escort**. | The prisoners were transported **under escort*** (=with an escort).

Es·ki·mo /ˈɛskəˌmoʊ/ *n.* (plural **Eskimos**) [C] an Inuit. Some people now consider this word offensive.

ESL *n.* [U] **English as a Second Language** the teaching of English to people whose first language is not English, but who are living in an English-speaking country

e·soph·a·gus /ɪˈsɑfəgəs/ *n.* [C] BIOLOGY the tube that goes from the mouth to the stomach [ORIGIN: 1300—1400 Greek *oisophagos*, from *oisein* "to be going to carry" + *phagein* "to eat"] → *see picture at* LUNG

es·o·ter·ic /ˌɛsəˈtɛrɪk/ *adj.* known and understood only by a few people

ESP *n.* [U] **extrasensory perception** the ability to know what another person is thinking

es·pe·cial·ly /ɪˈspɛʃəli/ *adv.* **1** used in order to emphasize that something is more important than other things, or that it happens more with one thing than with others: *Everyone's excited, especially Doug. | There may be feelings of dizziness, **especially when** walking or turning.* **2** to a particularly high degree, or more than usual: *The bread tasted especially good.* **3** for a particular purpose, reason, etc. → SPECIALLY: *Several songs were recorded especially for the new collection.*

es·pi·o·nage /ˈɛspiəˌnɑʒ/ *n.* [U] the activity of finding out secret information and giving it to a country's enemies or a company's competitors

ESPN *n.* a CABLE television company that broadcasts sports programs in the U.S.

es·pouse /ɛˈspaʊz, ɪ-/ *v.* [T] (formal) to believe in and support an idea, especially a political one: *The school board has espoused the new anti-drug policies.*

es·pres·so /ɛˈsprɛsoʊ/ *n.* (plural **espressos**) [C,U] very strong coffee that you drink in small cups [ORIGIN: 1900—2000 Italian *caffè espresso* "pressed-out coffee"]

es·say /ˈɛseɪ/ *n.* [C] a short piece of writing about a particular subject, especially as part of a course of study: *an **essay on/about** race relations* [ORIGIN: 1400—1500 Old French *essai*, from Late Latin *exagium* "act of weighing"]

THESAURUS

composition – an essay that you write as part of your school work: *We had to write a composition about one of our hobbies.*
paper – a piece of writing that is done as part of a course at school or university: *She's writing a paper on the Civil War.*
assignment – something that a teacher asks a student to do for homework: *For our assignment, we had to interview people about their eating habits.*
thesis – a long piece of writing that is part of an advanced university degree, for example an M.A.: *I wrote my thesis on the poems of Sylvia Plath.*
dissertation – a long piece of writing that you write for a Ph.D.: *He is currently working on his dissertation for his Ph.D. in Social Policy.*

es·sence /ˈɛsəns/ *n.* **1** [singular] the most basic and important quality of something: *Using scents to create a sense of well-being is the **essence of** aromatherapy. | **In essence** (=basically), these novels are all love stories.* **2** [U] a liquid that has a strong smell or taste and is obtained from a plant, flower, etc.: *vanilla essence* [ORIGIN: 1300—1400 French, Latin *essentia*, from *esse* "to be"]

es·sen·tial[1] /ɪˈsɛnʃəl/ *adj.* **1** important and necessary: *an essential element in the peace process | Good food is **essential for/to** your health.*

THESAURUS **important, of great/considerable importance, crucial, vital, major, key, paramount, significant, salient** → IMPORTANT
necessary, mandatory, compulsory, requisite, indispensable → NECESSARY

2 the essential parts, qualities, or features of something are the ones that are most important, typical, or easily noticed: *the **essential difference** between Democrats and Republicans*

THESAURUS **basic, fundamental, elementary, central, underlying** → BASIC

essential[2] *n.* [C usually plural] something that is important and necessary: *Elections are one of the essentials of democracy. | I packed only the **bare essentials*** (=the most necessary things).

es·sen·tial·ly /ɪˈsɛnʃəli/ *adv.* relating to the most important or basic qualities of something: *He is paid less for doing essentially the same job.*

es·tab·lish /ɪˈstæblɪʃ/ (Ac) *v.* [T] **1** to start something such as a company, system, situation, etc., especially one that will exist for a long time: *The school was established in 1922.* **2** to begin a relationship, conversation, etc. with someone: *In the 1980s, the two countries began to establish trade relations.* **3** to make people accept that you can do something, or that you have a particular quality: *He's **established himself as** the most powerful man in the state.* **4** to find out facts that will prove that something is true: *Several studies have **established that** good daycare does children no harm. | The blood test will **establish whether** the treatment has been successful.* [ORIGIN: 1300—1400 Old French *establir*, from Latin *stabilire* "to make firm"]

THESAURUS **demonstrate, show, indicate, suggest, prove, substantiate** → DEMONSTRATE

es·tab·lish·ment /ɪˈstæblɪʃmənt/ (Ac) *n.* **1** [C] (formal) an institution, especially a business, store, hotel, etc.: *an educational establishment* (=a school or college) **2 the Establishment** the organizations and people in a society who have a lot of power and who often are opposed to change

E

or new ideas: *the* ***political/medical/military Establishment*** **3** [U] the act of starting something such as a company, organization, system, etc.: *The case resulted in the establishment of new laws to protect children.*

es·tate /ɪ'steɪt/ (Ac) *n.* **1** [singular] LAW all of someone's property and money, especially everything that is left after s/he dies: *The house is part of his dead father's estate.* **2** [C] a large area of land in the country, usually with one large house on it ➔ REAL ESTATE

es·teem¹ /ɪ'stim/ *n.* [U] (formal) a feeling of respect and admiration for someone: *She was* ***held in high esteem*** *by everyone on the team.* ➔ SELF-ESTEEM

esteem² *v.* [T] (formal) to respect and admire someone: *a* ***highly esteemed*** (=greatly respected) *artist*

E

es·thet·ic /ɛs'θɛt̬ɪk/ *adj.* relating to beauty and the study of beauty —**esthetically** *adv.*

es·thet·ics /ɛs'θɛt̬ɪks/ *n.* [U] the study of beauty, especially beauty in art

es·ti·mate¹ /'ɛstəˌmeɪt/ (Ac) *v.* [T] to judge the value, size, etc. of something: *We* ***estimate that*** *75% of our customers are men.* | *Organizers* ***estimated*** *the crowd* ***at*** *50,000 people.* | *The tree is* ***estimated to*** *be at least 700 years old.* —**estimated** *adj.*: *The bridge was built at an estimated cost of $2 billion.*

es·ti·mate² /'ɛstəmɪt/ (Ac) *n.* [C] **1** a calculation or judgment of the value, size, etc. of something: ***a rough estimate*** (=a calculation that is not very exact) *of the distance* | *The figure is three times higher than previous estimates.* **2** a statement of how much it will probably cost to build or repair something: *Try to get three estimates.*

es·ti·ma·tion /ˌɛstə'meɪʃən/ (Ac) *n.* [U] a judgment or opinion about someone or something: ***In his estimation****, they had greatly improved.*

es·tranged /ɪ'streɪndʒd/ *adj.* **1** no longer living with your husband or wife **2** no longer having any relationship with a relative or friend: *Molly is* ***estranged from*** *her son.* —**estrangement** *n.* [C,U] (formal)

es·tro·gen /'ɛstrədʒən/ *n.* [U] BIOLOGY a HORMONE (=chemical substance) that is produced by a woman's body

es·tu·ar·y /'ɛstʃuˌɛri/ *n.* (plural **estuaries**) [C] EARTH SCIENCES the wide part of a river where it goes into the ocean ➔ *see picture at* DELTA

ETA *n.* [U] **estimated time of arrival** the time when an airplane, train, etc. is expected to arrive

e-tail·er /'i ˌteɪlɚ/ *n.* [C] **electronic retailer** a business that sells products or services on the Internet

et al. /ˌɛt̬ 'ɑl, -'æl/ *adv.* (formal) used after a list of names to mean that other people, who are not named, are also involved in something

etc. /ɛt 'sɛtrə, -t̬ərə/ *adv.* the written abbreviation of ET CETERA – used after a list to show that there are many other similar things or people that could be added

et cet·er·a /ɛt 'sɛtrə, -t̬ərə/ *adv.* (formal) the full form of ETC.

etch /ɛtʃ/ *v.* [I,T] to cut lines on a metal plate, piece of glass, stone, etc. to form a picture

e·ter·nal /ɪ'tɚnl/ *adj.* continuing for ever: *eternal life* —**eternally** *adv.*

e·ter·ni·ty /ɪ'tɚnət̬i/ *n.* **1 an eternity** a period of time that seems long because you are annoyed, anxious, etc.: *We waited for what seemed like an eternity.* **2** [U] time without any end, especially the time after death that some people believe continues for ever

e·ther /'iθɚ/ *n.* [U] **1** a clear liquid, used in past times to make people sleep during a medical operation **2** the air, considered as the place where computer information is

e·the·re·al /ɪ'θɪriəl/ *adj.* very delicate and light, in a way that does not seem real

eth·ic /'ɛθɪk/ (Ac) *n.* **1** [C] an idea or belief that influences people's behavior and attitudes: *an ethic of fairness* | *the Puritan work ethic* **2 ethics** [plural] moral rules or principles of behavior for deciding what is right and wrong: *medical ethics*

eth·i·cal /'ɛθɪkəl/ (Ac) *adj.* **1** relating to principles of what is right and wrong: *The use of animals in scientific tests raises difficult ethical questions.* **2** morally good and correct: *Is it ethical to use drugs to control behavior?* —**ethically** *adv.*

eth·nic /'ɛθnɪk/ (Ac) *adj.* relating to a particular race, nation, tribe, etc.: *Bosnia's three main* ***ethnic groups*** | *The students are from a wide variety of* ***ethnic backgrounds****.* [ORIGIN: 1300—1400 Late Latin *ethnicus*, from Greek *ethnos* "nation, people"]

ˌethnic 'cleansing *n.* [U] the use of violence in order to force people to leave an area because of their ethnic group

ˌethnic 'group *n.* [C] SOCIAL SCIENCE a group of people who share the same CULTURE, race, NATIONALITY, religion, or language

> THESAURUS **race, nation, people, tribe** ➔ RACE¹

eth·nic·i·ty /ɛθ'nɪsət̬i/ (Ac) *n.* (plural **ethnicities**) [C,U] the race or national group that someone belongs to

ˌethnic mi'nority *n.* [C] a group of people from a different ethnic group than the main group in a country

e·thos /'iθɑs/ *n.* [singular] the set of ideas and moral attitudes belonging to a person or group [ORIGIN: 1800—1900 Greek "custom, character"]

e-tick·et /'i ˌtɪkɪt/ *n.* [C] **electronic ticket** a ticket, especially for an airplane, that is stored in a computer and is not given to the customer in paper form

et·i·quette /ˈɛt̬ɪkɪt/ *n.* [U] the formal rules for polite behavior in society or in a particular group

et·y·mol·o·gy /ˌɛt̬əˈmɑlədʒi/ *n.* (plural **etymologies**) [C,U] ENG. LANG. ARTS the study of the origins, history, and meanings of words, or a description of the origins of a particular word [ORIGIN: 1300—1400 Latin *etymologia*, from Greek, from *etymon* "original meaning," from *etymos* "true" + *-logia* "study"] —**etymological** /ˌɛt̬əməˈlɑdʒɪkəl/ *adj.*

THESAURUS **origin, source, root** ➔ ORIGIN

EU *n.* **the EU** the EUROPEAN UNION

Eu·cha·rist /ˈyukərɪst/ *n.* **the Eucharist** the bread and wine that represent Christ's body and blood, used during a Christian ceremony, or the ceremony itself

eu·kar·y·a /yuˈkæriə/ *n.* [plural] BIOLOGY one of the classes into which scientists group animals, plants, and other living creatures whose cells have a NUCLEUS

eu·kar·y·ote /yuˈkæri͵out/ *n.* [C] BIOLOGY a living creature with a cell or cells that have its GENETIC material in a NUCLEUS —**eukaryotic** /yu͵kæriˈɑt̬ɪk/ *adj.*

eu·lo·gy /ˈyulədʒi/ *n.* (plural **eulogies**) [C,U] (formal) a speech or piece of writing that praises someone or something very much, especially at a funeral

eu·phe·mism /ˈyufə͵mɪzəm/ *n.* [C] ENG. LANG. ARTS a polite word or expression that you use instead of a more direct one, in order to avoid shocking or upsetting someone [ORIGIN: 1500—1600 Greek *euphemismos*, from *euphemos* "sounding good," from *pheme* "speech"] —**euphemistic** /͵yufəˈmɪstɪk◂/ *adj.* —**euphemistically** *adv.*

eu·pho·ri·a /yuˈfɔriə/ *n.* [U] a feeling of extreme happiness and excitement

eu·phor·ic /yuˈfɔrɪk/ *adj.* feeling very happy and excited: *After the game, the team was euphoric.* —**euphorically** *adv.*

eu·ro /ˈyʊroʊ/ *n.* (plural **euros**) [C] a unit of money that is used in most countries belonging to the European Union

Eu·rope /ˈyʊrəp/ *n.* one of the seven CONTINENTs that includes land north of the Mediterranean Sea and west of the Ural mountains

Eu·ro·pe·an¹ /͵yʊrəˈpiən◂/ *adj.* relating to or coming from Europe

European² *n.* [C] someone from Europe

͵European ˈUnion *n.* a European political and economic organization

eu·tha·na·sia /͵yuθəˈneɪʒə/ *n.* [U] the act of killing in a painless way someone who is very sick, in order to stop him/her suffering [ORIGIN: 1600—1700 Greek "easy death," from *thanatos* "death"] —**euthanize** /ˈyuθə͵naɪz/ *v.* [T]

e·vac·u·ate /ɪˈvækyu͵eɪt/ *v.* [I,T] to move people from a dangerous place to a safe place: *The police evacuated the building.* [ORIGIN: 1300—1400 Latin, past participle of *evacuare*, from *vacuus* "empty"] —**evacuation** /ɪ͵vækyuˈeɪʃən/ *n.* [C,U]

e·vac·u·ee /ɪ͵vækyuˈi/ *n.* [C] someone who has been evacuated

e·vade /ɪˈveɪd/ *v.* [T] **1** to avoid doing something you should do, or avoid talking about something ➔ EVASION: *Briggs evaded the issue.* **2** to avoid being caught by someone who is trying to catch you: *So far, he has evaded capture.*

e·val·u·ate /ɪˈvælyu͵eɪt/ (Ac) *v.* [T] **1** (formal) to judge how good, useful, or successful someone or something is: *a chance for students to evaluate teachers* | *Scientists are evaluating the results of the drug trials.*

THESAURUS **judge, assess, appraise, gauge** ➔ JUDGE²

2 MATH to calculate the value of a mathematical EXPRESSION

e·val·u·a·tion /ɪ͵vælyuˈeɪʃən/ (Ac) *n.* [C,U] the act of judging something or someone, or a document in which this is done: *an evaluation of new surgical techniques* | *The child was sent for a psychological evaluation.* [ORIGIN: 1700—1800 French *évaluation*, from *évaluer* "to evaluate," from *value* "value"]

e͵valuative ˈquestion *n.* [C] ENG. LANG. ARTS a question that asks someone to give his/her opinion or make a judgment about something, based on something s/he has read ➔ INFERENTIAL QUESTION, LITERAL QUESTION

ev·a·nes·cent /͵ɛvəˈnɛsənt/ *adj.* (literary) something that is evanescent disappears quickly

e·van·gel·i·cal /͵ivænˈdʒɛlɪkəl, ͵ɛvən-/ *adj.* SOCIAL SCIENCE evangelical Christians and beliefs emphasize a personal relationship with God, the importance of the Bible, and the importance of telling others about these ideas

e·van·ge·list /ɪˈvændʒəlɪst/ *n.* [C] someone who travels from place to place in order to try to persuade people to become Christians [ORIGIN: 1100—1200 Old French *evangeliste*, from Greek *euangelion* "good news, gospel"] —**evangelism** *n.* [U] —**evangelistic** /ɪ͵vændʒəˈlɪstɪk/ *adj.*

e·vap·o·rate /ɪˈvæpə͵reɪt/ *v.* **1** [I,T] CHEMISTRY if a liquid evaporates, or if something evaporates it, it changes into a gas **2** [I] to slowly disappear: *Support for the idea has evaporated.*

e·vap·o·ra·tion /ɪ͵væpəˈreɪʃən/ *n.* [U] CHEMISTRY the process by which a liquid changes into a gas, for example into a VAPOR such as steam ➔ CONDENSATION ➔ *see picture at* WATER CYCLE

E

e·va·sion /ɪˈveɪʒən/ *n.* [C,U] **1** the act of avoiding doing something you should do: *tax evasion* **2** the act of deliberately avoiding talking about something or dealing with something: *a speech full of lies and evasions*

e·va·sive /ɪˈveɪsɪv/ *adj.* **1** not willing to answer questions directly: *an evasive answer* **2 evasive action** an action someone does to avoid being injured or harmed —**evasively** *adv.*

eve /iv/ *n.* **1** [C usually singular] the night or day before a religious day or a holiday: *a party on New Year's Eve* **2 the eve of sth** the time just before an important event: *the eve of the election*

e·ven¹ /ˈivən/ *adv.* **1** used in order to emphasize that something is surprising or unexpected: *Even with the light on, it was hard to see.* | *Carrie doesn't even like cookies!* **2** used in order to make a comparison stronger: *That just made me feel even worse.* | *an even bigger house* **3 even if** used in order to show that what you have just said will not change for any reason: *If you ask a question, you'll get an answer, even if it's "I don't know."* **4 even though** used in order to emphasize that although one thing happens or is true, something else also happens or is true: *He still remembers it, even though it happened more than 20 years ago.* **5 even so** used in order to say that something is true, although it is different from something you have just said: *I knew he wasn't coming, but even so, I waited a few minutes more.*

E

even² *adj.* **1** flat, level, or smooth: *You need a flat, even surface to work on.*

THESAURUS **flat, level, smooth, horizontal**
→ FLAT¹

2 an even rate, temperature, etc. does not change much: *Store the chemicals at an even temperature.* **3** separated or divided by equal amounts, spaces, etc.: *his even white teeth* | *an even distribution of wealth* **4 be even** (informal) to no longer owe someone money: *If you give me $5, we'll be even.* **5** an even number can be divided by 2 (ANT) **odd** **6 get even (with sb)** (informal) to do something bad to someone to punish him/her for something s/he did to you → **break even** *at* BREAK¹ —**evenness** *n.* [U]

even³ *v.*

even (sth ↔) **out** *phr. v.* to become equal or level, or to make something do this: *If I give you two, that'll even things out.* | *Over the year, the rise and fall in share prices has tended to even out.*

even (sth ↔) **up** *phr. v.* to become equal or the same, or to make something do this: *O'Malley hit a home run to even up the score.*

ˌeven-ˈhanded *adj.* giving fair and equal treatment to everyone

THESAURUS **fair, just, reasonable, equitable, balanced, impartial, unbiased** → FAIR¹

eve·ning /ˈivnɪŋ/ *n.* **1** [C,U] the end of the day and the early part of the night: *Are you doing anything tomorrow evening?* | *I have a class **on** Thursday **evenings**.* | *She does her homework **in the evening**.* **2 (Good) Evening** (spoken) said in order to greet someone when you meet him/her in the evening: *Evening, Rick.* [ORIGIN: Old English *æfnung*, from *æfen* "evening"]

ˈevening gown *also* **ˈevening dress** *n.* [C] a dress worn by women for formal occasions in the evening

e·ven·ly /ˈivənli/ *adv.* **1** covering or affecting all parts of something equally: *Spread the paint evenly over the surface.* | *Make sure the weight is **evenly distributed**.* **2** divided in an equal way: *We split the money evenly.* **3** in a steady or regular way: *She was breathing evenly.* | *evenly spaced rows of young trees*

e·vent /ɪˈvɛnt/ *n.* [C] **1** something that happens, especially something important, interesting, or unusual: *a novel based on a historical event* | *the **sequence of events** leading up to the war*

THESAURUS

occurrence – something that happens: *a common occurrence*
incident – something unusual, serious, or violent that happens: *an upsetting incident*
affair – an event or set of related events, especially unpleasant ones: *the Watergate affair during Nixon's presidency*
happening – something that happens, especially a strange event: *There have been reports of strange happenings in the town.*
occasion – an important event or ceremony: *We're saving the champagne for a special occasion.*
phenomenon – something that happens or exists in society, science, or nature that is unusual or difficult to understand: *Homelessness is not a new phenomenon.*

2 a performance, sports competition, party, etc. that has been arranged for a particular date and time: *It was the **social event** of the summer.* | *Security is tight for large **sporting events**.* **3** one of the races or competitions that are part of a large sports competition: *"Which event are you entered in?" "The long jump."* **4 in any event** whatever happens or whatever the situation: *I'm planning to retire at the end of the year in any event.* **5 in the event of rain/fire/an accident etc.** used in order to tell people what they should do or what will happen if something else happens: *Britain agreed to support the U.S. in the event of war.* [ORIGIN: 1500—1600 Latin *eventus*, from the past participle of *evenire* "to happen"]

e·vent·ful /ɪˈvɛntˀfəl/ *adj.* full of interesting or important events: *an eventful meeting*

e·ven·tu·al /ɪˈvɛntʃuəl/ (Ac) *adj.* happening at the end of a process: *In the quarterfinals, the University of Kansas lost to the eventual winners of the tournament.* [ORIGIN: 1600—1700 French *éventuel*, from Latin *eventus* "what happens in the end"]

e·ven·tu·al·i·ty /ɪˌvɛntʃuˈæləṭi/ (Ac) *n.* (plural **eventualities**) [C] (formal) a possible event or result, especially an unpleasant one: *Fire crews have to be prepared for all possible eventualities.*

e·ven·tual·ly /ɪˈvɛntʃəli, -tʃuəli/ (Ac) *adv.* after a long time: *He eventually became one of the top salesmen.* | *Eventually, the pressure became too great and the volcano erupted.*

ev·er /ˈɛvɚ/ *adv.* **1** at any time – used mostly in questions, negatives, comparisons, or sentences with "if": *Nothing ever makes Paula angry.* | ***Have you ever** eaten snails?* | *If you're ever in Wilmington, give us a call.* | *That was one of the best meals I've ever had.* | *I **hardly ever** (=almost never) watch TV.* **2 ever since** continuously since: *He moved to Seattle after college and has lived there ever since.* **3 as good/much/long etc. as ever** as good, much, etc. as always or as usual: *The food was as good as ever.* **4 better/higher/more etc. than ever** even better, higher, etc. than before: *People are having to work harder than ever just to pay the rent.* **5 ever-growing/ever-increasing etc.** continuously becoming bigger, etc.: *the ever-growing population problem*

> **GRAMMAR**
> You use **ever** when you ask a question, but not when you answer a question: *"Have you ever eaten sushi?" "Yes, I have."*

ev·er·green /ˈɛvɚˌgrin/ *adj.* evergreen trees have leaves that do not fall off in winter → DECIDUOUS —**evergreen** *n.* [C]

ev·er·last·ing /ˌɛvɚˈlæstɪŋ◂/ *adj.* continuing for ever: *everlasting peace*

ev·ery /ˈɛvri/ *determiner* **1** each one of a group of people or things: *Every student will receive a certificate.* | *He told Jan **every single** thing* (=all the things) *I said.* | *If you play this hard **every time*** (=on each occasion), *you'll win every game.* **2** used in order to show how often something happens: *We get the newspaper every day.* | *Change the oil in the car every 5,000 miles.* | *He came to see us **every other day*** (=every two days). | *I still see her **every now and then/every so often*** (=sometimes but not often). **3 one in every 100/3 in every 5 etc.** used in order to show how often something affects a particular group of people or things: *One in every three couples live together without being married.* **4 every which way** (informal) in every direction: *People were running every which way.* [ORIGIN: Old English *æfre ælc* "ever each"]

> **GRAMMAR**
> **every, every one, everyone**
> These are all followed by a singular verb: *Almost every house has a computer nowadays.* | *She checked the weight of each bag, and found that every one was different.* | *Everyone wants to be famous.*
> **Every one** is used to emphasize that you mean each person or thing in a group: *I've read every one of his books.*
> **Everyone** means all the people in a group: *I want to thank everyone for their help.* → ALL[1]

ev·ery·bod·y /ˈɛvriˌbɑdi, -ˌbʌdi/ *pron.* everyone

ev·ery·day /ˈɛvriˌdeɪ/ *adj.* ordinary, usual, or happening every day: *Stress is just part of **everyday life**.*

ev·ery·one /ˈɛvriˌwʌn/ *also* **everybody** *pron.* **1** every person involved in a particular activity or in a particular place: *Is everyone ready to go?* | *They gave a small prize to everyone who played.* | *Where is everybody* (=where are the people that are usually here)*?* | *I was still awake but **everybody else*** (=all the other people) *had gone to bed.* | ***Everyone but*** (=all the people except) *Lisa went home.*

> **USAGE**
> Use **everyone** to mean all the people in a group: *Everyone has passed the test.*
> Use **every one** to mean each single person or thing in a group: *Every one of the songs was really good.*

2 all people in general: *Everyone has a bad day now and then.*

ev·ery·place /ˈɛvriˌpleɪs/ *adv.* (spoken) everywhere

> **THESAURUS** everywhere, all over sth, throughout sth, worldwide, nationwide → EVERYWHERE

ev·ery·thing /ˈɛvriˌθɪŋ/ *pron.* **1** each thing or all things → NOTHING: *I think everything is ready.* | *I've forgotten everything I learned about math in school.* | *There's only bread left. They've eaten **everything else*** (=all other things). **2** used when you are talking in general about your life or about a situation → NOTHING: *Everything was going wrong.* **3 be/mean everything** to be the thing that matters most: *Money isn't everything.* **4 and everything** (spoken) and a lot of similar things: *She's at the hospital having tests and everything.*

ev·ery·where /ˈɛvriˌwɛr/ *adv.* in or to every place → NOWHERE: *I've looked everywhere for my keys.* | *People here are the same as people **everywhere else**.*

> **THESAURUS**
> **all over sth** – everywhere on a surface or in a place: *Jack's clothes were all over the floor.*
> **throughout sth** – in every part of a place: *The incident shocked Americans throughout the country.*
> **worldwide** – everywhere in the world: *He has fans worldwide.*
> **nationwide** – everywhere in a particular nation: *The company has over 350 stores nationwide.*
> **everyplace** (spoken) – everywhere: *There you are. I've been looking for you everyplace.*

E

e·vict /ɪ'vɪkt/ *v.* [T] to legally force someone to leave the house s/he is renting from you: *Frank was **evicted from** his apartment four months ago.* —**eviction** /ɪ'vɪkʃən/ *n.* [C,U]

ev·i·dence /'ɛvədəns/ (Ac) *n.* **1** [U] facts, objects, or signs that show that something exists or is true: *The police **have evidence that** the killer was a woman.* | *scientists looking for **evidence of** life on other planets* | *I had to **give evidence** (=tell the facts) in my brother's trial.* | *The strongest **evidence for** the theory comes from ongoing studies of bacteria.* | *There was very little **evidence against** him.* | *medical/scientific evidence* ➔ COURT[1] **2 be in evidence** (formal) to be easily seen or noticed: *The police were very much in evidence at the march.*

GRAMMAR

Evidence does not have a plural form. You can say **some evidence**, **any evidence**, or **pieces of evidence:** *There is some evidence that foods rich in vitamin C can give protection against cancer.*

ev·i·dent /'ɛvədənt/ (Ac) *adj.* easily noticed or understood: ***It was** clearly **evident that** she was unhappy.* | *John's ability is **evident in** his grades.* [ORIGIN: 1300—1400 French, Latin *evidens*, from *e-* "out" + the present participle of *videre* "to see"] —**evidently** *adv.*

THESAURUS **noticeable, clear, obvious, apparent, conspicuous, unmistakable, manifest** ➔ NOTICEABLE

e·vil[1] /'ivəl/ *adj.* **1** deliberately cruel or harmful: *an evil dictator* **2** morally wrong: *Slavery was evil.*

THESAURUS **bad, wicked, immoral, wrong, depraved, reprehensible** ➔ BAD[1]

3 relating to the Devil: *evil spirits* [ORIGIN: Old English *yfel*]

evil[2] *n.* **1** [U] actions and behavior that are morally wrong and cruel: *the battle between **good and evil*** **2** [C] something that is very bad or harmful: *the **evils of** alcohol*

e·vince /ɪ'vɪns/ *v.* [T] (formal) to show a feeling or quality very clearly in what you do or say: *She had evinced her belief in my innocence.*

e·voc·a·tive /ɪ'vɑkət̬ɪv/ *adj.* making people remember something by reminding them of a feeling or memory: *the evocative smell of bread baking in the oven*

e·voke /ɪ'voʊk/ *v.* [T] to produce a strong feeling or memory in someone: *Hitchcock's movies can evoke a sense of terror.* —**evocation** /ˌɛvə'keɪʃən, ˌivoʊ-/ *n.* [C,U]

ev·o·lu·tion /ˌɛvə'luʃən/ (Ac) *n.* [U] **1** BIOLOGY the scientific idea that plants and animals develop gradually from simpler to more complicated forms: *the **evolution of** mammals* | *The process of biological evolution continues over millions of years.* **2** the gradual change and development of an idea, situation, or object: *the **evolution of** the home computer* —**evolutionary** *adj.*: *evolutionary change*

evoˌlutionary classifi'cation *n.* [U] BIOLOGY a scientific system of putting living things into particular groups or classes, according to the way they evolved

e·volve /ɪ'vɑlv/ (Ac) *v.* **1** [I] to develop and change gradually over a long period of time: *Did man **evolve from** apes?* | *Their relationship **evolved into** a strong friendship.* **2** [T] to develop something gradually: *In America, we have evolved legal structures to protect people's rights.*

ewe /yu/ *n.* [C] a female sheep

ex /ɛks/ *n.* [C usually singular] (informal) someone's former wife, husband, GIRLFRIEND, or BOYFRIEND

ex·ac·er·bate /ɪg'zæsəˌbeɪt/ *v.* [T] (formal) to make a bad situation worse: *Higher taxes exacerbated the problem.* [ORIGIN: 1600—1700 Latin, past participle of *exacerbare*, from *acerbus* "bitter"] —**exacerbation** /ɪgˌzæsə'beɪʃən/ *n.* [U]

ex·act[1] /ɪg'zækt/ *adj.* **1** correct and including all the necessary details: *The **exact time** is 2:47.* | *What were her **exact words**?* | *It has been nine months, **to be exact.*** **2 the exact opposite** someone or something that is as different as possible from another person or thing: *Unfortunately, today the exact opposite is true.*

exact[2] *v.* [T] (formal) **1** to punish someone or have a bad effect on him/her: *What is the penalty exacted for breaking the rules?* **2** to demand and get something from someone by using threats, force, etc.

ex·act·ing /ɪg'zæktɪŋ/ *adj.* demanding a lot of care, effort, and attention: *an exacting piece of work*

ex·act·ly /ɪg'zæktli/ *adv.* **1** used in order to emphasize that a particular number, amount, or piece of information is completely correct: *We got home at exactly six o'clock.* | *You're exactly right.* | *I don't know **exactly where** she lives.* | ***What exactly** did she say?*

SPOKEN PHRASES

2 said in order to emphasize that something is the same in every way: *That's **exactly what** I've been trying to tell you!* | *She's **exactly like** her mother.* | *The changes have had **exactly the opposite** effect from what was intended.* **3** said when you agree with what someone is saying: *"So we should spend more on education?" "Exactly!"* **4 not exactly a)** used as a reply to show that what someone has said is not completely correct or true: *"He told you?" "Not exactly. I heard him talking to Sarah."* **b)** used in order to show that you mean the opposite: *The report isn't exactly beach reading.*

ex·ag·ger·ate /ɪg'zædʒəˌreɪt/ *v.* [I,T] to make something seem better, larger, worse, etc. than it really is: *The danger should not be exaggerated.*

[ORIGIN: 1500—1600 Latin, past participle of *exaggerare* "to make into a pile"] —**exaggerated** *adj.* —**exaggeration** /ɪgˌzædʒəˈreɪʃən/ *n.* [C,U]

THESAURUS **emphasize, stress, highlight, underline, accentuate, underscore** → EMPHASIZE

ex·alt /ɪgˈzɔlt/ *v.* [T] (formal) to praise someone

ex·al·ta·tion /ˌɛgzɔlˈteɪʃən, ˌɛksɔl-/ *n.* [C,U] (formal) a very strong feeling of happiness

ex·alt·ed /ɪgˈzɔltɪd/ *adj.* (formal) **1** having a very high rank, and highly respected **2** filled with a feeling of great happiness

ex·am /ɪgˈzæm/ *n.* [C] **1** an official test of knowledge or ability in a particular subject: *a chemistry exam* | *When do you **take** your final **exams**?* | *How did you do **on the exam**?* **2** a set of medical tests: *an eye exam*

ex·am·i·na·tion /ɪgˌzæməˈneɪʃən/ *n.* [C] **1** the process of looking at something carefully in order to see what it is like or find out something: *a detailed **examination of** the photographs* | ***On closer examination**, the vases were seen to be cracked.* **2** (formal) an EXAM

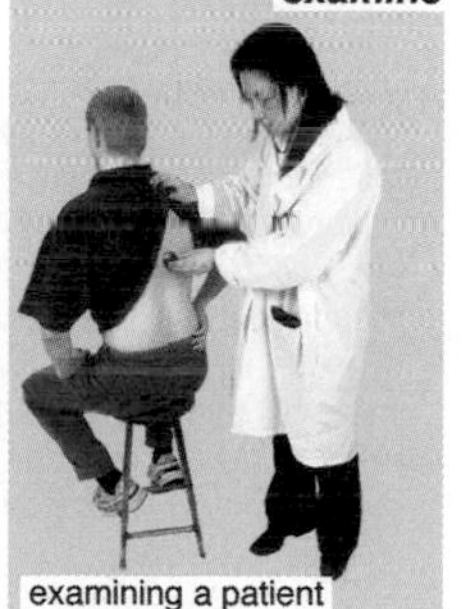

examining a patient

ex·am·ine /ɪgˈzæmɪn/ *v.* [T] **1** to look at something carefully in order to make a decision, find out something, etc.: *The doctor examined me thoroughly.* | *The study **examines how** alcohol abuse affects family relationships.* | *The police **examined** the room **for** fingerprints.*

THESAURUS

inspect – to examine something to make sure that it is correct, safe, etc., especially when it is your job to do this: *The building is regularly inspected by a fire safety officer.*

go through/go over – to examine something thoroughly from beginning to end, especially in order to check that it is correct: *You should ask your lawyer to go through the contract before you sign it.*

analyze – to carefully examine information, reports, the results of tests, etc., in order to understand something better: *When they analyzed the data, they found some surprising results.*

scrutinize – to examine something very closely and carefully in order to find out whether there is anything wrong: *Each part of the piano is carefully scrutinized, adjusted, and then tested again.*

2 (formal) to ask someone questions to get information or to test his/her knowledge about something: *You will be **examined on** everything covered this semester.* [ORIGIN: 1300—1400 French *examiner*, from Latin *examinare*, from *examen* "weighing out"] —**examiner** *n.* [C]

ex·am·ple /ɪgˈzæmpəl/ *n.* [C] **1** someone or something that you mention to show what you mean, show that something is true, or show what something is like: *an **example of** students' writing* | *These chairs are a **good/typical/classic example** of Shaker furniture.* | *Can anyone **give** me **an example** of a transitive verb?* | *Many countries, **for example*** (=as an example) *Mexico and Japan, have a lot of earthquakes.*

THESAURUS

case – an example of something that happens, especially something bad: *There have been a number of cases in which people have lost all their money.*

instance – an example of a particular kind of situation or event, especially one that does not happen very often: *I can't think of a single instance in which anyone has been hurt.*

2 someone whose behavior is very good and should be copied by other people: *Parents should **set an example for** their children* (=behave in the way they want their children to behave). | *She's an **example to** us all.* **3 make an example of sb** to punish someone so that other people are afraid to do the same thing [ORIGIN: 1300—1400 Old French, Latin *exemplum*, from *eximere* "to take out"]

ex·as·per·ate /ɪgˈzæspəˌreɪt/ *v.* [T] to make someone feel very annoyed by continuing to do something that upsets him/her: *His refusal to agree has exasperated his lawyers.* —**exasperating** *adj.* —**exasperation** /ɪgˌzæspəˈreɪʃən/ *n.* [U]

ex·as·pe·rat·ed /ɪgˈzæspəˌreɪtɪd/ *adj.* feeling annoyed because someone is continuing to do something that upsets you

ex·ca·vate /ˈɛkskəˌveɪt/ *v.* [I,T] **1** to dig a hole in the ground **2** to dig up the ground in order to find something that was buried there in an earlier time: *Archeologists are excavating an ancient city.* [ORIGIN: 1500—1600 Latin, past participle of *excavare*, from *cavus* "hollow"] —**excavation** /ˌɛkskəˈveɪʃən/ *n.* [C,U]

ex·ceed /ɪkˈsid/ (Ac) *v.* [T] (formal) **1** to be more than a particular number or amount: *The cost must not exceed $150.* | *Sales have **exceeded** our **expectations**.* **2** to go beyond an official or legal limit: *She received a fine for exceeding the speed limit.*

ex·ceed·ing·ly /ɪkˈsidɪŋli/ *adv.* (formal) extremely: *The show has done exceedingly well.*

ex·cel /ɪkˈsɛl/ *v.* (**excelled, excelling**) [I] (formal) to do something very well, or much better than most people: *He had **excelled in** volleyball and track.* [ORIGIN: 1400—1500 Latin *excellere*, from *ex* "out of" + *-cellere* "to rise, stick up"]

ex·cel·lence /ˈɛksələns/ *n.* [U] the quality of being excellent: *an honor given for academic excellence*

ex·cel·lent /'ɛksələnt/ *adj.* **1** extremely good or of very high quality: *Jim's in excellent health.* | *The food was excellent.*

THESAURUS **good, great, wonderful, fantastic, outstanding, exceptional, superb, first-class, ace** → GOOD[1]

2 (spoken) said when you approve of something: *"There's a party at Becky's house tonight." "Excellent!"* —**excellently** *adv.*

ex·cept[1] /ɪk'sɛpt/ *prep.* used in order to show the things or people who are not included in a statement: *We're open every day except Monday.* | *Everyone went to the show,* ***except for*** *Scott and Danny.* | *I don't know anything about it,* ***except what*** *I've read in the newspaper.*

except[2] *conjunction* used in order to show that the statement you have just made is not true or not completely true: *It is like all the other houses,* ***except that*** *it's painted bright blue.* | *I have earrings just like those, except they're silver.* | *I'd go, except it's too far.*

E

except[3] *v.* [T] (formal) to not include something

ex·cept·ed /ɪk'sɛptɪd/ *adj.* not included: *The cost is $5 per person, children excepted.*

ex·cept·ing /ɪk'sɛptɪŋ/ *prep.* (formal) not including

ex·cep·tion /ɪk'sɛpʃən/ *n.* [C,U] **1** someone or something that is not included in something: *It's been very cold, but today's an exception.* | *He was asked to* ***make an exception*** *to company policy* (=not include something in the policy). | *Everyone has improved,* ***with the*** *possible* ***exception of*** *Sam.* **2 be no exception** used in order to say that something is not different from before or from the other things mentioned: *March weather is usually changeable, and this year was no exception.* **3 without exception** (formal) used in order to say that something is true of all the people or things in a group: *Almost without exception, teachers said that students do not work hard enough.*

ex·cep·tion·al /ɪk'sɛpʃənəl/ *adj.* **1** unusually good: *an exceptional student*

THESAURUS **good, great, excellent, wonderful, fantastic, outstanding, superb, first-class, ace** → GOOD[1]

2 unusual and not likely to happen often: *The teachers were doing their best under* ***exceptional circumstances.*** —**exceptionally** *adv.*

ex·cerpt /'ɛksɚpt/ *n.* [C] a short piece of writing or music taken from a longer book, poem, etc.: *an* ***excerpt from*** *his poem* [ORIGIN: 1500—1600 Latin, past participle of *excerpere*, from *carpere* "to gather, pick"]

ex·cess[1] /'ɛksɛs, ɪk'sɛs/ *n.* **1** [singular, U] a larger amount of something than is needed, usual, or allowed: *There is* ***an excess of*** *alcohol in his blood.* **2 in excess of sth** more than a particular amount: *Our profits were in excess of $5 million.* **3 do sth to excess** to do something too much or too often: *Is it possible to exercise to excess?* **4 excesses** [plural] actions that are socially or morally unacceptable: *the worst* ***excesses of*** *capitalism*

excess[2] *adj.* additional and more than is needed or allowed: *There is a charge of $75 for excess baggage.*

ex·ces·sive /ɪk'sɛsɪv/ *adj.* much more than is reasonable or necessary: *excessive fees* —**excessively** *adv.*

ex·change[1] /ɪks'tʃeɪndʒ/ *n.* **1** [C,U] the act of giving someone something and receiving something else from him/her: *an* ***exchange of*** *political prisoners* | *The police offered him protection* ***in exchange for*** *information.* **2** [C] a short conversation, especially an angry one **3 exchange of ideas/information etc.** an action in which people discuss or share ideas, information, etc. **4** [C] an arrangement in which a student, teacher, etc. visits another country to work or study **5** [C] a place where things are bought, sold, or traded → STOCK EXCHANGE: *trading on the commodities exchange*

exchange[2] *v.* [T] **1** to give something to someone who gives you something else: *We still exchange gifts at Christmas.*

THESAURUS

trade – to exchange something that you have for something that someone else has: *He had traded milk and eggs from the farm for flour and sugar.*
swap – to give something to someone, who gives you something similar: *The two schools use the Internet to swap pictures, stories, and jokes.*
in exchange/return (for sth) – if you give something in exchange or in return for something else, you give it in order to get something else back: *Williams will plead guilty in exchange for a reduced sentence.*

2 to replace one thing with another: *This shirt is too big. Can I* ***exchange*** *it* ***for*** *a smaller one?* **3** if two people exchange words, information, looks, etc., they talk to each other, look at each other, etc. —**exchangeable** *adj.*

ex'change ˌrate *n.* [C] the value of the money of one country compared to the money of another country

ex·cheq·uer /'ɛksˌtʃɛkɚ, ɪk'stʃɛkɚ/ *n.* [C usually singular] ECONOMICS a government department in Great Britain and Northern Ireland that controls the money that the country collects and spends

ex·cise[1] /'ɛksaɪz, -saɪs/ *n.* [C,U] the government tax on particular goods produced and used inside a country

ex·cise[2] /ɪk'saɪz/ *v.* [T] (formal) to remove something completely by cutting it out —**excision** /ɪk'sɪʒən/ *n.* [C,U]

ex·cit·a·ble /ɪk'saɪṭəbəl/ *adj.* easily excited

ex·cite /ɪk'saɪt/ *v.* [T] **1** to make someone feel happy, eager, or nervous: *The thought of returning to Montana excited me.* **2** to make someone have strong feelings: *The murder trial has excited public interest.* [ORIGIN: 1300—1400 French *exciter*, from Latin *excitare*, from *citare* "to set in movement"]

ex·cit·ed /ɪk'saɪṭɪd/ *adj.* **1** happy, interested, or hopeful because something good has happened or will happen: *We're really* ***excited about*** *our trip to California.* | *These teachers want kids to* ***get excited*** *about learning.* **2** feeling sexual desire —**excitedly** *adv.*

ex·cite·ment /ɪk'saɪt˺mənt/ *n.* [U] the feeling of being excited: *people's* ***excitement about/over*** *the Olympics* | *Their eyes sparkled* ***with excitement.***

ex·cit·ing /ɪk'saɪṭɪŋ/ *adj.* making you feel happy or interested in something: *an exciting story*

THESAURUS

thrilling – very exciting: *a thrilling 3–2 victory*
gripping – a gripping movie, story, etc. is very exciting and interesting: *The novel is a gripping tale of power and corruption in ancient Rome.*
dramatic – used about something that is exciting to watch or hear about as it happens: *the dramatic events of the past week*
exhilarating – making you feel happy, excited, and full of energy: *an exhilarating ride*
electric – making you feel very excited: *There was an almost electric atmosphere in the stadium.*

ex·claim /ɪk'skleɪm/ *v.* [I,T] (written) to say something suddenly because you are surprised, excited, or angry: *"Oh!" exclaimed Stella. "What happened?"* —**exclamation** /ˌɛksklə'meɪʃən/ *n.* [C]

excla'mation ˌpoint *also* **excla'mation ˌmark** *n.* [C] ENG. LANG. ARTS the mark (!) used in writing after a sentence or word that expresses surprise, excitement, or anger

ex·clam·a·to·ry /ɪk'sklæməˌtɔri/ *adj.* ENG. LANG. ARTS an exclamatory sentence expresses a strong opinion or emotion and ends with an EXCLAMATION POINT (=!)

ex·clude /ɪk'sklud/ (Ac) *v.* [T] **1** to not allow someone to enter a place or to do something: *Women are* ***excluded from*** *the priesthood.* **2** to deliberately not include something: *Some of the data was* ***excluded from*** *the report.* [ORIGIN: 1300—1400 Latin *excludere*, from *ex* "out" + *claudere* "to close"]

ex·clud·ing /ɪk'skludɪŋ/ (Ac) *prep.* not including: *Figure out how much you spend each month, excluding set amounts such as housing or car payments.*

ex·clu·sion /ɪk'skluʒən/ (Ac) *n.* **1** [U] a situation in which someone is not allowed to do something or something is not used: *At that time, the judges upheld the* ***exclusion*** *of women* ***from*** *juries.* **2** [C] something that is deliberately not included in a contract or agreement: *a tax exclusion* **3 do sth to the exclusion of sth** to do something so much that you do not do, consider, or have time for something else: *History books have focused on the achievements of white men, to the exclusion of women and minorities.*

ex·clu·sive¹ /ɪk'sklusɪv, -zɪv/ (Ac) *adj.* **1** exclusive places, organizations, etc. are for people who have a lot of money, or who belong to a high social class: *an exclusive Manhattan hotel* **2** used by only one person or group, and not shared: *a car for the* ***exclusive use*** *of the Pope* **3 exclusive of sth** not including something: *The trip cost $450, exclusive of meals.*

exclusive² *n.* [C] an important news story that is in only one newspaper, magazine, television news program, etc.

ex·clu·sive·ly /ɪk'sklusɪvli, -zɪv-/ (Ac) *adv.* only: *Businesses should not focus exclusively on profit.*

exˌclusive 'powers *n.* [plural] POLITICS the legal right to do something that only one level of the government has. For example, one of the exclusive powers of the FEDERAL government is the ability to print money, which state governments are not allowed to do.

ex·com·mu·ni·cate /ˌɛkskə'myunəˌkeɪt/ *v.* [T] if a church excommunicates someone, it punishes him/her by not allowing him/her to continue to be a member —**excommunication** /ˌɛkskəˌmyunə'keɪʃən/ *n.* [C,U]

ex·cre·ment /'ɛkskrəmənt/ *n.* [U] (formal) the solid waste from a person's or animal's body

ex·crete /ɪk'skrit/ *v.* [I,T] BIOLOGY to get rid of waste from the body through the BOWELS, or to get rid of waste liquid through the skin [ORIGIN: 1600—1700 Latin *excretus*, past participle of *excernere* "to separate out"]

ex·cru·ci·at·ing /ɪk'skruʃiˌeɪṭɪŋ/ *adj.* **1** extremely painful **2** extremely boring or embarrassing: *He told us about his vacation in excruciating detail.* [ORIGIN: 1500—1600 *excruciate* "to cause great pain to" (16—21 centuries), from Latin *excruciare*, from *cruciare* "to crucify"] —**excruciatingly** *adv.*

ex·cul·pate /'ɛkskəlˌpeɪt/ *v.* [T] (formal) to prove or decide that someone is not guilty of something: *The jury exculpated the defendant.* —**exculpatory** /ɪk'skʌlpəˌtɔri/ *adj.*: *exculpatory evidence* —**exculpation** /ˌɛkskəl'peɪʃən/ *n.* [U]

ex·cur·sion /ɪk'skɚʒən/ *n.* [C] a short trip, usually made by a group of people: *an* ***excursion to*** *Sea World*

THESAURUS **trip, journey, voyage, tour, expedition, pilgrimage** → TRAVEL²

ex·cus·a·ble /ɪk'skyuzəbəl/ *adj.* behavior or words that are excusable are easy to forgive (ANT) **inexcusable**

ex·cuse¹ /ɪk'skyuz/ *v.* [T] **1 excuse me** (spoken) **a)** said when you want to politely get someone's attention in order to ask a question: *Excuse me, is this the right bus for the airport?* **b)** used in order to say you are sorry when you have done something that is embarrassing or rude: *Oh, excuse me, I didn't know anyone was in here.* **c)** used in order to politely tell someone that you are leaving a place: *Excuse me, I'll be right back.* **d)** used in order to ask someone to repeat what s/he has just said: *"What time is it?" "Excuse me?" "I asked what time it is."* **e)** used in order to ask someone to move so that you can go past him/her: *Excuse me, I need to get through.* **2** to forgive someone, usually for something not very serious: *Please excuse my bad handwriting.* | *Please* ***excuse me for*** *being so late.* **3** to not make someone do something that s/he is supposed to do: *She was* ***excused from*** *jury duty.* [ORIGIN: 1400—1500 Old French *excuser*, from Latin *excusare*, from *causa* "cause, explanation"]

E

ex·cuse² /ɪk'skyus/ *n.* [C] **1** a reason that you give to explain why you did something: *What's your* ***excuse for*** *being late?* | *There's* ***no excuse*** *for laziness.* | *You need to stop* ***making excuses*** *and take responsibility.* | *I was glad to* ***have an excuse*** *to put it off another day.*

THESAURUS **reason, explanation, motive, rationale, grounds** ➔ REASON¹

2 a false reason that you give to explain why you are or are not doing something: *I'll* ***make an excuse*** *and leave early.* | *They were looking for any* ***excuse to*** *start a fight.*

ex·ec /ɪg'zɛk/ *n.* [C] (informal) a business EXECUTIVE

ex·e·cra·ble /'ɛksɪkrəbəl/ *adj.* (formal) extremely bad: *an execrable movie*

ex·e·cute /'ɛksɪˌkyut/ *v.* [T] **1** to kill someone, especially as a legal punishment for a crime

THESAURUS **kill, murder, assassinate, slay** ➔ KILL¹

2 (formal) to do something that you have planned: *These ideas require money and materials to execute.*

ex·e·cu·tion /ˌɛksɪ'kyuʃən/ *n.* **1** [C,U] the act of killing someone, especially as a legal punishment for a crime **2** [U] (formal) a process in which you do something that you have planned to do: *We will need help with both the planning and the* ***execution of*** *the changes.*

ex·e·cu·tion·er /ˌɛksɪ'kyuʃənɚ/ *n.* [C] someone whose job is to kill someone else as a legal punishment for a crime

ex·ec·u·tive¹ /ɪg'zɛkyət̬ɪv/ *n.* [C] a manager in an organization or company who helps make important decisions

executive² *adj.* relating to making decisions, especially in a company, government, or other organization: *an executive committee*

ex'ecutive ˌbranch *n.* [C] POLITICS the part of a government that approves decisions and laws, and organizes how they will work ➔ JUDICIARY, LEGISLATURE

ex·ec·u·tor /ɪg'zɛkyət̬ɚ/ *n.* [C] LAW someone who deals with the instructions in a WILL

ex·em·pla·ry /ɪg'zɛmpləri/ *adj.* (formal) **1** excellent and providing a good example to follow: *the students' exemplary behavior* **2** severe and used as a warning: *an exemplary punishment*

ex·em·pli·fy /ɪg'zɛmpləˌfaɪ/ *v.* (**exemplified, exemplifies**) [T] (formal) **1** to be a very typical example of something: *This dish exemplifies her style of cooking.* **2** to give an example of something: *Exemplify each part of your argument.*

ex·empt¹ /ɪg'zɛmpt/ *adj.* having special permission not to do something or pay for something: *The money is* ***exempt from*** *state taxes.*

exempt² *v.* [T] to give someone special permission not to do or pay something: *Children are* ***exempted from*** *this rule.*

ex·emp·tion /ɪg'zɛmpʃən/ *n.* **1** [C] an amount of money that you do not have to pay tax on in a particular year: *a* ***tax exemption*** *for gifts to charity* **2** [C,U] permission not to do or pay something: *an* ***exemption from*** *military service*

ex·er·cise¹ /'ɛksɚˌsaɪz/ *n.* **1** [C,U] physical activity that you do in order to stay strong and healthy: *stretching exercises* | *I don't* ***get*** *much* ***exercise.*** | *Have you* ***done*** *your stomach* ***exercises*** *today?* **2** [C] a set of written questions that test your skill or knowledge: *For homework,* ***do exercises*** *1 and 2.* **3** [C] an activity or process that helps you practice a particular skill: *military exercises in the Pacific Ocean* | *We practiced relaxation exercises.* **4** [singular] an activity or situation that has a particular quality or result: *Trying to use public transportation to get downtown is an* ***exercise in*** *frustration.* **5 the exercise of sth** (formal) the use of power or a right: *laws that protect the exercise of freedom of speech* [ORIGIN: 1300—1400 French *exercice*, from Latin *exercere* "to drive on, keep busy"]

exercise² *v.* [I,T] **1** to do physical activities regularly so that you stay strong and healthy: *Eat right and exercise regularly.* | *Swimming exercises all the major muscle groups.*

TOPIC

People exercise so they can **stay/keep/get in shape** (=be healthy and strong). There are many different kinds of exercise, for example **jogging, lifting weights**, and **aerobics**. People often go to a **gym** or a **health club** to exercise. The series of exercises you do is called a **workout**. Before exercising, you **warm up** (=get your body ready) by **stretching** or jogging slowly.

2 (formal) to use power, a right, etc. to make something happen: *More young people need to exercise their right to vote.*

'exercise ˌbike *n.* [C] a bicycle that does not move and is used indoors for exercise

ex·ert /ɪg'zɚt/ *v.* [T] **1** to use your authority, power, influence, etc. to make something happen: *Powerful people* ***exerted pressure on*** *the paper not* *to run the story.* **2 exert yourself** to work very hard, using a lot of physical or mental energy

ex·er·tion /ɪg'zɚʃən/ *n.* [C,U] strong physical or mental effort

ex·hale /ɛks'heɪl, ɛk'seɪl/ *v.* [I,T] to breathe air, smoke, etc. out of your mouth SYN **breathe out**: *Take a deep breath, then exhale slowly.*

THESAURUS **breathe, take a breath, inhale, pant, wheeze** → BREATHE

ex·haust¹ /ɪg'zɔst/ *v.* [T] **1** to make someone very tired: *The effort exhausted her.* **2** to use all of something: *We are in danger of exhausting the world's oil supply.*

exhaust² *n.* **1** [U] the gas that is produced when a machine is working: *exhaust fumes* **2** [C] *also* **exhaust pipe** a pipe on a car or machine, that exhaust comes out of

ex·haust·ed /ɪg'zɔstɪd/ *adj.* extremely tired: *He was **exhausted by/from** the long day.*

THESAURUS **tired, worn out, weary, run-down, beat, fatigued** → TIRED

ex·haust·ing /ɪg'zɔstɪŋ/ *adj.* making you feel extremely tired: *an exhausting trip*

ex·haus·tion /ɪg'zɔstʃən/ *n.* [U] the state of being extremely tired

ex·haus·tive /ɪg'zɔstɪv/ *adj.* extremely thorough: *an exhaustive search* —**exhaustively** *adv.*

ex·hib·it¹ /ɪg'zɪbɪt/ (Ac) *v.* **1** [I,T] to put something in a public place so that people can see it: *The gallery will exhibit some of Dalí's paintings.* **2** [T] (formal) to show a quality, sign, emotion, etc. in a way that people easily notice: *The patient exhibited symptoms of heart disease.* [ORIGIN: 1400—1500 Latin *exhibitus*, past participle of *exhibere* "to hold out, show"]

exhibit² *n.* **1** [C] something that is put in a public place so that people can see it: *the museum's interactive exhibits* **2** [C,U] an object or a collection of objects that is put in a public place so that people can see it, learn about it, etc., or the act of doing this: *The exhibits date from the 17th century.* | *The painting is currently **on exhibit** in the Metropolitan Museum.* **3** [C] LAW something that is shown in a court of law to prove that someone is guilty or not guilty

ex·hi·bi·tion /ˌɛksə'bɪʃən/ (Ac) *n.* **1** [C] a public show where you put something so that people can see it: *an **exhibition of** historical photographs* **2** [U] the act of showing something such as a painting in a public place: *A collection of rare books is **on exhibition** at the city library.*

ex·hi·bi·tion·ism /ˌɛksə'bɪʃəˌnɪzəm/ *n.* [U] **1** behavior that makes people notice you, but that most people think is not acceptable **2** a mental problem that makes someone want to show his/her sexual organs in public places —**exhibitionist** *n.* [C]

ex·hil·a·rat·ed /ɪg'zɪləˌreɪtɪd/ *adj.* feeling extremely happy and excited: *Rita felt exhilarated by the crashing of the waves.*

ex·hil·a·ra·ting /ɪg'zɪləˌreɪtɪŋ/ *adj.* making you feel extremely happy and excited: *The balloon ride was exhilarating.*

THESAURUS **exciting, thrilling, gripping, dramatic, electric** → EXCITING

ex·hil·a·ra·tion /ɪgˌzɪlə'reɪʃən/ *n.* [U] a feeling of being extremely happy and excited —**exhilarate** /ɪg'zɪləˌreɪt/ *v.* [T]

ex·hort /ɪg'zɔrt/ *v.* [T] (formal) to try to persuade someone to do something —**exhortation** /ˌɛksɔr'teɪʃən, ˌɛgzɔr-/ *n.* [C,U]

ex·hume /ɪg'zum, ɛks'hyum/ *v.* [T] (formal) to remove a dead body from the ground after it has been buried —**exhumation** /ˌɛksyu'meɪʃən/ *n.* [C,U]

ex·i·gent /'ɛksədʒənt/ *adj.* (formal) an exigent situation is urgent, so that you must deal with it very quickly

ex·ile¹ /'ɛgzaɪl, 'ɛksaɪl/ *v.* [T] to force someone to leave his/her country and live in another country, usually for political reasons [ORIGIN: 1300—1400 French *exil*, from Latin *exul* "person sent away"] —**exiled** *adj.*

exile² *n.* **1** [U] a situation in which someone is exiled: *a writer who lives **in exile** in Canada* **2** [C] someone who has been exiled

ex·ist /ɪg'zɪst/ *v.* [I] **1** to happen or be present in a particular situation or place: *the gap that exists between rich and poor* **2** to be real or alive: *Do ghosts really exist?* ▸ Don't say "It is existing/They are existing." ◂ **3** to stay alive, especially in difficult conditions: *Wild birds **exist on** nuts, berries, and insects.* [ORIGIN: 1600—1700 Latin *exsistere* "to come into being, exist," from *sistere* "to stand"]

ex·ist·ence /ɪg'zɪstəns/ *n.* **1** [U] the state of existing: *Do you believe in the **existence of** God?* | *laws that are already **in existence*** **2** [C] the type of life that someone has, especially when it is difficult: *a terrible existence*

ex·ist·ing /ɪg'zɪstɪŋ/ *adj.* present now and available to be used: *Businesses want to hold on to existing customers.*

THESAURUS **present, current, prevailing** → PRESENT¹

ex·it¹ /'ɛgzɪt, 'ɛksɪt/ *n.* [C] **1** a door through which you can leave a room, building, etc.: *There are two exits at the back of the plane.* | *the theater's **emergency exit*** → *see picture at* ENTRANCE¹ **2** the act of leaving a room, stage, etc.: *The President **made a** quick **exit** after his speech.* **3** a place where vehicles can leave a large road such as a FREEWAY or HIGHWAY, and join another road: *Take the Spring Street exit.* [ORIGIN: 1500—1600

E

Latin *exitus*, from the past participle of *exire* "to go out"]

exit² *v.* [I,T] **1** to leave a place: *The band* ***exited through*** *a door behind the stage.* **2** IT to stop using a computer or computer program: *Press F3 to exit.*

ex·o·dus /'ɛksədəs/ *n.* [singular] a situation in which a lot of people leave a particular place at the same time: *the* ***exodus*** *of Russian scientists* ***to*** *America* [ORIGIN: 1600—1700 *Exodus*, the second book in the Bible, which describes how the Israelites left Egypt]

ex·on·er·ate /ɪg'zɑnəˌreɪt/ *v.* [T] (formal) to say officially that someone who has been blamed for something is not guilty: *Ross was* ***exonerated from*** *all charges of child abuse.* —**exoneration** /ɪgˌzɑnə'reɪʃən/ *n.* [U]

E

ex·or·bi·tant /ɪg'zɔrbət̬ənt/ *adj.* an exorbitant price, demand, etc. is much higher or greater than it should be

THESAURUS **high, extortionate, astronomical** → EXPENSIVE

ex·or·cize /'ɛksɔrˌsaɪz, -sɚ-/ *v.* [T] **1** to make yourself no longer be affected by a bad memory or experience **2** to force evil spirits to leave a place or someone's body by using special words and ceremonies —**exorcism** /'ɛksɔrˌsɪzəm/ *n.* [C,U] —**exorcist** *n.* [C]

ex·o·skel·e·ton /'ɛksoʊˌskɛlət̚n/ *n.* [C] BIOLOGY a hard structure on the outside of the body of some living creatures such as TURTLEs, that protects and supports the creature's body instead of a BACKBONE → ENDOSKELETON

ex·o·sphere /'ɛksoʊˌsfɪr/ *n.* **the exosphere** EARTH SCIENCES the upper part of the THERMOSPHERE, where some of the harmful energy from the Sun is reduced [ORIGIN: 1900—2000 from *exo*'outside' + *-sphere* (as in *atmosphere*)] → *compare* IONOSPHERE

ex·o·ther·mic /ˌɛksoʊ'θɚmɪk/ *adj.* CHEMISTRY relating to or describing a chemical reaction that produces or sends out heat → ENDOTHERMIC: *an exothermic process*

ex·ot·ic /ɪg'zɑt̬ɪk/ *adj.* unusual and exciting because of a connection with a foreign country: *an exotic flower* | *exotic places* [ORIGIN: 1500—1600 Latin *exoticus*, from Greek *exotikos*, from *exo* "outside"] —**exotically** *adv.*

ex·pand /ɪk'spænd/ (Ac) *v.* [I,T] **1** to become larger in size, area, or amount, or to make something become larger (ANT) **contract**: *The population of Texas* ***expanded rapidly*** *in the '60s.* **2** to open more shops, factories, etc.: *Starbucks coffee shops have* ***expanded into*** *Europe.* [ORIGIN: 1400—1500 Latin *expandere*, from *pandere* "to spread"] —**expandable** *adj.*

expand on/upon sth *phr. v.* (formal) to add more details or information to something that you have already said: *Could you expand on your last comment, please?*

ex·panse /ɪk'spæns/ *n.* [C] a very large area of water, sky, land, etc.

ex·pan·sion /ɪk'spænʃən/ (Ac) *n.* [U] the process of increasing in size, number, or amount: *a period of economic expansion* —**expansionism** *n.* [U] —**expansionist** *adj.*

ex·pan·sive /ɪk'spænsɪv/ (Ac) *adj.* **1** very friendly and willing to talk a lot: *an expansive mood* **2** very large and wide in area: *expansive beaches* **3** including a lot of information: *an expansive history book*

ex·pa·tri·ate /ɛks'peɪtriɪt/ *n.* [C] someone who lives in a foreign country —**expatriate** *adj.*

ex·pa·tri·a·tion /ɛksˌpeɪtri'eɪʃən/ *n.* [U] LAW a situation in which someone leaves or is forced to leave his/her country and go to live in another country —**expatriate** /ɛks'peɪtriˌeɪt/ *v.* [T]

ex·pect /ɪk'spɛkt/ *v.* [T] **1** to think that something will happen: *The hotel bill came to more than we expected.* | *I'm* ***expecting*** *her* ***to*** *arrive any day now.* | *Republicans* ***expect to*** *win a majority in the House.* | *He had a right to* ***expect (that)*** *his conversation would be private.* **2** to demand that someone should do something, because it is his/her duty: *Students are* ***expected to*** *return their homework on Friday.* | *Wanda's parents* ***expect too much of*** *her* (=think she can do more than she really can). **3 be expecting** if a woman is expecting, she is going to have a baby soon

ex·pect·an·cy /ɪk'spɛktənsi/ *n.* [U] the feeling that something exciting or interesting is about to happen: *There was a look of expectancy in her eyes.* → LIFE EXPECTANCY

ex·pect·ant /ɪk'spɛktənt/ *adj.* **1** hopeful that something good or exciting will happen: *An expectant crowd gathered.* **2 expectant mother/father** someone whose baby will be born soon —**expectantly** *adv.*

ex·pec·ta·tion /ˌɛkspɛk'teɪʃən/ *n.* **1** [C,U] the belief or hope that something will happen: *Sales of the car have* ***exceeded expectations*** (=have been better than expected). | *The stock market has fallen because of* ***expectations that*** *the dollar will drop in value.* | *We have a reasonable* ***expectation of*** *success.* **2** [C usually plural] a feeling or belief about the way something should be or how someone should behave: *We must meet customers'* ***expectations about*** *the quality of the products.* | *The movie didn't* ***live up to*** *our* ***expectations*** (=was not as good as we thought it would be). | *Her parents* ***have*** *very* ***high expectations*** *of her* (=believe she should succeed).

ex·pe·di·en·cy /ɪk'spidiənsi/ *also* **ex·pe·di·ence** /ɪk'spidiəns/ *n.* (plural **expediencies**) [C,U] the act of doing what is useful, easy, or necessary in a particular situation, even if it is morally wrong

ex·pe·di·ent /ɪk'spidiənt/ *adj.* helpful or useful, sometimes in a way that is morally wrong: *It would be* ***expedient to*** *consult a lawyer.* —**expedient** *n.* [C]

ex·pe·dite /ˈɛkspəˌdaɪt/ *v.* [T] to make a process, action, etc. happen more quickly

ex·pe·di·tion /ˌɛkspəˈdɪʃən/ *n.* [C] **1** a long and carefully organized trip, especially to a dangerous place: *an expedition to the North Pole*

THESAURUS **trip, journey, voyage, tour, excursion, pilgrimage** → TRAVEL²

2 a short trip, usually made for a particular purpose: *a shopping expedition*

ex·pel /ɪkˈspɛl/ *v.* (**expelled**, **expelling**) [T] **1** to officially make someone leave a school, organization, or country: *Larry was* ***expelled from*** *school for smoking.* **2** to force air, water, or gas out of something

ex·pend /ɪkˈspɛnd/ *v.* [T] (formal) to use money, time, energy, etc. to do something: *the time* ***expended on*** *meetings*

ex·pend·a·ble /ɪkˈspɛndəbəl/ *adj.* not needed enough to be kept or saved: *workers who are considered expendable*

ex·pend·i·ture /ɪkˈspɛndətʃə/ *n.* (formal) **1** [C,U] the total amount of money that a person or organization spends: ***Expenditure on*** *welfare programs went down by 5%.* **2** [U] the action of spending or using money, time, effort, etc.

ex·pense /ɪkˈspɛns/ *n.* **1** [C,U] the amount of money you spend on something: *Sally's parents* ***spared no expense*** (=spent a lot of money) *for her wedding.* | *$30,000 is needed for* ***medical/legal expenses.***

THESAURUS **cost, price, charge, fee, fare, rent, rate** → COST¹

2 at the expense of sb/sth if something is done at the expense of someone or something else, it is only achieved by doing something that could harm that person or thing: *The cars were produced quickly, at the expense of safety.* **3 at sb's expense a)** if you do something at someone's expense, that person pays for you to do it: *Education is provided at the public's expense.* **b)** if you make jokes at someone's expense, you make him/her seem stupid: *He kept making jokes at his wife's expense.* **4 expenses** [plural] money that you spend on travel, hotels, meals, etc. when you are working, and that your employer gives back to you later **5 all expenses paid** having all of your costs for hotels, travel, meals, etc. paid for by someone else

exˈpense acˌcount *n.* [C] money that is available to someone who works for a company so that s/he can pay for hotels, meals, etc. when traveling for work

ex·pen·sive /ɪkˈspɛnsɪv/ *adj.* something that is expensive costs a lot of money (ANT) **inexpensive, cheap**: *expensive jewelry* | *The car is* ***expensive to*** *maintain.*

THESAURUS

high – used about prices that are greater than normal or usual: *Gas prices are very high right now.*

pricey (informal) – expensive: *The hotel was a little bit pricey.*

costly – costing a lot of money: *costly car repairs*

overpriced – something that is overpriced is more expensive than it should be: *overpriced running shoes*

be a ripoff (informal) – if something is a ripoff, it is more expensive than it should be: *The restaurant was such a ripoff.*

extortionate/astronomical/exorbitant – used about prices that are much too high: *Housing prices in New York are exorbitant.*

fancy – used about fashionable restaurants, cars, clothes, etc. that look expensive: *a fancy hotel in Manhattan*

posh (informal) – used about expensive hotels, restaurants, schools, etc. that are used by rich people: *a posh five-star hotel* → CHEAP¹

E

ex·pe·ri·ence¹ /ɪkˈspɪriəns/ *n.* **1** [U] knowledge or skill that you gain from doing a job or activity: *Scott* ***has*** *a* ***lot*** *of* ***experience in*** *publishing.* | *a good way of* ***gaining/getting experience*** | *Do you have any* ***previous experience*** *in sales?* **2** [U] knowledge that you gain about life and the world by being in different situations and meeting different people: ***In*** *my* ***experience****, it is hard work, not luck, that brings success.* | *I know* ***from*** *personal* ***experience*** *that this is not easy.* **3** [C] something that happens to you and has an effect on how you feel or what you think: *Visiting Paris was a wonderful experience.* | *Other people have* ***had*** *similar* ***experiences.***

experience² *v.* [T] to be happening to you or affecting you: *The plane experienced engine problems.* | *Patients often experienced extreme pain.*

ex·pe·ri·enced /ɪkˈspɪriənst/ *adj.* having particular skills or knowledge because you have done something often or for a long time (ANT) **inexperienced**: *an experienced pilot*

ex·per·i·ment¹ /ɪkˈspɛrəmənt/ *n.* [C] **1** a scientific test done to show how something will react in a particular situation, or to prove that an idea is true: ***Experiments*** *were* ***performed/conducted/done*** *on rats to test the drug.* | ***experiments on/with*** *solar-powered vehicles*

THESAURUS **research, study** → RESEARCH¹

2 a process in which you try a new idea, method, etc. in order to find out if it is effective: *St. Mary's School is an* ***experiment in*** *bilingual education.* [ORIGIN: 1300—1400 Old French, Latin *experimentum*, from *experiri* "to try out"]

ex·per·i·ment² /ɪkˈspɛrəˌmɛnt/ *v.* [I] **1** to try using various ideas, methods, materials, etc. in order to find out how effective or good they are: *We encourage students to* ***experiment with*** *new ways of doing things.* **2** to do a scientific test in order to find out if a particular idea is true or to obtain more information: *Researchers* ***experimented on*** *animals when testing the treatment.* —**experimentation** /ɪkˌspɛrəmənˈteɪʃən/ *n.* [U]

ex·per·i·men·tal /ɪkˌspɛrəˈmɛntəl/ *adj.* **1** used for or related to experiments: *experimental research* **2** using or testing new ideas: *an experimental theater group* —**experimentally** *adv.*

ex·pert /ˈɛkspɚt/ (Ac) *n.* [C] someone with special skills or knowledge of a subject, gained as a result of training or experience: *an **expert on/in** Native American history* [ORIGIN: Old French, Latin *expertus*, past participle of *experiri* "to try out"] —**expert** *adj.*: *an expert teacher* | *very sick patients who need expert care* —**expertly** *adv.*

THESAURUS

specialist – someone who knows a lot about something because s/he has studied it for a long time: *Lowe is a specialist in immigration law.*
authority – someone who is very respected because s/he knows more about a subject than other people: *She is a leading authority on modern art.*
connoisseur – someone who knows a lot about something such as art, food, or music: *a connoisseur of fine wines*
pundit – someone who knows a lot about a particular subject, and is often asked for his/her opinion: *Most pundits think the Democrats' hold on Congress is secure.*

THESAURUS **skillful, accomplished, talented, gifted, adept, deft** → SKILLFUL

ex·per·tise /ˌɛkspɚˈtiz/ (Ac) *n.* [U] a special skill or knowledge that you learn by experience or training: *her **technical/medical/legal expertise** | his **expertise in** mathematics | Most people do not have the **expertise to** make wise investments.*

ex·pi·ate /ˈɛkspiˌeɪt/ *v.* [T] (formal) to do something to show that you are sorry and to improve the situation after you have done something wrong: *How can I expiate my sin?* —**expiation** /ˌɛkspiˈeɪʃən/ *n.* [U]

ex·pi·ra·tion /ˌɛkspəˈreɪʃən/ *n.* [U] the end of a period of time during which an official document or agreement is allowed to be used: *the expiration of the treaty*

expi'ration ˌdate *n.* [C] the date when something stops being safe to eat or to use

ex·pire /ɪkˈspaɪɚ/ *v.* [I] **1** if a document expires, you cannot legally continue to use it beyond a particular date: *My driver's license **expires in** September.* **2** (literary) to die

ex·plain /ɪkˈspleɪn/ *v.* [I,T] **1** to tell someone about something in a way that is easy to understand: *Dr. Brasco carefully explained the procedure.* | *Don **explained** the rules **to** me.* ►Don't say "explained me the rules."◄ | *Could you **explain how** this thing works?* ►Don't say "explain me how it works."◄

THESAURUS

tell – to give someone facts or information in speech or writing: *Can you tell me how to get to the Empire State Building?*
show – to tell someone how to do something or where something is: *Ellen showed me how to work the coffee maker.*
demonstrate – to show or describe how to use or do something: *Fred will now demonstrate how easy it is to use the drill.*
go through sth – to explain something carefully, especially one step at a time: *Mrs. Riddell went through the homework assignment.*
clarify – to make something easier to understand by explaining it in more detail: *He went on to clarify some of his earlier statements.*
elucidate (formal) – to explain very clearly something that is difficult to understand: *Each chapter elucidates some aspect of American life.*

2 to give or be the reason for something: *Brad never **explained why** he was late.* | *The doctor **explained that** he had to wait for the test results first.* [ORIGIN: 1500—1600 Latin *explanare* "to make level, unfold," from *planus* "level, flat"]

explain sth ↔ **away** *phr. v.* to make something seem to be less important or not your fault by giving reasons for it: *Claire tried to explain away the bruises on her arm.*

ex·pla·na·tion /ˌɛkspləˈneɪʃən/ *n.* **1** [C] a statement or piece of writing intended to make something easier to understand or to describe how something works: *an **explanation of** how the disease is passed to other people* **2** [C,U] the reasons you give for why something happened or why you did something: *an **explanation for** the changes in weather patterns* | *Smith refused to **give/provide an explanation for** his behavior.*

THESAURUS **reason, excuse, motive, rationale, grounds** → REASON[1]

ex·plan·a·to·ry /ɪkˈsplænəˌtɔri/ *adj.* giving information about something or describing how something works: *an explanatory booklet* → SELF-EXPLANATORY

ex·ple·tive /ˈɛkspləṭɪv/ *n.* [C] (formal) a rude word that you use when you are angry or in pain

ex·pli·ca·ble /ɪkˈsplɪkəbəl, ˈɛksplɪ-/ *adj.* able to be easily understood or explained (ANT) **inexplicable**

ex·plic·it /ɪkˈsplɪsɪt/ (Ac) *adj.* **1** expressed in a way that is very clear: *explicit directions* | *She was explicit about her reasons for changing jobs.* **2** language or pictures that are explicit describe or show a lot of sex or violence [ORIGIN: 1600—1700 French *explicite*, from Latin *explicare* "to unfold," from *plicare* "to fold"] —**explicitly** *adv.*

ex·plode /ɪkˈsploʊd/ *v.* **1** [I,T] to burst into small pieces, making a loud noise and causing damage, or to make something do this: *The car bomb exploded at 6:16.* | *In 1949, the USSR exploded its first atomic bomb.* **2** [I] to suddenly express strong emotions, especially anger: *John **exploded with/in** rage at the news.* **3** [I] if a situation explodes, it is suddenly no longer controlled: *Troops cannot control the violence that has exploded in the city.* **4** [I] to increase a lot in number, amount, or degree: *Florida's population exploded after World War II.* [ORIGIN: 1500—1600 Latin *explodere* "to drive off the stage by clapping," from *plaudere* "to clap"]

ex·ploit[1] /ɪk'splɔɪt/ (Ac) *v.* [T] **1** to treat someone unfairly in order to gain what you want: *employers who exploit their workers* **2** to use a situation to get an advantage for yourself, in a way that people disapprove of: *Republicans accused him of exploiting the issue for political purposes.* **3** to use something effectively and completely, or to get as much as you can out of a situation: *The country must exploit its resources more effectively.* —**exploitation** /ˌɛksplɔɪ'teɪʃən/ *n.* [U]: *We must protect children from exploitation in the labor market.* | *the exploitation of natural resources*

ex·ploit[2] /'ɛksplɔɪt/ (Ac) *n.* [C usually plural] a brave, exciting, and interesting action: *the young explorer's exploits*

ex·plo·ra·tion /ˌɛksplə'reɪʃən/ *n.* [C,U] **1** the activity of traveling through a place in order to find out about it or to find something such as oil or gold in it: *exploration for oil* | *space exploration* **2** an examination of or discussion about something to find out more about it: *an* ***exploration of*** *spiritual issues*

ex·plo·ra·to·ry /ɪk'splɔrəˌtɔri/ *adj.* done in order to find out more about something: *exploratory surgery*

ex·plore /ɪk'splɔr/ *v.* **1** [I,T] to travel around an area in order to find out what it is like: *We spent a week exploring the Oregon coastline.* **2** [T] to discuss or think about something carefully: *I want to make sure I've* ***explored*** *all my* ***options*** *before I decide.* | *The company is* ***exploring*** *the* ***possibility*** *of moving.*

ex·plor·er /ɪk'splɔrɚ/ *n.* [C] someone who travels to places that people have not visited before

ex·plo·sion /ɪk'sploʊʒən/ *n.* [C] **1** an occasion when something such as a bomb explodes, or the noise it makes: *We heard a huge explosion.* | *a nuclear explosion* **2** [usually singular] a sudden large increase: *the* ***population explosion*** | *an* ***explosion of*** *interest in organic foods*

ex·plo·sive[1] /ɪk'sploʊsɪv/ *adj.* **1** able or likely to explode: *Dynamite is highly explosive.* **2** likely to make people become violent or angry: *the explosive issue of abortion* | *the* ***explosive situation*** *in the Middle East* **3** likely to suddenly become violent and angry: *a man with an explosive temper* **4** increasing suddenly or quickly: *the* ***explosive growth*** *of the Internet*

explosive[2] *n.* [C] a substance that can cause an explosion

ex·po /'ɛkspoʊ/ *n.* (plural **expos**) [C] an EXPOSITION

ex·po·nent /ɪk'spoʊnənt, 'ɛkspoʊ-/ *n.* [C] an exponent of an idea or belief tries to persuade other people that it is good: *an* ***exponent of*** *socialism*

ex·po·nen·tial /ˌɛkspə'nɛnʃəl/ *adj.* **1** **exponential growth/increase** a rate of growth that becomes faster as the amount of the thing that is growing increases: *the exponential growth of the world's population* **2** MATH using a sign that shows how many times a number is to be multiplied by itself, such as y^3, which shows that y should be multiplied by itself three times —**exponentially** *adv.*

ex·port[1] /'ɛkspɔrt/ (Ac) *n.* [C,U] ECONOMICS a product that is sold to another country, or the business of selling goods to another country (ANT) **import**: *Coffee is an important export.* | *the* ***export of*** *lumber* [ORIGIN: 1400—1500 Latin *exportare*, from *portare* "to carry"]

ex·port[2] /ɪk'spɔrt/ (Ac) *v.* [I,T] **1** ECONOMICS to sell goods to another country (ANT) **import**: *The company* ***exports*** *machines* ***to*** *Russia.* **2** IT to move information from one computer to another one, using the Internet (ANT) **import** —**exporter** *n.* [C]: *The U.S. is the world's largest exporter of wheat.* —**exportation** /ˌɛkspɔr'teɪʃən/ *n.* [U]

ex·pose /ɪk'spoʊz/ (Ac) *v.* [T] **1** to show something that is usually covered or hidden: *It's best to keep babies' skin from being* ***exposed to*** *the sun.* **2** to put someone in a situation or place that could affect him/her in a harmful or dangerous way: *The test will tell you if you've been* ***exposed to*** *the virus.* **3** to make it possible for someone to experience new ideas, ways of life, etc.: *Field trips* ***expose*** *children* ***to*** *real examples of things they are learning about in the classroom.* **4** to tell people the truth about an event or situation that is not acceptable because it is dishonest or illegal: *We threatened to* ***expose*** *him* ***to*** *the police.* **5** to allow light onto a piece of film in a camera in order to produce a photograph [ORIGIN: 1400—1500 French *exposer*, from Latin *exponere* "to put out, explain"]

ex·po·sé /ˌɛkspoʊˌzeɪ/ *n.* [C] a story in a newspaper or on television that shows the truth about something, especially something dishonest or shocking

ex·posed /ɪk'spoʊzd/ (Ac) *adj.* **1** not protected from the weather: *an exposed coastline* **2** not covered: *exposed skin*

ex·po·si·tion /ˌɛkspə'zɪʃən/ *n.* **1** [C,U] (formal) a clear and detailed explanation **2** [C] a large public event at which you show or sell products, art, etc.

ex·pos·i·to·ry /ɪk'spɑzəˌtɔri/ *adj.* ENG. LANG. ARTS relating to a clear and detailed explanation in writing or speech

ex·po·sure /ɪk'spoʊʒɚ/ (Ac) *n.* **1** [C,U] the state of being put into a harmful or bad situation without any protection: *The disease does not show itself until a week to ten days after* ***exposure to*** *the virus.* **2** [singular, U] the chance to experience new

E

ideas, ways of life, etc.: *My first* ***exposure to*** *classical music was at college.* **3** [U] the attention that someone or something gets from newspapers, television, etc.: *The issue has* ***received*** *a lot of* ***exposure*** *in the press.* **4** [C,U] the action of telling people the truth about a dishonest person, event, or situation: *The school district has made changes since the newspaper's* ***exposure of*** *the scandal.* **5** [U] the harmful effects of staying outside for a long time when the weather is extremely cold: *Three climbers died of exposure.* **6** [C] a length of film, in a camera that is used to take one photograph: *This roll has 36 exposures.*

ex·press[1] /ɪk'sprɛs/ *v.* [T] to tell or show what you are feeling or thinking by using words, looks, or actions: *A number of people* ***expressed*** *their* ***concern.*** | *It's hard sometimes for children to* ***express themselves*** (=clearly say what they think or feel). | *His eldest son has* ***expressed an interest in*** *running the company.* [ORIGIN: 1300—1400 Early French *expresser*, from Latin *expressus*, past participle of *exprimere* "to press out"]

E

THESAURUS **say, mention, add, state, utter ➔** SAY[1]

express[2] *adj.* **1** clear and definite: *It was her* ***express wish*** *that you inherit her house.* **2 express train/bus** a train or bus that does not stop at many places and can therefore travel more quickly **3** [only before noun] designed to help you move through a place more quickly: *the* ***express lane*** *on the freeway* | *the* ***express*** *line at the supermarket* (=one for people who are buying a limited number of items) **4** [only before noun] delivered more quickly than normal: *express mail*

ex,pressed 'powers *n.* [plural] POLITICS powers given to the U.S. government that are clearly stated in the CONSTITUTION

ex·pres·sion /ɪk'sprɛʃən/ *n.* **1** [C] ENG. LANG. ARTS a word or phrase that has a particular meaning: *You use the expression "Break a leg" to wish an actor good luck.*

THESAURUS **phrase, idiom, cliché, saying, proverb, maxim ➔** PHRASE[1]

2 [C] a look on someone's face: *a cheerful expression* | *an* ***expression of*** *shock* **3** [C,U] something that you say, do, or write that shows what you think or feel: *I'm sending these flowers as an* ***expression of*** *my thanks.* | *Crying is a healthy expression of grief.* **4** [C] MATH a sign or group of signs that show a mathematical idea in a particular form: *$x^3 + 4$ is an algebraic expression.*

ex·pres·sion·less /ɪk'sprɛʃənlɪs/ *adj.* an expressionless face or voice does not show what someone is thinking or feeling

ex·pres·sive /ɪk'sprɛsɪv/ *adj.* showing what someone is thinking or feeling: *expressive eyes*

ex·press·ly /ɪk'sprɛsli/ *adv.* (formal) clearly and firmly: *Mr. Samson expressly asked you to leave.*

ex·press·way /ɪk'sprɛs,weɪ/ *n.* [C] a wide road in a city on which cars can travel fast

THESAURUS **road, street, main street, avenue, lane, main road, the main drag, highway, freeway, toll road, turnpike ➔** ROAD

ex·pro·pri·ate /ɛks'proupri,eɪt/ *v.* [T] (formal) to take away someone's private property for public use —**expropriation** /ɛks,proupri'eɪʃən/ *n.* [C,U]

ex·pul·sion /ɪk'spʌlʃən/ *n.* [C,U] the official act of making someone leave a place: *the* ***expulsion of*** *Communists from the government*

ex·punge /ɪk'spʌndʒ/ *v.* [T] (formal) to remove or deliberately forget something such as a name or piece of information: *The arrest was later expunged from his record.*

THESAURUS **remove, erase, efface ➔** REMOVE

ex·pur·gat·ed /'ɛkspɚ,geɪtɪd/ *adj.* (formal) an expurgated book, play, etc. has had some parts removed because they are considered harmful or offensive (ANT) **unexpurgated ➔** ABRIDGED —**expurgate** *v.* [T]

ex·quis·ite /ɪk'skwɪzɪt, 'ɛkskwɪ-/ *adj.* beautiful and delicate: *an exquisite piece of jewelry* —**exquisitely** *adv.*

ex·tant /'ɛkstənt, ɛk'stænt/ *adj.* (formal) still existing in spite of being very old (SYN) **surviving**: *The "Book of Changes" is perhaps the oldest extant Chinese work.*

ex·tem·po·ra·ne·ous /ɪk,stɛmpə'reɪniəs, ɛk-/ *adj.* spoken or done without any preparation or practice: *an extemporaneous speech*

ex·tend /ɪk'stɛnd/ *v.* **1** [I,T] to continue for a longer period of time, or to make something last longer: *The professor agreed to extend the deadline for the papers.* | *The warm weather extended into November.* | *The Department of Immigration is extending her visa by another six months.* **2** [I] to cover a particular distance or area: *The river* ***extends*** *more than 200 miles* ***through*** *the Grand Canyon.* **3** [T] to make a room, building, road, etc. bigger: *The developer plans to extend Thomas Road to meet Tenth Street.* **4** [I,T] to make something include or affect more things or people: *My insurance policy can be* ***extended to*** *cover my family too.* **5** [T] (formal) to officially offer someone help, thanks, sympathy, etc.: *I'd like to* ***extend a*** *warm* ***welcome*** *to our new members.* **6** [T] to stretch out your hand, arm, or leg: *"Hi, I'm Bill," he said, extending his hand.* [ORIGIN: 1300—1400 Latin *extendere*, from *tendere* "to stretch"]

ex,tended 'family *n.* [C] a family group that consists not only of parents and children but also of grandparents, AUNTs, etc. ➔ NUCLEAR FAMILY

ex·ten·sion /ɪk'stɛnʃən/ *n.* **1** [C] **a)** one of many telephone lines connected to a central system in a large building, which all have different numbers: *Hello, I'd like extension 1334, please.* | *What's your* ***extension number****?* **b)** one of the telephones in a house that all have the same number **2** [C usually singular] an extra period of time allowed for something: *The professor gave me a two-week extension on my paper.* **3** [C,U] the process of making something bigger or longer, or the part that is added in this process: *The city is building an* ***extension to*** *the subway line.* | *an* ***extension of*** *the museum* **4** [singular, U] the development of something so that it affects more things or people: *an* ***extension of*** *employee health care*

ex'tension ˌcord *n.* [C] an additional electric CORD that you attach to another cord in order to make it longer

ex·ten·sive /ɪk'stɛnsɪv/ *adj.* **1** containing a lot of information and details: *Doctors have done extensive research into the effects of stress.* | *The networks are planning* ***extensive television coverage*** **2** large in size, amount, or degree: *The flood caused* ***extensive damage*** *to the town.* | *the* ***extensive use*** *of pesticides*

ex·tent /ɪk'stɛnt/ *n.* **1** [U] how big, important, or serious something is: *What's the* ***extent of*** *the damage?* | *Medical tests were done to determine the extent of his injury.* **2 to ... extent** used to say how true something is: *I do agree with him* ***to some extent/a certain extent*** (=partly). | *Stock prices fell sharply in Asia and Europe and,* ***to a lesser/greater extent****, in the United States.* **3 to such an extent that/to the extent that** used to say how great an effect or change is: *The building was damaged to such an extent that it had to be knocked down.*

ex·te·ri·or¹ /ɪk'stɪriə/ *n.* [C] **1** the outside of something ANT **interior**: *the* ***exterior of*** *the house* **2 calm/confident etc. exterior** someone's behavior, that often does not show his/her real feelings or nature

exterior² *adj.* on the outside of something ANT **interior**: *the* ***exterior walls*** *of the church*

exˌterior 'angle *n.* [C] MATH an angle outside a POLYGON (=flat shape with straight sides) that is formed from one of the sides of the polygon and a line continuing out from a side that is next to the first side

ex·ter·mi·nate /ɪk'stəməˌneɪt/ *v.* [T] to kill all of a particular group of animals or people —**exterminator** *n.* [C] —**extermination** /ɪkˌstəmə'neɪʃən/ *n.* [C,U]

THESAURUS kill, murder, slaughter, massacre, slay → KILL¹

ex·ter·nal /ɪk'stənl/ Ac *adj.* **1** relating to the outside of something ANT **internal**: *This medicine is* ***for external use only*** (=you should put it on your skin and not eat it). | *a computer with an external modem* **2** from outside your organization, country, university, etc. ANT **internal**: *external threats to the country's security* [ORIGIN: 1500—1600 Latin *externus*, from *exter* "on the outside"]

ex·ter·nal·ize /ɪk'stənlˌaɪz/ Ac *v.* [T] to express your emotions in words or actions → INTERNALIZE

ex·tinct /ɪk'stɪŋkt/ *adj.* an extinct plant or animal no longer exists: *Activists fear that the tiger may* ***become extinct****.*

ex·tinc·tion /ɪk'stɪŋkʃən/ *n.* [U] the state of being extinct: *Greenpeace believes that whales are* ***in danger of extinction****.*

ex·tin·guish /ɪk'stɪŋgwɪʃ/ *v.* [T] to make a fire or light stop burning or shining: *Please extinguish all cigarettes.* [ORIGIN: 1500—1600 Latin *exstinguere*, from *stinguere* "to extinguish"]

ex·tin·guish·er /ɪk'stɪŋgwɪʃə/ *n.* [C] a FIRE EXTINGUISHER

ex·tol /ɪk'stoul/ *v.* (**extolled**, **extolling**) [T] (formal) to praise something very much: *Jack was* ***extolling the virtues of*** *being vegetarian.*

THESAURUS praise, commend → PRAISE¹

ex·tort /ɪk'stɔrt/ *v.* [T] to force someone to give you money by threatening him/her: *Rebel soldiers have been* ***extorting*** *money* ***from*** *local villages.* —**extortion** /ɪk'stɔrʃən/ *n.* [U]

ex·tor·tion·ate /ɪk'stɔrʃənɪt/ *adj.* (disapproving) extortionate prices, demands, etc. are much bigger than they should be

THESAURUS high, astronomical, exorbitant → EXPENSIVE

ex·tra¹ /'ɛkstrə/ *adj.* **1** [only before noun] more than the usual or standard amount of something: *a large mushroom pizza with extra cheese* | *The company gives employees extra time off to take care of sick family members.*

THESAURUS more, another, additional, further, supplemental, supplementary → MORE²

2 [not before noun] if something is extra, it is not included in the price of something and you have to pay more for it: *The catalog's prices are good, but shipping is extra.*

THESAURUS in addition, on top of sth, as well as sth → ADDITION

extra² *adv.* **1** in addition to the usual things or the usual amount: *You have to pay extra if you want to travel first class.* **2** used when emphasizing an adjective or adverb: *If you're extra good, I'll buy you an ice cream.* | *Henry's been working extra hard.*

extra³ *n.* [C] **1** something that can be added to a product or service, that makes it cost more: *The tour does not include extras, such as meals.* **2** an actor who has a small unimportant part in a movie

ex·tract¹ /ɪk'strækt/ Ac *v.* [T] **1** (formal) to remove something from a place or thing: *I have to* *have a* ***tooth extracted****.* | *Olive oil is* ***extracted from*** *green olives.* **2** to make someone give you information, money, etc. that s/he does not want to give: *The police couldn't* ***extract*** *any information* ***from*** *him.* [ORIGIN: 1400—1500 Latin, past participle of *extrahere*, from *ex* "out" + *trahere* "to pull"]

ex·tract² /'ɛkstrækt/ (Ac) *n.* **1** [C] a small part taken from a story, poem, etc.: *an* ***extract from*** *the article* **2** [C,U] a substance that is removed from a plant: *vanilla extract*

ex·trac·tion /ɪk'strækʃən/ (Ac) *n.* **1** [C,U] the process of removing something from something else: *the* ***extraction of*** *coal* **2 be of French/Irish etc. extraction** to be part of a family that came from France, Ireland, etc. in the past, though you were not born in that country

E

ex·tra·cur·ric·u·lar /ˌɛkstrəkə'rɪkyələ˞/ *adj.* [only before noun] extracurricular activities are those that you do for fun and are not part of the usual work you do for school

ex·tra·dite /'ɛkstrəˌdaɪt/ *v.* [T] LAW to send someone who may be guilty of a crime back to the country where the crime happened —**extradition** /ˌɛkstrə'dɪʃən/ *n.* [C,U]

ex·tra·ne·ous /ɪk'streɪniəs/ *adj.* (formal) not directly related to a particular subject: *extraneous details*

ex·traor·di·nar·y /ɪk'strɔrdnˌɛri/ *adj.* very unusual, special, or surprising: *an extraordinary talent* | *an extraordinary event* [ORIGIN: 1400—1500 Latin *extraordinarius*, from *extra ordinem* "out of the usual course," from *ordo* "order"]

> THESAURUS **surprising, amazing, shocking, astonishing, astounding, staggering, stunning** → SURPRISING

ex·trap·o·late /ɪk'stræpəˌleɪt/ *v.* [I,T] (formal) to use facts about a current situation in order to say what might happen in another

ex·tra·ter·res·tri·al /ˌɛkstrətə'rɛstriəl/ *adj.* in or from a place that is not the Earth: *the search for extraterrestrial life* —**extraterrestrial** *n.* [C]

ex·trav·a·gant /ɪk'strævəgənt/ *adj.* **1** spending or costing too much money: *extravagant parties* **2** extravagant claims, promises, etc. are not likely to be true [ORIGIN: 1300—1400 Medieval Latin, Latin *vagans*, present participle of *vagari* "to wander about"] —**extravagantly** *adv.* —**extravagance** *n.* [C,U]

ex·treme¹ /ɪk'strim/ *adj.* **1** very great in degree: *extreme violence* | *Mountain climbers face extreme danger.* **2** very unusual and severe or serious: *The soldiers were accused of using extreme methods to question prisoners.* | ***In extreme cases****, the spider's bite can kill.* **3** extreme opinions are very strong, and most people think they are unreasonable: *the party's extreme left wing* **4 extreme sport/skiing etc.** a sport that is done in a way that is more dangerous than usual

extreme² *n.* **1** [C] something that is much greater, more severe, etc. than usual: *the* ***extremes of*** *wealth and poverty* | *The temperature has gone* ***from one extreme to another*** (=from hot to cold or cold to hot). | *People were willing to* ***go to extremes*** (=do something to the greatest possible extent) *to prevent the prison from being built near their homes.* **2 in the extreme** extremely: *His new movie is violent in the extreme.*

ex·treme·ly /ɪk'strimli/ *adv.* to a very great degree: *She's extremely pretty.* | *an extremely difficult job*

ex·trem·ist /ɪk'strimɪst/ *n.* [C] (disapproving) someone with very strong political or religious opinions: *right-wing extremists* —**extremist** *adj.* —**extremism** *n.* [U]

ex·trem·i·ty /ɪk'strɛməṭi/ *n.* (plural **extremities**) **1** [C] the part that is furthest from the center of something: *the city's northern extremity* **2** [C, usually plural] one of the parts of your body that is furthest away from the center, for example your fingers or toes

ex·tri·cate /'ɛkstrəˌkeɪt/ *v.* [T] to get someone out of a place or a difficult situation: *They couldn't* ***extricate*** *themselves* ***from*** *the huge crowd of people.*

ex·tro·vert·ed /'ɛkstrəˌvə˞ṭɪd/ *adj.* confident and enjoying being with other people (ANT) **introverted** —**extrovert** *n.* [C]

> THESAURUS **sociable, outgoing, gregarious, affable, genial, convivial** → SOCIABLE

ex·u·ber·ant /ɪg'zubərənt/ *adj.* very happy, excited, and full of energy: *the exuberant bride* —**exuberance** *n.* [U]

ex·ude /ɪg'zud, ɪk'sud/ *v.* [T] to show that you have a lot of a particular feeling: *On the morning of the big game, the team exuded confidence.* [ORIGIN: 1500—1600 Latin *exsudare*, from *sudare* "to have liquid coming out through the skin"]

ex·ult /ɪg'zʌlt/ *v.* [I] (formal) to show that you are very happy and proud because you have achieved something: *The people* ***exulted over*** *the defeat of their enemy.* —**exultant** *adj.* —**exultation** /ˌɛgzʌl'teɪʃən, ˌɛksʌl-/ *n.* [U]

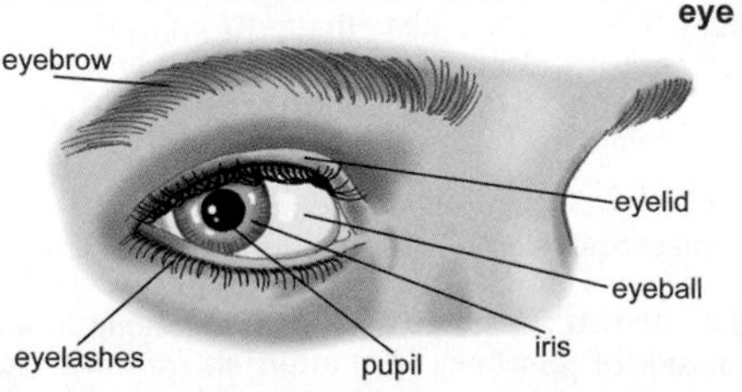

eye¹ /aɪ/ *n.* [C]
1 SEE one of the two parts of your face that you see with: *Gina has blue/brown etc. eyes.* | *My eyes are going bad; I think I need glasses.* | ***Close/shut*** *your eyes and go to sleep.* | *She* ***opened*** *her* ***eyes****.* | *He*

*spoke with **tears in** his **eyes**. | Dave is **blind in one eye**. | **blue-eyed/bright-eyed etc.***

COLLOCATIONS

If you **lower** your **eyes**, you look down.
Your **eyes narrow** if you are watching something carefully or thinking hard about something.
Your **eyes widen** if you are surprised, afraid, etc.
Your **eyes sparkle** if you are excited or very happy.

2 SEE/UNDERSTAND a particular way of seeing, judging, or understanding something: *The story is told **through the eyes of** a young boy. | a good **eye for** detail*
3 keep an eye on sb/sth (informal) to watch someone or something to make sure nothing bad happens: *Can you keep an eye on the baby while I go to the store?*
4 lay/set eyes on sb/sth (spoken) to see someone or something, especially for the first time: *The first time I laid eyes on him, I knew I liked him.*
5 cannot take your eyes off sb/sth to be unable to stop looking at someone or something because s/he or it is attractive or interesting: *When I watch him play, I just can't take my eyes off him.*
6 eye contact a situation in which you look directly at someone while s/he is looking at you: *I made a point of **making eye contact** with Marcus. | Tina **avoided eye contact** with her mother.*
7 keep an eye out for sb/sth to be ready to notice someone or something when he, she, or it appears: *Keep an eye out for Rick's car.*
8 in the eyes of the law/world/police etc. in the opinion or judgment of the law, world, etc.: *Divorce is a sin in the eyes of the Catholic Church.*
9 have your eye on sb to notice someone that you think is attractive or interesting: *Mark really has his eye on Yvonne.*
10 have your eye on sth to want something that you think might become available: *Harris has his eye on a two-story house in Woodside.*
11 see eye to eye if two people or groups see eye to eye, they have the same opinions about something: *Baker and Quinn don't always **see eye to eye on** every issue.*
12 close/open your eyes to sth to ignore something bad that is happening, or to start to realize that something bad is happening: *The trip opened his eyes to the poverty in the area.*
13 NEEDLE the hole in a needle, that you put thread through
14 the eye of a storm/hurricane/tornado the calm center of a big storm
15 an eye for an eye the idea that if people do something wrong, you should punish them by doing the same thing to them [ORIGIN: Old English *eage*] → **catch sb's eye** *at* CATCH¹, **look sb in the eye** *at* LOOK¹

eye² *v.* (past tense and past participle **eyed**, present participle **eyeing** *or* **eying**) [T] to look at someone or something with great interest: *Sarah kept eyeing my boyfriend all night.*

eye·ball /ˈaɪbɔl/ *n.* [C] the whole of your eye, including the part inside your head → *see picture at* EYE¹

eye·brow /ˈaɪbraʊ/ *n.* [C] the line of short hairs above your eye → *see picture at* EYE¹

ˈeye-ˌcatching *adj.* unusual, attractive, or noticeable: *an eye-catching dress*

THESAURUS **noticeable, obvious, striking, evident, conspicuous, unmistakable** → NOTICEABLE

eye·lash /ˈaɪlæʃ/ *n.* [C] one of the small hairs that grow on the edge of your eyelid → *see picture at* EYE¹

eye·lid /ˈaɪˌlɪd/ *n.* [C] the piece of skin that covers your eye when it is closed → *see picture at* EYE¹

eye·lin·er /ˈaɪˌlaɪnɚ/ *n.* [C,U] a type of MAKEUP that you put in a thin line along the edges of your eyelids

ˈeye-ˌopener *n.* [C usually singular] an experience from which you learn something new or surprising: *Seeing inside a prison was a real eye-opener for me.*

eye·piece /ˈaɪpis/ *n.* [C] SCIENCE the glass piece that you look through in a MICROSCOPE or TELESCOPE → *see picture at* MICROSCOPE

eye·shad·ow /ˈaɪˌʃædoʊ/ *n.* [U] colored MAKEUP that you put on your eyelids to make them look attractive

eye·sight /ˈaɪsaɪt/ *n.* [U] the ability to see: *Grandma is slowly **losing** her **eyesight**.*

eye·sore /ˈaɪsɔr/ *n.* [C] something that is very ugly, especially a building surrounded by other things that are not ugly

eye·wit·ness /ˌaɪˈwɪtˀnɪs, ˈaɪˌwɪtˀnɪs/ *n.* [C] someone who has seen a crime or accident: *an **eyewitness account** of the incident*

F, f /ɛf/ the sixth letter of the English alphabet

F¹ /ɛf/ *n.* **1** [C] a GRADE that a teacher gives to a student's work to show that s/he has failed: *Jill **got an F** in Physics.* **2** [C,U] ENG. LANG. ARTS the fourth note in the musical SCALE of C, or the musical KEY based on this note

F² **1** PHYSICS the written abbreviation of FAHRENHEIT **2** the written abbreviation of FEMALE

fa·ble /ˈfeɪbəl/ *n.* [C] a traditional story that teaches a moral lesson

THESAURUS **story, tale, myth, legend, yarn, narrative, anecdote** → STORY

fab·ric /ˈfæbrɪk/ *n.* **1** [C,U] cloth **2** [singular] the structure and CUSTOMS of a society: *Discrimination is threatening the whole **fabric of society**.* [ORIGIN: 1400—1500 Old French *fabrique*, from Latin *fabrica* "thing made, place where things are made"]

fab·ri·cate /ˈfæbrəˌkeɪt/ *v.* [T] to make up a story, piece of information, etc. in order to deceive someone: *He later admitted that he had fabricated the whole story.* —**fabrication** /ˌfæbrəˈkeɪʃən/ *n.* [C,U]

fab·u·lous /ˈfæbyələs/ *adj.* **1** very good: *You look fabulous!* **2** unusually large in amount or size: *a fabulous sum of money* —**fabulously** *adv.*

fa·cade, façade /fəˈsɑd/ *n.* [C] **1** [usually singular] a way of behaving that hides your real feelings or character: *Behind that cheerful facade she's really a lonely person.* **2** the front of a building

face¹ /feɪs/ *n.* [C] **1** the front of your head, where your eyes, nose, and mouth are: *Jodi has such a pretty face.* | *He had a surprised **look on his face**.* | *Keith was **lying face down*** (=with his face toward the ground) *on the bed.* | *a **round-faced** man* → *see picture on page A16* **2** an expression on someone's face: *the children's happy faces* | *Carl was **making faces at** Lisa* (=making expressions with his face to try to annoy her or make her laugh). | *I just couldn't **keep a straight face*** (=avoid laughing). | *When I told Garry I was quitting, **you should have seen** his **face*** (=used to say that someone was very angry, surprised, etc.). **3** a person: *There are a few new faces in class this year.* | *It was so nice to see a friendly face.* **4 face to face a)** while physically close to someone: *I've spoken to her on the phone but I've never **met** her **face to face**.* **b)** in a situation in which you experience something difficult and have to deal with it: *It was the first time he'd ever **come face to face with** death.* **5 in the face of sth** in a difficult or dangerous situation: *Delmore kept his composure in the face of racial threats.* **6** the front or surface of something: *a clock face* | *the north **face of** Mount Rainier* → *see picture at* WATCH² **7 lose/save face** to lose or avoid losing the respect of other people → FACE-SAVING **8 to sb's face** if you say something to someone's face, you say it directly to that person when you are with him/her **9 on the face of it** when you first consider something, before you know the details: *On the face of it, the data is not very helpful.* **10 in your face** (informal) behavior, remarks, etc. that are in your face are very direct and often shocking or surprising: *an "in your face" style of politics*

face² *v.* [T] **1** *also* **face up to sth** to accept that a difficult situation or problem exists: *Randy refuses to **face the fact that** he needs help.* | ***Let's face it** — nobody wants to hire someone my age.* | *It's time to **face up to the truth** and admit there is a problem.* **2** *also* **be faced with sth** to have to deal with a difficult situation: *She's faced with some very tough choices.* | *Jones is facing up to 20 years in jail.* **3 sb can't face (doing) sth** used in order to say that someone does not feel able to do something, especially because it upsets him/her: *I can't face going back to work again.* **4** to be looking at or pointing toward someone or something: *Dean **turned to face** me.* | *a north-facing window* | *My apartment faces the ocean.* **5** to talk to or deal with someone, when this is difficult: *You're going to **have to face** him sooner or later.* **6** to play against an opponent or team in a game or competition: *The Jets face the Dolphins in two weeks.*

face sb ↔ **down** *phr. v.* to deal in a strong and confident way with someone who opposes you: *Frost faced down a serious challenge from his opponent.*

face off *phr. v.* to get in a position in which you are ready to fight, argue, or compete with someone: *The two candidates will face off in the election in November.*

face·less /ˈfeɪslɪs/ *adj.* (disapproving) a faceless person, organization, etc. is not clearly known and seems unfriendly or not worth caring about

face·lift /ˈfeɪslɪft/ *n.* [C] **1** a medical operation to make your face look younger **2** work or repairs that make something look newer or better: *The offices were **given a facelift**.*

ˈface-ˌsaving *adj.* [only before noun] a face-saving action or arrangement prevents you from losing other people's respect: *a face-saving agreement*

fac·et /ˈfæsɪt/ *n.* [C] one of several parts of someone's character, a situation, etc.: *You've only seen one **facet of** his personality.*

fa·ce·tious /fəˈsiʃəs/ *adj.* (disapproving) saying things in order to be funny, in a way that is annoying or not appropriate —**facetiously** *adv.*

ˌface-to-ˈface *adj.* [only before noun] a face-to-face meeting, conversation, etc. is one where you are with another person and talking to them: *a face-to-face interview*

ˌface ˈvalue *n.* **1 take sth at face value** to accept what you are told without thinking carefully first: *Don't take anything Burgess tells you at face value.* **2** [singular, U] the value or cost shown on a coin, ticket, etc.

fa·cial¹ /ˈfeɪʃəl/ *adj.* on or relating to the face: *facial hair*

facial² *n.* [C] a beauty treatment to clean the skin on your face and make it softer

fac·ile /ˈfæsəl/ *adj.* (disapproving) too simple and showing a lack of careful thought or understanding: *a facile solution*

fa·cil·i·tate /fəˈsɪləˌteɪt/ (Ac) *v.* [T] (formal) to make it easier for something to happen: *The international network facilitates a quick exchange of information.*

THESAURUS **help, assist, aid, aid and abet** → HELP¹

fa·cil·i·ta·tor /fəˈsɪləˌteɪṭɚ/ (Ac) *n.* [C] (formal) someone or something that helps a process to take place, for example a discussion: *A facilitator needs to be a skilled listener.*

fa·cil·i·ty /fə'sɪləṭi/ (Ac) *n.* (plural **facilities**) **1 facilities** [plural] rooms, equipment, or services that are provided for a particular purpose: *The new office building has nursery facilities.* **2** [C] a place or building used for a particular purpose: *the prison's medical facility* **3** [C usually singular] a helpful service or feature that a machine or system has: *The phone is equipped with a call-back facility.*

fac·sim·i·le /fæk'sɪməli/ *n.* [C] an exact copy of a picture, piece of writing, etc.

fact /fækt/ *n.* [C] **1** something that is true: *I cannot accept **the fact that** our marriage is over.* | ***The fact remains that** people are still starving.* | *What are the **facts of/in** this case?* | *interesting **facts about** plants* | ***The fact of the matter is,** I don't have enough money.* | ***I know for a fact that** he was here last night.* **2 in (actual) fact a)** used in order to add information: *I know her really well. In fact, I had dinner with her last week.* **b)** used in order to emphasize that something is true, especially when it is surprising: *It's cheaper to fly, in actual fact.* **3 a fact of life** something bad that people must accept: *Violent crime seems to have become a fact of life.* **4 the facts of life** the details about sex and how babies are born [ORIGIN: 1400—1500 Latin *factum* "thing done," from *facere* "to do, make"] → **as a matter of fact** *at* MATTER[1]

fac·tion /'fækʃən/ *n.* [C] POLITICS a small group of people within a larger group, who have ideas that are different from those of the larger group: *a dispute between **rival factions** in the gang* —**factional** *adj.*

fac·tor[1] /'fæktɚ/ (Ac) *n.* [C] **1** one of several things that influence or cause a situation: *The weather could be an important/major/key **factor in** tomorrow's game.* | *Crime is due to **economic/social factors**.* | *We liked both houses, but the location was the **deciding factor*** (=most important factor). **2** a particular level on a scale that measures how strong or effective something is: *Strong north winds mean that the **windchill factor** will make the temperature seem much lower.* **3** MATH a number that divides into another number exactly: *3 is a factor of 15.* [ORIGIN: 1400—1500 French *facteur*, from Latin *factor* "doer, maker," from *facere* "to do, make"]

factor[2] (Ac) *v.* [T] MATH to divide a number into factors

factor sth ↔ **in** *phr. v.* to include a particular thing when you are deciding how long something will take, how much it will cost, etc.: *I made more money than my father had at my age, even factoring in inflation.*

factor sth ↔ **out** *phr. v.* to not include something when you are deciding how long something will take, how much it will cost, etc.: *If China is factored out, the number of children per family in the developing world is 4.4.*

fac·to·ri·al /fæk'tɔriəl/ *n.* [C] MATH the result when you multiply a whole number by all the numbers below or equal to it: *factorial 3 = 3 × 2 × 1*

fac·to·ry /'fæktəri/ *n.* (plural **factories**) [C] a building where goods are produced in large quantities: *a shoe factory*

fac·tu·al /'fæktʃuəl/ *adj.* based on or relating to facts: *The movie has many **factual errors**.* —**factually** *adv.*

fac·ul·ty /'fækəlti/ *n.* (plural **faculties**) **1** [C,U] all the teachers in a school or college, or in a particular department of a school or college: *a faculty meeting* | *the history faculty* **2** [C usually plural] a natural ability, such as the ability to see or think: *He wants to make out a will while he still has all his faculties* (=is still able to see, hear, think, etc. in the normal way).

fad /fæd/ *n.* [C] something that is very popular for a short period of time: *the newest fitness fad*

THESAURUS bestseller, blockbuster, hit, craze, cult → POPULAR

fade /feɪd/ *v.* **1** [I] *also* **fade away** to gradually disappear: *Hopes of a peace settlement are beginning to fade.* | *Their faces have **faded from** my memory now.* **2** [I,T] to lose color or brightness, or to make something do this: *faded jeans*

fade (sth ↔) **out** *phr. v.* to disappear slowly or become quieter, or to make a picture or sound do this: *The radio signal faded out.*

Fahr·en·heit /'færən,haɪt/ *n.* [U] PHYSICS (*written abbreviation* **F**) a temperature scale in which water freezes at 32° and boils at 212° → CELSIUS [ORIGIN: 1700—1800 Gabriel *Fahrenheit* (1686-1736), German scientist]

fail[1] /feɪl/ *v.* **1** [I] to be unsuccessful in what you are trying to do (ANT) **succeed**: *It looks likely that the peace talks will fail.* | *Doctors **failed to** save the girl's life.* | *President Clinton **failed in** his efforts to reform the health care system.* | *He **failed in** his **attempt** to regain the world title.* **2** [I] to not do what is expected, needed, or wanted: *Larry **failed to** present his proposal on time.* | *She felt she had **failed in** her **duty** as a parent.* **3** [I,T] if you fail a test, or if someone fails you, you do not pass it (ANT) **pass**: *I failed my math test.* | *The teacher had no choice but to fail her.* **4** [I] if a machine, a part of your body, etc. fails, it stops working: *The engine failed just after the plane took off.* | *her **failing eyesight*** **5** [I] if a business fails, it has to stop operating because of a lack of money **6 fail sb** to not do what someone has trusted you to do: *I feel I've failed my children by not spending more time with them.* **7 I fail to see/understand** (spoken, formal) used in order to show that you are annoyed by something that you do not accept or understand: *I fail to see the humor in this situation.* **8 sb's courage/nerve fails them** if your

F

courage, etc. fails you, you suddenly do not have it when you need it [ORIGIN: 1200—1300 Old French *faillir*, from Latin *fallere* "to deceive, disappoint"] —**failed** *adj.* [only before noun]: *a failed marriage*

fail² *n.* **without fail** if you do something without fail, you always do it: *Barry comes over every Friday without fail.*

fail·ing¹ /ˈfeɪlɪŋ/ *n.* [C] a fault or weakness: *He loved her in spite of her failings.*

failing² *prep.* used in order to say that if one thing is not possible, there is something else you could try: *You could try to fix it yourself, or, **failing that**, call a plumber.*

ˈfail-safe *adj.* **1** a fail-safe machine, piece of equipment, etc. will stop working if one part of it breaks or stops working correctly **2** a fail-safe plan is certain to succeed

fail·ure /ˈfeɪlyɚ/ *n.* **1** [U] a lack of success in achieving or doing something (ANT) **success**: *The recession caused the **failure of** many small businesses.* | *Poor soil can result in a plant's **failure to** grow.* | *The whole project **ended in failure**.* **2** [C] someone or something that is not successful (ANT) **success**: *I feel like such a failure.* | *The plan to expand the company overseas was a **complete/total failure**.* **3** [C,U] an occasion when a machine or part of your body stops working in the correct way: *He died of heart failure.* | *A mechanical failure caused the plane to crash.* **4 failure to do sth** the fact that someone has not done something that s/he should have done: *Failure to show proof of car insurance to an officer will result in a fine.*

faint¹ /feɪnt/ *adj.* **1** difficult to see, hear, or smell: *a faint sound* **2 a faint possibility/chance etc.** a very small possibility, etc.: *There's a faint hope that they're still alive.* **3** [not before noun] feeling weak and unsteady: *He was **faint with** hunger* **4 not have the faintest idea** to not know anything at all about something: *I **don't have the faintest idea what** you're talking about.* —**faintly** *adv.*

faint² *v.* [I] to become unconscious for a short time —**faint** *n.* [C]

fair¹ /fɛr/ *adj.*

1 REASONABLE reasonable, right, and accepted by most people (ANT) **unfair**: *What do you think is the fairest solution?* | *We paid what we think is a fair price.* | ***It's fair to say that** both sides were happy with the agreement.* | *I felt it was **fair to** let our employees know what was going on.*

2 EQUAL treating everyone equally or in the right way (ANT) **unfair**: *Why does Eric get to go and I don't? **It's not fair!*** | *The law isn't **fair to** women.*

THESAURUS

just – morally right and fair: *a just ruler*
reasonable – fair and sensible: *a reasonable request*
equitable (formal) – fair and equal to everyone involved: *an equitable solution*
balanced – fair and sensible: *balanced news coverage*
even-handed – giving fair and equal treatment to everyone: *He was very even-handed in the way he treated employees.*
impartial – not giving special attention or support to any one person or group: *A trial must have an impartial judge and jury.*
unbiased – fair, and not influenced by your own or other people's opinions: *accurate, unbiased information*

3 AVERAGE neither very good nor very bad (SYN) **average**: *Her written work is excellent but her lab work is only fair.*

4 ACCORDING TO RULES played or done according to the rules: *free and fair elections*

5 have more than your fair share of sth to have more problems than other people, in a way that seems unfair: *Tim's had more than his fair share of bad luck this year.*

6 HAIR/SKIN someone who is fair, or has fair skin or hair, has skin or hair that is light in color (ANT) **dark**

7 WEATHER weather that is fair is pleasant and not windy or rainy

8 fair game if someone or something is fair game, it is reasonable and right to criticize him/her or it: *If you're in show business, your personal life is considered fair game.*

9 give sb/get a fair shake (informal) to treat someone, or to be treated, in a way that gives everyone the same chances as everyone else: *Women don't always get a fair shake in business.* [ORIGIN: Old English *fæger* "beautiful"] —**fairness** *n.* [U]

fair² *adv.* **1 fair and square** in a fair and honest way: *They won fair and square.* **2 play fair** to play or behave in a fair and honest way

fair³ *n.* [C] **1** an outdoor event, at which there are large machines to ride on, games to play, and sometimes farm animals being judged and sold: *a **state/county fair*** **2** an event at which people or businesses show and sell their products: *a trade/book, etc. fair*

fair·ground /ˈfɛrgraʊnd/ *n.* [C] an open space on which a fair takes place

fair·ly /ˈfɛrli/ *adv.* **1** more than a little, but much less than very: *She speaks English fairly well.* | *The recipe is fairly simple.*

THESAURUS rather, pretty, quite, kind of
→ RATHER

2 in a way that is fair and reasonable: *I felt that I hadn't been treated fairly.*

fair·way /ˈfɛrweɪ/ *n.* [C] the part of a GOLF COURSE that you hit the ball along toward the hole

fair·y /ˈfɛri/ *n.* (plural **fairies**) [C] an imaginary magical creature like a very small person [ORIGIN:

1300—1400 Old French *faerie* "fairyland," from *fae* "fairy," from Latin *fatum* "fate"]

'fairy tale *n.* [C] a children's story in which magical things happen

faith /feɪθ/ *n.* **1** [U] a strong feeling of trust in someone or something: *My **faith in** his ability was justified.* | *I **have** great **faith** in her ability to succeed.* | *People seem to have **lost faith** in the justice system.* **2** [U] belief and trust in God: *a man of deep religious faith* | *his **faith in** God* **3 good faith** honest and sincere intentions: *He claimed he sold me the car **in good faith*** (=without meaning to deceive me). **4** [C] a religion: *the **Jewish/Muslim/Christian etc. faith***

THESAURUS

religion – belief in one or more gods, or a particular system of beliefs in one or more gods: *a book about world religions*
belief – an idea or set of ideas that you think are true: *She has strong religious beliefs.*
creed – a set of beliefs or principles: *The scholarship is available to anyone, regardless of race, creed, or color.*

faith·ful /'feɪθfəl/ *adj.* **1** remaining loyal and continuing to support someone or something: *a faithful friend* | *He remained **faithful to** his beliefs.*

THESAURUS

loyal – always supporting a particular person, set of beliefs, or country: *a loyal friend*
devoted – giving someone or something a lot of love, concern, and attention: *a devoted mother*
staunch – very loyal: *staunch supporters of the president*
steadfast – very loyal and continuing to support someone or something in spite of problems: *She had always been a steadfast Republican.*
true – faithful and loyal, and doing what you have promised to do: *She stayed true to her husband during the trial.*

2 loyal to your wife, BOYFRIEND, etc. by not having a sexual relationship with anyone else (ANT) **unfaithful**: *She hasn't always been **faithful to** me, but I love her anyway.* **3** representing an event or image exactly: *The movie is **faithful to** the book.* —**faithfulness** *n.* [U]

faith·ful·ly /'feɪθfəli/ *adv.* in a faithful way: *He visited his aunt faithfully.*

fake¹ /feɪk/ *n.* [C] **1** a copy of a valuable object that is intended to deceive people: *We thought it was a Picasso, but it was a fake.* **2** someone who does not really have the knowledge, skills, etc. that s/he claims to have: *It turned out her doctor was a fake.*

fake² *adj.* made to look or seem like something else in order to deceive people: *fake fur* | *She used a fake name to apply for a credit card.*

fake

THESAURUS

counterfeit – counterfeit money or a counterfeit product is made to look real in order to deceive people: *counterfeit credit cards* | *counterfeit lottery tickets* | *a million dollars in counterfeit bills*
phony – not real and intended to deceive people: *a phony birth certificate*
forged – used about writing or documents that have been illegally copied in order to deceive people: *forged passports*

THESAURUS **artificial, synthetic, simulated, man-made, imitation, false, virtual** → ARTIFICIAL

fake³ *v.* **1** [T] to make something seem real in order to deceive people: *He faked his uncle's signature on the check.* **2** [I,T] to pretend to be sick, interested, pleased, etc. when you are not: *I thought he was really hurt but he was just **faking it**.*

fal·con /'fælkən, 'fɔl-/ *n.* [C] a large bird that is often trained to hunt small animals

fall¹ /fɔl/ *v.* (past tense **fell** /fɛl/, past participle **fallen** /'fɔlən/)
1 MOVE DOWNWARD [I] to drop down toward the ground → PLUMMET: *Snow began to fall.* | *Apples had **fallen from** the trees.* | *A large tree **fell down** during the storm.*
2 STOP STANDING/WALKING, ETC. [I] to accidentally go down onto the ground when you are standing, walking, etc.: *Don't worry, I'll catch you if you fall.* | *She **fell down** the stairs.* | *Sam tripped and **fell into** a ditch.* → *see picture on page A22*

THESAURUS

trip – to hit your foot against something, so that you fall or nearly fall: *Be careful not to trip on that step.*
slip – to slide on something that is wet or icy, so that you fall or nearly fall: *She slipped on the ice and broke her leg.*
stumble – to put your foot down in an awkward way, so that you nearly fall: *She stumbled backwards and hit her head on the bed.*
lose your balance – to fall, for example, when

F

you are climbing a ladder or riding a bicycle: *He was walking on the top of the fence when he lost his balance.*

3 LOWER LEVEL/AMOUNT [I] to go down to a lower level or amount (ANT) **rise**: *Temperatures should fall below zero tonight.* | *The number of traffic deaths fell by 10% last year.* | *The unemployment rate* ***fell to*** *4.8%.*

THESAURUS **decrease, go down, drop, plummet, diminish, decline, dwindle** → DECREASE[1]

4 BECOME [I, linking verb] to begin to be in a new or different state: ***I fell asleep*** *at 8:30.* | *Your father and I* ***fell in love*** *when we were in college.* | *Everyone* ***fell silent*** *as Beth walked in.* | *The house* ***fell into*** *disrepair.*
5 GROUP [I] to be part of a particular group: *Most of his novels* ***fall into*** *the science fiction category.* | *The program* ***falls under*** *the authority of the Department of Education.*
6 fall into place if things fall into place, they become clear or start to happen as you want
7 HAPPEN [I] to happen on a particular day or date: *Christmas* ***falls on*** *a Monday this year.*
8 LIGHT/DARKNESS [I] if light or darkness falls, it makes something brighter or darker: ***Darkness/ Night fell on*** *the city.* | *A shadow* ***fell across*** *his face.*
9 HANG DOWN [I] to hang loosely: *Maria's hair fell over her shoulders.*
10 fall short (of sth) to be less than is needed or less than you want: *Her newest book fell short of my expectations.*
11 FACE [I] if your face falls, you suddenly look sad or disappointed
12 fall flat to fail to amuse or interest people: *His attempt at humor fell flat.*
13 DIE [I] (written) to be killed in a war
14 LOSE POWER [I] to lose power: *Saddam Hussein fell from power soon after the invasion.* [ORIGIN: Old English *feallan*]

fall apart *phr. v.*
1 to separate into many pieces: *The old book fell apart in my hands.*
2 to stop being effective or successful: *The economy was falling apart.*
3 to be unable to deal with your personal or emotional problems: *When Pam left, I thought I was going to fall apart.*

fall back on sth *phr. v.*
to use something or someone after other things or plans have failed: *Athletes need an education to fall back on.*

fall behind (sb/sth) *phr. v.*
to make progress more slowly than other people or than you should: *The older walkers soon fell behind.* | *The manufacturers have fallen behind schedule.*

fall for sb/sth *phr. v.*
1 to be tricked into believing something that is not true: *He said he was a police officer and I almost* ***fell for it.***
2 to start to love someone: *Samantha fell for a man half her age.*

fall off *phr. v.*
1 if part of something falls off, it becomes separated from the main part: *This button keeps falling off.*
2 to decrease: *The demand for cassette tapes has fallen off.*

fall out *phr. v.*
1 if a tooth or your hair falls out, it is no longer attached to your body
2 to argue or fight with someone: *Walker recently* ***fell out with*** *his publisher.*

fall over *phr. v.*
to fall to the ground or to fall from an upright position: *She fell over and cut her knee.* | *The Christmas tree fell over.*

fall through *phr. v.*
to fail to happen or be completed: *The deal fell through at the last minute.*

fall² *n.* **1** [C,U] the season between summer and winter, when the weather becomes cooler (SYN) **autumn**: *Brad's going to Georgia Tech* ***in the fall.*** | *Dad's going to retire* ***this fall.*** | ***last/next fall*** (=the fall before or after this one) **2** [C] a decrease in the level, quantity, price, etc. of something (ANT) **rise**: *a sudden* ***fall in*** *temperature* | *a* ***fall of*** *25% in unemployment* **3** [C] a movement down toward the ground: *He* ***had a*** *bad* ***fall*** *from a ladder.* | *He put his hand down to* ***break*** *his* ***fall*** (=prevent himself from falling too quickly and hurting himself). **4** [singular] a situation when someone or something is defeated or loses power: *the* ***fall of*** *Communism in East Germany* | *the party's* ***fall from*** *power* **5 falls** [plural] a WATERFALL

fal·la·cious /fəˈleɪʃəs/ *adj.* (formal) containing or based on false ideas: *a fallacious statement* —**fallaciously** *adv.*

fal·la·cy /ˈfæləsi/ *n.* (plural **fallacies**) [C] a false idea or belief: *the fallacy that money brings happiness*

fall·en /ˈfɔlən/ *v.* the past participle of FALL

ˈfall guy *n.* [C] (informal) someone who is punished for someone else's crime or mistake

fal·li·ble /ˈfæləbəl/ *adj.* able to make a mistake (ANT) **infallible**: *Steyer's murder trial showed that the justice system is fallible.* —**fallibility** /ˌfæləˈbɪləṭi/ *n.* [U]

fal·lo·pi·an tube /fəˌloʊpiən ˈtub/ *n.* [C] BIOLOGY one of the two tubes in a female's body through which her eggs move to her UTERUS

fall·out /ˈfɔlaʊt/ *n.* [U] **1** the bad results or effects of an event: *The* ***fallout from*** *the scandal cost him his job.* **2** the dangerous RADIOACTIVE dust that is in the air after a NUCLEAR explosion

false /fɔls/ *adj.* **1** untrue or wrong: *He gave the police false information.* | *Are these statements* ***true***

or false? | *The article gave a* ***false impression*** *of the company's finances.*

THESAURUS **wrong, incorrect, erroneous, inaccurate, misleading, fallacious** → WRONG[1]

2 not real, but intended to seem real: *He gave a false name.* | *false eyelashes*

THESAURUS **fake, counterfeit, phony, forged** → FAKE[2]
artificial, synthetic, fake, man-made, simulated, imitation → ARTIFICIAL

3 not sincere or honest: *Her smile and welcome seemed false.* **4 false alarm** a situation in which people wrongly think that something bad is going to happen **5 false start** an unsuccessful attempt to begin a process or event **6 under false pretenses** if you get something under false pretenses, you get it by deceiving people [ORIGIN: 900—1000 Latin *falsus*, from *fallere* "to deceive"] **—falsely** *adv.*: *a man falsely accused of murder*

false·hood /'fɔlshʊd/ *n.* [C] (formal) a statement that is untrue

THESAURUS **lie, fib, white lie, story, fabrication, slander, libel** → LIE[3]

ˌfalse 'teeth *n.* [plural] DENTURES

fal·set·to /fɔl'sɛt̮oʊ/ *n.* (plural **falsettos**) [C] a very high male voice **—falsetto** *adv.*

fal·si·fy /'fɔlsəˌfaɪ/ *v.* (**falsified, falsifies**) [T] to change figures, records, etc. so that they contain false information: *He was accused of falsifying the company's records.* **—falsification** /ˌfɔlsəfə'keɪʃən/ *n.* [C,U]

THESAURUS **lie, make sth up, tell (sb) a lie, invent, mislead, deceive, perjure yourself/commit perjury** → LIE[2]

fal·ter /'fɔltɚ/ *v.* [I] **1** to become weaker: *The economy is faltering.* **2** to speak or move in a way that seems weak or uncertain: *She faltered for a moment.*

fame /feɪm/ *n.* [U] the state of being known about by a lot of people because of your achievements: *Elizabeth Taylor's* ***rise to fame*** *came in the movie "National Velvet."* | *Johnny Depp first* ***gained/won/achieved fame*** *on the television program "21 Jump Street."* → **claim to fame** at CLAIM[2]

famed /feɪmd/ *adj.* (written) well-known: *The Rocky Mountains are* ***famed for*** *their beauty.*

fa·mil·iar /fə'mɪlyɚ/ *adj.* **1** well-known to you and easy to recognize: *Your face* ***looks familiar*** *to me.* | *a room full of* ***familiar faces*** (=people you know) | *The details are* ***familiar to*** *anyone who has followed the case.* | *The story covers* ***familiar ground/territory.*** **2 be familiar with sth** to know about something: *Are you familiar with his books?* **3** (disapproving) too informal and friendly with someone you do not know very well: *The waiter was a bit too familiar.* **—familiarly** *adv.*: *Robert is familiarly known as Bob.*

fa·mil·iar·i·ty /fəˌmɪl'yærət̮i, -ˌmɪli'ær-/ *n.* [U] **1** a good knowledge of something: *her* ***familiarity with*** *this software* **2** a relaxed feeling or way of behaving because you know a person or place well: *the familiarity of home*

fa·mil·iar·ize /fə'mɪlyəˌraɪz/ *v.* **familiarize yourself with sth** to learn about something so that you know it well: *I spent the first week familiarizing myself with my new job.* **—familiarization** /fəˌmɪlyərə'zeɪʃən/ *n.* [U]

fam·ily /'fæmli, -məli/ *n.* (plural **families**) **1** [C,U] a group of people who are related to each other, especially parents and their children: *Do you know the family next door?* | *The car will comfortably seat* ***a family of*** *five.* | *I know her* ***whole/entire family.*** | *Heart disease* ***runs in*** *our* ***family*** (=is common in our family).

COLLOCATIONS
Your **immediate family** includes the people you are very closely related to, such as your parents, brothers, sisters, and children.
A **nuclear family** is a family that has a father, mother, and children.
Your **extended family** includes all of your relatives such as aunts, uncles, cousins, and grandparents.

THESAURUS
relative – a member of your family: *Most of my relatives are in California.*
relation – a member of your family: *Hugh is a distant relation of mine.*
folks – your parents or family: *Where do your folks live?*
kin (old-fashioned) – your family: *We were her only kin.*

2 [C] children: *Steve and Linda want to* ***start a family*** (=have children). | *a great place to* ***raise a family*** **3** [C] ENG. LANG. ARTS a group of languages that share the same origin: *Spanish and Italian are part of the Romance language family.* **4** [C] BIOLOGY the groups into which scientists divide animals and plants. A family is larger than a GENUS but smaller than an ORDER: *tigers and other members of the cat family* [ORIGIN: 1400—1500 *familia* "people living in a house," from Latin *famulus* "servant"]

'family ˌname *n.* [C] the name someone shares with other members of his/her family SYN **last name**

ˌfamily 'planning *n.* [U] the practice of controlling the number of children you have by using CONTRACEPTION

'family ˌroom *n.* [C] a room in a house where the family can play games, watch television, etc.

ˌfamily 'tree *n.* [C] a drawing that shows the names of the members of a family over a period of time and how they are related to each other

F

fam·ine /ˈfæmɪn/ *n.* [C,U] a situation in which a large number of people have little or no food for a long time and many people die [ORIGIN: 1300—1400 French, Latin *fames* "hungry condition"]

fam·ished /ˈfæmɪʃt/ *adj.* (informal) [not before noun] very hungry: *What's for dinner? I'm famished.*

fa·mous /ˈfeɪməs/ *adj.* known about by a lot of people: *a famous actor* | *France is* ***famous for*** *its food and wine.* | *Lake Winnebago is* ***famous as*** *a fishing destination.* [ORIGIN: 1300—1400 Old French *fameus*, from Latin *fama* "report, fame"] —**famously** *adv.* → *see also* WORLD FAMOUS

THESAURUS

well-known fairly famous and known about by a lot of people: *a well-known actor* | *He is well-known for his charity work.* | *It's a well-known fact that smoking causes cancer.*
legendary – very famous and admired by many people for a long time: *the legendary blues guitarist, B.B. King*
infamous/notorious – famous for doing something bad: *Al Capone, the infamous criminal*
celebrated famous and often impressive or important: *the celebrated South African leader Nelson Mandela*
renowned/noted famous, especially for a particular quality, skill, etc.: *a renowned civil rights leader* | *The area is noted for its wildlife.*
distinguished/eminent well-known, especially for serious work in science, the arts, etc.: *a distinguished author* | *an eminent professor*

fan¹ /fæn/ *n.* [C] **1** someone who likes a particular sport, type of music, etc. very much, or who admires a famous person: *a* ***hockey/jazz/Yankee etc.*** *fan* | *He was a big* ***fan of*** *Elvis Presley.* **2** a machine with blades that turn and make the air move in order to make a room feel cooler **3** an object that you wave with your hand in order to make yourself feel cooler

fan² *v.* (**fanned**, **fanning**) [T] to make air move by waving a fan, piece of paper, etc.: *She fanned her face with a newspaper.*

fan out *phr. v.* if a group of people fan out, they walk forward while spreading over a wide area: *Thousands of soldiers and police fanned out across the state.*

fa·nat·ic /fəˈnæṭɪk/ *n.* [C] **1** someone who has extreme religious or political ideas and may be dangerous: *a religious fanatic* **2** someone who likes a particular thing or activity very much: *a fitness fanatic* —**fanatical** *adj.* —**fanaticism** /fəˈnæṭəˌsɪzəm/ *n.* [U]

fan·ci·ful /ˈfænsɪfəl/ *adj.* imagined rather than based on facts: *fanciful ideas*

ˈfan club *n.* [C] an organization for fans of a particular team, famous person, etc.

fan·cy¹ /ˈfænsi/ *adj.* (comparative **fancier**, superlative **fanciest**) **1** expensive and fashionable: *a fancy hotel*

THESAURUS **expensive, pricey, costly, overpriced, posh** → EXPENSIVE

2 unusual and complicated or having a lot of decorations: *I'd just like plain brown shoes,* ***nothing fancy****.*

fancy² *n.* [singular] (old-fashioned) a feeling that you like something or someone: *Grant's* ***taken a fancy to*** *you.*

fancy³ *v.* (**fancied**, **fancies**) **fancy yourself sth** to believe, usually wrongly, that something is true: *Hiram fancies himself a good writer.*

fan·fare /ˈfænfɛr/ *n.* [C] a short piece of music played on a TRUMPET to introduce an important person or event

fang /fæŋ/ *n.* [C] a long sharp tooth of an animal such as a snake or dog → *see picture on page A15*

ˈfan mail *n.* [U] letters sent to famous people by their fans

fan·ta·size /ˈfæntəˌsaɪz/ *v.* [I,T] to think about something that is pleasant or exciting, but unlikely to happen: *I used to* ***fantasize about*** *buying a boat and sailing around the world.*

THESAURUS **imagine, visualize, picture, daydream** → IMAGINE

fan·tas·tic /fænˈtæstɪk/ *adj.* **1** extremely good: *You look fantastic!* | *He's doing a fantastic job.* | *"I passed my math test!" "Fantastic!"*

THESAURUS **good, great, excellent, wonderful, outstanding, exceptional, superb, first-class, ace** → GOOD¹
nice, enjoyable, pleasant, great, wonderful → NICE

2 very large: *She spends fantastic amounts of money on clothes.* **3** a fantastic story, creature, or place is so strange that you think you must be imagining it: *a fantastic landscape that rivals any in our imaginations* —**fantastically** *adv.*

fan·ta·sy /ˈfæntəsi, -zi/ *n.* (plural **fantasies**) [C,U] an experience or situation that you imagine but is not real: *When I was young, I had* ***fantasies about*** *becoming a race car driver.* [ORIGIN: 1300—1400 Old French *fantasie*, from Latin *phantasia*, from Greek, "appearance, imagination"]

FAQ /fæk, ˌɛf eɪ ˈkjuː/ *n.* [C usually plural] **frequently asked question** a question that people often ask about something, which is shown together with its answer: *There's a section with tax FAQs.*

far¹ /fɑr/ *adv.* (comparative **farther** *or* **further**, superlative **farthest** *or* **furthest**)
1 DISTANCE a) a long distance: *I don't want to drive very far.* | *Let's see who can swim the farthest.* | *They found the body not too* ***far from*** *here.* | *His office is a little* ***farther down*** *the hallway.* | *The boat had moved* ***farther away*** *from the dock.* ▸Don't say "I walked far." say "I walked a long way."◂ **b)** used when asking the distance

between two places, or when talking about the distance between two places: ***How far** is Boston from here?*
2 A LOT/VERY MUCH very much, or to a great degree: *Our new car is **far better** than the old one.* | *Dinner cost **far more/less** than I expected.* | *It would take me **far too** long to explain.* | *This is **by far** the best movie she's ever made.*
3 PROGRESS used in order to talk about how much progress someone makes: *We only **got as far as** the first ten minutes of the video.* | *Republicans claimed that the bill did not **go far enough*** (=did not have a big enough effect). | *She's a good dancer and should **go far*** (=be very successful).
4 TIME in the past or in the future: *The church dates **as far back as** the 12th century.* | *They worked **far into** the night.* | *Let's not plan too **far ahead**.*
5 so far until now: *We haven't had any problems so far.*
6 go too far to do something that is too extreme: *He's always been a little rude, but this time he went too far.*
7 go so far as to do sth to do something that seems surprising or extreme: *He even went so far as to call her a liar.*
8 far from sth used to say that something is not at all true: *The deal is far from certain.*
9 not go far if money does not go far, you cannot buy very much with it: *A dollar doesn't go far anymore.*

SPOKEN PHRASES
10 as far as I know *also* **as far as I can remember/tell** used to say that you think something is true, but you may be wrong: *Cole wasn't even there, as far as I can remember.*
11 so far so good used to say that something has been successful until now: *"How's your new job?" "So far so good."*

→ **as far as sb's concerned** *at* CONCERNED

GRAMMAR
When you are talking about distances, you can use **far** in questions and negative sentences: *"How far is it to your house?" "It's not very far."* You can also use **far** after "too," "as," and "so": *It's too far to walk.* | *She ran as far as she could.* | *The star is so far away that you can only just see it.*
But do not use **far** in other kinds of sentence. For example, do not say "It's far to my house from here." Say: *"It's **a long way** to the next town from here."*

far² *adj.* (comparative **farther** *or* **further**, superlative **farthest** *or* **furthest**) **1** a long distance away (ANT) **near**: *We can walk if it's not far.* → *see picture at* NEAR² **2 the far side/end etc.** the side, etc. most distant from where you are: *the far side of the building* **3 the far north/south etc.** the part of an area that is furthest to the north, the south, etc.: *Nguyen was born in the far south of Vietnam.* **4 the far left/right** people who have extreme political opinions **5 be a far cry from sth** to be very different from something: *Europe was a far cry from what Tom had expected.*

far·a·way /ˈfɑrəˌweɪ/ *adj.* **1** (literary) distant: *faraway lands* **2 a faraway look** an expression on your face that shows that you are not thinking about what is around you

farce /fɑrs/ *n.* **1** [singular] an event or situation that is badly organized and does not happen in the way that it should: *The trial was a total farce.* **2** [C] ENG. LANG. ARTS a humorous play or movie in which a lot of silly things happen [ORIGIN: 1500—1600 French, Latin *farcire* "to stuff (= fill with a mixture of cut-up food);" because early religious plays often had humorous parts put into them] —**farcical** *adj.*

fare¹ /fɛr/ *n.* **1** [C] the price you pay to travel by train, airplane, bus, etc.: ***Air/Bus/Train fares** are going up again.*

THESAURUS cost, expense, price, charge, fee, rent, rate → COST¹

2 [U] food, especially food served in a restaurant: *vegetarian fare*

fare² *v.* **fare well/better/badly etc.** (formal) to be successful or unsuccessful in a particular situation: *Polls suggest Kramer will fare well in the election.*

ˌFar ˈEast *n.* **the Far East** the countries in the east of Asia, such as China, Japan, Korea, etc.

fare·well /ˌfɛrˈwɛl/ *n.* **1** [C] (old-fashioned) the action of saying goodbye: *We **bid farewell** to our friends.* | *a farewell speech* **2 a farewell party/drink** a party or drink that you have with someone who is leaving

ˌfar-ˈfetched *adj.* unlikely to be true, and so difficult to believe: *Her story was pretty far-fetched.*

ˌfar-ˈflung *adj.* very far away: *a far-flung region of Alaska*

farm¹ /fɑrm/ *n.* [C] an area of land used for raising animals or growing crops: *farm animals* | *I grew up **on a farm**.* | *a **dairy/hog/cattle etc.** farm* [ORIGIN: 1300—1400 Old French *ferme* "rent, lease," from Latin *firmus* "firm, fixed"]

farm² *v.* [I,T] to use land for raising animals or growing crops: *Our family has farmed here for years.*

farm·er /ˈfɑrmɚ/ *n.* [C] someone who owns or manages a farm

farm·hand /ˈfɑrmhænd/ *n.* [C] someone who works on a farm

farm·ing /ˈfɑrmɪŋ/ *n.* [U] the activity of raising animals or growing crops on a farm

farm·land /ˈfɑrmlænd/ *n.* [U] land used for farming

farm·yard /ˈfɑrmyɑrd/ *n.* [C] an area with farm buildings around it

ˌfar-ˈoff *adj.* (literary) a long distance away or a long time ago: *a far-off land*

ˌfar-ˈout *adj.* (informal) unusual or strange: *far-out clothes*

ˌfar-ˈreaching *adj.* having a big influence or effect: *far-reaching tax reforms*

far·sight·ed /ˈfɑrˌsaɪt̬ɪd/ *adj.* **1** able to see or read things clearly only when they are far away from you (ANT) **nearsighted** **2** (approving) considering what will happen in the future: *farsighted leaders*

fart /fɑrt/ *v.* [I] (informal) an impolite word meaning to make air come out of your BOWELS —**fart** *n.* [C]

far·ther /ˈfɑrðɚ/ *adj., adv.* the COMPARATIVE of FAR → FURTHER

USAGE

Use **farther** to talk about distance: *The restaurant's just a little farther down the street.*
Use **further** to talk about a greater amount or degree of something, or about a later time in the future: *There is likely to be a further increase in oil prices.* | *I don't want to discuss this matter any further.* | *No one knows what will happen further in the future.*
Many people use **further** in spoken English to talk about distance, but many teachers think that this is not correct.

far·thest /ˈfɑrðɪst/ *adj., adv.* the SUPERLATIVE of FAR → FURTHEST

fas·ci·nate /ˈfæsəˌneɪt/ *v.* [T] to interest you very much: *Mechanical things fascinate me.* | *We were **fascinated to learn** she had grown up in Kenya.* [ORIGIN: 1500—1600 Latin *fascinatus*, from *fascinum* "use of (evil) magic"]

fas·ci·nat·ing /ˈfæsəˌneɪt̬ɪŋ/ *adj.* extremely interesting: *a fascinating movie* | *I **found** her **fascinating**.*

THESAURUS interesting, intriguing, absorbing, enthralling, engrossing, compelling, gripping, riveting → INTERESTING

fas·ci·na·tion /ˌfæsəˈneɪʃən/ *n.* [singular, U] the state of being very interested in something: *Jan **had a fascination with/for** movie stars.*

fas·cism /ˈfæʃɪzəm/ *n.* [U] POLITICS an extreme RIGHT-WING political system in which people's lives are completely controlled by the state

fas·cist /ˈfæʃɪst/ *n.* [C] **1** POLITICS someone who supports fascism **2** someone who has extreme RIGHT-WING political opinions that you do not approve of, but who does not support fascism **3** someone who is cruel and unfair —**fascist** *adj.*

fash·ion[1] /ˈfæʃən/ *n.* **1** [C,U] something such as a style of clothes or hair that is popular at a particular time: *Hats are **in fashion** again.* | *Shoes like that **went out of fashion** years ago.* | *Miniskirts **come back into fashion** every few years.* | *She always buys **the latest fashions**.* **2** [U] the business or study of making or selling clothes: ***fashion show/model/magazine etc.*** **3 in a ... fashion** (formal) in a particular way: *Please return all phone calls in a timely fashion.* [ORIGIN: 1300—1400 Old French *façon*, from Latin *factio* "act of making"]

fashion[2] *v.* [T] (formal) to shape or make something with your hands or a few tools: *Many fans had fashioned home-made banners.*

fash·ion·a·ble /ˈfæʃənəbəl/ *adj.* popular, especially for a short time (ANT) **unfashionable**: *Long skirts are fashionable now.* | *a fashionable restaurant* | ***It's** become **fashionable to** wear fake fur.*

THESAURUS

trendy – modern and fashionable: *trendy restaurants*
stylish – attractive in a fashionable way: *a stylish blue suit*
designer – designer clothes, watches, etc. are made by someone who is famous for designing fashionable things: *a pair of designer jeans*
be in style/fashion – to be fashionable during a particular period of time: *At that time, plaid skirts were in fashion.*

ˈfashion show *n.* [C] an event at which new styles of clothes are shown to the public

fast[1] /fæst/ *adj.* **1** moving, happening, or doing something quickly (ANT) **slow**: *a fast runner* | *a fast car* | *The subway is the fastest way to get downtown.* **2** [not before noun] showing time that is later than the true time (ANT) **slow**: *I think my watch is fast.* **3 fast track** a way of achieving something more quickly than it is normally done: *young professionals **on the fast track** for promotion* **4 the fast lane a)** an exciting way of living that involves dangerous or expensive activities: *She loves **life in the fast lane**.* **b)** the part of a big road where people drive fastest [ORIGIN: Old English *fæst* "firm"]

fast[2] *adv.* **1** at a great speed, or in not much time: *He likes driving fast.* | *You're learning fast.*

THESAURUS

quickly/swiftly – used especially about movement: *I ran quickly down the stairs.* | *Anna looked swiftly up at him.*
rapidly/speedily – used especially about the speed at which something happens: *Unemployment rose rapidly.* | *Police reacted speedily to the calls.*
at high speed/at great speed – used about movement: *The car went around the corner at high speed.*
at a rapid rate – used especially about a change: *The world is changing at a rapid rate.*

2 fast asleep sleeping very deeply **3** firmly or tightly: *Walter **held fast** to the rope.* | *The boat's **stuck fast** in the mud.* **4 hold fast to sth** to continue to believe in or support an idea, principle, etc.: *In spite of everything, her father held fast to his religion.*

fastening a seat belt

fast[3] *v.* [I] to eat little or no food for a period of time, especially for religious reasons —**fast** *n.* [C]

fas·ten /ˈfæsən/ *v.* **1** [I,T] to join together the two sides of something so that it is closed, or to become joined (ANT) **unfasten, undo**: *Fasten your seat belts.* | *The skirt fastens at the back.*

THESAURUS

attach – to join something firmly to another object or surface: *A long lens was attached to the camera.*
secure (formal) – to fasten or tie something tightly in a particular position: *'Please fasten your seatbelt and secure all loose objects,' said the flight attendant.*
join – to make things connected
glue – to join things together using glue
tape – to fasten or attach something using tape
staple – to join things or attach something using staples (=small pieces of bent wire that go through paper)
clip – to join things together using a clip (=a small object that goes over paper to hold it together)
tie – to fasten a tie or shoes, etc. by making a knot: *Don't forget to tie your shoelaces.*
button (up) – to fasten the buttons on a shirt, coat, etc.
zip (up) – to fasten clothes, bags, etc. with a zipper

2 [T] to attach something firmly to another object or surface: *Jill **fastened** a flower **to/onto** her dress.* **3** [T] to firmly close and lock a window, gate, etc.

fas·ten·er /ˈfæsənɚ/ *n.* [C] something such as a button or pin that you use to join something together

ˈ**fast food** *n.* [U] food such as HAMBURGERS, that is prepared and served quickly in a restaurant

fast ˈforward *v.* [T] to wind a tape or video forward quickly in a machine without watching it ➔ PLAY —**fast-forward** *n.* [U]

fas·tid·i·ous /fæˈstɪdiəs, fə-/ *adj.* very careful about small details: *He is fastidious about hygiene.* —**fastidiously** *adv.*

fat[1] /fæt/ *adj.* **1** weighing too much because you have too much flesh on your body (ANT) **thin**: *Chris thinks he's **getting fat**.* | *a big fat guy*

THESAURUS

You can call yourself **fat**, but it is not polite to directly tell other people that they are fat: *I'm getting really fat.*
overweight – used as a more polite way of describing someone who is fat: *He's a little overweight.*
big/heavy/large – used as polite ways of describing someone who is big, strong, or fat: *a heavy woman in her fifties* | *He's a pretty big guy.*
obese – used about someone who is extremely fat in a way that is dangerous to their health
chubby – used about someone, especially a baby or a child, who is slightly fat
plump – used to say that someone, especially a woman or a child, is slightly fat in a pleasant way
stout – used to say that an adult is slightly fat
corpulent (formal) – very fat
rotund (formal) – having a fat round body

2 thick or wide (ANT) **thin**: *a fat cigar* **3** [only before noun] (informal) containing or worth a lot of money: *I should get a nice **fat check** at the end of the month.* **4 fat chance** (spoken) said when something is very unlikely to happen: *Sean said he'd be here at 5:00? Fat chance.* [ORIGIN: Old English *fætt*]

fat[2] *n.* **1** [U] the substance under the skin of people and animals that helps keep them warm **2** [C,U] an oily substance in some foods: *food that is **low/high in fat** | a **low-fat/high-fat** diet* **3** [C,U] an oily substance taken from animals or plants and used in cooking: *Fry the potatoes in oil or melted fat.*

fa·tal /ˈfeɪṭl/ *adj.* **1** resulting in someone's death: *a **fatal crash/accident** | a **fatal shooting** | The disease **proved fatal*** (=killed someone). **2** having a very bad effect: *Her **fatal mistake** was to marry too young.* | *There's a **fatal flaw** in his argument.* —**fatally** *adv.*

fa·tal·ism /ˈfeɪṭlˌɪzəm/ *n.* [U] the belief that there is nothing you can do to prevent events from happening —**fatalistic** /ˌfeɪṭlˈɪstɪk◂/ *adj.*

fa·tal·i·ty /feɪˈtæləṭi, fə-/ *n.* (plural **fatalities**) [C] a death in an accident or violent attack: *traffic fatalities*

fate /feɪt/ *n.* **1** [C] the things that happen to someone, especially bad events: *No one knows what the **fate of** the refugees will be.* | *He hopes his new restaurant doesn't **suffer** the same **fate** as his last one.* **2** [U] a power that is believed to control what happens in people's lives: *Fate brought us together.* | ***By a** lucky **twist of fate*** (=completely unexpected event), *we were on the same plane.* [ORIGIN: 1300—1400 French, Latin *fatum* "what has been spoken (by the gods)," from *fari* "to speak"]

fat·ed /ˈfeɪṭɪd/ *adj.* **be fated to do sth** certain to happen or to do something because a mysterious force is controlling events: *We were fated to meet.*

fate·ful /ˈfeɪtfəl/ *adj.* having an important, usually bad, effect on future events: *a fateful decision*

ˌ**fat-ˈfree** *adj.* containing no fat: *fat-free yogurt*

fa·ther[1] /ˈfɑðɚ/ *n.* [C] **1** a male parent: *a father* *of four* (=a man with four children) → RELATIVE[1] **2, Father** a priest, especially in the Roman Catholic Church: *Do you know Father Vernon?* **3 the father of sth** the man who was responsible for starting something: *George Washington is the father of our country.* [ORIGIN: Old English *fæder*]

father[2] *v.* [T] to become a male parent: *Taylor denies fathering her 4-month-old son.*

'father ˌfigure *n.* [C] an older man whom you trust and respect

fa·ther·hood /'fɑðɚˌhʊd/ *n.* [U] the state of being a father

'father-in-ˌlaw *n.* (plural **fathers-in-law**) [C] the father of your husband or wife

fa·ther·ly /'fɑðɚli/ *adj.* typical of a kind or concerned father: *fatherly advice*

'Father's Day *n.* a holiday in honor of fathers, celebrated in the U.S. and Canada on the third Sunday of June

F

fath·om[1] /'fæðəm/ *v.* [T] to understand what something means after thinking about it carefully: *I cannot fathom why it took them so long to respond.*

fathom[2] *n.* [C] a unit for measuring how deep water is, equal to 6 feet or 1.83 meters

fa·tigue /fə'tig/ *n.* [U] **1** extreme tiredness: *They were weak with fatigue after walking so far without food.* **2 fatigues** [plural] loose-fitting army clothes **3** PHYSICS weakness in a substance such as metal that may cause it to break —**fatigue** *v.* [T]

fat·ten /'fæt˺n/ *v.* [T] to make an animal become fatter so that it is ready to eat

fatten sb/sth ↔ **up** *phr. v.* to make a thin person or animal fatter: *Grandma's always trying to fatten me up.*

fat·ten·ing /'fæt˺n-ɪŋ/ *adj.* likely to make you fat: *I try to stay away from fattening foods.*

fat·ty /'fæṭi/ *adj.* containing a lot of fat: *fatty foods*

ˌfatty 'acid *n.* [C] BIOLOGY an acid that is obtained from natural substances, such as oil, fat, and plant material, which the cells of your body need to use food effectively

fat·u·ous /'fætʃuəs/ *adj.* very silly or stupid: *a fatuous remark*

fau·cet /'fɔsɪt/ *n.* [C] the thing that you turn on and off to control the flow of water from a pipe

fault[1] /fɔlt/ *n.* [C]
1 BLAME responsibility for a mistake: ***It's** not my **fault (that)** we missed the bus.* | *The car got dented, but it **was** my **own fault**.* | ***It's** my **fault for** not bringing enough money.*
2 be at fault to be responsible for something bad that has happened: *It was the other driver who was at fault.*
3 PROBLEM a problem with something that stops it working correctly: *a **fault in** the electrical system*

THESAURUS defect, problem, flaw, bug, imperfection → DEFECT[1]

4 find fault with sb/sth to criticize someone or something: *Why do you always have to find fault with my work?*
5 through no fault of my/his etc. own used in order to say that a bad thing that happened to someone was not caused by him/her: *Many Americans lost their jobs through no fault of their own.*
6 SB'S CHARACTER a bad part of someone's character: ***For all her faults*** (=in spite of her faults) *I still love her.*
7 CRACK EARTH SCIENCES a large crack in the rocks that form the Earth's surface, where EARTHQUAKES may start because the rocks on opposite sides of the crack are moving in different directions: *the San Andreas fault in California*
8 generous/loyal/honest etc. to a fault very generous, kind, etc. [ORIGIN: 1200—1300 Old French *faute*, from Latin *fallere* "to deceive, disappoint"]

fault[2] *v.* [T] to find a mistake in something: *We couldn't fault her singing.*

fault·less /'fɔltlɪs/ *adj.* having no mistakes SYN **perfect**: *a faultless performance*

fault·y /'fɔlti/ *adj.* **1** not working correctly: *faulty wires* **2** not correct: *faulty reasoning*

fau·na /'fɔnə/ *n.* [U] BIOLOGY all the animals living in a particular area → FLORA [ORIGIN: 1700—1800 Late Latin *Fauna*, wife or sister of Faunus (Roman god of nature and farms)]

faux pas /ˌfoʊ 'pɑ/ *n.* [C] an embarrassing mistake in a social situation

fa·vor[1] /'feɪvɚ/ *n.* **1** [C] something you do for someone to help or be kind to him/her: *Could you **do me a favor** and watch the baby for half an hour?* | *Can I **ask you a favor**?* | *She offered Willis a job **as a favor to** his mother.* **2 abandon/drop etc. sth in favor of sth** to decide not to have one thing and have something else instead: *Plans for a tunnel were rejected in favor of the bridge.* **3** [U] support, approval, or agreement for something: *All the board members were **in favor of** the idea.* **4 in sb's favor** to someone's advantage, or so that someone wins: *The vote was 60–59 in his favor.* **5 in favor/out of favor** liked and approved of, or no longer liked and approved of: *His books have gone out of favor.* **6** [C] a small gift that is given to guests at a party: *party favors such as balloons*

favor[2] *v.* [T] **1** to prefer something or someone to other things or people: *Blyth favors stricter gun control laws.* **2** to treat someone better than someone else, in a way that is not fair: *tax cuts that favor the rich* | *a judicial system that **favors** men **over** women* **3** to provide the right conditions for something to happen: *wind conditions that favor sailing*

fa·vor·a·ble /'feɪvərəbəl/ *adj.* **1** making people like or approve of someone or something: *Try to **make a favorable impression**.* **2** showing that you like or approve of something or someone: *I've heard favorable reports about your work.* **3** appropriate and likely to make something happen or succeed: *a favorable economic environment* —**favorably** *adv.*

fa·vor·ite[1] /ˈfeɪvrɪt, -vərɪt/ *adj.* your favorite person or thing is the one you like most: *Who's your favorite actor?* | *My favorite sport is baseball.* ►Don't say "most favorite."◄

favorite[2] *n.* [C] **1** something that you like more than others of the same kind: *I like all her books, but this one is my favorite.* **2** someone who is liked and treated better than others by a teacher or parent: *Katie was always Mom's favorite.* **3** the team, person, etc. that is expected to win a competition: *The Yankees are* ***favorites to*** *win the World Series.*

fa·vor·it·ism /ˈfeɪvrə,tɪzəm/ *n.* [U] the act of treating one person or group better than another, in a way that is not fair

fawn[1] /fɔn/ *v.* [I] (disapproving) to praise someone and be friendly to him/her because you want something: *I watched her* ***fawning over*** *him.*

fawn[2] *n.* [C] a young DEER

fax /fæks/ *n.* **1** [C] a document that is sent in electronic form down a telephone line and then printed using a special machine: *Did you get my fax?* **2** [C] *also* **fax machine** a machine used for sending and receiving faxes: *What's your fax number?* **3** [U] the system of sending documents using a fax machine: *You can send your résumé* ***by fax.*** —**fax** *v.* [T]: *Please fax me the contract.*

faze /feɪz/ *v.* [T] (informal) to make someone feel nervous or confused: *Nothing ever seemed to faze Rosie.* —**fazed** *adj.*

FBI *n.* **the FBI the Federal Bureau of Investigation** the U.S. police department that is controlled by the government and is concerned with crimes that happen in more than one state

FDA *n.* **the FDA the Food and Drug Administration** a U.S. government organization which makes sure that food and drugs are safe enough to be sold

fear[1] /fɪr/ *n.* **1** [C,U] the feeling you get when you are afraid or worried that something bad will happen: *a* ***fear of*** *heights* | *The refugees* ***live in fear of*** *being sent back to their own country.* | *There are* ***fears that*** *prices might continue to rise.* | *The rules help ease parents'* ***fears for*** *their children's safety.* | *Their* ***worst fears*** *became a reality.* **2 for fear of sth/for fear (that)** because you are worried that something bad will happen: *She kept quiet, for fear of saying the wrong thing.* [ORIGIN: Old English *fær* "sudden danger"]

fear[2] *v.* **1** [I,T] to feel afraid or worried that something bad will happen: *Fearing a snowstorm, many people stayed home.* | *When they heard about Heidi's car crash, they* ***feared the worst*** (=were afraid something very bad had happened). | *They left because they* ***feared for*** *their* ***lives.*** **2** [T] to be afraid of someone: *a dictator who was feared by his country*

fear·ful /ˈfɪrfəl/ *adj.* (formal) afraid: *Even doctors are* ***fearful of*** *getting the disease.* —**fearfully** *adv.*

THESAURUS **frightened, afraid, scared, terrified, petrified, phobic** → FRIGHTENED

fear·less /ˈfɪrlɪs/ *adj.* not afraid of anything: *a fearless soldier* —**fearlessly** *adv.* —**fearlessness** *n.* [U]

THESAURUS **brave, courageous, heroic, valiant, daring, bold, intrepid** → BRAVE[1]

fear·some /ˈfɪrsəm/ *adj.* very frightening: *his fearsome reputation* | *a fearsome weapon*

fea·si·ble /ˈfizəbəl/ *adj.* possible, and likely to work: *a feasible plan*

feast[1] /fist/ *n.* [C] a large meal for many people, especially a meal to celebrate a special occasion: *a wedding feast* [ORIGIN: 1100—1200 Old French *feste* "occasion of celebration," from Latin *festum*]

feast[2] *v.* **1 feast on sth** to eat a lot of a particular food with great enjoyment: *We feasted on chicken and roast potatoes.* **2 feast your eyes on sb/sth** to look at someone or something with great pleasure

feat /fit/ *n.* [C] an impressive achievement needing a lot of strength or skill: *The bridge is an amazing* ***feat of*** *engineering.* | *Getting your doctorate is* ***no mean feat*** (=difficult to do).

feath·er /ˈfɛðɚ/ *n.* [C] one of the light soft things that cover a bird's body [ORIGIN: Old English *fether*] → *see picture on page A15*

feath·er·y /ˈfɛðəri/ *adj.* soft and light like feathers: *feathery snow*

fea·ture[1] /ˈfitʃɚ/ (Ac) *n.* [C] **1** an important, interesting, or typical part of something: *Anti-virus software is a standard feature in all our computers.* | *One of the best* ***features of*** *this camera is its size.* | *An inability to sleep well is a* ***common feature*** *of depression.*

THESAURUS **characteristic, quality, trait, attribute, property, aspect** → CHARACTERISTIC[1]

2 a piece of writing about a subject in a newspaper or a magazine, or a special report on television or on the radio: *a* ***feature on*** *Johnny Depp* **3** a part of someone's face: *her delicate* ***facial features*** **4** a movie: *There's a* ***double feature*** (=two movies the same evening) *playing at the mall theater.* [ORIGIN: 1300—1400 Old French *feture* "shape, form," from Latin *facere* "to do, make"]

feature[2] (Ac) *v.* **1** [T] to show a particular person or thing in a film, magazine, show, etc.: *a new movie featuring Julia Roberts* | *The bakery was recently* ***featured in*** *the paper as one of the best in the area.* **2** [I] to be included in something and be an important part of it: *The theme of depression* ***features*** *strongly* ***in*** *the movie.* **3** [T] to advertise a particular product: *The supermarket's featuring a new ice cream.*

Feb·ru·ar·y /ˈfɛbyu,ɛri, ˈfɛbru,ɛri/ (*written abbreviation* **Feb.**) *n.* [C,U] the second month of the

F

year, between January and March: *Rick and Allison were married* ***on February 14th****.* | *The accident was* ***in February****.* | *She retired* ***last February****.* | *The book won't be finished until* ***next February****.* [ORIGIN: 1300—1400 Latin *Februarius*, from *Februa*, Roman religious ceremony in February to make things pure]

fe·ces /ˈfisiz/ *n.* [plural] (formal) solid waste material from the BOWELS —**fecal** /ˈfikəl/ *adj.*

feck·less /ˈfɛklɪs/ *adj.* a feckless person is not determined, effective, or successful

fe·cund /ˈfikənd, ˈfɛkənd/ *adj.* (formal) able to produce many children, young animals, or crops (SYN) **fertile** —**fecundity** /fɪˈkʌndəṭi/ *n.* [U]

Fed /fɛd/ *n.* **the Fed** ECONOMICS the FEDERAL RESERVE

fed *v.* the past tense and past participle of FEED

fed·er·al /ˈfɛdərəl/ (Ac) *adj.* **1** POLITICS relating to the central government of a country which consists of several states, rather than to the government of one of the states: *federal income tax* | *federal law* **2** consisting of a group of states that make some of their own decisions but are controlled by a central government: *the Federal Republic of Germany* [ORIGIN: 1600—1700 Latin *foedus* "formal agreement or joining together"]

ˌFederal ˌBureau of Investiˈgation *n.* the FBI

fed·er·al·ism /ˈfɛdərəˌlɪzəm/ *n.* [U] belief in or support for a federal system of government —**federalist** *n.* [C], *adj.*

ˌFederal Reˈserve *n.* **the Federal Reserve** ECONOMICS the group of banks in the U.S. that control the way all of the country's banks work

fed·er·a·tion /ˌfɛdəˈreɪʃən/ (Ac) *n.* [C] a group of states, countries, or organizations that have joined together to form a single group: *the American Federation of Teachers*

ˌfed ˈup *adj.* (informal) annoyed or bored, and wanting change: *I'm really* ***fed up with*** *all these meetings.*

fee /fi/ (Ac) *n.* [C] an amount of money that you pay for professional services or that you pay to do something: *medical/legal fees* | *college fees* | *The museum charges a small* ***entrance fee****.* | *Some companies charge a small* ***fee for*** *the catalogs.* [ORIGIN: 1300—1400 Old French *fé*, *fief*, from Medieval Latin *feudum* "land given in return for service"]

THESAURUS **cost, expense, price, charge, fare, rent, rate** → COST[1]

fee·ble /ˈfibəl/ *adj.* **1** extremely weak: *His voice sounded feeble.* **2** not good or effective: *a feeble attempt* [ORIGIN: 1100—1200 Old French *feble*, from Latin *flebilis* "causing tears, weak"]

ˌfeeble-ˈminded *adj.* unable to think clearly and decide what to do, or showing this quality

feed[1] /fid/ *v.* (past tense and past participle **fed** /fɛd/) **1** [T] to give food to a person or animal → WELL-FED: *Did you feed the dog?* | *She was too weak to feed herself.* | *Jimmy was* ***feeding*** *acorns* ***to*** *the squirrels.* **2** [T] to provide enough food for a group of people: *How can you feed a family on $80 a week?* **3** [I] if animals or babies feed, they eat: *Frogs feed at night.* | *Cows* ***feed on*** *grass.* **4** [T] to give a substance to a plant to help it grow: *Feed your violets once a month.* **5** [T] to put something slowly and continuously into something else: *The tube was fed into the patient's stomach.* **6** [T] to supply something in a continuous flow: *The sound is* ***fed*** *directly* ***to*** *the headphones.* [ORIGIN: Old English *fedan*; related to *food*]

feed[2] *n.* [U] food for animals: *cattle feed*

feed·back /ˈfidbæk/ *n.* [U] advice, criticism, etc. about how successful or useful something is, given so that something can be improved: *She's been* ***giving*** *me* ***feedback on*** *my presentation.*

feed·ing /ˈfidɪŋ/ *n.* [C] one of the times when you give milk to a small baby: *It's time for her noon feeding.*

feel[1] /fil/ *v.* (past tense and past participle **felt** /fɛlt/)
1 EMOTIONS [linking verb, T] to experience a particular physical feeling or emotion: *Let me know if you feel any pain.* | *We felt guilty for not asking her to come with us.* | *I'm feeling a little better today.* | *"How do you feel?" "Fine."* | *They didn't make us feel very welcome.* | *I walked through the door, and I* ***felt like/as if/as though*** *I had never been away.*
2 FEEL SMOOTH/DRY ETC. [linking verb] to seem to have a particular quality when touched or experienced by someone: *The ground still* ***feels damp****.* | *Her hands* ***felt cold****.* | *It* ***felt great*** *to see her after so many years.* | *How does* ***it feel*** *to be graduating?* | *It was a year ago, but it still* ***feels like*** *yesterday.*
3 OPINION [I,T] to have an opinion based on your feeling rather than on facts: *How do you* ***feel about*** *your new stepfather?* | ***I felt (that)*** *I could've helped more.* | ***I feel like*** *I'm being treated unfairly.*
4 TOUCH [T] to touch something with your fingers to find out about it: *Feel my forehead. Does it seem hot?*

THESAURUS **touch, handle, stroke, rub, scratch, pat, pet, caress, tickle** → TOUCH[1]

5 NOTICE STH [T] to notice something that is touching you or happening to you: *She felt a bug crawling up her leg.* | *Just feel that fresh sea air!* | *I felt her body brush against mine.*
6 feel the benefits/effects etc. of sth to experience the good or bad results of something: *We've started to feel the effects of the recession.*
7 feel your way a) to move carefully with your hands out in front of you because you cannot see well: *He felt his way across the room.* **b)** to do things slowly and carefully because you are unsure about a new situation: *Businesses are* ***feeling*** *their* ***way toward*** *a new relationship with their employees.*
8 feel around/in sth etc. (for sth) to try to find

something by using your fingers: *She felt around in her bag for a pen.*

SPOKEN PHRASES

9 feel like (doing) sth to want to have something or do something: *He didn't feel like going to work.* | *I feel like a Coke* (=feel like having a Coke).

10 feel free used in order to tell someone that you do not mind if s/he does something: *Feel free to come by my office.*

11 I know (just/exactly) how you feel said in order to show your sympathy with someone or with something s/he has just said: *"I can't seem to do anything right today." "I know exactly how you feel."*

[ORIGIN: Old English *felan*]

feel for sb *phr. v.*
to feel sympathy for someone: *All I could do was let him know that I felt for him.*

feel sb ↔ **out** *phr. v.* (informal)
to find out what someone's opinions or feelings are without asking him/her directly: *I'm not sure if he'll lend us the money. Let me feel him out.*

feel up to sth *phr. v.* (informal)
to have the strength, energy, etc. to do something: *I don't really feel up to going out tonight.*

feel² *n.* [singular] **1** the way something feels when you touch it: *the **feel of** the sand under our feet* | *Wet soap has a greasy feel.* **2** the quality something seems to have: *The beach has a kind of lonely feel.* | *The house had a nice **feel about it**.* **3 have/get a feel for sth** (informal) to have or develop an understanding of something or ability with something: *Pete has a real feel for music.*

feel·er /ˈfilɚ/ *n.* [C] **1 put/send out feelers** to start to try to discover what people think about something that you want to do: *Possible presidential candidates are already putting out feelers.* **2** one of the two long things on an insect's head that it uses to feel or touch things

ˈfeel-good *adj.* **feel-good movie/comedy/music etc.** a movie, etc. whose main purpose is to make you feel happy

feel·ing /ˈfilɪŋ/ *n.* **1 a)** [C,U] an emotion that you feel, such as anger or happiness: *It's always a great feeling to win a game at home.* | *My mother finds it hard to express her feelings.* | *a **feeling of** confidence* **b)** [C] something that you physically feel in your body: *He has no feeling in his legs.* | *feelings of **dizziness*** **2 sb's feelings** [plural] someone's feelings are his/her thoughts, emotions, and attitudes: *He doesn't care about my feelings.* | *Tell me the truth. You won't **hurt** my **feelings**.* **3** [C] a belief or opinion about something: *Many people have strong **feelings about/on** abortion.* | ***I have a feeling (that)** she's lying to us.* | *Mothers sometimes have **mixed feelings*** (=sometimes feel happy and sometimes feel sad) *about going to work.* **4** [U] a general attitude among a group of people about a subject: *a strong anti-war feeling* | *He had not understood the depth of **feeling against/in favor of** the changes.* **5 I know the feeling** (spoken) said when you understand how someone feels because you have had the same experience: *"I'm too tired to work today." "I know the feeling."* **6 bad/ill feeling** anger or lack of trust between people: *The divorce caused a lot of bad feeling between them.* **7 with feeling** in a way that shows you care very much about something: *She plays the violin with great feeling.*

feet /fit/ *n.* the plural of FOOT

feign /feɪn/ *v.* [T] (formal) to pretend to have a feeling, be sick, be asleep, etc.: *We feigned interest in Mr. Dixon's stamp collection.*

feint /feɪnt/ *n.* [C] a movement or an attack that is intended to deceive an opponent

feist·y /ˈfaɪsti/ *adj.* (approving) having a strong determined character and a lot of energy: *a feisty old man* [ORIGIN: 1800—1900 *feist* "small dog"]

fe·lic·i·tous /fɪˈlɪsət̬əs/ *adj.* (formal) well-chosen, appropriate, and pleasing: *the writer's felicitous phrases* **—felicitously** *adv.*

fe·line /ˈfilaɪn/ *n.* [C] BIOLOGY a cat or a member of the cat family **—feline** *adj.*

fell¹ /fɛl/ *v.* the past tense of FALL

fell² *v.* [T] (written) **1** to cut down a tree **2** to knock someone down

fel·low¹ /ˈfɛloʊ/ *n.* [C] **1** (old-fashioned) a man: *a nice young fellow from Iowa*

THESAURUS man, guy, gentleman, boy, youth, male → MAN¹

2 a GRADUATE student who has a fellowship in a university **3** a member of a society in a school or university

fellow² *adj.* **fellow workers/students/citizens etc.** people you work with, study with, etc.

fel·low·ship /ˈfɛloʊˌʃɪp, -lə-/ *n.* **1** [C] money given to a student to allow him/her to continue his/her studies at an advanced level: *a graduate fellowship* **2** [C] a group with similar interests or beliefs, who have meetings together: *a Christian youth fellowship* **3** [U] a feeling of friendship that people have because they have the same interests or experiences

fel·on /ˈfɛlən/ *n.* [C] LAW someone who is guilty of a serious crime: *a **convicted felon*** (=a criminal who is sent to prison)

fel·o·ny /ˈfɛləni/ *n.* (plural **felonies**) [C] LAW a serious crime such as murder

felt¹ /fɛlt/ *v.* the past tense and past participle of FEEL

felt² *n.* [U] a thick soft material made of wool, hair, or fur that has been pressed flat

ˌfelt tip ˈpen *n.* [C] a pen that has a hard piece of felt at the end that the ink comes through

fe·male¹ /ˈfimeɪl/ *n.* [C] a person or animal that belongs to the sex that can have babies or produce eggs ANT **male** [ORIGIN: 1300—1400 Old

French *femelle* (influenced by *male*), from Latin *femella* "girl"]

female² *adj.* **1** BIOLOGY belonging to the sex that can have babies or produce eggs ANT **male** → FEMININE: *a female horse* | *female athletes* **2** BIOLOGY a female plant or flower produces fruit → MALE

fem·i·nine /'fɛmənɪn/ *adj.* **1** having qualities that are considered to be typical of women → MASCULINE: *feminine clothes* **2** ENG. LANG. ARTS in grammar, a feminine noun or PRONOUN has a special form to show it is used to talk about a female, such as "actress" or "her"

fem·i·nin·i·ty /ˌfɛmə'nɪnəṭi/ *n.* [U] qualities that are thought to be typical of women → MASCULINITY

fem·i·nism /'fɛməˌnɪzəm/ *n.* [U] the belief that women should have the same rights and opportunities as men —**feminist** *n.* [C], *adj.*: *feminist authors*

fe·mur /'fimɚ/ *n.* [C] BIOLOGY the bone in the top part of your leg, above the knee

F

fence¹ /fɛns/ *n.* [C] **1** a structure made of wood, metal, etc. that surrounds a piece of land **2** a structure that horses jump over in a race or competition **3 sit/be on the fence** to avoid saying which side of an argument you support

fence² *v.* **1** [T] to put a fence around something **2** [I] to fight with a sword as a sport

fence sth ↔ **in** *phr. v.* to surround a place with a fence —**fenced-in** /ˌfɛnst 'ɪn◂ / *adj.*

fence sth ↔ **off** *phr. v.* to separate one area from another with a fence: *We fenced off part of the backyard.*

fencing

fenc·ing /'fɛnsɪŋ/ *n.* [U] **1** the sport of fighting with a long thin sword **2** fences, or the material used for making them

fend /fɛnd/ *v.* **fend for yourself** to take care of yourself without help from other people: *You'll have to fend for yourself while I'm gone.*

fend sb/sth ↔ **off** *phr. v.* to defend yourself when you are being attacked, asked difficult questions, etc.: *Mrs. Spector tried to fend off the other mugger.*

fend·er /'fɛndɚ/ *n.* [C] the side part of a car that covers the wheels

'fender-ˌbender *n.* [C] (informal) a car accident in which little damage is done

fe·ral /'fɛrəl, 'fɪrəl/ *adj.* feral animals used to live with humans but have become wild

fer·ment¹ /fɚ'mɛnt/ *v.* [I,T] if fruit, beer, or wine ferments or is fermented, the sugar in it changes to alcohol [ORIGIN: 1300—1400 Old French *fermenter*, from Latin *fermentum* "yeast"]

fer·ment² /'fɚmɛnt/ *n.* [U] excitement or trouble in a country, caused especially by political change

fer·men·ta·tion /ˌfɚmən'teɪʃən/ *n.* [U] CHEMISTRY a process in which the sugar contained in fruit, beer, wine, etc. is gradually changed into alcohol by the action of YEAST or BACTERIA

fern /fɚn/ *n.* [C] a plant with green leaves shaped like large feathers, but no flowers

fe·ro·cious /fə'roʊʃəs/ *adj.* extremely violent or severe: *a ferocious dog* | *a ferocious storm* [ORIGIN: 1600—1700 Latin *ferox* "wild-looking," from *ferus* "wild"] —**ferociously** *adv.*

fe·ro·ci·ty /fə'rɑsəṭi/ *n.* [U] extreme violence: *Felipe was shocked by the* ***ferocity of*** *her anger.*

fer·ret¹ /'fɛrɪt/ *n.* [C] a small animal, used for hunting rats and rabbits

ferret² *v.*

ferret sth ↔ **out** *phr. v.* (informal) to succeed in finding something, especially information: *Detectives managed to ferret out crucial details about the case.*

fer·ris wheel /'fɛrɪs ˌwil/ *n.* [C] a very large upright wheel with seats on it for people to ride on in an AMUSEMENT PARK

fer·rous /'fɛrəs/ *adj.* CHEMISTRY containing or relating to iron: *ferrous metals*

fer·ry¹ /'fɛri/ *n.* (plural **ferries**) [C] a boat that carries people, often with their cars, across a stretch of water → *see picture at* TRANSPORTATION

ferry² *v.* (**ferried**, **ferries**) [T] to carry people or goods a short distance from one place to another: *a bus that* ***ferries*** *tourists* ***from*** *the hotel* ***to*** *the beach*

fer·tile /'fɚṭl/ *adj.* **1** EARTH SCIENCES fertile land, soil, ground, etc. is able to produce good crops ANT **infertile** **2** BIOLOGY able to become PREGNANT or make someone pregnant ANT **infertile** **3 fertile imagination/mind** an imagination or mind that is able to produce a lot of unusual ideas [ORIGIN: 1400—1500 French, Latin *ferre* "to carry, bear"] —**fertility** /fɚ'tɪləṭi/ *n.* [U]

fer·til·ize /'fɚṭlˌaɪz/ *v.* [T] **1** to put fertilizer on the soil to help plants grow **2** BIOLOGY to make new animal or plant life develop by causing a female cell such as an egg to join with a male cell: *a fertilized egg* | *Fruit will not develop if the ovule is not fertilized by the pollination process.* —**fertilization** /ˌfɚṭlə'zeɪʃən/ *n.* [U]

fer·til·iz·er /'fɚṭlˌaɪzɚ/ *n.* [C,U] a substance that is put on the soil to help plants grow

fer·vent /ˈfɚvənt/ *adj.* believing or feeling something very strongly: *Marion's a* ***fervent believer in*** *working hard.* —**fervently** *adv.*

fer·vor /ˈfɚvɚ/ *n.* [U] very strong belief or feeling: *religious fervor*

fess /fɛs/ *v.*

fess up *phr. v.* (informal) to admit that you have done something wrong, although it is not serious: *He later* ***fessed up to*** *his mistake.*

fest /fɛst/ *n.* **beer/song/food etc. fest** an informal occasion when a lot of people do a fun activity together

fes·ter /ˈfɛstɚ/ *v.* [I] **1** if a bad situation or a problem festers, it gets worse because it has not been dealt with: *Letting your anger fester will only make things worse.* **2** if a wound festers, it becomes infected

fes·ti·val /ˈfɛstəvəl/ *n.* [C] **1** an occasion when there are performances of many films, plays, pieces of music, etc.: *the Cannes film festival* | *a* ***festival of*** *Japanese culture* **2** a special occasion when people celebrate something such as a religious event: *religious festivals* [ORIGIN: 1300—1400 Old French, Latin *festivus*, from *festum* "ceremony of celebration"]

fes·tive /ˈfɛstɪv/ *adj.* happy or cheerful in a way that seems appropriate for celebrating something: *Hollie was in a* ***festive mood.*** | *the* ***festive season*** (=Christmas)

fes·tiv·i·ties /fɛˈstɪvət̬iz/ *n.* [plural] things that people do to celebrate, such as dancing, eating, and drinking

fes·toon /fɛˈstun/ *v.* [T] to cover something with cloth, flowers, etc. as a decoration

fe·tal /ˈfit̬l/ *adj.* BIOLOGY relating to a FETUS: *fetal development*

ˈfetal poˌsition *n.* [singular] a body position in which your body is curled up, and your arms and legs are pulled up against your chest

fetch /fɛtʃ/ *v.* [T] **1** to be sold for a particular amount of money: *The tractor should fetch over $10,000.* **2** (old-fashioned) to go and get something and bring it back: *Rushworth went to fetch the key to the gate.*

fetch·ing /ˈfɛtʃɪŋ/ *adj.* (old-fashioned) attractive

fete¹ /feɪt/ *v.* [T] to honor someone by having a public celebration for him/her: *President Mandela was feted at a government banquet.*

fete² *n.* [C] a special occasion to celebrate something

fet·id /ˈfɛt̬ɪd/ *adj.* (formal) having a very bad smell: *the black fetid water*

fet·ish /ˈfɛt̬ɪʃ/ *n.* [C] **1** an object, thing, or activity that gives someone sexual pleasure, when this is not considered to be normal: *a foot fetish* **2** something that someone does too much or thinks about too much

fet·ter /ˈfɛt̬ɚ/ *v.* [T] (formal) to prevent someone from doing what s/he wants to do: *managers* ***fettered by*** *rules and regulations*

fet·ters /ˈfɛt̬ɚz/ *n.* [plural] **1** things that prevent someone from doing what s/he wants to do **2** chains that were put around a prisoner's feet in past times

fe·tus /ˈfit̬əs/ *n.* [C] BIOLOGY a young human or animal before it is born. In humans, an EMBRYO becomes a fetus after eight weeks of development.

feud /fyud/ *n.* [C] an angry and often violent argument between two people or groups that continues for a long time: *a bitter* ***feud between*** *neighbors* —**feud** *v.* [I]

feu·dal·ism /ˈfyudlˌɪzəm/ *n.* [U] HISTORY a social system in the Middle Ages, in which people received land and protection from someone of higher rank whom they worked and fought for —**feudal** *adj.*

fe·ver /ˈfivɚ/ *n.* **1** [C,U] an illness in which you have a very high temperature: *Andy* ***has a fever*** *and won't be coming into work today.* | *She's* ***running a fever*** (=has a fever). **2** [U] a situation in which people feel very excited or anxious: *Baseball fans are gripped by World Series fever.* | *When the TV crews arrived, the demonstration reached* ***fever pitch*** (=an extreme level of excitement or anxiety). [ORIGIN: 900—1000 Latin *febris*] —**fevered** *adj.* → HAY FEVER, SPRING FEVER

fe·ver·ish /ˈfivərɪʃ/ *adj.* **1** suffering from a fever **2** done extremely quickly by people who are very excited or worried: *working at a feverish pace* —**feverishly** *adv.*

few /fyu/ *quantifier, pron., adj.* **1 a few/the few** a small number of things or people: *Let's wait a few minutes and see if Carrie gets here.* | *I've seen* ***a few of*** *those new cars around.* | *Don has seemed really happy these* ***last few*** *weeks.* | *You'll have to work hard over the* ***next few*** *months.* | *There are* ***a few more*** *things I'd like to talk about before we go.* **2 quite a few** a fairly large number of things or people: *Quite a few people came to the meeting.* | ***Quite a few of*** *the customers got sick.* **3** not many: *There are few events that are as exciting as having a baby.* | *Women are having fewer children.* | *Grant's* ***one of the few*** *people I know who can tell stories well.* | ***Very few of*** *these players will play professionally.* **4 be few and far between** to be rare: *Good jobs are few and far between these days.* [ORIGIN: Old English *feawa*]

> GRAMMAR
>
> **few, a few**
>
> Use **few** when you mean "not many" or "not enough": *Very few people had heard of the disease.*
>
> Use **a few** when you mean "some" or "a small number": *There are still a few tickets left.*
>
> **Few** and **a few** are always used with plural noun forms. → LESS, LITTLE²

fi·an·c·é /ˌfiɑnˈseɪ, fiˈɑnseɪ/ *n.* [C] the man whom a woman is going to marry

F

fi·an·c·ée /ˌfiɑnˈseɪ, fiˈɑnseɪ/ *n.* [C] the woman whom a man is going to marry

fi·as·co /fiˈæskoʊ/ *n.* (plural **fiascoes** *or* **fiascos**) [C] an event that is completely unsuccessful, in a way that is very embarrassing or disappointing: *Their attempt to compete in the software market has been a total fiasco.*

fi·at /ˈfɪæt, -ɑt, -ət/ *n.* [C,U] (formal) an order that is given by someone in authority without considering what other people want: *Too often he governed* ***by fiat*** *rather than by the law.*

fib /fɪb/ *n.* [C] a small unimportant lie: *You shouldn't* ***tell fibs***. —**fib** *v.* [I] —**fibber** *n.* [C]

> THESAURUS lie, white lie, story, falsehood, fabrication, slander, libel ➔ LIE[3]

fi·ber /ˈfaɪbɚ/ *n.* **1** [U] parts of plants that you eat but do not DIGEST, that help food to move through your body: *The doctor said I need more fiber in my diet.* **2** [C,U] a mass of threads used to make rope, cloth, etc. **3** [C] a thin thread, or one of the thin parts like threads that form natural materials such as wood —**fibrous** /ˈfaɪbrəs/ *adj.*

F

fi·ber·glass /ˈfaɪbɚˌglæs/ *n.* [U] a light material made from small glass threads pressed together

ˌfiber ˈoptics *n.* [U] PHYSICS the use of long thin threads of glass to carry information in the form of light, especially on telephone lines —**fiber optic** *adj.*

fib·u·la /ˈfɪbyələ/ *n.* (plural **fibulas** *or* **fibulae** /-li/) [C] BIOLOGY the outer bone of the two bones in your leg below your knee ➔ TIBIA

fick·le /ˈfɪkəl/ *adj.* **1** someone who is fickle is always changing his/her opinion about people or things: *Voters are fickle.* **2** something that is fickle, such as the weather, often changes suddenly

fic·tion /ˈfɪkʃən/ *n.* **1** [U] ENG. LANG. ARTS books and stories about imaginary people and things (ANT) **nonfiction**: *a writer of children's fiction* | *detective fiction* | *After quitting the newspaper business, she wrote poetry and fiction.* **2** [C,U] something that someone wants you to believe is true, but that is not true: *The newspaper story turned out to be a complete fiction.*

fic·tion·al /ˈfɪkʃənəl/ *adj.* ENG. LANG. ARTS fictional people or events are from a book or story, and are not real

fic·tion·al·ize /ˈfɪkʃənəˌlaɪz/ *v.* [T] ENG. LANG. ARTS to tell the story of a real event, changing some details and adding imaginary characters

fic·ti·tious /fɪkˈtɪʃəs/ *adj.* not true, or not real: *a fictitious name*

fid·dle[1] /ˈfɪdl/ *n.* [C] (informal) a VIOLIN ➔ **play second fiddle to sb/sth** *at* PLAY[1]

fiddle[2] *v.*

fiddle around *phr. v.* to waste time by doing things that are not important: *Stop fiddling around or we'll be late!*

fiddle with sth *phr. v.* to keep moving and touching something, especially because you are bored or nervous: *She started fiddling with her hair.*

fid·dler /ˈfɪdlɚ/ *n.* [C] someone who plays the VIOLIN

fi·del·i·ty /fəˈdɛləṭi, faɪ-/ *n.* [U] (formal) **1** loyalty to your wife, husband, or partner by not having sex with other people (ANT) **infidelity** **2** loyalty to a person, organization, set of beliefs, etc.: *his* ***fidelity to*** *the Republican Party*

fidg·et /ˈfɪdʒɪt/ *v.* [I] to keep moving your hands or feet, especially because you are bored or nervous: *children fidgeting in their seats* —**fidgety** *adj.*

fi·du·ci·a·ry[1] /fɪˈduʃiˌɛri/ *n.* [C] LAW someone who has legal control of money or property that belongs to another person, a company, or an organization

fiduciary[2] *adj.* LAW relating to the legal control of someone else's money or property: *The board of directors has a* ***fiduciary duty/responsibility*** *to shareholders.*

fief /fif/ *n.* [C] HISTORY in past times, an area of land that a LORD gave to someone who promised to work and fight for him

field[1] /fild/ *n.* [C] **1** an area of land in the country where crops are grown or where animals feed on grass: *a corn field* | ***fields of*** *sunflowers* ➔ *see picture on page A24* **2** an area of ground where sports are played: *a* ***football/baseball/soccer etc. field***

> THESAURUS stadium, court, diamond, track ➔ SPORT[1]

3 a subject that people study or a type of work that they are involved in: *Professor Kramer is an expert in the* ***field of*** *ancient history.* | *Sullivan's an expert* ***in*** *his* ***field***. **4 the field** all the people, companies, or horses that are competing against each other: *They now* ***lead the field*** (=are the most successful company) *in making powerful computer chips.* **5 oil/gas/coal field** EARTH SCIENCES an area where there is a lot of oil, gas, or coal under the ground **6 magnetic/gravitational/force field** PHYSICS an area in which a strong natural force has an effect **7 field of view/vision** the whole area that you can see without turning your head [ORIGIN: Old English *feld*]

field[2] *v.* [T] **1** if you field a ball in a game of baseball, you stop it after it has been hit **2** if you field a team, an army, etc., they represent you or fight for you in a competition, election, or war: *There may not be enough healthy players to* ***field a team***. **3** to answer questions, telephone calls, etc., especially when there are a lot of them or they are difficult: *Riordan left without* ***fielding questions*** *from reporters.*

ˈfield day *n.* **1 have a field day** (informal) to have the chance to do something you enjoy a lot, especially a chance to criticize someone: *Talk radio hosts* ***had a field day with*** *the story.* **2** [C] a day when students at a school have sports competitions

field·er /ˈfildɚ/ *n.* [C] one of the players who tries to catch the ball in baseball

ˈfield eˌvent *n.* [C] a sports activity, such as the HIGH JUMP or the JAVELIN, that is part of an outdoor competition → TRACK EVENT

ˈfield ˌgoal *n.* [C] the action of kicking the ball over the bar of the GOAL for three points in football

ˈfield ˌhockey *n.* [U] HOCKEY played on grass

ˈfield ˌstudy *n.* [C] SCIENCE a piece of work to find out more about a particular subject, which takes place not inside a school or college but outside, in real conditions

ˈfield test *n.* [C] SCIENCE a test of a new product or system that is done in the place where it will be used rather than in a LABORATORY —**field-test** *v.* [T]

ˈfield trip *n.* [C] an occasion when students go somewhere to learn about a particular subject: *a field trip to the Maryland Science Center*

field·work /ˈfildwɚk/ *n.* [U] SCIENCE study which involves going somewhere in order to collect information, rather than working in a class or LABORATORY

fiend /find/ *n.* [C] **1** (informal) someone who likes something much more than other people normally do: *Isaac turns into a football fiend during the Super Bowl.* **2 dope/drug etc. fiend** (informal) someone who takes a lot of drugs **3** (literary) an evil spirit or person

fiend·ish /ˈfindɪʃ/ *adj.* **1** (literary) very bad or cruel: *a fiendish temper* **2** very difficult or complicated: *a fiendish puzzle*

fierce /fɪrs/ *adj.* **1** done with a lot of energy and strong feelings: *a **fierce debate** between the political parties* | ***fierce competition** between banks* | *The two teams are in a fierce battle for first place.* **2** a fierce person or animal looks very violent or angry and ready to attack: *fierce dogs* **3** fierce heat, cold, weather, etc. is very extreme or severe —**fiercely** *adv.*

fi·er·y /ˈfaɪəri/ *adj.* **1** full of strong or angry emotion: *a fiery speech* | *her fiery temper* **2** (written) involving fire, or on fire: *All perished* (=died) *in the fiery crash.* | *a fiery sunset*

fi·es·ta /fiˈɛstə/ *n.* [C] a religious holiday with dancing, music, etc., especially in Spain or Latin America

fif·teen /ˌfɪfˈtin◂/ *number* 15 —**fifteenth** *number*

fifth¹ /fɪfθ/ *number* **1** 5th **2** 1/5

fifth² *n.* [C] an amount of alcohol equal to 1/5 of a gallon, sold in bottles: *a fifth of bourbon*

fif·ty¹ /ˈfɪfti/ *number* **1** 50 **2 the fifties a)** the years between 1950 and 1959 **b)** the numbers between 50 and 59, especially when used for measuring temperature **3 be in your fifties** to be aged between 50 and 59: *She's **in** her **early/mid/late fifties**.* —**fiftieth** /ˈfɪftiəθ/ *number*

fifty² *n.* (plural **fifties**) [C] a piece of paper money worth $50

ˌfifty-ˈfifty *adj., adv.* (spoken) **1** divided equally between two people: *We should divide the profits fifty-fifty.* **2 a fifty-fifty chance** an equal chance that something will happen or not happen: ***a fifty-fifty chance of** winning*

fig /fɪg/ *n.* [C] a small soft sweet fruit, often eaten dried, or the tree on which this grows

fig. the written abbreviation of FIGURE

fight¹ /faɪt/ *v.* (past tense and past participle **fought** /fɔt/) **1** [I,T] to take part in a war or battle: *The country **fought** a three-year civil **war**.* | *Did your uncle **fight in** the war?* | *rebel forces **fighting against** the Russians* | *They **fought over/for** a small piece of land.* **2** [I,T] if people or animals fight, they use violence against each other: *Police **fought with** protesters in the streets.* | *dogs **fighting over** a bone* **3** [I] to argue: *Are the kids fighting again?* | *He was always **fighting with** his girlfriend.* | *They **fought over** custody of the children.*

> THESAURUS argue, have an argument, have a fight, quarrel, have a quarrel, squabble, bicker → ARGUE

4 [I] to try hard to do or get something: *The union **fought for** a better health care package.* | *Parents are **fighting to** save the school.* | *Perkins was lying in bed, **fighting for** his **life**.* **5** [I,T] to try hard to prevent something or to get rid of something: *Senator Redkin is fighting the proposal.* | *She spent her life **fighting against** poverty and injustice.* **6** [I,T] to take part in a BOXING match: *The boxers fought each other twice for the heavyweight title.* **7** [T] *also* **fight back** to try hard not to have or show a feeling: *He fought the impulse to yell at her.* | *Benson bit his lip and **fought back tears**.* **8 fight a fire/blaze etc.** to try to stop a fire from burning **9 fight your way** to move somewhere with difficulty: *We had to **fight** our **way through** the crowd.* **10 have a fighting chance** to have a chance to achieve something if you work very hard: *Davis believes he still has a fighting chance of winning the election.* **11 fight it out** to fight, argue, or compete until one person wins: *We left them alone to fight it out.* [ORIGIN: Old English *feohtan*]

fight back *phr. v.* **1** to work hard to achieve or oppose something, especially in a situation where you are losing: *Lewis fought back to win the match.* **2** to use violence or arguments against someone who has attacked you or criticized you: *The rebels are fighting back.*

fight sb/sth ↔ **off** *phr. v.* **1** to use violence to keep someone or something away, or to stop him/her from doing something to you: *They managed to fight off their attackers.* **2** to succeed in stopping other people from getting something, and to get it for yourself: *The president fought off a challenge from within his own party.* **3** to try hard to get rid of a feeling or illness: *I've been fighting off a cold for days.*

F

fight² *n.* **1** [C] an act of fighting between two people or groups: *He's always **getting into fights** at school.* | *A drunk tried to **pick/start** a **fight** with him.* | *a **fight between** rival gangs* | *The police were called in to **break up** (=stop) the **fight**.*

THESAURUS

brawl – a noisy fight among a lot of people
free-for-all – a fight or argument involving a lot of people
scuffle – a short fight
scrap (informal) – a short fight
boxing match
wrestling match

2 [C] an argument: *He's **had a fight** with his mother.* | ***fights over/about** money* **3** [singular] the process of trying very hard to achieve something or prevent something: *the union's **fight for** better working conditions.* | *the **fight against** drugs* | *the **fight to** reduce world hunger*

THESAURUS

battle – an attempt to stop something happening or to achieve something difficult: *the battle for equal rights*
campaign – a series of actions that are intended to achieve a particular result: *She helped lead the campaign against drunk driving.*
drive – a planned effort by an organization to achieve a particular result: *a drive to raise money for the school*
struggle – a long, hard fight for freedom, political rights, etc.: *the country's struggle for independence*
crusade – a determined attempt to change something because you think you are morally right: *an anti-smoking crusade that is aimed at teenagers*

4 [C] a battle between two armies: *a **fight for** control of the islands*

fight·er /ˈfaɪt̬ɚ/ *n.* [C] **1** (approving) someone who continues to try to do something although it is difficult **2** someone who fights, especially as a sport (SYN) **boxer** **3** *also* **fighter plane** a small fast military airplane that can destroy other airplanes

fight·ing /ˈfaɪt̬ɪŋ/ *n.* [U] an occasion when people or groups fight each other in a war, in the street, etc.: *seven days of **heavy fighting***

THESAURUS **war, warfare, conflict, combat, action, hostilities** ➔ WAR

fig·ment /ˈfɪɡmənt/ *n.* **a figment of sb's imagination** something you imagine to be real, but does not exist

fig·u·ra·tive /ˈfɪɡyərət̬ɪv/ *adj.* ENG. LANG. ARTS a figurative word or expression is used in a different way from its usual meaning, to give you a picture or idea in your mind. For example, in "a mountain of debt," "mountain" is used in a figurative way and means "a large amount" not "a high hill." (SYN) **metaphorical** ➔ LITERAL —**figuratively** *adv.*

ˌfigurative ˈlanguage *n.* [U] ENG. LANG. ARTS writing or speech that uses figurative words or expressions and gives people a particular picture or idea in their minds

fig·ure¹ /ˈfɪɡyɚ/ *n.* [C] **1 a)** [usually plural] a number representing an amount, especially an official number: ***sales/crime/population etc. figures*** **b)** a number from 0 to 9, written as a sign, not as a word: *a **six-figure** income* (=between $100,000 and $999,999) | *Five players scored in **double figures*** (=numbers between 10 and 99). | ***single figures*** (=numbers between 0 and 9) **2** ECONOMICS a particular amount of money: *The report quoted an estimated **figure of** $200 million.* **3** [usually singular] the shape of a woman's body: *She **has a** great **figure**.* **4 a)** someone who is important or famous in some way: *an important political figure* **b)** someone with a particular type of appearance or character, especially when s/he is difficult to see: *a dark figure in the distance* **c)** a person in a picture **5** (*written abbreviation* **fig.**) a numbered drawing in a book **6** MATH a shape in mathematics: *a six-sided figure*

figure² *v.* **1** [I] (informal) to be included as an important part of something: *Real events and real people always **figure** heavily **in** her books.*

SPOKEN PHRASES

2 [T] to have a particular opinion after thinking about a situation: *I **figured (that)** you'd need help moving.*

THESAURUS **think, believe, suspect, consider, guess** ➔ THINK

3 that figures/(it) figures said when something happens or someone behaves in a way that you expect, but do not like: *"I forgot to bring my checkbook again." "Figures."* **4 go figure** said to show that you think something is strange or difficult to explain: *"He didn't even say goodbye!" "Go figure."*

figure on sth *phr. v.* (spoken) to expect something or include it in your plans: *With traffic so heavy, we'd better figure on an extra hour.*

figure sb/sth ↔ **out** *phr. v.* to understand someone or something after thinking about him, her, or it: *Can you figure out how to open this?* | *I can't figure Betty out.*

ˌfigure ˈeight *n.* [C] the pattern or shape of a number eight, for example, in a dance

fig·ure·head /ˈfɪɡyɚˌhɛd/ *n.* [C] a leader who has no real power

ˌfigure of ˈspeech *n.* [C] ENG. LANG. ARTS a word or expression that is used in a different way from the usual one, to give you a picture in your mind: *"We died laughing" is a figure of speech.*

ˈfigure ˌskating *n.* [U] a sport in which you SKATE in patterns on ice

fil·a·ment /'fɪləmənt/ *n.* [C] a very thin thread or wire

filch /fɪltʃ/ *v.* [T] (informal) to steal something small or not very valuable: *teenagers filching cigarettes*

file¹ /faɪl/ (Ac) *n.* [C] **1** a set of papers, records, etc. that contain information about a particular person or subject: *The school* ***keeps files on*** *each student.* | *We'll keep your application* ***on file*** (=store it for later use). | *medical files*

THESAURUS **record, accounts, books, ledger, roll, log (book)** → RECORD¹

2 a box or folded piece of heavy paper in which you keep loose papers: *He took a file down from the shelf.* **3** IT information on a computer that is stored under a particular name: ***open/close*** *a file* | ***save/delete/copy/create*** *a file* → COMPUTER **4** a metal tool with a rough surface that you rub on something to make it smooth → NAIL FILE **5 in single file** moving in a line, with one person behind another

file² (Ac) *v.* **1** [T] to store papers or information in a particular order or a particular place: ***File*** *the contracts* ***alphabetically***.

THESAURUS **keep, store, save, reserve, collect, hoard** → KEEP¹

2 [I,T] LAW to give a document to a court or other organization so that it can be officially recorded and dealt with: *Some employees are* ***filing a claim*** *against the department.* | *The company was forced to* ***file for*** *bankruptcy.* | *The District Attorney's Office has* ***filed charges*** *against him.* **3** [I] to walk somewhere in a line of people, one behind the other: *The jury* ***filed into/filed out of*** *the courtroom.* **4** [T] to rub something with a metal tool to make it smooth or cut it: *I need to* ***file*** *my* ***nails***.

'file ˌcabinet *n.* [C] a piece of office furniture with drawers for storing important papers

fil·et /fɪ'leɪ/ *n.* [C,U] a FILLET¹

fil·i·bus·ter /'fɪləˌbʌstɚ/ *v.* [I,T] to try to delay action in Congress by making very long speeches —**filibuster** *n.* [C]

fil·i·gree /'fɪləˌgri/ *n.* [U] delicate decoration made of gold or silver wire

fil·ing /'faɪlɪŋ/ (Ac) *n.* **1** [U] the activity of putting papers into the correct FILES **2 filings** [plural] very small sharp pieces that come off a piece of metal when it is FILEd: *iron filings* **3** [C] a document, report, etc. that is officially recorded

'filing ˌcabinet *n.* [C] a FILE CABINET

fil·ings /'faɪlɪŋz/ *n.* [plural] very small pieces that come off a piece of metal when it is cut or FILEd

fill¹ /fɪl/ *v.* **1** *also* **fill up a)** [I,T] to become full of something, or to make something full: *He turned on the faucet and filled the bucket.* | *She kept filling up our glasses.* | *The kids* ***filled*** *their bags* ***with*** *candy.* **b)** [T] if something fills up a place, it takes up all of the space in that place: *The audience soon filled the theater.* | *The bedroom was* ***filled with*** *smoke.* **2** [T] *also* **fill in** to put something in a hole or crack in order to make a smooth surface: *Fill any cracks in the wall before you paint.* **3** [T] if a sound, smell, or light fills a place or space, you notice it because it is loud or strong: *The smell of fresh bread filled the kitchen.* **4** [T] to provide something that is needed or wanted: *Daycare centers* ***fill a need*** *for working parents.* | *The company is* ***filling a gap*** *in the market.* **5** [T] to do a particular job, or to find someone to do a job: *Anderson says he hopes to* ***fill the position*** *by spring.* | *Sorry, but the post has already been filled.* **6** [T] if you are filled with an emotion, you feel it strongly: *She was* ***filled with*** *excitement.* | *Her achievements* ***filled*** *him* ***with*** *pride.* **7** [T] if you fill a period of time with a particular activity, you spend that time doing it: *He filled his days playing golf and tennis.* [ORIGIN: Old English *fyllan*]

fill in *phr. v.* **1 fill** sth ↔ **in** to write all the necessary information on a document: *You'll have to fill in an application form.* **2 fill** sb ↔ **in** to tell someone about things that have happened recently: *I'll* ***fill*** *you* ***in on*** *all the news later.* **3** to do someone's job because s/he is not there: *Could you* ***fill in for*** *Bob while he's sick?*

fill out *phr. v.* **1 fill** sth ↔ **out 2** to write all the necessary information on a document **3** to get fatter or larger in a way that is considered attractive: *At puberty, a girl's body begins to fill out.*

fill² *n.* **your fill** as much of something as you want, or can deal with: *I've* ***had*** *my* ***fill of*** *screaming kids today!*

fil·let¹ *also* **filet** /fɪ'leɪ/ *n.* [C,U] a piece of meat or fish without bones: *a* ***fillet of*** *cod*

fillet² *v.* [T] to remove the bones from a piece of meat or fish

fill·ing¹ /'fɪlɪŋ/ *n.* **1** [C] a small amount of metal that is put into a hole in your tooth **2** [C,U] the food that is put inside a PIE, SANDWICH, etc.: *apple pie filling*

filling² *adj.* food that is filling makes your stomach feel full

fil·ly /'fɪli/ *n.* (plural **fillies**) [C] a young female horse

film¹ /fɪlm/ *n.* **1** [U] the material used in a camera for taking photographs or recording moving pictures: *a* ***roll of film*** | *The coach has the game* ***on film.*** → CAMERA **2** [C] a movie: *the Sundance Film Festival* | *We like to go see* ***foreign films.*** → MOVIE **3** [U] the art or business of making movies: *the film industry* **4** [singular] a very thin layer of liquid, powder, etc. on the surface of something [ORIGIN: Old English *filmen* "thin skin"]

film² *v.* [I,T] to use a camera to make a movie or a television program: *The movie was filmed in China.* —**filming** *n.* [U]: *The filming was completed in six weeks.*

film·mak·er /'fɪlmˌmeɪkɚ/ *n.* [C] someone who makes movies

film·strip /'fɪlmˌstrɪp/ *n.* [C] a short film that

F

shows photographs, pictures, etc. one at a time, not as moving pictures

fil·ter[1] /'fɪltɚ/ *n.* [C] a piece of equipment that removes unwanted solid substances as gas or liquid passes through it: *a water filter* [ORIGIN: 1300—1400 Old French *filtre* "piece of felt (=thick material) used as a filter," from Medieval Latin *filtrum*]

filter[2] *v.* **1** [T] to clean a liquid or gas using a filter: *filtered drinking water* **2** [I] if people filter somewhere, they gradually move in that direction: *The audience began to* ***filter into*** *the hall.* **3** [I] if information filters out to people, people gradually hear about it: *The news slowly* ***filtered through to*** *everyone in the office.* | *Eventually* ***word filtered out to*** *the guests that something was wrong.* **4** [I] if light or sound filters into a place, it can be seen or heard only slightly: *Hazy sunshine* ***filtered through*** *the curtains.*

filth /fɪlθ/ *n.* [U] **1** an extremely dirty substance: *Wash that filth off your shoes.* **2** very rude or offensive language, stories, or pictures about sex

F

filth·y[1] /'fɪlθi/ *adj.* (comparative **filthier**, superlative **filthiest**) **1** extremely dirty: *Doesn't he ever wash that jacket? It's filthy.*

THESAURUS **dirty, dusty, muddy, greasy, grimy, soiled, polluted** → DIRTY[1]

2 showing or describing sexual acts in a very rude or offensive way: *filthy language*

filthy[2] *adv.* **filthy rich** (informal) extremely rich

fil·tra·tion /fɪl'treɪʃən/ *n.* [U] CHEMISTRY the process of cleaning a liquid or gas by passing it through a FILTER: *a water filtration system*

fin /fɪn/ *n.* [C] one of the thin body parts that a fish uses to swim → *see picture on page A15*

fi·na·gle /fə'neɪgəl/ *v.* [T] (informal) to get something that is difficult to get by using unusual or unfair methods

fi·nal[1] /'faɪnl/ (Ac) *adj.* **1** [only before noun] last in a series of actions, events, parts of a story, etc.: *the final chapter of the book* **2** if a decision, offer, or agreement is final, it cannot be changed: *I don't think the* ***final decision*** *has been made.* | *You can't stay up late on a school night,* ***and that's final.*** **3** [only before noun] being the result at the end of a process: *The* ***final score*** *was 86 to 78.* [ORIGIN: 1300—1400 French, Latin *finalis*, from *finis* "end"]

final[2] (Ac) *n.* [C] **1** the last and most important game, race, etc. in a competition: *She skated very well in the final.* | *The Suns didn't* ***reach the*** *Western Conference* ***Finals.*** **2** an important test that students take at the end of each class in HIGH SCHOOL or college: *How did your finals go?* | *my chemistry final*

fi·nal·e /fɪ'næli, -'nɑ-/ *n.* [C] ENG. LANG. ARTS the last part of a piece of music or a performance, which is often the most exciting part: *the* ***grand finale*** *of a Broadway musical*

fi·nal·ist /'faɪnl-ɪst/ *n.* [C] one of the people or teams that reaches the last part of a competition

fi·nal·i·ty /faɪ'næləṭi, fə-/ (Ac) *n.* [U] the feeling or idea that something is finished and cannot be changed: *She closed the door with a finality that said she would not be coming back.*

fi·nal·ize /'faɪnl,aɪz/ (Ac) *v.* [T] to finish the last details or part of a plan, business deal, etc.: *Can we finalize the details tomorrow?*

fi·nal·ly /'faɪnl-i/ (Ac) *adv.* **1** after a long time: *After several delays, the plane finally took off at 6:00.* **2** as the last of a series of things: *And finally, I'd like to thank my teachers.* **3** in a way that does not allow further change: *I don't think anything has been finally decided.*

fi·nance[1] /fə'næns, 'faɪnæns/ (Ac) *n.* **1** [U] ECONOMICS the control of money that is earned and spent, especially for a company or a government: *She's an accountant in the Finance Department.* **2 finances** [plural] ECONOMICS the money that a person, company, organization, etc. has available, or the control of how this money is spent: *My finances are a mess.* | *The school's finances are limited.* **3** [U] ECONOMICS money provided by a bank, organization, etc. to help buy or do something: *mortgage finance companies* [ORIGIN: 1300—1400 French *finer* "to end, settle (a debt)"]

finance[2] *v.* [T] ECONOMICS to provide money, especially a large amount of money, to pay for something: *The program is financed by the government.*

fi·nan·cial /fə'nænʃəl, faɪ-/ (Ac) *adj.* ECONOMICS relating to money or the management of money: *a company that provides* ***financial services*** | *He had no* ***financial support*** *from his parents.* | *the company's* ***financial assets*** —**financially** *adv.*

fi,nancial 'aid *n.* [U] money that is given or lent to students at college to pay for their education

fi,nancial 'asset *n.* [C] ECONOMICS something such as STOCKS or BONDS which are owned by a person or a company, which are worth a particular amount of money, and which make a profit: *The crisis will affect people's savings and every other financial asset they own* | *You can compare the yield* (=profit received) *from stock dividends to other financial assets, like bonds.*

fin·an·cier /,faɪnæn'sɪr, fə,næn-, ,fɪnən-/ (Ac) *n.* [C] ECONOMICS someone who controls or lends large sums of money

fi·nanc·ing /'faɪnænsɪŋ/ (Ac) *n.* [U] ECONOMICS money that you borrow to start a business, buy something, etc., and which you pay back over an agreed period of time

finch /fɪntʃ/ *n.* [C] a small wild bird with a short beak

find[1] /faɪnd/ *v.* (past tense and past participle **found** /faʊnd/) [T]

1 GET BY SEARCHING to discover and get something that you have been looking for: *I can't find my keys.* | *He's having a hard time finding a job.* |

Can you find the kids something clean to wear?

THESAURUS

discover – to find something that was hidden or that people did not know about before: *They never discovered the truth about his past.*
detect – to notice or discover something, especially something that is not easy to see, hear, etc.: *The test can detect cancer at an early stage in the disease.*
trace – to find someone or something that has disappeared: *She had given up all hope of tracing her missing daughter.*
locate – to find the exact position of something: *We couldn't locate the source of the radio signal.*
track sb/sth down – to find someone or something after searching in different places: *Detectives finally tracked her down in California.*
turn sth up – to find something by searching for it thoroughly: *The investigation hasn't turned up any new evidence.*
unearth – to find out information or the truth about something: *It was years before the full story was unearthed.*

2 SEE BY CHANCE to discover something by chance: *She found a purse in the street.* | *We found a good restaurant near the hotel.*
3 LEARN STH to discover or learn new information: *Researchers have **found that** girls tend to speak earlier than boys.* | *We got there early **only to find that** the tickets had all been sold.* | *Scientists are still trying to find a cure for AIDS.*
4 OPINION to have an opinion or feeling about someone or something: *Do you find him attractive?* | ***I found it difficult/easy to** understand her.*
5 EXPERIENCE to learn or know something by experience: *I tried using oil, but I've **found that** butter works best.*
6 TIME/MONEY/ENERGY to have enough of something to be able to do what you want to do: *When do you find the time to read?*
7 be found to live or exist somewhere: *This type of grass is found only in the swamp.*
8 find yourself somewhere to be in a place although you did not plan to be there: *Suddenly I found myself back at the hotel.*
9 find your way (somewhere) to arrive at a place by discovering the way to get there: *Can you find your way, or do you need a map?*
10 find sb guilty/not guilty (of sth) to officially decide that someone is guilty or not guilty of a crime: *He was found guilty of murder.* [ORIGIN: Old English *findan*]

find out *phr. v.*
1 find (sth) **out** to learn information after trying to discover it or by chance: *If Dad ever **finds out about** this, he'll be furious.* | *He hurried off to **find out what** the problem was.* | *We need to find out everything we can about the disease.*
2 find sb **out** (informal) to discover that someone has been doing something dishonest or illegal: *What happens if we **get found out**?*

find² *n.* [C] something very good or valuable that you discover by chance: *That little Greek restaurant was **a real find**.*

find·ing /ˈfaɪndɪŋ/ *n.* [C usually plural] information that someone has learned as a result of studies, work, etc.: *the newest research findings*

fine¹ /faɪn/ *adj.* **1** good enough or acceptable SYN **all right**: *"What do you want for lunch?" "A sandwich is fine."* | *"More coffee?" "No, **I'm fine**, thanks."* | *"How about seeing a movie?" "That's **fine by me**."* **2** healthy and well: *"How are you?" "Fine, thanks."*

THESAURUS healthy, well, better, in (good) shape, physically fit → HEALTHY

3 very good: *He congratulated the team on a fine performance.* | *a selection of **fine wines*** **4** very thin or narrow, or made of very small pieces: *fine hair* | *a fine layer of dust* **5** fine differences, changes, or details are small or exact and difficult to see: *I didn't understand some of the **finer points** of his argument.* **6 a fine line** if you say that there is a fine line between two different things, you mean that they are so similar that one can easily become the other: *There's **a fine line between** genius and madness.*

fine² *adv.* (spoken) in a way that is satisfactory or acceptable SYN **well**: *"How's everything going?" "Fine."* | *The washer's working fine now.* | *Relax, you're **doing** just **fine**.*

fine³ *n.* [C] money that you have to pay as a punishment for breaking a law or rule: *a parking fine*

THESAURUS punishment, sentence, penalty → PUNISHMENT

fine⁴ *v.* [T] to make someone pay money as a punishment: *He was **fined** $50 **for** speeding.*

ˌfine ˈarts *n.* **the fine arts** ENG. LANG. ARTS activities such as painting, music, etc. that are concerned with making beautiful things

fine·ly /ˈfaɪnli/ *adv.* **1** in very thin or small pieces: *finely chopped onion* **2** to a very exact degree: *finely tuned instruments*

ˌfine ˈprint *n.* [U] the part of a contract or other document that has important information, often written in small print: *Before signing the contract, make sure you **read the fine print**.*

fi·nesse /fɪˈnɛs/ *n.* [U] if you do something with finesse, you do it with a lot of skill and style

ˌfine-ˈtune *v.* [T] to make small changes to something in order to make it as good as possible: *The team is still fine-tuning its game plan.*

fin·ger¹ /ˈfɪŋgɚ/ *n.* [C] **1** one of the four long thin parts at the end of your hand, not including your thumb: *Hold the thread **between** your **fingers**.* | *She has a ring **on** every **finger**.* → INDEX FINGER, LITTLE FINGER, MIDDLE FINGER → *see picture on page A16* **2 not lift a finger** to not make any effort to help someone: *I do all the work – Frank never lifts*

F

a finger. **3 keep/have your fingers crossed** (spoken) said when you hope that something will happen the way you want: *Keep your fingers crossed that the car makes it home.* **4 put your finger on sth** (informal) to realize exactly what is wrong, different, or unusual about something: *There's something strange about him, but I can't put my finger on what it is.* [ORIGIN: Old English]

finger² *v.* [T] to touch or feel something with your fingers

fin·ger·nail /ˈfɪŋgɚˌneɪl/ *n.* [C] the hard flat part that covers the top end of your finger ➔ *see picture at* HAND¹

fingerprint

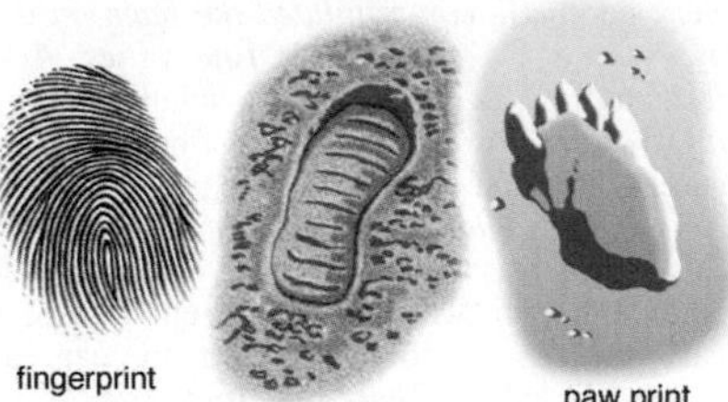

fin·ger·print /ˈfɪŋgɚˌprɪnt/ *n.* [C] the mark made by the pattern of lines at the end of someone's finger

fin·ger·tip /ˈfɪŋgɚˌtɪp/ *n.* [C] **1** the end of a finger **2 have sth at your fingertips** to have something easily available and ready to use, especially knowledge or information

fin·ick·y /ˈfɪnɪki/ *adj.* someone who is finicky only likes a few kinds of food, clothes, music, etc. and is difficult to please: *a finicky eater*

fin·ish¹ /ˈfɪnɪʃ/ *v.* **1** [I,T] to do the last part of something, or to stop when everything has been done (ANT) **start**: *Have you finished your homework?* | *Everyone applauded when she finished speaking.* | *What time does the show finish?*

> THESAURUS **end, stop, come to an end, be over** ➔ END²

2 [T] *also* **finish off/up** to eat, drink, or use all the rest of something: *Finish your breakfast before it gets cold.* | *Who finished off the cake?* | *Why don't you finish up the apple pie?* **3** [I,T] to be in a particular position at the end of a race, competition, etc.: *She* ***finished second*** *in the marathon.* **4** [T] to give the surface of something a smooth appearance by painting, POLISHing, etc. [ORIGIN: 1300—1400 French *finir*, from Latin *finire*, from *finis* "end"]

finish sth ↔ **up** *phr. v.* to end an event, situation, etc. by doing one final thing: *We finished up the evening with drinks in a bar downtown.*

finish with sth *phr. v.* **be finished with sth** to no longer need to use something: *Are you finished with the scissors?*

finish² *n.* **1** [C usually singular] the end or last part of something, especially a race: *It was* ***a close finish*** (=the race ended with the competitors close together), *but Jarrett won.* **2** [C,U] the way that a surface looks after it has been painted or POLISHed: *a table with a glossy finish* | *What kind of finish did you put on the deck?*

fin·ished /ˈfɪnɪʃt/ *adj.* **1** [only before noun] completed: *the finished product*

> THESAURUS **done, complete, over** ➔ DONE²

2 [not before noun] at the end of an activity: *I'm not quite finished.* **3** [not before noun] (informal) no longer able to do something successfully: *If the bank doesn't loan us the money, we're finished.*

ˈfinish line *n.* [C] the line at the end of a race that a competitor must cross first in order to win

fi·nite /ˈfaɪnaɪt/ (Ac) *adj.* having an end or a limit: *the Earth's finite resources*

fir /fɚ/ *n.* [C] a tree with leaves shaped like needles that do not fall off in winter ➔ *see picture on page A23*

fire¹ /faɪɚ/ *n.* **1** [C,U] uncontrolled flames and heat that destroy and damage things: *Fire destroyed part of the building.* | *a forest fire* | *Police are trying to find out who* ***started*** *the* ***fire.*** | *It took firefighters two days to* ***put out*** *the* ***fire*** (=stop it burning). | *The house is* ***on fire*** (=burning)*!* | *Some other buildings* ***caught fire*** (=started to burn). | *Rioters* ***set fire to*** *cars and stores* (=made them burn).

> COLLOCATIONS
> **verbs used with fire**
> **burn** – to produce heat and flames
> **break out** – to start burning suddenly
> **rage/blaze** – to burn strongly for a long time over a large area
> **die down** – to stop burning strongly
> **go out/die** – to stop burning completely
> **smolder** – to burn slowly with no flames and only a little smoke
> **extinguish/put out** – to make a fire stop burning

> THESAURUS
> **flames** – the bright parts of a fire that you see burning in the air
> **blaze** – the flames from a fire, or a large and dangerous fire: *Firemen fought to keep the blaze under control.*
> **inferno** (literary) – a very large and very dangerous fire: *Soon, the house became a raging inferno.*
> **bonfire** – a large outdoor fire: *a bonfire at the beach*
> **campfire** – a fire that you build outdoors when you are camping

2 [C] burning wood or coal used to heat a room or provide heat: *a campfire* | *Let's* ***light*** *a* ***fire*** *in the fireplace.* **3** [U] shooting by guns: *Troops* ***opened fire on*** (=started shooting at) *the rebels.* **4 be/come under fire** to be criticized very strongly [ORIGIN: Old English *fyr*]

F

fire² *v.* **1** [T] to make someone leave his/her job: *She didn't expect to **get fired**. | Brian was **fired from** his job at the bank. | My boss **fired** me **for** refusing to work over.* **2** [I,T] to shoot bullets from a gun: *Someone **fired** a **shot**. | Frank **fired at** the target.* **3 fire questions (at sb)** to ask someone a lot of questions very quickly **4 fire away** (spoken) said in order to show that you are ready to answer someone's questions

fire sth ↔ **off** *phr. v.* **1** to quickly send an angry letter to someone: *She fired off an angry e-mail to the manager.* **2** to shoot a weapon, often so that there are no bullets, etc. left

fire ↔ **up** *phr. v.* (informal) **1 fire** sth ↔ **up** to start a machine or piece of equipment, especially one that burns gas: *Let's fire up the grill.* **2 fire** sb ↔ **up** to make someone very excited and eager: *The kids were all fired up for the game.*

'fire a,larm *n.* [C] a piece of equipment that makes a loud noise to warn people of a fire in a building

fire·arm /'faɪɚɑrm/ *n.* [C] (formal) a gun

fire·brand /'faɪɚbrænd/ *n.* [C] (formal) someone who tries to make people angry about a law, government, etc. so that they will try to change it

fire·crack·er /'faɪɚ,krækɚ/ *n.* [C] a small FIREWORK that explodes loudly

'fire de,partment *n.* [C] an organization that works to prevent fires and stop them from burning

'fire drill *n.* [C] an occasion when people practice how to leave a burning building safely

'fire ,engine *n.* [C] a special large vehicle that carries people and equipment to stop fires from burning

'fire es,cape *n.* [C] metal stairs on the outside of a building that people can use in order to escape if there is a fire

'fire ex,tinguisher *n.* [C] a metal container with water or chemicals in it, used for stopping small fires

fire·fight·er /'faɪɚ,faɪt̬ɚ/ *n.* [C] someone whose job is to stop fires

fire·fly /'faɪɚflaɪ/ *n.* (plural **fireflies**) [C] an insect with a tail that shines in the dark

'fire ,hydrant *n.* [C] a water pipe in a street, used for getting water to stop fires

fire·man /'faɪɚmən/ *n.* (plural **firemen** /-mən/) [C] a man whose job is to stop fires

fire·place /'faɪɚpleɪs/ *n.* [C] an open place in the wall of a room where you can make a fire

fire·proof /'faɪɚpruf/ *adj.* something that is fireproof cannot be damaged by fire —**fireproof** *v.* [T]

fire·side /'faɪɚsaɪd/ *n.* [singular] the area close to a fireplace or around a small fire: *We were sitting by the fireside.*

'fire ,station *n.* [C] a building where the equipment used to stop fires from burning is kept, and where FIREFIGHTERS stay until they are needed

'fire truck *n.* [C] a FIRE ENGINE

fire·wall /'faɪɚwɔl/ *n.* [C] IT a system that protects a computer network from being used or looked at by people who do not have permission to do so

fire·wood /'faɪɚwʊd/ *n.* [U] wood that has been cut or collected in order to be burned on a fire

fire·work /'faɪɚwɚk/ *n.* [C usually plural] an object that burns or explodes to produce colored lights and noise in the sky: *a Fourth of July **fireworks display***

'firing squad *n.* [C] a group of soldiers whose duty is to shoot and kill a prisoner

firm¹ /fɚm/ *n.* [C] ECONOMICS a business or company, especially a small one that does not make goods: ***a law firm***

THESAURUS **company, business, corporation, subsidiary** → COMPANY

firm² *adj.* **1** not completely hard, but not soft and not easy to bend: *a bed with a firm mattress | Choose the ripest firmest tomatoes.*

THESAURUS **hard, stiff, solid, rigid** → HARD¹

2 [only before noun] definite and not likely to change: *No firm decision has been reached. | I'm a **firm believer** in the value of education.* **3** strong and in control: *You need to be **firm with** children.*

THESAURUS **strict, tough, stern** → STRICT

4 strongly fastened or placed in position and not likely to move: *Make sure the ladder feels firm before you climb up.* **5 a firm grip/grasp/hold etc.** a tight strong hold on something: *a firm handshake*

firm³ *v.*

firm sth ↔ **up** *phr. v.* to make arrangements, ideas, or plans more definite and exact: *We hope to firm up the deal later this month.*

first¹ /fɚst/ *adj.* **1** coming before all the other things or people in a series: *Susan was his first girlfriend. | **The first time** I flew on a plane I was really nervous. | I've only read the first chapter.* **2** most important SYN **main**: *Our first priority is to maintain the quality of the product.* **3 in the first place** (spoken) used in order to talk about the beginning of a situation: *Why did you agree to meet her in the first place?* **4 at first sight/glance** the first time that you look at someone or something, before you notice any details: *At first sight, there didn't appear to be much damage.* **5 first thing** (spoken) as soon as you wake up or start work in the morning: *I'll call you first thing tomorrow, okay?* **6 first things first** (spoken) used in order to say that something is important and must be dealt with before other things [ORIGIN: Old English *fyrst*] → **first/second/third string** *at* STRING¹, **in the first/second/third place** *at* PLACE¹

first² *adv.* **1** before anything or anyone else: *Who's going first?* **2** before doing anything else,

F

or before anything else happens: *I'll join you in a minute, but first I've got to make a phone call* | ***First of all**, we'd better make sure we have everything we need.* **3** done for the first time: *The book was first published in 1995.* **4 first come, first served** used in order to say that only the first people to arrive, ask for something, etc. will be given something: *Free movie tickets are being given away **on a first come, first served basis**.*

USAGE

Use **first** or **first of all** when you are giving a list of points, reasons, etc.: *There are three reasons for this. First of all it is too expensive...*
Use **first** or **first of all** to say what happens first in a series of actions: *First I checked my e-mail. Then I made a couple of calls.*
Use **at first** to say what happened at the beginning of a situation or time, when this changed later: *At first, we were very happy together.*

F

first³ *number, pron.* **1 at first** in the beginning: *At first I thought he was weird, but now I really like him.* **2 a first** something that has never happened before: *"Dad actually washed the dishes tonight." **"That's a first."*** **3** the first person or thing in a series: *My uncle was **the first** in my family to go to college.* | *the 1st of June* (=first day of June)

ˌfirst ˈaid *n.* [U] basic medical treatment that is given as soon as possible to someone who is injured or who suddenly becomes sick

ˌfirst ˈbase *n.* [U] in a game of baseball, the first of the four places that a player must touch before gaining a point

ˌfirst ˈclass *n.* [U] the best and most expensive place to sit on an airplane, train, or ship: *He was sitting **in first class**.*

ˌfirst-ˈclass² *adj.* **1** much better than other things of the same type: *a first-class educational system*

THESAURUS **good, great, excellent, wonderful, fantastic, outstanding, exceptional, superb, ace** → GOOD¹

2 using the FIRST CLASS on an airplane, train, or ship: *two first-class tickets to Hawaii* —**first class** *adv.*: *flying first class*

ˌfirst ˈfloor *n.* [C] the floor of a building that is at ground level (SYN) **ground floor**

first·hand /ˌfɚstˈhænd◂/ *adj.* [only before noun] firsthand knowledge is knowledge that you get or learn yourself, not from other people —**firsthand** *adv.*: *experience you have gained firsthand*

ˌfirst ˈlady *n.* **the First Lady** the wife of the President of the U.S.

first·ly /ˈfɚstli/ *adv.* used before saying the first of several things: *Firstly, I would like to thank everyone for coming.*

ˈfirst name *n.* [C] the name that, in English, comes before your family's name → LAST NAME, MIDDLE NAME: *Her first name is Caroline.*

ˌfirst ˈperson *n.* **1 the first person** ENG. LANG. ARTS the form of a verb or PRONOUN that you use to show that you are the speaker. "I," "we," "me," and "us" are all first person pronouns, and "am" is the first person singular of the verb "to be." → SECOND PERSON, THIRD PERSON **2 in the first person** ENG. LANG. ARTS a story in the first person is told by the writer or a speaker who is involved in the story → THIRD PERSON

ˌfirst-ˈperson *adj.* **first-person narrative/account/story** ENG. LANG. ARTS a story that is told by a first person narrator

ˌfirst person ˈnarrator *n.* [C] ENG. LANG. ARTS a person who writes or tells a story that s/he is involved in, and who refers to himself or herself as "I." A first person narrator only knows about the events s/he is involved in or is told about. → THIRD PERSON NARRATOR

ˌfirst-ˈrate *adj.* extremely good: *a first-rate performance*

fis·cal /ˈfɪskəl/ *adj.* ECONOMICS relating to money, taxes, debts, etc., especially those involving the government: *the budget for the forthcoming fiscal year* | *The country faces a fiscal crisis if the government fails to act immediately.* [ORIGIN: 1500—1600 Latin *fiscus* "basket, money bag"] —**fiscally** *adv.*

ˌfiscal ˈpolicy *n.* [C] ECONOMICS a government's plan for dealing with taxes, spending, and borrowing: *The Treasury's remedy for inflation is to tighten fiscal policies.*

ˌfiscal ˈyear *n.* [C] a period of 12 months, used by a government or business to calculate its accounts

fish¹ /fɪʃ/ *n.* (plural **fish** *or* **fishes**) **1** [C] an animal that lives in water and uses its FINs and tail to swim: *How many **fish** did you **catch**?* **2** [U] the flesh of a fish used as food: *We had fish for dinner.* [ORIGIN: Old English *fisc*; related to *Pisces*]

fish² *v.* **1** [I] to try to catch fish: *Dad's **fishing for** salmon.* **2** [I,T] to search for something in a bag, pocket, etc., or to bring it out when you have found it: *He **fished around in** his pocket for a quarter.* | *She finally **fished** a dime **out of** her jeans.* **3 be fishing for compliments** to be trying to make someone say nice things about you

fish·bowl /ˈfɪʃboʊl/ *n.* [C] **1** a place or situation in which you cannot do anything without people knowing about it **2** a glass container that pet fish are kept in

fish·er·man /ˈfɪʃɚmən/ *n.* (plural **fishermen** /-mən/) [C] a man who catches fish as a job or a sport

fish·er·y /ˈfɪʃəri/ *n.* (plural **fisheries**) [C] a part of the ocean that is used for catching fish as a business

fish·ing /ˈfɪʃɪŋ/ *n.* [U] the job or sport of catching fish: *Do you want to **go fishing**?*

ˈfishing pole *also* **ˈfishing rod** *n.* [C] a long thin pole with a long string and a hook tied to it, used for catching fish

fish·net /ˈfɪʃnɛt/ *n.* [U] a material with a pattern of threads and small holes like a net: *fishnet stockings*

fish·y /ˈfɪʃi/ *adj.* **1** (informal) seeming bad or dishonest: *There's something fishy about his business deals.* **2** tasting or smelling like fish

fis·sion /ˈfɪʃən/ *n.* [U] PHYSICS the process of splitting the NUCLEUS (=central part) of an atom to produce large amounts of energy or an explosion → FUSION [ORIGIN: 1600—1700 Latin *fissus*, past participle of *findere* "to split"]

fis·sure /ˈfɪʃɚ/ *n.* [C] EARTH SCIENCES a deep crack in rock or the ground

fist /fɪst/ *n.* [C] a hand with all the fingers bent tightly in toward the PALM: *She held the money tightly in her fist.*

fit¹ /fɪt/ *v* (past tense and past participle **fit** *or* **fitted**, present participle **fitting**) **1** [I,T] to be the right size and shape for someone or something: *The dress **fit** her **perfectly**. | This lid doesn't **fit** very **well**.* **2** [I] to be the right size and shape for a particular space, and not be too big or too small: *This key doesn't seem to fit in the lock. | All of these pieces are supposed to **fit together**.* **3** [I,T] if something fits into a place, there is enough space for it: *I don't think we'll be able to **fit** any more people **into** the car. | We can't get the table to **fit through** the door.* **4** [T] to put a piece of equipment into a place, or a new part onto a machine, so that it is ready to be used: *The windows and doors are all **fitted with** security locks.* **5** [I,T] if something fits another thing, it is similar to it or appropriate for it: *A man **fitting the** police **description*** (=looking like it) *was seen running from the park. | We wanted an experienced journalist, and Watts **fit the bill*** (=had the right experience).

fit in *phr. v.* **1** if someone fits in, s/he is accepted by the other people in a group: *New students often have a hard time fitting in.* **2 fit** sb/sth ↔ **in** to manage to do something or see someone, even though you have a lot of other things to do: *Dr. Tyler can fit you in on Monday at 3:30 p.m.*

fit² *n.* [C] **1 have/throw a fit** (spoken) to become very angry and shout a lot: *Mom's going to have a fit when she sees what you've done.* **2** a short period of time when someone stops being conscious and cannot control his/her body: *an epileptic fit* **3** a very strong emotion that you cannot control: *a **fit of** rage* **4** a period during which you laugh or cough a lot: *I had a **coughing fit** during the concert.* **5 be a good/tight/perfect etc. fit** to fit a person or a particular space well, tightly, perfectly, etc.: *The skirt's **a perfect fit**.*

fit³ *adj.* **1** appropriate or good enough for something (ANT) **unfit**: *This book is not **fit for** publication. | You're **in no fit state** to drive.* **2** healthy and strong: *He was young and **physically fit**.*

THESAURUS healthy, well, fine, better, in (good) shape → HEALTHY

3 see fit to do sth (formal) to decide that it is right to do something, even though many people disagree: *The government has seen fit to start testing more nuclear weapons.*

fit·ful /ˈfɪtfəl/ *adj.* always starting and stopping, not continuous or regular: ***a fitful sleep***

fit·ness /ˈfɪtˀnɪs/ *n.* [U] **1** the condition of being healthy or strong enough to do hard work or sports: *classes to improve your **physical fitness*** **2** the quality of being appropriate for something, especially a job: *They were unsure of his **fitness for** a job as a social worker.*

fit·ted /ˈfɪt̬ɪd/ *adj.* **1** fitted clothes are designed so that they fit closely to someone's body: *a fitted jacket* **2 be fitted with sth** to have or include something as a permanent part: *The food processor is fitted with three blades.*

fit·ting¹ /ˈfɪt̬ɪŋ/ *adj.* (formal) right or appropriate: ***It was fitting that** it rained the day of his funeral. | The game was a **fitting end** to the season.*

fitting² *n.* [C] an occasion when you put on clothes that are being made for you to find out if they fit

ˈfitting room *n.* [C] a DRESSING ROOM

five¹ /faɪv/ *number* **1** 5 **2** five o'clock: *I get off work **at five**.* **3** five years old: *My nephew is almost five.* [ORIGIN: Old English *fif*]

five² *n.* [C] **1** a piece of paper money worth $5 **2 give sb five** (informal) to hit the inside of someone's hand with the inside of your hand in order to show that you are very pleased about something

fix¹ /fɪks/ *v.* [T]

1 REPAIR to repair something that is broken or not working correctly: *I've fixed your bike. | Do you know how to **fix** the **problem**?*

THESAURUS repair, mend, renovate, restore, service, rebuild, recondition → REPAIR²

2 PREPARE to prepare a meal or drinks: *Let me fix you a drink. | Mom was **fixing dinner**.*

3 DECIDE to decide on an exact time, place, price, etc.: *Have you fixed a date for the wedding? | The interest rate was fixed at 6.5%*

4 HAIR/FACE to make your hair or MAKEUP look neat and attractive: *Let me fix my hair first and then we can go.*

5 RESULT to make dishonest arrangements so that an election, competition, etc. has the results that you want: *If you ask me, the game was fixed.* [ORIGIN: 1400—1500 Latin *fixus*, past participle of *figere* "to fasten"]

fix sb/sth ↔ **up** *phr. v.*

1 to decorate or repair a room or building: *We fixed up the guest bedroom.*

2 (informal) to find a romantic partner for someone: *Rachel keeps trying to fix me up with her brother.*

fix² *n.* **1 a quick fix** something that solves a problem quickly but is only a temporary solution **2 be in a fix** to have a problem that is difficult to solve: *We're going to be in a real fix if*

F

we miss the last bus. **3 get a fix on sb/sth a)** to find out exactly where someone or something is **b)** to understand what someone or something is really like **4** [singular] (slang) an amount of an illegal drug that someone needs to take regularly

fix·a·tion /fɪk'seɪʃən/ *n.* [C] a very strong interest in someone or something that is not healthy or natural: *Brian **has a fixation with** motorcycles.* —**fixated** /'fɪkseɪt̬ɪd/ *adj.*

fixed /fɪkst/ *adj.* **1** a fixed amount or time cannot be changed: *pensioners on a **fixed income** | fixed costs* **2** firmly fastened to something and in a particular position: *a mirror fixed to the wall* **3 have fixed ideas/opinions** (disapproving) to have opinions or ideas that will not change

fix·ed·ly /'fɪksɪdli/ *adv.* without looking at or thinking about anything else: *Ann **stared fixedly** at the screen.*

fix·ture /'fɪkstʃɚ/ *n.* **1** [C usually plural] a piece of equipment that is attached inside a house, such as an electric light or a FAUCET: *a bathroom with gold-plated fixtures* **2 be a (permanent) fixture** to always be present, and unlikely to move or go away: *He's been a fixture in the Senate since 1968.*

F

fizz /fɪz/ *n.* [singular, U] the BUBBLEs of gas in some types of drinks, or the sound they make → *see picture on page A20* —**fizz** *v.* [I] —**fizzy** *adj.*

fiz·zle /'fɪzəl/ *v.*

fizzle out *phr. v.* to gradually end in a weak or disappointing way: *The party fizzled out before midnight.*

FL the written abbreviation of FLORIDA

flab /flæb/ *n.* [U] (informal) soft loose fat on a person's body

flab·ber·gast·ed /'flæbɚˌgæstɪd/ *adj.* (informal) extremely shocked or surprised

> THESAURUS **surprised, amazed, shocked, astonished, astounded, stunned, dumbfounded, nonplussed, taken aback** → SURPRISED

flab·by /'flæbi/ *adj.* (informal) having too much soft loose fat instead of strong muscles: *flabby arms*

flac·cid /'flæsɪd/ *adj.* soft and weak instead of firm: *flaccid muscles*

flag¹ /flæg/ *n.* [C] **1** a piece of cloth with a picture or pattern that is used to represent a particular country or organization: *The children were **waving flags**. | the French flag* **2** a piece of colored cloth used as a signal: *The flag went down, and the race began.* [ORIGIN: (1) 1400—1500 Old Norse *flaga*]

flag² *v.* (**flagged**, **flagging**) [I] to become tired, weak, or less interested in something: *By the end of the meeting we had begun to flag.* —**flagging** *adj.*

flag sb/sth ↔ down *phr. v.* to make the driver of a vehicle stop by waving at him/her: *I flagged down a cab.*

fla·gel·lum /flə'dʒɛləm/ *n.* (plural **flagella** /-lə/) [C] BIOLOGY a thin part, like a hair, that grows from the surface of some cells and from BACTERIA, which helps them move around

flag·pole /'flægpoʊl/ *n.* [C] a tall pole used for hanging flags

fla·grant /'fleɪgrənt/ *adj.* a flagrant action is shocking because it is done in a very noticeable way and shows no respect for the law, the truth, etc.: *The arrests are a **flagrant violation** of human rights.* [ORIGIN: 1400—1500 Latin *flagrare* "to burn"] —**flagrantly** *adv.*

flag·ship /'flægˌʃɪp/ *n.* [C] **1** the most important ship in a group of Navy ships, on which the ADMIRAL sails **2** [usually singular] a company's best and most important product, building, etc.

flag·stone /'flægstoʊn/ *n.* [C] a smooth flat piece of stone used for floors, paths, etc.

flail /fleɪl/ *v.* [I,T] to wave your arms and legs in a fast but uncontrolled way

flair /flɛr/ *n.* [singular, U] a natural ability to do something very well: *He **has a flair for** languages.*

> THESAURUS **skill, talent, ability, knack, gift, aptitude** → SKILL

flak /flæk/ *n.* [U] (informal) strong criticism: *She **got a lot of flak** for that decision.*

flake¹ /fleɪk/ *v.* [I] to break or come off in small thin pieces: *The paint on the door is starting to flake off.*

flake out *phr. v.* (spoken) to do something strange or to not do what you said you were going to do: *Kathy kind of flaked out on us today.*

flake² *n.* [C] **1** a small flat thin piece that breaks off of something: *The paint was coming off the door in flakes.* **2** (slang) someone who easily forgets things or who does strange things

flak·y /'fleɪki/ *adj.* **1** tending to break into small thin pieces: *rich, flaky croissants* **2** (slang) someone who is flaky easily forgets things or does strange things

flam·boy·ant /flæm'bɔɪənt/ *adj.* **1** behaving in a loud, confident, or exciting way that makes people notice you: *flamboyant gestures* **2** noticeable because of being brightly colored, expensive, big, etc.: *a flamboyant red sequined dress* [ORIGIN: 1800—1900 French, present participle of *flamboyer* "to flame"] —**flamboyance** *n.* [U]

flame /fleɪm/ *n.* [C,U] **1** hot bright burning gas that you see when something is on fire: *Flames poured out of the windows.* **2 in flames** burning strongly: *By the time the firemen arrived, the house was in flames.*

fla·men·co /flə'mɛŋkoʊ/ *n.* [C,U] a very fast and exciting Spanish dance, or the music for this dance [ORIGIN: 1800—1900 Spanish "person from Flanders;" in former times the people of Flanders wore bright clothes and were often thought to look like gypsy dancers]

flam·ing /'fleɪmɪŋ/ *adj.* [only before noun] **1** very bright: *flaming red hair* **2** burning strongly and brightly: *flaming torches*

flamingo

fla·min·go /flə'mɪŋgoʊ/ *n.* (plural **flamingos** *or* **flamingoes**) [C] a tall tropical water bird with long thin legs, pink feathers, and a long neck [ORIGIN: 1500—1600 Portuguese *flamengo*, from Provençal *flamenc* "flamingo, fire-bird"]

flam·ma·ble /'flæməbəl/ *adj.* something that is flammable burns very easily (ANT) **nonflammable**

THESAURUS

Flammable and **inflammable** both describe something that burns very easily, but people usually use **flammable**.
Nonflammable describes something that does not burn easily.

flank¹ /flæŋk/ *n.* [C] **1** the side of a person's or animal's body between the RIBS and the HIP **2** the side of an army in a battle: *The enemy attacked us on our left flank.*

flank² *v.* [T] to be on both sides of someone or something: *The President arrived, flanked by bodyguards.*

flan·nel /'flænl/ *n.* [U] soft light cotton or wool cloth that is used for making warm clothes: *a flannel shirt*

flap¹ /flæp/ *v.* (**flapped**, **flapping**) **1** [T] if a bird flaps its wings, it moves them up and down **2** [I] if a piece of cloth, paper, etc. flaps, it moves around quickly and makes a noise: *The ship's sails flapped in the wind.*

flap² *n.* [C] a thin flat piece of cloth, paper, skin, etc. that is attached by one end to a surface, which you can lift up easily: *the **flap of** the envelope*

flare¹ /flɛr/ *v.* **1** [I] *also* **flare up** to suddenly begin to burn very brightly: *The fire flared up again.* **2** [I] *also* **flare up** if strong feelings flare or flare up, people suddenly become angry, violent, etc.: ***Tempers flared** during the debate.* **3** [I] *also* **flare up** if a disease or illness flares up, it suddenly becomes worse: *My allergies are flaring up.* **4** [I,T] to become wider at the bottom edge, or to make something do this: *a skirt that **flares out***

flare² *n.* [C] a very bright light used outdoors as a signal to show people where you are, especially because you need help

'flare-up *n.* [C] **1** a situation in which someone suddenly becomes angry or violent **2** a situation in which someone suddenly has problems because of a disease or illness after not having any problems for a long time: *a flare-up of her arthritis*

flash¹ /flæʃ/ *v.* **1** [I,T] to suddenly shine brightly for a short time, or to make something shine in this way: *Lightning flashed overhead.* | *Why did that guy **flash** his headlights **at** me?*

THESAURUS **shine, flicker, twinkle, glow, sparkle, shimmer, gleam, glint, glisten** → SHINE¹

2 [I] to move very quickly: *An ambulance **flashed by/past**.* **3** [T] to show something to someone suddenly and for a short amount of time: *Sergeant Wicks flashed his badge.* **4** [I] **flash through sb's mind/head/brain** if images, thoughts, memories, etc. flash through your mind, you suddenly remember or think about them: *The possibility that he was lying flashed through my mind.* **5 flash a smile/glance/look etc.** to smile or look at someone quickly

flash² *n.* [C] **1** a sudden quick bright light: *a **flash of** lightning* **2** a bright light on a camera that you use when taking photographs indoors or when there is not much light: *Did the flash go off?* → CAMERA **3 in a flash** very quickly: *Wait right here. I'll be back in a flash.* **4 a flash in the pan** someone or something that is successful only for a very short time

flash·back /'flæʃbæk/ *n.* **1** [C,U] ENG. LANG. ARTS part of a movie, play, book, etc. that shows something that happened earlier **2** [C] a very sudden memory of a past event

flash·card /'flæʃkɑrd/ *n.* [C] a card with a word or picture on it, used in teaching

flash·er /'flæʃɚ/ *n.* [C] (informal) someone who shows his or her sex organs in public

'flash flood *n.* [C] a sudden flood that is caused by a lot of rain falling in a short period of time

flash·light /'flæʃlaɪt/ *n.* [C] a small electric light that you carry in your hand → *see picture at* LIGHT¹

flash·y /'flæʃi/ *adj.* very big, bright, or expensive: *a flashy new sports car*

flask /flæsk/ *n.* [C] **1** a small flat container used for carrying alcohol in your pocket **2** a glass bottle with a narrow top used by scientists

flat¹ /flæt/ *adj.* (comparative **flatter**, superlative **flattest**) **1** smooth and level, with no slopes or raised parts: *The highway stays flat for the next 50 miles.* | *a flat roof*

THESAURUS

level – a surface or area that is level does not slope in any direction, so that every part of it is at the same height: *Make sure the shelves are level.*
smooth – having an even surface, without any holes or raised areas: *Sand the wood until it is smooth.*

even – flat, level, and smooth: *Make sure that the floor is even before laying tiles.*
horizontal – a horizontal line, position, or surface is straight, flat, and not sloping: *horizontal layers of rock*

2 flat rate/fee etc. an amount of money that is paid and that does not increase or decrease: *They charge a flat rate for delivery.* **3** a tire that is flat does not have enough air inside it **4** a drink that is flat does not taste fresh because it has no more BUBBLEs of gas: *This Coke is completely flat.* **5 a flat refusal/denial etc.** a refusal, etc. that is definite and which someone will not change **6** ENG. LANG. ARTS a musical note that is flat is played or sung slightly lower than it should be, in a way that is unpleasant ➔ SHARP **7 E flat/B flat etc.** ENG. LANG. ARTS a musical note that is lower than E, B, etc. by a specific amount ➔ SHARP

flat² *adv.* **1** in a straight position or stretched against a flat surface: *The box can be folded flat for storage.* | *I have to* ***lie flat on*** *my* ***back*** *when I sleep.* **2 in 10 seconds/two minutes etc. flat** (informal) very quickly, in 10 seconds, two minutes, etc.: *I was out of the house in 10 minutes flat.* **3 fall flat** if a joke, story, etc. falls flat, it does not achieve the effect that is intended: *All of her jokes fell flat.* **4** ENG. LANG. ARTS if you sing or play music flat, you sing or play slightly lower than the correct note so that the sound is unpleasant ➔ SHARP **5 flat out** (informal) in a direct and complete way: *She* ***asked*** *him* ***flat out*** *if he was seeing another woman.*

flat³ *n.* [C] **1** (informal) a tire that does not have enough air inside it: *The car* ***has a flat.*** **2** ENG. LANG. ARTS a musical note that is one HALF STEP lower than a particular note ➔ SHARP **3 flats** [plural] a type of women's shoes with very low heels

ˌflat ˈcharacter *n.* [C] ENG. LANG. ARTS a character (=person) in a book, movie, etc. with only one or two features or qualities, who is not interesting and does not have an effect on the way the story develops ➔ ROUND CHARACTER

flat·ly /ˈflætli/ *adv.* **1** said in a definite way that is not likely to change: *They* ***flatly refused*** *to help me.* **2** without showing any emotion: *"It's hopeless," he said flatly.*

ˈflat screen *n.* [C] IT a very thin flat television or computer screen with a very sharp clear picture ➔ *see picture on page A19*

flat·ten /ˈflætˀn/ *v.* [I,T] to make something flat or to become flat: *The hills* ***flatten out*** *near the coast.*

flat·ter /ˈflæt̬ɚ/ *v.* [T] **1 be/feel flattered** to be pleased because someone has shown you that s/he likes or admires you: *When they asked me to come, I felt flattered.* **2** to say nice things about someone or show that you admire him or her, sometimes when you do not really mean it: *He always flatters my mom by praising her cooking.*

THESAURUS **praise, congratulate, compliment sb/pay sb a compliment, extol, commend** ➔ PRAISE¹

3 to make someone look as attractive as s/he can: *That dress really flatters your figure.* **4 flatter yourself** to believe that your abilities or achievements are better than they really are: *"I think you like me more than you'll admit." "Don't flatter yourself."* [ORIGIN: 1100—1200 Old French *flater* "to move the tongue against, flatter"] —**flatterer** *n.* [C] —**flattering** *adj.*

flat·ter·y /ˈflæt̬əri/ *n.* [U] nice things that you say about someone or something, but which you do not really mean: *Flattery will get you nowhere!* (=will not help you get what you want)

flat·u·lence /ˈflætʃələns/ *n.* [U] (formal) the condition of having too much gas in your stomach

flaunt /flɔnt, flɑnt/ *v.* [T] to deliberately show your money, success, beauty, etc. in order to make other people notice it: *Pam was flaunting a new diamond ring.*

fla·vor¹ /ˈfleɪvɚ/ *n.* **1** [C] the particular taste of a food or a drink: *Which flavor do you want – chocolate or vanilla?* | *The wine* ***has*** *a smoky* ***flavor.*** | *the strong* ***flavor of*** *the cheese* **2** [U] the quality of tasting good: *The meat was cooked exactly right and full of flavor.* **3** [singular] a small amount of a particular quality that shows what the typical qualities of something are: *His book* ***gives*** *us the* ***flavor of*** *life on a midwestern farm.*

flavor² *v.* [T] to give something a particular taste or more taste: *The sauce is flavored with herbs.*

fla·vored /ˈfleɪvɚd/ *adj.* **strawberry-flavored/chocolate-flavored etc.** tasting like a STRAWBERRY, chocolate, etc.: *almond-flavored cookies*

fla·vor·ing /ˈfleɪvərɪŋ/ *n.* [C,U] a substance used to give food or drink a particular flavor

flaw /flɔ/ *n.* [C] **1** a mark or weakness that makes something not perfect: *I could see a* ***flaw in*** *the glass.*

THESAURUS **defect, problem, bug, fault, imperfection** ➔ DEFECT¹

2 a mistake in an argument, plan, etc.: *There is a fundamental* ***flaw in*** *his argument.* **3** a bad part of someone's character

flawed /flɔd/ *adj.* spoiled by having mistakes, weaknesses, or damage: *The whole system is* ***deeply flawed.***

flaw·less /ˈflɔlɪs/ *adj.* perfect, with no mistakes, marks, or weaknesses SYN **perfect**: *Lena has flawless skin.* —**flawlessly** *adv.*

flea /fli/ *n.* [C] a very small jumping insect that bites animals to drink their blood

flea·bag /ˈflibæg/ *adj.* (informal) cheap and dirty: *a fleabag hotel*

ˈflea ˌmarket *n.* [C] a market, usually in the street, where old or used goods are sold

fleck /flɛk/ *n.* [C] a small mark or spot: *a black beard with* ***flecks of*** *gray*

flecked /flɛkt/ *adj.* having small marks or spots: *His jeans were* ***flecked with*** *white paint.*

fledg·ling /ˈflɛdʒlɪŋ/ *adj.* a fledgling country, organization, etc. is new and still developing: *a fledgling republic*

flee /fli/ *v.* (past tense and past participle **fled** /flɛd/) [I,T] to leave somewhere very quickly in order to escape from danger: *The president was forced to **flee the country**.*

THESAURUS **escape, get away, get out, break out, break free/break away, abscond** → ESCAPE[1]

fleece¹ /flis/ *n.* [C] **1** the wool of a sheep **2** an artificial soft material used for making warm coats —**fleecy** *adj.*

fleece² *v.* [T] (informal) to charge someone too much money for something, usually by tricking him/her

fleet /flit/ *n.* [C] **1** a group of ships, or all the ships in a navy **2** a group of vehicles that are controlled by one company: *a **fleet of** trucks*

fleet·ing /ˈflit̬ɪŋ/ *adj.* happening for only a moment: *a fleeting smile*

flesh¹ /flɛʃ/ *n.* [U] **1** the soft part of the body of a person or animal, between the skin and the bones: *a freshwater fish with firm white flesh* **2** the soft part of a fruit or vegetable that you eat → *see picture on page 414* **3 (see/meet sb) in the flesh** to see someone whom you previously had only seen in a picture, on television, or in a movie: *He's more handsome in the flesh than on television.* **4 your own flesh and blood** someone who is part of your family

flesh² *v.*

flesh sth ↔ **out** *phr. v.* to add more details to something: *You need to flesh out your essay with more examples.*

flesh·y /ˈflɛʃi/ *adj.* having a lot of flesh: *a round fleshy face*

flew /flu/ *v.* the past tense of FLY

flex /flɛks/ *v.* [T] to bend and move part of your body so that your muscles become tight

flex·i·ble /ˈflɛksəbəl/ (Ac) *adj.* **1** able to change easily (ANT) **inflexible**: *flexible working hours* | *Teachers have to be flexible.* **2** easy to bend: *flexible plastic* [ORIGIN: 1400—1500 Latin *flexibilis*, from *flexus*, past participle of *flectere* "to bend"] —**flexibility** /ˌflɛksəˈbɪlət̬i/ *n.* [U]: *You need some flexibility in how you deal with bad behavior.* | *Stretching improves your flexibility.*

flex·time /ˈflɛksˌtaɪm/ *n.* [U] a system in which people can change the times at which they start and finish working

flick¹ /flɪk/ *v.* **1** [T] to make something move by hitting or pushing it quickly, especially with your thumb and finger: *Barry **flicked** the ash **from** his cigarette.* → *see picture on page A21* **2** [I,T] to move with a quick sudden movement, or to make something move in this way: *She flicked her hair back from her face.* **3** [T] to press a SWITCH to start or stop electrical equipment: *He **flicked** the light **switch on**.*

flick² *n.* [C] **1** (spoken) a movie: *That was a great flick!* → MOVIE **2** a short sudden movement or hit with your hand, a whip, etc.

flick·er¹ /ˈflɪkɚ/ *v.* [I] **1** to burn or shine with an unsteady light: *flickering candles*

THESAURUS **shine, flash, twinkle, glow, sparkle, shimmer, gleam, glint, glisten** → SHINE[1]

2 (literary) if an emotion or expression flickers on someone's face, it appears for only a short time: *A look of anger **flickered across** Andrea's face.*

flicker² *n.* **1** [singular] an unsteady light that goes on and off quickly: *the **flicker of** the old gas lamp* **2 a flicker of interest/guilt etc.** a feeling or an expression on your face that only continues for a short time: *Not even a flicker of emotion showed on his face.*

fli·er /ˈflaɪɚ/ *n.* [C] a sheet of paper advertising something

THESAURUS **advertisement, commercial, billboard, poster, junk mail** → ADVERTISEMENT

flight /flaɪt/ *n.* **1** [C] a trip in an airplane or space vehicle, or the airplane or vehicle that is making the trip: *We **caught** the next **flight** home.* | *Our **flight leaves** in 20 minutes.* | *We almost **missed** our **flight**.* | *I'm coming in on Flight 255 from Chicago.* **2** [U] the act of flying through the air: *a bird **in flight*** **3** [C] a set of stairs between one floor and the next: *She fell down a whole **flight of stairs**.* **4** [U] the act of avoiding a difficult situation by leaving or escaping: *The movie ends with the family's **flight from** Austria in World War II.* [ORIGIN: Old English *flyht*]

ˈflight atˌtendant *n.* [C] someone who is responsible for the comfort and safety of the passengers on an airplane

ˈflight deck *n.* [C] the place where the pilot sits to control the airplane

flight·less /ˈflaɪtlɪs/ *adj.* a bird that is flightless is unable to fly

flight·y /ˈflaɪt̬i/ *adj.* someone who is flighty changes his/her ideas or activities a lot without finishing them or being serious about them

flim·sy /ˈflɪmzi/ *adj.* **1** flimsy clothing or material is thin, light, and does not cover much of the body: *a flimsy summer blouse* **2** weak and not made very well: *a flimsy table* **3** a flimsy argument, excuse, etc. does not seem very likely and people do not believe it: *The **evidence** against him is very **flimsy**.*

flinch /flɪntʃ/ *v.* [I] **1** to make a sudden small backward movement when you are hurt or afraid of something: *He raised his hand, and the child flinched.* **2** to avoid doing something because it is difficult or unpleasant: *He **never flinches from** the truth, no matter how painful.*

fling[1] /flɪŋ/ *v.* (past tense and past participle **flung** /flʌŋ/) [T] to throw or move something quickly with a lot of force: *She **flung** her coat **onto** the bed and sat down.* | *Val **flung** her arms **around** my neck.*

> THESAURUS **throw, toss, chuck, hurl, cast, pass, pitch, lob** → THROW[1]

fling[2] *n.* [C] a short and not very serious sexual relationship

flint /flɪnt/ *n.* [C,U] a type of very hard black or gray stone that makes a small flame when you strike it with steel

flip[1] /flɪp/ *v.* (**flipped**, **flipping**) **1** [I,T] to turn over quickly, or to make something turn over: *The vehicle **flipped over** several times.* | *Let's **flip a coin** to see who goes first.* **2** [T] to change the position of something: *You just **flip** a **switch** and the machine does everything for you.* **3** *also* **flip out** [I] (informal) to suddenly become very angry or upset, or start behaving in a crazy way: *Harry flipped out when he found out that I'd wrecked his motorcycle.*

flip through sth *phr. v.* to look at a book, magazine, etc. quickly

flip[2] *n.* [C] a movement in which you jump up and turn over in the air, so that your feet go over your head

flip[3] *adj.* (informal) FLIPPANT

ˈflip chart *n.* [C] large pieces of paper which are connected at the top so that you can turn the pages over to present information to groups of people

ˈflip-flop *n.* [C] (informal) an occasion when someone changes his/her decision —**flip-flop** *v.* [I]

flip·pant /ˈflɪpənt/ *adj.* not serious about something that other people think you should be serious about: *a flippant answer*

flip·per /ˈflɪpɚ/ *n.* [C] **1** a flat part on the body of some large sea animals, used for pushing themselves through water **2** a large flat rubber shoe that you use in order to help you swim faster

ˈflip side *n.* [singular] (informal) the bad effects of something that also has good effects: *The flip side is that the medicine may cause hair loss.*

flirt[1] /flɚt/ *v.* [I] to behave toward someone as though you are sexually attracted to him/her, but not in a very serious way: *He's always **flirting with** the women in the office.*

flirt with sth *phr. v.* **1** to consider doing something, but not be very serious about it: *I've been flirting with the idea of moving to Greece.* **2 flirt with danger/disaster etc.** to do something that might be dangerous or have a very bad effect

flirt[2] *n.* [C] someone who flirts: *Dave is such a flirt!*

flir·ta·tion /flɚˈteɪʃən/ *n.* **1** [U] behavior that shows you are sexually attracted to someone, but not in a serious way **2** [C] a short period of time during which you are interested in someone or something

flir·ta·tious /flɚˈteɪʃəs/ *adj.* behaving as if you are sexually attracted to someone, but not in a serious way

flit /flɪt/ *v.* (**flitted**, **flitting**) [I] to move quickly from one place to another, never staying long in any one place: *birds flitting from branch to branch*

float

float[1] /floʊt/ *v.* **1 a)** [I] to stay or move on the surface of a liquid without sinking: *Leaves were **floating on** the surface of the water.* | *Their raft was **floating away**.* **b)** [T] to put something on the surface of a liquid so that it does not sink: *Children were floating small boats on the lake.* **2** [I] to stay in the air or move slowly through the air: *I watched a balloon **float up** into the sky.* **3** [T] to suggest an idea or plan, especially in order to find out what people think about it: *Bob **floated** the **idea** in a recent meeting.* **4** [T] ECONOMICS to sell SHAREs in a company or business to the public for the first time [ORIGIN: Old English *flotian*]

float[2] *n.* [C] **1** a large vehicle that is decorated to be part of a PARADE **2** a SOFT DRINK that has ICE CREAM floating in it

flock[1] /flɑk/ *n.* [C] **1** a group of sheep, goats, or birds: *a **flock of** geese* **2** a large group of people of the same type

flock[2] *v.* [I] if people flock to a place, a lot of them go there: *People are **flocking to** that new Thai restaurant.*

flog /flɑg, flɔg/ *v.* (**flogged**, **flogging**) [T] to beat a person or animal with a whip or stick as a punishment —**flogging** *n.* [C]

flood[1] /flʌd/ *v.* **1** [I,T] to make a place become covered with water, or to become covered with water: *The river floods the valley every spring.* | *The basement flooded and everything got soaked.* **2** [I,T] to arrive or go somewhere in large numbers or amounts: *Offers of help came **flooding in**.* **3 be flooded with sth** to receive so many letters, complaints, etc. that you cannot deal with them all: *After the show, the station was flooded with calls from angry viewers.* **4 flood the market** ECONOMICS to sell something in very large quantities, so that the price goes down **5** [I] if a memory or a feeling floods back, you remember it very strongly

flood[2] *n.* [C] **1** a very large amount of water that covers an area that is usually dry: *The town was destroyed by floods.* **2** a very large number of things or people that arrive at the same time: *A **flood of lawsuits** followed the plane crash.* **3** EARTH SCIENCES a FLOOD TIDE

flood·gate /ˈflʌdgeɪt/ *n.* **open the floodgates** to suddenly make it possible for a lot of people to do something: *The case could open the floodgates for thousands of other similar claims.*

flood·ing /ˈflʌdɪŋ/ *n.* [U] a situation in which an area that is usually dry becomes covered with water: *The heavy rain has caused more flooding.*

flood·light /ˈflʌdlaɪt/ *n.* [C] a very bright light, used at night to light the outside of buildings, sports fields, etc.

flood·lit /ˈflʌdˌlɪt/ *adj.* lit by floodlights

ˈflood plain *n.* [C] EARTH SCIENCES a large area of flat land on either side of a river that becomes covered with water when the river is too full

ˈflood tide *n.* [C] EARTH SCIENCES the flow of the ocean toward the land, when the TIDE comes in → EBB TIDE

floor¹ /flɔr/ *n.* [C] **1** the surface that you stand on when you are inside a building: *the kitchen floor* | *She found her keys **on the floor**.*

THESAURUS ground, land, earth → GROUND¹

2 one of the levels in a building: *My office is **on the third floor**.* **3 ocean/forest/valley etc. floor** the ground at the bottom of the ocean or in a forest → *see picture at* PHOTIC **4 the floor a)** the part of a public or government building where people discuss things: *an argument on the Senate floor* **b)** the people attending a public meeting: *Are there any questions from the floor?* **5** an area in a room where people can dance: *couples on the **dance floor*** **6** an area in a building where a lot of people do their job: *the **factory floor*** [ORIGIN: Old English *flor*]

floor² *v.* [T] **1** to surprise or shock someone so much that s/he does not know what to say or do: *I was completely floored by his question.* **2** to make a car go as fast as possible

floor·board /ˈflɔrbɔrd/ *n.* [C] **1** a board in a wooden floor **2** the floor in a car

floorboards

floor·ing /ˈflɔrɪŋ/ *n.* [U] a material used to make or cover floors

ˈfloor-length *adj.* long enough to reach the floor: *a floor-length skirt*

ˈfloor plan *n.* [C] a drawing that shows the shape of a room or rooms in a building and the positions of things in it, as seen from above

floo·zy /ˈfluzi/ *n.* (plural **floozies**) [C] (informal, disapproving) a woman who has sexual relationships with a lot of different men

flop¹ /flɑp/ *v.* (**flopped**, **flopping**) [I] **1** to sit or fall down quickly, especially because you are tired: *Jan **flopped down** on the bed.* **2** (informal) if something such as a product, play, or plan flops, it is not successful: *The musical flopped after its first week on Broadway.*

flop² *n.* [C] **1** (informal) a film, play, plan, etc. that is not successful: *Her last movie was a flop.* **2** a heavy falling movement or the noise that it makes: *He fell with a flop into the water.*

flop·house /ˈflɑphaʊs/ *n.* [C] (slang) a cheap hotel, especially one that has many beds in one room

flop·py /ˈflɑpi/ *adj.* soft and hanging loosely down: *a floppy hat*

ˌfloppy ˈdisk *also* **floppy** *n.* [C] IT a small flat piece of plastic, used for storing information from a computer

flo·ra /ˈflɔrə/ *n.* [U] BIOLOGY all the plants that grow in a particular place → FAUNA [ORIGIN: 1500—1600 Modern Latin, Latin *Flora*, Roman female god of flowers, from *flos* "flower"]

flo·ral /ˈflɔrəl/ *adj.* made of flowers or decorated with flowers: *fabrics with floral patterns*

flor·id /ˈflɔrɪd, ˈflɑrɪd/ *adj.* **1** florid language, writing, or music, etc. has too much decoration or detail: *florid language* **2** (literary) skin that is florid is red: *florid cheeks*

flo·rist /ˈflɔrɪst, ˈflɑr-/ *n.* [C] someone who owns or works in a store that sells flowers

floss /flɔs, flɑs/ *v.* [I,T] to clean between your teeth with DENTAL FLOSS

flo·til·la /floʊˈtɪlə/ *n.* [C] a group of small ships [ORIGIN: 1700—1800 Spanish *flota* "group of ships"]

flounce /flaʊns/ *v.* [I] to walk in a way that shows you are angry: *She frowned and **flounced out** of the room.*

floun·der /ˈflaʊndɚ/ *v.* [I] **1** to not know what to say or do because you feel confused or upset: *She floundered helplessly, unable to answer his question.* **2** to have a lot of problems and be likely to fail completely: *The economy is floundering.* **3** to move awkwardly or with difficulty, especially in water, mud, etc.

flour /flaʊɚ/ *n.* [U] a powder made from grain, usually wheat, that is used for making bread, cakes, etc.

flour·ish¹ /ˈflɚɪʃ, ˈflʌrɪʃ/ *v.* [I] to grow or develop well: *The plants flourished in the warm sun.* | *His business is flourishing.* [ORIGIN: 1200—1300 Old French *florir* "to produce flowers," from Latin *flos* "flower"]

flourish² *n.* **with a flourish** with a large confident movement that makes people notice you: *He handed us his coat with a flourish.*

F

flout /flaʊt/ *v.* [T] (formal) to deliberately disobey a rule or law

THESAURUS **disobey, break a rule/law, rebel, defy, violate, infringe, contravene** → DISOBEY

flow¹ /floʊ/ *v.* [I] **1** if a liquid flows, it moves in a steady continuous stream: *The river flows past our cabin.*

THESAURUS **pour, drip, leak, ooze, gush, spurt, run, come out** → POUR

2 to move easily, smoothly, and continuously from one place to another: *The cars flowed in a steady stream.* **3 a)** if conversation or ideas flow, people talk or have ideas without being interrupted **b)** if the ideas or words of a speech or piece of writing flow, they seem to go well together and make sense: *If I change this paragraph, do you think it will flow better?* **4** if clothing, hair, etc. flows, it hangs loosely and gracefully: *Her hair flowed down over her shoulders.* [ORIGIN: Old English *flowan*]

flow² *n.* **1** [C usually singular] a smooth steady movement of liquid: *They tried to stop the **flow of** blood.* **2** [C usually singular] a continuous movement of something from one place to another: *the constant **flow of** traffic in the street* **3** [U] actions, words, or ideas that are produced continuously: *I had **interrupted the flow of** their conversation.* **4 go with the flow** (spoken) to do what is easiest in your situation, and not try to do something difficult → CASH FLOW

'flow chart *n.* [C] a drawing that uses shapes and ARROWS to show how a series of actions or parts of a system are connected with each other → *see picture at* CHART¹

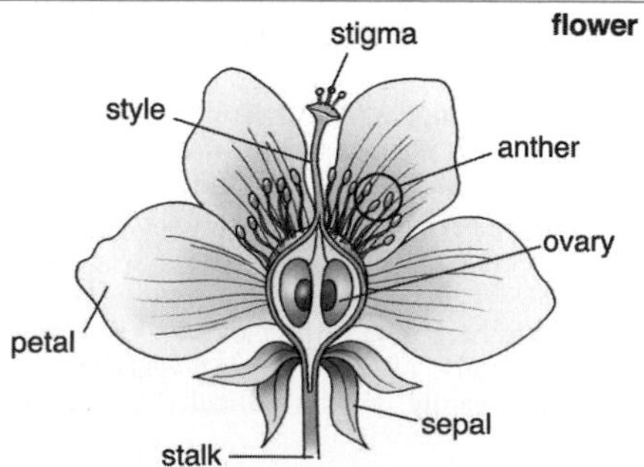

flow·er¹ /ˈflaʊɚ/ *n.* [C] **1** the colored part of a plant or tree that produces the seeds or fruit: *The tree has beautiful pink flowers in early spring.* → *see picture at* PLANT¹ **2** a small plant that produces beautiful flowers: *She's growing vegetables and flowers in the garden.* | *a **bouquet of flowers*** **3 in flower** a plant that is in flower has flowers on it [ORIGIN: 1100—1200 Old French *flor, flour*, from Latin *flos*]

flower² *v.* [I] to produce flowers

flow·er·bed /ˈflaʊɚˌbɛd/ *n.* [C] an area of ground in which flowers are grown

flow·ered /ˈflaʊɚd/ *adj.* decorated with pictures of flowers: *a flowered dress*

flow·er·pot /ˈflaʊɚˌpɑt/ *n.* [C] a pot in which you grow plants

flow·er·y /ˈflaʊəri/ *adj.* **1** decorated with pictures of flowers: *a flowery pattern* **2** flowery speech or writing uses complicated and unusual words instead of simple clear language

flown /floʊn/ *v.* the past participle of FLY

'flow ˌresource *n.* [C] EARTH SCIENCES a natural RESOURCE such as wind, light from the Sun, or flowing water, that must be used at the time or place that it exists

flu /flu/ *n.* [U] a common disease that is like a bad cold but is more serious: *Both of us have **had the flu** recently.* | *I was in bed **with the flu**.* | *She fell ill with **flu-like symptoms*** (=felt tired, had a sore throat, was coughing, etc.). | *a **flu bug/virus***

flub /flʌb/ *v.* (**flubbed**, **flubbing**) [I,T] (informal) to make a mistake or do something badly: *Several of the actors flubbed their lines.*

fluc·tu·ate /ˈflʌktʃuˌeɪt/ (Ac) *v.* [I] if a price or amount fluctuates, it keeps changing from a high level to a low one and back again: *Currency exchange rates fluctuate from day to day.* | *The price has **fluctuated between** $3 **and** $6 a share.* | *The temperature in the room **fluctuated wildly**.* [ORIGIN: 1600—1700 Latin *fluctuare*, from *fluere* "to flow"] —**fluctuation** /ˌflʌktʃuˈeɪʃən/ *n.* [C]: *fluctuations in oil prices*

flue /flu/ *n.* [C] a pipe through which smoke or heat from a fire can pass out of a building

flu·ent /ˈfluənt/ *adj.* able to speak or write a language very well: *Ted is **fluent in** French.* | *He spoke fluent English.* [ORIGIN: 1500—1600 Latin, present participle of *fluere* "to flow"] —**fluently** *adv.*: *She speaks Spanish fluently.* —**fluency** *n.* [U]

fluff¹ /flʌf/ *n.* [U] **1** small light pieces of waste wool, thread, etc. **2** (disapproving) news, music, writing, work, etc. that is not serious or important: *The movie is pure romantic fluff.* **3** very soft fur or feathers, especially from a young animal or bird

fluff² *also* **fluff up/out** *v.* [T] to make something soft appear larger by shaking or brushing it: *a bird fluffing out its feathers*

fluff·y /ˈflʌfi/ *adj.* made of or covered with something soft and light: *a fluffy kitten*

flu·id¹ /ˈfluɪd/ *n.* [C,U] a liquid: *My doctor told me to rest and drink plenty of fluids.*

fluid² *adj.* **1** fluid movements are smooth and graceful **2** a situation that is fluid is likely to change or is able to change —**fluidity** /fluˈɪdət̬i/ *n.* [U]

ˌfluid 'ounce (*written abbreviation* **fl oz**) *n.* [C] a unit for measuring liquid, equal to 1/16 of a PINT or 0.0296 liters

fluke /fluk/ *n.* [C] (informal) something that only happens because of chance or luck: *Their victory was a fluke.*

flung /flʌŋ/ *v.* the past tense and past participle of FLING

flunk /flʌŋk/ *v.* [I,T] (informal) to fail a test or course, or to give someone a low grade so s/he does this: *I flunked the history exam.* | *Mrs. Harris flunked me in English.*

flunk out *phr. v.* (informal) to be forced to leave a school or college because your work is not good enough: *Tim **flunked out of** Yale.*

flun·ky /ˈflʌŋki/ *n.* (plural **flunkies**) [C] (informal) someone who does the boring or physical work that someone else tells him or her to do

flu·o·res·cent /flʊˈrɛsənt, flɔ-/ *adj.* **1** a fluorescent light is a very bright electric light in the form of a tube **2** fluorescent colors shine very brightly [ORIGIN: 1800—1900 *fluorspar*, type of fluorescent mineral (18—21 centuries), from Modern Latin *fluor* "mineral used for melting," from Latin *fluere* "to flow"]

fluor·ide /ˈflɔraɪd/ *n.* [U] CHEMISTRY a chemical that helps to protect teeth against decay

fluor·ine /ˈflɔrin, ˈflʊr-/ *n.* [U] CHEMISTRY (*symbol* **F**) a chemical substance that is usually in the form of a poisonous gas. It is a chemical ELEMENT belonging to the HALOGEN group.

flur·ry /ˈflɚi, ˈflʌri/ *n.* (plural **flurries**) **1** [C usually singular] an occasion when there is suddenly a lot of activity for a short time: *His arrival produced a **flurry of** excitement.* **2** [C usually plural] an occasion when it snows for a short time: ***Snow flurries** are expected tonight.*

flush¹ /flʌʃ/ *v.* **1** [I,T] if a toilet flushes, or if you flush it, you make water go through it to clean it **2** [I] to become red in the face, especially because you are embarrassed or angry → FLUSHED: *Billy flushed and looked down.* **3** [T] *also* **flush out** to clean something by forcing water through it: *Drinking water helps flush out harmful substances from the body.*

flush² *n.* **1** [singular] the red color that appears on your face when you are embarrassed or angry **2 a flush of pride/embarrassment/happiness etc.** a sudden feeling of pride, embarrassment, etc.: *He felt a strong flush of pride as he watched his daughter on stage.*

flush³ *adj.* [not before noun] **1** if two surfaces are flush, they are at exactly the same level, so that the place where they meet is flat: *Is that cupboard **flush with** the wall?* **2** (informal) if someone is flush, s/he has plenty of money: *I'll buy dinner. I'm feeling flush right now.*

flushed /flʌʃt/ *adj.* **1** red in the face: *You look a little flushed.* **2 flushed with excitement/success** excited or pleased in a way that is easy to notice: *Jill ran in, flushed with excitement.*

flus·tered /ˈflʌstɚd/ *adj.* feeling nervous and confused: *Jay got flustered and forgot what he was supposed to say.*

flute /flut/ *n.* [C] a musical instrument shaped like a pipe that you play by holding it across your lips and blowing into it [ORIGIN: 1300—1400 Old French *flahute*, from Old Provençal *flaut*] → *see picture at* WOODWIND —**flutist** *n.* [C]

flut·ter /ˈflʌt̬ɚ/ *v.* **1** [I,T] if a bird or insect flutters, or flutters its wings, its wings move quickly and lightly up and down: *moths fluttering around the light* **2** [I] to wave or move gently in the air: *flags fluttering in the wind* **3** [I] if your heart or your stomach flutters, you feel very excited or nervous —**flutter** *n.* [singular]

flux /flʌks/ *n.* **be in (a state of) flux** to be changing a lot so that you cannot be sure what will happen: *The economy is in flux at the moment.*

fly¹ /flaɪ/ *v.* (past tense **flew** /flu/, past participle **flown** /floʊn/, third person singular **flies**)

1 THROUGH AIR [I,T] to move through the air, or to make something do this: *We watched the birds flying overhead.* | *He was flying a kite in the park.* | *The planes fly right over our house.*

2 TRAVEL [I] to travel by airplane: *Are you going to fly or drive?* | *Fran **flew to** Paris last week.*

3 AIRLINE [I,T] to use a particular AIRLINE or use a particular type of ticket when flying: *He usually flies first class.*

4 BE A PILOT [I,T] to be the pilot of an airplane: *Bill's learning to fly.*

5 SEND SB/STH BY AIRPLANE [T] to take goods or people somewhere by airplane: *Food and medicine are being **flown into** the area.*

6 MOVE [I] to suddenly move very quickly: *Timmy **flew down** the stairs and out the door.* | *The door suddenly **flew open**.*

7 TIME [I] (informal) if time flies, it seems to pass quickly: *Is it 5:30 already? Boy, time sure does fly!* | *Last week just **flew by**.*

8 fly off the handle (informal) to suddenly become angry for no good reason

9 FLAG [I,T] if a flag is flying, it is fixed to the top of a tall pole

fly² *n.* (plural **flies**) [C] **1** a common small flying insect with two wings: *There were flies all over the food.* **2** (informal) the part at the front of a pair of pants that you can open: *Your fly is unzipped.* **3** a hook that is made to look like a fly, used for catching fish

ˈfly-by-ˌnight *adj.* [only before noun] (informal, disapproving) a fly-by-night organization cannot be trusted and is not likely to exist very long: *fly-by-night operators who take your money and run*

fly·er /ˈflaɪɚ/ *n.* [C] a FLIER

fly·ing¹ /ˈflaɪ-ɪŋ/ *n.* [U] the activity of traveling by airplane or of being a pilot: *fear of flying*

flying² *adj.* **1** able to fly: *a type of flying insect* **2 with flying colors** if you pass a test with flying colors, you are very successful on it

ˌflying ˈsaucer *n.* [C] a space vehicle shaped like

a plate that some people believe carries creatures from another world (SYN) **UFO**

fly·swat·ter /ˈflaɪˌswɑt̬ɚ/ *n.* [C] a plastic square attached to a long handle, used for killing flies

FM *n.* [U] **frequency modulation** a system of broadcasting radio programs which produces a clear sound ➔ AM

foal /foʊl/ *n.* [C] a very young horse

foam[1] /foʊm/ *n.* [U] **1** a lot of very small BUBBLEs on the surface of something: *white foam on the tops of the waves* **2** a light solid substance filled with many very small BUBBLEs of air: *foam packing material* —**foamy** *adj.*

foam[2] *v.* [I] **1** to produce foam **2 foam at the mouth** to be very angry

ˌfoam ˈrubber *n.* [U] soft rubber full of air BUBBLEs that is used, for example, to fill PILLOWs

fo·cal point /ˈfoʊkəl ˌpɔɪnt/ *n.* [C] someone or something that you pay the most attention to: *Television has become* ***the focal point of*** *most American homes.*

F

fo·cus[1] /ˈfoʊkəs/ (Ac) *v.* [I,T] **1** to give all your attention to a particular thing: *In his speech he* ***focused on*** *the economy.* | *She tried to* ***focus*** *her* ***attention*** *on her work.* **2** to change the position of the LENS on a camera, TELESCOPE, etc. so you can see something clearly: *The telescopes are* ***focused on*** *a distant part of the galaxy.* ➔ CAMERA **3** if you focus your eyes, or if your eyes focus, you are able to see something clearly [ORIGIN: 1600—1700 Latin "hearth (=place for a fire in a house)"]

focus[2] (Ac) *n.* **1** [singular] the thing, person, situation, etc. that people pay special attention to: *He is the* ***focus of*** *intense media scrutiny.* | *She loves being* ***the focus of attention****.* **2** [U] special attention that you give to a particular person or subject: *Our main* ***focus*** *is* ***on*** *helping people get back to work.* **3 in focus/out of focus** if a photograph, camera, etc. is in focus, the edges of the things you see are clear; if it is out of focus, the edges are not clear

fo·cused (Ac) /ˈfoʊkəst/ *adj.* paying careful attention to what you are doing, in a way that shows you are determined to succeed: *You need to practice hard and stay focused.*

fod·der /ˈfɑdɚ/ *n.* [U] food for farm animals

foe /foʊ/ *n.* [C] (literary) an enemy

fog[1] /fɑg, fɔg/ *n.* [C,U] cloudy air near to the ground that is difficult for you to see through: *I could hardly see the road through* ***thick/heavy fog****.*

fog[2] *also* **fog up** *v.* (**fogged**, **fogging**) [I,T] if glass fogs or becomes fogged, it becomes covered with very small drops of water so you cannot see through it: *My glasses fogged up as soon as I stepped outside.*

fo·gey, **fogy** /ˈfoʊgi/ *n.* (plural **fogeys** *or* **fogies**) [C] (informal) someone who is old-fashioned and who does not like change: *Don't be such an* ***old fogey****.*

fog·gy /ˈfɑgi, ˈfɔgi/ *adj.* (comparative **foggier**, superlative **foggiest**) **1** not clear because of FOG: *a foggy morning* **2 I don't have the foggiest (idea)** (spoken, old-fashioned) said in order to emphasize that you do not know something: *I don't have the foggiest idea what his address is.*

fog·horn /ˈfɑghɔrn, ˈfɔg-/ *n.* [C] a loud horn used by ships in a FOG to warn other ships of their position

foi·ble /ˈfɔɪbəl/ *n.* [C] (formal) a habit that someone has that is slightly strange or silly

foil[1] /fɔɪl/ *n.* [U] metal sheets that are thin like paper, used for wrapping food: *Cover the pan tightly with* ***aluminum foil****.*

foil[2] *v.* [T] if you foil someone's plans, you stop him/her from doing something

foist /fɔɪst/ *v.*

foist sth **on/upon** sb *phr. v.* to make someone accept something that s/he does not want: *Marie is always trying to foist her religious beliefs on everyone.*

fold

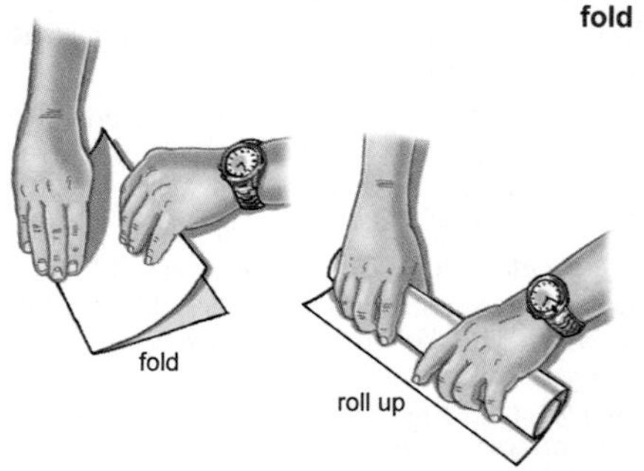

fold

roll up

fold[1] /foʊld/ *v.* **1** [T] to bend a piece of paper, cloth, etc. so that one part covers another part: *She folded her clothes and put them on a chair.* | ***Fold*** *the paper* ***in half*** (=fold it across the middle). **2** [I,T] to make something, for example a table or chair, smaller by bending it or closing it, so that it can be stored: *Be sure to fold up the ironing board when you're finished.* **3 fold your arms** to bend your arms so they are resting across your chest: *George stood silently with his arms folded.* **4** [I] if a business folds, it fails and is not able to continue [ORIGIN: Old English *fealdan*]

fold sth **in** *phr. v.* to gently mix another substance into a mixture when you are preparing food

fold[2] *n.* **1** [C] a line made in paper, cloth, etc. when you fold one part of it over another: *Bend the card and cut along the fold.* **2** [C usually plural] the folds in material, skin, etc. are the loose parts that hang over other parts of it: *She adjusted the folds of her dress.* **3 the fold** the group of people you belong to or have the same beliefs as: *The church will welcome him* ***back to the fold****.* **4** [C] a small area where sheep are kept for safety

fold·er /ˈfoʊldɚ/ *n.* [C] **1** a large folded piece of hard paper, in which you keep loose papers **2** a picture on a computer screen that shows you where a FILE is kept

fo·li·age /ˈfoʊliɪdʒ/ *n.* [U] BIOLOGY the leaves of a plant

folk[1] /foʊk/ *adj.* [only before noun] ENG. LANG. ARTS folk music, art, dancing, etc. is traditional and typical of the ordinary people who live in a particular area [ORIGIN: Old English *folc*]

folk[2] *n.* **1 sb's folks** your parents or family: *I need to call my folks sometime this weekend.* **2 folks** [plural] (spoken) said when you are talking to a group of people in a friendly way: *That's all for now, folks.* **3 folks** [plural] (informal) people: *Most folks around here are very friendly.* **4** [U] ENG. LANG. ARTS folk music

folk·lore /ˈfoʊk-lɔr/ *n.* [U] ENG. LANG. ARTS the traditional stories, CUSTOMs, etc. of the ordinary people of a particular area

ˈfolk ˌmusic *n.* [U] ENG. LANG. ARTS traditional music that is played by the ordinary people of a particular area

folk·sy /ˈfoʊksi/ *adj.* (informal) friendly and informal: *The town has a certain folksy charm.*

ˈfolk tale *n.* [C] ENG. LANG. ARTS a traditional spoken story from a particular area that is passed on by adults telling it to children. Folk tales usually form part of a particular society's CULTURE (=customs, beliefs, and way of life).

fol·li·cle /ˈfɑlɪkəl/ *n.* [C] **1** BIOLOGY one of the small holes in the skin that hair grows from. A follicle consists of a group of cells. **2** BIOLOGY a space that forms around an egg and the surrounding cells when the egg is developing inside a female's body [ORIGIN: 1400—1500 Modern Latin *folliculus*, from Latin *follis* "bag"]

fol·low /ˈfɑloʊ/ *v.*

1 COME BEHIND [I,T] to walk, drive, etc. behind or after someone else: *If you follow me, I'll show you to your room.* | *The president came in,* ***followed by*** *a crowd of photographers.* | *You go ahead – I'll follow later.*

2 IN ORDER TO WATCH SB [T] to go closely behind someone else in order to find out where s/he is going: *Marlowe looked over his shoulder to make sure no one was following him.*

THESAURUS

chase – to quickly follow someone or something in order to catch him, her, or it: *Police chased the thief down the street.*

pursue (formal) – to chase or follow someone or something in order to catch him, her, or it: *We ran faster, but he continued to pursue us.*

run after – to chase someone or something: *She started to leave, and Smith ran after her.*

tail (informal) – to secretly watch and follow someone such as a criminal: *Police have been tailing him.*

track – to search for a person or animal by following a smell or marks on the ground: *The police used dogs to track the missing girl.*

stalk – to follow a person or animal quietly in order to catch, attack, or kill him, her, or it: *a tiger stalking its prey*

3 HAPPEN AFTER [I,T] to happen or come immediately after something else: *There was a shout from the garage* ***followed by*** *a loud crash.* | *In the days that followed, Angie tried to forget about Sam.*

4 follow the instructions/rules/advice etc. to do something according to how the instructions, rules, etc. say it should be done: *Did you follow the instructions on the box?*

5 follow suit to do the same thing as someone else, after s/he has done it: *He praised Kim and encouraged others to* ***follow suit***. | *When Allied Stores reduced prices, other companies were forced to* ***follow suit***.

6 follow (in) sb's footsteps to do the same job that someone else did before you: *Toshi followed in his father's footsteps and started his own business.*

7 BE INTERESTED [T] to be interested in something, especially a sport, and pay attention to it: *Do you follow baseball at all?*

8 as follows used in order to introduce a list of names, instructions, etc.: *The winners are as follows: first place, Tony Gwynn; second place, ...*

9 UNDERSTAND [I,T] (spoken) to understand something such as an explanation or story: *Sorry, I* ***don't follow you***.

10 it follows that used in order to show that something must be true as a result of something else that is true: *If interest rates come down, it follows that more people will borrow money.*

11 GO IN A DIRECTION [T] to continue on a road or path, or go in the same direction as a river: *The road follows the river for the next six miles.*

12 BELIEVE/OBEY [T] to believe in or obey a particular set of religious or political ideas: *They still* ***follow*** *the* ***teachings*** *of Gandhi.* [ORIGIN: Old English *folgian*]

follow sb **around** *phr. v.*
to keep following someone everywhere s/he goes: *My little brother is always following me around.*

follow sth ↔ **through** *phr. v.*
to do what needs to be done to complete something or make it successful: *Harry was trained as an actor, but he never followed through with it.*

follow sth ↔ **up** *phr. v.*
to find out more about something, or to do more about something: *Did Jay ever* ***follow up on*** *that job possibility in Tucson?*

fol·low·er /ˈfɑloʊɚ/ *n.* [C] someone who believes in or supports a particular leader or set of ideas: *the early* ***followers of*** *Buddha*

fol·low·ing[1] /ˈfɑloʊɪŋ/ *adj.* **the following day/year/chapter etc.** the day, year, etc. after the one you have just mentioned: *Neil arrived on Friday, and his wife came the following day.*

THESAURUS **next, subsequent, succeeding, later, ensuing** → NEXT[1]

following[2] *n.* **1** [singular] a group of people who support or admire someone such as a performer:

The band has a big following in Europe. **2 the following** the people or things that you are going to mention next: *To open an account, you will need the following: ID, proof of residency and a minimum deposit of $50.*

following³ *prep.* immediately after: *There will be time for questions following the lecture.*

'follow-up *n.* **1** [C] a book, movie, article, etc. that comes after another one that has the same subject or characters: *The studio is planning to do a follow-up next year.* | *a* ***follow-up to*** *their successful first album* **2** [C,U] something that is done to make sure that earlier actions have been successful or effective —**follow-up** *adj.* [only before noun]

fol·ly /'fɑli/ *n.* (plural **follies**) [C,U] (formal) a very stupid thing to do: ***It would be*** *sheer* ***folly to*** *buy another car at this point.*

fo·ment /'foʊmɛnt, foʊ'mɛnt/ *v.* **foment war/revolution/trouble etc.** (formal) to do something that encourages people to cause a lot of trouble in a society

F

fond /fɑnd/ *adj.* **1 be fond of sb/sth** to like someone or something very much: *Mrs. Winters is very fond of her grandchildren.* **2 fond memories** memories that make you happy when you think of them: *Marie still* ***had fond memories of*** *their time together.* **3 be fond of doing sth** to enjoy doing something, and to do it often: *Dad is very fond of telling that story.* **4** [only before noun] a fond look, smile, action, etc. shows that you like someone very much: *As we left, we said a* ***fond farewell.*** —**fondness** *n.* [U]

fon·dle /'fɑndl/ *v.* [T] to gently touch and move your fingers over part of someone's body in a way that shows love or sexual desire

fond·ly /'fɑndli/ *adv.* **1** in a way that shows you like someone or something very much: *Greta smiled fondly at him from across the room.* **2 fondly remember/recall** to feel happy when you remember what you liked about a person or place: *That trip is still fondly remembered by all of us.*

font /fɑnt/ *n.* [C] **1** a set of printed letters that is a particular size and shape **2** a stone container in a church that holds the water used for the ceremony of BAPTISM

food /fud/ *n.* **1** [C,U] things that people and animals eat, such as vegetables or meat → FAST FOOD, HEALTH FOOD, JUNK FOOD: *I love Chinese food.* | *We didn't have enough food for everyone.* | *the frozen foods section of the supermarket*

COLLOCATIONS

fresh – recently picked or prepared, and not dried, put in cans, or frozen
stale – used about bread or cake that is not good any more because it has become hard and dry
sour – used about milk or cream that tastes and smells bad and is not good any more
frozen – packed and stored at very low temperatures
canned – stored and sold in cans
processed – processed food has chemicals in it to make it last longer
organic – produced without using harmful chemicals
vegetarian – containing no meat or fish
nutritious/nourishing/wholesome – good for your health

2 food for thought something that makes you think carefully about something: *The teacher's advice certainly* ***gave me food for thought.*** [ORIGIN: Old English *foda*]

'food bank *n.* [C] a place that gives food to people who need it

'food chain *n.* [singular] BIOLOGY animals and plants considered as a group in which one animal is eaten by another animal, which is eaten by another, etc.

'food ˌpoisoning *n.* [U] an illness caused by eating food that contains harmful BACTERIA

'food ˌprocessor *n.* [C] a piece of electrical equipment for preparing food, that cuts or mixes it very quickly

'food stamp *n.* [C usually plural] an official piece of paper, given by the government to poor people, that can be used instead of money to buy food

food·stuff /'fudstʌf/ *n.* [C usually plural] food – used especially when talking about the business of producing or selling food

'food web *n.* [C] BIOLOGY all the connected and dependent FOOD CHAINS in a particular place

fool¹ /ful/ *n.* [C] **1** a stupid person: ***I felt like a fool,*** *locking my keys in the car like that.* **2 make a fool of yourself** to do something stupid that you feel embarrassed about later: *Sorry if I made a fool of myself last night. I was drunk.* **3 make a fool of sb** to deliberately try to make someone seem stupid: *She made a fool of me in front of all the other students.* [ORIGIN: 1200—1300 Old French *fol*, from Latin *follis* "bag for blowing air"]

fool² *v.* **1** [T] to trick or deceive someone: *Don't* ***be fooled into*** *buying more insurance than you need.* **2 you could have fooled me** (spoken) said when you do not believe what someone has told you: *"Look, we're doing our best to fix it." "Well, you could have fooled me."* **3 be fooling yourself** to try to make yourself believe something that you know is not really true: *You're fooling yourself if you think he's going to come back to you.*

fool around *phr. v.* **1** to waste time behaving in a silly way or doing things that are not important: *Stop fooling around and start studying!* **2** to behave in a way which is careless and not responsible: *Stop* ***fooling around with*** *those scissors before someone gets hurt.* **3** to have a sexual relationship with someone else, especially when you should not

fool with sb/sth *phr. v.* (informal) to touch or play with something in a careless way: *Don't fool with that control panel unless you know what you're doing.*

fool·har·dy /'ful,hardi/ *adj.* taking risks that are not necessary

fool·ish /'fulɪʃ/ *adj.* not sensible or wise: *It was a very foolish thing to do.* | *a foolish woman* —**foolishly** *adv.*: *I foolishly agreed to go with them.* —**foolishness** *n.* [U]

fool·proof /'fulpruf/ *adj.* a foolproof plan, method, etc. is certain to be successful

foot¹ /fʊt/ *n.* [C]
1 BODY PART (plural **feet** /fit/) the part of your body that you stand on and walk on: *Turner kicks with his* ***left/right foot.*** | *He always walks around* ***in bare feet*** (=without shoes and socks). ➔ *see picture on page A16*
2 MEASUREMENT (plural **feet** *or* **foot**) (*written abbreviation* **ft.**) a unit for measuring length, equal to 12 INCHES or 0.3048 meters
3 on foot if you go somewhere on foot, you walk there: *We set out to explore the city on foot.*
4 the foot of sth the lowest part of something such as a mountain or tree, or the end of something such as a bed
5 on your feet a) to be standing for a long time without sitting down: *Waitresses are on their feet all day.* **b)** to be healthy again after being sick: *It's good to see you on your feet again!*
6 off your feet sitting or lying down, rather than standing or walking: *The doctor told me to stay off my feet for a few days.*
7 get/rise/jump etc. to your feet to stand up after you have been sitting: *The fans cheered and rose to their feet.*
8 set foot in sth to go into a place: *If that woman ever sets foot in this house, I'm leaving!*
9 put your foot down a) to say very firmly what someone must do or not do: *Brett didn't want to go to the doctor, but Dad put his foot down.* **b)** to make a car go faster
10 put your feet up to relax and rest, especially by having your feet supported on something
11 put your foot in your mouth to accidentally say something that embarrasses or upsets someone
12 have/keep both feet on the ground to be sensible and practical in the way you live your life
13 get your foot in the door to get your first opportunity to work in a particular organization or industry
14 have one foot in the grave (humorous) to be old
15 ON SEA/LAND ANIMAL BIOLOGY a muscle used to move forward, found on the lower part of a sea or land animal that has a soft body covered by a hard shell
16 POETRY ENG. LANG. ARTS a part of a line of poetry in which there is one strong BEAT and one or two weaker ones, to give the line a RHYTHM ➔ IAMB, ANAPEST, DACTYL, TROCHEE, SPONDEE
17 -footed having a particular number or type of feet: *a four-footed animal* | *a flat-footed man*
18 -footer being a particular number of feet in length: *Our sailboat's a twenty-footer.* [ORIGIN: Old English *fot*]

foot² *v.* **foot the bill** (informal) to pay for something: *Her father is footing the bill for flying lessons.*

foot·age /'fʊṭɪdʒ/ *n.* [U] film that shows a particular event: *black-and-white footage of the 1936 Olympics*

foot·ball /'fʊt˺bɔl/ *n.* **1** [U] a game in which two teams of 11 players carry, kick, or throw a ball into an area at the end of a field to win points: *a football game* ➔ *see picture on page A17* **2** [C] the ball used in this game

foot·bridge /'fʊt,brɪdʒ/ *n.* [C] a narrow bridge for people to walk over

foot·fall /'fʊtfɔl/ *n.* [C,U] (literary) the sound of each step when someone is walking (SYN) **footstep**

foot·hill /'fʊt,hɪl/ *n.* [C usually plural] EARTH SCIENCES one of the low hills at the bottom of a group of mountains: *the foothills of the Rockies* ➔ *see picture on page A24*

foot·hold /'fʊthoʊld/ *n.* [C] **1** a position from which you can start trying to get what you want: *The Republicans* ***gained a foothold*** *during the last elections.* **2** a space where you can safely put your foot when climbing a rock

foot·ing /'fʊṭɪŋ/ *n.* [singular] **1** the conditions or arrangements under which something exists or operates: *Most of all, the city needs to get on a* ***firm financial footing.*** | *The new rules will allow candidates to compete* ***on an equal footing*** (=with the same advantages and disadvantages). **2** a firm hold with your feet on a surface: *He* ***lost his footing*** *and fell down the stairs.*

foot·lights /'fʊtlaɪts/ *n.* [plural] a row of lights along the front of the stage in a theater

'foot ,locker *n.* [C] a large strong box that you keep your things in

foot·loose /'fʊtlus/ *adj.* able to do what you want and enjoy yourself because you are not responsible for anyone or anything: *No, I'm not married – still* ***footloose and fancy free.***

foot·note /'fʊt˺noʊt/ *n.* [C] ENG. LANG. ARTS a note in a book at the bottom of a page, which gives more information about something on that page

foot·path /'fʊtpæθ/ *n.* [C] a TRAIL

foot·print /'fʊt,prɪnt/ *n.* [C] a mark made by a foot or shoe: *a deer's footprints in the snow* ➔ *see picture at* FINGERPRINT

foot·rest /'fʊt˺rɛst/ *n.* [C] a part of a chair that you can raise or lower in order to support your feet when you are sitting down

foot·sie /'fʊtsi/ *n.* **play footsie (with sb)** (informal) to secretly touch someone's feet with your feet under a table, to show that you think s/he is sexually attractive

foot·step /'fʊtstɛp/ *n.* [C] the sound of each step

F

when someone is walking: *He heard someone's footsteps in the hall.* → **follow (in) sb's footsteps** *at* FOLLOW

foot·stool /ˈfʊtstul/ *n.* [C] a low piece of furniture used for supporting your feet when you are sitting down

foot·wear /ˈfʊt˺wɛr/ *n.* [U] things you wear on your feet, such as shoes or boots

foot·work /ˈfʊt˺wɚk/ *n.* [U] skillful use of your feet when dancing or playing a sport: *the dancer's **fancy footwork***

for¹ /fɚ; *strong* fɔr/ *prep.* **1** intended to be given to or used by a particular person or group: *Save a piece of cake for Noah.* | *Somebody left a message for you.* | *We made cookies for the party.* **2** used in order to show the purpose of an object, action, etc.: *a knife for cutting bread* | ***What** did you **do** that **for**?* (=why did you do it?) | ***What's** this gadget **for**?* (=what is its purpose) **3 for sale/rent** used in order to show that something is available to be sold or rented: *They've just put their house up for sale.* **4** in order to get or do something: *Alison is looking for a job.* | *We were waiting for the bus.* | *Let's **go for** a walk.* | ***For more information**, write to this address.*

THESAURUS in order to, to, so (that) → ORDER¹

5 used in order to show the time when something is planned to happen: *an appointment for 3:00* | ***It's time for** dinner* (=we're going to have dinner now). **6** in order to help someone: *Let me lift that box for you.* | ***What can I do for you?*** (=can I help you) **7** used in order to talk about a particular length of time: *I've known Kim for a long time.* | *Bake the cake for 40 minutes.* **8** because of or as a result of: *I got a ticket for going through a red light.* | *The award for the highest sales goes to Pete McGregor.* **9** used in order to show where a person, vehicle, etc. is going: *The plane for Las Vegas took off an hour late.* | *I was just leaving for church when the phone rang.* **10** used in order to express a distance: *We walked for miles.* **11** used in order to show a price or amount: *a check for $100* | *an order for 200 copies* | *I'm not working **for nothing/for free*** (=without being paid). **12 for breakfast/lunch/dinner** used in order to say what you ate or will eat at breakfast, LUNCH, etc.: ***"What's for lunch?"*** *"Hamburgers."* | *We **had** steak **for dinner** last night.* **13 for sb/sth to do sth** used when discussing what is happening, what may happen, or what can happen: *It's unusual **for** it **to** be this cold in June.* | *The plan is **for** us **to** leave on Friday morning and pick up Joe.* **14** if you are happy, sad, etc. for someone, you feel happy, sad, etc. because something has happened to him or her: *I'm really happy for you.* **15 for now** used in order to say that a situation can be changed later: *Just put the pictures in a box for now.* **16 work for/play for etc.** to work at a particular company, play a sport on a particular team, etc.: *She worked for Exxon until last year.* | *He plays for the Boston Red Sox.* **17** supporting or agreeing with someone or something: *How many people voted for Mulhoney?* | *I'm for getting a pizza, what about you?* **18 for all a)** considering how little: *For all the good I did, I shouldn't have tried to help.* **b)** in spite of: *For all his expensive education, Leo doesn't know very much.* **19 for all I know/care** (spoken) used in order to say that you really do not know or care: *He could be in Canada by now for all I know.* **20 for Christmas/for sb's birthday etc.** in order to celebrate Christmas, someone's BIRTHDAY, etc.: *What did you get for your birthday?* | *We went to my grandmother's for Thanksgiving last year.* **21** having the same meaning as another word, sign, etc.: *What's the Spanish word for oil?* **22** when you consider a particular fact: *Libby's very tall for her age.* **23 if it hadn't been for/if it weren't for sb/sth** if something had not happened, or if a situation were different: *If it weren't for Michelle's help, we'd never get this job done.*

for² *conjunction* (literary) because

for·age /ˈfɔrɪdʒ, ˈfɑr-/ *v.* [I] to go to a lot of places searching for food or other supplies: *animals **foraging for** food*

for·ay /ˈfɔreɪ, ˈfɑreɪ/ *n.* [C] **1** a short attempt at doing a particular job or activity: *a brief **foray into** politics* **2** a short sudden attack by a group of soldiers

for·bade /fɚˈbæd/ *v.* the past tense of FORBID

for·bear·ance /fɔrˈbɛrəns, fɚ-/ *n.* [U] (literary) the quality of being patient, having control over your emotions, and being willing to forgive someone

for·bid /fɚˈbɪd/ *v.* (past tense **forbade** /-ˈbæd/, past participle **forbidden** /-ˈbɪdn/, present participle **forbidding**) [T] **1** to order someone not to do something: *I **forbid** you **to** see that man again.*

THESAURUS

not allow/permit/let – to say that someone must not do something, and stop him/her doing it: *People are not allowed to sell food or drinks along the parade route.*
ban – to officially say that people must not do something or that something is not allowed: *The country's government has banned foreign journalists from the area.*
prohibit – to say officially that an action is illegal or not allowed: *Selling alcohol to people under 21 is prohibited.*
bar – to officially prevent someone from doing something: *During the drought, residents were barred from watering their lawns.*
proscribe (formal) – to officially stop the existence or use of something: *The laws proscribe child labor.*

2 God/Heaven forbid (spoken) said in order to emphasize that you hope that something will not happen: *God forbid you should have an accident.* [ORIGIN: Old English *forbeodan*]

for·bid·den /fɚˈbɪdn/ *adj.* not allowed, especially because of an official rule: ***It's forbidden to***

smoke in the hospital. | *This area is* ***forbidden to*** *everyone but the police.*

for·bid·ding /fɚˈbɪdɪŋ/ *adj.* looking frightening, unfriendly, or dangerous: *The mountains looked more forbidding as we got closer.*

force[1] /fɔrs/ *n.*

1 TRAINED GROUP [C] a group of people who have been trained to do military or police work → ARMED FORCES, AIR FORCE, POLICE FORCE: *Rebel forces are seeking to overthrow the government* | *A multinational* ***military force*** *will be sent to the region.*

2 VIOLENT ACTION [U] violent physical action used in order to achieve something: *The police* ***used force*** *to break up the demonstration.* | *an investigation into the excessive* ***use of force***

3 NATURAL POWER **a)** [U] the natural power that is used or produced when one thing moves or hits another thing: *Waves were hitting the rocks* ***with great force.*** | *The* ***force of*** *the explosion threw her backwards.* **b)** [C,U] PHYSICS a natural power that produces movement in another object: *the* ***force of*** *gravity*

THESAURUS

power – the physical strength of something such as an explosion, or the energy produced by a natural force: *wind power* | *Their home is heated by solar power.*
strength – the physical quality that makes you strong: *I don't have the strength to lift this.*

4 SB/STH THAT INFLUENCES [C] someone or something that has a strong influence or a lot of power: *Mandela was the* ***driving force*** *behind the changes* (=the one who made them happen). | *Technology can be a* ***force for*** *good* (=it can make good things happen).

5 STRONG EFFECT [U] the powerful effect of someone or something: *The* ***force of*** *public opinion stopped the new highway project.*

6 join/combine forces to work together to do something: *Various community groups have joined forces on the project.*

7 in force a) if a law or rule is in force, it must be obeyed **b)** in a large group: *The mosquitoes are going to be* ***out in force*** *tonight!*

8 by/from force of habit because you have always done a particular thing: *Ken puts salt on everything by force of habit.*

force[2] *v.* [T] **1** to cause someone to do something s/he does not want to do: *Nobody's* ***forcing*** *you* ***to*** *come, you know.* | *I had to* ***force myself*** *to get up this morning.* | *Bad health* ***forced*** *him* ***into*** *early retirement.*

THESAURUS

make – to force someone to do something: *I wish there were something I could do to make her quit smoking.*
coerce (formal) – to force someone to do something by threatening him/her: *Her parents tried to coerce her into an arranged marriage.*
compel – to force someone to do something: *The resulting scandal compelled her to resign.*
impel (formal) – to make you feel very strongly that you must do something: *I felt impelled to find out more.*
pressure – to try to make someone do something by using influence, arguments, threats, etc.: *Don't let them pressure you into making a donation.*

2 to use physical strength to move something or go somewhere: *Firefighters had to* ***force open*** *the door* (=open it using force). | *The doctor* ***forced*** *his* ***way through*** *the crowd.* **3 force the issue** to do something that makes it necessary for someone to make decisions or take action: *Don't force the issue; give them time to decide.*

force sth **on/upon** sb *phr. v.* to make someone accept something even though s/he does not want it: *They tried to force their own views on me.*

forced /fɔrst/ *adj.* **1** done because you must do something, not because of any sincere feeling: *a forced smile* **2** [only before noun] done suddenly and quickly because a situation makes it necessary: *The plane had to make a forced landing in a field.*

ˈforce-feed *v.* (past tense and past participle **force-fed**) [T] to force someone to eat by putting food or liquid down his/her throat

force·ful /ˈfɔrsfəl/ *adj.* powerful and strong: *a forceful personality* | *a forceful argument* —**forcefully** *adv.*

for·ceps /ˈfɔrsəps, -sɛps/ *n.* [plural] a medical tool used for picking up, holding, or pulling things

forc·i·ble /ˈfɔrsəbəl/ *adj.* done using physical force: *There aren't any signs of* ***forcible entry*** *into the building.* —**forcibly** *adv.*: *The demonstrators were forcibly removed from the embassy.*

ford[1] /fɔrd/ *n.* [C] EARTH SCIENCES a place in a river that is not deep, so that you can walk or drive across it

ford[2] *v.* [T] to walk or drive across a river at a place where it is not too deep

fore /fɔr/ *n.* **come to the fore** to become important or begin to have influence: *Environmental issues came to the fore in the 1980s.*

fore·arm /ˈfɔrɑrm/ *n.* [C] the lower part of the arm between the hand and the elbow

fore·bear /ˈfɔrbɛr/ *n.* [C usually plural] (formal) someone who was part of your family a long time ago SYN **ancestor**

fore·bod·ing /fɔrˈboʊdɪŋ/ *n.* [C,U] a feeling that something bad will happen soon: *We waited for news of the men with a* ***sense of foreboding.***

fore·cast[1] /ˈfɔrkæst/ *n.* [C] a description of what is likely to happen in the future, based on information you have now: *the* ***weather forecast*** | *the company's* ***sales forecast***

forecast[2] *v.* (past tense and past participle **forecast** *or* **forecasted**) [T] to say what is likely to happen in the future, based on information you have now:

Warm weather has been forecast for this weekend. —**forecaster** *n.* [C]: *a weather forecaster* | *a stock market forecaster*

THESAURUS predict, prophesy, foretell, foresee, have a premonition ➔ PREDICT

fore·close /fɔr'kloʊz/ *v.* [I] ECONOMICS to take away someone's property because s/he cannot pay back the money that s/he has borrowed to buy it —**foreclosure** /fɔr'kloʊʒɚ/ *n.* [C,U]

fore·fa·ther /'fɔr,fɑðɚz/ *n.* [C usually plural] someone who was part of your family a long time ago (SYN) **ancestor**

fore·fin·ger /'fɔr,fɪŋgɚ/ *n.* [C] the finger next to your thumb (SYN) **index finger**

fore·front /'fɔrfrʌnt/ *n.* **in/at/to the forefront of sth** in the main or most important position: *The company has always been at the forefront of science and technology.*

fore·gone con·clu·sion /,fɔrgɔn kən'kluʒən/ *n.* **be a foregone conclusion** if something is a foregone conclusion, the result of it is certain even though it has not happened yet

fore·ground /'fɔrgraʊnd/ *n.* **the foreground** the part of a picture, photograph, etc. nearest to you

fore·head /'fɔrhɛd, 'fɔrɪd, 'fɑrɪd/ *n.* [C] the part of the face above the eyes and below the hair: *He wiped his forehead with a handkerchief.* ➔ *see picture on page A16*

for·eign /'fɑrɪn, 'fɔrɪn/ *adj.* **1** not from your own country: *Can you speak a foreign language?* | *He was in a foreign country, far away from home.* **2** [only before noun] involving or dealing with other countries (ANT) **domestic**: *American **foreign policy*** | *The budget calls for cuts in **foreign aid**.* **3 foreign to sb** not familiar, or not typical: *Their way of life was **completely foreign** to her.* **4 foreign body/matter** something that has come into a place where it does not belong, especially someone's body: *foreign matter in someone's eye* [ORIGIN: 1200—1300 Old French *forein*, from Latin *foris* "outside"]

,foreign af'fairs *n.* [plural] POLITICS political matters that affect or concern the relationship between one country and other countries

for·eign·er /'fɑrənɚ, 'fɔr-/ *n.* [C] someone who is from a country that is not your own

,foreign ex'change *n.* **1** [U] the system of buying and selling foreign money: *The dollar is expected to fall in the **foreign exchange markets*** (=places where foreign money is bought and sold). **2** [C] an arrangement in which people, especially students, travel to another country to work or study for a particular length of time: *a **foreign exchange student***

,foreign 'minister *n.* [C] POLITICS a government official with a high rank who is in charge of a country's foreign affairs

,foreign 'policy *n.* [U] POLITICS a government's decisions, actions, etc. relating to other countries ➔ DOMESTIC POLICY: *The French president criticized American foreign policy in the Middle East.*

fore·leg /'fɔrlɛg/ *n.* [C] one of the two front legs of an animal that has four legs

fore·man /'fɔrmən/ *n.* (plural **foremen** /-mən/) [C] **1** someone who is in charge of a group of workers, for example, in a factory

THESAURUS boss, manager, head, chief, supervisor, forewoman ➔ BOSS[1]

2 the leader of a JURY

fore·most /'fɔrmoʊst/ *adj.* [only before noun] the most famous or important: *the foremost writer of her time*

fo·ren·sic /fə'rɛnsɪk, -zɪk/ *adj.* [only before noun] relating to methods for finding out about a crime: *Scientists are still examining the forensic evidence.* —**forensics** *n.* [U]

fore·play /'fɔrpleɪ/ *n.* [U] sexual activity, such as touching the sexual organs and kissing, that happens before having sex

fore·run·ner /'fɔr,rʌnɚ/ *n.* [C] someone or something that is an early example or a sign of something that comes later: *He described the machine as the **forerunner of** the modern computer.*

fore·see /fɔr'si/ *v.* (past tense **foresaw** /-'sɔ/, past participle **foreseen** /-,sin/) [T] (formal) to know that something will happen before it happens: *No one could have foreseen such a disaster.*

THESAURUS predict, prophesy, foretell, forecast, have a premonition ➔ PREDICT

fore·see·a·ble /fɔr'siəbəl/ *adj.* **1 for/in the foreseeable future** continuing for as long as you can imagine: *Leila will be staying here for the foreseeable future.* **2 in the foreseeable future** fairly soon: *There is a chance of water shortages in the foreseeable future.* **3** foreseeable difficulties, events, etc. should be planned for because they are very likely to happen in the future

fore·shad·ow /fɔr'ʃædoʊ/ *v.* [T] (literary) to be a sign of something that will happen in the future

fore·shad·ow·ing /fɔr'ʃædoʊɪŋ/ *n.* [U] ENG. LANG. ARTS a way of suggesting what will happen later in a story: *There was a lot of foreshadowing in the movie, so I wasn't surprised when the main character shot his wife.*

fore·sight /'fɔrsaɪt/ *n.* [singular, U] the ability to imagine what might happen in the future, and to consider this in your plans: *Luckily, we'd **had the foresight** to take plenty of food and warm clothing.*

fore·skin /'fɔr,skɪn/ *n.* [C] a loose fold of skin covering the end of a man's PENIS

for·est /'fɔrɪst, 'fɑr-/ *n.* [C,U] EARTH SCIENCES a very large area of land that is covered with trees: *tropical rain forests* | *a **virgin forest*** (=a forest that is still in its natural state and has not been used or changed by people) [ORIGIN: 1200—1300 Old French, Latin *foris* "outside" (because it was outside the main fenced area of woods)] → *see picture on page A24*

fore·stall /fɔr'stɔl/ *v.* [T] to prevent something from happening by doing something first: *The National Guard was sent in, to forestall trouble.*

ˌforest 'ranger *n.* [C] someone whose job is to protect or manage part of a public forest

for·est·ry /'fɔrəstri, 'fɑr-/ *n.* [U] EARTH SCIENCES the science and practice of planting and taking care of forests

fore·taste /'fɔrteɪst/ *n.* **be a foretaste of sth** to be a sign of something more important, more impressive, etc. that will happen in the future

fore·tell /fɔr'tɛl/ *v.* (past tense and past participle **foretold** /-'toʊld/) [T] to say what will happen in the future, especially by using special magic powers

THESAURUS **predict, prophesy, forecast, foresee, have a premonition** → PREDICT

fore·thought /'fɔrθɔt/ *n.* [U] careful thought or planning before you do something

for·ev·er /fə'rɛvɚ, fɔ-/ *adv.* **1** for all future time: *I wanted the holiday to **last forever**.* | *You can't avoid him forever.*

THESAURUS **always, permanently, for life, for good** → ALWAYS

2 (spoken) for a very long time: *Greg will probably be a student forever.* | *It'll **take forever** to drive to Helen's.* **3 go on forever** to be extremely long or large: *The roads out west seem to go on forever.*

fore·warn /fɔr'wɔrn/ *v.* [T] **1** to warn someone about something dangerous or unpleasant that may happen **2 forewarned is forearmed** used in order to say that if you know about something before it happens, you can be prepared for it

fore·wom·an /'fɔrˌwʊmən/ *n.* [C] **1** a woman who is the leader of a group of workers, for example in a factory

THESAURUS **boss, manager, head, chief, supervisor, foreman** → BOSS[1]

2 a woman who is the leader of a JURY

fore·word /'fɔrwɚd/ *n.* [C] ENG. LANG. ARTS a short piece of writing at the beginning of a book that introduces the book or the person who wrote it

for·feit[1] /'fɔrfɪt/ *v.* [T] to give something up or have it taken away from you because of a rule or law: *criminals who have **forfeited** their **right** to freedom.*

forfeit[2] *n.* [C] something that you have to give away or do as a punishment because you have broken a rule or law

for·gave /fɚ'geɪv/ *v.* the past tense of FORGIVE

forge[1] /fɔrdʒ/ *v.* [T] **1** to illegally copy something such as a document, a painting, or money in order to make people think it is real: *The signature on the check had been forged.*

THESAURUS **copy, reproduce, duplicate, replicate, pirate** → COPY[2]

2 to develop something new, especially a strong relationship with other people or groups: *A special alliance has been forged between the U.S. and Canada.* **3** to make something from a piece of metal by heating and shaping it

forge ahead *phr. v.* to make progress: *The organizers are **forging ahead with** a program of public events.*

forge[2] *n.* [C] a large piece of equipment that is used for heating and shaping metal objects, or the building where this is done

forg·er /'fɔrdʒɚ/ *n.* [C] someone who illegally copies documents, money, paintings, etc. and tries to make people think they are real

for·ger·y /'fɔrdʒəri/ *n.* (plural **forgeries**) **1** [C] a document, painting, or piece of paper money that has been illegally copied (SYN) **fake**: *An art dealer insisted that the portrait is a forgery.* **2** [U] the crime of illegally copying something

F

for·get /fɚ'gɛt/ *v.* (past tense **forgot** /-'gɑt/, past participle **forgotten** /-'gɑt˺n/, present participle **forgetting**) **1** [I,T] to be unable to remember facts, information, or something that happened: *I've forgotten her name.* ►Don't say "I am forgetting."◄ | *I know you told me, but I forgot.* | *He **forgot all about** our anniversary.* **2** [I,T] to not remember to do something that you should do: *I **forgot to** turn off my headlights.* | *David had **forgotten (that)** we had a meeting.* **3** [T] to not remember to bring something that you should have taken with you: *Oh, I forgot your book.*

USAGE
You can say "I forgot my passport."
You cannot say "I forgot my passport at home."
When you want to talk about the place where you left something by mistake, you must use "leave": *I left my passport at home.*

4 [I,T] to stop thinking or worrying about someone or something: *You'll **forget (that)** you're wearing contact lenses after a while.* | *I'll never forget her.* | *I can't just **forget about** the accident.* **5** [I,T] to stop planning to do or get something because it is no longer possible: *With this injury, you can **forget about** playing this season.*

SPOKEN PHRASES

6 forget it a) used in order to tell someone that something is not important: *"I'm sorry I broke your mug." "Forget it."* | *"Did you say something?" "No, forget it."* **b)** used in order to tell someone to stop asking or talking about something because it is annoying you: *I'm not buying you that bike, so just forget it.* **7 don't forget** used in order to remind someone about something: *Don't forget your lunchbox!* | *Don't forget to turn off the lights.* **8 I forget** said instead of "I have forgotten": *You know the guy we saw last week – I forget his* *name.* **9 forget it/you/that!** used in order to refuse to do something, or to say that something is impossible: *Drive to the airport in this snow? Forget it.* **10 ...and don't you forget it!** said in order to remind someone angrily about something important that should make him/her behave differently: *I'm your father, and don't you forget it!*

[ORIGIN: Old English *forgietan*]

for·get·ful /fɚ'gɛtfəl/ *adj.* often forgetting things —**forgetfulness** *n.* [U]

for'get-me-ˌnot *n.* [C] a plant with small blue flowers

for·give /fɚ'gɪv/ *v.* (past tense **forgave** /-'geɪv/, past participle **forgiven** /-'gɪvən/) [I,T] **1** to stop being angry and blaming someone, although s/he has done something wrong: *I can't **forgive** him **for** what he did to her.* | *"I'm sorry." "That's OK – **you're forgiven*** (=I forgive you)." | *If anything happened to the kids, I'd never **forgive myself**.* | *Maybe you can **forgive and forget**, but I can't* (=forgive someone and behave as if s/he had never done anything wrong). **2 forgive me** (spoken) said when you are going to say or ask something that might seem rude or offensive: ***Forgive me for saying so**, but that's nonsense.* **3 forgive a loan/debt** ECONOMICS if a country forgives a LOAN, it says that the country that borrowed the money does not have to pay it back

F

for·give·ness /fɚ'gɪvnɪs/ *n.* [U] (formal) the act of forgiving someone

for·giv·ing /fɚ'gɪvɪŋ/ *adj.* willing to forgive: *a forgiving person*

for·go /fɔr'goʊ/ *v.* (past tense **forwent** /-'wɛnt/, past participle **forgone**) [T] (formal) to decide not to do or have something

for·got /fɚ'gɑt/ *v.* the past tense of FORGET

for·got·ten /fɚ'gɑt˺n/ *v.* the past participle of FORGET

fork¹ /fɔrk/ *n.* [C] **1** a tool used for picking up and eating food, with a handle and three or four points: *knives, forks, and spoons* **2** a place where a road or river divides into two parts: *Turn left at the fork in the road.* **3** a tool with a handle and three or four points, used for digging and breaking up soil: *a gardening fork* **4** a PITCHFORK [ORIGIN: Old English *forca*, from Latin *furca*]

fork² *v.* **1** [I] if a road or river forks, it divides into two parts **2** [T] to pick up, carry, or turn something over using a fork

fork sth ↔ **over/out** *phr. v.* (informal) to spend a lot of money on something because you have to: *Fans are being asked to fork over $120 for tickets to see the concert.*

forked /fɔrkt/ *adj.* with one end divided into two or more parts: *a snake's forked tongue*

fork·lift /'fɔrkˌlɪft/ *n.* [C] a vehicle with special equipment on the front for lifting and moving heavy things, for example, in a factory

for·lorn /fɚ'lɔrn, fɔr-/ *adj.* (literary) sad and lonely: *The child looked forlorn.*

form¹ /fɔrm/ *n.* **1** [C] one type of something, that exists in many different varieties (SYN) **kind**: *ballet and other **forms of** dance* | *a severe **form of** cancer* **2** [C,U] the way in which something exists or appears: *You can get the vitamin C **in** tablet or liquid **form**.* | *The story is written **in the form of** a letter.* | *Language practice can **take the form of** drills or exercises.* **3** [C] an official document with spaces where you have to provide information: *an application form for college* | *Please **fill out** the **form** in black ink.* **4** [C] a shape: *dark forms behind the trees* | *The brooch is made of diamonds and rubies in the form of a butterfly.* **5** [C] ENG. LANG. ARTS in grammar, a way of writing or saying a word that shows its number, tense, etc. For example, "was" is a past form of the verb "to be."

form² *v.* **1** [I,T] to start to exist, or to make something start to exist (SYN) **develop**: *Ice was already **forming on** the roads.* | *the cloud of dust and gas that formed the universe* | *Reporters had already **formed the impression*** (=begun to think) *that Myers was guilty.* **2** [I,T, linking verb] to come together in a particular shape or a line, or to make something have a particular shape: ***Form** the dough **into** a circle, then roll it out.* | *The line forms to the right.* | *The birch trees formed a ring around a grassy hollow.* **3** [T] to start a new organization, committee, relationship, etc.: *Students formed a protest group.* | *Everett seemed unable to form close friendships.* **4** [T] to make something by combining two or more parts: *One way to form nouns is to add the suffix "-ness."* **5** [linking verb] to be the thing, or one of the things, that makes up something else: *Rice forms a basic part of their diet.* | *The Rio Grande forms the boundary between Texas and Mexico.*

for·mal¹ /'fɔrməl/ *adj.* **1** made or done officially or publicly (ANT) **informal**: *a formal announcement* | *The college made a formal request for extra funding.* | *His lawyer filed a formal complaint against the police.* **2 formal education/training/qualifications** education in a subject or skill that you get in school rather than by practical experience: *Most priests have no formal training in counseling.* **3** formal behavior is very polite, and is used in official situations, or with people you do not know well (ANT) **informal** **4** formal language is used in official or serious situations (ANT) **informal**: *a formal letter* **5** a formal event is important, and people who go to it wear special clothes and behave very politely: *Jack won't wear a tie, even on **formal occasions**.* **6** formal clothes, such as a TUXEDO or long dress, are worn to formal events (ANT) **casual**: *men's **formal wear*** —**formally** *adv.*: *The winner will be formally announced this afternoon.*

formal² *n.* [C] **1** a dance at which you have to wear formal clothes

THESAURUS **dance, ball, prom** → DANCE²

2 an expensive and usually long dress that women wear on formal occasions

for·mal·de·hyde /fəˈmældəˌhaɪd, fɔr-/ *n.* [U] CHEMISTRY a strong-smelling gas that can be mixed with water and used for preserving things such as parts of a body

for·mal·i·ty /fɔrˈmæləṭi/ *n.* (plural **formalities**) **1** [C usually plural] something formal or official that you must do as part of an activity or process, even though it may not have any practical importance: *I need your signature here, but it's* ***just a formality***. **2** [U] careful attention to polite behavior or language in formal situations

for·mal·ize /ˈfɔrməˌlaɪz/ *v.* [T] to make a plan or decision official and describe all its details: *The contracts must be formalized within one month.*

for·mat¹ /ˈfɔrmæt/ (Ac) *n.* [C] **1** the way something such as a computer document, television show, or meeting is organized or arranged: *The new show is slightly different from the usual talk-show format.* **2** IT used when talking about what type of equipment is needed to play a video, CD, tape, etc. **3** ENG. LANG. ARTS the size, shape, design, etc. in which something such as a book or magazine is produced: *a newsletter format* [ORIGIN: 1800—1900 French, German, from Latin *formatus*, past participle of *formare* "to form"]

format² *v.* (**formatted**, **formatting**) [T] **1** IT to organize the space on a computer DISK so that information can be stored on it **2** ENG. LANG. ARTS to arrange a book, document, page, etc. according to a particular design or plan: *The new text will be formatted in the same way as the previous paragraphs.* —**formatting** *n.* [U] —**formatted** *adj.*

for·ma·tion /fɔrˈmeɪʃən/ *n.* **1** [U] the process by which something develops into a particular thing or shape: *the* ***formation of*** *the solar system* **2** [U] the process of starting a new organization or group: *the* ***formation of*** *a democratic government* **3** [C,U] something that is formed in a particular shape, or the shape in which it is formed: *rock formations* | *soldiers marching* ***in formation*** (=in a special order)

form·a·tive /ˈfɔrməṭɪv/ *adj.* having an important influence on the way someone or something develops: *a child's* ***formative years*** (=when his/her character develops)

for·mer¹ /ˈfɔrmə/ *adj.* **1** having a particular position in the past, but not now (SYN) **last**, **previous**: *our former president* **2** happening or existing before, but not now: *the former Soviet Union*

former² *n.* **the former** (formal) the first of two people or things that are mentioned → LATTER: *Of the two possibilities, the former seems more likely.*

for·mer·ly /ˈfɔrməli/ *adv.* in earlier times: *New York was formerly called New Amsterdam.*

for·mi·da·ble /ˈfɔrmədəbəl, fɔrˈmɪdə-/ *adj.* **1** very powerful or impressive: *a formidable opponent* | *He had a formidable lead in the polls.* **2** difficult to deal with and needing a lot of skill: *the formidable task of working out a peace plan* —**formidably** *adv.*

form·less /ˈfɔrmlɪs/ *adj.* without a definite shape

ˈform ˌletter *n.* [C] a standard letter that is sent to many people, without any personal details in it

for·mu·la /ˈfɔrmyələ/ (Ac) *n.* (plural **formulas** *or* **formulae** /-li/) **1** [C] a method or set of principles that you use in order to solve a problem or to make sure that something is successful: *a* ***formula for*** *peace* | *There's no* ***magic formula for*** *a happy marriage.* **2** [C] MATH a series of numbers or letters that represent a mathematical or scientific rule: *What is the formula for calculating the area of a circle?* **3** [C] a list of substances used in order to make something, showing the amounts of each substance to use: *a formula for a perfect loaf of fresh bread* **4** [C,U] a liquid food for babies that is similar to a woman's breast milk [ORIGIN: 1600—1700 Latin "small form," from *forma*, perhaps from Greek *morphe* "form, shape"]

for·mu·late /ˈfɔrmyəˌleɪt/ (Ac) *v.* [T] **1** to develop something such as a plan or set of rules, and decide all the details of how it will be done: *What role does he have in formulating foreign policy?* **2** to think carefully about what you want to say, and say it clearly: *Ricardo asked for time to formulate a reply.* **3** to make something using particular amounts of different substances: *specially formulated baby lotions* —**formulation** /ˌfɔrmyəˈleɪʃən/ *n.* [C,U]

for·sake /fəˈseɪk, fɔr-/ *v.* (past tense **forsook** /-ˈsʊk/, past participle **forsaken** /-ˈseɪkən/) [T] (formal) **1** to leave someone, especially when s/he needs you **2** to leave a place or stop doing or having something: *We have forsaken our heritage.*

fort /fɔrt/ *n.* [C] a strong building or group of buildings used by soldiers or an army for defending an important place [ORIGIN: 1400—1500 French, Latin *fortis* "strong"]

forte¹ /fɔrt, ˈfɔrteɪ/ *n.* **be sb's forte** to be something that someone is good at doing: *Cooking isn't my forte.*

for·te² /ˈfɔrteɪ/ *adj., adv.* ENG. LANG. ARTS played or sung loudly (ANT) **piano**

forth /fɔrθ/ *adv.* **go forth** (literary) to go out or away from where you are → **back and forth** *at* BACK¹, **and so on/forth** *at* SO¹

forth·com·ing /ˌfɔrθˈkʌmɪŋ◂/ (Ac) *adj.* (formal) **1** happening or coming soon: *her forthcoming novel* **2** given or offered when needed: *If more money is not forthcoming, we'll have to close the theater.* **3** willing to give information about something: *Lassen was not very forthcoming.*

forth·right /ˈfɔrθraɪt/ *adj.* saying honestly what you think, in a way that may seem rude: *a forthright answer*

THESAURUS **honest, frank, candid, direct, upfront, straight, straightforward, blunt** → HONEST

F

for·ti·eth /ˈfɔrt̬iɪθ/ *number* 40th

for·ti·fi·ca·tion /ˌfɔrt̬əfəˈkeɪʃən/ *n.* **1** [U] the process of making something stronger **2 fortifications** [plural] towers, walls, etc. built around a place in order to protect it

for·ti·fy /ˈfɔrt̬əˌfaɪ/ *v.* (**fortified**, **fortifies**) [T] **1** to build towers, walls, etc. around a place in order to defend it: *a fortified city* **2** (formal, humorous) to make someone feel physically or mentally stronger: *He fortified himself with a glass of whiskey before going on stage.* **3** to make food or drinks more healthy by adding VITAMINS to them: *vitamin D fortified milk*

for·ti·tude /ˈfɔrt̬əˌtud/ *n.* [U] courage shown when you are in pain or having a lot of trouble

for·tress /ˈfɔrtrɪs/ *n.* [C] a large strong building used for defending an important place

for·tu·i·tous /fɔrˈtuət̬əs/ *adj.* (formal) lucky and happening by chance: *a fortuitous discovery*

THESAURUS **lucky, fortunate, miraculous, auspicious** → LUCKY

F

for·tu·nate /ˈfɔrtʃənɪt/ *adj.* **1** lucky (ANT) **unfortunate**: *We were **fortunate enough to** get tickets for the last show.* | *It was **fortunate that** the ambulance arrived so quickly.*

THESAURUS **lucky, fortuitous, miraculous, auspicious** → LUCKY

2 less fortunate people who are less fortunate are poor: *Less fortunate children should still get a good education.* | *Welfare should provide a safety net for **the less fortunate*** (=poor people).

for·tu·nate·ly /ˈfɔrtʃənɪtli/ *adv.* happening because of good luck: *Fortunately, firefighters quickly put out the blaze.*

for·tune /ˈfɔrtʃən/ *n.* **1** [C] a very large amount of money: *Hunter **made a fortune*** (=earned a lot of money) *in real estate.* | *Julia must've **spent a fortune** on her wedding dress.* | *He lost a **small fortune*** (=a lot of money) *playing the stock market.* **2** [U] chance or luck: *I **had the good fortune** to have Mrs. Dawson as my instructor.* **3** [C usually plural] the good or bad things that happen in life: *The loss marked a change in the team's fortunes.* **4 tell sb's fortune** to tell someone what will happen to him/her in the future, by using special cards, or looking at his/her hand, etc. [ORIGIN: 1200—1300 French, Latin *fortuna*]

ˈfortune ˌcookie *n.* [C] a Chinese-American cookie with a piece of paper inside it that tells you what will happen in your future

ˈfortune ˌteller *n.* [C] someone who tells you what is going to happen to you in the future

for·ty /ˈfɔrt̬i/ *number* **1** 40 **2 the forties a)** the years between 1940 and 1949 **b)** the numbers between 40 and 49, especially when used for measuring temperature **3 be in your forties** to be aged between 40 and 49: *He's in his **early/mid/late forties**.*

fo·rum /ˈfɔrəm/ *n.* [C] **1** an organization, meeting, report, etc. in which people have a chance to publicly discuss an important subject: *a **forum for** discussing ideas* | *a **forum on** neighborhood crime* **2** a group of computer users who are interested in a particular subject and discuss it using a website on the Internet

for·ward¹ /ˈfɔrwərd/ *also* **forwards** *adv.* **1** toward a place or position that is in front of you (ANT) **backward**: *The crowd moved forward.* | *He **leaned forward** to hear what they were saying.* **2** toward more progress, improvement, or development: *NASA's space project cannot **go forward** without more money.* | *The business is ready to **move forward**.* **3** toward the future (ANT) **backward**: *The company must **look forward*** (=make plans for the future) *and use the newest technology.* → FAST FORWARD, **look forward to sth** *at* LOOK¹, **step forward** *at* STEP²

forward² *adj.* **1 forward progress/planning/thinking etc.** progress, plans, ideas, etc. that are helpful in a way that prepares you for the future **2** [only before noun] closer to a person, place, etc. that is in front of you (ANT) **backward**: *Troops were moved to a forward position on the battlefield.* **3** [only before noun] at the front part of a ship, car, airplane, etc. (ANT) **rear**: *the forward cabin*

forward³ *v.* [T] to send a message or letter that you have received to the person it was intended for, usually at his/her new address: *The Post Office should be forwarding all my mail.*

forward⁴ *n.* [C] in basketball, one of two players whose main job is to SHOOT the ball at the other team's BASKET

ˈforwarding adˌdress *n.* [C] an address you give to someone when you move so that s/he can send your mail to you

ˈforward-ˌlooking *also* **ˈforward-ˌthinking** *adj.* thinking about and planning for the future in a positive way, especially by being willing to try new ideas

ˈforward slash *n.* [C] a line (/) used in writing to separate words, numbers, or letters, for example in a website address → BACKSLASH

fos·sil /ˈfɑsəl/ *n.* [C] part of an animal or plant that lived millions of years ago, or the shape of one of these plants or animals that is now preserved in rock [ORIGIN: 1500—1600 Latin *fossilis* "dug up," from *fodere* "to dig"] —**fossil** *adj.*

fossil

ˈfossil ˌfuel *n.* [C,U] EARTH SCIENCES a FUEL such as gas or oil that has been formed from plants and animals that lived millions of years ago

fos·sil·ize /ˈfɑsəˌlaɪz/ *v.* [I,T] EARTH SCIENCES to become a fossil by being preserved in rock, or to make something do this

ˈfossil ˌrecord *n.* [C] BIOLOGY information about the animals and other creatures that lived many thousands of years ago, what they looked like, what they ate, and the kind of environment they lived in, etc., which is obtained from their fossils

fos·ter¹ /ˈfɔstɚ, ˈfɑ-/ *v.* [T] **1** to help to develop an idea, skill, feeling, etc.: *Teachers want to foster a spirit of cooperation in their classrooms.* **2** to take care of someone else's child for a period of time without becoming his/her legal parent → ADOPT

foster² *adj.* **1 foster mother/father/parents/family** the person or people who foster a child **2 foster child** a child who is fostered **3 foster home** a person's or family's home where a child is fostered

fought /fɔt/ *v.* the past tense and past participle of FIGHT

foul¹ /faʊl/ *v.* **1** [I,T] to do something in a sport that is against the rules: *Rickey fouled the first pitch* (=hit it outside the legal area). | *Sal hit two free throws after being fouled.* **2** [T] to make something very dirty: *The water had been fouled by industrial waste.*

foul (sth ↔) **up** *phr. v.* (informal) to do something wrong or to ruin something by making a mistake: *Glen fouled up the seating arrangements.* | *You've totally fouled up this time.*

foul² *adj.* **1** very dirty or not having a pleasant smell or taste: *A foul smell filled the cell.* | *foul-tasting coffee*

THESAURUS **horrible, disgusting, awful, revolting, terrible, dreadful, horrendous →** HORRIBLE

2 foul language rude and offensive words **3 in a foul mood/temper** likely to get angry easily **4 foul weather** bad weather, with strong winds, rain, or snow

foul³ *n.* [C] an action in a sport that is against the rules

ˌfoul ˈplay *n.* [U] **1** murder or illegal violence: *Cattrell may have been the victim of foul play.* **2** an activity that is dishonest and unfair

ˈfoul-up *n.* [C] (informal) a mistake: *a bureaucratic foul-up*

found¹ /faʊnd/ *v.* the past tense and past participle of FIND [ORIGIN: 1300—1400 Old French *fonder*, from Latin *fundus* "bottom"]

found² *v.* [T] **1** to start an organization, town, or institution that is intended to continue for a long time: *The college was founded in 1701.* | *The Center for Auto Safety was founded by Ralph Nader.* **2 be founded on/upon sth** to base your ideas, beliefs, etc. on something: *The U.S. was founded on the idea of religious freedom.*

foun·da·tion /faʊnˈdeɪʃən/ (Ac) *n.* **1** [C] an idea, fact, or system from which a religion, way of life, etc. develops: *The Constitution* ***provided/laid the foundation for*** *the American government.* | *The children had a* ***solid foundation*** *in reading and writing.* **2** [C] an organization that gives or collects money to be used for special purposes: *a grant from the National Science Foundation* **3** [C] the solid base that is built under a building to support it: *Construction workers have begun to* ***lay the foundation*** (=build it). **4** [U] the action of establishing an organization, city, or institution **5 without foundation** not true, reasonable, or able to be proved: *Luckily my fears were without foundation.*

found·er¹ /ˈfaʊndɚ/ (Ac) *n.* [C] someone who establishes a business, organization, school, etc.: *the founders of Brandon College*

founder² *v.* [I] (formal) **1** to fail after a period of time: *His campaign foundered before the first primary.* **2** if a ship or boat founders, it fills with water and sinks

ˌfounding ˈfather *n.* **1** [C] someone who begins something such as a new way of thinking or a new organization: *one of the founding fathers of modern science* **2 the Founding Fathers** [plural] HISTORY the group of men who wrote the American Constitution and Bill of Rights and started the U.S. as a country → FRAMERS

found·ry /ˈfaʊndri/ *n.* (plural **foundries**) [C] a place where metals are melted and made into new parts for machines

foun·tain /ˈfaʊntˀn/ *n.* [C] a structure that sends water straight up into the air, built for decoration [ORIGIN: 1300—1400 French *fontaine*, from Latin *fons* "place where water comes out of the ground"] → DRINKING FOUNTAIN

four /fɔr/ *number* **1** 4 **2** four o'clock: *I'll meet you at four.* **3** four years old: *My son is four.* **4 on all fours** on your hands and knees: *Andy was on all fours looking for something.* [ORIGIN: Old English *feower*]

ˌfour-leaf ˈclover *n.* [C] a CLOVER plant with four leaves instead of the usual three, that is considered to be lucky

ˌfour-letter ˈword *n.* [C] a word that is considered offensive or shocking by most people

four·teen /ˌfɔrˈtin◂/ *number* 14 —**fourteenth** *number*

fourth /fɔrθ/ *number, n.* **1** [C] 4th **2** [C] 1/4 (SYN) **quarter**

ˌFourth of Juˈly *n.* a U.S. national holiday to celebrate the beginning of the United States as an independent nation

fowl /faʊl/ *n.* [C] a bird, especially one such as a chicken that is kept for its meat and eggs

FOX /fɑks/ *n.* one of the main companies that broadcasts television programs in the U.S.

fox /fɑks/ *n.* [C] **1** a wild animal like a small dog with dark red fur, a pointed face, and a thick tail → *see picture at* NOCTURNAL **2** (spoken) an attractive person: *He is such a fox!*

F

fox·trot /ˈfɑkstrɑt/ *n.* [C] a type of formal dance with quick movements, or the music for this dance

fox·y /ˈfɑksi/ *adj.* (informal) someone who is foxy is sexually attractive

foy·er /ˈfɔɪɚ/ *n.* [C] a room or hall at the entrance of a house, hotel, theater, etc.

fra·cas /ˈfrækəs, ˈfreɪ-/ *n.* [singular] a short noisy fight involving a lot of people [ORIGIN: 1700—1800 French, Italian *fracassare* "to break in pieces"]

frac·tion /ˈfrækʃən/ *n.* [C] **1** a very small amount of something: *For a **fraction of** a second, there was silence.* **2** MATH a number that is smaller than 1, such as 3/4 or 1/2, and that shows how many parts of a whole there are. For example, in 3/4, there are three of four equal parts. —**fractional** *adj.* —**fractionally** *adv.*

frac·tious /ˈfrækʃəs/ *adj.* someone who is fractious gets angry very easily and tends to start fights

frac·ture¹ /ˈfræktʃɚ/ *n.* [C] a crack or break in something hard such as a bone or rock

F

> THESAURUS **injury, wound, bruise, contusion, cut, laceration, scrape, sprain** → INJURY

fracture² *v.* [I,T] to crack or break something hard such as a bone or rock: *He fractured his arm when he fell.*

frag·ile /ˈfrædʒəl/ *adj.* **1** easily broken, damaged, harmed, or ruined: *a fragile china teapot* **2** weak, and likely to become worse: *the country's fragile peace* | *Mama's fragile health* [ORIGIN: 1400—1500 Latin *fragilis*, from *frangere* "to break"] —**fragility** /frəˈdʒɪləṭi/ *n.* [U]

frag·ment /ˈfrægmənt/ *n.* [C] **1** a part of something, or a small piece that has broken off of something: *Only **fragments of** the text have survived.* | *glass fragments*

> THESAURUS **piece, scrap, chunk, lump, crumb, slice, strip, block** → PIECE¹

2 *also* **sentence fragment** a sentence that is not complete, often because it does not have a verb → RUN-ON SENTENCE —**fragment** /ˈfrægˌmɛnt/ *v.* [T]

frag·ment·ed /ˈfrægˌmɛntɪd/ *adj.* separated into many parts, groups, or events and not seeming to have a main purpose: *Our society seems to be becoming more fragmented.*

fra·grance /ˈfreɪgrəns/ *n.* **1** [C,U] a pleasant smell: *the sweet fragrance of the flowers*

> THESAURUS **smell, aroma, scent, perfume** → SMELL²

2 [C] a PERFUME

fra·grant /ˈfreɪgrənt/ *adj.* having a pleasant smell: *a fragrant bouquet of red roses*

frail /freɪl/ *adj.* thin and weak, especially because of being old: *Grandpa looked tiny and frail in the hospital bed.* [ORIGIN: 1300—1400 Old French *fraile*, from Latin *fragilis*, from *frangere* "to break"]

frail·ty /ˈfreɪlti/ *n.* (plural **frailties**) [C,U] (formal) a lack of physical or moral strength: *human frailties*

frame¹ /freɪm/ *n.* [C] **1** a structure made of wood, metal, etc. that holds or surrounds something such as a picture, door, or window: *I should put this graduation picture in a frame.* | *Wes leaned against the door frame.* **2** the main structure that supports something such as a house, piece of furniture, or vehicle: *a bicycle frame* | *a frame house* (=with a wooden frame) → *see picture at* BICYCLE **3** an area of film that contains one photograph, or one of the series of separate photographs that make up a movie or video **4** IT one of the areas into which a WEB PAGE is divided **5** (literary) someone's body: *her slender frame* **6 frame of mind** a particular attitude or feeling that you have: *Melissa was **in a good frame of mind** when we visited.* **7 frame of reference** all your knowledge, experiences, etc. that influence the way you think **8 frames** [plural] the metal or plastic part of a pair of glasses that surrounds each LENS → TIME FRAME

frame² *v.* [T] **1** to put a picture in a frame: *a framed photo of her daughter* **2** to surround something or be surrounded by something: *Tammy's sweet face was framed by golden curls.* **3** to try to make someone seem guilty of a crime by deliberately giving false information: *His lawyers claimed he had been framed by the police.* **4** to organize and develop something in a particular way: *General Green was able to frame his battle plan on the basis of accurate information about the enemy's position.* | *He framed his response to the question carefully.* **5** to build or have a main structure that supports something: *iron-framed windows*

Fram·ers /ˈfreɪmɚz/ *n.* **the Framers** HISTORY the group of men who wrote the American Constitution and Bill of Rights and started the U.S. as a country → FOUNDING FATHERS

frame·work /ˈfreɪmwɚk/ (Ac) *n.* [C] **1** a set of rules, beliefs, knowledge, etc. that people use when making a decision or planning something: *a **framework for** further research* **2** the structure of something such as a society or organization: *the country's existing **legal/political/social framework*** **3** the main structure that supports a large thing such as a building or vehicle

fran·chise /ˈfræntʃaɪz/ *n.* [C] **1** ECONOMICS permission that a company gives a person or group to sell the company's products or services, or the business that has this permission: *a McDonald's franchise* **2** a sports team that has been given permanent permission to play in a particular LEAGUE, or the business that owns the sports team: *The Seahawks franchise has been in Seattle since 1974.* —**franchise** *v.* [T]

fran·ci·um /ˈfænsiəm/ *n.* [U] CHEMISTRY (*symbol* **Fr**) a heavy RADIOACTIVE metal that is an ELEMENT. It is found naturally in URANIUM or is produced as part of a NUCLEAR REACTION.

frank /fræŋk/ *adj.* honest and direct in the way that you speak: *Jane said she would be* ***frank with*** *me.* | *Well,* ***to be frank,*** *I don't think this is going well.* [ORIGIN: 1300—1400 French "free, generous," from Late Latin *Francus* "Frank" (because the Franks, an ancient German people, were given political freedom in France)]

THESAURUS **honest, candid, direct, upfront, straight, straightforward, blunt, forthright** → HONEST

frank·fur·ter /ˈfræŋkˌfɚtɚ/ *also* **frank** /fræŋk/ *n.* [C] a HOT DOG

frank·ly /ˈfræŋkli/ *adv.* **1** used in order to show that you are saying what you really think about something: *Frankly, it was boring.* **2** honestly and directly: *She spoke frankly about her problems.*

fran·tic /ˈfræntɪk/ *adj.* **1** extremely hurried and not very organized: *the frantic rush to get things ready* **2** very worried, frightened, or anxious: *His mother was* ***frantic with*** *worry.* —**frantically** *adv.*

frat *n.* [C] (informal) a fraternity

fra·ter·nal /frəˈtɚnl/ *adj.* **1** friendly because you share the same interests with someone: *a fraternal organization* **2** relating to brothers: *fraternal love* [ORIGIN: 1400—1500 Medieval Latin *fraternalis*, from Latin *frater* "brother"]

fra·ter·ni·ty /frəˈtɚnəṭi/ *n.* (plural **fraternities**) **1** [C] *also* **fraternity house** a club at a college or university that has only male members ➤ SORORITY **2** [U] a feeling of friendship among people who have the same interests, job, or nationality

frat·er·nize /ˈfræṭɚˌnaɪz/ *v.* [I] to be friendly with someone who is not allowed to be your friend: *Soldiers who* ***fraternize with*** *the enemy will be shot.*

fraud /frɔd/ *n.* **1** [C,U] LAW the crime of deceiving people in order to gain money or goods: *The police arrested him for* ***tax/credit card/insurance fraud.*** **2** [C] someone or something that is not what he, she, or it claims to be: *He wasn't a real doctor – he was a fraud.* | *The police proved that the letter was a fraud.* [ORIGIN: 1300—1400 Old French *fraude*, from Latin *fraus* "deceiving"]

fraud·u·lent /ˈfrɔdʒələnt/ *adj.* LAW intended to deceive people: *the sale of fraudulent bonds* | *fraudulent statements* —**fraudulently** *adv.*

fraught /frɔt/ *adj.* **fraught with problems/danger/pain etc.** full of problems, danger, pain, etc.

fray[1] /freɪ/ *v.* [I] if a cloth or rope frays, its threads become loose because it is old or torn —**frayed** *adj.*

fray[2] *n.* **the fray** a fight or argument: *Then, two junior congressmen* ***joined/entered the fray,*** *claiming the bill is unconstitutional.*

fraz·zled /ˈfræzəld/ *adj.* (informal) confused, tired, and worried

freak[1] /frik/ *n.* **1 bike/movie/health etc. freak** someone who is very interested in a particular thing or activity, or likes something a lot **2** someone or something that looks very strange or behaves in an unusual way: *He looked at me as if I were some kind of freak.* → CONTROL FREAK

freak[2] *adj.* unexpected and very unusual: *Her parents were killed in a freak accident.*

freak[3] *also* **freak out** *v.* [I,T] (spoken) to suddenly become very angry, frightened, or anxious, or to make someone do this: *When she heard the news, she just freaked.* | *Horror films always freak me out.*

freak·y /ˈfriki/ *adj.* (spoken) strange and slightly frightening

freck·le /ˈfrɛkəl/ *n.* [C usually plural] a small brown spot on someone's skin, especially the face: *a little girl with red hair and freckles* —**freckled** *adj.*

THESAURUS **blemish, pimple, zit, mole** → MARK[2]

free[1] /fri/ *adj.*

1 NOT RESTRICTED allowed to live, exist, or happen without being controlled or restricted: *Students are* ***free to*** *choose the activities they want to work on.* | *The media is* ***free from*** *governmental control.* | *the right to* ***free speech***

2 NO COST not costing any money: *I won free tickets to the concert.* | *Admission is free for children.*

3 NOT CONTAINING STH not having any of a particular substance: *sugar-free bubble gum* | *The water is* ***free from*** *chemical pollutants.*

4 NOT BUSY not busy doing other things: *Are you* ***free for*** *lunch?* | *Hansen does volunteer work in her* ***free time.***

5 NOT BEING USED not being used at this time: *Excuse me, is this seat free?*

THESAURUS **empty, deserted, uninhabited, vacant** → EMPTY[1]

6 feel free (spoken) used in order to tell someone that s/he is allowed to do something: *Feel free to ask me any questions after the class.*

7 NOT A PRISONER not a prisoner or SLAVE: *Muller will be free in three years.* | *The UN demanded that the three hostages be* ***set free*** (=be given their freedom).

8 NOT SUFFERING not suffering or not having to deal with something bad: ***free of*** *danger* | *Patients undergoing the treatment are now* ***free from*** *cancer.* | *a happy and trouble-free life*

9 TAX if something is free of tax, you do not have to pay tax: *the duty-free store at the airport*

10 free hand if someone has a free hand to do something, s/he is allowed to do what s/he wants or needs to do: *The police were* ***given a free hand*** *to deal with the gang problems.*

11 a free ride something you get without paying or working for it

free[2] *v.* [T] **1** to allow someone to leave prison or somewhere s/he has been kept as a prisoner: *After*

F

nine months, the hostages were finally freed. **2** to move someone or something that is trapped or stuck, or to make something loose: *Firefighters helped free two men trapped in the car.* **3** to stop someone or something from being controlled or restricted: *The farmers were* ***freed from*** *government controls on what they could plant.* **4** to stop someone suffering, or help someone by removing something bad or difficult: *The scholarship* ***freed*** *her* ***from*** *having to work while attending college.* **5** *also* **free up** to help someone be able to do something, or to make something be able to be used: *Hiring an assistant will free up your time to do other tasks.* | *I need to free up some space on the hard disk.*

free[3] *adv.* **1** without having to pay any money: *Students can visit the museum* ***free of charge.*** | *Kyle is fixing my car* ***for free.*** **2** not being restricted or controlled by someone: *He created music that* ***broke free*** *of tradition.* **3** not stuck or held in a particular place or position: *He grabbed my wrist but I managed to* ***struggle/pull free.***

F

ˌfree ˈagent *n.* [C] a professional sports player who can choose whether to sign a contract with a team

free·bie /ˈfribi/ *n.* [C] (informal) something that you are given free, especially by a business, store, etc.

free·dom /ˈfridəm/ *n.* **1** [C,U] the right to do what you want without being restricted or controlled by someone else: *The First Amendment guarantees* ***freedom of speech/religion/expression*** (=the legal right to say what you want, choose your own religion, etc.). | *The government must respect our basic freedoms.* | *Individual freedom is limited by social responsibilities.* **2** [U] the state of being free and allowed to do what you want: *I had a great sense of freedom when I first left home.* | *Thanks to the internet, many people have the* ***freedom to*** *work from home.* **3 freedom from sth** the state of not being hurt or affected by something: *freedom from hunger*

ˈfreedom ˌfighter *n.* [C] someone who fights in a war against a dishonest government, army, etc.

free ˈenterprise *n.* [U] ECONOMICS the freedom for companies to control their own business without being limited by the government very much

ˌfree-for-ˈall *n.* [C] (informal) a fight or noisy argument that a lot of people join: *The argument in the bar turned into a free-for-all.*

free·hand /ˈfrihænd/ *adj., adv.* drawn by hand without using any special tools

free·lance /ˈfrilæns/ *adj., adv.* doing work for one or more companies, rather than being employed only by one particular company: *a freelance journalist* | *She works freelance from home.* [ORIGIN: 1800—1900 *free lance* "soldier in former times who sold his fighting skills to anyone"] —**freelancer** *n.* [C] —**freelance** *v.* [I]

free·load·er /ˈfriˌloʊdɚ/ *n.* [C] (informal, disapproving) someone who takes food, money, or other things from other people, without giving them anything in return —**freeload** *v.* [I]

free·ly /ˈfrili/ *adv.* **1** without anyone or anything preventing or limiting something: *People can now travel freely across the border.* | *They were speaking freely, assuming we could not understand.* **2 freely admit/acknowledge** to say that something is true, even though this is difficult: *I freely admit I made a bad choice.* **3 freely available** very easy to get: *Information is freely available on the Internet.* **4** generously or in large amounts: *a company that gives freely to local charities*

ˌfree ˈmarket *n.* [singular] a situation in which prices are not controlled by the government or any other powerful group

Free·ma·son /ˈfriˌmeɪsən/ *n.* [C] a MASON

ˌfree-ˈrange *adj.* relating to a type of farming which allows animals such as chickens and pigs to move around and eat naturally, rather than being kept in cages: *free-range eggs*

ˌfree ˈspirit *n.* [C] someone who lives the way s/he wants to, rather than in the way society considers usual

ˌfree ˈthrow *n.* [C] an occasion in the game of basketball when a player is allowed to throw the ball toward the basket without anyone trying to prevent him/her because another player has FOULed him/her

ˌfree-ˈtrade ˌzone *n.* [C] ECONOMICS a place where goods can be IMPORTed (=brought in from another country to be sold) and EXPORTed (=sent to another country to be sold) without paying taxes

ˌfree ˈverse *n.* [U] ENG. LANG. ARTS poetry that does not have a definite RHYTHM or structure and that does not RHYME at the end of the lines

free·way /ˈfriweɪ/ *n.* [C] a very wide road in a city on which cars can travel very fast

> THESAURUS **road, street, main street, avenue, lane, main road, the main drag, highway, expressway, toll road, turnpike** → ROAD

free·wheel·ing /ˌfriˈwilɪŋ◂/ *adj.* (informal) not worrying about rules or what will happen in the future: *a freewheeling lifestyle*

ˌfree ˈwill *n.* **do sth of your own free will** to do something because you want to and not because someone forces you to: *She's offered to go of her own free will.*

freeze[1] /friz/ *v.* (past tense **froze** /froʊz/, past participle **frozen** /ˈfroʊzən/) **1** [I,T] if a liquid or thing freezes, or if something freezes it, it becomes solid and hard because it is so cold (ANT) **melt, thaw**: *The lake had frozen overnight.* | *One man got lost in the blizzard and* ***froze to death.*** | *The ground was* ***frozen solid.*** **2** [I,T] to preserve food for a long time by keeping it very cold in a freezer: *Do you want to freeze some of these pies?* **3 it's freezing**

(spoken) said when the temperature is extremely cold

THESAURUS cold, cool, chilly, frosty, icy (cold), bitter (cold), frigid → COLD[1]

4 [I] (spoken) to feel very cold: *Put on a coat – you'll freeze.* | *We almost **froze to death*** (=felt very cold) *at the football game.* 5 [I] to suddenly stop moving and stay very quiet and still: *Officer Greer shouted, "Freeze!"* 6 [T] to officially prevent money from being spent, or prevent prices, salaries, etc. from being increased [ORIGIN: Old English *freosan*]

freeze sb ↔ **out** *phr. v.* to deliberately prevent someone from being involved in something

freeze over *phr. v.* if an area of water freezes over, its surface turns into ice

freeze up *phr. v.* to suddenly be unable to speak normally because you are nervous: *He freezes up whenever she asks him a question.*

freeze² *n.* [C] 1 ECONOMICS an occasion when something is stopped or kept at a particular level: *a **freeze on** hiring new employees* | *a pay freeze* 2 a short period of time, especially at night, when the temperature is very low

ˌfreeze-ˈdried *adj.* freeze-dried food or drinks are preserved by being frozen and then dried very quickly: *freeze-dried coffee*

freez·er /ˈfrizɚ/ *n.* [C] a large piece of electrical equipment that is usually part of a REFRIGERATOR and is used for storing food at a very low temperature for a long time

freez·ing /ˈfriziŋ/ *n.* **above/below freezing** above or below the temperature at which water freezes

ˈfreezing ˌpoint *n.* [C] the temperature at which a liquid freezes

freight /freɪt/ *n.* [U] goods that are carried by train, airplane, or ship

freight·er /ˈfreɪt̬ɚ/ *n.* [C] an airplane or ship that carries goods

ˈfreight train *n.* [C] a train that carries goods

French¹ /frentʃ/ *adj.* 1 relating to or coming from France 2 relating to the French language

French² *n.* 1 [U] the language used in France 2 **the French** [plural] the people of France

ˌFrench ˈbread *n.* [U] white bread that is shaped like a long stick

ˌFrench ˈfry *n.* (plural **French fries**) [C usually plural] a FRY

ˌFrench ˈtoast *n.* [U] pieces of bread that are put into a mixture of egg and milk, then cooked in hot oil

fre·net·ic /frəˈnet̬ɪk/ *adj.* frenetic activity happens in a way that is fast and not very organized: *the frenetic pace of life in the city*

fren·zied /ˈfrenzid/ *adj.* frenzied activity is completely uncontrolled: *a frenzied attack*

fren·zy /ˈfrenzi/ *n.* [singular, U] 1 the state of being very anxious, excited, and unable to control your behavior: *The kids had worked themselves **into a frenzy** of anticipation.* 2 a period in which people do a lot of things very quickly: *The house was a **frenzy of activity** as we got ready for the party.* 3 **feeding frenzy** (informal) an occasion when a lot of people get involved in something in an uncontrolled way: *The media went into a feeding frenzy over this story.*

fre·quen·cy /ˈfrikwənsi/ *n.* (plural **frequencies**) 1 [U] the number of times that something happens within a particular period, or the fact that it happens a lot: *the **frequency of** fatal road accidents* | ***high frequency** names such as Smith or Johnson* | *Arguments began taking place **with increasing frequency**.* 2 [C] the number of radio waves broadcast per second by a particular station, used to find a station on the radio 3 [C,U] PHYSICS the number of sound, light, or radio WAVES that pass any point in a second, which is determined by the WAVELENGTH (=the distance between two points on the wave): ***high frequency sounds***

ˈfrequency distriˌbution *n.* [C] MATH a GRAPH or table showing how often a particular number or value appears in a set of DATA

fre·quent¹ /ˈfrikwənt/ *adj.* happening very often (ANT) **infrequent**: *He's **a frequent guest** on TV talk shows.* | *Her absences were becoming **more/less frequent**.*

fre·quent² /ˈfrikwənt, friˈkwent/ *v.* [T] to go to a particular place very often: *a restaurant **frequented by** students*

ˌfrequent ˈflier *n.* [C] someone who travels on airplanes very often, especially using a particular AIRLINE —**frequent-flier** *adj.*

fre·quent·ly /ˈfrikwəntˀli/ *adv.* very often: *We call each other frequently.*

THESAURUS often, a lot, regularly, repeatedly, constantly, continuously, again and again/over and over (again) → OFTEN

fresh /freʃ/ *adj.*
1 ADDED/REPLACING adding to or replacing what was there before: *Let me make some fresh coffee.* | *I put fresh sheets on the bed.*
2 RECENT recently done, made, or learned: *fresh tracks in the snow* | *fresh-squeezed orange juice* | *Researchers have presented fresh data.* | *Write about your trip while it's still **fresh in your mind**.*
3 NEW not done, seen, etc. before: *a new manager with fresh ideas* | *a fresh approach to teaching*
4 FOOD fresh food or flowers are in good condition because they have recently been produced, picked, or prepared: *fresh strawberries* | *bread fresh from the bakery*
5 CLEAN looking, feeling, smelling, or tasting clean, cool, and nice: *a fresh breeze* | *a fresh minty taste*
6 **fresh air** air from outside, especially clean air: *Let's go and **get some fresh air**.*

F

7 be fresh out of sth (spoken) **a)** to have used your last supplies of something: *I'm sorry, we're fresh out of bagels.* **b)** *also* **be fresh from sth** to have recently finished doing something: *He's fresh out of college.*
8 WATER fresh water has no salt and comes from rivers and lakes
9 fresh start the act of starting doing something again in a new or different way, especially after being unsuccessful: *immigrants who came to America to **make a fresh start*** (=start a new life) [ORIGIN: 1200—1300 Old French *freis*]

fresh·en /ˈfrɛʃən/ *v.* **1** [I] if the wind freshens, it becomes stronger **2** [T] *also* **freshen up** to add more liquid to a drink

freshen up *phr. v.* to wash your hands and face in order to feel comfortable: *Would you like to freshen up before dinner?*

fresh·ly /ˈfrɛʃli/ *adv.* very recently: *freshly mown grass*

THESAURUS **recently, just, a little/short while ago, lately, newly** → RECENTLY

F

fresh·man /ˈfrɛʃmən/ *n.* (plural **freshmen** /-mən/) [C] a student in the first year of HIGH SCHOOL or college → STUDENT

fresh·wa·ter /ˈfrɛʃˌwɔt̬ɚ, -ˌwɑt̬ɚ/ *adj.* EARTH SCIENCES relating to rivers or lakes rather than the ocean: *freshwater fish*

fret¹ /frɛt/ *v.* [I] to worry about small or unimportant things, or to make someone do this: *Don't **fret about** the delay – we'll get there on time.*

fret² *n.* [C] one of the raised lines on the long straight part of a GUITAR or similar instruments

fret·ful /ˈfrɛtfəl/ *adj.* (old-fashioned) worried, complaining, and unable to relax: *a fretful child*

Freud·i·an /ˈfrɔɪdiən/ *adj.* **1** relating to Sigmund Freud's ideas about the way the mind works **2 Freudian slip** something you say by mistake that shows a thought or feeling you did not mean to show, or did not know you had

fri·ar /ˈfraɪɚ/ *n.* [C] a man who belongs to a Roman Catholic group, whose members in past times traveled around teaching about religion and who were very poor

fric·tion /ˈfrɪkʃən/ *n.* [U] **1** disagreement, angry feelings, or lack of friendship between people: *the things that create **friction between** parent and child* **2** PHYSICS a force that tries to stop the movement of one surface against another. When things keep moving against each other, friction causes them to rub together and produce heat: *Moving parts subjected to constant friction eventually wear out.* [ORIGIN: 1500—1600 French, Latin *frictio*, from *fricare* "to rub"]

Fri·day /ˈfraɪdi, -deɪ/ (*written abbreviation* **Fri.**) *n.* [C,U] the sixth day of the week, between Thursday and Saturday: *Diane won't be here Friday.* | *I have class **on Friday**.* | ***Next Friday** is my birthday.* | *I talked to Jim **last Friday**.* | *Do you have plans for Friday night?* [ORIGIN: Old English *frigedæg* "day of Frigg, female god of love"]

fridge /frɪdʒ/ *n.* [C] (informal) a REFRIGERATOR

fried¹ /fraɪd/ *adj.* **1** cooked in hot fat: *a fried egg* **2** (slang) very tired: *My brain is fried today.*

fried² *v.* the past tense and past participle of FRY

friend /frɛnd/ *n.* [C] **1** someone whom you like very much and enjoy spending time with: *I'm meeting a friend for lunch.* | *Is she a **friend of yours**?* | *Tony's her **best friend**.* | *one of my **closest friends*** | *Lee's an **old friend**.*

COLLOCATIONS

You may have lots of **good/close friends** but your **best friend** is the one you like most.
An **old friend** is one you have known for a long time.
If you **have friends**, you know and like them already.
If you **make friends** with someone, you start to know and like him or her.
If **friends hang out together** (informal), or if you **hang out with friends** (informal), you spend time together in a relaxed way.
If **friends come over**, they visit you at home.

2 make friends (with sb) to become friendly with someone: *Kate makes friends easily.* **3 be friends (with sb)** to be someone's friend: *They've **been friends with** the Wilsons for years.* **4** someone who has the same beliefs or wants to achieve the same things: *our friends and allies around the world* **5** someone who supports a theater, MUSEUM, etc. by giving money or help **6 have friends in high places** to know important people who can help you [ORIGIN: Old English *freond*]

friend·ly /ˈfrɛndli/ *adj.* **1** showing that you like someone and are ready to talk to him/her: *Diane's **friendly to/with** everyone.* | *a friendly smile*

THESAURUS

warm – friendly: *Sonya's a very warm person.*
cordial – friendly and polite but formal: *The two nations have always maintained cordial relations.*
amiable – friendly and pleasant: *an amiable man*
genial (formal) – cheerful, kind, and friendly: *the genial host of the party*
affable (formal) – friendly and easy to talk to: *an affable young woman with plenty of friends*
welcoming – making you feel happy and relaxed: *Everyone was very welcoming.*
hospitable – friendly, welcoming, and generous to visitors: *They were very kind and hospitable to us.*

2 user-friendly/ozone-friendly etc. a) easy for people to use or be comfortable with: *user-friendly computers* | *a kid-friendly house* **b)** not damaging or harming something: *environmentally-friendly detergent* **3** not at war with you, or not your enemy or opponent: *The two countries have friendly relations.* **4 friendly fire** bombs, bullets, etc. that accidentally kill people who are fighting on the same side —**friendliness** *n.* [U]

friend·ship /ˈfrɛndʃɪp/ *n.* **1** [C] a relationship between friends: *Their friendship began in college.* | *his* ***friendship with*** *Bill* | *The two boys* ***formed/developed*** *a lasting* ***friendship***. | *a* ***close friendship*** **2** [U] the feelings that exist between friends: *I was grateful for her friendship and support.*

frieze /friz/ *n.* [C] a decoration that goes along the top of a wall

frig·ate /ˈfrɪgɪt/ *n.* [C] a small fast ship used especially for protecting other ships in a war

fright /fraɪt/ *n.* [singular, U] a sudden fear: *People screamed* ***in fright***. | *He was shaking* ***with fright***.

fright·en /ˈfraɪtˀn/ *v.* [T] to make someone feel afraid: *Libby was frightened by the thunder.* | *Don't stand so close to the edge – you're frightening me.*

frighten sb/sth ↔ **away** *phr. v.* to make a person or animal go away by making him, her, or it afraid: *Be quiet or you'll frighten away the birds.*

frighten sb ↔ **off** *phr. v.* to make someone so nervous or afraid that s/he goes away and does not do something s/he was going to do: *The company's poor results have frightened off investors.*

fright·ened /ˈfraɪtˀnd/ *adj.* feeling afraid: *a frightened child* | *He was* ***frightened of*** *losing her.* | *She was* ***frightened that*** *he might hit her.*

THESAURUS

afraid/scared – frightened because you think that you may get hurt or that something bad may happen: *I'm afraid to go out alone after dark.* | *I've always been scared of dogs.*
terrified – very frightened: *I'm terrified of heights.*
petrified – very frightened: *He's petrified of snakes.*
fearful (formal) – afraid: *Even doctors are fearful of getting the disease.*
phobic (formal) – having very strong and unreasonable fears: *My mother, who was phobic about leaving the apartment, never ventured outdoors.*

fright·en·ing /ˈfraɪtˀnɪŋ/ *adj.* making you feel afraid or nervous: *a frightening experience* —**frighteningly** *adv.*

frig·id /ˈfrɪdʒɪd/ *adj.* **1** a woman who is frigid does not like having sex **2** very cold

THESAURUS **cold, cool, chilly, frosty, freezing (cold), icy (cold), bitter (cold)** → COLD[1]

3 (literary) not friendly: *She gave me a frigid look.* —**frigidity** /frɪˈdʒɪdəṭi/ *n.* [U]

frill /frɪl/ *n.* **1** [C] a decoration on the edge of a piece of cloth, made of another piece of cloth with many small folds in it **2 frills** [plural] features that are nice but not necessary: *We saved money by cutting out frills like dining out.* | *a* ***no-frills*** *airline* → NO-FRILLS

frill·y /ˈfrɪli/ *adj.* with many frills: *a frilly blouse*

fringe[1] /frɪndʒ/ *n.* **1** [C] a small number of people whose ideas are more unusual or extreme than those of most other people: *the environmental fringe* **2** [C,U] an edge of hanging threads used as a decoration on a curtain, piece of clothing, etc.: *a cowboy jacket with leather fringe* **3** [C] the area that is furthest from the center of something: *the eastern fringe of Vancouver* **4 on the fringes of sth** not completely involved in or accepted by a particular group: *Cato lived on the fringes of society.*

fringe[2] *adj.* not representing or involving many people, and expressing unusual ideas: *a* ***fringe group*** *of political extremists*

ˈfringe ˌbenefit *n.* [C usually plural] a service or advantage that you are given with your job in addition to pay: *The job's many fringe benefits include a company car.*

fringed /frɪndʒd/ *adj.* **1** decorated with a fringe: *a large fringed shawl* **2** having something on the edge: *a palm-fringed beach*

Fris·bee /ˈfrɪzbi/ *n.* [C,U] (trademark) a piece of plastic shaped like a plate that people throw and catch as a game

frisk /frɪsk/ *v.* [T] to search someone for hidden weapons, drugs, etc. by passing your hands over his/her body

frisk·y /ˈfrɪski/ *adj.* full of energy, happiness, and fun: *a frisky kitten*

frit·ter[1] /ˈfrɪṭɚ/ *n.* [C] a piece of fruit, vegetable, or meat covered with a mixture of eggs and flour and cooked in oil: *corn fritters*

fritter[2] *v.*

fritter sth ↔ **away** *phr. v.* to waste time, money, or effort on something that is not important

fritz /frɪts/ *n.* (informal) **be on the fritz** if something electrical is on the fritz, it is not working correctly

fri·vol·i·ty /frɪˈvɑləṭi/ *n.* (plural **frivolities**) [C,U] behavior or activities that are not serious or sensible

friv·o·lous /ˈfrɪvələs/ *adj.* **1** not sensible: *pretty, frivolous clothes* **2** not important or necessary: *a frivolous request*

frizz·y /ˈfrɪzi/ *adj.* frizzy hair is very tightly curled in an unattractive way —**frizz** *v.* [I,T]

fro /froʊ/ *adv.* → TO AND FRO

frog /frɔg, frɑg/ *n.* [C] **1** a small animal with smooth skin that lives in or near water, makes a deep sound, and has long legs for jumping → TOAD **2 have a frog in your throat** (informal) to have difficulty in speaking because your throat is dry or sore [ORIGIN: Old English *frogga*]

frol·ic /ˈfrɑlɪk/ *v.* [I] to play in an active happy way —**frolic** *n.* [C]

from /frəm; *strong* frʌm/ *prep.*
1 WHERE SB/STH STARTS starting at a particular place, position, or condition: *He drove all the way*

F

from Colorado. | *I liked him from the first time I met him.* | *prices ranging from $80 to $250*
2 ORIGIN **a)** used in order to show the origin of someone or something: *lines from a play* | *I got the idea from Scott.* | *"Where do you **come from**?" "I'm from Norway."* **b)** sent or given by someone: *Who is the present from?* | *I got a phone call from Ernie today.*
3 MOVED/SEPARATED used in order to show that things or people are moved, separated, or taken away: *He pulled his shoes out from under the bed.* | *I'll **take** that **away from** you!* | *She needs some time **away from** the kids* (=time when she is not with them). | *Subtract $40 from the total.*
4 DISTANCE/TIME used in order to show distance or time: *We live about 3 miles from Des Moines.* | *It'll cost $400 to fly **from** Albuquerque **to** Atlanta.* | *The morning class is **from** 9:00 **to** 11:00.* | *One month **from now** we'll be in Mexico!*
5 from now on starting now and continuing into the future: *I decided that, from now on, I would keep a journal.*
6 from day to day/person to person/place to place etc. used in order to say that something continues or keeps changing: *The stock's value **varied/fluctuated from** week **to** week.*
7 from time to time sometimes, but not regularly (SYN) occasionally: *We talk on the phone from time to time.*
8 POSITION used in order to show where you are when you see, watch, or do something: *There's a man watching us from behind that fence.* | *From the top of the mountain, you can see the ocean.*
9 RESULT because of, or as a result of: *the number of injuries from car accidents* | *We could tell what he was thinking from the expression on his face.*
10 STOP STH HAPPENING used in order to say what is stopped, avoided, or prevented: *The fog **prevented** planes **from** landing.*
11 COMPARING used when comparing things: *Frieda is very different from her sister.* [ORIGIN: Old English]

frond /frɑnd/ *n.* [C] a leaf of a FERN or PALM TREE

front¹ /frʌnt/ *n.*
1 the front a) the part of something that is furthest forward, and closest to the direction it faces (ANT) back: *Good students tend to sit near the front.* | *Let's sit **at the front of** the bus.* **b)** the side or surface of something that faces or moves forward (ANT) back: *the large doors **at the front of** the building* | *He ran around the front of the car.* | *a sweatshirt with the college's name **on the front*** **c)** the most important side or surface of something, that you look at first (ANT) back: *a postcard with a picture of a lighthouse **on the front*** | *The author had signed his name **in the front of** the book* (=on one of the first pages).
2 in front of sb/sth a) further forward than or ahead of someone or something (ANT) behind: *A car suddenly pulled out in front of my truck.* | *two girls standing in front of me in line* **b)** facing someone or something (ANT) behind: *She sat in front of the mirror.* | *Mrs. Podell stood in front of the class.* **c)** near the entrance of a building (ANT) behind: *Drop me off in front of the theater.* | *a tree in front of their house* **d)** where someone can see or hear you: *He threatened her in front of several witnesses.* | *They won in front of 13,000 fans.*
3 in (the) front a) in the most forward or leading position (SYN) ahead: *Watch the car in front!* **b)** in the area nearest to the most forward part of something, or nearest to the entrance to a building: *The club has two bars, one in the front and one in the back.* **c)** in the part of a car where the driver sits: *Can I sit in front with you?*
4 in front of the TV/computer etc. watching a television or using a computer: *They'd eaten supper in front of the TV.*
5 out front in the area near the entrance to the building that you are in: *Jim's waiting out front.*
6 WEATHER [C] EARTH SCIENCES the place where two areas of air that have different temperatures meet each other: *The weather report says a **warm/cold front** is coming.*
7 on the publicity/money/health etc. front in a particular area of activity: *new developments on the economic front*
8 up front (informal) **a)** money that is paid up front is paid before work is done or goods are supplied: *We need the money up front before we can do anything.* **b)** directly and clearly from the start: *She told him up front she wasn't interested in marriage.*
9 ON YOUR BODY **sb's front** (informal) someone's chest, or the part of the body that faces forward: *Oh, I've just spilled milk down my front!*
10 BEHAVIOR [C, usually singular] a way of behaving that shows what you want people to see, rather than what you may feel: *Parents should try to present a **united front*** (=seem to agree with each other) *to their children.* | *Celia was nervous, but she **put up a** brave **front**.*
11 ILLEGAL ACTIVITIES [C] a legal business that someone operates in order to hide the illegal activities s/he is involved in
12 POLITICAL PARTY [singular] POLITICS used in the names of political parties or unofficial military organizations: *the Quebec Liberation Front*
13 WAR [C] a line along which fighting takes place during a war

front² *adj.* [only before noun] **1** at, on, or in the front of something (ANT) back: *the front door* | *tickets for front row seats* | *the magazine's front cover* | *one of the front wheels* **2** legally doing business as a way of hiding a secret or illegal activity: *a front organization for drug dealing*

front³ *v.* **1** [T] to lead something such as a musical group by being the person that the public sees most: *He's now fronting his own band.* **2** [I,T] to face something, or to be in front of something: *a building fronting Lake Michigan*

front·age /ˈfrʌntɪdʒ/ *n.* [C] the part of a building or piece of land that is along a road, river, etc.

fron·tal /ˈfrʌntəl/ *adj.* **1** toward the front of

something: *a frontal attack* **2** at the front part of something: *the frontal lobe of the brain*

fron·tier /frʌn'tɪr/ *n.* [C] **1 the frontier** the area beyond the places that people know well, especially in the western U.S. in the 19th century: *the settlement of the Oklahoma frontier* **2** the limit of what is known about something: *the frontiers of science* **3** the border of a country, or the area near the border

'front man *n.* [C] **1** someone who speaks for an organization, often an illegal one, but is not the leader of it **2** the leader of a JAZZ or ROCK band

front·run·ner /'frʌntˀ,rʌnɚ/ *n.* [C] the person or thing that is most likely to succeed in a competition: *the frontrunner for the Republican nomination*

frost[1] /frɔst/ *n.* **1** [U] ice that looks white and powdery and covers things that are outside when the temperature is very cold: *trees white with frost*

THESAURUS **snow, snowflakes, sleet, slush → SNOW**[1]

2 [C,U] very cold weather, when water freezes: *an early frost*

frost[2] *v.* **1** [T] to cover a cake with frosting **2** [I] to cover something with frost, or to become covered with frost: *All the windows had **frosted over** during the night.*

frost·bite /'frɔstbaɪt/ *n.* [U] a condition caused by extreme cold, in which your fingers, toes, etc. freeze, so that they swell, become darker, and sometimes drop off —**frostbitten** /'frɔst,bɪtˀn/ *adj.*

frost·ing /'frɔstɪŋ/ *n.* [U] a sweet substance that you put on cakes, made from sugar and liquid: *chocolate frosting*

frost·y /'frɔsti/ *adj.* **1** very cold or covered with FROST: *a frosty morning*

THESAURUS **cold, cool, chilly, freezing (cold), icy (cold), bitter (cold), frigid → COLD**[1]

2 unfriendly: *a frosty greeting*

froth[1] /frɔθ/ *n.* [singular, U] a lot of BUBBLES formed on top of a liquid

froth[2] *v.* [I] to produce froth

froth·y /'frɔθi, -ði/ *adj.* full of froth or covered with froth: *frothy beer*

frown[1] /fraʊn/ *v.* [I] to make an angry or unhappy expression by moving your EYEBROWS together, so that lines appear on your FOREHEAD: *Debbie's mother **frowned at** her.*

frown on/upon sth *phr. v.* to disapprove of something: *Even though divorce is legal, it's often frowned upon.*

frown[2] *n.* [C] the expression on your face when you frown

froze /froʊz/ *v.* the past tense of FREEZE

fro·zen[1] /'froʊzən/ *v.* the past participle of FREEZE

frozen[2] *adj.* **1** preserved by being kept at a very low temperature: *frozen peas* **2 be frozen (stiff)** (spoken) to feel very cold: *Can you turn up the heat? I'm frozen!* **3** made very hard or turned to ice because of the cold: *the frozen lake* → *see picture at* MELT **4 be frozen with fear/terror/fright** to be so afraid, shocked, etc. that you cannot move

fruc·tose /'frʊktoʊs, 'frʌk-/ *n.* [U] CHEMISTRY a type of natural sugar in fruit juices and HONEY → GLUCOSE, LACTOSE, SUCROSE

fru·gal /'frugəl/ *adj.* **1** careful to only buy what is necessary: *My parents were very frugal.* **2** small in quantity and cost: *a frugal lunch of cheese and bread* —**frugally** *adv.* —**frugality** /fru'gæləṭi/ *n.* [U]

fruit /frut/ *n.* (plural **fruit** *or* **fruits**) **1** [C,U] something that grows on a plant, tree, or bush, can be eaten as food, contains seeds, and is usually sweet: *Apples and bananas are Nancy's favorite fruits.* | *Would you like **a piece of fruit**?* *see picture on page 414* **2 the fruit(s) of sth** the good results that you have from something, after you have worked hard: *the fruits of his research* [ORIGIN: 1100—1200 Old French, Latin *fructus*, from *frui* "to enjoy, have the use of"] → **bear fruit** *at* BEAR[1]

fruit·cake /'frutˀkeɪk/ *n.* **1** [C,U] a cake that has dried fruit in it **2** [C] (informal) someone who seems to be mentally ill or behaves in a strange way

'fruit fly *n.* [C] a small fly that eats and lays eggs on fruit

fruit·ful /'frutfəl/ *adj.* producing good results: *a fruitful meeting*

fru·i·tion /fru'ɪʃən/ *n.* [U] (formal) the successful result of a plan, idea, etc.: *The community has worked hard for this plan to **come to/be brought to fruition**.*

fruit·less /'frutlɪs/ *adj.* failing to produce good results, especially after much effort: *a **fruitless attempt** to end the fighting* —**fruitlessly** *adv.*

fruit·y /'fruṭi/ *adj.* tasting or smelling strongly of fruit: *a fruity wine*

frump·y /'frʌmpi/ *adj.* someone, especially a woman, who is frumpy wears old-fashioned clothes and looks unattractive

frus·trate /'frʌstreɪt/ *v.* [T] **1** if something frustrates you, it makes you feel annoyed or angry because you are unable to do what you want: *The lack of public transportation frustrates commuters.* **2** to prevent someone's plans, efforts, or attempts from succeeding: *They feel the system frustrates their attempts to improve productivity.*

frus·trat·ed /'frʌ,streɪṭɪd/ *adj.* feeling annoyed or angry because you are unable to do what you want to do: *He **gets frustrated** and angry because he feels stupid.* | *I was **frustrated with** the lack of progress.*

frus·trat·ing /'frʌ,streɪṭɪŋ/ *adj.* making you feel annoyed or angry because you cannot do what you want to do: *Having a broken arm is really frustrating.*

F

frus·tra·tion /frʌ'streɪʃən/ *n.* **1** [C,U] the feeling of being annoyed or angry because you are unable to do what you want to do: *A toddler was kicking the ground* ***in frustration***. **2** [U] the fact of being prevented from achieving what you want to achieve: ***The frustration of*** *his ambitions left him bitter.*

fry¹ /fraɪ/ *n.* (plural **fries**) [C usually plural] a long thin piece of potato that has been cooked in hot oil [ORIGIN: 1200—1300 Old French *frire*, from Latin *frigere*]

fry² *v.* (**fried**) [I,T] to cook something in hot fat or oil, or to be cooked in hot fat or oil: *I fried some bacon for breakfast.*

THESAURUS cook, bake, roast, broil, grill, sauté, boil, steam, deep fry → COOK¹

'frying ˌpan *n.* [C] a round pan with a flat handle, used for frying food

ft. the written abbreviation of FOOT

F

fudge¹ /fʌdʒ/ *n.* [U] a soft creamy sweet food, usually made with chocolate

fudge² *v.* [I,T] to avoid giving exact figures or facts, in order to deceive people

fu·el¹ /'fyuəl, fyul/ *n.* [C,U] a substance such as coal, gas, or oil that can be burned to produce heat or energy [ORIGIN: 1100—1200 Old French *fouaille*, from *feu* "fire," from Latin *focus* "hearth"]

fuel² *v.* **1** [T] to make a situation worse or to make someone's feelings stronger: *The increase in property prices only fueled inflation.* **2** [I,T] *also* **fuel up** to take fuel into a vehicle, or to provide a vehicle with fuel

'fuel cell *n.* [C] CHEMISTRY a piece of equipment that combines a FUEL such as HYDROGEN with oxygen to produce electricity

fu·gi·tive /'fyudʒət̬ɪv/ *n.* [C] someone who is trying to avoid being caught, especially by the police: *a* ***fugitive from*** *justice* [ORIGIN: 1300—1400 French *fugitif*, from Latin *fugere* "to run away"]

ful·crum /'fʊlkrəm, 'fʌl-/ *n.* [C] the point on which a BAR that is being used for lifting something turns or is supported

ful·fill /fʊl'fɪl/ *v.* [T] **1** to get, do, or achieve something you wanted, promised, or hoped for: *The president fulfilled his election promise to cut taxes.* | *Learning to fly fulfilled a childhood dream.* | *an education that will help each child* ***fulfill*** *his* ***potential*** (=be as successful as he can be) **2** to do or provide what is necessary or needed: *The firm failed to fulfill its obligations under the contract.* | *The breakfast club fulfills a need in this poor neighborhood school.* **3** to make you feel satisfied because you are doing something useful and interesting and using your skills and qualities: *She wanted work that would fulfill her.*

ful·filled /fʊl'fɪld/ *adj.* satisfied with your life, job, etc. because you feel that it is interesting or useful and you are using all your skills

ful·fill·ing /fʊl'fɪlɪŋ/ *adj.* making you feel happy and satisfied because you are doing interesting, useful, or important things: *a fulfilling career*

ful·fill·ment /fʊl'fɪlmənt/ *n.* [U] **1** the feeling of being happy and satisfied with your life because you are doing interesting, useful, or important things: *Ann's work gives her a real* ***sense of fulfillment****.* **2** the act or state of meeting a need, demand, or condition: *This contract offer depends upon the fulfillment of certain conditions.*

full¹ /fʊl/ *adj.*

1 CONTAINER/ROOM/PLACE ETC. holding or containing as much or as many things or people as possible (ANT) **empty**: *Don't talk with your mouth full.* | *a full glass of milk* | *The bottle was only* ***half full****.* | *a box* ***full of*** *paper* ➔ see picture at EMPTY¹

THESAURUS

filled with sth – full of something: *a shopping cart filled with groceries*
packed – extremely full of people or things: *The trial took place in front of a packed courtroom.* | *The stadium was packed with fans.*
crammed – full of people or things: *The garage was crammed with junk.*
stuffed (full of sth) – full of things: *a suitcase stuffed full of clothes*
bursting (with sth) – very full of something: *a muffin bursting with blueberries*
overflowing – a container that is overflowing is so full that the liquid or things inside it come out over the top: *an overflowing trash basket*
overloaded – if a vehicle or ship is overloaded, too many people or things have been put in it: *The helicopter was overloaded and barely got off the ground.*
teeming with sth – full of people or animals that are all moving around: *The lake was teeming with fish.*
replete (formal) – full of something: *Books on the war were replete with references to him.*

2 COMPLETE [only before noun] including all parts or details: *Please write your* ***full name*** *and address in the boxes.* | *We will pay* ***the full cost*** *of repairs.*

3 HIGHEST AMOUNT/LEVEL [only before noun] the highest level or greatest amount of something that is possible: *The ship was going at* ***full speed****.* | *You have our* ***full support****.* | *I didn't pay* ***full price*** *for the jacket.*

4 be full of sth **a)** to contain many things of the same kind: *Eric's essay is full of mistakes.* | *a garden full of flowers* **b)** to feel or express a strong emotion: *Cathy woke up full of excitement.* | *He was full of praise for the children's achievement.* **c)** to think or talk about only one subject all the time: *She's full of plans for the wedding.*

5 FOOD [not before noun] having eaten so much food that you cannot eat any more: *"Would you like some more soup?" "No thanks.* ***I'm full****."*

6 CLOTHING a full skirt, pair of pants, etc. is made with a lot of material and fits loosely

7 BODY a full face, body, etc. is rounded or large: *clothes for the fuller figure*

8 TASTE/SOUND ETC. a full taste, sound, color, etc. is strong and pleasant: *a* ***full-bodied*** *wine*

9 RANK [only before noun] having or giving all the rights, duties, etc. that belong to a particular rank or position: *a full professor*

full² *n.* **1 in full** if you pay an amount of money in full, you pay the whole amount **2 to the full** in the best or most complete way: *Ronnie lived his life to the full.*

full³ *adv.* (literary) directly: *The sun shone* ***full on*** *her face.*

'full-blown *adj.* fully developed: *full-blown AIDS*

ˌfull-'fledged *adj.* completely developed, trained, or established: *a full-fledged lawyer*

ˌfull-'grown *adj.* a full-grown person, animal, or plant has developed to his, her, or its full size and will not grow any bigger

ˌfull 'house *n.* [C] an occasion at a concert hall, sports field, etc. when every seat has someone sitting in it

ˌfull-'length *adj.* **1 full-length mirror/photograph etc.** a mirror, etc. that shows all of a person, from his/her head to his/her feet **2 full-length skirt/dress** a skirt, etc. that reaches the ground **3 full-length play/book etc.** a play, etc. of the normal length

ˌfull 'moon *n.* [singular] the moon when it looks completely round

full·ness /'fʊlnɪs/ *n.* **1 in the fullness of time** (formal) when the right time comes: *I'm sure he'll tell us everything in the fullness of time.* **2** [U] the condition of having eaten enough food **3** [U] the quality of being large and round: *the fullness of her lips*

ˌfull-'scale *adj.* **1** as complete or thorough as possible: *a full-scale investigation* **2** a full-scale model, copy, picture, etc. is the same size as the thing it represents

ˌfull-'time *adj., adv.* working or studying for the number of hours that people usually work or study ➔ PART-TIME: *Andrea works full-time for an insurance company.* | *full-time students*

ful·ly /'fʊli/ *adv.* completely: *a fully trained nurse*

fum·ble /'fʌmbəl/ *v.* **1** [I] to try to hold, move, or find something with your hands in an awkward way: *Gary* ***fumbled for*** *the light switch in the dark.* **2** [I,T] to have difficulty saying something: *She* ***fumbled for*** *an appropriate response.* **3** [I,T] to drop a ball after catching it —**fumble** *n.* [C]

fume /fyum/ *v.* [I] to be very angry: *He was* ***fuming about/over/at*** *the repair costs.*

fumes /fyumz/ *n.* [plural] strong-smelling gas or smoke that is unpleasant to breathe in: *gasoline fumes*

F

fu·mi·gate /ˈfyuməˌgeɪt/ *v.* [T] to remove disease, BACTERIA, insects, etc. from somewhere using chemical smoke or gas —**fumigation** /ˌfyuməˈgeɪʃən/ *n.* [U]

fun¹ /fʌn/ *n.* [U] **1** pleasure, amusement, and enjoyment, or an activity that is enjoyable: *Swimming is a lot of fun.* | *Did you **have fun** at Phil's house?* | *I have to admit – **it's more fun** to win.* | *It's nice to have time to read something **for fun**.* | *The trip would be **no fun*** (=not fun) *with a bad back.*

USAGE

Use **fun** to talk about situations or activities that you enjoy: *Ice skating is a lot of fun.*
Use **funny** to describe someone or something that makes you laugh: *The movie was so funny we couldn't stop laughing.*

2 make fun of sb/sth to make unkind jokes about someone or something: *Some of the kids started making fun of Sarinder's accent.* **3 in fun** if you make a joke or say something about someone in fun, you do not intend it to be insulting: *I'm sorry, I only said it in fun.*

F

fun² *adj.* **1** a fun activity or experience is enjoyable: *It was a fun day.* **2** a fun person is enjoyable to be with: *Terry is always fun to be with.*

func·tion¹ /ˈfʌŋkʃən/ (Ac) *n.* [C] **1** the usual purpose of a thing, or the job that someone usually does: *What's **the** exact **function of** this program?* | *A manager has to **perform** many different **functions**.* **2** a large party or ceremonial event, especially for an important or official occasion: *The mayor has to attend all kinds of official functions.* **3** a mathematical quantity that changes according to how another mathematical quantity changes [ORIGIN: 1500—1600 Latin *functio*, from *fungi* "to perform"]

function² (Ac) *v.* [I] to work in a particular way or in the correct way: *Her kidneys had stopped functioning.*

function as sth *phr. v.* to be used or work as something: *The space station functions as a laboratory in space.*

func·tion·al /ˈfʌŋkʃənəl/ (Ac) *adj.* **1** designed to be useful rather than attractive: *functional furniture* **2** working in the way that something is supposed to: *There is a fully functional calculator on the key ring.* **3 functional illiteracy/illiterate** the quality of being able to read, but not well enough to perform skilled jobs, or someone who has this quality —**functionally** *adv.*

ˈfunction key *n.* [C] IT a key on the KEYBOARD of a computer that tells it to do something

ˈfunction word *n.* [C] ENG. LANG. ARTS a word such as a PRONOUN or PREPOSITION that is used in place of another word, or that shows the relationship between two words. For example, in the sentences "The cat is hungry. It hasn't been fed yet," "it" is a function word.

fund¹ /fʌnd/ (Ac) *n.* [C] **1** ECONOMICS an amount of money that is kept for a particular purpose: *candidates' campaign funds* | *a scholarship fund* **2 funds** [plural] ECONOMICS the money that an organization needs or has: *The PTO helps **raise funds** for the school.* | *federal funds for welfare programs* → MUTUAL FUND **3** an organization that is responsible for collecting and spending money for a particular purpose: *the Environmental Defense Fund* [ORIGIN: 1600—1700 Latin *fundus* "bottom, piece of land"]

fund² (Ac) *v.* [T] to provide money for an activity, organization, event, etc.: *Their medical research is federally funded.*

fun·da·men·tal¹ /ˌfʌndəˈmɛntəl◂/ (Ac) *adj.* **1** relating to the most basic and important parts of something: *People are demanding a **fundamental change** in the political system.* | *the fundamental democratic principle of free speech*

THESAURUS **basic, essential, elementary, central, underlying** → BASIC

2 necessary for something to exist or develop: *Education is **fundamental to** improving people's chances in life.*

fundamental² (Ac) *n.* [C usually plural] the most important ideas, rules, skills, etc. that something is based on: *the fundamentals of basketball*

fun·da·men·tal·ist /ˌfʌndəˈmɛntəlɪst/ *n.* [C] **1** someone who follows the rules of his/her religion very strictly **2** a Christian who believes that everything in the Bible is completely and actually true —**fundamentalist** *adj.* —**fundamentalism** *n.* [U]

fun·da·men·tal·ly /ˌfʌndəˈmɛntəl-i/ (Ac) *adv.* in every way that is important or basic: *Our political views are fundamentally different.*

fun·da·men·tals /ˌfʌndəˈmɛntəlz/ *n.* **the fundamentals of sth** the most important ideas, rules, etc. that something is based on: *a class in the fundamentals of computer programming*

fund·ing /ˈfʌndɪŋ/ (Ac) *n.* [U] ECONOMICS an amount of money used for a special purpose: *The university is providing **funding for** the research.*

ˈfund-ˌraising *adj.* fund-raising events collect money for a specific purpose

fu·ner·al /ˈfyunərəl/ *n.* [C] a ceremony, usually religious, for burying or burning a dead person: *The **funeral** will be **held** on Thursday at St. Patrick's church.* | *More than 150 people **attended the funeral**.* [ORIGIN: 1300—1400 Late Latin *funeralis*, from Latin *funus* "funeral"]

ˈfuneral diˌrector *n.* [C] someone whose job is to arrange funerals

ˈfuneral home *also* **ˈfuneral ˌparlor** *n.* [C] the place where a body is kept before a funeral and where sometimes the funeral is held

fun·gus /ˈfʌŋgəs/ *n.* (plural **fungi** /ˈfʌndʒaɪ, -gaɪ/ *or* **funguses**) [C,U] BIOLOGY a simple plant without leaves, such as MUSHROOMS, MOLD, and YEAST, that grows in dark warm slightly wet places —**fungal** /ˈfʌŋgəl/ *adj.*

funk /fʌŋk/ *n.* [U] **1** a type of popular music with a strong beat that is based on JAZZ and African music **2 in a funk** (informal) unhappy or worried about something

funk·y /ˈfʌŋki/ *adj.* (informal) **1** modern, fashionable, and interesting: *a funky website* **2** funky music is simple, with a strong RHYTHM that is easy to dance to

fun·nel[1] /ˈfʌnl/ *n.* [C] a tube with a wide top and a narrow bottom, used for pouring liquids or powders into a container

funnel

funnel[2] *v.* **1** [I,T] if you funnel something somewhere, or if it funnels there, it goes there by passing through a narrow opening: *The crowd* ***funneled through*** *the narrow streets.* **2** [T] to send things or money from different places to a particular place or person: *a policy of* ***funneling*** *the most talented students* ***into*** *special schools*

fun·nies /ˈfʌniz/ *n.* **the funnies** a number of different CARTOONS (=funny pictures) printed together in newspapers or magazines

fun·ni·ly /ˈfʌnəli/ *adv.* → **strangely/oddly/funnily enough** *at* ENOUGH

funny[1] /ˈfʌni/ *adj.* **1** amusing you and making you laugh: *John gave a funny little speech.* | *What's so funny?* | *He looked really funny.*

THESAURUS
hilarious/hysterical – extremely funny
witty – using words in a funny and intelligent way: *witty remarks*
amusing/humorous – slightly more formal ways to say that something is funny: *an amusing anecdote* (=a short, interesting, and funny story about an event or person)
comical – funny, especially in a strange or unexpected way: *a comical hat* → see USAGE box at FUN[1]

2 strange or unexpected, and difficult to understand or explain: *What's that funny noise?* | *The room smelled funny.* | *I got a funny feeling that someone was watching me.*

THESAURUS **strange, peculiar, curious, mysterious, odd, weird, bizarre, eccentric** → STRANGE[1]

3 slightly sick: *It makes my stomach* ***feel funny.***

SPOKEN PHRASES
4 it's funny used in order to say that you do not understand something that seems strange or unexpected: *"It's funny," she said. "You seem different somehow."* | ***It's funny how*** *you can affect people and not even realize it.* **5 that's funny** said when you are surprised by something that has happened, that you cannot explain: *That's funny! She was here just a minute ago.* **6 the funny thing is** used in order to say what the strangest or most amusing part of a story or situation is: *The funny thing is, once I stopped dieting I started to lose weight.* **7 very funny!** said when someone is laughing at you or making a joke that you do not think is funny

funny[2] *adv.* in a strange or unusual way: *Judy's been acting kind of funny lately.*

ˈ**funny bone** *n.* [singular] the soft part of your elbow that hurts a lot when you hit it against something

fur /fɚ/ *n.* **1** [U] the thick soft hair that covers the bodies of some animals, such as dogs and cats → *see picture on page A15* **2** [C,U] the skin of a dead animal with the fur still attached to it, or a piece of clothing made from this: *a fur coat* [ORIGIN: 1300—1400 *fur* "to cover the inside of with fur" (14—19 centuries), from Old French *forre* "inside covering"]

fu·ri·ous /ˈfyʊriəs/ *adj.* **1** very angry: *Jim'll be* ***furious with*** *me if I'm late.* | *Dad was* ***furious that*** *I had taken the car without asking.*

THESAURUS **angry, annoyed, irritated, livid, mad, indignant, irate, outraged, resentful** → ANGRY

2 done with a lot of uncontrolled energy or anger: *He woke up to a furious pounding at the door.* —**furiously** *adv.*

furled /fɚld/ *adj.* rolled or folded: *a furled umbrella* —**furl** *v.* [T]

fur·long /ˈfɚlɔŋ/ *n.* [C] (old-fashioned) a unit for measuring length that is used in horse racing. A furlong equals 201 meters and there are eight furlongs in a mile.

fur·lough /ˈfɚloʊ/ *n.* [C] a short period of time in which someone is allowed to be away from his/her job, especially in the military: *a soldier home* ***on furlough***

THESAURUS **vacation, holiday, break, leave, r & r, sabbatical** → VACATION

fur·nace /ˈfɚnɪs/ *n.* [C] a large container with a hot fire inside it, used for producing power or heat, or to melt metals and other materials

fur·nish /ˈfɚnɪʃ/ *v.* [T] **1** to put furniture and other things into a house or room: *a room* ***furnished with*** *two beds* **2** to supply something: *Your Internet provider will* ***furnish*** *you* ***with*** *e-mail software.* —**furnished** *adj.*: *a furnished apartment*

fur·nish·ings /ˈfɚnɪʃɪŋz/ *n.* [plural] the furniture and other things in a room, such as curtains, decorations, etc.

fur·ni·ture /ˈfɚnɪtʃɚ/ *n.* [U] large objects such as chairs, tables, and beds that you use in a room, office, etc.: *The room's only* ***piece of furniture*** *was an old sofa.* | *office furniture* [ORIGIN: 1500—1600 French *fourniture*, from Old French *furnir* "to complete, provide equipment"]

F

GRAMMAR

Furniture does not have a plural form. Do not say "furnitures". You can say **some furniture** or **any furniture:** *We need to buy some new furniture.* A single chair or table is **a piece of furniture**

fu·ror /ˈfyʊrɔr/ *n.* [singular] a sudden expression of anger or excitement among a large group of people: *His decision to resign* ***caused/created a furor.***

fur·row¹ /ˈfɚoʊ, ˈfʌroʊ/ *n.* [C] a long deep fold or line in the surface of something such as skin or the ground: *the furrows of a plowed field*

furrow² *v.* [T] to make a long deep fold or line in the surface of something such as skin or the ground: *Saks furrowed his brow.* **—furrowed** *adj.*

fur·ry /ˈfɚi/ *adj.* covered with fur, or looking or feeling as if covered with fur: *furry material*

fur·ther¹ /ˈfɚðɚ/ *adv.* **1** more, or to a greater degree: *I have nothing further to say.* | *Mark went* ***further into*** *debt.* | *He was falling* ***further and further*** *behind in his schoolwork.* **2** a longer way in time or space: *The records don't go any* ***further back*** *than 1960.* | *Their home is* ***further down*** *the street.* **3 take sth further** to do something at a more serious or higher level: *Hallas decided not to take the court case any further.* **4** (formal) in addition to what has already been written or said (SYN) **furthermore**

F

further² *adj.* additional: *Are there any further questions?* | ***Further information*** *is available on the website.*

THESAURUS **more, another, extra, additional, supplemental, supplementary** ➔ MORE²

further³ *v.* [T] (formal) to help something to succeed: *The training should help him further his career.*

fur·ther·more /ˈfɚðɚˌmɔr/ (Ac) *adv.* (formal) in addition to what has already been written or said: *Cycling to work is quicker than driving. Furthermore, it's a lot cheaper.*

fur·thest /ˈfɚðɪst/ *adj., adv.* **1** to the greatest degree or amount, or more than before: *Smith's book has probably* ***gone furthest*** (=done the most) *in explaining these events.* **2** at the greatest distance from a place or point in time: *the houses* ***furthest from*** *the center of town*

fur·tive /ˈfɚt̬ɪv/ *adj.* behaving as if you want to keep something secret: *a* ***furtive glance*** [ORIGIN: 1600—1700 French *furtif,* from Latin *fur* "thief"] **—furtively** *adv.*

fu·ry /ˈfyʊri/ *n.* **1** [singular, U] a state or feeling of extreme anger: *She was filled* ***with fury.*** | *Hanson left the meeting* ***in a fury.*** **2 the fury of the wind/storm etc.** used in order to describe very bad weather **3 a fury of sth** a state of great activity or strong feeling: *Joe went home in a fury of frustration.*

fuse¹ /fyuz/ *n.* [C] **1** a short wire inside a piece of electrical equipment that prevents damage to the equipment by melting if too much electricity tries to pass through it: *I went down to the basement and replaced a* ***blown fuse*** (=a fuse that had melted). **2** *also* **fuze** a part of a bomb, FIREWORK, etc. that delays it from exploding or makes it explode at a particular time **3** used in expressions relating to someone becoming angry: *Randy finally* ***blew a fuse*** (=got angry very suddenly) *and screamed at us.* | *Martina* ***has a short fuse*** (=gets angry easily) *when she's tired.*

fuse² *v.* [I,T] **1** to join together and become one thing, or to join two things together: *His novel fuses historical information with a romantic story.* **2** PHYSICS if metals, rocks, etc. fuse together, they melt and join together

fuse·box /ˈfyuzbɑks/ *n.* [C] a metal box that contains the fuses for the electrical system in a building

fu·se·lage /ˈfyusəˌlɑʒ, -lɪdʒ, -zə-/ *n.* [C] the main part of an airplane, in which people sit or goods are carried ➔ *see picture at* AIRPLANE

fu·sion /ˈfyuʒən/ *n.* [C,U] **1** PHYSICS the process of joining together the nuclei (NUCLEUS) of atoms, which produces heavier atoms and a lot of energy ➔ FISSION: *experiments in nuclear fusion* **2** the combination of separate things, groups, or ideas: *a fusion of French and Indian cuisine* [ORIGIN: 1500—1600 Latin *fusio,* from *fundere* "to pour, melt"]

fuss¹ /fʌs/ *n.* **1** [singular, U] attention, excitement, or activity that is not really necessary: *Hey, what's all the fuss about* (=why are people so excited, angry, busy, etc.)? | *They wanted a quiet wedding without any fuss.* **2 make a fuss/kick up a fuss** to complain or become angry about something that other people do not think is important: *Don't be afraid to make a fuss if you think you're not being treated right.* **3 make a fuss over sb/sth** to pay a lot of attention to someone or something that you like: *His mother made a fuss over him, stroking his hair.*

fuss² *v.* [I] to complain or become upset: *The baby woke up and started to fuss.*

fuss over sb/sth *phr. v.* to pay a lot of attention to someone or something that you like: *The women started fussing over Kate's baby.*

fuss with sth *phr. v.* to move or touch something again and again in a nervous way: *Stop fussing with your hair!*

fuss·y /ˈfʌsi/ *adj.* (comparative **fussier**, superlative **fussiest**) **1** concerned or worried about things that are not very important: *Many kids are fussy eaters.* **2** a fussy baby cries a lot **3** very detailed or decorated, in a way that is unpleasant

fu·tile /ˈfyut̬l/ *adj.* having no chance of being effective or successful: *a* ***futile attempt/effort*** *to prevent the war* **—futility** /fyuˈtɪlət̬i/ *n.* [U]

THESAURUS pointless, useless, a waste of time/money/effort, senseless → POINTLESS

fu·ton /'futan/ *n.* [C] a soft flat MATTRESS that can be used as a bed or folded into a chair

fu·ture¹ /'fyutʃɚ/ *n.* **1 the future** the time that will happen after the present: *Each story has a different vision of the future.* | *a feeling of hope* ***for the future*** | *The airport has room for another runway to be built* ***in the future*** (=at some time in the future). | *Investigators hope to wrap up the case* ***in the near/immediate future*** (=soon). | *The order will keep the company busy* ***for the foreseeable future*** (=for as long as you can plan for). | *a story set* ***in the not too distant future*** (=not too far in the future) **2 in the future** the next time you do the same activity: *In the future I'll be sure to reserve tickets.* **3** [C,U] what will happen to someone or something, or what he, she, or it will do in the future: *Parents want the best for their children's futures.* | *an issue that will affect* ***the future of*** *our country* | *Businesses must* ***look to the future*** (=plan for what will happen). **4 the future** ENG. LANG. ARTS in grammar, the tense of a verb that shows that an action or state will happen or exist at a later time. It is often shown in English by the MODAL VERB "will" followed by a verb. In the sentence "We will leave tomorrow," "will leave" is in the future. [ORIGIN: 1300—1400 Old French *futur*, from Latin *futurus* "going to be"]

future² *adj.* **1** likely to happen or exist during the time after the present: *The park will be preserved for future generations.* | *companies planning for future growth* | *I'd like you to meet my future wife* (=the person who will be your wife). **2** ENG. LANG. ARTS in grammar, being a tense of a verb that shows a future action or state: *the future tense* **3 for future reference** in order to be used again at a later time: *Can I* ***keep*** *that article* ***for future reference?***

ˌfuture 'perfect *n.* **the future perfect** ENG. LANG. ARTS in grammar, the tense of a verb that shows that an action will be completed before a particular time in the future. It is shown by the AUXILIARY VERBS "will have" followed by a past participle. In the sentence "I will have finished my finals by next Friday," "will have finished" is in the future perfect.

fu·tur·is·tic /ˌfyutʃə'rɪstɪk◂/ *adj.* futuristic ideas, books, movies, etc. describe what might happen in the future, especially because of scientific developments

fuze /fyuz/ *n.* [C] another spelling of FUSE¹

fuzz /fʌz/ *n.* [U] (informal) small soft thin hairs, or a similar material, on fruit such as PEACHes

fuzz·y /'fʌzi/ *adj.* **1** if a sound or picture is fuzzy, it is not clear: *Unfortunately, a lot of the photos are fuzzy.* **2** not easy to understand or not having very clear details: *The distinction between the two is fuzzy.* **3** having a lot of very small thin hairs, fur, etc. that are very soft: *a fuzzy sweater*

fwy. the written abbreviation of FREEWAY

FYI the abbreviation of **for your information**, used especially on MEMOs (=short business notes)

Gg

G, g /dʒi/ the seventh letter of the English alphabet

G /dʒi/ *n.* **1** [C,U] ENG. LANG. ARTS the fifth note in the musical SCALE of C, or the musical KEY based on this note **2** [C] PHYSICS an amount of force caused by GRAVITY on an object that is on the surface of the Earth **3** [C] PHYSICS a unit for measuring the rate at which an object increases speed as a result of GRAVITY **4** [C,U] **general** – used to show that a movie has been approved for people of any age

GA the written abbreviation of GEORGIA

gab /gæb/ *v.* (**gabbed**, **gabbing**) [I] (informal) to talk continuously, usually about things that are not important

G

ga·ble /'geɪbəl/ *n.* [C] the top part of a wall of a house where it joins with a pointed roof, making a shape like a TRIANGLE

gadg·et /'gædʒɪt/ *n.* [C] a small tool or machine that makes a particular job easier: *a handy kitchen gadget*

THESAURUS machine, appliance, device, mechanism, contraption → MACHINE¹

gaffe /gæf/ *n.* [C] an embarrassing mistake made in a social situation

gag¹ /gæg/ *v.* (**gagged**, **gagging**) **1** [I] to be unable to swallow and feel as if you are going to bring up the food from your stomach: *The smell made me gag.* | *I started* ***gagging on*** *a piece of my burrito.* **2** [T] to tie a piece of cloth over someone's mouth so that s/he cannot make any noise

gag² *n.* [C] **1** (informal) a joke or funny story

THESAURUS joke, wisecrack, one-liner, quip, witticism, pun, funny story → JOKE¹

2 a piece of cloth used in order to gag someone **3 gag gift** a present for someone that is meant to be funny → GAG ORDER

gagged /gægd/ *adj.* having your mouth tied with a piece of cloth so that you cannot make any noise

gag·gle /'gægəl/ *n.* [C] a group of GEESE, or a noisy group of people

'gag ˌorder *n.* [C] an order given by a court of law to prevent any public reporting of a case that is still being considered in the court

'gag rule *n.* [C] **1** POLITICS a rule or law that stops people from talking about a subject during a particular time or in a particular place **2** HISTORY a law passed by the House of Representatives in 1836 that prevented any speeches or documents that were against SLAVERY to be read or dealt with in the House

gai·e·ty /ˈgeɪəṭi/ *n.* [U] (old-fashioned) the state of having fun and being happy

gai·ly /ˈgeɪli/ *adv.* (old-fashioned) in a happy way

gain¹ /geɪn/ *v.* **1** [I,T] to get, win, or achieve something that you want or need (ANT) **lose**: *The Republicans gained control of Congress.* | *India gained independence in 1947.* | *What do you hope to **gain from** the course?*

USAGE

Gain means to get something useful or necessary: *I've gained a lot of useful experience.* Do not use **gain** to talk about getting money for the work you do. Use **earn**: *How much do you think he earns a year?*
Make is a less formal way of saying **earn**: *You can make a lot of money.*
Win means to get a prize in a game or competition: *I won second prize.*

G

2 [I,T] to gradually get more of a quality, feeling, etc.: *The ideas quickly gained popular support.* | *a chance to gain experience in publishing* | *The show has been **gaining in** popularity.* **3** [T] to increase in weight, speed, height, or value: *Bea has **gained** a lot of **weight** since Christmas.* | *The dollar gained 4% against the yen.* **4 gain access a)** to be able to enter a room or building: *Somehow the thief had gained access to his apartment.* **b)** to be allowed to see or use something: *Marston had difficulty gaining access to official documents.*

gain on sb/sth *phr. v.* to start getting closer to the person, car, etc. that you are chasing: *Hurry up! They're **gaining on** us!* [ORIGIN: 1400—1500 French *gagner*, from Old French *gaaignier* "to prepare the ground for growing crops, earn, gain"]

gain² *n.* **1** [C,U] an increase in the amount or level of something: *the program's **gain in** popularity* | *weight gain* | *the country's recent economic gains* **2** [C] an advantage or an improvement: ***gains in** medical science*

gait /geɪt/ *n.* [U] the way that someone walks

gal /gæl/ *n.* [C] (informal) a girl or woman

ga·la /ˈgælə, ˈgeɪlə/ *n.* [C] an event at which a lot of people are entertained and celebrate a special occasion [ORIGIN: 1600—1700 Italian, Old French *gale* "fun and enjoyment"] —**gala** *adj.*

ga·lac·tic /gəˈlæktɪk/ *adj.* PHYSICS relating to the galaxy

gal·ax·y /ˈgæləksi/ *n.* (plural **galaxies**) [C] **1** PHYSICS one of the large groups of stars that are in the universe → SPACE¹ **2 the Galaxy** PHYSICS the large group of stars that includes the Earth, the Sun, and the other PLANETS in our SOLAR SYSTEM [ORIGIN: 1300—1400 Late Latin *galaxias*, from Greek, from *gala* "milk;" because the galaxy looks milky white from the Earth]

gale /geɪl/ *n.* [C] a very strong wind: *a fierce gale*

THESAURUS **wind, breeze, gust, storm, hurricane, tornado, typhoon** → WIND¹

gall /gɔl/ *n.* **have the gall to do sth** to do something rude or unreasonable that most people would be embarrassed to do: *She had the gall to say that I looked fat!*

gal·lant /ˈgælənt/ *adj.* (old-fashioned) brave and kind: *a gallant soldier* —**gallantly** *adv.* —**gallantry** *n.* [U]

ˈgall ˌbladder *n.* [C] BIOLOGY the organ in your body that stores BILE

gal·ler·y /ˈgæləri/ *n.* (plural **galleries**) [C] **1** a room, hall, or building where people can look at paintings or other types of art: *the National Gallery of Art in Washington* **2** a small expensive store where people can look at and buy art: ***art galleries** in Manhattan* **3** an upper floor like a BALCONY inside a hall, church, or theater, where people can sit [ORIGIN: 1400—1500 Medieval Latin *galeria*]

gal·ley /ˈgæli/ *n.* [C] **1** a kitchen on a ship or an airplane **2** a long Greek or Roman ship that was rowed by SLAVES

gall·ing /ˈgɔlɪŋ/ *adj.* annoying: *a galling defeat*

gal·lon /ˈgælən/ *n.* [C] a unit for measuring liquid, equal to 4 QUARTS or 3.785 liters: *a **gallon of** gas* [ORIGIN: 1200—1300 Old North French, Medieval Latin *galeta* "liquid container, liquid measure"]

gallop

gal·lop¹ /ˈgæləp/ *v.* [I] if a horse gallops, it runs as fast as it can

gallop² *n.* [singular] the fastest speed that a horse can go, or the movement of a horse at this speed

gal·lop·ing /ˈgæləpɪŋ/ *adj.* increasing or developing very quickly: *galloping inflation*

gal·lows /ˈgæloʊz/ *n.* (plural **gallows**) [C] a structure that is used for killing criminals by hanging them

gall·stone /ˈgɔlstoʊn/ *n.* [C] BIOLOGY a hard stone that can form in your GALL BLADDER

ga·lore /gəˈlɔr/ *adj.* in large amounts or numbers:

He had toys and clothes galore. ►Don't say "He had galore clothes."◄ [ORIGIN: 1600—1700 Irish Gaelic *go leor* "enough"]

ga·losh·es /gə'lɑʃɪz/ *n.* [plural] (old-fashioned) rubber shoes you wear over your normal shoes when it rains or snows

gal·va·nize /'gælvə,naɪz/ *v.* [T] to shock someone so much that s/he realizes s/he needs to do something to solve a problem or improve the situation: *Martin Luther King's protests galvanized the nation.*

gal·va·nized /'gælvə,naɪzd/ *adj.* galvanized metal has been treated in a special way so that it does not RUST

gam·bit /'gæmbɪt/ *n.* [C] something you do or say in order to gain control in an argument, conversation, or meeting [ORIGIN: 1600—1700 Italian *gambetto* "act of making someone fall over," from *gamba* "leg"]

gam·ble¹ /'gæmbəl/ *v.* **1** [I] to risk money or possessions on the result of something such as a card game, race, etc. because you might win a lot more money if the race, etc. has the result you want: *Jack won $700 gambling in Las Vegas.* | *They* ***gambled on*** *the horses.* **2** [I,T] to do something that involves risk because you hope things will happen the way you want them to: *Many investors* ***gambled that*** *the market would continue to improve.*

gamble sth ↔ **away** *phr. v.* to lose money or possessions by gambling

gamble² *n.* [singular] an action or plan that involves risk because it might not be successful: *The coach* ***took a gamble*** *in playing the inexperienced young quarterback.*

gam·bler /'gæmblə/ *n.* [C] someone who gambles, especially as a habit

gam·bling /'gæmblɪŋ/ *n.* [U] the activity of risking money and possessions because you might win a lot more if a race, card game, etc. has the result you want: *Gambling is legal in Nevada.*

game¹ /geɪm/ *n.* **1** [C] an activity or sport that people play for fun or in a competition: *a good* ***card/video/board game*** | *The boys are outside,* ***playing*** *some kind of* ***game***.

THESAURUS

sport – a physical activity in which people or teams play against each other and try to win: *Her favorite sport is basketball.*
recreation – all the activities that people do in order to relax: *the city's parks and recreation department*
hobby – an activity that you do in your free time: *Her hobbies are reading and music.*
diversion (formal) – an activity that you do for pleasure or amusement: *Knitting is a relaxing diversion.*

2 [C] a particular occasion when you play a sport or activity: *Who* ***won/lost*** *the football* ***game***? | *The Aztecs* ***play*** *only two* ***games*** *this month.* | *How about a* ***game of*** *chess?* **3 games** [plural] a large sports event, where a variety of sports are played: *the Olympic Games* **4** [C] one of the parts of a competition, such as in tennis or BRIDGE: *Williams leads, two games to one.* **5 sb's game** how well someone plays a particular game or sport: *Ramone's* ***game*** *steadily* ***improved***. | *Abdul-Jabbar was* ***at the top of*** *his* ***game*** (=playing very well). **6 play games** to behave in a way that is not serious or that is dishonest or unfair: *Don't* ***play games with*** *me. I don't have time.* **7 be (just) a game** if something is just a game to you, you do not consider how serious or important it is: *Marriage is just a game to you, isn't it?* **8** [U] wild animals and birds that are hunted for food and as a sport [ORIGIN: Old English *gamen*]

game² *adj.* willing to do something dangerous, new, or difficult: *I'm game if you are.*

'game plan *n.* [C] a plan for achieving success, especially in business or politics: *the Senator's political game plan*

'game show *n.* [C] a television program in which people play games or answer questions in order to win money and prizes → TELEVISION

gam·ete /'gæmit/ *n.* [C] BIOLOGY a type of cell that joins with another cell, starting the development of a baby or other young creature [ORIGIN: 1800—1900 Modern Latin *gameta*, from Greek *gametes* "husband"]

gam·ma ray /'gæmə reɪ/ *n.* [C] PHYSICS a type of RADIATION that is the result of splitting the NUCLEUS (=central part) of an atom

gam·ut /'gæmət/ *n.* [singular] a complete range of possibilities: *His musical influences* ***ran the gamut from*** *Elvis* ***to*** *the Sex Pistols* (=included all the possibilities between two extremes). [ORIGIN: 1400—1500 Medieval Latin *gamma ut*, names given to the highest and lowest notes on the musical scale]

gan·der /'gændə/ *n.* **1** [C] a male GOOSE **2 have/take a gander at sth** (informal) to look at something

gang¹ /gæŋ/ *n.* [C] **1** a group of young people who often cause trouble and fight other similar groups: *teenage* ***gang members*** | *Chicago* ***street gangs*** | *the victims of* ***gang violence*** **2** a group of criminals who work together: *a* ***gang of*** *drug dealers* **3** a group of friends: *All the old gang will be there.*

gang² *v.*

gang up on sb *phr. v.* to join a group in order to criticize or attack someone: *My brothers used to gang up on me.*

gang·bust·ers /'gæŋ,bʌstəz/ *n.* **like gangbusters** (informal) very eargerly and with a lot of energy, or very quickly and successfully: *The town is growing like gangbusters.*

gang·land /'gæŋlænd/ *adj.* **a gangland killing/shooting/murder** a violent action that happens because of organized crime

gan·gly /ˈgæŋgli/ *also* **gan·gling** /ˈgæŋglɪŋ/ *adj.* very tall and thin and unable to move gracefully: *a gangly teenager*

gang·plank /ˈgæŋplæŋk/ *n.* [C] a board you walk on between a ship and the shore, or between two ships

gan·grene /ˈgæŋgrin, gæŋˈgrin/ *n.* [U] a medical condition in which your flesh decays on part of your body because blood has stopped flowing there as a result of an illness or injury

gang·ster /ˈgæŋstɚ/ *n.* [C] a member of a group of violent criminals

gang·way /ˈgæŋweɪ/ *n.* [C] a large gangplank

gap /gæp/ *n.* [C] **1** an empty space between two things or two parts of something: *a big* ***gap between*** *her two front teeth* | *a* ***gap in*** *the fence*

> THESAURUS **hole, space, leak, crack, opening, cavity** → HOLE[1]

2 a difference between two situations, groups, amounts, etc.: *a large age* ***gap between*** *Jorge and his sister* | *We should be trying to* ***bridge the gap between*** *rich and poor.* **3** something that is missing that stops something else from being good or complete: *His death left a* ***gap in*** *my life.* | *a* ***gap in*** *her memory* | *The company has* ***filled a gap in the market*** (=they produce a product or service that did not exist before). **4** a period of time in which nothing happens or nothing is said: *an uncomfortable* ***gap in*** *the conversation* **5** a low place between two higher parts of a mountain

gape /geɪp/ *v.* [I] **1** to look at something for a long time, usually with your mouth open, because you are very shocked or surprised: *She backed away from the children, who were* ***gaping at*** *her.*

> THESAURUS **look, glance, peek, peep, peer, stare, gaze, regard** → LOOK[1]

2 *also* **gape open** to be wide open or open widely: *Dan stood at the door, his shirt gaping open.*

gap·ing /ˈgeɪpɪŋ/ *adj.* a gaping hole, wound, or mouth is very wide and open

ga·rage /gəˈrɑʒ, gəˈrɑdʒ/ *n.* [C] **1** a building, usually connected to or next to your house, where you keep your car: *I think my tools are out in the garage.* | *a* ***one-car/two-car garage*** **2** a place where cars are repaired: *We took the car to a garage on Fourth Street.* [ORIGIN: 1900—2000 French *garer* "to shelter"] → PARKING GARAGE

gaˈrage ˌsale *n.* [C] a sale of used clothes, furniture, toys, etc. that you no longer want, usually held in your garage

garb /gɑrb/ *n.* [U] (literary) a particular style of clothing

gar·bage /ˈgɑrbɪdʒ/ *n.* **1** [singular, U] waste material such as old food, dirty paper, and empty bags, usually considered together with the container that holds it: *The place smelled of garbage.* | *Can somebody* ***take out the garbage***? | *We threw the paper plates* ***in the garbage.***

> THESAURUS
> **trash** – things that you throw away, such as old food, dirty paper, etc.: *a bag stuffed with trash*
> **refuse** (formal) – things that you throw away, such as old food, dirty paper, etc.: *the money spent on refuse collection*
> **litter** – garbage, especially pieces of paper, food containers, etc., that people leave on the ground in public places: *The Scouts picked up litter in the park.*
> **waste** – unwanted things or substances that are left after you have used something: *the safe disposal of nuclear waste*

2 [singular] (informal) something that is of very low quality: *Most of the stuff they sell is just garbage.* **3** [U] (informal) statements or ideas that are silly or wrong SYN **nonsense**: *I don't want to hear this garbage.* [ORIGIN: 1400—1500 Anglo-French]

ˈgarbage ˌcan *n.* [C] a large container with a lid in which you put waste materials, usually kept outside SYN **trash can**

ˈgarbage colˌlector *n.* [C] someone whose job is to remove waste from garbage cans

ˈgarbage disˌposal *n.* [C] a small machine in a kitchen SINK that cuts food waste into small pieces

ˈgarbage man *n.* [C] a garbage collector

ˈgarbage ˌtruck *n.* [C] a large vehicle used for carrying waste that is removed from people's garbage cans

gar·bled /ˈgɑrbəld/ *adj.* confusing and not giving correct information: *a garbled version of the story*

gar·den /ˈgɑrdn/ *n.* **1** [C] the part of someone's land used for growing flowers, or vegetable and fruit plants: *Jane was weeding the* ***vegetable/flower garden.*** **2 gardens** [plural] a public park where a lot of flowers and unusual plants are grown: *the Japanese Tea Gardens in Golden Gate park* [ORIGIN: 1300—1400 Old North French]

gar·den·er /ˈgɑrdnɚ/ *n.* [C] someone who does gardening as a job

gar·den·ing /ˈgɑrdn-ɪŋ/ *n.* [U] the activity or job of making a garden, yard, etc. look pretty by growing flowers, removing WEEDS, etc.: *gardening tools*

gar·gan·tu·an /gɑrˈgæntʃuən/ *adj.* extremely large: *a gargantuan bed* [ORIGIN: 1500—1600 *Gargantua*, name of a giant in the book Gargantua (1534) by François Rabelais]

gar·gle /ˈgɑrgəl/ *v.* [I] to move medicine or liquid around in your throat in order to make it stop feeling sore, or to clean the inside of your mouth: *If you have a sore throat,* ***gargling with*** *salt water might help.* —**gargle** *n.* [C,U]

gar·goyle /ˈgɑrgɔɪl/ *n.* [C] a stone figure shaped like the face of a strange creature, usually on the roofs of old buildings [ORIGIN: 1400—1500 Old French *gargouille* "throat;" because the water appears to come out of the creature's throat]

gar·ish /'gærɪʃ, 'gɛr-/ *adj.* very brightly colored and unpleasant to look at: *the garish carpet in the hotel lobby*

gar·land /'gɑrlənd/ *n.* [C] a ring of flowers or leaves, worn for decoration or in special ceremonies

gar·lic /'gɑrlɪk/ *n.* [U] a small plant like an onion with a very strong taste, used in cooking [ORIGIN: Old English *garleac*, from *gar* "spear" + *leac*]

gar·ment /'gɑrmənt/ *n.* [C] (formal) a piece of clothing

gar·ner /'gɑrnɚ/ *v.* [T] (formal) to take or collect something, especially information or support: *Harris garnered 54% of the vote.*

gar·net /'gɑrnɪt/ *n.* [C] a dark red stone used in jewelry

gar·nish[1] /'gɑrnɪʃ/ *v.* [T] **1** to decorate food with a small piece of a fruit or vegetable: ***Garnish** each plate **with** a slice of lemon.* **2** *also* **garnishee** /'gɑrnə'ʃi/ LAW to take money directly from someone's salary because s/he has not paid his/her debts

garnish[2] *n.* [C] a small piece of a fruit or vegetable that you use to decorate food

gar·ret /'gærɪt/ *n.* [C] (literary) a small room at the top of a house

gar·ri·son /'gærəsən/ *n.* [C] a group of soldiers who live in a particular area in order to defend it —**garrison** *v.* [T]

gar·ru·lous /'gærələs/ *adj.* always talking a lot: *her garrulous women friends*

gar·ter /'gɑrtɚ/ *n.* [C] a piece of ELASTIC (=material that stretches) attached to a woman's underwear and to her STOCKINGS to hold them up

gas[1] /gæs/ *n.* **1** [U] *also* **gasoline** a liquid that is used for producing power in the engines of cars, trucks, etc.: *How much is a gallon of gas?* | *The mechanic found a hole in the **gas tank*** (=container for holding gas). **2** (plural **gases** *or* **gasses**) [C,U] PHYSICS a substance such as air that is not solid or liquid and does not have a definite shape or VOLUME (=measurement of the amount of space it fills), and cannot usually be seen: *hydrogen gas* | *greenhouse gases* **3** [U] a clear substance like air that is burned to give heat for cooking and heating: *a gas stove* | *I think we might have a **gas leak** in here.* **4 the gas** the gas pedal on a car: ***Step on the gas*** (=push down the gas pedal and make the car go faster). **5** [U] the condition of having a lot of air in your stomach [ORIGIN: (2) 1600—1700 Modern Latin, Greek *khaos* "empty space"] → NATURAL GAS

gas[2] *v.* (**gassed**, **gassing**) [T] to attack or kill someone with poisonous gas

'gas ˌchamber *n.* [C] a large room in which people or animals are killed with poisonous gas

gas·e·ous /'gæsiəs, 'gæʃəs/ *adj.* consisting of gas or in the form of gas: *Jupiter is the largest gaseous planet in our solar system.*

gash /gæʃ/ *n.* [C] a deep cut —**gash** *v.* [T]

gas·ket /'gæskɪt/ *n.* [C] a flat piece of rubber between two surfaces of a machine that prevents steam, oil, etc. from escaping

'gas mask *n.* [C] a piece of equipment that you wear over your face to protect you from breathing poisonous gases

gas·o·line /ˌgæsə'lin, 'gæsəˌlin/ *n.* [U] GAS

gasp /gæsp/ *v.* [I] **1** to breathe in suddenly and loudly because you are surprised or in pain: *The audience **gasped in/with** surprise.* **2** to quickly breathe in a lot of air because you are having difficulty breathing normally: *Kim crawled out of the pool, **gasping for air/breath**.* —**gasp** *n.* [C]: *a **gasp of** disbelief*

'gas ˌpedal *n.* [C] the thing that you press with your foot to make a car go faster (SYN) **accelerator** → DRIVE[1]

'gas ˌstation *n.* [C] a place that sells gas for your car

gas·tric /'gæstrɪk/ *adj.* BIOLOGY relating to the stomach: *gastric ulcers*

gas·tro·nom·ic /ˌgæstrə'nɑmɪk◂/ *adj.* [only before noun] relating to cooking and eating good food: *the **gastronomic delights** of Chinatown*

G

gate /geɪt/ *n.* [C] **1** a door in a fence or outside wall → DOOR: *Who left the gate open?* | *Make sure the **front/back/rear/main gate** is locked.* **2** the place where you leave an airport building to get on the airplane: *Flight 207 to Chicago will be leaving from gate 16.* | *the **departure gate*** [ORIGIN: Old English *geat*]

gate-crasher, **gate·crash·er** /'geɪtˌkræʃɚ/ *n.* [C] someone who goes to a party that s/he has not been invited to —**gate-crash** *v.* [I,T]

gate·way /'geɪt˺weɪ/ *n.* [C] **1** an opening in a fence or wall that can be closed by a gate **2 the gateway to sth** a place, especially a city, that you go through in order to reach another place: *St. Louis was once the gateway to the West.* **3** IT a way of connecting two different computer networks that helps them to work together

gath·er /'gæðɚ/ *v.* **1** [I,T] if people gather somewhere, or if someone gathers them, they come together in the same place: *A **crowd gathered** to watch the fight.* | ***Gather around** and I'll tell you a story.* | *Jill gathered the children and lined them up.* | *Dozens of reporters were gathered outside the hotel.*

THESAURUS **meet, get together, assemble, come together, congregate, convene** → MEET[1]

2 [T] to bring things from different places together: *I'm currently trying to gather new ideas for my next novel.* | *"Wait for me," said Anna, **gathering up** her books.* **3** [T] to believe that something is true based on the information you have: ***From what I can gather/As far as I can gather*** (=I think it is true that) *he never intended to sell the house.* | ***I gather (that)** he won't be coming.* **4 gather steam/speed/momentum/force etc.** to become faster, stronger, etc.: *The car gathered speed as it rolled down the hill.* **5 gather dust** if something useful gathers dust, it is not being used: *The report has been gathering dust for 18 years.* [ORIGIN: Old English *gaderian*]

gath·er·ing /ˈgæðərɪŋ/ *n.* [C] a meeting of a group of people: *a family gathering* | *a* ***gathering of*** *war veterans*

gauche /goʊʃ/ *adj.* someone who is gauche says or does things that are considered impolite because s/he does not know the right way to behave

gaud·y /ˈgɔdi/ *adj.* something that is gaudy is too bright and looks cheap: *gaudy jewelry* [ORIGIN: 1400—1500 *gaud* "bright decorative object"]

gauge¹ /geɪdʒ/ *n.* [C] **1** an instrument that measures the amount or size of something: *a car's gas gauge* **2 a gauge of sth** something that helps you make a judgment about a person or situation: *The amount of money you make is not the only gauge of your success.* **3** a measurement of the width or thickness of something: *a 12-gauge shotgun*

gauge

G

gauge² *v.* [T] **1** to judge what someone is likely to do or how s/he feels: *It's difficult to* ***gauge*** *exactly* ***how*** *he's going to respond.*

THESAURUS judge, evaluate, assess, appraise → JUDGE²

2 to calculate the size or amount of something: *The thermostat will gauge the temperature and control the heat.*

gaunt /gɔnt, gɑnt/ *adj.* very thin, pale, and unhealthy

THESAURUS thin, slim, slender, slight, skinny, lean, underweight, emaciated, anorexic, skeletal → THIN¹

gaunt·let /ˈgɔntˀlɪt, ˈgɑntˀ-/ *n.* [C] **1 run the gauntlet** to be criticized or attacked by a lot of people: *There was no way to avoid running the gauntlet of media attention.* **2 throw down the gauntlet** to invite someone to fight, argue, or compete with you **3** a thick long GLOVE that you wear to protect your hand

gauze /gɔz/ *n.* [U] a very thin light cloth used for covering wounds and making clothes: *His hand was wrapped in a* ***gauze bandage****.*

gave /geɪv/ *v.* the past tense of GIVE

gav·el /ˈgævəl/ *n.* [C] a small hammer that someone in charge of a court of law, meeting, etc. hits on a table to get people's attention

gawk /gɔk/ *v.* [I] to look at someone or something for a long time, in a way that looks stupid: *Drivers slowed to* ***gawk at*** *the accident.*

gawk·y /ˈgɔki/ *adj.* tall and not graceful: *a tall gawky teenager*

gay¹ /geɪ/ *adj.* **1** sexually attracted to people of the same sex (SYN) **homosexual** → LESBIAN: *the gay community* | *He told me she's gay.* **2** (old-fashioned) bright and attractive: *a room painted in gay colors* **3** (old-fashioned) happy and cheerful: *gay laughter* [ORIGIN: 1200—1300 Old French *gai* "happy"]

gay² *n.* [C] someone, especially a man, who is sexually attracted to people of the same sex (SYN) **homosexual** → LESBIAN

gaze¹ /geɪz/ *v.* [I] to look at someone or something for a long time: *He sat for hours just* ***gazing out*** *the window.*

THESAURUS look, glance, peek, peep, peer, stare, gape, regard → LOOK¹

gaze² *n.* [singular] a long steady look: *Uncle John inspected us both with a clear and* ***steady gaze****.*

ga·ze·bo /gəˈziboʊ/ *n.* (plural **gazebos**) [C] a small building in a garden or park that you can sit in

gazebo

ga·zelle /gəˈzɛl/ *n.* [C] an animal like a small DEER

G.C.F. MATH the abbreviation of GREATEST COMMON FACTOR

GDP *n.* ECONOMICS **gross domestic product** the total value of all goods and services produced in a country in one year, not including income received from abroad → GNP

gear¹ /gɪr/ *n.* **1** [C,U] the machinery in a vehicle such as a car, truck, or bicycle that you use to go at different speeds: *There's a weird noise every time I* ***change/shift gears****.* | *The car's* ***in first/second etc. gear****.* → *see picture at* BICYCLE **2** [U] special equipment, clothing, etc. that you need for a particular activity: *camping gear* **3** [U] a piece of machinery that does a particular job: *the landing gear on a plane*

gear² *v.* **be geared to/toward sb/sth** to be organized in order to achieve a particular purpose: *All his training was geared to winning an Olympic gold medal.* | *concerts geared toward young children*

gear up *phr. v.* to prepare for something: *Congress is* ***gearing up for*** *a debate on Social Security.*

gear·box /ˈgɪrbɑks/ *n.* [C] the system of gears in a vehicle

ˈgear shift *n.* [C] a stick that you move to change gears in a vehicle

GED *n.* [C usually singular] **General Equivalency Diploma** a DIPLOMA that people who did not finish HIGH SCHOOL can get by taking a test

gee /dʒi/ *interjection* (spoken, old-fashioned) said when you are surprised or annoyed: *Aw, gee, Mom, I don't want to go to bed.*

geek /gik/ *n.* [C] (slang) someone who is not popular because s/he wears unfashionable clothes and does not know how to behave in social situations: *a computer geek* —**geeky** *adj.*

geese /gis/ *n.* the plural of GOOSE

gee·zer /ˈgizɚ/ *n.* [C] (informal) an old man

Gei·ger count·er /ˈgaɪgɚ ˌkaʊntɚ/ *n.* [C] an instrument that finds and measures RADIOACTIVITY [ORIGIN: 1900—2000 Hans W. *Geiger* (1882-1945), German scientist who invented it (with Walter M. Müller)]

gei·sha /ˈgeɪʃə, ˈgiʃə/ *n.* [C] a Japanese woman who is trained to dance, play music, and entertain men [ORIGIN: 1800—1900 Japanese *gei* "art" + *-sha* "person"]

gel[1] /dʒɛl/ *n.* [C,U] a thick liquid, used in beauty or cleaning products: *hair gel* | *shower gel*

gel[2] *v.* (**gelled**, **gelling**) [I] **1** if people gel, they begin to work together well as a group: *As yet, the team hasn't quite gelled.* **2** if an idea or plan gels, it becomes clearer or more definite: *These new trends have not yet gelled.* **3** if a liquid gels, it becomes thicker

gel·a·tin /ˈdʒɛlətən, -lət ˈn/ *n.* [U] a clear substance used for making liquid food more solid and in sweet foods such as Jell-O [ORIGIN: 1800—1900 French *gélatine*, from Italian *gelatina*, from *gelare* "to freeze"]

geld·ing /ˈgɛldɪŋ/ *n.* [C] a horse that has had its TESTICLES removed

gem /dʒɛm/ *n.* [C] **1** a valuable stone that has been cut into a particular shape: *precious gems* **2** (informal) someone or something that is very special: *a little* ***gem of*** *a movie*

Gem·i·ni /ˈdʒɛməˌnaɪ/ *n.* **1** [U] the third sign of the ZODIAC, represented by TWINS **2** [C] someone born between May 21 and June 21

gen·der /ˈdʒɛndɚ/ (Ac) *n.* **1** [C,U] (formal) the fact of being male or female: *A person cannot be denied a job because of age, race, or gender.* | *traditional* ***gender roles*** | *Showing the clothes were tall models of both genders* (=both men and women). **2** [U] ENG. LANG. ARTS the system in some languages of dividing nouns, adjectives, and PRONOUNS into MASCULINE, FEMININE, and NEUTER [ORIGIN: 1300—1400 Old French *gendre*, from Latin *genus* "birth, race, type"]

ˈgender ˌgap *n.* [C usually singular] SOCIAL SCIENCE a large difference between the life experiences of men and women, for example differences in the amounts of money men and women earn, or a difference in the way they think about politics

gene /dʒin/ *n.* [C] BIOLOGY a part of a cell in a living thing that controls how it develops. Parents pass genes on to their children. [ORIGIN: 1900—2000 German *gen*, from Greek *genos* "birth, kind"]

ge·ne·al·o·gy /ˌdʒiniˈɑlədʒi/ *n.* (plural **genealogies**) [C,U] the study of the history of a family, or document that explains how each person in a family is related to the other members of the family —**genealogist** *n.* [C] —**genealogical** /ˌdʒiniəˈlɑdʒɪkəl/ *adj.*

ˈgene map *n.* [C] BIOLOGY a drawing showing the position of all the known GENES along a CHROMOSOME (=the part of every living cell that is shaped like a thread and contains genes)

ˈgene pool *n.* [C] BIOLOGY all of the genes in a SPECIES of animal, plant, or other living thing in a particular area at a particular time

gen·er·al[1] /ˈdʒɛnərəl/ *adj.*
1 NOT DETAILED relating to the whole of something or its main features, not the details: *a general introduction to computers* | *The general standard of the students isn't very high.* | *I've got a* ***general idea*** *of how I want the room to look.* | *The mayor spoke* ***in general terms*** *about his plans for the next four years.*
2 in general **a)** usually, or in most situations: *In general, the Republicans favor tax cuts.* **b)** as a whole: *I love jazz, blues, and music in general.*
3 MOST PEOPLE including most people or situations: *How soon will the drug be available for* ***general use?*** | ***As a general rule****, you should call before visiting someone.* | *The service will soon become available to* ***the general public*** (=most ordinary people).
4 NOT LIMITED not limited to one subject, service, product, etc.: *a general education* | *Montreal* ***General Hospital***
5 JOB used in the job title of someone who has complete responsibility for a particular area of work: *the* ***general manager*** [ORIGIN: 1100—1200 French, Latin *generalis* "of the whole type," from *genus* "birth, race, type"]

general[2] *n.* [C] an officer with a very high rank in the Army, Air Force, or Marines

ˌgeneral anesˈthetic *n.* [C,U] a medicine that makes you unconscious during an operation so that you do not feel any pain

ˌgeneral eˈlection *n.* [C] an election in which all the voters in a country elect a government

gen·er·al·i·ty /ˌdʒɛnəˈræləṭi/ *n.* (plural **generalities**) [C usually plural] a general statement that does not mention specific facts, details, etc.: *Bryant spoke* ***in generalities*** *about his plans to protect the environment.*

gen·er·al·i·za·tion /ˌdʒɛnərələˈzeɪʃən/ *n.* [C,U] (disapproving) a statement that may be true in most situations, but is not true all of the time, or the act of making statements of this kind: *Don't* ***make*** *sweeping* ***generalizations.***

gen·er·al·ize /ˈdʒɛnərəˌlaɪz/ *v.* [I] **1** (disapproving) to form an opinion about something after considering only a few examples of it: *statements*

G

that ***generalize about*** *women* **2** to make a statement about people, events, or facts without mentioning any details: *It's difficult to* ***generalize about*** *a subject as big as American history.*

gen·er·al·ly /ˈdʒɛnərəli/ *adv.* **1** considering something as a whole, rather than its details: *Her school work is generally very good.* | ***Generally speaking,*** *movie audiences like happy endings.* **2** by or to most people: *It's generally believed that the story is true.* | *an agreement that is generally acceptable* **3** usually: *Megan generally works late on Fridays.*

ˈgeneral ˌstore *n.* [C] a store that sells a lot of different things, especially in a small town

gen·er·ate /ˈdʒɛnəˌreɪt/ (Ac) *v.* [T] **1** to produce or make something: *Our discussion generated a lot of new ideas.* | *The new game generated more than $1 million in sales.* | *Reed hopes the exhibit will* ***generate interest*** *in the museum.* **2** to produce energy, power, heat, etc.: *A solar panel helps generate power for the building.*

THESAURUS **make, produce, manufacture, build, construct, create** → MAKE[1]

G

gen·er·a·tion /ˌdʒɛnəˈreɪʃən/ (Ac) *n.* **1** [C] all the people in a society or family who are about the same age: *Three* ***generations of*** *Monroes have lived in this house.* | *music for the* ***younger/older generation*** | ***first-generation/second-generation etc.*** *Americans* (=being a member of the first, second, etc. generation to be born in America) **2** [C] the average period of time between your birth and the birth of your children: *A generation ago, no one had home computers.* | *This store has been here* ***for generations.*** **3** [C] machines that are at the same stage of development: *the next* ***generation of*** *TV technology* **4** [U] the process of producing power or energy: *the* ***generation of*** *electricity*

ˌgeneˈration ˌgap *n.* [singular] a lack of understanding between older and younger people

ˌGeneration ˈX *n.* [U] the group of people who were born during the late 1960s and 1970s in the U.S.

gen·er·a·tor /ˈdʒɛnəˌreɪt̬ɚ/ *n.* [C] a machine that produces electricity

ge·ner·ic /dʒəˈnɛrɪk/ *adj.* **1** CHEMISTRY a generic drug or other product is an exact copy of an existing drug or product, but does not have a BRAND NAME (=the name a company gives to each of its products): *the need for cheaper* ***generic drugs*** **2** ENG. LANG. ARTS relating to a whole group of similar things, rather than just one of them: *Fine Arts is a* ***generic term*** *for subjects such as painting, music, and sculpture.* —**generically** *adv.*

gen·er·os·i·ty /ˌdʒɛnəˈrɑsət̬i/ *n.* [U] a generous attitude, or generous behavior: *Thank you for your generosity.* | *The company is known for its* ***generosity toward*** *employees.*

gen·er·ous /ˈdʒɛnərəs/ *adj.* **1** someone who is generous is kind and enjoys giving people things or helping them: *She's always been* ***generous to*** *the kids.* | *Carl is* ***generous with*** *his time* (=is willing to spend time helping people). | ***It is*** *very* ***generous of*** *you* ***to*** *help.* **2** more than the usual amount: *a generous slice of cake* [ORIGIN: 1500—1600 French *généreux*, from Latin *generosus* "born into a high rank"] —**generously** *adv.*: *Clark* ***gives generously*** *to local charities.*

gen·e·sis /ˈdʒɛnəsɪs/ *n.* [singular] (formal) the beginning of something [ORIGIN: 1600—1700 Latin, Greek, from *gignesthai* "to be born"]

ge·net·ic /dʒəˈnɛt̬ɪk/ *adj.* BIOLOGY relating to GENES or genetics: *genetic research* | *genetic defects* —**genetically** *adv.*

geˌnetically ˈmodified *adj.* BIOLOGY genetically modified food, crops, etc. have been changed so that their GENE structure is different from the one they would have naturally

geˌnetic ˈcode *n.* [C] BIOLOGY the arrangement of chemicals in DNA or RNA that controls the way in which features are passed on from parents to their young

geˌnetic diˈversity *n.* [U] BIOLOGY the fact that there are many creatures, plants, etc. with slightly different GENES within a particular SPECIES (=group of animals or plants that can breed together)

geˌnetic enginˈeering *n.* [U] the science of changing the GENEs of a living thing

ge·net·ics /dʒəˈnɛt̬ɪks/ *n.* [plural] BIOLOGY the study of how GENES affect the development of living things —**geneticist** *n.* [C]

Ge·ne·va Con·ven·tion /dʒəˌnivə kənˈvɛnʃən/ *n.* HISTORY one of a series of international agreements containing rules for the treatment of prisoners of war, sick and wounded soldiers, and CIVILIANS in a time of war

ge·nial /ˈdʒinyəl, -niəl/ *adj.* cheerful, kind, and friendly: *a genial host*

THESAURUS **sociable, outgoing, extroverted, gregarious, affable, convivial** → SOCIABLE
friendly, warm, cordial, amiable, affable, welcoming, hospitable → FRIENDLY

ge·nie /ˈdʒini/ *n.* [C] a magical creature in old stories who can make wishes come true

gen·i·tals /ˈdʒɛnət̬lz/ *also* **gen·i·ta·lia** /ˌdʒɛnəˈteɪlyə/ *n.* [plural] BIOLOGY the outer sex organs —**genital** *adj.*

gen·i·tive /ˈdʒɛnət̬ɪv/ *n.* [C] ENG. LANG. ARTS a form of the noun in some languages, which shows a relationship of possession or origin between one thing and another —**genitive** *adj.*

ge·nius /ˈdʒinyəs/ *n.* **1** [U] a very high level of intelligence or ability: *a man* ***of genius*** | *Even the movie's title was* ***a stroke of genius*** (=a very smart idea). **2** [C] someone who has a very high level of intelligence or ability: *a musical genius* [ORIGIN: 1300—1400 Latin "spirit who guards a person or place," from *gignere*]

gen·o·cide /ˈdʒɛnəˌsaɪd/ *n.* [U] the deliberate murder of a whole race of people [ORIGIN: 1900—2000 Greek *genos* "birth, race, type" + English *-cide* "to kill"] —**genocidal** /ˌdʒɛnəˈsaɪdl/ *adj.*

ge·nome /ˈdʒinoʊm/ *n.* [C] BIOLOGY all the GENES in one cell of a living thing, containing all the GENETIC information about that particular living thing: *the human genome* [ORIGIN: 1900—2000 Greek *genos* "birth, race, type" + English *chromosome*]

ge·no·type /ˈdʒinəˌtaɪp/ *n.* [C] BIOLOGY the type and structure of the GENEs found in a living thing

gen·re /ˈʒɑnrə/ *n.* [C] ENG. LANG. ARTS a particular type of art, writing, music, etc.: *Science fiction is a relatively new literary genre.*

THESAURUS type, kind, sort, category, variety → TYPE[1]

gent /dʒɛnt/ *n.* [C] (informal) a GENTLEMAN

gen·teel /dʒɛnˈtil/ *adj.* polite, gentle, or graceful —**gentility** /dʒɛnˈtɪləṭi/ *n.* [U]

gen·tile /ˈdʒɛntaɪl/ *n.* [C] someone who is not Jewish —**gentile** *adj.*

gen·tle /ˈdʒɛntəl/ *adj.* **1** kind, and careful not to hurt anyone or anything: *Be **gentle with** the baby.* | *a gentle young man* **2** not strong, extreme, or violent: *a gentle voice* | *a gentle breeze* | *gentle persuasion* | *gentle humor* **3** a gentle hill or slope is not steep —**gentleness** *n.* [U] —**gently** *adv.*: *He gently lifted the baby from the cradle.*

gen·tle·man /ˈdʒɛntəlmən/ *n.* (plural **gentlemen** /-mən/) [C] **1** a man who is polite and behaves well: *Roland was a **perfect gentleman** last night.* **2** a polite word used for a man you do not know: *Can you show this gentleman to his seat?* | *Thank you, **ladies and gentlemen**.*

THESAURUS man, guy, fellow, boy, youth, male → MAN[1]

—**gentlemanly** *adj.*

gen·tri·fi·ca·tion /ˌdʒɛntrəfəˈkeɪʃən/ *n.* [U] a process in which a poor area improves after people who have money move there

gen·try /ˈdʒɛntri/ *n.* [plural] (old-fashioned) people of a high social class who owned land and employed others to work in their house or on their land

gen·u·flect /ˈdʒɛnyəˌflɛkt/ *v.* [I] to bend one knee when in a church or a holy place, as a sign of respect

gen·u·ine /ˈdʒɛnyuɪn/ *adj.* **1** a genuine feeling or desire is one that you really have, not one that you pretend to have SYN **sincere**: *He has a **genuine interest** in seeing his students succeed.* | *Mrs. Liu showed a **genuine concern** for Lisa's well-being.* **2** something that is genuine is real or true SYN **real**: *a genuine diamond* **3** someone who is genuine is honest and sincere —**genuinely** *adv.*: *She seemed genuinely surprised.*

ge·nus /ˈdʒinəs/ *n.* (plural **genera** /ˈdʒɛnərə/) [C] BIOLOGY of the groups into which scientists divide animals and plants. A genus is larger than a SPECIES but smaller than a FAMILY. [ORIGIN: 1500—1600 Latin "birth, race, type"]

ge·o·graph·i·cal /ˌdʒiəˈgræfɪkəl/ *also* **ge·o·graph·ic** /ˌdʒiəˈgræfɪk/ *adj.* relating to geography: *geographical maps of the area*

geoˌgraphic isoˈlation *n.* [U] BIOLOGY a situation in which a river, mountain, ocean, etc. keeps two populations of people, animals, plants, etc. apart, so that they develop different GENES and become a separate SPECIES

ge·og·ra·phy /dʒiˈɑgrəfi/ *n.* [U] EARTH SCIENCES the study of the countries, oceans, cities, populations, etc. of the world or of a particular area [ORIGIN: 1400—1500 Latin *geographia*, from Greek, "describing the Earth"] —**geographer** *n.* [C]

ge·o·log·ic time /ˌdʒiəlɑdʒɪk ˈtaɪm/ *n.* [U] EARTH SCIENCES the period of time from when the Earth first formed until the present day

ge·ol·o·gy /dʒiˈɑlədʒi/ *n.* [U] EARTH SCIENCES the study of materials such as rocks, soil, and minerals, and how they have changed over time [ORIGIN: 1700—1800 Modern Latin *geologia*, from Greek *ge* "Earth" + *logia* "study"] —**geologist** *n.* [C] —**geological** /ˌdʒiəˈlɑdʒɪkəl/ *adj.*

ge·o·met·ric /ˌdʒiəˈmɛtrɪk◂/ *also* **ge·o·met·ric·al** /ˌdʒiəˈmɛtrɪkəl/ *adj.* **1** having a regular pattern of shapes and lines: *geometric shapes* **2** relating to geometry

ˌgeometric ˈfigure *n.* [C] MATH a shape, such as a TRIANGLE, square, or PYRAMID, etc., that has lines, curves, or points. Geometric figures can be flat or THREE-DIMENSIONAL (=having length, depth, and height).

ˌgeometric ˈmean *n.* [singular] MATH an average value of a set of numbers

ˌgeometric ˈsequence *n.* [C] MATH a series of related numbers formed by multiplying or dividing each previous number in the list by one particular number. For example, in the geometric sequence 2, 4, 8, 16, each number is multiplied by 2 to get the next number in the series

ˌgeometric ˈseries *n.* [C] MATH the sum of the numbers in a geometric sequence

ge·om·e·try /dʒiˈɑmətri/ *n.* [U] MATH the mathematical study of angles, shapes, lines, etc. [ORIGIN: 1300—1400 French *géométrie*, from Greek *geometria* "measuring the Earth," from *ge* "Earth" + *metron* "measure"]

ge·o·pol·i·tic·al /ˌdʒioʊpəˈlɪṭɪkəl/ *adj.* SOCIAL SCIENCE relating to geopolitics: *geopolitical boundaries*

G

ge·o·pol·i·tics /ˌdʒioʊˈpɑlətɪks/ *n.* [plural] SOCIAL SCIENCE the study of the effects of a country's position, population, etc. on its political character and development

ge·o·ther·mal /ˌdʒioʊˈθɚməl/ *adj.* EARTH SCIENCES relating to or coming from the heat inside the Earth: *geothermal energy*

ge·ra·ni·um /dʒəˈreɪniəm/ *n.* [C] a common house plant with colorful flowers and large round leaves [ORIGIN: 1500—1600 Latin, Greek *geranion*, from *geranos* "crane;" because the plant's seed-case looks like a crane's long beak]

ger·bil /ˈdʒɚbəl/ *n.* [C] a small animal with soft fur and a long tail that is often kept as a pet

ger·i·at·ric /ˌdʒɛriˈætrɪk◂/ *adj.* relating to geriatrics: *geriatric patients* [ORIGIN: 1900—2000 Greek *geras* "old age" + English *-iatric*]

ger·i·at·rics /ˌdʒɛriˈætrɪks/ *n.* [U] the medical treatment and care of old people

germ /dʒɚm/ *n.* [C] **1** a very small living thing that can make you sick ➔ BACTERIA: *Sneezing spreads germs.* **2 the germ of an idea/hope etc.** the beginning of an idea, etc. that may develop into something else [ORIGIN: 1400—1500 French *germe*, from Latin *germen* "seed, bud, germ"]

G

Ger·man¹ /ˈdʒɚmən/ *adj.* relating to Germany, its people, or its language

German² *n.* **1** [U] the language used in Germany, Austria, and parts of Switzerland **2** [C] someone from Germany

ˌGerman ˈmeasles *n.* [plural] an infectious disease that causes red spots on the body (SYN) **rubella**

ˌGerman ˈshepherd *n.* [C] a large dog that looks like a WOLF, often used by the police and for guarding property

ger·mi·nate /ˈdʒɚməˌneɪt/ *v.* [I,T] BIOLOGY if a seed germinates, or if it is germinated, it begins to grow **—germination** /ˌdʒɚməˈneɪʃən/ *n.* [U]

ger·ry·man·der·ing /ˈdʒɛriˌmændərɪŋ/ *n.* [U] the practice of changing the borders of an area before an election, so that one person or party has an unfair advantage [ORIGIN: 1800—1900 Elbridge *Gerry* (1744-1818), U.S. politician + *salamander*; because a voting area he made to help his own party win an election was said to be shaped like a salamander] **—gerrymander** *v.* [I,T]

ger·und /ˈdʒɛrənd/ *n.* [C] ENG. LANG. ARTS in grammar, a noun formed from the PRESENT PARTICIPLE of a verb, such as "reading" in the sentence "He enjoys reading."

ges·ta·tion /dʒɛˈsteɪʃən/ *n.* [U] BIOLOGY the process during which a baby grows inside its mother's body, or the period when this happens: *a nine-month **gestation period***

ges·tic·u·late /dʒɛˈstɪkyəˌleɪt/ *v.* [I] to make movements with your arms and hands while speaking, usually because you are excited or angry

ges·ture¹ /ˈdʒɛstʃɚ, ˈdʒɛʃtʃɚ/ *n.* **1** [C,U] a movement of your head, arm, or hand to express your feelings: *He **made** a rude **gesture** at us as he drove by.* | *He made a fist in a **gesture of** disgust.* **2** [C] something you do or say to show that you care about someone or something: *The flowers were a **nice gesture**.* | *a **gesture of** friendship/support*

gesture² *v.* [I] to move your head, arm, or hand in order to tell someone something: *Tom **gestured for** me **to** move out of the way.*

get /gɛt/ *v.* (past tense **got** /gɑt/, past participle **gotten** /ˈgɑtˀn/, present participle **getting**)

1 RECEIVE/BUY [T] to receive, buy, or obtain something: *Did you get the job?* | *We haven't gotten any mail for three days.* | *I got an A in Spanish.* | *How much money did you **get from** Grandma?* | *My mom **got** these earrings **for** a dollar.* | *Jill knows a woman who can get the material for you.*

> THESAURUS buy, purchase, acquire, procure, snap sth up, pick sth up, stock up ➔ BUY¹

2 have got a) used to say that you have or possess something: *Mike's got a good job.* | *We've got tickets for tonight's game.* **b)** used to say that you need to do something or you must do something: *I've got a lot of work to do.*

3 BECOME [linking verb] to change from one state, feeling, etc. to another (SYN) **become**: *Vicky got really mad at him.* | *If I wear wool, my skin gets all red.* | *The weather had suddenly gotten cold.* | *I got lost on the way to the stadium.* | *Sean's getting married next week.* | *Hurry up and get dressed!*

4 CHANGE POSITION/STATE [I,T] to change or move from one place, position, or state to another, or to make something do this: *How did the burglar **get into** their house?* | *I can't **get** this jar **open**.* | *Everybody **get down** on the floor!*

5 REACH A PLACE [I] to reach a particular place or position: *When did you get home?* | *She got downstairs, and found that the room was full of smoke.* | *The thieves **got away*** (=escaped). | *You might be disappointed when you **get to** the end of the book.*

6 BRING/TAKE [T] to bring someone or something back from somewhere, or take something from somewhere: *Run upstairs and get me that book.* | *She **got** some money **out of** her purse.* | *I'm going to go **get** the kids **from** the babysitter's.*

7 MONEY [T] to receive money for doing work or selling something: *He gets $12 an hour at his job.* | *How much can you **get for** a house this size?*

> THESAURUS earn, make, be/get paid, gross, net ➔ EARN

8 get to do sth (informal) to have an opportunity to do something: *As you **get to know** the city, I'm sure you'll like it better.* | *I didn't **get to see** the game last night.*

9 MAKE STH HAPPEN [T] to make or arrange for someone or something to do a particular job or action: *I have to get this work done by tomorrow.* | *We'll have to get this room painted before they move in.*

10 **ILLNESS** [T] to begin to have an illness: *I got the flu when we were on vacation.*
11 **REACH A STAGE** [I] to reach a particular stage in a process successfully: *We didn't seem to be getting anywhere.* | *I started reading the book, but I didn't get very far.*
12 **get sb to do sth** to persuade or force someone to do something: *I tried to get Jill to come out tonight, but she was too tired.*
13 **get sth to do sth** to make something do something: *Bert couldn't get the light to work.*
14 **get the feeling/idea etc.** to start to have a feeling or an idea: *I get the feeling you don't like her.*
15 **get the bus/a flight etc.** to travel somewhere on a bus, airplane, etc.: *She managed to get a flight into Detroit.*
16 **RECEIVE A PUNISHMENT** [T] to receive a punishment: *He got ten years for robbery.*
17 **RADIO/TV** [I] to be able to receive a particular radio signal, television station, etc.: *Her TV doesn't get channel 24.*

SPOKEN PHRASES
18 [T] to understand something: *Tracey didn't* ***get the joke.*** | ***I don't get it!***
19 **you/we etc. get sth** used in order to say that something happens or exists: *We get a lot of rain around here in the summer.*
20 **get moving/going** to begin moving or going somewhere: *We have to get going, or we'll be late!*
21 **get the door/phone** to answer the door or telephone: *Can you get the phone, please?*
22 [T] to prepare a meal: *Are you hungry? Can I get you anything?*
23 **get sb** to attack, hurt, or catch someone: *I want to get him before he gets me.*

[ORIGIN: 1200—1300 Old Norse *geta*]

get sth ↔ **across** *phr. v.*
to be understood, or to make someone understand something: *The message isn't getting across.* | *It was difficult to* ***get*** *my idea* ***across to*** *the committee.*

get ahead *phr. v.*
to be successful in your job, work, etc.: *She lacks the business skills she'll need to get ahead.*

get along *phr. v.*
1 to have a friendly relationship with someone: *She* ***gets along with*** *Cy really well.*
2 **get along without sb/sth** to be able to continue doing something without having someone or something to help: *We'll have to get along without the car until the new part arrives.*

get around *phr. v.*
1 **get around** sth to avoid something that will cause problems: *There are ways of getting around the law.*
2 **get around** (sth) to go to different places: *His new wheelchair lets him get around more easily.*
3 if news or information gets around, a lot of people hear about it

get around to sth *phr. v.*
to do something you have been intending to do for a long time: *I meant to go to the bookstore, but I never got around to it.*

get at sth *phr. v.*
1 **be getting at sth** to be trying to explain an idea: *Did you understand what he was getting at?*
2 **get at the meaning/facts etc.** to discover information about something: *The judge asked a few questions to try to get at the truth.*
3 to be able to reach something: *I could see the ring stuck under the refrigerator, but I couldn't get at it.*

get away *phr. v.*
1 to leave a place: *Barney had to work late, and couldn't get away until 9:00.*
2 to escape from someone who is chasing you: *The two men got away in a blue pickup truck.*
3 to go on vacation: *Are you going to be able to get away this summer?*

get away with sth *phr. v.*
to not be noticed or punished when you have done something wrong: *He'll cheat if he thinks he can get away with it.*

get back *phr. v.*
1 to return to a place: *I didn't get back until after midnight.* | *Call me when you* ***get back to*** *Miami.*
2 **get** sth ↔ **back** to have something again after you had lost it or given it to someone: *Did you get your wallet back?*
3 **get** sb **back** *also* **get back at** sb to hurt or embarrass someone who has hurt or embarrassed you: *Jerry wants to* ***get back at*** *her* ***for*** *leaving him.*

get back to *phr. v.*
1 **get back to** sth to return to a previous state, condition, or activity: *It was hard to get back to work after my vacation.* | *Life is beginning to* ***get back to normal.***
2 **get back to** sb to talk to or telephone someone later in order to answer a question or give him/her information: *I'll try to get back to you later today.*

get behind *phr. v.*
if you get behind with work or a regular payment, you fail to do the work or pay the money in time: *They made people pay extra if they* ***got behind in/on*** *their rent.*

get by *phr. v.*
to have only just enough of something to be able to do the things you need to do: *I know enough French to get by.* | *He* ***gets by on*** *just $800 a month.*

get down *phr. v.*
1 **get** sth ↔ **down** to quickly write something down on paper: *Let me get your number down before I forget it.*
2 **get** sb **down** (informal) to make someone feel unhappy: *Don't let his criticism get you down.*
3 **get** sth ↔ **down** to be able to swallow food or drink: *I knew I'd feel better once I got some food down.*

get down to sth *phr. v.*
to start doing something that needs time or energy: *It's time to* ***get down to work.***

get in *phr. v.*
1 to be allowed or able to enter a place: *The door was locked, and he couldn't get in.* | *I applied to Princeton but I didn't get in.*

2 to arrive at a particular time or in a particular place: *What time does the plane get in?*
3 to arrive home: *Steve just got in a few minutes ago.*
4 **get** sth **in** to send or give something to a particular person, company, etc.: *Make sure you get your homework in by Thursday.*
get in on sth *phr. v.* (informal)
to become involved in something that other people are doing: *The kids saw us playing and wanted to get in on the game.*
get into sth *phr. v.*
1 to be allowed to go to a school, college, or university: *Liz got into the graduate program at Berkeley.*
2 to start being involved in a situation: *He's always **getting into trouble**.*
3 (informal) to start being interested in something: *When I was in high school I got into rap music.*
4 (informal) to begin to have a discussion about something: *Let's not get into it right now. I'm tired.*
get off *phr. v.*
1 **get off** (sth) to finish working: *What time do you **get off work**?*
2 **get** (sb) **off** to get little or no punishment for a crime, or to help someone escape punishment: *I can't believe his lawyers managed to get him off.* | *He **got off lightly*** (=received a very small punishment).
3 **where does sb get off (doing sth)?** (spoken) said when someone has done something that you think s/he does not have a right to do: *Where does he get off telling me how to raise my kids?*
get on *phr. v.*
1 **get on with sth** to continue or to make progress with a job, work, etc.: *Let's get on with the meeting, so we can go home on time.*
2 **be getting on (in years)** to be old
get onto sth *phr. v.*
to start talking about a particular subject: *Then, we got onto the subject of women, and Craig wouldn't shut up.*
get out *phr. v.*
1 **get** (sb) **out** to leave or escape from a place, or to help someone do this: *How did the dog **get out of** the yard?* | *We knew it was going to be difficult to get him out of the country.*
2 if secret information gets out, people find out about it: *Once **word gets out**, we're going to be in big trouble.*
get out of sth *phr. v.*
1 to avoid doing something that you should do: *She couldn't get out of the meeting, so she canceled our dinner.*
2 **get** sth **out of** sb to persuade someone to tell or give you something: *I was determined to get the truth out of her.*
3 **get** sth **out of** sth to enjoy an activity and feel you have gained something from it: *She gets a lot of pleasure out of acting.*
get over *phr. v.*
1 **get over** sth to feel better after an illness or bad experience: *It will take a couple of weeks to get over the infection.* | *Her son died suddenly, and she never **got over it**.*
2 **get** sth **over with** to finish something you do not like doing as quickly as possible: *"It should only hurt a little." "OK. Just get it over with."*
3 **sb can't/couldn't get over sth** (spoken) said when you are surprised, shocked, or amused by something: *I can't get over how much weight you've lost.*
get through *phr. v.*
1 **get** (sb) **through** sth to manage to deal with a difficult or bad experience until it ends, or to help someone do this: *I was so embarrassed. I don't know how I got through the rest of the dinner.*
2 to succeed in calling someone on the telephone: *When she finally got through, the department manager wasn't there.*
3 **get** (sth) **through** sth if a law gets through Congress, it is officially accepted
get through to sb *phr. v.*
to succeed in making someone understand you: *I tried to explain, but I couldn't get through to her.*
get to sb *phr. v.* (informal)
to upset someone: *Don't let him get to you, honey. He's just teasing you.*
get together *phr. v.*
1 to meet with someone or with a group of people: *We should get together for a drink.* | *Every time he **got together with** Murphy they argued.*
2 to start a romantic relationship with someone
3 **get yourself together/get it together** to change the way you live so that you are better organized, happier, etc.: *It took a year for me to get myself together after she left.*
get up *phr. v.*
1 **get** (sb) **up** to get out of your bed after sleeping, or to make someone do this: *I have to **get up at** 6:00 tomorrow.* | *Could you **get** me **up at** 8:00?*
2 to stand up: *Corrinne got up slowly and went to the window.*

get·a·way /ˈgɛt̬əˌweɪ/ *n.* [C] an escape from a place after doing something wrong: *a **getaway car*** (=a car used by criminals to escape after a crime) | *The bank robber **made** his **getaway** in a red truck.*

ˈget-toˌgether *n.* [C] an informal meeting or party: *a small get-together with friends*

get·up /ˈgɛt̬ʌp/ *n.* [C] (informal) strange or unusual clothes that someone is wearing

gey·ser /ˈgaɪzɚ/ *n.* [C] EARTH SCIENCES a natural spring that sends hot water and steam suddenly into the air from a hole in the ground

geyser

ghast·ly /ˈgæstli/ *adj.* extremely bad, shocking, or upsetting: *ghastly injuries* | *a ghastly noise*

G

ghet·to /ˈgɛt̬oʊ/ *n.* (plural **ghettos** *or* **ghettoes**) [C] a part of a city where poor people live in bad conditions, especially people of one particular race or social class [ORIGIN: 1600—1700 Italian]

THESAURUS **area, region, territory, zone, district, neighborhood, suburb, slum** ➔ AREA

ˈghetto ˌblaster *n.* [C] (informal) a BOOM BOX

ghost /goʊst/ *n.* [C] the spirit of a dead person that some people think they can see: *They say the captain's* ***ghost*** *still* ***haunts*** *the waterfront.* —**ghostly** *adj.*

THESAURUS
spirit – a creature without a physical body, such as an angel or ghost
phantom/specter/apparition (literary) – a ghost

ˈghost ˌstory *n.* [C] a story about ghosts that is intended to frighten people

ˈghost town *n.* [C] a town that is empty because most of its people have left

ghost writer, **ghost·writ·er** /ˈgoʊstˌraɪt̬ɚ/ *n.* [C] someone who is paid to write a book or story for another person, whose name then appears as the writer of the book —**ghostwrite** *v.* [T]

ghoul /gul/ *n.* [C] an evil spirit in stories that steals and eats dead bodies —**ghoulish** *adj.*

GI /ˌdʒi ˈaɪ/ *n.* [C] a soldier in the U.S. army

gi·ant¹ /ˈdʒaɪənt/ *adj.* much bigger than other things of the same type: *a* ***giant step*** *towards peace in the region* | *a giant TV screen* [ORIGIN: 1200—1300 Old French *geant*, from Greek *gigas*]

giant² *n.* [C] **1** a very tall strong man in stories **2** a very successful person or company: *one of the* ***giants of*** *the music industry*

gib·ber·ish /ˈdʒɪbərɪʃ/ *n.* [U] things you say or write that have no meaning or are difficult to understand

gibe /dʒaɪb/ *n.* [C] an unkind remark intended to make someone seem silly

gib·lets /ˈdʒɪblɪts/ *n.* [plural] organs such as the heart and LIVER that you remove from a bird before cooking it

gid·dy /ˈgɪdi/ *adj.* (comparative **giddier**, superlative **giddiest**) **1** behaving in a silly, happy, and excited way: *We were* ***giddy with*** *excitement.* **2** feeling slightly sick and unable to stand up because everything seems to be spinning around (SYN) **dizzy**

GIF /gɪf/ *n.* [C] IT **Graphics Interchange Format** a type of computer FILE used on the Internet that contains pictures, photographs, or other images

gift /gɪft/ *n.* **1** [C] something that you give to someone as a present: *a* ***birthday/Christmas/wedding etc.*** *gift* | *a* ***gift from*** *my mother* | *He sent her* ***gifts of*** *flowers and chocolate.* **2** [C, usually singular] a natural ability to do something: *Ekena sure* ***has*** *a* ***gift for*** *making people laugh.* [ORIGIN: 1200—1300 Old Norse]

THESAURUS **skill, talent, ability, knack, flair, aptitude** ➔ SKILL

ˈgift cerˌtificate *n.* [C] a special piece of paper that is worth a specific amount of money when it is exchanged at a store for goods

gift·ed /ˈgɪftɪd/ *adj.* having the natural ability to do something very well: *a gifted poet* | *a* ***gifted child*** (=a child who is extremely intelligent)

THESAURUS **intelligent, smart, bright, brilliant, wise, clever, intellectual, apt** ➔ INTELLIGENT
skillful, expert, accomplished, talented, adept, deft ➔ SKILLFUL

ˈgift wrap *n.* [U] attractive colored paper used for wrapping presents in —**gift wrap** *v.* [T]: *Would you like this gift wrapped?*

gig /gɪg/ *n.* [C] (informal) a concert at which musicians play popular music or JAZZ

gig·a·byte /ˈgɪgəˌbaɪt/ *n.* [C] IT a unit for measuring computer information, equal to 1024 MEGABYTES

G

gi·gan·tic /dʒaɪˈgæntɪk/ *adj.* extremely large: *a gigantic skyscraper*

THESAURUS **big, large, substantial, sizable, prodigious, huge, enormous, vast, massive, immense, colossal** ➔ BIG

gig·gle /ˈgɪgəl/ *v.* [I] to laugh quickly in a high voice, especially because you are nervous or embarrassed: *If you can't stop giggling, you'll have to leave the room.* —**giggle** *n.* [C]: *a nervous giggle*

THESAURUS **laugh, chuckle, cackle, snicker, titter, guffaw** ➔ LAUGH¹

gild /gɪld/ *v.* [T] to cover the surface of something with a thin layer of gold or gold paint

gill /gɪl/ *n.* [C] BIOLOGY one of the organs on the side of a fish through which it breathes ➔ *see picture on page A15*

gilt /gɪlt/ *adj.* covered with a thin layer of gold or gold-colored paint —**gilt** *n.* [U]

gim·mick /ˈgɪmɪk/ *n.* [C] (informal, disapproving) something unusual that is used to make people notice something: *advertising gimmicks* —**gimmicky** *adj.*

gin /dʒɪn/ *n.* [U] a strong clear alcoholic drink made from grain [ORIGIN: 1700—1800 *geneva* "gin" (18—20 centuries), from Dutch *genever*, from Latin *juniperus* "juniper," plant used to give gin its taste]

gin·ger /ˈdʒɪndʒɚ/ *n.* [U] a hot-tasting light brown root, or the powder made from this root, used in cooking

'ginger ale *n.* [U] a SOFT DRINK (=drink with no alcohol in it) with a ginger taste

gin·ger·bread /'dʒɪndʒɚˌbrɛd/ *n.* [U] a type of cookie or cake with ginger in it: *a **gingerbread house/man*** (=cookie in the shape of a house or person)

gin·ger·ly /'dʒɪndʒɚli/ *adv.* very slowly, carefully, and gently: *They gingerly loaded the patient into the ambulance.*

ging·ham /'gɪŋəm/ *n.* [U] cotton cloth that has a pattern of small white and colored squares on it

gi·raffe /dʒə'ræf/ *n.* [C] a tall African animal with a very long neck and legs and dark spots on its yellow-brown fur

gird·er /'gɚdɚ/ *n.* [C] an iron or steel beam that supports a floor, roof, or bridge

gir·dle /'gɚdl/ *n.* [C] a piece of women's underwear that fits tightly around her waist and HIPS

girl /gɚl/ *n.* [C] **1** a female child: *She's tall for a girl of her age.* | *a six-year-old girl* | *I've wanted to be in the movies since I was **a little girl**.* **2** a daughter ➔ BOY: *They have two boys and a girl.* **3** a word meaning a young woman, which is considered offensive by some women **4 the girls** (informal) a woman's female friends: *I'm going out with the girls tonight.*

G

girl·friend /'gɚlfrɛnd/ *n.* [C] **1** a girl or woman with whom you have a romantic relationship **2** a woman or girl's female friend

girl·hood /'gɚlhʊd/ *n.* [U] the time in a woman's life when she is a girl

'Girl Scout *n.* **1 the Girl Scouts** an organization for girls, that teaches them practical skills and helps develop their character ➔ BOY SCOUTS **2** [C] a member of the Girl Scouts

girth /gɚθ/ *n.* [C,U] the distance around the middle of something: *the girth of the tree's trunk*

GIS *n.* [singular] EARTH SCIENCES **geographic information system** a computer system for storing and examining information about the natural features of the Earth's surface

gist /dʒɪst/ *n.* **the gist** the main idea or meaning of what someone has said or written: *After a while I began to **get the gist of** his speech* (=understand the main ideas).

give¹ /gɪv/ *v.* (past tense **gave** /geɪv/, past participle **given** /'gɪvən/)
1 PROVIDE [T] to provide something for someone: *Dan gave me a ride to work.* | *She refused to give me any help.* | *They **gave** the job **to** that guy from Texas.*
2 PUT STH IN SB'S HAND [T] to put something in someone's hand (SYN) **hand**, **pass**: *Give me your coat.* | *He **gave** the books **to** Carl.*
3 LET SB DO STH [T] to allow or make it possible for someone to do something: *I was never **given a chance** to explain.* | *She **gave** me some **time** to finish the report.* | *Who **gave** you **permission** to come in here?* | *This bill will **give** more power **to** local authorities.*
4 PRESENT [T] to let someone have something as a present: *She gave Jen a CD for Christmas.*

THESAURUS

donate – to give money to an organization that uses it to help people: *Would you like to donate something to charity?*
leave/bequeath (formal) – to give something to people after you die: *This house was left to me by my aunt.*
award – to officially give money or a prize to someone: *Heaney was awarded the Nobel Prize for Literature.*
present – to formally or officially give something to someone who is with you: *The students presented her with a bouquet of flowers.*
grant (formal) – to give someone something that s/he as asked for or earned: *Ms. Chung was granted American citizenship last year.*

5 TELL SB STH [T] to tell someone information or details about something, or tell someone to do something: *Would you give Kim a message for me?* | *Let me **give** you some **advice**.* | *The police will ask him to **give** a **description** of the man.* | *Could you **give** me **directions** to the airport* (=tell me how to get there)*?* | *Harris walked into the room and started **giving orders**.*
6 PERFORM AN ACTION [T] to perform a particular action: *The boy gave Lydia a big smile.* | *The theater company gave performances in neighborhood schools and hospitals.* | ***Give** me a **call*** (=telephone me) *tonight.* | *Come on, give your Grandpa a hug.*
7 give sb trouble/problems etc. to make someone have problems: *The machines in the lab are giving us trouble.* | *Stop **giving** me **a hard time*** (=stop criticizing me)*!*
8 ILLNESS [T] to infect someone with the same illness that you have, or make someone feel a particular emotion or sensation: *The noise is giving me a headache.* | *My husband **gave** this cold **to** me.*
9 QUALITY [T] to make someone or something have a particular quality: *The color of the room gives it a warm cozy feeling.*
10 give (sb) an idea/feeling etc. to make someone think about something in a particular way: *She gave me the impression she wasn't interested.*
11 MONEY [T] to pay a particular amount of money for something: *I'll give you $75 for the oak desk.*
12 BEND/STRETCH [I] to bend, stretch, or break because of weight or pressure: *The leather will give slightly when you wear the boots.*
13 give or take a few minutes/a mile/a dollar etc. used in order to show that a number or amount is not exact: *The show lasts about an hour, give or take five minutes.*
14 give (sth) thought/attention/consideration etc. to spend some time thinking about something carefully
15 not give sth another/a second thought to not think or worry about something
16 BREAK/FALL [I] *also* **give way** to break or fall

down suddenly under pressure: *The branch suddenly gave way beneath him.*

SPOKEN PHRASES

17 sb would give anything/a lot/your right arm etc. for sth said in order to emphasize that you want something very much: *I'd give my right arm for his job.*

18 don't give me that! said when someone has just said something that you know is not true: *"I'm too tired." "Oh, don't give me that. You just don't want to come."*

[ORIGIN: Old English *giefan*] → GIVE AND TAKE, **give sb a (big) hand** *at* HAND[1], **give/lend sb a hand** *at* HAND[1]

give away *phr. v.*

1 give sth ↔ **away** to give someone something without asking for money: *I gave my old clothes away.* | *The store is* ***giving away*** *toasters* ***to*** *the first 50 customers.*

2 give sb/sth ↔ **away** to do or say something that lets someone know a secret: *They said they were English, but their New York accents gave them away* (=showed they were lying). → GIVEAWAY

give (sb) sth ↔ **back**

to return something to its owner: *Give him back his toy.* | *I gave her the book back.* | *I'll* ***give*** *the money* ***back to*** *you next week.*

give in *phr. v.*

1 to finally agree to do something that you did not want to do: *Randy asked her out for months until she finally gave in.* | *The government refused to* ***give in to*** *their demands.*

2 to accept that you have lost a fight, game, etc.: *Even when they fell behind by three goals, the team refused to give in.*

give in to sth *phr. v.*

to no longer try to stop yourself from doing something you want to do: *If you feel the need for a cigarette, don't give in to it.*

give off sth *phr. v.*

to produce a smell, light, heat, a sound, etc.: *The factory gives off a terrible smell.*

give out *phr. v.*

1 give sth ↔ **out** to give something to each person in a group: *She stood on the corner, giving out flyers.* | *He* ***gave out*** *candy* ***to*** *the kids.*

THESAURUS

hand out/pass out – to give something to each of the people in a group: *Mr. Goodmanson handed out the test.*

share – to divide something into equal parts and give a part to each person: *She made a cake and shared it with the children.*

distribute – to give things to a large number of people, especially on the street: *Anti-war protesters were distributing leaflets.*

dispense (formal) – to give or provide something to people, especially as part of an official activity: *Volunteers helped dispense food and blankets.*

allot (formal) – to give a particular share of something to someone: *Each person was allotted four tickets.*

2 to stop working correctly: *My voice gave out half way through the song.*

give up *phr. v.*

1 give (sth ↔) **up** to stop trying to do something: *I looked everywhere for the keys – finally, I just gave up.* | *Vladimir has given up trying to teach her Russian.*

2 give sth ↔ **up** to stop doing something, especially something that you do regularly: *I've been trying to give up smoking.* | *She gave up her job, and started writing full time.*

3 give yourself/sb **up** to allow yourself or someone else to be caught by the police or enemy soldiers

give up on sb *phr. v.*

to stop hoping that someone or something will change or improve: *His parents finally gave up on him.*

give[2] *n.* [U] the ability of a material to bend or stretch when it is under pressure

ˌgive and ˈtake *n.* [U] if there is give and take between two people, each person agrees to do some of the things that the other person wants: *In every successful marriage there is a certain amount of give and take.*

give·a·way /ˈgɪvəˌweɪ/ *n.* **1 be a giveaway** to make it very easy to guess something: *He's been smoking – the smell on his breath* ***is a dead giveaway.*** **2** [C] a product, prize, etc. that a store or company gives to its customers for free —**giveaway** *adj.*: *giveaway prices*

giv·en[1] /ˈgɪvən/ *adj.* **1 any/a given day/time/situation** any particular time, situation, etc., used when giving an example: *In any given year, over half of all accidents happen in the home.* **2** [only before noun] previously arranged: *Candidates will have to give a presentation on a given topic.*

given[2] *prep.* taking something into account: *Given the number of people we invited, I'm surprised that so few came.*

given[3] *v.* the past participle of GIVE

given[4] *n.* **a given** a basic fact that you accept as the truth: *It'll be a very difficult game – that's a given.*

ˈgiven name *n.* [C] FIRST NAME

giz·mo /ˈgɪzmoʊ/ *n.* (plural **gizmos**) [C] (informal) a GADGET

giz·zard /ˈgɪzɚd/ *n.* [C] BIOLOGY an organ near a bird's stomach that helps it break down food

gla·cial /ˈgleɪʃəl/ *adj.* EARTH SCIENCES relating to ice or glaciers, or formed by glaciers: *glacial streams*

gla·cier /ˈgleɪʃɚ/ *n.* [C] EARTH SCIENCES a large area of ice that moves slowly over an area of land

glad /glæd/ *adj.* [not before noun] **1** pleased and happy about something: *Mom's really* ***glad (that)*** *you came.* | *I'm* ***glad to*** *hear that you're feeling better.* | *I'll be* ***glad when*** *this is over.* ▶Don't say "She's a really glad person."◀

G

THESAURUS happy, pleased, content, delighted, thrilled, overjoyed, ecstatic, jubilant, elated → HAPPY

2 be glad to do sth to be willing to do something: *He said he'd be glad to help me.* [ORIGIN: Old English *glæd* "bright, shining, happy"]

glade /gleɪd/ *n.* [C] (literary) a small open space inside a forest

glad·i·a·tor /ˈglædiˌeɪt̬ɚ/ *n.* [C] HISTORY a man who had to fight other men or animals as entertainment in ancient Rome

glad·ly /ˈglædli/ *adv.* willingly or eagerly: *"Would you drive Jenny to school today?" "Gladly."*

glam·or·ize /ˈglæməˌraɪz/ *v.* [T] to make something seem more attractive or exciting than it really is: *Hollywood has always glamorized drinking.*

glam·or·ous /ˈglæmərəs/ *adj.* attractive, exciting, and relating to wealth and success: *a glamorous lifestyle*

glam·our, glamor /ˈglæmɚ/ *n.* [U] the attractive and exciting quality of being connected with wealth and success: *the **glamour of** Hollywood* [ORIGIN: 1700—1800 Scottish English "magic," from English *grammar*; because of an old association of knowledge with magic]

G

glance¹ /glæns/ *v.* [I] **1** to look at someone or something for a short time and then look quickly away: *He **glanced at** his watch.*

THESAURUS look, peek, peep, peer, stare, gaze, gape, regard → LOOK¹

2 to read something very quickly: *Paul **glanced at/through** the menu and ordered a sandwich.*

glance² *n.* [C] **1** a quick look: *He **gave** her a **glance** as she walked by.* **2 at a glance** immediately: *I knew at a glance that something was wrong.* **3 at first glance** when you first look at or think about something: *At first glance, the place seemed completely empty.*

gland /glænd/ *n.* [C] BIOLOGY an organ in the body that produces a substance such as SWEAT or SALIVA —**glandular** /ˈglændʒəlɚ/ *adj.*

glare¹ /glɛr/ *v.* [I] **1** to look angrily at someone or something for a long time: *They **glared at** each other across the room.* **2** to shine with a strong bright light that hurts your eyes: *Sunlight was **glaring off** the hood of the car.*

glare² *n.* **1** [singular, U] a strong bright light that hurts your eyes: *the **glare of** the sun* **2** [C] a long angry look: *a menacing glare*

glar·ing /ˈglɛrɪŋ/ *adj.* **1** too bright to look at: *a glaring white light*

THESAURUS bright, strong, brilliant, dazzling, blinding → BRIGHT

2 bad and very noticeable: *glaring mistakes*

glass /glæs/ *n.* **1** [U] a hard transparent material that is used for making windows, bottles, etc.: *a glass jar* | *a piece of **broken glass*** | *panes of glass* | *the cathedral's **stained-glass windows*** → *see picture at* MATERIAL¹ **2** [C] a container made of glass used for drinking, or the drink in it: *Did you put the wine glasses on the table?* | *a **glass of** milk* **3 glasses** [plural] two pieces of specially cut glass or plastic in a frame that you wear in front of your eyes in order to see better: *I need to buy a new **pair of glasses**.* | *He's just started **wearing glasses**.* **4** [U] objects made of glass: *a collection of Venetian glass* [ORIGIN: Old English *glæs*]

glass

a stained-glass window

ˌglass ˈceiling *n.* [C] the fact that women or people from MINORITY groups are not given jobs at the highest level in a company

ˌglassed-ˈin *adj.* surrounded by a glass structure: *a glassed-in porch*

glass·ware /ˈglæswɛr/ *n.* [U] glass objects, especially ones used for drinking and eating

glass·y /ˈglæsi/ *adj.* **1** smooth and shiny, like glass: *the glassy surface of the lake* **2** glassy eyes do not show any expression

glau·co·ma /glaʊˈkoʊmə, glɔ-/ *n.* [U] BIOLOGY an eye disease in which someone gradually loses the ability to see because of an increase in the pressure inside his/her eye

glaze¹ /gleɪz/ *v.* **1** [I] *also* **glaze over** if your eyes glaze, they show no expression because you are bored or tired: *Her eyes glazed over as if she were daydreaming.* **2** [T] to cover clay pots, bowls, etc. with a thin liquid that gives them a shiny surface **3** [T] to cover food with a liquid that gives it an attractive shiny surface **4** [T] to put glass into a window frame —**glazed** *adj.*

glaze² *n.* [C,U] **1** a liquid that is put on clay pots, bowls, etc. to give them a shiny surface **2** a liquid put on food to give it an attractive shiny surface

gleam¹ /glim/ *v.* [I] **1** to shine, especially after being cleaned: *Grandpa polished his shoes until they gleamed.*

THESAURUS shine, flash, flicker, twinkle, glow, sparkle, shimmer, glint, glisten → SHINE¹

2 if your eyes or face gleam with a feeling, they show it: *Her eyes **gleamed with** excitement.*

gleam² *n.* [C] **1** the shiny quality that something, especially something POLISHed, has when light shines on it **2** an emotion or expression that appears on someone's face for a short time: *There was a **gleam of** happiness on his face.*

glean /glin/ *v.* [T] to find out information slowly

and with difficulty: *Several lessons can be* ***gleaned from*** *our experience so far.*

glee /gli/ *n.* [U] a feeling of excitement and satisfaction: *The kids shouted with glee when they saw Santa.* —**gleefully** *adv.*

glen /glɛn/ *n.* [C] a deep narrow valley in Scotland or Ireland

glib /glɪb/ *adj.* (disapproving) **1** said in a way that makes something sound simple, easy, or true when it is not: *The doctor made some glib comment about my headaches being "just stress."* **2** speaking easily but not sincerely: *a glib salesman* —**glibly** *adv.*

glide /glaɪd/ *v.* [I] to move smoothly and quietly, as if without effort: *We watched the sailboats* ***glide across*** *the lake.* —**glide** *n.* [C]

glid·er /ˈglaɪdɚ/ *n.* [C] a light airplane that flies without an engine

glid·ing /ˈglaɪdɪŋ/ *n.* [U] the sport of flying a glider

glim·mer[1] /ˈglɪmɚ/ *n.* [C] **1 a glimmer of hope/doubt etc.** a small amount of hope, doubt, etc. **2** a light that is not very bright

glimmer[2] *v.* [I] to shine with a light that is not very bright

glimpse[1] /glɪmps/ *n.* [C] **1** a quick look at someone or something that does not allow you to see them clearly: *Dad only* ***got/caught a glimpse*** *of the guy who stole our car.* **2** a short experience of something that helps you to understand it: *Visitors to the museum get a glimpse of what life was like during the 1800s.*

glimpse[2] *v.* [T] to see someone or something for a moment without getting a complete view of them: *I glimpsed a figure at the window.*

glint /glɪnt/ *v.* [I] if something that is shiny or smooth glints, it flashes with a very small amount of light: *Her teeth glinted as she smiled.* —**glint** *n.* [C]

> THESAURUS **shine, flash, flicker, twinkle, glow, sparkle, shimmer, gleam, glisten** → SHINE[1]

glis·ten /ˈglɪsən/ *v.* [I] to shine and look wet or oily: *His back was* ***glistening with*** *sweat.*

> THESAURUS **shine, flash, flicker, twinkle, glow, sparkle, shimmer, gleam, glint** → SHINE[1]

glitch /glɪtʃ/ *n.* [C] a small problem that prevents something from working correctly: *Company records were lost due to a computer glitch.*

glit·ter[1] /ˈglɪt̬ɚ/ *v.* [I] to shine brightly with a lot of small flashes of light: *Fresh snow glittered in the morning light.* —**glittering** *adj.*

glitter[2] *n.* [U] **1** brightness consisting of many flashing points of light: *the glitter of her diamond ring* **2** the exciting attractive quality of a place, way of life, etc. that is connected with rich and famous people: *the glitter of Broadway* **3** very small pieces of shiny plastic, metal, or paper that are used for decoration

gloat /gloʊt/ *v.* [I] to show in an annoying way that you are proud of your success, or happy about someone else's failure: *The fans are still* ***gloating over*** *the team's victory.*

glob /glɑb/ *n.* [C] (informal) a small amount of a soft substance or thick liquid, that has a round shape: ***a glob of*** *ketchup*

glob·al /ˈgloʊbəl/ (Ac) *adj.* **1** affecting or including the whole world: *the* ***global economy*** | ***global climate change*** **2** IT affecting a whole computer system, program, or FILE: *a set of global changes to the file* **3** considering all the parts of a problem or a situation: *a global study on the company's weaknesses* —**globally** *adv.*

glob·al·i·za·tion /ˌgloʊbələˈzeɪʃən/ (Ac) *n.* [U] **1** ECONOMICS the process of operating a business in a lot of countries all over the world, or the result of this: *the globalization of world markets* **2** the idea that all the places in the world are becoming very similar, as large businesses become more powerful: *protests against globalization*

ˌglobal ˈwarming *n.* [U] EARTH SCIENCES an increase in the world temperatures, caused by an increase of CARBON DIOXIDE around the Earth → ENVIRONMENT

globe /gloʊb/ (Ac) *n.* [C] **1** a round object that has a map of the Earth painted on it **2 the globe** the world: *Carson traveled all over the globe.* **3** an object shaped like a ball [ORIGIN: 1500—1600 French, Latin *globus*]

glob·u·lar /ˈglɑbyəlɚ/ *adj.* shaped like a ball or a drop of liquid

glob·ule /ˈglɑbyul/ *n.* [C] a small drop of liquid or a melted substance

gloom /glum/ *n.* [singular, U] **1** (literary) darkness that you can hardly see through: *He was sitting alone in the gloom.* **2** a feeling of sadness, or having no hope → **doom and gloom** *at* DOOM[1]

gloom·y /ˈglumi/ *adj.* (comparative **gloomier**, superlative **gloomiest**) **1** making you feel that a situation will not improve: *The report* ***paints a gloomy picture*** *of the economy.* **2** sad because you do not have a lot of hope: *gloomy thoughts*

> THESAURUS **sad, unhappy, miserable, sorrowful, depressed, down, low, blue, downhearted, melancholy, morose, glum** → SAD

3 dark in a way that makes you feel sad: *the cold gloomy weather* —**gloomily** *adv.*

glo·ri·fied /ˈglɔrəˌfaɪd/ *adj.* [only before noun] made to seem like something more important: *My title is "Editorial Assistant," but I'm just a glorified secretary.*

glo·ri·fy /ˈglɔrəˌfaɪ/ *v.* (**glorified**, **glorifies**) [T] **1** to make someone or something seem more important or better than he, she, or it is: *movies that*

G

glorify violence **2** to praise someone or something, especially God —**glorification** /ˌglɔrəfəˈkeɪʃən/ *n.* [U]: *the glorification of war*

glo·ri·ous /ˈglɔriəs/ *adj.* **1** having or deserving praise and honor: *a glorious achievement* | *the country's* ***glorious past*** **2** very beautiful or impressive: *glorious views of the coast* | *a glorious fall morning* —**gloriously** *adv.*

glo·ry¹ /ˈglɔri/ *n.* (plural **glories**) **1** [U] the importance, praise, and honor that people give someone they admire: *At 19 he* ***won glory*** *as an Olympic champion.* **2** [C] an achievement that is greatly admired or respected, or that makes you feel proud: *Becoming a Supreme Court judge was the* ***crowning glory*** (=the final, most successful part) *of her legal career.* | *the* ***glories of*** *nature* | *the team's* ***past glories*** **3** [U] a beautiful and impressive appearance: *They spent $10 million on restoring the Grand Theater to its* ***former glory***.

glory² *v.* (**gloried**, **glories**)

glory in sth *phr. v.* to enjoy or be proud of the praise, attention, and success that you get: *The new mayor gloried in his victory.*

gloss¹ /glɔs, glɑs/ *n.* **1** [singular, U] a shiny attractive surface: *a hair gel that adds gloss to dull hair* **2** [C] a note in a piece of writing that explains a difficult word, phrase, or idea

G

gloss² *v.* [T] to provide a note in a piece of writing which explains a difficult word, phrase, or idea

gloss over sth *phr. v.* to avoid talking about something unpleasant, or to say as little as possible about it: *She glossed over the details of her divorce.*

glos·sa·ry /ˈglɑsəri, ˈglɔ-/ *n.* (plural **glossaries**) [C] ENG. LANG. ARTS a list of technical or unusual words with an explanation of their meaning, printed at the end of a book

gloss·y /ˈglɔsi, ˈglɑsi/ *adj.* **1** shiny and smooth: *glossy healthy hair* **2** a glossy magazine, book, or photograph is printed on shiny good quality paper

glot·tis /ˈglɑṭɪs/ *n.* [C] BIOLOGY the space between your VOCAL CORDS. When you open and close this space, the movement produces the sound of your voice. —**glottal** *adj.*

glove /glʌv/ *n.* [C] a piece of clothing worn on your hand, with separate parts to cover the thumb and each finger ➔ MITTEN: *a* ***pair of gloves*** [ORIGIN: Old English *glof*] ➔ *see picture at* CLOTHES

ˈglove comˌpartment *also* **ˈglove box** *n.* [C] a small cupboard in a car in front of the passenger seat, where small things such as maps can be kept

glow¹ /gloʊ/ *v.* [I] **1** to shine with a soft steady light: *The red tip of his cigarette was glowing in the dark*

THESAURUS **shine, flash, flicker, twinkle, sparkle, shimmer, gleam, glint, glisten ➔** SHINE¹

2 if your face glows, it is bright or hot because you are healthy, have been doing exercise, or are feeling a strong emotion **3 glow with happiness/pride/pleasure etc.** to show in your expression that you are very happy, proud, etc.: *Jodie was glowing with pride as she looked at the baby.*

glow² *n.* [singular] **1** a soft steady light: *the* ***glow of*** *candlelight* | *At sunset we could see an orange* ***glow from*** *the clouds.* **2** the bright color your face has when you are healthy, have been exercising, or are feeling a strong emotion: *the* ***healthy glow*** *in her cheeks* **3 a glow of pleasure/pride/satisfaction etc.** a strong feeling of pleasure, pride, etc.

glow·er /ˈglaʊə/ *v.* [I] to look at someone in an angry way: *Donna* ***glowered at*** *her husband but said nothing.* —**glower** *n.* [C]

glow·ing /ˈgloʊɪŋ/ *adj.* **glowing report/review/description etc.** a report, etc. that is full of praise for someone or something: *He spoke* ***in glowing terms*** *about the concert.* —**glowingly** *adv.*

glow·worm /ˈgloʊwəm/ *n.* [C] an insect that gives out light from its body

glu·cose /ˈglukoʊs/ *n.* [U] CHEMISTRY a natural form of sugar that is in fruits ➔ FRUCTOSE, LACTOSE, SUCROSE

glue¹ /glu/ *n.* [C,U] a sticky substance used for joining things together: *Stick the ribbon on with glue.*

glue² *v.* [T] **1** to join things together using glue: *The two pieces of leather were* ***glued together***.

THESAURUS **fasten, attach, secure, join, tape, staple, clip, tie, button (up), zip (up) ➔** FASTEN

2 be glued to sth to look at something with all your attention: *He was glued to the TV for the World Series.*

glum /glʌm/ *adj.* unhappy and quiet: *Anna looked glum.*

THESAURUS **sad, unhappy, miserable, sorrowful, depressed, down, low, blue, downhearted, melancholy, morose, gloomy ➔** SAD

glut¹ /glʌt/ *n.* [C] a supply of something that is more than you need: *a* ***glut of*** *new cars on the market*

glut² *v.* **be glutted with sth** to be supplied with too much of something: *The world market was glutted with oil.*

glut·ton /ˈglʌtˀn/ *n.* [C] **1** someone who eats too much food **2 a glutton for punishment** someone who seems to enjoy working very hard or doing something unpleasant

glut·ton·y /ˈglʌtˀn-i/ *n.* [U] (formal) the bad habit of eating and drinking too much

glyc·er·in /ˈglɪsərɪn/ *n.* [U] CHEMISTRY a sticky colorless liquid used in making soap, medicine, and EXPLOSIVES

glyph /glɪf/ *n.* [C] HISTORY a sign or picture, especially one cut into stone, used in a writing system

gm. the written abbreviation of GRAM

GMAT /ˈdʒi mæt/ *n.* [C] (trademark) **Graduate Management Admission Test** an examination taken by students who have completed a first degree and want to go to GRADUATE SCHOOL to study business

GMO *n.* [C] BIOLOGY **genetically modified organism** a plant or other living thing whose GENEs have been changed by scientists in order to make it stronger, less likely to get diseases, etc. —**GMO** *adj.*

gnarled /nɑrld/ *adj.* rough and twisted: *a gnarled branch*

gnash·ing /ˈnæʃɪŋ/ *n.* **gnashing of teeth** (humorous) used in order to say that people are very angry about something and are complaining loudly

gnat /næt/ *n.* [C] a small flying insect that bites

gnaw /nɔ/ *v.* [I,T] to keep biting something: *a dog **gnawing on** a bone*

gnaw at sb *phr. v.* to make you feel worried or anxious over a long time: *Guilt had been gnawing at him all day.*

gnaw·ing /ˈnɔ-ɪŋ/ *adj.* [only before noun] worrying or painful for a long time: *gnawing doubts*

gnome /noʊm/ *n.* [C] a creature in children's stories like a little old man, who lives under the ground

GNP *n.* ECONOMICS **Gross National Product** the total value of the goods and services produced in a country, including income received from abroad → GDP

go¹ /goʊ/ *v.* (past tense **went** /wɛnt/, past participle **gone** /gɔn, gɑn/, third person singular **goes** /goʊz/)
1 LEAVE [I] to leave a place → COME: *I wanted to go, but Craig wanted to stay.* | *Let's **go home**.* | *It's late – we should **be/get going**.*
2 VISIT (past participle **gone** *or* **been**) [I] to visit a place and then leave it: *Lucia **has gone to** Paris* (=she is in Paris now). | *Lucia **has been to** Paris* (=she has visited Paris in the past).

GRAMMAR
gone and been
Gone is the usual past participle of **go**: *She has gone to New York* (=she has traveled to New York and is there now).
Been is the past participle of the sense of **go** that means "visit": *I have been to New York many times* (=I have visited New York many times in the past, but I am not there now).

3 TRAVEL/MOVE [I] to travel or move in a particular way or for a particular distance: *The car was going much too fast.* | *We can **go by bus/car/train etc.***
4 be going to do sth used in order to say that something will happen, or is supposed to happen in the future: *It looks like it's going to rain.*
5 DO A PARTICULAR ACTIVITY [I] to leave the place where you are in order to do something: *Let's **go for** a walk.* | *I'll **go and** pick up the car for you.*
6 go shopping/swimming/clubbing etc. to leave somewhere in order to shop, swim, etc.
7 REACH [I] to reach as far as a particular place, or lead to a particular place: *The roots of the tree go very deep.* | *The belt won't go around my waist.*

THESAURUS reach, come → REACH¹

8 BE SENT [I] to be sent or passed on: *The email **went to** everyone in the company.*
9 USUAL POSITION [I] if something goes somewhere, that is its usual position: *"Where do the plates go?" "On the shelf."*
10 FIT [I] to be the right size, shape, or amount for a particular space: *I don't think all these bags will **go in** the trunk.*
11 CHANGE [linking verb] to change in some way, especially by becoming worse than before: *The company went bankrupt last year.* | *Her hair is starting to go gray.*
12 BE IN A STATE [linking verb] to be or remain in a particular state: *Many families are forced to **go hungry**.* | *His letter **went unanswered*** (=nobody replied to his letter).
13 ATTEND [I] **a)** to regularly attend school, a church, etc.: *Is Brett **going to** college next year?* **b)** to be at a concert, party, meeting, etc.: *Are you **going to** Gloria's party?*
14 HAPPEN [I] to happen or develop in a particular way: *How did your French test go?* | *The party **went well**.*
15 START [I] to start doing something: *It's time to **get going on** the cleaning.* | *The builders are **ready to go**, but their equipment isn't here yet.*
16 GET RID OF SB/STH [I] to be bad enough to be made to leave or be thrown away: *They knew that Parker **had to go**.* | *"Do you want all these magazines?" "No, they **can go**."*
17 MONEY [I] if money goes, it is spent: *The money **goes to** local charities.*
18 TIME [I] if time goes, it passes: *I just don't know where the time goes!*
19 BE SOLD [I] to be sold: *The painting should **go for** $2,000.*
20 SOUND/SONG [T] to make a particular sound, or have particular words or music: *Do you remember how that song goes?* | *The balloon suddenly went bang.*
21 MATCH [I] to look or taste good together: *Those colors don't **go together** very well.* | *Does red wine **go with** chicken?*
22 GET WORSE [I] to become weak and not work correctly: *He's old, and his hearing is going.*
23 to go **a)** remaining before something happens: *Only two weeks to go before we leave for South America!* **b)** food that is to go is bought from a restaurant and taken away to be eaten: *I'll have an order of fries to go, please.*

SPOKEN PHRASES
24 How's it going?/How are things going? said in order to ask someone how s/he is: *"Hey, Jimmy, how's it going?" "All right, I guess."*

G

25 go like this/that used in order to tell someone about what movement someone or something made: *He **went like this** and knocked the lamp over.*
26 don't (even) go there used in order to say that you do not want to think or talk about something: *"What if the two of them...?" "Don't even go there."*
27 it (just) goes to show used in order to emphasize what something proves or shows: *It just goes to show how important your first impression is.*
28 go (to the bathroom) to pass liquid or solid waste from your body: *Mommy, I **have to go**!*

[ORIGIN: Old English *gan*]

go about sth *phr. v.*
to do something or begin doing something: *I don't know how to go about this.* | *I didn't have the slightest idea how to go about making a movie.*

go after sb/sth *phr. v.*
1 to follow or chase someone: *Joe went after her to make sure she was okay.*
2 to try to get something: *I can't decide whether to go after the job or not.*

go against sb/sth *phr. v.*
G
1 if something goes against your beliefs, principles, etc., it is the opposite of what you believe in: *This goes against everything I've been brought up to believe in.*
2 to do the opposite of what someone wants or advises you to do: *She was scared to go against her father's wishes.*

go ahead *phr. v.*
1 (spoken) said in order to give someone permission to do something, or to let him/her speak before you: *You can **go ahead of** me – I'm waiting for someone.*
2 to start or continue to do something: *They've decided to **go ahead with** plans to build 50 new houses on the site.*
3 *also* **go on ahead** to go somewhere before the other people in your group: *You can go ahead and we'll catch up with you later.*

go along *phr. v.*
1 to continue doing something: *I went along making the same mistakes for weeks.*
2 if you do something as you go along, you do it without preparing or planning it: *I just made up the story as I went along.*

go along with sb/sth *phr. v.*
to agree with or support someone or something: *You'll never get Mom to go along with it.*

go around *phr. v.*
1 go around doing sth to behave or dress in a particular way: *You can't go around lying to people all the time!*
2 if something such as an illness or news is going around, it is being passed from one person to another: *There's a rumor going around that Hugh is having an affair.*
3 enough/plenty to go around enough for each person: *Is there enough ice cream to go around?*

go at sb/sth *phr. v.*
to attack someone or start a fight: *The dogs went at each other as soon as we let go.*

go away *phr. v.*
1 to leave a place or a person: *Go away! Leave me alone!*
2 to spend some time away from home, especially on vacation: *We're going away for two weeks in June.*
3 if a problem or bad feeling goes away, it disappears: *My headache hasn't gone away.*

go back *phr. v.*
1 to return to a place that you have just come from: *I think we ought to go back now.*
2 to continue something that you were doing before: *I'll **go back to** studying after the news is over.*
3 to have been made, built, or started at some time in the past: *Their family history **goes back to** the 16th century.*

go back on sth *phr. v.*
if you go back on a promise or agreement, you do not do what you promised to do: *We're not **going back on** our **word**.*

go by *phr. v.*
1 if time goes by, it passes: *Two months went by before Winton called.*
2 go by sth to use information, rules, etc. to help you decide what to do: *Don't go by that map. It's really old.*

go down *phr. v.*
1 BECOME LESS to become lower or less in level, amount, size, quality, etc.: *The temperature **went down to** freezing last night.* | *The swelling in her knee didn't go down for days.*
2 GO FROM ONE PLACE TO ANOTHER (spoken) to go to a place for a particular purpose: *We **went down to** Hudson's to buy a camera.*
3 SUN when the Sun goes down, it appears to move down until you cannot see it anymore
4 AIRPLANE if an airplane goes down, it crashes
5 SHIP if a ship goes down, it sinks
6 COMPUTER IT to stop working for a short time: *My computer went down an hour ago.*
7 go down well/badly etc. to get a particular reaction from someone: *Robbie's jokes didn't go down very well with her parents.*
8 BE REMEMBERED to be remembered or recorded in a particular way: *This day will **go down in history*** (=be remembered always).

go for sb/sth *phr. v.*
1 to try to get or win something: *a swimmer going for an Olympic record*
2 go for it (spoken) said when you want to encourage someone to do something: *Well, if you're sure you want to, go for it!*
3 I could/would go for sth (spoken) to want something: *I could really go for a taco right now.*
4 (spoken) to usually like a particular type of person or thing: *Kathy tends to go for older men.*

go into sth *phr. v.*
1 to start working in a particular profession or type of business: *Vivian wants to go into politics.*

2 to be used in order to make something work or happen: *A lot of money has gone into building this house.*
3 to describe or explain something thoroughly: *I don't want to **go into details** right now, but it was horrible.*
4 MATH if one number goes into another, it can divide it: *12 goes into 60 five times.*

go off *phr. v.*
1 to explode: *Fireworks went off all over the city that night.*
2 to make a loud noise: *My alarm clock didn't go off.*
3 to leave a place, especially in order to do something: *He **went off to** get something to eat.*
4 if a machine or light goes off, it stops working or stops shining: *Suddenly, all the lights went off.*

go on *phr. v.*
1 to continue without stopping or changing: *We can't go on fighting like this!* | *This guy **went on and on*** (=talked for a long time) *about himself all night.* | *We had to **go on with** our lives.*
2 to happen: ***What's going on** down there? Did something break?*
3 to do something new when you have finished something else: ***Go on to** question number 5 when you're done.*
4 to continue talking or explaining something, after you have stopped for a while: *After a minute, she stopped crying and **went on with** the story.*
5 (spoken) said in order to encourage someone to do something: *Go on, have another drink.*
6 to base an opinion or judgment on something: *The police don't have much to go on.*
7 be going on six o'clock/25 etc. to be nearly a time, age, number, etc.: *Aunt Tess must be going on 70 by now.*
8 if time goes on, it passes: *As time went on, he became more friendly.*
9 if a machine or light goes on, it starts working or starts shining

go out *phr. v.*
1 to leave your house, especially in order to do something you enjoy: *Are you going out tonight?* | *We **went out for dinner/lunch etc.** on Saturday.* | *Can I **go out and** play now?*
2 to have a romantic relationship with someone: *Leah used to **go out with** Dan's brother.*
3 if the TIDE goes out, the water moves away from the land (ANT) **come in**
4 if a light or fire goes out, it stops shining or burning

go over *phr. v.*
1 go over sth to look at or think about something carefully: *I've gone over the budget and I don't think we can afford a new computer.*
2 go over well if something goes over well, people like it: *His comments didn't go over very well with customers.*

go through *phr. v.*
1 go through sth to have a very upsetting or difficult experience: *She's just been through a divorce.*
2 go through sth to use all of something: *Jeremy goes through at least a quart of milk every day!*
3 if a deal, agreement, or law goes through, it is officially accepted: *My car loan has finally gone through.*
4 go through sth to look at, read, or explain something carefully: *She had to go through all her uncle's papers after he died.*

go through with sth *phr. v.*
to do something you had planned or promised to do: *I'm not sure if I can go through with the wedding.*

go to sth *phr. v.*
1 go to a lot of trouble/go to great lengths to use a lot of effort to get something or do something: *Suki went to a lot of trouble to get us the tickets.*
2 to begin to experience or do something, or begin to be in a particular state: *I lay down and went to sleep.*

go under *phr. v.*
ECONOMICS if a business goes under, it has serious problems and fails

go up *phr. v.*
1 to increase in number or amount: *Our rent has **gone up by** almost 20%.*
2 to be built: *All of those houses have gone up in the past six months.*
3 to explode or be destroyed by fire: *The factory **went up in flames** before the firemen got there.*

go with sb/sth *phr. v.*
1 to be included as part of something: *The car goes with the job.*
2 to accept someone's idea or plan: *Let's go with John's original proposal.*

go without sth *phr. v.*
1 to not have something you need or want: *We can go without a car in the city.*
2 it goes without saying used in order to say that something should be clear without needing to be said: ***It goes without saying that** you should stay with us when you're in Boston.*

go² *n.* (plural **goes**) [C] **1** an attempt to do something: *Don't worry about getting it right – just **give it a go**.* **2 on the go** (informal) very busy or working all the time: *Susan's three children really keep her on the go.*

goad /goʊd/ *v.* [T] to make someone do something by annoying him/her until s/he does it: *Kathy **goaded** him **into** confessing that he had lied.*

'go-a,head *n.* **give sb the go-ahead** (informal) to officially give someone permission to start doing something: *The bank finally **gave us the go-ahead to** start building.*

goal /goʊl/ (Ac) *n.* [C] **1** something that you hope to achieve in the future: *My **ultimate/long-term goal** is to become a doctor.* | *He will do anything it takes to **achieve/reach** his **goal**.*

THESAURUS

aim – something that you want to achieve when you do something: *His aim was to grow enough food to feed his family.*

objective – something that you are working hard to achieve, especially in business or politics: *The major objectives have been achieved.*
target – the number or amount that you want to achieve: *He set himself the target of raising over $1 million for cancer research.*
mission – the things that a person or organization wants to achieve, which forms the basis of all their activities: *The company says its mission is to organize the world's information and make it available to everyone.*

2 in a game or sport, the result of making the ball go into a particular area to win a point, or the point won by doing this: *He hasn't **scored a goal** in over four games.* **3** the area into which a player tries to put the ball in order to win a point [ORIGIN: 1500—1600 *gol* "limit," "boundary" (1300—1400)]

goal·ie /ˈgoʊli/ *n.* [C] (informal) a GOALKEEPER

goal·keep·er /ˈgoʊlˌkipɚ/ *also* **goal·tend·er** /ˈgoʊlˌtɛndɚ/ *n.* [C] the player on a sports team who tries to stop the ball from going into the goal

G

goal·post /ˈgoʊlpoʊst/ *n.* [C] one of the two upright BARS, with another bar along the top or across the middle, that form the goal in games like SOCCER and football

goat /goʊt/ *n.* [C] **1** a common farm animal with horns and with long hair under its chin ➔ *see picture at* FARM[1] **2 get sb's goat** (informal) to make someone very angry or annoyed [ORIGIN: Old English *gat*]

goat·ee /goʊˈti/ *n.* [C] a small BEARD on the end of a man's chin

gob·ble /ˈgɑbəl/ *also* **gobble up** *v.* [T] (informal) to eat something very quickly

gob·ble·dy·gook, **gobbledegook** /ˈgɑbəldiˌgʊk/ *n.* [U] (informal, disapproving) very complicated or technical language that seems to have no meaning

ˈgo-between *n.* [C] someone who takes messages from one person or group to another because the two sides do not want to meet or cannot meet: *The lawyer will **act as a go-between** for the couple.*

gob·let /ˈgɑblɪt/ *n.* [C] a cup made of glass or metal with a base and long stem but no handles

gob·lin /ˈgɑblɪn/ *n.* [C] a small and ugly creature in children's stories who likes to trick people

gobs /gɑbz/ *n.* [plural] (informal) a large amount of something: *They must have **gobs of** money.*

ˈgo-cart *n.* [C] a small car made of an open frame on four wheels that people race for fun

god /gɑd/ *n.* **1 God** the spirit or BEING whom Christians, Jews, Muslims, etc. pray to, and who they believe made the universe: *She **believes in God**.* **2** [C] a male spirit or BEING who is believed by some religions to control the world or part of it, or who represents a particular quality ➔ GODDESS: *Mars, the **god of** war*

THESAURUS

deity/divinity – a god or goddess
idol – an image or object that people pray to as a god

3 [C] someone or something that is given too much importance or respect: *Money became his god.* **4 a God-given duty/right/talent etc.** a duty, etc. received from God [ORIGIN: Old English]

god·child /ˈgɑdtʃaɪld/ *n.* (plural **godchildren** /-ˌtʃɪldrən/) [C] a child that a GODPARENT promises to help, usually by teaching him/her Christian values

god·dess /ˈgɑdɪs/ *n.* [C] a female spirit or BEING who is believed by some religions to control the world or part of it, or who represents a particular quality ➔ GOD: *Athena, the Greek goddess of wisdom*

god·fa·ther /ˈgɑdˌfɑðɚ/ *n.* [C] **1** a male GODPARENT **2** (slang) the leader of a criminal organization

ˈgod-ˌfearing *adj.* (old-fashioned) behaving according to the moral rules of a religion: *god-fearing men and women*

god·for·sak·en /ˈgɑdfɚˌseɪkən/ *adj.* a godforsaken place is far away from where people live, and does not have anything interesting or cheerful in it

god·less /ˈgɑdlɪs/ *adj.* not showing any respect for or belief in God

god·like /ˈgɑdlaɪk/ *adj.* having a quality like God or a god

god·ly /ˈgɑdli/ *adj.* (old-fashioned) showing that you obey God by behaving according to the moral rules of a religion

god·moth·er /ˈgɑdˌmʌðɚ/ *n.* [C] a female godparent

god·par·ent /ˈgɑdˌpɛrənt/ *n.* [C] someone who promises to help a child, usually by teaching him/her Christian values

god·send /ˈgɑdsɛnd/ *n.* [singular] something good that happens to you at a time when you really need it: *The drug has proved a **godsend to** people with the disease.*

go·fer /ˈgoʊfɚ/ *n.* [C] (informal) someone whose job is to get and carry things for other people

ˌgo-ˈgetter *n.* [C] (informal) someone who is very determined to succeed

ˌgoggle-ˈeyed *adj.* (informal) with your eyes wide open and looking at something that surprises you

gog·gles /ˈgɑgəlz/ *n.* [plural] special glasses that protect your eyes, for example when you are swimming

goggles

swimming goggles

go·ing¹ /ˈgoʊɪŋ/ *n.* [U] **1** the act of leaving a place: *His going will be a great loss to the company.* **2 rough/hard/good etc. going** (informal) the speed at which you do something: *I'm getting the work done, but it's slow going.*

going² *adj.* **1 the going rate** the usual cost of a service, or the usual pay for a job **2** [not before noun] available, or able to be found: *We think we make **the best** computers **going**.*

ˌgoing-ˈover *n.* [singular] a thorough examination of something to make sure it is all right: *Our lawyers will **give** the contract **a good going-over**.*

ˌgoings-ˈon *n.* [plural] (informal) activities or events that you think are strange or interesting

gold¹ /goʊld/ *n.* **1** [U] a valuable soft yellow metal that is used to make jewelry, coins, etc.: *The locket is made of **pure gold**.* **2** [C,U] a bright shiny yellow color [ORIGIN: Old English]

gold² *adj.* **1** made of gold: *a gold necklace* **2** having the color of gold: *a gold dress*

ˈgold ˌdigger *n.* [C] (informal) someone who marries someone else only for his/her money

gold·en /ˈgoʊldən/ *adj.* **1** having a bright shiny yellow color: *golden hair* **2 golden age** the time when something was at its best: *the **golden age of** television* **3 a golden opportunity** a good chance to get something valuable, or to be very successful **4** (literary) made of gold: *a golden crown*

gold·fish /ˈgoʊldˌfɪʃ/ *n.* [C] a small shiny orange fish often kept as a pet

ˌgold ˈmedal *n.* [C] a prize that is given to the winner of a race or competition, and that is usually made of gold: *He **won** three **gold medals** at the Olympics.* —**gold medalist** *n.* [C]

gold·mine /ˈgoʊldmaɪn/ *n.* [C] **1** (informal) a business or activity that produces a lot of money **2** a hole under the ground from which gold is taken

golf /gɑlf, gɔlf/ *n.* [U] a game in which you hit a small white ball into a hole in the ground with a golf club, using as few hits as possible: *I **play golf** every weekend.* ➔ *see picture on page A17* —**golfer** *n.* [C]

ˈgolf club *n.* [C] **1** a long wooden or metal stick used for hitting the ball in golf **2** a place where a group of people pay to play golf

ˈgolf course *n.* [C] an area of land on which you play golf

gol·ly /ˈgɑli/ *interjection* (old-fashioned) said when you are surprised

gon·do·la /ˈgɑndələ, gɑnˈdoʊlə/ *n.* [C] a long narrow boat, used on the CANALS of Venice

gone /gɔn, gɑn/ *v.* the past participle of GO

gon·er /ˈgɔnɚ, ˈgɑ-/ *n.* **be a goner** (informal, spoken) to be about to die, or in a lot of danger: *I heard an explosion, and I thought I was a goner.*

gong /gɔŋ, gɑŋ/ *n.* [C] a round piece of metal that hangs in a frame and is hit with a stick to make a loud sound as a signal

gon·na /ˈgɔnə, gənə/ *v.* (nonstandard) a way of writing "going to," used to show how people sound when they speak: *I'm gonna talk to her about it tomorrow.*

gon·or·rhe·a /ˌgɑnəˈriə/ *n.* [U] BIOLOGY a disease of the sex organs that is passed from one person to another during sex

goo /gu/ *n.* [U] a thick unpleasant sticky substance —**gooey** *adj.*: *gooey caramel*

good¹ /gʊd/ *adj.* (comparative **better**, superlative **best**)

1 HIGH IN QUALITY of a high standard (ANT) **bad, poor**: *The food was really good.* | *Who's the best player on the team?* | *His work just isn't **good enough**.*

THESAURUS

great (especially spoken): *We had a great time at camp.*
excellent: *It was an excellent concert.*
wonderful: *a wonderful place for a picnic*
fantastic: *That's fantastic news!*
outstanding: *an outstanding achievement*
exceptional: *She's an exceptional student.*
superb: *a superb performance*
first-class: *a first-class piece of work*
ace (informal): *an ace guitarist* ➔ BAD¹

USAGE

Use **good** to describe the quality of something or someone: *They did a good job.* | *He's a good actor.*
Use **well** to talk about the way someone does something: *He plays tennis very well.*

2 APPROPRIATE appropriate or convenient (ANT) **bad**: *When would be **a good time** for us to meet?* | *It was a good place to rest.*
3 SUCCESSFUL likely to be successful (ANT) **bad**: *That's a **good idea**.* | *We stand a **good chance** of winning.*
4 SKILLFUL smart or skillful: *a good swimmer* | *Andrea is very **good at** languages.*
5 NICE enjoyable and pleasant: *good weather* | ***It's good to** see you again.* | *We had such **a good time**.*
6 HEALTHY a) useful for your health or character: *Watching so much TV isn't **good for you**.* **b)** healthy: *"How do you feel today?" "Better, thanks."* | *I'm in reasonably **good health**.*
7 ABLE TO BE USED able to be used, and not broken or damaged: *There, now the table is **as good as new*** (=fixed so that it looks new again). | *The guarantee on my new watch is **good for** three years.*

G

8 WELL-BEHAVED behaving well, used especially about children: *Sit here and be a good girl.*
9 KIND kind and helpful: *It's* ***good of*** *you to come.* | *Dad was always* ***good about*** *helping me with my homework.*
10 as good as almost: *The work is as good as finished.*
11 a good deal (of sth) a lot: *I spent a good deal of time preparing for this test.*
12 RIGHT morally right: *He had always tried to lead a good life.*
13 LARGE/LONG large in amount, size, etc.: *a good-sized car* | *They've been gone* ***a good while*** (=a long time).
14 COMPLETE [only before noun] complete or thorough: *The car needs a good wash.* | ***Take a good look*** *at this picture.*
15 too good to be true/too good to last (informal) so good that you cannot believe it is real, or you expect something bad to happen: *Their relationship had always seemed too good to be true.*

SPOKEN PHRASES
16 good/oh good said when you are pleased that something has happened or has been done: *"I've finished." "Good, put your papers in the box."*
17 good luck used in order to say that you hope that someone is successful
18 good idea/question/point etc. used when someone says or suggests something interesting or important that you had not thought of before: *"But it's Sunday – the bank will be closed." "Good point."*
19 it's a good thing said when you are glad that something has happened: *It's a good thing you remembered to bring napkins.*
20 Good for sb! used in order to say that you approve of something that someone has done: *"I've decided to accept the job." "Good for you!"*
21 good God/grief/heavens etc. said in order to express anger, surprise, or other strong feelings. Saying "God" in this way is offensive to some people: *Good grief! Is it that late?*

[ORIGIN: Old English *god*]

good² *n.* [U] **1** something that improves a situation or gives you an advantage: *It'll* ***do you good*** (=make you feel better) *to take a vacation.* | *Take your medicine – it's* ***for*** *your* ***own good*** (=it will help you). **2 no good/not much good/not any good a)** not likely to be useful or successful: *It's no good trying to explain it to her – she won't listen.* **b)** bad: *That movie isn't any good.* **3 what's the good of...?/what good is...?** used in order to say that it is not worth doing or having something in a particular situation: ***What good is*** *an expensive house* ***if*** *you're always traveling?* **4 goods** [plural] ECONOMICS things that are produced in order to be sold: *furniture and other* ***household goods*** | *the tax payable on* ***consumer goods*** (=televisions, refrigerators, etc. that people buy) **5 for good** permanently: *I'd like to stay in Colorado for good.* **6 be up to no good** (informal) to be doing or planning to do something that is wrong or bad **7 deliver the goods/come up with the goods** (informal) to do what other people need or expect **8 make good on a promise/threat/claim etc.** to do what you say you are going to do or what you should do: *They're asking for more time to make good on their debts.* **9** behavior or actions that are morally right or follow religious principles: *the battle between good and evil*

good ˌafter'noon *interjection* used in order to say hello to someone in the afternoon

good·bye /gʊdˈbaɪ, gədˈbaɪ/ *interjection* said when you are leaving or being left by someone → HELLO: *Goodbye, Mrs. Anderson.* | *I just have to* ***say goodbye to*** *Erica.* [ORIGIN: 1500—1600 *God be with you*]

good 'evening *interjection* used in order to say hello to someone in the evening → GOOD NIGHT: *Good evening, ladies and gentlemen.*

ˌgood-for-'nothing *n.* [C] someone who is lazy or has no skills: *He's a lazy good-for-nothing.* —**good-for-nothing** *adj.*

ˌGood 'Friday *n.* the Friday before EASTER

ˌgood-'humored *adj.* cheerful and friendly

ˌgood-'looking *adj.* someone who is good-looking is attractive

> THESAURUS **attractive, nice-looking, pretty, beautiful, handsome, gorgeous, stunning, cute, hot** → ATTRACTIVE

ˌgood 'looks *n.* [plural] if someone has good looks, s/he is attractive

good 'morning *interjection* used in order to say hello to someone in the morning

ˌgood-'natured *adj.* naturally kind and helpful, and not easily made angry —**good-naturedly** *adv.*

good·ness /ˈgʊdnɪs/ *n.* [U] **1** (spoken) said when you are surprised or annoyed: ***My goodness,*** *you've lost a lot of weight!* | ***For goodness' sake,*** *will you be quiet!* **2** the quality of being good: *Anne believed in the basic goodness of people.*

good 'night *interjection* said when you are leaving or being left by someone at night, especially late at night → GOOD EVENING

good·will /gʊdˈwɪl/ *n.* [U] kind feelings toward or between people: *Christmas should be a time of peace and goodwill.*

good·y /ˈgʊdi/ *n.* (plural **goodies**) [C usually plural] (informal) something that is attractive, pleasant, or desirable, especially something good to eat: *We brought lots of goodies for the picnic.*

'goody-ˌgoody *also* **ˌgoody-'two-shoes** *n.* (plural **goody-goodies**) [C] (disapproving) someone who tries too hard to be good and helpful, in a way that others think is annoying

goof¹ /guf/ *v.* [I] (informal) to make a silly mistake
goof around/off *phr. v.* (informal) to spend time

doing silly things or not doing very much: *We spent the afternoon just goofing around at the mall.*

goof² *n.* [C] (informal) **1** a silly mistake **2** someone who is silly

goof·y /'gufi/ *adj.* (informal) stupid or silly: *a goofy smile*

goon /gun/ *n.* [C] (informal) **1** a violent criminal who is paid to frighten or attack people **2** a silly or stupid person

goop /gup/ *n.* [U] (informal) a thick slightly sticky substance: *What's that goop in your hair?*

goose /gus/ *n.* (plural **geese** /gis/) **1** [C] a common water bird that is similar to a duck but larger, and makes loud noises **2** [U] the meat from this bird [ORIGIN: Old English *gos*]

goose·bumps /'gusbʌmps/ *also* **'goose ˌpimples** *n.* [plural] a condition in which your skin is raised up in small points because you are cold, afraid, or excited: *I **get goosebumps** every time I think about playing in the championship.*

GOP *n.* **the GOP** Grand Old Party; another name for the Republican party in U.S. politics

go·pher /'goʊfɚ/ *n.* [C] a North and Central American animal like a SQUIRREL with a short tail, that lives in holes in the ground

gore¹ /gɔr/ *v.* [T] if an animal gores someone, it wounds him/her with its horns

gore² *n.* [U] blood that has flowed from a wound and become thicker and darker → GORY: *There's too much **blood and gore*** (=violence and blood) *in the movie.*

gorge¹ /gɔrdʒ/ *n.* [C] EARTH SCIENCES a deep narrow valley with steep sides → *see picture on page A24*

gorge² *v.* **gorge yourself on/with sth** to eat until you are too full: *We gorged ourselves on popcorn and hot dogs at the game.*

gor·geous /'gɔrdʒəs/ *adj.* very beautiful or pleasant: *What a gorgeous sunny day!* | *Liz looked gorgeous.*

THESAURUS **attractive, good-looking, nice-looking, pretty, beautiful, handsome, stunning, cute, hot** → ATTRACTIVE

go·ril·la /gə'rɪlə/ *n.* [C] the largest type of APE (=animal like a monkey) [ORIGIN: 1800—1900 Greek *Gorillai*, name of an African tribe of hairy women in old stories] → *see picture at* APE

gor·y /'gɔri/ *adj.* clearly describing or showing violence, blood, and killing: *a gory movie*

gosh /gɑʃ/ *interjection* said when you are surprised: *Gosh! I never knew that!*

gos·ling /'gɑzlɪŋ/ *n.* [C] a baby GOOSE

gos·pel /'gɑspəl/ *n.* **1** [C] *also* **Gospel** one of the four stories of Christ's life in the Bible **2** [U] *also* **gospel truth** something that is completely true: *Don't **take** what Ellen says **as gospel*** (=believe it to be completely true). **3** [U] *also* **'gospel ˌmusic** ENG. LANG. ARTS a type of Christian music, performed especially in African-American churches [ORIGIN: Old English *godspel*, from *god* "good" + *spell* "story, news"]

gos·sip¹ /'gɑsəp/ *n.* **1** [U] conversation or information about other people's behavior and private lives, often including unkind or untrue remarks: *People love hearing gossip about movie stars.* **2** [C] someone who likes talking about other people's private lives [ORIGIN: Old English *god-sibb* "godparent, close friend," from *god* "god" + *sibb* "relative"]

gossip² *v.* [I] to talk or write gossip about someone or something: *What are you **gossiping about**?*

THESAURUS **talk, have a conversation, chat (with/to sb)/have a chat, converse, visit with sb, discuss** → TALK¹

got /gɑt/ *v.* **1** the past tense of GET **2** a past participle of GET

got·cha /'gɑtʃə/ *interjection* (spoken) **1** a short form of "I've got you," said when you catch someone, or you have gained an advantage over him/her **2** a word meaning "I understand" or "all right": *"We have to be at the airport for five." "Gotcha."*

G

Goth·ic /'gɑθɪk/ *adj.* **1** ENG. LANG. ARTS a style of building that was common in Western Europe between the 12th and 16th centuries. Its main features were pointed ARCHes, tall PILLARs, and tall thin pointed windows.. *Gothic architecture* **2** ENG. LANG. ARTS a Gothic story, movie, etc. is about frightening things that happen in mysterious old buildings and lonely places, especially stories that were popular in the early 19th century **3** Gothic writing, printing, etc. has thick decorated letters

got·ta /'gɑt̬ə/ *v.* a way of writing "got to," used to show how people sound when they speak: *I gotta go now.* | *You've gotta admit he plays really well.*

got·ten /'gɑt˺n/ *v.* the usual past participle of GET

gou·ache /gʊ'ɑʃ, gwɑʃ/ *n.* **1** [U] ENG. LANG. ARTS a method of painting using colors that are mixed with water and made thicker with a type of GUM **2** [C] ENG. LANG. ARTS a picture produced using this method

gouge /gaʊdʒ/ *v.* [T] **1** to make a deep hole or cut in the surface of something **2** (informal) to charge someone too much money for something: *Hotels are ready to gouge Olympic visitors by raising their prices.* —**gouge** *n.* [C]

gouge sth ↔ **out** *phr. v.* to make a hole in something such as rock by removing material that is on its surface

gourd /gɔrd, gʊrd/ *n.* [C] a large fruit with a hard shell, that is sometimes used as a container

gour·mand /'gʊrmɑnd/ *n.* [C] (disapproving) someone who enjoys good food and drink very much, but who sometimes eats too much → GOURMET

gour·met¹ /gʊr'meɪ, 'gʊrmeɪ/ *adj.* [only before noun] relating to very good food and drink: *a gourmet restaurant*

gourmet² *n.* [C] someone who knows a lot about good food and drink, and who enjoys them

gout /gaʊt/ *n.* [U] a disease that makes your toes, knees, and fingers hurt and swell [ORIGIN: 1200—1300 Old French *goute*, from Latin *gutta* "drop;" because it used to be believed that it was caused by drops of disease in the blood]

gov·ern /'gʌvɚn/ *v.* **1** [I,T] to officially control a country, state, etc. and make all the decisions about things such as taxes and laws: *The same party governed for thirty years.* **2** [T] (formal) to control the way a system or situation works: *new rules governing immigration* [ORIGIN: 1200—1300 Old French *governer*, from Latin *gubernare*, from Greek *kybernan* "to control the direction of something"]

gov·er·nance /'gʌvɚnəns/ *n.* [U] POLITICS the act or process of governing

gov·ern·ess /'gʌvɚnɪs/ *n.* [C] a woman who lives with a family and teaches the children at home, especially in past times

G

gov·ern·ment /'gʌvɚmənt, 'gʌvɚnmənt/ *n.* **1** [C] *also* **Government** the group of people who govern a country, state, etc.: *The government will send aid to the disaster area.* | *the* ***British/German etc. government***

THESAURUS

democracy – a political system in which everyone can vote to choose the government, or a country that has this system
republic – a country that has an elected government, and does not have a king or queen
monarchy – a country that has a king or queen as the head of state, and which may or may not also have an elected government
regime – a government, especially one that was not elected fairly or that you disapprove of: *a brutal military regime*
dictatorship – a political system in which a dictator (=a leader who has complete power and who has not been elected) controls a country, or a country that has this system
totalitarian country/state, etc. – a country in which the government has complete control over everything
police state – a country where the government strictly controls people's freedom, for example to travel or to talk about politics → POLITICIAN

2 [U] the process of governing, or the system used for governing: *Voting is essential to democratic government.* —**governmental** /ˌgʌvɚn'mɛntl/ *adj.*

gov·er·nor, Governor /'gʌvənɚ, -vɚ-/ *n.* [C] the person in charge of governing a U.S. state: *the* ***Governor of*** *California* —**governorship** *n.* [U]

THESAURUS **politician, president, congressman/congresswoman, senator, mayor** → POLITICIAN

gown /gaʊn/ *n.* [C] **1** a long dress worn by a woman on formal occasions: *a silk evening gown* **2** a long loose piece of clothing worn for a particular activity or ceremony: *a graduation gown*

GPA *n.* [C] **grade point average** a number representing the average of all a student's grades, in which an A is 4 points, a B is 3 points, a C is 2 points, a D is 1 point, and an F is 0 points: *Kim has a really* ***high/low GPA***. | *He graduated with a 3.5 GPA.*

GPS *n.* (plural **GPSes**) **1** [U] **Global Positioning System** a system that uses radio signals from SATELLITES to show your exact position on the Earth **2** [C] a special piece of equipment that uses GPS to show your exact position, which people use in their cars to help them find places they are going to

grab¹ /græb/ *v.* (**grabbed, grabbing**) [T] **1** to take hold of someone or something with a sudden or violent movement: *He grabbed my bag and ran off.* | *Kay* ***grabbed hold*** *of my arm to stop me from going.* **2** (informal) to eat or sleep for a very short time: *I'll just grab a sandwich for lunch.* **3** (informal) to quickly take an opportunity to do something: *Try to get there early and grab a seat.* | *You should* ***grab the chance*** *to travel while you're young.* **4 how does sth grab you?** (spoken) used in order to ask if someone would be interested in doing a particular thing: *How does the idea of a trip to Hawaii grab you?*

grab at sth *phr. v.* to quickly and suddenly put out your hand in order to take hold of something: *I grabbed at the glass just before it fell.*

grab² *n.* **1 make a grab for/at sth** to suddenly try to take hold of something: *Parker made a grab for the knife.* **2 be up for grabs** (informal) if a job, prize, opportunity, etc. is up for grabs, it is available for anyone who wants to try to get it

grace¹ /greɪs/ *n.* [U] **1** a smooth way of moving that appears natural, relaxed, and attractive: *She moved with the grace of a dancer.* **2 a)** polite and pleasant behavior: *At least he* ***had the grace to*** *admit he was wrong.* | *Kevin accepted his defeat* ***with good grace*** (=without complaining). **b) graces** [plural] the skills needed to behave in a way that is considered polite and socially acceptable: *Her parents tried to teach her all the finer* ***social graces***. **3** *also* **grace period** more time that is added to the period you are allowed for finishing a piece of work, paying a debt, etc.: *The bill was supposed to be paid by Friday, but they're giving me* ***a week's grace***. **4** (formal) God's kindness that is shown to people: *Through* ***the grace of God*** *my dream became reality.* **5** a short prayer before a meal: *Who would like to* ***say grace***? [ORIGIN: 1100—1200 Old French, Latin *gratia* "pleasing quality, kindness," from *gratus*]

grace² *v.* [T] **1 grace sb/sth with your presence** (humorous) said when someone arrives late, or when someone who rarely comes to meetings or events arrives: *I'm so glad you've decided to grace* *us with your presence!* **2** (formal) to make a place or an object look more beautiful or attractive: *His new painting now graces the wall of the dining room.*

grace·ful /ˈgreɪsfəl/ *adj.* **1** moving in a smooth and attractive way, or having an attractive shape: *a graceful dancer* | *the car's* ***graceful curves*** **2** polite and exactly right for a situation: *They urged him to take the graceful way out and resign.* —**gracefully** *adv.*

gra·cious /ˈgreɪʃəs/ *adj.* **1** behaving in a polite, kind, and generous way: *a gracious host* **2** having the type of expensive style, comfort, and beauty that only rich people can afford: *gracious living* **3 (goodness) gracious!** (spoken, old-fashioned) used in order to express surprise or to emphasize "yes" or "no" —**graciously** *adv.*: *Valerie graciously agreed to let the group meet at her house.*

grad /græd/ *n.* [C] (spoken) a GRADUATE

gra·da·tion /greɪˈdeɪʃən, grə-/ *n.* [C] (formal) a small change in a set of changes: *gradations of color from dark red to pink*

grade¹ /greɪd/ (Ac) *n.* **1** [C] one of the 12 years you are in school in the U.S., or the students in a particular year: *My brother is* ***in the*** *eleventh* ***grade.*** | *a fourth-grade teacher* **2** [C] a number or letter that shows how well you have done at school, college, etc.: *She works hard and* ***gets good grades.*** **3** [C,U] a particular standard or level of quality that a product, material, etc. has: *Grade A beef* **4 make the grade** to succeed or reach the necessary standard: *I wanted to be an actress, but I was afraid I wouldn't make the grade.* **5** [C] a slope or a degree of slope, especially in a road or railroad tracks **6** [C,U] the level of importance you have or the level of pay you receive in a company or organization: *The pay depends on your grade.* [ORIGIN: 1500—1600 French, Latin *gradus* "step, degree"]

grade² (Ac) *v.* [T] **1** to separate things, or arrange them in order according to their quality or rank: *The eggs are graded according to size.* **2** to give a grade to an examination paper or to a piece of school work: *Grading essays takes time.* —**grading** *n.* [U]: *I have a lot of grading to do.*

grad·ed /ˈgreɪdɪd/ *adj.* **1** designed to suit different levels of learning: *The reading materials are graded.* **2** made level or less steep: *a graded road*

ˈgrade point ˌaverage *n.* [C] a GPA

-grader /greɪdɚ/ *n.* [C] a child in a particular grade: *a cute little first-grader*

ˈgrade ˌschool *n.* [C] an ELEMENTARY SCHOOL

gra·di·ent /ˈgreɪdiənt/ *n.* [C] a slope, or a measurement of how steep a slope is, especially in a road or railroad

ˈgrad school *n.* [C] (informal) a GRADUATE SCHOOL

grad·u·al /ˈgrædʒuəl/ *adj.* **1** happening, developing, or changing slowly over a long time (ANT) **sudden**: *gradual changes*

THESAURUS slow, leisurely, sluggish → SLOW¹

2 a gradual slope is not steep

grad·u·al·ly /ˈgrædʒuəli, -dʒəli/ *adv.* in a way that happens or develops slowly over time: *Gradually, his back got better.* | *The situation is gradually getting better.* | *The animals evolved gradually over millions of years.*

grad·u·ate¹ /ˈgrædʒuɪt/ *n.* [C] someone who has successfully completed his/her studies at a school, college, or university → UNDERGRADUATE: *high school graduates* | *a* ***graduate of*** *UCLA* → STUDENT

grad·u·ate² /ˈgrædʒuˌeɪt/ *v.* [I] to obtain a DIPLOMA or a degree by completing your studies at a school, college, or university: *Ruth has just* ***graduated from*** *Princeton.*

grad·u·at·ed /ˈgrædʒuˌeɪt̬ɪd/ *adj.* divided into different levels or sizes from lower to higher amounts or degrees: *graduated rates of income tax*

ˈgraduate ˌschool *n.* [C,U] a college or university where you can study for a MASTER'S DEGREE or a PH.D., or the period of time when you do this

ˈgraduate ˌstudent *n.* [C] a student who is studying for an advanced degree → STUDENT

grad·u·a·tion /ˌgrædʒuˈeɪʃən/ *n.* **1** [U] the time when you complete a college or university degree or HIGH SCHOOL education: *After graduation, Jayne went to nursing school.* **2** [C,U] a ceremony at which you receive a degree or DIPLOMA: *We're going to Sara's graduation today.*

graf·fi·ti /grəˈfit̬i/ *n.* [U] writing and pictures that are drawn illegally on the walls of buildings, trains, etc. [ORIGIN: 1800—1900 Italian *graffiare* "to make marks in a surface"]

graffiti

graft¹ /græft/ *n.* **1** [U] the practice of dishonestly using your position to get money or advantages: *politicians accused of graft* **2** [C] a piece of healthy skin or bone taken from someone's body and put on a damaged part of his/her body: *skin grafts* **3** [C] a piece cut from one plant and joined to another plant so that it grows where it is joined

graft² *v.* [I,T] **1** to put a piece of healthy skin or bone from one part of someone's body onto another part that has been damaged: *Doctors* ***grafted*** *skin from Mike's arm* ***onto*** *his burnt face.* **2** to join a part of a flower, plant, or tree onto another flower, plant, or tree

G

grain /greɪn/ *n.* **1** [C,U] a seed or seeds of crops such as corn, wheat, or rice that are used for food, or the crops themselves: *five-grain cereal* | *fields of grain* **2** [C] a very small piece or amount of something: *a* ***grain of*** *sand* | *There's not a* ***grain of truth*** *in what she said.* **3 the grain** the lines or patterns you can see in things such as wood or rock: *Split the wood along the grain.* **4 go against the grain** if something that you must do goes against the grain, you do not like doing it because it is not what you would naturally do **5 take sth with a grain of salt** to not completely believe what someone tells you because you know that s/he often lies or is wrong [ORIGIN: 1200—1300 Old French, Latin *granum* "seed"]

grain·y /ˈgreɪni/ *adj.* a photograph that is grainy has a rough appearance, as if the images are made up of spots

gram /græm/ *n.* [C] (*written abbreviation* **gm**) a unit for measuring weight, equal to 1/1000 of a kilogram or 0.035 OUNCES

gram·mar /ˈgræmɚ/ *n.* [U] ENG. LANG. ARTS the rules by which words change their form and are combined into sentences: *Check your spelling and grammar.* | *the rules of English grammar* [ORIGIN: 1300—1400 Old French *gramaire*, from Latin *grammatica*, from Greek *grammatikos* "of letters"]

G

gram·mat·i·cal /grəˈmæt̬ɪkəl/ *adj.* **1** [only before noun] ENG. LANG. ARTS relating to the use of grammar: *grammatical errors* **2** ENG. LANG. ARTS correct according to the rules of grammar: *a grammatical sentence* —**grammatically** *adv.*: *The sentence is grammatically correct.*

Gram·my /ˈgræmi/ *n.* (plural **Grammies**) [C] a prize given in the U.S. every year to the best song, the best singer, etc. in the music industry

grand[1] /grænd/ *adj.* **1** higher in rank than others of the same kind: *the grand prize* **2 grand total** the final total you get when you add up several numbers or amounts **3** (old-fashioned) very good or impressive: *a grand old house* [ORIGIN: 1500—1600 Old French "large, great," from Latin *grandis*] —**grandly** *adv.*

grand[2] *n.* (plural **grand**) [C] (informal) 1,000 dollars: *Bill only paid five grand for that car.*

grand·child /ˈgræntʃaɪld/ *n.* (plural **grandchildren** /-ˌtʃɪldrən/) [C] the child of your son or daughter

grand·dad /ˈgrændæd/ *n.* [C] (informal) a GRANDFATHER

grand·daugh·ter /ˈgrænˌdɔt̬ɚ/ *n.* [C] the daughter of your son or daughter

gran·deur /ˈgrændʒɚ, -dʒʊr/ *n.* [U] impressive beauty, power, or size: *the grandeur of the Pacific Ocean*

grand·fa·ther /ˈgrænd̮ˌfɑðɚ/ *n.* [C] the father of your mother or father → RELATIVE[1]

ˈgrandfather ˌclock *n.* [C] a tall clock in a wooden case that stands on the floor

gran·dil·o·quent /grænˈdɪləkwənt/ *adj.* (formal) using words that are too long and formal, in order to sound important SYN **pompous**: *a grandiloquent speech* —**grandiloquence** *n.* [U]

gran·di·ose /ˈgrændiˌoʊs, ˌgrændiˈoʊs/ *adj.* grandiose plans sound very important but are really not practical

ˌgrand ˈjury *n.* [C] a group of people who decide whether someone who may be guilty of a crime should be judged in a court of law

grand·ma /ˈgrændmɑ, ˈgræmɑ/ *n.* [C] (informal) a GRANDMOTHER

grand·moth·er /ˈgrændˌmʌðɚ/ *n.* [C] the mother of your mother or father → RELATIVE[1]

grand·pa /ˈgrændpɑ, ˈgræmpɑ/ *n.* [C] (informal) a GRANDFATHER

grand·par·ent /ˈgrændˌpɛrənt/ *n.* [C] the parent of your mother or father

ˌgrand piˈano *n.* [C] the type of large piano often used at concerts

grand prix /ˌgrɑn ˈpri/ *n.* [C] one of a set of international races, especially a car race

ˌgrand ˈslam *n.* [C] **1** a hit in baseball that gets four points because it is a HOME RUN and there are players on all the bases **2** the result of winning all of a set of important sports competitions in the same year

grand·son /ˈgrændsʌn/ *n.* [C] the son of your son or daughter

grandstand

grand·stand /ˈgrændstænd/ *n.* [C] a large structure that has many rows of seats and a roof, where people sit to watch sports competitions or races → BLEACHERS

gran·ite /ˈgrænɪt/ *n.* [U] EARTH SCIENCES a very hard gray rock, often used in buildings

gran·ny /ˈgræni/ *n.* (plural **grannies**) [C] (informal) a grandmother

gra·no·la /grəˈnoʊlə/ *n.* [U] a breakfast food made from nuts, OATS, and seeds

grant[1] /grænt/ (Ac) *n.* [C] an amount of money given to someone by an organization for a particular purpose: *They have* ***applied for*** *a research* ***grant***. | *a* ***grant from*** *the National Institute of Health* [ORIGIN: 1200—1300 Old French *creanter*, *graanter*, from Latin *credere* "to believe"]

grant² (Ac) *v.* **1 take it for granted (that)** to believe that something is true without making sure (SYN) **assume**: *You shouldn't take it for granted that your parents will pay for college.* **2 take sb for granted** to expect that someone will always be there when you need him/her, and never thank him/her: *He's so busy with his work that he takes his family for granted.* **3** [T] (formal) to give someone something that s/he has asked for or earned, especially official permission to do something: *The U.S. granted her permission to remain as a refugee.*

THESAURUS **give, award, present** → GIVE¹

4 granted (that) used in order to say that something is true, before you say something else about it: *Granted, he didn't practice much, but he played well anyway.*

gran·u·lat·ed /ˈgrænyəˌleɪt̬ɪd/ *adj.* granulated sugar is in the form of small white grains

gran·ule /ˈgrænyul/ *n.* [C] a very small hard piece of something: *coffee granules* —**granular** /ˈgrænyələ/ *adj.*

grape /greɪp/ *n.* [C] a small round green or purple fruit that grows on a VINE and is often used to make wine: *a* ***bunch of grapes*** [ORIGIN: 1200—1300 Old French *crape, grape* "hook, bunch of grapes"] → *see picture on page 414*

grape·fruit /ˈgreɪpfrut/ *n.* [C] a large yellow or pink CITRUS fruit with a thick skin, like a large orange

grape·vine /ˈgreɪpvaɪn/ *n.* **hear sth on/through the grapevine** to hear news because it has been passed from one person to another in conversation: *Sarah had heard through the grapevine that Larry was getting the job.*

graph /græf/ *n.* [C] a drawing that shows how two or more sets of measurements are related to each other: *a graph showing population growth over 50 years* → *see picture at* CHART¹

graph·ic /ˈgræfɪk/ *adj.* **1 a graphic account/description etc.** a very clear detailed description of an event **2** ENG. LANG. ARTS relating to drawing or printing: *graphic art* —**graphically** *adv.*: *She described the scene so graphically that we felt we were there.*

ˌgraphical ˈuser ˌinterface *n.* [U] IT GUI

ˌgraphic deˈsign *n.* [U] the art of combining pictures and words in the production of books, magazines, etc. —**graphic designer** *n.* [C]

ˌgraphic ˈnovel *n.* [C] ENG. LANG. ARTS a book that tells a story using a series of pictures, each of which is drawn inside a box, as they are in a COMIC STRIP —**graphic novelist** *n.* [C]

ˌgraphic ˈorganizer *n.* [C] a picture, GRAPH, DIAGRAM, etc. that helps you organize information in a way that is easy to see

graph·ics /ˈgræfɪks/ *n.* [plural] IT pictures or images, especially those produced on a computer: *the latest* ***computer graphics***

graph·ite /ˈgræfaɪt/ *n.* [U] EARTH SCIENCES a soft black substance that is a type of CARBON and is used in pencils

grap·ple /ˈgræpəl/ *v.* [I] to fight or struggle with someone, holding him/her tightly: *A young man was* ***grappling with*** *the guard.*

grapple with sth *phr. v.* to try hard to understand or solve a difficult problem: *The new governor will have to grapple with the problem of unemployment.*

grasp¹ /græsp/ *v.* [T] **1** to take and hold something firmly in your hands: *I grasped his arm firmly and led him away.*

THESAURUS **hold, grip, clutch, catch/take/keep/get (a) hold of sth, clasp, grab (hold of sth)/seize** → HOLD¹

2 to completely understand a fact or an idea, especially a complicated one: *They couldn't quite grasp the significance of the problem.* → **be grasping/clutching at straws** at STRAW

grasp at sth *phr. v.* to eagerly try to get or hold on to something: *He was desperately grasping at some way to stay in power.*

grasp² *n.* [singular] **1** the ability to understand a complicated idea or situation: *He* ***has*** *a* ***good grasp of*** *English grammar.* | *ideas that are* ***beyond*** *my* ***grasp*** (=too difficult to understand) **2** the possibility of being able to achieve or gain something: *Eve felt that success was finally* ***within*** *her* ***grasp***. **3** a hold on something, or your ability to hold it: *The bottle slipped out of his grasp and smashed on the floor.*

grasp·ing /ˈgræspɪŋ/ *adj.* (disapproving) too eager to get money: *a grasping man*

grass /græs/ *n.* **1** [U] a very common plant with thin green leaves that grows across fields, parks, hills, and yards: *Please keep off the grass.* | *a* ***blade of grass*** (=a single leaf) **2** [C,U] a particular type of grass: *mountain grasses* **3** [U] (informal) MARIJUANA [ORIGIN: Old English *græs*]

grass·hop·per /ˈgræsˌhɑpə/ *n.* [C] an insect that jumps with its long back legs and makes short loud noises

grass·land /ˈgræslænd/ *n.* [U] *also* **grasslands** [plural] EARTH SCIENCES a large area of land covered with wild grass

ˌgrass ˈroots *n.* **the grass roots** the ordinary people in an organization rather than the leaders —**grass-roots** *adj.*: *a grass-roots campaign*

gras·sy /ˈgræsi/ *adj.* covered with grass: *a grassy hill*

grate¹ /greɪt/ *v.* **1** [T] to rub food such as cheese, vegetables, etc. against a rough or sharp surface in order to break it into small pieces: *grated cheese*

G

THESAURUS cut, chop (up), slice, dice, peel, carve, shred → CUT[1]

2 [I] (informal) to annoy someone: *She's really beginning to **grate on** my **nerves**.*

grate² *n.* [C] **1** the frame and metal BARS that hold wood, coal, etc. in a FIREPLACE **2** a metal frame with bars across it that covers a hole, window, etc. (SYN) **grating**: *iron grates on the windows*

grate·ful /ˈgreɪtfəl/ *adj.* **1** feeling that you want to thank someone because of something kind that s/he has done (ANT) **ungrateful**: *I'm very **grateful for** the opportunity to study at Harvard.* | *Mona **was grateful to** Lorenzo **for** his support.* | *We're just **grateful that** you can help.* | *the thanks of a **grateful nation*** **2 I/we would be grateful if...** used in formal situations or letters to make a request: *I would be grateful if you would allow me to visit your school.* —**gratefully** *adv.*: *We gratefully accepted their offer.*

grat·er /ˈgreɪt̬ɚ/ *n.* [C] a kitchen tool used for grating food

grat·i·fy /ˈgræt̬əˌfaɪ/ *v.* (**gratified**, **gratifies**) [T] (formal) to make someone feel pleased and satisfied: *We were gratified by the result of the vote.* —**gratification** /ˌgræt̬əfəˈkeɪʃən/ *n.* [U]

G

grat·i·fy·ing /ˈgræt̬əˌfaɪ-ɪŋ/ *adj.* (formal) pleasing and satisfying: ***It's gratifying to** know that we have achieved so much.*

grat·ing¹ /ˈgreɪt̬ɪŋ/ *n.* [C] a metal frame with bars across it that covers a hole, window, etc.

grating² *adj.* a grating sound is unpleasant and annoying: *a grating voice*

gra·tis /ˈgræt̬ɪs, ˈgrɑ-/ *adj., adv.* (formal) provided without payment (SYN) **free**

grat·i·tude /ˈgræt̬əˌtud/ *n.* [U] the feeling of being grateful (ANT) **ingratitude**: *I would like to **express** my **gratitude** to everyone who helped us.*

gra·tu·i·tous /grəˈtuət̬əs/ *adj.* said or done without a good reason in a way that offends someone: *television programs full of **gratuitous violence***

gra·tu·i·ty /grəˈtuət̬i/ *n.* (plural **gratuities**) [C] (formal) a TIP

grave¹ /greɪv/ *n.* [C] **1** the place where a dead body is buried: *We visited my grandfather's grave.* | *They buried him in an **unmarked grave*** (=one with no name on it). **2 sb would turn/roll over in their grave** used in order to say that someone who is dead would strongly disapprove of something that is happening now **3 the grave** (literary) death: *He took the secret to the grave with him.* [ORIGIN: Old English *græf*]

grave² *adj.* **1** very serious and worrying: *I think he is making a **grave mistake**.* | *The war is a cause of **grave concern**.* **2** looking or sounding very serious: *My parents spoke quietly and **looked grave** for the rest of the day.* —**gravely** *adv.*

grave³ /greɪv, grɑv/ *adj.* ENG. LANG. ARTS a grave ACCENT is a mark put above a letter in some languages such as French to show how the letter is pronounced, for example è

grav·el /ˈgrævəl/ *n.* [U] small stones used in order to make a surface for paths or roads

grav·el·ly /ˈgrævəli/ *adj.* a gravelly voice sounds low and rough

grave·side /ˈgreɪvsaɪd/ *n.* [C usually singular] the area around a grave: *Mourners stood somberly **at his graveside*** (=beside it).

grave·stone /ˈgreɪvstoʊn/ *n.* [C usually singular] a stone on a grave that shows the name of the dead person and the dates of his/her birth and death

grave·yard /ˈgreɪvyɑrd/ *n.* [C] an area of ground where people are buried, often near a church → CEMETERY

ˈgraveyard ˌshift *n.* [C] a period of working time that begins late at night and continues until the early morning, or the people who work during this time

grav·i·tate /ˈgrævəˌteɪt/ *v.* [I] to be attracted to something and move toward it, or become involved with it: *Students **gravitate toward** others with similar interests.*

grav·i·ta·tion /ˌgrævəˈteɪʃən/ *n.* [U] PHYSICS the force that makes two objects, such as PLANETS, move toward each other because of their MASS

grav·i·ta·tion·al /ˌgrævəˈteɪʃənəl/ *adj.* PHYSICS relating to gravity: *the Earth's gravitational pull*

graviˌtational ˈfield *n.* [C] PHYSICS an area in space around every large mass such as a PLANET or star, that attracts other objects toward it

grav·i·ty /ˈgrævət̬i/ *n.* [U] **1** PHYSICS the force that makes objects fall to the ground: *the laws of gravity* **2** (formal) the seriousness or importance of an event, situation, etc.: *I don't think they understand the **gravity of** the situation.*

gra·vy /ˈgreɪvi/ *n.* [U] SAUCE made from the juice of cooked meat, flour, and milk: *mashed potatoes and gravy*

ˈgravy ˌtrain *n.* [singular] (informal) an organization, activity, or business from which many people can make money without much effort

gray¹ /greɪ/ *adj.* **1** having the color of black mixed with white: *He was wearing a gray suit.* **2** having gray hair: *Ryan's black hair is **turning/going gray**.* **3** if the weather is gray, the sky is full of clouds and the Sun is not bright: *a gray day* **4 gray area** a part of a subject such as law or science that is hard to deal with because the rules are not clear

gray² *n.* [U] a color made from black mixed with white: *The suit comes in gray or red.*

gray³ *v.* [I] if someone is graying, his/her hair is becoming gray

ˈgray ˌmatter *n.* [U] (informal) your intelligence, or the part of your brain that thinks

graze¹ /greɪz/ *v.* **1** [I,T] if an animal grazes, it eats grass: *cattle grazing in the field* **2** [T] to injure yourself by accidentally rubbing against something rough: *Billy grazed his knee when he fell.* **3** [T] to touch something lightly while passing it, sometimes damaging it: *The bullet grazed his arm.*

graze² *n.* [C] a wound caused by rubbing against something rough, which slightly breaks your skin: *minor cuts and grazes*

GRE *n.* [C] (trademark) **Graduate Record Examination** an examination taken by students who have completed a first degree and want to go to GRADUATE SCHOOL

grease¹ /gris/ *n.* [U] **1** a thick oily substance that is put on the moving parts of a car or machine to make it run smoothly **2** soft fat from animals or vegetables

grease² *v.* [T] to put grease on something: *Grease the pan lightly with butter.*

greas·y /ˈgrisi, -zi/ *adj.* covered in grease or oil: *greasy food* | *greasy hair*

THESAURUS **dirty, filthy, dusty, muddy, grimy, soiled, polluted** → DIRTY¹

ˌgreasy ˈspoon *n.* [C] (informal) a small cheap restaurant that mainly serves fried (FRY) food

great /greɪt/ *adj.*

1 USEFUL (informal) very useful or appropriate for something: *This stuff's **great for** getting stains out of clothes.*

2 LARGE very large in size, amount, or degree: *Willis caught a **great big** fish!* | ***A great many** people died in the earthquake.*

3 IMPORTANT very important, successful, or famous: *the great civilizations of the past* | *Ella Fitzgerald was the greatest jazz singer ever.*

SPOKEN PHRASES

4 EXCELLENT very good: *It's great to see you again!* | *We had a great time.*

THESAURUS **good, excellent, wonderful, fantastic, outstanding, exceptional, superb, first-class, ace** → GOOD¹
nice, enjoyable, pleasant, fantastic, wonderful → NICE

5 NOT GOOD said when you are annoyed and think that something is not good at all: *"Your car won't be ready until next week." "Oh, great!"*

6 a great deal a lot: *He's traveled a great deal.* | *The explosion caused **a great deal of** damage.*

7 great-grandmother/great-uncle etc. the grandmother, uncle, etc. of one of your parents

8 great-granddaughter/great-nephew etc. the GRANDDAUGHTER, NEPHEW, etc. of your child

9 (the) Great used in names to mean large or important: *Alexander the Great* | *the Great Lakes*

10 Greater Boston/New York etc. used to talk about a large city, including all the outer areas: *the Greater Los Angeles area* [ORIGIN: Old English] —**greatness** *n.* [U]

ˌgreatest ˌcommon ˈfactor (*abbreviation* **GCF**) *n.* [singular] MATH the largest positive number that divides exactly into each of a set of numbers

great·ly /ˈgreɪt˺li/ *adv.* (formal) extremely or very much: *The money you lent us was greatly appreciated.* ►Don't say "The money was appreciated greatly."◄

greed /grid/ *n.* [U] a strong desire for more food, money, power, possessions, etc. than you need

greed·y /ˈgridi/ *adj.* (comparative **greedier**, superlative **greediest**) always wanting more food, money, power, possessions, etc. than you need: *He was being selfish and greedy.* —**greedily** *adv.* —**greediness** *n.* [U]

Greek¹ /grik/ *adj.* **1** relating to or coming from Greece **2** relating to the Greek language

Greek² *n.* **1** [U] the language used in Greece **2** [C] someone from Greece

green¹ /grin/ *adj.* **1** having the color of grass: *green eyes* | *pale/dark green leaves* **2** covered with grass, trees, bushes, etc.: *green fields* **3** fruit that is green is not yet ready to be eaten: *green bananas* **4** relating to or concerned about the environment: *green issues* **5 be green with envy** to wish very much that you had something that someone else has **6 give sb/sth the green light** to allow a project, plan, etc. to begin: *The board just **gave us the green light** to begin research.* **7** (informal) young and lacking experience: *The trainees are still pretty green.*

THESAURUS **young, youthful, immature, underage** → YOUNG¹

8 have a green thumb to be good at making plants grow [ORIGIN: Old English *grene*]

green² *n.* **1** [C,U] the color of grass **2** [C] the smooth flat area of grass around a hole on a GOLF COURSE: *the 18th green* **3 greens** [plural] vegetables with large green leaves: *salad greens*

green·back /ˈgrinbæk/ *n.* [C] (informal) a dollar BILL

ˌgreen ˈbean *n.* [C] a long thin green vegetable that is picked and eaten before the beans inside it grow

ˌgreen ˈcard *n.* [C] a document that shows that someone who is not a citizen can live and work in the U.S.

green·er·y /ˈgrinəri/ *n.* [U] green leaves and plants

green·horn /ˈgrinhɔrn/ *n.* [C] (informal) someone who lacks experience in a job and can be easily deceived

green·house /ˈgrinhaʊs/ *n.* [C] a glass building in which you grow plants that need to be protected from the weather

greenhouse effect

① ② ③

1. incoming solar radiation
2. some energy is radiated out to space
3. greenhouse gases in the atmosphere retain a part of solar radiation

ˈgreenhouse efˌfect *n.* **the greenhouse effect** EARTH SCIENCES the gradual warming of the air around the Earth as a result of the Sun's heat being trapped by POLLUTION → ENVIRONMENT

G

ˈgreenhouse ˌgas *n.* [C] EARTH SCIENCES a gas, especially CARBON DIOXIDE or METHANE, that traps heat above the Earth and causes the greenhouse effect

ˌgreen ˈonion *n.* [C] a small white onion with a small round end and a long green stem that you eat raw (SYN) **scallion**

greet /grit/ *v.* [T] **1** to say hello to someone or welcome him/her: *Carol's mother **greeted** her **with** hugs and kisses.* **2** to react to something in a particular way: *The first speech **was greeted with** cheers and laughter.*

greet·ing /ˈgriṭɪŋ/ *n.* [C] **1** something that you say or do when you meet someone: *The two men **exchanged greetings*** (=said hello to each other). | *We received a **warm*** (=friendly) ***greeting**.* **2 holiday/birthday/Christmas etc. greetings** a message saying that you hope someone will be happy and healthy on his/her BIRTHDAY, at Christmas, etc.

ˈgreeting ˌcard *n.* [C] a card that you send to someone on his/her BIRTHDAY, at Christmas, etc.

gre·gar·i·ous /grɪˈgɛriəs/ *adj.* someone who is gregarious is friendly and enjoys being with other people [ORIGIN: 1600—1700 *gregarius*, from *grex* "group of animals"]

THESAURUS **sociable, outgoing, extroverted, affable, genial, convivial** → SOCIABLE

grem·lin /ˈgrɛmlən/ *n.* [C] an imaginary evil spirit that is blamed for problems in machinery

gre·nade /grəˈneɪd/ *n.* [C] a small bomb that can be thrown by hand or fired from a gun

grew /gru/ *v.* the past tense of GROW

grey /greɪ/ *adj.* another spelling of GRAY

grey·hound /ˈgreɪhaʊnd/ *n.* [C] a thin dog with long legs that can run very fast, often used in races

grid /grɪd/ *n.* [C] **1** a pattern of straight lines that cross each other and form squares: *streets organized in a grid system* **2** the system of squares with numbers on them that are printed on a map so the exact position of any place can be found **3** a network of CABLES that supply an area with electricity

grid·dle /ˈgrɪdl/ *n.* [C] an iron plate used for cooking food on top of a STOVE

grid·i·ron /ˈgrɪdaɪən/ *n.* [C] (informal) a football field

grid·lock /ˈgrɪdlɑk/ *n.* [U] **1** a situation in which the streets have so many cars, etc. using them that the cars cannot move **2** a situation in which nothing can happen, usually because people disagree strongly —**gridlocked** *adj.*: *Traffic was gridlocked in the downtown area.*

grief /grif/ *n.* [U] **1** extreme sadness, especially because someone you love has died: *His grief was obvious from the way he spoke.* **2 give sb grief** (informal) to say something that annoys or causes trouble for someone: *My mom's been giving me grief about not helping with my little sister.* [ORIGIN: 1200—1300 Old French *gref*, from Latin *gravis*]

griev·ance /ˈgrivəns/ *n.* [C,U] something that you complain about because you think it is unfair: *He has major **grievances against** his former employer.*

grieve /griv/ *v.* [I,T] to feel extremely sad, especially because someone you love has died: *We are still **grieving over** the death of our mother.* | *families **grieving for** their loved ones* | *grieving parents*

griev·ous /ˈgrivəs/ *adj.* (formal) very serious and likely to be harmful: *Lying to the police was a **grievous error/mistake**.* —**grievously** *adv.*

grift·er /ˈgrɪftə/ *n.* [C] (informal) someone who dishonestly obtains something, especially money

grill¹ /grɪl/ *v.* **1** [I,T] if you grill food, or if it grills, you cook it over a fire

THESAURUS **cook, bake, fry, roast, broil, sauté, boil, steam, deep fry** → COOK¹

2 [T] (informal) to ask someone a lot of difficult questions for a long period of time: *The police **grilled** him **about** the murder.*

grill² *n.* [C] **1** a flat metal frame with BARS across it that can be put over a fire so that food can be cooked on it: *Let's put a few steaks **on the grill**.* **2** *also* **grille** a frame of metal bars used for protecting something such as a window

grim /grɪm/ *adj.* **1** making you feel worried and unhappy: *grim news on the economy* | *We were running out of money and **things were looking** pretty **grim**.* **2** looking or sounding very serious: *a* *grim-faced judge* **3** a place that is grim is unattractive and unpleasant —**grimly** *adv.*

grim·ace /ˈgrɪməs/ *v.* [I] to twist your face in an ugly way because you feel pain, do not like something, or are trying to be funny: *Theo rolled around on the field **grimacing with** pain.* —**grimace** *n.* [C]

grime /graɪm/ *n.* [U] thick black dirt that forms a layer on surfaces

grim·y /ˈgraɪmi/ *adj.* covered in thick black dirt: *a grimy apartment building*

THESAURUS **dirty, filthy, dusty, muddy, greasy, soiled, polluted** → DIRTY[1]

grin[1] /grɪn/ *v.* (**grinned**, **grinning**) [I] **1** to smile continuously with a very big smile: *Sally was **grinning at** Martin from across the room.*

THESAURUS **smile, beam, smirk, simper** → SMILE

2 grin and bear it (informal) to accept a difficult situation without complaining because you cannot change it: *It won't be fun, but we'll have to grin and bear it.*

grin[2] *n.* [C] a wide smile: *He looked back at me with a **big grin** on his face.*

grind[1] /graɪnd/ *v.* (past tense and past participle **ground** /graʊnd/) [T] **1** to crush something such as coffee beans into small pieces or powder: *Could you grind some coffee for me?*

THESAURUS **press, squash, crush, mash, squeeze, compress, compact** → PRESS[1]

2 to cut food such as raw meat into small pieces, using a machine **3** to press something down into a surface and rub it with a strong twisting movement: *He paused and **ground** his cigarette butt **into** the ashtray.* **4** to make something smooth or sharp by rubbing it on a hard surface or by using a machine: *a stone for grinding knives and scissors* **5 grind your teeth** to rub your upper and lower teeth together, making a noise **6 grind to a halt** if something grinds to a halt, it stops moving or making progress: *Traffic slowly ground to a halt.*

grind[2] *n.* [singular] (informal) something that is hard, boring, and tiring: *The work has become a grind to them.*

grind·er /ˈgraɪndɚ/ *n.* [C] a machine used to crush or cut food into small pieces: *a coffee grinder*

grind·ing /ˈgraɪndɪŋ/ *adj.* **grinding poverty** the state of being extremely poor

grinder

a pepper grinder

grind·stone /ˈgraɪndstoʊn/ *n.* [C] a large round stone that is turned like a wheel and is used for making tools sharp → **keep your nose to the grindstone** *at* NOSE[1]

grip[1] /grɪp/ *n.* **1** [singular] a tight hold on something, or your ability to hold it: *Get a firm **grip on** the rope, and then pull.* **2** [singular] the control that you have over a person, a situation, or your emotions: *Come on, Dee, **get a grip on yourself** (=try to control your emotions)!* **3 come/get to grips with sth** to understand and deal with a difficult problem or situation: *Eric still hasn't come to grips with his drug problem.* **4 be in the grip of sth** to be experiencing a very unpleasant situation: *The economy is deep in the grip of a recession.*

grip[2] *v.* (**gripped**, **gripping**) **1** [T] to hold something very tightly: *I gripped his hand in fear.*

THESAURUS **hold, clutch, catch/take/keep/get (a) hold of sth, grasp, clasp, grab (hold of sth)/seize** → HOLD[1]

2 [T] to have a strong effect: *Unusually cold weather has gripped the northwest.* **3** [I,T] if something grips a surface, it stays on without slipping: *tires that grip the road* **4** [T] to hold all of your attention and interest: *a book that really grips you*

gripe[1] /graɪp/ *v.* [I] (informal) to complain about something continuously and in an annoying way: *Now what's Pete **griping about**?*

gripe[2] *n.* [C] something that you keep complaining about: *The students' main gripe is the dorm food.*

grip·ping /ˈgrɪpɪŋ/ *adj.* very exciting and interesting: *a gripping story*

THESAURUS **exciting, thrilling, dramatic, exhilarating, electric** → EXCITING
interesting, fascinating, intriguing, absorbing, enthralling, engrossing, compelling, riveting → INTERESTING

gris·ly /ˈgrɪzli/ *adj.* extremely unpleasant because death or violence is involved: *a grisly murder*

grist /grɪst/ *n.* **grist for the mill** something that is useful in a particular situation: *The president's comments provided journalists with plenty of **grist for** their mill.*

gris·tle /ˈgrɪsəl/ *n.* [U] the part of a piece of meat that is not soft enough to eat

grit[1] /grɪt/ *n.* **1** [U] very small pieces of stone **2** [U] (informal) determination and courage SYN **guts** **3 grits** [plural] a type of crushed grain that is cooked and eaten for breakfast, especially in the southern U.S. —**gritty** *adj.*

grit[2] *v.* (**gritted**, **gritting**) **grit your teeth** to use all your determination to continue doing something in spite of pain or difficulties: *Just grit your teeth; the worst is almost over.*

griz·zly bear /ˈgrɪzli ˌbɛr/ *also* **grizzly** *n.* [C] a large brown bear that lives in the northwest of North America

groan /groʊn/ *v.* [I] to make a long deep sound, for example because you are in pain or are not happy

G

about something: *Charlie was holding his arm and groaning.* —**groan** *n.* [C]: *Loud groans came from the crowd.*

gro·cer /ˈgrousɚ, -ʃɚ/ *n.* [C] someone who owns or works in a grocery store [ORIGIN: 1200—1300 Old French *grossier* "person who sells in large quantities," from *gros* "big, thick"]

gro·cer·ies /ˈgrousəriz, ˈgrouʃriz/ *n.* [plural] the food or other things that are sold in a grocery store or SUPERMARKET

gro·cer·y store /ˈgrousəri ˌstɔr, -ʃri-/ *also* **grocery** *n.* [C] a store that sells food and other things used in the home

grog·gy /ˈgrɑgi/ *adj.* weak and unable to walk steadily or think clearly because you are sick or very tired

groin /grɔɪn/ *n.* [C] the place where your legs join at the front of your body

groom¹ /grum/ *v.* [T] **1** to prepare someone for an important job or position by training him/her: *Sharon's being* ***groomed to*** *take over the business.* **2** to take care of your appearance by keeping your hair and clothes clean and neat: *a* ***well-groomed*** *young man* **3** to take care of animals by cleaning and brushing them —**grooming** *n.* [U]

G

groom² *n.* [C] **1** a man at the time he gets married, or just after he is married: *a wedding photo of* ***the bride and groom*** → WEDDING **2** someone whose job is to take care of horses

groove /gruv/ *n.* **1** [C] a thick line cut into a surface to hold something, or to make something move or flow where you want it to: *Plant the seeds in grooves about a foot apart.* **2** [singular] (informal) the way things should be done, so that it seems easy and natural: *It will take the players a while to* ***get back in the groove.***

grope /group/ *v.* **1** [I] to try to find something you cannot see, using your hands: *She* ***groped*** *in the dark* ***for*** *the flashlight.* **2 grope your way along/across etc.** to go somewhere by feeling the way with your hands because you cannot see **3 grope for sth** to have difficulty in finding the right words to say or the right solution to a problem **4** [T] (informal) to touch someone's body in a sexual way when s/he does not want to be touched

gross¹ /grous/ *adj.* **1** (spoken) very unpleasant to look at or think about: *There was one really gross part in the movie.* | *Oh, gross! I hate spinach!* **2** [only before noun] ECONOMICS a gross amount of money is the total amount before any tax or costs have been taken away → NET: *His* ***gross profit*** *was $300,000.* **3** a gross weight is the total weight of something, including its wrapping **4** [only before noun] wrong and unacceptable: *Workers are suing the company for* ***gross negligence.*** | *That's a* ***gross exaggeration.*** [ORIGIN: 1300—1400 Old French *gros* "big, thick," from Latin *grossus*] —**grossly** *adv.* —**grossness** *n.* [U]

gross² *v.* [T] ECONOMICS to earn an amount as a total profit or earn it as a total amount, before tax has been taken away: *The movie has already grossed over $10 million.*

> THESAURUS **earn, make, get, be/get paid, net** → EARN

gross sb ↔ **out** *phr. v.* if something grosses you out, it is very unpleasant and almost makes you feel sick: *His dirty fingernails really gross me out.*

ˌgross doˌmestic ˈproduct *n.* [singular, U] ECONOMICS GDP

ˌgross ˌnational ˈproduct *n.* [singular, U] ECONOMICS GNP

gro·tesque /grouˈtɛsk/ *adj.* ugly or strange in a way that is unpleasant or frightening: *drawings of grotesque monsters* [ORIGIN: 1500—1600 French, Old Italian *(pittura) grottesca* "cave painting," from *grotta*] —**grotesquely** *adv.*: *The movie is grotesquely violent.*

> THESAURUS **ugly, unattractive, unsightly, hideous, repulsive** → UGLY

grot·to /ˈgrɑt̬ou/ *n.* (plural **grottos** *or* **grottoes**) [C] a small CAVE

grouch¹ /grautʃ/ *n.* [C] (informal) someone who is always complaining

grouch² *v.* [I] (informal) to complain in a slightly angry way

grouch·y /ˈgrautʃi/ *adj.* feeling annoyed and complaining a lot

> THESAURUS **grumpy, cranky, crabby, cantankerous, irritable, touchy** → GRUMPY

ground¹ /graund/ *n.*

1 EARTH'S SURFACE [singular, U] **a)** the surface of the Earth: *We were all sitting* ***on the ground.*** | *People in the area were advised to move to* ***higher ground*** *in the event of a flood.* | *The fuel is stored* ***below ground.*** | *The pipes are laid* ***above ground.*** **b)** the soil on and under the surface of the Earth: *We put seeds in the ground.* → *see picture at* WATER CYCLE

> **USAGE**
>
> Use **on the ground** to say where someone or something is: *I saw the keys on the ground next to the car.*
>
> Use **to the ground** to show movement that goes down: *Eddie was knocked to the ground.*

> **THESAURUS**
>
> The **ground** is the surface under your feet when you are outside: *The ground was very muddy.*
>
> The **floor** is the surface under your feet when you are inside a building: *The floors all have carpets.*
>
> **Land** is an area of ground that is owned or controlled by someone: *He owns all the land around here.*

Earth or soil is the substance that plants grow in: *The soil is good for growing plants.*

2 AREA OF LAND **a)** [C] a large area of land or ocean that is used for a particular purpose: *a burial ground* **b) grounds** [plural] the land or gardens around a building: *prison grounds*
3 KNOWLEDGE [U] an area of knowledge, ideas, experience, etc.: *Scientists are* ***breaking new ground*** (=discovering new ideas) *in cancer research.* | *We* ***covered*** *a lot of* ***ground*** *in class today.*
4 OPINIONS [U] the general opinions you have about something: *There has to be a way we can find some* ***common/middle ground*** (=something that everyone can agree about). | *Neither side was willing to* ***give*** *any* ***ground*** (=agree that someone else is right).
5 hold/stand your ground a) to refuse to move when someone threatens you, in order to show that you are not afraid **b)** to refuse to change your opinion, belief, etc., even though people are trying to make you change it: *Joanne held her ground and made no apologies.*
6 REASON **grounds** [plural] a good reason for doing, believing, or saying something: *Mental cruelty can be* ***grounds for*** *divorce.* | *The committee rejected the proposal* ***on the grounds that*** *it would be too expensive.*
7 get off the ground to start being successful: *His company hasn't really gotten off the ground yet.*
8 gain/lose ground to become more or less successful or popular: *Republicans have been gaining ground in recent months.*
9 ELECTRICAL [singular] PHYSICS a wire that connects a piece of electrical equipment to the ground for safety
10 SMALL PIECES **grounds** [plural] the small pieces of something such as coffee which sink to the bottom of a liquid: *coffee grounds* [ORIGIN: Old English *grund*]

ground² *v.* [T] **1** to stop an aircraft or pilot from flying: *All planes were grounded due to the snow.* **2 be grounded in sth** to be based on something: *His theories about education are grounded in years of research.* **3** (informal) to stop a child from going out with his/her friends as a punishment for doing something wrong: *If you stay out that late again, you'll be grounded for a week.* **4** PHYSICS to make a piece of electrical equipment safe by connecting it to the ground with a wire

ground³ *adj.* **1 ground beef/turkey/pork etc.** meat that has been cut up into very small pieces **2** ground coffee, pepper, etc. has been crushed into small pieces: ***freshly ground*** *pepper*

ground⁴ *v.* the past tense and past participle of GRIND

ground·break·ing /ˈgraʊndˌbreɪkɪŋ/ *adj.* groundbreaking work involves making new discoveries, using new methods, etc.: *groundbreaking research*

ˈground crew *n.* [C] the group of people who work at an airport taking care of the aircraft

ˌground ˈfloor *n.* [C] the part of a building that is on the same level as the ground

ground·hog /ˈgraʊndˌhɔg/ *n.* [C] a small North American animal that has thick brown fur and lives in holes in the ground SYN **woodchuck** → *see picture at* RODENT

ˈGroundhog ˌDay *n.* February 2; according to American stories, the first day of the year that a groundhog comes out of its hole. If it sees its shadow, there will be six more weeks of winter; if it does not, good weather will come early.

ground·less /ˈgraʊndlɪs/ *adj.* not based on facts or reason: *They assured me that my fears were totally groundless.*

ˈground rule *n.* [C] a rule or principle on which future actions should be based

ground·swell /ˈgraʊndswɛl/ *n.* **a groundswell of support/enthusiasm** a sudden increase in how strongly people feel about something: *There has been a groundswell of support for change.*

ground·work /ˈgraʊndwɚk/ *n.* [U] work that needs to be done in order for an activity or plan to be successful: *Amelia is already* ***laying the groundwork*** *for her re-election campaign.*

ˌground ˈzero *n.* [U] **1** the place where an explosion happens, where a lot of damage has been done and a lot of people have been killed **2 Ground zero** HISTORY the place in New York City where the World Trade Center buildings were destroyed by TERRORISTS on September 11, 2001

group¹ /grup/ *n.* [C] **1** several people or things that are all together in the same place: *a* ***group of*** *children* | *The teacher asked everyone to get into groups of four.*

THESAURUS

group of people
crowd – a large group of people in one place
team – a group of people who work together: *a team of doctors* | *a successful baseball team*
crew – a group of people who all work together, especially on a ship or airplane: *the flight crew*
gang – a group of young people, especially a group that often causes trouble and fights
mob – a large noisy group of people, especially one that is angry and violent: *an angry mob* | *mob violence*
bunch (informal) – a group of people: *They're a nice bunch of kids*
flock – a large group of people of the same type: *a flock of tourists*
horde – a large group of people moving in a noisy uncontrolled way: *There were hordes of people coming out of the subway.*
mass – a large group of people all close together in one place: *As soon as the doors opened a mass of people pushed their way into the store.*

G

party – a group of people who have been organized to do something together: *a search party*

group of animals
herd of cows/deer/elephants
flock of sheep/birds
school/shoal of fish/dolphins/herring, etc.
pack of dogs
litter of puppies/kittens (=a group of baby animals born from the same mother at the same time)

group of things
bunch of flowers/grapes/keys, etc. (=several flowers, etc. tied or held together)
bundle of papers/clothes/sticks (=several papers, etc. tied or held together)
set of dishes/keys/rules, etc. (=several things that belong together or are related in some way)

2 several people or things that are connected with each other in some way: *a* ***terrorist group*** | *There should be equal treatment of all* ***racial*** *and* ***ethnic groups***. **3** musicians or singers who perform together, usually playing popular music: *a* ***rock group*** **4** CHEMISTRY a COLUMN of ELEMENTs in the PERIODIC TABLE, which all have similar ATOMIC structures and chemical properties (PROPERTY) [ORIGIN: 1600—1700 French *groupe*, from Italian *gruppo*]

G

group² *v.* [I,T] to come together to make a group, or to arrange people or things in a group: *The visitors* ***grouped*** *themselves* ***around*** *the statue.* | *Birds can be* ***grouped into*** *several types.*

group·ie /ˈgrupi/ *n.* [C] (informal) someone, especially a young woman, who follows popular musicians or other famous people around, hoping to meet them

group·ing /ˈgrupɪŋ/ *n.* [C] a set of people, things, or organizations that have the same interests, qualities, or features: *social groupings*

ˌgroup ˈtherapy *n.* [U] a method of treating people with emotional or PSYCHOLOGICAL problems by bringing them together in groups to talk about their problems

grouse¹ /graʊs/ *v.* [I] (informal, disapproving) to complain about something: *He's always* ***grousing about*** *the weather.*

grouse² *n.* (plural **grouse**) [C,U] a small fat bird that is hunted for food and sport, or the meat from this bird

grove /groʊv/ *n.* [C] a piece of land with trees growing on it: *a lemon grove*

grov·el /ˈgrɑvəl, ˈgrʌ-/ *v.* [I] to try too hard to please someone or to keep telling him/her that you are sorry: *I hate it when people start groveling to the boss.*

grow /groʊ/ *v.* (past tense **grew** /gru/, past participle **grown** /groʊn/)
1 PERSON/ANIMAL [I] to develop and become bigger over a period of time: *Jamie's grown two inches this year.*
2 HAIR/NAILS [I,T] to let your hair or nails become longer: *He's growing a beard.*
3 PLANTS [I,T] if plants grow, or if you grow them, they develop and become bigger: *Not many plants can grow in the far north.* | *We're trying to grow roses this year.*
4 INCREASE [I] to increase in amount, size, or degree: *a growing business* | *The number of students* ***grew by*** *5% last year.* | *A* ***growing number*** *of people are working from home.*

THESAURUS **increase, go up, rise, double, shoot up, multiply** → INCREASE¹

5 BECOME [linking verb] to become old, hot, worse, etc. over a period of time: *He became more conservative as he grew older.*
6 grow to like/fear/respect etc. to gradually start to like, fear, etc. someone or something: *She had grown to love the city.*
7 IMPROVE [I] to improve in ability or character: *Beth's really growing as a singer.*
8 BUSINESS [T] to make something such as a business become larger or more successful: *The president thinks cutting taxes will help* ***grow the economy.***

grow apart *phr. v.*
if two people grow apart, their relationship changes and they become less close

grow into sb/sth *phr. v.*
1 to develop over time and become a particular type of person or thing: *Gene's grown into a handsome young man.*
2 if a child grows into clothes, s/he becomes big enough to wear them: *The jacket's a little bit big for him now, but he'll soon grow into it.*

grow on sb *phr. v.*
if someone or something grows on you, you gradually start to like him, her, or it: *I didn't like blue cheese at first, but the taste has kind of grown on me.*

grow out of sth *phr. v.*
1 if a child grows out of clothes, s/he becomes too big to wear them
2 to stop doing something as you get older: *Sarah still sucks her thumb, but she'll grow out of it.*

grow up *phr. v.*
1 to develop from being a child to being an adult: *I grew up in San Diego.*
2 grow up! (spoken) said in order to tell someone to behave more like an adult

grow·er /ˈgroʊə/ *n.* [C] a person or company that grows fruit, vegetables, etc. in order to sell them

ˈgrowing ˌpains *n.* [plural] problems and difficulties that start at the beginning of a new activity, for example starting a business

ˈgrowing ˌseason *n.* [C] the period during the year from the time when crops start to grow until they become fully grown

growl /graʊl/ *v.* **1** [I] if an animal growls, it makes a deep angry sound: *dogs* ***growling at*** *a visitor* **2** [I,T] to say something in a low angry voice: *"Go away!" he growled.* —**growl** *n.* [C]

grown¹ /groʊn/ *adj.* **grown man/woman** an adult, used especially when you think someone is not behaving as an adult should: *I've never seen a grown man act like that.*

grown² *v.* the past participle of GROW

ˈgrown-up¹ *n.* [C] an adult, used especially by children or when talking to children: *Ask a grown-up to help you.*

ˈgrown-up² *adj.* fully developed as an adult: *a grown-up son*

growth /groʊθ/ *n.* **1** [singular, U] an increase in amount, size, or degree: *rapid population growth* | *There's been tremendous* ***growth in*** *the health food industry.* | *the* ***growth of*** *modern technology* **2** [U] the increase in the physical size and strength of a person, animal, or plant over a period of time: *Vitamins are necessary for healthy growth.* **3** [U] the development of someone's character, intelligence, or emotions: *a job that provides opportunities for* ***personal growth*** **4** [C] something that grows in your body or on your skin, caused by a disease: *a cancerous growth* **5** [C,U] something that is growing: *There are signs of new growth on the tree.*

grub /grʌb/ *n.* [U] (informal) food

grub·by /ˈgrʌbi/ *adj.* dirty: *grubby hands*

grudge¹ /grʌdʒ/ *n.* [C] a feeling of anger or dislike you have for someone who has harmed you: *Diane doesn't* ***hold grudges*** (=stay angry with people). | *Aunt Alice* ***bore a grudge against*** *him for 25 years.*

grudge² *v.* [T] BEGRUDGE

grudg·ing /ˈgrʌdʒɪŋ/ *adj.* done in a way that shows you do not really want to do something: *Some of the staff had grudging respect for her.* —**grudgingly** *adv.*: *They grudgingly agreed.*

gru·el·ing /ˈgruəlɪŋ/ *adj.* very difficult and tiring: *a grueling entrance exam* [ORIGIN: 1800—1900 *gruel* "to punish", from *gruel* "food;" because people were given gruel as a punishment]

grue·some /ˈgrusəm/ *adj.* very unpleasant to look at, and usually involving death or injury: *a gruesome accident* [ORIGIN: 1500—1600 *grue* "to shake (with fear)" (14—19 centuries), from Middle Dutch *gruwen*]

gruff /grʌf/ *adj.* unfriendly or annoyed: *a gruff answer* —**gruffly** *adv.*

grum·ble /ˈgrʌmbəl/ *v.* [I] to keep complaining in a quiet but slightly angry way: *He's always* ***grumbling about*** *how expensive everything is.*

grump·y /ˈgrʌmpi/ *adj.* (comparative **grumpier**, superlative **grumpiest**) easily annoyed and tending to complain: *a grumpy old man* —**grumpily** *adv.*

THESAURUS

cranky/crabby/grouchy (informal) – easily annoyed and complaining a lot: *I was feeling hungry and cranky.*
cantankerous – easily annoyed and complaining a lot: *a cantankerous old man*
irritable – easily annoyed or made angry: *He's been a little irritable lately.*
touchy – easily offended or annoyed: *She's touchy about her weight.*

grunge /grʌndʒ/ *n.* [U] (informal) dirt and GREASE —**grungy** *adj.*

grunt /grʌnt/ *v.* **1** [I,T] to make short sounds or say only a few words, especially because you do not want to talk: *He just grunted hello and kept walking.* **2** [I] if a pig grunts, it makes short low sounds —**grunt** *n.* [C]

G-string /ˈdʒi strɪŋ/ *n.* [C] very small underwear that does not cover the BUTTOCKS

gua·ca·mo·le /ˌgwɑkəˈmoʊleɪ/ *n.* [U] a Mexican dish made with crushed AVOCADOS [ORIGIN: 1900—2000 American Spanish, Nahuatl, from *ahuacatl* "avocado" + *molli* "sauce"]

guar·an·tee¹ /ˌgærənˈti/ (Ac) *v.* [T] **1** to promise that something will happen or be done: *We guarantee delivery within 48 hours.* | *Can you* ***guarantee (that)*** *it will arrive tomorrow?* | *It's impossible to guarantee everyone a job.*

THESAURUS **promise, give sb your word, swear, take/swear an oath, vow, pledge, undertake to do sth, commit** → PROMISE¹

2 to make a formal written promise to repair or replace a product if it has a problem within a specific time **3** to make it certain that something will happen: *Practicing guarantees that you'll play better, but it doesn't guarantee that you'll win.* **4 be guaranteed to do sth** to be certain to behave, work, or happen in a particular way: *This show is guaranteed to make you smile.* **5** if someone guarantees an amount of money, s/he is legally responsible for the payment of the money: *The city guaranteed the loan for the first five years.*

guarantee² (Ac) *n.* [C] **1** a formal written promise that a product will please the customer or perform in a particular way for a specific length of time: *a two-year guarantee* | *The breadmaker comes with a* ***money-back guarantee*** (=a promise that you will get your money back if it doesn't work). **2** a formal promise that something will be done or will happen: ***There's no guarantee that*** *the books will be delivered this week* (=it is not sure to happen). | *a* ***guarantee that*** *aid will be sent* **3** an action, situation, etc. that makes it certain that something else will happen: *A high school diploma is no* ***guarantee of*** *a job.* **4** an agreement to be responsible for someone else's promise, especially a promise to pay a debt: *a loan guarantee*

guar·an·tor /ˌgærənˈtɔr, ˈgærəntɚ/ *n.* [C] ECONOMICS someone who promises that s/he will pay for something if the person who should pay for it does not

guard¹ /gɑrd/ *n.* **1** [C] someone whose job is to guard people, places, or objects so that they are not attacked or stolen: *The guards stopped us at the gate.* | *a security guard* | *prison guards* **2** [U] the act of protecting a place or person, or preventing a prisoner from escape: *Soldiers are always **on guard** at the embassy.* | *The prisoners were held **under armed guard** at all times.* **3 catch/take sb off guard** to surprise someone by doing something that s/he is not ready to deal with: *The question caught the senator off guard.* **4** [C] something that covers and protects someone or something: *a hockey player's face guard* **5 sb's guard** the state of paying careful attention to what is happening in order to avoid being tricked or getting into danger: *These men are dangerous, so you'll need to **be on your guard*** (=be careful). | *He never **let down** his **guard*** (=relaxed and felt comfortable with others). **6** [C] **a)** one of two players in basketball whose main job is to defend his/her BASKET **b)** one of two football players who play on either side of the CENTER [ORIGIN: 1400—1500 French *garde*]

guard² *v.* [T] **1** to protect someone or something from being attacked or stolen, or to prevent a prisoner from escaping: *They have a dog to guard their house.* | *a **heavily-guarded** courtroom*

THESAURUS **protect, safeguard, shield, give/offer/provide protection, shelter, preserve, conserve** → PROTECT

G

2 to protect something such as a right or secret by preventing other people from taking it: *a **closely-guarded secret***

guard against sth *phr. v.* to try hard to prevent something from happening: *Exercise can help guard against a number of serious illnesses.*

guard·ed /'gɑrdɪd/ *adj.* careful not to show your emotions or give away information: *a guarded answer*

guard·i·an /'gɑrdiən/ *n.* [C] **1** someone who is legally responsible for a child, but who is not the child's parent: *His aunt is his **legal guardian**.* **2** (formal) a person or organization that tries to protect something —**guardianship** *n.* [U]

,guardian 'angel *n.* [C] an imaginary good spirit who protects a person

guard·rail /'gɑrd-reɪl/ *n.* [C] a long metal BAR that keeps cars or people from falling over the edge of a road, boat, or high structure

gua·va /'gwɑvə/ *n.* [C] a small tropical fruit with pink flesh and many seeds inside [ORIGIN: 1500—1600 Spanish *guayaba*, from Arawakan (a group of South American languages)]

gu·ber·na·to·ri·al /,gubərnə'tɔriəl/ *adj.* (formal) relating to the position of being a GOVERNOR

guer·ril·la, guerilla /gə'rɪlə/ *n.* [C] a member of a military group that is fighting for political reasons: *guerrilla warfare* [ORIGIN: 1800—1900 Spanish *guerra* "war"]

guess¹ /gɛs/ *v.* **1** [I,T] **a)** to try to answer a question or form an opinion when you are not sure whether you will be correct: *I'd say he's about 40, but I'm **just guessing**.* **b)** to guess something correctly: *"Don't tell me; you got the job." "How did you guess?"* | *I never would have **guessed that** they were sisters.* **2 keep sb guessing** to not tell someone what is going to happen next: *a film that really keeps the audience guessing*

SPOKEN PHRASES

3 I guess a) said when you think that something is true or likely: *I wasn't there, but I guess Mr. Radkin yelled at Jeannie.* | *His light's on, so I guess he's still up.* **b)** said in order to show that you do not feel very strongly about what you are planning or agreeing to do: *I guess I'll stay home tonight.*

THESAURUS **think, believe, suspect, consider, figure** → THINK

4 I guess so/not used in order to say yes or no to a question or statement, when you are not very sure: *"She wasn't happy?" "I guess not."* **5 guess what/you'll never guess who/what etc.** said when you are about to tell someone something that will surprise him/her: *You'll never guess who I saw today.*

guess² *n.* [C] **1** an attempt to guess something: *Just **take/make a guess**.* | *I can only **hazard a guess*** (=make a guess) *on how old she is.*

COLLOCATIONS

good guess – a guess that is likely to be right
educated guess – a guess that is likely to be correct because it is based on some information
wild guess – a guess that you make when you do not have any information, and that is likely to be wrong
lucky guess – a guess that is right, and that you made without very much information
rough guess – a guess that is not exact

2 an opinion formed by guessing: ***My guess is (that)** Don won't come.* **3 be anybody's guess** to be something that no one knows: *What she's going to do with her life now is anybody's guess.* **4 your guess is as good as mine** (spoken) said in order to tell someone that you do not know any more than s/he does about something

guess·ti·mate /'gɛstəmɪt/ *n.* [C] (informal) an attempt to judge a quantity by guessing it —**guesstimate** /'gɛstə,meɪt/ *v.* [I,T]

guess·work /'gɛswərk/ *n.* [U] a way of trying to find the answer to something by guessing

guest¹ /gɛst/ *n.* [C] **1** someone whom you invite to stay in your home, be at your party, etc.: *a dinner guest* | *He was a frequent **guest at** the White House.* **2** someone famous who is invited to take part in a television program, concert, etc.: *Tonight's **special guest** will be Justin Timberlake.* **3** someone who is paying to stay in a hotel: *Use of the swimming pool is free for guests.* **4 be my guest** (spoken) said when giving someone permission to do what s/he has asked to do: *"Could I use your phone?" "Be my guest."* [ORIGIN: 1200—1300 Old Norse *gestr*]

guest² *adj.* **1 guest speaker/artist/star etc.** someone famous who is invited to speak on a subject or take part in a performance **2** [only before noun] for guests to use: *the guest room* | *guest towels*

guf·faw /gə'fɔ/ *v.* [I] to laugh loudly —**guffaw** *n.* [C]

THESAURUS **laugh, giggle, chuckle, cackle, snicker, titter** → LAUGH[1]

GUI /'gui/ *n.* [U] IT **graphical user interface** a way of arranging information on a computer screen using pictures, which makes it easier for you to tell the computer what to do

guid·ance /'gaɪdns/ *n.* [U] helpful advice about work, education, etc.: *Ms. Norris has* ***given*** *me a lot of* ***guidance*** *about colleges and careers.*

THESAURUS **advice, tip, suggestion, recommendation, counseling, warning** → ADVICE

'guidance ˌcounselor *n.* [C] someone who works in a school, giving advice to students about what subjects to study and helping them with personal problems

guide[1] /gaɪd/ *n.* [C] **1** someone whose job is to take tourists to a place, or show a place to tourists: *a* ***tour guide*** **2** a book that provides information about a particular subject or explains how to do something: *a* ***guide for*** *new parents* **3** something that helps you decide what is likely to happen or helps you to make a decision: *The balance sheet is a fairly reliable guide to the company's financial position.*

guide[2] *v.* [T] **1** to take someone to or through a place that you know very well, showing him/her the way: *He offered to* ***guide*** *us* ***around/through*** *the city.*

THESAURUS **lead, direct, point, show, escort, usher** → LEAD[1]

2 to help someone or something to move in a particular direction: *The pilot guided the plane to a safe landing.* **3** to help someone to do something or to make a decision: *Children need parents to guide them.*

guide·book /'gaɪdbʊk/ *n.* [C] a special book about a city or country that gives details about the place and its history

guide·lines /'gaɪdlaɪnz/ *n.* [plural] rules or instructions about the best way to do something: *the* ***guidelines for*** *health and safety at work*

THESAURUS **rule, law, regulation, restriction, statute, code, precept** → RULE[1]

guild /gɪld/ *n.* [C] an organization of people who share the same interests, skills, or profession: *the writers' guild*

guile /gaɪl/ *n.* [U] (formal) the use of smart but dishonest methods to deceive someone

guile·less /'gaɪl-lɪs/ *adj.* behaving in an honest way, without trying to deceive people

guil·lo·tine /'gɪləˌtin, 'giə-, ˌgiə'tin/ *n.* [C] a piece of equipment that was used in past times to cut off the heads of criminals [ORIGIN: 1700—1800 French, from Joseph *Guillotin* (1738-1814), French doctor who invented it] —**guillotine** *v.* [T]

guilt /gɪlt/ *n.* [U] **1** a strong feeling of shame and sadness that you have when you know or believe you have done something wrong: *Marta felt a* ***sense of guilt*** *about leaving home.* | *He used to buy them expensive presents* ***out of guilt****.*

THESAURUS

shame – the feeling of being guilty or embarrassed that you have after doing something that is wrong: *I was too scared to help them, and I was filled with shame.*

remorse – a strong feeling of being sorry for doing something very bad: *a murderer who showed no remorse*

conscience – the set of feelings that tell you whether what you are doing is morally right or wrong: *My conscience wouldn't allow me to lie to her.*

2 **guilt trip** (informal) a feeling of guilt about something, when this is unreasonable: *I wish my parents would stop* ***laying a guilt trip on*** *me* (=making me feel guilty) *about not going to college.* **3** the fact that someone has broken an official law or moral rule ANT **innocence**: *The jury was sure of the defendant's guilt.* **4** the state of being responsible for something bad that has happened SYN **fault**: *Ron admitted that the guilt was his.*

'guilt-ˌridden *adj.* feeling extremely guilty about something

guilt·y /'gɪlti/ *adj.* **1** ashamed and sad because you have done something that you know is wrong: *I* ***feel guilty about*** *not inviting her to the party.* | *I don't think of watching TV as a* ***guilty pleasure*** (=something you like doing but feel guilty about). | *His* ***guilty conscience*** *kept him awake at night.*

THESAURUS

ashamed – unhappy and disappointed with yourself because you have done something wrong or unpleasant: *You should be ashamed of yourself for lying to your mother.*

embarrassed – feeling slightly worried about what people will think of you because you have done something stupid or silly: *I forgot his name, and I felt so embarrassed.* | *I'm embarrassed to say I voted for him.*

contrite (formal) – feeling guilty and sorry for something bad that you have done: *She felt suddenly contrite, and apologized.*

2 having broken a law or a rule ANT **innocent**: *I was not* ***guilty of*** *doing anything wrong.* | *The jury* ***found*** *him* ***guilty of*** *murder.* | *Her lawyers entered a* ***guilty plea****.* → COURT[1] —**guiltily** *adv.* —**guiltiness** *n.* [U]

guin·ea pig /'gɪni pɪg/ *n.* [C] **1** a small animal like a rat with fur, short ears, and no tail that is often kept as a pet **2** (informal) someone who is used in a test to see how successful or safe a new product, system, etc. is

guise /gaɪz/ *n.* [C] (formal) the way someone or something seems to be, which is meant to hide the truth: ***In/under the guise of** being protectors, the army took over the government.*

gui·tar /gɪˈtɑr/ *n.* [C] a musical instrument with six strings, a long neck, and a wooden body, which you play by pulling the strings [ORIGIN: 1600—1700 French *guitare*, from Spanish *guitarra*, from Arabic *qitar*, from Greek *kithara* type of stringed instrument] —**guitarist** *n.* [C]

gulch /gʌltʃ/ *n.* [C] EARTH SCIENCES a narrow deep valley formed by flowing water, but usually dry

gulf /gʌlf/ *n.* [C] **1** EARTH SCIENCES a large area of ocean partly enclosed by land: *the Gulf of Mexico* **2** a serious and important difference between two groups of people, where neither understands or is concerned about the other: *There is a widening **gulf between** the rich and the poor.*

ˈGulf Stream *n* **the Gulf Stream** EARTH SCIENCES a current of warm water that flows northeast in the Atlantic Ocean from the Gulf of Mexico toward Europe

G

gull /gʌl/ *n.* [C] a SEAGULL

gul·let /ˈgʌlɪt/ *n.* [C] (informal) the tube through which food goes down your throat

gul·li·ble /ˈgʌləbəl/ *adj.* a gullible person always believes what other people say, and is therefore easy to trick —**gullibility** /ˌgʌləˈbɪləṭi/ *n.* [U]

gul·ly /ˈgʌli/ *n.* (plural **gullies**) [C] **1** EARTH SCIENCES a small narrow valley, formed by a lot of rain flowing down the side of a hill **2** a deep DITCH

gulp¹ /gʌlp/ *v.* **1** [T] *also* **gulp down** to swallow something quickly: *She gulped her tea and ran to catch the bus.* **2** [T] *also* **gulp in** to take in large breaths of air quickly: *Steve leaned on the car and gulped in the night air.* **3** [I] to swallow suddenly because you are surprised or nervous: *Shula read the test questions, and gulped.*

gulp sth ↔ **back** *phr. v.* to stop yourself from expressing your feelings: *The boy was trying to gulp back his tears.*

gulp² *n.* [C] an act of swallowing something quickly: *He drank his beer **in one gulp**.*

gum /gʌm/ *n.* **1** [C] a sweet substance that you CHEW for a long time but do not swallow **2** [C usually plural] the pink part inside your mouth that holds your teeth **3** [U] BIOLOGY a sticky substance in the stems of some trees —**gummy** *adj.*

gum·bo /ˈgʌmboʊ/ *n.* [U] a thick soup made with meat, fish, and particular vegetables

gump·tion /ˈgʌmpʃən/ *n.* [U] (informal) the ability and determination to decide what needs to be done and to do it: *At least he had the gumption to call the police.*

gun¹ /gʌn/ *n.* [C] **1** a weapon from which bullets are fired: *He was **carrying a gun**. | a **loaded gun** | I've never **fired a gun** in my life. | He **had a gun** in the car.* **2 big/top gun** (informal) someone who controls an organization, or who is the most successful person in a group **3** a tool used in order to send out a liquid by pressure: *a spray gun* → **jump the gun** *at* JUMP¹, **stick to your guns** *at* STICK TO

gun² *v.* (**gunned**, **gunning**) [T] **1** (informal) to make the engine of a car go very fast by pressing the ACCELERATOR very hard **2 be gunning for sth** to be trying very hard to obtain something: *They're gunning for their third straight Superbowl win.* **3 be gunning for sb** (informal) to be trying to find an opportunity to criticize or harm someone

gun sb ↔ **down** *phr. v.* to shoot someone and badly injure or kill him/her: *He was gunned down outside his own home.*

gun·boat /ˈgʌnboʊt/ *n.* [C] a small military ship that carries several large guns

ˈgun conˌtrol *n.* [U] laws that restrict the possession and use of guns

gun·fire /ˈgʌnfaɪɚ/ *n.* [U] the repeated shooting of guns, or the noise made by this → GUNSHOT: *We **heard gunfire** in the distance. | an **exchange of gunfire*** (=when people are shooting at each other for a short time)

gung-ho /ˌgʌŋˈhoʊ/ *adj.* (informal) very eager, or too eager to do something: *a gung-ho supporter of the president* [ORIGIN: 1900—2000 Chinese *gonghe*, from *jongguo gongye hozo she* "Chinese Industrial Cooperatives Society," used as a battle cry (meaning "work together") by U.S. soldiers in World War II]

gunk /gʌŋk/ *n.* [U] (informal) any substance that is thick, dirty, and sticky: *There's a bunch of gunk clogging the drain.*

gun·man /ˈgʌnmən/ *n.* (plural **gunmen** /-mən/) [C] a criminal who uses a gun

gun·ner /ˈgʌnɚ/ *n.* [C] a soldier, sailor, etc. whose job is to aim or fire a large gun

gun·point /ˈgʌnpɔɪnt/ *n.* **at gunpoint** while threatening people with a gun, or being threatened with a gun: *She was robbed at gunpoint*

gun·pow·der /ˈgʌnˌpaʊdɚ/ *n.* [U] an explosive substance in the form of powder

gun·run·ning /ˈgʌnˌrʌnɪŋ/ *n.* [U] the activity of taking guns into a country secretly and illegally —**gunrunner** *n.* [C]

gun·shot /ˈgʌnʃɑt/ *n.* **1** [C] the action of shooting a gun, or the sound that this makes → GUNFIRE: *We **heard a gunshot** and a loud scream.* **2** [U] the bullets that are shot from a gun: *a **gunshot wound***

gup·py /ˈgʌpi/ *n.* (plural **guppies**) [C] a small brightly colored tropical fish

gur·gle /ˈgɚgəl/ *v.* [I] **1** if water gurgles, it flows along gently with a pleasant low sound **2** if a baby gurgles, it makes a happy low sound in its throat —**gurgle** *n.* [C]

gu·ru /ˈguru, ˈgʊru/ *n.* [C] **1** (informal) someone who knows a lot about a particular subject, and to whom people go for advice: *a fashion guru* **2** a Hindu religious teacher or leader

gush[1] /gʌʃ/ *v.* [I,T] **1** to flow or pour out quickly in large quantities: *Water **gushed out** of the broken pipe.* | *Blood was **gushing from** the wound.* | *His cheek was gushing blood.*

> THESAURUS **pour, flow, drip, leak, ooze, spurt, run, come out** ➔ POUR

2 to express your praise, pleasure, etc. in a way that other people think is too strong: *"This is so exciting," gushed Dana.*

gush[2] *n.* [C] a large quantity of liquid that suddenly flows from somewhere: *a **gush of** warm water*

gush·er /ˈgʌʃɚ/ *n.* [C] (informal) an oil WELL where the flow of oil is suddenly so strong that it shoots into the air

gush·ing /ˈgʌʃɪŋ/ *also* **gush·y** /ˈgʌʃi/ *adj.* expressing admiration, pleasure, etc. in a way that other people think is too strong: *He wrote in gushing terms about the poet well before he met him.*

gust[1] /gʌst/ *n.* [C] a sudden strong wind that blows for a short time: *A **gust of wind** blew our tent over.* —**gusty** *adj.*

> THESAURUS **wind, breeze, gale, storm, hurricane, tornado, typhoon** ➔ WIND[1]

gust[2] *v.* [I] if wind gusts, it blows strongly with sudden short movements: *Winds were gusting up to 70 mph.*

gus·to /ˈgʌstoʊ/ *n.* **with gusto** if you do something with gusto, you do it with a lot of eagerness and energy: *a band playing with gusto*

gut[1] /gʌt/ *n.* **1 gut reaction/feeling/instinct** (informal) a reaction or feeling that you are sure is right, although you cannot give a reason for it: *My gut reaction is that it's a bad idea.* **2 guts** [plural] (informal) the courage and determination you need to do something difficult or unpleasant: *He didn't **have the guts** to say what he really thought.* | *It **takes guts** to start a business on your own.* **3** [C] (informal) someone's stomach, especially when it is large: *He felt as if someone had just kicked him in the gut.* | *a **beer gut*** **4 a) guts** [plural] (informal) the organs inside your body **b)** [C] BIOLOGY the tube in your body through which food passes

gut[2] *v.* (past tense and past participle **gutted**, present participle **gutting**) [T] **1** to completely destroy the inside of a building, especially by fire **2** to remove the organs from inside a fish or animal in order to prepare it for cooking

gut·sy /ˈgʌtsi/ *adj.* (informal) brave and determined: *It was a gutsy performance.*

gut·ter /ˈgʌt̬ɚ/ *n.* [C] **1** the low place along the edge of a road, where water collects and flows away **2** an open pipe at the edge of a roof for collecting and carrying away RAINWATER **3 the gutter** the bad social conditions of the lowest and poorest people in society

gut·tur·al /ˈgʌt̬ərəl/ *adj.* a guttural sound is produced deep in the throat

guy /gaɪ/ *n.* [C] **1** (informal) a man: *He's a really nice guy.* | *There's some guy who wants to talk to you.*

> THESAURUS **man, gentleman, fellow, boy, youth, male** ➔ MAN[1]

2 you guys/those guys (spoken) said when talking to or about two or more people, male or female ➔ Y'ALL: *We'll see you guys Sunday, okay?*

guz·zle /ˈgʌzəl/ *v.* [I,T] (informal) to drink a lot of something eagerly and quickly: *Chris has been guzzling beer all evening.*

> THESAURUS **drink, sip/take a sip, slurp, gulp down, down, knock back, swig, take/have a swig, imbibe** ➔ DRINK[2]

gym /dʒɪm/ *n.* **1** [C] a special building or room that has equipment for doing physical exercise: *I **go to the gym** as often as I can.* **2** [U] sports and exercises done indoors, especially as a school subject: *gym class* [ORIGIN: 1500—1600 *gymnasium* Latin, Greek *gymnasion*, from *gymnazein* "to exercise with no clothes on"] ➔ EXERCISE[2]

gym·na·si·um /dʒɪmˈneɪziəm/ *n.* [C] a GYM [ORIGIN: 1500—1600 Latin, Greek *gymnasion*, from *gymnazein* "to exercise with no clothes on," from *gymnos* "naked"]

gymnast

gym·nast /ˈdʒɪmnæst, -nəst/ *n.* [C] someone who does gymnastics as a sport: *an Olympic gymnast*

gym·nas·tics /dʒɪmˈnæstɪks/ *n.* [plural] a sport involving physical exercises and movements that need skill and control, often performed in competitions

gym·no·sperm /ˈdʒɪmnəˌspɚm/ *n.* [C] BIOLOGY a plant producing seeds that are contained in a CONE

gy·ne·col·o·gy /ˌgaɪnəˈkɑlədʒi/ *n.* [U] BIOLOGY the study and treatment of medical conditions that affect women —**gynecologist** *n.* [C] —**gynecological** /ˌgaɪnəkəˈlɑdʒɪkəl/ *adj.*

gyp·sy /ˈdʒɪpsi/ *n.* (plural **gypsies**) [C] **1** a member of a group of people who traditionally live and travel around in CARAVANS. Most gypsies prefer to be called Romanies. **2** someone who does not like to stay in the same place for a long time

gy·rate /ˈdʒaɪreɪt/ *v.* [I] to turn around fast in circles: *dancers gyrating wildly*

G

Hh

H, h /eɪtʃ/ the eighth letter of the English alphabet

ha /hɑ/ *interjection* (spoken) said when you are surprised or pleased about something: *Ha! I knew I was right.* → HA HA

ha·be·as corpus /ˌheɪbiəs ˈkɔrpəs/ *n.* [U] LAW the right of someone who is in prison to come to a court of law so that the court can decide whether s/he should stay in prison or be freed

hab·er·dash·er·y /ˈhæbɚˌdæʃəri/ *n.* (plural **haberdasheries**) [C,U] (old-fashioned) a store or part of a store that sells men's clothing, or the clothes sold there

hab·it /ˈhæbɪt/ *n.* **1** [C,U] something that you do regularly, and usually without thinking: *healthy **eating habits** | Jen was **in the habit of** going to lunch with them every day. | Try to **get in the habit of** exercising regularly. | After my son moved out, I was still cleaning his room **out of habit*** (=because it was a habit).

THESAURUS

custom – something that people in a particular society do because it is traditional, or something that people think is the normal and polite thing to do: *It is a Japanese custom that you take off your shoes when you enter a house.*
tradition – a belief, custom, or way of doing something that has existed for a long time: *In many countries it's a tradition for the bride to wear white. | a family tradition*
practice – something that people often do, especially as part of their work or daily life: *The practice of punishing children by making them sit on a chair for a period of time is fairly common.*
convention – a rule of behavior that most people in a society accept: *Shaking hands to greet someone is a social convention.*

2 [C] something you do regularly that annoys other people or is bad for your health: *Biting your nails is a very **bad habit**. | He **has a habit of** being late. | Brad's been smoking for twenty years, and he just can't **break/kick** the **habit**. | a **drug habit*** **3 don't make a habit of (doing) sth** used in order to tell someone who has done something bad or wrong that s/he should not do it again: *You can turn your paper in late this time, but don't make a habit of it.* **4** [C] a set of long loose clothes worn by members of some religious groups

hab·it·a·ble /ˈhæbət̬əbəl/ *adj.* good enough for people to live in

hab·i·tat /ˈhæbəˌtæt/ *n.* [C] the natural environment in which a plant or animal lives: *We got a chance to see the gorillas in their **natural habitat**.*

hab·i·ta·tion /ˌhæbəˈteɪʃən/ *n.* [U] (formal) the act of living in a place: *There was no sign of habitation on the island.*

ha·bit·u·al /həˈbɪtʃuəl/ *adj.* **1** happening as a habit, or often doing something because it is a habit: *a habitual smoker* **2** [only before noun] usual or typical: *James took his habitual morning walk around the park.* —**habitually** *adv.*

ha·bit·u·ation /həˌbɪtʃuˈeɪʃən/ *n.* [U] BIOLOGY a basic learning process by which the reaction of a person, animal, or other living thing to a STIMULUS (=something that makes them move or react) gradually becomes less strong, so that after a period of time the person, animal, etc. does not react at all

hack[1] /hæk/ *v.* **1** [I,T] to cut something into pieces roughly or violently, or to hurt someone badly with a weapon such as a sword: *We hacked away the ivy that was growing over the wall. | He was **hacked to death** by the mob.* **2** [I,T] to use a computer in order to secretly and illegally enter someone else's computer system: *Somebody **hacked into** the company's central database.* **3 sb can't hack it** (informal) used in order to say that someone cannot continue to do something because it is too difficult or boring **4** [I] to cough very loudly and painfully: *a **hacking cough***

hack[2] *n.* [C] someone who writes low quality books, articles, etc.

hack·er /ˈhækɚ/ *n.* [C] (informal) someone who uses a computer to secretly use or change the information in another person's computer system —**hacking** *n.* [U]

hack·neyed /ˈhæknid/ *adj.* a hackneyed phrase is boring and does not have much meaning because it has been used too often

hack·saw /ˈhæksɔ/ *n.* [C] a small SAW (=cutting tool) used especially to cut metal

had /d, əd, həd; *strong* hæd/ *v.* **1** the past tense and past participle of HAVE **2 be had** to be tricked or made to look stupid: *She had the feeling she'd been had.*

had·dock /ˈhædək/ *n.* (plural **haddock**) [C,U] a common fish that lives in northern oceans, or the meat from this fish

had·n't /ˈhædnt/ *v.* the short form of "had not": *We hadn't been there long.*

hag /hæg/ *n.* [C] an ugly or mean woman, especially one who is old or looks like a WITCH

hag·gard /ˈhægɚd/ *adj.* having lines on your face and dark marks around your eyes because you are tired, sick, or worried: *He was thin and haggard.* [ORIGIN: 1500—1600 French *hagard* "wild"]

hag·gle /ˈhægəl/ *v.* [I] to argue about the amount of money you will pay for something: *The car dealer and I were **haggling over** the price for an hour.*

hah /hɑ/ *interjection* another spelling of HA

ha ha /hɑ ˈhɑ/ *interjection* used in writing to represent laughter

hail[1] /heɪl/ *v.* **1** [T] to call out to someone in order

H

to get his/her attention: *He was* ***hailing a taxi/cab*** (=waving at a taxi to make it stop). **2** [I] if it hails, frozen rain falls from the sky

hail sb/sth **as** sth *phr. v.* to publicly state how good someone or something is: *Their discovery was hailed as the most important event of the century.*

hail from sth *phr. v.* to come from a particular place: *The professor hailed from Massachusetts.*

hail² *n.* **1** [U] small hard drops of frozen rain that fall from the sky

THESAURUS **rain, hailstones, sleet** → RAIN¹

2 a hail of bullets/stones etc. a lot of bullets, stones, etc. that are shot or thrown at someone

hail·stone /ˈheɪlstoʊn/ *n.* [C usually plural] a small drop of hard frozen rain

hail·storm /ˈheɪlstɔrm/ *n.* [C] a storm when a lot of hail falls

hair /hɛr/ *n.* **1** [U] the things like thin threads that grow on your head: *He has brown hair and blue eyes.* | *She was* ***brushing*** *her* ***hair.*** | *I used to* ***have/wear my hair*** *very long.* → *see picture on page 462*

COLLOCATIONS

Describing hair
short/long hair
shoulder-length hair
blond/light hair
dark/brown/black/gray hair
red/auburn hair
straight/wavy/curly hair
frizzy hair – hair with many small curls in it
spiky hair – hair that sticks up from your head in thin stiff points
fine/thin/thick hair
white-haired/dark-haired/red-haired/long-haired/curly-haired, etc. (=used to describe someone)

Verbs you can use with hair
cut/trim your **hair**
wash/shampoo your **hair**
dry your **hair**
blow dry your **hair** – to dry your hair, using an electric hairdryer
comb/brush your **hair**
style your **hair** – to arrange your hair in a particular way
dye your **hair** – to change the color of your hair, using a dye
bleach your **hair** – to dye your hair a blond color, using chemicals → HEAD¹, SKIN¹

2 [C,U] the things like thin threads that grow on a person's or animal's skin → FUR: *An old blanket was covered with cat hair.* **3 short-haired/dark-haired etc.** having a particular type of hair or fur: *a long-haired cat* **4 let your hair down** (informal) to stop being serious and enjoy yourself **5 a hair** a small amount: *Larson won the race by a hair.* [ORIGIN: Old English *hær*]

hair·brush /ˈhɛrbrʌʃ/ *n.* [C] a brush you use on your hair to make it look neat → *see picture at* BRUSH¹

hair·cut /ˈhɛrkʌt/ *n.* [C] **1** the act of having your hair cut by someone: *I'm* ***getting a haircut*** *tomorrow.* **2** the style your hair has when it is cut: *Do you like my new haircut?*

hair·do /ˈhɛrdu/ *n.* (plural **hairdos**) [C] (informal) the style in which someone's hair is cut or shaped

hair·dress·er /ˈhɛrˌdrɛsɚ/ *n.* [C] someone who washes, cuts, and arranges people's hair

hair·dryer /ˈhɛrˌdraɪɚ/ *n.* [C] a machine that you sit under that blows out hot air, used for drying hair → BLOW DRYER

hair·line /ˈhɛrlaɪn/ *n.* [C] **1** the area around the top of your face where your hair starts growing **2 a hairline crack/fracture** a very thin crack in something hard such as glass or bone

hair·net /ˈhɛrnɛt/ *n.* [C] a thin net worn over your hair in order to keep it in place

ˈhair-ˌraising *adj.* frightening in an exciting way: *a hair-raising adventure*

hair·split·ting /ˈhɛrˌsplɪt̬ɪŋ/ *n.* [U] the act of paying too much attention to unimportant details and differences

ˈhair spray *n.* [C,U] a sticky liquid that you put onto your hair in order to make it stay in place

hair·style /ˈhɛrstaɪl/ *n.* [C] the particular style your hair has when it is cut, brushed, or arranged

hair·y /ˈhɛri/ *adj.* **1** having a lot of body hair: *a* ***hairy*** *chest* **2** (informal) dangerous or frightening: *I've had a few hairy moments when sailing.*

hal·cy·on /ˈhælsiən/ *adj.* **halcyon days** (literary) a time in the past when you were very happy

hale /heɪl/ *adj.* **hale and hearty** someone, especially an old person, who is hale and hearty is very healthy and active

half¹ /hæf/ *determiner, adj.* [only before noun] **1** 50% (½) of an amount, time, distance, number, etc.: *The wall is half a mile long.* | *Only half the guests had arrived by 7:00.* | *I'll wait another* ***half hour*** (=30 minutes), *but then I have to go.* **2 half the time/people etc.** a lot of the time, people, etc.: *I was up half the night worrying about you.* **3 be half the battle** (spoken) used in order to say that when you have done the most difficult part of an activity, the rest is easy: *Getting your children to listen to you is half the battle.* **4** if something or someone is half one thing and half something else, he, she, or it is a combination of those two things: *She's half Mexican and half German.* **5 half a dozen** *also* **a half dozen a)** six: *half a dozen eggs* **b)** a small number of people or things: *There were half a dozen other people in front of me.* **6 half a second/minute** (spoken) a very short time: *If you can wait half a second, I'll be ready to go.*

half² *n., pron.* [C] (plural **halves** /hævz/) **1** one of two equal parts of something: ***Half of*** *10 is 5.* | *Do* *you want the sandwich cut* ***in half*** (=in two equal pieces)? | ***Half of*** *the hotel's rooms have double beds in them.* ► Don't say "the half of the rooms." ◄ | *Our profits increased in the second half of the year.* | *My son's two and a half* (=2½) *now.* ► Don't say "two and one half." ◄ **2 half past one/two/three etc.** thirty minutes after the hour mentioned: *We should arrive there at half past three.* **3** one of two parts into which a sports event is divided: *The score was 21 to 10 at the end of the second half.*

half[3] *adv.* **1** partly but not completely: *I was half expecting her to say "no."* | *She sat up in bed, still half asleep.* | *There were several* ***half-empty*** *coffee cups on the table.* **2 half as good/interesting etc. (as sth)** much less good, less interesting, etc. than someone or something else: *The movie wasn't half as good as the book.* **3 not half bad** said when something that you expected to be bad is actually good: *The dinner wasn't half bad.* **4 half and half** partly one thing and partly something else: *The group was about half and half, men and women.*

ˌhalf-and-ˈhalf *n.* [U] a mixture of milk and cream, used in coffee

ˌhalf-ˈbaked *adj.* (informal) a half-baked idea, plan, or suggestion is not sensible or intelligent enough to be successful

ˈhalf-ˌbrother *n.* [C] a brother who is the child of only one of your parents

ˌhalf-ˈhearted *adj.* a half-hearted attempt is something that you do without really trying or wanting to be successful: *a half-hearted effort*

ˈhalf-life *n.* [singular] PHYSICS the amount of time it takes for a RADIOACTIVE substance to lose half of its RADIOACTIVITY

ˌhalf-ˈmast *n.* **fly/be at half-mast** if a flag flies or is at half-mast, it is lowered to the middle of its pole because someone important has died

ˈhalf note *n.* [C] ENG. LANG. ARTS a musical note that continues for half the length of a WHOLE NOTE → QUARTER NOTE

ˈhalf-ˌsister *n.* [C] a sister who is the child of only one of your parents

ˈhalf step *n.* [C] ENG. LANG. ARTS the difference in PITCH between any two notes that are next to each other on a piano

half·time /ˈhæftaɪm/ *n.* [U] a period of rest between two parts of a game such as football or

H

basketball: *Our team was in the lead **at halftime**.*

half·way /ˌhæf'weɪ◂/ *adj., adv.* at the middle point in space or time between two things: *I fell asleep **halfway through** the concert.* | *a town **halfway between** Los Angeles and San Francisco* | *Their boat was **halfway across** the lake when it started to rain.* | *We had reached **the halfway mark/point** of the trail.* → **meet (sb) halfway** *at* MEET[1]

hal·i·but /'hæləbət/ *n.* [C,U] a large flat sea fish, or the meat from this fish

hall /hɔl/ *n.* [C] **1** a passage in a house or building that leads to other rooms: *The bathroom's just down the hall.* **2** a public building or large room that is used for events such as meetings, concerts, and parties: *a concert at Carnegie Hall in New York* | *a dance hall* [ORIGIN: Old English *heall*]

hal·le·lu·jah /ˌhælə'luyə/ *interjection* said in order to express thanks or praise to God

hall·mark /'hɔlmɑrk/ *n.* [C] **1** a quality, idea, or method that is typical of a particular person or thing: *Excellent service has always been **the hallmark of** this hotel.* **2** an official mark put on silver, gold, or PLATINUM to prove that it is real

ˌHall of 'Fame *n.* (plural **Halls of Fame**) [C] a list of famous sports players, or a building in which the players' uniforms, sports equipment, and information about them is kept —**Hall of Famer** *n.* [C]: *baseball Hall of Famer, Roger Clemens*

hal·lowed /'hæloʊd/ *adj.* **1** made holy: *hallowed ground* **2** respected, honored, and important: *the hallowed walls of the U.S. Supreme Court*

Hal·low·een /ˌhælə'win, ˌhɑ-/ *n.* [U] a holiday on the night of October 31, when children wear COSTUMES, play tricks, and walk from house to house in order to get candy → TRICK OR TREAT [ORIGIN: 1700—1800 *All Hallow Even* "All Saints' Eve"]

hal·lu·ci·na·tion /həˌlusə'neɪʃən/ *n.* [C,U] something you see or hear that is not really there, or the experience of this, usually caused by a drug or mental illness —**hallucinate** /hə'lusəˌneɪt/ *v.* [I]

hal·lu·ci·no·gen·ic /həˌlusənə'dʒɛnɪk/ *adj.* hallucinogenic drugs cause hallucinations

hall·way /'hɔlweɪ/ *n.* [C] a HALL

ha·lo /'heɪloʊ/ *n.* (plural **halos**) [C] a circle of light that is painted above or around the head of a holy person in a religious painting

hal·o·gen[1] /'hælədʒən/ *n.* [U] CHEMISTRY one of a group of five simple chemical substances that make compounds easily. They are: CHLORINE, FLUORINE, IODINE, BROMINE, and ASTATINE. [ORIGIN: 1800—1900 Swedish, Greek *hals* "salt"]

halogen[2] *adj.* **a halogen lamp/light/bulb etc.** a type of lamp or LIGHT BULB that uses halogen gas to produce light

halt[1] /hɔlt/ *v.* [I,T] to stop or make something stop: *Safety concerns have halted work on the dam.*

halt[2] *n.* [singular] a stop or pause: *Traffic suddenly **came/ground to a halt**.* | *The project was **brought to a halt** (=ended) due to lack of money.*

hal·ter /'hɔltɚ/ *n.* [C] **1** *also* **halter top** a piece of women's clothing that ties behind the neck and does not cover the arms or back **2** a rope or leather band fastened around a horse's head in order to lead it

halt·ing /'hɔltɪŋ/ *adj.* stopping a lot when you move or speak, especially because you are nervous: *her halting voice*

halve /hæv/ *v.* [T] **1** to reduce the amount of something by half: *The number of people taking part in the 10k run has almost halved this year.* **2** to cut something into two equal parts: *Wash and halve the mushrooms.*

halves /hævz/ *n.* the plural of HALF

ham[1] /hæm/ *n.* [C,U] meat from the upper part of a pig's leg that is preserved with salt or smoke: *a ham sandwich* [ORIGIN: (1) Old English *hamm*]

ham[2] *v.* (**hammed, hamming**) **ham it up** (informal) to perform or behave with too much false emotion

ham·burg·er /'hæmˌbɚgɚ/ *n.* **1** [U] BEEF that is ground (GRIND) into very small pieces: *a pound of hamburger* **2** [C] BEEF that has been ground (GRIND) into very small pieces and is then cooked in a flat round shape and eaten between pieces of round bread → CHEESEBURGER [ORIGIN: 1800—1900 German "of Hamburg," city in Germany]

ham·let /'hæmlɪt/ *n.* [C] a very small VILLAGE

ham·mer[1] /'hæmɚ/ *n.* [C] a tool with a heavy metal part on a straight handle, used for hitting nails into wood

hammer[2] *v.* **1** [I,T] to hit something with a hammer in order to force it into a particular position or shape: *You'll have to **hammer** a few nails **into** the frame.* **2** [I] to hit something again and again, making a lot of noise: *They hammered on the door until I opened it.*

THESAURUS **hit, knock, bang, pound** → HIT[1]

hammer sth **into** sb *also* **hammer** sth **home** *phr. v.* to continue repeating something until people completely understand it: *The message must be hammered home that crime doesn't pay.*

hammer out sth *phr. v.* to finally agree on a solution, contract, etc. after arguing about details for a long time: *It took several days to hammer out an agreement.*

ham·mock /'hæmək/ *n.* [C] a large piece of material or a net you can sleep on that hangs between two trees or poles [ORIGIN: 1500—1600 Spanish *hamaca*, from Taino (a Caribbean language)]

ham·per[1] /'hæmpɚ/ *v.* [T] to make someone have difficulty moving, doing something, or achieving something: *The searches for the missing girl were hampered by the bad weather.*

H

hamper² *n.* [C] a large basket with a lid, used for holding dirty clothes until they can be washed

ham·ster /ˈhæmstɚ/ *n.* [C] a small animal with soft fur and no tail that is often kept as a pet ➔ *see picture at* PET¹

ham·string¹ /ˈhæmˌstrɪŋ/ *n.* [C] a TENDON behind your knee

hamstring² *v.* (past tense and past participle **hamstrung** /-ˌstrʌŋ/) [T] to make a person or group have difficulty doing or achieving something: *A lack of funds has hamstrung the research.*

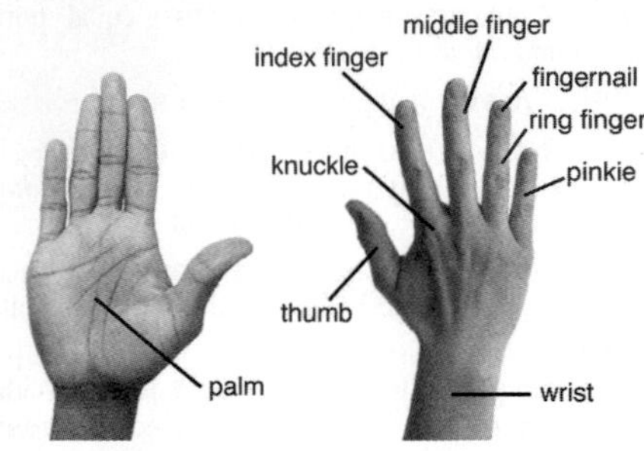

hand¹ /hænd/ *n.* [C]
1 BODY PART the body part at the end of a person's arm that includes the fingers and thumb, used for holding, etc. things: *Go wash your hands.* | *I write with my **right/left hand**.* | *I saw them **holding hands** and kissing.* | *Maria **took** the child **by the hand** and led him away.* | ***Raise your hand*** (=lift it up) *if you know the answer.* | *Here's a picture of me **shaking hands*** (=as a greeting or sign of friendship) *with the mayor.*
2 a hand help: *Can you **give/lend me a hand** with this box? It's really heavy.* | *Do you **need a hand** with the cooking?*
3 (on the one hand...) on the other hand used when comparing two different or opposite facts or ideas: *The movie was scary, but on the other hand it made me laugh.* | *On the one hand, they work slowly, but on the other hand they always finish the job.*
4 get out of hand to become impossible to control: *The demonstration seemed to be getting out of hand.*
5 in sb's hands/in the hands of sb being dealt with or cared for by someone: *The decision is in your hands.* | *Don't worry – the children are **in good hands**.* | *Most farmland is **in private hands*** (=owned or controlled by someone, not the government). | *The decision is now in the hands of the court.*
6 on hand close and ready when needed: *Our staff are always on hand to help.*
7 hand in hand a) holding each other's hands: *They strolled hand in hand through the rose garden.* **b)** if two things go hand in hand, they are closely connected: *Wealth and power **go hand in hand** in most societies.*
8 by hand a) done or made by a person, not a machine: *The rug was made by hand.* **b)** delivered from one person to another, not through the mail
9 out of sb's hands if something is out of your hands, you have no control over it: *The decision was out of her hands.*
10 get/lay your hands on sth to find or obtain something: *I read every book I could get my hands on at school.*
11 have a hand in sth to influence or be involved in something: *He scored one goal and had a hand in two others.*
12 at hand (formal) **a)** near in time or space: *Graduation day is **close at hand**.* **b)** needing to be dealt with now: *Let's discuss the case at hand, shall we?*
13 in hand being dealt with and controlled: *Lisa seemed to **have** things **in hand** by the time he returned.*
14 off your hands if someone or something is off your hands, you are not responsible for him, her, or it anymore: *Once this problem is off our hands we can relax.*
15 hands down easily: *He would have **won hands down** if he hadn't hurt his knee.*
16 have your hands full to be very busy or too busy: *You're going to have your hands full once you have the baby!*
17 give sb a (big) hand to CLAP loudly for a performer or speaker
18 CLOCK one of the long things that point to the numbers on a clock ➔ *see picture at* WATCH²
19 CARDS the cards that you are holding in a game
➔ FIRSTHAND, LEFT-HAND, RIGHT-HAND, SECONDHAND, **change hands** *at* CHANGE¹, **shake sb's hand/shake hands (with sb)** *at* SHAKE¹, **wait on sb hand and foot** *at* WAIT ON

hand² *v.* [T] **1** to pass something to someone else SYN **give**: *Can you hand me a towel?* **2 you have to hand it to sb** (spoken) said when you are admiring something that someone has done: *I have to hand it to you, Claire: you sure know how to cook!*

hand sth ↔ **back** *phr. v.* to give something back to the person who gave it to you: *Mr. Evans handed back our essays today.*

hand sth ↔ **down** *phr. v.* **1** to give something to a younger relative, or to people who live after you: *The ring was **handed down to** her from her grandmother.* **2** if a court of law hands down a decision or sentence, it officially announces a decision or punishment

hand sth ↔ **in** *phr. v.* to give something to someone in a position of authority: *Please hand in your application by September 30.*

hand sth ↔ **out** *phr. v.* to give something to everyone in a group: *They were handing out free t-shirts at the concert.*

THESAURUS **give out, pass out, distribute** ➔ GIVE¹

hand over *phr. v.* **1 hand** sth ↔ **over** to give something to someone with your hand, especially because s/he has asked for it or should have it: *She* *handed the phone over to me.* **2** to give someone power or responsibility over something which you used to be in charge of: *He will be handing over the business to his son.*

hand·bag /ˈhændbæg/ *n.* [C] a PURSE

hand·book /ˈhændbʊk/ *n.* [C] a small book with instructions and information about a particular subject: *an employee handbook*

hand·cuff /ˈhændkʌf/ *v.* [T] to put handcuffs on someone

hand·cuffs /ˈhændkʌfs/ *n.* [plural] two metal rings joined by a chain, used for holding a prisoner's wrists together: *Two people were arrested and taken away **in handcuffs**.*

hand·ful /ˈhændfʊl/ *n.* [C] **1** an amount that you can hold in your hand: *a **handful of** nuts* **2 a handful of sth** a small number of people or things: *Only a handful of people showed up.* **3 a handful** (informal) someone, especially a child, who is difficult to control: *She's a real handful!*

ˈhand greˌnade *n.* [C] a small bomb that is thrown by a person rather than shot from a machine

hand·gun /ˈhændgʌn/ *n.* [C] a small gun you hold in one hand when you shoot

hand·held /ˈhændhɛld/ *adj.* [only before noun] a handheld machine is small enough to hold in your hand when using it: *a handheld computer* —**handheld** *n.* [C]

hand·i·cap¹ /ˈhændiˌkæp/ *n.* [C] **1** something permanently wrong with a person's mind or body: *a severe physical handicap* **2** something that makes it difficult for you to do or achieve something: *Not being able to speak Spanish was a real handicap.* [ORIGIN: 1700—1800 *handicap* "game in which people put their hand, holding money for a bet, into a hat" (1600—1700), from *hand in cap*]

handicap² *v.* (**handicapped**, **handicapping**) [T] to make it difficult for someone to do something that s/he wants to do: *The charity is handicapped by a lack of funds.*

hand·i·capped /ˈhændiˌkæpt/ *adj.* **1** not able to use a part of your body or mind normally because it has been damaged. Many people think that this word is offensive ➔ DISABLED, IMPAIRED: *schools for **mentally/physically handicapped** children* **2 the handicapped** people who are mentally or physically handicapped

hand·i·work /ˈhændiˌwɚk/ *n.* [U] something that someone does or makes: *The documentary is the handiwork of a respected director.*

hand·ker·chief /ˈhæŋkɚtʃɪf, -ˌtʃif/ *n.* [C] a piece of cloth that you use for drying your nose or eyes

han·dle¹ /ˈhændl/ *v.* [T] **1** to deal with a situation or problem: *The principal handled the situation very well.* | *The job was so stressful, he couldn't handle it any longer.*

> THESAURUS deal with sth, tackle, cope, take care of sth ➔ DEAL²

2 to organize or be in charge of something: *Ms. Lee handled all of our travel arrangements.* **3** to pick up, hold, or touch something: *Please **handle** this package **with care**.* ➔ TOUCH¹ **4** to buy, sell, or deal with particular products or services: *Upton was charged with **handling stolen goods**.*

handle² *n.* [C] the part of something that is used for holding or opening it: *a door handle* | *a knife with an ivory handle*

han·dle·bars /ˈhændlˌbɑrz/ *n.* [plural] the metal BARS above the front wheel of a bicycle or MOTORCYCLE that you turn to control the direction you go in ➔ *see picture at* BICYCLE

han·dler /ˈhændlɚ/ *n.* [C] someone whose job is to deal with or be in charge of a particular kind of thing: *baggage handlers* | *a police dog and its handler*

hand·made /ˌhændˈmeɪd◂ / *adj.* made by a person and not a machine: *handmade quilts*

ˈhand-me-ˌdown *n.* [C] a piece of clothing that has been worn by someone and then given to his/her younger relative —**hand-me-down** *adj.*

hand·out /ˈhændaʊt/ *n.* [C] **1** money or food that is given to someone, usually because s/he is poor: *We're not looking for a handout from the government.* **2** a piece of paper with printed or copied information that is given to people in a class, meeting, etc.: *Let's look at the first page of the handout.*

H

hand·o·ver /ˈhændˌoʊvɚ/ *n.* [singular] the act of formally giving someone else control of a place or business: *The **handover of** the business to his daughter has gone smoothly.*

hand·picked /ˌhændˈpɪkt◂ / *adj.* someone who is handpicked has been carefully chosen for a particular purpose

hand·set /ˈhændsɛt/ *n.* [C] **1** the part of a telephone that you hold with your hand to your ear and mouth **2** a CELL PHONE

hands·free /ˌhændzˈfri◂ / *adj.* [only before noun] a handsfree machine is one that you operate without using your hands: *a handsfree headset for your cell phone*

hand·shake /ˈhændʃeɪk/ *n.* [C] the action of taking someone's right hand and shaking it, usually done when people meet or leave each other: *a **firm handshake***

hands ˈoff *interjection* said when warning someone not to touch something that is yours: *Hands off my cookies!*

ˈhands-off *adj.* **1 a hands-off approach/attitude etc.** a method, attitude, etc. taken by someone who likes to leave other people to make decisions and do all the work **2** someone who is hands-off does not like to be directly involved in a job and leaves other people to make the decisions and do all the work

hand·some /'hænsəm/ *adj.* **1 a)** a man who is handsome is attractive: *He was a handsome young man.* **b)** a woman who is handsome looks healthy and strong in an attractive way

THESAURUS **attractive, good-looking, nice-looking, pretty, beautiful** → ATTRACTIVE

2 a handsome gift/reward/profit a gift, etc. that is valuable or is a lot of money [ORIGIN: 1500—1600 *handsome* "easy to handle" (15—17 centuries), from *hand*]

'hands-on *adj.* **1 hands-on experience/training etc.** experience, training, etc. that you get by doing something rather than studying it **2** someone who is hands-on likes to be involved in a job and does not let other people make all the decisions and do all the work

hand·stand /'hændstænd/ *n.* [C] a movement in which you kick your legs up into the air so that you are upside down and supporting yourself on your hands

ˌhand to 'mouth *adv.* with just enough money and food to live, and nothing for the future: *For years they had been **living hand to mouth**.*

hand·writ·ing /'hændˌraɪṭɪŋ/ *n.* [U] the way someone writes when s/he uses a pen or a pencil: *She has very **neat handwriting**.*

hand·y /'hændi/ *adj.* **1** useful, or simple to use: *The extra key may **come in handy*** (=be useful in the future). **2** (informal) near and easy to reach: *You should always **keep** a first aid kit **handy**.* **3 be handy with sth** to be good at using something, especially a tool: *Terry's very handy with a needle and thread.*

hand·y·man /'hændiˌmæn/ *n.* (plural **handymen** /-ˌmɛn/) [C] someone who is good at making and repairing things

hang¹ /hæŋ/ *v.* (past tense and past participle **hung** /hʌŋ/) **1** [I,T] to put something somewhere so that its top part is fixed but its bottom part is free to move, or to be in this position: *You can hang your coat in the closet.* | *paintings **hanging on** the wall* **2 hang in the balance** to be in a situation in which the result is not certain, and something bad may happen: *The whole future of the airline is hanging in the balance.* **3 leave sb/sth hanging** to fail to finish something, or tell someone your decision about something: *The investigation should not be left hanging.* **4** [I] to stay in the air in the same place for a long time: *Dark clouds hung over the valley.* **5 hang your head** to look ashamed and embarrassed: *Kevin hung his head and left the room in silence.*

SPOKEN PHRASES

6 hang in there *also* **hang tough** to remain determined to succeed in a difficult situation: *Just hang in there, Midori, things will get better.* **7 hang a right/left** said in order to tell the driver of a car to turn right or left

hang around *phr. v.* (informal) **1** to stay in one place without doing very much, often because you are waiting for someone: *I hung around for about an hour and then left.* **2 hang around with sb** to spend a lot of time with someone: *He's been hanging around with Rick a lot lately.*

hang back *phr. v.* to be unwilling to say or do something, often because you are shy: *Stella ran out to see what was happening, but the others hung back.*

hang on *phr. v.* **1** (informal) to hold something tightly: *Hang on, everybody, the road's pretty bumpy.* **2 hang on!** (spoken) said in order to tell someone to wait for you: *Hang on, I'll be with you in a minute!*

hang onto sb/sth *phr. v.* (spoken) to keep something, or continue a relationship with someone: *I'd hang onto that letter. You might need it later.*

hang out *phr. v.* (informal) to spend a lot of time at a particular place or with particular people: *A lot of kids hang out at the mall.*

hang up *phr. v.* **1** to put the telephone down at the end of a conversation: *Please hang up and dial again.* | *She got mad and **hung up on** me* (=put the phone down before I was finished speaking). **2 hang** sth ↔ **up** to put something such as clothes on a hook or hanger

hang² *v.* (past tense and past participle **hanged**) [I,T] to kill someone by dropping him/her with a rope around his/her neck, as a punishment for a crime, or to die in this way: *Clayton **hanged himself** in his prison cell.* | *He was **hanged for** the killings.*

hang³ *n.* **get the hang of sth** (informal) to learn how to do something: *Driving a car is hard at first, but you'll get the hang of it.*

hang·ar /'hæŋɚ, 'hæŋgɚ/ *n.* [C] a very large building where aircraft are kept

hang·er /'hæŋɚ/ *n.* [C] a thing for hanging clothes on, made of a curved piece of metal, wood, or plastic with a hook on it

ˌhanger-'on *n.* (plural **hangers-on**) [C] (disapproving) someone who tries to spend a lot of time with important people, so that s/he can get some advantage

'hang ˌglider *n.* [C] a large frame covered with cloth, that you hang from and fly slowly through the air on, without an engine

'hang ˌgliding *n.* [U] the sport of flying using a hang glider

hang·ing /'hæŋɪŋ/ *n.* [C,U] the action of killing someone by dropping him/her with a rope around his/her neck as a punishment for a crime

hang·man /'hæŋmən/ *n.* (plural **hangmen** /-mən/) [C] someone whose job is to kill criminals by hanging them

hang·nail /'hæŋneɪl/ *n.* [C] a piece of dead skin that has become loose near the bottom of your FINGERNAIL

hang·out /'hæŋaʊt/ *n.* [C] (informal) a place that you like to go to often, especially with friends: *The coffee shop is our **favorite hangout**.*

hang·o·ver /ˈhæŋˌoʊvɚ/ *n.* [C] the feeling of sickness that someone has the day after s/he has drunk too much alcohol: *I **have** a really bad **hangover**.*

hang-up /ˈhæŋʌp/ *n.* [C] (informal) something that you are worried or embarrassed about: *She **has** a lot of **hang-ups about** relationships.*

hank·er /ˈhæŋkɚ/ *v.* [I] (informal) to have a very strong desire for something over a period of time: *The voters seem to be **hankering for** change.* —**hankering** *n.* [singular]

han·kie, **hanky** /ˈhæŋki/ *n.* (plural **hankies**) [C] (informal) a HANDKERCHIEF

han·ky-pan·ky /ˌhæŋki ˈpæŋki/ *n.* [U] (informal, humorous) sexual or criminal behavior that is not very serious

Ha·nuk·kah /ˈhɑnəkə/ *n.* an eight-day Jewish holiday in December

hap·haz·ard /ˌhæpˈhæzɚd/ *adj.* (disapproving) happening or done in a way that is not organized or planned —**haphazardly** *adv.*

hap·less /ˈhæplɪs/ *adj.* (literary) unlucky

hap·loid /ˈhæplɔɪd/ *n.* [C] BIOLOGY a cell that contains only one set of CHROMOSOMEs and one set of GENEs —**haploid** *adj.*: *haploid cells*

hap·pen /ˈhæpən/ *v.* [I] **1** if an event or situation happens, it exists and continues for a period of time, usually without being planned: *Did anything exciting happen while I was away?* | *We must do all we can to prevent such a disaster ever happening again.* | *We'll still be friends **whatever happens**.*

THESAURUS

Happen is mainly used to talk about things that have not been planned: *A funny thing happened on my way to work.* | *No one knows exactly what will happen.*
Take place is mainly used to talk about events that have been planned or that have already happened: *The next meeting will take place on Thursday.*
Occur is a formal word, used especially to say that something happens in a particular place or situation: *The accident occurred around 9 pm.*

2 happen to sb/sth to affect someone or something: *Strange things have been happening to me lately.* **3** to be the result of something you do: *When I try to turn on the motor, nothing happens.* | ***What happens if** your parents find out?* **4 happen to do sth** to do or to have something by chance: *I happened to see Hannah at the store today.* **5 sb/sth happens to be sth** (spoken) said when you are angry or annoyed, to add force to what you are saying: *That happens to be my foot that you just stepped on!* **6 as it happens/it (just) so happens** (spoken) used in order to say that something happens by chance, especially when this is surprising: *It just so happened that Mike and I had gone to the same school.* **7 what/whatever happened to sb/sth?** used in order to ask where a person or thing is now: *What happened to my blue sweater?* | *Whatever happened to Jenny Beale?* [ORIGIN: 1300—1400 *hap* "chance, luck" (13—20 centuries), from Old Norse *happ*]

happen on/upon sb/sth *phr. v.* to meet someone or find something by chance: *We just happened on the cabin when we were hiking one day.*

hap·pen·ing¹ /ˈhæpənɪŋ/ *adj.* (informal) fashionable and exciting: *a happening club*

happening² *n.* [C] something that happens: *The paper has a listing of the day's happenings.*

THESAURUS **event, occurrence, incident**
→ EVENT

hap·pi·ly /ˈhæpəli/ *adv.* **1** in a happy way: *Michelle smiled happily.* | *a **happily married** couple* | *Cinderella marries the prince and they **live happily ever after*** (=for the rest of his/her life). **2** fortunately: *Happily, no one was hurt in the fire.* **3** very willingly: *I'll happily watch the kids for you while you're gone.*

hap·pi·ness /ˈhæpinɪs/ *n.* [U] the state of being happy: *Her face was glowing with happiness.* | *They **found happiness** together at last.*

hap·py /ˈhæpi/ *adj.* (comparative **happier**, superlative **happiest**) **1** feeling pleased and cheerful, often because something good has happened to you (ANT) **unhappy**, **sad**: *He was a happy child.* | *I've never **felt happier** in my life.* | *I'm **happy (that)** everything worked out in the end.* | *I don't think he was too **happy about** having to stay late.* | *Congratulations! I'm so **happy for you**.*

THESAURUS

glad – pleased about a situation or something that has happened: *I'm so glad you were able to come.*
pleased – happy and satisfied with something that has happened: *Her parents were pleased that she had done so well.*
content – happy and satisfied: *We're usually content to stay at home and read or watch TV.*
delighted/thrilled/overjoyed – extremely happy because something good has happened: *We were delighted when she had a baby girl.*
ecstatic – extremely happy and excited: *When he heard he'd gotten the job, he was ecstatic.*
jubilant (formal) – extremely happy and pleased because you have been successful: *After the game, a jubilant crowd celebrated the win.*
elated (formal) – extremely happy and excited: *Ron was elated to hear that his wife was pregnant.*

2 be happy to do sth to be willing to do something, especially to help someone else: *I'll be happy to answer questions later.* **3** a happy time, place, etc. is one that makes you feel pleased or happy: *Those were the happiest years of my life.* | *They had a very happy marriage.* **4** [not before noun] satisfied or not worried: *Amy was not very **happy with** their decision.* **5 Happy Birthday/New Year etc.** used as a greeting, or to wish someone good luck on his/her BIRTHDAY or a special occasion

H

ˌhappy-go-ˈlucky *adj.* enjoying life and not worrying about things

ˈhappy hour *n.* [C,U] a short period of time when a BAR sells drinks at a lower price

ha·rangue /həˈræŋ/ *v.* [T] to speak in an angry way, often for a long time, to try to persuade someone that you are right —**harangue** *n.* [C]

ha·rass /həˈræs, ˈhærəs/ *v.* [T] to deliberately annoy or threaten someone, often over a long period of time: *They claim that they are being harassed by the police.*

ha·rass·ment /həˈræsmənt, ˈhærəs-/ *n.* [U] behavior that is threatening or offensive to other people: *Tina accused her boss of* ***sexual harassment****.*

har·bor¹ /ˈhɑrbɚ/ *n.* [C,U] an area of water next to the land, where ships can stay safely

harbor² *v.* [T] **1** to protect someone by hiding him/her from the police **2** to keep hopes, bad thoughts, or fears in your mind for a long time: *Ralph harbors no bitterness toward his ex-wife.*

hard¹ /hɑrd/ *adj.*
1 FIRM TO TOUCH firm and stiff, and difficult to cut, press down, or break (ANT) **soft**: *I can't sleep on a hard mattress.* | *hard candy* | *The plums are still too hard to eat.*

THESAURUS

firm – not completely hard, but not soft and not easy to bend: *Brownies are done when the edges are firm but the middle is still soft.*
stiff – difficult to bend or move: *a piece of stiff, brightly colored cardboard*
solid – firm and usually hard, without spaces or holes: *They blasted the tunnel through solid rock.*
rigid – stiff and impossible to bend: *Old airplanes had a rigid frame with cloth stretched tightly over it.*

2 DIFFICULT difficult to do or understand (ANT) **easy**: *Chemistry was one of the hardest classes I've ever taken.* | *The print was small and* ***hard to*** *read.* | ***I find it*** *extremely* ***hard to believe*** *that no one saw the accident.* | *It was* ***hard for*** *me to tell him the truth.* | *It's* ***hard to say*** (=difficult to know) *when Glenn will be back.*

THESAURUS **difficult, tough, awkward, challenging, demanding** ➔ DIFFICULT

3 A LOT OF EFFORT involving a lot of physical or mental effort: *I had a* ***hard day*** *at work.* | *Mowing the lawn is* ***hard work****.*
4 be hard on sb (informal) **a)** to treat someone in a way that is unfair or too strict: *Don't be too hard on the children – they were only playing.* **b)** to cause someone a lot of problems: ***It's hard on*** *her, having her husband in the hospital.*
5 be hard on sth (informal) to have a bad effect on something: *Aspirin can be pretty hard on your stomach.*
6 give sb a hard time (informal) **a)** to make someone feel embarrassed or uncomfortable, often by making jokes about him/her: *The guys were giving him a hard time about missing the ball.* **b)** to criticize someone a lot
7 NOT KIND showing no kindness or sympathy: *Mr. Katz is a hard man to work for, but he's fair.*
8 PROBLEMS full of problems, especially not enough money: ***Times were hard****, and we were forced to sell our house.* | *My mother has* ***had a hard life****.*
9 learn sth the hard way to learn about something by a bad experience or by making mistakes
10 no hard feelings (spoken) used in order to tell someone that you no longer feel angry with him/her
11 WATER hard water has a lot of minerals in it and does not mix easily with soap (ANT) **soft** [ORIGIN: Old English *heard*] —**hardness** *n.* [U]

hard² *adv.* **1** using a lot of effort: *She has* ***worked hard*** *all her life.* | *We try hard to keep our customers happy.* **2** with a lot of force: *You need to hit the ball hard.* | *It's raining hard outside.* **3 be hard pressed/put/pushed to do sth** (informal) to have difficulty doing something: *The painters will be hard pressed to finish by 6 o'clock.* **4 take sth hard** to feel very upset about something: *I didn't know that Joe would take the news so hard.*

ˌhard-and-ˈfast *adj.* **hard-and-fast rules/regulations** rules that cannot be changed

hard·back /ˈhɑrdbæk/ *n.* [C] a book that has a strong stiff cover ➔ BOOK¹

hard·ball /ˈhɑrdbɔl/ *n.* **play hardball** (informal) to be very determined to get what you want, especially in business or politics

ˌhard-ˈboiled *adj.* **1** a hard-boiled egg has been boiled until it becomes solid **2** (written) not showing or influenced by your emotions (SYN) **tough**: *a hard-boiled policeman*

ˌhard ˈcash *n.* [U] paper money and coins, not checks or CREDIT CARDS

ˈhard ˌcopy *n.* [C,U] information from a computer that is printed onto paper, or the printed papers themselves

hard·core /ˈhɑrdkɔr/ *adj.* [only before noun] extreme, and unlikely to change: *hardcore criminals*

hard·cov·er /ˈhɑrdˌkʌvɚ/ *n.* [C] a book that has a strong stiff cover ➔ BOOK¹ —**hardcover** *adj.*

ˌhard ˈcurrency *n.* [C,U] ECONOMICS money from a country that has a strong ECONOMY, that is unlikely to lose its value

ˌhard ˈdisk *n.* [C] IT a DISK inside a computer, used for permanently storing a large amount of information

ˈhard drive *n.* [C] IT the part of a computer where information and programs are stored, consisting of HARD DISKS and the electronic equipment that reads the information stored on them ➔ *see picture on page A19*

ˌhard ˈdrugs *n.* [plural] very strong illegal drugs such as COCAINE

hard·en /ˈhɑrdn/ *v.* [I,T] **1** to become firm or stiff, or to make something do this: *The glue takes about an hour to harden.* **2** to become less kind, less afraid, and more determined, or to make someone become this way: *Leslie's face hardened, and she turned away from him.* | *a* ***hardened criminal***

ˌhard ˈhat *n.* [C] a protective hat, worn by workers in places where buildings are being built ➔ *see picture at* HAT

ˌhard-ˈheaded *adj.* able to make difficult decisions without being influenced by your emotions

ˌhard-ˈhearted *adj.* not caring about other people's feelings

ˌhard-ˈhitting *adj.* criticizing someone or something in a strong and effective way: *a hard-hitting TV documentary*

hard·line /ˌhɑrdˈlaɪn◂ / *adj.* unwilling to change your extreme political opinions: *hardline conservatives* —**hardliner** *n.* [C]

ˌhard ˈliquor *n.* [U] strong alcohol such as WHISKEY

hard·ly /ˈhɑrdli/ *adv.* **1** almost not or almost none: *I hardly know the people I'm working with.* | *The children were so excited they* ***could hardly*** *speak.* | ***Hardly anyone*** (=very few people) *goes to the old theater anymore.* | *Katy is* ***hardly ever*** (=almost never) *at home.* **2** (formal) used in order to say that something is not at all true, surprising, etc.: *It's* ***hardly surprising*** *that she won't answer his calls after the way he's treated her.* | *You* ***can hardly blame*** *Tom for not waiting.*

ˌhard-ˈnosed *adj.* not affected by emotions, and determined to get what you want: *a hard-nosed negotiator*

ˌhard of ˈhearing *adj.* [not before noun] unable to hear well

ˌhard-ˈpressed *adj.* having a lot of problems and not enough money or time: *The program is meant to help hard-pressed families with young children.*

ˌhard ˈrock *n.* [U] loud ROCK music

ˌhard ˈsell *n.* [singular] a way of selling in which someone tries very hard to persuade you to buy something

hard·ship /ˈhɑrdˌʃɪp/ *n.* [C,U] something that makes your life difficult, especially the condition of having very little money: *Many families were* ***suffering*** *economic* ***hardship***. | *the* ***hardships of*** *war*

ˌhard ˈup *adj.* (informal) not having much money: *Scott was pretty hard up, so I gave him $20.*

hard·ware /ˈhɑrdwɛr/ *n.* [U] **1** IT computer machinery and equipment, as opposed to the programs that make computers work ➔ SOFTWARE **2** equipment and tools you use in your home and yard: *a* ***hardware store*** (=where you can buy these things)

ˌhard-ˈwired *adj.* IT computer systems that are hard-wired are controlled by HARDWARE rather than SOFTWARE and cannot be easily changed by the user

hard·wood /ˈhɑrdwʊd/ *n.* [C,U] strong heavy wood used for making furniture, or a type of tree that produces this kind of wood ➔ SOFTWOOD

ˌhard-ˈworking *adj.* working seriously with a lot of effort, and not wasting time (ANT) **lazy**: *a hard-working student*

har·dy /ˈhɑrdi/ *adj.* strong and healthy and able to live through difficult conditions: *hardy plants*

hare /hɛr/ *n.* [C] an animal like a rabbit, but larger, with longer ears and longer back legs

hare·brained /ˈhɛrbreɪnd/ *adj.* not sensible or practical: *a* ***harebrained scheme***

hare·lip /ˈhɛrˌlɪp/ *n.* [singular, U] the condition of having a top lip that is divided into two parts

har·em /ˈhɛrəm, ˈhærəm/ *n.* [C] **1** the group of wives or women who lived with a rich or powerful man in some Muslim societies in past times **2** the rooms in a Muslim home where the women live

hark /hɑrk/ *also* **hark·en** /ˈhɑrkən/ *v.*

hark/harken back to sth *phr. v.* to remember or to remind people of something from the past: *The band's music harks back to the 1950s.*

har·lot /ˈhɑrlət/ *n.* [C] (literary) a PROSTITUTE

harm¹ /hɑrm/ *n.* [U] **1** damage, injury, or trouble caused by someone's actions or by an event: *Some chemicals* ***cause harm to*** *the environment.* | *Just give it a taste; it won't* ***do*** *you any* ***harm***. | *Trying to lose weight can* ***do more harm than good*** (=cause problems). **2 there's no harm in doing sth** used in order to suggest that doing something may be helpful or useful: *There's no harm in asking.* **3 not mean any harm** used in order to say that even though someone hurt or upset someone else, this was not his/her intention: *I'm sure he didn't mean any harm.* **4 no harm done** (spoken) said in order to tell someone that you are not upset by what s/he has done or said: *"I'm sorry." "That's OK; no harm done."*

harm² *v.* [T] to damage or hurt something: *Too much sun will harm your skin.*

harm·ful /ˈhɑrmfəl/ *adj.* causing harm, or likely to cause harm: *the harmful effects of pollution* | *Some pesticides are* ***harmful to*** *the environment.*

THESAURUS

poisonous/toxic – containing a substance that can kill you or make you sick if you eat it, breathe it, etc.: *a poisonous snake* | *toxic fumes*
detrimental (formal) – harmful or damaging to something: *Fatty foods are detrimental to your health.*
damaging – having a bad effect on someone or something: *the damaging effects of alcohol on the brain*
destructive – causing something to be destroyed: *If the herd is too big, deer can be very destructive to woodlands.*
deleterious (formal) – damaging or harmful: *the deleterious effects of smoking*

harm·less /ˈhɑrmlɪs/ *adj.* **1** unable or unlikely

H

to hurt anyone or cause damage: *harmless bacteria* **2** not likely to upset or offend anyone: *harmless fun* —**harmlessly** *adv.*

har·mon·i·ca /hɑr'mɑnɪkə/ *n.* [C] a small musical instrument that you play by blowing into it and moving it from side to side

har·mo·nize /'hɑrmə,naɪz/ *v.* [I] **1** to work well or look good together: *Choose clothes that* ***harmonize with*** *your coloring.* **2** to sing or play music in harmony

har·mo·ny /'hɑrməni/ *n.* (plural **harmonies**) **1** [U] a situation in which people are friendly and peaceful, and agree with each other: *The students* ***lived/worked*** *together* ***in harmony****.* **2** [C,U] combinations of musical notes that sound good together: *four-part harmony* —**harmonious** /hɑr'moʊniəs/ *adj.*

har·ness¹ /'hɑrnɪs/ *n.* **1** [C,U] a set of leather bands fastened with metal, used in order to control a horse and attach it to a vehicle that it pulls **2** [C] a set of bands that is used to hold someone in a place, or to stop him/her from falling: *a safety harness*

harness² *v.* [T] **1** to control and use the natural force or power of something: *a dam to harness the power of the river* **2** to fasten two animals together, or to fasten an animal to something using a harness

H

harp¹ /hɑrp/ *n.* [C] a large musical instrument with strings stretched on a frame with three corners —**harpist** *n.* [C]

harp² *v.*

harp on sth *phr. v.* (informal, disapproving) to talk about something again and again, in a way that is annoying or boring: *My parents are always harping on my boyfriend's faults.*

har·poon /hɑr'pun/ *n.* [C] a weapon used for hunting WHALES

harp·si·chord /'hɑrpsɪ,kɔrd/ *n.* [C] a musical instrument like a piano, used especially in CLASSICAL MUSIC

har·row·ing /'hæroʊɪŋ/ *adj.* (formal) a harrowing sight or experience is one that frightens, shocks, or upsets you very much

harsh /hɑrʃ/ *adj.* **1** harsh conditions are difficult to live in and very uncomfortable: *harsh Canadian winters* | *the* ***harsh realities*** *of war* **2** too loud or too bright, and making you feel uncomfortable: *a harsh voice* | *the harsh street lights* **3** unkind, cruel, or strict: *harsh criticism* | *He had* ***harsh words*** *for the way the mayor has handled the issue.* —**harshly** *adv.* —**harshness** *n.* [U]

har·vest¹ /'hɑrvɪst/ *n.* **1** [C,U] the time when crops are gathered from the fields, or the act of gathering them: *It was harvest time.* | *the wheat harvest* **2** [C] the size or quality of the crops: *a good harvest*

harvest² *v.* [T] to gather crops from the fields

has /z, s, əz, həz; *strong* hæz/ *v.* the third person singular of the present tense of HAVE

'has-been *n.* [C] (informal) someone who was important or popular, but who has been forgotten

hash¹ /hæʃ/ *n.* **1** [C,U] a dish made with cooked meat and potatoes **2** [U] (informal) hashish

hash² *v.*

hash sth ↔ **out** *phr. v.* to discuss something very thoroughly and carefully: *It took them a long time to hash out a compromise.*

,hash 'browns *n.* [plural] potatoes that have been cut into very small pieces, pressed together, and cooked in oil

hash·ish /'hæʃiʃ, hæ'ʃiʃ/ *n.* [U] a form of the drug MARIJUANA

has·n't /'hæzənt/ *v.* the short form of "has not": *She hasn't seen Bruce in seven years.*

has·sle¹ /'hæsəl/ *n.* **1** [C,U] something that is annoying because it causes problems, or is difficult to do: *Driving downtown is just too much hassle.* | *legal hassles*

> THESAURUS **problem, difficulty, trouble** → PROBLEM

2 [C] (informal) an argument: *I've had a few hassles with the management.*

hassle² *v.* [T] (informal) to ask someone again and again to do something, in a way that is annoying: *She just kept* ***hassling*** *me* ***to*** *get a summer job.*

haste /heɪst/ *n.* [U] **1** great speed in doing something, especially because you do not have enough time: ***In her haste to*** *get to the airport, Pam forgot the tickets.* **2 in haste** quickly or in a hurry **3 haste makes waste** used in order to say that if you do something too quickly, it will not turn out well

has·ten /'heɪsən/ *v.* (formal) **1** [T] to make something happen faster or sooner: *The popularity of radio* ***hastened the end*** *of silent movies.* **2 hasten to do sth** to do or say something quickly or without delay

> THESAURUS **rush, speed** → RUSH¹

hast·y /'heɪsti/ *adj.* (formal) done in a hurry, especially with bad results: *a hasty decision* —**hastily** *adv.*: *a hastily written speech*

> THESAURUS **impulsive, rash, impetuous** → IMPULSIVE

hat /hæt/ *n.* [C] **1** a piece of clothing that you wear on your head: *a big straw hat* | *a cowboy hat* **2 keep sth under your hat** to keep information secret **3 throw/toss your hat into the ring** to officially announce that you will compete or take part in a competition

hatch¹ /hætʃ/ *v.* **1** [I,T] if an egg hatches or is hatched, it breaks and a baby bird, fish, or insect is

hats

born **2** [I] *also* **hatch out** to break through an egg in order to be born

hatch² *n.* [C] a hole in a ship or aircraft, used for loading goods, or the door that covers it

hatch·back /ˈhætʃbæk/ *n.* [C] a car with a door at the back that opens up

hatch·et /ˈhætʃɪt/ *n.* [C] **1** a small AX with a short handle **2 do a hatchet job on sb** (informal) to criticize someone severely and often unfairly → **bury the hatchet** *at* BURY

hate¹ /heɪt/ *v.* [T] **1** to dislike someone or some thing very much: *She hated my father.* | *I really hate spinach.* | *Tony **hates it when** people are late.*

THESAURUS

can't stand – to hate someone or something: *I can't stand being late.*
detest/loathe (formal) – to hate someone or something very much: *I was going out with a boy my mother detested.*
despise – to hate someone very much and not respect him/her at all: *She despised her neighbors.*
abhor (formal) – to hate something because you think it is morally wrong: *He abhors violence of any kind.* → LOVE¹

2 I hate to think what/how (spoken) used when you feel sure that something would have a bad result: *I hate to think what would happen if Joe got lost.* **3 hate sb's guts** (informal) to hate someone very much [ORIGIN: Old English *hete*] —**hated** *adj.*

hate² *n.* [U] an angry feeling of wanting to harm someone you dislike: *a look of hate*

ˈhate crime *n.* [C] a crime that is committed against someone only because s/he belongs to a particular race, religion, etc.

hate·ful /ˈheɪtfəl/ *adj.* very bad or unkind: *a hateful thought*

ha·tred /ˈheɪtrɪd/ *n.* [U] (formal) HATE: *his **hatred** of racism*

haugh·ty /ˈhɔt̬i/ *adj.* (literary, disapproving) proud and unfriendly —**haughtily** *adv.*

THESAURUS **proud, conceited, arrogant, stuck-up** → PROUD

haul¹ /hɔl/ *v.* [T] to carry or pull something heavy: *Trucks hauled cement to the site.*

THESAURUS **carry, tote, lug, cart** → CARRY
pull, tug, drag → PULL¹

haul sb **off** *phr. v.* (informal) to take someone somewhere s/he does not want to go: *Dave got **hauled off** to jail.*

haul² *n.* **1** [C] a large amount of illegal or stolen goods that are found by the police: *a huge drugs haul* **2 the long haul** the long time that it takes to achieve something difficult: *"We're **in this for the long haul**," said a government source.* **3 a long haul** a long distance to travel

haunch /hɔntʃ, hɑntʃ/ *n.* **1 haunches** [plural] the part of your body at the back between your waist and legs: *They squatted on their haunches playing dice.* **2** [C] one of the back legs of a four-legged animal, especially when it is used as meat

haunt¹ /hɔnt, hɑnt/ *v.* [T] **1** if the spirit of a dead person haunts a place, it appears there often: *The story is that the ship is haunted by ghosts of sea captains.* **2** if something haunts you, you keep remembering it or being affected by it, although you do not want this: *It's the kind of decision that **comes back to haunt** you later.*

haunt² *n.* [C] a place that someone likes to go to often: *Dan went back to visit his favorite old haunts.*

haunt·ed /ˈhɔntɪd, ˈhɑn-/ *adj.* a place that is haunted is one where the spirits of dead people are believed to live: *a **haunted** house*

haunt·ing /ˈhɔntɪŋ, ˈhɑn-/ *adj.* sad, beautiful, and staying in your thoughts for a long time: *a haunting memory* —**hauntingly** *adv.*

have¹ /v, əv, həv; *strong* hæv/ *auxiliary verb* (past tense and past participle **had**, third person singular **has**) **1** used with the past participle of a verb to make the perfect tenses: *Yes, I've read the book.* | *Have you seen the new Disney movie?* | *She had lived in Peru for 30 years.* | *Rick has not been honest with us.* **2** used with some MODAL VERBS and a past participle to make a past MODAL: *Carrie should have been nicer.* | *I must've left my wallet at home.* **3 had better** used in order to give advice, or to say what is the best thing to do: *You'd better take the popcorn off the stove or it'll burn.* | *I'd better not go out tonight – I'm too tired.* **4 have had it** (spoken) **a)** said when someone or something is old, broken, or not good any longer: *I think the car has had it. It wouldn't start this morning.* **b) I've had it with** said when you are so annoyed by someone or something that you do not want to deal with him, her, or it any longer: *I've*

H

had it with the noise here. Let's go! [ORIGIN: Old English *habban*]

have² /hæv/ *v.* [T not in passive]
1 FEATURES/QUALITIES used when saying what someone or something looks like, or what qualities or features he, she, or it possesses: *Rudy has brown eyes and dark hair.* | *My mother grew up in a house that didn't have an indoor toilet.* | *Japan has a population of over 120 million.*
2 OWN OR USE to own something, or be able to use something: *Kurt had a nice bike, but it got stolen.* | *The school doesn't **have room for** any more students.* | *We don't have enough money for a washing machine.* | *Dad, can I have the car tonight?*

THESAURUS own, possess → OWN²

3 have got used instead of "have" to mean "possess": *I've got four tickets to the opera.*
4 EAT/DRINK to eat, drink, or smoke something: *Do you want to come have a beer with us?* | *We're having steak for dinner tonight.* | *What time do you usually **have lunch/breakfast/dinner**?*
5 EXPERIENCE/DO to experience or do something: *I have a meeting in 15 minutes.* | *The kids will **have fun** at the circus.* | *Her secretary **had trouble/problems with** the copy machine.*
6 RECEIVE to receive something: *Jenny! You have a phone call!* | *I'm sure he had help from his father on his homework.*
7 IN A POSITION/STATE to put or keep something in a particular position or state: *He had his eyes closed.* | *Why do you always **have** the TV **on** so loud?*
8 may I have/can I have/I'll have (spoken) said when you are asking for something: *I'll have two hot dogs to go, please.* | *Could I have that pencil, please?*
9 SELL/MAKE AVAILABLE to sell something, or make it available for people to use: *Do they have lawn mowers at Sears?* | *The other pool has a water slide.*
10 FAMILY/FRIENDS ETC to know or be related to someone: *She has six brothers.* | *Chris has a friend who lives in Malta.*
11 AMOUNT OF TIME *also* **have got** to be allowed a particular amount of time to do something: *You have 30 minutes to finish the test.*
12 have time if you have time to do something, there is nothing else that you must do at that particular time: *Do you **have time to** come and have a cup of coffee with us?*
13 BE SICK/INJURED to become sick with a particular illness, or be injured in a particular way: *Sheila had the flu for a week.* | *He has a broken leg.*
14 CARRY WITH YOU to be carrying something with you: *Do you have your knife?* | *How much money do you **have on you**?*
15 IDEA/THOUGHT to think of something, or realize something: *Listen, I have an idea.*
16 have sth ready/done etc. to make something ready, or finish something: *They promised to have it done by Friday.*
17 GIVE BIRTH to give birth: *Sasha had twins!*
18 have your hair cut/have your house painted etc. to employ someone to cut your hair, paint your house, etc.
19 GUESTS to be with someone, or be visited by someone: *Sorry, I didn't realize you had guests.* | *Barry had an Australian guy with him.*
20 have an influence/effect etc. to influence someone or something, or cause a particular effect: *Folk songs **had** a great **influence on** his music.*
21 have nothing against used in order to say that you do not dislike someone or something: *I have nothing against hard work, but 80 hours a week is too much.* → **be had** *at* HAD

have on *phr. v.*
1 have sth **on** to be wearing something: *Marty had a blue shirt on.*
2 have sth **on** sb to know about something bad someone has done: *Do the police have anything on him?*

ha·ven /ˈheɪvən/ *n.* [C,U] a place where people go to be safe: *a **haven for** refugees*

have·n't /ˈhævənt/ *v.* the short form of "have not": *We haven't tried Indian food yet.* ▸Don't say "haven't to."◂

have to /ˈhæftə; *strong* ˈhæftu/ *also* **have got to** /v ˈgɑṭə, əv-, həv-/ *modal verb* **1** to be forced to do something because someone makes you do it, or because a situation makes it necessary: *We don't have to answer their questions.* | *Susan hates having to get up early.* | *I've got to go now. I'm already late!* **2** used when saying that it is important that something happens: *You'll have to be nice to Aunt Lynn.* **3** used when telling someone how to do something: *First you have to take the wheel off.* **4** used when saying that you are sure that something will happen or is true: *He has to be stuck in traffic – he wouldn't be late otherwise.*

GRAMMAR

have to, have got to, must
have to – used when a rule, law, situation, etc. forces you to do something and you do not have a choice about it: *You have to pay tax on your income* (=because the law says it is necessary). | *We have to be at the airport by 5:30* (=because the plane will leave soon after that time).
must – used especially in more formal writing when a law or person in authority forces you to do something: *All visitors must report to reception.*
must – used when you make yourself do something because you think it is a good idea or necessary: *You must come to Boston!* (=because we want to see you and we think it would be a good idea) | *I must study for tomorrow's test* (=because I know it is a good idea if I want to do well).
have got to – used in spoken English instead of **have to** or **must** to emphasize how important it is to do something: *I've got to be back by 8:00.*

hav·oc /ˈhævək/ *n.* [U] a situation in which there

is a lot of confusion and damage: *The bus strike **caused/created havoc** in the city's streets.* | *The war will **wreak havoc on** the country's economy.* [ORIGIN: 1400—1500 Anglo-French, Old French *havot* "destruction, disorder"]

hawk[1] /hɔk/ *v.* [T] to try to sell goods by carrying them around and talking about them —**hawker** *n.*

hawk[2] *n.* [C] a large wild bird that eats small birds and animals

hay /heɪ/ *n.* [U] a type of long grass that has been cut and dried, used as food for farm animals ➔ STRAW ➔ **hit the hay** *at* HIT[1]

'hay ˌfever *n.* [U] a medical condition like a bad COLD, caused by breathing in POLLEN (=dust from plants) ➔ ALLERGY

hay·ride /'heɪraɪd/ *n.* [C] an organized ride in a CART filled with hay, usually as part of a social event

hay·stack /'heɪstæk/ *n.* [C] a large firmly built pile of hay

hay·wire /'heɪwaɪɚ/ *adj.* **go haywire** (informal) to start working in completely the wrong way: *My computer's going haywire again.*

haz·ard[1] /'hæzɚd/ *n.* [C] **1** something that may be dangerous or cause accidents, problems, etc.: *a **health hazard*** | *the hazards of starting your own business*

THESAURUS danger, risk, threat ➔ DANGER

2 occupational hazard a problem or risk that cannot be avoided in the job that you do [ORIGIN: 1200—1300 Old French *hasard* "game of chance played with dice," from Arabic *az-zahr* "the chance"] —**hazardous** *adj.*: *hazardous waste from factories*

hazard[2] *v.* [T] to say something that is only a suggestion or guess: *I don't know, but I could **hazard a guess**.*

haze /heɪz/ *n.* [U] smoke, dust, etc. in the air that is difficult to see through ➔ HAZY, FOG, SMOG: *There was a gray haze of smoke over the mountains.*

ha·zel /'heɪzəl/ *adj.* eyes that are hazel are greenish-brown

ha·zel·nut /'heɪzəlˌnʌt/ *n.* [C] a sweet round nut

haz·ing /'heɪzɪŋ/ *n.* [C,U] the activity of making people who want to join a club or FRATERNITY do silly or dangerous things before they can join

haz·y /'heɪzi/ *adj.* **1** air that is hazy is not clear because there is a lot of smoke, dust, or mist in it: *a hazy sky* **2** an idea, memory, etc. that is hazy is not clear: *My memories of that night are a little hazy.*

he /i; *strong* hi/ *pron.* a male person or animal that has already been mentioned or is already known about: *"Does Matt still work here?" "No, he works in Ohio now."* | *How old is he?* | *He's* (=he is) *my brother.* [ORIGIN: Old English]

head[1] /hɛd/ *n.*

1 TOP OF BODY [C] the top part of your body that has your eyes, mouth, etc. in it: *He turned his head to kiss her.* ➔ *see picture on page A16*

COLLOCATIONS

turn your **head** – to look at something
shake your **head** (=move it from side to side) – to disagree or say "no"
nod your **head** (=move it up and down) – to agree or say "yes"
raise/lift your **head** – to look up
bend/lower your **head** – to look down
bow your **head** (=move it down) – to show respect for someone
hang your **head** (=lower it and keep it lowered) – if you are ashamed
scratch your **head** (=rub it with your fingers) – if you are thinking hard ➔ HAIR, EYE[1]

2 MIND [C] your mind: *Phil has some strange ideas **in his head**.* | *Ann has **a good head for math*** (=she is good at doing math). | *Why don't you **use your head*** (=think carefully and sensibly) *to find a solution?* | *I wish he'd **get it into his head*** (=realize or understand) *that school is important.*

3 LEADER [C] the leader or most important person in a group or organization: *the **head of** the biology department* | *the head waiter*

THESAURUS chief, supervisor, foreman, forewoman ➔ BOSS[1]

4 POSITION [singular] the top or front of something, or the most important part of it: *Edgar sat proudly **at the head of the table*** (=at the end where the most important people sit).

5 ON A TOOL [C] the widest or top part of something such as a piece of equipment or a tool: *a shower head*

6 PLANT [C] the top part of a plant with a lot of leaves: *a head of lettuce/cabbage*

7 (from) head to toe/foot over your whole body: *The kids were covered from head to toe in mud.*

8 put your heads together (spoken) to discuss a difficult problem together: *If we put our heads together, we'll think of a way.*

9 go over sb's head a) to be too difficult for someone to understand: *Most of the lecture went way over my head.* **b)** to ask a more important person to deal with something than the person you would normally ask

10 keep/lose your head to behave reasonably or stupidly in a difficult situation: *I guess I just lost my head for a minute.*

11 go to sb's head a) to make someone feel more important than s/he really is: *It's too bad Dave **let** his promotion **go to his head**.* **b)** to make someone quickly feel slightly drunk

12 come to a head if a problem comes to a head, it becomes worse and you have to do something about it immediately: *The situation came to a head when the workers went on strike.*

13 heads up! (spoken) used in order to warn

people that something is falling from above, or that something is being thrown to them

14 keep your head above water to just manage to live or keep your business working when you have money problems

15 laugh/shout/scream etc. your head off (informal) to laugh, shout, etc. very loudly

16 head over heels (in love) loving someone very much

17 COIN **heads** [U] the side of a coin that has a picture of a head on it (ANT) **tails** [ORIGIN: Old English *heafod*] ➔ *see also* BIGHEADED, REDHEAD

head² *v.* **1** [I,T] to go or make something go in a particular direction: *Where were they heading when you saw them?* | *A boat was* ***heading toward/for*** *the shore.* | *Roz headed the car down the hill.* **2** [T] to be in charge of a government, organization, or group: *The committee is headed by Jake Wilson.* | *Most single-parent families are headed by women.* **3 be heading/headed for sth** if you are heading for a situation, it is likely to happen: *They're heading for trouble.* **4 be headed** if a list, page, etc. is headed with particular words, those words are at the top: *The longest list was headed "Problems."*

head sb/sth ↔ **off** *phr. v.* to stop someone going in a particular direction by moving in front of him/her: *We'll try to head them off at the next intersection.*

H

head·ache /ˈhɛdeɪk/ *n.* [C] **1** a pain in your head: *I* ***have a*** *bad* ***headache***. **2** (informal) an annoying or worrying problem: *Balancing the checkbook is always a headache.*

head·band /ˈhɛdbænd/ *n.* [C] a band that you wear around your head to keep your hair off your face

head count, **head·count** /ˈhɛdkaʊnt/ *n.* [C usually singular] the process of counting the number of people in a particular place or event, or the actual number: *Hal* ***did a*** *quick* ***head count*** *before the meeting began.*

head·dress /ˈhɛd-drɛs/ *n.* [C] something that someone wears on his/her head for decoration on a special occasion

head·er /ˈhɛdɚ/ *n.* [C] **1** ENG. LANG. ARTS information at the top of a page, especially things such as page numbers or the titles that appear on each page in a document **2** IT information at the beginning of an EMAIL message that shows when it was written or sent, who wrote or sent it, etc. **3** a shot in SOCCER made by hitting the ball with your head

head·first /ˌhɛdˈfɚst/ *adv.* moving or falling forward with your head going first: *He fell down the stairs headfirst.*

head·gear /ˈhɛdgɪr/ *n.* [U] hats and similar things that you wear on your head

head·hunt·er /ˈhɛdˌhʌntɚ/ *n.* [C] someone who finds people with the right skills and experience to do a particular job

head·ing /ˈhɛdɪŋ/ *n.* [C] the title written at the top of a piece of writing

headland

head·land /ˈhɛdlənd, -lænd/ *n.* [C] EARTH SCIENCES an area of land that sticks out from the coast into the ocean

head·light /ˈhɛdlaɪt/ *n.* [C] one of the large lights at the front of a vehicle: *She* ***flashed*** *her* ***headlights*** (=quickly turned them on and off) *at me.*

head·line /ˈhɛdlaɪn/ *n.* [C] **1** the title of a newspaper article, printed in large letters above the article **2 make (the) headlines** to do something important, shocking, or new, so that newspapers, television shows, etc. talk about you: *The attacks made headlines around the world.*

head·long /ˈhɛdlɔŋ, ˌhɛdˈlɔŋ◂/ *adj. adv.* **1** without thinking carefully: *They* ***rushed headlong into*** *marriage.* **2** falling or moving quickly with your head going first: *He fell headlong from the window.*

head·mas·ter /ˈhɛdˌmæstɚ/, **head·mis·tress** /ˈhɛdˌmɪstrɪs/ *n.* [C] a PRINCIPAL in a private school

ˌhead of ˈstate *n.* (plural **heads of state**) [C] POLITICS the main representative of a country, such as a queen, king, or president

ˌhead-ˈon *adv.* **1 meet/hit/crash etc. head-on** if two vehicles meet or hit head-on, the front part of one vehicle comes toward or hits the front part of the other vehicle **2** if you deal with someone or something head-on, you deal with him, her, or it in a direct and determined way: *She intended to* ***face*** *her difficulties* ***head-on***. —**head-on** *adj.*: *a head-on crash*

head·phones /ˈhɛdfoʊnz/ *n.* [plural] a piece of equipment that you wear over your ears to listen to a radio or recording ➔ EARPHONES

headphones

head·quar·ters /ˈhɛdˌkwɔt̬ɚz/ *n.* [plural] **1** a building or office that is the center of a large organization, or the center of a particular activity: *the corporation's global headquarters in New York* **2** *also* **HQ** the place from which military operations are controlled

head·rest /ˈhɛd-rɛst/ *n.* [C] the top part of a chair or seat that supports the back of your head

head·room /ˈhɛd-rum/ *n.* [U] the amount of space above your head inside a car

ˌHead ˈStart *n.* POLITICS a government program for poor children, that helps prepare them to start school and that gives families advice about health and about other programs that may help them

ˌhead ˈstart *n.* [C] the advantage you gain in a particular activity by starting before other people: *We should* ***give*** *the younger kids* ***a head start*** *in the race.*

head·stone /ˈhɛdstoun/ *n.* [C] a GRAVESTONE

head·strong /ˈhɛdstrɔŋ/ *adj.* very determined to do what you want, even when other people advise you not to do it: *a headstrong child*

ˌhead-to-ˈhead *adj., adv.* directly competing with another person or group: *The new sitcom will* ***go head-to-head with*** *the top-rated show on Thursday nights.* | *head-to-head competition*

head·wa·ters /ˈhɛdˌwɔt̬ɚz/ *n.* [plural] EARTH SCIENCES the place or places where a stream starts, before it flows into a river

head·way /ˈhɛdweɪ/ *n.* **make headway** to make progress toward achieving something even when you have difficulties SYN **make progress**: *They have made little headway in the peace talks.*

head·wind /ˈhɛdˌwɪnd/ *n.* [C] a wind that blows directly toward you when you are moving

head·y /ˈhɛdi/ *adj.* (written) exciting in a way that makes you feel you can do anything: *the heady days of our youth*

heal /hil/ *v.* **1** [I] if a wound or broken bone heals, it becomes healthy again: *The scratch on her finger healed quickly.* **2** [T] to cure someone who is ill, or make a wound get better [ORIGIN: Old English *hælan*]

health /hɛlθ/ *n.* [U] **1** the general condition of your body, and how healthy you are: *You should take better care of your health.* | *a 68-year-old man* ***in good health*** | *serious* ***health problems*** **2** the state of being without illness or disease: *I wish you health and happiness.* **3** how successful an ECONOMY, business, or organization is [ORIGIN: Old English *hælth*, from *hal* "healthy, unhurt, complete"]

health care, health·care /ˈhɛlθkɛr/ *n.* [U] the service of taking care of the health of all the people in a country or area: *the high cost of health care*

ˈhealth club *n.* [C] a place where people go to exercise that you have to pay to use

ˈhealth food *n.* [C,U] food that contains only natural substances

health·ful /ˈhɛlθfəl/ *adj.* (written) likely to make you healthy

health·y /ˈhɛlθi/ *adj.* **1** physically strong and not likely to become sick: *a healthy baby girl* | *Rachel's always been* ***perfectly healthy***.

THESAURUS

well – healthy, used especially when describing how someone feels or looks: *I'm not feeling very well.*
fine (spoken) – healthy, used when someone has asked you how you feel and you are replying that you feel well: *"Hi, Tom, how are you?" "Fine, thanks."*
better – less sick than you were, or no longer sick: *I'm feeling a lot better now.*
in (good) shape – in a good state of health and physically strong: *Jogging keeps me in pretty good shape.*
physically fit – healthy and having a strong body: *Even kids need exercise to be physically fit.*

2 good for your body or your mind: *a* ***healthy diet/lifestyle*** | *It's not* ***healthy for*** *her to depend on him like that.* **3** successful and likely to stay that way: *a* ***healthy economy/business*** **4** (informal) fairly large or noticeable: *She seems to have a* ***healthy appetite***. | *a* ***healthy increase*** *in sales* | *Reed has a* ***healthy respect*** *for rattlesnakes.* **5** showing that you are healthy: *healthy skin* —**healthiness** *n.* [U]

heap¹ /hip/ *n.* [C] **1** a large messy pile of things: *a* ***heap of*** *newspapers* | *His clothes lay* ***in a heap*** *by the bed.*

THESAURUS **pile, mound, stack** → PILE¹

2 (informal) an old car that is in bad condition

heap² *v.* [T] **1** to put a lot of things on top of each other in a messy way: *Magazines were heaped on the table.* **2 be heaped with sth** to have a lot of things on top of something: *He held a plate heaped with food.*

heap·ing /ˈhipɪŋ/ *adj.* a heaping measurement of food is slightly more than the tool it is being measured with can hold: *two heaping teaspoons of sugar*

hear /hɪr/ *v.* (past tense and past participle **heard** /hɚd/) **1** [I,T] to know that a sound is being made, using your ears: *I love to hear the baby laugh like that.* | *Didn't you hear when I called you?*

THESAURUS

If a sound is **drowned out** by something, it prevents you from hearing the sound: *His voice was drowned out by the traffic.*
If someone cannot hear you because s/he is very far away from you, s/he is **out of earshot**: *"What are we going to do if you lose your job?" I asked John, as soon as the children were out of earshot.*
If someone is close enough to hear what you say, s/he is **within earshot**.
If someone says something **under his/her breath**, s/he makes a rude or angry statement very quietly because s/he does not want anyone to hear him/her: *"You rat," he muttered under his breath.*

H

If someone is **inaudible**, s/he speaks so quietly that you cannot hear him/her: *Her reply was inaudible.*
If someone is not able to hear very well because of a physical problem with his/her ears, you can say that s/he is **hard of hearing** or **hearing impaired**: *My grandmother's a little hard of hearing.*
If someone is **deaf**, s/he is not able to hear anything at all.
You **hear** a noise or something that someone says, often without trying to: *Did you hear that noise?* | *I could hear the phone ringing.*
If you **listen to** words, sounds, or music, you pay attention to them: *I enjoy watching movies and listening to music.* | *She listened carefully to his advice.* ➔ SEE

2 [T] to listen to music that is being played, to what someone is saying, etc.: *I heard a great song on the radio.* | *You should at least hear what she has to say.* **3** [I,T] to be told or find out a piece of information: *Have you* ***heard about*** *the new project?* | *"Mark's going to law school."* ***"So I've heard"*** (=said when you already know about something). **4 hear a case** to listen to what is said in a court of law, and make a decision: *The case will be heard on July 16.* **5 (do) you hear (me)?** (spoken) said when you are giving someone an order and want to be certain that s/he will obey you: *Be home by ten, you hear?* [ORIGIN: Old English *hieran*]

hear from sb *phr. v.* to get news or information from someone, usually by letter: *Have you heard from Jane yet?*

hear of sb/sth *phr. v.* **have heard of sb/sth** to know that someone or something exists because you have been told about him, her, or it: *"Do you know a guy named Phil Merton?" "I've never heard of him."*

hear sb **out** *phr. v.* to listen to all of someone's explanation for something, without interrupting: *Look, I know you're mad, but at least hear me out.*

hear·ing /ˈhɪrɪŋ/ *n.* **1** [U] the sense that you use to hear sounds: *My hearing's not as good as it used to be.* **2** [C] a meeting of a court or special committee to find out the facts about a case

ˈhearing aid *n.* [C] a small thing that you put in your ear if you cannot hear well, to make sounds louder

ˈhearing-imˌpaired *adj.* unable to hear well —**the hearing-impaired** *n.* [plural]

hear·say /ˈhɪrseɪ/ *n.* [U] something that you have heard about from other people, but do not know to be true ➔ GOSSIP: *Her opinions are based mainly on rumors and hearsay.*

hearse /hɚs/ *n.* [C] a large car in which a dead body in a CASKET is carried to or from a funeral [ORIGIN: 1200—1300 Old French *herce* "frame for holding candles, farm tool for breaking up soil," from Latin *hirpex*]

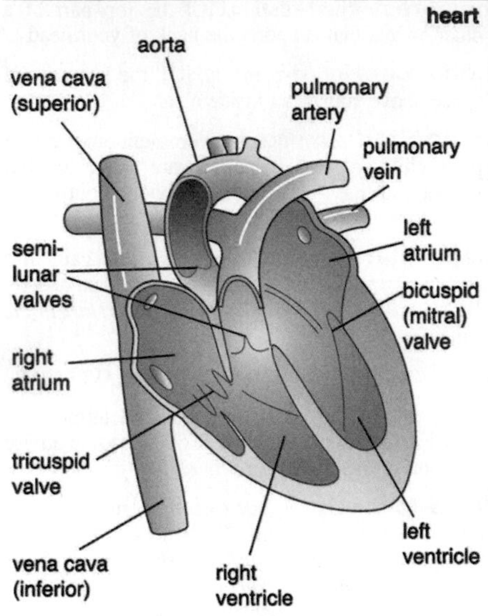

heart /hɑrt/ *n.*
1 BODY [C] BIOLOGY the body part inside a person's or animal's chest that pumps blood through the body: *He could feel his* ***heart beating*** *faster.* | *Dad's had some* ***heart trouble*** *this year.*
2 EMOTIONS [C,U] the part of you that is able to feel strong emotions such as love: *I knew* ***in my heart*** *that I wouldn't see her again.* | *I loved her* ***with all my heart****.*
3 SHAPE [C] a shape used for representing love
4 the heart of sth a) the main or most important part of something: *We talked for hours before we got to* ***the heart of the problem/matter****.* **b)** [singular] the middle or the busiest part of an area: *a big hotel* ***in the heart of*** *the city*
5 a sth at heart if you are a particular type of person at heart, that is the type of person you really are: *Bob can seem tough, but he's really a sweet guy at heart.*
6 know/learn/recite etc. sth by heart to correctly remember or say all of something that you have been taught, without needing to read it
7 GAME [C usually plural] a playing card with one or more red heart shapes on it ➔ *see picture at* PLAYING CARD
8 sb's heart sank used in order to say that someone suddenly became very sad or disappointed: *Nick's heart sank when he heard the news.*
9 do sth to your heart's content to do something as much as you want to: *You can go sailing to your heart's content at the resort.*
10 -hearted having a particular type of character: *a kind-hearted old lady*
11 have a heart of gold to be very generous and kind
12 take/lose heart to begin to have more hope, or to stop having hope [ORIGIN: Old English *heorte*]
➔ **cross my heart (and hope to die)** *at* CROSS[1]

heart·ache /ˈhɑrt̬eɪk/ *n.* [U] a strong feeling of sadness

ˈheart atˌtack *n.* [C] a serious medical condition in which a person's heart suddenly stops working: *Jo's dad **had a heart attack** last year.*

heart·beat /ˈhɑrt˺bit/ *n.* [C usually singular] the action or the sound of a heart pumping blood through the body

heart·break /ˈhɑrt˺breɪk/ *n.* [U] a strong feeling of sadness and disappointment

heart·break·ing /ˈhɑrt˺ˌbreɪkɪŋ/ *adj.* making you feel very upset: *a heartbreaking story*

heart·bro·ken /ˈhɑrt˺ˌbroʊkən/ *adj.* very sad because someone or something has disappointed you

heart·burn /ˈhɑrt˺bɚn/ *n.* [U] a slightly painful burning feeling in your stomach or chest caused by INDIGESTION

ˈheart disˌease *n.* [U] a medical condition in which a person's heart has difficulty pumping blood

heart·ened /ˈhɑrt˺nd/ *adj.* feeling happier and more hopeful (ANT) **disheartened** —**hearten** *v.* [T]

heart·en·ing /ˈhɑrt˺n-ɪŋ/ *adj.* making you feel happier and full of hope (ANT) **disheartening**: *heartening news*

ˈheart ˌfailure *n.* [U] the failure of the heart to continue working, which causes death

heart·felt /ˈhɑrtfɛlt/ *adj.* felt very strongly and sincerely: *heartfelt thanks*

hearth /hɑrθ/ *n.* [C] the part of the floor around a FIREPLACE

heart·i·ly /ˈhɑrt̬l-i/ *adv.* **1** loudly and cheerfully: *He laughed heartily.* **2** very much or completely: *I **heartily agree** with you.*

heart·land /ˈhɑrtlænd/ *n.* **the heartland** the part of a country where most of the food is produced and where people live in a way that represents the basic values of that country

heart·less /ˈhɑrtlɪs/ *adj.* cruel or unkind

heart·rend·ing /ˈhɑrtˌrɛndɪŋ/ *adj.* making you feel great pity: *heartrending sobs*

heart·strings /ˈhɑrtˌstrɪŋz/ *n.* **tug/pull on sb's heartstrings** to make someone feel a lot of pity or love

heart·throb /ˈhɑrtθrɑb/ *n.* [C] (humorous) a famous person whom many young people feel romantic love for: *a picture of the latest teen heartthrob*

ˌheart-to-ˈheart *n.* [C usually singular] a conversation in which two people honestly express their feelings or opinions about something: *I sat down and **had a heart-to-heart with** Emily.* —**heart-to-heart** *adj.*

heart·warm·ing /ˈhɑrt˺ˌwɔrmɪŋ/ *adj.* making you feel happy, calm, and hopeful: *a heartwarming story*

heart·wood /ˈhɑrt˺wʊd/ *n.* [U] BIOLOGY the older harder wood at the center of a tree which provides support but does not carry any SAP

heart·y /ˈhɑrt̬i/ *adj.* **1** very cheerful and friendly: *a hearty laugh* **2** a hearty meal or APPETITE is very large

heat¹ /hit/ *n.* **1** [U] warmth or the quality of being hot: *heat generated by the sun* **2** [U] very hot weather: *I can't work in this heat.* | *The heat has been almost unbearable.* **3** [U] the system in a house that keeps it warm, or the warmth that comes from this system: *Can you **turn the heat on/off**?* | *houses with no heat or electricity* **4 the heat of the moment/argument etc.** the period in a situation, argument, etc. when you feel extremely angry or excited: ***In the heat of the moment**, I said some things I didn't mean.* **5 take the heat** to deal with difficulties in a situation, especially by saying that you are responsible for them: *Coach Brown had to **take the heat for** the team's loss in the press.* **6** [C] one of the parts of a sports competition from which the winners are chosen to go on to the next part **7 in heat** if a female animal is in heat, she is able to become PREGNANT **8** [U] energy that moves from one object to another when there is a difference in temperature between the objects [ORIGIN: Old English *hætu*]

heat² *also* **heat up** *v.* [I,T] to become warm or hot, or to make something warm or hot: *I'll just heat some soup for dinner.* | *The oven heats up pretty quickly.*

heat up *phr. v.* if a situation, argument, etc. heats up, the people involved in it become angrier and more excited

ˈheat caˌpacity *n.* [C] CHEMISTRY the amount of heat needed in order to raise the temperature of one gram of an object or system by one degree CELSIUS

heat·ed /ˈhit̬ɪd/ *adj.* **1** kept warm by a heater: *a heated swimming pool* **2 heated argument/discussion etc.** an argument, etc. in which people become very angry and excited

heat·er /ˈhit̬ɚ/ *n.* [C] a machine used for heating air or water

hea·then /ˈhiðən/ *n.* (plural **heathen**) [C] (old-fashioned, disapproving) someone who does not belong to the Christian religion, or to any of the main world religions —**heathen** *adj.*

ˈheat wave *n.* [C] a period of unusually hot weather

heave¹ /hiv/ *v.* **1** [I,T] to pull, throw, or lift something with a lot of effort: *She heaved the box onto the back of the truck.*

THESAURUS **pull, tug, drag, haul** → PULL¹

2 heave a sigh to breathe out loudly, especially because you have stopped worrying about something: *We all **heaved a sigh of relief** when it was over.* **3** [I] if your chest heaves, it moves up and down quickly because it is difficult to breathe **4** [I] (informal) to VOMIT

H

heave² *n.* [C] a strong pulling, pushing, or throwing movement

heav·en /ˈhɛvən/ *n.* **1** [U] *also* **Heaven** the place where God or the gods are believed to live, and where good people go after they die ➔ HELL **2** [U] (informal) a very good thing, situation, or place: *Give Brad a TV and a comfortable chair, and he's **in heaven**.* **3 (Good) Heavens!** (spoken) said when you are surprised or slightly annoyed: *Good heavens! Where have you been?* **4 for heaven's sake** (spoken) said when you are annoyed or angry: *For heaven's sake, just shut up!* **5 heaven forbid** (spoken) said in order to emphasize that you hope something will not happen: *And if – heaven forbid – he has an accident, what do I do then?* **6 the heavens** (literary) the sky: *Their eyes lifted to the heavens.* [ORIGIN: Old English *heofon*]

heav·en·ly /ˈhɛvənli/ *adj.* **1** relating to heaven **2** very good or pleasing: *a heavenly dessert*

ˌheavenly ˈbody *n.* [C] a star, PLANET, or moon

heav·i·ly /ˈhɛvəli/ *adv.* **1** in very large amounts: *He's been **drinking heavily** recently.* **2** very or very much: ***heavily armed** rebels | The band's sound is **heavily influenced** by early punk rock.* **3** someone who is breathing heavily is breathing very slowly and loudly

H

heav·y /ˈhɛvi/ *adj.*

1 THINGS weighing a lot: *Be careful lifting that box – it's really heavy. | The suitcase feels heavier than before.*

2 PEOPLE used in order to politely describe someone who is fat: *He's gotten very heavy since we saw him last. | Tom's at least twenty pounds heavier than he was last year.*

THESAURUS **fat, overweight, big, large, obese, plump, stout** ➔ FAT¹

3 AMOUNT unusually large in amount or quantity: *Roads were closed due to **heavy rain/snow*** (=a large amount of rain or snow). *| Traffic is heavy on the 405 freeway.*

COLLOCATIONS

heavy losses – used especially in order to say that a company has earned a lot less money than it has spent

heavy casualties/losses – used in order to say that a lot of people have been injured or killed in a war, battle, etc.

4 BUSY very busy and full of activities: *a **heavy day/schedule***

5 heavy sleeper someone who does not wake up very easily

6 a heavy smoker/drinker someone who smokes a lot or drinks a lot of alcohol

7 SERIOUS very complicated or serious and involving a lot of mental effort: *a heavy discussion | For a comedy, that movie was **heavy going**.*

8 heavy breathing breathing that is slow and loud

9 a heavy workload/load/burden a problem or situation that is large or too difficult to deal with: *Three jobs! That's a heavy load for just one person.*

10 with a heavy heart (literary) feeling very sad [ORIGIN: Old English *hefig*] **—heaviness** *n.* [U] ➔ *compare* LIGHT²

ˌheavy-ˈduty *adj.* **1** strong enough to be used often or for hard work without being damaged: *heavy-duty plastic gloves* **2** (informal) said when you want to emphasize how complicated, serious, etc. someone or something is: *The movie deals with some heavy-duty issues.*

ˌheavy-ˈhanded *adj.* strict, unfair, and not considering other people's feelings: *heavy-handed demands*

ˌheavy ˈindustry *n.* [C,U] an industry that produces goods such as coal, steel, or chemicals, or large goods such as cars and machines

ˌheavy ˈmetal *n.* [U] a type of ROCK music with a strong beat that is played very loudly on electric GUITARS

heav·y·weight /ˈhɛviˌweɪt/ *n.* [C] **1** someone who BOXes or WRESTLEs, and is in the heaviest weight group ➔ LIGHTWEIGHT **2** someone who has a lot of power and experience in a particular business or job: *political heavyweights* **—heavyweight** *adj*

He·brew /ˈhibru/ *n.* [U] the official language of Israel, also used in many other places by Jewish people **—Hebrew, Hebraic** /hɪˈbreɪ-ɪk/ *adj.*

heck /hɛk/ *interjection* **1** said in order to emphasize a question, or when you are annoyed: ***Who/what/where etc. the heck** is that? | Ah, heck! I've lost my glasses.* **2 a/one heck of a sth** said in order to emphasize a statement: *That was one heck of a storm! | We had a heck of a time finding a parking space.* **3 what the heck!** said when you do something that you should not do: *"Want another piece of pie?" "Yeah, what the heck!"*

heck·le /ˈhɛkəl/ *v.* [T] to interrupt someone who is speaking or performing in front of a group of people **—heckler** *n.* [C] **—heckling** *n.* [U]

hec·tare /ˈhɛktɛr/ *n.* [C] a unit for measuring an area of land, equal to 10,000 square meters or 2.471 ACRES

hec·tic /ˈhɛktɪk/ *adj.* very busy, hurried, and slightly exciting: *It's been a really hectic week.*

he'd /id; *strong* hid/ **1** the short form of "he would": *Ed said he'd be a little late.* **2** the short form of "he had": *He'd never been a good dancer.*

hedge¹ /hɛdʒ/ *n.* [C] **1** a row of bushes used as a border around a yard or between two yards **2 a hedge against disaster/inflation etc.** something that helps avoid problems, losing a lot of money, etc.: *Putting your money into different stocks is a hedge against financial risk.*

hedge² *v.* **1** [I] to avoid giving a direct answer to a question: *She tried to hedge when Tom asked her age.* **2 hedge your bets** to reduce your chances of failing by trying several different possibilities instead of one: *It is a good idea to hedge your bets by applying to more than one college.*

hedge against sth *phr. v.* to protect yourself from having problems, losing a lot of money, etc.: *You could invest in bonds to hedge against sudden changes in interest rates.*

hed·o·nism /ˈhɛdnˌɪzəm/ *n.* [U] the belief that pleasure is the most important thing in life [ORIGIN: 1800—1900 Greek *hedone* "pleasure"] —**hedonist** *n.* [C] —**hedonistic** /ˌhɛdnˈɪstɪk◂/ *adj.*

heed[1] /hid/ *v.* [T] (formal) to pay attention to someone's advice or warning: *If she had* ***heeded*** *my* ***advice****, none of this would have happened.*

heed[2] *n.* [U] (formal) **take heed of sth/pay heed to sth** to pay attention to something and think about it seriously: *Congress has taken heed of voter dissatisfaction.*

heed·less /ˈhidlɪs/ *adj.* (literary) not paying attention to something important

heel[1] /hil/ *n.* **1** [C] the back part of your foot **2** [C] the back raised part of a shoe, or the back part of a sock that is under your heel: *shoes with* ***high/low heels*** ➔ *see picture at* SHOE[1] **3 heels** [plural] HIGH HEELS **4 -heeled** having a particular type of heel: *a high-heeled shoe* **5 on the heels of sth** very soon after something: *The team's loss* ***came on the heels of*** *another defeat in Dallas.* **6** the raised part of your hand near your wrist: *Use* ***the heel of your hand*** *to knead the bread dough.*

heel[2] *v.* **heel!** used in order to tell your dog to stay near you

heft·y /ˈhɛfti/ *adj.* **1** big, heavy, or strong: *a hefty man* **2 a hefty price/sum etc.** a large amount of money

he·gem·o·ny /hɪˈdʒɛməni, -ˈgɛ-, ˈhɛdʒəˌmoʊni/ *n.* [U] POLITICS a situation in which one state, country, or group has much more power than any other [ORIGIN: 1500—1600 Greek *hegemonia*, from *hegemon* "leader"]

heif·er /ˈhɛfɚ/ *n.* [C] a young female cow that has not yet given birth to a CALF (=baby cow)

height /haɪt/ *n.* **1** [C,U] how tall someone or something is: *Sue is about the same height as her mom.* | *Sunflowers can grow to* ***a height of*** *15 feet.* **2** [C] a particular distance above the ground: *The shelves were installed* ***at*** *the wrong* ***height.*** ➔ *see picture at* DIMENSION **3 the height of sth a)** the time when something is the strongest, most successful, etc. it can ever be: ***At the height of*** *the dotcom boom, web designers were in short supply.* **b)** the greatest degree or amount of something: *The hotel was the height of luxury.* **4 heights** [plural] high places: *I'm* ***afraid of heights.*** **5 to new heights** to an increased or more successful level: *Prices jumped to new heights last Wednesday.* [ORIGIN: Old English *hiehthu*]

height·en /ˈhaɪtˀn/ *v.* [I,T] to increase or make something become increased SYN **increase, intensify**: *Recent events have* ***heightened*** *residents'* ***awareness*** *of crime.*

hei·nous /ˈheɪnəs/ *adj.* extremely bad: *a heinous crime*

heir /ɛr/ *n.* [C] someone who will legally receive all of the money, property, etc. of a person who has died: *the sole* ***heir to*** *a vast fortune*

heir·loom /ˈɛrlum/ *n.* [C] a valuable object that a family owns for many years

heist /haɪst/ *n.* [C] a BURGLARY

he·jab /hɪˈdʒɑb/ *n.* [U] another spelling of HIJAB

held /hɛld/ *v.* the past tense and past participle of HOLD

hel·i·cop·ter /ˈhɛləˌkɑptɚ/ *n.* [C] a type of aircraft with metal blades on top of it that spin very fast [ORIGIN: 1800—1900 French *hélicoptère*, from Greek *heliko-* + *pteron* "wing"] ➔ *see picture at* TRANSPORTATION

he·li·o·cen·tric /ˌhilioʊˈsɛntrɪk/ *adj.* PHYSICS having the Sun at the center: *Copernicus described a heliocentric system, with the planets going around the Sun.*

hel·i·port /ˈhɛləˌpɔrt/ *n.* [C] an airport for helicopters

he·li·um /ˈhiliəm/ *n.* [U] CHEMISTRY (*symbol* **He**) a gas that is an ELEMENT and that is lighter than air, often used in order to make BALLOONS float [ORIGIN: 1800—1900 Greek *helios* "Sun;" because it was discovered in the Sun's spectrum]

he·lix /ˈhilɪks/ *n.* (plural **helices** /-lɪsiz/) [C] MATH a line that curves and rises around a central line SYN **spiral**

he'll /ɪl, il, hɪl; *strong* hil/ the short form of "he will": *I'm sure he'll get here soon.*

hell, Hell /hɛl/ *n.* [singular] the place where bad people will be punished after they die, according to some religions [ORIGIN: Old English]

Hel·le·nis·tic /ˌhɛləˈnɪstɪk◂/ *adj.* HISTORY relating to the ancient Greeks in the period between the fourth and the first century B.C.

hel·lo /həˈloʊ, hɛˈloʊ, ˈhɛloʊ/ *interjection* **1** used when meeting someone or greeting someone: *Hello, my name is Betty.* **2** said when answering the telephone or when starting a telephone conversation: *"Hello?" "Hello, is Chad there?"* **3** said when trying to get someone's attention: *Hello? Is anybody here?* **4 say hello** to have a quick conversation with someone: *I'll drop by later and say hello.*

helm /hɛlm/ *n.* [C] **1 at the helm (of sth)** controlling a group or organization: *With Ms. Mathis at the helm, the company has grown by 20%.* **2** a wheel used for guiding a ship's direction

hel·met /ˈhɛlmɪt/ *n.* [C] a hard hat that covers and protects your head: *a motorcycle helmet*

help[1] /hɛlp/ *v.* **1** [I,T] if you help people, you do something for them that makes it easier for them to do something: *Do you want me to help you move that table?* | *Mom, can you* ***help*** *me* ***with*** *my homework?* | *Is there anything I can do to help?*

THESAURUS

give sb a hand (with sth) – to help someone do something: *Can you give me a hand moving these boxes?*
need a hand – to need help doing something: *I need a hand to paint the house.*
lend a hand (with sth) – to help someone, especially when there are not enough people to do something: *I went over to see if I could lend a hand.*
assist/aid (formal) – to help someone, especially when you use special skills: *Dr. Taylor assisted in the research for this article.*
facilitate (formal) – to make it easier for something to happen: *Computers can be used to facilitate language learning.*
aid and abet (Law) – to help someone do something illegal: *He was accused of aiding and abetting the rioters.*

2 [I,T] to make it possible for something to become better, easier, or more developed: *It might* ***help to*** *talk to someone about your problems.* | *Brushing your teeth helps prevent cavities.*

SPOKEN PHRASES
3 can't/couldn't help said when you are unable to stop doing something: *I just couldn't help laughing.* **4 I can't help it** said when you think something is not your fault: *I can't help it if she lost the stupid book!* **5 help yourself** used when telling someone to take as much food or drink as s/he wants: ***Help yourself to*** *anything in the fridge.* **6 help!** said when you need someone to help you, especially because you are in danger

help (sb ↔) **out** *phr. v.* to help someone because s/he is very busy, has a lot of problems, etc.: *They did everything they could to help us out.* | *Do you need anyone to help out in the store?* [ORIGIN: Old English *helpan*]

help² *n.* **1** [U] the action of helping someone: *Do you* ***need*** *any* ***help*** *washing the dishes?* | *They* ***gave*** *us some* ***help*** *filling out the forms.* | *Dave built the garage* ***with the help of*** *his brother.* **2** [singular, U] someone or something that is useful or helpful: *The instructions* ***weren't much help***. | *Thanks a lot – you've been* ***a big help***. **3** [U] advice, treatment, money, etc. given in order to help someone: *She needs professional help from a psychiatrist.*

help·er /ˈhɛlpɚ/ *n.* [C] someone who helps another person

help·ful /ˈhɛlpfəl/ *adj.* **1** providing useful help in making a situation better or easier (ANT) **unhelpful**: *helpful advice* | *an extremely helpful guidebook* **2** willing to help: *Everyone was so helpful and friendly.* —**helpfully** *adv.*

help·ing¹ /ˈhɛlpɪŋ/ *n.* [C] the amount of food you are given or that you take: *Teri ate two* ***helpings of*** *pie.*

helping² *adj.* **lend/give a helping hand** to help someone

ˈhelping ˌverb *n.* [C] ENG. LANG. ARTS an AUXILIARY VERB

help·less /ˈhɛlplɪs/ *adj.* unable to take care of yourself or protect yourself: *The man lay helpless in the street.* —**helplessness** *n.* [U] —**helplessly** *adv.*

hel·ter-skel·ter /ˌhɛltɚˈskɛltɚ/ *adj., adv.* done in a disorganized, confusing, and hurried way

hem¹ /hɛm/ *n.* [C] the folded and sewn edge of a piece of clothing → EDGE¹

hem² *v.* (**hemmed**, **hemming**) [T] to fold and sew the edge of a piece of clothing

hem sb ↔ **in** *phr.v.* **1** to surround someone or something closely: *The valley is hemmed in by mountain ranges on both sides.* **2** to make someone feel that s/he is not free to do what s/he wants: *She felt hemmed in by her tight schedule.*

hem·i·sphere /ˈhɛməˌsfɪr/ *n.* [C] **1** EARTH SCIENCES one of the halves of the Earth, especially the northern or southern parts above and below the EQUATOR: *the* ***northern hemisphere*** (=the half of the Earth that is north of the equator) | *the* ***southern hemisphere*** (=the half of the Earth that is south of the equator) → *see picture at* GLOBE **2** BIOLOGY one of the two halves of your brain: *The right hemisphere of your brain controls the left side of your body.*

hem·line /ˈhɛmlaɪn/ *n.* [C] the bottom edge or length of a dress, skirt, or pair of pants

hem·lock /ˈhɛmlɑk/ *n.* [C,U] a very poisonous plant, or the poison of this plant

he·mo·glo·bin /ˈhiməˌgloʊbɪn/ *n.* [U] BIOLOGY a red substance in the blood that carries oxygen and iron [ORIGIN: 1800—1900 *hematoglobulin*, from Greek *haima* "blood"]

he·mo·phil·i·a /ˌhiməˈfɪliə, -ˈfilyə/ *n.* [U] BIOLOGY a serious disease that usually affects only men, in which the blood does not become thick, so that they lose too much blood after being cut or wounded [ORIGIN: 1800—1900 Modern Latin *hemo-* from Greek *haima* "blood" + *-philia* "fondness"] —**hemophiliac** /ˌhiməˈfɪliˌæk/ *n.* [C]

hem·or·rhage /ˈhɛmərɪdʒ/ *n.* [C] a serious medical condition in which an area in someone's body loses too much blood [ORIGIN: 1400—1500 French *hémorrhagie*, from Latin *haemorrhagia*, from Greek, from *haima* "blood" + "bursting out, flow"]

hem·or·rhoids /ˈhɛməˌrɔɪdz/ *n.* [plural] painfully swollen BLOOD VESSELS at the ANUS

hemp /hɛmp/ *n.* [U] a plant used for making a strong type of rope, and also for making the drug MARIJUANA

hen /hɛn/ *n.* [C] a fully grown female bird, especially a female chicken

hence /hɛns/ (Ac) *adv.* (formal) for this reason

→ THUS: *The sugar from the grapes remains in the wine, hence the sweet taste.* [ORIGIN: 1200—1300 *hen* "hence" (12—15 centuries) (from Old English *heonan*) + *-s* (as in backwards)]

hence·forth /ˈhɛnsfɔrθ, ˌhɛnsˈfɔrθ/ *adv.* (formal) from this time on: *Henceforth in this book, these people will be called "The Islanders."*

hench·man /ˈhɛntʃmən/ *n.* [C] someone who faithfully obeys a powerful person such as a politician or a criminal

hen·na /ˈhɛnə/ *n.* [U] a reddish-brown substance used to change the color of your hair or to DYE the skin —**henna** *v.* [T]

Hen·ry's law /ˈhɛnriz ˌlɔ/ *n.* CHEMISTRY a scientific principle that says the amount of gas that can be ABSORBed by a liquid will increase if the pressure of the gas above the liquid increases and the temperature remains the same

he·pat·ic /hɪˈpæt̬ɪk/ *adj.* [only before noun] BIOLOGY relating to your LIVER

hep·a·ti·tis /ˌhɛpəˈtaɪt̬ɪs/ *n.* [U] BIOLOGY a serious disease of the LIVER

hep·ta·gon /ˈhɛptəˌgɑn/ *n.* [C] MATH a flat shape with seven sides and seven angles —**heptagonal** /hɛpˈtægənəl/ *adj.*

THESAURUS **polygon, pentagon, hexagon, octagon, decagon, dodecagon** → POLYGON

hep·tath·lon /hɛpˈtæθlən, -lɑn/ *n.* [singular] a women's sports competition consisting of seven running, jumping, and throwing events → DECATHLON, PENTATHLON

her[1] /ɚ; *strong* hɚ/ *possessive adj.* **1** belonging to or relating to a female person or animal that has been mentioned or is known about: *Lori said her cat died last week.* | *Have you seen her new house?* **2** used when talking about a country, car, ship, etc. that has been mentioned: *Her top speed is 110 miles per hour.* [ORIGIN: Old English *hiere*]

her[2] *pron.* **1** the object form of "she": *I gave her $20.* | *Did you see her at the concert?* **2** a country, ship, car, etc. that has been mentioned

her·ald /ˈhɛrəld/ *v.* [T] **1** to say publicly that someone or something is likely to be successful: *He was* ***heralded as*** *the poet of his generation.* **2** to be a sign that something is going to come or happen soon: *The Internet heralded a new age of communications.*

herb /ɚb/ *n.* [C] a plant used in cooking to give food more taste, or to make medicine: *herbs and spices* [ORIGIN: 1200 — 1300 Old French *erbe*, from Latin *herba* "grass, herb"]

herb·al /ˈɚbəl/ *adj.* relating to herbs: *herbal tea*

herb·i·cide /ˈhɚbəˌsaɪd, ˈɚbə-/ *n.* [C, U] BIOLOGY a substance used to kill unwanted plants

herb·i·vore /ˈhɚbəˌvɔr, ˈɚbə-/ *n.* [C] BIOLOGY an animal that only eats plants [ORIGIN: 1800—1900 Latin *herbivorus* "plant-eating," from *herba* "grass, herb" + *-vorus*, from *vorare* "to eat"] → *compare* CARNIVORE

herd

a herd of deer

herd[1] /hɚd/ *n.* [C] a group of a particular type of animal that lives together: *a* ***herd of*** *cattle*

herd[2] *v.* [I,T] to form a group, or to make people or animals move together as a group: *The tour guide herded us onto the bus.*

here[1] /hɪr/ *adv.* **1** in or to this place (ANT) **there**: *I'm going to stay here with Kim.* | *How long have you lived here?* | *Chad said he's never been here before.* | *It's so dark* ***in/out here.*** | *Come* ***over here*** *so I can talk to you.* **2** if a period of time is here, it has begun: *Spring is here!* **3 here and there** scattered in several different places: *There were a few magazines lying around here and there.* **4** at this point in a discussion or piece of writing: *We might as well take a break here.* [ORIGIN: Old English *her*]

here[2] *interjection* said when you offer something to someone: *Here, use my pen.*

here·a·bouts /ˈhɪrəˌbaʊts, ˌhɪrəˈbaʊts/ *adv.* around or near the place where you are: *Everyone hereabouts thinks he's guilty.*

here·af·ter[1] /ˌhɪrˈæftɚ/ *adv.* (formal) from this time or in the future

hereafter[2] *n.* **the hereafter** life after you die: *Do you believe in the hereafter?*

here·by /ˌhɪrˈbaɪ, ˈhɪrbaɪ/ *adv.* (formal) as a result of this statement: *I hereby pronounce you man and wife.*

he·red·i·tar·y /həˈrɛdəˌtɛri/ *adj.* if a mental or physical quality, or a disease is hereditary, it is passed to a child from the GENEs of his/her parents: *a hereditary condition*

he·red·i·ty /həˈrɛdət̬i/ *n.* [U] BIOLOGY the process of passing on a mental or physical quality from a parent to a child through the GENES [ORIGIN: 1500 — 1600 French *hérédité*, from Latin *hereditas*]

here·in /ˌhɪrˈɪn/ *adv.* (formal) in this place, situation, or piece of writing

her·e·sy /ˈhɛrəsi/ *n.* (plural **heresies**) [C,U] **1** beliefs or behavior that are considered to be wrong by a particular political or social group **2** a belief or action that is so strongly

H

against the normal beliefs of a particular religion that it is considered to be evil

her·e·tic /'hɛrətɪk/ *n.* [C] someone whose beliefs are considered to be evil by a particular religion —**heretical** /hə'rɛtɪkəl/ *adj.*

here·with /ˌhɪr'wɪθ, -'wɪð/ *adv.* (formal) with this letter or document

he·ri·ta·ble /'hɛrətəbəl/ *adj.* **1** BIOLOGY a physical or mental feature that is heritable can be passed from a parent to his or her children: *a heritable cancer gene* **2** [usually before noun] LAW heritable property, land, etc. is property or land that you can legally give to someone when you die → INHERIT

her·it·age /'hɛrətɪdʒ/ *n.* [singular, U] the traditions, values, arts, etc. that are passed down over many years within a country, society, or family: *the immense variety of America's musical heritage*

her·ma·phro·dite /hɚ'mæfrəˌdaɪt/ *n.* [C] BIOLOGY a living thing that has both male and female sexual organs [ORIGIN: 1400 — 1500 Latin *hermaphroditus*, from Greek *Hermaphroditos*] —**hermaphrodite** *adj.* —**hermaphroditic** /hɚˌmæfrəˌdɪtɪk/ *adj.*

her·met·i·cal·ly /hɚ'mɛtɪkli/ *adv.* **hermetically sealed** very tightly closed so that no air can get in or out —**hermetic** *adj.*

her·mit /'hɚmɪt/ *n.* [C] someone who prefers to live far away from other people → RECLUSE [ORIGIN: 1100 — 1200 Old French *eremite*, from Greek *eremites* "living in the desert" from *eremos* "lonely"]

her·mit·age /'hɚmɪtɪdʒ/ *n.* [C] a place where a hermit lives or has lived

'hermit crab *n.* [C] a type of CRAB that lives in the empty shells of other sea creatures

her·ni·a /'hɚniə/ *n.* [C,U] BIOLOGY a medical condition in which an organ pushes through the skin or muscle that covers it

he·ro /'hɪroʊ/ *n.* [C] (plural **heroes**) **1** someone who is admired for doing something very brave or good: *one of America's **national heroes** | It was a chance to meet my hero in person.* **2** ENG. LANG. ARTS a man or boy who is the main character of a book, play, or movie → HEROINE: *The **hero of** the story is a young soldier.*

THESAURUS

main character – the most important person in a story, play, or movie, especially the person the story is about: *The main character is an eleven-year-old boy who finds out that he is a wizard.*
protagonist (formal) – the main character in a play, movie, or story: *The protagonist is based on the author's grandfather.*
anti-hero – the main character in a story, play, or movie who is an ordinary or unpleasant person and does not have the qualities that most people think a hero should have, such as being good or brave: *Hoffman plays Benjamin, the movie's anti-hero, who rebels against his parents' values more out of boredom than for any moral reasons.*
villain – the main bad character in a story, play, or movie: *Comic book villains such as Lex Luthor or The Joker are written as wholly evil characters.*

3 *also* **hero sandwich** a SANDWICH made of a long LOAF of bread filled with meat, cheese, etc. SYN **sub** [ORIGIN: 1500—1600 Latin *heros*, from Greek]

he·ro·ic /hɪ'roʊɪk/ *adj.* **1** admired for being brave, strong, and determined: *the firefighters' **heroic efforts** to rescue people from the fire*

THESAURUS **brave, courageous, valiant** → BRAVE[1]

2 a heroic story, poem, etc. has a hero in it

he·ro·ics /hɪ'roʊɪks/ *n.* [plural] brave actions or words that are meant to seem impressive to other people

her·o·in /'hɛroʊɪn/ *n.* [U] a strong illegal drug that some people take, usually by putting it into their arms with a special needle

her·o·ine /'hɛroʊɪn/ *n.* [C] a female hero

her·o·ism /'hɛroʊˌɪzəm/ *n.* [U] very great courage: *the soldiers' heroism in battle*

her·on /'hɛrən/ *n.* [C] a large wild bird with very long legs and a long beak that lives near water

her·pes /'hɚpiz/ *n.* [U] a very infectious disease that causes spots on the skin, especially on the face or sexual organs

her·ring /'hɛrɪŋ/ *n.* [C,U] (plural **herring** *or* **herrings**) a long thin silver sea fish, or the meat from this fish

hers /hɚz/ *pron.* the thing or things belonging to or relating to a female person or animal that has been mentioned or is known about: *That's my car. This is hers. | Tim is a friend of hers. | My boots are black. Hers are brown.*

her·self /ɚ'sɛlf; *strong* hɚ'sɛlf/ *pron.* **1** the REFLEXIVE form of "she": *Carol hurt herself. | She bought herself a new scarf.* **2** the strong form of "she," used in order to emphasize the subject or object of a sentence: *She installed the cabinets herself. | It's true! Vicky told me herself.* **3 (all) by herself a)** without help: *My daughter made dinner all by herself.* **b)** alone: *She went for a walk by herself.* **4 (all) to herself** for her own use: *Alison had the whole house to herself that night.* **5 not be herself** (spoken) if someone is not herself, she is not behaving or feeling the way she usually does because she is sick or upset: *Mom hasn't been herself lately.*

hertz /hɚts/ *n.* (plural **hertz**) [C] PHYSICS (*written abbreviation* **Hz**) a unit used to measure FREQUENCY. One hertz is one CYCLE each second. [ORIGIN: 1800 — 1900 Heinrich *Hertz* (1857-94), German scientist who worked on energy waves]

he's /iz; *strong* hiz/ **1** the short form of "he is": *He's a lawyer.* **2** the short form of "he has," used when "has" is an AUXILIARY VERB: *He's been in prison.*

hes·i·tant /ˈhɛzət̬ənt/ *adj.* not willing to do or say something because you are uncertain or worried: *He was **hesitant to** discuss the details.*

hes·i·tate /ˈhɛzəˌteɪt/ *v.* [I] **1** to pause before doing or saying something because you are uncertain: *She hesitated before answering his question.* **2 do not hesitate to do sth** (formal) used in order to tell someone not to worry about doing something: *Don't hesitate to call me if you need any help.* [ORIGIN: 1600 — 1700 Latin, past participle of *haesitare* "to stick firmly, hesitate," from *haerere* "to stick"]

hes·i·ta·tion /ˌhɛzəˈteɪʃən/ *n.* [U] the action of hesitating: ***Without hesitation** he said, "Yes!"*

het·er·o·ge·ne·ous /ˌhɛt̬ərəˈdʒiniəs, -nyəs/, **het·er·og·e·nous** /ˌhɛt̬əˈrɑdʒənəs/ *adj.* (formal) consisting of parts or members that are very different from each other ➔ HOMOGENEOUS: *a heterogeneous population* [ORIGIN: 1600—1700 Medieval Latin *heterogeneus*, from Greek, from *heteros* "other" + *genos* "type"] —**heterogeneity** /ˌhɛt̬əroʊdʒəˈniət̬i/ *n.* [U]

hetero,geneous 'mixture *n.* [C] CHEMISTRY a substance consisting of two or more different substances that remain physically separate, so that all parts of the mixture look different

het·er·o·sex·u·al /ˌhɛt̬ərəˈsɛkʃuəl/ *adj.* (formal) sexually attracted to people of the opposite sex (SYN) **straight** ➔ BISEXUAL, HOMOSEXUAL —**heterosexuality** /ˌhɛt̬ərəˌsɛkʃuˈæləti/ *n.* [U]

het·e·ro·troph /ˈhet̬ərəˌtrɑf, -ˌtroʊf/ *n.* [C] BIOLOGY a living creature that obtains the energy it needs in order to live, grow, and stay healthy from the foods it eats, rather than by PHOTOSYNTHESIS

he·te·ro·zy·gote /ˌhɛt̬əroʊˈzaɪgoʊt/ *n* [C] BIOLOGY a plant, animal, etc. that has two different GENES in a particular place on a pair of CHROMOSOMES that have the same series of genes ➔ HOMOZYGOTE

het·e·ro·zy·gous /ˌhɛt̬ərəˈzaɪgəs/ *adj.* BIOLOGY relating to a cell or ORGANISM that has two or more different forms of a particular GENE

heu·ris·tic /hyʊˈrɪstɪk/ *adj.* **1** heuristic education is based on discovering and experiencing things for yourself **2** helping you in the process of learning or discovery —**heuristically** *adv.*

heu·ris·tics /hjʊˈrɪstɪks/ *n.* [U] the study of how people use their experience to find answers to questions or to improve performance

hew /hyu/ *v.* (past participle **hewed** *or* **hewn** /hyun/) [T] (literary) to cut something with a cutting tool

hex·a·dec·i·mal /ˌhɛksəˈdɛsəməl/ *also* **hex** /heks/ *adj.* MATH hexadecimal numbers are based on the number 16 and are mainly used on computers

hex·a·gon /ˈhɛksəˌgɑn/ *n.* [C] MATH a flat shape with six sides and six angles [ORIGIN: 1500—1600 Latin, from Greek *hexagonon*, from *hex* "six" + *gonia* "angle"] ➔ *see picture at* POLYGON —**hexagonal** /hɛkˈsægənəl/ *adj.*

THESAURUS **polygon, pentagon, heptagon, octagon, decagon, dodecagon** ➔ POLYGON

hex·a·gram /ˈhɛksəˌgræm/ *n.* [C] MATH a star shape with six points, made from two TRIANGLES

hex·am·e·ter /hɛkˈsæmət̬ɚ/ *n.* [C] ENG. LANG. ARTS a line of poetry with six main beats

hey /heɪ/ *interjection* (informal) **1** said in order to get someone's attention, or to show someone you are surprised or annoyed: *Hey, you! Get away from my car!* **2** said in order to greet someone who you know well (SYN) **hi**: *Hey, Rob. How's it going?*

hey·day /ˈheɪdeɪ/ *n.* [C] the time when someone or something was most popular, successful, or powerful: *the **heyday of** silent movies* [ORIGIN: 1500 — 1600 *heyda* a shout of happiness (16 — 17 centuries), influenced by day]

HI the written abbreviation of HAWAII

hi /haɪ/ *interjection* (informal) hello: *Hi! How are you?*

hi·a·tus /haɪˈeɪt̬əs/ *n.* [C usually singular] (formal) a pause in an activity [ORIGIN: 1500 — 1600 Latin *hiare* "to yawn"]

hi·ber·nate /ˈhaɪbɚˌneɪt/ *v.* [I] if an animal hibernates, it sleeps all the time during the winter [ORIGIN: 1800—1900 Latin, past participle of *hibernare* "to pass the winter," from *hibernus* "of the winter"] —**hibernation** /ˌhaɪbɚˈneɪʃən/ *n.* [U]

hic·cup[1] /ˈhɪkʌp/ *n.* [C] **1** [usually plural] a sudden repeated stopping of the breath, usually caused by eating or drinking too fast: *I **have the hiccups**.* **2** a small problem or delay: *There's a slight **hiccup in** the schedule for today.*

hiccup[2] *v.* (**hiccupped**, **hiccupping**) [I] to have the hiccups

hick /hɪk/ *n.* [C] (disapproving) someone who lives in the country and is thought to be uneducated or stupid

hick·ey /ˈhɪki/ *n.* (plural **hickeys**) [C] (informal) a slight BRUISE (=dark mark on your skin) from being kissed too hard

hick·o·ry /ˈhɪkəri/ *n.* [U] a North American tree that produces nuts, or the hard wood from this tree [ORIGIN: 1600 — 1700 Algonquian *pawcohiccora* "food made from crushed nuts"]

hid /hɪd/ *v.* the past tense of HIDE

hid·den[1] /ˈhɪdn/ *v.* the past participle of HIDE

H

hidden² *adj.* **1** difficult to see or find: *Marcia* ***kept*** *her letters* ***hidden in*** *a box.* **2** not easy to notice or discover: *a hidden meaning*

hide¹ /haɪd/ *v.* (past tense **hid** /hɪd/, past participle **hidden** /ˈhɪdn/) **1** [T] to put something in a place where no one else can see or find it: *Jane* ***hid*** *the Christmas presents* ***in*** *the closet.*

hide

THESAURUS

conceal (formal) – to hide something carefully: *She dyes her hair to conceal the gray.*
cover/cover up – to put something over something else in order to hide it: *He covered his face with his hands.*
disguise/mask – to hide a smell or taste, your feelings, or the truth: *The scented candles masked the cooking smells from the kitchen.*
secrete (formal) – to hide something: *The money had been secreted somewhere within the house.*

2 [I] to go to or stay in a place where no one can see or find you: *I'll* ***hide behind/under*** *the bed.* **3** [T] to not show your feelings to people, or to not tell someone about something: *She could not hide her embarrassment.* **4** [T] to not tell someone about something: *The police knew Wilson was hiding something.* [ORIGIN: Old English *hydan*]

hide² *n.* [C] an animal's skin, especially when it is removed to be used for leather

ˌhide-and-ˈseek *n.* [U] a children's game in which one child shuts his/her eyes while the other children hide, and then s/he tries to find them

hide·a·way /ˈhaɪdəˌweɪ/ *n.* (plural **hideaways**) [C] a place where you can go to hide or be alone

hid·e·ous /ˈhɪdiəs/ *adj.* extremely ugly or disgusting: *a hideous monster* [ORIGIN: 1300—1400 Old French *hidous*, from *hide* "terror"] —**hideously** *adv.*

THESAURUS **ugly, unattractive, unsightly, repulsive, grotesque** ➔ UGLY

hide·out /ˈhaɪdaʊt/ *n.* [C] a place where you can hide

hid·ing /ˈhaɪdɪŋ/ *n.* **go into hiding** to stay somewhere in secret, often because you have done something illegal or you are in danger

hi·er·ar·chy /ˈhaɪəˌrɑrki/ (Ac) *n.* (plural **hierarchies**) **1** [C,U] SOCIAL SCIENCE a system of organization in which people have higher and lower ranks **2** [C] the most powerful members of an organization **3** [C] BIOLOGY the system in which animals are organized so that some are more important than others, which affects the way they behave [ORIGIN: 1300—1400 Old French *ierarchie*, from Latin, from Greek *hierarches*, from *hieros* "holy" + *-arches* "ruler"] —**hierarchical** /haɪəˈrɑrkɪkəl/ *adj.*

hier·o·glyph /ˈhaɪrəˌglɪf/ *n.* [C] HISTORY a sign or picture used in a writing system, for example by the ancient Egyptians

hier·o·glyph·ics /ˌhaɪrəˈglɪfɪks/ *n.* [U] ENG. LANG. ARTS a system of writing, especially one from ancient Egypt, that uses pictures to represent words [ORIGIN: 1500—1600 French *hiéroglyphique*, from Late Latin, from Greek, from *hieros* "holy" + *glyphein* "to cut marks in a surface"] —**hieroglyphic** *adj.*

hi-fi /ˌhaɪ ˈfaɪ/ *n.* [C] (old-fashioned) a piece of electronic equipment for playing recorded music

high¹ /haɪ/ *adj.*

1 TALL something that is high measures a long distance from its top to its bottom (ANT) **low** ➔ TALL: *the highest mountain in Colorado* | *a high wall*

2 ABOVE GROUND being a long way above the ground (ANT) **low**: *The nest was on a high branch.*

3 MORE THAN USUAL a high amount, number, or level is greater than usual (ANT) **low**: *clothes selling at* ***high prices*** | *high speed* | *a higher level of productivity* ➔ EXPENSIVE

4 RANK/POSITION having an important or powerful position or rank: *She was elected to* ***high office***. | *the highest levels of management*

5 GOOD very good (ANT) **low**: *Most items were of very* ***high quality***. | *We insist on* ***high standards***.

6 DRUGS under the effects of drugs: *He was* ***high on*** *drugs.* | *kids* ***getting high*** *on marijuana*

7 CONTAINING A LOT containing a lot of a particular substance or quality (ANT) **low**: *Candy bars are* ***high in*** *calories.*

8 SOUND/VOICE near the top of the range of sounds that humans can hear (ANT) **low**: *singing the high notes*

THESAURUS

high-pitched – higher than most sounds or voices: *a high-pitched voice*
piercing – very high and loud in a way that is not nice to listen to: *a piercing scream*
shrill – high and unpleasant: *a shrill whistle*
squeaky – making very high noises that are not loud: *squeaky floorboards*

9 knee-high/waist-high etc. having a particular height: *The grass was knee-high.*

10 high noon (old-fashioned) exactly 12 O'CLOCK in the day [ORIGIN: Old English *heah*]

high² *adv.* **1** at or to a level that is far above the ground: *kites flying* ***high in*** *the sky* | *She held her award high above her head.* **2** at or to a high value, amount, rank, etc.: *Jenkins has risen high in the company.* | *Ribas advised the students to "****aim high****"* (=try to be successful). **3 look/search high and low** to look everywhere for someone or something: *I searched high and low for the car* *keys.* **4 be left high and dry** (informal) to be left without any help in a difficult situation

high³ *n.* [C] **1** the highest level, number, temperature, etc. that has been recorded in a particular time period: *The price of gold* ***reached a new high*** *yesterday.* | *a high* (=high temperature) *in the mid 90s* **2** (informal) a feeling of great excitement caused by drugs or success, enjoyment, etc.

'high-born *adj.* (formal) born into the highest social class

high·brow /'haɪbraʊ/ *adj.* a highbrow book, movie, etc. is very serious and may be difficult to understand (ANT) **lowbrow**

high·chair /'haɪtʃɛr/ *n.* [C] a tall chair that a baby sits in to eat

ˌhigh-'class *adj.* of good quality and style, and usually expensive: *a high-class restaurant*

ˌhigh-defi'nition (*abbreviation* **HD**) *adj.* [only before noun] a high-definition television or computer MONITOR shows images very clearly

ˌhigher edu'cation *n.* [U] education at a college or university

ˌhighest ˌcommon 'factor *n.* [C] MATH the largest number that a set of numbers can all be divided by exactly: *The highest common factor of 12, 24, and 30 is 6.*

ˌhigh ex'plosive *n.* [C,U] a substance that explodes with great power and violence

high-ˌfrequency 'word *n.* [C] ENG. LANG. ARTS a word that is used much more often than most words in speaking or writing: *high-frequency words such as "the" and "and"*

ˌhigh-'grade *adj.* of high quality: *high-grade motor oil*

ˌhigh 'heels *n.* [plural] women's shoes with a high raised heel at the back —**high-heeled** *adj.* ➔ *see picture at* SHOE¹

'high jinks *n.* [U] (old-fashioned) noisy or excited behavior when people are having fun

'high jump *n.* **the high jump** a sport in which you run and jump over a BAR that is raised higher after each successful jump —**high jumper** *n.* [C]

high·lands /'haɪləndz/ *n.* [plural] EARTH SCIENCES an area with a lot of mountains ➔ LOWLANDS: *the Scottish highlands* —**highland** *adj* [only before noun] —**highlander** *n* [C]

ˌhigh-'level *adj.* involving important people, especially in the government: *high-level peace talks*

high·light¹ /'haɪlaɪt/ (Ac) *v.* [T] **1** to make a problem, subject, etc. easy to notice so people will pay attention to it: *The report highlights the problem of inner-city crime.*

THESAURUS **emphasize, stress, underline, underscore** ➔ EMPHASIZE

2 to mark written words with a pen or on a computer so that you can see them more easily

highlight² *n.* [C] the most important or exciting part of a movie, sports event, etc.: *the* ***highlights of*** *our trip*

high·light·er /'haɪˌlaɪt̬ɚ/ *n.* [C] a special pen that you use to mark written words so that you can see them more easily

high·ly /'haɪli/ *adv.* **1** very: *a* ***highly successful*** *meeting* | ***highly skilled*** *workers* **2** to a high level or degree: *a highly paid attorney*

ˌhigh-'minded *adj.* having high moral standards or principles

High·ness /'haɪnɪs/ *n.* **Your/His etc. Highness** a royal title used when speaking to a king, queen, etc.

ˌhigh-'pitched *adj.* a high-pitched song or voice is higher than most sounds or voices

ˌhigh-'powered *adj.* **1** very powerful: *a high-powered speedboat* **2** very important or successful: *a high-powered businessman*

ˌhigh 'pressure *n.* [C usually singular] EARTH SCIENCES an area of high air pressure in the sky, which usually brings warm weather

'high-pressure *adj.* **1** a high-pressure job or situation is one in which you need to work very hard to be successful **2** having or using a lot of pressure: *a high-pressure hose*

ˌhigh-'profile *adj.* attracting a lot of attention from people: *a high-profile court case*

'high-rise, high·rise /'haɪraɪz/ *n.* [C] a tall building —**high-rise** *adj.*: *high-rise apartment buildings*

ˌhigh 'roller *n.* [C] (informal) someone who spends a lot of money, especially by BETting on games, races, etc.

'high school *n.* [C,U] a school in the U.S. and Canada for students aged 14 and over: *Most* ***high school students*** *take three years of math.* | *Wendy and I were best friends* ***in high school.***

'high-speed *adj.* [only before noun] designed to travel or operate very fast: *a high-speed train*

ˌhigh-'spirited *adj.* having a lot of energy and liking to have fun: *a high-spirited four-year-old boy*

ˌhigh-'strung *adj.* nervous, and easily upset or excited: *a high-strung horse*

high-tech, hi-tech /ˌhaɪ 'tɛk◂/ *adj.* using the most modern information, machines, etc.: *a new high-tech camera*

THESAURUS **advanced, state-of-the-art, cutting-edge** ➔ ADVANCED

ˌhigh 'tide *n.* [C,U] EARTH SCIENCES the time when the ocean is at its highest level (ANT) **low tide** ➔ *see picture at* TIDE¹

'high-tops, high·tops /'haɪtɑps/ *n.* [plural] sports shoes that cover your ANKLEs

high·way /'haɪweɪ/ *n.* (plural **highways**) [C] a wide fast road that connects cities or towns: *There's always a lot of traffic* ***on that highway.***

H

THESAURUS freeway, expressway, toll road, turnpike → ROAD

hi·jab, hejab /hɪˈdʒɑb/ *n.* **1** [C] a SCARF worn by Muslim women that completely covers the head and sometimes includes a VEIL (=a thin piece of material) that covers the face except for the eyes **2** [U] SOCIAL SCIENCE the custom for some Muslim women to wear clothes that cover most of their body

hi·jack /ˈhaɪdʒæk/ *v.* [T] **1** to take control of an airplane, vehicle, etc. illegally: *The plane was hijacked by terrorists.* **2** to take control of something and use it for your own purposes: *The protesters tried to hijack the meeting.* —**hijacker** *n.* [C] —**hijacking** *n.* [C,U]

hike[1] /haɪk/ *n.* [C] **1** a long walk in the country, mountains, etc.: *We* ***went for a hike*** *on Sunday.* **2** (informal) a large increase in something: *a huge* ***tax hike*** **3 take a hike** (spoken) a rude way of telling someone to go away

hike[2] *v.* **1** [I,T] to take a long walk in the country, mountains, etc.

THESAURUS walk, march, stroll, trudge → WALK[1]

2 [T] *also* **hike up** to increase the price of something by a large amount SYN **raise**: *The governor plans to hike gasoline tax next month.*

H

hik·ing /ˈhaɪkɪŋ/ *n.* [U] an outdoor activity in which you take long walks in the country or mountains: *We could* ***go hiking*** *tomorrow.*

hi·lar·i·ous /hɪˈlɛriəs, -ˈlær-/ *adj.* extremely funny: *a hilarious video* [ORIGIN: 1800 — 1900 Latin *hilarus* "cheerful," from Greek *hilaros*] —**hilariously** *adv.* —**hilarity** /hɪˈlærət̬i/ *n.* [U]

THESAURUS funny, hysterical, amusing, humorous, comical → FUNNY[1]

hill /hɪl/ *n.* [C] **1** EARTH SCIENCES an area of high land, like a small mountain: *driving up a steep hill* **2 over the hill** (informal) no longer young, or too old to do a job well **3 the Hill** POLITICS another word for CAPITOL HILL, used especially by politicians and JOURNALISTS [ORIGIN: Old English *hyll*] —**hilly** *adj.*

hill·bil·ly /ˈhɪlˌbɪli/ *n.* (plural **hillbillies**) [C] someone who lives in the mountains and is thought to be uneducated or stupid

hill·side /ˈhɪlsaɪd/ *n.* [C] the side of a hill

hilt /hɪlt/ *n.* **1 to the hilt** completely or extremely: *Their house had been mortgaged to the hilt.* **2** [C] the handle of a sword or a large knife

him /ɪm; *strong* hɪm/ *pron.* the object form of "he": *Why don't you just ask him yourself?* | *The cop ordered him out of the car.* [ORIGIN: Old English]

him·self /ɪmˈsɛlf; *strong* hɪmˈsɛlf/ *pron.* **1** the REFLEXIVE form of "he": *Bill looked at himself in the mirror.* **2** the strong form of "he," used in order to emphasize the subject or object of a sentence: *It's true! He told me himself.* **3 (all) by himself a)** without help: *He tried to fix the car by himself.* **b)** alone: *Sam was all by himself on the mountain trail.* **4 (all) to himself** for his own use: *Ben had the house to himself for a week.* **5 not feel/look/seem like himself** if someone does not feel like himself, he is not behaving or feeling as he usually does, because he is sick or upset

hind /haɪnd/ *adj.* **hind legs/feet** the back legs or feet of an animal → *see picture on page A15*

hin·der /ˈhɪndɚ/ *v.* [T] to make it difficult for someone to do something: *The bad weather is hindering rescue efforts.*

Hin·di /ˈhɪndi/ *n.* [U] a language used in India

hind·quar·ters /ˈhaɪndˌkwɔrt̬ɚz/ *n.* [plural] (formal) the back part of an animal

hin·drance /ˈhɪndrəns/ *n.* [C] someone or something that makes it difficult for you to do something: *Students' family problems can be a* ***hindrance to*** *their education.*

hind·sight /ˈhaɪndsaɪt/ *n.* [U] the ability to understand something after it has happened: ***In hindsight****, it was a terrible mistake.*

Hin·du /ˈhɪndu/ *n.* [C] someone who believes in Hinduism —**Hindu** *adj.*

Hin·du·ism /ˈhɪnduˌɪzəm/ *n.* [U] the main religion in India, which includes belief in REINCARNATION

hinge[1] /hɪndʒ/ *n.* [C] a metal part that joins two things together, such as a door and a frame, so that one part can swing open and shut —**hinged** *adj.*

hinge[2] *v.*

hinge on/upon sth *phr. v.* to depend on something: *His political future hinges on this election.*

hint[1] /hɪnt/ *n.* [C] **1** something that you say or do that helps someone guess what you really want: *Come on,* ***give me a hint****.* | *Sue has been* ***dropping hints*** (=giving hints) *about what she wants for her birthday.* **2 a hint of sth** a small amount of something: *a hint of perfume in the air* **3** a useful piece of advice on how to do something: *a book full of* ***hints on*** *gardening*

hint[2] *v.* [I,T] to say something that helps someone guess what you want, or what will happen: *Irene* ***hinted that*** *I might get a raise.*

hin·ter·land /ˈhɪntɚˌlænd/ *n.* **the hinterland** the inner part of a country, usually away from cities or the coast

hip[1] /hɪp/ *n.* [C] one of the two parts on either side of your body, where your legs join your body: *She stood there with her* ***hands on*** *her* ***hips****.* [ORIGIN: (1) Old English *hype*] → *see picture on page A16*

hip[2] *adj.* (informal) modern and fashionable: *a hip new comedy on NBC*

ˈhip-hop *n.* [U] **1** a type of dance music with a strong regular beat and spoken words **2** a type of popular culture among young people in big cities, which includes RAP music, dancing, and GRAFFITI art

hip·pie, hippy /'hɪpi/ *n.* [C] someone, especially in the 1960s and 1970s, who usually had long hair, opposed the standards of society, and took drugs for pleasure

hip·po·pot·a·mus /ˌhɪpə'pɑṭəməs/ *also* **hip·po** /'hɪpoʊ/ *n.* (plural **hippopotamuses**) [C] a large African animal with a big head, fat body, and thick gray skin, that lives in and near water [ORIGIN: 1500—1600 Latin, Greek, from *hippos* "horse" + *potamos* "river"]

hire¹ /haɪɚ/ *v.* [T] to employ someone to work for you: *We're going to **hire** a lawyer **to** handle the case.*

hire² *n.* [C] someone who has recently been hired by a company: *All **new hires** will receive training.*

his¹ /ɪz; *strong* hɪz/ *possessive adj.* belonging to or relating to a male person or animal that has been mentioned or is known about: *Leo hates cleaning his room.* | *His mother is Spanish.*

his² *pron.* the thing or things belonging to or relating to a male person or animal that has been mentioned or is known about: *I think he has my suitcase, and I have his.* | *Dave is a friend **of his**.* | *My boots are black. His are brown.*

His·pan·ic /hɪ'spænɪk/ *adj.* from or relating to a country where Spanish or Portuguese is spoken [ORIGIN: 1500—1600 Latin *hispanicus*, from *Hispania* "Spain"] —**Hispanic** *n.* [C]

hiss /hɪs/ *v.* [I] to make a noise that sounds like "ssss": *Steam hissed from the pipe.* [ORIGIN: 1300—1400 from the sound] —**hiss** *n.* [C] → *see picture on page A20*

his·to·gram /'hɪstəˌgræm/ *n.* [C] MATH a type of BAR GRAPH in which the area of each bar represents how often a value appears in a set of information

his·to·ri·an /hɪ'stɔriən/ *n.* [C] someone who studies or writes about history

his·tor·ic /hɪ'stɔrɪk, -'stɑr-/ *adj.* a historic place or event is important as a part of history: *important **historic sites*** | *"This is a **historic moment**," he told journalists.*

his·tor·i·cal /hɪ'stɔrɪkəl, -'stɑr-/ *adj.* **1** relating to the study of history: *a collection of historical documents* **2** historical events, people, etc. really happened or existed in the past

his·to·ry /'hɪstəri/ *n.* (plural **histories**) **1** [U] all the things that happened in the past: ***Throughout history**, wars have been fought over religion.* | *Lincoln has an important place **in** American **history**.* **2** [U] the study of history, especially the political, social, or economic development of a particular country: *a class in European history* **3** [C] a book about events that happened in the past: *a **history of** the Roman empire* **4 be (ancient) history** (spoken) to not exist any more or not affect you any more: *One more losing season, and the coach will be history.* **5 have a history of sth** to have had illness, problems, etc. in the past: *Paul has a history of heart disease.* **6 make history/go down in history** to do something important that will be remembered [ORIGIN: 1400—1500 Latin *historia*, from Greek, from *histor* "knowing, learned"]

his·tri·on·ics /ˌhɪstri'ɑnɪks/ *n.* [plural] (disapproving) behavior that is very emotional but is not sincere —**histrionic** *adj.*

hit¹ /hɪt/ *v.* (past tense and past participle **hit**, present participle **hitting**) [T]
1 STRIKE to swing your hand, or something held in your hand, hard against someone or something: *He **hit** the boy **on the nose**.* | *She swung the bat and hit the ball.*

THESAURUS

punch – to hit someone hard with your closed hand, especially in a fight: *Steve punched him in the nose.*
slap – to hit someone with the flat part of your hand, especially because you are angry with him or her: *I felt like slapping his face.*
beat – to hit someone or something deliberately many times, or to hit against the surface of something continuously: *He had been robbed and beaten.* | *The wind howled and rain beat against the windows.*
smack – to hit someone or something, usually with your open hand: *Rick smacked him in the face.* | *Should a parent ever smack a child?*
whack (informal) – to hit someone or something very hard: *Edmonds whacked the ball over the fence.*
strike (formal) – to hit someone or something very hard: *She had been struck on the side of the head.*
knock – to hit a door or window with your closed hand in order to attract the attention of the people inside: *Someone was knocking on the door.*
bang – to make a loud noise, especially by hitting something against something hard: *A policeman was banging on the door.*
tap – to gently hit your fingers or foot against something: *I tapped him on the shoulder.*
pound – to knock very hard, making a lot of noise: *Thomas pounded on the door with his fist.*
rap – to knock quickly several times: *She rapped on his window angrily.*
hammer – to hit against something several times, making a lot of noise: *They hammered on my door until I opened up.*

2 CRASH to crash into someone or something quickly and hard: *Ann's car hit a tree.* | *I hit my head on the table.*

THESAURUS

bump – to hit or knock against something, especially by accident: *I bumped my head on the wall.*
collide – to crash violently into something or someone: *The two cars almost collided.*

bang – to hit a part of your body against something by accident: *I banged my toe on the dresser.*
strike (formal) – to hit someone or something: *The boys were struck and killed by a speeding car.*

3 BAD EFFECT to have a bad effect on someone or something: *The state's economy has been hit by budget cuts.*
4 BULLET/BOMB to wound someone or damage something with a bullet or bomb: *Over 90% of the bombs hit their intended targets.*
5 REACH STH to reach a particular level, number, position, etc.: *Unemployment has hit a new high, at 11.3%.* | *We'll hit the exit in three miles.*
6 hit it off (with sb) (informal) to like someone as soon as you meet him/her
7 THINK OF if an idea, thought, etc. hits you, you suddenly think of it: *It suddenly hit me that he was just lonely.*
8 hit the roof/ceiling (informal) to become very angry: *Cheryl really hit the roof when I told her.*
9 hit the road (informal) to start on a trip
10 hit the hay/sack (spoken) to go to bed
11 hit the spot (spoken) if a food or drink hits the spot, it tastes good and is exactly what you want [ORIGIN: 1000—1100 Old Norse *hitta* "to find, hit"] → **hit the bottle** *at* BOTTLE¹

hit back *phr. v.*
to attack or criticize someone who is attacking or criticizing you: *Today the President* ***hit back at*** *his critics.*

hit on sth *phr. v.*
to have a good idea about something, often by chance: *Turner may have hit on a solution.*

hit sb **up for** sth *phr. v.*
(spoken) to ask someone for something: *Mitch hit him up for a loan.*

hit² *n.* [C] **1** a movie, song, play, etc. that is very successful: *Her first novel was a* ***big hit.***

THESAURUS bestseller, blockbuster → POPULAR

2 the action of successfully striking something you are aiming at: *The missile scored a* ***direct hit.*** **3 be a hit (with sb)** to be liked very much by someone: *These brownies are always a hit.* **4** a quick hard blow with your hand, or with something in your hand

ˌhit-and-ˈmiss *also* **ˌhit-or-ˈmiss** *adj.* (informal) done in a way that is not planned or organized well

ˌhit-and-ˈrun *adj.* a hit-and-run accident is one in which a car driver hits someone and then drives away without stopping to help

hitch¹ /hɪtʃ/ *v.* **1** [I,T] (informal) to travel by asking for free rides in other people's cars (SYN) **hitchhike**: *We* ***hitched a ride with*** *a couple from Florida.* **2** [T] to fasten something to something else: *Dad finished* ***hitching*** *the trailer* ***to*** *the car.* **3 get hitched** (informal) to get married

hitch sth ↔ **up** *phr. v.* to pull a piece of clothing up: *Bill hitched up his pants.*

hitch² *n.* [C] **1** a small problem that causes a delay: *The performance* ***went off without a hitch*** (=happened with no problems).

THESAURUS problem, setback, difficulty, snag → PROBLEM

2 a part on a vehicle that is used to connect it to something it is pulling

hitch·hike /ˈhɪtʃhaɪk/ *v.* [I] to travel by asking for free rides in other people's cars —**hitchhiker** *n.* [C] —**hitchhiking** *n.* [U]

hi-tech /ˌhaɪ ˈtɛk◂/ *adj.* another spelling of HIGH-TECH

hith·er /ˈhɪðɚ/ *adv.* (literary) **1** (old-fashioned) here, to this place **2 hither and thither/yon** in many directions

hith·er·to /ˌhɪðɚˈtu, ˈhɪðɚˌtu/ *adv.* (formal) up until now: *a hitherto unexplored land*

ˈhit list *n.* [C usually singular] (informal) the names of people, organizations, etc. whom you would like to damage, hurt, or deal with

ˈhit man *n.* [C] (informal) a criminal whose job is to kill someone

HIV *also* **HIV/AIDS** /ˌeɪtʃ aɪ vi ˈeɪdz/ *n.* [U] BIOLOGY **Human Immunodeficiency Virus** a type of VIRUS that enters the body through the blood or through sexual activity, and that can develop into AIDS: *Brad tested* ***HIV positive*** (=he has HIV).

hive /haɪv/ *n.* **1** [C] *also* **beehive** a place where BEES live **2 hives** [plural] a condition in which someone's skin swells and becomes red, usually because s/he is ALLERGIC to something

hmm, hm /hm, hmh/ *interjection* a sound that you make to express doubt or disagreement

HMO *n.* [C] **health maintenance organization** a type of health insurance organization, in which members can only go to doctors and hospitals that are part of the organization

ho /hoʊ/ *interjection* used in writing to represent a shout of laughter in a deep voice

hoard¹ /hɔrd/ *also* **hoard up** *v.* [T] to collect things in large amounts and keep them in a secret place: *Fearful citizens were hoarding food in case of war.*

THESAURUS keep, store, save, collect → KEEP¹

hoard² *n.* [C] a group of valuable things that someone has hidden to keep safe: *a* ***hoard of*** *gold*

hoarse /hɔrs/ *adj.* someone who is hoarse has a voice that sounds rough, often because of a sore throat

hoax /hoʊks/ *n.* [C] a trick that makes someone believe something that is not true: *The bomb threat turned out to be a hoax.* —**hoaxer** *n.* [C]

hob·ble /ˈhɑbəl/ *v.* [I] to walk with difficulty, taking small steps, usually because you are injured

hob·by /ˈhɑbi/ *n.* (plural **hobbies**) [C] an activity that you enjoy doing in your free time: *Do you **have a hobby**? | I started painting **as a hobby**.*

THESAURUS **game, sport, recreation** → GAME[1]

ho·bo /ˈhoʊboʊ/ *n.* (plural **hoboes** *or* **hobos**) [C] (old-fashioned) someone who travels around and has no home or regular job

hock[1] /hɑk/ *v.* [T] (informal) to PAWN something

hock[2] *n.* **be in hock** (informal) to be in debt

hock·ey /ˈhɑki/ *n.* [U] *also* **ice hockey** a sport played on ice in which players use long curved sticks to try to hit a hard flat round object into a GOAL → FIELD HOCKEY: *a **hockey team/player/game*** → *see picture on page A17*

hodge·podge /ˈhɑdʒpɑdʒ/ *n.* [singular] a lot of things put together with no order or arrangement: *The cafe is decorated with a **hodgepodge of** little knick knacks and souvenirs.*

hoe /hoʊ/ *n.* [C] a garden tool with a long handle, used for making the soil loose and for removing wild plants —**hoe** *v.* [I,T]

hog[1] /hɔg, hɑg/ *n.* [C] **1** a large pig that is kept for its meat **2** (informal) someone who keeps or uses all of something for himself/herself **3 go (the) whole hog** (informal) to do something thoroughly or completely

hog[2] *v.* (**hogged, hogging**) [T] (informal) to keep or use all of something for yourself in a way that is unfair: *My sister was hogging the mirror.*

ho-hum /ˌhoʊ ˈhʌm/ *adj.* (informal) disappointing or boring: *a ho-hum movie*

hoist[1] /hɔɪst/ *v.* [T] to raise or lift something, especially using ropes or a special machine

hoist[2] *n.* [C] a piece of equipment used for lifting heavy things

ho·key /ˈhoʊki/ *adj.* (informal, disapproving) expressing emotions in a way that seems old-fashioned, silly, or too simple: *a hokey love song*

hold[1] /hoʊld/ *v.* (past tense and past participle **held** /hɛld/)

1 IN YOUR HANDS/ARMS [T] to have something firmly in your hands or arms: *Will you hold my purse for a minute? | Hold my hand when we cross the street. | He **held** it carefully **in** his hands. | **I held** her **tight**. | a couple **holding hands*** (=holding each other's hands) → *see picture on page A21*

THESAURUS

grip – to hold something very tightly: *I gripped the rail and tried not to look down.*

clutch – to hold something tightly, especially something you think might be taken away from you: *a child clutching a bag of candy*

catch/take/keep/get (a) hold of sth – to take something in your hands and hold it tightly: *Catch hold of the rope and pull.*

grasp – to take and hold something firmly in your hands: *I grasped his arm and led him away.*

clasp – to hold someone or something tightly, especially someone's hands: *The child clasped her mother's hand.*

grab (hold of sth)/seize – to take hold of someone or something suddenly or violently: *He grabbed the bag and ran.*

THESAURUS **hug, embrace, cuddle, wrap your arms around sb** → HUG[1]

2 EVENT [T] to have a meeting, party, etc., especially in a particular place or at a particular time: *a conference **held in** Las Vegas | Elections will be **held in** March. | The Senate will be **holding hearings** into the matter. | In April, the president **held talks** with Chinese leaders.*

3 MOVE IN YOUR HAND [T] to move your hand or something in your hand in a particular direction: *She **held** the picture **up** so we could see it. | **Hold out** your hand.*

4 KEEP IN POSITION [T] to make something stay in a particular position: *He **held** the door **open** for me. | Some tape **held** it **in place/position**. | **Hold still*** (=don't move) *for a minute.*

5 HAVE SPACE FOR [T] to have space for a particular amount of something: *The jug holds two gallons of liquid.*

6 KEEP/CONTAIN [T] to keep or contain something: *The files are held on computer. | That closet holds our winter clothes.*

7 POSITION/RANK/JOB [T] to have a particular position, job, or level of achievement: *The permit allows foreign workers to hold jobs in the U.S. | She was the first woman to **hold** high **office**. | He **holds the record** for the 10,000 meters race.*

8 CONTINUE/NOT CHANGE [I,T] to continue at a particular level, rate, or number, or to make something do this: ***Hold** your speed **at** fifty miles an hour. | Housing prices are **holding steady**.*

9 hold it! (spoken) used in order to tell someone to wait, or to stop doing something

10 TELEPHONE [I] to wait until the person you have telephoned is ready to answer: *Will you hold, please?*

11 hold sb's interest/attention to keep someone interested: *She knows how to hold her students' interest.*

12 hold sb responsible/liable/accountable etc. to think that someone is responsible for something bad that has happened: *Parents may be **held responsible for** their children's crimes.*

13 hold your own to succeed in a difficult situation, or to be good enough when compared to similar things: *The rebels held their own against the better-equipped army.*

14 HAVE A QUALITY [T] to have a particular quality: *The new drug **holds promise** for cancer sufferers.*

15 CAGE/PRISONER [T] to keep a person or animal in a place where he, she, or it cannot leave: *Police are holding two suspects. | The tigers are held in cages until they can be released in the wild. | He was **held hostage/prisoner/captive** for two years.*

16 SUPPORT WEIGHT [I,T] to support the weight of

H

something: *I wasn't sure the branch would hold him.*
17 THINK/BELIEVE [T] (formal) to think or believe something: *He disagrees with most of the* ***views/beliefs/opinions held*** *by Republican politicians.* | *The theory* ***holds that*** *tax cuts help economic growth.*
18 hold true/good (formal) to be true in particular situations: *I think her statement* ***holds true for*** *older women* (=is true about them). [ORIGIN: Old English *healdan*] ➔ **hold your breath** *at* BREATH, **hold your horses!** *at* HORSE[1], **hold sway** *at* SWAY[2]

hold sth **against** sb *phr. v.*
to blame someone for something s/he has done: *If the economy worsens, voters are likely to hold it against him.*

hold back *phr. v.*
1 hold sth ↔ **back** to control something or make it stay in one place: *The police couldn't hold the crowds back.*
2 hold (sth ↔) **back** to stop yourself from showing a particular feeling or saying something: *She struggled to hold back her tears.*
3 hold sb/sth **back** to prevent someone or something from developing or improving: *Your son's reading problems are holding him back.*

hold sth ↔ **down** *phr. v.*
1 to stop someone or something from moving, by pressing or holding him, her, or it: *Hold down the red button while lifting the handle.*
2 to keep something at a low level: *Insurance companies want to hold down health care costs.*
3 hold down a job to keep your job: *It's hard to hold down a job and go to college at the same time.*

hold off *phr. v.*
1 to delay doing something: *We* ***held off on*** *making the decision.*
2 hold sb ↔ **off** to prevent someone from attacking or defeating you: *The Jaguars held off the Buccaneers with a touchdown late in the game.*

hold on *phr. v.*
1 (spoken) said when you want someone to wait or stop talking for a short time: *Yeah, hold on, Mike is right here.* | ***Hold on a minute/second.*** *Let me put this in the car.*
2 to hold something tightly with your hand or arms: *She can hardly walk without* ***holding on to*** *something.* | *Okay, Becky,* ***hold on tight!***
3 to continue to do something difficult until it gets better: *The Rangers held on to win the game in the final period.*

hold on to sth *phr. v.*
to keep something, especially something that someone else wants: *People are holding on to their cars for longer.*

hold out *phr. v.*
1 to continue to defend yourself, or keep on refusing to do something: *Some of the council members are* ***holding out against*** *the changes.*
2 hold out hope/the prospect etc. to say that something may happen: *The doctors don't hold out much hope.*
3 if a supply of something holds out, there is still some of it left: *We talked for as long as the wine held out.*

hold out for sth *phr. v.*
to refuse to accept less than you have asked for: *He hasn't signed a contract; he's holding out for more money.*

hold out on sb *phr. v.*
to refuse to tell someone something s/he wants or needs to know

hold over *phr. v.*
be held over if a concert, play, or movie is held over, it is shown for longer than was planned because it is very good: *The play has been held over for another week.*

hold sb **to** sth *phr. v.*
to make someone do what s/he has promised to do: *"He said he would do it." "Well, you'd better hold him to it."*

hold together *phr. v.*
1 hold sth ↔ **together** if a group, family, organization, etc. holds together, or something holds it together, it stays together: *The children are the only thing holding their marriage together.*
2 to remain whole, without breaking: *I hope the car holds together long enough to get us to Fresno.*

hold up *phr. v.*
1 hold sb/sth ↔ **up** to make someone or something late: *I got held up in traffic.*
2 hold up sth to try to steal money from a store, bank, etc. using a gun: *Two men held up the convenience store.*
3 hold sth ↔ **up** to support something: *Posts hold up the tin roof.*
4 to remain strong or effective: *The theory didn't hold up in practice.*

hold[2] *n.* **1** [singular, U] the action of holding something: *He* ***grabbed/took/caught hold*** *of my arm.* **2 get (a) hold of sth** to find someone or something for a particular purpose: *Were you able to get a hold of Mike?* | *See if you can get hold of an overhead projector.* **3 on hold a)** waiting on the telephone before speaking to someone: *His secretary* ***put me on hold.*** **b)** if something is on hold, it is going to be done or dealt with later: *Her own plans had to be* ***put on hold*** *while she took care of her mother.* **4** [singular] control, power, or influence over something or someone: *The rebels were tightening their* ***hold over*** *the countryside.* **5 take hold** to start to have an effect on someone or something: *The ceasefire took hold in December.* **6** [C] the part of a ship where goods are stored

hold·er /'hoʊldɚ/ *n.* [C] **1** someone who has control of or owns a place, position, or thing: *Only* ***ticket holders*** *will be admitted.* **2** something that holds or contains something else: *a napkin holder*

hold·ing /'hoʊldɪŋ/ *n.* [C] something that you own or rent, especially land or part of a company

'holding ˌcompany *n.* [C] a company that owns a controlling number of SHARES in other companies

hold·o·ver /'hoʊldˌoʊvɚ/ *n.* [C] a feeling, idea, fashion, etc. from the past that has continued to the present: *The robes that judges wear are a* ***holdover from*** *a time when all important people wore robes.*

hold·up /ˈhoʊldʌp/ *n.* [C] **1** a delay, especially one caused by traffic **2** an attempt to rob someone, especially using a gun

hole¹ /hoʊl/ *n.* [C] **1** an empty or open space in something solid: *a* ***hole in*** *my sock | The dog* ***dug a hole*** *in the yard.*

THESAURUS

space – the empty area between two things, into which you can put something: *There's a space for that box on the shelf over there.*
gap – an empty space between two things or two parts of something: *A cold wind blew through the gap in the window.*
leak – a small hole that lets liquid or gas flow into or out of something: *a leak in the oil tank*
crack – a very narrow space between two things or two parts of something: *John peeked through the crack in the door.*
opening – a hole or space in something: *an opening in the fence*
cavity (formal) – a hole or space inside something solid, especially your body: *an infection in your nasal cavities*

2 the home of a small animal: *a rabbit hole* **3** one of the small holes in the ground that you try to hit the ball into in GOLF **4** a problem or fault in an idea, plan, or story, so that it can be proven wrong or does not make sense: *The witness's testimony was* ***full of holes.*** **5** (informal) a bad, ugly, or dirty place: *I have to get out of this hole.* **6 be in the hole** (spoken) to owe money: *We're still $600 in the hole.* [ORIGIN: Old English *hol*]

hole² *v.*

hole up *phr. v.* to hide somewhere, or find shelter somewhere: *The rebels are* ***holed up in*** *an army building.*

hol·i·day /ˈhɑləˌdeɪ/ *n.* (plural **holidays**) [C] a day when you do not have to go to work, school, etc.: *July 1 is a* ***national holiday*** *in Canada.* [ORIGIN: Old English *haligdæg* "holy day"]

THESAURUS **vacation, break, leave** → VACATION

ho·li·ness /ˈhoʊlinɪs/ *n.* **1** [U] the quality of being pure and holy **2 Your/His Holiness** a title used for talking to or about some religious leaders, especially the Pope

ho·lis·tic /hoʊˈlɪstɪk/ *adj.* concerning the whole of something, rather than its parts: *Some doctors are interested in* ***holistic medicine*** (=medicine that treats the whole person, not just the illness).

hol·ler /ˈhɑlɚ/ *v.* [I,T] (informal) to shout loudly: *Dad* ***hollered at*** *me to hurry up.* —**holler** *n.* [C]

THESAURUS **shout, scream, yell, bellow** → SHOUT¹

hollow

hol·low¹ /ˈhɑloʊ/ *adj.* **1** having an empty space inside: *a hollow chocolate bunny* **2** feelings or words that are hollow are not sincere: *His promises* ***ring hollow*** (=seem insincere). **3 hollow cheeks/eyes etc.** cheeks, eyes, etc. where the skin has sunk inward, especially because the person is sick or too thin

hollow² *n.* [C] **1** a hole in something, especially the ground, that is not very deep **2** a small valley

hollow³ *v.*

hollow sth ↔ **out** *phr. v.* to remove the inside of something

hol·ly /ˈhɑli/ *n.* [U] a small tree with dark shiny pointed green leaves and red berries, often used as a decoration at Christmas → *see picture on page A23*

Hol·ly·wood /ˈhɑliˌwʊd/ *n.* a city in California near Los Angeles, known as the center of the American movie industry

H

hol·o·caust /ˈhɑləˌkɔst, ˈhoʊ-/ *n.* [C] **1** an event that kills many people and destroys many things: *a nuclear holocaust* **2 the Holocaust** HISTORY the killing of millions of Jews by the Nazis in Europe in World War II [ORIGIN: 1200—1300 Old French *holocauste*, from Greek *holokaustos* "burnt whole," from *holos* "whole" + *kaiein* "to burn"]

hol·o·gram /ˈhoʊləˌgræm, ˈhɑ-/ *n.* [C] a special picture made with a LASER that looks as if it is not flat [ORIGIN: 1900—2000 Greek *holos* "whole" + English *-gram*]

hol·ster /ˈhoʊlstɚ/ *n.* [C] a leather object that you use for carrying a gun

ho·ly /ˈhoʊli/ *adj.* (comparative **holier**, superlative **holiest**) **1** relating to God or religion (SYN) **sacred**: *the holy city of Jerusalem* **2** very religious and morally pure: *a holy man* **3 holy cow/mackerel/moly** (spoken) used in order to express surprise, admiration, or fear [ORIGIN: Old English *halig*]

ˌHoly ˈGhost *n.* the HOLY SPIRIT

holy grail /ˌhoʊli ˈgreɪl/ *n.* [singular] **1** something that you try very hard to get or achieve: *A cure for AIDS has become something of a medical holy grail.* **2 the Holy Grail** the cup believed to have been used by Jesus Christ before his death. In stories, especially stories about King Arthur, people search for this cup.

ˈHoly Land *n.* **the Holy Land** the parts of the Middle East where the events in the Bible happened

ˌHoly ˈSpirit *n.* **the Holy Spirit** God in the form of a spirit, according to the Christian religion (SYN) **Holy Ghost**

hom·age /ˈhɑmɪdʒ, ˈɑ-/ *n.* [singular, U] (formal) something that you say or do to show respect for an important person: *The visitors* ***paid homage to*** *the war veterans.* [ORIGIN: 1200—1300 Old French *hommage*, from *homme* "man, man who owes duty to a ruler"]

home[1] /hoʊm/ *n.* **1** [C,U] the place where you usually live, especially with your family: *I decided just to stay* ***at home****.* | *I've been* ***living at home*** (=living with my parents) *for the past two years.*

THESAURUS

house – the house, apartment, or room where someone lives: *Let's go over to Dave's house.*
place (informal) – the house, apartment, or room where someone lives: *Do you want to come back to my place for coffee?*
residence (formal) – the place where you live: *a private residence*
dwelling (formal) – a house, apartment, etc. where people live: *the cliff dwellings in Colorado, where the Anasazi Indians used to live*
abode (formal) – the place where you live, used especially in literature: *In Norse mythology, Valhalla is the abode of fallen warriors.*

H

2 [C,U] the place where you come from or your country: *car sales* ***at home*** *and abroad* | *It even made the news* ***back home****.* **3 be/feel at home** to feel comfortable somewhere, or confident doing something: *I grew up in Manhattan, and this is where I feel at home.* | *It took a while before I felt at home using the new program.* **4 the home of sth** the place where something lives or comes from: *Australia is the home of the kangaroo.* **5 make yourself at home** (spoken) said in order to tell someone who is visiting that s/he should relax **6** [C] a place where people live who cannot take care of themselves because they are very old, sick, etc.: *I could never* ***put*** *Dad* ***into*** *a* ***home****.* **7** [C] *also* **home plate** the base that players must touch in baseball to gain a point [ORIGIN: Old English *ham* "village, home"]

home[2] *adv.* **1** to or at the place where you live: *Hi, honey,* ***I'm home****.* | *Come on, Andy, it's time to* ***go home****.* | *Many kids* ***come home*** *to an empty house.* | *I should* ***get home*** *in time for dinner.* ▸Don't say "go/get/come at home."◂ **2 take home** to earn a particular amount of money after tax has been taken away: *I take home about $200 a week.* **3 drive/hammer sth home** to make someone understand what you mean by saying it in a very clear and determined way: *We need to hammer home the message that drugs are dangerous.* **4 hit home** if something hits home, it makes you realize or understand something more clearly: *She said I was bullying her, and that really hit home.*

home[3] *adj.* **1** relating to or belonging to your home or family, or done at home: *My* ***home town*** *is Matamata.* | *What's your* ***home address****?* | *some good* ***home cooking*** (=meals cooked by your family) **2** playing on your own sports field rather than an opponent's field (ANT) **away**: *The* ***home team*** *is ahead by four runs.*

home[4] *v.*

home in on sth *phr. v.* to aim exactly at something and move directly toward it: *A rescue plane homed in on the location of the crash.*

home·boy /ˈhoʊmbɔɪ/ *n.* [C] (slang) a male HOMEY

home·com·ing /ˈhoʊmˌkʌmɪŋ/ *n.* [C] **1** an occasion when someone comes back to his/her home after being away for a long time **2** an occasion when former students return to their school or college

home·land /ˈhoʊmlænd/ *n.* [C] the country where you were born

home·less /ˈhoʊmlɪs/ *adj.* **1 the homeless** people who do not have a place to live, and who often live in the streets **2** without a home: *The war left a lot of people homeless.* —**homelessness** *n.* [U]

home·ly /ˈhoʊmli/ *adj.* a homely person is not very attractive —**homeliness** *n.* [U]

home·made /ˌhoʊmˈmeɪd◂/ *adj.* made at home and not bought from a store: *homemade jam*

home·mak·er /ˈhoʊmˌmeɪkɚ/ *n.* [C] someone who works at home cooking and cleaning, and does not have another job

ˌhome ˈoffice *n.* [C] an office you have in your house so that you can do your job at home

ho·me·op·a·thy /ˌhoʊmiˈɑpəθi/ *n.* [U] a system of medicine in which someone who is sick is given very small amounts of a substance that has the same effects as the disease [ORIGIN: 1800—1900 German *homöopathie*, from Greek *homoios* "like" + *pathos* "suffering"] —**homeopathic** /ˌhoʊmiəˈpæθɪk/ *adj.*

ho·me·o·sta·sis /ˌhoʊmioʊˈsteɪsɪs/ *n.* [U] BIOLOGY the process in which a living ORGANISM or cell stays in the same state even when its environment changes

home page, home·page /ˈhoʊmpeɪdʒ/ *n.* [C] IT the first page of a website on the Internet, which usually has LINKS to the other parts of the website

ˈhome plate *n* [U] in a game of baseball, the place where you stand to hit the ball, which is also the last place the player who is running must touch in order to get a point

hom·er /ˈhoʊmɚ/ *n.* [C] a HOME RUN —**homer** *v.* [I]

home·room /ˈhoʊmrum, -rʊm/ *n.* [C] the room where students go at the beginning of the school day, or at the beginning of each SEMESTER

ˌhome ˈrun *n.* [C] a long hit in baseball that lets the player run around all the bases and get a point

ˌhome 'shopping *n.* [U] shopping that you do at home by telephone, mail, or Internet, buying things that you have seen on the television or Internet

home·sick /'houmˌsɪk/ *adj.* feeling sad because you are away from your home: *I felt **homesick** already **for** my family.* —**homesickness** *n.* [U]

home·stead /'houmstɛd/ *n.* [C] a farm and the area of land and buildings around it, especially one that was originally given to someone by the government —**homestead** *v.* [I,T]

home·stead·er /'houmˌstɛdɚ/ *n.* [C] HISTORY in the past, homesteaders were people who owned an area of land that was given to them by the government according to a law called the Homestead Act

home·ward /'houmwɚd/ *adj.* going toward home —**homeward** *adv.*

home·work /'houmwɚk/ *n.* [U] **1** work for school that a student does at home → HOUSEWORK: *Have you **done** your **homework**? | my **math/history/English etc. homework*** **2 do (sb's) homework** to prepare for something by finding out information: *Before the interview, do some homework about the company.*

hom·ey¹ /'houmi/ *adj.* comfortable and pleasant, like home: *The restaurant had a nice homey atmosphere.*

homey² *n.* [C] (slang) a friend, or someone who comes from your area or GANG

hom·i·ci·dal /ˌhamə'saɪdl◂ , ˌhou-/ *adj.* likely to murder someone

hom·i·cide /'haməˌsaɪd, 'hou-/ *n.* [C,U] LAW the crime of murder [ORIGIN: 1200—1300 French, Latin *homicidium*, from *homo* "man" + *caedere* "to kill"]

hom·i·nid /'hamənɪd, 'hou-/ *n.* [C] BIOLOGY a member of a group of animals which includes humans and also the animals from which humans developed

hom·i·noid /'haməˌnɔɪd, 'hou-/ *adj.* **1** similar to a human **2** BIOLOGY belonging to a group of animals that includes humans and APES

ho·mo·ge·ne·ous /ˌhoumə'dʒiniəs, -nyəs/ *also* **ho·mog·e·nous** /hə'madʒənəs/ *adj.* (formal) consisting of parts or members that are all the same → HETEROGENEOUS [ORIGIN: 1600—1700 Medieval Latin *homogeneus*, from Greek *homo-* "same" + *genos* "type"] —**homogeneity** /ˌhoumoudʒə'niət̬i, -'neɪət̬i/ *n.* [U]

homoˌgeneous 'mixture *n.* [C] CHEMISTRY a chemical substance consisting of two or more different substances that have completely combined together, so that all parts of the mixture look the same (SYN) **solution**

ho·mo·ge·nize /hə'madʒəˌnaɪz/ *v.* [T] (formal) to change something so that its parts become similar or the same

ho·mo·ge·nized /hə'madʒəˌnaɪzd/ *adj.* homogenized milk has had its cream mixed in with the milk

hom·o·graph /'haməˌgræf, 'hou-/ *n.* [C] ENG. LANG. ARTS a word that is spelled the same as another, but is different in meaning, origin, grammar, or pronunciation. For example, the noun "record" is a homograph of the verb "record." [ORIGIN: 1800—1900 Greek *homo-* "same" + *-graphos* "written"]

ho·mol·o·gous /hə'maləgəs/ *adj.* **1** BIOLOGY relating to two CHROMOSOMEs that have the same form and structure **2** BIOLOGY relating to parts of a person's or animal's body which EVOLVED (=developed) from the same animal, and which now look different or have a different purpose: *a homologous structure*

hom·o·nym /'haməˌnɪm/ *n.* [C] ENG. LANG. ARTS a word that sounds the same and is spelled the same as another word, but has a different meaning. For example, the noun "bear" and the verb "bear" are homonyms. [ORIGIN: 1600—1700 Latin *homonymum*, from Greek, from *homos* + *onyma* "name"]

ho·mo·pho·bi·a /ˌhoumə'foubiə/ *n.* [U] hatred and fear of homosexuals [ORIGIN: 1900—2000 *homosexual* + *-phobia*] —**homophobic** *adj.*

> THESAURUS **prejudice, intolerance, sexism**
> → PREJUDICE¹

hom·o·phone /'haməˌfoun, 'hou-/ *n.* [C] ENG. LANG. ARTS a word that sounds the same as another word, but is different in spelling or meaning. For example, "pair" and "pear" are homophones.

ho·mo·sex·u·al /ˌhoumə'sɛkʃuəl/ *adj.* (formal) sexually attracted to people of the same sex (SYN) **gay** (ANT) **heterosexual** → BISEXUAL —**homosexual** *n.* [C] —**homosexuality** /ˌhouməˌsɛkʃu'ælət̬i/ *n.* [U]

ho·mo·zy·gous /ˌhoumou'zaɪgəs/ *adj.* BIOLOGY relating to a homologous CHROMOSOME which contains a pair of GENEs which are exactly the same

hon·cho /'hantʃou/ *n.* (plural **honchos**) [C] (informal) an important person who controls something: *Where's the **head honcho**?* [ORIGIN: 1900—2000 Japanese *hancho* "group leader"]

hone /houn/ *v.* [T] **1** to improve a skill: *Players must practice to hone their skills.* **2** to make a knife, sword, etc. sharp

hon·est /'anɪst/ *adj.* **1** someone who is honest does not lie, cheat, or steal (ANT) **dishonest**: *an honest, hardworking man* **2** not hiding the truth or the facts about something: *The **honest answer** was that I didn't know. | I need you to **be honest with** me.*

> THESAURUS
> **frank** – honest and direct in the way that you speak: *To be frank, I don't like him very much.*
> **candid** – telling the truth, even when the truth

H

may be unpleasant or embarrassing: *It sounds like you need to have a candid talk with him.*
direct – saying exactly what you mean in an honest and clear way: *direct criticism*
upfront – talking or behaving in a direct and honest way: *Parents need to be upfront with their kids about the risks of drugs and alcohol.*
straight – honest and direct and telling the truth: *Are you being straight with me?*
straightforward – honest and not hiding what you think: *He seems like a straightforward guy.*
blunt – speaking in an honest way even if it upsets people: *She was blunt about her feelings.*
forthright – saying honestly what you think, in a way that may seem rude: *She answered the questions in a forthright manner.*

3 honest/to be honest (spoken) said to emphasize that what you are saying is true: *We didn't think of that, to be honest with you.* **4 honest mistake** a mistake you make when you did not intend to deceive anyone or be cruel [ORIGIN: 1200—1300 Old French *honeste*, from Latin *honestus*]

hon·est·ly /ˈɑnɪstli/ *adv.* **1** (spoken) said to emphasize that what you are saying is true, even though it may seem surprising: *I honestly don't know what to do.* | *Honestly, it doesn't matter.* **2** in an honest way (ANT) **dishonestly**: *Walters spoke honestly about her problems.*

H

hon·es·ty /ˈɑnəsti/ *n.* [U] **1** the quality of being honest (ANT) **dishonesty**: *He has a reputation for honesty and decency.* **2 in all honesty** (spoken) said when you tell someone what you really think: *In all honesty, we made a lot of mistakes.*

hon·ey /ˈhʌni/ *n.* [U] **1** a sweet sticky substance made by BEEs, used as food **2** (spoken) a name that you call someone you love: *Have a good day, honey.* [ORIGIN: Old English *hunig*]

hon·ey·comb /ˈhʌniˌkoʊm/ *n.* [C] a structure made by BEEs to store honey in ➔ *see picture at* HIVE

hon·ey·moon /ˈhʌniˌmun/ *n.* [C] a vacation taken by two people who have just gotten married: *a picture of them **on** their **honeymoon*** [ORIGIN: 1500—1600 *honey* + *moon*; because the moon appears to get smaller, like the love of some newly married people] —**honeymooner** *n.* [C]

hon·ey·suck·le /ˈhʌniˌsʌkəl/ *n.* [C,U] a climbing plant with yellow or pink flowers that smell sweet

honk /hɑŋk, hɔŋk/ *v.* [I,T] to make a loud noise like a car horn or a GOOSE: *A taxi driver **honked** his **horn** behind her.* —**honk** *n.* [C]

hon·or¹ /ˈɑnɚ/ *n.* **1** [singular] something that makes you feel proud and glad: ***It's an honor to** meet you.* | *Being chosen to give the speech was a **great honor**.* **2** [U] the respect that someone or something receives from other people ➔ DISHONOR: *a statue **in honor of** (=to show respect for) Abraham Lincoln* **3** [C] something that is given to someone to show him/her that people respect and admire what s/he has done: *The medal is the government's **highest honor** for artists.* **4 with honors** if you finish high school or college with honors, you get one of the highest grades: *Sabrina **graduated with honors**.* **5** [U] strong moral beliefs and standards of behavior that make people respect and trust you: *a **man of honor*** **6 Your Honor** used when speaking to a judge

honor² *v.* [T] **1** to do something to show publicly that someone is respected and admired: *The team will be **honored with** a parade.* **2 be honored** to feel very proud and glad: ***I'm honored to** meet you.* **3 honor a contract/agreement etc.** to do what you have agreed to do in a contract, etc. **4 honor a check** to accept a check as payment

hon·or·a·ble /ˈɑnərəbəl/ *adj.* morally correct, and deserving respect and admiration (ANT) **dishonorable**: *an honorable action* —**honorably** *adv.*

hon·or·ar·y /ˈɑnəˌrɛri/ *adj.* **1** given to someone as an honor: *an honorary degree* **2** someone who has an honorary position does not receive payment for his/her work

ˈhonor roll *n.* [C] a list of the best students in a school: *Don **made the honor roll** for the first time.*

ˈhonor ˌstudent *n.* [C] a student whose name is included on the honor roll because his/her grades are among the highest in the school

hood /hʊd/ *n.* [C] **1** the metal cover over the engine of a car **2** the part of a coat that you pull up to cover your head **3** (slang) a NEIGHBORHOOD **4** (informal) a hoodlum

hood·ed /ˈhʊdɪd/ *adj.* having a hood or wearing a hood: *a hooded jacket*

hood·lum /ˈhudləm, ˈhʊd-/ *n.* [C] (old-fashioned) a young person who does bad, often illegal things [ORIGIN: 1800—1900 German dialect *hudellump* "lazy useless person"]

hoof /huf, hʊf/ *n.* (plural **hoofs** *or* **hooves** /huvz, hʊvz/) [C] the hard foot of an animal such as a horse ➔ *see picture on page A15*

hook¹ /hʊk/ *n.* [C] **1** a curved object that you hang things on: *a coat hook* **2** a curved piece of metal with a sharp point that you use for catching fish **3 let sb off the hook** to allow someone to get out of a difficult situation: *I'll let you off the hook today, but don't be late again.* **4 off the hook** if a telephone is off the hook, the part of the telephone that you speak into is not on its base, so no one can call you

hook² *v.* [T] **1** to fasten or hang something onto something else: ***Hook** the rope **over/on** the nail.* **2** (informal) to succeed in making someone interested in something or attracted to something: *The ads are designed to hook young people.* **3** to catch a fish with a hook

hook sth ↔ **up** *phr. v.* to connect something, especially a piece of equipment, to another piece of equipment or to an electricity supply: *Jen helped me **hook up** the printer **to** my computer.*

hook up with sb *phr. v.* to meet someone and become friendly with him/her or start a romantic relationship with him/her

hooked /hʊkt/ *adj.* **1 be/get hooked on sth** (informal) **a)** to be or become very interested in something and want to do or see it a lot: *We're trying to get kids hooked on books.* **b)** to be unable to stop taking a drug (SYN) **addicted** **2** shaped like a hook: *a hooked nose*

hook·er /ˈhʊkɚ/ *n.* [C] (informal) a PROSTITUTE

Hooke's law /ˌhʊks ˈlɔ/ *n.* PHYSICS a scientific rule stating that the amount an ELASTIC material stretches, is pressed, etc. is directly connected to the amount of force being used

hook·y /ˈhʊki/ *n.* (informal) **play hooky** to stay away from school without permission

hoo·li·gan /ˈhulɪgən/ *n.* [C] a noisy violent person who causes trouble by fighting or damaging things

hoop /hup/ *n.* **1** [C] a circular piece of wood, metal, plastic, etc.: *hoop earrings* | *a basketball hoop* (=what you throw the ball through) **2 hoops** [plural] (informal) basketball: *The guys are out* ***shooting hoops*** (=playing basketball).

hoo·ray /hʊˈreɪ/ *interjection* shouted when you are very excited and happy about something

hoot[1] /hut/ *n.* [C] **1** the sound made by an OWL or a ship's horn **2** a shout or laugh that shows you think something is funny, exciting, or stupid: *hoots of laughter* **3 be a hoot** (spoken) to be a lot of fun **4 not give a hoot** (spoken) to not care or be interested in something

hoot[2] *v.* [I,T] **1** if an OWL or a ship's horn hoots, it makes a loud clear noise **2** to shout or laugh loudly because you think something is funny or stupid

hooves /huvz, hʊvz/ *n.* a plural of HOOF

hop[1] /hɑp/ *v.* (**hopped, hopping**) [I] **1** to move by making short quick jumps ➔ *see picture at* JUMP[1]

> THESAURUS **jump, skip, leap, spring** ➔ JUMP[1]

2 (informal) to get into, onto, or out of something, for example a vehicle: ***Hop in*** *and I'll give you a ride.*

hop[2] *n.* [C] **1** a short jump **2 short hop** (informal) a short trip by airplane

hope[1] /hoʊp/ *v.* [I,T] to want something to happen or be true: ***I hope (that)*** *you feel better soon.* | *We* ***hope to*** *reduce our costs.* | *Leaders are* ***hoping for*** *a quick end to the fighting.* | *You just do what you can and* ***hope for the best*** (=hope a situation will end well). | *"Can I help you?"* ***"I hope so*** (=I hope this will happen)." | *"Do you think it's going to rain?"* ***"I hope not!"*** (=I hope this will not happen)

> USAGE
> Use **hope to** to talk about something that you or someone else wants to do: *She hopes to go to law school.*
> Use **hope that** to talk about what you hope will happen: *I hope that the weather will be sunny tomorrow.*

hope[2] *n.* **1** [C usually singular, U] the feeling that good things can or will happen: *The new treatment* ***gives/offers hope to*** *cancer patients* (=makes them have hope). | *The report expresses little* ***hope that*** *the economy will improve soon.* | *our* ***hopes for*** *peace* | *We have* ***high hopes*** (=strong feelings that something good will happen) *for this year's team.* **2** [C,U] a chance of succeeding or of something good happening: *Many of these children have no* ***hope of*** *going to college.* | *There is still a faint* ***hope that*** *the two sides will reach an agreement.* **3** [C] something that you hope will happen: *her hopes and fears for the future* **4 in the hope that/of sth** if you do something in the hope that you will get a particular result, you do it, even though you cannot be sure of this result: *Her parents put her in a new school,* ***in the hope that*** *her work would improve.* **5 don't get your hopes up** (spoken) used in order to tell someone that something s/he is hoping for is not likely to happen

hope·ful /ˈhoʊpfəl/ *adj.* **1** believing that what you want is likely to happen: *We're* ***hopeful about*** *our chances of winning.* | *I'm* ***hopeful that*** *the situation will improve.* **2** making you feel that what you want is likely to happen: *There are* ***hopeful signs*** *that an agreement will be reached.* —**hopefulness** *n.* [U]

hope·ful·ly /ˈhoʊpfəli/ *adv.* **1** a way of saying what you hope will happen, which some people think is not correct: *Hopefully, I'll be home early.* **2** in a hopeful way: *They talked hopefully about their futures.*

hope·less /ˈhoʊp-lɪs/ *adj.* **1** without any chance of success or improvement: *the hopeless poverty of the inner cities* **2** feeling no hope, or showing this —**hopelessly** *adv.* —**hopelessness** *n.* [U]

hop·scotch /ˈhɑpskɑtʃ/ *n.* [U] a game in which children jump on squares drawn on the ground

horde /hɔrd/ *n.* [C] a large crowd moving in a noisy uncontrolled way: ***hordes of*** *tourists*

ho·ri·zon /həˈraɪzən/ *n.* **1 the horizon** the place where the land or ocean seems to meet the sky: *a ship* ***on the horizon*** **2 horizons** [plural] the limit of your ideas, knowledge, and experience: *I took an evening class to* ***broaden my horizons.*** **3 on the horizon** seeming likely to happen in the future: *There may be a recession on the horizon.* [ORIGIN: 1300—1400 Late Latin, Greek, from *horizein* "to limit"]

hor·i·zon·tal /ˌhɔrəˈzɑntəl, ˌhɑr-/ *adj.* flat and level: *a horizontal surface* —**horizontally** *adv.* ➔ *see picture at* LINE[1]

> THESAURUS **flat, level** ➔ FLAT[1]

hor·mone /ˈhɔrmoʊn/ *n.* [C] BIOLOGY a substance

H

produced by your body that influences its growth, development, and condition —**hormonal** /hɔrˈmoʊnl/ *adj.*

horn /hɔrn/ *n.* **1** [C,U] a hard pointed thing that grows in pairs on the heads of cows, goats, etc., or the substance this is made of ➔ ANTLERS ➔ *see picture on page A15* **2** [C] the thing in a car, truck, etc. that you push to make a sound as a warning: *Someone was* ***honking/blowing a horn*** (=made a noise with the horn) *behind him.* **3** [C] a TRUMPET

hor·net /ˈhɔrnɪt/ *n.* [C] a large black and yellow insect that can sting you

hor·o·scope /ˈhɔrəˌskoʊp, ˈhɑr-/ *n.* [C] a description of your character and things that will happen to you, based on the position of the stars and PLANETS when you were born ➔ ZODIAC [ORIGIN: 1000—1100 French, Greek *horoskopos*, from *hora* "hour" + *skopein* "to look at"]

hor·ren·dous /həˈrɛndəs, hɔ-/ *adj.* **1** frightening and terrible: *a horrendous disaster*

THESAURUS **bad, awful, terrible, horrible, appalling, horrific** ➔ BAD[1]

2 extremely bad or difficult: *Traffic was horrendous on the freeway.*

THESAURUS **horrible, awful, terrible, dreadful** ➔ HORRIBLE

H

hor·ri·ble /ˈhɔrəbəl, ˈhɑr-/ *adj.* **1** very bad, and sometimes frightening (SYN) **terrible, awful**: *a horrible accident | The weather was horrible.*

THESAURUS

Describing a horrible taste or smell
disgusting: *It tastes disgusting.*
awful: *The wine was awful.*
revolting: *What's that revolting smell?*
foul: *the foul smell of the chemicals*

Describing a horrible experience, situation, or feeling
terrible: *I feel terrible.*
awful: *an awful headache*
dreadful: *What a dreadful thing to happen.*
horrendous: *The weather was horrendous.* ➔ BAD[1]

2 not polite or not friendly (SYN) **terrible, awful**: *horrible manners* —**horribly** *adv.*

hor·rif·ic /hɔˈrɪfɪk, hə-/ *adj.* very bad, frightening, and upsetting: *horrific violence*

THESAURUS **bad, awful, terrible, horrible, appalling, horrendous** ➔ BAD[1]

hor·ri·fied /ˈhɔrəˌfaɪd, ˈhɑr-/ *adj.* feeling very shocked or upset: *We were* ***horrified to hear/see/learn*** *how sick he was.* —**horrifying** *adj.* —**horrify** *v.* [T]

hor·ror /ˈhɔrɚ, ˈhɑrɚ/ *n.* **1** [U] a strong feeling of shock and fear: *I watched* ***in horror*** *as Ramsey hit her.* **2** [C] something that is very shocking or frightening: *the horrors of war*

hors d'oeu·vre /ɔr ˈdɚv/ *n.* [C] a small amount of food that is served before people sit down at the table for the main meal

horse[1] /hɔrs/ *n.* [C] **1** a large strong animal that people ride on and use for pulling heavy things ➔ PONY: *A girl was* ***riding a*** *white* ***horse.*** *| a horse race* ➔ *see picture at* FARM[1] **2 hold your horses!** (spoken) said when you want someone to wait or to stop doing something [ORIGIN: Old English *hors*]

horse[2] *v.*

horse around *phr. v.* (informal) to play in a rough and silly way

horse·back /ˈhɔrsbæk/ *n.* **1 horseback riding** the activity of riding a horse for pleasure **2 on horseback** riding a horse: *two men on horseback*

horse·play /ˈhɔrs-pleɪ/ *n.* [U] rough noisy play

horse·pow·er /ˈhɔrsˌpaʊɚ/ *n.* (plural **horsepower**) (*written abbreviation* **hp**) [C] a unit for measuring the power of an engine

horse·shoe /ˈhɔrʃ-ʃu, ˈhɔrs-/ *n.* **1** [C] a curved piece of iron that is attached to the bottom of a horse's foot to protect it **2 horseshoes** [U] an outdoor game in which horseshoes are thrown at a post

hor·ti·cul·ture /ˈhɔrt̬əˌkʌltʃɚ/ *n.* [U] the practice or science of growing plants [ORIGIN: 1600—1700 Latin *hortus* "garden" + English *culture*] —**horticultural** /ˌhɔrt̬əˈkʌltʃərəl/ *adj.*

hose[1] /hoʊz/ *n.* **1** [C,U] a long rubber or plastic tube that can be moved and bent, used to put water onto plants, fires, etc., or to allow liquids or air to flow through an engine, etc. **2** [plural] PANTYHOSE

hose[2] *v.*

hose sb/sth ↔ **down/off** *phr. v.* to wash or pour water over someone or something, using a hose: *Would you hose down the car for me?*

hos·pice /ˈhɑspɪs/ *n.* [C] a special hospital where people who are dying are cared for

hos·pi·ta·ble /hɑˈspɪt̬əbəl, ˈhɑspɪ-/ *adj.* **1** friendly, welcoming, and generous to visitors (ANT) **inhospitable** ➔ HOSPITALITY: *a hospitable family*

THESAURUS **friendly, warm, cordial, welcoming** ➔ FRIENDLY

2 providing a situation in which something can succeed or happen (ANT) **inhospitable**: *Nursing was a field* ***hospitable to*** *women.*

hos·pi·tal /ˈhɑspɪt̬l/ *n.* [C,U] a building where sick or injured people receive medical treatment: *Rick's dad is still* ***in the hospital*** (=being cared for in a hospital). *| He was unconscious and had to be* ***taken/rushed to the hospital.*** *| His wife had been* ***admitted to/released from the hospital*** *the day before.* [ORIGIN: 1200—1300 Old French, Medieval Latin *hospitale* "place to stay at," from Latin *hospitalis* "of a guest"]

hos·pi·tal·i·ty /ˌhɑspəˈtæləṭi/ *n.* [U] friendly behavior toward visitors

hos·pi·tal·ize /ˈhɑspɪṭlˌaɪz/ *v.* [T] to put someone into a hospital for medical treatment: *Two people were hospitalized with stab wounds.* —**hospitalization** /ˌhɑspɪṭl-əˈzeɪʃən/ *n.* [U]

host¹ /hoʊst/ *n.* [C] **1** the person at a party who invited the guests and organized the party → HOSTESS: *Our host greeted us at the door.* **2** someone who introduces and talks to the guests on a television or radio show: *a game show host* **3** a country or organization that provides the space, equipment, etc. for a special event: *The bookstore will **play host to** a poetry reading.* **4 a (whole) host of sth** a large number of things: *a host of possibilities* **5** BIOLOGY an animal or plant on which a smaller animal or plant is living as a PARASITE

host² *v.* [T] to be the host of an event, television program, etc.

hos·tage /ˈhɑstɪdʒ/ *n.* [C] someone who is kept as a prisoner by an enemy, so that the other side will do what the enemy demands (SYN) **captive**: *Three nurses were **taken/held hostage** (=caught and used as hostages) by the rebels.*

hos·tel /ˈhɑstl/ *n.* [C] a cheap place for young people to stay when they are traveling

THESAURUS **hotel, motel, inn, bed and breakfast (b&b), campground** → HOTEL

host·ess /ˈhoʊstɪs/ *n.* [C] **1** the woman at a party who invited the guests and organized the party **2** a woman who takes people to their seats in a restaurant

hos·tile /ˈhɑstl, ˈhɑstaɪl/ *adj.* **1** very unfriendly and ready to fight or argue with someone: *a hostile audience* **2** opposing a plan or idea very strongly: *Several unions are **hostile to** the proposals.* **3** belonging to an enemy: *hostile territory* **4** difficult to live in: *Plants such as cacti can survive in hostile environments.* **5 hostile takeover/bid** a situation in which a company tries to buy another company which does not want to be bought [ORIGIN: 1500—1600 French, Latin *hostilis*, from *hostis* "stranger, enemy"]

hos·til·i·ty /hɑˈstɪləṭi/ *n.* **1** [U] unfriendly and angry feelings or behavior: *Why is there so much **hostility toward** immigrants?* **2** [U] strong opposition to a plan or idea: *There's a certain amount of **hostility to** the changes.*

THESAURUS **opposition, antagonism, antipathy** → OPPOSITION

3 hostilities [plural] (formal) the fighting in a war: *an end to hostilities*

hot /hɑt/ *adj.* (comparative **hotter**, superlative **hottest**) **1** high in temperature (ANT) **cold**: *Be careful – the soup's hot.* | *a hot shower* | ***It's hot** (=the weather is hot) today.* | *The Mojave Desert is the hottest place in America.* | *We were all hot and tired.* | *a **steaming/piping/boiling hot** cup of coffee* | *a **scorching/broiling/boiling hot** day in August* | *The metal became **red hot** (=extremely hot).*

THESAURUS
warm – a little hot, especially in a pleasant way: *a warm summer evening*
humid – having air that feels hot and wet rather than dry: *the humid heat of the Brazilian rainforest*
boiling/baking/scorching (hot) – extremely hot: *a boiling hot weekend in August*
sweltering – hot in a very unpleasant, uncomfortable way: *the sweltering heat of the desert*
lukewarm – a liquid that is lukewarm is only slightly warm, and not as cold or hot as it should be: *a glass of lukewarm water*
scalding – a scalding liquid is extremely hot, and hot enough to burn you: *a cup of scalding coffee* → COLD¹, WEATHER¹

2 food that tastes hot has a burning taste (SYN) **spicy** (ANT) **mild**: *hot peppers*

THESAURUS **sweet, tasty, sour, salty, spicy** → TASTE¹

3 (informal) very good, popular, or exciting: *The tennis program has produced some hot young talents.* | *the hottest toy this Christmas* **4** difficult or dangerous to deal with: *Studio bosses decided her video was **too hot to handle** (=too much trouble to deal with).* | *Education has become the **hot topic/issue** (=the subject that people are arguing about) in this election.* **5** (informal) sexually exciting or attractive **6 not so hot** (spoken) slightly sick: *I'm not feeling so hot.* **7 be in hot water** (informal) to be in trouble because you have done something wrong: *He was always in hot water at school.* **8 hot air** (informal) things that someone says to sound important, but that do not really mean anything or are not true **9 be hot at sth** to be very good at doing something: *I wasn't too hot at math.* **10 a hot potato** (informal) a subject or problem that no one wants to deal with because any decision would make a lot of people angry **11 be in/on the hot seat** to be forced to deal with a difficult or bad situation, especially in politics [ORIGIN: Old English *hat*]

hot-ˈair balˌloon *n.* [C] a very large BALLOON made of cloth and filled with hot air, used for carrying people in the air

hot·bed /ˈhɑt˺bɛd/ *n.* **a hotbed of sth** a place where a lot of a particular type of activity happens: *At that time, the university was a hotbed of liberal ideas.*

hot·cake /ˈhɑt˺keɪk/ *n.* [C] **1 sell/go like hotcakes** (spoken) to sell very quickly and in large amounts **2** a PANCAKE

ˈ**hot dog, hot·dog** /ˈhɑtdɔg/ *n.* [C] a long SAUSAGE (=tube-shaped piece of cooked meat), eaten in a long BUN (=type of bread)

ho·tel /hoʊˈtɛl/ *n.* [C] a large building where people pay to stay for a short time: *I prefer to stay*

H

***in** a small **hotel**.* | *We **checked into** our **hotel** by six.* [ORIGIN: 1600—1700 French *hôtel*, from Old French *hostel*]

TOPIC

In order to arrange to stay at a hotel, you can **make a reservation** or **reserve a room**.
When you arrive at the hotel, you **check in** or **check into the hotel** by going to the **reception desk** and saying that you have arrived.
In many hotels, you can eat a meal in the restaurant or **call/order room service** in order to arrange for food to be delivered to your room.
When you leave the hotel, you **check out** or **check out of the hotel** and pay the bill.
→ ACCOMMODATION

THESAURUS

motel – a hotel for people traveling by car, usually with a place for the car near each room
inn – a small hotel, especially one where you can have breakfast and that is not in a city
bed and breakfast (B&B) – a house or a small hotel where you pay to sleep and have breakfast
hostel – a cheap place for young people to stay when they are traveling
campground – a place where you camp in a tent

hot 'flash *n.* [C] a sudden hot feeling that women have during MENOPAUSE

hot·head /'hɑthɛd/ *n.* [C] someone who gets angry or excited easily and does things too quickly, without thinking —**hotheaded** *adj.*

'hot key *n.* [C] IT one or more keys that you can press on a computer KEYBOARD to make the computer quickly do a particular set of actions

hot·line /'hɑt˺laɪn/ *n.* [C] a special telephone number that people can call for quick help with questions or problems: *a suicide hotline*

hot·ly /'hɑtli/ *adv.* **1** in an angry or excited way: *a **hotly debated/disputed** issue* **2** done with a lot of energy or effort: *the **hotly contested** race for governor*

'hot plate, hot·plate /'hɑtpleɪt/ *n.* [C] a small piece of equipment with a flat heated top, used for cooking food

'hot rod *n.* [C] (informal) a car that you have put a powerful engine into

hot·shot /'hɑt-ʃɑt/ *n.* [C] (informal, disapproving) someone who is very successful and confident —**hotshot** *adj.*: *a hotshot lawyer*

'hot spot *n.* [C] **1** a place where there is likely to be fighting or a particular problem: *hot spots around the globe* **2** PHYSICS a place where there is a lot of heat or RADIATION **3** IT an area on a computer screen that you CLICK on in order to make other pictures, words, etc. appear

,hot-'tempered *adj.* tending to become angry very easily

'hot tub *n.* [C] a heated bathtub that several people can sit in

hot-'water ,bottle *n.* [C] a rubber container filled with hot water, used to make a bed warm

'hot-wire *v.* [T] (informal) to start the engine of a vehicle without a key, by using the wires of the IGNITION system

hound[1] /haʊnd/ *v.* [T] to keep following someone and asking him/her questions in an annoying or threatening way: *Celebrities are hounded by reporters.*

hound[2] *n.* [C] a dog used for hunting

hour /aʊɚ/ *n.* **1** [C] a unit for measuring time. There are 60 minutes in one hour: *It **takes** two **hours** to get here from the airport.* | *I'll be home **in an hour**.* | *We met **for an hour** over lunch.* | *Paul should have been here **a half hour/half an hour*** (=30 minutes) *ago.* | *A bomb exploded in the airport just hours before* (=a few hours before) *the President's arrival.* | *a ten-hour trip* (=one that is ten hours long) | *a top speed of 120 **miles per hour*** ▸Don't say "a ten hours trip."◂ **2** [C] the distance you can travel in an hour: *The lake is **an hour from** Hartford.* **3** [singular] a time of day when a new hour starts: *Classes begin **on the hour*** (=exactly at 1 o'clock, 2 o'clock, etc.). **4** [C] a particular period or point in time during the day or night: *I'll go to the store **on** my **lunch hour**.* | *Parking is restricted during **daylight hours**.* | *I'm sorry to bother you **at this hour*** (=at this late time). **5** [C] an important time in history or in your life: *You were there **in my hour of need*** (=when I needed help). **6 hours** [plural] **a)** the period of time when a store or business is open, or when a particular activity happens: *The mall's **opening hours** are from 9 a.m. till 9 p.m.* | *Please phone during **office hours**.* | *What are the **visiting hours*** (=the time when you can visit) *at the hospital?* | *The inventory will be done **after hours*** (=when the store is closed). **b)** (informal) a long time: *She spends hours on the phone.* **7 at all hours** at any time during the day and night: *People wander through the lobby at all hours.* [ORIGIN: 1100—1200 Old French *heure*, from Latin *hora*, from Greek]

hour·glass /'aʊɚglæs/ *n.* [C] a glass container for measuring time, in which sand moves from the top half through a narrow middle part to the bottom half in exactly one hour

hour·ly /'aʊɚli/ *adj., adv.* **1** happening or done every hour: *an hourly news bulletin* | *Trains from Boston arrive hourly.*

THESAURUS **regular, daily, weekly, monthly, yearly** → REGULAR[1]

2 hourly pay/fees etc. the amount you earn or charge for every hour you work

house[1] /haʊs/ *n.* (plural **houses** /'haʊzɪz/) **1** [C] a building that you live in, especially one that is intended to be used by one family: *I'm going over to Dean's house.* | *a three-bedroom house* | *Every room **in the house** was cluttered with books.* | *You're welcome to stay **at** my **house**.*

THESAURUS

ranch house/ranch – a long narrow house built on one level
cottage – a small house in the country
row house – one of a row of houses that are joined together
mansion – a very large house
bungalow – a small house that is usually all on one level
duplex – a house that is divided into two separate homes
apartment – a set of rooms that is part of a bigger building
condominium/condo – one apartment in a building with several apartments, each of which is owned by the people living in it
townhouse a house in a group of houses that share one or more walls
mobile home/trailer – a type of house that can be pulled by a large vehicle and moved to another place
home, place, residence, dwelling, abode ➔ HOME[1]

2 [C] all the people who live in a house: *Be quiet, or you'll wake the whole house!* **3** [C] a building used for a particular purpose or to keep a particular thing in: *the Opera House* | *a hen house* **4** [C] **a)** POLITICS one of the groups of people who make the laws of a state or country: *The President will speak to both **houses of Congress** on Thursday.* **b) the House** POLITICS the HOUSE OF REPRESENTATIVES **5** [C] a company, especially one involved in a particular area of business: *America's oldest publishing house* **6** [C] the part of a theater where people sit, or the people in it: *There was a **full house*** (=every seat was full) *at Friday's performance.* **7 be on the house** (spoken) if drinks or meals in a restaurant are on the house, they are free **8** *also* **house music** [U] a type of modern dance music [ORIGIN: Old English *hus*]

house² /hauz/ *v.* [T] **1** to provide someone with a place to live: *More than 150,000 prisoners are **housed in** 32 prisons.* **2** if a building houses something, that thing is kept there

'house ar,rest *n.* **be under house arrest** to not be allowed to leave your house by the government or police

house·bound /'hausbaund/ *adj.* not able to leave your house, especially because you are sick or old

house·bro·ken /'haus,broukən/ *adj.* a pet animal that is housebroken has been trained not to make the house dirty with its URINE or other body waste

house·hold¹ /'haushould, 'hausould/ *n.* [C] all the people who live together in one house

household² *adj.* **1** relating to taking care of a house and the people in it: *household chores* **2 be a household name/word** to be famous or known about by many people

house·keep·er /'haus,kipɚ/ *n.* [C] someone whose job is to do the cooking, cleaning, etc. in a house or hotel

house·keep·ing /'haus,kipɪŋ/ *n.* [U] **1** the work that needs to be done in a house, hotel, etc. to keep it clean **2** the department in a large building such as a hotel or hospital that is in charge of keeping the building clean inside

,House of Repre'sentatives *n.* **the House of Representatives** POLITICS the larger of the two groups of people who are part of the government and who make the laws in countries such as the U.S. and Australia ➔ SENATE

house·plant /'hausplænt/ *n.* [C] a plant that is grown indoors for decoration

'house-sit *v.* [I] to take care of someone's house while s/he is away

house·wares /'hauswerz/ *n.* [plural] things used in the home, such as plates and lamps

house·warm·ing /'haus,wɔrmɪŋ/ *n.* [C] a party that you give to celebrate moving into a new house

house·wife /'hauswaɪf/ *n.* (plural **housewives** /-waɪvz/) [C] a married woman who works at home doing the cooking, cleaning, etc. ➔ HOMEMAKER

house·work /'hauswɚk/ *n.* [U] the work that you do to take care of a house, for example cleaning and washing clothes ➔ HOMEWORK

hous·ing /'hauzɪŋ/ *n.* **1** [U] the buildings that people live in: *affordable housing* **2** [U] the work of providing houses for people to live in: *a housing program* **3** [C] a protective cover for a machine: *the engine housing*

'housing de,velopment *n.* [C] a number of houses built in the same area at the same time, usually in a similar style

'housing ,project *n.* [C] a group of houses or apartments for poor families, usually built with money from the government

hov·el /'hʌvəl, 'hɑ-/ *n.* [C] (literary) a small dirty place where someone lives

hov·er /'hʌvɚ/ *v.* [I] **1** if a bird, insect, or HELICOPTER hovers, it stays in one place in the air **2** to stay in the same place, especially because you are waiting for something: *Her family hovered at her bedside.* **3** to stay close to a particular amount: *The temperature hovered just above freezing.*

how /hau/ *adv., conjunction* **1** used in order to ask about or explain the way something happens or is done: *How do you spell your name?* | *Martin explained how the system worked.* | *The advisor can show you **how to** apply for the loan.* **2** used in order to ask about the amount, size, or degree of something: *How old is Debbie?* | *How long have you been here?* | *How much are the tickets?* (=what do they cost) **3** used in order to ask about someone's health: *How is your mother these days?* **4** used in order to ask someone about his/her opinion or his/her experience of something: *"How do I look?" "Great!"* | *How was your*

H

vacation? **5** used in order to ask what someone or something looks like, behaves like, or the way something is expressed: *How does that song go?* | *How does she act with other children?* **6** used before an adjective or adverb to emphasize it: *How odd that they didn't tell anyone they were leaving.*

SPOKEN PHRASES

7 how are you?/how's it going?/how are you doing? used when asking if someone is well and happy: *So, how's it going at work?* **8 how about ...?** used when making a suggestion about what to do: *I'm busy tonight, but how about tomorrow?* **9 how come?** used when asking why something has happened (SYN) **why**: *How come you didn't tell me this before?* **10 how do you know?** used when asking why someone is sure about something: *"He's not back yet." "How do you know?"* **11 how can/could sb do sth?** said when you are very surprised by something or disapprove strongly of it: *How could you say that to her?* **12 how do you do?** (formal) said when you meet someone for the first time

how·dy /ˈhaʊdi/ (spoken, informal, humorous) used in order to say "hello" in an informal, usually humorous way

how·ev·er¹ /haʊˈɛvɚ/ *adv.* **1** used in order to add an idea or fact that is surprising or seems very different from what you have just said: *It is a serious disease that is, however, easy to treat.* → ALTHOUGH **2** used in order to say that it does not matter how big, good, serious, etc. something is because it will not change a situation in any way: *However difficult it is for you to accept, it is the truth.*

H

however² *conjunction* in whatever way: *However you do it, I'm sure it will be good.*

howl /haʊl/ *v.* [I] **1** to make a long loud crying sound like a dog or a WOLF → BARK **2** if the wind howls, it makes a loud high sound as it blows **3** to make a loud shouting or crying sound: *The jokes had the audience **howling with laughter**.* —**howl** *n.* [C]

HQ the abbreviation of HEADQUARTERS

hr. (plural **hrs.**) the written abbreviation of HOUR

HTML *n.* [U] IT **hypertext markup language** a computer language used to make documents that can be put on the Internet → SGML, XML

hub /hʌb/ *n.* [C] **1** the central part of an area, system, etc. that all the other parts are connected to: *the **hub of** a transit system* **2** the central part of a wheel

hub·bub /ˈhʌbʌb/ *n.* [singular, U] (informal) **1** the noise of a lot of people all talking at the same time **2** a situation in which there is a lot of activity or excitement: *the hubbub surrounding the trial*

hub·cap /ˈhʌbkæp/ *n.* [C] a metal cover for the center of a wheel on a vehicle

hu·bris /ˈhyubrɪs/ *n.* [U] (literary) too much PRIDE (=pleasure in what you have achieved)

hud·dle /ˈhʌdl/ *v.* [I] **1** *also* **huddle together/up** if a group of people huddle together, they gather very closely together: *A group of reporters were **huddled around** the door.* **2** to lie or sit with your arms and legs close to your body because you are cold or frightened: *Rosie huddled under the blankets.* —**huddle** *n.* [C]

hue /hyu/ *n.* [C] (literary) a color or type of color → SHADE: *a golden hue*

huff¹ /hʌf/ *n.* **in a huff** feeling angry: *Ray left in a huff.*

huff² *v.* (informal) **huff and puff** to breathe out in a noisy way, especially because you have been doing physical work

huff·y /ˈhʌfi/ *adj.* (informal) annoyed or slightly angry: *Don't **get huffy with** me.*

hug¹ /hʌg/ *v.* (**hugged**, **hugging**) [T] **1** to put your arms around someone and hold him/her tightly to show love or friendship: *Hug your children.*

THESAURUS

embrace – to put your arms around someone and hold him/her in a caring way: *Jason warmly embraced his son.*
cuddle – to put your arms around someone or something as a sign of love: *Dawn and her boyfriend were cuddling on the sofa.*
hold – to have something firmly in your hands or arms: *She held the baby in her arms.*
wrap your arms around sb – to hold someone in a loving way by putting your arms around his or her body: *I wrapped my arms around my daughter as she cried.*

2 to move along the side, edge, top, etc. of something, staying very close to it: *A boat was hugging the coast.*

hug² *n.* [C] the act of hugging: ***Give me a hug.***

huge /hyudʒ/ *adj.* very big: *Their house is huge.* | *a huge problem* —**hugely** *adv.*

THESAURUS **big, large, enormous, vast, gigantic, massive, immense, colossal** → BIG

huh /hʌ/ *interjection* **1** said when you have not heard or understood a question: *"What do you think, Bob?" "Huh?"* **2** said at the end of a question to ask for agreement: *Not a bad restaurant, huh?*

hull

hulk /hʌlk/ *n.* [C] **1** an old ship, airplane, or vehicle that is no longer used **2** a large heavy person or thing

hull /hʌl/ *n.* [C] the main outer structure or body of a ship

hul·la·ba·loo /ˈhʌləbəˌlu, ˌhʌləbəˈlu/ *n.* [singular, U] (informal) a lot of noise, excited talk, newspaper stories, etc., especially about something surprising or shocking: *There's always so much hullabaloo about the Olympics.*

hum /hʌm/ *v.* (**hummed**, **humming**) **1** [I,T] to sing a tune by making a continuous sound with your lips closed: *Mrs. Garner hummed while she worked.* **2** [I] to make a low continuous sound: *Air conditioners hummed in the windows.* **3** [I] if a place is humming, it is very busy and full of activity —**hum** *n.* [singular]

hu·man[1] /ˈhyumən/ *adj.* **1** belonging to or relating to people: *human behavior | the different cell types in **the human body** | Viruses are too small to be seen by **the human eye**. | NASA said the accident was a result of **human error*** (=a mistake made by a person, not a machine). | *the value of **human life*** **2** human weaknesses, emotions, etc. are typical of ordinary people ➔ INHUMAN: *The movie shows us **human nature*** (=the good and bad qualities that are typical of people) *at its best and worst.* **3 sb is only human** used in order to say that someone should not be blamed for what s/he has done **4 human interest** a quality that makes a story interesting because it is about people's lives, feelings, relationships, etc. [ORIGIN: 1300—1400 French *humain*, from Latin *humanus*]

human[2] *also* **human being** *n.* [C] a man, woman, or child

hu·mane /hyuˈmeɪn/ *adj.* treating people or animals in a way that is kind, not cruel (ANT) **inhumane** —**humanely** *adv.*

hu·man·ism /ˈhyuməˌnɪzəm/ *n.* [U] the belief that human problems can be solved through science rather than religion —**humanist** *n.* [C] —**humanistic** /ˌhyuməˈnɪstɪk◂/ *adj.*

hu·man·i·tar·i·an /hyuˌmænəˈtɛriən/ *adj.* [only before noun] concerned with improving bad living conditions and preventing unfair treatment of people: ***Humanitarian aid/relief/assistance** is flowing into the country.* —**humanitarian** *n.* [C] —**humanitarianism** *n.* [U]

hu·man·i·ty /hyuˈmænət̬i/ *n.* **1** [U] people in general ➔ HUMANKIND: *Pollution poses a danger to humanity.* **2** [U] kindness, respect, and sympathy toward other people (ANT) **inhumanity**: *a man of great humanity* **3 the humanities** [plural] subjects you study that are related to literature, history, art, etc. rather than mathematics or science **4** [U] the state of being human

hu·man·ize /ˈhyuməˌnaɪz/ *v.* [T] to make a system more pleasant for people: *The changes should help to humanize the prison.*

hu·man·kind /ˈhyumənˌkaɪnd/ *n.* [U] people in general (SYN) **mankind** ➔ HUMANITY

> THESAURUS man, mankind, people ➔ MAN[1]

hu·man·ly /ˈhyumənli/ *adv.* **humanly possible** able to be done using all your skills, knowledge, time, etc.: *The doctors **did everything humanly possible** to save his life.*

ˌhuman ˈrace *n.* **the human race** all people, considered as a single group

ˌhuman ˈresources *n.* [U] the department in a company that deals with employing, training, and helping people (SYN) **personnel**

ˌhuman ˈrights *n.* [plural] the basic rights that every person should have to be treated in a fair equal way without cruelty, especially by his/her government

hum·ble[1] /ˈhʌmbəl/ *adj.* **1** (approving) not considering yourself or your ideas to be as important as other people's (ANT) **proud** ➔ HUMILITY: *a quiet, humble man* **2** relating to a low social class or position: *The senator talked about his **humble beginnings/background** on a farm in Iowa.* [ORIGIN: 1200—1300 Old French, Latin *humilis* "low, humble," from *humus* "earth"] —**humbly** *adv.*

humble[2] *v.* [T] to make someone realize that s/he is not as important, good, kind, etc. as s/he thought: *The team was humbled by a surprise defeat.* —**humbling** *adj.*

hum·drum /ˈhʌmdrʌm/ *adj.* boring, ordinary, and having very little variety: *a humdrum job*

> THESAURUS boring, dull, tedious, not (very/that/all that) interesting, monotonous ➔ BORING

hu·mer·us /ˈhyumərəs/ *n.* (plural **humeri** /-raɪ/) [C] BIOLOGY the bone between your shoulder and elbow

hu·mid /ˈhyumɪd/ *adj.* if the weather is humid, the air feels warm and wet: *Summers here are **hot and humid**.* ➔ HOT ➔ DAMP

hu·mid·i·fier /hyuˈmɪdəˌfaɪɚ/ *n.* [C] a machine that makes the air in a room less dry —**humidify** *v.* [T]

hu·mid·i·ty /hyuˈmɪdət̬i/ *n.* [U] the amount of water that is contained in the air: *Atlanta is known for its heat and **high humidity** during the summer.*

hu·mil·i·ate /hyuˈmɪliˌeɪt/ *v.* [T] to make someone feel ashamed or stupid, especially when other people are present ➔ EMBARRASS: *Her husband abused and humiliated her.* —**humiliated** *adj.* —**humiliation** /hyuˌmɪliˈeɪʃən/ *n.* [C,U]

hu·mil·i·at·ing /hyuˈmɪliˌeɪt̬ɪŋ/ *adj.* making you feel ashamed or embarrassed: *a humiliating defeat at the polls*

hu·mil·i·ty /hyuˈmɪlət̬i/ *n.* [U] (approving) the quality of not being too proud about yourself

hu·mor[1] /ˈhyumɚ/ *n.* [U] **1** the ability to laugh at things and think that they are funny, or funny things you say that show you have this ability: *She has a great **sense of humor**. | Allen's **dry/black/wry humor*** (=humor with a particular quality) **2** the quality in something that makes it funny and makes people laugh: *a novel full of humor and intelligence* **3 good humor** a happy friendly attitude to people and events

H

humor² *v.* [T] to do what someone wants so that s/he will not become angry or upset: *Just humor me and listen, please.*

hu·mor·ist /ˈhyumərɪst/ *n.* [C] someone, especially a writer, who tells jokes and funny stories

hu·mor·less /ˈhyumɚlɪs/ *adj.* (disapproving) too serious and not able to laugh at things that are funny

hu·mor·ous /ˈhyumərəs/ *adj.* funny and enjoyable: *a humorous look at relationships* —**humorously** *adv.*

THESAURUS **funny, witty, amusing, comical** → FUNNY¹

hump /hʌmp/ *n.* [C] **1** a raised part on the back of a person or animal: *a camel's hump* **2** a round shape that rises above a surface: *Do you see that big hump of rock sticking out of the prairie?* **3 be over the hump** to have finished the most difficult part of something

hunch¹ /hʌntʃ/ *n.* [C] a feeling that something is true or that something will happen: ***My hunch is that** things will improve soon.* | *I **had a hunch** you'd call today.*

hunch² *v.* [I] to bend down and lean forward so that your back forms a curve: *Employees were **hunched over** their computer screens.* —**hunched** *adj.*

hunch·back /ˈhʌntʃbæk/ *n.* [C] (offensive) someone who has a large HUMP on his/her back

hun·dred¹ /ˈhʌndrɪd/ *number* **1** 100: *a hundred years* | *two hundred miles* **2** a very large number of things or people: ***Hundreds of** people marched in protest.* | *You've seen that program **a hundred times**!* **3 a/one hundred percent** completely: *I agree one hundred percent.* **4 give a hundred percent** to do everything you can in order to achieve something: *Everyone on the team gave a hundred percent.* [ORIGIN: Old English] —**hundredth** /ˈhʌndrɪdθ/ *number*

hundred² *n.* [C] a piece of paper money worth $100

hun·dred·weight /ˈhʌndrɪdˌweɪt/ (*written abbreviation* **cwt**) *n.* (plural **hundredweight**) [C] a measure of weight equal to 100 pounds or 45.36 kilograms

hung /hʌŋ/ *v.* the past tense and past participle of HANG

hun·ger¹ /ˈhʌŋgɚ/ *n.* **1** [U] the feeling that you want or need to eat → HUNGRY, THIRSTY: *He had **hunger pangs** (=feelings of being hungry) from missing lunch.* ►Don't say "I have hunger." Say "I am hungry."◄ **2** [U] a severe lack of food, especially for a long period of time SYN **starvation**: *People were **dying of hunger**.* **3** [singular, U] a strong need or desire for something: *a **hunger for** power*

hunger² *v.*

hunger for sth *phr. v.* to want something very much

ˈ**hunger strike** *n.* [C] a situation in which someone refuses to eat, in order to protest about something

ˌ**hung** ˈ**jury** *n.* [C usually singular] a JURY that cannot agree about whether someone is guilty of a crime

ˌ**hung** ˈ**over** *adj.* feeling sick because you drank too much alcohol the previous day → HANGOVER

hun·gry /ˈhʌŋgri/ *adj.* (comparative **hungrier**, superlative **hungriest**) **1** wanting to eat something → HUNGER, THIRST: *When's dinner? I'm hungry.* | *If you **get hungry**, there's some turkey in the fridge.* **2 go hungry** to not have enough food to eat: *Despite our country's wealth, many poor families still go hungry.* **3 be hungry for sth** to want something very much: *She was a lonely child who was hungry for a friend.* —**hungrily** *adv.*

ˌ**hung** ˈ**up** *adj.* (informal) worrying too much about someone or something: *Let's not **get hung up on** the details here.*

hunk /hʌŋk/ *n.* [C] **1** a thick piece of something that has been taken from a bigger piece: ***a hunk of** bread* **2** (informal) an attractive man who has a strong body

hun·ker /ˈhʌŋkɚ/ *v.*

hunker down *phr. v.* **1** (informal) to not do things that may be risky, so that you are safe and protected: *People are hunkering down and waiting for the economy to get better.* **2** to bend your knees so that you are sitting on your heels, close to the ground SYN **squat**

hunt¹ /hʌnt/ *v.* [I,T] **1** to chase animals or birds in order to catch and kill them: *This isn't the season for hunting deer.* **2** to look for someone or something very carefully: *She was **hunting for** the perfect wedding gown.* [ORIGIN: Old English *huntian*]

hunt sb/sth ↔ **down** *phr. v.* to find an enemy or criminal after searching hard: *The agency was created to hunt down war criminals.*

hunt² *n.* [C] **1** a careful search for someone or something: *The **hunt for** the missing child continues today.* **2** an occasion when people chase animals in order to catch or kill them

hunt·er /ˈhʌntɚ/ *n.* [C] **1** a person or animal that hunts wild animals **2** someone who is looking for a particular thing: *job hunters*

ˌ**hunter-**ˈ**gatherer** *n.* [C] SOCIAL SCIENCE a member of a society who live by hunting animals and collecting wild plants

hunt·ing /ˈhʌntɪŋ/ *n.* [U] **1** the act of chasing animals in order to catch or kill them: *Ed's going to **go** deer **hunting** next weekend.* **2 job-hunting/house-hunting etc.** the activity of looking for a job, a house to live in, etc. —**hunting** *adj.*

hur·dle¹ /ˈhɚdl/ *n.* [C] **1** a problem or difficulty

that you must deal with before you can achieve something: *The drug has **cleared the final hurdle** for FDA approval.* **2** a type of small fence that a person or a horse jumps over during a race

hurdle² *v.* [T] to jump over something while you are running —**hurdler** *n.* [C]

THESAURUS jump, skip, hop, leap, vault → JUMP¹

hurl /hɚl/ *v.* **1** [T] to throw something using a lot of force: *He **hurled** a brick **through/out** the window.*

THESAURUS throw, toss, chuck, fling, lob → THROW¹

2 hurl insults/abuse etc. at sb to shout at someone in a loud and angry way **3** [I] (spoken, humorous) to VOMIT

hur·ray /hə'reɪ, hʊ'reɪ/ *also* **hur·rah** /hʊ'rɑ/ *interjection* HOORAY

hur·ri·cane /'hɚɪˌkeɪn, 'hʌɪ-/ *n.* [C] a severe tropical storm that forms over the Atlantic Ocean at the end of summer and beginning of fall, with very strong winds of at least 74 miles per hour → TORNADO [ORIGIN: 1500—1600 Spanish *huracán*, from Taino (a Caribbean language) *hurakán*]

THESAURUS wind, gale, storm, tornado, typhoon → WIND¹

hur·ried /'hɚid, 'hʌrid/ *adj.* done more quickly than usual: *We are a hurried breakfast.* —**hurriedly** *adv.*

hur·ry¹ /'hɚi, 'hʌri/ *v.* (**hurried**, **hurries**) [I,T] to do something or go somewhere more quickly than usual, or to make someone or something do this (SYN) **rush**: *Students **hurried across/around etc.** campus.* | *The girls **hurried home** to tell their parents.* | *I spend so much time **hurrying** the kids **to/from** activities.*

THESAURUS rush, race, dash, hasten → RUSH¹

hurry up *phr. v.* **1** to do something or move somewhere more quickly: *I wish the bus would hurry up and get here.* | *Hurry up!* (=said when you want someone to hurry) *We're going to be late!* **2 hurry** sb/sth **up** to make someone do something more quickly, or to make something happen more quickly

hurry² *n.* **1 be in a hurry** to need to do something, go somewhere, etc. more quickly than usual: *Why is she in such a hurry?* | *He was **in a hurry to** get to town.* **2 (there's) no hurry** (spoken) said in order to tell someone that s/he does not have to do something quickly or soon: *Relax, there's no hurry.* **3 not be in any hurry/be in no hurry** to be able to wait because you have a lot of time in which to do something: *Take your time; I'm not in any hurry.* **4 what's (all) the hurry?** (spoken) said when you think someone is doing something too quickly

hurt¹ /hɚt/ *v.* (past tense and past participle **hurt**) **1** [T] to injure yourself or someone else: *She hurt her knee playing volleyball.* | *Did you hurt yourself?*

THESAURUS

Hurt and **injure** can mean the same, but **hurt** is usually used when the damage to your body is not very great: *Alex fell and hurt his knee.*
injure – used especially to say that someone has been hurt in an accident: *Three people were seriously injured in the crash.*
wound – to hurt someone using a weapon such as a gun or knife: *The gunman killed two people and wounded six others.*
maim (formal) – to injure someone very seriously and often permanently: *People are killed or maimed every day in the war.*
break – to damage a bone in your body
bruise – to get a dark mark on your skin after part of your body has hit against something hard
sprain/twist – to damage a joint in your body by suddenly twisting it
strain/pull – to hurt one of your muscles by stretching it or using it too much
dislocate – to move a bone out of its normal position in a joint

2 [I,T] to feel pain or cause pain in a part of your body: *My stomach hurts.* | *It hurts my knees to run.*

THESAURUS

ache – to feel a continuous pain: *My back was aching*
throb – if a part of your body throbs, you get a regular feeling of pain in it: *My throat was dry and my head was throbbing.*
sting – to feel a sudden sharp pain in your eyes, throat, or skin, or to make someone feel this: *The antiseptic might sting a little*
smart – to hurt with a stinging pain: *The smoke made my eyes smart.*
pinch – if something you are wearing pinches you, it is too tight and presses painfully on your skin: *These shoes pinch my toes.* → PAINFUL

3 [I,T] to make someone feel very upset or unhappy: *I'm sorry, I didn't mean to **hurt** your **feelings**.* **4** [T] to have a bad effect on someone or something: *The loss **hurts** the team's **chances** of getting to the playoffs.* **5 it won't/doesn't hurt to do sth** (spoken) said when you think someone should do something or something is a good idea: *It won't hurt him to clean his room.* **6 be hurting** (informal) to feel upset or unhappy about something —**hurt** *n.* [C,U]

hurt² *adj.* **1** suffering pain or injury: *It's okay, nobody **got hurt**.* | *Kerry was **badly/seriously/slightly hurt** in a skiing accident.* **2** very upset or unhappy: *Debra **felt hurt** and betrayed.* ► You say "seriously/badly/slightly hurt" about an injury, but "very hurt" when someone upsets you. ◄

hurt·ful /'hɚtfəl/ *adj.* making you feel upset or unhappy

hur·tle /'hɚtl/ *v.* [I] to move or fall very fast

H

hus·band /ˈhʌzbənd/ *n.* [C] the man that a woman is married to ➔ WIFE: *I'd like you to meet my husband Leon.* [ORIGIN: Old English *husbonda*, from Old Norse, from *hus* "house" + *bondi* "someone who lives in a house"]

hush¹ /hʌʃ/ *v.* [I] (spoken) said in order to tell someone to be quiet, or to comfort a child who is crying

hush sth ↔ **up** *phr. v.* to prevent people from knowing about something dishonest: *The senator denied that he had tried to hush up the story.*

hush² *n.* [singular] a peaceful silence: *A* ***hush fell*** *over the room* (=everyone suddenly became quiet).

hushed /hʌʃt/ *adj.* quiet: *They were speaking* ***in hushed tones.***

ˌhush-ˈhush *adj.* (informal) secret: *The whole project was very hush-hush.*

husk /hʌsk/ *n.* [C] the dry outer part of some grains, nuts, corn, etc.

husk·y¹ /ˈhʌski/ *adj.* **1** a husky voice is deep and sounds rough **2** a husky boy or man is big and strong

husky² *n.* (plural **huskies**) [C] a dog with thick hair, often used for pulling SLEDS over snow

hus·tle¹ /ˈhʌsəl/ *v.* **1** [T] to make someone move quickly, often by pushing him/her: *Jackson was* ***hustled into*** *his car by bodyguards.* **2** [I] to hurry in doing something or going somewhere: *Come on, you guys! Let's hustle!* **3** [I,T] (informal) to cheat someone in order to get money

H

hustle² *n.* **1 hustle and bustle** busy and noisy activity **2** [U] (informal) energy and determination in doing an activity: *She's a good worker with a lot of hustle.* **3** [C] (informal) a way of getting money that is illegal and dishonest

hus·tler /ˈhʌslɚ/ *n.* [C] someone who gets money in a way that is illegal and dishonest

hut /hʌt/ *n.* [C] a small wooden building with only one or two rooms

hutch /hʌtʃ/ *n.* [C] **1** a small wooden box in which you can keep rabbits **2** a piece of furniture used for storing and showing dishes

hwy. the written abbreviation of HIGHWAY

hy·brid /ˈhaɪbrɪd/ *n.* [C] BIOLOGY **1** an animal or plant that is produced from parents of different breeds or types **2** something that is a mixture of two or more things: *The book is a* ***hybrid of*** *fantasy and satire.* —**hybrid** *adj.*: *hybrid seed corn*

hy·brid·i·za·tion /ˌhaɪbrɪdəˈzeɪʃən/ *n.* [U] BIOLOGY a process in which a hybrid plant or animal is made —**hybridize** /ˈhaɪbrəˌdaɪz/ *v.* [I,T]

hy·drant /ˈhaɪdrənt/ *n.* [C] a FIRE HYDRANT

hy·drau·lic /haɪˈdrɔlɪk/ *adj.* moved or operated by the pressure of water or other liquids: *hydraulic brakes* —**hydraulically** *adv.*

hy·drau·lics /haɪˈdrɔlɪks/ *n.* [U] PHYSICS the study of how to use water pressure to produce power

hy·dro·car·bon /ˌhaɪdroʊˈkɑrbən/ *n.* [C usually plural] CHEMISTRY a chemical compound that consists only of hydrogen and CARBON, such as coal or NATURAL GAS

hy·dro·e·lec·tric /ˌhaɪdroʊɪˈlɛktrɪk/ *adj.* PHYSICS using water power to produce electricity —**hydroelectricity** /ˌhaɪdroʊɪlɛkˈtrɪsət̮i/ *n.* [U]: *Large hydroelectric dams generate most of the country's hydroelectricity.*

hy·dro·gen /ˈhaɪdrədʒən/ *n.* [U] CHEMISTRY (*symbol* **H**) a gas that is an ELEMENT and is lighter than air, and that forms water when it combines with oxygen [ORIGIN: 1700—1800 French *hydrogène*, from *hydro-* "water" + *-gène* "producing;" because it produces water when it is burned]

ˌhydrogen perˈoxide *n.* [U] CHEMISTRY a chemical liquid used for killing BACTERIA and for making hair and other substances lighter in color

hy·dro·plane /ˈhaɪdrəˌpleɪn/ *v.* [I] if a car hydroplanes, it slides on a wet road

hy·dro·ther·mal vent /ˌhaɪdroʊˌθɚməl ˈvɛnt/ *n.* [C] EARTH SCIENCES an opening in the ground at the bottom of the ocean, from which very hot water containing a lot of minerals is sent out with a lot of force

hy·drox·ide /haɪˈdrɑksaɪd/ *n.* [C] CHEMISTRY a chemical compound that contains one oxygen atom combined with one HYDROGEN atom

hyˌdroxide ˈion *n.* [C] CHEMISTRY a negative ION which has one oxygen atom and one HYDROGEN atom

hy·e·na /haɪˈinə/ *n.* [C] a wild animal like a dog that makes a loud sound like a laugh

hy·giene /ˈhaɪdʒin/ *n.* [U] the practice of keeping yourself and the things around you clean in order to prevent diseases: *The rules help to ensure* ***good hygiene*** *in school kitchens.* | *Good eating habits and* ***personal hygiene*** (=keeping your body clean) *can prevent infections.* [ORIGIN: 1600—1700 French *hygène*, from Greek *hygieina*, from *hygies* "healthy"]

hy·gi·en·ic /haɪˈdʒɛnɪk, -ˈdʒinɪk/ *adj.* clean and likely to prevent diseases from spreading

hy·gro·scop·ic /ˌhaɪgrəˈskɑpɪk◂/ *adj.* CHEMISTRY hygroscopic salts and other compounds are able or likely to take in water easily from the surrounding air

hymn /hɪm/ *n.* [C] a song of praise to God [ORIGIN: 800—900 Latin *hymnus* "song of praise," from Greek *hymnos*]

hym·nal /ˈhɪmnəl/ *n.* [C] a book of hymns

hype¹ /haɪp/ *n.* [U] attempts to make people think something is good or important by talking about it a lot on television, the radio, etc.: *The movie looks like it'll be good, but there is so much* ***media hype*** *around it!*

hype² *also* **hype up** *v.* [T] to try to make people think something is good or important by advertising or talking about it a lot on television, the radio, etc.: *The mayor's speech has been hyped for weeks.*

THESAURUS **advertise, promote, market, publicize, plug** ➔ ADVERTISE

ˌhyped 'up *adj.* (informal) very excited or anxious about something: *They're all* ***hyped up about*** *getting into the playoffs.*

hy·per /'haɪpɚ/ *adj.* (informal) extremely excited or nervous

hy·per·ac·tive /ˌhaɪpɚ'æktɪv/ *adj.* someone, especially a child, who is hyperactive is too active, and not able to keep still or quiet for very long —**hyperactivity** /ˌhaɪpɚæk'tɪvəṭi/ *n.* [U]

THESAURUS **energetic, vigorous, full of energy, dynamic, lively** ➔ ENERGETIC

hy·per·bo·la /haɪ'pɚbələ/ *n.* [C] MATH a pair of curved lines formed by a PLANE (=flat surface) crossing two CONEs, so that the difference of the distances between two fixed points inside the curves to any point on the curves is always the same ➔ CONIC SECTION —**hyperbolic** /ˌhaɪpɚ'bɑlɪk/ *adj*

hy·per·bo·le /haɪ'pɚbəli/ *n.* [C,U] ENG. LANG. ARTS a way of describing something by saying that it is much bigger, smaller, heavier, etc. than it really is

hy·per·in·fla·tion /ˌhaɪpɚɪn'fleɪʃən/ *n.* [U] ECONOMICS a very fast rise in prices that seriously damages a country's ECONOMY

hy·per·link /'haɪpɚˌlɪŋk/ *n.* [C] IT a word or picture on a WEBSITE or computer document that will take you to another page or document if you CLICK on it (SYN) **link**

hy·per·sen·si·tive /ˌhaɪpɚ'sɛnsəṭɪv/ *adj.* very easily offended or upset

hy·per·ten·sion /ˌhaɪpɚ'tɛnʃən, 'haɪpɚˌtɛnʃən/ *n.* [U] a medical condition in which someone's BLOOD PRESSURE is too high

hy·per·ton·ic /ˌhaɪpɚ'tɑnɪk/ *adj.* CHEMISTRY a hypertonic SOLUTION (=liquid with substances dissolved in it) contains more of a SOLUTE (=substance that is dissolved) than another solution that you are comparing it to ➔ HYPOTONIC

hy·per·ven·ti·late /ˌhaɪpɚ'vɛntlˌeɪt/ *v.* [I] to breathe too quickly because you are very excited or upset

hy·phen /'haɪfən/ *n.* [C] a mark (-) used in writing to join words or parts of words

hy·phen·ate /'haɪfəˌneɪt/ *v.* [T] to join words or parts of words with a hyphen —**hyphenated** *adj.* —**hyphenation** /ˌhaɪfə'neɪʃən/ *n.* [U]

hyp·no·sis /hɪp'noʊsɪs/ *n.* [U] a state similar to sleep, in which someone's thoughts and actions can be influenced by someone else ➔ HYPNOTIZE: *He remembered details of the crime* ***under hypnosis.***

hyp·not·ic /hɪp'nɑṭɪk/ *adj.* **1** making someone feel tired, especially because sound or movement is repeated **2** relating to hypnosis: *He was in a hypnotic trance.* —**hypnotically** *adv.*

hyp·no·tize /'hɪpnəˌtaɪz/ *v.* [T] to produce a sleep-like state in someone, so that you can influence his/her thoughts or actions —**hypnotism** /'hɪpnəˌtɪzəm/ *n.* [U] —**hypnotist** /'hɪpnətɪst/ *n.* [C]

hy·po·chon·dri·ac /ˌhaɪpə'kɑndriˌæk/ *n.* [C] someone who worries all the time about his/her health, even when s/he is not sick —**hypochondriac** *adj.* —**hypochondria** /ˌhaɪpə'kɑndriə/ *n.* [U]

hy·poc·ri·sy /hɪ'pɑkrəsi/ *n.* [U] (disapproving) the act of saying you have particular beliefs, feelings, etc., but behaving in a way that shows you do not really have these beliefs or feelings [ORIGIN: 1100—1200 Old French *ypocrisie*, from Greek *hypokrisis* "act of playing a part on stage, hypocrisy"]

hyp·o·crite /'hɪpəˌkrɪt/ *n.* [C] (disapproving) someone who pretends to believe something or behave in a good way when really s/he does not —**hypocritical** /ˌhɪpə'krɪṭɪkəl/ *adj.*

hy·po·der·mic /ˌhaɪpə'dɚmɪk◂/ *also* **hypodermic needle** *n.* [C] an instrument with a hollow needle used for putting drugs into someone's body through the skin ➔ SYRINGE —**hypodermic** *adj.*

hy·pot·e·nuse /haɪ'pɑt˺n-us/ *n.* [C] MATH the longest side of a TRIANGLE that has a RIGHT ANGLE

hy·po·thal·a·mus /ˌhaɪpoʊ'θæləməs/ *n.* (plural **hypothalami** /-ləmaɪ/) [C] BIOLOGY a small part of the brain that controls the temperature of your body, your desire for food and drink, and your need for sleep ➔ *see picture at* BRAIN[1]

hy·po·ther·mi·a /ˌhaɪpə'θɚmiə/ *n.* [U] a serious medical condition in which someone's body temperature becomes very low, caused by extreme cold

hy·poth·e·sis /haɪ'pɑθəsɪs/ (Ac) *n.* (plural **hypotheses** /-θəsiz/) [C] **1** SCIENCE an idea that is suggested as an explanation of something, but that has not yet been proven to be true ➔ THEORY: *research that supports this hypothesis*

THESAURUS **idea, concept, theory** ➔ IDEA

2 ENG. LANG. ARTS the idea that follows "if" or "unless" in a CONDITIONAL sentence (=sentence that expresses an idea, fact, etc. that causes something else to be true) [ORIGIN: 1500—1600 Greek *hypotithenai* "to put under"] —**hypothesize** /haɪ'pɑθəˌsaɪz/ *v.* [T]

hy·po·thet·i·cal /ˌhaɪpə'θɛṭɪkəl/ (Ac) *adj.* based on a situation that is not real, but that might happen (SYN) **theoretical**: *This is a hypothetical story that illustrates the difference in how rich and poor people are treated.* —**hypothetically** *adv.*

H

hy·po·ton·ic /ˌhaɪpoʊˈtɑnɪk/ *adj.* BIOLOGY a hypotonic SOLUTION (=liquid with substances dissolved in it) contains less of a SOLUTE (=substance that is dissolved) than another solution that you are comparing it to → HYPERTONIC

hys·ter·ec·to·my /ˌhɪstəˈrɛktəmi/ *n.* (plural **hysterectomies**) [C] a medical operation to remove a woman's UTERUS

hys·ter·i·a /hɪˈstɛriə, -ˈstɪriə/ *n.* [U] extreme excitement, anger, fear, etc. that you cannot control: *News stories like these could cause mass hysteria.* [ORIGIN: 1800—1900 *hysteric* "hysterical" (17—20 centuries), from Greek *hystera* "uterus;" because it was believed hysteria was caused by the uterus]

hys·ter·i·cal /hɪˈstɛrɪkəl/ *adj.* **1** (informal) extremely funny: *a hysterical comedy act*

THESAURUS **funny, hilarious, amusing, humorous** → FUNNY[1]

2 unable to control your behavior or emotions because you are very upset, afraid, excited, etc.: *Don't tell Rob – he'll just get hysterical.* —**hysterically** *adv.*

hys·ter·ics /hɪˈstɛrɪks/ *n.* [plural] **1** a state of being unable to control your behavior or emotions because you are very upset, afraid, excited, etc.: *As soon as she saw the rat she* ***went into hysterics.*** **2 be in hysterics** (informal) to be unable to stop laughing: *The audience was in hysterics.*

Hz PHYSICS the written abbreviation of HERTZ

I

Ii

I, i /aɪ/ **1** the ninth letter of the English alphabet **2** the number 1 in the system of ROMAN NUMERALS

I /aɪ/ *pron.* used as the subject of a verb when you are the person speaking: *I saw Mike yesterday.* | *I've been playing softball.* | *I'm thirsty.* | *My boyfriend and I went to Miami.* ►When you write or talk about yourself and another person, you should always mention the other person first, so don't say "I and my boyfriend... ." ◄

i *number* MATH an imaginary number that is equal to the SQUARE ROOT of negative 1

IA the written abbreviation of IOWA

i·amb /ˈaɪæmb/ *also* **i·am·bus** /aɪˈæmbəs/ *n.* (plural **iambuses** *or* **iambi**) [C] ENG. LANG. ARTS a RHYTHM in poetry in which a word or SYLLABLE that is not STRESSED is followed by one that is stressed, as in the word "alive"

i·am·bic pen·tam·e·ter /aɪˌæmbɪk pɛnˈtæmət̬ɚ/ *n.* [C,U] ENG. LANG. ARTS a common RHYTHM (=pattern of beats) used in English poetry, in which each line consists of five iambs. It was used more commonly in the past than it is today.

ice[1] /aɪs/ *n.* **1** [U] water that has frozen into a solid: *Do you want some ice in your drink?* | *There's too much ice and snow on the roads.* **2 break the ice** to begin to be friendly to someone by talking to him/her: *Stan tried to break the ice by asking her where she was from.* [ORIGIN: Old English *is*]

ice[2] *v.* [T] **1** to put ice on a part of your body that is injured **2** FROST

ice over/up *phr. v.* to become covered with ice: *The lake iced over during the night.*

ˈice age *n.* **1** [C] EARTH SCIENCES one of the periods in the Earth's history when temperatures were very cold and ice covered large parts of the Earth's surface **2 the Ice Age** HISTORY the most recent ice age, which happened thousands of years ago, when ice covered most northern countries

ice·berg /ˈaɪsbɚg/ *n.* [C] an extremely large piece of ice floating in the ocean → **tip of the iceberg** *at* TIP[1]

ice·break·er /ˈaɪsˌbreɪkɚ/ *n.* [C] **1** something you say or do to make someone less nervous **2** a ship that can sail through ice

ˈice cap *n.* [C usually singular] EARTH SCIENCES an area of thick ice that always covers the North and South Poles

ˌice-ˈcold *adj.* extremely cold: *ice-cold drinks*

ˈice cream *n.* [U] **1** a frozen sweet food made of milk or cream and sugar, usually with fruit, nuts, chocolate, etc. added to it: *vanilla ice cream* **2** [C] a small amount of this food for one person

ˈice cream ˌcone *n.* [C] a hard thin cookie shaped like a CONE, with ice cream in it

ˈice cube *n.* [C] a small block of ice that you put in cold drinks

ˌiced ˈcoffee *also* **ˌice ˈcoffee** *n.* [C,U] cold coffee that is served with ice, milk, and sometimes sugar, or a glass of this drink

ˌiced ˈtea *also* **ˌice ˈtea** *n.* [C,U] cold tea that is served with ice and sometimes LEMON or sugar, or a glass of this drink

ˈice ˌhockey *n.* [U] HOCKEY → *see picture on page A17*

ˈice pack *n.* [C] a bag of ice used for keeping something cold

ˈice skate[1] *n.* [C usually plural] one of two special boots with metal blades on the bottom that let you slide quickly on ice

ˈice skate[2] *v.* [I] to move along on ice for fun wearing ice skates —**ice skater** *n.* [C] —**ice skating** *n.* [U]

i·ci·cle /ˈaɪsɪkəl/ *n.* [C] a thin pointed piece of ice that hangs down from something such as a roof

ic·ing /ˈaɪsɪŋ/ *n.* [U] **1** FROSTING **2 sth is (the) icing on the cake** used to say that something makes a good situation even better: *Coe was delighted to win the race, but breaking the world record was the icing on the cake.*

ick·y /ˈɪki/ *adj.* (spoken) very disgusting to look at, taste, or feel: *The soup tasted icky.*

i·con /ˈaɪkɑn/ *n.* [C] **1** IT a small picture on a computer screen that makes the computer do something when you CLICK on it with the MOUSE **2** someone or something famous that people think represents an important idea: *The peace symbol is an icon of the sixties.* **3** a picture or figure of a holy person: *religious icons* [ORIGIN: 1500—1600 Latin, Greek *eikon*, from *eikenai* "to be like"]

i·con·o·clast /aɪˈkɑnəˌklæst/ *n.* [C] someone who attacks established ideas and traditional ways of doing things

ic·y /ˈaɪsi/ *adj.* (comparative **icier**, superlative **iciest**) **1** extremely cold: *a burst of icy air*

> THESAURUS **cold, cool, chilly, frosty, freezing (cold), bitter (cold), frigid** → COLD[1]

2 covered in ice: *an icy road* **3** unfriendly and frightening: *an icy stare* —**icily** *adv.* —**iciness** *n.* [U]

I'd /aɪd/ **1** the short form of "I had": *I'd never met Kurt before today.* **2** the short form of "I would": *I'd love to come!*

ID[1] *n.* [C,U] **identification** something that shows your name, address, the date you were born, etc., usually with a photograph: *Can I see your ID?* | *Pete got into the club with a fake ID.*

ID[2] the written abbreviation of IDAHO

i·de·a /aɪˈdiə/ *n.* **1** [C] a plan or suggestion that someone thinks of: *Braby got the* ***idea for*** *his book from some old letters.* | *That sounds like a* ***good/great idea.*** | *Ann thinks it's a* ***bad idea*** *to go today.* | ***I have an idea*** *– let's get Dad a set of golf clubs.*

> THESAURUS
>
> **An idea that explains something**
>
> **concept** – someone's general idea of what something is like: *our modern concept of love*
>
> **theory** – an idea or set of ideas that is intended to explain something, especially in science: *Einstein's theory of relativity*
>
> **hypothesis** – an idea that is suggested as an explanation of something, but has not yet been proven to be true: *He carried out a series of experiments in order to test his hypothesis.*
>
> **Something you think of**
>
> **thought** – something that you think of, think about, or remember: *Erika had a sudden thought: "Why don't you come with me?"*
>
> **inspiration** – something or someone that encourages you to do or produce something good: *People like Tara are an inspiration to us all.*

2 [C,U] understanding or knowledge of something: *The book gives you a pretty good* ***idea of*** *the basic principles of law.* | *Can you* ***give me a rough idea of*** (=a not very exact description of) *how much it will cost?* | ***I had no idea*** (=did not know at all) *what they were talking about.* | ***I don't have the faintest idea*** (=I don't know at all) *what to get Rachel for her birthday.* **3** [C,U] the aim or purpose of doing something: ***The idea of*** *the game is to hit the ball into the holes.* **4** [C] an opinion or belief: *Bill has some strange* ***ideas about*** *religion.* | *I don't want you to* ***get the idea*** (=begin to believe) *that I look like this all the time.*

i·de·al[1] /aɪˈdiəl/ *adj.* **1** being the best that something could possibly be: *ideal weather conditions* | *The beaches are* ***ideal for*** *evening strolls.*

> THESAURUS **perfect, just right** → PERFECT[1]

2 perfect, but not likely to exist: *In an* ***ideal world,*** *no one would ever get sick.*

ideal[2] *n.* [C] **1** a principle or standard that you would like to achieve: *the* ***ideal of*** *perfect equality* **2** a perfect example of something: *current* ***ideals of*** *beauty*

i·de·al·ism /aɪˈdiəˌlɪzəm/ *n.* [U] the belief that you should live according to your high standards or principles, even if it is difficult

i·de·al·ist·ic /ˌaɪdiəˈlɪstɪk/ *adj.* (approving) believing in principles and high standards, even if they cannot be achieved in real life: *idealistic young people* —**idealist** /aɪˈdiəlɪst/ *n.* [C]

i·de·al·ize /aɪˈdiəˌlaɪz/ *v.* [T] to imagine or suggest that something is perfect or better than it really is: *The show idealizes family life.* —**idealized** *adj.*

i·de·al·ly /aɪˈdiəli/ *adv.* **1** [sentence adverb] in a way that you would like things to be, even if it is not possible: *Ideally, I'd like to work at home.* **2** perfectly: *The job is* ***ideally suited to*** *Amy's circumstances.*

i·den·ti·cal /aɪˈdɛntɪkəl, ɪ-/ (Ac) *adj.* exactly the same: *The two pictures looked identical.* | *Jan's dress is* ***identical to*** *mine.* | *William and David are* ***identical twins*** (=two brothers or sisters who were born together and look the same). [ORIGIN: 1500—1600 Medieval Latin *identicus*, from Late Latin *identitas*, from Latin *idem* "same"] —**identically** *adv.*

> THESAURUS **similar, like, alike, matching** → SIMILAR

I

i·den·ti·fi·a·ble /aɪˌdɛntəˈfaɪəbəl, ɪ-/ (Ac) *adj.* able to be recognized: *The male birds are* ***easily/readily identifiable by*** *their bright colors.*

i·den·ti·fi·ca·tion /aɪˌdɛntəfəˈkeɪʃən, ɪ-/ (Ac) *n.* [U] **1** official documents that prove who you are: *You can use a passport as identification.* **2** the act of recognizing someone or something: *The victim's dental records were used in the identification process.* | *After* ***identification of*** *the child's learning problems, a program of help is developed.* **3** a strong feeling that you are like someone or something and share the qualities s/he or it has: *Freud discusses a child's* ***identification with*** *his or her mother.*

i·den·ti·fy /aɪˈdɛntəˌfaɪ, ɪ-/ (Ac) *v.* (**identified, identifies**) [T] to recognize and name someone or something: *The victims were* ***identified as*** *John and Louise Preston.* | *The tests help identify children with reading problems.* [ORIGIN: 1600—1700 Late Latin *identificare*, from Latin *idem* "same"]

identify with sb/sth *phr. v.* **1 identify with** sb to be able to share or understand the feelings of someone else: *It was easy to identify with the novel's main character.* **2 be identified with** sb/sth to be closely connected with an idea or organization: *He will always be identified with the Harry Potter movies.*

i·den·ti·ty /aɪˈdɛntəṭi, ɪ-/ (Ac) *n.* (plural **identities**) **1** [C,U] who someone is: *She refused to reveal the* ***identity of*** *the killer.* | *All passengers must provide* ***proof of identity*** *at check-in.* **2** [U] the qualities someone has that make him/her different from other people: *Many people's* ***sense of identity*** *comes from their job.* | *America has always had a strong sense of* ***national identity***. [ORIGIN: 1500—1600 Late Latin *identitas*, from Latin *idem* "same"]

I

iˈdentity ˌtheft *also* **iˈdentity ˌfraud** *n.* [U] any crime in which someone steals personal information about another person, for example his/her bank account number, and uses this information to deceive other people and get money or goods

i·de·o·log·i·cal /ˌaɪdiəˈlɑdʒɪkəl, ˌɪdiə-/ (Ac) *adj.* based on a particular set of beliefs or ideas: *the movie's ideological content* —**ideologically** *adv.*

i·de·ol·o·gy /ˌaɪdiˈɑlədʒi, ˌɪdi-/ (Ac) *n.* (plural **ideologies**) [C,U] a set of beliefs or ideas, especially political beliefs: *Communist ideology*

id·i·o·cy /ˈɪdiəsi/ *n.* [U] something that is extremely stupid ➔ IDIOT

id·i·om /ˈɪdiəm/ *n.* [C] ENG. LANG. ARTS a group of words that have a special meaning that is very different from the ordinary meaning of the separate words [ORIGIN: 1500—1600 French *idiome*, from Greek *idioma* "personal way of expressing yourself"] —**idiomatic** /ˌɪdiəˈmæṭɪk◂/ *adj.*: *an idiomatic expression*

> THESAURUS phrase, expression, cliché, saying, proverb, maxim ➔ PHRASE[1]

id·i·o·syn·cra·sy /ˌɪdiəˈsɪŋkrəsi/ *n.* (plural **idiosyncrasies**) [C] **1** an unusual habit or way of behaving that someone has: *Her husband is used to her idiosyncrasies.* **2** an unusual or unexpected feature that something has: *the idiosyncrasies of English spelling* —**idiosyncratic** /ˌɪdioʊsɪŋˈkræṭɪk/ *adj.*

id·i·ot /ˈɪdiət/ *n.* [C] a stupid person, or someone who has done something stupid: *You idiot! What did you say that for?* —**idiotic** /ˌɪdiˈɑṭɪk/ *adj.*

i·dle[1] /ˈaɪdl/ *adj.* **1** not working or being used: *Many aircraft* ***sat idle*** *during the strike.* **2** (old-fashioned) lazy

> THESAURUS lazy, indolent, shiftless, slack, slothful ➔ LAZY

3 having no useful purpose: *idle gossip* —**idleness** *n.* [U] —**idly** *adv.*

idle[2] *v.* [I] if an engine idles, it runs slowly because it is not doing much work

i·dol /ˈaɪdl/ *n.* [C] **1** someone or something that you admire very much: *Janet was always my idol when I was a kid.* **2** an image or object that people pray to as a god [ORIGIN: 1200—1300 Old French *idole*, from Greek *eidolon* "image, idol"]

> THESAURUS god, deity, divinity ➔ GOD

i·dol·a·try /aɪˈdɑlətri/ *n.* [U] **1** the practice of WORSHIPing idols **2** too much admiration for someone or something: *The fans' admiration of her seems to border on idolatry.* —**idolatrous** *adj.*

i·dol·ize /ˈaɪdlˌaɪz/ *v.* [T] to admire someone so much that you think s/he is perfect: *Susan idolizes her mother.*

> THESAURUS admire, worship, revere ➔ ADMIRE

i·dyl·lic /aɪˈdɪlɪk/ *adj.* very happy and peaceful

i.e. /ˌaɪ ˈi/ a written abbreviation used when you want to explain the exact meaning of something (SYN) **that is**: *Transfer the text via the clipboard (i.e. cut and paste).*

if[1] /ɪf/ *conjunction* **1** used in order to talk about something that might happen or that might have happened: *If I call her now, she should still be at home.* | *If I get the job, I'll move to New York.* ***If not****, I'll stay in Dallas.* | *The crew will work all weekend* ***if necessary***. | *I want to leave by 5 o'clock* ***if possible***. | *We would've canceled the game if the weather was too bad.* ▸Don't use the future tense with "will" in a clause beginning with "if."◂

> THESAURUS
> **as long as/provided that** – only if you do something, or only if something happens: *Hiking in the mountains is safe, as long as you follow some basic rules.*
> **on condition that** – only if someone agrees to do something: *They offered him the job on condition that he moved to Chicago.*

unless – if something does not happen, or if someone does not do something: *You won't pass your final exams unless you study hard.*
otherwise – used when saying that there will be a bad result if someone does not do something, or if something does not happen: *He had better hurry up, otherwise we'll be late.*
in case – in order to deal with something that might happen: *She did not think it would rain, but she took her umbrella just in case.*
whether or not – used when saying that it does not matter if something happens or not, or if something is true or not: *Her comments are always interesting, whether or not you agree with what she says.*

2 used in order to mean "whether," when you are asking or deciding something: *Do you mind if I close the door?* | *We really don't know if there's a problem with the phone line.* **3** used when you are talking about something that always happens (SYN) **whenever**: *If I drink milk, I get a stomach-ache.* **4** said when you are surprised, angry, or upset because something has happened or is true: *I'm sorry if I upset you.* **5 if I were you** used in order to give advice to someone: *If I were you, I'd call him instead of writing to him.* → **even if** *at* EVEN[1], **as if/though** *at* AS, **if only** *at* ONLY[1]

if² *n.* [C] **1** a condition or possibility: *There are still too many ifs to know if this will succeed.* | *Parry will start in Sunday's game if he's healthy – but **that's a big if*** (=it is unlikely). **2 no ifs, ands, or buts** used to say that you want something done quickly, without any disagreement

if·fy /'ɪfi/ *adj.* (informal) an iffy situation is one in which you do not know what will happen: *The weather looks iffy today.*

ig·loo /'ɪglu/ *n.* (plural **igloos**) [C] a round house made from blocks of hard snow and ice [ORIGIN: 1800—1900 Inuit *iglu* "house"]

ig·ne·ous /'ɪgniəs/ *adj.* EARTH SCIENCES igneous rocks are formed from LAVA (=hot liquid rock)

ig·nite /ɪg'naɪt/ *v.* (formal) **1** [T] to start a dangerous situation, angry argument, etc.: *These actions could ignite a civil war.* **2** [I,T] to start burning, or to make something do this: *A spark caused fuel vapors in the tank to ignite.*

ig·ni·tion /ɪg'nɪʃən/ *n.* **1** [singular] the electrical part of an engine in a car that makes it start working: *Put the key in the ignition.* → DRIVE[1] **2** [U] (formal) the act of making something start to burn

ig·no·min·i·ous /ˌɪgnə'mɪniəs/ *adj.* (formal) making you feel ashamed or embarrassed: *his ignominious failure* —**ignominiously** *adv.*

ig·no·rance /'ɪgnərəns/ (Ac) *n.* [U] **1** (disapproving) lack of knowledge or information about something: *Many mistakes were caused by **ignorance of/about** the law.* | *I would have remained **in ignorance** if Shaun hadn't mentioned it.* **2 ignorance is bliss** used in order to say that if you do not know about a problem, you cannot worry about it

ig·no·rant /'ɪgnərənt/ (Ac) *adj.* (disapproving) not knowing facts or information that you should know: *Many students seem **ignorant of** geography, and can't find even Canada on a map.* | *He was a brutal ignorant man.*

ig·nore /ɪg'nɔr/ (Ac) *v.* [T] to not pay any attention to someone or something: *Jeannie ignored me all night!* | *The school board has ignored our complaints.* [ORIGIN: 1600—1700 French *ignorer* "not to know," from Latin, from *ignarus* "not knowing, unknown"]

USAGE

ignore – to know about something but deliberately not pay any attention to it: *You must not ignore other people's feelings.*
be ignorant of sth – to not know about something: *We were ignorant of the dangers involved.*

i·gua·na /ɪ'gwɑnə/ *n.* [C] a large tropical American LIZARD [ORIGIN: 1500—1600 Spanish, Arawakan (a group of South American languages) *iwana*]

IL the written abbreviation of ILLINOIS

I'll /aɪl/ the short form of "I will": *I'll be there in a minute.*

ill¹ /ɪl/ *adj.* **1** [not usually before noun] suffering from a disease or not feeling well (SYN) **sick** → ILLNESS: *The doctor said Patty was **seriously/critically ill*** (=extremely ill). | *patients who are **terminally ill*** (=who are going to die from their illness) | *Don's brother is **mentally ill**.*

THESAURUS **sick, not very well, under the weather, ailing, infirm** → SICK

2 [only before noun] bad or harmful: *Has he suffered any **ill effects** from the treatment?* | *Anita felt no **ill will*** (=unkind feelings) *toward her ex-husband.* | *Several prisoners complained of **ill treatment**.* **3 ill at ease** nervous or embarrassed [ORIGIN: 1100—1200 Old Norse *illr*]

ill² *adv.* (formal) **1** badly or not enough: *We were **ill-prepared** for the cold weather.* **2 sb can ill afford (to do) sth** used in order to say that you cannot or should not do something because it would make your situation more difficult: *Congress can ill afford to raise taxes so close to an election.*

ill³ *n.* [C] (formal) a bad thing, especially a problem or something that makes you worry: *the **social ills** caused by poverty*

ˌill-ad'vised *adj.* (formal) not sensible or not wise: *an ill-advised decision to change the law*

il·le·gal¹ /ɪ'ligəl/ (Ac) *adj.* not allowed by the law (ANT) **legal**: *Did you know **it is illegal to** park your car here?* | ***illegal immigrants/aliens** in the U.S.* | *illegal drugs* —**illegally** *adv.*: *Most of the software had been illegally copied.* —**illegality** /ˌɪlɪ'gæləṭi/ *n.* [C,U]: *the illegality of what he had done*

I

illegal² *also* **illegal immigrant/alien** *n.* [C] someone who comes into a country to live or work without official permission

il·leg·i·ble /ɪ'lɛdʒəbəl/ *adj.* difficult or impossible to read: *His handwriting was completely illegible.* —**illegibly** *adv.*

il·le·git·i·mate /ˌɪlə'dʒɪt̬əmɪt/ *adj.* (formal) **1** born to parents who are not married to each other: *He admitted that he had an illegitimate son.* **2** not allowed by the rules or law: *an illegitimate use of public money* —**illegitimacy** /ˌɪlə'dʒɪt̬əməsi/ *n.* [U]

ˌill-e'quipped *adj.* not having the necessary equipment or skills for something: *Many companies are **ill-equipped to** survive in today's economy.*

ˌill-'fated *adj.* unlucky and leading to serious problems or bad results: *an ill-fated attempt to reach the South Pole*

> THESAURUS **unlucky, unfortunate, inauspicious** ➔ UNLUCKY

il·lic·it /ɪ'lɪsɪt/ *adj.* not allowed by the law, or not approved of by society, and kept secret: *an illicit love affair | illicit drugs* —**illicitly** *adv.*

il·lit·er·ate /ɪ'lɪt̬ərɪt/ *adj.* not able to read or write —**illiteracy** /ɪ'lɪt̬ərəsi/ *n.* [U]

ill·ness /'ɪlnɪs/ *n.* [C,U] a disease of the body or mind, or the state of having a disease or sickness: *Mrs. Elms died Friday after a long illness. | The research examines the connections between homelessness and **mental illness**. | a **serious/chronic/terminal illness***

> THESAURUS **disease, sickness** ➔ DISEASE

il·log·i·cal /ɪ'lɑdʒɪkəl/ (Ac) *adj.* not sensible or reasonable (ANT) **logical**: *The structure of your report is completely illogical.*

ˌill-'treat *v.* [T] to be cruel to a person or animal

il·lu·mi·nate /ɪ'lumə͵neɪt/ *v.* [T] to make a light shine on something: *Their faces were illuminated by the candle on the table.* [ORIGIN: 1400—1500 Latin, past participle of *illuminare*, from *lumen* "light"] —**illuminated** *adj.*

il·lu·mi·nat·ing /ɪ'lumə͵neɪt̬ɪŋ/ *adj.* (formal) making something easier to understand: *an illuminating lecture*

il·lu·mi·na·tion /ɪ͵lumə'neɪʃən/ *n.* [U] (formal) the light provided by a lamp, fire, etc.

il·lu·sion /ɪ'luʒən/ *n.* [C] **1** something that seems to be different from what it really is ➔ OPTICAL ILLUSION: *Large mirrors gave the room **an illusion of** space.* **2** an idea or belief that is false: *Terry **is under the illusion that*** (=wrongly believes that) *he's going to pass the test. | We **have no illusions about** the hard work that lies ahead* (=we know there will be a lot of hard work).

il·lu·so·ry /ɪ'lusəri, -zəri/ *adj.* (formal) false, but seeming to be true or real

il·lus·trate /'ɪlə͵streɪt/ (Ac) *v.* [T] **1** to explain or make something clear by giving examples: *The charts will help to illustrate this point. | The following examples **illustrate how** the system works.* **2** to draw, paint, etc. pictures for a book [ORIGIN: 1500—1600 Latin, past participle of *illustrare*, from *lustrare* "to make pure or bright"] —**illustrative** /ɪ'lʌstrət̬ɪv, 'ɪlə͵streɪt̬ɪv/ *adj.*: *The calculations here are for illustrative purposes.*

il·lus·tra·tion /͵ɪlə'streɪʃən/ (Ac) *n.* [C] **1** a picture in a book ➔ GRAPHIC, DIAGRAM: *watercolor illustrations*

> THESAURUS **picture, sketch, painting, snapshot, portrait, cartoon, caricature** ➔ PICTURE¹

2 an example that helps you understand something or shows the truth of something: *Saturday's game provided a vivid **illustration of** how popular soccer has become.*

il·lus·tra·tor /'ɪlə͵streɪt̬ɚ/ *n.* [C] someone whose job is to draw pictures for books, magazines, etc.

il·lus·tri·ous /ɪ'lʌstriəs/ *adj.* (formal) very famous and admired by a lot of people

I'm /aɪm/ the short form of "I am": *I'm not sure where he is. | Hi, I'm Tim, Ann's brother.*

im·age /'ɪmɪdʒ/ (Ac) *n.* [C] **1** the opinion that people have about someone or something, especially because of the way he, she, or it is shown on television, in newspapers, etc.: *The mayor did not want to spoil his **public image** so close to the election. | The party is trying to **improve its image**. | We need to **project** the right **image** in our advertising. | We want to change the old **image of** New York **as** an unfriendly city.* **2** a picture that you can see through a camera, on a television, in a mirror, etc.: *The baby was looking at his image in the mirror. | **images of** starving people on the news* ➔ PICTURE¹ **3** a picture that you have in your mind: *She had a clear **image of** how he would look in 20 years.* **4** a word, picture, or phrase that describes an idea in a poem, book, movie, etc.: *The **image of** the river represents change.* [ORIGIN: 1100—1200 Old French *imagene*, from Latin *imago*]

im·age·ry /'ɪmɪdʒri/ (Ac) *n.* [U] the use of words, pictures, or phrases to describe ideas or actions in poems, books, movies, etc.: *Some video games are full of violent imagery.*

i·mag·i·na·ble /ɪ'mædʒənəbəl/ *adj.* able to be imagined: *I had **the worst/best** day **imaginable**.*

i·mag·i·nar·y /ɪ'mædʒə͵nɛri/ *adj.* not real, but imagined ➔ IMAGINATIVE: *Many children have **imaginary friends**.*

i͵maginary 'number *n.* [C] MATH any number that can be written in the form bi, where i is the SQUARE ROOT of -1 and b is not zero ➔ COMPLEX NUMBER

i·mag·i·na·tion /ɪ͵mædʒə'neɪʃən/ *n.* [C,U] the ability to form pictures or ideas in your mind

→ FANTASY: *Use your **imagination** to come up with a new dessert.* | *Ben always had a **vivid/lively imagination**.* | *Sheila realized that her fears had all been **in her imagination*** (=were not true). | *It does not **take** much **imagination** to understand the depth of their grief.*

i·mag·i·na·tive /ɪ'mædʒənətɪv/ *adj.* **1** able to think of new and interesting ideas: *an imaginative writer* **2** containing new and interesting ideas: *an imaginative story* —**imaginatively** *adv.* → IMAGINARY

i·mag·ine /ɪ'mædʒɪn/ *v.* [T] **1** to form pictures or ideas in your mind → IMAGINARY, IMAGINATION: ***Imagine (that)*** *you're lying on a beach somewhere.* | *Just **imagine what** you could do with a million dollars.*

THESAURUS

visualize – to form a picture of someone or something in your mind: *Evans visualized every step he would take in the 400-meter race.*
picture – to imagine something, especially by making an image in your mind: *I had pictured him as short and dark, but he was actually very tall.*
conceive of sth – to imagine a situation or what something is like: *It's difficult to conceive of any reason why he would do something like that.*
fantasize – to think about something that is pleasant or exciting, but unlikely to happen: *I fantasized about losing weight and becoming a thin person.*
daydream – to think about nice things, so that you forget what you should be doing: *Eddie used to daydream about finding treasure in the woods.*
envision/envisage (formal) – to imagine something as a future possibility: *He envisions an America where poor children have just as many opportunities as richer ones.*

2 to have a false or wrong idea about something: *There's noone there – you must **be imagining things**.* **3** (spoken) to think that something may happen or may be true: *I imagine Kathy will be there tomorrow.*

im·ag·ing /'ɪmɪdʒɪŋ/ *n.* [U] the process of producing images or photographs of something using technical equipment

im·bal·ance /ɪm'bæləns/ *n.* [C,U] a lack of balance between two things, so they are not equal or correct: *a trade imbalance* —**imbalanced** *adj.*

im·be·cile /'ɪmbəsəl/ *n.* [C] someone who is extremely stupid (SYN) **idiot**

im·bibe /ɪm'baɪb/ *v.* [I,T] (formal, humorous) to drink something, especially alcohol

im·bue /ɪm'byu/ *v.*
imbue sb/sth **with** sth *phr. v.* to make someone feel an emotion very strongly, or to make something contain a strong emotion or other quality: *The movie is imbued with a real sense of optimism.*

im·i·tate /'ɪmə,teɪt/ *v.* [T] **1** to copy the way someone else speaks, moves, etc., especially in order to make people laugh: *Jerry started imitating his uncle, and everyone laughed.* **2** to copy something because you think it is good: *The first successful program was **widely imitated** in Latin America.* —**imitative** *adj.* —**imitator** *n.* [C]

im·i·ta·tion[1] /,ɪmə'teɪʃən/ *n.* **1** [C,U] a copy of someone's speech, behavior, etc., or the act of copying: *Harry **does an** excellent **imitation of** Elvis.* | *Children learn **by imitation**.* **2** [C] a copy of something: *It's not an antique; it's an imitation.*

imitation[2] *adj.* [only before noun] made to look and seem like something real (ANT) **genuine, real**: *an **imitation leather/fur** jacket*

THESAURUS **artificial, synthetic, fake, man-made, simulated** → ARTIFICIAL

im·mac·u·late /ɪ'mækyəlɪt/ *adj.* **1** very clean and neat: *Barb's house is always immaculate.* **2** perfect and without any mistakes: *They danced with immaculate precision.* [ORIGIN: 1400—1500 Latin *immaculatus*, from *in-* "not" + *macula* "spot of dirt"] —**immaculately** *adv.*

im·ma·te·ri·al /,ɪmə'tɪriəl/ *adj.* not important in a particular situation (SYN) **irrelevant**

im·ma·ture /,ɪmə'tʃʊr, -'tʊr/ (Ac) *adj.* **1** (disapproving) behaving in a way that is not sensible because it is typical of the behavior of someone much younger (SYN) **childish**: *He seemed immature compared to his classmates.* → YOUNG[1] **2** not fully formed or developed: *immature plants* —**immaturity** *n.* [U]

im·me·di·a·cy /ɪ'midiəsi/ *n.* [U] the quality of seeming to be important and urgent, and directly relating to what is happening now

im·me·di·ate /ɪ'midiɪt/ *adj.* [usually before noun] **1** happening or done with no delay: *Carla's first cafe was an immediate success.* | *Police demanded the immediate release of the hostages.* | *When we launched the new system, the results were immediate.* **2** existing now, and needing to be dealt with quickly: *Our immediate concern was to stop the fire from spreading.* | *Doctors knew his life was in **immediate danger**.* **3** near something or someone in time or place: *We have no plans to expand the business in **the immediate future**.* | *They closed the streets **in the immediate vicinity of*** (=very close to) *the sports arena.* **4 sb's immediate family** someone's parents, children, brothers, and sisters

im·me·di·ate·ly /ɪ'midiɪt˺li/ *adv.* **1** with no delay: *Mix in the other ingredients and serve immediately.* | *She realized her mistake almost immediately.* | *The rescue team immediately went to work.* | *The victims' names were not immediately available.*

THESAURUS

instantly – immediately, used when something happens at almost the same time as something else: *Data is available instantly over the computer network.*
right away (especially spoken) – immediately,

I

used especially when something needs to be done urgently: *Jill called him right away.*
at once – immediately, or without waiting: *I realized at once I had said the wrong thing.*
right now (spoken) – immediately, used especially when something needs to be done urgently: *I need it right now!*

2 very near to something in time or place: *Jon arrived* ***immediately before/after*** *the end of the show.*

im·mense /ɪ'mɛns/ *adj.* extremely large SYN **huge**: *an immense palace* [ORIGIN: 1400—1500 French, Latin *immensus*, from *in-* "not" + *mensus* "measured"]

THESAURUS **big, large, substantial, sizable, prodigious, huge, enormous, vast, gigantic, massive, colossal** ➔ BIG

im·mense·ly /ɪ'mɛnsli/ *adv.* very or very much: *Mountain bikes became* ***immensely popular*** *very quickly.* | *He* ***enjoyed*** *it* ***immensely***.

im·merse /ɪ'mɚs/ *v.* [T] **1 be immersed in sth/immerse yourself in sth** to be or become completely involved in something: *Grant is completely immersed in his work.* **2** to put something completely in a liquid: *First,* ***immerse*** *the jars* ***in*** *boiling water.* —**immersion** /ɪ'mɚʒən/ *n.* [U]

im·mi·grant /'ɪməgrənt/ Ac *n.* [C] someone who enters another country to live there permanently ➔ EMIGRANT, MIGRANT: *an* ***immigrant from*** *Russia* | *Chinese* ***immigrants to*** *the U.S.* | *the number of* ***legal/illegal immigrants*** *each year*

I

im·mi·grate /'ɪmə,greɪt/ Ac *v.* [I] to enter another country in order to live there permanently: *His family* ***immigrated to*** *Canada a few years ago.* [ORIGIN: 1600—1700 Latin, past participle of *immigrare* "to go in," from *migrare*]

THESAURUS

immigrate – to enter a new country in order to live there: *Yuko immigrated to the U.S. last year.*
emigrate – to leave your own country in order to live in a different one: *My grandparents emigrated from Italy.*
migrate – if birds **migrate**, they go to another part of the world in the fall and in the spring

im·mi·gra·tion /,ɪmə'greɪʃən/ Ac *n.* [U] **1** the process of entering another country in order to live there, or the total number of people who do this ➔ EMIGRATION, MIGRATION: *There has been a rise in* ***immigration to*** *the United States.* | *immigration from countries such as Mexico* **2** the place in an airport, at a border, etc. where officials check your documents, such as your PASSPORT

im·mi·nent /'ɪmənənt/ *adj.* likely to happen very soon: *We believe that an attack is imminent.* | *The city is not in* ***imminent danger***. [ORIGIN: 1500—1600 Latin, present participle of *imminere* "to stick out, threaten"] —**imminently** *adv.*

im·mis·ci·ble /ɪ'mɪsəbəl/ *adj.* CHEMISTRY immiscible liquids cannot combine together into one liquid ANT **miscible**: *Oil and water are immiscible.*

im·mo·bile /ɪ'moʊbəl/ *adj.* not moving, or not able to move

im·mod·est /ɪ'mɑdɪst/ *adj.* **1** (formal) too proud of yourself and your abilities, and always willing to tell people about your achievements or how smart you are ANT **modest** **2** clothes that are immodest show too much of someone's body ANT **modest** **3** immodest sexual behavior shocks or embarrasses

im·mor·al /ɪ'mɔrəl, ɪ'mɑr-/ *adj.* morally wrong, and not accepted by society: *Their church believes that dancing is sinful and immoral.* —**immorality** /,ɪmə'rælət̬i, ,ɪmɔ-/ *n.* [U]

THESAURUS **bad, evil, wicked, wrong** ➔ BAD[1]

im·mor·tal /ɪ'mɔrt̬l/ *adj.* **1** living or continuing forever: *your immortal soul* **2** an immortal phrase, song, etc. is so famous that it will never be forgotten: *In the immortal words of James Brown, "I feel good!"* —**immortality** /,ɪmɔr'tælət̬i/ *n.* [U]

im·mov·a·ble /ɪ'muvəbəl/ *adj.* impossible to move, change, or persuade

im·mune /ɪ'myun/ *adj.* **1** not able to be affected by a disease or illness: *Young children may not be* ***immune to*** *the virus.* **2** not affected by bad things that affect people, organizations, etc. in similar situations: *The company seems to be* ***immune to*** *economic pressures.* | *The Governor is popular, but not* ***immune from*** *criticism.*

im,mune re'sponse *also* **im,mune re'action** *n.* [C,U] BIOLOGY the reaction of the body's immune system to disease or infection

im'mune ,system *n.* [C] BIOLOGY the system by which your body protects itself against disease

im·mun·i·ty /ɪ'myunət̬i/ *n.* [U] **1** LAW the state or right of being protected from particular laws or punishment: *Congress* ***granted immunity*** (=gave immunity) *to both men.* **2** BIOLOGY the state of being immune to diseases or illnesses: *The disease causes a low* ***immunity to*** *infections.*

im·mu·ni·za·tion /,ɪmyənə'zeɪʃən/ *n.* [C,U] the act of immunizing someone: *Doctors are encouraging the* ***immunization*** *of babies in the U.S.* ***against*** *hepatitis B.*

im·mu·nize /'ɪmyə,naɪz/ *v.* [T] to protect someone from disease by giving him/her a VACCINE: *Have you been* ***immunized against*** *tuberculosis?*

im·mu·ta·ble /ɪ'myut̬əbəl/ *adj.* (formal) never changing, or impossible to change ANT **mutable**: *an immutable law of nature, such as gravity* —**immutability** /ɪ,myut̬ə'bɪlət̬i/ *n.* [U]

im·pact[1] /'ɪmpækt/ Ac *n.* **1** [C] the effect that an event or situation has on someone or something: *Every decision at work* ***has an impact on*** *profit.* | *What would be the* ***economic impact*** *of a possible* *strike?* | *Rising fuel costs could have a* ***major impact*** *on consumers.* **2** [C,U] the force of one object hitting another: *The impact of the crash made the car turn over.* **3 on impact** at the moment when one thing hits another: *The missile explodes on impact.* [ORIGIN: 1600—1700 Latin, past participle of *impingere*, from *pangere* "to fasten, drive in"]

im·pact² /ɪm'pækt/ (Ac) *v.* [I,T] to have an important or noticeable effect on someone or something: *The growth of the airport has impacted the city's economy.* | *Childcare is an issue that* ***impacts on*** *many women's lives.*

im·pair /ɪm'pɛr/ *v.* [T] to damage something, or make it less good: *Her sight was impaired as a result of the disease.* [ORIGIN: 1300—1400 Old French *empeirer*, from Vulgar Latin *impejorare*, from Late Latin *pejorare* "to make worse"] —**impairment** *n.* [U]

im·paired /ɪm'pɛrd/ *adj.* **1** damaged, less strong, or less good: *impaired kidney function* **2 hearing/visually/physically impaired** someone who is hearing impaired or visually impaired cannot hear, see, etc. well

im·pale /ɪm'peɪl/ *v.* [T] if someone or something is impaled on something, a sharp pointed object goes through him, her, or it

im·part /ɪm'pɑrt/ *v.* [T] (formal) **1** to give a particular quality to something: *Roasted chili peppers* ***impart*** *a smoky flavor* ***to*** *the dish.* **2** to give information, knowledge, etc. to someone: *He accused the universities of failing to* ***impart*** *moral values* ***to*** *students.*

im·par·tial /ɪm'pɑrʃəl/ *adj.* not giving special attention or support to any one person or group (SYN) **objective** (ANT) **biased**: *impartial advice* | *Rosen said he was unable to remain impartial in the case.* —**impartially** *adv.* —**impartiality** /ɪm,pɑrʃi'æləṭi/ *n.* [U]

> THESAURUS **fair, just, balanced, even-handed, unbiased** → FAIR¹

im·pass·a·ble /ɪm'pæsəbəl/ *adj.* impossible to travel along or through: *The road into the valley had become impassable.*

im·passe /'ɪmpæs/ *n.* [singular] a situation in which it is impossible to continue with a discussion or plan because the people involved cannot agree: *Discussions about pay have* ***reached an impasse****.*

im·pas·sioned /ɪm'pæʃənd/ *adj.* full of strong feelings and emotion: *an impassioned speech*

im·pas·sive /ɪm'pæsɪv/ *adj.* (formal) not showing any emotions: *His face was impassive as the judge spoke.* —**impassively** *adv.*

> THESAURUS **matter-of-fact, detached, dispassionate, cold** → MATTER-OF-FACT

im·pa·tient /ɪm'peɪʃənt/ *adj.* **1** annoyed because of delays or mistakes that make you wait: *After numerous delays in the project, some people began to* ***get/grow impatient****.* | *Rob's dad is very* ***impatient with*** *him sometimes.* **2** very eager for something to happen, and not wanting to wait: *Gary was* ***impatient to*** *leave.* —**impatience** *n.* [U] —**impatiently** *adv.*

im·peach /ɪm'pitʃ/ *v.* [T] LAW to say officially that a public official is guilty of a serious crime —**impeachment** *n.* [C,U]

im·pec·ca·ble /ɪm'pɛkəbəl/ *adj.* completely perfect and impossible to criticize: *She has impeccable taste in clothes.* [ORIGIN: 1500—1600 Latin *impeccabilis*, from *in-* "not" + *peccare* "to do bad things"] —**impeccably** *adv.*

im·pe·cu·ni·ous /,ɪmpɪ'kyuniəs/ *adj.* having very little money, especially over a long period of time (SYN) **penniless**, **poor**: *an impecunious student*

> THESAURUS **poor, needy, destitute, impoverished, broke, indigent, penurious** → POOR

im·pede /ɪm'pid/ *v.* [T] (formal) to make it difficult for someone or something to make progress: *Rescue attempts were impeded by storms.*

im·ped·i·ment /ɪm'pɛdəmənt/ *n.* [C] **1** a physical problem that makes speaking, hearing, or moving difficult: *Gina* ***has a*** *slight* ***speech impediment****.* **2** a fact or event that makes action difficult or impossible: *The current law is a major* ***impediment to*** *trade.*

im·pel /ɪm'pɛl/ *v.* (**impelled, impelling**) [T] (formal) to make you feel very strongly that you must do something: *He* ***felt impelled to*** *explain his actions.*

> THESAURUS **force, make, compel** → FORCE²

im·pend·ing /ɪm'pɛndɪŋ/ *adj.* [only before noun] likely to happen soon: *an impending oil shortage*

im·pen·e·tra·ble /ɪm'pɛnətrəbəl/ *adj.* **1** impossible to get through, see through, or get into → PENETRATE: *impenetrable fog* **2** very difficult or impossible to understand: *impenetrable business jargon*

im·per·a·tive¹ /ɪm'pɛrəṭɪv/ *adj.* **1** (formal) extremely important and urgent: ***It is imperative that*** *all fees be paid in full.* **2** ENG. LANG. ARTS an imperative verb expresses an order. In the sentence "Go to your room," "go" is an imperative verb. [ORIGIN: 1400—1500 Late Latin *imperativus*, from Latin *imperatus*, past participle of *imperare* "to command"]

imperative² *n.* [C] **1** (formal) something that must be done urgently: *Reducing air pollution has become an imperative.* **2** ENG. LANG. ARTS the form of a verb that expresses an order. In the sentence "Do it now!" the verb "do" is in the imperative.

im·per·cep·ti·ble /,ɪmpɚ'sɛptəbəl/ *adj.* impossible to notice: *an almost imperceptible change* —**imperceptibly** *adv.*

I

im·per·fect[1] /ɪm'pɚfɪkt/ *adj.* not completely perfect: *an imperfect legal system* —**imperfectly** *adv.*

imperfect[2] *n.* [singular] ENG. LANG. ARTS the form of a verb that shows an incomplete action in the past that is formed with "be" and the PRESENT PARTICIPLE. In the sentence "We were walking down the road," the verb phrase "were walking" is in the imperfect.

im·per·fec·tion /ˌɪmpɚ'fɛkʃən/ *n.* [C,U] the state of being imperfect, or something that is imperfect: *A few **slight/small imperfections** won't spoil the overall appearance.*

> THESAURUS defect, problem, flaw, fault → DEFECT[1]

im·pe·ri·al /ɪm'pɪriəl/ *adj.* relating to an EMPIRE or to the person who rules it

im·pe·ri·al·ism /ɪm'pɪriəˌlɪzəm/ *n.* [U] **1** POLITICS a political system in which one country controls a lot of other countries **2** (disapproving) the way in which a rich or powerful country's way of life, CULTURE, businesses, etc. influence and change a poorer country's way of life, etc.: *Small nations resent the West's **cultural/economic imperialism**.* —**imperialist** *n.* [C] —**imperialist, imperialistic** /ɪmˌpɪriə'lɪstɪk/ *adj.*

imˌperial 'state *n.* [C] HISTORY a state that was part of the Holy Roman Empire and had a vote in its PARLIAMENT

im·pe·ri·ous /ɪm'pɪriəs/ *adj.* giving orders and expecting to be obeyed: *his imperious personality* —**imperiously** *adv.*

im·per·son·al /ɪm'pɚsənəl/ *adj.* not showing any feelings of sympathy, friendliness, etc.: *an impersonal letter* —**impersonally** *adv.*

im·per·so·nate /ɪm'pɚsəˌneɪt/ *v.* [T] **1** to pretend to be someone else by copying his/her appearance, voice, etc. in order to deceive people: *Quinn was arrested for impersonating a police officer.* **2** to copy someone's voice and behavior in order to make people laugh: *a comedian who impersonates politicians* —**impersonator** *n.* [C] —**impersonation** /ɪmˌpɚsə'neɪʃən/ *n.* [U]

im·per·ti·nent /ɪm'pɚt̚n-ənt/ *adj.* impolite and not respectful, especially to someone who is older or more important (SYN) **rude, impudent**: *an impertinent child | impertinent questions* —**impertinence** *n.* [U]

> THESAURUS rude, impolite, offensive, insolent, disrespectful, impudent → RUDE

im·per·vi·ous /ɪm'pɚviəs/ *adj.* (formal) **1 impervious to sth** not affected or influenced by something: *He seemed impervious to the noise around him.* **2 impervious to sth** not allowing anything to pass through: *The container must be impervious to water.*

im·pet·u·ous /ɪm'pɛtʃuəs/ *adj.* (formal) tending to do things quickly, without thinking —**impetuously** *adv.* —**impetuousness** *n.* [U]

> THESAURUS impulsive, rash, hasty, precipitate → IMPULSIVE

im·pe·tus /'ɪmpət̬əs/ *n.* [U] (formal) an influence that makes something happen, or happen more quickly: *Much of the **impetus for** reform came from local activists. | The conference **gave** fresh **impetus to** change.*

im·pinge /ɪm'pɪndʒ/ *v.*

impinge on/upon sth *phr. v.* (formal) to have an unwanted or bad effect on someone or something: *International politics have impinged on decisions made in Congress.*

im·plac·a·ble /ɪm'plækəbəl/ *adj.* (formal) very determined to continue opposing someone or something: *an implacable enemy* —**implacably** *adv.*

im·plant[1] /ɪm'plænt/ *v.* [T] **1** to put something into someone's body in a medical operation: *Some healthy cells were **implanted in/into** the patient's brain.* **2** to influence someone so that s/he believes or feels something strongly: *His family **implanted in** him a strong sense of patriotism.*

im·plant[2] /'ɪmplænt/ *n.* [C] something that has been put into someone's body in a medical operation: *silicone breast implants*

im·plau·si·ble /ɪm'plɔzəbəl/ *adj.* difficult to believe and not likely to be true: *an implausible excuse*

im·ple·ment[1] /'ɪmpləˌmɛnt/ (Ac) *v.* [T] if you implement a plan, process, etc., you begin to make it happen: *Their recommendations may be difficult to implement.* —**implementation** /ˌɪmpləmən'teɪʃən/ *n.* [U]: *implementation of the new program*

im·ple·ment[2] /'ɪmpləmənt/ (Ac) *n.* [C] a tool, especially one used in farming or building: *agricultural implements*

im·pli·cate /'ɪmplɪˌkeɪt/ (Ac) *v.* [T] **1** to show that someone is involved in something wrong: *He pleaded guilty and **implicated** his cousin **in** the crime.* **2** to show that something is likely to be the cause of something bad or harmful: *Meat from this company was **implicated in** the food poisoning outbreak.* [ORIGIN: 1400—1500 Latin, past participle of *implicare* "to twist together, make complicated"]

im·pli·ca·tion /ˌɪmplɪ'keɪʃən/ (Ac) *n.* **1** [C] a possible effect or result of a plan, action, etc.: *What are the **implications of** their research? | This ruling will **have implications for** many people.* **2** [C,U] something you do not say directly but that you want people to understand: *I don't like the **implication that** I was lying.* **3** [U] a situation in which it is suggested that someone or something is involved in something wrong, illegal, or harmful: *the implication of the bank president in the theft | the implication of smoking in cases of lung disease*

im·plic·it /ɪm'plɪsɪt/ (Ac) *adj.* **1** suggested or understood but not stated directly → EXPLICIT:

There was implicit criticism in the principal's statement. **2** complete and containing no doubts: *She has **implicit faith** in her husband.* **3 be implicit in sth** (formal) to be a central part of something, without being stated: *Risk is implicit in owning a business.* —**implicitly** *adv.*

im,plied 'powers *n.* [plural] POLITICS powers given to the U.S. government that are not clearly stated in the CONSTITUTION, but which are accepted as necessary in order for the government to carry out its EXPRESSED POWERS (=those written down in the Constitution)

im·plode /ɪm'ploʊd/ *v.* [I] to explode inward

im·plore /ɪm'plɔr/ *v.* [T] (formal) to ask someone for something in an emotional way (SYN) **beg**: *Joan **implored** him **not to** leave.*

THESAURUS **ask, demand, beg, plead** → ASK

im·ply /ɪm'plaɪ/ (Ac) *v.* (**implied**, **implies**) [T] **1** to suggest that something is true without saying or showing it directly: *He **implied that** the money hadn't been lost, but had been stolen instead.* **2** to show that something is likely to exist or be true: *The chart implies that many purchases are not necessary.* [ORIGIN: 1300—1400 Old French *emplier*, from Latin *implicare* "to twist together, make complicated"]

im·po·lite /ˌɪmpə'laɪt/ *adj.* not polite (SYN) **rude**: ***It would be impolite to** leave in the middle of her recital.*

THESAURUS **rude, insulting, disrespectful** → RUDE

im·port¹ /'ɪmpɔrt/ *n.* **1** [C,U] ECONOMICS a product that is brought from one country into another so that it can be sold there, or the business of doing this (ANT) **export**: *Car imports have risen recently.* | *The government has banned the **import of** weapons.* **2** (formal) [U] importance or meaning: *a matter **of great import*** [ORIGIN: 1400—1500 Latin *importare*, from *portare* "to carry"]

im·port² /ɪm'pɔrt/ *v.* [T] ECONOMICS to bring something from one country into another so that it can be sold there (ANT) **export**: *Oil is imported from the Middle East.* —**importer** *n.* [C]

im·por·tance /ɪm'pɔrt˺ns, -pɔrtn̩s/ *n.* [U] the quality of being important: ***the importance of** regular exercise* | *The company **attaches great importance to** employee training.* | *These issues are **of great/critical/vital importance**.*

im·por·tant /ɪm'pɔrt˺nt, -'pɔrtn̩t/ *adj.* having a big effect or influence: *a very important meeting* | *Ellen's family is more **important to** her than anything else.* | ***It's important that** you look professional at the interview.* [ORIGIN: 1400—1500 French, Old Italian *importante* "carrying a meaning, significant," from Latin *importare*] —**importantly** *adv.*

THESAURUS

of great/considerable importance – very important: *Friends are of great importance to your child's development.*
crucial – very important: *The U.S. plays a crucial role in the region.*
vital – extremely important or necessary: *vital information*
essential – extremely important: *It's essential that you buy tickets in advance.*
major – very large or important, especially when compared to other things: *our major cities* | *a major problem*
key – very important and necessary for success or to understand something: *the team's key players* | *He plays a key role in the company.* | *The key question is whether to buy or sell.*
paramount (formal) – more important than anything else: *The needs of the customer should be paramount.*
significant – noticeable or important: *The new research is highly significant.*
salient (formal) – most noticeable or important: *the salient points of the plan*

im·por·ta·tion /ˌɪmpɔr'teɪʃən/ *n.* [U] the business of bringing goods from another country to sell in your country

im·pose /ɪm'poʊz/ (Ac) *v.* **1** [T] to introduce a rule, tax, punishment, etc. and force people to accept it: *City officials have **imposed** limits **on** commercial development.* **2** [T] to force someone to have the same ideas, beliefs, etc. as you: *Parents **impose** their values **on** their children.* **3** [I] to ask or expect someone to do something when it is not convenient for him/her to do it: *I didn't ask you because I didn't want to impose.* [ORIGIN: 1400—1500 French *imposer*, from Latin *imponere*, from *ponere* "to put"]

im·pos·ing /ɪm'poʊzɪŋ/ (Ac) *adj.* large and impressive: *an imposing statue*

THESAURUS **impressive, awe-inspiring, breathtaking, majestic, magnificent** → IMPRESSIVE

im·po·si·tion /ˌɪmpə'zɪʃən/ (Ac) *n.* **1** [C usually singular] something that someone expects or asks you to do for him/her, when it is not convenient for you to do it: *We want you to stay with us – it's not an imposition at all.* **2** [U] the introduction of something such as a rule, tax, or punishment: *the **imposition of** taxes **on** cigarettes*

im·pos·si·ble /ɪm'pɑsəbəl/ *adj.* **1** not able to be done or to happen: ***It was impossible for** us **to** answer all their questions.* | ***It is impossible to** predict what will happen.* | *The storm **made** driving **impossible**.* **2** extremely difficult to deal with: *an impossible situation* **3** behaving in an unreasonable and annoying way: *You're impossible!* —**impossibly** *adv.* —**impossibility** /ɪmˌpɑsə'bɪləṭi/ *n.* [C,U]

im·pos·ter /ɪm'pɑstɚ/ *n.* [C] someone who pretends to be someone else in order to trick people

im·po·tent /'ɪmpət̬ənt/ *adj.* **1** a man who is impotent is unable to have sex because he cannot have an ERECTION **2** unable to take effective action because you do not have enough power, strength, or control: *an impotent city government* —**impotence** *n.* [U]

im·pound /ɪm'paʊnd/ *v.* [T] LAW if the police or court of law impound your possessions, they take them and keep them until you go and get them

im·pov·er·ished /ɪm'pɑvərɪʃt/ *adj.* very poor: *an impoverished country*

THESAURUS **poor, needy, destitute, poverty-stricken, disadvantaged, underprivileged, deprived** → POOR

im·prac·ti·cal /ɪm'præktɪkəl/ *adj.* **1** an impractical plan, suggestion, etc. is not sensible because it would be too expensive or difficult **2** not good at dealing with ordinary practical matters —**impractically** *adv.* —**impracticality** /ɪm,præktɪ'kæləṭi/ *n.* [C,U]

im·pre·cise /,ɪmprɪ'saɪs/ (Ac) *adj.* not exact: *an imprecise measurement* —**imprecisely** *adv.* —**imprecision** /,ɪmprɪ'sɪʒən/ *n.* [U]

im·preg·na·ble /ɪm'prɛgnəbəl/ *adj.* very strong and unable to be entered: *an impregnable fort*

im·preg·nate /ɪm'prɛg,neɪt/ *v.* [T] (formal) **1** to make a woman or female animal PREGNANT **2** to make a substance spread completely through something, or to spread completely through something: *The paper is **impregnated with** perfume.*

I

im·press /ɪm'prɛs/ *v.* [T] **1** to make someone feel admiration and respect: *She dresses like that to impress people.* | *We were **impressed by/with** the size of his art collection.* **2** to make the importance of something clear to someone: *My parents **impressed on** me the value of an education.*

im·pres·sion /ɪm'prɛʃən/ *n.* **1** [C,U] the opinion or feeling you have about someone or something because of the way s/he or it seems: ***I get the impression that** something's wrong here.* | ***First impressions** can be wrong.* | *It's important to **make a** good **impression** at your interview.* **2 be under the impression (that)** to think that something is true when it is not true: *I was under the impression that Marcie was coming to dinner too.* **3** [C] the act of copying the speech or behavior of a famous person in order to make people laugh: *Eric **does** a great **impression of** Mick Jagger.* **4** [C] the mark left by pressing something into a soft surface

im·pres·sion·a·ble /ɪm'prɛʃənəbəl/ *adj.* easy to influence: *The girls are **at an impressionable age**.*

im·pres·sion·ism /ɪm'prɛʃə,nɪzəm/ *n.* [U] **1** *also* **Impressionism** ENG. LANG. ARTS a style of painting used especially in France in the 19th century, which uses color instead of details of form to produce effects of light or feeling **2** ENG. LANG. ARTS a style of music or literature from the late 19th and early 20th centuries that emphasizes feelings and images —**Impressionist** *adj.*: *Impressionist painters* —**Impressionist** *n.* [C]

im·pres·sion·is·tic /ɪm,prɛʃə'nɪstɪk/ *adj.* based on a general feeling of what something is like rather than on details: *an impressionistic account of the events*

im·pres·sive /ɪm'prɛsɪv/ *adj.* causing admiration: *an impressive performance on the piano* | *The view was impressive.* —**impressively** *adv.*

THESAURUS

imposing – large and impressive: *The judge sat behind an imposing desk.*
dazzling – very impressive, exciting, or interesting: *a dazzling display of Christmas decorations*
awe-inspiring – so impressive that you feel awe (=a feeling of respect and admiration): *The cathedral was an awe-inspiring sight.*
breathtaking – extremely impressive, exciting, or surprising: *breathtaking views of the Rocky Mountains*
majestic – looking very big and impressive: *the majestic pyramids at Giza in Egypt*
magnificent – very impressive because of being big, beautiful, etc.: *a magnificent cathedral*

im·press·ment /ɪm'prɛsmənt/ *n.* [U] HISTORY the action of forcing people to serve in the military

im·print¹ /'ɪm,prɪnt/ *n.* [C] the mark left by an object that has been pressed into or onto something: *the **imprint of** her thumb on the clay*

im·print² /ɪm'prɪnt/ *v.* **be imprinted on your mind/memory** if something is imprinted on your mind or memory, you can never forget it

im·print·ing /'ɪm,prɪntɪŋ/ *n.* [U] BIOLOGY a very early learning process in animals, in which a young animal learns patterns of behavior and its connection to members of its own kind, especially its parents

im·pris·on /ɪm'prɪzən/ *v.* [T] to put someone in prison or to keep him/her in a place s/he cannot escape from: *The opposition leaders were imprisoned and tortured.* —**imprisonment** *n.* [U]

im·prob·a·ble /ɪm'prɑbəbəl/ *adj.* **1** not likely to happen or to be true (SYN) **unlikely**: ***It is highly improbable that** you will find sharks in these waters.* **2** surprising and slightly strange: *an improbable partnership* —**improbably** *adv.* —**improbability** /ɪm,prɑbə'bɪləṭi/ *n.* [C,U]

im·promp·tu /ɪm'prɑmptu/ *adj.* done or said without any preparation or planning: *an impromptu speech* —**impromptu** *adv.*

im·prop·er /ɪm'prɑpɚ/ *adj.* unacceptable according to professional, moral, or social rules of behavior: *Many cases of "stomach flu" result from improper cooking of food.* | *the improper use of funds* —**improperly** *adv.*: *The car alarm had been improperly installed.*

im·pro·pri·e·ty /ˌɪmprəˈpraɪəṭi/ *n.* (plural **improprieties**) [C,U] (formal) behavior or an action that is unacceptable according to moral, social, or professional standards

im·prove /ɪmˈpruv/ *v.* [I,T] to become better, or to make something better: *Do some exercises to improve your muscle strength.* | *Your math skills have improved this year.* | *The situation* ***improved dramatically.*** [ORIGIN: 1500—1600 *emprowe* "to improve" (15—16 centuries), from Anglo-French *emprouer* "to make a profit"] —**improved** *adj.*

improve on/upon sth *phr. v.* to do something better than before, or to make it better: *No one's been able to improve on her Olympic record.*

im·prove·ment /ɪmˈpruvmənt/ *n.* **1** [C,U] an act of improving, or the state of being improved: *There's certainly been an* ***improvement in*** *Danny's behavior.* | *Your English is getting better, but there's still* ***room for improvement*** (=the possibility of more improvement). | *Jerry has* ***made*** *dramatic* ***improvement*** *since the surgery.* | *Ben's work is showing* ***signs of improvement.*** **2** [C] a change or addition that makes something better: ***home improvements***

im·pro·vise /ˈɪmprəˌvaɪz/ *v.* **1** [I,T] to make or do something without any preparation, using what you have: *I left my lesson plans at home, so I'll have to improvise.* **2** [I] to perform music, sing, etc. from your imagination: *Jazz musicians are good at improvising.* —**improvisation** /ɪmˌprɑvəˈzeɪʃən/ *n.* [C,U]

im·pu·dent /ˈɪmpyədənt/ *adj.* (formal) rude and not showing respect —**impudence** *n.* [U]

THESAURUS **rude, impolite, insulting, offensive, insolent, disrespectful, impertinent**
→ RUDE

im·pulse /ˈɪmpʌls/ *n.* **1** [C,U] a sudden desire to do something without thinking about the results: *She resisted the* ***impulse to*** *hit him.* | *I bought this shirt* ***on impulse****, and now I don't like it.* **2** [C] PHYSICS a short electrical signal sent in one direction along a wire or nerve, or through the air **3** [C] PHYSICS a measure of MOMENTUM that you get if you multiply the average value of a force by the length of time that the force acts

im·pul·sive /ɪmˈpʌlsɪv/ *adj.* tending to do things without thinking about the results, or showing this quality: *an impulsive shopper* | *an impulsive decision* —**impulsively** *adv.*

THESAURUS

rash – if you do something rash, especially something dangerous or stupid, you do it too quickly and without thinking carefully first. If you are rash, you behave like this: *Don't do anything rash!*
hotheaded – if someone is hotheaded, s/he gets angry or excited easily and does things too quickly, without thinking: *a hotheaded young man*
impetuous (formal) – tending to do things quickly, without thinking carefully first: *He is young and impetuous.*
hasty (formal) – done in a hurry, especially with bad results: *He soon regretted his hasty decision.*
spontaneous – done without being planned or organized, because you suddenly want to do it: *They began a spontaneous game of hide-and-seek.*
precipitate (formal) – done too quickly, without thinking carefully enough: *Perhaps I was too precipitate in my judgment.*

im·pu·ni·ty /ɪmˈpyunəṭi/ *n.* **with impunity** without risk of punishment: *We cannot let them break laws with impunity.*

im·pure /ɪmˈpyʊr/ *adj.* **1** mixed with other substances: *impure drugs* **2** (old-fashioned) morally bad, especially when relating to sex: *impure thoughts*

im·pu·ri·ty /ɪmˈpyʊrəṭi/ *n.* (plural **impurities**) **1** [C usually plural] a part of an almost pure substance that is of a lower quality: *The silver contained some impurities.* **2** [U] the state of being impure

im·pute /ɪmˈpyut/ *v.* (formal)

impute sth **to** sb *phr. v.* **1** to say that someone is responsible for something bad, often unfairly: *The police were not guilty of the violence imputed to them.* **2** to say that someone or something has a particular quality: *The author does not impute a modern way of thinking to her 19th-century characters.* —**imputation** /ˌɪmpyəˈteɪʃən/ *n.* [C,U]

IN the written abbreviation of INDIANA

in¹ /ɪn/ *prep.* **1** used with the name of a container, place, or area to show where something is: *The paper is in the top drawer.* | *I was still in bed at 11:30.* | *Cows were standing in the field.* | *He lived in Boston for 15 years.* **2** used with the names of months, years, seasons, etc. to say when something happens: *We bought our car in April.* | *In 1969 the first astronauts landed on the moon.* | *Sarah starts college in the fall.* **3** during a period of time: *We finished the whole project in a week.* **4** at the end of a period of time: *Gerry should be home in an hour.* | *I wonder if the business will still be going in a year.* **5** included as part of something: *One of the people in the story is a young doctor.* | *In the first part of the speech, he talked about the environment.* **6 sb has not done sth in years/months/weeks** if you have not done something in years, etc., you have not done it for that amount of time: *I haven't been to the circus in years!* **7** using a particular kind of voice, or a particular way of speaking or writing: *"Why?" she asked him in a whisper.* | *Their parents always talk to them in Italian.* | *Do not write in pen on this test.* **8** working at a particular kind of job: *She's in advertising.* **9** arranged in a particular way, often to form a group or shape: *Stand against the wall in a line.* | *He had made a bowl in the shape of a heart.* | *Put the words in alphabetical order.* **10** used in order to show the connection between two ideas or subjects: *I was never interested in sports as a kid.* **11** used before the bigger number when you are talking about a relationship between two numbers: *1 in 10 women* (=10% of all women) *has the disease.* **12 in shock/horror etc.** used in order to describe a strong feeling someone has when s/he does something: *She looked at me in shock as I told her how everything had gone wrong.* **13 in all** used when giving a total amount: *There were about 50 of us in all at the reunion.*

in² *adj., adv.* **1** so as to be contained inside or surrounded by something: *She pushed the box towards me so that I could put my money in.* **2** inside a building, especially the one where you live or work: *Mr. Linn should be in soon.* | *You're never in when I call.* **3** if an airplane, bus, train, or boat is in, it has arrived at the airport, station, etc.: *Her flight gets in at 5:30.* **4** given or sent to a particular place in order to be read or looked at: *Your final papers have to be in by Friday.* **5** if you write, paint, or draw something in, you write it, etc. in the correct place: *Fill in the blanks, using a number 2 pencil.* **6** if clothes, colors, etc. are in, they are fashionable: *Long hair is in again.* **7** if a ball is in during a game, it is inside the area where the game is played **8 be in for sth** if someone is in for something, something bad is about to happen to him/her: *She's in for a shock if she thinks we're going to help her pay for it.* **9 be in on sth** to be involved in doing, talking about, or planning something: *Everyone was in on the secret except Cheryl.* **10** if the TIDE comes in or is in, the ocean water is at its highest level **11 in joke** an in joke is one that is only understood by a small group of people

I

in·a·bil·i·ty /ˌɪnəˈbɪləṭi/ *n.* [singular, U] a lack of the ability, skill, etc. to do something: *an* ***inability to*** *remember details*

in·ac·ces·si·ble /ˌɪnəkˈsɛsəbəl/ (Ac) *adj.* difficult or impossible to reach: *The stairs make the building inaccessible to the disabled.*

in·ac·cu·ra·cy /ɪnˈækyərəsi/ (Ac) *n.* (plural **inaccuracies**) [C,U] a mistake, or when something is not correct: *There were several inaccuracies in the report.*

in·ac·cu·rate /ɪnˈækyərɪt/ (Ac) *adj.* **1** not completely correct: *an inaccurate description*

> THESAURUS **wrong, incorrect, erroneous, misleading** → WRONG¹

2 not aimed correctly, or not reaching the place aimed for: *an inaccurate throw to third base* —**inaccurately** *adv.*

in·ac·tion /ɪnˈækʃən/ *n.* [U] lack of action

in·ac·tive /ɪnˈæktɪv/ *adj.* not doing anything or not working: *inactive volcanoes* | *He injured his knee and was inactive for the rest of the season.* —**inactivity** /ˌɪnækˈtɪvəṭi/ *n.* [U]

in·ad·e·qua·cy /ɪnˈædəkwəsi/ (Ac) *n.* (plural **inadequacies**) **1** [U] a feeling that you are unable to deal with situations because you are not as good as other people: *Not having a job can cause strong* ***feelings of inadequacy***. **2** [C,U] the fact of not being good enough for a particular purpose, or something that is not good enough: *The research looked at the* ***inadequacy of*** *the children's diet.*

in·ad·e·quate /ɪnˈædəkwɪt/ (Ac) *adj.* not good enough, big enough, skilled enough, etc. for a particular purpose: *inadequate heating* | *She made me* ***feel*** *so* ***inadequate***. | *Both he and his wife work, but their wages are* ***inadequate to*** *lift the family out of poverty.* —**inadequately** *adv.*

in·ad·mis·si·ble /ˌɪnədˈmɪsəbəl/ *adj.* LAW not allowed to be used as EVIDENCE in a court of law: *Some of the evidence was inadmissible.*

in·ad·vert·ent·ly /ˌɪnədˈvɚtˀntli/ *adv.* without intending to do something: *She inadvertently hit the brakes.* —**inadvertent** *adj.*

in·al·ien·a·ble /ɪnˈeɪlyənəbəl/ *adj.* (formal) an inalienable right cannot be taken away from you

in·ane /ɪˈneɪn/ *adj.* extremely stupid, or without much meaning: *inane jokes*

in·an·i·mate /ɪnˈænəmɪt/ *adj.* not living: *Rocks are* ***inanimate objects***.

in·ap·pro·pri·ate /ˌɪnəˈproʊpriɪt/ (Ac) *adj.* not appropriate for a particular purpose or situation: *inappropriate behavior* | *The school board felt the book was* ***inappropriate for*** *fourth-grade children.* —**inappropriately** *adv.*

in·ar·tic·u·late /ˌɪnɑrˈtɪkyəlɪt/ *adj.* not able to express yourself or speak clearly

in·as·much as /ˌɪnəzˈmʌtʃ əz/ *conjunction* (formal) used in order to begin a phrase that explains the rest of your sentence by showing the limited way that it is true: *She's guilty, inasmuch as she knew what the other girls were planning to do.*

in·au·di·ble /ɪnˈɔdəbəl/ *adj.* too quiet to be heard: *Her reply was inaudible.* —**inaudibly** *adv.*

in·au·gu·rate /ɪˈnɔgyəˌreɪt/ *v.* [T] **1** to have an official ceremony in order to show that someone is beginning an important job: *The President is inaugurated in January.* **2** to open a new building or start a new service with a ceremony —**inaugural** /ɪˈnɔgyərəl/ *adj.*: *the president's inaugural speech* —**inauguration** /ɪˌnɔgyəˈreɪʃən/ *n.* [C,U]

in·aus·pi·cious /ˌɪnɔˈspɪʃəs◂/ *adj.* (formal) seeming to show that the future will be unlucky: *an* ***inauspicious start*** *to our trip* → UNLUCKY

ˌin-ˈbetween *adj.* (informal) in the middle of two points, sizes, etc.: *She's at that in-between age, neither a little girl nor a woman.*

in·born /ˌɪnˈbɔrn◂/ *adj.* an inborn quality or ability is one that you have had naturally since birth: *Humans have an almost inborn love of stories.*

in·bred /ˌɪnˈbrɛd◂/ *adj.* produced by the breeding of closely related members of a family, which often causes problems: *an inbred genetic defect* —**inbreeding** /ˈɪnˌbridɪŋ/ *n.* [U]

Inc. /ɪŋk, ɪn'kɔrpəˌreɪt̬ɪd/ the written abbreviation of INCORPORATED: *General Motors Inc.*

in·cal·cu·la·ble /ɪn'kælkyələbəl/ *adj.* too many or too great to be measured: *The scandal has done* ***incalculable damage*** *to the college's reputation.*

in·can·des·cent /ˌɪnkən'dɛsənt/ *adj.* giving a bright light when heated —**incandescence** *n.* [U]

in·can·ta·tion /ˌɪnkæn'teɪʃən/ *n.* [C,U] a set of special words that someone uses in magic, or the act of saying these words

in·ca·pa·ble /ɪn'keɪpəbəl/ (Ac) *adj.* unable to do something or to feel a particular emotion: *He seemed* ***incapable of*** *understanding how I felt.*

in·ca·pac·i·tate /ˌɪnkə'pæsəˌteɪt/ (Ac) *v.* [T] to make someone too sick or weak to live or work normally: *He was incapacitated for a while after the operation.*

in·ca·pac·i·ty /ˌɪnkə'pæsət̬i/ *n.* [U] lack of ability, strength, or power to do something, especially because you are sick

in·car·cer·ate /ɪn'kɑrsəˌreɪt/ *v.* [T] (formal) to put someone in a prison or keep him/her there —**incarceration** /ɪnˌkɑrsə'reɪʃən/ *n.* [U]

in·car·nate /ɪn'kɑrnɪt, -ˌneɪt/ *adj.* **evil/beauty/greed etc. incarnate** someone who is considered extremely evil, beautiful, etc.

in·car·na·tion /ˌɪnkɑr'neɪʃən/ *n.* **1** [C] according to some religions, the state of being alive in the form of a particular person or animal, or the period during which this happens **2 the incarnation of sth** someone who has a lot of a particular quality, or represents it: *She was the incarnation of wisdom.*

in·cen·di·ar·y /ɪn'sɛndiˌɛri/ *adj.* (formal) designed to cause a fire: *an* ***incendiary device/bomb***

in·cense /'ɪnsɛns/ *n.* [U] a substance that is burned in order to fill a room with a particular smell [ORIGIN: 1200—1300 Old French *encens*, from Latin *incensus*, past participle of *incendere* "to cause to start burning"]

in·censed /ɪn'sɛnst/ *adj.* extremely angry

in·cen·tive /ɪn'sɛntɪv/ (Ac) *n.* [C,U] something that encourages you to work harder, start new activities, etc.: *The government* ***provides incentives for*** *new businesses.* [ORIGIN: 1600—1700 Late Latin *incentivum*, from Latin *incinere* "to set the tune"]

in·cep·tion /ɪn'sɛpʃən/ *n.* [singular] (formal) the start of an organization or institution: *He has worked for the company* ***since its inception*** *in 1970.*

in·ces·sant /ɪn'sɛsənt/ *adj.* (formal) without stopping: *the incessant traffic noise* —**incessantly** *adv.*

in·cest /'ɪnsɛst/ *n.* [U] illegal sex between people who are closely related to each other —**incestuous** /ɪn'sɛstʃuəs/ *adj.* —**incestuously** *adv.*

inch¹ /ɪntʃ/ *n.* (plural **inches**) [C] **1** (*written abbreviation* **in**) a unit for measuring length, equal to 1/12 of a foot or 2.54 centimeters: *The females lay eggs that are about 5 inches long.* **2 every inch** all of someone or something: ***Every inch of*** *the closet was filled with boxes.* **3 inch by inch** very slowly or by a small amount at a time: *The old buses moved inch by inch toward the pyramids.* **4 not give/budge an inch** to refuse to change your opinions at all: *At first Will refused to give an inch in the argument.* [ORIGIN: 1000—1100 Latin *uncia* "one twelfth"]

inch² *v.* [I,T] to move very slowly and carefully, or to move something in this way: *I got a glass of wine and* ***inched*** *my* ***way*** *across the crowded room.*

in·cho·ate /ɪn'koʊɪt/ *adj.* (formal) inchoate ideas, plans, attitudes, etc. are just starting to develop or are not well formed

in·ci·dence /'ɪnsədəns/ (Ac) *n.* [singular] (formal) the number of times something happens: *Researchers found a high* ***incidence of*** *asthma in Detroit.*

in·ci·dent /'ɪnsədənt/ (Ac) *n.* [C] something unusual, serious, or violent that happens: *Any witnesses to the incident should speak to the police.* | *The protest finished* ***without incident*** (=without anything unusual or bad happening). [ORIGIN: 1400—1500 French, Latin, present participle of *incidere* "to fall into"]

> THESAURUS event, occurrence, affair, happening → EVENT

in·ci·den·tal /ˌɪnsə'dɛntl◂/ *adj.* happening or existing in connection with something else that is more important: *The issue that he brought up was* ***incidental to*** *the main debate.*

in·ci·den·tal·ly /ˌɪnsə'dɛntˀli/ (Ac) *adv.* **1** used when giving additional information, or when changing the subject of a conversation: *Incidentally, Jenny's coming over tonight.* **2** happening or existing as a result of something else, but in a way that is not planned and not the main purpose: *The dam was built for irrigation, but incidentally will control flooding.*

in·cin·er·ate /ɪn'sɪnəˌreɪt/ *v.* [T] (formal) to burn something in order to destroy it —**incineration** /ɪnˌsɪnə'reɪʃən/ *n.* [U]

in·cin·er·a·tor /ɪn'sɪnəˌreɪt̬ɚ/ *n.* [C] a machine that burns things at very high temperatures

in·ci·sion /ɪn'sɪʒən/ *n.* [C] (formal) a cut that a doctor makes in someone's body during an operation

in·ci·sive /ɪn'saɪsɪv/ *adj.* incisive words, remarks, etc. are very direct and deal with the most important part of a subject

in·ci·sor /ɪn'saɪzɚ/ *n.* [C] BIOLOGY one of your eight front teeth that has sharp edges

in·cite /ɪn'saɪt/ *v.* [T] to deliberately encourage people to fight, argue, etc.: *One man was jailed for* ***inciting a riot.*** [ORIGIN: 1400—1500 French

I

inciter, from Latin *citare* "to cause to start moving"]

in·cli·na·tion /ˌɪnklə'neɪʃən/ (Ac) *n.* **1** [C,U] the desire to do something: *I didn't have **the time or inclination to** go with them.* **2** [C,U] a tendency to think or behave in a particular way: *his **inclination to** act violently*

in·cline¹ /ɪn'klaɪn/ (Ac) *v.* [I,T] to slope at a particular angle, or make something do this [ORIGIN: 1300—1400 French *incliner*, from Latin *clinare* "to lean"]

in·cline² /'ɪnklaɪn/ (Ac) *n.* [C] a slope: *a steep incline*

in·clined /ɪn'klaɪnd/ (Ac) *adj.* **1 be inclined to agree/believe/think etc.** to have a particular opinion, but not have it very strongly: *I'm inclined to agree with you, but I don't really know.* **2** wanting to do something: *My client is not **inclined to** speak with reporters.* **3** likely or tending to do something: *He's **inclined to** get upset over small things.*

in·clude /ɪn'klud/ *v.* [T] **1** if one thing includes another, the second thing is part of the first: *The price includes your flight, hotel, and car rental.* | *Tim's job responsibilities include hiring new teachers.* | *Service is **included in** the bill.* **2** to make someone or something part of a larger group or set (ANT) **exclude**: *Homework exercises are **included in** the book.* | *You should **include** your educational background **on** your résumé.* [ORIGIN: 1400—1500 Latin *includere*, from *in* "in" + *claudere* "to close"]

I

in·clud·ing /ɪn'kludɪŋ/ *prep.* used in order to show that someone or something is part of a larger group or set that you are talking about (ANT) **excluding**: *There were 20 people in the room, including the teacher.* | *We only paid $12 each for dinner, including the tip.*

in·clu·sion /ɪn'kluʒən/ *n.* **1** [U] the action of including someone or something in a larger group or set, or the fact of being included in one: *I am surprised at his **inclusion in** the team.* | *Here's the list of books we're considering **for inclusion** on the reading list.* **2** [C] someone or something that is included

in·clu·sive /ɪn'klusɪv/ *adj.* including a wide variety of people, things, etc.: *American colleges try very hard to be inclusive.*

in·cog·ni·to /ˌɪnkɑg'niṭoʊ/ *adv.* if a famous person does something incognito, s/he is hiding who s/he really is [ORIGIN: 1600—1700 Italian, Latin *incognitus* "unknown"]

in·co·her·ent /ˌɪnkoʊ'hɪrənt/ (Ac) *adj.* **1** not clear, not organized, and hard to understand: *an incoherent letter* **2** speaking in a way that cannot be understood or that does not make sense: *Joey mumbled something incoherent.* —**incoherently** *adv.*

in·come /'ɪnkʌm, 'ɪŋ-/ (Ac) *n.* [C,U] the money that you earn from working or making INVESTMENTS: *a **good/high/low income*** | *She has an **annual income** of $40,000.* | *an elderly couple living on a **fixed income*** (=an income that does not change or grow)

> THESAURUS **pay, salary, wages, earnings, bonus, remuneration** → PAY²

'income distri,bution *n.* [U] ECONOMICS the way in which the total income earned by the population of a country exists in different amounts in different areas, depending on the number of people living in each place and their level of income

'income tax *n.* [U] ECONOMICS tax paid on the money you earn

in·com·ing /'ɪnˌkʌmɪŋ/ *adj.* **1 incoming call/letter/fax** a telephone call, letter, or FAX that you receive (ANT) **outgoing** **2** coming toward a place, or about to arrive (ANT) **outgoing**: *the incoming tide*

in·com·mu·ni·ca·do /ˌɪnkəˌmyunɪ'kɑdoʊ/ *adj., adv.* not allowed or not wanting to communicate with anyone

in·com·pa·ra·ble /ɪn'kɑmpərəbəl/ *adj.* so impressive, beautiful, etc. that nothing or no one is better: *the incomparable beauty of the landscape* —**incomparably** *adv.*

in·com·pat·i·ble /ˌɪnkəm'pæṭəbəl/ (Ac) *adj.* too different to be able to be accepted, work together well, or have a good relationship: *The two cellphones use incompatible systems.* | *Results of the two experiments were incompatible.* | *These new scientific facts are **incompatible with** each other.* | *Tony and I have always been incompatible.* —**incompatibility** /ˌɪnkəmˌpæṭə'bɪləṭi/ *n.* [U]

in·com·pe·tence /ɪn'kɑmpəṭəns/ *n.* [U] lack of ability or skill to do your job: *Police have been accused of incompetence.*

in·com·pe·tent /ɪn'kɑmpəṭənt/ *adj.* not having the ability or skill to do your job: *a totally incompetent waitress* —**incompetent** *n.* [C]

in·com·plete¹ /ˌɪnkəm'plit◂/ *adj.* not having all its parts or not finished yet: *an incomplete sentence* | *The report is still incomplete.*

incomplete² *n.* [C] a grade given to college students, which shows that they still have to finish some work for a course: ***I got an incomplete in** astronomy.*

in·com·pre·hen·si·ble /ˌɪnkɑmpri'hɛnsəbəl/ *adj.* impossible to understand: *His speech was incomprehensible.*

in·con·ceiv·a·ble /ˌɪnkən'sivəbəl/ (Ac) *adj.* too strange or unusual to seem real or possible: ***It was inconceivable that** such a quiet man could be violent.* —**inconceivably** *adv.*

in·con·clu·sive /ˌɪnkən'klusɪv/ (Ac) *adj.* not leading to any decision or result: *inconclusive research* | *The evidence the police provided was inconclusive* (=did not prove anything). —**inconclusively** *adv.*

in·con·gru·ous /ɪn'kɑŋgruəs/ *adj.* (formal) seeming to be wrong or unusual in a particular situation: *Her quiet voice seemed* ***incongruous with*** *her hard face.* —**incongruously** *adv.* —**incongruity** /ˌɪnkən'gruəṭi/ *n.* [C,U]

in·con·se·quen·tial /ˌɪnkɑnsə'kwɛnʃəl/ *adj.* (formal) not important (SYN) **insignificant**: *The issue is totally inconsequential.* —**inconsequentially** *adv.*

in·con·sid·er·ate /ˌɪnkən'sɪdərɪt/ *adj.* not caring about other people's needs or feelings: *It was really* ***inconsiderate of*** *you not to call and say you'd be late.* —**inconsiderately** *adv.*

in·con·sist·en·cy /ˌɪnkən'sɪstənsi/ (Ac) *n.* (plural **inconsistencies**) **1** [C,U] a situation in which two statements are different and cannot both be true: *The police became suspicious because of the* ***inconsistencies in*** *her story.* **2** [U] the quality of changing your ideas too often or of doing something differently each time, so that people do not know what to expect: *The team's inconsistency has resulted in a poor league position.*

in·con·sist·ent /ˌɪnkən'sɪstənt/ (Ac) *adj.* **1** two ideas or statements that are inconsistent are different and cannot both be true: *We're getting inconsistent results from the lab tests.* | *His story was* ***inconsistent with*** *the evidence.* **2** not doing things in the same way each time: *Inconsistent discipline can make children behave badly.* **3** not following an expected principle or standard: *What they have done is* ***inconsistent with*** *the agreement that they made with us.* —**inconsistently** *adv.*

in·con·sol·a·ble /ˌɪnkən'soʊləbəl/ *adj.* (literary) so sad that you cannot be comforted: *His widow was inconsolable.*

in·con·spic·u·ous /ˌɪnkən'spɪkyuəs/ *adj.* not easily seen or noticed: *I sat in the corner,* ***trying to look/be inconspicuous.***

in·con·ti·nent /ɪn'kɑntˀn-ənt, -tənənt/ *adj.* unable to control your BLADDER or BOWELS —**incontinence** *n.* [U]

in·con·tro·vert·i·ble /ˌɪnkɑntrə'vəṭəbəl/ *adj.* an incontrovertible fact is definitely true: *The police have* ***incontrovertible evidence*** *that he committed the crime.* —**incontrovertibly** *adv.*

in·con·ven·ience[1] /ˌɪnkən'vinyəns/ *n.* [C,U] something that causes you problems or difficulties, or the state of having problems or difficulties: *We apologize for any inconvenience caused by the delay to the bus service.*

inconvenience[2] *v.* [T] to cause problems or difficulties for someone: *"I'll drive you home." "Are you sure? I don't want to inconvenience you."*

in·con·ven·ient /ˌɪnkən'vinyənt/ *adj.* causing problems or difficulties, especially in an annoying way: *Is this an inconvenient time for you to talk?* —**inconveniently** *adv.*

in·cor·po·rate /ɪn'kɔrpəˌreɪt/ (Ac) *v.* [T] **1** to include something as part of a group, system, etc.: *Several safety features have been* ***incorporated into*** *the car's design.* **2** to form a CORPORATION [ORIGIN: 1300—1400 Late Latin, past participle of *incorporare*, from Latin *corpus* "body"] —**incorporation** /ɪnˌkɔrpə'reɪʃən/ *n.* [U]

In·cor·po·rat·ed /ɪn'kɔrpəˌreɪṭɪd/ (*written abbreviation* **Inc.**) *adj.* used after the name of a company in the U.S. to show that it is a CORPORATION

in·cor·rect /ˌɪnkə'rɛkt/ *adj.* not correct (SYN) **wrong**: *incorrect answers* —**incorrectly** *adv.*

THESAURUS **wrong, erroneous, inaccurate, misleading, false** → WRONG[1]

in·cor·ri·gi·ble /ɪn'kɔrədʒəbəl, -'kɑr-/ *adj.* someone who is incorrigible is bad in some way and cannot be changed: *an* ***incorrigible liar***

in·crease[1] /ɪn'kris/ *v.* [I,T] to become larger in number, amount, or degree, or make something do this (ANT) **decrease**: *The price of gas has* ***increased by*** *4%.* | *Immigration has* ***increased dramatically*** *in recent decades.* | *The waves were* ***increasing in*** *size.* | *Smoking increases your chances of getting cancer.* [ORIGIN: 1300—1400 Old French *encreistre*, from Latin *increscere*, from *crescere* "to grow"] —**increasing** *adj.*: *increasing concern about job security*

THESAURUS

go up – to increase in number, amount, or value: *Prices have gone up 2%.*
rise – to increase in number, amount, quality, or value: *Motor vehicle thefts rose from 145 to 312 last year.*
grow – to increase in amount, size, or degree: *The number of people working from home has grown substantially.*
double – to become twice as large or twice as much, or to make something do this: *The firm has doubled in size in ten years.*
shoot up – to quickly increase in number, size, or amount: *Unemployment shot up.*
multiply – to increase greatly, or to make something do this: *The company's problems have multiplied over the past year.*

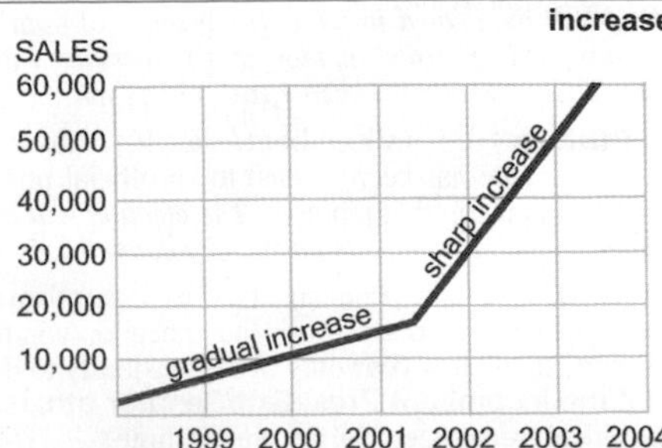

in·crease[2] /'ɪŋkris/ *n.* [C,U] a rise in number, amount, or degree (ANT) **decrease**: *an* ***increase in*** *sales* | *People are complaining about the large* ***tax increase.*** | *There has been a* ***dramatic/significant***

increase in housing prices. | *Crime in the city is* ***on the increase*** (=increasing).

in·creased /ɪnˈkrist/ *adj.* larger or more than before: *an increased awareness of environmental issues*

in·creas·ing·ly /ɪnˈkrisɪŋli/ *adv.* more and more: *It's becoming increasingly difficult to find employment.*

in·cred·i·ble /ɪnˈkrɛdəbəl/ *adj.* **1** extremely good, large, or impressive: *The view from our hotel window was incredible.* | *an incredible bargain* **2** very hard to believe: ***It's incredible that*** *he survived the fall.* | ***It's incredible to think*** *they actually lost the game.*

in·cred·i·bly /ɪnˈkrɛdəbli/ *adv.* **1** extremely: *It's incredibly beautiful here in the spring.* **2** in a way that is difficult to believe: *Incredibly, he was not injured.*

in·cred·u·lous /ɪnˈkrɛdʒələs/ *adj.* showing that you are unable or unwilling to believe something: *"You sold the car?" she asked, incredulous.* **—incredulously** *adv.* **—incredulity** /ˌɪnkrɪˈduləṭi/ *n.* [U]

in·cre·ment /ˈɪnkrəmənt, ˈɪŋ-/ *n.* [C] an amount by which a value, number, or amount of money increases: *an annual salary increment of 2.9%* | *He is paying off the $5,000 fine* ***in small increments.*** **—incremental** /ˌɪnkrəˈmɛntl◂/ *adj.*

in·crim·i·nate /ɪnˈkrɪməˌneɪt/ *v.* [T] to make someone seem guilty of a crime: *He refused to* ***incriminate himself*** *by answering questions.* **—incriminating** *adj.*: *incriminating evidence* **—incrimination** /ɪnˌkrɪməˈneɪʃən/ *n.* [U]

I

in·cu·bate /ˈɪŋkyəˌbeɪt/ *v.* [I,T] BIOLOGY if a bird incubates its egg or if an egg incubates, it is kept warm under a bird's body until the baby bird comes out **—incubation** /ˌɪŋkyəˈbeɪʃən/ *n.* [U]

in·cu·ba·tor /ˈɪŋkyəˌbeɪṭɚ/ *n.* [C] **1** a machine used by hospitals for keeping very small or weak babies alive **2** a machine for keeping eggs warm until the young birds come out

in·cul·cate /ˈɪnkʌlˌkeɪt, ɪnˈkʌlˌkeɪt/ *v.* [T] (formal) to make someone accept an idea or principle by repeating it to him/her frequently ➔ INSTILL: *Dad had inculcated in us a strong sense of family loyalty.* | *The army inculcates its recruits with patriotism.* **—inculcation** /ˌɪnkʌlˈkeɪʃən/ *n.* [U]

in·cum·bent[1] /ɪnˈkʌmbənt/ *n.* [C] (formal) someone who has been elected to an official position and is doing that job now: *The election will be tough for the incumbents on the city council.*

incumbent[2] *adj.* (formal) **1 it is incumbent on/upon sb to do sth** if it is incumbent on you to do something, it is your duty or responsibility to do it **2 the incumbent President/Senator etc.** the president, senator, etc. at the present time

in·cur /ɪnˈkɚ/ *v.* (**incurred, incurring**) [T] to have something bad, such as a punishment or debt, happen because of something you have done: *The oil company incurred a debt of $5 million last year.*

[ORIGIN: 1400—1500 Latin *incurrere* "to run into," from *currere* "to run"]

in·cur·a·ble /ɪnˈkyʊrəbəl/ *adj.* impossible to cure or change: *an incurable disease* | *I am an incurable optimist.* **—incurably** *adv.*

in·cur·sion /ɪnˈkɚʒən/ *n.* [C] (formal) a sudden attack or arrival into an area that belongs to other people: *There was heavy fighting after the army's* ***incursion into*** *the northern provinces.*

in·debt·ed /ɪnˈdɛṭɪd/ *adj.* **be indebted to sb** to be very grateful to someone for the help s/he has given you: *I am indebted to my friend Catherine, who edited my manuscript.* **—indebtedness** *n.* [U]

in·de·cent /ɪnˈdisənt/ *adj.* indecent behavior, clothes, or actions are likely to offend or shock people because they are against social or moral standards, or because they involve sex: *You can't wear a skirt that short – it's indecent!* | *indecent material on the Internet* **—indecency** *n.* [C,U]

in·de·ci·sion /ˌɪndɪˈsɪʒən/ *n.* [U] the state of not being able to make decisions: *After a week of indecision, we agreed to buy the house.*

in·de·ci·sive /ˌɪndɪˈsaɪsɪv/ *adj.* **1** unable to make decisions: *He was criticized for being a weak, indecisive leader.* **2** not having a clear result: *an indecisive battle* **—indecisiveness** *n.* [U]

in·deed /ɪnˈdid/ *adv.* **1** used when adding more information to a statement: *Most people at that time were illiterate. Indeed, only 8% of the population could read.* **2** used when emphasizing a statement or a question: *Jackson is indeed the best player in the league.*

in·de·fat·i·ga·ble /ˌɪndɪˈfæṭɪgəbəl/ *adj.* (formal) determined and never becoming tired SYN **tireless**: *an indefatigable worker*

in·de·fen·si·ble /ˌɪndɪˈfɛnsəbəl/ *adj.* too bad to be excused or defended: *indefensible behavior*

in·de·fin·a·ble /ˌɪndɪˈfaɪnəbəl/ *adj.* difficult to describe or explain: *For some indefinable reason she felt afraid.*

in·def·i·nite /ɪnˈdɛfənɪt/ Ac *adj.* **1** an indefinite action or period of time has no definite end arranged for it: *He was away in Alaska for an* ***indefinite period.*** **2** not clear or definite SYN **vague**: *The schedule is still indefinite.*

inˌdefinite ˈarticle *n.* [C] ENG. LANG. ARTS the words "a" and "an" ➔ DEFINITE ARTICLE

in·def·i·nite·ly /ɪnˈdɛfənɪtli/ Ac *adv.* for a period of time without an arranged end: *I'll be staying here indefinitely.*

inˌdefinite ˈpronoun *n.* [C] ENG. LANG. ARTS a word such as "some," "any," or "either" that is used instead of a noun, but that does not say exactly which person or thing is meant

in·del·i·ble /ɪnˈdɛləbəl/ *adj.* impossible to remove or forget SYN **permanent**: *indelible ink* |

The movie ***left an indelible impression*** *on her* (=she could not forget it). —**indelibly** *adv.*

in·del·i·cate /ɪn'dɛlɪkɪt/ *adj.* (literary) slightly impolite or offensive: *an indelicate question* —**indelicately** *adv.*

in·dem·ni·fy /ɪn'dɛmnə,faɪ/ *v.* (**indemnified, indemnifies**) [T] LAW to promise to pay someone if something s/he owns becomes lost or damaged, or if s/he is injured

in·dem·ni·ty /ɪn'dɛmnət̬i/ *n.* (plural **indemnities**) **1** [U] LAW protection in the form of a promise to pay for any damage or loss **2** [C] LAW money that is paid to someone for any damages, losses, or injury

in·dent /ɪn'dɛnt/ *v.* [T] to start a line of writing closer to the middle of the page than the other lines

in·den·ta·tion /,ɪndɛn'teɪʃən/ *n.* [C] **1** a space at the beginning of a line of writing **2** a cut or space in the edge of something

in·den·tured serv·ant /ɪn,dɛntʃə˞d 'sə˞vənt/ *n.* [C] HISTORY in past times, someone who agreed or was forced to work for his/her employer for a particular number of years before s/he could be free

in·de·pend·ence /,ɪndɪ'pɛndəns/ *n.* [U] **1** the freedom and ability to make your own decisions and take care of yourself without having to ask other people for help, money, or permission: *Many old people want to* ***keep/maintain*** *their* ***independence****. | Staying out late is one way teenagers try to* ***assert their independence****. | Having a job gives you* ***financial independence****.* **2** political freedom from control by another country: *The United States* ***declared independence*** *in 1776. | Mexico* ***gained independence from*** *Spain in 1821.*

Inde'pendence ,Day *n.* a U.S. national holiday on July 4th that celebrates the beginning of the United States as an independent nation

in·de·pend·ent /,ɪndɪ'pɛndənt◂/ *adj.* **1** confident, free, and not needing to ask other people for help, money, or permission to do something: *Women have become better educated and more independent. | He helps disabled people to lead independent lives.* **2** not controlled by another government or organization: *India became an independent nation in 1947. | a European army* ***independent of*** *NATO* **3** not influenced by other people: *an independent report on the experiment* —**independently** *adv.*

,independent 'clause *n.* [C] ENG. LANG. ARTS a CLAUSE that can make up a sentence by itself, for example "He woke up" in the sentence "He woke up when he heard the bell." SYN **main clause** → DEPENDENT CLAUSE

,independent 'variable *n.* [C] SCIENCE in a scientific EXPERIMENT (=test), one of the conditions you change, add, or remove in order to test its effect on something else involved in the experiment SYN **manipulated variable**

,independent 'voter *n.* [C] POLITICS someone who votes but who does not support one particular political party

'in-depth *adj.* **in-depth study/report** a study or report that is very thorough and considers all the details

in·de·scrib·a·ble /,ɪndɪ'skraɪbəbəl/ *adj.* too good, strange, frightening, etc. to be described: *My joy at seeing him was indescribable.*

in·de·struct·i·ble /,ɪndɪ'strʌktəbəl/ *adj.* impossible to destroy: *The tank was built to be indestructible.*

in·de·ter·mi·nate /,ɪndɪ'tə˞mənɪt/ *adj.* impossible to find out or calculate exactly: *a woman of indeterminate age*

in·dex¹ /'ɪndɛks/ (Ac) *n.* (plural **indexes** *or* **indices** /'ɪndə,siz/) [C] **1** an alphabetical list at the end of a book, that lists all the names, subjects, etc. in the book and the pages where you can find them: *Children should understand how to use an index.* **2** a set of cards with information, or a DATABASE, in alphabetical order: *Look up the book in the library's card index.* **3** a standard or level you can use for judging or measuring something: *the Consumer Price Index* **4** MATH the number that is written before and slightly above a RADICAL SIGN (√), which shows how many times a number was multiplied by itself to produce the number after the radical sign. The index of $^3\sqrt{5}$ is 3. [ORIGIN: 1500—1600 Latin "first finger, guide," from *indicare*]

index² *v.* [T] to make an index for something: *The software can index the documents on your computer.*

'index card *n.* [C] a small card that you write information on

'index ,finger *n.* [C] the finger next to the thumb SYN **forefinger** → *see picture at* HAND¹

In·di·an¹ /'ɪndiən/ *adj.* **1** relating to NATIVE AMERICANS **2** relating to or coming from India

Indian² *n.* [C] **1** a NATIVE AMERICAN **2** someone from India

,Indian 'Ocean *n.* **the Indian Ocean** the ocean surrounded by Africa in the west, India in the north, and Australia in the east

,Indian 'summer *n.* [C,U] a period of warm weather in the fall

in·di·cate /'ɪndə,keɪt/ (Ac) *v.* [T] **1** to show that something exists or is likely to be true: *Research* ***indicates that*** *women live longer than men. | Her writing indicated a deep understanding of science.*

> THESAURUS **demonstrate, show, suggest**
> → DEMONSTRATE

2 to point at something: *Indicating a chair, he said, "Please, sit down."* **3** to say or do something that shows what you want or intend to do: *He* ***indicated that*** *he had no desire to come with us.* [ORIGIN: 1600—1700 Latin, past participle of *indicare*, from *dicare* "to say publicly or officially"]

in·di·ca·tion /ˌɪndəˈkeɪʃən/ (Ac) *n.* [C,U] a sign that something exists or is likely to be true: *Did Rick ever* ***give any indication that*** *he was unhappy?* | *There has been no* ***indication of*** *improvement in his condition.*

in·dic·a·tive¹ /ɪnˈdɪkət̮ɪv/ (Ac) *adj.* (formal) **1 be indicative of sth** to show that something exists or is likely to be true: *His reaction is indicative of how frightened he is.* **2** ENG. LANG. ARTS relating to the indicative

indicative² (Ac) *n.* [C,U] ENG. LANG. ARTS the form of a verb that is used to make ordinary statements. For example, in the sentences "Penny passed her test," and "Mike likes cake," the verbs "passed" and "likes" are in the indicative. → IMPERATIVE, SUBJUNCTIVE

in·di·ca·tor /ˈɪndəˌkeɪt̮ɚ/ (Ac) *n.* [C] **1** an event, fact, etc. that shows that something exists, or shows you the way something is developing: *All the main* ***economic indicators*** *suggest that business is improving.* **2** something on a machine that shows the temperature, speed, etc.

in·di·ces /ˈɪndəˌsiz/ *n.* a plural of INDEX

in·dict /ɪnˈdaɪt/ *v.* [I,T] LAW to officially charge someone with a crime: *He was* ***indicted on charges of*** *perjury.* —**indictable** /ɪnˈdaɪt̮əbəl/ *adj.*

in·dict·ment /ɪnˈdaɪt˺mənt/ *n.* [C] **1** LAW an official written statement saying that someone has done something illegal

THESAURUS accusation, allegation, charge, complaint → ACCUSATION

2 be an indictment of sth something which shows that a system, method, etc. is very bad or wrong: *Bellow's novel can be read as* ***an indictment of*** *modern society.*

in·dif·ference /ɪnˈdɪfrəns/ *n.* [U] lack of interest or concern: *his* ***indifference to*** *the suffering of others*

in·dif·ferent /ɪnˈdɪfrənt/ *adj.* not interested in someone or something, or not having any feelings or opinions about him, her, or it: *The industry seems* ***indifferent to*** *environmental concerns.*

in·dig·e·nous /ɪnˈdɪdʒənəs/ *adj.* (formal) indigenous plants, animals, etc. have always lived or grown naturally in the place where they are (SYN) **native**: *These plants are* ***indigenous to*** *the Amazon region.* [ORIGIN: 1600—1700 Late Latin *indigenus*, from Latin *indigena* "someone born in a place"]

in·di·gent /ˈɪndɪdʒənt/ *adj.* (formal) not having much money or many possessions (SYN) **poor**: *money to help indigent hospital patients* —**indigent** *n.* [C] —**indigence** *n.* [U]

THESAURUS poor, needy, destitute, impoverished, impecunious, penurious, poverty-stricken → POOR

in·di·gest·i·ble /ˌɪndɪˈdʒɛstəbəl, -daɪ-/ *adj.* food that is indigestible cannot easily be broken down in the stomach → DIGEST

in·di·ges·tion /ˌɪndəˈdʒɛstʃən, -daɪ-/ *n.* [U] the pain caused by eating food that cannot easily be broken down in the stomach

in·dig·nant /ɪnˈdɪgnənt/ *adj.* angry because you feel you have been insulted or unfairly treated: *Marsha was* ***indignant about*** *the poor service she had received.* —**indignantly** *adv.*

THESAURUS angry, annoyed, irritated, livid, furious, mad, irate, outraged → ANGRY

in·dig·na·tion /ˌɪndɪgˈneɪʃən/ *n.* [U] feelings of anger and surprise because you feel insulted or unfairly treated: *her* ***indignation at*** *the suggestion that it was her fault* | *His eyes blazed* ***with indignation.***

in·dig·ni·ty /ɪnˈdɪgnət̮i/ *n.* (plural **indignities**) [C,U] a situation that makes you feel very ashamed and not respected: *Two of the diplomats* ***suffered the indignity of*** *being arrested.*

in·di·rect /ˌɪndəˈrɛkt◂, -daɪ-/ *adj.* **1** not directly caused by something or relating to it: *The accident was an* ***indirect result*** *of the heavy rain.* **2** not using the straightest or most direct way to get to a place: *an indirect route* **3** suggesting something without saying it directly or clearly: *He never mentioned my work, which I felt was an indirect criticism of its quality.* —**indirectly** *adv.*

ˌindirect ˈobject *n.* [C] ENG. LANG. ARTS in grammar, the person or thing that receives something as the result of the action of the verb in a sentence. In the sentence "Pete gave me the money," "me" is the indirect object. → DIRECT OBJECT

ˌindirect ˈreasoning *also* **ˌindirect ˈproof** *n.* [U] MATH the process of proving that a mathematical statement is true by first saying that it is false, and then showing that, if the statement is really false, other mathematical statements which are known or believed to be true must also be false

ˌindirect ˈrule *n.* [U] POLITICS the act of governing a COLONY (=a country or area ruled by a more powerful country) using local laws rather than the laws of the ruling country

ˌindirect ˈspeech *n.* [U] ENG. LANG. ARTS REPORTED SPEECH

in·dis·creet /ˌɪndɪˈskrit/ *adj.* careless about what you say or do, so that you let people know too much

in·dis·cre·tion /ˌɪndɪˈskrɛʃən/ (Ac) *n.* [C,U] an action, remark, or behavior that shows bad judgment and is usually considered socially or morally unacceptable: *his embarrassing sexual indiscretions* | *youthful indiscretion*

in·dis·crim·i·nate /ˌɪndɪˈskrɪmənɪt/ *adj.* an indiscriminate action is done without thinking about what harm it might cause: *indiscriminate acts of violence*

in·dis·pen·sa·ble /ˌɪndɪˈspɛnsəbəl/ *adj.* someone or something that is indispensable is so important or useful that you cannot manage without him, her, or it: *The information he provided was **indispensable to** our research.*

THESAURUS necessary, essential, vital → NECESSARY

in·dis·pu·ta·ble /ˌɪndɪˈspyuṭəbəl/ *adj.* a fact that is indisputable must be accepted because it is definitely true —**indisputably** *adv.*

in·dis·tinct /ˌɪndɪˈstɪŋkt/ (Ac) *adj.* not able to be seen, heard, or remembered very clearly (SYN) **unclear**: *We could hear indistinct voices in the next room.* —**indistinctly** *adv.*

in·dis·tin·guish·a·ble /ˌɪndɪˈstɪŋgwɪʃəbəl/ *adj.* things that are indistinguishable are so similar that you cannot see any difference between them: *This material is **indistinguishable from** real silk.*

in·di·vid·u·al¹ /ˌɪndəˈvɪdʒuəl/ (Ac) *adj.* **1** considered separately from other people or things in the same group: *Each individual drawing is slightly different.* | *the tasks given to the individual members of the group* **2** belonging to or intended for one person rather than a group: *Individual attention must be given to each student.* | *The gallery relies on both corporate and individual donations.* [ORIGIN: 1400—1500 Medieval Latin *individualis*, from Latin *individuus* "undividable"]

individual² (Ac) *n.* [C] one person, considered separately from the rest of the group or society that s/he lives in: *Thousands of homeless individuals and families use these shelters.* | *The substance can help prevent heart disease in some individuals.*

in·di·vid·u·al·ism /ˌɪndəˈvɪdʒuəˌlɪzəm/ (Ac) *n.* [U] **1** the behavior or attitude of someone who does things in his or her own way without being influenced by other people: *The culture of the western U.S. has always valued **rugged individualism**.* **2** the belief that the rights and freedom of individual people are the most important rights in society: *Japanese society promotes the group rather than individualism.* —**individualist** *n.* [C]: *He was an individualist who always spoke his mind.* —**individualistic** /ˌɪndəˌvɪdʒuəˈlɪstɪk/ *adj.*

in·di·vid·u·al·i·ty /ˌɪndəˌvɪdʒuˈæləṭi/ (Ac) *n.* [U] the quality that makes someone or something different from all others: *His individuality shows in his art work.*

in·di·vid·u·al·ly /ˌɪndəˈvɪdʒuəli, -dʒəli/ (Ac) *adv.* separately, not together in a group: *Mr. Wong met with each employee individually.*

in·di·vis·i·ble /ˌɪndəˈvɪzəbəl/ *adj.* not able to be separated or divided into parts —**indivisibly** *adv.*

in·doc·tri·nate /ɪnˈdɑktrəˌneɪt/ *v.* [T] (disapproving) to teach someone to accept a particular set of beliefs and not consider any others —**indoctrination** /ɪnˌdɑktrəˈneɪʃən/ *n.* [U]

in·do·lent /ˈɪndələnt/ *adj.* (formal) lazy —**indolently** *adv.* —**indolence** *n.* [U]

in·dom·i·ta·ble /ɪnˈdɑməṭəbəl/ *adj.* **indomitable spirit/courage etc.** (formal) determination, courage, etc. that can never be defeated

indoor

indoor swimming pool

in·door /ˈɪndɔr/ *adj.* [only before noun] used or happening inside a building (ANT) **outdoor**: *an indoor swimming pool*

in·doors /ˌɪnˈdɔrz/ *adv.* into or inside a building (ANT) **outdoors**: *He stayed indoors all morning.*

in·duce /ɪnˈdus/ (Ac) *v.* (formal) **1** [T] to make someone decide to do something: *What **induced** you **to** spend so much money on a car?*

THESAURUS cause, make, prompt → CAUSE²

2 [T] to cause a particular physical condition: *This drug may induce drowsiness.* **3** [I,T] to make a woman give birth to her baby by giving her a special drug

in·duce·ment /ɪnˈdusmənt/ *n.* [C,U] something that you are offered to persuade you to do something: *He was given $10,000 as an **inducement to** leave the company.*

in·duct /ɪnˈdʌkt/ *v.* [T] to officially make someone a member of a group or organization: *Joni Mitchell was **inducted into** the Rock and Roll Hall of Fame.* —**inductee** /ɪnˌdʌkˈti/ *n.* [C]

in·duc·tion /ɪnˈdʌkʃən/ (Ac) *n.* [C,U] the act or ceremony of officially making someone a member of a group or organization

in·duc·tive /ɪnˈdʌktɪv/ *adj.* using known facts or patterns to form the general principles of something or a general opinion about something: *inductive research*

inˌductive ˈreasoning *n.* [U] MATH the process of forming a general mathematical rule for solving a mathematical problem using an existing pattern of specific results or facts

in·dulge /ɪnˈdʌldʒ/ *v.* **1** [I,T] to let yourself do or have something that you enjoy, especially something that is considered bad for you: *We **indulged in** a piece of cheesecake after lunch.* | *Go ahead – **indulge yourself**.* **2** [T] to let someone do or have whatever s/he wants, even if it is bad for him/her: *She did not like her children to be indulged.*

in·dul·gence /ɪn'dʌldʒəns/ *n.* **1** [U] the habit of eating too much, drinking too much, etc.: *a life of indulgence* **2** [C] something that you do or have for pleasure, not because you need it: *Chocolate is my only indulgence.*

in·dul·gent /ɪn'dʌldʒənt/ *adj.* allowing someone to do or have whatever s/he wants, even if it is bad for him/her: *indulgent parents* —**indulgently** *adv.*

in·dus·tri·al /ɪn'dʌstriəl/ *adj.* **1** relating to industry or the people working in industry: *industrial waste* | *industrial production* **2** having many industries, or industries that are well developed: *an industrial region* —**industrially** *adv.*

in·dus·tri·al·ist /ɪn'dʌstriəlɪst/ *n.* [C] the owner of a factory, industrial company, etc.

in·dus·tri·al·ize /ɪn'dʌstriə,laɪz/ *v.* [I,T] if a country or place is industrialized, or if it industrializes, it develops a lot of industry —**industrialization** /ɪn,dʌstriələ'zeɪʃən/ *n.* [U]

in'dustrial ,park *n.* [C] an area of land that has offices, businesses, small factories, etc. on it

in,dustrial revo'lution *n.* **the Industrial Revolution** HISTORY the period in the 18th and 19th centuries in Europe, when machines and factories began to be used to produce goods in large quantities

I

in·dus·tri·ous /ɪn'dʌstriəs/ *adj.* (formal) tending to work hard: *an industrious young woman* —**industriously** *adv.*

in·dus·try /'ɪndəstri/ *n.* (plural **industries**) **1** [U] the production of goods, especially in factories ➔ INDUSTRIAL: *The country's economy is supported by industry.*

THESAURUS **business, commerce, trade, private enterprise** ➔ BUSINESS

2 [C] a particular type of trade or service that produces things: *He works in **the auto/retail/insurance industry**.* | *She's one of the most successful people in this industry.* [ORIGIN: 1400—1500 Old French *industrie* "skill, work involving skill," from Latin *industria* "willingness to work hard"]

in·e·bri·at·ed /ɪ'nibri,eɪt̬ɪd/ *adj.* (formal) drunk —**inebriation** /ɪ,nibri'eɪʃən/ *n.* [U]

in·ed·i·ble /ɪn'ɛdəbəl/ *adj.* not good enough to eat, or not appropriate for eating: *inedible mushrooms*

in·ef·fa·ble /ɪn'ɛfəbəl/ *adj.* (formal) too great to be described in words: *He felt an ineffable sadness.* —**ineffably** *adv.*

in·ef·fec·tive /,ɪnə'fɛktɪv/ *adj.* something that is ineffective does not achieve what it was intended to achieve: *Critics say that gun-control laws have been ineffective.* —**ineffectiveness** *n.* [U]

in·ef·fec·tu·al /,ɪnə'fɛktʃuəl/ *adj.* not achieving what someone or something is trying to do: *an ineffectual leader* —**ineffectually** *adv.*

in·ef·fi·cient /,ɪnə'fɪʃənt/ *adj.* not working well and wasting time, money, or energy: *an inefficient use of good farmland* —**inefficiently** *adv.* —**inefficiency** *n.* [C,U]

in·e·las·tic /,ɪnɪ'læstɪk/ *adj.* ECONOMICS if the demand for a particular product or service is inelastic, a change in the price produces only a small change in the amount people will buy (ANT) **elastic**

in·el·e·gant /ɪn'ɛləgənt/ *adj.* (formal) not graceful or well done: *inelegant manners* ➔ CLUMSY

in·el·i·gi·ble /ɪn'ɛlədʒəbəl/ *adj.* not allowed to do or have something: *Our family is **ineligible for** state aid.* —**ineligibility** /ɪn,ɛlədʒə'bɪlət̬i/ *n.* [U]

in·ept /ɪ'nɛpt/ *adj.* having no skill: *an inept driver* —**ineptitude** /ɪ'nɛptə,tud/ *n.* [U]

in·e·qual·i·ty /,ɪnɪ'kwɑlət̬i/ *n.* (plural **inequalities**) [C,U] an unfair situation, in which some groups in society have more money, opportunities, power, etc. than others ➔ UNEQUAL: *There are many **inequalities in** our legal system.*

in·eq·ui·ty /ɪn'ɛkwət̬i/ *n.* (plural **inequities**) [C,U] (formal) lack of fairness, or something that is unfair: *There are still **inequities in** the amount that men and women earn for the same job.*

in·ert /ɪ'nɚt/ *adj.* **1** CHEMISTRY not producing a chemical reaction when combined with other substances: *inert gases* **2** not moving: *He lay there, inert.* [ORIGIN: 1600—1700 Latin *iners* "unskilled, doing nothing," from *ars* "skill, art"]

in·er·tia /ɪ'nɚʃə/ *n.* [U] **1** a tendency for a situation to stay unchanged for a long time: *the problem of inertia in large bureaucracies* **2** a feeling that you do not want to do anything at all **3** PHYSICS the force that keeps an object in the same position or keeps it moving until it is moved or stopped by another force

in·es·cap·a·ble /,ɪnə'skeɪpəbəl/ *adj.* (formal) impossible to avoid or ignore: *The inescapable fact is that he has a drinking problem.* —**inescapably** *adv.*

in·es·ti·ma·ble /ɪn'ɛstəməbəl/ *adj.* (formal) too much or too great to be calculated —**inestimably** *adv.*

in·ev·i·ta·ble /ɪ'nɛvət̬əbəl/ (Ac) *adj.* **1** certain to happen and impossible to avoid: *A lawsuit seems inevitable.* | ***It was inevitable that** someone would get hurt.* **2 the inevitable** something that is certain to happen: *Finally, the inevitable happened and he lost his job.* [ORIGIN: 1400—1500 Latin *inevitabilis*, from *evitare* "to avoid"] —**inevitability** /ɪ,nɛvət̬ə'bɪlət̬i/ *n.* [U]

in·ev·i·ta·bly /ɪ'nɛvət̬əbli/ (Ac) *adv.* as was certain to happen: *Inevitably, there were a few mistakes.* | *Questions will inevitably arise.*

in·ex·act /ˌɪnɪgˈzækt◂/ *adj.* not exact: *Psychology is* ***an inexact science*** (=you cannot measure things exactly in it).

in·ex·cus·a·ble /ˌɪnɪkˈskyuzəbəl/ *adj.* inexcusable behavior is too bad to be excused: *Being late on your first day at a job is inexcusable.* —**inexcusably** *adv.*

in·ex·haust·i·ble /ˌɪnɪgˈzɔstəbəl/ *adj.* something that is inexhaustible exists in such large amounts that it can never be used up: *Warton seems to have an* ***inexhaustible supply*** *of energy.* —**inexhaustibly** *adv.*

in·ex·o·ra·ble /ɪnˈɛksərəbəl/ *adj.* (formal) an inexorable process cannot be stopped: *the inexorable process of aging* —**inexorably** *adv.*

in·ex·pen·sive /ˌɪnɪkˈspɛnsɪv/ *adj.* low in price: *an inexpensive vacation* —**inexpensively** *adv.*

THESAURUS cheap, reasonable, a good/great deal, good/great value → CHEAP[1]

in·ex·pe·ri·enced /ˌɪnɪkˈspɪriənst/ *adj.* not having much experience or knowledge: *an inexperienced driver* —**inexperience** *n.* [U]

in·ex·pli·ca·ble /ˌɪnɪkˈsplɪkəbəl/ *adj.* too unusual or strange to be explained or understood: *Police are investigating his inexplicable disappearance.* —**inexplicably** *adv.*

in·ex·tric·a·ble /ˌɪnɪkˈstrɪkəbəl, ɪnˈɛkstrɪk-/ *adj.* (formal) two or more things that are inextricable cannot be separated from each other: *the* ***inextricable link*** *between language and culture*

in·ex·tri·ca·bly /ˌɪnɪkˈstrɪkəbli/ *adv.* (formal) things that are inextricably connected or related cannot be separated from each other: *Their political beliefs and their religion are* ***inextricably linked.***

in·fal·li·ble /ɪnˈfæləbəl/ *adj.* **1** always right, and never making mistakes: *Many small children believe their parents are infallible.* **2** always having the intended effect: *an infallible cure for hiccups* —**infallibility** /ɪnˌfæləˈbɪləṭi/ *n.* [U]

in·fa·mous /ˈɪnfəməs/ *adj.* well known for being bad or evil → FAMOUS: *an infamous criminal* —**infamously** *adv.*

THESAURUS famous, legendary, notorious → FAMOUS

in·fa·my /ˈɪnfəmi/ *n.* [U] the state of being evil or of being well known for evil things

in·fan·cy /ˈɪnfənsi/ *n.* [U] **1** the period in a child's life before s/he can walk or talk: *Their son died* ***in infancy.*** **2 in its infancy** something that is in its infancy is just starting to be developed: *The project is still in its infancy.*

in·fant /ˈɪnfənt/ *n.* [C] (formal) a baby, especially one that cannot walk yet [ORIGIN: 1300—1400 French *enfant*, from Latin *infans* "unable to speak," from *fari* "to speak"]

in·fan·tile /ˈɪnfənˌtaɪl, -təl/ *adj.* **1** (disapproving) infantile behavior seems silly in an adult because it is typical of a child: *his infantile jokes* **2** [only before noun] affecting very small children: *infantile illnesses*

in·fan·try /ˈɪnfəntri/ *n.* [U] soldiers who fight on foot

in·farc·tion /ɪnˈfɑrkʃən/ *n.* [C] BIOLOGY a medical condition in which a blood VESSEL becomes blocked, so that no blood can go through

in·fat·u·at·ed /ɪnˈfætʃuˌeɪṭɪd/ *adj.* having unreasonably strong feelings of love for someone: *He's* ***infatuated with*** *her.* —**infatuation** /ɪnˌfætʃuˈeɪʃən/ *n.* [C,U]

in·fect /ɪnˈfɛkt/ *v.* [T] **1** BIOLOGY to give someone a disease: *People can feel well but still infect others.* | *a young man who is* ***infected with*** *the AIDS virus* **2** BIOLOGY to make food, water, etc. dangerous and able to spread disease: *bacteria that can infect fruit* **3** if a feeling that you have infects other people, it makes them begin to feel the same way: *Lucy's enthusiasm soon infected the rest of the class.* **4** IT if a computer VIRUS infects your computer or DISKS, it changes or destroys the information on them [ORIGIN: 1300—1400 Latin, past participle of *inficere* "to dip in, stain"]

in·fect·ed /ɪnˈfɛktɪd/ *adj.* **1** BIOLOGY a part of your body or a wound that is infected has harmful BACTERIA in it that prevent it from HEALing: *an infected finger* **2** BIOLOGY food, water, etc. that is infected contains BACTERIA that spread disease: *water* ***infected with*** *cholera* **3** IT if a computer or DISK is infected, the information on it has been changed or destroyed by a computer VIRUS

in·fec·tion /ɪnˈfɛkʃən/ *n.* [C,U] a disease or sickness in a part of your body, caused by BACTERIA or a VIRUS: *Wash the cut thoroughly to protect against infection.* | *an ear infection*

in·fec·tious /ɪnˈfɛkʃəs/ *adj.* **1** an infectious disease can be passed from one person to another: *Flu is* ***highly infectious.*** **2** someone who is infectious has a disease that could be passed to other people **3** infectious feelings or laughter spread quickly from one person to another

in·fer /ɪnˈfɚ/ (Ac) *v.* (**inferred**, **inferring**) [T] (formal) to form an opinion that something is probably true because of information that you have: *What can you* ***infer from*** *the available data?*

in·fer·ence /ˈɪnfərəns/ (Ac) *n.* [C,U] something that you think is true, based on information that you have: *You'll have to* ***draw*** *your own* ***inferences*** *from the evidence* (=decide what you think is true).

in·fer·en·tial ques·tion /ˌɪnfərɛnʃəl ˈkwɛstʃən/ *n.* [C] ENG. LANG. ARTS a question that asks someone to say what s/he thinks is true, based on something that s/he has read → EVALUATIVE QUESTION, LITERAL QUESTION

in·fe·ri·or[1] /ɪnˈfɪriɚ/ *adj.* **1** not good, or not as good as someone or something else (ANT) **superior**: *Larry always makes me feel inferior.* | *Her work is* ***inferior to*** *mine.* **2** (formal) lower in rank (ANT) **superior**: *an inferior court* [ORIGIN: 1400—

1500 Latin "lower," from *inferus* "below"] —**inferiority** /ɪnˌfɪriˈɑrət̬i, -ˈɔr-/ *n.* [U]

inferior² *n.* [C] someone who has a lower position or rank than you in an organization (ANT) **superior**

inˌferior ˈcourt *n.* [C] LAW a LOWER COURT → SUPERIOR COURT

in·fer·no /ɪnˈfɚnoʊ/ *n.* (plural **infernos**) [C] (literary) a very large and dangerous fire: *a* ***raging inferno*** (=an extremely violent fire)

THESAURUS **fire, flames, blaze** → FIRE[1]

in·fer·tile /ɪnˈfɚt̬l/ *adj.* **1** an infertile person or animal cannot have babies **2** infertile land or soil is not good enough to grow plants on —**infertility** /ˌɪnfɚˈtɪlət̬i/ *n.* [U]

in·fest /ɪnˈfɛst/ *v.* [T] if insects, rats, etc. infest a place, they are there in large numbers and usually cause damage: *The old carpet was* ***infested with*** *fleas.* —**infestation** /ˌɪnfɛˈsteɪʃən/ *n.* [C,U]

in·fi·del /ˈɪnfədl, -ˌdɛl/ *n.* (old-fashioned, disapproving) [C] someone who does not believe in what you consider to be the true religion

in·fi·del·i·ty /ˌɪnfəˈdɛlət̬i/ *n.* (plural **infidelities**) [C,U] an act of being unfaithful to your wife or husband by having sex with someone else

in·field /ˈɪnfild/ *n.* [singular] the part of a baseball field inside the four bases —**infielder** *n.* [C]

in·fight·ing /ˈɪnˌfaɪt̬ɪŋ/ *n.* [U] unfriendly competition and disagreement among members of the same group or organization: *political infighting*

I

in·fil·trate /ɪnˈfɪlˌtreɪt, ˈɪnfɪl-/ *v.* [I,T] to join an organization or enter a place, especially in order to find out secret information about it or to harm it: *The police have made several attempts to infiltrate the Mafia.* —**infiltrator** *n.* [C] —**infiltration** /ˌɪnfɪlˈtreɪʃən/ *n.* [U]

in·fi·nite /ˈɪnfənɪt/ (Ac) *adj.* **1** very great: *a teacher with infinite patience* | *There are an* ***infinite number*** *of devices to make preparing food easier.* **2** without limits in space or time: *The universe is infinite.* [ORIGIN: 1300—1400 Latin *in* "not" + *finitus*, past participle of *finire* "to end"]

in·fi·nite·ly /ˈɪnfənɪtli/ (Ac) *adv.* very much: *This stove is* ***infinitely better/worse*** *than the other one.*

in·fin·i·tes·i·mal /ˌɪnfɪnəˈtɛsəməl/ *adj.* extremely small: *infinitesimal changes in temperature* —**infinitesimally** *adv.*

in·fin·i·tive /ɪnˈfɪnət̬ɪv/ *n.* [C] ENG. LANG. ARTS in grammar, the basic form of a verb, used with "to." In the sentence "I forgot to buy milk," "to buy" is an infinitive. [ORIGIN: 1400—1500 Late Latin *infinitivus*, from Latin *infinitus*; because the verb is not limited by person or number]

in·fin·i·ty /ɪnˈfɪnət̬i/ *n.* **1** [U] a space or distance without limits or an end **2** [singular, U] MATH a number that is larger than all others

in·firm /ɪnˈfɚm/ *adj.* (formal) weak or sick, especially because of being old

THESAURUS **sick, ill, not very well, under the weather, ailing** → SICK

in·fir·ma·ry /ɪnˈfɚməri/ *n.* (plural **infirmaries**) [C] (formal) a place where sick people can receive medical treatment, especially in a place such as a school

in·fir·mi·ty /ɪnˈfɚmət̬i/ *n.* (plural **infirmities**) [C,U] (formal) bad health or a particular illness

in·flame /ɪnˈfleɪm/ *v.* [T] (literary) to make someone have strong feelings of anger, excitement, etc.

in·flam·ma·ble /ɪnˈflæməbəl/ *adj.* (formal) inflammable materials or substances will start to burn very easily (SYN) **flammable** (ANT) **nonflammable**: *Gasoline is* ***highly inflammable***.

THESAURUS **flammable, nonflammable** → FLAMMABLE

in·flam·ma·tion /ˌɪnfləˈmeɪʃən/ *n.* [C,U] swelling and soreness on or in a part of your body, which is often red and hot to touch —**inflamed** /ɪnˈfleɪmd/ *adj.*

in·flam·ma·to·ry /ɪnˈflæməˌtɔri/ *adj.* (formal) an inflammatory speech, piece of writing, etc. is likely to make people angry

in·flat·a·ble /ɪnˈfleɪt̬əbəl/ *adj.* an inflatable object has to be filled with air before you can use it: *an inflatable mattress*

in·flate /ɪnˈfleɪt/ *v.* **1** [I,T] to fill something with air or gas, so that it becomes larger, or to make something do this (ANT) **deflate**: *The machine quickly inflates the tires.* **2** [T] to make something larger in size, amount, or importance: *a policy that inflates land prices* [ORIGIN: 1400—1500 Latin, past participle of *inflare*, from *flare* "to blow"]

in·flat·ed /ɪnˈfleɪt̬ɪd/ *adj.* **1** greater or larger than is reasonable: *He has an inflated opinion of his own importance.* **2** filled with air or gas: *an inflated balloon*

in·fla·tion /ɪnˈfleɪʃən/ *n.* [U] **1** ECONOMICS a continuing increase in prices, or the rate at which prices increase: *countries with* ***high/low inflation*** | *an* ***inflation rate*** (=the rate at which prices rise over time) *of three percent* **2** the process of filling something with air or gas

in·fla·tion·a·ry /ɪnˈfleɪʃəˌnɛri/ *adj.* ECONOMICS relating to or causing price increases: *inflationary wage increases*

in·flect /ɪnˈflɛkt/ *v.* [I] ENG. LANG. ARTS if a word inflects, its form changes according to its meaning or use

in·flec·tion /ɪnˈflɛkʃən/ *n.* [C,U] ENG. LANG. ARTS the way in which a word changes its form to show differences in its meaning or use, such as the plural or a past tense, or one of the forms that is used in this way. For example, the inflections of "run" are "runs," "ran," and "running."

in·flex·i·ble /ɪn'flɛksəbəl/ (Ac) *adj.* **1** impossible to influence or change: *a school with inflexible rules* | *an inflexible boss* **2** inflexible material is stiff and will not bend —**inflexibility** /ɪnˌflɛksə'bɪləṭi/ *n.* [U]

in·flict /ɪn'flɪkt/ *v.* [T] to make someone suffer something bad: *Soldiers assessed the damage* ***inflicted on/upon*** *the enemy.* —**infliction** /ɪn'flɪkʃən/ *n.* [U]

in·flu·ence¹ /'ɪnfluəns/ *n.* **1** [C,U] the power to have an effect on the way someone or something develops, behaves, or thinks: *Diego Rivera* ***had*** *a profound* ***influence on*** *artists of the 1930s.* | *He has a lot of* ***political influence*** *in the community.* | *Lewis* ***used*** *his* ***influence*** *to avoid military service.* **2** [C] someone or something that has an effect on other people or things: *Alex's parents always thought that I was* ***a good/bad influence on*** *him.* | *The country remains untouched by* ***outside influences.*** **3 under the influence** drunk or feeling the effects of a drug [ORIGIN: 1300—1400 French, Medieval Latin *influentia*, from Latin *fluere* "to flow"]

influence² *v.* [T] to have an effect on the way someone or something develops, behaves, or thinks: *I don't want to influence your decision.* | *As a singer, she was strongly influenced by gospel music.*

THESAURUS **persuade, convince, coax, cajole, prevail on/upon sb** → PERSUADE

in·flu·en·tial /ˌɪnflu'ɛnʃəl/ *adj.* having a lot of influence: *an influential politician* | *Dewey was* ***influential in*** *shaping economic policy.* → POWERFUL —**influentially** *adv.*

in·flu·en·za /ˌɪnflu'ɛnzə/ *n.* [U] (formal) FLU

in·flux /'ɪnflʌks/ *n.* [C usually singular] the arrival of large numbers of people or things: *an* ***influx of*** *cheap imported goods*

in·fo /'ɪnfoʊ/ *n.* [U] (informal) information

in·fo·mer·cial /'ɪnfoʊˌməʃəl/ *n.* [C] a long television advertisement that is made to seem like a regular program

in·form /ɪn'fɔrm/ *v.* [T] to formally tell someone about something: *Please* ***inform*** *us* ***of*** *any progress.*
inform against/on sb *phr. v.* to tell the police, an enemy, etc. about what someone has done

in·for·mal /ɪn'fɔrməl/ *adj.* **1** relaxed and friendly: *an informal meeting* **2** appropriate for ordinary situations or conversations: *an informal letter to your family* —**informally** *adv.* —**informality** /ˌɪnfɔr'mæləṭi/ *n.* [U]

in·form·ant /ɪn'fɔrmənt/ *n.* [C] someone who gives secret information to the police, a government department, etc.: *a CIA informant*

in·for·ma·tion /ˌɪnfə'meɪʃən/ *n.* [U] **1** facts or details that tell you something about a situation, person, event, etc.: *I need some more* ***information about/on*** *this machine.* | *Goodwin was able to provide several new* ***pieces of information.*** | *For* ***further information,*** *call the number below.* **2** the telephone service that you can call to get someone's telephone number

GRAMMAR

Information is an uncountable noun and is never plural. Do not say "an information" or "some informations." Say **some information**, **any information**, or **a piece/bit of information:** *Do you have any information about places to stay in Seattle?* | *I found out an interesting piece of information.*

infor'mation techˌnology (*abbreviation* **IT**) *n.* [U] the use of electronic processes, especially computers, for gathering information, storing it, and making it available

in·form·a·tive /ɪn'fɔrməṭɪv/ *adj.* providing many useful facts or ideas: *a very informative book* —**informatively** *adv.*

in·formed /ɪn'fɔrmd/ *adj.* having a lot of knowledge or information about a particular subject or situation: *well-informed voters*

in·form·er /ɪn'fɔrmə/ *n.* [C] an INFORMANT

in·fo·tain·ment /ˌɪnfoʊ'teɪnmənt/ *n.* [U] television programs that present news and other types of information in an entertaining way

in·frac·tion /ɪn'frækʃən/ *n.* [C,U] (formal) an act of breaking a rule or law

in·fra·red /ˌɪnfrə'rɛd◂/ *adj.* infrared light produces heat but cannot be seen → ULTRAVIOLET

ˌinfrared radi'ation *n.* [U] PHYSICS energy in the form of waves that you cannot see, which are longer than waves of light that you can see and shorter than radio waves

in·fra·struc·ture /'ɪnfrəˌstrʌktʃə/ (Ac) *n.* [C] the basic systems that a country or organization needs in order to work in the right way, for example roads, COMMUNICATIONS, and banking systems: *Japan's economic infrastructure*

in·fre·quent /ɪn'frikwənt/ *adj.* not happening often (SYN) **rare**: *I met him on one of his infrequent visits to his parents.* —**infrequently** *adv.*

in·fringe /ɪn'frɪndʒ/ *v.* [T] to do something that is against the law or someone's legal rights —**infringement** *n.* [C,U]: *copyright infringement*

THESAURUS **disobey, break a rule/law, defy, flout, violate, contravene** → DISOBEY

infringe on/upon sth *phr. v.* to limit someone's freedom in some way: *The new law infringes on our basic right to freedom of speech.*

in·fu·ri·ate /ɪn'fyʊriˌeɪt/ *v.* [T] to make someone very angry: *He really infuriates me!*

THESAURUS **annoy, irritate, vex, irk** → ANNOY

in·fu·ri·at·ing /ɪn'fyʊriˌeɪṭɪŋ/ *adj.* very annoying: *an infuriating delay of four hours* —**infuriatingly** *adv.*

in·fuse /ɪn'fyuz/ *v.* **1** [T] to fill someone or something with a particular feeling or quality: *The coach has managed to **infuse** the team **with** new enthusiasm.* **2** [I,T] to put a substance such as tea in very hot water, so that its taste passes into the water

in·fu·sion /ɪn'fyuʒən/ *n.* **1** [C,U] the act of putting something new into something, especially a new feeling or quality: *I felt an **infusion of** spirituality.* | *A **cash infusion** helped save the company.* **2** [C] a medicine made with HERBS in hot water and usually taken as a drink

in·ge·nious /ɪn'dʒinyəs/ *adj.* **1** an ingenious plan, idea, etc. works well and is the result of intelligent thinking and new ideas: *an ingenious device* **2** an ingenious person is very good at inventing things, thinking of new ideas, etc. [ORIGIN: 1400—1500 French *ingénieux*, from Latin *ingenium* "natural ability"] —**ingeniously** *adv.*

in·ge·nu·i·ty /ˌɪndʒə'nuəṭi/ *n.* [U] skill at inventing things, thinking of new ideas, etc.

in·gen·u·ous /ɪn'dʒɛnyuəs/ *adj.* (formal) an ingenuous person trusts people too much and is honest, especially because they do not have experience in how badly people can behave (ANT) **disingenuous** —**ingenuously** *adv.* —**ingenuousness** *n.* [U]

in·gest /ɪn'dʒɛst/ *v.* [T] (formal) to eat something —**ingestion** /ɪn'dʒɛstʃən/ *n.* [U]

THESAURUS **eat, devour, gobble something up, wolf something down, nibble (on)** → EAT

in·grained /ɪn'greɪnd, 'ɪngreɪnd/ *adj.* ingrained attitudes or behavior are firmly established and difficult to change: *A sense of duty is **deeply ingrained in** most people.*

in·gra·ti·ate /ɪn'greɪʃiˌeɪt/ *v.* **ingratiate yourself (with sb)** (disapproving) to try to get someone's approval by doing things to please him/her, expressing admiration, etc., especially in a way that does not seem sincere: *Politicians try to ingratiate themselves with the voters.* —**ingratiating** *adj.* —**ingratiatingly** *adv.*

in·grat·i·tude /ɪn'græṭəˌtud/ *n.* [U] the quality of not being grateful for something

in·gre·di·ent /ɪn'gridiənt/ *n.* [C] **1** one of the things that goes into a mixture from which a type of food is made: *Combine all the ingredients in a large bowl.* | *Flour, water, and eggs are the **main ingredients**.* **2** a quality that helps to achieve something: *Jack seems to **have all the ingredients** to succeed in business.* [ORIGIN: 1400—1500 Latin, present participle of *ingredi*, from *in* "in" + *gradi* "to go"]

in·hab·it /ɪn'hæbɪt/ *v.* [T] to live in a particular place: *The forest is inhabited by bears and moose.*

in·hab·it·ant /ɪn'hæbəṭənt/ *n.* [C] one of the people who live in a particular place: *the **inhabitants of** large cities*

in·hale /ɪn'heɪl/ *v.* [I,T] to breathe in air, smoke, or gas: *Try not to inhale the fumes from the glue.* —**inhalation** /ˌɪnhə'leɪʃən/ *n.* [C,U]

THESAURUS **breathe, take a breath, exhale, pant, wheeze** → BREATHE

in·hal·er /ɪn'heɪlɚ/ *n.* [C] a plastic tube containing medicine that someone, especially someone with ASTHMA, inhales in order to make his/her breathing easier

in·her·ent /ɪn'hɪrənt, -'hɛr-/ (Ac) *adj.* a quality that is inherent in something is a natural part of it and cannot be separated from it: *The problem is **inherent in** the system.* —**inherently** *adv.*

inˌherent 'powers *n.* [plural] POLITICS powers given to the U.S. government that are not clearly stated in the CONSTITUTION, but which are accepted as necessary in order for the United States to be a completely independent country

in·her·it /ɪn'hɛrɪt/ *v.* **1** [I,T] to receive something from someone after s/he has died: *I **inherited** the house **from** my uncle.* **2** [T] to get a quality, type of behavior, appearance, etc. from one of your parents: *Suzy inherited her mother's good looks.*

in·her·i·tance /ɪn'hɛrɪṭəns/ *n.* [C,U] money, property, etc. that you receive from someone after s/he has died

in·hib·it /ɪn'hɪbɪt/ (Ac) *v.* [T] **1** to prevent something from growing or developing in the usual or expected way: *The new treatments inhibit the spread of the disease.* **2** to make someone feel embarrassed or less confident, so s/he cannot do or say what s/he wants to: *Fear of criticism may inhibit a child's curiosity.* **3** to make it more difficult or impossible for someone to do something: *The goal is to **inhibit** the virus **from** invading healthy cells.* [ORIGIN: 1400—1500 Latin, past participle of *inhibere* "to prevent," from *habere* "to have"]

in·hib·it·ed /ɪn'hɪbɪṭɪd/ (Ac) *adj.* not confident or relaxed enough to express how you really feel or do what you really want to do (ANT) **uninhibited**: *She wanted to dance with him, but felt too inhibited to tell him.*

in·hi·bi·tion /ˌɪnhɪ'bɪʃən, ˌɪnə-/ (Ac) *n.* [C,U] **1** a feeling of worry or embarrassment that stops you from expressing how you really feel or doing what you really want to do: *She seems to **lose** her **inhibitions*** (=stops feeling worried or embarrassed) *after a few drinks.* **2** the process of preventing something from working, growing, or developing in the usual or expected way: *Alcohol causes the **inhibition of** certain neurons in the brain, preventing them from communicating with other neurons.*

in·hos·pi·ta·ble /ˌɪnhɑ'spɪṭəbəl, ɪn'hɑspɪ-/ *adj.* (formal) **1** not friendly, welcoming, or generous to visitors **2** difficult to live or stay in because of severe weather conditions or lack of shelter: *an inhospitable climate* —**inhospitably** *adv.*

ˌin-ˈhouse *adj., adv.* within a company or organization rather than outside it: *an in-house training department*

in·hu·man /ɪnˈhyumən/ *adj.* **1** very cruel and without any normal feelings of pity: *inhuman treatment* **2** lacking any human qualities in a way that seems strange or frightening: *an inhuman scream*

in·hu·mane /ˌɪnhyuˈmeɪn/ *adj.* treating people or animals in a cruel and unacceptable way: *inhumane living conditions* —**inhumanely** *adv.* —**inhumanity** /ˌɪnhyuˈmænət̬i/ *n.* [U]

in·im·i·cal /ɪˈnɪmɪkəl/ *adj.* making it difficult for something to exist or happen: *This type of task is* ***inimical to*** *creativity.*

in·im·i·ta·ble /ɪˈnɪmət̬əbəl/ *adj.* too good for anyone else to copy: *Jerry gave the speech in his own inimitable style.*

in·iq·ui·ty /ɪˈnɪkwət̬i/ *n.* (plural **iniquities**) [C,U] (formal) the quality of being very unfair or evil, or an action that is very unfair or evil

i·ni·tial[1] /ɪˈnɪʃəl/ (Ac) *adj.* happening at the beginning (SYN) **first**: *the initial stages of the war* | *My initial reaction was shock.* [ORIGIN: 1500—1600 Latin *initialis*, from *initium* "beginning," from *inire* "to go in"] —**initially** *adv.*: *He initially refused the offer.*

initial[2] *n.* [C] the first letter of a name: *a suitcase with the initials S.H. on it*

initial[3] *v.* [T] to write your initials on a document: *Could you initial this form for me, please?*

i·ni·ti·ate /ɪˈnɪʃiˌeɪt/ (Ac) *v.* [T] **1** (formal) to arrange for something important to start: *The prison has recently initiated new security procedures.* **2** to introduce someone into an organization, club, etc., usually with a special ceremony: *This week, 11 students will be* ***initiated into*** *the school's honor society.*

i·ni·ti·a·tion /ɪˌnɪʃiˈeɪʃən/ (Ac) *n.* [C,U] **1** the process of introducing someone into an organization or club, or a young person into adult life: *an initiation ceremony* **2** the act of arranging for something important to start: *the initiation of legal proceedings*

i·ni·tia·tive /ɪˈnɪʃət̬ɪv/ (Ac) *n.* **1** [U] the ability to make decisions and take action without waiting for someone to tell you what to do: *I wish he would* ***show*** *more* ***initiative***. | *Try using* ***your own initiative*** (=doing something without being told what to do). **2** [C] a plan or process that has been started in order to achieve a particular aim or to solve a particular problem: *The state has several* ***initiatives to*** *reduce spending.* **3 take the initiative** to be the first one to take action to achieve a particular aim or solve a particular problem **4** [C] POLITICS a process by which citizens can suggest a change in a law by signing a form asking for the change to be voted on: *an effort to get the initiative on the ballot*

in·ject /ɪnˈdʒɛkt/ *v.* [T] **1** to put a liquid, especially a drug, into your body by using a special needle: *His shoulder was* ***injected with*** *a painkiller.* **2** to improve something by adding an important thing or quality to it: *Her remarks* ***injected*** *some humor* ***into*** *the situation.* [ORIGIN: 1500—1600 Latin, past participle of *inicere*, from *jacere* "to throw"]

injection

in·jec·tion /ɪnˈdʒɛkʃən/ *n.* **1** [C,U] an act of putting a liquid, especially a drug, into your body by using a special needle (SYN) **shot**: *The nurse* ***gave*** *me an* ***injection*** *of painkillers.* **2** [C] an addition of an important thing or quality to something in order to improve it: *The business received a* ***cash injection of*** *$20,000.*

in·junc·tion /ɪnˈdʒʌŋkʃən/ *n.* [C] LAW an official order given by a court, that stops someone from being allowed to do something

in·jure /ˈɪndʒɚ/ (Ac) *v.* [T] to hurt a person or animal: *She was* ***seriously/badly injured*** *in the accident.* | *Frank has injured his knee again.*

THESAURUS **hurt, wound, maim, break, bruise, sprain, twist, strain, pull, dislocate** → HURT[1]

in·jured /ˈɪndʒɚd/ (Ac) *adj.* **1** hurt or wounded: *his injured leg* | *injured civilians* **2 the injured** people who are hurt or wounded: *Doctors treated the injured.*

in·ju·ry /ˈɪndʒəri/ (Ac) *n.* (plural **injuries**) [C,U] physical harm or damage that is caused by an accident or attack, or a particular example of this: *a knee/back/head injury* | *serious/severe* ***injuries to*** *the head and neck* | *Luckily, she* ***suffered*** *only minor* ***injuries***.

THESAURUS

wound – an injury, especially a deep cut made in your skin by a knife or bullet: *He needed emergency treatment for a gunshot wound.*
bruise/contusion (formal) – a black or blue mark on your skin that you get when you fall or get hit: *There was a dark bruise on her cheek.*
cut – the small wound you get if a sharp object cuts your skin: *a cut on her finger*
laceration (formal) – a bad cut or tear on the skin: *She suffered facial lacerations in the attack.*
scrape – a mark or slight injury caused by rubbing your skin against a rough surface: *His legs were covered in scrapes and bruises.*
sprain – an injury to a joint in your body, caused by suddenly twisting it: *a slight ankle sprain*
bump – an area of skin that is swollen because you have hit it on something: *a bump on his forehead*
fracture – a crack or broken part in a bone: *X-rays revealed a small fracture.*

in·jus·tice /ɪnˈdʒʌstɪs/ *n.* [C,U] a situation in

which people are treated very unfairly: *Our country has a history of injustices against black people.*

ink /ɪŋk/ *n.* [U] a colored liquid used for writing, printing, etc.

ink·ling /ˈɪŋklɪŋ/ *n.* [singular] a slight idea about something: *We **had no inkling** that he was leaving.*

in·laid /ˈɪnleɪd, ɪnˈleɪd/ *adj.* having a thin layer of a material set into the surface for decoration: *a wooden box **inlaid with** gold*

in·land[1] /ˈɪnlənd/ *adj.* an inland area, city, etc. is not near the coast

in·land[2] /ɪnˈlænd, ˈɪnlænd, -lənd/ *adv.* in a direction away from the coast and toward the center of a country

ˌinland ˈsea *n.* [C] EARTH SCIENCES a sea that is completely surrounded by land

ˈin-laws *n.* [plural] your relatives by marriage, especially the mother and father of your husband or wife: *We're spending Christmas with my in-laws.*

in·lay /ˈɪnleɪ/ *n.* [C,U] a material that has been set into the surface of another material as a decoration, or the pattern made by this

in·let /ˈɪnlɛt, ˈɪnlət/ *n.* [C] **1** a narrow area of water reaching from the ocean or a lake into the land, or between islands **2** the part of a machine through which liquid or gas flows in

ˌin-line ˈskate *n.* [C] a special boot with a single row of wheels fastened under it (SYN) **Rollerblade** → ROLLERSKATE

I

in·mate /ˈɪnmeɪt/ *n.* [C] someone who is kept in a prison or in a hospital for people with mental illnesses

inn /ɪn/ *n.* [C] a small hotel, especially one that is not in a city

THESAURUS **hotel, motel, bed and breakfast (b&b), hostel** → HOTEL

in·nards /ˈɪnɚdz/ *n.* [plural] (informal) the parts inside your body, especially your stomach

in·nate /ˌɪˈneɪt◂/ *adj.* **1** an innate quality has been part of your character since you were born: *an innate sense of fun* **2 innate behavior** BIOLOGY the things that an animal or person does naturally from the time that they are first born, without having to learn to behave in this way —**innately** *adv.*

in·ner /ˈɪnɚ/ *adj.* [only before noun] **1** on the inside or close to the center of something (ANT) **outer**: *the inner ear* **2** inner feelings, thoughts, meanings, etc. are secret and not expressed **3 inner circle** the few people in an organization, political party, etc. who control it or share power with its leader

ˌinner ˈcity *n.* [C] the part of a city that is near the middle, especially the part where the buildings are in a bad condition and the people are poor —**inner city** *adj.*: *an inner city school*

ˌinner ˈear *n.* [C] BIOLOGY the part of your ear inside your head that you use for hearing and balance

in·ner·most /ˈɪnɚˌmoʊst/ *adj.* **1** your innermost feelings, desires, etc. are the ones you feel most strongly and keep private (ANT) **outermost**

THESAURUS **private, secret, personal, intimate** → PRIVATE[1]

2 (formal) farthest inside

ˈinner tube *n.* [C] the rubber tube that is filled with air inside a tire

in·ning /ˈɪnɪŋ/ *n.* [C] one of the nine playing periods in a game of baseball

inn·keep·er /ˈɪnˌkipɚ/ *n.* [C] (old-fashioned) someone who owns or manages an INN

in·no·cence /ˈɪnəsəns/ *n.* [U] **1** the fact of not being guilty of a crime (ANT) **guilt**: *How did they **prove her innocence**?* **2** the state of not having much experience of life, especially experience of bad or complicated things: *a child's innocence*

in·no·cent /ˈɪnəsənt/ *adj.* **1** not guilty of a crime (ANT) **guilty**: *Nobody would believe that I was innocent.* | *He was **found innocent of** murder by the jury* (=they decided he was innocent). **2 innocent victims/bystanders/people etc.** people who get hurt or killed in a war or as a result of a crime, though they are not involved in it **3** not having much experience of life, especially so that you are easily deceived: *I was 13 years old and very innocent.* **4** done or said without intending to harm or offend anyone: *It was a perfectly innocent question.* [ORIGIN: 1300—1400 French, Latin, from *in* "not" + *nocens* "evil," present participle of *nocere* "to harm"] —**innocently** *adv.*

in·noc·u·ous /ɪˈnɑkyuəs/ *adj.* not offensive, dangerous, or harmful: *an innocuous but boring movie* —**innocuously** *adv.*

in·no·vate /ˈɪnəˌveɪt/ (Ac) *v.* [I] to think of and begin to use new ideas, methods, or inventions: *Firms have to innovate to earn higher profits.* —**innovator** /ˈɪnəˌveɪtɚ/ *n.* [C]: *Parker was one of the great jazz innovators.*

in·no·va·tion /ˌɪnəˈveɪʃən/ (Ac) *n.* [C,U] a new idea, method, or invention, or the introduction and use of a new idea, method, etc.: ***innovations in** design* | *Too many regulations can discourage innovation.*

in·no·va·tive /ˈɪnəˌveɪt̬ɪv/ (Ac) *adj.* using new ideas, methods, or inventions: *an **innovative approach** to language teaching*

in·nu·en·do /ˌɪnyuˈɛndoʊ/ *n.* (plural **innuendoes** or **innuendos**) [C,U] a remark that suggests something sexual or unpleasant without saying it directly, or remarks like this in general: *He made some nasty innuendos about Laurie and the boss.* | *His writing is full of **sexual innuendoes**.*

in·nu·mer·a·ble /ɪˈnumərəbəl/ *adj.* (formal) very many

THESAURUS many, plenty, numerous, countless, myriad → MANY

in·oc·u·late /ɪ'nɑkyəˌleɪt/ *v.* [T] (formal) to protect someone against a disease by introducing a weak form of it into his/her body (SYN) **immunize**, **vaccinate**: *Children should be* ***inoculated against*** *measles.* [ORIGIN: 1400—1500 Latin, past participle of *inoculare* "to attach a bud to a plant," from *oculus* "eye, bud"] —**inoculation** /ɪˌnɑkyə'leɪʃən/ *n.* [C,U]

in·of·fen·sive /ˌɪnə'fɛnsɪv/ *adj.* unlikely to offend anyone: *a quiet, inoffensive man*

in·op·er·a·ble /ɪn'ɑpərəbəl/ *adj.* **1** something that is inoperable is not working and cannot be used (ANT) **operable**: *The airport is closed and will remain inoperable until Labor Day.* **2** an inoperable illness or condition cannot be treated by a medical operation (ANT) **operable**: *an inoperable brain tumor*

in·op·por·tune /ɪnˌɑpɚ'tun, ˌɪnɑ-/ *adj.* (formal) not appropriate or not good for a particular situation: *They arrived at* ***an inopportune moment.***

in·or·di·nate /ɪn'ɔrdn-ɪt/ *adj.* (formal) much greater than is reasonable: *an* ***inordinate amount*** *of work* —**inordinately** *adv.*

in·or·gan·ic /ˌɪnɔr'gænɪk◂/ *adj.* CHEMISTRY not consisting of anything that is living: *inorganic matter* —**inorganically** *adv.*

ˌinorganic 'chemistry *n.* [U] CHEMISTRY the science and study of substances that do not contain HYDROCARBONS. Usually, inorganic chemistry deals with substances that are not related to life processes. → ORGANIC CHEMISTRY

in·pa·tient /'ɪnˌpeɪʃənt/ *n.* [C] someone who stays and sleeps in a hospital while s/he is getting medical treatment → OUTPATIENT

in·put¹ /'ɪnpʊt/ (Ac) *n.* **1** [C,U] ideas, advice, money, or effort that you put into a job or activity in order to help it succeed: *I'd like to* ***get your input on*** *a few issues.* | *I'd like* ***input from*** *each of our employees.* **2** [U] IT information that is put into a computer (ANT) **output** **3** [C,U] electrical power that is put into a machine for it to use

input² (Ac) *v.* (past tense and past participle **input** *or* **inputted**, present participle **inputting**) [T] IT to put information into a computer: *The user inputs the data, and the computer stores it in its memory.*

in·quest /'ɪnkwɛst/ *n.* [C] LAW an official process to find out the cause of a sudden or unexpected death, especially if there is a possibility that the death is the result of a crime

in·quire /ɪn'kwaɪɚ/ *v.* [I,T] (formal) to ask someone for information: *I am writing to* ***inquire about*** *your advertisement in the New York Post.* | *She called to* ***inquire whether*** *her application had been received.* [ORIGIN: 1200—1300 Old French *enquerre*, from Latin *inquirere*, from *quaerere* "to look for"] —**inquirer** *n.* [C]

THESAURUS ask, question, interrogate → ASK

inquire into sth *phr. v.* to ask questions in order to get more information about something or to find out why something happened: *The investigation will inquire into the reasons for the disaster.*

in·quir·ing /ɪn'kwaɪərɪŋ/ *adj.* wanting to find out more about something: *Dad taught us to have* ***inquiring minds.*** —**inquiringly** *adv.*

in·quir·y /ɪn'kwaɪəri, 'ɪŋkwəri/ *n.* (plural **inquiries**) [C] **1** a question you ask in order to get information: *We're getting a lot of* ***inquiries about*** *our new train service.* **2** the official process of finding out why something happened, especially something bad

in·qui·si·tion /ˌɪnkwə'zɪʃən/ *n.* [singular] (formal) a series of questions that someone asks you in a way that seems threatening or not nice

in·quis·i·tive /ɪn'kwɪzət̬ɪv/ *adj.* interested in a lot of different things and wanting to find out more about them: *a very inquisitive little boy*

in·quis·i·tor /ɪn'kwɪzət̬ɚ/ *n.* [C] someone who asks you a lot of difficult questions and makes you feel very uncomfortable —**inquisitorial** /ɪnˌkwɪzə'tɔriəl/ *adj.* —**inquisitorially** *adv.*

in·roads /'ɪnroʊdz/ *n.* **make inroads into/on sth** to become more and more successful, powerful, or popular and so take away power, trade, votes, etc. from a competitor or enemy: *Their new soft drink is already making huge inroads into the market.*

INS *n.* **the INS the Immigration and Naturalization Service** the U.S. government department that deals with people who come to live in the U.S. from other countries

ˌins and 'outs *n.* **the ins and outs of sth** all the exact details of a complicated situation, system, problem, etc.: *I'm still learning the ins and outs of my new job.*

in·sane /ɪn'seɪn/ *adj.* **1** (informal) completely stupid or crazy, often in a way that is dangerous: *You must've been totally insane to go with him!* | *an insane idea* **2** someone who is insane is permanently and seriously mentally ill

THESAURUS crazy, mentally ill, disturbed, nuts, loony, demented, psychotic, unstable → CRAZY

—**insanely** *adv.*

in·san·i·ty /ɪn'sænət̬i/ *n.* [U] **1** very stupid actions that may cause you serious harm **2** the state of being seriously mentally ill: *A jury found him not guilty by reason of insanity.*

in·sa·tia·ble /ɪn'seɪʃəbəl/ *adj.* always wanting more and more of something: *an insatiable appetite*

I

inscribe

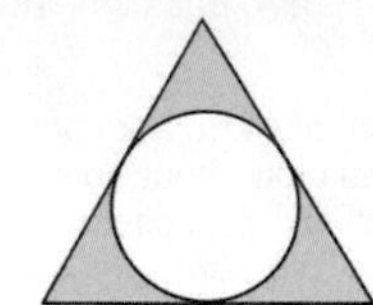

The circle is inscribed in the triangle.

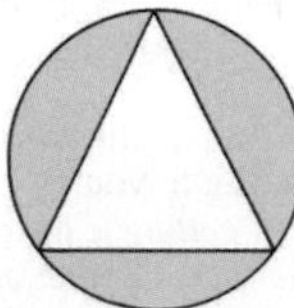

The triangle is inscribed in the circle.

in·scribe /ɪn'skraɪb/ *v.* [T] **1** to cut, print, or write words on something, especially on the surface of a stone or coin: *a tree **inscribed with** the initials J.S.* → WRITE **2 be inscribed in something a)** MATH if a circle is inscribed in another shape, the circle is inside the shape and each of the sides of the shape share one point with the circle **b)** MATH if a shape is inscribed in a circle, it is inside the circle and its angles are points on the circle —**inscription** /ɪn'skrɪpʃən/ *n.* [C]

in,scribed 'angle *n.* [C] MATH an angle formed inside a circle when two lines meet at a point on the edge of the circle

in·scru·ta·ble /ɪn'skruṭəbəl/ *adj.* (formal) someone who is inscrutable shows no reaction or emotion on his/her face so it is impossible to know what s/he is thinking or feeling: *an inscrutable smile* —**inscrutably** *adv.*

in·sect /'ɪnsɛkt/ *n.* [C] a small creature such as an ANT or a fly, with six legs and a body divided into three parts

in·sec·ti·cide /ɪn'sɛktə,saɪd/ *n.* [C,U] a chemical substance used for killing insects

in·sec·ti·vore /ɪn'sɛktə,vɔr/ *n.* [C] BIOLOGY a creature that eats insects —**insectivorous** /,ɪnsɛk'tɪvərəs/ *adj.*

in·se·cure /,ɪnsɪ'kyʊr/ (Ac) *adj.* **1** not feeling confident about yourself, your abilities, your relationships, etc. (ANT) **confident**: *Jane is **insecure about** her looks.* | *Children often behave badly when they **feel insecure**.*

THESAURUS

unsure of yourself – not very confident about yourself: *She's nervous and unsure of herself.*
lack confidence also **be lacking in confidence** – to not believe that you have the ability to do something well: *He is actually a pretty good player, but he lacks confidence.*

2 not safe or not protected: *She feels that her position in the company is insecure* (=she may lose her job). | *an insecure computer network* —**insecurity** *n.* [U] —**insecurely** *adv.*

in·sem·i·na·tion /ɪn,sɛmə'neɪʃən/ *n.* [U] the act of putting SPERM into a female's body in order to make her have a baby: *The cows are made pregnant by artificial insemination* (=using medical treatment, not sex).

in·sen·si·tive /ɪn'sɛnsəṭɪv/ *adj.* **1** not noticing other people's feelings, and not realizing that something that you do will upset them: *insensitive remarks* | *She's totally **insensitive to** my feelings.* **2** not affected by physical effects or changes —**insensitively** *adv.* —**insensitivity** /ɪn,sɛnsə'tɪvəṭi/ *n.* [U]

in·sep·a·ra·ble /ɪn'sɛpərəbəl/ *adj.* **1** people who are inseparable are always together and are very friendly with each other: *When they were younger, the boys were inseparable.* **2** unable to be separated, or not able to be considered separately: *The patient's mental and physical problems are inseparable.* —**inseparably** *adv.*

in·sert¹ /ɪn'sɚt/ (Ac) *v.* [T] **1** to put something inside or into something else: ***Insert** the key **in/into** the lock.* **2** to add something to something that already exists, especially a piece of writing: *The program will **insert** addresses **in** standard letters.* [ORIGIN: 1400—1500 Latin, past participle of *inserere*, from *serere* "to join"] —**insertion** /ɪn'sɚʃən/ *n.* [C,U]: *the insertion of a needle into a vein to withdraw blood*

insert

in·sert² /'ɪnsɚt/ (Ac) *n.* [C] **1** something that is designed to be put inside something else: *Put special inserts in your shoes to protect your heels.* **2** printed pages that are put inside a newspaper or magazine in order to advertise something

in·side¹ /ɪn'saɪd, 'ɪnsaɪd/ *adv., prep.* **1** in or into a container, room, building, etc. (ANT) **outside**: *He opened the box to find two kittens inside.* | *Go inside and get your jacket.* **2** if you have a feeling or thought inside you, you feel or think it but do not always express it: *You never know what's happening inside his head.* | *Don't keep the anger inside.* **3** used in order to emphasize that what is happening in a country or organization is known about there, but not outside it: *Sources inside the company confirmed that there will be more layoffs.* **4** in less time than: *We'll be there **inside of** an hour.*

inside² *n.* [C] **1 the inside** the inner part of something (ANT) **outside**: ***The inside of** the house was nicer than the outside.* | *The door had been locked **from the inside**.* **2 inside out** with the usual outside part on the inside: *Your shirt is on inside out.* **3 know/learn sth inside out** to know everything about a subject: *She knows the business inside out.*

inside³ *adj.* **1** on or facing the inside of something: *the inside pages of a magazine* **2 inside information/the inside story** information that is known only by people who are part of an organization, company, etc.

in·sid·er /ɪn'saɪdɚ/ *n.* [C] someone who has special knowledge of a particular organization because s/he is part of it

in·sid·i·ous /ɪn'sɪdiəs/ *adj.* happening gradually without being noticed, but causing great harm: *Breathing polluted air can have insidious effects on your health.* [ORIGIN: 1500—1600 Latin *insidiosus*, from *insidiae* "attack from a hiding-place"] —**insidiously** *adv.*

in·sight /'ɪnsaɪt/ (Ac) *n.* [C,U] a useful understanding of something that you did not have before, or the ability to understand something clearly: *The article gives us a real* ***insight into*** *Chinese culture.* | *We gained valuable* ***insight about*** *our relationship.*

in·sig·ni·a /ɪn'sɪgniə/ *n.* (plural **insignia** or **insignias**) [C] a BADGE or other object that shows what official or military rank someone has, or which group or organization s/he belongs to

insignia

in·sig·nif·i·cant /ˌɪnsɪg'nɪfəkənt/ (Ac) *adj.* too small or unimportant to consider or worry about: *an insignificant change in the unemployment rate* —**insignificantly** *adv.* —**insignificance** *n.* [U]

in·sin·cere /ˌɪnsɪn'sɪr/ *adj.* pretending to be pleased, sympathetic, etc., but not really meaning what you say: *an insincere smile* —**insincerely** *adv.* —**insincerity** /ˌɪnsɪn'sɛrət̬i/ *n.* [U]

in·sin·u·ate /ɪn'sɪnyuˌeɪt/ *v.* [T] to say something that seems to mean something unpleasant, without saying it directly: *Are you* ***insinuating that*** *she didn't deserve the promotion?* —**insinuation** /ɪnˌsɪnyu'eɪʃən/ *n.* [C,U]

in·sip·id /ɪn'sɪpɪd/ *adj.* (disapproving) not interesting, exciting, or attractive: *the movie's insipid story* —**insipidly** *adv.*

> THESAURUS **boring, dull, tedious, not (very/that/all that) interesting** → BORING

in·sist /ɪn'sɪst/ *v.* [I] **1** to say firmly and again and again that something is true, especially when other people think it may not be true: *The boys* ***insisted that*** *they were innocent.* **2** to demand that something happen: *I* ***insisted that*** *he leave.* | *They're* ***insisting on*** *your resignation.* [ORIGIN: 1500—1600 Latin *insistere* "to stand on, continue with determination," from *sistere* "to stand"]

in·sist·ence /ɪn'sɪstəns/ *n.* [U] the act of insisting that something should happen: *He came, but only* ***at my insistence.***

in·sist·ent /ɪn'sɪstənt/ *adj.* insisting that something should happen: *She's very* ***insistent that*** *we should all be on time.* —**insistently** *adv.*

in so far as, insofar as /ˌɪnsoʊ'fɑr əz/ *conjunction* (formal) to the degree that something affects another thing: *Insofar as sales are concerned, the company is doing very well.*

in·so·lent /'ɪnsələnt/ *adj.* (formal) rude and not showing any respect: *She gave me a cold, insolent look.* —**insolence** *n.* [U] —**insolently** *adv.*

> THESAURUS **rude, impolite, insulting, offensive, disrespectful, impertinent, impudent** → RUDE

in·sol·u·ble /ɪn'sɑlyəbəl/ *adj.* **1** CHEMISTRY an insoluble substance does not DISSOLVE when you put it into a liquid **2** *also* **insolvable** impossible to explain or solve: *a seemingly insoluble problem*

in·sol·vent /ɪn'sɑlvənt/ *adj.* (formal) not having enough money to pay what you owe —**insolvency** *n.* [U]

in·som·ni·a /ɪn'sɑmniə/ *n.* [U] the condition of not being able to sleep —**insomniac** /ɪn'sɑmniˌæk/ *n.* [C]

in·spect /ɪn'spɛkt/ (Ac) *v.* [T] **1** to examine something carefully: *She bent down to* ***inspect*** *the plant more* ***closely.*** | *The animals are* ***inspected for*** *quality.*

> THESAURUS **examine, go through/go over, scrutinize** → EXAMINE

2 to make an official visit to a building, organization, etc. to check that everything is satisfactory and that rules are being obeyed: *Nursing homes must be inspected once a year.* [ORIGIN: 1600—1700 Latin, past participle of *inspicere*, from *specere* "to look"]

in·spec·tion /ɪn'spɛkʃən/ (Ac) *n.* [C,U] the act of carefully checking a place, thing, or organization in order to be sure that it is in good condition or that rules are being obeyed: *The ship had recently passed a safety inspection.* | *a close* ***inspection of*** *the soldiers' living areas*

in·spec·tor /ɪn'spɛktɚ/ (Ac) *n.* [C] **1** an official whose job is to inspect something: *a health inspector* **2** a police officer of middle rank

in·spi·ra·tion /ˌɪnspə'reɪʃən/ *n.* [C,U] something or someone that encourages you to do or produce something good: *Dante was* ***the inspiration for*** *my book on Italy.* | *Her hard work and imagination should be* ***an inspiration to*** *everyone.* → IDEA —**inspirational** *adj.*: *an inspirational speech*

in·spire /ɪn'spaɪɚ/ *v.* [T] **1** to encourage someone to do or produce something good: *The church is trying to* ***inspire*** *more young men* ***to*** *become priests.* **2** to make someone have a particular feeling: *The captain* ***inspires*** *confidence* ***in*** *his men.* [ORIGIN: 1300—1400 French *inspirer*, from

Latin, from *spirare* "to breathe"] —**inspiring** *adj.*: *a powerful, inspiring story*

in·spired /ɪn'spaɪɚd/ *adj.* having very exciting special qualities: *an inspired leader*

in·sta·bil·i·ty /ˌɪnstə'bɪləṭi/ (Ac) *n.* [U] the state of being uncertain and likely to change suddenly ➔ UNSTABLE: *political instability in the region*

in·stall /ɪn'stɔl/ *v.* [T] **1** to put a piece of equipment somewhere and connect it so that it is ready to be used: *Many residents have installed new burglar alarms.* **2** IT to copy computer software onto a computer so that the software is ready to be used **3** to put someone in an important job or position, especially with a ceremony: *She will be installed as president of the college next week.* —**installation** /ˌɪnstə'leɪʃən/ *n.* [C,U]

instal'lation ˌart *n.* [C,U] ENG. LANG. ARTS modern art that can include objects, light, sound, etc., not just painting or SCULPTURE, or a particular example of this type of art

in·stall·ment /ɪn'stɔlmənt/ *n.* [C] **1** one of a series of regular payments that you make until you have paid all the money you owe: *You can pay for the computer* ***in*** *twelve monthly* ***installments.*** **2** one of the parts of a story that appears as a series in a magazine, newspaper, etc.

in·stance /'ɪnstəns/ (Ac) *n.* **1 for instance** for example: *There are some promising signs. For instance, high-school students' test scores have risen.* **2** [C] an example of a particular fact, event, etc. (SYN) **case**: *We are examining reports on* ***instances of*** *police brutality.*

in·stant¹ /'ɪnstənt/ *adj.* **1** happening or produced immediately: *The movie was an instant success.* **2** [only before noun] instant food, coffee, etc. is in the form of powder and is made ready to eat or drink by adding liquid to it

instant² *n.* **1** [C usually singular] a moment in time: *I didn't believe her for an instant.* **2 this instant** (spoken) now, without delay (SYN) **immediately**: *Come here this instant!*

in·stan·ta·ne·ous /ˌɪnstən'teɪniəs/ *adj.* happening immediately: *an instantaneous reaction to the drug* —**instantaneously** *adv.*

in·stant·ly /'ɪnstəntli/ *adv.* immediately: *He was killed instantly.*

THESAURUS **immediately, right away, at once** ➔ IMMEDIATELY

ˌinstant 'replay *n.* [C] the immediate repeating of an important moment in a sports game on television by showing the film or VIDEOTAPE again

in·stead /ɪn'stɛd/ *adv.* **1 instead of sb/sth** in place of someone or something: *Can I have chicken instead of beef? | You should do something instead of just sitting around all day.* **2** in place of someone or something that has just been mentioned: *I can't go, but Lilly could go instead.*

in·step /'ɪnstɛp/ *n.* [C usually singular] the raised part of your foot between your toes and your ANKLE, or the part of a shoe that covers this part of your foot

in·sti·gate /'ɪnstəˌgeɪt/ *v.* [T] to make something start to happen, especially something that will cause trouble: *Gang leaders were accused of instigating the riot.* —**instigator** *n.* [C] —**instigation** /ˌɪnstə'geɪʃən/ *n.* [U]

in·still /ɪn'stɪl/ *v.* [T] to teach someone a way of thinking or behaving over a long time: *Bonilla says he tries to* ***instill*** *hope* ***in*** *his students.*

in·stinct /'ɪnstɪŋkt/ *n.* [C,U] a natural tendency or ability to behave or react in a particular way, without having to learn it or think about it: *a lion's* ***instinct to*** *hunt | People have a natural* ***instinct for*** *survival.* [ORIGIN: 1400—1500 Latin *instinctus*, from *instinguere* "to make someone wish to do something"]

in·stinc·tive /ɪn'stɪŋktɪv/ *adj.* based on instinct: *an instinctive reaction* —**instinctively** *adv.*

in·sti·tute¹ /'ɪnstəˌtut/ (Ac) *n.* [C] an organization that has a particular purpose, such as scientific or educational work: *Walt Disney gave money to help found the California Institute of the Arts.* [ORIGIN: 1300—1400 Latin, past participle of *instituere*, from *statuere* "to set up"]

THESAURUS **organization, institution, association** ➔ ORGANIZATION

institute² *v.* [T] (formal) to introduce or start a system, rule, legal process, etc.: *The school has instituted changes in the lunch menu.*

in·sti·tu·tion /ˌɪnstə'tuʃən/ (Ac) *n.* **1** [C] a large organization that has a particular purpose, such as scientific, educational, or medical work: *financial/religious/educational, etc. institutions*

THESAURUS **organization, institute, association** ➔ ORGANIZATION

2 a place where people go to live when they need to be taken care of: *He was sent to a mental institution.* **3** [C] an established system or tradition in society: *The Civil War brought an end to the* ***institution of*** *slavery.* **4** [U] the act of introducing or starting a system, rule, legal process, etc.: *the* ***institution of*** *a new law* —**institutional** *adj.* ➔ MENTAL INSTITUTION

in·sti·tu·tion·al·ize /ˌɪnstə'tuʃənəˌlaɪz/ *v.* [T] to send someone to live in a mental hospital, a special home for old people, etc.

in·sti·tu·tion·al·ized /ˌɪnstə'tuʃənəˌlaɪzd/ (Ac) *adj.* **institutionalized violence/racism/corruption** violence, etc. that has happened for so long in an organization or society that it has become accepted as normal

in·struct /ɪn'strʌkt/ (Ac) *v.* [T] **1** to officially tell someone what to do: *The teacher* ***instructed*** *them* ***to*** *open their test sheets and begin.* **2** to teach someone or show him/her how to do something:

Diane ***instructs*** *senior citizens* ***in*** *basic computer skills.*

in·struc·tion /ɪn'strʌkʃən/ (Ac) *n.* **1 instructions** [plural] information or advice that tells you how to do something, how to use a piece of equipment or machine, etc. (SYN) **directions**: ***Follow the instructions*** *at the top of the paper.* | *Did you read the instructions first?* | *He gave us* ***instructions on/about how to*** *fix the toilet.* | *Inside, you'll find* ***instructions for*** *setting up your computer.* | *He gave* ***instructions to*** *keep the ball on the ground, not to kick it high.* **2** [U] teaching in a particular skill or subject: *She's never had any formal* ***instruction*** (=lessons or classes) ***in*** *music.* —**instructional** *adj.*

in·struc·tive /ɪn'strʌktɪv/ (Ac) *adj.* (formal) giving useful information: *an instructive story*

in·struc·tor /ɪn'strʌktɚ/ (Ac) *n.* [C] **1** someone who teaches a particular subject, sport, skill, etc.: *a swimming instructor*

THESAURUS **teacher, professor, lecturer, coach** → TEACHER

2 someone who teaches at a college or university and has a rank below that of PROFESSOR

in·stru·ment /'ɪnstrəmənt/ *n.* [C] **1** an object such as a piano, TRUMPET, VIOLIN, etc., used for producing musical sounds: *Can you play any* ***musical instruments****?* **2** a tool used in work such as science or medicine: *medical instruments*

in·stru·men·tal /ˌɪnstrə'mɛntl/ *adj.* **1 be instrumental in (doing) sth** to be important in making something happen: *Helen has been instrumental in organizing the festival.* **2** instrumental music is for instruments, not voices

in·sub·or·di·na·tion /ˌɪnsəˌbɔrdn'eɪʃən/ *n.* [U] (formal) refusal to obey someone who has a higher rank

in·sub·stan·tial /ˌɪnsəb'stænʃəl/ *adj.* not solid, large, strong, or not enough: *The evidence against him was insubstantial.*

in·suf·fi·cient /ˌɪnsə'fɪʃənt/ (Ac) *adj.* not enough: *insufficient supplies of food* | *His wages were* ***insufficient to*** *support his family.* —**insufficiently** *adv.* —**insufficiency** *n.* [singular, U]

in·su·lar /'ɪnsəlɚ, 'ɪnsyə-/ *adj.* (formal, disapproving) not interested in anything except your own group, country, way of life, etc. —**insularity** /ˌɪnsə'lærət̬i/ *n.* [U]

in·su·late /'ɪnsəˌleɪt/ *v.* [T] **1** to cover or protect something so that electricity, sound, heat, etc. cannot get in or out: *Insulate your garage to make it into a year-round workshop.* **2** to protect someone from bad experiences or unwanted influences: *College students are somewhat* ***insulated from*** *the hardships of real life.*

in·su·la·tion /ˌɪnsə'leɪʃən/ *n.* [U] the material used in order to insulate something, especially a building: *Insulation can save money on heating bills.*

in·su·lin /'ɪnsələn/ *n.* [U] BIOLOGY a substance produced naturally by your body that allows sugar to be used for energy

in·sult¹ /ɪn'sʌlt/ *v.* [T] to say or do something that offends someone, by showing that you do not respect him/her: *She didn't want to insult her hosts by leaving too early.* | *John would be insulted if we didn't go.* [ORIGIN: 1500—1600 French *insulter*, from Latin *insultare* "to jump on, insult"] —**insulting** *adj.*

in·sult² /'ɪnsʌlt/ *n.* [C] a rude or offensive remark or action: *Both groups screamed and shouted insults at each other.* | *The plan is an* ***insult to*** *teachers.* → **add insult to injury** *at* ADD

in·sur·ance /ɪn'ʃʊrəns/ *n.* [U] **1** an arrangement with a company in which you pay it money regularly and the company pays the costs if anything bad happens to you or your property, such as an illness or an accident: *Do you have* ***insurance on/for*** *your car?* | *The club* ***took out insurance*** *for all its members.* | *an* ***insurance policy*** | ***life/health/auto insurance*** *companies* | *It's a good idea to* ***buy*** *travel* ***insurance****.* **2** protection against something bad that might happen: *We bought an alarm as* ***insurance against*** *burglary.*

in·sure /ɪn'ʃʊr/ *v.* [T] **1** to buy or provide insurance: *Is your house* ***insured against*** *flooding?* | *This painting is* ***insured for*** *$5,000.* **2** to make something certain to happen: *The board will* ***insure that*** *all schools have adequate funds.*

in·sur·gent /ɪn'sɚdʒənt/ *n.* [C] one of a group of people fighting against the government of their own country —**insurgency** *n.* [U] —**insurgent** *adj.*

in·sur·mount·a·ble /ˌɪnsɚ'maʊnt̬əbəl/ *adj.* (formal) a difficulty or problem that is insurmountable is too large or too difficult to deal with

in·sur·rec·tion /ˌɪnsə'rɛkʃən/ *n.* [C,U] an attempt by a group of people within a country to take control using force and violence: *The armed insurrection was led by the army.*

THESAURUS **revolution, rebellion, revolt, insurgency, coup** → REVOLUTION

in·tact /ɪn'tækt/ *adj.* [not before noun] not broken, damaged, or spoiled: *Almost nothing was left intact by the storm.* | *The team's management system will* ***remain intact****.*

in·take /'ɪnteɪk/ *n.* [singular] the amount of food, FUEL, etc. that is taken in by someone or something: *I've been told to lower my* ***intake of*** *fat and alcohol.*

in·tan·gi·ble /ɪn'tændʒəbəl/ *adj.* an intangible quality or feeling cannot be clearly felt or described, although you know it exists —**intangibly** *adv.*

in·te·ger /'ɪnt̬ədʒɚ/ *n.* [C] MATH a number that is positive, negative, or zero, such as 3, -2, or 0

in·te·gral /ˈɪntəgrəl, ɪnˈtɛgrəl/ (Ac) *adj.* forming a necessary part of something: *an **integral part** of the contract* | *In this musical, the songs are **integral to** the story.*

in·te·grate /ˈɪntəˌgreɪt/ (Ac) *v.* **1** [I,T] to join in the life and traditions of a group or society, or to help someone do this: *It will take time for new members to **integrate into** the group.* **2** [T] to combine two or more things in order to make an effective system: *This software **integrates** moving pictures **with** sound.* **3** [I,T] to end the practice of separating people of different races in a place or institution (SYN) **desegregate** (ANT) **segregate**: *The Supreme Court decided that public schools should be integrated.* [ORIGIN: 1600—1700 Latin, past participle of *integrare*, from *integer* "whole, complete"]

in·te·grat·ed /ˈɪntəˌgreɪṭɪd/ (Ac) *adj.* combining many different groups, ideas, or parts in a way that works well: *an integrated world economy* | *integrated schools*

in·te·gra·tion /ˌɪntəˈgreɪʃən/ (Ac) *n.* [U] **1** the combining of two or more things so that they work together effectively: *economic integration* **2** the process of getting people of different races to live or work together instead of separately: *In 1963, Governor Wallace stood in the door to prevent the integration of the University of Alabama.* **3** the process by which people join in with a group or society and become members of it: *The book examines the integration of Jewish people into American life.*

in·teg·ri·ty /ɪnˈtɛgrəṭi/ (Ac) *n.* [U] **1** the quality of being honest and having high moral principles: *a man **of integrity*** **2** (formal) the state of being united as one complete thing: *the building's structural integrity*

in·tel·lect /ˈɪntəlˌɛkt/ *n.* [C,U] the ability to understand things and think intelligently: *an artist of great intellect*

in·tel·lec·tu·al[1] /ˌɪntəlˈɛktʃuəl/ *adj.* **1** concerning the ability to think and understand ideas and information: *the intellectual development of children* **2** an intellectual person is well-educated and interested in complicated ideas and subjects such as science, literature, etc.

THESAURUS **intelligent, smart, bright, brilliant** → INTELLIGENT

—**intellectually** *adv.*

intellectual[2] *n.* [C] someone who is well-educated and interested in complicated ideas and subjects such as science, literature, etc.

in·tel·li·gence /ɪnˈtɛlədʒəns/ (Ac) *n.* [U] **1** the ability to learn, understand, and think about things: *a child of average intelligence* **2** information about the secret activities of other governments, or the group of people who gather this: *intelligence on troop movements*

in·tel·li·gent /ɪnˈtɛlədʒənt/ (Ac) *adj.* having a high level of ability to learn, understand, and think about things (SYN) **smart** (ANT) **stupid**: *a young woman who is **highly intelligent*** | *an intelligent question* [ORIGIN: 1500—1600 Latin, present participle of *intelligere* "to understand," from *inter-* + *legere* "to gather, choose"] —**intelligently** *adv.*

THESAURUS

smart – intelligent: *a really smart guy*
bright – intelligent, used especially about children and young people: *a bright kid*
brilliant – extremely intelligent and good at the work you do: *a brilliant scientist*
wise – having a lot of experience and knowledge about people and the world: *a wise old man*
clever – intelligent, especially in a way that is unusual: *She's clever and creative.*
cunning/crafty – good at using your intelligence to trick people: *a cunning criminal*
intellectual – having a lot of education and interested in learning about art, science, literature, etc.
gifted – a gifted child is much more intelligent than most other children
apt (formal) – an apt pupil or student is able to learn or understand things quickly

in·tel·li·gi·ble /ɪnˈtɛlədʒəbəl/ *adj.* able to be understood (SYN) **clear** —**intelligibly** *adv.*

in·tend /ɪnˈtɛnd/ *v.* **1** [T] to have something in your mind as a plan or purpose (SYN) **mean**: *The work took longer than we intended.* | *Bob never **intended to** hurt him.* **2 be intended for sb/sth** to be provided or designed for someone or something: *The program is intended for the families of deaf children.* [ORIGIN: 1300—1400 Old French *entendre* "to have as a purpose," from Latin *intendere* "to stretch out, have as a purpose"] —**intended** *adj.*: *the movie's intended audience*

in·tense /ɪnˈtɛns/ (Ac) *adj.* **1** very extreme or having a very strong effect: *The department's researchers have been under intense pressure.* | *We weren't prepared for the intense heat.* **2** making you do a lot of work, think hard, etc.: *intense physical exercise* **3** serious and having very strong feelings or opinions: *an intense young woman* —**intensely** *adv.*

in·ten·si·fi·er /ɪnˈtɛnsəˌfaɪɚ/ *n.* [C] ENG. LANG. ARTS in grammar, a word that changes the meaning of another word, phrase, or sentence, in order to make its meaning stronger or weaker

in·ten·si·fy /ɪnˈtɛnsəˌfaɪ/ (Ac) *v.* (**intensified, intensifies**) [I,T] to increase in strength, size, or amount, etc., or to make something do this: *Spices will intensify the flavor.* | *Global competition has continued to intensify.* —**intensification** /ɪnˌtɛnsəfəˈkeɪʃən/ *n.* [U]

in·ten·si·ty /ɪnˈtɛnsəṭi/ (Ac) *n.* [U] the quality of being felt very strongly or of having a strong effect: *I was surprised by the intensity of his feelings.*

in·ten·sive /ɪnˈtɛnsɪv/ (Ac) *adj.* involving a lot of activity, effort, or attention in order to achieve something: *an intensive English course* —**intensively** *adv.*

in,tensive 'care *n.* [U] a department in a hospital that treats people who are very seriously sick or injured: *She's been **in intensive care** for two days.*

in·tent¹ /ɪn'tɛnt/ *n.* [C] **1** (formal) what you intend to do SYN **intention**: *Our intent is to become the market leader.* **2 for all intents and purposes** almost completely, or very nearly: *For all intents and purposes, their marriage was over.*

intent² *adj.* **be intent on (doing) sth** to be determined to do something: *Nick is intent on going to an Ivy League college.*

in·ten·tion /ɪn'tɛnʃən/ *n.* [C,U] something that you plan to do: *I **have no intention of** retiring anytime soon.*

in·ten·tion·al /ɪn'tɛnʃənəl/ *adj.* done deliberately: *If he did break the rules, I'm sure it was not intentional.* —**intentionally** *adv.*

in·ter /ɪn'tɚ/ *v.* (**interred**, **interring**) [T] (formal) to bury a dead body

in·ter·act /,ɪntə'rækt/ Ac *v.* [I] **1** to talk to other people and work together with them: *The website allows visitors to **interact with** other users.* | *Dinnertime is a good time for parents and children to interact.* **2** if two or more things interact, they have an effect on each other: *Alcohol **interacts with** nerve receptors in the brain.*

in·ter·ac·tion /,ɪntə'rækʃən/ Ac *n.* [C,U] **1** the activity of talking with other people and working together with them: *social **interaction between** teenagers* **2** a process in which two or more things have an effect on each other, or an occasion when this happens: *This medicine has fewer drug interactions than the other main drug used for the condition.*

in·ter·ac·tive /,ɪntə'ræktɪv/ Ac *adj.* **1** IT if a computer program, game, etc. is interactive, it does things as a reaction to the actions of the person using it: *an interactive software program for children* **2** involving people talking and working together: *interactive teaching methods*

in·ter·cept¹ /,ɪntɚ'sɛpt/ *v.* [T] to stop someone, or catch something that is going from one place to another before he, she, or it gets there: *O'Neill intercepted the ball.* —**interception** /,ɪntɚ'sɛpʃən/ *n.* [C,U]

in·ter·cept² /,ɪntɚ'sɛpt/ *n.* [C] MATH the point at which a line crosses an AXIS on a GRAPH

in·ter·change /'ɪntɚ,tʃeɪndʒ/ *n.* **1** [C] a place where two HIGHWAYS, FREEWAYS, or railroad tracks meet **2** [singular, U] an exchange of ideas, thoughts, etc.: *a friendly **interchange of** ideas*

in·ter·change·a·ble /,ɪntɚ'tʃeɪndʒəbəl/ *adj.* things that are interchangeable can be used instead of each other: *a toy with interchangeable parts* —**interchangeably** *adv.*

in·ter·com /'ɪntɚ,kɑm/ *n.* [C] a communication system by which people in different parts of a building, aircraft, etc. can speak to one another: *Suddenly, the captain's voice came **over the intercom**.*

in·ter·con·ti·nen·tal /,ɪntɚ,kɑntə'nɛntl, -,kɑntˀn'ɛntl/ *adj.* happening between or going from one CONTINENT to another: *an intercontinental flight*

in·ter·course /'ɪntɚ,kɔrs/ *n.* [U] (formal) the act of having sex

in·ter·de·pend·ent /,ɪntɚdɪ'pɛndənt/ *adj.* depending on or necessary to each other: *Plants and animals form an interdependent network of life.* —**interdependence** *n.* [U]

in·terest¹ /'ɪntrɪst/ *n.* **1** [singular, U] a feeling that makes you want to pay attention to something and find out more about it: *Both girls share an **interest in** politics.* | *Kelly **lost interest*** (=stopped being interested) *halfway through the movie.*

COLLOCATIONS

have an/no/some/little interest in sth: *Many young people have no interest in politics.*
show (an/no/some/little) interest in sth: *Joe has never shown any interest in baseball.*
express (an) interest in sth – to say that you are interested in something: *The airline has expressed an interest in buying the plane.*
attract/arouse (little/some) interest – to make people interested: *His first film attracted interest from the big Hollywood studios.*
lack interest (in sth) – to not have much interest in something: *It's hard to teach students if they lack interest in the subject.*

2 [C] a subject or activity that you enjoy studying or doing: *a list of your hobbies and interests* **3** [U] **a)** ECONOMICS money that you must pay for borrowing money: *You will be paying 12% on the unpaid balance of the loan.* | *interest payments* **b)** ECONOMICS money that a bank pays you when you keep your money there: *The more money you save, the more interest it will earn.* → INTEREST RATE **4** [U] a quality of something that attracts your attention and makes you want to know more about it: *a tourist guide to local places **of interest*** **5 be in sb's interest** to be an advantage to someone: *It would be in your interest to study the handbook carefully.*

interest² *v.* [T] to make someone want to pay attention to something and find out more about it: *I have some books that might interest you.*

in·terest·ed /'ɪntrɪstɪd, 'ɪntə,rɛstɪd/ *adj.* **1** giving a lot of attention to something because you want to find out more about it: *Tim's really **interested in** antique cars.* | *I'd be **interested to know** what you think about it.* **2** eager to do or have something: *Jill is **interested in** studying in Europe.*

'interest ,group *n.* [C] a group of people who join together to try to influence the government in order to protect their own particular rights, advantages, etc.

I

in·terest·ing /ˈɪntrɪstɪŋ, ˈɪntəˌrɛstɪŋ/ *adj.* unusual or exciting in a way that keeps your attention: *That's an interesting idea.* | *Amy's a very interesting person.* | ***It's interesting that*** *so many people choose to live in remote locations.* —**interestingly** *adv.*

THESAURUS

fascinating – very interesting: *He's had a fascinating life.*
intriguing – something that is intriguing is interesting because it is unusual or mysterious, and you want to find out more: *That raises some intriguing questions.*
absorbing/enthralling/engrossing – interesting and keeping your attention completely: *The book is an absorbing read.* | *She has written an engrossing memoir.*
compelling – very interesting or exciting: *a compelling story*
gripping/riveting – very interesting and exciting, and keeping your attention, used about stories and movies: *Money, power, and romance combine in this riveting story.* ➔ BORING

ˈinterest ˌperiod *n.* [C usually singular] ECONOMICS a period of time during which you are charged interest on a LOAN

ˈinterest ˌrate *n.* [C] ECONOMICS the PERCENTAGE amount that is charged by a bank, etc. on money that you borrow, or that is paid to you by a bank when you keep money in your account there: ***high/low interest rates*** | *The Federal Reserve decided to* ***cut interest rates*** (=make them lower).

in·ter·face /ˈɪntɚˌfeɪs/ *n.* [C] **1** the way a computer program looks on a screen, or the way you type or put information into the program **2** the way two subjects, events, etc. affect each other: *the* ***interface between*** *Islam and the West*

in·ter·fere /ˌɪntɚˈfɪr/ *v.* [I] to deliberately get involved in a situation when you are not wanted or needed: *It's better not to* ***interfere in*** *their arguments.* [ORIGIN: 1400—1500 Old French *entreferir* "to hit each other," from *ferir* "to hit"]
interfere with sth *phr. v.* **1** to prevent something from succeeding or happening in the way it was planned: *Don't let sports interfere with your schoolwork.* **2** to spoil the sound or picture of a radio or television broadcast

in·ter·fer·ence /ˌɪntɚˈfɪrəns/ *n.* [U] **1** the act of interfering: *I resented his* ***interference in*** *my personal life.* **2** in sports, the act of blocking or touching another player when you are not supposed to do this **3** unwanted noise, a spoiled picture, etc. on the radio, telephone, or television

in·ter·gov·ern·men·tal rev·e·nue /ˌɪntɚgʌvɚˌmɛntəl ˈrɛvənu/ *n.* [U] ECONOMICS money that one level of government gets from another level for a particular purpose or for financial support

in·ter·im¹ /ˈɪntərəm/ *adj.* [only before noun] an interim report, payment, manager, etc. is used or accepted for a short time until a final one is made or found (SYN) **temporary**

interim² *n.* **in the interim** in the period of time between two events: *The new stadium will not be ready until November, so games will be played at the university in the interim.*

in·te·ri·or¹ /ɪnˈtɪriɚ/ *n.* [C] the inner part or inside of something (ANT) **exterior**: *a car with a brown leather interior* [ORIGIN: 1400—1500 French *intérieur*, from Latin *interior*]

interior² *adj.* inside or indoor (ANT) **exterior**: *interior lighting*

inˌterior deˈsign *n.* [U] the job or skill of choosing and arranging furniture, colors, art, etc. for the inside of houses or buildings —**interior designer** *n.* [C]

in·ter·ject /ˌɪntɚˈdʒɛkt/ *v.* [I,T] (formal) to interrupt what someone is saying with a sudden remark [ORIGIN: 1500—1600 Latin, past participle of *intericere*, from *jacere* "to throw"]

in·ter·jec·tion /ˌɪntɚˈdʒɛkʃən/ *n.* [C] ENG. LANG. ARTS in grammar, a word or phrase that is used in order to express surprise, shock, pain, etc. In the sentence "Ouch! That hurt!," "ouch" is an interjection.

in·ter·lock·ing /ˌɪntɚˈlɑkɪŋ◂/ *adj.* connected firmly together: *the Olympic symbol of interlocking circles* —**interlock** *v.* [I,T]

in·ter·loc·u·tor /ˌɪntɚˈlɑkyət̬ɚ/ *n.* [C] (formal) the person someone is speaking with

in·ter·lop·er /ˈɪntɚˌloʊpɚ/ *n.* [C] (formal) someone who enters a place where s/he should not be

in·ter·lude /ˈɪntɚˌlud/ *n.* [C] a period of time between activities or events: *There was a brief interlude of peace before the fighting began again.*

in·ter·me·di·ar·y /ˌɪntɚˈmidiˌɛri/ *n.* (plural **intermediaries**) [C] someone who tries to help two other people or groups to agree with one another

in·ter·me·di·ate /ˌɪntɚˈmidiɪt/ (Ac) *adj.* done, existing, or happening between two other stages, levels, etc. ➔ BEGINNING, ELEMENTARY, ADVANCED: *an intermediate Spanish class* | *He was promoted to an intermediate-level position.* [ORIGIN: 1400—1500 Medieval Latin *intermediatus*, from Latin *intermedius*, from *medius* "middle"]

in·ter·mi·na·ble /ɪnˈtɚmənəbəl/ *adj.* very long and boring: *an interminable speech* —**interminably** *adv.*

THESAURUS **long, lengthy, prolonged, long-winded** ➔ LONG¹

in·ter·mis·sion /ˌɪntɚˈmɪʃən/ *n.* [C,U] a short period of time between the parts of a play, concert, etc.: *We talked for a while* ***during the intermission***. ➔ THEATER

in·ter·mit·tent /ˌɪntɚˈmɪtˀnt/ *adj.* happening at some times, but not regularly or continuously: *clouds and intermittent rain* —**intermittently** *adv.*

in·tern¹ /ˈɪntɚn/ *n.* [C] **1** someone, especially a student, who works for a short time in a particular job in order to gain experience → INTERNSHIP **2** someone who has almost finished training as a doctor and is working in a hospital → RESIDENT

in·tern² /ɪnˈtɚn/ *v.* **1** [I] to work as an intern: *Pena interned at the newspaper's Austin bureau for a year.* **2** [T] (formal) to put someone in prison, especially for political reasons → INTERNMENT

in·ter·nal /ɪnˈtɚnl/ (Ac) *adj.* **1** inside something such as your body (ANT) **external**: *internal bleeding | internal injuries* **2** within a particular company, organization, country, etc.: *the company's confidential internal documents | A major internal investigation is underway.* **3** inside something rather than outside (ANT) **external**: *an internal modem* [ORIGIN: 1400—1500 Medieval Latin *internalis*, from Latin *internus* "inward, inside"] —**internally** *adv.*: *This medicine should not be taken internally.*

in,ternal 'energy *n.* [U] PHYSICS the total amount of energy in or relating to all the atoms and MOLECULES in an object or substance

in·ter·na·lize /ɪnˈtɚnəˌlaɪz/ (Ac) *v.* [T] **1** if you internalize a belief, attitude, etc., it becomes part of your character: *She had internalized the work ethic of her parents.* **2** if you internalize emotions, you do not express them, but think about them → EXTERNALIZE: *Just allowing someone to talk can release internalized fears.*

In,ternal 'Revenue ,Service *n.* **the Internal Revenue Service** the IRS

in·ter·na·tion·al /ˌɪntɚˈnæʃənəl/ *adj.* relating to more than one country: *an international agreement | international trade | an international airport* —**internationally** *adv.*

in·ter·net /ˈɪntɚˌnɛt/ *n.* **the Internet** IT a system of connected computers that allows computer users around the world to exchange information (SYN) **the Net**, **the Web**: *I found information about the college **on the Internet**.*

TOPIC

To use the Internet, you first have to **connect** to it, using a **modem**. Some people use a **broadband** connection so that they can get Internet information faster. On the Internet, you can look for information using a **search engine**, or you can type in the **address** of a **website**. If you spend a lot of time looking at different websites, you can say that you are **surfing the net**. Many people also visit **chat rooms** (=sites where you can have a conversation with other people) and **newsgroups** (=sites where people with a shared interest exchange messages), and some people write **blogs** (=websites that you keep adding new information to). People use **email** to contact friends and family, or for work. More and more people and companies are using the Internet to send and receive work, and some people **work online**. → EMAIL, COMPUTER

in·ter·nist /ˈɪntɚnɪst/ *n.* [C] a doctor who treats medical conditions of the organs inside your body by using medicines, rather than by using SURGERY → SURGEON

in·tern·ment /ɪnˈtɚnmənt/ *n.* [C,U] the act of keeping someone in prison, especially for political reasons

in·tern·ship /ˈɪntɚnˌʃɪp/ *n.* [C] the period of time when an INTERN works, or the particular job s/he does: *an internship in a law firm*

in·ter·per·son·al /ˌɪntɚˈpɚsənəl/ *adj.* involving relationships between people: *interpersonal skills*

in·ter·plan·e·tar·y /ˌɪntɚˈplænəˌtɛri/ *adj.* [only before noun] happening or done between the PLANETS

in·ter·play /ˈɪntɚˌpleɪ/ *n.* [U] the way that two people or things affect each other: *the **interplay between** man and nature*

in·ter·po·late /ɪnˈtɚpəˌleɪt/ *v.* [T] (formal) to put additional words, ideas, information, etc. into something such as a piece of writing (SYN) **insert** —**interpolation** /ɪnˌtɚpəˈleɪʃən/ *n.* [C,U]

in·ter·pret /ɪnˈtɚprɪt/ (Ac) *v.* **1** [I,T] to change words spoken in one language into another → TRANSLATE: *Gina spoke enough Spanish to be able to interpret for me.* **2** [T] to explain or decide on the meaning of an event, statement, etc.: *His silence was **interpreted as** guilt. | A judge's main role is to interpret the law.* [ORIGIN: 1300—1400 French *interpréter*, from Latin *interpretari*, from *interpres* "someone who explains or translates"]

in·ter·pre·ta·tion /ɪnˌtɚprəˈteɪʃən/ (Ac) *n.* [C,U] an explanation for an event, someone's actions, etc.: *This is only one scientist's **interpretation of** the data; other scientists see it differently.*

in·ter·pret·er /ɪnˈtɚprət̬ɚ/ *n.* [C] someone who changes the spoken words of one language into another → TRANSLATOR

in·ter·pre·tive /ɪnˈtɚprət̬ɪv/ (Ac) *also* **in·ter·pre·ta·tive** /ɪnˈtɚprəˌteɪt̬ɪv/ *adj.* **1** relating to, explaining, or understanding the meaning of something: *an interpretive lecture on the park's geology* **2** relating to how feelings are expressed through music, dance, art, etc.: *interpretive dance*

in·ter·ra·cial /ˌɪntɚˈreɪʃəl◂/ *adj.* between different races of people: *an interracial marriage*

in·ter·re·lat·ed /ˌɪntɚrɪˈleɪt̬ɪd/ *adj.* things that are interrelated all have an effect on each other

in·ter·ro·gate /ɪnˈtɛrəˌgeɪt/ *v.* [T] to ask someone a lot of questions, sometimes in a threatening way: *Police are interrogating the suspect now.* —**interrogator** *n.* [C] —**interrogation** /ɪnˌtɛrəˈgeɪʃən/ *n.* [C,U]

THESAURUS **ask, question, inquire** → ASK

I

in·ter·rog·a·tive /ˌɪntəˈrɑgət̬ɪv/ *n.* **1 the interrogative** ENG. LANG. ARTS the form of a sentence or verb that is used for asking questions ➔ DECLARATIVE, EXCLAMATORY **2** [C] ENG. LANG. ARTS a word such as "who" or "what" that is used to ask questions —**interrogative** *adj.*: *an interrogative sentence*

in·ter·rupt /ˌɪntəˈrʌpt/ *v.* **1** [I,T] to stop someone from speaking by suddenly saying or doing something: *Sorry, I didn't mean to interrupt you.* | *One guy in the front row kept interrupting during Kay's talk.* **2** [T] to stop a process or activity for a short time: *The war interrupted the supply of oil.* [ORIGIN: 1300—1400 Latin, past participle of *interrumpere*, from *rumpere* "to break"]

THESAURUS stop, break, pause ➔ STOP[1]

—**interruption** /ˌɪntəˈrʌpʃən/ *n.* [C,U]: *Work on the bridge continued* ***without interruption***. | *several* ***interruptions in*** *the schedule*

in·ter·sect /ˌɪntəˈsɛkt/ *v.* [I,T] if two lines, roads, etc. intersect, they meet or go across each other [ORIGIN: 1600—1700 Latin, past participle of *intersecare*, from *inter* "between" + *secare* "to cut"]

in·ter·sec·tion /ˈɪntəˌsɛkʃən, ˌɪntəˈsɛkʃən/ *n.* [C] the place where two roads, lines, etc. meet and go across each other

in·ter·sperse /ˌɪntəˈspəs/ *v.* [T] to mix something together with something else: *The speeches were* ***interspersed with*** *short musical performances.*

I

in·ter·state[1] /ˈɪntəˌsteɪt/ *n.* [C] a road for fast traffic that goes between states

interstate[2] *adj.* [only before noun] between or involving different states in the U.S.: *interstate trade*

in·ter·twined /ˌɪntəˈtwaɪnd/ *adj.* twisted together or closely related: *several intertwined stories*

in·ter·val /ˈɪntəvəl/ (Ac) *n.* [C] **1** a period of time between two events, activities, etc.: *The Bijou Theater opened again after an interval of five years.* | *There was a brief* ***interval between*** *the battles.* **2 at intervals** with a particular amount of time or distance between things, activities, etc.: *Tickets let visitors in at half-hour intervals.* | *Look away from your screen* ***at regular intervals*** *to rest your eyes.* | *planes were landing* ***at intervals of*** *two minutes* **3** ENG. LANG. ARTS the amount of difference in PITCH between two musical notes [ORIGIN: 1300—1400 Old French *entreval*, from Latin *intervallum* "space between castle walls, interval"]

in·ter·vene /ˌɪntəˈvin/ (Ac) *v.* [I] **1** to do something to try to stop an argument, problem, war, etc.: *The police had to* ***intervene in*** *the march to stop the fighting.* **2** to happen between two events, especially in a way that interrupts or prevents something: *They had planned to get married, but the war intervened.* [ORIGIN: 1500—1600 Latin *intervenire*, from *inter* "between" + *venire* "to come"]

in·ter·ven·ing /ˌɪntəˈvinɪŋ◂ / (Ac) *adj.* relating to the amount of time between two events: *He had aged a lot in the intervening years.*

in·ter·ven·tion /ˌɪnt̬əˈvɛnʃən/ (Ac) *n.* [C,U] the act of becoming involved in an argument, problem, war, etc. in order to affect or change what happens: *Is military* ***intervention in*** *the region necessary?*

in·ter·view[1] /ˈɪntəˌvyu/ *n.* **1** [C] an occasion when someone famous is asked questions about his/her life, opinions, etc.: *The former president* ***gave an interview*** *to Barbara Walters* (=he answered her questions). | *an* ***interview with*** *several sports stars* **2** [C,U] *also* **job interview** a formal meeting in which someone is asked questions, usually to find out if s/he is good enough for a job: *I have an* ***interview for*** *a job as a project manager tomorrow.* [ORIGIN: 1500—1600 Early French *entrevue*, from *entrevoir* "to see each other, meet"]

interview[2] *v.* [T] to ask someone questions during an interview: *Kelly was interviewed on the radio after the game.* —**interviewer** *n.* [C]

in·ter·weave /ˌɪntəˈwiv/ *v.* (past tense **interwove** /-ˈwoʊv/, past participle **interwoven** /-ˈwoʊvən/, present participle **interweaving**) [T] if two or more ideas or situations are interwoven, they are too closely related to be separated easily: *The histories of the two countries are closely interwoven.*

in·tes·tine /ɪnˈtɛstɪn/ *n.* [C] BIOLOGY the long tube that takes food from your stomach out of your body: *bacteria that live in the intestines* | *the* ***large intestine*** (=the lower part of the intestines, in which water is removed from waste food as it passes through) | *the* ***small intestine*** (=the long tube that food goes through after it has passed through your stomach) [ORIGIN: 1400—1500 French *intestin*, from Latin *intestinum*, from *intus* "inside"] ➔ *see picture at* ORGAN —**intestinal** *adj.*

in·ti·ma·cy /ˈɪntəməsi/ *n.* [U] a state of having a close personal relationship with someone ➔ INTIMATE: *the intimacy of good friends*

in·ti·mate[1] /ˈɪntəmɪt/ *adj.* **1** having a very close relationship with someone: *a party for a few intimate friends* **2** (formal) relating to sex: *The virus can only be transmitted through intimate contact.* **3** relating to very private or personal matters: *intimate secrets* [ORIGIN: 1500—1600 Late Latin, past participle of *intimare* "to put in, announce," from Latin *intimus* "furthest inside"] —**intimately** *adv.*

in·ti·mate[2] /ˈɪntəˌmeɪt/ *v.* [T] (formal) to make someone understand what you mean without saying it directly

in·ti·ma·tion /ˌɪntəˈmeɪʃən/ *n.* [C,U] (formal) an indirect or unclear sign that something is true or may happen: *The narrator gives strong intimations that Johnson is unreliable.*

in·tim·i·date /ɪn'tɪmə,deɪt/ *v.* [T] to make someone afraid, often by using threats, so that s/he does what you want —**intimidation** /ɪn,tɪmə'deɪʃən/ *n.* [U]

in·tim·i·dat·ed /ɪn'tɪmə,deɪt̬ɪd/ *adj.* feeling worried or afraid because you are in a difficult situation: *Ben felt intimidated by the older boys.*

in·tim·i·dat·ing /ɪn'tɪmə,deɪt̬ɪŋ/ *adj.* making you feel worried and less confident: *Interviews can be an intimidating experience.*

in·to /'ɪntə; *before vowels* 'ɪntʊ; *strong* 'ɪntu/ *prep.* **1** in order to be inside something or in a place: *Amy went into the next room.* | *She put the fish back into the water.* **2** involved in a situation or activity: *He decided he would try to **go into** business for himself* (=start his own business). | *Try not to **get into** trouble.* **3** in a different situation or physical form: ***Make** the bread dough **into** a ball* (=the shape of a ball). | *Poe's house has been **turned into** a museum.* **4** to a point where you hit something, usually causing damage: *Dick drove his dad's car into a tree.* **5 be into sth** (spoken) to like and be interested in something: *I was really into music in high school.* **6** in a particular direction: *Look into my eyes.* **7** at or until a particular time: *We talked long into the night.*

in·tol·er·a·ble /ɪn'tɑlərəbəl/ *adj.* too difficult, bad, or painful for you to bear: *intolerable conditions* —**intolerably** *adv.*

in·tol·er·ant /ɪn'tɑlərənt/ *adj.* not willing to accept ways of thinking and behaving that are different from your own: *He's very **intolerant of** other people's political opinions.* —**intolerance** *n.* [U] ➔ PREJUDICE[1]

in·to·na·tion /,ɪntə'neɪʃən, -toʊ-/ *n.* [C,U] ENG. LANG. ARTS the rise and fall in the level of your voice when you speak

in·tox·i·cat·ed /ɪn'tɑksə,keɪt̬ɪd/ *adj.* (formal) **1** drunk: *He was intoxicated at the time of the accident.* **2** happy and excited because of success, love, power, etc. —**intoxicating** *adj.* —**intoxication** /ɪn,tɑksə'keɪʃən/ *n.* [U]

in·trac·ta·ble /ɪn'træktəbəl/ *adj.* (formal) very difficult to deal with or solve: *an intractable problem* —**intractability** /ɪn,træktə'bɪlət̬i/ *n.* [U]

in·tra·mu·ral /,ɪntrə'myʊrəl/ *adj.* intended for the students of one school: *intramural sports*

in·tran·si·gent /ɪn'trænsədʒənt, -zə-/ *adj.* (formal) unwilling to change your ideas or behavior in a way that seems unreasonable, or showing this quality: *intransigent attitudes* —**intransigence** *n.* [U] —**intransigently** *adv.*

in·tran·si·tive /ɪn'trænsətɪv, -zə-/ *adj.* ENG. LANG. ARTS in grammar, an intransitive verb has a subject but no object. In the sentence "They arrived early," "arrive" is an intransitive verb. ➔ TRANSITIVE

in·tra·ve·nous /,ɪntrə'vinəs◂/ *adj.* in or connected to a VEIN (=a tube that takes blood to your heart) ➔ IV: *an intravenous injection* —**intravenously** *adv.*

in·trep·id /ɪn'trɛpɪd/ *adj.* (literary) willing to do dangerous things or go to dangerous places: *intrepid travelers*

THESAURUS **brave, courageous, heroic, valiant, daring, bold, fearless** ➔ BRAVE[1]

in·tri·ca·cy /'ɪntrɪkəsi/ *n.* (plural **intricacies**) **1 the intricacies of sth** the complicated details of something: *You need an expert to help you with the intricacies of the tax system.* **2** [U] the state of containing a lot of parts or details: *the intricacy of the plot*

intricate

an intricate pattern

in·tri·cate /'ɪntrɪkɪt/ *adj.* containing a lot of parts or details: *an intricate pattern* [ORIGIN: 1400—1500 Latin, past participle of *intricare* "to mix up in a complicated way," from *tricae* "small unimportant things, things that get in your way"]

THESAURUS **complicated, complex, elaborate** ➔ COMPLICATED

in·trigue[1] /ɪn'trig/ *v.* [T] to interest someone a lot, especially by being strange or mysterious: *I was intrigued by her story.*

in·trigue[2] /'ɪntrig, ɪn'trig/ *n.* [C,U] the practice of making secret plans to harm or deceive someone: *a book about **political intrigue***

in·tri·guing /ɪn'trigɪŋ/ *adj.* very interesting because it is strange or mysterious: *an intriguing new book* —**intriguingly** *adv.*

THESAURUS **interesting, fascinating, absorbing, enthralling, engrossing, compelling, gripping, riveting** ➔ INTERESTING

in·trin·sic /ɪn'trɪnzɪk, -sɪk/ (Ac) *adj.* being part of the basic nature or character of someone or something: *the **intrinsic value** of good behavior* | *Meaning is **intrinsic to** a piece of writing; it is not wholly decided by the reader.* —**intrinsically** *adv.*

in·tro /'ɪntroʊ/ *n.* (plural **intros**) [C] (informal) a short part at the beginning of a song, piece of writing, etc. (SYN) **introduction**

in·tro·duce /,ɪntrə'dus/ *v.* [T] **1** if you introduce people to each other, you tell them each other's name for the first time ➔ INTRODUCTION: *Al,*

I

let me ***introduce*** *you* ***to*** *my parents.* | *Have you two been introduced yet?* **2** to make a change, plan, product, etc. happen, exist, or be available for the first time ➔ INTRODUCTION: *Over 60 new computer models were introduced last year.* **3 introduce sb to sth** to show someone something or tell him/her about it for the first time: *My aunt introduced me to cooking when I was 12.* **4** to speak at the beginning of a television program, public speech, etc. to say what will happen next ➔ INTRODUCTION [ORIGIN: 1400—1500 Latin *introducere*, from *ducere* "to lead"]

in·tro·duc·tion /ˌɪntrəˈdʌkʃən/ *n.* **1** [C,U] the act of making a change, plan, product, etc. happen, exist, or be available for the first time ➔ INTRODUCE: *the* ***introduction of*** *new drugs* **2** [C] the act of telling two people each other's names when they meet for the first time ➔ INTRODUCE **3** [C] a written or spoken explanation at the beginning of a book or speech ➔ INTRODUCE

in·tro·duc·to·ry /ˌɪntrəˈdʌktəri/ *adj.* relating to the beginning of a book, speech, course, etc.: *the introductory chapter*

in·tro·vert·ed /ˈɪntrəˌvɚt̬ɪd/ *adj.* thinking a lot about your own problems, interests, etc. and not wanting to be with other people (SYN) **shy** ➔ EXTROVERTED —**introvert** *n.* [C]

THESAURUS **shy, timid, bashful, demure, self-conscious, reserved** ➔ SHY[1]

in·trude /ɪnˈtrud/ *v.* [I] to go into a place or get involved in a situation where you are not wanted: *Newspaper stories often* ***intrude into/on*** *people's private lives.* ➔ ENTER[1]

in·trud·er /ɪnˈtrudɚ/ *n.* [C] someone who enters a building or area where s/he is not supposed to be

in·tru·sion /ɪnˈtruʒən/ *n.* [C,U] an unwanted person, event, etc. that interrupts or annoys you: *Some people feared the government's* ***intrusion into*** *their personal lives.* —**intrusive** /ɪnˈtrusɪv/ *adj.*

in·tu·i·tion /ˌɪntuˈɪʃən/ *n.* [C,U] the ability to understand or know that something is true, based on your feelings rather than facts: ***Trust*** *your* ***intuition*** *if you feel a situation is unsafe.* [ORIGIN: 1400—1500 Late Latin *intuitio*, from Latin *intueri* "to look at, think about"]

in·tu·i·tive /ɪnˈtuət̬ɪv/ *adj.* based on feelings rather than facts: *an intuitive understanding of the problem* —**intuitively** *adv.*

In·u·it /ˈɪnuɪt/ *n.* **the Inuit** [plural] a group of people who live in places such as northern Canada, Greenland, Alaska, and eastern Siberia —**Inuit** *adj.*

in·un·date /ˈɪnənˌdeɪt/ *v.* [T] **1 be inundated with/by sth** to receive so much of something that you cannot deal with all of it: *We were inundated with requests for tickets.* **2** (formal) to flood a place [ORIGIN: 1500—1600 Latin, past participle of *inundare*, from *unda* "wave"] —**inundation** /ˌɪnənˈdeɪʃən/ *n.* [C,U]

in·ure /ɪˈnʊr/ *v.*

inure sb **to** sth *phr. v.* (formal) to make people become used to something unpleasant, so they are no longer upset by it: *Doctors must never become inured to suffering.*

in·vade /ɪnˈveɪd/ *v.* **1** [I,T] to enter a place using military force ➔ INVASION: *A few days later, the island was invaded.* **2** [T] to go into a place in large numbers ➔ INVASION: *All the neighborhood kids invaded our pool yesterday.* [ORIGIN: 1400—1500 Latin *invadere*, from *in* "in" + *vadere* "to go"] —**invader** *n.* [C]

in·val·id[1] /ɪnˈvælɪd/ *adj.* not legally or officially acceptable (ANT) **valid**: *an invalid bus pass*

in·va·lid[2] /ˈɪnvələd/ *n.* [C] someone who needs to be cared for because s/he is sick, injured, or very old —**invalid** *adj.*

in·val·i·date /ɪnˈvæləˌdeɪt/ (Ac) *v.* [T] **1** to make a document, ticket, etc. not legally acceptable anymore ➔ VALID: *The Supreme Court invalidated a section of the new Immigration Act.* **2** to show that something such as a belief, explanation, etc. is wrong: *New research has invalidated the theory.*

in·val·u·a·ble /ɪnˈvælyəbəl, -yuəbəl/ *adj.* extremely useful (SYN) **valuable**: *Your advice has been invaluable.*

in·var·i·a·bly /ɪnˈvɛriəbli, -ˈvær-/ (Ac) *adv.* (formal) always, without changing: *The disease almost invariably ends in death.* ➔ ALWAYS —**invariable** *adj.*: *The pattern is invariable.*

in·va·sion /ɪnˈveɪʒən/ *n.* [C,U] **1** an occasion when an army enters a country using military force ➔ INVADE: *the* ***invasion of*** *Normandy* ➔ ATTACK[1] **2** the arrival of people or things at a place where they are not wanted ➔ INVADE: *Ron has tried everything to get rid of the invasion of ants in his kitchen.* **3 invasion of privacy** a situation in which someone tries to find out about someone else's personal life, in a way that is upsetting and often illegal —**invasive** /ɪnˈveɪsɪv/ *adj.*

inˌvasive ˈspecies *n.* [C] BIOLOGY a type of plant that does not naturally grow in a particular place, but which grows and spreads very quickly when planted there, stopping existing plants from growing successfully

in·vec·tive /ɪnˈvɛktɪv/ *n.* [U] (formal) impolite and insulting words that someone says when s/he is very angry

in·vent /ɪnˈvɛnt/ *v.* [T] **1** to make, design, or produce something for the first time ➔ INVENTION, INVENTOR: *Who invented the light bulb?*

THESAURUS

create – to invent or design something: *a dish created by our chef*

think up – to produce an idea, plan, etc. that is completely new: *Teachers constantly have to think up new ways to keep the kids interested.*

come up with sth – to think of a new idea, plan, reply, etc.: *Carson said he came up with the idea for the book about five years ago.*

I

conceive (formal) – to think of a new idea or plan: *It was Dr. Salk who conceived the idea of a polio vaccine.*
devise (formal) – to plan or invent a way of doing something: *The system was devised as a way of measuring students' progress.*
make up sth – to produce a new story, song, game, etc.: *Grandpa made up stories for us at bedtime.*
dream sth up – to think of a plan or idea, especially an unusual one: *The company's name was dreamed up by Harris' 15-year-old daughter.*

2 to think of an idea, story, etc. that is not true, usually to deceive people [ORIGIN: 1400—1500 Latin, past participle of *invenire* "to come upon, find," from *venire* "to come"]

THESAURUS **lie, make sth up, tell (sb) a lie, mislead, deceive** → LIE²

in·ven·tion /ɪn'vɛnʃən/ *n.* **1** [C,U] the act of inventing something, or the thing that is invented → INVENTOR: *The 20th century was a time when new inventions changed our lives.* | *the* ***invention of*** *television* **2** [C] an idea, story, etc. that is not true

in·ven·tive /ɪn'vɛntɪv/ *adj.* able to think of new and interesting ideas: *an inventive cook* —**inventiveness** *n.* [U]

in·ven·tor /ɪn'vɛntə/ *n.* [C] someone who has invented something

in·ven·to·ry /'ɪnvən,tɔri/ *n.* (plural **inventories**) **1** [U] all the goods in a store **2** [C,U] a list of all the things in a place: *The store will be closed on Friday to* ***take inventory*** (=make a list of its goods).

in·verse¹ /ɪn'vəs, 'ɪnvəs/ *adj.* **in inverse proportion/relation etc. to sth** getting larger as something else gets smaller, or getting smaller as something else gets larger —**inversely** *adv.*

in·verse² /'ɪnvəs, ɪn'vəs/ *n.* [singular] **1** MATH a number that is related to another number because an inverse operation has been done **2** (formal) the complete opposite of something

,inverse ope'ration *n.* [C] MATH a mathematical operation that does the opposite of another operation. For example, addition is the inverse operation of SUBTRACTION, and subtraction is the inverse operation of addition.

in·vert /ɪn'vət/ *v.* [T] (formal) to put something in the opposite position, especially by turning it upside down —**inversion** /ɪn'vəʒən/ *n.* [C,U]

in·ver·te·brate /ɪn'vəṭəbrɪt, -,breɪt/ *n.* [C] BIOLOGY an animal that does not have a BACKBONE → VERTEBRATE —**invertebrate** *adj.*

in·vest /ɪn'vɛst/ (Ac) *v.* **1** [I,T] to give money to a company, bank, etc., or to buy something, in order to get a profit later → INVESTMENT: *He recommended* ***investing in*** *stocks and bonds.* | *Greg invested his life savings in high-tech companies.* **2** [T] to use a lot of time or effort to make something succeed: *How much time are you prepared to* ***invest in*** *this project?* **3** [T] to give someone power or a position: *By the power invested in me, I pronounce you man and wife.* [ORIGIN: 1500—1600 Italian *investire* "to dress, invest," from Latin, "to dress," from *vestis* "piece of clothing"] —**investor** *n.* [C]: *investors in the local property market*

invest sb/sth **with** sth *phr. v.* (formal) to make someone or something seem to have a particular quality or character: *He invested his reply with scorn.*

in·ves·ti·gate /ɪn'vɛstə,geɪt/ (Ac) *v.* [I,T] to try to find out the truth about something, for example a crime, accident, etc.: *Police are currently investigating the case.* | *I heard a noise and went downstairs to investigate.* [ORIGIN: 1500—1600 Latin, past participle of *investigare* "to follow the track of," from *vestigium* "track"] —**investigator** *n.* [C]: *police investigators*

in·ves·ti·ga·tion /ɪn,vɛstə'geɪʃən/ (Ac) *n.* [C,U] an official attempt to find out the reasons for something, such as a crime or scientific problem: *an* ***investigation into*** *the plane crash* | *The issue is still* ***under investigation*** (=being investigated). | *a thorough* ***investigation of*** *the incident*

in·ves·ti·ga·tive /ɪn'vɛstə,geɪṭɪv/ (Ac) *adj.* intended to discover new details and facts about something, or relating to someone who does this: *investigative journalism*

in·vest·ment /ɪn'vɛstmənt/ (Ac) *n.* **1** [C,U] the use of money to get a profit or to make a business activity successful, or the money that is used to do this → INVEST: *a $5,000* ***investment in*** *stocks* | *Vietnam's economic development has been helped by* ***foreign investment****.* **2** [C] something that you buy or do because it will be valuable or useful later: *We bought the house* ***as an investment****.* | *Education is always a* ***good investment****.* **3** [C,U] a large amount of time, energy, emotion, etc. that you spend on something: *You cannot fully measure the investment of time and money that parents put into their children.*

in·vet·er·ate /ɪn'vɛṭərɪt/ *adj.* [only before noun] (formal) relating to doing or feeling something for a long time, and being unable or unwilling to change: *an inveterate gambler* —**inveterately** *adv.*

in·vig·o·rat·ing /ɪn'vɪgə,reɪṭɪŋ/ *adj.* making you feel more active and healthy: *an invigorating morning run* —**invigorate** *v.* [T] —**invigorated** *adj.*

in·vin·ci·ble /ɪn'vɪnsəbəl/ *adj.* too strong to be defeated or destroyed —**invincibly** *adv.*

in·vi·o·la·ble /ɪn'vaɪələbəl/ *adj.* (formal) an inviolable right, law, principle, etc. is extremely important and should not be gotten rid of —**inviolability** /ɪn,vaɪələ'bɪləṭi/ *n.* [U]

in·vis·i·ble /ɪn'vɪzəbəl/ (Ac) *adj.* not able to be seen, or not noticed: *These organisms are invisible without using a microscope.* | *It was as though my elderly mother were* ***invisible to*** *these young people; no one even said hello to her.* [ORIGIN: 1300—1400 Latin *visibilis*, from *in* "not" +

visus, past participle of *videre* "to see"] —**invisibly** *adv.* —**invisibility** /ɪnˌvɪzəˈbɪləti/ *n.* [U]

in·vi·ta·tion /ˌɪnvəˈteɪʃən/ *n.* [C] a request to someone that invites him/her to go somewhere or do something, or the card this is written on: *Mel didn't get an* ***invitation to*** *Tom's party.*

COLLOCATIONS

a party/wedding/dinner, etc. invitation
send out invitations – to send them to a number of people
get/receive an invitation
accept an invitation – to say yes
turn down/refuse an invitation – to say no

in·vite¹ /ɪnˈvaɪt/ *v.* [T] **1** to ask someone to come to a party, meal, wedding, etc. → INVITATION: *I* ***invited*** *the Rosens* ***to*** *dinner next Friday.* | *They've* ***invited*** *us* ***for*** *lunch.* | *"Why weren't you at Eva's party?" "I wasn't invited."* **2 invite trouble/criticism etc.** to make trouble, criticism, etc. more likely to happen to you [ORIGIN: 1500—1600 French *inviter*, from Latin *invitare*]

invite sb **along** *phr. v.* to ask someone to come with you when you go somewhere: *You can invite one of your friends along.*

invite sb **in** *phr. v.* to ask someone to come into your home, usually when s/he is standing at the door

invite sb **over** *phr. v.* to ask someone to come to your home for a party, meal, etc.: *You could* ***invite*** *the Chans* ***over for*** *dinner.*

I

in·vite² /ˈɪnvaɪt/ *n.* [C] (informal) an invitation

in·vit·ing /ɪnˈvaɪtɪŋ/ *adj.* an inviting sight, smell, etc. is attractive and makes you want to do something: *The lake looked inviting* (=made me want to swim in it). —**invitingly** *adv.*

in·voice /ˈɪnvɔɪs/ *n.* [C] a list that shows how much you owe for goods, work, etc. (SYN) **bill** [ORIGIN: 1500—1600 Early French *envois*, plural of *envoi* "message"] —**invoice** *v.* [T]: *We were* ***invoiced for*** *two parts that never arrived.*

THESAURUS **bill, check, tab** → BILL¹

in·voke /ɪnˈvoʊk/ (Ac) *v.* [T] (formal) **1** to use a law, principle, etc. to support your opinions or actions: *The reporter invoked the First Amendment when she refused to name her sources.* **2** to make a particular idea, image, or feeling appear in people's minds: *Her singing style invokes Billie Holiday, the great jazz singer.* **3** (literary) to ask for help from someone, especially a god: *St. Anthony is invoked against starvation.*

in·vol·un·tar·y /ɪnˈvɑlənˌtɛri/ *adj.* an involuntary movement, reaction, etc. is one that you make suddenly without intending to —**involuntarily** /ɪnˌvɑlənˈtɛrəli/ *adv.*

in·volve /ɪnˈvɑlv/ (Ac) *v.* [T] **1** to include or affect someone or something: *The riot involved 45 prisoners.* **2** to ask or allow someone to take part in something: *To improve kids' health, efforts should be made to* ***involve*** *them* ***in*** *sports activities.* **3** to include something as a necessary part or result of something else: *Taking the job involves moving to Texas.* [ORIGIN: 1300—1400 Latin *involvere* "to wrap," from *volvere* "to roll"]

in·volved /ɪnˈvɑlvd/ (Ac) *adj.* **1** taking part in an activity or event: *I don't want to* ***get involved in*** *her personal problems.* | *Parents need to be* ***involved with*** *their children's education.* **2** being a necessary part of an activity, event, etc.: *I hate the red tape* ***involved in*** *getting any project approved by the managers.* **3** difficult to understand because it is complicated or has a lot of parts: *a long involved answer* **4 be involved with sb** to be having a sexual relationship with someone

in·volve·ment /ɪnˈvɑlvmənt/ (Ac) *n.* [U] the act of taking part in an activity or event: *Brian's* ***involvement in*** *local politics has made a difference in our community.* | *The difference between kids who do well in school and those who don't is often parental involvement.*

in·vul·nerable /ɪnˈvʌlnərəbəl/ *adj.* not easy to harm, hurt, or attack

in·ward¹ /ˈɪnwəd/ *adj.* [only before noun] **1** felt in your own mind, but not expressed to other people (ANT) **outward**: *inward panic* **2** on or toward the inside of something —**inwardly** *adv.*: *Ginny was inwardly disappointed that she hadn't seen him at the party.*

inward² *also* **inwards** *adv.* toward the inside (ANT) **outward**

i·o·dine /ˈaɪəˌdaɪn, -dɪn/ *n.* [U] CHEMISTRY (*symbol* **I**) a dark red chemical substance, often used as a medicine for wounds. It is a chemical ELEMENT belonging to the HALOGEN group. [ORIGIN: 1800—1900 French *iode*, from Greek *ion* "dark bluish-red"]

i·on /ˈaɪən, ˈaɪɑn/ *n.* [C] PHYSICS an atom that has been given a positive or negative force

i·on·ic bond /aɪˌɑnɪk ˈbɑnd/ *n.* [C] CHEMISTRY a chemical BOND which is the result of atoms gaining and losing an ELECTRON, so that a negative ION and a positive ion are formed (SYN) **electrovalent bond**

i·on·ize /ˈaɪəˌnaɪz/ *v.* [I,T] CHEMISTRY to form ions or make them form —**ionization** /ˌaɪənəˈzeɪʃən/ *n.* [U]

i·on·o·sphere /aɪˈɑnəˌsfɪr/ *n.* **the ionosphere** EARTH SCIENCES the lower part of the THERMOSPHERE, where some of the harmful energy from the Sun is reduced [ORIGIN: 1900—2000 *ion* + *-sphere* (as in *atmosphere*)] → *compare* EXOSPHERE

i·o·ta /aɪˈoʊtə/ *n.* **not one/an iota of sth** not even a small amount of something: *There's not an iota of truth in what he says.*

IOU *n.* [C] (informal) **I owe you** a note that you sign to say that you owe someone some money

IPA *n.* [singular] ENG. LANG. ARTS **International Phonetic Alphabet** a system of signs that represent the sounds made in speech

iPod /ˈaɪpɑd/ *n.* [C] (trademark) IT a small piece of electronic equipment for playing and storing music that you DOWNLOAD from the Internet

IQ *n.* [C usually singular] **intelligence quotient** the level of someone's intelligence, with 100 being the average level: *He has an IQ of 130.*

IRA /ˈaɪrə/ *n.* **individual retirement account** a special bank account in which you can save money for your RETIREMENT without paying taxes on it until later

i·ras·ci·ble /ɪˈræsəbəl/ *adj.* (formal) easily becoming angry —**irascibly** *adv.*

i·rate /ˌaɪˈreɪt◂/ *adj.* extremely angry: *an irate customer* —**irately** *adv.*

THESAURUS **angry, livid, furious, mad, indignant, outraged** ➔ ANGRY

ir·i·des·cent /ˌɪrəˈdɛsənt/ *adj.* showing colors that seem to change in different lights —**iridescence** *n.* [U]

i·ris /ˈaɪrɪs/ *n.* [C] **1** BIOLOGY the round colored part of your eye ➔ *see picture at* EYE[1] **2** a tall plant with purple, yellow, or white flowers and long thin leaves

I·rish[1] /ˈaɪrɪʃ/ *adj.* relating to or coming from Ireland

Irish[2] *n.* **the Irish** [plural] the people of Ireland

irk /ɚk/ *v.* [T] to annoy someone

THESAURUS **annoy, irritate, get on sb's nerves, infuriate, bother, vex** ➔ ANNOY

i·ron[1] /ˈaɪɚn/ *n.* **1** [C] an object that is heated and that you push across a piece of clothing to make it smooth **2** [U] a common hard metal that is used to make steel, and is found in very small quantities in food and in blood [ORIGIN: Old English *isern, iren*]

iron[2] *v.* [T] to make your clothes smooth using an iron: *Can you iron my shirt for me?*

iron sth ↔ **out** *phr. v.* to solve a small problem: *Jim and Sharon are ironing out their differences.*

iron[3] *adj.* **1** made of iron: *iron bars on the gate* **2** very firm or strict: *He **ruled** the country **with an iron fist*** (=in a very strict and powerful way).

ˈIron Age *n.* **the Iron Age** HISTORY the period of time, about 3,500 years ago, when iron was first used for making tools, weapons, etc. ➔ BRONZE AGE, STONE AGE

ˌIron ˈCurtain *n.* **the Iron Curtain** HISTORY a name used in past times for the border between the Communist countries of Eastern Europe and the rest of Europe

i·ron·ic /aɪˈrɑnɪk/ *adj.* **1** using words that are the opposite of what you really mean, in order to be amusing or show that you are annoyed **2** an ironic situation is unusual or amusing because something strange or unexpected happens: ***It's ironic that** your car was stolen outside the police station.* —**ironically** *adv.*

i·ron·ing /ˈaɪɚnɪŋ/ *n.* [U] the activity of making clothes smooth with an iron

ˈironing ˌboard *n.* [C] a narrow board for ironing clothes ➔ *see picture at* BOARD[1]

i·ro·ny /ˈaɪrəni/ *n.* (plural **ironies**) **1** [U] ENG. LANG. ARTS the use of words that are the opposite of what you really mean, in order to be amusing or show that you are annoyed **2** [C,U] the part of a situation that is unusual or amusing because something strange happens, or the opposite of what is expected happens: ***The irony is that** the drug was supposed to save lives.* [ORIGIN: 1500—1600 Latin *ironia*, from Greek *eironeia*, from *eiron* "person who lies"]

ir·ra·tion·al /ɪˈræʃənəl/ (Ac) *adj.* not based on using sensible or clear reasons, or not thinking clearly: *an **irrational fear of** spiders* | *His decisions seemed irrational at the time.* —**irrationally** *adv.* —**irrationality** /ɪˌræʃəˈnæləṭi/ *n.* [U]

ir·rec·on·cil·a·ble /ɪˌrɛkənˈsaɪləbəl/ *adj.* irreconcilable opinions, positions, etc. are very different, making it impossible to reach an agreement: *They are getting divorced because of **irreconcilable differences**.* —**irreconcilably** *adv.*

ir·re·fut·a·ble /ˌɪrɪˈfyuṭəbəl/ *adj.* (formal) an irrefutable statement, argument, etc. cannot be proved wrong: *There was **irrefutable proof/evidence** that he had lied.*

ir·reg·u·lar /ɪˈrɛgyəlɚ/ *adj.* **1** having a shape, surface, etc. that is not even or smooth: *a face with irregular features* **2** not happening at regular times or at the usual time: *an **irregular heartbeat*** **3** ENG. LANG. ARTS an irregular verb or a form of a word does not follow the usual pattern in grammar. For example, the past tense "went" of the verb "go" is irregular. —**irregularly** *adv.* —**irregularity** /ɪˌrɛgyəˈlærəṭi/ *n.* [C,U]

ir·rel·e·vance /ɪˈrɛləvəns/ (Ac) *also* **ir·rel·e·van·cy** /ɪˈrɛləvənsi/ *n.* [U] a lack of importance in a particular situation: *the irrelevance of her remark*

ir·rel·e·vant /ɪˈrɛləvənt/ (Ac) *adj.* not useful or not relating to a particular situation, and therefore not important: *Large parts of the movie seemed irrelevant to the plot.* —**irrelevantly** *adv.*

ir·rep·a·ra·ble /ɪˈrɛpərəbəl/ *adj.* irreparable damage, harm, etc. is so bad that it can never be repaired or made better —**irreparably** *adv.*

ir·re·place·a·ble /ˌɪrɪˈpleɪsəbəl/ *adj.* too special, valuable, or rare to be replaced by anything else: *an irreplaceable work of art*

ir·re·press·i·ble /ˌɪrɪˈprɛsəbəl/ *adj.* always full of energy, happiness, or confidence, and never letting anything affect this: *Nathan's excitement was irrepressible.*

I

ir·re·proach·a·ble /ˌɪrɪˈproʊtʃəbəl/ *adj.* (formal) so good that you cannot criticize it: *Her behavior was irreproachable.*

ir·re·sist·i·ble /ˌɪrɪˈzɪstəbəl/ *adj.* **1** so attractive or desirable that you cannot stop yourself from wanting it: *The dessert looks irresistible.* | *The offer of so much money would be* ***irresistible to*** *most people.* **2** too strong or powerful to be stopped: *an* ***irresistible urge*** *to cry* —**irresistibly** *adv.*

ir·re·spec·tive /ˌɪrɪˈspɛktɪv/ *adv.* **irrespective of sth** used in order to show that a particular fact does not affect a situation at all: *Anyone can play, irrespective of age.*

ir·re·spon·si·ble /ˌɪrɪˈspɑnsəbəl/ *adj.* doing careless things without thinking about the possible bad results: *It was* ***irresponsible of*** *John to leave the kids alone.* —**irresponsibly** *adv.* —**irresponsibility** /ˌɪrɪˌspɑnsəˈbɪləṭi/ *n.* [U]

ir·rev·er·ent /ɪˈrɛvərənt/ *adj.* not showing enough respect for organizations, beliefs, etc.: *an irreverent sense of humor* —**irreverently** *adv.* —**irreverence** *n.* [U]

ir·re·ver·si·ble /ˌɪrɪˈvɚsəbəl/ (Ac) *adj.* something that has irreversible damage, change, etc. cannot be changed back to how it was before: *irreversible brain damage*

ir·rev·o·ca·ble /ɪˈrɛvəkəbəl/ *adj.* not able to be changed or stopped: *an irrevocable decision* —**irrevocably** *adv.*

ir·ri·gate /ˈɪrəˌgeɪt/ *v.* [T] to supply water to land or crops —**irrigation** /ˌɪrəˈgeɪʃən/ *n.* [U]: *an agricultural irrigation system*

I

ir·ri·ta·ble /ˈɪrəṭəbəl/ *adj.* easily annoyed or made angry: *He's always irritable in the morning.* —**irritably** *adv.* —**irritability** /ˌɪrəṭəˈbɪləṭi/ *n.* [U]

THESAURUS **grumpy, cranky, crabby, grouchy, cantankerous, touchy** → GRUMPY

ir·ri·tant /ˈɪrətənt/ *n.* [C] (formal) **1** something that makes you feel angry or annoyed: *Traffic noise is a constant irritant in the city.* **2** a substance that makes part of your body painful and sore

ir·ri·tate /ˈɪrəˌteɪt/ *v.* [T] **1** to make someone angry or annoyed: *Her voice really irritates me.*

THESAURUS **annoy, get on sb's nerves, infuriate, bother, vex, irk** → ANNOY

2 to make a part of your body painful and sore: *Wool* ***irritates*** *my* ***skin.***

ir·ri·tat·ed /ˈɪrəˌteɪṭɪd/ *adj.* feeling annoyed and impatient about something: *The teachers became increasingly* ***irritated by*** *Kevin's childish behavior.*

THESAURUS **angry, annoyed, mad, resentful** → ANGRY

ir·ri·tat·ing /ˈɪrəˌteɪṭɪŋ/ *adj.* annoying: *He has an* ***irritating habit*** *of always being late.* —**irritatingly** *adv.*

ir·ri·ta·tion /ˌɪrəˈteɪʃən/ *n.* **1** [C,U] the feeling of being annoyed, or something that makes you feel this way: *Tim made no secret of his* ***irritation with*** *me.* **2** [U] a painful sore feeling on a part of your body

IRS *n.* **the IRS the Internal Revenue Service** the government organization in the U.S. that deals with taxes

is /z, s, əz; *strong* ɪz/ *v.* the third person singular of the present tense of BE

Is·lam /ˈɪzlɑm, ɪzˈlɑm, ˈɪslɑm/ *n.* [U] the Muslim religion, which was started by Muhammad and whose holy book is the Koran [ORIGIN: 1600—1700 Arabic *islam* "obeying (the will of God)"] —**Islamic** /ɪzˈlɑmɪk, ɪs-/ *adj.*

is·land /ˈaɪlənd/ *n.* [C] a piece of land completely surrounded by water: *a hotel development* ***on the island*** | *the* ***island of*** *St. Kitts* [ORIGIN: Old English *igland*, from *ig* "island" + *land*]

is·land·er /ˈaɪləndɚ/ *n.* [C] someone who lives on an island

isle /aɪl/ *n.* [C] an island, used in poetry or in names of islands

is·n't /ˈɪzənt/ *v.* the short form of "is not": *That isn't true.*

i·so·late /ˈaɪsəˌleɪt/ (Ac) *v.* [T] **1** to make or keep one person or thing separate from others: *The town was isolated by the floods.* | *Computers seem to have* ***isolated*** *us* ***from*** *one another.* **2** to separate something from other things so that it can be examined, studied, or dealt with by itself: *It is difficult to isolate and measure the effect that this has had on the business.*

i·so·lat·ed /ˈaɪsəˌleɪṭɪd/ (Ac) *adj.* **1** far away from other things: *an isolated farm* **2** feeling alone or unable to meet or speak to other people: *New mothers often feel isolated.* **3 an isolated case/example etc.** a case, example, etc. that happens only once: *an isolated case of the disease* | *The violence was an* ***isolated incident.*** [ORIGIN: 1700—1800 French *isolé*, from Italian *isolata*, from *isola* "island"]

i·so·la·tion /ˌaɪsəˈleɪʃən/ (Ac) *n.* [U] **1** the state of being separate from other places, things, or people: *the city's geographical isolation* (=its location far away from other cities) **2 in isolation** separately: *These events cannot be examined in isolation from one another.* **3** a feeling of being lonely and unable to meet or talk to other people: *I buried the isolation I felt by working harder than ever.*

i·so·la·tion·ism /ˌaɪsəˈleɪʃəˌnɪzəm/ (Ac) *n.* [U] POLITICS beliefs or actions that are based on the political idea that your country should not be involved in the affairs of other countries: *America's isolationism before World War I* —**isolationist** *n.* [C] —**isolationist** *adj.*

i·so·mer /ˈaɪsəmɚ/ *n.* [C] CHEMISTRY one of two or more chemical compounds that have the same number of the same types of atoms, but different chemical structures and qualities

i·sos·ce·les trap·e·zoid /aɪˌsɑsəliz ˈtræpəˌzɔɪd/ *n.* [C] MATH a TRAPEZOID (=shape with four straight sides, two of which are parallel) in which the two angles at its base are the same size, and the two sides that are not parallel are the same length

i·sos·ce·les tri·an·gle /aɪˌsɑsəliz ˈtraɪˌæŋgəl/ *n.* [C] MATH a TRIANGLE in which two of the sides are the same length, and the two angles at the base are the same size → *see picture at* TRIANGLE

i·so·ton·ic /ˌaɪsəˈtɑnɪk◂/ *adj.* CHEMISTRY an isotonic SOLUTION has the same amount of a substance DISSOLVEd in it as another solution that you are comparing it to

i·so·tope /ˈaɪsəˌtoʊp/ *n.* [C] CHEMISTRY one of two or more atoms of a chemical ELEMENT that have the same number of PROTONs but a different number of NEUTRONS [ORIGIN: 1900—2000 *iso-* "equal" + Greek *topos* "place"]

is·sue¹ /ˈɪʃu/ (Ac) *n.* [C] **1** a subject or problem that people discuss: *We should **raise the issue** (=begin to discuss it) at our next meeting.* | *the controversial **issue of** abortion* | *Safety is the most **important issue**.* **2** a magazine, newspaper, etc. printed for a particular day, week, month, or year: *the April **issue of** Vogue* **3 make an issue (out) of sth** to argue about something **4 at issue** (formal) being discussed or considered: *At issue is whether the Senator improperly used campaign funds.* **5 take issue with sb/sth** to disagree or argue with someone about something: *He took issue with Mayor Farrell's statement.* **6 not be the issue** to not be the problem or subject that you are concerned about: *Money is not the issue here.* [ORIGIN: 1200—1300 Old French *issir* "to come out, go out," from Latin *exire*, from *ire* "to go"]

issue² (Ac) *v.* [T] **1** to officially make a statement or give a warning: *The President is expected to **issue a statement** later today.* **2** to officially provide or produce something: *Every player was **issued with** a new uniform.*

issue from sth *phr. v.* (formal) if something issues from a place or thing, it comes out of it: *Blood issued from the wound.*

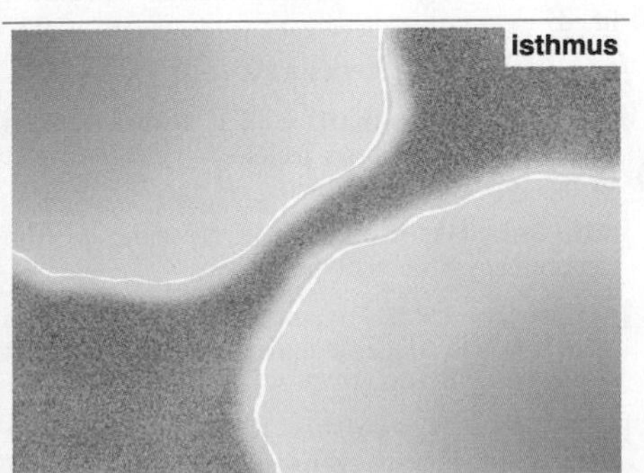

isth·mus /ˈɪsməs/ *n.* [C] EARTH SCIENCES a narrow piece of land with water on both sides, that connects two larger areas of land

IT *n.* [U] INFORMATION TECHNOLOGY

it /ɪt/ *pron.* [used as a subject or object] **1** a thing, situation, or idea that has been mentioned or is known about: *"Did you bring your umbrella?" "No, I left it at home."* | *"Where's the bread?" "It's* (=it is) *on the shelf."* | *In the summer, it must be beautiful here.* **2** the situation that someone is in now: *I can't stand it any longer. I'm resigning.* | *How's it going, Bob?* (=how are you?) **3** used as the subject or object of a sentence when the real subject or object is later in the sentence: *It costs less to drive than to take the bus.* **4** used with the verb "be" to talk about the weather, time, distance, etc.: *It's raining.* | *It's only a few miles from here to the beach.* **5** used in order to emphasize one piece of information in a sentence: *I don't know who took your book, but it wasn't me.* | *It was last year at this time that they went to Australia.* **6** used as the subject of the words "seem," "appear," "look," and "happen": *It seemed like she was angry.* **7 it's...** used in order to give the name of a person or thing when it is not already known: *"What's that?" "It's a pen."* | *"Who's on the phone?" "It's Jill."* **8** used in order to talk about a child or animal when you do not know what sex s/he is: *"Marilyn had a baby." "Is it a boy or girl?"* [ORIGIN: Old English *hit*] → **that's it** *at* THAT¹

I·tal·ian¹ /ɪˈtælyən/ *adj.* **1** relating to or coming from Italy **2** relating to the Italian language

Italian² *n.* **1** [U] the language used in Italy **2** [C] someone from Italy

i·tal·ics /ɪˈtælɪks, aɪ-/ *n.* [plural] a type of printed letters that lean to the right: *This example is printed **in italics**.* [ORIGIN: 1500—1600 Latin *italicus* "Italian;" because these letters were introduced by a 16th-century Italian printer, Aldus Manutius]

itch¹ /ɪtʃ/ *v.* **1** [I,T] if part of your body itches, you have an unpleasant feeling on your skin that makes you want to rub it with your nails: *My back is itching.* **2 be itching to do sth** (informal) to want to do something very much, as soon as possible: *Ian's been itching to try out his new bike.*

itch² *n.* [C] **1** an unpleasant feeling on your skin that makes you want to rub it with your nails **2** (informal) a strong desire to do or have something: *an **itch to** do something different*

itch·y /ˈɪtʃi/ *adj.* (comparative **itchier**, superlative **itchiest**) **1** if part of your body is itchy, it feels unpleasant and you want to rub it: *My eyes are really itchy.* **2** itchy clothes make your skin feel unpleasant and you want to rub it —**itchiness** *n.* [U]

it'd /ˈɪt̬əd/ **1** the short form of "it would": *It'd be easier if we both did it.* **2** the short form of "it had": *It'd been raining since Sunday.*

i·tem /ˈaɪt̬əm/ (Ac) *n.* [C] **1** a single thing in a set,

I

group, or list: *an **item of** clothing* | *There is one more **item on the agenda**.* | *household items*

THESAURUS **thing, object, article** → THING

2 a piece of news in the newspaper or on television: *I saw an item about the kidnapping in the paper.* [ORIGIN: 1500—1600 Latin "in the same way, also" (used to introduce things in a list), from *ita* "in this way"]

i·tem·ize /ˈaɪṭəˌmaɪz/ *v.* [T] to write down all of the parts of something in a list —**itemized** *adj.*

it·er·a·tive /ˈɪṭəˌreɪṭɪv, -rəṭɪv/ *adj.* MATH repeating a mathematical process or set of instructions for a computer program until a particular result is achieved: *an **iterative** process*

i·tin·er·ant /aɪˈtɪnərənt/ *adj.* (formal) traveling from place to place: *itinerant farm workers*

i·tin·er·ar·y /aɪˈtɪnəˌrɛri/ *n.* (plural **itineraries**) [C] a plan of a trip, usually including the places you want to see

it'll /ˈɪṭl/ the short form of "it will": *It'll be nice to see Martha again.*

it's /ɪts/ **1** the short form of "it is": *It's snowing!* **2** the short form of "it has": *It's been snowing all day.*

its /ɪts/ *possessive adj.* belonging or relating to a thing, situation, person, or idea that has been mentioned or is known about: *The tree has lost all of its leaves.*

it·self /ɪtˈsɛlf/ *pron.* **1** the REFLEXIVE form of "it": *The cat was licking itself.* **2 in itself** only the thing mentioned, and not anything else: *We're proud you finished the race. That in itself is an accomplishment.*

J

it·sy-bit·sy /ˌɪtsi ˈbɪtsi◂/ *also* **it·ty-bit·ty** /ˌɪṭi ˈbɪṭi◂/ *adj.* (informal) very small

IUD *n.* [C] **intrauterine device** a small plastic or metal object placed in a woman's UTERUS to prevent her from having a baby

IV *n.* [C] **intravenous** medical equipment that is used for putting liquid directly into your body

I've /aɪv/ the short form of "I have": *I've seen you somewhere before.*

i·vo·ry /ˈaɪvəri/ *n.* [U] **1** the hard smooth yellow-white substance from the TUSK (=long teeth) of an elephant **2** a pale yellow-white color —**ivory** *adj.*

i·vy /ˈaɪvi/ *n.* [U] a climbing plant with dark green shiny leaves → POISON IVY

ˈIvy ˌLeague *adj.* relating to a small group of old respected colleges in the northeast of the U.S.: *an Ivy League graduate* —**Ivy League** *n.* [singular]

J, j /dʒeɪ/ the tenth letter of the English alphabet

jab /dʒæb/ *v.* (**jabbed**, **jabbing**) [I,T] to quickly push something pointed into something else, or toward it: *The nurse **jabbed** a needle **into** his arm.* —**jab** *n.* [C]

jab·ber /ˈdʒæbɚ/ *v.* [I] to talk quickly, in an excited way, and not very clearly

jack¹ /dʒæk/ *n.* [C] **1** a piece of equipment used for lifting something heavy, such as a car, and supporting it **2** an electronic connection for a telephone or other electronic machine **3** a card used in card games which has a young man's picture on it: *the jack of clubs* → *see picture at* PLAYING CARD

jack² *v.*

jack sb/sth ↔ **up** *phr. v.* **1** to lift something heavy using a jack: *Dad jacked the car up so I could change the tire.* **2** (informal) to increase prices, sales, etc. by a large amount: *Stores have jacked up their prices since July.*

jack·al /ˈdʒækəl/ *n.* [C] a wild animal like a dog that lives in Africa and Asia

jack·ass /ˈdʒækæs/ *n.* [C] **1** (spoken) an impolite word meaning an annoying stupid person **2** a male DONKEY

jack·et /ˈdʒækɪt/ *n.* [C] **1** a short light coat: *a leather jacket* | *a rain jacket* → *see picture at* CLOTHES **2** the part of a suit that covers the top part of your body **3** a stiff piece of folded paper that fits over the cover of a book to protect it [ORIGIN: 1400—1500 French *jaquet*, from *jaque* "short coat"]

jack·ham·mer /ˈdʒækˌhæmɚ/ *n.* [C] a large powerful tool used for breaking hard materials such as the surface of a road

ˈjack-in-the-ˌbox *n.* [C] a toy shaped like a box, from which a figure jumps out when the box's lid is lifted

ˈjack knife *n.* [C] a POCKET KNIFE

jack·knife /ˈdʒæknaɪf/ *v.* [I] if a truck or train with two or more parts jackknifes, the back part swings toward the front part

jack-of-ˈall-trades *n.* [singular] someone who can do many different types of jobs

jack-o-lan·tern /ˈdʒæk ə ˌlæntɚn/ *n.* [C] a PUMPKIN with a face cut into it, usually with a light inside, made at HALLOWEEN

jack·pot /ˈdʒækpɑt/ *n.* [C] **1** a very large amount of money that you can win in a game **2 hit the jackpot a)** to win a lot of money **b)** to be very successful or lucky

Ja·cuz·zi /dʒəˈkuzi/ *n.* [C] (trademark) a HOT TUB

jade /dʒeɪd/ *n.* [U] a green stone used for making jewelry and ORNAMENTS [ORIGIN: 1500—1600 French from early Spanish *(piedra de la) ijada* "(stone of the) lower back"; because it was believed that jade cured pain in the kidneys]

jad·ed /ˈdʒeɪdɪd/ *adj.* not interested in or excited by things, usually because you have seen them or done them too much

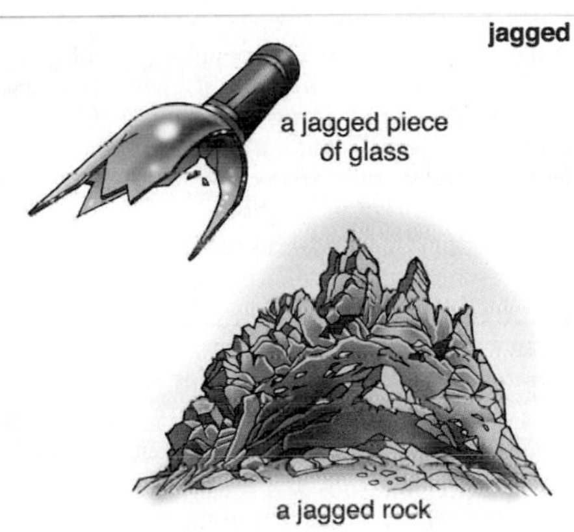

jag·ged /ˈdʒægɪd/ *adj.* having a rough uneven edge with a lot of sharp points: *jagged rocks*

jag·uar /ˈdʒægwɑr/ *n.* [C] a large wild cat with black spots from Central and South America [ORIGIN: 1600—1700 Spanish *yaguar* and Portuguese *jaguar*, from Guarani *yaguara* and Tupi (South American languages) *jaguara*]

jail¹ /dʒeɪl/ *n.* [C,U] a place where someone is sent to be punished for a crime (SYN) **prison**: *overcrowded jails* | *He was **in jail** for 15 years.* | *a two-year **jail sentence*** [ORIGIN: 1200—1300 Old French *jaiole*, from Latin *caveola*, from *cavea* "cage"]

COLLOCATIONS

go to jail: *If you commit a crime, you should go to jail.*
put sb in jail: *I hope they put him in jail and never let him out.*
send sb to jail: *He has a record of sending even petty criminals to jail.*
spend time in jail
release sb from jail: *She was released from jail and given parole.*
get out of jail: *We want to get these men out of jail and into a drug rehabilitation program.*
escape from jail: *He escaped from jail last year and has been on the run ever since.*
end up in jail: *I always said he'd end up in jail.*

jail² *v.* [T] to put someone in jail

jail·er, jailor /ˈdʒeɪlə/ *n.* [C] someone whose job is to guard a prison or prisoners

ja·lop·y /dʒəˈlɑpi/ *n.* (plural **jalopies**) [C] (informal) a very old car in bad condition

jam¹ /dʒæm/ *v.* (**jammed**, **jamming**) **1** [T] to push someone or something using a lot of force, especially into a small place: *Mr. Braithe jammed the letters into his pockets and left.*

THESAURUS shove, stick, thrust, cram → SHOVE

2 [I,T] *also* **jam up** if a machine jams up, or if you jam it, it stops working because something is stuck inside it: *Every time I try to use the Xerox machine, it jams.* **3** [T] to fill a place with a lot of people or things, so that nothing can move: *The roads **were jammed with** cars.* **4** [I] to play music for fun with a group of people without practicing first

jam² *n.* **1** [U] a thick sticky sweet substance made from fruit, usually eaten on bread: *strawberry jam* **2 be in a jam/get into a jam** (informal) to be or become involved in a difficult or bad situation: *Sarah, I'm in a jam — could you do me a favor?* **3** [C] a situation in which something is stuck somewhere: *a jam in the fax machine* → TRAFFIC JAM

jamb /dʒæm/ *n.* [C] the side post of a door or window

jam·bo·ree /ˌdʒæmbəˈri/ *n.* [C] a big noisy party or celebration

jammed /dʒæmd/ *adj.* impossible to move because of being stuck: *The stupid door's jammed again.*

jam-ˈpacked *adj.* (informal) completely full of people or things: *a cereal **jam-packed with** vitamins*

ˈjam ˌsession *n.* [C] an occasion when people meet to play music together for fun

Jane Doe /ˌdʒeɪn ˈdoʊ/ *n.* LAW a name used in legal forms, documents, etc. when a woman's name is not known

jan·gle /ˈdʒæŋgəl/ *v.* [I,T] to make a noise that sounds like metal objects hitting against each other: *His keys were jangling in his pocket.*

jan·i·tor /ˈdʒænət̬ə/ *n.* [C] someone whose job is to clean and take care of a large building: *the school janitor*

Jan·u·ar·y /ˈdʒænyuˌɛri/ (*written abbreviation* **Jan.**) *n.* [C,U] the first month of the year, between December and February: *Our wedding anniversary is **on January 6th**.* | *The baby's due sometime **in January**.* | *Mom was 60 **last January**.* | *I'm going to visit him **next January**.* [ORIGIN: 1200—1300 Latin *Januarius*, from *Janus*, ancient Roman god of doors, gates, and new beginnings]

Jap·a·nese¹ /ˌdʒæpəˈniz◂/ *adj.* **1** relating to or coming from Japan **2** relating to the Japanese language

Japanese² *n.* **1** [U] the language used in Japan **2 the Japanese** [plural] the people of Japan

J

jar¹ /dʒɑr/ *n.* [C] **1** a round glass container with a lid, used for storing food **2** the amount of food contained in a jar: *There's half a* ***jar of*** *peanut butter left.* [ORIGIN: 1500—1600 Old Provençal *jarra*, from Arabic *jarrah* "pot for carrying water"]

jar² *v.* (**jarred**, **jarring**) [I,T] **1** to shock someone, especially by making an unpleasant noise: *The alarm jarred her awake.* **2** to shake or hit something with enough force to damage it or make it become loose: *Alice jarred her knee when she jumped off the wall.*

jar·gon /ˈdʒɑrgən/ *n.* [U] technical words and phrases used by people in a particular profession that are difficult for other people to understand: *medical/legal/technical jargon*

THESAURUS **language, lingo, slang, terminology** ➔ LANGUAGE

jaun·dice /ˈdʒɔndɪs, ˈdʒɑn-/ *n.* [U] BIOLOGY a medical condition in which your skin and the white part of your eyes become yellow

jaun·diced /ˈdʒɔndɪst, ˈdʒɑn-/ *adj.* **1** tending to judge people, things, or situations in a negative way, often because of your own bad experiences in the past: *a jaundiced view of the world* **2** suffering from jaundice

jaunt /dʒɔnt, dʒɑnt/ *n.* [C] a short trip for pleasure

jaun·ty /ˈdʒɔnti, ˈdʒɑnti/ *adj.* showing that you feel confident and cheerful —**jauntily** *adv.*

jav·e·lin /ˈdʒævəlɪn, -vlɪn/ *n.* **1** [U] a sport in which you throw a SPEAR (=a long pointed stick) as far as you can **2** [C] the stick used in this sport

jaw /dʒɔ/ *n.* **1** [C] one of the two bones that form your mouth and that have all your teeth: *a broken jaw* ➔ *see picture on page A16* **2 sb's jaw dropped** used in order to say that someone looked very surprised or shocked: *Sam's jaw dropped when Katy walked into the room.* **3 jaws** [plural] the mouth of a person or animal, especially a dangerous animal [ORIGIN: 1300—1400 Old French *joe*]

J

jay·walk·ing /ˈdʒeɪˌwɔkɪŋ/ *n.* [U] the action of walking across a street in an area that is not marked for walking —**jaywalker** *n.* [C]

jazz¹ /dʒæz/ *n.* [U] **1** a type of popular music that usually has a strong beat and parts for performers to play alone **2 and all that jazz** (spoken) and things like that: *I'm sick of rules, responsibilities, and all that jazz.*

jazz² *v.*

jazz sth ↔ **up** *phr. v.* (informal) to make something more exciting and interesting: *You could jazz up that shirt with some accessories.*

jazzed /dʒæzd/ *adj.* (spoken) excited

jazz·y /ˈdʒæzi/ *adj.* (comparative **jazzier**, superlative **jazziest**) **1** bright, colorful, and easily noticed: *a jazzy tie* **2** similar to the style of jazz music

jeal·ous /ˈdʒɛləs/ *adj.* **1** feeling angry or unhappy because someone else has a quality, thing, or ability that you wish you had ➔ ENVIOUS: *Diane was* ***jealous of*** *me because I got better grades.* **2** feeling angry or unhappy because someone you love is paying attention to another person, or because another person is showing too much interest in someone you love: *It used to* ***make*** *me* ***jealous*** *when he danced with other women.* | *a jealous husband*

jeal·ous·y /ˈdʒɛləsi/ *n.* [U] the feeling of being jealous

jeans /dʒinz/ *n.* [plural] a popular type of pants made from DENIM: *a pair of jeans* [ORIGIN: 1800—1900 *jean* "strong cotton cloth" (15—21 centuries), from *Gene*, early form of the name *Genoa*, Italian city where the cloth was first made] ➔ *see picture at* CLOTHES

Jeep /dʒip/ *n.* [C] (trademark) a type of car made to travel over rough ground

jeer /dʒɪr/ *v.* [I,T] to shout, speak, or laugh in order to annoy or frighten someone you dislike: *The crowd* ***jeered at*** *the speaker.* —**jeer** *n.* [C]

jeez /dʒiz/ *interjection* said in order to express sudden feelings such as surprise, anger, or shock

Je·ho·vah /dʒɪˈhoʊvə/ *n.* a name for God in the OLD TESTAMENT (=first part of the Bible)

Jeˌhovah's ˈWitness *n.* [C] a member of a religious organization that believes the end of the world will happen soon and sends its members to people's houses to try to persuade them to join

je·june /dʒɪˈdʒun/ *adj.* (formal) **1** ideas and behavior that are jejune are too simple or childish: *jejune philosophical ideals* **2** writing or speech that is jejune is boring because it does not have any interesting details or humor

jell /dʒɛl/ *v.* [I] another spelling of GEL²

Jell-O, jello /ˈdʒɛloʊ/ *n.* [U] (trademark) a soft solid substance made from GELATIN and sweet fruit juice

jel·ly /ˈdʒɛli/ *n.* [U] a thick sticky sweet substance made from fruit but having no pieces of fruit in it, usually eaten on bread: *a peanut butter and jelly sandwich* [ORIGIN: 1300—1400 Old French *gelee*, from *geler* "to freeze," from Latin *gelare*]

jel·ly·fish /ˈdʒɛliˌfɪʃ/ *n.* [C] a round transparent sea animal with long things that hang down from its body

jeop·ard·ize /ˈdʒɛpɚˌdaɪz/ *v.* [T] to risk losing or destroying something that is valuable or important: *Junot was too worried about jeopardizing his career to say anything.*

jeop·ard·y /ˈdʒɛpɚdi/ *n.* **in jeopardy** in danger of being lost or destroyed: *My job is in jeopardy.* [ORIGIN: 1300—1400 Anglo-French *juparti*, from Old French *jeu parti* "divided game, uncertainty"]

jerk¹ /dʒɚk/ *v.* **1** [I,T] to move with a quick movement, or to make something move this way: *He* *jerked his head around to see her.* **2** [I,T] to pull something suddenly and quickly: *Tom* ***jerked open*** *the door.*

jerk sb **around** *phr. v.* (informal) to waste someone's time or deliberately make things difficult for him/her: *Don't jerk me around.*

jerk² *n.* [C] **1** (informal) someone, especially a man, who is stupid or who does things that annoy or hurt other people: *What a jerk!* **2** a quick movement, especially a pulling movement: *He pulled the cord* ***with a jerk.*** —**jerky** *adj.*

jerk·y /ˈdʒɚki/ *n.* [U] pieces of dried meat, usually with a salty or SPICY taste

jer·sey /ˈdʒɚzi/ *n.* (plural **jerseys**) [C] a shirt worn as part of a sports uniform

jest /dʒɛst/ *n.* **in jest** intending to be funny: *The comment was made in jest.*

jest·er /ˈdʒɛstɚ/ *n.* [C] a man employed in past times to entertain important people with jokes, stories, etc.

Je·sus /ˈdʒizəs/ *also* **ˌJesus ˈChrist** *n.* the man who Christians believe to be the son of God, and whose life and TEACHING Christianity is based on

jet¹ /dʒɛt/ *n.* [C] **1** a fast airplane with a jet engine **2** a narrow stream of liquid or gas that comes quickly out of a small hole, or the hole itself: *a strong* ***jet of*** *water*

jet² *v.* (**jetted, jetting**) [I] (informal) to travel in an airplane: *He* ***jetted off to*** *Paris yesterday.*

jet ˈengine *n.* [C] an engine that forces out a stream of hot air and gases, used in airplanes

ˈjet lag *n.* [U] the feeling of being very tired after traveling a long distance in an airplane —**jet-lagged** *adj.*

jet-proˈpelled *adj.* using a jet engine for power —**jet propulsion** *n.* [U]

ˈjet set *n.* [singular] rich and fashionable people who travel a lot —**jet setter** *n.* [C]

jet·ti·son /ˈdʒɛt̬əsən, -zən/ *v.* [T] **1** to get rid of someone or something, or decide not to use him/her anymore: *They're not likely to jettison their star player just because he's injured.* **2** to throw things away, especially from a moving airplane or ship

jet·ty /ˈdʒɛt̬i/ *n.* (plural **jetties**) [C] **1** a wide wall built out into the water, as protection against large waves **2** a WHARF

jew·el /ˈdʒuəl/ *n.* **1** [C] a small valuable stone, such as a DIAMOND **2 jewels** [plural] jewelry [ORIGIN: 1200—1300 Old French *juel*, from *jeu* "game, play"]

jew·eled /ˈdʒuəld/ *adj.* decorated with valuable stones

jew·el·er /ˈdʒuəlɚ/ *n.* [C] someone who buys, sells, makes, or repairs jewelry

jew·el·ry /ˈdʒuəlri/ *n.* [U] small decorations you wear that are usually made from gold, silver, and jewels, such as rings and NECKLACES

Jew·ish /ˈdʒuɪʃ/ *adj.* relating to Judaism —**Jew** *n.* [C]

jibe¹ /dʒaɪb/ *n.* [C] another spelling of GIBE

jibe² *v.* [I] if two statements, actions, etc. jibe with each other, they agree or make sense together: *Your statement to the police does not* ***jibe with*** *the facts.*

jif·fy /ˈdʒɪfi/ *n.* (spoken) **in a jiffy** very soon: *I'll be back in a jiffy.*

jig /dʒɪg/ *n.* [C] a type of quick dance, or the music for this dance

jig·ger /ˈdʒɪgɚ/ *n.* [C] a unit for measuring alcohol, equal to 1.5 OUNCES

jig·gle /ˈdʒɪgəl/ *v.* [I,T] to move from side to side with short quick movements, or to make something do this

jig·saw puz·zle /ˈdʒɪgsɔ ˌpʌzəl/ *n.* [C] a picture cut up into many small pieces that you try to fit together for fun

ji·had /dʒɪˈhɑd/ *n.* [C] SOCIAL SCIENCE a holy struggle to defend the Muslim faith against people, organizations, governments, etc. who are believed to be against Islam

jilt /dʒɪlt/ *v.* [T] to suddenly end a relationship with someone: *His girlfriend jilted him.* —**jilted** *adj.*

Jim Crow /ˌdʒɪm ˈkroʊ/ *n.* HISTORY a system of laws and practices used in the U.S. until the 1960s, that treated African-American people unfairly and separated them from white people → SEGREGATION: *One* ***Jim Crow law*** *said that separate railroad cars had to be provided for white and black passengers.*

jin·gle¹ /ˈdʒɪŋgəl/ *v.* [I,T] to shake small metal objects together so that they produce a noise, or to make this noise: *He jingled his keys in his pocket.*

jingle² *n.* **1** [C] a short song used in television and radio advertisements **2** [singular] the sound made by metal objects touching together

jinx¹ /dʒɪŋks/ *n.* [singular] someone or something that brings bad luck, or a period of bad luck that results from this

jinx² /dʒɪŋkst/ *v.* [I,T] to make someone have bad luck: *I don't want to talk about winning – I'm afraid I'll jinx myself.* —**jinxed** *adj.*

jit·ters /ˈdʒɪt̬ɚz/ *n.* **the jitters** the feeling of being nervous and anxious, especially before an important event: *I always* ***get the jitters*** *before I go on stage.*

jit·ter·y /ˈdʒɪt̬əri/ *adj.* worried and nervous: *The recession has made consumers jittery.*

jive¹ /dʒaɪv/ *v.* **1 sth doesn't jive (with sth)** (informal) to seem so strange or unusual that something does not make sense: *The newspaper report doesn't jive with the story on TV.* **2** [T] (slang) to try to make someone believe something that is not true: *You're jiving me!*

jive² *n.* **1** [C,U] a very fast type of dance, often performed to fast JAZZ music **2** [U] (slang) statements that you do not believe are true: *Don't you go giving me any of that jive!*

job /dʒɑb/ (Ac) *n.* [C]

1 WORK work that you do regularly in order to earn money: *She **applied for a job** at the bank.* | *a **part-time/full-time job*** | *Suzy **got a job as** a legal secretary.* | *He **quit/left his job** so he could go back to school.* | *I **lost my job** last week.* | *It is not your age which is important; it is your ability to do the job.*

THESAURUS

Your **job** is the particular work you do regularly to earn money.
Work is used in a more general way to talk about employment or the activities involved in it: *I started work when I was 18.*
Employment is a slightly formal word for any work that you do to earn money: *He's been looking for employment for six months.*
Position or **post** are more formal words for a job in a particular organization: *How long have you been in your current position?*
Occupation is used mainly on official forms to mean your **job**: *Please give your name, age, and occupation.*
A **profession** is a job for which you need special education and training: *the legal profession*
Your **career** is the work you do for most of your life: *I'm interested in a career in journalism.*
A **vocation** is a feeling that the purpose of your life is to do a particular job, or the job itself: *I accepted that nursing was both my job and my vocation.* ➔ WORK²

USAGE

Do not say "What is your job?" or "What is your work?" Say **"What do you do?"** or **"What kind of work do you do?"**

J

2 on the job while doing work or at work: *Our reporters are on the job now.* | *All our employees get on-the-job training.*
3 DUTY a particular duty or responsibility that you have: ***It's my job to** take care of my little brother.* | *Robots can carry out a wide variety of jobs in factories.*
4 IMPROVE STH something you do to fix or improve something: *The car needs a paint job.* | *a nose job* (=an operation to change the shape of your nose)
5 STH YOU MUST DO a piece of work you must do, usually without being paid: *I have a lot of **odd jobs*** (=different things) *to do on Saturday.*
6 do a good/great/bad etc. job to do something well or badly
7 Good job! (spoken) used to tell someone that s/he has done something well
8 KIND OF THING *also* **jobby** (spoken) used in order to say that something is of a particular type: *His new computer's one of those little portable jobs.*
9 do the job (informal) to make something have the result that you want or need: *A little more glue should do the job.*
10 CRIME (informal) a crime such as robbing a bank
11 COMPUTER an action done by a computer: *a print job*

jock /dʒɑk/ *n.* [C] (informal) a student who plays a lot of sports

jock·ey¹ /ˈdʒɑki/ *n.* (plural **jockeys**) [C] someone who rides horses in races

jockey² *v.* **jockey for position** to try to be in the best position or situation

jock·strap /ˈdʒɑkstræp/ *n.* [C] underwear that men wear to support their sex organs when playing sports

joc·u·lar /ˈdʒɑkyələ˞/ *adj.* (formal) joking or humorous —**jocularity** /ˌdʒɑkyəˈlærət̬i/ *n.* [U]

jog¹ /dʒɑg/ *v.* (**jogged**, **jogging**) **1** [I] to run slowly and in a steady way, especially for exercise: *Julie jogs every morning.* ➔ *see picture on page A17* **2 jog sb's memory** to make someone remember something: *This picture might jog your memory.* **3** [T] to knock or push something lightly by mistake: *Someone jogged my elbow and I dropped the plate.*

jog² *n.* [singular] a slow steady run, especially for exercise: *Let's **go for a jog**.*

jog·ging /ˈdʒɑgɪŋ/ *n.* [U] the activity of running as a way of exercising: *We **went jogging** in Central Park.* ➔ EXERCISE² —**jogger** *n.* [C]

john /dʒɑn/ *n.* [C] (spoken, informal) a toilet

ˌJohn ˈDoe *n.* LAW a name used in legal forms, documents, etc. when a man's name is not known

join /dʒɔɪn/ *v.* **1** [I,T] to become a member of an organization, society, or group: *Mary joined the gym last month.* | *It doesn't cost anything to join.* **2** [T] *also* **join in** to begin to take part in an activity that other people are involved in: *Joining a political campaign is a great experience.* **3** [I,T] to do something together with someone else: *Why don't you **join** us **for** dinner?* | *Please **join with** me **in** welcoming tonight's speaker.* **4** [I,T] to connect or fasten things together, or to be connected: *the place where the two roads join*

THESAURUS **fasten, attach, secure, glue, tape, staple, clip, tie, button (up), zip (up)** ➔ FASTEN

5 join hands if two or more people join hands, they hold each other's hands [ORIGIN: 1200—1300 Old French *joindre*, from Latin *jungere*]

joint¹ /dʒɔɪnt/ *adj.* **1** involving two or more people, or owned or shared by them: *They have to reach a joint decision.* | *a joint bank account* | *"Who cooked dinner?" "It was a **joint effort*** (=we did it together)." **2 joint resolution** POLITICS a decision or law agreed by both houses of the U.S. Congress and signed by the President —**jointly** *adv.*: *The company is **jointly owned** by Time Warner and Disney.*

joint² *n.* [C] **1** a part of the body where two bones meet, that can bend: *the knee joint* **2** (slang) a place, especially a BAR, club, or restaurant: *a* *fast-food joint* **3** (slang) a MARIJUANA cigarette **4** a place where two things or parts of an object are joined together: *One of the pipe joints was leaking.* **5 out of joint** a bone that is out of joint has been pushed out of its correct position

,joint 'venture *n.* [C] a business arrangement in which two or more companies work together to achieve something

joke¹ /dʒoʊk/ *n.* [C] **1** something funny that you say or do to make people laugh: *Let me* ***tell*** *you a* ***joke***.

COLLOCATIONS

inside joke – a joke that only a few people with knowledge about a particular subject or event will understand
running joke – a joke that continues or is repeated over a long period of time
practical joke – a trick that is intended to surprise someone or make other people laugh at him/her
dirty joke – a joke that is about sex
sick joke – a joke that is very cruel or disgusting

THESAURUS

gag – a short joke, especially one told by a professional entertainer: *His first job was writing gags for radio comedians.*
wisecrack – a quick, funny, and often slightly unkind remark: *She made the other kids laugh with her jokes and wisecracks.*
one-liner – a very short joke: *The play is full of hilarious one-liners.*
quip (formal) – an amusing remark: *She was always ready with a quip or funny story.*
witticism (formal) – a smart and amusing remark: *He is known for his witticisms.*
pun – an amusing use of a word or phrase that has two meanings, or of words with the same sound but different meanings: *The band is called Esso Es, a pun that to English-speakers sounds like a call for help, but in Spanish means "That's what it is."*
funny story – a short story that is told to make people laugh: *He was telling funny stories about his college days.*

2 (informal) a situation that is so silly or unreasonable that it makes you angry: *What a joke that meeting was.* **3 take a joke** to be able to laugh at a joke about yourself: *Come on – can't you take a joke?* [ORIGIN: 1600—1700 Latin *jocus*]

joke² *v.* [I] to say things that are intended to be funny: *Owen's always* ***joking about*** *something.* | *Davis was* ***joking with*** *reporters.* —**jokingly** *adv.*

jok·er /ˈdʒoʊkɚ/ *n.* [C] someone who makes a lot of jokes

jol·ly /ˈdʒɑli/ *adj.* (comparative **jollier**, superlative **jolliest**) happy and cheerful

jolt¹ /dʒoʊlt/ *n.* [C] **1** a sudden shock: *a* ***jolt of*** *electricity* | *Being fired came as quite a* ***jolt to*** *her.* **2** a sudden rough or violent movement: *We felt a big jolt, and then the room started shaking.*

jolt² *v.* **1** [I,T] to move suddenly and roughly, or to make someone or something do this: *The earthquake jolted southern California.* **2** [T] to give someone a sudden shock: *Companies have been jolted by the tax changes.*

jos·tle /ˈdʒɑsəl/ *v.* [I,T] to push or knock against someone in a crowd: *Spectators* ***jostled for*** *a better view.*

jot /dʒɑt/ *v.* (**jotted, jotting**)
jot sth ↔ **down** *phr. v.* to write something quickly: *She jotted down some ideas for her essay.*

joule /dʒul, dʒaʊl/ *n.* [C] PHYSICS (*written abbreviation* **J**) a unit of energy equal to the amount of energy used to move something one meter against a force of one NEWTON [ORIGIN: 1800—1900 James *Joule* (1818-89), English scientist]

jour·nal /ˈdʒɚnl/ (Ac) *n* [C] **1** a written record that you make of the things that happen to you each day

THESAURUS **record, diary, log (book)** → RECORD¹

2 a magazine or newspaper for people who are interested in a particular subject: *The Wall Street Journal* | *The report was published in a medical journal.* [ORIGIN: 1300—1400 French *journal* "daily," from Latin *diurnalis*, from *diurnus* "of the day"]

jour·nal·is·m /ˈdʒɚnl,ɪzəm/ *n.* [U] the job or activity of writing reports for newspapers, magazines, television, or radio

jour·nal·ist /ˈdʒɚnl-ɪst/ *n.* [C] someone who writes reports for newspapers, magazines, television, or radio → NEWSPAPER

jour·ney /ˈdʒɚni/ *n.* [C] a trip from one place to another, especially over a long distance: *a long* ***journey to*** *El Salvador* | *our* ***journey across*** *the United States* [ORIGIN: 1100—1200 Old French *journée* "day's journey," from *jour* "day," from Latin *diurnus*]

THESAURUS **travel, trip, voyage, tour, expedition, pilgrimage** → TRAVEL²

jo·vi·al /ˈdʒoʊviəl/ *adj.* friendly and cheerful: *a jovial face* [ORIGIN: 1500—1600 French, Late Latin *jovialis* "of the god Jove or Jupiter;" because people born under the influence of the planet Jupiter were thought likely to be happy]

jowls /dʒaʊlz/ *n.* [plural] loose skin on someone's lower jaw

joy /dʒɔɪ/ *n.* [C,U] great happiness and pleasure, or something that gives you this feeling: *She laughed* ***with joy*** *at the news.* | *I almost* ***jumped for joy*** (=I was very happy). [ORIGIN: 1100—1200 Old French *joie*, from Latin *gaudia*]

joy·ful /ˈdʒɔɪfəl/ *adj.* very happy, or likely to make people very happy: *joyful laughter* —**joyfully** *adv.*

joy·ous /ˈdʒɔɪəs/ *adj.* (literary) full of happiness,

J

or likely to make people happy: *a joyous song* —**joyously** *adv.*

joy·ride /ˈdʒɔɪraɪd/ *n.* [C] a fast dangerous drive in a car, often after someone has stolen it for fun —**joyriding** *n.* [U] —**joyrider** *n.* [C]

joy·stick /ˈdʒɔɪˌstɪk/ *n.* [C] a handle that you use in order to control something such as an aircraft or a computer game ➔ *see picture on page A19*

JPEG /ˈdʒeɪ pɛg/ *n.* [C] IT **Joint Photograph Experts Group** a type of computer FILE that contains pictures, photographs, or other images ➔ MPEG

Jr. the written abbreviation of JUNIOR

ju·bi·lant /ˈdʒubələnt/ *adj.* extremely happy and pleased because you have been successful —**jubilation** /ˌdʒubəˈleɪʃən/ *n.* [U]

THESAURUS **happy, glad, delighted, thrilled, overjoyed, ecstatic, elated** ➔ HAPPY

Ju·da·ism /ˈdʒudiˌɪzəm, -deɪ-, -də-/ *n.* [U] the Jewish religion based on the Old Testament, the Talmud, and later TEACHINGs of the RABBIS

Ju·de·o-Chris·tian /dʒuˌdeɪoʊ ˈkrɪstʃən/ *adj.* [only before noun] SOCIAL SCIENCE relating to the ideas and values that Jewish and Christian people share because of the relationship of their religions: *the morals taught within the Judeo-Christian tradition*

judge¹ /dʒʌdʒ/ *n.* [C] **1** the official in control of a court who decides how criminals should be punished ➔ COURT¹ **2** someone who decides on the result of a competition: *a **panel of judges** at the Olympics* **3 a good/bad etc. judge of sth** someone who is usually right or wrong about something: ***a good judge of character***

judge² *v.* **1** [I,T] to form or give an opinion about someone or something after thinking about all the information: *Employees should be **judged on** the quality of their work.* | ***Judging by** her clothes, I'd say she's rich.*

THESAURUS

evaluate (formal) – to judge how good, useful, or successful someone or something is: *The survey was meant to evaluate customer satisfaction.*
assess – to judge a person or situation after thinking carefully about it: *Psychologists will assess the child's behavior.*
appraise – to judge how valuable, effective, or successful someone or something is: *The company regularly appraises the performance of its employees.*
gauge – to judge what someone is likely to do or how s/he feels: *It can be difficult to gauge students' understanding.*

2 [T] to decide in court whether someone is guilty of a crime **3** [I,T] to decide the result in a competition: *Kim and I will be judging the writing competition.* **4** [I,T] to form an opinion about someone in an unfair or criticizing way: *I just want Mom to stop judging me.*

J

judg·ment /ˈdʒʌdʒmənt/ *n.* **1** [C,U] an opinion that you form after thinking about something: *It's still too early to **make a judgment about** the quality of her work.* | ***In my judgment*** (=in my opinion), *John is the best candidate.* **2** [U] the ability to make decisions about situations or people: *good/bad/poor judgment* | *I trust your judgment.* **3** [C,U] an official decision given by a judge or a court of law **4 judgment call** a decision you have to make yourself because there are no fixed rules in a situation

judg·ment·al /dʒʌdʒˈmɛntl/ *adj.* (disapproving) too quick to form opinions and criticize other people

ˈJudgment ˌDay *n.* a time after death when everyone is judged by God, according to some religions

ju·di·cial /dʒuˈdɪʃəl/ *adj.* relating to a court of law, judges, etc.: *the judicial system*

juˌdicial ˈbranch *n.* [singular] POLITICS the part of a government that decides whether laws are good and whether people have disobeyed these laws

juˌdicial reˈview *n.* [U] LAW a process in which a court decides if a law, another court's decision, or an official action is right or CONSTITUTIONAL

ju·di·ci·ar·y /dʒuˈdɪʃiˌɛri, -ʃəri/ *n.* **the judiciary** (formal) all the judges in a country who, as a group, form part of the system of government [ORIGIN: 1400—1500 Latin *judiciarius*, from *judicium*]

ju·di·cious /dʒuˈdɪʃəs/ *adj.* (formal) sensible and careful: *a judicious use of money*

ju·do /ˈdʒudoʊ/ *n.* [U] a Japanese method of defending yourself, in which you try to throw your opponent onto the ground, usually done as a sport [ORIGIN: 1800—1900 a Japanese word meaning "gentle way"]

jug /dʒʌg/ *n.* [C] a large deep container for liquids that has a narrow opening and a handle

jug·gle /ˈdʒʌgəl/ *v.* **1** [I,T] to keep three or more objects moving through the air by throwing and catching them very quickly **2** [T] to try to fit two or more jobs, activities, etc. into your life: *It's hard trying to juggle work and children.* [ORIGIN: 1300—1400 *juggler* (11—21 centuries), from Old French *jogleour*, from Latin *joculari* "to make fun"] —**juggler** *n.* [C]

juggle

jug·u·lar /ˈdʒʌgyələ/ *n.* [C] **1 go for the jugular** (informal) to criticize or attack someone very strongly **2** BIOLOGY the large VEIN in your neck that takes blood from your head to your heart

juice /dʒus/ *n.* **1** [C,U] the liquid that comes from fruit and vegetables, or a drink made from this: *a glass of orange juice* **2** [U] the liquid that comes out of meat when it is cooked [ORIGIN: 1200—1300 Old French *jus*, from Latin]

juic·y /ˈdʒusi/ *adj.* (comparative **juicier**, superlative **juiciest**) **1** containing a lot of juice: *a juicy peach* **2 juicy gossip/details** (informal) interesting or shocking information —**juiciness** *n.* [U]

juke box /ˈdʒuk bɑks/ *n.* [C] a machine in BARS, restaurants, etc. that plays music when you put money in it

Ju·ly /dʒʊˈlaɪ, dʒə-/ (*written abbreviation* **Jul.**) *n.* [C,U] the seventh month of the year, between June and August: *The package arrived **on July 3rd**.* | *Henry started working here **in July**.* | *We're getting married **next July**.* | *I haven't heard from him since **last July**.* [ORIGIN: 1100—1200 Latin *Julius*, from Gaius *Julius* Caesar who was born in this month]

jum·ble /ˈdʒʌmbəl/ *n.* [singular] a messy mixture of things: *a **jumble of** papers* —**jumble** *v.* [T]

jum·bo /ˈdʒʌmboʊ/ *adj.* (informal) larger than other things of the same type: *a jumbo jet*

jump¹ /dʒʌmp/ *v.*

1 UP [I,T] to push yourself suddenly up in the air using your legs, or to go across or over something by doing this: *A fan tried to **jump onto** the stage.* | *Lyle was **jumping up and down*** (=jumping many times) *and waving his arms.*

THESAURUS

skip – to move forward with little jumps between your steps
hop – to move around by jumping on one leg
leap – to jump high into the air or over something
spring – to jump or move suddenly and quickly in a particular direction
hurdle – to jump over something while you are running
dive – to jump into water with your head and arms first
vault – to jump over something in one movement, using your hands or a pole to help you

2 DOWN [I] to let yourself drop from a place that is above the ground: *During the fire, two people **jumped out** of a window.*

3 MOVE FAST [I] to move quickly or suddenly in a particular direction: *Paul **jumped up** to answer the door.*

4 IN SURPRISE/FEAR [I] to make a sudden movement because you are surprised or frightened: *The sudden ring of the telephone **made us jump**.*

5 INCREASE [I] if a number or amount jumps, it increases suddenly and by a large amount: *Profits jumped 20% last month.*

6 jump down sb's throat (informal) to suddenly speak angrily to someone: *All I did was ask a question, and he jumped down my throat!*

7 jump to conclusions to form an opinion about something before you have all the facts

8 jump the gun to start doing something too soon, especially without thinking about it carefully: *I know you wanted to tell Bill the news yourself, but I'm afraid I jumped the gun.*

jump at sth *phr. v.*
to eagerly accept the chance to do something: *Ruth **jumped at the chance** to study at Harvard.*

jump on sb *phr. v.* (informal)
to criticize or punish someone, especially unfairly: *Dad **jumps on** Jeff **for** every little mistake.*

jump² *n.* [C] **1** an act of pushing yourself suddenly up into the air using your legs **2** an act of letting yourself drop from a place that is above the ground: *a parachute jump* **3** a sudden large increase in an amount or value: *a **jump in** prices* **4 get a jump on sth** (informal) to gain an advantage by doing something earlier than usual or earlier than someone else: *I want to get a jump on my Christmas shopping.*

ˈjump drive *n.* [C] IT a USB DRIVE

jump·er /ˈdʒʌmpɚ/ *n.* [C] **1** a dress without SLEEVES, usually worn over a shirt **2** a person or animal that jumps

ˈjumper ˌcables *n.* [plural] thick wires used to connect the batteries (BATTERY) of two cars, in order to start one car that has lost power

ˈjump rope *n.* [C] a long piece of rope that you pass over your head and under your feet as you jump, either as a game or for exercise —**jump rope** *v.* [I] ➔ *see picture at* JUMP

ˈjump-start *v.* [T] **1** to help a process or activity start or become more successful: *The government has made efforts to jump-start the economy.* **2** to start a car whose BATTERY has lost power by connecting it to another BATTERY

jump·suit /ˈdʒʌmpsut/ *n.* [C] a single piece of clothing like a shirt attached to a pair of pants, worn especially by women

jump·y /ˈdʒʌmpi/ *adj.* worried or excited because you are expecting something bad to happen

J

junc·tion /ˈdʒʌŋkʃən/ *n.* [C] a place where one road, track, etc. meets another: *a railroad junction*

junc·ture /ˈdʒʌŋktʃɚ/ *n.* **at this juncture** (spoken, formal) at this point in an activity or time

June /dʒun/ (*written abbreviation* **Jun.**) *n.* [C,U] the sixth month of the year, between May and July: *Can you come to our party* ***on June 24th****?* | *Janet was born* ***in June****.* | *The movie will be released* ***next June****.* | *I graduated* ***last June****.* [ORIGIN: 1200—1300 French *juin*, from Latin *Junius*]

jun·gle /ˈdʒʌŋgəl/ *n.* [C,U] a thick tropical forest with many large plants that grow very close together [ORIGIN: 1700—1800 Hindi *jangal* "forest," from Sanskrit *jangala*]

Jun·ior /ˈdʒunyɚ/ *adj.* (*written abbreviation* **Jr.**) used after the name of a man who has the same name as his father ➔ SENIOR

junior[1] *n.* [C] **1** a student in the third year of HIGH SCHOOL or college ➔ STUDENT **2 be two/five/ten etc. years sb's junior** to be two, five, etc. years younger than someone else

junior[2] *adj.* [only before noun] younger, less experienced, or of a lower rank (ANT) **senior**: *the junior senator from Georgia* ➔ POSITION[1]

junior ˈcollege *n.* [C,U] a college where students can study for two years (SYN) **community college**

junior ˈhigh school *also* **junior ˈhigh** *n.* [C,U] a school in the U.S. and Canada for students who are between 12 and 14 or 15 years old ➔ MIDDLE SCHOOL, HIGH SCHOOL

junk /dʒʌŋk/ *n.* [U] old or unwanted things that have no use or value: *an attic filled with junk*

jun·ket /ˈdʒʌŋkɪt/ *n.* [C] (disapproving) an unnecessary trip made by a public official that is paid for by government money

ˈjunk food *n.* [U] (informal) food that is not healthy because it has a lot of fat or sugar

junk·ie /ˈdʒʌŋki/ *n.* [C] **1** (informal) someone who takes dangerous drugs and is dependent on them **2** (humorous) someone who likes something so much that s/he seems to need it: *a political junkie*

ˈjunk mail *n.* [U] mail that advertisers send to people who do not want it

THESAURUS **advertisement, flier, spam** ➔ ADVERTISEMENT

junk·yard /ˈdʒʌŋkˌyɑrd/ *n.* [C] a business that buys old cars, broken furniture, etc. and sells the parts of them that can be used again, or the place where this business keeps these things

jun·ta /ˈhʊntə, ˈdʒʌntə/ *n.* [C] a military government that has gained power by using force

Ju·pi·ter /ˈdʒupət̬ɚ/ *n.* PHYSICS the largest PLANET, which is fifth from the Sun ➔ *see picture at* SOLAR SYSTEM

jur·is·dic·tion /ˌdʒʊrɪsˈdɪkʃən/ *n.* [U] LAW the right to use an official power to make legal decisions, or the area where this right exists: *a matter outside the court's* ***jurisdiction***

jur·is·pru·dence /ˌdʒʊrɪsˈprudns/ *n.* [U] LAW the science or study of law

ju·ror /ˈdʒʊrɚ/ *n.* [C] a member of a jury

ju·ry /ˈdʒʊri/ *n.* (plural **juries**) [C] **1** LAW a group of 12 people who listen to details of a case in court and decide whether someone is guilty or not ➔ GRAND JURY ➔ COURT[1] **2** a group of people chosen to judge a competition

ˈjury ˌduty *n.* [U] a period of time during which you must be ready to be part of a jury if necessary

just[1] /dʒʌst/ *adv.* **1** exactly: *My brother looks* ***just like*** *my dad.* | *The temperature was* ***just right****.* | *The $250 TV is* ***just as*** *good* ***as*** *the $300 one.* | ***Just then*** *Mr. Struthers walked in.* **2** only: *He was just a little boy when his mother died.* | *Don't be upset – I was just joking.* | *Can you wait five minutes? I just have to iron this.* **3** if something has just happened, it happened only a short time ago: *I just got back from Marilyn's house.*

THESAURUS **recently, a little/short while ago, lately** ➔ RECENTLY

4 just about almost: *She calls her mother just about every day.* | *I'm just about finished.* **5 be just about to do sth** to be going to do something soon: *I was just about to call you.* **6 just before/after** only a short time before or after something else: *Theresa got home just before us.* **7 just (barely)** if something just happens, it does happen, but it almost did not: *Kurt just barely made it home before the storm.*

SPOKEN PHRASES

8 used when politely asking or telling someone something: ***Could/Can I just*** *use your phone for a minute?* **9 just a minute/second/moment** used in order to ask someone to wait for a short time while you do something: *Just a second – I'm getting dressed.* **10** used in order to emphasize something that you are saying: *The young woman just kept getting angrier and angrier.* | *Just be quiet, will you?* **11 it's just that** used in order to explain the reason for something when someone thinks there is a different reason: *Boulder is nice, it's just that I don't know anybody there.* **12 just now** a moment ago, or at this time: *He just now walked in the front door.* **13 I would just as soon do sth** if you would just as soon do something, you are saying in a polite way that you would prefer to do it: *I'd just as soon go with you, if that's okay.* **14 it's just as well** said when it is lucky that something has happened in the way it did because, if not, there may have been problems: *It's just as well Scott didn't go to the party, because Lisa was there.* **15 just because ... (it) doesn't mean ...** used to say that although one thing is true, another thing is not necessarily true: *Just because you're older than me doesn't mean you can tell me what to do!*

[ORIGIN: 1300—1400 French *juste*, from Latin *justus*, from *jus* "right, law"]

just² *adj.* morally right and fair (ANT) **unjust**: *a just punishment*

THESAURUS **fair, equitable, balanced, even-handed, impartial, unbiased** ➔ FAIR¹

jus·tice /ˈdʒʌstɪs/ *n.* **1** [U] fairness in the way people are treated (ANT) **injustice**: *If there were any justice in the world, teachers would earn more than athletes.* **2** [U] the system by which people are judged in courts of law and criminals are punished: *the criminal justice system* **3** [C] a judge in a court of law **4 do sb/sth justice** *also* **do justice to sb/sth** to treat or represent someone or something in a way that is fair and shows his, her, or its best qualities: *This picture doesn't do you justice.* [ORIGIN: 1100—1200 Old French, Latin *justitia*, from *justus*, from *jus* "right, law"]

ˌJustice of the ˈPeace *n.* [C] LAW someone who judges less serious cases in small courts of law and can perform marriage ceremonies

jus·ti·fi·a·ble /ˌdʒʌstəˈfaɪəbəl/ (Ac) *adj.* an action, decision, etc. that is justifiable is reasonable because it is done for good reasons: *The students take justifiable pride in what they have accomplished.* —**justifiably** *adv.*

jus·ti·fi·ca·tion /ˌdʒʌstəfəˈkeɪʃən/ (Ac) *n.* [C,U] a good and acceptable reason for doing something: *There is no* ***justification for*** *terrorism.* | *They argued,* ***with some justification***, *that the law was unconstitutional.*

jus·ti·fied /ˈdʒʌstəˌfaɪd/ (Ac) *adj.* having an acceptable explanation or reason: *Your complaints are certainly justified.* | *Violence can never be justified under any circumstances.*

jus·ti·fy /ˈdʒʌstəˌfaɪ/ (Ac) *v.* (**justified**, **justifies**) [T] to give an acceptable explanation for something that other people think is unreasonable: *How can you justify spending so much money on a coat?* | *People sometimes try to justify stealing on grounds of poverty.* [ORIGIN: 1300—1400 French *justifier*, from Late Latin *justificare*, from Latin *justus*, from *jus* "right, law"]

jut /dʒʌt/ *v.* (**jutted, jutting**) [I] *also* **jut out** to stick up or out farther than the other things in the same area: *The land* ***juts out into*** *the ocean at that point.*

ju·ve·nile /ˈdʒuvənl, -ˌnaɪl/ *adj.* **1** LAW relating to young people who are not yet adults: *juvenile crime* **2** typical of a child, rather than an adult (SYN) **childish**: *a juvenile sense of humor*

THESAURUS **child, kid, teenager, adolescent, youngster, minor** ➔ CHILD

—**juvenile** *n.* [C]

juvenile deˈlinquent *n.* [C] a child or young person who behaves in a criminal way —**juvenile delinquency** *n.* [U]

jux·ta·pose /ˈdʒʌkstəˌpouz, ˌdʒʌkstəˈpouz/ *v.* [T] (formal) to put things together, especially things that are not normally together, in order to compare them or make something new: *His art is made of photos* ***juxtaposed with*** *painted and drawn images.* [ORIGIN: 1800—1900 from French *juxtaposer*, from Latin *juxta* "near" + French *poser* "to put"] —**juxtaposition** /ˌdʒʌkstəpəˈzɪʃən/ *n.* [C,U]

K, k /keɪ/ the 11th letter of the English alphabet

K /keɪ/ **1** PHYSICS an abbreviation of **Kelvin** (=a measurement of temperature) **2** (informal) an abbreviation of **1,000**, especially 1,000 dollars: *He earns $50K a year.*

k /keɪ/ **1** IT an abbreviation of KILOBYTE (=a measurement of computer information) **2** an abbreviation of KILOMETER: *a 10k race*

ka·lei·do·scope /kəˈlaɪdəˌskoup/ *n.* [C] a tube with mirrors and pieces of colored glass at one end that shows colored patterns when you look into the tube and turn it [ORIGIN: 1800—1900 Greek *kalos* "beautiful" + *eidos* "form" + English *-scope* (as in telescope)]

kan·ga·roo /ˌkæŋgəˈru/ *n.* (plural **kangaroos**) [C] an Australian animal that has strong back legs for jumping and carries its babies in a pocket of skin on its stomach ➔ *see picture at* MARSUPIAL

ka·put /kəˈput/ *adj.* (spoken) broken: *The TV* ***went kaput*** *right during the game.* [ORIGIN: 1800—1900 German, French *capot* "having lost in a card game"]

kar·at /ˈkærət/ *n.* [C] a unit for measuring how pure a piece of gold is: *Pure gold is 24 karats.*

ka·ra·te /kəˈrɑt̬i/ *n.* [U] a Japanese fighting sport in which you use your hands and feet to hit and kick [ORIGIN: 1900—2000 a Japanese word meaning "empty hand"]

kar·ma /ˈkɑrmə/ *n.* [U] **1** (informal) the feeling you get from a person, place, or action: *This house has a lot of* ***good/bad karma***. **2** the force that is produced by the things you do in your life and that will influence you in the future, according to some religions [ORIGIN: 1800—1900 a Sanskrit word meaning "work"]

kay·ak /ˈkaɪæk/ *n.* [C] a type of boat, usually for one person, that has a hole for that person to sit in, and that is moved using a PADDLE [ORIGIN: 1700—1800 Inuit *qajaq*]

kay·ak·ing /ˈkaɪækɪŋ/ *n.* [U] the sport of making a kayak move through water using an OAR ➔ *see picture on page A17*

kcal PHYSICS a written abbreviation of KILOCALORIE

ke·bab /kə'bɑb/ *n.* [C] SHISH KEBAB

keel¹ /kil/ *n.* **stay/remain on an even keel** *also* **keep an even keel** to continue doing the things you always do, or feeling the way you always feel, without any sudden changes

keel² *v.*

keel over *phr. v.* to fall over sideways: *Rob looked as if he were ready to keel over.*

keen /kin/ *adj.* **1** very interested in something, or eager to do it: *Most people are* ***keen to*** *do a job well.* | *I was never very* ***keen on*** *science.* **2** a keen sense of smell, sight, or hearing is an extremely good ability to smell, etc. **3** (formal) intelligent and quick to understand things: *a keen mind* —**keenly** *adv.*

keep¹ /kip/ *v.* (past tense and past participle **kept** /kɛpt/)

1 NOT GIVE BACK [T] to have something and not give it back to the person who had it before: *You can keep that sweater – it's too small for me.*

2 NOT LOSE [T] to continue to have something and not lose it or get rid of it: *They're keeping the house in Colorado and selling this one.* | *I've kept her photograph all these years.*

3 NOT CHANGE/MOVE [linking verb] to continue to be in a particular condition or place and not change or move (SYN) **stay**: *This blanket should help you* ***keep warm.*** | ***Keep still*** *so I can cut your hair.*

4 MAKE SB/STH NOT CHANGE OR MOVE [T] to make someone or something continue to be in a particular state, situation, or place: *They kept him in jail for two weeks.* | *It's hard to keep the house clean with three kids.* | *Her son* ***kept*** *her* ***waiting*** *for an hour.* | *I don't know* ***what's keeping*** *her. It's 8:00 already.* | ***Keep*** *those kids* ***out*** *of my yard!*

5 keep (on) doing sth to continue doing something, or repeat an action many times: *If he keeps on growing like this, he'll be taller than Dad soon.* | *Keep driving – I'll tell you when we're almost there.*

6 STORE STH [T] to leave something in one particular place so that you can find it easily: *I* ***keep*** *my keys* ***in*** *the top drawer of my dresser.*

THESAURUS

store – to put things away and keep them there until you need them: *Canned goods can be stored at room temperature.*
save – to keep something so that you can use or enjoy it in the future: *I'm saving this bottle of champagne for a special occasion.*
reserve – to keep something separate so that it can be used for a particular purpose: *These seats are reserved for people with tickets.*
file – to store papers or information in a particular order or a particular place: *All the contracts are filed alphabetically.*
collect – to get and keep objects of the same type because you think they are attractive or interesting: *Kate collects old postcards.*
hoard – to collect things in large amounts and keep them, especially in a secret place: *The peasants hoarded rice and then sold it on the black markets.*

7 keep a record/diary etc. to regularly write down information in a particular place: *She's kept a diary since she was 13.*

8 keep going (spoken) used to encourage someone who is doing something and to tell them to continue: *Keep going, you're doing fine.*

9 keep your promise/word to do what you have promised to do: *The President kept his promise to appoint more women to his cabinet.*

10 keep sth quiet/keep quiet about sth to not say anything in order to avoid complaining, telling a secret, or causing problems: *I'll tell you what happened, but you have to keep it quiet.*

11 keep sb posted to continue to tell someone the most recent news about someone or something: *Keep me posted – I'd like to know about any changes.*

12 FOOD [I] if food keeps, it stays fresh enough to still be eaten: *How long do you think this milk will keep?* [ORIGIN: Old English *cepan*]

keep at sth *phr. v.*
to continue working hard at something: *Just* ***keep at it*** *until you get it right.*

keep (sb/sth ↔) **away** *phr. v.*
to avoid going somewhere or seeing someone, or to make someone or something do this: ***Keep away from*** *the fire.* | *Mom kept us away from school for a week.*

keep sth ↔ **down** *phr. v.*
1 to control something in order to prevent it from increasing: *They promised to keep the rents down.*
2 keep it down (spoken) said when you want someone to be quieter: *Keep it down! I'm on the phone.*
3 to succeed in keeping food in your stomach without VOMITing: *I haven't been able to keep anything down all day.*

keep from *phr. v.*
1 keep sth from sb to not tell someone something that you know: *He kept Angie's death from his family for three days.*
2 keep (sb/sth) from doing sth to prevent someone from doing something or prevent something from happening: *She had to cover her mouth to keep from laughing.* | *Put foil over the pie to keep it from burning.*

keep sth **off** *phr. v.*
to prevent something from affecting or damaging something else: *Wear a hat to keep the sun off your head.*

keep out *phr. v.*
1 Keep Out! used on signs to tell people that they are not allowed into a place
2 keep sb/sth out to prevent someone or something from getting into a place: *She closed the window to keep the dust out.*

keep out of sth *phr. v.*
to try not to become involved with something: *My father warned us to keep out of trouble.*

K

keep to *phr. v.*
1 keep to sth to continue to do, use, or talk about one thing and not change: *You're better off keeping to the main roads.* | *Mullin kept to the same strategy throughout the game.*
2 keep sth to yourself to not tell anyone else something that you know
3 keep to yourself to live a quiet private life, not doing things that involve other people: *Nina kept to herself at the party.*

keep up *phr. v.*
1 keep sth ↔ **up** to prevent something from going to a lower level: *The shortage of supplies is keeping the price up.*
2 keep sth ↔ **up** to continue doing something, or to make something continue: *Keep up the good work!*
3 to move as fast as someone else: *Hey, slow down. I can't keep up!*
4 to learn as fast or do as much as other people: *Davey's having trouble* ***keeping up with*** *the other students.*
5 to continue to learn about a subject: *It's hard to* ***keep up on/with*** *changes in computer technology.*
6 keep sb **up** to prevent someone from sleeping: *The dog has been keeping us up all night.*

keep² *n.* [C] **1 earn your keep** to do a job in order to pay for the basic things you need such as food, clothing, etc. **2 for keeps** (informal) forever

keep·ing /'kipɪŋ/ *n.* [U] **1 for safe keeping** so that something will not be damaged or lost: *I'll put the tickets here for safe keeping.* **2 in keeping with sth/out of keeping with sth** appropriate or not appropriate for a particular occasion or purpose: *In keeping with tradition, we opened our presents on Christmas Eve.*

keep·sake /'kipseɪk/ *n.* [C] a small object that reminds you of someone or something

keg /kɛg/ *n.* [C] a large round container, used especially for storing beer

Kel·vin /'kɛlvɪn/ *n.* [U] (*written abbreviation* **K**) PHYSICS a scale of temperature in which ABSOLUTE ZERO (=the lowest temperature that is possible) is represented as 0 K, water freezes at 273.15 K, and water boils at 373.15 K

ken·nel /'kɛnl/ *n.* [C] a place where dogs are cared for while their owners are away, or the CAGE where they sleep [ORIGIN: 1300—1400 From an unrecorded Old North French *kenil*, from Vulgar Latin *canile*, from Latin *canis* "dog"]

kept /kɛpt/ *v.* the past tense and past participle of KEEP

ker·nel /'kɚnl/ *n.* [C] **1** the center part of a nut or seed, usually the part you can eat **2** one of the small yellow parts of corn that you eat **3** something that is the most important part of a statement, idea, plan, etc.: *There may be a* ***kernel of truth*** *in what he says.*

ker·o·sene /'kɛrəˌsin, ˌkɛrə'sin/ *n.* [U] a type of oil that is burned for heat and light

ketch·up /'kɛtʃəp, 'kæ-/ *n.* [U] a red sauce made from tomatoes and used on food [ORIGIN: 1600—1700 Malay *kechap* "hot-tasting fish sauce"]

ket·tle /'kɛṭl/ *n.* [C] a special metal pot used for boiling and pouring water

key¹ /ki/ *n.* [C] **1** a specially shaped piece of metal that you put into a lock in order to lock or unlock a door, start a car, etc.: *I can't find my* ***car keys.*** **2 the key** the part of a plan, action, etc. that everything else depends on: *Exercise is* ***the key to*** *a healthy body.* **3** the part of a musical instrument, computer, or machine that you press with your fingers to make it work **4** ENG. LANG. ARTS a set of seven musical notes that have a particular base note, or the quality of sound these notes have: ***the key of*** *G* [ORIGIN: Old English *cæg*]

key² *adj.* very important and necessary for success or to understand something: *a key player*

> THESAURUS important, crucial, vital, essential, major → IMPORTANT

key³ *v.*
key sth ↔ **in** *phr. v.* to put information into a computer by using a keyboard: *Key in your password and press "Return."*

key·board /'kibɔrd/ *n.* [C] **1** IT a piece of equipment with buttons that have letters or numbers on them, which you press to put information into a computer → *see picture on page A19* **2** a row of keys on a musical instrument, such as a piano, that you press in order to play the instument **3** an electronic musical instrument similar to a piano, that can make the sounds of various musical instruments

ˌkeyed 'up *adj.* (informal) worried or excited: *I was so keyed up I couldn't sleep.*

key·hole /'kihoʊl/ *n.* [C] the hole in a lock that you put a key in

key·note /'kinoʊt/ *adj.* **1 keynote speech/address** the most important speech at an official event **2 keynote speaker** the person who gives the most important speech at an official event

'key ring *n.* [C] a metal ring that you keep keys on

kg the written abbreviation of KILOGRAM

kha·ki /'kæki/ *n.* **1** [U] a dull brown or green-brown color **2** [U] cloth of this color, especially when worn by soldiers **3 khakis** [plural] pants that are made from khaki [ORIGIN: 1800—1900 Hindi "dust-colored," from *khak* "dust"] —**khaki** *adj.*

kick¹ /kɪk/ *v.* **1** [T] to hit something with your foot: *Stop kicking me!* | *She* ***kicked*** *the pile of books* ***over.*** → *see picture on page A22* **2** [I,T] to move one or both of your legs with short quick movements as if you are hitting something with your foot: *a baby kicking its legs* | *Kyle collapsed on the floor* ***kicking and screaming.*** **3 kick the habit** (informal) to stop doing something, such as smoking, that is a harmful habit **4 kick yourself** (spoken) said when you are annoyed with yourself because you have made a mistake or missed an opportunity: *I wanted*

K

to kick myself for forgetting her name. **5 kick the bucket** (humorous) to die

kick around *phr. v.* **1 kick** sth ↔ **around** (informal) to think about something a lot or get people's opinions about it before making a decision: *We've been* ***kicking around*** *the* ***idea*** *of getting a dog.* **2 kick** sb **around** (informal) to treat someone badly or unfairly: *He won't be kicking me around anymore!*

kick back *phr. v.* (informal) to relax: *I thought I'd kick back and watch some TV.*

kick in *phr. v.* **1** (informal) to begin to have an effect: *Those pills should kick in any time now.* **2 kick in** sth (informal) to join with others to give money or help with something: *Everyone kicked in $5 for gas.* **3 kick** sth ↔ **in** to kick something so hard that it breaks open: *The police had to kick the door in.*

kick sth ↔ **off** *phr. v.* (informal) to start, or to make an event start: *The festivities will* ***kick off with*** *a barbecue dinner.*

kick sb ↔ **out** *phr. v.* (informal) to dismiss someone, or make him/her leave a place: *Sean was* ***kicked out of*** *school for cheating.*

kick² *n.* [C] **1** an act of hitting something with your foot: *If the gate won't open, just* ***give it a*** *good* ***kick*** (=kick it hard). **2** (informal) a strong feeling of excitement or pleasure: *I* ***get a*** *real* ***kick out of*** *watching my two cats play.* | *She started stealing* ***for kicks.*** **3 be on a health/wine/swimming etc. kick** (informal) to have a strong new interest in something

kick·back /ˈkɪkbæk/ *n.* [C,U] money that you pay someone for secretly or dishonestly helping you to make money (SYN) **bribe**

kick·off /ˈkɪk-ɔf/ *n.* [C,U] the time when a game of football or SOCCER starts, or the first kick that starts it: *Kickoff is at 3:00.*

K

kid¹ /kɪd/ *n.* **1** [C] (informal) a child: *Kim is really good with kids.* | *She's loved animals since she was a* ***little kid.***

THESAURUS child, baby, toddler, teenager, adolescent, youngster, minor, juvenile ➔ CHILD

2 [C] (informal) a son or daughter: *How many kids do you have?* **3** [C] (informal) a young person: *college kids* **4 kid stuff** (informal, disapproving) something that is very easy or boring **5** [C,U] a young goat, or the leather made from its skin

kid² *v.* (**kidded**, **kidding**) (informal) **1** [I,T] to say something that is not true, especially as a joke: *Don't get mad. I was* ***just kidding.***

SPOKEN PHRASES

2 no kidding used when you are surprised by what someone says: *"You lived in Baltimore? I did, too." "No kidding."* **3 You're kidding!** said when it is difficult for you to believe that what someone is telling you is true: *They fired you? You're kidding!* **4 kid yourself** to make yourself believe something that is not true or not likely: *Don't kid yourself; she'll never change.*

kid³ *adj.* **kid brother/sister** (informal) your brother or sister who is younger than you

kid·nap /ˈkɪdnæp/ *v.* (**kidnapped**, **kidnapping** *also* **kidnaped**, **kidnaping**) [T] to take someone away illegally and demand money for returning him/her: *She was kidnapped and held for ransom.* —**kidnapper** *n.* [C] —**kidnapping** *n.* [C,U]

kid·ney /ˈkɪdni/ *n.* (plural **kidneys**) [C] BIOLOGY one of the two organs in your lower back that separate waste liquid from blood and make URINE ➔ *see picture at* ORGAN

ˈkidney bean *n.* [C] a dark red bean with a curved shape

kill¹ /kɪl/ *v.* **1** [I,T] to make a person or living thing die: *Kerr is accused of killing three men.* | *Too much water could kill the plants.* | *Who knows when he might kill again?* | *Smoking kills.*

THESAURUS

murder – to deliberately kill someone
commit manslaughter – to kill someone without intending to
commit suicide – to deliberately cause your own death
assassinate – to deliberately kill an important person, especially a politician
slaughter/massacre – to kill a large number of people in a violent way
execute sb/put sb to death – to kill someone as a punishment for a crime
exterminate (formal) – to kill all of a particular group of animals or people
slay (formal) – to kill someone violently, used especially in newspapers ➔ CRIME

2 [T] to make something stop or fail, or turn off the power to something: *Nothing that the doctor gives me kills the pain.* | *A group of bankers persuaded lawmakers to kill the proposal.* **3** [T] (informal) to be very angry at someone: *My wife will kill me if I don't get home soon.* **4 sth is killing me** (spoken) used to say that a part of your body is hurting a lot: *My head is killing me.* **5 kill time** (informal) to do something that is not very useful or interesting while you are waiting for something to happen: *We hung out at the mall to kill time.* **6 kill two birds with one stone** to achieve two things with one action

kill sb/sth ↔ **off** *phr. v.* to cause the death of a lot of living things: *Pollution is rapidly killing off marine life in the lake.*

kill² *n.* **1** [singular] an animal killed by another animal, especially for food: *The lion dragged its kill into the bushes.* **2** [C usually singular] the act of killing a hunted animal: *The hawk swooped in* ***for the kill.***

kill·er¹ /ˈkɪlɚ/ *n.* [C] a person, animal, or thing that kills or has killed: *Police are still looking for the girl's killer.*

killer² *adj.* [only before noun] **1** (slang) very attractive or very good: *That looks like a killer movie.* **2** very harmful or likely to kill you: *a killer landslide*

kill·ing /ˈkɪlɪŋ/ *n.* [C] **1** a murder: *a series of brutal killings* **2 make a killing** (informal) to make a lot of money very quickly: *They planned to make a killing on the stock market.*

kiln /kɪln/ *n.* [C] a special OVEN for baking clay pots, bricks, etc. [ORIGIN: 700—800 Latin *culina* "kitchen," from *coquere* "to cook"]

ki·lo /ˈkiloʊ, ˈkɪ-/ *n.* (plural **kilos**) [C] a kilogram

ki·lo·byte /ˈkɪləˌbaɪt/ *n.* [C] IT a unit for measuring computer information, equal to 1,024 BYTES

kil·o·cal·o·rie /ˈkɪloˌkæləri/ *n.* [C] PHYSICS (*written abbreviation* **kcal**) a unit of heat. It equals the amount of heat needed to increase the temperature of one kilogram of water by 1°C.

kil·o·gram /ˈkɪləˌgræm/ *also* **kilo** *n.* [C] PHYSICS (*written abbreviation* **kg**) a unit for measuring weight, equal to 1,000 grams

ki·lo·me·ter /kɪˈlɑmət̬ɚ, ˈkɪləˌmit̬ɚ/ *n.* [C] (*written abbreviation* **km**) a unit for measuring length, equal to 1,000 meters

kil·o·watt /ˈkɪləˌwɑt/ *n.* [C] PHYSICS (*written abbreviation* **kW**) a unit for measuring electrical power, equal to 1,000 WATTS

kilt /kɪlt/ *n.* [C] a type of wool skirt with a pattern of lines and squares on it, traditionally worn by Scottish men

kil·ter /ˈkɪltɚ/ *n.* **out of kilter** *also* **off kilter** if something is out of kilter, it is not working the way it should be or not doing what it should

ki·mo·no /kəˈmoʊnoʊ/ *n.* (plural **kimonos**) [C] a traditional piece of Japanese clothing like a long coat, that is worn at special ceremonies

kin /kɪn/ *n.* [plural] **1 next of kin** (formal) your most closely related family **2** (old-fashioned) your family

> THESAURUS **family, relative, relation, folks** ➔ FAMILY

kind¹ /kaɪnd/ *n.* **1** [C] a type or sort of person or thing: *What* ***kind of*** *dog is that?* | *We sell* ***all kinds of*** *hats.* | *She met people* ***of all kinds*** *while traveling.* | *This camera is* ***the best of its kind.***

> THESAURUS **type, sort, category, genre, variety, species** ➔ TYPE¹

2 kind of (spoken) **a)** slightly, or in some ways: *You must be kind of disappointed.* **b)** used when you are explaining something and want to avoid giving the details: *I kind of made it look like it was an accident.* **3 (a) kind of (a)** (spoken) used in order to say that your description of something is not exact: *a kind of a reddish-brown color* **4 one of a kind** the only one of a particular type of something: *Each vase is handmade and is one of a kind.* **5 in kind** reacting by doing the same thing that someone else has just done: *The U.S. should* ***respond in kind*** *if other countries do not trade fairly.* [ORIGIN: Old English *cynd*]

kind² *adj.* helpful, friendly, and caring toward other people: *Thank you for your kind invitation.* | *That was very* ***kind of*** *you.* | *Janine has been very* ***kind to*** *me lately.*

> THESAURUS
> **nice** – friendly and kind: *It was really nice of him to give me a ride home.*
> **considerate** – thinking about other people's feelings: *How considerate of her, I thought, to leave a light on for me.*
> **thoughtful** – thinking of things you can do to make other people happy: *a thoughtful gift*
> **caring** – kind to someone and willing to help him/her: *caring parents*
> **warm-hearted** – friendly and kind: *a warm-hearted old lady*
> **compassionate** (formal) – feeling sympathy for people who are suffering: *My father was firm with us, but also warm and compassionate.*
> **sympathetic** – showing that you understand how sad, hurt, lonely, etc. someone feels: *He gave me a sympathetic look.* ➔ NICE

kind·a /ˈkaɪndə/ a short form of "kind of," used in writing to show how people sound when they speak: *I'm kinda tired.*

kin·der·gar·ten /ˈkɪndɚˌgɑrt¬n, -ˌgɑrdn/ *n.* [C] a class for young children who are about five years old that prepares them for school ➔ NURSERY SCHOOL [ORIGIN: 1800—1900 German "children's garden"]

ˌkind-ˈhearted *adj.* kind and generous: *a kind-hearted woman*

kin·dle /ˈkɪndl/ *v.* **1** [T] to make something start burning **2 kindle excitement/interest etc.** to make someone excited, interested, etc.

kin·dling /ˈkɪndlɪŋ/ *n.* [U] small pieces of dry wood, leaves, etc. that you use for starting a fire

kind·ly¹ /ˈkaɪndli/ *adv.* **1** in a kind way SYN **generously**: *Mr. Thomas has kindly offered to let us use his car.* **2 not take kindly to sth** to be annoyed or upset by something that someone says or does: *He didn't take kindly to having his picture taken.* **3** (spoken) a word meaning "please," often used when you are annoyed: ***Would you kindly*** *close that door?*

kindly² *adj.* (old-fashioned) kind and caring about other people: *a kindly woman*

kind·ness /ˈkaɪndnɪs/ *n.* [C,U] kind behavior, or a kind action: *We were overwhelmed by the* ***kindness of*** *the local people.*

kin·dred /ˈkɪndrɪd/ *adj.* **a kindred spirit** someone who thinks and feels the way you do

ki·net·ic /kɪˈnɛt̬ɪk/ *adj.* **1 kinetic art/sculpture/painting etc.** ENG. LANG. ARTS art that has moving parts **2** PHYSICS relating to movement: *the kinetic properties of each gas*

ki,netic 'energy *n.* [U] PHYSICS the energy that a moving object has as a result of its own movement → POTENTIAL ENERGY: *A rock rolling down a hill contains kinetic energy.*

ki,netic 'theory *n.* [U] PHYSICS a scientific THEORY used to describe and explain the behavior and properties of gases, based on the idea that all matter consists of PARTICLEs which are continuously moving around very quickly, and that energy and MOMENTUM are produced when particles hit each other

king /kɪŋ/ *n.* [C] **1** a man who is the ruler of a country because he is from a royal family → QUEEN: *the **king of** Spain | King Edward*

THESAURUS

queen – the female ruler of a country, or the wife of a king
prince the son of a king or queen, or the male ruler of some small countries
princess the daughter of a king or queen, or the wife of a prince
monarch – a king or queen
ruler – someone such as a king, who has official power over a country and its people
emperor – the ruler of an empire (=group of countries)
sovereign (formal) – a king or queen

2 someone who is considered to be the most important or best member of a group: *the **king of** comedy*

king·dom /'kɪŋdəm/ *n.* [C] **1** POLITICS a country ruled by a king or queen **2 the animal/plant/mineral kingdom** BIOLOGY the three parts into which scientists divide the natural world **3** BIOLOGY one of the six large groups into which scientists divide plants and animals

king·pin /'kɪŋ,pɪn/ *n.* [C] the most important person in a group: *a drug kingpin*

'king-size *also* **'king-sized** *adj.* very large, and usually the largest of its type: *a king-size bed*

kink /kɪŋk/ *n.* [C] **1** a twist in something that is normally straight: *The hose has a **kink in** it.* **2 work out the kinks** to solve all the problems in a plan, situation, etc.

kink·y /'kɪŋki/ *adj.* (informal) **1** someone who is kinky, or who does kinky things, has strange ways of getting sexual excitement **2** kinky hair has a lot of tight curls

ki·osk /'kiɑsk/ *n.* [C] a small building where you can buy things such as newspapers or tickets [ORIGIN: 1800—1900 French *kiosque*, from Turkish *kösk* "small building for sitting in"]

kiss¹ /kɪs/ *v.* **1** [I,T] to touch someone with your lips as a greeting, or to show love: *They stood on the beach and kissed. | She **kissed** me **on** the cheek. | He leaned forward and **kissed** her **goodnight**.* **2 kiss sth goodbye** (spoken) used in order to say that someone will lose his/her chance to get or do something: *If you don't start working harder, you can kiss medical school goodbye.* [ORIGIN: Old English *cyssan*]

kiss² *n.* [C] an act of kissing: *Come here and **give** me **a kiss**.*

kit /kɪt/ *n.* [C] **1** a set of tools, equipment, etc. that you use for a particular purpose or activity: *a first-aid kit* **2** something that you buy in parts and put together yourself: *a model airplane kit*

kitch·en /'kɪtʃən/ *n.* [C] the room where you prepare and cook food: *Jay's **in the kitchen** washing the dishes. | Put the groceries on the **kitchen table**.* [ORIGIN: Old English *cycene*]

kite /kaɪt/ *n.* [C] a toy that you fly in the air on the end of a long string, made from a light frame covered in paper or plastic

kitsch /kɪtʃ/ *n.* [U] decorations, movies, etc. that seem to be cheap and without style, and often amuse people because of this —**kitsch, kitschy** *adj.*

kit·ten /'kɪtˀn/ *n.* [C] a young cat [ORIGIN: 1300—1400 From an unrecorded Old North French *caton*, from *cat* "cat," from Late Latin *cattus*]

kit·ty /'kɪt̬i/ *n.* (plural **kitties**) [C] **1** (spoken) *also* **kit·ty·cat** /'kɪt̬u,kæt/ a word meaning a cat, used especially by children or when calling to a cat: *Here, kitty kitty!* **2** [usually singular] the money that people have collected for a particular purpose

'kitty-,corner *adv.* **kitty-corner from sth** on the other side of the street, and slightly to the left or the right, from a place: *His store is kitty-corner from the bank.*

ki·wi /'kiwi/ *also* **'kiwi fruit** *n.* [C] a soft green fruit with small black seeds and a thin brown skin → *see picture on page 414*

KKK *n.* the abbreviation of KU KLUX KLAN

Kleen·ex /'klinɛks/ *n.* [C,U] (trademark) a piece of soft thin paper, used especially for blowing your nose

klutz /klʌts/ *n.* [C] (informal) someone who often drops things and falls easily [ORIGIN: 1900—2000 Yiddish *klotz*, *klutz*, from German *klotz* "large piece of wood"] —**klutzy** *adj.*

km the written abbreviation of KILOMETER

knack /næk/ *n.* [singular] (informal) a natural ability to do something well: *Knight has always **had a knack for** teaching.*

THESAURUS **skill, talent, flair, gift, aptitude**
→ SKILL

knap·sack /'næpsæk/ *n.* [C] a bag that you carry on your shoulders (SYN) **backpack** [ORIGIN: 1600—1700 Low German *knappsack* or Dutch *knapzak* "food bag"]

knead /nid/ *v.* [T] to press DOUGH (=a mixture of flour, water, etc. for making bread) many times with your hands → *see picture on page A18*

knee¹ /ni/ *n.* [C] **1** the joint where your leg bends: *a knee injury | He actually got **down on** his **knees** and asked me to forgive him.* → *see picture on page*

A16 **2** the part of your pants that covers your knee: *Billy's jeans had holes in both knees.* **3 bring sb/sth to their knees a)** to defeat a country or group of people in a war **b)** to have such a bad effect on an organization, activity, etc. that it cannot continue [ORIGIN: Old English *cneow*]

knee² *v.* [T] to hit someone with your knee: *Victor* ***kneed*** *him* ***in*** *the stomach.*

knee·cap /ˈnikæp/ *n.* [C] the bone at the front of your knee → *see picture on page A16*

ˌknee-ˈdeep *adj.* **1 a)** deep enough to reach your knees **b)** in something that is deep enough to reach your knees: *The trails were* ***knee-deep in*** *snow.* **2 knee-deep in sth** (informal) very involved in something, or greatly affected by something that you cannot avoid: *Ralph lost his job, and we ended up knee-deep in debt.*

knee-deep

knee-deep in snow

ˌknee-ˈhigh *adj.* tall enough to reach your knees: *knee-high water*

ˈknee-jerk *adj.* (disapproving) a knee-jerk reaction, opinion, etc. is what you feel or say about a situation from habit, without thinking about it

kneel /nil/ *also* **kneel down** *v.* (past tense and past participle **knelt** /nɛlt/ *or* **kneeled**) [I] to be in or move into a position where your body is resting on your knees: *She* ***knelt down*** *on the floor to pray.* → *see picture on page A22*

knell /nɛl/ *n.* [C] (literary) the sound of a bell being rung slowly because someone has died

knew /nu/ *v.* the past tense of KNOW

knick·ers /ˈnɪkɚz/ *n.* [plural] short loose pants that fit tightly at your knees, worn especially in past times

knick-knack /ˈnɪk næk/ *n.* [C] (informal) a small object used as a decoration

knife¹ /naɪf/ *n.* (plural **knives** /naɪvz/) [C] a tool used for cutting or as a weapon, consisting of a metal blade attached to a handle: *a knife and fork* [ORIGIN: Old English *cnif*]

knife² *v.* [T] to put a knife into someone's body SYN **stab**: *The victim was* ***knifed in*** *the back.*

knight /naɪt/ *n.* [C] **1** a European man with a high rank in past times, who was trained to fight while riding a horse **2** the CHESS piece with a horse's head on it

knight·hood /ˈnaɪthʊd/ *n.* [C,U] a special title or rank that is given to someone by the British king or queen

knit

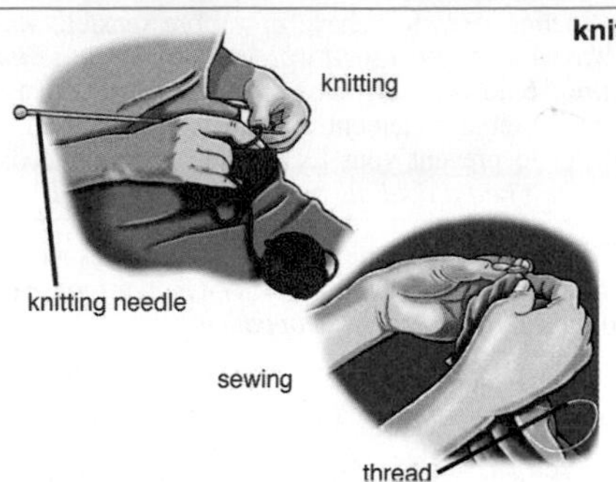

knit¹ /nɪt/ *v.* (past tense and past participle **knit** *or* **knitted**, present participle **knitting**) [I,T] **1** to make clothes out of YARN (=thick thread) using knitting needles or a special machine: *She's knitting me a sweater.* **2** to join people, things, or ideas more closely, or to be closely related: *The broken bone should* ***knit together*** *smoothly.* | *a* ***tightly/closely knit*** *community* **3 knit your brows** to show you are worried, thinking hard, etc. by moving your EYEBROWS together [ORIGIN: Old English *cnyttan*]

knit² *adj.* [only before noun] made by knitting: *a gray knit sweater*

knit·ting /ˈnɪt̬ɪŋ/ *n.* [U] something that is being knitted

ˈknitting ˌneedle *n.* [C] one of the two long sticks that you use to knit something → *see picture at* KNIT¹

knives /naɪvz/ *n.* the plural of KNIFE

knob /nɑb/ *n.* [C] a round handle that you turn or pull to open a door or drawer, turn on a radio, etc. → DOORKNOB

knob·by /ˈnɑbi/ *adj.* with hard parts that stick out from under the surface of something: *knobby knees*

knock¹ /nɑk/ *v.* **1** [I] to hit a door or window with your closed hand in order to attract the attention of the people inside: *I've been* ***knocking at/on*** *the door for five minutes.*

knock

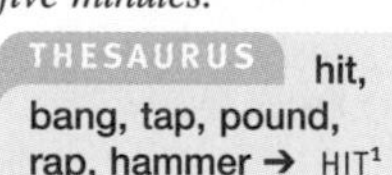

THESAURUS **hit, bang, tap, pound, rap, hammer** → HIT¹

2 [I,T] to hit someone or something with a quick hard hit, so that he, she, or it moves or falls down: *The ball was* ***knocked loose****, out of his hands.* | *A car* ***knocked into*** *a pole in the parking lot.* **3 knock sb unconscious** to hit someone so hard that s/he becomes unconscious

SPOKEN PHRASES

4 knock it off used in order to tell someone to stop doing something because it is annoying you **5 knock some sense into sb** to make

K

someone learn to behave in a more sensible way: *Maybe getting arrested will knock some sense into him.* **6 knock on wood** an expression that is used after a statement about something good, in order to prevent your luck from becoming bad: *I haven't had a cold all winter, knock on wood.*

---

7 [T] to criticize someone or something, especially in an unfair or annoying way: *The mayor took every opportunity to knock his opponent.*

THESAURUS **criticize, attack, find fault with, be disparaging about sb/sth** → CRITICIZE

knock sth ↔ **back** *phr. v.* (informal) to drink a large amount of alcohol very quickly: *He knocked back a few beers.*

knock sb/sth ↔ **down** *phr. v.* **1** to hit or push someone so that s/he falls to the ground: *The horse knocked Laura down while she was cleaning the stable.* **2** to destroy a building or structure: *My elementary school was knocked down so a mall could be built.* **3** (informal) to reduce the price of something: *The new stove we bought was* ***knocked down from*** *$800* ***to*** *$550.*

knock off *phr. v.* (informal) **1** to stop working: *We decided to knock off around 3.* **2 knock** sth ↔ **off** to reduce the price of something by a particular amount: *I got him to knock $10 off the regular price.*

knock out *phr. v.* **1 knock** sb ↔ **out** to make someone become unconscious: *He knocked out his opponent in the fifth round.* **2 knock** sb/sth ↔ **out** to defeat a person or team in a competition so that he, she, or it cannot continue to take part in the competition: *Indiana* ***knocked*** *Kentucky* ***out of*** *the tournament.* **3 knock yourself out** (informal) to work very hard in order to do something well, especially so that you are very tired when you finish: *He's been knocking himself out trying to find a job.*

knock sb/sth ↔ **over** *phr. v.* to hit or push someone or something so that he, she, or it falls down: *Scott knocked the lamp over.*

K

knock² *n.* [C] **1** the sound of something hard hitting a hard surface: *a loud knock at the door* **2** the action of something hard hitting your body: *a* ***knock on*** *the head* **3 take a knock** (informal) to have some bad luck or trouble: *Lee's* ***taken*** *quite a few* ***hard knocks*** *lately.*

knock·er /ˈnɑkɚ/ *n.* [C] a piece of metal on an outside door, that you use to knock loudly

knock·out /ˈnɑk-aʊt/ *n.* [C] **1** an act of hitting your opponent so hard in BOXING that s/he falls down and cannot get up again **2** (old-fashioned, informal) a woman who is very attractive

knoll /noʊl/ *n.* [C] a small round hill

knot¹ /nɑt/ *n.* [C] **1** a place where two ends or pieces of rope, string, etc. have been tied together: *Her Brownie troop is learning how to* ***tie knots.*** **2** many hairs, threads, etc. that are twisted together **3** a hard round place in a piece of wood where a branch once joined the tree **4** a tight painful place in a muscle, or a tight uncomfortable feeling in your stomach: *a* ***knot in*** *my back* | *My stomach is* ***in knots.*** **5 tie the knot** (informal) to get married **6** a small group of people standing close together **7** a unit for measuring the speed of a ship that is about 1,853 meters per hour [ORIGIN: Old English *cnotta*]

knot² *v.* (**knotted**, **knotting**) **1** [T] to tie together two ends or pieces of rope, string, etc. **2** [I,T] if hairs, threads, etc. knot, or if something knots them, they become twisted together

know¹ /noʊ/ *v.* (past tense **knew** /nu/, past participle **known** /noʊn/)

1 HAVE INFORMATION [I,T] to have information about something: *Do you know the answer?* | *I don't* ***know*** *much* ***about*** *art.* | *We don't* ***know what*** *we're supposed to be doing.* | *Did you* ***know that*** *Andy was fired?* | *He* ***wants to know*** (=wants to be told) *what happened.*

2 BE SURE [I,T] to be sure about something: *"Is Bob coming?" "I don't know."* | *I* ***knew that*** *she didn't like him.* | *Barry didn't* ***know what*** *to say.*

3 BE FAMILIAR WITH SB/STH [T] to be familiar with a person, place, system, etc.: *She knows the city pretty well.* | *I've known Jack since we were in the army.* | *He said he'd like to* ***get to know*** *us better* (=would like to know more about us).

4 REALIZE [T] to realize or understand something: *I don't think he* ***knows how*** *stupid he sounds.* | *I* ***know*** *exactly* ***what*** *you mean.* | *You* ***know full/perfectly well*** *what I'm talking about.*

5 RECOGNIZE [T] to be able to recognize someone or something: *She* ***knew*** *it was Gail* ***by*** *her voice* (=she recognized Gail because of her voice).

6 know better to be wise or experienced enough to avoid making mistakes: *He* ***should have known better than to*** *trust Rich.*

7 know your way around to be familiar with a place, organization, system, etc. so that you can use it effectively

---

SPOKEN PHRASES

8 you know a) said when you cannot quickly think of what to say next, but you want to keep someone's attention: *And then I told him he could, you know, call me whenever he wants.* **b)** said when you are trying to explain something by giving more information: *I have some clothes for Matthew, you know, for the baby, if Carrie wants them.* **c)** said when you begin talking about a subject: *You know, I spoke to Eric last night.* **d)** said in order to check if someone understands what you are saying: *I can't stand it when people are late, you know?*

9 I know a) used to agree with someone or to say that you feel the same way: *"That meeting was so boring!" "I know – I couldn't wait to get out of there."* **b)** said when you suddenly have an idea or think of the answer to a problem: *I know, let's ask Luis for a ride.*

10 as far as I know said when you think something is true, but you are not sure: *As far as I know, Bethany left at 6:00.*

11 you never know used to say that you are not

sure what will happen: *You never know, you might win!*

[ORIGIN: Old English *cnawan*]

know of sb/sth *phr. v.*
1 to have been told or to have read about someone or something, but not know much about him, her, or it: *I only know of him – I've never met him.*
2 used to ask for or give advice: *Do you know of any good restaurants around here?*
3 not that I know of used in order to say that the answer to a question is "No," but that there may be facts you do not know about: *"Does Chris smoke?" "Not that I know of."*

know² *n.* **in the know** having more information than most people about something: *Those in the know say that gas prices will be going up.*

'know-how *n.* [U] (informal) knowledge, practical ability, or skill

know·ing /'noʊɪŋ/ *adj.* [only before noun] showing that you know all about something: *a knowing smile*

know·ing·ly /'noʊɪŋli/ *adv.* **1** deliberately: *He'd never knowingly hurt you.* **2** in a way that shows you know all about something: *Tara nodded knowingly.*

'know-it-all *n.* [C] (informal, disapproving) someone who behaves as if s/he knows everything

knowl·edge /'nɑlɪdʒ/ *n.* [U] **1** the information and understanding that you have gained through learning or experience: *His **knowledge of** American history is impressive.* **2** what someone knows or has information about: ***To the best of my knowledge**, each of the victims survived* (=I think this is true, although I may not have all the facts). | *The decision to attack was made **without my knowledge*** (=I did not know about it). | *"Has there been any improvement in the patient's condition?" **"Not to my knowledge*** (=I do not think this is true, based on what I know)."

knowl·edge·a·ble /'nɑlɪdʒəbəl/ *adj.* knowing a lot: *Steve's very **knowledgeable about** politics.*

known¹ /noʊn/ *v.* the past participle of KNOW

known² *adj.* known about, especially by many people: *a known criminal*

knuck·le¹ /'nʌkəl/ *n.* [C] one of the joints in your fingers → *see picture at* HAND¹

knuckle² *v.*

knuckle under *phr. v.* (informal) to accept someone's authority or orders without wanting to: *She refused to **knuckle under to** company regulations.*

KO the abbreviation of KNOCKOUT

ko·a·la /koʊ'ɑlə/ *also* **ko'ala bear** *n.* [C] an Australian animal like a small bear that climbs trees and eats leaves → *see picture at* MARSUPIAL

Ko·ran /kə'ræn, -'rɑn/ *n.* **the Koran** the holy book of the Muslim religion [ORIGIN: 1600—1700 Arabic *qur'an*, from *qara'a* "to read"]

Ko·re·an¹ /kə'riən/ *adj.* **1** relating to or coming from Korea **2** relating to the Korean language

Korean² *n.* **1** [U] the language used in Korea **2** [C] someone from Korea

ko·sher /'koʊʃɚ/ *adj.* **1** kosher food is prepared according to Jewish law **2** kosher restaurants or stores sell food prepared in this way **3** (informal) honest and legal, or socially acceptable: *I don't think the way she broke up with him was kosher.*

kow·tow /'kaʊtaʊ/ *v.* [I] (informal, disapproving) to be too eager to please or obey someone who has more power than you: *I don't like the way this president **kowtows to** big business.* [ORIGIN: 1800—1900 Chinese *ke tou* "to hit your head;" because when you bow very low you hit your head on the floor]

Krem·lin /'kremlɪn/ *n.* **the Kremlin** the government of Russia and the former USSR, or the buildings that are this government's offices

KS the written abbreviation of KANSAS

ku·dos /'kudoʊs, -doʊz/ *n.* [U] admiration and respect that you get for being important or doing something important

Ku Klux Klan /ˌku klʌks 'klæn/ (*abbreviation* **KKK**) *n.* **the Ku Klux Klan** a U.S. political organization, whose members are Protestant white people, which believes that people of other races or religions should not have any power or influence in American society

kung fu /ˌkʌŋ 'fu/ *n.* [U] an ancient Chinese fighting art in which you attack people with your feet and hands

kW PHYSICS the written abbreviation of KILOWATT

Kwan·zaa /'kwɑnzə/ *n.* [C,U] a holiday celebrated by some African-Americans between December 26 and January 1

KY the written abbreviation of KENTUCKY

L

L, l /ɛl/ **1** the TWELFTH letter of the English alphabet **2** the number 50 in the system of ROMAN NUMERALS

LA 1 the written abbreviation of LOUISIANA **2 L.A.** Los Angeles

lab /læb/ *n.* [C] (informal) **1** a LABORATORY: *a **research lab** at Columbia University* **2** a LABRADOR

la·bel¹ /'leɪbəl/ (Ac) *n.* [C] **1** a piece of paper or other material that is attached to something and has information about that thing printed on it: *a beer label* | *Always read the instructions **on the label.*** | *The label should give clear information about how* *much salt and fat is in the product.* **2** a famous name that represents a company that is selling a product: *Fischer recorded two albums for the Victor label.* **3** a word or phrase that is used in order to describe someone or something: *As a writer, he's proud of his "liberal" label.* [ORIGIN: 1200—1300 Old French "long narrow piece of cloth"]

label² *v.* [T] **1** to attach a label to something or write information on something: *Make sure your charts are clearly labeled.* **2** to use a particular word or phrase in order to describe someone: *No one wants to be labeled a racist.* | *The principal* ***labeled*** *his behavior* ***as*** *inappropriate.*

THESAURUS **call, characterize, brand, portray** → CALL¹

la·bor¹ /ˈleɪbɚ/ (Ac) *n.* [U] **1** work, especially work using a lot of physical effort: *farm labor* | ***manual labor*** (=physical work) | *Marx defined the working class as people who sell their labor to employers.* **2** all the people who work for a company or in a country: *a shortage of* ***skilled labor*** (=trained workers) | *When there are labor shortages, employers have to raise wages.* **3** the process in which a baby is born by being pushed from its mother's body, or the period when this happens: *Sandra was* ***in labor*** *for 17 hours.* | *Twenty-four hours is a long labor for a second child.*

labor² *v.* [I] **1** (formal) to work very hard: *Farmers labored in the fields.* **2** to try to do something that is difficult: *Writers can spend hours* ***laboring over*** *a single sentence.*

lab·ora·to·ry /ˈlæbrəˌtɔri/ *n.* (plural **laboratories**) [C] a special room or building in which scientists do tests and RESEARCH [ORIGIN: 1600—1700 Medieval Latin *laboratorium*, from Latin *laborare* "to work"]

ˈlabor camp *n.* [C] a place where prisoners are forced to do hard physical work

ˈLabor Day *n.* a public holiday in the U.S. and Canada on the first Monday in September

la·bor·er /ˈleɪbərɚ/ *n.* [C] someone whose job involves a lot of physical work

la·bo·ri·ous /ləˈbɔriəs/ *adj.* needing to be done slowly, and with a lot of effort: *Filmmaking can be a* ***laborious process.***

ˈlabor ˌunion *n.* [C] SOCIAL SCIENCE an organization that represents the ordinary workers in a particular trade or profession, especially in meetings with employers

Lab·ra·dor /ˈlæbrəˌdɔr/ *n.* [C] a large dog with black or yellow fur

lab·y·rinth /ˈlæbəˌrɪnθ/ *n.* [C] a MAZE

lace¹ /leɪs/ *n.* **1** [U] a type of fine cloth made with patterns of very small holes: *lace curtains* **2** [C usually plural] a string that is pulled through special holes in shoes or clothing and tied, in order to pull the edges together and fasten them → *see picture at* SHOE¹ [ORIGIN: 1100—1200 Old French *laz* "net, string," from Latin *laqueus* "trap"]

lace² *also* **lace up** *v.* [T] to pull something together by tying a lace: *Paul laced up his boots.*

lac·er·ate /ˈlæsəˌreɪt/ *v.* [T] (formal) to badly cut or tear the skin

lac·er·a·tion /ˌlæsəˈreɪʃən/ *n.* [C,U] (formal) a serious cut in your skin or flesh

lack¹ /læk/ *n.* [singular, U] the state of not having something, or of not having enough of it: *a* ***lack of*** *interest* | *The project was canceled* ***for lack of*** *money* (=because there was not enough). [ORIGIN: 1200—1300 Middle Dutch *laken*]

lack² *v.* [T] to not have something, or to not have enough of it: *She's talented but lacks experience.*

lack·ing /ˈlækɪŋ/ *adj.* **1** not having enough of a particular thing or quality: *No one said she was* ***lacking in*** *determination.* **2** not existing or available: *Information about the cause of the crash was lacking.*

lack·lus·ter /ˈlækˌlʌstɚ/ *adj.* not very exciting or impressive: *a lackluster performance*

la·con·ic /ləˈkɑnɪk/ *adj.* using only a few words when you talk [ORIGIN: 1500—1600 Latin *laconicus* "of Sparta," from Greek *lakonikos*; because the people of ancient Sparta were famous for not using many words]

lac·quer /ˈlækɚ/ *n.* [U] a clear substance painted on wood or metal to give it a hard shiny surface —**lacquered** *adj.*: *a lacquered box*

lac·tose /ˈlæktoʊs/ *n.* [U] CHEMISTRY a type of sugar found in milk → FRUCTOSE, GLUCOSE, SUCROSE

lac·y /ˈleɪsi/ *adj.* decorated with LACE, or looking like lace: *black lacy underwear*

lad /læd/ *n.* [C] (old-fashioned) a boy or young man

lad·der /ˈlædɚ/ *n.* [C] **1** a piece of equipment used for climbing up to high places, consisting of two long BARS connected with RUNGS (=steps): *The painter* ***climbed up/down*** *the ladder.* **2** the jobs you have to do in an organization in order to gradually become more powerful or important: *Stevens worked his way to* ***the top of the*** *corporate* ***ladder***. [ORIGIN: Old English *hlæder*]

lad·en /ˈleɪdn/ *adj.* carrying or containing a lot of something: *The table was* ***laden with*** *food.*

ˈladies' room *n.* [C] a room in a public building with toilets for women

THESAURUS **toilet, bathroom, restroom, men's room, lavatory** → TOILET

la·dle /ˈleɪdl/ *n.* [C] a deep spoon with a long handle —**ladle** *v.* [T]: *I ladled soup into bowls.*

la·dy /ˈleɪdi/ *n.* (plural **ladies**) [C] a word meaning a woman, used in order to be polite: ***Ladies and gentlemen****, thank you for coming this evening.* | *a little old lady* [ORIGIN: Old English *hlæfdige*, from *hlaf* "bread" + *-dige* "one who kneads"]

la·dy·bug /ˈleɪdiˌbʌg/ *n.* [C] a small round insect that is red with black spots

lag¹ /læg/ *v.* (**lagged**, **lagging**) [I] to move or develop more slowly than other things or people: *Students' test scores are **lagging behind** last year's.*

lag² *n.* [C] a delay between two events → JET LAG

la·goon /lə'gun/ *n.* [C] EARTH SCIENCES an area of ocean that is not very deep, and is nearly separated from the ocean by rocks, sand, or CORAL

laid /leɪd/ *v.* the past tense and past participle of LAY

ˌlaid-'back *adj.* relaxed and not seeming to worry about anything: *He's a pretty laid-back guy.*

THESAURUS calm, relaxed, easygoing, mellow → CALM²

lain /leɪn/ *v.* the past participle of LIE

lair /lɛr/ *n.* [C] the place where a wild animal hides and sleeps: *a wolf's lair*

lais·sez-faire /ˌlɛseɪ 'fɛr/ *n.* [U] ECONOMICS the principle that the government should not control or INTERFERE with businesses or the economy

lake /leɪk/ *n.* [C] EARTH SCIENCES a large area of water surrounded by land: *We're going swimming in the lake.* | *Lake Michigan* [ORIGIN: 1200—1300 Old French *lac*, from Latin *lacus*] → *see picture on page A24*

lamb /læm/ *n.* [C,U] a young sheep, or the meat of a young sheep [ORIGIN: Old English]

lam·bast /læm'beɪst, 'læmbeɪst/ *v.* [T] to severely criticize someone or something

THESAURUS criticize, attack, knock → CRITICIZE

lame¹ /leɪm/ *adj.* **1** (old-fashioned) unable to walk easily because your leg or foot is injured **2** (informal) too silly or stupid to believe: *a lame excuse* **3** (spoken) boring or not very good: *The party was lame.*

lame² *v.* [T] to make a person or animal lame

ˌlame 'duck *n.* [C] someone such as a president who has no real power because his/her period in office will soon end

la·ment¹ /lə'mɛnt/ *v.* [I,T] to express feelings of great sadness or disappointment about something

lament² *n.* [C] something such as a song that expresses great sadness

lam·en·ta·ble /lə'mɛntəbəl/ *adj.* (formal) very disappointing

lam·i·nate /'læməˌneɪt/ *v.* [T] to cover paper or wood with a thin layer of plastic in order to protect it —**laminated** *adj.*

lamp /læmp/ *n.* [C] an object that produces light by using electricity, oil, or gas: *a desk lamp* [ORIGIN: 1100—1200 Old French *lampe*, from Latin *lampas*, from Greek *lampein* "to shine"] → *see picture at* LIGHT¹

lam·poon /læm'pun/ *v.* [T] to write about someone such as a politician in a funny way that makes him/her seem stupid —**lampoon** *n.* [C]

lamp·shade /'læmpʃeɪd/ *n.* [C] a cover put over the top of a lamp for decoration and in order to make the light less bright

LAN /læn, ˌɛl eɪ 'ɛn/ *n.* [C] IT **local area network** a small network of computers connected to each other within the same building or organization, so that people who work there can see and use the same information

lance /læns/ *n.* [C] a long thin pointed weapon used in past times by soldiers on horses

land¹ /lænd/ *n.* **1** [U] the ground, especially when owned by someone and used for buildings or farming → EARTH, SOIL: *A mall is being built on the land near the lake.* | *5,000 acres of agricultural land* → GROUND¹ **2** [U] the solid dry part of the Earth's surface: *Frogs live **on land** and in the water.* → EARTH **3** [C] (literary) a country or place: *a faraway land* [ORIGIN: Old English] → COUNTRY¹

land

land² *v.* **1** [I,T] if an airplane lands, or if a pilot lands an airplane, the airplane moves down until it is safely on the ground (ANT) **take off**: *My flight landed in Chicago an hour late.*

THESAURUS arrive, get to, reach, get in, come in → ARRIVE

2 [I] to fall or come down onto something after moving through the air: *Chris slipped and **landed on** his back.* **3** [T] to finally succeed in getting a particular job, contract, or deal: *Kelly landed a job with a big law firm.* **4** [I] to arrive somewhere in a boat, airplane, etc.: *The immigrants landed in New York.* **5** [T] to put someone or something on land from an airplane or boat: *They landed 1,200 troops on the beach.*

L

'land bridge *n.* [C] EARTH SCIENCES a narrow piece of land that connects two large areas of land: *People and animals migrated eastwards across the land bridge that is now covered by the Bering Sea.*

land·fill /'lændfɪl/ *n.* [C] a place where waste is buried in large amounts

land·form /'lændfɔrm/ *n.* [C] EARTH SCIENCES a natural physical feature of the Earth's surface, for example a mountain or valley

'land grant *n.* [C] a gift of public land from the government, usually used to build something such as a college, railroad, or HIGHWAY

land·ing /'lændɪŋ/ *n.* [C] **1** the floor at the top of a set of stairs **2** the action of arriving on land, or of making something such as an airplane or boat come onto land ➔ TAKEOFF: *an **emergency landing*** (=a sudden landing made by an airplane because it is having trouble)

'landing gear *n.* [U] an aircraft's wheels and wheel supports

'landing pad *n.* [C] the area where a HELICOPTER comes down to earth

'landing strip *n.* [C] a special road on which an airplane lands, especially one not at an airport ➔ RUNWAY

land·la·dy /'lænd,leɪdi/ *n.* (plural **landladies**) [C] a woman who owns a building or other property and rents it to people

land·locked /'lændlɑkt/ *adj.* surrounded by land: *a landlocked country*

land·lord /'lændlɔrd/ *n.* [C] someone who owns a building or other property and rents it to other people

land·mark /'lændmɑrk/ *n.* [C] **1** something that helps you recognize where you are, such as a famous building **2** one of the most important events, changes, or discoveries that influences someone or something: *The treaty is an important landmark in U.S.-Mexico relations.*

'land mine, land·mine /'lændmaɪn/ *n.* [C] a type of bomb hidden in the ground that explodes when someone walks or drives over it

land·own·er /'lænd,oʊnɚ/ *n.* [C] someone who owns a large amount of land

'land redistri,bution *n.* [U] a process in which land is taken away from people who own large farms and given to people who do not have any land at all or have very little land

'land re,form *n.* [C,U] POLITICS actions that are taken, especially by a government, to divide up farm land so that more people own some of it

land·scape¹ /'lændskeɪp/ *n.* [C] **1** a view across an area of land, including hills, forests, fields, etc. ➔ SCENERY: *the beautiful landscape of Sonoma Valley* **2** a photograph or painting of a landscape ➔ *see picture at* PAINTING

L

landscape² *v.* [T] to arrange where the plants should grow in a park, yard, or garden —**landscaping** *n.* [U]

land·slide /'lændslaɪd/ *n.* [C] **1** the sudden falling of a lot of soil and rocks down the side of a hill, cliff, or mountain: *Part of Highway 101 is blocked by a landslide.* **2** a victory in which a person or political party wins a lot more votes than the others in an election: *The president was re-elected **in/by a landslide**.*

lane /leɪn/ *n.* [C] **1** one of the parts of a main road that is divided by painted lines: *We drove **in the fast/slow lane*** (=in the lane that is farthest left or farthest right). **2** a narrow country road

THESAURUS **road, street, main street, avenue, main road** ➔ ROAD

3 one of the narrow areas that a pool or race track is divided into

lan·guage /'læŋgwɪdʒ/ *n.* **1** [C] ENG. LANG. ARTS a system of words, phrases, and grammar, used by people who live in a country or area to communicate with each other: *the English language | Her **native language*** (=the first language she learned) *is Tagalog. | "Do you speak any **foreign languages**?" "Yes, I speak Japanese."*

THESAURUS

dialect – a form of a language that is spoken in one area, which is different from the way it is spoken in other areas: *Cantonese is only one of many Chinese dialects.*
accent – a way of pronouncing words that someone has because of where s/he was born or lives: *She has a strong Southern accent.*
tongue – a particular language: *Winnie started school knowing only her native tongue.*
vernacular (formal) – the language or dialect that ordinary people in a country or area speak, especially when this is not the official language: *Much of the comedian's material is performed in the black vernacular.*
lingo (informal) – a language, especially a foreign one: *I've picked up some of the lingo, enough to be polite.*
slang – very informal and sometimes offensive language, used especially by people who belong to a particular group: *Mudbugs is Louisiana slang for crawfish.*
jargon – technical words and phrases used by people in a particular profession: *a document full of legal jargon*
terminology (formal) – the technical words or expressions that are used in a particular subject: *the basic terminology used by geologists*

2 [U] ENG. LANG. ARTS the use of words, grammar, etc. to communicate with other people: *language skills* **3** [U] ENG. LANG. ARTS the kind of words that someone uses, or that are used when talking or writing about a particular subject: *the language of business | poetic language | **bad language*** (=words that people consider offensive) **4** [C,U] IT a system of instructions used in computer programs **5** [C,U] any system of signs, movements, sounds, etc. that are used to express meanings or feelings: *the language of music* [ORIGIN: 1200—1300 Old French *langue* "tongue, language," from Latin *lingua*]

'language ,laboratory *also* **'language lab** *n.* [C] a room in a school or college where students can listen to TAPEs of a foreign language and practice speaking it

lan·guid /'læŋgwɪd/ *adj.* (literary) moving slowly and weakly, but in an attractive way

lan·guish /'læŋgwɪʃ/ *v.* [I] to be prevented from developing, improving, or being dealt with: *The case has languished for years in the courts.*

lank·y /'læŋki/ *adj.* someone who is lanky is very tall and thin

lan·tern /'læntɚn/ *n.* [C] a type of lamp you can

carry that usually has a metal frame and glass sides ➔ *see picture at* LIGHT[1]

lap[1] /læp/ *n.* [C] **1** the upper part of your legs when you are sitting down: *The little girl was sitting **on** her mother's **lap**.* **2** a single trip around a race track or between the two ends of a pool: *Patty swims 30 laps a day.*

lap[2] *v.* (**lapped**, **lapping**) **1** [I,T] if water laps something, or laps against something, it touches something with small waves: *Listen to the sound of the lake **lapping against** the shore.* **2** [T] *also* **lap up** to drink using quick movements of the tongue: *a cat lapping milk*

lap sth ↔ **up** *phr. v.* (disapproving) to enjoy or believe something without criticizing or doubting it at all: *She's flattering him and he's just **lapping it up**!*

la·pel /lə'pɛl/ *n.* [C] the front part of a coat or JACKET that is attached to the collar and folds back on both sides

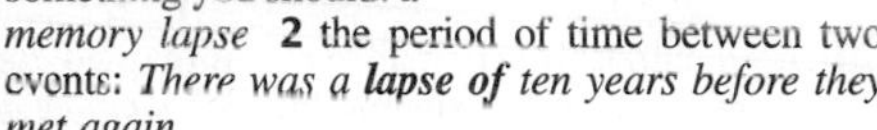

lapse[1] /læps/ *n.* [C] **1** a short period of time when you forget something, do not pay attention, or fail to do something you should: *a memory lapse* **2** the period of time between two events: *There was a **lapse of** ten years before they met again.*

lapse[2] *v.* [I] to end, especially because an agreed time limit is finished: *The insurance policy has lapsed.*

lapse into sth *phr. v.* **1** to start behaving or speaking in a very different way, especially one that is more normal or usual for you: *Without thinking, he lapsed into Spanish.* **2** to become very quiet, less active, or unconscious: *She **lapsed into silence**.*

lap·top /'læptɑp/ *also* **ˌlaptop com'puter** *n.* [C] IT a small computer that you can carry with you ➔ *see picture on page A19*

lar·ce·ny /'lɑrsəni/ *n.* [U] LAW the crime of stealing something

lard /lɑrd/ *n.* [U] the thick white fat from pigs, used in cooking

large /lɑrdʒ/ *adj.* **1** big, or bigger than usual in size, number, or amount (ANT) **small**: *a large pepperoni pizza | What's the largest city in Canada?*

THESAURUS big, huge, enormous, vast, gigantic, massive, immense, colossal ➔ BIG

2 a large person is tall and often fat: *Aunt Betsy was a very large woman.*

THESAURUS fat, overweight, big, heavy, obese, chubby, plump, stout, corpulent, rotund ➔ FAT[1]

3 at large in general: *The risk is to American society at large.* **4 be at large** if a dangerous person or animal is at large, he, she, or it has escaped from somewhere and may cause harm: *The suspect is still at large.* **5 larger than life** more attractive, exciting, or interesting than other people or things **6 by and large** used in order to say that something is generally true or usually happens, but not always: *By and large, the kids are well-behaved.* [ORIGIN: 1100—1200 Old French, Latin *largus*] —**largeness** *n.* [U]

ˌlarge in'testine *n.* [singular] BIOLOGY the lower part of your INTESTINES, where food is changed into solid waste matter ➔ SMALL INTESTINE ➔ *see picture at* ORGAN

large·ly /'lɑrdʒli/ *adv.* mostly or mainly: *The delay was largely due to bad weather.*

THESAURUS mainly, chiefly, principally, primarily ➔ MAINLY

ˌlarge-'scale *adj.* involving a lot of people, effort, money, supplies, etc.: *large-scale unemployment*

lar·gesse, largess /lɑr'dʒɛs, -'ʒɛs/ *n.* [U] (formal) the quality or act of being generous and giving money or gifts to people who have less than you, or the money or gifts that you give ➔ GENEROSITY: *The museum thanked him for his largess.*

lark /lɑrk/ *n.* [C] a small wild brown bird that sings and has long pointed wings

lar·va /'lɑrvə/ *n.* (plural **larvae** /'lɑrvi/) [C] BIOLOGY a young insect with a soft tube-shaped body that will become an insect with wings ➔ *see picture on page A15*

la·ryn·ges /lə'rɪndʒiz/ *n.* a plural of LARYNX

lar·yn·gi·tis /ˌlærən'dʒaɪt̮ɪs/ *n.* [U] BIOLOGY an illness in which your throat and larynx are swollen, making it difficult for you to talk

lar·ynx /'lærɪŋks/ *n.* (plural **larynges** /lə'rɪndʒiz/ *or* **larynxes**) [C] BIOLOGY the part of your throat from which your voice is produced [ORIGIN: 1500—1600 Modern Latin, Greek] ➔ *see picture at* LUNG

la·sa·gna /lə'zɑnyə/ *n.* [C,U] a type of Italian food made with flat pieces of PASTA, meat or vegetables, and cheese

las·civ·i·ous /lə'sɪviəs/ *adj.* (disapproving) showing a very strong sexual desire

la·ser /'leɪzɚ/ *n.* [C] a piece of equipment that produces a powerful narrow beam of light, or the beam of light itself: *laser surgery | a laser beam* [ORIGIN: 1900—2000 From *"light amplification by stimulated emission of radiation"*]

lash[1] /læʃ/ *v.* **1** [T] to hit someone very hard with a whip, stick, etc. **2** [T] to tie something tightly to something else using a rope: *The branches were lashed together.* **3** [I,T] to hit sharply against something: *Waves lashed against the rocks.*

lash out *phr. v.* **1** to suddenly speak loudly and angrily: *He **lashed out at** critics.* **2** to suddenly try to hit someone with a lot of violent uncontrolled movements

L

lash² *n.* [C] **1** a hit with a whip, especially as a punishment **2** an EYELASH

las·so /ˈlæsoʊ/ *n.* (plural **lassos** *or* **lassoes**) [C] a rope with one end tied in a circle, used for catching cattle and horses —**lasso** *v.* [T]

last¹ /læst/ *determiner, adj.* **1** most recent ➔ NEXT: *Did you go to the last football game?* | *I saw Tim* ***last night/week/Sunday****.* | *The* ***last time*** *I saw Ken, we got into an argument.*

USAGE

Use **last** to mean "the one that happened most recently" or "the one before the present one": *my last visit to Florida* | *my last boyfriend*
Use **latest** to mean "new and most recent": *the latest news* | *the latest version of the software*

THESAURUS

previous – happening or existing before the particular event, time, or thing mentioned: *Sales were higher than in the previous year.*
former – happening or existing before, but not now: *the former owner of the property*

2 at the end, after everyone or everything else: *The last part of the song is sad.* | *He's* ***the last person*** *I'd ask for help* (=I do not want to ask him). **3** remaining after all others have gone: *The last guests were just putting on their coats.* | *Do you want the last piece of cake?* **4 on its last legs** likely to fail or break: *The truck was on its last legs.* **5 have the last word** to make the last statement in an argument, which gives you an advantage

last² *adv.* **1** most recently before now: *When did you see her last?* **2** after everything or everyone else: *Harris is going to speak last.* **3 last but not least** said when making a final statement, to show that it is just as important as your other statements: *Last but not least, I'd like to thank my mother.*

last³ *n., pron.* [C] **1 the last** the person or thing that comes after all the others: *Joe was the last of nine children* (=he was born last). | *Les was the last to go to bed that night.* **2 at (long) last** if something happens at last, it happens after you have waited a long time: *At last, we were able to afford a house.* **3 the day/week/year before last** the day, week, etc. before the one that has just finished **4 the last I/we ...** (informal) used when telling someone the most recent news that you know: *The last we heard, Paul was in Brazil.* **5 the last of sth** the remaining part of something: *This is the last of the paint.*

L

last⁴ *v.* [I] **1** to continue to happen or exist: *Jeff's operation lasted three hours.* | *I wish this moment would last forever.* **2** to continue to be effective, useful, or in good condition: *Most batteries will* ***last for*** *up to eight hours.*

ˌlast-ˈditch *adj.* **last-ditch effort/attempt etc.** a final attempt to achieve something before it becomes impossible to do

last·ing /ˈlæstɪŋ/ *adj.* continuing for a long time: *It has been difficult to achieve lasting peace in the Middle East.*

THESAURUS **long, lengthy, long-running, prolonged** ➔ LONG¹

last·ly /ˈlæstli/ *adv.* (formal) used when telling someone the last thing in a series of statements: *Lastly, I'd like to suggest a few solutions.*

USAGE

Use **lastly** or **finally** to introduce the last point, action, or instruction in a list: *Lastly/Finally, I wanted to wish you all good luck.*
Use **finally** or **eventually** to say that something happens after a long time: *Finally/Eventually, we realized what the problem was.* | *She eventually/finally found her glasses case under the bed.*
Use **at last** to emphasize that you are glad when something happens because you have been waiting a long time for it: *At last some rain!*
➔ FIRST¹

ˌlast-ˈminute *adj.* [only before noun] happening or done as late as possible within a process, event, or activity: *a last-minute decision*

ˈlast name *n.* [C] your family's name, which in English comes after your other names ➔ FIRST NAME, MIDDLE NAME

latch¹ /lætʃ/ *n.* [C] a small metal BAR used for fastening a door, gate, window, etc. ➔ *see picture at* LOCK²

latch² *v.*

latch onto sth *phr. v.* (informal) if you latch onto an idea, style, phrase, etc., you think it is so good, important, etc. that you start using it too

late¹ /leɪt/ *adj.* **1** arriving, happening, or done after the expected time: *Sorry I'm late. I got stuck in traffic.* | *Peggy was* ***late for*** *school.* | *a late breakfast* | *Is it* ***too late to*** *send in my forms?*

THESAURUS

overdue – not done or happening when expected: *He recently paid two overdue tax bills.*
be behind with sth – to be late or slow in doing something: *They were three months behind with the rent.*
be delayed – to be made late by something: *The flight was delayed by bad weather.*
be held up – to be late because of something that has happened: *Sorry I'm late – I got held up.*
tardy – late, especially arriving after the expected time: *If you are tardy once more, you will have to stay after school.*
belated – happening or arriving late, used about things or actions: *a belated birthday card*

2 near the end of a period of time: *The house was built in the late 19th century.* **3** happening at night, especially when most people are asleep: *I watched the late show on TV.* **4** paid or given back after the arranged time: *I had to pay a fee because my payment was late.* **5** [only before noun] (formal) dead: *Marion and her late husband bought the house back in 1975.* [ORIGIN: Old English *læt*]

THESAURUS **dead, deceased** → DEAD[1]

late[2] *adv.* **1** after the usual or expected time: *I probably won't be home until late.* | *Our flight arrived two hours late.* **2** near the end of a period of time: ***late in** the afternoon* | *Would you ever take a walk **late at night**?*

late·ly /ˈleɪtli/ *adv.* recently: *It hasn't rained much lately.* | *Lately, I've been really busy.* → RECENTLY

USAGE

You must always use **lately** with the present perfect tense. It shows that the situation you are talking about is still continuing. You can use **recently** like this, too: *He hasn't been feeling very well lately.* | *There hasn't been much rain recently.* You can also use **recently** with the simple past tense to talk about something that happened not long ago: *They recently got married.*

la·tent /ˈleɪtˀnt/ *adj.* present but not yet noticeable, active, or completely developed: *latent racism*

lat·er[1] /ˈleɪtə/ *adv.* **1** after the present time or a time you are talking about: *I'll see you later.* | *They met in July, and two months later they got married.* → AFTER[1] **2 later on** at some time in the future, or after something else: *That's a decision we can make later on.*

later[2] *adj.* **1** coming in the future, or after something else: *This will be decided **at a later time/date**.*

THESAURUS **next, following, subsequent, succeeding, ensuing** → NEXT[1]

2 [only before noun] more recent: *Later models of the car are much improved.*

lat·er·al /ˈlætərəl/ *adj.* relating to the side of something, or movement to the side

lat·est[1] /ˈleɪtɪst/ *adj.* [only before noun] most recent or newest: *What's **the latest** news?* | ***the latest** fashions* → NEW

latest[2] *n.* **at the latest** no later than the time mentioned: *I want you home by 11 at the latest.*

la·tex /ˈleɪtɛks/ *n.* [U] a thick white liquid used for making products such as rubber, glue, and paint, and produced artificially or by some plants: *latex gloves*

lath·er[1] /ˈlæðə/ *n.* [singular, U] a lot of small white BUBBLEs produced by rubbing soap with water

lather[2] *v.* [I,T] to produce a lather, or cover something with lather

Lat·in[1] /ˈlætˀn/ *adj.* **1** relating to or coming from Mexico, Central America, or South America **2** relating to the Latin language

Latin[2] *n.* [U] an old language that is now used mostly for legal, scientific, or medical words

La·ti·na /ləˈtinə/ *n.* [C] a woman in the U.S. whose family comes from a country in Latin America —**Latina** *adj.*

ˌLatin Aˈmerica *n.* the land including Mexico, Central America, and South America —**Latin American** *adj.*

La·ti·no /ləˈtinoʊ/ *n.* (plural **Latinos**) [C] a man in the U.S. whose family comes from a country in Latin America ▸In the plural, Latinos can mean a group of men and women, or just men.◂ —**Latino** *adj.*

lat·i·tude /ˈlætəˌtud/ *n.* **1** [C,U] EARTH SCIENCES the distance north or south of the EQUATOR, measured in degrees → *compare* LONGITUDE → *see picture at* GLOBE **2** [U] (formal) freedom to do or say what you like: *Students now have greater **latitude in** choosing their classes.* [ORIGIN: 1300—1400 Latin *latitudo*, from *latus* "wide"] —**latitudinal** /ˌlætəˈtudn-əl/ *adj.*

la·trine /ləˈtrin/ *n.* [C] a toilet that is outside at a camp or military area

THESAURUS **toilet, lavatory, outhouse, privy** → TOILET

lat·ter[1] /ˈlætə/ *n.* **the latter** (formal) the second of two people or things that are mentioned → FORMER: *Either glass or plastic would be effective, but the latter* (=plastic) *weighs less.*

latter[2] *adj.* **1 the latter sth** (formal) being the last person or thing that has just been mentioned: *Of the phrases "go crazy" and "go nuts," the latter term is used less frequently.* **2 the latter sth** closer to the end of a period of time: *the latter part of the 19th century*

laud·a·ble /ˈlɔdəbəl/ *adj.* (formal) deserving praise or admiration

laud·a·to·ry /ˈlɔdəˌtɔri/ *adj.* (formal) expressing praise or admiration: *laudatory comments about his work*

laugh[1] /læf/ *v.* **1** [I] to make a sound with your voice, usually while smiling, because you think something is funny → LAUGHTER, SMILE: *How come no one ever **laughs at** my jokes?* | *The story **made** me **laugh** so hard I started crying.* | *Nancy and I **burst out laughing*** (=suddenly started laughing).

THESAURUS

giggle – to laugh quickly in a high voice, especially because you think something is very funny or because you are nervous or embarrassed
chuckle – to laugh quietly
cackle – to laugh in an unpleasant loud way
snicker – to laugh quietly in an unkind way
titter – to laugh quietly, especially in a nervous way
guffaw – to laugh loudly

2 no laughing matter something serious that should not be joked about [ORIGIN: Old English *hliehhan*]

laugh at sb/sth *phr. v.* to make unkind or funny

L

remarks about someone: *If I told them my real feelings, they would just laugh at me.*

laugh sth ↔ **off** *phr. v.* to joke about something in order to pretend that it is not very serious or important: *She laughed off their insults.*

laugh² *n.* **1** [C] the sound you make when you laugh → SMILE: *a loud laugh* **2 have the last laugh** to finally be successful after someone has criticized or defeated you

laugh·a·ble /ˈlæfəbəl/ *adj.* impossible to be treated seriously because of being so silly, bad, or difficult to believe (SYN) **ridiculous**

laugh·ing·stock /ˈlæfɪŋˌstɑk/ *n.* [C] someone who has done something silly or stupid, and whom people make jokes about and laugh at in a way that is not nice

laugh·ter /ˈlæftɚ/ *n.* [U] the action of laughing, or the sound of people laughing: *Everyone **burst into laughter*** (=started laughing). | *The audience **roared with laughter**.*

launch¹ /lɔntʃ, lɑntʃ/ *v.* [T] **1** to start something new, such as an activity, plan, or profession: *The movie launched his acting career.* **2** to send a weapon or a space vehicle into the sky or into space **3** to put a boat or ship into the water [ORIGIN: 1300—1400 Old North French *lancher*, from Late Latin *lanceare* "to throw a lance"]

launch into sth *phr. v.* to suddenly start describing something or criticizing something: *He launched into the story of his life.*

launch² *n.* [C] an occasion at which a new product is shown or made available

ˈlaunch pad *n.* [C] the area from which a space vehicle, ROCKET, etc. is sent into space

laun·der /ˈlɔndɚ, ˈlɑn-/ *v.* [T] **1** to put stolen money into legal businesses or bank accounts in order to hide it or use it **2** (formal) to wash clothes

Laun·dro·mat /ˈlɔndrəˌmæt, ˈlɑn-/ *n.* [C] (trademark) a place where you pay money to wash your clothes in machines

laun·dry /ˈlɔndri, ˈlɑn-/ *n.* (plural **laundries**) **1** [U] clothes, sheets, etc. that need to be washed, or that have already been washed: *I have to **do the laundry*** (=wash clothes, sheets, etc.). | *a **laundry basket*** **2** [C] a place or business where clothes etc. are washed and IRONed

lau·re·ate /ˈlɔriɪt, ˈlɑr-/ *n.* [C] (formal) someone who has been given an important prize: *a Nobel laureate*

lau·rel /ˈlɔrəl, ˈlɑr-/ *n.* [C] **1** a small tree with smooth shiny dark green leaves that do not fall off in winter **2 rest/sit on your laurels** to be satisfied with what you have achieved and therefore stop trying to achieve anything new

la·va /ˈlɑvə, ˈlævə/ *n.* [U] **1** EARTH SCIENCES hot melted rock that flows from a VOLCANO → *see picture at* VOLCANO **2** EARTH SCIENCES this rock when it becomes cold and solid

lav·a·to·ry /ˈlævəˌtɔri/ *n.* (plural **lavatories**) [C] (formal) a room with a toilet in it [ORIGIN: 1300—1400 Medieval Latin *lavatorium* "bowl for washing in," from Latin *lavare* "to wash"]

> THESAURUS **toilet, bathroom, restroom, women's/ladies' room, men's room, latrine** → TOILET

lav·en·der /ˈlævəndɚ/ *n.* **1** [C,U] a plant with purple flowers that have a strong pleasant smell **2** [U] a pale purple color [ORIGIN: 1300—1400 Anglo-French *lavendre*, from Medieval Latin *lavandula*]

lav·ish¹ /ˈlævɪʃ/ *adj.* very generous and often expensive or complicated: *lavish gifts* | *He is **lavish with** his praise.*

lavish² *v.*

lavish sth **on** sb *phr. v.* to give someone a lot of something good: *They lavish a lot of attention on their children.*

law /lɔ/ *n.* **1** [singular, U] the system of rules that people in a country, city, or state must obey → LEGAL: *Drunk driving is **against the law*** (=illegal). | *He never intended to **break the law*** (=do something illegal). **2** [C] a rule that people in a particular country, city, or local area must obey: ***Under** a new **law**, drivers may not use cell phones.*

> THESAURUS **rule, regulation, restriction** → RULE¹

3 [U] the study of law, or the profession involving laws: *She **practices law*** (=works as a lawyer) *in New York.* **4 the law** the police: *Is he in trouble with the law?* **5 law and order** a situation in which people respect the law, and crime is controlled by the police, the prison system, etc.: *The national guard was sent in to restore law and order.* **6** [C] a statement that describes and explains how something works: *the **law of** gravity* | *the economic law of supply and demand* [ORIGIN: Old English *lagu*]

ˈlaw-aˌbiding *adj.* respectful of the law and obeying it

law·ful /ˈlɔfəl/ *adj.* (formal) considered by the government or courts of law to be legal

law·less /ˈlɔlɪs/ *adj.* (formal) not obeying the law, or not controlled by law

lawn /lɔn/ *n.* [C] an area of ground around a house or in a park that is covered with grass: *I should **mow the lawn*** (=cut the grass) *today.* [ORIGIN: 1500—1600 Old French *launde* "open space between woods"]

lawn mower, lawn·mow·er /ˈlɔnˌmoʊɚ/ *n.* [C] a machine that you use to cut the grass

ˌlaw of deˈmand *n.* **the law of demand** ECONOMICS an idea which says that people will buy more of a product when its price decreases and buy less of a product when its price increases → LAW OF SUPPLY

ˌlaw of inˈertia *n.* **the law of inertia** PHYSICS another name for NEWTON'S FIRST LAW

ˌlaw of reˈflection *n.* **the law of reflection** PHYSICS a scientific rule which says that when a RAY of light hits a surface and then REFLECTS (=is sent back) off that surface, the angle between the light and the surface is the same when it hits as when it reflects off

ˌlaw of supˈply *n.* **the law of supply** ECONOMICS an idea which says that when the demand for a product stays the same, an increase in supply leads to a lower price, and a decrease in supply leads to a higher price ➔ LAW OF DEMAND

ˈlaw school *n.* [C,U] a part of a university or a special school where you study to become a lawyer after you get your B.A.

law·suit /ˈlɔsut/ *n.* [C] a problem or complaint that someone brings to a court of law to be settled, especially for money: *They have* ***filed*** *a* ***lawsuit*** *against the builders.*

law·yer /ˈlɔyɚ/ *n.* [C] someone whose job is to advise people about laws, write formal agreements, or represent people in court (SYN) **attorney**

lax /læks/ *adj.* not strict or careful about standards of behavior, work, safety, etc.: *The airport has been criticized for* ***lax security.*** ➔ STRICT —**laxity** *n.* [U]

lax·a·tive /ˈlæksət̬ɪv/ *n.* [C] a medicine or something that you eat that makes your BOWELS empty easily —**laxative** *adj.*

lay¹ /leɪ/ *v.* (past tense and past participle **laid**) **1** [T] to put someone or something carefully into a particular position: *Lay the peppers* ***on*** *the chicken.* | *Martha* ***laid*** *the baby* ***down.***

> **USAGE**
>
> **Lay** means to put something down in a flat position: *They laid the map on the table.*
> **Lie** has two different meanings:
> – to be in or move into a flat position on the floor, a bed, etc.: *She was lying on a sofa.* The past tense for this meaning of lie is **lay**: *He lay on the bed.*
> – to say something that is not true: *I know that he's lying.* The past tense for this meaning of lie is **lied**: *She lied because she didn't want to make him unhappy.*

2 lay bricks/carpet/cable etc. to put or attach something in the correct place, especially onto something flat or under the ground: ***laying down*** *a new bedroom carpet* **3** [I,T] if a bird, insect, etc. lays eggs, it produces them from its body **4 lay a finger/hand on sb** to hurt someone, especially to hit him/her: *He never laid a finger on her.* **5 lay blame/criticism/emphasis etc.** (formal) to blame, criticize, emphasize, etc. **6 lay yourself open to blame/criticism etc.** to do something that makes you likely to be blamed, criticized, etc.

lay sth ↔ **down** *phr. v.* to officially state rules, methods, etc. that someone must obey or use: *The rules have already been laid down.*

lay into sb *phr. v.* (informal) to attack someone physically or criticize him/her angrily: *You should have heard Dad laying into Tommy.*

lay off *phr. v.* **1 lay** sb ↔ **off** to stop employing someone, especially when there is not much work to do: *500 auto workers were laid off.* **2 lay off** sth (spoken) to stop doing, having, or using something: *Don't you think you should lay off alcohol for a while?* **3 lay off** sb to stop annoying, hurting, or criticizing someone: *Lay off him, he's just a kid.*

lay sth ↔ **out** *phr. v.* **1** to spread something out: *Pam laid her dress out on the bed.* **2** (informal) to explain or describe a plan, idea, etc.: *The mayor laid out her budget proposal at Tuesday's meeting.*

lay up *phr. v.* **be laid up (with sth)** to have to stay in bed because you are sick or injured: *He's laid up with a broken collarbone.*

lay² *v.* the past tense of LIE

lay³ *adj.* [only before noun] not trained in a particular profession or subject: *a lay preacher*

lay·a·way /ˈleɪəˌweɪ/ *n.* [U] a way of buying goods in which the goods are kept by the seller for a small amount of money until the full price is paid

lay·er¹ /ˈleɪɚ/ (Ac) *n.* [C] **1** an amount of a substance that covers all of a surface: *a* ***layer of*** *dust on the desk* **2** something that is placed on or between other things: *several* ***layers of*** *clothing* | *The lower layer of rock is normally older than the upper layer.*

layer² *v.* [T] to put something down in layers: *The lemon cake is* ***layered with*** *raspberries on top.*

lay·man /ˈleɪmən/ *n.* [C] someone who is not trained in a particular subject or type of work: *He has written a book on astronomy for* ***the layman*** (=people in general).

lay·off /ˈleɪɔf/ *n.* [C] the act of stopping a worker's employment because there is not enough work: *There have been layoffs in the computer industry.*

lay·out /ˈleɪaʊt/ *n.* [C,U] **1** the way things are arranged in a particular area or place: *changes in the office layout* **2** the way in which writing and pictures are arranged on a page

lay·o·ver /ˈleɪˌoʊvɚ/ *n.* [C] a short stay somewhere between parts of a trip: *We'll have a two-hour layover in Dallas.*

lay·per·son /ˈleɪˌpɚsən/ *n.* [C] a word meaning a LAYMAN that is used when the person could be a man or a woman

laze /leɪz/ *v.* [I] to relax and enjoy yourself without doing very much: *Jeff spent the morning just lazing in the yard.*

la·zy /ˈleɪzi/ *adj.* (comparative **lazier**, superlative **laziest**) **1** not liking to do work or to make an effort: *the laziest boy in the class* | *I've gotten a little lazy about cooking.*

> **THESAURUS**
>
> **idle** (old-fashioned) – lazy and wasting time when there is work to do: *In the story, Jack is an idle boy who would rather play than work.*
> **indolent** (formal) – lazy and living a comfortable

life: *The news startled him out of his state of indolent contentment.*
shiftless – lazy and not at all interested in working: *Some politicians seem to think that anyone who doesn't have a job is shiftless.*
slack – lazy and not taking enough care to do things correctly: *Some of the students were slack, not bothering to even turn in their homework.*
slothful (literary) – lazy and not doing the things you ought to do: *She tells slothful Americans to get out and exercise.*

2 a lazy time is spent relaxing: *lazy summer afternoons*

lb the written abbreviation of POUND [ORIGIN: 1300—1400 Latin *libra* "pound"]

lead¹ /lid/ *v.* (past tense and past participle **led** /lɛd/)
1 GUIDE [T] to take a person or animal to a place by going with or in front of the person or animal: *Isabel **led us up/down** some narrow stairs and into a small room.* | *We led the horses along the river.*

THESAURUS

guide – to take someone to or through a place you know well, especially in order to show him/her interesting things: *She guides tourists around the White House.*
direct (formal) – to explain to someone how to get somewhere: *He directed them to the station.*
point – to show someone which direction to go: *A sign pointed the way.*
show – to take someone somewhere, especially when it is hard for him or her to find the way: *Could you show Mrs. Wright the way to the university library?*
escort – to take someone somewhere, protecting him or her or showing him or her the way: *The president was escorted by his bodyguards.*
usher (formal) – to show someone the way to somewhere nearby, usually into or out of a room or building: *His secretary ushered us into his office.*

2 GO IN FRONT [I,T] to go in front of a group of people or vehicles: *The high school band is leading the parade.*
3 DOOR/ROAD [I] if a door, road, etc. leads somewhere, you can get there by using it: *The second door **leads to** the principal's office.*
4 CONTROL [T] to be in charge of something, especially an activity or a group of people: *Who is leading the investigation?*
5 WIN [I,T] to be winning a game or competition: *At half time, the Green Bay Packers were leading 12–0.*
6 CAUSE STH [T] to be the thing that makes someone do something or think something: *What **led** you **to** study geology?* | *Rick **led me to believe** (=made me believe) he was going to return the money.*
7 lead a normal/dull etc. life to have a normal, boring, etc. type of life
8 SUCCESS [I,T] to be more successful than other people, companies, or countries in a particular activity or area of business: *Georgia **leads** the nation **in** peanut production.*
9 lead the way a) to guide someone in a particular direction **b)** to be the first to do something good or successful: *The Japanese led the way in using robots in industry.*
10 CONVERSATION [I,T] to direct a conversation or discussion so that it develops in the way you want: *She finally led the topic around to pay raises.*

lead off ↔ sth *phr. v.*
to begin an event by doing something: *They **led off** the concert **with** a Beethoven overture.*

lead sb **on** *phr. v.*
to make someone believe something that is not true: *I thought he was in love with me, but he was just leading me on.*

lead to sth *phr. v.*
to make something happen or exist as a result of something else: *Opening the new lumber mill has led to the creation of 200 jobs.*

lead up to sth *phr. v.*
1 to come before something: *In the days leading up to the election, campaigners increased the number of phone calls to voters.*
2 to gradually introduce a subject into a conversation: *He made some remarks that were obviously leading up to a request for money.*

lead² *n.* **1** [singular] the position or situation of being in front of, or better than, everyone else in a race or competition: *Lewis is still **in the lead**.* | *Michael Phelps has **taken the lead*** (=moved into the front position in a race). **2** [singular] the distance, number of points, etc. by which one competitor is ahead of another: *The Bulls **have** a 5-point **lead over** the Celtics at halftime.* **3** [C] a piece of information that may help you to make a discovery or find the answer to a problem: *Police are pursuing all leads.* **4** [C] the main acting part in a play, movie, etc., or the main singer, dancer, etc. in a group: *Who has the lead in the school play?* | *the lead guitarist*

lead³ /lɛd/ *n.* **1** [U] a soft gray-blue metal that melts easily **2** [C,U] the substance in a pencil that makes the marks when you write

lead·er /ˈlidɚ/ *n.* [C] **1** the person who directs or controls a team, organization, country, etc.: *Most world leaders will attend the conference.* | *the **leader of** the Senate* **2** the person, organization, etc. that is better than all the others, especially in a race or competition: ***leaders in** the field of medical science*

lead·er·ship /ˈlidɚˌʃɪp/ *n.* **1** [U] the quality of being good at leading a team, organization, country, etc.: *Kids who are involved in Scouts learn leadership skills.* **2** [U] the position of being the leader of a team, organization, etc.: ***Under** Brown's **leadership**, the magazine attracted new readers.* **3** [singular] the people who lead a country, organization, etc.

lead·ing /ˈlidɪŋ/ *adj.* **1** best, most important, or most successful: *a leading athlete* **2 a leading**

question a question asked in a way that makes you give a particular answer

ˌleading ˈindicators *n.* [plural] ECONOMICS a list of important economic things that are likely to change over time, printed every month by the U.S. government and used as a sign of what is likely to happen in the U.S. ECONOMY

leaf¹ /lif/ *n.* (plural **leaves** /livz/) **1** [C] one of the flat green parts of a plant that are joined to its stem or branches: *There are still some leaves on the trees.* ➔ *see picture at* PLANT¹ **2** [C] a part of the top of a table that can be added to make the table larger **3** [U] gold or silver in a very thin sheet ➔ **turn over a new leaf** *at* TURN¹

leaf² *v.*

leaf through sth *phr. v.* to turn the pages of a book quickly, without reading it carefully

leaf·let /ˈliflɪt/ *n.* [C] a small piece of printed paper that gives information or advertises something

leaf·y /ˈlifi/ *adj.* having a lot of leaves: *green leafy vegetables*

league /lig/ *n.* [C] **1** a group of sports teams or players who play games against each other to see who is best: *major league baseball* **2** a group of people or countries that have joined together because they have similar aims, political beliefs, etc.: *the League of Nations* **3 not in the same league/out of sb's league** not having the same abilities or qualities as someone or something else: *He knows a lot more than I do – he's way out of my league.*

leak¹ /lik/ *v.* **1** [I,T] to let a liquid or gas in or out of a hole or crack: *Somebody's car must be leaking oil.* | *The roof's leaking!* **2** [I] to pass through a hole or crack: *Gas was* ***leaking out*** *of the pipes.*

THESAURUS **pour, flow, drip, ooze, gush, spurt, come out** ➔ POUR

3 [T] to deliberately give secret information to a newspaper, television company, etc.: *Details of the President's speech were* ***leaked to*** *reporters.* —**leakage** *n.* [C,U]

leak out *phr. v.* if secret information leaks out, a lot of people find out about it

leak² *n.* [C] **1** a small hole that lets liquid or gas flow into or out of something: *a leak in the water pipe*

THESAURUS **hole, crack** ➔ HOLE¹

2 a situation in which someone has secret information and gives it to someone else: *leaks from the White House*

leak·y /ˈliki/ *adj.* having a hole or crack so that liquid or gas can pass through: *a leaky faucet*

lean¹ /lin/ *v.* **1** [I] to move or bend your body in a particular position: *He* ***leaned over*** *and kissed his wife.* **2** [I] to support yourself or be supported in a position that is not straight or upright: *Brad was* ***leaning on/against*** *a wall.* ➔ *see picture on page A22* **3** [T] to put something in a sloping position against something else: *Dad* ***leaned*** *the ladder* ***against*** *the wall.*

THESAURUS

stand – to put something in an almost upright position: *He stood the Christmas tree against the wall.*

rest – to support an object by putting it on or against something: *I rested my head on the back of the chair.*

prop – to support something or keep it in a particular position: *A small mirror was propped against the wall.*

lean on sb/sth *phr. v.* to get support and encouragement from someone: *I know I can always lean on my friends.*

lean toward sth *phr. v.* to tend to agree with or support a particular set of opinions, beliefs, etc.: *Most of the church's members lean toward the political right.*

lean² *adj.* **1** thin in a healthy and attractive way. *She is lean and athletic-looking.*

THESAURUS **thin, slim, slender, slight, skinny** ➔ THIN¹

2 lean meat does not have much fat on it **3** difficult as a result of bad economic conditions or lack of money: *a lean year for the business*

lean·ing /ˈlinɪŋ/ *n.* [C] a tendency to prefer or agree with a particular set of beliefs, opinions, etc.: *liberal leanings*

leap¹ /lip/ *v.* (past tense and past participle **leaped** *or* **leapt** /lɛpt/) [I] **1** to jump high into the air or over something: *One by one, the kids were leaping into the river.*

THESAURUS **jump, spring, hurdle, vault** ➔ JUMP¹

2 to move very quickly and with a lot of energy: *Jon* ***leaped up*** *to answer the phone.*

leap at sth *phr. v.* to accept an opportunity very eagerly: *The manager needed an assistant, and Paula* ***leaped at the chance.*** [ORIGIN: Old English *hleapan*]

leap² *n.* **1** [C] a big jump **2 by/in leaps and bounds** very quickly: *Your English is improving in leaps and bounds.*

leap·frog /ˈlipfrɑg/ *n.* [U] a children's game in which someone bends over and someone else jumps over him/her

leapfrog

ˈleap year *n.* [C] a year when February has 29 days instead of

L

28, which happens every four years

learn /lɚn/ *v.* **1** [I,T] to gain knowledge of a subject or of how to do something, through experience or study: *Lisa's learning Spanish.* | *I'd like to* ***learn (how) to*** *sew.* | *We've been* ***learning about*** *electricity in school.*

USAGE

You **learn** a subject or skill when you study or practice it: *She's learning to drive.* | *Learning languages can be fun.*
If you **teach** someone a subject or skill, you help him/her learn it: *He taught me to play the guitar.* You cannot say "He learned me to ... "

THESAURUS

study – to spend time going to classes, reading, etc. to learn about a subject: *I studied French when I was in high school.*
pick sth up – to learn something without much effort, by watching or listening to other people: *I picked up some Korean when I was in the army.*
get the hang of sth – to learn how to do something, especially by practicing it: *She's fallen off the bike a lot, but she's beginning to get the hang of it.*
acquire (formal) – to develop or learn a skill: *The program helps adults acquire the skills they need to get into full-time work.*
master – to learn something so well that you understand it completely and have no difficulty with it: *It is a difficult piece of music, but she has mastered it.*

2 [T] to get to know something so well that you can easily remember it: *Have you learned your lines for the play?* **3** [I,T] (formal) to find out information, news, etc. by hearing it from someone else: *We only* ***learned about*** *the accident later.* **4 learn sth the hard way** to understand something by learning from your mistakes and experiences: *I've learned the hard way that it's better to keep business and friendship separate.* **5 learn your lesson** to suffer so much after doing something wrong that you will not do it again: *I didn't punish him because I thought he had learned his lesson.* [ORIGIN: Old English *leornian*] —**learner** *n.* [C]: *a* ***fast/quick/ slow learner***

L

learn·ed /ˈlɚnɪd/ *adj.* (formal) having a lot of knowledge because you have read and studied a lot

learn·ing /ˈlɚnɪŋ/ *n.* [U] knowledge gained through reading and study

ˈlearning curve *n.* [C] the rate at which you learn a new skill: *I like my new job, but it's been* ***a steep learning curve*** (=I had to learn a lot very quickly).

ˈlearning disaˌbility *n.* [C] a mental problem that affects a child's ability to learn

lease¹ /lis/ *n.* **1** [C] a legal agreement that allows you to use a building, property, etc. when you pay rent: *a two-year* ***lease on*** *the apartment* | *We* ***signed*** *the* ***lease*** *in December.* **2 a new/fresh lease on life** the feeling of being healthy, active, or happy again after being sick or unhappy

lease² *v.* [T] to use or let someone use buildings, property, etc. when s/he pays rent: *The lofts have been* ***leased to*** *artists.*

leash /liʃ/ *n.* [C] a piece of rope, leather, etc. fastened to a dog's collar in order to control the dog: *All dogs in the park must be kept* ***on a leash.***

least¹ /list/ *determiner, pron.* [the superlative of "little"] **1 at least a)** not less than a particular number or amount: *The thunderstorm lasted at least two hours.* **b)** used when mentioning an advantage to show that a situation is not as bad as it seems: *Well, at least you got your money back.* **c)** said when you want to correct or change something you have just said: *His name is Jerry. At least, I think it is.* **d)** even if nothing else is said or done: *Will you at least say you're sorry?* **2 the least sb could do** said when you think someone should do something to help someone else: *The least he could do is help you clean up.* **3 to say the least** used in order to show that something is more serious than you are actually saying: *Their relationship is unusual, to say the least.* **4** the smallest number or amount ➔ LESS: *Compared to the other cakes, this one has the least amount of calories.*

least² *adv.* **1** less than anything or anyone else: *It always happens when you least expect it.* | *I'm the least experienced person on the team.* **2 least of all** especially not: *I don't like any of them, least of all Debbie.*

ˌleast ˌcommon deˈnominator *n.* [C] MATH the smallest positive INTEGER (=whole number such as 1, 2, 3, 4, etc.) that can be divided exactly by all the DENOMINATORS (=bottom numbers) in a set of FRACTIONS

leath·er /ˈlɛðɚ/ *n.* [U] animal skin that has been treated to preserve it, and is used for making shoes, etc. ➔ SUEDE: *a leather belt* [ORIGIN: Old English *lether*] ➔ *see picture at* MATERIAL¹

leath·er·y /ˈlɛðəri/ *adj.* hard and stiff like leather: *leathery skin*

leave¹ /liv/ *v.* (past tense and past participle **left** /lɛft/, present participle **leaving**)
1 GO AWAY [I,T] to go away from a place or person: *Jones quickly left the room.* | *I'm* ***leaving for*** (=going to) *Milwaukee in an hour.* | *I feel a little lonely now the kids have all left home* (=are no longer living at home).

THESAURUS

Leave a place
go away – to leave a place, often for a long time or permanently: *The kids have gone away to summer camp.* | *Her husband went away and left her.*
set off – to start going somewhere: *What time do you set off?*
drive off/away – to leave somewhere in a car: *She got into her car and drove off.*

take off – if a plane takes off, it leaves the ground and goes up into the sky: *The plane took off two hours late.*
depart (formal) – if a plane, train or bus departs, it leaves a place: *The next train will depart at 10:30.*
withdraw – if an army withdraws from a place, it leaves: *U.S. forces will start to withdraw at the beginning of April.*

Leave your boyfriend/wife, etc.
split up with – to end your relationship with your boyfriend, wife, etc.: *She split up with her boyfriend after she saw him with another girl.*
walk out on sb – to suddenly end your relationship with someone in a way that seems unfair and unkind: *Her first husband walked out on her after just two years of marriage.*
leave your job or school → QUIT

2 leave sb alone (spoken) used in order to tell someone to stop annoying or upsetting someone else: *Just stop asking questions and leave me alone.* **3 leave sth alone** (spoken) used in order to tell someone to stop touching something: *Timmy! Leave that alone – you'll break it!* **4** STAY IN POSITION/STATE [T] to make or let something stay in a particular state, place, or position when you are not there. *We're going to leave the car at the airport.* **5** PUT STH IN A PLACE [T] to put something in a place for someone: *Just leave the map on the table.* | *Please* ***leave a message*** *and I'll get back to you.* **6** FORGET [T] to forget to take something with you when you leave a place: *I think I left my keys in the car.* **7 be left** to remain after everything else has been taken away: *Is there any coffee left?* **8** NOT DO STH [T] to not do something until later: *Let's* ***leave*** *the dishes* ***for*** *the morning.* **9** HUSBAND/WIFE [I,T] to stop living with your husband or wife: *Tammy's husband left her last year.* **10** LET SB DECIDE [T] to let someone decide something or be responsible for something: ***Leave*** *the details* ***to*** *me; I'll arrange everything.* **11** GIVE AFTER DEATH [T] to give something to someone after you die: *She* ***left*** *a lot of money* ***to*** *her son.*

THESAURUS give, bequeath → GIVE[1]

12 leave it at that (spoken) to not say or do anything more about a situation: *He's not going – let's just leave it at that.* **13 leave a mark/stain etc.** to make a mark, STAIN, etc. that remains afterward: *Make sure that you don't leave any footprints.* **14 leave a lot to be desired** to be very unsatisfactory: *Though the play leaves a lot to be desired, the costumes are beautiful.* **15 from where sb left off** from the place where you stopped: *Tomorrow, we'll start the reading from where we left off.* [ORIGIN: Old English]

leave sb/sth behind *phr. v.*
to forget to take something with you when you leave a place, or to not take something on purpose: *Did you leave your umbrella behind in the restaurant?*

leave sb/sth ↔ **out** *phr. v.*
1 to not include someone or something in a group, list, activity, etc.: *The stew will still taste okay if we leave out the wine.* **2 be/feel left out** to feel as if you are not accepted or welcome in a social group: *I always felt left out when my sister's friends were here.*

leave[2] *n.* **1** [U] time that you are allowed to spend away from your work because you are sick, have had a baby, etc.: *How much* ***sick leave*** *have you taken?*

THESAURUS vacation, holiday, break → VACATION

2 leave of absence a period of time that you are allowed to spend away from work for a particular purpose

leaves /livz/ *n.* the plural of LEAF

lech·er·ous /ˈlɛtʃərəs/ *adj.* (disapproving) a lecherous man is always thinking about sex

lec·tern /ˈlɛktən/ *n.* [C] a high desk that you stand behind when you give a speech

lec·ture[1] /ˈlɛktʃɚ/ (Ac) *n.* [C] **1** a long talk to a group of people about a particular subject: *She's* ***giving*** *a* ***lecture on*** *modern art.* | *Students take notes while* ***listening to lectures***.

THESAURUS lesson, course, seminar → CLASS[1]

2 a long serious talk that criticizes someone or warns him/her about something: *My parents* ***gave*** *me another* ***lecture about*** *my school work.* [ORIGIN: 1200—1300 Late Latin *lectura* "act of reading," from Latin *legere* "to read"]

lecture[2] *v.* **1** [T] to talk angrily or seriously to someone in order to criticize or warn him/her: *I wish you'd stop* ***lecturing*** *me* ***about*** *smoking.* **2** [I] to teach a group of people about a particular subject, especially at a college: *He lectures on psychiatry at the medical school.*

led /lɛd/ *v.* the past tense and past participle of LEAD

ledge /lɛdʒ/ *n.* [C] **1** a narrow flat surface like a shelf, that sticks out from the side of a building: *a window ledge* **2** a narrow flat surface of rock, that is parallel to the ground

ledg·er /ˈlɛdʒɚ/ *n.* [C] a book in which a bank, business, etc. records the money received and spent → RECORD[1]

THESAURUS record, file, accounts, books → RECORD[1]

leech /litʃ/ *n.* [C] a small soft creature that attaches itself to an animal in order to drink its blood

leek /lik/ *n.* [C] a vegetable with long straight green leaves, that tastes like an onion

leer /lɪr/ *v.* [I] to look at someone in an unpleasant way that shows that you think s/he is sexually attractive —**leer** *n.* [C]

leer·y /ˈlɪri/ *adj.* worried and unable to trust someone or something: *The girl was **leery of** strangers.*

lee·way /ˈliweɪ/ *n.* [U] freedom to do things in the way you want to: *Students **have** some **leeway** in what they can write about.*

left[1] /lɛft/ *adj.* **1** your left side is the side of your body that contains your heart (ANT) **right**: *He broke his left leg.* **2** on the same side of something as your left side (ANT) **right**: *Our house is the first one on the left side of the street.*

left[2] *adv.* toward the left side (ANT) **right**: ***Turn left** at the next street.*

left[3] *n.* [C] **1** the left side or direction (ANT) **right**: *It's the second door **on your/the left**.* **2 the left/Left** POLITICS political parties or other groups who believe that the government should use money received from taxes to pay for social services and should limit the power of businesses ➔ LIBERAL (ANT) **right**

left[4] *v.* the past tense and past participle of LEAVE

ˈleft field *n.* **1 in/from left field** (informal) unusual or strange compared to the way that people usually behave: *Some of his ideas are **way out in left field*** (=very strange). **2** [singular] the area in baseball in the left side of the OUTFIELD

ˌleft-ˈhand *adj.* on the left side of something: *the top left-hand drawer*

ˌleft-ˈhanded *adj.* **1** someone who is left-handed uses his/her left hand to do most things **2** done with the left hand: *a left-handed throw* **3** made to be used with the left hand: *left-handed scissors* —**left-handed** *adv.*

left·o·vers /ˈlɛftˌoʊvɚz/ *n.* [plural] food that remains at the end of a meal and is kept to be eaten later

ˌleft-ˈwing *adj.* POLITICS a left-wing person or group supports the ideas and beliefs of SOCIALISM or COMMUNISM (ANT) **right-wing**: *a left-wing newspaper* —**left-wing** *n.* [singular] —**left-winger** *n.* [C]

L

leg /lɛg/ *n.*

1 BODY PART [C] one of the two long parts of your body that you use to stand or walk, or a similar part on an animal or insect: *How did you hurt **your leg**? | Mia was sitting with her legs crossed. | She fell and broke her **left/right leg**.* ➔ *see picture on page A16*

2 FURNITURE [C] one of the upright parts that support a piece of furniture: *a table leg*

3 PANTS [C] the part of your pants that covers your leg

4 FOOD [C,U] the leg of an animal eaten as food: *roast leg of lamb*

5 TRIP/RACE ETC. [C] a part of a long trip, race, process, etc. that is done one part at a time: *She started the last leg of the tour last week.*

6 TRIANGLE [C] MATH one of the two sides of a TRIANGLE that meet and form an angle of 90°

7 -legged having a particular number or type of legs: *a three-legged cat*

8 leg room space in which to put your legs comfortably when you are sitting in a car, theater, etc.: *There wasn't enough leg room.*

9 not have a leg to stand on (informal) to be in a situation where you cannot prove or legally support what you say [ORIGIN: 1200—1300 Old Norse *leggr*] ➔ **on its last legs** *at* LAST[1]

leg·a·cy /ˈlɛgəsi/ *n.* (plural **legacies**) [C] **1** a situation that exists as a result of things that happened at an earlier time: *Racial tension in the country is a **legacy of** slavery.* **2** LAW money or property that you receive from someone after s/he dies

le·gal /ˈligəl/ (Ac) *adj.* **1** allowed, ordered, or approved by law (ANT) **illegal**: *Is it legal to park here overnight? | a legal agreement | Divorce finally **became legal** there in 1992.* **2** relating to the law: *the legal system | If you don't pay soon, we'll be forced to **take legal action*** (=go to court). *| Parents are **under a legal obligation** to ensure that their child receives an education.* [ORIGIN: 1400—1500 French, Latin *legalis*, from *lex* "law"] —**legally** *adv.*: *You can't legally buy alcohol until you're 21. | Teachers are legally responsible for the care of students.* —**legality** /lɪˈgæləṭi/ *n.* [U]: *The legality of his actions has been questioned.*

le·gal·ize /ˈligəˌlaɪz/ *v.* [T] to make something legal that was not legal before: *a campaign to legalize marijuana* —**legalization** /ˌligələˈzeɪʃən/ *n.* [U]

leg·end /ˈlɛdʒənd/ *n.* **1** [C,U] ENG. LANG. ARTS an old well-known story, often about brave people or adventures, or all stories of this kind: ***the legend of** King Arthur*

> THESAURUS **story, tale, myth, fable** ➔ STORY

2 [C] someone who is famous and admired for being extremely good at doing something: *Elvis Presley, the rock and roll legend*

leg·end·ar·y /ˈlɛdʒənˌdɛri/ *adj.* **1** famous and admired: *the legendary baseball player Joe DiMaggio*

> THESAURUS **famous, well-known, infamous, notorious, celebrated, renowned** ➔ FAMOUS

2 talked or read about in legends

leg·er·de·main /ˌlɛdʒɚdəˈmeɪn/ *n.* [U] (old-fashioned) skillful use of your hands when performing tricks

leg·gings /ˈlɛgɪŋz/ *n.* [plural] women's pants that stretch to fit the shape of the body

leg·i·ble /ˈlɛdʒəbəl/ *adj.* written or printed clearly enough for you to read (ANT) **illegible**: *His writing was barely legible.* —**legibly** *adv.*

le·gion /ˈlidʒən/ *n.* [C] a large group of soldiers or people

leg·is·late /ˈlɛdʒəˌsleɪt/ (Ac) *v.* [I,T] POLITICS to make a law about something: *The group wants to* ***legislate against*** *abortion.* | *Can Congress legislate a national minimum drinking age?*

leg·is·la·tion /ˌlɛdʒəˈsleɪʃən/ (Ac) *n.* [U] **1** LAW a law or set of laws: *human rights legislation* | *The new legislation has been widely supported by the business community.* **2** POLITICS the act of making laws: *Legislation can be an extremely lengthy process.*

leg·is·la·tive /ˈlɛdʒəˌsleɪt̬ɪv/ (Ac) *adj.* POLITICS relating to laws or to making laws: *legislative leaders* | *the legislative branch of government* | *The new assemblies will have no* ***legislative power***.

leg·is·la·tor /ˈlɛdʒəˌsleɪt̬ɚ/ (Ac) *n.* [C] POLITICS an elected government official who is involved in making laws: *A state legislator cannot stay in office for more than 12 years.* [ORIGIN: 1400—1500 Latin *legis lator* "suggester of a law"]

leg·is·la·ture /ˈlɛdʒəˌsleɪtʃɚ/ (Ac) *n.* [C] POLITICS an institution that has the power to make or change laws: *the Ohio state legislature* | *The legislature passed a law moving the election to April.*

le·git /lɪˈdʒɪt/ *adj.* (spoken) legitimate

le·git·i·mate /ləˈdʒɪt̬əmɪt/ *adj.* **1** fair or reasonable: *She has a legitimate reason for being late.* **2** operating legally or according to the law: *legitimate business activities* —**legitimacy** *n.* [U]

lei·sure /ˈliʒɚ/ *n.* [U] **1** time when you are not working and can do things you enjoy: *I spend most of my* ***leisure time*** *reading.* **2 at sb's leisure** as slowly as you want, and when you want: *Read it at your leisure.*

lei·sure·ly /ˈliʒɚli/ *adj.* moving or done in a relaxed way: *a leisurely walk around the park*

THESAURUS slow, sluggish, tardy → SLOW[1]

lem·on /ˈlɛmən/ *n.* [C,U] a yellow fruit that has a sour-tasting juice [ORIGIN: 1300—1400 French *limon*, from Medieval Latin *limo*, from Arabic *laymun*] → *see picture on page 414*

lem·on·ade /ˌlɛməˈneɪd/ *n.* [U] a drink made with lemon juice, sugar, and water

lend /lɛnd/ *v.* (past tense and past participle **lent** /lɛnt/) [T] **1** to let someone borrow money or something that belongs to you for a short time: *Could you lend me your bike?*

USAGE

If you **lend** something to someone, you give it to him/her so that s/he can use it for a short time: *I lent him my jacket.* | *Could you lend me some money?* You cannot say "Could you borrow me some money?"

If you **borrow** something from someone, you take something that belongs to him/her for a short time, with his/her permission, and then give it back: *Can I borrow your pen?* You cannot say "Can I lend your pen?"

2 if a bank lends money, it lets someone borrow it if s/he pays it back with an additional amount of money: *This bank* ***lends*** *a lot of money* ***to*** *local businesses.* **3 lend (sb) a hand** to help someone do something, especially something that needs physical effort: *Lend me a hand with this box.* **4 sth lends itself to sth** used to say that something is appropriate for being used in a particular way: *Nature lends itself to drawing and painting.* **5** to give something a particular quality: *The balloons lend a festive air to the park.* [ORIGIN: Old English *lænan*, from *læn*] —**lender** *n.* [C]

length /lɛŋkθ, lɛnθ/ *n.* **1** [C,U] the measurement of something from one end to the other: *The* ***length of*** *the room is five feet.* | *a pole about seven feet* ***in length*** → *see picture at* DIMENSION **2** [C,U] the amount of time that you spend doing something or that something continues for: *the* ***length of*** *your stay in the hospital* **3** [C,U] the amount of writing in a book, article, etc., or the amount of time that a movie, play, etc. continues for: *His new film is nearly twice the length of his last one.* **4 go to great lengths to do sth** to be willing to use many different methods to achieve something you want: *She went to great lengths to help us.* **5 at length** for a long time: *She spoke* ***at length*** *on the dangers of smoking.* **6** [C] a piece of something that is long and thin: *two* ***lengths of*** *rope*

length·en /ˈlɛŋkθən/ *v.* [I,T] to make something longer, or to become longer (ANT) **shorten**: *I need this dress lengthened.*

length·wise /ˈlɛŋkθwaɪz/ *also* **length·ways** /ˈlɛŋkθweɪz/ *adv.* in the direction or position of the longest side: *Fold the cloth lengthwise.*

length·y /ˈlɛŋkθi/ *adj.* continuing for a long time: *The magazine published a lengthy interview with the French president.* | *a lengthy period of economic growth*

le·ni·ent /ˈliniənt, ˈlinyənt/ *adj.* not strict in the way you punish someone or control his/her behavior: *She was too* ***lenient with*** *the children.* → STRICT —**leniency** *n.* [U]

lens /lɛnz/ *n.* [C] **1** SCIENCE a piece of curved glass or plastic that makes things look bigger, smaller, or clearer, for example in a pair of GLASSES, or in a TELESCOPE or a MICROSCOPE: *glasses with thick lenses* → *see picture at* MICROSCOPE **2** BIOLOGY the clear part inside your eye that FOCUSes so you can see things clearly

Lent /lɛnt/ *n.* the 40 days before Easter, when some Christians stop eating particular things or stop particular habits [ORIGIN: 1200—1300 *Lenten* "springtime, Lent" (11—17 centuries), from Old English *lengten*; because the days get longer in spring]

lent *v.* the past tense and past participle of LEND

len·til /ˈlɛntəl/ *n.* [C] a small round seed which has been dried and can be cooked

Le·o /ˈlioʊ/ *n.* **1** [U] the fifth sign of the ZODIAC, represented by a lion **2** [C] someone born between July 23 and August 22

leopard

leop·ard /ˈlɛpɚd/ *n.* [C] a large wild cat with yellow fur and black spots, from Africa and southern Asia [ORIGIN: 1200—1300 Old French *leupart*, from Late Latin *leopardus*, from Greek, from *leon* "lion" + *pardos* "leopard"]

le·o·tard /ˈliəˌtɑrd/ *n.* [C] a tight-fitting piece of women's clothing that covers the body from the neck to the top of the legs, worn especially while exercising [ORIGIN: 1800—1900 Jules *Léotard* (1830-70), French trapeze artist who invented it]

lep·er /ˈlɛpɚ/ *n.* [C] someone who has leprosy

lep·ro·sy /ˈlɛprəsi/ *n.* [U] a serious infectious disease in which someone's flesh is gradually destroyed —**leprous** /ˈlɛprəs/ *adj.*

les·bi·an /ˈlɛzbiən/ *n.* [C] a woman who is sexually attracted to other women → HOMOSEXUAL, GAY

le·sion /ˈliʒən/ *n.* [C] **1** BIOLOGY a wound or a sore infected area on someone's skin: *Many workers developed* ***skin lesions*** *from handling fiberglass.* **2** BIOLOGY a dangerous change in part of someone's body such as his/her lungs or brain, caused by injury or illness: *brain lesions found in Alzheimer's patients*

L

less /lɛs/ *quantifier, pron., adv.* [the comparative of "little"] **1** a smaller amount, or to a smaller degree (ANT) **more**: *The job involves much less stress than my last one.* | *I'm trying to exercise more and eat less.* | *Women generally earn* ***less*** *money* ***than*** *men.* | *She spends* ***less of*** *her time playing tennis now.* **2 less and less** gradually becoming smaller in amount or degree: *We seem to be spending less and less time together.* **3 no less than sth** used to emphasize that an amount or number is large: *I watched him eat no less than three pizzas.* **4 nothing less than sth** used to emphasize how serious or important something is: *Her death was nothing less than a tragedy.*

GRAMMAR

less, fewer

Use **less** before U nouns: *He earns less money than she does.*

Use **fewer** before plural noun forms: *There are fewer flights on Sundays.*

less·en /ˈlɛsən/ *v.* [I,T] to become smaller in size, amount, importance, or value, or to make something do this → REDUCE: *A low-fat diet can lessen the risk of heart disease.*

THESAURUS **relieve, alleviate, palliate** → REDUCE

less·er /ˈlɛsɚ/ *adj.* **1** (formal) not as large, as important, or as much as something else: *The same is true for Argentina, and to a* ***lesser extent*** *Chile.* | *These wounds would have killed* ***a lesser man*** (=someone not as strong or brave). **2 the lesser of two evils** the less bad or harmful of two bad choices —**lesser** *adv.*: *a lesser-known artist*

les·son /ˈlɛsən/ *n.* [C] **1** a period of time in which someone is taught a particular subject or skill: *I* ***have*** *a guitar* ***lesson*** *today.* | *Hannah is* ***taking*** *cooking* ***lessons from*** *a professional chef.*

THESAURUS **course, lecture, seminar** → CLASS[1]

2 an experience, especially a bad one, that makes you more careful in the future: *Our town's experience with the fire should serve as a lesson to the entire state.* [ORIGIN: 1100—1200 Old French *leçon*, from Latin *lectio* "act of reading"] → **learn your lesson** *at* LEARN, **teach sb a lesson** *at* TEACH

let /lɛt/ *v.* (past tense and past participle **let**, present participle **letting**) **1** [T] to allow someone to do something, or allow something to happen: *I wanted to go but my mother wouldn't let me.* | *Ed lets me borrow his car whenever I want.* | *Don't pick up the phone – let the answering machine get it.* | *Let me finish this, then we can go.*

THESAURUS **allow, permit, authorize, sanction, condone** → ALLOW

2 let go to stop holding someone or something: *You can* ***let go of*** *my hand when we've crossed the street.* **3 let sb go a)** to allow a person or animal to leave a place where they have been kept: *The police let her go after two hours.* **b)** to dismiss someone from his/her job: *I'm afraid we have to let you go.* **4 let sb know** to tell someone something: *Could you* ***let*** *me* ***know when*** *you're done?* **5 let alone** used to say that because one thing does not happen, is not true, etc. another thing cannot possibly happen or be true: *I don't have $10, let alone $10,000!* **6 let sth go/pass** to decide not to react to something bad or annoying that someone has said or done: *I'll let it go this time, but don't be late again.* **7 let sb/sth be** *also* **let sb/sth alone** to stop annoying someone, asking questions, or trying to change things: *Your mother's had a hard day, so just let her be.*

SPOKEN PHRASES

8 let's is the short form of "let us," used when you want to suggest that someone or a group of people do something with you: *I'm hungry; let's eat.* | ***Let's not** talk about this right now.* **9 let's see a)** said when you are going to try to do something: ***Let's see if/whether** Andy's home.* **b)** said when you pause because you cannot remember or find something: *Now let's see, where did I put it?* **c)** said to ask someone to show you something: *"I got a new dress." "Really? Let's see."* **10 let's hope (that)** said when you hope something is true or will happen: *Let's hope she didn't hear what we were saying.* **11 let me do sth** said when you are offering to help someone: *Let me carry that for you.* **12 let me tell you** said to emphasize a statement: *It was a really great party, let me tell you.*

[ORIGIN: Old English *lætan*]

let sb ↔ **down** *phr. v.* to make someone feel disappointed because you have behaved badly or have not done what you said you would do ➔ LETDOWN

let sb/sth ↔ **in** *phr. v.* **1** to open the door of a room, building, etc. so that someone can come in: *She unlocked the door to let him in.* **2** to allow light, water, etc. to enter a place: *The door opened, letting in a gust of wind.* **3 let sb in on sth** to tell someone a secret: *I'll let you in on a little secret.*

let sb ↔ **into** sth *phr. v.* to allow someone to come into a room or building: *Security guards refused to let reporters into the building.*

let sb ↔ **off** *phr. v.* to not punish someone, or to not make him/her do something: *The police officer **let us off with** a warning.*

let on *phr. v.* to behave in a way that shows you know a secret: *Don't **let on (that)** you know!*

let out *phr. v.* **1 let** sb ↔ **out** to allow someone to leave a building, room, etc.: *Let the dog out, please.* **2** if a school, college, movie, etc. lets out, it ends, and people can leave: *School lets out at 3:30.* **3 let** sth ↔ **out** to allow light, air, etc. to leave a place: *Close the door – you're letting all the heat out.* **4 let out a scream/cry etc.** to make a sound, especially a loud one

let up *phr. v.* if rain or snow lets up, it stops or there is less of it ➔ LETUP

let·down /ˈlɛtdaʊn/ *n.* [singular] (informal) something that makes you feel disappointed because it is not as good as you expected (SYN) **disappointment**: *Our hotel was a big letdown.*

le·thal /ˈliθəl/ *adj.* able to kill someone: *a lethal dose of heroin* [ORIGIN: 1500—1600 Latin *lethalis*, from *lethum* "death"]

le·thar·gic /ləˈθɑrdʒɪk/ *adj.* having no energy, so that you feel lazy or tired [ORIGIN: 1300—1400 Latin *lethargicus*, from Greek, from *lethargos* "forgetful, lazy"] —**lethargy** /ˈlɛθɚdʒi/ *n.* [U]

let's /lɛts/ the short form of "let us," used especially to make a suggestion: *I'm hungry. Let's eat!* | *Let's stay home tonight.* ➔ LET

let·ter /ˈlɛt̬ɚ/ *n.* [C] **1** a written message that you put into an envelope and send to someone by mail: *Ken **wrote a letter to** the local newspaper.* | *Can you **mail** this **letter** on your way to work?* **2** one of the signs in writing that represents a sound in speech: *There are 26 letters in the English alphabet.* **3 to the letter** exactly: *He followed their instructions to the letter.* [ORIGIN: 1200—1300 Old French *lettre*, from Latin *littera*]

let·ter·head /ˈlɛt̬ɚˌhɛd/ *n.* **1** [U] paper that has the name and address of a person or business printed at the top of it **2** [C] the name and address of a person or business printed at the top of a piece of paper

let·tuce /ˈlɛt̬ɪs/ *n.* [C,U] a round green vegetable with large thin leaves, eaten raw in SALADS [ORIGIN: 1200—1300 Old French *laitues*, plural of *laitue*, from Latin *lactuca*, from *lac* "milk;" because of its milky juice] ➔ *see picture at* VEGETABLE

let·up /ˈlɛt̬ʌp/ *n.* [singular, U] a pause or a reduction in a difficult, dangerous, or tiring activity: *We drove 24 hours straight without letup* (=without stopping).

leu·ke·mia /luˈkimiə/ *n.* [U] a serious disease that affects the blood and that can cause death [ORIGIN: 1800—1900 Greek *leukos* "white" + *-aimia* (from *haima* "blood")]

lev·ee /ˈlɛvi/ *n.* [C] a special wall built to stop a river from flooding

lev·el¹ /ˈlɛvəl/ *n.* [C] **1** the amount or degree of something, as compared to another amount or degree: *a **high/low level of** risk* | *The temperature will stay **at** these **levels** until Friday.* **2** the height or position of something in relation to the ground or another thing: *Check the water level in the radiator.* | *Hang the picture **at eye level*** (=at the same height as your eyes). ➔ SEA LEVEL **3** a standard of skill or ability in a particular subject, sport, etc.: *Students are given an exam to determine their level.* | *Few athletes can compete **at this level**.* **4** a particular position in a system that has different ranks: *The decision will be made at **local/state/federal etc. level**.* | *high-level talks* (=discussions between important people) **5** a floor in a building that has several floors: *Housewares is on Level 3.* **6** a tool used for checking if a surface is flat

L

level² *adj.* **1** flat and not sloping, with no surface higher than the rest: *The floor isn't level.*

> THESAURUS flat, even, horizontal ➔ FLAT¹

2 at the same height or position as something else: *My head was **level with** his chin.*

level³ *v.* [T] **1** to knock down or completely destroy a building or area: *An earthquake leveled several buildings in the city.* **2 level a charge/accusation/criticism etc.** to publicly criticize someone or say s/he is responsible for a crime, mistake, etc.: *Dunn **leveled** one criticism after another **at** the university.* **3** to make a surface flat and smooth: *Level the ground before laying the turf.*

level off/out *phr. v.* to stop going up or down, and

continue at the same height or amount: *The plane climbed to 20,000 feet, then leveled off.* | *Oil prices have* ***leveled off at*** *$55 a barrel.*

level with sb *phr. v.* (informal) to speak honestly with someone and tell him/her what you really think

ˌlevel-ˈheaded *adj.* calm and sensible in making judgments or decisions

lev·er /ˈlɛvɚ, ˈli-/ *n.* [C] **1** a stick or handle attached to a machine, that you move to make the machine work **2** a long thin piece of metal, wood, etc. that you put under a heavy object in order to lift it —**lever** *v.* [T]

lev·er·age /ˈlɛvərɪdʒ, ˈli-/ *n.* [U] influence that you can use to make people do what you want: *Small businesses have less leverage in dealing with banks.*

lev·i·tate /ˈlɛvəˌteɪt/ *v.* [I] to rise and float in the air as if by magic —**levitation** /ˌlɛvəˈteɪʃən/ *n.* [U]

lev·i·ty /ˈlɛvət̬i/ *n.* [U] (formal) the quality of telling jokes and having fun instead of being serious

lev·y[1] /ˈlɛvi/ (Ac) *v.* (**levied**, **levies**) **levy a tax/charge etc.** to officially make someone pay a tax, etc.: *A 15% tax is levied on most hotel services.*

levy[2] *n.* (plural **levies**) [C] an additional sum of money, usually paid as a tax: *A new levy on agricultural imports will be introduced.*

lewd /lud/ *adj.* using rude words or movements that make someone think of sex: *lewd jokes*

lex·i·cal /ˈlɛksɪkəl/ *adj.* ENG. LANG. ARTS relating to words

lex·i·con /ˈlɛksɪˌkɑn/ *n.* [C] **1** ENG. LANG. ARTS all the words used in a language or by people in a particular group, profession, etc. **2** ENG. LANG. ARTS a book containing lists of words and their meanings [ORIGIN: 1600—1700 Late Greek *lexikon*, from *lexikos* "of words," from Greek *lexis* "word, speech"]

li·a·bil·i·ty /ˌlaɪəˈbɪlət̬i/ *n.* (plural **liabilities**) **1** [U] LAW legal responsibility for something, especially for paying money that is owed, or for damage or injury: *The company has admitted* ***liability for*** *the accident.* **2** [C usually singular] someone or something that is likely to cause you problems: *He became a* ***liability to*** *the team.* **3 liabilities** [plural] ECONOMICS the amount of debt that a company owes ➔ ASSET

li·a·ble /ˈlaɪəbəl/ *adj.* **1 be liable to do sth** to be likely to do something, behave in a particular way, or be treated in a particular way: *Wayne and I are liable to start arguing if we discuss politics.* **2** LAW legally responsible for the cost of something: *The university was not* ***held liable for*** *the damage done by its students.*

li·aise /liˈeɪz/ *v.* [I] to work with other people and share information with them

li·ai·son /liˈeɪˌzɑn/ *n.* **1** [C] someone who talks to different people, departments, groups, etc. and tells each of them about what the others are doing: *He's the* ***liaison between*** *the ruler and the local people.* **2** [C] a secret sexual relationship **3** [singular, U] a working relationship between two groups, companies, etc.

li·ar /ˈlaɪɚ/ *n.* [C] someone who tells lies

li·bel /ˈlaɪbəl/ *n.* [C,U] LAW the act of writing or printing untrue statements about someone, so that other people are likely to have a bad opinion of him/her: *He is suing the magazine* ***for libel.*** [ORIGIN: 1300—1400 Old French, Latin *libellus*, from *liber* "book"] —**libel** *v.* [T]

THESAURUS **lie, fib, falsehood, fabrication, slander** ➔ LIE[3]

lib·eral[1] /ˈlɪbrəl, -bərəl/ (Ac) *adj.* **1** willing to understand or respect the different behavior, ideas, etc. of other people (ANT) **conservative**: *a liberal attitude toward sex* | *The role of the media is important in a liberal society.* **2** POLITICS supporting political ideas that include more involvement by the government in business and in people's lives, and willing to accept people's differences and changes in society (ANT) **conservative**: *the liberal wing of the Democratic party* **3** POLITICS allowing people or organizations a lot of political, economic, or social freedom: *a liberal democracy* | *The party supports a more liberal policy on crime and punishment.* **4** (formal) given in large amounts: *a liberal donation* [ORIGIN: 1300—1400 Old French, Latin *liberalis*, from *liber* "free"]

liberal[2] *n.* [C] POLITICS someone with liberal opinions or principles (ANT) **conservative**: *Liberals want Congress to introduce more programs to relieve child poverty.*

ˌliberal ˈarts *n.* [plural] subjects that develop someone's general knowledge and ability to think, rather than technical skills

lib·eral·is·m /ˈlɪbrəˌlɪzəm/ (Ac) *n.* [U] liberal opinions and principles, especially on social and political subjects ➔ CONSERVATISM

lib·eral·ize /ˈlɪbrəˌlaɪz/ (Ac) *v.* [T] to make a system, laws, or moral attitudes less strict: *Both candidates promised to liberalize trade policies.*

lib·eral·ly /ˈlɪbrəli/ (Ac) *adv.* **1** in large amounts: *The story was liberally illustrated with photographs.* **2** with liberal ideas or opinions: *a liberally-minded politician*

lib·er·ate /ˈlɪbəˌreɪt/ (Ac) *v.* [T] **1** to free someone from feelings or situations that make his/her life difficult: *These gadgets* ***liberated*** *housewives* ***from*** *many hard chores.* **2** to free prisoners, a city, a country, etc. from someone's control: *The city was liberated by the Allies in 1944.* —**liberator** *n.* [C] —**liberation** /ˌlɪbəˈreɪʃən/ *n.* [U]: *the liberation of Eastern Europe* | *Some human rights violations may have occurred immediately after the liberation of the country.*

lib·er·at·ed /ˈlɪbəˌreɪt̬ɪd/ (Ac) *adj.* free to do the things you want, and not controlled by rules or

L

other people: *The 1960s saw the beginning of a new liberated and permissive attitude.*

lib·er·tar·i·an /ˌlɪbɚˈtɛriən/ *n.* [C] someone who believes strongly that people should be free to live with little or no government involvement in their lives —**libertarian** *adj.*

lib·er·ty /ˈlɪbɚṭi/ *n.* (plural **liberties**) **1** [U] the freedom to do what you want without having to ask permission from people in authority: *principles of liberty and democracy* **2** [C usually plural] a particular legal right: *civil liberties* **3 be at liberty to do sth** to have the right or permission to do something: *I'm not at liberty to say where he is at the moment.* **4 take the liberty of doing sth** to do something without asking permission because you do not think it will upset or offend anyone: *I took the liberty of inviting Jeff along.* [ORIGIN: 1300—1400 French *liberté*, from Latin *libertas*, from *liber* "free"]

li·bi·do /lɪˈbidoʊ/ (plural **libidos**) *n.* [C,U] someone's desire to have sex

Li·bra /ˈlibrə/ *n.* **1** [U] the seventh sign of the ZODIAC, represented by a SCALE **2** [C] someone born between September 23 and October 23

li·brar·i·an /laɪˈbrɛriən/ *n.* [C] someone who works in a library

li·brar·y /ˈlaɪˌbrɛri/ *n.* (plural **libraries**) [C] a room or building containing books that you can borrow or read there [ORIGIN: 1300—1400 Medieval Latin *librarium*, from Latin *liber* "book"]

lice /laɪs/ *n.* the plural of LOUSE

li·cense¹ /ˈlaɪsəns/ (Ac) *n.* **1** [C] an official document that gives you permission to own something or do something: *a driver's license* | *He was charged with possessing firearms* ***without a license.*** | *The Tennessee Valley Authority applied for a license to operate the nuclear facility.* **2** [U] (formal) freedom to do or say whatever you want: *He thinks because he's famous he has* ***license to*** *be rude.* | *Teachers should be allowed greater license in choosing their teaching materials.* **3** [U] the way in which a writer or painter changes the facts of the real world to make his/her story, description, or picture of events more interesting or more beautiful: *The novelist allows himself considerable poetic license in his description of the town.*

license² *v.* [T] to give official permission for someone to own or do something: *Williams is not* ***licensed to*** *practice law in New York.* | *Medical personnel must be licensed by the state.*

li·censed /ˈlaɪsənst/ *adj.* having official permission to own or do something: *He had completed his studies to become licensed as a surveyor.*

ˈlicense plate *n.* [C] one of the signs with numbers and letters on it at the front and back of your car

li·cen·tious /laɪˈsɛnʃəs/ *adj.* (literary) sexually immoral or not controlling behavior in an acceptable way: *licentious books* —**licentiousness** *n.* [U]

lick¹ /lɪk/ *v.* [T] **1** to move your tongue across the surface of something in order to taste it, clean it, etc.: *Judy's dog jumped up to lick her face.* **2** (informal) to defeat an opponent or solve a problem: *"It looks like we have the fire licked," said Chief Grafton.* [ORIGIN: Old English *liccian*]

lick² *n.* [C usually singular] an act of licking something: *Can I have a lick of your ice cream cone?*

lick·ing /ˈlɪkɪŋ/ *n.* [singular] (informal) **1** a severe beating as a punishment **2** a heavy defeat in a sports competition

lic·o·rice /ˈlɪkərɪʃ/ *n.* [U] a type of strong-tasting black or red candy [ORIGIN: 1100—1200 Old French, Late Latin *liquiritia*, from Latin *glycyrrhiza*, from Greek, from *glykys* "sweet" + *rhiza* "root"]

lid /lɪd/ *n.* [C] **1** a cover for a pot, box, or other container: *He carefully lifted the* ***lid of*** *the box.*

> THESAURUS **cover, top, cap** → COVER²

2 keep a lid on sth (informal) to control a situation so that it does not become worse: *Police try to keep a lid on crime in the area.* **3** an EYELID [ORIGIN: Old English *hlid*]

lie¹ /laɪ/ *v.* (past tense **lay** /leɪ/, past participle **lain** /leɪn/, present participle **lying**) [I] **1 a)** to be in a position in which your body is flat on the floor, a bed, etc.: *We lay on the beach all day.* | *I* ***lay awake*** *worrying.* **b)** also **lie down** to put yourself in this position: *I'm going upstairs to lie down.* **2** to be in a particular place or position: *The town* ***lies to*** *the east of the lake.* | *The ship had* ***lain on*** *the ocean floor for decades.* **3** used to say where something such as a reason or answer can be found: *Mitchell's charm* ***lies in*** *his sense of humor.* **4** to be or remain in a particular condition or position: *The city* ***lay in ruins.*** | *The letters lay hidden in her attic for forty years.* **5 lie low** to remain hidden when someone is trying to find you: *Weaver decided to lie low at his sister's house.* **6 lie ahead** if something lies ahead, it is going to happen in the future: *There are difficulties that lie ahead.* → **not take sth lying down** *at* TAKE¹

lie around *phr. v.* **1** to be left out of the correct place, so that things look messy: *Books and papers were lying around everywhere.* **2** to spend time being lazy, not doing anything useful: *We lay around the house all afternoon, watching TV.*

lie behind sth *phr. v.* to be the true reason for an action, decision, etc.: *I wonder what really lay behind her decision to quit her job.*

lie² *v.* (past tense and past participle **lied** /laɪd/, present participle **lying**) [I] to deliberately tell someone something that is not true: *She's* ***lying about*** *her age.* | *Don't* ***lie to*** *me!*

> THESAURUS
> **make sth up** – to invent a story, explanation, etc. in order to deceive someone: *"What'll you tell your mother?" "I'll make something up."*

tell (sb) a lie – to lie: *Did he make a mistake, or did he tell a lie?*
invent – to think of an idea, story, etc. that is not true: *If I can't find a reason, I'll invent one.*
mislead – to make someone believe something that is not true by giving him/her false or incomplete information: *The ads were accused of misleading consumers.*
deceive – to make someone believe something that is not true: *In order to deceive the enemy, our troops first headed north, away from the bridge.*
perjure yourself/commit perjury (formal) – to tell a lie in a court of law: *Company executives may have perjured themselves in sworn testimony to Congress.*
falsify – to change figures, records, etc. so that they contain false information: *Apparently, he falsified the records in order to steal the money.*

lie³ *n.* [C] something that you say or write that you know is not true: *I've never known him to* ***tell lies.***

THESAURUS

fib (informal) – a small unimportant lie
white lie – a small lie that you tell someone, usually to avoid hurting his/her feelings
story – an excuse, explanation, or lie
falsehood (formal) – a statement that is not true
fabrication (formal) – a story, piece of information, etc. that you make up in order to deceive someone
slander (formal) – something untrue that is said about someone which could harm the opinion people have of him/her
libel (formal) – something untrue that is written about someone which could harm the opinion people have of him/her
perjury (formal) – the crime of telling a lie in a court of law

'lie deˌtector *n.* [C] a machine used by the police to find out if someone is lying

lieu /lu/ *n.* (formal) **in lieu of sth** instead of something else

lieu·ten·ant /lu'tɛnənt/ *n.* [C] **a)** a fairly low rank in the Army, Navy, Air Force, or Marines, or an officer who has this rank **b)** a fairly high rank in the police force, or an officer who has this rank

L

life /laɪf/ *n.* (plural **lives** /laɪvz/)
1 PERIOD OF LIFE [C,U] the period of time between someone's birth and death: *Charles lived in New York City* ***all his life****. | It was the happiest day* ***of my life****. | She* ***spent her life*** *helping others. | I've never felt better* ***in my life****.*
2 BEING ALIVE [C,U] the state of being alive: *Surgery could* ***save her life****. | Firemen* ***risked their lives*** (=did something during which they could have been killed) *to save him. | Tragically, she* ***took her own life*** (=killed herself).
3 WAY OF LIVING [C,U] all the experiences and activities that are typical of a particular way of living: *How's life in Japan? | He's spent most of his* ***working life*** (=time spent working) *with one company. |* ***Married life*** *has been an adjustment. | Violence is a* ***way of life*** *for many teenagers.*
4 EXPERIENCES [C] the type of experience that someone has during his/her life: *Tia had a full and happy life. | She wanted to save her son from* ***a life of*** *crime. | Then he started telling me his* ***life story*** (=all the things that happened in his life).
5 LIVING THINGS [U] BIOLOGY living things such as people, animals, or plants: *Do you think there is life on other planets?*
6 private/sex/social etc. life activities in your life that are private, relate to sex, are done with friends, etc.: *I don't have much time for a social life.*
7 MOVEMENT [U] activity or movement: *We looked around for any* ***signs of life****. | Katie was young and* ***full of life*** (=very cheerful and active).
8 EXISTENCE [U] human existence, and all the things that can happen during someone's life: *Life can be hard sometimes.*
9 PRISON [U] *also* **life in prison** a LIFE SENTENCE: *The defendants were* ***sentenced to life****.*
10 real life what really happens rather than what only happens in stories or someone's imagination: *Things like that don't happen* ***in real life****.*
11 quality of life the level or quality of health, success, and comfort in someone's life: *Crime affects everyone's quality of life.*
12 WORKING/EXISTING [singular] the period of time during which something exists or continues to happen: *long-life batteries*
13 bring sb/sth to life a) to make someone or something live: *Doctors fought to bring the baby back to life.* **b)** to make something more exciting or interesting: *The movie really brings 19th-century New York to life.*

SPOKEN PHRASES
14 that's life said when something bad has happened that you must accept
15 life is too short said when telling someone that something is not important enough to worry about: *Life's too short to hold grudges.*
16 Get a life! used to tell someone you think s/he is boring
17 Not on your life! used to say that you will definitely not do something
18 for the life of me said when you cannot do something, even when you try very hard: *I can't remember her name for the life of me!*

[ORIGIN: Old English *lif*]

life·boat /'laɪfbout/ *n.* [C] **1** a small boat that is used for helping people who are in danger on the ocean **2** a small boat carried by ships in order to save people if the ship sinks

'life ˌcycle *n.* [C] BIOLOGY all the different stages of development that an animal or plant goes through during its life

ˌlife ex'pectancy *n.* (plural **life expectancies**) [C] **1** BIOLOGY the average length of time that a person or animal is expected to live: *an insect with a life expectancy of only a week* **2** the age that a particular person is likely to live to, based on things such as his/her health, whether s/he smokes, etc., used to calculate the risk of insuring that person

life·guard /ˈlaɪfgɑrd/ *n.* [C] someone whose job is to help swimmers who are in danger at the beach or a pool

ˈlife inˌsurance *n.* [U] a type of insurance that someone buys so that when s/he dies, his/her family will receive money

ˈlife ˌjacket *n.* [C] a piece of equipment that you wear around your chest to prevent you from sinking in the water

life·less /ˈlaɪflɪs/ *adj.* **1** (literary) dead, or seeming to be dead: *His lifeless body was discovered in the river.* → DEAD[1] **2** lacking excitement, activity, or interest: *The team's performance was dull and lifeless.*

life·like /ˈlaɪflaɪk/ *adj.* very much like a real person or thing: *a lifelike statue*

life·line /ˈlaɪflaɪn/ *n.* [C] something that someone depends on completely: *Because I live so far from a town, the phone is my lifeline.*

life·long /ˈlaɪflɔŋ/ *adj.* continuing all through your life: ***lifelong friends***

life·sav·er /ˈlaɪfˌseɪvɚ/ *n.* [C] someone or something that helps you avoid a difficult or bad situation

ˌlife ˈsentence *n.* [C] the punishment of sending someone to prison for the rest of his/her life

ˈlife-size *also* **ˈlife-sized** *adj.* a life-size model, picture, etc. is the same size as the person or object it represents

life·style /ˈlaɪfstaɪl/ *n.* [C] the way someone lives, including his/her work and activities, and what things s/he owns: *an active, healthy lifestyle*

ˈlife supˌport *n.* [U] machines or methods that keep someone who is extremely sick alive

ˈlife-ˌthreatening *adj.* a life-threatening illness, injury, or situation could cause a person to die

life·time /ˈlaɪftaɪm/ *n.* [C] the period of time during which someone is alive: ***During her lifetime**, she had witnessed two world wars.*

ˈlife vest *n.* [C] a LIFE JACKET

lift[1] /lɪft/ *v.* **1** [T] to take something in your hands and raise it, move it, or carry it somewhere: *Can you help me lift this box?* → *see picture on page A22* **2** [I,T] *also* **lift up** to move something up into the air, or to move up into the air: *Lift up your feet so I can sweep the floor.* **3** [T] to remove a rule or a law that says that something is not allowed: *Does the government plan to **lift the ban** on Cuban cigars?* **4** [I] if clouds or FOG lift, they disappear **5** [T] (informal) to steal something, or to copy the words, ideas, music, etc. that someone else has written: *Parts of her essay were lifted directly from an encyclopedia.*

lift[2] *n.* [C] **1** if you give someone a lift, you take him/her somewhere in your car (SYN) **ride**: *Can you give me **a lift** to the nearest gas station?* **2 give sb/sth a lift** to make someone feel happier, or to make something more successful: *Lower interest rates should give the economy a lift.* **3** a movement in which something is lifted or raised

ˈlift-off *n.* [C,U] the moment when a vehicle that is about to travel in space leaves the ground → TAKE-OFF

lig·a·ment /ˈlɪgəmənt/ *n.* [C] BIOLOGY a band of strong material in your body that joins your bones together [ORIGIN: 1300—1400 Latin *ligamentum*, from *ligare* "to tie"]

light[1] /laɪt/ *n.*
1 LIGHT TO SEE [U] the energy from the Sun, a lamp, etc. that allows you to see things: *Light was streaming in through the window.* | ***The light** is better over here*
2 ELECTRIC LIGHT [C] something such as a lamp that uses electricity: *Can you **turn/switch the lights on/off** for me?*
3 TRAFFIC [C] one of a set of red, green, and yellow lights used for controlling traffic: *Turn left at the next light.* | *He was fined for **running a red light*** (=driving past a red light).
4 ON A VEHICLE [C] one of the lights on a car, bicycle, etc., especially the HEADLIGHTS
5 a light a match or lighter that you use to light a cigarette: *Excuse me, do you **have a light**?*
6 come to light/be brought to light if new information comes to light, it becomes known: *New evidence has come to light since the trial.*
7 in light of sth because of something: *The highway has been closed in light of heavy snow.*
8 in a new/different/bad etc. light if someone or something is seen or shown in a new, different, etc. light, people begin to have a different opinion of him, her, or it: *A recent biography shows the actor in a new light.*
9 shed/throw/cast light on sth to provide new information about something so it is easier to understand: *This sheds some light on the cause of the disease.*
10 light at the end of the tunnel something that gives you hope that a bad situation will end soon
11 see the light to suddenly realize and understand something: *We're hoping that one of these days he'll see the light and quit drinking.* [ORIGIN: Old English *leoht*]

L

light² *adj.*
1 COLOR a light color is pale and not dark (ANT) **dark**: *a light blue dress*

THESAURUS
pale – a pale color has more white in it than usual: *a dress made of pale yellow silk*
pastel – having a soft light color: *She was knitting a baby blanket in pastel blue yarn.*
faded – having lost color, for example by being washed many times or by being left out in the Sun: *a pair of faded jeans*
soft – soft colors are not too bright: *Use soft colors if you want the room to feel calm.*

2 WEIGHT not weighing very much (ANT) **heavy**: *My new cell phone is lighter than my old one.*
3 CLOTHES light clothes are thin and not very warm: *a light sweater*
4 ROOM if a room or building is light, a lot of light from the Sun gets into it: *The house was light and airy.*
5 TOUCH very gentle and soft: *She gave him a light kiss on the cheek.*
6 FOOD a) having less fat or fewer CALORIEs than usual: *light cream cheese* **b)** not having a strong taste: *a light wine*
7 NOT SERIOUS not serious in meaning or style: *light reading*
8 WIND blowing without much force ➔ STRONG: *a light breeze*
9 it is/gets light used to say that there is enough natural light outside to see by: *It was still light when we got home.*
10 SMALL AMOUNT small in amount, or less than you expected: *Traffic was lighter than usual today.*
11 make light of sth to joke about something, or to treat it as if it were not important

light³ *v.* (past tense and past participle **lit** /lɪt/ *or* **lighted**) **1** [I,T] to start burning, or to make something do this: *Derek stopped to light a cigarette.* **2** [T] to give light to something: *The room is lit by candles.* | *a **brightly-/poorly-/well-lit** room*

light up *phr. v.* **1** to become bright, or to make something bright: *Fireworks lit up the night sky.* **2** if your face or eyes light up, you show that you are pleased or excited: *Paula's eyes lit up when she saw all of her presents.* **3** (informal) to light a cigarette

light⁴ *adv.* **travel light** to travel without carrying too many clothes, etc.

ˈlight bulb *n.* [C] the glass object in a lamp, that produces light

light·en /ˈlaɪtˀn/ *v.* **1** [T] to reduce the amount of work, worry, debt, etc. that someone has: *Hiring extra men will **lighten the load**.* **2** [I,T] to become brighter, or make something become brighter (ANT) **darken**: *At 5 a.m., the sky started to lighten.* **3 lighten up!** (spoken) used in order to tell someone not to be so serious about something: *Hey, lighten up! It was just a joke.* **4** [I,T] to reduce the weight of something, or to become less heavy

light·er /ˈlaɪt̬ɚ/ *n.* [C] a small object that produces a flame to light cigarettes, CIGARs, etc.

ˌlight-ˈheaded *adj.* not able to think clearly or not able to move steadily because you are sick or have drunk too much alcohol (SYN) **dizzy**

ˌlight-ˈhearted *adj.* **1** not intended to be serious: *a light-hearted comedy* **2** cheerful and happy

light·house /ˈlaɪthaʊs/ *n.* [C] a tower with a bright light that guides ships away from danger near the shore

lighthouse

light·ing /ˈlaɪt̬ɪŋ/ *n.* [U] the lights in a room, building, etc., or the quality of the light: *soft/bright/dim lighting*

light·ly /ˈlaɪtli/ *adv.* **1** with only a small amount of weight or force: *I tapped her lightly on the shoulder.* **2** using or having only a small amount of something: *Sprinkle sugar lightly over the cake.* **3 take sth lightly** to do something without serious thought: *A bomb threat is not to be taken lightly.*

lightning

light·ning¹ /ˈlaɪtˀnɪŋ/ *n.* [U] a bright flash of light in the sky that happens during a storm: *The tree was **struck** (=hit) **by lightning**.*

lightning² *adj.* extremely fast or sudden: *a lightning attack*

ˈlight polˌlution *n.* [U] EARTH SCIENCES electric light from STREETLIGHTs, offices, houses, etc. that prevents you from being able to see the stars in the night sky clearly

light·weight¹ /ˈlaɪtˀweɪt/ *adj.* **1** weighing less than average: *a lightweight computer* **2** showing a lack of serious thought: *a lightweight novel*

lightweight² *n.* [C] (disapproving) **1** someone who you do not think has the ability to think about serious or difficult subjects **2** someone who has no importance or influence: *a political lightweight*

ˈlight year *n.* [C] PHYSICS the distance that light travels in one year

lik·a·ble /ˈlaɪkəbəl/ *adj.* likable people are nice, and are easy to like

L

like¹ /laɪk/ *prep.* **1** similar in some way to something else: *You two are behaving* ***just like*** *children.* | *I'd love a car like yours.* | *Ken* ***looks like*** *his brother.* | *It* ***tastes like*** *chicken.* | *Was the movie* ***anything like*** *the book* (=was it similar in any way)? | ***There's nothing like*** (=there is nothing better than) *a day at the beach.* **2** typical of a particular person: *It's not* ***like*** *Dad* ***to*** *be late* (=it is unusual that Dad is late). **3** (nonstandard) used to give an example of something (SYN) **such as**: *Foods like spinach and broccoli are high in iron.* **4 what is sb/sth like?** used when asking someone to describe or give his/her opinion on a person or thing: *What's the new house like?*

SPOKEN PHRASES

5 like this/so said when showing someone how to do something or how something is done: *He was leaning against the wall, like this.* **6 more like** said when giving a number that you think is more correct than the one already mentioned: *"He's been in there for 15 minutes." "More like half an hour!"*

GRAMMAR

like, such as

Many teachers think that using **like** to give an example is wrong. It is better to use **such as:** *Companies such as Toyota and General Motors are developing electric cars.*

like² *v.* [T] **1** to enjoy something, or think that someone or something is nice or good (ANT) **dislike:** *Do you like Mexican food?* | *I like Billy a lot.* | *He* ***really likes*** *camping.* | *Pam doesn't* ***like to*** *walk home late at night.* | *Mom doesn't* ***like it*** *when we argue.*

THESAURUS enjoy, love, relish → ENJOY

2 to prefer that something is done in one particular way or at one particular time rather than another: *Jim* ***likes to*** *get to the airport early.* | *How do you like your hamburger cooked?*

SPOKEN PHRASES

3 I/she etc. would like used to say politely what someone wants: *I'd like a large pizza with mushrooms.* | *He'd* ***like to*** *know how much it will cost.* | *We would like you to be there if you can.* **4 Would you like ...?** used to ask someone if s/he wants something: *Would you like some more coffee?* **5 How do you like sth?** used to ask someone for his/her opinion of something: *"How did you like the movie?" "It was okay."* **6 (whether you) like it or not** used to emphasize that something bad is true or will happen and cannot be changed: *They expect us to work together, whether we like it or not.*

[ORIGIN: Old English *lician*]

GRAMMAR

Do not say "I am liking it" or "I am liking to do it." Say "*I like it*" or "*I like to do it.*"
Do not say "I am liking very much this town." Say "*I like this town very much.*"

like³ *adv.* (spoken, nonstandard) **1 I'm like/he's like/Bob's like etc. a)** used in order to tell someone the exact words someone used: *He asked if he could use my car and I was like, no way.* **b)** said when describing an event, feeling, or person, when it is difficult to describe or when you use a noise instead of a word: *He was like, huh* (=he was really surprised)? | *We were like, oh no* (=we realized something was wrong)! **2** said when you pause because you do not know what to say, you are embarrassed, etc.: *Would it be OK if I, like, called you up sometime?* **3** said in order to give an example: *My neighbor's driving me crazy. Like last night I had to tell him to turn his radio down.* **4** said when what you are saying is not exact: *It was like 9 o'clock and she still wasn't home.* **5** said in order to emphasize something: *That's like so stupid.*

like⁴ *conjunction* **1** (nonstandard) as if: *He acts like he owns the place.* **2** (informal) **like I said/told you/was saying** said when you are repeating something you have already said: *Like I said, we'll be there around ten.* **3** in the same way as: *I don't want you to turn out like your father.*

like⁵ *adj.* **1** (formal) similar in some way: *a chance to meet people* ***of like minds*** (=who think in a similar way)

THESAURUS similar, alike, comparable → SIMILAR

2 -like typical of, or similar to something: *moving with cat-like grace*

like⁶ *n.* **sb's likes and dislikes** all the things you like and do not like

like·li·hood /ˈlaɪkliˌhʊd/ *n.* [singular, U] **1** how likely something is to happen: ***The likelihood of*** *being burglarized is very low.* **2 in all likelihood** almost definitely

like·ly /ˈlaɪkli/ *adj.* something that is likely will probably happen or is probably true: *It's* ***likely to*** *rain tomorrow.* | *Young drivers are* ***more likely*** *to have accidents than older drivers.* —**likely** *adv.*: *I'd* ***very likely*** *have done the same thing.*

ˌlike-ˈminded *adj.* having similar interests and opinions

lik·en /ˈlaɪkən/ *v.*

liken sb/sth **to** sb/sth *phr. v.* (formal) to say that someone or something is similar to someone or something else: *She likened the new hospital to a five-star hotel.*

like·ness /ˈlaɪknɪs/ *n.* **1** [U] the quality of being similar in appearance to someone or something else: *a strong* ***likeness to*** *his father* **2** [C] the image of someone in a painting or photograph: *It's a good* ***likeness of*** *Eva.*

like·wise /ˈlaɪk-waɪz/ (Ac) *adv.* **1** (formal) in the same way: *I fastened my seat belt and told the kids to* ***do likewise.*** | *Saturn was once thought to be unique, but we now know that Jupiter, Uranus, and Neptune likewise have rings.* **2** (spoken) said in order to return someone's greeting or polite remark: *"It's great to see you." "Likewise."*

lik·ing /ˈlaɪkɪŋ/ *n.* [C] **1 liking for sb/sth** the feeling when you like someone or something: *He always* ***had a liking for*** *whiskey.* **2 take a liking to sb** (informal) to begin to like someone or something

li·lac /ˈlaɪlək, -læk/ *n.* **1** [C] a small tree with pale purple or white flowers **2** [U] a pale purple color [ORIGIN: 1600—1700 Early French, from Arabic *lilak*, from Persian *nilak* "bluish"] —**lilac** *adj.*

lilt /lɪlt/ *n.* [singular] the pleasant rise and fall in the sound of someone's voice or a piece of music

lil·y /ˈlɪli/ *n.* (plural **lilies**) [C] a plant with large white flowers that are usually bell-shaped

li·ma bean /ˈlaɪmə ˌbin/ *n.* [C] a pale green flat bean

limb /lɪm/ *n.* [C] **1** a large branch of a tree **2 be/go out on a limb** to do something risky without any help or support **3** an arm or leg

lim·bo /ˈlɪmboʊ/ *n.* **be in limbo** to be in an uncertain situation in which it is difficult to know what to do: *I'm in limbo until I know which college I'm going to.*

lime /laɪm/ *n.* **1** [C] a bright green fruit with a sour taste, or the tree this grows on ➔ *see picture on page 414* **2** [U] a white substance used especially for making CEMENT [ORIGIN: (1) 1600—1700 French, Provençal *limo*, from Arabic *lim*]

lime·light /ˈlaɪmlaɪt/ *n.* **the limelight** the attention someone gets from newspapers and television [ORIGIN: 1800—1900 *lime* + *light*; because originally the light was produced by burning lime]

lim·er·ick /ˈlɪmərɪk/ *n.* [C] ENG. LANG. ARTS a humorous short poem with five lines

lime·stone /ˈlaɪmstoʊn/ *n.* [U] EARTH SCIENCES a type of rock that contains CALCIUM, often used to make buildings

lim·it¹ /ˈlɪmɪt/ *n.* [C] **1** the greatest or least amount, number, etc. that is allowed or is possible: *a 65 mph* ***speed limit*** | *There is a* ***limit on/to*** *the time you have to complete the test.* | ***There's no limit to*** *her potential.* | ***Set a limit*** *before you go shopping.* | *Our finances are* ***stretched to the limit*** (=we do not have any more money to spend). **2** the furthest point or edge of a place, often one that must not be passed: *Los Angeles* ***city limits*** **3 off limits** beyond the area where someone is allowed to go: *The beach is off limits after dark.* **4 within limits** within the time, level, amount, etc. considered acceptable: *Employees can dress how they like – within limits.*

L

limit² *v.* [T] **1** to stop an amount or number from increasing beyond a particular point: *Class size is* ***limited to*** *30.* **2** to allow someone to use only a particular amount of something: *Try to* ***limit*** *yourself* ***to*** *a glass of wine per night.* **3** to exist or happen only in a particular place or group: *The damage* ***was limited to*** *the roof.* —**limiting** *adj.*

lim·i·ta·tion /ˌlɪməˈteɪʃən/ *n.* **1** [C,U] the act or process of controlling or reducing something: *a nuclear limitation treaty* | *new* ***limitations on*** *parking* **2 limitations** [plural] things that limit how good something can be: *Computers* ***have*** *their* ***limitations.***

lim·it·ed /ˈlɪmɪt̮ɪd/ *adj.* not very great in amount, number, degree, etc.: *The organization has very* ***limited resources.*** | *There are only a* ***limited number*** *of tickets available.*

ˌlimited ˈgovernment *n.* [U] POLITICS a principle in the U.S. CONSTITUTION which says that the only powers the government should have are the powers the Constitution gives it

ˌlimited point of ˈview *n.* [singular] ENG. LANG. ARTS the style of telling a story in which the NARRATOR (=person telling the story) tells you what only one character or a limited number of characters experience, think, and feel ➔ OMNISCIENT POINT OF VIEW

lim·o /ˈlɪmoʊ/ *n.* (plural **limos**) (informal) [C] a limousine

lim·ou·sine /ˈlɪməˌzin, ˌlɪməˈzin/ *n.* [C] a big expensive car, driven by someone who is paid to drive [ORIGIN: 1900—2000 French "covering for the driver of a horse-drawn vehicle (as worn in Limousin)," from *Limousin* area of France]

limp¹ /lɪmp/ *adj.* not strong or firm: *The dog's body* ***went limp*** *as the drug took effect.*

limp² *v.* [I] to walk with difficulty because one leg is hurt ➔ WALK¹

limp³ *n.* [C] the way someone walks when s/he is limping: *After my surgery, I* ***walked with a limp.***

lim·pid /ˈlɪmpɪd/ *adj.* (literary) clear or transparent: *a limpid little stream in the woods* —**limpidly** *adv.* —**limpidness** *n.* [U] —**limpidity** /lɪmˈpɪdət̮i/ *n.* [U]

linch·pin /ˈlɪntʃˌpɪn/ *n.* **the linchpin of sth** the most important person or thing in a group, system, etc., on which everything depends: *My mother is the linchpin of the family.*

line¹ /laɪn/ *n.*

1 LONG THIN MARK [C] a long thin, usually continuous mark on a surface: *She* ***drew a line*** *on the map to show him how to get to the museum.* ➔ DOTTED LINE

THESAURUS

stripe – a long narrow line of color: *a tie with thin blue and white stripes*
streak – a colored line or thin mark, especially one that is not straight or has been made accidentally: *a streak of blood ran down his arm*
band – a narrow area of color that is different from the areas around it: *The fish has a black band on its fin.*

2 LIMIT/END [C] a long thin mark used to show a limit or end of something: *You're supposed to park*

lines

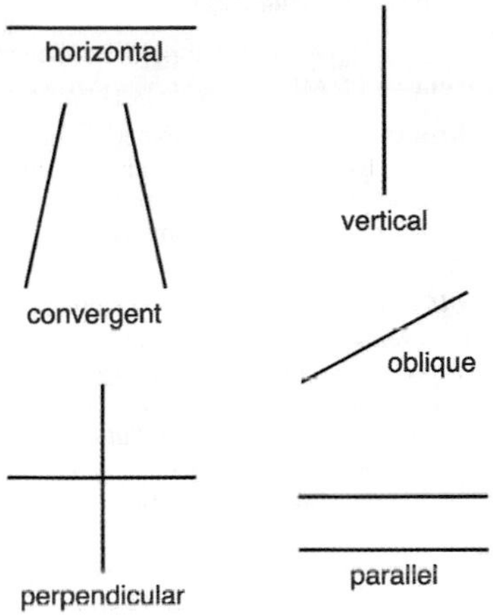

horizontal

vertical

convergent

oblique

perpendicular

parallel

between the white lines. | *crossing the **finish line*** → FINISH LINE
3 PEOPLE/THINGS [C] a row of people or things: *a **line of** cars* | *We **stood/waited in line** for more than two hours.*
4 DIRECTION [C] the direction something travels, or the imaginary path between two points in space: *Light travels **in a straight line**.*
5 COMPUTER on line IT using a computer that is connected to the Internet or a computer system to get information or communicate with other people: *You can buy airline tickets on line.* → ONLINE
6 LAND [C] an imaginary line on the surface of the Earth, for example one showing where one state or area of land stops and another begins: *I didn't stop driving until I crossed the **state line**.* | *lines of latitude/longitude*
7 line of action/thought/reasoning etc. a way or method of doing something or thinking about something: *That line of thinking will get you into trouble.*
8 WAY OF DOING STH [C] a way of thinking about or doing something: *This meeting will be organized **along the** same **lines*** (=in the same way) *as the last one.*
9 be out of line (informal) to say or do something that is not acceptable in a particular situation: *I thought what Kenny said was way out of line.*
10 be in line with sth if one thing is in line with another, they are similar to each other, or they operate in a similar way: *The company's actions are in line with state laws.*
11 ON SB'S FACE [C] a line on the skin of someone's face (SYN) **wrinkle**: *There were **fine lines** around her eyes.*
12 PLAY/POEM ETC. [C] **a)** ENG. LANG. ARTS a line of words in a poem, film, song, etc. **b)** ENG. LANG. ARTS the words of a play or performance that an actor learns: *He has trouble remembering his lines.*
13 PHONE [C] a telephone wire or connection → TELEPHONE, PHONE: *We were **on the line*** (=on the phone) *for almost two hours.* | *You'll have to try again later* – ***the line's busy*** (=someone is already using it).
14 RAILROAD [C] a track that a train travels along: *a **railroad line***
15 WAR [C] the edge of an area that is controlled by an army, where soldiers stay and try to prevent their enemy from moving forward: *a raid inside **enemy lines***
16 be (first/second/next etc.) in line for sth to be very likely to be the first, next, etc. person to get something: *Carl is next in line for a raise.*
17 PRODUCTS [C] ECONOMICS a type of goods for sale in a store: *a new **line of** computers*
18 COMPANY [C] a company that provides a system for moving goods by road, water, or air: *a large shipping line*
19 SHAPE [C usually plural] the outer shape of something long or tall: *the car's smooth, elegant lines*
20 the line a CLOTHESLINE
21 FAMILY [singular] the people that came or existed before you in your family: *She comes **from a long line of** politicians.*
22 SPORTS [C] a row of players with a particular purpose in a sport such as football: *the Bears' defensive line*
23 FISHING [C] a strong thin string, used to catch fish → **draw the line (at sth)** *at* DRAW[1], POVERTY LINE, **read between the lines** *at* READ, **somewhere along the line/way** *at* SOMEWHERE

line² *v.* [T] **1** to cover the inside of something with something else: *We **lined** the box **with** newspaper.* **2** to form rows along the edge of something: *Thousands of fans lined the streets.*

line up *phr. v.* **1 line** sb/sth ↔ **up** to make a row, or arrange people or things in a row: *Customers lined up hours before the show.* | *Line the chairs up in rows of ten.* **2 line** sb/sth ↔ **up** to make arrangements so that something will happen or someone will be available for an event: *They've lined up some dancers for the show.*

lin·e·age /ˈlɪniɪdʒ/ *n.* [C,U] (formal) the way in which members of a family are related to other members who lived in past times

lin·e·ar /ˈlɪniɚ/ *adj.* **1** consisting of lines, or in the form of a straight line: *a linear drawing* **2** related to length: *linear measurements* **3** involving a series of connected events, ideas, etc. that develop in stages

ˌlinear eˈquation *n.* [C] MATH an EQUATION that appears as a straight line when it is represented on a GRAPH

ˌlinear ˈfunction *n.* [C] MATH a mathematical FUNCTION, that can be represented by a linear equation, in which the VARIABLES are multiplied only by CONSTANTS and not by themselves, and are combined only by addition and SUBTRACTION

ˌlinear perˈspective *n.* [U] ENG. LANG. ARTS a method for making a picture appear to have distance and depth by having a series of straight lines from the edge that come together at a single point on the HORIZON (=line far away where the land or

L

ocean seems to meet the sky). The shape and size of each object in the picture is then drawn in relation to its position along one of these lines.

line·back·er /ˈlaɪnˌbækɚ/ *n.* [C,U] a football player whose job is to try to TACKLE the member of the other team who has the ball

lined /laɪnd/ *adj.* **1** a skirt, coat, etc. that is lined has a piece of material covering the inside: *a fur-lined coat* **2** lined paper has straight lines printed on it

line·man /ˈlaɪnmən/ *n.* (plural **linemen** /-mən/) [C] a player who plays in the front line of a football team

lin·en /ˈlɪnən/ *n.* [U] **1** sheets, TABLECLOTHS, etc.: *bed/table linen* **2** cloth used to make high quality clothes, home decorations, etc.

lin·er /ˈlaɪnɚ/ *n.* [C] **1** a large ship for carrying people: *an ocean liner* ➔ *see picture at* TRANSPORTATION, AIRLINER **2** a piece of material used inside something in order to protect it

line·up /ˈlaɪnʌp/ *n.* [C] **1** a set of events, programs, performers, etc. arranged to follow each other: *The lineup of performers included Madonna and Diana Ross.* **2** a group of people arranged in a row by the police so that a person who saw a crime can try to recognize the criminal ➔ STARTING LINEUP

lin·ger /ˈlɪŋɡɚ/ *v.* [I] **1** to stay somewhere for a little longer, especially because you do not want to leave: *We found a small cafe where we could* ***linger over*** *our coffee.* **2** *also* **linger on** if a smell, memory, etc. lingers, it does not disappear for a long time: *The smell of smoke lingered for days.*

lin·ge·rie /ˌlɑnʒəˈreɪ, ˌlɑndʒə-/ *n.* [U] women's underwear

lin·ger·ing /ˈlɪŋɡərɪŋ/ *adj.* slow to finish or disappear: *lingering questions about the murder*

lin·go /ˈlɪŋɡoʊ/ *n.* [C usually singular] (informal) **1** words used only by a group of people who do a particular job or activity: *computer lingo*

THESAURUS **language, slang, jargon, terminology** ➔ LANGUAGE

2 a language, especially a foreign one

lin·guist /ˈlɪŋɡwɪst/ *n.* [C] **1** ENG. LANG. ARTS someone who studies or teaches linguistics **2** ENG. LANG. ARTS someone who speaks several languages well

lin·guis·tic /lɪŋˈɡwɪstɪk/ *adj.* ENG. LANG. ARTS relating to language, words, or linguistics

lin·guis·tics /lɪŋˈɡwɪstɪks/ *n.* [U] ENG. LANG. ARTS the study of languages, including their structures, grammar, and history

lin·ing /ˈlaɪnɪŋ/ *n.* [C,U] a piece of material covering the inside of a box, a coat, etc.: *a jacket with a silk lining*

link¹ /lɪŋk/ (Ac) *v.* [T] **1** if two things are linked, they are related, often because one strongly affects or causes the other: *Lung cancer has been* ***linked to/with*** *smoking cigarettes.* | *Educational success is strongly linked to social class.*

THESAURUS **related, connected, relevant, pertinent** ➔ RELATED

2 *also* **link up** to connect computers, communication systems, etc. so that electronic messages can be sent between them: *Each computer is* ***linked to/with*** *the Internet.* **3** to connect one place to another: *a highway linking two major cities*

link² *n.* [C] **1** a relationship or connection between two or more events, people, ideas, etc.: *the* ***link between*** *poverty and crime* | *He is believed to have* ***links with*** *terrorist groups.* | *Scientists have established a clear link between pollution and lung disease.* **2** one of the rings in a chain **3 a satellite/telephone/rail etc. link** something that makes communication or travel between two places possible: *The administration is trying to improve road links in the south of the country.* **4** IT a word or picture on a WEBSITE or computer document that will take you to another page or document if you CLICK on it: *Click on a link to explore other related websites.* ➔ CUFF LINK

link·age /ˈlɪŋkɪdʒ/ (Ac) *n.* [C,U] a link or connection between two things: *It is claimed that there is a linkage between violence on TV and violence in the home.*

ˈlinking ˌverb *n.* [C] ENG. LANG. ARTS in grammar, a verb that connects the subject of a sentence to a word or phrase that describes it. In the sentence "She seems friendly," "seems" is the linking verb.

li·no·le·um /lɪˈnoʊliəm/ *n.* [U] smooth shiny material that is used to cover a floor

lint /lɪnt/ *n.* [U] soft light pieces of thread or wool that come off cotton, wool, or other material

li·on /ˈlaɪən/ *n.* [C] a large African and Asian wild cat, the male of which has long thick hair around his neck [ORIGIN: 1200—1300 Old French, Latin *leo*, from Greek *leon*]

li·on·ess /ˈlaɪənɪs/ *n.* [C] a female lion

lip /lɪp/ *n.* [C] **1** one of the two edges of your mouth where your skin is redder or darker: *a kiss* ***on the lips*** ➔ *see picture on page A16* **2** the top edge of a container such as a bowl or cup **3 my lips are sealed** (spoken) said when promising someone that you will not tell a secret **4 thin-lipped/full-lipped etc.** with lips that are thin, round, etc. **5 pay/give lip service to sth** to say that you support or agree with something, without doing anything to prove this [ORIGIN: Old English *lippa*]

ˈlip gloss *n.* [C,U] a substance used to make lips look very shiny

lip-read /ˈlɪp rid/ *v.* [I,T] to watch someone's lips move in order to understand what s/he is saying, especially because you cannot hear —**lip-reading** *n.* [U]

lip·stick /ˈlɪpˌstɪk/ *n.* [C,U] a substance used for adding color to your lips, or a small tube containing this

lip sync /ˈlɪp ˌsɪŋk/ *v.* [I] to pretend to sing by moving your lips at the same time as a recording is being played

liq·ue·fy /ˈlɪkwəˌfaɪ/ *v.* (**liquefied, liquefies**) [I,T] (formal) to become liquid, or make something become liquid

li·queur /lɪˈkɚ, lɪˈkyʊr/ *n.* [C,U] a strong sweet alcoholic drink usually drunk after a meal

liq·uid /ˈlɪkwɪd/ *n.* [C,U] a substance such as water that is not a solid or a gas: *Cook the rice until all the liquid is absorbed.* —**liquid** *adj.*: *liquid soap*

liq·ui·date /ˈlɪkwəˌdeɪt/ *v.* [I,T] ECONOMICS to close a business or company and sell the things that belong to it, in order to pay a debt —**liquidation** /ˌlɪkwəˈdeɪʃən/ *n.* [C,U]

li·quid·i·ty /lɪˈkwɪdət̬i/ *n.* [U] ECONOMICS a situation in which a business or a person has enough money to pay debts or owns goods that can be sold to pay debts

ˌLiquid ˈPaper *n.* [U] (trademark) white liquid that is used to correct mistakes in writing and TYPING

liq·uor /ˈlɪkɚ/ *n.* [U] a strong alcoholic drink such as WHISKEY [ORIGIN: 1200—1300 Old French *licour*, from Latin *liquor*, from *liquere* "to flow as a liquid"]

ˈliquor store *n.* [C] a store where alcohol is sold

lisp /lɪsp/ *n.* [C] someone who has a lisp pronounces "s" sounds like "th" —**lisp** *v.* [I,T]

list¹ /lɪst/ *n.* [C] a set of names, things, numbers, etc. written one below the other: *a **list of** questions* | ***Make a list** of the things you'll need.* | *a **shopping list*** | *Is my name **on the list**?* ▸Don't say "in the list." ◂

THESAURUS

Types of lists
grocery list or **shopping list** – a list of food you need to buy
mailing list – a list of people who are all sent information or advertising material by mail or email
price list – a printed list of a company's goods or services, and their prices
checklist – a list of things you need to check
waiting list – a list of people who want something but will have to wait for it
guest list – a list of people invited somewhere

list² *v.* [T] to write a list, or mention things one after the other: *Each Monday the newspaper lists the ten most popular films.*

lis·ten /ˈlɪsən/ *v.* [I] **1** to pay attention to what someone is saying or to something that you hear: *This is very important, so I need you to listen.* | *Have you **listened to** this CD?* **2** (spoken) used to tell someone to pay attention to what you are saying: *Listen, can I call you back later?* **3** to consider what someone says to you and accept his/her advice: *I told him it was dangerous, but he wouldn't listen.* [ORIGIN: Old English *hlysnan*]

listen for sth/sb *phr. v.* to pay attention so that you are sure you will hear a sound: *He put down the paper and listened for the telephone.*

listen in *phr. v.* to listen to what someone is saying without him/her knowing it: *I think someone's **listening in on** the other phone.*

listen up *phr. v.* (spoken) used in order to get people's attention so they will hear what you are going to say: *OK, people, listen up. I'm only going to say this once.*

lis·ten·er /ˈlɪsənɚ/ *n.* [C] **1** someone who listens, especially to the radio ➔ VIEWER **2 a good listener** someone who listens in a patient and sympathetic way to other people

list·ing /ˈlɪstɪŋ/ *n.* **1** [C] something that is on a list **2 listings** [plural] lists of movies, plays, and other events, with the times and places at which they will happen

list·less /ˈlɪstlɪs/ *adj.* feeling tired and not interested in things

lit¹ /lɪt/ *v.* the past tense and past participle of LIGHT

lit² *adj.* having light or burning: *a brightly lit hall way*

lit·a·ny /ˈlɪtˀn-i/ *n.* **a litany of sth** a long list of problems, questions, complaints, etc.

lite /laɪt/ *adj.* a way of spelling "light", often used as part of the name of food or drink that has fewer CALORIEs than usual: *lite beer*

li·ter /ˈlit̬ɚ/ *n.* [C] (*written abbreviation* **l**) a unit for measuring liquids, equal to 2.12 PINTS or 0.26 gallons: *a **liter of** vodka* [ORIGIN: 1700—1800 French *litre*, from Medieval Latin *litra*, a measure, from Greek, a weight]

lit·er·a·cy /ˈlɪt̬ərəsi/ *n.* [U] the ability to read and write

lit·er·al /ˈlɪt̬ərəl/ *adj.* the literal meaning of a word or expression is its basic or original meaning ➔ FIGURATIVE: *a literal interpretation of the Bible*

lit·er·al·ly /ˈlɪt̬ərəli/ *adv.* **1** according to the most basic meaning of a word or expression: *There are literally millions of students in these programs.* **2** (spoken) used in order to emphasize something you have just said: *The program has moved literally thousands of homeless people off the streets.* **3 take sb/sth literally** to think that a word or statement is literal when it is not: *Lou was joking, but Sara took it literally.*

ˌliteral ˈquestion *n.* [C] ENG. LANG. ARTS a question that asks for a fact or detail that is contained in a piece of writing ➔ EVALUATIVE QUESTION, INFERENTIAL QUESTION

lit·er·ar·y /ˈlɪt̬əˌrɛri/ *adj.* **1** ENG. LANG. ARTS relating to literature: *a literary critic* **2** ENG. LANG. ARTS typical of writing used in literature rather than in ordinary writing and talking

lit·er·ate /ˈlɪt̬ərɪt/ *adj.* **1** able to read and write (ANT) **illiterate** **2** well educated

lit·er·a·ture /ˈlɪt̬ərətʃɚ, ˈlɪtrə-/ *n.* [U] **1** ENG. LANG. ARTS books, plays, etc. that are considered to be very good and important: *the great classics of*

L

English literature **2** books, articles, etc. on a particular subject: *scientific literature* **3** printed information produced by organizations that want to sell something or tell people about something: *the candidate's campaign literature* | *sales literature* [ORIGIN: 1300—1400 Old French, Latin *litteratura*, from *litteratus*]

lithe /laɪð/ *adj.* able to bend and move your body easily and gracefully

lith·i·um /ˈlɪθiəm/ *n.* [U] CHEMISTRY (*symbol* **Li**) a soft silver-colored ELEMENT that is the lightest known metal [ORIGIN: 1800—1900 Greek *lithos* "stone"]

lith·o·sphere /ˈlɪθəˌsfɪr/ *n.* [C] EARTH SCIENCES the solid surface of the Earth, including the CRUST (=the surface layer of rocks, soil, etc.) and the upper MANTLE (=the layer directly below the Earth's crust)

lit·i·gant /ˈlɪt̬əgənt/ *n.* [C] LAW someone who is making a claim against someone else, or defending himself or herself against a claim in a court of law

lit·i·ga·tion /ˌlɪt̬əˈgeɪʃən/ *n.* [U] LAW the process of taking a legal case to a court of law —**litigate** /ˈlɪt̬əˌgeɪt/ *v.* [I,T]

lit·mus /ˈlɪt˺məs/ *n.* [U] CHEMISTRY a chemical that turns red when touched by acid, and blue when touched by an ALKALI

ˈlitmus ˌpaper *n.* [U] CHEMISTRY paper containing litmus, used to test whether a chemical is an acid or an ALKALI

ˈlitmus ˌtest *n.* **1** [singular] a single action, situation, or quality that allows you to measure someone's attitude, beliefs, etc.: *The elections will be* ***a litmus test of*** *the political mood in the U.S.* **2** [C] CHEMISTRY a test in which litmus paper is used to find out whether a chemical is an acid or an ALKALI

lit·ter¹ /ˈlɪt̬ɚ/ *n.* **1** [U] pieces of waste paper, etc. that people leave on the ground in public places

> THESAURUS **garbage, trash, refuse, waste** ➔ GARBAGE

2 [C] a group of baby animals born at the same time to one mother: ***a litter of*** *puppies*

litter² *v.* **1** [I,T] to leave pieces of waste paper, etc. on the ground in a public place: *The sign says: "Please Do Not Litter."* **2** [T] if a lot of things litter a place, they are spread all over it in a messy way: *The floor was* ***littered with*** *clothes.*

lit·tle¹ /ˈlɪt̬l/ *adj.* **1** small in size: *a little house*

> THESAURUS **small, tiny, minute, miniature, minuscule** ➔ SMALL

2 a little bit not very much: *It will only hurt a little bit.* | *Can I have* ***a little bit of*** (=a small amount of) *milk in my coffee, please?* **3** short in time or distance: *I'll wait* ***a little while*** *and then call again.* | *Anna walked* ***a little way*** *down the road with him.* **4** young and small: *a little boy* | *Amy's* ***little brother/sister*** (=younger brother or sister)

> THESAURUS **young, small** ➔ YOUNG¹

5 not important: *He gets angry over little things.* | *There is one little problem.* **6** (spoken) used in order to emphasize an adjective: *She owns a nice little restaurant in the city.* [ORIGIN: Old English *lytel*]

little² *quantifier* (comparative **less**, superlative **least**) **1** only a small amount of something: *Little is known about the disease.* | *We had* ***very little*** *money.* **2 a little** a small amount: *I only know a little Spanish.* | *She told him a little about it.* | *I need* ***a little more*** *time to finish the test.* | *Tony went out to see* ***a little of*** *the town.* **3** a short time or distance: *He must be* ***a little over*** *60* (=slightly older than 60). | *Phoenix is* ***a little under*** *50 miles from here* (=slightly fewer than 50 miles).

> GRAMMAR
> **little, a little**
> Use **little** when you mean "not much": *We have very little time.*
> Use **a little** when you mean "a small amount": *I only used a little salt.*
> **Little** and **a little** are always used with U nouns.
> ➔ FEW

little³ *adv.* **1** not much or only slightly ➔ LESS, LEAST: *He moved the table* ***a little*** *closer to the wall.* | *I was* ***a little*** *afraid of the dog.* | *She goes out very little.* **2 little by little** gradually: *Little by little, his playing improved.*

ˌlittle ˈfinger *n.* [C] the smallest finger on your hand

ˌLittle League ˈBaseball *n.* [U] (trademark) a group of baseball teams for children

lit·ur·gy /ˈlɪt̬ɚdʒi/ *n.* (plural **liturgies**) [C,U] prayers, songs, etc. that are said or sung in a particular order in a religious ceremony —**liturgical** /lɪˈtɚdʒɪkəl/ *adj.*

liv·a·ble, **liveable** /ˈlɪvəbəl/ *adj.* good enough to live in, but not very good (SYN) **habitable**

live¹ /lɪv/ *v.* **1** [I] to be alive or to continue to stay alive: *My grandmother lived to be 88.* | *Thoreau lived in the mid-1800s.* **2** [I] to have your home in a particular place: *Where do you live?* | *I* ***live in*** *Boston.* | *They* ***live on*** *Bergen Street.* | *Kitty still* ***lives at home*** (=lives with her parents). **3** [I,T] to have a particular type of life, or to live in a particular way: *We earn enough to live comfortably.* | *children* ***living in poverty*** [ORIGIN: Old English *libban*]

live sth **down** *phr. v.* **not live sth down** to not be able to make people forget about something bad or embarrassing you have done: *You'll never live this evening down!*

live for sb/sth *phr. v.* to consider someone or something to be the most important thing in your life: *She lives for her children.*

live off sb/sth *phr. v.* to get your food or money

from someone or something other than a job: *He's living off money from his investments.*
live on *phr. v.* **1 live on** sth to have a particular amount of money to buy food and other necessary things: *I don't know how he can live on $600 a month.* **2 live on** sth to eat a lot of a particular kind of food: *These animals live on insects.* **3** to continue to exist: *She will live on in our memories.*
live through sth *phr. v.* to experience difficult or dangerous conditions and continue living: *Don didn't expect to live through the war.*
live together *phr. v.* to live with another person in a sexual relationship without being married: *Mark and I have been living together for two years.*
live up to sth *phr. v.* to do something as well, or be as good as someone expects: *Charles could never* ***live up to*** *his father's* ***expectations.***
live with *phr. v.* **1 live with** sth to accept a difficult situation even when it continues for a long time: *living with pain* **2 live with** sb to live with another person, especially in a sexual relationship without being married: *Tim's living with a girl he met in college.*

live² /laɪv/ *adj.* **1** not dead or artificial ANT **dead**: *He fed the snake live rats.* **2** broadcast as an event happens: *a live broadcast of the Rose Parade* **3** performed for people who are watching: *The club has live music six nights a week.* **4** having electricity flowing through it: *a live wire* **5** ready to explode: *a live bomb* → **real live** *at* REAL¹

live³ /laɪv/ *adv.* **1** if something is broadcast live, it is broadcast on television or radio as it is actually happening: *The pictures were broadcast live across the world.* **2** performing in front of people: *The band is* ***playing live*** *in Houston this week.*

live·li·hood /ˈlaɪvliˌhʊd/ *n.* [C,U] the way you earn money in order to live: *Farming is their livelihood.*

live·ly /ˈlaɪvli/ *adj.* (comparative **livelier**, superlative **liveliest**) **1** very active and cheerful: *a lively group of children*

THESAURUS energetic, vigorous, full of energy, dynamic → ENERGETIC

2 very exciting and interesting: *a lively debate* —**liveliness** *n.* [U]

liv·en /ˈlaɪvən/ *v.*
liven (sth ↔) **up** *phr. v.* to become more exciting, or to make something more exciting: *Better music might liven the party up.*

liv·er /ˈlɪvɚ/ *n.* **1** [C] BIOLOGY a large organ in your body that cleans your blood → *see picture at* ORGAN **2** [U] the liver of an animal used as food

lives /laɪvz/ *n.* the plural of LIFE

live·stock /ˈlaɪvstɑk/ *n.* [U] animals that are kept on a farm

liv·id /ˈlɪvɪd/ *adj.* extremely angry

THESAURUS angry, furious, mad, indignant, irate, outraged → ANGRY

liv·ing¹ /ˈlɪvɪŋ/ *adj.* **1** [only before noun] alive now ANT **dead**: *She is one of our greatest living writers.* | *The ocean is full of* ***living things*** (=animals and plants). **2** existing or being used now: *a living language*

living² *n.* **1** [C usually singular] the way that you earn money: *What does he* ***do for a living?*** | *It's hard to* ***make a living*** (=earn enough money) *as an actor.* **2** [U] the way that someone lives his/her life: *Sometimes I want to give up city living and move to the country.* **3 the living** [plural] all the people who are alive → COST OF LIVING

ˈliving room *n.* [C] the main room in a house, where you relax, watch television, etc.

ˌliving ˈwill *n.* [C] LAW a document that explains what legal and medical decisions should be made for you if you are too sick to make them yourself

liz·ard /ˈlɪzɚd/ *n.* [C] a REPTILE that has rough skin, four short legs, and a long tail [ORIGIN: 1300—1400 Old French *lesard*, from Latin *lacerta*]

-'ll /l, əl/ the short form of "will": *He'll be here soon.*

lla·ma /ˈlɑmə/ *n.* [C] a large South American animal with thick hair like wool and a long neck [ORIGIN: 1600—1700 Spanish, Quechua (a South American language)]

Ln. the written abbreviation of LANE

load¹ /loʊd/ *n.* [C] **1** a large quantity of something that is carried by a person, a vehicle, etc.: *a ship carrying* ***a full load of*** *fuel and supplies* **2 carload/truckload etc.** the largest amount or number that a car, etc. can carry: *a busload of kids* **3** the amount of work that a machine or a person has to do: *a light/heavy* ***work load*** **4** a quantity of clothes that are washed at the same time: *Can you* ***do a load of*** *clothes later today?*

SPOKEN PHRASES
5 a load of sth/loads of sth a lot of something: *Don't worry, there's loads of time.* **6 get a load of sb/sth** said when you want someone to notice something funny or surprising

[ORIGIN: Old English *lad* "support, carrying"]

L

load² *v.* **1** [I,T] *also* **load up** to put a load of something on or into a vehicle or container: *They* ***loaded*** *all their luggage* ***into*** *the car.* | *He cleared the table and loaded the dishwasher.* **2** [T] to put bullets into a gun or film into a camera **3** [T] to put a program into a computer
load sb/sth ↔ **down** *phr. v.* to make someone carry too many things or do too much work: *Mom was* ***loaded down with*** *groceries.*

load·ed /ˈloʊdɪd/ *adj.* **1** containing bullets or film: *a loaded gun* **2** carrying a load of something: *a loaded truck* **3** [not before noun] (informal) very rich: *His grandmother is loaded.* **4 loaded question** a question that is unfair because it makes you give a particular answer **5 loaded with sth** full of a particular quality, or containing a lot of something: *a cake loaded with nuts*

loaf[1] /loʊf/ *n.* (plural **loaves** /loʊvz/) [C] bread that is shaped and baked in one large piece: ***a loaf of bread*** [ORIGIN: Old English *hlaf*] → *see picture at* BREAD

loaf[2] *v.* [I] (informal) to waste time in a lazy way when you should be working: *He spends his days **loafing around** the house.*

Loaf·er /ˈloʊfɚ/ *n.* [C] (trademark) a flat leather shoe without LACES

loan[1] /loʊn/ *n.* **1** [C] an amount of money that you borrow from a bank: *We'll **take out a loan** to buy the car.* | *I'll be **paying off/back** the **loan** for at least five years.* | ***student loans*** (=money that students borrow to pay for college) **2 on loan** being borrowed: *The book is on loan from the library.* **3** [singular] the act of lending something [ORIGIN: 1100—1200 Old Norse *lan*]

loan[2] *v.* [T] to lend someone something, especially money: *Can you loan me $20 until Friday?*

ˈloan shark *n.* [C] (disapproving) someone who lends money to people and charges a very high rate of INTEREST

loath /loʊθ, loʊð/ *adj.* **be loath to do sth** (formal) to be unwilling to do something

loathe /loʊð/ *v.* [T] (formal) to hate someone or something —**loathing** *n.* [U]

THESAURUS hate, can't stand, detest, despise, abhor → HATE[1]

loath·some /ˈloʊðsəm, ˈloʊθ-/ *adj.* (formal) very unpleasant (SYN) **disgusting**

loaves /loʊvz/ *n.* the plural of LOAF

lob /lɑb/ *v.* (**lobbed**, **lobbing**) [T] to throw or hit a ball so that it moves slowly in a high curve

THESAURUS throw, toss, chuck, hurl, fling, pass, pitch → THROW[1]

L

lob·by[1] /ˈlɑbi/ *n.* (plural **lobbies**) [C] **1** a large hall inside the entrance of a building: *waiting in the hotel lobby* **2** a group of people who try to persuade the government to change or approve a particular law: *the environmental lobby* [ORIGIN: 1500—1600 Medieval Latin *lobium* "covered way for walking"]

lobby[2] *v.* (**lobbied**, **lobbies**) [I,T] to try to persuade the government to change or approve a particular law: *a group **lobbying for/against** the law*

lob·by·ing /ˈlɑbiɪŋ/ *n.* [U] POLITICS the activity of trying to persuade someone with political power to change a law so that it is more favorable to a particular group of people

lob·by·ist /ˈlɑbiɪst/ *n.* [C] POLITICS someone whose paid job involves trying to persuade people with political power to change a law so that it is more favorable to the group of people that he or she represents

lobe /loʊb/ *n.* [C] your EARLOBE

lob·ster /ˈlɑbstɚ/ *n.* [C,U] an ocean animal with eight legs, a shell, and two large CLAWS, or the meat of this animal

lobster

lo·cal[1] /ˈloʊkəl/ *adj.* **1** [usually before noun] relating to a particular place or area, especially the place you live in: *a good local hospital* | *The story appeared in the local newspaper.* | *It costs a quarter to make a **local call*** (=a telephone call to someone in the same area as you). → NEAR[1] **2** affecting a particular part of your body: *a local anesthetic* [ORIGIN: 1300—1400 French, Late Latin *localis*, from Latin *locus* "place"]

local[2] *n.* **the locals** the people who live in a particular place

ˌlocal ˌarea ˈnetwork *n.* [C] IT a LAN

lo·cale /loʊˈkæl/ *n.* [C] (formal) the place where something happens

lo·cal·i·ty /loʊˈkæləṭi/ *n.* [C] (plural **localities**) (formal) a small area of a country, city, etc.

lo·cal·ized /ˈloʊkəˌlaɪzd/ *adj.* (formal) only within a small area: *localized pain*

lo·cal·ly /ˈloʊkəli/ *adv.* in or near the area where you are or the area you are talking about: *locally grown apples*

THESAURUS

nearby: *Do you live nearby?*
close by/close to here: *My folks live close by.*
around here: *Is there a bank around here?*
in the neighborhood: *Is there a good Chinese restaurant in the neighborhood?*
in/around these parts: *Most folk in these parts don't want the dam to be built.*
in close proximity (to) (formal) – near in distance: *the nations in close proximity to Russia*
→ NEAR[1]

ˈlocal time *n.* [U] the time of day in a particular part of the world: *We'll arrive in Boston at 4:00 local time.*

lo·cate /ˈloʊkeɪt/ (Ac) *v.* **1** [T] to find the exact position of something: *Divers have located the shipwreck.* | *If you have difficulty locating a particular book, ask a librarian for assistance.*

THESAURUS find, discover, trace, track sb/sth down, unearth → FIND[1]

2 be located to be in a particular place or position: *The bakery is located in the middle of town.* | *Many volcanoes are located along the coastal area.* **3** [I,T] to come to a place and start a business there: *The company **located** its offices **in** New Jersey when rents went up in New York.* | *Large retail companies are only prepared to locate stores* *in areas where there are a lot of people.* [ORIGIN: 1500—1600 Latin, past participle of *locare* "to place," from *locus*]

lo·ca·tion /loʊˈkeɪʃən/ (Ac) *n.* **1** [C] a particular place or position: *His apartment is in a really good location.* | *a map showing the **location of** the school* | *The climate of an area partly depends on its **geographical location**.*

THESAURUS place, position, spot, site → PLACE¹

2 [C,U] a place where a movie is filmed, away from the STUDIO: *scenes shot **on location** in Montana*

lock¹ /lɑk/ *v.* **1** [I,T] to be fastened with a lock, or to fasten something with a lock (ANT) **unlock**: *Lock the door when you leave.* **2 lock sth up/away/in etc.** to put something in a safe place and fasten it with a lock: *He **locked** the money **in** a safe.* **3** [I] to become set in one position and be unable to move: *The brakes locked and we skidded.*

lock sb **in** *phr. v.* to prevent someone from leaving a place by locking the door

lock into sth *phr. v.* **be locked into** sth to be unable to change a situation: *families who are locked into a cycle of poverty*

lock sb **out** *phr. v.* to prevent someone from entering a place by locking the door

lock up *phr. v.* **1** (informal) **lock** sb **up** to put someone in prison **2 lock** (sth ↔) **up** to make a building safe by locking all the doors

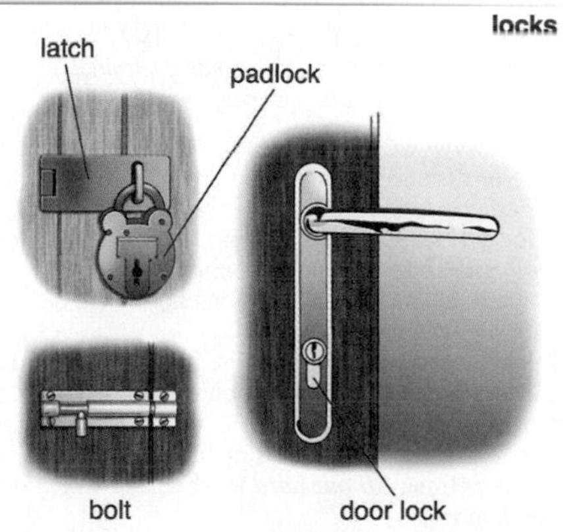

lock² *n.* [C] **1** a thing that keeps a door, drawer, etc. fastened or shut and is usually opened with a key: *There's no lock on the door.* **2 lock, stock, and barrel** including every part of something: *They sold everything, lock, stock, and barrel.* **3 under lock and key** kept safely in something that is locked **4** a small number of hairs on your head that hang together: *Carla twisted **a lock of hair** around her finger.* **5** a special area on a river where the water level can go up or down to raise or lower boats

lock·er /ˈlɑkɚ/ *n.* [C] a small cupboard with a lock where you leave books, clothes, etc., especially at school or when you are playing sports

ˈlocker room *n.* [C] a room where you change your clothes and leave them in a locker

lock·et /ˈlɑkɪt/ *n.* [C] a piece of jewelry like a small round box in which you put a picture of someone, worn on a chain around your neck

lock·smith /ˈlɑkˌsmɪθ/ *n.* [C] someone who makes and repairs locks

lo·co·mo·tive /ˌloʊkəˈmoʊt̬ɪv/ *n.* [C] a train engine

lo·cust /ˈloʊkəst/ *n.* [C] an insect similar to a GRASSHOPPER that flies in large groups and often destroys crops

lo·cu·tion /loʊˈkyuʃən/ *n.* [C] ENG. LANG. ARTS a phrase, especially one used in a particular area or by a particular group of people: *a Yiddish locution*

lodge¹ /lɑdʒ/ *v.* **1** [I] to become stuck somewhere (ANT) **dislodge**: *He had a fish bone **lodged in** his throat.* **2 lodge a complaint/protest etc.** to officially complain, protest, etc. about something: *He has lodged a formal complaint with the club.* **3** [I] to pay someone rent in order to live in a room in his/her house

lodge² *n.* [C] **1** a building in the country where people can stay for a short time, especially in order to do a particular activity: *a ski lodge* **2** a local meeting place for some organizations: *the Masonic lodge*

lodg·ing /ˈlɑdʒɪŋ/ *n.* [C,U] a place to stay: *The tourist office will give you information on lodging.*

loft /lɔft/ *n.* [C] **1** a space above a business, factory, etc. that was once used for storing goods, but has been changed into living space or work space for artists: *She's just bought a loft in Manhattan.* **2** a raised area above the main part of a room, usually used for sleeping **3** a raised level in a BARN, where HAY is kept [ORIGIN: 900—1000 Old Norse *lopt* "air, upstairs room"]

loft·y /ˈlɔfti/ *adj.* (comparative **loftier**, superlative **loftiest**) **1** showing high standards or high moral qualities: *lofty ideals* **2** (literary) high

log¹ /lɔg, lɑg/ *n.* [C] **1** a thick piece of wood cut from a tree → *see picture at* PLANT¹ **2** an official record of events on a ship or airplane

THESAURUS record, diary, journal → RECORD¹

log² *v.* (**logged**, **logging**) **1** [T] to make an official record of events, facts, etc., especially on a ship or airplane **2** [I,T] to cut down trees —**logger** *n.* [C]

log off/out *phr. v.* IT to stop using a computer or computer system by typing (TYPE) a special word

log on/in *phr. v.* IT to start using a computer or computer system by typing (TYPE) a special word

log·a·rithm /ˈlɑgəˌrɪðəm/ *also* **log** *n.* [C] MATH the number of times a number must be multiplied by itself to equal another number [ORIGIN: 1600—1700 Modern Latin *logarithmus*, from Greek *logos* "ratio, word" + *arithmos* "number"]

ˌlog ˈcabin *n.* [C] a small house made of logs

L

log·ger·heads /ˈlɔgɚˌhɛdz, ˈlɑ-/ *n.* **be at loggerheads (with sb)** to disagree very strongly with someone [ORIGIN: 1800—1900 *loggerhead* "stupid person, large head, type of heavy tool" (16—20 centuries), from *logger* "block of wood" (16—18 centuries) + *head*]

log·ging /ˈlɔgɪŋ, ˈlɑ-/ *n.* [U] the industry of cutting down trees for wood, paper, etc.

log·ic /ˈlɑdʒɪk/ (Ac) *n.* [U] **1** a set of sensible and correct reasons: *There is no* ***logic in*** *releasing criminals just because the prisons are crowded.* | *The* ***logic behind*** *that statement is faulty.* **2** the science or study of thinking carefully about something, using formal methods: *Logic was invented by the ancient Greeks over 3,000 years ago.* [ORIGIN: 1300—1400 French *logique*, from Latin *logica*, from Greek *logos* "speech, word, reason"]

log·i·cal /ˈlɑdʒɪkəl/ (Ac) *adj.* **1** seeming reasonable and sensible (ANT) **illogical**: *It's the logical place to build a new supermarket.* | *Is there a logical explanation for this unusual weather?* **2** based on the rules of logic: *a logical conclusion* | *Finding a new scientific theory is a creative act, not a process of logical analysis.* **—logically** *adv.*

lo·gi·cian /loʊˈdʒɪʃən/ (Ac) *n.* [C] someone who studies or is skilled in logic: *This is a problem that has puzzled logicians for centuries.*

lo·gis·tics /loʊˈdʒɪstɪks, lə-/ *n.* **the logistics of sth** the practical organizing that is needed to make a complicated plan or activity successful **—logistical** *adj.* **—logistically** *adv.*

log·jam /ˈlɔgdʒæm, ˈlɑg-/ *n.* [C] a lot of problems or other things that are preventing something from being done: *a logjam of work*

lo·go /ˈloʊgoʊ/ *n.* (plural **logos**) [C] a small design that is the official sign of a company or organization

loin·cloth /ˈlɔɪnklɔθ/ *n.* [C] a piece of cloth that men in some hot countries wear around their waist

loins /lɔɪnz/ *n.* [plural] (literary) the part of the body below your waist where the sexual organs are

loi·ter /ˈlɔɪt̬ɚ/ *v.* [I] to stand in a public place without having a reason to be there

loll /lɑl/ *v.* [I] **1** to sit or lie in a lazy or relaxed way: *We spent the afternoon* ***lolling around*** *on the beach.* **2** if someone's head or tongue lolls, it hangs down

lol·li·pop /ˈlɑliˌpɑp/ *n.* [C] a hard candy on the end of a stick

lone /loʊn/ *adj.* [only before noun] (literary) being the only person or thing in a place, or the only person or thing that does something: *a lone figure standing in the snow*

lone·ly /ˈloʊnli/ *adj.* **1** unhappy because you are alone: *She was very lonely after her husband died.* **2** far from where people live: *a lonely country road* **—loneliness** *n.* [U]

lon·er /ˈloʊnɚ/ *n.* [C] someone who wants to be alone or who has no friends

lone·some /ˈloʊnsəm/ *adj.* LONELY

long¹ /lɔŋ/ *adj.*
1 MEASUREMENT measuring a great length, distance, or time (ANT) **short**: ***long hair*** | *There was a* ***long line*** *at the bank.* | *The meeting was too long.* | *It* ***takes a long time*** *to drive to work.*
2 PARTICULAR LENGTH having a particular length: *The snake was at least three feet long.*
3 TIME continuing for a particular amount of time: ***How long*** *is the movie?* | *O'Keeffe lived* ***long enough*** *to see her artwork become successful.*

THESAURUS

lengthy – continuing for a long time, especially so that you have to wait before you can do something: *Finding the right job can be a lengthy process.*
long-running – use this about arguments, battles, events, or performances: *The two families have been involved in a long-running argument over land.*
lasting – strong enough to continue for a long time: *They formed a lasting friendship when they were in college.*
prolonged – continuing for much longer than people expected: *He was absent from school for prolonged periods.*
long-winded – too long and using too many words, in a way that is boring or confusing: *a long-winded explanation*
interminable – much too long in a way that is extremely boring: *The movie was interminable, and I couldn't wait till it ended.*

4 SEEMING LONG (informal) seeming too long in time or distance because you are tired, bored, etc.: *It's been a* ***long day***.
5 long hours a large amount of time: *She spent long hours working at the computer.*
6 BOOK/LIST/NAME ETC. a long book, list, etc. has a lot of pages, details, etc.
7 long weekend three days, including Saturday and Sunday, when you do not have to go to work or school
8 in the long run when something is finished, or at a later time: *All our hard work will be worth it in the long run.*
9 CLOTHES covering all of your arms or legs (ANT) **short**: *a long skirt* | *a* ***long-sleeved*** *shirt*
[ORIGIN: Old English *long*, *lang*]

long² *adv.* **1** for a long time: *Have you been waiting long?* **2 long before/after** for a long time before or after a particular time or event: *The farm was sold long before you were born.* **3 for long** for a long time: *Have you known the Garretts for very long?* **4 as long as** if: *You can go, as long as you're back by four o'clock.* **5 no longer** *also* **not any longer** used in order to show that something happened in the past, but does not happen now: *Mr. Allen no longer works for the company.* **6 so long** (spoken) goodbye **7 before long** soon: *It will be Christmas before long.*

long[3] *v.* [I] (formal) to want something very much: *The children* ***longed to*** *get outside.*

ˌlong-'distance *adj.* [only before noun] **1** a long-distance telephone call is to a place that is far away (ANT) **local** **2** traveling, running, etc. between two places that are far away from each other: *long-distance flights* —**long-distance** *adv.*

ˌlong di'vision *n.* [C,U] MATH a method of dividing one large number by another large number

ˌlong-drawn-'out *adj.* [only before noun] continuing for a longer time than is necessary: *a long-drawn-out discussion*

lon·gev·i·ty /lɑn'dʒɛvət̬i, lɔn-/ *n.* [U] (formal) long life

long·hand /'lɔŋhænd/ *n.* [U] writing full words by hand rather than using a machine such as a computer

long·ing /'lɔŋɪŋ/ *n.* [singular, U] a strong feeling of wanting someone or something very much: ***a longing for*** *peace* —**longing** *adj.* —**longingly** *adv.*

lon·gi·tude /'lɑndʒəˌtud/ *n.* [C,U] a position on the Earth measured in degrees east or west of an imaginary line from the top of the Earth to the bottom [ORIGIN: 1300—1400 Latin *longitudo* "length," from *longus* "long"] —**longitudinal** /ˌlɑndʒə'tudn-əl/ *adj.* ➔ compare LATITUDE ➔ see picture at GLOBE

'long johns *n.* [plural] (informal) warm underwear that covers your legs

'long jump *n.* [U] a sport in which you jump as far as possible

ˌlong-'lasting *adj.* continuing for a long time: *hopes for a long-lasting peace in the region* | *long-lasting batteries*

long-lived /ˌlɔŋ 'laɪvd◂ / *adj.* living or existing for a long time

ˌlong-'lost *adj.* [only before noun] lost or not seen for a long time: *a* ***long-lost friend***

ˌlong-'range *adj.* [usually before noun] **1** relating to a time that continues far into the future: *long-range development plans* **2** covering a long distance: *a long-range missile*

ˌlong-'running *adj.* [usually before noun] having existed or happened for a long time: *a long-running TV show*

long·shore·man /ˌlɔŋ'ʃɔrmən, 'lɔŋˌʃɔrmən/ *n.* (plural **longshoremen**) [C] someone whose job is to load and unload ships

'long shot *n.* [C usually singular] (informal) **1** someone or something with very little chance of success: *It's a long shot, but I may as well apply.* **2 not by a long shot** not at all, or not nearly: *This isn't over, not by a long shot.*

ˌlong-'standing *adj.* having continued or existed for a long time: *a long-standing agreement between the two countries*

ˌlong-'suffering *adj.* [usually before noun] patient in spite of problems or unhappiness

ˌlong-'term *adj.* continuing for a long period of time into the future ➔ SHORT-TERM: *The* ***long-term effects*** *of the drug are not known.* ➔ **in the long/short term** at TERM[1]

long·time /'lɔŋtaɪm/ *adj.* [only before noun] having existed for a long time, or having had a particular position for a long time: *a longtime friend of the family* | *longtime residents of Takoma Park*

ˌlong-'winded *adj.* continuing to talk for too long in a way that is boring: *a long-winded speech*

look[1] /lʊk/ *v.* **1** [I] to turn your eyes toward something so that you can see it: *I didn't see it. I wasn't looking.* | *"I have to go," Mel said,* ***looking at*** *his watch.*

USAGE

You **look at** a picture, person, thing, etc. because you want to: *She was looking at some old photographs.*
You **see** something without planning to: *I saw two men running out of the building.*
You **watch** TV, a movie, a game, or something that happens for a period of time: *He's watching the baseball game.* | *The kids are watching TV.*
You can also say that you saw a movie, a program, etc., but you cannot say "see television": *I saw a really good movie last night.*

THESAURUS

glance – to look at someone or something for a short time and then look quickly away: *Kevin glanced at the clock.*
peek/peep – to quickly look at something, especially something you are not supposed to see: *I peeked through the curtains, trying to see if they were home.*
peer – to look very carefully, especially because you cannot see something well: *Hansen peered through the windshield at the street signs.*
stare – to look at someone or something for a long time, especially without blinking your eyes: *He stood staring out into the street.*
gaze – to look at someone or something for a long time, often without realizing that you are doing it: *Helen gazed out the window at the shimmering water.*
gape – to look at something for a long time, usually with your mouth open, because you are very shocked or surprised: *She backed away as the children gaped at her.*
regard (formal) – to look at someone or something, especially in a particular way: *He regarded her steadily.*

2 [I] to try to find someone or something using your eyes: *I've* ***looked*** *everywhere* ***for*** *the money.* | *Have you looked in here?* | *Brad was* ***looking for*** *you last night.*

THESAURUS

search – to look carefully for someone or something: *We searched the whole house for the keys.*
try to find sb/sth – to look for someone or

L

something, especially when this is difficult: *He's been trying to find a job for several months.*
hunt for sb/sth – to look in a lot of places for someone or something: *I always seem to be hunting for my keys.*
seek (formal) – to try to find someone or something: *The new graduates are seeking employment.*
go through sth – to examine something very thoroughly when looking for something: *Security officers went through our bags.*
have a look for sb/sth (spoken) – to look quickly for someone or something: *I think I put it in the kitchen drawer; I'll take a look.*

3 [linking verb] to seem to be something, especially by having a particular appearance: *You* ***look nice/good*** *in that dress.* | *He* ***looks like*** *he hasn't slept for days.* | *Gina and Ron looked very happy.*

THESAURUS seem, appear → SEEM

4 -looking having a particular type of appearance: *That was a funny-looking dog!* | *weird-looking people* **5 look sb in the eye** to look directly at someone in order to show that you are not afraid of him/her

SPOKEN PHRASES

6 Look ... said when you are annoyed and you want to emphasize what you are saying: *Look, I'm very serious about this.* **7** [T] said in order to make someone notice something: *Look how skinny she is.* | *Mom, look what I made!* **8 (I'm) just looking** used in a store in order to tell someone who works there that you do not need help: *"Can I help you?" "No thanks, I'm just looking."*

[ORIGIN: Old English *locian*]

look after sb/sth *phr. v.* to take care of someone or something: *Paul helps look after his two younger brothers.*

look ahead *phr. v.* to think about what will happen in the future: *We need to look ahead and plan for next year.*

look around *phr. v.* **look around** sth to see, study, read, etc. many different things in order to find something or to learn about something: *We have about three hours to look around the downtown.*

look at *phr. v.* **1 look at sth** to read something quickly: *Jane was looking at a magazine while she waited.* **2 look at sth** to study and consider something in order to decide what to do: *The doctor looked at the cut on her head.* **3 look at** sb (spoken) used to give someone or something as an example of a situation: *Look at Eric. He didn't go to college and he's doing fine.*

look back *also* **look back on sth** *phr. v.* to think about something that happened in the past: *Looking back, I see my mistake.*

look down on sb/sth *phr. v.* to think that you are better than someone or something else: *He looks down on anyone who doesn't have a college education.*

look for sb/sth *phr. v.* **1** to try to find a particular type of thing or person that you need or want: *How long have you been looking for a job?* **2 be looking for trouble/a fight** (informal) to be behaving in a way that makes it likely that problems or a fight will happen

look forward to sth *phr. v.* to be excited and happy about something that is going to happen: *We're really looking forward to skiing in Tahoe.*

look into sth *phr. v.* to try to find out the truth about something: *The FBI will look into the cause of the fire.*

look on *phr. v.* **1** to watch something, without being involved in it: *Children ran through the playground as their mothers looked on.* **2 look on/upon** sth to think about something in a particular way: *My family* ***looks on*** *divorce* ***as*** *a sin.*

look out to pay attention to what is happening around you: *Look out! There's a car coming.*

look sth/sb ↔ **over** *phr. v.* to examine something or someone quickly: *Can you look over my résumé before I send it?*

look through *phr. v.* **1 look through** sth to look for something in a pile of papers, a drawer, someone's pockets, etc.: *I found her looking through my old letters.* **2 look right through sb** to pretend that you have not seen someone

look up *phr. v.* **1** if a situation is looking up, it is becoming better: *Things are looking up for me.* **2 look** sth ↔ **up** to try to find information in a book, on a computer, etc.: *If you don't know the word, look it up.* **3 look** sb ↔ **up** to visit someone you know, especially when you go to the place where s/he lives for another reason: *Don't forget to look up my parents when you're in Boston.*

look up to sb *phr. v.* to admire and respect someone: *Everybody looks up to him.*

look² *n.* **1** [C usually singular] an act of looking at something: *Let me* ***take/have a look at*** *that map again.* **2** [C] an expression that you make with your eyes or face to show how you feel: *She* ***gave*** *me an angry* ***look.*** **3** [C] the appearance of someone or something: *I* ***don't like the look of*** *that bruise – maybe you should see a doctor.* **4 looks** [plural] how attractive someone is: *He's got his father's* ***good looks.***

look·a·like /ˈlʊkəˌlaɪk/ *n.* [C] (informal) someone who looks very similar to someone else, especially someone famous: *a Madonna lookalike*

look·out /ˈlʊk-aʊt/ *n.* **1 be on the lookout (for sb/sth)** to continuously watch a place or pay attention to a situation because you are looking for someone or something: *Be on the lookout for snakes.* **2** [C] someone whose duty is to watch carefully for danger, or the place where s/he does this

loom¹ /lum/ *v.* [I] **1** to appear as a large unclear threatening shape: *The mountain loomed in front of us.* **2** if a problem or difficult situation looms, it is likely to happen soon: *The report warns that a crisis in the airline industry is looming.* **3 loom large** to seem important, worrying, and difficult to avoid: *Fear of failure loomed large in his mind.*

loom² *n.* [C] a frame or machine used for weaving cloth

loon·y /'luni/ *adj.* (informal) extremely silly or crazy

loop¹ /lup/ *n.* **1** [C] a shape like a curve or a circle, or a line, piece of wire, string, etc. that has this shape: *belt loops* (=cloth loops used for holding a belt on pants) **2 be out of the loop** to not be part of a group of people that has information and makes decisions about something

loop² *v.* [I,T] to make a loop, or to make something into a loop

loop·hole /'luphoʊl/ *n.* [C] a small mistake in a law or rule that makes it possible to legally avoid doing what the law says: *tax loopholes*

loose¹ /lus/ *adj.*

1 NOT FIRMLY ATTACHED not firmly attached to something: *a loose screw* | *The buttons on my shirt are coming loose.*

2 NOT TIED/FASTENED not tied or fastened very tightly: *My shoelaces are loose.*

3 CLOTHES loose clothes are big and do not fit tightly on your body (SYN) **baggy**

4 NOT CONTROLLED free from being controlled in a CAGE, prison, or institution: *Two of the prisoners* ***broke loose*** *from the guards.* | *Don't* ***let*** *your dog* ***loose*** *on the beach.*

5 not exact: *a* ***loose translation/interpretation***

6 loose ends parts of something such as work or an agreement that have not yet been completed: *I have to* ***tie up*** *a few* ***loose ends*** *before we go away.*

7 loose cannon someone who cannot be trusted because s/he says or does things you do not want him/her to

8 NOT MORAL (old-fashioned) behaving in a way that is considered to be sexually immoral: *The film portrayed her as a loose woman.* [ORIGIN: 1100—1200 Old Norse *lauss*] —**loosely** *adv.*: *A towel was loosely wrapped around his neck.*

loose² *n.* **on the loose** if a criminal is on the loose, s/he has escaped from prison

ˌloose-'leaf *adj.* [only before noun] having pages that can be put in or taken out easily: *a loose-leaf notebook*

loos·en /'lusən/ *v.* [I,T] to become less tight or less firmly attached to something, or to make something do this: *He loosened his tie.* | *The screws in the shelf had loosened.*

loosen (sb/sth ↔) **up** *phr. v.* **1** to become more relaxed and feel less worried, or to make someone feel this way: *Claire loosened up after she'd had a drink.* **2** if your muscles loosen up, or if you loosen them up, they stop feeling stiff

loot¹ /lut/ *v.* [I,T] to steal things, especially from stores that have been damaged in a war or RIOT: *Businesses were looted and burned in the riot.* —**looting** *n.* [U] —**looter** *n.* [C]

THESAURUS **steal, burglarize, rob, shoplift, plunder, pilfer** → STEAL¹

loot² *n.* [U] goods that are stolen by thieves or taken by soldiers who have won a battle

lop /lɑp/ *v.* (**lopped**, **lopping**) [T] *also* **lop off** to cut part of something off

lope /loʊp/ *v.* [I] (literary) to run easily using long steps

lop·sid·ed /'lɑpˌsaɪdɪd/ *adj.* having one side that is heavier, larger, or lower than the other side: *a lopsided smile*

lo·qua·cious /loʊ'kweɪʃəs/ *adj.* (formal) a loquacious person likes to talk a lot, sometimes too much —**loquaciousness** *also* **loquacity** /loʊ'kwæsəṭi/ *n.* [U]

Lord /lɔrd/ *n.* [C] **1** *also* **the Lord** a title used for God or Jesus Christ **2 good/oh/my Lord!** (spoken) said when you are surprised, worried, or angry

lord *n.* [C] a man who has a particular position in the ARISTOCRACY [ORIGIN: Old English *hlaford*, from *hlaf* "bread" + *weard* "keeper"]

lore /lɔr/ *n.* [U] knowledge and TRADITIONS that people learn from other people rather than from books

lose /luz/ *v.* (past tense and past participle **lost** /lɔst/, present participle **losing**)

1 NOT FIND [T] to be unable to find someone or something: *Danny's always losing his keys.*

USAGE

If you **lose** something, you cannot find it: *I've lost my keys.*

If you **miss** a class, meeting, etc. that you regularly attend, you do not go to it: *He didn't want to miss his class.* → LOST¹

2 NOT HAVE [I] to stop having something important that you need: *Michelle lost her job.* | *Anna's family* ***lost everything*** *in the war.*

3 NOT WIN [I,T] to not win a game, argument, war, etc.: *We* ***lost to*** *the Red Sox 5–0.* | *Sanders* ***lost*** *the election* ***by*** *371 votes.*

4 HAVE LESS [I] to have less of something than before: *I need to* ***lose weight.*** | *She's lost a lot of blood.*

5 lose your sight/memory/voice etc. to stop being able to see, remember things, talk, etc.

6 STOP HAVING A QUALITY [T] to no longer have a particular quality, belief, attitude, etc.: *The kids were* ***losing interest*** *in the game.* | *Jake* ***lost*** *his* ***temper/cool*** (=became angry) *and started shouting.* | *He* ***lost control*** *of the car and drove into a ditch.*

7 lose an arm/leg etc. to have a serious injury in which your arm, leg, etc. is cut off

8 lose your balance to become unsteady, especially so that you fall

9 lose your husband/mother etc. if you lose your husband, mother, etc., s/he dies: *Michael* ***lost*** *his wife* ***to*** *cancer.* | *Janet* ***lost the baby*** (=the baby died before being born).

10 lose your life to die: *5,000 soldiers lost their lives.*

11 WASTE [T] to waste time or opportunities: *Pam*

L

lost no time *in finding a new boyfriend.* | *You lost your chance!*

12 lose sb (informal) to confuse someone when explaining something to him/her: *You've lost me. Can you repeat that?*

13 have nothing to lose if you have nothing to lose, it is worth taking a risk because you cannot make your situation any worse: *You might as well apply for the job – you've got nothing to lose.*

14 lose touch (with sb/sth) a) to not speak to, see, or write to someone for so long that you do not know where s/he is: *I've lost touch with all my high school friends.* **b)** to not know the most recent information about a particular place, situation, event, etc.: *He's lost touch with his Mexican culture.*

15 lose it (spoken) **a)** to suddenly start shouting, laughing, or crying a lot because you think something is very bad, funny, or wrong: *When he started criticizing me again, I just completely lost it.* **b)** to become crazy

16 lose your mind (informal) to go crazy or to stop behaving sensibly: *What are you doing on the roof? Have you lost your mind?*

17 lose sight of sth to forget about the most important part of something you are doing: *We can't lose sight of our goals.*

18 lose your touch to stop having a special ability or skill

19 lose heart to become disappointed and unhappy

lose out *phr. v.*

to not get something important such as a job because someone else gets it: *He* ***lost out on*** *a scholarship because his grades were low.* [ORIGIN: Old English *losian* "to destroy or be destroyed, to lose"]

los·er /ˈluzɚ/ *n.* [C] **1** someone who does not win: *a* ***bad/sore loser*** (=someone who becomes too upset when s/he loses) **2** (informal, disapproving) someone who is never successful in life, work, or relationships: *Pam's boyfriend is such a loser!*

loss /lɔs/ *n.* **1** [C,U] the fact of not having something any longer, or the action of losing something: *weight loss* | *the* ***loss of*** *innocence* | *job losses*

L

COLLOCATIONS

loss of confidence – when you stop believing in your ability to do things well
loss of appetite – when you do not get hungry, for example because you are sick
loss of memory also **memory loss** – when you cannot remember things well
loss of blood also **blood loss** – when you bleed a lot, for example after an accident
weight loss – when you become thinner
hearing loss also **loss of hearing** – when you cannot hear as well as you could before
job losses – when a number of people lose their jobs in a company, industry, etc.

2 [C,U] ECONOMICS money that has been lost by a company, government, person, etc.: *The auto industry* ***reported losses of*** *$10 million last year.* **3** [C] an occasion when you do not win a game: *a record of 3 wins and 4 losses so far this season* **4** [C,U] the death of someone: *Troops suffered* ***heavy losses*** (=many deaths) *in the first battle.* **5** [singular, U] the sadness you feel or disadvantage you have because someone or something leaves: *She felt a great* ***sense of loss*** *when her son left home.* **6 be at a loss** to not know what you should do or say: *I'm* ***at a loss to explain*** *what happened.* **7 it's sb's loss** (spoken) said when you think someone is stupid for not taking a good opportunity: *Well, if he doesn't want to come, it's his loss.*

lost[1] /lɔst/ *adj.* **1** not knowing where you are or how to find your way: *We* ***got lost*** *driving around the city.*

USAGE

Use **lost** in order to describe something that someone cannot find, or someone who does not know where s/he is: *a lost ball* | *We took a wrong turn and got lost.*
Use **missing** in order to describe someone or something you have been looking for, especially when the situation is serious: *We're still trying to locate the missing money.* | *the search for the two missing boys*

2 unable to be found: *a lost dog* **3** wasted: *lost opportunities* **4 be/feel lost** to not feel confident or able to take care of yourself: *I'd be lost without all your help.* **5 be lost on sb** if humor or intelligent thinking is lost on someone, s/he cannot understand it or does not want to accept it: *Your sarcasm was lost on him.* **6 Get lost!** (spoken) used in order to tell someone rudely to go away **7 lost cause** something that has no chance of succeeding: *Trying to interest my son in classical music is a lost cause.*

lost[2] *v.* the past tense and past participle of LOSE

ˌlost-and-ˈfound *n.* [singular] an office used for keeping things that people have lost until their owners can get them

lot /lɑt/ *n.* **1 a lot** *also* **lots** (informal) **a)** a large amount, quantity, or number of something: ***A lot of*** *people at work have the flu.* | *Mrs. Ruiz has* ***lots of*** *money.* | ***A lot of times*** (=usually or often) *we just sat and talked.* **b)** much: *You'll get there a lot quicker if you drive.* **2 have a lot on your mind** to have many problems you are thinking about **3** [C] an area of land used especially for building on → PARKING LOT

GRAMMAR

a lot of, much, many
In negative sentences, you can use **much** or **many** instead of **a lot of**.
Much is used with uncountable nouns: *We never had much money.*
Many is used with plural noun forms: *There weren't many women musicians in those days.*
A lot of can be used with both types of noun: *I don't have a lot of time.* | *She doesn't have a lot of friends.*

lo·tion /ˈloʊʃən/ *n.* [C,U] a liquid mixture that you put on your skin in order to make it soft or to protect it: *hand lotion* [ORIGIN: 1300—1400 Latin *lotio* "act of washing," from *lavare* "to wash"]

lot·ter·y /ˈlɑt̬əri/ *n.* (plural **lotteries**) [C] a game of chance in which people buy tickets in order to try to win a lot of money: *Maybe I'll* ***win the lottery****.*

loud¹ /laʊd/ *adj.* **1** making a lot of noise (ANT) **quiet, soft**: *The TV's too loud!*

THESAURUS

noisy – making a lot of noise, or full of noise: *a classroom full of noisy kids* | *a noisy bar*
rowdy – behaving in a noisy and uncontrolled way: *rowdy football fans*
thunderous – extremely loud: *thunderous applause*
deafening – very loud, so that you cannot hear anything else: *a deafening roar*
ear-splitting – painfully loud: *The Saints scored and the crowd erupted in an ear-splitting din.*
shrill – a shrill sound is high and unpleasant: *a shrill voice*
raucous – a raucous voice or noise is very loud and unpleasant: *a raucous laugh*
resounding – a resounding noise is loud and clear and seems to continue for a few seconds: *a resounding cheer*
sonorous (formal) – having a deep pleasantly loud sound: *the singer's sonorous voice* ➔ QUIET¹

2 (disapproving) loud clothes are too brightly colored [ORIGIN: Old English *hlud*] —**loudly** *adv.*

loud² *adv.* loudly: *Can you talk a little louder, please?* ➔ **out loud** *at* OUT¹

ˈloud-mouth *n.* [C] (disapproving) someone who talks too much, too loudly, and often in an offensive way —**loud-mouthed** *adj.*

loud·speak·er /ˈlaʊdˌspikɚ/ *n.* [C] a piece of equipment that makes messages loud enough to be heard in a public place

lounge¹ /laʊndʒ/ *n.* [C] a room in a public building where people can relax, sit down, or drink: *We were watching TV in the student lounge.*

lounge² *v.* [I] to stand or sit in a lazy way: *We were lounging by the pool.*

louse¹ /laʊs/ *n.* (plural **lice** /laɪs/) [C] a very small insect that lives on the skin and hair of animals and people

louse² *v.*

louse sth ↔ **up** *phr. v.* to make a mistake or do something badly, especially so that it affects other people: *I don't want to louse things up in our relationship.*

lous·y /ˈlaʊzi/ *adj.* (informal) very bad: *What lousy weather!* | *I'm still* ***feeling*** *pretty* ***lousy*** (=feeling ill).

THESAURUS **bad, awful, terrible, horrible, horrendous, atrocious, abysmal** ➔ BAD¹

lov·a·ble /ˈlʌvəbəl/ *adj.* easy to love: *a lovable child*

love¹ /lʌv/ *v.* [T] **1** to care very much about someone, especially a member of your family or a close friend: *It's incredible how much she loves those two kids.*

THESAURUS

If you **are infatuated with** someone, you have unreasonably strong feelings of love for him/her.
If you **have a crush on** someone, you have a strong feeling of love for him/her, but it usually only continues for a short time: *Carrie has a crush on her brother's best friend.*
If you **are crazy about** someone, you love him/her very much, especially in a way that you cannot control.
If you **are devoted to** someone, you love him/her and are loyal to him/her: *He has always been devoted to his wife.*
If you **dote on** someone, you love him or her very much and show this by your actions: *They absolutely dote on their little boy.*
If you **adore** someone, you love him/her very much and are proud of him/her: *She adores her grandchildren.* ➔ HATE¹

2 to have a strong feeling of caring for and liking someone, combined with sexual attraction: *I love you, Betty.* | *Tom was the only man she had ever really loved.* **3** to like something very much, or enjoy doing something very much: *Tom loves to read.* | *I love being out in the woods.* | *Mom really loved her new dress.*

THESAURUS **enjoy, like, relish** ➔ ENJOY

4 to have a strong feeling of loyalty to your country, an institution, etc.: *He loves his country.* **5 I would love to/I'd love to (do sth)** (spoken) said when you really want to do something: *I'd love to come with you, but I have work to do.* [ORIGIN: Old English *lufu*]

love² *n.* **1** [U] a strong romantic feeling for someone: *He* ***is in love with*** *Laura.* | *They* ***fell in love****.* | *It was* ***love at first sight****.* **2** [U] the strong feeling of caring very much about someone or something: *a mother's* ***love for*** *her child* **3** [C,U] something that you like very much, or that you enjoy doing very much: *his* ***love of*** *music* **4** [C] someone whom you have romantic feelings about: *Mike was my* ***first love****.* **5 make love (to/with sb)** to have sex with someone you love **6 love/lots of love/all my love** (informal) written at the end of a letter to a friend, parent, husband, etc.: *Take care. Lots of love, Dad.*

ˈlove afˌfair *n.* [C] a romantic sexual relationship: *a secret love affair*

love·ly /ˈlʌvli/ *adj.* very nice, beautiful, or enjoyable: *Thank you for a lovely evening.*

lov·er /ˈlʌvɚ/ *n.* [C] **1** a sexual partner, usually someone whom you are not married to: *His wife* *had many lovers.* | *a pair of* ***young lovers*** **2** someone who enjoys something very much: *music lovers*

'love seat *n.* [C] a small SOFA for two people

love·sick /'lʌvˌsɪk/ *adj.* sad because the person you love is not with you or does not love you

lov·ing /'lʌvɪŋ/ *adj.* very caring: *a wonderful, loving husband*

low¹ /loʊ/ *adj.* **1** not high, or not far above the ground (ANT) **high**: *Move the toys onto a lower shelf.* | *a low ceiling* | *low clouds* **2** small in degree or amount (ANT) **high**: *low temperatures* | *Their profits were lower than expected.* **3** bad, or below an acceptable standard (ANT) **high**: *a low grade in math* | *a low opinion of his work* **4** if a supply is low, you have used almost all of it: *We're* ***running/getting low on*** *gas.* **5** unhappy: *I've been* ***feeling*** *pretty* ***low*** *since he left.*

THESAURUS **sad, unhappy, down, blue, depressed, miserable** → SAD

6 a low voice, sound, etc. is quiet or deep (ANT) **high**

THESAURUS **quiet, soft** → QUIET¹

7 lights that are low are not bright

low² *adv.* in a low position or at a low level (ANT) **high**: *The helicopters seemed to be flying very low.*

low³ *n.* [C] a low price, level, degree, etc.: *Prices dropped to an* ***all-time low*** (=the lowest they have ever been). | *Tomorrow's low will be 25°F.*

low·brow /'loʊbraʊ/ *adj.* (disapproving) a low-brow book, movie, etc. is not about serious ideas or not of very good quality

low-cal /ˌloʊ'kæl◂/ *adj.* (informal) low-cal food or drinks do not have many CALORIES

low·down /'loʊdaʊn/ *n.* **get the lowdown on sb/sth** (informal) to be given the important facts about someone or something

'low-end *adj.* [usually before noun] (informal) not the most expensive or not of the best quality: *low-end home computers*

L

low·er¹ /'loʊɚ/ *adj.* [only before noun] **1** below something else (ANT) **upper**: *He began to bite his lower lip.* **2** near or at the bottom of something (ANT) **upper**: *the lower floors of the building* **3** less important than other things (ANT) **upper**: *the lower levels of the organization*

lower² *v.* **1** [I,T] to become less, or to reduce something in amount, degree, strength, etc.: *We're lowering prices on all our products!* | *Please* ***lower your voice*** (=speak more quietly)*!*

THESAURUS **reduce, decrease, cut, slash** → REDUCE

2 [T] to move something down: *The flag was lowered at sunset.*

low·er·case /'loʊɚˌkeɪs/ *n.* [U] letters written in their small form, such as a, b, c, etc. (ANT) **uppercase**

ˌlower 'class *n.* **the lower class** SOCIAL SCIENCE the group of people in society who have less money, power, or education than anyone else → MIDDLE CLASS, UPPER CLASS, WORKING CLASS —**lower-class** *adj.*: *a lower-class family*

ˌlower 'court *n.* [C] LAW any court whose decisions can be considered and changed by a higher court (SYN) **inferior court** → SUPERIOR COURT

ˌlowest ˌcommon de'nominator *n.* [C,U] MATH the smallest number that the DENOMINATORS (=bottom numbers) of a group of FRACTIONS can be divided into exactly

ˌlow-'fat *adj.* low-fat food has very little fat: *low-fat milk* | *a low-fat diet*

ˌlow-'key *adj.* not intended to attract a lot of attention: *The reception was very low-key.*

low·lands /'loʊləndz/ *n.* [plural] EARTH SCIENCES an area of land that is lower than the land around it → HIGHLANDS: *the Bolivian lowlands* —**lowland** *adj.* [only before noun]: *a tropical lowland rainforest* —**lowlander** *n.* [C]

'low life *n.* [C] (informal) someone who is involved in crime or who is bad —**low-life** *adj.*

low·ly /'loʊli/ *adj.* low in rank or importance

ˌlow-'lying *adj.* **1** low-lying land is not much higher than the level of the ocean **2** not very high: *low-lying fog*

ˌlow 'pressure *n.* [U] EARTH SCIENCES a large area in the sky where there is low air pressure, which usually causes wet weather

ˌlow 'tide *n.* [C,U] EARTH SCIENCES the time when the ocean is at its lowest level (ANT) **high tide** → *see picture at* TIDE¹

loy·al /'lɔɪəl/ *adj.* always supporting a particular person, set of beliefs, or country (ANT) **disloyal**: *a loyal friend* | *The army has remained* ***loyal to*** *the government.* [ORIGIN: 1500—1600 Old French *leial, leel*, from Latin *legalis*, from *lex* "law"]

THESAURUS **faithful, staunch, steadfast, true** → FAITHFUL

loy·al·ist /'lɔɪəlɪst/ *n.* [C] **1** someone who continues to support a government or country when a lot of people want to change it **2 Loyalist** HISTORY an American who supported the British during the Revolutionary War

loy·al·ty /'lɔɪəlti/ *n.* (plural **loyalties**) **1** [U] the quality of being loyal to a particular person, set of beliefs, or country: *The company demands loyalty from its workers.* **2** [C usually plural] a feeling of wanting to help and encourage someone or something: *political loyalties*

loz·enge /'lɑzəndʒ/ *n.* [C] a small candy that has medicine in it

LSAT /'ɛlsæt/ *n.* [C] (trademark) **Law School Admission Test** an examination taken by students who have completed a first degree and want to go to LAW SCHOOL

LSD *n.* [U] an illegal drug that makes people have HALLUCINATIONS

lube /lub/ *v.* [T] (informal) to lubricate the parts of a car's engine

lu·bri·cant /ˈlubrəkənt/ *n.* [C,U] a substance such as oil that is used on things that rub together, making them move more smoothly and easily

lu·bri·cate /ˈlubrəˌkeɪt/ *v.* [T] to put a lubricant on something [ORIGIN: 1600—1700 Latin, past participle of *lubricare*, from *lubricus* "slippery"] —**lubrication** /ˌlubrəˈkeɪʃən/ *n.* [U]

lu·cid /ˈlusɪd/ *adj.* **1** clearly expressed and easy to understand: *a lucid speech* **2** able to think clearly and understand what is happening around you: *He was rarely lucid during his long illness.*

luck¹ /lʌk/ *n.* [U] **1** success or something good that happens by chance: *Have you **had any luck** finding a new roommate?* | ***Wish me luck!*** | ***Good luck** with your interview!*

USAGE

You can use **have** with **luck** only when luck has something before it such as "bad," "good," or "any": *He's had a lot of bad luck recently.*
Or you can use **be** with **lucky**: *She's lucky to be alive.* You cannot say you "have luck to do something."

2 the way in which good or bad things happen to people by chance: *I've had nothing but **good/bad luck** since moving here.* **3 be in luck/be out of luck** to get or not get something that you want: *You're in luck – there's one ticket left!* **4 just my luck!** (spoken) said when you are disappointed but not surprised that something bad has happened: *Just my luck! The guys just left.* **5 better luck next time** (spoken) said when you hope that someone will be more successful the next time s/he tries to do something [ORIGIN: 1400—1500 Middle Dutch *luk*] → **tough!/tough luck!** *at* TOUGH¹

luck² *v.*

luck out *phr. v.* (informal) to be lucky: *I lucked out and got an A.*

luck·y /ˈlʌki/ *adj.* (comparative **luckier**, superlative **luckiest**) **1** having good luck ANT **unlucky**: *He's **lucky to** be alive.* | *"I just got the last bus." "That was lucky!"* → see USAGE box at LUCK¹

THESAURUS

fortunate lucky: *It was fortunate that no one was injured in the accident.* | *a fortunate coincidence*
fortuitous (formal) lucky and happening by chance: *He made a fortuitous discovery.*
miraculous extremely lucky, especially because you avoid having something bad happen to you: *The woman had a miraculous escape after her car overturned on the freeway.*
auspicious (formal) an auspicious moment or start makes people feel hopeful that good things will happen: *The candidate could not have hoped for a more auspicious start to an election campaign.*

2 bringing good luck: *7 is my **lucky number**.* —**luckily** *adv.*: *Luckily, no one was hurt.*

lu·cra·tive /ˈlukrət̬ɪv/ *adj.* (formal) making you earn a lot of money: *lucrative business deals*

lu·di·crous /ˈludɪkrəs/ *adj.* silly, wrong, and unreasonable SYN **ridiculous** [ORIGIN: 1600—1700 Latin *ludicrus* "playful," from *ludus* "play"]

lug /lʌg/ *v.* (**lugged**, **lugging**) [T] (informal) to pull or carry something that is very heavy: *We **lugged** our suitcases **up** to our room.*

THESAURUS **carry, tote, cart, haul, schlep**
→ CARRY

lug·gage /ˈlʌgɪdʒ/ *n.* [U] the bags, etc. carried by people who are traveling SYN **baggage**: *We had lost our luggage.*

GRAMMAR

Luggage does not have a plural form. You can say **some luggage**, **any luggage**, or **a piece of luggage**: *Do you have any more luggage?*

lu·gu·bri·ous /ləˈgubriəs/ *adj.* (literary) very sad and serious

luke·warm /ˌlukˈwɔrm◂/ *adj.* **1** a liquid that is lukewarm is only slightly warm → HOT **2** not showing very much interest or excitement: *His idea got only a **lukewarm response** from the committee.*

lull¹ /lʌl/ *v.* [T] **1** to make someone feel calm or sleepy: *Singing softly, she **lulled** us **to sleep**.* **2** to make someone feel so safe and confident that you can easily deceive him/her: *She was **lulled into** believing that there was no danger.*

lull² *n.* [C] a short period when there is less activity or noise than usual: *a **lull in** the conversation*

lul·la·by /ˈlʌləˌbaɪ/ *n.* (plural **lullabies**) [C] a song that you sing to children in order to make them calm and sleepy [ORIGIN: 1500—1600 from *lu-lu*, a sound used to make a child sleepy + *by* (=bye-bye)]

lum·ber¹ /ˈlʌmbɚ/ *n.* [U] trees that are cut down and used as wood for building

lumber² *v.* [I] to move in a slow awkward way, usually because you are heavy

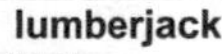

lum·ber·jack /ˈlʌmbɚˌdʒæk/ *n.* [C] someone whose job is to cut down trees for wood

lu·mi·nar·y /ˈluməˌnɛri/ *n.* (plural **luminaries**) [C] someone who is famous and respected because of his/her knowledge or skills

lu·mi·nous /ˈlumənəs/ *adj.* able to shine in the dark without being lit: *luminous paint*

lump[1] /lʌmp/ *n.* **1** [C] a small piece of something solid that does not have a definite shape: *a **lump of** clay*

THESAURUS piece, scrap, chunk, fragment, crumb → PIECE[1]

2 [C] a hard swollen area on someone's skin or in his/her body **3 a lump in your throat** the tight feeling in your throat that happens when you want to cry

lump[2] *v.* [T] to put two or more different people or things together and consider them as a single group: *Do you think I can **lump** these ideas **into** one paragraph?*

ˌlump ˈsum *n.* [C] an amount of money given in a single payment

lump·y /ˈlʌmpi/ *adj.* (comparative **lumpier**, superlative **lumpiest**) having lumps and therefore not smooth: *a lumpy mattress*

lu·na·cy /ˈlunəsi/ *n.* [U] actions or behavior that seem very stupid and unreasonable

lu·nar /ˈlunɚ/ *adj.* relating to the moon: *a lunar eclipse*

lu·na·tic /ˈlunətɪk/ *n.* [C] someone who behaves in a crazy, stupid, or very strange way [ORIGIN: 1200—1300 Old French *lunatique*, from Late Latin *lunaticus*, from Latin *luna* "moon;" because people thought mental illness was caused by the moon] —**lunatic** *adj.*

lunch /lʌntʃ/ *n.* [C,U] a meal eaten in the middle of the day, or that time of day: *What do you want **for lunch**? | When do you usually **eat lunch**? | We've already **had lunch**. | I'll see you **at lunch**. | **school lunches** for children* [ORIGIN: 1800—1900 *luncheon*]

COLLOCATIONS

have/eat lunch
have sth for lunch – to eat a particular food for lunch
go out for lunch – to go to eat lunch in a restaurant
take sb out to lunch – to take someone to a restaurant for lunch and pay the bill
be at lunch – to not be working because you are having lunch
break for lunch – to stop working in order to eat lunch
(brown) bag lunch also **sack lunch** – food, for example a sandwich, that you take to work or school for lunch → MEAL

lunch·eon /ˈlʌntʃən/ *n.* [C,U] (formal) lunch

lunch·time /ˈlʌntʃtaɪm/ *n.* [C,U] the time in the middle of the day when people usually eat lunch: *Is it lunchtime yet? | I usually go for a walk **at lunchtime**.*

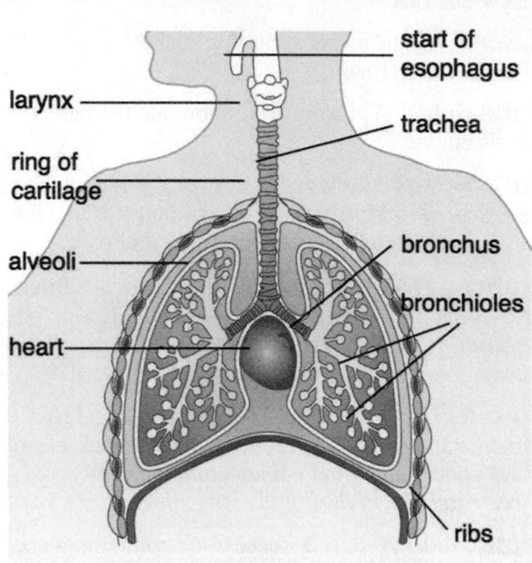

lung /lʌŋ/ *n.* [C] BIOLOGY one of two organs in your body that you use for breathing [ORIGIN: Old English]

lunge /lʌndʒ/ *v.* [I] to make a sudden forceful movement toward someone or something: *She suddenly **lunged at** me.* —**lunge** *n.* [C]

lurch[1] /lɚtʃ/ *v.* [I] to walk or move in an unsteady or uncontrolled way

lurch[2] *n.* **1** [C] a sudden movement **2 leave sb in the lurch** to leave someone at a time when you should stay and help him/her

lure[1] /lʊr/ *v.* [T] to persuade someone to do something by making it seem attractive, exciting, etc.: *Another company tried to lure him over by offering more money.*

lure[2] *n.* **1** [C usually singular, U] something that attracts people, or the quality of being able to do this: ***the lure of** power and money* **2** [C] an object used in order to attract animals or fish so that they can be caught

lu·rid /ˈlʊrɪd/ *adj.* (disapproving) a description, story, etc. that is lurid is deliberately shocking and involves sex or violence: *the lurid details of the murder* [ORIGIN: 1600—1700 Latin *luridus* "pale yellow," from *luror* "pale yellow color"]

lurk /lɚk/ *v.* [I] **1** to wait somewhere secretly, usually before doing something bad: *men lurking in the alley* **2** if you lurk in a CHAT ROOM on the Internet, you read what other people are writing to each other, but you do not write any messages yourself

lus·cious /ˈlʌʃəs/ *adj.* extremely good to eat: *luscious ripe strawberries* [ORIGIN: 1300—1400 *licious* (14—17 centuries), from *delicious*]

lush[1] /lʌʃ/ *adj.* having lots of very green and

L

healthy plants or leaves: *New Zealand is a country of lush green hills.*

lush² *n.* [C] (informal) someone who drinks too much alcohol

lust¹ /lʌst/ *n.* [C,U] a very strong feeling of sexual desire, or a strong desire for something such as power or money: *his **lust for** power*

lust² *v.*

lust after/for sb/sth *phr. v.* **1** to have a strong feeling of sexual desire for someone **2** to want something very much, especially something you do not really need: *Ever since I can remember, I've lusted for a Chevrolet Corvette.*

lus·ter /ˈlʌstɚ/ *n.* [singular, U] an attractive shiny appearance —**lustrous** /ˈlʌstrəs/ *adj.*

lust·y /ˈlʌsti/ *adj.* (literary) strong and healthy SYN **powerful**: *the lusty cry of a newborn baby* —**lustily** *adv.*

Lu·ther·an /ˈluθərən/ *adj.* relating to the Protestant church that follows the ideas of Martin Luther —**Lutheran** *n.* [C]

lux·u·ri·ant /lʌgˈʒʊriənt, lʌkˈʃʊ-/ *adj.* healthy and growing thickly and strongly

lux·u·ri·ate /lʌgˈʒʊriˌeɪt, lʌkˈʃʊ-/ *v.*

luxuriate in sth *phr. v.* to relax and enjoy the pleasure you feel: *She luxuriated in the hot bath.*

lux·u·ri·ous /lʌgˈʒʊriəs, lʌkˈʃʊ-/ *adj.* very comfortable, beautiful, and expensive: *a luxurious hotel*

lux·u·ry /ˈlʌkʃəri, ˈlʌgʒəri/ *n.* (plural **luxuries**) **1** [U] very great comfort and pleasure that you get from expensive food, beautiful houses, cars, etc.: *They lead **a life of luxury**.* | *a **luxury car/hotel*** **2** [C] something expensive that you want but do not need: *Back in the 1950s, a washing machine was a luxury.* [ORIGIN: 1300—1400 Old French *luxurie*, from Latin *luxuria* "too great quantity"]

Ly·cra /ˈlaɪkrə/ *n.* [U] (trademark) a cloth that stretches, used especially for making tight-fitting sports clothes

ly·ing /ˈlaɪ-ɪŋ/ *v.* the present participle of LIE

lymph /lɪmf/ *n.* [U] BIOLOGY a clear liquid that is formed in your body and that passes into your blood. This liquid contains cells that help to fight against infections. —**lymphatic** /lɪmˈfæt̬ɪk/ *adj.*

ˈlymph node *also* **ˈlymph gland** *n.* [C] BIOLOGY one of many small GLANDS in your body through which lymph passes in order to get rid of any BACTERIA before the lymph enters your BLOODSTREAM (=blood flowing around your body)

lynch /lɪntʃ/ *v.* [T] if a crowd of people lynch someone, they kill that person by HANGing him/her, without using the usual legal process [ORIGIN: 1800—1900 William *Lynch* (1724-1820), U.S. citizen who organized illegal trials in Virginia] —**lynching** *n.* [C]

lynch·pin /ˈlɪntʃˌpɪn/ *n.* [C] a LINCHPIN

lyr·ic /ˈlɪrɪk/ *n.* [C usually plural] ENG. LANG. ARTS the words of a song

lyr·i·cal /ˈlɪrɪkəl/ *adj.* ENG. LANG. ARTS expressing strong emotions in a beautiful way: *lyrical poetry*

lyr·i·cist /ˈlɪrəsɪst/ *n.* [C] ENG. LANG. ARTS someone who writes lyrics

M, m /ɛm/ **1** the thirteenth letter of the English alphabet **2** the number 1,000 in the system of ROMAN NUMERALS

M **1** the written abbreviation of MEDIUM, used especially in clothes **2** the written abbreviation of MILLION **3** the written abbreviation of MALE

m **1** the written abbreviation of METER **2** the written abbreviation of MILE **3** the written abbreviation of MARRIED **4** PHYSICS the written abbreviation of MASS, when written in ITALICS

MA the written abbreviation of MASSACHUSETTS

ma /mɑ, mɔ/ *n.* [C] (old-fashioned) mother

M.A. *n.* [C] **Master of Arts** a university degree in a subject such as history or literature that you can get after you have your first degree ➔ M.S.: *Eve **has an M.A. in** French.*

ma'am /mæm/ *n.* [C] (spoken) used in order to speak politely to a woman when you do not know her name ➔ MISS, SIR: *May I help you, ma'am?*

Mac /mæk/ *n.* **1** [C] *also* **(Apple) Mackintosh** IT a type of personal computer ➔ PC: *Will this software run on a Mac?* **2** (spoken) an impolite way of talking to a man whose name you do not know: *Hey, Mac, move your car out of the way!*

ma·ca·bre /məˈkɑbrə, məˈkɑb/ *adj.* (literary) strange, frightening, and relating to death or injury: *a macabre tale* | *macabre humor*

mac·a·da·mi·a /ˌmækəˈdeɪmiə/ *n.* [C] a sweet white nut that grows on a tropical tree, or the tree that produces this nut

mac·a·ro·ni /ˌmækəˈroʊni/ *n.* [U] a type of PASTA in the shape of small curved tubes: ***macaroni and cheese*** (=macaroni cooked with a cheese sauce)

Mace /meɪs/ *n.* [U] (trademark) a chemical that makes your eyes and skin sting painfully, which some people carry to defend themselves

ma·che·te /məˈʃɛt̬i, -ˈtʃɛ-/ *n.* [C] a large knife with a broad heavy blade, used as a tool for cutting or as a weapon

ma·chine¹ /məˈʃin/ *n.* [C] **1** a piece of equipment that uses power such as electricity to do a

M

particular job: *a **washing/sewing machine** | Just hit that button to stop the machine. | I left a message on her machine* (=answering machine).

THESAURUS

appliance – a machine that is used in the home: *kitchen appliances such as refrigerators*
device – a piece of equipment that is usually small and usually electronic, that does a special job: *A seismograph is a device that measures earthquake activity.*
gadget – a small piece of equipment that makes a particular job easier to do: *a new gadget for opening wine bottles*
mechanism – a part of a machine that does a particular job: *a car's steering mechanism*
contraption – a piece of equipment that looks strange: *What does that contraption do?*

2 IT a computer: *My machine just crashed again.* [ORIGIN: 1500—1600 Old French, Latin *machina*, from Greek *mechane*, from *mechos* "way of doing things"]

machine² *v.* [T] to make or shape something, especially metal parts, using a machine

ma'chine gun *n.* [C] a gun that fires a lot of bullets very quickly

ma,chine-'readable *adj.* IT able to be understood and used by a computer: *machine-readable text*

ma·chin·er·y /mə'ʃinəri/ *n.* [U] **1** machines, especially large ones: *farm machinery | You shouldn't drive or operate **heavy machinery** while taking this medication.* **2** the parts inside a machine that make it work **3** an official system or set of processes for organizing or achieving something: *The machinery of the law works slowly.*

ma·chin·ist /mə'ʃinɪst/ *n.* [C] someone who operates or makes machines

ma·cho /'mɑtʃoʊ/ *adj.* (informal) a man who is macho has qualities such as strength that are typical of men, but is not sensitive or sympathetic [ORIGIN: 1900—2000 Spanish "male," from Latin *masculus*]

mack·er·el /'mækərəl/ *n.* [C,U] a common sea fish that has a strong taste, or the meat from this fish

mac·ro·cos·m /'mækrə,kɑzəm/ *n.* [C] a large complicated system such as the whole universe or a society, considered as a single unit → MICROCOSM

mad /mæd/ *adj.* (comparative **madder**, superlative **maddest**) **1** (informal) angry: *Are you still **mad at** me? | You **make** me so **mad**! | Lucy **got mad** and told us all to leave.*

THESAURUS **angry, annoyed, irritated, livid, furious, indignant, irate, outraged, resentful** → ANGRY

2 do sth like mad (informal) to do something as quickly as you can: *Carlos was writing like mad at the end of the exam.* **3** behaving in a wild uncontrolled way, without thinking about what you are doing: *We made **a mad dash for*** (=ran wildly toward) *the door.* **4 power-mad/money-mad etc.** only thinking about power, money, etc.: *a power-mad dictator* [ORIGIN: Old English *gemæd*]

mad·am /'mædəm/ *n.* **1 Dear Madam** used at the beginning of a business letter to a woman whose name you do not know **2 Madam President/Ambassador etc.** used to address a woman who has an important official position **3** [C] a woman who is in charge of a BROTHEL [ORIGIN: 1200—1300 Old French *ma dame* "my lady"]

mad·den·ing /'mædn-ɪŋ, 'mædnɪŋ/ *adj.* very annoying: *maddening behavior*

made /meɪd/ *v.* **1** the past tense and past participle of MAKE **2 be made of sth** to be produced from a particular substance or material: *The frame is made of silver.*

USAGE

Use **made of** when you can clearly see what material has been used to make something: *a table made of wood | a handbag made of leather*
Use **made from** when the materials have been completely changed in the process of making something: *Paper is made from wood. | soap made from the finest ingredients*
Use **made by** to talk about the person or company that has made something: *furniture made by craftsmen*

3 be made for each other (informal) to be completely suitable for each other, especially as husband and wife: *I think Anna and Juan were made for each other.* **4 sb has (got) it made** (informal) to have everything that you need for a happy life or to be successful

mad·house /'mædhaʊs/ *n.* [C] a place that is very busy and noisy

mad·ly /'mædli/ *adv.* **1 madly in love (with sb)** very much in love **2** in a wild uncontrolled way: *Shoppers were rushing madly through the store.*

mad·man /'mædmæn, -mən/ *n.* [C] (plural **madmen** /-mɛn, -mən/) someone who behaves in a wild uncontrolled way: *He drives **like a madman**.*

mad·ness /'mædnɪs/ *n.* [U] very stupid and often dangerous behavior: ***It's madness to** spend that kind of money on a car.*

Ma·don·na /mə'dɑnə/ *n.* **1 the Madonna** Mary, the mother of Jesus Christ in the Christian religion **2** [C] a picture or figure of the Madonna

mael·strom /'meɪlstrəm/ *n.* [C] (literary) a situation full of events that you cannot control or strong emotions that make people feel confused or frightened

mae·stro /'maɪstroʊ/ *n.* (plural **maestros**) [C] someone who can do something very well, especially a musician

Ma·fi·a /'mɑfiə/ *n.* **the Mafia** a large organization of criminals who control many illegal activities

[ORIGIN: 1800—1900 Italian, Italian dialect, "great confidence, proud talk"]

mag·a·zine /ˌmægəˈzin, ˈmægəˌzin/ *n.* [C] **1** a large thin book with a paper cover, that contains news stories, articles, photographs, etc. and is sold weekly or monthly: *a* ***fashion/computer/news magazine*** | *He* ***subscribes to*** *several* ***magazines***. | *a* ***magazine article*** **2** the part of a gun that holds the bullets [ORIGIN: 1500—1600 Early French, "building where things are stored," from Old Provençal, from Arabic *makhazin*, plural of *makhzan* "storehouse"]

ma·gen·ta /məˈdʒɛntə/ *n.* [U] a dark purple-red color [ORIGIN: 1800—1900 *Magenta*, town in Italy where the substance the color is made from was discovered] —**magenta** *adj.*

mag·got /ˈmægət/ *n.* [C] the LARVA (=young insect) of a fly, that lives in decaying food or flesh

mag·ic¹ /ˈmædʒɪk/ *n.* [U] **1** a special power that makes strange or impossible things happen: *Do you believe in magic?*

THESAURUS

witchcraft – the use of magic, usually to do bad things: *Hundreds of women were accused of witchcraft in the 1600s.*
sorcery – magic, especially evil magic: *In the 18th and 19th centuries, missionaries sometimes suspected Native Americans of sorcery.*
black magic – magic that is believed to use the power of the Devil for evil purposes: *tales of black magic and adventure*
spell – a piece of magic that someone does, or the special words or ceremonies used in making it happen: *An evil witch cast a spell on him, turning him into a beast.*
curse – magic words that bring someone bad luck: *People believed the pharaoh would put a curse on anyone who broke into the tomb.*
the occult – the knowledge and study of magic and spirits: *stories that deal with the occult*
voodoo – magical beliefs and practices used as a form of religion, especially in parts of Africa, Latin America, and the Caribbean: *Folks say she's worked a voodoo spell on him.*

2 the skill of doing tricks that look like magic, or the tricks themselves **3** an attractive quality that makes someone or something interesting or exciting: *Christmas has lost some of its magic for me over the years.* [ORIGIN: 1300—1400 French *magique*, from Latin *magice*, from Greek *magos* "person with magic powers"]

magic² *adj.* [only before noun] **1** a magic word or object has special powers that make strange or impossible things happen: *a magic sword* | *a book of* ***magic spells*** **2** relating to the skill of doing tricks that look like magic: *He performed some* ***magic tricks*** *to keep us amused.*

mag·i·cal /ˈmædʒɪkəl/ *adj.* **1** very enjoyable and exciting, in a strange or special way: *a magical evening beneath the stars* **2** containing magic, or done using magic: *magical powers* —**magically** *adv.*

ma·gi·cian /məˈdʒɪʃən/ *n.* [C] someone who entertains people by doing magic tricks

ˌMagic ˈMarker *n.* [C,U] (trademark) a large pen with a thick soft point

ma·gis·trate /ˈmædʒɪˌstreɪt, -strɪt/ *n.* [C] someone who judges less serious crimes in a court of law [ORIGIN: 1300—1400 Latin *magistratus*, from *magister* "master"]

mag·ma /ˈmægmə/ *n.* [U] EARTH SCIENCES hot melted rock below the surface of the Earth → *see picture at* VOLCANO

Mag·na Car·ta /ˌmægnə ˈkɑrt̬ə/ *n.* HISTORY a document, signed by King John of England in 1215, which established the rights of NOBLEs, the church, and free citizens and limited the power of the king

mag·nan·i·mous /mægˈnænəməs/ *adj.* (formal) kind and generous toward other people —**magnanimity** /ˌmægnəˈnɪmət̬i/ *n.* [U]

mag·nate /ˈmægneɪt, -nɪt/ *n.* **steel/oil/shipping etc. magnate** a wealthy and powerful person in the steel, etc. industry

mag·ne·si·um /mægˈniziəm, -ʒəm/ *n.* [U] CHEMISTRY (*symbol* **Mg**) a light silver-white metal that is an ELEMENT and burns with a bright flame [ORIGIN: 1800—1900 Modern Latin *magnesia*]

mag·net /ˈmægnɪt/ *n.* [C] **1** PHYSICS a piece of iron or steel that can make other metal objects move toward it **2** a person or place that attracts many other people or things: *The city has become* ***a magnet for*** *many new industries.* [ORIGIN: 1400—1500 Old French *magnete*, from Latin *magnes*, from Greek *magnes (lithos)* "(stone) of Magnesia," ancient city in Turkey]

mag·net·ic /mægˈnɛt̬ɪk/ *adj.* **1** PHYSICS having the power of a magnet: *The compass needle points to the magnetic North Pole.* **2 magnetic tape/disk etc.** IT a special TAPE, etc. that contains electronic information which can be read by a computer or other machine **3 magnetic personality** a quality that someone has that makes other people feel strongly attracted to him/her

magˌnetic ˈfield *n.* [C] PHYSICS an area around an object that has magnetic power: *the Earth's magnetic field*

mag·net·ism /ˈmægnəˌtɪzəm/ *n.* [U] **1** a quality that makes other people feel attracted to you: *Raul's natural magnetism* **2** PHYSICS the power that a magnet has to attract things

mag·net·ize /ˈmægnəˌtaɪz/ *v.* [T] PHYSICS to make iron or steel able to pull other pieces of metal toward itself

mag·nif·i·cent /mægˈnɪfəsənt/ *adj.* very impressive because of being big, beautiful, etc.: *The view was magnificent.* [ORIGIN: 1400—1500 Latin *magnificus* "very impressive, excellent," from *magnus* "great"] —**magnificence** *n.* [U]

M

THESAURUS impressive, imposing, dazzling, awe-inspiring, breathtaking, majestic → IMPRESSIVE

mag·ni·fy /ˈmægnəˌfaɪ/ *v.* [T] (**magnified**, **magnifies**) **1** to make something appear larger than it is: *A microscope magnifies the image so you can see the cells.* **2** to make something seem more important or worse than it really is: *The reports tend to magnify the risks involved.* —**magnification** /ˌmægnəfəˈkeɪʃən/ *n.* [C,U]

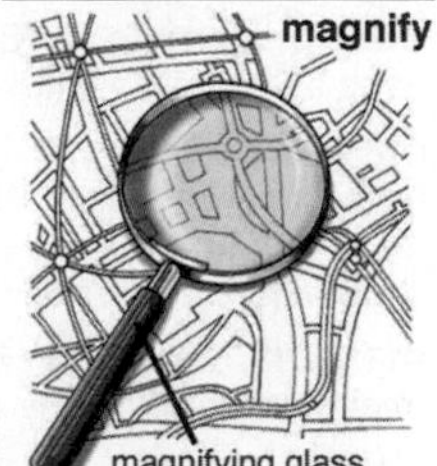

ˈmagnifying ˌglass *n.* [C] a round piece of glass with a handle, that magnifies things when you look through it → *see picture at* MAGNIFY

mag·ni·tude /ˈmægnəˌtud/ *n.* [U] **1** how large or important something is: *I hadn't realized* ***the magnitude of*** *the problem.* **2** EARTH SCIENCES how strong an EARTHQUAKE is **3** PHYSICS how bright a star is

mag·no·lia /mægˈnoʊlyə/ *n.* [C] a tree or bush with large white, yellow, pink, or purple sweet-smelling flowers

mag·pie /ˈmægpaɪ/ *n.* [C] a wild bird with black and white feathers and a loud cry

ma·hog·a·ny /məˈhɑgəni/ *n.* (plural **mahoganies**) [C,U] a tropical American tree, or the hard dark wood of this tree [ORIGIN: 1600—1700 Early Spanish *mahogani*]

maid /meɪd/ *n.* [C] **1** a woman whose job is to clean rooms, serve meals, wash clothes, etc. in a large house **2** a woman whose job is to clean rooms in a hotel

maid·en¹ /ˈmeɪdn/ *also* **maid** *n.* [C] (literary) a young woman or girl who is not married

maiden² *adj.* **maiden flight/voyage** the first trip that an airplane or ship makes

ˈmaiden name *n.* [C] the family name that a woman had before she got married and began using her husband's name

THESAURUS name, first name/given name, last name/family name/surname, middle name, full name → NAME¹

ˌmaid of ˈhonor *n.* [C] the main BRIDESMAID at a wedding → WEDDING

mail¹ /meɪl/ *n.* [U] **1** the system of collecting and delivering letters, packages, etc.: *What time does the mail come? | I just put the letter* ***in the mail****. | You can renew your passport* ***by mail****.* **2** the letters, packages, etc. that are delivered to a particular person or at a particular time: *They sent his mail to the wrong address.* **3** IT messages that are sent and received on a computer SYN **email** → AIRMAIL

mail² *v.* [T] **1** to send a letter, package, etc. to someone: *I'll* ***mail it to*** *you tomorrow.* **2** IT to send a document to someone using a computer SYN **email**: *Can you mail it to me as an attachment?*

mail·box /ˈmeɪlbɑks/ *n.* [C] **1** a box, usually outside a house, where someone's letters are delivered or collected **2** a special box outdoors or at a POST OFFICE, where you mail letters **3** IT the part of a computer's memory where email messages are stored

mail·ing /ˈmeɪlɪŋ/ *n.* [C,U] the act of sending a large number of letters, advertisements, etc. at the same time, or the total number of letters that you send

ˈmailing list *n.* [C] a list of people's names and addresses that a company keeps in order to send information or advertisements to them: *We have more than 1,000 names* ***on our mailing list****.*

mail·man /ˈmeɪlmæn, -mən/ *n.* (plural **mailmen** /-mɛn, -mən/) [C] a man who delivers mail to people's houses

ˌmail ˈorder *n.* [U] a method of buying and selling in which you buy goods from a company that sends them by mail: *a* ***mail order catalog***

maim /meɪm/ *v.* [T] (formal) to injure someone very seriously and often permanently: *The accident* ***maimed*** *her* ***for life****.*

THESAURUS hurt, injure, wound → HURT¹

main¹ /meɪn/ *adj.* [only before noun] **1** bigger or more important than all other things, ideas, etc. of the same kind: *Let's meet by the main entrance. | My main goal is to compete in the Olympics. | He left the job because of money – at least that was the* ***main reason****.* **2 the main thing** (spoken) used in order to say what the most important thing is in a situation: *As long as you're not hurt,* ***that's the main thing****.*

main² *n.* [C] a large pipe carrying water or gas, that is connected to people's houses by smaller pipes: *a frozen* ***water main***

ˌmain ˈclause *n.* [C] ENG. LANG. ARTS a CLAUSE that can form a sentence on its own SYN **independent clause**

main·frame /ˈmeɪnfreɪm/ *n.* [C] IT a large computer that can work very fast and that a lot of people can use at the same time

main·land /ˈmeɪnlænd, -lənd/ *n.* **the mainland** EARTH SCIENCES the main area of land that forms a country, as compared to islands near it that are also part of that country —**mainland** *adj.*: *mainland China*

main·ly /ˈmeɪnli/ *adv.* used in order to mention the main part or cause of something, the main reason for something, etc.: *Students in our program are mainly from Asia. | Their diet consists mainly of rice and beans. | I don't go out much,* ***mainly because*** *I have to look after the kids.*

M

THESAURUS

chiefly – mainly: *Their forest consists chiefly of fir trees.*
principally – firstly and most importantly: *Foreign aid was sent principally to the south of the region.*
largely – mainly, and because of a particular reason: *The school is in a largely black neighborhood.*
primarily – mainly because of one reason or situation, which is more important than any other: *We are primarily concerned with the effect this will have on the students here.*

main·stay /ˈmeɪnsteɪ/ *n.* [C] the most important part of something that makes it possible for it to work correctly or to continue to exist: *Farming is still* ***the mainstay of*** *our country's economy.*

main·stream /ˈmeɪnstrim/ *n.* **the mainstream** the beliefs and opinions that represent the most usual way of thinking about or doing something, or the people who have these beliefs and opinions: *The Green Party is still outside the mainstream in American politics.* —**mainstream** *adj.*: *mainstream Hollywood movies*

main·tain /meɪnˈteɪn/ (Ac) *v.* [T] **1** to make something continue in the same way or at the same standard as before: *The U.S. and Britain have maintained close ties.* | *It is important to maintain a healthy weight.* | *Strong controls must be maintained over important wildlife habitats.* **2** to keep something in good condition by taking care of it: *It costs a lot of money to maintain a big house.* | *The report found that safety equipment had been very poorly maintained.* **3** to strongly express an opinion or attitude: *I've always* ***maintained that*** *any changes in the law will hurt the poor more than the rich.* | *From the beginning, James has* ***maintained his innocence.*** [ORIGIN: 1200—1300 Old French *maintenir*, from Latin *manu tenere* "to hold in the hand"]

main·te·nance /ˈmeɪntˀn-əns/ (Ac) *n.* [U] the work that is necessary to keep something in good condition: *car maintenance* | *the* ***maintenance of*** *school buildings* | *The equipment needs very little maintenance.*

ma·jes·tic /məˈdʒɛstɪk/ *adj.* looking very big and impressive: *a majestic view of the lake* —**majestically** *adv.*

THESAURUS **impressive, imposing, dazzling, awe-inspiring, breathtaking, magnificent** → IMPRESSIVE

maj·es·ty /ˈmædʒəsti/ *n.* **1** [U] the quality of being impressive and beautiful: *the majesty of the Grand Canyon* **2 Your/Her/His Majesty** used when talking to or about a king or queen

ma·jor¹ /ˈmeɪdʒɚ/ (Ac) *adj.* [usually before noun] **1** very large or important, especially when compared to other things or people of a similar kind (ANT) **minor**: *major surgery* | *There were no* ***major problems.*** | *Training new employees is a major part of her job.* | *Carbon dioxide is a major factor in global warming.* ▸ Don't say "major than." Say "more important than" or "bigger than."◂

THESAURUS **important, of great/considerable importance, crucial, vital, essential, key** → IMPORTANT

2 ENG. LANG. ARTS based on a musical SCALE in which there are HALF STEPS between the third and fourth and the seventh and eighth notes [ORIGIN: 1200—1300 Latin "larger, greater," from *magnus* "large, great"]

major² (Ac) *n.* [C] **1** the main subject that you study at a college or university → MINOR: *His major is history.* | *Fewer students choose economics as a major.* → UNIVERSITY **2** someone who is studying a particular subject as his/her main subject at a college or university: *Darla was a biology major.* → STUDENT **3** a middle rank in the Army, Air Force, or Marines, or an officer who has this rank

major³ *v.*
major in sth *phr. v.* to study something as your main subject at a college or university: *I'm majoring in biology.*

ma·jor·i·ty¹ /məˈdʒɔrəṭi, -ˈdʒɑr-/ (Ac) *n.* (plural **majorities**) **1** [singular] most of the people or things in a particular group (ANT) **minority**: ***The majority of*** *people support the president.* | *The* ***vast majority of*** (=nearly all) *young people own a cell phone.* | *The overwhelming majority of the population were involved in farming.* **2** [C usually singular] the difference between the number of votes gained by the winning party or person in an election and the number gained by other parties or people: *He won by* ***a majority of*** *500 votes.* [ORIGIN: 1500—1600 French *majorité*, from Latin *major* "larger, greater," from *magnus* "large, great"]

majority² *adj.* [only before noun] happening as a result of the decision of most members of a group: *a* ***majority decision/ruling***

ˌmajor-ˈleague *adj.* [usually before noun] **1** relating to the Major Leagues: *a major-league pitcher* **2** important or having a lot of power: *a major-league player in Michigan politics*

ˌMajor ˈLeagues *also* **Majors** *n.* [plural] the group of teams that make up the highest level of American professional baseball → MINOR LEAGUES

ma·jor·ly /ˈmeɪdʒɚli/ *adv.* (spoken, slang) very or extremely: *When they broke up, he was majorly depressed.*

make¹ /meɪk/ *v.* (past tense and past participle **made** /meɪd/)
1 PRODUCE STH [T] to produce something by working or doing something: *Can I call you back? I'm making dinner.* | *She made the curtains herself.* | *My flute was made in Japan.*

THESAURUS

produce – to make or grow something in large quantities: *The cheese is produced in Italy.*

M

manufacture – to make things in large quantities in factories: *The vast majority of American consumer goods are manufactured in China.*
build – to make a house, tunnel, bridge, etc.: *John and his father built the cabin themselves.*
construct – to make something, especially something large, solid, and strong, by putting parts together: *The roof frames were constructed from thick, heavy timbers.*
create – to make something new and original in art, music, fashion, etc.: *Picasso created a completely new style of painting.*
generate – to produce electricity or power: *The building uses solar panels to generate electricity.*

2 DO STH [T] used before some nouns to show that someone does the action of the noun: *Maybe they* ***made*** *a* ***mistake****.* | *We've finally* ***made*** *a* ***decision****.* | *Do you want to* ***make*** *an* ***appointment*** *with the doctor?*
3 CAUSE [T] to cause a particular state or situation to happen: *Thanks for listening – you've really made me feel better.* | *That button makes the machine stop.* | *What made you decide to become a lawyer?* ▸Don't say "What made you to decide to become a lawyer?"◂

THESAURUS cause, bring about sth, result in sth, trigger, prompt → CAUSE[2]

4 FORCE [T] to force someone to do something: *Mom, make Billy stop it!* | *I wasn't hungry, but I made myself eat something.*

THESAURUS force, coerce, compel, impel, pressure → FORCE[2]

5 EARN MONEY [T] to earn or get money: *He's working Saturdays to make some extra money.*

THESAURUS earn, get, be/get paid → EARN

6 NUMBER [linking verb] MATH to be a particular number or amount when added together: *2 and 2 make 4.* | *If you include us, that makes eight people for dinner.*
7 make time (for sb/sth) to leave enough time to do something: *She always makes time for exercise.*
8 BE SUITABLE [linking verb] to have the qualities that are necessary for a particular job, use, or purpose: *John will make a good father.* | *Sonia's life would make a good movie.*
9 make a difference to cause a change, especially one that improves a situation: *Having a car has* ***made a big difference*** *in our lives.*
10 make it a) to arrive somewhere: *We just* ***made it to*** *the hospital before the baby arrived.* **b)** to be able to go to an event, meeting, etc.: *I'm sorry I can't* ***make it to*** *your play.* **c)** to be successful in a particular business or activity: *He's* ***made it big*** (=has been very successful) *in Hollywood.* **d)** to live after a serious illness or injury, or to deal with a very difficult situation: *Mom* ***made it through*** *the operation all right.*
11 make the bed to pull the sheets and BLANKETs over a bed to make it look neat when you are not sleeping in it
12 that makes two of us (spoken) used in order to say that you feel the same way that someone else does: *"I'm so tired!" "Yeah, that makes two of us."*
13 make or break to cause either great success or failure: *The first year can make or break a new business.*
14 make do to manage to do something using the things you already have, even though they are not exactly what you want: *We'll have to* ***make do with*** *a quick sandwich.*
15 make believe to pretend that something is true, especially as a game [ORIGIN: Old English *macian*] → **be made of** *at* MADE[2], **make a (big) difference/make all the difference** *at* DIFFERENCE, **make love** *at* LOVE[2], **make sense** *at* SENSE[1], **make the best of sth** *at* BEST[3], **make friends (with sb)** *at* FRIEND, **make up your mind** *at* MIND[1]

make for sth *phr. v.*
1 to go toward a place: *We made for the exit.*
2 to have a particular result or effect: *It should make for an interesting evening.* [ORIGIN: Old English *macian*] → **be made for each other** *at* MADE[2]

make sth ↔ **into** sth *phr. v.*
to change something into something else: *We can make your room into a study.*

make sth **of** sb/sth *phr. v.*
1 to have a particular opinion about someone or something, or a particular way of understanding something: *I really don't know what to make of him.*
2 make the most of sth to use an opportunity in a way that gives you as much advantage as possible: *I want to make the most of the time I have left in Europe.*
3 make too much of sth to treat a situation as if it is more important than it really is: *He doesn't like to make too much of his birthday.* → **make a fool of yourself** *at* FOOL[1]

make off with sth *phr. v.*
to steal something: *They made off with our TV.*

make out *phr. v.*
1 make (sth ↔) **out** to be able to hear, see, or understand something: *I can't make out what the sign says.*
2 make a check out to sb to write a check so that the money is paid to a particular person, company, store, etc.
3 make out (that) (informal) to say that something is true when it is not: *The situation was never as bad as the media made out.*
4 how did sb make out ...? (spoken) used in order to ask if someone did something well: *"How did you make out in the interview?" "I think it went well."*
5 (spoken) to kiss and touch someone in a sexual way

M

make up *phr. v.*
1 make (sth ↔) **up** to invent a story, explanation, etc. in order to deceive someone: *Ron made up an excuse so his mother wouldn't be mad.*
2 make (sth ↔) **up** to produce a new story, song, game, etc.: *"What are you singing?" "I don't know – I just made it up."*
3 make up sth to combine together to form a substance, group, system, etc.: *the rocks and minerals that make up the Earth's outer layer* | *Women make up 60% of our employees.*
4 make up sth to add to an amount in order to bring it up to the level that is needed: *We're going to have to charge more to* ***make up the difference.***
5 make (sth ↔) **up** to work at times when you do not usually work because you have not done enough work at some other time: *I have to leave early, but I'll* ***make up the time/work*** *tomorrow.*
6 make (sb ↔) **up** to put MAKEUP on someone's face in order to make him/her look better or different: *They made him up to look like an old man.*
7 make it up to sb to do something good for someone because you feel responsible for something bad that happened to him/her: *I'm sorry I forgot! I promise I'll make it up to you.*
8 make up to become friends with someone again, after you have had an argument: *Have you two made up?*

make up for sth *phr. v.*
1 to make a bad situation or event seem better: *He bought everyone a drink to make up for being late.*
2 to have so much of one quality that it does not matter that you do not have others: *Jay lacks experience, but he makes up for it with hard work.*
3 make up for lost time to do something very quickly because you started late or something made you work too slowly

make[2] *n.* **1** [C] a product made by a particular company: *"What make is your car?" "It's a Chevy."*

> THESAURUS **type, kind, sort, brand, model** → TYPE[1]

2 be on the make (disapproving) to be trying hard to get something such as money or sex

'make-be,lieve *adj., adv.* not real, but imagined or pretended: *Many small children have make-believe friends.*

mak·er /'meɪkɚ/ *n.* [C] **1** a person, company, or machine that makes something or does something: *U.S. auto makers* | *a coffee maker* **2 decision maker/peacemaker etc.** someone who is good at or responsible for making decisions, stopping arguments, etc.

make·shift /'meɪk,ʃɪft/ *adj.* [only before noun] made for temporary use when you need something and there is nothing better available: *a makeshift table made from boxes*

make·up /'meɪk-ʌp/ *n.* **1** [U] substances such as powder, creams, and LIPSTICK that some people, usually women or actors, put on their faces: *I waited for Ginny to* ***put on her makeup.*** **2** [singular] all the parts, members, or qualities that make up something: *We haven't yet been told what* ***the makeup of*** *the new government will be* (=who the members will be).

mak·ing /'meɪkɪŋ/ *n.* **1** [U] the process or business of making something: *He wrote a book about the making of the movie.* | *the art of rug making* **2 in the making** in the process of being made or produced: *The deal was 11 months in the making.* **3 have the makings of sth** to have the qualities or skills needed to become a particular type of person or thing: *Sandy has the makings of a good doctor.*

mal·a·dy /'mælədi/ *n.* (plural **maladies**) [C] (formal) **1** an illness **2** something that is wrong with a system or organization

mal·aise /mæ'leɪz/ *n.* [U] (formal) a feeling of anxiety, and a lack of confidence and satisfaction

ma·lar·i·a /mə'lɛriə/ *n.* [U] a serious disease that is common in hot countries and is caused by the bite of an infected MOSQUITO [ORIGIN: 1700—1800 Italian *mala aria* "bad air;" because it was believed that the disease came from gases rising from wet land]

male[1] /meɪl/ *adj.* **1** BIOLOGY belonging to the sex that cannot have babies (ANT) **female**: *a male lion* | *Many women earn less than their male colleagues.* **2** BIOLOGY typical of this sex (ANT) **female**: *a male voice* —**male** *n.* [C]: *Males under 25 pay the highest car insurance rates.*

> THESAURUS **man, guy, gentleman, fellow, boy, youth** → MAN[1]

,male 'chauvinist *also* **,male ,chauvinist 'pig** *n.* [C] a man who believes that men are better than women —**male chauvinism** *n.* [U]

mal·e·dic·tion /,mælə'dɪkʃən/ *n.* [C] (formal) a wish or prayer that something bad will happen to someone (SYN) **curse**

ma·lev·o·lent /mə'lɛvələnt/ *adj.* (formal) showing a desire to harm other people [ORIGIN: 1500—1600 Latin *malevolens* "wishing evil"] —**malevolence** *n.* [U]

mal·func·tion /mæl'fʌŋkʃən/ *n.* [C] a fault in the way a machine works: *a* ***malfunction in*** *the computer system* —**malfunction** *v.* [I]

mal·ice /'mælɪs/ *n.* [U] the desire to harm or upset someone: *The criticism was made* ***without malice.***

ma·li·cious /mə'lɪʃəs/ *adj.* showing a desire to harm or upset someone: *malicious gossip* —**maliciously** *adv.*

> THESAURUS **mean, cruel, unkind, nasty, thoughtless, spiteful, abusive, vicious** → MEAN[2]

ma·lign /mə'laɪn/ *v.* [T] (formal) to say or write unpleasant and untrue things about someone: *He's been* ***much maligned*** *by the press.*

M

ma·lig·nant /mə'lɪgnənt/ *adj.* BIOLOGY a malignant TUMOR (=a group of growing cells) contains CANCER and may kill someone (ANT) **benign** [ORIGIN: 1500—1600 Late Latin, present participle of *malignari*, from Latin *malignus*, from *male* "badly" + *gigni* "to be born"] —**malignancy** *n.* [U]

mall /mɔl/ *n.* [C] a very large building with a lot of stores in it (SYN) **shopping mall** ➔ STRIP MALL: *Suzy's **at the mall**. | Do you want to **go to the mall**?* [ORIGIN: 1700—1800 *mall* "long path used for playing a game called "pall-mall"" (17—19 centuries)]

mal·lard /'mælərd/ *n.* [C] a type of common wild duck

mal·le·a·ble /'mæliəbəl/ *adj.* **1** something that is malleable is easy to press, pull, or bend into a new shape: *a malleable metal* **2** (formal) someone who is malleable is easily influenced or changed by people

mal·let /'mælɪt/ *n.* [C] a wooden hammer

mal·nour·ished /ˌmæl'nərɪʃt, -'nʌrɪʃt/ *adj.* sick or weak because of not eating enough food, or because of not eating good food

mal·nu·tri·tion /ˌmælnu'trɪʃən/ *n.* [U] illness or weakness as a result of being malnourished

mal·prac·tice /ˌmæl'præktɪs/ *n.* [C,U] LAW the act of failing to do a professional duty, or of making a mistake while doing it

malt /mɔlt/ *n.* **1** [C] a drink made from milk, malt powder, ICE CREAM, and something such as chocolate **2** [U] grain, usually BARLEY, that is used for making beer, WHISKEY, etc.

malt·ed /'mɔltɪd/ *also* **ˌmalted 'milk** *n.* [C] a malt drink

mal·treat /mæl'trit/ *v.* [T] (formal) to treat an animal or person cruelly —**maltreatment** *n.* [U]

ma·ma /'mɑmə/ *n.* [C] (informal) a mother [ORIGIN: 1500—1600 From the sounds made by a baby]

'mama's boy *n.* [C] (informal, disapproving) a boy or man that people think is weak because his mother is too protective of him

mam·mal /'mæməl/ *n.* [C] BIOLOGY one of the group of animals, including humans, that drink milk from their mother's breasts when they are young [ORIGIN: 1800—1900 Late Latin *mammalis* "of the breast," from Latin *mamma* "breast"]

mam·ma·ry gland /'mæməri ˌglænd/ *n.* [C] BIOLOGY the part of a woman's breast that produces milk, or a similar part of a female animal

mam·mo·gram /'mæməˌgræm/ *n.* [C] an X-RAY picture of a woman's breast

mam·moth /'mæməθ/ *adj.* very large: *Replacing the bridge will be a mammoth construction project*

man[1] /mæn/ *n.* (plural **men** /mɛn/)
1 MALE [C] an adult male human ➔ WOMAN: *Carl is a really nice man. | A group of middle-aged men came into the restaurant.*

THESAURUS

guy (informal) – a man: *He's such a great guy. | One of the guys at work is from Mexico.*
gentleman – a polite word for a man, often used in formal situations: *Good evening, ladies and gentlemen.*
fellow (old-fashioned) – a man: *a nice young fellow*
boy – a young male person, usually a child or a teenager: *I took the boys swimming. | a teenage boy | The gang, including a boy of 10, had all been at the party.*
youth – a teenage boy or young man: *He teaches at a school for troubled youths in San Diego.*
male (formal) – a man, used especially by researchers or the police: *The suspect is a young white male.* ➔ WOMAN

2 STRONG/BRAVE [C usually singular] a man who has the qualities that people think a man should have, such as being brave, strong, etc.: *If someone has something to say, **be a man** and speak up.*
3 ALL PEOPLE [U] all people, both male and female, considered as a group: *This is one of the worst diseases **known to man**.*
4 PERSON [C] (old-fashioned) a person, either male or female: *All men are equal in the eyes of the law.*

THESAURUS

Man can mean "people in general": *Man has always tried to understand the stars.*
Mankind means "all people, considered as a group": *the darkest time in the history of mankind*
Some people think that using **man** and **mankind** in this way seems to not include women. To avoid this problem, you can use **people** to mean "people in general" and **humankind** instead of **mankind**: *People have always tried to understand the stars. | the darkest time in the history of humankind*

5 WORKER [C] a man who does a job for you, usually repairing something: *The telephone man is supposed to come this morning.*
6 SOLDIER [C usually plural] a soldier, SAILOR, police officer, etc. who has a low rank: *General Lee ordered his men to retreat.*
7 WHAT SB LIKES [C] used in order to say that a man likes, or likes doing, a particular thing: *a gambling man | He's a meat and potatoes man* (=likes eating plain traditional food).
8 GAMES [C] one of the pieces you use in a game such as CHESS
9 man and wife (formal) to be or become married: *I now pronounce you man and wife* (=you are now officially married).

SPOKEN PHRASES

10 [C] used in order to speak to someone, especially an adult male: *Hey, man! How're you doing?*

M

11 my man said by some men when talking to a male friend

[ORIGIN: Old English]

man² *v.* (**manned, manning**) [T] to use or operate a vehicle, piece of equipment, etc.: *the astronauts who manned the first spacecraft* → MANNED

man³ *interjection* used in order to emphasize what you are saying: *Oh man! I'm going to be really late.*

man·a·cle /ˈmænəkəl/ *n.* [C] an iron ring on a chain that is put around the hand or foot of a prisoner

man·age /ˈmænɪdʒ/ *v.* [I,T] **1** to succeed in doing something difficult, such as dealing with a problem or living in a difficult situation: *Don't worry – we'll manage somehow.* | *Did you* ***manage to*** *get any sleep on the plane?* **2** to direct or control a business and the people who work in it: *Katie manages a restaurant in town.* **3** (spoken) to be able to do something or carry something without help: *"Can I help you with that?" "That's okay – I can manage."*

man·age·a·ble /ˈmænɪdʒəbəl/ *adj.* easy to control or deal with: *Break the task down into manageable stages.*

man·age·ment /ˈmænɪdʒmənt/ *n.* **1** [U] the act or process of controlling and organizing the work of a company or organization and the people who work for it: *He studied Business Management.* **2** [singular, U] the people who are in charge of controlling and organizing a company or organization: *The management has agreed to talk with our union.* | *a member of the senior management team*

man·ag·er /ˈmænɪdʒɚ/ *n.* [C] someone who directs the work of something such as a business, organization, department, etc.: *That meal was terrible – I want to speak to the manager!* | *the* ***manager of*** *the store* | *the* ***general/sales/marketing etc.*** *manager*

> THESAURUS **boss, head, chief, principal, president, CEO, supervisor, foreman, forewoman, deputy manager/principal, etc.** → BOSS¹

man·a·ge·ri·al /ˌmænəˈdʒɪriəl/ *adj.* relating to the job of being a manager: *good managerial skills*

Man·da·rin /ˈmændərɪn/ *n.* [U] the official language of China

man·date /ˈmændeɪt/ *n.* **1** [C] (formal) an official order given to a person or organization to do something **2** [C] POLITICS the right or power that a government has to do something, which it has after winning an election or vote: *The governor was elected with a clear* ***mandate to*** *raise taxes.* **3** [C,U] POLITICS the power given to one country to govern another country, or the country that is being governed: *Lebanon became a French mandate after World War I.* **—mandate** *v.* [T]

man·da·to·ry /ˈmændəˌtɔri/ *adj.* something that is mandatory must be done: *mandatory safety inspections*

> THESAURUS **necessary, essential, vital, compulsory, requisite, indispensable** → NECESSARY

mane /meɪn/ *n.* [C] the long hair on the back of a horse's neck, or around the face and neck of a male lion

ma·neu·ver¹ /məˈnuvɚ/ *n.* **1** [C] a skillful movement or carefully planned action, especially to avoid something or go around it: *basic skiing maneuvers* **2 maneuvers** [plural] a military exercise like a battle, used for training soldiers

maneuver² *v.* [I,T] to move or turn skillfully, or to move or turn something skillfully: *It was hard to* ***maneuver*** *the piano* ***through*** *the door.*

ma·neu·ver·a·ble /məˈnuvərəbəl/ *adj.* easy to move or turn

man·ger /ˈmeɪndʒɚ/ *n.* [C] a long open container that horses, cows, etc. eat from

man·gle /ˈmæŋgəl/ *v.* [T] to damage something badly by crushing or twisting it: *The car was badly mangled in the accident.*

man·go /ˈmæŋgoʊ/ *n.* [C] (plural **mangos** or **mangoes**) a sweet juicy tropical fruit with a large seed [ORIGIN: 1500—1600 Portuguese *manga*, from Tamil *man-kay*] → *see picture on page 414*

man·grove /ˈmæŋgroʊv/ *n.* [C] a tropical tree that grows in or near water and grows new roots from its branches

mang·y /ˈmeɪndʒi/ *adj.* looking old, dirty, and in bad condition

man·han·dle /ˈmænˌhændl/ *v.* [T] to move someone or something roughly, using force

man·hole /ˈmænhoʊl/ *n.* [C] a hole on the surface of a road, covered by a lid, that people go down to examine pipes, wires, etc.

man·hood /ˈmænhʊd/ *n.* [U] **1** the qualities that people think a man should have: *He felt the need to prove* ***his manhood.*** **2** (formal) the state of being a man rather than a boy

man·hunt /ˈmænhʌnt/ *n.* [C] an organized search, usually for a criminal

ma·ni·a /ˈmeɪniə/ *n.* [C,U] **1** a very strong desire for or interest in something, especially among a lot of people **2** a type of mental illness in which someone is extremely excited and active

ma·ni·ac /ˈmeɪniˌæk/ *n.* [C] (informal) **1** someone who is not responsible and behaves in a stupid or dangerous way: *He drives* ***like a maniac.*** **2** someone who is considered strange because s/he is too involved or interested in something: *a sex maniac*

ma·ni·a·cal /məˈnaɪəkəl/ *adj.* behaving as if you are crazy: *maniacal laughter*

man·ic /ˈmænɪk/ *adj.* behaving in a very excited

and often anxious way: *She had a lot of manic energy.*

M

man·i·cure /ˈmænɪˌkyʊr/ *n.* [C,U] a treatment for the hands and FINGERNAILs that includes cleaning, cutting, etc. ➔ PEDICURE [ORIGIN: 1800—1900 French, Latin *manus* "hand" + *cura* "care"] —**manicure** *v.* [T] —**manicurist** *n.* [C]

man·i·fest[1] /ˈmænəˌfɛst/ *v.* (formal) **manifest itself** if something manifests itself, it appears or becomes easy to see: *The disease can manifest itself in many ways.*

manifest[2] *adj.* (formal) plain and easy to see (SYN) **obvious**: *a manifest error of judgment* —**manifestly** *adv.*: *The rules are manifestly unfair.*

THESAURUS noticeable, clear, obvious, striking, eye-catching, evident, apparent, conspicuous, unmistakable ➔ NOTICEABLE

man·i·fes·ta·tion /ˌmænəfəˈsteɪʃən/ *n.* [C,U] a very clear sign that a particular situation or feeling exists: *These latest riots are a clear* ***manifestation of*** *growing unhappiness.*

man·i·fes·to /ˌmænəˈfɛstoʊ/ *n.* (plural **manifestos**) [C] a written statement by a group, especially a political group, saying what it thinks and intends to do: *the Communist manifesto*

man·i·fold /ˈmænəˌfoʊld/ *adj.* (formal) many, and of different kinds: *The problems facing the government are manifold.*

ma·nil·a /məˈnɪlə/ *adj.* made of a strong brown paper: *a manila envelope*

ma·nip·u·late /məˈnɪpyəˌleɪt/ (Ac) *v.* [T] **1** to make someone do exactly what you want by deceiving or influencing him/her: *I don't like the way he manipulates people.* | *He knew he was being manipulated, but felt powerless to protest.* **2** to skillfully handle, control, or move something: *Babies investigate their world by manipulating objects.* [ORIGIN: 1800—1900 *manipulation* (18—21 centuries), from French, from *manipule* "handful," from Latin *manipulus*] —**manipulation** /məˌnɪpyəˈleɪʃən/ *n.* [U]

maˌnipulated ˈvariable *n.* [C] SCIENCE in a scientific EXPERIMENT (=test), one of the conditions you change, add, or remove in order to test its effect on something else involved in the experiment (SYN) **independent variable**

ma·nip·u·la·tive /məˈnɪpyələṭɪv/ (Ac) *adj.* (disapproving) good at controlling or deceiving people to get what you want: *She is very manipulative.* | *Manipulative behavior is learned at an early age.* —**manipulator** /məˈnɪpyəˌleɪṭɚ/ *n.* [C]

man·kind /ˌmænˈkaɪnd/ *n.* [U] all humans, considered as a group (SYN) **humankind**: *the worst war in* ***the history of mankind***

man·ly /ˈmænli/ *adj.* (approving) having qualities such as strength or courage that are considered to be typical of a man —**manliness** *n.* [U]

ˌman-ˈmade *adj.* made of substances such as plastic that are not natural ➔ ARTIFICIAL: *man-made fibers*

THESAURUS artificial, synthetic, fake, simulated, imitation ➔ ARTIFICIAL

manned /mænd/ *adj.* controlled or operated by people (ANT) **unmanned**: *a manned space flight*

man·ne·quin /ˈmænəkən/ *n.* [C] a model of a human body, used for showing clothes

man·ner /ˈmænɚ/ *n.* **1** [singular] (formal) the way in which something is done or happens: *The issue should be resolved* ***in a manner*** *fair to both parties.* **2** [singular] the way in which someone talks or behaves with other people: *She has an easygoing manner.* | *Greet the customer* ***in a*** *friendly and courteous* ***manner.***

THESAURUS behavior, conduct, demeanor ➔ BEHAVIOR

3 manners [plural] polite ways of behaving in social situations: *The girl had* ***good/bad manners.*** **4 all manner of sth** (formal) many different kinds of things or people: *The camp offers all manner of activities.* [ORIGIN: 1100—1200 Old French *maniere* "way of acting, way of handling," from Latin *manuarius* "of the hand"]

man·nered /ˈmænɚd/ *adj.* **well-mannered/bad-mannered etc.** (formal) polite or not polite to other people: *a nice mild-mannered young man*

man·ner·ism /ˈmænəˌrɪzəm/ *n.* [C,U] a way of speaking, behaving, moving, etc. that is typical of a particular person or group of people: *Some of his mannerisms are exactly like his father's.*

man·nish /ˈmænɪʃ/ *adj.* a woman who is mannish looks or behaves like a man

man·or /ˈmænɚ/ *n.* [C] **1** a large house with a large area of land around it **2** HISTORY in past times, the land that belonged to an important man of high rank

man·pow·er /ˈmænˌpaʊɚ/ *n.* [U] all the workers available to do a particular type of work: *We don't have enough manpower right now to start the project.*

man·sion /ˈmænʃən/ *n.* [C] a very large house ➔ HOUSE[1]

man·slaugh·ter /ˈmænˌslɔṭɚ/ *n.* [U] LAW the crime of killing someone without intending to ➔ MURDER

man·tel /ˈmæntl/ *also* **man·tel·piece** /ˈmæntlˌpis/ *n.* [C] the shelf above a FIREPLACE

man·tle /ˈmæntl/ *n.* [C] **1 take on/assume/wear the mantle of sth** to accept or have a particular duty or responsibility: *He assumed the mantle of leadership when the Prime Minister died.* **2 a mantle of snow/darkness etc.** (literary) something that covers or surrounds a surface or area **3** EARTH SCIENCES the part of the Earth around the central CORE ➔ *see picture at* GLOBE

M

man·tra /'mɑntrə/ *n.* [C] a repeated word or sound, used as a prayer or to help people MEDITATE

man·u·al¹ /'mænyuəl/ (Ac) *adj.* **1** manual work involves using your hands or your physical strength rather than your mind: *He makes a living doing **manual labor**.* | *People in manual occupations have a lower life expectancy.* **2** operated or done by hand or without the help of electricity, a computer, etc.: *a manual pump* | *It would take too long to do a manual search of all the data.* **3** relating to how well you use your hands to do or make things: *manual skills* [ORIGIN: 1400—1500 French *manuel*, from Latin *manualis*, from *manus* "hand"] —**manually** *adv.*

manual² *n.* [C] a book that gives instructions about how to do something such as use a machine: *a **computer manual***

man·u·fac·ture¹ /ˌmænyə'fæktʃə/ *v.* [T] ECONOMICS to use machines to make goods, usually in large numbers: *I work for a company that manufactures aircraft engine parts.* [ORIGIN: 1500—1600 French, Latin *manu factus* "made by hand"]

THESAURUS **make, produce, build, construct** ➔ MAKE¹

manufacture² *n.* [U] ECONOMICS the process of making goods, usually in large numbers

man·u·fac·tur·er /ˌmænyə'fæktʃərə/ *n.* [C] ECONOMICS a company that makes goods, usually in large numbers: *the world's largest shoe manufacturer*

man·u·fac·tur·ing /ˌmænyə'fæktʃərɪŋ/ *n.* [U] ECONOMICS the process of making goods in factories

ma·nure /mə'nʊr/ *n.* [U] waste matter from animals that is put into the soil to produce better crops

man·u·script /'mænyəˌskrɪpt/ *n.* [C] **1** a book or piece of writing before it is printed: *She sent a 350-page manuscript to the publisher.* **2** an old book written by hand before printing was invented: *an ancient Chinese manuscript* [ORIGIN: 1500—1600 Latin *manu scriptus* "written by hand"]

man·y /'mɛni/ *quantifier, pron.* (comparative **more**, superlative **most**) **1** a large number of people or things (ANT) **few**: *I don't have many friends.* | ***How many** people are in your class?* | *There **aren't many** tickets left.* | ***Many of** the staff work part-time.* | *I've missed **too many** days off work* (=more than I should) *already.* | *Why did you bring **so many** pencils?* ➔ *see Grammar box at* LOT

USAGE

many, a lot of

In sentences that are not negative and not questions, it is more usual to say **a lot of** instead of **many**, especially in spoken English: *You have a lot of books.*

THESAURUS

a large number: *They collected a large number of signatures on the petition.*
a lot/lots – a large amount, quantity, or number of something: *There are lots of other kids to play with in the neighborhood.* | *He has a lot of money.*
plenty – a large amount that is enough or more than enough: *Make sure you eat plenty of fruits and vegetables.*
numerous (formal) – many, but able to be counted: *There have been numerous studies showing that obese people do not necessarily overeat.*
countless/innumerable (formal) very many: *He had spent countless hours playing video games.*
a multitude of sb/sth (formal) – a very large number of things or people: *I had never seen such a multitude of stars.*
a plethora of sth (formal) – a very large number of something: *a plethora of diet books*
myriad (formal) a very large number of something, or being a large number of something: *the myriad plants and animal species that live in the forest*

2 as many the same number: *There weren't **as many** people at the meeting **as** we had hoped.* **3 a good/great many** (formal) a large number: *A great many men died in that battle.* [ORIGIN: Old English *manig*]

map¹ /mæp/ *n.* [C] a drawing of an area or country showing rivers, roads, cities, etc.: *a **map of** Texas* | *a **street/city map*** | *Do you see Smith Street **on the map**?* [ORIGIN: 1500—1600 Medieval Latin *mappa*, from Latin, "cloth, towel"]

COLLOCATIONS

You **look at a map** when you are trying to find your way to or around a place.
If you look very carefully at a map, you can say that you **study the map**.
If you can **read a map**, you can understand the information on a map.
If something is **on the map**, the map shows it: *I can't find Church Street on the map.*
A **detailed map** is one which includes a lot of information: *a detailed map showing the way to the campground*

map² *v.* (**mapped**, **mapping**) [T] to make a map of a particular area

map sth ↔ **out** *phr. v.* to plan something carefully: *His future had been mapped out by his parents.*

ma·ple /'meɪpəl/ *n.* [C,U] a tree in northern countries that has leaves with many points, or the wood from this tree ➔ *see picture on page 23*

ma·quette /mæ'kɛt/ *n.* [C] ENG. LANG. ARTS a small model or drawing that an artist produces in preparation for making a SCULPTURE

mar /mɑr/ *v.* (past tense and past participle **marred**, present participle **marring**) [T] (written) to make something less attractive or enjoyable (SYN) **spoil**: *His good looks were marred by a scar along his cheek.*

mar·a·thon¹ /'mærəˌθɑn/ *n.* [C] a race in which

M

competitors run 26 miles and 385 yards: *She* ***ran the marathon*** *in just under three hours.* [ORIGIN: 1800—1900 *Marathon*, place in Greece; from the story that in 490 B.C. a Greek soldier ran about 25 miles from the battlefield of Marathon to Athens, to bring news of the Athenian victory over the Persians]

marathon² *adj.* [only before noun] continuing for a very long time: *a marathon session of Congress*

ma·raud·ing /mə'rɔdɪŋ/ *adj.* searching for something to kill, steal, or destroy: *marauding soldiers*

mar·ble /'mɑrbəl/ *n.* **1** [U] EARTH SCIENCES a hard white rock that can be POLISHed and used for building, STATUEs, etc.: *a marble floor* **2** [C] a small colored glass ball that children roll along the ground as part of a game **3 marbles** a game played by children using marbles

March /mɑrtʃ/ (*written abbreviation* **Mar.**) *n.* [C,U] the third month of the year, between February and April: *We're going to meet* ***on March 15th.*** | *I might be going to California* ***in March.*** | *Julia had her baby* ***last March.*** | *The elections will take place* ***next March.*** [ORIGIN: 1200—1300 Old French, Latin *martius*, from *martius* "of Mars, god of war"]

march¹ *v.* [I] **1** to walk quickly and with firm regular steps like a soldier: *The Union army* ***marched across*** *the field.* → *see picture on page A22*

THESAURUS **walk, stride, stroll, amble, trudge, hike** → WALK¹

2 to walk quickly because you are angry or determined: *Mrs. Hawthorne stood up, turned around, and* ***marched out*** *the front door.* **3** to walk somewhere in a large group to protest about something: *The group plans to* ***march on*** *the White House next week.* [ORIGIN: 1300—1400 Old French *marchier* "to step heavily"]

THESAURUS **protest, demonstrate, riot** → PROTEST²

march² *n.* [C] **1** an organized event in which many people walk together to protest about something: *a civil rights march* **2** the act of walking with firm regular steps like a soldier **3** a piece of music with a regular beat for soldiers to march to

'marching ˌband *n.* [C] a group of musicians who march while they play instruments

Mar·di Gras /'mɑrdi ˌgrɑ/ *n.* the day before Lent, or the music, dancing, etc. that celebrate this day

mare /mɛr/ *n.* [C] a female horse or DONKEY → STALLION

mar·ga·rine /'mɑrdʒərɪn/ *n.* [U] a yellow food that is similar to butter [ORIGIN: 1800—1900 French, Greek *margaron* "pearl"]

mar·gin /'mɑrdʒɪn/ (Ac) *n.* [C] **1** the empty space at the side of a printed page: *I wrote some notes* ***in the margin.*** | *Word-processing software can set margins automatically.*

THESAURUS **edge, border, boundary, perimeter** → EDGE¹

2 ECONOMICS the difference in the number of votes, points, etc. that exists between the winners and the losers of an election or competition: *Polls show the senator leading by* ***a wide margin*** (=a lot of votes). | *The bill was approved by a margin of 45 votes.* **3 margin of error** the degree to which a calculation can be wrong without affecting the final results **4** the difference between what a business pays for something and what they sell it for (SYN) **profit margin** [ORIGIN: 1300—1400 Latin *margo* "border"]

mar·gin·al /'mɑrdʒənl/ (Ac) *adj.* small in importance or amount: *The film was a marginal success.* | *The figures show a marginal rise in the rate of inflation.* —**marginally** *adv.*: *The population of New Hampshire is only marginally larger than that of the city of Detroit.*

ˌmarginal 'cost *n.* [C] ECONOMICS the additional cost of producing one more of a particular product or thing

ˌmarginal 'revenue *n.* [C] ECONOMICS the additional money a business earns from selling one more of a particular product, which can be equal to the selling price of the product

mar·i·jua·na /ˌmærə'wɑnə/ *n.* [U] an illegal drug in the form of dried leaves that people smoke

ma·ri·na /mə'rinə/ *n.* [C] a small area of water where people keep boats used for pleasure

mar·i·nate /'mærəˌneɪt/ *also* **mar·i·nade** /ˌmærə'neɪd, 'mærəˌneɪd/ *v.* [T] to put meat or fish in a mixture of oil, wine, SPICEs, etc. before you cook it: ***Marinate*** *the chicken* ***in*** *soy sauce for one hour.* —**marinade** *n.*

ma·rine¹ /mə'rin/ *adj.* EARTH SCIENCES relating to the ocean and the animals and plants that live there: ***marine life*** (=animals and fish that live in the ocean) [ORIGIN: 1300—1400 Latin *marinus*, from *mare* "sea"]

marine² *n.* [C] someone who is in the Marines

mar·i·ner /'mærənɚ/ *n.* [C] (literary) a sailor

Ma·rines /mə'rinz/ *also* **Ma'rine ˌCorps** *n.* **the Marines** the military organization of the U.S. consisting of soldiers who are on ships

mar·i·o·nette /ˌmæriə'nɛt/ *n.* [C] a toy that looks like a person, animal, etc. that is moved by pulling strings attached to its body → *see picture at* PUPPET

mar·i·tal /'mærətl̩/ *adj.* relating to marriage: *marital problems* [ORIGIN: 1400—1500 Latin *maritalis*, from *maritus* "husband"]

mar·i·time /'mærəˌtaɪm/ *adj.* **1** relating to the ocean or ships: *the maritime industry* **2** near the ocean: *the maritime provinces* [ORIGIN: 1500—1600 Latin *maritimus*, from *mare* "sea"]

mark¹ /mɑrk/ *v.* **1** [T] to make a sign, shape, or word on something using a pen or pencil: *Check the envelopes that are marked "urgent" first.* | *The boxes are all **marked with** my name.* **2** [T] to show where something is or was: *The grave is marked by a stone cross.* **3** [T] if a particular year, month, or week marks an important event, the event happened on that date during a previous year: *This year marks the company's 50th anniversary.* **4** [T] to grade a student's work **5** [I,T] to make a mark on something in a way that spoils or damages it: *The heels of his boots had marked the floor.*

mark sth ↔ **down** *phr. v.* to reduce the price of things that are being sold: *Books have been marked down by 25%.* → MARKDOWN

mark sth ↔ **up** *phr. v.* to increase the price of something, so that you sell it for more than you paid for it → MARKUP

mark² *n.* [C]

1 DIRTY SPOT a spot or small dirty area on something that spoils its appearance: *What are these black marks on the couch?*

THESAURUS

Types of dirty marks

stain – a mark that is difficult to remove: *an ink stain on the shirt pocket*

spot – a small mark: *a grease spot on his shirt*

smudge – a dirty mark, made when something is rubbed against a surface: *a smudge of paint on her cheek*

smear – a mark that is left when a substance is spread on a surface: *There was a smear of blood on the chair.*

Types of marks on someone's skin

blemish – a mark on your skin that spoils its appearance

bruise – a purple or brown mark on your skin that you get because you have fallen or been hit

scar – a permanent mark on your skin, caused by a cut or by something that burns you

pimple – a small raised red mark or lump on your skin that teenagers often have

zit (informal) – a pimple

wart – a small hard raised mark on your skin caused by a virus (=a living thing that causes an infectious illness)

blister – a small area of skin that is swollen and full of liquid because it has been rubbed or burned

freckle – one of several small light brown marks on someone's skin

mole – a small usually brown mark on the skin that is often slightly higher than the skin around it

2 DAMAGE a small damaged area on someone or something: *Her injuries included scratch marks on her face.*

3 WRITING a sign or shape that is written or printed: *She **made a mark** on the map to show where her house was.*

4 make/leave your mark to become successful or famous: *He first made his mark as a pianist playing with Miles Davis.*

5 a mark of sth a sign that something is true or exists: *We'd like to give you this gift as **a mark of** our **respect**.*

6 be off the mark/be wide of the mark to be incorrect: *My estimate was **way off the mark**.*

7 on your mark(s), get set, go! (spoken) said in order to start a race

mark·down /ˈmɑrkdaʊn/ *n.* [C] a reduction in the price of something

marked /mɑrkt/ *adj.* very easy to notice: *a marked improvement* —**markedly** /ˈmɑrkɪdli/ *adv.*

mark·er /ˈmɑrkɚ/ *n.* [C] **1** an object, sign, etc. that shows the position of something: *a marker at the edge of the football field* **2** a large pen with a thick point → MAGIC MARKER

mar·ket¹ /ˈmɑrkɪt/ *n.*

1 PLACE TO BUY/SELL [C] **a)** an area outside where people buy and sell goods, food, etc.: *We buy all our vegetables from the **farmers' market**.* **b)** a GROCERY STORE → SUPERMARKET

2 the market ECONOMICS the STOCK MARKET

3 on the market ECONOMICS available for someone to buy: *Our house has been on the market for a year now.*

4 COUNTRY/AREA [C] ECONOMICS a particular country or area where a company sells its goods: *our biggest **overseas/domestic market*** | *the Japanese market*

5 BUYERS [singular] ECONOMICS the number or kind of people who want to buy something: *The **market for** used cars in the U.S. is getting smaller.* | *the youth market*

6 BUYING AND SELLING [C] ECONOMICS the activity of buying and selling goods, services, etc.: *Manufacturers are competing in an increasingly **global market**.* | *The **housing market** is beginning to recover.* | *the world's **financial markets***

7 the job/labor market the number of people looking for work or the number of jobs available

8 be in the market for sth to be interested in buying something: *I'm in the market for a new car.*

9 a buyer's/seller's market ECONOMICS a time that is better for buyers because prices are low, or better for sellers because prices are high [ORIGIN: 1100—1200 Old North French, Latin *mercatus* "buying and selling, marketplace," from *mercari* "to buy and sell," from *merx* "things to sell"] → **corner the market** at CORNER² → BLACK MARKET, FLEA MARKET, FREE MARKET

market² *v.* [T] ECONOMICS to try to persuade someone to buy something by advertising it in a particular way: *The game is being **marketed as** a learning toy.* —**marketer** *n.* [C]

THESAURUS **advertise, promote, publicize, hype, plug** → ADVERTISE

mar·ket·a·ble /ˈmɑrkɪt̬əbəl/ *adj.* marketable goods, skills, etc. are easy to sell because people want them: *The program is designed to provide students with real **marketable** skills.* —**marketability** /ˌmɑrkɪt̬əˈbɪlət̬i/ *n.* [U]

M

ˌmarket eˈconomy *n.* [C] ECONOMICS an economic system in which companies are not controlled by the government and decisions about what to produce or sell are based on profit

ˌmarket ˈforces *n.* [plural] ECONOMICS the conditions that exist when business and trade are not controlled by the government, which affect the level of prices and pay at a particular time

mar·ket·ing /ˈmɑrkɪt̬ɪŋ/ *n.* [U] ECONOMICS the activity of deciding how to advertise a product, what price to charge for it, etc., or the type of job in which you do this: *a large **marketing campaign** | Reed works in marketing.*

mar·ket·place /ˈmɑrkɪtˀˌpleɪs/ *n.* **1 the marketplace** ECONOMICS the business of buying and selling goods in competition with other companies **2** [C] a market

ˌmarket ˈvalue *n.* [C,U] **1** ECONOMICS the value of a product, building, etc. based on the price that people are willing to pay for it, rather than the cost of producing it or building it **2** ECONOMICS the total value of all the SHARES on a STOCK MARKET, or the value of the STOCK of a particular company

mark·ing /ˈmɑrkɪŋ/ *n.* [C usually plural] **1** marks painted or written on something: *line markings on the highway* **2** the colored patterns and shapes on an animal's fur or skin: *a cat with black and gray markings*

marks·man /ˈmɑrksmən/ *n.* (plural **marksmen** /-mən/) [C] someone who can shoot very well

mark·up /ˈmɑrk-ʌp/ *n.* [C] ECONOMICS an increase in the price of something: *The usual retail markup is 50%.*

mar·ma·lade /ˈmɑrməˌleɪd/ *n.* [U] a JAM made with fruit such as oranges [ORIGIN: 1400—1500 Portuguese *marmelada* "jam made from quinces," from *marmelo* "quince"]

ma·roon /məˈrun/ *n.* [U] a very dark red-brown color [ORIGIN: 1700—1800 French *marron* "chestnut"] —**maroon** *adj.*

ma·rooned /məˈrund/ *adj.* if you are marooned somewhere, you are in a place from which you cannot leave, and there are no people to help you: *The climbers were marooned on the mountain for three days.*

mar·quee /mɑrˈki/ *n.* [C] a large sign on a theater that gives the name of the movie or play

mar·riage /ˈmærɪdʒ/ *n.* **1** [C,U] the relationship between two people who are married, or the state of being married: *a long and happy marriage | She felt she wasn't ready for marriage. | She has two children from a **previous marriage**.*

COLLOCATIONS

a happy/good marriage
an unhappy/broken/troubled/failed/loveless marriage
sb's marriage breaks up – someone's marriage ends because of problems and disagreement
the breakup of sb's marriage – the end of someone's marriage
sb's marriage ends in divorce
a proposal of marriage – an occasion when one person asks another person to marry him or her
a mixed/interracial marriage – a marriage between people of different races
an arranged marriage – a marriage in which your parents choose the person you marry

2 [C] the ceremony in which two people get married SYN **wedding**

mar·ried /ˈmærid/ *adj.* having a husband or a wife: *How long have you been married? | Agnes and I have decided to **get married**. | Helen is **married to** a lawyer.* ➔ MARRY

THESAURUS

single – not married
engaged – having formally agreed to marry someone in the future
fiancée/fiancé – a woman or man who is engaged
separated – no longer living with your husband or wife because of problems in your marriage
divorced – no longer married because you have officially ended your marriage
divorcee – someone who is divorced
widowed – no longer married because your husband or wife has died
widow/widower – a woman or man who is widowed
living together – in a romantic relationship and sharing a home together, though not married
partner – one of two people who are living together or who are married
spouse (formal) – a husband or wife ➔ WEDDING

mar·row /ˈmæroʊ/ *n.* [U] BIOLOGY the soft substance in the hollow center of bones SYN **bone marrow**

mar·ry /ˈmæri/ *v.* (**married**, **marries**) **1** [I,T] to become someone's husband or wife: *I've asked Linda to marry me. | My uncle didn't marry until he was 50. | We **got married** last July. | She **married young*** (=at a young age). ►Don't say "married with."◄ **2** [T] to perform the ceremony at which two people get married: *Rabbi Feingold will marry us.* [ORIGIN: 1200—1300 French *marier*, from Latin *maritare*, from *maritus* "husband"]

marry into sth *phr. v.* to join a family by marrying someone who belongs to it: *She married into a rich family.*

Mars /mɑrz/ *n.* PHYSICS the fourth PLANET from the Sun ➔ *see picture at* SOLAR SYSTEM

marsh /mɑrʃ/ *n.* [C,U] an area of low ground that is soft and wet ➔ SWAMP —**marshy** *adj.*

mar·shal[1] /ˈmɑrʃəl/ *n.* [C] **1** a police officer in the U.S. whose job is to make sure that people obey an order that has been given by a court of law: *a U.S. marshal* **2** the officer in charge of a city's fire-fighting department: *the fire marshal*

marshal² *v.* **marshal your resources/forces etc.** to organize things or people so that they are used in the most effective way

marsh·mal·low /ˈmɑrʃˌmɛloʊ/ *n.* [C,U] a very soft white candy made of sugar

marsupials

mar·su·pi·al /mɑrˈsupiəl/ *n.* [C] a type of animal that carries its baby in a pocket of skin on its body

mart, Mart /mɑrt/ *n.* [C] a market or MALL, used especially in the names of stores: *Wall-Mart Stores Inc.* | *There wasn't a Pepsi machine or a convenience mart in sight.*

mar·tial /ˈmɑrʃəl/ *adj.* related to war and fighting [ORIGIN: 1300—1400 Latin *martialis* "of Mars," from *Mars*, god of war]

ˌmartial ˈart *n.* [C usually plural] a sport such as KARATE, in which you fight with your hands and feet

ˌmartial ˈlaw *n.* [U] POLITICS a situation in which the army takes control of an area and many citizens' rights are taken away, especially because of fighting against the government: *The country has been* ***under martial law*** *since the attempted coup.*

Mar·tian /ˈmɑrʃən/ *n.* [C] an imaginary creature from Mars

Mar·tin Lu·ther King Day /ˌmɑrt˺n ˌluθɚ ˈkɪŋ ˌdeɪ/ *n.* a public holiday in the U.S. on the third Monday in January, when people remember Dr. Martin Luther King, Jr.

mar·tyr /ˈmɑrt̬ɚ/ *n.* [C] someone who dies for his/her religious or political beliefs, and whose death makes people believe more strongly in those beliefs —**martyr** *v.* [T] —**martyrdom** *n.* [U]

mar·vel¹ /ˈmɑrvəl/ *v.* [I,T] to feel surprise or admiration for the quality of something: *We* ***marveled at*** *her courage.*

marvel² *n.* [C] something or someone that is extremely impressive: *Laser surgery is one of the* ***marvels of*** *modern medicine.*

mar·vel·ous /ˈmɑrvələs/ *adj.* extremely good, enjoyable, or impressive: *You are doing a marvelous job.* | *a marvelous opportunity*

Marx·is·m /ˈmɑrkˌsɪzəm/ *n.* [U] a political system based on Karl Marx's ideas that explains the changes in history as the result of the struggle between social classes —**Marxist** *n.* [C]

masc. the written abbreviation of MASCULINE

mas·car·a /mæˈskærə/ *n.* [U] a dark substance that you use to color your EYELASHes

mas·cot /ˈmæskɑt/ *n.* [C] an animal, toy, etc. that represents a team or organization, and is thought to bring it good luck [ORIGIN: 1800—1900 French *mascotte*, from Provençal *mascoto*, from *masco* "woman with magic powers"]

mas·cu·line /ˈmæskyəlɪn/ *adj.* **1** having qualities that are considered to be typical of men → FEMININE: *a masculine voice* **2** ENG. LANG. ARTS in grammar, a masculine noun or PRONOUN has a form that means it relates to a male, such as "widower" or "him" → FEMININE

mas·cu·lin·i·ty /ˌmæskyəˈlɪnət̬i/ *n.* [U] qualities that are considered typical of a man → FEMININITY

mash /mæʃ/ *v.* [T] to crush something, such as food that has been cooked, until it is soft: ***Mash the potatoes*** *until they're smooth.*

mask¹ /mæsk/ *n.* [C] something that covers all or part of your face, to protect or hide it: *a ski mask* | *The attackers wore masks.* → GAS MASK

mask² *v.* [T] **1** to hide the truth about a situation, about how you feel, etc.: *Small children find it hard to mask their emotions.*

THESAURUS **hide, conceal, cover/cover up, disguise** → HIDE¹

2 to prevent a smell, taste, sound, etc. from being noticed: *She turned on the radio to mask the noise.*

masked /mæskt/ *adj.* wearing a mask: *a masked gunman*

ˈmasking tape *n.* [U] a special type of tape, made of paper

mas·och·ism /ˈmæsəˌkɪzəm/ *n.* [U] sexual behavior in which someone gets pleasure from being hurt —**masochist** *n.* [C] —**masochistic** /ˌmæsəˈkɪstɪk◂/ *adj.*

ma·son /ˈmeɪsən/ *n.* [C] **1** someone who builds walls, buildings, etc. with bricks, stones, etc. **2 Mason** *also* **Freemason** a man who belongs to a society in which each member helps the other members to become successful, and in which they also do work to help other people

Ma·son-Dix·on line /ˌmeɪsən ˈdɪksən ˌlaɪn/ *n.* **the Mason-Dixon line** HISTORY the border between the states of Pennsylvania and Maryland, considered to be the dividing line between the northern and southern U.S.

ma·son·ry /ˈmeɪsənri/ *n.* [U] brick or stone from which a building, wall, etc. is made

M

mas·quer·ade¹ /ˌmæskəˈreɪd/ *n.* [C] a formal dance or party where people wear MASKS and unusual clothes

masquerade² *v.* [I] to pretend to be someone or something else: *Two men* ***masquerading as*** *police officers robbed a local bank.*

mass¹ /mæs/ *n.* **1** [C] a large amount or quantity of something: *The train wreck was* ***a mass of*** *twisted steel.* **2** [singular] a large crowd: *a* ***mass of*** *people* **3 Mass** [C,U] the main religious ceremony in some Christian churches, especially the Roman Catholic Church **4 the masses** [plural] all the ordinary people in a society **5** [U] PHYSICS the amount of material that a physical object contains. It is similar to its weight, but the mass of an object does not depend on GRAVITY: *the* ***mass of*** *a star*

mass² *adj.* involving or intended for a large number of people: *weapons of mass destruction* | *a mass grave*

mass³ *v.* [I,T] to come together in a large group, or to make people or things do this: *Troops are massing at the border.*

mas·sa·cre¹ /ˈmæsəkɚ/ *n.* [C,U] the killing of a lot of people, especially people who cannot defend themselves: *the* ***massacre of*** *17 unarmed peasants*

massacre² *v.* [T] to kill a lot of people, especially people who cannot defend themselves: *Government troops massacred hundreds of students.*

THESAURUS kill, murder, slaughter, exterminate, slay → KILL¹

mas·sage /məˈsɑʒ, -ˈsɑdʒ/ *n.* [C,U] the action of pressing and rubbing someone's body with your hands to reduce pain or help him/her relax: *I felt much calmer after the massage.* | *Larry* ***gave*** *me a gentle back* ***massage.*** [ORIGIN: 1800—1900 French *masser* "to massage," from Arabic *massa* "to stroke"] —**massage** *v.* [T]

mas·seur /mæˈsɚ, mə-/ *n.* [C] someone who gives people a massage

mas·seuse /mæˈsuz, mə-/ *n.* [C] a woman who gives people a massage

mas·sive /ˈmæsɪv/ *adj.* **1** very large, solid, and heavy: *a massive stone fireplace*

THESAURUS big, large, huge, enormous, vast, gigantic, immense, colossal → BIG

2 unusually large, powerful, or damaging: *Dad suffered a massive heart attack.* | *a massive tax bill*

ˌmass ˈmedia *n.* **the mass media** all the people and organizations that provide information and news for the public, including television, radio, and newspapers

ˌmass ˈmurderer *n.* [C] someone who has murdered a lot of people

ˈmass ˌnumber *n.* [C] PHYSICS the total number of PROTONS and NEUTRONS in the NUCLEUS (=central part) of an atom

ˌmass-proˈduced *adj.* produced in large numbers using machinery, so that each object is the same and can be sold cheaply: *The computers will be mass-produced in Korea.* —**mass production** *n.* [U] —**mass-produce** *v.* [T]

mast /mæst/ *n.* [C] **1** a tall pole on which the sails on a ship are hung **2** a tall pole on which a flag is hung

mas·ter¹ /ˈmæstɚ/ *n.* [C] **1** someone who is very skilled at something: *a* ***master of*** *disguise* **2** a document, record, etc. from which other copies are made **3** (old-fashioned) a man who has authority over people or animals → MISTRESS

master² *v.* [T] to learn something so well that you understand it completely and have no difficulty with it: *It only took him a few months to master French.*

THESAURUS learn, study, pick sth up, get the hang of sth, acquire → LEARN

master³ *adj.* **1 master copy/list/tape etc.** the original thing from which copies are made **2 master plumber/chef etc.** someone who is very skillful at doing a particular job **3** most important or main: *the* ***master bedroom***

mas·ter·ful /ˈmæstɚfəl/ *adj.* skillfully done, made, or dealt with: *a masterful performance*

ˈmaster key *n.* [C] a key that will open all the door locks in a building

mas·ter·mind /ˈmæstɚˌmaɪnd/ *n.* [C usually singular] someone who organizes a complicated plan, especially a criminal plan: *the* ***mastermind behind*** *the bombings* —**mastermind** *v.* [T]

ˌMaster of ˈArts *n.* an M.A.

ˌmaster of ˈceremonies *n.* [C usually singular] someone who introduces speakers or performers at a social or public occasion SYN **MC, emcee**

ˌMaster of ˈScience *n.* an M.S.

mas·ter·piece /ˈmæstɚˌpis/ *n.* [C] a work of art, piece of writing, music, etc. that is of the highest quality

ˈmaster's deˌgree *also* **master's** *n.* [C] a university degree that you get by studying for one or two years after your first degree

mas·ter·y /ˈmæstəri/ *n.* [U] complete control or power over someone or something: *Shakespeare's* ***mastery of*** *the English language*

mas·tur·bate /ˈmæstɚˌbeɪt/ *v.* [I,T] to touch or rub your sexual organs for pleasure —**masturbation** /ˌmæstɚˈbeɪʃən/ *n.* [U]

mat /mæt/ *n.* [C] **1** a small piece of thick material that covers part of a floor **2** a piece of thick soft material used in some activities for people to sit on, fall onto, etc.

mat·a·dor /ˈmæt̬əˌdɔr/ *n.* [C] someone who fights and tries to kill a BULL during a BULLFIGHT

match[1] /mætʃ/ *n.* **1** [C] a small wooden or paper stick with a special substance at the top, used to light a fire, cigarette, etc.: *a box of matches* | *He* ***lit/struck a match*** *so we could see.* **2** [C] a game or sports event: *a tennis/boxing/soccer match* | *a semi-final* ***match against*** *South Korea* **3 be no match for sb** to be much less strong, fast, etc. than an opponent: *Our defense was no match for theirs.* **4 a shouting match** a loud argument

match[2] *v.* **1** [I,T] if one thing matches another, or if two things match, they look good together because they have a similar color, pattern, etc.: *We found a carpet to match the curtains in this room.* | *Do these socks match?* **2** [I,T] if two things match, or if one matches the other, they look or seem the same: *Police say the murder weapon matches a knife belonging to the suspect.* **3** [T] to be appropriate for a particular person, thing, or situation: *We'll try to help you find a job to match your skills.* **4** [T] to put two people or things together that are somehow related to each other: ***Match*** *the title of each book* ***with*** *its author.* **5** [T] to be equal to something in value, size, or quality: *His ambition was matched by a devotion to his family.*

match up *phr. v.* **1** to be of a similar level or of similar quality to something: *If the product doesn't* ***match up to*** *our standards, we don't sell it.* **2** to belong with or fit together with something: *The edges of the cloth don't match up.*

match·book /ˈmætʃbʊk/ *n.* [C] a small piece of thick folded paper containing paper matches

match·box /ˈmætʃbɑks/ *n.* [C] a small box containing matches

match·ing /ˈmætʃɪŋ/ *adj.* having the same color, style, or pattern as something else: *She wore a green skirt with a matching jacket.*

THESAURUS **similar, like, alike, comparable, akin to sth, analogous, identical**
→ SIMILAR

match·less /ˈmætʃlɪs/ *adj.* (formal) better than all other things of the same kind

match·mak·er /ˈmætʃˌmeɪkɚ/ *n.* [C] someone who tries to find the right person for someone else to marry —**matchmaking** *n.* [U]

mate[1] /meɪt/ *n.* [C] **1 office/band/locker etc. mate** someone you work with, do an activity with, or share something with → CLASSMATE, ROOMMATE **2** a husband, wife, or sexual partner, used especially in magazines: *He's still searching for the perfect mate.* **3** BIOLOGY the sexual partner of an animal **4** one of a pair of objects: *I can't find the mate to this glove.*

mate[2] *v.* [I] BIOLOGY if animals mate, they have sex to produce babies: *The male* ***mates with*** *several females.*

materials

ma·te·ri·al[1] /məˈtɪriəl/ *n.* **1** [C,U] cloth used for making clothes, curtains, etc.: *Mom bought some velvet material to make a dress.* **2** [C,U] things such as wood, plastic, paper, etc. from which things can be made: *building materials* **3** [U] *also* **materials** [plural] the things that are used for making or doing something: ***reading/writing/teaching material*** **4** [U] information or ideas used in books, movies, etc.: *He's looking for new* ***material for*** *his next book.*

material[2] *adj.* **1** relating to your money, possessions, living conditions, etc. rather than the needs of your mind or soul: *We have very few* ***material possessions****, but we have each other.* **2** relating to the real world or to physical objects, rather than religious matters: *the material world* **3** LAW important and needing to be considered when making a decision: *a* ***material witness*** *for the defense* | *He was prosecuted for concealing facts* ***material to*** *the investigation.*

ma·te·ri·al·ism /məˈtɪriəˌlɪzəm/ *n.* [U] (disapproving) the belief that money and possessions are more important than art, religion, morality, etc. —**materialist** *adj.*, *n.* [C] —**materialistic** /məˌtɪriəˈlɪstɪk/ *adj.*

ma·te·ri·al·ize /məˈtɪriəˌlaɪz/ *v.* [I] **1** to happen or appear in the way that you expected: *The student*

M

protest ***failed to materialize/never materialized*** (=did not happen). **2** to appear in an unexpected and strange way: *A man materialized from the shadows.*

ma·ter·nal /mə'tɚnl/ *adj.* **1** typical of the way a good mother feels or acts → PATERNAL: *maternal feelings* **2 maternal grandfather/aunt etc.** your mother's father, sister, etc.

ma·ter·ni·ty /mə'tɚnəṯi/ *adj.* relating to a woman who is PREGNANT, or who has had a baby, or to the time when she is pregnant: *maternity clothes*

ma'ternity ˌleave *n.* [U] time that a woman is allowed away from her job when she has a baby: *Karen's still* ***on maternity leave.***

ma'ternity ˌward *n.* [C] a department in a hospital where a woman is cared for after having a baby

math /mæθ/ *n.* [U] (informal) the study or science of numbers and of the structure and measurement of shapes

math·e·mat·i·cal /mæθ'mæṯɪkəl, ˌmæθə-/ *adj.* related to or using mathematics: *a mathematical equation*

math·e·ma·ti·cian /ˌmæθmə'tɪʃən/ *n.* [C] someone who studies or teaches mathematics

math·e·mat·ics /ˌmæθ'mæṯɪks, ˌmæθə-/ *n.* [U] (formal) the study or science of numbers and of the structure and measurement of shapes (SYN) **math** [ORIGIN: 1500—1600 Latin *mathematicus*, from Greek, from *mathema* "learning, mathematics"]

mat·i·n·ée /ˌmæt˺n'eɪ/ *n.* [C] a performance of a play or movie in the afternoon

ma·tri·arch /'meɪtriˌɑrk/ *n.* [C] a woman who has the most influence or power in a family or social group → PATRIARCH —**matriarchal** /ˌmeɪtri'ɑrkəl/ *adj.*

ma·tri·ar·chy /'meɪtriˌɑrki/ *n.* [U] SOCIAL SCIENCE a social system in which women hold all the power → PATRIARCHY

ma·tric·u·late /mə'trɪkyəˌleɪt/ *v.* [I] (formal) to officially begin studying at a school or college: *He majored in theater after* ***matriculating to*** *Northwestern.* —**matriculation** /məˌtrɪkyə'leɪʃən/ *n.* [U]

mat·ri·lin·e·al /ˌmætrə'lɪniəl/ *adj.* SOCIAL SCIENCE a matrilineal society regards the connections between mothers and daughters as more important than the connections between fathers and sons → PATRILINEAL

mat·ri·mo·ny /'mætrəˌmoʊni/ *n.* [U] (formal) the state of being married [ORIGIN: 1200—1300 Old French *matremoine*, from Latin *matrimonium* "being a mother, marriage"] —**matrimonial** /ˌmætrə'moʊniəl/ *adj.*

ma·trix /'meɪtrɪks/ *n.* (plural **matrices** /-trəsiz/ *or* **matrixes**) [C] MATH an arrangement of numbers, letters, or signs on a GRID (=a background of regular crossed lines), used in mathematics, science, etc.

ma·tron /'meɪtrən/ *n.* [C] (literary) an older married woman

ma·tron·ly /'meɪtrənli/ *adj.* a polite word to describe a woman who is not thin, young, or attractive

matte /mæt/ *adj.* matte paint, color, or photographs are not shiny

mat·ted /'mæṯɪd/ *adj.* matted hair or fur is twisted and stuck together

mat·ter¹ /'mæṯɚ/ *n.*

1 SUBJECT/SITUATION [C] a subject or situation that you have to think about or deal with: *I need to speak with you about a* ***serious matter.*** | *The argument was strictly a* ***private/personal matter.*** | ***matters of*** *public concern* | *Whether he is guilty is* ***a matter for*** *the jury to decide.* | *financial matters*

> THESAURUS **subject, topic, theme, issue**
> → SUBJECT¹

2 matters [plural] a situation that you are in or have been describing: *She tried to apologize, but that only* ***made matters worse.*** | *It* ***didn't help matters*** (=made the situation worse) *when the money failed to arrive.*

SPOKEN PHRASES

3 the matter used to ask why something is not working normally, someone seems upset or sick, or something looks wrong: ***What's the matter?*** *Why are you crying?* | *Is there* ***something the matter with*** *the car?*

4 as a matter of fact said when giving a surprising or unexpected answer to a question or statement: *"Have you ever been to Paris?" "As a matter of fact, I just came from there."*

5 the fact of the matter is (that) used when saying what you think is really true concerning a situation: *The fact of the matter is the company has had financial problems for years.*

6 no matter how/where/what etc. used to say that something is always the same whatever happens, or in spite of someone's efforts to change it: *No matter how hard she tried, she couldn't get the door open.*

7 it's only/just a matter of time used to say that something will definitely happen in the future: *It's only a matter of time before he loses his job.*

8 SUBSTANCE [U] **a)** PHYSICS the material that everything in the universe is made of **b)** a substance that consists of a particular thing: ***waste/vegetable matter***

9 take matters into your own hands to deal with a problem yourself because other people have failed to deal with it: *Local people took matters into their own hands and hired their own security guards.*

10 sth is a matter of principle/money etc. used to say that what happens or what you decide depends on your judgment, how much something costs, how much time there is, etc.: *The money isn't important – it's a matter of principle.*

11 be a matter of doing sth used to say that you

only have to do a particular thing, or do something in a particular way, in order to be successful: *I have a place to stay. Now it's just a matter of booking my flight.*
12 sth is a matter of opinion used to say that people have different opinions about something
13 a matter of life and death a very dangerous or serious situation
14 a matter of seconds/days/inches etc. only a few seconds, days, inches, etc.: *The bullet missed him by a matter of inches.*
15 for that matter used to say that what you have said about one thing is also true about another: *We don't have a TV yet, or even a bed for that matter.*

matter[2] *v.* [I] **1** to be important, or to have an effect on what happens: *Money is the only thing that* ***matters to*** *him.* | *Does it* ***matter which*** *road I take?* | *No* ***matter how*** *much suntan lotion I put on, I still burn.* **2 it doesn't matter** (spoken) **a)** used to say that you do not care which one of two things you have: *"Do you want tea or coffee?" "Oh, it doesn't matter."* **b)** used to tell someone you are not angry or upset: *"I lost the book you loaned me." "It doesn't matter – I have another copy."*

ˌmatter-of-'fact *adj.* showing no emotion when you are talking about something, especially something exciting, frightening, upsetting, etc.: *Jerry was very* ***matter-of-fact about*** *losing his job.* **—matter-of-factly** *adv.*

THESAURUS
detached – not reacting to something in an emotional way: *She described what had happened in a detached way.*
impassive – not showing any emotions: *The witness remained impassive throughout questioning.*
dispassionate (formal) – not easily influenced by personal feelings: *a dispassionate analysis of the situation*
cold – without friendly feelings: *a cold and distant man*

mat·tress /ˈmætrɪs/ *n.* [C] the soft part of a bed that you lie on [ORIGIN: 1200—1300 Old French *materas*, from Arabic *matrah* "place where something is thrown"]

ma·ture[1] /məˈtʃʊr, məˈtʊr/ (Ac) *adj.* **1** behaving in a reasonable way like an adult – used especially about a child or young person (ANT) **immature**: *She's young, but she's very* ***mature for her age.*** **2** fully grown and developed: *Eagles aren't sexually mature until age five.* | *mature wine* | *The human brain isn't fully mature until about age 25.* **3** a polite way of describing someone who is not young anymore [ORIGIN: 1300—1400 Latin *maturus*]

mature[2] (Ac) *v.* [I] **1** to begin to behave in a reasonable way like an adult: *Pat's matured a lot since going to college.* **2** BIOLOGY to become fully grown or developed: *The fly matures in only seven days.* | *It will mature into a small tree.* | *Girls tend to mature more quickly than boys, both physically and emotionally.* **3** ECONOMICS if a financial arrangement, such as a BOND or POLICY, matures, it becomes ready to be paid **—maturation** *n.* [U]: *Scientists studied the maturation of the seeds under different weather conditions.*

ma·tur·i·ty /məˈtʃʊrət̬i, -ˈtʊr-/ (Ac) *n.* [U] **1** the quality of behaving in a sensible way like an adult: *He has a lot of maturity for a 15-year-old.* **2** BIOLOGY the time when a person, animal, or plant is fully grown or developed: *Rabbits* ***reach maturity*** *in only five weeks.* | *Few of the plants grew to maturity.* **3** ECONOMICS the time when a financial arrangement, such as a BOND or POLICY, is ready to be paid: *With these particular bonds, interest is paid* ***at maturity.***

maud·lin /ˈmɔdlɪn/ *adj.* (disapproving) talking or behaving in a sad and silly way: *moments of maudlin self-pity*

maul /mɔl/ *v.* [T] if an animal mauls someone, it injures him/her badly, tearing his/her flesh

mau·so·le·um /ˌmɔsəˈliəm, -zə-/ *n.* [C] a large stone building made specially to contain the body of a dead person or the dead bodies of an important family [ORIGIN: 1400—1500 Latin, Greek, from *Mausolos* king of Caria in ancient Turkey, for whom such a building was made]

mauve /moʊv/ *n.* [U] a pale purple color **—mauve** *adj.*

mav·er·ick /ˈmævərɪk/ *n.* [C] someone who thinks or behaves in a way that is different from most people: *a political maverick* [ORIGIN: 1800—1900 Samuel A. *Maverick* (1803-70), U.S. cattle owner who did not mark some of his young cattle] **—maverick** *adj.*

mawk·ish /ˈmɔkɪʃ/ *adj.* showing too much emotion in a way that is embarrassing (SYN) **sentimental**: *He writes movingly about his wife without becoming mawkish.* **—mawkishly** *adv.* **—mawkishness** *n.* [U]

max[1] /mæks/ (Ac) *n.* **1** (informal) the abbreviation of MAXIMUM: *Five people will fit, but that's the max.* **2 to the max** (slang) to the greatest degree possible **—max** *adj., adv.*: *It'll cost $50 max.*

max[2] *v.*
max sth ↔ **out** *phr. v.* (slang) to use something such as money or supplies so that there is none left: *I maxed out my credit card.*

max·im /ˈmæksɪm/ *n.* [C] a well-known phrase that gives a rule for sensible behavior

THESAURUS **phrase, expression, idiom, cliché, saying, proverb** → PHRASE[1]

max·i·mize /ˈmæksəˌmaɪz/ (Ac) *v.* [T] **1** to increase something as much as possible (ANT) **minimize**: *We want to maximize the services available to our customers.* | *The company's main function is to maximize profit.* **2** IT to CLICK on a special part of a WINDOW on a computer screen so that it becomes as big as the screen (ANT) **minimize**: *Users* *will need to maximize the window to see the full picture.*

M

max·i·mum¹ /ˈmæksəməm/ (Ac) *adj.* the maximum amount, quantity, speed, etc. is the largest that is possible or allowed (ANT) **minimum**: *The maximum penalty is five years in prison.* | *The maximum height of these trees is 25 feet.* [ORIGIN: 1500—1600 Latin *maximus* "greatest," from *magnus* "great"]

maximum² *n.* [C usually singular] the largest number, amount, etc. that is possible or is allowed (ANT) **minimum**: *The road was designed for **a maximum of** 35,000 vehicles a day.* | *The country's agricultural policies force farmers to exploit their land **to the maximum**.*

May /meɪ/ *n.* [C,U] the fifth month of the year, between April and June: *Our anniversary is **on** May 1st.* | *We might be going to Texas **in May**.* | *Construction is scheduled to begin **next May**.* | *We haven't seen Tania since **last May**.* [ORIGIN: 1100—1200 Old French *mai*, from Latin *Maius*, from *Maia* Roman goddess]

may *modal verb* **1** used to talk about what is or was possible ➔ MIGHT: *You may have to come back next week.* | *This may not be enough money.* ▸Don't say "mayn't."◂ **2 may I ...?** (spoken) used to ask politely if you can do something: *May I borrow your pen?* | *May I please speak to Carl?* **3** (formal) used to say that someone is allowed to do something: *You may start writing on your test forms now.* **4 may ..., but ...** used to say that although one thing is true, something else which seems very different is also true: *This may taste bad, but it's good for you.* **5 may as well ➔ might as well** *at* MIGHT¹

GRAMMAR

May is not used in questions about possible events or situations. Use **might** instead: *Might there be a connection between these two things?*

may·be /ˈmeɪbi/ *adv.* **1** used to say that something may be true or may happen, but that you are not sure (SYN) **perhaps**: *Maybe Anna's stuck in traffic.* | *"Will you be there tomorrow night?" "Maybe."* | *Maybe this wasn't such a good idea.* | *Maybe you're right, but **maybe not**.*

USAGE

Use **maybe** to talk about something that is possible, especially as a way of suggesting or explaining something. Maybe usually goes at the beginning of a sentence: *Maybe we can get together this weekend.*

May be is a modal verb followed by "be," used to show that something is possible but not sure: *We may be getting together this weekend.*

2 used to make a suggestion: *Maybe Jeff could help you.*

ˈMay Day *n.* the first day of May, when people traditionally celebrate the arrival of spring

may·day /ˈmeɪdeɪ/ *n.* [C usually singular] a radio signal used to ask for help when a ship or airplane is in danger [ORIGIN: 1900—2000 French *m'aider* "help me"]

may·hem /ˈmeɪhɛm/ *n.* [U] an extremely confused situation in which people are very frightened or excited: *There was complete mayhem after the explosion.*

may·o /ˈmeɪoʊ/ *n.* [U] (spoken) mayonnaise

may·on·naise /ˈmeɪəˌneɪz/ *n.* [U] a thick white sauce made of egg and oil [ORIGIN: 1800—1900 French]

may·or /ˈmeɪɚ, mɛr/ *n.* [C] someone who is elected to lead the government of a town or city

THESAURUS **politician, president, congressman/congresswoman, senator, governor** ➔ POLITICIAN

maze /meɪz/ *n.* [C] **1 a maze of streets/tunnels etc.** a complicated and confusing arrangement of streets, etc. **2** something that is complicated and difficult to understand: *a **maze of rules/laws/regulations*** **3** a specially designed system of paths that is difficult to find your way through, which people go to for fun [ORIGIN: 1200—1300 *maze* "to confuse"]

maze

M.B.A. *n.* [C] **Master of Business Administration** a GRADUATE degree that teaches you the skills you need to be in charge of a business

MC the abbreviation of MASTER OF CEREMONIES

MCAT /ˈɛmkæt/ *n.* [C] (trademark) **Medical College Admission Test** an examination taken by students who have completed a first degree and want to go to MEDICAL SCHOOL

Mc·Coy /məˈkɔɪ/ *n.* **the real McCoy** (informal) something that is real and not a copy

MD the written abbreviation of MARYLAND

M.D. *n.* [C] DOCTOR OF MEDICINE

ME the written abbreviation of MAINE

me /mi/ *pron.* **1** the object form of "I": *Cathy called me last night.* | *Give it to me.* **2 me too** (spoken) said when you agree with someone, or are going to do the same thing as s/he is: *"I'm hungry!" "Me too."* **3 me neither** (spoken) said when you agree with a negative statement someone has just made: *"I don't like fruitcake." "Me neither."*

mead·ow /ˈmɛdoʊ/ *n.* [C] a field with wild grass and flowers

mea·ger /ˈmigɚ/ *adj.* very small in amount: *a meager salary* [ORIGIN: 1300—1400 French *maigre*, from Latin *macer* "thin"]

M

meal /mil/ *n.* [C] a particular time when you eat food, or the food that is eaten then: *Would you like wine with your meal?* | *Don't **eat** a heavy **meal** before going to bed.* | *We **had** a nice **meal**.* [ORIGIN: Old English *mæl* "time, meal"]

COLLOCATIONS

evening meal – dinner or supper
main meal – the most important and largest meal you eat during a day
three/four/five-course meal – a large meal that has three, etc. courses (=separate parts of a meal)
light/quick meal – a small meal
decent/good/full meal – a large meal with good food
have/eat a meal
cook/prepare/make a meal
go (out) for a meal – to go to a restaurant to eat
ask sb out for a meal also **take sb out for a meal** – to ask someone to come to a restaurant with you to eat, or to take someone there
→ LUNCH

THESAURUS

Types of meals
breakfast – a meal that you eat in the morning
lunch – a meal that you eat in the middle of the day
brunch – a meal that you eat in the late morning, instead of breakfast or lunch
dinner/supper – a meal that you eat in the evening
picnic – a meal that you eat outdoors, consisting of food that you cook or prepare earlier
barbecue – a meal that you cook and eat outdoors
Parts of a large meal
appetizer – a small dish of food served at the beginning of a meal
hors d'oeuvre – a small amount of food that is served before people sit down at the table for the main meal
main course/entrée – the main part of a meal
side dish – food eaten with the main course
dessert – sweet food eaten at the end of the meal → CORNMEAL, OATMEAL

meal·time /ˈmiltaɪm/ *n.* [C] a time during the day when you have a meal

mean[1] /min/ *v.* (past tense and past participle **meant** /mɛnt/) [T] **1** to have or represent a particular meaning: ***What does** 'inoculate' **mean**?* | *This light means you're running low on fuel.* ►Don't say "is meaning."◄ **2** to intend a particular meaning when you say something: *I said Monday but I meant Tuesday.* | *I just **meant that** we need to think carefully about our options.* ►Don't say "I am meaning."◄ **3** to intend to do something or intend that someone else should do something: *I've been **meaning to** ask you something.* | *He says he didn't **mean for** her **to** get hurt.* **4** to have a particular result: *An airline strike **meant that** he was stuck in Athens for another week.*

SPOKEN PHRASES

5 I mean a) said when you want to explain or give an example of something, or when you stop to think about what to say next: *She's always late for work. I mean, yesterday she showed up at 10:30.* **b)** said when you want to quickly correct what you have just said: *She plays the violin, I mean the viola.* **6 (do) you mean ...?** said when you are checking that you understand something that someone has said: *You mean you want me to call you, or will you call me?* **7 (do) you know what I mean?** said when you are asking someone if s/he understands you: *He wore a hat like the one Sherlock Holmes had. You know what I mean?* **8 I know what you mean** used to tell someone that you understand or agree with what s/he is saying: *"I'm so tired of his complaining." "I know what you mean."* **9 I see what you mean** used to tell someone that you now understand what s/he has been saying **10 what do you mean (...)? a)** said when you do not understand someone **b)** said when you are very surprised or annoyed by something someone has said: *What do you mean, you sold the car?*

11 sb/sth means sth (to sb) used to say that someone or something is very important to someone: *It would **mean a lot to** your father if you offered to help.* **12 sb means business** to be determined to do something: *You have to be strict about the rules so they know you mean business.* **13 sth was meant to be** used to say that you think a situation was certain to happen and that no one could have prevented it: *Our marriage was never meant to be.* [ORIGIN: Old English *mænan*]

mean[2] *adj.* **1** cruel or not kind: *Why do you say such mean things to me?* | *Don't be **mean to** your sister.* | ***It** was **mean of** you not to invite her.*

THESAURUS

cruel – deliberately making someone suffer or feel unhappy: *Kids can be very cruel to each other.*
unkind – treating people in a way that makes them unhappy or hurts their feelings: *She never says an unkind word.*
nasty – not kind and not pleasant, often deliberately: *Their neighbors were really nasty.*
thoughtless – not thinking about the needs and feelings of other people: *a thoughtless remark*
spiteful – being unkind deliberately in order to annoy or upset someone: *Her reaction was spiteful.*
abusive – using cruel words or physical violence: *an abusive father*
vicious – very cruel and deliberately trying to upset someone: *a vicious rumor*
malicious (formal) – showing a desire to harm or upset someone: *malicious gossip*

2 no mean feat/trick/achievement etc. something that is very difficult to do, so that someone who does it deserves to be admired: *It was no mean*

M

achievement for a woman to become a doctor in 1920. **3 a mean sth** (informal) used to say that something is very good or someone is very good at doing something: *Ray plays a mean game of tennis.* **4** MATH average: *The mean age of the men in the study was 47.*

mean³ *n.* **1 means** [plural] a method, system, object, etc. that is used as a way of achieving a result: *We'll use any means we can to raise the money.* | *My bicycle is my main* ***means of*** *transportation.* | *The oil is transported* ***by means of*** (=using) *a pipeline.* **2 means** [plural] ECONOMICS the money or income that you have: *They don't have* ***the means to*** *buy a car.* | *Try to live* ***within*** *your* ***means*** (=only spending what you can afford). | *a man* ***of means*** (=who is rich) **3 by all means** (spoken) used to mean "of course" when politely allowing someone to do something or agreeing with a suggestion: *"Can I invite Clarence?" "Oh, by all means."* **4 by no means** (formal) not at all: *The results are by no means certain.* **5 a means to an end** something that you do only to achieve a result, not because you want to do it: *This job is just a means to an end.* **6 the mean** MATH the average amount, figure, or value → MEDIAN, MODE: *The mean of 7, 9, and 14 is 10.*

me·an·der /mi'ændɚ/ *v.* [I] to move in a slow relaxed way, not in any particular direction: *I spent the afternoon* ***meandering through*** *the city.* [ORIGIN: 1500—1600 Latin *maeander*, from Greek, from *Maiandros* (now Menderes), river in Turkey]

mean·ing /'minɪŋ/ *n.* **1** [C,U] the thing, idea, feeling, etc. that a word, phrase, or sign represents: *I don't understand the* ***meaning of*** *this word.* **2** [C,U] the thoughts or ideas that someone wants you to understand from what s/he says, does, writes, etc.: *The exact* ***meaning of*** *the king's statement was not clear.* **3** [U] the importance that something has in a particular situation: *Until today, I hadn't realized the full meaning of what had happened.* **4 (not) know the meaning of sth** to have, or not have, experience and understanding of a particular situation or feeling: *Those kids don't know the meaning of hard work.*

mean·ing·ful /'minɪŋfəl/ *adj.* **1** serious, useful, or important: *a meaningful relationship* | *meaningful work* **2** easy to understand: *The data isn't very meaningful to anyone but a scientist.* **3 a meaningful look/smile etc.** a look that clearly expresses the way someone feels

mean·ing·less /'minɪŋlɪs/ *adj.* having no purpose or importance and therefore not worth doing or having: *a meaningless job* | *a statistic that is* ***completely/totally/absolutely meaningless***

meant /mɛnt/ *v.* the past tense and past participle of MEAN

mean·time /'mintaɪm/ *n.* **in the meantime** in the period of time between now and a future event, or between two events in the past: *We want to buy a house, but in the meantime we're renting the apartment.*

mean·while /'minwaɪl/ *adv.* while something else is happening, or in the time between two events: *I was in the kitchen cleaning up. Meanwhile, Ray was in the living room watching TV.*

mea·sles /'mizəlz/ *also* **the measles** *n.* [U] an infectious illness in which you have a fever and small red spots on your face and body

mea·sly /'mizli/ *adj.* (informal) very small and disappointing in size, quantity, or value: *I only won a measly $5.*

meas·ur·a·ble /'mɛʒərəbəl/ *adj.* **1** able to be measured: *A manager should set measurable goals.* **2** important or large enough to have an effect: *The changes have not achieved any measurable results.* —**measurably** *adv.*

meas·ure¹ /'mɛʒɚ/ *v.* **1** [T] to find the size, length, or amount of something: *Measure the wall to see if the bookshelves will fit.* **2** [T] to judge the importance or value of something: *It is too early to measure the effectiveness of the drug.* | *Education cannot be measured by test scores alone.* **3** [linking verb] to be a particular size, length, or amount: *The table measures four feet by six feet.*

measure

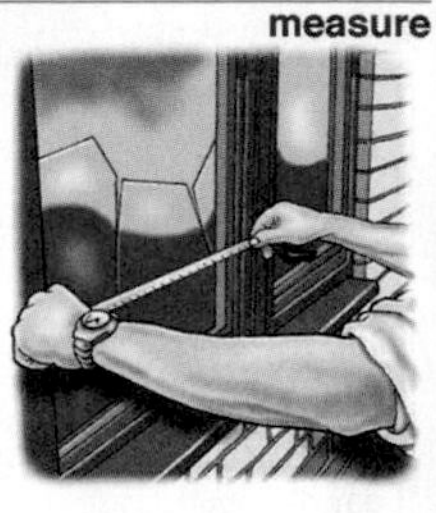

measure sb/sth **against** sth *phr. v.* to judge someone or something by comparing him, her, or it to another person or thing

measure up *phr. v.* to be good enough to do a particular job or to reach a particular standard: *The test will allow us to see how our students measure up.*

measure² *n.* **1** [C] an official action that is intended to deal with a problem: *Congress passed a measure to control spending today.* | *We have* ***taken measures*** *to limit smoking to one area in the building.* | *Officials said they were satisfied with* ***security measures****.* **2 a measure of sth** an amount of something good or something that you want: *Over time, they developed a measure of trust.* **3 be a measure of sth** (formal) to be a sign of the importance, strength, etc. of something: *Profits are often used as a measure of a company's success.* **4** [C,U] a system or unit for measuring the weight, length, etc. of something: *A kilo is a measure of weight.*

meas·ure·ment /'mɛʒɚmənt/ *n.* [C,U] the length, height, value, etc. of something, or the act of measuring this: *We* ***took measurements*** *and realized that the table wouldn't fit through the doorway.*

ˌmeasure of 'spread *also* **ˌmeasure of variaˈbility, ˌmeasure of variˈation** *n.* [C] MATH a measurement used to show how STATISTICAL information is spread across particular DATA

ˌmeasures 'of center *n.* [plural] MATH three standard units of measurement used when examining and describing DATA. The units are called the MEAN (=used to show the average quantity), the MODE (=used to show the most frequent quantity), and the MEDIAN (=used to show the middle quantity).

meat /mit/ *n.* [U] the flesh of animals and birds eaten as food: *She never eats meat on Fridays.* | ***red meat*** (=dark meat such as beef) | ***white meat*** (=pale meat such as chicken) [ORIGIN: Old English *mete* "food"]

THESAURUS

Types of meat
beef – the meat from a cow
veal – the meat from a young cow
pork – the meat from a pig
ham – meat from a pig, that has been preserved with salt or smoke
bacon – long thin pieces of meat from the back or sides of a pig, that have been preserved with salt or smoke
The meat from lamb, birds, or fish is called by the name of the animal: *We had chicken for dinner.* | *roast lamb* | *salmon steaks in tomato sauce*

meat·ball /'mitˀbɔl/ *n.* [C] a small round ball made from very small pieces of meat pressed together

meat·loaf /'mitlouf/ *n.* (plural **meatloaves**) [C,U] meat, egg, bread, etc. mixed and baked together in the shape of a LOAF

meat·y /'miṭi/ *adj.* containing a lot of meat or having a strong meat taste: *a meaty stew*

mec·ca /'mɛkə/ *n.* [singular] **1 Mecca** a city in Saudi Arabia which is the most important holy city of Islam **2** a place that many people want to visit for a particular reason: *Alaska is a **mecca for** nature lovers.*

me·chan·ic /mɪ'kænɪk/ *n.* **1** [C] someone whose job is to repair vehicles and machinery **2 mechanics** [U] the science that deals with the effects of forces on objects **3 the mechanics of (doing) sth** the way in which something works or is done: *The mechanics of bookkeeping can be complex.*

me·chan·i·cal /mɪ'kænɪkəl/ *adj.* **1** relating to machines, or using power from a machine: ***Mechanical failure*** *caused the jet to crash.* | *a mechanical device* **2** done or said without thinking, as if you were a machine: *a mechanical answer* [ORIGIN: 1400—1500 Late Latin *mechanicus*, from Greek, from *mechane* "machine"] —**mechanically** *adv.*

mech·a·nism /'mɛkəˌnɪzəm/ (Ac) *n.* [C] **1** the part of a machine, or a set of parts, that does a particular job: *a car's steering mechanism* **2** a way in which something works, or the process by which it is done: *the mechanisms of the brain* | *a **mechanism for** measuring employee performance* | *Alcohol affects the perception mechanism of the brain.*

mech·a·nized /'mɛkəˌnaɪzd/ *adj.* using machines instead of people or animals: *a highly mechanized factory* —**mechanize** *v.* [T]

med·al /'mɛdl/ *n.* [C] a round flat piece of metal given to someone who has won a competition or who has done something brave: *He **won** an Olympic gold **medal**.*

med·al·ist /'mɛdl-ɪst/ *n.* [C] someone who has won a medal in a competition: *a **gold/silver/bronze medalist***

me·dal·lion /mə'dælyən/ *n.* [C] a piece of metal shaped like a large coin, worn as jewelry on a chain around the neck

med·dle /'mɛdl/ *v.* [I] (disapproving) to try to influence a situation that does not concern you: *I don't want the government **meddling in** my affairs.* —**meddler** *n.* [C]

me·di·a /'midiə/ (Ac) *n.* [plural] all the organizations, such as television, radio, and newspapers, that provide news and information for the public, or the people who do this work: *the **news media*** | *The film attracted a lot of **media attention**.* | *The scandal was widely reported in the media.* → MASS MEDIA

me·di·an /'midiən/ *n.* **1** [C] something that divides a road or HIGHWAY, such as a thin piece of land **2** [singular] MATH the middle number in a set of numbers that are arranged in order of size → MEAN, MODE: *The median of 3, 9, 11, 13, and 14 is 11.* **3** [C usually singular] *also* **median of a triangle** MATH a line passing from one of the points of a TRIANGLE to the middle of the opposite side

me·di·ate /'midiˌeɪt/ (Ac) *v.* [I,T] to try to help two groups, countries, etc. to stop arguing and make an agreement: *The court had to **mediate between** Hassel and his neighbors.* | *He will be mediating talks between the two sides.* —**mediation** /ˌmidi'eɪʃən/ *n.* [U]

me·di·a·tor /'midiˌeɪṭɚ/ *n.* [C] someone who helps people, groups, countries, etc. to end an argument and reach an agreement

Med·i·caid /'mɛdɪˌkeɪd/ *n.* [U] a system by which the government helps to pay the cost of medical treatment for poor people

med·i·cal /'mɛdɪkəl/ (Ac) *adj.* relating to medicine and the treatment of disease or injury: *medical school* | *The clinic provides free **medical care**.* | *new types of **medical treatment*** | *the **medical profession*** (=doctors, nurses, etc.) | *More funding is needed for **medical research**.* [ORIGIN: 1600—1700 French *médical*, from Late Latin *medicalis*, from Latin *medicus* "doctor"] —**medically** *adv.*

'medical ˌschool *n.* [C,U] a part of a university, where people study to become doctors

Med·i·care /'mɛdɪˌkɛr/ *n.* [U] a system by which the government helps to pay for the medical treatment of old people

M

med·i·cat·ed /'mɛdɪˌkeɪt̬ɪd/ *adj.* containing medicine: *medicated shampoo*

med·i·ca·tion /ˌmɛdɪ'keɪʃən/ *n.* [C,U] medicine given to people who are sick: *Are you **taking** any **medication**?* | *He's **on medication** for his heart.*

> THESAURUS **medicine, pill, tablet, capsule, eye/ear drops, drug, dosage, prescription** → MEDICINE

me·dic·i·nal /mə'dɪsənəl/ *adj.* helping to cure illness or disease: *The herbs are used **for medicinal purposes**.*

med·i·cine /'mɛdəsən/ *n.* **1** [C,U] a substance used for treating illness: *Remember to **take** your **medicine**.* | *Medicines should be kept away from children.*

> THESAURUS
> **pill/tablet/capsule** – a small hard piece of medicine that you swallow
> **eye/ear drops** – liquid medicine that you put into your eye or ear
> **drug** – a medicine or a substance for making medicines: *a new drug in the treatment of breast cancer*
> **medication** – medicine given to people who are sick: *He's on medication for his heart.*
> **dosage** – the amount of medicine that you should take: *The usual dosage is 25 to 50 mg.*
> **prescription** – a type of medicine that a doctor says you should take, or the piece of paper on which a doctor writes this down: *I need to pick up my prescription at the pharmacy.*

2 [U] the treatment and study of illnesses and injuries: *She plans to study medicine at Harvard.*

me·di·e·val /mɪ'divəl, mɛ-, mi-/ *adj.* relating to the MIDDLE AGES: *medieval poetry* [ORIGIN: 1800—1900 Modern Latin *medium aevum* "middle age"]

me·di·o·cre /ˌmidi'oʊkɚ◂/ *adj.* not very good, but not extremely bad: *a mediocre student* [ORIGIN: 1500—1600 French, Latin *mediocris* "halfway up a mountain"] —**mediocrity** /ˌmidi'ɑkrət̬i/ *n.* [U]

med·i·tate /'mɛdəˌteɪt/ *v.* [I] to make yourself very calm by relaxing completely, and thinking only about one thing such as a sound or a religious idea —**meditation** /ˌmɛdə'teɪʃən/ *n.* [U]

med·i·ta·tive /'mɛdəˌteɪt̬ɪv/ *adj.* thinking deeply and seriously about something, or showing that you are doing this: *He was in a meditative mood.*

Med·i·ter·ra·ne·an /ˌmɛdɪtə'reɪniən/ *n.* **the Mediterranean** EARTH SCIENCES the areas of land surrounding the Mediterranean Sea (=sea between northern Africa and southern Europe), and the islands in it —**Mediterranean** *adj.*

me·di·um¹ /'midiəm/ (Ac) *adj.* of middle size or amount: *"What size do you wear?" "Medium."* | *Cook the soup over medium heat for 30 minutes.* | *a man **of medium height*** | *The study focused on medium-sized cities.*

medium² (Ac) *n.* [C] **1** (plural **media** /'midiə/) a way of communicating or expressing something: *The Internet is a powerful advertising medium.* | *In the modern age, television is the primary medium of communication.* **2** (plural **media**) the material, paints, etc. that an artist uses: *This sculptor's favorite medium is wood.* **3** (plural **mediums**) someone who claims to speak to dead people and receive messages from them

'medium-sized *also* **'medium-size** *adj.* not small, but not large either: *medium-sized apples* | *a medium-size city*

med·ley /'mɛdli/ *n.* (plural **medleys**) [C] ENG. LANG. ARTS tunes from different songs that are played one after the other as a single piece of music: *a **medley of** folk songs*

med school /'mɛd skul/ *n.* [C,U] (informal) a MEDICAL SCHOOL

me·dul·la ob·lon·ga·ta /məˌdʌlə ɑblɔŋ'gɑt̬ə/ *n.* [singular] BIOLOGY the lowest part of your brain, where it connects with your SPINAL CORD. The medulla oblongata controls your breathing and the flow of blood to and from your heart. → *see picture at* BRAIN¹

meek /mik/ *adj.* very quiet and gentle, and not willing to argue —**meekly** *adv.* —**meekness** *n.* [U]

meet¹ /mit/ *v.* (past tense and past participle **met** /mɛt/)

1 SEE SB FOR THE FIRST TIME [I,T] to see and talk to someone for the first time, or to be introduced to someone: *Mike and Sara met in college.* | *When did we first meet?* | *I saw Jim's wife once, but I never met her.*

2 BE IN THE SAME PLACE [I,T] to come to the same place as someone else because you have arranged to find him/her there: *Let's **meet for** lunch tomorrow.* | *I could meet you at the coffee shop at 11.*

> THESAURUS
> **get together** – to meet with someone or with a group of people: *Why don't we all get together and go out for a drink?*
> **gather** – if people gather somewhere, or if someone gathers them, they come together in the same place: *Fans have started to gather outside the stadium.*
> **assemble** – if you assemble people, or if people assemble, they are brought together in the same place: *The members of the tour group assembled at the airport before departure.*
> **come together** – if people come together, they meet in order to discuss things, exchange ideas, etc.: *People came together from miles away to attend his funeral.*
> **congregate** – to come together in a group: *A group of protesters had congregated outside.*
> **convene** (formal) – to come together for a

M

formal meeting, or to ask people to do this: *The committee will convene again in two weeks time.*

3 nice/good/pleased to meet you (spoken) said when you meet someone for the first time: *"Paul, this is Jack." "Nice to meet you."*
4 (it was) nice meeting you (spoken) used when saying goodbye to someone you have just met for the first time
5 MEETING [I] to be together in the same place in order to discuss something: *The committee met to discuss goals for the coming year.*
6 meet a need/demand etc. to have or do enough of what is needed, or be good enough to reach a particular standard: *We're trying to find a way to* ***meet the needs*** *of all students.*
7 SB ARRIVING [T] to be at an airport, station, etc. when someone arrives: *I'm going to meet John's plane.* | *Alice will meet us at the station.*
8 JOIN [I,T] to join together at a particular place: *the place where two roads meet*
9 meet (sb) halfway to do some of the things that someone wants, if s/he does some of the things you want [ORIGIN: Old English *metan*]

meet up *phr. v.*
to meet someone informally in order to do something together: *Let's meet up after the game.* | *We* ***met up with*** *Jan outside the museum.*

meet with sb/sth *phr. v.*
1 to have a meeting with someone: *The President met with European leaders today in Paris.*
2 to get a particular reaction or result: *His proposal* ***met with opposition/approval.***

meet² *n.* [C] a sports competition: *a* ***swim/track meet***

meet·ing /ˈmit̬ɪŋ/ *n.* [C] **1** an organized gathering of people for the purpose of discussing something: *We* ***have a meeting*** *at two.* | *a* ***meeting of*** *world business leaders* | *a* ***meeting with*** *my boss* | *John has been* ***in a meeting*** *all morning.* **2 a meeting of the minds** a situation in which people agree about something

ˈmeeting house *n.* [C] a building where Quakers go to WORSHIP

meg·a /ˈmɛgə/ *adj., adv.* (informal) very big, impressive, and enjoyable: *Their first record was a mega hit.*

meg·a·byte /ˈmɛgəˌbaɪt/ *n.* [C] IT a unit for measuring computer information equal to a million BYTES

meg·a·lo·ma·ni·a /ˌmɛgəloʊˈmeɪniə/ *n.* [U] the belief that you are extremely important and powerful —**megalomaniac** /ˌmɛgəloʊˈmeɪniˌæk/ *adj., n.* [C]

meg·a·phone /ˈmɛgəˌfoʊn/ *n.* [C] a thing like a large CONE, that you talk through when speaking to a crowd in order to make your voice sound louder

meg·a·ton /ˈmɛgəˌtʌn/ *n.* [C] a measure of the power of an explosive, that is equal to that of a million TONS of TNT (=a powerful explosive)

mei·o·sis /maɪˈoʊsɪs/ *n.* [U] BIOLOGY the process by which a cell divides to become two cells, each new cell having only half the number of CHROMOSOMES of the original cell → MITOSIS: *During meiosis, the paired genes separate to form sperm or eggs.*

mel·an·chol·y¹ /ˈmɛlənˌkɑli/ *adj.* sad, or making you feel sad: *a melancholy look*

THESAURUS **sad, unhappy, miserable, sorrowful, depressed, down, low, blue, downhearted, morose, gloomy, glum** → SAD

melancholy² *n.* [U] (literary) a feeling of sadness

mel·a·nin /ˈmɛlənɪn/ *n.* [U] BIOLOGY a natural substance in human skin, hair, and eyes that gives them a dark color

meld /mɛld/ *v.* [I,T] to mix or combine two or more different things together

mel·low¹ /ˈmɛloʊ/ *adj.* **1** pleasant and smooth in sound or taste: *mellow jazz* | *a mellow wine* **2** friendly, relaxed, and calm: *Tim's more mellow now that he's older*

THESAURUS **calm, relaxed, laid-back, easygoing, cool, placid, serene** → CALM²

mellow² *also* **mellow out** *v.* [I,T] to become more relaxed and calm, or to make someone do this: *She's mellowed over the years.*

me·lod·ic /məˈlɑdɪk/ *adj.* **1** having a pleasant tune or a pleasant sound like music: *a sweet melodic voice* **2** ENG. LANG. ARTS relating to the main tune in a piece of music: *the melodic structure of Beethoven's symphonies*

me·lo·di·ous /məˈloʊdiəs/ *adj.* (literary) having a pleasant tune or a pleasant sound like music: *a melodious voice*

mel·o·dra·ma /ˈmɛləˌdrɑmə/ *n.* [C,U] ENG. LANG. ARTS a story or play with many exciting events in which people's emotions are shown very strongly

mel·o·dra·mat·ic /ˌmɛlədrəˈmæt̬ɪk/ *adj.* (disapproving) having or showing emotions that are strong and unreasonable: *Stop being melodramatic!*

mel·o·dy /ˈmɛlədi/ *n.* (plural **melodies**) [C,U] ENG. LANG. ARTS a song or tune [ORIGIN: 1100—1200 Old French *melodie*, from Late Latin, from Greek *meloidia* "music"]

mel·on /ˈmɛlən/ *n.* [C,U] one of several types of large sweet juicy fruits with hard skins and flat seeds

melt /mɛlt/ *v.* **1** [I,T] to change something from solid to liquid by heating → FREEZE, THAW: *The snow's melting.* | *Melt the butter, and add the chopped onion.* → see picture on page 632 **2** [I] to suddenly feel love or sympathy: *My* ***heart melted*** *when I saw her crying.* **3 melt in your mouth** if food melts in your mouth, it is smooth and tastes good [ORIGIN: Old English *meltan*]

melt away *phr. v.* to disappear quickly and easily: *He began to exercise regularly, and the weight melted away.*

melt·down /'mɛltˀdaʊn/ *n.* [C,U] a very dangerous situation in which the material in a NUCLEAR REACTOR melts and burns through its container, allowing RADIOACTIVITY to escape

'melting pot *n.* [C] a place where people from different races, countries, or social classes come and live together: *People always refer to America as a melting pot.*

mem·ber /'mɛmbɚ/ *n.* [C] **1** someone who has joined a particular club, group, or organization: *Are you a **member of** the French club?* | *Ben treats his dog like a **member of the family**.* | *Frank has been a **staff member** for 20 years.* **2** one of a group of similar people or things: *Cats and tigers are **members of** the same species.* [ORIGIN: 1300—1400 Old French *membre*, from Latin *membrum*]

mem·ber·ship /'mɛmbɚˌʃɪp/ *n.* **1** [C,U] the state of being a member of a club, group, organization, or system: *Many countries have applied for **membership in** NATO.* | *I just **renewed** my gym **membership**.* | *The **membership fee*** (=money that you pay to become a member) *is $25.* **2** [singular] all the members of a club, group, or organization: *The membership will vote for a chairman tonight.*

mem·brane /'mɛmbreɪn/ *n.* [C,U] BIOLOGY a very thin substance similar to skin, that covers or connects parts of the body: *The **cell membranes** had been damaged.* | *the membrane that covers the spinal cord* | *the nuclear membrane* (=a layer covering the nucleus of a living cell) ➔ *see picture at* CELL

me·men·to /mə'mɛntoʊ/ *n.* (plural **mementos**) [C] a small object that you keep to remind you of someone or something: *I kept the picture as a **memento of** my college days.*

mem·o /'mɛmoʊ/ *n.* (plural **memos**) [C] a short official note to another person in the same company: *a **memo to** employees* | *I'll **send** you a **memo** when we set a date for the meeting.*

mem·oirs /'mɛmwɑrz/ *n.* [plural] a book written by a famous person about his/her life and experiences

mem·o·ra·bil·i·a /ˌmɛmərə'bɪliə, -'bil-/ *n.* [plural] things that you keep or collect because they relate to a famous person, event, or time: *sports memorabilia*

mem·ora·ble /'mɛmrəbəl/ *adj.* worth remembering: *a memorable evening* —**memorably** *adv.*

mem·o·ran·dum /ˌmɛmə'rændəm/ *n.* (plural **memoranda** /-'rændə/ *or* **memorandums**) [C] (formal) a MEMO

me·mo·ri·al¹ /mə'mɔriəl/ *adj.* [only before noun] made or done in order to remind people of someone who has died: *a **memorial service** for my grandfather*

memorial² *n.* [C] a public structure with writing on it that reminds people of someone who has died: *the Lincoln memorial* | *The wall was built as a **memorial to** soldiers who died in Vietnam.*

Me'morial ˌDay *n.* a U.S. national holiday on the last Monday in May, when people remember soldiers who were killed in wars

mem·o·rize /'mɛməˌraɪz/ *v.* [T] to learn and remember words, music, or other information: *You all should have your lines memorized by Friday.*

mem·o·ry /'mɛmri, -məri/ *n.* (plural **memories**) **1** [C,U] the ability to remember things, places, experiences, etc.: *My **memory** isn't as **good** as it used to be.* | *Could you draw the map **from memory*** (=from what you remember, without any other help)? **2** [C usually plural] something that you remember from the past about a person, place, or experience ➔ SOUVENIR: *John talked about his **memories of** the war.* | *I have such **fond/happy memories** of my grandmother.* | *That song really **brings back memories*** (=makes me remember something). **3** [U] IT the amount of space that can be used for storing information on a computer: *256 megabytes of memory* **4** [C,U] IT the part of a computer in which information can be stored **5 in memory of sb** for the purpose of remembering someone who has died: *We observed a moment of silence in memory of the bombing victims.* [ORIGIN: 1200—1300 Old French *memorie*, from Latin *memor* "remembering"]

memory card *n.* [C] IT a small piece of electronic equipment inside a DIGITAL camera, a CELL PHONE, or a small computer that you carry with you, used for storing photographs or information

'Memory Stick *n.* [C] (trademark) IT a small piece of equipment for storing information, that connects into a computer using a USB PORT. A Memory Stick can be removed and carried easily, and will fit into other computers. ➔ *see picture on page A19*

men /mɛn/ *n.* the plural of MAN

men·ace¹ /'mɛnɪs/ *n.* **1** [C] something or someone that is dangerous or extremely annoying: *That man is **a menace to society**!* **2** [U] a threatening quality or manner: *There was real menace in her voice.* [ORIGIN: 1300—1400 French, Latin *minacia*, from *minari* "to threaten"]

menace² *v.* [T] (formal) to threaten someone or something with danger or harm

men·ac·ing /'mɛnɪsɪŋ/ *adj.* making you expect something dangerous or bad (SYN) **threatening**: *a menacing laugh*

M

me·nag·er·ie /mə'nædʒəri, -ʒə-/ *n.* [C] (literary) a collection of animals kept privately or for people to see

mend¹ /mɛnd/ *v.* **1** [T] to repair a tear or hole in a piece of clothing: *You'd better mend that shirt.*

THESAURUS **repair, fix** → REPAIR²

2 mend your ways to improve the way you behave after behaving badly for a long time

mend² *n.* **be on the mend** to be getting better after an illness

men·da·cious /mɛn'deɪʃəs/ *adj.* (formal) not truthful: *The evidence was planted by mendacious police.* —**mendaciously** *adv.*

men·di·cant or·der /ˌmɛndɪkənt 'ɔrdɚ/ *n.* [C] a society of MONKs or NUNs (=men or women who live a holy life according to religious rules) who completely depend on the money or gifts that people give to them in order to live —**mendicant** *adj.*: *mendicant monks*

me·ni·al /'miniəl, -nyəl/ *adj.* (disapproving) menial work is boring and needs no skill

me·nin·ges /mə'nɪndʒiz/ *n.* [plural] BIOLOGY MEMBRANEs (=substance like very thin skin) that completely cover and protect the brain and the SPINAL CORD

men·o·pause /'mɛnəˌpɔz/ *n.* [U] BIOLOGY the time when a woman stops menstruating

me·no·rah /mə'nɔrə/ *n.* [C] a special CANDLESTICK that holds seven CANDLEs, used in Jewish ceremonies

'men's room *n.* [C] a room in a public place with toilets for men

THESAURUS **toilet, bathroom, restroom, women's/ladies' room, lavatory** → TOILET

men·stru·ate /'mɛnstruˌeɪt, -streɪt/ *v.* [I] BIOLOGY when a woman menstruates every month, blood flows from her body → PERIOD —**menstrual** *adj.* —**menstruation** /ˌmɛnstru'eɪʃən, mɛn'streɪʃən/ *n.* [U]

men·tal /'mɛntəl/ (Ac) *adj.* [only before noun] relating to the mind, or happening in the mind: *He has a history of severe **mental problems**.* | ***Mental illness** often runs in families.* | *The doctors were worried about her **mental health**.* | *I'm a little concerned about Jeremy's **mental state**.* | ***I made a mental note*** (=made an effort to remember) *to call Julie.* | *He conducted important research into the mental development of children.* [ORIGIN: 1400—1500 French, Late Latin *mentalis*, from Latin *mens* "mind"] —**mentally** *adv.*: *She is obviously **mentally ill**.*

'mental instiˌtution *n.* [C] a hospital for people who are mentally ill

men·tal·i·ty /mɛn'tæləṭi/ (Ac) *n.* (plural **mentalities**) [C,U] a particular type of attitude or way of thinking: *The crowd was gripped by a mob mentality.* | *The study investigates the mentality of people who commit violent crimes.*

men·thol /'mɛnθɔl, -θɑl/ *n.* [U] a substance that smells and tastes like MINT, used in medicine, candy, and cigarettes

men·tion¹ /'mɛnʃən/ *v.* [T] **1** to say or write about something in a few words: *I **mentioned** the idea **to** Joan, and she seemed to like it.* | *Helen **mentioned (that)** she had been feeling depressed.*

THESAURUS

refer to sth – to mention or speak about someone or something: *Palmer was referring to an article in the Times.*
note (formal) – to mention something because it is important or interesting: *His lawyer noted that Miller had no previous criminal record.*
raise – to begin to talk or write about something that you want someone to consider: *Becky raised the question of whether the students would learn better in smaller groups.*
allude to sth (formal) – to mention something in a way that is not direct: *Many stories and poems allude to this myth.*
bring sth up – to start to talk about a particular subject or person: *He waited until she was calmer to bring up the subject again.*
cite – to mention something as an example or proof of something else: *Collins cited the document as evidence that something had gone wrong.*

THESAURUS **say, add, state, utter, express** → SAY¹

2 don't mention it (spoken) used in order to say in a friendly way that there is no need for someone to thank you: *"Thanks for helping me out." "Don't mention it."* **3 not to mention sth** said when you are adding a piece of information that emphasizes what you have been saying: *He already has two houses and two cars, not to mention the boat.*

mention² *n.* [C,U] the act of mentioning someone or something in a conversation or piece of writing: *Any **mention of** the accident upsets her.* | *The report **made no mention of** any financial difficulties.*

men·tor /'mɛntɔr, -tɚ/ *n.* [C] an experienced person who advises and helps a less experienced person [ORIGIN: 1700—1800 *Mentor*, adviser of Odysseus's son Telemachus in the ancient Greek Odyssey by Homer]

men·tor·ing /'mɛntərɪŋ/ *n.* [U] a system of using people who have a lot of experience and knowledge to advise other people

men·u /'mɛnyu/ *n.* [C] **1** a list of all the kinds of food that are available in a restaurant: *Can we see a menu, please?* | *the most popular dish **on the menu*** → RESTAURANT **2** IT a list of things on a computer screen which you can ask the computer to do: *Go to the Edit menu and select Copy.* | *a **pull-down menu*** (=a list of choices which appears when you CLICK on a place on the screen)

M

me·ow /mi'aʊ/ *n.* [C] the crying sound that a cat makes —**meow** *v.* [I]

mer·can·til·ism /'mɚkəntil,ɪzəm/ *n.* [U] ECONOMICS the idea that trade produces wealth, EXPORTS (=goods sold to other countries) should be encouraged, and IMPORTS (=goods bought from other countries) should be restricted

mer·ce·nar·y[1] /'mɚsə,nɛri/ *n.* (plural **mercenaries**) [C] someone who fights for any country that pays him/her

mercenary[2] *adj.* (disapproving) only interested in making money, and not caring about whether your actions are right or wrong

mer·chan·dise /'mɚtʃən,daɪz, -,daɪs/ *n.* [U] ECONOMICS things that are for sale in stores: *Several thousand dollars' worth of merchandise was stolen.*

mer·chant /'mɚtʃənt/ *n.* [C] ECONOMICS someone who buys and sells large quantities of goods: *a wine merchant*

,merchant ma'rine *n.* **the merchant marine** all of a country's ships that are used for trade, not war, and the people who work on these ships

mer·ci·ful /'mɚsɪfəl/ *adj.* kind to people, rather than being cruel

mer·ci·ful·ly /'mɚsɪfli/ *adv.* fortunately, because a situation could have been much worse: *At least her death was mercifully quick.*

mer·cu·ri·al /mɚ'kyʊriəl/ *adj.* (literary) changing mood suddenly: *It would be difficult working for his mercurial brother-in-law.*

Mer·cu·ry /'mɚkyəri/ *n.* PHYSICS the smallest PLANET, which is nearest the Sun ➔ *see picture at* SOLAR SYSTEM

mercury *n.* [U] CHEMISTRY a liquid silver-white metal that is used in THERMOMETERS

mer·cy /'mɚsi/ *n.* **1** [U] kindness, pity, and a willingness to forgive: *The boy was **begging/pleading for mercy**. | The judge **showed** him **no mercy**.* **2 at the mercy of sb/sth** in a situation that is controlled by someone or something that has the power to hurt you: *We were at the mercy of the storm.* [ORIGIN: 1100—1200 Old French *merci*, from Latin *merces* "price paid, payment for work"]

'mercy ,killing *n.* [C,U] EUTHANASIA

mere /mɪr/ *adj.* [only before noun] **1** used in order to emphasize how small or unimportant someone or something is: *A mere 10% of the population voted in the last election.* **2** used in order to say that something small or unimportant has a big effect: ***The mere thought** of food made her feel sick.*

mere·ly /'mɪrli/ *adv.* (formal) used in order to emphasize that an action, person, or thing is very small, simple, or unimportant, especially when compared to what it could be (SYN) **only, just**: *For Ken, a job is merely a way to make money. | His behavior was **not merely** foolish but dangerous.*

merge /mɚdʒ/ *v.* **1** [I,T] to combine or join together to form one thing: *The two unions merged to form a larger one. | Her company **merged with** another.* **2** [I] if traffic merges, the cars from two roads come together onto the same road

merge into sth *phr. v.* to seem to disappear into something and become part of it: *a point where the mountains merged into the sky*

merg·er /'mɚdʒɚ/ *n.* [C] ECONOMICS the act of joining together two or more companies or organizations to form one larger one

me·rid·i·an /mə'rɪdiən/ *n.* [C] a line drawn from the North Pole to the South Pole to show the positions of places on a map

me·ringue /mə'ræŋ/ *n.* [C,U] a light sweet food made by baking a mixture of sugar and the white parts of eggs: *lemon meringue pie*

mer·it[1] /'mɛrɪt/ *n.* **1** [C usually plural] one of the good qualities or features of something or someone: *Living downtown **has its merits**.*

THESAURUS **advantage, benefit, good point** ➔ ADVANTAGE

2 [U] (formal) a good quality that makes something deserve praise or admiration: *a book **of** great **merit** | Each student will be judged **on merit**.*

merit[2] *v.* [T] (formal) to deserve something: *The idea merits serious consideration.*

mer·i·to·ri·ous /,mɛrə'tɔriəs/ *adj.* (formal) very good and deserving praise: *a medal for meritorious service* —**meritoriously** *adv.*

mer·maid /'mɚmeɪd/ *n.* [C] a woman in stories who has a fish's tail instead of legs

mer·ry /'mɛri/ *adj.* (comparative **merrier**, superlative **merriest**) **1 Merry Christmas!** used to say that you hope someone will have a happy time at Christmas **2** cheerful and happy

'merry-go-,round *n.* [C] a large round thing that children ride on for fun, which turns around and around

mesh[1] /mɛʃ/ *n.* [U] a piece of material made of threads or wires that have been woven together like a net: *a wire mesh screen*

mesh[2] *v.* [I] **1** if two or more ideas, qualities, people, etc. mesh, they go well together: *He wants a job that will **mesh with** his skills and interests.* **2** if two parts of an engine or machine mesh, they fit closely together

mes·mer·ize /'mɛzmə,raɪz/ *v.* [T] to make someone become completely interested in something: *The kids sat mesmerized in front of the TV.* [ORIGIN: 1800—1900 Franz *Mesmer* (1734-1815), Austrian doctor who developed hypnotism] —**mesmerizing** *adj.*

mes·o·sphere /'mɛzə,sfɪr/ *n.* **the mesosphere** EARTH SCIENCES the outer layer of the Earth's lower ATMOSPHERE, from about 30 to 50 miles above the Earth ➔ *see picture at* ATMOSPHERE

Mes·o·zo·ic /,mɛzə'zoʊɪk◂/ *n.* **the Mesozoic** EARTH SCIENCES the period of time in the Earth's history, from about 250 million until about 65

million years ago, when DINOSAURs, birds, and plants with flowers first started to exist —**Mesozoic** *adj.*: *the Mesozoic period* ➔ CENOZOIC, PALEOZOIC, PRECAMBRIAN

mess[1] /mɛs/ *n.* **1** [singular, U] a place or a group of things that is not organized or arranged neatly: *This house is a mess!* | *I'll help you* ***clean up*** *the* ***mess.*** | *The kids* ***made a mess*** *in their room again.* **2** [singular] (informal) a situation in which there are a lot of problems and difficulties, especially as a result of mistakes or people not being careful: *My life is such a mess.* | *How did we ever* ***get into this mess?*** **3** [singular] (informal) someone who has a lot of emotional problems: *Nell was a complete mess after the divorce.*

mess[2] *v.*

mess around *phr. v.* (informal) **1** to play or do silly things when you should be working or paying attention: *Stop messing around and do your homework.* **2** to have a sexual relationship with someone, especially when you should not: *Joe found his wife* ***messing around with*** *another man.*

mess up *phr. v.* (informal) **1 mess** sth ↔ **up** to spoil or ruin something: *I hope I haven't messed up your plans.* **2 mess** sth ↔ **up** to make something dirty or messy: *Stop it! You'll mess up my hair!* **3 mess** (sth ↔) **up** to make a mistake or do something badly: *"How did you do on the test?" "Oh, I really messed up."* ➔ MESSED UP

mess with *phr. v.* (informal) **1 mess with** sth to use something, or make small changes to it: *Who's been messing with my computer?* **2 mess with** sb to make someone angry, or argue with him/her: *I wouldn't mess with Nick if I were you.*

mes·sage /ˈmɛsɪdʒ/ *n.* **1** [C] written or spoken information that you leave for someone, especially when you cannot speak to him/her directly: *Did you* ***get*** *my* ***message?*** | *Hugh* ***left a message*** *saying he would be late.* | *Sorry, Tony's not home yet.* ***Can I take a message?*** (=used during phone calls) | *There's a* ***message from*** *your mother on the answering machine.*

COLLOCATIONS

telephone/phone message
email/mail message
fax message
text message – a written message on a cell phone
error message – a message on a computer screen, saying that the computer cannot do what you want it to do
message of thanks/congratulations/support/sympathy

2 [singular] the main idea or the most important idea in a movie, book, speech, etc.: *The message was clear: global warming will eventually affect us all.* | *an effective way of* ***getting*** *your* ***message across*** **3 get the message** (informal) to understand what someone means or what s/he wants you to do: *OK, I get the message – I'm going.* [ORIGIN: 1200—1300 Old French, Medieval Latin *missaticum*, from Latin *mittere* "to send"]

ˌmessed ˈup *adj.* (informal) if someone is messed up, s/he has a lot of emotional problems

mes·sen·ger /ˈmɛsəndʒɚ/ *n.* [C] someone who takes packages or messages to other people

ˌmessenger RNˈA *n.* [U] BIOLOGY (*written abbreviation* **mRNA**) a form of RNA that copies GENETIC information from DNA and carries it to RIBOSOMES

ˈmess hall *n.* [C] a large room where soldiers eat

mes·si·ah /məˈsaɪə/ *n.* **the Messiah** Jesus Christ in the Christian religion, or the leader sent by God to save the world in the Jewish religion

Messrs. /ˈmɛsɚz/ *n.* (formal) the written plural of Mr.

mess·y /ˈmɛsi/ *adj.* (comparative **messier**, superlative **messiest**) **1** dirty, or not arranged in an organized way: *a messy desk* **2** a messy situation is complicated and difficult to deal with, especially because it involves people's emotions: *a* ***messy divorce***

met /mɛt/ *v.* the past tense and past participle of MEET

me·tab·o·lism /məˈtæbəˌlɪzəm/ *n.* [C,U] BIOLOGY the chemical processes in your body that change food into the energy you need for working and growing —**metabolic** /ˌmɛt̮əˈbɑlɪk◂/ *adj.*

met·al /ˈmɛt̮l/ *n.* [C,U] a hard, usually shiny substance such as iron, gold, or steel: *a metal pipe* | *scrap metal* [ORIGIN: 1200—1300 Old French, Latin *metallum* "mine, metal," from Greek *metallon*]

ˈmetal deˌtector *n.* [C] a machine used for finding metal, especially one used at airports for finding weapons

me·tal·lic /məˈtælɪk/ *adj.* made of metal, or similar to metal in color, appearance, or taste: *a car painted metallic blue*

met·al·lur·gy /ˈmɛt̮lˌɚdʒi/ *n.* [U] EARTH SCIENCES the scientific study of metals and their uses —**metallurgical** /ˌmɛt̮lˈɚdʒɪkəl/ *adj.*

met·a·mor·phic /ˌmɛt̮əˈmɔrfɪk◂/ *adj.* EARTH SCIENCES metamorphic rock and other material is formed by the continuous effects of pressure, heat, or water: *This metamorphic rock has been compressed for millions of years.*

met·a·mor·phism /ˌmɛt̮əˈmɔrˌfɪzəm/ *n.* [U] EARTH SCIENCES changes in the structure of rock, caused by the continuous effects of pressure, heat, or water: *If the pressure and temperatures are high enough, the rocks can undergo metamorphism.*

met·a·mor·pho·sis /ˌmɛt̮əˈmɔrfəsɪs/ *n.* (plural **metamorphoses** /-siz/) [C,U] **1** the process in which something changes in a very noticeable way: *She underwent a metamorphosis to become the school's best tennis player.* **2** BIOLOGY the process in which a young insect, FROG, etc. changes as it moves on to the next stage in its development: *a caterpillar's* ***metamorphosis into*** *a butterfly*

met·a·phor /ˈmɛt̮əˌfɔr/ *n.* [C,U] ENG. LANG. ARTS a way of describing something by comparing it to

M

something else that has similar qualities, without using the words "like" or "as." For example, the phrase "a river of tears" is a metaphor. ➔ SIMILE —**metaphorical** /ˌmɛt̬əˈfɔrɪkəl/ *adj.* —**metaphorically** *adv.*

met·a·phys·i·cal /ˌmɛt̬əˈfɪzɪkəl/ *adj.* ENG. LANG. ARTS relating to a study of PHILOSOPHY that is concerned with trying to understand and describe what REALITY is —**metaphysics** *n.* [U] —**metaphysically** *adv.*

mete /mit/ *v.*

mete sth ↔ **out** *phr. v.* (formal) to give someone a punishment

me·te·or /ˈmit̬iə˞/ *n.* [C] PHYSICS a small piece of rock or metal that produces a bright burning line in the sky when it falls from space into the Earth's ATMOSPHERE ➔ SPACE[1]

me·te·or·ic /ˌmit̬iˈɔrɪk, -ˈɑr-/ *adj.* happening very suddenly and usually continuing for only a short time: *his* ***meteoric rise to*** *fame*

me·te·or·ite /ˈmit̬iəˌraɪt/ *n.* [C] PHYSICS a small meteor that has landed on the Earth's surface

me·te·o·roid /ˈmit̬iəˌrɔɪd/ *n.* [C] PHYSICS a piece of rock or similar material in space. When a meteoroid enters the Earth's ATMOSPHERE (=air surrounding the Earth), it becomes a meteor, and if it reaches the surface of the Earth, it is called a meteorite.

me·te·or·ol·o·gy /ˌmit̬iəˈrɑlədʒi/ *n.* [U] the scientific study of weather [ORIGIN: 1600—1700 French *météorologie*, from Greek, from *meteoron* "something in the sky," from *meteoros* "high in air"] —**meteorologist** *n.* [C]

meter /ˈmit̬ə˞/ *n.* **1** [C] (*written abbreviation* **m**) a unit for measuring length, equal to 100 centimeters or 39.37 inches **2** [C] a piece of equipment that measures the amount of gas, electricity, time, etc. you have used: *Someone from the gas company came to look at the meter.* | *The cab driver waited with the meter running.* ➔ PARKING METER **3** [C,U] the way that the words of a poem are arranged into a pattern of weak and strong beats [ORIGIN: (1) 1800—1900 French *mètre*, from Greek *metron* "measure"]

ˈmeter maid *n.* [C] (old-fashioned) a woman whose job is to check that cars are not parked illegally

meth·a·done /ˈmɛθəˌdoʊn/ *n.* [U] a drug that is often given to people who are trying to stop taking HEROIN

meth·ane /ˈmɛθeɪn/ *n.* [U] CHEMISTRY a gas with no color or smell, which can be burned to give heat

meth·od /ˈmɛθəd/ (Ac) *n.* [C] a planned way of doing something: *I think we should try again using a different method.* | *an effective* ***method of*** *birth control* | *traditional teaching methods* [ORIGIN: 1400—1500 Latin *methodus*, from Greek *methodos*, from *meta-* "after" + *hodos* "way"]

THESAURUS

way – a method of doing something: *Staying in a country is a great way to learn the language.*
technique – a particular way of doing something by using a special skill that you have learned: *The book teaches you some simple techniques which you can use to help you do well on the SATs.*
strategy – a carefully designed plan for achieving something that is difficult and may take a long time: *a meeting to discuss the company's business strategy*
procedure – the correct or official way of doing something, especially something that has several stages: *What is the procedure for getting a new passport?*
approach – a way of doing something or dealing with a problem: *We need a new approach to the problem of street crime.*

➔ SCIENTIFIC METHOD

me·thod·i·cal /məˈθɑdɪkəl/ (Ac) *adj.* done in a careful and well organized way, or always doing things this way: *They made a methodical search of the building.* | *He is very methodical in his research.* —**methodically** *adv.*

THESAURUS **careful, thorough, meticulous, systematic, painstaking, scrupulous, conscientious** ➔ CAREFUL

Meth·od·ist /ˈmɛθədɪst/ *adj.* relating to the Protestant church that follows the ideas of John Wesley —**Methodist** *n.* [C]

meth·od·ol·o·gy /ˌmɛθəˈdɑlədʒi/ (Ac) *n.* (plural **methodologies**) [C,U] a set of methods and principles used when studying a particular subject or doing a particular type of work: *More recently, studies have attempted to refine their research methodologies.* —**methodological** /ˌmɛθədəˈlɑdʒɪkəl/ *adj.*

me·tic·u·lous /məˈtɪkyələs/ *adj.* (approving) very careful about details, and always trying to do things correctly: *She kept meticulous records.* —**meticulously** *adv.*

THESAURUS **careful, methodical, thorough, systematic, painstaking, scrupulous, conscientious** ➔ CAREFUL

met·ric /ˈmɛtrɪk/ *adj.* MATH using the metric system, or relating to it: *All the tools are in metric sizes.*

ˈmetric ˌsystem *n.* **the metric system** MATH the system of weights and measures based on the meter, the liter, and the gram

met·ro /ˈmɛtroʊ/ *adj.* [only before noun] relating to or belonging to a very large city: *the metro area* | *Metro Detroit*

me·trop·o·lis /məˈtrɑpəlɪs/ *n.* [C] a very large city, or the most important city of a country or area [ORIGIN: 1500—1600 Late Latin, Greek, from *meter* "mother" + *polis* "city"] —**metropolitan**

/ˌmɛtrəˈpɑlətˀn/ *adj.*: *the New York metropolitan area*

met·tle /ˈmɛtl/ *n.* [U] (literary) courage and determination SYN **valor**: *an outstanding soldier who **proved** his **mettle** in battle many times*

Mex·i·can¹ /ˈmɛksɪkən/ *adj.* relating to or coming from Mexico

Mexican² *n.* [C] someone from Mexico

mez·za·nine /ˈmɛzəˌnin, ˌmɛzəˈnin/ *n.* [C] the floor or BALCONY just above the main floor in a theater, hotel, store, etc.

mg the written abbreviation of MILLIGRAM

MI the written abbreviation of MICHIGAN

mi·ca /ˈmaɪkə/ *n.* [U] EARTH SCIENCES a mineral that separates easily into small flat transparent pieces of rock, often used to make electrical instruments

mice /maɪs/ *n.* the plural of MOUSE

mi·crobe /ˈmaɪkroʊb/ *n.* [C] BIOLOGY an extremely small living creature that cannot be seen without a MICROSCOPE [ORIGIN: 1800—1900 *micro-* + Greek *bios* "life"]

mi·cro·bi·ol·o·gy /ˌmaɪkroʊbaɪˈɑlədʒi/ *n.* [U] BIOLOGY the scientific study of very small living things —**microbiologist** *n.* [C]

mi·cro·brew·er·y /ˈmaɪkroʊˌbruəri/ *n.* (plural **microbreweries**) [C] a small company that makes beer to sell, and often has a restaurant where its beer is served

mi·cro·chip /ˈmaɪkroʊˌtʃɪp/ *n.* [C] IT a computer CHIP

mi·cro·cli·mate /ˈmaɪkroʊˌklaɪmɪt/ *n.* [C] EARTH SCIENCES the general weather patterns in a small area, which are different from the weather patterns in the surrounding area

mi·cro·cosm /ˈmaɪkrəˌkɑzəm/ *n.* [C,U] a small group, society, etc. that has the same qualities as a much larger one → MACROCOSM: *San José's mix of people is **a microcosm of** America.*

mi·cro·fiche /ˈmaɪkroʊˌfiʃ/ *n.* [C,U] a sheet of microfilm that can be read using a special machine, especially in a library

mi·cro·film /ˈmaɪkrəˌfɪlm/ *n.* [C,U] film used for making very small photographs of important documents, newspapers, maps, etc.

mi·cro·or·ga·nism /ˌmaɪkroʊˈɔrgəˌnɪzəm/ *n.* [C] BIOLOGY an extremely small living creature that cannot be seen without a microscope

mi·cro·phone /ˈmaɪkrəˌfoʊn/ *n.* [C] a piece of electrical equipment that makes your voice sound louder when you hold it in front of your mouth while you are singing, giving a speech, etc.: *Please speak clearly **into the microphone**.*

mi·cro·proc·es·sor /ˌmaɪkroʊˈprɑsɛsɚ/ *n.* [C] IT the main CHIP in a computer that controls most of its operations

microscope

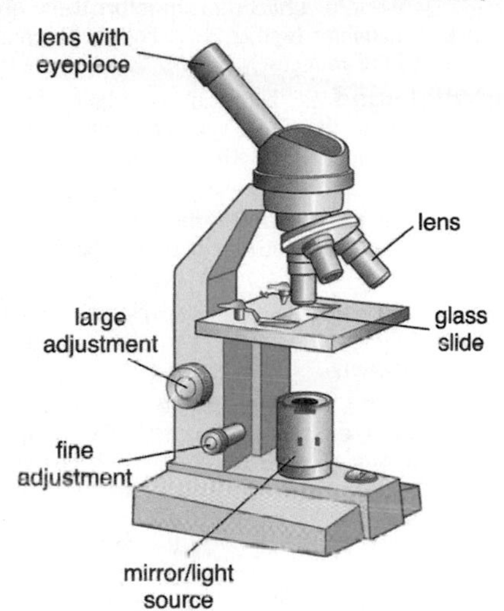

mi·cro·scope /ˈmaɪkrəˌskoʊp/ *n.* [C] a scientific instrument that makes extremely small things appear large enough to be seen: *We looked at the insects **under a microscope**.*

mi·cro·scop·ic /ˌmaɪkrəˈskɑpɪk◂/ *adj.* extremely small: *microscopic organisms*

mi·cro·wave¹ /ˈmaɪkrəˌweɪv/ *n.* [C] **1** *also* **microwave oven** a type of OVEN that cooks food very quickly by using electric waves instead of heat **2** PHYSICS a very short electric wave used especially for cooking food, sending radio messages, and in RADAR

microwave² *v.* [T] to cook something in a microwave

mid·air /ˌmɪdˈɛr◂/ *n.* **in midair** in the air or sky: *The plane exploded in midair.* —**midair** *adj.* [only before noun]: *a midair collision*

mid·day /ˈmɪd-deɪ/ *n.* [U] the middle of the day, around 12:00 p.m. SYN **noon** → MIDNIGHT

mid·dle¹ /ˈmɪdl/ *n.* **1 the middle** the part that is nearest the center of something, and furthest from the sides, edges, top, bottom, etc. SYN **center**: *Tom's the guy **in the middle**. | Hannah's toys were in the middle of the floor. | Why's your car parked **right in the middle of** the road?* **2 the middle** the part that is between the beginning and the end of a period of time or an event, story, etc.: *I fell asleep **in the middle of** class.* **3 be in the middle of (doing) something** to be busy doing something: *Can I call you back later? I'm **right in the middle of** cooking dinner.* [ORIGIN: Old English *middel*]

middle² *adj.* [only before noun] **1** nearest to the center of something: *The socks are in the middle drawer. | The middle lane was blocked off because of an accident.* **2** half way through an event, action, or period of time, or between the beginning

M

and the end: *I missed the middle act of the play.* **3 middle child/daughter/brother etc.** the child, daughter, brother, etc. who is between the oldest and the youngest

ˌmiddle-ˈaged *adj.* belonging or relating to the period of your life when you are about 45 to 65 years old: *a middle-aged woman* —**middle age** *n.* [U]

ˌMiddle ˈAges *n.* **the Middle Ages** HISTORY the period in European history between the 5th and 15th centuries A.D.

ˌMiddle Aˈmerica *n.* **1** the MIDWEST **2** SOCIAL SCIENCE average Americans who have traditional ideas and beliefs

ˌmiddle ˈclass *n.* **the middle class** *also* **the middle classes a)** SOCIAL SCIENCE the group of people in society who are neither rich nor poor, especially people who are educated and work in professional jobs ➔ LOWER CLASS, UPPER CLASS, WORKING CLASS **b)** HISTORY in the past, the social class in Europe between NOBLES (=rich royal people who owned land) and PEASANTS (=poor farmers), which included people who made or bought and sold things —**middle-class** *adj.*: *middle-class families*

ˌmiddle ˈear *n.* [singular] BIOLOGY the central part of the ear, between the EARDRUM and the COCHLEA. The middle ear contains parts that make the movement of the sound waves stronger.

ˌMiddle ˈEast *n.* **the Middle East** the part of Asia that is between the Mediterranean Sea and the Arabian Sea, including countries such as Turkey and Iran ➔ FAR EAST —**Middle Eastern** *adj.*

ˌmiddle ˈfinger *n.* [C] the longest finger in the middle of the five fingers on your hand ➔ *see picture at* HAND[1]

mid·dle·man /ˈmɪdlˌmæn/ *n.* (plural **middlemen** /-ˌmɛn/) [C] someone who buys things in order to sell them to someone else, or who helps to arrange business deals for other people

ˌmiddle ˈname *n.* [C] the name that, in English, comes between your first name and your family name

> THESAURUS **name, first name/given name, last name/family name/surname, full name, maiden name** ➔ NAME[1]

ˌmiddle-of-the-ˈroad *adj.* middle-of-the-road ideas, opinions, etc. are not extreme, so many people agree with them

ˈmiddle school *n.* [C] a school in the U.S. for students between the ages of 11 and 14

midg·et /ˈmɪdʒɪt/ *n.* [C] (offensive) a person who is very small because his/her body has not grown correctly

mid·life cri·sis /ˌmɪdlaɪf ˈkraɪsɪs/ *n.* [C usually singular] the worry and lack of confidence that some people feel when they are about 40 or 50 years old

mid·night /ˈmɪdnaɪt/ *n.* [U] 12 o'clock at night ➔ NOON, MIDDAY: *We arrived* ***at midnight.*** | *I fell asleep a little* ***after/before midnight.***

mid·point of a seg·ment /ˌmɪdpɔɪnt əv ə ˈsɛgmənt/ *n.* [C] MATH a point that is in the middle of a SEGMENT (=line connecting two points), so that the segment is divided into two parts of equal length

mid·riff /ˈmɪdrɪf/ *n.* [C] (formal) the front part of the body between your chest and your waist

midst /mɪdst/ *n.* **in the midst of sth** in the middle of something such as an event, situation, place, or group: *The city is* ***in the midst of a crisis.***

mid·term /ˈmɪdtɚm/ *n.* **1** [C] an examination that students take in the middle of a SEMESTER: *I have a biology* ***midterm*** *on Friday.* ➔ UNIVERSITY **2** [U] POLITICS the middle of the period when an elected government has power —**midterm** *adj.*

mid·way /ˌmɪdˈweɪ◂/ *adj., adv.* at the middle point between two places, or in the middle of a period of time or an event: *There's a gas station* ***midway between*** *here and Fresno.* | *He went silent* ***midway through*** *his speech.*

mid·week /ˌmɪdˈwik◂/ *adj., adv.* on one of the middle days of the week, such as Tuesday, Wednesday, or Thursday: *midweek classes* | *I can see you midweek.*

Mid·west /ˌmɪdˈwɛst/ *n.* **the Midwest** the central northern area of the U.S. —**Midwestern** /mɪdˈwɛstɚn/ *adj.*

mid·wife /ˈmɪdwaɪf/ *n.* (plural **midwives** /-waɪvz/) [C] a specially trained nurse, usually a woman, whose job is to help women when they are having a baby

miffed /mɪft/ *adj.* (informal) annoyed

might[1] /maɪt/ *modal verb* **1** used in order to talk about what was or is possible: *I might be able to get free tickets.* | *They might not come until tomorrow morning.* | *She might have tried calling, but I've been out.* **2** used instead of "may" when reporting what someone said or thought: *I thought he might still be mad at me.* **3 might as well** (spoken) used to suggest that someone should do something because there is no good reason to do anything else: *You might as well go fishing with your brother as sit around here all day.* **4** used in order to give advice or make a suggestion: *You might try calling the store.* | *You* ***might want to*** *get your blood pressure checked.*

might[2] *n.* [U] (literary) strength and power: *She tried* ***with all*** *her* ***might*** *to push him away.*

might·y[1] /ˈmaɪt̬i/ *adj.* strong and powerful: *mighty warriors*

mighty[2] *adv.* (informal) very: *That was a mighty fine meal.*

mi·graine /ˈmaɪgreɪn/ *n.* [C] an extremely bad HEADACHE [ORIGIN: 1300—1400 French, Late Latin *hemicrania* "pain in one side of the head"]

mi·grant /ˈmaɪgrənt/ (Ac) *n.* [C] **1** someone who goes to another area or country, especially in order to find work ➔ IMMIGRANT, EMIGRANT: ***migrant workers*** | *Texas has a large population of migrant and seasonal farm laborers.* **2** a bird or animal that travels from one part of the world to another, especially in the fall and spring: *Most species of geese are migrants.*

mi·grate /'maɪgreɪt/ (Ac) *v.* [I] **1** if birds or animals migrate, they travel to a different part of the world, especially in the fall and spring: *More than 2 million ducks* ***migrate to*** *the lake each fall.* **2** to go to another area or country for a short time, usually in order to find a place to live or work: *During the 1980s, over 27 million people migrated from rural to urban areas.* [ORIGIN: 1600—1700 Latin, past participle of *migrare*] ➔ IMMIGRATE

mi·gra·tion /maɪ'greɪʃən/ (Ac) *n.* [C,U] the action of a large group of birds, animals, or people moving from one area or country to another: *the yearly* ***migration of*** *geese* | *The railroads were built to make migration and settlement easier.* —**migratory** /'maɪgrəˌtɔri/ *adj.*

mike /maɪk/ *n.* [C] (informal) a MICROPHONE

mild /maɪld/ *adj.* **1** not too severe or serious: ***a mild case of*** *the flu* | *mild criticism* **2** not strong-tasting or spicy: *mild cheddar cheese* **3** if the weather is mild, it is not too cold or wet and not too hot: *a mild winter* **4** if a soap or beauty product is mild, it is gentle to your skin, hair, etc.

mil·dew /'mɪldu/ *n.* [U] a white or gray substance that grows on walls and other surfaces in warm, slightly wet places —**mildewed** *adj.*

mild·ly /'maɪldli/ *adv.* **1** slightly: *McKee was only mildly interested.* **2 to put it mildly** (spoken) said when you are saying something bad or severe in the most polite way that you can: *We were not welcome there, to put it mildly.* **3** in a gentle way without being angry: *"Perhaps," he answered mildly.*

mile /maɪl/ *n.* [C] **1** a unit for measuring distance, equal to 5,280 feet or about 1,609 meters: *Mark jogs at least five miles a day.* | *We're only a few hundred miles from Atlanta.* **2 miles** (informal) a very long distance: *We walked* ***for miles*** *without seeing anyone.* **3 talk a mile a minute** (spoken) to talk very quickly without stopping [ORIGIN: Old English *mil*, from Latin *milia passum* "thousands of paces"]

mile·age /'maɪlɪdʒ/ *n.* **1** [singular, U] the number of miles that a car has traveled since it was nade or since a particular time: *a used car with low mileage* **2** [U] the number of miles a car can travel using each gallon of gasoline: *Our car gets really* ***good mileage*** (=a lot of miles per gallon). **3 get a lot of mileage out of sth** to make something be as useful for you as it can be: *I've gotten a lot of mileage out of that old joke.*

mile·stone /'maɪlstoʊn/ *n.* [C] a very important event in the development of something: *a* ***milestone in*** *automotive history*

mi·lieu /mil'yu, mɪl'yʊ/ *n.* (plural **milieus**) [C,U] (formal) all the things and people that surround you and influence you

mil·i·tant[1] /'mɪlətənt/ *adj.* willing to use force or violence: *militant nationalists* —**militancy** *n.* [U]

militant[2] *n.* [C] someone who uses violence to achieve social or political change

mil·i·ta·ris·m /'mɪlɪtəˌrɪzəm/ *n.* [U] POLITICS the belief that a country should increase its army, navy, etc. and use them to get what it wants, or when a country increases and uses its military forces in this way —**militaristic** /ˌmɪlətə'rɪstɪk/ *adj.*

mil·i·tar·y[1] /'mɪləˌtɛri/ (Ac) *adj.* used by, involving, or relating to the army, navy, air force, or Marine Corps: *military aircraft* | *a military base in Greece* | *The U.S. is prepared to take* ***military action.*** [ORIGIN: 1400—1500 French *militaire*, from Latin *militaris*, from *miles* "soldier"] —**militarily** /ˌmɪlə'tɛrəli/ *adv.*

military[2] *n.* **the military** the military organizations of a country, such as the army and navy: *My father is* ***in the military.*** | *In some countries women are not allowed to join the military.*

mi·li·tia /mə'lɪʃə/ *n.* [C] a group of people trained as soldiers who are not members of the permanent army

milk[1] /mɪlk/ *n.* [U] **1** a white liquid that people drink, which is usually produced by cows or goats: *a glass of milk* | *Would you like milk in your coffee?*

THESAURUS

Types of milk
skim milk – milk that has had all the fat removed from it
low-fat/2% milk – milk that has had some of the fat removed from it
whole milk – milk that has not had any fat removed from it
buttermilk – the liquid that remains after butter has been made, used for drinking or cooking
half-and-half – a mixture of milk and cream, used in coffee

2 a white liquid produced by female animals and women for feeding their babies [ORIGIN: Old English *meolc, milc*]

milk[2] *v.* [T] **1** to take milk from a cow or goat **2 milk sb/sth for sth** (informal) to get all the money, advantages, etc. that you can from a person, thing, or situation: *I'm going to milk her for every penny she has.*

milk·man /'mɪlkmæn/ *n.* (plural **milkmen** /-mɛn/) [C] someone who delivers milk to houses each morning

milk·shake /'mɪlkʃeɪk/ *n.* [C] a thick drink made from milk and ICE CREAM: *a chocolate milkshake*

milk·y /'mɪlki/ *adj.* **1** water or a liquid that is milky is not clear and looks like milk **2** milky skin is white and smooth

M

ˌMilky 'Way *n.* **the Milky Way** PHYSICS the pale white band made up of large numbers of stars, that you can see across the sky at night

mill¹ /mɪl/ *n.* [C] **1** a large machine used for crushing food such as corn, grain, or coffee into a powder **2** a building where materials such as paper, steel, or cotton cloth are made **3** a small machine used for crushing pepper or coffee [ORIGIN: (1,2) Old English *mylen*, from Latin *mola* "mill, millstone"]

mill² *v.* [T] to crush grains in a mill

mill around *phr. v.* (informal) if a lot of people are milling around, they are moving around a place without any particular purpose: *Students were milling around waiting for their pictures to be taken.*

mil·len·ni·um /mə'lɛniəm/ *n.* (plural **millennia** /-niə/) [C] **1** a period of 1,000 years **2** the time when a new 1,000-year period begins: *the start of the new millennium*

mil·li·gram /'mɪləˌgræm/ *n.* [C] (*written abbreviation* **mg**) a unit for measuring weight, equal to 1/1,000th of a gram

mil·li·li·ter /'mɪləˌlit̬ɚ/ *n.* [C] (*written abbreviation* **ml**) a unit for measuring liquids, equal to 1/1,000th of a liter

mil·li·me·ter /'mɪləˌmit̬ɚ/ *n.* [C] (*written abbreviation* **mm**) a unit for measuring length, equal to 1/1,000th of a meter

mil·lion /'mɪlyən/ *number* **1** 1,000,000: *$350 million | 4 million people* ▸Don't say "4 million of people."◂ **2** *also* **millions** an extremely large number of people or things: *I've heard that excuse a million times.* **3 not/never in a million years** (spoken) said in order to emphasize how impossible or unlikely something is: *I never would have guessed in a million years.* **4 one in a million** the best of all possible people or things: *People like Sue are one in a million.* [ORIGIN: 1300—1400 French, Old Italian *milione*, from *mille* "thousand"] —**millionth** /'mɪlyənθ/ *number*

mil·lion·aire /ˌmɪlyə'nɛr/ *n.* [C] someone who is very rich and has at least one million dollars

mime¹ /maɪm/ *n.* [C] ENG. LANG. ARTS an actor who performs without using words, or a performance in which no words are used

mime² *v.* [I,T] to perform using actions and movements without any words: *She stretched out her arms, miming a swimmer.*

mim·ic¹ /'mɪmɪk/ *v.* (past tense and past participle **mimicked**, present participle **mimicking**) [T] **1** to copy the way someone speaks, moves, or behaves, usually to make people laugh: *Lily mimicked Sue's Boston accent.* **2** to behave or operate in exactly the same way as someone or something else: *The drug mimics the action of the body's own chemicals.* —**mimicry** *n.* [U]

mimic² *n.* [C] a person or animal that is good at mimicking someone's voice, appearance, etc. or something such as the sound of a machine

min. **1** the written abbreviation of MINIMUM **2** the written abbreviation of MINUTE or MINUTES

mince /mɪns/ *v.* **1** [T] to cut food into extremely small pieces: *Mince the onion and garlic.* **2 not mince words** to say exactly what you think, even if this may offend people: *Stella has never been one to mince words.* **3** [I] to walk, using very small steps and moving your HIPS a lot

mince·meat /'mɪnsmit/ *n.* [U] a sweet mixture of apples, dried fruit, and SPICEs, but no meat, used in PIES

mind¹ /maɪnd/ *n.*

1 BRAIN [C,U] your thoughts, or the part of your brain used for thinking and imagining things: *Grandma's mind is as sharp as ever. | What kind of plans did you* ***have in mind*** (=what have you thought of doing)*? | What's* ***on your mind*** (=what are you thinking about)*?*

2 change your mind to change your opinions or decision about something: *If you change your mind and want to come, give us a call.*

3 make up your mind to decide something, or become very determined to do something: *Have you made up your mind which college you want to go to? | Once she made up her mind to go, there was no stopping her.*

4 cross/enter your mind if something crosses your mind, you think about it for a short period: *It never* ***crossed*** *my* ***mind that*** *she might be unhappy.*

5 be out of your mind (informal) to behave in a crazy or stupid way: *Are you out of your mind?*

6 go out of your mind/lose your mind (informal) to start to become mentally ill or behave in a crazy way: *I'm going to lose my mind if I don't find a new apartment soon.*

7 on your mind if something is on your mind, you are thinking or worrying about it a lot: *Sorry I didn't call, but I've* ***had a lot on my mind*** *lately. | Is there something on your mind?*

8 have sb/sth in mind to have an idea about who or what you want for a particular purpose: *Did you have anyone in mind for the job?*

9 with sb/sth in mind while thinking about someone or something or considering that person or thing: *Racing cars weren't built with safety in mind.*

10 come/spring to mind if something comes to mind, you suddenly think of it: *She was so nervous she just started saying whatever came to mind.*

11 state/frame of mind the way you are feeling, such as how happy or sad you are: *I have to be in the right frame of mind before a game.*

12 -minded having a particular attitude, or believing that a particular thing is important: *He was a mean,* ***narrow-/closed-minded*** *old man* (=he did not accept other ideas and opinions). *| politically-minded students*

13 keep/bear sth in mind to remember something: ***Keep in mind that*** *the bank will be closed tomorrow.*

14 no one in his/her right mind (informal) no

M

one who is sensible: *No woman in her right mind would walk alone at night around here.*
15 have/keep an open mind to be willing to accept new ideas and opinions: *The mayor promises to keep an open mind on the issue of new schools.*
16 take/get/keep your mind off sth to make you stop thinking about something: *Dad needs a vacation to take his mind off work.*
17 keep your mind on sth to keep paying attention to something, even if you want to think about something else: *He could hardly keep his mind on what she was saying.*
18 put your mind to sth to decide to do something and use a lot of effort in order to succeed: *You can win if you just put your mind to it.* [ORIGIN: Old English *gemynd*] → ONE-TRACK MIND, **sth blows your mind** *at* BLOW¹, **slip your mind** *at* SLIP¹

mind² *v.* **1** [I,T] to feel annoyed, worried, or angry about something: *Do you mind if I open the window?* | *Chicago's a nice place to live if you don't mind cold winters.* | *He doesn't mind sleeping on the couch.* | *She doesn't* ***mind that*** *her book has not been selling well.*

SPOKEN PHRASES
2 do/would you mind used to ask politely if you can do something or if someone will do something: ***Do you mind if*** *I use your phone?* | *Would you mind waiting here a minute?* **3 mind your own business** to not ask questions about a situation that does not involve you, often used to tell someone rudely not to do this: *Why doesn't she mind her own business?* **4 I wouldn't mind (doing) sth** said when you would like something or would like to do something: *I wouldn't mind living in Minneapolis.*

5 mind your manners to behave or speak in a polite way → **never mind** *at* NEVER

'mind-ˌboggling *adj.* (informal) very difficult to imagine because of being so big, strange, or complicated: *The number of insects living in the rainforest is mind-boggling.*

mind·ful /ˈmaɪndfəl/ *adj.* behaving in a way that shows you remember a rule or fact: ***Mindful of*** *the guide's warning, they returned before dark.*

mind·less /ˈmaɪndlɪs/ *adj.* **1** so simple that you do not have to think about what you are doing: *mindless work* **2** stupid and without any purpose: *mindless violence/cruelty* —**mindlessness** *n.* [U]

mind·set /ˈmaɪndsɛt/ *n.* [C usually singular] someone's general attitude, and the way in which s/he thinks about things and makes decisions

mine¹ /maɪn/ *pron.* the thing or things belonging or relating to the person who is speaking: *Theresa's coat is black. Mine is blue.* | *He doesn't have a car, so I let him borrow mine.* | *Tom's a good* ***friend of mine.***

mine² *n.* [C] **1** a type of bomb that is hidden just below the ground or under water, which explodes when someone or something touches it **2** a deep hole or holes in the ground, from which gold, coal, etc. is dug: ***coal/gold etc. mines***

mine³ *v.* **1** [I,T] to dig into the ground in order to get gold, coal, etc.: *men* ***mining for*** *gold* **2** [T] to hide bombs under the ground or in the ocean: *The beaches were heavily mined.*

mine·field /ˈmaɪnfild/ *n.* [C] **1** an area of land that has mines hidden in it **2** a situation in which there are many hidden dangers: *The issue is a political minefield.*

min·er /ˈmaɪnɚ/ *n.* [C] someone who works in a mine: *a coal miner*

min·er·al /ˈmɪnərəl/ *n.* [C] **1** EARTH SCIENCES a natural substance such as coal, rock, or salt that is present in the Earth: *an area rich in minerals* **2** CHEMISTRY a substance such as CALCIUM or iron that is present in some foods and that is important for good health: *Milk is full of valuable* ***vitamins and minerals.***

'mineral ˌwater *n.* [C,U] water that comes from under the ground and contains minerals

min·gle /ˈmɪŋgəl/ *v.* **1** [I] to meet and talk with a lot of different people at a social event: *Reporters* ***mingled with*** *movie stars at the awards ceremony.* **2** [I,T] if smells, sounds, feelings, etc. mingle, they combine with each other: *anger* ***mingled with*** *disappointment and fear*

mini- /mɪni/ *adj.* (informal) small compared with others of the same type: *a minivan* | *a mini-market* (=a small food store)

min·i·a·ture¹ /ˈmɪniətʃɚ, ˈmɪnɪtʃɚ/ *adj.* very small: *a miniature camera*

THESAURUS small, little, tiny, minute, minuscule → SMALL

miniature² *n.* [C] **1** something that has the same appearance as someone or something, but is much smaller: *This painting is* ***a miniature of*** *the one in the museum.* **2 in miniature** exactly like someone or something but much smaller: *She has her mother's face in miniature.*

ˌminiature 'golf *n.* [U] a golf game, played for fun, in which you hit a small ball through passages, over small bridges and hills, etc.

min·i·mal /ˈmɪnəməl/ (Ac) *adj.* very small in degree or amount: *The damage caused by the fire was minimal.* | *Desert plants will stay healthy even with minimal watering.* —**minimally** *adv.*

min·i·mize /ˈmɪnəˌmaɪz/ (Ac) *v.* [T] **1** to make the degree or amount of something as small as possible (ANT) **maximize**: *To* ***minimize the risk*** *of getting heart disease, eat well and exercise daily.* **2** IT to make a document or program on your computer very small when you are not using it but still want to keep it open (ANT) **maximize**: *Click on the top of the window to minimize it.*

min·i·mum¹ /ˈmɪnəməm/ (Ac) *adj.* the minimum number, amount, or degree is the smallest that it is

M

possible to have (ANT) **maximum**: *You will need to make a minimum payment of $50 a month.* | *The factory owners wanted to get a minimum price fixed for their goods.* [ORIGIN: 1600—1700 Latin *minimus* "smallest"]

minimum² *n.* [C usually singular] the smallest number, amount, or degree that it is possible to have (ANT) **maximum**: *Jim works **a minimum of*** (=at least) *50 hours a week.* | *Costs were **kept to a minimum.*** | *We must try to keep the use of pesticides to an **absolute minimum.***

ˌminimum 'wage *n.* [singular, U] the lowest amount of money that can legally be paid per hour to a worker: *More than four million Americans earn **the minimum wage.***

min·ing /'maɪnɪŋ/ *n.* [U] the action or industry of digging gold, coal, etc. out of the ground

min·i·se·ries /'mɪniˌsɪriz/ *n.* (plural **miniseries**) [C] a television DRAMA that is divided into several parts and shown on different nights

min·i·skirt /'mɪniˌskɚt/ *n.* [C] a very short skirt

min·is·ter /'mɪnəstɚ/ *n.* [C] **1** a religious leader in some Christian churches ➔ PRIEST **2** a politician who is in charge of a government department in some countries: *the **Minister of** Defense* [ORIGIN: 1200—1300 Old French *ministre*, from Latin *minister* "servant"]

min·is·te·ri·al /ˌmɪnə'stɪriəl/ (Ac) *adj.* relating to a minister, or done by a minister: *The project was approved at ministerial level.*

min·is·try /'mɪnəstri/ (Ac) *n.* (plural **ministries**) **1 the ministry** the profession of being a church leader: *Our son **entered/joined the ministry*** (=became a minister) *two years ago.* **2** [C usually singular] the work done by a religious leader **3** [C] a government department in some countries: *the Foreign Ministry* [ORIGIN: 1300—1400 Latin *ministerium*, from *minister* "servant"]

min·i·van /'mɪniˌvæn/ *n.* [C] a large vehicle with seats for six or more people ➔ *see picture at* TRANSPORTATION

mink /mɪŋk/ *n.* [C,U] a small animal with soft brown fur, or the valuable fur from this animal: *a mink coat*

min·now /'mɪnoʊ/ *n.* [C] a very small fish that lives in rivers, lakes, etc.

mi·nor¹ /'maɪnɚ/ (Ac) *adj.* **1** small and not very important or serious, especially when compared with other things (ANT) **major**: *minor surgery* | *We made a few **minor changes** to the plan.* | *It's only a **minor injury.*** | *Most of the changes in the law were relatively minor.* ►Don't say "minor than."◄ **2** ENG. LANG. ARTS based on a musical SCALE in which the third note of the related MAJOR scale has been lowered by a HALF STEP [ORIGIN: 1200—1300 Latin "smaller"]

minor² *n.* [C] **1** LAW someone who is not old enough to be considered legally responsible for his/her actions: *It's illegal to sell cigarettes to minors.*

> **THESAURUS** child, kid, teenager, adolescent, youngster, juvenile ➔ CHILD

2 the second main subject that you study at college for your degree ➔ MAJOR: *She has **a minor in** history.* ➔ UNIVERSITY

minor³ *v.*

minor in sth *phr. v.* to study a second main subject as part of your college degree: *I'm minoring in history.*

mi·nor·i·ty¹ /mə'nɔrət̬i, maɪ-, -'nɑr-/ (Ac) *n.* (plural **minorities**) **1** [C usually plural] a group of people of a different race or religion than most people in a country, or someone in one of these groups: ***ethnic/racial/religious minorities*** | *The law prevents discrimination against minorities.* **2** [singular] a small part of a larger group of people or things ➔ MAJORITY: *Only **a** small **minority of** senators were in favor of a tax increase.* | *Opposition came from a small but vocal minority.* **3 be in the minority** to be less in number than any other group: *Male teachers are very much in the minority at public schools.*

minority² *adj.* relating to a group of people who do not have the same opinion, religion, race, etc. as most of the larger group that they are in: *help for minority groups* | *minority students*

ˌminor 'league *n.* **the minor leagues** *also* **the Minor Leagues** the groups of teams that form the lower levels of American professional sports, especially baseball ➔ MAJOR LEAGUES —**minor-league** *adj.* [only before noun]: *a minor-league team*

min·strel /'mɪnstrəl/ *n.* [C] **1** a white singer or dancer who tried to look like an African-American person, and who performed in shows in the early part of the 20th century **2** a singer or musician in the Middle Ages

mint¹ /mɪnt/ *n.* **1** [C] a candy with a strong fresh taste **2** [U] a plant with strong fresh-tasting leaves, used in cooking and making medicine ➔ PEPPERMINT **3** [C] a place where coins are officially made

mint² *adj.* **in mint condition** looking new and in perfect condition: *a 1957 Chevy in mint condition*

mint³ *v.* [T] to make a coin

mint·y /'mɪnt̬i/ *adj.* tasting or smelling of mint

mi·nus¹ /'maɪnəs/ *prep.* **1** MATH used in mathematics when you SUBTRACT one number from another ➔ PLUS: *17 minus 5 is 12 (17 – 5 = 12)* | *the value of your assets minus tax* ➔ CALCULATE **2** (informal) without something that would normally be there: *He came back from skate park minus a couple of front teeth.*

minus² *n.* [C] **1** MATH a minus sign **2** something bad about a situation ➔ PLUS: *There are **pluses and minuses** to living in a big city.*

minus³ *adj.* **1 A minus/B minus etc.** a GRADE used in a system of judging a student's work. A minus is lower than A, but higher than B PLUS. ➔ PLUS **2 minus 5/20/30 etc.** less than zero,

M

especially less than zero degrees in temperature → BELOW: *At night the temperature can go as low as minus 30.*

min·us·cule /ˈmɪnəˌskyul/ *adj.* extremely small: *Her allowance is minuscule.* | *a minuscule amount of food*

THESAURUS small, little, tiny, minute, miniature → SMALL

ˈminus ˌsign *n.* [C] MATH a sign (-) showing that a number is less than zero, or that the second of two numbers is to be SUBTRACTed from the first

min·ute¹ /ˈmɪnɪt/ *n.* **1** [C] a period of time equal to 60 seconds: *Ethel's train arrives in 15 minutes.* | *three **minutes to/before** 4:00* | *12 **minutes after/past** one* **2** [C] a very short period of time: ***For a minute** I thought he was serious.* | *I'll be ready **in a minute**.* **3 wait a minute/just a minute/hold on a minute** (spoken) **a)** used to ask someone to wait a short period of time while you do something: *"Are you coming with us?" "Yes. Just a minute."* **b)** used when you want to tell someone that you do not agree with something s/he has said or done: *Wait a minute – you said my car would be ready by 5:00!* **4 last minute** at the last possible time, just before something must be done or completed: *Frank changed his mind **at the last minute** and decided to come after all.* | *a few last-minute arrangements* **5 the minute (that)** as soon as: *I knew it was Jill the minute I heard her voice.* **6 any minute (now)** (spoken) very soon: *She should be here any minute now.* **7 minutes** [plural] an official written record of what is said and decided at a meeting **8** [C] MATH one of the 60 parts into which a degree of an angle can be divided. It can be shown as a SYMBOL after a number. For example, 78° 52' means 78 degrees 52 minutes.

mi·nute² /maɪˈnut/ *adj.* **1** extremely small: *You only need a minute amount.*

THESAURUS small, little, tiny, miniature, minuscule → SMALL

2 paying attention to the smallest things or parts: *Johnson explained the plan **in minute detail**.*

mir·a·cle /ˈmɪrəkəl/ *n.* [C] **1** something lucky that happens when you did not expect it to happen or did not think it was possible: ***It's a miracle (that)** you weren't killed!* | *the country's **economic miracle*** **2** an action or event believed to be caused by God, which is impossible according to the ordinary laws of nature **3 miracle cure/drug** an effective treatment for a serious medical illness

mi·rac·u·lous /mɪˈrækyələs/ *adj.* completely unexpected and very lucky: *The patient made a miraculous recovery.* —**miraculously** *adv.*

THESAURUS lucky, fortunate, fortuitous → LUCKY

mi·rage /mɪˈrɑʒ/ *n.* [C] something you think you see that is not actually there, caused by hot air in a desert

mire /maɪɚ/ *v.* **be mired in sth** **a)** to be in a very difficult situation: *an economy mired in recession* **b)** to be stuck in deep mud

mir·ror¹ /ˈmɪrɚ/ *n.* [C] **1** a piece of special flat glass that you can look at and see yourself in: *the bathroom mirror* | *a rearview mirror* (=a mirror in a car, for looking behind you) | *He looked at himself **in the mirror**.* **2 mirror image** a system or pattern that is almost exactly the same as another one: *This year's election is a mirror image of the one in 1984.* [ORIGIN: 1200–1300 Old French *mirour*, from *mirer* "to look at," from Latin *mirare*]

mirror² *v.* [T] to represent or be very similar to something else: *The election results mirrored public opinion.*

mirth /mɚθ/ *n.* [U] (literary) happiness and laughter

mis·ad·ven·ture /ˌmɪsədˈvɛntʃɚ/ *n.* [C,U] bad luck or an accident

mis·ap·pro·pri·ate /ˌmɪsəˈproʊpriˌeɪt/ *v.* [T] (formal) to dishonestly take something, especially money, that a company, organization, etc. has trusted you to keep safe —**misappropriation** /ˌmɪsəˌproʊpriˈeɪʃən/ *n.* [U]

mis·be·have /ˌmɪsbɪˈheɪv/ *v.* [I] to behave badly. *Anne's being punished for misbehaving in class.* —**misbehavior** /ˌmɪsbɪˈheɪvyɚ/ *n.* [U]

misc. the written abbreviation of MISCELLANEOUS

mis·cal·cu·late /ˌmɪsˈkælkyəˌleɪt/ *v.* [I,T] **1** to make a mistake in deciding how long something will take to do, how much money you will need, etc.: *We miscalculated the time it would take to drive to Long Island.* **2** to make a mistake when you are judging a situation: *Republicans seem to have miscalculated the mayor's popularity.* —**miscalculation** /mɪsˌkælkyəˈleɪʃən/ *n.* [C]

mis·car·riage /ˈmɪsˌkærɪdʒ, ˌmɪsˈkærɪdʒ/ *n.* [C,U] **1** the act of accidentally giving birth too early for the baby to live → ABORTION: *She **had a miscarriage** and nearly died.* **2 miscarriage of justice** a situation in which someone is wrongly punished by a court of law for something s/he did not do

mis·car·ry /ˌmɪsˈkæri/ *v.* (**miscarried**, **miscarries**) [I] to accidentally give birth to a baby too early for him/her to live

mis·cel·la·ne·ous /ˌmɪsəˈleɪniəs/ *adj.* made up of many different things or people that do not seem to be related to each other: *a stack of miscellaneous papers*

mis·chief /ˈmɪstʃɪf/ *n.* [U] bad behavior, especially by children, that causes trouble or damage but no serious harm: *A group of kids were running around and **making mischief*** (=behaving in a way that causes trouble). | *Sports **kept me out of mischief** when I was growing up.* [ORIGIN: 1200–1300 Old French *meschief* "something bad that happens"]

M

mis·chie·vous /'mɪstʃəvəs/ *adj.* a mischievous child likes to have fun by playing tricks on people or doing things to annoy or embarrass them —**mischievously** *adv.*: *He smiled mischievously.*

mis·ci·ble /'mɪsəbəl/ *adj.* CHEMISTRY miscible liquids or gases are able to mix and combine together completely into one liquid or gas (ANT) **immiscible**: *Miscible liquids such as water and ethanol will diffuse* (=mix together).

mis·con·cep·tion /ˌmɪskən'sɛpʃən/ *n.* [C,U] an idea that is wrong or untrue, but that people still believe: *It's a **misconception that** red meat cannot be part of a healthy diet.*

mis·con·duct /ˌmɪs'kɑndʌkt/ *n.* [U] (formal) bad or dishonest behavior by someone in a position of authority or trust: *an investigation into police misconduct*

mis·con·strue /ˌmɪskən'stru/ *v.* [T] (formal) to not understand correctly what someone has said or done: *The research results have been misconstrued.*

mis·deed /ˌmɪs'did/ *n.* [C] (formal) a wrong or illegal action

mis·de·mean·or /ˌmɪsdɪ'minɚ/ *n.* [C] LAW a crime that is not very serious

mis·di·rect /ˌmɪsdə'rɛkt/ *v.* [T] (formal) to use your efforts, emotions, or abilities in a way that is wrong or not appropriate: *misdirected anger*

mi·ser /'maɪzɚ/ *n.* [C] (disapproving) someone who hates spending money and likes saving it —**miserly** *adj.*

mis·er·a·ble /'mɪzərəbəl/ *adj.* **1** very unhappy, especially because you are lonely or sick: *I saw Dana last week, and she looked miserable.* | *She **made my life miserable**.*

THESAURUS **sad, unhappy, sorrowful, depressed, down, low, blue, downhearted, melancholy, morose, gloomy, glum** ➔ SAD

2 very bad in quality: *miserable weather* [ORIGIN: 1400—1500 Old French, Latin *miserabilis*] —**miserably** *adv.*

mis·er·y /'mɪzəri/ *n.* (plural **miseries**) [C,U] great suffering or unhappiness, caused for example by being very poor or very sick: *The conflict is causing **human misery** on an unprecedented scale.* | *the suffering and **misery of** the poor*

mis·fit /'mɪsˌfɪt/ *n.* [C] someone who does not seem to belong in a place because s/he is very different from the other people there: *a social misfit*

mis·for·tune /mɪs'fɔrtʃən/ *n.* [C,U] bad luck, or something that happens to you as a result of bad luck: *We **had the misfortune of** being in an airport when the snowstorm hit.*

mis·giv·ing /mɪs'gɪvɪŋ/ *n.* [C usually plural, U] a feeling of doubt or fear about what might happen, or about whether something is right: *He **had** some **misgivings about** letting me use his car.*

mis·guid·ed /mɪs'gaɪdɪd/ *adj.* **1** intended to be helpful but actually making a situation worse: *a misguided attempt to impress her boss* **2** wrong because of being based on a wrong understanding of a situation: *He became a teacher on the misguided belief that the hours were short.*

mis·han·dle /ˌmɪs'hændl/ *v.* [T] to deal with a situation badly, or not skillfully: *The government has mishandled the crisis.*

mis·hap /'mɪshæp/ *n.* [C,U] a small accident or mistake that does not have a very serious effect: *The rest of the flight continued **without mishap**.* | *We had a few mishaps, nothing serious.* ➔ ACCIDENT

mis·in·form /ˌmɪsɪn'fɔrm/ *v.* [T] to give someone information that is not correct: *Patients were misinformed about their treatment.*

mis·in·ter·pret /ˌmɪsɪn'tɚprɪt/ (Ac) *v.* [T] to not understand the correct meaning of something that someone says or does: *They may misinterpret your actions as a sign of weakness.* —**misinterpretation** /ˌmɪsɪnˌtɚprə'teɪʃən/ *n.* [C,U]

mis·judge /ˌmɪs'dʒʌdʒ/ *v.* [T] **1** to form a wrong or unfair opinion about a person or situation: *The White House has badly misjudged Congress's support for his bill.* **2** to guess an amount, distance, etc. wrongly: *Don misjudged the turn and wrecked his car.* —**misjudgment** *n.* [C,U]

mis·lead /mɪs'lid/ *v.* (past tense and past participle **misled** /-'lɛd/) [T] to make someone believe something that is not true by giving him/her false or incomplete information: *a deliberate attempt to mislead the public*

THESAURUS **lie, make sth up, tell (sb) a lie, invent, deceive, perjure yourself/commit perjury, falsify** ➔ LIE[2]

mis·lead·ing /mɪs'lidɪŋ/ *adj.* likely to make someone believe something that is not true: *Statistics can be very misleading.* —**misleadingly** *adv.*

THESAURUS **wrong, incorrect, erroneous, inaccurate, false** ➔ WRONG[1]

mis·man·age /ˌmɪs'mænɪdʒ/ *v.* [T] if someone mismanages something s/he is in charge of, s/he deals with it badly: *This project's been completely mismanaged from the beginning.* —**mismanagement** *n.* [U]: *financial mismanagement*

mis·match /'mɪsmætʃ/ *n.* [C] a combination of things or people that do not work well together or are not appropriate for each other: *There seems to be a **mismatch between** skills and jobs.* —**mismatched** *adj.*

mis·no·mer /ˌmɪs'noʊmɚ/ *n.* [C] a wrong or inappropriate name: *The term "dry cleaning" is **something of a misnomer**, as fluids are actually used.*

mi·sog·y·nist /mɪ'sɑdʒənɪst/ *n.* [C] (formal) a man who hates women —**misogyny** *n.* [U] —**misogynistic** /mɪˌsɑdʒə'nɪstɪk/ *adj.*

Finding Words in the Dictionary

Exercise 1

To find a word in the dictionary, you will need to know the correct spelling, especially the first two or three letters. If you can't find a word, you may have the wrong spelling. Think what other spellings may be possible.

These words all contain spelling mistakes in the first two or three letters. What are the correct spellings?

1 fysics	3 reath	5 ryme	7 accademic
2 skale	4 neel	6 tiranny	8 cumpassion

Exercise 2

The dictionary lists words in alphabetical order. Sometimes a word is made up of two words that are written separately (**horse race**) or joined with a hyphen (**role-play**). In this dictionary, these words are listed alphabetically as if they were one word. Write these groups of words in alphabetical order.

1	market	4	separate	5	conflict	2	knife	3	wise	6	although	1
2	ballot		piece		mass number		modal		obvious		smack	
3	segregate		secondary		select		secularize		season		semester	
4	connect		concave		confidence		confusion		conman		con artist	

Exercise 3

Some words are made from other words. For example, the adjective **overwhelmed** comes from the verb **overwhelm**, so it appears in the same entry.

The following words do not have separate entries in this dictionary. Which main entry would you go, to to find them?

1 cynically ......cynical........	5 pharmacologist ....
2 hemophiliac	6 transparently ....
3 assimilation	7 procedural ....
4 sarcastically	8 nutritionally ....

Red Key Words

Exercise 4

Some entries begin with a word that is **red**. These are the most important words to learn and remember. In the following groups of words, one word is *not* a "red" word and is less frequently used than the other words. Circle the word that is not a key word.

1 noisy loud [deafening]
2 find locate trace discover
3 admire respect idolize
4 fare fee expense cost

Checking Spellings

Exercise 5

Use the dictionary to check words if you are unsure of their spelling.

Each of the following words has one letter missing. Correct the spelling. Look the words up in the dictionary if necessary.

1 reconize ....recognize....
2 acess ....
3 rythm ....
4 embarassed ....
5 labratory ....
6 comittee ....
7 artic ....
8 libary ....

Exercise 6

These content words are each misspelled. Correct the spelling. Look the words up in the dictionary if necessary.

1 abalition ....
2 conducter ....
3 corralation ....
4 deductable ....
5 governunce ....
6 morain ....
7 nuron ....
8 seizmograph ....

Finding and Understanding Meanings

Exercise 7

The definitions in this dictionary use a selected vocabulary of 2,000 words. This means that even definitions of difficult words are easy to understand.

The following verbs all describe ways of throwing something. Try and match them to the definitions below.

pitch hurl toss fling pass chuck

1 to throw something in a careless or relaxed way (*informal*) ....chuck....
2 to throw or move something quickly with a lot of force ....
3 to throw a ball or other object to another member of your team ....
4 to throw something without much force ....
5 to throw something using a lot of force ....
6 to aim and throw the ball toward the batter in baseball ....

Words with More Than One Meaning

Exercise 8

Many words in English have more than one meaning. Different meanings are listed separately in the entry, each preceded by a number in bold type: **1**, **2**, **3** …

When a word has more than one part of speech, you will often find completely separate entries for each function.

Look up these words in the dictionary. How many meanings does each one have?

1 modest ....3....	4 fierce	7 rocky ....
2 develop	5 chorus	8 barrier ....
3 settlement	6 wherever	9 appreciation ....

Exercise 9

Read the following pairs of definitions. Each pair refers to the same word, but used in different meanings. What is the word?

square litter fine bear long silence spring bitter

1 *n* a large strong animal with thick fur *v* to be responsible for something	........bear........
2 *n* a shape with four straight equal sides forming four right angles *n* a broad open area with buildings around it, in the middle of a town	....
3 *n* pieces of waste paper, etc. that people leave on the ground in public places *n* a group of baby animals born at the same time to one mother	....
4 *adj* angry and upset because you feel something bad or unfair has happened to you *adj* having a strong taste, like coffee without sugar	....
5 *n* the season between winter and summer, when leaves and flowers appear *v* to jump or move suddenly and quickly in a particular direction	....
6 *n* money that you have to pay as a punishment for breaking a law or rule *adj* good enough or acceptable	....
7 *n* complete quiet because no one is talking, or a period of complete quiet *v* to make someone stop criticizing or giving their opinions	....
8 *adj* measuring a great length, distance, or time *v* to want something very much	....

Exercise 10

To help you find the meaning of a word that you need, this dictionary lists the different meanings of words in order of frequency. The first definition is the most frequently used meaning of the word, but read all the meanings to make sure you have found the right one.

Read these pairs of sentences. Put a check mark next to the sentence that shows the more frequent use of the word in **red** type.

1 a Native Americans believe that all living **creatures** should be respected. ☑
  b The story is about **creatures** from outer space. ☐
2 a There were a lot of good **points** in his speech. ☐
  b Teachers should try to focus on a learner's strong **points**, and then work on his or her weak points. ☐
3 a She fell down a whole **flight** of stairs. ☐
  b Our **flight** leaves in 20 minutes. ☐
4 a Her heart rate was 80 **beats** a minute. ☐
  b As a journalist, he covers the political **beat**. ☐
5 a I **searched** the Web for a cheap flight. ☐
  b Denise began to **search** for her keys. ☐
6 a We **watched** the game on TV. ☐
  b **Watch** your head; the door's low. ☐

Vocabulary Building (Thesaurus Boxes)

Exercise 11

The Thesaurus boxes in this dictionary help students to build their vocabulary by grouping together words with a similar meaning or which are used to talk about a particular topic. Go to the Thesaurus box at the word **thin**, read the definitions for the various adjectives, then look at the exercise below without referring to the Thesaurus box.

gaunt **skinny** **anorexic** **slim**

Fill in the blanks with the best adjective from the list above.

1 The hospital treats ......*anorexic*...... girls by trying to change their eating habits.
2 Elise was tall and .... and very attractive.
3 The old man was very pale and .... , and he looked as if he had been sick for a very long time.
4 He was a .... boy whose clothes looked too big.

Exercise 12

This time, go to the Thesaurus box at the word **fire**, read the definitions for the various nouns, then look at the exercise below without referring to the Thesaurus box.

campfire inferno flames blaze

Fill in the blanks with the best noun from the list above.

1 We watched the .... dance in the fireplace.
2 Fire fighters were called to a .... in an abandoned house.
3 The boys built a .... and toasted marshmallows over it.
4 No one could have survived the .... that the building became.

Exercise 13

Now go to the Thesaurus box at the word **piece**, read the definitions for the various nouns, then look at the exercise below without referring to the Thesaurus box.

fragment lump scrap crumb

Fill in the blanks with the best noun from the list above.

1 The table was covered in bread ....
2 .... of glass were scattered over the sidewalk.
3 Each child was given a .... of clay to make into a pot.
4 She wrote her telephone number on a .... of paper.

Using Words Together Correctly (Collocations)

Collocations are pairs or groups of words that are frequently used together. For example, the verb **commit** is often used with the noun **crime**. You can find Collocation boxes throughout the dictionary. They give important information that will help you to sound natural in English.

Exercise 14

The words in **red** below have their own Collocation box in the dictionary. Study the relevant Collocation boxes, then choose a word from the list below and use it in the correct form to complete these sentences.

split best tumbled expired dirty seize late window/aisle

1 The company's stock **prices** ......*tumbled*...... as they began having difficulties.
2 If you get a chance to go to the workshop, you should .... the **opportunity**.
3 Teenagers often **sleep** .... on Saturday mornings.
4 My friend and I .... the **check** when we go out for pizza.
5 I've known my .... **friend** since I was two years old.
6 The woman at the ticket desk asked if I wanted a .... **seat** on the plane.
7 I don't like him much. He's always telling .... **jokes**.
8 You'd better make sure your **passport** hasn't .... before we buy these tickets.

Exercise 15

In addition to Collocation boxes, the dictionary shows many examples of the correct collocations to use with particular words. Fill in the blank with the correct collocation for the word shown in **red** in these sentences. Compare your answers to the examples given in the dictionary.

1 If you ....*break*......... the **rules**, you will be sent to the principal's office.
2 We .... a lot of **pictures** when we were on vacation.
3 I've been looking for work ever since I .... my **job** last December.
4 Brianna .... a **habit** of interrupting people.
5 We got completely soaked by the .... **rain**.
6 I .... a lot of **weight** by exercising more and eating less.
7 The party was a .... **success**.
8 I have .... **news**! Maria had a baby boy.

Prepositions

Exercise 16

The dictionary shows many examples of the correct prepositions to use with particular words. Choose the correct preposition for these sentences. Compare your answers to the examples given in the dictionary.

to down away after as under with at

1 She **attached** a photograph ....*to*............. her letter.
2 Juan **looked** .... me and smiled.
3 Marta **described** him .... looking athletic.
4 He tried to talk to her, and she **pushed** him ....
5 The classroom is **equipped** .... 15 computers.
6 Paul **ran** .... the stairs.
7 Jordan has been .... a lot of **stress** at work.
8 I don't like walking home .... **dark**.

Idioms

Exercise 17

An idiom is an expression that has a special meaning that is different from the meanings of all the individual words put together. Look at these idioms. The words in **red** type show you where you can find the idiom. What do they mean?

a **hit** the roof ....
b hold your **horses** ....
c get the **show** on the road ....
d be in hot **water** ....
e **drag** your feet ....
f be/go over somebody's **head** ....
g be a **piece** of cake ....
h be no **picnic** ....

Match the idioms to the sentences below by writing the correct idiom in each blank (change the word forms where necessary).

1 He explained the math problem, but it ......*went over my head*...... .
2 When I told him I'd broken the window, he ....
3 Mom asked the kids to clean out the garage, but they're ....
4 You might think being a stay-at-home mom is great, but believe me, it's
....
5 .... ! We can't do everything at once.
6 That test was a .... I'm sure I got an A.
7 Come on, let's .... We have a lot to do today.
8 My brother misbehaves a lot and is always .... at home.

Etymology

Exercise 18

English words have developed over a long period of time. For example, the words **eat** and **drink** come from the Old English words *etan* and *drinkan*. Match each of the following words with its etymology.

1 safari	A from Old Norse *uggligr*, meaning "frightening"
2 binoculars	B from Latin *caput*, meaning "head"
3 ethnic	C from Latin *bini*, meaning "two by two," and *oculus*, meaning "eye"
4 arithmetic	D from Greek *arithmein*, meaning "to count"
5 captain	E from Latin *Ceres*, who was the Roman goddess of grain and farming
6 graffiti	F from Arabic *safariy*, meaning "of a trip"
7 orange	G from Italian graffiare, meaning "to make marks on a surface"
8 husband	H from Greek *ethnos*, meaning "nation, people"
9 ugly	I from Old Norse *hus*, meaning "house," and *bondi*, meaning "someone who lives in a house"
10 cereal	J from Sanskrit *naranga*, meaning "orange tree"

Exercise 19

Many scientific and academic words originally came from Latin or Greek. Fill in the table with the words below that come from the Latin or Greek root. Some words may appear in more than one column.

assume **genocide** **biography** **geography** **commune** **contradict**
community **geometry** **contraband** **parameter** **topography** **geology**
trigonometry **gene** **presume** **genus** **diameter** **communicate**
contravene **genome** **consume** **gender**

Greek ***communis*** **"common"**	**Latin** ***contra*** **"against"**	**Greek** ***ge*** **"Earth"**	**Greek** ***graphia*** **"writing"**	**Greek** ***metria*** **or** ***metron*** **"measure"**	**Greek** ***genos*** **"birth, race, type"**	**Latin** ***sumere*** **"to take up"**
		geology				

Parts of Speech

Exercise 20

The dictionary tells you the grammatical function of each word. These functions are called "parts of speech." What word classes do the following words belong to?

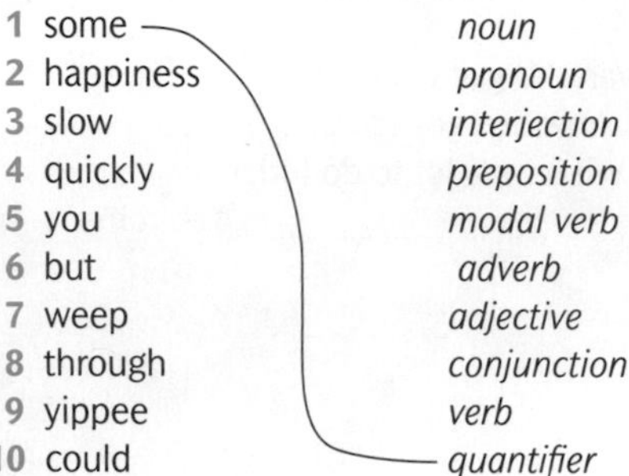

Exercise 21

Sometimes the same word may have more than one part of speech. There is an entry for each different grammatical function of the same word. If you see a small raised number after the main word that begins an entry (**chip**[1]), it means there is more than one entry for this word.

Read the sentences and circle the correct word class for the word in **bold** type.

1 The audience **cheered** as the band came onto the stage. *noun / verb*
2 They greeted the news with **cheers** and shouts. *adjective / noun*
3 Let me know if you **feel** any pain. *adjective / verb*
4 The table had a greasy **feel**. *noun / adjective*
5 Go **inside** and get your jacket. *noun / adverb*
6 The door was locked from the **inside**. *noun / adjective*
7 The floor didn't look very **clean**. *verb / adjective*
8 I need to **clean** the house on Saturday. *noun / verb*
9 They used a **chemical** to kill the bacteria. *noun / adjective*
10 A **chemical** reaction occurs when the two substances are mixed. *verb / adjective*
11 Do you **mind** if I close the window? *verb / adjective*
12 Have you made up your **mind** about which college to go to? *verb / noun*
13 The prices seem really **high** in this store. *adjective / noun*
14 Birds were flying **high** in the sky. *adverb / adjective*
15 He tried with all his **might** to lift away the rocks. *noun / verb*
16 I **might** not be able to play in the next game. *modal verb / adverb*

Word Families

Exercise 22

Not every word has its own entry in the dictionary. Sometimes the entry for a very common word will have less common related words shown at the end of the entry. Look up the words in the first column below in the dictionary. At the end of the entry for the main word, you will find words that are related to it. Write the related words in the columns on the right. The first one has been done for you.

word	adjective	adverb	noun	verb
angry		angrily		
chemical				
authentic				
statistic				
perplex				
creative				
procedure				
magnet				
permanent				

Countable and Uncountable Nouns

Exercise 23

Most English nouns (like *chair*, *house*, and *computer*) have plural forms (*chairs*, *houses*, *computers*). These are called *countable nouns* and are marked [C] in this dictionary. Nouns that don't have plurals (*laughter*, *money*, *information*) are *uncountable nouns* and are marked [U]. Some nouns can be either countable or uncountable, depending on how they are used (*wine*, *cheese*, *coincidence*), and are marked [C, U].

Is the noun in **red** type in each sentence countable or uncountable? Write C or U next to it.

1 Do you have any **pets**? [C]
2 Her **joy** at the news was clear to see. [ ]
3 Have you heard the latest **news**? [ ]
4 If you have any **problems**, just let me know. [ ]
5 Can you give me some **help** with this? [ ]
6 My only concern is your **happiness**. [ ]
7 I never eat **fish**. [ ]
8 **Fish** such as salmon travel a long distance in order to lay eggs. [ ]

Irregular Plurals

Exercise 24

To form the plural of nouns in English, we usually add *-s* or *-es* to the singular form.

A few nouns have irregular plurals. These irregular forms are always shown in the dictionary at the beginning of the entry.

Here are eight irregular plural nouns. What are their singular forms?

1 alumni ......alumnus......
2 wives ....
3 children ....
4 shelves ....
5 diagnoses ....
6 deer ....
7 media ....
8 lice ....

Compound Nouns

Exercise 25

Look through the dictionary and you will notice two-word entries, for example *foul play*. This is because compounds are nouns in their own right.

How many of these compounds do you recognize and understand? Try to match them to the definitions below.

police department coral reef minor league junk mail
high jump draft dodger life cycle simple sentence

1 the group of teams that form the lower levels of American professional sports, especially baseball ...minor league...
2 someone who illegally avoids joining the military, even though s/he has been ordered to join ....
3 a long hard structure formed of coral in warm ocean water that is not very deep ....
4 the official police organization in a particular area or city ....
5 all the different stages of development that an animal or plant goes through during its life ....
6 a sport in which you run and jump over a bar that is raised higher after each successful jump ....
7 mail that advertisers send to people who do not want it ....
8 a sentence that consists of one main clause, for example "He ate the cake." ....

Transitive and Intransitive Verbs

Exercise 26

Many verbs normally have a direct object (noun or pronoun or clause). These are called *transitive* verbs and are marked [T] in this dictionary. Examples of these verbs include *hit*, *see*, *enjoy*, *contain*, and *need*.

We can't say *Did you see?* But we can say *Did you see the game?*

Many verbs do not normally have a direct object. These are called *intransitive* verbs and are marked [I] in this dictionary. Examples of these verbs include *happen*, *wait*, *snow*, *sleep*, *arrive*, and *rain*.

We can't say *Wait the others here*. We can only say *Wait here*. (or *Wait for the others here.*)

Some verbs can be used transitively and intransitively. They are marked [I,T] in this dictionary. Examples of these verbs include *begin*, *drop*, *open*, *win*, and *ring*.

We can say *Williams won the game* (transitive) or *Williams won* (intransitive).

Are the grammar codes for these verbs [I], [T], or [I, T]? Put a direct object (noun or pronoun) after these verbs wherever possible.

1 We sold ......the car...... . [T]
2 My mother shouted .... [ ]
3 He prefers .... [ ]
4 We began .... [ ]
5 It's snowing .... [ ]
6 Are you going to watch .... ? [ ]
7 Will he win .... ? [ ]
8 Sarah cried .... [ ]

Irregular Verbs

Exercise 27

For all irregular verbs, the dictionary gives the past tense, the past participle, and the present participle (see the Irregular Verbs table at the end of the book).

Complete this chart of irregular verbs. If necessary, check the verbs in the dictionary by looking up the infinitive form.

Infinitive	Past tense	Past participle	Present participle
begin	began	begun	beginning
catch	caught	caught	1 ....
pay	2	paid	paying
break	3	4	breaking
send	sent	5	sending
6	grew	grown	growing

Phrasal Verbs

Exercise 28

Phrasal verbs are special verbs that are made up of a verb + an adverb or preposition. Phrasal verbs can be found in this dictionary at the end of the entries for the verbs that they begin with. Try keeping your own lists of phrasal verbs. You will be surprised how soon you start to see verbs from your lists in different contexts.

Complete the sentences.

blow fall drop sell lock spread die look

1 The concert .....*sold out*..... so quickly I couldn't get tickets.
2 "My book is ...." "Why don't you tape the cover back on?"
3 The teacher asked the children to .... so that they had more room to move.
4 Terrorists set a bomb to .... the bridge.
5 My aunt .... after work to talk to my mother.
6 I .... a magazine while I waited for my brother.
7 Oh no! I left my keys in the car and now I'm .... of the house!
8 The dinosaurs all .... , probably because of a huge meteor that hit the Earth.

Exercise 29

Write each phrasal verb from the previous exercise in the blank next to its definition.

1 to move apart from the other people in a group in order to cover a wide area .....*spread out*.....
2 to disappear or stop existing completely ....
3 to destroy something, or to be destroyed, by an explosion ....
4 to prevent someone from entering a place by locking the door ....
5 to sell all of something, so there is none left ....
6 to visit someone when you have not arranged to come at a particular time ....
7 to separate into many pieces ....
8 to read something quickly ....

Modal Verbs

Exercise 30

A modal verb is a special kind of verb that is usually used with another main verb to change its meaning somehow. Write the correct modal verb in these sentences.

can could may must should will would

1 My mom .....*could*..... run really fast when she was young.
2 A lot of people will be there. It .... be a great party.
3 We .... not be able to visit Grandma on Sunday.
4 My brother .... be so annoying sometimes.
5 You .... have worked really hard on this.
6 I .... go to the store later.
7 He .... love to help if he can get the time off work.

Pronunciation

Pronunciations in this dictionary are shown at the beginning of entries between slanting lines / / using the International Phonetic Alphabet (IPA). Learning the IPA will help you pronounce English, since the normal spelling of English words does not always show you clearly how to pronounce them. The pronunciation table can be found on the inside front cover of this dictionary.

Exercise 31

Put the words below under the correct vowel symbol by looking in the dictionary to see which sound each word uses.

red seed paw blue too set bleed ought root creed
cough mean bed crew do neat dread caught fault

/i/	/ɛ/	/ɔ/	/u/
seed	red	paw	blue

Exercise 32

Put the words below under the correct consonant symbol, by looking in the dictionary to see which sound each word starts with.

scientist kitchen newspaper pneumonia creation psychology circuit
common kilobyte knock career snake cyberspace negative

/s/	/k/	/n/
scientist	kitchen	newspaper

Exercise 33

Circle the correct pronunciation of these six words.

1 waves weɪfz / weɪvz
2 usual 'yuʒuəl / 'uʒuəl
3 true tru / troʊ
4 gospel 'gʌspəl / 'gɑspəl
5 blouse bloʊs / bləʊs
6 answer 'ænsɚ / 'ænswɚ

Exercise 34

There are many irregularities in English spelling. Words can sound the same, yet be spelled differently. Find the pairs of words in these lists that rhyme.

1 doll	said
2 dead	crane
3 rain	off
4 cough	kite
5 might	drawl

6 date	note
7 sea	plum
8 crumb	high
9 fly	straight
10 goat	free

Stress

Exercise 35

If a word has two or more syllables we put a stress on one of the syllables. In this dictionary, the symbol /ˈ/ appears before the main stressed syllable. For example, the phonetic transcription of *discuss*, [dɪˈskʌs], shows that the second syllable is stressed. Circle the stressed syllable in the following words.

1 deposit
2 hamburger
3 notable
4 impress
5 strategy
6 vaccine
7 century
8 challenge

Exercise 36

Words may change their stress when they are used for different grammatical functions. Read these sentences and circle the correct stress pattern for the words in **bold** type.

1 What sort of man would **desert** his children? deSERT / DESert
2 Plants in the **desert** get very little water. deSERT / DEsert
3 I won't let you **insult** my mother! INsult / inSULT
4 He shouted an **insult** at her. INsult / inSULT
5 There was some sort of sharp **object** in the bottom of the bag. obJECT/ OBject
6 Many students **object** to the tuition increase. obJECT / OBject
7 He is a **suspect** in the robbery. SUSpect / susPECT
8 I **suspect** that she is lying. SUSpect / susPECT

Syllables and Hyphenation

Exercise 37

It helps to learn the pronunciation of a long word by starting to say it one syllable at a time. This dictionary uses dots (=small round marks) between the syllables of a word to show where the syllable breaks are: **in·her·i·tance** /ɪnˈherɪtəns/ *n*

Say each syllable slowly: **in her i tance** ɪnˈherɪtəns

Now say the word quickly. Remember to put the stress on /her/: **inheritance**.

Look up the words below and mark the syllable breaks.

1 child|hood
2 community
3 respect
4 drummer
5 another
6 mumble

Animals

Jaguar
tail
hind leg
whiskers
fangs
front leg
claws
paw
Salmon
scales
dorsal fin
gill
fin
tail
Moose
antler
muzzle
hoof
Puffin
beak
webbed feet
Lobster
leg
claw
pincer
antennae
Butterfly
antennae
chrysalis
wing
larva/ caterpillar
eggs
Mockingbird
beak
breast
wing
claws
tail feathers
Eagle
wing
talon
Buffalo/Bison
fur
horn
Alligator
tail
nostrils
teeth
jaw
feet

Body

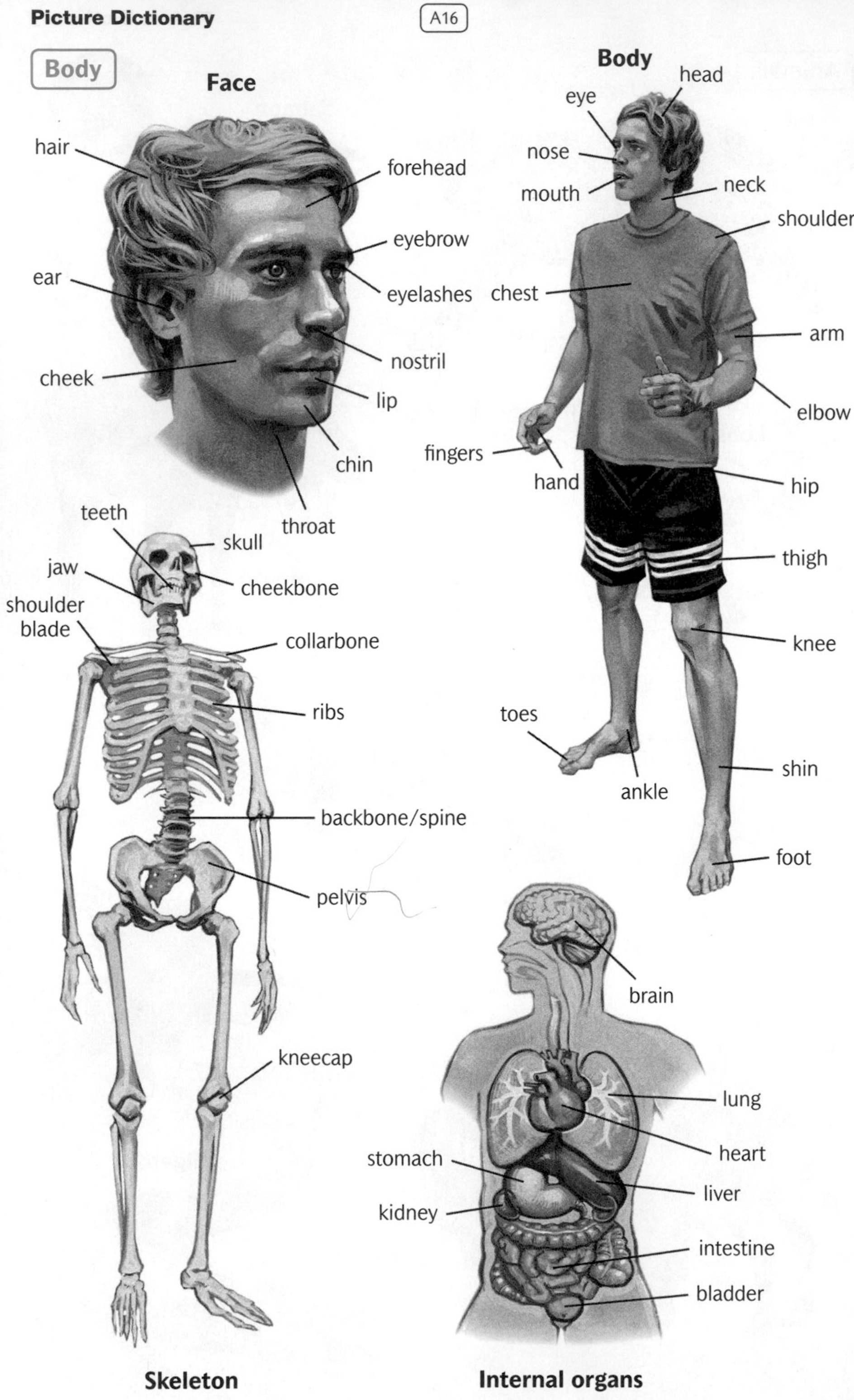
Face
hair
forehead
eyebrow
ear
eyelashes
nostril
cheek
lip
chin
throat
Body
head
eye
nose
mouth
neck
shoulder
chest
arm
elbow
fingers
hand
hip
thigh
knee
toes
ankle
shin
foot
teeth
skull
jaw
cheekbone
shoulder blade
collarbone
ribs
backbone/spine
pelvis
kneecap
Skeleton
brain
lung
heart
stomach
liver
kidney
intestine
bladder
Internal organs

Sports

baseball

track

gliding

parachuting

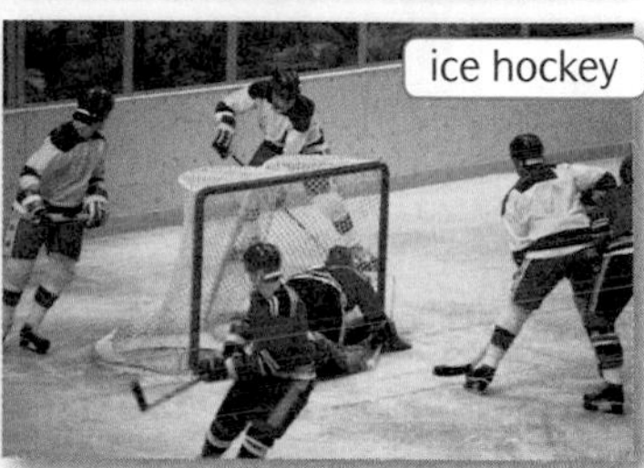
ice hockey

golf

mountain biking

kayaking

swimming

football

rowing

climbing

sailing

skiing

surfing

wind surfing

Kitchen Verbs

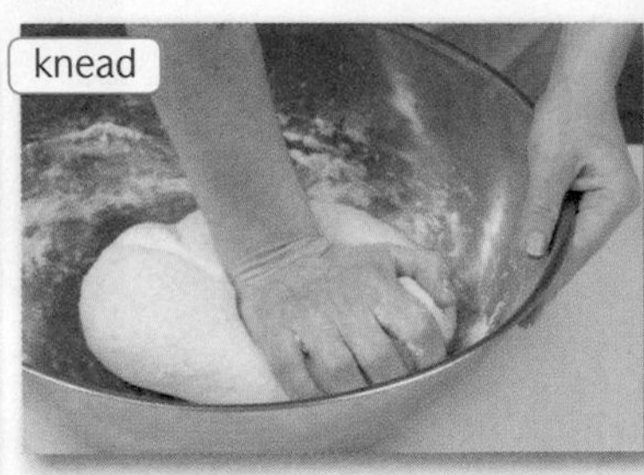

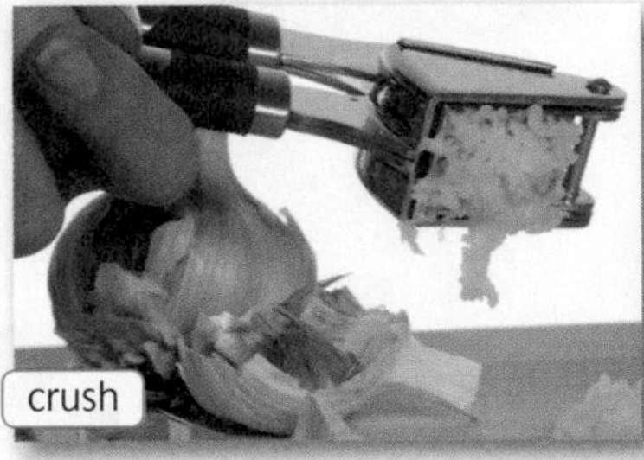

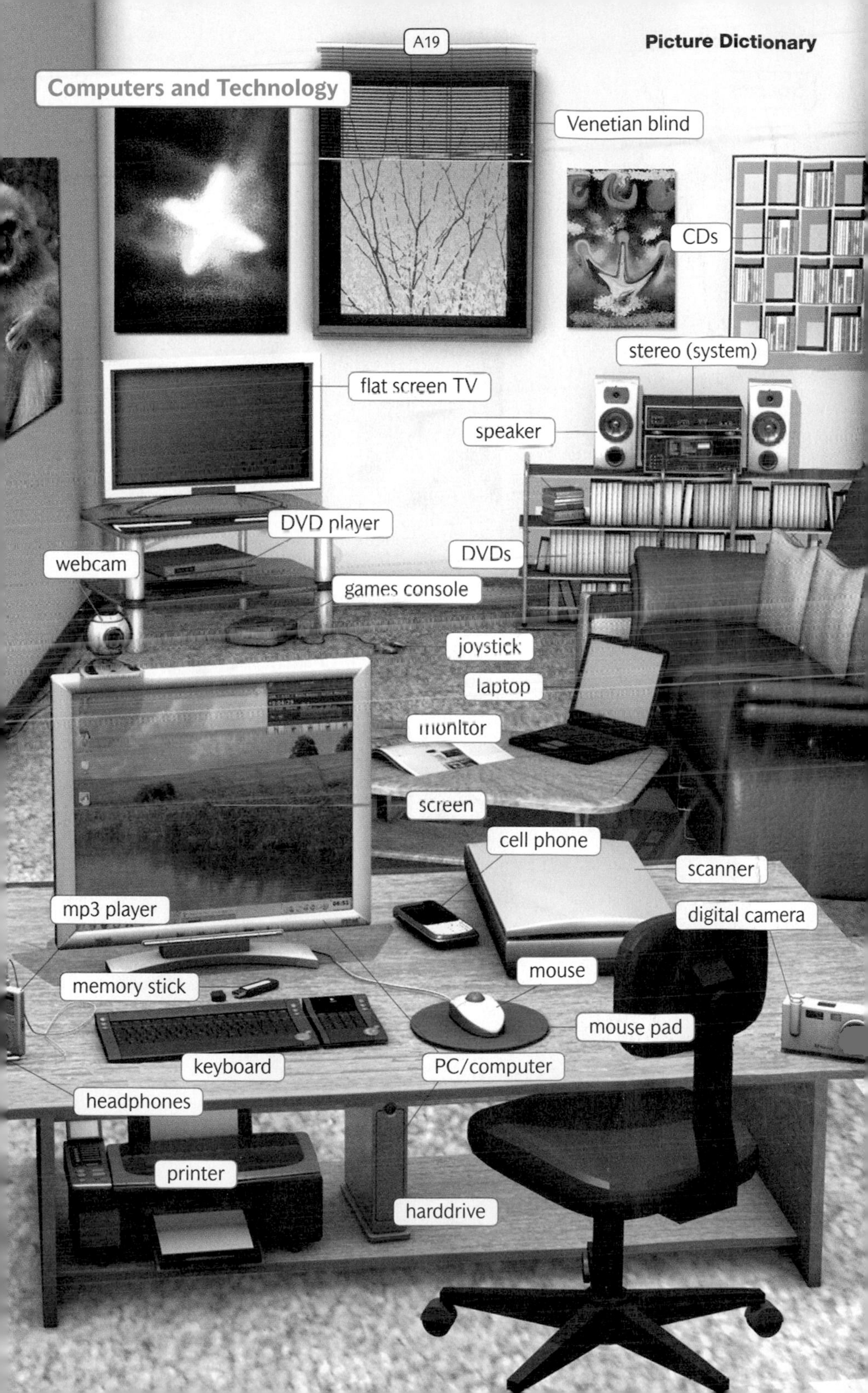
A19
Computers and Technology
Venetian blind
CDs
stereo (system)
flat screen TV
speaker
DVD player
webcam
DVDs
games console
joystick
laptop
monitor
screen
cell phone
scanner
mp3 player
digital camera
mouse
memory stick
mouse pad
keyboard
PC/computer
headphones
printer
harddrive

Sounds

ring
crash
squeak
creak
bang
splash
buzz
rustle
rattle
crunch
click
sizzle
fizz
crackle
hiss

Verbs of Movement (hands)

flick

clap

hold hands

pinch

tap

point

scratch

poke

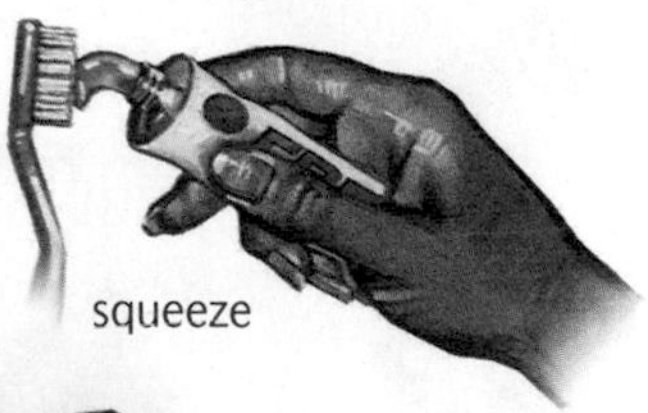

squeeze

pet/stroke

wave

Verbs of Movement (body)

Plants and Trees

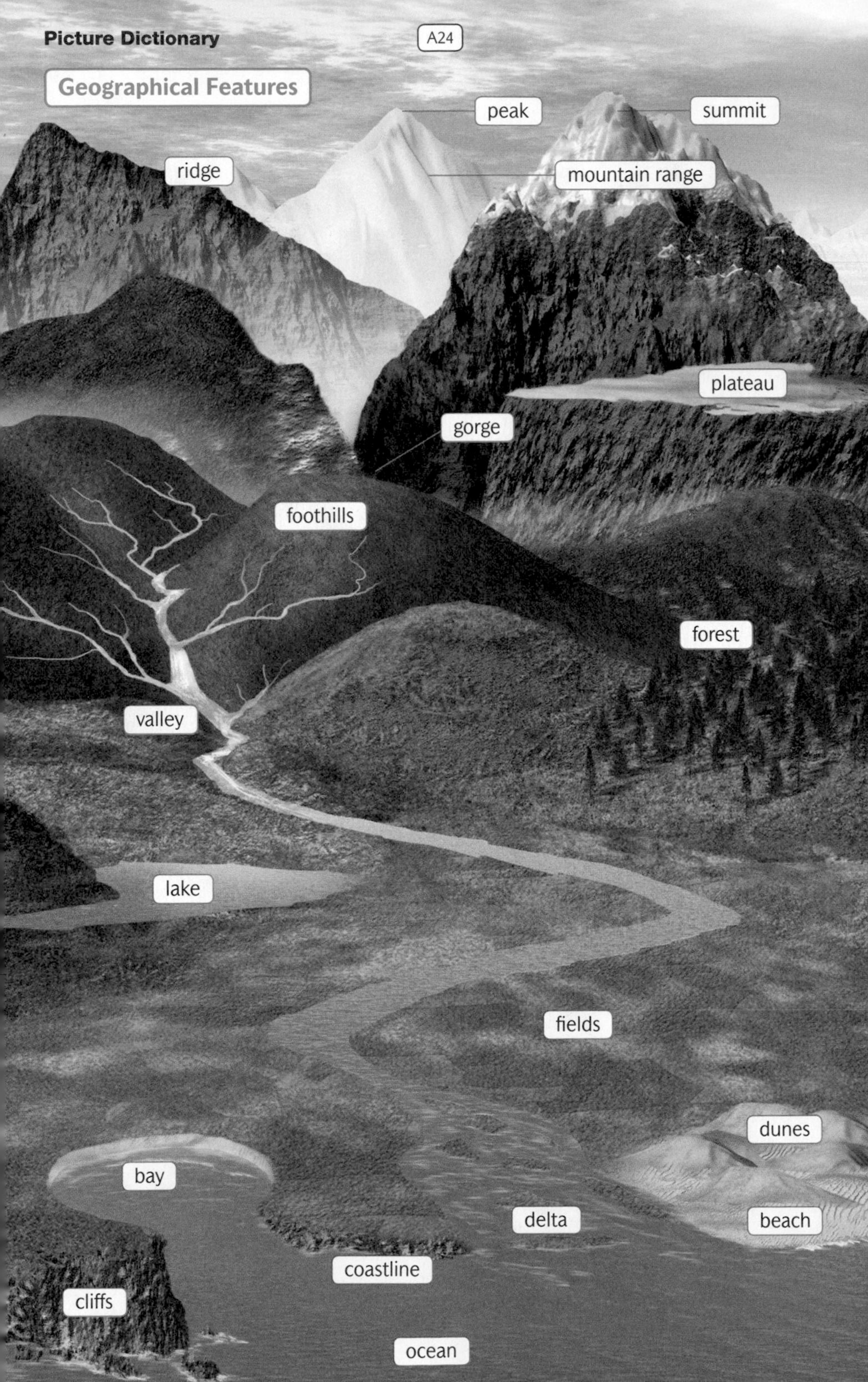
Geographical Features
peak
summit
ridge
mountain range
plateau
gorge
foothills
forest
valley
lake
fields
dunes
bay
delta
beach
coastline
cliffs
ocean

Map of USA

New England
Middle Atlantic States/The East Coast
Southern States/The South
Southwestern States/The Southwest
Midwestern States/The Midwest
Rocky Mountain States
Pacific Coast States/The West Coast
ALASKA
CANADA
CANADA
Rocky Mountains
Seattle
WASHINGTON
Portland
OREGON
MONTANA
Helena
NORTH DAKOTA
Bismarck
MINNESOTA
Minneapolis
WISCONSIN
MICHIGAN
Lake Superior
Lake Huron
Lake Michigan
Lake Ontario
Lake Erie
Boise
IDAHO
SOUTH DAKOTA
Pierre
WYOMING
Cheyenne
NEBRASKA
Omaha
IOWA
Chicago
Milwaukee
Detroit
Cleveland
OHIO
INDIANA
Indianapolis
ILLINOIS
Cincinnati
Louisville
Carson City
NEVADA
Great Salt Lake
Salt Lake City
UTAH
Sacramento
San Francisco
CALIFORNIA
Sierra Nevada Mountains
Las Vegas
Grand Canyon
COLORADO
Denver
Kansas City
KANSAS
Missouri River
St. Louis
MISSOURI
KENTUCKY
Nashville
TENNESSEE
Los Angeles
San Diego
Albuquerque
Santa Fe
NEW MEXICO
ARIZONA
Phoenix
Tucson
El Paso
Odessa
TEXAS
Oklahoma City
OKLAHOMA
Dallas
Austin
San Antonio
Houston
Memphis
ARKANSAS
Little Rock
Jackson
MISSISSIPPI
Mississippi River
LOUISIANA
New Orleans
ALABAMA
Birmingham
Atlanta
GEORGIA
Tallahassee
FLORIDA
Tampa
Jacksonville
Miami
Charleston
SOUTH CAROLINA
NORTH CAROLINA
Charlotte
VIRGINIA
Norfolk
WEST VIRGINIA
Appalachian Mountains
PENNSYLVANIA
Philadelphia
NEW YORK
Buffalo
New York
NEW HAMPSHIRE
VERMONT
MAINE
Augusta
Concord
MASSACHUSETTS
Boston
RHODE ISLAND
CONNECTICUT
NEW JERSEY
DELAWARE
MARYLAND
WASHINGTON, DC
Pacific Ocean
Atlantic Ocean
Gulf of Mexico
MEXICO
0 400 km
0 250 miles
N
S
E
W
N north
S south
E east
W west
HAWAII

Capitalization and Punctuation

WRITING TIP

› Learn the basic rules of capitalization and punctuation. They make your writing clearer and allow your readers to focus on what you are trying to say.

Capitalization

Use a capital letter at the start of:

- Every sentence:
  He works on Saturdays. | *Where do you go to school?* | *How much does it cost?*
- Names of places, people, organizations, languages, religions, and nationalities:
  Dallas, Texas | *Maria Hernandez* | *the Red Cross* | *Spanish* | *Catholicism* | *Brazilian*
- Words like *college*, *high school*, and *place*, when they are part of a name:
  I go to City College. (but: *I go to college.*) | *We live on Victory Street.*
- The first word of the title of a book, movie, etc., and all the following words except for articles, prepositions, coordinating conjunctions, and the *to* in infinitives:
  The Catcher in the Rye | *Lord of the Rings* | *Journey to the Center of the Earth*
- Names of days of the week and months of the year:
  Wednesday | *April*
- Titles and ranks used with people's names:
  Mrs. Davis | *Professor Jones* | *Colonel Bedell*
- Titles of family members, when they are used as names:
  Where are the car keys, Mom? (but *My mom works in a bank.*)
- The pronoun *I*, no matter where it is in the sentence:
  I heard that. | *Can I help you?*

Punctuation

Use a **period** (**.**):

- At the end of a sentence that makes a statement:
  The homework is due tomorrow. | *The tickets cost $30.*
- After some abbreviations, and after each letter of the intials in some abbreviations:
  Mr. Lewis | *3 p.m.* | *etc.*

Use a **question mark** (**?**):

- At the end of a question:
  Why did you do that? | *When are they coming?*

Use an **exclamation point** (**!**):

- At the end of a sentence that shows a strong emotion, or that uses a verb in the imperative in a forceful way:
  This is so much fun! | *Come on!*

Use a **comma** (**,**):

- Before a coordinating conjunction such as *and*, *or*, *so*, or *but* that joins two main clauses (each with a subject and verb) in one sentence:
  Josh went to Brad's house, and Lisa went to the pool with her friends. | *You can spend the money now, or you can save it.* | *I was going to call Brianna, but I couldn't find her number.*

- After a word or phrase that introduces a sentence, such as *however*, *for example*, or *furthermore*:
  The chips are lower in fat. However, they do not taste as good as ordinary ones. | *In the next six weeks, we will be reading two important American novels.*
- After a clause at the beginning of a sentence that begins with a subordinating conjunction, such as *if*, *while*, *when*, or *although*:
  If I'm going to be late, I'll call you. | *Although a hundred people were invited, only twenty came to the meeting.*
- To separate spoken words from the rest of the sentence:
  "Hello," he said. | *Emily asked, "Where did you get your hair cut?"*

Use a **colon** (:):

- After a sentence, to introduce a list or example:
  Which of the following animals are mammals: dolphins, sharks, whales, or jellyfish?

Use a **semicolon** (;):

- Between two closely related sentences that are joined together in a single sentence:
  Twenty people came; over a hundred people were invited.

Use an **apostrophe** ('):

- To represent missing letters:
  can't, haven't, he'll, I'm, there's
- To show a possessive:
  Andy's car

Use **quotation marks** (" "):

- To show words which are spoken:
  "I'm sorry I'm late," she said.
- Around titles of short stories, essays, articles, chapters etc.:
  Mark Twain wrote about the contest in his story "The Celebrated Jumping Frog of Calaveras County."
- Around words that are being treated in a special way or used with an ironic meaning:
  The word "rural" is difficult for many foreigners to pronounce. | *The "airplanes" her father made turned out to be models.*

Commas and periods always go inside quotation marks. Question marks, exclamation points, and semicolons go inside or outside, depending on the meaning of the sentence.

Use **parentheses** (( )):

- Around extra information that you want to set off from the rest of the sentence.
  Gutenberg's printing press (completed in 1440) changed the way people got information.

Use a **dash** (—):

- To set extra information off from the rest of the sentence. A dash draws more attention to the information than parentheses. If the extra information comes in the middle of a sentence, use a dash on both sides of the information.
  Hoover Dam — sometimes also known as Boulder Dam — is still one of the largest dams in the world.

Vocabulary Building: Using the Thesaurus Boxes

WRITING TIPS

- Use synonyms in your writing to avoid repeating the same basic word again and again.
- Choose words with precise meanings.
- Choose words with the appropriate level of formality for what you are writing.

Throughout this dictionary, you will find thesaurus boxes at different entries. These boxes list words that are related in meaning to the word you are looking up. Using these thesaurus boxes can help you build your vocabulary and improve your writing. Specifically, use the boxes to help you:

1. Vary Your Word Choice

English has more words than any other language, so there are always many words to choose from. If you choose one basic word and repeat it again and again, people will understand what you are writing. However, your writing will not be as interesting as it could be if you varied your vocabulary and used synonyms. For example, read the following paragraph:

> One **fat** woman told me that she had been trying different diets for years. "I was a little bit **fat** as a child," she said, but it wasn't until I was a teenager that I became really **fat**." Now she is so **fat** that it is dangerous to her health, and her doctor is helping her to lose weight.

fat[1] /fæt/ *adj.* **1** weighing too much because you have too much flesh on your body (ANT) **thin**: *Chris thinks he's **getting fat**.* | *a big fat guy*

THESAURUS

You can call yourself **fat**, but it is not polite to directly tell other people that they are fat: *I'm getting really fat.*
overweight – used as a more polite way of describing someone who is fat: *He's a little overweight.*
big/heavy/large – used as polite ways of describing someone who is big, strong, or fat: *a heavy woman in her fifties* | *He's a pretty big guy.*
obese – used about someone who is extremely fat in a way that is dangerous to their health
chubby – used about someone, especially a baby or a child, who is slightly fat
plump – used to say that someone, especially a woman or a child, is slightly fat in a pleasant way
stout – used to say that an adult is slightly fat
corpulent (formal) – very fat
rotund (formal) – having a fat round body

2 thick or wide (ANT) **thin**: *a fat cigar* **3** [only before

The adjective *fat*, which is a very basic word, is used four times. After looking at the thesaurus box for *fat* you could rewrite the paragraph like this:

> One **large** woman told me that she had been trying different diets for years. "I was **chubby** as a child," she said, "but it wasn't until I was a teenager that I became seriously **overweight**." Now she is **obese**, and her doctor is helping her to lose weight.

2. Write More Precisely

Some words have very general meanings and others have more specific meanings. In general, it is best to use precise words with specific meanings so that your readers know exactly what you mean. The thesaurus boxes can help you find precise words and understand small differences in meaning. Using more precise words makes your writing clearer and more interesting.

For example, *make* is a very general word. It is not wrong to write a sentence such as "The two boys made a dog house," but it is more interesting to write "The two boys built a dog house." The thesaurus box at *make* lists six different words to describe different ways of making something. Using any of these words will give your readers much more precise information than using *make* alone.

make[1] /meɪk/ *v.* (past tense and past participle **made** /meɪd/)
1 PRODUCE STH [T] to produce something by working or doing something: *Can I call you back? I'm making dinner.* | *She made the curtains herself.* | *My flute was made in Japan.*

THESAURUS

produce – to make or grow something in large quantities: *The cheese is produced in Italy.*
manufacture – to make things in large quantities in factories: *The vast majority of American consumer goods are manufactured in China.*
build – to make a house, tunnel, bridge, etc.: *John and his father built the cabin themselves.*
construct – to make something, especially something large, solid, and strong, by putting parts together: *The roof frames were constructed from thick, heavy timbers.*
create – to make something new and original in art, music, fashion, etc.: *Picasso created a completely new style of painting.*
generate – to produce electricity or power: *The building uses solar panels to generate electricity.*

2 DO STH [T] used before some nouns to show that someone does the action of the noun: *Maybe they* ***made*** *a* ***mistake***. | *We've finally* ***made*** *a* ***decision***. |

Sentences with Precise Vocabulary	What the Sentences Tell Us
They have begun **producing** ethanol from corn.	They are making a lot of ethanol, using corn, and they are making it in a factory.
The toys are **manufactured** in China.	The toys are being made in large amounts in factories in China.
They lived in cabins **constructed** from strong logs.	They lived in cabins made from large logs, which they built themselves.
Denise **created** the costumes for the show.	Denise made the costumes using her own ideas.
Wind and sun **generate** clean power.	Wind and sun make electricity that does not hurt the environment.

3. Choose the Appropriate Level of Formality

Some words are more formal or informal than others. When you are writing, it is important to choose words that match the level of formality of your writing. For example, if you look at the thesaurus box for *angry*, you will see that *furious* and *mad* mean the same thing. However, *mad* is an informal word. If you were writing an essay or a story for a class, you could use the word *furious* (*Environmentalists are furious that the law is not being followed.*). The word *mad* would not be appropriate, though, because it is too informal. On the other hand, you could use *mad* if you were writing an email to a friend (*My dad was really mad about the dent in the car.*).

Collocations

STUDY TIP

› When you learn a new noun, make a note of the verbs and the adjectives that are often used with it.

Verbs That Go with Nouns

Some pairs of verbs and nouns sound right when they are used together and others do not. For example, you cannot say ***do*** *a mistake*. You have to say ***make*** *a mistake*. If you say ***do*** *a mistake*, people will understand what you mean, but your English will sound unnatural.

Common Mistakes with Verb + Noun Collocations

✗ He keeps ~~saying~~ jokes that are not funny.
✓ He keeps **telling** jokes that are not funny.

✗ I ~~did~~ a lot of mistakes on my essay.
✓ I **made** a lot of mistakes on my essay.

✗ Why do we have to ~~do~~ so many tests?
✓ Why do we have to **take** so many tests?

This dictionary shows you the correct verbs to use with particular nouns. Look at the entry for **test**. The main collocations are shown in bold:

test[1] /tɛst/ *n.* [C] **1** a set of questions or exercises to measure someone's skill or knowledge: *I have a history test tomorrow.* | *Paul* ***passed/failed*** *his driver's* ***test.*** | *All students must* ***take a*** *placement* ***test.*** ▸ Don't say "make a test." Say "take a test." ◂ **2** a medical examination on a part of your body: *a blood test* | *a* ***test for*** *HIV* | *They don't know what's wrong with her yet – they're* ***running/doing*** *some* ***tests.*** **3** a process used to find out whether something works, whether it is safe, etc.: *In science, we did a* ***test for*** *chemicals in the water.* **4** a situation in which the qualities of something are clearly shown: *Today's race is a real* ***test of*** *skill.* | *Living together will really* ***put*** *their relationship* ***to the test*** (=find out how good it is).

make and *do*, *have* and *take*

Learning *verb* + *noun* combinations will improve your English and make it sound more correct and natural. Look at the following table. It shows collocations for *make*, *do*, *have*, and *take*.

make	have	do	take
preparations	an operation	damage	a picture
a decision	a baby	research	a bath/shower
a discovery	a party	harm	lessons
a phone call	fun	work	a test
a noise	a problem	business	a look
a promise	a cold	the dishes	a walk

make	have	do	take
a complaint	an argument	the shopping	a break
a choice	a headache	good	notes
breakfast			risks
progress			a breath
an effort			
a comment			
a suggestion			
a list			

Adjectives That Go with Nouns

If you want to describe a noun, there are many adjectives to choose from. Some adjectives are always used with particular nouns. Somebody who eats a lot is *a* ***big*** *eater*, but somebody who smokes a lot is *a* ***heavy*** *smoker* (NOT *a* ***big*** *smoker*). When you look up a noun in the dictionary, the entry tells you if there are adjectives that often go with it. Look at the entry for **sign** In the actual entry, you will see some collocations in bold. But there is also a collocations box after the entry that lists a large number of *adjective + noun* collocations. These collocation boxes can be found throughout the dictionary.

sign[1] /saɪn/ *n.* [C] **1** a piece of paper, metal, etc. with words or a picture that gives people information, a warning, or instructions: *Follow the* ***signs*** *that* ***say*** *"Montlake Bridge."* | *a no smoking sign* **2** an event, fact, etc. that shows that something exists or is happening, or that it will happen in the future: *The house* ***showed*** *no* ***signs of*** *a forced entry.* | *That's a* ***good/bad sign!*** | *Extreme tiredness is an early* ***sign of*** *the disease.* | ***There are*** *worrying* ***signs*** *that the agreement will fail.*

COLLOCATIONS

clear/obvious/visible sign – one that you can clearly see or understand
good/positive/encouraging sign – one that tells you that something good might happen
bad/warning sign – one that tells you that something bad might happen
early sign – one that shows what is happening at the beginning of a process, situation, etc.
sure sign – one that proves that something is true

3 a picture or shape that has a particular meaning

Nouns That Go with Nouns

Sometimes, when two or more nouns often appear together, they only sound correct in English if they are used in a particular order. For example, you always say **bread and butter**. If you say **butter and bread** it sounds very strange.

Here are examples of nouns matched with their correct partners (look them up in the dictionary if you are not sure what they mean):

knife and fork **black and white** **room and board** **dos and don'ts**
law and order **cup and saucer** **pros and cons** **ladies and gentlemen**
salt and pepper

›› See also **Grammar Guide** on **Intensifying Adjectives** and **Intensifying Adverbs**

Idioms

Using idioms in your writing can make your writing more natural and interesting. However, idioms are sometimes tricky to use, and not all idioms are appropriate for all types of writing. In fact, many idioms are best used only in spoken English or informal English. Most of the idioms below should not be used when writing essays or formal letters.

STUDY TIPS

- Always look idioms up in the dictionary and make sure you have understood their meaning.
- Check if the idiom is informal or slang. If it is, be careful when you use it, and do not use it in formal writing.
- Remember that you cannot usually translate idioms directly from one language into another.
- Learning and using idioms can be fun, but remember not to use too many idioms together, as this can sound strange or unnatural.

What Is an Idiom?

An idiom is a group of two or more words that have a special meaning. This meaning is different from the meanings of the individual words when they are used separately. For example, if you are told that somebody is **up the creek**, you cannot guess the meaning from the usual meanings of **up** + **the** + **creek**. This idiom actually means "in a difficult situation."

In this dictionary, each idiom is shown in **bold** at the beginning of a new sense. For example, the entry for **head** shows these five idioms after the main senses:

7 (from) head to toe/foot over your whole body: *The kids were covered from head to toe in mud.*
8 put your heads together (spoken) to discuss a difficult problem together: *If we put our heads together, we'll think of a way.*
9 go over sb's head a) to be too difficult for someone to understand: *Most of the lecture went way over my head.* **b)** to ask a more important person to deal with something than the person you would normally ask
10 keep/lose your head to behave reasonably or stupidly in a difficult situation: *I guess I just lost my head for a minute.*
11 go to sb's head a) to make someone feel more important than s/he really is: *It's too bad Dave **let** his promotion **go to his head**.* **b)** to make someone quickly feel slightly drunk
12 come to a head if a problem comes to a head, it becomes worse and you have to do something about it immediately: *The situation came to a head when the workers went on strike.*

Idiom Meanings

We saw above that **up the creek** means "in a difficult situation." You could also say that someone was **in hot water** or **in a fix**. Often, there are many idioms that mean something similar, but are used in slightly different situations. For example, there are many idioms that people use to talk about anger. The following table shows just a few of them. Look up the words in **bold** in the dictionary to find out exactly what they mean.

ANGRY		
to angrily criticize or insult someone – • **bite** someone's head off • give someone a **piece** of your mind • **jump** down someone's throat	**to become suddenly very angry –** • blow a **fuse** • **fly** off the handle • go **ballistic** • go **bananas** • have/throw a **fit** • see **red**	**to angrily say something or complain about something –** • be up in **arms** (about something) • let/blow off **steam**

When you learn a new idiom it is very important to make sure that you understand what it means. Do you know the difference between **going ballistic** and **seeing red**? The dictionary will make it clear.

Metaphor in Idioms

If we say that someone is **up the creek**, we do not mean that they are actually in a stream of water far away from any bridges. **Up the creek** has a metaphorical meaning – it is understood as a difficult situation to be in. A metaphor is a way of describing something by comparing it to something else that has similar qualities. Many idioms use metaphor in this way. For example, words relating to movement, especially beginning to drive or fly, are often used as a metaphor for starting something:

- get off the **ground**
- get under **way**
- get the **show** on the road
- set the **ball** rolling

Similarly, stopping a movement or work, or not being able to move, are metaphors for something ending:

- put the **brakes** on something
- call it a **day**
- go down the **tubes**
- have your **back** against the wall

Many idioms are formed with verbs that are not used with their literal meanings. It can be very difficult to guess what these idioms mean. For example, ***sweep*** *someone off his/her feet* means "to make someone feel strongly attracted to you in a romantic way." It does not have anything to do the ordinary meanings of sweep: "to clean the dirt from a floor using a broom" or "to move somewhere quickly or move something quickly."

Sometimes, two idioms can use the same verb, which makes them look very similar. However, they may still have very different meanings. For example:

- ***hit*** *the roof* means "to become very angry."
- ***hit*** *the road* means "to start on a trip."

By contrast, sometimes several different idioms can mean the same thing. For example, the following idioms all describe a situation in which someone does not know or understand something:

- *not have a* ***clue***
- *go/be over your* ***head***
- *be in the* ***dark***

» If you want more information on idioms, the ***Longman American Idioms Dictionary*** shows clearly the meaning and use of thousands of spoken and written idioms.

Writing Essays

WRITING TIPS

- Give your essay a clear structure with a beginning (introduction), middle (body), and end (conclusion).
- Use clear, short sentences. Use common words that you know well, but avoid very informal words.
- Do not use contracted forms such as *don't* and *can't*. These are used in spoken and informal English.
- After you write the first draft, reread your essay and make changes.
- Remember to proofread and check your punctuation, capitalization, and spelling.

There are many things you can do in an essay, but you should decide what type of essay you are writing before you start. Doing this will help you organize your ideas. In your essay, you can:

1. Compare two or more things and decide which is best
2. Discuss the advantages and disadvantages of doing something
3. Discuss a problem and suggest a solution

Make sure that the topic you choose includes an opinion and is not just a collection of facts that everyone already knows. Remember your readers and make your essay as interesting or surprising as possible.

Organizing Your Essays

Your completed essay should have an introduction, a body, and a conclusion. Each part of the essay has a specific purpose:

Introduction (usually one paragraph)	1. Introduce the subject and say why it is important and of interest to your readers. 2. Describe in a general way the areas that you will discuss in your essay. 3. Give your thesis statement, usually at the end of the introduction. The thesis statement is a clear opinion that you will prove in your essay.
Body (one paragraph for each main idea)	1. Describe the main points of the situation or problem in a sensible order. Save your strongest points for the end of the essay. 2. Organize your discussion into paragraphs and give each main point its own paragraph. 3. Write a topic sentence for each paragraph, that states the main point of the paragraph. Use the rest of the paragraph to give facts, details, and examples that support the topic sentence.
Conclusion (usually one paragraph)	1. Give a summary of the points you have made and present your conclusion. 2. Make sure your conclusion matches your thesis statement in the introduction. If they express different opinions, you need to make changes until they do match. 3. Do not introduce any major new ideas in the conclusion. If there is another idea you want to discuss, put it in the body of the essay.

Linking Your Ideas

You can use the following useful phrases to organize your essay and link your ideas together. If you understand and learn these useful phrases, it will make your arguments clearer. These phrases can all come at the beginning of sentences or paragraphs. Try to vary your use of these phrases and avoid using the same one over and over.

To Introduce the Subject	*It is a well-known fact that …* *Many people believe that …* *It is often claimed that …* *There are several ways of looking at the problem of …* *One of the most important issues in society today is …*
To Start the Discussion	*First of all, / Firstly, / To begin with, /* *In the first place, …* (**NOT** *Firstly of all*) *Let us begin by looking at …* *First of all, let us consider …* *The first thing that should be noted is …* *It is worth stating from the outset that …*
To Continue the Discussion	*Secondly, …* (**NOT** *Second* or *Secondly of all*) *Thirdly, …* (It is rare to use *Fourthly, Fifthly*, etc.) *Lastly, / Finally, …* (**NOT** *In the last / final place*) *As far as … is concerned / As regards … / As for …* *This brings us to the question of whether/how/ who etc. …* *It should also be noted/stressed that …* *Furthermore, / Moreover, / In addition, / Besides this, / What is more, …*
To Show the Other Side of the Discussion	*However, / Nevertheless, …* *The opposite may also be true.* *There is more than one way of looking at this problem.* *(On the one hand …) On the other hand, …* If you use *On the one hand …*, you should also use *On the other hand …* in the following sentence or paragraph.
To Show Similarities	*Likewise, / Similarly, / In the same way, …*
To Give Examples	*For example, …* *For instance, …*
To State a Result or Effect	*Therefore, / As a result, / Consequently, …*
To Present a Conclusion or a Solution to the Problem	*On balance, …* *To sum up, / In summary, / In conclusion, it would seem that …* *This brings us to the conclusion that …* *To conclude, it seems likely that …*
To Express Your Personal Opinion	*In my opinion, …* (do NOT write *I think* after this phrase) *My personal opinion is that …* *My own view of this is that …* *It is my opinion that …*

Writing Letters and E-mails

WRITING TIPS

- Choose the appropriate level of formality and make sure that you use the same level of formality from the beginning to the end. Use the boxes below to guide you.
- For a formal style, do not use contractions like *I'm*, *I've*, or *you'd*, and avoid abbreviations like *etc.* and *e.g.*
- Use paragraphs to organize the main points in your letter.

Writing Letters

You use different styles for different kinds of letters. The box below will help you to decide how to start and finish your letter.

	Formal Letters	Informal Letters
Ways of Opening a Letter (The Greeting or Salutation)	**In formal or business letters, use a colon (:) after the salutation:** ***Dear Mr./Mrs./Ms./Miss*** + family name: (In a business context, it is best to use **Ms.** rather than **Mrs.** or **Miss** as a title for a woman, and it should always be used when you do not know if the woman is married or not) ***Dear Dr./Professor*** + family name: (do **NOT** use the person's first name with **Dear Dr./Professor**) ***Dear Sir or Madam***: or ***Dear Sir/Madam***: (use this when you do not know whether you are writing to a man or a woman) ***Dear Sir***: (use this when you do not know the man's name) ***Dear Madam***: (use this when you do not know the woman's name) ***To Whom It May Concern***: (use this when you do not know the person's name and the letter is very formal)	**In informal or personal letters, use a comma (,) after the salutation:** ***Dear*** + first name, (use this when you know the person well enough to use their first name only) ***Hi/Hello*** (+ first name), (use this in letters to friends and people that you know well)

	Formal Letters	Informal Letters
Phrases Used in the Body of a Letter	*With regard to your letter of July 18 …* *I am writing to enquire about …* *I am writing to confirm that …* *I am writing to apologize for …* *I am writing to inform you that …* *I am writing in response to your advertisement in …* *I would appreciate it if you could …* *Please accept my apologies for …* *I am enclosing …* *Please do not hesitate to contact me if you have any questions/ problems.* *I can be contacted at the address above or at (555) 555-1234.* *I look forward to hearing from you.* *Thank you in advance for …*	*I was really pleased to get your letter. / Thanks for your letter.* *It was great to see you/hear from you.* *Sorry it's been so long since I last wrote. / Sorry I haven't written for so long.* *I hope everything is fine. / How are you? / How're things?* *Just a quick note to let you know …* *Give me a call and let me know whether you can make it.* *Let me know when you are free so we can get together.* *It would be great to hear from you.* *Hope to see you soon. / Really looking forward to seeing you. / Talk to you soon.* *Write soon. / Keep in touch. / Drop me a line when you get a chance.* *Give my love/regards to …*
Ways of Ending a Letter (The Closing)	**Use one of these before signing your first and last name:** ***Sincerely,*** ***Yours truly,*** ***Sincerely yours,***	**Use one of these before signing your first name:** ***Love, / Lots of love (from),*** (use this in letters to your close friends and family) ***All the best, / Best wishes,*** ***Take care,*** ***Regards, / Best regards,*** (use this in letters to people you work with or do not know very well)

Writing E-mails

E-mails to companies and organizations are usually formal, and you can use the same beginnings and endings as in a formal letter. E-mails to friends and colleagues are usually written in a very brief and informal style:

Informal E-mails:

You can open the email with:
Hi, *Hi* + first name, *Dear* + first name, (slightly more formal)
first name only, no name, and no greeting

You can end the e-mail with:
All the best, + your first name *Best wishes,* + your first name
Regards, (slightly more formal) + your first name
Love, (only to friends and family) + your first name
Talk to you soon/later, + your first name
your first name only the first letter of your first name only (informal)

2334 Greenwood Road, Los Angeles, CA 90014

March 3, 2008

Ms. Ashley Hanson
Director of Human Resources
Northern Publishing
8671 Johnson Avenue
Minneapolis, MN 55403

Dear Ms. Hanson:

Thank you for taking the time to meet with me this morning and tell me more about the technical support manager position. I really liked everyone I met and am excited about the possibility of working at your company. I feel sure that I could be an asset to your IT team.

As we discussed in the interview, I would be able to begin working as early as next month. If you have any further questions, please do not hesitate to contact me. My phone number, once again, is (213) 555-4965. I look forward to speaking with you again soon.

Sincerely,

Michael Woods

Michael Woods

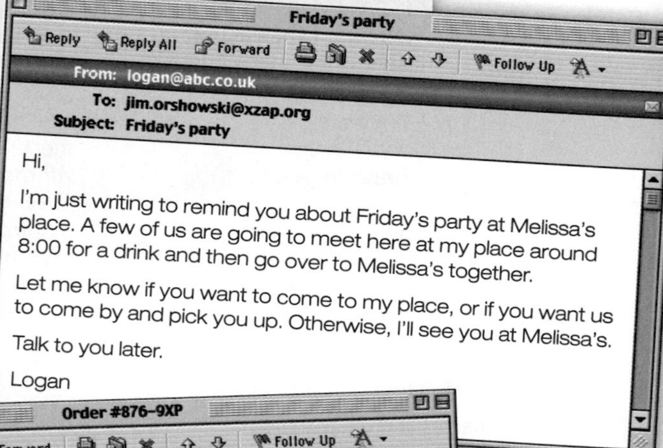

Friday's party

Reply | Reply All | Forward | Follow Up

From: logan@abc.co.uk
To: jim.orshowski@xzap.org
Subject: Friday's party

Hi,

I'm just writing to remind you about Friday's party at Melissa's place. A few of us are going to meet here at my place around 8:00 for a drink and then go over to Melissa's together.

Let me know if you want to come to my place, or if you want us to come by and pick you up. Otherwise, I'll see you at Melissa's.

Talk to you later.

Logan

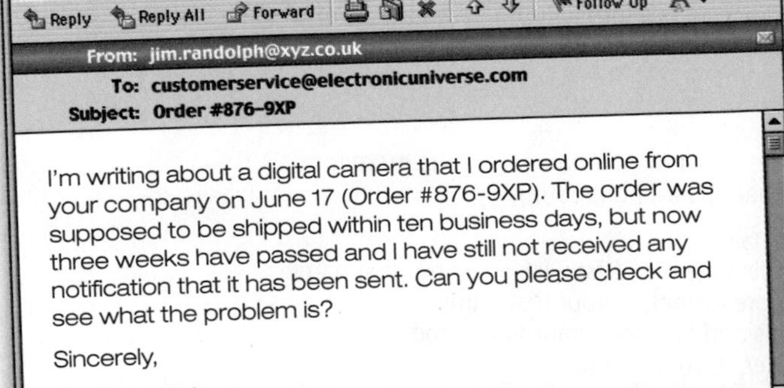

Order #876-9XP

Reply | Reply All | Forward | Follow Up

From: jim.randolph@xyz.co.uk
To: customerservice@electronicuniverse.com
Subject: Order #876-9XP

I'm writing about a digital camera that I ordered online from your company on June 17 (Order #876-9XP). The order was supposed to be shipped within ten business days, but now three weeks have passed and I have still not received any notification that it has been sent. Can you please check and see what the problem is?

Sincerely,

Jim Randolph

Writing Résumés and Cover Letters

WRITING TIPS

- Make your résumé and cover letter as concise as possible.
- Focus on your relevant work experience and your strongest points.
- Use short, clear sentences. Do not use contractions and informal language.

Writing a Résumé (See Résumé on page A41)

A résumé is a document that lists your experience and qualifications. You should give each section a clear heading, keep explanations short, focus on what is relevant, and put the most important or relevant information first. Résumés should usually be no more than one page.

It is a good idea to modify your résumé slightly, depending on the job you are applying for, in order to highlight your most relevant qualifications.

Section Heading	Information to Include
Personal Information	Include your name, address, phone number, and email address at the top of the first page. Do NOT include your age or birth date, height, weight, or marital status. It is not usual to attach a picture of yourself.
Objective	Give a brief statement of the type of position that you are looking for. Make sure this statement matches the job you are applying for. It is common to include an objective, but not required.
Work Experience	List your work experience in reverse order, starting with your most recent job. Give the title of your position, the name and location of your employer, and the dates you worked there. If you have had many previous jobs, you can list only your most relevant work experience.
Education	List the degrees you have earned in reverse order, and the names and locations of academic institutions you have attended. If you have attended a college or university, you do not usually mention your high school or earlier schools.
Awards and Achievements	List, in reverse order, any special awards or achievements that are relevant to the field of work you are applying for.
Skills	List skills that would be helpful in the job you are applying for. These can include foreign language skills or experience with different types of software.
Related Coursework	List any courses you have taken that would be helpful in the job you are applying for.
Interests	List any interests or hobbies you want the employer to know about.
References	You can list the names and phone numbers of two or three people who have worked with you or who know you and your work history well. You should also explain their relationship to you. Alternatively, you may simply write "Available upon request" under this heading.

Writing a Cover Letter (See Cover Letter on page A41)

A cover letter is a formal letter you write to accompany your résumé when you are applying for a job. It is your chance to highlight the most important points in your résumé and explain why you should be interviewed for the job. It should not be handwritten and should not be longer than one page.

Section	Information to Include	Sample Phrases
Your Address	Include your address (but not your name) at the top of the page.	*2334 Greenwood Road* *Los Angeles, CA 90014*
Date	Include the date on a separate line below your address.	*February 4, 2008*
The Company's Address	Include the name and title of the person you are writing to (if you have it), the name of the company, and its address.	*Ms. Ashley Hanson* *Director of Human Resources* *Northern Publishing* *8671 Johnson Avenue* *Minneapolis, MN 55403*
Opening or Salutation	Write directly to the person who will look at your application. If the person's name does not appear in the job advertisement and you cannot find out the name by calling the company, use the appropriate title.	*Dear Ms. Hanson:* *Dear Mr. Matsunami:* *Dear Human Resources Director:*
First Paragraph	State clearly the job you are applying for and how you learned about it. You can also state why you are particularly well qualified for the job.	*I am writing to apply for the technical support manager position that was advertised in today's* Post.
Body Paragraph(s)	Talk about the highlights of your résumé here. List strongest qualities first. Explain in more detail experience or qualifications that are particularly relevant. Do not simply repeat the information in your résumé, and do not list details that are not relevant to the job you are applying for.	*As you can see from my enclosed/attached résumé,* *I hold a B.S. in Computer Science from Southridge State University.* *I have worked in a number of technical positions in the publishing field.*
Last Paragraph	Emphasize the qualities and skills that you will bring to the company you are applying to. State your availability for an interview and provide contact information. (See model letter)	*I am confident that I can bring many new ideas, technical expertise, and a dynamic management style to your team.* *I would enjoy meeting with you in person to discuss my qualifications, etc.*
Closing	Close with "Sincerely." Type your first and last name below your signature.	*Sincerely,* *Michael Woods* *Michael Woods*

2334 Greenwood Road, Los Angeles, CA 90014

February 4, 2008

Ms. Ashley Hanson
Director of Human Resources
Northern Publishing
8671 Johnson Avenue
Minneapolis, MN 55403

Dear Ms. Hanson:

I am writing to apply for the technical support manager position that was advertised in today's *Post*. I believe that my technical background, work experience, and managerial skills make me an ideal candidate for the job.

As you can see from my enclosed résumé, I hold a B.S. in Computer Science from Southridge State University and have worked, since my graduation in 2002, in a number of technical positions in the publishing field. Most recently, I managed a team of eleven support staff at Pearl Publishing in Los Angeles, which I built up over the past three years from a team of eight. During that time, I completely redesigned the company's help desk procedures and led regular training seminars.

I have spent the past 12 years on the West Coast, but I am originally from the Midwest. I am very familiar with Minneapolis and would welcome the opportunity to move back closer to home and work in that vibrant city.

While I have enjoyed my time at Pearl and have learned a great deal, I am now ready for the challenges that a larger office such as Northern Publishing could provide. It has been exciting to be a part of a growing company at Pearl, and I am confident I could bring that same level of excitement to your team at Northern with my technical expertise and dynamic management style.

I would enjoy meeting with you in person to discuss my qualifications and learn more about the opening at your company. You can reach me by phone at (213) 555-4965 or by email at mwz@woods.com to set up an appointment. I look forward to hearing from you.

Sincerely,

Michael Woods

Michael Woods

2334 Greenwood Road, Los Angeles, CA 90014

Michael Woods

Tel: (213) 555-4965
E-mail: mwz@woods.com

Objective: To find a technical support position in the field of publishing

Experience: **2004 – present** Pearl Publishing Los Angeles, CA
Technical Support Manager
- Managed IT support staff of eleven people.
- Led regular training seminars.
- Redesigned company-wide help desk procedures.

2003–2004 Mayfair Books Southridge, WA
Systems Administrator
- Managed LAN network.
- Implemented training courses for new analysts.

2002–2003 Mayfair Books Southridge, WA
Information Technology Associate
- Maintained computer system of editorial and design staff.
- Worked on team of twenty IT associates to improve overall operations.

Education: **1998–2002** Southridge State University Southridge, WA
- B.S., Computer Science.
- Graduated Summa Cum Laude.

Interests: Salsa dancing, running, gardening, carpentry, computers

References: Available upon request.

Word Building

Prefix	Meaning	Example
a-, an-	opposite; without; not	amoral, atypical, antonym
anti-	opposed to; against	antifreeze, antidote
audi-, audio-	relating to sound; relating to hearing	audiovisual, auditorium
auto-	of or by yourself	autobiography, automobile
bi-	two; twice	bilingual, biannual
bio-	relating to living things	biology, biochemistry
cent-, centi-	100; 100th part of something	centipede, centimeter
circum-	all the way around something	circumstance, circumference
co-, col-, com-, con-, cor-	with; together	coexist, collect, compassion, confederation, correlation
contra-	against	contraceptive
counter-	opposite; against	counterproductive
cyber-	relating to computers	cyberspace, cyberpunk
de-	to do or make the opposite of; remove from; reduce	decriminalize, decaffeinated, devalue
dis-	opposite	disapprove, dishonesty
down-	to a lower position; to or toward the bottom	downturn, downriver, downstairs
eco-	relating to the environment	ecological
electri-, electro-	relating to electricity	electrify, electrocute
em-, en-	to make something have a quality	empower, enlarge
ex-	no longer being or doing	ex-wife, ex-football player
ex-	out; from	exit, export
extra-	outside; beyond	extraterrestrial, extracurricular
geo-	relating to the earth	geology, geography
hydr-, hydro-	relating to or using water	hydroelectric, hydrant
il-, im-, in-, ir-	not	illogical, impossible, inconvenient, irrational
im-, in-	in; into	immerse, incoming
inter-, intro-, intra-	between; together; within	international, introduce, intravenous
mis-	bad; badly	misfortune, misbehave
mono-	one	monogram, monologue
multi-	many	multicolored, multicultural
non-	not	nonsmoking, nonstandard
over-	too much; beyond; outer; additional	overpopulate, overhang, overcoat, overtime
poly-	many	polygon
post-	later than; after	postgraduate, postpone
pre-	before	prewar, preview
pro-	in favor of	pro-American
re-	again	rewrite, redo, rewind
semi-	half; partly	semicircle, semiprecious
sub-	under; below; less important or powerful	subway, substandard, subcommittee
super-	larger; greater; more powerful	supermarket, superhuman, supervisor
sym-, syn-	with; together	sympathy, synthesis
tele-	at or over a long distance	telescope, television
theo-	relating to God or gods	theology
therm-, thermo-	relating to heat	thermostat, thermometer
trans-	on or to the far side of something; between two things	transatlantic, transportation
tri-	three	tricycle, triangle
ultra-	beyond; extremely	ultrasonic, ultramodern
un-	not; opposite	unhappy, unfair, undress
under-	too little	underdeveloped, underage
uni-	one	unilateral
vice-	next in rank below the most important person	Vice-President, vice-captain

Suffix	Meaning	Example
-ability, -ibility	used in order to make nouns from adjectives that end in -able and -ible	accountability, flexibility
-able, -ible	capable of; having a particular quality	manageable, comfortable, reversible, responsible
-al, -ial	relating to something; the act of doing something	electrical, financial, refusal, denial
-an, -ian, -ean	from or relating to a place; someone who has a particular job or knows about a particular subject; relating to, or similar to, a time, thing, or person; someone who has a particular belief	American, suburban, librarian, historian, subterranean, Victorian, Christian
-ant, -ent	someone or something that does something	servant, disinfectant, resident, repellent
-ar	relating to something	muscular, stellar
-ary	relating to something	customary, planetary
-ation, -tion, -ion	the act of doing something; the state or result of doing something	examination, combination, completion, election
-cy	used in order to make nouns	accuracy
-en	made of something; to make something have a particular quality	wooden, golden, darken, strengthen
-ence, -ance, -ency, -ancy	a state or quality; the act of doing something	intelligence, obedience, performance, tendency, presidency, pregnancy
-er, -or, -ar, -r	someone or something that does something	teacher, actor, beggar, writer, photocopier, accelerator
-ery, -ry	an act; a quality; a place where something is done or made	bribery, bravery, snobbery, distillery, bakery
-ful	full of	beautiful, harmful
-goer	someone who goes somewhere regularly	moviegoer, churchgoer
-graph, -graphy	something that is written or drawn	autograph, biography
-hood	the state or time of being something	childhood, manhood, womanhood
-ial, -al	relating to something	managerial, coastal
-ic, -ical	of; like; relating to a particular thing	photographic, historical
-ify	to affect in a particular way	purify, clarify, terrify
-ish	people or language; having a quality	Spanish, English, childish, selfish
-ism	a belief or set of ideas; the act of doing something	Buddhism, capitalism, criticism
-ist	relating to a political or religious belief	socialist, Methodist
-ity	having a particular quality	stupidity, regularity
-ive	having a particular quality	creative, descriptive
-ize	to make something have a quality; to change something into a different state	modernize, crystallize
-less	without something	childless, careless, endless
-logue, -log	relating to words	monologue, catalog
-ly	in a particular way; at regular times	slowly, quickly, hourly
-ment	the act or result of doing something	government, development
-ness	used in order to make nouns	happiness, softness
-ology	the study or science of something	geology, technology
-or	someone or something that does something	doctor, actor, inventor, radiator, incinerator, incubator
-ory	a place or thing used for doing something; having a particular quality	laboratory, satisfactory, obligatory
-ous, -ious	used in order to make adjectives from nouns	dangerous, furious
-proof	not allowing something to come in, come through, or destroy something	soundproof, waterproof, fireproof
-ship	having a particular position; an art or skill	membership, friendship, scholarship
-wear	clothes of a particular type	menswear, womenswear, sportswear
-y	full of or covered with something; tending to do something	hairy, fuzzy, sleepy, curly

Etymology

Etymology is the study and description of the origin of words. Etymology can tell us a lot about the long history of the English language. Many everyday words go back to the 5th and 6th century AD, when English was first starting to develop as a language. For example, **eat** and **drink** come from the Old English words *etan* and *drinkan*. **House** and **town** come from the Old English words *hus* and *tun*. When England was invaded by the Normans in 1066, many French words started to come into the English language, for example **parliament** and **jail**.

Etymology also shows that words have come into English from almost every language in the world. For example, **sugar** comes from the Arabic word *sukkar*, **tomato** comes from the Nahuatl word *tomatl*, and **shampoo** comes from the Hindi word *capo*.

Some words are named after a particular person or place, for example **teddy bear** is named after President Theodore Roosevelt, whose nickname was "Teddy," and who liked hunting bears. The **turkey** is named after the country Turkey, because it looked like another type of bird that came from that country.

The evolution of language

People sometimes talk about the "original" meaning of a word, and believe that the meaning of the word is fixed. In fact, language does not stand still, and the meaning of words can change dramatically over a long period of time. The study of etymology shows a number of cases of this.

For example, the word **nice** comes from an old French word that meant "stupid," which came from the Latin word *nescius*, which meant "lacking in knowledge." The word **hospital** comes from the old French word *hospitale*, which meant simply "a place to stay." This later came to be used about a place where poor people could stay, before being used about places for medical treatment.

Why is etymology useful when studying scientific and academic words?

Etymology can also help us understand new words and predict what they might mean. Many scientific and academic words come from Latin and Greek. Often the same Latin or Greek part of the word are used for different words.

For example, in geometry, there are several words that are formed from the Greek word *gonia*, which means "angle."

Word	Meaning	Other Greek Word
penta<u>gon</u>	a flat shape with five sides and five angles	In Greek, *pente* means "five."
hexa<u>gon</u>	a flat shape with six sides and six angles	In Greek, *hex* means "six."
hepta<u>gon</u>	a flat shape with seven sides and seven angles	In Greek, *hepta* means "seven."
octa<u>gon</u>	a flat shape with eight sides and eight angles	In Greek, *okto* means "eight."
poly<u>gon</u>	a flat shape with three or more sides and angles	In Greek, *poly* means "many."

There are also a number of words that are formed from the Greek word *onyma*, which means "name:"

Word	Meaning	Other Greek Word
synonym	a word that has the same meaning as another word	In Greek, *syn* means "together" or "same."
antonym	a word that has the opposite meaning	In Greek, *anti-* means "opposite."
homonym	a word that has the same sound and spelling, for example **bear** (*noun*) and **bear** (*verb*)	In Greek, *homos* means "same."

There are several words that are formed from the Latin word *vorare*, which means "to eat:"

Word	Meaning	Other Latin Word
herbivore	an animal that only eats plants	In Latin, *herba* means "plants."
carnivore	an animal that only eats meat	In Latin, *caro* means "meat."
omnivore	an animal that eats everything	In Latin, *omnis* means "everything."
have a voracious appetite	you want to eat or do something a lot	In Latin, *vorax* means "greedy." This originally came from *vorare*, meaning "to eat."

In medicine, there are several words formed from the Greek word *haima*, which means "blood."

Word	Meaning	Other Word
hemoglobin	a red substance in the blood that carries oxygen and iron	In Latin, *globulus* means "a small globe" or "a drop."
hemophilia	a serious disease in which people lose a lot of blood after getting a cut	In Greek, *philia* means "fondness."
hemorrhage	a medical condition in which an area in someone's body loses too much blood	In Greek, *rhegnynai* means "to burst out or flow."

Lastly, many the names of scientific subjects are based on the Greek word *logia*, which means "study."

Word	Meaning	Other Greek Word
geology	the study of rocks	In Greek, *ge* means "earth."
psychology	the study of the mind	In Greek, *psykhe* means "soul" or "mind."
anthropology	the scientific study of people and societies	In Greek, *anthropos* means "human being."
paleontology	the study of fossils (ancient animals preserved in rock)	In Greek, *palois* means "ancient" and *onta* means "living things."

Countable and Uncountable Nouns

Countable Nouns

Things that you can count are called **countable nouns**. These are often (but not always) objects such as *apple* and *house*:

a phone **two phones** **a desk** **six desks**

In this dictionary, countable nouns appear with a label like this: [**C**]

REMEMBER

1 Countable nouns can be both singular (*table*) and plural (*tables*).
2 A singular countable noun is almost always used with an article or other determiner (for example, *a*, *another*, or *the*).
3 A plural countable noun is often used without a determiner. For example, when you are talking in general about something, *the* is not used: *Apples are sweeter than lemons*.
4 When a noun is singular, the following verb is also singular: *A tiger has black stripes.*
5 When a noun is plural, the following verb is also plural: *Tigers have black stripes.*

Uncountable Nouns

Things that you cannot count are called **uncountable nouns**. Uncountable nouns are usually the names of substances (such as *water*, *grass*), qualities (such as *happiness*), collections (such as *furniture*, *money*), and other things that we do not see as individual objects (such as *electricity*).

In this dictionary, uncountable nouns appear with a label like this: [**U**]

Common Mistakes with Uncountable Nouns

Here are some common mistakes that students make with uncountable nouns:

✗ I want to give you ~~an~~ **advice**.
✓ I want to give you a **piece of advice**.

✗ We have ~~many **homeworks**~~ in this class.
✓ We have **a lot of homework** in this class.

✗ I need more ~~**informations**~~ for my paper.
✓ I need more **information** for my paper.

REMEMBER

1 Uncountable nouns NEVER have a plural form. You say *some furniture* (NOT *some furnitures*).
2 You do not use *a*, *an*, or *another*, or words such as *many*, *these*, or *three* with uncountable nouns. These determiners are only used with countable nouns.
3 You DO use *the* with uncountable nouns when you are referring to a particular thing: *The weather was cold* (NOT *Weather was cold*) or *She finally had the luck she needed* (NOT *She finally had luck she needed*).
4 The verb that follows an uncountable noun is always singular. You say *The music was beautiful* (NOT *The music were beautiful*).

Quantity

As we have already seen, you use different words and expressions in English to describe the *number* of countable nouns and *amount* of uncountable nouns. The table below will help you to learn and remember the correct way to describe these two types of nouns:

Countable Nouns	Uncountable Nouns
How **many** students?	How **much** fruit?
a student	**fruit**, **a piece of** fruit
some / **several** / **a few** / **not many** students	**some** / **a little** / **not much** fruit
fewer students	**less** fruit
not ... any / **no** students	**not ... any** / **no** fruit
none	**none**

Note that some nouns that are **countable** in your language may be **uncountable** in English. The nouns in the list below are all uncountable nouns in English.

advice, **equipment**, **furniture**, **hardware/software**, **homework**, **housework**, **information**, **knowledge**, **machinery**, **money**, **scenery**, **stuff**, **traffic**, **weather**

Counting Uncountable Nouns with *A Piece of ...*

If you want to talk about one or more individual examples of an uncountable noun, you cannot use *a* or *an*. For example, you cannot say *an advice*, you have to say *a piece of advice*. Here are some more uncountable nouns that can be used with *a piece of*:

information an interesting *piece of* information
paper a blank *piece of* paper
advice a helpful *piece of* advice
cake Would you like *a piece of* cake?
research an interesting *piece of* research

Nouns That Are Countable AND Uncountable

Some nouns can have both a countable [**C**] and an uncountable [**U**] meaning. This often happens with the names of animals that are also a type of food:

> **fish**[1] /fɪʃ/ *n.* (plural **fish** *or* **fishes**) **1** [C] an animal that lives in water and uses its FINS and tail to swim: *How many **fish** did you **catch**?* **2** [U] the flesh of a fish used as food: *We had fish for dinner.* [ORIGIN: Old English *fisc*; related to *Pisces*]

Some nouns are countable and uncountable in the same meaning. These are often things we eat and drink. You can talk about an amount of the food or drink (uncountable), or about different types of the food or drink (countable). In this dictionary, these nouns appear with a label like this: [**C, U**]:

> **cheese** /tʃiz/ *n.* [C,U] a solid food made from milk, that is usually white or yellow: *a **grilled cheese sandwich** | a **piece/slice/wedge of cheese** | I'd like a bagel with **cream cheese**.* [ORIGIN: Old English *cese*]

Verb Patterns

STUDY TIP

- Whenever you learn a new verb, look it up in the dictionary and study the grammatical patterns that can follow it.
- Use the example sentences in the dictionary to help you to learn these patterns. There are many different patterns that can follow verbs but not all of them can be used with every verb.

Read the passage below:

> Juan **wanted to enter** the school science fair. He **finished reading** the requirements and **asked his friend to work** with him and **help him decide** what to do. He **thought about making** a robot, but they **couldn't afford** the materials. His friend **advised him** to choose something cheaper to do.

The patterns for the verbs in this passage are:

want **to do** sth, finish **doing** sth, ask sb **to do** sth, help (sb) **decide** sth, think **about doing** sth, (can't) **afford** sth, advise sb **to do** sth

Common Mistakes with Verb Patterns

✗ I want ~~that you do~~ more research.
✓ I **want you to do** more research.

✗ I am ~~waiting a call~~ from my sister.
✓ I am **waiting for a** call from my sister.

✗ You can ~~to~~ go there by bus.
✓ You **can go** there by bus.

The box below gives examples of different patterns that are used when one verb follows another in a sentence. In this dictionary, the prepositions and to-infinitives used in patterns are shown in bold type:

Types of Verb Patterns	Examples
verb + verb-*ing* (enjoy doing sth)	I **enjoy dancing**. She **suggested using** a new software program. The baby **started crying**.
verb + infinitive with *to*	I **want to** study English. He **plans to** work before going to college. **Remember to** send your forms in!
verb + direct object + infinitive with *to* (advise sb to do sth)	The doctor **advised** me **to** rest. I **warned** her not **to** go out alone at night.
verb + direct object + infinitive without *to* (+ object) (let sb do sth)	My dad **let** me **borrow** his car. I love to **hear** the baby **laugh**. He **watched** her **lock** the door.
verb + preposition + verb-*ing* (think about doing sth)	He **thought about calling** the police. She **began by thanking** everyone for coming.
verb + direct object + preposition + verb-*ing* (stop sb/sth from doing sth)	He **stopped** me **from leaving**. A knee injury **prevented** him **from playing**.

Adjective Patterns

Choosing the Right Preposition or Pattern

When you use an adjective such as **interested**, you need to know which preposition or pattern to use with it. Do you say *happy about* something or *happy in* something? Do you say *happy to do* something or *happy in doing* something?

This dictionary shows you clearly which prepositions and patterns to use. Here is the entry for **happy**:

> **hap·py** /ˈhæpi/ *adj.* (comparative **happier**, superlative **happiest**) **1** feeling pleased and cheerful, often because something good has happened to you (ANT) **unhappy, sad**: *He was a happy child.* | *I've never **felt happier** in my life.* | *I'm **happy (that)** everything worked out in the end.* | *I don't think he was too **happy about** having to stay late.* | *Congratulations! I'm so **happy for you**.*
>
> THESAURUS
>
> **glad** – pleased about a situation or something that has happened: *I'm so glad you were able to come.*
> **pleased** – happy and satisfied with something that has happened: *Her parents were pleased that she had done so well.*
>
> **2 be happy to do sth** to be willing to do something, especially to help someone else: *I'll be happy to answer questions later.*

As you can see, the usual preposition to use with **happy** is **about**. The verb pattern that you choose depends on the meaning of **happy**. If you want to talk about "being willing to do something," you say **happy to do something**. If you want to talk about "feeling pleased or cheerful," you say **happy about something**.

Common Mistakes with Adjectives

✗ She is good ~~in~~ math.
✓ She is **good at** math.

✗ New York is different ~~of~~ Los Angeles.
✓ New York is **different from** Los Angeles.

✗ I had the pleasure ~~to meet~~ her yesterday.
✓ I had the **pleasure of** meet**ing** her yesterday.

✗ She's only concerned ~~in~~ making money.
✓ She's only **concerned with** making money.

✗ Are you interested ~~about~~ politics?
✓ Are you **interested in** politics?

✗ We were afraid ~~to miss~~ the plane.
✓ We were **afraid of** miss**ing** the plane.

Choosing the Right Pattern

Here is a list of some common adjectives and the patterns that can follow them:

+ Preposition + Verb-*ing*	+ Infinitive Verb Form	+ *that*
tired of wait**ing**	**difficult to finish** on time	**important (that)** you do well
excited about learn**ing** new things	**necessary to buy** new textbooks	**possible (that)** she did not know
nervous about start**ing** a new job	**impossible to see** without a microscope	**obvious (that)** he was not hurt
exhausted from work**ing** so hard	**glad to see** her friends	**confident (that)** they would win
pleased about pass**ing** the test	**determined to go** to college	**afraid (that)** he would fail
scared of be**ing** alone	**easy to** understand	
	surprised to see us there	

Prepositions

Prepositions are words that come before nouns and show the relationship between those nouns and the rest of the sentence. They can show location, direction, time, possession etc. For example, in the sentence "The tree is behind the house," *behind* is a preposition. The pictures on these pages show some of the most common prepositions of location.

The glasses are **in** the cabinet **on** the top shelf. The plates are **on** the bottom shelf. The cabinet is **on** the wall **above/over** the counter. The toaster is **on** the counter. There is a drawer **under/below** the counter. The silverware is **in** the drawer.

There's a campground **below** the hill, **beside** the river. The campground is **near** the bridge that goes **over** the river. Cars are **on** the bridge, driving **over** it. The river flows **through** the valley **under** the bridge **past** the campground. There's a tent **under** a tree and a small campfire **next to** the tent. There's a rowboat **on** the river and someone is fishing **in** the river.

There is a large vase **on** the table. There are flowers **in** the vase. There is a candle **beside/next to** the vase. There are chairs **around** the table.

Shawn and Terry live **in** a city. They live **in** this apartment building. They live **on** East 135th Street. They live **on** the corner of East 135th Street and Ferndale Avenue. They live **at** 2963 East 135th Street **in** apartment 7B.

The truck is **in front of** the station wagon. The convertible is **between** the truck and the motorcycle. All the other vehicles are **behind** the motorcycle.

A woman is coming **out of** the bookstore. Two teenagers are going **into** the shoe store. A group of children are walking **toward** the toy store. A man is walking **away from** it.

The post office is **next to** the library. The library is **between** the post office and the clothes store. There are three buildings **across from** these buildings. The movie theater is directly **opposite** the library. The bank is **kitty-corner from** the park.

Phrasal Verbs

What Is a Phrasal Verb?

Read the passage below:

> My alarm **went off** at 7:00, but I didn't **get up** until 7:45. That's when my roommate yelled, "**Hurry up** if you want a ride – I'm about to leave." So I jumped out of bed, **threw on** some clothes, and ran out the door.

In this passage, **go off**, **get up**, **hurry up**, and **throw on** are phrasal verbs, but *jump out of* and *run out* are not. Why?

A phrasal verb is a verb that is made up of two or three words. The first word is a verb, and the second word (and the third, if there is one) is a *particle*. A particle can be an adverb or a preposition.

But that is not all that is necessary to make a phrasal verb. In some verbs such as **fall down**, the particle does not change the meaning of the main verb. In phrasal verbs, however, the addition of the particle creates a completely new meaning. For example, the phrasal verb **get up to** (which means "to do something that might be slightly bad") is not connected with the usual meanings of the words **get** + **up** + **to**. It is often difficult to guess the meaning of a phrasal verb.

NOTE

- If a verb is followed by a preposition but keeps its ordinary meaning, it is *not* a phrasal verb. This is why *jump out of* and *run out* in the passage above are not phrasal verbs.

In this dictionary, phrasal verbs are labeled *phr. v.* and appear in blue at the end of the main verb entry. Some phrasal verbs must have an object, and the object can come either before or after the particle.

Different Types of Phrasal Verbs	
Phrasal Verbs with No Object	take off *phr. v.* **3** *informal* to leave a place *We packed everything in the car and* ***took off****.*
Phrasal Verbs with One Object	1 With some phrasal verbs, the object can come *either* before *or* after the particle. The ***Longman Dictionary of American English*** uses a special symbol **↔** to show this is possible. take **sth ↔** down *phr. v.* to remove something from its place, especially by separating it into pieces *We* ***take*** *the Christmas tree* ***down*** *on January 6.* You can also say: *We* ***take down*** *the Christmas tree on January 6.* **Note** If the object is a pronoun (it/them/her/him etc.), the pronoun MUST always come before the particle: *We* ***take*** *it* ***down***. NOT *We* ***take down*** *it.*

Different Types of Phrasal Verbs	
	2 With some phrasal verbs, the object must always come *between* the verb and the particle. **take sb out** *phr. v.* **1** to go with someone to a restaurant, movie, party, etc., and pay for his/her meal and entertainment: *We're **taking** Sabina **out** for dinner.*
	3 With some phrasal verbs, the object must always come after the particle. **take in** *phr. v.* **5 take in** sth to go to see something, such as a movie, play etc.: *tourists **taking in** the sights*
Phrasal Verbs with Two Objects	With phrasal verbs that have two objects, one object comes after the verb and the other comes after the particle. **take sb up on sth** *phr. v.* to accept an offer, invitation, etc.: *A number of students **have taken** him **up on** his offer of extra help.*

Expand Your Vocabulary

Often there is a single word that has a similar meaning to a particular phrasal verb. For example, the single word **distribute** means the same as the phrasal verb **hand out** (they both mean "to give something to everyone in a group"). However, you should be careful when you use a single-word verb, because they are often more formal or more technical than the equivalent phrasal verb. Always check whether a verb is formal or informal, so that you use words that are appropriate for the situation. Here are some verbs that you can use when talking about stopping something.

STOP			
to make a machine, light etc. stop working – • switch off • turn off • turn out • shut off	**when a machine stops working –** • break down • go down • go off • give out	**to stop talking –** • shut up • clam up • break off	**to stop doing something –** • give up • pack up

Modal Verbs

The modal verbs in English are **can**, **could**, **must**, **will**, **would**, **should**, **may**, **shall**, and **might**. These verbs are used before an infinitive verb without *to*. They are used to give extra information about the main verb. **Need (to)**, **ought to**, **have to**, and **have got to** are also often used in similar ways.

Modal verbs are often contracted (=shortened), especially in speech and informal writing. So we say *I can't* rather than *I cannot*, *you shouldn't* rather than *you should not*, *they wouldn't* rather than *they would not*.

You can use modal verbs for offering help, advice, or suggestions, and for asking for and giving permission:

Making Requests: **can, will, could, would**	Offering to Help: **can, may, shall, will**	Asking for and Giving Permission: **can, could, may**	Making Suggestions and Giving Advice: **should, ought to, shall, have to**
Can I borrow your notes? **Will** you meet me after class? **Could** you tell me what time it is? **Would** you close the door, please? **Note: could** and **would** are more formal and polite.	**Can** I carry those for you? **May** I help you? **Shall** I open the window? **I'll** drive you home.	You **can** borrow my notes. **Can** I tape the lecture? **Could** I use the car tonight? **May** I speak to Professor Jensen, please? **Note: could** is more polite than **can**, and **may** is used in more formal English.	You **should** exercise more. You **ought to** plan your essays first. **Shall** we go? You really **have to** read this – it's so good.

You can also use modal verbs for expressing certainty, probability, or possibility:

Certainty: **must, can't, will**	Probability: **should, ought to**	Possibility: **may, could, might**
He **must** be here already – there's his car. She wasn't in class today; she **must** be sick. You **can't** be finished already! **You use will/won't to say whether something is certain to happen in the future.** It **will** be finals week soon. They **won't** do that again. I **won't** forget you.	They **should** be in New York by now. The movie **ought to** end around10:00. It's only a headache – I **should** feel better in the morning.	I **may** have dropped it on campus. It **could** be in the basement – I'm not sure. I **might** have left it in my locker at school.

You can also use modal verbs for talking about somebody's abilities or about necessity and obligations:

Ability: **can, could**	Necessity and Obligation: **need to, have to, have got to, must**
She **can** speak Chinese. **Can** you hear me at the back of the room? I **can't** get a dorm room this year. **Could** you understand what he was saying? I **could** see him on the running track.	I **need to** go to class now. I **have to** call my parents today. **I've got to** get up early in the morning. Students **must** sign in before using the exercise room. **You use will have to or will need to to say that it is necessary to do something in the future.** You**'ll have to** help me move this – it's too heavy. You**'ll need to** learn some Japanese before you go to Tokyo.

Common Problems with Modal Verbs

Modal verbs are followed by a verb in the infinitive, without "to":

✗ I should ~~to~~ do my homework.
✓ I should **do** my homework.

They do not take "s" in the 3rd person singular:

✗ She ~~cans~~ answer your questions.
✓ She **can** answer your questions.

They cannot follow another verb. If you want to talk about the future, simply use the modal verb without *will*, or another verb or verb phrase such as *will be able to* or *will have to*:

✗ I ~~will can~~ meet you tomorrow.
✓ I **can** meet you tomorrow.
✓ I **will be able to** meet you tomorrow.

✗ He ~~will must~~ take the class again.
✓ He **will have to** take the class again.

STUDY TIP

- Avoid repetition by using different modal verbs to express the same meaning. For example, you can say: *Tonight **I have to** do my homework, then **I need to** write to Sally, and then **I've got to** go to bed early.*

Intensifiers

STUDY TIP

› When you look up a word in the dictionary, pay attention to the example sentences and to the examples in bold. This will help you learn which words belong together.

Intensifying Adjectives

You can make your English sound more natural and interesting by using a wider variety of adjectives and adverbs to emphasize what you are saying. Instead of saying that something is a **big problem** or a **big surprise**, you can say that it is a **serious problem** or a **complete surprise**.

Common Mistakes with Intensifying Adjectives

Sometimes it is hard to choose the correct adjective. For example, you can say that something is of **great importance**, but you can't say that it is of **big importance**.

✗ a ~~strong~~ lie	✗ a ~~big~~ interest in something	✗ a ~~strong~~ illness/infection/disease
✓ a **big** lie	✓ a **great** interest in something	✓ a **serious** illness/infection/disease

The lists below show you some of the different adjectives that are used to emphasize some common nouns:

difference
big difference **great** difference **huge** difference

difficulty
great difficulty **huge** difficulty **serious** difficulty

disaster
complete disaster **huge** disaster **total** disaster

importance
great importance **huge** importance

lack of sth
complete lack of sth **serious** lack of sth **total** lack of sth

mistake
big mistake **complete** mistake **great** mistake **huge** mistake **total** mistake **serious** mistake

possibility
distinct possibility **strong** possibility

problem
big problem **huge** problem **serious** problem

surprise
big surprise **complete** surprise **huge** surprise **total** surprise

Intensifying Adverbs

Instead of saying that something is **very difficult** or that somebody is **very intelligent**, you can say **extremely difficult**, or **highly intelligent**.

Common Mistakes with Intensifying Adverbs

Sometimes it is hard to choose the correct adverb. For example, you can say **highly intelligent**, but NOT **highly smart** (you have to say **very smart**).

✗ ~~strongly~~ sure
✓ **absolutely** sure

✗ ~~absolutely~~ different
✓ **completely** different

✗ ~~highly~~ certain
✓ **absolutely** certain

✗ ~~completely~~ hungry
✓ **very** hungry

✗ ~~strongly~~ disappointed
✓ **deeply** disappointed

The lists below show you some of the different adverbs that are used to emphasize some common adjectives:

different
completely different **really** different **totally** different **very** different

difficult
extremely difficult **really** difficult **very** difficult

exhausted
absolutely exhausted **completely** exhausted **really** exhausted **totally** exhausted

funny
extremely funny **really** funny **very** funny

ill
extremely ill **really** ill **seriously** ill **very** ill

important
extremely important **highly** important **really** important **very** important

impossible
absolutely impossible **completely** impossible **totally** impossible

interesting
extremely interesting **highly** interesting **really** interesting **very** interesting

sorry
extremely sorry **really** sorry **very** sorry

successful
completely successful **extremely** successful **totally** successful
really successful **very** successful

upset
extremely upset **really** upset **very** upset

NOTE

› Often, different meanings of a word will collocate with different intensifying adjectives and adverbs. So you say:

- She was ***badly/seriously*** hurt (= injured) in the accident.

but

- I was ***deeply/very*** hurt (= upset) by her comments.

» See also **Writing Guide** on **Collocations**

Articles

Articles are special words that come before nouns that show which person, place, or thing you are talking about. The articles in English are **a** or **an**, and **the**. Adjectives come between articles and nouns, but do not use an article without a noun:

✗ He's ~~a~~ great. ✓ He's **a** great professor.

Use *The*:

- When it is clear which person, place, or thing you are talking about:
  *I'm not going to **the** party* (= the person you are talking to knows which party you mean).
- When you refer to a particular thing, or when there is only one thing of this kind:
  *I live in **the** house with **the** blue door* (= there is only one house with a door like this).
  ***The** sun shone all day* (= there is only one sun).

Use *A* or *An*:

- When you refer to someone or something for the first time and it may not be clear which person, place, or thing you are talking about:
  *Would you like to go to **a** party* (= the person you are talking to does not know about the party yet)?
- When you are talking about one of several things in a general way:
  *I live in **a** house with **a** blue door* (= there is more than one house like this).
- When you talk about a type of person or thing:
  *My mother is **a** doctor.* | *Do you want **an** umbrella?*

A or *An*?

- Use **an** instead of **a** before a word that starts with a vowel sound:
  ✗ I bought ~~a~~ orange. ✓ I bought **an** orange.
  ✗ I bought ~~an~~ big orange. ✓ I bought **a** big orange.
- The choice between **a** or **an** depends on pronunciation, not spelling, so use **an** before any word that starts with a vowel sound, even if it is spelled with a consonant:
  ✗ I got there ~~a~~ hour early. ✓ I got there **an** hour early.
- The letter "u" is a vowel. But when a "u" at the beginning of a word is pronounced like "you" (as in *unit*) the word starts with a consonant sound. In this case, use **a** not **an**:
  ✗ ~~A~~ uncle ✓ **An** uncle
  BUT
  ✗ ~~An~~ university ✓ **A** university
- The letters *f*, *h*, *l*, *m*, *n*, *r*, *s*, and *x* are consonants, but the pronunciation of their names starts with vowel sounds (e.g., "eff" and "aitch"). Use **an** before the NAMES of these letters:
  ✗ Do you spell "rise" with ~~a~~ *s* or ~~a~~ *z*? ✓ Do you spell "rise" with **an** *s* or **a** *z*?

›› You can Test Yourself on **a** or **an** by doing the exercises on Articles on the CD-ROM
See also **Grammar Guide** on **Countable and Uncountable Nouns**.

M

mis·place /ˌmɪsˈpleɪs/ *v.* [T] to put something somewhere and then forget where you put it: *I've misplaced my glasses again.*

mis·placed /ˌmɪsˈpleɪst/ *adj.* misplaced feelings of trust, love, etc. are inappropriate because the person that you have these feelings for does not deserve them: *a misplaced sense of loyalty*

mis·print /ˈmɪsˌprɪnt/ *n.* [C] a mistake in a book, magazine, etc.

mis·pro·nounce /ˌmɪsprəˈnaʊns/ *v.* [T] to pronounce a word or name wrongly —**mispronunciation** /ˌmɪsprəˌnʌnsiˈeɪʃən/ *n.* [C,U]

mis·quote /ˌmɪsˈkwoʊt/ *v.* [T] to make a mistake in reporting what someone else has said or written: *Morales claims the magazine misquoted him.*

mis·read /ˌmɪsˈrid/ *v.* (past tense and past participle **misread** /-ˈrɛd/) [T] **1** to make a wrong judgment about a situation or person → MISINTERPRET: *The UN badly misread the situation.* **2** to read something in the wrong way: *I misread the schedule and missed my bus.*

mis·rep·re·sent /ˌmɪsrɛprɪˈzɛnt/ *v.* [T] to deliberately give a wrong description of someone's opinions or of a situation (SYN) **distort, twist**: *Our aims have been misrepresented in the press.* —**misrepresentation** /mɪsˌrɛprɪzənˈteɪʃən/ *n.* [C,U]

miss¹ /mɪs/ *v.* **1** [T] to not go somewhere or do something, especially when you want to but cannot: *Sorry I missed your call.* | *She didn't want to* ***miss a chance/opportunity to*** *work in Hollywood.* **2** [T] to be too late for something: *By the time we got there, we'd missed the beginning of the movie.* | *You'll* ***miss*** *your* ***plane/train/bus*** *unless you leave now.* **3** [T] to feel sad because you are not with a particular person, or because you no longer have something or are no longer doing something: *Did you miss me while I was gone?* | *I miss living in London.* **4** [I,T] to not hit or catch something: *She fired at the target but missed.* | *Jackson missed an easy catch and the A's scored.* **5 miss the point** to not understand the main point of what someone is saying **6** [T] to not see, hear, or notice something: *Jody found an error that everyone else had missed.* | *It's a big red house with a small pond in front –* ***you can't miss it.*** **7** [T] to notice that something or someone is not in the place you expect him, her, or it to be: *I didn't miss my key until I got home.* **8 miss the boat** (informal) to fail to take an opportunity that will give you an advantage: *Investors who failed to buy the stock when it was first listed have missed the boat.*

miss out *phr. v.* to not have the chance to do something that you enjoy: *You're the one who'll miss out if you don't come.* | *She got married very young, and now she feels she's* ***missing out on*** *life.*

miss² *n.* **1 Miss Smith/Jones etc.** used in front of the family name of a woman who is not married in order to speak to her politely, write to her, or talk about her → MRS., MS. **2** [C] a failed attempt to hit, catch, or hold something **3** used to speak politely to a young woman when you do not know her name: *Excuse me, miss, you've dropped your umbrella.*

mis·shap·en /ˌmɪsˈʃeɪpən, ˌmɪˈʃeɪ-/ *adj.* not the normal or natural shape: *He was born with a misshapen spine.*

mis·sile /ˈmɪsəl/ *n.* [C] **1** a weapon that can fly over long distances and that explodes when it hits something: *a* ***nuclear missile*** **2** (formal) an object that is thrown at someone in order to hurt him/her

miss·ing /ˈmɪsɪŋ/ *adj.* **1** someone or something that is missing is not in the place where you would normally expect him, her, or it to be: *Police are still searching for the missing child.* | *A button on his shirt was missing.* | *$200 was* ***missing from*** *my desk drawer.*

> **USAGE**
>
> Use **lost** in order to describe something that someone cannot find, or someone who does not know where s/he is: *a lost ball* | *We took a wrong turn and got lost.*
>
> Use **missing** in order to describe someone or something you have been looking for, especially when the situation is serious: *We're still trying to locate the missing money.* | *the search for the two missing boys*

2 not included, although it ought to have been: *Why is my name* ***missing from*** *the list?* **3 missing in action** a soldier who is missing in action has not been seen after a battle, and is probably dead

mis·sion /ˈmɪʃən/ *n.* [C] **1** an important job that someone has been given to do: *His mission was to help the president win re-election.* **2** a group of people who are sent by their government to another country for a particular purpose: *a Canadian trade mission to Japan* **3** the purpose or the most important aim of an organization: *Each school's central mission should be to teach reading, writing, and arithmetic.*

> **THESAURUS** goal, aim, objective, target → GOAL

4 something that you feel you must do because it is your duty: *She feels her* ***mission in life*** *is to help poor people.* **5** a special trip made by a space vehicle or military airplane: *a mission to Mars* **6** the work of a missionary, or a building where s/he does this work [ORIGIN: 1500—1600 Latin *missio* "act of sending," from *mittere* "to send, throw"]

mis·sion·ar·y /ˈmɪʃəˌnɛri/ *n.* (plural **missionaries**) [C] someone who has gone to a foreign country in order to teach people about Christianity

mis·spell /ˌmɪsˈspɛl/ *v.* [T] to spell a word incorrectly —**misspelling** *n.* [C,U]

mis·step /ˈmɪs-stɛp/ *n.* [C] (written) a mistake, especially one that offends or upsets people: *political missteps*

mist¹ /mɪst/ *n.* [C,U] cloud that is close to the

M

ground, making it difficult to see very far ➔ FOG: *The sun had burned through the early morning mist.*

mist² *v.* [I,T] to become covered with very small drops of water, or to make something do this: *The windows are all* ***misted up/over.***

mis·take¹ /mɪ'steɪk/ *n.* [C] **1** something that has been done in the wrong way, or an opinion or statement that is incorrect: *spelling mistakes* | *I think you've* ***made a mistake*** *– I ordered fish, not beef.* | *The bill is $500?* ***There must be some mistake.***

THESAURUS

A **mistake** is something that you do by accident, or that is the result of a bad judgment: *I took Larry's coat by mistake.* | *We made a mistake in buying this car.*
An **error** is a mistake that you do not realize you are making, and that causes problems: *He made several errors when adding up the bill.*

2 something you do that you later realize was not the right thing to do: *Marrying him was a* ***big mistake.*** | ***I made the mistake of*** *giving him my phone number.* | *We need to start* ***learning from*** *our* ***mistakes.*** **3 by mistake** if you do something by mistake, you do it without intending to: *I brought the wrong book home by mistake.* [ORIGIN: 1300—1400 Old Norse *mistaka*]

mistake² *v.* (past tense **mistook** /-'stʊk/, past participle **mistaken** /-'steɪkən/)

mistake sb/sth **for** sb/sth *phr. v.* to think that one person or thing is someone or something else: *I mistook him for his brother.*

mis·tak·en /mɪ'steɪkən/ *adj.* wrong about something: *I think the party is next week, but I might be mistaken.* | *We bought the rug in Turkey,* ***if I'm not mistaken.*** **—mistakenly** *adv.*

mis·ter /'mɪstɚ/ *n.* **1** the full form of MR. **2** (spoken, old-fashioned) said in order to speak to a man when you do not know his name ➔ SIR: *Hey, mister, is this your wallet?*

mis·tle·toe /'mɪsəl,toʊ/ *n.* [U] a plant with small white berries that is often used as a decoration at Christmas

mis·took /mɪ'stʊk/ *v.* the past tense of MISTAKE

mis·treat /,mɪs'trit/ *v.* [T] to treat a person or animal cruelly: *The hostages said they had not been mistreated.* **—mistreatment** *n.* [U]

mis·tress /'mɪstrɪs/ *n.* [C] **1** a woman that a man has a sexual relationship with, even though he is married to someone else **2** (old-fashioned) a woman who has authority over servants or animals ➔ MASTER

mis·tri·al /'mɪstraɪl/ *n.* [C] LAW a TRIAL during which a mistake in the law is made, so that a new trial has to be held

mis·trust /mɪs'trʌst/ *n.* [U] the feeling that you cannot trust someone: *Some Americans admit to deep* ***mistrust of*** *the media.* **—mistrust** *v.* [T]

mist·y /'mɪsti/ *adj.* **1** misty weather is weather with a lot of mist **2** (literary) full of tears: *her eyes became misty*

mis·un·der·stand /,mɪsʌndɚ'stænd/ *v.* (past tense and past participle **misunderstood** /-'stʊd/) [I,T] to fail to understand someone or something correctly: *I think you misunderstood what I was trying to say.*

mis·un·der·stand·ing /,mɪsʌndɚ'stændɪŋ/ *n.* **1** [C,U] a failure to understand a question, situation, or instruction: *There must be some misunderstanding. I didn't order all these books.* | *We've called a meeting to clear up any* ***misunderstandings about*** *the project.* **2** [C] an argument or disagreement that is not very serious: *We've had our misunderstandings in the past, but we're good friends now.*

mis·un·der·stood /,mɪsʌndɚ'stʊd/ *adj.* if someone is misunderstood, s/he has been treated unfairly because people have decided that they do not like him/her, without knowing what s/he is really like: *Albert's really a nice guy; he's just misunderstood.*

mis·use¹ /,mɪs'yuz/ *v.* [T] to use something in the wrong way or for the wrong purpose: *He faces a charge of misusing state funds for his re-election campaign.*

mis·use² /,mɪs'yus/ *n.* [C,U] the use of something in the wrong way or for the wrong purpose: *a* ***misuse of*** *power*

mite /maɪt/ *n.* [C] **1** BIOLOGY a very small insect that lives in plants, CARPETS, etc.: *dust mites* **2 a mite** (old-fashioned) a little: *The hotel was a mite expensive.*

mit·i·gate /'mɪt̬ə,geɪt/ *v.* [T] (formal) to make a situation or the effects of something less bad, harmful, or serious: *Only foreign aid can mitigate the terrible effects of the war.* **—mitigation** /,mɪt̬ə'geɪʃən/ *n.* [U]

mi·to·chon·dri·on /,maɪt̬ə'kɑndriən/ *n.* (plural **mitochondria** /-driə/) [C] BIOLOGY a very small part of a cell in a plant, animal, or FUNGUS, which changes ORGANIC MATTER (=natural material that is going through the process of decaying) into energy

mi·to·sis /maɪ'toʊsɪs/ *n.* [U] BIOLOGY the process by which a cell divides to become two cells, each new cell having the same number of CHROMOSOMES as the original cell ➔ MEIOSIS

mi·tral valve /'maɪtrəl ,vælv/ *n.* [C] BIOLOGY a BICUSPID VALVE ➔ *see picture at* HEART

mitt /mɪt/ *n.* [C] **1** a type of leather GLOVE used for catching a ball in baseball **2** a GLOVE made of thick material, worn to protect your hand: *an oven mitt*

mit·ten /'mɪt˺n/ *n.* [C] a type of GLOVE that does not have separate parts for each finger

mix¹ /mɪks/ *v.* **1** [I,T] if you mix two or more substances, or if they mix, they combine to become a single substance: *Oil and water don't mix.* | ***Mix***

the butter ***and*** *sugar* ***together****, and then add the milk.* | ***Mix*** *the beans thoroughly* ***with*** *the sauce.*
➔ see picture on page A18

THESAURUS

combine – to join two or more things together, or to be joined together with another thing: *Combine the ingredients and beat until smooth.*
stir – to mix a liquid or food by moving a spoon around in it: *Reduce the heat and stir until thickened.*
blend – to mix together soft or liquid substances to form a single smooth substance: *Blend the yogurt with fresh fruit for a wonderful drink.*
beat – to mix food together quickly and thoroughly using a fork or kitchen tool: *Beat the eggs and add to the sugar mixture.*

2 [I,T] to combine two or more different activities, ideas, groups of things, etc.: *Their music* ***mixes*** *jazz* ***and*** *rock.* | *I don't* ***mix*** *business* ***with*** *pleasure.* **3** [I] to enjoy meeting, talking, and spending time with other people, especially people you do not know very well: *Joey* ***mixed*** *easily* ***with*** *the other children.*

mix up *phr. v.* **1 mix** sb/sth ↔ **up** to make the mistake of thinking that someone or something is another person or thing: *I keep* ***mixing*** *him* ***up with*** *his brother.* **2 mix** sth ↔ **up** to change the way things have been arranged so that they are no longer in the same order: *Don't mix up those papers, or we'll never find the ones we need.* **3 mix** sb **up** (informal) to make someone feel confused: *Too many people were giving her advice and mixing her up.* ➔ MIXED UP, MIX-UP

mix² *n.* **1** [C,U] a combination of substances that you mix together to make something: *cake mix* **2** [singular] the particular combination of things or people that form a group: *There was a strange* ***mix of*** *people at Larry's party.*

mixed /mɪkst/ *adj.* **1** consisting of many different types of things or people: *a can of mixed nuts* | *They were a mixed group, predominantly young, but there were some older people too.* **2 have mixed emotions/feelings (about sth)** to be unsure about whether you like or agree with something: *We had mixed feelings about moving to New York.* **3 a mixed blessing** something that is good in some ways but bad in others: *Having children is a mixed blessing.* **4 mixed response/reaction** if something gets a mixed response, some people say that they like it, but others do not like it

ˌmixed 'marriage *n.* [C,U] a marriage between two people from different races or religions

ˌmixed 'up *adj.* **1** confused: *I got mixed up and went to the wrong restaurant.* **2 be mixed up with sb** to be involved with someone who has a bad influence on you: *If you get mixed up with those people, you'll end up in jail.* **3 be mixed up in sth** to be involved in an illegal or dishonest activity: *I don't want my kids getting mixed up in drugs.*

mix·er /'mɪksɚ/ *n.* [C] a piece of equipment used for mixing different substances together: *Beat the eggs and sugar with an electric mixer.*

mix·ture /'mɪkstʃɚ/ *n.* **1** [C,U] a single substance made by mixing several substances together: *Pour the cake mixture into a pan and bake it for 45 minutes.*

THESAURUS

combination – two or more different things, substances, etc. that are used or put together: *Doctors use a combination of drugs to combat the disease.*
blend – a mixture of two or more things: *The salad dressing is an interesting blend of oil, vinegar, and spices.*
compound – a chemical compound is a substance that consists of two or more different substances: *Carbon dioxide is a common compound found in the air.*
solution – a liquid mixed with a solid or a gas: *a weak sugar solution*

2 [C usually singular] a combination of two or more people, things, feelings, or ideas that are different: *I listened to his excuse with* ***a mixture of*** *amusement and disbelief.*

'mix-up *n.* [C] (informal) a mistake that causes confusion about details or arrangements: *There was a mix-up at the station and Eddie got on the wrong bus.*

ml the written abbreviation of MILLILITER

mm the written abbreviation of MILLIMETER

MN the written abbreviation of MINNESOTA

MO the written abbreviation of MISSOURI

mo. the written abbreviation of MONTH

moan¹ /moʊn/ *v.* [I] **1** to make the sound of a moan: *The victim was bleeding and moaning in pain.* **2** (informal) to complain in an annoying way, especially in an unhappy voice: *Stop* ***moaning about*** *your problems and get to work!* —**moaner** *n.* [C]

moan² *n.* [C] a long low sound expressing pain or sadness

moat /moʊt/ *n.* [C] a deep wide hole, usually filled with water, that was dug around a castle as a defense

mob¹ /mɑb/ *n.* [C] **1** a large noisy crowd, especially one that is angry and violent: *A* ***mob of*** *protesters attacked the police.* | *The thieves were lynched by an angry mob.* **2 the Mob** (informal) the MAFIA

mob² *v.* (**mobbed**, **mobbing**) [T] **1** to form a crowd around someone in order to express admiration or to attack him/her: *She's mobbed by her fans wherever she goes.* **2** if a place is mobbed, it has a lot of people in it: *The beach was* ***mobbed with*** *people.*

mo·bile¹ /'moʊbəl/ *adj.* able to move or be moved easily (ANT) **immobile**: *I'm much more mobile now that I have a car.* [ORIGIN: 1400—1500 French,

M

Latin *mobilis*, from *movere* "to move"] —**mobility** /moʊˈbɪləṭi/ *n.* [U]: *elderly people with limited mobility*

mo·bile² /ˈmoʊbil/ *n.* [C] a decoration made of small objects tied to string and hung up so that they move when air blows around them

ˌmobile ˈhome *n.* [C] a type of house made of metal, that can be pulled by a large vehicle and moved to another place → HOUSE¹

ˌmobile ˈphone *n.* [C] a CELL PHONE

mo·bi·lize /ˈmoʊbəˌlaɪz/ *v.* [I,T] **1** to gather together, or be brought together, in order to work to achieve something difficult: *Forces have been mobilized to defend the capital.* **2 mobilize support/opposition** to encourage people to support or oppose something —**mobilization** /ˌmoʊbələˈzeɪʃən/ *n.* [C,U]

mob·ster /ˈmɑbstɚ/ *n.* [C] (informal) a member of the Mafia

moc·ca·sin /ˈmɑkəsən/ *n.* [C] a flat comfortable shoe made of soft leather [ORIGIN: 1600—1700 Virginia Algonquian *mockasin*]

mock¹ /mɑk/ *v.* [I,T] to laugh at someone or something and try to make him, her, or it seem stupid, especially by copying his, her, or its actions or speech: *Wilson mocked Joe's southern accent.* | *Are you mocking me?* —**mockingly** *adv.*

mock² *adj.* not real: *a mock debate* | ***mock horror/surprise***

mock·er·y /ˈmɑkəri/ *n.* **1 make a mockery of sth** to make something such as a plan or system seem completely useless or ineffective: *The trial made a mockery of justice.* **2** [U] the act of laughing at someone or something and trying to make him, her, or it seem stupid or silly

mock·ing·bird /ˈmɑkɪŋˌbɚd/ *n.* [C] an American bird that copies the songs of other birds

ˌmodal ˈverb *also* **modal** *n.* [C] ENG. LANG. ARTS in grammar, a verb that is used with other verbs to change their meaning by expressing ideas such as possibility, permission, or intention. In English, the modals are "can," "could," "may," "might," "shall," "should," "will," "would," "must," "ought to," "used to," "have to," and "had better." → AUXILIARY VERB

mode /moʊd/ (Ac) *n.* **1** [C] (formal) a particular way or style of behaving, living, or doing something: *a very efficient* ***mode of*** *transportation* | *Artists use various modes of expression, such as painting and poetry.* **2** [singular] MATH the middle number in a set of numbers that are arranged in order of size → MEAN, MEDIAN

mod·el¹ /ˈmɑdl/ *n.* [C] **1** someone whose job is to show clothes, hair styles, etc. by wearing them and being photographed: *a top* ***fashion model*** **2** a small copy of a vehicle, building, machine, etc., especially one that can be put together from separate parts: *They showed us a* ***model of*** *the building.* **3** someone who is employed by an artist or photographer in order to be painted or photographed **4** a person or thing that is a perfect example of something good and is therefore worth copying: *It served as a* ***model for*** *other cities.* | *Shelly's essay is a* ***model of*** *care and neatness.* → ROLE MODEL **5** a particular type or design of a vehicle, machine, weapon, etc.: *Ford has two new models coming out in October.*

THESAURUS **type, kind, sort, category, brand, make** → TYPE¹

6 SCIENCE a description of a system or structure that is used to help people understand similar systems or structures: *Early astronomers constructed a model of the universe in purely geometric terms.*

model² *adj.* **1 model airplane/train/car etc.** a small copy of an airplane, etc., especially one that can be put together from separate parts **2 model wife/employee/school etc.** a person or thing that is a perfect example of its type

model³ *v.* **1** [I,T] to wear clothes in order to show them to possible buyers **2** [I,T] to be employed by an artist or photographer in order to be painted or photographed **3** [T] to copy a system or way of doing something: *Their education system is* ***modeled on*** *the French one.* **4 model yourself after sb** to try to be like someone else because you admire him/her: *The young singer modeled himself after Frank Sinatra.* **5** [T] to make small objects from materials such as wood or clay

mod·el·ing /ˈmɑdl-ɪŋ/ *n.* [U] **1** the work of a fashion model: *a career in modeling* **2** the activity of making models or objects: *clay modeling*

mo·dem /ˈmoʊdəm/ *n.* [C] IT a piece of electronic equipment that allows information from one computer to be sent along telephone wires to another computer → INTERNET

mod·er·ate¹ /ˈmɑdərɪt/ *adj.* **1** neither very big nor very small, very hot nor very cold, very fast nor very slow, etc.: *a moderate temperature* | *Moderate exercise can reduce the risk of heart disease.* **2** having opinions or beliefs, especially about politics, that are not extreme and that most people consider reasonable: *a* ***moderate Republican/Democrat*** | ***moderate voters***

mod·e·rate² /ˈmɑdəˌreɪt/ *v.* [I,T] to make something less extreme or violent, or to become less extreme or violent: *To lose weight, moderate the amount of food you eat.*

mod·e·rate³ /ˈmɑdərɪt/ *n.* [C] someone whose opinions or beliefs, especially about politics, are not extreme and are considered reasonable by most people

mod·er·ate·ly /ˈmɑdərɪtli/ *adv.* fairly but not very: *a moderately successful company*

mod·er·a·tion /ˌmɑdəˈreɪʃən/ *n.* **1 in moderation** if you do something in moderation, you do not do it too much: *You've got to learn to drink in moderation.* **2** [U] (formal) control of your behavior, so that you keep your actions, feelings, habits, etc. within reasonable or sensible limits

mod·er·at·or /ˈmɑdəˌreɪtɚ/ *n.* [C] someone whose job is to control a discussion or argument and to help people reach an agreement

mod·ern /ˈmɑdɚn/ *adj.* **1** belonging to the present time or the most recent time ➔ CONTEMPORARY: *modern American history* | *Computers are an essential part of **modern life**.* | *The country is suffering one of its worst economic crises **in modern times**.*

THESAURUS **advanced, sophisticated, high-tech, state-of-the-art, cutting-edge** ➔ ADVANCED

2 using or willing to use very recent ideas, fashions, or ways of thinking: *The school is very modern in its approach to sex education.* **3** made or done using the most recent methods: *advances in **modern medicine*** | ***modern technology*** [ORIGIN: 1500—1600 Late Latin *modernus*, from Latin *modo* "just now"]

THESAURUS **new, recent, original, latest** ➔ NEW

—modernity /mɑˈdɚnət̬i, -ˈdɛr-/ *n.* [U]

mod·ern·i·za·tion /ˌmɑdɚnəˈzeɪʃən/ *n.* [C,U] **1** the process or act of modernizing something: *the modernization of the railroads* **2** ECONOMICS the process by which a country becomes more developed through new TECHNOLOGY, social change, and better government

mod·ern·ize /ˈmɑdɚˌnaɪz/ *v.* [T] to change something so that it is more modern, by using new equipment or methods: *We're modernizing the whole house, starting with a new bathroom.*

mod·est /ˈmɑdɪst/ *adj.* **1** (approving) unwilling to talk proudly about your abilities and achievements (ANT) **immodest**: *He was extremely **modest about** his achievements.* **2** not very big in size, quantity, value, etc.: *a modest salary* | *The film was only a **modest success**.* **3** shy about showing your body or attracting sexual interest [ORIGIN: 1500—1600 Latin *modestus*] **—modestly** *adv.*

mod·es·ty /ˈmɑdəsti/ *n.* [U] **1** (approving) the quality of being modest about your abilities or achievements **2** the quality of being modest about your body

mod·i·cum /ˈmɑdɪkəm/ *n.* (formal) **a modicum of sth** a small amount of something, especially a good quality: *Walker had a modicum of success as a football player.*

mod·i·fi·ca·tion /ˌmɑdəfəˈkeɪʃən/ (Ac) *n.* **1** [C] a small change made in something such as a design, plan, or system: *We've made a few **modifications to** the original design.* | *In 2007, a further modification to the system was agreed.* **2** [U] the act of modifying something, or the process of being modified: *Modification of a patient's environment can sometimes speed up recovery.*

mod·i·fi·er /ˈmɑdəˌfaɪɚ/ *n.* [C] ENG. LANG. ARTS in grammar, an adjective, adverb, or phrase that gives additional information about another word. In the sentence "The dog is barking loudly," "loudly" is a modifier.

mod·i·fy /ˈmɑdəˌfaɪ/ (Ac) *v.* (**modified**, **modifies**) [T] **1** to make small changes to something in order to improve it: *The car's been **modified to** go faster.* | *Many of these ideas, in modified form, still interest scientists today.*

THESAURUS **change, alter, adapt, adjust, revise, amend** ➔ CHANGE[1]

2 ENG. LANG. ARTS to act as a modifier: *In English, an adjective usually immediately precedes the noun it modifies.* [ORIGIN: 1300—1400 French *modifier*, from Latin *modificare* "to measure, moderate," from *modus* "measure, way"]

mod·u·lar /ˈmɑdʒəlɚ/ *adj.* based on modules or made using modules: *modular furniture*

mod·u·late /ˈmɑdʒəˌleɪt/ *v.* [T] to change the sound of your voice or another sound **—modulation** /ˌmɑdʒəˈleɪʃən/ *n.* [U]

mod·ule /ˈmɑdʒul/ *n.* [C] **1** one of several separate parts that can be combined to form a larger object, such as a machine or building **2** a part of a SPACECRAFT that can be separated from the main part and used for a particular purpose ➔ SPACE[1]

mo·gul /ˈmoʊgəl/ *n.* **media/business/movie etc. mogul** someone who has great power and influence in a particular industry or activity [ORIGIN: 1600—1700 *Mogul* "member of a Muslim group that ruled India in former times" (16—21 centuries), from Persian *Mughul*, from Mongolian *Mongol*]

mo·hair /ˈmoʊhɛr/ *n.* [U] expensive wool made from ANGORA

Mo·ham·med /moʊˈhæməd/ *n.* MUHAMMAD

moi·e·ty /ˈmɔɪət̬i/ *n.* (plural **moieties**) [C] (formal) a half of something

moist /mɔɪst/ *adj.* slightly wet, in a pleasant way: *Make sure the soil is moist before planting the seeds.* | *a moist chocolate cake* [ORIGIN: 1300—1400 Old French *moiste*, from Latin *mucidus* "wet and slippery"] ➔ DAMP

moist·en /ˈmɔɪsən/ *v.* [I,T] to become slightly wet, or to make something become slightly wet: *Moisten the clay with a little water.*

mois·ture /ˈmɔɪstʃɚ/ *n.* [U] small amounts of water that are present in the air, in a substance, or on a surface: *The roots of the trees are not getting enough moisture.*

mois·tur·iz·er /ˈmɔɪstʃəˌraɪzɚ/ *n.* [C] a creamy liquid you put on your skin to keep it soft

mol /moʊl/ CHEMISTRY another spelling of MOLE

mo·lar /ˈmoʊlɚ/ *n.* [C] BIOLOGY one of the large teeth at the back of the mouth, used for crushing food [ORIGIN: 1300—1400 Latin *molaris* "crushing like a mill," from *mola*]

mo·las·ses /məˈlæsɪz/ *n.* [U] a thick dark sweet liquid that is obtained from raw sugar plants when they are being made into sugar

M

mold¹ /mould/ *n.* **1** [U] a soft green or black substance that grows on old food and on objects that are in warm, slightly wet places **2** [C] a hollow container that you pour liquid into, so that when the liquid becomes solid, it takes the shape of the container: *a candle mold shaped like a star*

mold² *v.* [T] **1** to shape a solid substance by pressing or rolling it, or by putting it into a mold: *a figure of a man **molded out of** clay* **2** to influence the way someone's character or attitudes develop: *I try to take young athletes and **mold** them **into** team players.*

mold·ing /'mɔldɪŋ/ *n.* [C,U] a thin line of stone, wood, plastic, etc. used as decoration around the edge of something such as a wall, car, or piece of furniture

mold·y /'mouldi/ *adj.* covered with mold: *moldy bread*

mole /moul/ *n.* [C] **1** a small brown mark on the skin that is sometimes slightly higher than the skin around it

THESAURUS **mark, blemish, bruise, scar, pimple, zit, wart, blister, freckle** → MARK²

2 a small animal with brown fur that lives in holes in the ground, and that cannot see well → *see picture at* RODENT **3** someone who works for an organization, especially a government, in order to secretly give information about it to its enemy **4** *also* **mol** CHEMISTRY an amount of a substance that contains 6.0225 × 10^{23} atoms, molecules, etc., which is equal to the number of atoms in 12 grams of CARBON-12

mol·e·cule /'mɑlə,kyul/ *n.* [C] CHEMISTRY one or more atoms that form the smallest unit of a particular substance: *a single water molecule* [ORIGIN: 1700—1800 French *molécule*, from Latin *moles* "mass"] —**molecular** /mə'lɛkyələ/ *adj.*

mo·lest /mə'lɛst/ *v.* [T] to attack or harm someone, especially a child, by touching him/her in a sexual way or trying to have sex with him/her: *She was sexually molested by her uncle.* —**molester** *n.* [C]: *a child molester* —**molestation** /,moulə'steɪʃən, ,mɑ-/ *n.* [U]

mol·li·fy /'mɑlə,faɪ/ *v.* (**mollified, mollifies**) [T] to make someone feel less angry and upset about something: *'I'm sorry,' Mike said, trying to mollify her.* —**mollification** /,mɑləfə'keɪʃən/ *n.* [U]

mol·lusk /'mɑləsk/ *n.* [C] a type of sea or land animal with a soft body covered by a hard shell, for example a SNAIL or CLAM

molt /moult/ *v.* [I] BIOLOGY when a bird or animal molts, it loses hair, feathers, skin, or shell so that new hair, etc. can grow

mol·ten /'moult¬n/ *adj.* EARTH SCIENCES molten metal or rock is liquid because it has been heated to a very high temperature

molt·ing /'moultɪŋ/ *n.* [U] BIOLOGY a process in which a bird or animal loses its hair, feathers, skin, or shell so that new hair, etc. can grow

mom /mɑm/ *n.* [C] (informal) mother: *Can I go to David's house, Mom?* | *I called my mom.* → RELATIVE¹

mo·ment /'moumənt/ *n.* [C] **1** a very short period of time → MINUTE: *Robert paused **for a moment**.* | *I'll be back **in a moment**.* | *Could you wait **just a moment**?* | *He was here **a moment ago**.* | *Denise arrived moments later.* **2** a particular point in time: *Just **at that moment**, Shelly came in.* | *I knew it was you **the moment (that)** I heard your voice.* | *He said he loved her **from the moment (that)** he met her.* | ***At that very/exact/precise moment**, the phone rang.* **3 at the moment** now: *Japanese food is popular at the moment.* **4 any moment** soon: *The attack could come **at any moment**.* **5 for the moment** used in order to say that something is happening now but will probably change in the future: *For the moment, she decided not to argue.* **6** a particular period of time when you have a chance to do something: *It was her **big moment*** (=important chance)*; she took a deep breath and began to play.* | *Jo speaks out against sexism, but knows she has to **choose** her **moments*** (=choose the best time) *carefully.*

mo·men·tar·i·ly /,moumən'tɛrəli/ *adv.* **1** for a very short time: *The car slowed down momentarily.* **2** very soon: *I'll be with you momentarily.*

mo·men·tar·y /'moumən,tɛri/ *adj.* continuing for a very short time: *a momentary silence*

mo·men·tous /mou'mɛntəs, mə-/ *adj.* a momentous event, occasion, decision, etc. is very important, especially because of the effects it will have in the future: *the momentous events of the past year*

mo·men·tum /mou'mɛntəm, mə-/ *n.* [U] **1** the ability to keep increasing, developing, or being more successful: *Leconte won the first set, then seemed to **lose momentum**.* | *Cellular phone use has **gained/gathered momentum** in the past few years.* **2** the force that makes a moving object keep moving: *I'd **gained/gathered** so much **momentum*** (=moved faster and faster) *that I couldn't stop.* [ORIGIN: 1600—1700 Latin "movement, moment," from *movere* "to move"]

mom·ma /'mɑmə/ *n.* [C] (spoken) mother

mom·my /'mɑmi/ *n.* (plural **mommies**) [C] (spoken) mother → RELATIVE¹

mon·arch /'mɑnək, 'mɑnɑrk/ *n.* [C] a king or queen [ORIGIN: 1400—1500 Late Latin *monarcha*, from Greek, from *mono-* + *-archos* (from *archein* "to rule")]

THESAURUS **king, queen, prince, princess, ruler, emperor, sovereign** → KING

mon·ar·chy /'mɑnəki/ *n.* (plural **monarchies**) **1** [U] the system in which a country is ruled by a king or queen → REPUBLIC

THESAURUS **government, democracy, republic, regime, dictatorship, totalitarian** country/state, etc., police state ➔ GOVERNMENT

2 [C] a country that is ruled by a king or queen

mon·as·ter·y /ˈmɑnəˌstɛri/ *n.* (plural **monasteries**) [C] a building or group of buildings in which MONKS live ➔ CONVENT [ORIGIN: 1300—1400 Late Latin *monasterium*, from Greek, from *monazein* "to live alone"]

mo·nas·tic /məˈnæstɪk/ *adj.* relating to MONKS or a monastery

Mon·day /ˈmʌndi, -deɪ/ (*written abbreviation* **Mon.**) *n.* (plural **Mondays**) [C,U] the second day of the week, between Sunday and Tuesday: *The results will be announced Monday.* | *It snowed* ***on Monday.*** | *We'll see you* ***next Monday.*** | *Kelly arrived* ***last Monday.*** | *I'll call you first thing* ***Monday morning.*** [ORIGIN: from Old English *monandæg*, from a translation of Latin *lunae dies* "day of the moon"]

mon·e·tar·y /ˈmɑnəˌtɛri/ *adj* ECONOMICS relating to money, especially all the money in a particular country: *France's monetary policy*

mon·ey /ˈmʌni/ *n.* [U] **1** what you earn by working and use in order to buy things, for example coins or special pieces of paper ➔ CASH, CURRENCY: *$250 is a lot of money.* | *the* ***amount of money*** *California spends on schools* | *Teachers don't* ***make/earn*** *a lot of* ***money.*** | *We're trying to* ***save*** *enough* ***money*** *for a trip to Europe.* | *Women tend to* ***spend*** *their* ***money*** *on their families.* | *I forgot my wallet – do you* ***have*** *enough* ***money*** *to pay for the meal?* | *Buying a used truck is a* ***waste of money.*** | *The raffle is to* ***raise money*** *for the school.* | *Plumbers can make* ***good money*** (=good wages). | *a business that is* ***losing money*** (=earning less money than it spends)

THESAURUS

Types of money
bill – paper money: *a $20 bill*
coin – metal money: *old coins*
penny – a coin worth 1 cent
nickel – a coin worth 5 cents
dime – a coin worth 10 cents
quarter – a coin worth 25 cents
cash – money in the form of coins and bills: *I didn't have enough cash, so I paid by check.*
change – money in the form of coins: *Do you have any change for the phone?*
currency – the money used in a particular country: *He had $500 worth of Japanese currency.*

2 all the money that a person, country, or organization owns: *Is Ed just marrying her for her money?* | *I think he* ***made*** *his* ***money*** *on the stock market.* **3 get your money's worth** to think that something you have paid to do or see was worth the price that you paid: *Fans should get their money's worth.*

SPOKEN PHRASES

4 this/that kind of money a phrase meaning a lot of money, used when you think something costs too much, when someone earns a lot more than other people, etc.: *The rent was $5,250, and I just* ***don't have that kind of money.*** **5 pay good money for sth** to spend a lot of money on something: *I paid good money for those shoes!* **6 for my money** used when giving your opinion about something, to emphasize that you believe it strongly: *For my money, Williams was a much better ballplayer.* **7 put your money where your mouth is** to show by your actions that you really believe what you say: *The legislature needs to put its money where its mouth is regarding the environment.* **8 money is no object** used in order to say that you can spend as much money as you want to on something

[ORIGIN: 1200—1300 Old French *moneie*, from Latin *moneta* "mint, money," from *Moneta*, name given to Juno, the goddess in whose temple the ancient Romans produced money]

mon·ey·mak·er /ˈmʌniˌmeɪkɚ/ *n.* [C] ECONOMICS a product or business that earns a lot of money

ˈmoney ˌmarket *n.* [C] ECONOMICS the banks and other financial institutions that buy and sell BONDS, CURRENCY (=paper money), etc.

ˈmoney ˌorder *n.* [C] a special type of check that you buy and send to someone so that s/he can exchange it for money

ˈmoney supˌply *n.* [singular] ECONOMICS all the money that exists in a country's ECONOMY at a particular time, and the speed at which it is used

mon·grel /ˈmɑŋgrəl, ˈmʌŋ-/ *n.* [C] a dog that is a mix of several breeds ➔ MUTT

mon·i·tor¹ /ˈmɑnət̬ɚ/ (Ac) *n.* [C] **1** IT a piece of equipment, especially computer equipment, that looks like a television and shows information or pictures: *the regular beeps from the patient's heart monitor* | *a flat-screen monitor* ➔ *see picture on page A19* **2** someone whose job is to make sure that something happens fairly or in the right way: *UN monitors will oversee the elections.* **3** a child who is chosen to help a teacher in some way [ORIGIN: 1500—1600 Latin *monere* "to warn"]

monitor² *v.* [T] to carefully watch, listen to, or examine something over a period of time, to check for any changes or developments: *Nurses are monitoring the patient's condition.* | *Army intelligence has been* ***closely monitoring*** *the enemy's radio broadcasts.*

monk /mʌŋk/ *n.* [C] a man who is a member of a group of religious men who live together in a MONASTERY (=special building) ➔ NUN

mon·key¹ /ˈmʌŋki/ *n.* (plural **monkeys**) [C] **1** a type of active animal that lives in hot countries and has a long tail that it uses with its hands to climb trees **2** (informal) a small child who is active and likes to play tricks **3 monkey business** behavior that may cause trouble or be dishonest

monkey² *v.* (**monkeyed, monkeys**)

monkey (around) with sth *phr. v.* to touch or change something, usually when you do not know how to do it correctly: *They should stop monkeying around with the tax system.*

M

'monkey bars *n.* [plural] a structure of metal bars for children to climb on

'monkey wrench *n.* [C] a tool that is used for holding or turning things of different widths, especially NUTS

mon·o /'manoʊ/ *n.* [U] (informal) an infectious illness that makes you feel weak and tired for a long time

mon·o·chro·mat·ic /ˌmanəkroʊ'mæt̬ɪk/ *adj.* PHYSICS monochromatic light has only one WAVELENGTH

mon·o·cot·y·le·don /ˌmanəkat̬l'idn/ *also* **mon·o·cot** /'manəˌkat/ *n.* [C] BIOLOGY a type of plant that has seeds which produce one COTYLEDON (=first leaf) when it first starts to grow. An example of a monocotyledon is grass. ➔ DICOTYLEDON

mo·nog·a·my /mə'nagəmi/ *n.* [U] the CUSTOM or practice of being married to only one person at one time ➔ POLYGAMY —**monogamous** /mə'nagəməs/ *adj.*

mon·o·gram /'manəˌgræm/ *n.* [C] a design made from the first letters of someone's names that is put on things such as shirts or writing paper —**monogrammed** *adj.*

mon·o·lith·ic /ˌmanl'ɪθɪk◂/ *adj.* a monolithic organization, political system, etc. is very large and difficult to change —**monolith** /'manl-ɪθ/ *n.* [C]

mon·o·logue, **monolog** /'manlˌɔg, -ˌag/ *n.* [C] a long speech by one character in a play, movie, or television show

mon·o·mer /'manəmɚ/ *n.* [C] CHEMISTRY a MOLECULE with a simple chemical structure, which can combine with other molecules to form a POLYMER

mo·no·mi·al /ma'noʊmiəl/ *n.* [C] MATH an EXPRESSION in ALGEBRA that consists of only a single group of numbers, letters, or INDEXes. For example, y, 5x, or $5x^2y$ is a monomial, but 2x + 9y is not. ➔ POLYNOMIAL

mon·o·nu·cle·o·sis /ˌmanoʊˌnukli'oʊsɪs/ *n.* [U] (formal) MONO

mo·nop·o·lize /mə'napəˌlaɪz/ *v.* [T] (disapproving) to have complete control over something, especially a type of business, so that other people cannot get involved: *Big farming corporations are starting to monopolize the industry.* —**monopolization** /məˌnapələ'zeɪʃən/ *n.* [U]

Mo·nop·o·ly /mə'napəli/ *n.* [U] (trademark) a game using artificial money in which you try to get more money and property than your opponents

monopoly *n.* (plural **monopolies**) [C usually singular] **1** ECONOMICS the control of all or most of a business activity, or the company that has this control: *The train company has a* ***monopoly on/over*** *services to New Jersey.* **2 have a monopoly on sth** to have complete control or possession of something, so that other people cannot have it: *No country has a monopoly on bravery.* —**monopolistic** /məˌnapə'lɪstɪk/ *adj.*

mon·o·rail /'manəˌreɪl/ *n.* [C] a type of railroad that uses a single RAIL, or the train that travels on this type of railroad

mon·o·sac·cha·ride /ˌmanoʊ'sækəˌraɪd/ *n.* [C] CHEMISTRY a type of natural sugar, such as GLUCOSE, that has a very simple chemical structure ➔ POLYSACCHARIDE

mon·o·syl·lab·ic /ˌmanəsɪ'læbɪk/ *adj.* **1** ENG. LANG. ARTS a monosyllabic word has only one SYLLABLE ➔ POLYSYLLABIC **2** someone who is monosyllabic, or makes monosyllabic remarks, seems impolite because s/he does not say much: *a monosyllabic response*

mon·o·the·ism /'manəθiˌɪzəm/ *n.* [U] SOCIAL SCIENCE the belief that there is only one God ➔ POLYTHEISM —**monotheistic** /ˌmanəθi'ɪstɪk/ *adj.*

mon·o·tone /'manəˌtoʊn/ *n.* [singular] a way of talking that is boring because it does not get louder or softer: *She read aloud in a monotone.*

mo·not·o·nous /mə'nat¬n-əs/ *adj.* boring because nothing changes: *a monotonous job* —**monotony** *n.* [U] —**monotonously** *adv.*

THESAURUS **boring, dull, tedious** ➔ BORING

mon·soon /man'sun/ *n.* [C] EARTH SCIENCES the season, from April to October, when it rains a lot in India and other southern Asian countries, or the rain or wind that happens during this season [ORIGIN: 1500—1600 Early Dutch *monssoen*, from Portuguese *monçao*, from Arabic *mawsim* "time, season"]

mon·ster /'manstɚ/ *n.* [C] **1** an imaginary large ugly frightening creature: *a sea monster* **2** someone who is cruel and evil: *Only a monster could kill an innocent child.* **3** an object, animal, etc. that is unusually large: *The storm was a monster.* —**monster** *adj.*

mon·stros·i·ty /man'strasət̬i/ *n.* (plural **monstrosities**) [C] something large that is very ugly, especially a building

mon·strous /'manstrəs/ *adj.* **1** very wrong, immoral, or unfair: *a monstrous crime* **2** unusually large: *a monstrous animal* —**monstrously** *adv.*

mon·tage /man'taʒ, moʊn-/ *n.* **1** [U] ENG. LANG. ARTS an art form in which a picture, movie, etc. is made by combining parts of different pictures, etc. **2** [C] ENG. LANG. ARTS a picture, movie, etc. made using this process

month /mʌnθ/ *n.* [C] **1** one of the 12 periods of time that a year is divided into: *the month of May* | *He's starting college at the end of* ***this month.*** | *the meeting* ***last/next month*** (=the month before or after this one) | *We see my parents* ***once/twice etc. a month.*** **2** any period of time equal to about four weeks: *a six-month-old baby* | *We'll be back* ***a***

M

month from today/tomorrow/Friday. **3 months** a long time: *He was in the hospital **for months**.* [ORIGIN: Old English *monath*]

GRAMMAR

Talking about months
Use **in** to talk about a month but not about a particular date in that month: *The concert is in August.*
Use **on** to talk about a particular date in a month: *The concert is on August 20th.* | *She finishes school on the nineteenth of July.*
You can use **next** to talk about a month in the year after the present one: *They're getting married next June.*
You can also use **this** or **this coming** to talk about a month in the very near future: *This coming October, my daughter turns 15.*
You can use **last** to talk about a month before the present one: *She left last October.*
You can also use **this** or **this past** to talk about a month in the very recent past: *He returned to Los Angeles this past July.*

month·ly /ˈmʌnθli/ *adj., adv.* **1** happening or done every month: *a monthly meeting* | *The windows are cleaned monthly.*

THESAURUS **regular, hourly, daily, weekly, yearly, annual** → REGULAR[1]

2 relating to a single month: *his monthly income*

mon·u·ment /ˈmɑnyəmənt/ *n.* [C] a building or other large structure that is built to remind people of an important event or famous person → STATUE: *a **monument to** soldiers killed in the war* [ORIGIN: 1200—1300 Latin *monumentum*, from *monere* "to remind"]

mon·u·men·tal /ˌmɑnyəˈmɛntl◂/ *adj.* [usually before noun] **1** extremely large, bad, good, impressive, etc.: *a monumental task* **2** very important and having a lot of influence: *Darwin's monumental work on evolution*

moo /mu/ *n.* [C] the sound that a cow makes —**moo** *v.* [I]

mood /mud/ *n.* **1** [C] the way you feel at a particular time: *You're certainly **in a good/bad mood** today.* **2 be in the mood** to want to do something or feel that you would enjoy something: *He wasn't **in the mood for** jokes.* **3** [singular] the way a group of people feels about something or about life in general: *The mood of the country has changed.* **4** [C usually singular] the way that a place, book, movie, etc. makes you feel: *The opening shot of dark, rainy streets sets the mood for the whole movie.* **5 mood swings** occasions when someone's mood changes from being happy to being sad or angry, usually for no reason **6** [C,U] ENG. LANG. ARTS in grammar, one of the sets of verb forms that show whether the speaker is describing facts, giving orders, or expressing a wish or doubt. These verb forms are called the INDICATIVE (=used to express a fact or action), the IMPERATIVE (=used to express a command), and the SUBJUNCTIVE (=used to express a doubt or wish).

mood·y /ˈmudi/ *adj.* (comparative **moodier**, superlative **moodiest**) **1** (disapproving) someone who is moody becomes angry or sad quickly: *a moody teenager* **2** making people feel sad, worried, or frightened: *the song's moody lyrics*

moon[1] /mun/ *n.* **1 the Moon** *also* **the moon** PHYSICS the round object that shines in the sky at night: ***The moon rose** over the frozen lake.* | *the craters on the surface of the Moon* → SPACE[1] → *see picture at* SOLAR SYSTEM **2** [singular] the shape of this object as it appears at a particular time: *There's no moon tonight* (=it cannot be seen). | *a **full moon*** (=the moon when it looks completely round) | *the **new moon*** (=the moon when it first appears again in the sky as a thin CRESCENT) **3** [C] PHYSICS a large round object that moves around PLANETS other than the Earth: *Saturn has several moons* [ORIGIN: Old English *mona*] → **once in a blue moon** *at* ONCE[1]

moon[2] *v.* [I,T] (informal) to bend over and show your uncovered BUTTOCKS to someone as a rude joke

moon·less /ˈmunlɪs/ *adj.* without the moon showing in the sky: *a cloudy moonless night*

moon·light[1] /ˈmunlaɪt/ *n.* [U] the light of the moon: *The water looked silver **in the moonlight**.*

moonlight[2] *v.* [I] (informal) to have a second job in addition to your main job: *Clayton's been **moonlighting as** a security guard.* —**moonlighting** *n.* [U]

moon·lit /ˈmunˌlɪt/ *adj.* made brighter by the light of the moon: *a beautiful moonlit night*

moon·shine /ˈmunʃaɪn/ *n.* [U] (informal) strong alcohol that is produced illegally

moor /mʊr/ *v.* [I,T] to fasten a ship or boat to the land or the bottom of the sea, lake, etc. with a rope or chain

moor·ing /ˈmʊrɪŋ/ *n.* [C] the place where a ship or boat moors

moose /mus/ *n.* [C] a large wild North American, European, or Asian animal with large ANTLERS (=flat horns that look like branches) and a head like a horse

moot /mut/ *adj.* a situation or possible action that is moot is no longer likely to happen or exist, or is no longer important: *I've already handed in my notice, so whether it was the right thing to do is a **moot point**.*

mop[1] /mɑp/ *n.* [C] **1** a thing for washing floors, made of a long stick with thick strings or a SPONGE fastened to one end **2** (informal) a large amount of thick messy hair: *a **mop of** curly **hair***

mop[2] *v.* (**mopped**, **mopping**) [T] **1** to wash a floor with a wet mop

THESAURUS **clean, do the housework, vacuum, sweep (up), scrub** → CLEAN[2]

M

2 to remove liquid from a surface by rubbing it with a cloth or something soft: *He mopped his face with a napkin.*

mop sth ↔ **up** *phr. v.* to clean liquid off a surface using a mop, cloth, or something soft: *We mopped up the spill with a rag.*

mope /moʊp/ *also* **mope around** *v.* [I] to pity yourself and feel sad, without trying to be happier: *Jack just moped around the house all day feeling guilty.*

mo·ped /ˈmoʊpɛd/ *n.* [C] a vehicle like a bicycle with a small engine

mo·raine /məˈreɪn/ *n.* [C,U] EARTH SCIENCES rock, sand, clay, etc. that is pushed along in front of a GLACIER when it moves forward, and that is left in place when the glacier melts

mor·al[1] /ˈmɔrəl, ˈmɑrəl/ *adj.* [usually before noun] **1** relating to the principles of what is right and wrong behavior, and the difference between good and evil (ANT) **immoral**: *a moral issue such as the death penalty* | *There are doubts about his ethical and* ***moral standards/values***. | *a* ***moral responsibility/obligation/duty*** *to help the poor* **2 moral support** encouragement that you give by expressing approval or interest, rather than by giving practical help: *I went along to offer moral support.* **3 moral victory** a situation in which you show that your beliefs are right and fair, even if you do not win **4** always behaving in a way that is based on strong principles about what is right and wrong: *a moral man*

moral[2] *n.* **1 morals** [plural] principles or standards of good behavior, especially in matters of sex: *You're dealing with someone who has no morals or ethics.*

THESAURUS

ethics – moral rules or principles of behavior for deciding what is right and wrong: *Corporations should learn to care about ethics as much as profit.*
standards – moral principles about what kind of behavior and attitudes are acceptable: *Are the country's moral standards lower than in the past?*
values – your beliefs about what is right and wrong, or about what is important in life: *Children should learn values from their parents.*
principles – a set of rules or ideas about what is right and wrong that influences how you behave: *He tries to live according to his Christian principles.*
scruples – a belief about what is right and wrong that prevents you from doing something bad: *No one should set aside their moral scruples when they go to work.*
mores (formal) – the customs, social behavior, and moral values of a particular group: *During the 1960's, American sexual mores began to change.*

2 [C] a practical lesson about how to behave that you learn from a story or from something that happens to you: ***The moral of the story is*** *that crime doesn't pay.*

mo·rale /məˈræl/ *n.* [U] a person's or group's morale is how good, bad, or confident they feel about their situation: *The employees'* ***morale*** *is* ***low/high*** (=bad/good).

mor·al·ist·ic /ˌmɔrəˈlɪstɪk◂, ˌmɑr-/ *adj.* (disapproving) having very strong beliefs about what is right and wrong, and about how people should behave —**moralist** /ˈmɔrəlɪst, ˈmɑ-/ *n.* [C]

mo·ral·i·ty /məˈræləṭi/ *n.* [U] **1** beliefs or ideas about what is right and wrong, and about how people should behave: *declining standards of morality* **2** the degree to which something is right or acceptable: *a discussion on the* ***morality of*** *the death penalty*

mor·al·ize /ˈmɔrəˌlaɪz, ˈmɑr-/ *v.* [I] (disapproving) to tell other people your ideas about right and wrong behavior, and about how people should behave

mor·al·ly /ˈmɔrəli, ˈmɑr-/ *adv.* **1** according to moral principles about what is right and wrong: *It wasn't against the law, but it was* ***morally wrong***. **2** in a way that is good and right: *He tried to act morally.*

mo·rass /məˈræs/ *n.* [singular] **1** a complicated and confusing situation that is very difficult to get out of: *the country's economic morass* **2** a complicated amount of information: *a* ***morass of*** *details*

mor·a·to·ri·um /ˌmɔrəˈtɔriəm, ˌmɑr-/ *n.* [C usually singular] an official announcement stopping an activity for a period of time: *a* ***moratorium on*** *nuclear weapons testing*

mor·bid /ˈmɔrbɪd/ *adj.* (disapproving) having a strong interest in unpleasant subjects, especially death: *The newspapers printed all the morbid details of the murder.* [ORIGIN: 1600—1700 Latin *morbidus* "diseased," from *morbus* "illness"] —**morbidly** *adv.*

more[1] /mɔr/ *adv.* **1** [used before an adjective or adverb to form the comparative] having a particular quality to a greater degree (ANT) **less**: *The second test was more difficult.* | *It was* ***more*** *expensive* ***than*** *I thought it would be.* | *People change careers* ***much/a lot/far more*** *frequently now.* | *Teenagers rely* ***more and more*** *on their friends.* | *Children are* ***no more*** *likely* ***than*** *adults to develop the disease.* **2** happening a greater number of times, or for longer (ANT) **less**: *I promised I'd help more in the house.* | *We see our grandchildren* ***more than*** *we used to.* | *He's been working* ***a lot more*** *lately.* **3 not ... any more** used in order to show that something that used to happen or be true does not happen or is not true now ➔ ANYMORE: *Sarah doesn't live here any more.* ➔ **once more** *at* ONCE[1]

more[2] *quantifier* [the comparative of "many" and "much"] **1** a greater amount or number: ***More*** *new jobs were created* ***than*** *were lost in the industry.* | *The bus was* ***more than*** *two hours late.* | ***More and more*** *schools have their own website.* **2** an additional number or amount: *Would you like some* *more coffee?* | *I have* ***some/a few/many etc. more*** *phone calls to make.* | *Is there* ***any more*** *cake?* | *We had* ***no more*** *questions.* | *We had* ***5/12/20 more*** *people at the meeting* ***than*** *we expected.* | *Scott needed to see* ***more of*** *his father.*

THESAURUS

another – something in addition to a particular amount, distance, period of time, etc.: *Do you want another cup of coffee?*
extra – more than the usual or standard amount of something: *I always carry an extra key, in case I lose my other one.*
additional – more than you already have, or more than was agreed or expected: *Additional troops will be sent to the region.*
further – more, used especially when something happens again or is done again: *Further research is needed.*
supplemental/supplementary – additional, used especially when the original amount is not quite enough: *Colleges can help students who need more money to get supplemental loans.*

3 more or less almost: *This report says more or less the same thing as the other one.*

more·o·ver /mɔr'oʊvɚ/ *adv.* (formal) a word meaning "in addition to this" that is used in order to add information to something that has just been said: *The rent is reasonable, and, moreover, it's close to work.*

mo·res /'mɔreɪz/ *n.* [plural] (formal) the CUSTOMS, social behavior, and moral values of a particular group: *American social mores*

THESAURUS **moral, ethics, standards, values** → MORAL[2]

morgue /mɔrg/ *n.* [C] a building or room where dead bodies are kept before they are buried or burned

Mor·mon /'mɔrmən/ *adj.* relating to a religious organization called The Church of Jesus Christ of Latter-Day Saints, that has strict moral rules such as not allowing its members to drink alcohol and coffee —**Mormon** *n.* [C] —**Mormonism** *n.* [U]

morn·ing /'mɔrnɪŋ/ *n.* **1** [C,U] the early part of the day, especially from when the Sun rises until the middle of the day: *I got a letter from Wayne* ***this morning.*** | *The freeway is usually jammed* ***in the morning.*** | *Andy woke up at* ***two/three etc. in the morning*** (=during the night). | *the TV programs that are on* ***Saturday/Tuesday etc. morning*** | *a meeting* ***yesterday/tomorrow morning*** | *a* ***sunny/cloudy/foggy etc. morning*** | *I had my* ***morning coffee/walk/routine etc.*** (=coffee, etc. that you have in the morning) **2 (Good) Morning** (spoken) said in order to greet someone when you meet him/her in the morning: *Morning, Rick.*

'morning ˌsickness *n.* [U] a feeling of sickness that some women have when they are PREGNANT

mo·ron /'mɔrɑn/ *n.* [C] someone who is very stupid —**moronic** /mə'rɑnɪk/ *adj.*

mo·rose /mə'roʊs/ *adj.* (literary) unhappy, silent, and in a bad mood —**morosely** *adv.*

THESAURUS **sad, unhappy, miserable, sorrowful, depressed, down, low, blue, downhearted, melancholy, gloomy, glum** → SAD

morph /mɔrf/ *v.* **1** [I,T] IT to make one image gradually change into a different image by using a computer, or to gradually change into a different image **2** [I] (informal) to gradually change into something different: *At that time, I was* ***morphing into*** *being a single mom.*

mor·pheme /'mɔrfim/ *n.* [C] ENG. LANG. ARTS the smallest unit of language that has meaning, consisting of a word or part of a word that cannot be divided without losing its meaning. For example, "gun" contains one morpheme, but "gunfighter" contains three: "gun," "fight," and "-er." → PHONEME

mor·phine /'mɔrfin/ *n.* [U] a powerful drug used for stopping pain [ORIGIN: 1800—1900 French *Morpheus* ancient Roman god of sleep]

mor·phol·o·gy /mɔr'fɑlədʒi/ *n.* [U] **1** ENG. LANG. ARTS the study of the morphemes of a language and of the way in which they are joined together to make words → SYNTAX **2** BIOLOGY the scientific study of how animals, plants, and their parts are formed

Morse code /ˌmɔrs 'koʊd/ *n.* [U] a system of sending messages in which the alphabet is represented by short and long signals of sound or light

mor·sel /'mɔrsəl/ *n.* [C] a small piece of food: *a* ***morsel of*** *bread*

mor·tal[1] /'mɔrtl/ *adj.* **1** not living forever (ANT) **immortal**: *mortal creatures* **2 mortal injuries/blow/danger etc.** injuries, etc. that will cause death or are likely to cause death **3 mortal fear/terror/dread** extreme fear [ORIGIN: 1300—1400 Old French, Latin *mortalis*, from *mors* "death"] —**mortally** *adv.*: *He was mortally wounded.*

mortal[2] *n.* **1 lesser/ordinary/mere mortals** (humorous) an expression meaning ordinary people, as compared with people who are more important or more powerful **2** [C] (literary) a human

mor·tal·i·ty /mɔr'tæləti/ *n.* [U] **1** *also* **mortality rate** the number of deaths during a particular period of time among a particular group of people or from a particular cause: *a decrease in the* ***infant mortality rate*** (=the rate at which babies die) **2** the condition of being human and having to die

mor·tar /'mɔrtɚ/ *n.* **1** [C] a heavy gun that fires explosives in a high curve **2** [U] a mixture of LIME, sand, and water, used in building for sticking bricks or stones together

mortarboard

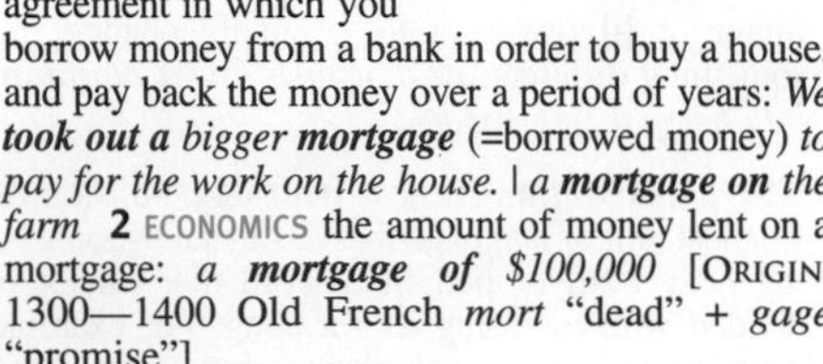

mor·tar·board /ˈmɔrt̬ɚˌbɔrd/ *n.* [C] a cap with a flat square top that you wear when you GRADUATE from a HIGH SCHOOL, college, or university

mort·gage¹ /ˈmɔrgɪdʒ/ *n.* [C] **1** ECONOMICS an agreement in which you borrow money from a bank in order to buy a house, and pay back the money over a period of years: *We* ***took out a*** *bigger* ***mortgage*** (=borrowed money) *to pay for the work on the house.* | *a* ***mortgage on*** *the farm* **2** ECONOMICS the amount of money lent on a mortgage: *a* ***mortgage of*** *$100,000* [ORIGIN: 1300—1400 Old French *mort* "dead" + *gage* "promise"]

mortgage² *v.* [T] ECONOMICS to borrow money by giving someone, usually a bank, the right to own your house, land, or property if you do not pay back the money the person or bank lent you within a certain period of time

mor·ti·cian /mɔrˈtɪʃən/ *n.* [C] someone whose job is to arrange funerals and prepare bodies before they are buried

mor·ti·fy /ˈmɔrt̬əˌfaɪ/ *v.* **be mortified** to feel extremely embarrassed or ashamed: *Harry was mortified by his mistake.* **—mortifying** *adj.* **—mortification** /ˌmɔrt̬əfəˈkeɪʃən/ *n.* [U]

mor·tu·ar·y /ˈmɔrtʃuˌɛri/ *n.* (plural **mortuaries**) [C] the place where a body is kept before a funeral and where the funeral is sometimes held

mo·sa·ic /moʊˈzeɪ-ɪk/ *n.* [C,U] a pattern or picture made by fitting together small pieces of colored stone, glass, etc.

mosh /mɑʃ/ *v.* [I] (informal) to dance using a lot of energy at a concert with loud ROCK or PUNK music

Mos·lem /ˈmɑzləm, ˈmɑs-/ *n.* [C] a MUSLIM **—Moslem** *adj.*

mosque /mɑsk/ *n.* [C] a building where Muslims go to have religious services [ORIGIN: 1400—1500 Old French *mosquee*, from Old Spanish *mezquita*, from Arabic *sajada* "to lie face downward"]

mos·qui·to /məˈskit̬oʊ/ *n.* (plural **mosquitoes**) [C] a small flying insect that bites and sucks the blood of people and animals, making you ITCH and sometimes spreading diseases [ORIGIN: 1500—1600 Spanish *mosca* "fly," from Latin *musca*]

moss /mɔs/ *n.* [U] a small flat green or yellow plant that looks like fur and often grows on trees and rocks **—mossy** *adj.*

most¹ /moʊst/ *adv.* **1** [used before an adjective or adverb to form the superlative] having the greatest amount of a particular quality: *Basketball is the most popular sport.* | *She has lived in France, Italy, and, most recently, Spain.* | *the most powerful man in the world* **2** to a greater degree, or more times than anything else: *Which do you like most?* | *It's been challenging, but* ***most of all****, it's been fun.* **3** (spoken, informal) almost: *We eat at Joe's* ***most every*** *weekend.*

most² *quantifier* [the superlative of "many" and "much"] **1** almost all of the people or things in a group ➔ MAJORITY: ***Most of the*** *books were old.* | *Polls show that most Americans don't eat enough fruit.* **2** a larger amount or number than anyone or anything else: *Which class has* ***the most*** *children?* | *The team that scores* ***the most*** *points wins.* **3** the largest number or amount possible: *How can we get* ***the most*** *power from the engine?* **4 at (the) most** used in order to say that a number or amount will not be larger than you say: *It'll take twenty minutes at the most.* **5 for the most part** used in order to say that something is generally true but not completely true: *For the most part, they did a pretty good job.* **6 make the most of sth/get the most out of sth** to get the greatest possible advantage from a situation: *It's your only chance, so make the most of it.*

GRAMMAR

most, most of

Use **most** immediately before a plural noun form or an uncountable noun when you are talking about something in general: *I like most kinds of music.* | *Most oil comes from the Middle East.*

Use **most of** before "the," "this," "my," etc. and a noun when you are talking about a particular group or thing: *Most of the houses are new.* | *Most of her friends still lived with their parents.*

most·ly /ˈmoʊstli/ *adv.* in most cases, or most of the time: *The room was full of athletes, mostly football players.* | *Mostly, we talked about marriage and kids.* ▸Don't say "mostly all," "mostly everybody," etc. Say "almost all," "almost everybody," etc.◂

mo·tel /moʊˈtɛl/ *n.* [C] a hotel for people traveling by car, with a place for the car near each room

THESAURUS **hotel, inn, bed and breakfast (b&b), hostel** ➔ HOTEL

moth /mɔθ/ *n.* [C] an insect similar to a BUTTERFLY, that usually flies at night, especially toward lights ➔ *see picture at* BUTTERFLY

moth·ball¹ /ˈmɔθbɔl/ *v.* [T] (informal) to close a factory or operation, and keep all its equipment or plans for a long time without using them

mothball² *n.* [C] a small ball made of a strong-smelling chemical, used for keeping moths away from clothes

moth·er /ˈmʌðɚ/ *n.* [C] **1** a female parent: *My mother said I have to be home by 9:00.* | *a* ***mother of three*** (=with three children) | *a mother hen and her chicks* ➔ RELATIVE¹ **2** (spoken) something that is a very good or very bad example of its type, or that is very impressive: *I woke up with* ***the mother***

of all hangovers. [ORIGIN: Old English *modor*] —**mother** *v.* [T]

moth·er·board /ˈmʌðɚˌbɔrd/ *n.* [C] IT the main CIRCUIT BOARD inside a computer

moth·er·hood /ˈmʌðɚˌhʊd/ *n.* [U] the state of being a mother

moth·er·ing /ˈmʌðərɪŋ/ *n.* [U] the activity of a mother taking care of her children

ˈmother-in-ˌlaw *n.* (plural **mothers-in-law**) [C] the mother of your husband or wife

moth·er·ly /ˈmʌðɚli/ *adj.* typical of a kind or concerned mother: *The teacher was a motherly woman.*

ˌMother ˈNature *n.* [U] an expression used in order to talk about the Earth, its weather, and the living creatures and plants on it

ˌmother-of-ˈpearl *n.* [U] a pale-colored smooth shiny substance on the inside of some shells, used for making buttons, jewelry, etc.

ˈMother's Day *n.* a holiday in honor of mothers, celebrated in the U.S. and Canada on the second Sunday of May

ˌmother-to-ˈbe *n.* (plural **mothers-to-be**) [C] a woman who is going to have a baby

mo·tif /moʊˈtif/ *n.* [C] ENG. LANG. ARTS an idea, subject, or pattern that is regularly repeated and developed in a book, movie, work of art, etc.

mo·tion¹ /ˈmoʊʃən/ *n.* **1** [U] the process of moving, or the way that someone or something moves: *the gentle rolling* ***motion of*** *the ship* **2** [C] a single movement of your head, hand, etc.: *One of the soldiers* ***made a*** *chopping* ***motion*** *with his hand.* **3** [C] a proposal that is made formally at a meeting and then decided on by voting: *The* ***motion to*** *increase the charges was* ***passed/carried*** *by 15 votes to 10.* | *Janke* ***made/proposed a motion*** *that the meeting be adjourned.* | *The* ***motion*** *was* ***seconded*** *by Levin.* **4 in slow motion** if something on television or in the movies is shown in slow motion, it is shown more slowly than usual so that all the actions can be clearly seen: *Let's look at that touchdown in slow motion.* **5 set sth in motion** to start a process or series of events that will continue: *The kidnapping set in motion a massive police investigation.* **6 go through the motions** to do something because you have to do it, without being very interested in it: *Too many of our top players are just going through the motions.*

motion² *v.* [I,T] to give someone directions or instructions by moving your head, hand, etc.: *The police officer* ***motioned for*** *me* ***to*** *stop the car.*

mo·tion·less /ˈmoʊʃənlɪs/ *adj.* not moving at all: *Kemp sat motionless as the verdict was read.*

ˌmotion ˈpicture *n.* [C] a movie

mo·ti·vate /ˈmoʊt̬əˌveɪt/ (Ac) *v.* [T] **1** to make someone feel determined or eager to do something: *Praise, rather than criticism,* ***motivates*** *children* ***to*** *do well.* **2 motivating factor/force** the reason why someone behaves in a particular way: *Money was the main* ***the motivating factor behind*** *their decision.*

mo·ti·vat·ed /ˈmoʊt̬əˌveɪt̬ɪd/ (Ac) *adj.* **1** very eager to do or achieve something: *an intelligent and* ***highly motivated*** *student* **2** done for a particular reason: *The killings were thought to be* ***racially motivated*** (=done because someone hates other races).

mo·ti·va·tion /ˌmoʊt̬əˈveɪʃən/ (Ac) *n.* **1** [U] the determination and desire to do something: *Jack is smart, but he lacks motivation.* | *If the task is too difficult, learners lose motivation.* **2** [C] the reason why you want to do something: *a student's* ***motivation for*** *learning* | *What was the* ***motivation behind*** *his actions?* —**motivational** *adj.*: *a motivational speech*

mo·tive /ˈmoʊt̬ɪv/ (Ac) *n.* [C] the reason that makes someone do something, especially when this reason is kept hidden: *Police are trying to find out the* ***motive for*** *the attack.* | *The people began to question the motives of their leaders.* → **ulterior motive** *at* ULTERIOR

THESAURUS **reason, explanation, excuse, rationale, grounds** → REASON¹

mot·ley /ˈmɑtli/ *adj.* (disapproving) **a motley crew/bunch/assortment etc.** a group of people or other things that do not seem to belong together

mo·tor¹ /ˈmoʊt̬ɚ/ *n.* [C] the part of a machine that makes it work or move → ENGINE: *The drill is powered by a small electric motor.*

motor² *adj.* **1** using power provided by an engine: *a motor vehicle* **2** relating to the way muscles are controlled: *a child's motor skills*

mo·tor·bike /ˈmoʊt̬ɚˌbaɪk/ *n.* [C] a motorcycle, especially a small one → *see picture at* TRANSPORTATION

mo·tor·cade /ˈmoʊt̬ɚˌkeɪd/ *n.* [C] a group of cars and other vehicles that travel together and surround a very important person's car

mo·tor·cy·cle /ˈmoʊt̬ɚˌsaɪkəl/ *n.* [C] a fast, usually large, two-wheeled vehicle with an engine

ˈmotor home *n.* [C] a large vehicle with beds, a kitchen, etc. in it, used for traveling (SYN) **RV** → MOBILE HOME

mo·tor·ist /ˈmoʊt̬ərɪst/ *n.* [C] (formal) someone who drives a car

mo·tor·ized /ˈmoʊt̬əˌraɪzd/ *adj.* having an engine, especially when something does not usually have an engine: *a motorized wheelchair*

ˈmotor ˌscooter *n.* [C] a SCOOTER

ˈmotor ˌvehicle *n.* [C] (formal) a car, bus, truck, etc.

mot·tled /ˈmɑt̬ld/ *adj.* covered with spots of light and dark colors of different shapes: *mottled skin*

mot·to /ˈmɑt̬oʊ/ *n.* (plural **mottoes**) [C] a short statement that expresses the aims or beliefs of a

M

person, school, or institution: *The motto of the Boy Scouts is "Be Prepared."*

mound /maʊnd/ *n.* [C] **1** a pile of dirt, stones, sand, etc. **2** a large pile of something: *a* ***mound of*** *papers*

THESAURUS pile, heap, stack, drift → PILE[1]

mount[1] /maʊnt/ *v.* **1** [I] *also* **mount up** to increase gradually in size, degree, or amount → MOUNTING: *His debts continued to mount up.* | ***Tensions mounted*** *as we waited for the result.* **2** [T] to plan, organize, and begin an event or a course of action: *The gallery mounted an exhibition of Weston's photographs.* | *Guerrillas* ***mounted an attack*** *on the village.* **3** [I,T] (formal) to get on a horse or bicycle ANT **dismount** **4** [T] (formal) to go up something such as a set of stairs: *He mounted the steps and shook hands with Bianchi.* **5 be mounted on sth** to be attached to something and supported by it: *paintings mounted on the wall* [ORIGIN: 1200—1300 Old French *monter* "to go up," from Latin *mons*]

mount[2] *n.* **1 Mount** part of the name of a mountain: *Mount Everest* **2** [C] (literary) an animal, especially a horse, that you ride on

moun·tain /ˈmaʊntˀn/ *n.* [C] **1** EARTH SCIENCES a very high hill: *the highest mountain in California* | *She was the first British woman to* ***climb*** *the* ***mountain***. | *the* ***mountain ranges*** (=lines of mountains) *in the west* | *snow-capped* ***mountain peaks*** (=tops of mountains) → *see picture on page A24* **2** a very large pile or amount of something: *a* ***mountain of*** *work to do*

ˈmountain ˌbike *n.* [C] a strong bicycle with wide thick tires that you can ride on rough ground

ˈmountain ˌbiking *n.* [U] the activity of riding a mountain bike on rough ground → *see picture on page A17*

moun·tain·eer·ing /ˌmaʊntˀnˈɪrɪŋ/ *n.* [U] an outdoor activity in which you climb mountains —**mountaineer** *n.* [C]

ˈmountain goat *n.* [C] a type of goat that lives in the western mountains of North America

ˈmountain ˌlion *n.* [C] a COUGAR

moun·tain·ous /ˈmaʊntˀn-əs/ *adj.* having a lot of mountains: *a mountainous region of Europe*

moun·tain·side /ˈmaʊntˀnˌsaɪd/ *n.* [C] the side of a mountain

moun·tain·top /ˈmaʊntˀnˌtɑp/ *n.* [C] the top part of a mountain

Mount·ie /ˈmaʊnti/ *n.* [C] a member of the national police force of Canada

mount·ing /ˈmaʊntɪŋ/ *adj.* gradually increasing or becoming worse: *There was* ***mounting pressure*** *from the country's political leaders.*

mourn /mɔrn/ *v.* [I,T] to feel very sad because someone has died, and show this in the way you behave: *The whole country mourned Kennedy's death.* | *She was still* ***mourning for*** *her sister.*

mourn·er /ˈmɔrnɚ/ *n.* [C] (written) someone who attends a funeral, especially a relative of the dead person

mourn·ful /ˈmɔrnfəl/ *adj.* (literary) very sad: *slow mournful music*

mourn·ing /ˈmɔrnɪŋ/ *n.* [U] **1** great sadness because someone has died: *People wore black as a sign of mourning.* **2 be in mourning** to be very sad because someone has died: *She's still* ***in mourning for*** *her son.*

mouse /maʊs/ *n.* [C] **1** (plural **mouses** *or* **mice** /maɪs/) IT a small object connected to a computer by a wire, that you move with your hand to give instructions to the computer → *see picture on page A19* **2** (plural **mice**) a small furry animal with a long tail and a pointed nose that lives in buildings or in fields [ORIGIN: Old English *mus*] → *see picture at* RODENT

ˈmouse pad *n.* [C] IT a small piece of flat material on which you move a computer mouse → *see picture on page A19*

mousse /mus/ *n.* [U] **1** a cold sweet food made from a mixture of cream, eggs, and fruit or chocolate: *chocolate mousse* **2** a slightly sticky substance that you put in your hair to make it look thicker or to hold it in place

mous·tache /ˈmʌstæʃ, məˈstæʃ/ *n.* [C] a MUSTACHE

mous·y /ˈmaʊsi, -zi/ *adj.* (disapproving) **1** mousy hair is a dull brownish-gray color **2** a mousy girl or woman is small, quiet, not interesting, and not attractive

mouth[1] /maʊθ/ *n.* (plural **mouths** /maʊðz/) [C] **1** the part of your face that you use for speaking and eating: *his round face and wide mouth* | *The beginnings of a smile touched the* ***corners of*** *her* ***mouth***. | *Don't talk with your* ***mouth full*** (=full of food). → *see picture on page A16* **2 open/shut your mouth** to start to speak, or to stop speaking: *Shut your mouth, Tonya!* | *He was afraid to open his mouth during the meeting.* **3 keep your mouth shut** (informal) to not say what you are thinking, or not tell someone a secret: *I was getting really mad, but I kept my mouth shut.* **4** an opening, entrance, or way out: *the mouth of a river* (=where it joins the ocean) | *the mouth of a jar* **5 big mouth** (informal) someone who is a big mouth or has a big mouth often says things that s/he should not say **6 make your mouth water** if food makes your mouth water, it smells or looks so good you want to eat it immediately → MOUTH-WATERING **7 open-mouthed/wide-mouthed etc.** with an open, wide, etc. mouth [ORIGIN: Old English *muth*] → **shoot your mouth off** *at* SHOOT[1]

mouth[2] /maʊð/ *v.* [T] to move your lips as if you are saying words, but without making any sound: *Kim looked at me and mouthed, "It's O.K."* → BAD-MOUTH

M

mouth off *phr. v.* (informal) to talk angrily or rudely to someone: *a boxer* ***mouthing off to*** *his opponent*

mouth·ful /ˈmaʊθfʊl/ *n.* [C] an amount of food or drink that you put into your mouth at one time: *He swallowed a* ***mouthful of*** *coffee.*

mouth·piece /ˈmaʊθpis/ *n.* [C] **1** the part of a musical instrument, telephone, etc. that you put in your mouth or next to your mouth **2** a person, newspaper, etc. that expresses the opinions of a government or a political organization, especially without ever criticizing these opinions: *The newspaper is the* ***mouthpiece of/for*** *the ruling party.*

mouth·wash /ˈmaʊθwɑʃ, -wɔʃ/ *n.* [U] a liquid you can use to make your mouth smell fresh or to get rid of an infection in your mouth

ˈmouth-ˌwatering *adj.* food that is mouth-watering looks or smells extremely good

mov·a·ble /ˈmuvəbəl/ *adj.* able to be moved (ANT) **immovable**: *dolls with movable arms and legs*

move¹ /muv/ *v.*

1 CHANGE POSITION [I,T] to change from one place or position to another, or to make something do this → MOTION: *Molly sat down and refused to move.* | *Could you move your car, please?* | *Pat* ***moved closer to/toward*** *her.* | *She* ***moved slowly/quickly etc.*** *to the door.* | *The kids were* ***moving around*** *the classroom, choosing activities.*

2 NEW PLACE [I,T] to go to a new place to live, work, or study, or to make someone do this: *Her parents are* ***moving into*** *a retirement home.* | *The army paid to* ***move*** *our family* ***to*** *Germany.*

3 CHANGE JOB/CLASS ETC. [I,T] to change to a different job, class, etc., or to make someone do this: *He* ***moved*** *easily* ***from*** *teaching* ***into*** *administration.* | *Some students were* ***moved into*** *the intermediate class.*

4 get moving *also* **move it** (spoken) used in order to say that someone needs to hurry: *If you don't get moving, you'll miss the bus.*

5 PROGRESS [I] to progress or change in a particular way: *The talks seem to be* ***moving*** *swiftly* ***toward*** *a deal.*

6 START DOING STH [I] to start doing something in order to achieve something: *U.S. leaders should* ***move*** *quickly* ***to*** *outlaw these weapons.* | *The Senate has not yet* ***moved on*** (=not done anything as a result of) *the suggestions from the committee.*

7 FEEL EMOTION [T] to make someone feel a strong emotion, especially sadness or sympathy → MOVING: *The mourners were all* ***moved to tears*** *by the poem.* | *The audience,* ***deeply/genuinely moved****, was silent.*

8 CHANGE ARRANGEMENTS [T] to change the time or order of something: *The meeting's been* ***moved to*** *Tuesday.*

9 MEETING [I] (formal) to make an official suggestion at a meeting: *Dr. Reder* ***moved that*** *the proposal be accepted.*

10 GO FAST [I] (informal) to travel very fast: *That truck was really moving.* [ORIGIN: 1200—1300 Old French *mouvoir*, from Latin *movere*]

move away *phr. v.*
to go to live in a different area: *I lost touch with her when her family moved away.*

move in *phr. v.*
1 *also* **move into** to start living in a new house (ANT) **move out**: *When are you moving into your new house?*
2 to start living with someone in the same house: *After her father died, she* ***moved in with*** *her aunt.* | *Al and Bridget have* ***moved in together****.*
3 to start being involved in and controlling a situation that someone else controlled previously: *huge companies* ***moving in on*** *small businesses*

move on *phr. v.*
1 to leave your present job, class, or activity and start doing another one: *After 12 years as principal here, Garcia will* ***move on to*** *a new school this fall.*
2 to leave a place where you have been staying or doing something in order to continue to another place: *We stayed in Singapore for a few days and then decided to move on.*
3 to start talking or writing about a new subject in a speech, book, discussion, etc.: *Before we move on, does anyone have any questions?*
4 to develop in your life, and change your relationships, interests, activities, etc.: *Harry left you a year ago; it's time for you to move on.*
5 to progress, improve, or become more modern as time passes: *By the time the software was ready, the market had moved on.*

move out *phr. v.*
to leave the house where you are living in order to go to live somewhere else (ANT) **move in**: *When did Bob move out?* | *I* ***moved out of*** *my folk's place when I turned 18.*

move over *phr. v.*
to change position so that there is space for someone or something else: *Move over a little, so I can sit down.*

move up *phr. v.*
to get a better job, or change to a more advanced group, higher rank, or higher level: *Students have to pass oral and written exams before moving up.* | ***Moving up the*** *economic* ***ladder*** *is everyone's dream.*

move² *n.* [C] **1** something that you decide to do in order to achieve something or make progress: *The White House says the statement is a* ***move toward*** *peace.* | *I'm not sure that's a* ***good/bad/wise etc. move****.* | *The government* ***made no move to*** *end the conflict.* **2** an action in which someone moves in a particular direction: *dancers practicing their moves* | *Grover* ***made a move toward*** *the door.* | *They watched us, but* ***made no move to*** *stop us.* **3 be on the move** to travel or move a lot: *These little fish are always on the move.* **4 get a move on** (spoken) said when you want someone to hurry: *Get a move on, or we'll be late!* **5** the process of leaving the place where you live or work and going to live or work somewhere else: *We visited Seattle several times before deciding to* ***make the move****.* **6** the act of changing the position

M

of one of the objects in a game: *It's your move, Jane.*

move·ment /'muvmənt/ *n.* **1** [C,U] an action in which something or someone changes position or moves from one place to another: *the dancer's graceful movements | troop movements in the desert | the* ***movement of*** *goods across the border* **2** [C] a group of people who share the same ideas or beliefs and work together to achieve a particular aim: *the* ***civil rights/antiwar/feminist etc. movement*** *| the* ***movement for*** *democracy* **3** [C] a change or development in a situation or in people's attitudes or behavior: *a* ***movement away from/toward*** *fairness in employment* **4** [C] one of the main parts into which a piece of music such as a SYMPHONY is divided **5** [C] the moving parts of a piece of machinery, especially a clock **6** [C] (formal) the action of getting rid of waste matter from your BOWELS

mov·er /'muvɚ/ *n.* [C] **1** someone whose job is to help people move from one house to another **2 mover and shaker** an important person who has power and influence over what happens in a situation

mov·ie /'muvi/ *n.* [C] **1** a story that is told using sound and moving pictures (SYN) **film**: *I was* ***watching a movie*** *on television when the phone rang. | I've* ***seen*** *that* ***movie*** *twice. | She appeared in several* ***TV movies****.*

THESAURUS

Types of movies
feature film – a movie made to be shown in movie theaters
comedy – a movie intended to make people laugh
romantic comedy – a movie about love that is intended to make the people who watch it feel happy
thriller – an exciting movie about murder or serious crimes
western – a movie with cowboys in it
action movie – a movie that has lots of fighting, explosions, etc.
horror movie – a frightening movie about ghosts, murders, etc.
science fiction movie – a movie about imaginary events in the future or in outer space
animated movie/cartoon – a movie with characters that are drawn or made using a computer
flick (informal) – a movie: *an action flick*
film – a movie, especially one that people think is very good or important: *a foreign film*

People who make movies
actor – a man or woman who acts in a movie
actress – a woman who acts in a movie
star – a famous actor or actress
director – the person who tells the actors and actresses in a movie what to do
producer – the person who makes the arrangements for a movie to be made and controls the movie's budget (=the money available to make the film)
film/movie crew – the people operating the camera, lights, etc. who help the director make a movie

2 the movies the theater where you go to watch a movie: *Do you want to* ***go to the movies*** *with us?*

'movie star *n.* [C] a famous movie actor or actress

'movie ˌtheater *n.* [C] a building where you go to watch movies

mov·ing /'muvɪŋ/ *adj.* **1** making you feel strong emotions, especially sadness or sympathy: *a moving story | a* ***deeply/very moving*** *experience*

THESAURUS **emotional, touching, poignant, emotive, sentimental, schmaltzy** ➔ EMOTIONAL

2 [only before noun] changing from one position to another: *the* ***moving parts*** *of an engine |* ***fast/slow moving*** *traffic* —**movingly** *adv.*: *She spoke movingly about her father's last days.*

'moving ˌvan *n.* [C] a large vehicle used for moving furniture from one house to another

mow /moʊ/ *v.* (past tense **mowed**, past participle **mowed** *or* **mown** /moʊn/) [I,T] to cut grass with a machine: *When are you going to* ***mow the lawn****?*

THESAURUS **cut, trim, snip** ➔ CUT[1]

mow sb ↔ **down** *phr. v.* to kill people or knock them down, especially in large numbers: *soldiers mowed down by machine-gun fire*

mow·er /'moʊɚ/ *n.* [C] a LAWN MOWER

MP3 /ˌem pi 'θri/ *n.* [C] IT a type of computer FILE containing recorded music

MP'3 ˌplayer *n.* [C] IT a small piece of equipment used to play MP3 music FILES ➔ *see picture on page A19*

MPEG /'ɛmpɛg/ *n.* [C] IT **Moving Picture Experts Group** a type of computer FILE that contains sound and VIDEO ➔ JPEG

mpg miles per gallon – used when describing the amount of gasoline used by a car: *a car that gets 35 mpg*

mph miles per hour – used when describing the speed of a vehicle: *a 65 mph speed limit*

Mr. /'mɪstɚ/ **1 Mr. Smith/Jones etc.** used before a man's family name to be polite when you are speaking to him, writing to him, or talking about him **2** a title used when speaking to a man in an official position: *Mr. Chairman | Mr. President* **3 Mr. Right** (informal) a man who would be the perfect husband for a particular woman: *Jill's still looking for Mr. Right.*

MRI *n.* **1** [U] **magnetic resonance imaging** the use of strong MAGNETIC FIELDS to make an image of the inside of the body **2** [C] a picture of the inside of someone's body made using MRI equipment

mRNA BIOLOGY the abbreviation of MESSENGER RNA

Mrs. /ˈmɪsɪz/ **Mrs. Smith/Jones etc.** used before a married woman's family name to be polite when you are speaking to her, writing to her, or talking about her ➔ MISS, MS.

MS the written abbreviation of MISSISSIPPI

Ms. /mɪz/ **Ms. Smith/Jones etc.** used before a woman's family name when she does not want to be called "Mrs." or "Miss," or when you do not know whether she is married or not

M.S., M.Sc. *n.* [C] **Master of Science** a university degree in science that you can earn after your first degree ➔ M.A.

MSG *n.* [U] a chemical that is added to food to make it taste better

MT the written abbreviation of MONTANA

Mt. the written abbreviation of MOUNT: *Mt. Everest*

much¹ /mʌtʃ/ *adv.* **1** [used before comparatives or superlatives] a lot: *I'm feeling much better.* | *This one is* ***much higher/bigger/longer etc.*** | *The job was* ***much more*** *difficult than I expected.* | *He was driving* ***much too*** *fast.* **2 too much/so much/very much/how much etc.** used in order to talk about the amount or degree to which someone does something or something happens: *Thank you very much!* | *How much further is it?* | *He's feeling so much better today.* **3 not ... much a)** only a little or hardly at all: *"Did you enjoy it?" "No, not much."* | *She isn't much younger than me.* | *Rob didn't like the movie very much.* **b)** used in order to say that something does not happen very often: *Kids* ***don't*** *play outside* ***as much as*** *they used to.* ➔ *see Grammar box at* LOT **4 much like/as sth** *also* **much the same (as sth)** used in order to say that something is very similar to something else: *It tastes* ***very much like*** *butter.* **5 much less** used in order to say that one thing is even less true or less possible than another: *You'll never see him in a tie, much less a suit.*

much² *quantifier* **1** ["much" is used mainly in questions and negatives] a lot of something: *Was there much traffic?* | *We don't have much time.* | *The storm will bring rain to* ***much of*** *the state.* **2 how much** used in order to ask or talk about the amount or cost of something: *How much were the groceries* (=what did they cost)*?* | *It is not clear how much of the crime problem is gang-related.* **3 so much/too much** used in order to talk about an amount that is very large, especially one that is larger than it should be: *There was so much smoke we couldn't see anything.* | *Ray drinks too much.* **4 not much/nothing much** used in order to say that something is not important, interesting, good, etc.: *"What's going on?" "Not much."* | *I didn't think much of the book* (=I didn't like it). **5 as much (...) as** an amount that is equal and not less: *I hope you have as much fun as we did.* | *Just try to eat as much as you can.* **6 so much for sth** (spoken) said when a particular action, idea, statement, etc. was not useful or did not produce the result that was hoped for: *She wouldn't discuss it. So much for trying to compromise.* **7 be too much for sb** to be too difficult for someone: *The stairs were too much for her.*

> GRAMMAR
>
> **much, a lot of**
>
> In sentences that are not negative and not questions, use **a lot of** rather than **much**: *She has a lot of money.* Do not say "She has much money." ➔ LOT

muck /mʌk/ *n.* [U] something such as dirt, mud, or another sticky substance: *the muck near the water's edge*

muck·rak·er /ˈmʌkˌreɪkɚ/ *n.* [C] (disapproving) a writer for a newspaper who tells the public about the bad things that important or famous people have done or are supposed to have done —**muckraking** *n.* [U], *adj.*

mu·cus /ˈmyukəs/ *n.* [U] BIOLOGY a sticky liquid produced by parts of your body such as your nose —**mucous** *adj.*

mud /mʌd/ *n.* [U] **1** wet earth that is soft and sticky: *His boots were covered in mud.* **2 sb's name is mud** (spoken) said when people are annoyed at someone because s/he has caused trouble

mud·dle¹ /ˈmʌdl/ *v.*

muddle through (sth) *phr. v.* to continue doing something even though it is confusing or difficult

muddle² *n.* [C usually singular] a state in which things are confused, not organized correctly, or done badly: *a bureaucratic muddle*

mud·dled /ˈmʌdld/ *adj.* confused, messy, or not organized correctly: *a muddled line between reality and fantasy*

mud·dy¹ /ˈmʌdi/ *adj.* covered with mud, or containing mud: *muddy boots* | *muddy water*

> THESAURUS **dirty, filthy, grimy, soiled** ➔ DIRTY¹

muddy² *v.* (**muddied**, **muddies**) [T] **1 muddy the issue/waters** to make a situation more complicated or more confusing than it was before **2** to make something dirty with mud

mud·slide /ˈmʌdslaɪd/ *n.* [C] EARTH SCIENCES a lot of very wet mud that has slid down the side of a hill

mud·sling·ing /ˈmʌdˌslɪŋɪŋ/ *n.* [U] the practice of saying bad things about someone so that other people will have a bad opinion of him/her: *political mudslinging* —**mudslinger** *n.* [C]

muf·fin /ˈmʌfən/ *n.* [C] a small, slightly sweet type of bread that often has fruit in it: *a blueberry muffin*

muf·fle /ˈmʌfəl/ *v.* [T] to make a sound less loud or clear: *Thick curtains muffled the traffic noise.*

M

—**muffled** *adj.*: *the muffled sound of a TV in the next room*

muf·fler /ˈmʌflɚ/ *n.* [C] **1** a piece of equipment on a vehicle that makes the noise from the engine quieter **2** (old-fashioned) a SCARF

mug¹ /mʌg/ *n.* [C] a large cup with straight sides and a handle: *a **mug of** coffee*

mug

mug² *v.* (**mugged**, **mugging**) [T] to attack and rob someone in a public place: *She was mugged in front of her apartment.* —**mugging** *n.* [U] —**mugger** *n.* [C]

THESAURUS steal, burglarize, rob → STEAL¹

THESAURUS offender, thief, robber, burglar, attacker → CRIME

mug·gy /ˈmʌgi/ *adj.* (comparative **muggier**, superlative **muggiest**) (informal) muggy weather is unpleasant because it is too warm and wet → HUMID —**mugginess** *n.* [U]

mug·shot /ˈmʌgʃɑt/ *n.* [C] (informal) a photograph of a criminal's face taken by the police

Mu·ham·mad /moʊˈhæməd/ *n.* a religious leader, born in Mecca, who started the religion of Islam and is its most important PROPHET. According to Islam, God told him many things, which were later written down to form the holy book called the Koran.

mu·lat·to /məˈlɑt̬oʊ/ *n.* (plural **mulattoes**) [C] (old-fashioned) a word for someone with one black parent and one white parent, now considered offensive

mulch /mʌltʃ/ *n.* [singular, U] decaying leaves that you put on the soil to improve its quality and to protect the roots of plants

mule /myul/ *n.* [C] an animal that has a DONKEY and a horse as parents

mull /mʌl/ *v.* [T] to heat wine or beer with sugar and SPICES

mull sth ↔ **over** *phr. v.* to think about something carefully: *I decided to mull over his offer.*

mul·lah /ˈmʌlə/ *n.* [C] a religious leader or teacher in Islam

mul·ti·col·ored /ˈmʌltɪˌkʌlɚd/ *adj.* having many different colors: *a multicolored shirt*

mul·ti·cul·tur·al /ˌmʌltiˈkʌltʃərəl/ *adj.* involving people or ideas from many different countries, races, religions, etc.: *The U.S. is a multicultural society.*

mul·ti·cul·tu·ral·ism /ˌmʌltiˈkʌltʃərəˌlɪzəm/ *n.* [U] SOCIAL SCIENCE the belief that it is important and right to include and respect people who have come to a country from many other countries, and who may be a different race or religion or have different customs than most of the people in their new country —**multiculturalist** *n.* [C]

mul·ti·far·i·ous /ˌmʌltɪˈfɛriəs/ *adj.* of very many different kinds: *He hired assistants to help with these multifarious projects.* —**multifariously** *adv.* —**multifariousness** *n.* [U]

mul·ti·lat·er·al /ˌmʌltɪˈlæt̬ərəl/ *adj.* involving several different countries, companies, etc. → BILATERAL, UNILATERAL: *a **multilateral agreement** to stop the fighting*

mul·ti·me·di·a /ˌmʌltɪˈmidiə/ *adj.* [only before noun] IT using a mixture of sounds, words, pictures, etc. to give information, especially on a computer program —**multimedia** *n.* [U]

mul·ti·na·tion·al /ˌmʌltɪˈnæʃənl/ *adj.* **1** ECONOMICS a multinational company has offices, businesses, etc. in several different countries

THESAURUS company, firm, business, corporation, subsidiary → COMPANY

2 involving people from several different countries: *a multinational peace-keeping force*

mul·ti·ple¹ /ˈmʌltəpəl/ *adj.* including or involving many parts, people, events, etc.: *He suffered multiple injuries to his legs.* | *She ordered multiple copies of the book.* [ORIGIN: 1600—1700 French, Latin *multiplex*]

multiple² *n.* [C] MATH a number that can be divided by a smaller number an exact number of times. For example, 20 is a multiple of 4 and 5.

ˌmultiple ˈchoice *adj.* a multiple choice test or question shows several possible answers and you must choose the correct one

mul·ti·plex /ˈmʌltɪˌplɛks/ *n.* [C] a movie theater that has several rooms in which different movies are shown

mul·ti·pli·ca·tion /ˌmʌltəpləˈkeɪʃən/ *n.* [U] **1** MATH a method of calculating in which you multiply numbers → ADDITION, DIVISION, MULTIPLICATION **2** (formal) a large increase in the size, amount, or number of something

mul·ti·plic·i·ty /ˌmʌltəˈplɪsət̬i/ *n.* [singular, U] (formal) a large number or great variety of things: *a **multiplicity of** views on the issue*

mul·ti·ply /ˈmʌltəˌplaɪ/ *v.* (**multiplied**, **multiplies**) [I,T] **1** to increase greatly, or to make something do this: *The company's problems have multiplied over the past year.*

THESAURUS increase, go up, rise, grow, double, shoot up → INCREASE¹

2 MATH to do a calculation in which you add one number to itself a particular number of times: *4 **multiplied by** 5 is 20* (=4 x 5 = 20) → CALCULATE

mul·ti·pur·pose /ˌmʌltɪˈpɚpəs◂/ *adj.* having

many different uses or purposes: *a multipurpose room*

mul·ti·ra·cial /ˌmʌltɪˈreɪʃəl◂/ *adj.* including or involving many different races of people ➔ MULTICULTURAL: *a multiracial society*

mul·ti·tude /ˈmʌltəˌtud/ *n.* (formal) **a multitude of sb/sth** a very large number of people or things: *a multitude of possible interpretations*

mum·ble /ˈmʌmbəl/ *v.* [I,T] to say something too quietly or not clearly enough, so that other people cannot understand you: *He mumbled something and left.*

mum·bo-jum·bo /ˌmʌmboʊ ˈdʒʌmboʊ/ *n.* [U] (informal) something that is difficult to understand or that makes no sense: *legal mumbo-jumbo*

mum·mi·fy /ˈmʌməˌfaɪ/ *v.* (**mummified, mummifies**) [T] to preserve a dead body by putting special oils on it and wrapping it with cloth

mum·my /ˈmʌmi/ *n.* (plural **mummies**) [C] a dead body that has been preserved and often wrapped in cloth, especially in ancient Egypt [ORIGIN: 1600—1700 Old French *momie*, from Medieval Latin *mumia*, from Arabic *mumiyah*, from Persian *mum* "wax"]

mumps /mʌmps/ *n.* **the mumps** an infectious illness in which your throat swells and becomes painful

munch /mʌntʃ/ *v.* [I,T] to eat something in a noisy way: *The kids were **munching on** popcorn.*

munch·ies /ˈmʌntʃiz/ *n.* [plural] (informal) **1 have the munchies** to feel hungry, especially for food such as cookies or POTATO CHIPS **2** foods such as cookies or POTATO CHIPS that are served at a party

mun·dane /mʌnˈdeɪn/ *adj.* ordinary and not interesting or exciting (SYN) **boring**: *Initially, the job was pretty mundane.* —**mundanely** *adv.*

mu·nic·i·pal /myuˈnɪsəpəl/ *adj.* relating to the government of a town or city: *municipal elections*

mu·nic·i·pal·i·ty /myuˌnɪsəˈpæləti/ *n.* (plural **municipalities**) [C] a town or city that has its own government

mu·nif·i·cent /myuˈnɪfəsənt/ *adj.* (formal) very generous: *a munificent gift* —**munificence** *n.* [U] —**munificently** *adv.*

mu·ni·tions /myuˈnɪʃənz/ *n.* [plural] military supplies such as bombs and large guns

mu·ral /ˈmyʊrəl/ *n.* [C] ENG. LANG. ARTS a painting that is painted on a wall

mur·der¹ /ˈmɚdɚ/ *n.* **1** [C,U] the crime of deliberately killing someone: *Lowe has been **charged with murder**. | Police don't know who **committed** the **murders**. | the brutal **murder of** a young woman | Investigators have not yet found the **murder weapon**.*

THESAURUS crime, robbery, assault, mugging ➔ CRIME

2 get away with murder (informal) to not be punished for doing something wrong, or to be allowed to do anything you want: *The parents just let him get away with murder!* [ORIGIN: Partly from Old English *morthor*, partly from Old French *murdre*]

murder² *v.* [T] to kill someone deliberately and illegally: *John Lennon was murdered in 1980.* —**murderer** *n.* [C]: *a convicted murderer*

THESAURUS kill, commit manslaughter, commit suicide, assassinate, execute sb/put sb to death, exterminate, slay ➔ KILL¹

THESAURUS offender, thief, robber, burglar, attacker, mugger ➔ CRIMINAL²

mur·der·ous /ˈmɚdərəs/ *adj.* very dangerous or violent and likely to kill someone: *He went into a murderous rage.*

murk·y /ˈmɚki/ *adj.* (comparative **murkier**, superlative **murkiest**) dark and difficult to see through: *murky water*

mur·mur¹ /ˈmɚmɚ/ *v.* [I,T] to say something in a soft quiet voice: *He softly murmured her name.* —**murmuring** *n.* [C,U]

murmur² *n.* [C] **1** a soft quiet sound made by someone's voice: *She answered in a low murmur.* **2 a murmur of approval/dissent/disbelief etc.** approval, etc. that is expressed in a soft or quiet way

mus·cle /ˈmʌsəl/ *n.* **1** [C,U] BIOLOGY one of the pieces of flesh inside your body that join bones together and make your body move: *stomach/leg/thigh etc. muscles | Weightlifting will strengthen your muscles. | I think I've **pulled a muscle*** (=injured a muscle). **2 military/political etc. muscle** military, etc. power or influence **3** [U] physical strength and power: *It **takes muscle** to move a piano.* **4 not move a muscle** to not move at all

mus·cu·lar /ˈmʌskyəlɚ/ *adj.* **1** having a lot of big muscles: *strong muscular arms* **2** related to or affecting the muscles: *a muscular disease*

muse /myuz/ *v.* [I] (formal) to imagine or think a lot about something

mu·se·um /myuˈziəm/ *n.* [C] a building where important objects are kept and shown to the public: *the Museum of Modern Art* [ORIGIN: 1600—1700 Latin, Greek *Mouseion*, from *Mousa*]

mush /mʌʃ/ *n.* [singular, U] a soft food that is part solid and part liquid

mush·room¹ /ˈmʌʃrum/ *n.* [C] one of several kinds of FUNGUS with stems and round tops, some of which can be eaten and some of which are poisonous [ORIGIN: 1400—1500 French *mousseron*, from Latin *mussirio*] ➔ *see picture at* VEGETABLE

mushroom² *v.* [I] to grow in size or numbers very

quickly: *The city's population has mushroomed to over one million.*

'mushroom ˌcloud *n.* [C] a large cloud shaped like a mushroom that is caused by a NUCLEAR explosion

mush·y /'mʌʃi/ *adj.* **1** soft and wet: *a mushy banana* **2** expressing love in a silly way: *He gets all mushy when he's around you.* | *mushy love stories*

mu·sic /'myuzɪk/ *n.* [U] **1** the arrangement of sounds made by instruments or voices in a way that is pleasant or exciting: *What kind of music does your band play?* | ***pop/country/classical etc. music*** | *I like to* ***listen to music****.* | *My favorite* ***piece of music*** *is Bach's "Magnificat."* | *Why don't you* ***put*** *some* ***music on*** (=turn on the radio or start playing a CD)*?*

THESAURUS

tune – a series of musical notes that are nice to listen to: *Suzy was humming a tune.*
melody – a song or tune: *a lovely melody*
song – a short piece of music with words: *pop songs*
arrangement – a piece of music that has been written or changed for a particular instrument: *an arrangement for flute and guitar*
composition – a piece of music or art, or a poem: *one of Schubert's early compositions*
number – a piece of popular music, a song, a dance, etc. that forms part of a larger performance: *She sang several numbers from her most recent album.*
piece – a piece of music: *This is a piece I'm learning for my piano recital.*
track – one of the songs or pieces of music on a CD: *The first track is my favorite.*

Types of music
pop (music), rock (music), rock'n'roll, heavy metal, reggae, house (music), hip-hop, rap (music), jazz, classical (music), country (music), folk (music)

2 the art of writing or playing music: *music lessons* **3** a set of written marks representing music, or the paper that this is written on: *Jim plays the piano well, but he can't* ***read music****.* **4 face the music** to admit that you have done something wrong and accept punishment: *If he took the money, he'll have to face the music.* [ORIGIN: 1200—1300 Old French *musique*, from Latin, from Greek *mousike* "art of the Muses"]

mu·si·cal¹ /'myuzɪkəl/ *adj.* **1** [only before noun] relating to music or consisting of music: *musical instruments* **2** good at playing or singing music: *I wasn't very musical as a child.* —**musically** *adv.*

musical² *n.* [C] ENG. LANG. ARTS a play or movie that uses songs and music to tell a story ➔ THEATER

mu·si·cian /myu'zɪʃən/ *n.* [C] someone who plays a musical instrument very well or as a job: *classical musicians*

musk /mʌsk/ *n.* [U] a strong-smelling substance used to make PERFUME —**musky** *adj.*

mus·ket /'mʌskɪt/ *n.* [C] a type of gun used in past times

Mus·lim /'mʌzləm, 'mʊz-, 'mʊs-/ *adj.* relating to Islam [ORIGIN: 1600—1700 An Arabic word meaning "someone who surrenders (to God)"] —**Muslim** *n.* [C]

muss /mʌs/ *v.* [T] (informal) to make something messy, especially hair

mus·sel /'mʌsəl/ *n.* [C] a small sea animal with a black shell and a soft body that can be eaten ➔ *see picture at* SHELLFISH

must¹ /məst; *strong* mʌst/ *modal verb* (*negative short form* **mustn't**) **1** (past tense **had to**) used in order to say that something is necessary because of a rule, or because it is the best thing to do: *The $60 passport fee must accompany your application.* | *It's getting late – I really must go.* ➔ *see Grammar box at* HAVE TO

USAGE

If an action is not necessary, you can say that you **don't need to** do it: *I don't need to leave until 10.*
If someone **must not** do something, s/he is not allowed to do it. **Must not** is quite formal and is used especially in written English: *You must not take any sharp objects on the plane.*
Do not say **don't need to** to mean **must not**.

2 (past tense **must have**) used in order to say that something is very likely to be true: *George must be almost 80 years old now.* | *We must have gone the wrong way.* **3** used in order to suggest that someone do something: ***You must*** *see his new film.*

must² /mʌst/ *n.* **a must** (informal) something that you must do or must have: *The Greens Cookbook is a must for any serious vegetarian.*

mus·tache /'mʌstæʃ, mə'stæʃ/ *n.* [C] hair that grows on a man's upper lip [ORIGIN: 1500—1600 French *moustache*, from Italian *mustaccio*, from Medieval Greek *moustaki*] ➔ *see picture on page 462*

mus·tang /'mʌstæŋ/ *n.* [C] a small wild horse

mus·tard /'mʌstɚd/ *n.* [U] a yellow SAUCE with a strong taste, usually eaten in small amounts with meat

mus·ter¹ /'mʌstɚ/ *v.* **muster (up) courage/support etc.** to find or gather as much courage, etc. as you can in order to do something difficult: *I'm still trying to muster up the courage to speak to her.*

muster² *n.* **pass muster** to be accepted as good enough for something

must·n't /'mʌsənt/ *modal verb* the short form of "must not": *You mustn't forget to tell her what I said.*

must·y /'mʌsti/ *adj.* having a wet unpleasant smell: *musty old books*

M

mu·ta·ble /ˈmyut̬əbəl/ *adj.* (formal) able or likely to change ANT **immutable** —**mutability** /ˌmyut̬əˈbɪləṭi/ *n.* [U]

mu·tant /ˈmyutˀnt/ *n.* [C] BIOLOGY an animal or plant that is different from others of the same kind because of a change in its GENES —**mutant** *adj.*

mu·tate /ˈmyuteɪt/ *v.* [I] BIOLOGY if an animal or plant mutates, it becomes different from others of the same kind because of a change in its GENES —**mutation** /myuˈteɪʃən/ *n.* [C,U]

mute¹ /myut/ *v.* [T] to make a sound quieter, or to make it disappear completely: *I usually mute the TV during the commercials.*

mute² *adj.* unable to speak —**mutely** *adv.*

mut·ed /ˈmyut̬ɪd/ *adj.* **1 muted criticism/response etc.** criticism, etc. that is not expressed strongly **2** quieter than usual: *the muted sound of snoring from the next room* **3** a muted color is less bright than usual

mu·ti·late /ˈmyut̬lˌeɪt/ *v.* [T] to damage someone or something severely, especially by removing part of it: *bodies mutilated in the explosion* —**mutilation** /ˌmyut̬lˈeɪʃən/ *n.* [C,U]

mu·ti·nous /ˈmyutˀn-əs/ *adj.* involved in a mutiny: *mutinous soldiers*

mu·ti·ny /ˈmyutˀn-i/ *n.* (plural **mutinies**) [C,U] a situation in which soldiers or SAILORS refuse to obey someone in authority and try to take control for themselves —**mutiny** *v.* [I]

mutt /mʌt/ *n.* [C] (informal) a dog that does not belong to a particular breed

mut·ter /ˈmʌt̬ɚ/ *v.* [I,T] to speak in a quiet voice, especially when you are complaining about something but do not want other people to hear you: *What are you muttering about?*

mut·ton /ˈmʌtˀn/ *n.* [U] the meat from a sheep [ORIGIN: 1200—1300 Old French *moton* "(male) sheep"]

mu·tu·al /ˈmyutʃuəl/ Ac *adj.* **1** a feeling that is mutual is felt by two or more people toward one another: *A good marriage is marked by **mutual respect**.* | *European nations can live together in a spirit of **mutual trust**.* | *There is a need to promote **mutual understanding** between people of different faiths.* **2 mutual agreement/consent** a situation in which two or more people both agree to something: *He has left the company **by mutual agreement**.* **3** shared by two or more people: *We were introduced by a mutual friend* (=someone we both know). | *Members of the organization share a **mutual interest** in science.* **4 the feeling is mutual** (spoken) said when you have the same feeling about someone as s/he has toward you: *"You really drive me crazy sometimes!" "The feeling's mutual!"* [ORIGIN: 1400—1500 French *mutuel*, from Latin *mutuus* "lent, borrowed, mutual"] —**mutuality** /ˌmyutʃuˈæləṭi/ *n.* [U]

ˈmutual fund *n.* [C] a company through which you can buy SHARES of other companies

mu·tu·al·ly /ˈmyutʃuəli, -tʃəli/ Ac *adv.* **1** done, felt, or experienced by two or more people: *They have mutually agreed to go their separate ways.* | *a solution that was mutually beneficial to both sides* **2 mutually exclusive** if two ideas, beliefs, etc. are mutually exclusive, they cannot both exist or be true at the same time: *The beliefs of Christians and atheists are mutually exclusive.*

Mu·zak /ˈmyuzæk/ *n.* [U] (trademark) recorded music that is played continuously in airports, offices, etc.

muz·zle¹ /ˈmʌzəl/ *n.* [C] **1** BIOLOGY the nose and mouth of an animal, especially a dog or horse → *see picture on page A15* **2** the end of the BARREL of a gun **3** something that you put over a dog's mouth so it cannot bite someone

muzzle² *v.* [T] **1** to prevent someone from speaking freely or from expressing his/her opinions: *an attempt to muzzle the press* **2** to put a muzzle over a dog's mouth so that it cannot bite someone

my /maɪ/ *possessive adj.* belonging or relating to the person who is speaking: *That's my car over there.* | *I tried not to let my feelings show.* | *My son is in college.*

my·e·lin sheath /ˌmaɪəlɪn ˈʃiθ/ *n.* [C] BIOLOGY a MEMBRANE (=material like a very thin piece of skin) in a nerve cell that covers and protects the AXON (=part that carries messages to muscles and other parts of the body)

my·o·car·di·um /ˌmaɪoʊˈkɑrdiəm/ *n.* (plural **myocardia**) [C usually singular, U] BIOLOGY the layer of muscle surrounding the heart

my·o·pi·a /maɪˈoʊpiə/ *n.* [U] BIOLOGY a medical condition which stops you seeing things clearly when they are far away SYN **nearsightedness**

my·op·ic /maɪˈɑpɪk, -ˈoʊ-/ *adj.* BIOLOGY unable to see things clearly when they are far away SYN **nearsighted**

my·o·sin /ˈmaɪəsɪn/ *n.* [U] BIOLOGY a PROTEIN in muscle cells that makes the muscle become tighter or relaxed

myr·i·ad /ˈmɪriəd/ *n.* [C] (literary) a very large number of something: ***a myriad of** stars in the sky* —**myriad** *adj.*

> **THESAURUS** many, a large number, a lot/lots, plenty, numerous, countless, innumerable, a multitude of sb/sth, a plethora of sth → MANY

my·self /maɪˈsɛlf/ *pron.* **1** used by the person speaking or writing to show that s/he is affected by his/her own action: *I made myself a cup of coffee.* | *I blame myself for what has happened.* **2** used in order to emphasize "I" or "me": *They say it's a beautiful place, but I myself have never been there.* **3 (all) by myself a)** without help: *Look, Mommy – I tied my shoes all by myself!* **b)** alone: *I went to the movie by myself.* **4 (all) to myself** for my own use: *I **had** the whole swimming pool **to***

myself today. **5 not be myself** (spoken) said when you are not behaving or feeling as you usually do because you are sick or upset: *I'm sorry for what I said – I'm not myself these days.*

mys·te·ri·ous /mɪˈstɪriəs/ *adj.* **1** strange and difficult to explain or understand: *the mysterious disappearance of our neighbor*

THESAURUS **strange, peculiar, curious, odd, weird, bizarre** → STRANGE¹

2 not saying much about something because you want it to be a secret: *Oliver is being very* ***mysterious about*** *his plans.* —**mysteriously** *adv.*: *Modotti died mysteriously in 1945.*

mys·ter·y /ˈmɪstəri/ *n.* (plural **mysteries**) **1** [C] something that is difficult to explain or understand: *The location of the stolen money* ***remains a mystery.*** | *It won't be easy to* ***solve*** *the* ***mystery.*** **2** [C] a story, especially about a murder, in which events are not explained until the end: *the Sherlock Holmes mystery stories* **3** [U] a quality that makes someone or something seem strange, interesting, and difficult to explain or understand: *There's an* ***air of mystery*** *about him that intrigues people.* [ORIGIN: 1300—1400 Latin *mysterium*, from Greek, from *mystos* "keeping silent"]

mys·ti·cal /ˈmɪstɪkəl/ *also* **mys·tic** /ˈmɪstɪk/ *adj.* relating to religious or magical powers that people cannot understand —**mystically** *adv.*

mys·ti·cism /ˈmɪstəˌsɪzəm/ *n.* [U] a religious practice in which someone tries to gain knowledge about God and truth by praying and thinking very seriously —**mystic** /ˈmɪstɪk/ *n.* [C]

mys·ti·fy /ˈmɪstəˌfaɪ/ *v.* (**mystified**, **mystifies**) [T] to make someone feel confused and unable to explain or understand something: *a case that mystified the police* —**mystifying** *adj.*

mys·tique /mɪˈstik/ *n.* [U] (formal) the quality that makes something seem mysterious, special, or interesting

myth /mɪθ/ *n.* [C,U] **1** ENG. LANG. ARTS an ancient story, especially one that explains a natural or historical event, or this type of story in general: *Greek myths*

THESAURUS **story, tale, legend, fable** → STORY

2 an idea or story that many people believe, but that is not true: ***the myth that*** *older workers are not productive* [ORIGIN: 1800—1900 Greek *mythos* "story, speech, myth"]

myth·i·cal /ˈmɪθɪkəl/ *adj.* **1** ENG. LANG. ARTS existing only in a myth: *mythical creatures such as the Minotaur* **2** imagined or invented

my·thol·o·gy /mɪˈθɑlədʒi/ *n.* [U] **1** ENG. LANG. ARTS ancient myths in general, or the beliefs that they represent: *stories from Greek mythology* **2** ideas or stories that many people have, but that are not true —**mythological** /ˌmɪθəˈlɑdʒɪkəl/ *adj.*

Nn

N, n /ɛn/ the fourteenth letter of the English alphabet

N *also* **N.** the written abbreviation of NORTH or NORTHERN

n. the written abbreviation of NOUN

'n' /n, ən/ *conjunction* a short form of "and": *rock 'n' roll music*

N/A not applicable – used on a form to show that you do not need to answer a particular question

nab /næb/ *v.* (**nabbed**, **nabbing**) [T] (informal) to catch someone doing something illegal: *The police nabbed him for speeding.*

na·dir /ˈneɪdɚ/ *n.* [singular] (literary) the time when a situation is at its worst, or when something is at its lowest level (ANT) **zenith**: *The series has* ***reached a nadir*** *with this unconvincing and ridiculous episode.*

nag¹ /næg/ *v.* (**nagged**, **nagging**) [I,T] **1** to continuously ask someone to do something in an annoying way: *Shawna has been* ***nagging me to*** *fix the kitchen sink.* **2** to make someone feel continuously worried or uncomfortable over a period of time: *A problem had been* ***nagging at*** *me for days.*

nag² *n.* [C] (informal) someone who keeps complaining or asking someone to do something, in an annoying way

nag·ging /ˈnægɪŋ/ *adj.* [only before noun] making you worry or feel pain all the time: *I have this* ***nagging feeling*** *that he's lying.* | *a* ***nagging injury***

nail¹ /neɪl/ *n.* [C] **1** a thin pointed piece of metal with a flat end, that you push into a piece of wood, etc. using a hammer **2** the hard flat part that covers the top end of your fingers and toes: *Stop* ***biting*** *your* ***nails!*** | *I need to* ***cut/file/paint*** *my* ***nails.*** [ORIGIN: Old English *nægl*] → **fight (sb/sth) tooth and nail** *at* TOOTH

COLLOCATIONS

You **cut/clip** your **nails** with **scissors** or **nail clippers**.
You **file** your **nails** (=rub them) with a **nail file** to make them the right shape.
Some women put **nail polish** on their nails.
If you **have a manicure**, someone shapes and polishes your nails for you.

nail² *v.* [T] **1** to fasten something to something else with a nail: *The windows were* ***nailed shut.*** | *She* ***nailed*** *the poster* ***to*** *the wall.* **2** (informal) to catch someone who has done something wrong and prove that s/he is guilty: *They finally* ***nailed*** *him* ***for*** *fraud.* **3** (informal) to do something exactly right, or to be exactly correct: *Jackson nailed his final shot, and the Bulls won the game.*

nail sth ↔ **down** *phr. v.* (informal) to reach a final and definite decision about something: *The contract hasn't been nailed down yet.*

nail·brush /ˈneɪlbrʌʃ/ *n.* [C] a small stiff brush used for cleaning your nails

ˈnail file *n.* [C] a thin piece of metal with a rough surface, used for shaping your nails

ˈnail ˌpolish *n.* [U] colored or clear liquid that you paint on your nails to make them look attractive

na·ive /nɑˈiv/ *adj.* lacking any experience of life, so that you believe most people are honest and kind and that only good things will happen to you ➔ INNOCENT: *a naive young girl* —**naively** *adv.* —**naivety, naiveté** /nɑˌivəˈteɪ, nɑˈivˌteɪ/ *n.* [C,U]

na·ked /ˈneɪkɪd/ *adj.* **1** not wearing any clothes: *The child was running naked through the backyard.* | *He was **stark naked*** (=completely naked).

THESAURUS

nude – not wearing any clothes, used especially when talking about people in paintings, movies, etc.: *a nude photograph of a beautiful woman*
undressed – not wearing any clothes, especially because you have just taken them off in order to go to bed, take a bath, etc.: *Rachel got undressed and ready for bed.*
bare – not covered by clothes: *Their long, bare legs dangled over the edge of the porch.*
have nothing on also **not have anything on**: *He didn't have anything on except a towel.*

2 the naked eye if you can see something with the naked eye, you can see it without using something such as a TELESCOPE to help you: *On a clear night, many other planets are **visible to the naked eye**.* —**nakedness** *n.* [U] —**nakedly** *adv.*

name¹ /neɪm/ *n.* **1** [C] the word that someone or something is called or known by: *My **first name** is Vera and my **last name** is Smith.* | *She **called** him **by** his first **name*** (=she used his first name when talking to him). | *Please write your **full name*** (=complete name) *and address.* | *I can't remember the **name of** the hotel.* | *They don't have a **name for** the baby yet.*

THESAURUS

Types of names
first name/given name – for example "Bret" in the name Bret Stern
last name/family name/surname – for example "Potter" in the name Harry Potter
middle name – the name between your first and last names
full name – your complete name
maiden name – a woman's family name before she got married and changed it
nickname – a name your friends and family use for you, not your real name
stage name – the name an actor uses that is not his/her real name
pen name/pseudonym – a name a writer uses that is not his/her real name
assumed name/alias – a false name, often one used by a criminal

2 a big/famous/household name (informal) someone who is famous: *the biggest names in Hollywood* **3** [singular] the opinion that people have about a person, company, etc. SYN **reputation**: *He has **given** baseball **a bad name*** (=made people have a bad opinion about it). | *He is determined to **clear his** family's good **name*** (=make people respect them again). **4 be in sb's name** to officially belong to someone: *The house is in my wife's name.* **5 (do sth) in the name of science/religion etc.** to use science, religion, etc. as the reason for doing something, even if it is wrong **6 call sb names** to say something insulting to someone **7 the name of the game** the most important thing or quality in a particular activity [ORIGIN: Old English *nama*]

name² *v.* [T] **1** to give someone or something a particular name: *They named their son Jacob.* | *We **named** the baby Henry, **after** his grandfather* (=gave him the same name as his grandfather). | *RFK Stadium was **named for** Robert F. Kennedy* (=it was given his name to show respect for him). **2** to say what the name of someone or something is: *He refused to name his clients.* | *Wells was **named as** the leading suspect.* **3** to officially choose someone for a particular job: *Roy Johnson was **named as** the new manager.* **4 you name it** (spoken) said after a list of things to mean that there are many more that you could mention: *Beer, whiskey, wine – you name it and I've **got it**!* **5 name names** to give the names of people who are involved in something, especially something wrong or something they want to hide: *She did not name names, but I think she was referring to Richard.*

ˈname-ˌcalling *n.* [U] the act of using an unpleasant or insulting word to describe someone in order to hurt or embarrass him/her

name·drop·ping /ˈneɪmˌdrɑpɪŋ/ *n.* [U] (disapproving) the act of mentioning the name of a famous or important person to make it seem that you know them well —**namedrop** *v.* [I]

name·less /ˈneɪmlɪs/ *adj.* **1** not known by a name SYN **anonymous**: *a gift from a nameless businessman* **2 sb who shall remain nameless** (spoken) used when you want to say that someone has done something wrong, but without saying his/her name **3** having no name: *millions of nameless stars*

name·ly /ˈneɪmli/ *adv.* used when saying the name of the person or thing you are talking about: *The movie won two Oscars, namely "Best Actor" and "Best Director."*

name·sake /ˈneɪmseɪk/ *n.* **sb's namesake** someone or something that has the same name as someone or something else

ˈname tag *n.* [C] a small sign with your name on

it, that you attach to your clothes so that people know who you are

nan·ny /'næni/ *n.* (plural **nannies**) [C] a woman whose job is to take care of a family's children, usually in the children's own home

nan·o·me·ter /'nænə,mitər/ *n.* [C] SCIENCE a unit for measuring distance. There are a BILLION (=1,000,000,000) nanometers in a meter.

nan·o·sec·ond /'nænoʊ,sɛkənd/ *n.* [C] SCIENCE a unit for measuring time. There are a BILLION (=1,000,000,000) nanoseconds in a second.

nan·o·tech·nol·o·gy /,nænətɛk'nɑlədʒi/ *n.* [U] SCIENCE the science of making extremely small electronic equipment from atoms or MOLECULES that measure less than 100 nanometers

nap /næp/ *n.* [C] a short sleep during the day: *Dad usually **takes a nap** in the afternoon.* —**nap** *v.* [I]

na·palm /'neɪpɑm/ *n.* [U] a liquid used in bombs to burn people and things

nape /neɪp/ *n.* [singular] the back of your neck: *He kissed **the nape of** her **neck**.*

nap·kin /'næpkɪn/ *n.* [C] a small piece of cloth or paper used for cleaning your mouth or hands when you are eating [ORIGIN: 1600—1700 *nape* "cloth" (1400—1500), from Old French, from Latin *mappa* "cloth, towel"]

narc /nɑrk/ *n.* [C] (informal) a police officer who deals with catching people who use and sell illegal drugs

nar·cis·sis·tic /,nɑrsə'sɪstɪk/ *adj.* (formal) having too much admiration for your own appearance or abilities —**narcissism** /'nɑrsə,sɪzəm/ *n.* [U] —**narcissist** *n.* [C]

nar·cot·ic /nɑr'kɑtɪk/ *n.* [C] a strong drug such as HEROIN that stops pain and makes people sleep [ORIGIN: 1300—1400 French *narcotique*, from Greek *narkotikos*, from *narkoun* "to make numb"] —**narcotic** *adj.*

nar·rate /'næreɪt, næ'reɪt/ *v.* [T] ENG. LANG. ARTS if someone narrates a movie or television program, s/he describes or explains what is happening in the pictures: *a documentary narrated by Robert Redford* —**narration** /næ'reɪʃən/ *n.* [C,U]

nar·ra·tive /'nærətɪv/ *n.* **1** [C,U] ENG. LANG. ARTS a description of events that is told as a story

> THESAURUS **story, tale, yarn** → STORY

2 [U] ENG. LANG. ARTS the skill or process of telling a story —**narrative** *adj.*

nar·ra·tor /'næ,reɪtər/ *n.* [C] ENG. LANG. ARTS someone who tells the story in a movie, book, etc.

nar·row[1] /'næroʊ/ *adj.* **1** only measuring a small distance from side to side (ANT) **wide**: *a long narrow street* | *The stairs were very narrow.* **2 narrow defeat/victory etc.** a defeat, victory, etc. that is achieved with difficulty or happens by only a small amount: *France finished in first place after a narrow victory over Brazil.* | *Bush **won** the election **by a narrow margin*** (=by a very small amount). **3** (disapproving) a narrow attitude or way of looking at a situation is too limited and does not consider enough possibilities: *She has a very **narrow view** of life.* **4 narrow escape** an occasion when you just avoid something bad or dangerous that almost happens to you [ORIGIN: Old English *nearu*] —**narrowness** *n.* [U] → **the straight and narrow** at STRAIGHT[3]

narrow[2] *v.* [I,T] **1** to become more narrow, or to make something do this: *The road narrows here.* | *She **narrowed** her **eyes** and frowned.* **2** also **narrow down** to reduce the number of possibilities or choices: *The police have narrowed down their list of suspects.*

nar·row·ly /'næroʊli/ *adv.* **1** only by a small amount: *Smith narrowly lost the election* | *They narrowly escaped death in the accident.* **2** in a limited way: *The law is being interpreted too narrowly.*

,narrow-'minded *adj.* (disapproving) not willing to accept ideas or beliefs that are new and different → PREJUDICED

na·sal /'neɪzəl/ *adj.* **1** a nasal sound or voice comes mostly through your nose **2** [only before noun] BIOLOGY relating to the nose: *the nasal cavity* —**nasally** *adv.*

nas·cent /'næsənt, 'neɪ-/ *adj.* [only before noun] (formal) coming into existence or starting to develop: *a developing country's nascent car market*

nas·ty /'næsti/ *adj.* (comparative **nastier**, superlative **nastiest**) **1** unkind or unpleasant: *Matt has been saying some nasty things about me.* | *a nasty old man* | *I don't understand why Stacy was so **nasty to** us.* | *nasty weather* | *a nasty habit*

> THESAURUS **mean, cruel, unkind, thoughtless, spiteful, abusive, vicious, malicious** → MEAN[2]

2 (spoken) having a bad appearance, smell, or taste: *That looks like a nasty bruise.* | *Those toilets are so nasty.* —**nastiness** *n.* [U] —**nastily** *adv.*

na·tion /'neɪʃən/ *n.* [C] **1** POLITICS a country and its people, used especially when considering its political and economic structures: *The President is addressing the nation tomorrow.* | *People all across the nation were protesting against the war.* | *the major industrialized nations*

> THESAURUS **country, state, power, land, realm** → COUNTRY[1]

2 a large group of people of the same race who speak the same language: *the Cherokee nation* [ORIGIN: 1200—1300 French, Latin *natio*, from *natus*, past participle of *nasci* "to be born"]

> THESAURUS **race, people, tribe, ethnic group** → RACE[1]

na·tion·al[1] /'næʃənl/ *adj.* **1** relating to a whole nation rather than to part of it or to other nations → INTERNATIONAL: *the national news* | *an issue of* *national importance* **2** [only before noun] owned or controlled by the government: *Yosemite National Park*

national² *n.* [C] someone who is a citizen of one country but is living in another country ➔ ALIEN, CITIZEN: *a Korean national living in the U.S.*

ˌnational ˈanthem *n.* [C] the official song of a nation that is sung or played at public occasions

na·tion·al·ism /ˈnæʃənlˌɪzəm/ *n.* [U] **1** POLITICS the belief that your country is better than any other country **2** POLITICS the desire by a group of people of the same race or origin to have their own country: *the rise of nationalism in Eastern Europe*

na·tion·al·ist /ˈnæʃənl-ɪst/ *adj.* POLITICS wanting to become politically independent, or wanting to remain this way —**nationalist** *n.* [C]: *Quebec nationalists*

na·tion·al·is·tic /ˌnæʃnəˈlɪstɪk/ *adj.* believing that your country is better than other countries ➔ PATRIOTIC

na·tion·al·i·ty /ˌnæʃəˈnæləṭi/ *n.* (plural **nationalities**) [C,U] **1** the legal right of belonging to a particular country (SYN) **citizenship**: *He has British/Swiss etc.* ***nationality***. ▸Don't say "My nationality is Mexican/Swedish etc." Say "I come from Mexico/Sweden etc."◂ **2** a large group of people who have the same race, language, or culture: *There are children of many different nationalities at our school.*

na·tion·al·ize /ˈnæʃənəˌlaɪz/ *v.* [T] ECONOMICS if a government nationalizes a large company or an industry, it buys it or takes control of it ➔ PRIVATIZE

na·tion·al·ly /ˈnæʃənl-i/ *adv.* by or to everyone in a nation: *a series of nationally televised debates*

ˌnational ˈmonument *n.* [C] a building or a special place that is protected by the government for people to visit

ˌnational seˈcurity *n.* [U] the ways in which a country protects its citizens or keeps its secrets safe, for example by having a strong army

na·tion·wide /ˌneɪʃənˈwaɪd◂ / *adj.* happening or existing in every part of a nation: *nationwide price increases* —**nationwide** *adv.*: *The brewery employs about 3,000 people nationwide.*

THESAURUS everywhere, all over sth, throughout sth, worldwide ➔ EVERYWHERE

na·tive¹ /ˈneɪṭɪv/ *adj.* **1 native country/land etc.** the place where you were born: *He returned to his native Poland.* **2 native Californian/New Yorker etc.** someone who was born in California, etc. **3** growing, living, or produced in a particular area: *a plant* ***native to*** *Ecuador* **4 native language/tongue** the language you first learned to speak

native² *n.* [C] **1** someone who was born in a particular country: *Andrea is a* ***native of*** *Brazil.* **2** [usually plural] a word used by white people in the past to refer to the people who lived in Africa, America, etc. before Europeans arrived. Many people now consider this word offensive.

ˌNative Aˈmerican *n.* [C] someone who belongs to one of the tribes who were living in North America before the Europeans arrived —**Native American** *adj.*

ˌnative ˈspeaker *n.* [C] someone who has learned a particular language as his/her first language, rather than as a foreign language (ANT) **non-native speaker**: *a* ***native speaker of*** *English*

NATO /ˈneɪṭoʊ/ *n.* **North Atlantic Treaty Organization** a group of countries in North America and Europe that give military help to each other

nat·u·ral¹ /ˈnætʃərəl/ *adj.* **1** normal or usual, and what you would expect in a particular situation (ANT) **unnatural**: ***It's only natural to*** *have doubts before your wedding.* | *It's not* ***natural for*** *a four-year old* ***to*** *be so quiet.* **2** existing in nature, not caused, made, or controlled by people: *earthquakes and other* ***natural disasters*** | *natural fibers like cotton* | *He died of* ***natural causes*** (=because of illness or old age). | *The storm of meteorites was rare, but it was a* ***natural phenomenon*** (=something unusual that happens naturally).

THESAURUS

Describing things that are natural

wild – used about flowers, plants, and animals that are not controlled by people: *Wild dogs roamed the streets.*

pure – used about food or drink that has not had anything added to it: *pure orange juice*

organic – used about fruit, vegetables, meat, etc. that is produced without using chemicals: *organic tomatoes*

3 [only before noun] having a particular skill or ability without being taught: *a* ***natural athlete*** **4** behaving in a way that is normal and shows you are relaxed and not trying to pretend: *Just be natural – you'll do fine.* —**naturalness** *n.* [U]

natural² *n.* **be a natural** to be very good at doing something without being taught

ˌnatural ˈgas *n.* [U] gas used for cooking or heating that is taken from under the earth or ocean

ˌnatural ˈhistory *n.* [U] EARTH SCIENCES the study of plants, animals, and minerals

nat·u·ral·ism /ˈnætʃərəˌlɪzəm, ˈnætʃrə-/ *n.* [U] ENG. LANG. ARTS a style of art or literature that tries to show the world and people exactly as they are

nat·u·ral·ist /ˈnætʃərəlɪst/ *n.* [C] EARTH SCIENCES someone who studies plants, animals, and other living things

nat·u·ral·ize /ˈnætʃərəˌlaɪz/ *v.* [T usually passive] to officially make someone who was born outside a particular country a legal citizen of that country

nat·u·ral·ized /ˈnætʃərəˌlaɪzd/ *adj.* a naturalized citizen is someone who becomes a citizen of a country that s/he was not born in —**naturalization** /ˌnætʃərələˈzeɪʃən/ *n.* [U]

N

ˌnatural ˈlaw *n.* [C,U] SOCIAL SCIENCE a rule or set of rules for moral behavior that people naturally believe in, rather than laws made by governments or religious laws

nat·u·ral·ly /ˈnætʃərəli/ *adv.* **1** in a way that you would expect: *Naturally, you'll want to discuss this with your wife.* | ***Naturally enough**, she wants her child to grow up fit and strong.* **2** (spoken) used in order to agree with what someone has said, or to answer "Of course" to a question: *"Are you excited to be home?" "Naturally."* **3** as a natural feature or quality, not made or done by people: *Allison's hair is naturally curly.* | *Golf seemed to **come naturally** to him* (=he was good at it without being taught). **4** in a relaxed manner, without trying to look or sound different from usual: *Just **speak naturally** and pretend the microphone isn't there.* | *Try to **act naturally**.*

ˌnatural ˈresource *n.* [C usually plural] things such as land, minerals, energy, etc. that exist in a country

ˌnatural seˈlection *n.* [U] BIOLOGY the process by which only the plants and animals that are naturally appropriate for life in their environment will continue to live

na·ture /ˈneɪtʃɚ/ *n.* **1** [U] everything that exists in the world that is not made or controlled by humans, such as animals, plants, weather, etc.: *All of these minerals are found **in nature**.* | *the **forces of nature*** (=wind, rain, etc.) | *a nature walk/trail* **2** [C,U] the character or particular qualities of someone or something: *He was an optimist **by nature**.* | *The **nature of** my work requires a lot of traveling.* | *Of course she's jealous – it's **human nature*** (=the feelings and qualities that all people have). **3** [singular] a particular type of thing: *He provided support **of a** financial **nature**.* **4 let nature take its course** to allow events to happen without doing anything to change the results → SECOND NATURE

ˈnature reˌserve *n.* [C] EARTH SCIENCES an area of land in which animals and plants are protected

naught /nɔt/ *n.* [U] (old-fashioned) nothing: *All their plans **came to naught*** (=failed).

naugh·ty /ˈnɔt̬i/ *adj.* (comparative **naughtier**, superlative **naughtiest**) a naughty child behaves badly and is rude or does not obey adults —**naughtiness** *n.* [U] —**naughtily** *adv.*

nau·se·a /ˈnɔziə, ˈnɔʒə, ˈnɔʃə/ *n.* [U] (formal) the feeling you have when you think you are going to VOMIT [ORIGIN: 1400—1500 Latin, Greek *nausia* "seasickness," from *nautes* "sailor," from *naus* "ship"]

nau·se·at·ed /ˈnɔziˌeɪt̬ɪd/ *adj.* feeling that you are going to VOMIT: *When I was pregnant, I felt nauseated all the time.* —**nauseate** *v.* [T]

nau·se·at·ing /ˈnɔziˌeɪt̬ɪŋ/ *adj.* making you feel that you are going to VOMIT: *the nauseating smell of cigar smoke*

nau·seous /ˈnɔʃəs, -ʒəs/ *adj.* **1** feeling that you are going to VOMIT: *I suddenly **felt nauseous**.* **2** (literary) making you feel that you are going to VOMIT: *nauseous odors*

nau·ti·cal /ˈnɔt̬ɪkəl/ *adj.* relating to ships or sailing: *a distance of 300 **nautical miles*** [ORIGIN: 1500—1600 Latin *nauticus*, from Greek, from *nautes* "sailor," from *naus* "ship"] —**nautically** *adv.*

na·val /ˈneɪvəl/ *adj.* relating to the navy: *a naval battle*

na·vel /ˈneɪvəl/ *n.* [C] BIOLOGY a small hollow or raised place in the middle of your stomach SYN **belly button**

nav·i·ga·ble /ˈnævɪgəbəl/ *adj.* a river, lake, etc. that is navigable is deep and wide enough for ships to travel on

nav·i·gate /ˈnævəˌgeɪt/ *v.* **1** [I,T] to plan the way a car, ship, or airplane travels to a place, using a map: *Rick usually drives and I navigate.* **2** [I,T] IT to find your way around a particular WEBSITE, or to move from one website to another: *The university's website is really easy to navigate.* **3** [I,T] to find your way through a complicated system, set of rules, etc.: *A social worker is helping Kelly navigate the legal system.* **4** [T] to sail a boat or ship along a river or other area of water [ORIGIN: 1500—1600 Latin, past participle of *navigare*, from *navis* "ship"] —**navigation** /ˌnævəˈgeɪʃən/ *n.* [U]

nav·i·ga·tor /ˈnævəˌgeɪt̬ɚ/ *n.* [C] the officer on a ship or aircraft who plans the way along which it travels

na·vy /ˈneɪvi/ *n.* (plural **navies**) **1** *also* **Navy** [C usually singular] the part of a country's military forces that is organized for fighting a war at sea → AIR FORCE, ARMY, MARINES: *My dad was 20 when he **joined the navy**.* | *Frank is **in the navy**.* **2** [U] navy blue [ORIGIN: 1300—1400 Old French *navie* "group of ships," from Latin *navigia* "ships"]

ˌnavy ˈblue *adj.* very dark blue —**navy blue** *n.* [U]

NBC *n.* **National Broadcasting Company** one of the national television and radio companies in the U.S.

NC the written abbreviation of NORTH CAROLINA

NCAA *n.* **National Collegiate Athletic Association** the organization that is in charge of sports at American colleges and universities

NCO *n.* [C] **Noncommissioned Officer** a soldier such as a CORPORAL or SERGEANT

ND the written abbreviation of NORTH DAKOTA

NE 1 the written abbreviation of NORTHEAST **2** the written abbreviation of NEBRASKA

neap tide /ˈnip taɪd/ *n.* [C] EARTH SCIENCES a TIDE in which the rise and fall of the level of the ocean is smaller than normal, that takes place at the first and third quarters of the moon → SPRING TIDE

near¹ /nɪr/ *adv., prep.* **1** only a short distance from someone or something: *Why don't we meet near the library?* | *I'd like to live* ***nearer to*** *the ocean.* | *Is there a bank near here?*

USAGE

Near and **close** are both used to talk about short distances between things.
Near can be followed directly by a noun: *Is the hotel near the beach?*
Close cannot be followed directly by a noun. **Close** must be followed by the preposition "to" and then a noun: *They live close to the park.*

THESAURUS

close – not far from someone or something: *He sat close to his mom.*
not far (away) – not a long distance away: *The park's not far away.*
nearby – near here or near a particular place: *Do you live nearby?* | *a nearby farm*
within walking distance (of sth) – easy to walk to from somewhere: *The beach is within walking distance of the hotel.*
local – used about stores, schools, etc. that are in the area where you live: *your local library*
neighboring – used about towns, countries, etc. that are very near a particular place: *discussions between Egypt and neighboring states*

2 close in time to a particular event: *She got more and more nervous as the wedding* ***drew near*** (=became closer in time). | *The construction work is now near completion.* **3 nowhere near** not at all close to a particular quality or state: *His latest movie is nowhere near as good as the last one.* | *We're nowhere near finished.* **4 near perfect/impossible etc.** (informal) almost perfect, impossible, etc. (SYN) **nearly**: *a near perfect test score*

near

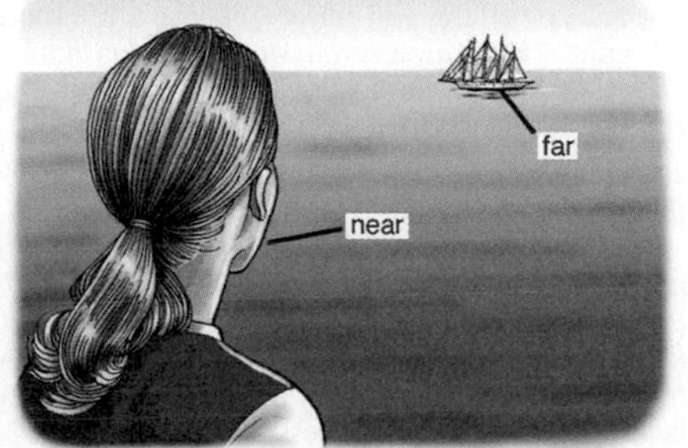

near² *adj.* **1** only a short distance from someone or something: *The nearest town* (=the town that is the closest) *is 20 miles away.* **2** very close to having a particular quality or being a particular thing: *His explanation is as* ***near to*** *the truth as we'll get.* **3 in the near future** at a time that is not very far in the future: *We will have a new teacher joining us in the near future.* **4 near miss** a situation in which something almost hits something else

near·by /ˌnɪrˈbaɪ◂/ *adj.* [only before noun] not far away: *Rita was taken to a nearby hospital.* —**nearby** *adv.*: *The teacher stood nearby.*

THESAURUS **near, close, not far (away), within walking distance (of sth), local, neighboring** → NEAR¹

THESAURUS **locally, close by/close to here, in close proximity (to)** → LOCALLY

near·ly /ˈnɪrli/ *adv.* almost, but not completely or exactly: *It took me nearly five hours to write the essay.* | ***Nearly all*** *of our students go on to college.* | *The team is* ***not nearly as*** *good as it could have been.*

near·sight·ed /ˈnɪrˌsaɪt̬ɪd/ *adj.* unable to see things clearly unless they are close to you (ANT) **far-sighted** —**nearsightedness** *n.* [U]

neat /nit/ *adj.* **1** (spoken) very good, enjoyable, interesting, etc.: *What a neat idea!* | *He's a really neat guy.* **2** carefully arranged and not messy: *Chris looked neat and well shaven.* | *They keep their house* ***neat and clean***. **3** a neat person does not like his/her things or house to be messy **4** simple and effective: *a neat solution to the problem* —**neatly** *adv.* —**neatness** *n.* [U]

neb·u·la /ˈnɛbyələ/ *n.* (plural **nebulas** *or* **nebulae** /-li/) [C] **1** PHYSICS a mass of gas and dust among the stars, that looks similar to a bright cloud in the sky at night **2** PHYSICS a GALAXY (=large group of stars) that looks like a bright cloud in the sky at night [ORIGIN: 1600—1700 Latin "mist, cloud"]

neb·u·lous /ˈnɛbyələs/ *adj.* (formal) **1** not clear or exact at all (SYN) **vague**: *The guidance the students were given was fairly nebulous.* **2** a nebulous shape cannot be seen clearly and has no definite edges —**nebulously** *adv.* —**nebulousness** *n.* [U]

nec·es·sar·i·ly /ˌnɛsəˈsɛrəli/ *adv.* **not necessarily** used to say that something may not be true or may not always happen, even if it might be reasonable to expect it to: *Expensive restaurants do not necessarily have the best food.*

nec·es·sar·y /ˈnɛsəˌsɛri/ *adj.* **1** needed in order for you to do something or have something → ESSENTIAL: *Will you make all the necessary arrangements?* | *Don't call me unless it's* ***absolutely necessary***. | *He will do anything* ***necessary to*** *win.* | *It might be* ***necessary for*** *me to have an operation.* | *We're prepared to go to war,* ***if necessary***.

THESAURUS

essential – important and necessary: *Education is essential if you want a good job.*
vital – extremely important and necessary: *He was accused of withholding vital information from the police.*
mandatory – if something is mandatory, it must be done because of a rule or law: *Parents do not want school uniform to become mandatory.*

N

compulsory – if something is compulsory, you must do it: *Service in the army was compulsory.*
requisite (formal) – needed for a particular purpose: *He lacked the requisite skills for the job.*
indispensable (formal) – something or someone that is indispensable is so important or useful that something cannot be done without that person or thing: *The accounting program is indispensable for small businesses.*

2 a necessary evil something bad or unpleasant that you have to accept in order to achieve what you want: *He regarded work as a necessary evil.* [ORIGIN: 1300—1400 Latin *necessarius*, from *necesse* "necessary," from *ne-* "not" + *cedere* "to give up"]

ne·ces·si·tate /nə'sɛsə͵teɪt/ *v.* [T] (formal) to make something necessary

ne·ces·si·ty /nə'sɛsət̬i/ *n.* (plural **necessities**) **1** [C] something that you need to have or that must happen: *A car is an **absolute necessity** in the suburbs.* | *A valid driver's license is a **necessity for** renting a car.* | ***basic necessities** like food and shelter* **2** [U] the fact of something being necessary: *Many parents are questioning **the necessity of** standardized tests.* | *She went back to work, but only **out of necessity**.*

neck¹ /nɛk/ *n.* [C] **1** the part of your body that joins your head to your shoulders: *She was wearing a gold chain **around** her **neck**.* | *Swans have long slender necks.* → *see picture on page A16* **2 V-necked/open-necked etc.** *also* **V-neck/open-neck** if a piece of clothing is V-necked, open-necked, etc., it has that type of neck: *a V-neck sweater* | *an open-necked shirt* **3** the long narrow part of something such as a bottle or a musical instrument **4 neck and neck** (informal) if two people, teams, etc. are neck and neck in a competition, they both have an equal chance of winning **5 in this neck of the woods** (informal) in this area or part of the country: *What are you doing in this neck of the woods?* **6 be up to your neck in sth** (informal) to be in a very difficult situation, or to be very busy doing something: *Mason is up to his neck in debt.* [ORIGIN: Old English *hnecca*]

neck² *v.* [I] (informal, old-fashioned) if two people neck, they kiss for a long time in a sexual way

neck·lace /'nɛk-lɪs/ *n.* [C] a piece of jewelry that hangs around your neck: *a pearl necklace* → *see picture at* JEWELRY

neck·line /'nɛk-laɪn/ *n.* [C] the shape made by the edge of a woman's dress, shirt, etc. around or below the neck: *a low neckline*

neck·tie /'nɛktaɪ/ *n.* [C] (formal) a tie

nec·tar /'nɛktɚ/ *n.* [U] **1** thick juice made from some fruits: *peach nectar* **2** the sweet liquid that BEEs collect from flowers

nec·ta·rine /͵nɛktə'rin/ *n.* [C] a round juicy yellow-red fruit that has a large rough seed and smooth skin

née /neɪ/ *adj.* used in order to show the family name that a woman had before she was married: *Lorna Brown, née Wilson*

need¹ /nid/ *v.* [T] **1** to feel that you must have or do something, or that something is necessary: *I need a vacation.* | *What do you **need** the money **for**?* | *He knows exactly what **needs to** be done.* | *David, I **need** you **to** pick up the dry cleaning.* | *Affordable housing is **badly/desperately needed** in the city.*

THESAURUS

could use sth/could do with sth (spoken) – to need or want something: *Let's stop. I could use a rest.*
be desperate for sth – to need something urgently: *a little boy who is desperate for attention*
can't do without sth – to be unable to manage without something: *I can't do without my morning coffee.*
be dependent on sth/sb – to be unable to live or continue normally without something or someone: *The refugees are dependent on outside food supplies.*
require – to need something in order to be successful: *This sport requires a lot of skill and strength.*

2 to have to do something: *There's something I **need to** tell you.* | *Do we **need to** bring anything?* | *You **don't need to** make a reservation.*

USAGE

Use **must not** or **mustn't** when saying that someone should not do something: *You mustn't tell anyone about this.* **Must not** is quite formal and is used mainly in written English.
Use **don't have to** when saying that it is not necessary for someone to do something: *You don't have to stay if you don't want to.* → MUST¹

3 sb does not need sth (spoken) used in order to say that something will make someone's life more difficult: *"He's always questioning everything I do." "Yeah, you don't need that."* [ORIGIN: Old English *nied*, *ned*]

need² *n.* **1** [singular,U] a situation in which something must be done, especially to improve the situation: *I've never felt the **need to** diet.* | ***There is no need to** apologize.* | *a **need for** change* | *There's an **urgent need** for more nurses.* | *We will work all night **if need be*** (=if it is necessary). **2** [C usually plural] something that you need in order to be healthy, comfortable, successful, etc.: *We aim to **meet** the **needs** of our customers.* | *children with **special needs*** (=physical or learning problems) **3 in need of sth** needing attention, help, money, etc.: *a large population in need of doctors* **4 in need** not having enough food or money: *We're collecting donations for families in need.*

nee·dle¹ /'nidl/ *n.* [C] **1** a small thin piece of steel used for sewing, that has a point at one end and a hole at the other end: *a needle and thread* **2** the sharp hollow metal part on the end of a SYRINGE: *Drug users are at risk when they share* needles. **3** a small thin pointed leaf, especially from a PINE tree ➔ *see picture at* PLANT[1] **4** the very small pointed part in a RECORD PLAYER, that picks up sound from the records **5 sth is like looking for a needle in a haystack** used in order to say that something is almost impossible to find [ORIGIN: Old English *nædl*]

needle² *v.* [T] to deliberately annoy someone by making a lot of unkind remarks or stupid jokes

need·less /ˈnid-lɪs/ *adj.* **1 needless to say** used when you are telling someone something that s/he probably already knows or expects: *Needless to say, with four children we're always busy.* **2** not necessary, and often easily avoided: *Why take needless risks?* —**needlessly** *adv.*

nee·dle·work /ˈnidlˌwɚk/ *n.* [U] the activity or art of sewing, or things made by sewing

need·y /ˈnidi/ *adj.* **1** having very little food or money: *a needy family*

THESAURUS poor, destitute, impoverished, indigent, poverty-stricken, deprived ➔ POOR

2 the needy people who do not have enough food or money

ne·far·i·ous /nɪˈfɛriəs, -ˈfær-/ *adj.* (formal) evil or criminal: *a nefarious plot to kill the mayor* —**nefariously** *adv.* —**nefariousness** *n.* [U]

ne·gate /nɪˈgeɪt/ (Ac) *v.* [T] (formal) to prevent something from having any effect: *The decision would effectively negate last year's Supreme Court ruling.* | *The drug's side effects negate any possible benefit to the patient.* [ORIGIN: 1600—1700 Latin, past participle of *negare* "to say no"] —**negation** /nɪˈgeɪʃən/ *n.* [U]

neg·a·tive¹ /ˈnɛgətɪv/ (Ac) *adj.* **1** bad or harmful (ANT) **positive**: *The divorce had a* ***negative effect*** *on the children.* **2** considering only the bad qualities of a situation, person, etc. (ANT) **positive**: *a* ***negative attitude*** | *He has always been very* ***negative about*** *the U.S.* **3** saying or meaning no (ANT) **affirmative**: *The response was negative.* **4** SCIENCE a medical or scientific test that is negative does not show any sign of what was being looked for (ANT) **positive**: *She* ***tested negative*** *for HIV.* | *The blood tests* ***came back/up/out negative.*** **5** PHYSICS having the type of electrical charge that is carried by ELECTRONS, shown by a (-) sign on a BATTERY (ANT) **positive**: *Make the connection to the negative terminal on the battery.* **6** MATH a negative number or quantity is lower than zero. (-) is the negative sign. (ANT) **positive**: *They had a negative return on their investment.* **7** BIOLOGY not having RHESUS FACTOR in your blood (ANT) **positive**: *Her blood type is O negative.* —**negatively** *adv.*

negative² *n.* **1** [C] a piece of film that shows dark areas as light and light areas as dark, from which a photograph is printed: *A copy of the photograph was made from the negative.* **2** [U] a statement or expression that means no (ANT) **affirmative**: *He replied* ***in the negative.*** **3** [C] something bad or harmful (ANT) **positive**: *Another negative was the increase in unemployment.* | *In this case, the negatives outweigh the positives.*

ne·glect¹ /nɪˈglɛkt/ *v.* [T] **1** to not pay enough attention to someone or something, or to not take care of him, her, or it very well: *Each year, 700,000 children are abused or neglected.* **2** to not do something, or forget to do it, especially because you are lazy or careless: *Sarah* ***neglected to*** *tell us of the change in plans.* —**neglected** *adj.*

neglect² *n.* [U] **1** failure to take care of something or someone well: *cases of child abuse or neglect* **2** the condition something or someone is in when he, she, or it has not been taken care of: *inner cities in a state of neglect*

ne·glect·ful /nɪˈglɛktfəl/ *adj.* (formal) not taking care of something or someone very well: *neglectful parents*

neg·li·gee /ˌnɛglɪˈʒeɪ, ˈnɛglɪˌʒeɪ/ *n.* [C] a very thin pretty piece of clothing that a woman wears over a NIGHTGOWN

neg·li·gence /ˈnɛglɪdʒəns/ *n.* [U] the failure to do something that you are responsible for in a careful enough way, so that something bad happens or may happen: *They're suing the doctor for negligence.*

neg·li·gent /ˈnɛglɪdʒənt/ *adj.* not being careful enough about something that you are doing, so that serious mistakes are made: *The company had been* ***negligent in*** *its safety procedures.* —**negligently** *adv.*

neg·li·gi·ble /ˈnɛglɪdʒəbəl/ *adj.* too slight or unimportant to have any effect (SYN) **insignificant** —**negligibly** *adv.*

ne·go·tia·ble /nɪˈgoʊʃəbəl/ *adj.* prices, agreements, etc. that are negotiable can be discussed and changed: *Is the salary negotiable?*

ne·go·ti·ate /nɪˈgoʊʃiˌeɪt/ *v.* **1** [I,T] to discuss something in order to reach an agreement: *UN representatives are trying to negotiate a ceasefire.* | *The government refuses to* ***negotiate with*** *terrorists.* **2** [T] to succeed in getting past or over a difficult place on a road, path, etc.: *an old man carefully negotiating the steps* [ORIGIN: 1500—1600 Latin, past participle of *negotiari* "to do business"] —**negotiator** *n.* [C]

ne·go·ti·a·tion /nɪˌgoʊʃiˈeɪʃən/ *n.* [C usually plural, U] official discussions between two groups who are trying to agree on something: *We can't discuss the details because they are still* ***under negotiation.*** | *Baseball owners have begun* ***negotiations with*** *the players' union.* | *budget* ***negotiations between*** *the White House and Congress*

Ne·gro /ˈnigroʊ/ *n.* (plural **Negroes**) [C] (old-fashioned) a word used in the past for a black person. This word is now considered offensive. [ORIGIN: 1500—1600 Spanish, Portuguese, from *negro* "black," from Latin *niger*] —**Negro** *adj.*

neigh /neɪ/ *v.* [I] to make a loud sound like a horse —**neigh** *n.* [C]

N

neigh·bor /ˈneɪbɚ/ *n.* [C] **1** someone who lives in a house or apartment very near you: *The Nelsons are our **next-door neighbors*** (=they live in the house next to ours). **2** someone who is sitting or standing next to you: *Discuss the questions with your neighbor.* **3** a country that has a border with another country: *Germany and its European neighbors* [ORIGIN: Old English *neahgebur*]

neigh·bor·hood /ˈneɪbɚˌhʊd/ *n.* [C] **1** a small area of a town, or the people who live there: *a nice neighborhood in Boston | a neighborhood school | Are there any good restaurants **in the neighborhood*** (=in this area of town)*?*

THESAURUS **area, district, suburb, slum, ghetto** → AREA

2 in the neighborhood of sth either a little more or a little less than a particular number or amount: *The car cost **something/somewhere in the neighborhood of** $60,000.*

neigh·bor·ing /ˈneɪbərɪŋ/ *adj.* near the place where you are or the place you are talking about: *neighboring towns*

THESAURUS **near, close, not far (away), nearby, within walking distance (of sth), local** → NEAR[1]

neigh·bor·ly /ˈneɪbɚli/ *adj.* friendly and helpful toward your neighbors —**neighborliness** *n.* [U]

nei·ther[1] /ˈniðɚ, ˈnaɪ-/ *determiner, pron.* not one or the other of two people or things → EITHER, NONE: ***Neither of** them was hungry, but they had a cup of coffee. | Neither leader would admit to being wrong.*

GRAMMAR

neither, neither of

Neither is used with a singular noun form and a singular verb: *Neither answer is right.*

Neither of is used with a plural noun form or pronoun, and the verb is usually singular: *Neither of them understood what she was saying.*

neither[2] *adv.* used in order to agree with a negative statement that someone has made, or to add a negative statement to one that has just been made: *"I don't like coffee." "Neither do I." | Bill can't sing at all, and neither can his brother. | "I haven't seen Greg in a long time." "Me neither."*

neither[3] *conjunction* **neither ... nor ...** used when mentioning two statements, facts, actions, etc. that are not true or possible: *Neither his mother nor his father spoke English. | The equipment is neither accurate nor safe.*

ne·o·con·ser·va·tive /ˌnioʊkənˈsɚvət̬ɪv/ *adj.* [usually before noun] POLITICS supporting political ideas that include strict moral behavior and the importance of being responsible for your own actions and not being dependent on the government —**neoconservative** *n.* [C]

Ne·o·lith·ic, neolithic /ˌniəˈlɪθɪk◂/ *adj* EARTH SCIENCES relating to the last period of the STONE AGE, about 10,000 years ago, when people began to live together in small groups and make stone tools and weapons: *Neolithic art* → PALEOLITHIC

ne·ol·o·gism /niˈɑləˌdʒɪzəm/ *n.* [C] ENG. LANG. ARTS a new word or expression, or a word used with a new meaning

ne·on /ˈniɑn/ *n.* [U] CHEMISTRY a gas that shines brightly when electricity goes through it, used in lights and signs: *neon lights*

ne·o·phyte /ˈniəˌfaɪt/ *n.* [C] someone who has just started to learn a particular skill, art, job, etc.: *a collection of CDs for jazz neophytes to listen to* —**neophyte** *adj.* [only before noun]

neph·ew /ˈnɛfyu/ *n.* [C] the son of your brother or sister, or the son of your husband's or wife's brother or sister → NIECE → RELATIVE[1]

nep·o·tism /ˈnɛpəˌtɪzəm/ *n.* [U] (disapproving) the practice of giving the best jobs to members of your family when you are in a position of power

Nep·tune /ˈnɛptun/ *n.* PHYSICS the eighth PLANET from the Sun → *see picture at* SOLAR SYSTEM

nerd /nɚd/ *n.* [C] (informal) someone who is not fashionable and does not know how to behave in social situations: *a computer nerd* (=someone who is interested only in computers) —**nerdy** *adj.*

nerve /nɚv/ *n.* **1** [U] the ability to stay calm in a dangerous, difficult, or frightening situation: *It **takes a lot of nerve** to give a speech in front of so many people. | He would've won if he hadn't **lost** his **nerve*** (=suddenly become very nervous).

THESAURUS **courage, bravery, guts, valor, mettle** → COURAGE

2 nerves [plural] the feeling of being nervous because you are worried or a little frightened: *"What's wrong?" "It's just nerves. My exam is tomorrow."* **3** [C] BIOLOGY one of the thin parts like threads inside your body that help control your movements, and along which your brain sends and receives feelings of heat, cold, pain, etc.: *He has some **nerve damage** in his left hand.* **4 get on sb's nerves** (informal) to annoy someone, especially by doing something again and again: *Joyce's complaining is getting on my nerves.* **5 have the nerve to do sth** (informal) to be rude without being ashamed or embarrassed about it: *He had the nerve to criticize my cooking.* **6 hit/touch/strike a (raw) nerve** (informal) to mention something that people feel strongly about or that upsets people: *I must have hit a raw nerve by asking him about his ex-wife.* [ORIGIN: 1300—1400 Latin *nervus*]

ˈnerve-ˌracking, nerve-wracking *adj.* very worrying or frightening: *a nerve-racking wait for test results*

nerv·ous /ˈnɚvəs/ *adj.* **1** worried or frightened about something, and unable to relax: *Sam's **nervous about** taking his driving test again. | Would you stop staring? You're **making** me **nervous**. | nervous laughter | By the time I got to the interview, I was a **nervous wreck*** (=was extremely nervous).

> **THESAURUS** worried, anxious, concerned, uneasy, stressed (out), tense, apprehensive
> → WORRIED

2 often becoming worried or frightened and easily upset: *a thin nervous man* **3** relating to the nerves in your body: *a nervous disorder* —**nervously** *adv.* —**nervousness** *n.* [U]

ˌnervous ˈbreakdown *n.* [C] a mental illness in which someone becomes extremely anxious and tired and cannot live and work normally: *He almost **had/suffered a nervous breakdown** last year.*

ˈnervous ˌsystem *n.* [C usually singular] BIOLOGY the system of nerves in your body, through which you feel pain, heat, etc. and control your movements

ˈnervous ˌtissue *n.* [U] BIOLOGY TISSUE (=matter in the body made from many cells) that is made up of NEURONS (=cells that send messages to parts of the body and the brain)

nest¹ /nɛst/ *n.* [C] **1** a hollow place made or chosen by a bird to lay its eggs in and to live in: *The robins were **building** a **nest** in our backyard.* **2** a place where insects or small animals live: *a hornets' nest* **3 leave/fly the nest** (informal) to leave your parents' house when you are an adult [ORIGIN: Old English]

nest² *v.* [I] to build or use a nest: *owls nesting in a tree hole*

ˈnest egg *n.* [C] an amount of money that you have saved

nes·tle /ˈnɛsəl/ *v.* **1** [I,T] to move into a comfortable position by pressing against someone or something: *She nestled her head against his shoulder.* **2** [I] (literary) to be in a position that is protected from wind, rain, etc.: *a village **nestling among** the hills*

net¹ /nɛt/ *n.* **1** [C,U] a material made of strings, wires, or threads woven across each other with regular spaces between them: *a fishing net* **2** [C usually singular] a net used in particular games: *The ball went straight **into the net**.* **3 the Net** the INTERNET: *I read about it **on the Net**.*

net

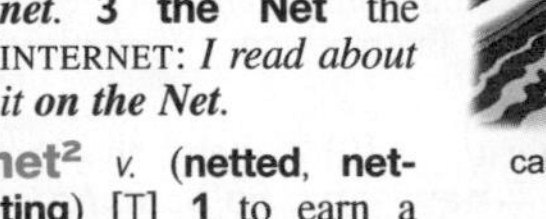

casting a fishing net

net² *v.* **(netted, netting)** [T] **1** to earn a particular amount of money as a profit after paying taxes → GROSS: *Last year, they netted $52,000.*

> **THESAURUS** earn, make, get, be/get paid, gross → EARN

2 to catch a fish in a net

net³ *adj.* [only before noun] **1** ECONOMICS a net amount of money is the amount that remains after things such as taxes, etc. have been taken away → GROSS: *a **net profit/loss** of $500,000* **2 net weight** the weight of something without its container **3 net worth** ECONOMICS the value of a company or business after all its debts have been taken away from its profits, and the things it owns **4 net result** the final result, after all the effects are known: *The net result of the policy was higher prices in the stores.*

net·i·quette, Netiquette /ˈnɛt̮ɪkɪt/ *n.* [U] IT the commonly accepted rules for polite behavior when communicating with other people on the Internet

net·ting /ˈnɛt̮ɪŋ/ *n.* [U] material consisting of string, wire, etc. that has been woven into a net

net·tle /ˈnɛt̮l/ *n.* [C] a wild plant with rough leaves that sting you

net·work¹ /ˈnɛtˀwɚk/ (Ac) *n.* [C] **1** a group of radio or television stations that broadcasts many of the same programs in different parts of the country: *the four biggest TV networks* **2** IT a set of computers that are connected to each other so that they can share information: *network administrators* | *I wasn't able to log onto the network.* | *Three-quarters of the traffic on their network consisted of emails.* **3** a system of lines, tubes, wires, roads, etc. that cross each other and are connected to each other: *the freeway network* | *the **network of** blood vessels in the body* | *The GPS system is based on a network of 24 satellites sending out radio signals.* **4** a group of people, organizations, etc. that are connected or that work together: *Trina had developed a good **network of** business contacts.*

network² *v.* **1** [I] to meet other people who do the same type of work, in order to share information, help each other, etc.: *Conferences can be a great opportunity to network.* **2** [I] IT to connect several computers together so that they can share information: *This system allows you to network all your computers.*

net·work·ing /ˈnɛtˀˌwɚkɪŋ/ (Ac) *n.* [U] the practice of meeting other people who do the same type of work, in order to share information, help each other, etc.: *Networking may give you the opportunity to find another job.*

neu·rol·o·gy /nʊˈrɑlədʒi/ *n.* [U] BIOLOGY the scientific study of the NERVOUS SYSTEM and the diseases that are related to it —**neurologist** *n.* [C] —**neurological** /ˌnʊrəˈlɑdʒɪkəl/ *adj.*

neu·ron /ˈnʊrɑn/ *n.* [C] BIOLOGY a type of cell in the NERVOUS SYSTEM that sends messages to muscles, the brain, and other parts of the body [ORIGIN: 1800—1900 Greek "nerve"]

neu·ro·sis /nʊˈroʊsɪs/ *n.* (plural **neuroses** /-ˈroʊsiz/) [C,U] a mental illness that makes someone worried or frightened in an unreasonable way

neu·rot·ic /nʊˈrɑt̮ɪk/ *adj.* **1** unreasonably anxious or afraid: *My aunt is **neurotic about** cleanliness.* **2** relating to a neurosis: *neurotic disorders* —**neurotically** *adv.* —**neurotic** *n.* [C]

neu·ter¹ /ˈnut̮ɚ/ *adj.* ENG. LANG. ARTS in English grammar, a neuter PRONOUN such as "it" relates to

N

something that has no sex, or does not show the sex of the person or animal that it relates to [ORIGIN: 1300—1400 Latin "neither," from *ne-* "not" + *uter* "which of two"]

neuter² *v.* [T] BIOLOGY to remove part of the sex organs of a male animal so that it cannot produce babies → SPAY

N

neu·tral¹ /ˈnutrəl/ (Ac) *adj.* **1** not supporting either side in an argument, competition, or war: *Switzerland was neutral during World War II.* | *The French government acted as a neutral observer during the talks.* **2** not showing any strong feelings or opinions: *"I see," she said in a* ***neutral tone.*** **3** a neutral color such as gray or brown is not strong or bright: *Neutral tones give the room a feeling of space.*

neutral² *n.* [U] the position of the GEARS of a car or machine when it will not move forward or backward: *Start the car* ***in neutral.***

neu·tral·i·ty /nuˈtræləṭi/ (Ac) *n.* [U] the state of not supporting either side in an argument, competition, or war: *Switzerland was determined to maintain its traditional neutrality.*

neu·tral·ize /ˈnutrəˌlaɪz/ (Ac) *v.* [T] to prevent something from having any effect: *Air freshener can help neutralize pet odors.* | *Higher taxes will neutralize increased wages.* —**neutralization** /ˌnutrələˈzeɪʃən/ *n.* [U]

neu·tron /ˈnutrɑn/ *n.* [C] PHYSICS a part of an atom that has no electrical CHARGE [ORIGIN: 1900—2000 Probably from *neutral*] → *see picture at* ATOM

nev·er /ˈnɛvɚ/ *adv.* **1** not at any time, or not once: *I've never been to Hawaii.* | *We waited until 11:00, but they never came.* | *I'll* ***never*** *make that mistake* ***again.*** | ***I never knew*** (=I did not know until now) *that you played the guitar!*

THESAURUS

never ever (spoken) – used to emphasize that you mean never: *I'll never ever forgive him.*
not in a million years (spoken) – used to say that something is completely impossible: *She wouldn't go without me – not in a million years!*
not once – used to show that you are surprised or annoyed, or to emphasize something: *Craig didn't phone all week – not once!* → OFTEN, RARELY, SOMETIMES

2 never mind (spoken) used in order to tell someone that something was not important or that you do not want to say something again: *"What did you say?" "Never mind, it doesn't matter."* **3 you never know** (spoken) used in order to say that something that seems unlikely could happen: *You never know, maybe you'll win.*

GRAMMAR

Use **never** before a verb, unless the verb is "be": *I never thought that this would happen.* | *He's never late.*
If there are two or more verbs together, **never** comes after the first one: *She has never wanted to live anywhere else.*

nev·er·the·less /ˌnɛvɚðəˈlɛs◂/ (Ac) *adv.* in spite of what has just been mentioned: *I know he's telling the truth. Nevertheless, I don't trust him.*

THESAURUS **however, in spite of/despite, nonetheless** → ALTHOUGH

new /nu/ *adj.* **1** recently made, built, invented, or developed (ANT) **old**: *The city is building a new football stadium.* | *Can the new drugs help her?* | *technology that is completely new*

THESAURUS

recent – used about something that was new or that happened a short time ago: *recent news reports*
modern – used about things that are different from earlier things of the same kind: *modern technology*
original – completely new and different from anything that has been done or thought of before: *original ideas*
fresh – recently made or picked, or not done, seen etc. before: *fresh bread*
latest – used about a film, book, fashion, etc. that is the newest one: *his latest movie* → OLD

2 recently bought: *Do you like my new dress?* **3** not used or owned by anyone before (ANT) **used**: *A used car costs a lot less than a new one.* | *a* ***brand new*** (=completely new) *CD player* **4** not experienced by someone before: *Do you like your new teacher?* | *Learning a new language is always a challenge.* | *The idea was* ***new to*** *me.* **5** having recently arrived in a place, or started a different job or activity: *Are you a new student here?* | *Charlie is* ***new to*** *the area and eager to meet people.* | *It's hard being* ***the new kid on the block*** (=the newest person in a job, school, etc.). **6** recently discovered: *new evidence* | *a new planet* **7 what's new?** (spoken) used as a friendly greeting to ask what is happening in someone's life [ORIGIN: Old English *niwe*] —**newness** *n.* [U]

ˈNew Age *adj.* relating to a set of beliefs about religion, medicine, and ways of life that are not part of traditional Western religions, etc.

new·bie /ˈnubi/ *n.* [C] (informal, humorous) someone who has just started doing something, especially using the Internet or computers (SYN) **beginner**

new·born /ˈnubɔrn/ *n.* [C] a baby that has recently been born —**newborn** /ˌnuˈbɔrn◂/ *adj.*

new·com·er /ˈnuˌkʌmɚ/ *n.* [C] someone who has recently arrived somewhere or recently started a particular activity: *a* ***newcomer to*** *the real estate business*

new·fan·gled /ˈnuˌfæŋgəld/ *adj.* [only before noun] (disapproving) newfangled ideas, machines, etc. have been recently invented but seem complicated or unnecessary: *newfangled ideas about raising children*

new·ly /ˈnuli/ *adv.* **newly elected/formed etc.** elected, etc. very recently: *the newly appointed chairman*

THESAURUS recently, just, lately → RECENTLY

new·ly·weds /ˈnuliˌwɛdz/ *n.* [plural] a man and a woman who have recently gotten married

news /nuz/ *n.* **1** [U] information about something that has happened recently: *Have you* ***heard*** (=received) *any* ***news about*** *your job application?* | *I have some* ***good/bad news*** *for you.* | *We were shocked by the* ***news that*** *Tom had left his wife.* | *I don't know how I'm going to* ***break the news*** *to her* (=tell her about something bad that has happened). | *an interesting* ***piece of news*** **2** [U] reports of recent events in the newspapers or on the radio or television: *There is more* ***news of*** *fighting in the area.* | *a* ***news story/report/item*** *on the plane crash* | ***local/national/international news*** | *20 years ago, environmental issues rarely* ***made the news*** (=were reported in newspapers, etc.). **3 the news** a regular television or radio program that gives you reports of recent events: *the 11 o'clock news* | *We usually* ***watch the*** *evening* ***news.*** | *The teachers' strike was* ***on the news.*** **4 that's news to me** (spoken) said when you are surprised or annoyed because you were not told something earlier: *The meeting's been canceled? That's news to me.*

GRAMMAR

News is always followed by a singular verb: *The news was good.* You can say **some news**, **any news**, etc., or **a piece of news**: *I have some news for you.*

ˈnews ˌagency *n.* [C] a company that supplies reports on recent events to newspapers, television, and radio

ˈnews ˌbulletin *n.* [C] a very short news program about something important that has just happened, that is broadcast suddenly in the middle of a television or radio program

news·cast /ˈnuzkæst/ *n.* [C] a news program on television or the radio

news·cast·er /ˈnuzˌkæstɚ/ *n.* [C] someone who reads the news on television or the radio

news·let·ter /ˈnuzˌlɛt̬ɚ/ *n.* [C] a short written report of news about a club, organization, or particular subject, that is sent regularly to people: *our church newsletter*

news·pa·per /ˈnuzˌpeɪpɚ/ *n.* **1** [C] *also* **paper** a set of large folded sheets of paper containing news, pictures, advertisements, etc. that is printed and sold daily or weekly: *the local newspaper* | *I saw your picture* ***in the newspaper.*** | *a* ***newspaper article***

THESAURUS

Newspapers in general

the papers, **the press**, **the media** (=newspapers, TV, radio, etc.)
tabloid – a newspaper that has small pages, a lot of photographs, short stories, and not much serious news
broadsheet – a serious newspaper printed on large sheets of paper

Parts of a newspaper

front page – the first page, which usually contains the most important news
sports/entertainment/food etc. sections – the set of pages dealing with sports, entertainment, etc.
the comics page/the funnies – the page with many different cartoons
editorial/opinion/op-ed page – the page or pages in which the editor and other people express their opinions about the news, rather than just giving facts
headlines – the titles of newspaper articles, printed in large letters above the article, and which usually show the most important pieces of news
article – a piece of writing about a particular subject
report – a piece of writing in a newspaper about an event
story – a report in a newspaper about a recent event
column – an article on a particular subject or by a particular writer, that appears regularly

People who write newspapers

editor – the person who is in charge of a newspaper, magazine, etc. and decides what should be included in it, or the person who prepares an article for printing by deciding what to include and checking for mistakes
reporter – someone whose job is to report on events for a newspaper or magazine, or on television or the radio
journalist – someone who writes reports for newspapers and magazines
correspondent – someone whose job is to report news from a distant area or about a particular subject
columnist – someone who writes articles, especially about a particular subject, that appear regularly

2 [U] sheets of paper from old newspapers: *We packed the dishes in newspaper.* **3** [C] a company that produces a newspaper

news·print /ˈnuzˌprɪnt/ *n.* [U] cheap paper used mostly for printing newspapers

news·stand /ˈnuzˌstænd/ *n.* [C] a place on a street where newspapers are sold

news·wor·thy /ˈnuzˌwɚði/ *adj.* important or interesting enough to be reported as news: *newsworthy events*

news·y /ˈnuzi/ *adj.* (informal) a newsy letter is from a friend or relative and contains a lot of information about him/her

newt /nut/ *n.* [C] a small animal with a long body, four legs, and a tail, that lives in water

N

ˌNew ˈTestament *n.* **the New Testament** the part of the Bible that is about Jesus Christ's life and what he taught → OLD TESTAMENT

new·ton /ˈnutˀn/ *n.* [C] PHYSICS (*written abbreviation* **N**) a unit for measuring force. One newton is equal to the force needed to make an object that weighs one kilogram move at a speed that increases every second by one meter a second.

ˌNewton's First ˈLaw *n.* PHYSICS a scientific rule which says that an object will not start to move, or will not move forward faster, unless it is made to do so by an outside force

ˌnew ˈwave *n.* [C usually singular] people who are trying to introduce new ideas in music, movies, art, politics, etc.: *a **new wave of** Hong Kong filmmakers* **—new-wave** *adj.*

ˌNew ˈWorld *n.* **the New World** HISTORY North, Central, and South America, used when talking about the time that Europeans first discovered these areas

ˌnew ˈyear *n.* [C] **1 New Year** *also* **New Year's** the time when you celebrate the beginning of the year: ***Happy New Year!*** | *Have you made any **New Year's resolutions*** (=promises to improve yourself)*?* **2 the new year** the year after the present year, especially the months at the beginning of it: *We're opening three new stores **in the new year**.*

ˌNew Year's ˈDay *n.* a holiday on January 1, the first day of the year in Western countries

ˌNew Year's ˈEve *n.* a holiday on December 31, the last day of the year in Western countries, when many people have parties to celebrate the start of the new year

next¹ /nɛkst/ *determiner, adj.* **1** the next day, time, event, etc. is the one that happens after the present one: ***The next** flight leaves in 45 minutes.* | *They returned to New York **the next day**.* | ***Next time*** (=when this happens again), *be more careful.* | *See you **next week**.* | *School starts **next Monday**.* ▸Don't say "the next Monday/month/year, etc."◂

THESAURUS

following – immediately after the one you have just been talking about: *The following day, she invited me to dinner.*
subsequent (formal) – coming after or following something else: *In subsequent years, Dr. Kim devoted all of his time to research.*
succeeding – coming after something else: *In the succeeding weeks, he gradually grew stronger.*
later – coming in the future, or after something else: *We'll discuss this at a later time.*
ensuing (formal) – happening after something, often as a result of it: *He realized, in the ensuing silence, that he had said the wrong thing.*

2 the next place is the one closest to where you are now: *Turn left at the next corner.* | *the people at the next table* **3** the next person or thing on a list, in a series, etc. is the one that comes after the present one: *Who's the next person in line?* | *Read the next two chapters by Friday.* **4 the next best thing** the thing or situation that is almost as good as the one you really want: *If we can't be together, talking on the phone is the next best thing.*

next² *adv.* **1** immediately afterward: *What should we do next?* | *First, write your name at the top of the page. Next, read the instructions.*

THESAURUS **after, afterward, later, subsequently** → AFTER¹

2 next to sb/sth very close to someone or something, with nothing in between: *I sat next to a really nice lady on the plane.* | *The baby sleeps in the room next to ours.* **3 next to nothing** very little: *Phil earns next to nothing.* **4 next to impossible** very difficult: *It's next to impossible to get tickets for the game.*

next³ *pron.* **1** the person or thing in a list, series, etc. that comes after the person or thing you are dealing with now: *What's next on the shopping list?* | *We're next in line.* **2 the day/week etc. after next** the day, week, etc. that follows the next one: *The week after next is our spring break.*

next ˈdoor *adv.* in the room, building, etc. that is next to yours or someone else's: *Deanna's office is right next door.* | *The Garcias just bought the house **next door to** my mother's.*

ˈnext-door *adj.* [only before noun] relating to the room, building, etc. that is next to yours: *Our **next-door neighbor** will take care of the cats for us.*

ˌnext of ˈkin *n.* [U] LAW your closest living relative or relatives, for example your mother, father, son, or daughter: *The victim will not be named until her next of kin are informed.*

NFC *n.* **National Football Conference** a group of teams that is part of the NFL

NFL *n.* **National Football League** the organization that is in charge of professional football in the U.S.

NH the written abbreviation of NEW HAMPSHIRE

NHL *n.* **National Hockey League** the organization that is in charge of professional HOCKEY in the U.S. and Canada

nib·ble /ˈnɪbəl/ *v.* [I,T] to eat a small amount of food by taking very small bites: *Guests were **nibbling on** cheese and crackers.* **—nibble** *n.* [C]

THESAURUS **eat, pick at, ingest** → EAT

nice /naɪs/ *adj.* **1** good, pleasant, attractive, or enjoyable: *Did you have a **nice time** last night?* | *That's a nice sweater.* | *Their apartment is much nicer than ours.* | *You **look nice** today.* | ***It's nice to** see you again.* | ***It would be nice if** Chris could come.* | ***It's** really **nice out*** (=the weather is good) *today.* | *Let's sit by the fire where it's **nice and warm**.*

THESAURUS

enjoyable – used for describing something that gives you pleasure because it is interesting, exciting, etc.: *an enjoyable day at the beach*

pleasant – used for describing something that you like, especially something that is peaceful or relaxing: *It had been a pleasant evening.*
great/fantastic/wonderful – used for describing something that you like very much: *"How was your vacation?" "Wonderful!"*
→ HORRIBLE

2 friendly or kind: *Matt is a really nice guy.* | ***It was nice of you to** stop by.* | ***Be nice to** your little sister!*

THESAURUS **kind, considerate, thoughtful, caring, warm-hearted, sympathetic** → KIND[2]

SPOKEN PHRASES

3 (it's) nice to meet you a polite phrase used when you meet someone for the first time **4 (it was) nice meeting you** a polite phrase used when you say goodbye after meeting someone for the first time **5 Have a nice day!** a phrase used when you say goodbye to someone, especially to a customer in a store, restaurant, etc. **6 Nice going/move/one!** said as a joke when someone makes a mistake or does something wrong: *"I just spilled my coffee!" "Nice going!"*

[ORIGIN: 1200—1300 Old French "stupid," from Latin *nescius* "lacking knowledge"] **—niceness** *n.* [U]

ˌnice-ˈlooking *adj.* fairly attractive: *He's a really nice-looking guy.* → ATTRACTIVE

nice·ly /ˈnaɪsli/ *adv.* **1** in a satisfactory, pleasing, or skillful way SYN **well**: *Belinda is always so nicely dressed* (=wearing attractive clothes). | *His arm is healing nicely.* **2** in a polite or friendly way: *I'm sure he'll help if you ask him nicely.*

ni·ce·ty /ˈnaɪsət̬i/ *n.* (plural **niceties**) [C] something small that is nice to have, but not necessary: *The car includes such niceties as GPS and cruise control.*

niche /nɪtʃ/ *n.* [C] a job or activity that is perfect for the skills, abilities, and character that you have: *After many years, she **found her niche** as a fashion designer.*

nick[1] /nɪk/ *n.* [C] **1 in the nick of time** just before it is too late or before something bad happens: *The doctor arrived just in the nick of time.* **2** a very small cut on the surface or edge of something

nick[2] *v.* [T] to accidentally make a small cut on the surface or edge of something: *I nicked my chin when I was shaving.*

nick·el /ˈnɪkəl/ *n.* **1** [C] a coin used in the U.S. and Canada worth five cents (=1/20 of a dollar)

THESAURUS **money, bill, coin, penny, dime, quarter** → MONEY

2 [U] CHEMISTRY a hard silver-white metal that is an ELEMENT and is used for making other metals [ORIGIN: 1700—1800 German *kupfernickel* substance containing nickel, from *kupfer* "copper" + *nickel* "spirit that plays tricks;" because the substance contains no copper, even though it looks like copper]

nick·name /ˈnɪkneɪm/ *n.* [C] a silly name or a shorter form of someone's real name, usually given by friends or family: *The kids had nicknames for all the teachers.* **—nickname** *v.* [T]: *The puppy was soon nicknamed "Trouble."*

THESAURUS **name, first name/given name, last name/family name/surname, middle name, full name, stage name, pen name/pseudonym, assumed name/alias** → NAME[1]

nic·o·tine /ˈnɪkəˌtin/ *n.* [U] a dangerous substance in tobacco [ORIGIN: 1800—1900 Jean *Nicot* (1530-1604), French diplomat who first brought tobacco into France]

niece /nis/ *n.* [C] the daughter of your brother or sister, or the daughter of your husband's or wife's brother or sister → NEPHEW → RELATIVE[1]

nif·ty /ˈnɪfti/ *adj.* (informal) very good, fast, or effective: *a nifty little machine*

nig·gling /ˈnɪglɪŋ/ *adj.* [only before noun] not very important, but continuing to annoy someone: ***a niggling doubt***

night /naɪt/ *n.* **1** [C,U] the dark part of each 24-hour period, when the Sun cannot be seen → DAY: *a cold night* | *I stayed up **all night** to finish the paper.* | *You can see the stars really clearly here **at night**.* **2** [C,U] the evening → TONIGHT: *Some friends are coming over **tomorrow night**.* | *What did you do **last night**?* | *I fly back to New Orleans **on Thursday night**.* | *I don't want to walk home alone **late at night**.* ▸Don't say "this night," say "tonight."◂ **3** [C,U] the time when most people are sleeping: *The baby cried **all night long**.* | *We'll **spend the night*** (=sleep) *at my parents' and come back Sunday.* | *I woke up **in the middle of the night**.* | *What you need is a **good night's sleep*** (=to sleep well all night). **4 nights** [plural] if you do something nights, you do it regularly or often at night: *Peter **works nights**.* **5 night and day** *also* **day and night** all the time: *We had to work night and day to get it finished.* **6 night after night** every night for a long period: *He goes out drinking night after night.* [ORIGIN: Old English *niht*]

night·club /ˈnaɪt˺klʌb/ *n.* [C] a place where people can drink and dance that is open late at night

night·fall /ˈnaɪtfɔl/ *n.* [U] (literary) the time in the evening when the sky becomes darker SYN **dusk**

night·gown /ˈnaɪt˺gaʊn/ *n.* [C] a piece of loose clothing, like a dress, that women wear in bed

night·ie /ˈnaɪt̬i/ *n.* [C] (informal) a nightgown

night·in·gale /ˈnaɪt˺nˌgeɪl, ˈnaɪt̬ɪŋ-/ *n.* [C] a small European wild bird that sings very beautifully, especially at night

night·life /ˈnaɪt˺laɪf/ *n.* [U] entertainment in places where you can dance, drink, etc. in the evening: *Las Vegas is famous for its nightlife.*

N

'night light *n.* [C] a small not very bright light, often used in a child's room at night, so that s/he will not be afraid of the dark

night·ly /'naɪtli/ *adj., adv.* happening every night: *the nightly news* | *The restaurant is open nightly.*

night·mare /'naɪt˺mɛr/ *n.* [C] **1** a very frightening dream: *I still* ***have*** *terrible* ***nightmares*** *about the accident.* **2** (informal) a person, thing, situation, etc. that is very bad or very difficult to deal with: *Living with my parents again would be a total nightmare!* —**nightmarish** *adj.*

'night owl *n.* [C] (informal) someone who enjoys being awake or working late at night

'night school *n.* [U] classes taught at night, for people who work during the day: *I was working every day and going to night school.*

night·stand /'naɪtstænd/ *also* **'night ˌtable** *n.* [C] a small table beside a bed

night·time /'naɪt-taɪm/ *n.* [U] the time during the night when the sky is dark (ANT) **daytime**

ni·hil·ism /'niəˌlɪzəm, 'naɪ-/ *n.* [U] the belief that nothing in life has any meaning or value, and that all social and political institutions should be destroyed —**nihilist** *n.* [C] —**nihilistic** /ˌniə'lɪstɪk◂ / *adj.*

nil /nɪl/ *n.* [U] (formal) nothing or zero: *His chances of winning the election are* ***almost/practically/virtually nil.***

nim·ble /'nɪmbəl/ *adj.* able to move quickly and skillfully (SYN) **agile**: *nimble fingers*

nim·bus /'nɪmbəs/ *n.* (plural **nimbuses** *or* **nimbi** //) [C,U] EARTH SCIENCES a dark cloud that may bring rain or snow ➔ CIRRUS, CUMULONIMBUS, CUMULUS, STRATUS

nin·com·poop /'nɪŋkəmˌpup/ *n.* [C] (old-fashioned, informal) a stupid person (SYN) **idiot**

nine /naɪn/ *number* **1** 9 **2** nine o'clock: *I have to be in the office by nine.* | *The store opens at nine.* **3** nine years old: *Larry will be nine next July.* [ORIGIN: Old English *nigon*]

nine·teen /ˌnaɪn'tin◂ / *number* 19 —**nineteenth** *number*

ˌnine-to-'five *adj., adv.* from 9:00 a.m. until 5:00 p.m., the hours that most people work in an office: *I* ***work nine-to-five*** *most days.* | *a nine-to-five job*

nine·ty /'naɪnti/ *number* **1** 90 **2 the nineties a)** the years between 1990 and 1999 **b)** the numbers between 90 and 99, especially when used for measuring temperatures **3 be in your nineties** to be between 90 and 99 years old —**ninetieth** /'naɪntiɪθ/ *number*

ninth /naɪnθ/ *number* **1** 9th **2** 1/9

nip¹ /nɪp/ *v.* (**nipped**, **nipping**) **1** [I,T] to bite someone or something with small sharp bites, or to try to do this: *This stupid dog keeps* ***nipping at*** *my ankles.* **2 nip sth in the bud** to prevent something from becoming a problem by stopping it as soon as it starts

nip² *n.* [C] a small sharp bite

nip·ple /'nɪpəl/ *n.* [C] **1** the dark raised circle in the middle of a woman's breast that a baby sucks in order to get milk **2** one of the two dark raised circles on a man's chest **3** the small piece of rubber on the end of a baby's bottle

nip·py /'nɪpi/ *adj.* (informal) weather that is nippy is a little cold (SYN) **chilly**

nir·va·na, Nirvana /nɚ'vɑnə, nɪr-/ *n.* [U] SOCIAL SCIENCE the final state of complete knowledge and understanding that is the aim of believers in Buddhism [ORIGIN: 1800—1900 Sanskrit *nis-* "out" + *vati* "it blows"]

nit /nɪt/ *n.* [C] the egg of a LOUSE (=small insect)

nit·pick·ing /'nɪtˌpɪkɪŋ/ *n.* [U] (informal, disapproving) the act of criticizing people about unimportant details —**nitpick** *v.* [I] —**nitpicking** *adj.*

ni·trate /'naɪtreɪt/ *n.* [C,U] CHEMISTRY a chemical compound that is mainly used for improving the soil that crops are grown in

ni·tro·gen /'naɪtrədʒən/ *n.* [U] (*symbol* **N**) CHEMISTRY a gas that is an ELEMENT and is the main part of the Earth's air

'nitrogen ˌcycle *n.* [singular] EARTH SCIENCES a continuous process by which nitrogen in the air is taken in by plants, soil, and some living creatures and is then passed back out into the air

nit·ty-grit·ty /'nɪṭi ˌgrɪṭi, ˌnɪṭi 'grɪṭi/ *n.* **the nitty-gritty** (informal) the basic and practical facts and details of an agreement or activity: *Let's* ***get down to the nitty-gritty*** *and work out the cost.*

nit·wit /'nɪt˺ˌwɪt/ *n.* [C] (informal) a silly stupid person

nix /nɪks/ *v.* [T] (informal) to answer no to something or refuse something: *They immediately nixed my idea.*

NJ the written abbreviation of NEW JERSEY

NM the written abbreviation of NEW MEXICO

no¹ /noʊ/ *adv.* **1** said in order to give a negative reply to a question, offer, or request (ANT) **yes**: *"Is she married?" "No, she's not."* | *"Do you want some more coffee?"* ***"No thanks."*** | *When I asked him, he* ***said no.*** **2** (spoken) said when you disagree with a statement (ANT) **yes**: *"Gary's weird." "No, he's just shy."* **3** (spoken) said when you do not want someone to do something (ANT) **yes**: *No, Jimmy, don't touch that.*

no² *determiner* **1** not any, or not at all: *There was no evidence that a crime had been committed.* | *There's no more milk.* | *He had no intention of returning the money.* | *There's no reason to be afraid.* **2** used on a sign in order to show that something is not allowed: *No smoking* | *No pets* ➔ **no good** *at* GOOD², **in no time** *at* TIME¹

no³ *n.* (plural **noes**) [C usually singular] a negative answer or decision: *Her answer was a definite no.*

no. (plural **nos.**) the written abbreviation of NUMBER

no·bil·i·ty /noʊˈbɪləṭi/ *n.* **1 the nobility** the group of people in particular countries who have the highest social class and have special titles **2** [U] the quality of being noble

no·ble¹ /ˈnoʊbəl/ *adj.* **1** morally good or generous in a way that should be admired: *The money is going to a noble cause.* | *a noble ideal/goal* **2** belonging to the group of people in particular countries who have the highest social class and special titles: *noble families* —**nobly** *adv.*

noble² *also* **no·ble·man** /ˈnoʊbəlmən/, **no·ble·wom·an** /ˈnoʊbəlˌwʊmən/ *n.* (plural **noblemen** /-mən/, **noblewomen** /-ˌwɪmɪn/) [C] someone who belongs to the nobility

ˌnoble ˈgas *n.* [C] CHEMISTRY a gas that is an ELEMENT and that combines with only a small number of other gases or not at all

no·bod·y¹ /ˈnoʊˌbʌdi, -ˌbɑdi/ *pron.* no person (SYN) **no one**: *I knocked on the door, but nobody answered.*

nobody² *n* (plural **nobodies**) [C] someone who is not important, successful, or famous

ˌno-ˈbrainer *n.* [C usually singular] (informal) something that you do not have to think about because it is easy to understand: *The decision is a no-brainer – take the job.*

nocturnal animals

1. bat 2. owl 3. fox 4. raccoon

noc·tur·nal /nɑkˈtɚnl/ *adj.* **1** BIOLOGY nocturnal animals are active at night **2** (formal) happening at night [ORIGIN: 1400—1500 Late Latin *nocturnalis*, from Latin *nocturnus* "by night," from *nox* "night"]

nod /nɑd/ *v.* (**nodded**, **nodding**) **1** [I,T] to move your head up and down, especially to show that you agree with or understand something: *Dora **nodded** her **head** in agreement.* | *He nodded and smiled.* **2** [I] to move your head up and down once toward someone or something, in order to greet someone or to give him/her a sign to do something: *I **nodded to** the waiter and asked for the bill.* | *"Sally's in there," Jim said, **nodding toward** the door.* —**nod** *n.* [C]: *He gave a nod of agreement.*

nod off *phr. v.* to begin to sleep, often without intending to: *His speech was so boring I kept nodding off.*

node /noʊd/ *n.* [C] **1** MATH a place where lines in a network, GRAPH, etc. meet or join **2** BIOLOGY a LYMPH NODE

ˌno-ˈfault *adj.* [only before noun] **1** no-fault car insurance will pay for the damage done in an accident, even if you caused the accident **2** a no-fault DIVORCE does not blame either the husband or the wife

ˌno-ˈfrills *adj.* [only before noun] without any features that are not completely necessary: *a no-frills airline*

Noh /noʊ/ *n.* [U] ENG. LANG. ARTS a type of traditional Japanese musical play

noise /nɔɪz/ *n.* [C,U] a sound or sounds that is or are too loud, annoying, or not intended: *the **noise of** the traffic* | *You're **making** too much **noise**.* | *Do you hear that squeaking noise?* | *There was **a lot of noise** outside.*

THESAURUS

A **sound** is anything that you can hear: *the sound of voices*
A **noise** is usually a loud, unpleasant, or unexpected sound: *the deafening noise of overhead planes*

noise·less /ˈnɔɪzlɪs/ *adj.* (literary) not making any sound —**noiselessly** *adv.*

ˈnoise polˌlution *n.* [U] very loud continuous noise in the environment, that is considered unpleasant and harmful to people

noi·some /ˈnɔɪsəm/ *adj.* (literary) extremely bad, ugly, etc.: *The poor were forced to live in noisome slums.*

nois·y /ˈnɔɪzi/ *adj.* (comparative **noisier**, superlative **noisiest**) making a lot of noise, or full of noise: *a noisy crowd* | *a noisy restaurant* | *Their lawn mower is really noisy.* —**noisily** *adv.*

THESAURUS **loud, rowdy, thunderous, deafening, ear-splitting, raucous** → LOUD¹

no·mad /ˈnoʊmæd/ *n.* [C] **1** a member of a tribe that travels from place to place, especially to find food for their animals: *the desert nomads* **2** someone who often travels from place to place, or who changes jobs, homes, etc. often —**nomadic** /noʊˈmædɪk/ *adj.*: *nomadic tribes*

ˈno-man's ˌland *n.* [singular, U] land that no one owns or controls, especially between two opposing armies

no·men·cla·ture /ˈnoʊmənˌkleɪtʃɚ/ *n.* [C,U] SCIENCE a system of naming things

N

nom·i·nal /ˈnɑmənl/ *adj.* **1 a nominal price/fee/sum etc.** a small amount of money: *You can get the new telephone service for a nominal fee.* **2 nominal leader/head etc.** someone who has the title of leader, etc. but does not actually do that job

nom·i·nal·ly /ˈnɑmənl-i/ *adv.* (formal) officially described as something or as doing something, although the truth may be different: *The country is nominally Catholic.*

nom·i·nate /ˈnɑməˌneɪt/ *v.* [T] **1** to officially choose someone so that s/he can be one of the competitors in an election, competition, etc.: *Ferraro was the first woman to be **nominated for** the job of vice president.* **2** to choose someone for a particular job or position: *Margaret was **nominated (as)** club representative.*

nom·i·na·tion /ˌnɑməˈneɪʃən/ *n.* [C,U] **1** the act of officially choosing someone to be a competitor in an election, competition, etc., or the official choice: *Who will get the Republican **nomination for** president?* **2** the act of choosing someone for a particular job, or the person chosen: *Judge Howard's **nomination to** the United States Supreme Court | The Senate voted to confirm his **nomination as** defense secretary.*

nom·i·na·tive /ˈnɑmənət̬ɪv, ˈnɑmnə-/ *n.* [singular] ENG. LANG. ARTS a particular form of a noun in some languages, such as Latin and German, which shows that the noun is the SUBJECT of the verb —**nominative** *adj.*

nom·i·nee /ˌnɑməˈni/ *n.* [C] someone who has been nominated for a prize, duty, etc.: *the Democratic Party's presidential nominee*

non·ag·gres·sion /ˌnɑnəˈgrɛʃən/ *n.* [U] the state of not fighting or attacking: *a **nonaggression pact/treaty*** (=a promise not to attack another country)

non·a·gon /ˈnɑnəˌgɑn/ *n.* [C] MATH a flat shape with nine sides ➔ POLYGON

non·al·co·hol·ic, non-alcoholic /ˌnɑnælkəˈhɔlɪk/ *adj.* nonalcoholic drinks do not contain any alcohol: *nonalcoholic beer*

non·cha·lant /ˌnɑnʃəˈlɑnt/ *adj.* calm and not seeming interested in or worried about anything: *She tried to look nonchalant.* —**nonchalance** *n.* [U] —**nonchalantly** *adv.*

non·com·bat·ant /ˌnɑnkəmˈbætˀnt/ *n.* [C] someone who is in the military during a war but does not actually fight, for example a doctor

non·com·mit·tal /ˌnɑnkəˈmɪt̬l/ *adj.* (formal) not giving a definite answer, or not willing to express your opinions: *The lawyer was **noncommittal about** his chances of going to prison.* —**noncommittally** *adv.*

non·con·form·ist /ˌnɑnkənˈfɔrmɪst/ (Ac) *n.* [C] someone who deliberately does not accept the beliefs and ways of behaving that most people in a society accept: *Nonconformists are not tolerated in corporate environments.*

non·count /nɑnˈkaʊnt/ *adj.* **noncount noun** ENG. LANG. ARTS an UNCOUNTABLE noun

ˌnon-ˈdairy *adj.* containing no milk, and used instead of a product that contains milk: *non-dairy creamer*

ˌnon-denomiˈnational *adj.* not related to a particular religion or religious group: *a non-denominational chapel*

non·de·script /ˌnɑndɪˈskrɪpt◂ / *adj.* not having any noticeable or interesting qualities: *a nondescript man in a plain gray suit*

none[1] /nʌn/ *quantifier, pron.* **1** not any of something: *"Can I have some more pie?" "Sorry, there's none left."* **2** not one person or thing: ***None of** my friends has a bike. | An old car is better than **none at all**.* **3 none other than sb** used in order to emphasize a fact when you are surprised that it is true: *Pam's writing was praised by none other than Toni Morrison.*

GRAMMAR

When you use **none** with an uncountable noun, the verb is singular: *None of the money has been spent.*
When you use **none** with a plural noun form, the verb can be singular or plural: *None of the rooms is being used. | None of my friends were there.*

none[2] *adv.* **1 none the worse/wiser etc.** not any worse than before, not knowing any more than before, etc.: *She seems **none the worse for** her experience.* **2 none too soon/likely etc.** not at all soon, not at all likely, etc.: *Consumers are none too happy about the price increase.*

non·en·ti·ty /nɑnˈɛntət̬i/ *n.* (plural **nonentities**) [C] someone who has no importance, power, or ability

none·the·less /ˌnʌnðəˈlɛs◂ / (Ac) *adv.* (formal) in spite of what has just been mentioned (SYN) **nevertheless**: *Although some residents protested, the council nonetheless voted to demolish the building. | The influence of the media was small, but nonetheless significant.*

THESAURUS however, in spite of/despite, nevertheless ➔ ALTHOUGH

non·ex·ist·ent /ˌnɑnɪgˈzɪstənt◂ / *adj.* not existing at all in a particular place or situation: *Airplanes were practically nonexistent in those days.*

non·fat /ˌnɑnˈfæt◂ / *adj.* nonfat milk, YOGURT, etc. has no fat in it

non·fic·tion /ˌnɑnˈfɪkʃən/ *n.* [U] ENG. LANG. ARTS articles, books, etc. about real facts or events, not imagined ones (ANT) **fiction** —**nonfiction** *adj.*

non·flam·ma·ble /ˌnɑnˈflæməbəl/ *adj.* difficult or impossible to burn (ANT) **flammable, inflammable**

non·im·mi·grant /nɑnˈɪməgrənt/ *n.* [C] someone who is living in or visiting a foreign country, but is not planning to live there permanently —**nonimmigrant** *adj.*: *a nonimmigrant student visa*

non·in·ter·ven·tion /ˌnɑnɪntɚˈvɛnʃən/ *n.* [U] the refusal of a government to become involved in the affairs of other countries

non·lin·e·ar pro·gres·sion /nɑnˌlɪniɚ prəˈgrɛʃən/ *also* **nonˌlinear ˈsequence** *n.* [C] MATH a series of numbers, for example 1, 3, 4, 8, with different increases between them. If you showed them on a GRAPH, they would not form a straight line. ➔ ARITHMETIC SEQUENCE, GEOMETRIC SEQUENCE

ˌnon-ˌnative ˈspeaker *n.* [C] someone who has learned a particular language as a foreign language

ˈno-no *n.* (plural **no-nos** *or* **no-no's**) (informal) something that is not allowed, or not socially acceptable: *Chewing gum during a job interview is a definite no no.*

ˌno-ˈnonsense *adj.* very practical, direct, and unwilling to waste time: *a no-nonsense attitude toward work*

non·pay·ment /ˌnɑnˈpeɪmənt/ *n.* [U] ECONOMICS failure to pay bills, taxes, or debts: ***nonpayment of** rent*

non·plussed /ˌnɑnˈplʌst/ *adj.* so surprised that you do not know what to say or do

> THESAURUS **surprised, amazed, shocked, astonished, astounded, flabbergasted, stunned, dumbfounded, taken aback** ➔ SURPRISED

non·prof·it /ˌnɑnˈprɑfɪt/ *adj.* ECONOMICS a nonprofit organization, school, hospital, etc. uses the money it earns to help people instead of making a profit, and therefore does not have to pay taxes —**nonprofit** *n.* [C]: *Danson works for a Seattle nonprofit.*

non·pro·lif·er·a·tion /ˌnɑnprəˌlɪfəˈreɪʃən/ *n.* [U] the act of limiting the number of NUCLEAR or chemical weapons that are being made across the world

non·re·fund·a·ble /ˌnɑnrɪˈfʌndəbəl/ *adj.* if something you buy is nonrefundable, you cannot get your money back after you have paid for it: *nonrefundable airline tickets*

non·re·new·a·ble /ˌnɑnrɪˈnuəbəl/ *adj.* nonrenewable types of energy, such as coal or gas, cannot be replaced after they have been used (ANT) **renewable**: *Demand for many **nonrenewable resources** is still growing.*

non·res·i·dent /ˌnɑnˈrɛzɪdənt/ *n.* [C] someone who does not live permanently in a particular place or country

non·re·stric·tive clause /ˌnɑnrɪˌstrɪktɪv ˈklɔz/ *also* **ˌnonrestrictive ˌrelative ˈclause** *n.* [C] ENG. LANG. ARTS a CLAUSE that gives additional information about a particular person or thing, rather than saying which person or thing is being mentioned. For example, in the sentence "Perry, who is 22, worked at the company," the phrase "who is 22" is a nonrestrictive clause. ➔ RELATIVE CLAUSE, RESTRICTIVE CLAUSE

non·sec·tar·i·an /ˌnɑnsɛkˈtɛriən/ *adj.* not relating to a particular religion or religious group (ANT) **sectarian**: *a nonsectarian charity*

non·sense /ˈnɑnsɛns, -səns/ *n.* [U] **1** ideas, statements, or opinions that are not true or that seem very stupid: *That's **complete/total/utter nonsense!*** **2** behavior that is stupid and annoying: *She won't **take any nonsense** from the kids in her class.* **3** speech or writing that has no meaning or cannot be understood: *nonsense words* —**nonsensical** /nɑnˈsɛnsɪkəl/ *adj.*

non se·qui·tur /ˌnɑn ˈsɛkwɪtɚ/ *n.* [C] (formal) a statement that does not seem related to the statements that were made before it [ORIGIN: 1500—1600 Latin "it does not follow"]

non·smok·er /ˌnɑnˈsmoʊkɚ/ *n.* [C] someone who does not smoke

non·smok·ing /ˌnɑnˈsmoʊkɪŋ◂/ *adj.* a nonsmoking area, building, etc. is one where people are not allowed to smoke

non·stand·ard /ˌnɑnˈstændɚd◂/ *adj.* ENG. LANG. ARTS nonstandard words, expressions, or pronunciations are usually considered incorrect by educated speakers of a language ➔ STANDARD

non·stick /ˌnɑnˈstɪk◂/ *adj.* nonstick pans have a special surface inside that food will not stick to

non·stop /ˌnɑnˈstɑp◂/ *adj., adv.* without stopping, or without a stop: *Dan worked nonstop for 12 hours.* | *a nonstop flight to New York*

non·vi·o·lence /ˌnɑnˈvaɪələns/ *n.* [U] the practice of opposing a government without fighting, for example by not obeying laws

non·vi·o·lent /ˌnɑnˈvaɪələnt/ *adj.* not using or not involving violence: *nonviolent protests*

noo·dle /ˈnudl/ *n.* [C usually plural] a long thin piece of soft food made from flour, water, and usually eggs, that is cooked by being boiled: *egg noodles*

nook /nʊk/ *n.* [C] **1** a small quiet place or corner: *a shady nook* **2 every nook and cranny** every part of a place: *We've searched every nook and cranny for that key.*

noon /nun/ *n.* [U] 12 o'clock in the middle of the day ➔ MIDNIGHT: *Lunch will be right **at noon**.* | *The gallery is open from noon to 5:00 p.m.* [ORIGIN: Old English *non* "ninth hour from sunrise," from Latin *nonus* "ninth"]

ˈno one *pron.* not anyone: *I tried calling last night, but no one was home.* | *No one could remember her name.*

noose /nus/ *n.* [C] a circle of a rope that becomes tighter as it is pulled, used for killing someone by hanging

nope /noʊp/ *adv.* (spoken, informal) no: *"Aren't you hungry?" "Nope."*

no·place, **'no place** /ˈnoʊpleɪs/ *adv.* (informal) nowhere

nor /nɚ; *strong* nɔr/ *conjunction* **1 neither ... nor** used in order to show that not one of a set of facts, people, qualities, actions, etc. is true: *My mother's family was neither rich nor poor.* | *Neither Julie nor Mark said anything.* **2** (formal) used after a negative statement when adding another negative statement: *She didn't reply, nor did she look at him.*

norm /nɔrm/ (Ac) *n.* [C] the usual or generally accepted way of doing something: *Working at home is becoming* ***the norm*** *for many employees.* | *the* ***social/cultural norms*** *of American society* | *Kerouac's style of writing was a* ***departure from the norm.***

nor·mal¹ /ˈnɔrməl/ (Ac) *adj.* **1** usual, typical, or expected: *The store is open during normal business hours.* | ***It's normal to*** *feel nervous when you start a new job.* | *Under normal circumstances, such children grow into healthy adults.*

THESAURUS

ordinary – not special or unusual: *an ordinary day*
average – typical of a normal person or thing: *the average family*
standard – used about products or methods that are the most usual type: *shoes in standard sizes*
routine – used about something that is done regularly and is part of a normal system: *a routine check of the plane*
conventional – used when comparing a piece of equipment, method, etc. that has been used for a long time with something that is new and different: *microwaves and conventional ovens*
orthodox (formal) – officially accepted, and considered to be normal by most people: *orthodox methods of treating disease* → NATURAL¹

2 a normal person is mentally and physically healthy and does not behave strangely (ANT) **abnormal**: *He seems like a* ***perfectly normal*** *child to me.* | *Sometimes his behavior doesn't seem entirely normal.* [ORIGIN: 1400—1500 Latin *normalis*, from *norma*]

normal² *n.* [U] the usual state, level, or amount: *The temperatures have been slightly* ***above/below normal.*** | *Things are finally getting* ***back to normal.***

nor·mal·i·ty /nɔrˈmæləṭi/ (Ac) *also* **nor·mal·cy** /ˈnɔrməlsi/ *n.* [U] a situation in which everything happens in the usual or expected way: *The country returned to normality after years of civil war.*

nor·mal·ize /ˈnɔrməˌlaɪz/ (Ac) *v.* [I,T] to become normal again, or to make a situation become normal again: *The two countries have* ***normalized relations*** (=become friendly again after a period of disagreement). —**normalization** /ˌnɔrmələˈzeɪʃən/ *n.* [U]

nor·mal·ly /ˈnɔrməli/ (Ac) *adv.* **1** usually: *I normally go to bed around 11.* | *Normally, it takes me about 20 minutes to get to work.* **2** in the usual or expected way: *Try to relax and breathe normally.* | *The engine began to run normally again.*

Norse /nɔrs/ *adj.* relating to the people of ancient Scandinavia or their language: *Norse mythology*

north

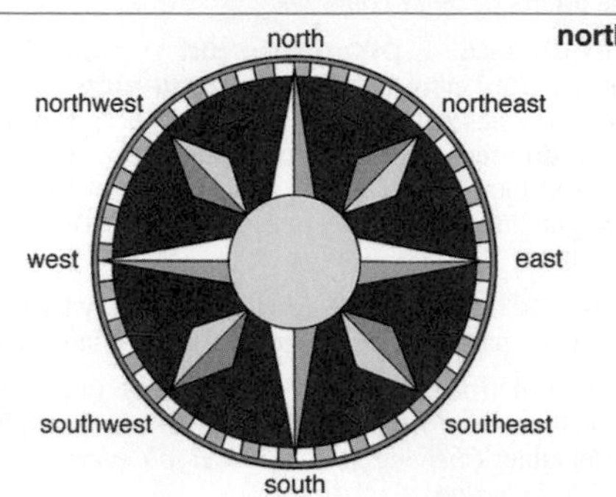

north¹, **North** /nɔrθ/ *n.* [singular, U] **1** the direction toward the top of the world, or to the left of someone facing the rising Sun: *Which way is north?* **2 the north** the northern part of a country, state, etc.: *My relatives live* ***in the north*** *of the state.* **3 the North** the part of the U.S. east of the Mississippi River and north of Washington, D.C. [ORIGIN: Old English]

USAGE

Use **north/south/east/west of sth** in order to describe where a place is in relation to another place: *Chicago is south of Milwaukee.*
Use **in the north/south/east/west of sth** in order to say which part of a place you are talking about: *The mountains are in the west of the province.*
Use **northern**, **southern**, **eastern**, **western** with the name of a place: *They have a cabin in northern Ontario.*
Don't say "in the north of Ontario."

north² *adj.* **1** in, to, or facing north: *a town 20 miles* ***north of*** *Salem* | *the north side of the street* **2 north wind** a wind coming from the north

north³ *adv.* **1** toward the north: *Go north on I-5 to Portland.* | *The window faces north.* **2 up North** in or to the northern part of the U.S.: *He lives most of the year up North but winters in Florida.*

ˌNorth Aˈmerica *n.* one of the seven CONTINENTS, that includes land between the Arctic Ocean and the Caribbean Sea —**North American** *adj.*

north·bound /ˈnɔrθbaʊnd/ *adj.* traveling or leading toward the north: *northbound traffic*

north·east¹ /ˌnɔrθˈist◂/ *n.* [U] **1** the direction that is exactly between north and east → *see picture at* NORTH¹ **2 the northeast** the northeast part of a country, state, etc. **3 the Northeast** the area of the U.S. that includes New England and the states of New Jersey, New York, and Pennsylvania —**northeastern** *adj.*

N

northeast² *adj., adv.* in, from, or toward the northeast: *traveling northeast* | *a northeast wind*

north·er·ly /ˈnɔrðəli/ *adj.* **1** in or toward the north: *sailing in a northerly direction* **2** a northerly wind comes from the north

north·ern /ˈnɔrðən/ *adj.* in or from the north part of an area, country, state, etc.: *northern California* ➔ see USAGE box at NORTH¹

north·ern·er, Northerner /ˈnɔrðənə/ *n.* [C] someone who comes from the northern part of a country

ˌNorthern ˈLights *n.* **the Northern Lights** EARTH SCIENCES bands of colored lights that are seen in the night sky in the most northern parts of the world

north·ern·most /ˈnɔrðənˌmoust/ *adj.* farthest north: *the northernmost tip of Maine*

ˌNorth ˈPole *n.* **the North Pole** EARTH SCIENCES the most northern point on the surface of the Earth, or the area around it ➔ *see picture at* GLOBE

north·ward /ˈnɔrθwəd/ *adj., adv.* toward the north

north·west¹ /ˌnɔrθˈwɛst◂/ *n.* [U] **1** the direction that is exactly between north and west ➔ *see picture at* NORTH¹ **2 the northwest** the northwest part of a country, state, etc. **3 the Northwest** the area of the U.S. that includes the states of Idaho, Oregon, and Washington —**northwestern** *adj.*

northwest² *adj., adv.* in, from, or toward the northwest: *driving northwest* | *a northwest wind*

nose¹ /nouz/ *n.* [C]
1 FACE the part of your face that you use for smelling and breathing: *a broken nose* | *He took out a tissue and **blew his nose*** (=cleared it by blowing). | *Don't **pick your nose*** (=clean it with your finger). ➔ *see picture on page A16*
2 sb's nose is running/sb has a runny nose if someone's nose is running, or if s/he has a runny nose, liquid is slowly coming out of it because s/he has a cold
3 red-nosed/long-nosed etc. having a nose that is red, long, etc.
4 (right) under sb's nose so close to someone that s/he should notice but does not: *Lynn's husband had been having an affair right under her nose.*
5 stick/poke your nose into sth (informal) to show too much interest in private matters that do not concern you: *Jana's always sticking her nose into other people's business.*
6 keep your nose out (of sth) (informal) to avoid becoming involved in a situation that should not involve you
7 look down your nose at sb (informal) to think that you are much better than someone else
8 turn your nose up (at sth) (informal) to refuse to accept something because you do not think it is good enough for you
9 on the nose (informal) exactly: *Tanya guessed the price right on the nose.*
10 AIRPLANE the pointed front end of an airplane, ROCKET, etc.
11 keep your nose to the grindstone to continue working very hard, without stopping to rest [ORIGIN: Old English *nosu*] ➔ **pay through the nose** *at* PAY¹

nose² *v.* [I,T] to move forward, or move something forward, slowly and carefully: *The ship nosed forward.*

nose around (sth) *phr. v.* to try to find out private information about someone or something: *Why were you nosing around my office?*

nose·bleed /ˈnouzblid/ *n.* [C] blood that is coming out of your nose: *Bill **has a nosebleed.***

nose·dive /ˈnouzdaɪv/ *n.* [C] **1** a sudden drop in amount, price, rate, etc.: *The company's profits **took a nosedive** last year.* **2** a sudden steep drop by an airplane, with its front end pointing toward the ground —**nosedive** *v.* [I]

ˈnose job *n.* [C] (informal) a medical operation on someone's nose in order to improve its appearance

ˌno-ˈshow *n.* [C] (informal) someone who does not arrive at a place or event where s/he was expected to be: *The first baseman has been a no-show at spring training.*

nos·tal·gia /nɑˈstældʒə, nə-/ *n.* [U] the slightly sad feeling you have when you remember happy events from the past: ***nostalgia for** the good old days* [ORIGIN: 1700—1800 Modern Latin, Greek *nostos* "returning home" + *algos* "pain"] —**nostalgic** *adj.* —**nostalgically** *adv.*

nos·tril /ˈnɑstrəl/ *n.* [C] one of the two holes at the end of your nose, through which you breathe ➔ *see picture on page A16*

nos·y /ˈnouzi/ *adj.* (disapproving) always trying to find out private information about someone or something: *Our neighbors are really nosy.* —**nosiness** *n.* [U]

not /nɑt/ *adv.* **1** used in order to make a word, statement, or question negative ➔ NO: *The museum is not open on Mondays.* | *She's not a very nice person.* | *I don't* (=do not) *smoke.* **2** used instead of a whole phrase to mean the opposite of what has been mentioned before it: *No one knows if the story is true **or not**.* | *"Is Mark still sick?" **"I hope not."*** **3** used in order to make a word or phrase have the opposite meaning: *The food is **not very good** there.* | ***Not a lot/not much*** (=little) *is known about the disease.* | *Most of the hotels were **not that** cheap* (=they were fairly expensive). **4 not only** in addition to being or doing something: *She's **not only** funny, she's **also** smart.* **5 not a sth/not one sth** not any person or thing SYN **no**: *Not one of the students knew the answer.* | *There wasn't* (=was not) *a cloud in the sky.* **6 not bad!** (spoken) said when you want to praise something, or when something is better than you expected: *"See, I got a B+ on my test!" "Not bad!"* **7 not that...** used before a negative sentence: *Sarah has a new boyfriend – **not that I care*** (=I do not care).

no·ta·ble /ˈnoʊṯəbəl/ *adj.* [usually before noun] important, interesting, or unusual enough to be noticed: *Freeman is the most notable player on the Texas team.* | *Most teachers agreed with the principal, with a few* ***notable exceptions*** (=a few teachers did not).

N

no·ta·bly /ˈnoʊṯəbli/ *adv.* especially or particularly: *Some politicians, most notably the President, refused to comment.*

no·ta·rize /ˈnoʊṯəˌraɪz/ *v.* [T] if a document is notarized, a notary puts an official stamp on it: *Have these witness statements been notarized?* —**notarized** *adj.*: *a notarized statement*

no·tar·y /ˈnoʊṯəri/ *n.* (plural **notaries**) *also* **ˌnotary ˈpublic** [C] LAW someone who has the legal power to make a signed document official

no·ta·tion /noʊˈteɪʃən/ *n.* [C,U] a system of written marks or signs used for representing musical sounds, mathematical problems, or scientific ideas

notch¹ /nɑtʃ/ *n.* [C] **1** a V-shaped cut in a surface or edge: *Cut a notch near one end of the stick.* **2** a level of achievement or a social position: *Losing the game* ***brought*** *the team* ***down a few notches.***

notch² *v.* [T] **1** to cut a V-shaped mark into something **2** *also* **notch up** to win or achieve something: *Craven just notched the third goal of the season.*

note¹ /noʊt/ *n.* **1** [C] a short informal letter: *I* ***wrote/sent*** *Tina* ***a note*** *to thank her for helping.* | *Renee wasn't there, so we* ***left a note*** *on her door.* **2** [C] something that you write down in order to remind you of something: *She* ***made a note of*** *my new address.* **3 notes** [plural] information that a student writes down during a class, from a book, etc., so s/he will remember it: *Did you* ***take*** *any* ***notes*** (=write them) *in history class?* **4** [C] ENG. LANG. ARTS a particular musical sound or PITCH, or the sign in written music that represents this **5 take note (of sth)** to pay careful attention to something: *Take note of the instructions at the top of the page.* **6** [singular] a particular quality or feeling that you notice in a particular person or situation: *You could hear* ***a note of*** *weariness in her voice.* | *The story ended* ***on a*** *happy* ***note.*** **7 sb/sth of note** (formal) someone or something that is important or famous: *a writer of note*

note² *v.* [T] **1** (formal) to notice or pay careful attention to something: *Please* ***note that*** *these prices may change.* **2** (formal) to mention something because it is important or interesting: *The judge* ***noted that*** *Miller had no previous criminal record.*

> THESAURUS mention, refer to sth, raise, allude to sth, bring sth up, cite → MENTION¹

3 *also* **note down** to write something down so you will remember it: *He noted my telephone number.*

note·book /ˈnoʊt˺bʊk/ *n.* [C] **1** a book of plain paper in which you write notes **2** IT a small computer that is about the size of a book → LAPTOP

not·ed /ˈnoʊṯɪd/ *adj.* well-known or famous: *a noted author*

> THESAURUS famous, well-known, legendary, celebrated, renowned, distinguished, eminent → FAMOUS

note·pa·per /ˈnoʊt˺ˌpeɪpɚ/ *n.* [U] paper used for writing letters or notes

note·wor·thy /ˈnoʊt˺ˌwɚði/ *adj.* (formal) important or interesting enough to deserve your attention: *It is noteworthy that the recommendations have already been implemented in California's state schools.*

noth·ing¹ /ˈnʌθɪŋ/ *pron.* **1** not anything or no thing: *There's nothing in the bag.* | *I know nothing about her family.* | *Nothing you can say will change my mind.* | *There was* ***nothing else*** *the doctors could do.* | *I* ***have nothing against*** *New York* (=I have no reason for not liking it) – *I just don't want to live there.* **2** something that you do not consider to be important or interesting: *There's nothing on TV tonight.* | *I have nothing to wear to the wedding.* **3** zero: *The Red Sox won the game three nothing* (=the Red Sox had 3; the other team had no points). **4 for nothing a)** without getting the results you expected or wanted: *We drove all the way down there for nothing* **b)** without paying or being paid: *My dad said he'd fix it for nothing.* **5 have nothing to do with sb/sth a)** if something has nothing to do with a fact or situation, it is not related to that fact or situation: *She claims that the timing of the bill has nothing to do with her coming election.* **b)** if someone has nothing to do with a situation or person, s/he is not involved in that situation or with that person: *"What happened?" "I don't know. I had nothing to do with it."* **6 nothing special** having no very good or very bad qualities: *The play was good, but nothing special.* **7 nothing but sth** only: *We've had nothing but rain for two weeks now.* | *He's nothing but trouble.*

SPOKEN PHRASES

8 nothing much (spoken) very little: *"What did you do last weekend?" "Oh, nothing much."* **9 it was nothing** used when someone thanks you, in order to say that you did not mind helping: *"Thanks a lot." "It was nothing."* **10 (there's) nothing to it/sth** used in order to say that something is easy to do: *Anyone can use a computer. There's nothing to it.* **11** (nonstandard) anything: *I never said nothing about buying you a ring.*

[ORIGIN: Old English *nan thing, nathing* "no thing"]

nothing² *adv.* **1 be nothing like sb/sth** to have no qualities that are similar to someone or something else: *Tommy is nothing like his father.* **2 be nothing less than sth** *also* **be nothing short of sth** if something is nothing less than or nothing short of a particular quality, then it has that quality: *She thought his ideas were nothing less than ridiculous.*

noth·ing·ness /ˈnʌθɪŋnɪs/ *n.* [U] **1** empty space, or the complete absence of anything: *He stared into nothingness.* **2** the state of not existing: *With death, each person returns to nothingness.*

no·tice¹ /ˈnoʊt̬ɪs/ *v.* [I,T] to see, feel, or hear someone or something: *I don't think I've ever noticed that painting before.* | *I* ***noticed that*** *his hands were trembling.* | *Did you* ***notice how*** *tired Frances looked?*

THESAURUS **see, spot, catch sight of sb/sth, behold, observe** → SEE

notice² *n.* **1** [C] a written or printed statement that gives information or a warning to people: *Put the notice up here so everyone can see it.* **2** [U] information or a warning about something that will happen: *You must* ***give*** *the bank* ***three days'/two weeks'/a month's notice*** *before closing the account.* **3 take notice (of sb/sth)** to pay attention to someone or something: *Critics are really starting to take notice of Gwen's poetry.* | *Mother kept talking, but nobody took any notice.* **4 give notice/hand in your notice** to tell your employer that you will be leaving your job soon SYN **resign**: *Ross gave notice yesterday.* **5 on short notice** without much warning, so that you have only a short time to do something: *It will be hard to find a substitute teacher on such short notice.* **6 until further notice** from now until another change is announced: *The store will be closed until further notice.*

no·tice·a·ble /ˈnoʊt̬ɪsəbəl/ *adj.* easy to notice: *There's been a noticeable improvement in your work.* —**noticeably** *adv.*

THESAURUS

clear – impossible to doubt or make a mistake about: *clear evidence of his guilt*
obvious – easy to notice: *an obvious mistake*
striking – unusual or interesting enough to be noticed: *He bears a striking resemblance to his father.*
eye-catching – noticeable and attractive: *an attractive eye-catching design*
evident (formal) – easily noticed or understood: *It was clearly evident that she was unhappy.*
apparent (formal) – easily seen or understood: *It was apparent that the enemy was stronger than they had believed.*
conspicuous – very noticeable, especially because something is different from other things: *I felt conspicuous in my red coat.*
unmistakable – easy to notice and recognize: *the unmistakable taste of garlic*
manifest (formal) – plain and easy to notice: *a manifest error in his judgment*

no·ti·fi·ca·tion /ˌnoʊt̬əfəˈkeɪʃən/ *n.* [C,U] (formal) an act of officially telling someone about something

no·ti·fy /ˈnoʊt̬əˌfaɪ/ *v.* (**notified**, **notifies**) [T] (formal) to tell someone something formally or officially SYN **inform**: *Have you notified the police?*

no·tion /ˈnoʊʃən/ Ac *n.* [C] an idea, belief, or opinion about something, especially one that you think is wrong: *She rejects* ***the notion that*** *women are weaker than men.* | *People can have very different notions of what is right or good in a situation.* [ORIGIN: 1300—1400 Latin *notio*, from *notus* "known"]

no·to·ri·e·ty /ˌnoʊt̬əˈraɪət̬i/ *n.* [U] the state of being famous for doing something bad

no·to·ri·ous /noʊˈtɔriəs/ *adj.* famous for something bad: *The city is* ***notorious for*** *rainy weather.* | *a notorious criminal* —**notoriously** *adv.*: *Their statistics are notoriously unreliable.*

THESAURUS **famous, legendary, infamous, celebrated** → FAMOUS

not·with·stand·ing /ˌnɑtˀwɪθˈstændɪŋ/ Ac *prep., adv.* (formal) if something is true notwithstanding something else, it is true even though the other thing has happened: *Their friendship notwithstanding, the two senators have very different ideas.* | *Notwithstanding his youth, his poetry was mature and profound.*

noun /naʊn/ *n.* [C] ENG. LANG. ARTS in grammar, a word or group of words that represents a person, place, thing, quality, action, or idea. In the sentence "Pollution is a problem in some cities," "pollution," "problem," and "cities" are nouns. [ORIGIN: 1300—1400 Anglo-French "name, noun," from Old French *nom*, from Latin *nomen*]

nour·ish /ˈnɚɪʃ, ˈnʌrɪʃ/ *v.* [T] to give a person or plant the food that is needed in order to live, grow, and be healthy: *healthy* ***well-nourished*** *children*

nour·ish·ing /ˈnɚɪʃɪŋ, ˈnʌr-/ *adj.* food that is nourishing makes you strong and healthy: *a nourishing meal*

nour·ish·ment /ˈnɚɪʃmənt, ˈnʌr-/ *n.* [U] (formal) food that is needed so you can live, grow, and be healthy

no·va /ˈnoʊvə/ *n.* [C] PHYSICS a star that explodes and suddenly becomes much brighter for a short time → SUPERNOVA

nov·el¹ /ˈnɑvəl/ *n.* [C] ENG. LANG. ARTS a long book in which the characters and events are usually imaginary: *a novel by Hemingway* | *She's written several novels.* | *a* ***romance/historical/mystery novel*** [ORIGIN: 1500—1600 Italian *novella*, from *storia novella* "new story"]

novel² *adj.* new, different, and unusual: *a novel idea*

nov·el·ist /ˈnɑvəlɪst/ *n.* [C] ENG. LANG. ARTS someone who writes novels

no·vel·la /noʊˈvɛlə/ *n.* [C] ENG. LANG. ARTS a story that is shorter than a novel, but longer than a short story

nov·el·ty /ˈnɑvəlti/ *n.* (plural **novelties**) **1** [U] the quality of being new, different, and unusual: *It* *was fun for a while, but the* ***novelty wore off*** (=it became boring). **2** [C] something new and unusual that attracts people's attention and interest: *I remember when the Internet was still a novelty.*

No·vem·ber /noʊˈvɛmbɚ, nə-/ (*written abbreviation* **Nov.**) *n.* [C,U] the eleventh month of the year, between October and December: *The festival starts* ***on November 6th.*** | *Valerie's turning 30* ***in November.*** | *Ben will be three years old* ***next November.*** | *The project began* ***last November.*** [ORIGIN: 1200—1300 Old French *Novembre*, from Latin *November*, from *novem* "nine;" because it was the ninth month of the ancient Roman year]

nov·ice /ˈnɑvɪs/ *n.* [C] someone who has just begun learning a skill or activity: *I'm still a novice at chess.*

No·vo·cain /ˈnoʊvəˌkeɪn/ *n.* [U] (trademark) a drug used in order to stop pain during a small operation or treatment, especially on your teeth

now¹ /naʊ/ *adv.* **1** at the present time: *Where is Heather working now?* | *Judy should have been home* ***by now*** (=before now). | *Mom says we have to be home by 9:00* ***from now on*** (=starting now and continuing into the future). | *Let's leave the boxes in the closet* ***for now*** (=for a short time).

THESAURUS

at the moment – now: *Both men are in jail at the moment.*
for the moment – happening now but likely to change in the future: *The business is not for sale, at least for the moment.*
at present/at the present time – happening or existing now: *At present, my kids are all at college.*
currently – happening or existing now: *I'm currently writing a new novel.*
presently (formal) – at this time: *The company presently employs over 1,000 people.*

2 immediately: *You'd better go now – you're late.* | *Call her* ***right now*** *before she leaves.* **3** used when you know or understand something because of something you have just seen, just been told, etc.: *Having met his family, she now knew where his temper came from.* **4 three weeks/two years etc. now** used in order to say how long ago something started: *I've been here for four years now.* **5 (every) now and then** used in order to say that something happens sometimes but not very often: *We go out to dinner every now and then.*

SPOKEN PHRASES

6 said when you pause because you cannot think what to say, or when you want to get someone's attention: *Now, what did you say your name was?* | *OK, now. Watch me.* **7 any day/minute etc. now** very soon: *She's going to have the baby any day now.* **8 now you tell me!** said when you are annoyed because someone has just told you something s/he should have told you before

[ORIGIN: Old English *nu*]

now² *also* **now that** *conjunction* because or after something has happened: *I don't see as much of Mona now that she's married.*

now·a·days /ˈnaʊəˌdeɪz/ *adv.* in the present, compared to what happened in past times: *There's a lot more violence on television nowadays.*

no·where /ˈnoʊwɛr/ *adv.* **1** not any place: *There was nowhere to sit.* | *There are plants on the island that grow* ***nowhere else*** (=in no other place). **2 get/go nowhere** to have no success, or make no progress: *His career is going nowhere.* **3 be nowhere to be seen/found** *also* **be nowhere in sight** to be impossible to find: *We looked everywhere, but the money was nowhere to be found.* **4 nowhere near a)** far from a particular place: *Buffalo is in New York State, but it's nowhere near New York City.* **b)** not at all: *They've sold a lot of bikes, but nowhere near as many as they needed to.* **5 out of/from nowhere** happening or appearing suddenly and without warning: *The car came out of nowhere, and just missed hitting her.*

nox·ious /ˈnɑkʃəs/ *adj.* (formal) harmful or poisonous: *a noxious gas* [ORIGIN: 1400—1500 Latin *noxius*, from *noxa* "harm"]

noz·zle /ˈnɑzəl/ *n.* [C] a short tube attached to the end of a pipe or HOSE, that controls the flow of liquid coming out

NPR *n.* **National Public Radio** a company in the U.S. that broadcasts radio programs without advertisements

-n't /ənt/ *adv.* the short form of "not": *He isn't* (=is not) *here.* | *She can't* (=cannot) *see him.* | *I didn't* (=did not) *do it.*

nu·ance /ˈnuɑns/ *n.* [C,U] a very slight difference in meaning, color, or feeling [ORIGIN: 1700—1800 French, Old French *nuer* "to make shades of color," from *nue* "cloud"] —**nuanced** *adj.*

nu·cle·ar /ˈnukliɚ/ (Ac) *adj.* **1** relating to or involving the use of nuclear weapons: *nuclear war* **2** PHYSICS using nuclear power, or relating to nuclear energy: *a nuclear submarine* | *a nuclear reactor* **3** PHYSICS relating to the NUCLEUS (=central part) of an atom: *nuclear physics*

ˌnuclear disˈarmament *n.* [U] the activity of getting rid of NUCLEAR WEAPONS

ˌnuclear ˈenergy *n.* [U] PHYSICS the powerful force that is produced when the NUCLEUS of an atom is either split or joined to another atom

ˌnuclear ˈfamily *n.* [C] a family that has a father, mother, and children → EXTENDED FAMILY

ˌnuclear ˈfission *n.* [U] PHYSICS the splitting of the NUCLEUS of an atom, that results in a lot of power being produced

ˌnuclear ˈfusion *n.* [U] PHYSICS a nuclear reaction in which the NUCLEI (=central parts) of light atoms join with the nuclei of heavier atoms, which produces power without any waste

ˌnuclear ˈpower *n.* [U] power, usually in the

form of electricity, produced from NUCLEAR ENERGY

ˌnuclear reˈaction *n.* [C] PHYSICS a process in which the parts of the NUCLEUS (=central part) of an atom become arranged in a different way to form new substances

ˌnuclear reˈactor *n.* [C] a large machine that produces NUCLEAR ENERGY, especially as a means of producing electricity

ˌnuclear ˈwaste *n.* [U] waste from NUCLEAR REACTORS, which is RADIOACTIVE

ˌnuclear ˈweapon *n.* [C] a very powerful weapon that uses NUCLEAR ENERGY to destroy large areas

nu·cle·o·lus /nuˈkliələs/ *n.* (plural **nucleoli** /-laɪ/) [C] BIOLOGY a small round body of PROTEIN and RNA (=an important chemical that exists in all living things) contained in the NUCLEUS of most cells. It is involved in making proteins. → *see picture at* CELL

nu·cle·on /ˈnukliɑn/ *n.* [C] PHYSICS a PROTON or a NEUTRON

nu·cle·us /ˈnukliəs/ *n.* (plural **nuclei** /-kliaɪ/) [C] **1** PHYSICS the central part of an atom **2** BIOLOGY the central part of a living cell **3 the nucleus of sth** the central or most important part of something: *Moore and Lane form the nucleus of the team.* [ORIGIN: 1700—1800 Latin "center of a nut," from *nux* "nut"] → *see picture at* CELL

nude[1] /nud/ *adj.* not wearing any clothes —**nudity** *n.* [U]

THESAURUS naked, undressed, bare, have nothing on, not have anything on → NAKED

nude[2] *n.* **1 in the nude** without wearing any clothes: *sleeping in the nude* **2** [C] ENG. LANG. ARTS a painting or STATUE of someone who is not wearing clothes

nudge /nʌdʒ/ *v.* [T] to push someone or something gently, especially with your elbow: *Ken nudged me and said, "Look, there's Cindy."* —**nudge** *n.* [C]

THESAURUS push, poke, shove, elbow → PUSH[1]

nu·dist /ˈnudɪst/ *n.* [C] someone who enjoys not wearing any clothes because s/he believes it is natural and healthy —**nudist** *adj.*

nug·get /ˈnʌgɪt/ *n.* [C] a small rough piece of a valuable metal found in the earth: *a gold nugget*

nui·sance /ˈnusəns/ *n.* [C usually singular] someone or something that annoys you or causes problems: *Jon* ***made a nuisance of himself*** *at Rachel's birthday party.*

nuke[1] /nuk/ *v.* [T] (informal) **1** to attack a place using NUCLEAR WEAPONS **2** (spoken) to cook food in a MICROWAVE

nuke[2] *n.* [C usually plural] (informal) a NUCLEAR WEAPON

null and void /ˌnʌl ən ˈvɔɪd/ *adj.* LAW an agreement, contract, etc. that is null and void has no legal force

nul·li·fy /ˈnʌləˌfaɪ/ *v.* (**nullified**, **nullifies**) [T] LAW to state officially that something will have no legal force: *The election results were nullified because of voter fraud.*

numb[1] /nʌm/ *adj.* **1** unable to feel anything: *My feet are* ***getting numb*** *from the cold.* **2** unable to think, feel, or react in a normal way: *She was* ***numb with*** *grief after her mother's death.* —**numbness** *n.* [U] —**numbly** *adv.*

numb[2] *v.* [T] to make someone unable to feel anything: *The cold wind numbed my face.*

num·ber[1] /ˈnʌmbɚ/ *n.*

1 SIGN [C] a word or sign that represents an amount or quantity: *Pick any number between one and ten.* | *Add the numbers 7, 4, and 3.* | *an* ***even number*** (=2, 4, 6, 8, etc.) | *an* ***odd number*** (=1, 3, 5, 7, etc.)

2 ON A PHONE [C] a set of numbers that you press on a telephone when you are calling someone: *Ann's phone number is 555–3234.* | *I think I dialed the* ***wrong number***. | *He gave me his* ***work/home number***.

3 IN A SERIES [C] a number used in order to show the position of something in an ordered set, list, series, etc.: *Look at question number five.* | *What's his room number?*

4 FOR RECOGNIZING PEOPLE/THINGS [C] a set of numbers used in order to name or recognize someone or something: *a social security number* | *What's your account number?*

5 AMOUNT [C,U] an amount of something that can be counted: ***The number of*** *smokers is decreasing.* | *We have been friends for* ***a number of*** (=several) *years.* | *People are moving to the southwest* ***in increasing/growing numbers***. | *Doctors believe that* ***a large/great/small number of*** *people are at risk.*

6 number one (informal) the best or most important person or thing in a group: *California continues to be the number one travel destination in the U.S.*

7 MUSIC [C] a piece of popular music, a song, a dance, etc. that forms part of a larger performance [ORIGIN: 1200—1300 Old French *nombre*, from Latin *numerus*]

number[2] *v.* [T] **1** to give a number to something that is part of a set or list: ***Number*** *the items* ***from***

N

one to ten. **2** if people or things number a particular amount, that is how many there are: *The crowd numbered around 20,000.* **3 sb's/sth's days are numbered** used in order to say that someone or something cannot live or continue much longer: *These injuries mean his days as a player are numbered.*

nu·mer·al /ˈnuməral, ˈnumrəl/ *n.* [C] MATH a written sign that represents a number, such as 5, 22, etc.

nu·mer·a·tor /ˈnuməˌreɪt̬ɚ/ *n.* [C] MATH the number above the line in a FRACTION. For example, in the fraction ¾, 3 is the numerator. ➔ DENOMINATOR

nu·mer·i·cal /nuˈmɛrɪkəl/ *adj.* expressed in numbers, or relating to numbers: *Are the pages* ***in numerical order*** (=numbered 1, 2, 3, etc.)? —**numerically** *adv.*

num·er·ous /ˈnumərəs/ *adj.* (formal) many: *We discussed the plans* ***on numerous occasions***.

> THESAURUS many, a large number, a lot/lots, plenty, countless, innumerable, myriad ➔ MANY

nun /nʌn/ *n.* [C] a woman who is a member of a group of women who live together in a CONVENT ➔ MONK

nup·tials /ˈnʌpʃəlz/ *n.* [plural] (formal) a wedding

nurse¹ /nɚs/ *n.* [C] someone whose job is to take care of people who are sick or injured, usually in a hospital: *The nurse is coming to give you an injection.* [ORIGIN: 1200—1300 Old French *nurice*, from Latin *nutricius*, from Latin *nutrire* "to nourish"]

nurse² *v.* **1** [T] to take care of people who are sick or injured: *Michael* ***nursed*** *his wife* ***back to health***. **2** [T] to rest a part of your body when you have an illness or injury, so you will get better: *He's nursing a sprained ankle.* **3** [I,T] to BREAST-FEED

nurs·er·y /ˈnɚsəri/ *n.* (plural **nurseries**) [C] **1** a place where plants and trees are grown and sold **2** (old-fashioned) a bedroom for a baby

ˈnursery rhyme *n.* [C] a short well-known song or poem for children

ˈnursery ˌschool *n.* [C] a school for children from three to five years old ➔ KINDERGARTEN, PRESCHOOL

nurs·ing /ˈnɚsɪŋ/ *n.* [U] the job of taking care of people who are sick, injured, or very old: *Joanne plans to go into nursing.*

ˈnursing home *n.* [C] a place where people who are too old or sick to take care of themselves can live ➔ RETIREMENT HOME

nur·ture¹ /ˈnɚtʃɚ/ *v.* [T] (formal) **1** to feed and take care of a child or a plant while it is growing: *children nurtured by loving parents* **2** to help a plan, idea, feeling, etc. develop: *Reading to your child helps nurture a love of books.*

nurture² *n.* [U] (formal) the education and care that are given to a child who is growing and developing

nut /nʌt/ *n.* [C] **1** a large seed that you can eat that usually grows in a hard brown shell: *a cashew nut* **2** a small piece of metal with a hole in the middle, that is screwed onto a BOLT to fasten things together: *Use a wrench to loosen the nut.* **3 golf/opera etc. nut** (informal) someone who is very interested in golf, etc.: *a golf nut* **4** (informal) someone who is crazy or behaves strangely **5 the nuts and bolts of sth** the practical details of a subject, plan, job, etc. [ORIGIN: Old English *hnutu*]

nut·crack·er /ˈnʌtˀˌkrækɚ/ *n.* [C] a tool for cracking the shells of nuts

nut·meg /ˈnʌtˀmɛg/ *n.* [U] a brown powder used as a spice to give a particular taste to food [ORIGIN: 1200—1300 Old Provençal *noz muscada* "musky nut"]

nu·tri·ent /ˈnutriənt/ *n.* [C] BIOLOGY a chemical or food that helps plants, animals, or people to live and grow: *Plants take nutrients from the soil.* [ORIGIN: 1600—1700 Latin, present participle of *nutrire* "to feed, nourish"]

nu·tri·tion /nuˈtrɪʃən/ *n.* [U] the process of getting the right types of food for good health and growth: ***good/poor nutrition*** —**nutritional** *adj.*: *food that has little nutritional value* —**nutritionally** *adv.*

nu·tri·tious /nuˈtrɪʃəs/ *adj.* food that is nutritious has a lot of substances that your body needs to stay healthy and grow

nuts /nʌts/ *adj.* (informal) crazy, silly, or angry: *His stupid comments* ***drive me nuts*** (=annoy me very much).

> THESAURUS crazy, mentally ill, insane, loony ➔ CRAZY

nut·shell /ˈnʌtˀʃɛl/ *n.* [C] **1 (to put it) in a nutshell** (informal) used in order to show that you are going to give the main facts about something in a way that is short and clear **2** the hard outer part of a nut

nut·ty /ˈnʌt̬i/ *adj.* **1** tasting like nuts: *a nutty flavor* **2** (informal) crazy: *a nutty idea*

nuz·zle /ˈnʌzəl/ *v.* [I,T] to gently rub your face or head against someone in a loving way: *When I took him from his crib, he nuzzled his head into my neck.*

NV the written abbreviation of NEVADA

NW the written abbreviation of NORTHWEST

NY the written abbreviation of NEW YORK

ny·lon /ˈnaɪlɑn/ *n.* **1** [U] a strong artificial material that is used for making plastic, cloth, rope, etc.: *a colorful nylon tent* **2 nylons** [plural] a piece of clothing that women wear on their legs, that is very thin and made of nylon

nymph /nɪmf/ *n.* [C] **1** one of the spirits of nature who appears in the form of a young girl, in ancient Greek and Roman stories **2** BIOLOGY the LARVA of some insects, that looks like the adult but without full wings, and that develops into the adult without passing through any other stages

nym·pho·ma·ni·ac /ˌnɪmfəˈmeɪniˌæk/ *n.* [C] a woman who wants to have sex often, usually with a lot of different men —**nymphomania** /ˌnɪmfəˈmeɪniə/ *n.* [U]

O, o /oʊ/ the fifteenth letter of the English alphabet

O /oʊ/ *n.* [U] **1** (spoken) zero: *room 203* (=two o three) **2** a common type of blood

oaf /oʊf/ *n.* [C] (old-fashioned) a large stupid awkward man or boy —**oafish** *adj.*

oak /oʊk/ *n.* [C,U] a large tree that is common in northern countries, or the hard wood of this tree [ORIGIN: Old English *ac*]

oar /ɔr/ *n.* [C] a long pole with a wide blade at one end, used for rowing a boat [ORIGIN: Old English *ar*]

oasis

o·a·sis /oʊˈeɪsɪs/ *n.* (plural **oases** /oʊˈeɪsiz/) [C] a place with trees and water in a desert

oat /oʊt/ *n.* **oats** [plural] a grain that is eaten by people and animals —**oat** *adj.* [only before noun]: *hot oat cereal*

oath /oʊθ/ *n.* (plural **oaths** /oʊðz, oʊθs/) **1 be under oath** LAW to have made an official promise to tell the truth in a court of law: *The witness **testified under oath**.* **2** [C] a formal and serious promise: *New U.S. citizens **take/swear an oath** of allegiance* (=promise to be loyal to the U.S.). **3 oath of office** POLITICS a formal and serious promise that someone in an official position makes to do his or her job well because of loyalty to his or her country: *The president **took the oath of office** for his second presidential term.*

oat·meal /ˈoʊt˺mil/ *n.* [U] crushed oats that are boiled and eaten for breakfast, or used in cooking

ob·du·rate /ˈɑbdərət/ *adj.* (formal) very determined not to change your beliefs or feelings, in a way that seems unreasonable (SYN) **stubborn**: *He has remained obdurate in his opposition to the changes.* —**obduracy** *n.* [U]

o·be·di·ence /əˈbidiəns, oʊ-/ *n.* [U] doing what you are supposed to do, according to a law or to someone in authority (ANT) **disobedience** → OBEY: ***Obedience to** authority is an essential part of their culture.*

o·be·di·ent /əˈbidiənt, oʊ-/ *adj.* always obeying laws, rules, or people in authority (ANT) **disobedient** → OBEY: *an obedient child* —**obediently** *adv.*

o·bese /oʊˈbis/ *adj.* very fat in a way that is unhealthy —**obesity** *n.* [U]

THESAURUS **fat, overweight, big, heavy, large, corpulent, rotund** → FAT[1]

o·bey /əˈbeɪ, oʊ-/ *v.* (**obeyed**, **obeys**) [I,T] to do what you are supposed to do, according to the law or to what someone in authority says (ANT) **disobey** → OBEDIENT: *Children should be taught to **obey the law**.* | *"Sit!" he said, and the dog obeyed him immediately.* [ORIGIN: 1200—1300 Old French *obeir*, from Latin *oboedire*, from *audire* "to hear"]

THESAURUS
do what sb says: *I don't ask questions – I just do what the coach says.*
do what you are told/do as you are told: *Maybe next time you'll do what you are told.*
follow sb's orders/instructions: *Follow the manufacturer's instructions.* | *You must follow your doctor's orders.*
comply (formal) – to do what you are asked to do or what a law or rule tells you to do: *Those who fail to comply with the law will be fined.*
observe (formal) – to obey a law, agreement, or religious rule: *Both sides are observing the ceasefire.*

ob·fus·cate /ˈɑbfəˌskeɪt/ *v.* [T] (formal) to deliberately make something unclear or difficult to understand: *The manual is written in technical language that obfuscates the safety warnings.* —**obfuscation** /ˌɑbfəˈskeɪʃən/ *n.* [U]

o·bit·u·ar·y /əˈbɪtʃuˌɛri, oʊ-/ *n.* (plural **obituaries**) [C] a report of someone's death in a newspaper [ORIGIN: 1700—1800 Medieval Latin *obituarium*, from Latin *obitus* "death"]

ob·ject[1] /ˈɑbdʒɪkt, ˈɑbdʒɛkt/ *n.* **1** [C] a thing that you can see, hold, or touch: *a small metal object*

THESAURUS **thing, something, item, article** → THING

2 [singular] the purpose of a plan, action, or activity: ***The object of** the game is to improve children's math skills.* **3 an object of desire/pity etc.** someone or something that you desire, pity, etc. **4** [C] **a)** ENG. LANG. ARTS in grammar, the person or thing that is affected by the action of the verb, for example "door" in the sentence "Sheila closed the door." (SYN) **direct object** **b)** ENG. LANG. ARTS in grammar, the person who is involved in the result of an action, for example "her" in the sentence "I gave her a book." (SYN) **indirect object** **c)** ENG. LANG. ARTS in grammar, the person or thing that is connected by a PREPOSITION to another word, for example "table" in the sentence "We sat at the table."

O

ob·ject² /əbˈdʒɛkt/ *v.* [I] to say that you do not like or approve of something: *Reynolds* ***objected to*** *the plan.*

ob·jec·tion /əbˈdʒɛkʃən/ *n.* [C] a reason you give for not approving of an idea or plan: *The group* ***has*** *strong* ***objections to*** *the death penalty.* | *Several Senators* ***raised objections*** (=they objected) *to the bill.*

COLLOCATIONS

have an objection: *I have no objection to comedians making fun of politicians.*
raise an objection: *Opponents of the plan have raised other objections.*
state an objection: *The President stated three main objections to the legislation.*
voice an objection: *The church has voiced strong objections to the movie.*
make an objection: *She was granted bail after the prosecution made no objection.*
lodge/register an objection (formal) (=make one): *Players have registered their strong objection to the new contracts.*

THESAURUS **opposition, antagonism, hostility, antipathy** ➔ OPPOSITION

ob·jec·tion·a·ble /əbˈdʒɛkʃənəbəl/ *adj.* likely to offend people (SYN) **offensive**: *The program contains material that some people may* ***find objectionable.***

ob·jec·tive¹ /əbˈdʒɛktɪv/ (Ac) *n.* [C] something that you are working hard to achieve: *The company's* ***main objective*** *is to increase sales overseas.* | *How can you* ***achieve*** *your* ***objectives****?*

THESAURUS **goal, aim, target, mission** ➔ GOAL

objective² (Ac) *adj.* not influenced by your own feelings, beliefs, or ideas (ANT) **subjective**: *objective news reporting* | *Students must try to be objective when doing an experiment.* —**objectively** *adv.*: *We need to look at the situation objectively.* | *Scientists prefer to make judgments about things they can objectively measure.* —**objectivity** /ˌɑbdʒɛkˈtɪvət̬i/ *n.* [U]

ob·li·gat·ed /ˈɑbləˌgeɪt̬ɪd/ *adj.* **be/feel obligated (to do sth)** to feel that it is your duty to do something: *I don't want them to feel obligated to pay for dinner.*

ob·li·ga·tion /ˌɑbləˈgeɪʃən/ *n.* [C,U] a moral or legal duty to do something: *Every father* ***has an obligation to*** *take care of his child.* | *You are* ***under no obligation to*** (=do not have to) *answer these questions.*

o·blig·a·to·ry /əˈblɪgəˌtɔri/ *adj.* (formal) having to be done because of a law, rule, etc. (SYN) **mandatory**

o·blige /əˈblaɪdʒ/ *v.* **1 be/feel obliged (to do sth)** to feel that it is your duty to do something: *You shouldn't feel obliged to work overtime.* **2** [I,T] (formal) to do something that someone has asked you to do: *He asked to borrow my car, and I was* ***happy/glad to oblige.*** **3 (I'm/we're) much obliged** (spoken, old-fashioned) said in order to thank someone very politely [ORIGIN: 1200—1300 Old French *obliger*, from Latin *obligare*, from *ligare* "to tie"]

o·blig·ing /əˈblaɪdʒɪŋ/ *adj.* willing and eager to help: *a cheerful and obliging woman* —**obligingly** *adv.*

o·blique /əˈblik, oʊ-/ *adj.* **1** (formal) not expressed in a direct way (SYN) **indirect**: *She made an oblique reference to his drinking problem.* **2** an oblique line is sloping ➔ *see picture at* LINE¹

obˈlique ˌangle *n.* [C] MATH an angle that is not 90°, 180°, or 270° ➔ ACUTE ANGLE, OBTUSE ANGLE

ob·lit·er·ate /əˈblɪt̬əˌreɪt/ *v.* [T] to destroy something completely: *Large areas of the city were obliterated during World War II.* —**obliteration** /əˌblɪt̬əˈreɪʃən/ *n.* [U]

ob·liv·i·on /əˈblɪviən/ *n.* [U] (formal) **1** the state of being completely forgotten: *Old movie stars who have* ***faded into oblivion.*** **2** the state of being unconscious or of not knowing what is happening: *He spent the night drinking himself* ***into oblivion.*** [ORIGIN: 1300—1400 Old French, Latin *oblivio*, from *oblivisci* "to forget"]

ob·liv·i·ous /əˈblɪviəs/ *adj.* not knowing about or not noticing something happening around you (SYN) **unaware**: *She seemed completely* ***oblivious to/of*** *the danger.*

ob·long /ˈɑblɔŋ/ *adj.* having a shape that is longer than it is wide: *an oblong mirror* [ORIGIN: 1400—1500 Latin *oblongus*, from *ob-* "toward" + *longus* "long"] —**oblong** *n.* [C]

ob·nox·ious /əbˈnɑkʃəs/ *adj.* very offensive or rude: *Her friends were loud and obnoxious.* [ORIGIN: 1500—1600 Latin *obnoxius*, from *noxa* "harm"] —**obnoxiously** *adv.*

o·boe /ˈoʊboʊ/ *n.* [C] a wooden musical instrument, shaped like a narrow tube, that you play by blowing into it ➔ *see picture at* WOODWIND

ob·scene /əbˈsin, ɑb-/ *adj.* **1** offensive and shocking in a sexual way: *obscene photographs* | *He made an* ***obscene gesture.*** **2** extremely immoral or unfair: *Some players earn obscene amounts of money.*

ob·scen·i·ty /əbˈsɛnət̬i/ *n.* (plural **obscenities**) **1** [C usually plural] a sexually offensive word or action: *kids shouting obscenities* **2** [U] offensive language or behavior involving sex, especially in a book, play, etc.: *laws against obscenity*

ob·scure[1] /əb'skyʊr/ *adj.* **1** unclear or difficult to understand: *Jarrett didn't like the plan for some obscure reason.* **2** known about only by a few people: *an obscure poet*

obscure[2] *v.* [T] **1** to prevent something from being seen or heard clearly: *Parts of the coast were obscured by fog.* **2** to make something difficult to know or understand: *Recent successes have **obscured the fact that** the company is still in trouble.*

ob·scur·i·ty /əb'skyʊrət̬i/ *n.* (plural **obscurities**) **1** [U] the state of not being known or remembered: *O'Brien retired from politics and died **in obscurity**.* **2** [C,U] something that is difficult to understand, or the quality of being difficult to understand

ob·se·qui·ous /əb'sikwiəs/ *adj.* too eager to please people and agree with them: *The waiter was helpful but not obsequious.* —**obsequiously** *adv.*

ob·serv·a·ble /əb'zɚvəbəl/ *adj.* able to be seen or noticed

ob·serv·ance /əb'zɚvəns/ *n.* [U] the practice of obeying laws or doing something because it is part of a religion or CUSTOM: *Stores were closed **in observance of** Christmas.*

ob·serv·ant /əb'zɚvənt/ *adj.* **1** good or quick at noticing things: *I can see you're very observant.* **2** obeying laws, religious rules, etc.: *observant Hindus*

ob·ser·va·tion /ˌɑbzɚ'veɪʃən, -sɚ-/ *n.* **1** [C,U] the act or process of carefully watching someone or something, or one of the facts you learn from doing this: *The psychologist's theories are based on his **observation of** children's behavior.* | *The patient is **under** close **observation*** (=being continuously watched). **2** [C] a remark about something that you have noticed: *I'd like to **make an observation**.*

ob·serv·a·to·ry /əb'zɚvəˌtɔri/ *n.* (plural **observatories**) [C] a special building from which scientists watch the moon, stars, weather, etc.

ob·serve /əb'zɚv/ *v.* [T] **1** to watch someone or something carefully: *The police have been observing his movements.*

> THESAURUS **see, notice, spot, witness, behold** → SEE

2 (formal) to see or notice something in particular: *Doctors **observed that** the disease only occurs in women over 50.* **3** to obey a law, agreement, or religious rule: *Both sides are observing the cease-fire.* [ORIGIN: 1300—1400 Old French *observer*, from Latin *observare* "to guard, watch"]

> THESAURUS **obey, do what sb says, do what you are told/do as you are told, follow sb's orders/instructions, comply** → OBEY

ob·serv·er /əb'zɚvɚ/ *n.* [C] **1** someone who goes to a meeting, class, event, etc. to officially watch or check what is happening: *International observers monitored the elections.* **2** someone who sees or notices something

ob·sess /əb'sɛs/ *v.* **1** [T] to think about someone or something all the time, so that you cannot think of anything else: *William **is obsessed with** making money.* **2** [I] (informal) to think about something or someone much more than is necessary and sensible: *Stop **obsessing about/over** your weight. You look great!*

O

ob·ses·sion /əb'sɛʃən/ *n.* [C,U] an extreme unhealthy interest in something or worry about something, which prevents you from thinking about other things: *She developed an **obsession with** food.*

ob·ses·sive /əb'sɛsɪv/ *adj.* thinking or worrying too much about someone or something so that you do not think about other things enough: *She's **obsessive about** exercise.* —**obsessively** *adv.*

ob·so·lete /ˌɑbsə'lit◂/ *adj.* no longer useful or needed because something newer and better has been made: *Floppy disks have **become obsolete**.* [ORIGIN: 1500—1600 Latin, past participle of *obsolescere* "to grow old, become disused"] —**obsolescence** /ˌɑbsə'lɛsəns/ *n.* [U]

> THESAURUS **old-fashioned, outdated, outmoded, dated, antiquated** → OLD-FASHIONED

ob·sta·cle /'ɑbstɪkəl/ *n.* [C] **1** something that makes it difficult for you to succeed: *Lack of confidence can be a big **obstacle to** success.* | *The team has had to **overcome obstacles** this season.* **2** something that blocks your way, so that you must go around it: *an obstacle in the road* [ORIGIN: 1300—1400 Old French, Latin *obstaculum*, from *obstare* "to stand in the way, stand in front of"]

'obstacle course *n.* [C] a line of objects that a runner must jump over, go under, etc.

ob·stet·rics /əb'stɛktrɪks, ɑb-/ *n.* [U] BIOLOGY the part of medical science that deals with the birth of children —**obstetrician** /ˌɑbstə'trɪʃən/ *n.* [C]

ob·sti·nate /'ɑbstənɪt/ *adj.* refusing to change your opinions, ideas, behavior, etc. (SYN) **stubborn** —**obstinacy** *n.* [U]

ob·strep·er·ous /əb'strɛpərəs/ *adj.* noisy and refusing to agree or to do what someone else tells you to do, or showing this quality: *an obstreperous group of teenagers*

ob·struct /əb'strʌkt/ *v.* [T] **1** to block a road, path, passage, or someone's view of something: *The truck was on its side, obstructing two lanes of traffic.* **2** to try to prevent someone from doing something by making it difficult: *Federal officers accused Robbins of obstructing their investigation.* [ORIGIN: 1600—1700 Latin, past participle of *obstruere* "to build in the way"] —**obstructive** *adj.*

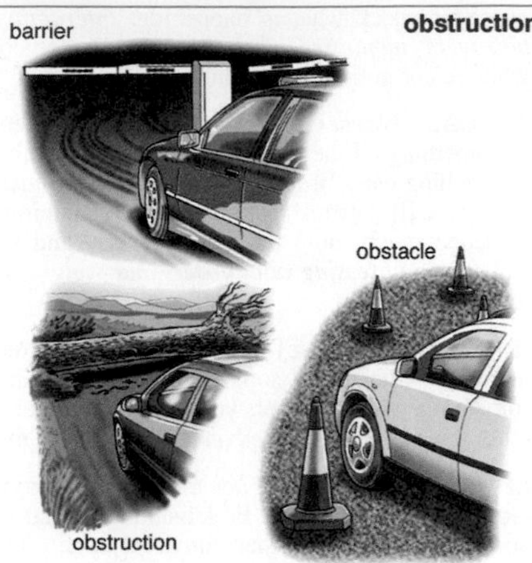

ob·struc·tion /əb'strʌkʃən/ *n.* **1** [C,U] something that blocks a road, passage, tube, etc., or the fact of blocking a road, etc.: *The accident* ***caused an obstruction*** *on the freeway.* **2** [U] the act of preventing something from happening: *Powell could be charged with* ***obstruction of justice.***

ob·tain /əb'teɪn/ (Ac) *v.* [T] (formal) to get something that you want: *Information about passports can be* ***obtained from*** *the embassy.* | *Weisner is hoping to obtain funding for a second study of the children.* [ORIGIN: 1400—1500 Old French *obtenir*, from Latin *obtinere* "to hold on to, own, obtain"]

ob·tain·a·ble /əb'teɪnəbəl/ (Ac) *adj.* able to be obtained: *The application form is obtainable from the secretary.*

ob·tru·sive /əb'trusɪv/ *adj.* (formal) noticeable in a bad or annoying way (ANT) **unobtrusive**: *The waitresses were friendly but never obtrusive.*

ob·tuse /əb'tus, ɑb-/ *adj.* (formal) stupid or slow to understand something

ob,tuse 'angle *n.* [C] MATH an angle between 90° and 180° → *see picture at* ANGLE[1]

ob,tuse 'triangle *n.* [C] MATH a TRIANGLE with one angle that is between 90 and 180 degrees

ob·vi·ous /'ɑbviəs/ (Ac) *adj.* easy to notice or understand: *the obvious choice* | ***It was obvious (that)*** *he hadn't actually read the book.* | *The need for change seemed* ***obvious to*** *everyone.* | *The need to recycle glass and other materials is obvious.* [ORIGIN: 1500—1600 Latin *obvius*, from *obviam* "in the way"]

> THESAURUS noticeable, clear, evident, apparent, conspicuous, unmistakable, manifest → NOTICEABLE

ob·vi·ous·ly /'ɑbviəsli/ (Ac) *adv.* used when something is easily noticed or understood: *Obviously, I was scared.* | *Patrick is obviously a good father.*

oc·ca·sion /ə'keɪʒən/ *n.* **1** [C] a time when something happens: *I met with him* ***on*** *several* ***occasions.*** **2** [C] an important event or ceremony: *We're saving the champagne for* ***a special occasion.*** | ***a joyous/happy/solemn etc. occasion***

> THESAURUS event, occurrence, affair, happening → EVENT

3 on occasion sometimes, but not often: *Craig helps out on occasion.* **4** [U] a cause or reason to do something: *I'm sure we will* ***have occasion to*** *discuss this further.*

oc·ca·sion·al /ə'keɪʒənl/ *adj.* happening sometimes but not often: *He has* ***the/an occasional*** *drink.*

oc·ca·sion·al·ly /ə'keɪʒənl-i/ *adv.* sometimes, but not regularly or often: *We occasionally see each other.* | *Heat the soup, stirring occasionally.*

oc·cult /ə'kʌlt/ *n.* **the occult** the knowledge and study of magic and spirits —**occult** *adj.*

oc·cu·pan·cy /'ɑkyəpənsi/ (Ac) *n.* [U] (formal) someone's use of a building or other space for living or working: *The new college dormitory is ready for occupancy.*

oc·cu·pant /'ɑkyəpənt/ (Ac) *n.* [C] (formal) someone who lives in a building, room, etc., or who is in it at a particular time: *a letter addressed to the occupant* | *The occupants of the condominium were unhappy with the rise in rent.*

oc·cu·pa·tion /,ɑkyə'peɪʃən/ (Ac) *n.* **1** [C] (formal) a job or profession → EMPLOYMENT, WORK: *the occupations available to women* | *Workers in low-paid occupations often suffer from poor health.*

> THESAURUS job, work, employment, profession, career, vocation → JOB

2 [U] the act of entering a place and getting control of it, especially by military force → OCCUPY: *the German* ***occupation of*** *France in the war* | *London became an important town during the Roman occupation of Britain.* **3** [C] (formal) a way of spending your time: *One of his childhood occupations was collecting baseball cards.*

oc·cu·pa·tion·al /,ɑkyə'peɪʃənəl/ (Ac) *adj.* relating to your job: *Occupational injuries are common in the coal mining industry.*

oc·cu·pied /'ɑkyə,paɪd/ *adj.* **1** busy doing or thinking about something: *Bring some games to* ***keep*** *the kids* ***occupied.*** | *His father was* ***occupied with*** *work.* **2** being used: *All the rooms on the first floor are occupied.* **3** an occupied place is controlled by an army: *Jewish settlements in the occupied territories*

oc·cu·py /'ɑkyə,paɪ/ (Ac) *v.* (**occupied**, **occupies**) [T] **1** to live, work, stay, etc. in a particular place: *Salem Press occupies the seventh floor of the building.* **2** if something occupies you or your time, you are busy doing it: *Work occupies most of my day.* | *Only six percent of police time is occupied with criminal incidents.* **3** to fill a particular amount of space: *Family photos occupied almost* *the entire wall.* | *At present, the government occupies some 70 million square feet in the Washington area.* **4** to enter a place and get control of it, especially by military force ➔ INVADE: *Kuwait was occupied by Iraq from August 1990 to February 1991.* [ORIGIN: 1300—1400 French *occuper*, from Latin *occupare*]

oc·cur /ə'kɚ/ (Ac) *v.* (**occurred**, **occurring**) [I] (formal) **1** to happen, especially without being planned first (SYN) **take place**: *Earthquakes occur without any warning signs.* | *A third of accidental deaths occur in the home.* **2** to exist or be present in a particular place: *The disease mainly* ***occurs in*** *young children.* | *Chromium and nickel occur commonly in areas which are also rich in magnesium.* [ORIGIN: 1500—1600 Latin *occurrere*, from *currere* "to run"] **—occurrence** *n.* [C, singular]: *Stress-related illness is now a fairly common occurrence.* | *An increase in the occurrence of heart disease was reported.*

occur to sb *phr. v.* to suddenly come into your mind: ***It never occurred to me to ask.***

o·cean /'oʊʃən/ *n.* **1** [C] EARTH SCIENCES a particular area of salt water somewhere on Earth: *the Indian Ocean* ➔ *see picture at* WATER CYCLE **2 the ocean** EARTH SCIENCES the great quantity of salt water that covers most of the Earth's surface [ORIGIN: 1200—1300 Latin *oceanus*, from Greek *Ōkeanos* name of a river believed to flow around the world] **—oceanic** /ˌoʊʃi'ænɪk◂/ *adj.*

o·cean·og·ra·phy /ˌoʊʃə'nɑgrəfi/ *n.* [U] EARTH SCIENCES the scientific study of the ocean **—oceanographer** *n.* [C]

o'clock /ə'klɑk/ *adv.* **one/two/three etc. o'clock** one of the times when the clock shows the exact hour as a number from 1 to 12 [ORIGIN: 1400—1500 *of the clock*]

oc·ta·gon /'ɑktəˌgɑn/ *n.* [C] MATH a flat shape with eight sides and eight angles [ORIGIN: 1500—1600 Latin, from Greek *octagonon*, from *okto* "eight" + *gonia* "angle"] **—octagonal** /ɑk'tægənəl/ *adj.* ➔ *see picture at* POLYGON

THESAURUS **polygon, pentagon, hexagon, heptagon, decagon, dodecagon** ➔ POLYGON

oc·tave /'ɑktəv/ *n.* [C] **1** ENG. LANG. ARTS the range of musical notes between the first note of a musical SCALE and the last one **2** ENG. LANG. ARTS the first and last notes of a musical SCALE played together [ORIGIN: 1300—1400 Medieval Latin *octava*, from Latin *octo* "eight;" because there are eight notes in the range]

oc·tet /ɑk'tɛt/ *n.* [C] **1** ENG. LANG. ARTS eight singers or musicians performing together **2** ENG. LANG. ARTS a piece of music for an octet

Oc·to·ber /ɑk'toʊbɚ/ (*written abbreviation* **Oct.**) *n.* [C,U] the tenth month of the year, between September and November: *The group will be performing* ***on October 22nd.*** | *Clare's going to be two* ***in October.*** | *We have been in this apartment since* ***last October.*** | *Our membership expires* ***next October.*** [ORIGIN: 1000—1100 Old French *Octobre*, from Latin *October*, from *octo* "eight;" because it was the eighth month of the ancient Roman year]

oc·to·pus /'ɑktəpəs/ *n.* (plural **octopuses** *or* **octopi** /'ɑktəpaɪ/) [C] a sea creature with a soft body and eight TENTACLES (=arms) [ORIGIN: 1700—1800 Modern Latin, Greek *oktopous* "scorpion," from *okto* "eight" + *pous* "foot"]

OD *v.* (past tense and past participle **OD'd**, present participle **OD'ing**) [I] (slang) **overdose** to take too much of a dangerous drug

odd /ɑd/ (Ac) *adj.* **1** different from what is expected or normal (SYN) **strange**: *an odd guy* | ***It's odd*** *that she hasn't phoned by now.*

THESAURUS **strange, funny, peculiar, curious, weird, bizarre, eccentric** ➔ STRANGE[1]

2 odd jobs small jobs of different types, for example fixing or cleaning things **3** an odd number cannot be divided by 2. For example, 1, 3, 5, etc. are odd numbers ➔ EVEN **4** [only before noun] separated from its pair or set: *an odd sock* **5 20-odd/30-odd etc.** (informal) a little more than 20, 30, etc. ➔ ODDS

odd·ball /'ɑdbɔl/ *adj.* (informal) strange or unusual **—oddball** *n.* [C]

odd·i·ty /'ɑdət̮i/ *n.* (plural **oddities**) [C] a strange or unusual person or thing

odd·ly /'ɑdli/ *adv.* in a strange or unusual way ➔ **strangely/oddly/funnily enough** *at* ENOUGH

odds /ɑdz/ (Ac) *n.* [plural] **1 the odds** how likely it is that something will or will not happen (SYN) **chance**: ***The odds are*** *about 1 in 12* ***that*** *a boy will be colorblind.* | *Doctors have improved* ***the odds of*** *survival for these babies.* **2** difficulties that make a good result seem very unlikely: *Our team won the title* ***against all the odds*** (=in spite of difficulties). **3 at odds (with sb)** disagreeing with someone: *Mark's account of what happened is at odds with Dan's.*

ˌodds and 'ends *n.* [plural] (informal) various small things that have little value

ode /oʊd/ *n.* [C] a long poem that is written in order to praise a person or thing

o·di·ous /'oʊdiəs/ *adj.* (formal) very bad or disgusting

o·dor /'oʊdɚ/ *n.* [C] a smell, especially a bad one

THESAURUS **smell, stink, stench** ➔ SMELL[2]

o·dor·less /'oʊdɚlɪs/ *adj.* not having a smell: *an odorless gas*

od·ys·sey /'ɑdəsi/ *n.* (plural **odysseys**) [C] (literary) a long trip with many difficulties or adventures

of /əv, ə; *strong* ʌv/ *prep.* **1** used in order to show a quality or feature that someone or something has: *the color of his shirt* | *the size of the building* | *It* *was stupid of me to say that.* **2** used in order to show that something is a part of something else: *the first part of the story | the tips of your fingers* **3** used in order to show that something belongs to or relates to someone or something: *an old shirt of his | a friend of Bobby's* **4** used with words that show a particular type of group: *a bunch of grapes | a herd of elephants* **5** used in order to show an amount or measurement: *a cup of coffee | lots of room | a drop of water* **6** used in order to show that someone or something is from a larger group: *That's one of her best poems. | members of a rock group* **7** used in dates: *the 23rd of January, 2004* **8** (spoken) used in giving the time, to mean "before": *It's ten of five* (=ten minutes before 5:00). **9** used when giving the name of something: *the city of New Orleans | the game of chess* **10** used when giving the reason for or the cause of something: *She died of cancer.* **11** used in order to say what something shows: *a picture of his family | a map of the world* **12** used in order to say what something is about or what type of thing it is: *Do you know the story of Tom Thumb? | the problem of crime in schools* **13** used in order to show direction or distance: *I live just north of here. | The school is within a mile of the park* (=it is less than a mile from the park). **14** used after nouns describing actions, to show to whom the action is done or who did the action: *the testing of river water for chemicals | the crying of a child* **15** (literary) made from: *a dress of pure silk* **16** written, made, produced, etc. by someone or something: *the early plays of Shakespeare* **17** used in order to say where someone lives: *the people of Malaysia* [ORIGIN: Old English] → **of course** *at* COURSE

off /ɔf/ *adv., prep., adj.* **1** away from or out of a place or position: *She waved and drove off. | Get your feet off the couch! | He took his shoes off. | The bus stopped, and she got off.* **2** a machine, light, etc. that is off is not working or operating (ANT) **on**: *Why are all the lights off? | **Turn** the lights **off** when you leave. | Does the machine **shut** itself **off**?* **3** lower in price: *You **get 10%/15% off** if you buy $100 worth of groceries.* **4** how far away something is, or how much time there is between now and a future event: *Spring is still **a long way off**. | mountains **way off** in the distance* **5** away from a particular place: *Oak Hills – isn't that off Route 290? | a hotel **just off** the main street* **6** not at work or school because you are sick or on vacation: *Dave's off tomorrow. | Monday is my **day off**. | I'm **taking the day/week off**.* **7** if an event is off, it will not now take place: *The wedding's off.* **8** not as good as usual: *Sales are a little off compared with last year.* **9** not correct or not of good quality: *His calculations are off by 20%.* **10 have an off day/week etc.** (spoken) to have a day, week, etc. when you are not doing something as well as you usually do **11 off and on/on and off** for short periods of time, but not regularly: *We've been going out together for two years, off and on.* → WELL-OFF

ˌoff-ˈbalance *adj.* [not before noun] **1** in an unsteady position and likely to fall: *He staggered back, off-balance.* **2 catch/throw sb off-balance** to surprise or shock someone because s/he is not prepared: *American forces were caught off-balance by the tactics.*

off·beat /ˌɔfˈbit◂/ *adj.* (informal) unusual and not what people expect, in an interesting way: *an offbeat style of comedy*

of·fend /əˈfɛnd/ *v.* **1** [T] to make someone angry or upset → OFFENSIVE: *The senator's remarks offended many women.* **2** [I] LAW to do something that is a crime

of·fend·er /əˈfɛndɚ/ *n.* [C] LAW someone who is guilty of a crime: *As a **first-time offender**, Joe received a fine.*

> THESAURUS **criminal, thief, robber, burglar, shoplifter, pickpocket, attacker, mugger** → CRIMINAL²

of·fense¹ /əˈfɛns/ *n.* **1** [C] LAW a crime: *Drinking and driving is a **serious offense**. | Anyone charged with a **criminal offense** is entitled to a trial. | programs to prevent teenagers from **committing** more serious **offenses*** **2 no offense** (spoken) said in order to show that you hope what you are saying will not offend someone: *No offense, but how old are you?* **3 take offense/cause offense** to feel offended or to offend someone: *Many women **took offense at** the tone of his speech.*

of·fense² /ˈɔfɛns/ *n.* [U] the action of trying to get points and win in a sports game, or the group of players responsible for doing this (ANT) **defense**: *The team needs to work on their offense.*

of·fen·sive¹ /əˈfɛnsɪv/ *adj.* **1** used or intended for attacking (ANT) **defensive**: *offensive weapons* **2** very insulting and likely to upset people (ANT) **inoffensive**: *offensive jokes*

> THESAURUS **rude, impolite, insulting, tactless** → RUDE

3 relating to trying to get points and win in sports games, or relating to the players who do this (ANT) **defensive**: *the Bears' offensive lineup* —**offensively** *adv*

offensive² *n.* [C] **1** an attack made on a place by an army: *a **military offensive*** **2 be/go on the offensive** *also* **take the offensive** to attack or criticize people

of·fer¹ /ˈɔfɚ, ˈɑfɚ/ *v.* **1** [T] to say that you are willing to give something to someone, or to hold something out to someone so that s/he can take it: *Can I offer you a drink? | Did they offer you the job? | They **offered** us $175,000 **for** the house. | The company **offers** scholarships **to** inner-city students. | Stewart **offers advice/help/support** to women in this difficult position.* **2** [I,T] to say that you are willing to do something: *She didn't even **offer to** help.* [ORIGIN: 1200—1300 Old French *offrir*, from Latin *offerre*, from *ob* "to" + *ferre* "to carry"]

offer² *n.* [C] **1** a statement that you are willing to give something to someone or do something for someone: *an* ***offer*** *of help* | *a* ***job offer***

COLLOCATIONS

make someone an **offer**
have/receive an **offer** from someone
consider an **offer** – to think about an offer carefully before making a decision
accept/take an **offer** – to say yes
refuse/reject an **offer** or **turn** it **down** – to say no → ACCEPT, REFUSE[1]

2 something that is offered, especially an amount of money: *The company* ***made an offer of*** *$5 million for the site.*

of·fer·ing /ˈɔfrɪŋ, ˈɑ-/ *n.* [C] something you give someone, especially God

off ˈguard *adj.* **catch/take sb off guard** to surprise someone by doing something or happening when s/he is not expecting anything: *The storm caught everyone off guard.*

off·hand[1] /ɔfˈhænd/ *adv.* immediately, without time to think: *I can't give you an answer offhand.*

off·hand[2] /ˌɔfˈhænd◂ / *adj.* said or done without thinking, or said in a way that makes something seem unimportant: *an offhand remark*

of·fice /ˈɔfɪs, ˈɑ-/ *n.* **1** [C] a room with a desk, telephone, etc. in it where you do your work: *the manager's office* | *Is Shaw* ***in his office?*** | *a small* ***home office*** **2** [C] the building of a company or organization where people work: *Are you going to* ***the office*** *today?* | *the* ***main/central office*** *of the company* | *the* ***branch/local office*** *of the FBI*

TOPIC

Many modern offices are not divided into separate rooms. Instead, people sit at **desks** in small **cubicles** or **cubes**. The part of an office where you work, including your **desk**, **computer/PC**, etc. is your **workstation**. Somewhere in the office there is a **printer**, a **photocopier**, a **fax (machine)**, and **file/filing cabinets**. The office building may have several **floors**. There is often a **cafeteria** where you can eat.

3 [C,U] an important job or position, especially in government: *Richardson's achievements* ***in office*** | *Muller* ***took/left office*** *in 2007.* | *It takes a lot of money to* ***run for office*** (=try to be elected). **4** [C] the place where a doctor or DENTIST sees patients [ORIGIN: 1200—1300 Old French, Latin *officium* "service, duty, office," from *opus* "work" + *facere* "to do"] → BOX OFFICE, POST OFFICE

of·fi·cer /ˈɔfəsɚ, ˈɑ-/ *n.* [C] **1** someone who has a position of authority in the army, navy, etc. **2** a member of the police: *the officers at the scene* | *Officer Johnson will take your statement.* **3** someone who has an important position in an organization → CEO, OFFICIAL[2]

of·fi·cial[1] /əˈfɪʃəl/ *adj.* approved of or done by someone in authority, especially the government: *an official investigation* | *The governor was on an official visit to Mexico.*

official[2] *n.* [C] someone who has a responsible position in an organization: *senior bank officials*

of·fi·cial·ly /əˈfɪʃəli/ *adv.* **1** publicly and formally: *The new bridge was officially opened this morning.* **2** according to what you say publicly, even though this may not be true: *Officially, they are not counted as unemployed.*

of·fi·ci·ate /əˈfɪʃiˌeɪt/ *v.* [I] (formal) to perform special duties, especially at a religious ceremony

of·fi·cious /əˈfɪʃəs/ *adj.* (disapproving) someone who is officious is always telling other people what to do

off·ing /ˈɔfɪŋ/ *n.* **be in the offing** to be about to happen: *Big changes are in the offing.*

off·line /ˌɔfˈlaɪn◂ / *adv.* **1** IT with your computer not connected to the Internet → ONLINE: *writing emails offline* **2** IT not connected to or controlled by a computer: *Problems with the server kept the system offline until noon.* —**offline** *adj*

ˈoff-ramp *n.* [C] a road for driving off a HIGHWAY or FREEWAY (ANT) **on-ramp**

ˌoff ˈseason *n.* [singular] the time in the year when a sport is not usually played —**off-season** *adj.* [only before noun]

off·set /ˌɔfˈsɛt, ˈɔfsɛt/ (Ac) *v.* (past tense and past participle **offset**, present participle **offsetting**) [T] if something offsets another thing, it has an opposite effect so that the situation remains the same: *The new contracts should help to offset the recent losses.* | *Congress is required to offset the revenue lost through lowered taxes with federal spending cuts.*

off·shoot /ˈɔfʃut/ *n.* [C] an organization, system of beliefs, etc. that has developed from a larger or earlier one: *The business was an* ***offshoot of*** *IBM.*

off·shore /ˌɔfˈʃɔr◂ / *adj., adv.* in the water, at a distance from the shore: *America's offshore oil reserves*

off·spring /ˈɔfˌsprɪŋ/ *n.* (plural **offspring**) [C] (formal) **1** someone's child or children **2** an animal's baby or babies

off·stage /ˌɔfˈsteɪdʒ/ *adv.* **1** just behind or to the side of a stage in a theater: *There was a loud crash offstage.* **2** when an actor is not acting: *Offstage, he was very shy.*

ˌoff-the-ˈrecord *adj.* an off-the-record remark is not supposed to be made public → **off/on the record** *at* RECORD[1]

ˌoff-the-ˈwall *adj.* (informal) strange or unusual: *an off-the-wall TV comedy*

ˌoff-year ˈelection *n.* [C] POLITICS an election to choose members of the SENATE and the HOUSE OF REPRESENTATIVES, held in one of the years between elections for the U.S. president

of·ten /ˈɔfən, ˈɔftən/ *adv.* **1** if something happens often, it happens regularly, many times, or in many situations (SYN) **frequently**: *She often works weekends.* | ***How often*** *do you come to New*

O

Orleans? | *This happens* **more often** *than you might think.*

THESAURUS

a lot (informal) – very often: *I've been to Boston a lot of times.*
frequently – very often: *He's frequently late for work.*
regularly – often and at regular times, for example every day, every week, or every month: *You should exercise regularly.*
repeatedly – use this to emphasize that someone did something many times: *I asked him repeatedly to tell me what was wrong.*
constantly – very often over a long period of time: *He talked constantly about his old girlfriend.*
continuously – without stopping: *He's been sick almost continuously for the last year.*
again and again/over and over (again) – many times, and more often than you would expect: *Fans of the show go to see it again and again.* | *I get bored doing the same thing over and over again.* ➔ NEVER, RARELY, SOMETIMES

2 all too often used in order to say that something sad or wrong happens too much: *All too often, fathers don't see their children much after a divorce.* **3 every so often** sometimes, but not regularly: *We go out for coffee every so often.* [ORIGIN: 1200—1300 *oft*]

GRAMMAR

often, very often
Use **often** before a verb, unless the verb is "be": *She often makes her own clothes.* | *He's often tired in the evenings.*
If there are two or more verbs together, **often** comes after the first one: *You can often see bears in the forest.*
Very often is used at the end of a negative sentence: *I don't speak to him very often.*

of·ten·times /ˈɔfənˌtaɪmz/ *adv.* (informal) often: *Oftentimes the situation can get out of control.*

o·gle /ˈoʊgəl/ *v.* [I,T] to look at someone in an offensive way that shows you think s/he is sexually attractive

o·gre /ˈoʊgɚ/ *n.* [C] **1** someone who seems cruel and frightening **2** a large ugly person in children's stories who eats people

OH the written abbreviation of OHIO

oh /oʊ/ *interjection* **1** used in order to express strong emotions or to emphasize what you think about something: *Oh, thank goodness you're safe!* | ***Oh, no!*** *My wallet is gone!* **2** said in order to make a slight pause, especially before replying to a question or giving your opinion on something: *"Why did you do it?" "Oh, I don't know."* | *"I'm finished."* ***"Oh, yeah,*** *how does it look?"* | *"We lost."* ***"Oh, well,*** *better luck next time."*

ohm /oʊm/ *n.* [C] PHYSICS a unit for measuring electrical RESISTANCE

ˈOhm's ˌlaw *n.* PHYSICS a scientific rule that says that the VOLTAGE in an electric current can be calculated by multiplying the RESISTANCE by the current

oil[1] /ɔɪl/ *n.* **1** [U] a thick dark liquid from under the ground, from which GASOLINE and other products are made (SYN) **petroleum**: *the price of oil* | *the oil industry* **2** [U] a smooth thick liquid that is burned to produce heat or used for making machines run easily: *motor oil* **3** [C,U] a smooth thick liquid made from plants or animals, used in cooking or for making beauty products: *Fry the chicken in oil.* | *a tablespoon of* ***olive/sunflower/vegetable oil*** **4 oils** [plural] paints that contain oil [ORIGIN: 1100—1200 Old French *oile*, from Latin *oleum* "olive oil"]

oil[2] *v.* [T] to put oil into or onto something

oiled /ɔɪld/ *adj.* covered with oil: *Place the fish in a lightly oiled pan.*

ˈoil ˌpainting *n.* [C,U] ENG. LANG. ARTS a picture painted with paint that contains oil, or the art of painting with oil paint

ˈoil slick *n.* [C] a layer of oil floating on water

ˈoil well *n.* [C] a special hole dug in the ground so that oil can be taken out

oil·y /ˈɔɪli/ *adj.* **1** covered with oil, or containing a lot of oil: *shampoo for oily hair* | *oily fish* **2** looking or feeling like oil: *an oily liquid*

oink /ɔɪŋk/ *n.* [C] the sound that a pig makes —**oink** *v.* [I]

oint·ment /ˈɔɪntˀmənt/ *n.* [C,U] a soft oily substance that you rub into your skin, especially as a medical treatment

OJ *n.* [U] (spoken) orange juice

OK the written abbreviation of OKLAHOMA

okay[1], OK /oʊˈkeɪ/ *adj., adv.* (spoken) **1** not sick, injured, unhappy, etc.: *Do you* ***feel okay*** *now?* **2** satisfactory or acceptable: *Does my hair look okay?* | *I did okay on the test.* **3** used in order to ask if you can do something, or to tell someone that s/he can do something: ***Is it okay*** *if I leave early?* | ***It's okay*** *for you to go.*

okay[2], OK *interjection* **1** said when you start talking, or continue to talk after a pause: *OK, can we go now?* **2** said when you agree with someone or when you give permission: *"We'd better be there by four." "Okay."* **3** said to ask if someone agrees or will give permission: *I'll go first, okay?*

okay[3], OK *v.* (**okayed, okays**) [T] (informal) to say officially that you will agree to something or allow it to happen: *Are you sure the bank will okay the loan?*

okay[4], OK *n.* (informal) **give the okay/get the okay** to give or get permission to do something: *I got the okay to leave early.*

old /oʊld/ *adj.* **1** having existed or been used for a long time (ANT) **new**: *We sell old and new books.* | *an old building*

THESAURUS

ancient – used about buildings, cities, languages, etc. that existed long ago: *ancient history* | *ancient cultures*
antique – used about furniture, jewelry, etc. that is old and valuable: *an antique rug*
vintage – used about things that are old but of high quality: *vintage cars*
classic – used about movies, books, television programs, and cars that are old but of very good quality: *Lumet's classic film "12 Angry Men"*
secondhand – used about cars, books, clothes, etc. that were owned by someone else and then sold
used – used about cars or other products which are being sold that are not new: *a used car dealer*
stale – used about bread, cakes, etc. that are no longer fresh
rotten – used about food, especially fruit or eggs, that is no longer good to eat ➔ NEW, YOUNG[1]

2 a) having lived for a long time (ANT) **young** ➔ ELDERLY: *an old man* | *My parents are **getting old**.* **b) the old** old people **3** having a particular age: *Our dog is three years old.* | *my ten-year-old daughter* | ***How old** is Kenny?* **4 old house/job/teacher etc.** (informal) a house, etc. that you had before but do not have now (SYN) **former**: *I saw your old girlfriend last night.* **5 good/poor/silly old etc. sb** (spoken) used in order to talk to or about someone you know and like: *Good old Larry hadn't changed a bit.* **6** experienced, heard, or seen many times before (SYN) **familiar**: *all the old familiar faces* | *I'm tired of listening to **the same old** music all the time.* **7 an old friend/enemy etc.** a friend, etc. that you have known for a long time **8 the old days** times in the past: ***In the old days**, only a few people were well educated.* | *She sat listening to her mother talk about **the good old days**.* [ORIGIN: Old English *eald*]

old·en /ˈoʊldən/ *adj.* (literary) **in olden days/times** a long time ago

ˌold-ˈfashioned *adj.* not considered to be modern or fashionable anymore: *old-fashioned values* | *a good old-fashioned ghost story*

THESAURUS

outdated/out-of-date/outmoded – no longer useful or modern: *They are still using computer equipment that is hopelessly outdated.* | *outdated laws* | *If the rules are out-of-date or unrealistic, they should be changed.*
dated – looking old-fashioned: *The film looks a bit dated now, but the story is still very contemporary.*
antiquated (formal) – old-fashioned and not appropriate for modern needs or conditions: *antiquated lab equipment*
obsolete – no longer useful or needed because something newer and better has been made: *The textbooks had become obsolete.*

old·ie /ˈoʊldi/ *n.* [C] (informal) someone or something that is old, especially a song or movie

ˌOld ˈTestament *n.* **the Old Testament** the part of the Bible that tells about the time before the birth of Jesus Christ ➔ NEW TESTAMENT

ˌold-ˈtimer *n.* [C] (informal) someone who has been in a particular job, place, etc. for a long time

ˌOld ˈWorld *n.* **the Old World** Europe, and parts of Asia and Africa ➔ NEW WORLD —**Old World** *adj.*

ol·i·gar·chy /ˈɑləˌɡɑrki/ *n.* (plural **oligarchies**) **1** [U] POLITICS government or control by a small group of people **2** [C] POLITICS a small group of people who run a country or state, or a country or state that is run by a small group of people [ORIGIN: 1400—1500 Greek *oligarchia*, from *oligos* "few" + *-archia* (-ARCHY)]

ol·ive /ˈɑlɪv/ *n.* **1** [C] a small black or green fruit, eaten as a vegetable or used for making oil **2** [U] *also* **olive green** a dull pale green color —**olive** *adj.*

O·lym·pic Games /əˌlɪmpɪk ˈɡeɪmz/ *n.* **the Olympic Games** [plural] *also* **the Olympics** an international sports event held every four years —**Olympic** *adj.*

ome·let, omelette /ˈɑmlɪt/ *n.* [C] eggs that have been beaten together and cooked, often with other foods added: *a cheese omelet* [ORIGIN: 1600—1700 French *omelette*, from Latin *lamella* "thin plate"]

o·men /ˈoʊmən/ *n.* [C] a sign of what will happen in the future: *a **good/bad omen***

om·i·nous /ˈɑmənəs/ *adj.* making you feel that something bad is going to happen: *ominous black clouds* —**ominously** *adv.*

o·mis·sion /oʊˈmɪʃən, ə-/ *n.* **1** [U] the act of not including or doing something **2** [C] something that has been omitted: *The report is full of mistakes and omissions.*

o·mit /oʊˈmɪt, ə-/ *v.* (**omitted**, **omitting**) [T] (formal) to not include something, either deliberately or because you forgot to do it (SYN) **leave out**: *Important details had been omitted.*

om·nip·o·tent /ɑmˈnɪpət̬ənt/ *adj.* (literary) able to do everything [ORIGIN: 1200—1300 Old French, Latin, from *omni-* "all" + *potens*, present participle of *potere* "to be powerful"] —**omnipotence** *n.* [U]

om·ni·scient /ɑmˈnɪʃənt/ *adj.* (literary) **1** knowing everything **2 omniscient narrator** ENG. LANG. ARTS if a story has an omniscient narrator, the person telling the story knows everything that happens and how every character thinks, feels, or experiences things [ORIGIN: 1600—1700 Medieval Latin, from Latin *omni-* "all" + *scire* "to know"] —**omniscience** *n.* [U]

omˌniscient point of ˈview *n.* [U] ENG. LANG. ARTS the style of telling a story in which the NARRATOR is not a character in the story but knows everything that happens and what all the characters experience, think, and feel ➔ LIMITED POINT OF VIEW

om·ni·vore /ˈɑmnɪˌvɔr/ *n.* [C] BIOLOGY an animal that eats both plants and other animals → CARNIVORE, HERBIVORE [ORIGIN: 1800–1900 Latin *omnivorus*, from *omni* "all" + *vorus*, from *vorare* "to eat"]

on /ɔn, ɑn/ *prep., adj., adv.* **1** touching, being supported by, or hanging from something: *I got mud on my pants.* | *pictures hanging on the wall* | *a child sitting on her dad's shoulders* **2** if you have a piece of clothing on, you are wearing it: *He came to the door with his coat on.* **3** in a particular place or area of land: *The answer is on page 44.* | *They built a fence on our land.* **4** at the side of something such as a street, road, or river: *a restaurant on the river* | *the stores on Rodeo Drive* **5** at some time during a particular day: *Is there a meeting on Monday?* | *a party on her birthday* | *On May 10, Jo had a baby girl.* **6** continuing without stopping: *Go on, Cheryl. What happened next?* | *The peace talks dragged on* (=continued slowly) *for months.* **7** forward or ahead, toward a particular place: *We drove on to Kansas City.* | *You guys go on without me.* **8** later or after a particular time: ***From that day/point/time on**, he started eating healthy foods and exercising.* **9** being broadcast by a television or radio station, or recorded on something: *Keillor's program on the radio* | *a movie available on video* | *The news will be on at six.* **10** about a particular subject: *a book on China*

> **THESAURUS** about, concerning, regarding
> → ABOUT[1]

11 used in order to show who or what is affected by an action: *a new tax on imported wine* | *The divorce was hard on Jill.* | *medical testing done on rats* **12** using something: *Sam's on the phone.* | *a piece featuring Hawkins on saxophone* | *a report done on the computer* | *I cut myself on a piece of glass.* **13** in a particular direction: *The Mayor was sitting on my right.* **14** in or into a vehicle such as a bus, airplane, train, etc.: *Did you sleep on the plane?* | *I **got on** at Vine Street.* **15** taking part in an activity or traveling somewhere: *They met on a trip to Spain.* **16** included in a team or group, or in a list: *She's on the volleyball team.* | *an item on the agenda* **17** operating or working (ANT) **off**: *The TV was on.* | ***Turn on** the light.* **18** taking a medicine or drugs: *She's on antibiotics.* **19 have/carry sth on you** (informal) to have something with you now: *Do you have a pen on you?* **20** (spoken) used in order to say that someone is paying for something: *Dinner's on me tonight.* **21** if an event is on, it will happen: *There's a jazz festival on this weekend.* **22** (informal) if something bad happens on someone, it happens when s/he is not expecting it: *You can't just quit on me!* → HEAD-ON, **later on** *at* LATER[1], **on and off** *at* OFF

once[1] /wʌns/ *adv.* **1** on one occasion, or at a time in the past: *I've only met her once.* | *I once ran 21 miles.* | *He tried skiing **once before**, but he didn't like it.* **2 once a week/year etc.** one time every week, year, etc. as a regular activity: *She goes to the gym once a week.* **3 (every) once in a while** sometimes, but not often: *We see each other every once in a while.* **4 once more** one more time (SYN) **again**: *I'll call him once more, but then we have to leave.* **5 at once a)** at the same time: *I can't do two things at once!* **b)** (formal) immediately or without waiting: *I recognized him at once.* **6 all at once a)** suddenly: *All at once, the room went quiet.* **b)** at the same time: *A lot of things needed to be dealt with all at once.* **7** in the past, but not now: *They were once good friends.* **8 for once** (spoken) used in order to say that something should happen more often: *For once, try telling me the truth.* **9 once and for all** definitely and finally: *Let's settle this once and for all.* **10 once upon a time** a long time ago – used at the beginning of children's stories **11 once in a blue moon** very rarely: *He comes to see us once in a blue moon.*

once[2] *conjunction* from the time something happens: *Once you try this, you'll never want to stop.*

on·com·ing /ˈɔnˌkʌmɪŋ, ˈɑn-/ *adj.* **oncoming car/traffic etc.** a car, etc. that is coming toward you

one[1] /wʌn/ *number* **1** 1 **2** one o'clock: *I have a meeting at one.* **3** one year old: *Katie's almost one.* [ORIGIN: Old English *an*]

one[2] *pron.* **1** someone or something that has been mentioned or is known about: *"Do you have a bike?" "No, but I'm getting one for my birthday."* | *"Where are those books?" "Which ones?"* | *"Which candy bar do you want?" **"This/that one."*** | *Jane's **the one** with the red hair.* **2 one by one** if people do something one by one, first one person does it, then the next, etc.: *One by one, the passengers got off the bus.* **3 one after the other/one after another** if events or actions happen one after the other, they happen without much time between them: *He's had one problem after another this year.* **4 (all) in one** if someone or something is many different things all in one, s/he or it is all those things: *This is a TV, radio, and VCR all in one.* **5** (formal) **a)** people in general: *One must be careful to keep exact records.* **b)** (old-fashioned) used in order to mean "I": *One is tempted to ignore the whole problem.*

> **GRAMMAR**
> **One of** is followed by a plural noun form but a singular verb: *One of her legs is shorter than the other.*

one[3] *determiner* **1** used to emphasize a particular person or thing: *One reason I like the house is because of the big kitchen.* | ***One of** the children is sick.* ▸Don't say "One of the children are sick."◂ **2 one day/afternoon etc. a)** a particular day, etc. in the past: *There was one week in April when we had two feet of snow.* **b)** any day, etc. in the future: *We should go for a meal one evening.* **3 for one thing** used in order to introduce a reason for what you have just said **4** (spoken) used in order to emphasize your description of someone or something: *That is one cute kid!*

one[4] *n.* [C] a piece of paper money worth $1: *Do you have five ones?*

ˌone anˈother *pron.* (formal) EACH OTHER

ˌone-diˈmensional *adj.* a one-dimensional character in a book, movie, etc. does not seem like a real person because s/he has only one quality ➔ THREE-DIMENSIONAL

ˌone-ˈliner *n.* [C] a very short joke ➔ GAG

ˌone-night ˈstand *n.* [C] an occasion when two people have sex, but do not intend to meet each other again

ˌone-of-a-ˈkind *adj.* special because no one or nothing else is like him, her, or it: *one-of-a-kind handmade carpets*

ˌone-on-ˈone *adj.* between only you and one other person: *one-on-one English lessons* —**one-on-one** *adv.*

on·er·ous /ˈɑnərəs, ˈoʊ-/ *adj.* (formal) difficult and tiring: *an **onerous task/job***

ˌone-ˈsided *adj.* **1** considering or showing only one side of a question, subject, etc. in a way that is unfair: *a one-sided account of the war* **2** an activity or competition that is one-sided is one in which one person or team is much stronger or does more than the other: *a one-sided football game*

one·time /ˈwʌntaɪm/ *adj.* former: *a onetime TV star*

ˌone-to-ˈone *adj.* **1** between only two people: *one-to-one talks* **2** matching one other person, thing, etc. exactly: *a one-to-one correspondence between sound and symbol*

ˌone-track ˈmind *n.* **have a one-track mind** (disapproving) to think about only one thing all the time

ˌone-ˈway *adj.* **1** moving or allowing movement in only one direction: *one-way traffic | a one-way street* **2** a one-way ticket is for taking a trip from one place to another, but not back again ➔ ROUND-TRIP

on·go·ing /ˈɔnˌgoʊɪŋ, ˈɑn-/ (Ac) *adj.* continuing: *ongoing discussions*

on·ion /ˈʌnyən/ *n.* [C,U] a round white vegetable with brown, red, or white skin and many layers, that has a strong taste and smell [ORIGIN: 1100—1200 Old French *oignon*, from Latin *unio*] ➔ *see picture at* VEGETABLE

on·line /ˌɔnˈlaɪn◂, ˌɑn-/ *adj., adv.* **1** IT connected to other computers through the Internet, or available through the Internet (ANT) **offline**: *All the city's schools will **be/go online** by the end of the year.* ➔ INTERNET **2** IT directly connected to or controlled by a computer (ANT) **offline**: *an online printer*

on·look·er /ˈɔnˌlʊkɚ, ˈɑn-/ *n.* [C] someone who watches something happening without being involved in it: *A crowd of onlookers had gathered at the scene of the accident.*

on·ly[1] /ˈoʊnli/ *adv.* **1** not more than a particular amount, number, age, etc., especially when this is unusual: *Tammy was only 9 months old when she started walking. | It's only eight o'clock.* **2** nothing or no one except the person or thing mentioned: *You're only wearing a T-shirt. No wonder you're cold. | parking for restaurant customers only* **3** in one place, situation, or way and no other, or for one reason and no other: *You can only exit through this door. | The contract will be renewed **only if** the work has been done to the correct standard. | Lasting security will come to the region **only when** the two sides make peace.* **4** not very important, serious, good, etc. compared to something else: *The job's interesting, but it's only temporary. | I was only kidding.* **5 not only ... (but also)** used in order to say that something is even better, worse, or more surprising than what you have just said: *Math is not only easy for her, it's fun.* **6** (formal) no earlier than a particular time: *Congress passed the law only last year. | She finally tapped his shoulder, and **only then** did he look up.* **7 if only a)** used in order to give a reason for something, and say that it is not the best one: *He was thinking about joining the navy, if only to get away from his parents.* **b)** used in order to express a strong wish: *If only they'd let us know in time!* **8 only too** very or completely: *He was only too ready to leave.*

only[2] *adj.* **1** used in order to say that there is one person, thing, or group in a particular situation and no others: *Walking is the only exercise I get. | He's **the only one** who did a good job.* **2 an only child** a child who does not have any brothers or sisters **3 the only thing is...** (spoken) used before you begin to talk about something that might be a problem: *The only thing is, I have to be back by eight.*

only[3] *conjunction* except that (SYN) **but**: *I'd help, only I'm really busy that day.*

on·o·mat·o·poe·ia /ˌɑnəmɑṭəˈpiə/ *n.* [U] ENG. LANG. ARTS the use of words that sound like the thing that they are describing, such as "hiss" or "boom" [ORIGIN: 1500—1600 Late Latin, Greek *onomatopoiia*, from *onoma* "name" + *poiein* "to make"]

ˈon-ramp *n.* [C] a road for driving onto a HIGHWAY or FREEWAY (ANT) **off-ramp**

on·set /ˈɔnsɛt, ˈɑn-/ *n.* **the onset of sth** the beginning of something, especially something bad: *the onset of a bad cold*

on·slaught /ˈɑnslɔt, ˈɔn-/ *n.* [C usually singular] a very strong attack or criticism

ˈon-the-job *adj.* [only before noun] while working, or at work: *on-the-job training*

on·to /*before consonants* ˈɔnṭə, ˈɑn-; *before vowels and strong* ˈɔntu, ˈɑn-/ *prep.* **1** used in order to show movement to a position on a surface, area, or object: *The cat leaped onto the table. | Turn onto River Road. | Claire jumped **out/back/over onto** the sidewalk.* **2 be onto sb** (informal) to know who did something wrong or illegal: *Briggs knew the cops were onto him.*

o·nus /'oʊnəs/ *n.* **the onus** the RESPONSIBILITY for something: ***The onus is on** the company **to** provide safety equipment.*

on·ward[1] /'ɔnwəd, 'ɑn-/ *also* **onwards** *adv.* **1 from ... onward** beginning at a particular time and continuing after that: *European history from 1900 onward* **2** (formal) forward: *The ship moved onward through the fog.*

onward[2] *adj.* (formal) moving forward, continuing, or developing: *the onward march of scientific progress*

O

oo·dles /'udlz/ *n.* (informal) **oodles of sth** a large amount of something: *She earns oodles of money.*

oops /ʊps, ups/ *interjection* said when someone has fallen, dropped something, or made a small mistake: *Oops! I spilled the milk.*

ooze /uz/ *v.* [I,T] **1** if a liquid oozes from something, or if something oozes a liquid, liquid flows from it very slowly: *Blood was **oozing from** the cut.*

THESAURUS pour, flow, drip, leak, run, come out ➔ POUR

2 (informal) to show a lot of a particular quality: *Leo positively oozes charm.*

o·pal /'oʊpəl/ *n.* [C,U] a white stone with changing colors in it, used in jewelry

o·paque /oʊ'peɪk/ *adj.* **1** difficult to see through (ANT) **transparent** **2** hard to understand [ORIGIN: 1400—1500 Latin *opacus* "dark"]

o·pen[1] /'oʊpən/ *adj.*
1 DOOR/BOOK/BOX ETC. not closed or covered (ANT) **closed, shut**: *an open door* | *A book lay open on the table.* | *All the windows were **wide open**.*
2 EYES/MOUTH not closed, so that your EYELIDS or LIPS are apart: *I can barely **keep** my **eyes open**, I'm so tired.*
3 STORES/BANKS ETC. ready or available for people to use, visit, etc.: *The museum is open daily* | *When is the new library going to be open?* | *The restaurant's **open for** lunch and dinner.* | *Stores were **open for business** as usual.* | *The pool is only **open to the public** in the summer.*
4 NOT RESTRICTED available to anyone, so that anyone can take part: *The competition is **open to** children aged 7 to 14.* | *an open meeting*
5 NOT ENCLOSED not enclosed or covered by buildings, walls, etc.: *Lang grew up in the **open spaces** of the prairie.* | *classes held out in the **open air*** (=outdoors) | *an open fire*
6 NOT SECRET not hiding anything: *Ralph looked at her with open admiration.* | *testimony given in open court* (=in a court where everything is done in public) | *My husband and I try to be **open with** each other.*
7 WILLING TO LISTEN willing to listen to other people: ***Keep an open mind*** (=listen without judging) *until you've heard everyone's ideas.* | *We're **open to suggestions** on how to improve our service.*
8 be open to criticism/blame/suspicion etc. likely to be criticized, blamed, etc.: *By accepting the money, she has left herself open to criticism.*
9 NOT DECIDED not finally decided: *The location of the peace talks is still **an open question**.* | *The wisdom of cutting taxes is **open to** debate.* | *It's a possibility. I'm **keeping** my **options open*** (=not deciding between the things I might do).
10 an open mind if you have an open mind, you deliberately do not make a decision or form a definite opinion about something: *Jurors must try to **keep an open mind** during the trial.*
11 keep your eyes/ears open (spoken) to keep looking or listening so that you will notice anything that is important
12 welcome/greet sb with open arms to greet someone with happiness and excitement [ORIGIN: Old English]

open[2] *also* **open up** *v.* **1** [I,T] to move something so that something is not closed or covered, or to be moved in this way: *Dan's opening his birthday presents.* | *a door that opens automatically* | *Meg opened her eyes wide.* | *She opened the curtains.* | ***Open up** the window, will you?*

USAGE

Do not use **open** and **close** to talk about things that use electricity or things that provide water or gas. Use **turn on/off** instead: *Can you turn off the stove?* | *I turned on the TV.*
For things that use electricity, you can also use **switch on/off**: *Don't forget to switch off the lights.*

THESAURUS

unlock – to open a door, drawer, etc. with a key
unscrew – to open a lid on a bottle, container, etc. by turning it
unwrap – to open a package by removing the paper that covers it
unfold – to open a piece of paper, a cloth, etc. that was folded
unfasten/undo – to open something that is fastened or tied, for example a seat belt or a piece of clothing ➔ CLOSE[1]

2 [I] if a store, bank, or public building opens at a particular time, it begins to allow people inside at that time: *What time does the bookstore open on Sundays?* **3** [I,T] to start, or to make something start: *The restaurant opens next month.* | *a new play opening on Broadway* | *He **opened up** a checking account.* **4** [I,T] to spread something out, or become spread out: *I can't open my umbrella.* | *The roses are starting to **open up**.* | *Open your books to page 153.* **5** [T] to make something available to be used or visited: *Snowplows were out **opening up** the streets.* | *Parts of the White House will be opened to the public.* **6 open fire (on sb/sth)** to start shooting at someone or something

open up *phr. v.* **1 open** sth ↔ **up** to become available or possible, or to make something available or possible: *Education opens up all kinds of opportunities.* **2** to stop being shy and say what you really think

open[3] *n.* **(out) in the open a)** outdoors **b)** not hidden or secret: *The truth is finally out in the open.*

open-air

an open-air concert

ˌopen-ˈair *adj.* outdoor: *open-air concerts*

ˌopen-ˈended *adj.* without a definite ending time, rules, or an answer: *an open-ended investigation*

ˌopen-ended ˈquestion *n.* [C] ENG. LANG. ARTS a question that does not have a single definite answer or result

o·pen·er /ˈoupənɚ/ *n.* [C] **1** a tool or machine used in order to open letters, bottles, or cans: ***a can opener*** **2** the first of a series of things such as sports games: *the season opener against the Celtics*

ˌopen-heart ˈsurgery *n.* [U] a medical operation in which doctors operate on someone's heart

ˌopen ˈhouse *n.* [C] **1** an occasion when a school or business allows the public to come in and see the work that is done there **2** a party that you can come to or leave at any time during a particular period

o·pen·ing¹ /ˈoupənɪŋ/ *n.* [C] **1** an occasion when a new business, building, etc. is ready for use: *the **opening of** the exhibition* **2** the beginning of something: *the **opening of** the concert season* **3** a job or position that is available: ***job openings** for high school graduates* **4** a hole or space in something: *an **opening in** the fence*

THESAURUS hole, space, gap, crack → HOLE¹

5 a chance to do or say something: *This provides an opening for you to praise the student's effort.*

opening² *adj.* first or beginning: *the opening paragraph | Are you going to **opening night*** (=the first night of a new play, movie, etc.)*?*

o·pen·ly /ˈoupənli/ *adv.* honestly and not secretly: *They talk openly about their problems.*

ˌopen-ˈminded *adj.* willing to consider and accept new ideas, opinions, etc. **—open-mindedness** *n.* [U]

o·pen·ness /ˈoupənnɪs/ *n.* [U] **1** the quality of being honest and not keeping things secret: *the openness of a small child* **2** the quality of being willing to accept new ideas or people: *the country's **openness to** change*

op·er·a /ˈɑprə, ˈɑpərə/ *n.* [C,U] ENG. LANG. ARTS a musical play in which all of the words are sung, or these plays considered as a form of art → MUSICAL → THEATER [ORIGIN: 1600—1700 Italian, from Latin "works," plural of *opus*] **—operatic** /ˌɑpəˈræṭɪk◂/ *adj.*

op·er·a·ble /ˈɑprəbəl/ *adj.* **1** able to be treated by a medical operation (ANT) **inoperable**: *The cancer is operable.* **2** working and ready to use (ANT) **inoperable**: *an operable machine*

op·er·ate /ˈɑpəˌreɪt/ *v.* **1** [I,T] if a machine operates or you operate it, it works or you make it work: *technicians who are trained to operate the scanning equipment | The engine seems to be operating smoothly.* **2** [I] to cut open someone's body in order to repair or remove a part that is damaged: *Surgeons **operated on** his knee.* **3** [I,T] if a business or organization operates, or if you operate it, it is organized to do its work: *an agreement to build and operate a cellular phone network | factories **operating in** Mexico* **4** [I,T] if a system, process, or service operates, or if you operate it, it works or has a particular purpose: *How does the new security system operate? | The cloth **operates as** a filter.*

ˈoperating ˌsystem *n.* [C] IT a system in a computer that helps all the programs to work

op·er·a·tion /ˌɑpəˈreɪʃən/ *n.* **1** [C] the process of cutting into someone's body to repair or remove a part that is damaged: *a knee operation | He needed an **operation on** his brain. | Taylor has **had/undergone** a heart bypass **operation**.* **2** [C] a set of planned actions or activities for a particular purpose: *a rescue operation* **3** [U] the way the parts of a machine or system work together: *Wear protective glasses when the machine is **in operation**.* **4** [C,U] a business or company, or the work of a business: *The company is expanding its overseas operations. | A literacy program has been **in operation*** (=been working) *for ten years.* **5** [C] IT an action done by a computer: *a machine performing millions of operations per second* **6** [U] the way something such as a law has an effect or achieves a result: *the operation of the tax laws*

op·er·a·tion·al /ˌɑpəˈreɪʃənl/ *adj.* **1** working and ready to be used: *The system is now **fully operational**.* **2** relating to the operation of a business, government, etc.: *operational costs* **—operationally** *adv.*

op·er·a·tive /ˈɑpərəṭɪv/ *n.* [C] someone who does work that is secret in some way: *a CIA operative*

op·er·a·tor /ˈɑpəˌreɪṭɚ/ *n.* [C] **1** someone who works for a telephone company giving information to people and helping to connect calls **2** someone who operates a machine or piece of equipment: *a radio operator*

oph·thal·mol·o·gy /ˌɑfθəlˈmɑlədʒi, -θəˈmɑ-, ˌɑp-/ *n.* [U] the medical study of the eyes and diseases that affect them **—ophthalmologist** *n.* [C]

o·pin·ion /əˈpɪnyən/ *n.* **1** [C,U] your ideas or beliefs about a particular subject: *What's your **opinion on/of** the death penalty? | Teachers were not asked their **opinions about** the curriculum. | **In***

my opinion**, getting a divorce is too easy.* | *people who aren't afraid to **express/give their opinions | *Polls are taken to discover **public opinion*** (=what ordinary people think about something).

THESAURUS

view – your opinion about something: *What are your views about global warming?*
point of view – a particular way of thinking about or judging something: *The story is told from the man's point-of-view.*
position – used especially about the opinion of a government or organization: *The president has made his position perfectly clear.*
stance – an opinion that is stated publicly: *What is your stance on abortion?*
attitude – your opinions and feelings about something: *If you go into the game with a positive attitude, you have more chance of winning.* | *the French attitude toward food*
sentiment (formal) – an opinion or feeling that you have about something: *Public sentiment against the war grew steadily over the next year.*
conviction (formal) – a very strong belief or opinion: *At the beginning of World War II, he had the strong conviction that America should go to Britain's aid and fight.*

2 [C] judgment or advice from a professional person about something: *We got **a second opinion*** (=we asked two people) *before replacing the furnace.* **3 have a high/low/good etc. opinion of sb/sth** to think that someone or something is very good or very bad: *On the whole, people have a low opinion of politicians.* [ORIGIN: 1300—1400 French, Latin *opinio*]

o·pin·ion·at·ed /əˈpɪnyəˌneɪt̬ɪd/ *adj.* (disapproving) expressing very strong opinions about things

oˈpinion poll *n.* [C] a POLL

o·pi·um /ˈoʊpiəm/ *n.* [U] an illegal drug made from POPPY seeds

o·pos·sum /əˈpɑsəm, ˈpɑsəm/ *n.* [C] an American animal that looks like a large rat and can hang from trees by its tail ➔ *see picture at* MARSUPIAL

op·po·nent /əˈpoʊnənt/ *n.* [C] **1** someone who tries to defeat another person or team in a competition, game, argument, etc.: *This week, the team faces its toughest opponent.* **2** someone who disagrees with a plan, idea, etc.: ***opponents of** abortion*

op·por·tune /ˌɑpɚˈtun/ *adj.* (formal) **an opportune moment/time/place etc.** a time, etc. that is appropriate for doing something

op·por·tun·ist /ˌɑpɚˈtunɪst/ *n.* [C] (disapproving) someone who uses every chance to gain power or advantages over others —**opportunism** *n.* [U] —**opportunistic** /ˌɑpɚtuˈnɪstɪk/ *adj.*

op·por·tu·ni·ty /ˌɑpɚˈtunət̬i/ *n.* (plural **opportunities**) [C] **1** an occasion when it is possible for you to do something ➔ CHANCE: *Children will **get/have** an **opportunity to** try several different sports.* | *The program **gives** students **the/an opportunity to** see live drama.* | *I'd like to **take this opportunity to** thank everyone who helped me.* | *Under the law, women were guaranteed **equal opportunities*** (=chances to do things that are equal to men's chances). | *This is a **great/good opportunity** for investors.*

COLLOCATIONS

An **opportunity comes along/up** or **arises**.
You **have/are given** the **opportunity** to do something.
You **take/seize/use** an **opportunity** by doing something when you have the chance to do it.
A **wasted/lost/missed opportunity** is a good opportunity that you did not take.
An **ideal/perfect/unique/golden opportunity** is one that is very good or special, and may not happen again.
A **rare opportunity** is one that does not happen very often.

2 a chance to get a job: *There are good opportunities for graduates in your field.*

op·pose /əˈpoʊz/ *v.* [T] to disagree strongly with an idea or action: *A local group opposes the plan for environmental reasons.*

op·posed /əˈpoʊzd/ *adj.* **1** disagreeing strongly with someone or something, or feeling strongly that someone or something is wrong: *militants who are **opposed to** the peace process* | *groups that are **strongly opposed to** abortion* **2 as opposed to sth** used in order to show that two things are different from each other: *The teaching is geared to practical problems, as opposed to theory.*

op·pos·ing /əˈpoʊzɪŋ/ *adj.* **1** opposing teams, groups, etc. are competing, arguing, etc. with each other **2** opposing ideas, opinions, etc. are completely different from each other

op·po·site[1] /ˈɑpəzɪt, -sɪt/ *n.* [C] a person or thing that is completely different from someone or something else: *Hot and cold are opposites.* | *Most people think work and play are **the opposite of** each other.* | *the **exact opposite** of the truth* | *He said he'd do one thing, and then did **the opposite**.*

opposite[2] *adj.* **1** completely different: *Ray walked off in the opposite direction.* | *the two men are at **opposite ends** of the political spectrum* **2** facing something or directly across from something: *a building on the opposite side of the river* **3 the opposite sex** the other sex. If you are a man, women are the opposite sex.

opposite[3] *prep., adv.* if one thing or person is opposite another, they are facing each other: *the wall opposite the door* | *He's moved into the house opposite.*

ˌopposite ˈangles *n.* [plural] MATH two equal angles that are formed when two lines cross, and which are opposite each other ➔ *see picture at* ANGLE[1]

op·po·si·tion /ˌɑpəˈzɪʃən/ *n.* [U] strong disagreement with, or protest against, something: *the* residents' **opposition to** plans for a new highway | There was **stiff/strong/intense opposition** from the teachers' union.

THESAURUS

objection – a reason you give for not approving of an idea or plan: *Lawyers raised no objections to the plan.*
antagonism (formal) – strong opposition to or hatred of someone else: *antagonism between the two political parties*
hostility – strong opposition to a plan or idea: *There has been a certain amount of hostility to the proposed reform.*
antipathy (formal) – a feeling of strong dislike or opposition: *a growing antipathy towards the government*

op·press /ə'prɛs/ *v.* [T] to treat people in an unfair and cruel way —**oppressor** /ə'prɛsɚ/ *n.* [C]

op·pressed /ə'prɛst/ *adj.* treated unfairly or cruelly: *oppressed minority groups | the poor and* ***the oppressed*** (=people who are oppressed)

op·pres·sion /ə'prɛʃən/ *n.* [U] the act of oppressing people, or the state of being oppressed

op·pres·sive /ə'prɛsɪv/ *adj.* **1** cruel and unfair: *an oppressive military government* **2** making you feel uncomfortable: *oppressive heat*

opt /ɑpt/ *v.* [T] to choose one thing or do one thing instead of another: *If you prefer quiet,* ***opt for*** *a smaller resort. | More high school students are* ***opting to*** *go to college.*
opt out *phr. v.* to choose not to join in a group or system: *Parents can* ***opt out of*** *the public school system by home schooling.*

op·tic /'ɑptɪk/ *adj.* BIOLOGY relating to the eyes

op·ti·cal /'ɑptɪkəl/ *adj.* relating to the way light is seen, or relating to the eyes: *an optical instrument* —**optically** *adv.*

ˌoptical ilˈlusion *n.* [C] a picture or image that tricks your eyes and makes you see something that is not actually there

op·ti·cian /ɑp'tɪʃən/ *n.* [C] someone who makes glasses

op·ti·mism /'ɑptəˌmɪzəm/ *n.* [U] a tendency to believe that good things will happen (ANT) **pessimism**: ***optimism about*** *the country's economic future | The results give* ***reason/cause/grounds for optimism.***

op·ti·mist /'ɑptəmɪst/ *n.* [C] someone who believes that good things will happen (ANT) **pessimist**

op·ti·mist·ic /ˌɑptə'mɪstɪk/ *adj.* believing that good things will happen in the future (ANT) **pessimistic**: *The coach is* ***optimistic about*** *the team's chances of winning. | Police remain* ***optimistic that*** *the child will be found.* —**optimistically** *adv.*

op·ti·mum /'ɑptəməm/ *adj.* best or most appropriate for a particular purpose: *the optimum diet for good health*

op·tion /'ɑpʃən/ (Ac) *n.* [C] **1** a choice you can make in a particular situation: *career options | The jury* ***had the option of*** *finding him guilty but mentally ill. | Dropping out of school* ***is not an option*** (=you cannot do it). *| Press 4 to select the printer control option* (=on a computer). **2 keep/leave your options open** to wait before making a decision: *Leave your options open until you have the results of the test.* **3** ECONOMICS the right to buy or sell something in the future: *stock options | All employees are given an option on 100 shares of stock.* [ORIGIN: 1500—1600 French, Latin *optio* "free choice"]

op·tion·al /'ɑpʃənl/ (Ac) *adj.* something that is optional is something you do not need to do or have, but can choose if you want it (ANT) **mandatory**: *Attendance at the meeting is optional. | If they wish, students can attend an optional philosophy class.*

op·tom·e·trist /ɑp'tɑmətrɪst/ *n.* [C] someone who examines people's eyes and orders glasses for them —**optometry** /ɑp'tɑmətri/ *n.* [U]

op·u·lent /'ɑpyələnt/ *adj.* decorated in an expensive way: *an opulent hotel* —**opulence** *n.* [U]

OR the written abbreviation of OREGON

or /ɚ; *strong* ɔr/ *conjunction* **1** used between two possibilities or before the last in a series of possibilities ➔ EITHER: *Would you like pie, cake, or some ice cream? | Will the project receive state or federal funds? | You can use* ***either*** *milk* ***or*** *cream in the sauce. | They speak only a little Spanish,* ***or else*** *none at all.* **2 or anything/something** (spoken) something that is similar to what you have just mentioned: *Do you want to go out for a drink or anything?* **3** used after a negative verb when you mean not one thing and not another thing: *Elena never learned to read or write English.* **4** used in order to warn or advise someone: *Hurry, or you'll miss your plane. | Businesses will have to raise prices,* ***or else*** *their profits will drop. | Don't be late,* ***or else... !*** (=used as a threat) **5** used when you are guessing at a number, time, distance, etc. because you cannot be exact: *a little girl four or five years old | There's a gas station a mile* ***or so*** *down the road.* **6** used in order to give more specific information or to correct what has been said before: *biology, or the study of living things* **7** used in order to explain why something happened or why something must be true: *She must be tired, or she wouldn't be so crabby.* [ORIGIN: Old English *oththe*]

or·a·cle /'ɔrəkəl, 'ɑr-/ *n.* [C] **1** HISTORY someone the ancient Greeks believed could communicate with the gods, who gave advice to people or told them what would happen in the future **2** HISTORY the holy place where an oracle could be found [ORIGIN: 1300—1400 French, Latin *oraculum*, from *orare*; ORATION]

o·ral[1] /'ɔrəl/ *adj.* **1** spoken, not written: *an oral report* **2** relating to the mouth: *oral hygiene* [ORIGIN: 1600—1700 Late Latin *oralis*, from Latin *os* "mouth"]

oral[2] *n.* [C] a test in a university in which questions and answers are spoken rather than written

or·ange /'ɔrɪndʒ, 'ɑr-/ *n.* **1** [C] a round fruit that has sweet juice and thick skin which you do not eat: *orange juice* ➔ *see picture on page 414* **2** [U] the color of an orange [ORIGIN: 1200—1300 Old French, Arabic *naranj*, from Sanskrit *naranga* "orange tree"] **—orange** *adj.*

O

o·rang·u·tan /ə'ræŋəˌtæn/ *also* **o·rang·u·tang** /ə'ræŋəˌtæŋ/ *n.* [C] a large APE that has long arms and long orange-brown hair [ORIGIN: 1600—1700 Malay *orang hutan* "man of the forest"] ➔ *see picture at* APE

o·ra·tion /ə'reɪʃən, ɔ-/ *n.* [C] a formal public speech

or·a·tor /'ɔrət̬ɚ, 'ɑr-/ *n.* [C] (formal) someone who makes speeches and is good at persuading people

or·a·tory /'ɔrəˌtɔri, 'ɑr-/ *n.* [U] (formal) the skill of making public speeches

or·bit[1] /'ɔrbɪt/ *n.* [C] PHYSICS the path traveled by an object that is moving around a larger object: *the Moon's orbit around the Earth* [ORIGIN: 1500—1600 Latin *orbita* "wheel-track"] **—orbital** *adj.* ➔ *see picture at* APOGEE

orbit[2] *v.* [I,T] PHYSICS to travel in a circle around a larger object: *a satellite that orbits the Earth*

or·chard /'ɔrtʃɚd/ *n.* [C] a place where fruit trees are grown: *a cherry orchard*

or·ches·tra /'ɔrkɪstrə/ *n.* [C] a large group of musicians who play CLASSICAL MUSIC on different instruments

TOPIC

Sections of an orchestra
the woodwind/wind section also **the winds** – the instruments made mostly of wood that you blow through
the strings/the string section – the instruments that have strings
the brass (section) – the instruments made of metal that you blow through
the percussion (section) – the instruments such as drums

People in an orchestra:
conductor – the person who directs the music and musicians
cellist – a person who plays the cello
flutist – a person who plays the flute
violinist – a person who plays the violin
percussionist – a person who plays percussion

—orchestral /ɔr'kɛstrəl/ *adj.*

'orchestra pit *n.* [C] the space below the stage in a theater where the musicians sit ➔ *see picture at* THEATER

or·ches·trate /'ɔrkɪˌstreɪt/ *v.* [T] to organize an important event or a complicated plan, especially secretly: *Was the rebellion orchestrated by the army?*

or·chid /'ɔrkɪd/ *n.* [C] a tropical, often brightly colored flower with three PETALS

or·dain /ɔr'deɪn/ *v.* [T] to officially make someone a religious leader ➔ ORDINATION: *John was ordained a priest.*

or·deal /ɔr'dil/ *n.* [C] a very bad experience that continues for a long time: *She had to* ***go through*** *a terrible* ***ordeal***. [ORIGIN: Old English *ordal* "trial, judgment"]

or·der[1] /'ɔrdɚ/ *n.*
1 in order (for sb/sth) to do sth so that something can happen, or so that someone can do something: *In order for you to graduate next year, you'll have to go to summer school.* | *Plants need light in order to live.*

THESAURUS

to – a shorter way of saying **in order to**: *I went to the bank to get some money.*
so (that) – in order to do something to make something possible: *She's studying Japanese so that she can get a job in Japan.*
for – so that you can get or do something: *They were waiting for the school bus.*

2 ARRANGEMENT [U] the way that several things are arranged, organized, or put on a list: *Are all the slides* ***in order***? | *The names were written* ***in alphabetical order***. | *I think these pages are* ***out of order*** (=not correctly arranged). | *State the main points* ***in order of*** *importance.* | *We've got to* ***get*** *our finances* ***in order*** (=organize them).
3 REQUEST FOR GOODS [C] a request for goods from a company or for food in a restaurant, or the goods or food that you ask for: *We've received more* ***orders for*** *car alarms this year than ever before.* | *The school's just* ***placed an order*** *for more books.* | *May I* ***take*** *your* ***order*** (=used to ask what a customer in a restaurant wants)? | *Your order will be ready soon.*
4 NO CRIME/TROUBLE [U] a situation in which people obey rules and respect authority: *Police are working hard to maintain* ***law and order*** *in the area.*
5 COMMAND [C] a command given by someone in authority: *Captain Marshall* ***gave*** *the* ***order*** *to advance.* | *The soldiers had been trained to* ***obey/follow orders***.
6 out of order a phrase meaning "not working," used especially on signs: *The pay phone was out of order.*
7 in order legal and correct: *Your passport seems to be in order.*
8 POLITICS ETC. [singular] the political, social, or economic situation at a particular time: *the present economic order*
9 ANIMALS/PLANTS [C] one of the groups into which scientists divide animals and plants. An order is larger than a FAMILY but smaller than a CLASS. ➔ **in short order** *at* SHORT[1]

order² *v.* **1** [I,T] ask for food or drink in a restaurant, bar, etc.: *Are you ready to order?* | *We ordered coffee and dessert.*

THESAURUS **ask, request, demand** → ASK

2 [T] to ask a company to make or send you something: *They've ordered a new carpet for the bedroom.* **3** [T] to tell someone that s/he must do something: *The judge **ordered** him **to** pay $1 million.* **4** [T] to arrange something in a particular way: *Order the list of names alphabetically.*

order sb around *phr. v.* to continuously tell someone what to do, in a way that is annoying: *I wish she'd stop ordering me around.*

ˌordered ˈpair *n.* [C] MATH two numbers that are used to represent a point on a GRID. The first number shows which HORIZONTAL line of the grid the point is on, and the second number shows which VERTICAL line it is on.

or·der·ly¹ /ˈɔrdɚli/ *adj.* **1** peaceful or behaving well: *Please leave the building **in an orderly fashion**.* **2** arranged or organized in a neat way: *an orderly desk*

orderly² *n.* (plural **orderlies**) [C] someone who does unskilled jobs in a hospital

ˈordinal ˌnumber *n.* [C] MATH one of the numbers such as first, second, third, etc. that show the order of things → CARDINAL NUMBER

or·di·nance /ˈɔrdn-əns/ *n.* [C] LAW a law of a city or town: *parking ordinances*

ˈOrdinance ˌPowers *n.* [plural] POLITICS the official powers that the American president has to make certain types of decisions. These powers are given to the president by Congress and are in the U.S. CONSTITUTION. → EXCLUSIVE POWERS, RESERVED POWERS

or·di·nar·i·ly /ˌɔrdnˈɛrəli/ *adv.* usually: *I don't ordinarily go to sleep so early.*

or·di·nar·y /ˈɔrdnˌɛri/ *adj.* **1** average or usual, and not different or special in any way: *All the candidates are trying to reach out to **ordinary people**.* | *Art should be part of **ordinary life**.* | *It was just an ordinary day.*

THESAURUS **normal, average, standard, conventional** → NORMAL¹

2 out of the ordinary very different from what is usual: *Did you notice anything out of the ordinary?*

or·di·na·tion /ˌɔrdnˈeɪʃən/ *n.* [C,U] the act or ceremony of making someone a religious leader → ORDAIN

ore /ɔr/ *n.* [C,U] EARTH SCIENCES rock or earth from which metal can be obtained

o·reg·a·no /əˈrɛgəˌnoʊ/ *n.* [U] a plant used in cooking, especially Italian cooking

organs

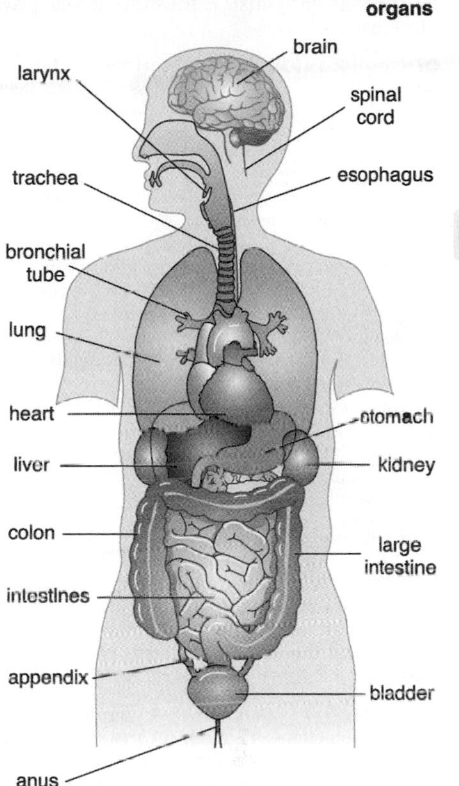

or·gan /ˈɔrgən/ *n.* [C] **1** a part of the body of an animal or plant that has a particular purpose: *an organ transplant* **2** a large musical instrument like a piano, with large pipes to make the sound, or an electric instrument that makes similar sounds [ORIGIN: 1200—1300 Old French *organe*, from Latin, from Greek *organon* "tool, instrument"]

or·ga·nelle /ˌɔrgəˈnɛl/ *n.* [C] BIOLOGY one of several structures in a cell that has a particular purpose, similar to the different purposes that organs have in the body. The NUCLEUS is an organelle.

or·gan·ic /ɔrˈgænɪk/ *adj.* **1** BIOLOGY living, or relating to living things, and containing CARBON in some form ANT **inorganic**: ***Organic matter** such as leaves, grass, and vegetable peelings can be used as compost.* | *organic chemistry* **2** using farming methods that do not use chemicals, or produced by these methods: *organic vegetables* —**organically** *adv.*: *organically grown vegetables*

orˌganic ˈchemistry *n.* [U] CHEMISTRY the study of compounds that contain CARBON. Usually, organic chemistry deals with substances that are related to life processes. → INORGANIC CHEMISTRY

or·ga·nism /ˈɔrgəˌnɪzəm/ *n.* [C] BIOLOGY a living thing: *a microscopic organism*

O

or·gan·ist /ˈɔrgənɪst/ *n.* [C] someone who plays the organ

or·ga·ni·za·tion /ˌɔrgənəˈzeɪʃən/ *n.* **1** [C] a group, such as a club or business, that has been formed for a particular purpose: *student organizations | a non-profit organization*

THESAURUS

institution – a large important organization such as a bank or university
institute – an organization that has a particular purpose, such as scientific or educational work
association – an organization for people who do the same kind of work or have the same interests
(political) party – an organization of people with the same political aims
club/society – an organization for people who share an interest
union – an organization formed by workers in order to protect their rights
agency – an organization, especially within a government, that does a specific job

2 [U] the act of planning and arranging things effectively: *Anne is responsible for the **organization of** the reception.* **3** [U] the way in which the different parts of a system are arranged and work together: *I still need to work on the **organization of** my essay.* —**organizational** *adj.*

or·ga·nize /ˈɔrgəˌnaɪz/ *v.* **1** [T] to plan or arrange something: *I agreed to help organize the company picnic. | Organize your ideas on paper before you write your essay.* **2** [I,T] to form a UNION (=an organization that protects workers' rights), or persuade people to join one

or·ga·nized /ˈɔrgəˌnaɪzd/ *adj.* **1** planned or arranged in an effective way (ANT) **disorganized**: *Her presentation was **well organized**.*

THESAURUS

efficient – working well, without wasting time or energy: *an energy efficient refrigerator | efficient workers*
well-run – organized efficiently: *a well-run hotel*
businesslike – sensible and practical in the way you do things: *a businesslike attitude*

2 an organized person is able to plan and arrange things in an effective way (ANT) **disorganized**: *Barbara's a very organized person. | I need to **get** more **organized**.* **3** an organized activity is arranged for and done by many people: *organized religion*

ˌorganized ˈcrime *n.* [U] illegal activities involving powerful well-organized groups of criminals → MAFIA

or·ga·niz·er /ˈɔrgəˌnaɪzɚ/ *n.* [C] someone who organizes an event or group of people: *The organizers had expected about 50,000 people to attend the event.*

or·gasm /ˈɔrˌgæzəm/ *n.* [C,U] the moment when you have the greatest sexual pleasure during sex

or·gy /ˈɔrdʒi/ *n.* (plural **orgies**) [C] a wild party with a lot of sexual activity

O·ri·ent /ˈɔriənt/ *n.* **the Orient** (old-fashioned) the eastern part of the world, especially China and Japan

o·ri·ent /ˈɔriˌɛnt/ (Ac) *v.* [T] **1** to make someone familiar with a place or situation: *It takes a while to **orient yourself** in a new city. | There are several organizations which exist to help orient new students.* **2** to find your position using a map or a COMPASS [ORIGIN: 1300—1400 Old French, Latin, present participle of *oriri* "to rise"]

O·ri·en·tal /ˌɔriˈɛntl◂/ *adj.* **1** relating to the eastern part of the world, especially China or Japan **2** (old-fashioned) a word for someone from Asia, now considered offensive → ASIAN

o·ri·en·ta·tion /ˌɔriənˈteɪʃən/ (Ac) *n.* **1** [C,U] the beliefs, aims, or interests that a person or group chooses to have: *their political orientation* **2** [U] training and preparation for a new job or activity: *It's orientation week for new students.* **3 sexual orientation** the fact of being HETEROSEXUAL or HOMOSEXUAL: *Discrimination on the grounds of sexual orientation is still far too widespread.* **4** [C] the direction in which something faces: *This chapter deals with the orientation of the Earth's magnetic field.*

o·ri·ent·ed /ˈɔriˌɛntɪd/ *adj.* giving attention to a particular type of person or thing: *She's very career-oriented. | We provide a service **oriented towards** the needs of business people.*

or·i·gin /ˈɔrədʒɪn, ˈɑr-/ *n.* [C,U] **1** when, where, or how something began: *a word **of** Latin **origin** | The theory explains **the origins of** the universe.*

THESAURUS

source – the thing, place, or person that you get something from: *Tourism is the country's main source of income. | a source of energy*
root – the most important reason or cause of something, especially a problem or something bad: *The root of the problem is money.*
etymology – the origin of a word, or the study of the origins of words in general: *What is the etymology of the word "sugar?"*
birthplace – the place where someone, especially someone famous, was born: *We visited Martin Luther King's birthplace in Atlanta.*

2 the country, race, or social class from which someone comes: *Nine percent of the city's population is **of** Hispanic **origin**.* [ORIGIN: 1500—1600 French *origine*, from Latin *origo*, from *oriri* "to rise"]

o·rig·i·nal[1] /əˈrɪdʒənl/ *adj.* **1** [only before noun] first or earliest: *Our original plan was to go to Florida. | The original version of the song is much better.*

THESAURUS **new, recent, modern, fresh, latest** → NEW

2 completely new and different: *Steve comes up*

with a lot of ***original ideas.*** | *Her writing is truly original.* **3** [only before noun] not copied, or not based on something else: *an original screenplay*

original² *n.* [C] a painting, document, etc. that is not a copy: *I'll keep a copy of the lease and you can have* ***the original.***

o·rig·i·nal·i·ty /əˌrɪdʒəˈnæləti/ *n.* [U] the quality of being completely new and different: *Marie's work* ***shows*** *a lot of* ***originality.***

o·rig·i·nal·ly /əˈrɪdʒənl-i/ *adv.* in the beginning: *I'm originally from Texas.* | *Originally, we hoped to be finished by June.*

o·rig·i·nate /əˈrɪdʒəˌneɪt/ *v.* [I] (formal) to start to develop in a particular place or from a particular situation: *The custom of having a Christmas tree* ***originated in*** *Germany.*

o·ri·ole /ˈɔriˌoʊl, ˈɔriəl/ *n.* [C] a wild bird that is black with a red and a yellow STRIPE on its wings

or·na·ment /ˈɔrnəmənt/ *n.* [C] an object that you use for decoration because it is beautiful rather than useful: *Christmas ornaments*

or·na·men·tal /ˌɔrnəˈmɛntl◂ / *adj.* designed to decorate something: *ornamental vases*

or·nate /ɔrˈneɪt/ *adj.* having a lot of decoration: *ornate furniture* [ORIGIN: 1500—1600 Latin, past participle of *ornare* "to decorate"] —**ornately** *adv.*

ornate

an ornate clock

or·ne·ry /ˈɔrnəri/ *adj.* (informal) behaving in an unreasonable and angry way

or·ni·thol·o·gy /ˌɔrnəˈθɑlədʒi/ *n.* [U] BIOLOGY the scientific study of birds [ORIGIN: 1600—1700 Modern Latin *ornithologia*, from Greek *ornis* "bird"] —**ornithologist** *n.* [C]

or·phan¹ /ˈɔrfən/ *n.* [C] a child whose parents are dead

orphan² *v.* **be orphaned** to become an orphan

or·phan·age /ˈɔrfənɪdʒ/ *n.* [C] a place where orphans live

or·tho·don·tist /ˌɔrθəˈdɑntɪst/ *n.* [C] a DENTIST who makes teeth straight when they have not been growing correctly [ORIGIN: 1900—2000 *ortho-* (from Greek *orthos* "straight, correct") + Greek *odous* "tooth"] —**orthodontics** *n.* [U] —**orthodontic** *adj.*

or·tho·dox /ˈɔrθəˌdɑks/ *adj.* **1** officially accepted, or considered to be normal by most people: *orthodox methods of treating disease*

THESAURUS **normal, ordinary, standard, conventional** → NORMAL¹

2 following the traditional beliefs of a religion: *an orthodox Jew* [ORIGIN: 1500—1600 French *orthodoxe*, from Late Latin, from Late Greek *orthodoxos*, from Greek *ortho-* (from *orthos* "straight, correct") + *doxa* "opinion"]

THESAURUS **religious, devout, pious, god-fearing, practicing** → RELIGIOUS

—**orthodoxy** *n.* [C,U]

ˌOrthodox ˈChurch *n.* **the Orthodox Church** one of the Christian churches in eastern Europe and parts of Asia

O

or·thog·o·nal draw·ing /ɔrˌθɑgənl ˈdrɔ-ɪŋ/ *also* **orˌthogonal proˈjection, ˌorthographic proˈjection** *n.* [C] MATH a drawing that shows what a THREE-DIMENSIONAL object looks like when you look at it directly from different directions (usually the top, the front, and one side), or a drawing that shows a collection of views of the different sides

or·thog·ra·phy /ɔrˈθɑgrəfi/ *n.* [U] ENG. LANG. ARTS the system for spelling words in a language, or the way in which a word is spelled —**orthographic** /ˌɔrθəˈgræfɪk◂ / *adj.*

or·tho·pe·dics /ˌɔrθəˈpidɪks/ *n.* [U] the area of medicine that treats problems that affect people's bones —**orthopedic** *adj.*

Os·car /ˈɑskə/ *n.* [C] one of the prizes given each year to the best movies, actors, etc. in the movie industry: *Who won the* ***Oscar for*** *best actor?*

os·cil·late /ˈɑsəˌleɪt/ *v.* [I] **1** (formal) to keep changing between two extreme amounts or limits SYN **fluctuate**: *For several days, the world's stock markets oscillated wildly.* **2** (formal) to keep moving regularly from side to side, between two limits: *an oscillating fan* **3** PHYSICS if an electric current, light wave, or sound wave oscillates, it changes frequently in size, strength, direction, etc. —**oscillation** /ˌɑsəˈleɪʃən/ *n.* [C,U] —**oscillatory** /ˈɑsələˌtɔri/ *adj.*

os·mo·sis /ɑzˈmoʊsɪs, ɑs-/ *n.* [U] BIOLOGY a gradual process in which the liquid contained in one substance passes through a MEMBRANE into a substance that contains less liquid. The process continues until the amount of liquid in each substance is equal. —**osmotic** /ɑzˈmɑtɪk/ *adj.*

os·ten·si·ble /ɑˈstɛnsəbəl/ *adj.* [only before noun] (written) the ostensible purpose or reason for something is the one which is openly stated, but which is probably not the true reason or purpose —**ostensibly** *adv.*

os·ten·ta·tious /ˌɑstənˈteɪʃəs/ *adj.* (disapproving) designed or done in order to be impressive to other people: *a big ostentatious engagement ring* —**ostentation** /ˌɑstənˈteɪʃən/ *n.* [U]

os·tra·cism /ˈɑstrəˌsɪzəm/ *n.* [U] **1** the action or result of ostracizing someone from a group: *In those days, a pregnant woman who was unmarried faced ostracism.* **2** HISTORY the process in ancient Greece by which citizens could vote to send another citizen away from their society for a limited period of time → BANISHMENT

os·tra·cize /ˈɑstrəˌsaɪz/ *v.* [T] to behave in a

very unfriendly way toward someone, and not allow him/her to be part of a group: *He was ostracized by the other students.* [ORIGIN: 1800—1900 Greek *ostrakizein* "to send away by voting with broken pieces of pot," from *ostrakon* "broken piece of pot"]

os·trich /'ɑstrɪtʃ, 'ɔs-/ *n.* [C] a very large African bird with long legs, that runs very quickly but cannot fly

O

oth·er¹ /'ʌðɚ/ *determiner, adj.* **1** used in order to mean one or more of the rest of a group of people or things, when you have already mentioned one person or thing: *I could do it, but none of* ***the other*** *boys in the class could.* | *Here's one sock, but where's* ***the other one****?* **2** used in order to mean someone or something that is different from, or exists in addition to, the person or thing you have already mentioned: *He shares an apartment with three other guys.* | *Sue went to the mall with some of her other friends.* | *Does anyone have* ***any other*** *questions?* | *Let's discuss this* ***some other*** *time.* | *A taxi stopped on* ***the other side*** *of the road.* **3 the other day/morning etc.** (spoken) recently: *I talked to Ted the other day.* **4 other than** except: *I know she has brown hair, but other than that I don't remember much about her.* **5 every other day/week etc.** on one of every two days, weeks, etc.: *The class meets every other Thursday.* **6 in other words** used in order to express an idea or opinion in a way that is easier to understand: *There are TV sets in 68.5 million homes; in other words, 97 percent of the population watches TV.* → EACH OTHER, **on the one hand ... on the other hand** *at* HAND¹

> **GRAMMAR**
> Do not use **other** after "an." Use **another**: *He lived in another part of the city.*

other² *pron.* **1** one or more people or things that form the rest that you are talking about: *We ate one pizza and froze the other.* | *It looks like* ***all the others*** *have left.* | *Some MP3 players are better than others.* **2 someone/something etc. or other** used when you cannot be certain or definite about what you are saying: *We'll get the money somehow or other.*

oth·er·wise /'ʌðɚˌwaɪz/ *adv.* **1** a word meaning "if not," used when there will be a bad result if something does not happen: *You'd better go now, otherwise you'll be late.*

> **THESAURUS** **if, as long as/provided that, on condition that, unless, in case, whether or not** → IF¹

2 except for what has just been mentioned: *The sleeves are too long, but otherwise the dress fits.* **3** in a different way: *Adam was ready to buy the house, but his wife decided otherwise.*

ot·ter /'ɑt̬ɚ/ *n.* [C] a small animal that can swim, has brown fur, and eats fish

ouch /aʊtʃ/ *interjection* said when you feel sudden pain: *Ouch! That hurt!*

ought to /'ɔt̬ə; *strong* 'ɔtu/ *modal verb* **1** used to say that someone should do something: *We ought to give Jane a call.* | *You ought to be ashamed of yourself.* **2** used in order to say that you expect something to happen or be true: *The weather ought to be nice there in October.*

ounce /aʊns/ *n.* [C] **1** (*written abbreviation* **oz**) a unit for measuring weight, equal to 1/16 of a pound or 28.35 grams → FLUID OUNCE **2 an ounce of truth/sense etc.** a small amount of a particular quality: *Don't you have even an ounce of sense?*

our /ɑr; *strong* aʊɚ/ *possessive adj.* belonging or relating to the person who is speaking and one or more other people: *We don't have curtains on our windows.* | *Our daughter is in college.*

ours /aʊɚz, ɑrz/ *pron.* the thing or things belonging or relating to the person who is speaking and one or more other people: *"Whose car is that?" "It's ours."* | *They have their tickets, but ours haven't come yet.*

our·selves /aʊɚ'sɛlvz, ɑr-/ *pron.* **1** the REFLEXIVE form of "we": *It was strange seeing ourselves on television.* **2** the strong form of "we," used in order to emphasize the subject or object of a sentence: *We started this business ourselves.* **3 (all) by ourselves a)** without help: *Amy and I made supper all by ourselves.* **b)** alone: *Dad left us by ourselves for an hour.* **4 to ourselves** not having to share with other people: *We'll have the house to ourselves next week.*

oust /aʊst/ *v.* [T] (written) to force someone out of a position of power: *Several other senators attempted to* ***oust*** *him* ***from*** *the chairmanship.*

out¹ /aʊt/ *adv., adj.* **1** away from the inside of a place or container (ANT) **in**: *Close the door on your way out.* | *The keys must have fallen* ***out of*** *my pocket.* **2** away from the place where you usually are, such as home or work (ANT) **in**: *Did anyone call while I was out?* | *He* ***asked*** *me* ***out*** *for dinner tonight* (=invited me to dinner). | *We* ***eat out*** (=eat in a restaurant) *all the time.*

> **USAGE**
> **out** – away from the building where you live or work: *Tom's out. He should be back soon.*
> **outside** – not inside a room or building but near it: *I'll wait for you outside.*
> **outdoors** – not inside a building: *We spent most of the summer outdoors.*
> **outdoor** (without an -s) – used to describe things that are outside, or that happen outside: *an outdoor swimming pool* | *outdoor sports*

3 outside: *Why don't you go out and play?* **4** in or to a place that is far away or difficult to get to: *a little hotel out in the country* | *He's moved out to Arizona.* **5** completely or carefully: *Clean out the cupboard before you put the dishes in.* | *I'm worn out* (=very tired). **6** if power, electricity, etc. is out, it is not working correctly, or not on: *The electricity was out for an hour last night.* | *The lights are out – I don't think anyone's home.* **7** not having power any more: *The only way to lower taxes is to vote the*

Democrats out! | *He may face prosecution when he is* ***out of office***. **8** used in order to say that something has appeared: *It looks like the sun is finally going to come out.* **9 out loud** done in a way so that people can hear your voice: *parents reading out loud to their kids* **10** available to be bought: *Morrison has a new book out this month.* **11** (spoken) not possible: *"Where should we go?" "Well, skiing's out because it costs too much."* **12 be out for sth/be out to do sth** (informal) to intend to do or get something: *Don't listen to Danny – he's just out to get attention.* **13** (informal) **a)** asleep: *Billy was* ***out like a light*** *by 6:00.* **b)** not conscious: *You must have hit him pretty hard – he's* ***out cold***. **14** a player in a game who is out is no longer allowed to play, or has lost one of his/her chances to get a point **15** clothes or styles that are out are no longer fashionable **16** someone who is out has told people that s/he is HOMOSEXUAL **17** if the TIDE is out, the ocean is at its lowest level

out² *prep.* **1** from inside something, or through something: *He was looking out the window at the beach.* **2 out of a)** from a particular place or time: *I got a Coke out of the refrigerator.* | *A nail was sticking out of the wall.* | *The tango is a dance that comes out of Buenos Aires.* **b)** from a larger group of the same kind: *Three out of four dentists recommend the toothpaste.* | *Kathy was chosen out of all the kids in her class.* **c)** having none of something that you had before: *We're almost out of gas.* | *The car was completely out of control.* **d)** used in order to show what something is made from: *a box made out of wood* **3 out of it** (informal) not able to think clearly because you are very tired, drunk, etc.: *I'm really out of it today.* **4 out of the way** finished: *Good. Now that's out of the way, we can start working.*

out³ *n.* **1** [C] an act of making a player in baseball lose the chance to get a RUN **2 an out** (informal) an excuse for not doing something: *I'm busy Sunday, so that gives me an out.*

out⁴ *v.* [T] to publicly say that someone is HOMOSEXUAL when that person wants it to be a secret

out·age /ˈaʊt̬ɪdʒ/ *n.* [C] a period of time when a service, especially the electricity supply, is not provided: *a* ***power outage***

ˌout-and-ˈout *adj.* [only before noun] having all the qualities of a particular type of person or thing (SYN) **complete**: *an out-and-out lie*

out·back /ˈaʊt˺bæk/ *n.* **the outback** the Australian COUNTRYSIDE far away from cities, where few people live

out·bid /aʊt˺ˈbɪd/ *v.* (past tense and past participle **outbid**, present participle **outbidding**) [T] to offer more money than someone else for something that you want to buy

out·bound /ˈaʊt˺baʊnd/ *adj.* moving away from you or away from a city, country, etc.: *outbound flights*

out·break /ˈaʊt˺breɪk/ *n.* [C] the start or sudden appearance of something bad such as a war or disease: *an* ***outbreak of*** *malaria*

out·burst /ˈaʊt˺bɚst/ *n.* [C] a sudden powerful expression of strong emotion: *an angry outburst*

out·cast /ˈaʊt˺kæst/ *n.* [C] someone who is not accepted by other people: *a social outcast*

out·class /aʊt˺ˈklæs/ *v.* [T] to be much better than someone or something else

out·come /ˈaʊt˺kʌm/ (Ac) *n.* [singular] the final result of a meeting, process, etc.: *We were eager to know what the* ***outcome of*** *the experiment would be.* | *Several factors influenced the outcome of the war.*

O

> THESAURUS **result, consequences, upshot**
> → RESULT¹

out·cry /ˈaʊt˺kraɪ/ *n.* [singular, U] an angry protest by a lot of people: *There was a* ***public outcry against*** *the war.*

out·dat·ed /ˌaʊtˈdeɪt̬ɪd◂/ *adj.* no longer useful or modern: *The textbooks were outdated and needed to be replaced.*

> THESAURUS **old-fashioned, outmoded, dated, antiquated, obsolete** → OLD-FASHIONED

out·dis·tance /aʊtˈdɪstəns/ *v* [T] to go faster or farther than someone else in a race

out·do /aʊtˈdu/ *v.* (past tense **outdid** /-ˈdɪd/, past participle **outdone** /-ˈdʌn/, third person singular **outdoes** /-ˈdʌz/) [T] to be better or more successful than someone else: *The skaters were trying to outdo each other.* | *You've really* ***outdone yourself*** (=done something extremely well) *this time!*

out·door /ˈaʊtdɔr/ *adj.* [only before noun] happening, existing, or used outside and not in a building (ANT) **indoor**: *outdoor activities* | *an outdoor swimming pool*

out·doors /aʊtˈdɔrz/ *adv.* outside, not inside a building (ANT) **indoors**: *I prefer working outdoors.*

out·door·sy /aʊtˈdɔrzi/ *adj.* (informal) someone who is outdoorsy enjoys outdoor activities, such as HIKING and camping

out·er /ˈaʊt̬ɚ/ *adj.* [only before noun] **1** on the outside of something (ANT) **inner**: *Peel off the outer leaves of lettuce.* **2** far from the middle of something (ANT) **inner**: *the outer suburbs*

out·er·most /ˈaʊt̬ɚˌmoʊst/ *adj.* [only before noun] farthest from the middle (ANT) **innermost**: *the outermost planets*

ˌouter ˈspace *n.* [U] the space outside the Earth's air, where the stars and PLANETS are

out·field /ˈaʊtfild/ *n.* [singular] the part of a baseball field that is farthest from the player who is batting (BAT) —**outfielder** *n.* [C]

out·fit¹ /ˈaʊtˌfɪt/ *n.* [C] **1** a set of clothes worn together: *She bought a new outfit for the party.* **2** (informal) a group of people who work together as an organization: *a small advertising outfit in San Diego*

outfit² *v.* (**outfitted**, **outfitting**) [T] to provide someone or something with the clothes or equipment s/he needs for a special purpose

out·fit·ter /ˈaʊtˌfɪt̬ɚ/ *n.* [C] a store that sells equipment for outdoor activities such as camping

out·go·ing /ˈaʊt˺ˌgoʊɪŋ/ *adj.* **1** wanting to meet and talk to new people, or showing this quality: *Sally is really outgoing and easy to talk to.* | *an outgoing personality*

THESAURUS **sociable, extroverted, gregarious** → SOCIABLE

2 the outgoing president/CEO etc. someone who is finishing a job as president, etc. **3** [only before noun] going out from or leaving a place (ANT) **incoming**: *outgoing phone calls*

out·grow /aʊt˺ˈgroʊ/ *v.* (past tense **outgrew** /-ˈgru/, past participle **outgrown** /-ˈgroʊn/) [T] **1** to grow too big for something: *Kara's already outgrown her shoes.* **2** to no longer enjoy something that you used to enjoy

out·growth /ˈaʊt˺groʊθ/ *n.* [C] a natural result of something: *Crime is often an* ***outgrowth of*** *poverty.*

out·house /ˈaʊthaʊs/ *n.* [C] a small building over a hole in the ground, that is used as a toilet

out·ing /ˈaʊt̬ɪŋ/ *n.* [C] a short enjoyable trip for a group of people: *a Sunday* ***outing to*** *the park*

out·land·ish /aʊtˈlændɪʃ/ *adj.* strange and unusual: *outlandish clothes*

out·last /aʊtˈlæst/ *v.* [T] to continue to exist or do something longer than someone else: *The whole point of the game is to outlast your opponent.*

out·law¹ /ˈaʊt˺lɔ/ *v.* [T] to say officially that something is illegal: *The agreement outlaws chemical weapons.*

outlaw² *n.* [C] (old-fashioned) a criminal who is hiding from the police

out·lay /ˈaʊt˺leɪ/ *n.* (plural **outlays**) [C,U] an amount of money that is spent for a particular purpose: *There will be an initial outlay of $2,500 for tools and equipment.*

out·let /ˈaʊt˺lɛt, -lɪt/ *n.* [C] **1** a place on a wall where you can connect electrical equipment to the electricity supply **2** a store that sells things for less than the usual price: *an outlet mall* **3** a way of expressing or getting rid of strong feelings: *I use judo as* ***an outlet for*** *stress.* **4** a way out through which something such as a liquid or gas can flow

out·line¹ /ˈaʊt˺laɪn/ *n.* **1** [C,U] the main ideas or facts about something, without all the details: *Here is an* ***outline of*** *the company's plan.* **2** [C] a plan for a piece of writing in which each new idea is separately written down: *The teacher wants an* ***outline of*** *our essays by Friday.* **3** [C,U] a line around the edge of something that shows its shape

outline² *v.* [T] **1** to describe the main ideas or facts about something, but not all the details: *The president outlined his peace plan for the Middle East.* **2** to draw or put a line around the edge of something to show its shape: *We could see the huge ferris wheel* ***outlined in*** *colored lights.*

out·live /aʊt˺ˈlɪv/ *v.* [T] to live longer than someone else: *She outlived her husband by ten years.*

out·look /ˈaʊt˺lʊk/ *n.* **1** [C] your general attitude to life and the world: *Nels has a very* ***positive outlook on*** *life.* **2** [singular] what is expected to happen in the future: *The* ***outlook for*** *the health care professions is good.*

out·ly·ing /ˈaʊt˺ˌlaɪ-ɪŋ/ *adj.* [only before noun] far from cities, people, etc.: *Housing prices are lower in some* ***outlying areas.***

out·ma·neu·ver /ˌaʊt˺məˈnuvɚ/ *v.* [T] to gain an advantage over someone by using skillful movements or plans

out·mod·ed /aʊt˺ˈmoʊdɪd/ *adj.* OUTDATED

THESAURUS **old-fashioned, outdated, dated, antiquated, obsolete** → OLD-FASHIONED

out·num·ber /aʊt˺ˈnʌmbɚ/ *v.* [T] to be more in number than another group: *Men outnumber women in Congress.*

ˌout of ˈbounds *adj.* **1** not inside the official playing area in a sports game: *The referee said the ball was out of bounds.* **2** not allowed or acceptable: *Some topics, such as sex, are out of bounds for discussion.* **—out of bounds** *adv.*: *The ball was knocked out of bounds.*

ˌout-of-ˈdate *adj.* OUTDATED → OLD-FASHIONED

ˌout-of-ˈstate *adj., adv.* from, to, or in another state: *out-of-state license plates*

ˌout-of-the-ˈway *adj.* far from cities and people, and often difficult to find: *They met in an out-of-the-way hotel.*

out·pa·tient /ˈaʊt˺ˌpeɪʃənt/ *n.* [C] someone who goes to the hospital for treatment, but does not stay there → INPATIENT

out·per·form /ˌaʊt˺pɚˈfɔrm/ *v.* [T] to do something better than other things or people

out·place·ment /ˈaʊt˺ˌpleɪsmənt/ *n.* [U] a service that a company provides to help its workers find other jobs when it cannot continue to employ them

out·post /ˈaʊt˺poʊst/ *n.* [C] a small town or group of buildings in a place that is far away from big cities

out·pour·ing /ˈaʊt˺ˌpɔrɪŋ/ *n.* [C] a large amount of something that is produced suddenly, such as strong emotions, ideas, or help: *an* ***outpouring of*** *grief*

out·put /ˈaʊt˺pʊt/ (Ac) *n.* [C,U] **1** ECONOMICS the amount of work, goods, etc. produced by someone or something (SYN) **production**: *Economic output is down 10% this year.* | *In the manufacturing sector, smaller firms account for a quarter of the total* output. **2** IT the results produced by a computer or other process: *Output from and input to the serial port can be controlled by either software or hardware.*

out·rage¹ /ˈaʊt˺reɪdʒ/ *n.* [C,U] a feeling of great anger or shock, or something that causes this: *a deep sense of **moral outrage** | The prices they charge are an outrage!*

outrage² *v.* [T] to make someone feel very angry or shocked: *I was outraged by his sexist comments.* —**outraged** *adj.*

out·ra·geous /aʊt˺ˈreɪdʒəs/ *adj.* very shocking or unreasonable: *outrageous lies* —**outrageously** *adv.*: *outrageously expensive clothes*

out·reach /ˈaʊt˺ritʃ/ *n.* [U] the practice of trying to help people with particular problems, especially through an organization: *the church's community outreach program*

out·right¹ /ˈaʊt˺raɪt/ *adj.* [only before noun] **1** complete and total: *an outright refusal* **2** clear and direct: *an outright lie*

out·right² /aʊt˺ˈraɪt, ˈaʊt˺raɪt/ *adv.* **1** clearly and directly: *Nadine laughed outright at the suggestion.* **2 buy/own sth outright** to own something such as a house completely because you have paid the full price with your own money

out·run /aʊt˺ˈrʌn/ *v.* (past tense **outran** /-ˈræn/, past participle **outrun**, present participle **outrunning**) [T] **1** to run faster or farther than someone **2** to develop more quickly than something else: *The company's spending was outrunning its income*

out·set /ˈaʊtsɛt/ *n.* **at/from the outset** at or from the beginning of an event or process: *The rules were agreed **at the outset of** the game.*

out·shine /aʊtˈʃaɪn/ *v.* (past tense and past participle **outshone** /-ˈʃoʊn/) [T] to be much better at something than someone else

out·side¹ /ˌaʊtˈsaɪd, ˈaʊtsaɪd/ *adv., prep also* **outside of** *prep.* **1** not inside a building or room, but near it (ANT) **inside**: *Mom, can I **go outside** and play? | He left an envelope outside my door.* **2** beyond the limits of a city, country, etc.: *We live **just outside** Pittsburgh.* **3** beyond the limits of a situation, activity, etc.: *Teachers can't control what students do outside school. | I'm afraid that subject is outside the scope of this discussion.*

outside² *adj.* [only before noun] **1** not inside a building: *We turned off the outside lights.* **2** involving people who do not belong to the same group or organization as you: *We may need some **outside help**.* **3 the outside world** the rest of the world: *Since the attack, the city has been cut off from the outside world.* **4 outside interests** things that you do or are interested in that are not related to your work

outside³ *n.* **1 the outside** the outer part or surface of something (ANT) **inside**: *They painted **the outside of** the building pink. | **From the outside**, the house looked very nice.* **2 on the outside** used in order to describe the way someone or something appears to be: *Their marriage seemed so perfect on the outside.*

out·sid·er /aʊtˈsaɪdɚ/ *n.* [C] someone who does not belong to a particular group, organization, etc.: *Corran is a Washington outsider who has never been in office before.*

out·skirts /ˈaʊtskɚts/ *n.* [plural] the parts of a city or town that are farthest from the center: *He lived **on the outskirts of** town.*

O

out·smart /aʊtˈsmɑrt/ *v.* [T] to gain an advantage over someone using tricks or your intelligence

out·sourc·ing /ˈaʊtˌsɔrsɪŋ/ *n.* [U] ECONOMICS the practice of using workers from outside a company, or of buying supplies, parts, etc. from another company instead of producing them yourself —**outsource** *v.* [T]

out·spo·ken /aʊtˈspoʊkən/ *adj.* expressing your opinions honestly and directly, even if they shock or offend other people: *an outspoken critic of the program* —**outspokenness** *n.* [U]

out·stand·ing /aʊtˈstændɪŋ/ *adj.* **1** better than anyone or anything else (SYN) **excellent**: *an outstanding performance*

> THESAURUS **good, great, excellent, wonderful, fantastic, exceptional, superb, first-class, ace** → GOOD¹

2 not yet done, paid, or solved: *an outstanding debt*

out·stretched /ˌaʊtˈstrɛtʃt◂/ *adj* reaching out to full length: *I took hold of his **outstretched arm/hand**.*

out·strip /aʊtˈstrɪp/ *v.* (past tense and past participle **outstripped**, present participle **outstripping**) [T] to be larger, greater, or better than someone or something else: *The gains will outstrip the losses.*

out·ward¹ /ˈaʊt˺wɚd/ *adj.* **1** relating to how people, things, etc. seem to be rather than how they are (ANT) **inward**: *Amy answered with a look of outward calm.* **2** going away from a place, or toward the outside: *The outward flight was bumpy.*

outward² *also* **outwards** *adv.* toward the outside (ANT) **inward**: *The door opens outward.*

out·ward·ly /ˈaʊt˺wɚdli/ *adv.* according to how people, things, etc. seem to be rather than how they are inside (ANT) **inwardly**: *Outwardly, he seems to be very happy.*

out·weigh /aʊt˺ˈweɪ/ *v.* [T] to be more important or valuable than something else: *The advantages **far outweigh** the disadvantages.*

out·wit /aʊt˺ˈwɪt/ *v.* (past tense and past participle **outwitted**, present participle **outwitting**) [T] OUTSMART

ova *n.* the plural of OVUM

o·val /ˈoʊvəl/ *n.* [C] a shape that is like a circle, but longer than it is wide → *see picture at* SHAPE¹ [ORIGIN: 1500—1600 Medieval Latin *ovalis*, from Latin *ovum* "egg"] —**oval** *adj.*

THESAURUS shape, square, circle, semicircle, triangle, rectangle, cylinder → SHAPE[1]

ˌOval ˈOffice *n.* **the Oval Office** the office of the U.S. President, in the White House in Washington, D.C.

o·var·i·an /oʊˈvɛriən/ *adj.* [only before noun] BIOLOGY relating to the ovaries: *ovarian cancer*

O

o·va·ry /ˈoʊvəri/ *n.* (plural **ovaries**) [C] **1** BIOLOGY the part of a female that produces eggs **2** BIOLOGY the part of a flower that produces seeds → *see picture at* FLOWER[1]

o·va·tion /oʊˈveɪʃən/ *n.* (formal) [C] if people give someone an ovation, they CLAP their hands to show approval: *The performance received a* ***standing ovation*** (=people stood up and clapped their hands).

ov·en /ˈʌvən/ *n.* [C] a piece of equipment that food is cooked inside, shaped like a metal box with a door on it: *Preheat the oven to 350 degrees.* [ORIGIN: Old English *ofen*]

o·ver[1] /ˈoʊvɚ/ *prep.* **1** above or higher than something, without touching it (ANT) **under**: *I leaned over the desk.* | *The sign over the door said "No Exit."* | *The ball went* ***way over*** (=a long way above) *my head.* **2** moving across the top of something, or from one side of it to the other: *We walked over the hill.* | *One of the men jumped over the counter and grabbed the money.* **3** on something or someone so that he, she, or it is covered (ANT) **under**: *I put the blanket over the baby.* **4** more than a particular amount, number, or age: *Mike makes over $100,000 a year.* | *The game is designed for children over seven years old.* **5** during: *Where did you go over summer vacation?* **6** down from the edge of something: *Hang the towel over the back of the chair.* **7 be/get over sth** to feel better after being sick or upset: *He's mad, but he'll get over it.* **8** about or concerning something: *They had an argument over who would take the car.* **9** using the telephone or a radio: *The salesman explained it to me over the phone.* → **all over** at ALL[2]

over[2] *adv.* **1** down from an upright position: *Kate fell over and hurt her ankle.* | *The wind blew the table over.* **2** used in order to show where someone or something is: *I'm over here!* | *There's a mailbox* ***over on*** *the corner.* **3** to or in a particular place: *Pat came over to our place last night.* | *The weather's awful. Why don't you* ***stay over*** (=spend the night at my house)? **4** above: *You can't hear anything when the planes fly over.* **5** again: *I got mixed up and had to* ***start over.*** | *If you make a mistake in the recording, we can always* ***do it over.*** | *They just keep playing the same songs* ***over and over again*** (=repeatedly). **6 think/read/talk sth over** to think, read, or talk about something carefully or thoroughly before deciding what to do: *I'll need to read the contract over before I sign it.* **7** so that another side is showing: ***Turn*** *your papers* ***over*** *and begin.* | *He rolled over and went to sleep.* **8** from one person or group to another: *The land was* ***handed over*** (=given) *to the government.* **9** more or higher than a particular amount, number, or age: *"Did you guess the right number?" "No, I was* ***over by*** *two."* (=the number I guessed was two higher) | *The game is best for children ages six* ***and over.***

over[3] *adj.* **1** finished: *The game's over – Dallas won.*

THESAURUS done, finished, complete, through → DONE[2]

2 get sth over with (informal) to do something that you do not want to do, but that is necessary, so that you do not have to worry about it anymore: *Well, call her and get it over with.*

o·ver·all[1] /ˈoʊvɚˌɔl/ (Ac) *adj.* including everything: *The overall cost of the trip is $500.* | *The overall level of unemployment is approximately 12% of the population.*

o·ver·all[2] /ˌoʊvɚˈɔl/ (Ac) *adv.* **1** generally: *Overall, the situation looks good.* | *Overall, females performed better than males in tests.* **2** including everything: *Inflation is growing at 3% a year overall.* | *Although there are now women in positions of power, their numbers overall are still few.*

o·ver·alls /ˈoʊvɚˌɔlz/ *n.* [plural] heavy cotton pants with a piece that covers your chest, held up by two bands that go over your shoulders → *see picture at* CLOTHES

o·ver·bear·ing /ˌoʊvɚˈbɛrɪŋ/ *adj.* (disapproving) always trying to control other people without considering their feelings or needs (SYN) **domineering**

o·ver·board /ˈoʊvɚˌbɔrd/ *adv.* **1** over the side of a ship into the water: *He* ***fell overboard*** *in the storm.* **2 go overboard** to do or say something that is too extreme for a particular situation, for example by being too emotional or expensive: *She managed to find a nice present, without going overboard.*

o·ver·bur·dened /ˌoʊvɚˈbɚdnd/ *adj.* carrying or doing too much: *Some of the managers are overburdened with work.* | *the overburdened court system*

o·ver·cast /ˈoʊvɚˌkæst/ *adj.* dark because of clouds: *a gray overcast sky*

o·ver·charge /ˌoʊvɚˈtʃɑrdʒ/ *v.* [I,T] to charge someone too much money for something (ANT) **undercharge**

o·ver·coat /ˈoʊvɚˌkoʊt/ *n.* [C] a long thick warm coat

o·ver·come /ˌoʊvɚˈkʌm/ *v.* (past tense **overcame** /-ˈkeɪm/, past participle **overcome**) **1** [T] to succeed in controlling a feeling or problem: *I'm trying to overcome my fear of flying.* **2** [T] to make someone very emotional, sick, or weak: *She was* ***overcome by*** *smoke.* | *Charles was* ***overcome with*** *grief.* **3** [I,T] to fight and win against someone or something: *Union troops finally overcame rebel forces in the south.*

THESAURUS beat, defeat, vanquish, conquer → BEAT[1]

o·ver·com·pen·sate /ˌoʊvɚˈkɑmpənˌseɪt/ v. [I] to try to correct a weakness or mistake by doing too much of the opposite thing: *She overcompensates for her shyness by talking too much.* —**overcompensation** /ˌoʊvɚˌkɑmpənˈseɪʃən/ n. [U]

o·ver·crowd·ed /ˌoʊvɚˈkraʊdɪd◂ / adj. filled with too many people or things: *an overcrowded bus*

o·ver·do /ˌoʊvɚˈdu/ v. (past tense **overdid** /-ˈdɪd/, past participle **overdone** /-ˈdʌn/, third person singular **overdoes** /-ˈdʌz/) [T] to do or use too much of something: *When exercising, you have to be careful not to* ***overdo it****.*

o·ver·done /ˌoʊvɚˈdʌn/ adj. cooked too much: *an overdone steak*

o·ver·dose /ˈoʊvɚˌdoʊs/ n. [C] too much of a drug taken at one time: *He died from a heroin overdose.* —**overdose** v. [I]

o·ver·drawn /ˌoʊvɚˈdrɔn/ adj. having spent more money than you have in the bank, so you owe the bank money: *If you are overdrawn, there's a $50 fee to pay.* → ACCOUNT[1]

o·ver·due /ˌoʊvɚˈdu◂ / adj. **1** not done or happening when expected SYN **late**: *an overdue library book*

THESAURUS late, tardy, belated → LATE[1]

2 something that is overdue should have happened or been done a long time ago: *Salary increases are* ***long overdue****.*

o·ver·eat /ˌoʊvɚˈit/ v. (past tense **overate** /-ˈeɪt/, past participle **overeaten** /-ˈitˀn/) [I] to eat too much, or more than is healthy

o·ver·es·ti·mate /ˌoʊvɚˈɛstəˌmeɪt/ Ac v. [I,T] to think that someone or something is larger, more expensive, or more important than he, she, or it really is: *Rosa had overestimated the strength of her opponent.* | *The importance of education* ***cannot be overestimated*** (=it is very important). —**overestimate** /ˌoʊvɚˈɛstəmɪt/ n. [C]: *The figure of 30% is clearly an overestimate.*

o·ver·ex·tend /ˌoʊvɚɪkˈstɛnd/ v. [T] to try to do too much or use too much of something, causing problems: *Even with extra people working, they're* ***overextending themselves****.* —**overextended** adj.

o·ver·flow[1] /ˌoʊvɚˈfloʊ/ v. [I,T] **1** if a liquid or river overflows, it goes over the edges of the container or place where it is: *The sink was* ***overflowing with*** *water.* **2** if people overflow a place, or if a place overflows with people, there are too many people to fit into it

o·ver·flow[2] /ˈoʊvɚˌfloʊ/ n. [C,U] the people, water, etc. that cannot be contained in a place because it is already full: *The* ***overflow of*** *people from the concert was standing outside in the street.*

o·ver·graz·ing /ˌoʊvɚˈgreɪzɪŋ/ n. [U] a situation in which animals are allowed to eat too much of the grass in an area, with the result that the land becomes damaged

o·ver·grown /ˌoʊvɚˈgroʊn◂ / adj. covered with plants that have grown without being controlled: *Their yard was* ***overgrown with*** *weeds.*

o·ver·hand /ˈoʊvɚˌhænd/ adj., adv. thrown with your arm above the level of your shoulder ANT **underhand**: *an overhand pitch*

o·ver·hang /ˌoʊvɚˈhæŋ/ v. (past tense and past participle **overhung** /-ˈhʌŋ/) [I,T] to hang over something or stick out above it: *Tree branches overhung the path.*

o·ver·haul /ˌoʊvɚˈhɔl, ˈoʊvɚˌhɔl/ v. [T] to repair or change all the parts of a machine, system, etc. that need it —**overhaul** /ˈoʊvɚˌhɔl/ n. [C]: *The truck needs a complete overhaul.*

o·ver·head[1] /ˌoʊvɚˈhɛd◂ / adj., adv. above your head: *A plane flew overhead.* | *We put our bags in the overhead compartment.*

o·ver·head[2] /ˈoʊvɚˌhɛd/ n. [U] ECONOMICS money that you spend for rent, etc. to keep a business operating: *He's trying to lower our overhead.*

o·ver·hear /ˌoʊvɚˈhɪr/ v. (past tense and past participle **overheard** /-ˈhɚd/) [T] to hear by accident what other people are saying when they do not know that you are listening → EAVESDROP: *I overheard some people saying that the food was bad.*

o·ver·joyed /ˌoʊvɚˈdʒɔɪd/ adj. extremely happy because something good has happened: *We were* ***overjoyed to hear*** *that they are getting married.*

THESAURUS happy, glad, pleased, delighted, thrilled, ecstatic, jubilant, elated → HAPPY

o·ver·kill /ˈoʊvɚˌkɪl/ n. [U] (informal) more of something than is necessary or desirable: *If your speech were any longer, it would be overkill.*

o·ver·land /ˈoʊvɚˌlænd/ adj., adv. across land, not by sea or air: *overland travel*

o·ver·lap /ˌoʊvɚˈlæp/ Ac v. (**overlapped**, **overlapping**) [I,T] **1** if two or more things overlap, part of one thing covers part of another thing: *a pattern of overlapping circles* **2** if two subjects, activities, ideas, etc. overlap, they share some but not all of the same parts or qualities: *Our jobs overlap in certain areas.* | *The study of history overlaps with the study of politics.* —**overlap** /ˈoʊvɚˌlæp/ n. [C,U]

o·ver·load /ˌoʊvɚˈloʊd/ v. [T] **1** to load something with too many things or people: *Don't* ***overload*** *the washing machine* ***with*** *clothes.* **2** to give someone too much work to do **3** to damage an electrical system by causing too much electricity to flow through it —**overload** /ˈoʊvɚˌloʊd/ n. [C,U]

o·ver·look /ˌoʊvɚˈlʊk/ v. [T] **1** to not notice something, or to not realize how important it is: *It's* *easy to overlook mistakes when reading your own writing.* **2** to forgive someone's mistake, bad behavior, etc.: *I can't overlook his drinking any longer.* **3** to have a view of something from above: *Our room overlooked the beach.*

o·ver·ly /ˈoʊvɚli/ *adv.* too much, or very: *It is a problem, but we are **not overly** concerned about it.*

o·ver·night¹ /ˌoʊvɚˈnaɪt/ *adv.* **1** for or during the night: *She's **staying overnight** at a friend's house.* **2** (informal) suddenly: *You can't expect to lose the weight overnight.*

O

o·ver·night² /ˈoʊvɚˌnaɪt/ *adj.* [only before noun] continuing all night: *an overnight flight to Japan*

o·ver·pass /ˈoʊvɚˌpæs/ *n.* [C] a structure like a bridge, that allows one road to go over another road

o·ver·pop·u·lat·ed /ˌoʊvɚˈpɑpyəˌleɪt̬ɪd/ *adj.* an overpopulated place has too many people: *an overpopulated city* —**overpopulation** /ˌoʊvɚˌpɑpyəˈleɪʃən/ *n.* [U]

o·ver·pow·er /ˌoʊvɚˈpaʊɚ/ *v.* [T] to defeat someone because you are stronger

o·ver·pow·er·ing /ˌoʊvɚˈpaʊərɪŋ/ *adj.* very strong SYN **intense**: *an overpowering smell*

o·ver·priced /ˌoʊvɚˈpraɪst◂ / *adj.* too expensive: *overpriced restaurants*

THESAURUS **expensive, high, pricey, costly, extortionate, exorbitant** → EXPENSIVE

o·ver·qual·i·fied /ˌoʊvɚˈkwɑləˌfaɪd/ *adj.* having more experience or education than is needed for a particular job: *Sara's **overqualified for** most sales jobs.*

o·ver·ran /ˌoʊvɚˈræn/ *v.* the past tense of OVERRUN

o·ver·rat·ed /ˌoʊvɚˈreɪt̬ɪd◂ / *adj.* not as good or important as some people think or say ANT **underrated**: *I think her books are overrated.* —**overrate** *v.* [T]

o·ver·re·act /ˌoʊvɚriˈækt/ *v.* [I] to react to something with too much anger or surprise, or by doing more than is necessary: *You always **overreact to** criticism.* —**overreaction** /ˌoʊvɚriˈækʃən/ *n.* [C,U]

o·ver·ride /ˌoʊvɚˈraɪd/ *v.* (past tense **overrode** /-ˈroʊd/, past participle **overridden** /-ˈrɪdn/) [T] **1** to change someone's decision because you have the authority to do so: *Congress has overridden the President's veto.* **2** to be more important than something else: *The state of the economy seems to override other political and social questions.*

o·ver·rid·ing /ˌoʊvɚˈraɪdɪŋ/ *adj.* [only before noun] more important than anything else: *Security is of overriding importance.*

o·ver·rule /ˌoʊvɚˈrul/ *v.* [T] to officially change someone's order or decision because you think that it is wrong: *The Supreme Court overruled the lower court's decision.*

o·ver·run /ˌoʊvɚˈrʌn/ *v.* (past tense **overran** /-ˈræn/, past participle **overrun**) [T] to spread over a place quickly and in great numbers: *During the summer, the town is **overrun with** tourists.*

o·ver·seas /ˌoʊvɚˈsiz/ Ac *adj., adv.* to or in a foreign country that is across the ocean → ABROAD: *overseas travel* | *Apparel retailers in the U.S. buy roughly half their merchandise overseas each year.*

o·ver·see /ˌoʊvɚˈsi/ *v.* (past tense **oversaw** /-ˈsɔ/, past participle **overseen** /-ˈsin/) [T] to watch a group of workers to be sure that a piece of work is done correctly SYN **supervise**: *Bentley is overseeing the project.* —**overseer** /ˈoʊvɚˌsiɚ/ *n.* [C]

o·ver·shad·ow /ˌoʊvɚˈʃædoʊ/ *v.* [T] to make someone seem less important: *His work has been overshadowed by that of newer writers.*

o·ver·shoot /ˌoʊvɚˈʃut/ *v.* (past tense and past participle **overshot** /-ˈʃɑt/) [I,T] to accidentally go a little further or spend more than you intended: *The plane overshot the runway.*

o·ver·sight /ˈoʊvɚˌsaɪt/ *n.* **1** [C,U] a mistake in which you forget something or do not notice something: *If Butler didn't receive the report, it was an oversight.* **2** [U] if someone has oversight of something, s/he must make sure it is done correctly

ˈoversight ˌfunction *n.* [C] POLITICS an official check by a special government committee of the decisions made by the EXECUTIVE BRANCH of the U.S. government to make sure that the government acted legally and correctly

o·ver·sim·pli·fy /ˌoʊvɚˈsɪmpləˌfaɪ/ *v.* (**oversimplified**, **oversimplifies**) [I,T] (disapproving) to make a problem or situation seem more simple than it really is, by ignoring important facts —**oversimplification** /ˌoʊvɚˌsɪmpləfəˈkeɪʃən/ *n.* [C,U]

o·ver·sleep /ˌoʊvɚˈslip/ *v.* (past tense and past participle **overslept** /-ˈslɛpt/) [I] to sleep for longer than you intended

o·ver·spend /ˌoʊvɚˈspɛnd/ *v.* (past tense and past participle **overspent** /-ˈspɛnt/) [I,T] to spend more money than you can afford

o·ver·state /ˌoʊvɚˈsteɪt/ *v.* [T] to talk about something in a way that makes it seem more important, serious, etc. than it really is SYN **exaggerate** ANT **understate**: *A child's need for a routine **cannot be overstated*** (=it is very important).

o·ver·step /ˌoʊvɚˈstɛp/ *v.* (**overstepped**, **overstepping**) [T] to go beyond an acceptable limit: *Wilson has clearly **overstepped his authority**.*

o·vert /oʊˈvɚt, ˈoʊvɚt/ *adj.* (formal) done or shown in public or in an open way ANT **covert**: *overt discrimination* —**overtly** *adv.*

o·ver·take /ˌoʊvɚˈteɪk/ *v.* (past tense **overtook** /-ˈtʊk/, past participle **overtaken** /-ˈteɪkən/) [T] **1** to have a sudden strong effect on someone: *He was overtaken by exhaustion.* **2** to develop or increase more quickly than someone or something else: *DVDs rapidly overtook video.*

ˌover-the-ˈcounter *adj.* over-the-counter medicines can be bought without a PRESCRIPTION (=written order) from a doctor

o·ver·throw /ˌoʊvɚˈθroʊ/ *v.* (past tense **overthrew** /-ˈθru/, past participle **overthrown** /-ˈθroʊn/) [T] to remove a leader or government from power by force: *Rebel forces have made an attempt to overthrow the government.* —**overthrow** /ˈoʊvɚˌθroʊ/ *n.* [U]

o·ver·time /ˈoʊvɚˌtaɪm/ *n.* [U] time that you work on your job in addition to your usual working hours: *Tom's been **working/doing** a lot of **overtime** lately.*

o·ver·took /ˌoʊvɚˈtʊk/ *v* the past tense of OVERTAKE

o·ver·ture /ˈoʊvɚtʃɚ, -ˌtʃʊr/ *n.* [C] **1** a piece of music written as an introduction to a longer musical piece, especially an OPERA **2** [usually plural] an attempt to be friendly with a person, group, or country: *They began **making overtures to** the Japanese government.*

o·ver·turn /ˌoʊvɚˈtɚn/ *v.* **1** [I,T] if something overturns, or you overturn it, it turns upside down or falls over on its side: *an overturned car* **2 overturn a ruling/verdict/law etc.** to change a decision made by a court so that it becomes the opposite of what it was before

o·ver·view /ˈoʊvɚˌvyu/ *n* [C] a short description of a subject or situation, that gives the main ideas without explaining all the details: *The article gave **an overview of** developments in the Middle East.*

o·ver·weight /ˌoʊvɚˈweɪt◂/ *adj.* too heavy or too fat: *He was **10/20 etc. pounds overweight**.*

> THESAURUS fat, big, heavy, large, obese, chubby, plump, stout, corpulent, rotund ➔ FAT[1]

o·ver·whelm /ˌoʊvɚˈwɛlm/ *v.* [T] **1** if work, a problem, etc. overwhelms someone, it is too much or too difficult to deal with: *Maia is a sensitive child who is **overwhelmed by** the demands of school.* **2** if a feeling overwhelms someone, s/he feels it very strongly: *I was **overwhelmed by/with** grief.* —**overwhelmed** *adj.*

o·ver·whelm·ing /ˌoʊvɚˈwɛlmɪŋ/ *adj.* **1** affecting someone very strongly: *an overwhelming sense of guilt* **2** extremely large or great: *an **overwhelming number/majority** of voters* —**overwhelmingly** *adv.*

o·ver·worked /ˌoʊvɚˈwɚkt◂/ *adj.* working too much and for too long: *an overworked teacher* —**overwork** /ˈoʊvɚˌwɚk/ *n.* [U]

ov·ule /ˈɑvyul/ *n.* [C] BIOLOGY a very small structure in plants that develops into a seed after the plant has been FERTILIZED

o·vum /ˈoʊvəm/ *n.* (plural **ova** /ˈoʊvə/) [C] BIOLOGY an egg, especially one that develops inside a woman's or a female animal's body

ow /aʊ/ *interjection* said in order to show that something hurts you: *Ow! That hurt!*

owe /oʊ/ *v.* [T] **1** to need to pay someone because s/he has allowed you to borrow money: *Bob owes me $20.* | *How much do you still owe on your college loans?*

> THESAURUS
> **be in debt** – to owe an amount of money
> **be overdrawn** – to owe money to your bank, as a result of spending more money than you have in your bank account
> **be in the red** – to have spent more money than you have

2 to feel that you should do something for someone or give something to someone, especially because s/he has done something for you: *Jane will watch the kids – she **owes me a favor** anyway.* | *You **owe it to** your kids to teach them about healthy eating.* | *I think I **owe** you **an apology**.*

ˈowing to *prep.* (formal) because of: *Greely was unable to accept the job, owing to a serious illness.*

owl /aʊl/ *n.* [C] a bird that hunts at night and has large eyes and a loud call ➔ *see picture at* NOCTURNAL

owl

own¹ /oʊn/ *determiner, pron.* **1** belonging to or done by a particular person and no one else: *his own car* | *She makes a lot of her own clothes.* | *I'd love a place **of** my **own**.* **2 (all) on your own a)** alone: *Many older people still live on their own.* **b)** without help: *It's a decision you have to make on your own.*

own² *v.* [T] to legally have something because you bought it or have been given it (SYN) **possess**: *The city owns the buildings.*

> THESAURUS
> **possess** (formal) – to own or have something: *Philips was charged with possessing cocaine.*
> **have** – to own something: *How many students have a cell phone?*
> **belong to sb** – if something belongs to you, you own it: *The ring belonged to my grandmother.*

own up *phr. v.* to admit that you have done something wrong: *He'll never **own up to** his mistakes.*

own·er /ˈoʊnɚ/ *n.* [C] someone who owns something: *pet owners* | *the **owner of** the business* —**ownership** *n.* [U]

ox /ɑks/ *n.* (plural **oxen** /ˈɑksən/) [C] a male cow that has had part of its sex organs removed

ox·i·da·tion /ˌɑksəˈdeɪʃən/ *n.* [U] CHEMISTRY the process in which a chemical combines with oxygen, losing one or more ELECTRONS

ox·ide /ˈɑksaɪd/ *n.* [C,U] CHEMISTRY a substance that is produced when a substance is combined with oxygen

ox·i·dize /ˈɑksəˌdaɪz/ *v.* [I,T] **1** CHEMISTRY to combine with oxygen, or to make something combine with oxygen, especially in a way that causes RUST **2** CHEMISTRY to lose ELECTRONS or make another chemical compound lose electrons

ˈoxidizing ˌagent *n.* [C] CHEMISTRY a chemical substance that oxidizes another substance and gives up oxygen or gains ELECTRONs in the process

ox·y·gen /ˈɑksɪdʒən/ *n.* [U] CHEMISTRY (*symbol* **O**) a gas in the air that has no color, smell, or taste, and that all plants and animals need in order to live [ORIGIN: 1700—1800 French *oxygène*, from Greek *oxys* "sharp, acid" + French *-gène* "forming;" because it was believed that oxygen forms part of all acids]

ox·y·mo·ron /ˌɑksiˈmɔrɑn/ *n.* [C] ENG. LANG. ARTS a combination of words that seem to mean the opposite of each other, such as "new classics"

oys·ter /ˈɔɪstɚ/ *n.* [C,U] a small sea animal that has a shell and can produce a jewel called a PEARL, or the meat of this animal → *see picture at* SHELLFISH

oz the written abbreviation of OUNCE

o·zone /ˈoʊzoʊn/ *n.* [U] CHEMISTRY a poisonous blue gas that is a type of oxygen

ˈozone ˌlayer *n.* [singular] EARTH SCIENCES a layer of ozone above the Earth that prevents harmful RADIATION from the Sun from reaching the Earth's surface

P, p /pi/ the sixteenth letter of the English alphabet

p. (plural **pp.**) the written abbreviation of PAGE and PAGES

PA[1] the written abbreviation of PENNSYLVANIA

PA[2] *n.* [C usually singular] **public address system** electronic equipment that makes someone's voice loud enough to be heard by a large group of people

Pa CHEMISTRY the written abbreviation of PASCAL

pa /pɑ/ *n.* [C] (old-fashioned) father

PAC /pæk/ *n.* POLITICS **political action committee** an organization that tries to influence politicians so that they will support the organization's aims

pace[1] /peɪs/ *n.* **1** [singular] the speed or rate at which something happens or is done: *We started walking uphill* ***at a steady/slow/rapid/fast etc. pace.*** | *Students are encouraged to work* ***at*** *their* ***own pace.***

COLLOCATIONS

pace of life – the amount of activity in people's lives and how busy they are
pace of change/reform/growth – how quickly change, reform, or growth happens
at your own pace – at a pace that is comfortable for you
at a rapid/slow/steady etc. pace
at a snail's pace – very slowly
keep up the pace – continue to do something or happen as quickly as before
keep pace with sth – do something at the same speed or rate as something else

2 keep pace (with sb/sth) to move or change as fast as something or someone else

pace[2] *v.* [I,T] **1** to walk first in one direction and then in another, again and again, when you are waiting or worried about something: *Darren* ***paced back and forth*** *in the waiting room.* **2 pace yourself** to do something at a steady speed so you do not get tired too quickly

pace·mak·er /ˈpeɪsˌmeɪkɚ/ *n.* [C] a very small machine that is attached to someone's heart to help it beat regularly

Pa·cif·ic /pəˈsɪfɪk/ *n.* [U] (spoken) a short form of Pacific Time, the TIME ZONE in the western part of the U.S.

pa·cif·ic /pəˈsɪfɪk/ *adj.* (literary) peaceful, loving peace, or helping peace to happen: *a pacific settlement to the argument*

Paˌcific ˈOcean *n.* **the Pacific Ocean, the Pacific** the large ocean between Asia and Australia in the west, and North and South America in the east

Paˌcific ˈRim *n.* **the Pacific Rim** the land and islands that are around the edges of the Pacific Ocean, especially in Asia

pac·i·fi·er /ˈpæsəˌfaɪɚ/ *n.* [C] a plastic or rubber object that a baby sucks on so that s/he does not cry

pac·i·fism /ˈpæsəˌfɪzəm/ *n.* [U] the belief that all wars and forms of violence are wrong —**pacifist** *n.* [C]

pac·i·fy /ˈpæsəˌfaɪ/ *v.* (**pacified, pacifies**) [T] to make someone calm and quiet after s/he has been angry or upset, or to make a group or area peaceful: *"You're right," Rita said, in order to pacify him.*

pack[1] /pæk/ *v.* **1** [I,T] *also* **pack up** to put things into boxes, SUITCASEs, bags, etc. in order to take or store them somewhere: *The Olsons* ***packed*** *their* ***bags/suitcases.*** | *I still need to pack tonight.* | *They packed up and moved back to Tucson.* | *eggs packed in cartons* **2** [I,T] if a crowd of people packs a place, there are so many of them that the place is too full: *50,000 fans packed the stadium.* **3** [T] to cover, fill, or surround something closely with material to protect it: ***Pack*** *some newspaper* ***around*** *the bottles.* **4** [T] to press soil, snow, etc.

down firmly: ***Pack** the soil firmly **around** the roots.*

pack sb/sth ↔ **in** *phr. v.* **1** (informal) to fit a lot of people, information, ideas, etc. into a limited space: *Any movie starring Brad Pitt always packs in the fans.* **2 pack it in** (informal) to stop doing something: *Mike was ready to pack it in for the night.*

pack sth **into** sth *phr. v.* to fit a lot of something into a space, place, or period of time: *We packed a lot of sightseeing into two weeks.*

pack sb/sth **off** *phr. v.* (informal) to send someone or something away quickly, especially in order to get rid of him/her: *Our folks **packed** us **off to** camp every summer.*

pack up *phr. v.* (informal) to finish work and put things away: *The band packed up at midnight.*

pack² *n.* [C] **1** a small container that holds a set of things: *a **pack of cigarettes/cards/gum*** **2** a group of wild animals that live and hunt together: *a wolf pack* **3** a group of people: *A **pack of** reporters was yelling questions.* **4** several things wrapped or tied together to make them easy to sell, carry, or send: *a **pack of** three T-shirts | a six pack of beer*

pack·age¹ /ˈpækɪdʒ/ *n.* [C] **1** something packed into a box and wrapped in paper, especially for mailing **2** the box, bag, etc. that food is put into in order to be sold: *Nutrition information is listed on the side of the package.* **3** a set of related things or services that are sold or offered together: *a new software package | a financial aid package for students*

package² *v.* [T] **1** to put something in a special package, ready to be sold or sent: *Meat is packaged and dated in this area here.* **2** to try to make an idea, person, etc. seem interesting or attractive so that people will like it or buy it: *The company is packaging the band to appeal to teenage girls.*

pack·ag·ing /ˈpækɪdʒɪŋ/ *n.* [U] the container or material that a product is sold in: *cardboard packaging*

packed /pækt/ *adj.* **1** extremely full of people or things: *The theater was packed. | The forest is **tightly/densely/closely packed** with pine trees.*

> THESAURUS **full, filled with sth, crammed, stuffed (full of sth), bursting (with sth), overflowing, overloaded** → FULL¹

2 if you are packed, you have put everything you need into boxes or SUITCASEs before going on a trip

pack·er /ˈpækɚ/ *n.* [C] someone whose job is to pack things that are to be moved or sold

pack·et /ˈpækɪt/ *n.* [C] **1** a small envelope containing something: *a **packet of** sugar* **2** IT a quantity of information that is sent as a single unit from one computer to another on a network or on the Internet

ˈpack ice *n.* [U] EARTH SCIENCES a large area of ice floating in the ocean, formed by smaller pieces joining together when the ocean is very cold

pack·ing /ˈpækɪŋ/ *n.* [U] **1** the act of putting things into boxes, cans, SUITCASEs, etc. so that you can send or take them somewhere: *I've still got to **do my packing.*** **2** paper, plastic, cloth, etc. used for packing things

ˈpack rat *n.* [C] (informal) someone who collects and stores things that s/he does not really need

pact /pækt/ *n.* [C] a formal or serious agreement between two groups, nations, or people: *The U.S. signed a trade **pact with** Canada. | We **made a pact to** help each other out.* [ORIGIN: 1400—1500 French *pacte*, from Latin *pactum*, from *pacisci* "to agree"]

pad¹ /pæd/ *n.* [C] **1** a thick piece of soft material, used for protecting or cleaning something, or for making something more comfortable: *the helmets and pads of a football player | a heating pad* **2** many sheets of paper fastened together, used for writing or drawing: *a **sketch pad*** → LAUNCH PAD

pad² *v.* (**padded**, **padding**) **1** [I] to walk softly and quietly: *The cat padded across the floor.* **2** [T] to fill or cover something with a soft material in order to protect it or make it more comfortable **3** [T] (informal) to add something unnecessary to a document or speech to make it longer, or to a price to make it higher: *He was padding his expense accounts.*

pad·ded /ˈpædɪd/ *adj.* filled or covered with a soft material: *a padded jacket*

pad·ding /ˈpædɪŋ/ *n.* [U] material that fills or covers something to make it softer or more comfortable

pad·dle¹ /ˈpædl/ *n.* [C] **1** a short pole with a wide flat end, used for moving a small boat along → OAR **2** an object used for hitting the ball in PING-PONG, consisting of a round flat top on a short handle

paddle² *v.* **1** [I,T] to move a small boat through water, using a paddle **2** [T] to hit a child with a piece of wood as a punishment → DOG PADDLE

pad·dy /ˈpædi/ *also* **rice paddy** *n.* (plural **paddies**) [C] a field in which rice is grown in water

pad·lock /ˈpædlɑk/ *n.* [C] a lock with a curved bar at the top that you can put on a door, bicycle, etc. —**padlock** *v.* [T] → *see picture at* LOCK²

pa·gan /ˈpeɪgən/ *n.* [C] someone who does not believe in any of the main modern religions of the world [ORIGIN: 1300—1400 Late Latin *paganus*, from Latin, "someone who lives in the country"] —**pagan** *adj.*

page¹ /peɪdʒ/ *n.* [C] **1** one side of a sheet of paper in a book, newspaper, etc., or the sheet of paper itself: *Do the exercises **on page** 10 for homework. | The story was on the **front page** of every newspaper. | Callie **turned** the **page** and continued reading.* **2** all the writing and pictures that you can see at one time on a computer screen: *a **web***

page **3** a young person who works in a government office for a short time in order to gain experience [ORIGIN: (1) 1500—1600 French, Latin *pagina*]

page² *v.* [T] **1** to call someone's name in a public place, especially using a LOUDSPEAKER: *We couldn't find Jan at the airport, so we had her paged.* **2** to call someone using a BEEPER (=small machine that receives messages)

page down/up *phr. v.* to press a special key on a computer that makes the screen show the page after or before the one you are reading

P

pag·eant /'pædʒənt/ *n.* [C] **1** a competition for young women in which their beauty and other qualities are judged: *a **beauty pageant*** **2** a public show or ceremony that usually shows an event in history

pag·eant·ry /'pædʒəntri/ *n.* [U] (formal) impressive ceremonies or events, involving many people wearing special clothes: *the pageantry of a royal wedding*

pag·er /'peɪdʒɚ/ *n.* [C] a BEEPER

pa·go·da /pə'goʊdə/ *n.* [C] an Asian TEMPLE that has several levels, with a decorated roof at each level [ORIGIN: 1500—1600 Portuguese *pagode*]

paid /peɪd/ *v.* the past tense and past participle of PAY

pail /peɪl/ *n.* [C] **1** a container with a handle, used for carrying liquids or by children when playing on the beach (SYN) **bucket**: *a pail of water* **2** a container used for carrying or holding something: *a garbage pail* | *a lunch pail*

pain¹ /peɪn/ *n.* **1** [C,U] the feeling you have when part of your body hurts: *Soldiers lay groaning **in pain*** (=feeling pain) *on the ground.* | *She was given drugs to **ease/relieve the pain*** (=make it hurt less). | *These patients suffer from **shoulder/chest/back pain**.* | *As soon as I stood up, I **felt the pain**.*

COLLOCATIONS

A **terrible, severe, intense**, or **unbearable pain** is very bad.
A **sharp pain** is short but severe.
A **dull pain** is not severe, but it continues for a long time.
If you have pain over a long period of time, you can call it **chronic pain**.
Another word for a pain that continues but is not very strong is an **ache**.
If you are **in pain**, you take **medicine** or **painkillers** to **lessen/ease/relieve/kill the pain**.

2 be a pain (in the neck/butt) (spoken) to be very annoying: *This pan is a pain to wash.* **3** [C,U] the feeling of unhappiness you have when you are sad, upset, etc.: *Children feel a lot of pain when their parents divorce.* **4 take pains to do sth** to make a special effort to do something well: *I took **great pains** not to upset them.* **5 be at pains to do sth** (formal) to be very careful to do something [ORIGIN: 1200—1300 Old French *peine*, from Latin *poena*, from Greek *poine* "payment, punishment"]

pain² *v.* [T] (formal) to make someone feel unhappy: ***It pains me to** see my mother growing old.*

pained /peɪnd/ *adj.* worried, upset, or slightly annoyed: *a **pained look/expression***

pain·ful /'peɪnfəl/ *adj.* **1** making you feel physical pain: *a painful injury* | *He was finding it **painful** to walk.*

THESAURUS

tender – a tender part of your body is painful if someone touches it: *Her feet still felt tender.*
stiff – if a part of your body is stiff, your muscles hurt and it is difficult to move, usually because you have exercised too much or you are sick: *My legs are so stiff!*
sore – painful as a result of a wound, infection, or too much exercise: *a sore throat and fever*
raw – skin that is raw is red and sore: *Eczema is a skin condition that can leave your skin raw and itchy.* ➔ HURT¹

2 making you feel very upset or unhappy: ***painful memories** of the war* | *The divorce was **painful for** both of us.* | *I made the **painful decision** to leave.* **3** very bad and embarrassing for other people to watch, hear, etc.: *The acting in the movie was so bad that it was painful to watch.*

pain·ful·ly /'peɪnfəli/ *adv.* **1** with pain, or causing pain: *Mike walked slowly and painfully to the door.* | *People can be painfully cruel to each other.* **2** very – used to emphasize a bad or harmful quality or that something makes you upset: *It was **painfully obvious** that she wasn't well.* **3** needing a lot of effort, or causing a lot of trouble: *Real change is a painfully slow process.*

pain·kill·er /'peɪn,kɪlɚ/ *n.* [C] a medicine that reduces or removes pain

pain·less /'peɪnlɪs/ *adj.* **1** without pain, or causing no pain: *a painless death* **2** (informal) needing no effort or hard work: *There is no painless way to learn another language.*

pains·tak·ing /'peɪnz,teɪkɪŋ, 'peɪn,steɪ-/ *adj.* very careful and thorough: *painstaking research* —**painstakingly** *adv.*

THESAURUS **careful, methodical, thorough, meticulous, systematic, scrupulous, conscientious** ➔ CAREFUL

paint¹ /peɪnt/ *n.* **1** [U] a colored liquid that you put on a surface to make it a particular color: *a can of yellow paint* | *The kitchen needs a fresh **coat of paint*** (=layer of paint). **2** [C,U] a colored substance in a small tube or block, used for painting pictures: *a set of oil paints* [ORIGIN: 1100—1200 Old French *peint*, past participle of *peindre* "to paint," from Latin *pingere*]

paint² *v.* [I,T] **1** to put paint on a surface: *How much will it cost to paint the house?* | *The door had* *been painted blue.* | *the* ***freshly painted*** (=recently painted) *walls* **2** to make a picture of someone or something using paint: *He painted a portrait of Allen's wife.* **3 paint a picture/portrait of sth** to describe something in a particular way: *The report paints a grim picture of family life.*

paint·brush /ˈpeɪntˀbrʌʃ/ *n.* [C] a special brush used for painting pictures or for painting rooms, houses, etc. → *see picture at* BRUSH[1]

paint·er /ˈpeɪntɚ/ *n.* [C] **1** someone who paints pictures (SYN) **artist**: *a landscape painter* **2** someone whose job is painting houses, rooms, etc.

painting

still life

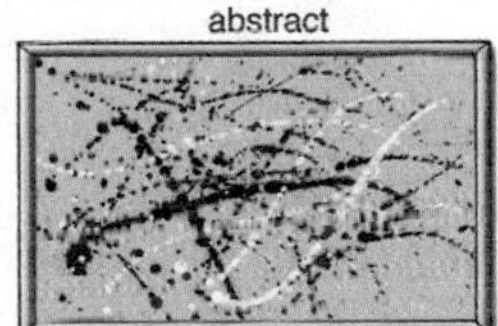
abstract

landscape

portrait

paint·ing /ˈpeɪntɪŋ/ *n.* **1** [C] a painted picture: *a* ***painting of*** *Thomas Jefferson* (=that shows Thomas Jefferson) | *a* ***painting by*** *Mondrian* (=painted by him)

THESAURUS **picture, sketch, portrait, cartoon, illustration** → PICTURE[1]

2 [U] the act or skill of making a picture using paint: *Monet's style of painting*

THESAURUS **art, drawing, photography, sculpture, pottery, ceramics** → ART

3 [U] the act of covering a wall, house, etc. with paint

ˈpaint ˌthinner *n.* [U] a liquid that you add to paint to make it less thick

pair

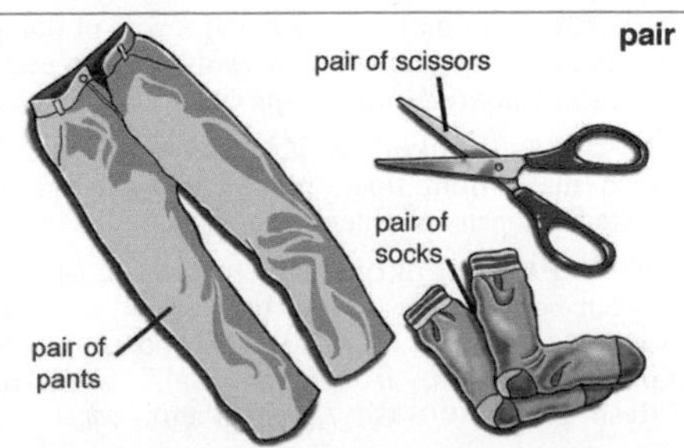

pair¹ /pɛr/ *n.* (plural **pairs** *or* **pair**) [C] **1** something made of two similar parts that are joined together: *a* ***pair of*** *scissors* | *two pairs of jeans* | *a pair of glasses* **2** two things of the same kind that are used together: *a* ***pair of*** *earrings* | *She has 12 pairs of shoes!* **3** two people who are standing or doing something together: *a* ***pair of*** *dancers* | *Work* ***in pairs*** (=in groups of two) *on the next exercise.* [ORIGIN: 1200—1300 Old French *paire*, from Latin *paria* "equal things"]

pair² *also* **pair up** *v.* [I,T] to form or be put into groups of two: *We were each* ***paired with*** *a newcomer to help with training.*

pair (sb ↔) **off** *phr. v.* to come together or bring two people together: *The guests paired off for the first dance.*

P

pa·ja·mas /pəˈdʒɑməz, -ˈdʒæ-/ *n.* [plural] a pair of loose pants and a loose shirt that you wear in bed [ORIGIN: 1800—1900 Hindi *pajama* (singular), from Persian *pa* "leg" + *jama* "piece of clothing"]

pal /pæl/ *n.* [C] (old-fashioned) a close friend: *a college pal* [ORIGIN: 1600—1700 Romany *phral, phal* "brother, friend," from Sanskrit *bhratr* "brother"] → PEN PAL

pal·ace /ˈpælɪs/ *n.* [C] a large house where a king or queen officially lives: *Buckingham Palace in England* [ORIGIN: 1200—1300 Old French *palais*, from Latin *palatium*, from *Palatium* the Palatine Hill in Rome where the ruler's palace was]

pal·at·a·ble /ˈpælət̬əbəl/ *adj.* (formal) **1** palatable food or drinks have an acceptable taste: *a palatable wine* **2** an idea, suggestion, etc. that is palatable is acceptable: *Can they come up with a plan that is more palatable to local residents?*

pal·ate /ˈpælɪt/ *n.* [C] **1** BIOLOGY the top inside part of the mouth **2** [usually singular] (formal) someone's ability to taste things: *The flavors must please the palate.*

pa·la·tial /pəˈleɪʃəl/ *adj.* very large and beautifully decorated: *a palatial hotel*

pale¹ /peɪl/ *adj.* **1** having a much lighter skin color than usual because you are sick, frightened, etc.: *Her father looked pale and nervous.* **2** a pale color has more white in it than usual: *pale green walls* [ORIGIN: 1300—1400 Old French, Latin *pallidus*]

THESAURUS **light, pastel** → LIGHT²

pale² *v.* [I] **1 pale in/by comparison** to seem less important, good, etc. when compared to something else: *Recent economic problems* ***pale in comparison with*** *those of the 1930s.* **2 pale into insignificance** to seem much less important when compared to something else: *All our troubles paled into insignificance when we heard about the war.* **3** (literary) if you pale, your face becomes much whiter than usual because you are sick, frightened, etc.

Pa·le·o·lith·ic, paleolithic /ˌpeɪliəˈlɪθɪk/ *adj.* EARTH SCIENCES relating to the earliest period of the STONE AGE (=the period many thousands of years ago when people made stone tools and weapons): *the Paleolithic era* ➔ NEOLITHIC

pa·le·on·tol·o·gy /ˌpeɪliənˈtɑlədʒi, -liɑn-/ *n.* [U] EARTH SCIENCES the study of FOSSILS (=ancient animals and plants that have been preserved in rock) [ORIGIN: 1800—1900 *paleo-* + Greek *onta* "living things" + English *-ology*] **—paleontologist** *n.* [C]

Pa·le·o·zo·ic /ˌpeɪliəˈzoʊɪk/ *n.* **the Paleozoic** EARTH SCIENCES the period of time in the Earth's history, from about 570 million until about 250 million years ago, when fish, insects, REPTILES, and some plants first started to exist **—Paleozoic** *adj.*: *the Paleozoic period* ➔ CENOZOIC, MESOZOIC, PRECAMBRIAN

P

pal·ette /ˈpælɪt/ *n.* [C] **1** a board with a curved edge and a hole for the thumb, on which a painter mixes colors **2** the particular set of colors a painter uses: *a bright palette*

pal·in·drome /ˈpælənˌdroʊm/ *n.* [C] ENG. LANG. ARTS a word or phrase such as "deed" or "level," which is the same when you read it backward

pall¹ /pɔl/ *n.* **1** [C] a low dark cloud of smoke, dust, etc.: *a **pall of** black **smoke*** **2** [singular] something that spoils an event or occasion that should have been happy: *The drug scandal **cast a pall over*** (=spoiled the happy feelings at) *the Olympics.*

pall² *v.* [I] (literary) to become less interesting or enjoyable: *Gradually, the novelty of city life began to pall.*

pall·bear·er /ˈpɔlˌbɛrɚ/ *n.* [C] someone who helps to carry a CASKET (=a box with a dead body inside) at a funeral

pal·let /ˈpælɪt/ *n.* [C] a large flat wooden frame on which heavy goods can be lifted, stored, or moved

pal·li·ate /ˈpæliˌeɪt/ *v.* [T] (formal) to make a bad situation or illness better, but not make it go away completely **—palliation** /ˌpæliˈeɪʃən/ *n.* [U] **—palliative** *adj.*: *cancer patients receiving palliative care*

THESAURUS **relieve, ease, lessen, soothe, alleviate** ➔ REDUCE

pal·lid /ˈpælɪd/ *adj.* (literary) looking pale and unhealthy: *pallid skin*

pal·lor /ˈpælɚ/ *n.* [singular] (literary) a pale unhealthy color of your skin or face

palm¹ /pɑm/ *n.* [C] **1** the inside surface of your hand between the base of your fingers and your wrist: *The boy held a penny **in the palm of** his **hand**.* ➔ *see picture at* HAND¹ **2** a palm tree

palm² *v.* [T]

palm sth ↔ **off** *phr. v.* to persuade someone to accept or buy something, especially by deceiving him/her

ˌPalm ˈSunday *n.* the Sunday before Easter in Christian religions

palm·top /ˈpɑmtɑp/ *n.* [C] IT a very small computer that you can hold in your hand

ˈpalm tree *n.* [C] a tall tropical tree with large pointed leaves at its top that grows near beaches or in deserts ➔ *see picture on page A23*

pal·pa·ble /ˈpælpəbəl/ *adj.* (formal) easily and clearly noticed: *Rosanne's disappointment was palpable.* **—palpably** *adv.*

pal·pi·ta·tions /ˌpælpəˈteɪʃənz/ *n.* [plural] irregular or extremely fast beating of your heart

pal·try /ˈpɔltri/ *adj.* (disapproving) too small to be useful or important: *a paltry pay raise*

pam·per /ˈpæmpɚ/ *v.* [T] to give someone a lot of care and attention, sometimes in a way that is bad for him/her: *a pampered dog*

pam·phlet /ˈpæmflɪt/ *n.* [C] a very thin book with paper covers, giving information about something

pan¹ /pæn/ *n.* [C] **1** a round metal container used for cooking, usually with a handle: *a large **pan of** boiling water* | ***pots and pans*** | *a **frying pan*** **2** a metal container used for baking food, or the food that this contains: *Spoon half the batter into a greased pan.* | *a **pan of** sweet rolls* **3** a container with low sides, used for holding liquids: *an oil pan* [ORIGIN: Old English *panne*]

pan² *v.* (**panned**, **panning**) **1** [T] (written) to strongly criticize a movie, play, etc. in a newspaper or on television or radio: *The critics panned his first play.* **2** [I,T] to move a camera while taking a picture, or follow a moving object with a camera: *The camera panned across the crowd.* **3** [I] to wash soil in a pan in order to separate gold from it: *Men were **panning for** gold in the stream.*

pan out *phr. v.* (informal) to happen or develop in the expected way: *I got a few job interviews, but nothing panned out.*

pan·a·ce·a /ˌpænəˈsiə/ *n.* [C usually singular] something that people think will make everything better or cure any illness: *Money is not a **panacea for** the problems in our schools, but it can help.*

THESAURUS **solution, answer, cure, remedy** ➔ SOLUTION

pa·nache /pəˈnæʃ, -ˈnɑʃ/ *n.* [U] a way of doing things that is exciting and makes them seem easy: *Mr. Seaton danced **with** real **panache**.*

pan·cake /ˈpænkeɪk/ *n.* [C] a flat round type of bread made from flour, milk, and eggs that is cooked in a pan and eaten for breakfast

pan·cre·as /ˈpæŋkriəs/ *n.* [C] BIOLOGY a GLAND in your body that helps your body to use the food you eat [ORIGIN: 1500—1600 Modern Latin, Greek *pankreas*, from *pan-* "all" + *kreas* "flesh"] **—pancreatic** /ˌpæŋkriˈæt̬ɪk/ *adj.*

pan·da /ˈpændə/ *n.* [C] a large black and white animal, similar to a bear, that lives in China

pan·dem·ic /pæn'dɛmɪk/ *n.* [C] an illness or disease that affects the population of a very large area ➔ EPIDEMIC: *the virus that caused the deadly Spanish flu pandemic in 1918* —**pandemic** *adj.*: *New strains of influenza could cause pandemic disease.*

pan·de·mo·ni·um /ˌpændə'moʊniəm/ *n.* [U] a situation in which there is a lot of noise and movement because people are angry, frightened, excited, etc.: *For the next hour, there was pandemonium in the auditorium.* [ORIGIN: 1600—1700 *Pandaemonium* city of evil spirits in the poem Paradise Lost (1667) by John Milton, from Greek *pan-* "all" + *daimon* "evil spirit"]

pan·der /'pændɚ/ *v.*

pander to sth/sb *phr. v.* (disapproving) to try to please someone by doing what s/he wants you to do, even though you know this is wrong: *Do we want a president who panders to big business?*

pane /peɪn/ *n.* [C] a piece of glass in a window or door: ***a window pane*** | ***a pane of glass***

pan·el[1] /'pænl/ (Ac) *n.* [C] **1** a group of people who are chosen to discuss something, decide something, or answer questions: *Six congressmen are* ***on the panel*** *looking into the issue.* | ***a panel of*** *experts* | *An independent review panel was set up to investigate the complaints.* **2** a flat sheet of wood, glass, etc. that fits into a frame to form part of a door, wall, or ceiling: *an oak door with three panels* **3 instrument/control panel** the place in an airplane, boat, etc. where the instruments or controls are

panel[2] *v.* [T] to cover or decorate something such as a wall with flat pieces of wood, glass, etc.: *an oak-paneled room*

pan·el·ing /'pænl-ɪŋ/ *n.* [U] wood in long pieces that is used for covering walls, etc.: *pine paneling*

pan·el·ist /'pænl-ɪst/ *n.* [C] a member of a panel, especially on a radio or television program

pang /pæŋ/ *n.* [C] a sudden strong and unpleasant feeling: *strong* ***hunger pangs*** | ***a pang of*** *regret*

pan·han·dle[1] /'pænˌhændl/ *v.* [I] to ask people for money in the streets (SYN) **beg** —**panhandler** *n.* [C]

panhandle[2] *n.* [C] a thin piece of land that is joined to a larger area: *the Texas panhandle*

pan·ic[1] /'pænɪk/ *n.* [C,U] a sudden feeling of fear or anxiety that makes you do things without thinking carefully about them: *People fled the area* ***in (a) panic.*** | *The announcement caused widespread panic.* [ORIGIN: 1600—1700 French *panique* "caused by panic," from Greek *panikos*, from *Pan* ancient Greek god of nature, who caused great fear]

panic[2] *v.* (past tense and past participle **panicked**, present participle **panicking**) [I,T] to suddenly feel so frightened that you do things without thinking clearly, or to make someone feel this way: *Johnson panicked and ran.* | ***Don't panic*** (=stay calm) – *we're getting you out of there right now.* —**panicky** *adj.*

'panic-ˌstricken *adj.* so frightened that you cannot think clearly: *Panic-stricken parents swarmed around the school.*

pan·o·ram·a /ˌpænə'ræmə, -'rɑ-/ *n.* [C] an impressive view over a wide area of land: ***a panorama of*** *the Rocky Mountains* [ORIGIN: 1700—1800 *pan-* "all" + Greek *horama* "sight"] —**panoramic** /ˌpænə'ræmɪk◂ / *adj.*: *a panoramic view of the valley*

pan·sy /'pænzi/ *n.* (plural **pansies**) [C] a small flat brightly colored garden flower

pant[1] /pænt/ *v.* [I] to breathe quickly with short noisy breaths, especially after exercising or because it is hot: *Eddie was panting with the effort of the climb.*

> THESAURUS **breathe, take a breath, inhale, exhale, wheeze, be short of breath, be out of breath, gasp for breath, gasp for air** ➔ BREATHE

pant[2] *adj.* [only before noun] relating to, or part of, a pair of pants: *We rolled up our* ***pant legs*** *and waded in the creek.*

pan·the·ism /'pænθiˌɪzəm/ *n.* [U] the religious idea that God is present in all natural things in the universe

pan·ther /'pænθɚ/ *n.* [C] a large wild black cat that is good at hunting

pant·ies /'pæntiz/ *n.* [plural] a piece of women's underwear that covers the area between the waist and the top of the legs ➔ *see picture at* CLOTHES

pan·to·mime /'pæntəˌmaɪm/ *n.* [C,U] a method of performing using only actions and not words, or a play performed using this method

pan·try /'pæntri/ *n.* (plural **pantries**) [C] a small room near a kitchen, where food, dishes, etc. are kept

pants /pænts/ *n.* [plural] a piece of clothing that covers you from your waist to your feet and has a separate part for each leg: *a black* ***pair of pants*** | *He put it in his* ***pants pocket.*** [ORIGIN: 1800—1900 *pantaloons*] ➔ *see picture at* CLOTHES

pant·suit /'pæntsut/ *n.* [C] a women's suit consisting of a JACKET and matching pants

pan·ty·hose /'pæntiˌhoʊz/ *n.* [plural] a very thin piece of women's clothing that covers the legs from the feet to the waist, usually worn with dresses or skirts

pan·ty·lin·er /'pæntiˌlaɪnɚ/ *n.* [C] a very thin SANITARY NAPKIN

pa·pa /'pɑpə/ *n.* [C] (old-fashioned) father

pa·pa·cy /'peɪpəsi/ *n.* **the papacy** the position and authority of the POPE

pa·pal /'peɪpəl/ *adj.* relating to the POPE

pa·pa·raz·zi /ˌpɑpə'rɑtsi/ *n.* [plural] people who take photographs of famous people by following

P

them around [ORIGIN: 1900—2000 Italian, from the name of a character in the film La Dolce Vita (1960)]

pa·pa·ya /pə'paɪə/ *n.* [C,U] a sweet juicy tropical fruit with many small seeds inside it

pa·per[1] /'peɪpɚ/ *n.* **1** [U] material in the form of thin sheets, used for writing or drawing, wrapping things, etc.: *Her letter was written on blue paper.* | *Kellen looked at the **piece/sheet of paper** on his desk.* | *She jotted her phone number on a **slip/scrap of paper*** (=small piece of paper). | *a piece of **wax/tissue/wrapping etc. paper*** | *a brown paper bag* **2** [C] a newspaper: *Have you seen today's paper?* | *an article **in the paper*** | *an ad in the **local paper*** (=the newspaper for the area you live in) **3** [C] a piece of writing that is done as part of a class: *My history paper is due tomorrow.*

THESAURUS essay, composition, assignment, thesis, dissertation → ESSAY

4 papers important or official documents or letters, such as documents you use in your work, your WILL, your PASSPORT, etc.: *legal papers* | *a set of identity papers* **5 on paper a)** if an idea seems good on paper, it seems good or true but has not been tested or does not work in a real situation: *On paper, the company's policy of flexible working hours sounded great.* **b)** if you put ideas or information on paper, you write them down **6** [C] a piece of writing or a speech by someone who has studied a particular subject: *Einstein's first **paper on** relativity* **7** [C,U] WALLPAPER [ORIGIN: 1300—1400 Old French *papier*, from Latin *papyrus*]

paper[2] *v.* [T] to decorate the walls of a room by covering them with WALLPAPER

pa·per·back /'peɪpɚˌbæk/ *n.* [C] a book with a stiff paper cover: *Her novel's available **in paperback**.* → BOOK[1]

'paper boy *n.* [C] a boy who delivers newspapers to people's houses

'paper clip *n.* [C] a small piece of curved wire used for holding sheets of paper together

'paper girl *n.* [C] a girl who delivers newspapers to people's houses

pa·per·weight /'peɪpɚˌweɪt/ *n.* [C] a small heavy object that you put on top of papers so that they stay on a desk

pa·per·work /'peɪpɚˌwɚk/ *n.* [U] **1** work such as writing letters or reports, which must be done but is not very interesting: *Social workers have far too much paperwork to do.* **2** the documents that you need for a business deal, a trip, etc.: *I went to the insurance office to fill out the paperwork.*

pa·pier-mâ·ché /ˌpeɪpɚ mə'ʃeɪ/ *n.* [U] a soft substance made from a mixture of paper, water, and glue, which becomes hard when it dries

Pap smear /'pæp smɪr/ *n.* [C] a medical test that takes cells from a woman's CERVIX and examines them for signs of CANCER

par /pɑr/ *n.* **1 be on a par (with sth)** to be of the same standard as something else: *Their military forces are on a par with ours.* **2 not be up to par** *also* **be below par** to be less good or well than usual: *Several students are not performing up to par.* **3 be par for the course** to be what you would normally expect to happen: *"Lisa was late again." "That's par for the course."* **4** [U] the number of STROKES a good player should take to hit the ball into a hole in golf

par·a·ble /'pærəbəl/ *n.* [C] a short simple story that teaches a moral or religious lesson

pa·rab·o·la /pə'ræbələ/ *n.* [C] MATH a curved shape that looks like the curve a ball makes when it is thrown high in the air and comes down a short distance away. It is formed by a PLANE (=flat surface) crossing through the side of a CONE, so that the distances from the curve to fixed points inside and outside the curve are always the same. → CONIC SECTION —**parabolic** /ˌpærə'bɑlɪk◂/ *adj.*: *a parabolic curve* → *see picture at* HYPERBOLA

parabola

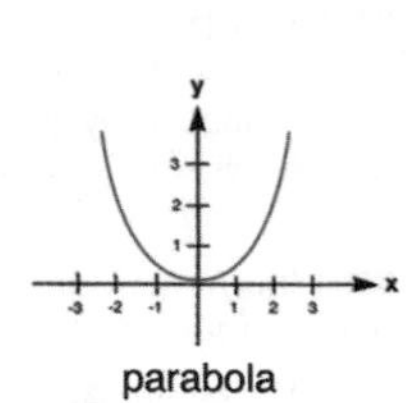

parabola

par·a·chute[1] /'pærəˌʃut/ *n.* [C] a large piece of cloth that is attached to the back of someone who jumps out of an AIRPLANE, which makes him/her fall slowly and safely to the ground

parachute

parachute[2] *v.* **1** [I] to jump from an AIRPLANE using a parachute: *A group of soldiers **parachuted into** the field during the night.* **2** [T] to drop something from an AIRPLANE with a parachute: *Supplies were **parachuted into** the area.*

pa·rade[1] /pə'reɪd/ *n.* [C] **1** a public celebration when musical bands, decorated vehicles, etc. move down the street: *The Rose Parade is always held on New Year's Day.* | *Their high school band was marching in the parade.* **2** a military ceremony in which soldiers stand or march together so that they can be examined: *cadets **on parade***

parade[2] *v.* **1** [I] to march together to celebrate or protest something: *Peace demonstrators **paraded through/along/in** the streets.* **2** [I] (disapproving) to walk around an area in order to attract attention: *A couple of teenage girls were **parading around** the pool in their bikinis.* **3** [T] to show someone to the public, especially in order to prove that you have control or power over him/her: *The prisoners were paraded in front of the TV cameras.* **4** [T] to show a particular quality or possession in order to make people notice you: *Young athletes will get a chance to parade their skills.*

par·a·digm /ˈpærəˌdaɪm/ (Ac) *n.* [C] (formal) a model or typical example of something that explains an idea or process very clearly: *The Holocaust of World War II is a* ***paradigm of*** *evil.* | *Pius XII remained the paradigm of what a pope should be.* [ORIGIN: 1400—1500 Late Latin *paradigma*, from Greek *paradeigma*, from *paradeiknynai* "to show side by side"] **—paradigmatic** /ˌpærədɪgˈmæţɪk/ *adj.*

par·a·dise /ˈpærəˌdaɪs, -ˌdaɪz/ *n.* **1** [U] a place or situation that is extremely pleasant, beautiful, or enjoyable: *an island paradise* **2** [singular] a place that has everything you need to do a particular activity: *This mall is a shopper's paradise.* **3** [U] heaven [ORIGIN: 1100—1200 Old French, Late Latin, from Greek *paradeisos* "enclosed park"]

par·a·dox /ˈpærəˌdɑks/ *n.* [C] a statement or situation that seems strange or impossible because it contains two ideas or qualities that are very different but are both true: *It's a paradox that such a very rich country has so many extremely poor people.* **—paradoxical** /ˌpærəˈdɑksɪkəl/ *adj.* **—paradoxically** *adv.*

par·af·fin /ˈpærəfɪn/ *n.* [U] a soft white substance used for making CANDLES

par·a·gon /ˈpærəˌgɑn/ *n.* [C] someone who is a perfect example of something: *Alice was a* ***paragon of*** *wifely* ***virtue.***

par·a·graph /ˈpærəˌgræf/ (Ac) *n.* [C] ENG. LANG. ARTS a group of several sentences that start on a new line and deal with one idea in a piece of writing: *I've only read the first paragraph of the article.* | *Your closing paragraph should sum up your argument.* [ORIGIN: 1400—1500 Old French, Medieval Latin, from Greek, from *paragraphein* "to write beside"]

par·a·keet /ˈpærəˌkit/ *n.* [C] a small brightly colored bird with a long tail, that is often kept as a pet [ORIGIN: 1500—1600 Spanish *periquito*, from Old French *perroquet*]

par·a·le·gal /ˌpærəˈligəl/ *n.* [C] someone whose job is to help a lawyer do his/her work

par·al·lel¹ /ˈpærəˌlɛl/ (Ac) *n.* [C] **1** a relationship or similarity between two things, especially things that happen or exist in different places or at different times: *The article* ***draws a parallel between*** *the political situation now and the situation in the 1930s* (=it shows how they are similar). | *The administration would like us to see* ***parallels with*** *World War II in today's conflict.* | *The close parallels between the two stories suggest that they come from the same source.* **2** an imaginary line drawn on a map of the Earth that is parallel to the EQUATOR: *The 42nd parallel is the northern border of Pennsylvania.* [ORIGIN: 1500—1600 Latin *parallelus*, from Greek *parallelos*, from *para* "beside" + *allelon* "of one another"]

parallel² *adj.* **1** two lines that are parallel to each other are the same distance apart along their whole length: *a street* ***parallel to/with*** *the railroad* | *Draw* ***parallel lines*** *from the top to the bottom of the page.* → *see picture at* LINE¹ **2** similar and happening at the same time: *two parallel murder investigations* | *The novel has two parallel story lines.*

parallel³ *v.* [T] (formal) to be very similar to something else: *The movie's plot closely parallels a play by Shakespeare.* | *The increase in the birds' population has been paralleled elsewhere.*

ˌparallel ˈcircuit *n.* [C] PHYSICS an electrical CIRCUIT (=complete circle that an electric current travels in) in which electricity travels to each light or SWITCH by a straight line, without going through other lights, etc. → SERIES CIRCUIT

par·al·lel·ism /ˈpærəlɛˌlɪzəm/ *n.* [U] ENG. LANG. ARTS the use of sentences or phrases that have similar GRAMMATICAL structures in writing or poetry

par·al·lel·o·gram /ˌpærəˈlɛləˌgræm/ *n.* [C] MATH a flat shape with four straight sides, in which each side is the same length as the side parallel to it → *see picture at* POLYGON

ˌparallel ˈstructure *n.* [U] ENG. LANG. ARTS a way of connecting different ideas in a piece of writing or a speech by expressing them in the same GRAMMATICAL structure

pa·ral·y·sis /pəˈræləsɪs/ *n.* [U] **1** the loss of the ability to move or feel part of your body: *Such injuries can cause permanent paralysis.* **2** a lack of ability to operate correctly or to do anything: *Congress's lack of cooperation with the White House has caused political paralysis.*

par·a·lyze /ˈpærəˌlaɪz/ *v.* [T] **1** to make someone lose the ability to move part of his/her body, or to feel anything in it **2** to make something or someone unable to operate normally: *Heavy snow has paralyzed several cities in the eastern States.* | *He was paralyzed by fear.* **—paralyzed** *adj.*: *The stroke left him paralyzed and unable to feed himself.*

par·a·med·ic /ˌpærəˈmɛdɪk/ *n.* [C] someone who usually works in an AMBULANCE, and is trained to help sick or injured people but is not a doctor or nurse

pa·ram·et·er /pəˈræməţɚ/ (Ac) *n.* [C usually plural] a limit that controls the way that something should be done: *Congress will decide on* ***parameters for*** *the investigation.* | *Business parameters are set by the market and the customers' demands.* [ORIGIN: 1600—1700 Modern Latin *para-* "beside" + Greek *metron* "measure"]

par·a·mil·i·tar·y /ˌpærəˈmɪləˌtɛri/ *adj.* organized like an army, but not part of the legal military

P

forces of a country: *extremist paramilitary groups* —**paramilitary** *n.* [C]

par·a·mount /ˈpærəˌmaʊnt/ *adj.* more important than anything else: *The needs of the customer should be paramount.*

THESAURUS **important, of great/considerable importance, crucial, vital, essential, major, key** → IMPORTANT

par·a·noid /ˈpærəˌnɔɪd/ *adj.* **1** believing unreasonably that you cannot trust other people, or that they are trying to harm you: *All the stress about job losses is making me a little paranoid.* **2** suffering from a mental illness that makes you believe that other people are trying to harm you —**paranoia** /ˌpærəˈnɔɪə/ *n.* [U]

par·a·pher·na·lia /ˌpærəfɚˈneɪlyə, -fəˈneɪl-/ *n.* [U] a lot of small things that belong to someone or that are used for a particular activity: *photographic paraphernalia* [ORIGIN: 1600—1700 Medieval Latin, Greek *parapherna* "things brought to a marriage by a woman apart from the agreed amount of money"]

par·a·phrase /ˈpærəˌfreɪz/ *v.* [T] ENG. LANG. ARTS to express what someone has written or said in a way that is shorter or easier to understand: *Write a paragraph that paraphrases the story.* —**paraphrase** *n.* [C]

par·a·ple·gic /ˌpærəˈplidʒɪk/ *n.* [C] someone who is unable to move the lower part of his/her body

par·a·site /ˈpærəˌsaɪt/ *n.* [C] **1** BIOLOGY a plant or animal that lives on or in another plant or animal and gets food from it **2** (disapproving) a lazy person who does not work but depends on other people —**parasitic** /ˌpærəˈsɪṭɪk◂/ *adj.*

par·a·sol /ˈpærəˌsɔl, -ˌsɑl/ *n.* [C] a type of UMBRELLA used for protection from the Sun

par·a·troop·er /ˈpærəˌtrupɚ/ *n.* [C] a soldier who is trained to jump out of an AIRPLANE using a PARACHUTE

par·cel¹ /ˈpɑrsəl/ *n.* [C] **1** a package **2** an area of land that is part of a larger area that has been divided: *a 50-acre parcel in the foothills*

parcel² *v.*

parcel sth ↔ **out** *phr. v.* to divide or share something among several people or groups: *The foundation receives the money, then parcels it out to various projects.*

ˈparcel post *n.* [U] the slowest and cheapest way of sending packages by mail in the U.S.

parched /pɑrtʃt/ *adj.* **1** (literary) extremely dry: *parched fields* **2 be parched** (informal) to be very THIRSTY: *I'm parched!*

par·don¹ /ˈpɑrdn/ *v.* [T] **1 pardon me** (spoken) **a)** used in order to politely say sorry after you have made an impolite sound such as a BURP or a YAWN **b)** used in order to politely say sorry when you have accidentally pushed someone, interrupted him/her, etc.: *Oh, pardon me, I didn't realize you were on the phone.* **c)** *also* **Pardon?** used in order to politely ask someone to repeat what s/he has just said because you did not hear it correctly **d)** used in order to politely get someone's attention in order to ask a question: *Pardon me, do you know what time it is?* **e)** used before you politely correct someone or disagree with him/her: *Pardon me, but I don't think that's true.* **2** to officially allow someone to be free without being punished, although a court has decided s/he is guilty of a crime: *Before he could serve his full term, he was pardoned by the governor.* [ORIGIN: 1200—1300 Old French *pardoner*, from Late Latin *perdonare* "to give freely"]

pardon² *n.* [C] an official order allowing someone to be free without being punished, although a court has decided s/he is guilty of a crime: *The governor was persuaded to **grant/give** Davis **a pardon**.* → **I beg your pardon** *at* BEG

par·don·a·ble /ˈpɑrdn-əbəl/ *adj.* (formal) possible to forgive or excuse: *a pardonable error*

pare /pɛr/ *v.* [T] to cut off the thin outer part of a fruit or vegetable: *Pare the apples and slice them into chunks.*

pare sth ↔ **down** *phr. v.* to gradually reduce an amount or number: *Production costs have to be pared down.*

par·ent /ˈpɛrənt, ˈpær-/ *n.* [C] the father or mother of a person or animal: *My parents are coming to visit next week.* | *Many **single parents** (=who do not live with their child's other parent) cannot afford childcare.* [ORIGIN: 1400—1500 Old French, Latin, present participle of *parere* "to give birth to"] —**parental** /pəˈrɛntl/ *adj.*: *parental rights*

par·ent·age /ˈpɛrəntɪdʒ, ˈpær-/ *n.* [U] (formal) someone's parents and the country they are from: *children of French-Canadian parentage*

pa·ren·the·sis /pəˈrɛnθəsɪs/ *n.* (plural **parentheses** /-siz/) [C usually plural] ENG. LANG. ARTS one of the marks ( ), used in writing to separate additional information from the main information: *The numbers **in parentheses** refer to page numbers.* [ORIGIN: 1500—1600 Late Latin, Greek, from *parentithenai* "to put in"]

par·ent·hood /ˈpɛrəntˌhʊd, ˈpær-/ *n.* [U] the state of being a parent: *They felt that they were not yet ready for parenthood.*

pa·ri·ah /pəˈraɪə/ *n.* [C] a person, organization, country, etc. that is hated and avoided by others: *The regime was treated as an international pariah and subjected to international sanctions.*

par·ish /ˈpærɪʃ/ *n.* **1** [C] the area that a priest in some Christian churches is responsible for **2 the parish** the members of a particular church —**parishioner** /pəˈrɪʃənɚ/ *n.* [C]

par·i·ty /ˈpærəṭi/ *n.* [U] the state of being equal, especially having equal pay, rights, or power: *Our* *employees are demanding* ***parity with*** *other workers in the industry.*

park¹ /pɑrk/ *n.* [C] **1** a large open area with grass and trees in a town, where people can walk, play games, etc.: *We went for a walk* ***in the park.*** | *a park bench* | *Central Park* **2** a large area of land in the country, that has been kept in its natural state to protect the plants and animals there: *a* ***state/national park*** **3** a field where baseball is played: *Fenway Park* [ORIGIN: 1200—1300 Old French *parc*, from Medieval Latin *parricus*] → AMUSEMENT PARK, BALL PARK, THEME PARK, TRAILER PARK

park² *v.* [I,T] to put a car or other vehicle in a particular place for a period of time: *Is it okay if I park here?* | *Park your car in the back lot.* → DRIVE¹

par·ka /'pɑrkə/ *n.* [C] a thick warm coat with a HOOD [ORIGIN: 1700—1800 Aleut (a language spoken in the Aleutian Islands) "skin, outer clothing," from Russian, "animal skin and fur," from Yurak (a language spoken in Siberia)]

ˌpark and 'ride *n.* [U] a system in which you leave your car in a special place in one part of a city, and then take a bus or train from there to the center of town

park·ing /'pɑrkɪŋ/ *n.* [U] **1** the act of parking a car: *The sign said "No Parking."* **2** spaces in which you can leave a car: *Parking is available on Lemay Street.* | *We found a* ***parking space/place*** *near the door.*

'parking gaˌrage *n.* [C] a building with several floors where cars can be parked: *an underground parking garage*

'parking lot *n.* [C] an open area where cars can be parked

'parking ˌmeter *n.* [C] a machine that you put money into when you park your car next to it

park·way /'pɑrkweɪ/ *n.* [C] a wide road, usually with grass and trees in the middle or along the sides

par·lay /'pɑrleɪ, -li/ *v.* (**parlayed**, **parlays**)
parlay sth **into** sth *phr. v.* (written) to use something that you already have, such as your skills, experience, or money, to become successful or get something that you want: *She parlayed a $600 investment into the state's largest home decorating company.*

par·lia·ment /'pɑrləmənt/ *n.* [C] the group of people in some countries who are elected to make laws and discuss important national affairs [ORIGIN: 1200—1300 Old French *parlement*, from *parler* "to speak"] —**parliamentary** /ˌpɑrlə'mɛntri◂, -'mɛntəri◂/ *adj.*

ˌparliamentary de'mocracy *n.* [C,U] POLITICS a system of government in which citizens vote to elect representatives to a PARLIAMENT, or a country that has this system

par·lor /'pɑrlɚ/ *n.* [C] **1** a store or type of business that provides a particular service: *a beauty parlor* | *a funeral parlor* **2** (old-fashioned) a room in a house, that has comfortable chairs and is used for meeting guests

Par·me·san /'pɑrməˌzɑn/ *also* **'Parmesan ˌcheese** *n.* [U] a hard strong-tasting Italian cheese [ORIGIN: 1500—1600 French "of Parma," city in Italy where the cheese was first made]

pa·ro·chi·al /pə'roʊkiəl/ *adj.* **1** relating to a particular church: *a* ***parochial school*** (=a private school that is run by a particular church) **2** (disapproving) only interested in the things that affect you and your local area: *Brian has a very parochial world view.*

par·o·dy¹ /'pærədi/ *n.* (plural **parodies**) [C,U] ENG. LANG. ARTS a performance or a piece of writing or music that copies a particular well-known style in a funny way: *a* ***parody of*** *a romance novel*

parody² *v.* (**parodied**, **parodies**) [T] to copy someone's style or attitude in a funny way

pa·role /pə'roʊl/ *n.* [U] LAW permission for someone to leave prison before the end of his/her sentence. People who are on parole must behave well and report regularly to the police or other authority. If they do not, they are sent back to prison: *He was released* ***on parole*** *after serving five years.* | *She is appearing before the* ***parole board*** (=the official group that can give a prisoner parole) *next week.* [ORIGIN: 1400—1500 French "speech, word, word of honor," from Late Latin *parabola*] —**parole** *v.* [T]

par·quet /pɑr'keɪ, 'pɑrkeɪ/ *n.* [U] small flat blocks of wood laid in a pattern that cover the floor of a room

par·rot¹ /'pærət/ *n.* [C] a brightly colored tropical bird with a curved beak, that can be taught to copy human speech

parrot² *v.* [T] (disapproving) to repeat someone else's words or ideas without really understanding them

par·si·mo·ni·ous /ˌpɑrsə'moʊniəs◂/ *adj.* (formal) extremely unwilling to spend money (SYN) stingy —**parsimoniously** *adv.* —**parsimony** /'pɑrsəˌmoʊni/ *n.* [U]

pars·ley /'pɑrsli/ *n.* [U] a plant with groups of curled leaves, used in cooking or as a decoration on food

part¹ /pɑrt/ *n.*
1 OF A WHOLE [C,U] one of the pieces or features of something, such as an object, place, event, or period of time: *Which* ***part of*** *town do you live in?* | ***The best/worst part*** *of the movie was the ending.* | *Getting Dad to agree will be* ***the hard/easy part.*** | ***A large/good part of*** (=a lot of) *my time is spent reading.* | *We waited for* ***the better part of*** (=most of) *an hour.*

THESAURUS

piece – one of several different parts that you join together to make something: *One of the pieces of the jigsaw puzzle was missing.*
section – one of several parts that something is divided into: *the sports section of the newspaper*

segment – a part of something that is different from or divided from the whole: *Teenagers form a distinct segment of the market for this product.*
portion – a part of something larger: *The newspaper printed only a small portion of the interview.*
chapter – one of the parts that a book is divided into: *I've read the first two chapters.*
scene – one of the parts that a play or movie is divided into: *the opening scene | a love scene*
department – one part of a large organization, which is responsible for a particular kind of work: *the marketing department*
stage, step, phase, point, round → STAGE[1]

P

2 SEPARATE PIECE [C usually plural] one of the separate pieces that a machine or piece of equipment is made of: *Do you sell parts for Ford cars?*
3 play/have a part (in sth) to be one of several things that make something happen or be successful: *The college's excellent reputation **played a big/important/major part in** her decision to go there.*
4 take part to be involved in an activity, event, etc. together with other people (SYN) **participate**: *Ten runners **took part in** the race.*
5 WHAT SB DID [C,U] what someone did in an activity, especially one that was shared by several people: *We'd like to thank Walter for his **part in** organizing the concert. | It was a huge mistake **on her part*** (=that she made).
6 IN A PLAY/MOVIE [C] the words and actions of a particular character in a play, movie, etc., performed by an actor: *Kessler **played/had the part of** Hamlet.*
7 QUANTITY [C] used to say how much of each particular substance there is or should be in a mixture containing two or more substances: *Mix two parts sand to one part cement.*
8 HAIR [C] the line on your head made by dividing your hair with a comb
9 for the most part *also* **in large part** mostly, in most places, or most of the time: *She is, for the most part, a fair person.*
10 in part (formal) to some degree, but not completely: *The accident was due in part to the bad weather.*

part[2] *v.* **1** [I,T] to pull the two sides of something apart, or to move apart in this way, making a space in the middle: *He parted the curtains and looked out into the street.* **2** [I] (formal) to separate from someone, or end a relationship with him/her: *Sharon and I parted on friendly terms.* **3** [T] if you part your hair, you comb some of your hair in one direction and the rest in the other direction **4 part company a)** to separate from someone, or end a relationship with someone: *Dick **parted company with** Rogers after a property deal that lost money.* **b)** to no longer agree with someone
part with sth *phr. v.* to get rid of something although you do not want to: *She couldn't bear to part with the dress.*

part[3] *adv.* **part sth, part sth** if something is part one thing, part another, it consists of both those things: *The English test is part written, part spoken.*

par·tial /ˈpɑrʃəl/ *adj.* **1** not complete: *The airline released a partial list of the flight's passengers.* **2 be partial to sth** (formal) to like something very much: *The Beals are partial to country music.* **3** unfairly supporting one person or one side against another (ANT) **impartial**

par·ti·al·i·ty /ˌpɑrʃiˈæləṭi/ *n.* [U] unfair support of one person or group more than another

par·tial·ly /ˈpɑrʃəli/ *adv.* not completely: *He's only partially to blame.*

par·tic·i·pant /pɑrˈtɪsəpənt, pɚ-/ (Ac) *n.* [C] someone who is taking part in an activity or event: *The Chinese will be **participants in** the negotiations. | Jesse is an **active participant** in class.*

par·tic·i·pate /pɑrˈtɪsəˌpeɪt, pɚ-/ (Ac) *v.* [I] to take part in an activity or event: *If you'd like to participate, send us your name and address. | Thanks to everyone who **participated in** the festival. | It is only in a democracy that all citizens participate equally.* [ORIGIN: 1400—1500 Latin, past participle of *participare*, from *particeps* "taking part"]

par·ti·ci·pa·tion /pɑrˌtɪsəˈpeɪʃən, pɚ-/ (Ac) *n.* [U] the act of taking part in something: *The suspect was charged with **participation in** an illegal organization.*

par·tic·i·pa·to·ry /pɑrˈtɪsəpəˌtɔri, pɚ-/ (Ac) *adj.* [usually before noun] (formal) a participatory way of organizing something, making decisions, etc. is one that involves everyone who will be affected: *Participatory management involves workers as well as managers.*

par·ti·cip·i·al /ˌpɑrṭəˈsɪpiəl/ *adj.* ENG. LANG. ARTS using a participle, or having the form of a participle: *a participial phrase | participial structures*

par·ti·ci·ple /ˈpɑrṭəˌsɪpəl/ *n.* [C] ENG. LANG. ARTS in grammar, the form of a verb, usually ending in "-ing" or "-ed," that is used in compounds to make verb tenses, or as an adjective or GERUND → PAST PARTICIPLE, PRESENT PARTICIPLE

par·ti·cle /ˈpɑrṭɪkəl/ *n.* [C] **1** a very small piece of something: *dust particles* **2** PHYSICS one of the very small pieces of matter that an atom consists of: *particles such as protons and electrons* **3** ENG. LANG. ARTS an adverb or PREPOSITION that combines with a verb to form a PHRASAL VERB

par·tic·u·lar[1] /pɚˈtɪkyəlɚ/ *adj.* **1** [only before noun] a particular thing or person is the one that you are talking about, and not any other: *There's one particular song I've been trying to find. | Consumers can easily find out how much caffeine a particular product contains.* **2** [only before noun] special or important enough to mention separately: *Police say there was **no particular reason** why the victim was attacked. | There was nothing in the letter **of particular importance**.* **3** very careful about choosing exactly what you like, and not easily satisfied SYN **fussy**: *He's very **particular about** what he eats.*

particular² *n.* **in particular** special or specific: *Is there **anything/something in particular** I can help you with?*

par·tic·u·lar·ly /pɚˈtɪkyələli, -ˈtɪkyəli/ *adv.* **1** especially: *We are hoping to expand our business, particularly in China.* **2 not particularly a)** not very: *She's not particularly pretty.* **b)** (spoken) not very much, or not really: *"Do you like cats?" "No, not particularly."*

part·ing¹ /ˈpɑrt̬ɪŋ/ *n.* [C,U] (literary) an occasion when two people leave each other: *an emotional parting at the airport*

parting² *adj.* **1 parting kiss/gift/glance etc.** something that you give someone as you leave **2 parting shot** a cruel or severe remark that you make just as you are leaving: *As a parting shot, Ashley told him never to call her again.*

par·ti·san¹ /ˈpɑrt̬əzən, -sən/ *adj.* POLITICS showing support for a particular political party, plan, or leader, and criticizing all others: *The Democrats were accused of partisan politics in refusing to support the bill.*

par·ti·san² *n.* [C] **1** POLITICS someone who supports a particular political party, plan, or leader: *a well-known partisan of the democratic movement in China* **2** HISTORY a member of an armed group that fights against an enemy that has taken control of its country: *Italian partisans fought against the Nazis during World War II.*

par·ti·san·ship /ˈpɑrt̬əzənˌʃɪp/ *n.* [U] POLITICS the act of showing strong support for a particular political party, plan, or leader

par·ti·tion¹ /pɑrˈtɪʃən, pɚ-/ *n.* **1** [C] a thin wall that separates one part of a room from another **2** [U] POLITICS the separation of a country into two or more independent countries: *the conflict led to the **partition of** the country into three separate states.*

partition² *v.* [T] to divide a country, room, or building into two or more parts

THESAURUS separate, divide ➔ SEPARATE²

partition sth ↔ **off** *phr. v.* to divide part of a room from the rest, using a partition

part·ly /ˈpɑrtli/ *adv.* to some degree, but not completely: *The accident was partly my fault.* | *The company's success is **partly due to** a strong economy.* | *The forecast is for **partly cloudy** skies.*

part·ner /ˈpɑrt˺nɚ/ Ac *n.* [C] **1** someone with whom you do a particular activity, for example dancing, or playing a game against two other people: *my tennis partner* **2** one of the owners of a business: *She's a partner in a law firm.* **3** one of two people who are married, or who live together and have a sexual relationship: *Discuss your worries with your partner.* | *In some cultures, parents choose the marriage partner for their daughter.* [ORIGIN: 1300—1400 Anglo-French *parcener* "heir sharing half," from Old French *parçon* "share;" influenced by *part*]

part·ner·ship /ˈpɑrt˺nɚˌʃɪp/ Ac *n.* **1** [U] the state of being a partner, especially in business: *We've been **in partnership with** them for five years.* | *One big advantage of partnership is the ability to share decision-making and risk-taking.* **2** [C] a relationship in which two or more people, organizations, etc. work together to achieve something: *a **partnership between** the college and the local business community* | *Leaders of the two countries worked in close partnership throughout the 20th century.* **3** [C] ECONOMICS a business owned by two or more partners: *There is always some compromise involved in operating any business partnership.*

ˌpart of ˈspeech *n.* (plural **parts of speech**) [C] ENG. LANG. ARTS in grammar, any of the types into which words are divided according to their use, such as noun, verb, or adjective

par·tridge /ˈpɑrtrɪdʒ/ *n.* [C,U] a fat brown bird with a short tail, that some people shoot as a sport or for food

ˌpart-ˈtime *adj., adv.* someone who has a part-time job works for only part of each day or week ➔ FULL-TIME: *I **worked part-time** at a bookstore when I was in college.* | *a part-time job*

part·way /ˌpɑrt˺ˈweɪ◂/ *adv.* after part of a distance has been traveled, or after part of a period of time has passed: *Dave arrived **partway through** the lecture.*

par·ty¹ /ˈpɑrt̬i/ *n.* (plural **parties**) [C] **1** an occasion when people meet together to enjoy themselves by eating, drinking, dancing, etc.: *We're **having/giving/throwing a party** on Saturday.* | *a birthday party* | *a surprise party*

THESAURUS

get-together – a small informal party
bash (informal) – a party
dinner party – a party where people are invited to someone's house for an evening meal
birthday party – a party to celebrate someone's birthday, especially a child's
house-warming party – a party that you have when you move into a new house
cocktail party – a party that people go to in order to talk and drink together for a few hours
bachelor party – a social event that is just for men, which happens before a wedding
baby/wedding/bridal shower – an event at which people give presents to a woman who is going to have a baby or get married
reception – a large formal party, for example after a wedding
celebration – a party that is organized in order to celebrate something

2 an organization of people with the same political aims, that you can vote for in elections: *the Democratic Party* **3** a group of people that has been organized in order to do something: *A **search party***

P

was formed to find the missing girl. | *Foster,* ***party of*** *six, your table is ready.* **4** (formal) one of the people or groups involved in an argument, agreement, etc., especially a legal one: *The two parties will meet to discuss a settlement.* **5 party animal** (informal) someone who enjoys parties a lot [ORIGIN: 1200—1300 Old French *partie* "part, party," from *partir* "to divide"]

party² *v.* (**partied**, **parties**) [I] (informal) to enjoy yourself, especially by drinking alcohol, eating, dancing, etc.: *We were out partying until 4 a.m.*

pas·cal /pæ'skæl/ *n.* [C] PHYSICS (*written abbreviation* **Pa**) a unit of pressure which is equal to a force of one NEWTON in a square meter (=square area measuring one meter high by one meter wide)

P

pass

pass¹ /pæs/ *v.*

1 GO PAST [I,T] *also* **pass by** to move to a particular point, object, person, etc. and go past him, her, or it: *Angie waved at me as she passed.* | *A car passed us doing at least 90 miles an hour.* | *I pass by her house every day.*

USAGE

Passed is the past tense and past participle of the verb **pass**: *We've just passed Tim's house.*
Past is an adjective or noun that is used to talk about a period of time before now: *The past year has been very difficult.* | *things that happened in the past*
Past is also an adverb and a preposition used in order to describe something's movement or position in relation to other things: *She drove past us on her way to work.* | *The hotel is just past the church.*

2 MOVE IN A DIRECTION [I] to move from one place to another, following a particular direction: *We* ***passed through*** *Texas on our way to Mexico.* | *A plane* ***passed over*** *the fields.*
3 GO THROUGH/ACROSS ETC. [I,T] to go across, through, around, etc. something else, or to make something do this: *The road* ***passes through*** *some pretty little towns.* | *She was* ***just passing through*** (=traveling through a place) *on her way to Miami.* | *Pass the rope around the tree.*
4 GIVE [T] to take something and put it in someone's hand SYN **hand**: *Please pass the salt.* | *Can you pass me a napkin?*
5 SPORTS [I,T] to kick, throw, or hit a ball or other object to another member of your team: *My dad taught me how to pass a football.*

THESAURUS **throw, toss, chuck, hurl, fling** → THROW¹

6 TIME a) [I] if time passes, it goes by: *A year passed before I learned the truth.* **b)** [T] to spend time in a particular way: *I cleaned my apartment to* ***pass the time****.*
7 TEST/CLASS a) [I,T] to succeed in a test or class ANT **fail**: *You'll never pass if you don't start studying.* | *He's worried he won't pass history.* **b)** [T] to officially decide that someone has passed a test ANT **fail**: *Do you think Mrs. Cox will pass us?*
8 LAW/DECISION [T] to officially accept a law or proposal, especially by voting: *The motion was passed, 15 votes to 3.*

THESAURUS **approve, ratify, sanction, endorse** → APPROVE

9 let sth pass to deliberately not say something when someone says or does something that you do not like: *Carla made some comment about my work, but I decided to* ***let it pass****.*
10 END [I] to stop existing or happening SYN **end**: *The storm soon passed.* | *Ann will be upset for a while, but it'll pass.*
11 pass judgment (on sb) to say whether you think someone or something is right or wrong: *I'm only here to listen, not to pass judgment.*
12 DON'T KNOW THE ANSWER [I] (spoken) to say that you do not know the answer to a question: *I had to* ***pass on*** *the last question.*

pass sth ↔ **around** *phr. v.*
to give something to one person in a group, who then gives it to another person, etc.: *Pass these papers around, will you?*

pass away *phr. v.*
to die – used in order to avoid saying this directly

pass sb **by** *phr. v.*
if something passes you by, it happens, but you are not involved in it: *Robin felt that* ***life was passing*** *her* ***by****.*

pass sth ↔ **down** *phr. v.*
to give or teach something to people who are younger than you or who live after you: *These traditions have been* ***passed down from*** *one generation* ***to*** *the next.*

pass for sb/sth *phr. v.*
to seem very similar to someone or something else, so that people might not realize what or who they are looking at: *With her hair cut like that, she could pass for a boy.*

pass sb/sth **off as** sth *phr. v.*
to try to make people think that someone or something is something that he, she, or it is not: *He tried to pass himself off as a police officer.*

pass sth ↔ **on** *phr. v.*
1 to tell someone a piece of information that someone else has told you: *She said she'd* ***pass*** *the message* ***on to*** *Ms. Chen.*

2 to give something to someone else: *Take one and **pass** the rest **on to** the next person.*

pass out *phr. v.*
1 to become unconscious
2 pass sth ↔ **out** to give something to each one of a group of people: *Please **pass out** the dictionaries to the class.*

THESAURUS give out, hand out, share, distribute → GIVE[1]

pass sb ↔ **over** *phr. v.*
if you pass over someone for a job, you give the job to someone else who is younger or lower in the organization than s/he is

pass sth ↔ **up** *phr. v.*
pass up a chance/opportunity/offer etc. to not use a chance to do something: *I couldn't pass up an opportunity to meet the president.*

pass² *n.* [C] **1** the act of kicking, throwing, or hitting a ball or other object to another member of your team during a game: *a 30-yard pass* **2** an official document that proves you are allowed to enter a building or travel on something without paying: *a bus pass* | *a museum pass* **3** a road or path that goes between mountains to the other side: *a narrow mountain pass* **4 make a pass at sb** (informal) to try to kiss or touch another person with the intention of having sex with him/her

pass·a·ble /ˈpæsəbəl/ *adj.* **1** (formal) good enough to be acceptable, but not very good: *Al speaks passable Spanish.*

THESAURUS satisfactory, good enough, acceptable, all right/okay, reasonable, respectable, adequate → SATISFACTORY

2 a road or river that is passable is not blocked, so you can travel along or across it (ANT) **impassable**

pas·sage /ˈpæsɪdʒ/ *n.* **1** [C] *also* **pas·sage·way** /ˈpæsɪdʒˌweɪ/ a narrow area with walls on each side that connects one room or place to another: *a dark passage at the back of the building* **2** [C] a short part of a book, poem, speech, piece of music, etc.: *a **passage from** the Bible* **3** [U] the process of having a new law accepted by Congress or a similar organization: *Supporters say that passage of the bill will reduce crime.* **4** [U] (formal) the action of going across, over, or along something: *The bridge isn't strong enough to allow the **passage of** heavy vehicles.* **5** [C] a tube in your body that air or liquid can pass through: *nasal passages* **6 the passage of time** the passing of time: *Her condition improved with the passage of time.*

pass·book /ˈpæsbʊk/ *n.* [C] a book for keeping a record of the money you put into and take out of your bank account

pas·sé /pæˈseɪ/ *adj.* no longer modern or fashionable: *a writing style that has become passé*

pas·sen·ger /ˈpæsəndʒɚ/ *n.* [C] someone who is traveling in a car, AIRPLANE, boat, etc., but is not driving it: *There were only a few other passengers.* | *Police found a gun under the car's **passenger seat*** (=the seat next to the driver).

pass·er·by /ˌpæsɚˈbaɪ/ *n.* (plural **passersby**) [C] someone who is walking past a place by chance: *Several passersby saw the accident.*

pass·ing¹ /ˈpæsɪŋ/ *adj.* **1** going past: *A passing motorist gave her a ride.* **2** continuing or lasting for only a short time: *He gave the report only a passing glance.* | *It's just a passing fad.*

passing² *n.* **1 in passing** if you say something in passing, you mention it while you are mainly talking about something else: *The actress **mentioned in passing** that she had once worked in a factory.* **2** [U] (formal) someone's death – used in order to avoid saying this directly

pas·sion /ˈpæʃən/ *n.* **1** [C,U] a very strongly felt emotion, especially of love, hatred, or anger: *He spoke **with passion** about the situation in his country.* | *her **passion for** two men* **2** [C] a strong liking for something: *a **passion for** golf*

pas·sion·ate /ˈpæʃənɪt/ *adj.* showing passion, or full of passion: *a passionate kiss* | *a passionate speech* —**passionately** *adv.*

THESAURUS enthusiastic, eager, ardent, zealous → ENTHUSIASTIC

pas·sive¹ /ˈpæsɪv/ (AC) *adj.* **1** tending to accept situations or things that other people do, without attempting to change or fight against them: *"I'm a very passive person," she admitted.* **2** not actively involved in something that is happening: *Children tend to learn more in an active situation, rather than a passive one.* [ORIGIN: 1300—1400 Latin *passivus*, from *pati* "to suffer"] —**passively** *adv.* —**passivity** /pæˈsɪvət̬i/ *n.* [U]

passive² *n.* **the passive (voice)** ENG. LANG. ARTS in grammar, in the passive voice, the action of the verb has an effect on the subject of the sentence. It is shown in English by the verb "be" followed by a past participle. In the sentence "Oranges are grown in California," the verb is in the passive voice. → ACTIVE: *Change the verbs in the following sentences into the passive.*

ˌpassive ˈsmoking *n.* [U] the act of breathing in smoke from someone else's cigarette, pipe, etc., although you do not want to

Pass·o·ver /ˈpæsˌoʊvɚ/ *n.* an important Jewish holiday in the spring, when people remember the escape of the Jews from Egypt [ORIGIN: 1500—1600 Translation of Hebrew *pesah* "to pass without affecting;" because, according to the Bible, God did not kill Jewish children when he killed children of other races]

pass·port /ˈpæspɔrt/ *n.* [C] a small official document given by a government to a citizen, which proves who that person is and allows them to leave the country and enter other countries

COLLOCATIONS
A **passport holder** is the person who a passport belongs to.

If you travel to a foreign country, you must **show** your **passport** at immigration (=the place in an airport, at a border, etc. where officials check your documents) when you enter the country and may **have/get** your **passport stamped**.
A **valid passport** is officially acceptable.
A **passport** that has **expired** is too old to be acceptable.

pass·word /ˈpæswɚd/ *n.* [C] **1** a secret group of letters or numbers that you must type into a computer before you can use a system or program: *Enter your username and password.* | *I've **forgotten** my **password**.* **2** a secret word or phrase that you must use before being allowed to enter a place that is guarded

P

past¹ /pæst/ *adj.* **1** [only before noun] having happened, existed, or been experienced before now: *He knew from past experience not to argue.* | *Our current problems are the result of past mistakes.* **2** [only before noun] a little earlier than the present, or up until now: *Tim's been out of town for the past week.* | *the past six months* **3** finished or having come to an end: *The time for discussion is past.* **4** [only before noun] achieving something in the past, or holding an important position in the past (SYN) **former**: *She's a past president of the club.*

past² *prep.* **1** farther than: *My house is **just past** the bridge.* **2** up to and beyond: *She walked **right past** me without saying hello.* | *We drove past Al's old house.* **3** after a particular time: *It's ten past nine* (=ten minutes after nine o'clock). | *It was **way past** midnight when the party ended.* **4 I wouldn't put it past sb (to do sth)** (spoken) used in order to say that you would not be surprised if someone did something bad or unusual because it is typical of him/her: *I wouldn't put it past Mark to lie to his wife.*

past³ *n.* **1 the past** the time that existed before now, and the things that happened during that time: *People travel more now than they did **in the past**.* | *We should ignore the past and concentrate on the future.* **2** [singular] all the things that have happened to you in the time before now: *I'd like to forget my past and start all over.*

past⁴ *adv.* **1** up to and beyond a particular place: *Hal and his friends drove past at top speed.* **2 go past** if a period of time goes past, it passes: *Several weeks went past without any news from home.*

pas·ta /ˈpɑstə/ *n.* [U] an Italian food made from flour, water, and sometimes eggs, and cut into various shapes, usually eaten with a sauce

paste¹ /peɪst/ *n.* **1** [U] a type of thick glue that is used for sticking paper onto things **2** [C,U] a soft thick mixture that can be easily shaped or spread: *Mix the water and the powder into a smooth paste.* | *tomato paste*

paste² *v.* **1** [I,T] IT to make words that you have removed or copied appear in a new place on a computer screen → COPY, CUT **2** [T] to stick something to something else using paste

pas·tel /pæˈstɛl/ *n.* **1** [C] a soft pale color, such as pale blue or pink

THESAURUS **light, pale** → LIGHT²

2 [C,U] a small colored stick used for drawing pictures, made of a substance like CHALK —**pastel** *adj.*: *soft **pastel colors***

pas·teur·ize /ˈpæstʃəˌraɪz, -stəˌraɪz/ *v.* [T] to heat a liquid, especially milk, in a special way that kills any harmful BACTERIA in it —**pasteurization** /ˌpæstʃərəˈzeɪʃən/ *n.* [U]

pas·tiche /pæˈstiʃ/ *n.* **1** [C] ENG. LANG. ARTS a work of art that consists of a variety of different styles put together: *The novel is a **pastiche of** diary entries, letters, and interviews.* **2** [C] ENG. LANG. ARTS a piece of writing or music, or a film, etc. that is deliberately made in the style of another artist **3** [U] ENG. LANG. ARTS the style or practice of making a pastiche

pas·time /ˈpæs-taɪm/ *n.* [C] something enjoyable that you do when you are not working: *His pastimes include watching TV and reading.* [ORIGIN: 1400—1500 Translation of French *passe-temps* "pass time"]

pas·tor /ˈpæstɚ/ *n.* [C] a minister in some Protestant churches [ORIGIN: 1300—1400 Old French *pastour*, from Latin *pastor* "someone who takes care of sheep"]

pas·tor·al /ˈpæstərəl/ *adj.* **1** SOCIAL SCIENCE relating to the duties of a priest, minister, etc. toward the members of his/her religious group: *Father Murphy made pastoral visits to all the older members of his congregation.* **2** ENG. LANG. ARTS typical of the simple peaceful life in the country: *a pastoral scene depicting* (=showing) *a group of peasants working the fields*

ˌpast ˈparticiple *n.* [C] ENG. LANG. ARTS in grammar, a PARTICIPLE that is usually formed by adding "-ed" to a verb, but that can be IRREGULAR. It can be used in compounds to make PERFECT tenses, or as an adjective. In the sentence "Look what you have done," "done" is a past participle.

ˌpast ˈperfect *n.* **the past perfect** ENG. LANG. ARTS in grammar, the tense of a verb that shows that an action was completed before another event or time in the past. In the sentence "I had finished my breakfast before Rick called," "had finished" is in the past perfect.

pas·tra·mi /pæˈstrɑmi/ *n.* [U] smoked BEEF that contains a lot of spices and is usually eaten in sandwiches

pas·try /ˈpeɪstri/ *n.* (plural **pastries**) **1** [U] a mixture of flour, fat, and milk or water, used for making the outer part of baked foods such as PIES → CRUST, DOUGH **2** [C] a small sweet cake

ˌpast ˈtense *n.* **the past tense** ENG. LANG. ARTS in grammar, the tense of a verb that shows that an action or state began and ended in the past. In the sentence "We walked to school yesterday," "walked" is in the past tense.

pas·ture /ˈpæstʃɚ/ *n.* [C,U] land that is covered with grass and is used for cattle, sheep, etc. to eat

past·y /ˈpeɪsti/ *adj.* looking very pale and unhealthy: *a pasty face*

pat[1] /pæt/ *v.* (**patted**, **patting**) **1** [T] to touch someone or something lightly again and again, with your hand flat: *He knelt down to pat the dog.*

THESAURUS **touch, feel, stroke, rub, scratch, pet, caress** ➔ TOUCH[1]

2 pat sb/yourself on the back (informal) to praise someone or yourself for doing something well

pat[2] *n.* [C] **1** an act of touching someone or something with your hand flat, especially in a friendly way: *She **gave** the little boy **a pat** on the head.* **2 a pat on the back** (informal) praise for something that you have done well: *Alex deserves a pat on the back for all his hard work.* **3 a pat of butter** a small flat piece of butter

pat[3] *adv.* **have sth down pat** to know something thoroughly so that you can say it, perform it, etc. without thinking about it

patch[1] /pætʃ/ *n.* [C] **1** a small piece of material used for covering a hole in something, especially clothes: *There were **patches on** the elbows of his jacket.* **2** a part of an area that is different or looks different from the parts that surround it: *We finally found a **patch of** grass to sit down on.* **3** a small area of ground for growing fruit or vegetables: *a cabbage patch*

patch[2] *also* **patch up** *v.* [T] to put a small piece of material over a hole, especially in a piece of clothing

patch sth ↔ **up** *phr. v.* **1** to end an argument and become friendly with someone: *I've **patched things up with** my girlfriend.* **2** to fix something quickly but not carefully: *We patched up his wound until we could get him to a hospital.*

patch·work /ˈpætʃwɚk/ *n.* [U] a type of sewing in which many different-colored pieces of cloth are sewn together to make one large piece: *a patchwork quilt*

patch·y /ˈpætʃi/ *adj.* **1** happening or existing in some areas but not in others: *patchy fog* **2** not complete enough to be useful: *My knowledge of biology is pretty patchy.*

pâ·té /pɑˈteɪ, pæ-/ *n.* [U] a thick smooth food made from meat or fish, that you spread on bread

pa·tel·la /pəˈtɛlə/ *n.* [C] BIOLOGY your KNEECAP

pa·tent[1] /ˈpætˀnt/ *n.* [C] ECONOMICS a special document that gives you the right to make or sell a new invention or product that no one else is allowed to copy for a set period of time: *The designers **took out** a **patent** on the machine.*

patent[2] *v.* [T] to obtain a patent for a new invention or product: *He developed and patented a device that is still used around the world in steel production.*

patent[3] *adj.* (formal) clear and easy to notice SYN **obvious**: *a patent lie*

ˌpatent ˈleather *n.* [U] thin shiny leather that is usually black

pa·tent·ly /ˈpætˀntli/ *adv.* (formal) **patently obvious/false/unfair etc.** completely clear, untrue, unfair, etc., in a way that anyone can notice: *patently offensive language*

pa·ter·nal /pəˈtɚnl/ *adj.* **1** typical of the way a father feels or acts ➔ MATERNAL **2 paternal grandmother/uncle etc.** your father's mother, brother, etc. ➔ MATERNAL [ORIGIN: 1400—1500 Latin *paternus* "of a father," from *pater* "father"] —**paternally** *adv.*

pa·ter·nal·ism /pəˈtɚnlˌɪzəm/ *n.* [U] (disapproving) the practice of making decisions for people or organizations, so that they are never able to be responsible themselves —**paternalistic** /pəˌtɚnlˈɪstɪk/ *adj.*

pa·ter·ni·ty /pəˈtɚnəṭi/ *n.* [U] LAW the state of being a father ➔ MATERNITY

path /pæθ/ *n.* (plural **paths** /pæðz, pæθs/) [C] **1** a track that people walk along over an area of ground: *a path through the woods* | *I **followed** the **path** until I came to the river.* **2** a way through something, made by opening a space to allow you to move forward: *The police cleared a **path through** the crowd.* | *There was a truck blocking our path.* **3** the direction or line along which someone or something moves: *The storm destroyed everything **in** its **path**.* [ORIGIN: Old English *pæth*]

pa·thet·ic /pəˈθɛṭɪk/ *adj.* very bad, useless, or weak: *Vicky made a pathetic attempt to apologize.* —**pathetically** *adv.*

path·o·gen /ˈpæθədʒən/ *n.* [C] BIOLOGY a living thing, such as a VIRUS, that can cause disease

path·o·log·i·cal /ˌpæθəˈlɑdʒɪkəl/ *adj.* **1** pathological behavior or feelings are unreasonable and impossible to control: *a **pathological liar*** **2** a mental or physical condition that is pathological is caused by disease: *a pathological condition*

pa·thol·o·gy /pəˈθɑlədʒi, pæ-/ *n.* [U] BIOLOGY the study of the causes and effects of diseases —**pathologist** *n.* [C]

pa·thos /ˈpeɪθoʊs, -θɑs, ˈpæ-/ *n.* [U] (literary) the quality that a person or a situation has that makes you feel pity and sadness: *The pathos of the play is reminiscent of Shakespeare or Chekhov.*

path·way /ˈpæθweɪ/ *n.* [C] a path

pa·tience /ˈpeɪʃəns/ *n.* [U] the ability to wait calmly for a long time, or deal with difficulties without becoming annoyed or anxious ANT **impatience**: *Finally, I **lost my patience with** him and started shouting.* | *The kids are beginning to **try my patience*** (=make me stop being patient). | *She **has** no **patience for** people who make excuses.*

pa·tient[1] /ˈpeɪʃənt/ *n.* [C] someone who is getting

medical treatment: *cancer patients* | *Dr. Ross is very popular with his patients.*

patient² *adj.* able to wait calmly for a long time or to deal with difficulties without becoming annoyed or anxious (ANT) **impatient**: ***Be patient** – I'll be off the phone in a minute.* | *Wendy is very **patient with** her students.* —**patiently** *adv.*: *Simpson **waited patiently** for his chance.*

pat·i·o /ˈpæṭiˌoʊ/ *n.* (plural **patios**) [C] a flat hard area next to a house, where people can sit outside: *Sylvia was sitting **out on the patio**.* [ORIGIN: 1800—1900 Spanish]

P

pa·tri·arch /ˈpeɪtriˌɑrk/ *n.* [C] (formal) a man who is respected as the head of a family or tribe → MATRIARCH

pa·tri·arch·al /ˌpeɪtriˈɑrkəl◂/ *adj.* (formal) **1** ruled or controlled only by men: *a patriarchal society* **2** relating to being a patriarch, or typical of a patriarch

pa·tri·arch·y /ˈpeɪtriˌɑrki/ *n.* [U] a social system in which men hold all the power → MATRIARCHY

pa·tri·cian¹ /pəˈtrɪʃən/ *n.* [C] **1** someone who is from the highest class in society (SYN) **aristocrat** **2** HISTORY someone belonging to the high class of people who governed in ancient Rome → PLEBEIAN

patrician² *adj.* **1** having the appearance, behavior, way of speaking, etc. that is typical of people from the highest social class (SYN) **aristocratic**: *his patrician background* **2** HISTORY belonging to the high class of people who governed in ancient Rome → PLEBEIAN

pat·ri·lin·e·al /ˌpætrəˈlɪniəl/ *adj.* SOCIAL SCIENCE a patrilineal society is one in which connections between the fathers and sons are regarded as the most important → MATRILINEAL

pa·tri·ot /ˈpeɪtriət/ *n.* [C] (approving) someone who loves his/her country and is willing to defend it

pa·tri·ot·ic /ˌpeɪtriˈɑṭɪk/ *adj.* (approving) having or expressing a great love of your country: *a patriotic citizen* | *patriotic songs* —**patriotism** /ˈpeɪtriəˌtɪzəm/ *n.* [U]

pat·rol¹ /pəˈtroʊl/ *v.* (**patrolled**, **patrolling**) [I,T] to regularly check an area in order to prevent problems or crime: *Two tanks patrolled the city center.*

patrol² *n.* **1** [C,U] the action of regularly checking different parts of an area to prevent problems or crime: *Guards were **on patrol** throughout the night.* **2** [C] a group of police, soldiers, AIRPLANES, etc. that patrol a particular area: *the California Highway Patrol*

paˈtrol car *n.* [C] a police car that drives around the streets of a city

pa·trol·man /pəˈtroʊlmən/ *n.* (plural **patrolmen** /-mən/) [C] a police officer who patrols a particular area

pa·tron /ˈpeɪtrən/ *n.* [C] **1** someone who supports an organization, artist, musical performer, etc., especially by giving money: *a **patron of** the arts* **2** (formal) someone who uses a particular store, restaurant, company, etc. (SYN) **customer**

> THESAURUS **customer, client, shopper** → CUSTOMER

pa·tron·age /ˈpeɪtrənɪdʒ, ˈpæ-/ *n.* [U] **1** (formal) the support that you give a particular store, restaurant, company, etc. by buying their goods or using their services: *Thank you for your patronage.* **2** the support that a patron gives to an organization, etc. **3** SOCIAL SCIENCE a system in which a powerful person gives money or important jobs to people who support him/her

pa·tron·ize /ˈpeɪtrəˌnaɪz, ˈpæ-/ *v.* [T] **1** (disapproving) to talk to someone in a way that seems friendly but shows that you think s/he is less important or intelligent than you: *Don't patronize me.* | *Some of his employees believed that he patronized women.* **2** (formal) to regularly use a particular store, restaurant, company, etc.

pa·tron·iz·ing /ˈpeɪtrəˌnaɪzɪŋ, ˈpæ-/ *adj.* (disapproving) talking to someone or treating someone as if you think s/he is less important or intelligent than you: *a patronizing attitude*

pat·ter /ˈpæṭɚ/ *n.* **1** [singular] the sound of something lightly hitting a hard surface again and again: *the **patter of** footsteps* **2** [singular, U] very fast and continuous talk: *a car salesman's patter* —**patter** *v.* [I]

pat·tern /ˈpæṭɚn/ *n.* [C] **1** the regular way in which something happens, develops, or is done: ***patterns of** behavior* | *Romantic novels tend to **follow** a similar **pattern**.* **2** a regularly repeated arrangement of shapes, colors, lines, etc.: *a **pattern of** red and white squares* | *a dress with a rose pattern*

> THESAURUS
> **design** – a pattern used for decorating something: *curtains with a floral design*
> **markings** – the colored patterns and shapes on an animal's fur, feathers, or skin: *the tiger's black and orange markings*
> **motif** – a pattern that is regularly repeated: *a light blue wallpaper with a rose motif*

3 a shape that you copy onto cloth, paper, etc. when making something, especially clothing: *a skirt pattern*

pat·terned /ˈpæṭɚnd/ *adj.* decorated with a pattern: *a gold and black patterned tie*

pat·ty /ˈpæṭi/ *n.* (plural **patties**) [C] a round flat piece of cooked meat or other food: *beef patties*

pau·ci·ty /ˈpɔsəṭi/ *n.* **a/the paucity of sth** (formal) less than is needed of something: *a paucity of evidence*

paunch /pɔntʃ, pɑntʃ/ *n.* [C] a man's fat stomach —**paunchy** *adj.*

pau·per /ˈpɔpɚ/ *n.* [C] (old-fashioned) someone who is very poor

pause¹ /pɔz/ *v.* **1** [I] to stop speaking or doing something for a short time before starting again: *Tom **paused for** a moment, and then asked, "So what should I do?"* | *Amanda **paused to** admire the view.*

THESAURUS **stop, have/take a break, break** → STOP¹

2 [I,T] to push a button on a CD PLAYER, TAPE RECORDER, computer, etc. in order to make a CD, tape, etc. stop playing for a short time [ORIGIN: 1400—1500 Latin *pausa*, from Greek *pausis*, from *pauein* "to stop"]

pause² *n.* [C] a short time when you stop speaking or doing something: *a **pause in** the conversation* | *After a **long pause**, Rick said, "You're right."*

pave /peɪv/ *v.* [T] **1** to cover a path, road, etc. with a hard level surface such as CONCRETE **2 pave the way** to do something that will make an event, development, etc. possible in the future: *Galileo's achievements **paved the way for** Newton's scientific laws.*

pave·ment /ˈpeɪvmənt/ *n.* [U] the hard surface of a road: *As she fell off the bike, her arm hit the pavement.*

pa·vil·ion /pəˈvɪlyən/ *n.* [C] a structure built in a park or at a FAIR, and used as a place for public entertainment, EXHIBITIONS, etc.

ˈpaving stone *n.* [C] one of the flat pieces of stone used to make a hard surface to walk on

paw¹ /pɔ/ *n.* [C] an animal's foot that has nails or CLAWS: *a lion's paw* → *see picture on page A15*

paw² *v.* [I,T] **1** if an animal paws something, it touches the thing with its paw: *The dog's **pawing at** the door again.* **2** (informal) to touch someone in a way that is too rough or too sexual: *He kept trying to paw me in the car.*

pawn¹ /pɔn/ *n.* [C] **1** one of the eight smallest and least valuable pieces in the game of CHESS **2** someone who is used by a more powerful person or group: *We're just **pawns in** a big political game.*

pawn² *v.* [T] to leave a valuable object with a pawnbroker in order to borrow money

pawn·bro·ker /ˈpɔnˌbroʊkɚ/ *n.* [C] someone whose business is to lend people money in exchange for valuable objects

pay¹ /peɪ/ *v.* (past tense and past participle **paid**, third person singular **pays**)

1 GIVE MONEY [I,T] to give someone money for something in order to buy it, or for something s/he has done for you: *They ran off without paying.* | *Have you paid the babysitter yet?* | *The company's **paying for** my plane tickets.* | *The government agreed to **pay** them **for** their land in the east.* | *How much did you **pay for** those shoes?* | *You can **pay by check**.*

2 BILL/DEBT [T] to give a person, company, etc. the money that you owe for a bill or debt: *We need to **pay** the electricity **bill** soon.*

3 JOB [I,T] to give someone money for the job s/he does: *How much do they pay you?* | *Plumbers **get paid** $40 an hour.* | *workers who are **well/highly/poorly paid***

4 pay attention (to sb/sth) to carefully listen to or watch someone or something, or to be careful about what you are doing: *Sorry, I wasn't paying attention. What did you say?*

5 pay a visit to sb *also* **pay sb a visit** to go to see a particular person: *It's about time you paid a visit to the dentist.*

6 pay sb a compliment to say nice things about someone's appearance, behavior, etc.

7 pay your way to pay for your bills, food, etc. without needing to use anyone else's money: *She paid her own way through law school.*

8 GOOD RESULT [I] to be worth doing, and result in an advantage for you: *Crime doesn't pay.* | ***It pays to** be on time.*

9 PROFIT [I] ECONOMICS if a shop or business pays, it makes a profit: *We worked hard but couldn't **make** the business **pay**.*

10 pay tribute to sb/sth to show how much you admire or respect someone or something

11 pay your respects (to sb) (formal) to greet someone politely or visit a place, especially in order to say or show that you are sorry that someone has died: *Sam came over to pay his respects to the family.*

12 pay your dues to work at the lowest levels of a profession or organization in order to earn the right to move up to a better position

13 pay through the nose (for sth) (informal) to pay far too much money for something → **pay/give lip service** *at* LIP

pay sb/sth ↔ **back** *phr. v.*
to give someone the money that you owe him/her (SYN) **repay**: *Can I borrow $10? I'll pay you back tomorrow.*

pay for sth *phr. v.*
to suffer or be punished for doing something: *If you drink any more, you'll be paying for it in the morning.*

pay sth ↔ **in** *also* **pay** sth **into** sth *phr. v.*
to put money into a bank account: *The check was paid into your account on Friday.* | *How much do you pay in each month?*

pay off *phr. v.*
1 pay sth ↔ **off** to pay all the money that you owe for something: *We've finally paid off the mortgage.*
2 if something that you try to do pays off, it is successful after a long time: *My efforts finally paid off when they called me in for an interview.*
3 pay sb ↔ **off** to give someone money so that s/he will not tell people about something illegal or dishonest

pay sth ↔ **out** *phr. v.*
to pay a lot of money for something: *Last year, $123 million was paid out in health benefits.*

pay up *phr. v.*
(informal) to pay all the money that you owe

P

pay² *n.* [U] money that you are given for working (SYN) **salary**: *The pay will be better at my new job.* | *Workers say they haven't had a* ***pay raise/increase*** *in two years.* | *Teachers have refused to accept a* ***pay cut.***

COLLOCATIONS

base pay – the pay that you always receive, without payment for any extra hours
overtime pay – payment for extra hours that you work
take-home pay – the money you receive after tax, etc. has been taken away
vacation pay – payment for the time when you are on vacation
sick pay – payment for the times when you are sick and not at work → MONEY, PENSION

THESAURUS

income – money that you receive from working, investments, etc.: *families on a low income*
salary – the pay that professional people such as teachers or lawyers earn every year: *a salary of $34,000 a year*
wages – the pay that someone earns every hour or every week: *Her wages barely cover the rent.*
earnings – all the money that you earn by working: *Record your earnings on the income tax form.*
bonus – money added to someone's pay, especially as a reward for good work: *The company offers performance bonuses to every employee.*
remuneration (formal) – the pay that someone receives for his or her work: *The work was hard and the remuneration was low.*

pay·a·ble /'peɪəbəl/ *adj.* **1** a bill, debt, etc. that is payable must be paid: *A standard fee of $35 is payable every three months.* **2 payable to sb** able to be paid to a particular person or organization: *Please* ***make the check payable to*** *Al's Service Station* (=write this name on the check).

pay·check /'peɪtʃɛk/ *n.* [C] a check that pays a worker his/her salary: *a weekly paycheck*

pay·day /'peɪdeɪ/ *n.* [C usually singular] the day when you get your paycheck

'pay dirt *n.* **hit/strike pay dirt** (informal) to make a valuable or useful discovery: *Crash investigators struck pay dirt when they found the aircraft's flight recorder.*

pay·ee /peɪ'i/ *n.* [C] ECONOMICS the person who should be paid money, especially by check

pay·load /'peɪloʊd/ *n.* [C,U] the amount of goods or passengers carried by a vehicle or aircraft

pay·ment /'peɪmənt/ *n.* **1** [C] an amount of money that must be paid or has been paid: *How much are your* ***car/house/loan payments****?* | *He couldn't afford to* ***make*** *the* ***payments on*** *his house.* | *She agreed to repay the loan in* ***monthly payments*** *of $200.* **2** [U] the act of paying: *Late payment will result in a $10 fine.*

pay·off /'peɪɔf/ *n.* [C] **1** the good result or the advantage that you get because of doing something: *With electric cars, the development costs are high, but there is a big environmental payoff.* **2** a payment that is made to someone, often illegally, in order to stop him/her from causing you trouble

'pay phone *n.* [C] a public telephone that you can use when you put in coins or a CREDIT CARD number

pay·roll /'peɪroʊl/ *n.* [C usually singular] **1** the people who are employed by a company: *We have 127 staff* ***on the payroll.*** **2** ECONOMICS the total amount of money that a company pays the people who work there

PBS *n.* **Public Broadcasting System** a company in the U.S. that broadcasts television programs without advertisements

PC¹ *n.* [C] IT **personal computer** a small computer that is used by one person at a time, at work or at home → *see picture on page A19*

PC² *adj.* POLITICALLY CORRECT

pdf, PDF /ˌpi di 'ef/ *n.* [C] IT **portable document format** a type of computer FILE that can be opened on most personal computers, even those that do not have the same software program that was used to produce the file

PE *n.* [U] **physical education** sports and exercises that are taught as a school subject

pea /pi/ *n.* [C] a small round green seed that is cooked and eaten as a vegetable

peace /pis/ *n.* **1** [singular,U] a situation or period of time in which there is no war or fighting: *The country's nuclear program is a threat to* ***world peace.*** | *Germany has been* ***at peace with*** *France since 1945.* | *My hope is that one day our countries can* ***live in peace.*** | *The prime minister promised to* ***bring peace to*** *the region.* **2** [U] a situation that is very calm, quiet, and pleasant: *All I want is some* ***peace and quiet.*** | *Mary, let your sister read* ***in peace*** (=without being interrupted). **3** [U] a feeling of being calm, happy, and not worried: *I decided to see a doctor, just for* ***peace of mind.*** **4 disturbing the peace** LAW the crime of being too noisy or too violent in a public place **5 make (your) peace** to agree to stop fighting with a person or group: *He was anxious to* ***make peace with*** *Jill before she left.* [ORIGIN: 1100—1200 Old French *pais*, from Latin *pax*]

peace·a·ble /'pisəbəl/ *adj.* not liking to argue, or not causing any arguments or fights: *peaceable subjects who paid their taxes and posed no threat to public order* —**peaceably** *adv.*

'Peace Corps *n.* **the Peace Corps** a U.S. government organization that helps poorer countries by sending VOLUNTEERS to teach skills in education, health, farming, etc.

peace·ful /'pisfəl/ *adj.* **1** calm, quiet, and without problems or excitement: *It's peaceful out here in the woods.*

THESAURUS quiet, calm, tranquil, still → QUIET[1]

2 not fighting a war, or deliberately not being violent: *a peaceful relationship between countries* | *a peaceful protest* —**peacefully** *adv.*

peace·keep·ing /'pis,kipɪŋ/ *adj.* trying to prevent fighting or violence: *peacekeeping troops* —**peacekeeper** *n.* [C]

peace·mak·er /'pis,meɪkɚ/ *n.* [C] someone who tries to persuade people or countries to stop fighting

peace·time /'pis-taɪm/ *n.* [U] a period of time when a country is not fighting a war (ANT) **wartime**

peach /pitʃ/ *n.* **1** [C] a round juicy yellow-red fruit that has a large rough seed and skin that feels FUZZY, or the tree that it grows on → *see picture on page 414* **2** [U] a pale pink-orange color [ORIGIN: 1200—1300 Old French *peche* from Latin *persicus* "Persian"]

pea·cock /'pikɑk/ *n.* [C] a large bird, the male of which has long blue and green tail feathers that it can spread out

peacock

peak[1] /pik/ *n.* [C] **1** the time when someone or something is biggest, most successful, or best: *Trenton is now **at the peak of** his career.* | *The company's profits **reached a peak** in 1992.* **2** the pointed top of a mountain, or a mountain with a pointed top: *the Alps' snow-covered peaks*

peak[2] *v.* [I] to become the biggest, most successful, or best that someone or something can be: *In the 1950s, Chicago's population **peaked at** around 3.6 million.*

peal /pil/ *n.* [C] (literary) a sudden loud repeated sound, such as laughter, THUNDER, or bells ringing: *I could hear **peals of laughter** coming from upstairs.* —**peal** *v.* [I]

pea·nut /'pinʌt/ *n.* **1** [C] a small nut you can eat that has a soft light brown shell **2 peanuts** [plural] (informal) a very small amount of money: *I'm tired of **working for peanuts**.*

'peanut ,butter *n.* [U] a soft food made from crushed peanuts, usually eaten on bread: *a peanut butter and jelly sandwich*

pear /pɛr/ *n.* [C] a sweet juicy fruit with a round wide bottom that becomes thinner on top near the stem, or the tree on which it grows → *see picture at* FRUIT

pearl /pɚl/ *n.* [C] a valuable small white round object, that forms inside an OYSTER and is used in jewelry: *a pearl necklace*

peas·ant /'pɛzənt/ *n.* [C] a poor farmer who owns or rents a small amount of land, either in past times or in poor countries

peas·ant·ry /'pɛzəntri/ *n.* **the peasantry** all the peasants of a particular country: *The land tax was bitterly resented by the peasantry.*

peat /pit/ *n.* [U] EARTH SCIENCES a substance formed under the surface of the ground from decaying plants, used as soil or as FUEL

peb·ble /'pɛbəl/ *n.* [C] a small smooth stone that is usually in a river or on a beach

pe·can /pɪ'kɑn, -'kæn/ *n.* [C] a long thin sweet nut with a dark smooth shell, or the tree on which these nuts grow: *pecan pie* [ORIGIN: 1700—1800 French *pacane*, from an Algonquian language]

peck[1] /pɛk/ *v.* [I,T] if a bird pecks something or pecks at something, it quickly moves its beak to hit, bite, or pick up that thing

peck[2] *n.* [C] **1** a quick kiss: *He gave Jill a **peck on the cheek**.* **2** the action of a bird pecking something with its beak

pe·cu·liar /pɪ'kyulyɚ/ *adj.* **1** strange and a little surprising: *This cheese has a peculiar smell.* | *Something very peculiar is going on here.*

THESAURUS strange, funny, curious, odd, weird → STRANGE[1]

2 be peculiar to sth to be a quality that only one particular person, place, or thing has: *The problem of racism is not peculiar to this country.* —**peculiarly** *adv.*

pe·cu·li·ar·i·ty /pɪ,kyuli'ærət̬i/ *n.* (plural **peculiarities**) [C,U] an unusual or slightly strange habit or quality, especially one that only a particular person, place, etc. has: *the **peculiarities of** the newspaper business* | *Over time, she grew to love his peculiarities.*

pe·cu·ni·ar·y /pɪ'kyuni,ɛri/ *adj.* (formal) relating to or consisting of money: *He was accused of obtaining a pecuniary advantage by deception.*

ped·a·go·gi·cal /,pɛdə'gɑdʒɪkəl/ *adj.* (formal) relating to methods of teaching —**pedagogy** /'pɛdə,gɑdʒi/ *n.* [U]

ped·al[1] /'pɛdl/ *n.* [C] the part of a bicycle, car, or MOTORCYCLE that you push with your foot in order to make it move: *the gas pedal* [ORIGIN: 1600—1700 French *pedale*, from Italian, from Latin *pedalis* "of the foot"] → *see picture at* BICYCLE

pedal[2] *v.* [I,T] to ride a bicycle by pushing the pedals with your feet

pe·dan·tic /pə'dæntɪk/ *adj.* (disapproving) paying too much attention to small details and rules: *The book is fascinating, although some readers will find it pedantic.*

ped·dle /'pɛdl/ *v.* [T] to go from place to place trying to sell something, especially something illegal or cheap: *Eric was caught **peddling drugs**.* —**peddler** *n.* [C]

ped·es·tal /'pɛdəstl/ *n.* [C] **1** the base on which a STATUE or a PILLAR stands **2 put/place sb on a pedestal** (disapproving) to admire someone so

P

much that you treat him/her or talk about him/her as though s/he is perfect

pe·des·tri·an¹ /pəˈdɛstriən/ *n.* [C] someone who is walking instead of driving a car, riding a bicycle, etc. [ORIGIN: 1700—1800 Latin *pedester* "going on foot," from *pes* "foot"]

pedestrian² *adj.* (formal) ordinary, and not very interesting or exciting: *I thought the orchestra's overall performance was poor and the choice of music was fairly pedestrian.*

pe·di·a·tri·cian /ˌpidiəˈtrɪʃən/ *n.* [C] a doctor who treats children → DOCTOR¹

P

pe·di·at·rics /ˌpidiˈætrɪks/ *n.* [U] the area of medicine that deals with children and their illnesses

ped·i·cure /ˈpɛdɪˌkyʊr/ *n.* [C,U] a treatment for the feet that includes cleaning them and cutting the TOENAILS → MANICURE

ped·i·gree /ˈpɛdəˌgri/ *n.* [C,U] the parents and other past family members of an animal or person, or the written record of them —**pedigree** *adj.*: *a pedigree Great Dane*

pee /pi/ *v.* [I] (informal) to pass liquid waste from your body (SYN) **urinate** —**pee** *n.* [U]

peek¹ /pik/ *v.* [I] to quickly look at something, especially something you are not supposed to see: *Paula opened the box and peeked inside.*

THESAURUS **look, glance, peep, peer** → LOOK¹

peek² *n.* [C] a quick look at something: ***Take a peek*** *down the hall and see if anyone's coming.*

peek·a·boo /ˈpikəˌbu/ *interjection, n.* [U] a game played with babies and young children, in which you hide your face and then show it again and again, saying "peekaboo!"

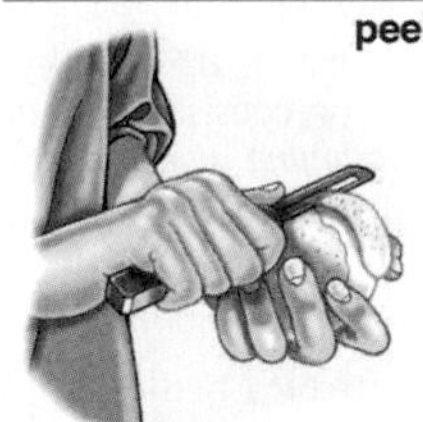

peeling a potato

peel¹ /pil/ *v.* **1** [T] to remove the skin of a fruit or vegetable: *Peel the potatoes and cut them in half.*

THESAURUS **cut, chop (up), slice, dice, carve, shred, grate** → CUT¹

2 [T] to remove a thin outside layer from the surface of an object: ***Peel*** *the labels* ***off/from*** *the jars before recycling.* **3** [I] if skin, paper, or paint is peeling, it is loose and coming off in small thin pieces: *I got sunburned and now my face is peeling.*

peel sth ↔ **off** *phr. v.* to take off your clothes, especially if they are wet or tight: *He peeled off his damp uniform and stepped into the shower.*

peel² *n.* [U] the thick skin of a fruit or vegetable, such as an orange, a potato, or a BANANA: *orange peel* → *see picture on page 414*

peel·ings /ˈpilɪŋz/ *n.* [plural] pieces of skin that have been removed from a fruit or vegetable: *carrot peelings*

peep¹ /pip/ *v.* [I] **1** to look at something quickly and secretly: *I saw Joe* ***peeping through*** *the curtains.*

THESAURUS **look, glance, peek, peer** → LOOK¹

2 to appear from behind or under something: *The sun finally* ***peeped out*** *from behind the clouds.*

peep² *n.* [C] **1** [usually singular] a sound: ***I didn't hear a peep out of*** *the kids all afternoon.* **2** [usually singular] a quick or secret look at something: *Did you* ***get/take a peep at*** *the audience?* **3** a short weak high sound that some young birds make

peep·hole /ˈpiphoʊl/ *n.* [C] a small hole in a door that you can look through

peeping Tom /ˌpipɪŋ ˈtɑm/ *n.* [C] someone who secretly watches people, especially people who are taking off their clothes

peer¹ /pɪr/ *n.* **sb's peer** someone who is the same age as another person, or who has the same type of job, rank, etc.: *Barton has gained the respect of his peers.*

peer² *v.* [I] to look very carefully, especially because you cannot see something well: *Harris* ***peered into*** *the dark closet.*

THESAURUS **look, glance, peek, peep** → LOOK¹

ˈpeer group *n.* [C] SOCIAL SCIENCE a group of people who are the same age, are from the same social class, or have the same type of job, etc.: *Peer groups and popular culture both have a strong influence on teenage children.*

peer·less /ˈpɪrlɪs/ *adj.* (formal) better than anyone or anything else: *B.B. King's peerless guitar playing*

ˈpeer ˌpressure *n.* [U] the strong feeling that young people have that they should do the same things that their peers are doing: *It can be difficult not to* ***give in to peer pressure*** (=do something just because other people are doing it).

peeve /piv/ *n.* **pet peeve** (informal) something that always annoys you, but that may not annoy other people: *One of my pet peeves is people being late for meetings.*

peg¹ /pɛg/ *n.* [C] **1** a short piece of wood or metal that fits into a hole or is fastened to a wall, and can be used for fastening furniture together, for hanging things, etc.: *a coat peg* **2** *also* **tent peg** a pointed piece of wood or metal used for keeping a tent attached to the ground

peg² *v.* (**pegged, pegging**) [T] **1** to believe or say that someone has a particular type of character: *Teachers* ***had*** *him* ***pegged as*** *a troublemaker.* **2** ECONOMICS to set prices, salaries, etc. in relation to a particular value: *loan payment rates that are* ***pegged to*** *the national rates*

pe·jor·a·tive /pɪˈdʒɔrət̬ɪv, -ˈdʒɑr-/ *adj.* (formal) a pejorative word or phrase is used in order to insult someone or to show disapproval [ORIGIN: 1800—1900 Late Latin *pejoratus*, past participle of *pejorare* "to make worse," from *pejor* "worse"]

pel·i·can /ˈpɛlɪkən/ *n.* [C] a large bird that catches fish for food and holds them in the part of its large beak that is shaped like a bag [ORIGIN: 1000—1100 Late Latin *pelecanus*, from Greek]

pel·let /ˈpɛlɪt/ *n.* [C] a small hard ball made from metal, ice, paper, food, etc.

pel·lu·cid /pəˈlusɪd/ *adj.* (literary) very clear, so that it can be seen through easily or understood easily → TRANSLUCENT: *the pellucid air of the mountains*

pelt[1] /pɛlt/ *v.* [T] to attack someone by throwing a lot of things at him/her: *Two kids were* ***pelting*** *each other* ***with*** *snowballs.*

pelt[2] *n* [C] BIOLOGY the skin of a dead animal with the fur or hair still on it

pel·vis /ˈpɛlvɪs/ *n.* [C] BIOLOGY the set of large wide curved bones at the base of your SPINE, to which your legs are joined [ORIGIN: 1600—1700 Latin "basin"] → *see picture on page A16* —**pelvic** *adj.*

pen[1] /pɛn/ *n.* **1** [C,U] an instrument used for writing and drawing in ink: *a ballpoint pen* | *Write your essays* ***in pen*** (=using a pen), *not pencil.* **2** [C] a small area surrounded by a fence that farm animals are kept in → PIGPEN [ORIGIN: (1) 1200—1300 Old French *penne* "feather, pen," from Latin *penna* "feather"]

pen[2] *v.* (**penned**, **penning**) [T] (literary) to write a letter, note, etc. with a pen → WRITE

pen sb/sth **in/up** *phr. v.* to prevent a person or animal from leaving an enclosed area: *The protesters were kept penned up behind the fence.*

pe·nal /ˈpinl/ *adj.* **1** LAW relating to the legal punishment of criminals: *the penal system* **2 penal offense** LAW a crime

ˈpenal ˌcode *n.* [C] a set of laws and the punishments for not obeying these laws

pe·nal·ize /ˈpinlˌaɪz, ˈpɛn-/ *v.* [T] **1** to punish someone or treat him/her unfairly: *I'm being* ***penalized for*** *something that isn't my fault.* **2** to punish a player or sports team by giving an advantage to the other team: *The Bears were* ***penalized for*** *taking too much time.*

pen·al·ty /ˈpɛnlt̬i/ *n.* (plural **penalties**) [C] **1** LAW a punishment for not obeying a law, rule, or legal agreement: *The maximum* ***penalty for*** *the crime is five years in prison.* | *He was given* ***the death penalty*** (=killed as a punishment).

> THESAURUS **punishment, sentence, fine, community service** → PUNISHMENT

2 a disadvantage given to a player or sports team for not obeying the rules [ORIGIN: 1500—1600 Medieval Latin *poenalitas*, from Latin *poena* "punishment"]

pen·ance /ˈpɛnəns/ *n.* [C,U] (literary) a punishment that you accept, especially for religious reasons, to show that you are sorry for doing a bad thing

pen·chant /ˈpɛntʃənt/ *n.* [C] a liking for something that you do as a habit: *Bill* ***has a penchant for*** *fast cars.*

pen·cil[1] /ˈpɛnsəl/ *n.* [C,U] a thing that you use for writing and drawing, made of wood containing a black or colored center: *Do the math problems* ***in pencil*** (=using a pencil), *not pen.* | *a sharp pencil* [ORIGIN: 1300—1400 Old French *pincel* "paintbrush," from Latin *penicillus* "little tail"]

pencil[2] *v.* [T] to write something with a pencil or make a mark with a pencil

pencil sb/sth ↔ **in** *phr. v.* to make an arrangement for a meeting or other event, knowing that it might have to be changed later: *I'll* ***pencil in*** *a meeting for next Tuesday.*

ˈpencil ˌsharpener *n.* [C] an object with a small blade inside it, used for making the pointed end of a pencil sharp

pend·ant /ˈpɛndənt/ *n.* [C] a jewel or small decoration that hangs from a NECKLACE: *a diamond pendant*

pend·ing[1] /ˈpɛndɪŋ/ *prep.* (formal) until something happens, or while something happens: *The decision has been delayed pending further research.*

pending[2] *adj.* (formal) not yet decided, agreed on, or finished: *Their divorce is still pending.*

pen·du·lum /ˈpɛndʒələm/ *n.* [C] a long stick with a weight on the end of it that hangs down and swings from side to side, especially in a large clock [ORIGIN: 1600—1700 Modern Latin, Latin *pendulus* from *pendere* "to hang"]

pen·e·trate /ˈpɛnəˌtreɪt/ *v.* **1** [I,T] to enter something or pass through it, especially when this is difficult: *bullets that can penetrate metal* | *Explorers* ***penetrated*** *deep* ***into*** *unknown regions.*

> THESAURUS **enter, go in, come in, get in, trespass, intrude** → ENTER[1]

2 [T] to join and be accepted by an organization, business, etc. in order to find out secret information: *Spies had penetrated the highest ranks of both governments.* **3** [T] to understand something difficult: *scientists trying to penetrate the mysteries of nature* —**penetration** /ˌpɛnəˈtreɪʃən/ *n.* [U]

pen·e·trat·ing /ˈpɛnəˌtreɪt̬ɪŋ/ *adj.* **1 penetrating eyes/look/gaze etc.** someone who has penetrating eyes, etc. seems able to see what another person is thinking **2** a penetrating noise or voice is so loud that you hear it very clearly **3** showing an ability to understand things quickly and completely: *a penetrating mind*

pen·guin /ˈpɛŋgwɪn/ *n.* [C] a large black and white Antarctic sea bird that cannot fly but uses its wings for swimming

pen·i·cil·lin /ˌpɛnəˈsɪlən/ *n.* [U] BIOLOGY a substance used as a medicine to destroy BACTERIA

pe·nin·su·la /pəˈnɪnsələ/ *n.* [C] EARTH SCIENCES a piece of land that is almost completely surrounded by water [ORIGIN: 1500—1600 Latin *paeninsula*, from *paene* "almost" + *insula* "island"] —**peninsular** *adj.*

pe·nis /ˈpinɪs/ *n.* [C] BIOLOGY the outer sex organ of a male

pen·i·tent /ˈpɛnətənt/ *adj.* (literary) feeling sorry about doing something bad, and showing you do not intend to do it again —**penitence** *n.* [U]

pen·i·ten·tia·ry /ˌpɛnəˈtɛnʃəri/ *n.* (plural **penitentiaries**) [C] a prison: *the state penitentiary*

P

pen·knife /ˈpɛn-naɪf/ *n.* (plural **penknives** /-naɪvz/) [C] a POCKET KNIFE

ˈpen name *n.* [C] a name used by a writer instead of his/her real name (SYN) **pseudonym**

pen·nant /ˈpɛnənt/ *n.* [C] a long pointed flag used by schools, sports teams, etc., or on ships as a sign

pen·ni·less /ˈpɛnɪlɪs/ *adj.* having no money

pen·ny /ˈpɛni/ *n.* (plural **pennies**) [C] **1** a coin worth one cent (=1/100 of a dollar), used in the U.S. and Canada

THESAURUS **money, coin, nickel, dime, quarter** → MONEY

2 not a penny no money at all: *I don't owe her a penny!* **3 every (last) penny** all of your money: *He spent every penny on his car.* | *The new carpet wasn't cheap, but it was* ***worth every penny*** (=I am happy I bought it).

ˈpen pal *n.* [C] someone to whom you write letters in order to become his/her friend

pen·sion /ˈpɛnʃən/ *n.* [C] the money that a company pays regularly to someone after s/he RETIRES (=stops working after reaching a particular age): *Howe* ***draws*** *a yearly* ***pension*** *of $15,000.*

ˈpension fund *n.* [C] ECONOMICS a large amount of money that a company, organization, etc. INVESTS and uses for paying pensions

ˈpension plan *n.* [C] ECONOMICS a system organized by a company for paying pensions to its workers when they RETIRE (=stop working after reaching a particular age)

pen·sive /ˈpɛnsɪv/ *adj.* (literary) thinking about something a lot and seeming slightly sad [ORIGIN: 1300—1400 French *pensif*, from *penser* "to think"]

Pen·ta·gon /ˈpɛntəˌgɑn/ *n.* **the Pentagon** the U.S. government building in Washington, D.C. from which the army, navy, etc. are controlled, or the military officers who work in this building

pentagon *n.* [C] MATH a flat shape with five sides and five angles [ORIGIN: 1500—1600 Latin, from Greek *pentagonon*, from *pente* "five" + *gonia* "angle"] —**pentagonal** /pɛnˈtægənl/ *adj.* → *see picture at* POLYGON

THESAURUS **polygon, hexagon, heptagon, octagon, decagon, dodecagon** → POLYGON

pen·tam·e·ter /pɛnˈtæmət̬ɚ/ *n.* [C] ENG. LANG. ARTS a line of poetry with five main beats → IAMBIC PENTAMETER

pen·tath·lon /pɛnˈtæθlən, -lɑn/ *n.* [singular] a sports competition consisting of five different sports → DECATHLON, HEPTATHLON

Pen·te·cos·tal /ˌpɛntɪˈkɑstl/ *adj.* relating to the Christian church whose members believe that the spirit of God can help them to cure diseases and pray in special languages —**Pentecostal** *n.* [C]

pent·house /ˈpɛnthaʊs/ *n.* [C] a very expensive and comfortable apartment on the top floor of a tall building

ˌpent-ˈup *adj.* pent-up emotions are not expressed for a long time: *pent-up anger and frustration*

pe·nul·ti·mate /pɪˈnʌltəmɪt/ *adj.* [only before noun] (formal) next to the last: *the penultimate game of the season* [ORIGIN: 1600—1700 Latin *paenultimus*, from *paene* "almost" + *ultimus* "last"]

pe·nu·ri·ous /pəˈnʊriəs/ *adj.* (formal) very poor → POOR

pe·on /ˈpiɑn/ *n.* [C] (informal) someone who works at a boring or physically hard job for low pay: *the office peons*

peo·ple¹ /ˈpipəl/ *n.* **1** [plural] the usual plural form of PERSON: *I like the people I work with.* | *How many people were at the wedding?* **2 the people** [plural] all the ordinary people in a country or a state: *The mayor should remember that he was elected to serve the people.*

THESAURUS

the public – ordinary people, not people who work for the government or other special organizations: *It's the job of the media to inform the public.*
society – all the people who live in a country: *responsible members of society*
the human race/mankind/humankind – all the people in the world, considered as a group: *the origins of the human race*
populace (formal) – the ordinary people living in a country: *Surveys say that almost 90% of the American populace believe in God.*
population – the number of people or animals living in a particular area, country, etc.: *What's the population of Los Angeles?* | *the planet's rapid population growth*

3 [plural] people in general, or people other than yourself: *People sometimes make fun of my name.* | *Computer people seem to speak a language of their own.*

THESAURUS **man, mankind, humankind** → MAN¹

4 of all people (spoken) used in order to say that someone is the only person who you would not have expected to do something: *You of all people* *should have realized the risks.* **5** [C] (formal) a race or nation: *all the peoples of the world*

THESAURUS race, nation, tribe, ethnic group → RACE[1]

people² v. **be peopled with/by sb** (literary) to be filled with people of a particular type

pep¹ /pɛp/ v. (**pepped**, **pepping**)

pep sb/sth ↔ **up** phr. v. (informal) to make something or someone more active, interesting, or full of energy: *I had some coffee to pep myself up.*

pep² n. [U] (informal) physical energy —**peppy** adj.

pep·per¹ /ˈpɛpɚ/ n. **1** [U] a spicy black, pale yellow, or red powder, used in cooking: *salt and pepper* **2** [C] a hollow red, green, or yellow fruit with a sweet or spicy taste, that is eaten as a vegetable or added to other foods → *see picture at* VEGETABLE [ORIGIN: Old English *pipor*, from Latin *piper*, from Greek *peperi*]

pepper² v. [T] **1** to scatter things all over or all through something: *The article is **peppered with** quotations.* **2** to put pepper in food

pep·per·mint /ˈpɛpɚˌmɪnt/ n. **1** [U] a MINT plant with sweet-smelling strong-tasting leaves, used in making candy, tea, and medicine **2** [C] a candy that has a taste like peppermint

pep·pe·ro·ni /ˌpɛpəˈroʊni/ n. [U] a spicy dry Italian SAUSAGE

ˈpep ˌrally n. [C] an event at a school before a sports event, when people give speeches or shout to encourage and support a team

ˈpep talk n. [C] (informal) a speech that is intended to encourage people to work harder, win a game, etc.: *The coach was **giving** the team a **pep talk**.*

pep·tide /ˈpɛptaɪd/ n. [C] CHEMISTRY a compound consisting of two or more AMINO ACIDS joined together in a chain

per /pɚ/ prep. for each: *Bananas are 60 cents per pound.* | *You need at least half a bottle of wine per person for the party.*

per ca·pi·ta /pɚ ˈkæpət̬ə/ adj., adv. ECONOMICS calculated by dividing the total amount of something by the number of people in a particular place: *The average per capita income in the area is $40,000 a year.* [ORIGIN: 1600—1700 Latin "by heads"]

per ˌcapita ˈincome n [U] ECONOMICS the total amount earned by all the people living in a place divided by the number of people living there, used to show how rich or poor people are on average: *The average per capita income in the area is $40,000 a year.* | *Rapid economic growth drove per capita income up.*

per·ceive /pɚˈsiv/ (Ac) v. [T] (formal) **1** to understand or think about something in a particular way: *The government was widely **perceived as** corrupt.* | *Investors will pull out if they **perceive that** the economy is failing.* **2** to notice something that is difficult to notice: *The sound is too high to be perceived by humans.* [ORIGIN: 1200—1300 Old French *perceivre*, from Latin *percipere*] —**perceived** adj.: *This proposal addresses a widely perceived need to expand health care for children.*

per·cent¹ /pɚˈsɛnt/ (Ac) n. **five/ten etc. percent** also **5%/10% etc.** five, ten, etc. in every hundred: *The interest rate at the bank is six percent* (=6%, or six cents on every dollar). | *Five percent of $250 is $12.50.* [ORIGIN: 1500—1600 Latin from *per* "by" + *centem* "hundred"]

percent² (Ac) adj., adv. **1** (symbol %) equal to a particular amount in every hundred: *Figures showed there had been a 43 percent reduction in crime.* **2 a/one hundred percent** completely: *I agree with you a hundred percent.*

per·cent·age /pɚˈsɛntɪdʒ/ (Ac) n **1** [C,U] a particular amount out of every hundred: *What **percentage of** the population is elderly?* | *A **small/large percentage** of students receive financial aid.* **2** [C usually singular] ECONOMICS a share of profits equal to a particular amount in every dollar: *He gets a percentage for every book that is sold.*

per·cep·ti·ble /pɚˈsɛptəbəl/ adj. (formal) noticeable (ANT) **imperceptible**: *The sound was **barely perceptible**.*

per·cep·tion /pɚˈsɛpʃən/ (Ac) n. **1** [C,U] the way you understand something and your beliefs about what it is like: *A child's **perception of** the world is not the same as an adult's.* | *There's a **perception that** Margaret is not an effective leader.* | *We need to challenge many popular perceptions of old age.* **2** [U] the way you use your sight, hearing, feeling, taste, or smell to notice things: *drugs that alter perception* | *One theory is that caffeine somehow counteracts the perception of pain.* **3** [U] the natural ability to understand or notice something quickly: *I was impressed by her perception and her grasp of the facts.*

per·cep·tive /pɚˈsɛptɪv/ adj. good at noticing and understanding what is happening or what someone is thinking or feeling: *a perceptive young man* | *perceptive comments*

perch¹ /pɚtʃ/ n. **1** [C] a branch, stick, etc. where a bird sits **2** [C] (informal) a high place where someone can sit or where a building is placed: *He watches from his perch halfway up the mountain.* **3** [C,U] (plural **perch**) a fish with sharp pointed FINS that lives in rivers, lakes, etc., or the meat from this fish

perch² v. **1 be perched on/over etc. sth** to be in a position on top of, or on the edge of, something: *a house perched on a hill* **2 perch (yourself) on sth** to sit on top of, or on the edge of something: *Wally perched on the gate and stared at us.* **3** [I] if a bird perches on something, it sits on it

per·co·late /ˈpɚkəˌleɪt/ v. [I] if a liquid percolates through something, it passes slowly through a material that has small holes in it

per·co·la·tor /ˈpɚkəˌleɪt̬ɚ/ n. [C] a pot in which

P

coffee is made by passing hot water again and again through crushed coffee beans

per·cus·sion /pə'kʌʃən/ *n.* [U] ENG. LANG. ARTS drums and other musical instruments which you play by hitting or shaking them —**percussionist** *n.* [C]

pe·ren·ni·al[1] /pə'rɛniəl/ *adj.* **1** [only before noun] happening again and again, or existing for a long time: *the perennial problem of poverty* **2** BIOLOGY a plant that is perennial lives for more than two years [ORIGIN: 1600—1700 Latin *perennis*, from *per-* "through" + *annus* "year"]

perennial[2] *n.* [C] BIOLOGY a plant that lives for more than two years

P

per·fect[1] /'pɚfɪkt/ *adj.* **1** complete and without any mistakes or problems (ANT) **imperfect** ➔ PERFECTLY: *a car in perfect condition* | *Your English is perfect.* **2** as good as possible, or the best of its kind ➔ PERFECTLY: *John was in perfect health.* | *a perfect solution to the problem* **3** exactly right for a particular purpose: *This rug's* ***perfect for*** *the living room.* | *a perfect day for a picnic*

THESAURUS

ideal – being the best that something could possibly be: *It's an ideal vacation spot for families.*
just right – being the best or most appropriate for something: *The dress was just right for the occasion.*

4 used in order to emphasize what you are saying: *Why did you give your phone number to a* ***perfect stranger****?* | *I'm sorry, I've been a* ***perfect fool/idiot.*** **5 nobody's perfect** (spoken) used when you are answering someone who has criticized you: *Yes, I made a mistake – nobody's perfect.* [ORIGIN: 1200—1300 Old French *parfit*, from Latin *perfectus*, past participle of *perficere* "to do completely, finish"]

per·fect[2] /pɚ'fɛkt/ *v.* [T] to make something perfect or as good as you are able to: *She's spending a year in France to perfect her French.*

per·fect[3] /'pɚfɪkt/ *n.* **the perfect** ENG. LANG. ARTS in grammar, the tense of a verb used when talking about a period of time up to and including the present, formed using "have" with a PAST PARTICIPLE ➔ FUTURE PERFECT, PAST PERFECT, PRESENT PERFECT

per·fec·tion /pɚ'fɛkʃən/ *n.* [U] **1** the state of being perfect: *Claire's parents demanded perfection from her.* | *The steak was cooked* ***to perfection.*** **2** the process of making something perfect: *the* ***perfection of*** *his golf swing*

per·fec·tion·ist /pɚ'fɛkʃənɪst/ *n.* [C] someone who is not satisfied with anything unless it is completely perfect: *You look fine. Don't be such a perfectionist.*

per·fect·ly /'pɚfɪktli/ *adv.* **1** used in order to emphasize what you are saying: *It's perfectly normal to feel nervous before a performance.* | *They had thrown away a* ***perfectly good*** *stereo.* **2** in a perfect way: *She speaks English perfectly.*

ˌperfect 'square *n.* [C] MATH a number whose SQUARE ROOT is a WHOLE NUMBER (=1, 3, 6, etc.), not a FRACTION (=¼, ½, etc.). For example, 25 is a perfect square whose square root is 5.

per·fid·i·ous /pɚ'fɪdiəs/ *adj.* (literary) disloyal and not able to be trusted: *his perfidious acts* —**perfidy** /'pɚfədi/ *n.* [U]

per·fo·rat·ed /'pɚfəˌreɪt̬ɪd/ *adj.* a piece of paper that is perforated has a line of small holes in it so that part of it can be torn off easily

per·form /pɚ'fɔrm/ *v.* **1** [I,T] ENG. LANG. ARTS to do something to entertain people: *The drama group performed "Hamlet" last week.* | *Karen will be performing with her band on Friday.* **2** [T] to do something such as a job or piece of work, especially something difficult or complicated: *Surgeons performed an emergency operation.* | *software that performs a specific function* **3 perform well/badly etc.** to work or do something well, badly, etc.: *The bike performs well on mountain trails.* | *The team has been performing poorly.*

per·form·ance /pɚ'fɔrməns/ *n.* **1** [C] ENG. LANG. ARTS an act of performing a play, piece of music, etc., or the occasion when something is performed: *a beautiful* ***performance of*** *Swan Lake* | *The next performance is at 8 o'clock.* **2** [U] how well or badly someone or something does something: *Linda's performance at school has greatly improved.* | *I was impressed with the car's performance on wet roads.* **3** [U] the act of doing something, especially your work: *the* ***performance of*** *his official duties*

per·form·er /pɚ'fɔrmɚ/ *n.* [C] ENG. LANG. ARTS an actor, musician, etc. who performs in order to entertain people: *a circus performer*

perˌforming 'arts *n.* **the performing arts** ENG. LANG. ARTS arts such as dance, music, or DRAMA, that are performed to entertain people

per·fume /'pɚfyum, pɚ'fyum/ *n.* [C,U] **1** a liquid with a strong pleasant smell that women put on their skin: *She never* ***wears perfume.*** **2** a pleasant smell: *the rose's sweet perfume* [ORIGIN: 1500—1600 French *parfum*]

THESAURUS **smell, aroma, scent, fragrance** ➔ SMELL[2]

—**perfumed** *adj.*: *perfumed soap*

per·func·to·ry /pɚ'fʌŋktəri/ *adj.* (formal) a perfunctory action is done quickly or without interest, and only because people expect it: *He shook my hand in a perfunctory way.* —**perfunctorily** *adv.*

per·haps /pɚ'hæps/ *adv.* **1** possibly (SYN) **maybe**: *Perhaps it'll be warmer tomorrow.* | *This is perhaps Irving's finest novel.* **2** (spoken) used in order to ask or suggest something politely (SYN) **maybe**: *Perhaps you'd like to join us?* [ORIGIN: 1400—1500 *per* "by" + *haps*, plural of *hap* "chance"]

per·i·gee /'pɛrədʒi/ *n.* [C] PHYSICS the point where the moon, a SATELLITE, or other object that is traveling in a curved path through space around the Earth is nearest the Earth → *see picture at* APOGEE

per·il /ˈpɛrəl/ *n.* (literary) **1** [U] danger of being harmed or killed: *Everyone feared that the sailors were* ***in great peril.***

THESAURUS danger, risk, threat → DANGER

2 the perils of sth the dangers involved in a particular activity: ***the perils of*** *drug use*

per·il·ous /ˈpɛrələs/ *adj.* (literary) very dangerous: *a perilous journey*

pe·rim·e·ter /pəˈrɪmət̬ɚ/ *n.* [C] **1** the border around an area of land: *the* ***perimeter of*** *the airfield*

THESAURUS edge, border, boundary → EDGE[1]

2 MATH the whole length of the border around an area or shape → CIRCUMFERENCE: *the* ***perimeter of*** *a triangle*

pe·ri·od /ˈpɪriəd/ (Ac) *n.* [C] **1** a length of time: *We worked together over a 15-month period.* | *James finished the research within a short* ***period of time.*** **2** a particular length of time in history or in a person's life: *We're studying the Civil War period.* | *the blue period in Picasso's painting* | *These years are a critical period in the child's development.* **3** the monthly flow of blood from a woman's body **4** ENG. LANG. ARTS the mark (.) used in writing that shows the end of a sentence or an abbreviation **5** one of the equal parts that the school day is divided into: *I have a history test during* ***first/second/third etc. period*** *on Tuesday.*

THESAURUS class, lesson → CLASS[1]

6 one of the equal parts that a game is divided into in a sport such as HOCKEY **7 period!** (spoken) said at the end of a sentence when you have made a decision and you do not want to discuss the subject any more: *I just won't do it, period!* [ORIGIN: 1300—1400 French *période*, from Latin, from Greek, from *peri-* + *hodos* "way"]

pe·ri·od·ic /ˌpɪriˈɑdɪk◂/ (Ac) *also* **periodical** *adj.* happening again and again, usually at regular times: *Dale gets periodic headaches.* | *Periodic reforms of the voting system took place during the 19th century.*

pe·ri·od·i·cal /ˌpɪriˈɑdɪkəl/ (Ac) *n.* [C] ENG. LANG. ARTS a magazine, especially one about a serious or technical subject: *The article appeared in a scholarly periodical.*

pe·ri·od·i·cally /ˌpɪriˈɑdɪkli/ *adv.* happening again and again, usually at regular times: *The river periodically floods the valley.* | *Athletes are periodically tested for drugs.*

ˌperiodic ˈtable *n.* **the periodic table** CHEMISTRY a specially arranged list of the ELEMENTS (=simple chemical substances)

pe·riph·e·ral[1] /pəˈrɪfərəl/ *adj.* **1** (formal) relating to the main idea, question, activity, etc., but less important than it: *He had only a peripheral role in the negotiations.* **2 peripheral vision** what you can see to the side of you when you look straight ahead **3** IT peripheral equipment can be connected to a computer and used with it

peripheral[2] *n.* [C] IT a piece of equipment that is connected to a computer and used with it

pe·riph·er·y /pəˈrɪfəri/ *n.* [singular] the outside area or edge of something: *a new neighborhood* ***on the periphery of*** *the city* [ORIGIN: 1500—1600 Old French *periferie*, from Late Latin, from Greek, from *peripherein* "to carry around"]

per·i·scope /ˈpɛrəˌskoʊp/ *n.* [C] a long tube with mirrors inside it, used for looking over the top of something, especially in a SUBMARINE [ORIGIN: 1800—1900 from Greek *peri-* "around" + *skopos* "look"]

per·ish /ˈpɛrɪʃ/ *v.* [I] (literary) to die: *Hundreds perished when the Titanic sank.*

per·ish·a·ble /ˈpɛrɪʃəbəl/ *adj.* food that is perishable can become bad quickly: *milk and other perishable items* —**perishables** *n.* [plural]

per·jure /ˈpɚdʒɚ/ *v.* **perjure yourself** LAW to tell a lie in a court of law

per·ju·ry /ˈpɚdʒəri/ *n.* [U] LAW the crime of telling a lie in a court of law

THESAURUS lie, fib, falsehood, fabrication → LIE[3]

perk[1] /pɚk/ *n.* [C] money, goods, or other advantages that you get from your work in addition to your pay: *a few extra perks like a company car and travel expenses*

perk[2] *v.* (informal)

perk (sb ↔) **up** *phr. v.* to become more cheerful and interested in what is happening around you, or to make someone feel this way: *A cup of coffee will perk you up.* | *Meg perked up when the music started.*

perk (sth ↔) **up** *phr. v.* to become better, more interesting, etc., or to make something do this: *A little more pepper will perk up the sauce.*

perk·y /ˈpɚki/ *adj.* (informal) confident, happy, and full of interest: *a perky little girl*

perm[1] /pɚm/ *n.* [C] a way of putting curls into straight hair by treating it with chemicals

perm[2] *v.* [T] to put curls into straight hair using chemicals: *Did you* ***have*** *your* ***hair permed****?*

per·ma·frost /ˈpɚməˌfrɔst/ *n.* [U] EARTH SCIENCES a thick layer of permanently frozen ground just below the top layer of soil, in countries such as Alaska where it is very cold for most of the year

per·ma·nent /ˈpɚmənənt/ *adj.* continuing to exist for a long time or for all time (ANT) **temporary**: *There was not any* ***permanent damage*** *to the muscle.* | *The UN Security Council has five permanent members.* [ORIGIN: 1400—1500 Latin,

P

present participle of *permanere* "to stay until the end"] —**permanence** *n.* [U]

per·ma·nent·ly /ˈpɚmənəntli/ *adv.* always, or for a very long time: *Do you plan to live here permanently?* | *The accident left him permanently disabled.*

THESAURUS always, all the time/the whole time ➔ ALWAYS (1)
always, forever, for life, for good ➔ ALWAYS (2)

ˌpermanent ˈpress *n.* [U] a way of treating cloth so that it stays smooth, or cloth that has been treated in this way

P

per·me·ate /ˈpɚmiˌeɪt/ *v.* [I,T] (formal) to spread through every part of something: *The smell of smoke permeated the house.* | *A feeling of sadness permeates his music.*

per·mis·si·ble /pɚˈmɪsəbəl/ *adj.* (formal) allowed by law or by the rules: *In some religions, divorce is not permissible.*

per·mis·sion /pɚˈmɪʃən/ *n.* [U] the act of allowing someone to do something: *You have to* ***ask permission*** *if you want to leave class early.* | *You must* ***have permission*** *to enter these areas.* | *Did your dad* ***give*** *you* ***permission*** *to use the car?* ▸Don't say "the permission."◂

per·mis·sive /pɚˈmɪsɪv/ *adj.* allowing actions or behavior that many people disapprove of: *permissive parents*

per·mit¹ /pɚˈmɪt/ *v.* (**permitted**, **permitting**) (formal) **1** [T] to allow something to happen, especially by a rule or law: *Smoking is not permitted inside the building.* | *Each employee is* ***permitted to*** *bring a guest to the party.*

THESAURUS allow, let, authorize, sanction ➔ ALLOW

2 [I] to make it possible for something to happen: *We'll probably go to the beach,* ***weather permitting.*** [ORIGIN: 1400—1500 Latin *permittere* "to let through, allow"]

per·mit² /ˈpɚmɪt/ *n.* [C] an official written statement giving you the right to do something: *You can't park here without a permit.* | *a* ***travel/work permit***

per·mu·ta·tion /ˌpɚmyʊˈteɪʃən/ *n.* [C] one of the different ways in which a set of things can be arranged, or put together to make something else

per·ni·cious /pɚˈnɪʃəs/ *adj.* (formal) very harmful, especially in a way that is not easily noticeable: *the pernicious effects of advertising*

per·o·ra·tion /ˌpɛrəˈreɪʃən/ *n.* [C] ENG. LANG. ARTS the last part of a speech, especially a part in which the main points are repeated

per·ox·ide /pəˈrɑkˌsaɪd/ *n.* [U] CHEMISTRY a chemical liquid used in order to make dark hair lighter, or to kill BACTERIA

per·pen·dic·u·lar /ˌpɚpənˈdɪkyəlɚ/ *adj.* **1** MATH if one line is perpendicular to another line, they form an angle of 90° ➔ HORIZONTAL, VERTICAL: *perpendicular lines* | *Main Street* ***is perpendicular to*** *First Street.* ➔ *see picture at* LINE¹ **2** exactly upright and not leaning to one side or the other SYN **vertical**: *a perpendicular pole*

per·pe·trate /ˈpɚpəˌtreɪt/ *v.* [T] (formal) to do something that is wrong or illegal: *crimes perpetrated by young people* [ORIGIN: 1500—1600 Latin, past participle of *perpetrare* "to achieve something"]

per·pe·tra·tor /ˈpɚpəˌtreɪt̬ɚ/ *n.* [C] someone who does something illegal

per·pet·u·al /pɚˈpɛtʃuəl/ *adj.* continuing forever or for a long time: *the perpetual noise of the machinery* | *her perpetual complaining* —**perpetually** *adv.*

per·pet·u·ate /pɚˈpɛtʃuˌeɪt/ *v.* [T] to make a situation, attitude, etc., especially a bad one, continue to exist for a long time: *The movie perpetuates stereotypes about women.*

per·plex /pɚˈplɛks/ *v.* [T] if a problem perplexes you, it confuses you and worries you, because it is difficult to understand: *Shea's symptoms perplexed the doctors.* —**perplexed** *adj.*

per·qui·site /ˈpɚkwəzɪt/ *n.* [C] (formal) a PERK

per se /ˌpɚ ˈseɪ/ *adv.* (formal) used in order to show that something is being considered alone, apart from anything else: *Money, per se, is not usually why people change jobs.*

per·se·cute /ˈpɚsɪˌkyut/ *v.* [T] to treat someone cruelly and unfairly, especially because of his/her religious or political beliefs: *a writer* ***persecuted for*** *criticizing the government* [ORIGIN: 1400—1500 French *persécuter*, from Latin *persecutus*, past participle of *persequi* "to pursue, follow"] —**persecutor** *n.* [C]

per·se·cu·tion /ˌpɚsɪˈkyuʃən/ *n.* [U] the act of persecuting someone: *the* ***persecution of*** *religious groups*

per·se·ver·ance /ˌpɚsəˈvɪrəns/ *n.* [U] (approving) determination to keep trying to do something difficult: *It took perseverance to overcome his reading problems.*

per·se·vere /ˌpɚsəˈvɪr/ *v.* [I] (approving) to continue trying to do something difficult in a determined way: *The team has persevered through a lot of tough times.*

per·sist /pɚˈsɪst/ Ac *v.* [I] (formal) **1** to continue to do something, even though it is difficult or other people do not like it: *Students must* ***persist in*** *their efforts if they wish to do well.* | *She* ***persisted with*** *her studies in spite of financial problems.* **2** to continue to exist or happen: *Call a doctor if the pain persists for more than a few days.* [ORIGIN: 1500—1600 French *persister*, from Latin *persistere*, from *sistere* "to stand firm"]

per·sist·ence /pɚˈsɪstəns/ Ac *n.* [U] **1** determination to do something even though it is difficult or other people oppose it: *Claudia's persistence paid off and she got the job.* **2** when something continues to exist or happen, especially for longer than is usual or desirable: *The bank needed to act because of the persistence of high inflation.*

per·sist·ent /pɚˈsɪstənt/ (Ac) *adj.* **1** continuing to exist or happen, especially for longer than is usual or desirable: *persistent problems | There have been **persistent rumors** that the chairman is going to quit.* **2** continuing to do something even though it is difficult or other people oppose it: *You have to be persistent if you want to get a job.* —**persistently** *adv.*: *He persistently denies doing anything wrong.*

per·son /ˈpɚsən/ *n.* (plural **people** /ˈpipəl/) [C] **1** a man, woman, or child: *Diane is a really nice person. | I was the last person to be called. | Abby's a **computer/cat/night etc. person*** (=someone who likes computers, cats, etc.).

USAGE

person – a man, woman, or child: *She's a really generous person.*
persons (formal) – more than one man, woman, or child – used only in official language: *Police are looking for the person or persons responsible for her death.*
people – many men, women, and children. In this meaning, **people** is the plural of **person**: *There were about 100 people at the wedding*
people – a particular race or group that lives in a particular country. In this meaning, the plural is **peoples**: *the peoples of the Caribbean*

2 in person if you do something in person, you do it when you are in a place, not by sending a letter or using the telephone: *You'll have to apply for your passport in person.* [ORIGIN: 1100—1200 Old French *persone*, from Latin *persona* "actor's mask, character in a play, person"] → FIRST PERSON, SECOND PERSON, THIRD PERSON

per·so·na /pɚˈsoʊnə/ *n.* [C] **1** (plural **personas** *or* **personae** /-ni/) the way you behave when you are with other people: *You always wonder how different movie stars are from their **public personas**.* **2** (plural **personae**) ENG. LANG. ARTS the character or voice that NARRATES (=tells) the story in a book, movie, etc.: *The author used the persona of a teenage girl to tell the story.* **3** (plural **personae**) ENG. LANG. ARTS any of the characters in a book, play, etc.

per·son·a·ble /ˈpɚsənəbəl/ *adj.* having a pleasant way of talking and behaving

per·son·al /ˈpɚsənəl/ *adj.*
1 RELATING TO YOU [only before noun] belonging or relating to one particular person, rather than to other people or to people in general: *Please keep all bags and other **personal belongings** with you. | I know **from personal experience** how difficult this kind of work can be. | My **personal opinion** is that we began the project too late.*
2 PRIVATE private and concerning only you: *Can I ask you a **personal question**? | He won't talk about his **personal life**. | Beth had a lot of **personal problems** at that time.*

THESAURUS private, secret, intimate → PRIVATE[1]

3 DONE BY YOU used in order to emphasize that someone does something directly, instead of asking someone else to do it: *The president made a personal visit to the scene of the accident. | I will give this my **personal attention**.*
4 CRITICISM involving rude or upsetting criticism of someone: *Making **personal remarks** like that isn't professional. | **It's nothing personal*** (=I am not criticizing you) – *I just don't agree with you.*
5 personal friend someone you know well, especially someone famous or important: *The editor is **a personal friend of** his.*
6 NOT WORK not relating to your work or business: *We're not allowed to make personal phone calls at work.*
7 YOUR BODY [only before noun] relating to your body or the way you look: *personal hygiene*

ˌpersonal comˈputer *n.* [C] IT a PC → *see picture on page A19*

per·son·al·i·ty /ˌpɚsəˈnæləṭi/ *n.* (plural **personalities**) **1** [C,U] someone's character, especially the way s/he behaves toward other people: *an ambitious woman with a strong personality | Childhood experiences can affect personality.* **2** [C] someone who is well known to the public: *a TV personality* **3** [U] (informal) the qualities that make someone or something interesting: *We liked the name because we thought it had personality.*

per·son·al·ize /ˈpɚsənəˌlaɪz/ *v.* [T] **1** to put your name or INITIALS on something: *cars with personalized license plates* **2** to decorate something in a way you like: *Becky has personalized her office with photos and drawings.* **3** to make something appropriate for what a particular person needs: *All products can be personalized to the client's requirements.*

per·son·al·ly /ˈpɚsənəli/ *adv.* **1** (spoken) used in order to emphasize that you are giving your own opinion: *Personally, I think it's a bad idea.* **2** doing or having done something yourself: *I delivered the letter personally. | She's **personally responsible** for all the arrangements.* **3 take sth personally** to get upset by the things other people say or do because you think their remarks or behavior are directed at you: *Don't take it personally – he's rude to everyone.* **4** as a friend, or as someone you have met: *I don't **know** her **personally**, but I like her books.*

ˌpersonal ˈpronoun *n.* [C] ENG. LANG. ARTS in grammar, a PRONOUN used for the person who is speaking, being spoken to, or being spoken about, such as "I,' "you," and "they"

ˌpersonal ˈproperty *n.* [U] money, property, jewelry, etc. that belongs to one particular person, rather than to several people or to people in general

per·so·nals /ˈpɚsənəlz/ *n.* **the personals** [plural] a part of a newspaper in which people can have private messages printed

P

persona non gra·ta /pə˞ˌsoʊnə nɑn ˈgrɑt̬ə/ *n.* [U] **1** (formal) someone who is not welcome in a particular place or in a particular group: *After the court case, he found himself persona non grata in the business community.* **2** POLITICS a DIPLOMAT (=government representative) who has been ordered to leave the country where he or she has been sent to work [ORIGIN: 1800—1900 Latin "person not acceptable"]

per·son·i·fi·ca·tion /pə˞ˌsɑnəfəˈkeɪʃən/ *n.* **1 the personification of sth** someone who has a lot of a particular quality, so that s/he is used as an example of that quality: *Mrs. Grant is the personification of kindness.* **2** [C,U] the REPRESENTATION of a thing or a quality as a person: *the personification of Justice as a woman holding scales*

P

per·son·i·fy /pə˞ˈsɑnəˌfaɪ/ *v.* (**personified, personifies**) [T] **1** to have a lot of a particular quality or be a typical example of something: *An earthquake personifies the force of nature.* **2 sb is sth personified** used in order to say that someone perfectly represents a quality or idea: *Theresa was kindness personified.* **3** ENG. LANG. ARTS to think of or represent a quality or thing as a person: *Time is usually personified as an old man with a beard.*

per·son·nel /ˌpə˞səˈnɛl/ *n.* **1** [plural] the people who work in a company or for a particular kind of employer: *All personnel need to have identification cards.* | *military personnel* **2** [U] HUMAN RESOURCES: *the personnel department*

per·spec·tive /pə˞ˈspɛktɪv/ (Ac) *n.* **1** [C] a way of thinking about something that is influenced by the type of person you are or by your experiences: *Becoming a mother gave Helen a whole new* ***perspective on*** *life.* | *The novel is written* ***from*** *a child's* ***perspective.*** | *We are trying to develop a broader perspective on Third World development.* **2** [U] the ability to think about something sensibly, so that it does not seem worse than it is: *I think Tony's* ***lost*** *all* ***sense of perspective.*** | *You've got to* ***keep*** *things* ***in perspective.*** **3** [U] ENG. LANG. ARTS a method of drawing a picture that makes objects look solid and shows distance and depth: *the artist's use of perspective*

per·spi·ca·cious /ˌpə˞spɪˈkeɪʃəs◂ / *adj.* (formal) good at judging and understanding people and situations, or showing this quality: *a perspicacious critic* —**perspicaciously** *adv.* —**perspicacity** /ˌpə˞spɪˈkæsət̬i/ *n.* [U]

per·spi·ra·tion /ˌpə˞spəˈreɪʃən/ *n.* [U] (formal) SWEAT

per·spire /pə˞ˈspaɪə˞/ *v.* [I] (formal) to SWEAT

per·suade /pə˞ˈsweɪd/ *v.* [T] **1** to make someone agree to do something by giving good reasons why s/he should: *We eventually* ***persuaded*** *Mark* ***to*** *come with us.*

THESAURUS

talk sb into sth – to persuade someone to do something: *I should never have let my mother talk me into buying this dress.*
get sb to do sth – to persuade or force someone to do something: *I tried to get Jill to come, but she said she was too tired.*
encourage sb to do sth – to persuade someone to do something, especially by telling him/her that it is good for him/her: *More high schools are encouraging their students to do community service.*
influence – to have an effect on what someone does or thinks: *Sports figures influence kids' ideas about what's cool.*
convince – to persuade someone to do something, especially something s/he does not want to do: *I convinced him to stay another night.*
coax – to persuade someone to do something by talking gently and kindly: *"Come for Christmas," Jody coaxed over the phone.*
cajole – to persuade someone to do something by praising him/her or making promises to him/her: *I managed to cajole Miguel into directing the movie.*
prevail on/upon sb (formal) – to persuade someone: *Her father prevailed upon her not to marry immediately.*

2 to make someone believe something or feel sure about something (SYN) **convince**: *Members of the jury were not persuaded by the lawyer's arguments.* | *She'll only take me back if I can* ***persuade*** *her* ***(that)*** *I've changed.* [ORIGIN: 1500—1600 Latin *persuadere*, from *suadere* "to advise"]

per·sua·sion /pə˞ˈsweɪʒən/ *n.* **1** [U] the act or skill of persuading someone to do something: *With a little persuasion, Debbie agreed to come with us.* | *It took all of my* ***powers of persuasion*** *to convince him.* **2** [C] a particular belief, especially a political or religious one: *Jake and his brother are of different political persuasions.*

per·sua·sive /pə˞ˈsweɪsɪv/ *adj.* able to influence other people to believe or do something: *Erin can be very persuasive.* | *It was not a very* ***persuasive argument.***

pert /pə˞t/ *adj.* **1** small and attractive: *a pert nose* **2** (literary) amusing in a way that shows a slight lack of respect: *a pert answer*

per·tain /pə˞ˈteɪn/ *v.*

pertain to sth *phr. v.* (formal) to relate directly to something: *laws pertaining to welfare benefits*

per·ti·na·cious /ˌpə˞t˺nˈeɪʃəs/ *adj.* (formal) continuing to believe something or to do something in a very determined way —**pertinaciously** *adv.* —**pertinacity** /ˌpə˞t˺nˈæsət̬i/ *n.* [U]

per·ti·nent /ˈpə˞t˺n-ənt/ *adj.* (formal) directly relating to something that is being considered (SYN) **relevant**: *Reporters asked a few pertinent questions.*

THESAURUS **related, connected, linked, relevant** ➔ RELATED

per·turbed /pə˞ˈtə˞bd/ *adj.* (formal) worried and annoyed: *We weren't too perturbed by the delay.* —**perturb** *v.* [T]

THESAURUS upset, unsettled, troubled, disturbed → UPSET[1]

pe·ruse /pə'ruz/ *v.* [T] (formal or humorous) to read something in a careful way: *Anne looked at the book he'd been perusing.* —**perusal** *n.* [C,U]

THESAURUS read, flip/thumb through sth, browse through sth, skim/scan (through) sth → READ

per·vade /pɚ'veɪd/ *v.* [T] (formal) to spread through all parts of something: *A feeling of hopelessness pervaded the country.*

per·va·sive /pɚ'veɪsɪv/ *adj.* existing or spreading everywhere: *the pervasive influence of violence on TV*

per·verse /pɚ'vɚs/ *adj.* behaving in an unreasonable way by doing the opposite of what people want you to do: *He takes perverse pleasure in arguing with everyone.*

per·ver·sion /pɚ'vɚʒən/ *n.* [C,U] **1** a type of sexual behavior that is considered unnatural and unacceptable **2** the act of changing something so that it is no longer right, reasonable, or true: *a **perversion of** the truth*

per·vert[1] /pɚ'vɚt/ *v.* [T] to change someone or something in a harmful way: *Athletes who cheat by taking drugs are perverting traditional Olympic values.*

per·vert[2] /'pɚvɚt/ *n.* [C] someone whose sexual behavior is considered unnatural and unacceptable

per·vert·ed /pɚ'vɚt̬ɪd/ *adj.* **1** relating to unacceptable and unnatural sexual thoughts or behavior **2** morally wrong or unnatural: *perverted logic*

pes·ky /'pɛski/ *adj.* (informal) annoying and causing trouble: *Those pesky kids!*

pes·si·mis·m /'pɛsə,mɪzəm/ *n.* [U] a tendency to believe that bad things will happen (ANT) **optimism**: *a feeling of **pessimism about** the future* [ORIGIN: 1700—1800 French *pessimisme*, from Latin *pessimus* "worst"]

pes·si·mist /'pɛsəmɪst/ *n.* [C] someone who always expects that bad things will happen (ANT) **optimist**

pes·si·mis·tic /,pɛsə'mɪstɪk/ *adj.* expecting that bad things will happen or that a situation will have a bad result (ANT) **optimistic**: *Jonathan is **pessimistic about** his chances.*

pest /pɛst/ *n.* [C] **1** a small animal or insect that destroys crops or food **2** (informal) an annoying person: *The kids next door can be real pests.*

pes·ter /'pɛstɚ/ *v.* [T] to annoy someone by asking for something again and again: *She kept pestering her parents to let her go out.*

pes·ti·cide /'pɛstə,saɪd/ *n.* [C] a chemical substance that kills insects that destroy crops

pets

pet[1] /pɛt/ *n.* [C] an animal that you keep at home: *Do you have any pets?* → TEACHER'S PET

pet[2] *v.* (**petted**, **petting**) [T] to touch and move your hand gently over an animal's fur: *Our cat loves being petted.* → *see picture on page A21*

THESAURUS touch, feel, stroke, rub, scratch, pat, caress → TOUCH[1]

pet[3] *adj.* [only before noun] **1 pet project/subject etc.** a plan, subject, etc. that you particularly like or are interested in: *Congressmen are always looking for funding for their pet projects.* **2** a pet animal is one that someone keeps at home: *a pet hamster* **3 pet peeve** something that always annoys you, that may not annoy other people: *One of my pet peeves is people being late for meetings.*

pet·al /'pɛt̬l/ *n.* [C] the colored part of a flower that is shaped like a leaf: *rose petals* → *see picture at* FLOWER[1]

pe·ter /'pit̬ɚ/ *v.*

peter out *phr. v.* to gradually become smaller, fewer, quieter, etc. and then no longer exist or happen: *After a few minutes, the conversation began to peter out.*

pet·i·ole /'pɛti,oʊl/ *n.* [C] BIOLOGY a thin narrow part of a plant, that supports a leaf and keeps it attached to the stem

pe·tite /pə'tit/ *adj.* (approving) a woman who is petite is short and thin in an attractive way

THESAURUS small, little, tiny, diminutive → SMALL

pe·ti·tion[1] /pə'tɪʃən/ *v.* [I,T] to formally ask someone in authority to do something, especially by sending him/her a petition: *Residents are **petitioning against** a new prison in the area.* [ORIGIN: 1300—1400 Old French, Latin *petitio*, from *petere* "to try to get or find"]

petition[2] *n.* [C] a piece of paper that asks someone in authority to do or change something, and is signed by a lot of people: *Will you* ***sign*** *our* ***petition****?* | *a* ***petition against*** *nuclear testing*

Pe·tri dish /ˈpitri ˌdɪʃ/ *n.* [C] SCIENCE a small clear dish with a cover, used especially by scientists for growing BACTERIA

pet·ri·fied /ˈpɛtrəˌfaɪd/ *adj.* **1** extremely frightened: *I'm absolutely* ***petrified of*** *dogs.*

THESAURUS **frightened, afraid, scared, terrified, fearful, phobic** → FRIGHTENED

2 petrified wood wood that has changed into stone over millions of years [ORIGIN: 1400—1500 French *pétrifier*, from Greek *petra* "rock"] —**petrify** *v.* [T]

P

pet·ro·chem·i·cal /ˌpɛtroʊˈkɛmɪkəl/ *n.* [C] CHEMISTRY a chemical substance obtained from petroleum or natural gas: *the petrochemical industry*

pe·tro·le·um /pəˈtroʊliəm/ *n.* [U] oil that is obtained from below the surface of the Earth and is used in order to make GASOLINE and other chemical substances: *petroleum-based products*

pet·ty /ˈpɛt̬i/ *adj.* **1** something that is petty is not serious or important: *Don't bother me with petty details.* **2** someone who is petty cares too much about things that are not very important or serious: *Sometimes he's so petty about money* (=he thinks too much about exactly how much people owe him). **3 petty crime** a crime that is not serious, for example stealing things that are not expensive —**pettiness** *n.* [U]

ˌpetty ˈcash *n.* [U] money that is kept in an office for making small payments

ˌpetty ˈofficer, Petty Officer *n.* [C] an officer who has the lowest rank in the navy

pet·u·lant /ˈpɛtʃələnt/ *adj.* behaving in an impatient and angry way for no reason at all, like a child: *My ex-husband is behaving like a petulant child.* —**petulantly** *adv.* —**petulance** *n.* [U]

pew¹ /pyu/ *n.* [C] a long wooden seat in a church

pew² *interjection* said when something smells very bad: *Pew! There must be a farm near here.*

pew·ter /ˈpyut̬ɚ/ *n.* [U] a gray metal made by mixing LEAD and TIN

PG *n.* [C,U] **parental guidance** – used in order to show that a movie may include parts that are not suitable for young children

PG-13 /ˌpi dʒi θɚˈtin/ *n.* [C,U] **parental guidance-13** – used in order to show that a movie may include parts that are not suitable for children under the age of 13

pH /piˈeɪtʃ/ *also* **pˈH ˌvalue** *n.* [C usually singular] CHEMISTRY a number on a scale of numbers from 0 to 14, that shows how acid or ALKALINE a substance is

phag·o·cyte /ˈfægəˌsaɪt/ *n.* [C] BIOLOGY a blood cell that protects the body by destroying harmful BACTERIA, VIRUSes, etc.

phal·lic /ˈfælɪk/ *adj.* like a PENIS, or relating to the PENIS

phal·lus /ˈfæləs/ *n.* [C] the male sex organ, or a model of it

phan·tom /ˈfæntəm/ *n.* [C] (literary) **1** a GHOST

THESAURUS **ghost, spirit, specter, apparition** → GHOST

2 something that exists only in your imagination

Phar·aoh /ˈfɛroʊ, ˈfær-/ *n.* [C] a ruler of ancient Egypt

phar·ma·ceu·ti·cal /ˌfɑrməˈsut̬ɪkəl/ *n.* [C usually plural] CHEMISTRY a medicine or drug [ORIGIN: 1600—1700 Late Latin *pharmaceuticus*, from Greek *pharmakeuein* "to give drugs"] —**pharmaceutical** *adj.* [only before noun]: *large pharmaceutical companies*

phar·ma·cist /ˈfɑrməsɪst/ *n.* [C] someone whose job is to prepare drugs and medicines in a store or hospital

phar·ma·col·o·gy /ˌfɑrməˈkɑlədʒi/ *n.* [U] CHEMISTRY the scientific study of drugs and medicines —**pharmacologist** *n.* [C]

phar·ma·cy /ˈfɑrməsi/ *n.* (plural **pharmacies**) [C] a store, or a part of a store, where medicines are prepared and sold [ORIGIN: 1300—1400 Late Latin *pharmacia* "giving drugs," from Greek, from *pharmakeuein* "to give drugs"]

phar·ynx /ˈfærɪŋks/ *n.* (plural **pharynges** /fəˈrɪndʒiz/ *or* **pharynxes**) [C] BIOLOGY the tube that goes from the back of your mouth to your ESOPHAGUS

phase¹ /feɪz/ (Ac) *n.* [C] **1** one of the stages of a process of development or change: *The first* ***phase of*** *renovation should be finished by January.* | *The work will be carried out* ***in phases****.* | *Your child is just* ***going through a phase****.*

THESAURUS **stage, part, step** → STAGE¹

2 PHYSICS one of the changes in the appearance of the moon or a PLANET when it is seen from the Earth **3 in phase/out of phase** PHYSICS two or more waves of sound, light, energy, etc. are in phase if their highest parts and lowest parts reach the same place at the same time. They are out of phase if these points do not match. [ORIGIN: 1800—1900 Modern Latin *phasis*, from Greek, "appearance of a star, phase of the moon"]

phase² *v.*

phase sth ↔ **in** *phr. v.* to introduce something gradually: *New rules are being phased in over the next two months.* | *The state plans to phase in alternative sources of energy.*

phase sth ↔ **out** *phr. v.* to gradually stop using or providing something: *Leaded gas was phased out in the 1970s.*

Ph.D. /ˌpi eɪtʃ ˈdi/ *n.* [C] **Doctor of Philosophy** the highest university degree that can be earned, or someone who has this degree

pheas·ant /ˈfɛzənt/ *n.* [C,U] a large colorful bird with a long tail that is hunted for food and sport, or the meat from this bird [ORIGIN: 1200—1300 Anglo-French *fesaunt*, from Latin, from Greek *phasianos*, from *Phasis* ancient river in Asia]

phe·nom·e·nal /fɪˈnɑmənl/ (Ac) *adj.* very great or impressive: *New York's* ***phenomenal success*** *in reducing crime* | *The growth in California's population during this period was phenomenal.* —**phenomenally** *adv.*: *phenomenally popular*

phe·nom·e·non /fɪˈnɑmənən, -ˌnɑn/ (Ac) *n.* (plural **phenomena** /-mənə/) [C] **1** something that happens or exists in society, science, or nature that is unusual or difficult to understand: *Homelessness is not a* ***new phenomenon.*** | ***natural phenomena*** *such as earthquakes* | *Language is a social and cultural phenomenon.*

THESAURUS **event, occurrence, incident**
➔ EVENT

2 a person or thing that has a rare ability or quality [ORIGIN: 1500—1600 Late Latin from Greek *phainomenon*, from *phainein* "to show"]

phe·no·type /ˈfinəˌtaɪp/ *n.* [C] BIOLOGY the physical appearance of a living thing, that results from its GENES and the environment in which it lives ➔ GENOTYPE

phew /fyu, hyu/ *interjection* said when you feel tired, hot, or RELIEVED: *Phew! I'm glad that's over.*

phi·lan·der·er /fɪˈlændərə/ *n.* [C] (disapproving) a man who has sex with many women but does not want a serious relationship —**philandering** *n.* [U]

phil·an·throp·ic /ˌfɪlənˈθrɑpɪk◂/ *adj.* a philanthropic person or institution gives money to people who are poor or who need money in order to do something good or useful —**philanthropically** *adv.*

phi·lan·thro·pist /fɪˈlænθrəpɪst/ *n.* [C] a rich person who gives a lot of money to help poor people

phi·lan·thro·py /fɪˈlænθrəpi/ *n.* [U] the practice of giving money and help to people who need it

phil·is·tine /ˈfɪləˌstin/ *n.* [C] (disapproving) someone who does not like or understand art, music, literature, etc. [ORIGIN: 1800—1900 *Philistine*; because the Philistines were thought by the Israelites in the Bible to be uncivilized people]

phi·los·o·pher /fɪˈlɑsəfə/ (Ac) *n.* [C] someone who studies or teaches philosophy: *ancient Greek philosophers*

phil·o·soph·i·cal /ˌfɪləˈsɑfɪkəl/ (Ac) *adj.* **1** relating to philosophy: *a philosophical discussion* | *The debate never became philosophical.* **2** accepting difficult or bad situations calmly: *Anderson remains* ***philosophical about*** *his defeat.* —**philosophically** *adv.*

phi·los·o·phize /fɪˈlɑsəˌfaɪz/ (Ac) *v.* [I] to talk or think about important subjects and ideas in a serious way

phi·los·o·phy /fɪˈlɑsəfi/ (Ac) *n.* (plural **philosophies**) **1** [U] the study of what it means to exist, what good and evil are, what knowledge is, or how people should live: *She graduated from Yale with a degree in philosophy.* | *Her work explores the connections between language and philosophy.* **2** [C] a set of ideas about these subjects: *the* ***philosophy of*** *Plato* **3** [C] a set of beliefs about how you should live your life, do your job, etc.: *a new business philosophy* | *We share a similar* ***philosophy of life.*** | *Jefferson had to reconcile two competing philosophies of government.* [ORIGIN: 1300—1400 Old French *philosophie*, from Latin, from Greek *philo-* "loving" + *sophia* "knowledge"]

P

phish·ing /ˈfɪʃɪŋ/ *n.* [U] IT an illegal activity in which someone sends an email or has a WEBSITE that is intended to trick people into giving away information such as their bank account number or their computer PASSWORD. This information is then used to get money or goods.

phlegm /flɛm/ *n.* [U] BIOLOGY a thick sticky substance produced in your nose and throat, especially when you have a cold (SYN) **mucus**

phleg·mat·ic /flɛgˈmæṭɪk/ *adj.* (formal) calm and not easily excited or worried

phlo·em /ˈfloʊɛm/ *n.* [U] BIOLOGY the TISSUE (=material consisting of cells) in plants that carries food substances from the leaves to all parts of the plant

pho·bi·a /ˈfoʊbiə/ *n.* [C] a strong unreasonable fear of something: *Holly* ***has a phobia about*** *snakes.* [ORIGIN: 1700—1800 Modern Latin, Late Latin *-phobia*, from Greek, from *phobos* "fear"] —**phobic** *adj.*

phoe·nix /ˈfinɪks/ *n.* [C] ENG. LANG. ARTS a bird in ancient stories that burns itself at the end of its life and is born again from the ASHes [ORIGIN: 800—900 Latin, from Greek *phoinix* "red, Phoenician, phoenix," from *phoinos* "blood-red"]

phone[1] /foʊn/ *n.* [C] **1** a piece of equipment that you use in order to talk with someone in another place: *I got up to* ***answer the phone.*** | *I was* ***on the phone*** (=talking to someone else using a telephone) *for an hour, talking to Lynn.* | *Will you get* ***off the phone****? I'm expecting a call.* | *What's your* ***phone number****?* | *Just as we sat down to dinner, the* ***phone rang.*** | *Tickets can be ordered* ***by phone.*** **2** the part of a telephone that you hold close to your ear and mouth: *She* ***picked up the phone*** *and dialed.*

TOPIC

When you want to **make a phone call/call sb/phone sb**, you **lift/pick up** the **receiver** (=part you speak into) and **dial** the **number** you want. If the telephone **rings**, someone may **answer** it, or there may be **no answer**. If the number is **busy**, someone is already speaking on that **line**, and you cannot **get through**. If the person you are **calling** has an **answering machine** or **voice mail**, you can **leave a message** for the person to listen to later. If you **get the wrong number** by mistake, try **dialing** again. When you finish speaking on the phone, **hang up** (=put the receiver down). → CELL PHONE

phone² *v.* [I,T] to talk to someone using a phone SYN **call**: *Several people phoned the radio station to complain.*

'phone book *n.* [C] a book containing an alphabetical list of the names, addresses, and telephone numbers of all the people and businesses that have a telephone in the area

'phone booth *n.* [C] a partly enclosed structure containing a telephone that the public can use

phone booth

'phone card *n.* [C] a special card that you buy and use to make phone calls on a public phone

pho·neme /'foʊnim/ *n.* [C] ENG. LANG. ARTS the smallest speech sound that can be used to make one word different from another word, such as the "b" and the "p" in "big" and "pig" —**phonemic** /fə'nimɪk/ *adj.* → MORPHEME

pho·ne·mics /fə'nimɪks/ *n.* [U] ENG. LANG. ARTS the study and description of the phonemes of languages

pho·net·ic /fə'nɛt̬ɪk/ *adj.* ENG. LANG. ARTS relating to the sounds of human speech: *a phonetic alphabet* (=one that uses signs to represent the sounds) [ORIGIN: 1800—1900 Modern Latin *phoneticus*, from Greek *phonetikos*, from *phonein* "to speak"] —**phonetically** *adv.*

pho·net·ics /fə'nɛt̬ɪks/ *n.* [U] ENG. LANG. ARTS the science and study of speech sounds

phon·ics /'fɑnɪks/ *n.* [U] ENG. LANG. ARTS a method of teaching people to read in which they are taught to recognize the sounds that letters represent

pho·no·graph /'foʊnə,græf/ *n.* [C] (old-fashioned) a RECORD PLAYER

pho·nol·o·gy /fə'nɑlədʒi/ *n.* [U] ENG. LANG. ARTS the study of the system of speech sounds in a language, or the system of sounds itself —**phonological** /,foʊnə'lɑdʒɪkəl/ *adj.* —**phonologically** *adv.*

pho·ny /'foʊni/ *adj.* (informal) false or not real, and intended to deceive someone SYN **fake**: *Dirk gave the cops a phony address.* | *a phony passport* —**phony** *n.* [C]: *She's such a phony!*

phoo·ey /'fui/ *interjection* (old-fashioned) used in order to express strong disbelief or disappointment

phos·phate /'fɑsfeɪt/ *n.* [C,U] CHEMISTRY one of the various forms of a salt of phosphorus, used in industry [ORIGIN: 1700—1800 French *acide phosphorique* "phosphoric acid"]

phos·pho·res·cent /,fɑsfə'rɛsənt/ *adj.* CHEMISTRY shining slightly in the dark but producing little or no heat —**phosphorescence** *n.* [U]

phos·pho·rus /'fɑsfərəs/ *n.* [U] CHEMISTRY a poisonous chemical that starts to burn when it is brought out into the air —**phosphoric** /fɑs'fɔrɪk, -'fɑr-/ *adj.*

photic zone

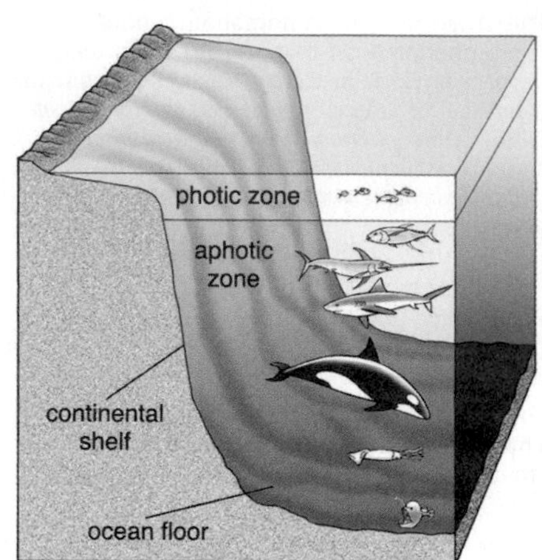

pho·tic zone /'foʊt̬ɪk ,zoʊn/ *n.* **the photic zone** BIOLOGY the upper layer of an ocean or a lake where there is enough light from the Sun for PHOTOSYNTHESIS to take place

pho·to /'foʊt̬oʊ/ *n.* [C] (informal) a photograph: *Who's the girl in this photo?* | *a* ***photo of*** *Babe Ruth* | *This camera* ***takes*** *quite good* ***photos***.

pho·to·cop·i·er /'foʊt̬ə,kɑpiə/ *n.* [C] a machine that quickly copies documents onto paper by photographing them

pho·to·cop·y /'foʊt̬ə,kɑpi/ *n.* (plural **photocopies**) [C] a copy of a document made by a photocopier: ***Make a photocopy of*** *this article for me.* —**photocopy** *v.* [T]

THESAURUS **copy, reproduce, duplicate, xerox** → COPY²

pho·to·e·lec·tric /,foʊt̬oʊ-ɪ'lɛktrɪk◂/ *adj.* PHYSICS using an electric current that is controlled by light: *Photoelectric panels in the roof of the building help to maintain a constant temperature.*

,photo 'finish *n.* [C] the end of a race in which the leaders finish so close together that a photograph has to be taken to show who won

pho·to·gen·ic /,foʊt̬ə'dʒɛnɪk/ *adj.* a photogenic person always looks attractive in photographs: *Julie is very photogenic.*

pho·to·graph¹ /'foʊt̬ə,græf/ *n.* [C] a picture that is made using a camera: *The book includes more* *than 100 color photographs.* | *an old* ***photograph of*** *my grandfather* | *Visitors are not allowed to* ***take photographs***. [ORIGIN: 1800—1900 *photo-* + *-graph* (from Greek *phos* "light" + *graphein* "to write")] → PICTURE[1]

photograph² *v.* [T] to take a photograph of someone or something: *She was photographed by Vogue.*

pho·tog·ra·pher /fə'tɑgrəfə/ *n.* [C] someone who takes photographs, especially as a job: *a news photographer*

pho·to·graph·ic /ˌfoʊt̬ə'græfɪk◂/ *adj.* **1** relating to photographs: *a photographic image* **2 photographic memory** an ability that some people have to remember exactly every detail of something s/he has seen

pho·tog·ra·phy /fə'tɑgrəfi/ *n.* [U] the art, profession, or process of producing photographs or the scenes in movies: *fashion photography*

THESAURUS **art, painting, drawing, sculpture, pottery, ceramics** → ART

pho·ton /'foʊtɑn/ *n.* [C] PHYSICS the smallest PARTICLE of light or other form of RADIATION, that has energy but no electric charge or MASS

'photo opporˌtunity *n.* [C] an occasion when someone such as a politician is photographed by the newspapers or filmed for television doing something that will make him/her look good

pho·to·syn·the·sis /ˌfoʊt̬oʊ'sɪnθəsɪs/ *n.* [U] BIOLOGY the way that green plants make their food using the light from the Sun

pho·tot·ro·pism /foʊ'tɑtrəˌpɪzəm/ *n.* [U] BIOLOGY the way that a plant moves as a reaction to light, usually by growing toward the light → TROPISM

ˌphrasal 'verb *n.* [C] ENG. LANG. ARTS in grammar, a verb that changes its meaning when it is used with an adverb or PREPOSITION. In the sentence "The rocket blew up," "blew up" is a phrasal verb.

phrase¹ /freɪz/ *n.* [C] **1** a group of words that together have a particular meaning: *Darwin's famous phrase, "the survival of the fittest"*

THESAURUS

expression – a word or phrase that has a particular meaning
idiom – a group of words that have a special meaning that is different from the usual meaning of each word
cliché – a phrase that has been repeated so often that it is not interesting
saying/proverb – a phrase that many people know, that expresses a sensible idea and is used to give advice
maxim – a well-known phrase that gives a rule for sensible behavior

2 ENG. LANG. ARTS in grammar, a group of words without a main verb that together make a subject, an object, or a verb tense. In the sentence "We have a brand new car," "a brand new car" is a noun phrase. → CLAUSE, SENTENCE [ORIGIN: 1500—1600 Latin *phrasis*, from Greek, from *phrazein* "to point out, explain, tell"]

phrase² *v.* [T] to express something in a particular way: *He phrased his question politely.* —**phrasing** *n.* [U]: *I don't remember her exact phrasing.*

phras·e·ol·o·gy /ˌfreɪzi'ɑlədʒi/ *n.* [U] ENG. LANG. ARTS the way that words and phrases are chosen and used in a particular language or subject: *People such as computer technicians use a particular phraseology.*

phy·lum /'faɪləm/ *n.* (plural **phyla** /-lə/) [C] BIOLOGY one of the groups into which scientists divide plants and animals. A phylum is larger than a CLASS but smaller than a KINGDOM.

P

phys·i·cal¹ /'fɪzɪkəl/ (Ac) *adj.* **1** relating to someone's body rather than his/her mind or soul → MENTAL: *a woman of great physical strength* | *She was in constant physical pain.* | *your* ***physical appearance*** (=the way you look) **2** relating to real things that can be seen, tasted, felt, etc.: *our physical environment* | *There is no* ***physical evidence*** *to connect him to the crime scene.* **3** someone who is physical touches people a lot **4** involving touching someone in a rough or violent way: *Hockey is a very physical game.* **5** relating to or following the laws of nature: *The world is governed by physical laws.* **6** SCIENCE a science such as PHYSICS or CHEMISTRY, that studies things that are not living → ORGANIC: *physical chemistry* [ORIGIN: 1400—1500 Medieval Latin *physicalis*, from Latin *physica*, from Greek *physikos* "of nature"]

physical² *also* **ˌphysical exami'nation** *n.* [C] a medical examination by a doctor to check that you are healthy, especially when you start a new job

ˌphysical edu'cation *n.* [U] PE

phys·i·cally /'fɪzɪkli/ (Ac) *adv.* **1** in relation to the body rather than the mind or soul → MENTALLY: *He was physically exhausted.* | *I try to keep myself* ***physically fit*** (=having strong muscles and not much fat). | *Most people have little contact with mentally or* ***physically handicapped*** *people.* **2 physically impossible** not possible according to the laws of nature: *It's physically impossible for penguins to fly.*

ˌphysical 'therapy *n.* [U] a treatment for injuries and muscle problems that uses special exercises, rubbing, heat, etc. —**physical therapist** *n.* [C]

phy·si·cian /fɪ'zɪʃən/ *n.* [C] (formal) a doctor

THESAURUS **doctor, surgeon, specialist, psychiatrist, pediatrician** → DOCTOR[1]

phys·ics /'fɪzɪks/ *n.* [U] the science that deals with the study of physical objects and substances, and natural forces such as light, heat, and movement —**physicist** /'fɪzəsɪst/ *n.* [C]

phys·i·ol·o·gy /ˌfɪzi'ɑlədʒi/ *n.* [U] BIOLOGY a science that deals with the study of how the bodies of living things work **—physiological** /ˌfɪziəˈlɑdʒɪkəl/ *adj.*

phys·i·o·ther·a·py /ˌfɪzioʊˈθɛrəpi/ *n.* [U] PHYSICAL THERAPY

phy·sique /fɪˈzik/ *n.* [C] the shape, size, and appearance of someone's body: *a man with a powerful physique*

phy·to·plank·ton /ˌfaɪtoʊˈplæŋktən/ *n.* [U] BIOLOGY the very small floating plants that are part of PLANKTON ➔ ZOOPLANKTON

pi /paɪ/ *n.* [U] MATH a number, about 3.1416, that is represented by the Greek letter (π) and is equal to the distance around a circle divided by its width. Pi is used to calculate the area of a circle.

P

pi·an·o¹ /piˈænoʊ/ *n.* [C] a large musical instrument that you play by pressing the KEYs (=narrow black and white bars) **—pianist** *n.* [C]

pi·a·no² /piˈɑnoʊ/ *adj., adv.* ENG. LANG. ARTS played or sung quietly (ANT) **forte**

pick¹ /pɪk/ *v.* [T]

1 CHOOSE to choose something or someone from a group of people or things: *In the end, Katie picked the blue dress.* | *Have you **picked** a date **for** the wedding yet?* | *He **picked** the Giants **to** win the division.* | *The board **picked** Kertzman **as** the man to run the company.* | *She can **pick and choose** her jobs* (=she can choose only the ones she likes).

THESAURUS choose, select, opt for sth, decide on sth ➔ CHOOSE

2 FLOWER/FRUIT to pull off or break off a flower, fruit, etc. from a plant or tree: *We're going out to the farm on Saturday to pick apples.* | *Amy picked a bunch of flowers from her garden.*

3 REMOVE/PULL OFF to remove small things from something, or to pull off small pieces from something: *She got up and started **picking** dishes **off** the table.* | *Michael, stop **picking** your **nose*** (=cleaning the inside of it with your finger).

4 pick your way through/across/among etc. sth to move carefully through an area, choosing exactly where to walk or drive: *Rescue workers picked their way through the rubble.*

5 pick a fight (with sb) to deliberately begin an argument or fight with someone: *Adam's always picking fights with the younger kids.*

6 pick sb's pocket to quietly steal something from someone's pocket, bag, etc.

7 pick sb's brain(s) to ask someone who knows a lot about a subject for information or advice about it: *Can I pick your brains about a legal issue?*

8 pick a lock to use something that is not a key to unlock a door, window, etc. ➔ PICKPOCKET

pick at sth *phr. v.*

to eat only a small amount of your food because you do not feel hungry or do not like the food: *I was so nervous I could only pick at my lunch.*

pick sb/sth ↔ **off** *phr. v.*

to shoot people or animals one at a time from a long distance away: *Snipers were picking off anyone who came outdoors.*

pick on sb *phr. v.*

to treat someone in a way that is not kind: *Greg, stop picking on your sister!*

pick sb/sth ↔ **out** *phr. v.*

1 to choose someone or something carefully from a group: *We had a lot of fun picking out a present for Leslie's baby.*

2 to recognize someone or something in a group of people or things: *The victim was able to pick out her attacker from a police lineup.*

pick sth ↔ **over** *phr. v.*

to examine a group of things carefully in order to choose the ones you want: *Wash and pick over the beans.*

pick up *phr. v.*

1 LIFT UP **pick** sb/sth ↔ **up** to lift something or someone up: *Pick me up, Daddy!* | *I **picked up the phone*** (=answered the phone) *just as it stopped ringing.* | *He knelt down to pick up his keys.* ➔ *see picture on page A22*

2 GO GET SB/STH **pick** sb/sth ↔ **up** to go somewhere, usually in a vehicle, in order to get someone or something: *I'll pick up my stuff around six, okay?* | *What time should we pick you up at the airport?*

3 BUY **pick** sth ↔ **up** to buy something: *Will you pick up something for dinner on your way home?* | *The company is **picking up the bill/tab*** (=paying) *for my computer.*

4 CLEAN A PLACE **pick** sth ↔ **up** to put things away neatly, or to clean a place by doing this: *Straighten your room and pick all those papers up.* | *Pick up the living room, please.* | *He never **picks up after** himself* (=puts away the things he has used).

5 GET BETTER to improve: *Sales should pick up before Christmas.*

6 INCREASE **pick up** (sth) to increase or get faster: *The car was gradually picking up speed* (=going faster). | *The wind had picked up considerably.*

7 LEARN **pick** sth ↔ **up** to learn something without much effort by watching or listening to other people: *I picked up some Korean when I was in the army.*

8 ILLNESS **pick** sth ↔ **up** to get an illness from someone, or to become sick: *She's picked up a cold from a child at school.*

9 NOTICE **pick** sth ↔ **up** to notice, smell, or hear something, especially when this is difficult: *The dogs were able to pick up the scent.*

10 RADIO/SIGNALS **pick** sth ↔ **up** if a machine picks up a sound, movement, or signal, it is able to notice it or receive it: *We didn't pick anything up on radar.* | *Our TV doesn't pick up channel 26 very well.*

11 START AGAIN **pick** (sth ↔) **up** to begin a conversation, meeting, etc. again, starting from the point where it stopped earlier: *We'll **pick up where we left off** after lunch.*

12 POLICE **pick** sb ↔ **up** if the police pick someone up, they find him/her and take him/her to the police station: *Carr was picked up and taken in for questioning.*

13 SEX **pick** sb ↔ **up** to talk to someone you do not know because you want to have sex with

him/her: *Some guy at the bar was trying to pick up Audrey.*
14 pick up the pieces (of sth) to get a situation back to normal after something bad has happened: *Republicans will try to pick up the pieces after major losses in the last election.*

pick up on sth *phr. v.*
to notice something about the way someone is behaving, especially when it is not easy to notice: *Children quickly pick up on tensions between their parents.*

pick² *n.* **1** [U] choice: *There are four kinds of cake, so you can **take** your **pick**. | She'll be able to **have** her **pick of** colleges* (=choose any one she wants). **2 the pick of sth** (informal) the best thing or things in a group: *The Doles will get the pick of the puppies.* **3** [C] a pickax **4** [C] a small flat object that you use for playing an instrument such as a GUITAR

pick·ax /ˈpɪk-æks/ *n.* [C] a large tool that you use for breaking up the ground. It consists of a curved iron bar with a sharp point on each end, and a long handle.

pick·er /ˈpɪkɚ/ *n.* [C] a person or machine that picks things such as fruit, cotton, etc.

pick·et¹ /ˈpɪkɪt/ *also* **ˈpicket line** *n.* [C] a group or line of people who picket a factory, store, etc.: *Two workers were hurt today trying to **cross the picket line*** (=trying to work during a STRIKE).

picket² *v.* [I,T] to stand or march in front of a factory, store, etc. to protest something, or to stop people from going in to work during a STRIKE (=time when a group of workers refuse to work): *Protesters are still picketing outside the White House gates.*

ˈpicket ˌfence *n.* [C] a fence made of a line of strong pointed sticks fastened in the ground

pick·le¹ /ˈpɪkəl/ *n.* **1** [C,U] a CUCUMBER preserved in VINEGAR or salt water, or a piece of this: *a dill pickle* **2 be in a pickle** (old-fashioned) to be in a difficult situation

pickle² *v.* [T] to preserve food in VINEGAR or salt water —**pickled** *adj.*: *pickled onions*

ˈpick-me-up *n.* [C] (informal) something that makes you feel cheerful or gives you more energy, especially a drink or medicine

pick·pock·et /ˈpɪkˌpɑkɪt/ *n.* [C] someone who steals things from people's pockets, especially in a crowd

THESAURUS **offender, thief, robber, burglar, shoplifter** → CRIMINAL²

pick·up /ˈpɪkʌp/ *n.* **1** [C] *also* **pickup truck** a small truck with low sides that is used for carrying goods **2** [C] an occasion when someone or something is taken away from a place: *There is a regular garbage pickup on Tuesdays.* **3** [U] the ability of a car to reach a high speed in a short time: *My old car didn't have much pickup.* **4** [C] an increase or improvement in something: *a **pickup in** sales*

pick·y /ˈpɪki/ *adj.* (comparative **pickier**, superlative **pickiest**) (informal, disapproving) someone who is picky is difficult to make happy because s/he only likes certain things SYN **fussy**: *He's not a very **picky eater**.*

pic·nic¹ /ˈpɪknɪk/ *n.* [C] **1** an occasion when people take food and eat it outdoors, for example in a park: *We used to **have picnics** down by the creek. | Do you want to **go for a picnic** this Saturday?* **2 be no picnic** (informal) to be difficult or unpleasant: *A two-hour bus ride to work every day is no picnic!* [ORIGIN: 1700—1800 French *pique-nique*]

picnic² *v.* (past tense and past participle **picnicked**, present participle **picnicking**) [I] to have a picnic

pic·to·ri·al /pɪkˈtɔriəl/ *adj.* relating to or using pictures: *a pictorial history of Montana*

pic·ture¹ /ˈpɪktʃɚ/ *n.*
1 IMAGE [C] a painting, drawing, or photograph: *a **picture of** Nelson Mandela | **Draw/paint a picture of** your house. | a group of tourists **taking pictures*** (=taking photographs) | *Leo's picture* (=photograph of him) *is in the newspaper.*

THESAURUS
sketch – a picture that is drawn quickly
painting – a picture made using paint
snapshot – a photograph that is taken quickly
portrait – a painting, drawing, or photograph of a person
cartoon – a funny drawing in a newspaper or magazine that tells a story or a joke
caricature – a funny drawing of someone that makes a particular feature of his/her face or body look bigger, worse, etc. than it really is
illustration – a picture in a book
poster – a large picture printed on paper, used in order to advertise something or as a decoration on a wall
image – a picture seen on a screen, or a formal word for what is in a picture → CAMERA
drawing, doodle, comic strip → DRAWING

2 SITUATION [singular] the general situation in a place, organization, etc.: *The **political picture** has greatly changed since March. | You're missing the **big/bigger/wider picture*** (=the situation considered as a whole).
3 DESCRIPTION [C usually singular] a description that gives you an idea of what something is like: *To get a better **picture of** how the company is doing, look at sales. | The book **paints a** clear **picture** of life in ancient Rome.*
4 be in/out of the picture (informal) to be involved or not be involved in a situation: *With his main rival out of the picture, the mayor has a chance of winning the election.*
5 ON A SCREEN [C] the image that you see on a television or in a movie: *Something's wrong with the picture.*
6 get the picture (spoken) to understand something: *I don't want you around here any more – get the picture?*

P

7 MOVIE [C] (old-fashioned) a movie: *Grandma loved going to the pictures.* [ORIGIN: 1400—1500 Latin *pictura*, from *pictus*, past participle of *pingere* "to paint"]

picture² *v.* [T] **1** to imagine something, especially by making an image in your mind: *I can still picture him standing there with his uniform on.* | *I can't **picture** myself **as** a mother.*

THESAURUS **imagine, visualize, envision, envisage** → IMAGINE

2 to show something or someone in a photograph, painting, or drawing: *The governor is pictured here with his wife and children.*

P

'picture book *n.* [C] a children's story book that has a lot of pictures in it

pic·tur·esque /ˌpɪktʃəˈrɛsk◂/ *adj.* attractive and interesting: *a picturesque seaside town*

pid·dling /ˈpɪdlɪŋ/ *adj.* (informal) small and unimportant: *a piddling amount of money*

pidg·in /ˈpɪdʒən/ *n.* [C,U] ENG. LANG. ARTS a language that is a mixture of two other languages, which people who do not speak each other's languages will use to talk to each other [ORIGIN: 1800—1900 from a Chinese pronunciation of the English word "business"]

pie /paɪ/ *n.* **1** [C,U] a food usually made with fruit baked inside a covering of PASTRY: *a **piece/slice** of apple pie* **2 as easy as pie** (informal) very easy **3 a piece/share/slice of the pie** (informal) a share of something such as money or profit: *Landers wants a bigger slice of the pie.* **4 pie in the sky** (informal) a good plan or promise that you do not think will happen: *Hope of a cure is just pie in the sky.*

piece¹ /pis/ *n.* [C]
1 PART OF A WHOLE a part of something that has been separated, broken, or cut off from the rest of it: *Do you want a **piece of** pizza?* | *There were pieces of broken glass everywhere.* | *The vase lay **in pieces*** (=in small parts) *on the floor.* | ***Cut** the chicken **into pieces**, and put it in a roasting pan.*

THESAURUS

scrap – a small piece of paper, cloth, etc.: *He took out the scrap of paper on which he'd written the address.*
chunk – a thick piece of something solid that does not have an even shape: *a stew filled with large chunks of chicken*
lump – a small piece of something solid that does not have a definite shape: *a lump of metal*
fragment – a small piece that has broken off something, especially glass or metal: *Fragments of glass from the crash were still on the street.*
crumb – a very small piece of bread, cake, etc.: *She scattered crumbs for the birds.*
slice – a thin, flat piece of bread, meat, etc. cut from a larger piece: *a slice of blueberry pie*
strip – a long narrow piece of paper, cloth, etc.: *She tore a strip off her shirt to make a bandage.*
block – a piece of a hard material such as wood or stone with straight sides: *a block of wood*

2 PART OF A SET a single thing of a particular type, often part of a set of things or part of a larger thing: *a **piece of** paper* | *a chess piece* | *We found this perfect piece of land on the river.* | *a **five-piece band*** (=one with five members) → PART¹
3 CONNECTED PART one of several different parts that can be connected together to make something: *the **pieces of** a jigsaw puzzle* | *The cars were shipped **in pieces*** (=separated into pieces) *and then reassembled.*
4 a piece of advice/information/gossip etc. some advice, information, etc.: *Let me give you a piece of advice: don't ask her about her mother.*
5 go to pieces to become so upset or nervous that you cannot think or behave normally: *When he died, Liz just went to pieces.*
6 smash/tear/rip etc. sth to pieces to damage something severely by breaking it into many parts: *A dog had torn the bird to pieces.*
7 (all) in one piece not damaged or injured: *I'm glad the china arrived all in one piece.*
8 give sb a piece of your mind (informal) to tell someone that you are very angry with him/her: *I went back to the store and gave the manager a piece of my mind.*
9 be a piece of cake (informal) to be very easy to do: *Raising four children hasn't been a piece of cake.*
10 ART/MUSIC ETC. something that has been written or made by an artist, musician, or writer: *an impressive **piece of** art* | *They performed a piece by Mozart.*

piece² *v.*
piece sth ↔ **together** *phr. v.* **1** to use all the facts or information that you have in order to understand a situation: *Police are still trying to piece together a motive for the shooting.* **2** to put all the parts of something back into the correct position or order

piece·meal /ˈpismil/ *adj., adv.* happening or done slowly in separate stages that are not planned or related: *Changes were introduced in piecemeal fashion.* | *The house was filled with old furniture they'd bought piecemeal.*

piece·work /ˈpiswɚk/ *n.* [U] work for which you are paid according to the number of things you produce rather than the number of hours you work

'pie ˌchart *n.* [C] MATH a circle divided into several parts that shows how big the different parts of a total amount are → *see picture at* CHART¹

pier /pɪr/ *n.* [C] **1** a structure that is built out into the water so that boats can stop next to it or people can walk along it: *We were standing at the end of the pier, watching the boats.* **2** a thick stone, wooden, or metal post used for supporting something such as a bridge

pierce /pɪrs/ *v.* [T] **1** to make a hole in or through something, using an object with a sharp point: *Tiffany's **getting** her **ears pierced*** (=having a hole put in her ears for wearing jewelry). | *A bullet pierced his body.*

THESAURUS

make a hole in sth – to cause a hole to appear in something: *Make a hole in the bottom of the can using a hammer and nail.*
prick – to make a small hole in the surface of something, using a sharp point: *She pricked her finger with the needle.*
punch – to make a hole in something using a metal tool or other sharp object: *I had to punch an extra hole in the belt to get it to fit.*
puncture – to make a small hole in something, so that air or liquid can get out: *One bullet punctured his lung.*
drill – to make a hole using a special tool: *They drilled a 180-foot-deep well.*
bore – to make a deep round hole in a hard surface: *Workers bored a hole in the wall.*

2 (literary) if light or sound pierces something, you suddenly see or hear it: *The car's headlights pierced the darkness.*

pierc·ing /ˈpɪrsɪŋ/ *adj.* **1** a piercing sound is high, loud, and not nice to listen to: *a piercing cry/scream*

THESAURUS **high, high-pitched, shrill, squeaky** → HIGH[1]

2 a piercing wind is very cold **3** someone with piercing eyes seems to know what you are thinking when s/he looks at you: *her piercing gaze*

pi·e·ty /ˈpaɪəṭi/ *n.* [U] respect for God and religion, shown in the way you behave

pig[1] /pɪg/ *n.* [C] **1** a farm animal with short legs, a fat body, and a curled tail. Pigs are kept for their meat. **2** (spoken) an impolite word meaning someone who eats too much, is very dirty, or is offensive in some way: *You ate all the pizza, you pig.*

pig[2] *v.* (**pigged**, **pigging**)
pig out *phr. v.* (informal) to eat a lot of food all at once: *We **pigged out on** ice cream last night.*

pi·geon /ˈpɪdʒən/ *n.* [C] a gray bird with short legs that is common in cities [ORIGIN: 1300—1400 Old French *pijon*, from Late Latin *pipio* "young bird"]

pi·geon·hole[1] /ˈpɪdʒənˌhoʊl/ *n.* [C] one of a set of small boxes built into a desk, or into a frame on a wall, into which letters or papers can be put

pigeonhole[2] *v.* [T] to decide unfairly that someone or something belongs to a particular group or type: *Hijuelos resists being **pigeonholed as** strictly a "Latino writer."*

ˈpigeon-ˌtoed *adj.* having feet that point in rather than straight forward when you walk

pig·gy /ˈpɪgi/ *n.* (plural **piggies**) [C] (spoken) a pig – used especially by children or when talking to children

pig·gy·back ride /ˈpɪgiˌbæk ˌraɪd/ *n.* [C] a way of carrying a child by putting him/her on your back —**piggyback** *adv.*

ˈpiggy bank *n.* [C] a small container, sometimes in the shape of a pig, used especially by children for saving coins

pig·head·ed /ˈpɪgˌhɛdɪd/ *adj.* (disapproving) determined to do things the way you want even if there are good reasons not to SYN **stubborn**

pig·let /ˈpɪglɪt/ *n.* [C] a young pig

pig·ment /ˈpɪgmənt/ *n.* [C,U] BIOLOGY a natural substance that makes skin, hair, plants, etc. a particular color

pig·men·ta·tion /ˌpɪgmənˈteɪʃən/ *n.* [U] the natural color of living things

pig·pen /ˈpɪgpɛn/ *also* **pig·sty** /ˈpɪgstaɪ/ (plural **pigsties**) *n.* [C] **1** a place on a farm where pigs are kept **2** (informal) a place that is very dirty or messy: *Your bedroom is a pigpen!*

pig·tail /ˈpɪgteɪl/ *n.* [C] one of two long lengths of hair that has been pulled together and tied at either side of the head, worn especially by young girls: *a girl with her hair **in pigtails*** → BRAID[1], HAIRSTYLE, PONYTAIL

pike /paɪk/ *n.* [C] **1** (plural **pike**) a large fish that eats other fish and lives in rivers and lakes **2** (informal) a TURNPIKE

pile[1] /paɪl/ *n.* **1** [C] a large mass of things collected or thrown together in the shape of a small hill: *huge **piles of** garbage* | *a pile of snow* | *He raked the leaves **into small piles**.*

THESAURUS

heap – a large messy pile of things: *A heap of books and papers lay on the floor.*
mound – a pile of something with a round shape: *a small mound of rice on the plate*
stack – a neat pile of things: *a stack of books on the table*
drift – a large pile of snow, sand, etc. that has been blown by the wind: *a ten-foot snow drift by the side of the road*

2 [C] a neat collection of similar things put one on top of the other SYN **stack**: *a **pile of** folded clothes* **3 piles of sth/a pile of sth** (informal) a lot of something: *I have piles of work to do tonight.* | *She's making **piles of money** at her new job.*

pile[2] *v.* **1** [I,T] *also* **pile up** to make a pile by collecting things together: *A lot of dishes had piled up in the sink.* **2** [T] to fill something or cover a surface with a lot of something: *a plate **piled high with** spaghetti*
pile in/into sth *phr. v.* (informal) if a group of people pile into a place or vehicle, they all try to get into it quickly and at the same time: *We all piled into the car and left.*
pile out *phr. v.* (informal) if a group of people pile out of a place or vehicle, they all try to get out of it quickly and at the same time: *As soon as we stopped, the kids piled out and ran to the beach.*

pile up *phr. v.* to become larger in quantity or amount, in a way that is difficult to manage: *Debts from the business were piling up quickly.*

pile·up /ˈpaɪlʌp/ *n.* [C] a traffic accident involving many vehicles: *a 16-car pileup*

THESAURUS **accident, crash, collision, wreck** → ACCIDENT

pil·fer /ˈpɪlfɚ/ *v.* [I,T] to steal things that are not worth much: *He was caught **pilfering from** the office.*

THESAURUS **steal, burglarize, rob, shoplift, rip off sth** → STEAL¹

P

pil·grim /ˈpɪlgrəm/ *n.* [C] a religious person who travels a long way to a holy place [ORIGIN: 1100—1200 Old French *peligrin*, from Latin *peregrinus* "foreigner"]

pil·grim·age /ˈpɪlgrəmɪdʒ/ *n.* [C,U] a trip to a holy place for a religious reason: *Every year, about two million Muslims **make the pilgrimage to** Mecca.* → TRAVEL²

pil·ing /ˈpaɪlɪŋ/ *n.* [C] a heavy post made of wood, cement, or metal, used for supporting a building or bridge

pill /pɪl/ *n.* [C] **1** a small solid piece of medicine that you swallow: *She's **taking pills** to control her blood pressure.* | *sleeping pills*

THESAURUS **medicine, tablet, capsule, drug, medication, prescription** → MEDICINE

2 the pill a pill taken regularly by some women in order to avoid having babies: *Mary has been **on the pill** for years now.* [ORIGIN: 1400—1500 Latin *pilula*, from *pila* "ball"]

pil·lage /ˈpɪlɪdʒ/ *v.* [I,T] if soldiers pillage a place in a war, they steal a lot of things and do a lot of damage

pil·lar /ˈpɪlɚ/ *n.* [C] **1** a tall solid post used as a support for part of a building: *Eight massive stone pillars supported the roof.* **2 a pillar of the community/church etc.** an active and important member of a group, organization, etc.

pil·low /ˈpɪloʊ/ *n.* [C] a cloth bag filled with soft material that you put your head on when you sleep [ORIGIN: Old English *pyle*, from Latin *pulvinus*] → *see picture at* BED¹

pil·low·case /ˈpɪloʊˌkeɪs/ *n.* [C] a cloth cover for a pillow

pi·lot /ˈpaɪlət/ *n.* [C] **1** someone who operates the controls of an aircraft or spacecraft: *an airline pilot* **2** a television program that is made in order to test whether people like it and would watch it again in the future **3 pilot program/project/study etc.** a test that is done to see if an idea or product will be successful [ORIGIN: 1500—1600 French *pilote*, from Italian *pedota*, from Greek *pedon* "oar"] —**pilot** *v.* [T]

ˈpilot light *n.* [C] a small gas flame that burns all the time and is used for lighting larger gas BURNERS

pimp /pɪmp/ *n.* [C] a man who makes money by controlling PROSTITUTES (=women who have sex with men for money)

pim·ple /ˈpɪmpəl/ *n.* [C] a small raised red spot on your skin, especially on your face —**pimply** *adj.*

THESAURUS **blemish, bruise, scar, zit, wart, blister, freckle, mole** → MARK²

PIN /pɪn/ *n.* **Personal Identification Number** a number that you use when you get money from a machine using a plastic card

pin¹ /pɪn/ *n.* [C] **1** a short thin piece of metal with a sharp point at one end, used especially for fastening pieces of cloth together **2** a piece of metal, sometimes containing jewels, that you fasten to your clothes to wear as a decoration **3** one of the bottle-shaped objects that you try to knock down in a game of BOWLING **4** a thin piece of metal used to fasten things together, especially broken bones: *He has to have pins put in his ankle.* [ORIGIN: Old English *pinn*] → CLOTHESPIN, PINS AND NEEDLES, ROLLING PIN, SAFETY PIN

pin² *v.* (**pinned**, **pinning**) **1** [T] to fasten something somewhere, or join things together with a pin or pins: *Can you **pin** this announcement **on** the bulletin board for me?* | *He wore campaign buttons **pinned to** his lapels.* **2 pin your hopes on sth/sb** to hope that something will happen or someone will help you because all your plans depend on this: *I hope she's not pinning all her hopes on winning.* **3** [T] to make someone unable to move by putting a lot of pressure or weight on him/her: *He **pinned** her arms **to** her sides.* | *He was **pinned under** the car.*

pin sb/sth **down** *phr. v.* **1** to make someone decide something or tell you what the decision is: *I couldn't pin him down to a definite date for the meeting.* **2** to understand something clearly or be able to describe exactly what it is: *I can't pin down his accent.*

pin·ball /ˈpɪnbɔl/ *n.* [U] a game played on a machine with a sloping board. You push buttons to try to keep a ball from rolling off the board: *a pinball machine*

pin·cer /ˈpɪnsɚ, ˈpɪntʃɚ/ *n.* [C] one of the pair of CLAWS (=sharp curved nails) that some insects and SHELLFISH have → *see picture on page A15*

pinch¹ /pɪntʃ/ *v.* **1** [T] to press a part of someone's skin very tightly between your finger and thumb: *She leaned over and pinched his cheeks.* → *see picture on page A21* **2** [I,T] if your clothes, shoes, etc. pinch you, they are too tight and hurt you

THESAURUS **hurt, sting, smart** → HURT¹

3 pinch pennies to be careful to spend as little money as possible

pinch² *n.* [C] **1 pinch of salt/pepper etc.** a small amount of salt, pepper, etc. that you can hold between your finger and thumb **2** an act of pinching someone: *She **gave him a pinch** on the cheek.* **3 in a pinch** if necessary in a difficult or urgent situation: *I have room for four more people, five in a pinch.*

pinched /pɪntʃt/ *adj.* **1** not having enough money to do what you want: *financially pinched schools* **2** a pinched face looks thin and unhealthy, for example because the person is sick, cold, or tired

'pinch-hit *v.* [I] **1** to BAT² instead of another player in a game of baseball **2** to do something for someone else because s/he is suddenly not able to do it: *Could you pinch-hit for Larry in the meeting today?* —**pinch-hitter** *n.* [C]

pin·cush·ion /'pɪn,kʊʃən/ *n.* [C] a small soft object into which you stick pins until you need to use them

pine¹ /paɪn/ *also* **'pine tree** *n.* [C,U] a tree with long leaves shaped like needles, or the wood of this tree [ORIGIN: 1000—1100 Latin *pinus*]

pine² *also* **pine away** *v.* [I] to gradually become weaker, less active, and less healthy because you are very unhappy

pine for sb/sth *phr. v.* to be unhappy because you cannot be with a person, be in a place, or experience something that happened in the past again: *Ten years after Amanda left, he was still pining for her.* | *After two months in France, I was pining for home.*

pine·ap·ple /'paɪn,æpəl/ *n.* [C,U] a large yellow-brown tropical fruit, or its sweet yellow flesh → *see picture on page 414*

'pine cone *n.* [C] the brown seed container of the pine

ping /pɪŋ/ *n.* [C] a short high RINGing sound —**ping** *v.* [I]

ping-pong, **Ping Pong** /'pɪŋpɑŋ, -pɔŋ/ *n.* [U] (trademark) an indoor game played on a large table, in which two people use PADDLEs to hit a small ball to each other across a low net (SYN) **table tennis**

pink /pɪŋk/ *adj.* pale red: *a pink dress* —**pink** *n.* [C,U]

pink·ie, **pinky** /'pɪŋki/ *n.* (plural **pinkies**) [C] the smallest finger on your hand → *see picture at* HAND¹

,pink 'slip *n.* [C] (informal) a written warning telling you that your job is going to end because there is not enough work

pin·na·cle /'pɪnəkəl/ *n.* **1** [singular] the most successful, powerful, or exciting part of something: *It took Carlson only eight years to **reach the pinnacle of** his profession.* **2** [C] EARTH SCIENCES the top of a high mountain **3** [C] a pointed stone decoration like a small tower on top of a church or castle

pin·point¹ /'pɪnpɔɪnt/ *v.* [T] to say exactly what something is, or exactly where someone or something is: *It was impossible to pinpoint the cause of the crash.* | *Can you **pinpoint where** you last saw him?*

pinpoint² *adj.* **with pinpoint accuracy** very exactly: *the plane's ability to drop bombs with pinpoint accuracy*

pinpoint³ *n.* [C] a very small area or amount of something: *a tiny **pinpoint of** light*

pin·prick /'pɪn,prɪk/ *n.* [C] a very small hole or mark in something, like one made by a pin

,pins and 'needles *n.* **1** [U] an uncomfortable feeling that you get, especially when you have not moved part of your body for a long time and the supply of blood has stopped flowing correctly **2 be on pins and needles** to be very nervous: *Mom's been on pins and needles waiting to hear from you.*

pin·stripe /'pɪnstraɪp/ *n.* [C] one of the thin light-colored lines that form a pattern on dark cloth: *a blue pinstripe suit* —**pinstriped** *adj.*

pint /paɪnt/ *n.* [C] a unit for measuring liquid, equal to 2 cups or 0.4732 liters: *a **pint of** milk*

pin·up /'pɪnʌp/ *n.* [C] **1** a picture of an attractive or famous person, often a woman wearing little clothing **2** someone who appears in one of these pictures

pi·o·neer¹ /,paɪə'nɪr/ *n.* [C] **1** one of the first people to do something that other people will later develop or continue to do: *one of the **pioneers of** the personal computer industry* **2** one of the first people to travel to a new or unknown place and begin living there, farming, etc. [ORIGIN: 1500—1600 Old French *peonier* "soldier," from *peon*]

pioneer² *v.* [T] to be the first person to do, invent, or use something: *a hospital pioneering a new type of surgery*

pi·ous /'paɪəs/ *adj.* having strong religious beliefs, and showing this in the way you behave

THESAURUS **religious, devout, god-fearing, orthodox** → RELIGIOUS

pipe¹ /paɪp/ *n.* [C] **1** a tube through which a liquid or gas flows: *a **water pipe*** | *The **pipes** had **frozen** and we had no water.* **2** a thing used for smoking tobacco, consisting of a small tube with a container shaped like a bowl at one end: *Harry stood on the porch, **smoking** his **pipe**.* **3** one of the metal tubes that air is forced through in an ORGAN **4** a simple musical instrument like a tube, that you blow through

pipe² *v.* [T] to send a liquid or gas through a pipe to another place: *oil piped from Alaska*

pipe down *phr. v.* (spoken) to stop talking or making a noise, and become calmer and less excited: *Pipe down! I'm trying to listen to this!*

pipe up *phr. v.* (informal) to suddenly say something, especially when you have been quiet until then: *Dennis piped up, saying he didn't agree.*

P

'pipe dream *n.* [C] a hope, idea, plan, etc. that will probably never work or happen: *Money and fame – isn't that all a pipe dream?*

pipe·line /'paɪp-laɪn/ *n.* [C] **1** a long line of connecting pipes, used for carrying gas, oil, etc. over long distances **2 be in the pipeline** if a plan, idea, or event is in the pipeline, it is still being prepared, but it will happen or be completed soon

pi·pette /paɪ'pɛt/ *n.* [C] CHEMISTRY a thin glass tube for sucking up exact amounts of liquid, used especially in chemistry

pip·ing¹ /'paɪpɪŋ/ *n.* [U] **1** several pipes, or a system of pipes, used for carrying a liquid or gas: *copper piping* **2** thin cloth CORDS used as decorations on clothes and furniture

P

piping² *adv.* **piping hot** very hot: *a pot of piping hot tea*

pip·squeak /'pɪpskwik/ *n.* [C] (spoken, old-fashioned) someone who you think is not worth attention or respect, especially because s/he is small or young: *Shut up, you little pipsqueak!*

pi·quant /pi'kɑnt, 'pikənt/ *adj.* (formal) **1** having a pleasantly spicy taste: *a piquant chili sauce* **2** interesting and exciting: *piquant photos of life in Paris* —**piquancy** /'pikənsi/ *n.* [U]

pique¹ /pik/ *v.* [T] **1 pique sb's interest/curiosity** to make someone very interested in something: *Emker's life story piqued the public's interest.* **2** (formal) to make someone feel annoyed or upset

pique² *n.* [U] (formal) a feeling of being annoyed or upset: *Greta left **in a fit of pique**.*

pi·ra·cy /'paɪrəsi/ *n.* [U] **1** the act of illegally copying and selling books, tapes, videos, computer programs, etc.: *software piracy* **2** the crime of attacking and stealing from ships at sea

pi·ra·nha /pə'rɑnə, -'ræn-/ *n.* [C] a South American fish with sharp teeth that lives in rivers and eats flesh

pi·rate¹ /'paɪrɪt/ *n.* [C] **1** someone who sails on the oceans, attacking other boats and stealing things from them **2** someone who illegally copies and sells another person's work: *We're losing thousands of dollars to video pirates.* [ORIGIN: 1200—1300 Latin *pirata*, from Greek *peirates*, from *peiran* "to attack"]

pirate² *v.* [T] to illegally copy and sell another person's work: *pirated CDs*

> THESAURUS **copy, reproduce, duplicate, forge** ➔ COPY²

pir·ou·ette /,pɪru'ɛt/ *n.* [C] a dance movement in which the dancer turns very quickly, standing on one toe or the front part of one foot —**pirouette** *v.* [I]

Pis·ces /'paɪsiz/ *n.* **1** [U] the twelfth sign of the ZODIAC, represented by two fish **2** [C] someone born between February 19 and March 20

pis·ta·chi·o /pɪ'stæʃi,oʊ/ *n.* (plural **pistachios**) [C] a small green nut

pis·tol /'pɪstl/ *n.* [C] a small gun that you can use with one hand [ORIGIN: 1500—1600 French *pistole*, from German, from Czech *pišťal* "pipe"]

pis·ton /'pɪstən/ *n.* [C] a part of an engine, consisting of a short solid piece of metal inside a tube, that moves up and down to make the other parts of the engine move

pit¹ /pɪt/ *n.*

1 HOLE [C] a hole in the ground, especially one made by digging: *a barbecue pit*

2 MARK [C] a small hollow mark in the surface of something: *There are tiny scratches and pits on the windshield.*

3 MESSY PLACE [singular] (spoken) a house or room that is dirty, messy, or in bad condition: *Erica's house is a total pit!*

4 be the pits (spoken) to be very bad: *My job is the pits.*

5 in the pit of your stomach if you have a feeling in the pit of your stomach, you have a sick or tight feeling in your stomach, usually because you are nervous or afraid: *The strange noises gave her a funny feeling in the pit of her stomach.*

6 IN FRUIT [C] BIOLOGY the single large hard seed in some fruits: *a peach pit* ➔ *see picture on page 414*

7 FOR CARS the pit/pits [C] a place beside a racetrack where a race car can quickly get more gas or be repaired

8 an ORCHESTRA PIT

9 a MINE²

pit² *v.* (**pitted**, **pitting**) [T] **1** to take out the single large hard seed inside some fruits **2** to put small marks or holes in the surface of something: *The disease had pitted and scarred his skin.*

pit sb/sth **against** sb/sth *phr. v.* to test your strength, ability, power, etc. against someone else: *This week's big game pits Houston against Miami.*

pi·ta /'pitə/ *also* **'pita bread** *n.* [C,U] a type of flat bread that can be opened so you can put food into it

'pit bull *also* **,pit bull 'terrier** *n.* [C] a short dog that is extremely strong and often violent

pitch¹ /pɪtʃ/ *v.*

1 BASEBALL [I,T] to aim and throw the ball to the BATTER in baseball: *Who's pitching for the Red Sox today?* | *He **pitched** three **innings** in Monday night's game.*

> THESAURUS **throw, toss, chuck, hurl, fling, pass, lob** ➔ THROW¹

2 THROW [T] to throw something, especially with a lot of force: *Carl tore up Amy's letter and **pitched it into the fire**.*

3 FALL [I,T] to fall suddenly and heavily in a particular direction, or to make someone or something fall in this way: *A sudden stop **pitched** her **into the windshield**.* | *Daley **pitched forward** and fell from the stage.*

4 VOICE/MUSIC [T] to make a sound be produced at

a particular level: *The song is pitched too high for me.*
5 pitch a tent to set up a tent
6 SELL/PERSUADE [I,T] (informal) to try to persuade someone to buy or do something: *The meeting is your chance to* ***pitch*** *your ideas* ***to*** *the boss.*
7 SAY/WRITE [T] to aim a product, film, etc. at a particular group of people, or to describe something in a particular way in order to sell it: *a TV show* ***pitched at*** *children*
8 SHIP/PLANE [I] if a ship or an aircraft pitches, it moves up and down in an uncontrolled way with the movement of the water or air
pitch in *phr. v.* (informal)
to join others and help with an activity: *If we all pitch in, it won't take very long to finish.*

pitch² *n.* **1** [C] a throw of the ball to the BATTER in baseball: *The first pitch was a strike.* **2** [C] how high or low someone's voice is **3** [C,U] ENG. LANG. ARTS a musical note, or how high or low a musical note is: *The high notes rang out* ***on pitch.*** **4** [C] (informal) the things someone says in order to persuade people to buy or do something: *a sales pitch* **5** [singular, U] the strength of your feelings or opinions about something: *Their excitement rose to* ***fever pitch*** (=a very excited level). **6** [U] a dark sticky substance that is used on roofs, the bottoms of ships, etc. to stop water coming through

ˌpitch 'black *adj.* completely black or dark: *She turned off the lights, and suddenly it was pitch black.*

pitch·er /'pɪtʃɚ/ *n.* [C] **1** a container used for holding and pouring liquids, with a handle and a SPOUT (=shaped part for pouring): *a* ***pitcher of*** *beer* **2** the baseball player who throws the balls to the BATTER

pitch·fork /'pɪtʃfɔrk/ *n.* [C] a farm tool with a long handle and two or three long curved metal points, used especially for lifting HAY (=dried cut grass)

pit·e·ous /'pɪt̬iəs/ *adj.* (literary) making you feel pity: *a piteous cry*

pit·fall /'pɪtfɔl/ *n.* [C] a problem or difficulty that is likely to happen: *the* ***pitfalls of*** *fame*

pith·y /'pɪθi/ *adj.* spoken or written in strong clear language without wasting any words: *pithy comments*

pit·i·ful /'pɪt̬ɪfəl/ *adj.* **1** making you feel pity or sympathy: *a pitiful sight* **2** very bad in quality: *His grades this semester are pitiful.* —**pitifully** *adv.*

pit·i·less /'pɪt̬ɪlɪs/ *adj.* showing no pity: *a pitiless dictator*

'pit stop *n.* **1 make a pit stop** (spoken) to stop when driving on a long trip in order to get food, gas, etc., or to use the toilet **2** [C] a time when a race car stops beside the track in order to get more gas or be quickly repaired

pit·tance /'pɪtˀns/ *n.* [singular] a very small or unfairly small amount of money: *She works for a pittance.*

pi·tu·i·tar·y /pə'tuəˌtɛri/ *n.* (plural **pituitaries**) *also* **pi'tuitary ˌgland** [C] BIOLOGY the small organ at the base of your brain which produces HORMONEs that control the growth and development of your body —**pituitary** *adj.*: *The growth hormone somatotropin is a pituitary protein essential to the growth process.* → *see picture at* BRAIN¹

pit·y¹ /'pɪt̬i/ *n.* **1** [U] sympathy you feel for someone who is suffering or unhappy: *I don't need your pity! | He doesn't appear to have any* ***pity for*** *the victims of the war.* **2** [singular] used to show that you are disappointed about something and you wish things could happen differently: ***It's a pity (that)*** *so much time was wasted. | "We're leaving tomorrow."* ***"What a pity!"*** **3 take/have pity on sb** to feel sympathy for someone and do something to help him/her [ORIGIN: 1200—1300 Old French *pité*, from Latin *pietas* "piety, pity"]

pity² *v.* (**pitied**, **pities**) [T] to feel sympathy for someone because s/he is in a bad situation: *I pity anyone who has to live with Sherry.*

piv·ot¹ /'pɪvət/ *n.* [C] **1** a central point or pin on which something balances or turns **2** *also* **pivot point** the most important idea or event on which all the other parts of a plan, situation, process, etc. are based

pivot² *v.* [I,T] to turn or balance on a central point, or to make something do this: *The table-top* ***pivots on*** *two metal pins.*
pivot on sth *phr. v.* to depend on or be planned around one important thing, event, idea, etc.: *Her future pivoted on their answer.*

piv·ot·al /'pɪvət̬əl/ *adj.* a pivotal time, event, or person has a very important effect on the way something develops: *Parker played* ***a pivotal role*** *in getting the deal.*

pix·el /'pɪksəl/ *n.* [C] IT the smallest unit of an image on a computer screen

pix·ie /'pɪksi/ *n.* [C] a very small imaginary creature with magic powers that looks like a person

piz·za /'pitsə/ *n.* [C,U] a thin flat round bread, baked with TOMATO, cheese, and usually vegetables or meat on top: *a slice of pizza* [ORIGIN: 1800—1900 Italian "pie"]

piz·zazz /pə'zæz/ *n.* [U] (informal) an exciting quality or style: *a theater show that needs more pizzazz*

piz·ze·ri·a /ˌpitsə'riə/ *n.* [C] a restaurant that serves pizza

pj's, PJ's /'pi dʒeɪz/ *n.* [plural] (spoken) PAJAMAS

plac·ard /'plækɚd, -kɑrd/ *n.* [C] a large sign or advertisement that you carry or put on a wall

pla·cate /'pleɪkeɪt, 'plæ-/ *v.* [T] (formal) to make someone stop feeling angry: *The airline gave out free drinks in an effort to placate angry customers.*

place¹ /pleɪs/ *n.* [C]
1 AREA/SPACE/BUILDING ETC. any space or area, for example a particular point on a surface or a room, building, town, city, etc.: *Keep your money*

in a safe **place**. | *a beautiful place surrounded by mountains* | *She was born in a place called Black River Falls.* | *The water is 30 feet deep* **in places** (=in some areas). | *a sore place on my knee*

THESAURUS

position – the exact place where someone or something is, in relation to other things: *We need to know the enemy's position.*
spot (informal) – a place, especially a pleasant one where you spend time: *It's a favorite spot for picnics.*
point – an exact place, for example on a map: *At this point the path gets narrower.*
location – the place where a hotel, store, office, etc. is, or where a movie is made: *The apartment's in an ideal location.*
site – a place where something is going to be built, or where something important happened: *the site for the new airport* | *an archeological site*
scene – a place where an accident or crime happened: *Firefighters arrived at the scene within minutes.*

2 WHERE YOU DO STH a building or area that is used for, or is suitable for, a particular purpose or activity: *I spent 20 minutes trying to find a* **place to** *park.* | *a* **place of worship** (=a church, mosque, etc.) | *There's a nice Korean place* (=restaurant) *on the corner.* | *Mexico's a great* **place for** *a vacation.* | *A library* **is no place** *for a party.*
3 take place to happen: *The earthquake took place at about 5:00 this morning.*
4 WHERE SB LIVES (informal) the house, apartment, or room where someone lives: *I'm going over to Jeff's place* (=his house) *for dinner.* | *For months I've been looking for a new* **place to live**.

THESAURUS **home, house, residence, dwelling, abode** → HOME[1]

5 SEAT/POSITION IN LINE a space where you can sit, or a position in a line: *Is this place taken* (=being used)? | *Can you* **save my place** (=not let anyone else use it)?
6 RIGHT POSITION/ORDER the right or usual position or order: *Put the CDs back in their place.* | *By six o'clock, everything was* **in place** *for the party.*
7 in place of sb/sth instead of someone or something: *Try using mixed herbs in place of salt on vegetables.*
8 in sb's place used when talking about what you would do if you were in someone else's situation: *What would you do in my place?*
9 IMPORTANCE the importance or position that someone or something has, compared to other people or things: *No one could ever* **take her place** (=be as important or loved as she is). | *Carla has friends* **in high places** (=with important ranks in society). | *By the 1950s, cars had* **taken the place of** (=were used instead of) *trains.* | *There will always be* **a place for** *you here* (=a position for you to have).
10 RIGHT OCCASION the right occasion or situation: *This* **isn't the place to** *talk business.*
11 first/second/third etc. place first, second, etc. position in a race or competition: *Jerry finished* **in** *third* **place**.
12 in the first/second/third place (spoken) used in order to introduce a series of points in an argument or discussion: *Well, in the first place, I can't afford it, and in the second place, I'm not really interested.*
13 all over the place (informal) everywhere: *There were children all over the place!*
14 it is not sb's place (to do sth) if it is not your place to do something, you do not have the duty or right to do it: *It's not her place to tell me how to raise my kids.*
15 out of place not appropriate for or comfortable in a particular situation: *I felt really out of place at Cindy's wedding.*
16 put sb in his/her place to show someone that s/he is not as important, intelligent, etc. as s/he thinks s/he is
17 go places (informal) to become successful: *Work hard and you could really go places.*
18 *also* **Place** used in the names of short streets: *I live at 114 Seaview Place.*

place[2] *v.* [T] **1** to put something somewhere, especially with care (SYN) **put**: *Seth* **placed** *his trophy* **on** *the top shelf.* | *She* **placed** *the money* **in** *a large brown envelope.* **2** to put someone or something in a particular situation: *You'll be placed with the advanced students.* | *This places me in a very difficult position.* **3** to decide that someone or something is important or valuable: *Your father has placed great trust in you.* **4 can't place sb** to recognize someone, but be unable to remember where you have met him/her before: *I know the name, but I can't quite place her.* **5** to arrange for something to be done: *The police department* **placed an order** *for six new cars.* | *He* **placed an ad/advertisement** *in the local paper.* **6** to find a job or place to live for someone: *The agency had* **placed** *her* **in** *a local firm.* | *He was later* **placed with** *a foster family.*

pla·ce·bo /plə'siboʊ/ *n.* (plural **placebos**) [C] BIOLOGY a harmless substance such as water, that is given to a patient instead of medicine without telling him/her it is not a medicine, often as part of a test [ORIGIN: 1700—1800 Latin "I shall please," from *placere*]

place·ment /'pleɪsmənt/ *n.* [C,U] **1** the act of finding a place for someone to live, work, or go to college: *a job placement* | *the college* **placement office** (=where they help you find work) **2** the act of putting something or someone in a position: *He wasn't satisfied with the furniture placement.* | *You'll need to take a* **placement test** (=test that decides which level of class you can take).

place·name /'pleɪsneɪm/ *n.* [C] the name of a particular city, mountain, etc.

pla·cen·ta /plə'sɛntə/ *n.* [C] BIOLOGY an ORGAN that forms inside a woman's UTERUS to feed a baby that has not been born yet

plac·id /'plæsɪd/ *adj.* calm and peaceful: *There*

was a placid expression on her face. | *the placid waters of the lake* —**placidly** *adv.*

THESAURUS calm, relaxed, laid-back, easygoing, mellow, cool, serene → CALM[2]

pla·gia·rism /ˈpleɪdʒəˌrɪzəm/ *n.* [C,U] ENG. LANG. ARTS the act of using someone else's words, ideas, or work and pretending they are your own, or the words, etc. themselves: *She was accused of plagiarism in writing her thesis.* | *an article full of plagiarisms* [ORIGIN: 1600—1700 *plagiary* "plagiarism" (17—19 centuries), from Latin *plagiarius* "thief"] —**plagiarist** *n.* [C]

pla·gia·rize /ˈpleɪdʒəˌraɪz/ *v.* [I,T] ENG. LANG. ARTS to take someone else's words, ideas, etc. and copy them, pretending that they are your own: *The teacher accused me of having plagiarized.*

plague[1] /pleɪg/ *n.* **1** [C,U] any disease that causes death and spreads quickly to a large number of people **2 a plague of rats/locusts etc.** a very large and dangerous number of rats, etc.

plague[2] *v.* [T] to make someone suffer over a long period of time, or to cause trouble again and again: *Gloria had always been plagued by ill health.*

plaid /plæd/ *n.* [C,U] a pattern of crossed lines and squares, used especially on cloth —**plaid** *adj.*: *a plaid work shirt*

plain[1] /pleɪn/ *adj.* **1** very clear, and easy to understand or recognize: ***It's** quite **plain that** you don't agree.* | *Why don't you tell me **in plain English*** (=without using technical or difficult words)*?* **2** without anything added or without decoration (SYN) **simple**: *plain yogurt* | *a plain blue suit* | *a sheet of **plain paper*** (=paper with no lines on it) **3** showing clearly and honestly what you think about something: *Albright was known for her plain speaking.* **4** a woman or girl who is plain is unattractive – used in order to avoid saying this directly [ORIGIN: 1200—1300 Old French, Latin *planus* "flat, level, clear"]

plain[2] *n.* [C] *also* **plains** a large area of flat land: *a grassy plain* | *countless miles of plains*

plain[3] *adv.* **plain stupid/wrong/rude etc.** (spoken) clearly and simply stupid, wrong, etc.: *They're just plain lazy.*

plain·clothes /ˈpleɪnklouz, -klouðz/ *adj.* plainclothes police wear ordinary clothes so that they can work without being recognized

plain·ly /ˈpleɪnli/ *adv.* **1** in a way that is easy to see, hear, or understand: *Tony was plainly nervous as he began his speech.* **2** simply or without decoration: *a plainly dressed young girl*

plain·tiff /ˈpleɪntɪf/ *n.* [C] LAW the person who brings a legal action against another person in a CIVIL COURT (=court of law that deals with the affairs of private citizens rather than crime) → DEFENDANT

plain·tive /ˈpleɪntɪv/ *adj.* (literary) a plaintive sound is high, like someone crying, and sounds sad: *the **plaintive cry** of the wolf*

plan[1] /plæn/ *n.* [C] **1** something that you have decided to do or achieve: *She has no **plans to** retire.* | *Brown's **plans for** the future* | *We **made plans** to go out and see him in the fall.* | *Do you **have** any **plans** for Friday night?*

THESAURUS

plot/conspiracy – a secret plan to do something bad or illegal, especially a plan that involves a lot of people: *a plot to assassinate the President*
scheme – a plan, especially to do something bad or illegal: *He created an elaborate scheme to steal from his employer.*
strategy – a careful plan aimed at achieving something difficult: *the government's economic strategy*
schedule – a plan of what someone is going to do and when s/he is going to do it: *My schedule looks pretty busy.*
timetable – a plan that shows the exact times when something should happen: *We had to adjust the timetable for construction.*

2 a set of actions for achieving something in the future: ***plans for** dealing with a major earthquake* | ***Under the plan**, 700 acres will become a park.* | *a **business plan*** (=what your business will do) *for the 21st century* | *the zoo's **master plan*** (=main plan for the future) **3 health/pension/retirement etc. plan** ECONOMICS an arrangement in which you pay money to a company, and they give you money back if you need medical care, stop working, etc. **4** a drawing of something such as a building, room, or machine, as it would be seen from above, showing the shape, size, parts, etc.: *the **plans for** the new library*

plan[2] *v.* (**planned**, **planning**) **1** [I,T] *also* **plan out** to think about something you want to do, and how you will do it: *Mary's planning a 21st birthday party for her son.* | *Most problems can be avoided by **careful/good planning**.* **2** [T] to intend to do something: *How long do you **plan on** staying?* | *David **plans to** work part-time.* **3** [T] to think about something you are going to make or build, and decide what it will look like: *Planning a small garden is often difficult.*

plane /pleɪn/ *n.* [C] **1** a vehicle that flies in the air and has wings and at least one engine (SYN) **airplane**: *What time does your **plane take off**?* | *The **plane landed** at O'Hare Airport.* | *My son held my hand as we **boarded the plane**.* **2** a level or standard of thought, conversation, etc.: *a **higher plane** of intellectual curiosity* **3** a tool that has a flat bottom with a sharp blade in it, used for making wooden surfaces smooth **4** MATH a completely flat surface in GEOMETRY

plan·et /ˈplænɪt/ *n.* [C] **1** PHYSICS a very large round object in space, that moves around a star, such as the Sun: *Mercury is the smallest planet.* → SPACE[1] **2 the planet** the Earth: *weapons capable of destroying the planet* | *the richest goldmine **on the planet*** [ORIGIN: 1100—1200 Old French *planete*, from Late Latin *planeta*, from Greek

P

planes "wanderer"] —**planetary** /ˈplænəˌtɛri/ *adj.*

plan·e·tar·i·um /ˌplænəˈtɛriəm/ *n.* [C] a building where lights on a curved ceiling show the movements of planets and stars

plank /plæŋk/ *n.* [C] **1** a long narrow flat piece of wood, used for building **2** a feature or principle that a political party says is one of its aims ➔ PLATFORM: *Education is a **central plank** in the candidate's platform.*

plank·ton /ˈplæŋktən/ *n.* [U] BIOLOGY very small plants and animals that live in the ocean and are eaten by fish [ORIGIN: 1800—1900 German, Greek, from *planktos* "wandering," from *plazesthai* "to wander"]

plan·ner /ˈplænɚ/ *n.* [C] someone who plans something, especially someone who plans the way cities grow and develop: ***city planners*** | *He works **as a financial planner**.*

plant¹ /plænt/ *n.* [C] **1** BIOLOGY a living thing that has leaves and roots and grows in the ground, especially one that is smaller than a tree ➔ HOUSEPLANT: *a plant that grows well in the shade* | *a bean plant* **2** ECONOMICS a factory and all its equipment: *a manufacturing plant*

plant² *v.* [T] **1** to put plants or seeds in the ground to grow: *Plant tomatoes in a sunny place.* | *a hillside **planted with** pine trees* **2** (informal) to hide stolen or illegal goods in someone's clothes, bags, room, etc. in order to make him/her seem guilty of a crime: *The police were accused of planting evidence against him.* **3** to put something firmly somewhere: *He stood, his feet planted slightly apart.* **4 plant an idea/doubt/suspicion (in sb's mind)** to mention something that makes someone begin to have an idea, doubt, etc.: *Don't plant ideas in the boy's head!* —**planting** *n.* [C,U]

Plan·tae /ˈplænti/ *n.* BIOLOGY the KINGDOM (=largest group into which scientists divide living things) that consists of all the plants ➔ ANIMALIA

plan·ta·tion /plænˈteɪʃən/ *n.* [C] **1** a large farm, especially in a hot country, where a single crop such as tea, cotton, or sugar is grown: *a rubber plantation* **2** HISTORY in the past, a large farm in the U.S. South that used SLAVES to grow cotton, tobacco, etc.

plant·er /ˈplæntɚ/ *n.* [C] **1** a container in which plants are grown **2** someone who owns or is in charge of a plantation

plaque /plæk/ *n.* **1** [C] a piece of flat metal or stone with writing on it: *A bronze plaque on the house read: "Walt Whitman was born here."* **2** [U] BIOLOGY a harmful substance that forms on your teeth, that BACTERIA can live and grow in [ORIGIN: 1800—1900 French, Dutch *plak*, from *plakken* "to stick"]

plas·ma /ˈplæzmə/ *n.* [U] **1** BIOLOGY the yellowish liquid part of the blood that contains the blood cells **2** PHYSICS a gas that exists at very high

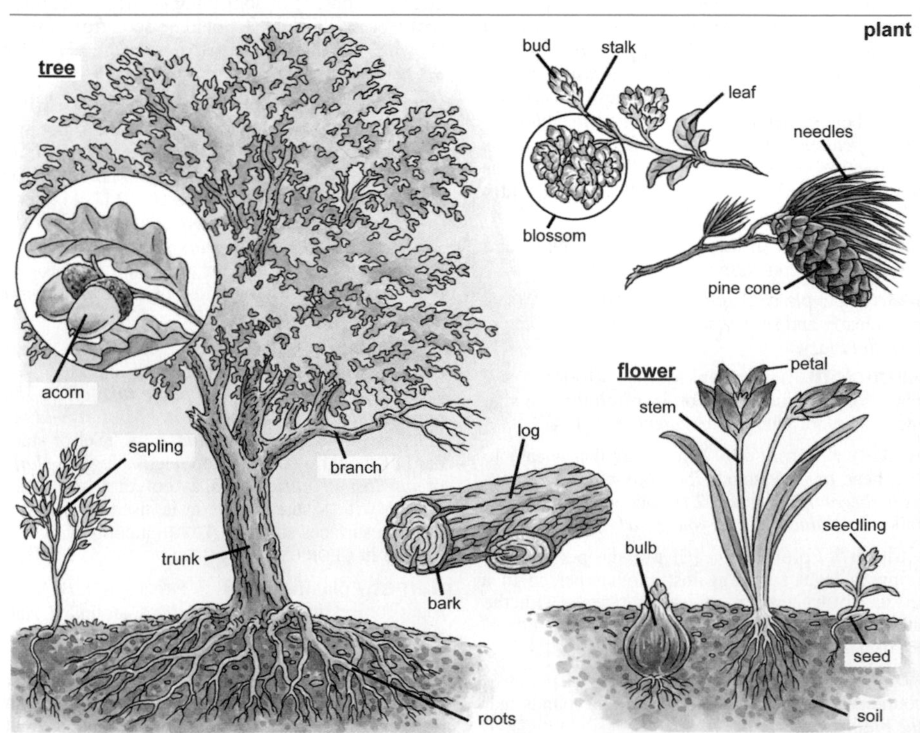

temperatures, for example in stars, which consists of IONS and ELECTRONS

plas·ter¹ /ˈplæstɚ/ *n.* [U] a substance used for covering walls and ceilings to give them a smooth surface

plaster² *v.* [T] **1** to spread or stick something all over a surface so that it is thickly covered: *a wall **plastered with** posters* **2** to cover a surface with plaster

plas·tered /ˈplæstɚd/ *adj.* (informal) very drunk

plaster of Par·is /ˌplæstɚ əv ˈpærɪs/ *n.* [U] a mixture of a white powder and water that dries quickly, used especially for making STATUES or MOLDS

plas·tic¹ /ˈplæstɪk/ *n.* **1** [C,U] a light strong material that is produced by a chemical process, that can be made into different shapes when it is soft: *toys made of plastic* **2** [U] (informal) a CREDIT CARD: *Some customers are worried about paying with plastic on the Internet.*

plastic² *adj.* **1** made of plastic: *a plastic bag* | *plastic cups* → *see picture at* MATERIAL¹ **2** (disapproving) seeming artificial or not natural: *a plastic smile* | *plastic-tasting food* **3** a plastic substance such as clay can be formed into many different shapes and then keeps the shape until someone changes it

plas·tic·i·ty /plæˈstɪsət̬i/ *n.* [U] the quality of being easily made into any shape

ˌplastic ˈsurgery *n.* [U] the medical practice of changing the appearance of people's faces or bodies, either to improve their appearance or to repair injuries

plate /pleɪt/ *n.* **1** [C] a flat, usually round dish that you eat from or serve food on: *a china plate* | *Even Jon **cleaned his plate*** (=ate all the food that was on his plate). **2** [C] *also* **plateful** /ˈpleɪtfʊl/ the amount of food on a plate → DISH: *a **plate of** scrambled eggs and toast* **3** [C] a flat piece of metal, glass, bone, etc.: *A brass plate on the door had the director's name on it.* **4 gold/silver etc. plate** [U] ordinary metal with a thin covering of gold, silver, etc. **5** [C] (informal) a LICENSE PLATE: *New Jersey plates* **6** [singular] the place where the person hitting the ball stands in the sport of baseball: *Reid **stepped up to the plate**, swung, and hit the ball.* **7** [C] a thin piece of plastic with FALSE TEETH in it

pla·teau /plæˈtoʊ/ *n.* [C] **1** EARTH SCIENCES a large area of flat land that is higher than the land around it **2** a period during which the level or amount of something does not change: *I had **reached a plateau** in my career.* → *see picture on page A63* —**plateau** *v.* [I]

-plat·ed /ˈpleɪt̬ɪd/ *adj.* **gold-plated/silver-plated/brass-plated etc.** covered with a thin layer of gold, silver, or other metal: *a silver-plated spoon*

ˌplate ˈglass *n.* [U] clear glass made in large thick sheets, used especially in store windows —**plate-glass** *adj.*: *a **plate-glass window***

plate·let /ˈpleɪtlət/ *n.* [C] BIOLOGY a type of cell in your blood that helps it to CLOT (=become solid) when you bleed, so that you stop bleeding

ˌplate tecˈtonics *n.* [U] EARTH SCIENCES a scientific idea that explains how movement in the very large sheets of rock that form the surface of the Earth produces mountains and causes VOLCANOS and EARTHQUAKES, etc. → TECTONIC PLATE

plat·form /ˈplætfɔrm/ *n.* [C] **1** a raised structure for people to stand or work on: *He climbed onto the wooden platform and began to speak.* | *an oil platform* **2** POLITICS the main ideas and aims of a political party, especially the ones that they state just before an election: *Tax cuts may be included in the **party platform** for the next election.* **3** IT the type of computer system or software that someone uses: *a multimedia platform* **4** a chance for someone to express his/her opinions: *He used the TV interview as a **platform for** his views on education.* **5** the place in a railroad station or SUBWAY where you get on and off a train: *We were waiting **on the platform**.*

P

plat·ing /ˈpleɪt̬ɪŋ/ *n.* [U] a thin layer of metal that covers another metal surface: *silver plating*

plat·i·num /ˈplætˀnəm, ˈplætˀn-əm/ *n.* [U] CHEMISTRY (*symbol* **Pt**) an expensive heavy silver-white metal that is an ELEMENT and is used in making jewelry [ORIGIN: 1800—1900 Modern Latin, Spanish *platina*, from *plata* "silver"]

plat·i·tude /ˈplæt̬əˌtud/ *n.* [C] (disapproving) a boring statement that has been made many times before: *a speech full of platitudes*

pla·ton·ic /pləˈtɑnɪk/ *adj.* a relationship that is platonic is friendly, but not sexual

pla·toon /pləˈtun/ *n.* [C] a small group of soldiers that is part of a COMPANY [ORIGIN: 1600—1700 French *peloton* "ball, small group," from *pelote* "little ball"]

plat·ter /ˈplæt̬ɚ/ *n.* [C] **1** a large plate, used for serving food **2 chicken/seafood etc. platter** chicken, etc. arranged on a plate with other foods and served in a restaurant

plat·y·pus /ˈplæt̬əpəs/ *n.* [C] a small Australian animal that lays eggs and has a beak, but also has fur and feeds milk to its babies [ORIGIN: 1700—1800 Modern Latin, Greek *platypous* "flat-footed"]

plau·dits /ˈplɔdɪts/ *n.* [plural] (formal) praise and admiration: *Her ideas have **won plaudits** from scientists.*

plau·si·ble /ˈplɔzəbəl/ *adj.* easy to believe and likely to be true (ANT) **implausible**: *a plausible story* [ORIGIN: 1500—1600 Latin *plausibilis* "worth applauding," from *plaudere* "to applaud"]

play¹ /pleɪ/ *v.* (**played**, **plays**)
1 SPORT/GAME a) [I,T] to take part or compete in a game or sport: *men playing poker* | *Kara played*

basketball in college. | *Garcia* ***plays for*** *the Hornets.* | *The 49ers are playing the Vikings on Saturday* (=they are competing against the Vikings). **b)** [T] to use a particular piece, card, person, etc. in a game or sport: *Coach Nelson will play Williams at quarterback.*

2 CHILDREN/TOYS [I,T] to do things that you enjoy, especially to pretend things or to use toys: *a little girl who likes* ***playing with*** *dolls* | *Outside, the kids were* ***playing tag/catch/house etc.*** | *Parents need to spend time just* ***playing with*** *their children.*

3 MUSIC a) [I,T] ENG. LANG. ARTS to perform a piece of music on an instrument: *The band played for 10,000 people at the Newport Festival.* | *Matt plays drums.* **b)** [I,T] to make a radio, STEREO, etc. produce sounds, especially music: *a story tape to play for the kids in the car* | *an entertainment center capable of playing CDs, DVDs and games*

P

4 play a part/role to have an effect or influence on something: *Police believe he may have* ***played a role in*** *the boy's death.*

5 THEATER/MOVIE a) [T] ENG. LANG. ARTS to act as one of the characters in a movie, television, or theater performance: *Kidman* ***plays the role/part of*** *Virginia Woolf in the movie.* | *He plays a shy, nervous man.* **b)** [I] to be performed or shown at a theater, etc.: *Where's the movie playing?*

6 BEHAVE [linking verb, T] (informal) to behave in a particular way, or pretend to have a particular quality, in order to achieve something: *If he asks, just* ***play dumb*** (=pretend you do not know the answer). | *the accusation that scientists are* ***playing God*** | *Doctors warned parents to* ***play it safe*** (=do the safest thing) *by immunizing their children.* | *Tracy forced herself to* ***play it cool*** (=stay calm and not be too eager) *with Brad.*

7 play ball a) to throw, hit, kick, or catch a ball as a game or activity: *Just don't play ball in the house.* **b)** (informal) to agree to do something that someone wants you to do: *They threatened to stop advertising if the magazine didn't play ball.*

8 play a trick/joke/prank on sb to do something to surprise or deceive someone, and make other people laugh

9 play tricks (on you) if your mind, memory, sight, etc. plays tricks on you, you feel confused and not sure about what is happening

10 play it by ear (informal) to decide what to do as things happen, instead of planning anything: *We'll see what the weather's like and play it by ear.*

11 play sth by ear to be able to play music after you have heard it instead of by reading the notes

12 play games (disapproving) to not be serious about what you are doing, or not say what you really think, especially in a way that tricks or deceives other people: *Stop playing games and just tell me what you want.*

13 play with fire to do something that could have a very bad result: *If you invest in high-risk stocks, you're playing with fire.*

14 play your cards right to behave in an effective way in a situation, in order to get what you want: *If you play your cards right, eventually you'll get promoted.*

15 play second fiddle to sb/sth to be involved in an activity, but not be as important as the main person or group that is involved in it [ORIGIN: Old English *plegan*]

GRAMMAR

Do not use a preposition or "the" after **play** when you are talking about playing a game or sport. Say: *They're playing football.*
Do not say "They're playing at football" or "They're playing the football."
Always use "the" after the verb **play** and before the names of musical instruments: *Anna plays the piano.*

play around *phr. v.*

1 to spend time having fun, but without having a particular purpose: *I didn't get good grades because I played around a lot.*

2 (informal) to have a sexual relationship with someone who is not your husband or wife

play sth ↔ **back** *phr. v.*

to let someone hear or see again something that has been recorded on a TAPE, VIDEO, etc.: *Jody rewound the tape and played it back.*

play sth ↔ **down** *phr. v.*

to make something seem less important or bad than it really is: *The White House tried to play down the latest economic figures.*

play on sth *phr. v.*

to use a feeling or idea in order to get what you want, often in an unfair way: *His campaign plays on people's fear of crime.*

play sth ↔ **up** *phr. v.*

to make something seem better or more important than it really is: *The town has played up its location to attract tourists.*

play with sth *phr. v.*

1 to keep touching or moving something: *Stop playing with the remote control!*

2 *also* **play around with** sth to organize or think about something in different ways, to see what works: *I've been playing with the design of the newsletter.*

play² *n.* **1** [C] ENG. LANG. ARTS a story that is written to be performed by actors, especially in a theater: *a play by Shakespeare* | *a* ***play about*** *two men on trial for murder* | *Each year, the drama department* ***puts on/performs a play*** *in the spring.* → THEATER **2** [C,U] the actions of the people who are playing a game or sport: *On the next play, Johnson ran fifteen yards for a touchdown.* **3** [U] the things that people, especially children, do for fun, such as using toys: *the shouts of children* ***at play*** | *Children learn* ***through play***. | *a play area with slides and swings* **4** [U] the effect or influence of something: *All of these factors are* ***at play*** (=having an effect) *in any human relationship.* | *Cultural differences* ***come into play*** (=begin to have an effect) *when trying to sell a product in a foreign country.* | *A complex system of muscles is* ***brought into play*** (=begun to be used) *for each body movement.* **5 play on words** a use of a word or phrase that is interesting or funny because it has more than one meaning ➔ PUN

play·act·ing /ˈpleɪˌæktɪŋ/ *n.* [U] (disapproving) behavior in which someone pretends to be serious or sincere, but is not

play·boy /ˈpleɪbɔɪ/ *n.* (plural **playboys**) [C] (old-fashioned) a rich man who does not work and who spends time enjoying himself with beautiful women, fast cars, etc.

ˌplay-by-ˈplay *adj.* **play-by-play commentary/description** a description of the action in a sports game as it happens, given on television or the radio

ˈPlay-Doh *n.* [U] (trademark) a soft substance like colored clay, used by children for making shapes

play·er /ˈpleɪɚ/ *n.* [C] **1** someone who plays a game, sport, or musical instrument: *a piano player* | *a basketball player* **2** one of the people, companies, organizations, etc. that is involved in a situation: *a **major/dominant/key player** in the stock market* **3 a CD/record/cassette etc. player** a machine that is used to play CDs, etc.

play·ful /ˈpleɪfəl/ *adj.* **1** intended to be fun rather than serious, or showing that you are having fun: *playful tunes* | *She gave him a playful poke.* **2** very active and happy: *playful children tumbling in the snow* —**playfully** *adv.* —**playfulness** *n.* [U]

play·ground /ˈpleɪgraʊnd/ *n.* [C] an area where children can play, especially at a school or in a park, that often has special equipment that children can climb on, ride on, etc.

play·house /ˈpleɪhaʊs/ *n.* [C] **1** a theater, often used as part of a theater's name: *the Pasadena Playhouse* **2** a small structure like a house, that children can play in

playing card

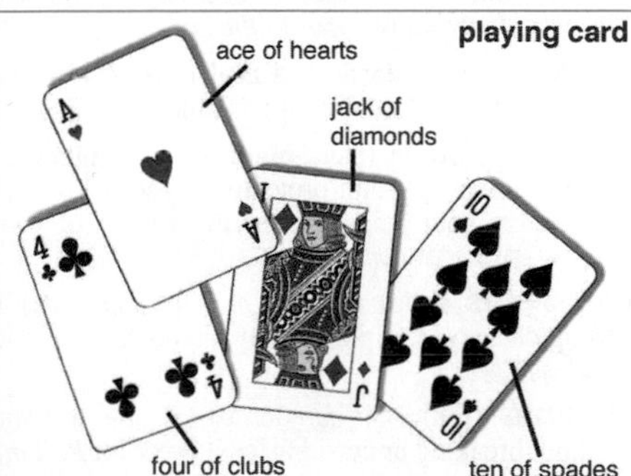

ˈplaying card *n.* [C] a CARD

ˈplaying field *n.* **1** [C] a large piece of ground with particular areas marked on it for playing football, baseball, etc. **2 a level playing field** a situation in which different people, companies, countries, etc. can all compete fairly with each other because no one has special advantages: *Canada limits election spending in an attempt to create a level playing field.*

play·mate /ˈpleɪmeɪt/ *n.* [C] (old-fashioned) a friend you play with when you are a child

play·off /ˈpleɪɔf/ *n.* [C usually plural] a game or series of games played by the best teams or players in a sports competition, in order to decide the final winner: *The Chicago Cubs are **in the playoffs**.*

THESAURUS **competition, championship, tournament** ➔ COMPETITION

play·pen /ˈpleɪpɛn/ *n.* [C] an enclosed area like an open box with a net or wooden BARS around it, in which very young children can play safely

play·room /ˈpleɪrum/ *n.* [C] a room for children to play in

play·thing /ˈpleɪˌθɪŋ/ *n.* [C] a toy

play·time /ˈpleɪtaɪm/ *n.* [U] a period of time during which a child can play: *Don't let TV take up too much playtime.*

play·wright /ˈpleɪraɪt/ *n.* [C] ENG. LANG. ARTS someone who writes plays

pla·za /ˈplɑzə, ˈplæzə/ *n.* [C] an outdoor public place, usually with a lot of stores and small businesses

plea /pli/ *n.* [C] **1** a request that is urgent and full of emotion: *a **plea for** help* | *They **made a plea** for more resources.* **2** LAW a statement by someone in a court of law saying whether s/he is guilty or not: *The defendant **entered a plea of** "not guilty."*

ˈplea-ˌbargain *v.* [I] LAW to avoid punishment for a serious crime by agreeing to say you are guilty of a less serious one

plead /plid/ *v.* **1** [I] (past tense and past participle **pleaded**) to ask for something you want very much, in an urgent and emotional way (SYN) **beg**: *Mother **pleaded with** Dad **to** be gentler with us.* | *He **pleaded for** forgiveness.*

THESAURUS **ask, beg, implore** ➔ ASK

2 [I,T] (past tense and past participle **pleaded** *or* **pled** /plɛd/) LAW to officially say in a court of law whether or not you are guilty of a crime: *"How do you plead?" "Not guilty."* | *Parker **pled guilty to** four charges of theft.*

pleas·ant /ˈplɛzənt/ *adj.* **1** enjoyable, nice, or good: *It had been a pleasant evening.* | *a pleasant surprise*

THESAURUS **nice, enjoyable** ➔ NICE

2 polite, friendly, or kind: *a really nice, pleasant man* —**pleasantly** *adv.*: *We were pleasantly surprised by how welcoming everyone was.*

pleas·ant·ry /ˈplɛzəntri/ *n.* (plural **pleasantries**) [C] (formal) something that you say in order to be polite

please[1] /pliz/ *interjection* **1** used in order to be polite when asking someone to do something: *Patty, sit down, please.* | *Could you please hold the line?* **2** used in order to be polite when asking for something: *Can I have a cookie, please?* | *Can I* *please go to Becky's party?* **3** (spoken) said in order to politely accept something that someone offers you: *"Coffee?" "Yes, please."*

please² *v.* **1** [I,T] to make someone feel happy or satisfied: *a business that wants to please its customers* | *a boss who is* ***hard to please*** | *Children are often* ***eager to please****.* **2** [I] used in some phrases to show that someone can do or have what s/he wants: *Students can study* ***whatever*** *they* ***please****.* | *You can come and go* ***as you please****.*

pleased /plizd/ *adj.* **1** happy or satisfied: *Your mom will be really pleased.* | *We're very* ***pleased with*** *the results.* | *Ellen was* ***pleased that*** *Toby had remembered.* | *I was* ***pleased to hear/see/learn etc.*** *that things had improved.*

> THESAURUS happy, glad, content, delighted ➔ HAPPY

2 (I'm) pleased to meet you (spoken) said in order to be polite when you meet someone for the first time

P

pleas·ing /'plizɪŋ/ *adj.* (formal) giving pleasure, enjoyment, or satisfaction: *a pleasing flavor* | *The design of the car is very* ***pleasing to the eye*** (=nice to look at).

pleas·ur·a·ble /'plɛʒərəbəl/ *adj.* (formal) enjoyable: *pleasurable activities*

pleas·ure /'plɛʒɚ/ *n.* **1** [U] a feeling of happiness, satisfaction, or enjoyment ➔ PLEASANT: *Marie laughed* ***with pleasure****.* | *I'd like more time to read* ***for pleasure****.* | *He* ***took pleasure in*** *his work.* | *The park has* ***given pleasure to*** *many people.* | *The kids yelled for the* ***sheer/pure pleasure*** *of it.* **2** [C] an activity or experience that you enjoy very much: *Chocolate is one of my chief pleasures.* | ***It's a pleasure to*** *finally meet you.* **3 (it is) my pleasure** (spoken) a polite phrase used in order to say that you are glad you can do something nice for someone: *"Thanks for walking me home." "It was my pleasure."*

pleat /plit/ *n.* [C usually plural] a flat fold in a piece of clothing —**pleat** *v.* [T]

pleat·ed /'plit̬ɪd/ *adj.* a pleated skirt, pair of pants, dress, etc. has a lot of flat narrow folds

ple·be·ian¹ /plɪ'biən/ *n.* [C] HISTORY an ordinary person who had no special rank in ancient Rome ➔ PATRICIAN [ORIGIN: 1500—1600 Latin *plebeius*, from *plebs* "common people"]

plebeian² *adj.* **1** (disapproving) relating to ordinary people and what they like, rather than to people from a high social class **2** HISTORY relating to plebeians in ancient Rome

pled /plɛd/ *v.* a past tense and past participle of PLEAD

pledge¹ /plɛdʒ/ *n.* [C] **1** a serious promise or agreement to do something or give money to something: *a pledge of support* | *Parents* ***make a pledge*** *to take their children to rehearsals.* | *a pledge of $100 to the public television station* **2** someone who promises to become a member of a college FRATERNITY or SORORITY

pledge² *v.* [T] **1** to make a formal, usually public, promise: *Canada* ***pledged to*** *provide medical aid.*

> THESAURUS promise, give sb your word, swear, take/swear an oath, vow, undertake to do sth, guarantee, commit ➔ PROMISE¹

2 to make someone formally promise something: *Employees were* ***pledged to*** *secrecy.* **3** to promise to become a member of a college FRATERNITY or SORORITY

ˌPledge of Al'legiance *n.* **the Pledge of Allegiance** an official statement said by Americans in which they promise to be loyal to the United States. It is usually said by children every morning at school.

plen·i·tude /'plɛnəˌtud/ *n.* (literary) **1 a plenitude of sth** a large amount of something: *Hunters in the 1800s found a plenitude of beaver.* **2** [U] the condition of being complete or full

plen·ti·ful /'plɛntɪfəl/ *adj.* more than enough in amount or number: *a plentiful supply* —**plentifully** *adv.*

plen·ty¹ /'plɛnti/ *pron.* a large amount that is enough or more than enough: *Eat* ***plenty of*** *fruits and vegetables.* | *We have* ***plenty to*** *worry about.* [ORIGIN: 1200—1300 Old French *plenté*, from Latin *plenitas* "fullness"]

> THESAURUS many, a large number, a lot/lots, a multitude of sb/sth, a plethora of sth, myriad ➔ MANY
> enough, ample, sufficient ➔ ENOUGH

plenty² *adv.* (spoken) more than enough SYN **a lot**: *There's* ***plenty more*** *room in the car.*

pleth·o·ra /'plɛθərə/ *n.* **a plethora of sth** (formal) a very large number of something

pleu·ra /'plʊrə/ *n.* (plural **pleurae** /-ri/ *or* **pleuras**) [C] BIOLOGY a very thin protective layer of material that covers your lungs and the inner walls of your chest —**pleural** *adj.*

Plex·i·glas /'plɛksiˌglæs/ *n.* [U] (trademark) a strong clear type of plastic that can be used instead of glass

pli·a·ble /'plaɪəbəl/ *adj.* (formal) **1** able to bend without breaking or cracking SYN **flexible**: *Roll the clay until it is soft and pliable.* **2** *also* **pli·ant** /'plaɪənt/ easily influenced by others, or willing to accept new ideas: *a pliant legislature*

pli·ers /'plaɪɚz/ *n.* [plural] a small metal tool used for bending wire or cutting it: *a pair of pliers*

plight /plaɪt/ *n.* [C usually singular] a bad, serious, or sad situation that someone is in: *the* ***plight of*** *women in that society* | *the university's financial plight*

plod /plɑd/ *v.* (**plodded**, **plodding**) [I] to move or do something very slowly, especially in a way that is boring or that shows you are tired: *We plodded* *uphill.* | *The movie* ***plods along*** *without very much ever happening.* —**plodding** *adj.*

plop¹ /plɑp/ *v.* (**plopped**, **plopping**) [I,T] to sit down, fall down, or drop something somewhere in a careless way: *Jaime* ***plopped down*** *on the bed.* | *I plopped a couple of ice cubes into a glass.*

plop² *n.* [C] the sound made by something when it falls or is dropped into liquid

plot¹ /plɑt/ *n.* [C] **1** the events that form the main story of a book, movie, or play: *The movie has a very complicated plot.* **2** a secret plan you make with other people to do something illegal or harmful: *a plot to kill the President*

THESAURUS plan, conspiracy, scheme → PLAN¹

3 a small piece of land for building or growing things on: *a two-acre* ***plot of land***

plot² *v.* (**plotted**, **plotting**) **1** [I,T] to make a secret plan, especially one intended to harm a particular person or organization: *The group had* ***plotted to*** *smuggle explosives into the country.* | *Rebels* ***plotted against*** *the dictator.* **2** [T] *also* **plot out** to make lines and marks on a CHART or map that represent facts, numbers, etc.: *These graphs plot the company's progress.*

plow¹ /plaʊ/ *n.* [C] **1** a large piece of equipment used on farms that cuts up the surface of the ground so that seeds can be planted **2** (informal) a SNOWPLOW

plow² *v.* **1** [I,T] to use a plow in order to cut earth, push snow off streets, etc.: *newly plowed fields* **2** [I] to move with a lot of effort or force: *A ship* ***plowed through*** *the waves.*

plow ahead *phr. v.* to continue to do something in spite of difficulties or opposition: *She was silent, but I* ***plowed ahead with*** *my questions.*

plow sth ↔ **back** *phr. v.* to use money that you have earned from a business to make the business bigger and more successful: *Profits are* ***plowed back into*** *equipment and training.*

plow into sth *phr. v.* to hit something hard with a car, truck, etc.: *We plowed into a parked car.*

plow through sth *phr. v.* to read or look at all of something even though it is difficult, long, or boring: *Investigators plowed through the phone records.*

ploy /plɔɪ/ *n.* (plural **ploys**) [C] a way of tricking someone in order to gain an advantage: *It was just a* ***ploy to*** *advance his political career.*

pluck¹ /plʌk/ *v.* [T] **1** to pull something quickly in order to remove it: *She put flowers plucked from the garden into a vase.* | *She* ***plucks her eyebrows*** (=pulls out hairs from the edges of them). **2** to take someone away from a place or situation: *Rescue teams* ***plucked*** *people* ***from*** *the rooftops as the water rose.* **3 pluck up the courage** to make yourself be brave or confident enough to do something: *I finally* ***plucked up the courage to*** *ask for a raise.* **4** to pull the feathers off a chicken or other bird before cooking it **5** to quickly pull the strings of a musical instrument

pluck² *n.* [U] (old-fashioned) courage and determination to do something that is difficult: *It* ***takes*** *a lot of* ***pluck*** *to do what he's done.* —**plucky** *adj.*

plug¹ /plʌg/ *n.* [C] **1** the small object at the end of a wire, that is used for connecting a piece of electrical equipment to a SOCKET (=supply of electricity) **2** a round flat piece of rubber, used for blocking the hole in a bathtub or SINK **3** (informal) a way of advertising a book, movie, etc. by talking about it on a radio or television program

plug² *v.* (**plugged**, **plugging**) [T] **1** *also* **plug up** to fill a hole or block it: *The drain was plugged up with paper.* **2** to advertise a book, movie, etc. by talking about it on a radio or television program: *Susan was on the show to plug her new novel.*

THESAURUS advertise, promote, market, publicize, hype → ADVERTISE

plug away *phr. v.* to continue working hard at something: *Scientists have been* ***plugging away at*** *the problem.*

plug sth ↔ **in** *phr. v.* to connect a piece of electrical equipment to a SOCKET (=supply of electricity) ANT **unplug**: *Is the TV plugged in?*

plug sth **into** sth *phr. v.* to connect one piece of electrical equipment to another: *Can you plug the speakers into the stereo for me?*

plum /plʌm/ *n.* [C] **1** a soft round usually purple fruit with a single large seed, or the tree on which it grows → *see picture on page 414* **2** something very good that other people wish they had, such as a good job, part in a play, etc.: *The governorship of California is a bigger political plum than a seat in Congress.* —**plum** *adj.* [only before noun]: *a* ***plum job/role/assignment***

plum·age /ˈplumɪdʒ/ *n.* [U] (formal) the feathers covering a bird's body

plumb /plʌm/ *adv.* (spoken, informal) exactly or completely: *He's plumb crazy.* | *Sorry, I just plumb forgot.*

plumb·er /ˈplʌmɚ/ *n.* [C] someone whose job is to repair water pipes, SINKs, toilets, etc. [ORIGIN: 1300—1400 Old French *plommier* "worker in lead," from Latin *plumbarius*, from *plumbus* "lead;" because water pipes were originally made of lead]

plumb·ing /ˈplʌmɪŋ/ *n.* [U] the system of water pipes in a house or building

plume /plum/ *n.* [C] **1** a small cloud of smoke, dust, gas, etc.: ***Plumes of*** *black smoke were coming from the garage.* **2** a large feather

plum·met /ˈplʌmɪt/ *v.* [I] **1** to suddenly and quickly decrease in value: *House prices have plummeted.*

THESAURUS decrease, go down, drop, fall → DECREASE¹

2 to fall suddenly and very quickly from a very

P

high place: *The plane plummeted to the ground.*

plump¹ /plʌmp/ *adj.* **1** attractively round and slightly fat: *plump juicy strawberries* **2** fat – used in order to be polite: *He was 67, short, and a little plump.*

THESAURUS **fat, overweight, big, heavy, large, obese, chubby, stout, corpulent, rotund** → FAT¹

plump² *also* **plump up** *v.* [T] to make a PILLOW rounder and softer by shaking or hitting it

plun·der¹ /'plʌndɚ/ *v.* [I,T] to steal money or property from a place while fighting in a war: *The Vikings invaded and plundered the town.*

THESAURUS **steal, burglarize, loot** → STEAL¹

plunder² *n.* [U] things that are stolen during an attack or war

plunge¹ /plʌndʒ/ *v.* **1** [I,T] to move, fall, or be thrown or pushed suddenly forward or downward: *The plane* ***plunged into*** *the Atlantic shortly after takeoff.* → DIVE¹ **2** [I] to suddenly decrease in amount or value: *The stock market plunged more than 1,200 points.*

plunge (sb/sth) **into** sth *phr. v.* to suddenly experience a bad or difficult situation, or to make someone or something do this: *The company was plunged into bankruptcy.*

plunge² *n.* **1 take the plunge** to decide to do something risky, usually after delaying or worrying about it: *Deming took the plunge and started his own business.* **2** [C] a sudden decrease in amount, or a sudden fall

plung·er /'plʌndʒɚ/ *n.* [C] a tool used for clearing waste that is blocking a kitchen or bathroom pipe. It consists of a straight handle with a large rubber cup on the end.

plunk /plʌŋk/ *v.* [I,T] (informal) to put something somewhere in a noisy, sudden, or careless way, or to suddenly sit down: *Grover* ***plunked down*** *in front of the TV.*

plunk sth ↔ **down** *phr. v.* to spend a lot of money for something: *He plunked down $30 for a box of chocolates.*

plu·per·fect /ˌplu'pɚfɪkt/ *n.* **the pluperfect** ENG. LANG. ARTS the PAST PERFECT

plu·ral /'plʊrəl/ *n.* **the plural** ENG. LANG. ARTS in grammar, the form of a word that represents more than one person or thing. For example, "dogs" is the plural of "dog." → SINGULAR [ORIGIN: 1300—1400 Old French *plurel*, from Latin *pluralis*, from *plus* "more"] —**plural** *adj.*: *a* ***plural noun/verb***

plu·ral·i·ty /plʊ'ræləṭi/ *n.* (plural **pluralities**) [C,U] the largest number of votes in an election, especially when this is less than the total number of votes that all the other people or parties have received

plus¹ /plʌs/ (Ac) *prep.* used when one number or amount is added to another: *Three plus six equals nine (3 + 6 = 9).* | *The jacket costs $49.95 plus tax.* → CALCULATE [ORIGIN: 1500—1600 Latin "more" (adjective and adverb)]

plus² (Ac) *conjunction* and also: *He's going to college, plus he's working 20 hours a week.*

plus³ (Ac) *adj., adv.* **1 A plus/B plus/C plus etc.** a grade used in a system of marking students' work. For example, a C plus is higher than a C, but lower than a B MINUS. → MINUS **2** greater than zero or than a particular amount → MINUS: *a temperature of plus 12°* | *She makes $50,000 a year plus.* **3 plus or minus** used in order to say that a number may be more or less by a certain amount: *The poll's margin of error was plus or minus 3 percentage points.* | *We expect a variation of plus or minus 5% in these figures.* **4 plus sizes** sizes for women's clothes that are larger than regular sizes

plus⁴ *n.* [C] **1** MATH a plus sign **2** something that is an advantage or a quality that you think is good: *The restaurant's location is* ***a big/major plus.***

plush¹ /plʌʃ/ *adj.* comfortable, expensive, and of good quality: *a plush resort*

plush² *n.* [U] a type of cloth with a thick soft surface: *a plush rabbit*

'plus sign *n.* [C] MATH the sign (+)

Plu·to /'pluṭoʊ/ *n.* PHYSICS an object in space that was considered to be the smallest PLANET until 2006, when scientists decided that it was a DWARF PLANET rather than a planet

plu·to·ni·um /plu'toʊniəm/ *n.* [U] CHEMISTRY (*symbol* **Pu**) a metal that is an ELEMENT and is used for producing NUCLEAR power

ply¹ /plaɪ/ *n.* [U] a unit for measuring the thickness of thread, rope, plywood, etc. based on the number of threads or layers that it has: ***two-/three-ply etc.*** *toilet paper*

ply² *v.* (**plied, plies**) **1 ply your trade/craft** (written) to work at your business or special skill: *He is now in his eighties, but still plying his trade.* **2** [I,T] (literary) a boat or vehicle that plies between two places travels to those two places regularly

ply sb **with** sth *phr. v.* to continue giving someone large amounts of something, especially food and drinks

ply·wood /'plaɪwʊd/ *n.* [U] a material made of thin sheets of wood stuck together to form a hard board

p.m. used when talking about times that are between NOON and MIDNIGHT: *I get off work at 5:30 p.m.* [ORIGIN: 1600—1700 Latin *post meridiem* "after noon"]

PMS *n.* [U] **premenstrual syndrome** the uncomfortable physical and emotional feelings that many women have before their PERIOD starts

pneu·mat·ic /nʊ'mæṭɪk/ *adj.* **1** filled with air: *a pneumatic tire* **2** able to work using air pressure: *a pneumatic drill* —**pneumatically** *adv.*

pneu·mo·nia /nʊ'moʊnyə/ *n.* [U] a serious illness that affects your lungs and makes it difficult to breathe

P.O. the written abbreviation of POST OFFICE

P.O. Box /ˌpi 'oʊ ˌbɑks/ *n.* [C] **post office box** a box in a post office that has a special number, to which you can have mail sent instead of to your home

P.O.W. *n.* [C] PRISONER OF WAR: *a P.O.W. camp*

poach /poʊtʃ/ *v.* **1** [T] to cook food such as eggs or fish in a small amount of boiling liquid **2** [I,T] to illegally catch or shoot animals, birds, or fish, especially from private land

poach·er /'poʊtʃɚ/ *n.* [C] someone who illegally catches or shoots animals, birds, or fish, especially on private land

pock·et[1] /'pɑkɪt/ *n.* [C] **1** a small bag sewn into or onto shirts, coats, pants, or skirts, that you can put keys, money, etc. in: *a key in his pants pocket* **2** the amount of money you have that you can spend: *Over $20 million was taken **out of the pockets** of American taxpayers.* | *a corporation with **deep pockets*** (=a lot of money) **3** a small bag or piece of material that is attached to something such as a car seat, used for holding maps, magazines, etc. **4** a small area or amount that is different from what surrounds it: ***pockets of** poverty in the city* [ORIGIN: 1400—1500 Old North French *pokete*, from *poke* "bag"]

pocket[2] *v.* [T] **1** to put something in your pocket **2** to get money in a way that is very easy or dishonest: *One judge pocketed $500,000 in bribes.*

pocket[3] *also* **'pocket-sized** *adj.* small enough to fit into a pocket: *a pocket calendar*

pock·et·book /'pɑkɪtˌbʊk/ *n.* [C] **1** the amount of money you have, or your ability to pay for things: *Some voters are worried that the changes could hurt their pocketbooks* (=cause them to have less money). **2** (old-fashioned) a WALLET or PURSE

pock·et·ful /'pɑkɪtfʊl/ *n.* [C] the amount that will fill a pocket, or a large amount: *a **pocketful of** small change*

'pocket knife *n.* [C] a small knife with a blade that you can fold into its handle

pod /pɑd/ *n.* [C] **1** the long green part of plants such as beans and PEAS that the seeds grow in **2** a group of sea animals, such as WHALES or DOLPHINS, that swim together

pod·cast /'pɑdkæst/ *n.* [C] IT a television or radio show in DIGITAL form, that you can DOWNLOAD from a website and watch on your computer or listen to on equipment such as an MP3 PLAYER —**podcasting** *n.* [U]

po·di·a·trist /pə'daɪətrɪst/ *n.* [C] a doctor who takes care of people's feet and treats foot diseases —**podiatry** *n.* [U]

po·di·um /'poʊdiəm/ *n.* [C] **1** a tall narrow desk that you stand behind when giving a speech to a lot of people: *Several speakers **took the podium*** (=spoke from it) *that night.* **2** a small raised area for a performer, speaker, or musical CONDUCTOR to stand on

po·em /'poʊəm/ *n.* [C] a piece of writing that expresses emotions, experiences, and ideas, especially in short lines using words that RHYME (=have a particular pattern of sounds) [ORIGIN: 1400—1500 French *poème*, from Latin, from Greek *poiein* "to make, create"]

po·et /'poʊɪt/ *n.* [C] ENG. LANG. ARTS someone who writes poems

po·et·ess /'poʊət̬ɪs/ *n.* [C] (old-fashioned) ENG. LANG. ARTS a female poet

po·et·ic /poʊ'ɛt̬ɪk/ *adj.* **1** ENG. LANG. ARTS relating to poetry, or typical of poetry: *poetic language* **2** graceful and expressing deep emotions: *a poetic and powerful ballet* —**poetically** *adv.*

poˌetic 'justice *n.* [U] a situation in which someone who has done something bad suffers in a way that you think s/he deserves

poˌetic 'license *n.* [U] the freedom to change facts, not obey grammar rules, etc. because you are writing poetry or making art

po·et·ry /'poʊətri/ *n.* [U] ENG. LANG. ARTS poems, or the art of writing them → PROSE: *a book of Emily Dickinson's poetry*

po·grom /'poʊgrəm/ *n.* [C] a planned killing of large numbers of people, especially Jews, done for reasons of race or religion → GENOCIDE

poign·ant /'pɔɪnyənt/ *adj.* making you feel sad or full of pity: *a simple melody and poignant lyrics* [ORIGIN: 1300—1400 French, present participle of *poindre* "to prick, sting," from Latin *pungere*] —**poignancy** *n.* [U] —**poignantly** *adv.*

THESAURUS **emotional, moving, touching, emotive** → EMOTIONAL

poin·set·ti·a /pɔɪn'sɛt̬iə/ *n.* [C] a plant with groups of large bright red or white leaves that look like flowers

point[1] /pɔɪnt/ *n.*

1 ONE IDEA [C] a single fact, idea, or opinion in an argument or discussion: *There were a lot of **good points** in his speech.* | *I **made** that **point** at a staff meeting last week.* | *I didn't like his attitude, but I could **see his point*** (=understand his idea). | *I had to admit that he **had a point*** (=his opinion is correct).

2 MAIN IDEA the point the main meaning or idea in something that is said or done: *Come on, Charlie, **get to the point*** (=say your idea directly)! | ***The point is (that)** he had been proven wrong.* | ***What's your point**, Rob?* | *I think you're **missing the point*** (=do not understand the most important thing). | *He's a nice guy, but **that's beside/not the point**.* | ***The important/main/crucial point** is that no one is wholly good or wholly evil.*

3 PURPOSE [U] the purpose or aim of doing something: ***The whole point of** traveling is to experience* *new things.* | ***There's no point in*** *continuing.* ▸Don't say "There's no point to continue."◂

4 IN TIME/DEVELOPMENT [C] a specific moment, time, or stage in something's development: ***At this/that/one/some point****, Moore decided to tell him.* | *She had* ***reached the point*** *where she knew something had to change.* | *It's a good* ***starting point*** *for any future negotiations.* | *the* ***turning point*** *in the investigation* (=the time when it changed)

> THESAURUS stage, part, step, phase → STAGE[1]

5 PLACE [C] a particular position or place: *the point where two lines cross each other*

> THESAURUS place, position, spot, location → PLACE[1]

6 QUALITY [C] a particular quality or feature that someone or something has: *Teachers try to focus on a learner's* ***strong points*** (=best qualities or abilities), *and then work on his or her* ***weak points****.*

7 GAME/SPORT [C] a unit used for showing the SCORE in a game or sport: *The Rams beat the Giants by six points.*

8 IN NUMBERS [C] MATH the sign (.) used for separating a whole number from the DECIMALS that follow it: *four point five percent* (=4.5%)

9 MEASURE [C] a measure on a scale: *Stocks were down 12 points today at 8,098.*

10 the high/low point of sth the best or worst part of something, or the best or worst moment: *It was the high point of their trip.*

11 SHARP END [C] the sharp end of something (SYN) **tip**: *the point of a needle*

12 up to a point partly, but not completely: *He believed her story, up to a point.*

13 make a point of doing sth to deliberately do something: *Don makes a point of spending Saturdays with his kids.*

14 SMALL SPOT [C] a very small spot: *a tiny point of light*

15 LAND [C] a long thin piece of land that stretches out into the ocean

16 to the point only talking about the most important facts or ideas: *Your business letters should be short and to the point.*

17 the point of no return a stage in a process or activity when it becomes impossible to stop it or do something different: *We've* ***reached the point of no return****, so we might as well finish the project.*
→ GUNPOINT, POINT OF VIEW

point[2] *v.* **1** [I] to show someone something by holding your finger out toward it: *John* ***pointed to/toward*** *two of the players.* | *"That's my car," she said,* ***pointing at*** *a white Ford.* → *see picture on page A21* **2** [I,T] to aim something, or to be aimed, in a particular direction: *He* ***pointed*** *a gun* ***at*** *the old man's head.* | *Dozens of cameras were* ***pointed toward*** *them.* | *What time is it when the little hand* ***points to*** *the 8, and the big hand points to the 12?* **3** [T] to show someone which direction to go: *There should be signs* ***pointing the way*** *to the beach.*

> THESAURUS lead, guide, direct, show → LEAD[1]

4 point the finger at sb (informal) to blame someone (SYN) **accuse**

point out *phr. v.* **1 point** sth↔ **out** to tell someone something that s/he does not already know or has not yet noticed: *The manager* ***pointed out that*** *he would have to raise rents to pay for the improvements.* **2 point** sb/sth ↔ **out** to show a person or thing to someone by pointing at him, her, or it: *The little girl* ***pointed out*** *her mother* ***to us****.*

point to/toward sb/sth *phr. v.* to show that something is probably true: *The report points to stress as a cause of heart disease.*

ˌpoint-ˈblank *adv., adj.* **1** if you say something point-blank, you say it in a very direct way: ***I asked/told*** *him* ***point-blank*** *what was going on.* **2** if you shoot a gun point-blank, the person or thing you are shooting is directly in front of you: *Ralston was* ***shot point-blank*** *in the chest.* | ***He was shot at point-blank range.***

point·ed /ˈpɔɪntɪd/ *adj.* **1** having a point at the end: *cowboy boots with pointed toes* **2 a pointed question/look/remark etc.** a direct question, look, etc. that deliberately shows that you are bored, annoyed, or do not approve of something

point·ed·ly /ˈpɔɪntɪdli/ *adv.* deliberately, so that people notice that you are bored, annoyed, or do not approve of something: *Wilton looked pointedly at the clock.*

point·er /ˈpɔɪntɚ/ *n.* [C] **1** a helpful piece of advice (SYN) **tip**: *I* ***gave*** *him some* ***pointers on*** *his golf technique.* **2** the thin ARROW on a piece of equipment such as a computer or scale, that points to a particular place, number, or direction **3** a long stick used for pointing at things on a map, board, etc.

point·less /ˈpɔɪntlɪs/ *adj.* without any purpose or meaning, or not likely to have an effect: *pointless violence on TV* | ***It's pointless*** *trying to call him; he isn't home.*

> THESAURUS
> **futile** – having no chance of being effective or successful: *a futile attempt to prevent the war*
> **useless** – not useful or effective in any way: *The information he provided was useless.*
> **be a waste of time/money/effort** – to be not worth doing or spending money on because little or nothing is achieved or gained: *I thought the class was a waste of time.*
> **senseless** – happening or done for no good reason or with no purpose: *the senseless killing of innocent civilians*

ˈpoint man *n.* [C usually singular] **1** a soldier who goes ahead of a group to see if there is any danger **2** someone who is in charge of a particular subject in a company or organization: *the administration's* ***point man on*** *health care*

ˌpoint of ˈview *n.* [C] **1** a particular way of

thinking about or judging a situation: *I began writing about families* ***from** a father's* ***point of view***. **2** someone's own personal opinion or attitude about something: *My parents never seem to be able to see my point of view.*

THESAURUS **opinion, view, position, stance, attitude** → OPINION

3 ENG. LANG. ARTS if a story is told from the NARRATOR'S or a character's point of view, it is written as though that person is telling the story: *a novel written from the point of view of a teenage boy*

poin·ty /'pɔɪnti/ *adj.* (informal) POINTED: *a pointy beard*

poise¹ /pɔɪz/ *n.* [U] **1** a calm confident way of behaving, and the ability to control how you feel: *She spoke to the police* ***with perfect poise***. **2** a graceful way of moving or standing: *the poise of a dancer*

poise² *v.* [T] to put something in a carefully balanced position, or to hold it there: *He* ***poised*** *the bottle* ***over*** *her glass, ready to pour.*

poised /pɔɪzd/ *adj.* **1** completely prepared to do something or for something to happen, when it is likely to happen soon: *The team is* ***poised to*** *win the championships.* **2** not moving, but completely ready to move: *I could sense that she was* ***poised to*** *run at any second.* | *a rocket* ***poised for*** *launch* **3** behaving in a calm confident way, and able to control your feelings and reactions: *a poised and talented girl*

poi·son¹ /'pɔɪzən/ *n.* [C,U] **1** a substance that can kill you or make you sick if you eat it, breathe it, etc.: *rat poison* **2** a person, feeling, idea, etc. that makes you behave badly or makes you feel very unhappy: *Hatred is a poison for the soul.* [ORIGIN: 1200—1300 Old French "drink, poisonous drink, poison," from Latin *potio*]

poison² *v.* [T] **1** to kill or harm someone by giving him/her poison: *She poisoned the neighbor's dog.* **2** to make land, lakes, rivers, air, etc. dirty and dangerous, especially by using harmful chemicals: *Pesticides are poisoning our rivers.* **3** to have harmful effects on someone's mind or emotions, or on a situation: *Money has poisoned American politics.*

poi·son·ing /'pɔɪzənɪŋ/ *n.* [C,U] an illness that is caused by swallowing, touching, or breathing a poisonous substance: *The children were suffering from* ***food/lead poisoning***.

ˌpoison 'ivy *n.* [U] a plant with an oily substance on its leaves that makes your skin hurt and ITCH if you touch it

ˌpoison 'oak *n.* [U] a plant that has leaves that make your skin hurt and ITCH

poi·son·ous /'pɔɪzənəs/ *adj.* containing poison or producing poison: *a poisonous chemical* | *poisonous snakes* —**poisonously** *adv.*

THESAURUS **harmful, toxic, detrimental, damaging, destructive** → HARMFUL

poke /poʊk/ *v.* **1** [I,T] to quickly push your finger or some other pointed object into something or someone: *Polly* ***poked*** *me* ***in*** *the ribs.* | *David* ***poked at*** *the campfire with a stick.* → *see picture on page A21*

THESAURUS **push, shove, nudge, elbow** → PUSH¹

2 [I,T] to push something through a space or out of an opening, so that you can see part of it, or to be partly through a space or opening: *Eve* ***poked*** *her head* ***around*** *the door and told us to be quiet.* | *Weeds were* ***poking through*** *the cracks.* **3 poke a hole** to make a hole in something by pushing a pointed object through it **4 poke fun at sb** to joke about someone in an unkind way: *The article pokes fun at Hollywood celebrities.* —**poke** *n.* [C]

poke along *phr. v.* (informal) to move or travel slowly

poke around *phr. v.* to look for something, especially by moving things: *I began poking around in the cupboard.*

pok·er /'poʊkɚ/ *n.* **1** [U] a card game that people usually play for money **2** [C] a metal stick used for moving coal or wood in a fire to make it burn better

pok·ey, poky /'poʊki/ *adj.* (informal) doing things very slowly, especially in a way that you find annoying: *a pokey driver*

po·lar /'poʊlɚ/ *adj.* **1** EARTH SCIENCES relating to the North Pole or the South Pole: *polar ice* **2 polar opposite** someone or something that is completely opposite to another person or thing in character or style: *Presidents Kennedy and Johnson were polar opposites in terms of style and background.*

polar bear

'polar ˌbear *n.* [C] a large white bear that lives near the North Pole

po·lar·ize /'poʊləˌraɪz/ *v.* [I,T] (formal) to divide into two opposing groups, or to make people do this: *The trial polarized the city.* —**polarization** /ˌpoʊlərə'zeɪʃən/ *n.* [U]

Po·lar·oid /'poʊləˌrɔɪd/ *n.* [C] (trademark) a camera that uses a special film to produce a photograph very quickly, or a photograph taken with this kind of camera

'polar ˌzone *n.* [C] EARTH SCIENCES one of the two parts of the Earth that are near the NORTH POLE and

P

the SOUTH POLE, where the weather is always very cold → TEMPERATE ZONE, TROPICS

Pole /poʊl/ *n.* [C] someone from Poland

pole *n.* [C] **1** a long stick or post: *a telephone pole* (=holding up telephone wires outside) | *a fishing pole* **2** EARTH SCIENCES the most northern and southern point on a PLANET: *an expedition to the North Pole* **3 be poles apart** to be very different from someone or something else: *The two classes were poles apart in atmosphere.* **4** PHYSICS one of two points at the end of a MAGNET where its power is strongest **5** PHYSICS one of the two points at which wires can be attached to a BATTERY in order to use its electricity

P

po·lem·ic /pə'lɛmɪk/ *n.* [C,U] strong arguments that criticize or defend a particular idea, opinion, or person —**polemical** *adj.*

'pole vault *n.* **the pole vault** a sport in which you jump over a high BAR using a special long pole —**pole vaulter** *n.* [C]

po·lice¹ /pə'lis/ *n.* **1 the police** an official organization whose job is to catch criminals, make sure that people obey the law, and protect people and property: *Her neighbors called the police.*

THESAURUS

People in the police
police officer/policeman/policewoman
detective – a police officer whose job is to discover who is responsible for crimes
plain-clothes police officer – a police officer who is wearing ordinary clothes instead of a uniform
cop (informal) – a police officer

Things the police do
investigate crimes
find/collect evidence
arrest sb
question/interrogate/interview sb
hold/keep sb in custody – to keep someone in prison while collecting more information about a crime, or before s/he goes to court
charge sb with a crime – to state officially that someone might be guilty of a crime

2 [plural] the people who work for this organization: *Police broke down the door.* | *police records/reports* [ORIGIN: 1400—1500 French, Late Latin *politia* "government," from *polites* "citizen"]

police² *v.* [T] **1** to keep control over a place using police **2** to control a particular activity or industry by making sure people obey the rules: *The agency is responsible for policing the nuclear power industry.* —**policing** *n.* [U]

po'lice de,partment *n.* [C] the official police organization in a particular area or city

po'lice force *n.* [C] the official police organization in a country or area

po·lice·man /pə'lismən/ *n.* (plural **policemen** /-mən/) [C] a male police officer

po'lice ,officer *n.* [C] a member of the police

po'lice state *n.* [C] POLITICS a country where the government strictly controls most of the activities of its citizens

THESAURUS **government, democracy, republic, monarchy, regime, dictatorship, totalitarian country/state, etc.** → GOVERNMENT

po'lice ,station *n.* [C] the local office of the police in a town or city

po·lice·wom·an /pə'lis,wʊmən/ *n.* (plural **policewomen** /-,wɪmɪn/) [C] a female police officer

pol·i·cy /'pɑləsi/ (Ac) *n.* (plural **policies**) **1** [C,U] a way of doing things that has been officially agreed and chosen by a political party, business, or organization: *our* ***foreign/economic/immigration etc. policy*** | *the company's* ***policy on*** *maternity leave* | *government officials who* ***make policy*** | *monetary policy* | *a leading authority on welfare policies* **2** [C] a written agreement with an insurance company: *a health* ***insurance policy*** **3** [C,U] a particular principle that you believe in: ***It's*** *my* ***policy*** *not* ***to*** *gossip.* [ORIGIN: (2) 1500—1600 French *police* "document, certificate," from Old Italian *polizza*, from Greek *apodeixis* "proof"]

po·li·o /'poʊli,oʊ/ *n.* [U] a serious infectious disease of the nerves in the SPINE, that often results in someone being permanently unable to move particular muscles

po·li sci /,pɑli 'saɪ/ *n.* [U] (informal) POLITICAL SCIENCE

Po·lish¹ /'poʊlɪʃ/ *adj.* relating to or coming from Poland

Polish² *n.* **1** [U] the language used in Poland **2 the Polish** [plural] the people of Poland

pol·ish¹ /'pɑlɪʃ/ *v.* [T] to make something smooth, bright, and shiny by rubbing it: *He polished his shoes each night.*

THESAURUS **clean, do the housework, dust, vacuum, sweep (up), scrub, mop** → CLEAN²

polish sth ↔ **off** *phr. v.* (informal) to finish food, work, etc. quickly or easily: *The kids polished off the rest of the cake.*

polish² *n.* **1** [C,U] a liquid, powder, or other substance that you rub into a surface to make it shiny: *furniture polish* | *shoe polish* **2** [U] a high level of skill and style in the way someone performs, writes, or behaves: *Meeting new people will help give you social polish.* **3** [singular] the smooth shiny appearance of something, that is produced by polishing → NAIL POLISH

pol·ished /'pɑlɪʃt/ *adj.* **1** shiny because of being rubbed with polish: ***highly polished*** *wood* **2** done with great skill and style, or doing something with skill and style: *a polished performance* | *a polished ballerina* **3** polite and confident: *a polished and sophisticated woman*

po·lite /pə'laɪt/ *adj.* behaving or speaking in a way

that is correct for the social situation you are in, or showing good manners: *polite young people* | ***It's not polite to** talk with your mouth full.* | *a polite smile* | *Len sipped at his drink to be polite.* | *They weren't just making **polite conversation**; they really wanted to know.* —**politely** *adv.* —**politeness** *n.* [U]

THESAURUS

have good manners – to behave in a polite way in social situations: *Parents want to teach their children to have good manners.*
well-behaved – behaving in a polite or socially acceptable way: *My kids are generally well-behaved.*
courteous – polite and respectful: *You should be courteous to other drivers.*
civil – polite but not very friendly: *I know you don't like him, but try to be civil.*

po·lit·i·cal /pəˈlɪt̬ɪkəl/ *adj.* **1** relating to the government, politics, and the public affairs of a country: *The U.S. has two main political parties.* | *the political issues that are important to senior citizens* **2** relating to the way that different people or groups have power within a system, organization, etc.: *He was promoted for political reasons.* **3** [not before noun] interested in or active in politics: *Mike's never been political.* —**politically** *adv.*: *She's becoming more politically active.*

poˌlitically corˈrect (*abbreviation* **P.C.**) *adj.* politically correct language, behavior, and attitudes are carefully chosen so that they do not offend or insult anyone —**political correctness** *n.* [U]

poˌlitical ˈprisoner *n.* [C] someone who is put in prison because s/he criticizes the government

poˌlitical ˈscience *also* **poli sci** (informal) *n.* [U] the study of politics and government

pol·i·ti·cian /ˌpɑləˈtɪʃən/ *n.* [C] someone who works in politics, especially an elected member of the government

THESAURUS

president – someone who is elected to be the official leader of a country that does not have a king or queen
congressman/congresswoman – someone who is elected to be in Congress
senator – someone who is elected to be a member of the Senate
governor – someone who is elected to lead the government of a state
mayor – someone who is elected to lead the government of a town or city → GOVERNMENT

po·lit·i·cize /pəˈlɪt̬əˌsaɪz/ *v.* [T] to make a situation, position, or organization more political or more involved in politics: *The Olympic Games should not be politicized.* —**politicized** *adj.*

pol·i·tics /ˈpɑlətɪks/ *n.* **1** [U] ideas and activities relating to gaining and using power in a country, city, etc.: *an important figure in American politics* | *a debate about **local/national/international politics*** | *They like to **talk/discuss politics**.* **2** [U] the profession of being a politician: *Smith **went into politics** as a young man.* **3** [plural] the activities of people who are concerned with gaining personal advantage within a group: *Working at home frees you from **office politics**.* **4** [plural] someone's political beliefs and opinions: *I don't agree with her politics.* [ORIGIN: 1500—1600 Greek *politika* (plural), from *politikos*]

pol·ka /ˈpoʊlkə, ˈpoʊkə/ *n.* [C] a very quick simple dance for people dancing in pairs, or the music for this dance —**polka** *v.* [I]

ˈpolka dot *n.* [C] one of a number of round spots that form a pattern, especially on cloth used for clothing: *a white dress with red polka dots* —**polka-dot** *adj.*: *a polka-dot scarf*

poll¹ /poʊl/ *n.* **1** [C] the process of finding out what people think about something by asking many people the same question, or the record of the result: *a recent **opinion poll*** | *a **poll conducted/taken/done** by the New York Times*

THESAURUS

survey – a set of questions that you ask a large number of people in order to find out about their opinions and behavior: ***According to a recent survey**, most Americans think there is too much violence on television.*
questionnaire – a written set of questions about a particular subject that is given to a large number of people, in order to collect information: *Would you have a moment to **fill out** this **questionnaire**?*

2 the polls [plural] the voting in an election: *Voters will **go to the polls*** (=vote) *on Tuesday.*

poll² *v.* [T] to ask a lot of people the same questions in order to find out what they think about a subject: *35% of those polled had been on a diet recently.*

THESAURUS **ask, question, interrogate, inquire** → ASK

ˈpoll book *n.* [C] POLITICS an official record of all the people in a PRECINCT (=area of a town or city with its own local government) who have the legal right to vote

pol·len /ˈpɑlən/ *n.* [U] BIOLOGY a powder produced by flowers, which is carried by the wind or insects to make other flowers of the same type produce seeds

pol·li·nate /ˈpɑləˌneɪt/ *v.* [T] BIOLOGY to make a flower or plant produce seeds by giving it pollen: *Bees pollinate flowers.* —**pollination** /ˌpɑləˈneɪʃən/ *n.* [U]

ˈpolling place *also* **ˈpolling ˌstation** *n.* [C] the place where you can go to vote in an election

poll·ster /ˈpoʊlstɚ/ *n.* [C] someone who works for a company that prepares and asks questions to find out what people think about a particular subject

pol·lut·ant /pə'lutˀnt/ *n.* [C] a substance that makes air, water, soil, etc. dangerously dirty

pol·lute /pə'lut/ *v.* [I,T] to make air, water, soil, etc. dangerously dirty: *Toxic waste is **polluting** the **air/ocean/environment**.* —**polluter** *n.* [C]

pol·lut·ed /pə'luṭɪd/ *adj.* full of pollution: ***heavily/highly/badly polluted** air*

THESAURUS dirty, filthy, soiled → DIRTY[1]

pol·lu·tion /pə'luʃən/ *n.* [U] **1** the process of polluting a place: *Toxic waste is a major cause of pollution.* → ENVIRONMENT **2** substances that pollute a place: *a plan to reduce pollution*

po·lo /'poʊloʊ/ *n.* [U] an outdoor game played between two teams riding horses, who use long wooden hammers to hit a small ball → WATER POLO

'polo shirt *n.* [C] a shirt with short SLEEVES and a collar, usually made of cotton

pol·y·es·ter /'pɑliˌɛstɚ, ˌpɑli'ɛstɚ/ *n.* [U] an artificial material used especially to make cloth: *a polyester suit*

pol·y·eth·yl·ene /ˌpɑli'ɛθəˌlin/ *n.* [U] strong light plastic used for making bags, small containers, etc.

po·lyg·a·my /pə'lɪgəmi/ *n.* [U] the practice of having more than one husband or wife at the same time —**polygamous** *adj.* —**polygamist** *n.* [C]

polygons

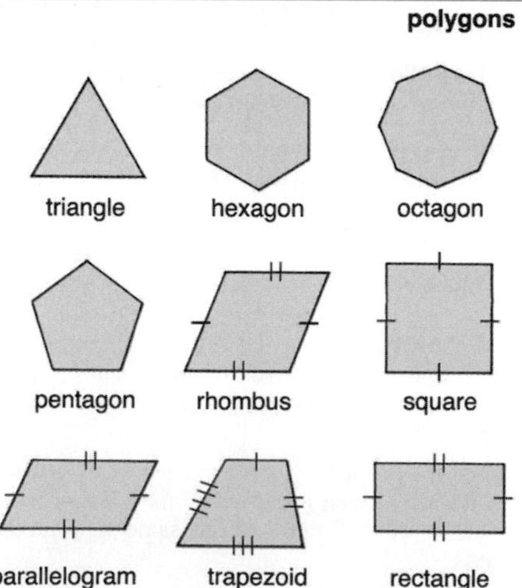

pol·y·gon /'pɑliˌgɑn/ *n.* [C] MATH a flat shape with three or more straight sides [ORIGIN: 1500—1600 Latin, from Greek *polygonon*, from *poly* "many" + *gonia* "angle"]

THESAURUS

pentagon – a flat shape with five sides and five angles
hexagon – a flat shape with six sides and six angles
heptagon – a flat shape with seven sides and seven angles
octagon – a flat shape with eight sides and eight angles
decagon – a flat shape with ten sides and ten angles
dodecagon – a flat shape with twelve sides and twelve angles

pol·y·graph /'pɑliˌgræf/ *n.* [C] a LIE DETECTOR: *The suspect later passed a **polygraph test**.*

pol·y·he·dron /ˌpɑli'hidrən/ *n.* [C] MATH a solid shape with many sides, each of which is a polygon

pol·y·mer /'pɑləmɚ/ *n.* [C] CHEMISTRY a chemical compound that has a simple structure of large MOLECULES

pol·y·no·mi·al /ˌpɑlɪ'noʊmiəl/ *n.* [C] MATH in ALGEBRA, a mathematical expression consisting of two or more MONOMIALS (=a single group of numbers or letters) added together or SUBTRACTed from each other. For example, $7x - 4x + 11$ or $3x^3 + 2x^2 + x - 5$ are polynomials. —**polynomial** *adj.*: *a polynomial equation*

pol·yp /'pɑləp/ *n.* [C] **1** BIOLOGY a small LUMP that grows inside someone's body and is caused by an illness **2** BIOLOGY a sea animal that has a body like a tube, and TENTACLES around an opening in its body that it uses both for eating and for getting rid of waste: *a coral polyp* [ORIGIN: 1300—1400 French *polype*, from Latin *polypus* "octopus," from Greek, from *poly-* "many" + *pous* "foot"]

pol·y·sac·cha·ride /ˌpɑli'sækəˌraɪd/ *n.* [C] BIOLOGY a CARBOHYDRATE consisting of simple sugar MOLECULES that have joined together → MONOSACCHARIDE

pol·y·syl·lab·ic /ˌpɑlisə'læbɪk/ *adj.* ENG. LANG. ARTS a polysyllabic word contains more than three SYLLABLES → DISYLLABIC, MONOSYLLABIC

pol·y·tech·nic /ˌpɑli'tɛknɪk/ *n.* [C] a college where you can study technical or scientific subjects

pol·y·the·ism /'pɑliθiˌɪzəm/ *n.* [U] SOCIAL SCIENCE the belief that there is more than one god —**polytheistic** *adj.*: *polytheistic faiths, such as Hinduism*

pol·y·un·sat·u·rat·ed /ˌpɑliʌn'sætʃəˌreɪṭɪd/ *adj.* polyunsaturated fats or oils come from vegetables and plants, and are considered to be better for your health than animal fats → SATURATED FAT

pom·e·gran·ate /'pɑməˌgrænɪt/ *n.* [C] a round fruit with thick red skin and many juicy red seeds that you can eat

pomp /pɑmp/ *n.* [U] (formal) all the impressive clothes, decorations, music, etc. that are traditional for an important public ceremony

pom·pom /'pɑmpɑm/ *also* **pom·pon** /'pɑmpɑn/ *n.* [C] **1** a large round ball of loose plastic strings connected to a handle, used by CHEERLEADERS **2** a small wool ball used as a decoration on clothing, especially hats

pomp·ous /'pɑmpəs/ *adj.* (disapproving) trying to

make people think you are important, especially by using a lot of formal words: *pompous politicians* —**pomposity** /pɑm'pɑsəṭi/ *n.* [U]

pon·cho /'pɑntʃoʊ/ *n.* (plural **ponchos**) [C] a type of coat that is made from a single piece of thick cloth, with a hole in the middle for your head, and sometimes a HOOD (=cover for your head) [ORIGIN: 1700—1800 American Spanish, Araucanian (a group of South American languages) *pontho* "woolen cloth"]

pond /pɑnd/ *n.* [C] a small area of fresh water that is smaller than a lake [ORIGIN: 1200—1300 Old English *pund*, from Latin *pondo*]

pon·der /'pɑndɚ/ *v.* [I,T] (formal) to spend time thinking carefully and seriously about something: *Travers took a deep breath as he* ***pondered*** *the* ***question.*** [ORIGIN: 1300—1400 Old French *ponderer* "to weigh," from Latin *ponderare*, from *pondus* "weight"]

pon·der·ous /'pɑndərəs/ *adj.* **1** moving slowly or awkwardly because of being very big and heavy: *an elephant's ponderous walk* **2** boring and too serious: *His films are ponderous.*

pon·tiff /'pɑntɪf/ *n.* [C] (formal) the POPE

pon·tif·i·cate /pɑn'tɪfəˌkeɪt/ *v.* [I] to give your opinion about something in a way that shows you think you are always right: *Anthony likes to* ***pontificate about*** *politics.*

pon·toon /pɑn'tun/ *n.* [C] one of the floating metal containers that are attached to bridges, airplanes, etc. in order to make them float

po·ny[1] /'poʊni/ *n.* (plural **ponies**) [C] a small horse

pony[2] *v.* (**ponied**, **ponies**)

pony up (sth) *phr. v.* (informal) to pay for something: *Fans will have to pony up $34.95 to see the boxing match.*

ˌPony Ex'press *n.* HISTORY a mail service in the 1860s that used horses and riders to carry the mail

po·ny·tail /'poʊniˌteɪl/ *n.* [C] long hair that you tie together at the back of your head: *Chrissy pulled her hair back* ***in a ponytail.*** ➔ *see picture on page 462*

pooch /putʃ/ *n.* [C] (informal) a dog

poo·dle /'pudl/ *n.* [C] a dog with thick curly hair [ORIGIN: 1800—1900 German *pudel*, from *pudelhund* "dog that splashes in water"]

pooh-pooh /ˌpu 'pu/ *v.* [T] (informal) to say that you think that an idea, suggestion, etc. is not very good: *At first, they pooh-poohed the idea.*

pool[1] /pul/ *n.* **1** [C] *also* **swimming pool** a structure that has been specially built and filled with water so that people can swim or play in it: *They have a nice pool in their backyard.* **2** [U] a game in which you use a stick to hit numbered balls into holes in the sides and corners of a table: *Let's* ***play/shoot*** *some* ***pool.*** **3 pool of blood/water/oil etc.** a small area of liquid on a surface: *Creighton lay there in a pool of blood.* **4 pool of light** a small area of light shining on something **5** [C] a small area of still water in the ground: *Mosquitoes breed in stagnant pools of water.* **6** [C] a group of people who are available to work or to do an activity when they are needed: *a* ***pool of*** *volunteers* | *a jury pool* **7** [C] a group of things or an amount of money that is owned or shared by a group of people: *Banks lend money from the huge* ***pool of*** *money that people have saved with them.*

pool[2] *v.* [T] to combine your money, ideas, skills, etc. with those of other people so that you can all use them: *If we* ***pool*** *our* ***resources,*** *we can start our own business.*

'pool hall *n.* [C] a building where people go to play pool

'pool ˌtable *n.* [C] a cloth-covered table with pockets at the corners and sides, used for playing pool

poop[1] /pup/ *n.* [singular, U] (spoken) solid waste from your BOWELS, or the act of passing waste: *dog poop*

poop[2] *v.* [I,T] (informal) to pass solid waste from your BOWELS

pooped /pupt/ *also* **ˌpooped 'out** *adj.* (spoken) very tired: *I'm pooped!*

poop·er scoop·er /'pupɚ ˌskupɚ/ *n.* [C] (informal) a small SHOVEL and a container, used by dog owners for removing their dogs' solid waste from the streets

poor /pʊr, pɔr/ *adj.* **1** having very little money and not many possessions: *She comes from a poor family.* | *a poor country*

THESAURUS

needy – having very little food or money: *The program provides health care to needy families.*
destitute (formal) – having no money, no place to live, no food, etc.: *The Depression left many farmers completely destitute.*
impoverished (formal) – very poor: *an impoverished neighborhood in Chicago*
broke – not having any money for a period of time: *I'm broke and I need a job.*
impecunious (formal) – having very little money, especially over a long period of time: *an impecunious student*
indigent (formal) – not having much money or many possessions: *The funding is for indigent hospital patients.*
penurious (formal) – lacking money and therefore poor: *my penurious financial status*
poverty-stricken (written) – extremely poor: *a poverty-stricken neighborhood*

Poor and having social problems
disadvantaged – having social problems, such as a lack of money, that make it difficult to succeed: *students from disadvantaged backgrounds*
underprivileged – poor and not having the advantages of most other people in society: *The center helps underprivileged children.*
deprived – not having the things that are

considered necessary for a comfortable or happy life: *a deprived area in the inner city*

2 the poor people who are poor: *The charity distributes food to the poor.* **3** not as good as it could be or should be: *The soil in this part of the country is poor.* | *poor health* **4** [only before noun] (spoken) said in order to show pity for someone because s/he is unlucky, unhappy, etc.: *Poor Stacy – her mother's very sick.* | *The* ***poor thing*** *looks like she hasn't eaten in days.* **5** not good at doing something: *a poor student* [ORIGIN: 1100—1200 Old French *povre*, from Latin *pauper*]

P

poor·ly /ˈpʊrli, ˈpɔr-/ *adv.* badly: *a poorly lit room*

pop[1] /pɑp/ *v.* (**popped**, **popping**) **1** [I,T] to suddenly make a short sound like a small explosion, especially when something bursts, or to make something do this: *Jody squeezed the* ***balloon*** *until it* ***popped.***

THESAURUS **break, burst** ➔ BREAK[1]

2 [I] (spoken) to go somewhere quickly, suddenly, or without planning: *I need to* ***pop into*** *the drugstore for a second.* | *Maybe I'll just* ***pop in on*** *Terry* (=visit him for a short time). **3** [I] to come suddenly or without warning out of or away from something: *A button* ***popped off*** *my jacket.* | *The ball* ***popped out*** *of her hands and rolled under the sofa.* **4** [T] to cook popcorn until it bursts open **5** [I] if your ears pop, you feel the pressure in them suddenly change, for example when you go up in an airplane **6 pop the question** (informal) to ask someone to marry you: *Has Dan popped the question yet?* **7** [T] (informal) to hit someone: *If you say that again, I'll pop you.* [ORIGIN: 1300—1400 From the sound]

pop out *phr. v.* (informal) to say something suddenly without thinking about it first: *I didn't mean to say that – it just popped out.*

pop up *phr. v.* (informal) to happen or appear suddenly or without warning: *Her name keeps popping up in the newspapers.*

pop[2] *n.* **1** [U] *also* **ˈpop ˌmusic** modern music that is popular with young people: *a pop concert* **2** [C usually singular] (old-fashioned) father **3** [U] (informal) a sweet drink with bubbles but no alcohol

THESAURUS **soft drink, soda, soda pop** ➔ SOFT DRINK

4 [C] a sudden short sound like a small explosion: *the pop of an air rifle* **5 pops** [U] CLASSICAL MUSIC that is known and liked even by people who do not usually like classical music: *the Boston Pops Orchestra*

pop·corn /ˈpɑpkɔrn/ *n.* [U] a type of corn that swells and bursts open when heated, usually eaten warm with butter and salt

Pope /poʊp/ *n.* [C] the leader of the Roman Catholic Church: *the Pope's recent visit* | *Pope Paul VI* [ORIGIN: 800—900 Late Latin *papa*, from Greek *papas* "father," used as a title of bishops]

pop·lar /ˈpɑplɚ/ *n.* [C] a very tall thin tree that grows very fast ➔ *see picture on page A23*

ˌpop psyˈchology *n.* [U] the ways in which people's personal problems are dealt with on television or in books, but which are not considered scientific

pop·py /ˈpɑpi/ *n.* (plural **poppies**) [C] a brightly colored flower, usually red, with small black seeds

ˈpop quiz *n.* [C] a short test that is given without any warning in order to check that students have been studying

Pop·si·cle /ˈpɑpsɪkəl/ *n.* [C] (trademark) frozen fruit juice on a stick

pop·u·lace /ˈpɑpyələs/ *n.* [singular] (formal) the ordinary people living in a country

THESAURUS **people, the public, society, population** ➔ PEOPLE[1]

pop·u·lar /ˈpɑpyəlɚ/ *adj.* **1** liked by a lot of people: *His movies have become very popular.* | *the most popular kid in school* | *Tom is very* ***popular with*** *women.*

THESAURUS

bestseller – a book that a lot of people buy
blockbuster – a movie that a lot of people watch, especially an exciting movie
hit – a movie, song, play, etc. that a lot of people pay to see or listen to
craze/fad – a fashion, game, etc. that is very popular for a short time
cult – used about a movie or a performer that is very popular among a certain group of people: *cult movies*

2 shared, accepted, or done by a lot of people: *The party had managed to gain massive popular support.* | *Despite* ***popular opinion/belief*** (=what most people think), *not everybody in Fayette County is rich.* **3** relating to ordinary people, or intended for ordinary people: *Ramsay believes there's too much violence in American* ***popular culture*** (=TV, pop music, action films, etc.). [ORIGIN: 1400—1500 Latin *popularis*, from *populus* "people"]

pop·u·lar·i·ty /ˌpɑpyəˈlærət̬i/ *n.* [U] the quality of being liked or supported by a large number of people: *the growing* ***popularity of*** *electronic music*

pop·u·lar·ize /ˈpɑpyələˌraɪz/ *v.* [T] to make something well known and liked: *His books have helped popularize science.*

pop·u·lar·ly /ˈpɑpyəlɚli/ *adv.* by most people: *It's popularly believed that people need eight hours of sleep every night.*

pop·u·late /ˈpɑpyəˌleɪt/ *v.* [T] if an area is populated by a particular group of people, they live there: *They live in a neighborhood that is* ***densely/***

heavily populated *by students* (=has a lot of students living there). | *a* ***sparsely populated*** *area* (=with few people)

pop·u·la·tion /ˌpɑpyəˈleɪʃən/ *n.* [C,U] **1** the number of people or animals living in a particular area, country, etc.: *What's the* ***population of*** *New York?* | *There was a* ***population explosion*** (=a sudden large increase in population) *between 1944 and 1964 in the U.S.* **2** all of the people who live in a particular area or share a particular condition: *Most of the population of Canada lives fairly near the U.S. border.* | *Florida has a large Hispanic population.*

THESAURUS people, the public, society, populace → PEOPLE[1]

pop·u·lous /ˈpɑpyələs/ *adj.* (formal) having a large population: *the most populous country in Africa*

ˈpop-up *n.* [C] IT a window, often containing an advertisement, that suddenly appears on a computer screen when you are looking at a WEBSITE —**pop-up** *adj.* [only before noun]: *Google does not allow* ***pop-up ads*** *of any kind on its site.*

por·ce·lain /ˈpɔrsəlɪn/ *n.* [U] a hard shiny white substance that is used for making expensive plates, cups, etc., or objects made of this

porch /pɔrtʃ/ *n.* [C] a structure built onto a house at its front or back entrance, with a floor and roof but no walls [ORIGIN: 1200—1300 Old French *porche*, from Latin *porticus*, from *porta* "gate"]

por·cu·pine /ˈpɔrkyəˌpaɪn/ *n.* [C] an animal with long sharp needle-like parts growing all over its back and sides

pore[1] /pɔr/ *n.* [C] one of the small holes in your skin or in a leaf, that liquid can pass through

pore[2] *v.*

pore over sth *phr. v.* to read or look at something very carefully for a long time: *We spent all day poring over wedding magazines.*

pork /pɔrk/ *n.* [U] **1** the meat from pigs: *pork chops* **2** (slang, disapproving) government money spent in a particular area in order to get political advantages [ORIGIN: 1200—1300 Old French *porc* "pig," from Latin *porcus*]

por·nog·ra·phy /pɔrˈnɑgrəfi/ *also* **porn** /pɔrn/ *n.* [U] magazines, movies, etc. that show sexual acts and images in a way that is intended to make people feel sexually excited —**pornographer** *n.* [C] —**pornographic** /ˌpɔrnəˈgræfɪk◂/ *adj.*

po·rous /ˈpɔrəs/ *adj.* allowing liquid, air, etc. to pass through slowly: *porous soil*

por·poise /ˈpɔrpəs/ *n.* [C] a large sea animal, similar to a DOLPHIN, that breathes air

por·ridge /ˈpɔrɪdʒ, ˈpɑ-/ *n.* [U] cooked OATMEAL

port /pɔrt/ *n.* **1** [C,U] a place where ships can be loaded and unloaded: *The ship was back* ***in port*** *after a week at sea.* **2** [C] a town or city with a HARBOR: *the port of Veracruz* **3** [C] IT a place on the outside of a computer where you can connect another piece of equipment, such as a PRINTER **4** [U] a strong sweet Portuguese wine **5** [U] the left side of a ship or aircraft when you are looking toward the front → STARBOARD [ORIGIN: (5) 1500—1600 *port side*; because it was the side from which ships were unloaded.]

port·a·ble /ˈpɔrt̬əbəl/ *adj.* light and easily carried or moved: *a portable phone/computer* —**portable** *n.* [C]

portable

a portable TV

por·tal /ˈpɔrt̬l/ *n.* [C] **1** IT a website that helps you find other websites **2** (literary) a large gate or entrance to a building

por·tend /pɔrˈtɛnd/ *v.* [T] (literary) to be a sign that something is going to happen, especially something bad: *Do these strange events portend some great disaster?*

por·tent /ˈpɔrtɛnt/ *n.* [C] (literary) a sign or warning that something is going to happen: *I hope their cooperation is a* ***portent of*** *the future.* → OMEN

por·ter /ˈpɔrt̬ɚ/ *n.* [C] **1** someone whose job is to carry travelers' bags at airports, hotels, etc. **2** someone whose job is to take care of the part of a train where people sleep

port·fo·li·o /pɔrtˈfoʊliˌoʊ/ *n.* (plural **portfolios**) [C] **1** a large flat case used especially for carrying pictures, documents, etc. **2** ENG. LANG. ARTS a collection of pictures or other pieces of work by an artist, photographer, etc.: *You'll need to submit a* ***portfolio of*** *your work along with your application.* **3** ECONOMICS a collection of STOCK owned by a particular person or company: *an investment portfolio* [ORIGIN: 1700—1800 Italian *portafoglio*, from *portare* "to carry" + *foglio* "leaf, sheet"]

port·hole /ˈpɔrthoʊl/ *n.* [C] a small window on the side of a ship or airplane

por·ti·co /ˈpɔrt̬ɪˌkoʊ/ *n.* (plural **porticoes** *or* **porticos**) [C] a covered entrance to a building, consisting of a roof supported by PILLARS

por·tion[1] /ˈpɔrʃən/ (Ac) *n.* [C] **1** a part of something larger: *The news showed only a* ***portion of*** *the interview.* | *He sends a* ***large portion*** *of his salary home to El Salvador.* | *Only a* ***small portion*** *of the total data was examined.* → PART[1] **2** an amount of food for one person, especially when served in a restaurant: *Do you have children's portions?* | *Everyone was given a small* ***portion of*** *rice and beans.* **3** a share of something such as blame or a duty: *Both drivers must bear a* ***portion of*** *the blame.*

portion[2] *v.*

portion sth ↔ **out** *phr. v.* to divide something into

P

parts and give them to several people: *Land was portioned out to new settlers.*

port·ly /ˈpɔrtli/ *adj.* (written) someone who is portly, especially an old man, is fat and round: *a portly gentleman*

por·trait /ˈpɔrtrɪt/ *n.* [C] **1** a painting, drawing, or photograph of a person: *a family portrait* → *see picture at* PAINTING

> THESAURUS **picture, sketch, painting, cartoon, caricature, illustration** → PICTURE[1]

2 a description of someone or something in a book, movie, etc.: *The movie is a* ***portrait of*** *life in Harlem in the 1940s.*

P

por·trai·ture /ˈpɔrtrɪtʃɚ/ *n.* [U] (formal) the art of painting or drawing pictures of people

por·tray /pɔrˈtreɪ, pɚ-/ *v.* (**portrayed, portrays**) [T] **1 portray sb/sth as sth** to describe or show someone or something in a particular way, according to your opinion of him/her: *Each candidate portrayed himself as an enemy of big business.*

> THESAURUS **call, describe, characterize, label, brand** → CALL[1]

2 to describe or represent something or someone: *The movie portrays the life of Charlie Chaplin.* **3** to act the part of a character in a play: *Dan Radcliffe portrayed Harry Potter in the movies.*

por·tray·al /pɔrˈtreɪəl, pɚ-/ *n.* [C,U] the way someone or something is described or shown in a book, film, play, etc.: *an* ***accurate portrayal*** *of pioneer life*

Por·tu·guese[1] /ˌpɔrtʃəˈgiz◂ / *adj.* relating to or coming from Portugal

Portuguese[2] *n.* **1** [U] the language of Portugal, Brazil, and some other countries **2 the Portuguese** [plural] the people of Portugal

pose[1] /poʊz/ (Ac) *v.* **1 pose a problem/threat/challenge etc.** to exist in a way that may cause a problem, danger, difficulty, etc.: *Nuclear waste poses a threat to the environment.* | *The list of problems posed by global warming is growing.* **2** [I,T] to sit or stand in a particular position in order to be photographed or painted, or to make someone do this: *The astronauts* ***posed for*** *pictures near the shuttle.* **3 pose a question** to ask a question that needs to be thought about carefully: *Nielsen's essay poses some tough questions.* **4 pose as sb** to pretend to be someone else in order to deceive people: *The thief got in by posing as a repairman.*

pose[2] *n.* [C] the position in which someone deliberately stands or sits, especially in a painting or photograph: *She* ***struck a pose*** (=stood or sat in a particular position) *with her head to one side.*

pos·er /ˈpoʊzɚ/ *n.* [C] someone who pretends to have a quality or social position s/he does not have, in order to seem impressive to other people

posh /pɑʃ/ *adj.* expensive and used by rich people: *a posh hotel*

> THESAURUS **expensive, high, pricey, overpriced, fancy** → EXPENSIVE

po·si·tion[1] /pəˈzɪʃən/ *n.*

1 STANDING/SITTING [C] the way someone stands, sits, or lies, or the direction in which an object is pointing: *You should be* ***in*** *a comfortable* ***position*** *when driving.* | *This exercise is done in* ***a sitting/standing/kneeling position.***

2 SITUATION [C usually singular] the situation that someone or something is in: *The company is in a dangerous financial position right now.* | *I'm not sure what I would do if I were* ***in*** *your* ***position.*** | *I'm afraid I'm* ***not in a position to*** *help you* (=do not have the power or money to help you).

3 OPINION [C] an opinion about a particular subject: *The senator has changed his* ***position on*** *abortion.*

> THESAURUS **opinion, view, point of view, stance, attitude** → OPINION

4 PLACE [C,U] the place where someone or something is, in relation to other things: *Help me put the furniture back* ***in position.*** | *The army took up* ***strategic positions*** *around the capital.*

> THESAURUS **place, spot, point, location, site, scene** → PLACE[1]

5 JOB [C] a job: *He decided to give up his* ***position as*** *coach of the football team.*

> THESAURUS
>
> **Describing types of positions**
>
> **senior** – used about someone who has an important position in a company or organization: *a senior executive*
>
> **chief** – used about someone who has the most important or one of the most important positions in a company or organization, used especially in job titles: *the company's chief financial officer*
>
> **high-ranking** – used about someone who has a high position in an organization such as the police, the army, or the government: *high-ranking military officers*
>
> **top** – used about someone who is in a very high position in a large company or organization, or someone in an important profession, for example a lawyer or a doctor, who is very successful in his/her job: *the top executives of some of the country's biggest corporations* | *one of the agency's top lawyers*
>
> **junior** – used about someone who does not have an important position or who has less experience than someone doing the same job: *the junior senator from Mississippi*
>
> **assistant** – an assistant manager, director, editor, etc. has a position just below a manager, etc.: *the store's assistant manager*
>
> **job, work, employment, post, occupation** → JOB

6 RANK [C] the level or rank someone has in a society or organization: *Ask someone in a* ***position***

of authority. | *a study on the* ***position of*** *minorities in our society*

7 SPORTS [C] the area where someone plays in a sport, or the type of actions s/he is responsible for doing in a game: *"What* ***position*** *do you* ***play****?" "Second base."*

8 RACE/COMPETITION [C,U] the place of someone or something in a race or competition in relation to the other people or things (SYN) **place**: *Paldi has moved into* ***first/second/third etc. position****.*

position² *v.* [T] to put something or someone in a particular place: *Police positioned themselves around the bank.*

pos·i·tive¹ /ˈpɑzət̮ɪv/ (Ac) *adj.* **1** [not before noun] very sure that something is right or true: *"Are you sure you don't want a drink?" "Positive."* | *I'm* ***positive that*** *I told her to meet us here at 2 o'clock.*

THESAURUS sure, certain, convinced, confident → SURE¹

2 hopeful and confident, and thinking about what is good in a situation rather than what is bad (ANT) **negative**: *The president sounded very* ***positive about*** *the state of the economy.* | *I always try to have a* ***positive attitude****.* **3** good or useful (ANT) **negative**: *At least* ***something positive*** *has come out of the situation.* | *Living abroad has been* ***a positive experience*** *for Jim.* | *We need to provide girls with more* ***positive role models*** (=good or successful people that they will want to be like). **4** expressing support, agreement, or approval (ANT) **negative**: *So far, we've had mostly positive reactions to the new show.* **5** a medical or scientific test that is positive shows signs of what is being looked for (ANT) **negative**: *He was banned after* ***testing positive*** *for drugs.* | *Her pregnancy test* ***came back/up/out positive****.* **6** MATH a positive number or quantity is higher than zero. (+) is the positive sign. (ANT) **negative**: *If you square any number, it gives you a positive number.* **7** PHYSICS having the type of electrical charge that is carried by PROTONS, shown by a (+) sign on a BATTERY (ANT) **negative**: *Each battery has a positive and negative terminal.* **8** BIOLOGY having RHESUS FACTOR in your blood (ANT) **negative**: *His blood type is AB positive.*

positive² *n.* [C] a quality or feature that is good or useful (ANT) **negative**: *You can find positives in any situation.*

pos·i·tive·ly /ˈpɑzət̮ɪvli, ˌpɑzəˈtɪvli◂/ (Ac) *adv.* **1** (informal) used in order to emphasize what you are saying: *Some patients positively enjoy being in the hospital.* | *This is positively the last time I'm going to say this.* **2** in a way that shows you agree with something and want it to succeed: *News of the changes was received positively.* **3** in a way that leaves no doubt: *Don't tell anyone unless you're positively certain you can trust them.* **4** PHYSICS having the type of electrical charge that is carried by PROTONS: *A positively charged ion has lost some electrons.* → **think positively** *at* THINK

pos·it·ron /ˈpɑzəˌtrɑn/ *n.* [C] PHYSICS a PARTICLE (=very small piece of matter) that has the same mass as an ELECTRON but has a positive electrical CHARGE

pos·se /ˈpɑsi/ *n.* [C] **1** a group of men gathered together in past times by a SHERIFF (=local law officer) to help catch criminals **2** (informal) someone's group of friends – used especially by young people

pos·sess /pəˈzɛs/ *v.* [T] **1** (formal) to own or have something: *Neither of them possessed a credit card.* | *Bauer was charged with possessing illegal weapons.*

THESAURUS own, have → OWN²

2 what possessed sb (to do sth)? (spoken) said when you cannot understand why someone did something stupid: *What possessed you to buy such an expensive gift?* [ORIGIN: 1300–1400 Old French *possesser*, from Latin *possidere*] —**possessor** *n.* [C]

pos·sessed /pəˈzɛst/ *adj.* controlled by an evil spirit

pos·ses·sion /pəˈzɛʃən/ *n.* **1** [C usually plural] something that you own (SYN) **belongings**: *When they left, they had to sell most of their possessions.* **2** [U] (formal) the state of having or owning something: *He was found* ***in possession of*** *stolen property.* | *China* ***took possession of*** *Hong Kong in 1997.*

pos·ses·sive¹ /pəˈzɛsɪv/ *adj.* **1** (disapproving) wanting someone to have feelings of love or friendship only for you: *I love Dave, but he's very possessive.* **2** unwilling to let other people use something you own: *As a child, she was very* ***possessive of*** *her toys.*

possessive² *n.* **the possessive** ENG. LANG. ARTS in grammar, a word such as "my," "its," "their," etc., used in order to show that one thing or person belongs to another thing or person, or is related to that thing or person —**possessive** *adj.*: *a possessive adjective/pronoun*

pos·si·bil·i·ty /ˌpɑsəˈbɪlət̮i/ *n.* (plural **possibilities**) **1** [C,U] if there is a possibility that something is true or that something will happen, it might be true or it might happen: *There's always the* ***possibility (that)*** *we may all lose our jobs.* | *There's a* ***strong possibility*** *he won't be able to play on Sunday.* | *Is there a* ***possibility of*** *getting a scholarship?* **2** [C] an opportunity to do something, or something that can be done or tried: *We want to* ***explore*** *all the* ***possibilities****.* | *the almost endless* ***possibilities for*** *sales growth*

pos·si·ble /ˈpɑsəbəl/ *adj.* **1 as long/much/soon etc. as possible** as long, much, etc. as you can: *They need the information as quickly as possible.* | *Keep him busy for as long as possible.* **2** able to be done, or likely to happen, exist, or be true → IMPOSSIBLE: *Icy conditions are possible along the coast.* | ***Is it possible to*** *use the*

P

program on a Macintosh? | *Computer technology now* ***makes it possible*** *for people to work at home.* | *This is the* ***best/worst possible*** *result* (=it can be no better or worse). **3 would it be possible (for sb) to do sth?** (spoken) said when asking politely if you can do or have something: *Would it be possible to exchange these gloves?* **4 whenever/wherever possible** every time you have an opportunity to do something: *She visits her grandmother whenever possible.* [ORIGIN: 1300—1400 French, Latin *possibilis*, from *posse* "to be able"]

pos·si·bly /'pɑsəbli/ *adv.* **1** used when saying that something may be true or likely SYN **perhaps**: *The trial will take place soon, possibly next week.* | *This new drug could* ***quite possibly*** (=very likely) *save thousands of lives.* **2** used with MODAL VERBS, especially "can" and "could," to emphasize that something is or is not possible: *I couldn't possibly eat all that!* | *We did everything we possibly could to help them.* **3 could/can you possibly...?** (spoken) said when politely asking someone to do something: *Could you possibly turn the radio down?*

pos·sum /'pɑsəm/ *n.* [C] (informal) an OPOSSUM

post[1] /poʊst/ *n.* [C] **1** a strong upright piece of wood, metal, etc. that is set into the ground, especially to support something: *a fence post* | *the goal posts* **2** (formal) an important job, especially in the government or military: *She decided to leave her post at the Justice Department.*

THESAURUS **job, work, employment, position** ➔ JOB

3 the place where a soldier, guard, etc. is expected to be in order to do his/her job: *The guards cannot* ***leave*** *their* ***posts***. **4** a military BASE (=place where soldiers live and work)

post[2] *v.* [T] **1 a)** to put a public notice about something on a wall or BULLETIN BOARD: *They've posted warning signs on the gate.* **b)** IT to put a message or computer document on the Internet so that other people can see it: *FBI agents have posted a message on the Internet describing the suspect.* **2** if someone who works for the government or military is posted somewhere, s/he is sent to work there, usually for several years: *His regiment have been* ***posted to*** *Germany.* **3** ECONOMICS if a company posts its profits, sales, losses, etc., it records the money gained or lost in its accounts: *In the final quarter, the company posted $12.4 million in earnings.*

post·age /'poʊstɪdʒ/ *n.* [U] the money charged for sending a letter, package, etc. by mail: *Please add $3.95 for* ***postage and handling*** (=the charge for packing and sending something you have bought).

'postage stamp *n.* [C] (formal) a STAMP

post·al /'poʊstl/ *adj.* relating to the official mail system that takes letters from one place to another: *postal workers*

'postal ˌservice *n.* **the postal service** the public service for carrying letters, packages, etc. from one part of the country to another

post·card /'poʊstkɑrd/ *n.* [C] a card, often with a picture on the front, that can be sent in the mail without an envelope: ***Send*** *me* ***a postcard*** *while you're away.*

post·date /ˌpoʊst'deɪt/ *v.* [T] to write a check with a date that is later than the actual date, so that it cannot be used until that time

post·er /'poʊstɚ/ *n.* [C] a large printed notice, picture, etc. used in order to advertise something or as a decoration: *a poster of Bob Marley*

THESAURUS **advertisement, commercial, billboard** ➔ ADVERTISEMENT
picture, sketch, painting, snapshot, portrait, cartoon, caricature, illustration ➔ PICTURE[1]

pos·te·ri·or /pɑ'stɪriɚ, poʊ-/ *n.* [C] (humorous) the part of the body you sit on

pos·ter·i·ty /pɑ'stɛrət̬i/ *n.* [U] all the people in the future who will be alive after you are dead: *I'm saving these pictures* ***for posterity***.

post·grad·u·ate /ˌpoʊst'grædʒuɪt/ *adj.* relating to the work people do when studying to obtain a higher degree after college: *a postgraduate scholarship* ➔ STUDENT

post·hu·mous /'pɑstʃəməs/ *adj.* happening after someone's death: *a posthumous award* —**posthumously** *adv.*

'Post-it *n.* [C] (trademark) a small piece of paper that sticks to things, used for leaving notes for people

post·man /'poʊstmən/ *n.* (plural **postmen** /-mən/) [C] a MAILMAN

post·mark /'poʊstmɑrk/ *n.* [C] an official mark made on a letter, package, etc. that shows the place and time it was sent —**postmark** *v.* [T]: *The card is postmarked Dec. 2.*

post·mas·ter /'poʊstˌmæstɚ/ *n.* [C] the person in charge of a post office

post·mor·tem /ˌpoʊst'mɔrt̬əm/ *n.* [C] an examination of a dead body to discover why the person died

'post ˌoffice *n.* [C] a place where you can buy stamps, and send letters, packages, etc.

'post office ˌbox *n.* [C] a P.O. BOX

post·par·tum /ˌpoʊst'pɑrt̬əm◂/ *adj.* relating to the time just after a woman has a baby: *postpartum depression*

post·pone /poʊst'poʊn/ *v.* [T] to change an event to a later time or date ➔ CANCEL: *The game was postponed because of rain.* [ORIGIN: 1400—1500 Latin *postponere*, from *post* "after" + *ponere* "to put"] —**postponement** *n.* [C,U]

THESAURUS **delay, put off, procrastinate, defer** ➔ DELAY[1]

post·script /ˈpoʊstˌskrɪpt/ (*written abbreviation* **P.S.**) *n.* [C] a message written at the end of a letter below the place where you sign your name [ORIGIN: 1500—1600 Modern Latin *postscriptum*, from Latin *postscribere* "to write after"]

pos·tu·late /ˈpɑstʃəˌleɪt/ *v.* [T] (formal) to suggest that something might have happened or might be true

pos·ture /ˈpɑstʃɚ/ *n.* [C,U] the position you hold your body in when you sit or stand: *Poor posture can lead to back trouble.*

post·war /ˈpoʊstwɔr/ *adj.* [only before noun] happening or existing after a war: *the postwar years* | *postwar prosperity*

po·sy /ˈpoʊzi/ *n.* (plural **posies**) [C] (literary) a small BUNCH of flowers

pot¹ /pɑt/ *n.* **1** [C] a container used for cooking, that is round, deep, and usually made of metal, or the amount this container holds ➔ JAR, PAN, SAUCEPAN: *pots and pans* | *a* ***pot of*** *soup* **2** [C] a container with a handle and a small tube for pouring, used for making coffee or tea ➔ JUG: *a coffee pot* **3** [C] a container for a plant (SYN) **flowerpot**: *The plant needs a new pot.* **4 go to pot** (informal) if an organization or a place goes to pot, its condition becomes worse because no one takes care of it: *The farm has gone to pot since my uncle died.* **5 the pot** (informal) all the money that people have risked in a game of cards **6** [U] (informal) MARIJUANA [ORIGIN: Old English *pott*]

pot² *v.* (**potted**, **potting**) [T] to put a plant in a pot filled with soil

po·ta·ble /ˈpoʊt̬əbəl/ *adj.* (formal) potable water is safe to drink

po·tas·si·um /pəˈtæsiəm/ *n.* [U] CHEMISTRY (*symbol* **K**) a silver-white soft metal that is an ELEMENT and is used in making soaps and FERTILIZERS [ORIGIN: 1800—1900 Modern Latin, English *potash*]

po·ta·to /pəˈteɪt̬oʊ, -t̬ə/ *n.* (plural **potatoes**) [C,U] a hard round white root with a brown, red, or pale yellow skin, cooked and eaten as a vegetable: ***mashed/baked/fried/boiled potatoes*** [ORIGIN: 1500—1600 Spanish *batata*, from Taino (a Caribbean language)] ➔ *see picture at* VEGETABLE

po'tato chip *n.* [C] one of many thin hard pieces of potato that have been cooked in oil, and that are sold in packages: *a* ***bag of potato chips***

pot·bel·ly /ˈpɑt˺ˌbɛli/ *n.* (plural **potbellies**) [C] a large round stomach that sticks out —**potbellied** *adj.*

po·ten·cy /ˈpoʊt˺nsi/ *n.* [U] **1** the strength of the effect of a drug, medicine, alcohol, etc. on your mind or body: *high-potency vitamins* **2** a man's ability to have sex

po·tent /ˈpoʊt˺nt/ *adj.* powerful and effective: *a potent weapons system* | *potent drugs*

po·ten·tate /ˈpoʊt˺nˌteɪt/ *n.* [C] (literary) a ruler with direct power over his people

po·ten·tial¹ /pəˈtɛnʃəl/ (Ac) *adj.* likely to develop into a particular type of person or thing in the future: *Brush regularly and avoid potential problems with your teeth.* | ***potential customers/buyers*** | *Today, acid rain is a potential threat to crops in the region.* [ORIGIN: 1300—1400 Late Latin *potentialis*, from Latin *potentia* "power"]

potential² *n.* **1** [singular, U] the possibility that something will develop or happen in a particular way: *There's* ***a potential for*** *conflict in the area.* | *It hasn't lived up to its potential.* | *The area has great economic potential.* **2** [U] a natural ability that could develop to make you very good at something: *She* ***has/shows potential*** *as a singer.* | *We want a society in which children can grow and achieve their potential.*

P

poˌtential 'difference *n.* [C] PHYSICS the difference in electrical force between two points in an electric CIRCUIT, measured in VOLTS

poˌtential 'energy *n.* [U] PHYSICS the energy that is stored in physical matter when it is not moving ➔ KINETIC ENERGY

po·ten·tial·ly /pəˈtɛnʃəli/ (Ac) *adv.* something that is potentially dangerous, useful, etc. is not dangerous, etc. now, but may become so in the future: *a potentially embarrassing situation* | *a potentially fatal disease* (=one that could kill you) | *Wind power would bring potentially significant environmental benefits.*

pot·hold·er /ˈpɑtˌhoʊldɚ/ *n.* [C] a piece of thick material used for holding hot cooking pans

pot·hole /ˈpɑthoʊl/ *n.* [C] a hole in the surface of a road that makes driving difficult

po·tion /ˈpoʊʃən/ *n.* [C] (literary) a drink intended to have a special or magic effect on the person who drinks it: *a love potion*

pot·luck¹ /ˌpɑtˈlʌk◂/ *n.* **take potluck** (informal) to choose something without knowing very much about it: *Nobody knew about any good restaurants, so we took potluck.*

potluck² *adj.* **a potluck meal/dinner etc.** a meal in which everyone who is invited brings something to eat

ˌpot 'pie *n.* [C] meat and vegetables covered with PASTRY and baked in a deep dish: *chicken pot pie*

pot·pour·ri /ˌpoʊpʊˈri/ *n.* [U] a mixture of dried flowers and leaves kept in a bowl to make a room smell nice

pot·ter·y /ˈpɑt̬əri/ *n.* [U] **1** the activity of making objects out of baked clay ➔ CERAMICS: *a pottery class* **2** objects made out of baked clay: *Native American pottery* —**potter** *n.* [C]

pot·ty /ˈpɑt̬i/ *n.* (plural **potties**) [C] (spoken) a word meaning a toilet, used when speaking to children

pouch /paʊtʃ/ *n.* [C] **1** a small leather or cloth bag that you can keep things in **2** a pocket of skin on the stomach that MARSUPIALS keep their babies in

poul·try /ˈpoʊltri/ *n.* [U] birds such as chickens, that are kept on farms for supplying eggs and meat, or the meat from these birds

pounce

pounce /paʊns/ *v.* [I] to suddenly jump on a person or animal after waiting to catch him, her, or it: *He **pounced on** my back, forcing me to the ground.*

pounce on sb/sth *phr. v.* to criticize someone's mistakes or ideas very quickly and eagerly: *Republicans quickly pounced on the president's proposal.*

pound¹ /paʊnd/ *n.* [C] **1** (*written abbreviation* **lb**) a unit for measuring weight, equal to 16 OUNCEs or 453.6 grams: *a **pound of** apples* | *Jim **weighs** 175 **pounds**.* | *She's **lost/gained** ten **pounds** this year* (=her weight has gone down or up by 10 pounds). **2 the pound** a place where lost dogs and cats are kept until the owner claims them **3** the standard unit of money in the U.K. and some other countries: *It cost three pounds.* | *a ten-pound note* [ORIGIN: (3) Old English *pund*, from Latin *pondo*]

pound² *v.* **1** [I,T] to hit something several times to make a lot of noise, damage it, make it lie flat, etc.: *Thomas **pounded on** the desk with his fist.* | *The man suddenly began **pounding** his head **against** the wall.* | *The women pounded the grain to make flour.*

> THESAURUS **hit, beat, strike, knock, bang, rap, hammer** → HIT¹

2 [T] to attack a place continuously for a long time with bombs: *Enemy guns pounded the city until morning.* **3** [I] if your heart pounds, it beats very quickly **4** [I] to walk or run quickly with heavy loud steps: *I heard the sound of heavy boots pounding on the floor.*

ˈpound cake *n.* [C] a heavy cake made from flour, sugar, eggs, and butter

pour /pɔr/ *v.* **1** [T] to make a liquid or a substance such as salt or sand flow out of or into something: *She poured coffee for everyone.* | *Could you pour me a glass of lemonade, please?* → *see picture on page A18* **2** [I] to rain heavily without stopping: *It's been pouring all afternoon.* **3** [I] to flow quickly and in large amounts: *Fuel **poured out of** the plane.*

> THESAURUS
> **flow** – to move in a steady continuous stream: *This is the place where the river flows into the ocean.*
> **drip** – to produce small drops of liquid, or to fall in drops: *Water dripped onto the floor.*
> **leak** – if a liquid leaks, it passes through a hole or crack: *Oil leaked from the damaged tanker.*
> **ooze** – to flow from something very slowly: *Blood oozed through the bandages.*
> **gush** – to flow or pour out quickly in large quantities: *Water gushed from the fountain.*
> **spurt** – to flow out suddenly with a lot of force: *Blood spurted from the wound.*
> **run** – to flow: *Tears ran down her cheeks.*
> **come out** – to pour out of a container, place, etc.: *I turned on the faucet, but no water came out.*

4 [I] if people or things pour into or out of a place, a lot of them arrive or leave at the same time: *Letters are **pouring in** from people all over the state.* | *People **poured out of** their houses into the streets.* **5 pour money/aid etc. into sth** to invest a lot of money in something over a period of time in order to make it successful: *Thomas has poured thousands of dollars into his store.*

pour sth ↔ **out** *phr. v.* to tell someone everything about your thoughts, feelings, etc.: *Sonia **poured out** all her frustrations **to** Val.*

pout /paʊt/ *v.* [I,T] to push out your lower lip because you are annoyed, or in order to look sexually attractive: *Stop pouting; you're not going, and that's final.* —**pout** *n.* [C]

pov·er·ty /ˈpɑvəṭi/ *n.* [U] the situation or experience of being poor: *families **living in poverty*** | *I was shocked by the **abject/extreme poverty** that I saw.*

ˈpoverty ˌline *also* **ˈpoverty ˌlevel**, **ˈpoverty ˌthreshold** *n.* [C] ECONOMICS the income below which someone is officially considered to be very poor and in need of help: *Fifteen percent of the city's residents live **below the poverty level**.*

ˈpoverty-ˌstricken *adj.* extremely poor: *a poverty-stricken neighborhood*

> THESAURUS **poor, needy, destitute, impoverished, indigent, penurious, deprived** → POOR

pow·der¹ /ˈpaʊdə/ *n.* [C,U] a dry substance in the form of very small grains: *talcum powder* | *baking powder* [ORIGIN: 1200—1300 Old French *poudre*, from Latin *pulvis* "dust"]

powder² *v.* [T] **1** to put powder on your skin **2 powder your nose** a phrase meaning to go to the toilet, used by women in order to be polite

pow·dered /ˈpaʊdəd/ *adj.* produced or sold in the form of powder: *powdered milk*

ˈpowder room *n.* [C] (old-fashioned) a polite phrase meaning a women's public toilet

pow·der·y /ˈpaʊdəri/ *adj.* like powder, or easily broken into powder: *powdery snow*

pow·er¹ /ˈpaʊə/ *n.*
1 CONTROL SB/STH [U] the ability or right to control people or events → POWERFUL, POWERLESS: *We all felt that the chairman had too much power.* |

I resented my father's ***power over*** *me.* | ***the power of*** *the media*
2 POLITICAL [U] POLITICS political control of a country or government: *The current leader has been* ***in power*** *for ten years.* | *He* ***came to power*** (=began to control the country) *after the revolution.*
3 ENERGY [U] PHYSICS energy such as electricity, that can be used to make a machine, car, etc. work: *The plane* ***lost power*** *and had to make an emergency landing.* | *The storm caused a* ***power failure/cut*** (=a time when there is no electricity) *in our area.* | *The area uses electricity produced by* ***nuclear/solar/wind power****.*
4 AUTHORITY [C,U] the legal right or authority to do something: *Congress has the* ***power to*** *declare war.* | *Only the police have the* ***power of*** *arrest.*

THESAURUS **ability, capacity** → ABILITY

5 COUNTRY [C] a country that is very strong and important: *Germany is a major* ***industrial power*** *in Europe.* | *a meeting of* ***world powers*** (=the strongest countries in the world)

THESAURUS **country, nation, state, land, realm** → COUNTRY[1]

6 PHYSICAL [U] the physical strength of something such as an explosion, natural force, or animal: *The* ***power of*** *the eruption blew away the whole mountainside.*

THESAURUS **force, strength** → FORCE[1]

7 NATURAL ABILITY [C,U] a natural or special ability to do something: *the* ***power of*** *sight/speech* | *She has the* ***power to*** *make an audience laugh or cry.*
8 do everything in your power to do everything that you are able or allowed to do: *I did everything in my power to save her.*
9 a power struggle a situation in which groups or leaders try to defeat each other and get complete control
10 earning/purchasing etc. power ECONOMICS the ability to earn money, buy things, etc.: *the purchasing power of middle-class teenagers*
11 be in sb's power to be in a situation in which someone has control over you
12 the powers that be (informal) the people who have positions of authority, and whose decisions affect your life: *The hardest part will be persuading the powers that be at City Hall to agree.*
13 to the power of 3/4/5 etc. MATH if a number is increased to the power of three, four, five, etc., it is multiplied by itself three, four, five, etc. times

power[2] *v.* **1 solar-powered/nuclear-powered etc.** working or moving by means of the Sun, etc.: *a battery-powered flashlight* **2** [T] to supply power to a vehicle or machine: *Can a car be* ***powered by*** *solar energy?* **3** [I,T] to do something quickly and with a lot of strength: *North Carolina* ***powered*** *its way* ***through*** *the tournament.*

power sth ↔ **up** *phr. v.* to make a machine start working: *Never move a computer while it is powered up.*

'power base *n.* [C] the group of people in a particular area that supports a politician or leader

pow·er·boat /'paʊɚˌboʊt/ *n.* [C] a boat with a powerful engine that is used for racing

pow·er·ful /'paʊɚfəl/ *adj.* **1** able to control and influence events and other people's actions: *a meeting of the world's most powerful leaders* | *the most powerful political party in the country*

THESAURUS
influential – having a lot of power to influence what happens: *a meeting of influential business leaders*
strong – having a lot of power, influence, or ability: *He is a strong voice in the state assembly.*
dominant – more powerful than other people or groups, and able to control what happens: *England was once the dominant power in the world.*

2 having a lot of power, strength, or force: *a powerful engine* | *a powerful man* | *a powerful explosion* **3** having a strong effect on someone's feelings or ideas: *a powerful speech* | *a* ***powerful argument*** *against eating meat* **4** having a strong effect on your body: *a powerful drug/medicine* —**powerfully** *adv.*

pow·er·house /'paʊɚˌhaʊs/ *n.* [C] (informal) **1** a country, company, organization, etc. that has a lot of power or influence **2** someone who has a lot of energy

pow·er·less /'paʊɚlɪs/ *adj.* unable to stop or control something because you do not have the power, strength, or right to do so: *The small group of soldiers was* ***powerless to*** *stop the attack.* —**powerlessness** *n.* [U]

'power line *n.* [C] a large wire carrying electricity above or under the ground

ˌpower of at'torney *n.* (plural **powers of attorney**) [C,U] LAW the legal right to do things for someone else in his/her business or personal life, or the document that gives this right

'power plant *also* **'power ˌstation** *n.* [C] a building where electricity is produced to supply a large area

'power ˌsteering *n.* [U] a special system that makes it easier for the driver of a vehicle to STEER (=change the direction of the vehicle)

'power tool *n.* [C] a tool that works by using electricity

pow·wow /'paʊwaʊ/ *n.* [C] **1** (humorous) a meeting or discussion **2** a meeting or council of Native American tribes

pp. the written abbreviation of PAGES: *Read pp. 20–35.*

PR *n.* **1** [U] PUBLIC RELATIONS **2** the written abbreviation of **Puerto Rico**

prac·ti·ca·ble /ˈpræktɪkəbəl/ *adj.* (formal) possible in a particular situation: *The only practicable course of action is to sell the company.*

prac·ti·cal /ˈpræktɪkəl/ *adj.* **1** relating to real situations and events rather than ideas: *Do you have a lot of* ***practical experience*** *as a mechanic?* | *I deal with* ***practical matters****, like finding people places to stay.* **2** practical plans, methods, etc. are likely to succeed or be effective: *Is that a practical solution to the problem?* | *Treganowan's book gives* ***practical advice*** *for keeping your car on the road.* **3** a practical person is good at dealing with problems and making decisions based on what is possible and what will really work: *Be practical – at least wait for the storm to pass.* **4** useful, or appropriate for a particular purpose: *practical gifts, such as clothes* | *a practical car for a family* **5 for all practical purposes** used in order to describe what the real effect of a situation is: *For all practical purposes, the election is over* (=we already know who the winner is).

P

prac·ti·cal·i·ty /ˌpræktɪˈkæləṭi/ *n.* **1 practicalities** [plural] the real facts of a situation, rather than ideas about how it might be: *The* ***practicalities of*** *raising children can be quite different from what the books say.* **2** [U] how appropriate something is, and whether it will work: *You need to think about comfort and practicality when choosing walking shoes.*

ˌpractical ˈjoke *n.* [C] a trick that is intended to surprise someone and make other people laugh —**practical joker** *n.* [C]

prac·ti·cally /ˈpræktɪkli/ *adv.* **1** (spoken) almost: *Practically everyone was there.* | *She practically jumped out of her chair.* | *I've read* ***practically all*** *of his books.* **2** in a sensible way: *Vasko just doesn't think practically.*

prac·tice¹ /ˈpræktɪs/ *n.*
1 SKILL a) [U] regular activity that you do in order to improve a skill or ability: *It* ***takes*** *a lot of* ***practice*** *to be a good piano player.* | *Your English will improve* ***with practice****.* **b)** [C,U] the period of time in which you do this: ***football/choir etc. practice***
2 STH THAT IS USUALLY DONE [C,U] **a)** something that people do often and in a particular way: *It's* ***common/standard/normal practice*** *to do the payroll in this way.* **b)** something that you do often because of your religion or your society's tradition (SYN) **custom**: ***The practice of*** *kissing someone as a greeting is common in other countries.*

THESAURUS **habit, custom, tradition, convention** → HABIT

3 in practice used in order to describe what the real situation is rather than what seems to be true: *Annette is the head of the company, but in practice Sue runs everything.*
4 DOCTOR/LAWYER [C] the work of a doctor or lawyer, or the place where s/he works: *She has a successful* ***medical/legal practice****.*
5 be out of practice to be unable to do something well because you have not done it for a long time: *I'd like to play with you, but I'm really out of practice.*
6 put sth into practice if you put an idea, plan, etc. into practice, you start to use it and see if it is effective: *Now's your chance to put the skills you've learned into practice.*

practice² *v.* **1** [I,T] to do an activity regularly to improve your skill or ability: *Gail practices the piano more than an hour every day.* | *The Giants spent the afternoon* ***practicing for*** *their game on Sunday.*

THESAURUS
rehearse – to practice something such as a play or concert before giving a public performance: *The band was rehearsing for the show that night.*
work on sth – to practice a skill, musical instrument, etc. in order to improve: *Jessie has been working on her tennis serve.*
train – to prepare for a sports event by exercising and practicing: *Olympic swimmers train for hours every day.*
drill – to teach people something by making them repeat the same exercise, lesson, etc. many times: *The program allows you to drill yourself on grammar, vocabulary, and dictation.*

2 [I,T] to work as a doctor or lawyer: *Bill is* ***practicing law/medicine*** *in Ohio now.* **3** [T] to do an activity as a habit, or to live according to the rules of a religion: *The posters encourage young people to practice safe sex.*

prac·ticed /ˈpræktɪst/ *adj.* good at doing something because you have done it many times before: *a practiced pilot*

prac·tic·ing /ˈpræktɪsɪŋ/ *adj.* **1 a practicing Catholic/Jew/Muslim etc.** someone who obeys the rules of a particular religion

THESAURUS **religious, devout, pious, god-fearing, orthodox** → RELIGIOUS

2 a practicing doctor/lawyer/architect etc. someone who is working as a doctor, lawyer, etc.

prac·ti·tion·er /prækˈtɪʃənə/ (Ac) *n.* [C] (formal) someone who is trained to do a particular type of work that involves a lot of skill: *a tax practitioner* | *a medical practitioner* | *This sort of surgery can only be undertaken by highly skilled practitioners.*

prag·mat·ic /prægˈmæṭɪk/ *adj.* dealing with problems in a sensible practical way, instead of strictly following a set of ideas: *The diet gives you pragmatic suggestions for eating healthily.*

prag·mat·ics /prægˈmæṭɪks/ *n.* [U] ENG. LANG. ARTS the study of how words and phrases are used with special meanings in particular situations, for example the way "I know" can be used to agree with someone

prag·ma·tism /ˈprægməˌtɪzəm/ *n.* [U] a tendency to deal with problems in a pragmatic way —**pragmatist** *n.* [C]

prai·rie /ˈprɛri/ *n.* [C] a large area of flat land in North America that is covered in grass

ˈprairie dog *n.* [C] a North American animal with a short tail, that lives in holes on a prairie

praise[1] /preɪz/ *v.* [T] **1** to say publicly that someone has done something well or that you admire him/her: *Mr. Bonner **praised** Jill **for** the quality of her work.* | *a **highly praised** speech*

THESAURUS

congratulate – to tell someone that you are happy that s/he has achieved something
flatter – to say nice things about someone, sometimes when you do not really mean it, often in order to get something you want
compliment sb/pay sb a compliment – to say something nice to someone in order to praise him or her
extol (formal) – to praise something very much: *One of his colleagues extolled him as "a very fine human being."*
commend (formal) – to praise someone or something publicly or formally: *The children were commended for their behavior.*

2 to give thanks or honor to God [ORIGIN: 1200—1300 Old French *preisier*, from Late Latin *pretiare* "to value highly"]

praise[2] *n.* [U] **1** words that you say or write to praise someone or something: *The papers **were full of praise for** the quick actions of the fire department.* | *Teachers try to **give** plenty of **praise and encouragement** to students.* **2** an expression of respect or thanks to God: *Let us give praise unto the Lord.*

praise·wor·thy /ˈpreɪzˌwɚði/ *adj.* (formal) deserving praise

prance /præns/ *v.* [I] (disapproving) to walk or dance with high steps or large movements, in a way that makes people notice you: *He started **prancing around** in front of the video camera.*

prank /præŋk/ *n.* [C] a trick that is intended to make someone look silly: *Chris and Keith love to **play/pull pranks** on each other.*

prank·ster /ˈpræŋkstɚ/ *n.* [C] someone who plays pranks on people

prawn /prɔn/ *n.* [C] a sea animal like a large SHRIMP, that is used for food

pray /preɪ/ *v.* [I,T] **1** to speak to a god or gods in order to ask for help or give thanks: *You don't have to go to church to pray.* | *People are **praying for** peace.* | *She got down on her knees and **prayed to** God.* **2** to wish or hope for something very strongly: *We're **praying for** good weather tomorrow.* | *I'm just **praying that** I finish on time.* [ORIGIN: 1200—1300 Old French *preier*, from Latin *precari*, from *prex* "request, prayer"]

prayer /prɛr/ *n.* **1** [C] words that you say when praying to a god or gods: *I closed my eyes and **said a prayer**.* | *Our thoughts and prayers go out to the victims.* | *a **prayer for** the dead* **2** [U] the act or regular habit of praying: *a time of prayer* | *They bowed their heads **in prayer**.* **3 not have a prayer** (informal) to have no chance of succeeding: *The Seahawks **don't have a prayer of** winning.*

preach /pritʃ/ *v.* **1** [I,T] to give a speech, usually in a church, about a religious subject: *The minister **preaches to** large crowds every Sunday.* **2** [T] to talk about how good or important something is and to try to persuade other people to do or accept it: *He's always preaching **the value/virtue/gospel etc. of** hard work.* **3** [I] to give advice in a way that annoys people: *I wish you would stop **preaching at** me like this.*

preach·er /ˈpritʃɚ/ *n.* [C] someone who talks about religious subjects, usually in a church

preach·y /ˈpritʃi/ *adj.* (informal) trying very hard to persuade people to accept a particular opinion, in a way that annoys them: *I don't like the preachy tone in her writing.*

pre·am·ble /ˈpriˌæmbəl/ *n.* [C] (formal) a statement at the beginning of a book, speech, etc.: *the **preamble to** the Constitution*

pre·ar·ranged /ˌpriəˈreɪndʒd◂/ *adj.* planned before: *We can have a driver pick you up at a prearranged time.*

Pre·cam·bri·an /priˈkæmbriən/ *n.* **the Precambrian** EARTH SCIENCES the period of time in the Earth's history from when the hard outer surface of the Earth first formed about 4,600 million years ago until about 570 million years ago when simple forms of life first appeared on the Earth —**Precambrian** *adj.*: *Precambrian rock* → CENOZOIC, MESOZOIC, PALEOZOIC

pre·car·i·ous /prɪˈkɛriəs, -ˈkær-/ *adj.* **1** a precarious situation may easily or quickly become worse: *The newspaper is in a **precarious** financial **position**.* **2** likely to fall, or likely to cause something to fall: *We had to cross a precarious rope bridge.* —**precariously** *adv.*

pre·cau·tion /prɪˈkɔʃən/ *n.* [C] something that you do to prevent something bad or dangerous from happening: *safety precautions* | *People were warned to stay inside **as a precaution**.* | *You have to **take precautions** when working with chemicals.*

pre·cau·tion·a·ry /prɪˈkɔʃəˌnɛri/ *adj.* done as a precaution: *The doctors have put him in the hospital as a **precautionary measure**.*

pre·cede /prɪˈsid/ (Ac) *v.* [T] (formal) to happen or exist before something else: *The fire was preceded by a loud explosion.* [ORIGIN: 1300—1400 French *précéder*, from Latin *praecedere* "to go in front"]

prec·e·dence /ˈprɛsədəns/ (Ac) *n.* **take/have precedence (over sth)** to be more important or urgent than something else: *This project takes precedence over everything else.* | *Federal laws take precedence over local laws.*

prec·e·dent /ˈprɛsədənt/ (Ac) *n.* [C] an action or official decision that is used as an example for a similar action or decision at a later time: *The trial* *set a precedent for civil rights legislation.* | *The judge's ruling was an important precedent.*

pre·ced·ing /prɪˈsidɪŋ, ˈprisidɪŋ/ (Ac) *adj.* [only before noun] (formal) happening or coming before something else: *The events of the preceding week worried him.* | *The preceding chapter discussed the economic effects of slavery in the Southern states.*

pre·cept /ˈprisɛpt/ *n.* [C] (formal) a rule that helps you decide how to think or behave in a situation: *basic moral precepts*

THESAURUS **rule, law, regulation, restriction** ➔ RULE[1]

P

pre·cinct /ˈprisɪŋkt/ *n.* [C] **1** POLITICS a part of a city that has its own police force, government officials, etc.: *the 12th precinct* **2** POLITICS the smallest voting area in a U.S. election [ORIGIN: 1400—1500 Medieval Latin *praecinctum*, from Latin *praecingere* "to put a belt around"]

pre·cious[1] /ˈprɛʃəs/ *adj.* **1** something that is precious is valuable or important and should not be wasted: *We cannot afford to waste **precious time/days/minutes etc.*** **2** precious memories or possessions are very important to you because they remind you of people or events in your life: *The doll is **precious to** me because it was my grandmother's.* **3** valuable because of being rare or expensive: *a **precious jewel/stone/metal***

THESAURUS **valuable, priceless, worth a lot/a fortune** ➔ VALUABLE

4 (spoken) used in order to describe someone or something that is small and pretty: *What a precious little girl!* [ORIGIN: 1200—1300 Old French *precios*, from Latin *pretiosus*, from *pretium* "price, money"]

precious[2] *adv.* **precious little/few** (informal) very little or very few: *We had precious little time to prepare for the trip.*

prec·i·pice /ˈprɛsəpɪs/ *n.* [C] a very steep side of a mountain or cliff

pre·cip·i·tate[1] /prɪˈsɪpəˌteɪt/ *v.* [T] (formal) to make something happen suddenly: *The President's death precipitated a political crisis.*

pre·cip·i·tate[2] /prɪˈsɪpətɪt/ *adj.* (formal) done too quickly, especially without thinking carefully enough

THESAURUS **impulsive, rash, hotheaded, impetuous, hasty** ➔ IMPULSIVE

pre·cip·i·ta·tion /prɪˌsɪpəˈteɪʃən/ *n.* [C,U] EARTH SCIENCES rain or snow

pre·cip·i·tous /prɪˈsɪpət̬əs/ *adj.* (formal) **1** very sudden: *a **precipitous drop/decline** in property values* **2** dangerously high or steep: *precipitous cliffs*

pré·cis /ˈpreɪsi/ *n.* (plural **précis** /-siz/) [C] ENG. LANG. ARTS a short piece of writing that gives the main points from another piece of writing ➔ SUMMARY —**précis** *v.* [T]

pre·cise /prɪˈsaɪs/ (Ac) *adj.* **1** exact or correct in every detail: *The precise cause of the accident is unknown.* | *What is the **precise location** of the ship?* | *At that **precise moment**, the telephone rang.* | *a **precise figure/number/amount*** | *No method of measuring intelligence can be precise.* **2 to be precise** used when you add exact details about something: *He was born in April, on the 4th to be precise.* [ORIGIN: 1500—1600 French *précis*, from Latin *praecisus*, from *praecidere* "to cut off"]

pre·cise·ly /prɪˈsaɪsli/ (Ac) *adv.* **1** exactly or correctly: *I do not remember **precisely what** happened.* | *at precisely 4 o'clock* | *Often, the children who need help most are precisely those who are afraid to ask for it.* **2** (spoken) used in order to agree with what someone has just said: *"So Clark is responsible for the mistake." "Precisely."*

pre·ci·sion /prɪˈsɪʒən/ (Ac) *n.* [U] the quality of being very exact: *The weight of an atom can be measured **with** great **precision**.* | *The audience was impressed by the clarity and precision of his arguments.* —**precision** *adj.*: *precision bombing* | *The factory produces precision instruments such as microscopes.*

pre·clude /prɪˈklud/ *v.* [T] (formal) to prevent something or make it impossible to happen: *Poor eyesight may **preclude** you **from** driving.*

pre·co·cious /prɪˈkoʊʃəs/ *adj.* a precocious child shows skill or intelligence at a young age, or behaves in an adult way [ORIGIN: 1600—1700 Latin *praecox* "becoming ripe early," from *coquere* "to cook, ripen"]

pre·con·ceived /ˌprikənˈsivd◂/ *adj.* [only before noun] preconceived ideas are formed about something before you know what it is really like: *He has a lot of **preconceived ideas/notions** about what living in America is like.*

pre·con·cep·tion /ˌprikənˈsɛpʃən/ *n.* [C] an idea that is formed about something before you know what it is really like

pre·con·di·tion /ˌprikənˈdɪʃən/ *n.* [C] something that must happen before something else can happen: *An end to the fighting is a **precondition for** peace negotiations.*

pre·cur·sor /ˈpriˌkɚsɚ, prɪˈkɚsɚ/ *n.* [C] (formal) something that happened or existed before something else and influenced its development: *This machine is **a precursor of** the computer.*

pre·date /priˈdeɪt/ *v.* [T] to happen or exist earlier than something else: *His troubles actually predated the arrest.*

pred·a·tor /ˈprɛdət̬ɚ/ *n.* [C] an animal that kills and eats other animals

pred·a·to·ry /ˈprɛdəˌtɔri/ *adj.* **1** predatory animals kill and eat other animals **2** (disapproving) trying to use someone's weakness to get an advantage for yourself

ˌpredatory ˈpricing *n.* [U] ECONOMICS the practice of selling a product or service for less than the cost of producing it. Companies do this in order to increase their share of sales in a market and to force competitors out of the market.

pred·e·ces·sor /ˈprɛdəˌsɛsɚ/ *n.* [C] **1** the person who had a job before someone else began to do it: *My predecessor worked here for ten years.* **2** something such as a machine or system that existed before another one: *The new computer is similar to its predecessors, but even faster.* [ORIGIN: 1300—1400 French *prédécesseur*, from Late Latin, from Latin *pre* "before" + *decedere* "to go away, leave your job"]

pre·des·ti·na·tion /ˌpridɛstəˈneɪʃən/ *n.* [U] **1** SOCIAL SCIENCE the belief that God or FATE has decided everything that will happen and that no one can change this **2** SOCIAL SCIENCE the belief in some Christian churches that God decided before the beginning of the world who would go to heaven and who would not

pre·des·tined /priˈdɛstɪnd/ *adj.* something that is predestined is certain to happen and cannot be changed

pre·de·ter·mined /ˌpridɪˈtɚmɪnd/ *adj.* (formal) decided or arranged before: *The doors unlock at a predetermined time.*

pre·dic·a·ment /prɪˈdɪkəmənt/ *n.* [C] a difficult situation in which you do not know what is the best thing to do: *It was Raoul who got us **in this predicament** in the first place.*

pred·i·cate /ˈprɛdɪkɪt/ *n.* [C] ENG. LANG. ARTS in grammar, the part of a sentence that has the main verb, and that tells what the subject is doing or describes the subject. In the sentence "He ran out of the house," "ran out of the house" is the predicate. → SUBJECT

pred·i·ca·tive /ˈprɛdɪkət̬ɪv, -ˌkeɪt̬ɪv/ *adj.* ENG. LANG. ARTS in grammar, a predicative adjective or phrase comes after a verb and describes the subject, such as "sad" in "She is sad."

pre·dict /prɪˈdɪkt/ (Ac) *v.* [T] to say that something will happen before it happens: *The newspapers are predicting a close election.* | *Analysts **predict (that)** college costs will continue to rise.* | *It's difficult to **predict** exactly **what** the effects will be.* [ORIGIN: 1500—1600 Latin, past participle of *praedicere* "to say beforehand"]

THESAURUS

prophesy/foretell – to use religious or magical knowledge to say what will happen in the future: *The priestess at Delphi prophesied that Laius would be killed by his own son.*
forecast – to say what is likely to happen in the future, based on information you have: *The number of passengers using the airport is forecast to rise.*
foresee – to know that something will happen before it happens: *No one could have foreseen what happened next.*
have a premonition – to have a feeling that something bad is about to happen: *He had a premonition of impending danger.*

pre·dict·a·ble /prɪˈdɪktəbəl/ (Ac) *adj.* behaving or happening in a way that you expect: *You're so predictable!* | *The ending of the movie was too predictable.* | *The disease develops in a way that follows a predictable pattern.* | *The results of the experiment were **highly predictable**.* —**predictably** *adv.* —**predictability** /prɪˌdɪktəˈbɪlət̬i/ *n.* [U]

pre·dic·tion /prɪˈdɪkʃən/ (Ac) *n.* [C,U] a statement saying that something is going to happen, or the act of making statements of this kind: *It's hard to **make a prediction** about who will win.* | ***predictions of** climate change* | *Despite all our modern technology, **weather prediction** is still unreliable.* —**predictive** *adj.*

pred·i·lec·tion /ˌprɛdlˈɛkʃən, ˌprid-/ *n.* [C] (formal) the tendency to like a particular kind of person or thing: *a **predilection for** apple pie*

pre·dis·posed /ˌpridɪˈspoʊzd/ *adj.* **predisposed to/toward sth** likely to behave or think in a particular way, or to have a particular health problem: *Some people are predisposed to depression.*

pre·dis·po·si·tion /ˌpridɪspəˈzɪʃən/ *n.* [C] a tendency to behave in a particular way or suffer from a particular health problem: *a **predisposition to/toward** skin cancer*

pre·dom·i·nance /prɪˈdɑmənəns/ (Ac) *n.* (formal) **1** [singular] if there is a predominance of one type of thing or person in a group, there are more of them than any other type of person or thing: *the **predominance of** male students in the class* **2** [U] the most power or importance in a particular group or area: *American **predominance in** world economics* | *Rival supermarkets are constantly fighting to achieve predominance.*

pre·dom·i·nant /prɪˈdɑmənənt/ (Ac) *adj.* more powerful, common, or noticeable than others: *Racism in American society is a predominant theme in Wright's novels.* | *The predominant mode of instruction is lectures and seminars.* | *These two political parties were predominant in the 19th century.*

pre·dom·i·nant·ly /prɪˈdɑmənəntli/ (Ac) *adv.* mostly or mainly: *a predominantly middle-class neighborhood* | *Throughout this region, the economy is based predominantly on agriculture.*

pre·dom·i·nate /prɪˈdɑməˌneɪt/ (Ac) *v.* [I] to have the most importance, or to be the most in number: *Democrats predominate in this district.* | *Sometimes, passing tests predominates over the importance of learning.*

pree·mie /ˈprimi/ *n.* [C] (informal) a PREMATURE baby

pre·em·i·nent /priˈɛmənənt/ *adj.* much more important or powerful than all others in a particular group: *a preeminent political figure* —**preeminence** *n.* [U]

P

pre·empt /pri'ɛmpt/ *v.* [T] to make what someone is about to do unnecessary or not effective, by doing something else first: *Approval of the plan would preempt the strike.* —**preemptive** *adj.*: *a preemptive attack*

preen /prin/ *v.* **1** [I,T] if a bird preens, or preens itself, it cleans itself and makes its feathers smooth **2 preen yourself** (disapproving) to spend a lot of time making yourself look good: *He's always preening himself in the mirror.*

pre-ex·ist·ing /ˌpriɪg'zɪstɪŋ◂/ *adj.* [only before noun] existing already, or before something else: *a pre-existing medical condition*

P

pre·fab·ri·cat·ed /pri'fæbrəˌkeɪt̬ɪd/ also **pre·fab** /pri'fæb, 'prifæb/ *adj.* built from parts made in a factory and put together somewhere else: *prefabricated homes*

pref·ace[1] /'prɛfɪs/ *n.* [C] an introduction at the beginning of a book or speech: *the **preface to** the novel*

preface[2] *v.* [T] (formal) to say or do something first before saying or doing something else: *He **prefaced** his remarks **with** an expression of thanks to the audience.*

pre·fer /prɪ'fɚ/ *v.* (**preferred**, **preferring**) [T] **1** to like someone or something more than someone or something else: *Which color do you prefer?* | *Many companies **prefer to** hire young workers.* | *I **would prefer** not to talk about it at the moment.* | *She **prefers** walking **to** driving.* **2 I would prefer it if** (spoken) used in order to tell someone politely not to do something: *I'd prefer it if you didn't smoke in the house.* [ORIGIN: 1300—1400 French *préférer*, from Latin *praeferre* "to put in front, prefer"]

pref·er·a·ble /'prɛfərəbəl/ *adj.* better or more appropriate: *Anything is **preferable to** war.*

pref·er·a·bly /'prɛfərəbli/ *adv.* used in order to show which person, thing, place, or idea you think would be the best choice: *You should see a doctor, preferably a specialist.*

pref·er·ence /'prɛfrəns, -fərəns/ *n.* **1** [C,U] if someone has a preference for something, s/he likes it more than another thing: *We have always **had a preference for** small cars.* | *It's a matter of **personal preference.*** **2 give/show preference (to sb)** to treat someone better than you treat other people: *Doctors should give preference to patients who are seriously ill.*

pref·er·en·tial /ˌprɛfə'rɛnʃəl◂/ *adj.* treating one person or group better than others: *Why should she get **preferential treatment**?*

pre·fix /'prifɪks/ *n.* [C] ENG. LANG. ARTS in grammar, a group of letters that is added to the beginning of a word in order to make a new word, such as "mis-" in "misunderstand" ➔ SUFFIX [ORIGIN: 1600—1700 Modern Latin *praefixum*, from Latin *praefigere* "to fasten before"]

preg·nan·cy /'prɛgnənsi/ *n.* (plural **pregnancies**) [C,U] the condition of being pregnant, or the period of time when a woman is pregnant: *You should not drink alcohol during your pregnancy.* | *a pregnancy test*

preg·nant /'prɛgnənt/ *adj.* **1** having a baby that has not been born yet growing in your body: *a pregnant woman* | *She's three months pregnant.* | *Marie **got pregnant** soon after the wedding.* | *She's **pregnant with** her first child.* **2 a pregnant silence/pause** (literary) a silence or pause that is full of meaning or emotion [ORIGIN: 1400—1500 Latin *praegnans*, from *praegnas*, from *prae-* "before" + *gnatus* "born"]

pre·heat /pri'hit/ *v.* [T] to heat an OVEN to a particular temperature before cooking food in it

pre·his·tor·ic /ˌprihɪ'stɔrɪk◂/ *adj.* relating to the time in history before anything was written down: *prehistoric cave drawings* —**prehistory** /pri'hɪstəri/ *n.* [U]

pre·judge /ˌpri'dʒʌdʒ/ *v.* [T] (disapproving) to form an opinion about someone or something before knowing all the facts

prej·u·dice[1] /'prɛdʒədɪs/ *n.* [C,U] an unreasonable dislike of someone who is different from you in some way, especially because of his/her race, sex, or religion: ***racial prejudice*** | ***prejudice against** single mothers* [ORIGIN: 1200—1300 Old French, Latin *praejudicium*, from *judicium* "judgment"]

THESAURUS

Types of prejudice

racism – unfair treatment of people because they belong to a different race: *accusations of police brutality and racism*
discrimination – the practice of treating one group of people differently from another in an unfair way: *She accused the company of sexual discrimination.*
intolerance – the fact of not being willing to accept ways of thinking or behaving that are different from your own: *religious intolerance*
bigotry – behavior or beliefs that show that you have unreasonable opinions, especially about race or religion: *In the 1930s, bigotry against immigrants increased.*
sexism – the belief that one sex, especially the female sex, is weaker, less intelligent, or less important than the other, especially when this results in someone being treated unfairly: *The armed forces have worked to reduce sexism in their policies.*
homophobia – hatred and fear of homosexuals: *Homophobia is common, and had been the cause of some serious crimes.*
anti-Semitism – a strong feeling of hatred toward Jewish people: *Is anti-Semitism on the rise in America and Europe?*

People who are prejudiced

racist – someone who believes that people of his/her own race are better than others, and treats people of other races unfairly: *When he expressed his opinion, he was branded a racist.*
bigot – someone who has strong unreasonable

opinions, especially about race or religion: *He was known to be a bigot.*

prejudice² *v.* [T] to influence someone so that s/he has an unfair opinion about someone or something before s/he knows all the facts: *Watson's wild appearance may* ***prejudice*** *the jury* ***against*** *him.*

prej·u·diced /ˈprɛdʒədɪst/ *adj.* having an unfair feeling of dislike for someone who is of a different race, sex, religion, etc.: *Kurt is so* ***prejudiced against*** *gay people!*

prej·u·di·cial /ˌprɛdʒəˈdɪʃəl/ *adj.* (formal) influencing people so that they have a bad opinion of someone or something: *prejudicial remarks*

pre·lim·i·nar·y¹ /prɪˈlɪməˌnɛri/ (Ac) *adj.* happening before something that is more important, often in order to prepare for it: *a preliminary investigation* | *preliminary talks/discussions* | *In this preliminary study, a small number of texts were examined.* [ORIGIN: 1600—1700 French *préliminaire*, from Medieval Latin *praeliminaris*, from Latin *limen* "threshold"]

preliminary² *n.* (plural **preliminaries**) [C usually plural] something that is done at the beginning of an activity, event, etc., often in order to prepare for it: *the preliminaries of the competition*

prel·ude /ˈprɛlyud, ˈpreɪlud/ *n.* **1 be a prelude to sth** to happen just before something else, often as an introduction to it: *The attack may be a prelude to full-scale war.* **2** [C] a short piece of music that comes before a large musical piece: *Chopin's preludes*

pre·mar·i·tal /priˈmærətl/ *adj.* happening or existing before marriage: *premarital sex*

pre·ma·ture /ˌpriməˈtʃʊr◂, -ˈtʊr◂ / *adj.* **1** happening too early or before the right time: *a premature death* **2** a premature baby is born before the usual time: *The baby was six weeks premature.* —**prematurely** *adv.*: *The sun causes your skin to age prematurely.* | *The baby was born prematurely.*

pre·med, pre-med /ˈprimɛd/ *adj.* (informal) relating to classes that prepare a student for medical school, or to students who are taking these classes: *a premed student*

pre·med·i·tat·ed /priˈmɛdəˌteɪt̬ɪd/ *adj.* a premeditated action has been planned and done deliberately: *a premeditated murder* —**premeditation** /priˌmɛdəˈteɪʃən/ *n.* [U]

pre·men·strual /priˈmɛnstrəl/ *adj.* happening just before a woman's PERIOD (=monthly flow of blood)

preˌmenstrual ˈsyndrome *n.* [U] PMS

pre·mier¹, Premier /prɪˈmɪr, -ˈmyɪr, ˈprimɪr/ *n.* [C] the leader of a government

premier² *adj.* (formal) best or most important: *a premier wine from California*

pre·miere, première /prɪˈmɪr, -ˈmyɪr, -ˈmyɛr/ *n.* [C] the first public performance of a movie or play: *the 1955* ***premiere of*** *"Cat on a Hot Tin Roof"* —**premiere** *v.* [I,T]

prem·ise /ˈprɛmɪs/ *n.* **1 premises** [plural] the buildings and land that a store, company, etc. uses: *He was ordered* ***off the premises*** (=out of the building). | *Do not smoke* ***on the premises*** (=in the building). **2** [C] (formal) a statement or idea that you think is true and use as a base for developing other ideas: *His theory is based on the* ***premise that*** *there may be life on other planets.*

pre·mi·um /ˈprimiəm/ *n.* [C] **1** an amount of money that you pay for something such as insurance: *annual premiums* **2 be at a premium** difficult to get because a lot of people want it: *Hotel rooms are at a premium around major holidays.* **3 put/place a premium on sth** to think that one quality or activity is much more important than others: *My grandparents put a premium on education.*

P

pre·mo·ni·tion /ˌpriməˈnɪʃən, ˌprɛ-/ *n.* [C] a feeling that something bad is about to happen: *She* ***had*** *a horrible* ***premonition that*** *something would happen to the children.*

pre·na·tal /ˌpriˈneɪt̬l◂ / *adj.* relating to unborn babies and the care of women who are PREGNANT ➜ POSTPARTUM: *prenatal care*

pre·oc·cu·pa·tion /priˌɑkyəˈpeɪʃən/ *n.* **1** [singular, U] the state of being preoccupied: *His growing* ***preoccupation with*** *his health began to affect his work.* **2** [C] something that you give all your attention to: *Brad's main preoccupations were eating and sleeping.*

pre·oc·cu·pied /priˈɑkyəˌpaɪd/ *adj.* thinking or worrying about something a lot, so that you do not pay attention to other things: *What's wrong? You seem* ***preoccupied with*** *something today.*

pre·oc·cu·py /priˈɑkyəˌpaɪ/ *v.* (**preoccupied**, **preoccupies**) [T] if something preoccupies you, you think or worry about it a lot

pre·or·dained /ˌpriɔrˈdeɪnd/ *adj.* (formal) certain to happen because God or FATE has already decided it

prep /prɛp/ *v.* (**prepped**, **prepping**) [T] (informal) to prepare for something

pre·paid /ˌpriˈpeɪd◂ / *adj.* if something is prepaid, it is paid for before it is needed or used: *a prepaid phone card*

prep·a·ra·tion /ˌprɛpəˈreɪʃən/ *n.* **1** [U] the act or process of preparing something: *Flowers have been ordered* ***in preparation for*** *the wedding.* | *the* ***preparation of*** *the report* | *income tax preparation* **2** *also* **preparations** [plural] arrangements for something that is going to happen: *They are* ***making preparations for*** *the President's visit.*

pre·par·a·to·ry /prɪˈpærəˌtɔri, -ˈpɛr-, ˈprɛprə-/ *adj.* [only before noun] done in order to get ready for something: *preparatory work*

pre·pare /prɪˈpɛr/ *v.* **1** [T] to make something

ready to be used: *The rooms still need to be* ***prepared for*** *the guests.* | *You need to prepare the soil before planting the seeds.*

THESAURUS

get sth ready – to prepare something for what you are going to do: *I've been getting everything ready for the party.*
set sth up – to make a piece of equipment ready to be used: *Kim's setting up the computer in the meeting room.*
make preparations – to prepare for an important event: *They spent six months making preparations for the trip.*

P

2 [I,T] to make plans or arrangements for something that will happen soon: *I hope you've begun to* ***prepare for*** *the test.* | *The Bears are* ***preparing to*** *play the Redskins next week.* | *We need to prepare a plan for raising the money.* **3** [T] to make yourself or someone else ready to deal with something that will happen soon: *You should probably* ***prepare yourself for*** *some bad news.* **4** [T] to give someone the training, skill, etc. that s/he needs to do something: *The program* ***prepares*** *students* ***for*** *a career in business.* **5** [T] to make food or a meal ready to eat: *This dish can be prepared the day before.* [ORIGIN: 1400—1500 French *préparer*, from Latin *praeparare*, from *prae* "before" + *parare* "to get, make ready"]

pre·pared /prɪˈpɛrd/ *adj.* **1** [not before noun] ready to do something or to deal with a particular situation: *He wasn't really* ***prepared for*** *all their questions.* **2 be prepared to do sth** to be willing to do something if it is necessary: *Is he prepared to accept the offer?* | *I am not prepared to discuss this any further.* **3** [only before noun] arranged and ready to be used, before it is needed: *The police read out a* ***prepared statement*** *to the press.*

pre·par·ed·ness /prɪˈpɛrɪdnɪs/ *n.* [U] the state of being ready for something: *military preparedness*

pre·pon·der·ance /prɪˈpandərəns/ *n.* [singular] (formal) a larger number or amount of one type of thing or person in a group than of any other type: *There's* ***a preponderance of*** *women in the orchestra.*

prep·o·si·tion /ˌprɛpəˈzɪʃən/ *n.* [C] ENG. LANG. ARTS in grammar, a word or phrase that is used before a noun, PRONOUN, or GERUND to show place, time, direction, etc. In the phrase "at the bank," "at" is a preposition. —**prepositional** *adj.*: *a prepositional phrase*

ˌprepositional ˈphrase *n.* [C] ENG. LANG. ARTS in grammar, a phrase consisting of a preposition and the noun, PRONOUN, or GERUND following it, such as "in bed" or "about traveling"

pre·pos·sess·ing /ˌpripəˈzɛsɪŋ◂/ *adj.* (formal) looking attractive or pleasant: *He was small and not prepossessing.*

pre·pos·ter·ous /prɪˈpastərəs/ *adj.* completely unreasonable or silly (SYN) **absurd**: *That's a preposterous story!* [ORIGIN: 1500—1600 Latin *praeposterus* "with the back part in front"]

prep·py /ˈprɛpi/ *adj.* (informal) preppy styles or clothes are very neat and CONSERVATIVE in a way that is typical of people who go to expensive private schools

ˈprep school *n.* [C] (informal) a private school that prepares students for college

pre·quel /ˈprikwəl/ *n.* [C] a book or movie that tells the story of what happened before the story told in a previous popular book or movie

pre·reg·is·ter /priˈrɛdʒɪstɚ/ *v.* [I] to put your name on a list for a particular course of study, school, etc. before the official time to do so —**preregistration** /ˌprirɛdʒɪˈstreɪʃən/ *n.* [U]

pre·req·ui·site /priˈrɛkwəzɪt/ *n.* [C] (formal) something that is necessary before something else can happen or be done: *A degree in biology is a* ***prerequisite for*** *the job.*

pre·rog·a·tive /prɪˈragət̬ɪv/ *n.* [C] a special right that someone has: *If you want to leave early, that's your prerogative.*

pres·age /ˈprɛsɪdʒ, prɪˈseɪdʒ/ *v.* [T] (literary) to be a sign that something is going to happen, especially something bad

Pres·by·te·ri·an /ˌprɛzbəˈtɪriən, ˌprɛs-/ *adj.* relating to the Protestant church that is one of the largest churches in the U.S. and the national church of Scotland —**Presbyterian** *n.* [C]

pre·school /ˈpriskul/ *n.* [C] a school for young children between two and five years of age: *Emma is* ***in preschool*** *now.* —**preschool** *adj.*: *preschool children* —**preschooler** *n.* [C]

pre·sci·ent /ˈprɛʃiənt, -ʃənt/ *adj.* (formal) able to imagine or know what will happen in the future: *his prescient analysis of what would happen after the elections* —**prescience** *n.* [U]

pre·scribe /prɪˈskraɪb/ *v.* [T] **1** to say what medicine or treatment a sick person should have: *Doctors commonly* ***prescribe*** *steroids* ***for*** *children with asthma.* **2** (formal) to state officially what should be done in a particular situation: *a punishment prescribed by the law* [ORIGIN: 1400—1500 Latin *praescribere* "to write at the beginning, order"]

pre·scrip·tion /prɪˈskrɪpʃən/ *n.* **1** [C] a piece of paper on which a doctor writes what medicine a sick person should have, or the medicine itself: *a* ***prescription for*** *painkillers*

THESAURUS **medicine, pill, tablet, capsule, eye/ear drops, drug, medication** → MEDICINE

2 by prescription a drug that you get by prescription can only be obtained with a written order from the doctor (ANT) **over the counter**

pre·scrip·tive /prɪˈskrɪptɪv/ *adj.* (formal) saying how something should be done or what someone should do

pres·ence /ˈprɛzəns/ *n.* **1** [U] the state of being present in a particular place (ANT) **absence**: *The ambassador's presence at the reception was a surprise.* | *Tests revealed **the presence of** poison in the blood.* **2 in sb's presence/in the presence of sb** with someone, or in the same place as him/her: *Everyone was afraid to voice an opinion in his presence.* | *He blushed whenever he was in the presence of women.* **3** [singular] a group of people, especially the army or the police, who are in a place to watch or control what is happening: *the American **military presence** in Vietnam* | *There's a heavy **police presence** at the embassy.* **4 have the presence of mind to do sth** to have the ability to deal with a dangerous situation calmly and quickly: *Bill had **the presence of mind to** call 911 after the fire started.* **5 make your presence felt** to have a strong effect on other people or situations: *Hanley has made his presence felt since joining the company.* **6** [U] the ability to appear impressive to people with your appearance or manner: *As an actor, he has a powerful stage presence.*

pres·ent¹ /ˈprɛzənt/ *adj.* **1 be present** (formal) to be in a particular place (ANT) **absent**: *How many people were **present at** the board meeting?* **2** [only before noun] happening or existing now: *We are unable to answer your questions **at the present time**.* | *Many people are unhappy with the **present situation**.*

THESAURUS
current – happening, existing, or being used now: *What is your current address?*
existing – present now and available to be used: *The existing system is not working.*
prevailing – very common in a particular place at a particular time: *the prevailing market price for corn*

3 the present day (formal) in modern times: *Traditional Indian pottery designs are still used in the present day.*

pre·sent² /prɪˈzɛnt/ *v.* [T] **1** to give something to someone, especially at an official or public occasion: *Mr. Davis **presented** the winning team **with** a gold cup.*

THESAURUS **give, award, grant** → GIVE¹

2 to give or show information in a particular way: *The evidence was **presented to** the court by Conor's lawyer.* **3 present yourself** the way you present yourself is the way you talk and behave when you meet new people: *She presents herself as confident and experienced.* **4** to cause something such as a problem or difficulty to happen or exist: *The heavy rains **presented** a new **difficulty** for the rescue workers.* **5** to give a performance in a theater, etc., or broadcast it on television or radio: *The Roxy is presenting a production of "Waiting for Godot" this week.* **6** (formal) to introduce someone formally to someone else: *May I present my parents, Mr. and Mrs. Benning.*

pre·sent³ /ˈprɛzənt/ *n.* **1** [C] something that you give to someone on a special occasion (SYN) **gift**: *a **birthday/Christmas/anniversary present*** | *He didn't even **give** me a **present**.* **2 the present** the time that is happening now: *Live in the present – don't worry about the past!* **3 at present** at this time: *We have no plans at present for closing the factory.*

pre·sent·a·ble /prɪˈzɛntəbəl/ *adj.* attractive and neat enough to be seen or shown in public: *Do I **look presentable**?* | *Let me try to **make** the house a little bit more **presentable**.*

pres·en·ta·tion /ˌprizənˈteɪʃən, ˌprɛ-/ *n.* **1** [C] the act of giving someone a prize or present at a formal ceremony: *the **presentation of** the awards* **2** [C] a formal talk about a particular subject: *She **gave** a short **presentation on/about** the new product.* **3** [U] the way in which something is shown, said, etc. to others: *As a chef, I care about the **presentation of** food as well as its taste.*

ˈpresent-day *adj.* modern or existing now: *The colonists settled near present-day Charleston.*

pres·ent·ly /ˈprɛzəntli/ *adv.* (formal) **1** at this time: *I presently live in Berlin.*

THESAURUS **now, at the moment, for the moment, at present/at the present time, currently** → NOW¹

2 (old-fashioned) in a short time: *The doctor will see you presently.*

THESAURUS **soon, in a minute, any minute now, before long, shortly** → SOON

ˌpresent ˈparticiple *n.* [C] ENG. LANG. ARTS in grammar, a PARTICIPLE that is formed by adding "-ing" to a verb. It can be used in compounds to make CONTINUOUS tenses, as in "She's sleeping," as an adjective, as in "the sleeping child," or as a GERUND, as in "I like cooking."

ˌpresent ˈperfect *n.* **the present perfect** ENG. LANG. ARTS in grammar, the tense of a verb that shows a time up to and including the present, and is formed with "have" and the past participle. In the sentence "Ken has traveled all over the world," "has traveled" is in the present perfect.

ˌpresent ˈtense *n.* **the present tense** ENG. LANG. ARTS in grammar, the form of a verb that shows what is true, what exists, or what is happening now. In the sentence "I always leave for work at 8:00," "leave" is in the present tense.

pres·er·va·tion /ˌprɛzɚˈveɪʃən/ *n.* [U] the act of keeping something unharmed or unchanged, or the degree to which it is unharmed or unchanged: *the **preservation of** the rainforest* | *The painting was **in a good/bad state of preservation**.*

pre·serv·a·tive /prɪˈzɚvət̬ɪv/ *n.* [C,U] a chemical substance that prevents food or wood from decaying: *The bread contains no **artificial preservatives**.*

pre·serve¹ /prɪˈzɚv/ *v.* [T] **1** to keep something

P

or someone from being harmed, destroyed, or changed too much: *The group is dedicated to preserving historic buildings.* | *We want to preserve as much open land as possible.*

THESAURUS **protect, guard, safeguard, give/offer/provide protection, conserve** → PROTECT

2 to add something to food so that it will stay in good condition for a long time: *Cucumbers* ***preserved in*** *vinegar are called pickles.*

preserve² *n.* **1** [C] an area of land or water in which animals, fish, or trees are protected: *Yellowstone was the nation's first wilderness preserve.* **2** [singular] an activity that only one particular group of people can do, or a place that only those people can use: *Politics is no longer the* ***preserve of*** *wealthy white males.* **3 preserves** [plural] a sweet food such as JAM, made from large pieces of fruit boiled with sugar: *strawberry preserves*

P

pre·side /prɪ'zaɪd/ *v.* [I] to be in charge of a formal meeting, ceremony, important situation, etc.: *Judge Baxter* ***presided over*** *the trial.*

pres·i·den·cy /'prɛzədənsi/ *n.* (plural **presidencies**) [C] the job of being a president, or the period of time when someone is a president: *He decided to run for the presidency.*

pres·i·dent, **President** /'prɛzədənt/ *n.* [C] **1** the official leader of a country that does not have a king or queen: *the* ***President of*** *Mexico* | *President Lincoln*

THESAURUS **politician, congressman/congresswoman, senator, governor, mayor** → POLITICIAN

2 someone who is in charge of a business, bank, club, college, etc.: *the* ***President of*** *Brown University* [ORIGIN: 1300—1400 French *président*, from Latin, present participle of *praesidere* "to sit in front of, guard, preside over"]

THESAURUS **boss, manager, head, chief, CEO** → BOSS¹

pres·i·den·tial /ˌprɛzə'dɛnʃəl◂/ *adj.* relating to the job or office of president: *the presidential campaign/election* | *the presidential nominee/candidate/contender*

ˌpresident pro 'tempore *also* **ˌpresident pro 'tem** *n.* (plural **presidents pro tempore**) [C usually singular] POLITICS a member of the U.S. SENATE who is elected by other SENATORS to be in control of the Senate's meetings when the VICE PRESIDENT is not there

'Presidents' Day *n.* a U.S. holiday on the third Monday in February, to remember the BIRTHDAYS of George Washington and Abraham Lincoln

pre'siding ˌofficer *n.* [C] POLITICS the person who is officially in charge of controlling the meetings in the U.S. SENATE or the HOUSE OF REPRESENTATIVES

pre·si·di·o /prɪ'sidioʊ, -'sɪd-/ *n.* [C] HISTORY a group of buildings that is protected by walls, built by Spanish SETTLERS (=people who go to live in an area where not many people like them have lived before) in areas that are now the southwest United States

press¹ /prɛs/ *v.*

1 WITH FINGER [T] to push something with your finger in order to make a machine start, a bell ring, etc.: *What happens if I* ***press*** *this* ***button****?* | *Mrs. Mott pressed the doorbell again.* | *Press F3 to save the document.*

2 PUSH AGAINST [T] to push something firmly against a surface: *He* ***pressed*** *some money* ***into*** *her hand.* | *Their faces were* ***pressed against*** *the window.*

3 IRON [T] to make clothes smooth using heat SYN **iron**: *I need to have this suit cleaned and pressed.*

4 press charges to say officially that someone has done something illegal so that a court must decide if s/he is guilty

5 PERSUADE [T] to try very hard to persuade someone to do something or tell you something: *He* ***pressed*** *me* ***to*** *accept the job.* | *Detectives had been* ***pressing*** *him* ***for*** *details.*

6 MOVE [I] to move in a particular direction by pushing: *The crowd* ***pressed forward*** *to see what was happening.*

7 HEAVY WEIGHT [T] to put pressure or weight on something to make it flat, crush it, etc.: *a machine for pressing grapes*

THESAURUS

squash – to press something and damage it by making it flat: *Put the tomatoes where they won't get squashed.*
crush – to press something very hard so that it is broken or destroyed: *His leg was crushed in the accident.*
mash – to press fruit or cooked vegetables until they are soft and smooth: *Mash the potatoes well.*
grind – to press something into powder using a special machine: *Can you grind the coffee beans?*
squeeze – to press something from both sides, usually with your fingers: *Squeeze the toothpaste tube from the bottom.* | *fresh-squeezed orange juice*
compress (formal) – to press something so that it takes up less space: *The pump compresses the air, forcing it through a tube into the tire.*
compact (formal) – to press something together so that it becomes smaller or more solid: *The machine compacts household trash.*

press on/ahead *phr. v.*
to continue doing something without stopping: *The army crossed the river and pressed on to the border.*

press² *n.* **1 the press** newspapers, magazines, etc., or the people who work for them: *Taylor refuses to speak to the press.* | *the* ***freedom of the press*** | *Mary's new play is getting the attention of* ***the national/local press.*** **2 good/bad press** the praise or criticism that someone is given by newspapers, radio, or television: *I don't think Kurt deserves all the **bad press** that he's **getting**.* **3** [C] a business that prints and sometimes sells books: *the University Press* **4** [C] a PRINTING PRESS **5 go to press** if a newspaper, magazine, or book goes to press, it begins to be printed: *All information was correct at the time we went to press.* **6** [C] a piece of equipment that makes something flat or forces liquid out of something: *a flower press* | *a wine press*

'press ˌagent *n.* [C] someone whose job is to give photographs or information about a famous person to newspapers, radio, or television

'press ˌconference *n.* [C] a meeting at which someone makes official statements to people who write news reports: *The Governor **held a press conference** last night.*

'press corps *n.* [C] a group of people who usually write the news reports that come from a particular place: *the White House press corps*

pressed /prɛst/ *adj.* **be pressed for time/money etc.** to not have enough time, money, etc.: *I can't stop now – I'm pressed for time.*

press·ing /'prɛsɪŋ/ *adj.* a pressing problem, matter, question, etc. needs to be dealt with very soon SYN **urgent**: *Poverty is the country's most **pressing problem**.*

'press reˌlease *n.* [C] an official statement that gives information to the newspapers, radio, or television

pres·sure¹ /'prɛʃɚ/ *n.* **1** [U] an attempt to make someone do something by using influence, arguments, threats, etc.: *Kay's family is **putting pressure on** her to get married.* | *The company is **under pressure** to reduce costs.* | *The president faces **pressure from** militants in his own party.* **2** [C,U] the conditions of your work, family, or way of living that make you anxious, and cause problems: *I've been **under** a lot of **pressure** at work lately.* | *There is a lot of **pressure on** children these days.* | *the **pressures of** modern life* **3** [C,U] the force that a gas or liquid has when it is pushed and held inside a container: *The air pressure in the tires might be low.* **4** [U] the force produced by pressing on someone or something: *She felt the comforting **pressure of** his hand on her shoulder.*

pressure² *v.* [T] to try to make someone do something by using influence, arguments, threats, etc.: *She was **pressured into** signing the statement.*

> THESAURUS **force, make, coerce, compel** → FORCE²

'pressure ˌcooker *n.* [C] a tightly covered cooking pot that cooks food very quickly using hot steam

pres·sured /'prɛʃɚd/ *adj.* feeling a lot of worry because of the number of things that you have to do: *Her job makes her **feel pressured** all the time.*

'pressure group *n.* [C] a group of people or an organization that tries to influence what the public thinks about things, and what the government does about things

pres·sur·ized /'prɛʃəˌraɪzd/ *adj.* if an aircraft is pressurized, the air pressure inside it is similar to the pressure on the ground

pres·tige /prɛ'stiʒ, -'stidʒ/ *n.* [U] if you have prestige, you are respected and admired because of your job or something that you have achieved: *My present job has a certain amount of prestige attached to it.*

pres·tig·ious /prɛ'stɪdʒəs, -'sti-/ *adj.* admired or respected as one of the best and most important: *a prestigious award for writers*

pre·sum·a·bly /prɪ'zuməbli/ (Ac) *adv.* used in order to say that something is likely to be true, although you are not certain: *Presumably, he's going to come back and get this stuff.*

pre·sume /prɪ'zum/ (Ac) *v.* **1** [T] to think that something is likely to be true, although you are not certain: *I **presume (that)** this price includes all transportation and hotels.* | *Many of these diseases are now widely presumed to be under control.*

> THESAURUS **assume, be under the impression that ..., take it for granted (that)** → ASSUME

2 [T] to accept that something is true until it is proved untrue, especially in law: *She is missing and **is presumed dead**.* **3** [I] (formal) to behave rudely by doing something that you do not have the right to do: *Don't **presume to** tell me how to raise my children!* [ORIGIN: 1300—1400 French *présumer*, from Latin *praesumere*, from *prae* "before" + *sumere* "to take"]

pre·sump·tion /prɪ'zʌmpʃən/ (Ac) *n.* **1** [C] something that you think must be true or is very likely to be true: *There should always be **a presumption of** innocence until someone is proven guilty.* | *This idea is based on the **presumption that** the brain is like a digital computer.* **2** [U] (formal) behavior that seems rude and too confident

pre·sump·tu·ous /prɪ'zʌmptʃuəs/ (Ac) *adj.* doing something that you have no right to do and that seems rude: ***It would be presumptuous** of me to try to tell you what to do.* | *It is perhaps presumptuous to think that we will one day understand the purpose of the universe.*

pre·sup·pose /ˌprisə'poʊz/ *v.* [T] (formal) to depend on something that is thought to be true SYN **assume**: *All your plans **presuppose that** the bank will be willing to lend us the money.* —**presupposition** /ˌprisʌpə'zɪʃən/ *n.* [C,U]

pre·teen /'pritin/ *n.* [C] someone who is 11 or 12 years old —**preteen** *adj.*: *my preteen daughter*

pre·tend¹ /prɪ'tɛnd/ *v.* [I,T] **1** to behave as if something is true when you know it is not: *Terry **pretended to** be asleep.* | *We can't go on **pretending***

(that) everything is OK. **2** to imagine that something is true or real, as a game: *Let's **pretend (that)** we're on the moon!*

pretend² *adj.* a word meaning IMAGINARY, used especially by children, or when talking to children: *We sang songs around a pretend campfire.*

pre·tense /ˈpritɛns, prɪˈtɛns/ *n.* **1** [singular, U] an attempt to pretend that something is true: *Kevin **made no pretense of** being surprised.* | *We had to **keep up the pretense** that we were married.* **2 under false pretenses** if you do something under false pretenses, you do it by pretending that something is true when it is not: *He entered the country on a Japanese passport obtained under false pretenses.*

P

pre·ten·sion /prɪˈtɛnʃən/ *n.* [C usually plural, U] an attempt to seem more important, rich, or intelligent than you really are: *his honesty and lack of pretension*

pre·ten·tious /prɪˈtɛnʃəs/ *adj.* trying to seem more important, rich, or intelligent than you really are: *There were a bunch of pretentious people at the gallery opening.*

pret·er·ite, **preterit** /ˈpreṭərɪt/ *n.* **the preterite** ENG. LANG. ARTS the PAST TENSE

pre·text /ˈpritɛkst/ *n.* [C] a false reason that is given for doing something, in order to hide the real reason: *He got into the building **on the pretext** of checking the heating.*

pret·ty¹ /ˈprɪṭi/ *adv.* (informal) **1** fairly, but not completely: *I thought the test was pretty easy.* | *"How are you feeling?" "Oh, pretty good."* | *That car was going pretty quickly.*

THESAURUS rather, fairly, quite, kind of → RATHER

2 very: *Dad was pretty angry about it.* **3 pretty much** almost completely: *I'm pretty much done with my homework.* [ORIGIN: Old English *prættig* "tricky," from *prætt* "trick"]

pretty² *adj.* (comparative **prettier**, superlative **prettiest**) **1** a woman or child who is pretty is attractive: *a very pretty little girl* | *Laura is much prettier than her sister.*

THESAURUS attractive, good-looking, nice-looking, beautiful, gorgeous, stunning, cute → ATTRACTIVE

2 attractive or pleasant to look at or listen to: *a pretty pink dress* | *a song with a pretty tune* **3 not a pretty picture/sight** very ugly, upsetting, or worrying: *The plane was completely destroyed – it's not a pretty picture.*

pret·zel /ˈprɛtsəl/ *n.* [C] a salty type of bread, baked in the shape of a loose knot [ORIGIN: 1800—1900 German *pretzel*, *bretzel*, from Latin *brachiatus* "having branches like arms"]

pre·vail /prɪˈveɪl/ *v.* [I] (formal) **1** if a person, idea, or principle prevails, they achieve success after a struggle: *Justice prevailed in the end.*

THESAURUS win, be victorious, triumph → WIN¹

2 if a belief or opinion prevails, it is common among a group of people: *After the riots, a mood of uncertainty still **prevails in** the neighborhood.* [ORIGIN: 1300—1400 Latin *praevalere*, from *prae* "before" + *valere* "to be strong"]

prevail on/upon sb *phr. v.* (formal) to persuade someone: *I might be willing to prevail upon the committee to reconsider its decision.*

pre·vail·ing /prɪˈveɪlɪŋ/ *adj.* **1** very common in a particular place at a particular time (SYN) **current**: *Williams' books challenged prevailing views of U.S. history.*

THESAURUS present, current, existing → PRESENT¹

2 prevailing wind the direction in which the wind usually blows over a particular area at a particular time of the year

prev·a·lent /ˈprɛvələnt/ *adj.* common at a particular time, in a particular place, or among a particular group of people: *The disease is more **prevalent among** young people.* —**prevalence** *n.* [U]: *the prevalence of crime in the inner city*

pre·vent /prɪˈvɛnt/ *v.* [T] to stop something from happening, or stop someone from doing something: *It was an accident that could have been prevented.* | *A knee injury **prevented** him **from** playing.* [ORIGIN: 1400—1500 Latin, past participle of *praevenire* "to come before"] —**preventable** *adj.*: *preventable diseases*

pre·ven·ta·tive /prɪˈvɛnṭəṭɪv/ *adj.* preventive

pre·ven·tion /prɪˈvɛnʃən/ *n.* [U] the act of preventing something, or the actions that you take in order to prevent something: *crime prevention* | *the **prevention of** accidents*

pre·ven·tive /prɪˈvɛntɪv/ *adj.* intended to prevent something you do not want to happen: *preventive medicine* (=treatment to prevent people from becoming sick)

pre·view /ˈprivyu/ *n.* [C] **1** an occasion when you see a movie, play, etc. before it is shown to the public **2** an advertisement for a movie or television program that often consists of short parts of it —**preview** *v.* [T]

pre·vi·ous /ˈpriviəs/ (Ac) *adj.* [only before noun] happening or existing before a particular event, time, or thing: *She has two children from a previous marriage.* | *Have you had any previous experience in accounting?* | *In previous generations, the elderly depended on their children.* [ORIGIN: 1600—1700 Latin *praevius* "leading the way," from *via* "way"]

THESAURUS last, former → LAST¹

pre·vi·ous·ly /ˈpriviəsli/ (Ac) *adv.* before now, or before a particular time: *She previously worked* at Bank of Boston. | Previously, people had believed that the sun orbited around the Earth.

THESAURUS before, earlier → BEFORE[1]

pre·war /ˌpriˈwɔr◂ / *adj., adv.* happening or existing before a war, especially World War I or World War II: *the country's prewar population*

prey[1] /preɪ/ *n.* **1** [U] an animal that is hunted and eaten by another animal: *On TV, a tiger stalked its prey.* **2 fall prey to sth** to be affected by something unpleasant: *More teenagers are falling prey to gang violence.*

prey[2] *v.*

prey on sb/sth *phr. v.* **1** if an animal or bird preys on another animal or bird, it hunts and eats it **2** to try to influence or deceive weaker people: *The police issued a warning about dishonest salesmen who prey on old people.*

price[1] /praɪs/ *n.* **1** [C,U] the amount of money that must be paid in order to buy something: *What's the **price of** this book?* | *Gas **prices** have **gone up** again.* | *I can't believe how **high/low** their **prices** are.* | *Stock **prices fell** yesterday.* | *We could rent a car or take the train – there's almost no difference **in price**.* | *price cuts*

COLLOCATIONS

go up/rise/increase – to become higher
increase/raise prices – to make them higher
go down/fall/drop – to become lower
cut/lower/slash prices – to make them lower
rocket/soar – to suddenly become much higher
tumble/plummet – to suddenly become much lower
fluctuate – to keep becoming higher and then lower
level out/off – to stop going up or down, and continue at the same amount
cost, expense, charge, fee, rate → COST[1]

2 [U] something bad that you must deal with in order to have or do something else: *He's very busy, but I guess that's the **price of** success.* | *She's gotten the job she wanted, but **at what price**?* **3 at/for a price** used in order to say that you can buy something, but only if you pay a lot of money: *You can buy excellent wine here – at a price.* **4 at any price** even if something is extremely difficult: *They were determined to have a child at any price.* **5 asking price** the price that someone who is selling something says s/he wants for it: *The asking price was $500, but we paid $350 for it.* [ORIGIN: 1200—1300 Old French *pris*, from Latin *pretium* "price, money"]

price[2] *v.* [T] **1** to give a price to something that is for sale: *a reasonably priced pair of shoes* **2** to put a sign on goods that shows how much they cost

ˈprice ˌindex *n.* [C] ECONOMICS a list of particular goods and services, showing how much their prices change each month. It is used as a way of measuring INFLATION (=the rate at which prices increase over a period of time).

price·less /ˈpraɪslɪs/ *adj.* **1** so valuable that you cannot calculate a financial value: *priceless antiques*

THESAURUS valuable, precious, worth a lot/a fortune → VALUABLE

2 extremely important or useful: *priceless information* **3** (informal) very funny or silly: *The look on his face when I walked in the room was priceless.*

ˈprice war *n.* [C] ECONOMICS a situation in which companies that are competing against each other reduce the prices of products or services they sell, because each company is trying to get the most customers

pric·ey, pricy /ˈpraɪsi/ *adj.* (informal) expensive: *a pricey restaurant*

THESAURUS expensive, overpriced, fancy, posh → EXPENSIVE

prick[1] /prɪk/ *v.* **1** [T] to make a small hole in the surface of something, using a sharp point: *Prick the pie dough all over with a fork.* | *She **pricked** her **finger** with the needle.*

THESAURUS pierce, make a hole in sth, punch, puncture → PIERCE

2 prick up its ears if an animal pricks up its ears, it raises them and points them toward a sound **3 prick up your ears** to start listening to what someone is saying because it is interesting

prick[2] *n.* [C] **1** a slight pain you get when something sharp goes into your skin: *She felt a sharp prick when the needle went into her finger.* **2** a small hole in the surface of something, made by a sharp point

prick·le[1] /ˈprɪkəl/ *n.* [C] **1** a long thin sharp point on the skin of some plants and animals **2** a stinging feeling on your skin

prickle[2] *v.* [I,T] if your skin prickles, or if something prickles your skin, you feel a slight stinging pain on your skin: *That sweater always prickles me.*

prick·ly /ˈprɪkli/ *adj.* **1** covered with prickles: *prickly bushes* **2** causing a stinging feeling on your skin: *a prickly wool jacket*

prickly

a prickly cactus

pride[1] /praɪd/ *n.* [U] **1** a feeling of satisfaction and pleasure in what you have done, or in what someone connected with you has done → PROUD: *Everyone on our team **takes** great **pride in** (=is very proud of) the quality of their work.* | *They always talk about their son **with pride**.* **2** a feeling that you like and respect yourself, and that you deserve to be respected by other people: *Losing his job really **hurt** his **pride**.* **3** a feeling that you are better than other people: *I had too much pride to ask for money.* **4 sb's pride and joy** someone or something that is very important to someone: *Ken's new car is his pride and joy.* **5 swallow your pride** to ignore your feelings of pride and do something that seems necessary, even though you do not want to do it: *You're just going to have to swallow your pride and apologize.*

pride² *v.* **pride yourself on sth** to be very proud of something that you do well, or of a quality that you have: *Sandy prides herself on her ability to speak four languages.*

priest /prist/ *n.* [C] someone who performs religious duties and ceremonies in some religions → MINISTER

P

priest·ess /ˈpristɪs/ *n.* [C] a woman with religious authority and duties in some non-Christian religions

priest·hood /ˈpristhʊd/ *n.* **the priesthood** the position of being a priest: *Angelo has decided to* ***enter the priesthood*** (=become a priest).

prim /prɪm/ *adj.* very formal in the way you behave, and easily shocked by anything rude: *Janet's much too* ***prim and proper*** *to laugh at a joke like that.* —**primly** *adv.*

pri·ma·cy /ˈpraɪməsi/ (Ac) *n.* [U] the state of being the thing or person with the most importance or authority: *No one ever questioned* ***the primacy of*** *the church.*

pri·ma don·na /ˌprimə ˈdɑnə, ˌprɪmə-/ *n.* [C] (disapproving) someone who thinks that s/he is very good at what s/he does, and demands a lot of attention and admiration from other people

pri·mal /ˈpraɪməl/ *adj.* [only before noun] primal feelings are basic and seem to come from ancient times when humans were more like animals: *primal instincts*

pri·mar·i·ly /praɪˈmɛrəli/ (Ac) *adv.* mainly: *We do sell paintings, but this is primarily a furniture store.* | *Natural gas consists primarily of methane.*

THESAURUS **mainly, chiefly, principally, largely** → MAINLY

pri·mar·y¹ /ˈpraɪˌmɛri, -məri/ (Ac) *adj.* [only before noun] **1** most important (SYN) **main**: *Our primary concern is the safety of the children.* | *The primary goal of the campaign was to win the next election.* **2** relating to the education of children who are between 5 and 11 years old: *primary education* [ORIGIN: 1400—1500 Latin *primarius*, from *primus* "first"]

primary² *n.* (plural **primaries**) [C] POLITICS an election in the U.S. in which people vote to decide who will be their political party's CANDIDATE for a political position

ˌprimary ˈcare *n.* [U] the main medical help that you get, unless your doctor decides that you need to see a SPECIALIST (=doctor with special skills)

ˌprimary ˈcell *n.* [C] PHYSICS a piece of equipment that makes electricity from the energy that is produced when two or more chemicals are mixed together. This process can only happen once, and when the electricity is used up, the cell is dead. (SYN) **voltaic cell**

ˌprimary ˈcolor *n.* [C] one of the three colors – red, yellow, and blue – that you can mix together to make any other color

ˌprimary eˈlection *n.* [C] POLITICS a PRIMARY

ˌprimary ˈgrowth *n.* [U] BIOLOGY new growth in the stem of a plant, that happens at the top of its stem and at the end of its roots

ˈprimary ˌschool *n.* [C] an ELEMENTARY SCHOOL

ˌprimary ˈsource *n.* [C] HISTORY a written or spoken description of an event by someone who was actually there when it happened → SECONDARY SOURCE

ˌprimary ˈstress *n.* [C,U] ENG. LANG. ARTS the strongest STRESS (=force) that you give to part of a long word when you are speaking, for example like the force given to "pri" when you say "primary." It is shown in this dictionary by the mark (/ˈ/). → SECONDARY STRESS

pri·mate /ˈpraɪmeɪt/ *n.* [C] BIOLOGY a member of the group of MAMMALs that includes humans and monkeys

prime¹ /praɪm/ (Ac) *adj.* [only before noun] **1** most important: *Smoking is the prime cause of lung disease.* **2** very good: *The house is in a* ***prime location.*** | *The church is a* ***prime example*** *of Gothic architecture.* [ORIGIN: 1300—1400 French, Latin *primus* "first"]

prime² *n.* **1 be in your prime/be in the prime of life** to be at the time in your life when you are strongest and most active **2** [C] a PRIME NUMBER

prime³ *v.* [T] **1** to prepare someone for a situation so that s/he knows what to do: *The senators were primed to ask some tough questions.* **2** to put a special layer of paint on a surface, to prepare it for the main layer **3** to prepare a pump to work by filling it with a liquid

ˌprime ˈminister *n.* [C] the leader of the government in countries that have a PARLIAMENT

ˌprime ˈnumber *n.* [C] MATH a number that can only be divided by itself and the number one

prim·er /ˈpraɪmɚ/ *n.* [C,U] a special paint that you put on wood, metal, etc. before you put on the main layer of paint

ˈprime ˌtime *n.* [U] the time in the evening when the largest number of people are watching television

pri·me·val /praɪˈmivəl/ *adj.* EARTH SCIENCES belonging to the earliest time in the existence of the Earth or the universe: *primeval forests*

prim·i·tive /ˈprɪmət̬ɪv/ *adj.* **1** belonging to a simple way of life that existed in the past, or to an early stage in the development of humans or animals (ANT) **modern**: *primitive societies* **2** very simple, uncomfortable, or without modern features: *primitive living conditions*

pri·mor·di·al /praɪˈmɔrdiəl/ *adj.* EARTH SCIENCES existing at the beginning of time or the beginning of the Earth: *the primordial seas*

prince /prɪns/ *n.* [C] **1** the son of a king or queen, or one of his or her close male relatives

THESAURUS **king, queen, princess, monarch, ruler, emperor, sovereign** → KING

2 a male ruler of some small countries: *Prince Albert of Monaco* [ORIGIN: 1100—1200 Old French, Latin *princeps* "leader," from *primus* "first" + *capere* "to take"]

prince·ly /ˈprɪnsli/ *adj.* impressive or large: *a **princely sum** of money*

prin·cess /ˈprɪnsɪs, -sɛs/ *n.* [C] **1** the daughter of a king or queen, or one of his or her close female relatives

THESAURUS **king, queen, prince, monarch, ruler, emperor, sovereign** → KING

2 the wife of a prince

prin·ci·pal¹ /ˈprɪnsəpəl/ (Ac) *n.* **1** [C] someone who is in charge of a school: *a high school principal* | *Helen Davies is the **principal of** Ferry Elementary School.* **2** [U] ECONOMICS the original amount of money that is lent to someone or saved by someone, not including any of the INTEREST: *The principal amounts to $50,000.* **3** [C] the main person in a business or organization, who can make business decisions [ORIGIN: 1200—1300 Old French, Latin *principalis*, from *princeps* "leader," from *primus* "first" + *capere* "to take"]

principal² *adj.* most important (SYN) **main**: *Magic is a principal ingredient in fairy tales.* | *Oil is the country's principal source of income.*

prin·ci·pal·i·ty /ˌprɪnsəˈpæləṭi/ *n.* (plural **principalities**) [C] a country ruled by a prince

prin·ci·pally /ˈprɪnsəpli/ (Ac) *adv.* mainly: *The audience was principally made up of women.* | *The data is derived principally from national surveys.*

THESAURUS **mainly, chiefly, largely, primarily** → MAINLY

prin·ci·ple /ˈprɪnsəpəl/ (Ac) *n.* **1** [C,U] a moral rule or set of ideas about what is right and wrong, that influences how you behave: *the **principle that** everyone is equal* | *I refused to sign the contract as a **matter of principle*** (=because the contract included things I believed were wrong). | *our society's values and **moral principles*** | *Schools try to teach children a set of principles.* **2** [C] the basic idea that a plan or system is based on: *the **principles of** business management* | *The law is a violation of the **basic principles** of a free society.* | *The **management principles** used by the Japanese provided valuable lessons for American labor.* **3** [C] a rule that explains the way something works: *the **basic/fundamental principles** of physics* | *Scientific inquiry enabled man to relate the visible changes in nature with the permanent **principles underlying** them.* **4 in principle a)** if something is possible in principle, there is no good reason why it should not happen: *In principle, you can leave work early on Friday, but it's not always possible.* | *The class is, in principle, open to all ages.* **b)** if you agree to something in principle, you agree about a general plan or idea without the details: *The arrangement has been agreed to in principle.* | *Approval in principle was all that was needed to get the negotiations started.* [ORIGIN: 1300—1400 French *principe*, from Latin *principium* "beginning"]

prin·ci·pled /ˈprɪnsəpəld/ (Ac) *adj.* (written) having strong beliefs about what is morally right and wrong: *a **strongly/highly principled** woman* | *Sadly, those high ideals and principled declarations had led to war, not peace.*

P

print¹ /prɪnt/ *v.* **1** [I,T] to produce words, numbers, or pictures on paper, using a machine that puts ink onto the surface: *The books are printed in China.* | *Why isn't my document printing?* **2** [T] to produce many copies of a book, newspaper, etc.: *About 100 copies of the report have been printed.* **3** [T] to print an article, letter, speech, etc. in a newspaper, book, or magazine: *The Times printed a story about it this week.* **4** [I,T] to write words by hand without joining the letters: *Please print your name in capital letters.* **5** [T] to produce a photograph on special paper

print sth ↔ **off/out** *phr. v.* to produce a printed copy of a computer document [ORIGIN: 1200—1300 Old French *preinte*, from *preint*, past participle of *preindre* "to press," from Latin *premere*]

print² *n.* **1** [U] writing that has been printed in books, newspapers, etc.: *The print is awfully small.* | *People learn many words by seeing them **in print**, rather than hearing them said.* **2 be in print/be out of print** if a book is in print, it is available to buy, and if it is out of print, it is not available to buy anymore **3 the fine/small print** the details of a legal document which are often in very small writing: *the fine print in the contract* **4** [C] a picture that has been printed from a small sheet of metal or block of wood, or a copy of a painting **5** [C] a photograph printed on paper: *Why don't you order an extra **set of prints**?* **6** [C] a mark made on a surface or in a soft substance by something that has been pressed onto it → FOOTPRINT: *There were muddy paw prints all over the floor.* **7 prints** [plural] someone's FINGERPRINTS **8** [C,U] cloth that has a colored pattern on it: *a print dress*

print·er /ˈprɪnṭɚ/ *n.* [C] **1** a machine connected to a computer, that can copy documents from a computer onto paper: *a laser printer* → *see picture on page A19* **2** someone who owns or works in a printing business

print·ing /ˈprɪnṭɪŋ/ *n.* **1** [U] the act or process of making a book, magazine, etc. using a machine: *a printing error* **2** [C] an act of printing a number of copies of a book: *The novel is in its third printing.* **3** [U] a method of writing, in which you write each letter of a word separately rather than joining them together

'printing press *n.* [C] a machine that prints newspapers, books, etc.

print·out /'prɪntaʊt/ *n.* [C,U] paper with printed information on it, produced by a computer printer

pri·or /'praɪɚ/ (Ac) *adj.* (formal) **1 prior to sth** before: *the week prior to the election* | *The AIDS virus may not have existed prior to the 1960s.* **2** [only before noun] done, planned, or existing earlier than something else (SYN) **previous**: *No change can be made without prior approval.* [ORIGIN: 1700—1800 Latin "earlier, older, higher in rank," from Latin *pri* "before"]

P

pri·or·i·tize /praɪ'ɔrə,taɪz/ (Ac) *v.* [T] to deal with something important first, or to list several things, problems, etc. in order of importance: *Ask your boss to prioritize your projects.* | *The city needs to prioritize the needs of children in the budget.* —**prioritization** /praɪ,ɔrət̬ə'zeɪʃən/ *n.* [U]

pri·or·i·ty /praɪ'ɔrət̬i/ (Ac) *n.* (plural **priorities**) **1** [C,U] the thing that you think is most important and that needs attention before anything else: *Education is his* ***top priority****.* | *The company considers training to be a* ***high/low priority****.* | *The development of new fuel sources is* ***of high priority****.* | *Increasing market share is high on the corporation's* ***list of priorities****.* **2** [U] the right to be given attention first and before other people or things: *Children who live near the school are* ***given priority over*** *those who live farther away.* | *Industry should* ***place a higher priority on*** *reducing pollution.*

prism /'prɪzəm/ *n.* [C] **1** PHYSICS a transparent block of glass that breaks up white light into different colors **2** MATH a solid GEOMETRIC shape with two matching ends and three or more sides that are the same width from the bottom to the top

pris·on /'prɪzən/ *n.* [C,U] a large building where people are kept as a punishment for a crime, or while waiting to go to court for their TRIAL: *He spent ten months* ***in prison****.* | *Williams was* ***sent to prison*** *for rape.* | *a* ***prison sentence/term*** (=time that must be spent in prison)

COLLOCATIONS

go to prison: *He could go to prison for 25 years.*
put sb in prison: *If he's caught, they'll put him in prison.*
send sb to prison: *Her husband was sent back to prison after violating his parole* (=disobeying the rules which allowed him to leave prison early).
spend time in prison – to be in prison for committing a crime: *He will spend the rest of his life in prison.*
release sb from prison – to let someone leave prison: *He was released from prison after serving a two-year sentence.*
get out of prison – to be released from prison: *The day he got out of prison, he stole a car.*
escape from prison: *He was killed while trying to escape from prison.* → CRIME, CRIMINAL[1], PUNISHMENT

pris·on·er /'prɪzənɚ/ *n.* [C] **1** someone who is kept in a prison as a punishment for a crime (SYN) **convict** **2** someone who is taken by force and kept somewhere, for example during a war: *Six soldiers were* ***taken prisoner****.* | *They* ***kept/held*** *her* ***prisoner*** *for three months.*

THESAURUS

captive – someone who is kept as a prisoner, especially in a war: *The rebels are holding 54 captives.*
hostage – someone who is kept as a prisoner by an enemy, so that the other side will do what the enemy demands: *The group demanded that 400 prisoners be released in exchange for the hostages.*

,prisoner of 'war *n.* (plural **prisoners of war**) (*abbreviation* **P.O.W.**) [C] a member of the military who is caught by the enemy during a war and kept as a prisoner

pris·sy /'prɪsi/ *adj.* (informal, disapproving) behaving very correctly, and easily shocked by anything rude

pris·tine /'prɪ,stin, prɪ'stin/ *adj.* extremely clean, and not spoiled at all by use: *She owns a 1973 Volkswagen Beetle* ***in pristine condition****.* | *the pristine white sand*

pri·va·cy /'praɪvəsi/ *n.* [U] **1** the state of being able to be alone, and not seen or heard by other people: *If he wants to smoke* ***in the privacy of*** *his own home, that's fine, but he can't smoke in my house.* **2** the state of being able to keep your own affairs secret: *Reporters* ***invade*** *the* ***privacy*** *of celebrities.*

pri·vate[1] /'praɪvɪt/ *adj.* **1** for use by one person or group, not for everyone (ANT) **public**: *a private jet* | *Rooms are available for private parties.* | *They were arrested for trespassing on* ***private property****.* **2** secret or personal, and not for sharing with others: *her private thoughts* | *You had no right to look at my private papers.*

THESAURUS

secret – known or felt only by you, and not talked about or shown to anyone else: *Dreams may reveal our secret desires.*
personal – concerning only you: *He asked a lot of personal questions.*
innermost – your innermost feelings, desires, etc. are the ones you feel most strongly and keep private: *Collins expressed her innermost feelings in her poetry.*
intimate – relating to very private or personal matters: *all my intimate secrets*
be none of sb's business – if something is none of your business, it is private and you should not ask about it: *It's none of your business what I do in my free time.* → SECRET[1]

3 not relating to, owned by, or paid for by the

government (ANT) **public**: *a private college* **4** separate from your work or your official position, and not related to it: *Should reporters be prying into the* ***private lives*** *of politicians?* **5** quiet and without lots of people: *Is there a private corner where we can talk?* —**privately** *adv.*: *Is there someplace we can talk privately?*

private² *n.* **1 in private** without other people listening or watching: *Miss Schultz, I need to speak to you in private.* **2** [C] a soldier of the lowest rank in the Army or the Marines

ˌprivate ˈenterprise *n.* [U] ECONOMICS the economic system in which private businesses can compete and the government does not control industry

THESAURUS **business, commerce** → BUSINESS

ˌprivate inˈvestigator *also* **ˌprivate deˈtective, ˌprivate ˈeye** (informal) *n.* [C] someone whom you pay to do things such as look for information or missing people, or follow someone and report on what s/he does

ˌprivate ˈparts *also* **pri·vates** /ˈpraɪvɪts/ *n.* [plural] (informal) the sex organs – used in order to avoid naming them directly

ˈprivate school *n.* [C] a school that is not supported by government money, where education must be paid for by the children's parents → PUBLIC SCHOOL

pri·va·tion /praɪˈveɪʃən/ *n.* [C,U] (formal) a lack of the things that everyone needs, such as food, warmth, and shelter

pri·vat·ize /ˈpraɪvəˌtaɪz/ *v.* [T] ECONOMICS if a government privatizes an industry, service, etc. that it controls or owns, it sells it or gives contracts to private companies → NATIONALIZE —**privatization** /ˌpraɪvət̬əˈzeɪʃən/ *n.* [U]

priv·i·lege /ˈprɪvlɪdʒ, -vəlɪdʒ/ *n.* **1** [C] a special advantage that is given only to one person or group of people: *These soldiers were given* ***special privileges.*** | *Good health care should not be just a* ***privilege of*** *the wealthy.* **2** [singular] something that you are lucky to have the chance to do, and that you enjoy very much: ***It's*** *been* ***a privilege to*** *meet you, sir.* | *I* ***had the privilege of*** *working with some very interesting people.* **3** [U] a situation in which people who are rich or of a high social class have many more advantages than other people: *a life of wealth and privilege* —**privileged** *adj.*

priv·y¹ /ˈprɪvi/ *adj.* (formal) **be privy to sth** to share secret knowledge of something: *I was not privy to the discussion.*

privy² *n.* (plural **privies**) [C] (old-fashioned) an OUTHOUSE → TOILET

prize¹ /praɪz/ *n.* [C] something that is given to someone who is successful in a competition, race, game of chance, etc.: *Her roses won* ***first/second/third prize*** *at the flower show.* | *Bohr* ***won*** *the Nobel* ***Prize*** *in 1922.* | *the Pulitzer* ***Prize for*** *fiction*

prize² *adj.* **1** good enough to win a prize or to have won a prize: *prize cattle* **2 prize money** money that is given to the person who wins a competition, race, etc.

prize³ *v.* [T] to think that someone or something is very important or valuable: *He gave her a necklace that his mother had prized.*

prized /praɪzd/ *adj.* very important or valuable to someone: *Education is* ***highly prized.*** | *All her most* ***prized possessions*** *were lost in the fire.*

prize·fight /ˈpraɪzfaɪt/ *n.* [C] a BOXING match in which the competitors are paid —**prizefighter** *n.* [C]

pro /proʊ/ *n.* (plural **pros**) [C] **1** (informal) a PROFESSIONAL: *a golf pro* **2** something that is an advantage: *We discussed* ***the pros and cons*** (=the advantages and disadvantages) *of starting our own business.* —**pro** *adj.*: *pro basketball*

pro·ac·tive /proʊˈæktɪv/ *adj.* taking action to influence events in advance, rather than dealing with things after they happen: *We need to adopt a more proactive approach to the problem of global warming.*

prob·a·bil·i·ty /ˌprɑbəˈbɪlət̬i/ *n.* (plural **probabilities**) **1** [singular, U] how likely it is that something will happen, exist, or be true: *the* ***probability of*** *delay* | *a* ***high/low probability*** *of success* **2 in all probability** very probably: *There will, in all probability, be parts that you do not understand.* **3** [singular] something that is likely to happen or exist: *War is a real probability unless the talks succeed.* **4** [C,U] MATH how likely something is to happen, measured in a mathematical calculation: *The blood test shows a 99.4 percent probability that Hill is the child's father.*

prob·a·ble /ˈprɑbəbəl/ *adj.* likely to happen, exist, or be true: ***It is probable that*** *both genes and the environment play a role in the disease.* | *the probable cause of the accident*

prob·a·bly /ˈprɑbəbli/ *adv.* likely to happen, exist, or be true: *It will probably take about a week.* | *"Is Julie going?"* ***"Probably not."***

pro·bate /ˈproʊbeɪt/ *n.* [U] LAW the legal process of deciding that someone's WILL has been made correctly, or the court where this takes place

pro·ba·tion /proʊˈbeɪʃən/ *n.* [U] **1** LAW a system that allows some criminals to leave prison early or not to go to prison at all, if they promise to behave well for a specific period of time: *Preston's been* ***on probation*** *for three years.* **2** a period of time during which an employer can see if a new worker is good enough —**probationary** /proʊˈbeɪʃəˌneri/ *adj.*

proˈbation ˌofficer *n.* [C] LAW someone whose job is to watch, advise, and help people who have broken the law and are on probation

probe¹ /proʊb/ *v.* [I,T] **1** to ask questions in order to find things out: *Reporters have* ***probed into*** *the senator's personal life.* **2** to look for something or examine something, using a long thin instrument —**probing** *adj.*: *probing questions*

probe² *n.* [C] **1** a long thin instrument that doctors and scientists use to examine parts of the body **2** a SPACECRAFT without people in it that is sent into space to collect information → SPACE¹ **3** (written) a process of asking many questions in order to find the truth about something

pro·bi·ty /ˈproʊbət̬i/ *n.* [U] (formal) completely moral behavior: *a man known for his probity*

prob·lem /ˈprɑbləm/ *n.* [C] **1** a difficult situation or person that has to be dealt with or thought about: *I've been **having** a few **problems** with my car.* | *There are **problems with** the equipment.* | *The governor has done nothing to **solve** these **problems**.* | *Is there a **drug problem** in the school?* | *the **problem of** teen pregnancy* | *Unemployment remains a **serious problem**.* ►Don't say "an important problem."◄

THESAURUS

setback – a problem that stops you from making progress: *The space program suffered a major setback when the space shuttle, Discovery, exploded.*
difficulty – a problem or something that causes trouble: *the country's financial difficulties*
snag (informal) – a problem, especially one that you had not expected: *The project has hit a major snag.*
hitch – a small problem that delays or prevents something: *There have been a few last-minute hitches.*
trouble – when something does not work in the way it should: *The plane developed engine trouble.*
hassle (spoken) – a situation that is annoying because it causes problems: *I wish clothes shopping was less of a hassle.* | *You get the smoky barbecue flavor without the hassle of getting a fire started.*
flaw, **bug**, **fault** → DEFECT¹

2 something wrong with your health or with part of your body: *a woman with serious **health problems*** | *He has a **back/heart/knee etc. problem**.* **3** a question that must be answered, especially one relating to numbers or facts: *The test will have 20 algebra problems.*

SPOKEN PHRASES

4 no problem a) used in order to say that you are very willing to do something: *"Can you help?" "Sure, no problem."* **b)** used after someone has thanked you or said s/he is sorry: *"Thanks a lot." "Oh, no problem."* **5 that's your/his/their etc. problem** used in order to say that someone else is responsible for dealing with a situation, not you: *If you can't get yourself there on time, that's your problem.* **6 what's your problem?** used in order to ask someone what is wrong, in a way that shows you think s/he is not being reasonable: *Look, what's your problem? It's my decision!*

[ORIGIN: 1300—1400 French *problème*, from Latin *problema*, from Greek, "something thrown forward"]

prob·lem·at·ic /ˌprɑbləˈmæt̬ɪk/ *adj.* full of problems and difficult to deal with: *Painkillers can be problematic when combined with other medicines.* —**problematically** *adv.*

pro bo·no /ˌproʊ ˈboʊnoʊ/ *adj.* LAW used to describe work that someone, especially a lawyer, does without getting paid for it: *Turner has agreed to handle the case on a pro bono basis.*

pro·car·y·ote /proʊˈkæriˌoʊt/ *n.* [C] another spelling of PROKARYOTE

pro·ce·dure /prəˈsidʒɚ/ (Ac) *n.* [C,U] a way of doing something, especially the correct or normal way → PROCESS: *What is the **procedure for** dealing with a fire.* | *Officials must **follow** the correct **procedure**.* | *a common **medical procedure*** —**procedural** *adj.*

THESAURUS **method, way, technique, strategy, approach** → METHOD

pro·ceed /prəˈsid, proʊ-/ (Ac) *v.* [I] **1** to continue to do something that has already been planned or started: *We will **proceed with** the negotiations.* | *The project seemed to be proceeding smoothly.* **2 proceed to do sth** to do something next: *He took out his wallet, and proceeded to count out enough money to pay for the meal.* **3** (formal) to move in a particular direction: *Please **proceed to** the nearest exit.* [ORIGIN: 1300—1400 Old French *proceder*, from Latin *procedere* "to go forward"]

pro·ceed·ings /prəˈsidɪŋz, proʊ-/ (Ac) *n.* [plural] **1** an event or series of actions: *A crowd gathered to watch the proceedings.* **2** LAW actions taken in a court of law or in a legal case: *legal proceedings*

pro·ceeds /ˈproʊsidz/ (Ac) *n.* [plural] the money that has been gained from doing something or selling something: *The **proceeds from** the carnival will **go to** local children's charities.*

pro·cess¹ /ˈprɑsɛs, ˈproʊ-/ (Ac) *n.* [C] **1** a series of actions, developments, or changes that happen naturally: *the aging process* | *the **natural process** of evolution* | *Describe some of the key processes that occur in plant and animal cells.* **2** a series of actions that someone does to achieve a particular result: *the peace process* | *Medical research is a **slow process**.* | *The process of applying to a college is often very time-consuming.* **3 be in the process of doing sth** to have started doing something and not yet be finished: *Grady is in the process of collecting data for the study.* **4 in the process** while you are doing something or something is happening: *I spilled my coffee, burning myself in the process.* **5** a system or a treatment of materials that is used for producing goods: *an industrial process* [ORIGIN: 1300—1400 Old French *proces*, from Latin *processus*, from *procedere* "to go forward"]

process² (Ac) *v.* [T] **1** to deal with information in an official way: *This department processes mail* *order requests.* **2** to make food, materials, or goods ready to be used or sold, for example by preserving or improving them in some way: *In the early 1900s, companies began to process food and distribute it using the railroads.* **3** IT to put information into a computer to be examined —**processed** *adj.*: *processed cheese* —**processing** *n.* [U]

pro·ces·sion /prəˈsɛʃən/ *n.* [C] **1** a line of people or vehicles moving slowly as part of a ceremony ➔ PARADE: *a funeral procession* **2** several people or things of the same kind, appearing or happening one after the other: *a* ***procession of*** *legal experts*

pro·ces·sor /ˈprɑsɛsɚ/ *n.* [C] IT a CPU ➔ FOOD PROCESSOR

ˌpro-ˈchoice *adj.* believing that women have a right to have an ABORTION ➔ PRO-LIFE

pro·claim /proʊˈkleɪm, prə-/ *v.* [T] (formal) to say officially or publicly that something is true or exists: *In 1948, Israel proclaimed its independence.*

proc·la·ma·tion /ˌprɑkləˈmeɪʃən/ *n.* [C] an official public statement about something important: *the Emancipation Proclamation* (=the speech about freeing the SLAVEs in the U.S. in 1863)

pro·cliv·i·ty /proʊˈklɪvət̬i/ *n.* (plural **proclivities**) [C] (formal) a tendency to behave in a particular way, or like a particular thing, especially something bad: *Does watching violent TV shows produce a* ***proclivity for*** *violence?*

pro·cras·ti·nate /prəˈkræstəˌneɪt/ *v.* [I] to delay doing something that you ought to do: *People tend to* ***procrastinate about*** *paperwork.* [ORIGIN: 1500—1600 Latin, past participle of *procrastinare*, from *cras* "tomorrow"] —**procrastinator** *n.* [C] —**procrastination** /prəˌkræstəˈneɪʃən/ *n.* [U]

THESAURUS **delay, postpone, put off, defer** ➔ DELAY[1]

pro·cre·ate /ˈproʊkriˌeɪt/ *v.* [I,T] (formal) to produce children or baby animals —**procreation** /ˌproʊkriˈeɪʃən/ *n.* [U]

pro·cure /proʊˈkyʊr, prə-/ *v.* [T] (formal) to obtain something, especially something that is difficult to get: *Senator Craven helped to procure funding to build the new library.* —**procurement** *n.* [U]

THESAURUS **buy, purchase, acquire, get** ➔ BUY[1]

prod /prɑd/ *v.* (**prodded**, **prodding**) [I,T] **1** POKE **2** to strongly encourage someone to do something, especially when s/he is lazy or not willing: *Her parents are having to* ***prod*** *her* ***into*** *completing her homework.*

pro·di·gious /prəˈdɪdʒəs/ *adj.* (formal) very large or skillful in a surprising or impressive way: *The Internet contains* ***prodigious amounts*** *of information.* —**prodigiously** *adv.*

THESAURUS **big, large, substantial, huge, enormous, vast, gigantic, massive, immense, colossal** ➔ BIG

prod·i·gy /ˈprɑdədʒi/ *n.* (plural **prodigies**) [C] a young person who has a great natural ability in a subject or skill ➔ GENIUS: *Mozart was a* ***child prodigy***. [ORIGIN: 1400—1500 Latin *prodigium* "sign telling the future, monster"]

pro·duce¹ /prəˈdus/ *v.* [T] **1** to grow something or make it naturally ➔ PRODUCT, PRODUCTION: *Cotton is produced in the southern states.* | *Trees produce carbon dioxide.* **2** to make something happen or develop, or have a particular result or effect: *The drug can produce side effects in some people.* **3** to show something so it can be seen or considered: *Officer Ryan asked the suspect to produce his driver's license.* **4** to make something, especially using an industrial process ➔ PRODUCT: *the costs of producing goods and services*

THESAURUS **make, manufacture, build, generate** ➔ MAKE[1]

5 if someone produces a movie, play, or television program, s/he finds the money for it and controls the way it is made ➔ PRODUCER **6** to make something using skill and imagination: *Diane produced a fantastic meal.* **7** to give birth to a baby or young animals

prod·uce² /ˈprɑdus, ˈproʊ-/ *n.* [U] food, especially fruit or vegetables, that has been grown on a farm to be sold ➔ PRODUCT: *The restaurant uses* ***fresh*** *local* ***produce***.

pro·duc·er /prəˈdusɚ/ *n.* [C] **1** a person, company, or country that makes or grows goods, foods, or materials: *Scotland is a* ***producer of*** *high-quality wool.* | *oil producers in Venezuela* **2** someone whose job is to control the preparation of a play, movie, etc., but who does not direct the actors: *a TV producer* ➔ MOVIE **3** BIOLOGY a living thing, such as a plant or BACTERIA, that produces its own food using the energy from the Sun or from a chemical process (SYN) **autotroph**

prod·uct /ˈprɑdʌkt/ *n.* **1** [C,U] something that is grown, made in a factory, or taken from nature, usually in order to be sold ➔ PRODUCE, PRODUCTION: *None of our products are tested on animals.* | *milk and other* ***dairy products*** **2 be the product of sth** to be the result of particular experiences, situations, or processes: *Abusive husbands tend to be the product of violent homes.* | *The report was the product of four years' hard work.* **3** [C] MATH the number you get by multiplying two or more numbers

pro·duc·tion /prəˈdʌkʃən/ *n.* **1** [U] the process of making or growing things, or the amount that is produced: *Steel production has decreased by 35%.* **2** [C,U] a play, movie, etc. that is produced for the public, or the process of producing it: *a new Broadway production of "My Fair Lady"*

pro·duc·tive /prəˈdʌktɪv/ *adj.* producing or achieving a lot (ANT) **unproductive**: *productive*

P

land | *Some workers become* ***more/less productive*** *under this system.* —**productively** *adv.*

pro·duc·tiv·i·ty /ˌproʊdəkˈtɪvət̬i, ˌprɑ-/ *n.* [U] the rate at which goods are produced, and the amount produced: *ways of* ***increasing/raising/improving productivity***

prof /prɑf/ *n.* **1** [C] (spoken) a PROFESSOR **2 Prof.** the written abbreviation of PROFESSOR

pro·fane /proʊˈfeɪn, prə-/ *adj.* showing a lack of respect for God or for holy things, by using rude words or religious words wrongly → OBSCENE: *profane language*

P

pro·fan·i·ty /proʊˈfænət̬i, prə-/ *n.* (plural **profanities**) [C,U] a swear word, or a religious word used wrongly, that shows a lack of respect for God or for holy things → OBSCENITY

pro·fess /prəˈfɛs, proʊ-/ *v.* [T] (formal) **1** to say that you do something or are something, often when it is not really true (SYN) **claim**: *He* ***professed to*** *be surprised by the verdict.* **2** to express a personal feeling or belief openly: *Soon, Frank was* ***professing*** *his* ***love*** *and asking her to marry him.* —**professed** *adj.*

pro·fes·sion /prəˈfɛʃən/ *n.* **1** [C] a job that needs special education and training: *professions such as nursing or teaching* | *He's a lawyer* ***by profession*** (=as his job).

THESAURUS **job, work, employment, occupation, career, vocation** → JOB

2 [singular] all the people in a particular profession: *the medical/legal/teaching etc. profession* **3** [C] (formal) a statement of your belief, opinion, or feeling

pro·fes·sion·al¹ /prəˈfɛʃənl/ (Ac) *adj.* **1** doing a job, sport, or activity for money (ANT) **amateur**: *professional athletes* | *a professional army* **2** professional sports are played by people who are paid (ANT) **amateur**: *professional hockey* **3** relating to a job that needs special education and training: *You should speak to a lawyer for professional advice.* **4** showing that someone has been well trained and is good at his/her work: *This report looks very professional.* —**professionally** *adv.*: *The service uses volunteers rather than professionally trained staff.*

professional² *n.* [C] **1** someone who works in a job that needs special education and training: *a health care professional* **2** someone who earns money by doing a job, sport, or activity that other people do just for enjoyment (ANT) **amateur**: *In this competition, the amateurs play alongside the professionals.*

pro·fes·sion·al·ism /prəˈfɛʃənlˌɪzəm/ (Ac) *n.* [U] the skill and high standards of behavior expected of a professional person: *Gossiping about your co-workers shows a lack of professionalism.*

pro·fes·sor /prəˈfɛsɚ/ *n.* [C] a teacher at a university or college, especially one who has a high rank: *Thank you, Professor Drexler.* | *my history professor* | *a* ***professor of*** *economics*

THESAURUS **teacher, lecturer, instructor** → TEACHER

prof·fer /ˈprɑfɚ/ *v.* [T] (formal) to offer something to someone

pro·fi·cien·cy /prəˈfɪʃənsi/ *n.* [U] the ability to do something with a high level of skill: *a student's* ***proficiency in*** *math* | *The classes were geared to our* ***level of proficiency***.

pro·fi·cient /prəˈfɪʃənt/ *adj.* able to do something with a high level of skill: *a proficient typist* —**proficiently** *adv.*

profile

pro·file¹ /ˈproʊfaɪl/ *n.* **1** [C,U] a side view of someone's head: *Callan photographed her* ***in profile***. **2** [C] a short description that gives important details about someone or something: *a* ***profile of*** *her career* **3 keep a low profile** to behave quietly and avoid doing things that would make people notice you **4 high profile** something that is high profile is noticed by many people and gets a lot of attention: *Luria has a high profile in the arts community.*

profile² *v.* [T] to write or give a short description of someone or something: *The artists who are profiled in his book are major 20th-century figures.*

pro·fil·ing /ˈproʊˌfaɪlɪŋ/ *n.* [U] the process of examining information about a particular group, in order to know what they might want or do, or in order to know who might belong to that group: *Profiling has helped U.S. Customs officers spot drug smugglers.*

prof·it¹ /ˈprɑfɪt/ *n.* **1** [C,U] money that you gain by selling things or doing business: *NovaCorp* ***made a profit*** *of $39 million.* | *They sold the company* ***at a huge profit***. **2** [U] an advantage that you gain from doing something: *reading for profit and pleasure*

profit² *v.* (formal) **1** [I,T] to be useful or helpful to someone: *Everyone* ***profits from*** *an education.* **2** [I] to get money from doing something: *The states have* ***profited from*** *cigarette taxes.*

prof·it·a·bil·i·ty /ˌprɑfɪt̬əˈbɪlət̬i/ *n.* [U] the state of producing a profit, or the degree to which a business or activity is profitable

prof·it·a·ble /ˈprɑfɪt̬əbəl/ *adj.* producing a profit or a useful result: *The company has had a profitable year.* —**profitably** *adv.*

prof·it·eer /ˌprɑfəˈtɪr/ *n.* [C] someone who makes an unfairly large profit by selling something that is difficult to get at a very high price: *black market profiteers* —**profiteering** *n.* [U]: *As food* *supplies began to run low, some merchants were criticized for profiteering.*

'profit ˌmargin *n.* [C] ECONOMICS the difference between the cost of producing something and the price you sell it at to make a profit

'profit ˌmotive *n.* [U] ECONOMICS the desire to make money, which is the reason why a person or business wants to take part in a business activity

'profit ˌsharing *n.* [U] ECONOMICS a system in which workers are allowed to share some of their company's profits

prof·li·gate /'prɑfləgɪt/ *adj.* (formal) wasting money in a careless way

pro·found /prə'faʊnd/ *adj.* **1** very great, important, or strong: *Davis had a **profound impact/effect/influence** on jazz music.* **2** showing strong serious feelings SYN **deep**: *a profound sense of guilt* **3** showing great knowledge and understanding SYN **deep**: *a profound book* —**profoundly** *adv.*: *Their lives had been profoundly affected by the war.* —**profundity** /prə'fʌndəṭi/ *n.* [C,U]

pro·fuse /prə'fyus, proʊ-/ *adj.* given, flowing, or growing freely and in large amounts: *profuse sweating* | *profuse apologies* —**profusely** *adv.*: *He thanked them profusely.* —**profuseness** *n.* [U]

pro·fu·sion /prə'fyuʒən/ *n.* [singular, U] (formal) a very large amount: *a **profusion of** wild flowers*

prog·e·ny /'prɑdʒəni/ *n.* [U] (literary) the babies of a person or animal

prog·no·sis /prɑg'noʊsɪs/ *n.* (plural **prognoses** /-siz/) [C] (formal) **1** a doctor's opinion of how an illness or disease will develop ➔ DIAGNOSIS **2** a judgment about what will happen in the future, based on information or experience

pro·gram¹ /'proʊgræm, -grəm/ *n.* [C] **1** a show on television or radio: *a popular TV program* | *a **program about** whales* ➔ TELEVISION **2** IT a set of instructions given to a computer to make it do a particular job: *an educational software program* **3** a series of actions, services, courses, etc. which are designed to achieve something: *Stanford's MBA program* | *government programs that benefit poor people* | *an exercise program* **4** a small book or piece of paper that gives information about a play, concert, etc. and who the performers are ➔ THEATER **5 get with the program** (spoken) used in order to tell someone to pay attention to what needs to be done, and do it

program² *v.* (**programmed**, **programming**) [T] **1** to set a machine to operate in a particular way: *I programmed the VCR to record that movie you wanted.* **2 be programmed** if a person or animal is programmed socially or BIOLOGICALLY to do something, he, she, or it does it without thinking: *Our bodies seem **programmed to** want the types and amounts of foods we need.* **3** IT to give a set of instructions to a computer to make it do a particular job: *The computer is **programmed to** play chess.*

pro·gram·mer /'proʊˌgræmɚ, -grəmɚ/ *n.* [C] IT someone whose job is to write programs for computers

pro·gram·ming /'proʊˌgræmɪŋ/ *n.* [U] **1** television or radio programs, or the planning of these broadcasts: *children's programming* **2** IT the activity of writing programs for computers, or something written by a programmer

prog·ress¹ /'prɑgrəs, -grɛs/ *n.* [U] **1** the process of developing or improving, or getting closer to achieving something: *The country has **made** great economic **progress**.* | *The tests measure the **progress of** individual students.* | *The patients with eating disorders had made **progress in** changing their eating habits.* | ***Progress on** the report has been slow.* **2 in progress** happening now, and not yet finished: *Please do not enter while there is a class in progress.* **3** movement toward a place: *The ship **made** slow **progress through** the rough sea.* [ORIGIN: 1400—1500 Latin, past participle of *progredi* "to go forward"]

pro·gress² /prə'grɛs/ *v.* [I] **1** to develop, improve, or become more complete over a period of time: *Work on the new building progressed quickly.* **2** if an activity, event, time, etc. progresses, it continues and time passes: *As the talks progressed, a deal became certain.*

pro·gres·sion /prə'grɛʃən/ *n.* [singular, U] a process of change or development: *the rapid progression of her illness*

pro·gres·sive¹ /prə'grɛsɪv/ *adj.* **1** supporting new or modern ideas and methods: *Dewey developed some of the ideas behind progressive education.* **2** becoming better, worse, or more complete over a period of time: *a progressive disease* —**progressively** *adv.*

progressive² *n.* **the progressive** ENG. LANG. ARTS the CONTINUOUS

pro·hib·it /proʊ'hɪbɪt, prə-/ Ac *v.* [T] **1** to say that an action is illegal or not allowed, especially officially: *Smoking is strictly prohibited.* | *Stores are **prohibited from** selling alcohol to people under 21.* | *Many countries prohibit the use of cell phones while driving.*

THESAURUS **forbid, not allow/permit/let, ban, bar, proscribe** ➔ FORBID

2 to make something impossible or prevent it from happening [ORIGIN: 1400—1500 Latin, past participle of *prohibere* "to hold away, prevent"]

pro·hi·bi·tion /ˌproʊə'bɪʃən/ Ac *n.* **1** [C,U] LAW the act of saying that something is illegal or not allowed, or an order that does this: *a **prohibition on** cigarette advertising* **2 Prohibition** HISTORY the period from 1919 to 1933 in the U.S., when it was illegal to produce or sell alcoholic drinks

pro·hib·i·tive /proʊ'hɪbəṭɪv, prə-/ Ac *adj.* preventing people from doing or buying something: *The **cost** of the trip was **prohibitive*** (=too high). —**prohibitively** *adv.*

proj·ect¹ /ˈprɑdʒɛkt, -dʒɪkt/ (Ac) *n.* **1** [C] a carefully planned piece of work: *the new highway project* | *Her research project involves studying people with cancer.* | *The project aims to provide an analysis of children's emotions.* **2 the projects** [plural] (informal) HOUSING PROJECTS [ORIGIN: 1300—1400 Latin *projectum*, from the past participle of *proicere* "to throw forward"]

project

overhead projector

pro·ject² /prəˈdʒɛkt/ (Ac) *v.* **1** [T] to calculate or plan what will happen in the future, using the information you have now: *The new freeway is projected to cost $230 million.* | *A national tour is projected for 2010.* | *The company projected an annual growth rate of 3%.* **2** [T] to make other people have a particular idea about you: *Jim always* ***projects an image*** *of self-confidence.* **3** [I,T] to speak or sing loudly enough to be heard by everyone in a big room or theater **4** [T] to make the picture of a movie, photograph, etc. appear in a larger form on a screen or flat surface **5** [I,T] to stick out beyond an edge or surface: *The roof projects over the driveway.* **6** [T] (formal) to make something move up or forward with great force

pro·jec·tile /prəˈdʒɛktl, -ˌtaɪl/ *n.* [C] (formal) an object that is thrown or fired from a weapon

pro·jec·tion /prəˈdʒɛkʃən/ (Ac) *n.* **1** [C] a statement about something you think will happen, based on information you have now: *this year's sales projections* | *The graph shows a projection of housing needs over the next 10 years.* **2** [C] something that sticks out beyond an edge or surface **3** [C,U] the act of making a movie, photograph, etc. appear on a screen, or the image itself: *film projection*

pro·jec·tion·ist /prəˈdʒɛkʃənɪst/ *n.* [C] someone whose job is to operate a projector

pro·jec·tor /prəˈdʒɛktɚ/ *n.* [C] a piece of equipment that uses light to make a movie, photograph, etc. appear on a screen

pro·kar·y·ote, procaryote /proʊˈkæriˌoʊt/ *n.* [C] BIOLOGY a type of living thing whose cells do not have a NUCLEUS (=central part). Most prokaryotes, for example BACTERIA, have only one cell. —**prokaryotic** /proʊˌkæriˈɑt̬ɪk/ *adj.*: *prokaryotic cell structure*

pro·le·tar·i·at /ˌproʊləˈtɛriət/ *n.* **the proletariat** the people in a society who are poor, own no property, etc. —**proletarian** *adj.*

ˌpro-ˈlife *adj.* opposing ABORTION ➔ PRO-CHOICE

pro·lif·er·ate /prəˈlɪfəˌreɪt/ *v.* [I] (formal) to increase very quickly in number and spread to many different places: *In the Triassic period, dinosaurs proliferated.* —**proliferation** /prəˌlɪfəˈreɪʃən/ *n.* [singular, U]

pro·lif·ic /prəˈlɪfɪk/ *adj.* producing a lot of something: *Danielle Steel is a prolific writer.* —**prolifically** *adv.*

pro·logue /ˈproʊlɑg, -lɔg/ *n.* [C] ENG. LANG. ARTS the introduction to a book, movie, or play

pro·long /prəˈlɔŋ/ *v.* [T] to make something such as a feeling, activity, or state continue longer (SYN) **lengthen**: *In hospitals, high-tech machinery prolongs people's lives.* —**prolonged** *adj.*: *a prolonged illness*

prom /prɑm/ *n.* [C] a formal dance party for HIGH SCHOOL students, usually held at the end of a school year: *the* ***senior prom*** (=dance for students in their last year of school)

THESAURUS: **dance, ball, formal** ➔ DANCE²

prom·e·nade /ˌprɑməˈneɪd, -ˈnɑd/ *n.* [C] (old-fashioned) a walk for pleasure in a public place, or a wide path where you can do this —**promenade** *v.* [I]

prom·i·nence /ˈprɑmənəns/ *n.* [U] the fact of being important and famous: *Condoleezza Rice* ***rose to prominence*** (=became famous) *during George W. Bush's administration.*

prom·i·nent /ˈprɑmənənt/ *adj.* **1** famous or important: *a prominent biotech company* **2** large and sticking out: *prominent cheekbones* **3 a prominent place/position** somewhere that is easily seen: *The sculpture has a prominent position in the park.* [ORIGIN: 1400—1500 Latin, present participle of *prominere* "to stick out"] —**prominently** *adv.*

pro·mis·cu·ous /prəˈmɪskyuəs/ *adj.* (formal) having sex with a lot of people —**promiscuity** /ˌprɑmɪˈskyuət̬i/ *n.* [U]

prom·ise¹ /ˈprɑmɪs/ *v.* **1** [I,T] to tell someone that you will definitely do something, or that something will definitely happen: *Police have promised a full investigation.* | ***I promised*** *Barbara* ***(that)*** *I'd meet her after work.* | ***I promise (that)*** *I'll never do that again.* | *Both candidates* ***promised to*** *get tougher on crime.* | *I've already promised them a ride to the dance.*

THESAURUS

give sb your word – to promise someone very sincerely that you will do something: *He gave us his word and I believe him.*

swear – to make a very serious promise: *He had sworn not to reveal her secret.*
take/swear an oath – to make a very serious promise in public: *You must take an oath of loyalty to your country.*
vow – to make a serious promise, often to yourself: *She vowed that she would never drink alcohol again.*
pledge – to make a formal, usually public, promise: *Canada pledged to provide medical aid.*
undertake to do sth (formal) – to promise or agree to do something: *I undertook to support her, clothe her, and protect her.*
guarantee – to promise something that you feel very sure about: *I can guarantee you a ten percent increase on your current salary.*
commit – to say that you will definitely do something: *The company had committed to finishing the project by June 20.*

2 [T] to make people expect that something will happen: *The game **promises to be** exciting.* **3 I can't promise anything** (spoken) used in order to tell someone that you will try to do what s/he wants, but you may not be able to do it [ORIGIN: 1300—1400 Latin *promissum*, from the past participle of *promittere* "to send out, promise"]

promise² *n.* **1** [C] a statement that you will definitely do something, or that something will definitely happen: *She **made a promise** to take care of her neighbor's dog.* | *I didn't want to **break** my **promise*** (=not do what I said I would do). | *Has the president **kept** his **promise** to increase funding for education?* | *a **promise of** help* **2** [U] signs that something or someone will be good or successful: *He **shows** a lot of **promise** as a writer.*

prom·is·ing /'prɑmɪsɪŋ/ *adj.* showing that someone or something is likely to be successful in the future: *a promising young singer* —**promisingly** *adv.*

pro·mo /'proʊmoʊ/ *n.* (plural **promos**) [C] (informal) a PROMOTION

prom·on·to·ry /'prɑmən,tɔri/ *n.* (plural **promontories**) [C] EARTH SCIENCES a high piece of land that goes out into the ocean

pro·mote /prə'moʊt/ (Ac) *v.* [T] **1** to help something develop and be successful: *The bureau's job is to promote tourism to the area.* | *A balanced diet promotes good health.* **2** to give someone a better, more responsible position at work (ANT) **demote**: *Ted was **promoted to** senior sales manager.* **3** to advertise a product or event: *The author went on a national tour to promote the book.*

THESAURUS **advertise, market, publicize, hype, plug** ➔ ADVERTISE

4 to be responsible for arranging a large public event such as a concert or a sports game [ORIGIN: 1300—1400 Latin, past participle of *promovere* "to move forward"]

pro·mot·er /prə'moʊt̬ɚ/ (Ac) *n.* [C] someone whose job is to arrange large public events such as concerts or sports games

pro·mo·tion /prə'moʊʃən/ (Ac) *n.* [C,U] **1** a move to a better, more responsible position at work: *She received a **promotion to** lieutenant.* **2** an activity intended to advertise a product or event, or the thing that is being advertised: *a sales promotion*

pro·mo·tion·al /prə'moʊʃənl/ *adj.* promotional products and activities are made or organized in order to advertise something

prompt¹ /prɑmpt/ *v.* **1** [T] to make someone do something, or to help him/her remember to do it: *The changes prompted several people to resign from the committee in protest.*

THESAURUS **cause, make, result in sth, lead to sth, trigger, induce** ➔ CAUSE²

2 [I,T] to remind someone, especially an actor, of the next words in a speech [ORIGIN: 1300—1400 Medieval Latin *promptare*, from Latin *promptus*, from the past participle of *promere* "to bring out"]

prompt² *adj.* **1** done quickly, immediately, or at the right time: *Prompt payment is requested.* **2** someone who is prompt arrives at the right time or does something on time —**promptly** *adv.*: *Callan dealt with the problem promptly.*

prompt³ *n.* [C] IT a sign on a computer screen that shows that the computer has finished one operation and is ready to begin the next

prom·ul·gate /'prɑməl,geɪt/ *v.* [T] **1** (formal) to spread an idea or belief to as many people as possible: *Family customs tend to be promulgated by women.* **2** LAW to make a new law come into effect by announcing it officially —**promulgator** *n.* [C] —**promulgation** /,prɑməl'geɪʃən/ *n.* [U]

prone /proʊn/ *adj.* **1** likely to do something or suffer from something: *This narrow river is **prone to** flooding.* | *He seems **accident prone*** (=he often has accidents). **2** (formal) lying down flat, with the front of your body facing down —**prone** *adv.*

prong /prɔŋ, prɑŋ/ *n.* [C] **1** one of the thick sharp pointed parts on the end of something, such as a PLUG or a PITCHFORK ➔ TINE **2** one of two or three ways of achieving something, that are used at the same time: *the second **prong of** the attack* —**pronged** *adj.*: *a two-pronged fork*

pro·noun /'proʊnaʊn/ *n.* [C] ENG. LANG. ARTS in grammar, a word that is used instead of a noun or noun phrase, such as "he" instead of the name "Peter" or the noun phrase "the man"

pro·nounce /prə'naʊns/ *v.* [T] **1** to make the sound of a letter, word, etc. in the correct way ➔ PRONUNCIATION: *Her name is Tea, pronounced "Tay-uh."* **2** to state something officially and formally: *He was **pronounced dead** at 11:00 p.m.*

pro·nounced /prə'naʊnst/ *adj.* very strong or noticeable: *Jan still has a pronounced Czech accent.*

pro·nounce·ment /prə'naʊnsmənt/ *n.* [C] (formal) an official public statement

pron·to /'prɑntoʊ/ *adv.* (spoken) quickly or immediately – used especially when you are annoyed: *Get in the house, pronto!*

pro·nun·ci·a·tion /prə,nʌnsi'eɪʃən/ *n.* **1** [C,U] the way in which a language or a particular word is pronounced: *the correct pronunciation of English words* **2** [singular, U] a particular person's way of pronouncing a word or words

proof /pruf/ *n.* **1** [U] facts, information, documents, etc. that prove something is true: *There is no* ***proof that*** *the suspect was home when he said he was.* | *Drivers should carry* ***proof of*** *insurance.* | *The tests are used* ***as proof*** *that the students are making progress.* **2** [C] a printed copy of a piece of writing that is checked carefully before the final printing is done **3** [U] a measurement of how much alcohol is in a drink. For example, 40 proof is 20% alcohol. **4** [C] MATH a test in mathematics of whether a calculation is correct, or a list of reasons that shows a THEOREM (=statement) in GEOMETRY to be true

proof·read /'pruf-rid/ *v.* (past tense and past participle **proofread** /-rɛd/) [I,T] to read something in order to correct any mistakes in it —**proofreader** *n.* [C]

P

prop[1] /prɑp/ *v.* (**propped**, **propping**) [T] to support something or keep it in a particular position: *He* ***propped*** *his bike* ***against*** *the fence.* | *The gate had been* ***propped open*** *with a brick.*

THESAURUS lean, stand, rest → LEAN[1]

prop sth ↔ **up** *phr. v.* **1** to prevent something from falling by putting something against it or under it: *Steel poles prop up the crumbling walls.* | *Frank propped himself up on his elbows.* **2** to help something to continue to exist: *Military spending props up the economies of several states.*

prop[2] *n.* [C] **1** an object placed under or against something to hold it in a position **2** an object such as a book, weapon, etc. used by actors in a play or movie

prop·a·gan·da /,prɑpə'gændə/ *n.* [U] information that is false or which emphasizes just one part of a situation, used by a government or other group to make people agree with them: *Soviet propaganda about the evils of capitalism* —**propagandist** *n.* [C] —**propagandize** *v.* [I,T]

prop·a·gate /'prɑpə,geɪt/ *v.* (formal) **1** [T] to share ideas, information, or beliefs with many people **2** [I,T] BIOLOGY to grow or produce new plants, or to make a plant do this —**propagation** /,prɑpə'geɪʃən/ *n.* [U]

pro·pane /'proʊpeɪn/ *n.* [U] a colorless gas used for cooking and heating

pro·pel /prə'pɛl/ *v.* (**propelled**, **propelling**) [T] **1** to make someone achieve something, or to make something happen or develop: *Pearl Harbor was the attack that* ***propelled*** *America* ***into*** *World War II.* **2** to move, drive, or push something forward: *Paddle wheel ships were propelled by steam.*

pro·pel·ler /prə'pɛlɚ/ *n.* [C] a piece of equipment that consists of two or more blades that spin around to make an airplane or ship move

pro·pen·si·ty /prə'pɛnsət̬i/ *n.* (plural **propensities**) [C] (formal) a natural tendency to behave or develop in a particular way: *Doug* ***has a propensity to*** *gain weight.*

prop·er /'prɑpɚ/ *adj.* **1** correct, or right for a particular situation: *You need the proper tools for the job.*

THESAURUS appropriate, right, suitable, suited → APPROPRIATE[1]

2 socially correct and acceptable: *proper behavior for young girls* **3** [only after noun] inside the limits of an area or subject: *We don't live in Boston proper; it's a suburb of Boston.*

prop·er·ly /'prɑpɚli/ *adv.* correctly, in a way that is right or appropriate: *When used properly, car airbags save lives.*

,proper 'noun *also* **,proper 'name** *n.* [C] ENG. LANG. ARTS in grammar, a noun that is the name of a particular person, place, or thing and is spelled with a capital letter, such as "Mike," "Paris," or "Easter"

prop·er·ty /'prɑpɚt̬i/ *n.* (plural **properties**) **1** [U] something that someone owns: *Police recovered some of the* ***stolen property.*** | *his* ***personal property***

THESAURUS

possessions – the things that you own: *The fire destroyed most of their possessions.*
things – the things that you own or are carrying: *Just put your things over there.*
stuff (informal) – the things that you own or are carrying with you: *All our stuff is still in cardboard boxes.*
belongings – things you own, especially things you are carrying with you: *The bell rang, and the students began gathering up their belongings.*
effects (formal) – the things that someone owns: *After Harding's death, the army sent his personal effects to his parents.*
valuables – things that you own that are worth a lot of money, such as jewelry, cameras, etc.: *Please make sure you take any valuables with you when you leave.*

2 [C,U] land, a building, or both together: *The property is worth about $5 million.* | *The building is* ***private/public property*** (=it is owned by a person or business/it is owned by the government). **3** [C usually plural] SCIENCE a quality that a plant or substance has naturally: *an herb with* ***healing properties*** | *the* ***chemical/physical properties*** *of the compound*

THESAURUS characteristic, quality, trait, attribute, feature → CHARACTERISTIC[1]

proph·e·cy /ˈprɑfəsi/ *n.* (plural **prophecies**) [C] a statement that tells what will happen in the future, often made by someone with religious or magical power

proph·e·sy /ˈprɑfəˌsaɪ/ *v.* (**prophesied**, **prophesies**) [I,T] to use religious or magical knowledge to say what will happen in the future

THESAURUS **predict, foretell, forecast, foresee** → PREDICT

proph·et /ˈprɑfɪt/ *n.* **1** [C] someone who says what will happen in the future and teaches people more about a religion **2 the Prophet** Mohammed, who began the religion of Islam

pro·phet·ic /prəˈfɛt̬ɪk/ *adj.* correctly saying what will happen in the future: *His words turned out to be prophetic.* —**prophetically** *adv.*

pro·pi·tious /prəˈpɪʃəs/ *adj.* (formal) good and likely to bring good results: *It seemed a* ***propitious moment*** *to ask her a question.* —**propitiously** *adv.*

pro·po·nent /prəˈpoʊnənt/ *n.* [C] someone who supports something or persuades people to do something (ANT) **opponent**: *a* ***proponent of*** *the new airport*

pro·por·tion /prəˈpɔrʃən/ (Ac) *n.* **1** [C,U] a part or share of a larger amount or number of something: *The* ***proportion of*** *adults who smoke is lower than before. | He won a* ***large/high proportion*** *of the vote. | The proportion of people living below the poverty line declined to 30%.* **2** [C,U] the relationship between the amounts, numbers, or sizes of related things: *Girls outnumber boys at the school by a* ***proportion of*** *three* ***to*** *one. | Taxes rise* ***in proportion to*** *the amount you earn. | The bird's eggs are unusually small in proportion to its size.* **3 proportions** [plural] the size or importance of something: *The flu outbreak has* ***reached*** *epidemic* ***proportions****.* **4** [U] the correct relationship between the size or shape of the different parts of something: *Her head seems large* ***in proportion to*** *her thin figure.* **5 get/blow things out of proportion** to react to a situation as if it is worse or more serious than it really is **6 sense of proportion** the ability to judge what is most important in a situation **7** [U] MATH a mathematical statement showing that the relationship is the same between two pairs of numbers, as in the statement "8 is to 6 as 32 is to 24"

pro·por·tion·al /prəˈpɔrʃənl/ (Ac) also **pro·por·tion·ate** /prəˈpɔrʃənɪt/ *adj.* staying in a particular relationship with another thing in size, amount, or importance: *The number of Representatives each state has* ***is proportional to*** *its population. | Inner cities have more than a proportionate share of social problems.* —**proportionally** *adv.*

pro·pos·al /prəˈpoʊzəl/ *n.* **1** [C,U] a plan or idea that is officially suggested for someone to consider, or the act of suggesting this: *a* ***proposal to*** *raise bus fares* **2** [C] the act of asking someone to marry you

pro·pose /prəˈpoʊz/ *v.* **1** [T] to officially suggest that something be done: *Smith* ***proposes that*** *the rules be changed.* **2** [I] to ask someone to marry you: *Has he proposed yet?* **3** [T] (formal) to intend to do something: *What does the candidate* ***propose to*** *do about unemployment?*

prop·o·si·tion¹ /ˌprɑpəˈzɪʃən/ *n.* [C] **1** a statement in which you express a judgment or opinion: *The Founding Fathers supported the* ***proposition that*** *all people are created equal under the law.* **2** an offer, plan, or idea, especially in business or politics: *Jack went to Robards with a proposition. | Proposition 13 on the ballot*

proposition² *v.* [T] to suggest to someone that s/he have sex with you, especially in exchange for money

pro·pri·e·tar·y /prəˈpraɪəˌtɛri/ *adj.* (formal) information or products that are proprietary can only be known about or sold by a particular company

pro·pri·e·tor /prəˈpraɪətɚ/ *n.* [C] (formal) an owner of a business

pro·pri·e·ty /prəˈpraɪət̬i/ *n.* [singular, U] (formal) correct social or moral behavior (ANT) **impropriety**: *There is a debate over the* ***propriety of*** *spanking children.*

pro·pul·sion /prəˈpʌlʃən/ *n.* [U] the force that moves a vehicle forward, or the system used in order to make this happen: *jet propulsion*

pro ra·ta /ˌproʊ ˈreɪt̬ə, -ˈrɑt̬ə/ *adj.* [only before noun] (technical) a pro rata payment or share is calculated according to exactly how much of something is used, how much work is done, etc. —**pro rata** *adv.*

pro·rate /ˈproʊreɪt, proʊˈreɪt/ *v.* [T] to calculate a price, salary, etc. according to exactly how much of something is used or how much work is done

pro·rogue /proʊˈroʊg/ *v.* [T] LAW if an institution that makes laws is prorogued, the institution's meetings officially stop for a period of time → ADJOURN, DISSOLVE

pro·sa·ic /proʊˈzeɪ-ɪk/ *adj.* (formal) boring, ordinary, or lacking in imagination: *a prosaic style of writing* —**prosaically** *adv.*

pro·sce·ni·um /proʊˈsiniəm, prə-/ *n.* [C] ENG. LANG. ARTS the part of a theater stage that is in front of the curtain [ORIGIN: 1600—1700 Latin, Greek *proskenion*, from *skene* "building in front of which plays are performed"]

pro·scribe /proʊˈskraɪb/ *v.* [T] LAW to officially stop the existence or use of something: *The laws proscribe child labor.* —**proscription** /proʊˈskrɪpʃən/ *n.* [C,U]

THESAURUS **forbid, not allow/permit/let, ban, prohibit, bar** → FORBID

P

prose /prouz/ *n.* [U] ENG. LANG. ARTS written language in its usual form, not as poetry

pros·e·cute /'prasə,kyut/ *v.* [I,T] to say officially that you think someone is guilty of a crime and must be judged by a court of law: *He was **prosecuted for** theft.*

pros·e·cu·tion /,prasə'kyuʃən/ *n.* **1 the prosecution** LAW the lawyers who try to prove in a court of law that someone is guilty of a crime → DEFENSE: *His ex-partner will appear as a **witness for the prosecution.*** → COURT[1] **2** [C,U] LAW the process or act of prosecuting someone

P

pros·e·cu·tor /'prasə,kyutə/ *n.* [C] LAW a lawyer who is trying to prove in a court of law that someone is guilty of a crime → DISTRICT ATTORNEY

pros·pect[1] /'praspɛkt/ (Ac) *n.* **1** [C,U] something that is possible or likely to happen in the future: *I was excited at **the prospect of** going to Europe.* | *a company with good **prospects for** growth* **2 prospects** [plural] chances of success in the future: *Going to college will improve your **job prospects**.* [ORIGIN: 1400—1500 Latin *prospectus*, from the past participle of *prospicere* "to look forward"]

prospect[2] *v.* [I,T] to look for things such as gold, silver, or oil in the ground or under the ocean: *Men came to California to **prospect for** gold.* —**prospector** *n.* [C]

pro·spec·tive /prə'spɛktɪv/ (Ac) *adj.* **1** likely to do a particular thing: *a prospective buyer for the house* **2** likely to happen: *the prospective annual costs*

pro·spec·tus /prə'spɛktəs/ *n.* [C] a document that describes a business opportunity or advertises something

pros·per /'praspə/ *v.* [I] to grow and develop in a successful way, especially by making money: *Under his leadership, the company had prospered.*

pros·per·i·ty /pra'spɛrəti/ *n.* [U] the condition of having money and being successful: *a time of peace and prosperity*

pros·per·ous /'praspərəs/ *adj.* successful and rich: *a prosperous community*

THESAURUS **rich, well-off, wealthy, affluent, well-to-do, rolling in it/loaded** → RICH

pros·tate /'prasteɪt/ *n.* [C] BIOLOGY a part in the body of a man or a male animal, that produces a liquid in which SPERM are carried

pros·ti·tute /'prastə,tut/ *n.* [C] someone who has sex with people to earn money

pros·ti·tu·tion /,prastə'tuʃən/ *n.* [U] the work of prostitutes

pros·trate[1] /'prastreɪt/ *adj., adv.* (formal) **1** lying flat on the ground with your face down **2** so shocked or upset that you cannot do anything: *Mrs. Klinkman was **prostrate with** grief.*

prostrate[2] *v.* **prostrate yourself** (literary) to lie flat on the ground with your face down, in order to show praise or respect

pro·tag·o·nist /prou'tægənɪst/ *n.* [C] ENG. LANG. ARTS the main character in a play, movie, or story

THESAURUS **hero, main character, anti-hero, villain** → HERO

pro·te·an /'proutiən, prou'tiən/ *adj.* (literary) having the ability to change your appearance or behavior again and again: *an actor's protean talents*

pro·tect /prə'tɛkt/ *v.* [T] to keep someone or something safe from harm, damage, or illness: *We must protect the environment.* | *The vaccine **protects** you **against** disease.* | *The laws are meant to **protect** minorities **from** discrimination.* —**protected** *adj.*: *a protected species* —**protector** *n.* [C]: *a chest protector*

THESAURUS

guard – to protect someone or something from being attacked or stolen: *The building is guarded by security officers.*
safeguard – to protect someone or something from possible dangers or problems, especially by making a law or agreement: *laws to safeguard wildlife*
shield – to protect someone or something from being hurt, damaged, or upset: *She brought up her arms to shield her face.*
give/offer/provide protection – to protect someone from something harmful: *Sun lotions provide protection from the Sun's harmful rays.*
shelter – to provide a place where someone is protected from the weather or from danger: *At great risk to themselves, they sheltered Jews from the Nazis.*
preserve – to keep someone or something from being harmed, destroyed, or changed too much: *Efforts are being made to preserve the reef.*
conserve – to prevent something from being wasted, damaged, or destroyed: *Europe has successfully conserved many of its ancient buildings.*

pro·tec·tion /prə'tɛkʃən/ *n.* [C,U] something that protects someone or something, or the act of protecting something: *environmental protections* | *the **protection of** civil rights* | *a hat **offers/provides/gives protection against** the sun*

pro·tec·tion·ism /prə'tɛkʃə,nɪzəm/ *n.* [U] ECONOMICS the practice in which a government tries to protect an industry in its own country by putting a tax on foreign goods entering the country —**protectionist** *adj., n.* [C]

pro·tec·tive /prə'tɛktɪv/ *adj.* **1** used or intended for protection: *a crab's protective shell* **2** wanting to protect someone from danger or harm: *She's fiercely **protective of** her children.*

pro·tec·tor·ate /prə'tɛktərɪt/ *n.* [C] POLITICS a country with its own government, that is protected and controlled by a more powerful country

pro·té·gé /ˈproʊt̬əˌʒeɪ, ˌproʊt̬əˈʒeɪ/ *n.* [C] a young person who is taught or helped by an older more experienced person

pro·tein /ˈproʊtin/ *n.* [C,U] BIOLOGY a substance in foods such as meat and eggs that helps your body to grow and be healthy. Proteins are formed by a chain of AMINO ACIDS.

pro·test¹ /ˈproʊtɛst/ *n.* **1** [C] a strong complaint that shows you disagree with something that you think is wrong or unfair: *Almirez led a* ***protest against*** *the new road.* | *Six managers quit* ***in protest*** *of the board's decision.* | *He cleaned his room* ***without protest.*** **2 do sth under protest** to do something in a way that shows you do not want to do it because you think it is wrong or unfair

pro·test² /ˈproʊtɛst, prəˈtɛst/ *v.* **1** [I,T] to say or do something publicly to show that you disagree with something or think that it is wrong or unfair: *Demonstrators were* ***protesting against*** *changes in the law.* | *Students carried signs protesting the war.*

THESAURUS

march – to protest while walking with a group of people from one place to another: *Over a million people marched to protest against the war.*
demonstrate – to protest while walking or standing somewhere with a group of people: *A crowd of people were demonstrating outside the embassy.*
riot – to protest by behaving in a violent and uncontrolled way: *People were rioting in the streets in reaction to the elections.*
hold/stage a sit-in – to protest by refusing to leave a place: *Hundreds of students staged a sit-in.*
go on a hunger strike – to protest by refusing to eat: *The prisoners went on a hunger strike.*
boycott – to protest about the actions of a company or country by refusing to buy something, go somewhere, etc.: *In 1980, some countries boycotted the Olympic Games.*

2 [T] to state very strongly that something is true, especially when other people do not believe you: *Throughout the trial, he kept* ***protesting*** *his* ***innocence.*** —**protestation** /ˌprɑt̬əˈsteɪʃən, ˌproʊ-/ *n.* [C]

Prot·es·tant /ˈprɑt̬əstənt/ *adj.* relating to a part of the Christian church that separated from the Roman Catholic church in the 16th century —**Protestant** *n.* [C] —**Protestantism** *n.* [U]

pro·test·er, protestor /ˈproʊˌtɛstɚ, proʊˈtɛstɚ/ *n.* [C] someone who takes part in a public event to show his/her opposition to something: *anti-war protesters*

pro·to·col /ˈproʊt̬əˌkɔl, -ˌkɑl/ (Ac) *n.* **1** [singular, U] the system of rules for the correct way to behave on official occasions: *Even touching the Queen is a* ***breach of protocol*** (=it is not allowed). **2** [C] an official statement of the rules that a group of countries have agreed to follow in dealing with a particular problem: *the Montreal Protocol on greenhouse gases* [ORIGIN: 1400—1500 Old French *prothocole*, from Late Greek *protokollon* "first page of a document"]

pro·ton /ˈproʊtɑn/ *n.* [C] PHYSICS a part in the NUCLEUS of an atom, that has a positive electrical CHARGE [ORIGIN: 1800—1900 Greek "first thing," from *protos* "first"] → *see picture at* ATOM

pro·to·type /ˈproʊt̬əˌtaɪp/ *n.* [C] a model of a new car, machine, etc., used in order to test the design before it is produced in large numbers

pro·tract·ed /proʊˈtræktɪd, prə-/ *adj.* continuing for a long time, usually longer than necessary: *a protracted strike*

pro·trac·tor /proʊˈtræktɚ, prə-/ *n.* [C] MATH a flat tool shaped like a half circle, used for measuring and drawing angles

P

pro·trude /proʊˈtrud/ *v.* [I] (formal) to stick out from somewhere: *Rocks* ***protruded from*** *the water.* —**protrusion** /proʊˈtruʒən/ *n.* [C,U]

proud /praʊd/ *adj.* **1** feeling pleased because you think that something you have achieved or are connected with is very good → PRIDE: *My husband and I are very* ***proud of*** *her.* | *We're* ***proud to*** *announce the birth of our son.* | *I'm* ***proud (that)*** *the team's done so well.* **2** (disapproving) thinking that you are better, more important, more skillful, etc. than other people

THESAURUS

conceited/big-headed (informal) – very proud of yourself, especially of what you can do, in a way that other people dislike
vain – very proud of yourself, especially of your appearance, in a way that other people dislike
arrogant – showing that you think you are better than other people
stuck-up (informal) – proud and unfriendly because you think you are better and more important than other people
egotistical (formal) – believing that you are more interesting or important than other people
haughty (formal) – proud and unfriendly

3 too embarrassed or ashamed to allow other people to help you when you need help: *Terry was too proud to ask his family for money.* **4 do sb proud** to make someone feel proud of you by doing something well: *Vicki hopes to do her school proud.* —**proudly** *adv.* → PRIDE¹

prove /pruv/ *v.* (past tense **proved**, past participle **proved** *or* **proven** /ˈpruvən/) [T] **1** to show that something is definitely true → PROOF: *They have enough evidence to* ***prove that*** *she is guilty.* | *I know he's innocent, and I'm going to* ***prove it to*** *you.*

THESAURUS **demonstrate, show, indicate, establish, substantiate** → DEMONSTRATE

2 to show over time that someone or something has a particular quality: *Any delay will prove costly.* | *The weather* ***proved to be*** *beautiful.* **3 prove yourself** *also* **prove sth to sb** to show that you are able to do something well: *At seventeen years old, she had yet to prove herself on the pro golf* *tour.* [ORIGIN: 1100—1200 Old French *prover*, from Latin *probare* "to test, prove"] —**provable** *adj.*

prov·en[1] /ˈpruvən/ *adj.* shown to be real or true: *a proven method of learning*

proven[2] *v.* a past participle of PROVE

prov·erb /ˈprɑvɚb/ *n.* [C] ENG. LANG. ARTS a short statement that most people know, that contains advice about life. For example, "A penny saved is a penny earned" is a proverb.

THESAURUS **phrase, expression, idiom, cliché, saying, maxim** → PHRASE[1]

P

pro·ver·bi·al /prəˈvɚbiəl/ *adj.* **the proverbial sth** used when you describe something using a well-known expression: *Ice cream was selling like the proverbial hotcakes.* —**proverbially** *adv.*

pro·vide /prəˈvaɪd/ *v.* [T] **1** to give or supply something to someone: *The charity **provides** shelter **for** the homeless.* | *Rescuers **provided** the lost hikers **with** blankets and food.* **2 provide that** (formal) if a law or rule provides that something must happen, it states that it must happen

provide for sb/sth *phr. v.* **1** to give someone the things s/he needs, such as money, food, or clothing: *Dad always thought a man should provide for his family.* **2** to make plans in order to deal with something that might happen in the future: *The hotel is examining ways to provide for the disabled.*

pro·vid·ed /prəˈvaɪdɪd/ *also* **proˈvided that** *conjunction* used in order to say that something will only happen if another thing happens first: *Talks will take place in July, provided that enough progress has been made.*

prov·i·dence /ˈprɑvədəns/ *n.* [singular, U] a force that some people believe controls our lives in the way God wants: *an act of **divine providence***

pro·vid·er /prəˈvaɪdɚ/ *n.* [C] **1** a person or company that provides a service: *a health-care provider* **2** someone who supports a family

pro·vid·ing /prəˈvaɪdɪŋ/ *also* **proˈviding that** *conjunction* used in order to say that something will only happen if another thing happens first: *You can borrow the car, providing that I have it back by six o'clock.*

prov·ince /ˈprɑvɪns/ *n.* **1** [C] one of the large areas into which some countries are divided: *the provinces of Canada* **2 the provinces** [plural] the parts of a country that are not near a large city, especially the capital city: *In Boston, he received a more sophisticated schooling than he had **in the provinces**.*

pro·vin·cial /prəˈvɪnʃəl/ *adj.* **1** (disapproving) not interested in anything new or different: *provincial attitudes* **2** relating to a province, or the parts of a country that are not near the capital: *the provincial government of Quebec*

pro·vi·sion /prəˈvɪʒən/ *n.* **1** [C,U] the act of providing something that someone needs now or will need in the future: *the **provision of** services for the elderly* | *He has **made provisions for** his wife in his will* (=he arranged for her to have money when he dies). **2** [C] a condition in an agreement or law: *the **provisions of** the treaty* **3 provisions** [plural] food supplies, especially for a trip: *We had enough provisions for two weeks.*

pro·vi·sion·al /prəˈvɪʒənl/ *adj.* intended to exist for only a short time and likely to be changed in the future: *a provisional government*

pro·vi·so /prəˈvaɪzoʊ/ *n.* (plural **provisos**) [C] (formal) something that you say must happen before another thing is allowed to happen: *Tom's grandson inherited his money **with the proviso that** he go to college.*

prov·o·ca·tion /ˌprɑvəˈkeɪʃən/ *n.* [C,U] an action or event that makes someone angry, or that is intended to do this: *My client was attacked **without provocation**.*

pro·voc·a·tive /prəˈvɑkət̬ɪv/ *adj.* **1** intending to make someone angry or cause a lot of discussion: *provocative comments* **2** intending to make someone sexually excited: *a provocative dress* —**provocatively** *adv.*

pro·voke /prəˈvoʊk/ *v.* [T] **1** to make someone very angry, especially by deliberately annoying him/her: *She did hit him, but he **provoked** her **into** doing it.* **2** to cause a sudden reaction or feeling: *The president's speech provoked criticism from Democrats.*

pro·vost /ˈproʊvoʊst/ *n.* [C] an important official at a university

prow /praʊ/ *n.* [C] the front part of a ship or boat

prow·ess /ˈpraʊɪs/ *n.* [U] (formal) great skill at doing something: *a man of great athletic prowess*

prowl[1] /praʊl/ *v.* [I,T] to move around an area quietly, trying not to be seen or heard: *Tigers prowled through the jungle.*

prowl[2] *n.* **1 be on the prowl** if an animal is on the prowl, it is hunting **2 be on the prowl for sth/sb** if someone is on the prowl for something, s/he is moving around looking for something or someone in different places: *She's always on the prowl for bargains.*

prowl·er /ˈpraʊlɚ/ *n.* [C] someone who moves around quietly at night, especially near your house, in order to steal something or harm you

prox·im·i·ty /prɑkˈsɪmət̬i/ *n.* [U] (formal) nearness in distance or time: *We chose this house because of its **proximity to** the school.*

prox·y /ˈprɑksi/ *n.* (plural **proxies**) **1** [C] someone whom you choose to represent you, especially to vote for you **2 by proxy** if you do something by proxy, you arrange for someone else to do it for you

prude /prud/ *n.* [C] (disapproving) someone who is very easily shocked by anything relating to sex —**prudish** *adj.*

pru·dence /ˈprudns/ *n.* [U] a sensible and careful

attitude that makes you avoid unnecessary risks: *The situation demanded prudence.*

pru·dent /'prudnt/ *adj.* sensible and careful, especially by avoiding risks that are not necessary: *It would not **be prudent to** invest all of your money in the same place.*

prune[1] /prun/ *also* **prune back** *v.* [T] to cut some of the branches of a tree or bush to make it grow better

prune[2] *n.* [C] a dried PLUM (=type of fruit)

pru·ri·ent /'pruriənt/ *adj.* (formal) showing too much interest in sex

pry /praɪ/ *v.* (**pried**, **pries**) **1** [T] to force something open, or to force it away from something else: *They finally **pried** the window **open**. | I had to use a screwdriver to **pry** the lid **off** the paint can.* **2** [I] to try to find out details about someone's private life in an impolite way: *I don't want to pry, but I need to ask you one or two questions.*

P.S. *n.* [C] **postscript** a note that you add to the end of a letter, that gives more information

psalm /sɑm/ *n.* [C] a song or poem praising God

pseu·do·nym /'sudn,ɪm, 'sudə,nɪm/ *n.* [C] a false name used by someone, especially a writer, instead of his/her real name [ORIGIN: 1800—1900 French *pseudonyme*, from Greek *pseudonymos*, from *pseudes* "false" + *onoma* "name"]

psych /saɪk/ *v.*

psych sb ↔ **out** *phr. v.* (informal) to do or say things that will make your opponent feel nervous or confused: *He would psych out opponents by screaming and jumping up and down before each game.*

psych sb/yourself **up** *phr. v.* (informal) to build up your confidence before doing something difficult by telling yourself or someone else that you can do it: *Soldiers have to psych themselves up for combat.*

psy·che /'saɪki/ *n.* [C usually singular] someone's mind or basic nature that controls how s/he thinks or behaves [ORIGIN: 1600—1700 Greek "breath, life, soul, mind"]

psyched /saɪkt/ *also* **,psyched 'up** *adj.* (spoken) **be psyched (up)** to be mentally prepared for an event and excited about it: *Bryony's totally **psyched about/for** her date.*

psy·che·del·ic /,saɪkə'dɛlɪk◂/ *adj.* **1** psychedelic drugs such as LSD make you see things that do not really exist **2** psychedelic art, clothing, etc. has a lot of bright colors and patterns

psy·chi·a·trist /saɪ'kaɪətrɪst, sə-/ *n.* [C] a doctor who studies and treats mental illness ➔ PSYCHOLOGIST

THESAURUS **doctor, physician, surgeon, specialist, pediatrician** ➔ DOCTOR[1]

psy·chi·a·try /saɪ'kaɪətri, sə-/ *n.* [U] the study and treatment of mental illness [ORIGIN: 1800—1900 French *psychiatrie*, from Greek *psykhe* "soul, mind" + *iatreia* "cure"] —**psychiatric** /,saɪki'ætrɪk◂/ *adj.*: *a psychiatric hospital*

psy·chic[1] /'saɪkɪk/ *adj.* **1** relating to strange events involving the power of the human mind: *a mysterious **psychic phenomenon** | She claims to have **psychic powers**.* **2** someone who is psychic has the ability to know what other people are thinking or what will happen in the future **3** affecting the mind rather than the body: *psychic pain/scar/wound | people who are in **psychic pain***

psychic[2] *n.* [C] someone who has strange powers such as the ability to know what will happen in the future

P

psy·cho /'saɪkoʊ/ *n.* (plural **psychos**) [C] (informal) someone who is likely to behave in a violent or crazy way

psy·cho·a·nal·y·sis /,saɪkoʊə'næləsɪs/ *n.* [U] a way of treating someone who is mentally ill by talking to him/her about his/her life, feelings, etc. to find out the cause of the illness —**psychoanalyze** /,saɪkoʊ'ænl,aɪz/ *v.* [T]

psy·cho·an·a·lyst /,saɪkoʊ'ænl-ɪst/ *n.* [C] someone who treats people using psychoanalysis

psy·cho·log·i·cal /,saɪkə'lɑdʒɪkəl/ (Ac) *adj.* **1** relating to the way people's minds work and the way this affects their behavior: *The patient has a history of **psychological problems**.* **2** relating to the science of psychology: *a psychological test* —**psychologically** *adv.*: *psychologically disturbed patients*

psy·chol·o·gist /saɪ'kɑlədʒɪst/ (Ac) *n.* [C] someone who is trained in psychology ➔ PSYCHIATRIST

psy·chol·o·gy /saɪ'kɑlədʒi/ (Ac) *n.* (plural **psychologies**) **1** [U] the study of the mind and how it works: *a professor of psychology* **2** [C usually singular,U] what someone thinks or believes, and how this affects what s/he does: *the **psychology of** a serial killer* [ORIGIN: 1600—1700 Modern Latin *psychologia*, from Greek *psykhe-* "soul, mind" + *logia* "study"]

psy·cho·path /'saɪkə,pæθ/ *n.* [C] someone who has a mental illness that makes him/her behave in a violent or criminal way —**psychopathic** /,saɪkə'pæθɪk/ *adj.*

psy·cho·sis /saɪ'koʊsɪs/ *n.* (plural **psychoses** /-siz/) [C,U] a serious mental illness that may cause changes in someone's behavior

psy·cho·so·mat·ic /,saɪkoʊsə'mæṭɪk/ *adj.* a psychosomatic illness is caused by fear or anxiety, not by any physical problem

psy·cho·ther·a·py /,saɪkoʊ'θɛrəpi/ *n.* [U] the treatment of mental illness by talking to someone and discussing problems, rather than by using drugs or medicine —**psychotherapist** *n.* [C]

psy·chot·ic /saɪ'kɑṭɪk/ *adj.* relating to mental illness, or resulting from it: *psychotic behavior* —**psychotic** *n.* [C] ➔ CRAZY

PTA *n.* [C] **Parent-Teacher Association** an organization of teachers and parents that works to improve a particular school

pub /pʌb/ *n.* [C] a comfortable BAR that often serves food

pu·ber·ty /ˈpyubɚṭi/ *n.* [U] BIOLOGY the time when your body develops from being a child to being an adult: *Our daughter is just* ***reaching puberty*** (=starting to develop physically).

pu·bes·cent /pyuˈbɛsənt/ *adj.* BIOLOGY a pubescent boy or girl is going through puberty

pu·bic /ˈpyubɪk/ *adj.* relating to or near the sex organs: *pubic hair*

P

pub·lic¹ /ˈpʌblɪk/ *adj.* **1** relating to all the ordinary people in a country or city: *We acted out of concern for public welfare.* | *The judge ruled that allowing the broadcast of the trial would be* ***in the public interest.*** | *The mayor seems to have* ***public opinion*** *on his side.* **2** available for anyone to use ANT **private**: *a public restroom* | *public transportation* **3** relating to the government and the services that it provides ANT **private**: *It has been eight years since she was elected to* ***public office*** (=a job in the government). | *Republicans want to cut* ***public spending*** (=money the government spends on roads, hospitals, etc.). **4** known about by most people: *Last night the name of the killer was* ***made public.*** | *a* ***public figure*** (=well-known person) **5** intended for anyone to know, see, or hear ANT **private**: ***public display of affection/emotion/anger etc.*** (=showing your emotions so that everyone can see) **6 go public** to tell everyone about something that was secret: *They finally went public with news of their engagement.* [ORIGIN: 1400—1500 French *publique*, from Latin *publicus*] → PUBLICLY

public² *n.* **1 the public** all the ordinary people in a country or city: *The museum is* ***open to the public*** *five days a week.* | *This product is not for sale to* ***the general public.*** **2 in public** in a place where anyone can know, see, or hear ANT **in private**: *She was careful not to criticize him in public.* **3** [singular, U] the people who like a particular singer, writer, etc.: *A star has to try to please her public.*

ˌpublic ˈaccess *n.* [U] a situation in which anyone can enter a place or use a service: *Public access to the beach is blocked by private property.*

ˌpublic adˈdress ˌsystem *n.* [C] a PA

ˌpublic afˈfairs *n.* [plural] events or questions, especially political ones, that affect everyone

ˌpublic asˈsistance *n.* [U] the government programs that help poor people get food, homes, and medical care → WELFARE

pub·li·ca·tion /ˌpʌbləˈkeɪʃən/ AC *n.* **1** [U] the process of printing a book, magazine, etc. and offering it for sale → PUBLISH: *She was in New York for the* ***publication of*** *her new book.* | *There may be a delay of up to eight weeks before publication.* **2** [C] a book, magazine, etc.: *a monthly publication for stamp collectors* **3** [U] the act of making something known to the public: *The authorities tried to stop the publication of the test results.*

ˌpublic ˈdebt *n.* [U] ECONOMICS the total amount of money owed by the government of a country

ˌpublic deˈfender *n.* [C] LAW a lawyer who is paid by the government to defend people who cannot pay for a lawyer themselves

ˌpublic ˈfigure *n.* [C] someone who is well known because s/he is on television or in the newspapers a lot

ˌpublic ˈhousing *n.* [U] houses or apartments built by the government for poor people

pub·li·cist /ˈpʌbləsɪst/ *n.* [C] someone whose job is to make sure that famous people or new products, movies, books, etc. get a lot of publicity

pub·lic·i·ty /pəˈblɪsəṭi/ *n.* [U] **1** the attention that someone or something gets from newspapers, television, etc.: *His new novel has* ***received*** *a lot of* ***publicity.*** | ***good/bad/negative publicity*** **2** the business of making sure that people know about what a famous person is doing, or about a new product, movie, book, etc.: *a publicity campaign*

pub·li·cize /ˈpʌbləˌsaɪz/ *v.* [T] to tell people about a new movie, book, event, etc.: *a* ***well-publicized*** *movie*

THESAURUS **advertise, promote, market, hype, plug** → ADVERTISE

pub·lic·ly /ˈpʌblɪkli/ *adv.* **1** in a way that is intended for anyone to know, see, or hear: *None of the players were willing to comment publicly.* | *Lozansky was jailed for publicly criticizing the government.* **2** by the government, as part of its services: *The hospitals are publicly operated in cities, suburbs, and rural areas.* **3** ECONOMICS a company that is publicly owned has sold STOCK in it to the public **4** among the ordinary people in a country or city: *publicly elected bodies*

ˌpublicly ˌheld corpoˈration *n.* [C] ECONOMICS a large company that sells its STOCK on an official STOCK EXCHANGE

ˌpublic reˈlations (*written abbreviation* **PR**) *n.* **1** [plural] the relationship between an organization and the public: *Organizing events for charity is always good for public relations.* **2** [U] the work of explaining what a company does, so the public will approve of it: *the public relations department*

ˌpublic ˈschool *n.* [C] a free local school that is controlled and paid for by the government → PRIVATE SCHOOL

ˌpublic ˈtelevision *n.* [U] a television program or service that is paid for by the government, large companies, and the public

ˌpublic transporˈtation *n.* [U] buses, trains, etc. that are available for everyone to use

ˌpublic ˈworks *n.* [plural] buildings, roads, etc. built by the government for the public to use

pub·lish /ˈpʌblɪʃ/ (Ac) *v.* **1** [I,T] to arrange for a book, magazine, etc. to be written, printed, and sold: *Huckleberry Finn was first published in 1884.* | *We publish mainly educational materials.* **2** [T] if a newspaper, magazine, etc. publishes something such as a letter, it prints it for people to read: *The article was published in the Los Angeles Times.* **3** [T] to make official information available for everyone to use: *New guidelines for social studies education were published this year.* [ORIGIN: 1300—1400 French *publier*, from Latin *publicare* "to make public, publish"] —**publishing** *n.* [U]: *I work in publishing.*

pub·lish·er /ˈpʌblɪʃɚ/ (Ac) *n.* [C] a person or company that arranges the writing, printing, and sale of books, newspapers, etc.

puck /pʌk/ *n.* [C] a hard flat circular piece of rubber that you hit with a stick in the game of HOCKEY

puck·er /ˈpʌkɚ/ *also* **pucker up** *v.* **1** [I,T] (informal) if your mouth puckers, or if you pucker it, your lips are pulled together tightly, for example because you are going to kiss someone **2** [I] if cloth puckers, it gets folds in it so that it is no longer flat —**puckered** *adj.*

pud·ding /ˈpʊdɪŋ/ *n.* [C,U] a thick sweet creamy food made with milk, eggs, sugar, and flour, that is eaten cold: *chocolate pudding* [ORIGIN: 1200—1300 Old French *boudin*, from Latin *botellus* "sausage"]

pud·dle /ˈpʌdl/ *n.* [C] a small pool of rain on a road, path, etc.: *Children were splashing in the puddles.*

pudg·y /ˈpʌdʒi/ *adj.* fatter than usual: *short pudgy fingers* —**pudginess** *n.* [U]

Pueb·lo /ˈpwɛbloʊ/ *n.* a group of Native American tribes from the southwest U.S., who built homes made of ADOBE —**Pueblo** *adj.*

pueblo *n.* [C] **1** a small town or group of Native American homes in the southwest U.S., usually with more than one level, made of stone or ADOBE (=building material made from earth and STRAW) **2** a small town in the southwest U.S.

pu·er·ile /ˈpyʊrəl, -raɪl/ *adj.* (formal) silly and stupid (SYN) **childish**: *puerile humor*

puff¹ /pʌf/ *v.* **1** [I,T] to breathe in and out while smoking a cigarette, pipe, etc.: *William sat there **puffing on** his pipe.* **2** [I] to breathe quickly and with difficulty after running, carrying something heavy, etc.: *Max was puffing heavily after climbing the stairs.* **3** [I,T] to blow steam or smoke out of something: *The boiler was puffing thick black smoke.*

puff sth ↔ **out** *phr. v.* to make something bigger by filling it with air: *The frog had its throat puffed out.*

puff up *phr. v.* **1** *also* **puff** sth ↔ **up** to become bigger by filling with air, or to make something do this: *Birds puff up their feathers to stay warm.* **2** if your eye, face, etc. puffs up, it swells: *My eye puffed up where he hit me.*

puff² *n.* [C] **1** the action of breathing smoke into your mouth and blowing it out again: *He **took a puff on** his cigar.* **2** a sudden short movement of air, smoke, or wind: *Puffs of smoke came from the chimney.*

puf·fin /ˈpʌfɪn/ *n.* [C] a North Atlantic bird with a black and white body and a large brightly colored beak

puff·y /ˈpʌfi/ *adj.* puffy eyes, cheeks, or faces are swollen: *Her eyes were red and puffy from crying.* —**puffiness** *n.* [U]

pug·na·cious /pʌgˈneɪʃəs/ *adj.* (formal) very eager to argue or fight with people

puke /pyuk/ *v.* [I,T] (slang) VOMIT —**puke** *n.* [U]

pul·chri·tude /ˈpʌlkrəˌtud/ *n.* [U] (formal) beauty, especially of a woman

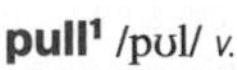
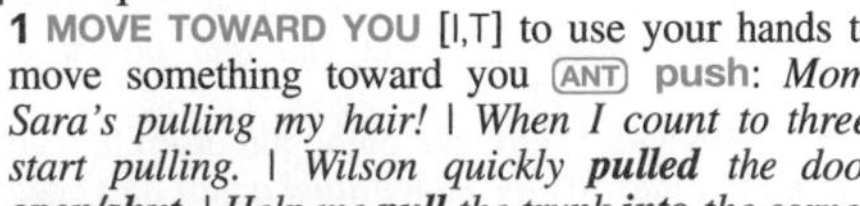

pull¹ /pʊl/ *v.*

1 MOVE TOWARD YOU [I,T] to use your hands to move something toward you (ANT) **push**: *Mom, Sara's pulling my hair!* | *When I count to three, start pulling.* | *Wilson quickly **pulled** the door **open/shut**.* | *Help me **pull** the trunk **into** the corner.*

THESAURUS

tug – to pull something suddenly, especially several times with small movements: *The little boy was tugging at her sleeve.*

drag – to pull something somewhere, usually along the ground: *I dragged the chair upstairs.*

haul – to pull something heavy, often using a rope: *Fishermen hauled in their nets.*
tow – to pull another vehicle or boat: *Some pickup trucks were towing trailers.*
heave – to pull or lift something very heavy, especially with one movement: *We managed to heave the piano into position.* → PUSH[1]

2 REMOVE [T] to remove something from its place, especially by using force: *She has to have her wisdom teeth pulled.* | *The baby's **pulled** everything **out** of the cupboards.*
3 MAKE STH FOLLOW YOU [I,T] to use a rope, chain, your hands, etc. to make something move behind you in the direction you are moving (ANT) **push**: *The car was pulling a camper behind it.*
4 MUSCLE [T] to injure a muscle by stretching it too much during physical activity: *Martinez **pulled** a groin **muscle** and had to leave the game.*

THESAURUS **hurt, injure, break, bruise, sprain, twist, strain, dislocate** → HURT[1]

5 pull sb's leg (informal) to tell someone something that is not true, as a joke: *I think he was just pulling your leg.*
6 pull strings to secretly use your influence with important people in order to get something or to help someone: *Barry pulled some strings and got us tickets for the football game.*
7 MOVE YOUR BODY a) [I,T] to move your body or part of your body away from someone or something: *She **pulled away from** him in horror.* **b)** [T] to use force to move your body somewhere: *The kids **pulled** themselves **up** onto the platform.*
8 CLOTHING [I,T] to put on or take off clothing, usually quickly: *He **pulled off** his gloves and placed them on the dresser.*
9 pull your weight to do your share of the work: *If you don't start pulling your weight around here, you'll be fired!*
10 pull a stunt/trick/joke/prank (informal) to do something that annoys or harms other people: *Don't you ever pull a stunt like that again!*
11 TRICK [T] (spoken) to deceive or trick someone: *What are you trying to pull?* | *Are you trying to **pull a fast one** on me?*
12 pull the strings to control something, especially when you are not the person who is supposed to be controlling it: *Who is really pulling the strings in the White House?*
13 SWITCH [T] to move a control such as a SWITCH or TRIGGER toward you to make a piece of equipment work: *She raised the gun and pulled the trigger.*
14 GUN/KNIFE [T] to take out a gun or knife ready to use it: *Suddenly the man **pulled** a **gun** and began shooting.*
15 pull the rug out from under sb to suddenly take away something that someone was depending on to achieve what s/he wanted

pull sth ↔ **apart** *phr. v.*
to separate something into two or more pieces or groups: *Loosen the roots and gently pull the plants apart.* | *the ethnic problems that pulled Yugoslavia apart*

pull away *phr. v.*
1 to move ahead of a competitor by going faster or being more successful: *Chicago pulled away in the third quarter to win 107–76.*
2 to start to drive away from the place where your car was stopped: *Grant **pulled away from** the curb.*

pull sth ↔ **down** *phr. v.*
to destroy a building, wall, etc.: *Many of the houses were pulled down to make way for a new highway.*

pull for sb *phr. v.* (informal)
to encourage a person or team to succeed: *Which team are you pulling for?*

pull in *phr. v.*
1 pull (sth ↔) **in** to move a car into a particular space and stop it: *Kevin pulled in behind me and parked.*
2 pull sth ↔ **in** (informal) if you pull in a lot of money, you earn it

pull off *phr. v.*
1 pull sth ↔ **off** (informal) to succeed in doing something difficult: *Cruz expects to win the fight, but no one else thinks he can **pull it off**.*
2 pull off sth to leave a road in order to stop or to turn into another road

pull out *phr. v.*
1 to drive a car onto a road from where you have stopped
2 to get out of a bad situation or dangerous place: *Investors pulled out, selling all their shares.*
3 pull sb/sth ↔ **out** to get someone out of a bad situation or dangerous place: *We plan to pull our troops out of the area.*

pull (sb/sth ↔) **over** *phr. v.*
to drive to the side of a road and stop your car, or to make someone do this: *We didn't realize we were speeding until the highway patrol pulled us over.*

pull through *phr. v.*
1 pull sb through (sth) to stay alive after a serious injury or illness, or to help someone do this: *We all prayed that he would pull through.*
2 pull through sth to continue to live or exist after being in a difficult or upsetting situation: *The city managed to pull through its financial crisis.*

pull together *phr. v.*
1 to work hard with other people to achieve something: *After the hurricane, neighbors pulled together to help each other.*
2 pull yourself together (informal) to force yourself to stop being nervous, afraid, or disorganized: *A year after the accident, she's finally starting to pull herself together.*

pull up *phr. v.*
1 to stop the vehicle you are driving: *A red Buick pulled up at the stop lights.*
2 pull up a chair/stool etc. to get a chair and sit down near someone who is already sitting

pull[2] *n.* **1** [C] an act of using force to move something toward you or in the same direction as you are going: ***Give the rope a good pull.*** **2** [C usually singular] a strong force such as GRAVITY, that makes things move in a particular direction: *the* *pull of the ocean's tide* **3** [singular, U] (informal) power that gives you an unfair advantage: *a family with a lot of political pull*

pul·ley /ˈpʊli/ *n.* (plural **pulleys**) [C] a piece of equipment used for lifting heavy things, consisting of a wheel over which you pull a chain or rope

pull·out /ˈpʊlaʊt/ *n.* [C] **1** the act of an army, business, etc. leaving a particular place: *the pullout of NATO troops from the region* **2** part of a book or magazine that can be removed

pull·o·ver /ˈpʊlˌoʊvɚ/ *n.* [C] a SWEATER without buttons

ˈpull-up *n.* [C] an exercise in which you use your arms to pull yourself up toward a BAR that is above your head

pul·mo·nar·y /ˈpʊlməˌnɛri, ˈpʌl-/ *adj.* BIOLOGY relating to or affecting the lungs: *pulmonary disease* | ***the pulmonary vein/artery*** (=tubes that carry blood from the heart to the lungs)

pulp¹ /pʌlp/ *n.* [U] **1** the soft inside part of a fruit or vegetable: *Cut the melon in half and scoop out the pulp.* **2** a very soft substance that is almost liquid: ***Mash** the bananas **to a pulp**.* | *Timber is grown for **wood pulp**, which is used for making paper.* **3 beat sb to a pulp** (informal) to hit someone until s/he is seriously injured

pulp² *adj.* pulp magazines, stories, etc. are usually of poor quality and tell stories about sex and violence: *pulp fiction*

pul·pit /ˈpʊlpɪt, ˈpʌl-/ *n.* [C] a structure like a tall box at the front of a church, that a priest or minister stands behind when s/he speaks: *Reverend Dawson addressed the congregation **from the pulpit**.*

pul·sate /ˈpʌlseɪt/ *v.* [I] to make sounds or movements that are strong and regular like a heart beating: *loud pulsating music* —**pulsation** /pʌlˈseɪʃən/ *n.* [C,U]

pulse¹ /pʌls/ *n.* **1** [C usually singular] the regular beat that can be felt as your heart pumps blood around your body: *He doesn't **have a pulse**.* | ***Her pulse rate*** (=the number of beats per minute) *is high.* | *A nurse came in and **took** my **pulse*** (=counted the number of beats in a minute). **2** [C] an amount of light, sound, or energy that continues for a very short time: *an electric pulse*

pulse² *v.* [I] to move or flow quickly with a steady beat or sound: *Blood **pulses through** the veins.*

pul·ver·ize /ˈpʌlvəˌraɪz/ *v.* [T] **1** to crush something into powder: *a machine that pulverizes rocks* **2** (informal) to defeat someone completely

pu·ma /ˈpumə, ˈpyumə/ *n.* [C] a COUGAR

pum·mel /ˈpʌməl/ *v.* [T] to hit someone or something many times with your FISTS

pump¹ /pʌmp/ *n.* [C] **1** a machine that forces liquid or gas into or out of something: ***a water/fuel/gas etc. pump*** | *an air/a bicycle pump* ➔ *see picture at* BICYCLE **2** a woman's plain shoe that does not fasten: *a pair of black pumps* **3** *also* **gas pump** a machine at a GAS STATION, used to put gasoline into a car [ORIGIN: (1) 1400—1500 Middle Low German *pumpe* or Middle Dutch *pompe*]

pump² *v.* **1** [T] to make liquid or gas move in a particular direction, using a pump: *That's the machine that **pumps** water **into** the fields.* **2** [I] to move liquid very quickly in and out or up and down: *His heart was pumping fast.* **3 pump sb (about sth)** (informal) to ask someone a lot of questions in order to find out information **4 pump iron** (informal) to do exercise by lifting heavy weights

pump sth **into** sth *phr. v.* **pump money into sth** (informal) to spend a lot of money on something such as a project: *He had to pump $10,000 of his own money into the company.*

pump sth ↔ **out** *phr. v.* **1** to remove liquid from something using a pump: *We had to pump the basement out after the pipes burst.* **2** to produce or supply something in large amounts: *I pump out a new novel every year.*

pump up *phr. v.* **1 pump** sth ↔ **up** to fill something such as a tire or ball with air until it is full SYN **inflate** **2 pump** sb ↔ **up** to increase someone's interest or excitement about something: *Hutchison traveled around the state the day before the election to pump up voters.*

pum·per·nick·el /ˈpʌmpɚˌnɪkəl/ *n.* [U] a heavy dark brown bread

pump·kin /ˈpʌmpkɪn, ˈpʌŋkɪn/ *n.* [C,U] a very large orange fruit that grows on the ground, or the inside of this eaten as food: *pumpkin pie* [ORIGIN: 1600—1700 *pumpion* "pumpkin" (16—19 centuries), from French *pompon* "melon, pumpkin"] ➔ *see picture at* VEGETABLE

pun /pʌn/ *n.* [C] ENG. LANG. ARTS an amusing use of a word or phrase that has two meanings, or of words with the same sound but different meanings —**pun** *v.* [I]

THESAURUS **joke, gag, wisecrack, one-liner, quip, witticism** ➔ JOKE¹

punch¹ /pʌntʃ/ *v.* [T] **1** to hit someone or something hard with your FIST (=closed hand): *Bill was suspended from school for punching another student.* ➔ *see picture on page A22*

THESAURUS **hit, slap, beat, smack, whack, strike, pound** ➔ HIT¹

2 to make a hole in something using a metal tool or other sharp object: *The conductor came along and punched our tickets.*

THESAURUS **pierce, make a hole in sth, prick, puncture** ➔ PIERCE

3 punch a clock to record the time that you start or finish work by putting a card into a special machine [ORIGIN: 1300—1400 Old French *poinçonner* "to make a hole in," from *poinçon* "tool for making holes"]

punch in *phr. v.* to record the time that you arrive at work by putting a card into a special machine

punch out *phr. v.* to record the time that you leave work by putting a card into a special machine

punch² *n.* **1** [C] a quick strong hit made with your FIST (=closed hand): *a punch in the stomach* **2** [U] a drink made from fruit juice, sugar, water, and sometimes alcohol: *fruit punch* **3** [C] a metal tool for cutting holes or for pushing something into a small hole **4** [U] a strong effective quality that makes people interested: *We need something to give the ad campaign some punch.*

'punching bag *n.* **1** [C] a heavy leather bag that hangs from a rope, that is punched for exercise **2 use sb as a punching bag** (informal) to hit someone hard, or to criticize someone a lot, even though s/he has done nothing wrong

P

punch line, punch·line /'pʌntʃlaɪn/ *n.* [C] the last few words of a joke or story that make it funny or surprising

punc·til·i·ous /pʌŋk'tɪliəs/ *adj.* (formal) very careful to behave correctly and keep exactly to rules: *her punctilious attention to instructions* —**punctiliously** *adv.* —**punctiliousness** *n.* [U]

punc·tu·al /'pʌŋktʃuəl/ *adj.* arriving, happening, etc. at exactly the time that has been arranged: *My boss demands that we be punctual for work.* —**punctuality** /ˌpʌŋktʃu'æləṭi/ *n.* [U]

punc·tu·ate /'pʌŋktʃuˌeɪt/ *v.* [T] **1** ENG. LANG. ARTS to divide written work into sentences, phrases, etc. using COMMAS, PERIODS, etc. **2 be punctuated by/with sth** to be interrupted many times by something: *The president's speech was punctuated by occasional cheers.*

punc·tu·a·tion /ˌpʌŋktʃu'eɪʃən/ *n.* [U] ENG. LANG. ARTS the way that punctuation marks are used in a piece of writing

ˌpunctu'ation mark *n.* [C] ENG. LANG. ARTS a sign, such as a COMMA or QUESTION MARK, that is used in dividing a piece of writing into sentences, phrases, etc.

punc·ture¹ /'pʌŋktʃɚ/ *n.* [C] a small hole made when something is punctured

puncture² *v.* [I,T] to make a small hole in something, so that air or liquid can get out: *One bullet punctured his lung.*

> THESAURUS pierce, make a hole in sth, prick, punch → PIERCE

pun·dit /'pʌndɪt/ *n.* [C] someone who knows a lot about a particular subject, and is often asked for his/her opinion: *political pundits* [ORIGIN: 1600—1700 Hindi *pandit*, from Sanskrit *pandita* "wise"]

> THESAURUS expert, specialist, authority → EXPERT

pun·gent /'pʌndʒənt/ *adj.* having a strong smell or taste: *the pungent smell of onions*

pun·ish /'pʌnɪʃ/ *v.* [T] to make someone suffer because s/he has done something wrong or broken the law: *We will catch the people responsible for this crime, and we will punish them.* | *Don't* ***punish*** *him* ***for*** *one small mistake.* | *Any student caught destroying school property will be* ***severely punished.*** [ORIGIN: 1300—1400 Old French *punir*, from Latin *punire*, from *poena*, from Greek *poine* "payment, punishment"]

pun·ish·a·ble /'pʌnɪʃəbəl/ *adj.* deserving legal punishment: *Murder is* ***punishable by*** *life imprisonment.*

pun·ish·ing /'pʌnɪʃɪŋ/ *adj.* difficult, tiring, or extreme: *a punishing walk*

pun·ish·ment /'pʌnɪʃmənt/ *n.* **1** [C] something that is done to punish someone: *Mason wants tougher* ***punishments for*** *youths involved with gangs.* | *A year in prison seems like a* ***harsh/severe punishment*** *for a minor offense.* ▸ Don't say "strict/strong punishments." ◂

> THESAURUS
> **sentence** – a punishment given by a judge in a court: *a prison sentence* | *He faces a death sentence* (=death as punishment for a crime).
> **penalty** – a punishment given to someone who has broken a law, rule, or agreement: *Drug dealers face severe penalties.* | *The prosecution will seek the death penalty* (=death as punishment for a crime) *for the murder.*
> **fine** – an amount of money that you must pay as a punishment for breaking a rule or law: *I got a fine for speeding.*
> **community service** – unpaid work helping other people that someone does as punishment for a crime: *He was ordered to do 60 hours of community service.*
> **corporal punishment** – the act of punishing a child by hitting him/her: *Corporal punishment is illegal in schools.*
> **capital punishment** – the practice of killing someone as punishment for a crime

2 [U] the act of punishing someone, or the process of being punished: *The terrorists will not escape punishment.* | ***As punishment****, Marshall had to stay after school.*

pu·ni·tive /'pyunəṭɪv/ *adj.* intended as punishment: *The company will seek* ***punitive damages*** (=money that a court orders someone to pay as a punishment) *related to the fraud conviction.*

punk /pʌŋk/ *n.* **1** [U] *also* **punk rock** a type of loud music popular in the late 1970s and 1980s **2** [C] (informal) a boy or young man who likes to start fights, do things that are illegal, etc. **3** [C] *also* **punk rocker** someone who likes punk music and wears things that are typical of it, such as torn clothes, metal chains, and colored hair

punt /pʌnt/ *n.* [C] in football, a long kick that you make after dropping the ball from your hands —**punt** *v.* [I,T]

pu·ny /'pyuni/ *adj.* small, thin, and weak: *a puny little kid*

pup /pʌp/ *n.* [C] **1** a PUPPY **2** a young SEAL or OTTER

pu·pa /ˈpyupə/ *n.* (plural **pupas** *or* **pupae** /-pi/) [C] BIOLOGY a young insect that is at the stage of its development in which it does not eat and is protected inside a special cover, before it becomes an adult —**pupal** *adj.*

pu·pil /ˈpyupəl/ *n.* [C] **1** (formal) a child or young person in school ➔ STUDENT **2** BIOLOGY the small black round area in the middle of your eye ➔ *see picture at* EYE[1] [ORIGIN: (1) 1300—1400 French *pupille*, from Latin *pupillus* "young boy who is looked after"]

puppet

pup·pet /ˈpʌpɪt/ *n.* [C] **1** a model of a person or animal that you can move by pulling strings that are attached to parts of its body, or by putting your hand inside it: *a puppet show* **2** (disapproving) a person or organization that is controlled by someone else and does not make any independent decisions: *a puppet government*

pup·pet·eer /ˌpʌpɪˈtɪr/ *n.* [C] someone who performs with puppets

pup·pet·ry /ˈpʌpɪtri/ *n.* [U] **1** the art of controlling how puppets move **2** the activity of making puppets

pup·py /ˈpʌpi/ *n.* (plural **puppies**) [C] a young dog

ˈpuppy love *n.* [U] a young boy's or girl's romantic love for someone, that people do not think of as serious

pur·chase[1] /ˈpɚtʃəs/ (Ac) *v.* [T] (formal) to buy something: *The couple recently purchased a $4 million mansion in Beverly Hills.* | *Tickets may be* ***purchased from*** *the box office.* | *There is a growing demand to purchase goods on credit.* | *Eighty percent of men's clothing is purchased by women.* [ORIGIN: 1200—1300 Old French *purchacier* "to try to get," from *chacier* "to run after and try to catch"] —**purchaser** *n* [C]

THESAURUS **buy, acquire, get, procure, snap sth up, pick sth up** ➔ BUY[1]

purchase[2] *n.* (formal) **1** [C,U] the act of buying something: *Please have your credit card ready when* ***making*** *your* ***purchase***. | *The law requires a five-day waiting period for the* ***purchase of*** *handguns.* | *A personal computer is often a family's third-biggest purchase after the house and the car.* **2** [C] something that has been bought: *The store will deliver your purchases.*

pure /pyʊr/ *adj.* **1** not mixed with anything else (ANT) **impure**: *rings made of* ***pure gold*** | *pure wool blankets* ➔ NATURAL[1] **2** [only before noun] complete: *a smile of* ***pure joy*** | *It was* ***pure chance*** *that we were there at the same time.* **3** clean, without anything harmful or unhealthy (ANT) **impure**: *pure drinking water* | *In the mountains, the air is purer.* **4 pure and simple** used to emphasize that there is only one thing involved or worth considering: *This was murder, pure and simple.* **5** (literary) without any sexual experience or evil thoughts (ANT) **impure** **6 pure science/math etc.** work done in order to increase our knowledge of something rather than to make practical use of it ➔ APPLIED [ORIGIN: 1200—1300 Old French *pur*, from Latin *purus*]

pu·rée /pyʊˈreɪ/ *n.* [C,U] food that is boiled or crushed until it is almost a liquid: *tomato purée* —**purée** *v.* [T]

pure·ly /ˈpyʊrli/ *adv.* completely and only: *He did it for purely selfish reasons.* | *We met purely by chance.*

pur·ga·to·ry /ˈpɚgəˌtɔri/ *n.* [U] **1 Purgatory** a place where, according to Roman Catholic beliefs, the souls of dead people must suffer for the bad things they have done, until they are good enough to enter heaven **2** a place, situation, or time when you suffer a lot

purge /pɚdʒ/ *v.* [T] **1** to force people to leave a place or organization because the people in power do not like them: *The army was* ***purged of*** *anyone the government considered dangerous.* **2** (formal) to get rid of something bad that is in your body **3** (literary) to remove bad feelings: *We must purge ourselves of hatred.* —**purge** *n.* [C]

pu·ri·fy /ˈpyʊrəˌfaɪ/ *v.* (**purified**, **purifies**) [T] to remove the dirty or unwanted parts from something: *The water should be purified before drinking.* —**purification** /ˌpyʊrəfəˈkeɪʃən/ *n.* [U]

pur·ist /ˈpyʊrɪst/ *n.* [C] someone who has very strict ideas about what is right or correct in a particular subject

pur·it·an /ˈpyʊrətən, -rətˀn/ *n.* [C] **1** someone with strict moral views who thinks that pleasures such as sex or drinking alcohol are wrong **2 Puritan** HISTORY a member of a Protestant religious group in the 16th and 17th centuries, who wanted to make religion simpler

pu·ri·tan·i·cal /ˌpyʊrəˈtænɪkəl/ *adj.* (disapproving) having strict attitudes about religion and moral behavior: *a puritanical and deeply religious woman*

pu·ri·ty /ˈpyʊrət̬i/ *n.* [U] the quality or state of being pure: *the purity of the water* | *religious purity*

pur·ple /ˈpɚpəl/ *n.* [U] a dark color made from red mixed with blue [ORIGIN: 900—1000 Latin *purpura*, from Greek *porphyra* type of shellfish from which purple coloring was obtained] —**purple** *adj.*

ˌPurple ˈHeart *n.* [C] a MEDAL given to U.S. soldiers who have been wounded in battle

pur·port /pɚˈpɔrt/ *v.* [I,T] (formal) to claim to be or do something, even if this is not true: *He **purports to be** the son of the wealthy Italian banker.* | *The painting **is purported to be** the work of Monet.* —**purportedly** *adv.*

pur·pose /ˈpɚpəs/ *n.* **1** [C] the thing that an event, process, or activity is supposed to achieve: *The **purpose of** this exercise is to increase your strength.* | *The Red Cross sent supplies **for** medical **purposes**.* | ***For the purposes** of the report, low income was defined as $30,000 a year for a family of four.* | *He came here **with the purpose of** carrying out the attack.* **2 on purpose** deliberately: *Firefighters believe the fire was started on purpose.* **3** [U] determination to succeed in what you want to do: *She came back from vacation with a new sense of purpose.*

P

pur·pose·ful /ˈpɚpəsfəl/ *adj.* having a clear aim or purpose (SYN) **determined**: *She kept walking, with long, purposeful strides.*

pur·pose·ly /ˈpɚpəsli/ *adv.* deliberately: *They purposely left him out of the discussion.*

THESAURUS **deliberately, on purpose, intentionally** ➔ DELIBERATELY

purr /pɚ/ *v.* [I] if a cat purrs, it makes a soft low sound in its throat to show that it is pleased —**purr** *n.* [C]

purse¹ /pɚs/ *n.* **1** [C] a bag used by women to carry money and personal things: *I think my glasses are still in my purse.* ➔ *see picture at* BAG¹ **2 control/hold the purse strings** to control the money in a family, company, etc. [ORIGIN: 1200—1300 Late Latin *bursa* "bag (for money)"]

purse² *v.* **purse your lips** to bring your lips together tightly in a circle, especially to show disapproval

purs·er /ˈpɚsɚ/ *n.* [C] an officer who is responsible for the money on a ship and is in charge of the passengers' rooms, comfort, etc.

pur·sue /pɚˈsu/ (Ac) *v.* [T] **1** to continue doing an activity or trying to achieve something over a long time: *He left home to **pursue** a **career** in acting.* | *Students should **pursue** their own **interests**, as well as do their school work.* | *The program allows adult learners to pursue their studies in their own time.* **2** to chase or follow someone or something in order to catch him, her, or it: *A police car pursued the suspect along Nordhoff Blvd.*

THESAURUS **follow, chase, run after** ➔ FOLLOW

3 pursue the matter/question/argument to continue trying to ask about, find out about, or persuade someone about a particular subject: *The company plans to pursue the matter in court.* [ORIGIN: 1300—1400 Anglo-French *pursuer*, from Old French *poursuir*, from Latin *prosequi* "to follow and try to catch"]

pur·suit /pɚˈsut/ (Ac) *n.* **1** [U] the act of chasing or following someone: *With the officers **in (hot) pursuit** (=following close behind), Parker pulled off the freeway and ran into the woods.* **2** [U] (formal) the act of trying to achieve something in a determined way: *the right to life, liberty, and the **pursuit of** happiness* | *People are having to move to other areas in pursuit of work.* **3** [C usually plural] (formal) an activity that you spend a lot of time doing: *Nancy enjoys outdoor pursuits.*

pur·vey·or /pɚˈveɪɚ/ *n.* [C] (formal) a business that supplies information, goods, or services: *purveyors of fine cheeses* —**purvey** *v.* [T]

pus /pʌs/ *n.* [U] a thick yellowish liquid produced in an infected part of your body

push¹ /pʊʃ/ *v.*

1 MOVE [I,T] to move a person or thing away from you by pressing him, her, or it with your hands (ANT) **pull**: *A couple of guys were pushing an old Volkswagen down the street.* | *Lisa **pushed** Amy **into** the pool.* | *She tried to **push** him **away**.* | *Can you push harder? It's not moving.* ➔ *see picture on page A22*

THESAURUS

roll – to push a round object so that it moves forward: *He rolled the wheel over to the car.*
poke – to push someone or something with your finger or something sharp: *Jill poked the fish to see if it was alive.*
shove – to push someone or something roughly: *He shoved her against a wall.*
nudge – to push someone gently with your elbow to get his or her attention: *"Move over," she said, nudging my arm.*
elbow – to push someone with your elbows, especially in order to move past him/her: *As he left the field, he elbowed jeering spectators out of his way.* ➔ PULL¹

2 MAKE STH START/STOP [I,T] to press a button, SWITCH, etc. to make a machine start or stop working: *Push the green button to start the engine.*

3 TRY TO GET PAST SB [I,T] to move somewhere by pushing people away from you: *Heather **pushed past** us without speaking.* | *People were trying to **push** their **way** to the front.*

4 PERSUADE [I,T] to try to persuade someone to accept or do something: *The agency is **pushing to** increase U.S. exports.* | *Concerned citizens are **pushing for** stricter gun controls.* | *My parents **pushed** me **into** going to college.*

5 WORK HARD [T] to make someone work very hard: *Royce has been **pushing himself** too much lately.* | *Coach Koepple **pushes** his players pretty **hard**.*

6 INCREASE/DECREASE [I,T] to increase or

decrease an amount, number, or value: *New medical technology has **pushed** the cost of health care **up/higher**.* | *The recession has **pushed** stock market prices **down/lower**.*

7 DRUGS [T] (informal) to sell illegal drugs

8 push your luck/push it (informal) to do something or ask for something again, when this is likely to annoy someone or be risky: *I want to ask my boss for another day off, but I don't want to push my luck.* [ORIGIN: 1300—1400 Old French *poulser* "to hit, push," from Latin *pulsare*, from *pellere* "to drive, hit"]

push ahead *phr. v.*
to continue with a plan or activity in a determined way: *The airport is **pushing ahead with** its program to expand.*

push sb ↔ **around** *phr. v.*
(informal) to tell someone what to do in a rude or threatening way: *Don't let your boss push you around.*

push on *phr. v.*
to continue traveling somewhere or doing an activity: *The others stopped for a rest, but I pushed on to the top of the mountain.* | *Even with disagreement growing, they decided to **push on with** the negotiations.*

push sth ↔ **through** *phr. v.*
to get a plan, law, etc. officially accepted, especially quickly: *The governor pushed through a measure to increase the state sales tax.*

push² *n.* [C usually singular] **1** the act of pushing someone or something: *Just **give** the door **a push** if it's stuck.* **2** an attempt to get or achieve something: *Eastern Europe then started a **push to** modernize its economies.* | *a **push for** longer prison terms* **3 if/when push comes to shove** when or if a situation becomes extremely difficult: *If push comes to shove, I can always rent out the house.*

push·er /ˈpʊʃɚ/ *n.* [C] (informal) someone who sells illegal drugs

push·o·ver /ˈpʌʃˌoʊvɚ/ *n.* (informal) **be a pushover** to be easy to persuade, influence, or defeat

ˈpush-up *n.* [C] an exercise in which you lie on the floor facing the ground, and push yourself up with your arms: *I can only do about twenty push-ups.*

push·y /ˈpʊʃi/ *adj.* (disapproving) so determined to succeed and get what you want that you behave in a rude way: *pushy salespeople*

puss·y·cat /ˈpʊsiˌkæt/ *n.* [C] **1** a word meaning cat, used by children, or when speaking to children **2** (informal) someone who is kind and gentle: *Jake's a real pussycat once you get to know him.*

puss·y·foot /ˈpʊsiˌfʊt/ *v.* [I] (informal) to be too careful and afraid to do something: *Stop **pussyfooting around** and decide!*

put /pʊt/ *v.* (past tense and past participle **put**, present participle **putting**) [T]
1 MOVE TO PLACE/POSITION to move someone or something into a particular place or position: *Where did you put the newspaper?* | *Put the scissors in the drawer when you're finished.* | *I put some money into our account.* | *It's time to **put** the kids **to bed*** (=make them go into their beds).
2 CHANGE to change someone's situation or the way s/he feels: *Ohio State's win put them in the playoffs.* | *The recent layoffs put 250 people out of work.* | *Higher insurance costs may **put** many companies **out of business*** (=make the companies close down). | *Politics **puts** me **to sleep**.* | *He **put** himself **in danger** to save the lives of others.* | *Listen to music to **put** you **in a** relaxed **mood*** (=make you feel relaxed).
3 WRITE to write or print something: *Put your name at the top of your answer sheet.* | *We put an ad in the paper.*
4 put emphasis/pressure/blame etc. on sb/sth to emphasize something, make someone feel pressure, blame someone, etc.: *We want to put more pressure on Congress to pass gun control laws.*
5 put an end/a stop to sth to stop an activity that is harmful or not acceptable: *We want the president to put an end to this war.*
6 EXPRESS to say or express something in a particular way: ***How can I put this?*** (=said to someone when you want to tell them something that they may not like) | ***To put it bluntly**, a lot of people just don't like her.* | *Well, let me **put it this way**: he's lied to us before.*
7 HAVE IMPORTANCE/QUALITY to consider something to have a particular level of importance or quality: *Responsible parents always put their children first.* | *The new study puts UCLA among the top five research universities in the U.S.*
8 put sth behind you to try to forget about a bad experience or a mistake so that it does not affect you now: *Vietnam veterans talked of the need to put the war behind them.*

P

9 put faith/confidence/trust etc. in sb/sth to trust or believe in someone or something: *These people put little trust in doctors.* [ORIGIN: Old English *putian*] ➔ **put your mind to sth** *at* MIND[1]

put sth ↔ **across** *phr. v.*
to explain your ideas, beliefs, etc. in a way that people can understand: *I had a hard time putting my message across to the students.*

put sth ↔ **aside** *phr. v.*
1 to ignore a problem or disagreement because you want to achieve something: *Try to put your feelings aside and look at the facts.*
2 to save money regularly, usually for a particular purpose: *I have money put aside for emergencies.*

P

put sth ↔ **away** *phr. v.*
to put something in the place where it is usually kept: *Could you put the dishes away before you go to bed?*

put sth ↔ **back** *phr. v.*
to put things or people in the place or situation they were before: *Put the milk back in the fridge, please.* | *The program helps put people back to work.*

put down *phr. v.*
1 put sth ↔ **down** to put something you are holding onto a surface: *She put her case down on the floor.* ➔ *see picture on page A22*
2 put sb ↔ **down** (informal) to criticize someone and make him/her feel silly or stupid: *Her father is always putting her down.*
3 put sth ↔ **down** (informal) to write something on a piece of paper: *I put down that I'd be available to work on Saturdays.*
4 put sb/sth ↔ **down** to use force to stop people who are fighting against a government: *Soldiers were sent to put down the rebellion.*

put sth ↔ **forward** *phr. v.*
to suggest a plan, idea, etc.: *The treaty was put forward by the Dutch.*

put sth ↔ **in** *phr. v.*
1 to put a piece of equipment somewhere and connect it so that it is ready to be used: *We had to have a new furnace put in.*
2 to spend time or effort doing something: *Doug is putting in a lot of hours at work* (=he is working a lot).
3 to ask for something in an official way: *Sawyer put in his expenses claim last week.* | *Jones put in a request for a transfer to our Dallas office.*

put sth **into** sth *phr. v.*
1 to make money available to be used for a particular purpose: *The company plans to put more money into computer technology.*
2 put energy/effort/enthusiasm etc. into sth to use energy, etc. when you are doing something: *Koskoff put a lot of time and effort into this project.*
3 put sth into action/effect/practice to start using something such as a plan: *The college hopes to put the changes into effect by August 1.*

put off *phr. v.*
1 put sth ↔ **off** to delay something, or to delay doing something: *Many Americans put off filling out their tax forms as long as possible.* | *We've decided to put off our trip to Europe until next year.*
2 put sb ↔ **off** to make you dislike something or not want to do something: *Don't be put off by the restaurant's decor; the food is excellent.*

put sth ↔ **on** *phr. v.*
1 to put a piece of clothing on your body ➔ TAKE OFF: *Put your coat on – it's cold.*
2 put sth ↔ **on** sth to do something that affects or influences something else: *The government put a freeze on the construction of new nuclear power plants* (=they stopped it).
3 put on weight/5 pounds etc. to become fatter and heavier
4 to make a piece of equipment begin working: *It's cold in here. Why don't you put on the heat?*
5 to begin to play a record, tape, video, etc.: *Let's put on some music.*
6 to use MAKEUP, etc. on your skin: *I hardly ever put on lipstick.*
7 to arrange an event, concert, play, etc., or to perform in one: *The orchestra is putting on a concert for charity.*
8 to start cooking something: *Let me just put the potatoes on.*

put out *phr. v.*
1 put sth ↔ **out** to make a fire, cigarette, etc. stop burning: *It took nearly three hours to put out the fire.*
2 put sth ↔ **out** to produce something, such as a book, record, movie, etc.: *They've put out three books now on vegetarian cooking.*
3 put sth ↔ **out** to place things where people can find and use them: *I'm just going to put out cold cuts, bread, and stuff for lunch.*
4 put sth ↔ **out** to put something outside the house: *Has anybody put the trash out yet?*
5 put sth ↔ **out** to broadcast or produce something for people to read or listen to: *The company has put out a statement saying that they will replace all the defective products.*
6 put sb ↔ **out** to make more work or cause problems for someone: *Will it put you out if I bring another guest?*
7 put your hand/foot/arm out to move your hand, etc. away from your body: *Jack put out his foot and tripped her.*

put through *phr. v.*
1 put sb **through** sth to make someone do something that is very bad or difficult: *My father's drinking problem put my mother through hell.*
2 put sb through school/college/university to pay for someone to go to school, etc.: *He worked part-time to put himself through school.*
3 put sb **through** to connect someone to someone else on the telephone

put sth **to** sb *phr. v.*
to suggest something such as a plan to a person or group: *The proposal was put to the committee on January 9.*

put sth ↔ **together** *phr. v.*

1 to build or fix something by joining its different parts together: *The store will put the bicycle together for you.*

2 to prepare or produce something by collecting pieces of information, ideas, etc.: *Franklin has put together a program to help families in need.*

3 put together combined: *He earns* ***more than*** *the rest of us* ***put together***.

put up *phr. v.*

1 put sth ↔ **up** to build something such as a wall or building, or to raise something so that it is upright: *The developers plan to put up a 15-story office building.*

2 put sth ↔ **up** to attach a picture, etc. to a wall or decorate things, so people can see them: *Stores are already putting up Christmas decorations.*

3 put sth up for sale/discussion/review etc. to make something available to be sold, discussed, etc.: *We put our house up for sale.*

4 put sb ↔ **up** (informal) to let someone stay in your house: *I can put Jared up for the night.*

5 put up money/$500/$3 million etc. to give money to be used for a particular purpose: *Furth put up $42,000 in prize money for the contest.*

6 put up resistance/a fight/a struggle to argue against or oppose something in a determined way, or to fight against someone who is attacking you: *Opponents of the bill are putting up a good fight in the Assembly.*

put sb **up to** sth *phr. v.*
to encourage someone to do something wrong, silly, or dangerous: *Jim wouldn't usually play such a stupid trick; someone must have put him up to it.*

put up with sb/sth *phr. v.*
to accept a bad situation or person without complaining: *I'm not going to put up with being treated like that.*

'put-down *n.* [C] (informal) something you say that is intended to make someone feel stupid and unimportant

pu·tre·fy /ˈpyutrəˌfaɪ/ *v.* (**putrefied**, **putrefies**) [I,T] (formal) to decay and smell very bad (SYN) **rot**

pu·trid /ˈpyutrɪd/ *adj.* decaying and smelling very bad

putt /pʌt/ *v.* [I,T] to hit a GOLF ball gently a short distance along the ground toward the hole —**putt** *n.* [C]

put·ter /ˈpʌt̬ɚ/ *v.* [I] to spend time doing things that are not very important, in a relaxed way: *He's been* ***puttering around*** *the yard all morning.*

put·ty /ˈpʌt̬i/ *n.* [U] a soft substance that becomes hard when it dries, used especially for fixing glass into window frames

'put up,on *adj.* **be/feel put upon** to think that other people are treating you unfairly by expecting you to do too much

puz·zle¹ /ˈpʌzəl/ *n.* [C] **1** a game or toy that has a lot of pieces that you have to fit together: *a 500-piece* ***jigsaw puzzle*** **2** a game in which you have to think hard to answer a difficult question or solve a problem: *a book of crossword puzzles* **3** something that is difficult to understand or explain: *The way the stock market works has always been a puzzle to me.*

puzzle

crossword puzzle

puzzle² *v.* **1** [T] to confuse someone because s/he does not understand something: *The results of the study puzzled scientists.* **2** [I,T] to think for a long time about something because you cannot understand it: *Jill* ***puzzled over*** *the first question on the test for ten minutes.*

puz·zled /ˈpʌzəld/ *adj.* confused and unable to understand something: *a puzzled look*

THESAURUS **confused, bewildered, baffled**
→ CONFUSED

puz·zling /ˈpʌzlɪŋ/ *adj.* difficult to understand: *a puzzling question | I find his work puzzling.*

pyg·my /ˈpɪgmi/ *n.* (plural **pygmies**) [C] **1** *also* **Pygmy** someone who belongs to a race of very small people from parts of Asia and Africa **2** a very small type of animal: *a pygmy rabbit*

py·lon /ˈpaɪlɑn/ *n.* [C] a tall metal structure that supports wires carrying electricity

pyramid

pyr·a·mid /ˈpɪrəmɪd/ *n.* [C] **1** a large stone building with a flat base and sides shaped like TRIANGLES that form a point at the top → *see picture at* SHAPE¹ **2** something that has this shape

pyre /paɪɚ/ *n.* [C] a high pile of wood on which a dead body is placed to be burned in a funeral ceremony: *a funeral pyre*

Py·rex /ˈpaɪrɛks/ *n.* [U] (trademark) a special type of strong glass that does not break at high temperatures and is used for making cooking dishes

Py·thag·o·re·an The·o·rem /pɪˌθægəriən ˈθiərəm/ *n.* MATH a rule for calculating the length of one side of a RIGHT TRIANGLE (=one with one angle of 90°), that states that the SQUARE of the

HYPOTENUSE (=longest side) is equal to the sum of the squares of the other two sides. It is written as $a^2 + b^2 = c^2$.

py·thon /ˈpaɪθɑn, -θən/ *n.* [C] a large tropical snake that kills animals for food by crushing them

Qq

Q, q /kyu/ the 17th letter of the English alphabet

Q., q. the written abbreviation of QUESTION

q PHYSICS a sign for heat

Q-tip /ˈkyu tɪp/ *n.* [C] (trademark) a small thin stick with soft cotton at each end, used for cleaning parts of your body that are small, such as your ears

quack¹ /kwæk/ *v.* [I] to make the sound that ducks make

quack² *n.* [C] **1** (informal) someone who pretends to be a doctor **2** the sound a duck makes

quad /kwɑd/ *n.* (informal) **1** [C] a square open area with buildings all around it, especially in a school or college **2 quads** [plural] QUADRICEPS

quad·ran·gle /ˈkwɑdræŋgəl/ *n.* [C] **1** a flat shape that has four straight sides **2** a quad

quad·rant /ˈkwɑdrənt/ *n.* [C] **1** MATH a quarter of a circle → *see picture at* CIRCLE¹ **2** a quarter of an area, especially of land: *the town's southwest quadrant* **3** a tool for measuring angles **4** MATH one of four equal parts into which a PLANE is divided by two straight lines that cross each other at an angle of 90 degrees [ORIGIN: 1300—1400 Latin *quadrans* "fourth part"]

quad·rat·ic e·qua·tion /kwɑˌdræt̬ɪk ɪˈkweɪʒən/ *n.* [C] MATH an EQUATION which includes numbers or quantities multiplied by themselves, for example $ax^2 + bx + c = y$

quad·ri·ceps /ˈkwɑdrəˌsɛps/ *n.* [plural] BIOLOGY the large muscle at the front of your THIGH

quad·ri·lat·er·al /ˌkwɑdrəˈlæt̬ərəl/ *n.* [C] MATH a flat shape with four straight sides —**quadrilateral** *adj.*

quad·ri·ple·gic /ˌkwɑdrəˈplidʒɪk/ *n.* [C] someone who is permanently unable to move any part of his/her body below his/her neck → PARAPLEGIC —**quadriplegic** *adj.*

quad·ru·ped /ˈkwɑdrəˌpɛd/ *n.* [C] BIOLOGY an animal that has four feet

quad·ru·ple¹ /kwɑˈdrupəl/ *v.* [I,T] to increase and become four times as big or as high, or to make something do this: *The city's population has quadrupled since the 1930s.*

quadruple² *adj., quantifier* four times as big, as many, or as much: *quadruple the normal dose*

quad·ru·plet /kwɑˈdruplɪt/ *n.* [C] one of four babies born at the same time to the same mother

quag·mire /ˈkwægmaɪɚ, ˈkwɑg-/ *n.* [C] **1** a difficult or complicated situation: *Vietnam became a political and military quagmire.* **2** an area of soft wet muddy ground

quail /kweɪl/ *n.* [C,U] a small fat bird with a short tail that is hunted and shot for food and sport, or the meat from this bird

quaint /kweɪnt/ *adj.* unusual and attractive, especially in an old-fashioned way: *a quaint little restaurant*

quake¹ /kweɪk/ *v.* [I] **1** to shake, usually because you are afraid: *He quaked in terror.* **2** if the earth, a building, etc. quakes, it shakes violently

quake² *n.* [C] (informal) an EARTHQUAKE

Quak·er /ˈkweɪkɚ/ *n.* [C] a member of the Society of Friends, a Christian religious group that opposes violence, has no religious leaders or ceremonies, and holds its religious meetings in silence —**Quaker** *adj.*

qual·i·fi·ca·tion /ˌkwɑləfəˈkeɪʃən/ *n.* **1** [C usually plural] a skill, personal quality, or type of experience that makes you right for a particular job or position: *What are the key* ***qualifications for*** *the presidency? | Does he have the right* ***qualifications to*** *become a Supreme Court Justice?* **2** [C,U] the official standard that must be achieved in order to do a job, enter a sports competition, etc., or the achievement of this standard: *The injury puts her* ***qualification for*** *the Olympic swimming team into doubt. | educational qualifications* **3** [C,U] something that you add to a statement to limit its effect or meaning: *You have the right to refuse without qualification.*

qual·i·fied /ˈkwɑləˌfaɪd/ *adj.* **1** having the right knowledge, experience, skills, etc. for a particular job: *a qualified teacher | The employees here are* ***highly qualified.*** **2** [usually before noun] qualified agreement, approval, etc. is limited in some way because you do not completely agree: *Is it worth the money? The answer is* ***a qualified yes.***

qual·i·fi·er /ˈkwɑləˌfaɪɚ/ *n.* [C] **1** someone who has reached the necessary standard for entering a competition **2** ENG. LANG. ARTS a word or phrase that limits or adds to the meaning of another word or phrase. In the phrase "her new red bike," "new" and "red" are qualifiers.

qual·i·fy /ˈkwɑləˌfaɪ/ *v.* (**qualified, qualifies**) **1** [I] to pass an examination, or reach the standard of knowledge or skill that you need in order to do something: *I* ***qualified as*** *a pilot. | She has* ***qualified for*** *the 100-meter race.* **2** [I,T] to have the right to have or do something, or to give someone this right: *They* ***qualify for*** *food stamps.* **3** [I] to have all the necessary qualities to be considered a particular thing: *The organization* ***qualifies as*** *a charity.* **4** [T] to add something to what has already been said, in order to limit its effect or meaning: *Let me qualify that statement.*

qual·i·ta·tive /ˈkwɑləˌteɪt̬ɪv/ (Ac) *adj.* relating to the quality or standard of something, rather than the amount or number → QUANTITATIVE: *a qualitative study of the health care program* | *This test allows us to make a qualitative analysis of a student's performance.*

qual·i·ty¹ /ˈkwɑləṭi/ *n.* (plural **qualities**) **1** [C,U] the degree to which something is good or bad: *today's air quality* | *The* ***quality of*** *education they received was on the whole fairly good.* | ***high-/low-quality*** *recording equipment* | *These new drugs may improve* ***the quality of life*** *for cancer sufferers.* **2** [C usually plural] something that someone has as part of his/her character, especially good things → CHARACTERISTIC: *She has many of the qualities he lacks.* | *leadership qualities* | *the* ***qualities of*** *honesty and independence*

THESAURUS **characteristic, trait, attribute, feature** → CHARACTERISTIC¹

3 [C] something that is typical of something and makes it different from other things: *the qualities of the rock* **4** [U] a high standard: *a guarantee of quality*

quality² *adj.* [only before noun] of a high standard: *quality products*

ˈquality conˌtrol *n.* [U] the practice of checking goods as they are produced, to make sure their quality is good enough

ˈquality ˌtime *n.* [U] the time that you spend giving someone your full attention, especially time you spend with your children

qualm /kwɑm, kwɔm/ *n.* [C usually plural] a feeling of slight worry or doubt because you are not sure that what you are doing is right: *He* ***has no qualms about*** *proceeding.*

quan·da·ry /ˈkwɑndəri/ *n.* [C] **be in a quandary about/over sth** to be unable to decide what to do about a difficult problem or situation: *We were* ***in a quandary*** *over whether to go or not.*

quan·ta /ˈkwɑnt̬ə/ *n.* the plural of QUANTUM

quan·ti·fi·er /ˈkwɑnt̬əˌfaɪɚ/ *n.* [C] ENG. LANG. ARTS in grammar, a word or phrase that is used with a noun to show quantity. In the sentence "There were only a few people at the party," "few" is a quantifier.

quan·ti·fy /ˈkwɑnt̬əˌfaɪ/ *v.* (**quantified**, **quantifies**) [T] to measure something and express it as a number: *The damage to the company is difficult to quantify.* —**quantifiable** /ˌkwɑnt̬əˈfaɪəbəl/ *adj.*

quan·ti·ta·tive /ˈkwɑnt̬əˌteɪt̬ɪv/ *adj.* relating to amounts rather than to the quality or standard of something → QUALITATIVE: *a quantitative improvement in production*

quan·ti·ty /ˈkwɑnt̬əṭi/ *n.* (plural **quantities**) [C,U] an amount of something that can be counted or measured: *You cannot ignore the* ***quantity of*** *evidence proving his guilt.* | ***large/great quantities*** *of natural gas*

quan·tum /ˈkwɑnt̬əm/ *n.* (plural **quanta** /-t̬ə/) [C] PHYSICS the smallest unit that can be used to measure something such as light or energy. For example, a quantum of light is a PHOTON.

ˌquantum ˈleap *n.* [C] a very large and important improvement

ˌquantum meˈchanics *also* **ˌquantum ˈphysics** *n.* [U] PHYSICS the scientific study of the way that atoms and the parts of an atom behave and how they affect each other

ˈquantum ˌtheory *n.* [singular] PHYSICS the scientific idea that energy, especially light, travels in very small separate pieces, not in a continuous form, used to explain how atoms and the parts of an atom behave

quar·an·tine /ˈkwɔrənˌtin, ˈkwɑr-/ *n.* [C,U] a time when a person or animal is kept apart from others in case he, she, or it has a disease: *The dogs were kept* ***in quarantine*** *for three months.* [ORIGIN: 1600—1700 Italian *quarantina* "period of forty days," from Old French *quarante* "forty"] —**quarantine** *v.* [T]

quark /kwɑrk/ *n.* [C] PHYSICS one of a group of PARTICLES that form the parts of an atom

quar·rel¹ /ˈkwɔrəl, ˈkwɑrəl/ *n.* [C] **1** an angry argument: *He'd* ***had a quarrel*** *with his wife.* | *a* ***quarrel over*** *money* **2** (formal) a reason to dislike someone or disagree with an idea, decision, etc.: *We* ***have no quarrel with*** *the court's decision.* [ORIGIN: 1300—1400 Old French *querele* "complaint," from Latin *querela*, from *queri* "to complain"]

quarrel² *v.* [I] to have an angry argument: *I had* ***quarreled with*** *my parents.* | *Downstairs, the children were* ***quarreling over*** *a game.*

THESAURUS **argue, have an argument, fight, have a fight, have a quarrel, squabble, bicker** → ARGUE

quar·rel·some /ˈkwɔrəlsəm, ˈkwɑr-/ *adj.* too ready to argue about things

quar·ry /ˈkwɔri, ˈkwɑri/ *n.* (plural **quarries**) [C] **1** a place where large amounts of stone, sand, etc. are dug out of the ground **2** an animal or person that you are hunting or chasing [ORIGIN: (1) 1300—1400 Old French *quarriere*, from *quarre* "square stone," from Latin *quadrum* "square"] —**quarry** *v.* [T]

quart /kwɔrt/ *n.* [C] a unit for measuring liquid, equal to 2 PINTS or 0.9463 liters: *a* ***quart of*** *milk*

quar·ter /ˈkwɔrt̬ɚ/ *n.* [C] **1** one of four equal parts into which something can be divided → HALF, THIRD: *Cut the sandwiches into quarters.* | ***A quarter of*** *Canada's population is French-speaking.* | ***three-quarters of*** *(=75%) the country's voters* **2** a period of fifteen minutes: *Can you be ready in* ***a quarter (of an) hour****?* | *It's* ***a quarter to/after five*** (=15 minutes before or after 5 o'clock). | *The unloading took* ***three-quarters of an hour*** (=45 minutes). **3** a coin used in the U.S. and Canada worth 25 cents (=1/4 of a dollar)

> THESAURUS **money, coin, penny, nickel, dime** → MONEY

4 a period of three months – used when discussing business and financial matters: *Profits were down in the fourth quarter.* **5** one of the four periods into which a year at school or college is divided → SEMESTER **6** one of the four equal periods of time into which games of some sports are divided: *The score was 66–58 in the third quarter.* **7 quarters** [plural] the house or rooms where you live, especially if you are a servant or in the army: *Upstairs were spacious **living quarters**.*

quar·ter·back /ˈkwɔrt̬ɚˌbæk/ *n.* [C] the player in football who directs the OFFENSE and throws the ball

Q

quar·ter·fi·nal /ˌkwɔrt̬ɚˈfaɪnl/ *n.* [C] one of the set of four games near the end of a competition, whose winners play in the two SEMIFINALS

quar·ter·ly /ˈkwɔrt̬ɚli/ *adj., adv.* produced or happening four times a year: *a quarterly report*

ˈquarter note *n.* [C] ENG. LANG. ARTS a musical note that continues for a quarter of the length of a WHOLE NOTE → HALF NOTE

quar·tet /kwɔrˈtɛt/ *n.* [C] **1** ENG. LANG. ARTS four singers or musicians who perform together: *a **woodwind/string/brass quartet*** **2** ENG. LANG. ARTS a piece of music written for four performers **3** a group of four things or people

quar·tile /ˈkwɔrtaɪl, -t̬l/ *n.* [C] **1** MATH one of four equal parts that a set of numbers representing facts or measurements can be divided into **2** MATH one of the three values dividing a set of numbers representing facts or measurements into four equal parts

quartz /kwɔrts/ *n.* [U] EARTH SCIENCES a hard mineral substance that is used in making electronic watches and clocks

qua·sar /ˈkweɪzɑr/ *n.* [C] PHYSICS a very bright, very distant object similar to a star

quash /kwɑʃ/ *v.* [T] (formal) **1** to officially state that a judgment or decision is no longer legal or correct: *The judge quashed the decision of a lower court.* **2** to say or do something to stop something from continuing: *an attempt to quash rumors*

quat·rain /ˈkwɑtreɪn/ *n.* [C] ENG. LANG. ARTS a group of four lines in a poem

qua·ver /ˈkweɪvɚ/ *v.* [I,T] if your voice quavers, it shakes as you speak, especially because you are nervous

quay /keɪ, ki/ *n.* [C] a place where boats can be tied up or loaded

quea·sy /ˈkwizi/ *adj.* feeling that you are going to VOMIT (SYN) **nauseous** —**queasiness** *n.* [U]

queen /kwin/ *n.* [C] **1** *also* **Queen** the female ruler of a country who is from a royal family, or the wife of a king: *Queen Elizabeth II of Great Britain*

> THESAURUS **king, prince, princess, monarch, ruler, emperor, sovereign** → KING

2 a large female BEE, ANT, etc. that lays the eggs for a whole group **3** the woman who wins a beauty competition [ORIGIN: Old English *cwen* "woman, queen"]

ˈqueen-size *adj.* larger than the standard size: *a queen-size bed*

queer /kwɪr/ *adj.* (old-fashioned) strange: *a queer expression*

quell /kwɛl/ *v.* [T] **1** to make a violent situation end: *The military were sent in to **quell the rioting**.* **2** to stop feelings of doubt, worry, and anxiety from getting stronger: *I struggled to quell my sense of panic.*

quench /kwɛntʃ/ *v.* **quench your thirst** if a drink quenches your thirst, it makes you stop feeling thirsty

quer·u·lous /ˈkwɛrələs, -yələs/ *adj.* (formal) complaining all the time in an annoying way: *a querulous tone of self-pity in her voice* —**querulously** *adv.* —**querulousness** *n.* [U]

que·ry /ˈkwɪri/ *n.* (plural **queries**) [C] (formal) a question: *Staff members will be available to **answer** your **queries**.* —**query** *v.* [T]

quest /kwɛst/ *n.* [C] (literary) a long search for something —**quest** *v.* [I]

ques·tion¹ /ˈkwɛstʃən, ˈkwɛʃtʃən/ *n.* **1** [C] a sentence or phrase used in order to ask for information (ANT) **answer**: *Can I **ask** you a **question**? | Does anyone **have** any **questions**? | **questions about/on** health habits | I'm not sure I can **answer** that **question**.*

> COLLOCATIONS
> **ask a question**
> **answer a question**
> **have a question** – to want to ask one
> **put a question to sb** – to ask someone a question in a formal situation
> **pose a question** – to ask a difficult question
> **bombard sb with questions** – to ask someone a lot of questions
> **rephrase a question** – to ask it in a different way
> **avoid/evade/sidestep a question** – to avoid giving a direct answer

2 [C] a subject or problem that needs to be discussed or dealt with (SYN) **issue**: ***The question of** what should be done with nuclear waste has not been satisfactorily answered. | Their actions **raise the question** of whether they should be treated as war criminals.* **3** [U] a feeling of doubt about something: *The accuracy of the data has been **called into question*** (=people have doubts about it). | ***There is no question** that teachers prefer smaller classes.* **4 without question a)** definitely: *The most beautiful fish here is, without question, the angelfish.* **b)** without complaining or asking why: *He followed Dennison's advice without question.* **5 in question** the person or thing that is in question is the one that is being discussed: *The document in question is a report dated June 18, 1948.* **6 be a question of sth** used in order to say what the most important fact, part, or feature of something is: *It's a question of all working together to solve these problems.* **7 be out of the question** if something is out of the question, it is definitely not possible or not allowed: *Ticket prices are so high that going to the game is out of the question.* **8 (that's a) good question** (spoken) said when you are admitting you do not know the answer to a question: *"How did she and Luke meet?" "Good question."* [ORIGIN: 1200—1300 Old French, Latin *quaestio*, from *quaestus*, past participle of *quaerere* "to ask"]

question² *v.* [T] **1** to ask someone questions, especially about a crime: *Police are **questioning** three men **about** the murder.*

THESAURUS **ask, interrogate, inquire** → ASK

2 to have or express doubts about whether something is true, good, or necessary: *Are you questioning my honesty?* | *Fans are **questioning whether** the team can win.*

ques·tion·a·ble /ˈkwɛstʃənəbəl/ *adj.* **1** not likely to be good, honest, or morally correct: *questionable business activities* **2** not certain, or possibly not correct: ***It is questionable whether** the tests are worthwhile.*

ques·tion·ing¹ /ˈkwɛstʃənɪŋ/ *n.* [U] the process of asking questions: *A witness is currently undergoing questioning.*

questioning² *adj.* a questioning look or expression shows that you need more information or that you doubt something

ˈquestion mark *n.* [C] ENG. LANG. ARTS the mark (?), used in writing at the end of a question

ques·tion·naire /ˌkwɛstʃəˈnɛr/ *n.* [C] a written set of questions about a particular subject, that is given to a large number of people in order to collect information

THESAURUS **poll, survey** → POLL¹

quib·ble /ˈkwɪbəl/ *v.* [I] to argue about something that is not very important —**quibble** *n.* [C]

quiche /kiʃ/ *n.* [C] a type of food that consists of PASTRY filled with a mixture of eggs, cheese, vegetables, etc.

quick¹ /kwɪk/ *adj.* **1** quick actions or events continue for, or are done, in a short time (ANT) **slow**: *I'll just take a quick shower first.* | *a quick response* | *It'd be quicker to drive.*

THESAURUS **short, brief, cursory** → SHORT¹

2 moving or doing something fast (ANT) **slow**: *I promise I'll be quick.* | *People are **quick to** complain but slow to help.* **3** able to learn and understand things in a short time (SYN) **intelligent**: *Carolyn's a **quick learner**.* [ORIGIN: Old English *cwic* "alive"]

quick² *adv.* (spoken, nonstandard) quickly: *Come quick! Larry's on TV!* | *It was all over pretty quick.*

quick·en /ˈkwɪkən/ *v.* [I,T] (written) to become quicker, or to make something do this: *Elaine **quickened** her **pace*** (=walked faster).

quick·ie /ˈkwɪki/ *adj.* (informal) happening or done quickly: *a quickie divorce* (=one that is done cheaply and quickly) —**quickie** *n.* [C]

quick·ly /ˈkwɪkli/ *adv.* **1** fast, or done in a short amount of time: *Don't eat too quickly.* | *Firefighters quickly put out the blaze.*

THESAURUS **fast, swiftly, rapidly, speedily, at high speed/at great speed, at a rapid rate** → FAST²

2 after a very short time: *I quickly realized it wasn't going to be easy.* **3** for a short amount of time: *I'll just run into the store quickly, and then we can go.*

Q

quicksand

quick·sand /ˈkwɪksænd/ *n.* [C,U] wet sand that is dangerous because it pulls you down into it if you walk on it

ˌquick-ˈwitted *adj.* able to understand things quickly and say things that are funny and smart

quid pro quo /ˌkwɪd proʊ ˈkwoʊ/ *n.* [C] (formal) something that you give or do in exchange for something else, especially when this arrangement is not official

qui·et¹ /ˈkwaɪət/ *adj.* **1** not making much noise: ***Be quiet!** I'm on the phone.* | *a quiet car* | *The classroom suddenly became quiet.*

THESAURUS

Words used to describe a quiet voice or sound

low – a low voice or sound is quiet and deep: *A low humming noise was coming from the refrigerator.*
soft – quiet in a way that is pleasant: *He spoke with a soft southern accent.*
muffled – a muffled sound is very difficult to hear: *the muffled sound of voices in the next room*
hushed – if people speak in **hushed tones**, they speak with quiet voices, especially so that other

people cannot hear them: *They huddled together in a corner, speaking in hushed tones.*
inaudible – too quiet to be heard: *We were so far away from the stage that the actors were inaudible.* ➔ LOUD[1]

2 not busy, or not full of people or activity: *a quiet neighborhood* | *Finally, the house was quiet.* | *Business has been really quiet recently.*

THESAURUS

Words to describe a quiet place
calm – quiet and without activity or trouble: *The streets remained calm again after last week's riots.*
tranquil/peaceful – quiet in a way that is pleasant and relaxing: *a tranquil spot for a picnic*
sleepy – quiet with very little happening: *a sleepy little town*
still – quiet and calm, without any movement: *The forest was completely still.* ➔ CALM[2]

Q

3 not speaking, or not likely to say much: *a quiet, hard-working boy* | *Why are you so quiet tonight?* ➔ **keep (sth) quiet** *at* KEEP[1]

quiet[2] *also* **quiet down** *v.* [I,T] to become calmer and less active or noisy, or to make someone do this: *Quiet down and get ready for bed!*

quiet[3] *n.* [U] the state of being quiet and not active: *I was looking for some* ***peace and quiet.***

qui·et·ly /ˈkwaɪətli/ *adv.* **1** without making much or any noise: *Ron shut the door quietly.* | *"I'm sorry," he said quietly.* **2** in a way that does not attract attention: *The council has been quietly preparing for the changes.*

quill /kwɪl/ *n.* [C] **1** a large feather, or a pen made from a large feather, used in past times **2** one of the sharp needles on the backs of some animals, such as the PORCUPINE

quilt /kwɪlt/ *n.* [C] a warm thick cover for a bed, made by sewing two layers of cloth together with a filling of cloth or feathers: *a patchwork quilt* [ORIGIN: 1200—1300 Old French *cuilte*, from Latin *culcita* "mattress"]

quilt·ed /ˈkwɪltɪd/ *adj.* quilted cloth consists of layers held together by lines of stitches that cross each other

quint·es·sen·tial /ˌkwɪntəˈsɛnʃəl/ *adj.* being a perfect example of a particular type of person or thing: *New York is the quintessential big city.* —**quintessentially** *adv.* —**quintessence** /kwɪnˈtɛsəns/ *n.* [U]

quin·tet /kwɪnˈtɛt/ *n.* [C] ENG. LANG. ARTS five singers or musicians who perform together

quin·tu·plet /kwɪnˈtʌplɪt, -ˈtu-/ *n.* [C] one of five babies who are born at the same time to the same mother

quip /kwɪp/ *v.* (**quipped**, **quipping**) [I] to make an amusing remark —**quip** *n.* [C] ➔ JOKE[1]

quirk /kwɚk/ *n.* [C] **1** a strange habit or feature that someone or something has: *a* ***quirk in*** *the law* **2** something strange that happens by chance: *Years later, by a strange* ***quirk of fate***, *she met him again on a plane.*

quirk·y /ˈkwɚki/ *adj.* slightly strange or unusual: *a quirky comedy*

quit /kwɪt/ *v.* (**quit**, **quitting**) **1** [I,T] (informal) to leave a job, school, etc., usually without finishing it, especially because you are annoyed or unhappy: *He quit school when he was 16.* | *Betty quit her job to stay home with the children.*

THESAURUS

give up – to stop doing something, or stop trying to do something: *She gave up her job to care for her ailing parents.*
resign – to officially leave your job or position: *Three board members have resigned.*
retire – to leave your job, especially because you have reached the age when most people stop working: *My father retired when he was 62.*
give notice – to officially tell your employer that you will be leaving your job soon: *She left without giving notice.*
drop out – to stop going to school or stop an activity before you have finished it: *Tucker dropped out of high school when he was 16.*
withdraw – to stop taking part in a competition, race, etc., or to leave an organization or class: *He decided to withdraw from the senate race.*

2 [T] (informal) to stop doing something that is bad: *I quit smoking three years ago.*

quite /kwaɪt/ *adv.*, *quantifier* **1** very, but not extremely (SYN) **pretty**: *He's quite fat.* | *It became quite clear that we needed help.*

THESAURUS **rather, fairly, pretty, kind of** ➔ RATHER

2 not quite not completely or not exactly: *I'm not quite ready.* | *It wasn't quite the way he had imagined it.* | *Lewis* ***isn't quite as*** *fast as he used to be.* **3** used when an amount or number is large, but not extremely large: *They've had* ***quite a bit*** *of snow this year* (=a lot of snow). | *There were* ***quite a few*** *people at the party* (=a lot of people). | *We saved* ***quite a lot*** *of money.* | *We haven't seen each other in* ***quite a while*** (=a long time). **4** used in order to emphasize the fact that something is unusually good, bad, etc.: *That's* ***quite a*** *coat; where did you buy it?* | *Ruby made* ***quite an*** *impression on the kids.*

quits /kwɪts/ *adj.* (informal) **call it quits** to stop doing something: *Baird will call it quits after two terms as mayor.*

quit·ter /ˈkwɪt̬ɚ/ *n.* [C] (informal, disapproving) someone who stops doing a job, activity, or duty because it becomes difficult

quiv·er[1] /ˈkwɪvɚ/ *v.* [I] to shake slightly because you are angry, upset, or anxious: *Diana's voice* ***quivered with*** *emotion.*

THESAURUS **shake, tremble, shiver, wobble** ➔ SHAKE[1]

quiver² *n.* [C] **1** a slight shaking movement **2** a long case used for carrying ARROWS

quix·ot·ic /kwɪk'sɑt̬ɪk/ *adj.* (formal) having ideas and plans that are based on hopes and are not practical [ORIGIN: 1700—1800 Don *Quixote*, main character of the book Don Quixote de la Mancha (1605) by Spanish writer Cervantes]

quiz¹ /kwɪz/ *n.* (plural **quizzes**) [C] **1** a short test: *a math quiz* | *Mr. Wilson gave us a* ***pop quiz*** (=an unexpected test). **2** a competition or game in which you have to answer questions: *a love quiz in a magazine*

quiz² *v.* (**quizzed**, **quizzing**) [T] to ask someone a lot of questions: *Webster quizzed 20 possible jurors.*

quiz·zi·cal /'kwɪzɪkəl/ *adj.* **a quizzical look/smile/expression** a look, etc. that shows you have a question

quo·rum /'kwɔrəm/ *n.* [C usually singular] the smallest number of people that must be at a meeting in order for official decisions to be made

quo·ta /'kwoʊt̬ə/ *n.* [C] **1** an official limit on the number or amount of something that is allowed in a particular period: *a* ***quota on*** *the amount of fish you may catch* **2** an amount of something that someone is expected to do or achieve: *The department is* ***meeting*** *its sales* ***quota****.* **3** POLITICS the number of jobs or PROMOTIONS (=moves to a more important job or rank) that a law or rule says an organization must give to people from groups who have been treated unfairly in the past because of their race or sex [ORIGIN: 1600—1700 Medieval Latin *quota pars* "how large a part"]

quo·ta·tion /kwoʊ'teɪʃən/ (Ac) *n.* **1** [C] words from a book, poem, etc. that you repeat in your own speech or piece of writing: *a Biblical quotation* | *When writing a literary essay, always include quotations from the text.* **2** [C] a written statement of the exact amount of money that a service will cost ➔ ESTIMATE: *Get quotations from two or more insurance companies.* **3** [U] the act of quoting something

quo'tation ˌmark *n.* [C usually plural] ENG. LANG. ARTS a mark (" or ") used in writing before and after any words that are being quoted

quote¹ /kwoʊt/ (Ac) *v.* **1** [I,T] to repeat exactly what someone else has said or written: *A doctor was* ***quoted as saying*** *he would not give the vaccine to his children.* | *He* ***quoted*** *a verse* ***from*** *the Bible.* **2** [T] to give something as an example to support what you are saying: *Dr. Morse quoted three successful cases in which patients used the new drug.* | *He quoted a figure of 220 deaths each year from accidents in the home.* **3** [T] to tell a customer the price you will charge him/her for a service or product: *The airline has been quoting a standard fare of $358.* **4 quote ... unquote** (spoken) used when you are repeating the exact words someone else used: *He said it was the fault of quote "those people" unquote.* [ORIGIN: 1300—1400 Medieval Latin *quotare*, from Latin *quot* "how many"]

quote² (Ac) *n.* [C] (informal) a quotation: *He used a quote from Mark Twain at the beginning of his essay.*

quo·tid·i·an /kwoʊ'tɪdiən/ *adj.* (formal) daily or ordinary: *our quotidian responsibilities of work and family*

quo·tient /'kwoʊʃənt/ *n.* [C] MATH a number that is the result of one number being divided by another

R, r the eighteenth letter of the English alphabet

R /ɑr/ *n.* [C,U] **restricted** – used in order to show that no one under the age of 17 can go to a particular movie unless an adult goes with him/her

rab·bi /'ræbaɪ/ *n.* [C] (plural **rabbis**) a Jewish religious leader [ORIGIN: 1000—1100 Late Latin, Greek, from Hebrew, "my master"]

rab·bit /'ræbɪt/ *n.* [C] a small animal with long ears and soft fur that lives in a hole in the ground ➔ *see picture at* PET¹

rab·ble /'ræbəl/ *n.* [singular] a noisy crowd of people who are likely to cause trouble

rab·id /'ræbɪd/ *adj.* **1** very extreme and often unreasonable: *rabid anti-Americanism* **2** suffering from RABIES: *a rabid dog*

ra·bies /'reɪbiz/ *n.* [U] a disease that affects animals, that people can catch if they are bitten by an infected animal

rac·coon /ræ'kun/ *n.* [C] an animal with black fur around its eyes and black and white bands on its tail ➔ *see picture at* NOCTURNAL

race¹ /reɪs/ *n.* **1** [C] a competition to find out who can run, drive, swim, etc. the fastest: *The colt has* ***won*** *nine* ***races*** *already.* | *She finished second* ***in the race****.* **2** [C,U] one of the groups that humans can be divided into, based on their skin color and other physical features: *The census has questions about race and ethnicity.*

THESAURUS

nation – a country and its social and political structure, or a group of people with the same history and language: *The leaders of several Western nations are meeting in Paris this week.* | *the Mandan tribe of the Sioux nation*
race – one of the groups that people are divided into, based on skin color and other physical features: *The survey was given to people of different races and ages.*
people – a race or group of people that live in a particular country. The plural of this meaning of "people" is "peoples": *the native peoples of the United States*
tribe – a group of people within a country who are the same race, and who have the same traditions and the same leader: *The Navajo tribe is the second largest in the U.S.*
ethnic group – a group of people of the same race, nation, or tribe: *Many different ethnic groups call the city home.*

R

3 [C] a competition for power, a prize, or a political position: *the presidential race* **4** [C] a situation in which one group tries to obtain or achieve something before another group does: *the* ***race to*** *put a man on the moon* **5 a race against time** a situation in which something difficult must be done before a particular time **6 the races** an event at which horses are raced against each other → ARMS RACE, HUMAN RACE

race² *v.* **1** [I,T] to compete in a race: *I'll race you to the corner!* | *She'll be* ***racing against*** *some of the world's top athletes.* **2** [I,T] to go very quickly, or to make someone or something do this: *I raced home after school.* | *Victims were* ***raced to*** *the hospital.*

THESAURUS **run, sprint, dash, tear** → RUN¹
rush, dash, hurry, charge, speed, hasten → RUSH¹

3 [I] to try to do something very quickly, especially because there is little time or you want to be the first: *Doctors* ***raced to*** *solve this medical mystery.* **4** [I] if your heart or mind races, it is working harder and faster than usual: *Her mind was racing – would David be there?* **5** [I,T] if an engine races, or you race it, its parts are moving too fast

'race re,lations *n.* [plural] the relationship between two groups of people who are from different races but who live in the same city, country, or area

race·track /'reɪs-træk/ *n.* [C] a track around which runners, cars, horses, etc. race

ra·cial /'reɪʃəl/ *adj.* **1** relating to the relationships between different races of people: *a fight against* ***racial discrimination*** (=unfair treatment of people because of their race) **2** relating to people's race: *racial groups* —**racially** *adv.*: *a racially motivated attack*

rac·ing /'reɪsɪŋ/ *n.* **horse/car/bicycle etc. racing** the sport of racing horses, cars, etc.

rac·ism /'reɪsɪzəm/ *n.* [U] **1** unfair treatment of people, or violence against them, because they belong to a different race from yours: *the struggle against racism and poverty*

THESAURUS **prejudice, discrimination, intolerance, bigotry, sexism, homophobia, anti-semitism** → PREJUDICE¹

2 the belief that some races of people are better than others

rac·ist /'reɪsɪst/ *n.* [C] someone who believes that people of his/her own race are better than others, and treats people of other races unfairly: *He is accused of making racist remarks.* —**racist** *n.* [C] → PREJUDICE¹

rack¹ /ræk/ *n.* [C] a frame or shelf for holding things, usually with BARS or hooks: *a coat rack*

rack² *v.* [T] **1 rack your brain(s)** to think very hard or for a long time **2** to make someone feel great physical or mental pain: *Afterwards, he was* ***racked with*** *guilt and shame.*

rack sth ↔ **up** *phr. v.* (informal) to make the value, amount, or level of something increase: *They racked up a nine-game winning streak.*

rack·et /'rækɪt/ *n.* **1** [singular] (informal) a loud noise: *Laura was* ***making*** *a terrible* ***racket*** *in the kitchen.* **2** [C] a thing used for hitting the ball in games such as tennis, consisting of a light stick with a circle filled with tight strings at the top **3** [C] (informal) a dishonest way of obtaining money – sometimes used about an ordinary business to show that you think it is somehow unfair: *the insurance racket* [ORIGIN: (2) 1500—1600 French *raquette*, from Italian *racchetta*, from Arabic *rahah* "front of the hand"]

rack·et·ball /'rækɪt˺,bɔl/ *n.* [U] an indoor game in which two players use rackets to hit a small rubber ball against the four walls of a square court

rack·et·eer·ing /,rækə'tɪrɪŋ/ *n.* [U] LAW a crime that consists of getting money dishonestly, using a carefully planned system —**racketeer** *n.* [C]

rac·y /'reɪsi/ *adj.* exciting in a sexual way

ra·dar /'reɪdɑr/ *n.* [C,U] a piece of equipment that uses radio waves to find the position of things and watch their movement, or the process of doing this: *The missile didn't show up* ***on radar***.

ra·di·al tire /,reɪdiəl 'taɪɚ/ *also* **radial** *n.* [C] a car tire with wires inside the rubber to make it stronger and safer

ra·di·ance /'reɪdiəns/ *n.* [U] **1** soft shining light: *the moon's radiance* **2** great happiness or love that shows in the way someone looks: *the radiance of youth*

ra·di·ant /'reɪdiənt/ *adj.* **1** full of happiness and love, in a way that shows in your face: *a radiant smile* **2** PHYSICS sending out light or heat —**radiantly** *adv.*

ra·di·ate /'reɪdi,eɪt/ *v.* **1** [I,T] if someone radiates a feeling or quality, or if it radiates from him/her, s/he shows it in a way that is easy to see:

Janine radiates confidence. **2** [I,T] if something radiates light or heat, or if light or heat radiates, it is sent out in all directions: *The fireplace radiated a comforting warmth.* **3** [I] to spread out from a central point: *The pain* ***radiated down*** *his leg.*

ra·di·a·tion /ˌreɪdiˈeɪʃən/ *n.* [U] **1** energy in the form of heat or light sent out as waves that you cannot see ➔ RADIOACTIVE: *cancer treated with radiation* **2** a form of energy that comes from NUCLEAR reactions, which in large amounts is harmful to living things ➔ RADIOACTIVE: *radiation exposure*

ra·di·a·tor /ˈreɪdiˌeɪt̬ɚ/ *n.* [C] **1** the part of a car or airplane that stops the engine from getting too hot **2** a piece of equipment used for heating a room, consisting of a hollow metal container fastened to a wall, through which hot water passes

rad·i·cal¹ /ˈrædɪkəl/ (Ac) *adj.* **1** thorough and complete, so that something is very different: ***radical changes*** *in family life* | *These proposals may sound radical, but we need to do far more to decrease pollution.* **2** relating to a political or social idea that is very different from what exists now, or supporting these ideas: *Radical demonstrators clashed with riot police.* [ORIGIN: 1300—1400 Late Latin *radicalis*, from Latin *radix* "root"] **—radically** *adv.*: *a radically different idea*

radical² *n.* [C] someone who wants thorough and complete social and political change **—radicalism** *n.* [U]

ˌradical eˈquation *n.* [C] MATH an EQUATION containing one or more radical expressions

ˌradical exˈpression *n.* [C] MATH a set of numbers or letters that have a radical sign (√) before them in an EQUATION

ˈradical ˌsign *n.* [C] MATH a mathematical sign (√) that appears before a number or letter, showing that you must find its SQUARE ROOT. If there is a small number before the sign, for example ³√, you must find that particular ROOT, in this case the CUBE ROOT.

rad·i·cand /ˈrædɪˌkænd/ *n.* [C] MATH the number or letter that appears after a radical sign, for example 3 in √3

ra·di·i /ˈreɪdiaɪ/ *n.* the plural of RADIUS

ra·di·o¹ /ˈreɪdiˌoʊ/ *n.* (plural **radios**) **1** [C,U] a piece of electronic equipment that you use to listen to music or programs that are broadcast, or the programs themselves: *the latest hits* ***on the radio*** | *Kelly was* ***listening to the radio.*** | *J.D.* ***turned on the radio.*** **2** [U] the activity of making and broadcasting programs that can be heard on a radio: *He'd like a job* ***in radio.*** | *a San Diego* ***radio station*** **3** [C,U] a piece of electronic equipment that can send and receive spoken messages, or the sending or receiving of these messages: *We've lost radio contact.*

radio² *v.* (**radioed**, **radios**, **radioing**) [I,T] to send a message using a radio: *The ship* ***radioed for*** *help.*

ra·di·o·ac·tive /ˌreɪdioʊˈæktɪv◂/ *adj.* **1** PHYSICS containing or producing RADIATION: *Plutonium is highly radioactive.* | *radioactive waste* **2** PHYSICS relating to or caused by RADIATION: *radioactive decay*

ra·di·o·ac·tiv·i·ty /ˌreɪdioʊækˈtɪvət̬i/ *n.* [U] PHYSICS the sending out of RADIATION, when the NUCLEUS (=central part) of an atom has broken apart

ra·di·og·ra·ph·y /ˌreɪdiˈɑgrəfi/ *n.* [U] SCIENCE the process of taking X-RAY photographs of the inside of someone's body for medical purposes

ra·di·o·i·so·tope /ˌreɪdioʊˈaɪsəˌtoʊp/ *n.* [C] PHYSICS an ISOTOPE (=one of the different possible forms of a RADIOACTIVE atom)

ra·di·ol·o·gist /ˌreɪdiˈɑlədʒɪst/ *n.* [C] a hospital doctor who is trained in the use of RADIATION to find out what is causing an illness and to treat people

ra·di·ol·o·gy /ˌreɪdiˈɑlədʒi/ *n.* [U] the study of the use of RADIATION and X-RAYS in medical treatment

R

ˌradio ˈtelescope *n.* [C] PHYSICS a piece of equipment that receives RADIO WAVES coming from space, which scientists use to find the exact position of stars and other objects in space

ra·di·o·ther·a·py /ˌreɪdioʊˈθɛrəpi/ *n.* [U] the treatment of illnesses using RADIATION

rad·ish /ˈrædɪʃ/ *n.* [C] a small red or white root that has a slightly hot taste and is eaten raw as a vegetable

ra·di·um /ˈreɪdiəm/ *n.* [U] CHEMISTRY (*symbol* **Ra**) a RADIOACTIVE white metal that is an ELEMENT, used in the treatment of diseases such as CANCER

ra·di·us /ˈreɪdiəs/ *n.* (plural **radii** /ˈreɪdiaɪ/) [C] **1** MATH the distance from the center to the edge of a circle, or a line drawn from the center to the edge ➔ *see picture at* CIRCLE¹ **2 within a 10-mile/100-meter etc. radius** within a distance of 10 miles, etc. in all directions from a particular place: *The bomb caused damage within a half-mile radius.*

ra·don /ˈreɪdɑn/ *n.* [U] CHEMISTRY (*symbol* **Rn**) a RADIOACTIVE gas that is an ELEMENT

raf·fle¹ /ˈræfəl/ *n.* [C] a type of competition or game in which people buy tickets with numbers on them in order to try to win prizes

raffle² *also* **raffle off** *v.* [T] to offer something as a prize in a raffle

raft /ræft/ *n.* [C] **1** a small flat rubber boat filled with air: *He helped her onto the* ***life raft*** (=used when a boat sinks). **2** a flat floating structure, usually made of pieces of wood tied together, used as a boat **3 a raft of sth** a large number of things or a large amount of something: ***A whole raft of*** *popular players will attend.*

raf·ter /ˈræftɚ/ *n.* [C] one of the large sloping pieces of wood that form the structure of a roof

raft·ing /ˈræftɪŋ/ *n.* [U] the sport of traveling down a fast-flowing river in a rubber raft

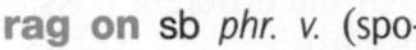
rafting

rag¹ /ræg/ *n.* [C] **1** a small piece of old cloth: *a dirty rag* **2 in rags** wearing old torn clothes **3 from rags to riches** becoming very rich after starting your life very poor

rag² *v.* **(ragged, rag-ging)**

rag on sb *phr. v.* (spoken, informal) **1** to make jokes and laugh at someone in order to embarrass him/her SYN **tease** **2** to criticize someone in an angry way: *The coach was ragging on me for missing my free throws.*

ˌrag ˈdoll *n.* [C] a soft DOLL made of cloth

rage¹ /reɪdʒ/ *n.* [C,U] a strong feeling of anger that you cannot control: *She was shaking* ***with rage.*** [ORIGIN: 1200—1300 Old French, Latin *rabies* "anger, wildness," from *rabere* "to be wild with anger"]

rage² *v.* [I] **1** to continue happening with great force or violence: *The rioting raged for four days.* | *a raging blizzard* **2** to feel extremely angry about something, and to show this in the way you behave or speak: *Tom raged at himself for having been so stupid.*

rag·ged /ˈrægɪd/ *also* **rag·ged·y** /ˈrægɪdi/ *adj.* **1** torn and in bad condition: *a ragged shirt* **2** not straight or neat, but with rough uneven edges: *a ragged beard* **3** wearing clothes that are old, torn, and dirty: *ragged children* **4** not regular or smooth, or not done together: *ragged breathing*

rag·tag /ˈrægtæg/ *adj.* looking messy and wearing dirty torn clothes: *a ragtag army*

rag·time /ˈrægtaɪm/ *n.* [U] a type of JAZZ music with a quick strong beat, popular in the U.S. in the early 1900s

raid¹ /reɪd/ *n.* [C] **1** a short attack on a place by soldiers, airplanes, or ships, intended to cause damage but not to take control: *an air raid*

THESAURUS **attack, invasion, ambush, counterattack** → ATTACK¹

2 a sudden visit by the police to search for something illegal: *an FBI* ***raid on*** *the apartment*

raid² *v.* [T] **1** if the police raid a place, they enter it suddenly to search for something illegal: *Police raided his home and seized his computer.* **2** (informal) to take or use something that does not belong to you: *Governors have raided education budgets to pay for more prisons.* | *The kids* ***raided the refrigerator*** *after school* (=ate a lot of food from it). **3** to make a sudden attack on a place **4** (informal) to go into a place and steal things —**raider** *n.* [C]

rail¹ /reɪl/ *n.* **1** [C] a bar that is fastened along or around something, especially to keep you from falling, hang something on, etc.: *Tourists stood at the rail taking pictures of the falls.* | *a towel rail* **2** [U] a railroad system: *The city is promoting* ***light rail*** (=a railroad that only carries passengers) *as an alternative to cars.* **3** [C] one of the two long metal tracks attached to the ground, that trains move along

rail² *v.* [I] (formal) to complain angrily about something that you think is unfair: *Business leaders have been* ***railing against*** *the proposed tax increases.*

rail·ing /ˈreɪlɪŋ/ *n.* [C] *also* **railings** [plural] a short fence consisting of upright bars or lengths of wood or metal supported by upright posts, which keeps people from falling over an edge, supports them going up stairs, etc.: *the porch railing*

rail·road¹ /ˈreɪlroʊd/ *n.* **1** [U] a method of traveling or moving things around using trains, and things relating to this: *Livestock is shipped* ***by railroad.*** | *a* ***railroad station*** **2** [C] the tracks and ground that a train travels on **3** [C] a company that owns trains and tracks: *the Southern Pacific railroad* **4 the railroad** the system of trains, and all the companies, work, equipment, etc. relating to it: *My grandfather* ***worked on/for the railroad*** *all his life.*

railroad² *v.* [T] to force or persuade someone to do something without giving him/her enough time to think about it: *The workers were* ***railroaded into*** *signing the agreement.*

rain¹ /reɪn/ *n.* **1** [U] water that falls in small drops from clouds in the sky: *I hate going out* ***in the rain.*** | *He walked through* ***the pouring/driving/heavy rain*** (=a lot of rain). | *A* ***light rain*** (=a small amount of rain) *fell on the crowd.* → *see picture at* WATER CYCLE

THESAURUS

drizzle – light rain with very small drops of water: *a steady drizzle*
shower – a short period of rain: *a light shower*
downpour – a lot of rain that falls in a short period of time: *a heavy downpour*
storm – very bad weather with a lot of wind and rain: *violent storms* | *a tropical storm*
hail – frozen rain that falls in the form of **hailstones** (=small balls of ice): *A hail storm flattened crops.*
sleet – a mixture of snow and rain: *sleet and snow showers*

2 the rains a time in the year when there is a lot of rain in tropical countries SYN **monsoon** [ORIGIN: Old English *regn*]

rain² *v.* [I] if it rains, drops of water fall from clouds in the sky: *Is it still raining?* | *It suddenly started* ***raining hard*** (=raining a lot).

THESAURUS

It's pouring (rain) – it's raining very heavily
It's drizzling – a small amount of rain is falling
It's sprinkling – it is raining lightly

It's sleeting – it's raining and snowing at the same time
It's hailing – small balls of ice are falling
→ WEATHER[1]

rain down (sth) *phr. v.* if something rains down or is rained down, it falls in large quantities: *Bombs rained down on the city.*

rain sth ↔ **out** *phr. v.* if an event is rained out, it has to stop because there is too much rain

rainbow

rain·bow /ˈreɪnboʊ/ *n.* [C] a large curve of different colors that can appear in the sky when there is both Sun and rain

ˈrain check *n.* [C] **1 take a rain check** (spoken) used in order to say that you would like to accept an invitation or offer later, but you cannot right now: *I'm sorry, but I'm busy on Saturday – can I take a rain check?* **2** a piece of paper that allows you to buy something at a special price, given to people when the thing they want to buy is not available **3** a ticket for an outdoor event, game, etc. that you can use again if the event has to stop because of rain

rain·coat /ˈreɪnkoʊt/ *n.* [C] a coat that you wear to protect yourself from the rain

rain·drop /ˈreɪndrɑp/ *n.* [C] a single drop of rain

rain·fall /ˈreɪnfɔl/ *n.* [C,U] the amount of rain that falls on an area in a particular time: *six inches of annual rainfall*

ˈrain ˌforest *n.* [C] EARTH SCIENCES an area of thick forest with tall trees that are very close together, growing in a place where it rains a lot

rain·storm /ˈreɪnstɔrm/ *n.* [C] a storm with a lot of rain and strong winds

rain·water /ˈreɪnˌwɔt̬ɚ, -ˌwɑ-/ *n.* [U] water that has fallen as rain

rain·y /ˈreɪni/ *adj.* **1** having a lot of rain: *a rainy weekend* **2 rainy day** a difficult time when you will need money that you do not need now: *We have a little extra money **saved for a rainy day**.*

raise¹ /reɪz/ *v.* [T]
1 MOVE to move or lift something to a higher position or to an upright position ANT **lower**: *The flag is raised at school every morning.* | ***Raise** your **hand** if you know the answer.*
2 INCREASE to increase an amount, number, or level ANT **lower**: *a plan to raise taxes* | *She hopes the story will raise awareness of mental illness* (=increase people's understanding of it). | *In my family, no one ever **raised** their **voices*** (=spoke loudly and angrily).
3 IMPROVE to improve the quality or standard of something ANT **lower**: *Public schools have been trying hard to raise standards.*
4 CHILDREN to take care of your children until they are adults: *Michelle is a single parent raising her children alone.*
5 GET MONEY/SUPPORT to collect money, support, etc. so that you can use it to help people: *The dinner is being held to **raise** money **for** cancer research.*
6 FARMING to grow plants or keep animals, especially to sell: *The chickens are raised in cages.*
7 CAUSE A REACTION to cause a particular emotion or reaction: *The accident has raised concerns about safety.*
8 START A SUBJECT to begin to talk or write about something that you want someone to consider SYN **bring up**: *The article raises questions about the fairness of the trial.*

THESAURUS mention, allude to sth, bring sth up, cite → MENTION[1]

9 raise your eyebrows to show surprise, a question, doubt, disapproval, etc. by moving your EYEBROWS upward
10 raise eyebrows if something raises eyebrows, it surprises and shocks people: *The police chief's actions have raised eyebrows.*

raise

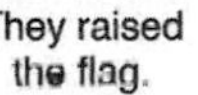

They raised the flag.

The balloon rose up into the sky.

raise² *n.* [C] an increase in the money you earn: *a raise of $100 a month*

rai·sin /ˈreɪzən/ *n.* [C] a dried GRAPE [ORIGIN: 1300—1400 French "grape," from Latin *racemus* "bunch of grapes"]

rake¹ /reɪk/ *n.* [C] a tool used for removing dead leaves from areas of grass or making soil level

rake² *v.* **1** [I,T] *also* **rake up** to move a rake across a surface in order to remove dead leaves from an area of grass or make the soil level **2** [T]

R

to move something such as a gun or a light across an area: *Soldiers raked the building with gunfire.* **3 rake your fingers/nails** to pull your fingers or nails through something or across a surface: *She raked his face with her nails.* **4 rake sb over the coals** to speak angrily to someone who has done something wrong

rake sth ↔ **in** *phr. v.* (informal) to earn a lot of money without trying very hard: *One lawyer raked in $3.5 million on a case.*

ral·ly[1] /ˈræli/ *n.* (plural **rallies**) [C] **1** a large public meeting to support a political idea, sports event, etc.: *a campaign rally* **2** an occasion when something becomes stronger or better again, after a period of weakness or defeat: *The Cubs scored three runs in a late rally.*

rally[2] *v.* (**rallied**, **rallies**) **1** [I,T] to come together or bring people together to support an idea, a political party, etc.: *Women's groups* ***rallied to*** *her defense.* **2** [I] to become stronger or better again after a time of weakness or defeat: *The Miami Heat rallied to beat the Chicago Bulls.*

R

rally around (sb/sth) *phr. v.* if a group of people rally around, they all try to help you in a difficult situation: *Her friends all rallied around when her father died.*

RAM /ræm/ *n.* [U] **random access memory** IT the part of a computer that keeps information for a short time so that it can be used immediately ➔ ROM

ram[1] /ræm/ *v.* (**rammed**, **ramming**) **1** [I,T] to run or drive into something, or to push something using a lot of force: *A truck* ***rammed into*** *a line of cars.* | *We had to turn hard to starboard to avoid ramming the ship.* **2 ram sth down sb's throat** to try to make someone accept an idea or opinion by repeating it again and again

ram sth ↔ **through** *phr. v.* to try to make someone accept something, without giving him/her time to consider it carefully: *Democrats were trying to ram the bill through Congress.*

ram[2] *n.* [C] a fully grown male sheep

Ram·a·dan /ˈrɑməˌdɑn/ *n.* the ninth month of the Muslim year, during which no food may be eaten during the hours of the day when it is light

ram·ble[1] /ˈræmbəl/ *v.* [I] **1** to talk in a way that is not clearly organized, and move from one subject to another in a confusing way: *His speeches tend to ramble.* **2** to go on a walk for pleasure

ramble on *phr. v.* to talk or write for a long time in a way that other people think is boring: *Sara rambled on about her trip.*

ramble[2] *n.* [C] a long walk for pleasure

ram·bling /ˈræmblɪŋ/ *adj.* **1** speech or writing that is rambling is very long and does not seem to have any clear organization or purpose: *a long rambling letter* **2** a building that is rambling has an irregular shape and covers a large area: *a rambling old house*

ram·bunc·tious /ræmˈbʌŋkʃəs/ *adj.* noisy, full of energy, and behaving in a way that cannot be controlled: *a rambunctious kid*

ram·i·fi·ca·tion /ˌræməfəˈkeɪʃən/ *n.* [C usually plural] (formal) a result of something you do, that affects things in a way that you may not have expected: *What are the ramifications of oil prices rising so quickly?*

ramp /ræmp/ *n.* [C] **1** a road for driving onto or off a large main road ➔ OFF-RAMP, ON-RAMP **2** a slope that has been built to connect two places that are at different levels: *ramps for wheelchair users*

ram·page /ˈræmpeɪdʒ, ræmˈpeɪdʒ/ *v.* [I] to behave wildly or violently, especially in groups: *Rioters* ***rampaged through*** *the city, destroying property.* —**rampage** *n.* [C]: *a gunman* ***on*** *a bloody* ***rampage***

ramp·ant /ˈræmpənt/ *adj.* spread across or affecting a large area, and difficult to control: *rampant inflation* —**rampantly** *adv.*

ram·rod /ˈræmrɑd/ *n.* **ramrod stiff/straight** sitting or standing with your back straight and your body stiff

ram·shack·le /ˈræmˌʃækəl/ *adj.* badly built and needing to be repaired: *a ramshackle farm house*

ran /ræn/ *v.* the past tense of RUN

ranch /ræntʃ/ *n.* [C] a very large farm where cattle, horses, or sheep are raised [ORIGIN: 1800—1900 Mexican Spanish *rancho*, from Spanish, "camp, small building, small farm"]

ranch·er /ˈræntʃɚ/ *n.* [C] someone who owns or works on a ranch: *a cattle rancher* —**ranch** *v.* [I] —**ranching** *n.* [U]

ˈranch house *n.* [C] a type of house built on one level, with a roof that does not slope much

ran·cho /ˈræntʃoʊ/ *n.* [C] **a)** a ranch in the SOUTHWEST U.S. **b)** a simple building or group of buildings where the workers on a ranch sleep and eat

ran·cid /ˈrænsɪd/ *adj.* food such as milk, butter, or meat that is rancid smells or tastes unpleasant because it is no longer fresh: *rancid butter*

ran·cor /ˈræŋkɚ/ *n.* [U] (formal) a feeling of hatred, especially when you cannot forgive someone (SYN) **resentment**: *Political rancor has marked this election campaign.* —**rancorous** /ˈræŋkərəs/ *adj.*

R & B *n.* [U] **rhythm and blues** a type of popular music that is a mixture of BLUES and JAZZ

R & D *n.* [U] **research and development** the part of a business concerned with studying new ideas and planning new products

ran·dom /ˈrændəm/ (Ac) *adj.* **1** happening or chosen without any definite plan, aim, or pattern: *a* ***random sample*** *of 635 patients* **2 at random** in a completely unplanned way: *The winning numbers will be chosen at random.* —**randomly** *adv.*: *The lottery numbers are randomly chosen.*

ˌrandom ˈaccess ˌmemory *n.* [U] IT RAM

ˌrandom ˈvariable *n.* [C] MATH a VARIABLE (=mathematical quantity that is not fixed and can be any of several amounts) whose value cannot be known certainly, but can be described using a mathematical calculation

R & R *n.* [U] **rest and relaxation** a vacation given to people in the army, navy, etc. after a long time of hard work or during a war

rang /ræŋ/ *v.* the past tense of RING

range¹ /reɪndʒ/ (Ac) *n.*
1 GROUP [C] a number of people or things that are different, but belong to the same general type: *students with a* ***range of*** *interests* | *books on a* ***wide/broad range*** *of subjects* | *The drug is effective against a range of bacteria.*
2 NUMBER LIMITS [C] the limits within which amounts, levels, ages, etc. can be different from each other: *games for the 8–12 age range* | *The house is* ***beyond/out of*** *our* ***price range*** (=more than our limit). | *Music has a wider frequency range than speech.*
3 PRODUCTS [C] a set of similar products made by a particular company or available in a particular store: *a new range of mountain bikes*
4 DISTANCE **a)** [singular,U] the distance within which something can be seen or heard: *Luckily, we were not* ***within range*** *when they began firing.* | *I was* ***out of her range*** *of vision.* | *A typical radio signal has a range of about 100 miles.* **b)** [singular,U] the distance at which a weapon can hit something: *short-range ballistic missiles* **c)** [C] the distance a vehicle such as an aircraft can travel before it needs more FUEL: *The plane has* ***a range of*** *more than 3,000 miles.*
5 LIMITS TO POWER/ACTIVITY [C] the limits to the amount of power or RESPONSIBILITY that a person or organization has, or the types of activity they are allowed to do: *The issue falls outside the range of the investigation.*
6 MOUNTAINS [C] EARTH SCIENCES a line of mountains or hills: *the Cascade Range* ➔ *see picture on page A59*
7 LAND [C,U] EARTH SCIENCES a large area of land covered with grass, used by cattle
8 FOR PRACTICE [C] an area of land where you can practice using weapons: *a rifle range*
9 COOKING [C] a STOVE
10 DATA [C] *also* **range of a set of data** MATH a measure of the difference between the largest and smallest quantities in a set of DATA (=information or facts)
11 RELATED VALUES [C] MATH all the different possible values that can be produced by a mathematical FUNCTION ➔ DOMAIN

range² *v.* [I] **1** to include the two things mentioned and other things in between them: *The men are serving prison sentences* ***ranging from*** *10 to twenty years.* | *toys* ***ranging in*** *price from $5 to $25* | *The population of the city* ***ranges between*** *3.5 and 4 million.* **2** to deal with a large number of subjects: *Republicans challenged him on issues* ***ranging from*** *abortion* ***to*** *taxes.* **3** if animals range somewhere, they move over a wide area of land

rang·er /ˈreɪndʒɚ/ *n.* [C] someone whose job is to watch and take care of a forest or area of public land and the people and animals that use it: *a park ranger*

rank¹ /ræŋk/ *n.* [C,U] the position or level that someone has in an organization: *an officer of* ***high/low rank*** | *He* ***held the rank*** *of sergeant.* [ORIGIN: 1300—1400 Old French *renc, reng* "line, place, row"]

rank² *v.* **1** [I] to have a particular position in a list of people or things that are put in order of quality or importance: *The team is ranked fourth in the city.* **2** [T] to decide the position someone or something should have on a list, based on quality or importance: *The wines are ranked by quality and price.*

rank³ *adj.* having a very strong and unpleasant smell or taste: *rank meat*

ˌrank and ˈfile *n.* **the rank and file** the ordinary members of an organization rather than the leaders

R

rank·ing¹ /ˈræŋkɪŋ/ *n.* [C] the position or level that someone has on a list of people who have a particular skill: *the skater's national ranking*

ranking² *adj.* a ranking person has a high position in an organization, or is one of the best at an activity: *the ranking officer*

ran·kle /ˈræŋkəl/ *v.* [I,T] if something rankles, or rankles you, it still annoys you a long time after it happened

ran·sack /ˈrænsæk/ *v.* [T] **1** to go through a place stealing things and causing damage: *The victim's house had been ransacked.* **2** to search a place very thoroughly: *She ransacked her closet for something to wear.*

ran·som /ˈrænsəm/ *n.* [C,U] an amount of money paid to free someone who is held as a prisoner: *a ransom note* | *The kidnappers demanded $200,000* ***in ransom.*** —**ransom** *v.* [T]

rant /rænt/ *v.* [I] to talk or complain in a loud excited confused way: *She* ***ranted about*** *the misleading claims of diet books.* —**rant** *n.* [C]

rap¹ /ræp/ *n.* **1** [U] *also* **ˈrap music** a type of popular music in which the words are not sung, but spoken in time to music with a steady beat **2** [C] a quick light hit or knock: *a rap on the door* **3** [singular] blame or punishment for a mistake or crime: *a murder rap* | *He got himself a good lawyer to* ***beat the rap*** (=avoid punishment). | *I'd rather drive while he reads the map, so I don't have to* ***take the rap*** (=be blamed) *for getting lost.* **4 get a bad/bum rap** (informal) to be unfairly criticized, or to be treated badly: *Diet food has gotten a bad rap for the way it tastes.*

rap² *v.* (**rapped**, **rapping**) **1** [I,T] to hit or knock something quickly and lightly: *Henry* ***rapped on*** *the door.*

THESAURUS hit, beat, strike, knock, bang, tap → HIT[1]

2 [T] to criticize or blame someone: *The movie was rapped by critics for its violence.* **3** [I] to say the words of a rap song

rape[1] /reɪp/ *v.* [T] to force someone to have sex, especially by using violence

rape[2] *n.* **1** [C,U] the crime of forcing someone to have sex, especially by using violence: *a rape victim* **2** [singular] unnecessary destruction, especially of the environment: *the rape of our rain forests*

rap·id /ˈræpɪd/ *adj.* done very quickly, or happening in a short time SYN **fast, quick**: *rapid population growth* [ORIGIN: 1600—1700 Latin *rapidus* "seizing, sweeping away," from *rapere* "to seize"] —**rapidly** *adv.*: *Technology is rapidly changing.* —**rapidity** /rəˈpɪdəṭi/ *n.* [U]

rap·ids /ˈræpɪdz/ *n.* [plural] part of a river where the water looks white because it is moving very fast over rocks

R

ˌrapid ˈtransit *also* **ˌrapid ˈtransit ˌsystem** *n.* [C] a system of trains, buses, etc. for moving people around a city

rap·ist /ˈreɪpɪst/ *n.* [C] someone who has forced someone else to have sex, especially by using violence

rap·per /ˈræpɚ/ *n.* [C] someone who speaks the words of a RAP song

rap·port /ræˈpɔr, rə-/ *n.* [singular U] friendly agreement and understanding between people: *She's a very good teacher, who has a* ***rapport with*** *her students.*

rap·proche·ment /ˌræproʊʃˈmɑn/ *n.* [singular, U] (formal) the establishment of good relations between two countries or groups of people, after a time of unfriendly relations: *the U.S.* ***rapprochement with*** *China in the 1970s*

rapt /ræpt/ *adj.* so interested in something that you do not notice anything else: *The children listened with* ***rapt attention***.

rap·ture /ˈræptʃɚ/ *n.* [U] great excitement, pleasure, and happiness: *He looked* ***with/in rapture*** *at her face.* —**rapturous** *adj.*

rare /rɛr/ *adj.* **1** not seen or found very often, or not happening very often ANT **common**: *a rare form of cancer* | ***It is rare for*** *her* ***to*** *miss school.*

USAGE

Use **rare** when something is valuable and there is not much of it: *a rare coin worth a lot of money*
Use **scarce** when there is not enough of something available at a particular time: *During the war, food was scarce.*

2 meat that is rare has only been cooked for a short time and is still red [ORIGIN: (1) 1400—1500 Latin *rarus*]

rar·e·fac·tion /ˌrɛrəˈfækʃən/ *n.* [U] PHYSICS a process in which the pressure of a gas decreases ANT **compression**

rare·ly /ˈrɛrli/ *adv.* not often ANT **frequently**: *She's rarely home.*

THESAURUS

not very often: *I go to the movies, but not very often.*
hardly ever – almost never: *The kids hardly ever call* (=telephone) *me.*
seldom (more formal) – very rarely: *We seldom see her nowadays.*
infrequently – not happening often: *She visited her parents only infrequently.* → NEVER, OFTEN, SOMETIMES

rar·ing /ˈrɛrɪŋ/ *adj.* **raring to go** (informal) very eager to start an activity: *We got up early, raring to go.*

rar·i·ty /ˈrɛrəṭi/ *n.* **be a rarity** to not happen or exist very often: *In 1975, women lawyers were a rarity.*

ras·cal /ˈræskəl/ *n.* [C] (humorous) a child who behaves badly but whom you still like

rash[1] /ræʃ/ *adj.* done too quickly without thinking carefully first, or behaving in this way: *rash promises* | *a rash young man*

THESAURUS impulsive, hotheaded, impetuous, hasty, spontaneous, precipitate → IMPULSIVE

rash[2] *n.* **1** [C] a lot of red spots on someone's skin, caused by an illness or a reaction to food, plants, medicine, etc. **2 a rash of sth** (informal) a large number of unpleasant events, changes, etc. within a short time: *There's been a rash of injuries on the team.*

rasp·ber·ry /ˈræzˌbɛri/ *n.* (plural **raspberries**) [C] a soft sweet red BERRY → *see picture on page 414*

rasp·y /ˈræspi/ *adj.* making a rough unpleasant sound: *his raspy voice* —**rasp** *v.* [I] —**rasp** *n.* [singular]

rat[1] /ræt/ *n.* [C] **1** an animal that looks like a large mouse with a long tail **2** (informal) someone who has been disloyal to you or has deceived you: *That rat Bruce just did it for the money.* [ORIGIN: Old English *ræt*] → RAT RACE

rat[2] *v.* (**ratted**, **ratting**) [I] (old-fashioned) to tell someone in authority about something wrong that someone has done, in a way that is considered disloyal: *I never* ***ratted on*** *Huey.*

rate[1] /reɪt/ *n.* [C] **1** the number of times something happens over a period of time: *a country with a low* ***birth/unemployment/crime etc. rate*** | *an area with a* ***low/high rate*** *of crime* **2** a charge or payment set according to a standard scale: *The Federal Reserve lowered* ***interest rates*** *today.* | *the hourly* ***rate of*** *pay*

THESAURUS **cost, expense, price, charge, fee, fare** → COST[1]

3 the speed at which something happens over a period of time: *Children learn* ***at different rates.*** | *Car thefts have increased* ***at an alarming rate.*** **4 at any rate** (spoken) used when you are giving one definite fact in a situation that is not sure or not satisfactory: *He's what, 17? At any rate, he's old enough to go on his own.* **5 at this rate** (spoken) used in order to say what will happen if things continue to happen in the same way: *At this rate, we'll never afford a vacation.* **6 first-rate/second-rate/third-rate** of good, bad, or very bad quality: *a third-rate movie*

rate² *v.* **1** [T] to have a particular opinion about the value or worth of someone or something: *38% rated him a weak leader.* **2 X-rated/rated R etc.** used in order to show that a movie has been officially approved for people of a particular age to see **3** [T] (informal) to deserve something: *You all rate a big thank-you for your work.*

rath·er /ˈræðɚ/ *adv., quantifier* **1 rather than** a phrase meaning instead of, used when you are comparing two things or situations: *We usually travel by train, rather than by plane.* **2 would rather** used when you would prefer to do or have one thing more than another: *I hate sitting doing nothing; I'd rather be busy.* | *Dave* ***would rather*** *have a dog* ***than*** *a cat, but I like cats.* | *"Why don't you ask her?"* ***"I'd rather not."*** **3** (formal) used in order to give more correct or specific information about what you have said: *Lucy, or Susie rather, asked me to come tonight.* **4** fairly, or to some degree: *The photograph is rather blurred.*

THESAURUS

fairly: *The test was fairly easy.* | *It's a fairly long way.*
pretty (spoken): *Her Spanish is pretty good.* | *It's pretty tough work.*
quite (formal): *It's quite late.* | *That's quite an interesting problem.*
kind of (informal): *It was kind of cold out.*

rat·if·i·ca·tion /ˌræṭəfəˈkeɪʃən/ *n.* [U] **1** POLITICS the act of giving official approval to an agreement: *Ratification of the treaty led to a reduction in nuclear weapons.* **2** POLITICS the act of approving an AMENDMENT to the U.S. CONSTITUTION

rat·i·fy /ˈræṭəˌfaɪ/ *v.* (**ratified, ratifies**) [T] POLITICS to make a written agreement official by signing it: *Both nations ratified the treaty.*

THESAURUS **approve, pass, sanction, endorse** → APPROVE

rat·ing /ˈreɪṭɪŋ/ *n.* **1** [C] a level on a scale that shows how popular, good, important, etc. someone or something is: *The governor's* ***approval rating*** *is high.* **2** [singular] a letter that shows what age someone should be before s/he can see a particular movie, television show, etc.: *The movie received an R rating.* | *There's a rating system for video games.* **3 the ratings** [plural] a list that shows which movies, television programs, etc. are the most popular: *The show finished 20th* ***in the ratings.***

ra·ti·o /ˈreɪʃiˌoʊ, ˈreɪʃoʊ/ (Ac) *n.* (plural **ratios**) [C] a relationship between two amounts, represented by two numbers that show how much bigger one amount is than the other → PROPORTION: *The* ***ratio of*** *boys* ***to*** *girls in the class is 2:1* (=two boys for each girl). | *If the ratio of spending to income is too high, you will end up in debt.* [ORIGIN: 1600—1700 Latin "calculation, reason," from *ratus* past participle of *reri* "to calculate"]

ra·tion¹ /ˈræʃən, ˈreɪ-/ *n.* **1** [C] a limited amount of something such as food or gas that you are allowed to have when there is not much available: *a ration of sugar* **2 rations** [plural] a particular amount of food given to a soldier or a member of a group

ration² *v.* [T] to control the supply of something by allowing people to have only a limited amount of it: *Gas may have to be rationed in the future.* —**rationing** *n.* [U]

R

ra·tion·al /ˈræʃənəl/ (Ac) *adj.* **1** rational thoughts, decisions, etc. are based on reason rather than on emotion (ANT) **irrational**: *a rational decision* | *Your analysis of the situation must be rational if you are going to make a fair judgment.* **2** a rational person is able to think clearly and make good decisions (SYN) **sensible** (ANT) **irrational**: *Let's try to discuss this like rational human beings.* [ORIGIN: 1300—1400 Latin *rationalis*, from *ratio* "calculation, reason"] —**rationally** *adv.*: *We were too shocked to think rationally.* —**rationality** /ˌræʃəˈnæləṭi/ *n.* [U]

ra·tion·ale /ˌræʃəˈnæl/ *n.* [C,U] (formal) the reasons and principles on which a decision, plan, etc. is based: *What is the Pope's* ***rationale for*** *not allowing women to be priests?*

THESAURUS **reason, explanation, motive, grounds** → REASON[1]

ˌrational eˈquation *n.* [C] MATH an EQUATION that has a rational expression on at least one side of the equal sign

ˌrational exˈpression *n.* [C] MATH a mathematical statement containing a POLYNOMIAL (=several different numbers and signs which are equal to a specific amount) divided by another polynomial

ra·tion·al·ism /ˈræʃənəˌlɪzəm/ *n.* [U] SOCIAL SCIENCE the belief that your actions should be based on scientific thinking, not on emotions or religious beliefs: *scientific rationalism*

ra·tion·al·ize /ˈræʃənəˌlaɪz/ (Ac) *v.* [I,T] if you rationalize behavior that is wrong, you think of reasons for it so that it does not seem as bad: *We rationalize that junk food is part of childhood, but we're setting our kids up for health problems.* —**rationalization** /ˌræʃnələˈzeɪʃən/ *n.* [C,U]

ˌrational ˈnumber *n.* [C] MATH a REAL NUMBER (=number that is not the square root of a negative number) which can be written as the exact RATIO of two WHOLE NUMBERS (=1, 2, 3, etc.)

ˈrat race *n.* **the rat race** (informal) the unpleasant situation in business, politics, etc. in which people are always competing against each other

rat·tle¹ /ˈrætl/ *v.* **1** [I,T] if you rattle something, or it rattles, it shakes and makes a short repeated knocking sound: *There was something **rattling around** in the trunk.* ➔ SHAKE¹ **2** [T] (informal) to make someone lose his/her confidence and become nervous: *She's a good player, but **gets rattled** easily.*

rattle sth ↔ **off** *phr. v.* to say something very quickly and easily, especially from memory: *He rattled off his phone number.*

rattle² *n.* [C] **1** a baby's toy that makes a noise when it is shaken **2** [usually singular] the noise that you hear when the parts of something knock against each other ➔ *see picture on page A20*

rat·tler /ˈrætlɚ, ˈrætl-ɚ/ *n.* [C] (informal) a rattlesnake

rat·tle·snake /ˈrætlˌsneɪk/ *n.* [C] a poisonous American snake that makes a noise with its tail

rau·cous /ˈrɔkəs/ *adj.* a raucous voice or noise is very loud and unpleasant: *a raucous laugh* —**raucously** *adv.*

> THESAURUS **loud, noisy, thunderous, deafening, ear-splitting, shrill** ➔ LOUD¹

raun·chy /ˈrɔntʃi, ˈrɑn-/ *adj.* (informal) intended to make you think about sex, in a way that seems shocking: *a raunchy movie*

rav·age /ˈrævɪdʒ/ *v.* [T] to destroy, ruin, or damage something badly (SYN) **devastate**: *a forest **ravaged by** fire*

rav·ag·es /ˈrævɪdʒɪz/ *n.* **the ravages of sth** (literary) damage or destruction caused by something such as war, disease, time, etc.: *The country has not recovered from **the ravages of war**.*

rave¹ /reɪv/ *v.* [I] **1** to talk in an excited way about something because you think it is very good: *Customers **rave about** their chili.* **2** to talk in an angry or crazy way: *He was **ranting and raving** about something she'd done.* —**raving** *adj., adv.*: *raving drunk*

rave² *adj.* **rave reviews** strong praise for something such as a new movie, book, etc.: *The book has **won rave reviews**.*

rave³ *n.* [C] **1** an event at which young people dance all night to music with a strong beat **2** strong praise for a new movie, book, etc.

ra·ven /ˈreɪvən/ *n.* [C] a large black bird

rav·en·ous /ˈrævənəs/ *adj.* extremely hungry

ra·vine /rəˈvin/ *n.* [C] a deep narrow valley with steep sides

rav·ish·ing /ˈrævɪʃɪŋ/ *adj.* (literary) very beautiful – used especially to describe people

raw /rɔ/ *adj.* **1** not cooked: *raw onions* **2** raw substances are in a natural state and have not been treated or prepared for people to use: *The paper company imports its **raw materials**.* **3** skin that is raw is red and sore

> THESAURUS **painful, tender, sore** ➔ PAINFUL

4 not experienced or not fully trained: ***raw recruits** in the army* (=people who have just joined the army) **5** not organized, examined, or developed: *raw data* | *This idea was the **raw material*** (=an idea that is not developed) *for his new play.* **6** a raw emotion or quality is strong, natural, and easy to notice: *raw courage* **7 a raw deal** unfair treatment: *She deserved a raise – I think she's **getting a raw deal**.*

ray /reɪ/ *n.* [C] **1** a narrow beam of light from the Sun, a lamp, etc.: *the **rays of** the Sun* **2 ray of hope/comfort etc.** something that provides a small amount of hope, comfort, etc.

ray·on /ˈreɪɑn/ *n.* [U] a smooth artificial material like silk, used for making clothes

raze /reɪz/ *v.* [T] to destroy a city, building, etc. completely: *The old theater had been razed.*

ra·zor /ˈreɪzɚ/ *n.* [C] a sharp instrument for removing hair from the body: *an electric razor*

ˈrazor blade *n.* [C] a small flat blade with a very sharp cutting edge, used in some razors

ˌrazor-ˈsharp *adj.* **1** very sharp **2** showing intelligence and the ability to think quickly: *a razor-sharp sense of humor*

Rd. the written abbreviation of ROAD

RDA *n.* [singular] **recommended daily allowance** the amount of substances such as VITAMINS that you should have every day

-'re /ɚ/ *v.* the short form of "are": *We're* (=we are) *ready to go.*

re /ri/ *prep.* used in business letters to introduce the main subject: *Re your letter of June 10...*

> THESAURUS **about, on, concerning, regarding, with regard to** ➔ ABOUT¹

reach¹ /ritʃ/ *v.* **1** [I,T] to move your hand or arm in order to touch, hold, or pick up something: *David **reached for** the butter.* | *He **reached out** and took her hand.* | *Jean can't reach the cans on the top shelf.* **2** [T] to increase, decrease, or develop to a particular level, standard, or situation over time: *The temperature will reach 95° today.* | *John had **reached the point*** (=reached a situation) *in his life at which he knew he had to make some changes.* **3 reach a decision/agreement/verdict etc.** to succeed in deciding something, agreeing on something, etc. **4** [T] to speak to someone, especially by telephone: *Hughes could not be reached for comment.* **5** [T] to arrive at a particular place: *Peary's first attempt to reach the North Pole was in 1898.*

THESAURUS arrive, get to → ARRIVE

6 [I,T] to be big enough, long enough, etc. to get to a particular level or point: *Will the ladder reach the roof?*

THESAURUS

go: *The water went up almost to the top of the dam.* | *The road only goes as far as the farmhouse.*
come: *Alex is taller; he comes up to Pat's shoulder now.*

7 [T] if a message, television program, etc. reaches a lot of people, they hear or see it: *The TV program reaches millions of homes.* [ORIGIN: Old English *ræcan*]

reach² *n.* **1** [singular, U] the distance that you can stretch out your arm to touch something: *The boat floated away, **out of reach.*** | *He breaks everything **within reach.*** **2 within reach (of sth) a)** within a distance that you can easily travel: *We live **within easy reach of** the city.* **b)** *also* **in reach** able to be achieved or gotten with the skills, power, money, etc. that you have: *An agreement is **within reach.*** **3 beyond the reach/out of reach** difficult to achieve or get because you do not have enough skill, power, or money: *A permanent solution is still **out of reach.***

re·act /ri'ækt/ Ac *v.* [I] **1** to behave in a particular way because of what someone has done or said to you → OVERREACT: *How did she **react to** the news?* | *The audience **reacted by** shouting and booing.* **2** to become ill when a chemical or drug goes into your body, or when you eat a particular food: *Health workers sometimes react to the latex in gloves.* **3** CHEMISTRY if a chemical substance reacts, it changes when mixed with another substance: *The calcium reacts with sulfur in the atmosphere.* **4** if a machine or a piece of equipment reacts, it performs a particular action because of what is happening in or around it: *The thermometer is very accurate, reacting to very small temperature differences.*

react against sth *phr. v.* to show that you do not like or agree with something by deliberately doing the opposite: *He reacted against his religious upbringing.* | *Feminists reacted against the limitations of women's traditional roles.*

re·ac·tant /ri'æktənt/ *n.* [C] CHEMISTRY a chemical substance which combines with another substance to form a chemical compound

re·ac·tion /ri'ækʃən/ Ac *n.* **1** [C,U] something that you feel or do because of something that has happened or been said: *The public **reaction to** the decision was furious.* | *My **first/initial/immediate reaction** to the book was quite negative.* | *An emergency fund was set up **in reaction to** the famine.* **2** [C] if you have a reaction to a drug or to something you have eaten, it makes you sick: *an **allergic reaction** to seafood* | *Less than 1% of patients experience a reaction.* **3 reactions** [plural] your ability to move quickly when something dangerous happens: *an athlete with quick reactions* **4** [singular] a change in someone's attitudes, behavior, etc. that happens because s/he disapproves of the way things were done in the past: *The attitudes of my generation are a **reaction against** the selfish values of the 1980s.* **5** [C,U] CHEMISTRY a change that happens when two or more chemical substances are mixed together: *A chemical reaction takes place in the soil.* → **gut reaction/feeling etc.** *at* GUT¹

re·ac·tion·ar·y /ri'ækʃəˌnɛri/ Ac *adj.* (disapproving) strongly opposed to social or political change —**reactionary** *n.* [C]: *Reactionaries protested against giving civil rights to all citizens.*

re·ac·ti·vate /ri'æktəˌveɪt/ Ac *v.* [T] to make something start working again: *The California legislature reactivated the death penalty in 1977.*

re·ac·tive /ri'æktɪv/ Ac *adj.* **1** reacting to events or situations rather than starting or doing new things yourself: *Many businesses follow a reactive strategy rather than creating new products.* **2** CHEMISTRY a reactive substance changes when it is mixed with another substance: *Oxygen is a highly reactive gas.*

re·ac·tor /ri'æktə/ Ac *n.* [C] a NUCLEAR REACTOR

read /rid/ *v.* (past tense and past participle **read** /rɛd/) **1** [I,T] to look at written words, numbers, or signs and understand what they mean: *Children start learning to read in kindergarten.* | *She sat reading a magazine.* | *I can't read music.*

THESAURUS

flip/thumb through sth – to look at parts of a book, magazine, etc. quickly
browse through sth – to look at parts of a book, magazine, etc. slowly
skim/scan (through) sth – to read something quickly to get the main ideas or to find what you want
pore over sth – to read something very carefully for a long time
devour sth – to read something quickly and eagerly
plow/wade through sth – to read something long and boring
peruse (formal) – to read something → WRITE

2 [I,T] to find out information from books, newspapers, etc.: *The class has been **reading about** the Mayans.* | *He had **read that** walking was good for your health.* **3** [I,T] to say written or printed words to other people: *Will you read me a story?* | ***Read to** your kids every day.* | *a good book to **read aloud*** **4 read between the lines** to guess what someone really feels or means, even when his/her words do not show it **5 read sb's mind/thoughts** to guess what someone is thinking: *"Coffee?" "You must have read my mind."* **6** [T] if a measuring instrument reads a particular number, it shows that number: *The thermometer read 46 degrees.* **7** [T] to understand a remark, situation, etc. in a particular way: *The movie could be read as*

R

a protest against the Catholic Church. **8 well-read** having read a lot of books [ORIGIN: Old English *rædan*]

read sth **into** sth *phr. v.* to think that a situation, action, etc. means more than it really does: *People shouldn't read too much into the court's decision.*

read sth ↔ **out** *phr. v.* to read and say words that are written down, so that people can hear: *He read out the name of the winner.*

read up on sth *phr. v.* to read a lot about something so that you know a lot about it: *Patients should try to read up on their illness.*

read·a·ble /ˈridəbəl/ *adj.* **1** interesting, enjoyable, or easy to read: *a very readable book* **2** clear and able to be read → MACHINE-READABLE

read·er /ˈridɚ/ *n.* [C] **1** someone who reads a lot, or reads in a particular way: *an **avid/voracious reader*** (=someone who likes to read a lot) | *a book for young readers* | *a fast/slow reader* **2** someone who reads a particular book, newspaper, etc.: *a newspaper with 30,000 readers*

R

read·er·ship /ˈridɚˌʃɪp/ *n.* [C,U] the people who read a particular newspaper, magazine, etc.

read·i·ly /ˈrɛdl-i/ *adv.* **1** quickly and easily: *The information is **readily available** on the Internet.* **2** quickly, willingly, and without complaining: *Chip readily agreed to help.*

read·i·ness /ˈrɛdinɪs/ *n.* **1** [singular,U] willingness to do something: *I admire his **readiness to** help people.* **2** [U] the state of being prepared and ready for something that might happen: *The army was standing by **in readiness for** an attack.*

read·ing /ˈridɪŋ/ *n.* **1** [U] the activity of looking at and understanding written words: *Paula loves reading.* **2** [U] the books, articles, etc. that you read: *I have a lot of reading to do for class.* | *It's **light reading*** (=easy to read and not very serious). **3** [singular] the act of reading something: *a **close reading** of the book* **4** [C] your way of understanding what a particular statement, situation, event, etc. means (SYN) **interpretation**: *What's your **reading of** the situation, Herb?* **5** [C] a number or amount shown on a measuring instrument: *The man came to **take** a **reading** from the electric meter.* **6** [C] an occasion when something is read to people: *a poetry reading*

re·ad·just /ˌriəˈdʒʌst/ (Ac) *v.* **1** [I] to change the way you do things because of a new job, situation, or way of life: *After living in the dorms, I needed time to **readjust to** life at home.* | *After leaving the army, soldiers often struggle to readjust.* **2** [T] to make a small change to something, or move something to a new position: *We lifted him up and readjusted the back of the chair.* | *The figures had to be slightly readjusted.* —**readjustment** *n.* [C,U]

ˌread-only ˈmemory *n.* [U] IT ROM

read·out /ˈrid-aʊt/ *n.* [C] IT a record of information produced by a computer, that is shown on a screen or in print

read·y /ˈrɛdi/ *adj.* [not before noun] **1** someone who is ready is prepared or able to do something: *Aren't you ready yet?* | *We're just about **ready to** eat.* | *Go **get ready** for bed.* | *I don't think he's **ready for** marriage yet.* **2** something that is ready has been prepared and can be used, eaten, etc. immediately: *Is supper ready?* | *The computer is now set up and **ready to** use.* | *Is everything **ready for** the party?* | *I've got to **get** a room **ready** for our guests.* | ***Have** your passport **ready** when you go through immigration.* **3** willing or likely to do something: *She's always **ready to** help.* [ORIGIN: 1100—1200 Old English *ræde* "prepared"]

ˌready-ˈmade *adj.* already prepared and ready to be used immediately: *ready-made curtains*

real¹ /ril/ *adj.* **1** not imaginary but actually existing: *The new system has real advantages.* | *There is a **very real danger/possibility/risk** of an explosion.* **2** [only before noun] true and not pretended: *What's the real reason you were late?* | *That's not her real name.* **3** not false or artificial (ANT) **fake**: *real leather* | *I don't want a plastic Christmas tree – I want **the real thing*** (=a real Christmas tree). **4** (informal) used in order to emphasize what you are saying: *Matt's a real jerk.* | *It's a real pleasure to meet you.* **5 the real world** *also* **real life** the world that people actually live in, as opposed to an imaginary one: *Things don't happen like that in the real world.*

SPOKEN PHRASES

6 said when something is the way you think it should be: *Now that's real coffee!* **7 real live** used in order to emphasize how rare or unusual something is: *Wow! A real live movie star!* **8 are you for real?** used when you are very surprised or shocked by what someone has done or said **9 for real** seriously, not just pretending: *He quit smoking? For real?* **10 get real!** used in order to tell someone that s/he is being silly or unreasonable: *Get real! He'll never make the team.* **11 keep it real** (slang) something young people say when they mean to behave in an honest way and not pretend to be different from how they really are

[ORIGIN: 1400—1500 Old French, Medieval Latin *realis* "of things (in law)," from Latin *res* "thing"]

real² *adv.* (spoken, nonstandard) very: *I'm real sorry!*

ˈreal esˌtate *n.* [U] **1** property such as houses or land: *Real estate prices fell again last year.* **2** the business of selling houses or land

ˈreal estate ˌagent *n.* [C] someone whose job is to sell houses or land

re·al·ism /ˈriəˌlɪzəm/ *n.* [U] **1** the ability to deal with situations in a practical or sensible way **2** the quality of seeming real: *The program's bleak realism made it seem very authentic.* **3** *also* **Realism** a style of art and literature in which everything is shown or described as it really is in life

re·al·ist /ˈriəlɪst/ *n.* [C] someone who thinks in a realistic way

re·al·is·tic /ˌriəˈlɪstɪk/ *adj.* **1** practical and sensible, or dealing with situations in this way: *You have to be **realistic about** your chances of winning* (=realize that you may not win). | *realistic goals* (=sensible ones, that can be achieved) **2** showing things as they are in real life: *His paintings are so realistic they look like photographs.*

re·al·is·tic·ally /ˌriəˈlɪstɪkli/ *adv.* **1** in a realistic way: *We can't realistically hope for any improvement so soon.* **2** in a way that is very similar to real life: *a realistically drawn picture*

re·al·i·ty /riˈæləṭi/ *n.* (plural **realities**) **1** [C,U] what is true or what actually happens, not what is imagined or not real: *Crime is one of the **realities of** living in the city.* | *She refuses to **face reality**.* | ***The reality is that** we can't depend on him.* **2 in reality** used in order to say that something is different from what seems to be true: *He said he'd retired, but in reality he was fired.* **3 become a reality/make sth a reality** to begin to exist or happen, or to make something do this: *Frank's dream of opening a restaurant became a reality last May.* **4 reality check** (informal) an occasion when you consider the facts of a situation, as opposed to what you would like or what you have imagined

re·al·i·za·tion /ˌriələˈzeɪʃən/ *n.* [singular, U] **1** the act of understanding or realizing something that you did not know before: *We finally **came to the realization that** the business wasn't going to work.* **2** (formal) the act of achieving what you had planned or hoped to do: ***the realization of** a lifelong ambition*

re·al·ize /ˈriəˌlaɪz/ *v.* [T] **1** to know or understand the importance of something that you did not know before: *Do you **realize (that)** you're an hour late?* | *It was only later that I realized my mistake.*

THESAURUS

become aware – to gradually realize that something is happening or is true: *I became aware that two girls were watching me.*
dawn on sb – to realize something for the first time: *It dawned on me that he was making fun of me.*
sink in – to begin to understand something or realize its full meaning: *It took a few minutes for the doctor's words to sink in.*

2 realize a hope/goal/dream etc. to achieve something you have been hoping to achieve **3 sb's (worst) fears were realized** used in order to say that the thing that you were afraid of has actually happened: *Morris's worst fears were realized when the police came to his door.*

real·ly /ˈrili/ *adv.* **1** very or very much: *Tom's a really nice guy.* | *His letter really irritated me.* | *I'm **really, really** sorry.* **2** used when you are talking about what actually happened or is true, rather than what people might wrongly think: *Kevin's not really his brother.* | *What do you really think?*

SPOKEN PHRASES

3 used in order to emphasize something you are saying: *I really don't mind.* | *No, really, I'm fine. Don't worry.* **4 really?** used when you are surprised about or interested in what someone has said: *"Meg's getting married." "Really? When?"* **5 not really** used in order to say "no," especially when something is not completely true: *"Are you hungry yet?" "Not really."* **6 (yeah) really** used in order to agree with someone: *"Greg can be such a jerk sometimes." "Yeah, really."*

realm /rɛlm/ *n.* [C] **1** (formal) an area of knowledge, interest, or thought: *new discoveries in the **realm of** science* **2** (literary) a country ruled over by a king or queen

THESAURUS country, nation, state, power, land → COUNTRY[1]

ˌreal ˈnumber *n.* [C] MATH any number that is not the square root of a negative number

ˈreal-time *adj.* [only before noun] IT a real-time computer system deals with information as fast as it receives it —**real time** *n.* [U]

Real·tor /ˈriltɚ/ *n.* [C] (trademark) a REAL ESTATE AGENT who belongs to the National Association of Realtors

real·ty /ˈrilti/ *n.* [U] REAL ESTATE

ream /rim/ *n.* **1 reams of sth** (informal) a lot of something: *He took reams of notes.* **2** [C] 500 sheets of paper

reap /rip/ *v.* **1** [T] to get something good because of the hard work that you have done: *Paula is starting to **reap the benefits** of all her hard work.* **2** [I,T] to cut and gather a crop of grain

rear[1] /rɪr/ *n.* [C] **1 the rear** the back part of an object, vehicle, building, etc.: *There are more seats **at the rear of** the theater.* **2** *also* **rear end** (informal) the part of your body that you sit on **3 bring up the rear** to be at the back of a line or group of people that is moving forward: *The kids came around the corner, with Donny bringing up the rear.*

rear[2] *v.* **1** [T] to care for a person, animal, or plant until he, she, or it is fully grown (SYN) **raise**: *She reared seven children by herself.* **2** [I] *also* **rear up** if an animal rears, it rises up on its back legs: *The horse reared and threw me off.*

rear[3] *adj.* [only before noun] relating to the back of something (ANT) **front**: *the rear wheels of the car* | *the rear entrance of the hospital*

ˈrear end *n.* [C] (spoken) the part of your body that you sit on

ˈrear-end *v.* [T] (informal) to hit the back of someone's car with another car: *Someone rear-ended us on the freeway.*

re·ar·range /ˌriəˈreɪndʒ/ *v.* [T] to change the position or order of things: *We rearranged the furniture in the living room.* —**rearrangement** *n.* [C,U]

rear·view mir·ror /ˌrɪrvyu ˈmɪrɚ/ *n.* [C] the mirror in a car that you use to see what is behind you

R

rear·ward /ˈrɪrwɚd/ *adv.* in, toward, or at the back of something

rea·son¹ /ˈrizən/ *n.* **1** [C] the cause or fact that explains why something happens or exists: *Did he give any **reason for** quitting? | There are many **reasons why** people develop heart disease. | One of the **reasons (that)** she came to Boston is her family.*

THESAURUS

explanation – a reason that you give for why something happened or why you did something: *Is there any explanation for his behavior?*
excuse – a reason that you give for why you did something bad: *I hope she has a good excuse for being late again.*
motive – a reason that makes someone do something, especially something bad: *The police have found no motive for the attack.*
rationale (formal) – the reasons and principles on which a decision, plan, etc. is based: *What is the Pope's rationale for not allowing women to be priests?*
grounds – a good reason for doing, believing, or saying something: *Abusive behavior is grounds for divorce.*

R

2 [C,U] a fact that makes it right or fair to do something: *There is **no reason to** panic. | You **had every reason** to be suspicious.* **3** [U] sensible judgment or advice: *He won't **listen to reason*** (=be persuaded by sensible advice). *| You can go anywhere you want, **within reason*** (=within sensible limits). **4** [U] the ability to think, understand, and make good judgments → LOGIC: *a conflict between reason and emotion* **5 all the more reason to do sth** used in order to say that what has just been mentioned is another reason for doing what you have suggested: *"We can't agree about anything." "Well, that's all the more reason for us to sit down and talk."* [ORIGIN: 1200—1300 Old French *raison*, from Latin *ratio* "calculation, reason"]

reason² *v.* **1** [T] to form a particular judgment about something after thinking about the facts: *The jury **reasoned that** he could not have committed the crimes.* **2** [I] to think about facts clearly and make judgments: *the ability to reason*

reason with sb *phr. v.* to talk to someone in order to persuade him/her to be more sensible: *I tried to reason with her, but she wouldn't listen.*

rea·son·a·ble /ˈriznəbəl/ *adj.* **1** fair and sensible ANT **unreasonable**: *a reasonable request | **Be reasonable** – you can't expect her to do all the work on her own! | He seemed like a reasonable guy.* → FAIR¹ **2** a reasonable amount, number, or price is not too much or too big: *good food at a reasonable price*

THESAURUS **inexpensive, good/great value, competitive** → CHEAP¹
satisfactory, good enough, acceptable → SATISFACTORY

—**reasonableness** *n.* [U]

rea·son·a·bly /ˈriznəbli/ *adv.* **1** fairly but not completely: *I did reasonably well on the test.* **2** in a way that is fair or sensible: *"I'm sure we can find an answer," Steve said reasonably.*

rea·soned /ˈrizənd/ *adj.* based on careful thought SYN **logical**: *a reasoned argument*

rea·son·ing /ˈrizənɪŋ/ *n.* [U] the process of thinking carefully about something in order to make a judgment: *What's the **reasoning behind** this proposal?* → INDIRECT REASONING

re·as·sur·ance /ˌriəˈʃʊrəns/ *n.* [C,U] something that you say or do to make someone feel less worried about a problem: *People sought **reassurance that** their pensions would still be paid, despite the failure of the company.*

re·as·sure /ˌriəˈʃʊr/ *v.* [T] to make someone feel calm and less worried about a problem: *Kids need to be **reassured that** their parents love them no matter what. | She **reassured** me **that** everything would be okay.*

re·as·sur·ing /ˌriəˈʃʊrɪŋ/ *adj.* making someone feel less worried: *a reassuring smile* —**reassuringly** *adv.*

re·bate /ˈribeɪt/ *n.* [C] an amount of money that is paid back to you when you have paid too much rent, taxes, etc.: *a tax rebate*

reb·el¹ /ˈrɛbəl/ *n.* [C] **1** someone who opposes or fights against people in authority: *Rebels have overthrown the government.* **2** someone who does not do things in the way that other people want him/her to do them: *She was a rebel at school.* [ORIGIN: 1300—1400 *rebel* "rebellious" (13—21 centuries), from Old French *rebelle*, from Latin, from *bellum* "war"]

re·bel² /rɪˈbɛl/ *v.* (**rebelled**, **rebelling**) [I] to oppose or fight against someone who is in authority: *It's part of being a teenager to **rebel against** your parents.*

THESAURUS **disobey, break a rule/law, defy** → DISOBEY

re·bel·lion /rɪˈbɛlyən/ *n.* [C,U] **1** an organized attempt to change the government by using violence → REVOLUTION: *He led an armed **rebellion against** the government.*

THESAURUS **revolution, revolt, uprising, insurrection, insurgency** → REVOLUTION

2 opposition to someone in authority: *teenage rebellion*

re·bel·lious /rɪˈbɛlyəs/ *adj.* **1** deliberately disobeying someone in authority: *a rebellious child* **2** fighting against the government by using violence: *rebellious troops*

re·birth /riˈbɚθ, ˈribɚθ/ *n.* [singular] (formal) a change that results in an old idea, method, etc. becoming popular again

re·boot /riˈbut/ *v.* [I,T] IT if you reboot a computer, you start it again after it has stopped working

re·bound¹ /ˈribaʊnd, rɪˈbaʊnd/ *v.* [I] **1** if a ball

rebounds, it moves quickly back after hitting something solid: *The ball* ***rebounded off*** *the hoop.* **2** to increase again after decreasing SYN **recover**: *Oil prices rebounded this week.*

re·bound² /'ribaʊnd/ *n.* **on the rebound** if someone is on the rebound, s/he has recently stopped being in a romantic relationship, and is likely to start another romantic relationship soon

re·buff /rɪ'bʌf/ *v.* [T] (formal) to be unkind to someone who is trying to be friendly or helpful —**rebuff** *n.* [C]

re·build /ri'bɪld/ *v.* (past tense and past participle **rebuilt** /-'bɪlt/) [T] **1** to build something again, after it has been damaged or destroyed: *The freeway system was quickly rebuilt after the earthquake.*

THESAURUS **repair, fix, renovate, restore** → REPAIR²

2 to make something strong and successful again: *We try to help drug addicts* ***rebuild*** *their* ***lives.***

re·buke /rɪ'byuk/ *v.* [T] (formal) to criticize someone because s/he has done something wrong [ORIGIN: 1300—1400 Old North French *rebuker*, from *bukier* "to hit, cut down"] —**rebuke** *n.* [C,U]

THESAURUS **criticize, scold, admonish, reprimand** → CRITICIZE

re·but /rɪ'bʌt/ *v.* (**rebutted, rebutting**) [T] (formal) to give reasons to show that a statement or a legal charge that has been made against you is false —**rebuttal** /rɪ'bʌtl/ *n.* [C]

re·cal·ci·trant /rɪ'kælsətrənt/ *adj.* (formal) refusing to obey or be controlled, even after being punished —**recalcitrance** *n.* [U]

re·call¹ /rɪ'kɔl/ *v.* [T] **1** to remember something: *I don't recall meeting him.* | *I seem to* ***recall (that)*** *we had problems finding the place.* **2** if a company recalls a product, it asks people to return the product because something is wrong with it

re·call² /rɪ'kɔl, 'rikɔl/ *n.* **1** [U] the ability to remember something you have learned or experienced: *She has* ***total recall*** (=ability to remember everything) *of what she has read.* **2** [C] a situation in which a company recalls a product

re·cant /rɪ'kænt/ *v.* [I,T] (formal) to say publicly that you no longer have a particular religious or political belief

re·cap /'rikæp/ *n.* [C usually singular] (informal) the act of repeating the main points of something that has just been said: *And now for a recap of tonight's news.* —**recap** /'rikæp, ri'kæp/ *v.* [I,T]

re·ca·pit·u·late /ˌrikə'pɪtʃəˌleɪt/ *v.* [I,T] (formal) to repeat the main points of something that has just been said SYN **recap** —**recapitulation** /ˌrikəpɪtʃə'leɪʃən/ *n.* [C,U]

re·cap·ture /ri'kæptʃɚ/ *v.* [T] **1** to make someone experience or feel something again: *The movie recaptures the innocence of childhood.* **2** to catch a prisoner or animal that has escaped

re·cede /rɪ'sid/ *v.* [I] **1** if something you see, feel, or hear recedes, it gets further and further away until it disappears: *The sound of her footsteps* ***receded into the distance.*** **2** if your hair recedes, you gradually lose the hair at the front of your head: *He has a* ***receding hairline.*** **3** if water recedes, it moves back from an area that it was covering

re·ceipt /rɪ'sit/ *n.* **1** [C] a piece of paper that shows that you have received money or goods: *Keep your receipts for tax purposes.* | *credit card receipts* **2** [U] (formal) the act of receiving something: *The contract becomes valid* ***on/upon receipt of*** (=when we receive) *your letter.*

re·ceive /rɪ'siv/ *v.* [T] **1** to be given something officially: *He* ***received*** *an award* ***from*** *the college.* **2** (formal) to get a letter, telephone call, etc.: *Have you received my letter?* **3** to react to something in a particular way: *Her first novel was* ***well received*** (=people said it was good). **4** (formal) if you receive medical treatment, an injury, etc., it happens or is done to you: *He is still in the hospital* ***receiving treatment*** *for the cuts on his hands.* **5** (formal) to accept or welcome someone officially as a guest or member of a group: *Perez was received at the White House and given the award.* [ORIGIN: 1300—1400 Old North French *receivre*, from Latin *recipere*, from *capere* "to take"]

re·ceiv·er /rɪ'sivɚ/ *n.* [C] **1** the part of a telephone that you hold next to your mouth and ear → PHONE¹ **2** a piece of electronic equipment in a STEREO, that changes electrical signals into sound, then makes them loud enough to hear **3** in football, the player who catches the ball

re·cent /'risənt/ *adj.* having happened or begun to exist only a short time ago: *a recent photo* | *the* ***most recent*** *edition of the magazine* | *The situation has improved* ***in recent years/months.***

THESAURUS **new, modern, latest** → NEW

re·cent·ly /'risəntli/ *adv.* not long ago: *We recently moved from Ohio.* | *Have you seen Anna recently?* | *He worked as a teacher* ***until recently.***

THESAURUS

just – only a few minutes, hours, or days ago: *The show just started.* | *They just got back from Portland.*

a little/short while ago – only a few minutes, hours, or days ago: *Ned called a little while ago.*

lately – in the recent past: *I haven't been to the movies lately.*

freshly – used to say that something was recently made, picked, etc.: *freshly baked bread* | *freshly cut flowers*

newly – used to say that something happened recently, or that something was made, done, etc.

R

recently: *the newly elected governor of New York* | *a newly married couple* | *newly built homes*

re·cep·ta·cle /rɪ'sɛptəkəl/ *n.* [C] (formal) a container

re·cep·tion /rɪ'sɛpʃən/ *n.* **1** [C] a large formal party to celebrate something or to welcome someone: *a wedding reception* | *a reception for the visiting professors* **2** [C usually singular] a way of reacting to a person or idea that shows what you think of him, her, or it: *He got a **warm reception*** (=a friendly greeting) *from the crowd.* **3** [U] the quality of the sound of your radio or the picture of your television: *My TV **gets good/poor reception**.* **4 reception desk/area** the desk or area where visitors who are arriving in a hotel or large organization go first

re·cep·tion·ist /rɪ'sɛpʃənɪst/ *n.* [C] someone whose job is to answer the telephone and help people when they arrive at an office

re·cep·tive /rɪ'sɛptɪv/ *adj.* willing to listen to new ideas or new opinions: *Ron isn't very **receptive to** other people's suggestions.*

R

re·cess /'risɛs, rɪ'sɛs/ *n.* **1** [U] a time when children are allowed to go outside to play during the school day: *Charlie got into a fight **during/at recess**.* **2** [C,U] the time between when work stops and starts again in a court of law or other institution where people have been elected to make laws: *Congress is **in recess** until January.* **3** [C] a space in the wall of a room for shelves, cupboards, etc.

re·ces·sion /rɪ'sɛʃən/ *n.* [C] a period of time when there is less business activity, trade, etc. than usual: *an **economic recession*** | *The economy is going **into recession**.* | *The country is struggling **out of recession**.*

THESAURUS

depression – a long period when businesses do not buy, sell, or produce very much and many people do not have jobs: *During the depression, many young people were unable to find any work at all.*
slump – a period when there is a reduction in business and many people lose their jobs: *a slump in the airline industry*
downturn – a time during which business activity is reduced and economic conditions become worse: *Government projects helped the construction industry survive the downturn.*
crash – an occasion when the value of stocks on a stock market falls suddenly and by a large amount, causing economic problems: *the effects of the 1987 stock market crash*

re·ces·sive /rɪ'sɛsɪv/ *adj.* BIOLOGY a recessive GENE is passed to a child from his/her parents only if both parents have the gene (ANT) **dominant**: *Blue eyes are recessive.*

re·charge /ri'tʃɑrdʒ/ *v.* [T] to put a new supply of electricity into a BATTERY **—rechargeable** *adj.*

rec·i·pe /'rɛsəpi/ *n.* **1** [C] a set of instructions that tells you how to cook something: *recipes from a vegetarian cookbook* | *a **recipe for** chocolate cake* **2 be a recipe for sth** (informal) to be likely to cause a particular result: *Inviting Paul and his ex-wife to the party was a **recipe for disaster**.*

re·cip·i·ent /rɪ'sɪpiənt/ *n.* [C] (formal) someone who receives something: *Bauer has been the **recipient of** many honors.*

re·cip·ro·cal /rɪ'sɪprəkəl/ *adj.* (formal) a reciprocal agreement, relationship, etc. is one where two groups of people do or give the same things to each other [ORIGIN: 1500—1600 Latin *reciprocus* "returning the same way," from *re-* "back" + *pro-* "forward"]

re·cip·ro·cate /rɪ'sɪprə,keɪt/ *v.* [I,T] (formal) to do or give something because something similar has been done for or given to you

re·cit·al /rɪ'saɪtl/ *n.* [C] a public performance of a piece of music or poetry, usually by one person: *a piano recital*

re·cite /rɪ'saɪt/ *v.* [I,T] to say something such as a poem, story, etc. that you know by memory **—recitation** /,rɛsə'teɪʃən/ *n.* [C,U]

reck·less /'rɛklɪs/ *adj.* not caring about danger or the bad results of your behavior, or showing this quality: ***reckless driving*** **—recklessly** *adv.* **—recklessness** *n.* [U]

reck·on /'rɛkən/ *v.* [T] **1** to guess a number, amount, etc. without calculating it exactly: *The software company reckons it will sell 2.5 million units this year.* **2** (spoken) to think or suppose: *I reckon they'll be late.*

reckon with sb/sth *phr. v.* to consider a possible problem when you think about the future: *The new team is a **force to be reckoned with*** (=something to consider seriously).

reck·on·ing /'rɛkənɪŋ/ *n.* [U] calculation that is not exact: ***By my reckoning**, we should be there by now.*

re·claim /rɪ'kleɪm/ *v.* [T] **1** to ask for something to be given back to you: *reclaiming lost luggage* **2** to make land able to be used for farming, building, etc., when it has never been used or has not been used for a while: *Large areas of land will be reclaimed for a new airport.* **—reclamation** /,rɛklə'meɪʃən/ *n.* [U]

re·cline /rɪ'klaɪn/ *v.* **1** [I,T] to push the back of a seat or chair so that it slopes backward, so that you can lean back in it: *The front seats of the car recline.* **2** [I] to lie or sit back in a relaxed way: *People **reclined on** the grass in the sunshine.*

rec·luse /'rɛklus/ *n.* [C] someone who chooses to live alone, and avoids seeing or talking to other people: *Hudson became a recluse after her husband's death.* [ORIGIN: 1100—1200 Old French *reclus* "shut up," from Late Latin *recludere* "to shut up"] **—reclusive** /rɪ'klusɪv/ *adj.*: *the reclusive novelist Thomas Pynchon*

rec·og·ni·tion /,rɛkəg'nɪʃən/ *n.* **1** [singular, U] public admiration and thanks for someone's work or achievements: *She was given an award* ***in recognition of*** *25 years of service.* | *He* ***gained*** *international* ***recognition*** *after winning the competition.* **2** [singular,U] the act of realizing and accepting that something is important or true: *There is a growing* ***recognition of*** *the importance of early childhood education.* **3** [U] the act of recognizing someone or something: *He looked past me with no sign of recognition.* | *The city had changed* ***beyond recognition*** (=so much that I could not recognize it).

rec·og·nize /'rɛkəg,naɪz/ *v.* [T] **1** to realize when you see someone that you know him/her because you have seen him/her before: *He'd lost so much weight I hardly recognized him!* | *Social workers have been trained to recognize the signs of child abuse.* **2** to accept officially that an organization, government, etc. is legal: *The UN has refused to recognize the new government.* **3** to accept and admit that something is true or real: *It's important to* ***recognize that*** *stress can affect your health.* **4** to thank someone officially for something s/he has done: *His contribution to classical music should be recognized.* [ORIGIN: 1400—1500 Old French *reconoistre*, from Latin *recognoscere*, from *cognoscere* "to know"] —**recognizable** /,rɛkəg'naɪzəbəl, 'rɛkəg,naɪ-/ *adj.* —**recognizably** *adv.*

re·coil /'rikɔɪl, rɪ'kɔɪl/ *v.* [I] **1** to feel a strong dislike for something and want to avoid it: *Most people* ***recoil from*** *such racist views.* **2** to move back suddenly from something that you do not like or are afraid of: *Emily* ***recoiled at*** *the sight of the snake.*

rec·ol·lect /,rɛkə'lɛkt/ *v.* [T] to remember something: *I don't recollect her name.*

rec·ol·lec·tion /,rɛkə'lɛkʃən/ *n.* [C,U] (formal) something from the past that you remember, or the act of remembering it: *He* ***has no recollection*** *of the crash.*

rec·om·mend /,rɛkə'mɛnd/ *v.* [T] **1** to advise someone to do something: *Dentists* ***recommend that*** *you change your toothbrush every few months.* | *We* ***strongly recommend*** *buying a bicycle helmet.*

> **THESAURUS** advise, urge, suggest →
> ADVISE

2 to say that someone or something is good: *Can you recommend a local restaurant?* | *I* ***recommend*** *this book* ***to*** *anyone who likes adventure stories.* **3 sth has little/nothing etc. to recommend it** used in order to say that something has few or no good qualities: *The hotel has little to recommend it except that it's cheap.*

rec·om·men·da·tion /,rɛkəmən'deɪʃən/ *n.* **1** [C] advice given to someone, especially about what to do: *The committee was able to* ***make*** *detailed* ***recommendations*** *to the school.* | *The* ***recommendation that*** *babies should sleep on their backs has decreased the number of crib deaths.*

> **THESAURUS** advice, tip, suggestion →
> ADVICE

2 [U] a suggestion that someone or something is appropriate or useful for a particular situation: *We took the tour* ***on a friend's recommendation.*** **3** [C] *also* **letter of recommendation** a letter which states that someone would be a good person to do a job, study at a college, etc.: *Can you* ***write a recommendation*** *for me?*

rec·om·pense /'rɛkəm,pɛns/ *v.* [T] (formal) to give someone a payment for trouble or losses that you have caused —**recompense** *n.* [singular, U]

rec·on·cile /'rɛkən,saɪl/ *v.* **1 be reconciled (with sb)** to have a good relationship with someone again after arguing with him/her: *His parents are now reconciled with each other.* **2** [T] to show that two different ideas, situations, etc. can exist together and are not opposed to each other: *How can he* ***reconcile*** *his religious beliefs* ***with*** *all this gambling?*

reconcile sb to sth *phr. v.* to make someone able to accept a bad situation: *I've reconciled myself to the fact that our marriage is over.*

rec·on·cil·i·a·tion /,rɛkən,sɪli'eɪʃən/ *n.* [singular,U] a situation in which two people, countries, etc. become friendly again after arguing or fighting with each other: *There are signs of a* ***reconciliation between*** *the two countries.*

re·con·di·tion /,rikən'dɪʃən/ *v.* [T] to repair a machine so that it can be sold again

re·con·nais·sance /rɪ'kɑnəsəns, -zəns/ *n.* [C,U] the activity of sending out aircraft or soldiers in order to get information about the enemy —**reconnoiter** /,rikə'nɔɪtə/ *v.* [I,T]

re·con·sid·er /,rikən'sɪdə/ *v.* [I,T] to think again about something in order to decide if you should change your opinion: *Won't you reconsider our offer?* —**reconsideration** /,rikən,sɪdə'reɪʃən/ *n.* [U]

re·con·sti·tute /ri'kɑnstə,tut/ *v.* [T] **1** to make a group, organization, etc. exist in a different form: *The four political groups will be reconstituted as a new party.* **2** to change dried food to its original form by adding water to it

re·con·struct /,rikən'strʌkt/ (Ac) *v.* [T] **1** to produce a complete description of something that happened by collecting pieces of information: *Police have reconstructed the events leading up to the crime.* **2** to build something again after it has been destroyed or damaged

re·con·struc·tion /,rikən'strʌkʃən/ (Ac) *n.* **1** [U] work that is done to repair damage to a city, industry, etc., especially after a war: *The reconstruction of the South after the Civil War took many years.* **2** [C usually singular] a description or copy of something that you produce by collecting information about it: *a* ***reconstruction of*** *the crime*

re·con·struc·tive /,rikən'strʌktɪv/ *adj.* [only before noun] a reconstructive operation is one done to make a part of someone's body the right shape, for example after a bad injury: ***reconstructive surgery***

re·cord¹ /ˈrɛkɚd/ *n.* **1** [C,U] information about something or someone, which is either written on paper or stored on a computer: ***Keep a record of*** *how much you spend on this trip.* | ***medical records*** | *This summer has been the dryest* ***on record*** (=that has been written in records).

THESAURUS

diary/journal – a book in which you write down the things that have happened to you each day
file – a set of written records, or information stored on a computer under a particular name
accounts – an exact record of the money that a company has received and spent
books – written records of a company's financial accounts
ledger – a book in which a company's financial records are kept
roll – an official list of names, for example of the people attending a school
log (book) – an official record of events, especially on a ship or airplane

R

2 [C] the fastest speed, longest distance, highest or lowest level, etc. ever: *a* ***record high/low*** *temperature* | *She* ***holds*** *the world* ***record*** *for the long jump.* | *The movie* ***broke*** *all box office* ***records***. **3** [singular] the known facts about someone's past behavior and how good or bad it has been: *an airline with a* ***good/bad*** *safety* ***record*** | *Does he have a* ***criminal record*** (=has he committed any crimes)? **4** [C] a round flat piece of plastic on which music is stored: *a huge* ***record collection*** **5 off/on the record** not official and not meant to be repeated, or official and able to be repeated **6 for the record** used in order to tell someone that what you are saying should be remembered

re·cord² /rɪˈkɔrd/ *v.* **1** [T] to write information down so that it can be looked at in the future: *All the events were recorded.* **2** [I,T] to store music, sound, television programs, etc. on tape or DISKS, etc. so that people can listen to them or watch them again: *The group has just recorded a new album.* | *Are we recording yet?* **3** [T] to measure the size, speed, temperature, etc. of something so that it can be seen

ˈrecord-ˌbreaking *adj.* better, higher, faster, etc. than anything done before: *record-breaking temperatures*

re·cord·er /rɪˈkɔrdɚ/ *n.* [C] **1** a TAPE RECORDER **2** a small wooden musical instrument shaped like a tube, that you play by blowing into it

re·cord·ing /rɪˈkɔrdɪŋ/ *n.* [C] a piece of music, speech, etc. that has been recorded: ***a recording of*** *Vivaldi's "Gloria"*

ˈrecord ˌlabel *n.* [C] a company that records and produces a singer's, group of musicians', etc. music

ˈrecord ˌplayer *n.* [C] a piece of equipment for playing records

re·count¹ /rɪˈkaʊnt/ *v.* [T] (formal) to tell a story or describe a series of events

re·count² /ˈrikaʊnt/ *n.* [C] a process of counting votes again

re·coup /rɪˈkup/ *v.* [T] to get back money you have lost or spent

re·course /ˈrikɔrs, rɪˈkɔrs/ *n.* [U] (formal) something you can do to help yourself in a difficult situation, or the act of doing this: *The police* ***had no recourse but to*** *shoot* (=shooting was their only choice).

re·cov·er /rɪˈkʌvɚ/ (Ac) *v.* **1** [I] to get better after an illness, injury, shock, etc.: *My uncle is* ***recovering from*** *a heart attack.* **2** [I] to return to a normal condition after a period of trouble or difficulty: *The economy will take years to recover.* **3** [T] to get back something that was taken from you, lost, or almost destroyed: *The stolen paintings have been recovered.* **4** [T] to get back your ability to control your feelings or your body: *He never recovered the use of his arm.* [ORIGIN: 1200—1300 Old French *recovrer*, from Latin *recuperare*, from *capere* "to take"]

re·cov·er·y /rɪˈkʌvəri/ (Ac) *n.* **1** [singular,U] the process of getting better after an illness, injury, etc.: *His* ***recovery from*** *the knee injury has been slow.* | *Doctors expect Kelly to* ***make a full recovery***. **2** [singular,U] the process of returning to a normal condition after a period of trouble or difficulty: *economic recovery* **3** [U] the act of getting back something that is lost, stolen, or owed: *the* ***recovery of*** *the stolen jewels*

re·cre·ate /ˌrikriˈeɪt/ (Ac) *v.* [T] to make something exist again or be experienced again: *The zoo tries to recreate the animals' natural habitats.*

rec·re·a·tion /ˌrɛkriˈeɪʃən/ *n.* [C,U] an activity that you do for pleasure or fun: *outdoor recreation* [ORIGIN: 1300—1400 French *récréation*, from Latin, from *recreare* "to make new, refresh"] —**recreational** *adj.*

THESAURUS **game, sport, hobby, diversion**
→ GAME¹

re·crim·i·na·tion /rɪˌkrɪməˈneɪʃən/ *n.* [C usually plural,U] a situation in which people blame each other, or the things they say when they are blaming each other

re·cruit¹ /rɪˈkrut/ *v.* [I,T] to find new people to work in a company, join an organization, do a job, etc.: *The coaches are visiting high schools in order to recruit new players.* [ORIGIN: 1600—1700 French *recrute* "new growth, new soldiers," from Old French *recroistre* "to grow up again"] —**recruitment** *n.* [U] —**recruiter** *n.* [C]

recruit² *n.* [C] someone who has recently joined a company or an organization: *You could tell he was* ***a new recruit***.

rec·tan·gle /ˈrɛkˌtæŋgəl/ *n.* [C] a shape with four straight sides, two of which are usually longer than the other two, and four RIGHT ANGLES [ORIGIN: 1500—1600 Medieval Latin *rectangulus* "having a right angle," from Latin *rectus* "right" + *angulus* "angle"] —**rectangular** /rɛk'tæŋgyələ/ *adj.* ➔ *see picture at* POLYGON

THESAURUS **shape, square, circle, semicircle, triangle, oval, cylinder** ➔ SHAPE[1]

rec·ti·fy /'rɛktə,faɪ/ *v.* (**rectified**, **rectifies**) [T] (formal) to correct something that is wrong: *All efforts to rectify the problem have failed.* [ORIGIN: 1300—1400 French *rectifier*, from Latin *rectus* "right, straight"]

rec·ti·tude /'rɛktə,tud/ *n.* [U] (formal) behavior that is honest and morally correct: *He was admired for his personal rectitude.*

rec·tor /'rɛktə/ *n.* [C] **1** a priest who is in charge of a local Episcopal church **2** the person in charge of some colleges or schools

rec·tum /'rɛktəm/ *n.* [C] BIOLOGY the lowest part of your BOWELS —**rectal** /'rɛktəl/ *adj.*

re·cu·per·ate /rɪ'kupə,reɪt/ *v.* [I] to get better after an illness, injury, etc.: *Jan is still **recuperating from** her operation.* —**recuperation** /rɪ,kupə'reɪʃən/ *n.* [U]

re·cur /rɪ'kə/ *v.* (**recurred**, **recurring**) [I] to happen again, or to happen several times: *a recurring dream* —**recurrence** /rɪ'kʌrəns, rɪ'kə-/ *n.* [C,U]

re·cur·rent /rɪ'kʌrənt, -'kə-/ *adj.* happening or appearing several times: *a recurrent infection* | *The dangers of pride are a **recurrent theme** in these stories.*

re·cy·cla·ble /ri'saɪkləbəl/ *adj.* able to be recycled: *recyclable bottles* —**recyclable** *n.* [C usually plural]

re·cy·cle /ri'saɪkəl/ *v.* [I,T] to put used objects or materials through a special process, so that they can be used again: *Can these bottles be recycled?* ➔ ENVIRONMENT —**recycled** *adj.*: *recycled paper* —**recycling** *n.* [U]

red[1] /rɛd/ *adj.* **1** having the color of blood: *a red dress* | ***bright red** lipstick* **2** hair that is red is an orange-brown color **3** skin that is red is a bright pink color [ORIGIN: Old English *read*] —**redness** *n.* [U]

red[2] *n.* **1** [C,U] a red color **2 be in the red** ECONOMICS to owe more money than you have (ANT) **be in the black** **3 see red** to become very angry

,red 'blood cell *also* **,red 'corpuscle** *n.* [C] BIOLOGY one of the cells in your blood that carry oxygen to every part of your body ➔ WHITE BLOOD CELL

,red-'blooded *adj.* **red-blooded male/American etc.** (humorous) used in order to emphasize that someone has all of the qualities that a typical man, American, etc. is supposed to have

,red 'carpet *n.* **the red carpet** special treatment that you give someone important who is visiting you

,Red 'Cross *n.* an international organization that helps people who are suffering as a result of war, floods, disease, etc.

red·den /'rɛdn/ *v.* [I,T] to become red, or to make something do this

re·dec·o·rate /ri'dɛkə,reɪt/ *v.* [I,T] to change the way a room looks by painting, changing the furniture, etc.

re·deem /rɪ'dim/ *v.* [T] (formal) **1 redeem yourself** to do something to improve other people's opinion of you, after you have behaved badly or failed **2** to exchange a piece of paper representing an amount of money for the money that it is worth: *You can redeem the coupon at any store.* **3 redeeming quality/value etc.** a good quality, etc. that keeps someone or something from being completely bad or wrong: *Maybe she has redeeming qualities, but I can't see them.* **4** to make something less bad: *Nothing could redeem this awful movie.* —**redeemable** *adj.*

re·demp·tion /rɪ'dɛmpʃən/ *n.* [U] **1 past/beyond redemption** too bad to be saved or improved **2** the state of being freed from the power of evil, believed by Christians to be made possible by Jesus Christ

re·de·vel·op /,ridə'vɛləp/ *v.* [T] to make an area more modern by putting in new buildings or changing old ones —**redevelopment** *n.* [C,U]

'red-eye *n.* [U] (informal) an airplane with passengers on it that flies at night and arrives early in the morning: *I **took the red-eye** from Chicago to Seattle.*

,red 'flag *n.* [C] something that shows or warns you that something might be wrong, illegal, etc.

,red-'handed *adj.* **catch sb red-handed** (informal) to catch someone at the moment when s/he is doing something wrong: *She was caught red-handed taking money from the register.*

red·head /'rɛdhɛd/ *n.* [C] someone who has red hair

,red 'herring *n.* [C] a fact or idea that is not important but is introduced in order to take your attention away from something that is important, especially in a story

,red-'hot *adj.* extremely hot: *red-hot metal*

re·di·rect /,ridɪ'rɛkt, -daɪ-/ *v.* [T] to send something in a different direction, or use something for a different purpose: *She needs to redirect her energy into something more useful.*

re·dis·tri·bu·tion /,ridɪstrə'byuʃən/ *n.* [U] the act of sharing something between people in a way that is different from in the past: *the **redistribution of wealth/income/land etc.*** —**redistribute** /,ridɪ'strɪbyut/ *v.* [T]: *One of the purposes of taxes is to redistribute some wealth to the poor.*

,red-'light ,district *n.* [C] the area of a city where there are many PROSTITUTES

R

ˌred ˈmeat *n.* [U] dark-colored meat such as BEEF

red·neck /ˈrɛdnɛk/ *n.* [C] (informal, disapproving) someone who lives in a country area, is not educated, and has strong unreasonable opinions

re·do /riˈdu/ *v.* (past tense **redid** /-ˈdɪd/, past participle **redone** /-ˈdʌn/, third person singular **redoes** /-ˈdʌz/) [T] to do something again: *You'll have to redo this essay.*

re·dou·ble /riˈdʌbəl/ *v.* **redouble your efforts** to greatly increase your efforts as you try to do something

re·doubt·a·ble /rɪˈdaʊt̬əbəl/ *adj.* (literary) someone who is redoubtable is a person you respect or fear (SYN) **formidable**: *No one would argue with this redoubtable professor.*

re·dress /rɪˈdrɛs/ *v.* [T] (formal) to correct something that is wrong, not equal, or unfair —**redress** /ˈridrɛs, rɪˈdrɛs/ *n.* [U]

R

ˌred ˈshift *n.* [U] PHYSICS a change in the light given off by an object such as a star in space, in which the light appears more red as the object is moving away from the person looking at it ➔ BLUE SHIFT

ˌred ˈtape *n.* [U] official rules that seem unnecessary and that delay action: *The new policies are intended to* ***cut red tape****.*

re·duce /rɪˈdus/ *v.* [T] to make something become less in amount, size, price, etc.: *Reduce the heat and simmer the rice for another 10 minutes.* | *I bought a new jacket that was* ***reduced from*** *$75* ***to*** *$35.*

THESAURUS

To reduce prices, numbers, or amounts

lower: *The candidate promised to lower tax rates.*
decrease: *Salaries of middle managers have decreased in the last few years.*
cut: *Stores cut prices after Christmas to get rid of excess merchandise.*
slash – to reduce an amount or price by a large amount: *State spending was slashed in an attempt to balance the budget.*
roll back (informal) – to reduce prices, costs, etc. to a previous level: *There's a proposal to roll back the gas tax.*

To reduce pain

relieve – to make pain less severe or make it stop: *Aspirin is effective at relieving headaches.*
ease – to reduce pain and make someone feel more comfortable: *Massage can ease the pain from tight muscles.*
lessen – to reduce pain, but not make it go away: *drugs to lessen pain*
soothe – to make a pain stop hurting so much: *A hot bath will soothe aching muscles.*
alleviate (formal): *Sitting in a warm bath may alleviate the discomfort.*
palliate (formal) – to make a bad illness better, but not make it go away completely: *Can acupuncture palliate breathing difficulties?*

reduce to *phr. v.* **1 reduce sb to tears/silence etc.** to make someone cry, be silent, etc.: *Many of us were reduced to tears by the tragedy.* **2 reduce sb to doing sth** to make someone do something that s/he would prefer not to, especially behaving or living in a way that is not as good as before: *They were reduced to begging on the streets.* **3 reduce sth to rubble/ashes/ruins** to destroy something completely, especially a building or city [ORIGIN: 1300—1400 Latin *reducere* "to lead back," from *ducere* "to lead"]

re·duc·tion /rɪˈdʌkʃən/ *n.* [C,U] a decrease in size, amount, price, etc.: *a* ***reduction in*** *the price of gasoline* | *a* ***reduction of*** *30% on all sale items* | *an* ***arms reduction*** *treaty*

re·dun·dant /rɪˈdʌndənt/ *adj.* not necessary because something else means or does the same thing. —**redundancy** *n.* [U]

red·wood /ˈrɛdwʊd/ *n.* [C,U] a very tall tree that grows near the coast in Oregon and California, or the wood from this tree ➔ *see picture on page A23*

reed /rid/ *n.* [C] **1** a tall plant like grass that grows near water **2** a thin piece of wood in some musical instruments that produces a sound when you blow over it

reef /rif/ *n.* [C] a line of sharp rocks or a raised area of sand near the surface of the ocean

reek /rik/ *v.* [I] to have a strong bad smell: *His breath* ***reeked of*** *garlic.* —**reek** *n.* [singular]

reel¹ /ril/ *n.* [C] **1** a round object onto which things such as film or string for fishing can be wound **2** the amount that one of these objects will hold: *a* ***reel of*** *film*

reel² *v.* **1** [I] to walk in an unsteady way and almost fall over, as if you are drunk: *A guy* ***came reeling*** *down the hallway.* **2** [I] to be confused or shocked: *People* ***are*** *still* ***reeling from*** *the hurricane that hit the town on Sunday.* **3** [T] to wind or unwind the string on the reel of a fishing ROD: *It took almost an hour to* ***reel*** *the fish* ***in****.*

reel sth ↔ **off** *phr. v.* (informal) to repeat a lot of information quickly and easily: *Andy can reel off the names of all the state capitals.*

re·e·lect /ˌriəˈlɛkt/ *v.* [T] to elect someone again —**reelection** /ˌriəˈlɛkʃən/ *n.* [C,U]

re-en·act /ˌriɪˈnækt/ *v.* [T] to perform the actions of a story, crime, etc. that happened in the past: *In church, the smaller children re-enacted the Christmas story.* —**re-enactment** *n.* [C]

re·en·try /riˈɛntri/ *n.* (plural **reentries**) [C,U] an act of entering a place or situation again: *The* *spacecraft made a safe* ***reentry into*** *the Earth's atmosphere.*

ref /rɛf/ *n.* [C] (spoken) a referee

re·fer /rɪ'fɚ/ *v.* (**referred**, **referring**)

refer to *phr. v.* **1 refer to** sb/sth to mention or speak about someone or something: *Rachel didn't mention names, but everyone knew who she was referring to.* | *He likes to be* ***referred to as*** *"Doctor Mills."* **2 refer to** sth to look at a book, map, piece of paper, etc. for information: *Refer to page 14 for instructions.* **3 refer to** sb/sth if a statement, number, report, etc. refers to someone or something, it is about that person or thing: *The blue line on the graph refers to sales.* **4 refer** sb/sth **to** sb/sth to send someone or something to another place or person for information, advice, or a decision: *My doctor referred me to a specialist.*

ref·er·ee¹ /ˌrɛfə'ri/ *n.* [C] someone who makes sure that the rules are followed during a game in sports such as football, basketball, or BOXING

THESAURUS

Referee and **umpire** mean the same but are used for different sports.
Use **referee** when you are talking about football, soccer, ice hockey, basketball, boxing, wrestling, or volleyball.
Use **umpire** when you are talking about baseball or tennis.

referee² *v.* [I,T] to be the referee for a game

ref·erence /'rɛfrəns/ *n.* **1** [C,U] something you say or write that mentions another person or thing: *Her writing is full of* ***references to*** *Chicago.* | *The article* ***made no reference to*** *previous research.* **2** [C,U] the act of looking at something for information, or the book, magazine, etc. you get the information from: *I'll keep a copy of the document* ***for future reference****.* | *the reference section of the library* **3** [C] **a)** a letter containing information about you, written by a former employer or someone who knows you well to a new employer **b)** the person who writes this letter **4** [C] a note that tells you where the information that is used in a book, article, etc. comes from: *a list of references at the end of the article*

'reference book *n.* [C] a book such as a dictionary that you look at to find information → BOOK¹

'reference ˌlibrary *also* **'reference ˌroom** *n.* [C] a public library, or a room in a library, that contains reference books that you can use but not take away

ref·er·en·dum /ˌrɛfə'rɛndəm/ *n.* (plural **referenda** /-də/ *or* **referendums**) [C,U] POLITICS an occasion when you vote in order to make a decision about a particular subject, rather than voting for a person: *In Quebec, the party is campaigning for a* ***referendum on*** *independence.*

re·fer·ral /rɪ'fʌrəl, -'fɚ-/ *n.* [C,U] (formal) an act of sending someone or something to another place for help, information, etc.: *The doctor will* ***give*** *you a* ***referral to*** *a specialist.*

re·fill /ri'fɪl/ *v.* [T] to fill something again: *A waiter refilled our glasses.* —**refill** /'rifɪl/ *n.* [C]: *Would you like a refill?*

re·fi·nance /ri'faɪnæns, ˌrifə'næns/ *v.* [T] to replace a LOAN that you have with another loan: *We plan to refinance our mortgage.*

re·fine /rɪ'faɪn/ (Ac) *v.* [T] **1** to make a substance more pure using an industrial process: *The sugar is refined and then shipped abroad.* **2** to improve a method, plan, system, etc. by making small changes to it: *Refine your analysis as you get more data.*

re·fined /rɪ'faɪnd/ (Ac) *adj.* **1** made more pure using an industrial process: *refined flour* **2** improved and made more effective: *a more refined technique* **3** polite and well-educated

re·fine·ment /rɪ'faɪnmənt/ (Ac) *n.* **1** [U] the process of improving something or making a substance more pure: *the* ***refinement of*** *sugar* | *the* ***refinement of*** *their economic theories* **2** [C] a change to an existing product, plan, system, etc. that improves it: *We've added a number of refinements to the design.* **3** [U] the quality of being polite and well-educated

re·fin·er·y /rɪ'faɪnəri/ *n.* (plural **refineries**) [C] a factory where something such as oil, sugar, or metal is refined

re·fin·ish /ri'fɪnɪʃ/ *v.* [T] to give the surface of something, especially wood, a new appearance by painting or POLISHing it: *The hardwood floors were sanded and refinished.*

re·flect /rɪ'flɛkt/ *v.* **1 be reflected in sth** if an object, person, view, etc. is reflected in a mirror or in the water, you can see the person or thing in it: *We could see the mountains* ***reflected in*** *the lake.* **2** [T] if a surface reflects light, heat, or sound, it sends back the light, etc. that hits it: *Wear something white – it reflects the heat.* **3** [T] to show or be a sign of a particular situation, idea, or feeling: *The fact that people are living longer is reflected in the latest census statistics.* **4** [I] to think carefully: *Please take some time to* ***reflect on*** *our offer.* [ORIGIN: 1300—1400 Latin *reflectere* "to bend back," from *flectere* "to bend"]

reflect on sb/sth *phr. v.* to influence people's opinion of someone or something, especially in a bad way: *Some children's behavior* ***reflects badly on*** *their parents.*

re·flec·tion /rɪ'flɛkʃən/ *n.* **1** [C] an image that is reflected in a mirror, glass, or water: *We looked at our reflections in the pool.* **2** [C,U] careful thought, or an idea or opinion based on this: *The book includes the writer's* ***reflections on*** *America in the 1920s, when he was a boy.* | *At first I disagreed, but* ***on/upon reflection*** (=after thinking carefully about it) *I realized she was right.* **3** [singular] something that shows, or is a sign of, a particular situation, fact, or feeling: *The rise in crime is a* ***reflection of*** *a violent society.* | *If your kids are bad, it's a* ***reflection on*** *you* (=a sign that you are a bad parent). **4** [U] the light or heat that is reflected from something

reflection

reflection

distortion

re·flec·tive /rɪˈflɛktɪv/ *adj.* **1** a reflective surface reflects light: *reflective tape* **2** thinking quietly, or showing that you are doing this: *He was in a reflective mood.*

R

re·flec·tor /rɪˈflɛktɚ/ *n.* [C] a small piece of plastic that REFLECTS light ➔ *see picture at* BICYCLE

re·flex /ˈriflɛks/ *n.* [C usually plural] a sudden physical reaction that you have without thinking about it: *Basketball players tend to have* ***good reflexes*** (=the ability to react quickly).

re·flex·ive /rɪˈflɛksɪv/ *adj.* ENG. LANG. ARTS in grammar, a reflexive verb or PRONOUN refers back to the person or thing that does the action. In the sentence "I enjoyed myself," "myself" is reflexive.

re·form¹ /rɪˈfɔrm/ *v.* **1** [T] to improve an organization or system by making a lot of changes to it: *The plans to reform the health care system are controversial.*

THESAURUS **change, alter, reorganize, restructure, transform** ➔ CHANGE¹

2 [I,T] to improve your behavior by making a lot of changes to it, or to make someone do this: *a* ***reformed alcoholic/smoker etc.*** (=someone who is no longer an alcoholic, etc.)

reform² *n.* [C,U] a change made to an organization or system in order to improve it: *the* ***reform of*** *the legal system* | ***economic/political/educational reform***

re·form·er /rɪˈfɔrmɚ/ *n.* [C] someone who works hard to make a lot of changes in order to improve a government or society

reˈform school *n.* [C] a special school where young people who have broken the law are sent

re·fract /rɪˈfrækt/ *v.* [I,T] PHYSICS to change the direction of light or sound, for example when light goes from the air into a liquid or through a transparent substance: *Light is refracted when it hits the surface of the water.*

re·frac·tion /rɪˈfrækʃən/ (Ac) *n.* [U] PHYSICS a change in the direction of light or sound, for example when it goes from the air into a liquid or through a transparent substance

re·frain¹ /rɪˈfreɪn/ *v.* [I] (formal) to stop yourself from doing something: *Please* ***refrain from*** *smoking.* [ORIGIN: 1300—1400 Old French *refrener*, from Latin *refrenare*, from *frenum* "bridle" (a leather band used by a rider to control a horse)]

refrain² *n.* [C] ENG. LANG. ARTS part of a song that is repeated, especially at the end of each VERSE

re·fresh /rɪˈfrɛʃ/ *v.* **1** [T] to make someone feel less tired or hot: *A shower will refresh you.* **2 refresh sb's memory** to say something that makes someone remember something: *Please refresh my memory – what was your last job?* —**refreshed** *adj.*

reˈfresher ˌcourse *n.* [C] a training class that teaches you about new developments in a subject or skill you have already studied or learned

re·fresh·ing /rɪˈfrɛʃɪŋ/ *adj.* **1** making you feel less tired or less hot: *a refreshing drink* **2** pleasantly different from what is familiar and boring: *The movie is a* ***refreshing change*** *from the usual Hollywood blockbusters.* —**refreshingly** *adv.*

re·fresh·ment /rɪˈfrɛʃmənt/ *n.* **1** [C usually plural] food and drinks that are provided at a meeting, party, sports event, etc.: *Refreshments will be served after the concert.* **2** [U] food and drinks in general

re·fried beans /ˌrifraɪd ˈbinz/ *n.* [plural] a Mexican dish in which beans that have already been cooked are crushed and FRIED with spices

re·frig·er·ate /rɪˈfrɪdʒəˌreɪt/ *v.* [T] to make something such as food and drinks cold in order to preserve them: *Refrigerate the sauce overnight.* [ORIGIN: 1500—1600 Latin, past participle of *refrigerare*, from *frigerare* "to make cold"] —**refrigeration** /rɪˌfrɪdʒəˈreɪʃən/ *n.* [U]

re·frig·er·a·tor /rɪˈfrɪdʒəˌreɪt̬ɚ/ *n.* [C] a large piece of kitchen equipment used for keeping food and drinks cold, shaped like a metal cupboard and kept cold by electricity (SYN) **fridge**

re·fuel /riˈfyul/ *v.* [I,T] to fill a vehicle or airplane with FUEL again before it continues on a trip

ref·uge /ˈrɛfyudʒ/ *n.* [C,U] a place that provides protection or shelter from bad weather or danger: *About 50 families have* ***taken refuge*** (=found protection) *in a Red Cross shelter.* | *We* ***sought refuge*** (=looked for protection) *from the 110-degree heat.*

ref·u·gee /ˌrɛfyʊˈdʒi◂/ *n.* [C] someone who has been forced to leave his/her country, especially during a war: *Refugees were streaming across the border.* | ***refugee camps***

re·fund /ˈrifʌnd/ *n.* [C] an amount of money that is given back to you if you are not satisfied with the goods or services you have paid for: *If you're not completely satisfied, we'll* ***give*** *you* ***a refund.*** —**refund** /rɪˈfʌnd, ˈrifʌnd/ *v.* [T]

re·fur·bish /rɪˈfɚbɪʃ/ *v.* [T] to repair and improve a building: *The hotel was recently refurbished.* —**refurbishment** *n.* [C,U]

re·fus·al /rɪˈfyuzəl/ *n.* [C,U] an act of saying or

showing that you will not do, accept, or allow something: *His **refusal to** pay the fine means he may go to prison.*

re·fuse¹ /rɪˈfyuz/ *v.* **1** [I,T] to say firmly that you will not do or accept something: *I asked her to marry me, but she refused.* | *Steen **refused to** answer any questions.* | *The offer was **too good to refuse*** (=so good that you cannot say no).

THESAURUS **reject, turn down, say no, decline** ➔ REJECT¹

2 [T] to not give or allow someone to have something that s/he wants, especially when s/he has asked for it officially: *We were refused permission to enter the country.*

ref·use² /ˈrɛfjus/ *n.* [U] (formal) waste material

THESAURUS **garbage, trash, litter, waste** ➔ GARBAGE

re·fute /rɪˈfyut/ *v.* [T] (formal) to prove that a statement or idea is not correct or fair: *Several scientists have attempted to refute Moore's theories.*

re·gain /rɪˈgeɪn/ *v.* [T] to get something back, especially an ability or quality that you have lost: *The doctors don't know if Maria will ever regain the use of her legs.*

re·gal /ˈrigəl/ *adj.* typical of a king or queen and therefore very impressive [ORIGIN: 1300—1400 Old French, Latin *regalis*, from *rex* "king"]

re·ga·lia /rɪˈgeɪlyə/ *n.* [U] traditional clothes and decorations, used at official ceremonies: *a Native American chief **in full regalia*** (=wearing traditional clothes, decorations, etc.)

re·gard¹ /rɪˈgɑrd/ *n.* (formal) **1** [U] respect for someone or something, or when you show respect to someone or something: *Doctors are **held in high regard*** (=respected very much) *by society.* | *You have no **regard for** my feelings!* **2 with/in regard to sth** (formal) used in order to say what you are talking or writing about: *Several changes have been made with regard to security.* **3 regards** [plural] used in order to send good wishes to someone in a polite and slightly formal way: ***Give my regards** to your parents.*

regard² *v.* [T] **1** [not in progressive] to think about someone or something in a particular way: *I've always **regarded** you **as** my friend.* | *Carl's work is **highly regarded** by critics.* **2** (formal) to look at someone or something, especially in a particular way: *She regarded him thoughtfully.*

THESAURUS **look, glance, stare, gaze** ➔ LOOK¹

re·gard·ing /rɪˈgɑrdɪŋ/ *prep.* (formal) a word used especially in business letters to introduce the particular subject you are writing about: *Regarding your recent inquiry, I've enclosed our new brochure.*

THESAURUS **about, concerning, with regard to, re** ➔ ABOUT¹

re·gard·less /rɪˈgɑrdlɪs/ *adv.* **1 regardless of sth** without being affected by different situations, problems, etc.: *The law requires equal treatment for all, regardless of race, religion, or sex.* **2** if you continue doing something regardless, you do it in spite of difficulties or people telling you not to do it: *He does what he wants **regardless of** what I say.*

re·gat·ta /rɪˈgɑṭə, -ˈgæ-/ *n.* [C] a race for rowing or sailing boats [ORIGIN: 1600—1700 Italian *regattare* "to compete"]

re·gen·er·ate /rɪˈdʒɛnəˌreɪt/ *v.* [I,T] (formal) to develop and grow strong again, or to make something do this: *Given time, the forest will regenerate.* —**regeneration** /rɪˌdʒɛnəˈreɪʃən/ *n.* [U]

re·gent /ˈridʒənt/ *n.* [C] a member of a small group of people that makes decisions about education in a U.S. state, or that governs a university

reg·gae /ˈrɛgeɪ/ *n.* [U] a type of popular music from Jamaica [ORIGIN: 1900—2000 Jamaican English *rege* "rags"]

re·gime /reɪˈʒim, rɪ-/ (Ac) *n.* [C] POLITICS a government, especially one that was not elected fairly, or that you disapprove of: *a brutal **military regime*** [ORIGIN: 1400—1500 French *régime*, from Latin *regimen*, from *regere* "to rule"]

THESAURUS **government, democracy, republic, monarchy, dictatorship, totalitarian country/state etc., police state** ➔ GOVERNMENT

re·gi·men /ˈrɛdʒəmən/ *also* **regime** *n.* [C] a special plan for eating, exercising, etc. that is intended to improve your health

reg·i·ment /ˈrɛdʒəmənt/ *n.* [C] a large group of soldiers consisting of several BATTALIONS —**regimental** /ˌrɛdʒəˈmɛntl/ *adj.*

reg·i·ment·ed /ˈrɛdʒəˌmɛnṭɪd/ *adj.* controlled very strictly: *Prisoners follow a highly regimented schedule.* —**regimentation** /ˌrɛdʒəmənˈteɪʃən/ *n.* [U]

re·gion /ˈridʒən/ (Ac) *n.* [C] **1** a fairly large area of a state, country, etc., usually without exact limits: *Snow is expected in mountain regions.* | *the Burgundy **region of** France*

THESAURUS **area, territory, zone, district** ➔ AREA

2 the area around a particular part of your body: *He has some pain in the lower back region.* **3 (somewhere) in the region of sth** about (SYN) **approximately**: *It will cost in the region of $750.* [ORIGIN: 1300—1400 Old French, Latin *regio*, from *regere* "to rule"]

re·gion·al /ˈridʒənl/ (Ac) *adj.* relating to a particular region: *a regional accent* —**regionally** *adv.*

ˌregional ˈcouncil *n.* [C] POLITICS a COUNCIL OF GOVERNMENTS

re·gion·al·ism /ˈridʒənl̩ˌɪzəm/ *n.* [U] POLITICS loyalty to a particular part of a country and the desire for it to be more politically independent

reg·is·ter¹ /ˈrɛdʒəstɚ/ (Ac) *n.* **1** [C] a book containing an official list or record of something: *He signed the register at the hotel.* **2** [C] the place where the warm or cool air of a heating system comes into a room, with a metal cover you can open or close (SYN) **vent** **3** [C,U] ENG. LANG. ARTS a way of speaking or writing that is formal, informal, humorous, etc. that you use when you are in a particular situation **4** [C] a CASH REGISTER

register² (Ac) *v.* **1** [I,T] to record a name, details about something, etc. on an official list: *The car is registered in my sister's name.* **2** [I,T] to officially arrange to attend a particular school, university, or course (SYN) **enroll**: *How many students have* ***registered for*** *Beginning Japanese?* **3** [T] (formal) to express a feeling or opinion about something: *Her face registered surprise and shock.* **4** [I,T] if an instrument registers an amount, or if an amount registers on it, the instrument shows or records that amount: *The thermometer registered 74°F.*

ˌregistered ˈmail *n.* [U] a service in which the post office records the time when your mail is sent and delivered

ˌregistered ˈnurse (*abbreviation* **RN**) *n.* [C] someone who has been trained and is officially allowed to work as a nurse

reg·is·trar /ˈrɛdʒəˌstrɑr/ *n.* [C] someone who is in charge of official records, especially in a college

reg·is·tra·tion /ˌrɛdʒəˈstreɪʃən/ (Ac) *n.* **1** [U] the process of officially arranging to attend a particular school, university, or class (SYN) **enrollment** **2** [U] the act of recording names and details on an official list: *laws requiring the* ***registration of*** *handguns* **3** [C] an official piece of paper containing details about a vehicle and the name of its owner: *May I see your* ***license and registration****, Ma'am?*

reg·is·try /ˈrɛdʒəstri/ *n.* (plural **registries**) [C] a place where official records are kept

re·gress /rɪˈgrɛs/ *v.* [I] to go back to an earlier, less developed state (ANT) **progress** —**regression** /rɪˈgrɛʃən/ *n.* [U]

re·gret¹ /rɪˈgrɛt/ *v.* (**regretted**, **regretting**) [T] **1** to feel sorry about something you have done and wish you had not done it: *We've always regretted selling that car.* | *He* ***regrets that*** *he never went to college.* | *You'll* ***regret it*** *if you leave your job now.* **2** (formal) [not in progressive] to be sorry and sad about a situation: *I* ***regret that*** *I will be unable to attend.*

regret² *n.* [C,U] sadness that you feel about something because you wish it had not happened or that you had not done it: *The company* ***expressed*** *deep* ***regret at*** *the accident.* | *Carl said he* ***had*** *no* ***regrets about*** *his decision.* —**regretfully** *adv.* —**regretful** *adj.*

re·gret·ta·ble /rɪˈgrɛt̬əbəl/ *adj.* something that is regrettable is something that you wish had not happened: *a regrettable mistake* —**regrettably** *adv.*

re·group /ˌriˈgrup/ *v.* [I,T] to form a group again in order to be more effective, or to make people do this: *The party needs time to regroup politically.*

reg·u·lar¹ /ˈrɛgyəlɚ/ *adj.*
1 REPEATED happening every hour, every week, every month, etc., usually with the same amount of time in between: *His heartbeat is strong and regular.* | *We hear from him* ***on a regular basis.*** | *Planes were taking off* ***at regular intervals.***

THESAURUS

hourly – happening or done every hour: *Legal advisors usually charge an hourly fee.* | *The tour of the studio departs hourly.*
daily – happening or done every day: *a daily newspaper* | *The park is open daily from 10:00 am.*
weekly – happening or done every week: *She writes a weekly column for the Boston Globe.* | *Our website is updated weekly.*
monthly – happening or done every month: *regular monthly meetings* | *The magazine is published monthly.*
yearly – happening or done every year: *yearly visits to his mother* | *The hospital keeps a record of the number of the operations performed yearly.*
annual – happening every year: *We hold our annual convention in May.*

2 OFTEN happening or doing something very often: *He's one of our regular customers.* | *Regular exercise will help you lose weight.*
3 USUAL normal or usual: *She's not our regular babysitter.*
4 ORDINARY ordinary, without any special features or qualities: *He's just* ***a regular guy.***
5 NORMAL SIZE of standard size: *fries and a regular Coke*
6 EVENLY SHAPED evenly shaped, with parts or sides of equal size: *regular features* (=an evenly shaped face)
7 GRAMMAR ENG. LANG. ARTS a regular verb or noun changes its forms in the same way as most verbs or nouns. The verb "walk" is regular, but "be" is not. [ORIGIN: 1300—1400 Old French *reguler*, from Latin *regula* "edge for drawing straight lines, rule"] —**regularity** /ˌrɛgyəˈlærət̬i/ *n.* [U]

regular² *n.* **1** [C] (informal) a customer who goes to the same store, restaurant, etc. very often: *The bartender knows all the regulars by name.* **2** [U] gas that contains LEAD

reg·u·lar·ly /ˈrɛgyəlɚli, ˈrɛgyɚli/ *adv.* **1** at regular times, for example every day, week, or month: *Brush your teeth and see your dentist regularly.* **2** often: *Janet comes to visit regularly.*

THESAURUS **often, a lot, frequently, repeatedly** → OFTEN

reg·u·late /ˈrɛgyəˌleɪt/ (Ac) *v.* [T] **1** to control an activity or process, usually by having rules: *The use of these drugs is strictly regulated.* **2** (formal) to make a machine or your body work at a particular speed, temperature, etc.: *People sweat to regulate their body heat.*

reg·u·la·tion /ˌrɛgyəˈleɪʃən/ *n.* **1** [C] an official rule or order: *safety regulations* | *There seem to be so many* ***rules and regulations****.*

THESAURUS **rule, law, restriction, guidelines, statute** → RULE[1]

2 [C,U] ECONOMICS government control over the sale of particular goods or services in a country, or official limits on particular goods coming into or going out of a country: *The total amount of bank credit is restricted by* ***federal government regulations****.* | *the* ***regulation of*** *trade*

reg·u·la·tor /ˈrɛgyəˌleɪtɚ/ (Ac) *n.* [C] **1** someone or something that makes sure that an activity, system, or process operates in the right way: *regulators of the banking system* **2** an instrument or system for controlling the temperature, speed, etc. of something: *Scuba divers breathe through a regulator so that they get the right amount of oxygen.*

reg·u·la·to·ry /ˈrɛgyələˌtɔri/ (Ac) *adj.* (formal) having the purpose of controlling an activity or process, especially by rules: *the Nuclear Regulatory Commission*

re·gur·gi·tate /rɪˈgɚdʒəˌteɪt/ *v.* (formal) **1** [I,T] VOMIT **2** [T] (disapproving) to repeat facts, ideas, etc. that you have heard or read without understanding them clearly yourself —**regurgitation** /rɪˌgɚdʒəˈteɪʃən/ *n.* [U]

re·hab /ˈrihæb/ *n.* [U] (informal) treatment to help someone who takes drugs or drinks too much alcohol. *Frank's been* ***in rehab*** *for six weeks.*

re·ha·bil·i·tate /ˌriəˈbɪləˌteɪt, ˌrihə-/ *v.* [T] **1** to help someone to live a healthy or useful life again after s/he has been sick or in prison: *The program helps to rehabilitate young criminals.* **2** to improve a building or area so that it is in a good condition again —**rehabilitation** /ˌriəˌbɪləˈteɪʃən, ˌrihə-/ *n.* [U]

re·hash /riˈhæʃ/ *v.* [T] (informal, disapproving) to use the same ideas again in a new form that is not really different or better: *He keeps rehashing the same old speech.* —**rehash** /ˈrihæʃ/ *n.* [C]

re·hears·al /rɪˈhɚsəl/ *n.* [C,U] ENG. LANG. ARTS a period of time or a particular occasion when all the people in a play, concert, etc. practice it before giving a public performance: *a* ***rehearsal for*** *"Romeo and Juliet"*

re·hearse /rɪˈhɚs/ *v.* [I,T] to practice something such as a play or concert before giving a public performance: *They* ***rehearsed*** *the* ***scene*** *in her dressing room.* [ORIGIN: 1200—1300 Old French *rehercier*, from *herce* "farm tool for breaking up soil"]

THESAURUS **practice, work on sth** → PRACTICE[2]

Reich /raɪk/ *n.* HISTORY the German state or EMPIRE during a particular period of its history

reign[1] /reɪn/ *n.* **1** [C] the period of time during which someone rules a country: *the* ***reign of*** *Queen Anne* **2** [singular] a period of time during which someone is in control of an organization, business, etc.: *his four-year reign as team coach* **3 reign of terror** a period during which a government, army, etc. uses violence to control people [ORIGIN: 1200—1300 Old French *regne*, from Latin *regnum*, from *rex* "king"]

reign[2] *v.* [I] **1** to be the ruler of a country **2 the reigning champion** the most recent winner of a competition **3** (literary) if a feeling or quality reigns, it is the main feature of the situation: *For a few moments* ***confusion reigned****.*

re·im·burse /ˌriɪmˈbɚs/ *v.* [T] (formal) to pay money back to someone: *The company will* ***reimburse*** *you* ***for*** *your travel expenses.* —**reimbursement** *n.* [U]

rein /reɪn/ *n.* **1** [C usually plural] a long narrow band of leather that is fastened around a horse's head in order to control it **2 give sb (a) free rein** to give someone complete freedom to say or do things the way s/he wants to **3 keep a tight rein on sb/sth** to control someone or something strictly: *The government is trying to keep a tight rein on public spending.* [ORIGIN: 1200—1300 Old French *rene*, from Latin *retinere*, from *tenere* "to hold"]

re·in·car·nate /ˌriɪnˈkɑrˌneɪt/ *v.* **be reincarnated** to be born again in another body after you have died

re·in·car·na·tion /ˌriɪnkɑrˈneɪʃən/ *n.* **1** [U] the belief that people return to life in another body after they have died **2** [C] the person or animal that a person becomes when they are reincarnated

rein·deer /ˈreɪndɪr/ *n.* [C] a type of DEER with long horns that lives in very cold places

re·in·force /ˌriɪnˈfɔrs/ (Ac) *v.* [T] **1** to support an opinion, feeling, system, etc. and make it stronger: *The fire safety rules will be reinforced by regular drills.* **2** to make something stronger, such as a part of a building, a piece of clothing, etc.: *The concrete wall is reinforced with steel rods.*

re·in·force·ment /ˌriɪnˈfɔrsmənt/ (Ac) *n.* **1** [U] the act of doing something to make an opinion, statement, feeling, etc. stronger: *Parents should* ***give*** *their children* ***positive reinforcement*** *when their behavior is good* (=praise them so that they will behave well again). **2 reinforcements** [plural] more soldiers or police who are sent to help make a group stronger: *The police* ***called for reinforcements****.* **3** [U] the act of making something stronger: *The bridge needs some structural reinforcement.*

re·in·state /ˌriɪnˈsteɪt/ *v.* [T] **1** to put someone back into a job that s/he had before: *Two employees who were wrongfully fired will be reinstated.* **2** if a law, system, or practice is reinstated, it begins to be used after not being used —**reinstatement** *n.* [C,U]

R

re·in·ter·pret /ˌriɪnˈtɚprɪt/ (Ac) *v.* [T] (formal) to think about or perform something again in a slightly different way, especially to understand it in a new way: *The book reinterprets the Dracula legend.* —**reinterpretation** /ˌriɪntɚprəˈteɪʃən/ *n.* [C,U]

re·in·vent /ˌriɪnˈvɛnt/ *v.* [T] **1 reinvent yourself** to completely change your appearance and image: *To stay popular, pop stars must often reinvent themselves.* **2** to make changes to an existing idea, method, system, etc. in order to improve it or make it more modern: *The changes are an attempt to reinvent the American educational system.* **3 reinvent the wheel** (informal) to waste time trying to find a way of doing something, when someone else has already discovered the best way to do it

re·is·sue /riˈɪʃu/ *v.* [T] to produce a record, book, etc. again, after it has not been available for some time —**reissue** *n.* [C]

R

re·it·e·rate /riˈɪt̬əˌreɪt/ *v.* [T] (formal) to say something more than once: *Lawyers* ***reiterated that*** *there was no direct evidence against Mr. Evans.* —**reiteration** /riˌɪt̬əˈreɪʃən/ *n.* [C,U]

re·ject¹ /rɪˈdʒɛkt/ (Ac) *v.* [T] **1** to not accept someone or something: *She rejected our offers of help.* | *Tom was rejected by several law schools.*

THESAURUS

reject – to say firmly that you will not accept an offer or suggestion: *Morse's book was rejected by many publishers.*
refuse – to say firmly that you do not want something that you have been offered: *They refused all offers of help.*
turn down (informal) – to say that you do not want something that you have been offered – use this especially when this is surprising: *An advertising company offered her a job, but she turned it down.*
say no (spoken) – to say you do not want something or will not accept a suggestion: *I asked him if he wanted a drink, but he said no.*
decline (formal) – to say politely that you cannot or will not accept an offer: *Mr. and Mrs. Forester declined the invitation.* → ACCEPT, AGREE, REFUSE¹

2 to decide that you do not believe in or agree with something: *Kim has rejected her parents' religious beliefs.* **3** to not give someone love or attention: *She feels rejected by her parents.* **4** if your body rejects an organ that doctors have put in your body to replace your own, your body produces substances that attack the organ [ORIGIN: 1400—1500 Latin, past participle of *reicere* "to throw back"]

re·ject² /ˈridʒɛkt/ (Ac) *n.* [C] **1** a product that is thrown away because it is damaged or imperfect **2** (spoken) someone who is not accepted or liked by other people

re·jec·tion /rɪˈdʒɛkʃən/ (Ac) *n.* **1** [C,U] the act of not accepting something: *The council's* ***rejection of*** *the proposal was unexpected.* | *She received many rejections before the novel was published.* **2** [U] a situation in which someone stops giving you love or attention: *fear of rejection* **3** [U] a situation in which your body rejects an organ

re·joice /rɪˈdʒɔɪs/ *v.* [I] (literary) to feel or show that you are very happy —**rejoicing** *n.* [U]

re·join /rɪˈdʒɔɪn/ *v.* [T] to return to a group or person: *She rejoined her friends in the lobby.*

re·join·der /rɪˈdʒɔɪndɚ/ *n.* [C] (formal) a reply, especially one that is rude

re·ju·ve·nate /rɪˈdʒuvəˌneɪt/ *v.* [T] **1** to make someone feel or look young and strong again: *After a workout, I feel rejuvenated.* **2** to make a system or place better again: *the rejuvenated downtown area* —**rejuvenation** /rɪˌdʒuvəˈneɪʃən/ *n.* [singular, U]

re·kin·dle /riˈkɪndl/ *v.* [T] to make someone have a particular feeling, thought, etc. again: *Was this a chance to rekindle an old romance?*

re·lapse /rɪˈlæps/ *n.* [C,U] a situation in which someone feels sick again after seeming to improve: *He's* ***had/suffered a relapse.*** [ORIGIN: 1400—1500 Latin, past participle of *relabi* "to slide back"] —**relapse** *v.* [I]

re·late /rɪˈleɪt/ *v.* **1** [T] to show or prove a connection between two or more things: *I don't understand how the two ideas relate.* **2** [I] to be concerned with or directly connected to a particular subject: *How does this job* ***relate to*** *your career goals?* **3** [T] (formal) to tell someone about something that has happened: *He later* ***related*** *the whole story* ***to*** *us.*

relate to sb/sth *phr. v.* to understand how someone feels: *I find it hard to relate to kids.*

re·lat·ed /rɪˈleɪt̬ɪd/ *adj.* **1** connected by similar ideas or dealing with similar subjects: *Police believe the murders are related.* | *Lung cancer and other diseases are* ***related to*** *smoking.* | *Politics and economics are* ***closely related.***

THESAURUS

connected/linked – related: *These two problems are closely connected with each other.* | *Police think that the crimes may be linked.*
relevant – related to what you are talking about: *Are you sure this is relevant to our discussion?*
pertinent (formal) – if something is pertinent to what is being discussed, it is directly related to it and it is important to consider it: *They asked some very pertinent questions.*
have nothing to do with sth (spoken) – to have no relation or effect on what you are discussing: *They deserved to win. Luck has nothing to do with it.*

2 stress-related/drug-related etc. caused by or relating to stress, drugs, etc.: *alcohol-related violence* **3** connected by a family relationship: *Are you* ***related to*** *Paula?*

re·la·tion /rɪˈleɪʃən/ *n.* **1 in relation to sb/sth** used when comparing two things or showing the relationship between them: *The area of land is tiny* *in relation to the population.* **2 relations** [plural] official connections and attitudes between countries, organizations, groups, etc.: *Are the **relations between** the staff and students good?* | *Israel's **relations with** its Arab neighbors* | *The U.S. has maintained **diplomatic relations** with Laos.* **3** [C,U] a connection between two things: *Is there any **relation between** the medication he was taking and his death?* | *This case **bears no relation to*** (=is not connected with or similar to) *the Goldman trial.* **4** [C] a member of your family SYN **relative**

THESAURUS family, relative, folks, kin → FAMILY

re·la·tion·ship /rɪˈleɪʃən,ʃɪp/ *n.* **1** [C] the way in which two people or groups behave toward each other: *They seem to **have** a good **relationship**.* | *A mother's **relationship with** her children is important to their development.* | *In his speech, he mentioned the special **relationship between** the U.S. and Britain.* **2** [C] a situation in which two people have sexual or romantic feelings for each other: *a **sexual relationship*** | *He's much happier now that he's **in a relationship**.* **3** [C,U] the way in which two or more things are related to each other: *The study looked at the **relationship between** pay and performance at work.*

rel·a·tive¹ /ˈrɛlət̬ɪv/ *n.* [C] a member of your family: ***a close relative*** (=mother, brother, cousin, etc.) | ***distant relatives*** (=second or third cousins, etc. that you rarely see)

THESAURUS family, relation, folks, kin → FAMILY

relative² *adj.* **1** having a particular quality when compared with something else: *The 1950s were a time of **relative peace/calm/prosperity** for the country.* **2 relative to sth** relating to or compared with a particular subject: *Demand for corn is low relative to the supply.*

,relative 'clause *n.* [C] ENG. LANG. ARTS a part of a sentence that has a verb in it and is joined to the rest of the sentence by a RELATIVE PRONOUN. In the sentence "The dress that I bought is too small," "that I bought" is the relative clause.

rel·a·tive·ly /ˈrɛlət̬ɪvli/ *adv.* to a particular degree, especially when compared to something similar: *It's a relatively inexpensive restaurant.*

,relative 'pronoun *n.* [C] ENG. LANG. ARTS a PRONOUN such as "who," "which," or "that," which connects a relative clause to the rest of the sentence. In the sentence "The dress that I bought is too small," "that" is the relative pronoun.

rel·a·tiv·i·ty /,rɛləˈtɪvət̬i/ *n.* [U] PHYSICS the relationship between time, space, and movement: *Einstein's theory of relativity*

re·lax /rɪˈlæks/ Ac *v.* **1** [I,T] to become more calm and less worried, especially by resting or doing something enjoyable, or to make someone do this: *What do you do to relax?* | *Taking long, deep, regular breaths can help to relax you.* **2** [I,T] if a part of your body relaxes, or if you relax it, it becomes less stiff and tight: *Try to relax your neck.* | *Let your muscles relax.* **3** [T] to make rules, controls, etc. less strict: *Are there plans to relax the law?* [ORIGIN: 1300—1400 Latin *relaxare* "to loosen," from *laxus* "loose"]

re·lax·a·tion /,rilækˈseɪʃən/ Ac *n.* **1** [C,U] the state of being relaxed in your mind and body, or the process of becoming this way: *I like to cook **for relaxation**.* **2** [U] the process of making rules, controls, etc. less strict: *the **relaxation of** travel restrictions*

re·laxed /rɪˈlækst/ Ac *adj.* **1** calm and not worried or angry: *He looked much more relaxed when I saw him last week.*

THESAURUS calm, laid-back, easygoing, mellow, cool, serene → CALM²

2 a situation or attitude that is relaxed is informal and not strict: *There's a **relaxed atmosphere** in class.*

re·lax·ing /rɪˈlæksɪŋ/ Ac *adj.* making you feel calm: *relaxing music*

re·lay¹ /ˈrileɪ, rɪˈleɪ/ *v.* (**relayed**, **relays**) [T] to send a message or information from one person, thing, or place to another person, thing, or place: *Could you **relay** the message **to** Mary for me?*

re·lay² /ˈrileɪ/ *also* **'relay race** *n.* [C] a race in which each member of a team runs or swims part of the distance

re·lease¹ /rɪˈlis/ Ac *v.* [T] **1** to allow someone to be free after you have kept him/her somewhere: *Three hostages were released this morning.* | *With this type of operation, patients are usually **released from** the hospital the same day..* **2** to stop holding something: *He released her arm when she screamed.* **3** to let news or information be known publicly: *Details of the crime have not been released.* **4** to make a movie, record, etc. available for people to buy or see: *The movie will be released in time for Christmas.* [ORIGIN: 1200—1300 Old French *relessier*, from Latin *relaxare* "to loosen"]

release² Ac *n.* **1** [singular] the act of allowing someone to be free after s/he has been kept somewhere: *After his **release from** prison, he worked as a carpenter.* **2** [C] a new movie, record, etc. that is available for people to see or buy: *the singer's latest release* **3** [U] a feeling that you are free from worry or pain: *a sense of emotional release* **4** [C,U] an official statement, report, etc. that can be printed or broadcast, or the act of making this available: *a press release* | *the release of previously secret information*

rel·e·gate /ˈrɛlə,geɪt/ *v.* [T] (formal) to make someone or something less important than before: *He's been **relegated to** the role of assistant.* [ORIGIN: 1400—1500 Latin, past participle of *relegare* "to send back to do a job"]

re·lent /rɪˈlɛnt/ *v.* [I] to let someone do something

that you refused to let him/her do before: *At last, her father relented and she moved into her own apartment.* [ORIGIN: 1300—1400 Latin *lentare* "to bend"]

re·lent·less /rɪ'lɛntlɪs/ *adj.* **1** if something bad is relentless, it continues without stopping or getting less severe: *There's relentless pressure on top athletes.* | *the relentless heat of the desert* **2** someone who is relentless continues to do something in a determined way: *We will be **relentless in** our pursuit of criminals.* —**relentlessly** *adv.*

rel·e·vant /'rɛləvənt/ (Ac) *adj.* directly relating to the subject or problem being discussed (ANT) **irrelevant**: *The question is not **relevant to** my point.* | *We told the police all the relevant facts.* —**relevance** *n.* [U]

THESAURUS **related, connected, linked, pertinent** → RELATED

re·li·a·ble /rɪ'laɪəbəl/ (Ac) *adj.* someone or something that is reliable can be trusted or depended on (SYN) **dependable** (ANT) **unreliable**: *a reliable car* | *Our babysitter is very reliable.* —**reliably** *adv.* —**reliability** /rɪˌlaɪə'bɪləṭi/ *n.* [U]

R

re·li·ance /rɪ'laɪəns/ (Ac) *n.* [singular, U] the state of being dependent on something: *We need to reduce our **reliance on** imported oil.*

re·li·ant /rɪ'laɪənt/ (Ac) *adj.* **be reliant on/upon sb/sth** to depend on something or someone → RELY: *She's still reliant on her parents for money.*

rel·ic /'rɛlɪk/ *n.* [C] something from the past that still exists: ***relics of** ancient Egypt* [ORIGIN: 1200—1300 Old French *relique*, from Latin *reliquiae* "things left behind"]

re·lief /rɪ'lif/ *n.* **1** [singular, U] the happy feeling you have when something frightening, worrying, or painful has ended or has not happened: *Final exams are finally over. **What a relief!*** | ***It was a relief** to finally be alone.* | *No one was hurt, and we all **breathed a sigh of relief**.* | *She listened to the news **with relief**.* **2** [U] the reduction of pain: *a medicine for **pain relief*** | ***relief from** the intense heat* **3** [U] money, food, clothing, etc. given to people who need them by a government or other organization: ***disaster/earthquake/flood relief** operations* | ***Relief workers** distributed bottles of water.* **4** [C] a person or group of people that replaces another one and does their work after they have finished: *a relief pitcher*

re·lieve /rɪ'liv/ *v.* [T] **1** to make a pain, problem, bad feeling, etc. less severe: *The county is building a new school to relieve overcrowding.* | *We tried to **relieve the boredom/tension** by singing.*

THESAURUS **reduce, ease, lessen, soothe, alleviate, palliate** → REDUCE

2 to replace someone else at a job or duty: *The guards are relieved at six o'clock.*

relieve sb of sth *phr. v.* (formal) to help someone by carrying something heavy or by doing something difficult for him/her: *He rose and relieved her of her bags.*

re·lieved /rɪ'livd/ *adj.* feeling happy because something bad did not happen or is finished → RELIEF: *I was **relieved to be** out of the hospital.* | *We were **relieved that** Brian was home safe.*

re·li·gion /rɪ'lɪdʒən/ *n.* [C,U] belief in one or more gods, or a particular system of beliefs in one or more gods: *the study of religion* | *people **of different religions*** [ORIGIN: 1100—1200 Latin *religio*]

THESAURUS **faith, belief, creed** → FAITH

re·li·gious /rɪ'lɪdʒəs/ *adj.* **1** relating to religion: *We don't share the same **religious beliefs**.* **2** believing strongly in your religion and obeying its rules: *a very religious woman*

THESAURUS

devout – having very strong religious beliefs: *a devout Catholic*
pious – believing strongly in a religion, and showing this in how you behave: *a pious woman attending church*
God-fearing (old-fashioned) – behaving according to the moral rules of a religion: *the God-fearing men and women of this town*
practicing – obeying the rules of a particular religion: *a practicing Muslim*
orthodox – believing in all the traditional beliefs, laws, and practices of a religion: *orthodox Jews*

re·li·gious·ly /rɪ'lɪdʒəsli/ *adv.* **1** regularly and thoroughly or completely: *He exercises religiously.* **2** in a way that is related to religion: *a religiously diverse country* (=one with many different religions)

re·lin·quish /rɪ'lɪŋkwɪʃ/ *v.* [T] (formal) to give up your position, power, rights, etc.

rel·ish[1] /'rɛlɪʃ/ *v.* [T] to enjoy something or like it: *Jamie **didn't relish the idea of** getting up early.*

THESAURUS **enjoy, like, love** → ENJOY

relish[2] *n.* **1** [C,U] a cold SAUCE eaten especially with meat to add taste: *pickle relish* **2** [U] great enjoyment of something: *Barry ate **with great relish**.*

re·live /ˌri'lɪv/ *v.* [T] to experience something again that happened in past times, or to remember it clearly: *I'm focusing on the future, not reliving the past.*

re·load /ˌri'loʊd/ *v.* [I,T] **1** to put something into a container again, especially bullets into a gun **2** IT if you reload a page on the Internet, you ask for the information shown on that page to be sent to your computer again

re·lo·cate /ri'loʊˌkeɪt/ (Ac) *v.* [I,T] to move to a new place: *Our company **relocated to** the West Coast.* —**relocation** /ˌriloʊ'keɪʃən/ *n.* [U]

re·luc·tant /rɪˈlʌktənt/ (Ac) *adj.* unwilling and slow to do something: *a reluctant nod* | *She was* ***reluctant to*** *ask for help.* —**reluctance** *n.* [singular, U] —**reluctantly** *adv.*

re·ly /rɪˈlaɪ/ (Ac) *v.* (**relied**, **relies**) [ORIGIN: 1300—1400 Old French *relier*, from Latin *religare* "to tie back"]

rely on/upon sb/sth *phr. v.* to trust or depend on someone or something: *We're relying on him to help.* | *The country's economy relies heavily on agricultural exports.*

re·main /rɪˈmeɪn/ *v.* **1** [I, linking verb] to stay in the same place or condition: *The others left, while I remained at home.* | *Veltman* ***remained silent.*** **2** [I] to continue to exist after other things or parts have gone or been destroyed: *Only half the statue remains.* **3** [I] if something remains to be done, said, etc., it still needs to be done, said, etc.: *Many questions remain to be answered.* | *It* ***remains to be seen*** *whether the operation was successful* (=we do not know yet whether it was successful). [ORIGIN: 1300—1400 Old French *remaindre*, from Latin *remanere*, from *manere* "to stay"]

re·main·der /rɪˈmeɪndɚ/ *n.* **the remainder (of sth)** the rest of something after everything else has gone or been dealt with: *the remainder of the semester*

re·main·ing /rɪˈmeɪnɪŋ/ *adj.* still left when other similar things or people have gone or been dealt with: *The remaining puppies were given away.*

re·mains /rɪˈmeɪnz/ *n.* [plural] **1** the parts of something that are left after the rest has been destroyed: *We visited* ***the remains of*** *the temple.* **2** (formal) a person's body after s/he has died

re·make /ˈrimeɪk/ *n.* [C] a movie or song that has the same story as one that was made before: *a* ***remake of*** *"The Wizard of Oz"* —**remake** /riˈmeɪk/ *v.* [T]

re·mand /rɪˈmænd/ *v.* [T] **1** LAW if a court remands someone, it sends him/her to prison to wait for a TRIAL: *The prosecutor asked the judge to* ***remand*** *Nelson* ***into*** *federal* ***custody.*** **2** LAW to send a case to be dealt with in another court

re·mark[1] /rɪˈmɑrk/ *n.* [C] something that you say: *Carl* ***made*** *a sarcastic* ***remark.***

remark[2] *v.* [T] to say something, especially your opinion about something: *One woman* ***remarked that*** *he was handsome.* | *Several people* ***remarked on/upon*** *the poor service.*

re·mark·a·ble /rɪˈmɑrkəbəl/ *adj.* very unusual or noticeable in a way that deserves attention or praise: *Josephine was a truly remarkable woman.*

re·mark·a·bly /rɪˈmɑrkəbli/ *adv.* in a way that is surprising: *Charlotte and her cousin look remarkably similar.*

re·mar·ry /riˈmæri/ *v.* (**remarried**, **remarries**) [I,T] to marry again: *After her husband's death, Carol never remarried.* —**remarriage** *n.* [C,U]

re·mas·ter /riˈmæstɚ/ *v.* [T] to improve the quality of a movie or musical recording, using a computer

re·me·di·al /rɪˈmidiəl/ *adj.* **1 remedial class/education etc.** a special class, etc. for students who are having difficulty learning something **2** (formal) intended to provide a cure or improvement in something

rem·e·dy[1] /ˈrɛmədi/ *n.* (plural **remedies**) [C] **1** a successful way of dealing with a problem: *a* ***remedy for*** *unemployment*

THESAURUS **solution, answer, cure** → SOLUTION

2 a medicine that cures pain or illness: *a cold remedy* [ORIGIN: 1200—1300 Anglo-French *remedie*, from Latin *remedium*, from *mederi* "to heal"]

remedy[2] *v.* (**remedied**, **remedies**) [T] to deal successfully with a problem or improve a bad situation: *The hospital is trying to remedy the problem.*

re·mem·ber /rɪˈmɛmbɚ/ *v.* **1** [I,T] to have a picture or idea in your mind of people, events, etc. from the past: *Do you remember that guy Anthony from school?* | *I don't remember meeting her before.* | ***I remember (that)*** *he had a broken leg that summer.* | *Mr. Daniels has lived there* ***for as long as I can remember.*** **2** [I,T] to bring information or facts that you know back into your mind: *She suddenly* ***remembered (that)*** *she had to go to the dentist.* | *I can't remember her phone number.* **3** [I,T] to not forget to do something: ***Remember to*** *get some milk at the store today!* **4** [T] to think about someone who has died, with special respect and honor: *On Memorial Day, we remember those who have died in wars.* **5 be remembered for/as sth** to be famous for something important that you did [ORIGIN: 1300—1400 Old French *remembrer*, from Latin *memor* "remembering"]

USAGE

remember – to think of something that you must do, and not forget about it: *I hope he remembers to bring the wine.*

remind – to make someone remember something s/he must do or something s/he needs to know: *Remind me to take a bottle of wine to the party.*

re·mem·brance /rɪˈmɛmbrəns/ *n.* [U] the act of remembering and giving honor to someone who has died: *She planted a tree* ***in remembrance of*** *her husband.*

re·mind /rɪˈmaɪnd/ *v.* [T] to make someone remember something that s/he must do: ***Remind*** *me* ***to*** *tell you the story sometime.* | *Let me call Frank to* ***remind*** *him* ***that*** *we're picking him up at 8:00.* → see USAGE box at REMEMBER

remind sb **of** sb/sth *phr. v.* to seem similar to

someone or something else: *Carl reminds me of his father.*

re·mind·er /rɪˈmaɪndɚ/ *n.* [C] something that makes you notice or remember something else: *a painful* ***reminder of*** *the war*

rem·i·nisce /ˌrɛməˈnɪs/ *v.* [I] to talk or think about pleasant events in your past: *We sat* ***reminiscing about*** *our college days.* —**reminiscence** *n.* [C,U]

rem·i·nis·cent /ˌrɛməˈnɪsənt/ *adj.* **reminiscent of sth** reminding you of something: *His voice is reminiscent of Frank Sinatra's.*

re·miss /rɪˈmɪs/ *adj.* (formal) careless about doing something that you ought to do: *Investigators would* ***be remiss*** *if they didn't pursue every possible lead.*

re·mis·sion /rɪˈmɪʃən/ *n.* [C,U] a period of time when an illness improves: *Her cancer* ***is in remission.***

re·mit /rɪˈmɪt/ *v.* (**remitted, remitting**) [I,T] (formal) to send a payment by mail

R

re·mit·tance /rɪˈmɪt˺ns/ *n.* [C,U] (formal) the act of sending money by mail, or the amount of money that is sent

rem·nant /ˈrɛmnənt/ *n.* [C] a small part of something that remains after the rest has been used or destroyed: *In New Mexico, there are* ***remnants of*** *old Spain in the street names.*

re·mod·el /ˌriˈmɑdl/ *v.* [T] to change the shape or appearance of something: *We've had the kitchen remodeled.*

rem·on·strate /ˈrɛmənˌstreɪt, rɪˈmɑnˌstreɪt/ *v.* [I] (formal) to tell someone that you strongly disapprove of what s/he has done

re·morse /rɪˈmɔrs/ *n.* [U] a strong feeling of being sorry for doing something very bad: *Keating* ***showed/expressed no remorse*** *for his crime.* —**remorseless** *adj.*: *a remorseless killer* —**remorseful** *adj.*

re·mote /rɪˈmoʊt/ *adj.* **1** far away in distance or time: *a remote forest area | the remote past* **2** very slight or small: *There's* ***a remote possibility/chance that*** *the operation will not work. | The prospects for peace seem very remote.* **3** very different from something else, or not closely related to it: *Political subjects seemed* ***remote from*** *my everyday life.* **4** unfriendly, and not interested in people: *Her father was a remote, stern man.* —**remoteness** *n.* [U]

reˌmote conˈtrol *also* **remote** *n.* [C] a piece of equipment that you use to control a television, video, etc. from a distance → TELEVISION —**remote-controlled** *adj.*: *a remote-controlled car*

re·mote·ly /rɪˈmoʊtli/ *adv.* used in order to emphasize a negative statement: *This is* ***not even remotely*** *funny.*

re·mov·a·ble /rɪˈmuvəbəl/ (Ac) *adj.* able to be removed: *a child's bed with removable railings*

re·mov·al /rɪˈmuvəl/ (Ac) *n.* [C,U] the act of removing something: *the* ***removal of*** *diseased trees from the park | his* ***removal from*** *power*

re·move /rɪˈmuv/ (Ac) *v.* [T] **1** to take something away from, out of, or off the place where it is: *He removed his glasses and rubbed his eyes. |* ***Remove*** *the pan* ***from*** *the oven to cool.*

THESAURUS

Informal ways of saying "remove"

take off – to remove clothing: *She began to take off her clothes.*

tear off – to remove part of a piece of paper or cloth by tearing it: *Tear off the coupon below.*

break off – to remove a part of something by breaking it: *Ted broke off a piece of chocolate.*

cut off – to remove a part of something by cutting it: *Tree surgeons cut off the dead branches.*

cut out – to remove a part of something by cutting around it: *The kids were cutting pictures out of magazines.*

scrape off – to remove something using a knife or sharp tool: *We began by scraping off the wallpaper.*

wipe off/up – to remove dirt, liquid, etc. with a cloth: *He wiped the sweat off his forehead. | Julie wiped up the spilled milk.*

rub off – to remove dirt, marks, etc. with a cloth or brush: *He rubbed off some of the rust.*

More formal ways of saying "remove"

erase – to remove writing from paper, recorded sounds from tape, or information from a computer's memory: *Write in pencil so you can erase your mistakes.*

efface (formal) – to remove something so that it cannot be seen or noticed: *The country has tried to efface the incident, and it is not mentioned in textbooks.*

expunge (formal) – to deliberately remove something such as a name or piece of information from a piece of writing: *The arrest and charge were later expunged from his record.*

2 to get rid of something so it does not exist anymore: *Chocolate ice cream stains are difficult to remove.* **3 be (far) removed from sth** to be very different from something else: *This job is far removed from anything that I've done before.* **4** (formal) to make someone leave a job: *They voted to* ***remove*** *her* ***from*** *office.* [ORIGIN: 1200—1300 Old French *removoir*, from Latin *removere*, from *movere* "to move"]

re·mov·er /rɪˈmuvɚ/ *n.* **paint/stain etc. remover** a substance that removes paint, etc. from something else

re·mu·ner·ate /rɪˈmyunəˌreɪt/ *v.* [T] (formal) to pay someone for something s/he has done —**remuneration** /rɪˌmyunəˈreɪʃən/ *n.* [C,U]

ren·ais·sance /ˈrɛnəˌzɑns, -ˌsɑns, ˌrɛnəˈsɑns/ *n.* **1** [singular] a new interest or development in something that has not been popular: *the* ***renaissance in*** *women's sports* **2 the Renaissance** the time in Europe between the 14th and

17th centuries when a lot of new art and literature was produced

re·nal /ˈrinl/ *adj.* [only before noun] BIOLOGY relating to the KIDNEYS: *renal failure*

re·name /riˈneɪm/ *v.* [T] to change the name of something

ren·der /ˈrɛndɚ/ *v.* [T] (formal) **1** to cause someone or something to be in a particular state: *The accident rendered her left leg useless.* **2** to give someone something: *It is the jury's responsibility to render a fair verdict.* | *payment **for services rendered*** (=for work someone has done)

ren·der·ing /ˈrɛndərɪŋ/ *n.* [C] the particular way a painting, story, etc. is expressed

ren·dez·vous /ˈrɑndeɪˌvu, -dɪ-/ *n.* (plural **rendezvous** /-ˌvuz/) [C] an arrangement to meet someone at a particular time and place, or the place where you meet: *a midnight **rendezvous with** her lover* —**rendezvous** *v.* [I]

ren·di·tion /rɛnˈdɪʃən/ *n.* [C] the way that a play, piece of music, art, etc. is performed or made: *a powerful **rendition of** "America the Beautiful"*

ren·e·gade /ˈrɛnəˌgeɪd/ *n.* [C] someone who joins the opposing side in a war, argument, etc. [ORIGIN: 1400—1500 Spanish *renegado*, from Medieval Latin *renegare* "to say that something is not true"] —**renegade** *adj.*: *renegade soldiers*

re·nege /riˈnɛg, -ˈnɪg/ *v.* [I] to not do something that you promised to do: *He **reneged on** his **promise** to send the money.*

re·new /rɪˈnu/ *v.* [T] **1** to arrange for something such as a contract to continue: *It's time to renew our insurance.* | *Library books can be renewed by phone.* **2** (formal) to begin to do something again (SYN) **resume**: *The search will be renewed in the morning.* —**renewal** *n.* [C,U]

re·new·a·ble /rɪˈnuəbəl/ *adj.* **1** a renewable contract, ticket, etc. can be made to continue after the date that it is supposed to end **2** able to be replaced by natural processes so that it is never used up (ANT) **nonrenewable**: *Water is a natural **renewable resource**.* | ***renewable energy**, for example solar power*

re·newed /rɪˈnud/ *adj.* increasing again after not being very strong: *his **renewed interest** in religion*

re·nounce /rɪˈnaʊns/ *v.* [T] **1** to say publicly that you will no longer try to keep something, or will not stay in an important position: *Grayson **renounced his claim to** the family fortune.* **2** to say publicly that you no longer believe in or support something: *We absolutely renounce all forms of terrorism.*

ren·o·vate /ˈrɛnəˌveɪt/ *v.* [T] to repair something such as a building so that it is in good condition again [ORIGIN: 1400—1500 Latin, past participle of *renovare*, from *novare* "to make new"] —**renovation** /ˌrɛnəˈveɪʃən/ *n.* [C,U]

> THESAURUS **repair, fix, restore, rebuild, recondition** → REPAIR²

re·nown /rɪˈnaʊn/ *n.* [U] the quality of being famous and admired because of some special skill or achievement: *an artist **of** great **renown***

re·nowned /rɪˈnaʊnd/ *adj.* known and admired by a lot of people (SYN) **famous**: *a renowned architect* | *She was **renowned for** her beauty.*

> THESAURUS **famous, well-known, legendary, celebrated, noted, distinguished, eminent** → FAMOUS

rent¹ /rɛnt/ *v.* **1** [I,T] to pay money regularly to live in a place that belongs to someone else: *They're renting an apartment near the beach.* | *I rented for years before buying a place.*

> TOPIC
> When you rent a house or apartment, you are called the **tenant**. You usually have to **pay a deposit** before moving in. The **deposit/security deposit** is usually an amount of money equal to a month's rent, or equal to the first and last month's rent. After that you **pay the rent** every month to the **landlord/landlady** (=owner). If you do not pay the rent or behave well, the landlord can **evict** you (=force you to leave). If you want to stop renting the house or apartment, you have to **give notice** (=tell the landlord you want to leave), usually a month before you want to leave.

2 [T] to pay money for the use of something for a short period of time: *We're probably going to rent a car while we're there.* | *Do you want to rent a movie?* **3** [I,T] *also* **rent out** to let someone live in a place that you own, in return for money: *They've rented out their house for the summer.* | *He refused to **rent to** unmarried couples.* —**renter** *n.*

rent² *n.* [C,U] **1** the amount of money you pay for the use of a house, room, car, etc. that belongs to someone else: *I don't know how we're going to **pay the rent** next month.*

> THESAURUS **cost, expense, price, charge, fee, fare** → COST¹

2 for rent available to be rented: *She put the house up for rent a month ago.*

rent·al¹ /ˈrɛntl/ *n.* **1** [C,U] an arrangement by which you rent something: *car rental companies* **2** [U] the money that you pay to rent something: *Ski rental is $14.*

rental² *adj.* available to be rented, or being rented: *a rental car* | *rental properties*

ˈrent conˌtrol *n.* [U] official action taken by a city or state to limit the price of renting apartments

re·nun·ci·a·tion /rɪˌnʌnsiˈeɪʃən/ *n.* [C,U] (formal) the act of renouncing (RENOUNCE) something

re·or·ga·nize /riˈɔrgəˌnaɪz/ *v.* [I,T] to arrange or organize something in a new and better way: *The filing system needs to be reorganized.* —**reorganization** /riˌɔrgənəˈzeɪʃən/ *n.* [U]

> THESAURUS **change, alter, reform, restructure** → CHANGE¹

R

rep /rɛp/ *n.* [C] (informal) someone who represents an organization or a company and its products (SYN) **representative**: *a sales rep*

re·pair¹ /rɪˈpɛr/ *n.* **1** [C usually plural, U] something that you do to fix something that is broken or damaged: *They're **doing repairs** on/to the bridge.* | *The roof is badly **in need of repair**.* | *It's damaged **beyond repair*** (=so damaged that it cannot be repaired). **2 in good/bad repair** (formal) in good or bad condition [ORIGIN: 1300—1400 Old French *reparer*, from Latin *reparare*, from *parare* "to prepare"]

repair

repair² *v.* [T] to fix something that is broken or damaged: *I have to **get** the TV **repaired**.* | *Jones had surgery to **repair** the **damage** to his knees.*

R

THESAURUS

fix – to repair something that is broken or not working correctly: *Someone's coming to fix the washing machine.*
mend – to repair a hole in something, especially a piece of clothing: *She was mending a pair of jeans.*
renovate – to repair a building or furniture so that it is in good condition again: *a renovated 19th century hotel*
restore – to repair something so that it looks new: *The church was carefully restored after the war.*
service – to examine a machine or vehicle and repair it if necessary: *I need to take the car in to get it serviced.*
rebuild – to build something again, after it has been damaged or destroyed: *This government aid will help rebuild homes damaged by the storm.*
recondition – to repair a machine so that it can be sold again: *a VW camper with a reconditioned engine*

re·pair·man /rɪˈpɛrmæn/ *n.* (plural **repairmen** /-mɛn/) [C] someone whose job it is to fix a particular type of thing: *a TV repairman*

rep·a·ra·tion /ˌrɛpəˈreɪʃən/ *n.* [C,U] (formal) payment made to someone for damage, injury, etc. that you have caused: *The government agreed to **pay reparations** to victims.*

re·pa·tri·ate /riˈpeɪtriˌeɪt/ *v.* [T] to send someone back to his/her own country —**repatriation** /riˌpeɪtriˈeɪʃən/ *n.* [U]

re·pay /riˈpeɪ/ *v.* (past tense and past participle **repaid**, third person singular **repays**) [T] **1** to pay back money that you have borrowed: *How long will it take to repay the loan?* **2** to show someone that you are grateful for his/her help: *How can I ever repay you?* —**repayment** *n.* [C,U]

re·peal /rɪˈpil/ *v.* [T] to officially end a law: *In 1933, Prohibition was finally repealed.* —**repeal** *n.* [U]

re·peat¹ /rɪˈpit/ *v.* [T] **1** to say or do something again: *Sally kept repeating, "It wasn't me, it wasn't me."* | *You'll have to repeat the class.* | *He's always **repeating himself*** (=saying the same thing again). **2** to say something that you have heard someone else say: *Please don't **repeat** any of this **to** Bill.*

repeat² *n.* [C] an event that is just like something that happened before: *I don't want to see **a repeat performance** of last year* (=have the same thing happen).

re·peat·ed /rɪˈpit̬ɪd/ *adj.* done or happening again and again: *She has made repeated attempts to lose weight.* —**repeatedly** *adv.*: *He has repeatedly denied the rumor.*

re·pel /rɪˈpɛl/ *v.* (**repelled**, **repelling**) **1** [T] to use force to make someone who is attacking you go away: *Tear gas was used to repel the rioters.* **2** [T] if something repels you, you dislike it a lot and want to avoid it **3** [I,T] PHYSICS if two things repel each other, they push each other away with a MAGNETIC force: *Two positive electrical charges will repel each other.* [ORIGIN: 1400—1500 Latin *repellere*, from *pellere* "to drive"]

re·pel·lent¹ /rɪˈpɛlənt/ *n.* [C,U] a substance that keeps insects away from you: *mosquito repellent*

repellent² *adj.* disgusting: *The sight of blood is repellent to some people.*

re·pent /rɪˈpɛnt/ *v.* [I,T] (formal) to be sorry for something that you have done, especially something that breaks a religious law —**repentance** *n.* [U]

re·pen·tant /rɪˈpɛntˀnt/ *adj.* sorry for something wrong that you have done (ANT) **unrepentant**: *His apology was sincerely repentant.* —**repentantly** *adv.*

re·per·cus·sions /ˌripɚˈkʌʃən/ *n.* [plural] the effects of an action or event, especially bad effects that happen much later: *The collapse of the company will **have repercussions** for the whole industry.*

THESAURUS **result, consequences, aftereffects** → RESULT¹

rep·er·toire /ˈrɛpɚˌtwɑr/ *n.* [C usually singular] all the plays, pieces of music, etc. that a performer or group can perform

rep·e·ti·tion /ˌrɛpəˈtɪʃən/ *n.* [C,U] the act of saying or doing the same thing again or many times → REPEAT: *We don't want a **repetition of** last year's disaster.* | *Kids learn the times tables **by repetition**.*

rep·e·ti·tious /ˌrɛpəˈtɪʃəs/ *adj.* saying or doing the same thing many times, so that people become bored: *a repetitious speech*

re·pet·i·tive /rɪˈpɛt̬ət̬ɪv/ *adj.* done many times in the same way: *repetitive exercises*

re·phrase /ri'freɪz/ *v.* [T] to express something in different words so that its meaning is clearer or more acceptable: *Let me* ***rephrase*** *the* ***question.***

re·place /rɪ'pleɪs/ *v.* [T] **1** to start doing something, or being used instead of another person or thing: *Typewriters have been replaced by computers.* **2** to remove someone from his/her job or something from its place, and put a different person or thing there: *They have* ***replaced*** *thousands of full-time workers* ***with*** *part-timers.* **3** to buy something that is newer or better, in order to use it instead of something that is old or broken: *The tires need to be replaced.* **4** to put something back in its correct place: *Please replace the books when you are finished.*

re·place·ment /rɪ'pleɪsmənt/ *n.* **1** [C] someone or something that replaces another person or thing: *We're waiting for Mr. Dunley's replacement.* **2** [U] the act of replacing something

re·play /'ripleɪ/ *n.* [C] a sports game, or particular part of the game, that has been recorded and is shown again: *an* ***instant replay*** (=immediate replay) *of the touchdown*

re·plen·ish /rɪ'plɛnɪʃ/ *v.* [T] (formal) to put new supplies into something, or to fill something again [ORIGIN: 1600—1700 Old French *replenir*, from *plein* "full"] —**replenishment** *n.* [U]

re·plete /rɪ'plit/ *adj.* (formal) full of something: *a new car* ***replete with*** *leather seats*

rep·li·ca /'rɛplɪkə/ *n.* [C] a very good copy of a piece of art, a building, etc. [ORIGIN: 1800—1900 Italian "something repeated," from Latin *replicare*]

rep·li·cate /'rɛplə,keɪt/ *v.* [T] (formal) to do or make something again, so that you get the same result or make an exact copy: *Scientists are trying to replicate Hudson's experiment.*

THESAURUS **copy, reproduce, duplicate** → COPY[2]

rep·li·ca·tion /,rɛplə'keɪʃən/ *n.* [U] BIOLOGY the process by which a cell or DNA (=substance in a cell, that contains GENETIC information) makes an exact copy of itself: *During replication, each strand of DNA generates a new strand.*

re·ply[1] /rɪ'plaɪ/ *v.* (**replied**, **replies**) [I,T] to answer someone by saying or writing something: *"Of course," she replied.* | *He never* ***replied to*** *our letters.* | *Deagal* ***replied that*** *he had not known what would happen.*

THESAURUS **answer, respond** → ANSWER[1]

reply[2] *n.* (plural **replies**) [C,U] something that is said, written, or done in order to reply to someone: *There haven't been any* ***replies to*** *the ad.* | *Billy* ***made*** *no* ***reply.***

re·port[1] /rɪ'pɔrt/ *n.* [C] **1** a written or spoken description of a situation or event, giving people information: *a police* ***report on*** *the accident* | *a weather report* → NEWSPAPER **2** a piece of writing in which someone carefully examines a particular subject: *a book report* | *an environmental impact report* **3** (formal) the noise of an explosion or shot

report[2] *v.* **1** [I,T] to tell someone about something, especially in newspapers and on television: *The Daily Gazette reported the story.* | *A journalist* ***reporting on*** *the election wrote the story.* **2** [T] to tell someone in authority that a crime or accident has happened: *Three boys were reported missing.* | *Only 4% of burglaries are* ***reported to*** *police.* **3 be reported to be/do sth** used in order to say that a statement has been made about someone or something, but you do not know if it is true: *Cummings was reported to be furious.* **4** [I,T] to tell someone, especially your manager, about what has been happening or what you are doing, as part of your job: *Each naval station* ***reports to*** *an admiral.* **5** [I] to state officially to someone in authority that you have arrived in a place: *Visitors should* ***report to*** *reception.* | *One of the soldiers had not* ***reported for duty.*** **6** [T] to complain officially about someone to people in authority: *A customer reported her to her supervisor.*

report back *phr. v.* to bring someone information that s/he asked you to find: *The committee* ***reported back to*** *Congress.*

re'port card *n.* [C] a written statement by teachers about a child's work at school

re·port·ed·ly /rɪ'pɔrtɪdli/ *adv.* according to what some people say, but when it is not known for certain: *Two soldiers reportedly were injured.*

re,ported 'speech *n.* [U] ENG. LANG. ARTS the style of speech or writing used for reporting what someone says, without repeating the actual words. The sentence "She said she didn't feel well." is an example of reported speech. SYN **indirect speech** → DIRECT SPEECH

re·port·er /rɪ'pɔrtɚ/ *n.* [C] someone whose job is to write or tell about events in a newspaper or on radio or television → JOURNALIST: *a newspaper reporter* → NEWSPAPER

re·pose /rɪ'poʊz/ *n.* [U] (formal) a state of calm or comfortable rest SYN **rest**: *She looked pale and tired* ***in repose.*** —**reposeful** *adj.*

re·pos·i·to·ry /rɪ'pɑzə,tɔri/ *n.* (plural **repositories**) [C] (formal) a place where things are kept safely: *a repository for nuclear waste*

re·pos·sess /,ripə'zɛs/ *v.* [T] to take back something such as a car or furniture that someone has paid part of the money for because s/he cannot pay the rest of the money

rep·re·hen·si·ble /,rɛprɪ'hɛnsəbəl/ *adj.* (formal) reprehensible behavior is very bad and deserves criticism

THESAURUS **bad, immoral, wrong** → BAD[1]

rep·re·sent /,rɛprɪ'zɛnt/ *v.* **1** [T] to do things or speak officially for someone else, or to express

R

his/her views or opinions: *She represents the 5th congressional district of Texas.* | *They want a school board that represents their educational values.* **2** [linking verb] to form or be something: *The talks represent a significant step toward peace.* **3** [T] to be a sign or mark for something else SYN **stand for**: *The green triangles on the map represent campgrounds.* **4** [T] if art represents something, it shows or means a thing or idea: *Paintings representing heaven and hell were common in medieval art.* **5** [T] to describe someone or something in a particular way, especially in a way that is not true: *The author was criticized for the way he represents women.*

rep·re·sen·ta·tion /ˌrɛprɪzɛnˈteɪʃən, -zən-/ *n.* **1** [U] the state of having someone to speak, vote, or make decisions for you: *There is no representation on the council for the Hispanic community.* **2** [U] the state of being present in a place, or of taking part in something: *The representation of minorities among the faculty should be increased.* **3** [C] something, for example a painting or sign, that shows or describes something else: *The model is a* ***representation of*** *a water molecule.*

R

rep·re·sent·a·tive¹ /ˌrɛprɪˈzɛntət̬ɪv/ *n.* [C] **1** someone who is chosen to act, speak, vote, etc. for someone else **2** *also* **Representative** POLITICS a member of the House of Representatives in the U.S. Congress

representative² *adj.* **1** like other members of the same group SYN **typical**: *The sample is* ***representative of*** *the total population.* **2** relating to a system of government in which people elect other people to represent them: *representative democracy*

re·press /rɪˈprɛs/ *v.* [T] **1** to stop yourself from expressing a feeling, remembering something, or doing something you want to do: *Boys learn to repress their need to cry.* **2** to control people by using force

re·pressed /rɪˈprɛst/ *adj.* (disapproving) having feelings or desires that you do not express

re·pres·sion /rɪˈprɛʃən/ *n.* [U] **1** the use of force to control people: *Stalin's repression of religious groups* **2** the action of stopping yourself from feeling an emotion, or the state of having done this

re·pres·sive /rɪˈprɛsɪv/ *adj.* controlling people in a cruel and severe way: *a repressive society*

re·prieve /rɪˈpriv/ *n.* [C] **1** a delay before something bad happens or continues: *a* ***reprieve from*** *the pain* **2** an official order that prevents a prisoner from being killed as a punishment → PARDON —**reprieve** *v.* [T]

rep·ri·mand /ˈrɛprəˌmænd/ *v.* [T] to tell someone officially that s/he has done something wrong: *He was* ***reprimanded for*** *failing to do his duty.* —**reprimand** *n.* [C,U]

THESAURUS **scold, rebuke, admonish** → CRITICIZE

re·pris·al /rɪˈpraɪzəl/ *n.* [C,U] a violent action that punishes your enemy for something bad that s/he has done

re·prise /rɪˈpriz/ *v.* [I,T] to act the same part again, play the same tune again, etc.

re·proach¹ /rɪˈproʊtʃ/ *n.* **1** [C,U] criticism or disapproval, or a remark that expresses this: *The reproach in her voice made me pause.* **2 above/beyond reproach** impossible to criticize SYN **perfect**: *The actions of the police should be above reproach.*

reproach² *v.* [T] to criticize someone and try to make him/her sorry for doing something: *His daughter* ***reproached*** *him* ***for*** *not telling her the truth.* —**reproachful** *adj.*

rep·ro·bate /ˈrɛprəˌbeɪt/ *n.* [C] (formal *or* humorous) someone who behaves in an immoral way

re·pro·duce /ˌriprəˈdus/ *v.* **1** [I,T] BIOLOGY to produce young plants or animals: *Most fish reproduce by laying eggs.* **2** [T] to make a copy of something: *The colors were difficult to reproduce.*

THESAURUS **copy, duplicate, replicate** → COPY²

re·pro·duc·tion /ˌriprəˈdʌkʃən/ *n.* **1** [U] BIOLOGY the act or process of producing babies, young animals, or plants: *We studied the reproduction and diet of the elephants in the forest* **2** [C,U] the act of copying something such as a book or painting, or the copy itself: *a reproduction of Homer's painting*

re·pro·duc·tive /ˌriprəˈdʌktɪv/ *adj.* BIOLOGY relating to the process of producing babies, young animals, or plants: *the reproductive system of mammals*

reproˌductive isoˈlation *n.* [U] BIOLOGY conditions that prevent one population of living things from breeding with another, for example a physical difference between creatures or when a river, ocean, or mountain, etc. separates them

re·prove /rɪˈpruv/ *v.* [T] (formal) to criticize someone for doing something bad

rep·tile /ˈrɛptaɪl, ˈrɛptl/ *n.* [C] BIOLOGY a type of animal, such as a snake or LIZARD, that lays eggs, and whose body temperature changes according to the temperature around it [ORIGIN: 1300—1400 Old French, Late Latin *reptilis* "creeping," from Latin *repere* "to creep"] —**reptilian** /rɛpˈtɪliən/ *adj.*

re·pub·lic /rɪˈpʌblɪk/ *n.* [C] POLITICS a country governed by elected representatives and led by a president → MONARCHY [ORIGIN: 1500—1600 French *république*, from Latin *respublica*, from *res* "thing" + *publica* "public"]

THESAURUS **government, democracy, monarchy, regime, dictatorship, totalitarian country/state, etc., police state** → GOVERNMENT

re·pub·li·can¹ /rɪˈpʌblɪkən/ *adj.* **1 Republican** POLITICS relating to or supporting the Republican Party of the U.S. → DEMOCRATIC: *a Republican* *candidate for the Senate* **2** POLITICS relating to or supporting a system of government that is not led by a king or queen and is elected by the people: *a republican government* —**Republicanism** *n.* [U]

republican² *n.* [C] **1 Republican** POLITICS a member or supporter of the Republican Party of the U.S. → DEMOCRAT **2** POLITICS someone who believes in government by elected representatives only, with no king or queen

Re'publican ˌParty *n.* **the Republican Party** POLITICS one of the two main political parties of the U.S. → DEMOCRATIC PARTY

re·pu·di·ate /rɪ'pyudiˌeɪt/ *v.* [T] (formal) to refuse to accept or continue with something, especially because you disagree strongly with it (SYN) **reject**: *The senator repudiated the allegation* (=statement saying that someone has done something wrong or illegal). —**repudiation** /rɪˌpyudi'eɪʃən/ *n.* [U]

re·pug·nance /rɪ'pʌgnəns/ *n.* [U] (formal) a feeling of strong dislike (SYN) **disgust**

re·pug·nant /rɪ'pʌgnənt/ *adj.* (formal) very unpleasant and offensive: *Slavery is* ***morally repugnant.***

re·pulse /rɪ'pʌls/ *v.* [T] **1** if something or someone repulses you, you think that he, she, or it is so unpleasant that it makes you feel sick: *The terrorist attacks repulsed the nation.* **2** to defeat a military attack

re·pul·sion /rɪ'pʌlʃən/ *n.* **1** [singular, U] a sick feeling that you get from seeing or thinking about something extremely unpleasant (SYN) **revulsion** **2** [U] PHYSICS the electric or MAGNETIC force by which one object pushes another one away from it

re·pul·sive /rɪ'pʌlsɪv/ *adj.* extremely unpleasant, so that you almost feel sick: *a repulsive crime*

THESAURUS **ugly, unattractive, unsightly, hideous, grotesque** → UGLY

rep·u·ta·ble /'rɛpyət̬əbəl/ *adj.* respected for being honest and doing good work: *a reputable construction company*

rep·u·ta·tion /ˌrɛpyə'teɪʃən/ *n.* [C] the opinion that people have of someone or something because of what has happened in the past: *Denver has a* ***reputation as*** *a livable city.* | *a* ***reputation for*** *honesty*

re·pute /rɪ'pyut/ *n.* [U] (formal) reputation: *a pianist* ***of*** *great* ***repute***

re·put·ed /rɪ'pyut̬ɪd/ *adj.* (formal) according to what most people think or say: *He* ***is reputed to be*** *a millionaire.* —**reputedly** *adv.*

re·quest¹ /rɪ'kwɛst/ *n.* [C] the act of asking for something politely or formally: *a* ***request for*** *more funding* | *The Citizenship and Immigration Service rejected his* ***request to*** *remain in the U.S.* | *The governor of New Orleans* ***made an*** *official* ***request*** *for aid.* | *a* ***formal/polite/written request*** | *Drinks are available* ***on request*** (=if you ask for them). [ORIGIN: 1300—1400 Old French *requeste*, from Vulgar Latin, from *requaerere* "to try to find, need"]

request² *v.* [T] to ask for something politely or formally: *She* ***requested that*** *everyone attend a meeting at 2 p.m.* | *Harris* ***requested permission/information/aid.***

THESAURUS **ask, order, demand** → ASK

req·ui·em /'rɛkwiəm/ *n.* [C,U] a Christian ceremony of prayers for someone who has died, or a piece of music written for this ceremony

re·quire /rɪ'kwaɪɚ/ (Ac) *v.* [T] **1** to need something: *The program requires 16 megabytes of memory.* **2** (formal) to demand officially that someone do something because of a law or rule: *Doctors are* ***required to*** *report certain serious diseases.* | *The law* ***requires that*** *the milk be pasteurized.* [ORIGIN: 1300—1400 Old French *requerre*, from Vulgar Latin *requaerere* "to try to find, need"]

re·quire·ment /rɪ'kwaɪɚmənt/ (Ac) *n.* [C] **1** something that someone needs or asks for: *The refugees' main requirements are food and shelter.* | *a vitamin pill that* ***meets*** *all your daily* ***requirements*** **2** something that must be done because of a rule or law: *English 4 is a* ***requirement for*** *English majors* (=they must take this class). | *the* ***legal requirements*** *regarding marriage*

req·ui·site /'rɛkwəzɪt/ *adj.* (formal) needed for a particular purpose

THESAURUS **necessary, essential, vital, mandatory, compulsory, indispensable** → NECESSARY

req·ui·si·tion /ˌrɛkwə'zɪʃən/ *n.* [C,U] (formal) an official demand to have something, usually made by the army —**requisition** *v.* [T]

re·route /ri'raʊt, ri'rut/ *v.* [T] to make vehicles, aircraft, etc. go a different way from the way they usually go: *Traffic has been rerouted across the bridge.*

re·run /'rirʌn/ *n.* [C] a television program or a movie that is being shown again: *reruns of "Friends"* —**rerun** /ri'rʌn/ *v.* [T]

re·sale /'riseɪl/ *n.* [U] the state of being sold again: *the* ***resale value*** *of the house*

re·sched·ule /ri'skɛdʒəl/ (Ac) *v.* [T] to arrange for something to happen at a different time from the time that was originally planned: *The meeting will be* ***rescheduled for*** *March 19.*

re·scind /rɪ'sɪnd/ *v.* [T] to officially end a law, agreement, or decision

R

rescue

a mountain rescue

res·cue¹ /ˈrɛskyu/ *v.* [T] to save someone or something from harm or danger: *Survivors of the crash were rescued by helicopter.* | *He **rescued** two people **from** the fire.* —**rescuer** *n.* [C]

rescue² *n.* [C,U] an act of saving someone or something from harm or danger: *a **rescue mission/operation*** | *A nearby boat **came to the rescue*** (=saved or helped someone).

R

re·search¹ /ˈrisɚtʃ, rɪˈsɚtʃ/ (Ac) *n.* [U] serious study of a subject, that is intended to discover new facts about it: *scientific **research on/into** heart disease* | *Holmes is **doing research*** (=finding information) *for a book on the Middle Ages.* [ORIGIN: 1500—1600 Old French *recerche*, from *recercher* "to find out about something thoroughly"]

THESAURUS

study – a piece of research on a particular subject: *The study showed that children who ate a good breakfast did better at school.*
experiment – a scientific test done to find out how something reacts under certain conditions, or to find out if a particular idea is true: *Skinner carried out a series of experiments to test his theory.*
results/findings – the information that someone has discovered as a result of research: *The results of the study will be published in the New England Journal of Medicine.*
conclusion – something that someone has decided after examining a subject carefully, especially when this is written at the end of an official report: *Their conclusion was that the drug was effective in most cases.*

re·search² /rɪˈsɚtʃ, ˈrisɚtʃ/ (Ac) *v.* [I,T] to study a subject in detail, in order to discover new facts about it: *She has been researching her family's history for several years.* —**researcher** *n.* [C]

re·sem·blance /rɪˈzɛmbləns/ *n.* [C,U] if there is a resemblance between two things or people, they are similar to each other: *There's a slight **resemblance between** Mike and his cousin* (=they look like each other).

re·sem·ble /rɪˈzɛmbəl/ *v.* [T] to look like, or be similar to, someone or something: *She resembles her mother in many ways.* [ORIGIN: 1300—1400 Old French *resembler*, from *sembler* "to be like, seem," from Latin *similare* "to copy"]

re·sent /rɪˈzɛnt/ *v.* [T] to feel angry and upset about something that you think is unfair: *The law was **bitterly/deeply resented** by voters.* [ORIGIN: 1500—1600 French *ressentir* "to feel strongly about," from *sentir* "to feel," from Latin *sentire*]

re·sent·ful /rɪˈzɛntfʊl/ *adj.* feeling angry and upset about something that you think is unfair: *a resentful look*

THESAURUS **angry, annoyed, irritated, mad, indignant** → ANGRY

re·sent·ment /rɪˈzɛntˀmənt/ *n.* [U] a feeling of anger about something that you think is unfair

res·er·va·tion /ˌrɛzɚˈveɪʃən/ *n.* **1** [C] an arrangement that you make so that a place in a hotel, on an airplane, etc. is kept for you to use: *a plane reservation* | *Have you **made reservations** at the restaurant yet?* **2** [C,U] a feeling of doubt because you do not agree completely with a plan, idea, etc.: *They **have** serious **reservations about** the proposal.* **3** [C] an area of land in the U.S. that is kept separate, especially an area for Native Americans to live on

re·serve¹ /rɪˈzɚv/ *v.* [T] **1** to arrange for a place in a hotel, on an airplane, etc. to be kept for you to use: *I'd like to reserve a table for 8:00.* **2** to keep something separate so that it can be used for a particular purpose: *a parking space **reserved for** the disabled* [ORIGIN: 1300—1400 Old French *reserver*, from Latin *reservare* "to keep back"]

THESAURUS **keep, store, save** → KEEP¹

reserve² *n.* **1** [C usually plural] an amount of something that is kept to be used if it is needed: *oil reserves* | *A month's supply of food is **kept in reserve** for emergencies.* **2** [U] the quality of not liking to express your emotions or talk about your problems → SHYNESS: *John's natural reserve* **3** [C] EARTH SCIENCES an area of land where wild animals, plants, etc. are protected: *a wetlands reserve* **4** [U] *also* **reserves** [plural] a military force that a country has in addition to its usual army

re·served /rɪˈzɚvd/ *adj.* not liking to express your emotions or talk about your problems: *a quiet reserved man*

THESAURUS **shy, self-conscious, retiring** → SHY¹

Reˌserved ˈPowers *n.* [plural] POLITICS the power that each U.S. state has to make decisions and pass laws, when the decision or law is not one that the U.S. CONSTITUTION says must be made by Congress → EXCLUSIVE POWERS, ORDINANCE POWERS

res·er·voir /ˈrɛzəˌvwɑr, -zɚ-, -ˌvwɔr/ *n.* [C] **1** EARTH SCIENCES a special lake where water is stored to be used by people in a city **2** a large amount of something that has not been used yet: *a reservoir of oil beneath the desert*

re·shuf·fle /ri'ʃʌfəl/ *v.* [T] to REORGANIZE something

re·side /rɪ'zaɪd/ (Ac) *v.* [I] (formal) to live in a particular place [ORIGIN: 1400—1500 French *résider*, from Latin *residere* "to sit back, remain, stay," from *sedere* "to sit"]

res·i·dence /'rɛzədəns/ (Ac) *n.* (formal) **1** [C] the place where you live: *a private residence*

THESAURUS **home, house, place, dwelling, abode** → HOME[1]

2 [U] the state of living in a place: *What is your usual place of residence?* **3 in residence** living or working in a place: *the job of **artist/poet etc. in residence** at UCLA*

res·i·den·cy /'rɛzədənsi/ *n.* [U] **1** a period of time during which a doctor receives special training in a particular type of medicine **2** the state of living in a place, or legal permission to live in a country: *After five years of residency, you may apply for citizenship.*

res·i·dent¹ /'rɛzədənt/ (Ac) *n.* [C] **1** someone who lives in a particular place: *a park for local residents* **2** a doctor working at a hospital where s/he is being trained

resident² (Ac) *adj.* **1** working regularly for a particular organization, and sometimes living in the place where you work: *She had a job as the resident nurse at the resort.* **2** living in a place: *noncitizens who are lawfully **resident in** this country*

res·i·den·tial /ˌrɛzə'dɛnʃəl◂/ (Ac) *adj.* **1** a residential area consists of private houses, with no offices or businesses: *a typical house in a residential neighborhood* **2** relating to homes, or people who live in homes, rather than to businesses: *electricity prices for residential customers*

re·sid·u·al /rɪ'zɪdʒuəl/ *adj.* (formal) remaining after a process, event, etc. is finished: *the residual effects of radiation exposure*

res·i·due /'rɛzəˌdu/ *n.* [C,U] a substance that remains after something else has disappeared or been removed: *an oily residue*

re·sign /rɪ'zaɪn/ *v.* **1** [I,T] to officially leave your job or position: *Burton **resigned from** the company yesterday.*

THESAURUS **quit, give up, retire** → QUIT

2 resign yourself to (doing) sth to accept something that is unpleasant but cannot be changed: *I resigned myself to paying the fees.* [ORIGIN: 1300—1400 Old French *resigner*, from Latin *resignare* "to unseal, cancel, give back"]

res·ig·na·tion /ˌrɛzɪg'neɪʃən/ *n.* **1** [C,U] the act of resigning, or a written statement to say you are doing this: *Morris **handed in/submitted** his **resignation*** (=gave his resignation to the manager). **2** [U] the feeling of accepting an unpleasant situation that you cannot change: *I could hear the resignation in his voice.*

re·signed /rɪ'zaɪnd/ *adj.* accepting an unpleasant situation that you cannot change, or showing that you feel this: *patients who seem **resigned to** the pain* | *a resigned voice/look*

re·sil·ient /rɪ'zɪliənt/ *adj.* **1** able to become strong, happy, or successful again after a difficult situation or event: *a resilient economy* **2** strong and not easily damaged by being pulled, pressed, etc.: *resilient materials* —**resilience** *n.* [U]

res·in /'rɛzən/ *n.* **1** [U] a thick sticky liquid that comes from some trees **2** [C,U] CHEMISTRY a chemical substance used for making plastics

re·sist /rɪ'zɪst/ *v.* **1** [I,T] to stop yourself from having something that you like or doing something that you want to do: *I **couldn't resist** the temptation to peek.* | *Carter found their offer **hard/difficult to resist**.* **2** [I,T] to not accept changes, or to try to prevent changes from happening: *People generally resist change.* **3** [I,T] to use force to stop something from happening: *The suspect resisted arrest.* | *I pulled her to me and she did not resist.* **4** [T] to not be changed or harmed by something: *Vitamin C is supposed to help you resist colds.* [ORIGIN: 1300—1400 Latin *resistere*, from *sistere* "to stop"]

R

re·sist·ance /rɪ'zɪstəns/ *n.* **1** [singular, U] a refusal to accept new ideas or changes: *people's **resistance to** change* | *The plan met with **resistance from** the U.S. ambassador.* **2** [singular, U] fighting against someone or something: *a resistance fighter* | *The rebels **put up** fierce **resistance**.* **3** [singular, U] BIOLOGY the natural ability of a person, animal, or GERM (=small living thing that can make you ill), etc. to stop a disease or drug from harming it: *Some types of infections have developed a **resistance to** antibiotics.* **4** [U] PHYSICS the degree to which a substance can stop electricity from going through it

re·sis·tant /rɪ'zɪstənt/ *adj.* **1** not easily harmed or damaged by something: *flame-resistant pajamas* **2** unwilling to accept something: *companies that are **resistant to** change*

re·sis·tor /rɪ'zɪstɚ/ *n.* [C] PHYSICS a piece of wire or other material used for increasing electrical resistance

res·o·lute /'rɛzəˌlut/ *adj.* doing something because you feel very strongly that you are right —**resolutely** *adv.*

res·o·lu·tion /ˌrɛzə'luʃən/ (Ac) *n.* **1** [C] POLITICS a formal or official decision agreed on by a group, especially after a vote: *A Congressional resolution allowed the U.S. to enter the war.* **2** [singular, U] the final solution to a problem or difficulty: *This method means that children can find a **resolution to** their differences without adult help.* **3** [C] a promise that you make to yourself to do something: *Have you made any **New Year's resolutions**?* **4** [U] the quality of having strong beliefs and determination: *his resolution to continue* **5** [C,U] the power of a television, camera, TELESCOPE, etc. to give a clear picture of things: *a high-resolution telescope* **6** [C] POLITICS a formal decision or statement from the U.S. SENATE or the HOUSE OF REPRESENTATIVES, that does not have the force of law and does not need to be signed by the American president **7** [singular] ENG. LANG. ARTS the point near the end of a story, book, play, etc. when the CONFLICT between important characters or forces that have opposed each other during the story is fully dealt with

re·solve[1] /rɪ'zɑlv/ (Ac) *v.* **1** [T] to find an answer to a problem or a way of dealing with it: *The training helps children resolve conflicts without fighting.* | *They are trying to* ***resolve*** *their* ***differences*** (=stop arguing and become friendly again) *with the help of a counselor.* **2** [I] to make a definite decision to do something: *I* ***resolved to*** *lose weight.*

R

THESAURUS decide, make up your mind, choose, determine ➔ DECIDE

3 [I,T] to make a formal decision to do something, especially by voting: *The transportation board resolved to rename the highway in his honor.*

resolve[2] *n.* [U] (formal) strong determination to succeed in doing something: *His words only strengthened her* ***resolve to*** *persevere.*

res·o·nant /'rɛzənənt/ *adj.* having a deep clear loud sound that continues for a long time: *a resonant voice* —**resonance** *n.* [U]

res·o·nate /'rɛzəˌneɪt/ *v.* [I] **1** to make a deep clear loud sound that continues for a long time **2** if an event or idea resonates with people, it seems important to them or means a lot to them

re·sort[1] /rɪ'zɔrt/ *n.* **1** [C] a place where many people can go for a vacation, with hotels, swimming pools, etc.: *a beach resort* **2 last resort** what you will do if everything else fails: ***As a last resort****, doctors will try an experimental drug.*

resort[2] *v.*

resort to sth *phr. v.* to do something or use something in order to succeed, even if it is bad: *Police fear the demonstrators will resort to violence.*

re·sound /rɪ'zaʊnd/ *v.* [I] **1** to be full of sound: *The room* ***resounded with*** *laughter.* **2** if a sound resounds, it continues loudly and clearly for a long time

re·sound·ing /rɪ'zaʊndɪŋ/ *adj.* **1** a resounding noise is loud and clear: *a resounding crash*

THESAURUS loud, noisy, thunderous, deafening, sonorous ➔ LOUD[1]

2 a resounding success/victory etc. a very great and complete success, victory, etc. —**resoundingly** *adv.*

re·source /'risɔrs, rɪ'sɔrs/ (Ac) *n.* **1** [C usually plural] something such as land, minerals, or natural energy that exists in a country and can be used in order to increase its wealth: ***natural resources*** *such as timber and oil* **2** [C] something that can be used in order to make a job or activity easier, especially by providing information: *an electronic resource for lesson plans* **3 resources** [plural] all the money, property, skills, etc. that you have available to use: *the organization's financial resources* [ORIGIN: 1600—1700 French *ressource*, from Old French *resourdre* "to rise again, relieve," from Latin *resurgere*] ➔ HUMAN RESOURCES

re·source·ful /rɪ'sɔrsfəl/ (Ac) *adj.* good at finding ways to deal with problems effectively: *a resourceful leader* —**resourcefulness** *n.* [U]

re·spect[1] /rɪ'spɛkt/ *n.* **1** [U] the attitude of believing that something or someone is important, and so being careful not to be rude or not to harm him, her, or it (ANT) **disrespect**: *In Japan, people* ***show*** *more* ***respect to*** *the elderly.* | *These kids* ***have*** *no* ***respect for*** *other people's property.* | ***Out of respect for*** *the flag, you should stand.* **2** [U] admiration for someone because of his/her knowledge, skill, personal qualities, etc.: *I* ***have*** *a lot of* ***respect for*** *this team.* | *Earhart had* ***earned the respect of*** *the other pilots.* **3 in one respect/in some respects/in every respect** used in order to say that something is true in one way, in some ways, or in every way: *In some respects, very little has changed.* **4 respects** [plural] (formal) polite greetings: ***Give my respects to*** *your parents.* **5 pay your (last/final) respects** to go to a funeral to show that you liked and respected someone **6 with (all due) respect** (formal) used before disagreeing with someone when you want to be polite: *With all due respect, I don't think that will work.* **7 with respect to sth** (formal) relating to a particular thing, or relating to something that has just been mentioned (SYN) **regarding**: *The article examines what the Bible says with respect to marriage.*

respect[2] *v.* [T] **1** to admire someone because of his/her knowledge, skill, personal qualities, etc.: *The students like and respect him.*

THESAURUS admire, look up to sb, hold sb in high esteem ➔ ADMIRE

2 to be careful not to do anything against someone's wishes, rights, etc.: *Parents should respect a teenager's need for privacy.* | *When traveling abroad, I always try to respect local customs.* **3 respect the law/Constitution etc.** to be careful not to disobey the law, Constitution, etc.

re·spect·a·ble /rɪ'spɛktəbəl/ *adj.* **1** showing standards of behavior or appearance that people approve of and admire: *a respectable family* **2** good or satisfactory: *She jumped a respectable five and a half feet.*

THESAURUS satisfactory, good enough, acceptable, reasonable ➔ SATISFACTORY

—**respectably** *adv.* —**respectability** /rɪˌspɛktə'bɪləṭi/ *n.* [U]

re·spect·ed /rɪ'spɛktɪd/ *adj.* admired by many people because of your work, skills, etc.: *a **highly/widely respected** musician*

re·spect·ful /rɪ'spɛktfəl/ *adj.* feeling or showing respect (ANT) **disrespectful** —**respectfully** *adv.*

re·spec·tive /rɪ'spɛktɪv/ *adj.* people's respective jobs, houses, etc. are the separate ones that each of them has: *the two sisters and their respective husbands*

re·spec·tive·ly /rɪ'spɛktɪvli/ *adv.* each separately in the order mentioned: *The dollar and yen rose 2% and 3% respectively.*

res·pi·ra·tion /ˌrɛspə'reɪʃən/ *n.* [U] the process of breathing → ARTIFICIAL RESPIRATION → BREATHE

res·pi·ra·tor /'rɛspəˌreɪt̬ɚ/ *n.* [C] a piece of equipment that covers the nose and mouth and helps someone to breathe

res·pira·to·ry /'rɛsprəˌtɔri/ *adj.* BIOLOGY relating to breathing: *the respiratory system*

res·pite /'rɛspɪt/ *n.* [singular, U] a short time when something bad stops happening: *a brief **respite from** the rain*

re·splend·ent /rɪ'splɛndənt/ *adj.* (formal) very beautiful in appearance, in a way that looks expensive

re·spond /rɪ'spɑnd/ (Ac) *v.* **1** [I] to react to something that has been said or done: *Engine Company 29 **responded to** the fire.* | *The Federal Reserve **responded by** raising interest rates.* **2** [I,T] to say or write something as a reply: *He **responded that** he didn't want to see her.* | *The mayor's office has not **responded to** requests for comments.*

THESAURUS answer, reply → ANSWER[1]

3 [I] to improve as a result of a particular medical treatment: *Her cancer is **responding** well **to** the drugs.* [ORIGIN: 1500—1600 Latin *respondere* "to promise in return, answer," from *spondere*]

re·spond·ent /rɪ'spɑndənt/ (Ac) *n.* [C] someone who answers questions, especially as part of a study: *93% of the respondents agreed with the statement.*

reˌsponding 'variable *n.* [C] SCIENCE in a scientific EXPERIMENT (=test), a result that is likely to change depending on the different conditions used in the experiment (SYN) **dependent variable**

re·sponse /rɪ'spɑns/ (Ac) *n.* **1** [C,U] something that is said, written, or done as a reaction or reply to something else: *"No," Thompson said **in response to** the question.* | *We've had a good **response to** our appeal for help.* **2** [C] BIOLOGY a single reaction to a STIMULUS (=something that causes a reaction in living things), for example the way your body reacts to a particular infection

re·spon·si·bil·i·ty /rɪˌspɑnsə'bɪlət̬i/ *n.* (plural **responsibilities**) **1** [U] a duty to be in charge of or take care of something: *Do you think he's ready for more responsibility?* | *It's your **responsibility to** inform us of any changes.* | *The students **take responsibility for** planning their projects.* | *The federal government **has responsibility for** enforcing immigration laws.* **2** [C] something that you have a duty to do, be in charge of, or take care of: *a single parent trying to balance work and family responsibilities* **3** [U] blame for something bad: *No one has **accepted/taken responsibility for** the bombing.*

re·spon·si·ble /rɪ'spɑnsəbəl/ *adj.* **1** if you are responsible for something bad, it is your fault: *the people **responsible for** the murder* | *Can parents be **held responsible** when their children commit a crime?* **2** in charge of or taking care of something: *The Forest Service is **responsible for** fighting fires in national forests.* | *Mills is responsible for a budget of over $5 million.* **3** sensible and able to be trusted: *a responsible young man* **4 responsible job/position/post** a job in which the ability to make good judgments and decisions is needed **5 be responsible to sb** if you are responsible to someone, that person is in charge of your work and you must explain your actions to him/her

re·spon·si·bly /rɪ'spɑnsəbli/ *adv.* in a sensible way that makes people trust you: *Are reporters acting responsibly?*

re·spon·sive /rɪ'spɑnsɪv/ (Ac) *adj.* **1** reacting quickly, in a useful or helpful way: *a company that is **responsive to** your business needs* **2** able or eager to communicate with people, and to react to them in a positive way: *a happy and responsive baby* —**responsiveness** *n.* [U]

rest[1] /rɛst/ *n.* **1 the rest** the part of a group, thing, etc. that is left after everything else has been used, dealt with, etc.: *I'll read you the rest tomorrow night.* | *Each child does a dance while the rest watch.* | *He will have to take the medication for **the rest of** his life.* **2** [C,U] a period of time when you can relax or sleep: *You'd better **get some rest**.* **3 put/set sb's mind at rest** to make someone feel less anxious or worried **4 come to rest** to stop moving: *The ball came to rest near the hole.* **5 lay/put sth to rest** to stop people from believing, talking, or worrying about something: *He has put to rest speculation that he would run for president.* **6 at rest** not moving **7** [C] ENG. LANG. ARTS a period of silence of a particular length in a piece of music, or the written sign that shows this [ORIGIN: (1) 1400—1500 French *reste*, from *rester* "to remain," from Latin *restare*]

rest[2] *v.* **1** [I] to stop doing something and relax or sleep for a period of time: *I usually rest for a while after lunch.* **2 rest your feet/legs/eyes etc.** to stop using a part of your body for a period of time because it is feeling sore or tired: *The snow is so bright you have to close your eyes to rest them.* **3** [T] to support an object or part of your body by putting it on or against something: *The baby **rested** his head **on** my shoulder.* | *His briefcase **rested against** his chair.*

THESAURUS lean, stand, prop → LEAN[1]

4 rest assured (that) (formal) used in order to tell someone not to worry because what you say is true: *You can rest assured that we'll do all we can.* **5 sb will not rest until...** (literary) if someone will not rest until something happens, s/he will not be satisfied until it happens **6** [I] if a dead person rests somewhere, s/he is buried there: *My mother, may she **rest in peace**, is buried there.*

rest on/upon sth *phr. v.* (formal) to depend on or be based on something: *Their chance of going to the playoffs rests on this game.*

rest with sb *phr. v.* if a decision rests with someone, s/he is responsible for it: *The final decision rests with the Public Health Service.*

re·state /ri'steɪt/ *v.* [T] to say something again in a different way, so that it is clearer or more strongly expressed: *Jackson restated his intention to retire.* —**restatement** *n.* [C,U]

res·tau·rant /'rɛsˌtrɑnt, 'rɛstəˌrɑnt, 'rɛstərənt/ *n.* [C] a place where you can buy and eat a meal: *a small Italian restaurant* [ORIGIN: 1800—1900 French *restaurer* "to restore," from Latin *restaurare* "to renew, rebuild"]

R

THESAURUS

cafe/coffee shop – a place where you can get drinks, cakes, and small meals
fast food restaurant – one where you can get meals such as hamburgers, french fries, etc.
diner – a restaurant where you can eat cheap and simple food
cafeteria – a place at work or school where you can get a meal which you take to a table yourself

TOPIC

In a restaurant, the **waiter** or **waitress** brings you the **menu** and you choose what you want to eat. The menu may be divided into **appetizers** (=first courses), **main courses/entrées**, and **desserts** (=sweet food eaten at the end). When you have finished your meal, you ask for the **check/bill**. People usually **leave a tip** unless waiter **service** is **included** in the cost.

rest·ful /'rɛstfəl/ *adj.* peaceful and quiet: *a restful weekend*

'rest home *n.* [C] a NURSING HOME

res·ti·tu·tion /ˌrɛstə'tuʃən/ *n.* [U] (formal) the act of giving back to the owner something that was lost or stolen, or of paying for damage

res·tive /'rɛstɪv/ *adj.* (formal) bored or not satisfied with your situation, and wanting it to change

rest·less /'rɛstlɪs/ *adj.* **1** unable to keep still, especially because you are nervous or bored: *The kids have been inside all day, and they're **getting restless**.* **2** not satisfied and wanting new experiences: *a restless man, always changing jobs* —**restlessness** *n.* [U] —**restlessly** *adv.*

re·store /rɪ'stɔr/ (Ac) *v.* [T] **1** to make something exist again or return to its former state: *The army was called in to **restore order**.* | *ways to **restore** her **confidence*** **2** to repair something so that it is in its original condition: *They're restoring a Victorian house.*

THESAURUS **repair, renovate, rebuild, recondition** → REPAIR[2]

3 (formal) to give something back to someone: *The change in the law will **restore** benefits **to** legal immigrants.* [ORIGIN: 1200—1300 Old French *restorer*, from Latin *restaurare* "to renew, rebuild"] —**restoration** /ˌrɛstə'reɪʃən/ *n.* [C,U]: *a building in need of restoration*

re·strain /rɪ'streɪn/ (Ac) *v.* [T] **1** to prevent someone from doing something, often by using physical force: *They attacked a policeman who tried to **restrain** them **from** driving drunk.* | *He could not restrain a sigh.* **2** to control or limit something: *Raising prices should restrain consumer spending.*

re·strained /rɪ'streɪnd/ (Ac) *adj.* behavior that is restrained is calm and controlled

re·straint /rɪ'streɪnt/ (Ac) *n.* **1** [U] calm and controlled behavior: *He urged the protesters to **show restraint**.* **2** [C,U] something that controls what you can say or do: *Budget cuts have put **restraints on** public spending.* **3** [C] something that prevents someone from moving freely: *a prisoner in restraints*

re·strict /rɪ'strɪkt/ (Ac) *v.* [T] to control something or keep it within limits: *regulations that **restrict** the sale of alcohol **to** minors* [ORIGIN: 1400—1500 Latin, past participle of *restringere*, from *stringere* "to tie tightly, press together"]

re·strict·ed /rɪ'strɪktɪd/ (Ac) *adj.* **1** controlled or limited: *The sale of alcohol is restricted.* **2** only allowed to be seen or used by a particular group of people: *a restricted area*

re·stric·tion /rɪ'strɪkʃən/ (Ac) *n.* [C,U] a rule or set of laws that limits what you can do or what is allowed to happen: ***restrictions on** cigarette advertising* | *freedom to travel without restriction*

THESAURUS **rule, law, regulation, guidelines, statute** → RULE[1]

re·stric·tive /rɪ'strɪktɪv/ (Ac) *adj.* stopping people from doing something, or limiting what they can do: *restrictive trade policies*

reˌstrictive 'clause *also* **reˌstrictive ˌrelative 'clause** *n.* [C] ENG. LANG. ARTS a part of a sentence that says exactly which person or thing is meant. For example, in "the man who came to dinner," the phrase "who came to dinner" is a restrictive clause because it tells someone exactly which man you mean. → NONRESTRICTIVE CLAUSE, RELATIVE CLAUSE

rest·room /'rɛstrum/ *n.* [C] a room with a toilet, in a public place such as a restaurant or theater: *Employees must wash their hands after using the restroom.*

THESAURUS bathroom, women's/ladies' room, men's room, lavatory → TOILET

re·struc·ture /ˌri'strʌktʃɚ/ (Ac) *v.* [T] to change the way in which something such as a business or system is organized: *companies that are cutting jobs and restructuring* —**restructuring** *n.* [U]

THESAURUS change, alter, reform, reorganize → CHANGE[1]

re·sult[1] /rɪ'zʌlt/ *n.* **1** [C,U] something that happens or exists because of something that happened before: *The **end/final result** will be a delicious loaf of bread.* | *Will more students attend college **as a result of** the tax breaks?* | *Some teachers already use the system, **with** excellent **results**.*

THESAURUS

consequences – the things that happen as a result of an action, event, etc.: *the tragic consequences of the accident*
effect – a change that is the result of something: *the harmful effects of pollution*
aftereffects – bad effects that continue for a long time after the thing that caused them: *The country is still suffering from the aftereffects of the war.*
side effect – an unwanted effect, especially of a type of drug or medical treatment: *The drug's side effects can include headaches and nausea.*
outcome – the final result of a meeting, election, war, etc.: *the final outcome of the talks*
upshot – the final result of a situation: *The upshot of higher interest rates is that products cost more to manufacture.*
repercussions – bad effects caused by an event, action, or decision, which happen much later: *The scandal could have serious repercussions for her political career.*

2 [C] information or answers that are produced by examining something carefully, especially in a scientific way: *a blood test result* | *the **results of** the police investigation* [ORIGIN: 1400—1500 Latin *resultare* "to jump back, result," from *saltare* "to jump"]

result[2] *v.* [I] to happen or exist because of something: *injuries **resulting from** car accidents*
result in sth *phr. v.* to make something happen: *The fire resulted in the death of two children.*

re·sult·ant /rɪ'zʌltənt, -tˀnt/ *adj.* (formal) happening or existing because of something else

re·sume /rɪ'zum/ *v.* [I,T] (formal) to start doing something again after a pause: *The mayor hopes to resume his duties soon.* —**resumption** /rɪ'zʌmpʃən/ *n.* [singular, U]

ré·su·mé /'rɛzəˌmeɪ, ˌrɛzə'meɪ/ *n.* [C] a written list and description of your education and your previous jobs that you use when you are looking for a job: *I'll put this job **on** my **résumé**.*

re·sur·face /ˌri'sɚfɪs/ *v.* **1** [I] to appear again: *The issue resurfaced again during the last election.* **2** [I] to come back up to the surface of the water **3** [T] to put a new surface on a road

re·sur·gence /rɪ'sɚdʒəns/ *n.* [singular, U] if there is a resurgence of a belief or activity, it appears again and becomes stronger, after a time when it was not common: *a **resurgence of** racism* [ORIGIN: 1800—1900 *resurgent* (18—21 centuries), from Latin *resurgere* "to rise again"] —**resurgent** *adj.*

res·ur·rect /ˌrɛzə'rɛkt/ *v.* [T] to bring an old practice, belief, etc. back into use or fashion: *Designers have resurrected the styles of the 1960s.*

res·ur·rec·tion /ˌrɛzə'rɛkʃən/ *n.* **1 the Resurrection** the return of Jesus Christ to life after his death on the cross, which is one of the main beliefs of the Christian religion **2** [U] the act of bringing an old practice, belief, etc. back into use or fashion

re·sus·ci·tate /rɪ'sʌsəˌteɪt/ *v.* [T] to make someone breathe again after s/he has almost died [ORIGIN: 1500—1600 Latin, past participle of *resuscitare*, from *suscitare* "to cause to move around"] —**resuscitation** /rɪˌsʌsə'teɪʃən/ *n.* [U]

R

re·tail[1] /'riteɪl/ *n.* [U] ECONOMICS the sale of goods in stores to people for their own use → WHOLESALE: *retail stores* | *a retail price of $16.95* [ORIGIN: 1300—1400 Old French *retaillier* "to divide into pieces," from *taillier* "to cut"] —**retailing** *n.* [U]

retail[2] *v.* **retail for/at sth** ECONOMICS to be sold at a particular price in stores: *The wine retails for $8.95 a bottle.*

retail[3] *adv.* ECONOMICS if you buy or sell something retail, you buy or sell it in a shop

re·tail·er /'riˌteɪlɚ/ *n.* [C] ECONOMICS someone who sells goods to the public, using a store → WHOLESALER

re·tain /rɪ'teɪn/ (Ac) *v.* [T] **1** to keep something, or to continue to have something: *Steamed vegetables retain more of their flavor.* | *The Republicans retained control of Congress.* **2** to keep facts in your memory: *She retains most of what she reads.* [ORIGIN: 1300—1400 Old French *retenir*, from Latin *retinere*, from *tenere* "to hold"] —**retention** /rɪ'tɛnʃən/ *n.* [U]: *The retention of good employees is vital for a healthy corporation.*

re·tain·er /rɪ'teɪnɚ/ (Ac) *n.* [C] **1** ECONOMICS an amount of money that you pay regularly to someone such as a lawyer, so that s/he will continue to work for you **2** a small plastic and wire object that you wear in your mouth to make your teeth stay straight

re·take /ˌri'teɪk/ *v.* (past tense **retook** /-'tʊk/, past participle **retaken** /-'teɪkən/) [T] **1** to get control of something again: *Rebels have retaken the city.* **2** to take a test or class again because you failed it before → SCHOOL[1]

re·tal·i·ate /rɪ'tæliˌeɪt/ *v.* [I] to do something bad to someone because s/he has done something bad to you: *Police **retaliated by** using tear gas.* [ORIGIN: 1600—1700 Late Latin, past participle of *retaliare*, from *talio* "suitable punishment"]

re·tal·i·a·tion /rɪˌtæli'eɪʃən/ *n.* [U] the act of retaliating: *The shooting appeared to be **in retaliation for** an attack last week.*

re·tard /rɪ'tɑrd/ *v.* [T] (formal) to delay the development of something, or to make something happen more slowly —**retardation** /ˌritɑr'deɪʃən/ *n.* [U]

re·tard·ed /rɪ'tɑrdɪd/ *adj.* less mentally developed than other people

retch /rɛtʃ/ *v.* [I] if you retch, you feel like you are VOMITing but nothing comes out of your stomach

re·ten·tive /rɪ'tɛntɪv/ (Ac) *adj.* (formal) someone with a retentive memory or mind is able to remember information clearly

re·think /ˌri'θɪŋk/ *v.* (past tense and past participle **rethought** /-'θɔt/) [I,T] to think about a plan or idea again in order to decide if any changes should be made

R

ret·i·cent /'rɛṭəsənt/ *adj.* not willing to talk about what you know or how you feel —**reticence** *n.* [U]

ret·i·na /'rɛtˀnə/ *n.* [C] BIOLOGY the area at the back of your eye that sends an image of what you see to your brain

ret·i·nue /'rɛtˀnˌu/ *n.* [C] a group of helpers or supporters who are traveling with an important person: *a retinue of aides*

re·tire /rɪ'taɪɚ/ *v.* **1** [I,T] to stop working, usually because of old age, or to make someone do this: *Quigley retired from the army in September.*

> TOPIC
>
> In the United States, most people retire when they are 65. This is the usual **retirement age**, but some people **take early retirement**. When you retire, you must live on your **pension**, **Social Security**, or your **savings**. → PENSION, WORK[1], QUIT

2 [I] (formal) to go away to a quiet place: *He **retired to** his room.* **3** [I] (formal) to go to bed

re·tired /rɪ'taɪɚd/ *adj.* retired people have stopped working, usually because they are old: *a retired teacher*

re·tire·ment /rɪ'taɪɚmənt/ *n.* **1** [C,U] the act of retiring from your job: *his **retirement from** the Senate* **2** [singular, U] the period of time after you have retired: *a long and happy retirement*

re'tirement ˌhome *n.* [C] a place where old people can live, where various services are provided such as food, social activities, and medical care → NURSING HOME

re·tir·ing /rɪ'taɪərɪŋ/ *adj.* **1** not wanting to be with other people: *a shy and retiring woman*

> THESAURUS **shy, timid, reserved** → SHY[1]

2 the retiring president/manager etc. a president, etc. who is soon going to retire

re·tort¹ /rɪ'tɔrt/ *v.* [T] to reply quickly, in an angry or humorous way: *"None of your business!" he retorted.*

retort² *n.* [C] **1** a short reply, that usually expresses anger or humor **2** CHEMISTRY a bottle with a long narrow bent neck, used for heating chemicals

re·trace /ri'treɪs/ *v.* [T] **1** to go back the way you have come: *I tried to **retrace** my **steps**, but I can't find the campsite.* **2** to repeat exactly the same trip that someone else has made: *The ships retraced Columbus's route.*

re·tract /rɪ'trækt/ *v.* **1** [T] to make an official statement saying that something you said earlier is not true: *He confessed to the crime but later retracted his statement.* **2** [I,T] if a part of something retracts or is retracted, it moves back into the main part —**retraction** /rɪ'trækʃən/ *n.* [C,U]

re·tract·a·ble /rɪ'træktəbəl/ *adj.* a retractable part of something can be pulled back into the main part: *a knife with a retractable blade*

re·treat¹ /rɪ'trit/ *v.* [I] **1** to decide not to do what you have planned, because it seems too difficult or not popular: *The president seems to be **retreating from** his pledge to cut taxes.* **2** to move away from a place or person: *He shouted, and the dogs retreated.* **3** to stop being involved with society or other people: *His way of coping is to **retreat into** his own world.* **4** if an army retreats, it stops fighting and moves away from the enemy

retreat² *n.* **1** [singular, U] the act of deciding to not do what you had planned, because it is too difficult or not popular: *The United States must not **retreat from** its international responsibilities.* **2** [C,U] an army's movement away from the enemy: *Napoleon's **retreat from** Moscow* **3** [C] a place you can go to that is quiet or safe: *a mountain retreat* **4** [C,U] an occasion when you go away from people, especially to pray or study, or the action of doing this: *a weekend retreat for people who do yoga* **5** [singular, U] a movement away from a place or person

re·tri·al /ˌri'traɪl, 'ritraɪl/ *n.* [C] LAW the process of judging a law case in court again: *My lawyer demanded a retrial.*

ret·ri·bu·tion /ˌrɛtrə'byuʃən/ *n.* [singular, U] punishment that is deserved: *The victims' families are demanding **retribution for** the attacks.*

re·trieve /rɪ'triv/ *v.* [T] **1** to find something and bring it back: *I ran to retrieve the ball.* | *It took four days to **retrieve** all the bodies **from** the crash.* **2** IT to get back information that has been stored in the memory of a computer [ORIGIN: 1400—1500 Old French *retrover* "to find again," from *trover* "to find"] —**retrieval** *n.* [U]

re·triev·er /rɪ'trivɚ/ *n.* [C] a type of dog that can be trained to find and bring back birds that its owner has shot

ret·ro·ac·tive /ˌrɛtroʊˈæktɪv/ *adj.* a law or decision that is retroactive is effective from a particular date in the past: *a retroactive pay increase* —**retroactively** *adv.*

ret·ro·spect /ˈrɛtrəˌspɛkt/ *n.* **in retrospect** thinking back to a time in the past, and knowing more now than you did then: *In retrospect, I should have left him much earlier.*

re·tro·spec·tive /ˌrɛtrəˈspɛktɪv/ *adj.* relating to or thinking about the past: *a retrospective look at Capra's movies*

ret·ro·vi·rus /ˌrɛtroʊˈvaɪrəs/ *n.* [C] BIOLOGY a VIRUS (=very small living thing that causes an infectious illness) that holds its GENETIC information in the chemical substance RNA rather than in DNA: *No one has yet produced a vaccine for the retrovirus that causes AIDS.*

re·turn[1] /rɪˈtɚn/ *v.*

1 GO BACK [I] to go or come back to a place where you were before: *Kevin has just* ***returned from*** *Texas.* | *Are you planning to* ***return to*** *Spain?* | *She didn't return until after 8 o'clock.* ►Don't say "return back."◄

2 PREVIOUS STATE [I] to be in a previous state or condition again: *Her heartbeat* ***returned to*** *normal.* | *Will the Democrats* ***return to*** *power in the next election?*

3 GIVE BACK [T] to give something back, or put something back in its place: *I have to* ***return*** *these books* ***to*** *the library.* | *It didn't fit, so I returned it* (=took it back to the store).

4 HAPPEN AGAIN [I] to start to happen or exist again: *Take two of these pills if the pain returns.*

5 START AGAIN [I] to go back to an activity, discussion, etc. that was stopped or interrupted: *He smiled and* ***returned to*** *his book.* | *Hannah* ***returned to*** *work part-time.*

6 DO STH SIMILAR [T] to react to something someone has done by doing something similar: *Why didn't you return my call?* | *Lisa returned his smile.*

7 return a verdict if a JURY returns a VERDICT, they say whether someone is guilty or not

8 MONEY [T] if an INVESTMENT returns a particular amount of money, that is how much profit it produces

return[2] *n.*

1 GOING BACK [singular, U] the act of going or coming back to a place where you were before: *Jefferson's* ***return from*** *France* | *I want you to have dinner ready* ***on/upon*** *my* ***return*** (=when I come back).

2 GIVING STH BACK [U] the act of giving, putting, or sending something back: *the safe* ***return of*** *the prisoners of war*

3 CHANGING BACK [singular] a change back to a previous state or situation: *We must prevent a* ***return to*** *Communist rule.*

4 STH HAPPENING AGAIN [singular, U] the fact of something starting to happen or to exist again: *the* ***return of*** *spring*

5 STH STARTING AGAIN [singular, U] the act of starting an activity, discussion, etc. again after stopping for a time: *her* ***return to*** *full-time work*

6 PROFIT [U] *also* **returns** [plural] ECONOMICS the amount of profit you receive from money you have INVESTed (–used to buy things such as STOCK, goods, or property, etc.): *Most people get fairly low* ***returns from*** *their personal investments.* | *These investments bring a high* ***rate of return*** (=level of profit).

7 COMPUTER [U] the key that you press on a computer at the end of an instruction or to move to a new line SYN enter

8 in return (for sth) in exchange for, or as payment for something: *One student does childcare in return for room and board.*

9 STATEMENT [C] a statement or set of figures given as a reply to an official demand: *a tax return*

re·turn·a·ble /rɪˈtɚnəbəl/ *adj.* returnable bottles, containers, etc. can be given back to the store

re·u·ni·fy /riˈyunəˌfaɪ/ *v.* (**reunified**, **reunifies**) [T] to join the parts of something together again, especially a country that was divided → REUNITE —**reunification** /riˌyunəfəˈkeɪʃən/ *n.* [U]: *the reunification of Germany*

re·un·ion /riˈyunyən/ *n.* **1** [C] a meeting of people who have not met for a long time: *a high-school reunion* | *a family reunion* **2** [U] the state of being brought together again after a period of being separated: *a day of* ***reunion with*** *friends*

re·u·nite /ˌriyuˈnaɪt/ *v.* [I,T] to come together again, or to be brought together again after a period of being separated: *The children were* ***reunited with*** *their families.*

Rev. the written abbreviation of REVEREND

rev[1] /rɛv/ *n.* [C usually plural] (informal) one REVOLUTION of an engine

rev[2] *also* **rev up** *v.* (**revved**, **revving**) [I,T] if you rev an engine, or if it revs, it works faster

re·vamp /riˈvæmp/ *v.* [T] (informal) to change something in order to improve it: *a promise to revamp the welfare system*

re·veal /rɪˈvil/ Ac *v.* [T] **1** to show something that was previously hidden: *The magician pulled off the covering to reveal a black box.* **2** to make something known that was previously secret: *The company has not revealed the name of the prospective buyer.* | *The report* ***revealed that*** *many children were not reading at grade level.* [ORIGIN: 1300—1400 Old French *reveler*, from Latin *revelare* "to uncover"]

re·veal·ing /rɪˈvilɪŋ/ Ac *adj.* **1** showing something about someone's character, thoughts, or feelings: *a revealing comment* **2** revealing clothes show parts of your body that are usually kept covered

rev·el /ˈrɛvəl/ *v.*

revel in sth *phr. v.* to enjoy something very much: *Bobby reveled in my undivided attention.*

rev·e·la·tion /ˌrɛvəˈleɪʃən/ Ac *n.* [C,U] a surprising and previously secret fact that suddenly

R

becomes known, or the act of making this fact known: *strange **revelations about** her past* | ***revelations that** two senior officers had lied in court*

rev·el·er /ˈrɛvələ/ *n.* [C] someone who is enjoying singing, dancing, etc. in a noisy way

rev·el·ry /ˈrɛvəlri/ *n.* [U] wild noisy dancing, eating, drinking, etc., usually to celebrate something

re·venge[1] /rɪˈvɛndʒ/ *n.* [U] something you do in order to punish someone who has harmed or offended you: *The voters **took revenge** on election day.* | *He vowed that someday he would **get revenge**.*

revenge[2] *v.* [T] to punish someone who has harmed or offended you ➔ AVENGE

rev·e·nue /ˈrɛvəˌnu/ (Ac) *n.* [U] **1** money that is earned by a company: *The company earns $30 billion in annual revenue.* **2** money that the government receives from tax [ORIGIN: 1400—1500 French, past participle of *revenir* "to return"]

R

re·ver·ber·ate /rɪˈvɚbəˌreɪt/ *v.* [I] **1** if a loud sound reverberates, it is heard many times as it is sent back from different surfaces: *Their voices **reverberated around** the empty church.* **2** to have a strong effect that continues for a long time: *News of the verdict reverberated through the city.* [ORIGIN: 1400—1500 Latin, past participle of *reverberare* "to hit back, repel," from *verberare* "to hit"] —**reverberation** /rɪˌvɚbəˈreɪʃən/ *n.* [C,U]

re·vere /rɪˈvɪr/ *v.* [T] (formal) to greatly respect and admire someone

> THESAURUS **admire, respect, look up to sb, idolize, worship, hold sb in high esteem** ➔ ADMIRE

rev·er·ence /ˈrɛvrəns/ *n.* [U] (formal) respect and admiration (ANT) **irreverence**: *reverence for tradition* —**reverent** *adj.* —**reverently** *adv.*

Rev·er·end /ˈrɛvrənd, -ərənd/ used in the title of a minister in a Christian church: *Reverend Larson*

rev·er·ie /ˈrɛvəri/ *n.* [C,U] a state of imagining or thinking about pleasant things (SYN) **daydream**

re·ver·sal /rɪˈvɚsəl/ (Ac) *n.* [C,U] the act of changing an arrangement, process, or action in order to do the opposite: *a **reversal of** the court's decision* | *Their **role reversal**, in which Mike is the stay-at-home parent, benefits everyone.*

re·verse[1] /rɪˈvɚs/ (Ac) *v.* **1** [T] to change something, such as a decision, judgment, or process, so that it is the opposite of what it was before: *The court reversed the original ruling.* | *Unions want to reverse the decline in membership.* **2 reverse yourself** to change your opinion or position in an argument **3** [T] to change around the usual order of the parts of something, or the usual things two people do: *Our roles as teacher and pupil had been reversed.* **4** [I,T] to move backward, especially in a vehicle (SYN) **back up** **5** [T] to turn something over, so that it shows the back of it or so that it faces the opposite way: *The image in the mirror is reversed.*

reverse[2] *n.* **1 the reverse** the opposite: *Some people get sleepy after one drink; for others it's the reverse.* **2 in reverse** done in the opposite way or with the opposite effect: *We went from the east coast to the west coast last year, and did the trip in reverse this year.* **3** [U] the control in a vehicle that makes it go backward: *I started the car and put it **in reverse**.*

reverse[3] *adj.* opposite to what is usual or to what has just been stated: *She answered their questions in reverse order.*

reˌverse discrimiˈnation *n.* [U] the practice of giving a particular number of jobs, places at university, etc. to people who are often treated unfairly because of their race, sex, etc. ➔ AFFIRMATIVE ACTION

re·vers·i·ble /rɪˈvɚsəbəl/ *adj.* **1** if something that has changed is reversible, the thing that was changed can be changed back to the way it was before: *Are the effects of the decision reversible?* **2** a piece of clothing that is reversible can be worn with the part that is normally on the inside showing on the outside: *a reversible coat*

reˌversible reˈaction *n.* [C] CHEMISTRY a chemical reaction in which the substance that the reaction has produced is able to react again to return to its original state

re·vert /rɪˈvɚt/ *v.* **revert to sth** to go back to a previous situation, condition, use, or habit: *Leningrad reverted to its former name of St. Petersburg.* —**reversion** /rɪˈvɚʒən/ *n.* [singular, U]

re·view[1] /rɪˈvyu/ *n.* **1** [C,U] a careful examination of a situation or process: *an urgent **review of** safety procedures* | *the main issue **under review*** (=being considered) | *a review committee* **2** [C] an article that gives an opinion about a new book, play, movie, etc.: *His book got very good reviews.* [ORIGIN: 1400—1500 French *revue*, from *revoir* "to look over"]

review[2] *v.* **1** [T] to examine, consider, and judge a situation or process carefully: *The policy is being reviewed by federal wildlife officials.* **2** [I,T] to write an article describing and judging a new book, play, movie, etc.: *He writes a column reviewing computer software.* **3** [I,T] to prepare for a test by studying books, notes, reports, etc.

re·view·er /rɪˈvyuɚ/ *n.* [C] someone who writes articles that give his/her opinion about new books, plays, movies, etc.

re·vile /rɪˈvaɪl/ *v.* [T] (formal) to express hatred of someone or something

re·vise /rɪˈvaɪz/ (Ac) *v.* [T] **1** to change your opinions, plans, etc. because of new information or ideas: *Plans for the building are being revised.*

> THESAURUS **change, alter, adapt, adjust, modify, amend** ➔ CHANGE[1]

2 ENG. LANG. ARTS to improve a piece of writing:

Students should be encouraged to revise their writing. [ORIGIN: 1500—1600 French *réviser*, from Latin *revisere* "to look at again"]

re·vi·sion /rɪˈvɪʒən/ (Ac) *n.* **1** [C,U] the process of changing something to improve it, especially a piece of writing: *a **revision of** the labor laws* **2** [C] ENG. LANG. ARTS a piece of writing that has been improved

re·vi·tal·ize /riˈvaɪtl̩ˌaɪz/ *v.* [T] to make something become strong, active, or powerful again: *The city has begun to revitalize the downtown area* (=make businesses stronger, rebuild buildings, etc.). **—revitalization** /riˌvaɪtl̩-əˈzeɪʃən/ *n.* [U]

re·viv·al /rɪˈvaɪvəl/ *n.* **1** [C,U] a process in which something becomes active, strong, or popular again: *a **revival of** interest in traditional crafts* **2** [C] ENG. LANG. ARTS a new performance of a play that has not been performed for a long time: *a revival of "Oklahoma!"* **3** [C] *also* **revival meeting** a public religious meeting that is intended to make people interested in Christianity

re·vive /rɪˈvaɪv/ *v.* **1** [I,T] to become conscious, healthy, or strong, or to make someone or something do this: *measures to revive a sagging economy* **2** [T] to bring something back into use or existence: *The workshop will help revive the ancient craft of storytelling.* [ORIGIN: 1400—1500 Old French *revivre*, from Latin *revivere* "to live again"]

re·voke /rɪˈvoʊk/ *v.* [T] LAW to officially state that a law, decision, etc. is no longer effective (SYN) **cancel**: *Her driver's license has been revoked.* [ORIGIN: 1300—1400 Old French *revoquer*, from Latin *revocare* "to call back"]

re·volt[1] /rɪˈvoʊlt/ *v.* **1** [I] to refuse to obey a government, law, etc., often using violence against it (SYN) **rebel** → REVOLUTION: *Rebels in the south **revolted against** the government.* **2** [T] to make you feel sick and shocked → REVULSION: *The idea revolted me.* [ORIGIN: 1500—1600 French *révolter*, from Old Italian *rivoltare* "to defeat and remove from power"]

revolt[2] *n.* [C,U] a refusal to obey a government, law, etc., sometimes expressed by violent action against it: *a **revolt against** an unfair tax* | *The people rose **in revolt**.* | *a slave revolt in 1791*

THESAURUS **revolution, rebellion, uprising, insurrection, insurgency, coup** → REVOLUTION

re·volt·ing /rɪˈvoʊltɪŋ/ *adj.* extremely unpleasant: *a revolting stench*

THESAURUS **horrible, disgusting, awful, foul, terrible, dreadful, horrendous** → HORRIBLE

rev·o·lu·tion /ˌrɛvəˈluʃən/ (Ac) *n.* **1** [C,U] POLITICS a time when people change a ruler or political system by using force or violence: *the American Revolution*

THESAURUS

rebellion – an organized attempt to change the government of a country using violence: *an armed rebellion*
revolt – a refusal to obey a government, law, etc., or an occasion when people try to change the government of a country, often by using violence: *Troops loyal to the President crushed the revolt.*
uprising – an occasion when a large group of people use violence to try to change the rules, laws, etc. in an institution or country: *a popular uprising* (=involving ordinary people, not the army)
insurrection (formal) – an attempt by a group of people within a country to take control using force and violence: *an armed insurrection led by the army*
insurgency (formal) – the action of fighting against the government of your own country: *the Communist insurgency in Vietnam in the 1950s and 60s*
coup – an action in which a group of people, especially soldiers, suddenly take control of their country: *The President was deposed in a violent military coup.*

2 [C] a complete change in ways of thinking, methods of working, etc.: *Computer technology has caused a revolution in business practices.* | *the sexual revolution* **3** [C,U] one complete circular movement or spin around a central point → REVOLVE: *The earth makes one **revolution around** the sun each year.* [ORIGIN: 1300—1400 Old French, Latin *revolutio*, from *revolvere* "to roll back, cause to return"]

R

rev·o·lu·tion·ar·y[1] /ˌrɛvəˈluʃəˌnɛri/ (Ac) *adj.* **1** completely new and different: *a revolutionary new treatment for cancer* **2** POLITICS relating to a political or social revolution: *a revolutionary army*

revolutionary[2] *n.* (plural **revolutionaries**) [C] someone who joins in or supports a political or social revolution

rev·o·lu·tion·ize /ˌrɛvəˈluʃəˌnaɪz/ (Ac) *v.* [T] to completely change the way people think or do things: *His work revolutionized the treatment of this disease.*

THESAURUS **change, alter, adjust, modify, revise, reform, transform** → CHANGE[1]

re·volve /rɪˈvɑlv/ *v.* [I,T] to spin around a central point, or to make something do this: *The wheels began to revolve slowly.* [ORIGIN: 1300—1400 Latin *revolvere* "to roll back, cause to return," from *volvere* "to roll"]

THESAURUS **turn, twist, spin, whirl, twirl, swivel, go around, rotate** → TURN[1]

—revolving *adj.*: *a revolving door*

revolve around *phr. v.* **1 revolve around** sb/sth to have something as a main subject or purpose:

Jess's life has revolved around basketball. **2 revolve around** sth to move in circles around something: *The moon revolves around the earth.*

re·volv·er /rɪˈvɑlvɚ/ *n.* [C] a type of small gun that you hold in one hand

re·vue /rɪˈvyu/ *n.* [C] a show in a theater that includes singing, dancing, and telling jokes

re·vul·sion /rɪˈvʌlʃən/ *n.* [U] a strong feeling of shock and strong dislike SYN **disgust**

re·ward¹ /rɪˈwɔrd/ *n.* [C,U] something that you get because you have done something good or helpful or have worked hard ➔ AWARD, PRIZE: *The police are offering a* ***reward for*** *information.*

reward² *v.* [T] to give something to someone because s/he has done something good or helpful or has worked for it: *The students are* ***rewarded for*** *hard work.* | *They* ***rewarded*** *him* ***with*** *a free ticket.*

re·ward·ing /rɪˈwɔrdɪŋ/ *adj.* making you feel happy and satisfied: *a rewarding job*

R

re·wind /riˈwaɪnd/ *v.* (past tense and past participle **rewound** /-ˈwaʊnd/) [I,T] to make a TAPE go back to the beginning

re·work /riˈwɚk/ *v.* [T] to change or improve a plan, piece of music, story, etc.: *He spent some time reworking the last paragraph.*

re·write /riˈraɪt/ *v.* (past tense **rewrote** /-ˈroʊt/, past participle **rewritten** /-ˈrɪtˀn/) [T] to write something again using different words, in order to make it clearer or more effective —**rewrite** /ˈriraɪt/ *n.* [C]

rhap·so·dize /ˈræpsəˌdaɪz/ *v.* [I] to talk about something in an eager, excited, and approving way: *Helen* ***rhapsodized about*** *the wild strawberries she had found.*

rhap·so·dy /ˈræpsədi/ *n.* (plural **rhapsodies**) [C] ENG. LANG. ARTS a piece of music that is written to express emotion, and does not have a regular form

Rhe·sus fac·tor /ˈrisəs ˌfæktɚ/ *n.* [singular] BIOLOGY a substance that some people have in their red blood cells

rhet·o·ric /ˈrɛt̬ərɪk/ *n.* [U] **1** speech or writing that sounds impressive, but is not actually sincere or very useful: *slick speeches and political rhetoric* **2** ENG. LANG. ARTS the art of speaking or writing in order to persuade or influence people

rhe·tor·i·cal /rɪˈtɔrɪkəl, -ˈtɑ-/ *adj.* ENG. LANG. ARTS using speech or writing in special ways in order to persuade people or to produce an impressive effect: *The poem is deliberately direct, with far fewer* ***rhetorical devices*** (=particular examples of rhetorical language) *than in his early work.* | *the president's rhetorical skills* [ORIGIN: 1300—1400 Old French *rethorique*, from Latin, from Greek *rhetorike*, from *rhetor* "public speaker," from *eirein* "to say, speak"] —**rhetorically** *adv.*

rheˌtorical ˈquestion *n.* [C] a question that you ask as a way of making a statement, without expecting an answer

rheu·ma·tism /ˈruməˌtɪzəm/ *n.* [U] a disease that makes your joints or muscles painful and stiff

rhine·stone /ˈraɪnstoʊn/ *n.* [C,U] a jewel made from glass or a rock, that is intended to look like a DIAMOND

rhi·noc·er·os /raɪˈnɑsərəs/ *also* **rhi·no** /ˈraɪnoʊ/ *n.* [C] a large heavy animal with thick rough skin and one or two horns on its nose [ORIGIN: 1200—1300 Latin, Greek, from *rhis* "nose" + *keras* "horn"]

rho·do·den·dron /ˌroʊdəˈdɛndrən/ *n.* [C] a large bush with groups of red, purple, pink, or white flowers [ORIGIN: 1600—1700 Modern Latin, Greek, from *rhodon* "rose" + *dendron* "tree"]

rhom·boid /ˈrɑmbɔɪd/ *n.* [C] MATH a PARALLELOGRAM in which the opposite sides are equal and the ADJACENT sides are not equal

rhom·bus /ˈrɑmbəs/ *n.* [C] MATH a flat shape with four equal straight sides, especially a shape that is not a square ➔ *see picture at* POLYGON

rhu·barb /ˈrubɑrb/ *n.* [U] a plant with long thick red stems that are cooked and eaten as a fruit [ORIGIN: 1300—1400 Old French *reubarbe*, from Medieval Latin *reubarbarum*, from *rha* "rhubarb" (from Greek) + *barbarus* "foreign"]

rhyme¹ /raɪm/ *v.* **1** [I] ENG. LANG. ARTS if two words or lines of poetry rhyme, they end with the same sound: *"House"* ***rhymes with*** *"mouse."* **2** [T] ENG. LANG. ARTS to put two or more words together to make them rhyme: *You can't* ***rhyme*** *"box"* ***with*** *"backs."*

rhyme² *n.* **1** [U] ENG. LANG. ARTS the use of words that rhyme in poetry, especially at the ends of lines: *Parts of Shakespeare's plays are written* ***in rhyme.*** **2** [C] ENG. LANG. ARTS a short poem or song, especially for children, using words that rhyme ➔ NURSERY RHYME **3** [C] a word that ends with the same sound as another word: *I can't find a* ***rhyme for*** *"donkey."* **4 rhyme or reason** used in negative statements to say there does not seem to be a sensible reason for something: *There seemed to be* ***no rhyme or reason*** *to the court's decision.* | *The facts were presented one after the other,* ***without rhyme or reason.***

rhythm /ˈrɪðəm/ *n.* [C,U] ENG. LANG. ARTS a regular repeated pattern of sounds in music, speech, etc.: *the* ***rhythm of*** *the music* [ORIGIN: 1500—1600 Latin *rhythmus*, from Greek, from *rhein* "to flow"]

ˌrhythm and ˈblues *n.* [U] R & B

rhyth·mic /ˈrɪðmɪk/ *adj.* having rhythm: *a rhythmic swinging motion*

RI the written abbreviation of RHODE ISLAND

rib¹ /rɪb/ *n.* [C] **1** one of the 12 pairs of curved bones that surround your lungs, or one of the similar bones in an animal ➔ *see picture on page A16* **2** a piece of meat that includes an animal's rib: *barbecued ribs*

rib² *v.* (**ribbed**, **ribbing**) [T] (informal) to make jokes about someone and laugh at him/her, but in a friendly way (SYN) **tease** —**ribbing** *n.* [U]

ri·bald /ˈraɪbɔld, ˈrɪbəld/ *adj.* ribald jokes, remarks, songs, etc. are humorous and usually about sex

ribbed /rɪbd/ *adj.* having a pattern of raised lines: *a ribbed sweater*

rib·bon /ˈrɪbən/ *n.* **1** [C,U] a long narrow piece of cloth, used for tying things or as a decoration: *Her braids were tied with bright red ribbons.* **2** [C] a colored ribbon that is given as a prize in a competition ➔ BLUE RIBBON [ORIGIN: 1500—1600 *riband* "ribbon" (14—21 centuries), from Old French *riban, ruban*]

ˈrib cage *n.* [C] BIOLOGY the structure of ribs around your lungs and heart

ri·bo·so·mal RNA /ˌraɪbəsoʊməl ˌɑr ɛn ˈeɪ/ (*abbreviation* **rRNA**) *n.* [U] BIOLOGY RNA that is part of a ribosome

ri·bo·some /ˈraɪbəˌsoʊm/ *n.* [C] BIOLOGY a small part of every living cell, consisting of PROTEIN and the chemical substance ribosomal RNA. Ribosomes change AMINO ACIDS into PROTEIN. ➔ *see picture at* CELL

rice /raɪs/ *n.* [U] a white or brown grain grown in wet fields that is eaten after it has been boiled [ORIGIN: 1200—1300 Old French *ris*, from Greek *oryza, oryzon*]

ˈrice ˌpaddy *n.* [C] a PADDY

rich /rɪtʃ/ *adj.* **1** having a lot of money or valuable possessions (ANT) **poor**: *one of the richest women in America* | *a rich and powerful nation* | *a bright young lawyer who wants to **get rich***

THESAURUS

well-off – fairly rich, so that you can live very comfortably
wealthy – used especially about people whose families have been rich for a long time
prosperous (formal) – rich and successful
affluent (formal) – having a lot of money, nice houses, expensive things, etc.
well-to-do – rich and having a high position in society
rolling in it/loaded (informal) – extremely rich
➔ POOR

2 rich foods contain a lot of butter, cream, or eggs, and make you feel full very quickly (ANT) **light**: *rich desserts* **3** containing a lot of something good: *Oranges are **rich in** vitamin C.* | *a rich cultural heritage* **4 the rich** people who have a lot of money or valuable possessions **5** very deep, strong, and pleasant: *the rich colors of Brett's illustrations* | *the rich tone of a cello* | *the wine's rich flavor* **6** good for growing plants in: *rich soil* **7** expensive and beautiful: *rich silk* [ORIGIN: Old English *rice*] —**richness** *n.* [U]

rich·es /ˈrɪtʃɪz/ *n.* [plural] (literary) a lot of money or valuable possessions

rich·ly /ˈrɪtʃli/ *adv.* **1** in a beautiful or expensive way: *a richly colored window* | *The woman was richly dressed.* **2** in large amounts: *Their efforts were richly rewarded.* | *a richly forested area* **3 richly deserve** to completely deserve something: *They got the punishment they so richly deserved.*

Rich·ter scale /ˈrɪktɚ ˌskeɪl/ *n.* [singular] EARTH SCIENCES a scale that shows how strong an EARTHQUAKE is, with 1 being very weak and 10 being the strongest

rick·et·y /ˈrɪkəṭi/ *adj.* a rickety piece of furniture, set of stairs, etc. is in bad condition and is likely to break if you use it

rick·shaw /ˈrɪkʃɔ/ *n.* [C] a small vehicle used in Asia for carrying one or two passengers that is pulled by someone walking or riding a bicycle [ORIGIN: 1800—1900 Japanese *jinrikisha*, from *jin* "man" + *riki* "strength" + *sha* "vehicle"]

ric·o·chet /ˈrɪkəˌʃeɪ/ *v.* [I] if something such as a bullet or a thrown rock ricochets, it changes direction when it hits a surface —**ricochet** *n.* [C]

rid¹ /rɪd/ *adj.* **1 get rid of sb/sth a)** to throw away something you do not want or use: *Get rid of all your old clothes that don't fit.* **b)** to make something that is unpleasant go away, stop happening, or stop existing: *I can't get rid of this cold.* **c)** to make someone leave because s/he annoys you or causes problems: *It can be difficult to get rid of under-performing employees.* **2 be rid of sb/sth** to have gotten rid of someone who annoys you or something that is unpleasant: *He's gone, and I'm glad to be rid of him.* [ORIGIN: 1100—1200 Old Norse *rythja* "to clear land"]

rid² *v.* (past tense and past participle **rid**, **ridding**)
rid sb/sth **of** sth *phr. v.* **1** to remove someone or something that is bad or harmful from a place, organization, etc.: *The diet is supposed to rid the body of toxins* (=poisonous substances that can cause illness). **2 rid yourself of sth** to stop having a feeling, thought, or problem that was causing you trouble: *She's taking classes to rid herself of her Southern accent.*

rid·dance /ˈrɪdns/ *n.* **good riddance** (spoken) said when you are glad that someone or something has gone away

rid·dle /ˈrɪdl/ *n.* [C] **1** a difficult and amusing question that you must guess the answer to **2** a mysterious action, event, or situation that you do not understand and cannot explain: *His disappearance is a riddle.*

rid·dled /ˈrɪdld/ *adj.* **riddled with sth** very full of something, especially something bad or unpleasant: *a street riddled with potholes*

ride¹ /raɪd/ *v.* (past tense **rode** /roʊd/, past participle **ridden** /ˈrɪdn/) **1** [I,T] to sit on an animal, especially a horse, or on a bicycle, and make it move along: *He rode his bike to school.* | *In the movies, the bad guys **ride on** black horses.* **2** [I,T] to travel in a car, train, or other vehicle ➔ DRIVE: *We rode* *the bus into New York City.* | *Mrs. Turnbull rode in silence.* | *My three-year-old loves to ride the escalators in Bloomingdale's.* **3 let sth ride** (spoken) to take no action about something that is wrong or unpleasant: *I didn't like what he was saying, but I let it ride.* **4** [T] (spoken) to annoy someone by continuously criticizing him/her or asking him/her to do a lot of things: *Why are you riding her so hard?* [ORIGIN: Old English *ridan*]

ride on sth *phr. v.* if something is riding on something else, it depends on it: *My chances of making the team are riding on tomorrow's tryouts.*

ride sth ↔ **out** *phr. v.* if you ride out a difficult situation or experience, you are not badly harmed by it: *The company managed to ride out the recession.*

ride² *n.* [C] **1** a trip in a car, train, or other vehicle, when you are not driving: *Have you* ***gone for a ride in*** *Peggy's new car yet?* | *a 30-minute* ***train/bus/car etc. ride*** | *Mick* ***gave*** *me* ***a ride*** *to work.* **2** a large machine that people ride on for pleasure at a FAIR or AMUSEMENT PARK: *a new ride at Disneyland* **3** a trip on an animal, especially a horse, or on a bicycle: *a fifteen-mile* ***bike ride*** | *Want to* ***go for a ride****?*

R

rid·er /ˈraɪdɚ/ *n.* [C] someone who rides a horse, bicycle, etc.

ridge /rɪdʒ/ *n.* [C] **1** EARTH SCIENCES a long area of high land, especially at the top of a mountain: *a ridge overlooking the valley* → *see picture on page A24* **2** something long and thin that is raised above the things around it: *There are still ridges and ruts left in the ground by wagon wheels.*

rid·i·cule¹ /ˈrɪdəˌkyul/ *n.* [U] unkind laughter, or remarks intended to make someone or something seem stupid: *The other children made her an* ***object/target of ridicule.*** [ORIGIN: 1600—1700 French, Latin *ridiculum* "something funny," from *ridere* "to laugh"]

ridicule² *v.* [T] to laugh at a person, idea, etc., or to make unkind remarks about him, her, or it: *At the time, his ideas were ridiculed.*

ri·dic·u·lous /rɪˈdɪkyələs/ *adj.* silly or unreasonable: *That's ridiculous! I never even met him.* | *He looked ridiculous.* —**ridiculously** *adv.*

rid·ing /ˈraɪdɪŋ/ *n.* [U] the sport of riding horses: *Let's* ***go riding.***

rife /raɪf/ *adj.* **1 rife with sth** full of something bad: *The office is rife with rumors.* **2** if something bad is rife, it is very common

riff /rɪf/ *n.* [C] a repeated series of notes in popular music

ri·fle¹ /ˈraɪfəl/ *n.* [C] a long gun that you hold up to your shoulder to shoot [ORIGIN: 1700—1800 *rifle* "to cut grooves on the inside of something, especially a gun barrel" (17—21 centuries), from Old French *rifler* "to cut into a surface, steal"]

rifle² *v.* [T] *also* **rifle through** to search through a place and steal things from it: *Someone had been rifling through my desk.*

rift /rɪft/ *n.* [C] **1** a serious disagreement: *a growing* ***rift between*** *the two countries* **2** a crack or narrow opening in a large piece of rock, group of clouds, etc.

ˈrift ˌvalley *n.* [C] EARTH SCIENCES a valley with very steep sides, formed by the cracking and moving of the Earth's surface

rig¹ /rɪg/ *v.* (**rigged**, **rigging**) [T] **1** to dishonestly arrange or influence the result of an election, competition, etc., or the price that will be charged for something: *The opposition charged that the election had been rigged.* **2** *also* **rig sth ↔ up** to arrange something so that it will do something in a particular way: *She rigged a mosquito net over the bed.* **3** to provide a ship with ropes, sails, etc.

rig sth ↔ **up** *phr. v.* to make a piece of equipment, furniture, etc. from objects that you find around you: *He'd rigged up a buzzer by his bed so he could call his wife.*

rig² *n.* [C] **1** a large structure used for digging to find oil **2** (informal) a large truck

rig·a·ma·role /ˈrɪgəməˌroʊl/ *n.* [singular, U] another spelling of RIGMAROLE

rig·ging /ˈrɪgɪŋ/ *n.* [U] all the ropes, sails, etc. on a ship

right¹ /raɪt/ *adj.* **1** correct or true (ANT) **wrong**: *Did you get the right answer?* | *You were right – it's really busy tonight.*

> THESAURUS
>
> **correct** – used about answers, facts, etc. that are right: *Is this information correct?*
> **accurate** – used about measurements, descriptions, etc. that are completely right: *Can you give us an accurate description of the man?*
> **true** – based on facts, and not imagined or invented: *a true understanding of the problem*
> → WRONG¹

2 on the right, which is the side of the body that has the hand most people write with (ANT) **left**: *Make a right turn after the gas station.* | *Raise your right hand.* **3** best or most appropriate for a particular situation or purpose (ANT) **wrong**: *the right choice* | *the right person for the job*

> THESAURUS **appropriate, suitable, suited, proper** → APPROPRIATE¹

4 morally correct, or done according to the law (ANT) **wrong**: *I'm only trying to do what's right.* | *Was I* ***right to*** *report him to the police?* **5 be in the right place at the right time** to be in a place or position where something useful becomes available or is being offered

SPOKEN PHRASES

6 that's right said in order to agree with what someone says, to answer "yes" to a question, or when you remember something or are reminded of it: *"You're Steve?" "That's right."* | *"No, it's on Friday." "Oh, that's right."* **7** said in order to check if what you have said is correct: *There's a meeting at two, right?* **8 yeah, right** said when you do not believe what has just been said: *He says, "I'll call you," and I'm like, "yeah, right."* **9** used in order to check that someone understands and agrees with what you have said: *If people are comfortable, they're more likely to talk, right?*

[ORIGIN: Old English *riht*] → *see also* ALL RIGHT

right² *adv.* **1** exactly in a particular position or place: *Shut up, he's **right behind** you!* | *I left the keys **right there/here**.* **2** immediately: *Call me back **right away**.* | *I need it **right now**!* | *It's on **right after** the six o'clock news.* | *I'll **be right there*** (=I am coming now). | *She'll **be right back*** (=come back soon). **3** correctly ANT **wrong**: *They didn't spell my name right.* **4** toward the right side ANT **left**: ***Turn right** at the lights.* **5** all the way to something, through something, etc.: *The school is right on the other side of town.* | *You can see right through her bathing suit!* **6 sb will be right with you** used in order to say that someone will come soon to help or talk to you: *Your waitress will be right with you.*

right³ *n.* **1** [C] something that you are allowed to do or have according to the law or according to moral ideas: *Women didn't **have the right to** vote until 1920.* | *a defendant's **right to** a trial* | *the fight for **equal rights*** (=rights that are the same for everyone) → CIVIL RIGHTS, HUMAN RIGHTS **2** [singular] the side of your body that has the hand that most people write with, or the direction toward this side ANT **left**: *Traffic in the U.S. drives **on the right**.* | *the door **to your right*** **3** [U] behavior that is morally correct: *Teach your kids to **know right from wrong*** (=know what is morally correct and what is not). **4 in his/her/its own right** considered alone, without depending on anyone or anything else: *San José is a city in its own right, not just a suburb of San Francisco.* **5 have a right to be/do sth** to have a good reason to do something, feel something, expect something, etc.: *Weil **has every right to be** angry.* | *You **have no right to** tell me what to do!* **6 the right/Right** POLITICS political parties or other groups who believe that the government should keep taxes low and encourage private business rather than businesses owned by the state → CONSERVATIVE ANT **left** **7 rights** [plural] LAW legal permission to print or use a story, movie, etc. in another form: ***the** movie **rights to** his new book*

right⁴ *v.* [T] **1** to put something back in an upright position: *We righted the canoe.* **2** to correct something: *an attempt to **right the wrong*** (=correct something bad that was done) *of discrimination*

'right ˌangle *n.* [C] MATH an angle of 90°, like the angles at the corners of a square —**right-angled** *adj.*

ˌright-'click *v.* [I,T] IT to press the right button on a computer MOUSE to make the computer do something

right·eous /ˈraɪtʃəs/ *adj.* **1 righteous indignation/anger etc.** strong feelings of anger when you think a situation is not morally right or fair **2** (literary) morally good and fair: *a righteous man* —**righteousness** *n.* [U] —**righteously** *adv.*

'right field *n.* [singular] the area in baseball in the right side of the OUTFIELD

right·ful /ˈraɪtfəl/ *adj.* according to what is legally and morally correct: *Racism denied them their rightful place in society.* —**rightfully** *adv.*

ˌright-'hand *adj.* **1** on your right side: *Make a right-hand turn.* **2 sb's right-hand man** the person who supports and helps someone the most, especially in his/her job

ˌright-'handed *adj.* **1** someone who is right-handed uses his/her right hand for most things **2** done with the right hand: *right-handed pitching* —**right-handed** *adv.*

right·ly /ˈraɪtli/ *adv.* correctly, or for a good reason: *The book has rightly been called "an American Classic."* | *The organization decided, **rightly or wrongly**, that the problem was limited.*

ˌright of 'way *n.* (plural **rights of way**) **1** [U] the right to drive into or across a road before other vehicles: *You **have the right of way** at this intersection.* **2** [C,U] the right to go across private land, or a place where you can do this

ˌright 'triangle *also* **ˌright-angled 'triangle** *n.* [C] MATH a TRIANGLE in which the angle opposite the longest side measures 90° → *see picture at* TRIANGLE

ˌright-'wing *adj.* POLITICS a right-wing person or group supports the ideas and beliefs of CAPITALISM ANT **left-wing**: *a right-wing newspaper* —**right-winger** *n.* [C] —**right wing** *n.* [singular]

rig·id /ˈrɪdʒɪd/ AC *adj.* **1** rigid methods, systems, etc. are very strict and difficult to change ANT **flexible**: *parents who set rigid rules*

THESAURUS **strict, firm, rigorous, stringent** → STRICT

2 someone who is rigid is very unwilling to change his/her ideas ANT **flexible** **3** stiff and not moving or bending ANT **flexible**: *a tent supported on a rigid frame* [ORIGIN: 1400—1500 Latin *rigidus*, from *rigere* "to be stiff"]

THESAURUS **hard, firm, stiff** → HARD¹

—**rigidly** *adv.* —**rigidity** /rɪˈdʒɪdəṭi/ *n.* [U]

rig·ma·role /ˈrɪgməˌroʊl/ *n.* [singular, U] a set of actions that seems silly: *the rigmarole of filling out all these forms* [ORIGIN: 1700—1800 *ragman roll* "document containing a long list, used in a game called "ragman"" (15—18 centuries)]

rig·or /ˈrɪgɚ/ *n.* **1** [U] the action of taking great care and being thorough in making sure that something is correct: *students who lack intellectual rigor* **2 the rigors of sth** the problems and difficulties of a situation: *the rigors of a Canadian winter*

rig·or mor·tis /ˌrɪgɚ 'mɔrt̬ɪs/ *n.* [U] BIOLOGY the condition in which someone's body becomes stiff after s/he dies

rig·or·ous /'rɪgərəs/ *adj.* **1** careful and thorough: *rigorous safety checks*

THESAURUS **strict, tough, firm, stringent** → STRICT

2 very strict or severe: *rigorous education standards* —**rigorously** *adv.*

rile /raɪl/ *also* **rile up** *v.* [T] (informal) to make someone very angry

rim /rɪm/ *n.* [C] **1** the outside edge of something, especially something circular such as a glass: *the rim of the Grand Canyon*

THESAURUS **edge, border, boundary, perimeter, margin, hem, curb** → EDGE[1]

R

2 -rimmed with a particular type of rim: *gold-rimmed glasses*

rind /raɪnd/ *n.* [C,U] the thick outer skin of some foods, such as cheese or fruit

ring[1] /rɪŋ/ *n.* [C] **1** a piece of jewelry that you wear on your finger: *a **wedding ring** | a **diamond ring*** → *see picture at* JEWELRY **2** a circular line or mark: *a dirty ring around the tub* **3** an object in the shape of a circle: *a key ring* **4** a group of people or things arranged in a circle: *a ring of young birch trees* **5** a group of people who illegally control a business or criminal activity: *a drug ring* **6** the sound made by a bell, or the act of making this sound: *a ring at the door* → *see picture on page A20* **7** a small square area where people BOX or WRESTLE, or the large circular area surrounded by seats at a CIRCUS [ORIGIN: (1) Old English *hring*]

ring[2] *v.* (past tense **rang** /ræŋ/, past participle **rung** /rʌŋ/) **1** [I,T] to make a bell make a sound, especially to call someone's attention to you: *Benjy rang the doorbell.* **2** [I] if a bell rings, it makes a noise: *The telephone's ringing.* **3** [I] if your ears ring, they are filled with a continuous sound that only you can hear **4 ring a bell** (informal) if something rings a bell, you think you have heard it before: *Frank Gordon – the name rings a bell, but I can't be sure.* **5 not ring true** if something does not ring true, you do not believe it: *None of these explanations rang true.*

ring out *phr. v.* if a voice, bell, etc. rings out, it makes a loud and clear sound: *Shouts rang out from the schoolyard.*

ring sth ↔ **up** *phr. v.* to press buttons on a CASH REGISTER to record how much money needs to be put inside it: *She rang up our purchases.*

ring[3] *v.* (past tense and past participle **ringed**) [T] to surround something: *a house ringed by trees*

ring·lead·er /'rɪŋˌlidɚ/ *n.* [C] someone who leads a group that is doing something illegal or wrong

ring·let /'rɪŋlɪt/ *n.* [C] a long curl of hair that hangs down

ring·side /'rɪŋsaɪd/ *n.* [singular] the area nearest to the performance in a CIRCUS or BOXING match: *a ringside seat*

ring·worm /'rɪŋwɚm/ *n.* [U] a common disease that gives you red rough circles on your skin

rink /rɪŋk/ *n.* [C] a building with a specially prepared area with a smooth surface where you can SKATE: *an ice rink*

rinse[1] /rɪns/ *v.* [T] to use running water and no soap in order to remove dirt, soap, etc.: *He used a hose to **rinse off** the car.* | ***Rinse** the lettuce **in** cold water.* [ORIGIN: 1200—1300 Old French *rincer*]

rinse sth ↔ **out** *phr. v.* to wash something with clean water but not soap: *Chuck rinsed out his cup.*

rinse[2] *n.* **1** [C,U] a product used for slightly changing the color of hair: *a brown rinse* **2** [C] an act of rinsing something: *Add fabric softener during the final rinse.*

ri·ot[1] /'raɪət/ *n.* **1** [C] a situation in which a crowd of people behaves in a violent and uncontrolled way: *the **race riots*** (=caused by problems between different races of people) *of the late 1960s* **2** [singular] someone or something that is very funny or enjoyable **3 read sb the riot act** (informal) to warn someone angrily that s/he must stop doing something wrong [ORIGIN: 1100—1200 Old French "quarrel"]

riot[2] *v.* [I] if a crowd of people riots, they all behave violently in a public place → PROTEST[2] —**rioter** *n.* [C]

ri·ot·ing /'raɪət̬ɪŋ/ *n.* [U] violent and uncontrolled behavior from a crowd that is out of control: ***Rioting broke out** in the city late last night.*

ri·ot·ous /'raɪət̬əs/ *adj.* **1** noisy, exciting, and fun in an uncontrolled way: *the kids cheered with riotous pleasure* **2** noisy, possibly dangerous, and not controlled: *riotous crowds*

RIP Rest in Peace – written on a GRAVESTONE

rip[1] /rɪp/ *v.* (**ripped**, **ripping**) [I,T] to tear something, or be torn, quickly and violently: *Dave ripped his jacket on the fence.* | *Don't pull on it; it'll rip.* | *I ripped a sheet of paper from my notebook.* | *Impatiently, Sue **ripped** the letter **open**.*

rip sth ↔ **apart** *phr. v.* to destroy something by separating it into pieces: *Their family has been ripped apart by the murder.* | *The bomb ripped apart a bus.*

rip into sb *phr. v.* to criticize someone angrily

rip off *phr. v.* (spoken) **1 rip** sb ↔ **off** to charge someone too much money for something: *The cab driver tried to rip me off!* **2 rip** sth ↔ **off** to steal something: *Someone ripped off the liquor store.*

rip through sth *phr. v.* to move through a place quickly and violently: *typhoons that rip through the islands*

rip sth ↔ **up** *phr. v.* to tear something into several pieces: *In frustration, she ripped up her story.*

rip² *n.* [C] a long tear or cut

ripe /raɪp/ *adj.* **1** ripe food or crops are ready to eat: *ripe peaches* **2 be ripe for sth** to be in the right condition for something: *The company is weak and ripe for a takeover.* **3 the time is ripe (for sth)** used in order to say it is the right time for something to happen: *She'll grab for power when the time is ripe.* **4 ripe old age** if you live to a ripe old age, you are very old when you die [ORIGIN: Old English] —**ripeness** *n.* [U]

rip·en /'raɪpən/ *v.* [I,T] to become ripe, or to make something do this

rip·off, rip-off /'rɪpɔf/ *n.* [C] (spoken) **1** something that is unreasonably expensive, and makes you feel cheated: *Most diet products are a complete ripoff.* **2** a piece of music or art or a movie that copies something else without admitting it

rip·ple¹ /'rɪpəl/ *v.* **1** [I,T] to move in small waves, or to make something do this: *a soft breeze rippled the wheat* **2** [I] to make a noise like water that is flowing gently: *water rippling over rocks* **3** [I] to pass from one person to the next like a wave: *Laughter **rippled through/around** the crowd.*

ripples

ripple² *n.* [C] **1** a small low wave on the surface of a liquid: *ripples on the pond* **2** a feeling or sound that spreads through a person or group because of something that happens: *A **ripple of** laughter ran through the audience.* **3 ripple effect** a situation in which one action causes another, which then causes a third, etc.

rise¹ /raɪz/ *v.* (past tense **rose** /roʊz/, past participle **risen** /'rɪzən/) [I]
1 INCREASE to increase in number, amount, quality, or value (ANT) **fall**: *Ocean temperatures are rising.* | *Tourism **rose by** 4% last year.* | *The population has **risen steadily/sharply** since the 1950s.* | *rising crime/unemployment*

THESAURUS increase, go up, grow, double, shoot up, multiply → INCREASE¹

2 GO UP to go up (ANT) **fall**: *Smoke rose from the chimney.* | *The tide had risen.* → *see picture at* RAISE¹

USAGE
Rise is not followed by an object: *The balloon rose high into the air.*
Raise is always followed by an object: *Raise your hand if you know the answer.*

3 STAND to stand up: *Thornton **rose to his feet** and turned to speak to them.*
4 BECOME SUCCESSFUL to become important, powerful, successful, or rich: *Presley **rose to** fame in the 1950s.*
5 VOICE/SOUND to be heard, especially by getting louder or stronger: *The sound of traffic rose from the street below.*
6 SUN/MOON/STAR to appear in the sky (ANT) **set**: *The moon rose over the lake.*
7 EMOTION to get stronger: *You could feel the excitement rising as we waited.*
8 MOUNTAIN/BUILDING to be or seem taller than anything else around: *the skyscrapers that **rise above** the Manhattan skyline*
9 BREAD/CAKES if bread, cakes, etc. rise, they become bigger as they bake because there is air inside them
10 rise to the occasion/challenge to deal with a difficult situation or problem successfully by doing things better than you have done them before
11 all rise (spoken, formal) used in order to tell people to stand up when a judge enters a court of law
12 BED (literary) to get out of bed in the morning
13 AGAINST A GOVERNMENT (literary) *also* **rise up** to try to defeat the government or army that is in control of your country (SYN) **rebel**

rise above sth *phr. v.*
to be good or wise enough to not let a bad situation or influence affect you: *He rose above his poverty-stricken childhood to become a top lawyer.* [ORIGIN: Old English *risan*]

rise² *n.* **1** [C] an increase in number, amount, or value (ANT) **fall**: *a **rise in** college costs* | *price rises* **2** [singular] the achievement of importance, success, or power (ANT) **fall**: *a book about his **rise to fame/power/prominence*** **3 give rise to sth** to be the reason something happens or begins to exist: *The book's popularity gave rise to a number of imitations.* **4** [C] a movement upward: *the rise and fall of her chest as she breathed* **5** [C] an upward slope: *a slight rise in the road* **6 get a rise out of sb** (informal) to make someone annoyed or embarrassed by making a joke about him/her

ris·er /'raɪzɚ/ *n.* **1 early/late riser** someone who usually wakes up very early or very late **2 risers** [plural] a set of steps for a group of people to stand on

risk¹ /rɪsk/ *n.* **1** [C,U] the chance that something bad may happen: *the **risk of** injury to workers* | *There was a **risk (that)** the herd would stampede.* | *There is no **risk to** public health.* | *Healthy eating **reduces the risk of** cancer.*

THESAURUS danger, threat, hazard → DANGER

2 take a risk to do something even though there is a chance that something bad will happen: *We knew we were taking a risk when we lent him the*

R

money. **3 at risk** likely to be harmed or put in a bad situation: *The firm's reputation is at risk.* | *Small children may be* ***at risk from*** *car airbags.* | *men* ***at risk of/for*** *diabetes* | *people whose lifestyles* ***put them at risk*** *for AIDS* **4 run a risk** to be in a situation where something bad may happen to you: *The nurses run the risk of infection.* **5 at your own risk** if you do something at your own risk, no one else is responsible if something bad happens: *Parking is at your own risk.* **6** [C] something that is likely to hurt you or be dangerous: *Oily rags are a fire risk.* | *the* ***risk factors*** *for heart disease* (=things that make you likely to get sick) **7** [C] a person or business to whom it is a good or bad idea to give insurance or lend money: *Drivers under 21 are considered poor* ***insurance risks.*** [ORIGIN: 1600—1700 French *risque*, from Italian *risco*]

risk² *v.* [T] **1** to put something in a situation in which it could be lost, destroyed, or harmed: *I'm not going to* ***risk*** *my life* ***to*** *save a cat!* | *If you don't make the loan payments, you risk losing your home.* **2** to do something that you know may have bad results: *She risked a glance back over her shoulder.*

R

risk·y /ˈrɪski/ *adj.* involving a risk that something bad will happen: *Doctors said that operating would be too risky.* | *Investing in the stock market is* ***risky business*** (=a risky thing to do). —**riskiness** *n.* [U]

ris·qué /rɪsˈkeɪ/ *adj.* a joke, remark, etc. that is risqué is slightly shocking because it is about sex

rite /raɪt/ *n.* [C] **1** a ceremony that is always performed in the same way, often for a religious purpose: *funeral rites* **2 rite of passage** a special ceremony or action that is a sign of a new time in someone's life

rit·u·al¹ /ˈrɪtʃuəl/ *n.* [C,U] a ceremony or set of actions that is always done in the same way: *religious rituals* | *the Christmas ritual of decorating the tree*

ritual² *adj.* **1** done as part of a rite or ritual: *ritual sacrifice* **2** done in a particular expected way, but without real meaning: *ritual campaign promises*

ritz·y /ˈrɪtsi/ *adj.* (informal) fashionable and expensive: *a ritzy neighborhood*

ri·val¹ /ˈraɪvəl/ *n.* [C] a person, group, or organization that you compete with: *a business rival* [ORIGIN: 1500—1600 Latin *rivalis* "someone who uses the same stream as another, rival in love," from *rivus* "stream"]

rival² *adj.* **rival company/team/player etc.** a person, group, or organization that competes against you: *rival airlines*

rival³ *v.* [T] to be as good or important as someone or something else: *The band rivaled The Doors as L.A.'s finest rock band.*

ri·val·ry /ˈraɪvəlri/ *n.* (plural **rivalries**) [C,U] competition over a long period of time: *sibling rivalry* | *the* ***rivalry between*** *the two teams*

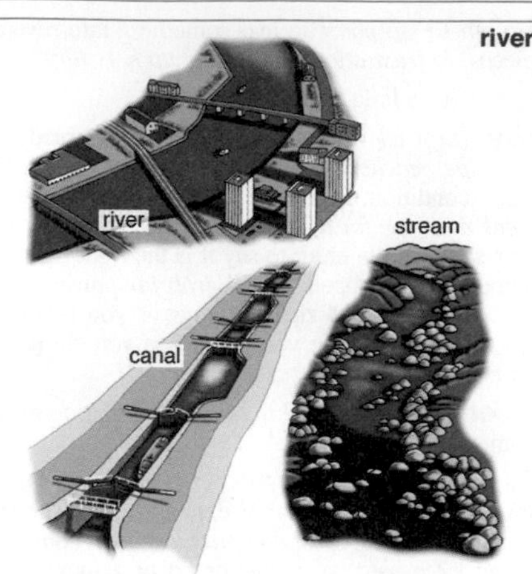

riv·er /ˈrɪvɚ/ *n.* [C] **1** EARTH SCIENCES a natural and continuous flow of water in a long line that goes into an ocean, lake, etc.: *the Colorado River* | *trees on the* ***river bank*** (=land on the edge of a river) | *a boat sailing* ***up/down river*** (=in the opposite direction that a river is flowing, or in the same direction) **2** a large amount of moving liquid: *a* ***river of*** *tears* [ORIGIN: 1200—1300 Old French *rivere*, from Latin *riparius* "of a river bank"]

riv·er·bed /ˈrɪvɚˌbɛd/ *n.* [C] EARTH SCIENCES the ground over which a river flows

riv·er·side /ˈrɪvɚˌsaɪd/ *n.* [singular] the land on the sides of a river: *a cottage on the riverside*

riv·et¹ /ˈrɪvɪt/ *n.* [C] a metal pin for fastening flat pieces of metal together

rivet² *v.* [T] **1** to attract and hold someone's attention: *People sat* ***riveted to*** *their TVs during the trial.* **2** to fasten something with rivets

riv·et·ing /ˈrɪvət̬ɪŋ/ *adj.* extremely interesting: *a riveting tale of suspense*

> THESAURUS **interesting, fascinating, absorbing, enthralling, engrossing, compelling, gripping** → INTERESTING

R.N. the abbreviation of REGISTERED NURSE

RNA *n.* [U] BIOLOGY **ribonucleic acid** an important chemical that exists in all living cells and controls chemical activity in cells → DNA

roach /routʃ/ *n.* [C] (informal) a COCKROACH

road /roud/ *n.* **1** [C,U] a specially prepared hard surface for vehicles to travel on: *Tom's dad lives just* ***up/down the road*** (=farther along the road). | *the* ***main road*** *out of town* | *a* ***side/back road*** (=a small one that is not used very much) | *the traffic on Mission Road* | *ice* ***on the roads*** (=on all the streets and roads in an area)

> THESAURUS
>
> **Types of road**
>
> **street** – a road in a town, with houses or stores on each side

main street – a road in the middle of a town where many stores, offices, etc. are
avenue – a road in a town, often with trees on each side
lane – a narrow road in the country, or one of the two or three parallel areas on a road which are divided by painted lines to keep traffic apart
main road – a large and important road
the main drag (informal) – the main road through a town
highway – a very wide road for traveling fast over long distances
freeway/expressway – a very wide road in a city or between cities, on which cars can travel very fast without stopping
toll road – a road that you pay to use
turnpike – a large road for fast traffic that you pay to use

2 on the road **a)** traveling for a long distance, especially in a car: *We've been on the road since 7:00 a.m.* **b)** if a sports team, group of actors, etc. are on the road, they are traveling to different places playing games or giving performances: *Oregon had two losses on the road.* **3 on the road to success/recovery etc.** developing in a way that will result in success, health, etc. **4 down the road** in the future: *That may cause problems further down the road.* [ORIGIN: Old English *rad* "ride, journey"]

road·block /ˈroʊdblɑk/ *n.* [C] **1** something that stops the progress of a plan: *Lack of education is a* ***roadblock to*** *success.* **2** a place where the police are blocking the road to stop traffic: *Police* ***put/set up roadblocks*** *to catch drunk drivers.*

road·house /ˈroʊdhaʊs/ *n.* [C] a restaurant or BAR on a road outside a city

road·kill /ˈroʊdkɪl/ *n.* [U] (informal) animals that are killed by cars on a road or HIGHWAY

road·run·ner /ˈroʊdˌrʌnɚ/ *n.* [C] a small bird that runs very fast and lives in the southwest U.S.

road·side /ˈroʊdsaɪd/ *n.* [singular] the edge of a road: *a roadside restaurant*

ˈroad trip *n.* [C] **1** a long trip in a car, taken for pleasure **2** an occasion when a sports team travels to other places to play: *a four-game road trip*

road·way /ˈroʊdweɪ/ *n.* [singular] the part of the road that is used by vehicles

roam /roʊm/ *v.* [I,T] to walk or travel for a long time with no clear purpose: *Buffalo roamed the prairie.* | *I spent the summer* ***roaming around/through*** *Europe.*

roar¹ /rɔr/ *v.* **1** [I] to make a deep, very loud noise: *lions roaring* | *Jets roared overhead.* **2** [I] if a vehicle roars somewhere, it moves very quickly and in a noisy way: *Two motorcycles* ***roared down*** *the street.* **3** [I,T] to say something or laugh with a loud voice: *"What are you doing?" he roared.* | *The audience* ***roared with laughter.***

roar² *n.* [C] a deep loud continuous sound: *a roar of laughter* | *the roar of the engine*

roar·ing /ˈrɔrɪŋ/ *adj.* **roaring fire** a fire that burns with a lot of flames and heat

roast¹ /roʊst/ *v.* [I,T] to cook meat or vegetables in an OVEN or over a fire

THESAURUS cook, bake, fry, broil, grill, sauté, boil, steam, deep fry → COOK¹

roast² *n.* [C] **1** a large piece of roasted meat **2** an outdoor party at which food is cooked on an open fire: *a hot dog roast* **3** an occasion at which people celebrate someone by telling funny stories and giving speeches about him/her

roast³ *adj.* having been roasted: *roast beef*

rob /rɑb/ *v.* (**robbed**, **robbing**) [T] to steal money or things from a person, bank, etc.: *The boys robbed a convenience store.*

THESAURUS steal, burglarize, mug, shoplift, loot, plunder, pilfer → STEAL¹

rob sb/sth **of** sth *phr. v.* to take away an important quality, ability, etc. from someone or something: *A hamstring injury robbed him of his speed.*

rob·ber /ˈrɑbɚ/ *n.* [C] someone who steals things, especially from stores or banks: *a bank robber*

THESAURUS criminal, offender, thief, burglar, shoplifter, pickpocket → CRIMINAL²

rob·ber·y /ˈrɑbəri/ *n.* (plural **robberies**) [C,U] the crime of stealing money or things from a person or place: *Most home robberies are drug-related.* | *the* ***armed robbery*** (=robbery using a gun) *of a bank*

THESAURUS crime, theft, burglary, shoplifting → CRIME

robe /roʊb/ *n.* [C] a long loose piece of clothing: *pajamas and a robe* | *a judge's black robe*

rob·in /ˈrɑbɪn/ *n.* [C] a common wild bird with a red chest and brown back [ORIGIN: 1500—1600 *robin redbreast* "robin," from *Robin*, form of the male name *Robert*]

ro·bot /ˈroʊbɑt, -bʌt/ *n.* [C] a machine that can move and do some of the work of a person, and is controlled by a computer: *industrial robots* [ORIGIN: 1900—2000 Czech *robota* "work"] —**robotic** /roʊˈbɑt̬ɪk, rə-/ *adj.*

ro·bot·ics /roʊˈbɑt̬ɪks/ *n.* [U] SCIENCE the study of how robots are made and used

ro·bust /roʊˈbʌst, ˈroʊbʌst/ *adj.* strong and healthy, or not likely to have problems: *a robust 70-year-old man* | *robust economic growth* [ORIGIN: 1500—1600 Latin *robustus* "strong (like an oak tree)," from *robur* "oak, strength"]

rock¹ /rɑk/ *n.* **1** [U] EARTH SCIENCES a type of stone that forms part of the Earth's surface: *a tunnel cut through solid rock* **2** [C] a large piece of stone: *A ship hit the rocks in the storm.* | *He sat on a rock by the river, fishing.* **3** [U] *also* **rock music** a type of popular modern music with a strong loud beat, played on GUITARS and drums: *a rock band* | *a rock* *concert* **4 be between a rock and a hard place** to have a choice between two things, both of which are unpleasant **5 on the rocks a)** alcoholic drinks that are served on the rocks have ice in them **b)** a relationship or marriage that is on the rocks is failing [ORIGIN: (2) 1900—2000 Old English *roccian*]

rock² *v.* **1** [I,T] to move gently, leaning from one side to the other, or to make something do this: *She rocked the cradle until the baby slept.* | *Hilda rocked back and forth, crying.* | *The boat rocked gently.* **2** [T] to make the people in a place feel very shocked or surprised: *a city rocked by violence* **3 rock the boat** (informal) to cause problems for other members of a group by criticizing something or trying to change the way something is done **4 sb/sth rocks** (spoken) said in order to show that you strongly approve of someone or something

ˌrock and ˈroll *n.* [U] another spelling of ROCK'N'ROLL

R

ˌrock ˈbottom *n.* **hit/reach rock bottom** (informal) to become as bad as something can possibly be: *By June, their marriage had hit rock bottom.*

ˈrock-bottom *adj.* rock-bottom prices are as low as they can possibly be

ˈrock ˌcycle *n.* **the rock cycle** EARTH SCIENCES the series of events in which rocks are formed, changed, destroyed, and formed again as the result of different natural processes

rock·er /ˈrɑkɚ/ *n.* **1** [C] a ROCKING CHAIR **2 be off your rocker** (spoken) to be crazy

rock·et¹ /ˈrɑkɪt/ *n.* [C] **1** a vehicle used for traveling or carrying things into space, which is shaped like a big tube **2** a weapon shaped like a big tube ➔ MISSILE: *They began **firing rockets** at the ship.* **3** a type of FIREWORK [ORIGIN: 1600—1700 Italian *rocchetta* "small stick used in spinning thread," from *rocca* "stick used in spinning"]

rocket² *v.* [I] **1** to move somewhere very fast: *Her serve rocketed over the net.* **2** to achieve a successful position very quickly: *The song rocketed to number one in the charts.* **3** *also* **rocket up** if a price or amount rockets, it increases quickly and suddenly: *The company's shares rocketed up 46%.*

ˈrocking chair *n.* [C] a chair that has two curved pieces of wood fixed under it, so that it ROCKS ➔ *see picture at* SEAT¹

ˈrocking horse *n.* [C] a toy horse for children that ROCKs when you sit on it

rock'n'roll /ˌrɑkənˈroʊl/ *n.* [U] a type of music with a strong loud beat, played on GUITARs and drums, that first became popular in the 1950s

rock·y /ˈrɑki/ *adj.* **1** covered with rocks, or made of rock: *the rocky coast of Maine* **2** (informal) a relationship or situation that is rocky is difficult and may not continue or be successful: *The team has **gotten off to a rocky start** this season.*

rod /rɑd/ *n.* [C] a long thin pole or stick: *a fishing rod* [ORIGIN: Old English *rodd*]

rode /roʊd/ *v.* the past tense of RIDE

rodents

1. beaver 2. groundhog 3. chipmunk 4. squirrel 5. mouse

ro·dent /ˈroʊdnt/ *n.* [C] BIOLOGY one of a group of small animals with long sharp front teeth, such as rats or rabbits [ORIGIN: 1800—1900 Latin, present participle of *rodere* "to chew with the front teeth"]

ro·de·o /ˈroʊdiˌoʊ, roʊˈdeɪoʊ/ *n.* (plural **rodeos**) [C] a competition in which COWBOYs ride wild horses and catch cattle with ropes [ORIGIN: 1800—1900 Spanish *rodear* "to surround"]

roe /roʊ/ *n.* [C,U] fish eggs eaten as a food

rogue¹ /roʊg/ *adj.* [only before noun] a rogue person or organization does not follow the usual rules or methods, and often causes trouble: *The government is concerned about **rogue states** that may have nuclear weapons.*

rogue² *n.* [C] (old-fashioned) a man who often behaves in a slightly bad or dishonest way, but whom people still like

rogu·ish /ˈroʊgɪʃ/ *adj.* typical of a rogue, or behaving like a rogue: *the actor's roguish image*

role /roʊl/ (Ac) *n.* [C] **1** the position, job, or purpose that someone or something has in a particular situation or activity: *The company has **played a major/key role in** medical research over the years.* | *He has traditional views about the **role of** women in society.* | *Parents should **take an active role** in their child's education.* **2** ENG. LANG. ARTS the character played by an actor: *Who will **play the role of** Dorothy?* | *Kate has a **leading/starring role** in the movie.* [ORIGIN: 1600—1700 French *rôle* "roll, role," from Old French *rolle* "rolled up document"]

ˈrole ˌmodel *n.* [C] someone whose behavior or

attitude people try to copy because they admire him/her: *She's a **good/bad/positive role model** for teenagers.*

'role-play *n.* [C,U] an exercise in which you behave in the way that someone else would behave in a particular situation: *ideas for classroom role-plays* —**role-play** *v.* [I,T]

roll¹ /roʊl/ *v.*

roll

1 ROUND OBJECT [I,T] to move by turning over and over, or from side to side, or to make something do this: *The ball **rolled down** the street.* | *One of the eggs **rolled off** the counter.* | ***Roll** the chicken breasts **in** flour.* ➔ PUSH¹

2 PERSON/ANIMAL [I,T] *also* **roll over** to turn your body over when you are lying down, or to turn someone else's body over: *We tried to **roll** him **onto** his side.* | *Beth's dog has been **rolling in** the mud.*

3 SHAPE OF TUBE/BALL [T] to make something into the shape of a tube or ball: ***Roll** the dough **into** small balls.*

4 STH WITH WHEELS [I,T] to move on wheels, or make something that has wheels move: *The van was starting to **roll backwards**.* | *The waitress **rolled** the dessert cart **over** to our table.*

5 MAKE STH FLAT [T] *also* **roll out** to make something flat by moving something round and heavy over it: *Roll the pie crust thin.* ➔ *see picture on page A18*

6 DROP OF LIQUID [I] to move over a surface smoothly without stopping: *A tear **rolled down** her cheek.*

7 roll your eyes to move your eyes around and up to show that you think someone or something is stupid

8 WAVES/CLOUDS [I] to move continuously in a particular direction: *We watched the waves **rolling onto** the beach.* | *We could see the fog starting to **roll in**.*

9 GAME [I,T] if you roll DICE, you throw them as part of a game

10 SOUND [I] if a drum or THUNDER rolls, it makes a long deep sound

11 MACHINE/CAMERA [I] if a machine such as a movie camera or a PRINTING PRESS rolls, it operates: *Quiet! The cameras are rolling!*

12 (all) rolled into one including several things in one thing: *The class was a history, art, and language course all rolled into one.*

SPOKEN PHRASES

13 be ready to roll used in order to say that you are ready to do something or go somewhere: *After months of planning, we were finally ready to roll.*

14 let's roll used in order to suggest to a group of people that you all begin doing something or go somewhere

15 be rolling in money/dough/cash/it to have or earn a lot of money

roll around *phr. v.* (informal)
if a regular time or event rolls around, it arrives or happens again: *By the time Friday night rolled around, we were too tired to go out.*

roll sth ↔ **back** *phr. v.*
to reduce the price of something: *a promise to roll back taxes*

roll sth ↔ **down** *phr. v.*
roll a window down to open a car window

roll in *phr. v.* (informal)
1 to arrive in large numbers or quantities: *Investors will expect profits to start rolling in soon.*
2 to arrive later than expected: *They finally rolled in at 4:00.*

roll up *phr. v.*
1 roll sth up to curl something so that it is in the shape of a ball or a tube: *Painters arrived and rolled up the carpet.*
2 roll your sleeves up to start doing a job even though it is difficult or you do not want to do it
3 roll a window up to close a car window

roll² *n.* [C] **1** a piece of paper, film, money, etc. that has been curled into the shape of a tube: *I need to buy a **roll of film*** | *rolls of toilet paper* **2** a small round LOAF of bread for one person: *The soup comes with a roll.* **3** an official list of the names of people at a meeting, in a class, etc. ➔ ROLL CALL, HONOR ROLL **4 be on a roll** (informal) to be having a lot of success with what you are trying to do: *I don't want to stop playing – I'm on a roll!* **5** a thick layer of skin or fat, usually just below your waist: *the **rolls of fat** on his stomach* **6** a long deep sound: *There was a **roll of thunder** and then the rain started coming down.* **7** an action of throwing DICE as part of a game

'roll call *n.* [C,U] the act of reading out an official list of names to check who is present at a meeting or in a class

roll·er /ˈroʊlɚ/ *n.* [C] **1** a tube-shaped piece of wood, metal, etc. that can be rolled over and over: *paint rollers* **2** a CURLER

Roll·er·blade /ˈroʊlɚˌbleɪd/ *n.* [C] (trademark) a special boot with a single row of wheels fixed under it that you wear for skating (SKATE) ➔ ROLLER SKATE —**rollerblade** *v.* [I] —**rollerblading** *n.* [U]

'roller ˌcoaster *n.* [C] **1** a track with sudden steep slopes and curves, that people ride on in special cars at FAIRS and AMUSEMENT PARKS **2** a situation that is impossible to control because it keeps changing very quickly: *I feel like I'm on an **emotional roller coaster**.*

'roller skate *n.* [C] a special boot with four wheels fixed under it that you wear for skating (SKATE) —**rollerskate** *v.* [I] —**rollerskating** *n.* [U]

rol·lick·ing /ˈrɑlɪkɪŋ/ *adj.* [only before noun] noisy and cheerful: *a rollicking good time*

R

roll·ing /ˈroʊlɪŋ/ *adj.* rolling hills have many long gentle slopes

ˈrolling pin *n.* [C] a long tube-shaped piece of wood used for making PASTRY flat and thin before you cook it

ro·ly-po·ly /ˌroʊli ˈpoʊli/ *adj.* a roly-poly person is short and fat

ROM /rɑm/ *n.* [U] IT **read-only memory** the part of a computer where permanent instructions and information are stored → RAM

Ro·man Cath·olic /ˌroʊmən ˈkæθlɪk/ *adj.* relating to the part of the Christian religion whose leader is the Pope: *the Roman Catholic Church* —**Roman Catholic** *n.* [C]

ro·mance /ˈroʊmæns, roʊˈmæns/ *n.* **1** [C] an exciting relationship between two people who love each other: *a summer romance* **2** [C] ENG. LANG. ARTS a story, book, or movie about two people who fall in love with each other **3** [U] the feeling of excitement and adventure that is related to a particular place, activity, etc.: *the **romance of** traveling to distant places* [ORIGIN: 1200—1300 Old French *romans* "French, something written in French," from Latin *romanicus* "Roman"]

R

ˌRoman ˈnumeral *n.* [C] a number in a system that was used in ancient Rome, that uses combinations of the letters I, V, X, L, C, D to represent numbers: *XXVII is the Roman numeral for 27.*

ro·man·tic¹ /roʊˈmæntɪk/ *adj.* **1** showing strong feelings of love: *"Paul gave me roses for our anniversary." "How romantic!"* **2** involving feelings of love: *I'm not ready for a romantic relationship.* **3** a romantic story or movie is about love: *a new romantic comedy* **4** (disapproving) romantic ideas are not practical because they are based on how you would like things to be rather than how they really are (ANT) **realistic**: *the **romantic notion** that Christmas shopping is a magical event* —**romantically** *adv.*: *They were never romantically involved.*

romantic² *n.* [C] **1** someone who shows strong feelings of love and likes doing things that are related to love, such as buying flowers, presents, etc. **2** someone who is not practical and bases his/her actions too much on an imagined idea of the world (ANT) **realist**

ro·man·ti·cism, Romanticism /roʊˈmæntəˌsɪzəm/ *n.* [U] ENG. LANG. ARTS a way of writing or painting that was popular in the late 18th and early 19th centuries, in which feelings and wild natural beauty were considered more important than anything else

ro·man·ti·cize /roʊˈmæntəˌsaɪz/ *v.* [T] to talk or think about things in a way that makes them seem more attractive than they really are: *a romanticized idea of country life*

romp /rɑmp/ *v.* [I] **1** to play in a noisy way by running, jumping, etc.: *They could hear the children romping around upstairs.* **2** to win a race, competition, election, etc. very easily —**romp** *n.* [C]: *the Yankees' 12–1 romp over the Red Sox*

roof¹ /ruf, rʊf/ *n.* [C] **1** the part of a building or vehicle that covers the top of it: *They finally found the cat up on the roof.* | *The roof is leaking.* | *We can probably strap the bikes to the **roof of** the car.* **2** the top of a passage under the ground: *The roof of the tunnel suddenly collapsed.* **3 the roof of your mouth** the top part of the inside of your mouth **4 a roof over your head** a place to live: *I may not have a job, but at least I've got a roof over my head.* **5 under one roof/under the same roof** in the same building or house: *If we're going to live under the same roof, we need to get along.* [ORIGIN: Old English *hrof*]

roof² *v.* [T] to put a roof on a building: *a house **roofed with** tiles*

roof·ing /ˈrufɪŋ/ *n.* [U] material for making or covering roofs

roof·top /ˈruftɑp/ *n.* [C] the top surface of a building: *People were standing on rooftops to watch the parade.*

rook·ie /ˈrʊki/ *n.* [C] someone who has just started doing a job or playing a professional sport, and has little experience: *a rookie policeman*

room¹ /rum, rʊm/ *n.* **1** [C] a part of the inside of a building that has its own walls, floor, and ceiling: *The room is quite big.* | *the **living room/dining room*** | *a **hotel/motel room*** | *Amanda, can you clean up **your room*** (=your bedroom), *please?* **2** [U] enough space for a particular purpose: *There isn't any more **room in** the closet.* | *Save **room for** dessert!* | *The kids don't have much **room to** play in the yard.* **3** [U] the possibility that something may exist or will happen: *I always try to **make room** for exercise.* | *There was little **room for doubt** that he was guilty.* | *Good work is being done, but there's still **room for improvement*** (=the possibility of doing better). **4** [singular] all the people in a room: ***The whole room** started singing "Happy Birthday."* [ORIGIN: Old English *rum*]

room² *v.* **room with sb** to share the room that you live in with someone, for example at college

ˌroom and ˈboard *n.* [U] a room to sleep in, and meals: *Room and board at school costs $600 a month.*

room·mate /ˈrum-meɪt/ *n.* [C] someone with whom you share a room, apartment, or house: *college roommates*

ˈroom ˌservice *n.* [U] a service provided by a hotel, by which food, drinks, etc. can be brought to a guest's room: *We decided to **order room service**.*

room·y /ˈrumi, ˈrʊmi/ *adj.* with plenty of space inside: *a roomy car*

roost /rust/ *n.* [C] a place where birds rest and sleep —**roost** *v.* [I]

roost·er /ˈrustɚ/ *n.* [C] a male chicken

root¹ /rut, rʊt/ *n.* [C]
1 PLANT the part of a plant or tree that grows under

the ground: *Cover the roots with plenty of soil.* → *see picture at* PLANT[1]
2 PROBLEM the basic or main part of a problem or idea: *The love of money is* ***the root of*** (=is the cause of) *all evil.* | *the* ***root causes*** *of crime.* | *A good mechanic will* ***get to the root of*** *the problem.*

THESAURUS **origin, source** → ORIGIN

3 roots [plural] the origin or main part of something such as a CUSTOM, law, activity, etc. from which other things have developed: *Jazz* ***has its roots in*** *African music.*
4 sb's roots someone's connection with a place because s/he was born there or his/her family lived there: *She's proud of her Polish roots.*
5 put down roots to start to feel that a place is your home
6 TOOTH/HAIR BIOLOGY the part of a tooth, hair, etc. that is fixed to the rest of the body
7 take root a) if an idea takes root, people begin to accept or believe it: *helping democracy take root* **b)** if a plant takes root, it grows into the ground
8 LANGUAGE *also* **root word** ENG. LANG. ARTS a word that is used as a base to make other longer words by adding a PREFIX or a SUFFIX to it. For example, "undrinkable" includes the root "drink."
9 MATHEMATICS MATH the root of a number is a smaller number that, when it is multiplied by itself a particular number of times, equals the number that you have: *2 is the fourth root of 16* (=2 × 2 × 2 × 2 = 16). [ORIGIN: 1100—1200 Old Norse *rot*]
→ SQUARE ROOT, CUBE ROOT, GRASS ROOTS

root[2] *v.* **1 be rooted in sth** to have developed from something and be strongly influenced by it: *The country's problems are rooted in a series of economic blunders.* **2** [I] to search for something by moving things around: *I* ***rooted through*** *my purse for a pen and paper.* **3** [I,T] to grow roots, or to fix a plant firmly by its roots: *The bulbs will root in spring.*
root for sb *phr. v.* (informal) to support and encourage someone to succeed in a competition, test, or difficult situation: *We're all rooting for you, Bill.*
root sth ↔ **out** *phr. v.* to find out where a particular problem exists and get rid of it: *efforts to root out corruption in the police force*

'root beer *n.* [C,U] a sweet non-alcoholic drink made from the roots of some plants

'root hair *n.* [C] BIOLOGY one of very many small hairs that stick out from the surface of a plant's root

root·less /'rutlɪs/ *adj.* having nowhere that you feel is really your home

rope[1] /roʊp/ *n.* **1** [C,U] very strong thick string, made by twisting together many threads: *They tied a piece of rope around my waist and pulled me up.* **2 the ropes** [plural] the things someone needs to know in order to do a job: *I spent the first month* ***learning the ropes.*** | *New employees are assigned a buddy to* ***show them the ropes.*** **3 be at/near the end of your rope** to have no more strength or ability to deal with a difficult situation

rope[2] *v.* [T] to tie things together using rope: *Harvey* ***roped*** *his horse* ***to*** *a nearby tree.* | *The climbers were* ***roped together*** *for safety.*
rope sb ↔ **in/into** sth *phr. v.* (informal) to persuade someone to help you in a job or activity: *My wife and I have been roped into going to this fund-raising dinner.*
rope sth ↔ **off** *phr. v.* to surround an area with ropes in order to separate it from another area: *Police roped off the area of the robbery.*

ro·sa·ry /'roʊzəri/ *n.* (plural **rosaries**) [C] a string of BEADS used by Roman Catholics for counting prayers

rose[1] /roʊz/ *n.* [C] a common sweet-smelling flower that grows on a bush that has THORNS (=sharp points on a stem): *a dozen* ***red roses*** [ORIGIN: Old English, Latin *rosa*]

rose[2] *v.* the past tense of RISE

ro·sé /roʊ'zeɪ/ *n.* [U] pink wine

Rosh Ha·sha·nah /ˌrɑʃ hə'ʃɑnə/ *n.* Jewish New Year, in late September or early October

ros·ter /'rɑstə/ *n.* [C] **1** a list of the names of people on a sports team, in an organization, etc.: *the company's* ***roster of*** *top executives* | *Williams took Carney's place* ***on the*** *Miami Dolphin* ***roster.*** **2** a list of people's names showing the jobs they must do and when they must do them [ORIGIN: 1700—1800 Dutch *rooster* "frame for cooking things on, list," from *roosten* "to roast"]

ros·trum /'rɑstrəm/ *n.* [C] a small PLATFORM (=raised area) that you stand on in front of an AUDIENCE [ORIGIN: 1500—1600 Latin "beak, front part of a ship," from *rodere* "to chew with the front teeth"]

ros·y /'roʊzi/ *adj.* (comparative **rosier**, superlative **rosiest**) **1** seeming to offer hope of success or happiness: *The company has a* ***rosy future.*** **2** pink: *rosy cheeks*

rot[1] /rɑt/ *v.* (**rotted**, **rotting**) [I,T] to decay by a gradual natural process, or to make something do this SYN **decompose**: *Sugar rots your teeth.* | *old buildings that were left to rot*

rot[2] *n.* [U] the natural process of decaying, or the part of something that has decayed: *a tree full of rot*

ro·ta·ry /'roʊt̬əri/ *adj.* turning in a circle around a fixed point, like a wheel

ro·tate /'roʊteɪt/ *v.* **1** [I,T] to turn around a fixed point, or to make something do this: *The Earth rotates every 24 hours.* | ***Rotate*** *the handle* ***to*** *the right.*

THESAURUS **turn, twist, spin, whirl, twirl, swivel, go around, revolve** → TURN[1]

2 [I,T] if a job rotates, or if people rotate jobs, they each do the job for a fixed period of time: *We try to rotate the boring jobs.* **3** [T] EARTH SCIENCES to regularly change the crops grown on a piece of land

R

[ORIGIN: 1600—1700 Latin, past participle of *rotare*, from *rota* "wheel"] —**rotation** /roʊˈteɪʃən/ *n.* [C,U]: *crop rotation*

ROTC /ˈrɑtsi, ˌɑr oʊ ti ˈsi/ *n.* **Reserve Officers Training Corps** an organization that trains students to be U.S. army officers

rote /roʊt/ *n.* **learn sth by rote** to learn something by repeating it until you remember it, without really understanding it

ro·tis·ser·ie /roʊˈtɪsəri/ *n.* [C] a piece of equipment for cooking meat by turning it around and around on a metal ROD

ro·tor /ˈroʊt̬ɚ/ *n.* [C] the part of a machine that turns around on a fixed point

rot·ten /ˈrɑt̚n/ *adj.* **1** badly decayed: *rotten apples* **2** (informal) very bad: *I'm a rotten cook.* | *She felt rotten about having to fire him.* [ORIGIN: 1200—1300 Old Norse *rotinn*]

ro·tund /roʊˈtʌnd/ *adj.* having a fat round body ➔ FAT¹

R

ro·tun·da /roʊˈtʌndə/ *n.* [C] a round building or hall, especially one with a DOME

rouge /ruʒ/ *n.* [U] pink or red powder or cream that women put on their cheeks (SYN) **blush**

rough¹ /rʌf/ *adj.* **1** having an uneven surface ➔ FLAT, SMOOTH: *Our Jeep's good for traveling over rough ground.* **2** not exact, or not containing many details: *Can you give us a* ***rough idea*** *of the cost?* | *a* ***rough draft*** *of an essay* **3** using force or violence: *Ice hockey is a rough sport.* **4** a rough area has a lot of violence and crime: *a rough part of the city* **5** a rough period of time is one when you have a lot of problems and difficulties: *It sounds like you had a* ***rough day*** *at work.* | *I had a* ***rough night*** (=I did not sleep well). | *We've been through some* ***rough times*** *together.* **6** with strong winds or storms: *Their boat sank in* ***rough seas***. **7** not fair or kind: *Don't be so* ***rough on*** *her* (=be kinder). [ORIGIN: Old English *ruh*] —**roughness** *n.* [U]

rough² *v.* **rough it** (informal) to live in conditions that are not very comfortable: *We're going to rough it in the mountains for a few days.*

rough sb ↔ **up** *phr. v.* (informal) to attack someone by hitting him/her

rough³ *adv.* **play rough** to play in a fairly violent way

rough·age /ˈrʌfɪdʒ/ *n.* [U] BIOLOGY a substance in some foods that helps your BOWELS to work (SYN) **fiber**

ˌrough-and-ˈtumble *adj.* full of people competing, often in a cruel way: *the rough-and-tumble world of politics*

rough·house /ˈrʌfhaʊs/ *v.* [I] to play in a noisy physical way

rough·ly /ˈrʌfli/ *adv.* **1** not exactly (SYN) **approximately**, **about**: *Roughly 100 people came.*

THESAURUS about, approximately, around, or so, in the region of ➔ ABOUT²

2 not gently or carefully: *Don't pet the cat so roughly!*

rough·shod /ˈrʌfʃɑd/ *adv.* **ride roughshod over sb/sth** to behave in a way that ignores other people's feelings or opinions

rou·lette /ruˈlɛt/ *n.* [U] a game in which people try to win money by guessing which hole a small ball on a spinning wheel will fall into

round¹ /raʊnd/ *adj.* **1** shaped like a circle or a ball: *a round table* | *a tree with round berries* | *the baby's round cheeks*

THESAURUS oval, circular, triangular, rectangular, cylindrical ➔ SHAPE¹

2 a round number is a whole number, often ending in 0, that is usually not exact: *Let's make it a round number – $50.* | ***In round numbers*** (=to the nearest 10, 100, 1,000, etc.), *we supply 50% of the trucks in the area.* [ORIGIN: 1200—1300 Old French *roont*, from Latin *rotundus*] —**roundness** *n.* [U]

round² *n.* [C]

1 CONNECTED EVENTS a number of events that are related: *the latest* ***round of*** *peace talks*

THESAURUS stage, part, step, phase ➔ STAGE¹

2 DRINKS if you buy a round of drinks, you buy an alcoholic drink for all the people in your group: *I'll buy the next round.*

3 COMPETITION one of the parts of a competition that you have to finish or win before you can go to the next part: *She made it to the second round.* | *the final* ***round of*** *the championship*

4 round of applause a time when people CLAP to show that they enjoyed a performance: *Let's* ***give*** *them* ***a round of applause***.

5 rounds [plural] the usual visits or checks that someone makes as a part of his/her job, especially a doctor: *The theft was discovered by a security guard who was* ***making*** *his* ***rounds***.

6 SHOT a single shot from a gun: *The soldier fired several rounds before escaping.*

7 GOLF a complete game of golf

8 BOXING one of the periods in a BOXING match: *a 15-round heavyweight bout*

9 SONG ENG. LANG. ARTS a song for three or four singers who each start the same tune at different times until all of them are singing

round³ *v.* [T] **1** to go around something such as a bend or the corner of a building: *The Porsche* ***rounded the bend*** *at 120 mph.* **2** to make something round: *The edges of the counter have been rounded to make them safer.*

round sth ↔ **off** *phr. v.* to change an exact figure to the nearest whole number

round sth ↔ **out/off** *phr. v.* to do something pleasant at the end of an activity or event that makes the experience more satisfying: *Chocolate* *cake served with vanilla ice cream rounded out the meal.*

round up *phr. v.* **1 round** sb ↔ **up** to find and gather together a group of people or things: *Police rounded up 20 people for questioning.* **2 round** sth ↔ **up** to increase an exact figure to the next highest whole number

round[4] *adv.* AROUND → **all year round** *at* YEAR

round·a·bout /ˈraʊndəˌbaʊt/ *adj.* [only before noun] not done in the shortest most direct way: *a roundabout route to avoid heavy traffic*

ˌround ˈcharacter *also* **ˌrounded ˈcharacter** *n.* [C] ENG. LANG. ARTS a character (=person) in a book, movie, etc. with many features or qualities, who is interesting and often has an effect on the way the story develops → FLAT CHARACTER

ˌround-the-ˈclock *adj.* all the time, both day and night: *round-the-clock hospital care*

ˈround-trip *adj.* a round-trip ticket is for taking a trip from one place to another and back again (ANT) **one-way** —**round trip** *n.* [C]

round·up /ˈraʊndʌp/ *n.* [C] **1** an occasion when a lot of people or animals are brought together, often by force: ***a roundup of*** *criminal suspects* **2** a short description of the main parts of the news, on the radio or on television

rouse /raʊz/ *v.* [T] **1** to make someone want to do something: *The speech **roused** King's supporters **to** action.* **2** (formal) to wake up, or wake someone up

rous·ing /ˈraʊzɪŋ/ *adj.* making people feel excited and eager to do something: *a rousing speech*

rout /raʊt/ *v.* [T] to defeat someone completely —**rout** *n.* [C]

route[1] /rut, raʊt/ (Ac) *n.* [C] **1** the way from one place to another: *What is the shortest **route from** Memphis **to** Atlanta?* | *the most **direct route** home* | *We had to **take a** longer **route** because of the snow.* **2** a particular road or direction that something follows to get from one place to another: *the parade route* **3** a way of doing something or achieving a particular result: *This school has chosen a different route to establishing discipline.* [ORIGIN: 1100—1200 Old French, Vulgar Latin *rupta (via)* "broken way," from Latin *ruptus* "broken"]

route[2] *v.* [T] to send something or someone by a particular route → EN ROUTE: *All the military supplies were **routed through** Turkey.*

rout·er /ˌruṭɚ/ *n.* [C] IT a piece of electronic equipment that sends messages between different computers or between different networks very quickly

rou·tine[1] /ruˈtin/ *n.* **1** [C,U] the usual or normal way in which you do things: *Harry doesn't like any change in his **daily routine**.* | *It took us a little while to **get into** our old **routine**.* **2** [C] a series of movements performed one after the other: *an exercise routine*

routine[2] *adj.* **1** regular and usual: *a routine medical test* | *a few routine questions* **2** ordinary and boring: *a routine job* —**routinely** *adv.*

> THESAURUS **normal, ordinary, average, standard** → NORMAL[1]

rov·ing /ˈroʊvɪŋ/ *adj.* traveling or moving from one place to another: *a roving reporter*

row[1] /roʊ/ *n.* [C] **1** a line of things or people next to each other: ***a row of*** *houses* | *children standing **in a row*** **2** a line of seats in a theater, large room, etc.: *I sat **in the front row**.* **3 three/four etc. in a row** happening three times, four times, etc. in exactly the same way or with the same result: *We've lost four games in a row.*

row[2] *v.* [I,T] to make a boat move by using OARS: *Slowly, she **rowed across** the lake.*

row·boat /ˈroʊboʊt/ *n.* [C] a small boat that you move by using OARS → *see picture at* TRANSPORTATION

row·dy /ˈraʊdi/ *adj.* behaving in a noisy way that is not controlled: *a group of rowdy children* → LOUD[1] —**rowdiness** *n.* [U]

ˈrow house *n.* [C] a house that is part of a line of houses that are joined to each other → HOUSE[1]

row·ing /ˈroʊɪŋ/ *n.* [U] the sport or activity of making a boat move through water using OARS → *see picture on page A17*

roy·al /ˈrɔɪəl/ *adj.* relating to or belonging to a king or queen: *the royal family* [ORIGIN: 1200—1300 Old French *roial*, from Latin *regalis*]

roy·al·ty /ˈrɔɪəlti/ *n.* (plural **royalties**) **1** [C usually plural] ECONOMICS payments made to the writer of a book or piece of music **2** [U] members of a royal family

rpm **revolutions per minute** a measurement of the speed at which an engine turns

rRNA BIOLOGY the abbreviation of RIBOSOMAL RNA

RSI *n.* [U] **repetitive strain injury** pain in your hands or arms caused by doing the same movement many times, especially typing (TYPE)

RSVP an abbreviation that is written on invitations in order to ask someone to reply [ORIGIN: 1800—1900 French *répondez, s'il vous plaît* "please reply"]

rub[1] /rʌb/ *v.* (**rubbed**, **rubbing**) [I,T] **1** to move your hand, a cloth, etc. over a surface while pressing against it: *Laura took off her glasses and rubbed her eyes.* | *The stain will come out if you **rub harder**.* | *Can you **rub** some lotion **on** my back, please?*

> THESAURUS **touch, feel, stroke, scratch, pat, pet, caress** → TOUCH[1]

2 to press something against something else and move it around: *The cat was **rubbing against** my legs.* | *They were **rubbing** their hands **together**, trying to stay warm.* **3 rub it in** (informal) to remind someone of something embarrassing that

R

you know s/he wants to forget: *Okay, I was wrong – there's no need to keep rubbing it in!* **4 rub sb the wrong way** (informal) if someone rubs you the wrong way, s/he annoys you, usually without intending to **5 rub shoulders with sb** *also* **rub elbows with sb** (informal) to meet and spend time with important or famous people

rub off on sb *phr. v.* if a feeling, quality, or habit rubs off on someone, s/he starts to have it because someone else has it: *Her positive attitude seemed to rub off on everyone.*

rub² *n.* [C] an act of rubbing something or someone: *Could you* ***give*** *me a back* ***rub****?*

rub·ber /ˈrʌbɚ/ *n.* **1** [U] a substance used for making tires, boots, etc. that is made from chemicals or the liquid that comes out of tropical trees: *rubber gloves* ➔ *see picture at* MATERIAL¹ **2** [C] (informal) a CONDOM

ˌrubber ˈband *n.* [C] a thin circular piece of rubber used to hold things together

rub·ber·neck /ˈrʌbɚˌnɛk/ *v.* [I] (informal) to look around at something such as an accident while you are driving or walking past

ˌrubber-ˈstamp *v.* [T] (disapproving) to give official approval to something without really thinking about it

rub·ber·y /ˈrʌbəri/ *adj.* looking or feeling like rubber

rub·bish /ˈrʌbɪʃ/ *n.* [U] GARBAGE

rub·ble /ˈrʌbəl/ *n.* [U] broken stones or bricks from a building, wall, etc. that has been destroyed: *a pile of rubble*

rub·down /ˈrʌbdaʊn/ *n.* **give sb a rubdown** to give someone a MASSAGE in order to make him/her relax, especially after exercise

ru·bel·la /ruˈbɛlə/ *n.* [U] (formal) GERMAN MEASLES

ru·bid·i·um /ruˈbɪdiəm/ *n.* [U] CHEMISTRY (*symbol* **Rb**) a soft silver-white metal that is an ELEMENT

ru·bric /ˈrubrɪk/ *n.* [C] **1** (formal) a title for a group of things that all have the same particular qualities **2** ENG. LANG. ARTS the title written at the top of a piece of writing **3** (formal) a set of rules that are used to judge something

ru·by /ˈrubi/ *n.* (plural **rubies**) [C,U] a dark red jewel, or the color of this jewel [ORIGIN: 1300—1400 Old French *rubis*, *rubi*, from Latin *rubeus* "reddish"] **—ruby** *adj.*

ruck·us /ˈrʌkəs/ *n.* [singular] (informal) a noisy argument or confused situation: *What's all the ruckus about?*

rud·der /ˈrʌdɚ/ *n.* [C] a flat part at the back of a boat or aircraft, that is turned in order to change the direction in which the vehicle moves

rud·dy /ˈrʌdi/ *adj.* a ruddy face looks pink and healthy

rude /rud/ *adj.* **1** speaking or behaving in a way that is not polite: *a rude remark* | *Don't be* ***rude to*** *your grandmother!* ▸Don't say "rude with."◂ | ***It's rude to*** *stare.*

THESAURUS

impolite (formal) – not polite: *You might touch the person next to you and that would be impolite.*
insulting – saying or doing something that insults someone: *comments that are insulting to women*
tactless – carelessly saying or doing things that are likely to upset someone: *a tactless remark*
offensive – likely to upset or offend people: *His remarks are offensive to African Americans.*
insolent (formal) – deliberately rude, especially to someone in authority: *He was insolent toward the teacher.*
disrespectful – not showing respect for someone or something, when you should: *The players should not be disrespectful to the coach.*
impertinent (formal) – impolite and not respectful, especially to someone who is older or more important: *an impertinent child*
impudent (formal) – rude and not showing respect, especially to someone older than you: *He felt that some of the trainees were impudent.*

2 a rude awakening a situation in which someone suddenly realizes something upsetting or bad [ORIGIN: 1200—1300 Old French, Latin *rudis* "raw, rough"] **—rudely** *adv.* **—rudeness** *n.* [U]

ru·di·men·ta·ry /ˌrudəˈmɛntri, -ˈmɛntəri/ *adj.* (formal) very simple and basic: *a* ***rudimentary knowledge of*** *geometry*

ru·di·ments /ˈrudəmənts/ *n.* [plural] (formal) the most basic parts of a subject: *I learned* ***the rudiments of*** *the language before visiting Mexico.*

rue /ru/ *v.* [T] (literary) to wish that you had not done something (SYN) **regret**: *She'll* ***rue the day that*** *she met him.*

rue·ful /ˈrufəl/ *adj.* showing that you wish something had not happened but you accept it: *a rueful smile* **—ruefully** *adv.*

ruf·fle¹ /ˈrʌfəl/ *v.* [T] **1** to make a smooth surface uneven or messy: *He reached over and* ***ruffled*** *my* ***hair***. **2** to offend, annoy, or upset someone: *I don't want to* ***ruffle*** *his* ***feathers*** (=upset him).

ruffle² *n.* [C] a band of cloth sewn in folds as a decoration around the edges of a shirt, skirt, etc. **—ruffled** *adj.*

rug /rʌg/ *n.* [C] a piece of thick cloth or wool that covers part of a floor, used for warmth or as a decoration ➔ CARPET

rug·by /ˈrʌgbi/ *n.* [U] an outdoor game played by two teams with an OVAL ball that you kick or carry [ORIGIN: 1800—1900 *Rugby* School in England, where the game is said to have been invented]

rug·ged /ˈrʌgɪd/ *adj.* **1** land that is rugged is rough and uneven, with a lot of rocks: *a rugged terrain full of wildlife* **2** a man who is rugged is attractive and has strong features that may not be perfect: *his rugged good looks*

rug

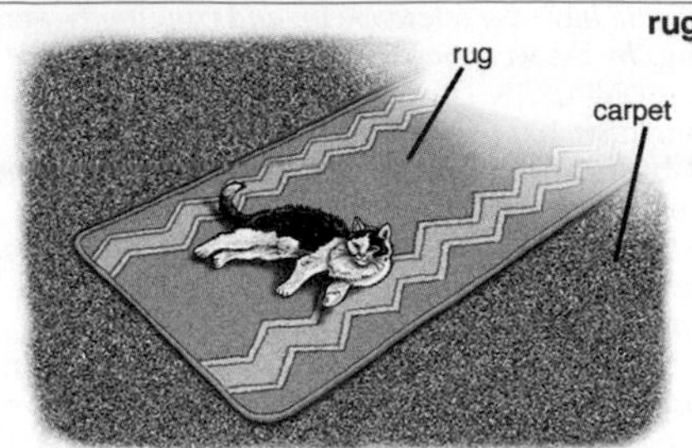

ru·in¹ /'ruɪn/ *v.* [T] **1** to spoil or destroy something completely: *The new road will ruin the countryside.* | *One stupid comment had ruined everything.* **2** ECONOMICS to make someone lose all his/her money: *A long strike would ruin the company.* [ORIGIN: 1300—1400 Old French *ruine*, from Latin *ruina*]

ruin² *n.* **1** [U] ECONOMICS a situation in which someone loses his/her social position or money, especially because of a business failure: *small businesses facing **financial ruin*** **2** [C] *also* **ruins** [plural] the part of a building that is left after the rest has been destroyed: *the **ruins of** the temple* **3 be/lie in ruins** to be badly damaged or destroyed: *The country's economy is in ruins.* **4 fall into ruin** if something falls into ruin, it becomes damaged or destroyed because no one is taking care of it: *The 18th-century mansion has fallen into ruin.*

ru·in·ous /'ruɪnəs/ *adj.* causing great destruction or loss of money: *a ruinous decision*

rule¹ /rul/ *n.* **1** [C] an official instruction that says how something is to be done or what is allowed, especially in a game, organization, or job: *Erin knows the **rules of** the game.* | ***strict rules** about what you can wear* | *If you **follow** the **rules**, you won't get into trouble.* | *Well, that's what happens if you **break** the **rules*** (=disobey them). | *It's **against the rules** to pick up the ball* (=it is not allowed). | *Can't we **bend the rules*** (=allow something that is usually not allowed) *just this once?*

THESAURUS

law – a rule that people in a particular country, city, or state must obey: *The law requires motorcyclists to wear helmets.*
regulation – an official rule or order: *environmental regulations on air pollution*
restriction – a rule or set of laws that limits what you can do or what is allowed to happen: *new restrictions on immigration*
guidelines – rules or instructions about the best way to do something: *the Department of Health's guidelines for a healthy diet*
statute (formal) – a law or rule: *a federal statute prohibiting sex discrimination*
code – a set of rules, laws, or principles that tells people how to behave: *the school's dress code*
precept (formal) – a general rule or idea that helps you decide how to think or behave in a situation: *our basic moral precepts*

2 [U] the government of a country by a particular group of people or by using a particular system: *At that time, Vietnam was **under** French **rule**.* | ***majority rule*** (=government by the political party that most people voted for) → INDIRECT RULE **3** [singular] something that is the case or is usually true: ***As a general rule**, vegetable oils are much better for you than animal fats.* | *I worked last weekend, but that's **the exception rather than the rule**.* **4** [C] a statement about what is usually allowed in the grammar of a language, or according to a particular system: *the **rules of** grammar* **5 rule of thumb** a principle that is based on practical experience, and that works most of the time: *As a rule of thumb, chicken should be cooked 15 minutes for each pound.* [ORIGIN: 1200—1300 Old French *reule*, from Latin *regula* "edge for drawing straight lines, rule"]

rule² *v.* **1** [I,T] to have the official power to control a country and its people: *The king ruled for 30 years.* | *Alexander the Great **ruled over** a huge empire.* **2** [I,T] to make an official decision about something such as a legal problem: *The judge **ruled that** the mother should have custody of the children.* | *The Supreme Court has not **ruled on** the case yet.* **3** [T] if a feeling or desire rules someone, it controls his/her life, so that s/he does not have time for other things: *Don't let your job **rule** your **life**.* **4 sb/sth rules** (spoken) used in order to say that the team, school, place, etc. mentioned is better than any other: *Jefferson High rules!*

rule sb/sth ↔ **out** *phr. v.* to decide that someone or something is not possible or appropriate: *We can't **rule out the possibility** that he has left the country.*

ruled /ruld/ *adj.* ruled paper has parallel lines printed across it

rul·er /'rulɚ/ *n.* [C] **1** someone such as a king who has official power over a country and its people

THESAURUS **king, queen, prince, princess, monarch, emperor, sovereign** → KING

2 a flat narrow piece of plastic, wood, or metal that you use for measuring things and drawing straight lines

rul·ing¹ /'rulɪŋ/ *n.* [C] an official decision, especially one made by a court of law: *the Supreme Court's **ruling on** the case*

ruling² *adj.* **the ruling class/party** the group that controls a country or organization

rum /rʌm/ *n.* [C,U] a strong alcoholic drink made from sugar

rum·ble /'rʌmbəl/ *v.* [I] to make a lot of long low sounds: *Thunder rumbled in the distance.* —**rumble** *n.* [singular]

ru·men /'rumən/ *n.* (plural **rumens** *or* **rumina** /-mənə/) [C] BIOLOGY a separate enclosed part in the stomach of an animal such as a cow, that stores and partly changes food the animal has just eaten, before passing it into the other part of the stomach

R

ru·mi·nate /ˈruməˌneɪt/ *v.* [I] (formal) to think carefully about something

rum·mage /ˈrʌmɪdʒ/ *v.* [I] to search for something by moving things around: *Kerry was **rummaging through** a drawer looking for a pen.*

ˈrummage sale *n.* [C] an event at which old clothes, furniture, toys, etc. are sold

ru·mor /ˈrumɚ/ *n.* [C,U] information that is passed from one person to another and which may not be true: *Have you heard the **rumor about** Sam and Kelly?* | *Knox denied **rumors that** he might be running for office.* | ***Rumor has it (that)*** (=people are saying that) *Jean's getting married again.* [ORIGIN: 1300—1400 Old French *rumour*, from Latin *rumor*]

ru·mored /ˈrumɚd/ *adj.* if something is rumored to be true, people are saying that it may be true but no one knows for certain: ***It was rumored that** a magazine had offered a lot of money for her story.* | *He's **rumored to** be running for president.*

R

rump /rʌmp/ *n.* [C,U] BIOLOGY the part of an animal's back that is just above its legs

rum·pled /ˈrʌmpəld/ *adj.* rumpled hair, clothes, etc. are messy

run¹ /rʌn/ *v.* (past tense **ran** /ræn/, past participle **run**, present participle **running**)

1 MOVE [I] to move very quickly, moving your legs faster than when you walk: *If we run, we can still catch the bus.* | *I **ran down** the stairs as fast as I could.* | *Billy **ran over** to the playground.* | *Stephen **came running** into the house.* ➔ *see picture on page A22*

THESAURUS

sprint – to run as fast as you can for a short distance: *I sprinted toward the end zone.*
dash/tear – to run very fast in a hurried way: *He's always dashing off somewhere.*
jog/go jogging – to run quite slowly for exercise over a long distance
race – to go somewhere very quickly: *I raced home from school.*
bolt – to suddenly run somewhere very fast, especially in order to escape or because you are frightened: *At the sound of the bell, the kids bolted for the door.* ➔ WALK¹

2 BE IN CHARGE OF STH [T] to control, organize, or operate a business, organization, etc.: *Ann runs a restaurant in Atlanta.* | *The hotel is **well run/badly run**.*

3 IN A RACE [I,T] to run in a race: *I'm **running in** a marathon at the end of this month.*

4 GO SOMEWHERE QUICKLY [I] (spoken) to go somewhere quickly, either walking or in a car: *I need to run out to my car – I left my books in it.* | *I need to **run to** the store for some milk.*

5 MACHINES [I,T] if a machine runs, or if you run it, it is operating: *The radio **runs on/off** batteries* (=uses batteries to work). | *I forgot to run the dishwasher.* | *Nate left the engine running.* | *We should have the telescope **up and running*** (=working) *by the weekend.*

6 COMPUTER [T] IT to start or use a computer program: *You can run this software on any PC.*

7 be running late to be doing things late: *Sorry you had to wait – I've been running late all day.*

8 ELECTION [I] POLITICS to try to be elected: *It looks like he is going to **run for** president.* | *Johnstone is **running against** Pershing.*

9 NEWS/STORIES/ADVERTISEMENTS [I,T] to print or broadcast a story, etc.: *What does it cost to run an ad in the local paper?* | *They ran the item on the 6 o'clock news.*

10 run a check/test/experiment etc. to arrange for someone or something to be checked or tested: *The doctors say they need to run a few tests first.*

11 MONEY/NUMBERS [I,T] to be at a particular level, length, amount, price, etc.: *Unemployment is **running at** 5%.* | *The cost of repairs could **run to** $500.*

12 WATER/LIQUIDS [I] to flow: *Tears ran down her face.* | *Who left the water running* (=still flowing from a pipe)? | *My **nose is running*** (=liquid is coming out).

THESAURUS **pour, flow, drip, leak, ooze** ➔ POUR

13 HAPPEN [I] to happen in a particular way or for a particular time: *The play **ran for*** (=was performed for) *two years* | *The teacher kept things **running smoothly**.*

14 STH LONG [I,T] if something long such as a road or wire runs in a particular direction, that is its position, or that is where you put it: *Developers want to run a road right through his farm.* | *Run the cables under the carpet.*

15 BUSES/TRAINS [I] to take people from one place to another: *The bus doesn't run on Sunday.* | *The trains should **run on time*** (=arrive and leave at the correct time).

16 be running short of sth *also* **be running low on sth** to have very little of something left: *I'm **running low on** money.*

17 TOUCH [T] to touch something by moving your hand along its surface: *She ran her fingers through her hair.*

18 sth runs in the family if something such as a quality, disease, or skill runs in the family, many people in that family have it

19 run drugs/guns to bring drugs or guns illegally into a country in order to sell them

20 COLOR [I] if color or MAKEUP runs, it spreads from one area of cloth or skin to another when it gets wet

21 HOLE IN CLOTHES [I] if a hole in PANTYHOSE runs, it gets longer in a straight line

22 be running a temperature/fever to have a body temperature that is higher than normal because you are sick

23 FEELING [I] if thoughts or feelings run through you, you feel them in a very strong way: *I felt a sharp pain run down my leg.* [ORIGIN: Old English *rinnan*]

run across sb/sth *phr. v.*
to meet or find someone or something by chance: *I ran across some old love letters the other day.*

run after sb/sth *phr. v.*
to chase someone or something: *She started to leave, but Smith ran after her.*

run around *phr. v.*
to be very busy doing many small jobs: *She's been running around all day getting things ready for the wedding.*

run away *phr. v.*
1 to leave a place in order to escape from someone or something: *Kathy* ***ran away from home*** *at the age of 16.*
2 to try to avoid an unpleasant situation: *You can't* ***run away from*** *your problems.*

run sth **by** sb *phr. v.*
to tell someone about something so that s/he can give you his/her opinion: *Can you run that by me again* (=repeat what you said because I did not understand)*?*

run down *phr. v.*
1 run sb/sth **down** to hit a person or animal with a car while you are driving, and kill or injure him, her, or it: *A drunk driver ran down a 14-year-old girl.*
2 run sth ↔ **down** to gradually lose power, or to make something do this: *Don't leave it switched on you'll run down the batteries.*
3 run sb/sth ↔ **down** (informal) to criticize someone or something: *Her boyfriend's always running her down.*

run into *phr. v.*
1 run into sb (informal) to meet someone by chance: *I ran into him in town.*
2 run into sb/sth to hit someone or something with a car: *He lost control and ran into another car.*
3 run into trouble/problems/debt etc. to begin to have trouble, problems, etc.: *She ran into trouble when she couldn't pay the hospital bills.*

run off *phr. v.*
1 to leave your husband or wife and live with or marry someone else: *Her husband had run off, leaving her and the children.*
2 run sth ↔ **off** to quickly print copies of something: *I'll need to run off 100 copies of this.*

run off with *phr. v.*
1 run off with sb to go away with someone because you are having a sexual relationship with him/her and other people do not approve: *Her husband ran off with an old girlfriend.*
2 run off with sth to steal something and leave on foot: *A thief ran off with her cell phone.*

run out *phr. v.*
1 to use all of something, so that there is none left: *We've* ***run out of*** *sugar.* | *I'm running out of ideas.*
2 if something is running out, there will soon be none left: *They need to make a deal, but* ***time is running out.***
3 to come to the end of a period of time when something is allowed to be done or used: *My membership runs out in September.*

run sb/sth ↔ **over** *phr. v.*
to hit someone or something with a car or other vehicle, and drive over him, her, or it: *My dog was run over by a car.*

run through sth *phr. v.*
1 to read, check, or practice something quickly: *I'd like to run through the agenda with you before the meeting.*
2 if a quality or feature runs through something, it exists in all parts of it: *a theme which runs through the book*

run up sth *phr. v.*
to spend or borrow so much money that you have a lot to pay back: *We* ***ran up*** *a huge phone* ***bill.***

run up against sth *phr. v.*
to suddenly have to deal with a problem when you are trying to do something: *The school board has run up against opposition to its proposals.*

run² *n.*
1 ON FOOT [C] a period of time spent running, the act of running, or a distance that you run: *He usually* ***goes for a run*** *before breakfast.* | *It was still raining, but we decided to* ***make a run for*** *the car.* | *a 5-mile run*
2 in the short/long run in the near future, or later in the future: *I think in the long run you'll be happier without him.*
3 BASEBALL [C] a point in a baseball game: *The Cubs* ***scored*** *three* ***runs*** *in the sixth inning.*
4 be on the run a) to be trying to escape from someone, especially the police: *He's been* ***on the run from*** *the police for years.* **b)** to be very busy doing a lot of different things and going to different places: *It's hard to eat well when you're on the run all day.*
5 PLAY/MOVIE ETC. [C] a period of time during which a play, movie, or television show is shown or performed regularly: *The play starts an eight-week run on Friday.*
6 a run of good/bad luck several lucky or unlucky things happening quickly one right after another: *Losing my job was the start of a run of bad luck that year.*
7 a run on sth a situation in which a lot of people take their money out of a bank or buy a lot of one particular thing at the same time: *There's always a run on chocolates and flowers on Mother's Day.*
8 ELECTION [C usually singular] an attempt to be elected: *Turner is* ***making*** *his first* ***run for*** *public office.*
9 HOLE IN CLOTHES [C] a long hole in a pair of PANTYHOSE
10 make a run for it to suddenly start running in order to escape
11 have the run of sth to be allowed to go anywhere or do anything in a place: *We had the run of the house for the weekend.*
12 REGULAR TRIP [C usually singular] a regular trip made by a person or a vehicle that carries a lot of people: *the daily ferry run*
13 give sb a run for his/her money to make an opponent or competitor work very hard to beat you:

The White Sox gave the A's a run for their money, but lost in the ninth inning.

run·a·round /ˈrʌnəˌraʊnd/ *n.* **give sb the runaround** (informal) to deliberately avoid giving someone the information or help s/he has asked for: *I keep calling to find out about my insurance, but they just keep giving me the runaround.*

run·a·way¹ /ˈrʌnəˌweɪ/ *n.* [C] someone, especially a child, who has left home or the place where s/he is supposed to be

runaway² *adj.* [only before noun] **1** a runaway vehicle is out of control **2** happening quickly and suddenly: *The movie was a* ***runaway success.***

ˌrun-ˈdown *adj.* **1** a building or area that is run-down is in very bad condition: *a run-down motel* **2** [not before noun] someone who is run-down is very tired and not very healthy: *He's been feeling run-down lately.*

THESAURUS **tired, exhausted, worn out, fatigued** → TIRED

R

run·down /ˈrʌndaʊn/ *n.* [singular] a quick report or explanation of a situation, event, etc.: *Can you* ***give*** *me* ***a rundown on*** *what happened while I was gone?*

rung¹ /rʌŋ/ *v.* the past participle of RING

rung² *n.* [C] **1** one of the steps of a LADDER **2** (informal) a particular level or position in an organization: *I started on the bottom rung of the company.*

ˈrun-in *n.* [C] (informal) an argument or disagreement with someone in authority: *Barry* ***had a run-in with*** *the police.*

run·ner /ˈrʌnɚ/ *n.* [C] **1** someone who runs as a sport: *a long-distance runner* **2** one of the long thin blades of metal on the bottom of a SLED **3 drug/gun runner** someone who brings drugs or guns illegally into a country in order to sell them

ˌrunner-ˈup *n.* (plural **runners-up**) [C] the person or team that finishes in second place in a race or competition

run·ning¹ /ˈrʌnɪŋ/ *n.* **1** [U] the activity of running: *running shoes | Do you want to* ***go running?*** **2 be in the running/be out of the running** to have some chance of winning or being successful, or to have no chance: *Is Sam still* ***in the running for*** *the swim team?* **3 the running of sth** the way that a business, organization, etc. is managed or organized: *He is not involved in* ***the day-to-day running of*** *the business.*

running² *adj.* **1 running water** water that comes from a FAUCET: *a house with no running water* **2 running battle/argument** an argument that continues over a long period of time **3 running commentary** a spoken description of an event while it is happening, especially a sports event **4 running total** a total that is always being increased as new costs, amounts, etc. are added to it

running³ *adv.* **three years/five times etc. running** for three years, five times, etc. without a change: *This is the fourth day running that it has rained.*

ˌrunning ˈback *n.* [C] in football, a player whose main job is to run with the ball

ˈrunning mate *n.* [C] POLITICS the person who is chosen by someone who is trying to become president, who will then be the VICE PRESIDENT if s/he wins the election

run·ny /ˈrʌni/ *adj.* (informal) **1** a runny nose has liquid coming out of it because you are sick **2** food that is runny is not as thick as normal or as you want: *runny eggs*

ˈrun-off *n.* **1** [C] POLITICS an election or competition that is arranged when there is no clear winner of the first one **2** [U] EARTH SCIENCES rain or other liquid that flows off the land into rivers and lakes → *see picture at* WATER CYCLE

ˌrun-of-the-ˈmill *adj.* not special or interesting (SYN) **ordinary**: *a run-of-the-mill job*

ˈrun-on ˌsentence *n.* [C] a sentence that has two main CLAUSEs without connecting words or correct PUNCTUATION

runt /rʌnt/ *n.* [C] the smallest and least developed baby animal of a group born at the same time

ˈrun-through *n.* [C] a short practice before a performance, test, etc.

ˈrun-up *n.* **the run-up to sth** the period of time just before an important event: *Most stores are hiring more staff in the run-up to Christmas.*

run·way /ˈrʌnweɪ/ *n.* [C] a very long surface like a wide road, that aircraft leave from and come down on

rup·ture¹ /ˈrʌptʃɚ/ *n.* [C,U] an occasion when something suddenly breaks apart or bursts: *the* ***rupture of*** *a blood vessel*

rupture² *v.* [I,T] to break or burst, or to make something do this: *An oil pipeline ruptured early this morning.*

ru·ral /ˈrʊrəl/ *adj.* relating to country areas rather than the city (ANT) **urban**: *a peaceful rural setting* [ORIGIN: 1400—1500 Old French, Latin *ruralis*, from *rus* "open land"]

ruse /ruz/ *n.* [C] (formal) something you do in order to deceive someone (SYN) **trick**

rush¹ /rʌʃ/ *v.* **1** [I,T] to move somewhere or do something very quickly: *David* ***rushed into*** *the room. | There's no need to rush – we have plenty of time. | Everyone was* ***rushing to*** *catch the last bus.*

THESAURUS

race – to go somewhere as fast as you can: *Carter raced downstairs.*
dash – to run somewhere very fast, especially only a short distance: *I dashed into my bedroom and grabbed my notebook.*
hurry – to do something or go somewhere more quickly than usual, especially because there is

not much time: *People hurried into stores to escape the rain.*
charge – to move quickly forward: *The boys charged up the trail, laughing and yelling.*
speed – to move very fast, used about cars, trains, etc., or the people traveling in them: *The train sped toward San Francisco.*
hasten (formal) – to move or do something quickly or without delay: *Mr. Samuels hastened toward him.* → RUN[1]

2 [T] to take or send something somewhere very quickly: *We had to **rush** Helen **to** the hospital.* **3** [I,T] to do or decide something too quickly, without taking the time to think carefully, or to make someone do this: *Don't rush me – let me think.* | *My mother's worried that I'm **rushing into** getting married.*
rush around *phr. v.* to try to do a lot of things quickly in a short period of time
rush sth ↔ **through** *phr. v.* to get something such as a new law approved more quickly than usual

rush² *n.* **1** [singular] a sudden fast movement of things or people: *There was **a rush for** the door.* **2** [singular, U] a situation in which you need to hurry, especially because a lot of people want to do or get something: *We have plenty of time – there's no rush.* | *I can't stop – I'm **in a rush.*** | *There's a big **rush to** get tickets.* **3 the rush** the time when a place or group of people are very busy: *the Christmas rush* **4** [singular] a sudden strong feeling: *Mark felt **a rush of** anger.*

'rush hour *n.* [C,U] the time of day when there are a lot of vehicles on the road because people are going to and from work: *rush hour traffic*

Rus·sian¹ /'rʌʃən/ *adj.* **1** relating to or coming from Russia **2** relating to the Russian language

Russian² *n.* **1** [U] the language used in Russia **2** [C] someone from Russia

rust¹ /rʌst/ *n.* [U] the reddish-brown substance that forms on iron, steel, etc. when it gets wet

rust² *v.* [I,T] to become covered with rust, or to make something do this: *a lock that has rusted shut*

rus·tic /'rʌstɪk/ *adj.* simple and old-fashioned in a way that is attractive and typical of the COUNTRYSIDE: *a rustic mountain cabin*

rus·tle¹ /'rʌsəl/ *v.* [I,T] if leaves, papers, etc. rustle, or if you rustle them, they make a soft noise as they rub against each other
rustle sth ↔ **up** *phr. v.* to find or make something quickly, especially food for a meal

rustle² *n.* [singular] the noise made when something rustles: *the **rustle of** dry leaves* → *see picture on page A20*

rust·proof /'rʌstpruf/ *adj.* metal that is rustproof will not rust

rust·y /'rʌsti/ *adj.* **1** covered with rust: *rusty nails* **2** if a skill that you have is rusty, you are not as good at something as you used to be because you have not practiced it for a long time: *My tennis is a little rusty.*

rut /rʌt/ *n.* **1 in a rut** (informal) living or working in a situation that does not change, and so is boring: *I was **stuck in a rut** and decided to look for a new job.* **2** [C] a deep narrow track left in the ground by a wheel

ru·ta·ba·ga /'ruṭəˌbeɪgə/ *n.* [C] a large round yellow vegetable that grows under the ground [ORIGIN: 1700—1800 Swedish *rotabagge*, from *rot* "root" + *bagge* "bag"]

ruth·less /'ruθlɪs/ *adj.* not caring if you have to harm other people to get what you want: *a ruthless dictator* | *ruthless determination* —**ruthlessly** *adv.* —**ruthlessness** *n.* [U]

RV *n.* [C] **recreational vehicle** a large vehicle with cooking equipment, beds, etc., that a family uses for traveling or camping

rye /raɪ/ *n.* [U] a type of grain that is used for making bread and WHISKEY (=alcohol)

S, s /ɛs/ the nineteenth letter of the English alphabet

S *also* **S.** the written abbreviation of SOUTH or SOUTHERN

-'s /z, s, ɪz/ **1** the short form of "is": *What's that?* **2** the short form of "has": *He's gone out.* **3** used in order to show the POSSESSIVE form of nouns: *Bill is one of Jason's friends.* | *the company's profits* **4** the short form of "us," used only with "let" to form "let's": *Let's go, or we'll be late.*

S&L *n.* [C] ECONOMICS SAVINGS AND LOAN

Sab·bath /'sæbəθ/ *n.* **the Sabbath** the day of the week that Jews or Christians consider to be a day for resting and praying, either Saturday or Sunday [ORIGIN: 900—1000 Latin *sabbatum*, from Hebrew *shabbath* "rest"]

sab·bat·i·cal /sə'bæṭɪkəl/ *n.* [C,U] a period when someone who teaches stops doing his/her usual work in order to study or travel: *Prof. Morris **is on sabbatical** this semester.* | *She **took a sabbatical** from her job at Stanford University to coach the U.S. Olympic team.*

THESAURUS **vacation, holiday, break, leave** → VACATION

sa·ber /'seɪbɚ/ *n.* [C] a military sword

sa·ble /'seɪbəl/ *n.* [C,U] an expensive fur used for

making coats, or the small animal this fur comes from

sab·o·tage¹ /ˈsæbəˌtɑʒ/ *v.* [T] **1** to secretly damage or destroy something so that an enemy cannot use it: *Soldiers sabotaged road and rail lines.* **2** to deliberately spoil someone's plans because you do not want him/her to succeed: *Outside forces are trying to sabotage the Middle East peace process.* [ORIGIN: 1800—1900 French *saboter* "to walk along noisily, do work badly, sabotage," from *sabot* "wooden shoe"] —**saboteur** /ˌsæbəˈtɚ/ *n.* [C]

sabotage² *n.* [U] deliberate damage done to equipment, vehicles, etc., in order to prevent an enemy or opponent from using them: *an **act of sabotage** at the factory*

sac /sæk/ *n.* [C] BIOLOGY a part shaped like a small bag inside a plant or animal, that contains air or liquid

sac·cha·rin /ˈsækərɪn/ *n.* [U] a chemical substance that tastes very sweet and is used instead of sugar [ORIGIN: 1800—1900 Latin *saccharum* "sugar," from Greek *sakcharon*, from Sanskrit *sarkara* "small stones, sugar"]

S

sac·cha·rine /ˈsækəˌrin/ *adj.* very romantic or involving a lot of emotion, in a way that seems silly and not sincere: *a saccharine view of motherhood*

sack¹ /sæk/ *n.* [C] **1** a large bag made of strong cloth, plastic, or paper in which you carry or keep things: *a **sack of** potatoes* **2** *also* **sackful** the amount that a sack can contain [ORIGIN: Old English *sacc*, from Latin *saccus*, from Greek *sakkos* "bag, sackcloth"] → **hit the sack** *at* HIT¹

sack² *v.* [T] **1** to steal and destroy things in a city that has been defeated by an army: *The Vandals sacked Rome in 455 A.D.* **2** to knock down the QUARTERBACK in football

sack out *phr. v.* (informal) to go to sleep: *Karl was **sacked out on** the sofa.*

sac·ra·ment /ˈsækrəmənt/ *n.* [C] an important Christian ceremony such as marriage or COMMUNION

sa·cred /ˈseɪkrɪd/ *adj.* **1** relating to a god or religion, and believed to be holy: *The temple is one of the most sacred places for Hindus.* | *sacred text/book/writing* **2** extremely important or greatly respected: *Human life is sacred.* [ORIGIN: 1300—1400 Past participle of *sacre* "to make holy" (13—17 centuries), from Old French *sacrer*]

ˌsacred ˈcow *n.* [C] (disapproving) a belief, object, etc. that is so important to someone that s/he will not let anyone criticize or change it

sac·ri·fice¹ /ˈsækrəˌfaɪs/ *n.* [C,U] **1** something that you decide not to have or not to do in order to get something that is more important: *Her parents **made** a lot of **sacrifices** to put her through college.* **2** the act of offering something to a god, or an object or animal that is killed in order to be offered to a god —**sacrificial** /ˌsækrəˈfɪʃəl◂/ *adj.*

sacrifice² *v.* [T] **1** to willingly stop having or doing something in order to get something that is more important: *Ellis **sacrificed** a high-paying legal career **to** work in the inner city.* | *Rugiero was willing to **sacrifice** his life **for** his country.* **2** to offer something to a god as part of a ceremony, often by killing it

sac·ri·lege /ˈsækrəlɪdʒ/ *n.* [C,U] an occasion when someone treats something holy or important in a way that does not show respect —**sacrilegious** /ˌsækrəˈlɪdʒəs/ *adj.*

sac·ro·sanct /ˈsækroʊˌsæŋkt/ *adj.* something that is sacrosanct is considered to be so important that noone is allowed to criticize or change it: *Marriage no longer seems to be sacrosanct.* [ORIGIN: 1600—1700 Latin *sacrosanctus*, probably from *sacro sanctus* "made holy by religious ceremonies"]

sad /sæd/ *adj.* (comparative **sadder**, superlative **saddest**) **1** unhappy, especially because something unpleasant has happened ANT **happy**: *Ted **looked** tired and **sad**.* | *We **were sad to** see him go.* | *a sad face*

THESAURUS

unhappy – not happy: *an unhappy marriage* | *We're unhappy with your performance.*
miserable – very sad, especially because you are lonely or sick: *I couldn't help feeling miserable.* | *I had a miserable time at college.*
sorrowful (formal) – feeling great sadness, especially because someone has died or something very bad has happened: *the sorrowful mothers of the soldiers who were killed*
depressed – sad for a long time because things are wrong in your life: *Patients will get depressed over their symptoms.*
down/low/blue (informal) – a little sad about things in your life: *Whenever I felt down, I'd read his letter.*
downhearted (literary) – sad about something that has happened: *A friendly word can mean a lot to someone who is downhearted.*
melancholy (formal) – sad and slightly depressed: *His letters seemed increasingly melancholy.*
morose (formal) – unhappy, silent, and in a bad mood: *She was morose, and he could do nothing to cheer her up.*
gloomy – sad because you think a situation will not improve: *a gloomy mood*
glum – used especially to say that someone looks sad: *You look glum.*

2 a sad event, story, etc. makes you feel unhappy: *sad news* | *It was a sad day for us all.* | *a story with a sad ending* | ***It's sad that** James couldn't come.* **3** very bad or unacceptable: *The house was in a **sad state of** neglect.* | ***It's sad that** these patients don't get the help they need.* [ORIGIN: Old English *sæd* "having had enough"] —**sadness** *n.* [singular, U]

sad·den /ˈsædn/ *v.* [T] (formal) to make someone feel sad or disappointed: *We were deeply **saddened by** her death.*

sad·dle¹ /ˈsædl/ *n.* [C] **1** a seat made of leather that is put on a horse's back so that you can ride it **2** a seat on a bicycle or a MOTORCYCLE

saddle² *v.* [T] *also* **saddle up** to put a saddle on a horse

saddle sb **with** sth *phr. v.* to give someone a job, problem, etc. that is difficult or boring: *small businesses saddled with debts*

sad·dle·bag /ˈsædlˌbæg/ *n.* [C] a bag that you carry things in, that is attached to a saddle on a horse or a bicycle

sa·dism /ˈseɪˌdɪzəm/ *n.* [U] behavior in which someone gets pleasure, especially sexual pleasure, from being cruel to someone → MASOCHISM —**sadist** *n.* [C] —**sadistic** /səˈdɪstɪk/ *adj.*: *a sadistic ruler*

sad·ly /ˈsædli/ *adv.* **1** in a way that shows you are sad: *Jimmy nodded sadly.* **2** in a way that you wish were not true (SYN) **unfortunately**: *Sadly, most small businesses fail in the first year.*

sa·fa·ri /səˈfɑri/ *n.* [C] a trip through the country areas of Africa in order to watch wild animals: *tourists **on safari** in Zaire* [ORIGIN: 1800—1900 Arabic *safariy* "of a trip"]

safe¹ /seɪf/ *adj.* **1** not in danger of being harmed or stolen: *People don't **feel safe** in their own homes.* | *Nothing can **keep** a city **safe from** terrorist attacks.* | *Both children were found, **safe and sound*** (=unharmed). **2** not likely to cause or allow any physical injury or harm: *safe drinking water* | ***It's** not **safe to** walk there at night.* | *Have a **safe trip**.* | *He stopped the car **a safe distance** away.* **3** a safe place is one where something is not likely to be stolen or lost: *Keep your passport in a safe place.* **4** not involving any risk and very likely to be successful: *a safe investment* | *U.S. Treasury bonds are a **safe bet**.* **5** not likely to cause disagreement: *I think **it's safe to say** that few people read the entire document.* **6 to be on the safe side** (spoken) used when you are being very careful in order to avoid an unpleasant situation: *We'll each keep a copy of the lease to be on the safe side.* **7 better (to be) safe than sorry** (spoken) used in order to say that it is better to be careful, even if this takes time or effort, than to take a risk [ORIGIN: 1200—1300 Old French *sauf*, from Latin *salvus* "safe, healthy"] —**safely** *adv.*: *Drive safely!*

safe² *n.* [C] a strong metal box or cupboard with a lock on it, where you keep money and valuable things

ˈsafe-deposit ˌbox *n.* [C] a small box used for keeping valuable objects, usually in a special room in a bank

safe·guard /ˈseɪfgɑrd/ *n.* [C] a law, agreement, etc. that is intended to protect someone or something from possible dangers or problems: ***safeguards against** the exploitation of children* —**safeguard** *v.* [T]

THESAURUS protect, guard, shield, give/offer/provide protection → PROTECT

ˌsafe ˈhaven *n.* [C] a place where someone can go in order to escape from possible danger or attack

safe·keep·ing /ˌseɪfˈkipɪŋ/ *n.* **for safekeeping** if you put something somewhere for safekeeping, you put it in a place where it will not get damaged, lost, or stolen

ˌsafe ˈsex *n.* [U] ways of having sex that reduce the risk of getting a sexual disease, especially by using a CONDOM

safe·ty /ˈseɪfti/ *n.* [U] **1** the state of being safe from danger or harm: *Some students are concerned about safety on campus.* **2** how safe someone or something is: *Police have expressed **fears for** the girl's **safety**.* | *People have questioned the **safety of** the fireworks show*

ˈsafety belt *n.* [C] a SEAT BELT

ˈsafety net *n.* [C] **1** SOCIAL SCIENCE a system or arrangement that helps people if they get into a difficult situation or have serious problems: *a safety net for the country's poorest people* **2** a large net that is placed below someone who is performing high above the ground, to catch him/her if s/he falls **3** ECONOMICS actions taken by a government to help or protect companies or financial institutions that have serious financial problems

ˈsafety pin *n.* [C] a curved metal pin for fastening things together. The point of the pin fits into a cover so that it cannot hurt you.

safety pin

ˈsafety valve *n.* [C] **1** something you do that allows you to express strong feelings such as anger without doing any harm: *Exercise is a good safety valve for stress.* **2** a part of a machine that allows gas, steam, etc. to be let out when the pressure is too high

sag /sæg/ *v.* (**sagged**, **sagging**) [I] **1** to hang down or bend in the middle, especially because of the weight of something: *The bookcases sagged under the weight of hundreds of books.* **2** to become weaker or less valuable: *a sagging economy*

sa·ga /ˈsɑgə/ *n.* [C] ENG. LANG. ARTS a long story or description of events

sa·gac·i·ty /səˈgæsət̬i/ *n.* [U] (formal) good judgment and understanding (SYN) **wisdom**

sage /seɪdʒ/ *n.* **1** [C] (literary) someone, especially someone old, who is very wise **2** [U] an HERB with gray-green leaves **3** [U] EARTH SCIENCES sagebrush —**sage** *adj.*: *sage advice*

sage·brush /ˈseɪdʒbrʌʃ/ *n.* [U] EARTH SCIENCES a small bush with a strong smell, that grows on dry land in western North America

S

Sag·it·tar·i·us /ˌsædʒəˈtɛriəs/ *n.* **1** [U] the ninth sign of the ZODIAC, represented by a man with a BOW and ARROWS **2** [C] someone born between November 22 and December 21

said[1] /sɛd/ *v.* the past tense and past participle of SAY[1]

said[2] *adj.* used when giving more information about someone or something that has just been mentioned: *The said robbery happened about 5:00.*

sail[1] /seɪl/ *v.* **1** [I] to travel across an area of water in a boat or ship: *Melville* ***sailed to*** *Hawaii.* | *the first Europeans to* ***sail across*** *the Atlantic* **2** [I,T] to direct or control the movement of a boat or ship: *We sailed the boat along the coast.* | *I'd like to learn how to sail.* **3** [I] to start a trip by boat or ship: *We sail at high tide.* | *The Dawn Princess will sail from San Juan.*

sail through sth *phr. v.* to succeed in doing something very easily

sail[2] *n.* [C] **1** a large piece of strong cloth attached to a boat, so that the wind will push the boat along **2 set sail** to begin a trip by boat or ship: *The ship will set sail at dawn.*

S

sail·boat /ˈseɪlboʊt/ *n.* [C] a small boat with one or more sails

sail·ing /ˈseɪlɪŋ/ *n.* [U] the sport of traveling through water in a sailboat → *see picture on page A17*

sail·or /ˈseɪlɚ/ *n.* [C] **1** someone who works on a ship **2** someone who is in the Navy → *see picture at* ARMED FORCES

saint /seɪnt/ *n.* [C] **1** *also* **Saint** someone who is given a special honor by the Catholic Church after he or she has died, because s/he was very good or holy: *Saint Jude* **2** (spoken) someone who is very good, kind, or patient: *I'm certainly no saint!* [ORIGIN: 1100—1200 Old French, Late Latin *sanctus*, from Latin, "holy"] —**sainthood** /ˈseɪnthʊd/ *n.* [U]

Saint Ber·nard /ˌseɪnt˺ bɚˈnɑrd/ *n.* [C] a very large strong dog with long hair

sake /seɪk/ *n.* [U] **1 for the sake of sb** *also* **for sb's sake** in order to help, improve, or please someone or something: *She stayed in the marriage for the sake of the children.* | *Be nice to her, for Kathy's sake.* **2 for goodness'/Pete's/heaven's etc. sake** (spoken) said when you are annoyed, surprised, etc., or when you want to emphasize what you are saying: *Why didn't you tell me, for heaven's sake?*

sal·a·ble, **saleable** /ˈseɪləbəl/ *adj.* something that is salable can be sold, or is easy to sell

sal·ad /ˈsæləd/ *n.* [C,U] **1** a mixture of raw vegetables, for example LETTUCE, CUCUMBER, and TOMATO **2** raw or cooked food cut into small pieces and served cold: *potato salad* [ORIGIN: 1300—1400 Old French *salade*, from Old Provençal *salada*, from *salar* "to add salt to"]

ˈsalad bar *n.* [C] a place in a restaurant where you can make your own salad

ˈsalad ˌdressing *n.* [C,U] a liquid mixture for putting on salads to give them a special taste

sal·a·man·der /ˈsæləˌmændɚ/ *n.* [C] a small animal similar to a LIZARD, that can live in water and on land

sa·la·mi /səˈlɑmi/ *n.* [C,U] a large SAUSAGE with a strong taste, that is eaten cold

sal·a·ried /ˈsælərid/ *adj.* receiving a salary: *salaried workers*

sal·a·ry /ˈsæləri/ *n.* (plural **salaries**) [C,U] money that you receive every month as payment from the organization you work for → WAGES: *the average* ***yearly/annual salary*** | *The university may need to* ***pay*** *higher* ***salaries*** *to attract top faculty.* [ORIGIN: 1200—1300 Latin *salarium* "money to pay for salt," from *sal* "salt"]

THESAURUS **pay, income, wages, earnings, remuneration** → PAY[2] → WORK[1]

sale /seɪl/ *n.* **1** [C,U] the act of selling something, or an occasion when you sell something: *The* ***sale of*** *alcohol is strictly controlled.* | *a* ***yard/garage sale*** (=an occasion when you sell things you no longer need) **2 sales a)** [plural] ECONOMICS the total number of products that are sold during a particular period of time: *a company with* ***sales of*** *$60 million per year* | *Sales of the album have been strong.* **b)** [U] the part of a company that deals with selling products: *Sally got a job as sales manager.* **3 for sale** available to be bought: *They had to* ***put*** *their home* ***up for sale.*** | *postcards for sale in the gift shop* **4 on sale a)** available to be bought: *Tickets* ***go on sale*** *Monday.* **b)** available to be bought for a lower price than usual: *The sweaters were on sale.* **5** [C] a time when stores sell their goods at lower prices than usual: *Nordstrom's summer sale*

ˈsales clerk *n.* [C] someone who sells things in a store

sales·man /ˈseɪlzmən/ *n.* (plural **salesmen**) [C] a man whose job is to sell things: *a used car salesman*

sales·person /ˈseɪlzˌpɚsən/ *n.* [C] someone whose job is to sell things

ˈsales repreˌsentative *also* **ˈsales rep** *n.* [C] someone who travels around selling his/her company's products

ˈsales slip *n.* [C] a small piece of paper that you are given in a store when you buy something (SYN) **receipt**

ˈsales tax *n.* [C,U] ECONOMICS a tax that you pay in addition to the cost of something you are buying

sales·wom·an /ˈseɪlzˌwʊmən/ *n.* (plural **saleswomen**) [C] a woman whose job is selling things

sa·li·ent /ˈseɪliənt/ *adj.* (formal) most noticeable or important: *the* ***salient points*** *of the plan* —**salience** *n.* [U]

THESAURUS important, crucial, vital, essential, major, key, significant → IMPORTANT

sa·line /'seɪlin, -laɪn/ *adj.* CHEMISTRY containing or consisting of salt: *a **saline solution*** (=liquid with salt in it) [ORIGIN: 1400—1500 Latin *salinus*, from *sal* "salt"] —**saline** *n.* [U]

sa·lin·i·ty /sə'lɪnət̬i/ *n.* [U] CHEMISTRY the amount of salt which something contains

sa·li·va /sə'laɪvə/ *n.* [U] BIOLOGY the liquid that is produced naturally in your mouth

sal·i·vate /'sælə,veɪt/ *v.* [I] **1** BIOLOGY to produce more saliva in your mouth than usual, because you see or smell food **2** (informal) to show interest in something in a way that shows you like or want it: *Newspapers are **salivating over** the story.*

sal·low /'sæloʊ/ *adj.* sallow skin looks slightly yellow and unhealthy

salm·on /'sæmən/ *n.* [C,U] a large ocean fish with silver skin and pink flesh, or the meat from this fish [ORIGIN: 1200—1300 Anglo-French *salmun*, from Latin *salmo*]

sal·mo·nel·la /,sælmə'nɛlə/ *n.* [U] BIOLOGY a type of BACTERIA in food that makes you sick [ORIGIN: 1900—2000 Modern Latin, from Daniel E. *Salmon* (1850-1914), U.S. scientist]

sa·lon /sə'lɑn/ *n.* [C] a place where you can get your hair cut, have a MANICURE, etc.: *a beauty salon* [ORIGIN: 1600—1700 French, from Italian *salone* "large hall"]

sa·loon /sə'lun/ *n.* [C] a place where alcoholic drinks were sold and drunk in the western U.S. in the 19th century

sal·sa /'sælsə, 'sɔl-/ *n.* [U] **1** a sauce made from onions, tomatoes, and hot-tasting peppers, which you put on Mexican food **2** a type of Latin American dance music

salt[1] /sɔlt/ *n.* **1** [U] a natural white mineral that is added to food to make it taste better: *Add some salt and pepper.* **2** [C] CHEMISTRY a type of chemical, formed by combining an acid with another substance **3 salts** [plural] a mineral substance like salt that is used as a medicine or to make your bath smell good [ORIGIN: Old English *sealt*]

salt[2] *v.* [T] to add salt to food to make it taste better

salt sth ↔ **away** *phr. v.* to save money for future use, especially dishonestly

salt[3] *adj.* **1** preserved by salt: *salt pork* **2** containing salt or saltwater: *a salt lake*

salt marsh *n.* [C] EARTH SCIENCES an area of flat wet ground near the ocean with many different varieties of grass growing on it, that is regularly flooded by saltwater

salt ,shaker *n.* [C] a small container for salt

salt·wa·ter /'sɔlt˺,wɔtɚ, -,wɑ-/ *adj.* EARTH SCIENCES living in salty water: *saltwater fish*

salt·y /'sɔlti/ *adj.* tasting like or containing salt —**saltiness** *n.* [U]

THESAURUS sweet, tasty, sour, hot, spicy → TASTE[1]

sal·u·ta·tion /,sælyə'teɪʃən/ *n.* [C,U] (formal) a word or phrase used to greet someone at the beginning of a letter or speech, such as "Dear Mr. Roberts"

sa·lute[1] /sə'lut/ *v.* [I,T] to move your right hand to your head in order to show respect to an officer in the Army, Navy, etc.: *He turned around and saluted the captain.* [ORIGIN: 1300—1400 Latin *salutare*, from *salus* "health, safety, greeting"]

salute[2] *n.* [C] **1** an act of saluting **2** an occasion when guns are fired into the air in order to show respect for someone: *a 21-gun salute*

sal·vage[1] /'sælvɪdʒ/ *v.* [T] to save something from a situation in which other things have already been damaged, destroyed, or lost: *He's trying to salvage his political reputation.* | *a sofa **salvaged from** the dump*

salvage[2] *n.* [U] the act of salvaging something, or the things that are salvaged

sal·va·tion /sæl'veɪʃən/ *n.* [U] **1** the state of being saved from evil by God, according to the Christian religion **2** something that prevents danger, loss, or failure: *Education seemed their best chance of salvation.*

Sal,vation 'Army *n.* **the Salvation Army** a Christian organization that tries to help poor people

salve /sæv/ *n.* [C,U] a substance that you put on sore skin to make it less painful —**salve** *v.* [T]

sal·vo /'sælvoʊ/ *n.* (plural **salvos**) [C] (formal) **1** one of a series of actions or statements, especially in a situation in which people are arguing: *the **opening salvo** of the election campaign* **2** the act of shooting several guns in a battle or as part of a ceremony

Sa·mar·i·tan /sə'mærət˺n/ *also* **good Samaritan** *n.* [C] someone who helps you when you have problems [ORIGIN: 1600—1700 From the Bible story of a person from Samaria (an area of ancient Palestine) who stopped and helped a man who had been attacked and robbed]

same[1] /seɪm/ *adj.* [only before noun] **1 a)** one particular person, place, etc. and not a different one: *We work at **the same** place.* | *Their birthdays are on **the same** day.* **b)** used in order to say that two or more people, things, etc. are exactly like each other (SYN) **identical**: *I told him **the same** thing.* | *The two of them looked **exactly the same**.* | *She does **the same** job **as** I do, but in a bigger company.* ▸Don't say "She does the same job like I do."◂ **2** used in order to say that a particular person or thing does not change: *He's still **the same** old Peter!* **3 at the same time** if two things happen at the same time, they happen together: *I wanted to laugh and cry at the same time.* **4 the same old story/excuse etc.** (informal, disapproving) something that you have heard many times

S

before: *politicians repeating the same old promises* **5 same difference** (spoken) used in order to say that different actions, behavior, etc. have the same result: *"Should I e-mail them or fax a letter?" "Same difference."* **6 by the same token** in the same way or for the same reasons: *Some mothers are committed to their careers. By the same token, some fathers want to spend more time with their families.* **7 be in the same boat** to be in the same difficult situation that someone else is in [ORIGIN: 1100—1200 Old Norse *samr*]

GRAMMAR

Do not say "a same." Say "the same sort of": *I'd like the same sort of car as that.*

same² *pron.* **1 the same a)** used in order to say that two or more people, actions, or things are exactly like each other: *Thanks – I'll do the same for you sometime.* | *The houses look the same, but one's slightly larger.* **b)** used in order to say that a particular person or thing does not change: *It won't be the same without you.* | *"How's Danny?" "Oh, he's the same as ever."* ►Don't say "He's same as ever."◄ **2 (and the) same to you!** (spoken) used as a reply to a greeting, or as an angry reply to a rude remark: *"Happy New Year!" "Same to you!"* **3 same here** (spoken) said in order to tell someone that you feel the same way as him/her: *"I'd love to see you again." "Same here."*

S

same·ness /ˈseɪmnɪs/ *n.* [U] a boring lack of variety, or the quality of being very similar to something else: *the sameness of the landscape*

ˌsame-ˈsex *adj.* **same-sex marriage/relationship etc.** a marriage, etc. between two men or two women

sam·ple¹ /ˈsæmpəl/ *n.* [C] **1** a small part or amount of something that is examined or used in order to find out what the rest is like: *Do you have a **sample of** your work?* | *a **blood/urine/tissue sample*** (=one that a doctor examines for a disease) | *a **free sample** of shampoo* **2** a group of people who have been chosen to give information by answering questions: *a **random sample of** 500 college students* **3** a small part of a song from a CD or record that is used in a new song [ORIGIN: 1200—1300 Old French *essample*, from Latin *exemplum*]

sample² *v.* [T] **1** to taste a food or drink, go to a place, try an activity, etc. in order to see what it is like: *We sampled several kinds of cheese.* **2** to choose some people from a larger group in order to ask them questions: *A quarter of the people sampled were college-educated.* **3** to use a small part of a song from a CD or record in a new song —**sampling** *n.* [C]

ˈsampling ˌmethod *n.* [C] MATH one of several methods that can be used to collect information about people. The methods are different from each other in the way they choose the people to collect information about.

sam·u·rai /ˈsæmʊˌraɪ/ *n.* (plural **samurai**) [C] HISTORY a member of a powerful military class in Japan in past times

sanc·ti·fy /ˈsæŋktəˌfaɪ/ *v.* (**sanctified**, **sanctifies**) [T] to make something holy

sanc·ti·mo·ni·ous /ˌsæŋktəˈmoʊniəs/ *adj.* (disapproving) behaving as if you are morally better than other people

sanc·tion¹ /ˈsæŋkʃən/ *n.* **1 sanctions** [plural] official orders or laws stopping trade, communication, etc. with another country, as a way of forcing its leaders to make political changes: *Trade **sanctions** were **imposed on** South Africa before apartheid ended.* | *U.S. **sanctions against** Cuba* **2** [U] official permission, approval, or acceptance: *The protest march was held without government sanction.* **3** [C] something, such as a punishment, that makes people obey a rule or law: *Sex outside of marriage was punished by powerful social sanctions.*

sanction² *v.* [T] (formal) to officially accept or allow something: *The UN refused to sanction the use of force.*

THESAURUS **allow, let, permit, authorize** → ALLOW
approve, pass, endorse → APPROVE

sanc·ti·ty /ˈsæŋktət̬i/ *n.* **the sanctity of sth** the quality that makes something so important that it must be respected and preserved: *the sanctity of marriage*

sanc·tu·ar·y /ˈsæŋktʃuˌɛri/ *n.* (plural **sanctuaries**) **1** [C,U] a peaceful place that is safe and provides protection, especially for people who are in danger: *The rebel leader **took sanctuary** in an embassy.* **2** [C] an area for birds or animals where they are protected and cannot be hunted **3** [C] the room where Christian religious services take place [ORIGIN: 1300—1400 Old French *sainctuarie*, from Late Latin *sanctuarium*, from Latin *sanctus* "holy"]

sanc·tum /ˈsæŋktəm/ *n.* **1 the inner sanctum** (humorous) a place that only a few important people are allowed to enter **2** [C] a holy place inside a TEMPLE

sand¹ /sænd/ *n.* [U] the substance that forms deserts and beaches, and consists of many small grains of rock [ORIGIN: Old English]

sand² *v.* [T] **1** to make a surface smooth by rubbing it with SANDPAPER or a special piece of equipment **2** to put sand on a frozen road to make it safer

san·dal /ˈsændl/ *n.* [C] a light open shoe that you wear in warm weather [ORIGIN: 1300—1400 Latin *sandalium*, from Greek, from *sandalon*] → *see picture at* SHOE¹

sand·bag /ˈsændbæg/ *n.* [C] a bag filled with sand, used for protection from floods, explosions, etc.

sand·bank /ˈsændbæŋk/ *n.* [C] EARTH SCIENCES a raised area of sand in a river, ocean, etc.

sand·blast /ˈsændblæst/ *v.* [T] to clean or polish metal, stone, glass, etc. with a machine that sends out a powerful stream of sand

sand·box /ˈsændbɑks/ *n.* [C] a special area of sand for children to play in

sand·cas·tle /ˈsændˌkæsəl/ *n.* [C] a small model of a castle made out of sand, usually by children on a beach

ˈsand dune *n.* [C] EARTH SCIENCES a DUNE

sand·man /ˈsændmæn/ *n.* [singular] a man in children's stories who makes children sleep by putting sand in their eyes

sand·pa·per /ˈsændˌpeɪpɚ/ *n.* [U] strong paper covered on one side with sand or another rough substance, used for rubbing wood in order to make it smooth —**sandpaper** *v.* [T]

sand·pip·er /ˈsændˌpaɪpɚ/ *n.* [C] a small bird with long legs and a long beak, that lives by the ocean

sand·stone /ˈsændstoʊn/ *n.* [U] EARTH SCIENCES a type of soft yellow or red rock

sand·storm /ˈsændstɔrm/ *n.* [C] EARTH SCIENCES a storm in the desert in which sand is blown around by strong winds

sand·wich¹ /ˈsændwɪtʃ/ *n.* [C] two pieces of bread with cheese, meat, egg, etc. between them, usually eaten for LUNCH: *tuna fish sandwiches* [ORIGIN: 1700—1800 Earl of *Sandwich* (1718-92), who ate sandwiches so that he could continue gambling without leaving the table]

sandwich² *v.* **be sandwiched between sth** to be in a very small space between two other things: *a motorcycle sandwiched between two vans*

sand·y /ˈsændi/ *adj.* **1** covered with sand: *a sandy beach* **2** sandy hair is dark BLONDE

sane /seɪn/ *adj.* **1** able to think in a normal and reasonable way (ANT) **insane** **2** reasonable and based on sensible thinking: *a sane solution to a difficult problem*

sang /sæŋ/ *v.* the past tense of SING

san·guine /ˈsæŋgwɪn/ *adj.* (formal) happy and hopeful about the future (SYN) **optimistic**: *Smith's lawyers aren't very sanguine about the outcome of the trial.* [ORIGIN: 1300—1400 French *sanguin*, from Latin *sanguineus*, from *sanguis* "blood"]

san·i·tar·i·um /ˌsænəˈtɛriəm/ *n.* [C] a hospital for sick people who are getting better but still need rest and care

san·i·tar·y /ˈsænəˌtɛri/ *adj.* **1** relating to the ways that dirt, infection, and waste are removed, so that places are clean and healthy for people to use: *the lack of* ***sanitary facilities*** (=toilets and sinks) **2** clean and not involving any danger to your health: *All food should be stored under sanitary conditions.*

ˈsanitary ˌnapkin *n.* [C] a piece of soft material that a woman wears in her underwear when she has her PERIOD

san·i·ta·tion /ˌsænəˈteɪʃən/ *n.* [U] the protection of public health by removing and treating waste, dirty water, etc.

san·i·tize /ˈsænəˌtaɪz/ *v.* [T] **1** to make news, literature, etc. less offensive by taking out anything unpleasant: *a sanitized version of the story* **2** to clean something thoroughly, removing dirt and BACTERIA

san·i·ty /ˈsænət̬i/ *n.* [U] **1** the ability to think in a normal and reasonable way: *I went away for the weekend to try and* ***keep*** *my* ***sanity***. **2** the condition of being mentally healthy: *I feared for my mother's fragile sanity.* | *She wondered if she was* ***losing*** *her* ***sanity***.

sank /sæŋk/ *v.* the past tense of SINK

San·ta Claus /ˈsæntə ˌklɔz/ *also* **Santa** *n.* an old man with red clothes and a long white BEARD, who children believe brings them presents at Christmas [ORIGIN: 1700—1800 Dutch *Sinterklaas*, from *Sint Nikolaas* "Saint Nicholas," patron saint of children]

sap¹ /sæp/ *n.* **1** [U] BIOLOGY the substance like water that carries food through a plant **2** [C] (informal) a stupid person who is easy to deceive or treat badly

sap² *v.* (**sapped**, **sapping**) [T] to gradually make something weak or destroy it: *The heat and humidity* ***sapped*** *my* ***strength***.

sap·ling /ˈsæplɪŋ/ *n.* [C] a young tree ➔ *see picture at* PLANT¹

sap·phire /ˈsæfaɪɚ/ *n.* [C,U] a transparent bright blue jewel [ORIGIN: 1200—1300 Old French *safir*, from Latin, from Greek, from Hebrew *sappir*, from Sanskrit *sanipriya* "dear to the planet Saturn"]

sap·py /ˈsæpi/ *adj.* (disapproving) expressing love and emotions in a way that seems silly: *a sappy love song*

sap·wood /ˈsæpwʊd/ *n.* [U] BIOLOGY the younger outer wood in a tree, that is not as dark or hard as the wood in the middle, through which water, SAP, and other liquids are moved around the plant

Sa·ran Wrap /səˈræn ˌræp/ *n.* [U] (trademark) thin transparent plastic used for wrapping food

sar·casm /ˈsɑrˌkæzəm/ *n.* [U] a way of speaking or writing in which you say the opposite of what you really mean in order to make an unkind joke or to show that you are annoyed: *There was a hint of sarcasm* (=a little sarcasm) *in his letter.* | *His voice* ***dripped with sarcasm*** (=showed a lot of sarcasm). [ORIGIN: 1500—1600 French *sarcasme*, from Late Latin, from Greek *sarkazein* "to tear flesh, bite your lip angrily, sneer"]

sar·cas·tic /sɑrˈkæstɪk/ *adj.* using sarcasm: *He can be very sarcastic.* —**sarcastically** *adv.*

S

sar·coph·a·gus /sɑr'kɑfəgəs/ *n.* (plural **sarcophagi**) a decorated stone box for a dead body, used in ancient times ➔ MUMMY

sarcophagus

sar·dine /sɑr'din/ *n.* **1** [C] a young HERRING (=a type of fish), or the meat from this fish, usually sold in cans **2 be packed like sardines** to be packed tightly together in a small space

sar·don·ic /sɑr'dɑnɪk/ *adj.* speaking or smiling in an unpleasant way that shows you do not have a good opinion of someone or something [ORIGIN: 1600—1700 French *sardonique*, from Greek *sardonios*, from *sardanios*; influenced by *Sardonios* "Sardinian," because of a plant from Sardinia (an Italian island) which causes the face to twist into a smile]

sa·ri /'sɑri/ *n.* [C] a type of loose clothing worn by many Indian and Bangladeshi women, and some Pakistani women

S

SASE *n.* [C] **self-addressed stamped envelope** an envelope that you put your name, address, and a stamp on, so that someone else can send you something

sash /sæʃ/ *n.* [C] **1** a long piece of cloth that you wear around your waist like a belt: *a white dress with a blue sash* **2** a long piece of cloth that you wear over one shoulder and across your chest as a sign of a special honor [ORIGIN: 1500—1600 Arabic *shash* "fine cloth"]

sass /sæs/ *v.* [T] (spoken) to talk in a rude way to someone you should respect: *Don't sass me, young lady!* —**sass** *n.* [U]

sass·y /'sæsi/ *adj.* (informal) **1** a sassy child is rude to someone s/he should respect **2** a sassy woman is confident and does not really care what other people think about her

SAT /sæt/ *n.* [C] (trademark) **Scholastic Aptitude Test** an examination that high school students take before they go to college

sat /sæt/ *v.* the past tense and past participle of SIT

Sa·tan /'seɪt˺n/ *n.* the Devil, considered to be the main evil power and God's opponent

sa·tan·ic /sə'tænɪk, seɪ-/ *adj.* **1** relating to practices that treat the Devil like a god: *satanic rites* **2** (literary) extremely cruel or evil: *satanic laughter*

sa·tan·is·m /'seɪt˺n,ɪzəm/ *n.* [U] the practice of treating the Devil like a god —**satanist** *n.* [C]

satellite

a satellite photo

sat·el·lite /'sæṭl,aɪt/ *n.* [C] **1** a machine that has been sent into space and goes around the Earth in order to send and receive electronic information: *a live broadcast coming in* ***by/via satellite*** | *a satellite communications network* ➔ SPACE¹ **2** PHYSICS a natural object such as the moon that moves around a PLANET ➔ *see picture at* APOGEE **3** a country, town, or organization that is controlled by or is dependent on another larger one: *the former Soviet satellites of eastern Europe* [ORIGIN: 1500—1600 French, Latin *satelles* "personal servant or guard"]

'satellite ,dish *n.* [C] a large circular piece of metal that receives the signals for satellite television

,satellite 'television *also* **,satellite T'V** *n.* [U] television programs that are broadcast using SATELLITES in space

sa·ti·ate /'seɪʃi,eɪt/ *v.* [T usually passive] (literary) to completely satisfy a desire or need for something, for example food: *They rested,* ***satiated with*** *the big meal.* —**satiated** *adj.* —**satiety** /sə'taɪəṭi/ *n.* [U]

sat·in /'sæt˺n/ *n.* [U] a type of cloth that is very smooth and shiny [ORIGIN: 1300—1400 Old French]

sat·in·y /'sæt˺n-i/ *adj.* smooth, shiny, and soft like satin: *satiny material*

sat·ire /'sætaɪɚ/ *n.* **1** [U] ENG. LANG. ARTS a way of criticizing someone or something, in which you show his, her, or its faults in a funny way: *a comedian who does* ***political satire*** | *a* ***satire of*** *the movie industry* **2** [C] ENG. LANG. ARTS a play, story, etc. written in this way —**satirical** /sə'tɪrɪkəl/ *adj.* —**satirically** *adv.*

sat·i·rist /'sæṭərɪst/ *n.* [C] ENG. LANG. ARTS someone who writes satire

sat·i·rize /'sæṭə,raɪz/ *v.* [T] ENG. LANG. ARTS to use satire to make people see someone's or something's faults: *a movie satirizing the fashion industry*

sat·is·fac·tion /,sæṭɪs'fækʃən/ *n.* **1** [C,U] a feeling of happiness or pleasure because you have achieved something or gotten what you wanted (ANT) **dissatisfaction**: *He looked around the room* ***with satisfaction.*** | *Liz found* ***satisfaction in*** *her job.* | *the* ***satisfaction of*** *knowing that I was* *right* **2** [U] the act of getting something you want, need, or have demanded: *the satisfaction of basic physical needs* **3 to sb's satisfaction** as well or completely as someone wants: *I'm not sure I can answer that question to your satisfaction.*

sat·is·fac·to·ry /ˌsæt̬ɪs'fæktəri, -tri/ *adj.* good enough for a particular situation or purpose, or good enough to please you (ANT) **unsatisfactory** → SATISFYING: *a satisfactory explanation* | *Progress has been satisfactory.* | *a satisfactory result* | *an agreement that is* ***satisfactory to*** *both sides*

THESAURUS

good enough – having a standard that is satisfactory for a particular purpose or situation: *Well, that coat's a little big, but it's good enough.*
acceptable – good enough for a particular purpose: *Some students said it was easy to get acceptable grades without doing much work.*
passable (formal) – good enough to be acceptable, but not very good: *Al speaks passable Spanish.*
all right/okay – acceptable, but not excellent: *The food was all right, I guess, nothing special.*
reasonable – fairly good, large, or high: *a reasonable level of pay*
respectable – good or satisfactory: *She jumped a respectable five and a half feet.*
adequate – enough in quantity or of a good enough quality for a particular purpose: *Are they given adequate training before starting work?*

sat·is·fied /'sæt̬ɪsˌfaɪd/ *adj.* **1** pleased because something has happened in the way that you want, or because you have achieved something (ANT) **dissatisfied**: *satisfied customers* | *Are you* ***satisfied with*** *your job?* **2** feeling sure that something is right or true: *I'm* ***satisfied (that)*** *he's telling the truth.*

THESAURUS **sure, certain, convinced, confident** → SURE[1]

3 satisfied? (spoken) said in an annoyed way when you say or do something that you do not really want to say or do: *Okay, okay, I was wrong – satisfied?*

sat·is·fy /'sæt̬ɪsˌfaɪ/ *v.* (**satisfied**, **satisfies**) [T] **1** to make someone happy by providing what s/he wants or needs: *One bite satisfied my craving for chocolate.* | *Can the school* ***satisfy the needs*** *of special learners?* **2** to make someone feel sure that something is true or has been done correctly: *The evidence did not* ***satisfy*** *the jury* ***that*** *he was guilty.* **3** (formal) to be good enough for a particular purpose, standard, etc.: *students who have not satisfied the requirements for graduation* [ORIGIN: 1400—1500 Old French *satisfier*, from Latin *satisfacere*, from *satis* "enough" + *facere* "to make"]

sat·is·fy·ing /'sæt̬ɪsˌfaɪ-ɪŋ/ *adj.* **1** making you feel pleased and happy, especially because you have got what you wanted: *a satisfying victory* **2** food that is satisfying makes you feel that you have eaten enough: *a satisfying meal*

sat·u·rate /'sætʃəˌreɪt/ *v.* [T] **1** to make something completely wet: *The ground is completely* ***saturated with*** *rain.* **2** to make something very full of a particular type of thing: *an area* ***saturated with*** *radio stations* —**saturation** /ˌsætʃə'reɪʃən/ *n.* [U]

ˌsaturated 'fat *n.* [C,U] a type of fat from meat and milk products

Sat·ur·day /'sæt̬ɚdi, -deɪ/ (*written abbreviation* **Sat.**) *n.* [C,U] the seventh day of the week, between Friday and Sunday: *The documents were released Saturday.* | *Jim's going to Phoenix* ***on Saturday.*** | *Would* ***next Saturday*** *be a good time for me to visit?* | *I went out and played golf* ***last Saturday.*** | *What are you doing* ***Saturday night?*** [ORIGIN: 800—900 Translation of Latin *Saturni dies* "day of Saturn"]

Sat·urn /'sæt̬ɚn/ *n.* PHYSICS the second largest PLANET, which is sixth from the Sun → *see picture at* SOLAR SYSTEM

sauce /sɔs/ *n.* [C,U] a thick cooked liquid that is served with food to give it a particular taste: *spaghetti with tomato sauce* [ORIGIN: 1300—1400 Old French, Latin *salsa*, from *sallere* "to add salt to"]

sauce·pan /'sɔs-pæn/ *n.* [C] a deep round metal container with a handle, used for cooking

sau·cer /'sɔsɚ/ *n.* [C] a small round plate that you put a cup on

sau·cy /'sɔsi/ *adj.* about sex or relating to sex, in a way that is amusing but not shocking: *a saucy comedy*

sau·er·kraut /'saʊɚˌkraʊt/ *n.* [U] a salty German food made of CABBAGE

sau·na /'sɔnə/ *n.* [C] **1** a room that is filled with steam to make it very hot, in which people sit because it is considered healthy **2** a time when you sit or lie in a room like this

saun·ter /'sɔntɚ, 'sɑn-/ *v.* [I] to walk in a slow and confident way: *Myers sauntered up to her desk.*

sau·sage /'sɔsɪdʒ/ *n.* [C,U] a mixture of meat and SPICES, usually in a small tube shape, that is cooked and often eaten for breakfast [ORIGIN: 1400—1500 Old North French *saussiche*, from Late Latin *salsicia*, from Latin *salsus* "salted"]

sau·té /sɔ'teɪ/ *v.* [T] to cook something quickly in a little hot oil or fat: *sautéed mushrooms*

sav·age[1] /'sævɪdʒ/ *adj.* **1** very cruel and violent: *a savage murder* **2** criticizing someone or something very severely: *a savage attack on the newspaper industry* **3** very severe and harmful: *savage budget cuts* **4** (old-fashioned) PRIMITIVE [ORIGIN: 1200—1300 Old French *sauvage*, from Latin *silvaticus* "of the woods, wild"] —**savagely** *adv.*

savage[2] *n.* [C] (old-fashioned, offensive) someone from a country where the way of living seems simple and undeveloped

S

savage³ *v.* [T] **1** to criticize someone or something very severely: *a movie savaged by the critics* **2** if an animal savages someone, it attacks him/her, and causes serious injuries

sav·age·ry /ˈsævɪdʒri/ *n.* [U] extremely cruel and violent behavior

sa·van·na, savannah /səˈvænə/ *n.* [C,U] EARTH SCIENCES a large flat area of land covered in grass in a warm part of the world

save¹ /seɪv/ *v.*
1 FROM HARM/DANGER [T] to make someone or something safe from danger, harm, or destruction: *We are working to* ***save*** *the rain forest* ***from*** *destruction.* | *The new treatment could* ***save*** *his* ***life***.
2 MONEY [I,T] *also* **save up** to keep money so that you can use it later: *We're trying to* ***save*** *money* ***to*** *buy a house.* | *I'm* ***saving up for*** *a trip to Europe.*
3 NOT WASTE [T] to use less time, money, energy, etc. so that you do not waste any: *We'll save time if we take a cab.* | *Buying new equipment will actually save the company money.*
4 TO USE LATER [T] to keep something so that you can use or enjoy it in the future: *I'm* ***saving*** *this bottle of champagne* ***for*** *a special occasion.*

THESAURUS keep, store, reserve → KEEP¹

5 HELP TO AVOID [T] to help someone by making it unnecessary for him/her to do something that is inconvenient or difficult: *If you could pick up Lori's birthday cake, it would save me a trip to the bakery.*
6 COLLECT [T] *also* **save** (sth ↔) **up** to keep all the objects of a particular kind that you can find so that they can be used for a special purpose: *I'm* ***saving*** *all the bottles and cans* ***for*** *recycling.*
7 KEEP FOR SB [T] to stop people from using something so that it is available for someone else: *We'll* ***save*** *some dinner* ***for*** *you.* | *Will you save me a seat?*
8 COMPUTER [I,T] IT to make a computer keep the work that you have done on it: *Don't forget to save before you close the file.* → COMPUTER
9 SPORT [T] to stop the other team from scoring a GOAL in games such as SOCCER or HOCKEY
10 saving grace the one good thing that makes someone or something acceptable: *His sense of humor was his only saving grace.* → **lose/save face** *at* FACE¹
save on sth *phr. v.*
to avoid wasting something by using as little as possible of it: *We turn the heat down during the day to save on electricity.* [ORIGIN: 1200—1300 Old French *salver*, from Late Latin *salvare*, from Latin *salvus*]

save² *n.* [C] an action by the GOALKEEPER in SOCCER, HOCKEY, etc. that prevents the other team from getting a point

sav·er /ˈseɪvɚ/ *n.* **1 time-saver/money-saver/energy-saver etc.** something that prevents loss or waste: *Shopping by mail is a great time-saver.* **2** [C] someone who saves money in a bank

sav·ing /ˈseɪvɪŋz/ *n.* **1 savings** [plural] all the money that you have saved, especially in a bank: *She lost their* ***life savings*** *in a Vegas casino.* **2** [C] an amount of something that you have not used or do not have to spend: *Enjoy 25%* ***savings on*** *our regular prices.* | *a* ***saving of*** *$15*

ˈsavings acˌcount *n.* [C] ECONOMICS a bank account that pays INTEREST on the money you have in it

ˌsavings and ˈloan (*abbreviation* **S&L**) *n.* [C] ECONOMICS a business similar to a bank where you can save money, and that also lends money for things such as houses

ˈsavings bank *n.* [C] ECONOMICS a bank whose business is mostly from savings accounts and from LOANs on houses

sav·ior /ˈseɪvyɚ/ *n.* **1** [C] someone or something that saves you from a difficult or dangerous situation: *Many believed he would be the* ***savior of*** *the organization.* **2 the/our Savior** another name for Jesus Christ, used in the Christian religion

sa·vor /ˈseɪvɚ/ *v.* [T] to make an activity or experience last as long as you can, because you are enjoying every moment of it: *Drink it slowly and savor every drop.*

sa·vor·y /ˈseɪvəri/ *adj.* savory food has a pleasant spicy or salty smell or taste: *savory snacks* [ORIGIN: 1200—1300 Old French *savouré*, past participle of *savourer*, from *savour*]

sav·vy /ˈsævi/ *n.* [U] practical knowledge and ability: *marketing savvy* —**savvy** *adj.*: *a savvy businesswoman*

saw¹ /sɔ/ *v.* the past tense of SEE

saw² *n.* [C] a tool that has a flat blade with a row of sharp points, used for cutting wood

saw³ *v.* (past tense **sawed**, past participle **sawed** *or* **sawn** /sɔn/) [I,T] to cut something using a saw: *We decided to* ***saw off*** *the lower branches of the apple tree.* → CUT¹

saw·dust /ˈsɔdʌst/ *n.* [U] very small pieces of wood that are left when you cut wood with a saw

saw·mill /ˈsɔmɪl/ *n.* [C] a factory where trees are cut into boards

sawn /sɔn/ *v.* a past participle of SAW³

sax /sæks/ *n.* [C] (informal) a saxophone

sax·o·phone /ˈsæksəˌfoʊn/ *n.* [C] a metal musical instrument that you play by blowing into it and pressing special KEYS [ORIGIN: 1800—1900 French, from Adolphe *Sax* (1814-94), Belgian musician who invented the instrument]

say¹ /seɪ/ *v.* (past tense and past participle **said** /sɛd/, third person singular **says** /sɛz/)
1 EXPRESS STH [T] to express a thought or feeling in words: *"I'm so tired," she said.* | *They left without* ***saying goodbye***. | *Dave* ***said (that)*** *he'd call back.* | *Did she* ***say what*** *happened?* | *Tom didn't* ***say why*** *he was angry.* | *That was* ***a nice/mean/strange*** *thing* ***to say***. | *What did you* ***say to*** *them?*

S

USAGE

Say cannot have a person as its object. Do not use "say me." Use " **tell** me" instead. Compare these sentences: *He said that he was tired.* | *He told me that he was tired.*

THESAURUS

mention – to say something but without giving many details: *He mentioned something about a party.*
add – to say something more about something: *Is there anything you'd like to add?*
state (formal) – to give a piece of information or your opinion, especially by saying it clearly: *The witness stated that he had never seen the woman before.*
utter (literary) – to say something: *No one uttered a word.*
express – to say how you feel about something: *It's hard to express how I felt.*

2 PRONOUNCE [T] to pronounce a word or sound: ***How do** you **say** your last name?*
3 WITHOUT WORDS [I,T] to express something without using words: *What is Hopper trying to say in this painting?* | *Her smile **says it all*** (=her smile expresses her happiness).
4 GIVE INFORMATION [T] to give information in writing, pictures, or numbers: *The clock said quarter after six.* | *The instructions **say (that)** you cook it for ten minutes.*
5 sth goes without saying used when what you have said or written is so clear that it really did not need to be stated: ***It goes without saying** that a well-rested person is a better worker.*
6 say to yourself to think something: *I was worried about it, but I said to myself, "You can do this."*
7 to say the least used when what you have said could have been stated much more strongly: *The house needs work, to say the least.*
8 having said that used before saying something that makes the opinion you have given seem less strong: *The movie is poorly made, but having said that, it's still a cute picture to take the kids to.*
9 that is to say used before describing what you mean in more detail or more clearly: *Things still aren't equal. That is to say, women still are not paid as much as men.*

SPOKEN PHRASES

10 be saying used in phrases to emphasize that you are trying to explain what you mean in a way that someone will understand better, especially in a situation in which you are arguing with someone and do not want him/her to be angry: ***All I'm saying is** that he should have been more careful.* | ***I'm not saying** it's a bad idea, just that we need to think about it.* | ***I'm just saying** it would be easier if we made a copy.* | *Maybe if you stopped shouting at him, he might actually tell you what's wrong, **(do you) know what I'm saying*** (=do you understand me)*?*
11 [T] to suggest or suppose that something might happen or might be true: *Say you were going to an interview. What would you wear?* | ***Let's say** they don't approve our plan. What do we do then?*
12 what do you say? used in order to ask someone if s/he agrees with a suggestion: ***What do you say we** all go to a movie?*
13 you can say that again used in order to say that you completely agree with someone: *"It's cold in here." "You can say that again."*
14 say when used when you want someone to tell you when you have given him/her the correct amount of something, especially a drink

[ORIGIN: Old English *secgan*]

say² *n.* **1** [singular, U] the right to help decide something: *Citizens should **have a say in** how their tax money is spent.* | *Members felt that they **had no say in** the proposed changes.* | *The chairman **has the final say*** (=has the right to make the final decision about something). **2 have your say** to have the opportunity to give your opinion about something: *You'll all have the chance to have your say.*

say·ing /'seɪ-ɪŋ/ *n.* [C] a well-known statement that expresses an idea most people believe is true and wise

THESAURUS phrase, expression, idiom, cliché, proverb, maxim → PHRASE¹

SC the written abbreviation of SOUTH CAROLINA

scab /skæb/ *n.* [C] **1** a hard layer of dried blood that forms over a cut or wound **2** (informal) an insulting word for someone who works in a place where other people are on STRIKE (=refusing to work because of a disagreement with an employer)

scads /skædz/ *n.* [plural] (informal) large numbers or quantities of something: ***scads of** money*

scaf·fold /'skæfəld, -foʊld/ *n.* [C] **1** a structure built next to a building or high wall, for people to stand on while they work on the building or wall **2** a structure used in past times for killing criminals by hanging them from it [ORIGIN: 1200—1300 Old North French *escafaut*, from Vulgar Latin *catafalicum* "stage, platform, scaffold"]

scaf·fold·ing /'skæfəldɪŋ/ *n.* [U] poles and boards that are built into a structure for people to stand on when they are working on a high wall or the outside of a building

scaffolding

scald /skɔld/ *v.* [T] to burn yourself with hot liquid or steam [ORIGIN: 1100—1200 Old North French *escalder*, from Late Latin *excaldare* "to wash in warm water"]

scald·ing /'skɔldɪŋ/ *adj., adv.* extremely hot: ***scalding hot** coffee*

S

> **THESAURUS** hot, boiling/baking/scorching (hot) → HOT

scale¹ /skeɪl/ *n.*
1 SIZE [singular, U] the size or level of something, when compared to what is normal: *The **scale of** the problem soon became clear.* | *There has been housing development **on a** massive **scale** since 1980.* | *a **large/small scale** research project*
2 MEASURING SYSTEM [C usually singular] a system for measuring the force, speed, amount, etc. of something, or for comparing it with something else: *The earthquake measured 7 **on** the Richter **scale**.* | *Your performance will be judged **on a scale of** 1 to 10.*
3 RANGE [C usually singular] the whole range of different types of people, things, ideas, etc. from the lowest level to the highest: *Some rural schools have 50 students while **at the other end of the scale** are city schools with 5,000 students.*
4 FOR WEIGHING [C] a machine or piece of equipment for weighing people or objects: *The nurse asked me to get **on the scale**.* → *see picture at* WEIGH
5 MEASURING MARKS [C] a set of marks with regular spaces between them on an instrument that is used for measuring: *a ruler with a metric scale*
S
6 MAP/DRAWING [C,U] the relationship between the size of a map, drawing, or model and the actual size of the place or thing that it represents: *a **scale of** 1 inch to the mile*
7 MUSIC [C] ENG. LANG. ARTS a series of musical notes that have a fixed order and become gradually higher or lower in PITCH
8 ON FISH [C usually plural] one of the small flat pieces of hard skin that cover the bodies of fish, snakes, etc. → *see picture on page A15*

scale² *v.* [T] to climb to the top of something that is high: *They scaled a 40-foot wall and escaped.*

scale sth ↔ **back/down** *phr. v.* to reduce the size of something such as an organization or plan: *Military operations in the area have been scaled down.*

'scale ˌdrawing *n.* [C] a drawing of an object, building, or areas, etc. that is larger or smaller than the actual object, building, etc.

sca·lene tri·an·gle /ˌskeɪlin 'traɪˌæŋgəl/ *n.* [C] MATH a TRIANGLE with three sides that are all different lengths → *see picture at* TRIANGLE

scal·lion /'skælyən/ *n.* [C] a small white onion with a small round end and a long green stem that you eat raw (SYN) **green onion**

scal·lop /'skæləp, 'skɑləp/ *n.* [C] a small sea animal that has a hard flat shell, or the meat from this animal

scal·loped /'skæləpt, 'skɑ-/ *adj.* cloth or objects that have scalloped edges are cut in a series of small curves as a decoration

scalp¹ /skælp/ *n.* [C] BIOLOGY the skin on the top of your head, where your hair grows

scalp² *v.* [T] **1** (informal) to buy tickets for an event and sell them again at a much higher price **2** to cut the scalp off a dead enemy as a sign of victory

scal·pel /'skælpəl/ *n.* [C] a small and very sharp knife used by doctors during operations

scalp·er /'skælpɚ/ *n.* [C] someone who makes money by buying tickets for an event and selling them again at a very high price

scal·y /'skeɪli/ *adj.* **1** an animal that is scaly is covered with small flat pieces of hard skin **2** scaly skin is dry and rough

scaly

scam /skæm/ *n.* [C] (informal) a smart but dishonest plan to get money: *an insurance scam*

scam·per /'skæmpɚ/ *v.* [I] to run with short quick steps, like a small animal: *A mouse **scampered into** its hole.*

scan¹ /skæn/ *v.* (**scanned**, **scanning**) **1** [I,T] *also* **scan through** to read something quickly in order to understand its main meaning or to find a particular piece of information → SKIM: *I had a chance to scan through the report on the plane.* **2** [T] to examine an area carefully, because you are looking for a particular person or thing: *They anxiously **scanned** the streets **for** Billy.* **3** [T] if a machine scans an object or a part of your body, it produces a picture of what is inside → SCANNER: *All luggage has to be scanned at the airport.* **4** [T] to copy a picture or piece of writing onto a computer by putting it into a machine attached to the computer → SCANNER [ORIGIN: 1300—1400 Late Latin *scandere*, from Latin, "to climb"]

scan² *n.* [C] a medical test in which a special machine produces a picture of something inside your body: *a bone/brain scan*

scan·dal /'skændl/ *n.* [C,U] something that has happened that people think is immoral or shocking: *He was involved in a major **financial scandal**.* [ORIGIN: 1100—1200 Late Latin *scandalum* "offense," from Greek *skandalon*]

scan·dal·ize /'skændlˌaɪz/ *v.* [T] to do something that shocks people very much

scan·dal·ous /'skændl-əs/ *adj.* completely immoral and shocking: *scandalous behavior*

scan·ner /'skænɚ/ *n.* [C] **1** PHYSICS a machine that passes a beam of ELECTRONS over an object or a part of your body in order to produce a picture of what is inside **2** IT a piece of computer equipment that copies an image from paper onto the computer → *see picture on page A19*

scant /skænt/ *adj.* not enough: *The story has received **scant attention** in the press.*

scant·y /'skænti/ *adj.* very little in size or amount: *a scanty bikini* —**scantily** *adv.*: *scantily dressed*

scape·goat /ˈskeɪpgoʊt/ *n.* [C] someone who is blamed for something bad that happens, even if it is not his/her fault: *He's been made a* ***scapegoat for*** *their lack of success.* [ORIGIN: 1500—1600 *scape* (from *scape* "to get away" (13—20 centuries), from *escape*) + *goat*] —**scapegoat** *v.* [T]

scar¹ /skɑr/ *n.* [C] **1** a permanent mark on your skin from a cut or wound: *The cut will* ***leave a*** *permanent* ***scar***.

THESAURUS blemish, bruise, pimple, zit, wart, blister, freckle, mole ➔ MARK²

2 a feeling of fear and sadness that stays with a person after a bad experience: *The war has* ***left*** *a deep* ***scar*** *on this community.* [ORIGIN: 1300—1400 Old French *escare*, from Late Latin *eschara*, from Greek]

scar² *v.* (**scarred, scarring**) [T] **1** to have or be given a permanent mark on your skin from a cut or wound: *The fire had left him* ***scarred for life***. **2** if a bad experience scars you, it leaves you with a feeling of sadness and fear that continues for a long time: *She was* ***deeply scarred*** *by her father's suicide.*

scarce /skɛrs/ *adj.* if food, clothing, water, etc. is scarce, there is not enough of it available

scarce·ly /ˈskɛrsli/ *adv.* **1** almost not at all, or almost none at all (SYN) **hardly**: *Their teaching methods have scarcely changed in the last 10 years.* | *The country has* ***scarcely any*** *industry.* **2** definitely not, or almost certainly not: *Owen is really angry, and you can scarcely blame him.*

scar·ci·ty /ˈskɛrsət̬i/ *n.* [singular, U] a situation in which there is not enough of something: *a* ***scarcity of*** *medical supplies*

scare¹ /skɛr/ *v.* **1** [T] to make someone feel frightened: *I didn't mean to scare you.* | *We were* ***scared to death*** (=very scared). | *The alarm* ***scared the life out of*** *me* (=scared me very much)*!* **2** [I] to become frightened: *I don't* ***scare easily****, you know.* [ORIGIN: 1100—1200 Old Norse *skirra*, from *skjarr* "shy, fearful"]

scare sb/sth ↔ **off/away** *phr. v.* **1** to make someone or something go away by frightening him, her, or it: *A barking dog had scared the attackers away.* **2** to make someone uncertain or nervous so that s/he does not do something s/he was going to do: *I'd like to call him, but I don't want to scare him off.*

scare sth ↔ **up** *phr. v.* (spoken) to make something although you have very few things to make it from: *I'll try to scare up some breakfast.*

scare² *n.* **1** [singular] a sudden feeling of fear: *You really* ***gave us a scare***. **2** [C] a situation in which a group of people become frightened about something: *a* ***bomb scare***

scare·crow /ˈskɛrkroʊ/ *n.* [C] an object made to look like a person, that is put in a field to frighten birds away

scared /skɛrd/ *adj.* frightened by something or nervous about something (SYN) **afraid**: *A lot of people are* ***scared of*** *flying.* | *She was* ***scared (that)*** *she might slip and fall on the ice.* | *Steve heard some noise, and he was* ***scared stiff/scared to death*** (=extremely frightened).

THESAURUS frightened, afraid, terrified, petrified, fearful, phobic ➔ FRIGHTENED

scarf¹ /skɑrf/ *n.* (plural **scarves** /skɑrvz/ or **scarfs**) [C] a piece of material that you wear around your neck, head, or shoulders to keep you warm or to make you look attractive [ORIGIN: 1500—1600 Old North French *escarpe*, from Old French *escherpe* "bag hung around the neck"] ➔ *see picture at* CLOTHES

scarf² *v.* (slang)

scarf sth ↔ **down/up** *phr. v.* to eat something very quickly: *I scarfed down a candy bar between classes.*

scar·let /ˈskɑrlɪt/ *n.* [U] a very bright red color [ORIGIN: 1200—1300 Old French *escarlate*, from Medieval Latin *scarlata*, from Persian *saqalat*, type of cloth] —**scarlet** *adj.*

scarves /skɑrvz/ *n.* a plural of SCARF¹

scar·y /ˈskɛri/ *adj.* (comparative **scarier**, superlative **scariest**) frightening: *a scary movie*

scath·ing /ˈskeɪðɪŋ/ *adj.* scathing remarks, COMMENTS, etc. criticize someone or something very severely: *a* ***scathing attack*** *on the president* [ORIGIN: 1700—1800 *scathe* "to harm" (12—20 centuries), from Old Norse *skatha*]

scat·ter /ˈskæt̬ɚ/ *v.* **1** [T] to throw or drop a lot of things over a wide area: ***Scatter*** *the seeds* ***over*** *the soil.* **2** [I,T] if people or animals scatter, or if something scatters them, they move quickly in different directions: *The sound of gunfire made the crowd scatter.*

scat·ter·brained /ˈskæt̬ɚˌbreɪnd/ *adj.* (informal) tending to forget or lose things because you do not think in a practical way

scat·tered /ˈskæt̬ɚd/ *adj.* spread over a wide area or over a long period of time: *The weather forecast is for* ***scattered showers*** (=short periods of rain).

scav·enge /ˈskævɪndʒ/ *v.* [I,T] to search for food or useful objects among things that have been thrown away [ORIGIN: 1600—1700 *scavenger* (16—21 centuries), from *scavager* "tax collector, someone who cleans streets"] —**scavenger** *n.* [C]

sce·nar·i·o /sɪˈnɛriˌoʊ, -ˈnær-/ (Ac) *n.* (plural **scenarios**) [C] a situation that could possibly happen but has not happened yet: *Even in the **worst-case scenario** (=if the worst possible thing happens), we'll still get the money back.* | *A **likely scenario** is that the college will hire a new head coach by June.*

scene /sin/ *n.*
1 PLAY/MOVIE [C] ENG. LANG. ARTS a part of a play or movie during which the action all happens in one place over a short period of time: *She comes on in Act 2, Scene 3.* | *a love scene*
2 ACCIDENT/CRIME [singular] the place where an accident or crime happened: *Firefighters arrived **on/at the scene** within minutes.* | *the **scene of the crime***
3 VIEW/PICTURE [C] a view or picture of a place: *a peaceful country scene* ►Don't say "There's a nice scene from my window." Say "There's a nice view from my window."◄
4 the music/fashion/political etc. scene a particular set of activities and the people who are involved in them: *a newcomer to the political scene*
5 ARGUMENT [C] a loud angry argument, especially in a public place: *Sit down and stop **making a scene**!*
6 not sb's scene (informal) not the type of thing someone likes: *Loud parties aren't really my scene.*
7 behind the scenes secretly, while other things are happening publicly: *People are working hard behind the scenes.*
8 set the scene a) to provide the conditions in which an event can happen: *This agreement **sets the scene for** democratic elections.* **b)** to describe the situation before you begin to tell a story [ORIGIN: 1500—1600 French *scène*, from Latin *scena, scaena* "stage, scene"]

sce·ner·y /ˈsinəri/ *n.* [U] **1** the natural features of a place, such as mountains, forests, etc.: *What beautiful scenery!* **2** ENG. LANG. ARTS the painted background, furniture, etc. used on a theater stage

sce·nic /ˈsinɪk/ *adj.* with beautiful views of nature: *Let's take the **scenic route** home.*

scent /sɛnt/ *n.* [C] **1** a particular smell, especially a pleasant one: *the **scent of** roses*

THESAURUS smell, aroma, fragrance, perfume → SMELL²

2 the smell left behind by an animal or person [ORIGIN: 1300—1400 Old French *sentir* "to feel, smell," from Latin *sentire* "to feel"]

scent·ed /ˈsɛntɪd/ *adj.* having a pleasant smell: *scented soap*

sched·ule¹ /ˈskɛdʒəl, -dʒul/ (Ac) *n.* **1** [C,U] a plan of what someone is going to do and when s/he is going to do it: *What's your schedule like on Wednesday?* | *I have a very **busy/full/tight schedule** this week* (=I am very busy). | *The project is six months **behind schedule*** (=progressing more slowly than planned). | *The building was finished **ahead of schedule*** (=earlier than the planned time). | *We are right **on schedule*** (=doing things at the planned times). → PLAN¹ **2** [C] a list showing the times that buses, trains, etc. leave or arrive at a particular place [ORIGIN: 1300—1400 Old French *cedule* "piece of paper, note," from Late Latin *schedula*, from Latin *scheda* "sheet of papyrus"]

schedule² (Ac) *v.* [T] to plan that something will happen at a particular time: *The meeting has been **scheduled for** Friday.* | *Another new store is **scheduled to** open in three weeks.*

sche·mat·ic¹ /skiˈmæt̬ɪk/ *adj.* showing the main parts of something in a simple way: *a schematic drawing of a circuit*

schematic² *n.* [C] a simple drawing of a structure, especially of an electrical or MECHANICAL system, that shows its main parts

scheme¹ /skim/ (Ac) *n.* [C] **1** a plan, especially to do something bad or illegal: *a **scheme to** avoid paying taxes*

THESAURUS plan, plot, conspiracy → PLAN¹

2 a system that you use to organize information, ideas, etc.: *a classification scheme that divided the stories by genre* **3 color scheme** the different colors in which a room or house is painted

scheme² *v.* [I] to secretly make dishonest plans to get or achieve something: *politicians **scheming to** win votes* —**schemer** *n.* [C]

schism /ˈsɪzəm, ˈskɪzəm/ *n.* [C,U] (formal) the separation of a group of people into two groups as the result of a disagreement

schiz·o·phre·ni·a /ˌskɪtsəˈfriniə/ *n.* [U] a serious mental illness in which someone's thoughts and feelings become separated from what is really happening around him/her [ORIGIN: 1900—2000 German *schizophrenie*, from Greek *schizo-* "split" + *phren* "mind"] —**schizophrenic** /ˌskɪtsəˈfrɛnɪk/ *adj., n.* [C]

schlep /ʃlɛp/ *v.* (**schlepped**, **schlepping**) [T] (informal) to carry or pull something heavy: *I don't want to **schlep** this bag all the way **across** town.* [ORIGIN: 1900—2000 Yiddish *shleppen*, from Middle High German *sleppen*]

THESAURUS carry, tote, lug, haul → CARRY

schlock /ʃlɑk/ *n.* [U] (informal) things that are cheap, bad, or useless

schmaltz·y /ˈʃmɔltsi, ˈʃmɑl-/ *adj.* (informal, disapproving) dealing with strong emotions such as love and sadness in a way that seems silly: *a schmaltzy love song* [ORIGIN: 1900—2000 *schmaltz* "schmaltzy quality" (20—21 centuries), from Yiddish *shmalts* "melted fat"] —**schmaltz** *n.* [U]

schmooze /ʃmuz/ *v.* [I] (informal, disapproving) to talk about unimportant things at a social event in a friendly way that is not always sincere [ORIGIN: 1800—1900 Yiddish *shmuesn* "to talk"]

schmuck /ʃmʌk/ *n.* [C] (informal) a stupid person [ORIGIN: 1800—1900 Yiddish *shmok* "penis, stupid person," from German *schmuck* "decoration"]

schnapps /ʃnæps/ *n.* [U] a strong alcoholic drink [ORIGIN: 1800—1900 German *schnaps*, from Low German *snappen* "to snap"]

schol·ar /ˈskɑlɚ/ *n.* [C] someone who studies a subject and knows a lot about it

schol·ar·ly /ˈskɑlɚli/ *adj.* **1** relating to the serious study of a particular subject: *a scholarly journal* **2** someone who is scholarly spends a lot of time studying, and knows a lot about a particular subject

schol·ar·ship /ˈskɑlɚˌʃɪp/ *n.* **1** [C] an amount of money that is given to someone by an organization to help pay for his/her education: *a football/music/academic, etc. scholarship* | *Michael **got a scholarship** to college.* **2** [U] the knowledge, work, or methods used in serious studying: *Burns's book is a work of great scholarship.*

scho·las·tic /skəˈlæstɪk/ *adj.* (formal) relating to schools or teaching → ACADEMIC: *an excellent scholastic record*

school¹ /skul/ *n.*

1 BUILDING [C,U] a place where children are taught: *Which **school** did you **go to*** (=attend)? | *I can get some work done while the kids are **at school*** (=studying in the school building).

TOPIC

At school, **schoolchildren/students** have classes with a **teacher** and **study/learn** a range of **subjects**. In class, students **do classwork**. After school, they **do homework**. Students **take tests/exams**. If they **pass a test/an exam**, they succeed in the test. If they **fail a test/an exam**, they do not succeed in the test, and may have to **retake** it.

2 TIME AT SCHOOL [U] **a)** the time spent at school: *What are you doing **after school**?* **b)** the time during your life when you go to a school: *Joanne's one of my old friends from school.*

GRAMMAR

Do not use "the" before **school** when you are talking about someone studying or teaching there: *What time do you leave for school in the morning?*
Use "the" before **school** if someone goes there for some other reason, not to study or teach: *We all went to see the play at the school.*
You must also use "the" if you describe exactly which school you are talking about: *the school on Court Street*

3 in school attending a school, as opposed to having a job: *Are your boys still in school?*
4 UNIVERSITY a) [C,U] (informal) a college or university, or the time when you study there: *"Where did you go to school?" "UC San Diego."* **b)** [C] a department that teaches a particular subject at a university: *the Harvard **School of** Law* | *I worked my way through **law/medical/graduate school**.*
5 FOR ONE SUBJECT [C,U] a place where a particular subject or skill is taught: *an art school*
6 TEACHERS/STUDENTS [singular,U] the students and teachers at a school: *The whole school was sorry when she left.*
7 ART/IDEAS [C] ENG. LANG. ARTS a number of artists, writers, etc. who are considered as a group because their style of work or their ideas are very similar: *the Dutch school of painting*
8 school of thought an opinion or way of thinking about something that is shared by a group of people: *There are many schools of thought on how yoga should be taught.*
9 FISH [C] BIOLOGY a large group of fish or other sea creatures that are swimming together: *a **school of** dolphins* [ORIGIN: Old English *scol*, from Latin *schola*, from Greek *schole* "discussion, school"]

school² *v.* [T] (formal) to train or teach someone: *The children are **schooled in** music and art from a very early age.*

school·ing /ˈskulɪŋ/ *n.* [U] education at school

schoo·ner /ˈskunɚ/ *n.* [C] a fast sailing ship with two sails

sci·ence /ˈsaɪəns/ *n.* **1** [U] knowledge about the physical world that is based on testing and proving facts, or work that results in this knowledge: *the teaching of science in schools* | *developments in **science and technology*** **2** [C,U] the study of a particular type of human behavior: *political science* [ORIGIN: 1300—1400 Old French, Latin *scientia* "knowledge," from *scire* "to know"]

ˌscience ˈfiction *n.* [U] ENG. LANG. ARTS books and stories about the future, for example about traveling in time and space → BOOK¹

sci·en·tif·ic /ˌsaɪənˈtɪfɪk◂/ *adj.* **1** relating to science: *scientific discoveries* | *a **scientific experiment*** **2** using an organized system: *We do keep records, but we're not very scientific about it.*

ˌscientific ˈmethod *n.* [U] SCIENCE a thorough method for doing scientific study, in which scientists test their ideas about how things work by doing EXPERIMENTS

ˌscientific noˈtation *n.* [U] SCIENCE a way of writing very small and very large numbers. For example, $1x10^9$ means one billion or 1,000,000,000; $1x10^{-9}$ means one billionth or 0.000000001.

sci·en·tist /ˈsaɪəntɪst/ *n.* [C] someone who works in science

sci-fi /ˌsaɪˈfaɪ/ *n.* [U] (informal) SCIENCE FICTION

scin·til·lat·ing /ˈsɪntlˌeɪt̬ɪŋ/ *adj.* (formal) very interesting, exciting, and impressive: *a scintillating speech*

scis·sors /ˈsɪzɚz/ *n.* [plural] a tool for cutting paper, cloth, etc., made of two sharp blades fastened together in the middle, and handles with

S

holes for your finger and thumb: *Hand me that **pair of scissors**, please.* [ORIGIN: 1300—1400 Old French *cisoires*, from Late Latin *cisorium* "cutting tool"]

scle·ra /ˈsklɪrə/ *n.* [C] BIOLOGY the white outer layer of your eye

scoff /skɔf, skɑf/ *v.* [I] to laugh at a person or idea, or to say something in a way that shows you think he, she, or it is stupid: *David **scoffed at** my fears.*

scold /skoʊld/ *v.* [T] to tell someone in an angry way that s/he has done something wrong: *Mom **scolded** the boys **for** taking the candy without asking first.* —**scolding** *n.* [C,U]

THESAURUS **rebuke, admonish, reprimand**
→ CRITICIZE

scoop¹ /skup/ *n.* [C] **1** a deep spoon for serving food, or the amount that a scoop contains: *two **scoops of** ice cream* **2** an important or exciting news story that is reported by one newspaper, television station, etc. before any of the others know about it

scoop² *v.* [T] to pick something up with a scoop, a spoon, or with your curved hand: *Cut the melon and **scoop out** the seeds.*

scoot /skut/ *v.* [I] (informal) **1** to move to one side, especially to make room for someone or something else: *Can you **scoot over**?* **2** to move quickly: *Go to bed, Andrew – scoot!*

scoot·er /ˈskut̬ɚ/ *n.* [C] **1** a small two-wheeled vehicle like a bicycle with an engine → *see picture at* TRANSPORTATION **2** a child's vehicle with two small wheels, an upright handle, and a narrow board that you stand on with one foot, while the other foot pushes the vehicle along the ground

scope¹ /skoʊp/ (Ac) *n.* [U] **1** the range of things that a subject, activity, book, etc. deals with: *A thorough discussion of this subject is **beyond the scope of** this paper.* **2** the opportunity to do or develop something: *I want a job with **scope for** promotion.* [ORIGIN: 1500—1600 Italian *scopo* "purpose," from Greek *skopos*]

scope² *v.*

scope sb/sth ↔ **out** *phr. v.* (informal) to look at someone or something to see what he, she, or it is like: *A couple of guys were scoping out the girls.*

scorch /skɔrtʃ/ *v.* [I,T] if you scorch something, or if it scorches, its surface burns slightly and changes color: *Turn down the iron or you'll scorch your shirt.* —**scorch** *n.* [C]: *scorch marks from the fire*

scorch·er /ˈskɔrtʃɚ/ *n.* [C usually singular] (informal) an extremely hot day

scorch·ing /ˈskɔrtʃɪŋ/ *adj.* (informal) extremely hot: *the **scorching heat** of summer in New Orleans*

score¹ /skɔr/ *n.* [C] **1** the number of points that each team or player has won in a game or competition: *What's the score? | The **final score** was 35 to 17. | Who's going to **keep score*** (=keep a record of the points won)? **2** the number of points that a student has earned for correct answers on a test: *Average **test scores** have fallen in recent years. | I got a **higher/lower score** than Tracy on the geometry test.* **3 sb knows the score** (informal) if someone knows the score, s/he knows the real facts of a situation, including any unpleasant ones: *He knew the score when he decided to get involved.* **4** ENG. LANG. ARTS a printed copy of a piece of music, or the music itself: *a jazz score* **5 on that score** (spoken) concerning the subject you have just mentioned: *We've got plenty of money, so don't worry on that score.* **6 scores of sth** a large number of people or things: *Scores of reporters gathered outside the courthouse.* **7 settle a score** to do something to harm someone who has harmed you in the past [ORIGIN: 1000—1100 Old Norse *skor* "mark cut into a surface, count, twenty"]

score² *v.* **1** [I,T] to win or earn points in a game, competition, or test: *How many **goals** has he **scored** this year? | Dallas scored in the final minute of the game. | Anyone who scored under 70% has to take the exam again.* **2** [T] to give a particular number of points in a game, competition, or test: *The exams will be scored by computer.* **3 score points (with sb)** (informal) to do or say something to please someone or to make him/her feel respect for you: *You'll score points with your girlfriend if you send her flowers.* **4** [I,T] (slang) to manage to get something such as sex or illegal drugs

score·board /ˈskɔrbɔrd/ *n.* [C] a sign on which the score of a game is shown as it is played

score·card /ˈskɔrkɑrd/ *n.* [C] a printed card used for writing the score of a game as it is played

scor·er /ˈskɔrɚ/ *n.* [C] **1** someone who scores a GOAL, point, etc. in a game **2** *also* **scorekeeper** someone who records the number of points won in a game or competition as it is played

scorn¹ /skɔrn/ *n.* [U] strong criticism of someone or something that you think is stupid or not as good as other people or things: *He could barely disguise his **scorn for** her.* —**scornful** *adj.*

scorn² *v.* [T] (formal) to show in an unkind way that you think that a person, idea, or suggestion is stupid or not worth considering: *Skinner's ideas were scorned by many American psychologists.*

Scor·pi·o /ˈskɔrpiˌoʊ/ *n.* **1** [U] the eighth sign of the ZODIAC, represented by a scorpion **2** [C] someone born between October 24 and November 21

scor·pi·on /ˈskɔrpiən/ *n.* [C] a tropical creature like an insect with a curving tail and a poisonous sting

Scotch /skɑtʃ/ *n.* [C,U] a type of WHISKEY (=a strong alcoholic drink) made in Scotland, or a glass of this drink

ˌScotch ˈtape *n.* [U] (trademark) sticky thin clear plastic in a long narrow band, used for sticking paper and other light things together

scot-free /ˌskɑt ˈfri/ *adv.* **get off scot-free** (informal) to avoid being punished although you deserve to be [ORIGIN: 1200—1300 *scot* "tax" (13—19 centuries), from Old Norse *skot* "shot, payment"]

Scot·tish /ˈskɑṭɪʃ/ *adj.* relating to or coming from Scotland

scoun·drel /ˈskaʊndrəl/ *n.* [C] (old-fashioned) a bad or dishonest man

scour /skaʊɚ/ *v.* [T] **1** to search very carefully and thoroughly through an area or a document: *Police have **scoured** the area **for** evidence.* **2** to clean something very thoroughly by rubbing it with a rough material

THESAURUS clean, do/wash the dishes, scrub, do the housework, dust, polish, sweep (up), mop → CLEAN[2]

scourge /skɚdʒ/ *n.* [C] (formal) something that causes a lot of harm or suffering: *the **scourge of** war* [ORIGIN: 1100—1200 Anglo-French *escorge*, from Old French *escorgier* "to whip"] —**scourge** *v.* [T]

scout[1] /skaʊt/ *n.* [C] **1** a soldier who is sent to search an area in front of an army and get information **2** someone whose job is to look for good sports players, musicians, etc. in order to employ them: *a talent scout* **3** a member of the GIRL SCOUTS or BOY SCOUTS [ORIGIN: 1300—1400 Old French *escouter* "to listen," from Latin *auscultare*]

scout[2] *v.* **1** [I] *also* **scout around** to look for something in a particular area: *I'll **scout around for** a place to eat.* **2** [T] *also* **scout for** to look for good sports players, musicians, etc. in order to employ them

scowl /skaʊl/ *v.* [I] to look at someone in an angry or disapproving way: *Tom **scowled at** me from across the room.* —**scowl** *n.* [C]

Scrab·ble /ˈskræbəl/ *n.* [U] (trademark) a game using a special board and small objects with letters on them, in which you try to make words out of the letters

scrabble *v.* [I] to quickly feel around with your fingers in order to find something

scrag·gly /ˈskrægli/ *adj.* growing in a way that looks uneven and messy: *a scraggly beard*

scram /skræm/ *v.* (**scrammed**, **scramming**) [I] (informal) to leave a place very quickly, used especially to tell someone to leave: *Get out of here! Scram!*

scram·ble[1] /ˈskræmbəl/ *v.* **1** [I] to climb up or over something quickly and with difficulty, using your hands to help you: *The kids were **scrambling over** the rocks.* | *They tried to **scramble up** the cliff.* **2** [I] to compete and struggle with other people in order to get or reach something: *people **scrambling for** safety* **3** [I] to try to do something difficult very quickly: *Builders are **scrambling to** keep up with demand for their services.* **4** [T] to mix electronic signals so that they cannot be understood without a special piece of equipment: *All messages are scrambled for security reasons.* **5** [T] to mix up the order of letters, words, etc., so that the meaning is not clear

scramble[2] *n.* [singular] **1** a quick and difficult climb in which you have to use your hands to help you: *a rough scramble over loose rocks* **2** a situation in which people rush and struggle with each other in order to get or reach something: *a **scramble for** the best seats*

ˌscrambled ˈeggs *n.* [plural] eggs that have been cooked after mixing the white and yellow parts together

scrap[1] /skræp/ *n.* **1** [C] a small piece of paper, cloth, etc.: *He wrote his address on a **scrap of** paper.*

THESAURUS piece, fragment, strip → PIECE[1]

2 [C] a small amount of information, truth, etc.: *There isn't a **scrap of** evidence to support her story.* **3** [U] materials or objects that are damaged or not used anymore, but can be used again in another way: *He collects and sells **scrap metal*** (=metal from old cars, machines, etc. that is melted and used again). **4 scraps** [plural] pieces of food that are left after you have finished eating: *scraps for the dog* **5** [C] (informal) a short fight or argument that is not very serious: *Katie got into a little scrap at school.*

THESAURUS fight, brawl, scuffle → FIGHT[2]

scrap[2] *v.* (**scrapped**, **scrapping**) [T] **1** (informal) to decide not to do or use something because it is not practical: *We've decided to **scrap** the whole **idea** of renting a car.* **2** to get rid of an old machine, vehicle, etc., and use its parts in some other way: *equipment to be sold or scrapped*

scrap·book /ˈskræpbʊk/ *n.* [C] a book with empty pages in which you can stick pictures, newspaper articles, or other things you want to keep

scrape[1] /skreɪp/ *v.* **1** [T] to remove something from a surface, using the edge of a knife, stick, etc.: *Jerry bent to **scrape** the mud **off** his boots.* **2** [I,T] to rub against a rough surface in a way that causes slight damage or injury, or to make something do this: *I **scraped** my knee **on** the sidewalk.* **3** [I,T] to make an unpleasant noise by rubbing roughly against a surface: *She couldn't hear him over the racket of chairs scraping and trays being put away.*

scrape by *phr. v.* to have just enough money to live: *They just manage to scrape by on her salary.*

scrape sth ↔ **together/up** *phr. v.* to get enough money for a particular purpose, when this is difficult: *We're trying to scrape together enough money for a vacation.*

scrape[2] *n.* [C] **1** a mark or slight injury caused by rubbing against a rough surface: *Steve only got a few **cuts and scrapes**.*

THESAURUS injury, wound, bruise, contusion, cut, laceration, bump → INJURY

2 (informal) a situation in which you get into trouble or have difficulties: *Harper has had previous* ***scrapes with*** *the law.* 3 the noise made when one surface rubs roughly against another: *the scrape of chalk on the blackboard*

ˈscrap ˌpaper *n.* [U] used paper on which you can write notes, lists, etc.

scrap·py /ˈskræpi/ *adj.* (informal, approving) having a determined character and always willing to compete, argue, or fight

scratch¹ /skrætʃ/ *v.* **1** [I,T] to rub your skin with your nails → ITCH: *Will you scratch my back? | Try not to scratch those mosquito bites.* → *see picture on page A21*

THESAURUS touch, feel, stroke, rub → TOUCH¹

2 [T] to cut someone's skin slightly with your nails or with something sharp: *Did the cat scratch you? | The tree's branches had scratched her hands.* **3** [T] to damage a surface by pulling something sharp against it: *Don't drag the chair – you'll scratch the floor.* **4** [I] if an animal scratches, it rubs its foot against something, making a noise: *The dog kept* ***scratching at*** *the door to be let in.* **5 scratch the surface** to deal with only a very small part of a subject: *He believes that we've only scratched the surface of what we can do with the internet.* **6** [T] (informal) to stop planning to do something because it is no longer possible or practical: *I guess we can scratch that idea.* **7** [T] to remove a person or thing from a list: *Her name had been* ***scratched from/off*** *the list of competitors.*

scratch² *n.* **1** [C] a long thin cut or mark on the surface of something or on someone's skin: *Where did this scratch on the car come from?* **2 from scratch** without using anything that was prepared before: *I made the cake from scratch.* **3 without a scratch** (informal) without being injured at all: *Stuart was hurt in the accident, but Max escaped without a scratch.*

ˈscratch ˌpaper *n.* [U] cheap paper, or paper that has already been used on one side, that you can write notes or lists on

scratch·y /ˈskrætʃi/ *adj.* **1** scratchy clothes or materials have a rough surface and are uncomfortable to wear or touch: *a scratchy pair of wool socks* **2** a voice that is scratchy sounds deep and rough **3** a scratchy throat is sore

scrawl /skrɔl/ *v.* [T] to write something in a fast, careless, or messy way: *a telephone number scrawled on a piece of paper* —**scrawl** *n.* [C,U]

scraw·ny /ˈskrɔni/ *adj.* thin and weak: *a scrawny little kid*

scream¹ /skrim/ *v.* **1** [I] to make a loud high noise with your voice because you are hurt, frightened, excited, etc.: *There was a loud bang and people started screaming. | She lay there* ***screaming in pain.***

THESAURUS shout, shriek, yell, bellow, holler → SHOUT¹

2 [I,T] to shout something in a very loud high voice because you are angry or afraid (SYN) **yell**: *I* ***screamed for*** *help. | The girls were* ***screaming at*** *each other.*

scream² *n.* [C] **1** a loud high noise that you make when you are hurt, frightened, excited, etc.: *He* ***let out a scream.***

COLLOCATIONS

shrill/piercing – very loud, high, and annoying
high-pitched – very high
ear-splitting – very loud
bloodcurdling – very frightening

2 a very loud high sound: *the scream of the jet engines* **3 be a scream** (informal) to be very funny: *"How was the show?" "It was a scream."*

screech /skritʃ/ *v.* **1** [I,T] to shout loudly in a high voice, especially because you are upset: *"Get out of my way!" she screeched.* **2** [I] if a vehicle screeches, its wheels make a loud high noise: *The car* ***screeched to a halt.*** [ORIGIN: 1500—1600 *scritch* "to screech" (13—20 centuries), from the sound] —**screech** *n.* [C]

screen¹ /skrin/ *n.* **1** [C] the flat glass part of a television or a computer, on which you see words, pictures, etc.: *a computer with an 18-inch screen | It's easier to correct your work* ***on screen*** *than on paper.* → *see picture on page A19* **2** [C] a large flat white surface that movies are shown on in a movie theater **3** [singular, U] movies in general: *his first appearance* ***on screen*** *| Her play was adapted for* ***the big screen.*** **4** [C] a wire net that covers an open door or window so that air can get inside a house but insects cannot: *screens on the windows | a screen door* **5** [C] a piece of furniture like a thin wall that can be moved around and is used for dividing one part of a room from another **6** [C] something that hides a place or thing: *The house was hidden behind a* ***screen of*** *bushes.* [ORIGIN: 1300—1400 Old French *escren*, from Middle Dutch *scherm*]

screen² *v.* [T] **1** to do medical tests on people in order to discover whether they have a particular illness: *Women over the age of 50 are* ***screened for*** *breast cancer.* **2** to find out information about people in order to decide whether they can be trusted in a particular job: *People wanting to work with children are thoroughly screened.* **3** *also* **screen off** to hide or protect something by putting something in front of it: *The hedge screens the back yard from the street.* **4 screen (your) calls** to let your telephone calls be answered by an ANSWERING MACHINE, so that you can decide whether or not to talk to the person who calls you **5** to show a movie or television program

screen·ing /ˈskrinɪŋ/ *n.* **1** [C,U] the showing of

S

a film or television program: *a screening of Spielberg's new movie* **2** [C,U] medical tests that are done on a lot of people to make sure that they do not have a particular disease: *new guidelines on **screening for** breast cancer* | *The group received mammograms, then follow-up screenings in succeeding months.* **3** [U] tests or checks that are done to make sure that people or things are acceptable or useful for a particular purpose: *security screening of airline passengers*

screen·play /ˈskrinpleɪ/ *n.* [C] ENG. LANG. ARTS a story written for a movie or a television show

ˈscreen ˌsaver *n.* [C] IT a moving picture that appears on a computer screen while you are not using the computer

screen·writ·er /ˈskrinˌraɪt̬ɚ/ *n.* [C] ENG. LANG. ARTS someone who writes screenplays

screw¹ /skru/ *n.* **1** [C] a thin pointed piece of metal that you push and turn in order to fasten pieces of wood or metal together → NAIL, SCREWDRIVER **2 have a screw loose** (informal) to be slightly crazy [ORIGIN: 1400—1500 Old French *escroe* "inner screw, nut," from Latin *scrofa* "female pig"]

screw² *v.* **1** [T] to fasten one thing to another, using a screw: *Screw the shelf **to** the wall.* **2** [T] to fasten or close something by turning it until it cannot be turned any more: *Don't forget to **screw** the top back **on**.*

screw around *phr. v.* (spoken) to waste time or behave in a silly way: *Stop screwing around and get back to work!*

screw up *phr. v.* **1 screw** sth ↔ **up** (informal) to make a bad mistake that ruins what you intended to do: *You'd better not screw up again!* | *He's always screwing everything up.* **2 screw** sb ↔ **up** (informal) to make someone feel extremely unhappy, confused, or anxious, especially for a long time: *Carole's family really screwed her up.*

screw·ball /ˈskrubɔl/ *n.* **1** [C] (informal) someone who seems very strange, silly, or crazy **2 screwball comedy** a film or television program that is funny because silly or crazy things happen

screw·driv·er /ˈskruˌdraɪvɚ/ *n.* [C] a tool that you use to turn screws

ˌscrewed ˈup *adj.* (informal) **1** very unhappy, confused, or anxious because you have had bad experiences in the past: *These poor kids, they're so screwed up from their parents' divorce.* **2** not working, or in a bad condition: *My left leg **got screwed up** playing football.*

screw·y /ˈskrui/ *adj.* (informal) slightly strange or crazy: *a screwy plan*

scrib·ble /ˈskrɪbəl/ *v.* **1** [T] *also* **scribble down** to write something quickly in a messy way: *He scribbled down his phone number on a business card.* **2** [I] to draw marks that do not mean anything

THESAURUS **draw, sketch, doodle, trace** → DRAW¹

—**scribble** *n.* [C,U]

scribe /skraɪb/ *n.* [C] someone in past times whose job was to copy or record things by writing them

scrimp /skrɪmp/ *v.* **scrimp and save** to try to save as much money as you can, even though you have very little

script /skrɪpt/ *n.* **1** [C] ENG. LANG. ARTS the written form of a speech, play, movie, etc. **2** [C,U] ENG. LANG. ARTS the set of letters used in writing a language (SYN) **alphabet**: *Arabic script*

script·ed /ˈskrɪptɪd/ *adj.* a scripted speech or broadcast has been planned and written down so that it can be read

scrip·ture /ˈskrɪptʃɚ/ *n.* **1** [U] *also* **the (Holy) Scripture** the Bible **2** [C,U] the holy books of a particular religion —**scriptural** *adj.*

script·writ·er /ˈskrɪptˌraɪt̬ɚ/ *n.* [C] someone who writes scripts for movies, television programs, etc.

scroll¹ /skroʊl/ *n.* [C] a document that is rolled up, especially an official document from the past [ORIGIN: 1400—1500 *scrow* "scroll" (13—17 centuries), from Old French *escroue* "piece of paper, scroll;" influenced by *roll*]

scroll² *v.* [I,T] IT to move information up or down a computer screen so that you can read it

scrooge /skrudʒ/ *n.* [C] (informal) someone who hates to spend money [ORIGIN: 1800—1900 Ebenezer *Scrooge*, character in A Christmas Carol (1843) by Charles Dickens]

scro·tum /ˈskroʊt̬əm/ *n.* [C] BIOLOGY the bag of flesh on a man or male animal that contains the TESTICLES

scrounge /skraʊndʒ/ *v.* (informal) **1** [T] to get money or something you want by asking other people to give it to you instead of earning it or paying for it yourself: *We managed to **scrounge up** enough money to pay the bills.* **2** [I] to search for something such as food or supplies: *We saw children **scrounging around for** food in garbage cans.*

scrub¹ /skrʌb/ *v.* (**scrubbed**, **scrubbing**) [I,T] to clean something by rubbing it very hard with a stiff brush or rough cloth: *Tom was on his knees, scrubbing the floor.*

THESAURUS **clean, do/wash the dishes, scour, do the housework, dust, polish, sweep (up), mop** → CLEAN²

scrub² *n.* [U] EARTH SCIENCES low bushes and trees that grow in very dry soil

scruff /skrʌf/ *n.* **by the scruff of the neck** by the back of a person's or animal's neck: *The cat had a kitten by the scruff of its neck.*

scruff·y /ˈskrʌfi/ *adj.* dirty and messy: *a scruffy kid*

S

scrump·tious /ˈskrʌmpʃəs/ *adj.* (informal) food that is scrumptious tastes very good

scrunch /skrʌntʃ/ *v.*
scrunch sth ↔ **up** *phr. v.* to twist and press a piece of paper into a ball

scru·ple /ˈskrupəl/ *n.* [C usually plural] a belief about what is right and wrong that prevents you from doing something bad: *He* ***has no scruples*** *about lying.*

scru·pu·lous /ˈskrupyələs/ *adj.* **1** taking a lot of care to make sure that every detail is correct: *This job requires scrupulous attention to detail.*

THESAURUS **careful, methodical, thorough, meticulous, systematic, painstaking, conscientious** → CAREFUL

2 careful to be honest and fair —**scrupulously** *adv.*

scru·ti·nize /ˈskrutˀnˌaɪz/ *v.* [T] to examine someone or something very carefully and completely

THESAURUS **examine, inspect, go through/go over** → EXAMINE

S

scru·ti·ny /ˈskrutˀn-i/ *n.* [U] the process of examining something carefully and completely: ***Closer scrutiny*** *shows that the numbers don't add up.* | *The senator's office later* ***came under scrutiny*** *from the Justice Department.*

scu·ba div·ing /ˈskubə ˌdaɪvɪŋ/ *n.* [U] the sport of swimming under water while breathing from a container of air on your back

scuff /skʌf/ *v.* [T] to make a mark on a smooth surface by rubbing something rough against it: *I've already scuffed my new shoes.*

scuf·fle /ˈskʌfəl/ *n.* [C] a short fight: *A policeman was injured in a scuffle with demonstrators yesterday.* —**scuffle** *v.* [I,T]

THESAURUS **fight, brawl, scrap** → FIGHT²

sculp·tor /ˈskʌlptɚ/ *n.* [C] ENG. LANG. ARTS an artist who makes sculptures

sculp·ture /ˈskʌlptʃɚ/ *n.* **1** [C,U] ENG. LANG. ARTS a work of art made from stone, wood, clay, etc.: *a bronze sculpture by Peter Helzer* **2** [U] ENG. LANG. ARTS the art of making objects out of stone, wood, clay, etc.: *a sculpture class* [ORIGIN: 1300—1400 Latin *sculptura*, from *sculpere* "to carve"] → ART

sculp·tured /ˈskʌlptʃɚd/ *adj.* **1** cut or formed from wood, clay, stone, etc., or decorated with sculptures **2 sculptured muscles/features etc.** muscles, etc. that have a smooth attractive shape

scum /skʌm/ *n.* [singular, U] the thick dirty substance that forms on the surface of a liquid: *a pond covered with green scum*

scur·ri·lous /ˈskɚələs, ˈskʌr-/ *adj.* (formal) scurrilous remarks, articles, etc. contain damaging and untrue statements about someone

scur·ry /ˈskɚi, ˈskʌri/ *v.* (**scurried**, **scurries**) [I] to move very quickly with small steps: *workers* ***scurrying around*** *the factory floor*

scut·tle /ˈskʌṭl/ *v.* **1** [T] (informal) to ruin someone's plans or chance of being successful: *The issue threatens to scuttle the peace talks.* **2** [I] to run quickly with small steps, especially because you are afraid: *Eddie scuttled down the hall.* **3** [T] to sink a ship, especially in order to prevent it from being used by an enemy

scythe /saɪð/ *n.* [C] a farming tool with a long curved blade, used for cutting grain or long grass

SD the written abbreviation of SOUTH DAKOTA

SE the written abbreviation of SOUTHEAST

sea /si/ *n.* **1** [C] EARTH SCIENCES a large area of salty water that is smaller than an ocean, or that is enclosed by land: *the Mediterranean Sea* | *an* ***inland sea*** (=a sea that is completely surrounded by land) **2** [singular, U] a word meaning the ocean that is used when talking about traveling in a ship or boat: *The boat was heading* ***out to sea*** (=away from land). | *four days* ***at sea*** (=on a boat in the ocean) **3 a sea of sth** a large number or amount of something: *a sea of people* **4 the seas** (literary) the ocean [ORIGIN: Old English *sæ*]

sea·bed /ˈsibɛd/ *n.* **the seabed** EARTH SCIENCES the SEA FLOOR

sea·board /ˈsibɔrd/ *n.* [C] the east side of the U.S., next to the Atlantic Ocean: *the* ***eastern/Atlantic seaboard***

ˌsea ˈfloor *n.* **the sea floor** EARTH SCIENCES the land at the bottom of the sea

sea·food /ˈsifud/ *n.* [U] ocean animals such as fish and SHELLFISH that can be eaten

sea·gull /ˈsigʌl/ *n.* [C] a common gray and white bird that lives near the ocean and has a loud cry

sea·horse /ˈsihɔrs/ *n.* [C] a small sea fish that has a head and neck that look like those of a horse

seal¹ /sil/ *n.* [C] **1** a large sea animal that has smooth fur, eats fish, and lives around coasts **2** an official mark that is put on documents, objects, etc. in order to prove that they are legal or real: *the seal of the Department of Justice* **3** a piece of rubber or plastic used on something such as a pipe, machine, or container in order to prevent something such as water or air from going into or out of it: *a leak in the rubber seal* **4** a piece of paper, plastic, WAX, etc., that you break in order to open a letter or container: *Do not use this product if the* ***seal*** *on the bottle is* ***broken***. **5 seal of approval** if you give something your seal of approval, you say that you accept or approve of it, especially officially: *a diet that has the Medical Association's seal of approval*

seal² *v.* [T] **1** *also* **seal up** to close an entrance, container, or hole with something that stops air, water, etc. from coming in or out of it: *Many of the* *tombs have remained sealed since the 16th century.* **2** to close an envelope, package, etc. using something sticky, such as TAPE or glue **3 seal a deal/agreement etc.** to do something that makes a promise, agreement, etc. seem more definite or official: *We shook hands, sealing the bargain.*

seal sth ↔ **in** *phr. v.* to stop something from going out of the thing it is contained in: *Fry the steak quickly to seal in the flavor.*

seal sth ↔ **off** *phr. v.* to stop people entering a particular area or building, especially because it is dangerous: *Police sealed off the street to traffic.*

sealed /sild/ *adj.* something that is sealed is completely closed and cannot be opened unless it is broken, cut, or torn: *a sealed envelope*

'sea ˌlevel *n.* [U] the average level of the sea, used as a standard for measuring the height of an area of land, such as a mountain: *Its highest ridge is 6,000 feet above sea level.*

'sea ˌlion *n.* [C] a large type of SEAL that lives on the coasts of the Pacific Ocean

seam /sim/ *n.* [C] **1** the line where two pieces of cloth have been sewn together **2** EARTH SCIENCES a layer of a mineral, such as coal, that is under the ground **3** the line where two pieces of metal, wood, etc. have been joined together

sea·man, Seaman /'simən/ *n.* [C] someone who has the lowest rank in the Navy

seam·less /'simlɪs/ *adj.* done or made so well, that you do not notice where one part ends and another part begins: *The show is a seamless blend of song, dance, and storytelling.*

seam·stress /'simstrɪs/ *n.* [C] a woman whose job is to make and sew clothes

seam·y /'simi/ *adj.* involving unpleasant things such as crime, violence, or immoral behavior: *the seamy side of politics* [ORIGIN: 1800—1900 *seamy* "having the rough side of the seam showing" (17—19 centuries), from *seam*]

sé·ance /'seɪɑns/ *n.* [C] a meeting where people try to talk to the spirits of dead people, or to receive messages from them

'sea plane *n.* [C] an airplane that can land on water

sear /sɪr/ *v.* **1** [I,T] to burn something with a sudden very strong heat: *The firestorm seared the ground.* **2** [T] to cook the outside of a piece of meat quickly at a very high temperature **3** [I,T] to have a very strong unpleasant effect on you: *The images sear themselves into the viewer's mind.*

search¹ /sɚtʃ/ *n.* **1** [C] an attempt to find someone or something that is difficult to find: *The company has begun a **search for** a new president.* | *The tiger goes **in search of** food.* | *Police have **called off the search** for* (=officially stopped looking for) *the missing children.* **2** [C] IT a series of actions done by a computer to find information: *I **ran a search** for information on diabetes.* **3** [singular] an attempt to find the answer to or explanation of a difficult problem: *the **search for** genetic causes of disease* [ORIGIN: 1300—1400 Old French *cerchier* "to go around, examine, search," from Late Latin *circare* "to go around"]

search² *v.* **1** [I,T] to try to find someone or something by looking very carefully: *Denise **searched** her purse **for** a photo of Ben.* | *Jackie's **searching for** a job.* | *I **searched through** the papers on my desk, looking for the receipt.*

> THESAURUS **look, try to find sb/sth, hunt for sb/sth, go through sth, have a look for sb/sth** → LOOK¹

2 [T] if the police or someone in authority searches you or your house, bags, etc., they look for things you might be hiding: *Police **searched** the house **for** weapons.* **3** [T] IT to use a computer to find information, especially on the Internet: *Try **searching** the Web **for** a cheap flight.* **4** [I] to try to find an answer or explanation for a difficult problem: *The Center is **searching for** solutions to campus overcrowding.*

'search ˌengine *n.* [C] IT a computer program that helps you find information on the Internet → INTERNET

search·ing /'sɚtʃɪŋ/ *adj.* trying hard to find out details, facts, or someone's feelings and thoughts: *searching questions*

search·light /'sɚtʃlaɪt/ *n.* [C] a large bright light used for finding people, vehicles, etc. at night

'search ˌparty *n.* [C] a group of people who are organized to look for someone who is lost or missing

'search ˌwarrant *n.* [C] a legal document that officially allows the police to search a building

sear·ing /'sɪrɪŋ/ *adj.* **1** searing pain is very severe **2** extremely hot: *the searing heat of the desert*

sea·shell /'siʃɛl/ *n.* [C] an empty shell that once covered some types of ocean animals

sea·shore /'siʃɔr/ *n.* **the seashore** the land along the edge of the ocean → BEACH

> THESAURUS **shore, coast, beach** → SHORE¹

sea·sick /'siˌsɪk/ *adj.* feeling sick because of the movement of a boat or ship —**seasickness** *n.* [U]

sea·side /'sisaɪd/ *adj.* relating to the land next to a sea or ocean: *a seaside restaurant*

sea·son¹ /'sizən/ *n.* **1** [C] one of the four main periods in the year, which are winter, spring, summer, and fall: *the change of the seasons* **2** [C usually singular] a period of time in a year when something happens most often or when something is usually done: *The **rainy/wet season** usually starts in May.* | *the first game of the season* (=the time when a particular sport is played) | *the **hunting/football etc. season*** | *the **holiday season*** (=the period from Thanksgiving to New Year) **3 be in season** if particular vegetables or fruit are in

S

season, it is the time of year when they are ready to be eaten **4 out of season** if someone hunts or catches fish out of season, s/he is doing it when it is not legal [ORIGIN: 1300—1400 Old French *saison*, from Latin *satio* "act of planting seeds"]

season² *v.* [T] to add salt, pepper, etc. to food in order to make it taste better

sea·son·a·ble /ˈsizənəbəl/ *adj.* **seasonable weather/temperatures** weather that seems typical for a particular season (ANT) **unseasonable**

sea·son·al /ˈsizənəl/ *adj.* only happening, available, or needed during a particular season: *seasonal farm workers*

sea·soned /ˈsizənd/ *adj.* [only before noun] having a lot of experience of something: *a seasoned diplomat*

sea·son·ing /ˈsizənɪŋ/ *n.* [C,U] salt, pepper, SPICES, etc. that you add to food to make it taste better

ˈseason ˌticket *n.* [C] a ticket that allows you to go on a trip, go to a theater, watch a sports team, etc. as often as you want during a period of time

ˈsea stack *n.* [C] EARTH SCIENCES a tall thin upright rock structure in the ocean near an island or large area of land, formed by the gradual effect of the wind and waves moving against the land

seat¹ /sit/ *n.* **1** [C] a place where you can sit, especially one in a vehicle, restaurant, theater, etc.: *Lucy sat **in the front/back seat**.* | *We had great seats at the Giants game.*

COLLOCATIONS

back/rear/front seat – the back or front seat in a car
driver's seat – where the driver sits
passenger seat – the seat next to the driver's
window/aisle seat – a seat next to the window or aisle on an airplane
front row seat – a seat in a theater, stadium, etc. that is closest to the stage, field, etc.
good seat – one in a theater, stadium, etc. from which you can see well
empty/vacant seat – one that is not being used
book/reserve a seat – to arrange to have a seat in a theater, on an airplane, etc. at a particular time in the future

2 take/have a seat to sit down **3** [C] the part of a chair, bicycle, etc. that you sit on: *the toilet seat* **4** [C] a position as a member of the government or a group that makes official decisions: *Republicans hold a majority of the **seats in** the Senate.* | *a **seat on** the school board* **5** [singular] the part of your pants that you sit on **6 baby/child/car/safety seat** a special seat that you put in a car for a baby or small child **7 seat of learning/government etc.** (formal) a place, usually a city, where a university or government is based [ORIGIN: 1100—1200 Old Norse *sæti*] ➔ **take a back seat** *at* BACK SEAT

seat² *v.* [T] **1 seated** sitting down: *We **were seated** at the table.* | *Please **be seated**.* | ***Remain seated** and fasten your seat belts.* | *The boy seated next to me had red hair.* **2 seat yourself** to sit down somewhere **3** to make someone sit in a particular place: *The hostess will seat you soon.* **4** if a room, vehicle, theater, etc. seats a number of people, it has enough seats for that number: *The new Olympic stadium seats over 70,000.*

ˈseat belt *n.* [C] a strong belt attached to the seat of a car or airplane, that you fasten around yourself for protection in an accident: *Please **fasten** your **seat belts**.*

seat·ing /ˈsiṭɪŋ/ *n.* [U] **1** all the seats in a theater, restaurant, etc. **2** the places where people will sit, according to an arrangement: *a **seating plan** for the reception*

ˈsea ˌurchin *n.* [C] a small round sea animal that is covered with sharp points

sea·weed /ˈsiwid/ *n.* [U] a common plant that grows in the ocean

se·ba·ceous /sɪˈbeɪʃəs/ *adj.* BIOLOGY related to a part of the body that produces special oils

se·bum /ˈsibəm/ *n.* [U] BIOLOGY a special oil that is produced by the skin

sec /sɛk/ *n.* [C] (spoken) a short form of "second": *Wait a sec, will you?*

se·cede /sɪˈsid/ *v.* [I] (formal) to formally stop being part of a country, especially because of a disagreement: *The southern states wanted to* ***secede from*** *the U.S. in the 1850s.* —**secession** /sɪˈsɛʃən/ *n.* [singular, U]

se·ces·sion·ist /sɪˈsɛʃənɪst/ *n.* [C] HISTORY someone who wants an area to formally stop being part of a country, especially someone who wanted the South to stop being part of the U.S. around the time of the CIVIL WAR

se·clud·ed /sɪˈkludɪd/ *adj.* very private and quiet: *a secluded beach*

se·clu·sion /sɪˈkluʒən/ *n.* [U] the state of being private and away from other people: *The family lives* ***in seclusion.***

sec·ond[1] /ˈsɛkənd/ *number, pron.* **1** 2nd; someone or something that is after the first one: *September 2nd | Jane's second husband | She* ***came in second*** *in the women's marathon.* **2** another example of the same thing, or another in addition to the one you have: *A second woman came into the room.* **3 have second thoughts** to start having doubts about a decision you have made: *I had second thoughts about going to graduate school.* **4 a second chance** an opportunity to try to do something again, after you failed the first time **5 be second to none** to be better than anyone or anything else: *His generosity is second to none.*

second[2] *n.* **1** [C] a unit for measuring time. There are 60 seconds in a minute: *Players have five seconds to take a shot.* **2** [C usually singular] (spoken) a very short period of time: ***For a second,*** *I thought he was joking. | I'll be off the phone* ***in a second!*** *|* ***Just a second,*** *I'm almost ready.* **3 seconds** [plural] **a)** another serving of the same food, after you have eaten your first serving **b)** goods sold cheaply because they are not perfect: *factory seconds* [ORIGIN: (1) 1300—1400 Medieval Latin *secunda*, from *secunda pars minuta* "second small part, one sixtieth of a minute," from Latin *secundus*]

sec·ond·ar·y /ˈsɛkənˌdɛri/ *adj.* **1** not as important or valuable as something else: *Some of the students behave as though studying is* ***secondary to*** *their social life.* **2** developing from something of the same type, or coming from it: *a secondary infection* **3** relating to secondary schools: *secondary education*

ˌsecondary ˈgrowth *n.* [U] BIOLOGY an additional increase in the width of the roots and stems of large plants or trees which supports the growing plant and helps it develop → PRIMARY GROWTH

ˈsecondary ˌschool *n.* [C] a school that children go to after ELEMENTARY SCHOOL and before college → HIGH SCHOOL

ˌsecondary ˈsource *n.* [C] **1** ENG. LANG. ARTS a book, article, etc. that deals with a piece of literature or a historical event and that can be used to support your ideas in an ESSAY **2** HISTORY a description of an event by someone who was not there when it happened → PRIMARY SOURCE

ˌsecondary ˈstress *n.* [C,U] ENG. LANG. ARTS the second strongest STRESS that you give to part of a word or sentence when you speak it, for example the "dar" in "secondary." It is shown in this dictionary by the mark (/ˌ/). → PRIMARY STRESS

ˌsecond ˈbase *n.* [U] in a game of baseball, the second of the four places that a player must touch before gaining a point

ˌsecond ˈclass *n.* [U] a way of traveling, especially on trains, that is cheaper but not as comfortable as FIRST CLASS

ˌsecond-ˈclass *adj.* **1** considered to be less important than other people or things: *They treated us like* ***second-class citizens*** (=people who are not as important as other people in society). **2** relating to cheaper and less comfortable seats on a train, bus, etc.: *second-class tickets*

ˌsecond-ˈguess *v.* [T] **1** to criticize something after it has already happened, by saying what should have been done: *A lot of people have been second-guessing the police investigation.* **2** to try to say what will happen or what someone will do before s/he does it

sec·ond·hand /ˌsɛkəndˈhænd◂ / *adj.* **1** secondhand clothes, furniture, books, etc. have already been owned or used by someone else: *a cheap secondhand car* **2** a secondhand report, secondhand information, etc. is told to you by someone who is not the person who originally said it —**secondhand** *adv.*

sec·ond·ly /ˈsɛkəndli/ *adv.* used in order to give a second fact, reason, etc.: *Firstly, I need the extra money, and secondly, I like working in a bar.*

ˌsecond ˈnature *n.* [U] something you have done so often that you now do it without thinking a lot about it: *After you get used to driving a car, it becomes second nature.*

ˌsecond ˈperson *n.* **the second person** ENG. LANG. ARTS in grammar, a form of a verb or PRONOUN that you use to show the person you are speaking to. "You" is a second person pronoun, "you are" is the second person singular of the verb "to be." → FIRST PERSON, THIRD PERSON

ˌsecond-ˈrate *adj.* not very good: *second-rate artists*

second wind /ˌsɛkənd ˈwɪnd/ *n.* [singular] a new feeling of energy after you have been working or exercising very hard, and had thought you were too tired to continue

se·cre·cy /ˈsikrəsi/ *n.* [U] the act of keeping something such as information secret, or the state of being secret: *She* ***swore*** *him* ***to secrecy*** (=made him promise to keep a secret). | *talks conducted* ***in secrecy***

se·cret[1] /ˈsikrɪt/ *adj.* known about by only a few people: *The deal was* ***kept secret*** *until the contracts were signed. | He* ***kept*** *his marriage* ***secret from*** *his parents* (=he did not tell his parents about it). | *secret government files* [ORIGIN: 1300—1400 Old

S

French, Latin *secretus*, past participle of *secernere* "to separate"] —**secretly** *adv.*: *I secretly recorded our conversation.*

THESAURUS

Confidential information is secret and not intended to be shown or told to other people: *confidential FBI files*
Classified information, documents, etc. are kept secret by the government or an organization: *a spy who passed classified documents to the enemy*
Sensitive information is kept secret because there would be problems if the wrong people knew it: *The report contained sensitive information on the situation in Iraq.*
Covert activities are done secretly, especially by a government or official organization: *covert operations run by the CIA*
Undercover work is done secretly by the police in order to catch criminals or find out information: *The police mounted an undercover operation to break the drug-smuggling ring.*
Clandestine meetings, arrangements, actions, etc. are organized and carried out in secret: *a clandestine nuclear weapons program* → PRIVATE[1]

S

secret[2] *n.* [C] **1** something that is kept hidden or that is known about by only a few people: *Can you **keep a secret*** (=not tell a secret)? **2 in secret** in a private way or place that other people do not know about: *The meetings took place **in secret**.* **3** a particular way of achieving a good result: ***The secret to** good French bread is steam in the oven.*

ˌsecret 'agent *n.* [C] someone who secretly collects information or watches people for a government

sec·re·tar·y /ˈsɛkrəˌtɛri/ *n.* (plural **secretaries**) [C] **1** someone whose job is to TYPE letters, keep records, arrange meetings, answer telephones, etc. in an office **2** an official who is in charge of a large government department in the U.S.: *the Secretary of Defense* **3** an official in an organization whose job is to write down notes from meetings, write letters, etc.: *the secretary of the PTA* —**secretarial** /ˌsɛkrəˈtɛriəl/ *adj.*

se·crete /sɪˈkrit/ *v.* [T] **1** BIOLOGY if part of a plant or animal secretes a substance, it produces that substance: *The male secretes a scent to mark out its territory.* **2** (formal) to hide something

THESAURUS **hide, conceal** → HIDE[1]

—**secretion** /sɪˈkriʃən/ *n.* [C,U]

se·cre·tive /ˈsikrət̬ɪv/ *adj.* behaving in a way that shows you do not want to tell people your thoughts, plans, etc.

ˌsecret 'service *n.* **the Secret Service** a U.S. government department whose main purpose is to protect the President

sect /sɛkt/ *n.* [C] a group of people who have their own set of beliefs or religious habits, especially a group that has separated from a larger group [ORIGIN: 1300—1400 Old French *secte* "group, sect," from Latin *secta* "way of life, type of people"]

THESAURUS **church, denomination, cult** → CHURCH

sec·tar·i·an /sɛkˈtɛriən/ *adj.* supporting a particular religious group and its beliefs, or relating to the differences between religious groups (ANT) **nonsectarian**: *sectarian violence*

sec·tion[1] /ˈsɛkʃən/ (Ac) *n.* [C] **1** one of the parts that an object, group, place, etc. is divided into: *the eastern **section of** the city* | *the reference section of the library* | *The rocket is built **in sections*** (=in parts that are then fitted together). | *the brass section of the orchestra* | *the poor section of society* → PART[1] **2** one of the parts of a book or newspaper: *the **sports/travel/business etc. section*** | *the topic discussed in section 3* [ORIGIN: 1300—1400 Latin *sectio*, from *secare* "to cut"] —**sectional** *adj.*

section[2] *v.* [T] to separate something into parts
section sth ↔ **off** *phr. v.* to divide an area into parts: *The old part of the graveyard had been sectioned off by trees.*

sec·tion·al·ism /ˈsɛkʃənlˌɪzəm/ *n.* [U] POLITICS when someone, especially a politician, shows that he or she is concerned only with what is best for one part of a country, not what is best for the whole country

sec·tor /ˈsɛktɚ/ (Ac) *n.* [C] **1** a part of an area of activity, especially of business, industry, or trade: *jobs in the **public/private sector*** (=the part controlled by the government or by private companies) **2** one of the parts that an area is divided into for military purposes: *the former eastern sector of Berlin*

sec·u·lar /ˈsɛkyəlɚ/ *adj.* not religious or not controlled by a religious authority: *a secular government*

sec·u·lar·ize /ˈsɛkyələˌraɪz/ *v.* [T] SOCIAL SCIENCE to remove the control or influence of religious groups from a society or an institution —**secularization** /ˌsɛkyələrəˈzeɪʃən/ *n.* [U]

se·cure[1] /sɪˈkyʊr/ (Ac) *adj.* **1** not likely to change or be at risk: *a secure job* **2** safe and protected from danger: *The bank's deposits remain secure.* **3** fastened, locked, or guarded: *Keep your passport in a secure place.* **4** confident about yourself and your abilities (ANT) **insecure**: *children who feel **secure in** their parents' love* **5** feeling certain about a situation and not worried that it might change: *He was successful and **financially secure*** (=did not need to worry about having enough money). [ORIGIN: 1500—1600 Latin *securus*, from *se* "without" + *cura* "care"] —**securely** *adv.*: *The door was securely locked.*

secure[2] *v.* [T] **1** to get or achieve something important, especially after a lot of effort: *a treaty designed to secure peace* **2** to make something safe from being attacked or harmed: *Troops* *secured the border.* **3** to fasten or tie something tightly in a particular position: *Her ponytail was secured with an elastic band.*

THESAURUS **fasten, attach, join, glue, tape, staple, clip, tie, button (up), zip (up)** → FASTEN

se·cu·ri·ty /sɪˈkyʊrət̬i/ (Ac) *n.* [U] **1** the state of being safe, or the things you do to keep someone or something safe: *national security | airport security checks | security cameras | **tight security** at the conference | the security of Internet purchases* **2** protection from change, risks, or bad situations: *employees with **job security** | Rules and order can give a child a **sense of security**.* **3** the guards who protect a business's buildings, equipment, and workers: *The receptionist called security.*

se·dan /sɪˈdæn/ *n.* [C] a large car that has seats for at least four people and has a TRUNK

se·date /sɪˈdeɪt/ *adj.* slow, formal, or not very exciting: *a sedate private club*

se·dat·ed /sɪˈdeɪt̬ɪd/ *adj.* made sleepy or calm by being given a sedative

sed·a·tive /ˈsɛdət̬ɪv/ *n.* [C] a drug used in order to make someone sleepy or calm

sed·en·tar·y /ˈsɛdnˌtɛri/ *adj.* a sedentary job involves sitting down or not moving very much [ORIGIN: 1500—1600 French *sédentaire*, from Latin *sedentarius*, from *sedere* "to sit"]

sed·i·ment /ˈsɛdəmənt/ *n.* [singular, U] EARTH SCIENCES the solid material, such as dirt, that settles at the bottom of a liquid

sed·i·ment·a·ry /ˌsɛdəˈmɛntri, -ˈmɛntəri/ *adj.* EARTH SCIENCES made of the sediment at the bottom of lakes, oceans, etc.: *sedimentary rock*

se·di·tion /sɪˈdɪʃən/ *n.* [U] LAW speech, writing, or actions that try to encourage people to disobey a government —**seditious** *adj.*

se·duce /sɪˈdus/ *v.* [T] **1** to persuade someone to do something, especially to have sex, by making it seem extremely attractive: *Are you trying to seduce me?* **2** to make someone want to do something by making it seem very attractive or interesting: *young people who are seduced by Hollywood* [ORIGIN: 1400—1500 Latin *seducere* "to lead away," from *ducere* "to lead"] —**seduction** /sɪˈdʌkʃən/ *n.* [C,U]

se·duc·tive /sɪˈdʌktɪv/ *adj.* **1** sexually attractive: *a seductive look* **2** very attractive to you: *a seductive job offer*

see /si/ *v.* (past tense **saw** /sɔ/, past participle **seen** /sin/)

1 NOTICE [T] to notice someone or something, using your eyes: *He saw her go into the house. | Can I see your ticket, please? | Did you **see where** the car went off the road?*

USAGE

You **look at** a picture, person, thing, etc. because you want to: *Hey, look at these jeans.*

You **see** something without planning to: *Two people saw him take the bag.*

You **watch** TV, a movie, or something that happens for a period of time: *Did you watch the football game last night? | The kids are watching TV.*

You can also say that you **saw** a movie, a program, etc., but you cannot say "see television": *I saw a great movie on TV last night.*

THESAURUS

notice – to see something interesting or unusual: *I noticed a police car outside their house.*

spot – to notice or recognize someone or something that is difficult to see: *Nick spotted the advertisement in the paper.*

glimpse/catch a glimpse of sth/sb – to see something or someone, but only for a short time: *I caught a glimpse of his face as he ran past the window.*

make sth out – to see something, but only with difficulty: *Ahead, I could just make out the figure of a woman.*

catch sight of sb/sth – to suddenly see someone or something: *She caught sight of Alec, waiting in a doorway.*

witness – to see something bad happen, especially an accident or a crime: *Several people witnessed the attack.*

behold (literary) – to see something: *The northern lights are an awesome sight to behold.*

observe (formal) – to see or notice something in particular: *He observed that the fuel gauge was not working.* → HEAR

2 UNDERSTAND [I,T] to understand or realize something: *Do you **see how** it works? | I could **see (that)** something was terribly wrong. | **(You) see,** you have to put in this part first* (=used when you are explaining something). *| "It goes in the red box." "Oh, **I see*** (=I understand)." *| At 14, he couldn't **see the point of*** (=understand the reason for) *staying in school. | It's all coming apart here, **see what I mean/see what I'm saying?*** (=used to check that someone understands)

3 ABILITY TO SEE [I,T] to be able to use your eyes to look at things and know what they are: *I **can't see** a thing without my glasses.*

4 VISIT/MEET [T] to visit, meet, or have a meeting with someone: *I'm seeing Margo and Rod on Saturday. | You ought to see a doctor.*

5 FIND OUT [T] to find out information or a fact: *Plug it in and **see if** it's working. | Marion looked out to **see what** was happening. | We could see that it was dangerous.*

6 WATCH [T] to watch a television program, play, movie, etc.: *Karl's seen "Star Wars" about eight times.*

7 CONSIDER [T] to consider someone or something in a particular way: *I thought I'd done the right thing, but Bill saw it differently. | Fights on TV can make children **see** violence **as** normal. | Well, **the way I see it**, that school is no worse than any other.*

S

8 EXPERIENCE [T] to have experience of something: *The attorney said he had never seen a case like this before.*
9 HAPPEN [T] to be the time when something happens, or the place where something happens: *This year has seen a 5% increase in burglaries.*
10 FUTURE [I,T] to find out something about the future, or to imagine what might happen in the future: *Just **wait and see** if anything improves.* | *Call them and **see if** we can schedule a meeting.* | *I don't know – I'll **see how it goes/things go**.* | ***I can't see** her **as** a teacher.*
11 MAKE SURE [T] to make sure or check that something is done correctly: *Their duty is to **see that** the rules are kept.*
12 be seeing sb to be having a romantic relationship with someone
13 see eye to eye to agree with someone: *My mother and I have never really seen eye to eye.*
14 see fit to do sth (formal) to decide that it is right to do something, even though many people disagree: *The government has seen fit to start testing more nuclear weapons.*

SPOKEN PHRASES
15 see you used in order to say goodbye to someone you will meet again: *Okay, I'll **see you later**.* | *See you, Ben.*
16 let's see/let me see said when you are trying to remember something or think about something: *Let me see, that's two per person, so 24.*
17 I don't see why not said when you mean yes: *"Would that be possible?" "I don't see why not."*
18 I'll/we'll see said when you do not want to make a decision immediately, especially when you are talking to a child: *"Can Denise come too?" "We'll see."*
19 you should have seen sb/sth said when you think someone or something you have seen was very funny, surprising, etc.: *You should've seen the look on her face!*
20 we'll see about that said when you intend to stop someone doing something: *"She says she's leaving early today." "Really? We'll see about that."*

[ORIGIN: Old English *seon*]
see about sth *phr. v.*
to make arrangements for someone to do something: *I made some phone calls to see about getting him a job.*
see sb ↔ **off** *phr. v.*
to go to an airport, station, etc. to say goodbye to someone who is leaving: *My friends came to see me off at the airport.*
see sb ↔ **out** *phr. v.*
to go with someone to the door when s/he leaves: *No, that's okay, I'll **see myself out*** (=leave without anyone coming with me).
see through *phr. v.*
1 see through sb/sth to be able to recognize the truth when someone is trying to deceive you: *I can't lie to her; she sees right through me.*
2 see sb/sth **through** (sth) to continue doing something difficult until it is finished, or to give help and support to someone during a difficult time: *I managed to earn enough to see me through the rest of the year.* | *He'd promised to stay long enough to see it through.*
3 see sth through sb's eyes to see something or think about it in the way that someone else does
see to sth *phr. v.*
to deal with something or make sure that it happens: *Klein **saw to it** that she got free tickets.*

seed[1] /sid/ *n.* **1 a)** [C] a small hard object produced by plants, from which a new plant will grow: *an apple seed* → *see picture at* PLANT[1] **b)** [U] a quantity of seeds: *grass seed* **2 (the) seeds of sth** the beginning of something that will grow and develop: *The World War I peace agreement **sowed the seeds of** World War II.* [ORIGIN: Old English *sæd*]

seed[2] *v.* [T] to plant seeds in the ground

'seed coat *n.* [C] BIOLOGY a protective cover surrounding the seeds of a plant, that prevents it from becoming too dry

'seed cone *n.* [C] BIOLOGY in a tree that produces both male and female cells, a container for holding the female cells during the time when male cells are developing

seed·ling /ˈsidlɪŋ/ *n.* [C] BIOLOGY a young plant grown from seed → *see picture at* PLANT[1]

seed·y /ˈsidi/ *adj.* (informal) looking dirty or poor, and often being related to illegal or immoral activity: *a seedy bar*

see·ing /ˈsiɪŋ/ *conjunction* because a particular fact or situation is true: *You can stay out later tonight, **seeing that/as** it's Friday.*

ˌSeeing 'Eye ˌdog *n.* [C] (trademark) a dog that is trained to guide blind people

Seeing Eye dog

seek /sik/ (Ac) *v.* (past tense and past participle **sought** /sɔt/) [T] **1** to try to find or get something: *graduates seeking employment* | *Ted **sought advice/approval/help** from his parents.* | *Refugees **sought refuge** from the civil war.*

THESAURUS **look, search, try to find sb/sth, hunt for sb/sth, have a look for sb/sth** → LOOK[1]

2 (formal) to try to achieve or do something: *The governor will seek re-election.* | *Schools are **seeking to** improve test scores.* [ORIGIN: Old English *secan*]

seem /sim/ *v.* [linking verb] **1** to appear to exist or be true, or to have a particular quality or feeling: ***It seemed** very strange.* | *The nausea **seems to be** a side effect from the medication.* | ***It seems to** me you* *don't have much choice.* | *He* ***seems to*** *like his job.* | *The town* ***seemed like*** *a nice place.* | *It just didn't* ***seem*** *right* ***to*** *me.*

THESAURUS

appear (formal) – to seem to have particular qualities: *Light colors make a room appear bigger than it is.*
look – to seem to be something, especially by having a particular appearance: *William looked very tired.*
sound – to seem to have a particular quality when you hear or read about someone or something: *It sounds like a wonderful trip.*
come across as sth – to seem to have certain qualities: *She comes across as a really happy person.*

2 can't/couldn't seem to do sth used to say that you have tried to do something but cannot do it: *I can't seem to relax.* **3** used to make what you are saying less strong or certain, and more polite: *We* ***seem to*** *have turned onto the wrong road.* [ORIGIN: 1100—1200 Old Norse *sœma* "to be appropriate to," from *sœmr* "appropriate"]

seem·ing /'simɪŋ/ *adj.* (formal) appearing to be true even though it may not be: *Your seeming lack of concern worries me.*

seem·ing·ly /'simɪŋli/ *adv.* in a way that appears to be true but may not be (SYN) **apparently**: *a seemingly endless road* | *a seemingly simple task*

seen /sin/ *v.* the past participle of SEE

seep /sip/ *v.* [I] to flow slowly through small holes or cracks: *Blood* ***seeped through/into*** *the bandages.* —**seepage** *n.* [singular, U]

see·saw[1] /'sisɔ/ *n.* [C] a long board on which children play, that is balanced in the middle so that when one end goes up the other end goes down

seesaw[2] *v.* [I] to move suddenly up and down or from one condition to another and back again: *Stock prices seesawed throughout the morning.*

seethe /sið/ *v.* [I] to be so angry that you are almost shaking: *Holly was* ***seething with*** *rage.* —**seething** *adj.*

seg·ment /'sɛgmənt/ *n.* [C] **1** a part of something that is different from or divided from the whole: *a* ***segment of*** *the entertainment market* | *an orange segment* ➔ PART[1] **2** MATH the part of a line between two points **3** MATH a part of a circle that is separated from the rest of the circle by a straight line across it [ORIGIN: 1500—1600 Latin *segmentum,* from *secare* "to cut"] —**segmentation** /ˌsɛgmən'teɪʃən/ *n.* [U] —**segmented** /'sɛgmɛntɪd/ *adj.*

seg·re·gate /'sɛgrəˌgeɪt/ *v.* [T] to separate one group of people from others, usually because they are a different race, sex, religion, etc. (ANT) **integrate**: *The classes are segregated by ability.* | *Not long ago, schools in the South were racially segregated.* [ORIGIN: 1500—1600 Latin, past participle of *segregare,* from *se-* "apart" + *grex* "herd"]

THESAURUS **separate, divide, split, partition** ➔ SEPARATE[2]

seg·re·gat·ed /'sɛgrəˌgeɪt̬ɪd/ *adj.* segregated buildings or areas can only be used by members of a particular race, sex, religion, etc.: *racially segregated schools*

seg·re·ga·tion /ˌsɛgrə'geɪʃən/ *n.* [U] the practice of keeping people of different races or religions apart and making them live, work, or study separately (ANT) **integration**: *racial segregation*

seis·mic /'saɪzmɪk/ *adj.* EARTH SCIENCES relating to or caused by EARTHQUAKES: *a period of seismic activity* | *seismic waves* [ORIGIN: 1800—1900 Greek *seismos* "shock, earthquake," from *seiein* "to shake"]

seis·mo·graph /'saɪzməˌgræf/ *n.* [C] EARTH SCIENCES an instrument that measures and records the movement of the Earth during an EARTHQUAKE —**seismographic** /ˌsaɪzmə'græfɪk◂/ *adj.*

seis·mol·o·gy /saɪz'mɑlədʒi/ *n.* [U] EARTH SCIENCES the scientific study of EARTHQUAKES —**seismologist** *n.* [C]

seize /siz/ *v.* [T] **1** to take hold of something quickly and in a forceful way (SYN) **grab**: *Thomas seized her hand.* **2** to take control of a place suddenly, using military force: *Rebels* ***seized control*** *of the embassy.* **3** to take away something such as illegal guns, drugs, etc.: *Police seized 10 kilos of cocaine.* [ORIGIN: 1200—1300 Old French *saisir* "to take possession of," from Medieval Latin *sacire*]

sei·zure /'siʒɚ/ *n.* **1** [U] the act of taking control or possession of something suddenly: *the seizure of illegal firearms* **2** [C] a short time when someone is unconscious and cannot control the movements of his/her body: *an epileptic seizure*

sel·dom /'sɛldəm/ *adv.* very rarely: *Glenn seldom eats breakfast.* [ORIGIN: Old English *seldan*]

THESAURUS **rarely, not very often, hardly ever, infrequently** ➔ RARELY

se·lect[1] /sɪ'lɛkt/ (Ac) *v.* [T] to choose something or someone (SYN) **pick**: *The entertainers were* ***selected to*** *appeal to both adults and children.* | *the five students* ***selected for*** *the program* | *The university* ***selected*** *Garrett* ***as*** *athletics director.* [ORIGIN: 1500—1600 Latin, past participle of *seligere* "to select," from *legere* "to gather, choose"]

THESAURUS **choose, pick, opt for sth, decide on sth** ➔ CHOOSE

select[2] *adj.* (formal) consisting of or used by a small group of specially chosen people: *a select club*

seˌlect com'mittee *n.* [C] POLITICS a small group of politicians and advisers from various parties, chosen to examine a particular subject

se·lec·tion /sɪ'lɛkʃən/ (Ac) *n.* **1** [C,U] the act of choosing something or someone, or the thing or person that is chosen (SYN) **choice**: *his **selection as** the Democratic candidate | the **selection of** a new leader | **Make** a **selection** from the list.* **2** [C] a collection of things of one type, especially things for sale: *a wide **selection of** jewelry* **3** [C usually singular] a number of things that have been chosen from among a group of things of the same type: *a selection of Simon and Garfunkel songs*

se·lec·tive /sɪˈlɛktɪv/ (Ac) *adj.* careful about what you choose to do, buy, etc.: *a **highly selective** university*

se,lective 'breeding *n.* [U] BIOLOGY the deliberate mating (MATE) of two animals in order to produce better animals than existing ones

self /sɛlf/ *n.* (plural **selves** /sɛlvz/) **1** [C usually singular] the type of person you are, including your character, abilities, etc.: *He's starting to feel like his **old/usual self** again* (=feel normal again, after feeling bad or sick). **2** [U] your feeling of being a separate person, different from other people: *the need for a child to develop a **sense of self***

,self-ab'sorbed *adj.* interested only in yourself and the things that affect you

,self-ap'pointed *adj.* (disapproving) giving yourself a duty or job without the agreement of other people: *a self-appointed guardian of morality*

S

,self-as'sured *adj.* confident about what you are doing —**self-assurance** *n.* [U]

> THESAURUS **confident, self-confident, assertive** → CONFIDENT

,self-'centered *adj.* interested only in yourself and never thinking about other people (SYN) **selfish**: *a vain, self-centered man*

,self-'confident *adj.* sure that you can do things well, that people like you, etc. (SYN) **confident** —**self-confidence** *n.* [U]

> THESAURUS **confident, self-assured, assertive** → CONFIDENT

,self-'conscious *adj.* worried and embarrassed about what you look like or what other people think of you: *"Hi," I said, suddenly **self-conscious about** my accent.*

> THESAURUS **shy, timid, bashful** → SHY[1]

,self-con'tained *adj.* complete in itself and not needing other things to make it work: *a self-contained army base*

,self-con'trol *n.* [U] the ability to control your feelings and behavior even when you are angry, excited, or upset: *children learning to **exercise self-control***

,self-de'feating *adj.* making a situation have a bad result for you: *the self-defeating attempt to stay young*

,self-de'fense *n.* [U] the use of force to protect yourself from attack: *She shot him **in self-defense**.*

,self-de'nial *n.* [U] the practice of not having or doing the things that you enjoy, either because you cannot afford them or for moral or religious reasons

,self-de'structive *adj.* self-destructive actions are likely to harm or kill the person who is doing them

,self-'discipline *n.* [U] the ability to make yourself do the things that you ought to do, without someone else making you do them: *Working at home takes self-discipline.* —**self-disciplined** *adj.*

,self-ef'facing *adj.* (formal) not wanting to attract attention to yourself or your achievements (SYN) **modest**

,self-em'ployed *adj.* working for yourself rather than for a company

,self-es'teem *n.* [U] the feeling of being satisfied with your own abilities, and that you deserve to be liked or respected: *Lack of success at school often leads to **low/poor self-esteem**.*

,self-'evident *adj.* clearly true and needing no proof (SYN) **obvious**

,self-ex'planatory *adj.* clear and easy to understand, with no need for explanation: *The controls are pretty self-explanatory.*

,self-ful,filling 'prophecy *n.* [C] a statement about what will happen in the future, that becomes true because you changed your behavior to make it happen

,self-'government *n.* [U] POLITICS the government of a country or part of a country by its own citizens, rather than by another country or group

,self-'help *n.* [U] the use of your own efforts to deal with your problems instead of depending on other people: *self-help books*

,self-'image *n.* [C] the idea that you have of your own abilities, appearance, and character: *a **poor/good/positive self-image***

,self-im'portant *adj.* (disapproving) thinking you are more important than other people

,self-im'provement *n.* [U] the activity of trying to learn more skills or deal with your problems better

,self-in'dulgent *adj.* (disapproving) allowing yourself to have or enjoy something that you do not need: *He's irresponsible and self-indulgent.* —**self-indulgence** *n.* [singular, U]

,self-in'flicted *adj.* a self-inflicted injury, problem, etc. is one that you have caused yourself: *a self-inflicted gunshot wound*

,self-'interest *n.* [U] the state of caring most about what is best for you, and less about what is best for other people: *an action that is **in** the national **self-interest***

self·ish /ˈsɛlfɪʃ/ *adj.* (disapproving) caring only about yourself and not about other people (ANT) **unselfish**: *Don't be selfish.* —**selfishness** *n.* [U] —**selfishly** *adv.*

self·less /ˈsɛlflɪs/ *adj.* caring about other people more than about yourself

ˌself-ˈmade *adj.* successful and rich because of your own efforts: *a self-made millionaire*

ˌself-ˈpity *n.* [U] the feeling of being too sorry for yourself

ˌself-ˈportrait *n.* [C] a picture that you make of yourself

ˌself-posˈsessed *adj.* calm and confident because you are in control of your feelings

ˌself-preserˈvation *n.* [U] keeping yourself from being harmed or killed: *the instinct for self-preservation*

ˌself-reˈliance *n.* [U] the ability to act and make decisions by yourself without depending on other people —**self-reliant** *adj.*

ˌself-reˈspect *n.* [U] a feeling of confidence and happiness about your abilities, ideas, and character: *She needs to regain her confidence and self-respect.* —**self-respecting** *adj.*

ˌself-reˈstraint *n.* [U] the ability to control what you do or say in situations that upset you

ˌself-ˈrighteous *adj.* (disapproving) very proud and sure that your beliefs, attitudes, etc. are right, in a way that annoys other people

ˌself-ˈsacrifice *n.* [U] (approving) the act of giving up what you need or want in order to help someone else —**self-sacrificing** *adj.*

ˌself-ˈsatisfied *adj.* SMUG

self-ˈservice *also* **ˌself ˈserve** *adj.* relating to stores, restaurants, etc. where you get things for yourself, rather than being served: *a self-service gas station*

ˌself-ˈserving *adj.* (disapproving) showing that you will only do something if it gains you an advantage: *self-serving politicians*

ˈself-styled *adj.* (disapproving) having given yourself a title, position, etc. without having a right to it: *a self-styled expert*

ˌself-sufˈficient *adj.* able to provide all the things you need without help from other people: *a country that is **self-sufficient in** food production* —**self-sufficiency** *n.* [U]

ˌself-supˈporting *adj.* able to earn enough money to support yourself: *a self-supporting museum*

sell /sɛl/ *v.* (past tense and past participle **sold** /soʊld/) **1** [I,T] to give something to someone in exchange for money (ANT) **buy**: *I sold him my baseball card collection.* | *We **sold** the car **for** $5,000.* | *It is illegal to **sell** alcohol **to** minors.* **2** [I,T] to offer something for people to buy: *a store selling hand-crafted jewelry* | *Avocados **sell for** only a few cents each in Mexico.* **3** [I,T] to make someone want to buy something: *Advertisers know that sex sells.* **4** [T] to be bought by people: *Her novels have sold millions of copies.* | *Lower-priced homes continue to **sell well/badly**.* **5** [I,T] to try to make someone accept a new plan, idea, etc., or to become accepted: *the candidate's attempts to **sell** his policies **to** the voters* [ORIGIN: Old English *sellan*]

sell sth ↔ **off** *phr. v.* to sell something, especially cheaply, because you need the money or want to get rid of it: *The company is selling off everything but its core business.*

sell out *phr. v.* **1** to sell all of something, so that there is none left: *The concert is almost sold out.* **2** (informal) to do something that is against your beliefs or principles, in order to get power or money: *a politician who has sold out to the gun lobby*

sell·er /ˈsɛlɚ/ *n.* [C] **1** a person or company that sells something (ANT) **buyer** **2 good/best/biggest etc. seller** a product that a company sells a lot of ➔ BEST-SELLER

ˈselling point *n.* [C] a special feature of a product that will make people want to buy it

sell·out /ˈsɛlaʊt/ *n.* [singular] **1** a performance, sports event, etc. for which all the tickets have been sold: *a sellout crowd* **2** (informal) a situation in which someone does not do something s/he promised, or in which s/he does something that is against his/her beliefs or principles: *Environmental groups labeled the deal a sellout.*

selves /sɛlvz/ *n.* the plural of SELF

se·man·tics /səˈmæntɪks/ *n.* [U] **1** ENG. LANG. ARTS the meaning of a word or phrase **2** ENG. LANG. ARTS the study of the meanings of words and phrases —**semantic** *adj.*

sem·a·phore /ˈsɛməˌfɔr/ *n.* [U] a system of sending messages using two flags, that you hold in different positions to represent letters and numbers

sem·blance /ˈsɛmbləns/ *n.* **a/some semblance of sth** a condition or quality that is similar to another one: *Life was returning to some semblance of normality.*

se·men /ˈsimən/ *n.* [U] BIOLOGY the liquid that is produced by the male sex organs and contains SPERM

se·mes·ter /səˈmɛstɚ/ *n.* [C] one of two periods into which a year at school or college is divided ➔ QUARTER: *the **spring/fall semester*** ➔ UNIVERSITY [ORIGIN: 1800—1900 German, Latin *semestris* "half-yearly," from *sex* "six" + *mensis* "month"]

sem·i /ˈsɛmi/ *n.* [C] (informal) **1** a very large heavy truck consisting of two connected parts **2** a SEMIFINAL

sem·i·cir·cle /ˈsɛmiˌsɚkəl/ *n.* [C] **1** MATH half a circle ➔ *see picture at* CIRCLE[1]

> THESAURUS **shape, square, circle, triangle, rectangle, oval** ➔ SHAPE[1]

2 a group arranged in a curved line: *chairs arranged **in a semicircle*** —**semicircular** /ˌsɛmiˈsɚkyəlɚ/ *adj.*

semiˌcircular caˈnal *n.* [C] BIOLOGY one of three

S

tubes inside your INNER EAR that gives your brain information about your body's position and direction and helps to keep you balanced

sem·i·co·lon /ˈsɛmiˌkoʊlən/ *n.* [C] ENG. LANG. ARTS the mark (;) used in writing to separate independent parts of a sentence or list

sem·i·con·duct·or /ˈsɛmikənˌdʌktɚ/ *n.* [C] PHYSICS a substance such as SILICON that is used in electronic equipment to allow electricity to pass through it

sem·i·fi·nal /ˈsɛmiˌfaɪnl, ˈsɛmaɪ-, ˌsɛmiˈfaɪnl/ *n.* [C] one of two sports games whose winners then compete against each other to decide who wins the whole competition ➔ QUARTERFINAL

sem·i·lu·nar valve /ˌsɛmilunɚ ˈvælv, ˌsemai-/ *n.* [C] BIOLOGY one of two small parts in your heart that open and close to prevent blood flowing back into the left and right VENTRICLES ➔ *see picture at* HEART

sem·i·nal /ˈsɛmənəl/ *adj.* new and important, and influencing the way something develops in the future: *Darwin's seminal work on evolution*

sem·i·nar /ˈsɛməˌnɑr/ *n.* [C] a short course or a special meeting that people attend in order to study a particular subject: *a **seminar on** effective management*

S

THESAURUS **lesson, course, period, lecture** ➔ CLASS[1]

sem·i·nary /ˈsɛməˌnɛri/ *n.* (plural **seminaries**) [C] a college at which people study religion and can train to be priests or ministers

se·mi·ot·ics /ˌsɛmiˈɑt̬ɪks/ *also* **sem·i·ol·o·gy** /ˌsɛmiˈɑlədʒi/ *n.* [U] ENG. LANG. ARTS the way in which people communicate through signs and images, or the study of this —**semiotic** /ˌsɛmiˈɑt̬ɪk/ *adj.*

Se·mit·ic /səˈmɪt̬ɪk/ *adj.* relating to the race of people that includes Jews, Arabs, and, in ancient times, Babylonians and Assyrians ➔ ANTI-SEMITIC

Sen·ate /ˈsɛnɪt/ *n.* **the Senate** POLITICS the smaller of the two groups of people who make the laws in countries such as the U.S. and Australia ➔ HOUSE OF REPRESENTATIVES [ORIGIN: 1100—1200 Old French *senat*, from Latin *senatus*, from *senex* "old man"]

sen·a·tor, Senator /ˈsɛnət̬ɚ/ *n.* [C] a member of the Senate: *Senator Feinstein* —**senatorial** /ˌsɛnəˈtɔriəl/ *adj.*

THESAURUS **politician, congressman/congresswoman, governor, mayor** ➔ POLITICIAN

send /sɛnd/ *v.* (past tense and past participle **sent** /sɛnt/) [T] **1** to arrange for something to go or be taken to another place, especially by mail: *Taryn sent some pictures of the baby.* | *I sent you an e-mail yesterday.* | *Do you want me to **send** a copy **to** you?* | *a letter **sent by** fax* **2** to ask or tell someone to go somewhere: *The UN is **sending** troops **to** the region.* | *The refugees were **sent back** to Sudan.* | *Frank came, but I **sent** him **away**.* **3** to arrange for someone to go somewhere and stay there: *Morrison was **sent to** jail for five years.* **4 send your love/best wishes etc.** to ask someone to give your greetings, good wishes, etc. to someone else: *Mark sends his love.* **5** to make someone or something do something: *The blast sent people running for safety.* | *The film sent me to sleep.* [ORIGIN: Old English *sendan*]

send away for sth *phr. v.* to order something through the mail

send sth ↔ **down** *phr. v.* to make something lose value: *The news sent shares down.*

send for sb/sth *phr. v.* to ask or order someone to come to you, or that something be brought or mailed to you: *An ambulance was sent for.* | *Send now for your free catalog.*

send sb/sth ↔ **in** *phr. v.* **1** to send something, usually by mail, to a place where it can be dealt with: *Did you send in your application?* **2** to send soldiers, police, etc. somewhere to deal with a dangerous situation: *The FBI sent in agents to investigate.*

send sb/sth ↔ **off** *phr. v.* **1** to mail something somewhere: *She sent off the completed book to her publisher.* **2** to make someone go somewhere: *We got sent off to camp every summer.*

send sb/sth ↔ **out** *phr. v.* to make something or someone go from one place to various other places: *The wedding invitations were sent out weeks ago.*

ˈsend-off *n.* [C] (informal) an occasion when people gather together to say goodbye to someone who is leaving: *We wanted to **give** you a big **send-off**.*

se·nile /ˈsinaɪl/ *adj.* mentally confused or behaving strangely, because of old age —**senility** /sɪˈnɪlət̬i/ *n.* [U]

Se·nior /ˈsinyɚ/ (*written abbreviation* **Sr.**) *adj.* used after the name of a man who has the same name as his son ➔ JUNIOR: *Robert Burrelli, Sr.*

senior[1] *n.* [C] **1** a student in the last year of HIGH SCHOOL or college ➔ STUDENT **2 be two/five/ten etc. years sb's senior** to be two, five, ten, etc. years older than someone [ORIGIN: 1300—1400 Latin "older," from *senex* "old"]

senior[2] *adj.* older, or of higher rank (ANT) **junior**: *a senior officer*

THESAURUS **chief, high-ranking, top** ➔ POSITION[1]

ˌsenior ˈcitizen *n.* [C] an old person, especially someone over the age of 65

ˌsenior ˈhigh school *n.* [C] a HIGH SCHOOL

se·nior·i·ty /ˌsinˈyɔrət̬i, -ˈyɑr-/ *n.* [U] **1** if you have seniority in a company or organization, you have worked there a long time and have some official advantages: *a worker with ten years' seniority at the plant* **2** the state of being older or higher in rank than someone else: *a position of seniority*

sen·sa·tion /sɛn'seɪʃən/ *n.* **1** [C,U] the ability to feel, or a feeling that you get from one of your five senses: *Matt **had a** burning **sensation** in his arm.* | *Jerry realized that he had no sensation in his legs.* **2** [C] a feeling that is difficult to describe, caused by a particular event, experience, or memory: *I **had the** strangest **sensation that** I was being watched.* **3** [C usually singular] extreme excitement or interest, or someone or something that causes this: *The band's first album **caused a sensation** among rap fans.*

sen·sa·tion·al /sɛn'seɪʃənl/ *adj.* **1** very interesting or exciting: *a sensational finish to the race* **2** (disapproving) intended to excite or shock people: *sensational news stories* **3** (informal) very good: *She looked sensational.*

sen·sa·tion·al·ism /sɛn'seɪʃənl,ɪzəm/ *n.* [U] (disapproving) a way of reporting events or stories that is intended to excite or shock people

sense¹ /sɛns/ *n.*
1 JUDGMENT [U] good understanding and judgment, especially about practical things, that allows you to make sensible decisions → COMMON SENSE: *Earl **had the sense** not **to** move the injured man much.* | ***There's no sense in** waiting any longer* (=it is not sensible to continue waiting).
2 FEELING [singular] a feeling about something: *She **felt a** strong **sense of** accomplishment.* | *A sense of panic has spread over the country.*
3 make sense a) to have a clear meaning and be easy to understand: *Do these instructions make any sense to you?* | *I can't **make sense of*** (=understand) *the report.* **b)** if something makes sense, there seems to be a good reason for it: *Why would she wander off alone? It doesn't make sense.* **c)** to be a sensible thing to do: *It **makes sense to** take care of your health while you're young.*
4 SIGHT/SMELL ETC. [C] BIOLOGY one of the five natural powers of sight, hearing, touch, taste, and smell: *Dogs have a keen **sense of smell**.*
5 sense of humor the ability to understand and enjoy things that are funny, or to make people laugh: *Larry **has a** great **sense of humor**.*
6 in a sense/in one sense/in some senses used to say that something is true or correct in a particular way but there may be other ways in which it is not true or correct: *We're all competitors in a sense but we also want each other to succeed.*
7 sb's senses someone's ability to know and do what is sensible in a situation: *I'm glad that Lisa finally **came to** her **senses*** (=realized what was sensible) *and sold that car.* | *Have you **lost your senses*** (=are you crazy)? | *It's too bad it took a lawsuit to **bring** them **to** their **senses*** (=make them think clearly and behave sensibly).
8 ABILITY [singular] a natural ability to judge something: *When we were in the woods, I lost all **sense of direction*** (=ability to know where I was).
9 in the sense that used in order to say that something you have just said is true in a particular way: *The experiment was a success in the sense that we got the results we were looking for.*
10 MEANING [C] ENG. LANG. ARTS the meaning of a word, phrase, sentence, etc.: *The word "record" has many senses.* | *In what sense is the term used?* [ORIGIN: 1300—1400 Old French *sens*, from Latin *sensus*, from *sentire* "to feel"]

sense² *v.* [T] to feel that something exists or is true without being told or having proof: *I could sense something was wrong.* | *Sonya **sensed that** David wanted to be alone.* | *I could **sense how** disappointed she was.*

sense·less /'sɛnslɪs/ *adj.* **1** happening or done for no good reason or with no purpose: *the senseless killing of innocent people*

> THESAURUS pointless, futile, useless → POINTLESS

2 (informal) if someone is knocked, beaten, etc. senseless, s/he is hit until s/he is unconscious

sen·si·bil·i·ty /,sɛnsə'bɪləṭi/ *n.* (plural **sensibilities**) [C,U] the way that someone reacts to particular subjects or types of behavior: *We apologize if we have **offended the sensibilities of** our viewers.* | *our moral sensibility*

sen·si·ble /'sɛnsəbəl/ *adj.* **1** showing good judgment: *Come on, be sensible.* | *a sensible approach to the problem*

> **USAGE**
> Use **sensible** in order to talk about someone who makes good reasonable decisions and who does not behave in a stupid or dangerous way: *She's sensible enough not to drive when she's had a drink.*
> Use **sensitive** in order to talk about someone who is easily upset or offended: *He's a little sensitive about his height.*

2 suitable for a particular purpose, and practical rather than fashionable: *Wear sensible shoes.* —**sensibly** *adv.*

sen·si·tive /'sɛnsəṭɪv/ *adj.* **1** a sensitive person is able to understand the feelings, problems, etc. of other people (ANT) **insensitive**: *a husband who is **sensitive to** his wife's needs* **2** easily offended or hurt by the things that other people do or say: *a very sensitive child* | *Chrissy is very **sensitive about** her weight.* | *Alan is very **sensitive to** criticism.* → see USAGE box at SENSIBLE **3** easily affected, hurt, or damaged by a substance or temperature: *My teeth are really **sensitive to** cold.* | ***sensitive skin*** **4** a sensitive situation or subject needs to be dealt with very carefully because it is secret or because it may offend people: *a sensitive issue/subject/topic* | ***highly sensitive** information*

> THESAURUS secret, confidential → SECRET¹

5 reacting to very small changes in light, temperature, sound, etc.: *a **highly sensitive** listening device* —**sensitively** *adv.* —**sensitivity** /,sɛnsə'tɪvəṭi/ *n.* [U]

sens·or /'sɛnsɚ, -sɔr/ *n.* [C] a piece of equipment

that is used to find light, heat, movement, etc., even in very small amounts

sen·so·ry /ˈsɛnsəri/ *adj.* BIOLOGY relating to your SENSE of sight, hearing, smell, taste, or touch: *a baby's sensory perception*

sen·su·al /ˈsɛnʃuəl/ *adj.* relating to or enjoying physical pleasure, especially sexual pleasure: *a sensual massage* | *She believes that food can be a* ***sensual pleasure***. —**sensuality** /ˌsɛnʃuˈæləṭi/ *n.* [U]

sen·su·ous /ˈsɛnʃuəs/ *adj.* **1** pleasing to your SENSE of sight, hearing, smell, taste, or touch: *the sensuous feel of silk* **2** attractive in a sexual way: *her sensuous curves*

sent /sɛnt/ *v.* the past tense and past participle of SEND

sen·tence¹ /ˈsɛntˀns, -təns/ *n.* [C] **1** ENG. LANG. ARTS a group of written or spoken words that has a subject and a verb, and expresses a complete thought or asks a question. Sentences written in English begin with a capital letter and end with a PERIOD, a QUESTION MARK, or an EXCLAMATION POINT. **2** a punishment that a judge gives to someone who is guilty of a crime: *a 10-year* ***prison sentence*** | *Harris is* ***serving a*** *28-year* ***sentence*** (=spending 28 years in prison). | *He has just begun a* ***life sentence*** *for murder.* | *The defendant faces a possible* ***death sentence*** (=punishment by death). [ORIGIN: 1200—1300 Old French, Latin *sententia* "feeling, opinion, sentence," from *sentire* "to feel"]

THESAURUS punishment, penalty, fine ➔ PUNISHMENT

sentence² *v.* [T] if a judge sentences someone who is guilty of a crime, s/he gives him/her a punishment: *He was* ***sentenced to*** *life in prison for the murder.*

sen·ti·ment /ˈsɛnṭəmənt/ *n.* **1** [C,U] (formal) an opinion or feeling that you have about something: ***Public/Popular sentiment*** (=what many people believe) *against the war was growing.* | *"Anderson ought to be fired."* ***"My sentiments exactly*** (=I completely agree)."

THESAURUS opinion, view, position, attitude ➔ OPINION

2 [U] feelings such as pity, love, or sadness that are considered to be too strong or not appropriate for a particular situation: *There's no room for sentiment in business!*

sen·ti·men·tal /ˌsɛnṭəˈmɛnṭl◂/ *adj.* **1** showing emotions such as love, pity, and sadness too strongly: *a sentimental movie* | *Laurie still gets* ***sentimental about*** *our old house.*

THESAURUS emotional, moving, touching, schmaltzy ➔ EMOTIONAL

2 based on or relating to feelings rather than being practical: *a sentimental view of the past* | *The watch wasn't worth much, but it had great* ***sentimental value***. —**sentimentality** /ˌsɛnṭəmɛnˈtæləṭi/ *n.* [U]

sen·try /ˈsɛntri/ *n.* (plural **sentries**) [C] (old-fashioned) a soldier standing outside a building as a guard

se·pal /ˈsipəl, ˈsɛ-/ *n.* [C] BIOLOGY one of the small leaves that contains a young flower before the flower opens, and which stays directly under the flower ➔ *see picture at* FLOWER¹

sep·a·ra·ble /ˈsɛpərəbəl/ *adj.* able to be separated from something else (ANT) **inseparable**

sep·a·rate¹ /ˈsɛprɪt/ *adj.* **1** not related to or not affected by something else: *He keeps his professional life* ***separate from*** *his private life.* | *It's a completely separate issue.* **2** different: *a word with four separate meanings* | *My wife and I have separate bank accounts.* **3** not joined to each other or touching something else: *There is a small smoking area* ***separate from*** *the main dining room.* [ORIGIN: 1400—1500 Latin, past participle of *separare*, from *se-* "apart" + *parare* "to prepare, get"] —**separately** *adv.*

sep·a·rate² /ˈsɛpəˌreɪt/ *v.* **1** [I,T] to divide or split something into two or more parts, or to make something do this: *Ms. Barker* ***separated*** *the class* ***into*** *four groups.* | *At this point the satellite* ***separates from*** *the rocket.*

THESAURUS

divide – to separate something into a number of smaller parts: *The teacher divided the class into groups.*
split – to separate something into two or more groups, parts, etc.: *We split the money between us.*
break up – to separate something into smaller parts: *The phone company was broken up to encourage competition.*
segregate – to separate one group of people from others because of race, sex, religion, etc.: *Schools were racially segregated.*
partition (formal) – to divide a country, room, or building into two or more parts: *After World War II, Germany was partitioned into East and West Germany.*
apportion (formal) – to decide how something should be divided between various people: *The funds are apportioned to each of the schools in the district.*

2 [T] to be between two things so that they cannot touch each other or connect to each other: *A curtain* ***separated*** *one patient's area* ***from*** *another.* **3** [I] to start to live apart from your husband, wife, or sexual partner: *When did Lyle and Jan separate?*

THESAURUS divorce, split up/break up, leave sb ➔ DIVORCE²

4 [I,T] to move apart, or to make people do this: *Police moved in to separate the crowd.* | *In the fog, they got* ***separated from*** *the rest of their group.*

sep·a·rat·ed /ˈsɛpəˌreɪṭɪd/ *adj.* no longer living

with your husband, wife, or sexual partner: *Her parents are separated.*

sep·a·ra·tion /ˌsɛpəˈreɪʃən/ *n.* **1** [U] (formal) the act of separating or the state of being separate: *the **separation of** powers between Congress and the President* **2** [C,U] a period of time when two or more people live apart from each other: *Separation from the family is hard on children.* **3** [C] a situation in which a husband and wife agree to live apart even though they are still married

sepaˌration of ˈpowers *n.* [singular, U] POLITICS the situation that exists when each of the three parts of government, the EXECUTIVE, LEGISLATIVE, and JUDICIAL branches, are independent of each other and do different things

Sep·tem·ber /sɛpˈtɛmbɚ/ (*written abbreviation* **Sept.**) *n.* [C,U] the ninth month of the year, between August and October: *School starts **in September**.* | *We have to turn in the papers **on September 2nd**.* | *Laura moved here **last September**.* | *They're getting married **next September**.* [ORIGIN: 1000—1100 Old French *Septembre*, from Latin *September*, from *septem* "seven;" because it was the seventh month of the ancient Roman year]

se·quel /ˈsikwəl/ *n.* [C] **1** ENG. LANG. ARTS a movie, book, etc. that continues the story of an earlier one: *They've made several **sequels to** "Batman".* **2** an event that is related to an earlier event

se·quence /ˈsikwəns/ (Ac) *n.* [C,U] **1** the order in which things happen, or are supposed to happen: *Two of the pages were **out of sequence*** (=not in the correct order). | *Try to place the following pictures **in sequence*** (=in the correct order). **2** a series of related events, actions, etc. that happen in a particular order: *the **sequence of events** that led to World War I* [ORIGIN: 1300—1400 Late Latin *sequentia*, from Latin *sequi* "to follow"]

se·quen·tial /sɪˈkwɛnʃəl/ (Ac) *adj.* (formal) relating to or happening in a sequence —**sequentially** *adv.*

se·quin /ˈsikwɪn/ *n.* [C] a small shiny flat round piece of metal that is sewn on clothes for decoration

se·quoi·a /sɪˈkwɔɪə/ *n.* [C] a REDWOOD → *see picture on page A23*

ser·e·nade /ˌsɛrəˈneɪd/ *n.* [C] ENG. LANG. ARTS a love song —**serenade** *v.* [T]

ser·en·dip·i·ty /ˌsɛrənˈdɪpəṭi/ *n.* [U] (literary) the process of accidentally discovering something that is interesting or valuable: *Many scientific discoveries are pure serendipity.*

se·rene /səˈrin/ *adj.* very calm or peaceful [ORIGIN: 1400—1500 Latin *serenus* "clear, calm"] —**serenity** /sɪˈrɛnəṭi/ *n.* [U]

THESAURUS **calm, relaxed, laid-back, easygoing, mellow** → CALM²

serf /sɚf/ *n.* [C] HISTORY someone who lived and worked on land that s/he did not own and who had to obey the owner of this land, during the Middle Ages in Europe

ser·geant /ˈsɑrdʒənt/ *n.* [C] a low rank in the Army, Air Force, police, etc., or an officer who has this rank

se·ri·al¹ /ˈsɪriəl/ *adj.* **1** arranged or happening one after the other in the correct order: *serial processing on a computer* **2 serial killer/rapist etc.** someone who commits the same crime several times

serial² *n.* [C] a story that is broadcast or printed in several separate parts on television, in a newspaper, etc.

ˈserial ˌnumber *n.* [C] a number put on things that are produced in large quantities, so that each one has its own different number

se·ries /ˈsɪriz/ (Ac) *n.* (plural **series**) [C] **1** a group of events, actions, or things of the same kind that happen one after the other: *There has been a **series of** accidents along this road.* | *the first novel in a series* **2** a set of television or radio programs with the same characters or on the same subject: *a new comedy series* **3** a set of sports games played between the same two teams: *the World Series* (=in baseball) [ORIGIN: 1600—1700 Latin *serere* "to join"]

ˈseries ˌcircuit *n.* [C] PHYSICS an electrical CIRCUIT (=complete circle that an electric current travels in) in which electricity travels through all the lights or SWITCHes one after the other → PARALLEL CIRCUIT

se·ri·ous /ˈsɪriəs/ *adj.* **1** a serious problem, situation, etc. is extremely bad or dangerous: *Luckily, the damage was not serious.* | *Drugs are a **serious problem** in many communities.* | *Her mother's been in a **serious accident**.* **2 be serious** to say what you really mean, and not joke or pretend: *John is **serious about** finding a new career.* | *You can't be serious* (=I do not believe you)*!* **3** important and deserving a lot of attention: *Raising children is a **serious business**.* **4** a serious romantic relationship is intended to continue for a long time [ORIGIN: 1400—1500 French *sérieux*, from Late Latin *seriosus*, from Latin *serius*] —**seriousness** *n.* [U]

se·ri·ous·ly /ˈsɪriəsli/ *adv.* **1** in a way that is bad or dangerous: *Two of the victims were **seriously injured**.* | *Something was **seriously wrong**.* **2** in a way that shows that you think something is important: *He's thinking seriously about running for governor.* | *Don't **take** everything he says so **seriously*** (=think that it is important). **3** [sentence adverb] (spoken) used to show that what you say next is not a joke: *Seriously, I really need you to be there on time.*

ser·mon /ˈsɚmən/ *n.* [C] **1** a talk about a religious subject, usually given at a church and based on the Bible **2** (informal, disapproving) a long talk in which someone tries to give you unwanted moral advice: *I don't need another **sermon on** the virtues of hard work!* → PREACH

ser·pent /ˈsɚpənt/ *n.* [C] (literary) a snake [ORIGIN: 1200—1300 Old French, Latin, present participle of *serpere* "to creep"]

ser·rat·ed /səˈreɪt̬ɪd, ˈsɛˌreɪt̬ɪd/ *adj.* having a sharp edge made of a row of connected V-shaped points: *a serrated knife*

se·rum /ˈsɪrəm/ *n.* [C,U] BIOLOGY a liquid containing substances that fight infection or poison, that is put into a sick person's blood

serv·ant /ˈsɚvənt/ *n.* [C] someone who is paid to clean someone's house, cook food for him/her, etc.

serve[1] /sɚv/ *v.*

1 FOOD/DRINKS [I,T] to give someone food or drinks as part of a meal: *Dinner will be served at 8:00.* | *The crab was* ***served with*** *melted butter and a slice of lemon.* | *Why aren't you out there serving the guests?*

2 BE USED [I,T] to be appropriate for a particular purpose: *The couch can also* ***serve as*** *a bed.* | *Critics claim that the weapon* ***serves*** *no useful military* ***purpose****.*

3 DO A JOB [I,T] to spend time doing a particular job, especially one that is helpful: *Kelly* ***served*** *a three-year term* ***in*** *the Army.* | *In 1993, Campbell became the first woman to* ***serve as*** *Canada's prime minister.*

S

4 PROVIDE STH [T] to provide an area or a group of people with something that they need or use: *Its Southwestern Bell subsidiary serves customers in Texas, Missouri, Oklahoma, Kansas and Arkansas.*

5 IN PRISON [T] to spend time in prison: *Baxter* ***served a*** *five-year* ***sentence for*** *theft.*

6 LEGALLY [T] to officially give or send someone a legal document to appear in court: *Jones was* ***served a summons*** *to appear in court.*

7 SPORTS [I,T] to start playing a game such as tennis by throwing the ball into the air and hitting it to your opponent

8 it serves sb right (spoken) used in order to say that someone deserves something bad, because s/he has done something stupid or unkind: *"I failed my test." "Serves you right for not studying."*

serve[2] *n.* [C] the action in a game such as tennis in which you throw the ball into the air and hit it to your opponent

serv·er /ˈsɚvɚ/ *n.* [C] **1** IT the main computer on a network that controls all the others **2** someone who brings you food in a restaurant

serv·ice[1] /ˈsɚvɪs/ *n.*

1 IN A STORE ETC. [U] the help that people who work in a restaurant, hotel, store, etc. give you: *The food is terrific but the service is lousy.* | *the* ***customer service*** *department*

2 WORK DONE [C,U] the work that you do for someone or an organization: *He retired after 20* ***years of service****.* | *You may need the* ***services of*** *a lawyer.* | *She was given an award in honor of her years of* ***service to*** *the Democratic Party.*

3 BUSINESS [C] a business that provides help or does jobs for people rather than producing things: *a cleaning service*

4 public services things such as hospitals, schools, etc. that are provided by the government for the public to use

5 CEREMONY [C] a formal religious ceremony, especially in a church: *The funeral service will be held on Friday.*

6 HELP [singular, U] (formal) help that you give to someone: *"Thank you so much." "I'm glad to* ***be of service*** *(=to help)."* | *We're* ***at your service*** (=available to help), *Ma'am.*

7 the service a country's military forces, especially considered as a job

8 GOVERNMENT [C] an organization that works for the government: *the foreign service*

9 SPORTS [C] an act of hitting the ball to your opponent to start a game such as tennis

10 CAR/MACHINE [C] a regular examination of a car or machine to make sure that it works correctly

11 in service/out of service to be available or not available for people to use: *Two of the Fire Department's trucks were out of service for much needed repairs.*

service[2] *v.* [T] **1** to examine a machine or vehicle and fix it if necessary: *When's the last time you had the car serviced?*

> THESAURUS **repair, fix** → REPAIR[2]

2 to provide people with something that they need: *buses that service the local community*

serv·ice·a·ble /ˈsɚvɪsəbəl/ *adj.* ready or able to be used

ˈservice ˌcharge *n.* [C] an amount of money that is added to the price of something in order to pay for extra services that you use when buying it: *For phone orders, there's a $1 service charge.*

ˈservice eˌconomy *n.* [C] ECONOMICS a country or an economic system in which most people work for businesses that provide services, rather than businesses involved in MANUFACTURING (=producing goods)

serv·ice·man /ˈsɚvɪsˌmæn, -mən/ *n.* (plural **servicemen** /-ˌmɛn, -mən/) [C] a man who is a member of the military

ˈservice ˌstation *n.* [C] a GAS STATION

serv·ice·wom·an /ˈsɚvɪsˌwʊmən/ *n.* (plural **servicewomen** /-ˌwɪmɪn/) [C] a woman who is a member of the military

ser·vile /ˈsɚvəl, -vaɪl/ *adj.* (disapproving) very eager to obey and please someone

serv·ing /ˈsɚvɪŋ/ *n.* [C] an amount of food that is enough for one person

ser·vi·tude /ˈsɚvəˌtud/ *n.* [U] the condition of being a SLAVE or being forced to obey someone

ses·sion /ˈsɛʃən/ *n.* [C] **1** a period of time used for a particular purpose, especially by a group of people: *a question-and-answer session* | *teacher-training sessions* **2** a formal meeting or group of meetings, especially of a court of law or government organization: *The State Court is now* ***in session****.* **3** a part of the year when classes are given at a university [ORIGIN: 1300—1400 Old French, Latin *sessio* "act of sitting, session," from *sedere* "to sit"]

set[1] /sɛt/ *v.* (past tense and past participle **set**, present participle **setting**)

1 PUT STH SOMEWHERE [T] to carefully put something down somewhere: *Just* ***set*** *that bag* ***down*** *on the floor.* | *He took off his watch and* ***set*** *it* ***on*** *the dresser.*

2 STANDARD [T] to decide something that other things are compared to or measured against: *The agency has* ***set standards*** *for water cleanliness.* | *Parents should* ***set an example*** *for their children* (=behave in the way they want their children to behave).

3 PRICE/TIME ETC. [T] to decide that something will happen at a particular time, cost a particular amount, etc.: *The judge plans to* ***set*** *a* ***date*** *for the trial.* | *Officials have not yet* ***set*** *a* ***price*** *on how much the study will cost.*

4 CLOCK/MACHINE [T] to move part of a clock or a piece of equipment so that it will do what you want it to do: *I* ***set*** *my* ***alarm*** *for 6:30.* | *Do you know how to set the VCR?*

5 START STH HAPPENING [I,T] to make something start happening or to make someone start doing something: *Angry mobs* ***set*** *the building* ***on fire.*** | *Careless campers* ***set fire to*** *the dry brush.* | *A study by military experts was immediately* ***set in motion.*** | *Volunteers set to work clearing trash from the field.*

6 MOVIE/STORY ETC. [T] ENG. LANG. ARTS if a play, movie, story, etc. is set in a place or at a particular time, the action takes place there or then: *Clavell's epic novel is* ***set in*** *17th-century Japan.*

7 set a record to run faster, jump higher, etc. than anyone else: *He set a new world record in the 100 meters at the games.*

8 set the table to put knives, forks, etc. on a table so that you can eat a meal

9 set sb/sth straight to correct something or someone: *The company wants to* ***set the record straight*** (=explain the true situation) *about its safety procedures.*

10 set the stage/scene to make it possible for something to happen: *Recent pay cuts set the stage for a strike.*

11 SUN/MOON [I] when the Sun or Moon sets, it moves lower in the sky and disappears (ANT) **rise**

12 set your mind/sights/heart on (doing) sth to be determined to achieve something or decide that you definitely want to have it: *Heath had set her sights on the U.S. Senate seat for Colorado.*

13 set foot in/on sth to go into or onto a place: *The event is attracting people who have never before set foot in a museum.*

14 set sb/sth free/loose to allow a person or animal to be free: *All the other hostages were finally set free.*

15 set sail to start sailing somewhere

16 BECOME SOLID [I] if a substance sets, it becomes hard: *The concrete will set within two hours.*

17 set sth to music a) ENG. LANG. ARTS to write music for a story or poem: *poems set to music by Lloyd Webber* **b)** to arrange something so that it can be done while music plays: *exercise routines set to music*

18 set a trap a) to make a trap ready to catch an animal **b)** to invent a plan that will catch someone doing something wrong: *Police set a trap for the thieves.*

19 BONE **a)** [T] to move the ends of a broken bone into position so that they are in the right place to grow together again **b)** [I] if a broken bone sets, it joins together again

20 HAIR [T] to arrange someone's hair while it is wet, so that it will have a particular style when it is dry

set about sth *phr. v.*

set about (doing) sth to begin doing something: *Johnny set about improving his Spanish before his trip.*

set sb **against** sb *phr. v.*

to make someone start to argue or fight with someone else: *The civil war set brother against brother.*

set sb/sth **apart** *phr. v.*

to make someone or something different from or better than other similar people or things: *The movie's realistic characters* ***set*** *it* ***apart from*** *other gangster pictures.*

set sth ↔ **aside** *phr. v.*

1 to save something for a special purpose: *Hotels must* ***set aside*** *50% of their rooms* ***for*** *non-smokers.*

2 to decide not to be affected by a particular belief, idea, etc. because something else is more important: *They should set politics aside and do what is best for the country.*

set back *phr. v.*

1 set sb/sth ↔ **back** to delay the progress or development of someone or something: *Officials fear that the incident will set back race relations.*

2 set sb **back** (informal) to cost someone a lot of money: *My new stereo set me back $2,000.*

set sth ↔ **down** *phr. v.*

to write about something so that you have a record of it, such as a set of rules: *The rules of the game were clearly set down.*

set in *phr. v.*

if something unpleasant sets in, it begins and is likely to continue: *Winter seems to be setting in early this year.*

set off *phr. v.*

1 to start to go somewhere: *Thousands of people* ***set off for*** *the West during the 1800s.*

2 set sth ↔ **off** to make something start happening: *The attack set off another round of fighting.* | *The rains set off a mudslide that killed 15 people.*

3 set sth ↔ **off** to make something explode: *The bomb was set off by a remote control device.*

4 set sth ↔ **off** to make an ALARM start working: *A fire in the kitchen set off the smoke alarms.*

set forth *phr. v.*

1 set sth ↔ **forth** (formal) to write or talk about an idea, rule, etc. in a clear and organized way, especially in an official document or speech (SYN) **set out**: *the principles set forth in the treaty*

2 (literary) to start a trip (SYN) **set out**

S

set out *phr. v.*
1 to start a trip, especially a long trip: *The couple **set out for** Fresno at 9:30.*
2 set out to do sth to deliberately start doing something in order to achieve a particular result: *He set out to make a movie about his experiences in Vietnam.*
3 set out sth to write or talk about ideas, rules, etc. in a clear and organized way: *He is the first candidate to set out his foreign policy proposals.*
set up *phr. v.*
1 set sth ↔ **up** to start a company, organization, business, etc.: *The county has set up a special education program for teenage mothers.*
2 set sth ↔ **up** to prepare equipment so that it is ready for an event, activity, or situation: *Chris, could you help me set up the computer?*
3 set sth ↔ **up** to arrange for something to happen: *Call the doctor's office and set up an appointment.*
4 set sth ↔ **up** to build or place something somewhere: *The police have set up a roadblock.*
5 set sb ↔ **up** to deliberately make people think that someone has done something wrong: *Hudson accused his partners of setting him up.*
6 set up shop to start a business: *They set up shop in 1993 in Mason's basement.*

S

set² *n.* [C] **1** a group of things that belong together or are related in some way: *a **set of** dishes* | *a set of rules* | *a chess set* ➔ *see picture at* COLLECTION **2** a television: *a TV set* **3 a)** a place where a movie or television program is filmed: *OK, everybody, quiet **on the set**!* **b)** the SCENERY, furniture, etc. used in a play, movie, or television show **4** one part of a game such as tennis or VOLLEYBALL: *Hewitt leads two sets to one.* **5** a performance by a band, singer, or DJ: *They played a 90-minute set.*

set³ *adj.* **1** [only before noun] a set time, amount, price, etc. is fixed and is never changed: *We meet at a set time each week.* | *I invest a set amount of money each month.* **2** [not before noun] (informal) ready to do something: *If everyone is **all set**, we'll start the meeting.* | *I was just **set to** leave when the phone rang.* **3 be set on/upon/against (doing) sth** (informal) to be very determined about something: *Jerry's **dead set against** paying the extra money for the trip.* **4** in a particular place or position: *a castle **set on** a hill*

set·back /ˈsɛt˺bæk/ *n.* [C] something that delays your progress or makes things worse than they were: *Losing their drummer is a **major setback** for the band.* | *The peace talks **suffered a setback** when fighting resumed this week.*

THESAURUS problem, difficulty, snag, hitch ➔ PROBLEM

set·ting /ˈsɛṭɪŋ/ *n.* [C] **1** the place where something is or where something happens, and all the things that surround it: *a cabin in a mountain setting* | *the **perfect setting** for a wedding* **2** the position in which you put the controls on a machine or instrument: *Turn the microwave to its **highest setting**.* **3** ENG. LANG. ARTS the place or time in which the events in a book, movie, etc. happen: *London is the setting for his most recent novel.*

set·tle /ˈsɛṭl/ *v.*
1 END ARGUMENT [I,T] to end an argument or solve a disagreement: *an attempt to **settle** the **case/claim/lawsuit*** | *The union finally **settled with** management after a two-day strike.* | *They might be willing to **settle out of court*** (=come to an agreement without going to a court of law). | *They met recently to try and **settle their differences*** (=agree to stop arguing).
2 COMFORTABLE POSITION [I,T] to move into a comfortable position: *Dave **settled back** and turned on the TV.* | *Roger settled himself on a park bench for a photograph.*
3 DECIDE STH [T] to decide on something, or organize the details of something that will happen in the future: *So it's settled — I'll meet you in front of the theater at 7:00.*
4 IN A NEW PLACE a) [I,T] to go to a place where no people have lived permanently before and start to live there: *the men and women who settled Alaska* **b)** [I] to begin to live in a place where you intend to live for a long time: *My family moved around a lot before **settling in** Los Angeles.*
5 SNOW/DUST [I] if snow, dust, etc. settles, it falls to the ground and stays there
6 BILL/DEBT [T] if you settle a bill, account, debt, etc., you pay all the money that you owe
7 settle a score to do something bad to someone because s/he has done something bad to you
8 STOMACH [I,T] if your stomach settles, or if something settles it, it stops feeling uncomfortable or making you sick
9 settle your nerves to do something to make yourself stop being nervous or upset: *He took a deep breath to settle his nerves.*
settle down *phr. v.*
1 settle (sb) **down** to become quiet and calm, or to make someone quiet and calm: *Kids, settle down and eat your dinner.* | *Sometimes we take the baby for a ride in the car to settle him down.*
2 to start living a quiet and calm life in one place, especially when you get married: *My parents want me to marry Jim and settle down.*
3 to begin to do something and to give it all your attention: *When he finally **settled down to** work, it was 10:30.*
settle for sth *phr. v.*
to accept something that is less than what you wanted: *We looked at some nice apartments, but we had to settle for the cheapest one.*
settle in *also* **settle into** sth *phr. v.*
to become happier and more comfortable in a new situation or place: *Adam seems to have settled in at his new school.*
settle on/upon sth *phr. v.*
to decide or agree on something: *They haven't settled on a name for the baby yet.*
settle up *phr. v.* (informal)
to pay money that you owe for something: *I'll **settle up with** the bartender, then let's go.*

set·tled /ˈsɛt̬ld/ *adj.* **1 feel/be settled** to feel comfortable about living or working in a particular place: *We don't feel settled in our new house yet.* **2** unlikely to change: *the settled life of a farmer*

set·tle·ment /ˈsɛt̬lmənt/ *n.* **1** [C,U] an official agreement or decision that ends an argument: *The two sides have **reached a settlement*** (=made an agreement) *in the land dispute.* **2** [C,U] ECONOMICS a payment of money that you owe someone or that someone owes to you: *He accepted a financial settlement of $500.* **3** [U] the movement of a large number of people into a new place in order to live there: *the **settlement of** the Oklahoma territory* **4** [C] a group of houses and buildings where people live, in a place where no group lived before: *a Stone Age settlement*

set·tler /ˈsɛtlɚ, ˈsɛt̬l-ɚ/ *n.* [C] someone who goes to live in a new place, usually where there were few people before: *early **settlers of** the American West*

set·up /ˈsɛt̬ʌp/ *n.* [C usually singular] **1** a way of organizing or arranging something: *Do you like the new setup at work?* **2** (informal) a dishonest plan that is intended to trick someone: *I knew immediately that the whole thing was a setup.*

sev·en /ˈsɛvən/ *number* **1** 7 **2** seven o'clock: *The movie starts at seven.* **3** seven years old: *Patty was seven on her last birthday.* [ORIGIN: Old English *seofon*]

sev·en·teen /ˌsɛvənˈtin◂/ *number* 17 —**seventeenth** *number*

sev·enth /ˈsɛvənθ/ *number* **1** 7th **2** 1/7 **3 be in seventh heaven** (informal) to be extremely happy

sev·en·ty /ˈsɛvənt̬i/ *number* **1** 70 **2 the seventies a)** the years between 1970 and 1979 **b)** the numbers between 70 and 79, especially when used for measuring temperature **3 be in your seventies** to be aged between 70 and 79: *She's **in** her **early/mid/late seventies**.* —**seventieth** /ˈsɛvənt̬iɪθ/ *number*: *her seventieth birthday*

sev·er /ˈsɛvɚ/ *v.* [T] (formal) **1** to cut through something completely: *His finger was severed in the accident.* **2** to end a relationship or agreement with someone: *The deal **severs all ties** between the two organizations.* —**severance** *n.* [U]

sev·eral /ˈsɛvrəl/ *quantifier* a number of people or things that is more than a few, but not a lot ➔ FEW: *I called her several times on the phone.* | *I've talked to **several of** my students about this.*

sev·erance pay /ˈsɛvrəns ˌpeɪ/ *n.* [U] money you get from a company that you worked for when they no longer have a job for you

se·vere /səˈvɪr/ *adj.* **1** very bad or serious: *severe head injuries* | *severe problems* **2** very strict or extreme: *severe criticism* | *The president's plan calls for severe penalties for underage criminals.* **3** not kind or friendly: *a severe look on her face* [ORIGIN: 1500—1600 French *sévère*, from Latin *severus*] —**severity** /sɪˈvɛrət̬i/ *n.* [C,U]

se·vere·ly /səˈvɪrli/ *adv.* very badly or to a great degree: *The building was severely damaged in the fire.* | *She was punished severely for her actions.*

sew /soʊ/ *v.* (past tense **sewed**, past participle **sewn** /soʊn/ *or* **sewed**) [I,T] to use a needle and thread to make or repair clothes, or to attach something such as a button to them: *My mother taught me to sew.* | *Can you **sew** a button **on** this shirt for me?* [ORIGIN: Old English *siwian*] —**sewing** *n.* [U] ➔ *see picture at* KNIT[1]

sew sth ↔ **up** *phr. v.* (informal) to gain control over a situation so that you are sure to win or get an advantage: *The Republicans think they **have** the election **sewn up**.*

sew·age /ˈsuɪdʒ/ *n.* [U] the waste material and used water that is carried away from houses by sewers: *a sewage treatment plant*

sew·er /ˈsuɚ/ *n.* [C] a pipe or passage under the ground that carries away waste material and used water from houses, factories, etc. [ORIGIN: 1400—1500 Old French *esseweur*, from *essewer* "to carry away water," from Vulgar Latin *exaquare*]

sewn /soʊn/ *v.* a past participle of SEW

sex /sɛks/ (Ac) *n.* **1** [U] BIOLOGY the physical activity that people do together in order to produce babies or for pleasure: *They believe it's wrong to **have sex** before they're married.* | *the need to practice **safe sex*** (=wear something that will protect you from sexual diseases) **2** [U] BIOLOGY the condition of being male or female: *I don't care what sex the baby is, as long as it's healthy.* **3** [C] one of the two groups of people or animals, male and female: *He isn't comfortable with members of **the opposite sex*** (=people that are not his own sex). | *people of **both sexes*** (=men and women)

ˈsex ˌchromosome *n.* [C] BIOLOGY either of the two CHROMOSOMEs in humans and some animals that directly influence whether someone is male or female

ˈsex drive *n.* [C usually singular] someone's ability or need to have sex regularly

ˈsex eduˌcation *n.* [U] education in schools about sexual activity and sexual relationships

sex·ism /ˈsɛkˌsɪzəm/ (Ac) *n.* [U] the belief that one sex is weaker, less intelligent, or less important than the other, especially when this results in women being treated unfairly: *programs to lessen sexism in the workplace*

THESAURUS **prejudice, racism, discrimination, intolerance, bigotry, homophobia, anti-Semitism** ➔ PREJUDICE[1]

sex·ist /ˈsɛksɪst/ *adj.* relating to or showing sexism: *sexist remarks* —**sexist** *n.* [C]

ˈsex life *n.* [C] someone's sexual activities

ˈsex ˌsymbol *n.* [C] someone famous who many people think is very sexually attractive

sex·u·al /ˈsɛkʃuəl/ (Ac) *adj.* **1** relating to sex:

S

sexual contact | *a sexual relationship* **2** relating to the social relationships between men and women: *a commitment to greater sexual equality* —**sexually** *adv.*: *the age when teenagers become sexually active* (=start having sex)

ˌsexual 'harassment *n.* [U] sexual remarks, looks, or touching done to someone who does not want it, especially from someone s/he works with

ˌsexual 'intercourse *n.* [U] (formal) the physical act of sex between two people

sex·u·al·i·ty /ˌsɛkʃu'æləṭi/ (Ac) *n.* [U] the things people do and feel that are related to their desire or ability to have sex: *A person's sexuality is constrained by the rules of society.*

sex·y /'sɛksi/ *adj.* (comparative **sexier**, superlative **sexiest**) sexually exciting or attractive: *sexy clothes*

SGML *n.* [U] IT **Standard Generalized Markup Language** a computer language that allows you to write documents in a structure that can be read on different computer systems ➔ HTML, XML

Sgt. the written abbreviation of SERGEANT

sh, shh /ʃʃ/ *interjection* used in order to tell someone to be quiet: *Shh! I can't hear what he's saying.*

shab·by /'ʃæbi/ *adj.* **1** shabby clothes, places, or objects are old and in bad condition: *shabby hotel rooms* **2** unfair or wrong: *I don't deserve this kind of* ***shabby treatment***. —**shabbily** *adv.*

shack¹ /ʃæk/ *n.* [C] a small building that has not been built very well

shack² *v.*

shack up *phr. v.* (informal, disapproving) to start living with someone who you have sex with but are not married to: *I found out that she was* ***shacked up with*** *some guy from Florida.*

shack·le¹ /'ʃækəl/ *n.* [C usually plural] **1** one of a pair of metal rings joined by a chain, that is used for keeping a prisoner's hands or feet together **2 the shackles of sth** (written) limits that something puts on your freedom: *We need to free ourselves from the shackles of the past.*

shackle² *v.* [T] **1** to restrict what someone can do: *a company shackled by debts* **2** to put shackles on someone

shade¹ /ʃeɪd/ *n.* **1** [singular, U] an area that is cooler and darker because the light of the Sun cannot reach it ➔ SHADOW: *Let's find a table* ***in the shade***. | *boys sitting* ***in the shade of*** *a tree* ➔ *see picture at* SHADOW¹ **2** [C] something that reduces or blocks light, especially a cover that you pull across a window **3** [C] a particular degree of a color: *a darker* ***shade of*** *red* **4 shades** [plural] (informal) SUNGLASSES **5 shade of meaning/opinion etc.** a meaning, etc. that is slightly different from other ones: *The word can have many shades of meaning, depending on the context.* **6 a shade** very slightly, a little bit: *The room is a shade too hot for me.* [ORIGIN: Old English *sceadu*]

shade² *v.* [T] to protect something from direct light or heat: *She used her hand to* ***shade*** *her eyes* ***from*** *the Sun.*

shadow

shadow

shade

shad·ow¹ /'ʃædoʊ/ *n.* **1** [C] a dark shape that an object or a person makes on a surface when he, she, or it is between that surface and the light: *The sun began to* ***cast*** *long* ***shadows*** (=make long shadows) *across a grassy field.* **2** [C,U] darkness caused when light is prevented from coming into a place: *Margaret's face was half hidden* ***in shadow***. | *He waited* ***in the shadows***. **3 without/beyond a shadow of a doubt** without any doubt at all: *I think he's guilty beyond a shadow of a doubt.* **4 cast a shadow over/on sth** to make something seem less attractive or impressive: *The scandal cast a shadow over his reputation for the rest of his career.*

shadow² *v.* [T] to follow someone closely in order to watch what s/he is doing

shad·ow·y /'ʃædoʊi/ *adj.* **1** mysterious and secret: *a* ***shadowy figure*** *from his past* **2** full of shadows and difficult to see: *a shadowy corner*

shad·y /'ʃeɪdi/ *adj.* **1** protected from the Sun or producing shade: *a shady spot for a picnic* **2** (informal) not honest or legal: *a* ***shady*** *business* ***deal***

shaft /ʃæft/ *n.* [C] **1** a passage that goes up through a building or down into the ground, so that someone or something can get in or out: *an elevator shaft* **2** a long handle on a tool, SPEAR, etc. **3 shaft of light/sunlight** a narrow beam of light

shag·gy /'ʃægi/ *adj.* **1** shaggy hair or fur is long and messy: *a shaggy beard* **2** having shaggy hair

shake

shaking hands

shake¹ /ʃeɪk/ *v.* (past tense **shook** /ʃʊk/, past participle **shaken** /'ʃeɪkən/, present participle **shaking**) **1** [I,T] to move up and down or from side to side with quick movements, or to make someone or something do this: *His hands were shaking.* | *Shake the bottle before you open it.* | *She shook him by the shoulders and told him to wake up.*

THESAURUS

tremble – to shake because you are frightened or upset: *The dog was trembling with fear.*
shiver – to shake because you are very cold: *I jumped up and down to stop myself shivering.*
wobble – to shake from side to side: *The pile of books wobbled and fell.*
vibrate – to shake continuously with small fast movements: *The music was so loud that the whole room vibrated.*
quiver – if a person's voice or a part of their body quivers, it shakes slightly, especially because s/he is angry, upset, or anxious: *The boy's top lip began to quiver* (=because he was going to cry).
rattle – to shake and make a noise: *The windows rattled in the wind.*

2 shake your head to move your head from side to side as a way of saying no, or to show disapproval or sadness ➔ NOD **3 shake sb's hand/shake hands (with sb)** to hold someone's hand in your hand and move it up and down, as a greeting or a sign that you have agreed on something **4** [I] if your voice shakes, it sounds unsteady, usually because you are nervous or angry **5** [T] to make someone feel less confident or certain about something: *This experience has* ***shaken*** *my* ***confidence/faith/belief*** *in the legal system.* **6 be/look/feel shaken** to be frightened, shocked, or upset: *Mark looked shaken as he put down the phone.* [ORIGIN: Old English *sceacan*]

shake sb ↔ **down** *phr. v.* (informal) to get money from someone by using threats

shake off *phr. v.* **1 shake** sth ↔ **off** to get rid of an illness, problem, etc.: *I can't seem to shake off this cold.* **2 shake** sb ↔ **off** to escape from someone who is chasing you

shake sth ↔ **out** *phr. v.* to shake something such as a cloth so that small pieces of dirt, dust, etc. come off

shake sb/sth ↔ **up** *phr. v.* **1** if an unpleasant experience shakes someone up, s/he is shocked or upset by it: *The accident really shook her up.* **2** to make changes to an organization, country, etc. to make it more effective ➔ SHAKEUP

shake² *n.* [C] **1** an act of shaking: ***Give*** *the ketchup bottle* ***a*** *good* ***shake***. **2** a MILKSHAKE: *a vanilla shake*

shake·down /ˈʃeɪkdaʊn/ *n.* [C] **1** (informal) the act of getting money from someone by using threats **2** a final test of a vehicle or system for problems before it is put into general use, to find any remaining problems

shak·en /ˈʃeɪkən/ *v.* the past participle of SHAKE¹

shake·up /ˈʃeɪk-ʌp/ *n.* [C] a process in which an organization, company, etc. makes a lot of changes in a short time in order to be more effective

shak·y /ˈʃeɪki/ *adj.* **1** weak and unsteady because of illness, old age, or shock: *a shaky voice* | *She stood up, still feeling a little bit shaky.* **2** likely to fail or be unsuccessful: *a shaky marriage* | *The team got off to a* ***shaky start*** (=they started badly). **3** not solid or firm: *a shaky ladder*

shall /ʃəl; *strong* ʃæl/ *modal verb* **1** (formal) used in official documents to state an order, law, promise, etc.: *The right to a trial by jury shall be preserved.* **2 shall I/we?** used in order to ask a question, especially as a way of suggesting something: *Shall I turn on the air conditioner?* **3** (formal) used in order to say what will happen in the future: *I shall keep her picture always.* [ORIGIN: Old English *sceal*]

shallow

shal·low /ˈʃæloʊ/ *adj.* **1** measuring only a short distance from the top to the bottom (ANT) **deep**: *a shallow baking dish* | *The rice is planted in shallow water.* **2** (disapproving) not interested in or not showing any understanding of important or serious matters (ANT) **deep**: *a shallow argument* | *If he's only interested in your looks, that shows how shallow he is.*

sham¹ /ʃæm/ *n.* [singular] (disapproving) someone or something that is not what s/he is claimed to be: *Our marriage is a sham.*

sham² *adj.* made to appear real in order to deceive people: *sham jewelry*

sham·bles /ˈʃæmbəlz/ *n.* (informal) **be (in) a shambles a)** to be very badly organized, and fail completely: *The whole evening was a shambles – the food never even arrived.* **b)** to be very messy or damaged: *The apartment was a shambles.*

shame¹ /ʃeɪm/ *n.* [U] **1 it's/what a shame** (spoken) used in order to say that a situation is disappointing, and you wish things had happened differently: ***It's such a shame (that)*** *Margaret couldn't come.* | *"Our game was cancelled because of the rain." "Oh,* ***that's a shame.****"* | ***What a shame*** *we missed the wedding.* **2** the feeling of being guilty or embarrassed that you have after doing something that is wrong ➔ ASHAMED: *a deep sense of shame*

THESAURUS guilt, remorse ➔ GUILT

3 Shame on you! (spoken) used in order to tell someone that s/he should feel ashamed of something that s/he has done: *Shame on you, Patrick. I* *trusted you.* **4 put sb/sth to shame** to be so much better than someone or something else that it makes the other thing seem very bad or ordinary: *This party puts my little dinner to shame.* **5** loss of honor: *His behavior* ***brought shame on*** *the whole family.* | ***There's no shame in*** *finishing second* (=it should not make you feel ashamed).

shame² *v.* [T] to make someone feel ashamed: *It shames me to say it, but I lied.*

shame·ful /ˈʃeɪmfəl/ *adj.* so bad that someone should be ashamed: *a shameful secret* —**shamefully** *adv.*

shame·less /ˈʃeɪmlɪs/ *adj.* not seeming to be ashamed of your bad behavior, although other people think you should be ashamed: *a shameless liar* —**shamelessly** *adv.*

sham·poo¹ /ʃæmˈpu/ *n.* (plural **shampoos**) [C,U] a liquid soap used for washing your hair [ORIGIN: 1700—1800 Hindi *cāpo*, from *cāpna* "to press, shampoo"]

shampoo² *v.* [T] to wash something with shampoo: *She showered and* ***shampooed*** *her* ***hair***.

shan·ty /ˈʃænti/ *n.* (plural **shanties**) [C] a small building that has not been built very well

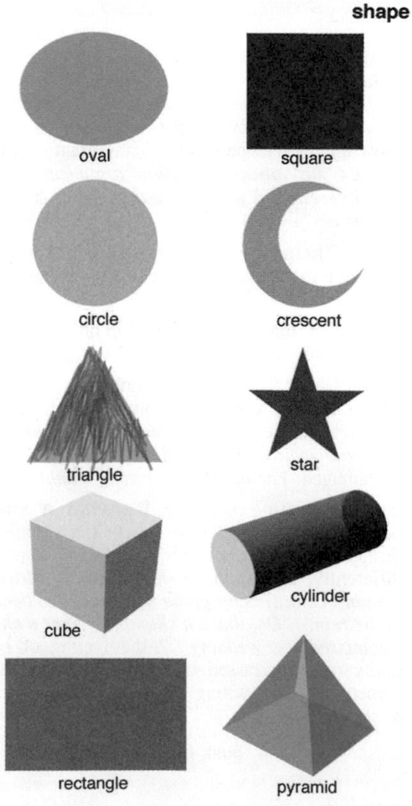

shape

oval square circle crescent triangle star cube cylinder rectangle pyramid

shape¹ /ʃeɪp/ *n.* **1** [C,U] the form that something has, for example round, square, TRIANGULAR, etc. → SHAPED: *a cake* ***in the shape of*** *a heart* | *What shape is your kitchen table?*

THESAURUS

Types of shapes

square – a shape with four straight sides that are equal in length and four angles of 90 degrees

circle – a round shape that is like an O

semicircle – half a circle

triangle – a shape with three straight sides and three angles

rectangle – a shape with four straight sides and four angles of 90 degrees

oval – a shape like a circle, but which is longer than it is wide

cylinder – an object in the shape of a tube

Describing types of shapes

square – shaped like a square: *a square box*

circular/round – shaped like a circle: *a circular table*

semicircular – shaped like a semicircle: *a semicircular arch above the door*

triangular – shaped like a triangle: *sails divided into triangular sections*

rectangular – shaped like a rectangle: *a simple rectangular building*

oval – shaped like an oval: *an oval swimming pool*

cylindrical – shaped like a cylinder: *The statue is on top of a tall cylindrical column.*

2 in good/bad/poor shape in good, bad, etc. condition or health: *The old car's still in good shape.* **3 in shape/out of shape** in a good or bad state of health or physical FITNESS: *I need to* ***get in shape***. **4 take shape** to develop into a clear and definite form **5** [C] something or someone that you cannot see clearly enough to recognize: *He was just a shape in the mist.*

shape² *v.* [T] **1** to influence something such as a belief or opinion and make it develop in a particular way: *an event that shaped public opinion* **2** to make something have a particular shape: ***Shape*** *the clay* ***into*** *small balls.*

shape up *phr. v.* (informal) **1** to improve your behavior or work: *You better shape up, John, or you're off the team.* **2** to make progress in a particular way: *The team is starting to shape up nicely.*

shaped /ʃeɪpt/ *adj.* having a particular shape: ***heart-shaped/star-shaped etc.*** *flowers* | *a trophy* ***shaped like*** *a football*

shape·ly /ˈʃeɪpli/ *adj.* having an attractive shape: *her long shapely legs*

share¹ /ʃɛr/ *v.* **1** [I,T] to have or use something with other people: *She* ***shares*** *an office* ***with*** *her boss.* | *There's only one book – we'll have to share.* **2** [T] to let someone have or use something that belongs to you: *Will you* ***share*** *your toys* ***with*** *Ronnie?* **3** [I,T] to divide something between two or more people: *I took the cookies to work to* ***share with*** *everybody.*

THESAURUS **give out, hand out/pass out, distribute** → GIVE[1]

4 [T] to have the same interest, opinion, etc. as someone else: *We **share** an **interest in** cooking.* 5 [T] to tell someone else about an idea, secret, problem, etc.: *Thank you for **sharing** your feelings **with** me.*

share² *n.* 1 [singular] the part of something that you own or are responsible for: *I paid my **share of** the bill and left.* | *Becky deserves a large share of the credit.* **2 have/get your (fair) share** to get as much of something as you could reasonably expect to have: *Rob's certainly **getting** his **share of** attention from the women.* | *Don't worry – you'll get your fair share.* 3 [C] ECONOMICS one of the equal parts into which the OWNERSHIP of a company is divided, that people can buy and sell → STOCK: *He wants to **buy/sell** 500 **shares** in CNN.* | ***shares in** General Electric*

share·crop·ping /ˈsɛrˌkrɑpɪŋ/ *n.* [U] a type of farming in which the farmer rents the land from the owner and is paid a share of the value of the crop —**sharecropper** *n.* [C]

share·hold·er /ˈʃɛrˌhoʊldɚ/ *n.* [C] ECONOMICS someone who owns STOCK

shark /ʃɑrk/ *n.* [C] a large sea fish with very sharp teeth

sharp¹ /ʃɑrp/ *adj.*
1 ABLE TO CUT something that is sharp has a very thin edge or point that can cut things easily ANT **dull, blunt**: *a sharp knife* | *The blade is **razor sharp*** (=very sharp).

sharp

sharp

dull

2 DIRECTION a sharp turn or bend changes direction suddenly: *a **sharp turn** in the road* | *Make a **sharp left/right** onto Grant Avenue.*
3 CHANGE a sharp increase, fall, etc. is very sudden and very big: *a **sharp rise/increase** in prices* | *a **sharp decline/drop** in the number of smokers*
4 DIFFERENCE clear and definite, so that there is no doubt: *The crowd's support was in **sharp contrast*** (=very different) *to the criticism he has received lately.* | *a **sharp difference** of opinion*
5 INTELLIGENT able to think and understand things very quickly: *She's a very sharp lawyer.* | *her **sharp wit***
6 PAIN sudden and very bad: *a **sharp pain** in my chest*
7 REMARK criticizing in a severe and angry way: *The proposal has drawn **sharp criticism** from the president.* | *He's known for his **sharp tongue**.*
8 EYES able to see or notice things very easily: *Lenny has **a sharp eye for detail**.*
9 CLOTHES attractive and stylish: *My grandfather was a sharp dresser* (=wore stylish clothes).
10 SOUNDS loud, short, and sudden: *a sharp cry*
11 PICTURE if an image or picture is sharp, you can see all the details very clearly: *a sharp picture on the TV*
12 MUSIC **a) F/C etc. sharp** ENG. LANG. ARTS a musical note that is a HALF STEP higher than the note F, C, etc., and is shown by the sign (#) → FLAT **b)** ENG. LANG. ARTS a musical note that is sharp is played or sung slightly higher than it should be → FLAT
13 TASTE having a strong taste: *sharp Cheddar cheese* [ORIGIN: Old English *scearp*] —**sharply** *adv.* —**sharpness** *n.* [U]

sharp² *adv.* **1 at 8 o'clock/two-thirty etc. sharp** at exactly 8:00, 2:30, etc.: *I expect you to be here at 10:30 sharp.* 2 ENG. LANG. ARTS if you sing or play music sharp, you sing or play slightly higher than the correct note so that it sounds bad

sharp·en /ˈʃɑrpən/ *v.* [I,T] to make something sharper, or become sharper: *sharpening a pencil*

sharp·en·er /ˈʃɑrpənɚ/ *n.* [C] a tool or machine that sharpens pencils, knives, etc.

shat·ter /ˈʃæt̬ɚ/ *v.* 1 [I,T] to break suddenly into very small pieces, or to make something do this: *My cup fell to the floor and shattered.*

THESAURUS **break, smash** → BREAK[1]

2 [T] to completely destroy someone's hopes, beliefs, or confidence: *A knee injury shattered his hopes of becoming a baseball player.*

shave¹ /ʃeɪv/ *v.* [I,T] to cut off hair very close to the skin, especially from your face or legs, using a RAZOR: *Brian had **cut** himself **shaving**.* | *She **shaves her legs**.* [ORIGIN: Old English *scafan*]

shave² *n.* 1 [C usually singular] an act of shaving: *I need a shave.* **2 a close shave** a situation in which you only just avoid an accident or something bad

shav·er /ˈʃeɪvɚ/ *n.* [C] a tool used for shaving

shav·ings /ˈʃeɪvɪŋz/ *n.* [plural] very thin pieces of something such as wood that are cut from a surface

shawl /ʃɔl/ *n.* [C] a piece of cloth that is worn around the shoulders or head for warmth, especially by women

s/he /ˌʃi ɚ ˈhi/ *pron.* used in writing when the subject of the sentence can be either male or female

she¹ /ʃi/ *pron.* a female person or animal who has been mentioned or is known about: *"Where's Kate?" "She went out to the car."* | *"I saw Suzy today." "Oh really, how is she?"* | *She's* (=she is) *a nurse.*

she² *n.* [singular] a female: *What a cute dog! Is it a she or a he?*

sheaf /ʃif/ *n.* (plural **sheaves** /ʃivz/) [C] several pieces of paper held or tied together

shear /ʃɪr/ *v.* (past tense **sheared**, past participle **sheared** *or* **shorn** /ʃɔrn/) [T] to cut the wool off a sheep

shears /ʃɪrz/ *n.* [plural] a tool like a large pair of scissors

sheath /ʃiθ/ *n.* (plural **sheaths** /ʃiðz, ʃiθs/) [C] a cover for the blade of a knife or sword

sheaves /ʃivz/ *n.* the plural of SHEAF

she'd /ʃid/ **1** the short form of "she had": *She'd forgotten to close the door.* **2** the short form of "she would": *She said she'd love to come.*

shed¹ /ʃɛd/ *n.* [C] a small building used especially for storing things: *a tool shed*

shed² *v.* (past tense and past participle **shed**) [T] **1** to get rid of something that you do not want: *I'd like to **shed** a few **pounds*** (=lose some weight) *before summer.* **2** BIOLOGY to allow something to fall off, especially as part of a natural process: *Snakes regularly shed their skin.* **3 shed tears** to cry: *She had not shed a single tear during the funeral.* **4 shed blood** to kill someone **5 shed light on sth** to make something easier to understand: *Recent research has shed light on the causes of the disease.*

sheen /ʃin/ *n.* [singular, U] a smooth shiny appearance

S

sheep /ʃip/ *n.* (plural **sheep**) [C] a farm animal that is kept for its wool and its meat [ORIGIN: Old English *sceap*] ➔ *see picture at* FARM¹

sheep·ish /ˈʃipɪʃ/ *adj.* uncomfortable or embarrassed because you have done something silly or wrong: *Renny apologized, looking sheepish.* —**sheepishly** *adv.*

sheer /ʃɪr/ *adj.* **1 sheer joy/luck/bliss etc.** joy, luck, etc. with no other feeling or quality mixed with it: *people dancing and singing with sheer joy* **2 the sheer size/weight/numbers etc.** used in order to emphasize that something is very big, heavy, etc.: *The most impressive thing about Alaska is its sheer size.* **3** a sheer drop, cliff, etc. is extremely steep **4** material that is sheer is fine or thin, so that you can almost see through it

sheet /ʃit/ *n.* [C] **1** a large piece of thin cloth that you put on a bed to lie on or under: *Have you **changed the sheets*** (=put clean sheets on the bed)*?* ➔ *see picture at* BED¹ **2** a thin flat piece of something such as paper, metal, or glass: *a **sheet of** paper* **3** a large flat area of something such as ice or water that is spread over a surface: *The road was covered with a **sheet of** ice.*

sheik, sheikh /ʃik, ʃeɪk/ *n.* [C] **1** an Arab chief or prince **2** a Muslim religious teacher or leader

shelf /ʃɛlf/ *n.* (plural **shelves** /ʃɛlvz/) [C] a long flat board attached to a wall, in a frame, etc., that you can put things on: *shelves of books* | *Could you get me that bowl off the **top shelf**?* [ORIGIN: 1300—1400 Middle Low German *schelf*]

she'll /ʃil/ the short form of "she will"

shell¹ /ʃɛl/ *n.* [C] **1** the hard outer part that covers and protects nuts, eggs, seeds, and some types of animals: *sea shells* | *peanut shells* **2** a metal tube containing a bullet and an explosive substance, which is fired from a large gun [ORIGIN: Old English *sciell*]

shell² *v.* [T] to fire shells at something, using a large gun

shell out *phr. v.* (informal) to pay money for something, often when you do not want to: *We had to shell out over $400 to get the car fixed.*

shellfish

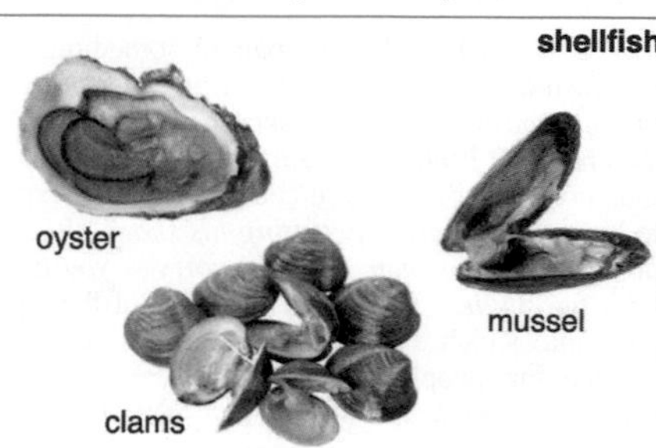

shell·fish /ˈʃɛlˌfɪʃ/ *n.* (plural **shellfish**) [C,U] a small sea or water animal that has a shell, or this animal eaten as a food

shel·ter¹ /ˈʃɛltɚ/ *n.* **1** [C,U] a place with a roof over it that protects you from danger or the weather, or the protection that it gives: *a bomb shelter* | *a bus shelter* | *The family **took shelter** in the cellar when the tornado hit.* **2** [C] a place where people or animals can go if they have no home or are in danger from someone who treats them badly: *a shelter for battered women* **3** [U] a place to live, considered as one of the basic needs of life: *providing food and shelter for the homeless*

shelter² *v.* **1** [T] to provide a place where someone is protected from the weather or from danger: *families who **sheltered** Jews **from** the Nazis*

THESAURUS protect, guard, shield, give/offer/provide protection ➔ PROTECT

2 [I] to stay somewhere in order to be protected from bad weather or danger: *People were sheltering in doorways, under bridges, anywhere.*

shel·tered /ˈʃɛltɚd/ *adj.* **1** protected from anything that might hurt, upset, or shock you: *Gina had a sheltered childhood.* **2** protected from the weather: *a sheltered valley*

shelve /ʃɛlv/ *v.* [T] to decide not to continue with a plan, although you might continue with it later: *The project has been shelved due to lack of funding.*

shelves /ʃɛlvz/ *n.* the plural of SHELF

shelv·ing /ˈʃɛlvɪŋ/ *n.* [U] a set of shelves, or the material used for them

she·nan·i·gans /ʃəˈnænɪgənz/ *n.* [plural] (informal) tricks or slightly dishonest behavior

shep·herd /ˈʃɛpɚd/ *n.* [C] someone whose job is to take care of sheep

sher·bet /ˈʃɚbət/ *n.* [U] a frozen sweet food made from water, fruit, sugar, and milk

sher·iff /ˈʃɛrɪf/ *n.* [C] a chief police officer in a COUNTY who is elected [ORIGIN: Old English *scirgerefa*, from *scir* "area with its own government" + *gerefa* "person in charge of an area"]

sher·ry /'ʃɛri/ *n.* (plural **sherries**) [C,U] a strong Spanish wine, or a glass of this drink [ORIGIN: 1500—1600 *sherris* "sherry" (16—18 centuries), from *Xeres* (now *Jerez*), city in southwestern Spain]

she's /ʃiz/ **1** the short form of "she is": *She's my little sister.* **2** the short form of "she has": *She's invited us to a party.*

shield[1] /ʃild/ *n.* [C] **1** something that protects someone or something from being hurt or damaged: *police carrying riot shields* | *the heat shield on a rocket* **2** a broad piece of metal or leather used in past times by soldiers to protect themselves in battle

shield[2] *v.* [T] to protect someone or something from being hurt, damaged, or upset: *Of course, you try to **shield** your children **from** bad influences.* | *a hat to **shield** your face **from** the sun*

THESAURUS **protect, guard, safeguard, give/offer/provide protection** → PROTECT

shift[1] /ʃɪft/ (Ac) *v.* [I,T] **1** to change your opinion or attitude: *Washington's policy toward Taiwan appears to have shifted.* **2** to move from one place or position to another, or make something do this: *Jan shifted uncomfortably in her seat.* | *Amos shifted his chair around to get a better look.* **3** to change the GEARS when you are driving: *I pulled away and **shifted into** second gear.*

shift[2] (Ac) *n.* [C] **1** a change in the way most people think about something, or in the way something is done: *Polls show a **shift in** public opinion.* | *the **shift from** communism to capitalism* **2** one of the periods during each day and night when workers in a factory, hospital, etc. are at work: *Lou's on the **night/day shift** this week.* → GEAR SHIFT

shift·less /'ʃɪftlɪs/ *adj.* lazy and not at all interested in working

THESAURUS **lazy, idle, indolent, slack, slothful** → LAZY

shift·y /'ʃɪfti/ *adj.* someone who is shifty looks dishonest

shim·mer /'ʃɪmɚ/ *v.* [I] to shine with a soft light that seems to shake slightly: *a lake shimmering in the moonlight* —**shimmer** *n.* [singular]

THESAURUS **shine, gleam, glint, glisten** → SHINE[1]

shin /ʃɪn/ *n.* [C] the front part of your leg between your knee and your foot → *see picture on page A16*

shine[1] /ʃaɪn/ *v.* (past tense and past participle **shone** /ʃoʊn/, present participle **shining**) **1** [I] to produce light: ***The Sun** was **shining**.* | *The bright TV lights were **shining in** her eyes.*

THESAURUS

flash – to shine brightly for a very short time: *Lightning flashed across the sky.*
flicker – to shine with an unsteady light: *The candle flickered and went out.*
twinkle – to shine in the dark but not very brightly or continuously: *stars twinkling in the sky*
glow – to shine with a warm soft light: *I could see a lamp glowing in the window.*
sparkle – to shine with many small bright points of light: *diamonds sparkling in the light*
shimmer – to shine with a soft light that seems to shake slightly: *The lake shimmered in the moonlight.*
gleam – if something smooth and clean gleams, it shines: *The silverware had been polished until it gleamed.*
glint – if something that is shiny glints, it reflects light very strongly: *The Sun glinted off the windows.*
glisten – to shine and look wet or oily: *Tears glistened on her cheeks.*

2 [I] to look bright and smooth: *Dan polished the car until it shone.* **3** (past tense and past participle **shined**) [T] to make something bright by rubbing it: *When's the last time you **shined** your **shoes**?* **4** [T] to point a light toward a particular place or in a particular direction: *Shine the flashlight over here.* **5** [I] if your eyes or face shine, they show you are happy **6** [I] to be very good at something: *The concert will give young musicians a chance to shine.* [ORIGIN: Old English *scinan*]

shine[2] *n.* [singular, U] the brightness that something has when light shines on it: *Lucy's dark hair seemed to have lost its shine.*

shin·gle /'ʃɪŋgəl/ *n.* [C,U] one of many thin pieces of wood or other material used for covering a roof or a wall

shin·ny /'ʃɪni/ *v.* (**shinnied**, **shinnies**) **shinny up/down** (informal) to climb quickly up or down a tree or a pole

shin·y /'ʃaɪni/ *adj.* (comparative **shinier**, superlative **shiniest**) bright and smooth looking: *shiny hair* | *shiny leather boots*

ship[1] /ʃɪp/ *n.* [C] **1** a large boat used for carrying people and things on the ocean: *a cruise ship* | *Supplies came **by ship**.*

THESAURUS

Ships that carry people
cruise ship, liner, ferry

Ships that carry goods
freighter, tanker, barge

Fighting ships
aircraft carrier, battleship, cruiser, submarine, warship

2 a space vehicle: *a rocket ship* [ORIGIN: Old English *scip*]

ship[2] *v.* (**shipped**, **shipping**) [T] **1** to deliver goods: *The books will be shipped out to you within*

S

24 hours. **2** to send or carry something by sea

ship·load /'ʃɪploʊd/ *n.* [C] the number of people or things a ship can carry

ship·ment /'ʃɪpmənt/ *n.* [C,U] a load of goods being delivered, or the act of sending them: *a **shipment of** grain | The goods are ready for shipment.*

ship·ping /'ʃɪpɪŋ/ *n.* **1 shipping and handling** the price charged for delivering goods: *Please add $2.95 to cover **shipping and handling**.* **2** [U] ships considered as a group, or anything that is related to business done by ships: *The canal has been closed to shipping.*

ship·wreck[1] /'ʃɪp-rɛk/ *n.* [C,U] the destruction of a ship by a storm or an accident, or a ship that has been destroyed in this way: *survivors of a shipwreck*

shipwreck[2] *v.* **be shipwrecked** to have been in a ship that has been destroyed by a storm or an accident

ship·yard /'ʃɪp-yard/ *n.* [C] a place where ships are built or repaired

shirk /ʃɚk/ *v.* [I,T] (formal) to avoid doing something you should do: *parents who **shirk** their **duties/responsibilities** towards their children*

shirt /ʃɚt/ *n.* [C] a piece of clothing that covers the upper part of your body and your arms, and has a collar and usually buttons down the front → BLOUSE, T-SHIRT: *She was wearing a white silk shirt. | I have to wear a **shirt and tie** to work.* [ORIGIN: Old English *scyrte*] → *see picture at* CLOTHES

shirt·sleeves /'ʃɚtslivz/ *n.* **in (your) shirtsleeves** wearing a shirt but no JACKET

shish ke·bab /'ʃɪʃ kə,bab/ *n.* [C] small pieces of meat and sometimes vegetables, cooked on a stick

shiv·er[1] /'ʃɪvɚ/ *v.* [I] to shake slightly because you are cold or frightened: *Come inside – you're shivering.*

> THESAURUS **shake, tremble, wobble, quiver** → SHAKE[1]

shiver[2] *n.* [C] a shaking movement of your body that happens when you are cold or afraid: *A **shiver ran down** my **spine*** (=I felt afraid). —**shivery** *adj.*

shoal /ʃoʊl/ *n.* [C] BIOLOGY a large group of fish that swim together

> THESAURUS **group, flock, herd, school, pack, litter** → GROUP[1]

shock[1] /ʃak/ *n.* **1** [C usually singular] an unexpected and unpleasant event or piece of news that makes you extremely upset: *Rob's death **came as a** complete **shock** to us.* **2** [singular,U] the feeling of surprise and DISBELIEF you have when something unexpected and unpleasant happens: *She looked like she was **in shock**. | **the shock of** seeing someone in such pain* **3** [C] a sudden painful feeling caused by a flow of electricity passing through your body: *Ow! The toaster **gave me a shock**.* **4** [U] a medical condition in which someone is very weak, often after an unpleasant experience: *The crash victims are **suffering from shock**. | He is clearly **in a state of shock**.* **5** [C] EARTH SCIENCES SHOCK WAVE **6** [C] a SHOCK ABSORBER [ORIGIN: (1) French *choc*, from *choquer* "to strike against"]

shock[2] *v.* **1** [I,T] to make someone feel very surprised, and usually upset or offended: *We were **shocked to hear** of his arrest.* **2** [T] to give someone an electric shock —**shocked** *adj.*

'shock ab,sorber *n.* [C] a piece of equipment connected to each wheel of a vehicle to make it travel smoothly over uneven ground

shock·ing /'ʃakɪŋ/ *adj.* very offensive or upsetting: *a shocking crime*

> THESAURUS **surprising, astonishing, astounding, staggering, stunning** → SURPRISING

'shock wave *n.* [C] **1** a strong feeling of shock that people have when something bad happens without warning: *The news **sent shock waves through** the world's stock markets.* **2** EARTH SCIENCES a strong movement of air, heat, or the earth from an explosion, EARTHQUAKE, etc.

shod[1] /ʃad/ *adj.* (literary) wearing shoes

shod[2] *v.* the past tense and past participle of SHOE

shod·dy /'ʃadi/ *adj.* **1** badly or cheaply made, or not done well: *shoddy goods* **2** unfair and dishonest: *He treated me in a pretty shoddy way.* [ORIGIN: 1800—1900 *shoddy* "cloth made from reused wool" (19—20 centuries)]

shoes

shoe[1] /ʃu/ *n.* [C] **1** something that you wear to cover your feet, that is made of leather or some other strong material: ***a pair of shoes** | high-heeled shoes* **2 be in sb's shoes** to be in the situation that someone else is in: ***I wouldn't like to be in** his **shoes** when his wife finds out what happened.* [ORIGIN: Old English *scoh*]

shoe[2] *v.* (past tense and past participle **shod** /ʃɑd/) [T] to put a HORSESHOE (=curved piece of metal) on a horse's foot

shoe·horn /ˈʃuhɔrn/ *n.* [C] a curved piece of plastic or metal that you use to help you put a shoe on easily

shoe·lace /ˈʃuleɪs/ *n.* [C] a thin piece of string or leather that you use to tie your shoes (SYN) **lace**

shoe·string /ˈʃuˌstrɪŋ/ *n.* **on a shoestring** done or made without spending very much money: *a movie made on a shoestring*

shone /ʃoun/ *v.* the past tense and past participle of SHINE[1]

shoo /ʃu/ *interjection* said in order to tell an annoying child or animal to go away —**shoo** *v.* [T]: *Aunt Betty shooed us out of the kitchen.*

ˈshoo-in *n.* [C usually singular] (informal) someone who is expected to win an election or race easily: *He looked like a shoo-in to win the election.*

shook /ʃʊk/ *v.* the past tense of SHAKE[1]

ˌshook-ˈup *adj.* [not before noun] (spoken) very frightened, shocked, or upset because of something that has happened

shoot[1] /ʃut/ *v.* (past tense and past participle **shot** /ʃɑt/)
1 GUN [I,T] to fire a gun at someone, or kill or injure someone with a gun: *Stop or I'll shoot!* | *She pulled out a gun and shot him.* | *Someone on the roof was* ***shooting at*** *her.* | *He had been shot in the leg while trying to escape.* | *One police officer was* ***shot dead*** *in the incident.*
2 MOVE QUICKLY [I,T] to move quickly in a particular direction, or to make something move in this way: *The fountain shoots water 20 feet into the air.* | *A sharp pain suddenly* ***shot through*** *his right arm.*
3 PHOTO/MOVIE [I,T] to take photographs or make a movie: *The movie was shot in Rome.*
4 SPORTS [I,T] to throw, kick, or hit a ball toward the place where you can make points: *We were waiting for him to shoot.*
5 shoot (spoken) used in order to tell someone to start speaking: *"I've got a question." "Okay, shoot."*
6 shoot the breeze (informal) to have a friendly conversation about unimportant things: *Cal and I were sitting on the porch, shooting the breeze.*
7 shoot your mouth off (informal) to talk too much, especially about your opinions or a secret: *Don't go shooting your mouth off about this.*
shoot sb/sth ↔ **down** *phr. v.*
1 to destroy an enemy airplane while it is flying: *The plane was shot down over the ocean.*
2 to say that what someone suggests is wrong or stupid: *Terry's boss shot down all her ideas.*
shoot for sth *phr. v.* (informal)
to try to achieve something: *Okay, we'll shoot for 1:30* (=try to do something by then).
shoot up *phr. v.*
to quickly increase in number, size, or amount: *Prices shot up by 60%.*

shoot[2] *n.* [C] **1** an occasion when someone takes photographs or makes a movie: *a* ***photo shoot*** **2** BIOLOGY a new part of a plant

shoot[3] *interjection* said when you are annoyed, disappointed, or surprised: *Oh shoot, I forgot to go to the bank.*

shoot·ing /ˈʃut̬ɪŋ/ *n.* [C] a situation in which someone is killed or injured by a gun

ˌshooting ˈstar *n.* [C] PHYSICS a piece of rock or metal from space that burns brightly as it falls toward the Earth

shop[1] /ʃɑp/ *n.* **1** [C] a small store that sells only a particular type of goods: *a card shop* **2** [C] a place where things are made or repaired: *a bicycle repair shop* **3** [U] a subject taught in school, in which students use tools and machinery to make or repair things [ORIGIN: Old English *sceoppa* "stall"] → **set up shop** *at* SET UP

shop[2] *v.* (**shopped**, **shopping**) [I] to go to one or more stores to buy things: *I was out* ***shopping for*** *food.* —**shopper** *n.* [C]: *Christmas shoppers*
shop around *phr. v.* to compare the price and quality of different things before you decide which to buy

shop·lift /ˈʃɑpˌlɪft/ *v.* [I,T] to take something from a store without paying for it —**shoplifting** *n.* [U] —**shoplifter** *n.* [C]

THESAURUS steal, burglarize, pilfer → STEAL[1]

THESAURUS offender, thief, robber, burglar, pickpocket → CRIMINAL[2]

shop·ping /ˈʃɑpɪŋ/ *n.* **1** [U] the activity of going to stores to buy things: *I've got to* ***do some shopping*** (=buy the food, etc. that you use regularly). | *Christmas shopping* **2 go shopping** to go to stores to buy things, often for enjoyment **3** [singular] the things you have bought, usually food: *The boys helped me bring the shopping in from the car.*

ˈshopping ˌcenter *n.* [C] a group of stores built together in one area

ˈshopping mall *n.* [C] a MALL

shore[1] /ʃɔr/ *n.* [C,U] EARTH SCIENCES the land along the edge of a large area of water: *We could see a boat about a mile from shore.* | *The cabin stood* ***on the shores of*** *Lake Erie.* [ORIGIN: 1300—1400 Middle Dutch, Middle Low German *schore*] → *see picture on page A24*

THESAURUS

coast – the land next to the ocean: *The island is 15 miles off the coast of Newfoundland.*
beach – an area of sand or small stones at the edge of an ocean or lake: *We spent the day at the beach.* | *Let's take a walk on the beach at sunset.* | *Palm Beach, Florida*
seashore – the area of land next to the ocean: *hotels directly on the seashore*

bank – the edge of a river: *the banks of the Mississippi river*

shore² *v.*
shore sth ↔ **up** *phr. v.* **1** to support a wall with large pieces of wood, metal, etc. to stop it from falling down **2** to help or support something that is likely to fail or is not working well: *The money is needed to shore up the failing bank.*

shore·line /ˈʃɔrlaɪn/ *n.* [C,U] EARTH SCIENCES the land on the edge of a lake, river, or ocean (SYN) **coastline**: *the island's rocky shoreline* ➔ *see picture on page A24*

shorn /ʃɔrn/ *v.* a past participle of SHEAR

short¹ /ʃɔrt/ *adj.*
1 LENGTH/DISTANCE not very long in length or far in distance (ANT) **long**: *His hair is very short.* | *a short skirt* | *It's only a* ***short distance*** *from here to the river.*
2 TIME happening for only a little time or for less time than usual (ANT) **long**: *a short meeting* | *I've just been living here* ***a short time.*** | ***Life's too short*** *to stay angry.*

THESAURUS

Lasting only a short time
brief – lasting only a short time, especially because there is not much time available: *We made a brief visit to the Museum of Modern Art.*
quick – doing something very quickly, especially because you are in a hurry: *He had a quick shower and left for work.*
cursory – a cursory look or check is done very quickly, without much attention to details: *The officer took a cursory look inside the trunk.*
temporary – something that is **temporary** is expected to continue for only a short time, and will not be permanent: *I'm sure it's only a temporary problem.*
ephemeral (formal) – existing only for a short time, and changing quickly: *Fashion is very ephemeral.*
using only a few words
brief – using only a few words: *He left a brief note saying that he would be late.*
concise – short and clear, and with no unnecessary words: *Try to keep your answers as concise as possible.*
succinct – expressing something well but with very few words: *His instructions were always short and succinct.*
curt – replying in very few words, in a way that seems rude: *I received a rather curt letter saying that my application had been unsuccessful.*

3 PERSON not as tall as average height (ANT) **tall**: *a short fat man*
4 NOT ENOUGH not having enough of something you need: *I'm* ***short of cash*** *right now.* | *I'm five dollars short.*
5 on short notice with very little warning that something is going to happen: *Sorry – we can't come on such short notice.*
6 in the short run/term during a short period of time after the present: *The crisis will affect the peace process, at least in the short term.*
7 be short for sth to be a shorter way of saying a name: *Her name is Becky, short for Rebecca.*
8 short of breath unable to breathe easily, especially because of being unhealthy
9 be in short supply to not be available in large quantities: *Fruit and sugar were in short supply then.*
10 be short with sb to speak to someone in a rude or unfriendly way: *Sorry I was so short with you on the phone.*
11 in short order very quickly: *His demands were met in short order.*
12 get the short end of the stick (informal) to be given something difficult or bad to do, especially when other people have been given something better [ORIGIN: Old English *scort*] —**shortness** *n.* [U]

short² *adv.* **short of (doing) sth** without actually doing something: *They've cut the budget and the workforce – everything short of canceling the project altogether.* ➔ **cut sth short** *at* CUT¹, **fall short (of sth)** *at* FALL¹, **be running short of sth** *at* RUN¹, **stop short of sth** *at* STOP¹

short³ *n.* **1 shorts** [plural] **a)** short pants that end at or above the knees: *a* ***pair of shorts*** **b)** loose underwear for men (SYN) **boxer shorts** **2 in short** used when you want to say the most important point in a few words: *In short, I don't think we can do it.* **3 for short** as a shorter way of saying a name: *It's called the Message Handling System – MHS for short.* **4** [C] (informal) a short movie that is shown before the main movie in a theater **5** [C] (informal) a SHORT CIRCUIT

short⁴ *v.* [I,T] (informal) to have a bad electrical connection that makes a machine stop working correctly, or to make something do this

short·age /ˈʃɔrtɪdʒ/ *n.* [C,U] a situation in which there is not enough of something that people need: *food shortages* | *a* ***shortage of*** *medicine*

short·bread /ˈʃɔrt˺brɛd/ *n.* [U] a hard sweet cookie made with a lot of butter

short·cake /ˈʃɔrt˺ˌkeɪk/ *n.* [U] cake over which a sweet fruit mixture is poured: *strawberry shortcake*

ˌshort-ˈchange *v.* [T] **1** to treat someone unfairly by not giving him/her what s/he deserves: *The miners felt short-changed by the new contract.* **2** to give back too little money to someone who has paid you for something

ˌshort ˈcircuit *n.* [C] the failure of an electrical system caused by bad wires or a fault in a connection in the wires

short·com·ing /ˈʃɔrt˺ˌkʌmɪŋ/ *n.* [C usually plural] a fault in something or someone, that makes it, him, or her less effective: *the* ***shortcomings of*** *the new law* | ***shortcomings in*** *his research*

ˌshort ˈcut *n.* [C] **1** a quicker more direct way of going somewhere: *Let's* ***take a short cut*** *across the* park. **2** a quicker way of doing something: *There are no **short cuts to** finding a job.*

short·en /ˈʃɔrtˀn/ *v.* [I,T] to become shorter, or to make something shorter (ANT) **lengthen**: *Her name is often shortened to Pat.* | *It was fall, and the days had begun to shorten.*

short·en·ing /ˈʃɔrtˀn-ɪŋ, -nɪŋ/ *n.* [U] fat made from vegetable oil that you mix with flour when making PASTRY

short·fall /ˈʃɔrtfɔl/ *n.* [C] the difference between the amount you have and the amount you need or expect: ***shortfalls in** the city's budget*

short·hand /ˈʃɔrthænd/ *n.* [U] a fast method of writing using special signs and short forms of words: *taking notes **in shorthand***

ˈshort list *n.* [C] a list of the most appropriate people for a job, chosen from all the people who were first considered for it

short-lived /ˌʃɔrtˈlɪvd◂/ *adj.* existing only a short time: *a short-lived fashion*

short·ly /ˈʃɔrtli/ *adv.* **1** very soon: *I expect him home shortly.* | *The president left for Washington shortly before noon.*

THESAURUS soon, in a minute, any minute now, before long, presently → SOON

2 speaking in a way that is not patient: *"Yes, yes, I understand," he said shortly.*

ˌshort-order ˈcook *n.* [C] someone in a restaurant kitchen who makes the food that can be prepared easily or quickly

ˌshort-ˈrange *adj.* [only before noun] short-range weapons are designed to travel or be used over a short distance

short·sight·ed, short-sighted /ˌʃɔrtˈsaɪṭɪd◂/ *adj.* **1** not considering the future effects of something: *The company's decision was short-sighted.* | *the shortsighted option* **2** NEARSIGHTED

short·stop /ˈʃɔrtstɑp/ *n.* [C,U] the position in baseball between SECOND BASE and THIRD BASE, or the person who plays this position

ˌshort ˈstory *n.* [C] ENG. LANG. ARTS a short written story, usually about imaginary events

ˌshort-ˈterm *adj.* continuing for only a short time into the future (ANT) **long-term**: *a short-term solution* → **in the long/short term** *at* TERM[1]

ˈshort wave *n.* [U] a range of radio waves used for broadcasting around the world

shot[1] /ʃɑt/ *n.* [C]
1 GUN an act of firing a gun, or the sound that this makes: *We heard a shot.* | *He quickly **fired** three **shots**.*
2 SPORTS an attempt to throw, kick, or hit the ball toward the place where you can get a point: ***Nice shot!*** | *Shaw **made the shot** and turned to run down the court.*
3 MOVIES/PHOTOGRAPHS a) a photograph: *a beautiful **shot of** the countryside around Prague* **b)** the view of something in a movie, television program, or photograph: *a **close-up shot*** | *In the **opening shot**, we see a man walking down a street.*
4 ATTEMPT (informal) an attempt to do something or achieve something: *Marty always wanted to **take a shot at** acting.* | *I'll **give it** my **best shot*** (=try as hard as possible).
5 DRINK a small amount of a strong alcoholic drink: *a **shot of** whiskey*
6 DRUG the act of putting medicine into your body using a needle: *Have you **had** your tetanus **shot**?*
7 a shot in the dark an attempt to guess something without having any facts or definite ideas: *My answer to the last question was a complete shot in the dark.*
8 like a shot very quickly: *He jumped up like a shot and ran to the door.* → BIG SHOT, LONG SHOT

shot[2] *adj.* **be shot** (informal) to be in bad condition or useless: *This battery is shot – do we have another one?*

shot[3] *v.* the past tense and past participle of SHOOT[1]

shot·gun /ˈʃɑtˀgʌn/ *n.* [C] a long gun, used for shooting animals and birds

ˌshotgun ˈwedding *n.* [C] a wedding that has to take place immediately because the woman is going to have a baby

ˈshot put *n.* **the shot put** a sport in which you throw a heavy metal ball as far as you can —**shot putter** *n.* [C]

should /ʃəd; *strong* ʃʊd/ *modal verb* **1** used when giving or asking for advice or an opinion: *You **should have** called me right away.* | *Should I wear my gray dress?* | *Children shouldn't* (=should not) *take candy from strangers.* **2** used in order to say that you expect something to happen or be true: *Yvonne **should be** back by 8:00.* | *It should be a nice day tomorrow.* **3** (formal) used like "if" in formal CONDITIONAL sentences that use the present tense: *Should you decide to accept the offer, please return the enclosed form.*

shoul·der[1] /ˈʃoʊldɚ/ *n.* [C] **1** one of the two parts of the body at each side of the neck where the arm is connected: *Andy put his arm around his wife's shoulders.* | *When we asked him what was wrong, he just **shrugged his shoulders*** (=raised them to show that he did not know or care). → *see picture on page A16* **2 watch/look over sb's shoulder** to watch carefully what someone is doing, sometimes so that you can criticize him/her: *I can't work at the computer when someone is watching over my shoulder.* **3** the part of a shirt, coat, etc. that covers your shoulders **4 a shoulder to cry on** someone who gives you sympathy: *Diane's always there when I **need a shoulder to cry on**.* **5** an area of ground beside a road where drivers can stop their cars if they are having trouble

shoulder[2] *v.* **1 shoulder the responsibility/blame/cost etc.** to accept a difficult or unpleasant

S

RESPONSIBILITY, duty, etc.: *Carrie shouldered the burden of taking care of three young kids alone.* **2 shoulder your way through/into etc.** to move through a large crowd of people by pushing with your shoulders: *He shouldered his way through the crowd.*

'shoulder bag *n.* [C] a woman's PURSE that hangs from the shoulder by a long piece of material

'shoulder blade *n.* [C] BIOLOGY one of the two flat bones on each side of your back ➔ *see picture on page A16*

should·n't /'ʃʊdnt/ *modal verb* the short form of "should not"

should've /'ʃʊdəv/ *modal verb* the short form of "should have"

shout¹ /ʃaʊt/ *v.* [I,T] to say something very loudly: *"Get out of the way!" she shouted.* | *I wish he'd stop* ***shouting at*** *the children.* | *They* ***shouted for*** *help.*

THESAURUS

call (out) – to shout in order to get someone's attention
scream – to shout in a very loud high voice because you are so angry, excited, etc. that you cannot control your voice
shriek – to shout in a loud high unpleasant voice, because you are frightened, angry, excited, etc.
yell – to shout, for example because you are angry or excited, or because you want to get someone's attention
cry out – to make a sudden loud noise, for example when you are suddenly hurt or afraid
raise your voice – to say something more loudly than usual, often because you are angry about something
cheer – to shout to show that you like a team, performance, etc.
bellow – to shout loudly in a deep voice
holler (informal) – to shout loudly ➔ SCREAM¹

shout sb ↔ **down** *phr. v.* to shout so that someone who is speaking cannot be heard: *She tried to argue, but was quickly shouted down.*

shout sth ↔ **out** *phr. v.* to say something suddenly in a loud voice: *Don't shout out the answer.*

shout² *n.* **1** [C] a loud call that expresses anger, excitement, etc.: *She heard a shout from upstairs.* **2 give sb a shout** (spoken) to go and find someone and tell him/her something: *Give me a shout if you need any help.*

shove /ʃʌv/ *v.* **1** [I,T] to push someone or something in a rough or careless way, using your hands or shoulders: *People were* ***pushing and shoving*** *to get a better view.* | *They searched him and shoved him into a cell.*

THESAURUS **push, poke, nudge, elbow** ➔ PUSH¹

2 [T] (informal) to put something somewhere quickly and carelessly: *Just shove those papers into the drawer for now.*

THESAURUS

stick – to put something somewhere in a careless way: *Just stick the books on the table for now.*
thrust – to push something somewhere suddenly or forcefully: *David thrust his hands into his pockets.*
dump – to drop or put something somewhere in a careless way: *Don't just dump your coat on the floor!*
cram/jam – to force a lot of something into a small space: *Josh crammed his books and coat into his locker.*

3 shove it (spoken) an impolite phrase said when you are very annoyed or angry and you do not want to talk to someone any longer: *They can take their job and shove it.* —**shove** *n.* [C]

shove off *phr. v.* to push a boat away from the land, usually with a pole

shov·el¹ /'ʃʌvəl/ *n.* [C] a tool with a long handle, used for digging or moving earth, stones, etc.

shovel² *v.* **1** [I,T] to dig or move earth, stones, etc. with a shovel: *I'm going out to* ***shovel the driveway/sidewalk*** (=shovel snow from the driveway or sidewalk). **2 shovel sth into/onto sth** to put something into a place quickly: *He sat at the table shoveling his dinner into his mouth.*

show¹ /ʃoʊ/ *v.* (past tense **showed**, past participle **shown** /ʃoʊn/)

1 LET SB SEE [T] to let someone see something: *Karen showed us her wedding pictures.* | *I* ***showed*** *the letter* ***to*** *Ruth.*

2 MAKE STH CLEAR [T] to make it clear that something is true or exists by providing facts or information: *The report shows a rise in employment.* | *Studies have* ***shown (that)*** *consumers are buying more organic produce.* | *Applicants must* ***show how*** *their qualifications make them suitable for the job.*

THESAURUS **demonstrate, indicate, suggest, prove, establish** ➔ DEMONSTRATE

3 HOW YOU FEEL [T] to show how you feel by the way that you behave: *Alan tried not to show his disappointment.*

4 EXPLAIN STH [T] to tell someone how to do something or where something is: *I'll show you what to do.* | *My grandma* ***showed*** *me* ***how to*** *make cornbread.*

THESAURUS **explain, tell, demonstrate** ➔ EXPLAIN

5 GUIDE SB [T] to go with someone and guide him/her to a place: *Did Rachel show you where to leave your coat?* | *I'll* ***show*** *you* ***the way.***

THESAURUS **lead, guide, escort, usher** ➔ LEAD¹

6 CAN BE SEEN [I,T] if something shows, people can see or notice it easily: *His anger showed on his face.* | *Ellen was tired, and **it showed**.*
7 MOVIE [I,T] if a movie or television program is shown, people are able to see it at a theater or on television: *The movie was shown on HBO.*
8 show signs of sth used in order to say that something is starting to become noticeable: *At 65, Nelson **shows no signs of** slowing down.* | *Data from the second quarter **showed some signs of** improvement.*
9 INFORMATION [T] if a picture, map, etc. shows something, you can see it on the picture, map, etc.: *a map showing all the stations*
10 have something/nothing to show for sth to have achieved something or nothing as a result of your efforts: *I've been practicing so hard, and I still have nothing to show for it.* [ORIGIN: Old English *sceawian* "to look, look at, see"]

show sb **around** *phr. v.*
to go with someone around a place and show him/her what is important, interesting, etc.: *His wife showed us around the house.*

show off *phr. v.*
1 (disapproving) to try to make people admire your abilities, achievements, or possessions: *Ignore him. He's just showing off.*
2 show sth ↔ **off** to show something to many people because you are very proud of it: *Jen proudly showed off her engagement ring.*

show up *phr. v.*
1 (informal) to arrive at the place where someone is waiting for you: *It was 9:20 when he finally showed up.*
2 to be easy to see or notice: *The bacteria showed up under the microscope.*
3 show sb ↔ **up** to do something that embarrasses someone or make him/her seem stupid when other people are there

show² *n.* [C] **1** a performance in a theater or on radio or television: *a new show opening on Broadway* | *a popular TV show* ➔ TELEVISION **2** a collection of things for the public to look at: *the spring flower show* | *a Paris **fashion show*** **3 a show of sth** something that someone does in order to make a particular feeling or quality clear to someone else: *The army marched through the town **in a show of force**.* **4 make a show of sth** (disapproving) to do something in a very clear way so that other people notice that you are doing it: *She made a show of interest.* **5 on show** if something is on show, it is in a place where it can be seen by the public: *The photographs will be on show until the end of the month.* **6 let's get this show on the road** (spoken) said when you want to tell people it is time to start working or start a trip

ˌshow and ˈtell *n.* [U] an activity for children in which they bring an object to school and tell the other children about it

show biz /ˈʃoʊ bɪz/ *n.* [U] (informal) SHOW BUSINESS

ˈshow ˌbusiness *n.* [U] the entertainment industry

show·case /ˈʃoʊkeɪs/ *n.* [C] an event or situation that is designed to show the good qualities of a person, organization, etc.: *a **showcase for** new musical talent* —**showcase** *v.* [T]

show·down /ˈʃoʊdaʊn/ *n.* [C] a meeting, argument, fight, etc. that will settle a disagreement or competition that has continued for a long time: *a **showdown between** the top two teams in the league*

show·er¹ /ˈʃaʊɚ/ *n.* [C] **1** a thing that you stand under to wash your whole body: *The phone always rings when I'm **in the shower**.* **2** an act of washing your body while standing under the shower: *Hurry up! I want to **take a shower** too.* **3** a short period of rain: *Showers are expected later today.*

THESAURUS **rain, drizzle, downpour, sleet**
➔ RAIN¹

4 a party at which presents are given to a woman who is going to get married or have a baby: *We're having a **baby shower** for Paula on Friday.*

shower² *v.* **1** [I] to wash your whole body while standing under a shower **2** [I,T] to cover a person or place with a lot of small things: *People standing near the window were showered with broken glass.* **3** [T] to give someone a lot of something: *Mother **showered** us **with** gifts.*

show·ing /ˈʃoʊɪŋ/ *n.* **1** [C] an occasion when a movie, art show, etc. can be seen or looked at: *a special **showing of** Georgia O'Keeffe's paintings* **2** [C usually singular] something that shows how well or badly you are doing: *The senator **made** a strong **showing** at the polls.*

show·man /ˈʃoʊmən/ *n.* (plural **showmen** /-mən/) [C] someone who is good at entertaining people and getting a lot of public attention —**showmanship** *n.* [U]

shown /ʃoʊn/ *v.* the past participle of SHOW¹

ˈshow-off *n.* [C] (informal, disapproving) someone who always tries to show how smart s/he is or how much skill s/he has so that other people will admire him/her: *Don't be such a show-off!*

show·piece /ˈʃoʊpis/ *n.* [C] something that an organization, government, etc. wants people to see because it is a successful example of what they are doing

show·room /ˈʃoʊrum/ *n.* [C] a large room where you can look at things that are for sale: *a car showroom*

show·y /ˈʃoʊi/ *adj.* very colorful, big, expensive, etc. in a way that attracts people's attention: *a showy ring*

shrank /ʃræŋk/ *v.* the past tense of SHRINK¹

shrap·nel /ˈʃrapnəl/ *n.* [U] small pieces of metal from a bomb or bullet that has exploded [ORIGIN: 1800—1900 Henry *Shrapnel* (1761-1842), British army officer who invented such bombs]

shred¹ /ʃrɛd/ *n.* [C] **1** a small thin piece that is

torn or cut roughly from something: *The kitten had **torn/ripped** the toy **to shreds**.* **2** a very small amount: *There's **not a shred of evidence** against him* (=there is none at all).

shred² *v.* (**shredded**, **shredding**) [T] **1** to cut or tear something into shreds → *see picture at* CUT¹

THESAURUS **cut, chop (up), slice, dice, peel, carve, grate** → CUT¹

2 to put a document into a shredder

shred·der /ˈʃrɛdɚ/ *n.* [C] a machine that cuts documents into small pieces so that no one can read them

shrewd /ʃrud/ *adj.* good at judging what people or situations are really like, especially in a way that makes you successful: *a shrewd businesswoman* [ORIGIN: 1200—1300 *shrew* in the old meaning "very bad man"]

shriek /ʃrik/ *v.* [I,T] to shout loudly, or to say something in a very loud voice, especially because you are frightened, excited, angry, etc. SYN **scream**: *They were dragged from their homes, shrieking and weeping.* | *"I'll kill you," Anne **shrieked at** him.* —**shriek** *n.* [C]

THESAURUS **shout, scream, yell, holler** → SHOUT¹

shrill /ʃrɪl/ *adj.* a shrill sound is high and unpleasant: *shrill voices*

THESAURUS **high, high-pitched, piercing** → HIGH¹
loud, noisy, ear-splitting → LOUD¹

shrimp /ʃrɪmp/ *n.* [C,U] a small curved sea animal that has ten legs and a soft shell, or the meat from this animal

shrine /ʃraɪn/ *n.* [C] **1** a place that is related to a holy event or holy person, and that people visit for religious reasons **2** a place that people visit and respect because it is related to a famous person: *Elvis Presley's home has become a shrine.* [ORIGIN: Old English *scrin*, from Latin *scrinium* "case, box"]

shrink¹ /ʃrɪŋk/ *v.* (past tense **shrank** /ʃræŋk/, past participle **shrunk** /ʃrʌŋk/) **1** [I,T] to become smaller, or to make something smaller: *My sweater shrank in the dryer.* **2** [I,T] to become smaller in amount, size, or value: *Profits have been shrinking over the last year.* **3** [I] to move away because you are afraid: *She **shrank back** in fright.*

shrink from sth *phr. v.* to avoid doing something difficult or unpleasant: *Many people shrink from discussing such personal issues.*

shrink² *n.* [C] (informal, humorous) a PSYCHIATRIST

shrink·age /ˈʃrɪŋkɪdʒ/ *n.* [U] the act of shrinking, or the amount that something shrinks

ˌshrink-ˈwrapped *adj.* goods that are shrink-wrapped are wrapped tightly in plastic —**shrink-wrap** *n.* [U]

shriv·el /ˈʃrɪvəl/ *also* **shrivel up** *v.* [I,T] if something shrivels, or if it is shriveled, it becomes smaller and its surface is covered in lines because it is dry or old: *The flowers had shriveled up.* —**shriveled** *adj.*: *her shriveled hands*

shroud¹ /ʃraʊd/ *n.* [C] **1** a cloth that is wrapped around a dead person's body before it is buried **2** something that hides or covers something: *a **shroud of** fog*

shroud² *v.* **1 be shrouded in darkness/mist/cloud etc.** to be so dark that you cannot see anything, or be completely covered and hidden by mist, cloud, etc.: *mountains shrouded in clouds* **2 be shrouded in mystery/secrecy etc.** to be mysterious, secret, etc.

shrub /ʃrʌb/ *n.* [C] a small bush

shrub·ber·y /ˈʃrʌbəri/ *n.* [U] shrubs planted close together in a group

shrug /ʃrʌg/ *v.* (**shrugged**, **shrugging**) [I,T] to raise and then lower your shoulders in order to show that you do not know something or do not care about something: *Dan shrugged and went back to what he was doing.* | *Melanie **shrugged** her **shoulders**.* —**shrug** *n.* [C]: *"I don't know," he said with a shrug.*

shrug sth ↔ **off** *phr. v.* to treat something as unimportant and not worry about it: *Marge tried to shrug off her failure.*

shrunk /ʃrʌŋk/ *v.* the past participle of SHRINK¹

shrunk·en /ˈʃrʌŋkən/ *adj.* having become smaller or been made smaller: *a shrunken sweater*

shuck /ʃʌk/ *v.* [T] to remove the outer cover of a vegetable such as corn or PEAS, or the shell of OYSTERS or CLAMS

shucks /ʃʌks/ *interjection* (old-fashioned) said in order to show you are a little disappointed about something

shud·der /ˈʃʌdɚ/ *v.* [I] to shake because you are frightened or cold, or because you think something is very unpleasant: *She **shuddered at** the thought.* —**shudder** *n.* [C]

shuf·fle¹ /ˈʃʌfəl/ *v.* **1** [I] to walk slowly and in a noisy way, without lifting your feet off the ground: *an old man **shuffling across** the room* **2 shuffle your feet** to keep moving your feet slightly because you are bored or embarrassed: *Ernie looked nervous and shuffled his feet.* **3** [T] to move something such as papers into a different order or into different positions: *Ginny shuffled the papers on her desk.* **4** [I,T] to mix playing cards into a different order before playing a game with them

shuffle² *n.* **be/get lost in the shuffle** to not be noticed or considered because there are so many other things to deal with

shuf·fle·board /ˈʃʌfəlˌbɔrd/ *n.* [U] a game in which you use a long stick to push a flat round object along a smooth surface toward an area with numbers on it

shun /ʃʌn/ *v.* (**shunned**, **shunning**) [T] to avoid someone or something deliberately: *She shuns publicity.*

shunt /ʃʌnt/ *v.* [T] to move someone or something to another place or position, especially in a way that seems unfair: *Some of the children had been **shunted aside** into slower classes.*

shush /ʃʌʃ, ʃʊʃ/ *v.* **1 shush!** (spoken) said in order to tell someone, especially a child, to be quiet **2** [T] to tell someone to be quiet: *She started to complain, but Betty shushed her.*

shut[1] /ʃʌt/ *v.* (past tense and past participle **shut**, present participle **shutting**) [I,T] to close something, or to become closed: *Do you want me to shut the window?* | *I heard the back door shut.* | *She leaned back and **shut** her **eyes**.* [ORIGIN: Old English *scyttan*]

shut sb/sth **away** *phr. v.* to put someone or something in a place away from other people: *He **shut himself away** in his office.*

shut down *phr. v.* **shut** sth ↔ **down** if a company, factory, machine, etc. shuts down, or if you shut it down, it stops operating: *Three nuclear generators were shut down for safety reasons.* | *How do I shut down this machine?*

shut off *phr. v.* **1 shut** sth ↔ **off** if a machine, tool, etc. shuts off, or if you shut it off, it stops operating: *We shut the engine off before it overheated.* | *The heat shuts off automatically.* **2 shut** sth ↔ **off** to prevent goods or supplies from being available or being delivered: *Food, oil, and gas supplies were shut off during the fighting.* **3 shut yourself off** to avoid meeting and talking to other people: *After his wife's death, Pete **shut himself off from** the rest of the family.*

shut out *phr. v.* **1 shut** sb ↔ **out** to deliberately not let someone join in an activity, process, etc.: *Many of the working poor are being shut out of the health care system.* **2 shut** sth ↔ **out** to stop yourself from seeing, hearing, or thinking about something: *He can shut out the rest of the world when he's working.* **3 shut out** sb to defeat an opposing team and prevent them from getting any points: *The Blue Jays shut out the Phillies 3–0.*

shut up *phr. v.* **1 shut up!** (spoken) said in order to tell someone rudely to stop talking **2 shut** sb **up** to make someone stop talking or be quiet: *I wish I could say something that would calm him down and shut him up.*

shut[2] *adj.* [not before noun] not open (SYN) **closed**: *We heard the door **slam shut** behind us.* | *Squeeze your **eyes shut**.*

shut·down /ˈʃʌtdaʊn/ *n.* [C] the closing of a factory, business, or piece of machinery: *a **shutdown of** the paper mill*

ˈshut-eye *n.* [U] (informal) sleep: *I really need to **get/catch some shut-eye*** (=go to sleep).

shut·ter /ˈʃʌtə/ *n.* [C] **1** a wooden or metal cover that can be closed over the outside of a window **2** a part of a camera that opens to let light onto the film

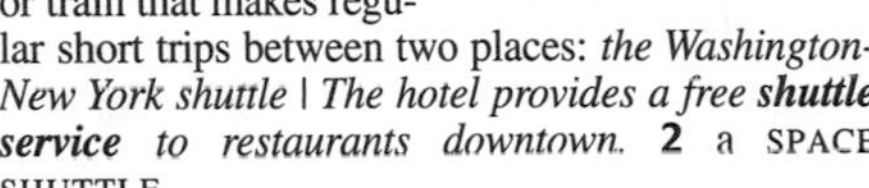
shutter

shut·tle[1] /ˈʃʌtl/ *n.* [C] **1** an airplane, bus, or train that makes regular short trips between two places: *the Washington-New York shuttle* | *The hotel provides a free **shuttle service** to restaurants downtown.* **2** a SPACE SHUTTLE

shuttle[2] *v.* [T] to travel or move people regularly between two places: *The visitors were **shuttled between** the hotel and the conference center twice a day.*

shut·tle·cock /ˈʃʌtl,kɑk/ *n.* [C] a small light object that you hit over the net in the game of BADMINTON (SYN) **birdie**

shy[1] /ʃaɪ/ *adj.* **1** nervous and embarrassed about meeting and speaking to other people, especially people you do not know: *As a teenager, I was **painfully shy*** (=extremely shy). | *She's **too shy** to speak up for herself.*

THESAURUS

timid – not brave or confident: *She's a good player, but timid on the court.*
bashful – shy and not willing to say very much: *Rachel blushed and gave me a bashful smile.*
demure (formal) – a girl or woman who is demure is shy, quiet, and always behaves well: *Tammy was quiet and demure.*
self-conscious – worried and embarrassed about what you look like or what other people think of you: *I was too self-conscious to be a good actor.*
reserved – not liking to express your emotions or talk about your problems: *a quiet, reserved man*
introverted – thinking a lot about your own interests, problems, etc., and not liking to be with other people: *She was an introverted person who did not become involved in campus activities.*
retiring (formal) – not wanting to be with other people: *a shy and retiring woman* → INSECURE, SOCIABLE

2 sb is not shy about sth used in order to say that someone is very willing to do something or get involved in something: *John has strong opinions, and he's **not shy about** voicing them.* [ORIGIN: Old English *sceoh*] —**shyly** *adv.*: *She smiled shyly.* —**shyness** *n.* [U]

shy[2] *v.* (**shied**, **shies**) [I] if a horse shies, it makes a sudden movement away from something because it is frightened

shy away from sth *phr. v.* to avoid doing something because you are not confident enough about it: *Erik had always shied away from speaking in public.*

S

shy·ster /ˈʃaɪstɚ/ *n.* [C] (informal) a dishonest person, especially a lawyer or politician

sib·ling /ˈsɪblɪŋ/ *n.* **1** [C] (formal) your brother or sister: *All of her siblings are still in Korea.* **2 sibling rivalry** competition between brothers and sisters for the attention of their parents

sic /sɪk/ *adv.* ENG. LANG. ARTS used after a word that you have copied into a piece of writing in order to show that you know it was not spelled or used correctly

sick /sɪk/ *adj.* **1** suffering from a disease or illness: *His mother's very sick.* | *Everyone ate the same thing, but I was the only one who **got sick**.* | *Leslie **called in sick*** (=telephoned to say she would not come to work because she was sick) *today.*

THESAURUS

feel sick – to feel sick in your stomach and as if you might vomit
not feel good/well – to feel sick: *Mommy, I don't feel good.*
ill – sick: *More than 50 school children became ill.*
not very well: *You don't look very well* (=you look sick).
under the weather (spoken) – slightly sick: *I've been a little under the weather lately.*
ailing (formal) – weak and sick: *his ailing grandmother*
infirm (formal) – weak or sick, especially because of being old: *They looked at nursing homes for their elderly and infirm father.*

2 be sick to bring food up from your stomach through your mouth (SYN) **vomit**: *I think I'm going to be sick.* **3 the sick** people who are sick: *nurses taking care of the sick and wounded* **4 feel sick (to your stomach)** to feel as if you are going to VOMIT: *I felt so sick after eating all that popcorn.* **5 be sick (and tired) of/be sick to death of** to be angry and bored with something that has been happening for a long time: *I'm sick and tired of her excuses.* **6 make me sick** (spoken) **a)** to make you feel strong anger and disapproval: *People who treat animals like that make me sick.* **b)** to make someone feel very JEALOUS – used humorously: *He's so smart and successful it makes me sick!* **7 be worried sick** to be extremely worried: *Why didn't you call? We were worried sick about you.* **8** someone who is sick does things that are strange and cruel: *The murders are obviously the work of a **sick mind**.* **9** sick stories, jokes, etc. deal with death and suffering in a cruel or unpleasant way [ORIGIN: Old English *seoc*]

sick·en /ˈsɪkən/ *v.* **1** [T] to make you feel strong anger and disapproval: *We were sickened by newspaper reports of child abuse.* **2** [I] to become sick

sick·en·ing /ˈsɪkənɪŋ/ *adj.* **1** very shocking, annoying, or upsetting: *It's sickening to see so many poor people in such a wealthy country.* **2** disgusting and making you feel as if you want to VOMIT: *the sickening smell of rotting meat*

sick·le /ˈsɪkəl/ *n.* [C] a tool with a blade in the shape of a hook, used for cutting wheat or long grass

ˈsick leave *n.* [U] the time you are allowed to be away from work because of sickness

sick·ly /ˈsɪkli/ *adj.* **1** weak, unhealthy, and often sick: *a sickly child* **2** a sickly smell, taste, etc. is disgusting and makes you feel sick —**sickly** *adv.*: *the sickly sweet smell of cheap perfume*

sick·ness /ˈsɪknɪs/ *n.* **1** [U] the state or feeling of being sick: *soldiers suffering from hunger and sickness* | ***motion/car/sea etc. sickness*** (=sickness caused by traveling in a car, boat, etc.)

THESAURUS **disease, illness** → DISEASE

2 [C] a particular illness: *common sicknesses such as colds and ear infections* → MORNING SICKNESS

sick·o /ˈsɪkoʊ/ *n.* (plural **sickos**) [C] (informal) someone who gets pleasure from things that most people find disgusting or upsetting: *What kind of sicko would write something like that?*

ˈsick pay *n.* [U] money paid by an employer to a worker who cannot work because of illness

side¹ /saɪd/ *n.* [C]
1 PART OF AN AREA one of the two areas that something is divided into: *Jim grew up on Detroit's east side.* | *They own a house **on the other side of** the lake.* | *She tilted her head **to one side**, considering the question.*
2 NEXT TO STH [usually singular] the place or area directly next to someone or something: *Stand on this side of me so Dad can get a photo.* | *Her mother was always **at/by** her **side** in the hospital.*
3 side by side a) next to each other: *They walked side by side.* **b)** if people live, work, etc. side by side, they do it together, have a good relationship, and help each other: *Doctors and scientists are working side by side to find a cure for AIDS.*
4 EDGE the part of an object or area that is farthest from the middle, at or near the edge: *We pulled over to **the side of the road**.*
5 OF A BUILDING/VEHICLE ETC. a part of something that is not the front, back, top, or bottom: *A truck ran into the left **side of** the bus.*
6 OF A THIN OBJECT one of the two surfaces of a thin flat object: *You can write on both **sides of** the paper.*
7 FLAT SURFACE one of the flat surfaces of something: *A cube has six sides.* | *a five-sided shape*
8 from side to side moving continuously from right to left: *The boat swayed from side to side as waves hit it.*
9 from all sides from every direction: *enemy gunfire coming from all sides*
10 SUBJECT/SITUATION one part of a subject, problem, or situation: *I'd like to hear her side of the story.* | *You should **look on the bright side*** (=think about the positive parts of the situation). | *Who's in charge of the creative side of the project?*
11 ARGUMENT/WAR ETC. one of the people, groups, teams, or countries opposing each other in an argument, war, etc.: *Nancy's **on our side***

S

(=agrees with us). | *We were on* ***the winning/losing side***. | *Teachers should never* ***take sides*** (=support just one person or opinion).

12 FOOD a dish that you eat in addition to the main dish of a meal in a restaurant (SYN) **side dish, side order**: *I'll have the roast beef sandwich with* ***a side of*** *fries.*

13 on the side a) in addition to your regular job: *He runs a little business on the side.* **b)** in addition to the main dish that you order in a restaurant: *Could I have a salad on the side?*

14 PART OF YOUR BODY the left or right part of your body from your shoulder to the top of your leg: *Turn over and* ***lie on*** *your right* ***side***.

15 OF A FAMILY the parents, grandparents, etc. of your mother or father: *There's a history of heart disease* ***on*** *my mother's* ***side***.

16 MOUNTAIN/VALLEY one of the sloping areas of a hill, valley, etc.

side[2] *adj.* [only before noun] **1** in or on the side of something: *You can leave by the side door.* **2 side street/road etc.** a street, road, etc. that is smaller than a main street: *We parked the car on a side street.* **3** from the side of something: *a side view of the statue*

side[3] *v.*

side against sb *phr. v.* to argue against a person or group in an argument, fight, etc.

side with sb *phr. v.* to support a person or group in an argument, fight, etc.: *It seems like Frank always sides with Dad.*

side·board /ˈsaɪdbɔrd/ *n.* [C] a long low piece of furniture in a DINING ROOM that you store dishes and glasses in

side·burns /ˈsaɪdbɚnz/ *n.* [plural] hair that grows down the sides of a man's face in front of his ears [ORIGIN: 1800—1900 *burnsides* type of beard in which the chin is shaved, from Ambrose *Burnside* (1824-81), U.S. general who wore such a beard]

side·car /ˈsaɪdkɑr/ *n.* [C] an enclosed seat that is joined to the side of a MOTORCYCLE and has a separate wheel

ˈside dish *n.* [C] a dish that is served along with the main food at a meal

ˈside efˌfect *n.* [C] **1** an effect that a drug has on your body in addition to the intended effect: *The drug has no* ***harmful side effects***. **2** an unexpected result of an activity, situation, or event

THESAURUS **result, consequences, aftereffects** → RESULT[1]

side·kick /ˈsaɪdˌkɪk/ *n.* [C] (informal) someone who is a close friend or helper of a more important person, especially in a movie or on a television show

side·line[1] /ˈsaɪdlaɪn/ *n.* [C] **1** one of the two lines that form the edges of a field where sports are played, and the area just outside these lines **2** something that you do to earn money in addition to your regular job: *Mark does translation work* ***as a sideline***. **3 on the sidelines** not taking part in an activity even though you want to: *There are still buyers on the sidelines waiting to get stocks.*

sideline[2] *v.* **be sidelined** to not be included in a game or event because you are injured or because you are not as good as someone else: *Their quarterback was sidelined with a knee injury.*

side·long /ˈsaɪdlɔŋ/ *adj.* **a sidelong look/glance** a way of looking at someone by moving your eyes to the side, done secretly or when you are nervous

ˈside ˌorder *n.* [C] a small amount of a food ordered in a restaurant to be eaten with a meal, but served on a separate dish: *a* ***side order of*** *onion rings*

side·show /ˈsaɪdʃoʊ/ *n.* [C] a separate small part of a CIRCUS or fair, that often has very unusual performers

side·step /ˈsaɪdstɛp/ *v.* (**sidestepped, sidestepping**) [T] to avoid a difficult question or decision: *Congressman Howell sidestepped the reporters' questions.*

side·swipe /ˈsaɪdswaɪp/ *v.* [T] to hit the side of a car or other vehicle with the side of your car

side·track /ˈsaɪdtræk/ *v.* [T] to make someone stop doing or saying something by making him/her interested in something else: *I think we're* ***getting sidetracked*** *from the main issue here.*

ˌside-view ˈmirror *n.* [C] a mirror attached to the side of a car

side·walk /ˈsaɪdwɔk/ *n.* [C] a hard surface or path for people to walk on along the side of a street

side·ways /ˈsaɪdweɪz/ *adv.* toward one side, or with the side facing forward: *Mel's car slid sideways as it hit the ice.*

sid·ing /ˈsaɪdɪŋ/ *n.* [U] wood, metal, or plastic in long narrow pieces, used for covering the sides of houses: *They've put new* ***aluminum siding*** *on their home.*

si·dle /ˈsaɪdl/ *v.* [I] to walk toward someone or something slowly, as if you do not want to be noticed: *Theo* ***sidled up to*** *me with an embarrassed look.*

siege /sidʒ/ *n.* [C,U] a situation in which an army surrounds a place and stops supplies of food, weapons, etc. from getting to it: *a city* ***under siege*** (=surrounded by an army)

si·es·ta /siˈɛstə/ *n.* [C] a short sleep in the afternoon, often taken by people in warm countries → NAP [ORIGIN: 1600—1700 Spanish, Latin *sexta (hora)* "sixth hour, noon"]

sieve /sɪv/ *n.* [C] a kitchen tool that looks like a wire net, used for separating solids from liquids —**sieve** *v.* [T]

sift /sɪft/ *v.* [T] **1** to put flour, sugar, etc. through a sifter in order to remove large pieces **2** *also* **sift through** to examine something very carefully in order to find something: *The commission will have*

S

to sift through thousands of White House documents.

sift·er /ˈsɪftɚ/ *n.* [C] a kitchen tool made of a tube with a wire net inside, through which you put flour, sugar, etc. in order to remove or break up large pieces

sigh¹ /saɪ/ *v.* [I] to breathe out loudly and slowly, especially when you are tired or in order to express a strong emotion: *She **sighed deeply** and shook her head.*

sigh² *n.* [C] an act or sound of sighing: *Judy sat down with a **sigh of** relief.*

sight¹ /saɪt/ *n.*

1 ABILITY TO SEE [U] the physical ability to see ➔ EYESIGHT: *My grandmother is **losing** her **sight*** (=going blind).

2 ACT OF SEEING [singular,U] the act of seeing something: *He can't stand **the sight of** blood.* | *We **caught sight of*** (=suddenly saw) *Henry as we turned the corner.*

3 STH YOU SEE [C] something you can see, especially if it is something beautiful, unusual, etc.: *The Wrigley Building is one of the most famous sights in Chicago.* | *It was a **common sight** to see children begging on the streets.*

4 in/within sight (of sth) a) inside the area that you can see: *There was nobody in sight.* | *We camped within sight of the lake.* **b)** likely to happen soon: *Peace is in sight.*

5 out of sight (of sth) outside the area that you can see: *Keep your car windows rolled up and your valuables out of sight.*

6 not let sb out of your sight to make sure that someone stays near you: *Stay here, and don't let the baby out of your sight.*

7 lose sight of sth to forget an important part of something because you are too concerned about the details: *We have **lost sight of the fact that** the computer is only a tool.*

8 out of sight, out of mind used to say that you will soon forget someone or something if you do not see him, her, or it for a short period of time

9 ON A WEAPON [C usually plural] the part of a gun or weapon that helps you aim at something [ORIGIN: Old English *gesiht*]

sight² *v.* [T] to see something from a long distance away, especially something you have been looking for: *Two bears have been sighted in the area.*

sight·ed /ˈsaɪt̬ɪd/ *adj.* able to see (ANT) **blind**

sight·ing /ˈsaɪt̬ɪŋ/ *n.* [C] an occasion when something is seen, especially when it is something unusual or rare

sight-read /ˈsaɪt˺rid/ *v.* (past tense and past participle **sight-read** /-rɛd/) [I,T] ENG. LANG. ARTS to play or sing written music that you are looking at for the first time, without practicing it first

sight·see·ing /ˈsaɪtˌsiɪŋ/ *n.* [U] the activity of visiting famous or interesting places, especially as a tourist: *We **went sightseeing** and saw a play.* —**sightseer** *n.* [C]

ˈsight word *n.* [C] ENG. LANG. ARTS a word which a reader recognizes immediately as a whole without needing to examine its different parts

sign¹ /saɪn/ *n.* [C] **1** a piece of paper, metal, etc. with words or a picture that gives people information, a warning, or instructions: *Follow the **signs** that **say** "Montlake Bridge."* | *a no smoking sign* **2** an event, fact, etc. that shows that something exists or is happening, or that it will happen in the future: *The house **showed** no **signs of** a forced entry.* | *That's a **good/bad sign**!* | *Extreme tiredness is an early **sign of** the disease.* | ***There are** worrying **signs** that the agreement will fail.*

COLLOCATIONS

clear/obvious/visible sign – one that you can clearly see or understand
good/positive/encouraging sign – one that tells you that something good might happen
bad/warning sign – one that tells you that something bad might happen
early sign – one that shows what is happening at the beginning of a process, situation, etc.
sure sign – one that proves that something is true

3 a picture or shape that has a particular meaning (SYN) **symbol**: *A dollar sign looks like "$."* **4** a movement or sound that you make without speaking, in order to tell someone something: *'I'm ready to go,' he said, giving the crowd a thumbs-up sign.* **5** one of the SYMBOLS of the ZODIAC [ORIGIN: 1200—1300 Old French *signe*, from Latin *signum* "mark, sign, image, seal"]

sign² *v.* **1** [I,T] to write your name on a letter or document to show that you wrote it or agree with it, or to make it official: *Rundon signed the agreement last week.* | *Underneath, she had **signed** her **name**.* | *The players **signed autographs** after the game.* ➔ *see picture at* CHECK² **2** [T] to officially agree to employ someone: *Columbia Records **signed** her **to** a three-year contract.* **3** [I] to tell someone something by using movements: *She **signed to us to** get out of the way.*

sign sth ↔ **away** *phr. v.* to sign a document that gives your property or legal rights to someone else: *The Puyallup Tribe signed away much of their land rights.*

sign for sth *phr. v.* to sign a document to prove that you have received something: *I need you to sign for this package.*

sign (sb) ↔ **in** *phr. v.* to write your name or someone's name in a book when you enter a hotel, an office building, etc.

sign off *phr. v.* **1** to officially say or show that you approve of a document, plan, or idea: *Both sides **signed off on** the agreement.* **2** to say goodbye at the end of a radio or television broadcast, or at the end of a letter

sign on *phr. v.* to agree to work for someone or to do something, and usually to sign a document showing this: *Several boys **signed on as** volunteers.*

sign out *phr. v.* **1 sign** (sb) **out** to write your name in a book when you leave a hotel, an office building, etc. **2 sign** sth ↔ **out** to write your name on a form or in a book to show that you have taken or borrowed something

sign sth ↔ **over** *phr. v.* to sign an official document that gives your property or legal rights to someone else: *Daley **signed over** his shares **to** his partner.*

sign up *phr. v.* **1 sign** sb ↔ **up** if someone is signed up by an organization, s/he signs a contract and agrees to work for that organization: *Navy recruiters want to sign up people with technical abilities.* **2** to put your name on a list because you want to take a class, belong to a group, etc.: *500 children have **signed up for** the music classes.*

sig·nal[1] /ˈsɪgnəl/ *n.* [C] **1** a sound, action, or event that gives information or tells someone to do something: *He **gave the signal** to start.* | *I phoned, but only got a **busy signal*** (=a sound telling you the phone is being used). | *The governor is sending **signals that** he will run for president.* **2** PHYSICS a series of light waves, sound waves, etc. that carry an image, sound, or message to something such as a radio or television: *After landing on the asteroid, the spacecraft will continue to **send/transmit signals** to Earth.* | *The 18-inch dish is able to **receive signals** directly from a satellite.*

signal[2] *v.* **1** [I,T] to make a movement or sound, without speaking, that gives information or tells someone to do something: *Marshall **signaled for** coffee.* **2** [T] to make something clear by what you say or do: *Carter has signaled his intention to run for mayor.* **3** [T] to be a sign or proof that something is going to happen: *Bad behavior may signal a learning problem.* **4** [I] to show the direction you intend to turn in a car, by using lights (SYN) **indicate**: *Don't forget to signal before you change lanes.*

sig·na·to·ry /ˈsɪgnəˌtɔri/ *n.* (plural **signatories**) [C] (formal) one of the people or countries that sign an agreement

sig·na·ture /ˈsɪgnətʃɚ/ *n.* [C] your name written the way you usually write it, for example at the end of a letter, on a check, etc.: *We need your signature on these documents.* ➔ WRITE

sig·nif·i·cance /sɪgˈnɪfəkəns/ (Ac) *n.* [U] the importance or meaning of something, especially something that might affect you in the future: *the historical **significance of** the battle*

sig·nif·i·cant /sɪgˈnɪfəkənt/ (Ac) *adj.* **1** noticeable or important (ANT) **insignificant**: *a significant 20th century artist* | *significant differences between the two groups*

THESAURUS **important, crucial, vital, essential, major, key** ➔ IMPORTANT

2 having a special meaning that is not known to everyone: *Tom gave her a significant look.* [ORIGIN: 1500—1600 Latin, present participle of *significare*, from *signum* "mark, sign, image, seal"] —**significantly** *adv.*

sigˌnificant ˈother *n.* [C] (humorous) your husband, wife, girlfriend, or boyfriend

sig·ni·fy /ˈsɪgnəˌfaɪ/ (Ac) *v.* (**signified, signifies**) [T] **1** to represent, mean, or be a sign of something: *The image of a dove signifies peace.* | *The flag **signified that** the ship was Japanese.* **2** to express a wish, feeling, or opinion by doing something: *Everyone nodded to signify their agreement.*

sign·ing /ˈsaɪnɪŋ/ *n.* [U] the act of writing your name on something such as an agreement or a contract: *the **signing of** the peace agreement*

ˈsign ˌlanguage *n.* [C,U] ENG. LANG. ARTS a language that uses hand movements instead of spoken words, used by people who cannot hear

sign·post /ˈsaɪnpoʊst/ *n.* [C] **1** something that is used for holding a street sign up **2** something that shows you what is happening or what you should do: *The employment figures are a key signpost of the economy's performance.*

si·lence[1] /ˈsaɪləns/ *n.* **1** [C,U] complete quiet because no one is talking, or a period of complete quiet: *There was a **stunned/awkward/embarrassed etc. silence**.* | *a **brief/short/long silence*** | *The family sat eating **in silence**.* **2** [U] complete absence of sound or noise: ***the silence of** space* | *A blackbird's call **broke the silence**.*

silence[2] *v.* [T] **1** (written) to make someone stop criticizing or giving his/her opinions: *Critics of the government were silenced.* **2** to make someone stop talking, or to stop something making noise: *A shout from the soldier silenced everybody.*

si·lenc·er /ˈsaɪlənsɚ/ *n.* [C] a thing that is put on the end of a gun so that it makes less noise when it is fired

si·lent /ˈsaɪlənt/ *adj.* **1** not saying anything or making any noise (SYN) **quiet**: *silent prayer* | *The crowd **fell silent*** (=became quiet) *when the President appeared.* **2** failing or refusing to talk about something: *Those closest to the actress are **remaining silent** about the affair.* **3** [only before noun] a silent movie has pictures but no sound **4** a silent letter in a word is not pronounced [ORIGIN: 1400—1500 Latin, present participle of *silere* "to be silent"] —**silently** *adv.*

ˌsilent ˈpartner *n.* [C] someone who owns part of a business but does not make decisions about how it operates

sil·hou·ette[1] /ˌsɪluˈɛt, ˈsɪluˌɛt/ *n.* [C] a dark shape or shadow, seen against a light background [ORIGIN: 1700—1800 French, from Étienne de *Silhouette* (1709-67), French politician famous for not liking to spend money whose name became assocated with a cheap simple picture]

silhouette[2] *v.* [T] to appear as a silhouette: *skyscrapers **silhouetted against** the sky*

sil·i·cate /ˈsɪləˌkeɪt, -kət/ *n.* [C,U] EARTH SCIENCES one of a group of common solid mineral substances that exist naturally in the Earth's surface

sil·i·con /ˈsɪlɪˌkɑn, -kən/ *n.* [U] CHEMISTRY an ELEMENT that is often used for making glass, bricks, parts for computers, etc.

ˌsilicon ˈchip *n.* [C] IT a computer CHIP

S

silk /sɪlk/ *n.* [C,U] a thin thread produced by a silkworm, or the soft, usually shiny cloth made from this thread: *a silk shirt*

silk·en /ˈsɪlkən/ *adj.* (literary) soft and smooth like silk, or made of silk: *her silken hair*

silk·worm /ˈsɪlk-wɚm/ *n.* [C] a type of CATERPILLAR (=insect) that produces silk

silk·y /ˈsɪlki/ *adj.* soft and smooth like silk: *silky fur*

sill /sɪl/ *n.* [C] the narrow flat piece of wood at the base of a window frame

sil·ly /ˈsɪli/ *adj.* (comparative **sillier**, superlative **silliest**) not sensible or serious: *a silly thing to do* | *You're being silly.* [ORIGIN: Old English *sælig* "happy"] —**silliness** *n.* [U]

si·lo /ˈsaɪloʊ/ *n.* (plural **silos**) [C] **1** a tall round building used for storing grain, animal food, etc. **2** a large structure under the ground from which a MISSILE can be fired

silt /sɪlt/ *n.* [U] EARTH SCIENCES sand or mud that is carried by the water in a river, and settles in a bend of the river or in the entrance to a port

S

sil·ver¹ /ˈsɪlvɚ/ *n.* [U] **1** CHEMISTRY a valuable shiny white metal that is an ELEMENT and is used for making jewelry, spoons, etc. **2** the color of this metal [ORIGIN: Old English *seolfor*]

silver² *adj.* **1** made of silver: *a silver spoon* → *see picture at* MATERIAL¹ **2** colored silver: *a silver dress*

ˌsilver anniˈversary *n.* [C] the date that is exactly 25 years after an important event, especially a wedding

ˌsilver ˈmedal *n.* [C] a prize made of silver that is given to someone who finishes second in a race or competition

sil·ver·ware /ˈsɪlvɚˌwɛr/ *n.* [U] objects such as knives, spoons, and forks that are made of silver or a similar metal

sim·i·lar /ˈsɪmələ/ (Ac) *adj.* almost the same but not exactly the same (ANT) **dissimilar** → ALIKE: *kids with similar backgrounds* | *The system is* ***similar to*** *one used in other schools.* | *The two cheeses are* ***similar in*** *flavor.* [ORIGIN: 1500—1600 French *similaire*, from Latin *similis* "like, similar"]

THESAURUS

like – similar in some way to something else: *It tastes a little like chicken.*
alike – very similar: *She and her sister look alike.*
comparable (formal) – similar to something else in size, number, quality, etc.: *Is the pay rate comparable to that of other companies?*
akin to sth – similar to something: *He looked at me with something akin to awe.*
analogous (formal) – similar to another situation or thing, so that you can compare them or use one thing to help you understand the other: *The communication system is analogous to the body's nervous system.*
identical – exactly the same: *The two pictures were identical.*
matching – having the same color, style, or pattern as something else: *The twins were dressed in matching outfits.*

sim·i·lar·i·ty /ˌsɪməˈlærət̬i/ (Ac) *n.* (plural **similarities**) [C,U] the quality of being similar, or a particular way in which things or people are similar: ***There are similarities*** *with German, but Yiddish is a distinct language.* | *his* ***similarity to*** *my brother* | *Discuss the* ***similarities and differences*** *between the two writers.*

sim·i·lar·ly /ˈsɪmələli/ (Ac) *adv.* in a similar way: *The two cities are laid out similarly.*

ˌsimilar ˈpolygons *n.* [plural] MATH similar POLYGONS (=flat shapes with three or more sides) have the same shape and equal angles, but do not have to be the same size

sim·i·le /ˈsɪməli/ *n.* [C] ENG. LANG. ARTS an expression in which you compare two things using the words "like" or "as," for example "as red as blood" → METAPHOR

sim·mer /ˈsɪmɚ/ *v.* **1** [I,T] to cook food in liquid and not allow it to boil **2 simmer down** (spoken) to become less excited or angry and more calm —**simmer** *n.* [singular]

sim·per /ˈsɪmpɚ/ *v.* [I] to smile in a way that is silly and annoying

THESAURUS **smile, grin, beam, smirk** → SMILE

sim·ple /ˈsɪmpəl/ *adj.* **1** not difficult or complicated (SYN) **easy**: *a simple math problem* | *The solution is* ***fairly/pretty/relatively simple.*** | *It's* ***simple to*** *make.*

THESAURUS

easy – not difficult: *It was an easy class.*
straightforward – simple and easy to understand: *a straightforward task*
uncomplicated – not difficult to understand or deal with, and not having many parts: *The instructions are clear and uncomplicated.*
facile (formal) – too simple and showing a lack of careful thought or understanding: *a facile explanation*

2 made in a plain style, without a lot of decoration or things that are not necessary: *a simple white dress* **3** not involving anything else: *He plays for the love of music,* ***pure/plain and simple.*** | ***The simple fact/truth is*** *we don't have the money.* ►Don't say "The fact is simple."◄ **4** consisting of only one or a few necessary parts: *simple tools like a hammer and saw* **5** ordinary and not special in any way: *I live a very simple life.* **6 simple past/present/future** ENG. LANG. ARTS a tense of a verb that is not formed with an AUXILIARY such as "have" or "be" [ORIGIN: 1200—1300 Old French "plain, uncomplicated," from Latin *simplus*, from *sim-* "one" + *-plus* "multiplied by"]

ˌsimple ˈinterest *n.* [U] ECONOMICS INTEREST that is calculated on the sum of money that you first

INVESTED, and does not include the interest it has already earned ➔ COMPOUND INTEREST

ˌsimple-ˈminded *adj.* not able to understand complicated things

ˌsimple ˈsentence *n.* [C] ENG. LANG. ARTS a sentence that consists of one main CLAUSE, for example: "He ate the cake."

sim·plic·i·ty /sɪmˈplɪsət̬i/ *n.* [U] the quality of being simple and not complicated, especially when this is attractive or useful: *the simplicity of his writing style* | ***For simplicity*** (=to make something easy), *divide the class into three groups.*

sim·pli·fy /ˈsɪmpləˌfaɪ/ *v.* (**simplified, simplifies**) [T] **1** to make something clearer and easier to do or understand ➔ OVERSIMPLIFY: *a promise to simplify the tax forms* **2** MATH to change an EQUATION, FRACTION, or other mathematical expression into its simplest form, using ARITHMETIC and ALGEBRA —**simplification** /ˌsɪmpləfəˈkeɪʃən/ *n.* [U]

sim·plis·tic /sɪmˈplɪstɪk/ *adj.* (disapproving) treating difficult subjects in a way that is too simple: *a simplistic view of the problem*

sim·ply /ˈsɪmpli/ *adv.* **1** only (SYN) **just**: *You shouldn't buy something* ***simply because*** *it's on sale.* **2** used in order to emphasize what you are saying: *The movie simply isn't any good.* **3** in a way that is easy to understand: ***To put it simply*** (=explain it in a simple way), *inflation means that prices rise.* **4** in a plain and ordinary way: *Alanna was dressed quite simply.*

sim·u·late /ˈsɪmyəˌleɪt/ (Ac) *v.* [T] to make or do something that is not real but looks, sounds, or feels as though it is real: *Computer models have simulated conditions on Mars.* [ORIGIN: 1400—1500 Latin, past participle of *simulare* "to copy," from *similis* "like, similar"] —**simulator** *n.* [C]: *a flight simulator* —**simulated** *adj.* ➔ ARTIFICIAL

sim·u·la·tion /ˌsɪmyəˈleɪʃən/ (Ac) *n.* [C,U] something you do or make in order to practice what you would do in a real situation: *a computer simulation used to train airline pilots*

si·mul·ta·ne·ous /ˌsaɪməlˈteɪniəs/ *adj.* happening or done at exactly the same time: *a simultaneous broadcast on TV and radio* [ORIGIN: 1600—1700 Medieval Latin *simultaneus*, from Latin *simul* "at the same time"] —**simultaneously** *adv.*

sin¹ /sɪn/ *n.* **1** [C] something you do that is against religious laws: *He* ***confessed*** *his* ***sins*** *to one of the priests.* **2** [singular] (informal) something that you do not approve of: ***It's a sin*** *to waste food.*

sin² *v.* (**sinned, sinning**) [I] to do something wrong that is against religious laws

sin³ MATH the written abbreviation of SINE

since /sɪns/ *conjunction, prep., adv.* **1** at or from a particular time in the past until now: *I haven't seen him since we graduated from high school.* | *Paul had been waiting since 2 o'clock.* | *His ex-wife has since remarried, but he's still single.* | *We've lived here* ***ever since*** *we got married.* | *He had a car accident in 2002.* ***Since then****, he has been unemployed.* **2** because: *You'll have to get up early, since the bus leaves at 7 a.m.* **3 since when?** (spoken) used in questions to show anger or surprise: *Since when did you start smoking?* ➔ *see Grammar box at* AGO

sin·cere /sɪnˈsɪr/ *adj.* honest and true, or based on what you really feel or believe (ANT) **insincere**: *a sincere apology* [ORIGIN: 1500—1600 Latin *sincerus* "clean, pure"]

sin·cere·ly /sɪnˈsɪrli/ *adv.* **1** in a sincere way: *Both men sincerely admired each other's work.* **2 Sincerely/Sincerely yours/Yours sincerely** an expression you write at the end of a formal letter before you sign your name

sin·cer·i·ty /sɪnˈsɛrət̬i/ *n.* [U] the quality of being honest, and really meaning or believing what you say: *I don't doubt her sincerity, but I think she's got her facts wrong.*

sine /saɪn/ *n.* [C] MATH the FRACTION that you calculate for an angle in a RIGHT TRIANGLE, by dividing the length of the side opposite the angle by the length of the HYPOTENUSE (=longest side)

sin·ew /ˈsɪnju/ *n.* [C,U] BIOLOGY a strong CORD in the body that connects a muscle to a bone

sin·ew·y /ˈsɪnyui/ *adj.* showing strong muscles

sin·ful /ˈsɪnfəl/ *adj.* **1** morally wrong (SYN) **wicked**: *a sinful man* **2** (informal) very bad or wrong: *a sinful waste of money*

sing /sɪŋ/ *v.* (past tense **sang** /sæŋ/, past participle **sung** /sʌŋ/) **1** [I,T] to make musical sounds, songs, etc. with your voice: *The kids* ***sang songs*** *about peace.* | *Jana sings in the church choir.* | *She started* ***singing*** *Georgie* ***to sleep****.* **2** [I] if birds sing, they produce high musical sounds —**singing** *n.* [U]

sing along *phr. v.* to sing with someone else who is already singing or playing music: ***Sing along to/with*** *all your favorite tunes.*

sing out *phr. v.* to sing or shout loudly and clearly

sing. the written abbreviation of SINGULAR

singe /sɪndʒ/ *v.* [I,T] to burn something slightly on the surface or edge, or to be burned in this way

sing·er /ˈsɪŋɚ/ *n.* [C] someone who sings, especially as a job: *an opera singer*

sin·gle¹ /ˈsɪŋgəl/ *adj.* **1** only one: *We lost the game by a single point.* | *a single sheet of paper* **2** not married: *Is he single?* | *a club for single men/women* **3 single parent/mother/father** a mother or father who takes care of her/his children by herself or himself, because s/he is not married **4** used in order to emphasize a separate thing: *Smoking is the* ***single most*** *important cause of lung cancer.* | *This is the* ***single biggest/greatest*** *problem we face.* | *She visits her mother* ***every single*** *day.* **5** intended to be used by only one person ➔ DOUBLE: *a single bed* ➔ *see picture at* BED¹ [ORIGIN: 1200—1300 Old French, Latin *singulus*]

single² *n.* [C] **1** a musical recording of only one song: *her hit single* **2** a one-dollar bill: *Do you have any singles?* **3 singles** [plural] people who are not married: *a singles bar* (=where single people can go to drink and meet people)

ˌsingle ˈfile *n.* [U] a line with one person behind the other: *The children* ***walked in single file*** *to the field.*

ˌsingle-ˈhandedly *also* **ˌsingle-ˈhanded** *adv.* done by one person with no help from anyone else

THESAURUS alone, on your own, (all) by yourself, solo, independently, unaided → ALONE

ˌsingle ˈmarket *n.* [C] ECONOMICS a group of countries in which there is freedom of movement of goods, services, money, and workers, and with an agreement on rules for production and trade. The European Union is a single market.

ˌsingle-ˈminded *adj.* having one clear purpose and working hard to achieve it: *a* ***single-minded determination*** *to succeed*

sin·gly /ˈsɪŋgli/ *adv.* alone, or one at a time: *people walking singly or in groups*

S

sing·song /ˈsɪŋsɔŋ/ *n.* [singular] a way of speaking in which your voice keeps rising and falling —**singsong** *adj.*

sin·gu·lar¹ /ˈsɪŋgyələ˞/ *adj.* **1** ENG. LANG. ARTS relating to the singular **2** [usually before noun] very great or noticeable: *a singular achievement*

singular² *n.* **the singular** ENG. LANG. ARTS in grammar, the form of a word that represents only one person or thing. For example, "child" is in the singular. → PLURAL

sin·gu·lar·ly /ˈsɪŋgyələ˞li/ *adv.* (formal) in a way that is very noticeable or unusual: *She wore a singularly inappropriate dress.*

sin·is·ter /ˈsɪnɪstə˞/ *adj.* seeming to be bad or evil: ***There was something/nothing sinister*** *about his financial dealings.* [ORIGIN: 1400—1500 Old French *sinistre*, from Latin *sinister* "left-handed, unlucky"]

sink¹ /sɪŋk/ *v.* (past tense **sank** /sæŋk/ *or* **sunk** /sʌŋk/, past participle **sunk**)
1 IN WATER [I,T] to go down below the surface of water, mud, etc., or to make something do this: *The Titanic* ***sank to*** *the bottom of the ocean.* | *Submarines were ordered to sink enemy ships.* → *see picture at* FLOAT¹ → DIVE¹
2 FALL/SIT DOWN [I] to fall down heavily, especially because you are weak or tired: ***I sank down into*** *one of the soft chairs.*
3 MOVE LOWER [I] to move down slowly to a lower level: *The sun* ***sank beneath*** *the horizon.*
4 GET WORSE [I] to gradually get into a worse state: *In the 1930s, America* ***sank*** *deeper* ***into*** *the Depression.*
5 DECREASE [I] to decrease in amount, number, value, etc.: *House prices in the area are sinking fast.*
6 be sunk (informal) to be in a situation in which you are certain to fail or have a lot of problems: *If he doesn't lend us the money, we're sunk!*
7 your heart sinks/your spirits sink if your heart or spirits sink, you lose your hope or confidence
8 a sinking feeling a feeling that you get when you realize that something very bad is beginning to happen
9 sink or swim to succeed or fail without help from anyone else
10 MONEY [T] to spend a lot of money on something (SYN) **invest**: *They had* ***sunk*** *thousands* ***into*** *that house.*
11 SPORTS [T] to get a basketball or GOLF ball into a basket or hole

sink in *phr. v.*
if information, facts, etc. sink in, you begin to understand them or realize their full meaning: *At first, what she said didn't really sink in.*

sink² *n.* [C] an open container in a kitchen or BATHROOM that you fill with water to wash dishes, your hands, etc.: *There was a pile of dirty dishes in the sink.*

sin·ner /ˈsɪnə˞/ *n.* [C] someone who SINs

sin·u·ous /ˈsɪnyuəs/ *adj.* curving and twisting smoothly, like the movements of a snake: *a tree with sinuous branches*

si·nus /ˈsaɪnəs/ *n.* [C] BIOLOGY one of the pair of hollow spaces in the bones of your face behind your nose

sip¹ /sɪp/ *v.* (**sipped**, **sipping**) [I,T] to drink something slowly, swallowing only small amounts: *Mrs. Hong sipped her tea.*

sip² *n.* [C] a very small amount of a drink: *He* ***took a sip of*** *coffee.*

si·phon¹ /ˈsaɪfən/ *v.* [T] **1** to take something away from the person, organization, etc. for which it was intended, especially to dishonestly take money: *Aid was* ***siphoned off*** *by government officials for their own use.* **2** SCIENCE to remove liquid from a container using a siphon

siphon² *n.* [C] SCIENCE a bent tube that you use to get liquid out of a container, by holding one end of the tube at a lower level than the container

sir /sə˞/ *n.* **1** (spoken) used in order to speak politely to a man when you do not know his name or when you want to show respect: *Can I help you, sir?* | *"Do you understand, Louise?" "Yes, sir."* | *Dear Sir* (=used at the beginning of a business letter to a man when you do not know his name) **2 Sir** a title used before the name of a KNIGHT: *Sir Lancelot* [ORIGIN: 1200—1300 Old French, Latin *senior* "older"]

sire /saɪə˞/ *v.* [T] (written) **1** to be the father of a child **2** to be the father of an animal —**sire** *n.* [C]

si·ren /ˈsaɪrən/ *n.* [C] a piece of equipment that makes very loud warning sounds, used on police cars, fire engines, etc.: *I heard police sirens in the distance.*

sir·loin /ˈsɚlɔɪn/ *also* ˌ**sirloin ˈsteak** *n.* [C,U] a good piece of meat cut from the back of a cow

sis·sy /ˈsɪsi/ *n.* (plural **sissies**) [C] (informal) a boy that other boys do not approve of because he likes doing things that girls do —**sissy** *adj.*

sis·ter /ˈsɪstɚ/ *n.* [C] **1** a girl or woman who has the same parents as you ➔ BROTHER: *Mary is my* ***big/older*** *sister, and Kim is my* ***little/younger sister.*** ➔ RELATIVE[1] **2** used by women to talk about other women and to show that they have feelings of friendship and support toward them: *Susan B. Anthony and other sisters fought for our right to vote.* **3** *also* **Sister** a NUN: *Sister Frances* [ORIGIN: Old English *sweostor*] —**sisterly** *adj.*

sis·ter·hood /ˈsɪstɚˌhʊd/ *n.* [U] a strong loyalty among women who share the same ideas and aims ➔ BROTHERHOOD

ˈ**sister-in-ˌlaw** *n.* (plural **sisters-in-law**) [C] **1** the sister of your husband or wife **2** the wife of your brother, or the wife of your husband's or wife's brother

sit /sɪt/ *v.* (past tense and past participle **sat** /sæt/, present participle **sitting**)

1 ON A SEAT [I] **a)** to be on a chair, a seat, or the ground with the top half of your body upright and your weight resting on your BUTTOCKS: *The children* ***sat around*** *her* ***on*** *the floor.* | *I was* ***sitting at*** *my desk writing a letter.* | ***Sit still*** (=sit without moving) *and let me fix your hair.* **b)** *also* **sit down** to move to a sitting position after you have been standing: *He came and* ***sat beside/next to*** *her.* ➔ *see picture on page A22*

2 OBJECTS/BUILDINGS [I] to lie or be in a particular position or condition: *Several books* ***sat on*** *the desk.* | *The house sat empty for two years.*

3 NOT DO ANYTHING [I] to stay in one place for a long time, especially doing nothing useful: *I can't* ***sit here*** *all day, I have work to do.* | *He was just* ***sitting there****, staring into space.*

4 MAKE SB SIT [T] *also* **sit sb down** to make someone sit somewhere: *She* ***sat*** *the boy* ***in*** *a corner.*

5 TAKE CARE OF [I] to take care of a baby or child while his/her parents are not home (SYN) **babysit**

6 sit tight to stay where you are and not move, or to stay in the same situation and not do anything, while you are waiting for something: *Investors should sit tight and not panic.*

7 not sit well with sb if a situation, plan, etc. does not sit well with someone, s/he does not like it: *A tax raise won't sit well with the voters.*

8 sit on the fence to avoid saying which side of an argument you support or what your opinion is about something

9 MEET [I] to have an official meeting: *The court sits once a month.* [ORIGIN: Old English *sittan*]

sit around *phr. v.*
to spend time resting or not doing anything useful or to spend a lot of time sitting and doing nothing useful: *We were just sitting around talking.*

sit back *phr. v.*
1 to get into a comfortable position and relax: *Just sit back and relax – I'll make dinner.*
2 to make no effort to get involved in something: *You can't just sit back and then complain about what happens.*

sit in *phr. v.*
to be present somewhere but not get involved in the activity: *I* ***sat in on*** *one of his classes.*

sit in for sb *phr. v.*
to do a job, go to a meeting, etc. instead of the person who usually does it: *He's sitting in for Sally while she's gone.*

sit on sth *phr. v.*
to be a member of an organization or other official group: *Hawkins sits on several committees.*

sit sth ↔ **out** *phr. v.*
to stay where you are and not take part in something until it finishes: *Due to injuries, Herrera sat out the last two games.*

sit through sth *phr. v.*
to go to a meeting, performance, etc. and stay until it finishes, even if it is very long or boring: *We had to sit through a three-hour meeting this morning.*

sit up *phr. v.*
1 to be in a sitting position or move to a sitting position after you have been lying down: *He finally was able to sit up in bed and eat something.* | *Tommy,* ***sit up straight*** *and stop slouching.*
2 to stay awake and not go to bed: *He sat up all night reading it.*
3 sit up and take notice to suddenly start paying attention to someone or something: *Their live gigs became so popular that record companies began to sit up and take notice.*

sit·com /ˈsɪtˀkɑm/ *n.* [C,U] a funny television program in which the same characters appear in different situations each week ➔ TELEVISION

ˈ**sit-down** *adj.* **1** a sit-down meal or restaurant is one in which you sit at a table and eat a formal meal **2 sit-down protest/strike etc.** POLITICS an occasion when a large group of people protest something by not moving from a particular area until their demands are listened to

site[1] /saɪt/ (Ac) *n.* [C] **1** a place where something important or interesting happened: *the site where the Pilgrims landed* | *archeological digs at historical sites* | *the* ***site of*** *an important battle*

> THESAURUS **place, position, spot, point, location** ➔ PLACE[1]

2 an area where something is being built or will be built: *a construction site* **3** a WEBSITE **4** a place that is used for a particular purpose: *a Navajo burial site* [ORIGIN: 1300—1400 Old French, Latin *situs*, from *sinere* "to leave, put"]

site[2] *v.* **be sited** to be put or built in a particular place: *The zoo is sited in the middle of the city.*

ˈ**sit-in** *n.* [C] POLITICS a protest in which people sit down and refuse to leave a place until their demands are listened to

sit·ter /ˈsɪtɚ/ *n.* [C] (spoken) a BABYSITTER

sit·ting /ˈsɪtɪŋ/ *n.* **at/in one sitting** during one continuous period of time when you are sitting in a chair: *Morris read the whole book in one sitting.*

sit·u·at·ed /ˈsɪtʃuˌeɪtɪd/ *adj.* **be situated** to be in a particular place or position: *The hotel is **situated in/near** the old market district.*

sit·u·a·tion /ˌsɪtʃuˈeɪʃən/ *n.* [C] a combination of all the things that are happening and all the conditions that exist at a particular time and place: *the present **economic/political situation** in the country* | *He asked himself what his father would have done **in** the same **situation**.*

COLLOCATIONS

difficult/bad/dangerous/tough situation – one that is bad and difficult to deal with
economic/political/financial situation
present/current situation – one that exists now
no-win situation – one that will end badly no matter what you decide to do
win-win situation – one that will end well for everyone involved in it
If a **situation improves**, it becomes better.
If a **situation worsens** or **deteriorates**, it becomes worse.

S

ˌsituation ˈcomedy *n.* [C] a SITCOM

ˈsit-up *n.* [C usually plural] an exercise for your stomach, in which you sit up from a lying position while keeping your feet on the floor ➔ CRUNCH

six /sɪks/ *number* **1** 6 **2** six o'clock: *I get out of class at six.* **3** six years old: *My folks moved here when I was six.* [ORIGIN: Old English]

ˈsix-pack *n.* [C] six bottles or cans of a drink sold together as a set: *a six-pack of beer*

six·teen /ˌsɪkˈstin◂/ *number* 16 —**sixteenth** *number*

sixth /sɪksθ/ *number* **1** 6th **2** 1/6

ˌsixth ˈsense *n.* [singular] a special ability to feel or know something without using any of your five SENSES (=sight, hearing, smell, taste, or touch) ➔ INTUITION

six·ty /ˈsɪksti/ *number* **1** 60 **2 the sixties a)** the years between 1960 and 1969 **b)** the numbers between 60 and 69, especially when used for measuring temperature **3 be in your sixties** to be aged between 60 and 69: *He's **in** his **early/mid/late** sixties.* —**sixtieth** /ˈsɪkstiɪθ/ *number*

siz·a·ble, sizeable /ˈsaɪzəbəl/ *adj.* fairly large: *a sizable crowd*

THESAURUS **big, large, substantial** ➔ BIG

size¹ /saɪz/ *n.* **1** [C,U] how big or small something is: *Class sizes are smaller at private schools.* | *an orange that is **the size of*** (=the same size as) *a softball* | *Abby and Kate are about **the same size**.* | *Shrimp vary **in size**.* **2** [U] the fact of being very big: *You should see the size of their house!* | *The company's **sheer size** gives it an advantage.* **3** [C] one of the standard measures in which clothes, goods, etc. are made and sold: *This shirt is the wrong size.* ►Don't say "have a size."◄ | *They didn't have anything **in my size**.* | *a size 10 shoe* **4 large-sized/medium-sized etc.** large, average, etc. in size: *a pocket-sized calculator*

size² *v.*

size sb/sth ↔ **up** *phr. v.* (informal) to look at or consider a person or situation and make a judgment about them: *He sized up the situation in a glance.*

siz·zle /ˈsɪzəl/ *v.* [I] to make a sound like water falling on hot metal: *bacon sizzling in the pan* —**sizzle** *n.* [singular,U] ➔ *see picture on page A20*

skate¹ /skeɪt/ *n.* [C] **1** an ICE SKATE **2** a ROLLER SKATE

skate² *v.* [I] to move on skates —**skating** *n.* [U]: *Let's **go skating**.* —**skater** *n.* [C]

skate·board /ˈskeɪtˀbɔrd/ *n.* [C] a short board with two wheels at each end, on which you stand and ride, pushing your foot along the ground in order to move —**skateboarding** *n.* [U] ➔ *see picture at* BOARD¹

ˈskate park *n.* [C] a special place where children can ride skateboards

skel·e·ton /ˈskɛlətˀn/ *n.* **1** [C] BIOLOGY the structure consisting of all the bones in a human or animal body: *the human skeleton* ➔ *see picture on page A16* **2 have a skeleton in the closet** to have a secret about something embarrassing or unpleasant that happened to you in the past **3 skeleton staff/crew/service** only enough people to keep an operation or organization working [ORIGIN: 1500—1600 Modern Latin, Greek, from *skeletos* "dried up"] —**skeletal** *adj.*

skep·tic /ˈskɛptɪk/ *n.* [C] someone who does not believe something unless s/he has definite proof [ORIGIN: 1500—1600 Greek *skeptikos* "thoughtful," from *skeptesthai* "to look, consider"]

skep·ti·cal /ˈskɛptɪkəl/ *adj.* doubting or not believing something: *Voters are highly **skeptical about/of** the proposal.* —**skepticism** /ˈskɛptəˌsɪzəm/ *n.* [U]

THESAURUS **doubtful, dubious, unconvinced** ➔ DOUBTFUL

sketch¹ /skɛtʃ/ *n.* [C] **1** a drawing that you do quickly and without a lot of details: *a pencil **sketch of** a bird*

THESAURUS **drawing, picture, doodle, comic strip, cartoon** ➔ DRAWING
picture, caricature, illustration ➔ PICTURE¹

2 a short humorous scene that is part of a longer performance: *a comedy sketch* **3** a short written or spoken description without a lot of details: *a brief sketch of each candidate* [ORIGIN: 1600—1700 Dutch *schets*, from Italian *schizzo*, from *schizzare* "to splash"]

sketch² *v.* **1** [I,T] to draw a sketch of something

THESAURUS draw, doodle, scribble → DRAW[1]

2 [T] *also* **sketch out** to describe something in a general way, giving the basic ideas: *Deming sketched out his plans for the new business.*

sketch·y /ˈskɛtʃi/ *adj.* not thorough or complete, and not having enough details to be useful: *sketchy information*

skew /skyu/ *v.* [T] if something skews the result of a test, election, RESEARCH, etc. it affects the results, making them incorrect: *Money is skewing our political system.* —**skewed** *adj.*: *Sometimes the data can be badly skewed.*

skew·er /ˈskyuɚ/ *n.* [C] a long metal or wooden stick that you put through a piece of raw food that you want to cook —**skewer** *v.* [T]

ski[1] /ski/ *n.* (plural **skis**) [C] one of a pair of long narrow pieces of wood or plastic that you fasten to boots so you can move easily on snow [ORIGIN: 1700—1800 Norwegian, Old Norse *skith* "stick of wood, ski"]

ski[2] *v.* (**skied**, **skies**) [I] to move over snow on skis —**skier** *n.* [C] —**skiing** /ˈskiɪŋ/ *n.* [U]: *We're **going skiing** this weekend.* → *see picture on page A17*

skid[1] /skɪd/ *v.* (**skidded**, **skidding**) [I] if a vehicle skids, it suddenly slides sideways and it is difficult to control: *A car **skidded on** the ice.* → *see picture at* SLIDE[1]

skid[2] *n.* [C] **1** a sudden sliding movement of a vehicle, that you cannot control: *skid marks* | *He **went into a skid** on an icy road.* **2 be on the skids/hit the skids** (informal) to begin to fail: *That was when his career hit the skids.*

skill /skɪl/ *n.* [C,U] an ability to do something very well, especially because you have learned and practiced it → TALENT: *a test of basic **skills in** reading and math* | *a child's **reading/writing/communication skills*** | *We are beginning to question his **managerial/leadership etc. skills**.* | *The men rode their horses **with** great **skill**.* [ORIGIN: 1100—1200 Old Norse *skil* "good judgment, knowledge"]

THESAURUS

talent – a natural ability to do something well: *He has a remarkable musical talent.*
ability – your level of skill at doing something: *She has great athletic ability.*
knack (informal) – a natural ability to do something well: *Kate has a knack for making people feel at ease.*
flair/gift – a natural ability to do something very well: *He has a flair for languages.*
aptitude (formal) – a natural ability or skill, especially in learning: *If you want to be an accountant, you should have an aptitude for mathematics.* → ABILITY

skilled /skɪld/ *adj.* having the training and experience needed to do something well (ANT) **unskilled**: *a **highly skilled** mechanic*

skil·let /ˈskɪlɪt/ *n.* [C] a FRYING PAN

skill·ful /ˈskɪlfəl/ *adj.* good at doing something that you have learned and practiced: *a skillful painter*

THESAURUS

expert very skillful and experienced at doing something: *He's an expert cook.*
accomplished very skillful, especially at artistic or creative things: *an accomplished musician*
talented very good at doing something because you have a natural ability: *His coach saw that he was a talented young player.*
gifted extremely good at doing something because you have a great natural ability: *Atwood is one of the most gifted writers of her generation.*
adept good at doing something that needs a lot of care and skill: *She became adept at dealing with difficult customers.*
cunning skillful at tricking people in order to get what you want: *a cunning politician*
deft moving in a quick and skillful way: *He finished the portrait with a few deft brush strokes.*

—**skillfully** *adv.*

skim /skɪm/ *v.* (**skimmed**, **skimming**) **1** [I] to remove something that is floating on the surface of a liquid: ***Skim** the fat **off** the soup.* **2** [I,T] *also* **skim through** to read something quickly to find the main facts or ideas in it: *Helen opened the newspaper and skimmed the headlines.* **3** [T] to move along quickly, nearly touching the surface of something: *birds skimming the trees*

skim sth ↔ **off** *phr. v.* to take the best people, best part of something, or money for yourself: *Corrupt leaders have skimmed off much of the country's wealth.*

ˈskim milk *n.* [U] milk that has had most of its fat removed from it

skimp /skɪmp/ *v.* [I,T] to not use enough money, time, effort, etc. on something, so it is unsuccessful or of bad quality: *Don't **skimp on** buying good shoes for your children.*

skimp·y /ˈskɪmpi/ *adj.* too small in size or quantity: *a skimpy little dress*

skin[1] /skɪn/ *n.*
1 ON A BODY [C,U] BIOLOGY the natural outer covering of a human's or animal's body: *her beautiful dark skin* | *The snake was shedding its skin.*

COLLOCATIONS

fair/pale skin
dark/olive skin
dry/oily/sensitive skin
smooth/soft skin
rough/leathery skin
good/bad skin – healthy or unhealthy skin
→ HAIR

2 FOOD [C,U] the natural outer layer of some fruits and vegetables: *banana skins*
3 ANIMAL SKIN [C,U] the skin of an animal used as leather, clothes, etc.: *a tiger skin rug*

S

4 dark-skinned/smooth-skinned etc. having a particular type or color of skin: *a fair-skinned woman*
5 LAYER [C,U] a thin solid layer that forms on the top of a liquid such as paint or milk when it gets cool or is left uncovered
6 COMPUTER [C,U] IT the way particular information appears on a computer screen, especially when this can be changed quickly and easily
7 get under sb's skin (informal) to annoy someone, especially by the way you behave: *I could tell my comment had gotten under his skin.*
8 have thin/thick skin to be easily upset or not easily upset by criticism
9 (do sth) by the skin of your teeth (informal) to succeed in doing something, when you have almost failed to do it: *We made it there by the skin of our teeth.*
10 make sb's skin crawl to make someone feel uncomfortable, nervous, or slightly afraid
11 sth is only skin deep used in order to say that something may seem important or effective, but it really is not because it only affects the way things appear: *Beauty is only skin deep.* [ORIGIN: 1100—1200 Old Norse *skinn*]

S

skin[2] *v.* (**skinned**, **skinning**) [T] to remove the skin from an animal, fruit, or vegetable

skin·flint /ˈskɪnˌflɪnt/ *n.* [C] (informal, disapproving) someone who hates spending or giving away money SYN **miser**

skin·head /ˈskɪnhɛd/ *n.* [C] a young person who SHAVES off his/her hair and often behaves violently toward people who are not white

skin·ny /ˈskɪni/ *adj.* (comparative **skinnier**, superlative **skinniest**) very thin, especially in a way that is not attractive: *a tall, skinny kid*

THESAURUS **thin, slim, slender, slight, lean, underweight, gaunt** ➔ THIN[1]

ˈskinny ˌdipping *n.* [U] (informal) swimming without any clothes on

ˌskin-ˈtight *adj.* clothes that are skin-tight fit tightly against your body: *skin-tight jeans*

skip /skɪp/ *v.* (**skipped**, **skipping**) **1** [T] to not do something that you would usually do or that you should do: *I'd skipped breakfast.* | *Brad got in trouble for **skipping school**.* **2** [I] to move forward with quick jumps from one foot to the other: *children **skipping down/across** the street*

THESAURUS **jump, hop, leap** ➔ JUMP[1]

3 [I,T] to not read, mention, or deal with something that would normally come or happen next: *I skipped question four.* | *Readers occasionally **skip over** a word they don't know.* **4** [I] to go from one subject, place, etc. to another in no particular order: *She **skips from** one topic **to** another.*

skip·per /ˈskɪpɚ/ *n.* [C] (informal) someone who is in charge of a ship SYN **captain**

skir·mish /ˈskɚmɪʃ/ *n.* [C] a military fight between small groups of people or soldiers: *a border skirmish*

skirt[1] /skɚt/ *n.* [C] a piece of women's clothing that fits around the waist and hangs down like the bottom part of a dress: *She was wearing a white blouse and a plain black skirt.* | *a **short/long skirt*** [ORIGIN: 1200—1300 Old Norse *skyrta* "shirt"] ➔ *see picture at* CLOTHES

skirt[2] *also* **skirt around** *v.* [T] **1** to go around the outside edge of a place: *The soldiers skirted around the town and crossed the river.* **2** to avoid talking about an important problem, subject, etc.: *The company spokesman skirted the question.* **3** if you skirt the rules or the law, you do something that is not illegal, but that does not exactly follow the rules

skit /skɪt/ *n.* [C] a short funny play

skit·tish /ˈskɪt̮ɪʃ/ *adj.* nervous, frightened, or not sure about something: *a skittish horse*

skulk /skʌlk/ *v.* [I] to hide or move around quietly because you do not want to be seen: *Two men were **skulking in** the shadows.*

skull /skʌl/ *n.* [C] BIOLOGY the bones of a person's or animal's head ➔ *see picture on page A16*

skull·cap /ˈskʌlkæp/ *n.* [C] a YARMULKE

skunk /skʌŋk/ *n.* [C] a small black and white animal that produces a very bad smell if it feels threatened

sky /skaɪ/ *n.* (plural **skies**) **1** [C,U] the space above the Earth where the Sun, clouds, and stars are: *a **clear/cloudless/overcast etc.** sky* | *a few clouds **in the sky*** **2 skies** [plural] the sky – used especially when talking about the weather: *clear skies* **3 the sky's the limit** (spoken) used to say that there is no limit to what someone can achieve, spend, etc. [ORIGIN: 1200—1300 Old Norse "cloud"]

sky·div·ing /ˈskaɪˌdaɪvɪŋ/ *n.* [U] the sport of jumping from an aircraft and falling through the sky before opening a PARACHUTE —**skydiver** *n.* [C]

ˌsky-ˈhigh *adj.* (informal) extremely high or expensive: *Prices at the auction were sky-high.* —**sky-high** *adv.*

sky·light /ˈskaɪlaɪt/ *n.* [C] a window in the roof of a building

skyline

sky·line /ˈskaɪlaɪn/ *n.* [C] the shape made by tall buildings or hills against the sky: *the New York City skyline*

ˈsky ˌmarshall *n.* [C] a specially trained person who carries a gun and whose job is to travel on an airplane and protect it from attack by TERRORISTS SYN **air marshall**

sky·rock·et /ˈskaɪˌrɑkɪt/ *v.* [I] to increase suddenly and by large amounts: *Property values have skyrocketed.*

sky·scrap·er /ˈskaɪˌskreɪpɚ/ *n.* [C] a very tall building in a city

slab /slæb/ *n.* [C] a thick flat piece of a hard material such as stone: *a concrete slab*

slack[1] /slæk/ *adj.* **1** hanging loosely, or not pulled tight: *a slack rope* **2** with less business activity than usual: *People get laid off when things are slack.* **3** (disapproving) not taking enough care to do things correctly: *The waiters were slack.*

slack[2] *n.* **1 slacks** [plural] a pair of pants **2 take/pick up the slack a)** to do something that needs to be done because the person or organization that usually does it is no longer doing it: *As the government cuts programs, charities try to pick up the slack.* **b)** to make a rope tighter **3 cut/give sb some/any slack** (informal) to allow someone to do something without criticizing him/her or making it more difficult: *They have no reason to cut the opposing team any slack.* **4** [U] looseness in the way something such as a rope hangs or is fastened: *He **gave** the line **some slack**, then slowly began reeling it in.*

slack[3] *also* **slack off** *v.* [I] to not work as quickly as you should on your job: *Everything was going well, and I thought I could slack off a little.* —**slacker** *n.* [C]

slack·en /ˈslækən/ *v.* [I,T] to gradually become slower, weaker, or less active, or to make something do this: *The rain slackened briefly.*

slag /slæg/ *n.* [U] waste material that is left when metal is obtained from rock

slain /sleɪn/ *v.* the past participle of SLAY

slake /sleɪk/ *v.* (literary) **slake your thirst** to drink so that you are not THIRSTY

slam[1] /slæm/ *v.* (**slammed**, **slamming**) **1** [I,T] if a door, gate, etc. slams, or if someone slams it, it shuts loudly with a lot of force: *Baxter left the room, slamming the door.* | *The door **slammed shut**.* **2** [I,T] to hit something or someone against a surface with a lot of force, or to hit something with a lot of force: *Manya **slammed** the phone **down**.* | *He was going 50 mph when he **slammed into** the back of a car stopped at a red light.* **3** [T] (informal, written) to criticize someone strongly: *Watson was slammed for not acting sooner.*

slam[2] *n.* [C usually singular] the noise or action of hitting or closing something hard

ˈslam dunk *n.* [C] an action in basketball when a player jumps up high and throws the ball down through the basket —**slam dunk** *v.* [I]

slan·der /ˈslændɚ/ *n.* [C,U] a spoken statement about someone that is not true and is intended to damage the good opinion that people have of him/her —**slander** *v.* [T] —**slanderous** *adj.*

THESAURUS **lie, fib, falsehood, libel, perjury** → LIE[3]

slang /slæŋ/ *n.* [U] very informal, sometimes offensive, language that is used especially by people who belong to a particular group —**slangy** *adj.*

THESAURUS **language, lingo, jargon, terminology** → LANGUAGE

slant[1] /slænt/ *v.* **1** [I,T] to slope, or to make something slope in a particular direction: *a hat slanted over his forehead* **2** [T] to provide information in a way that unfairly supports one opinion, gives an advantage to one group, etc.

slant[2] *n.* [singular] **1** a sloping position or angle: *The house seems to be built **at/on a slant**.* **2** a way of writing or thinking about a subject that shows support for a particular set of ideas or beliefs: ***a** feminist **slant on** Dickens's novels*

slan·ted /ˈslæntɪd/ *adj.* **1** (disapproving) providing facts or information in a way that unfairly supports only one side of an argument or one opinion SYN **biased**: *The article was slanted.* **2** sloping: *a slanted roof*

slap[1] /slæp/ *v.* (**slapped**, **slapping**) [T] **1** to hit someone quickly with the flat part of your hand: *She **slapped** his **face**.*

THESAURUS **hit, punch, beat, smack, whack, strike** → HIT[1]

2 (informal) to suddenly make someone do something more, pay more money, etc.: *In 1990, the U.S. **slapped** sanctions **on** Iraq.* **3 slap sb on the back** to hit someone on the back in a friendly way, often as a way of praising him/her

slap sth ↔ **on** *phr. v.* to put or spread something quickly on a surface in a careless way: *Just slap on a coat of paint.*

slap[2] *n.* [C] **1** a quick hit with the flat part of your hand **2 a slap in the face** an action that seems to be deliberately intended to offend or upset someone: *The offer was so low as to be a slap in the face.* **3 a slap on the wrist** (informal) a punishment that is not very severe

slap·dash /ˈslæpdæʃ/ *adj.* careless and done too quickly: *a slapdash job*

slap·stick /ˈslæpˌstɪk/ *n.* [U] humorous acting in which the actors fall over, throw things at each other, etc.

slash[1] /slæʃ/ *v.* **1** [I,T] to cut or try to cut something in a violent way with a sharp weapon, making a long deep cut: *Someone had slashed the car's front tire.* **2** [T] (informal, written) to greatly reduce an amount or price: *a campaign promise to slash taxes*

THESAURUS **reduce, lower, decrease, cut** → REDUCE

slash[2] *n.* [C] **1** *also* **slash mark** a line (/) used in writing to separate words, numbers, or letters **2** a long narrow cut in something

slat /slæt/ *n.* [C] a thin flat piece of wood, plastic, or metal, used especially in furniture

slate¹ /sleɪt/ *n.* **1** [U] EARTH SCIENCES a dark gray rock that can be easily split into thin flat pieces **2** [C] POLITICS a list of people that voters can choose in an election

slate² *v.* **be slated to do sth/be slated for sth** if something is slated to happen, it is planned to happen in the future: *The committee is slated to vote on the bill next week.* | *The corner office buildings are slated for demolition.*

slath·er /ˈslæðɚ/ *v.* [T] (informal) to cover something with a thick layer of a soft substance: *fresh bread slathered with butter*

slaugh·ter /ˈslɔt̬ɚ/ *v.* [T] **1** to kill a lot of people in a cruel or violent way: *Hundreds of innocent civilians had been slaughtered by government troops.*

THESAURUS **kill, murder, massacre, exterminate, slay** ➔ KILL¹

2 to kill an animal for food **3** (informal) to defeat an opponent by a large number of points: *New York slaughtered Boston, 11–2.* —**slaughter** *n.* [U]: *the slaughter of innocent people*

S

slaugh·ter·house /ˈslɔt̬ɚˌhaʊs/ *n.* [C] a building where animals are killed for their meat

slave¹ /sleɪv/ *n.* [C] **1** someone who is owned by another person and is forced to work without pay for him/her **2 be a slave to/of sth** (disapproving) to be so strongly influenced by something that you cannot make your own decisions: *a* ***slave to fashion*** [ORIGIN: 1200—1300 Old French *esclave*, from Medieval Latin *sclavus*, from *Sclavus* "Slavic person;" because in the early Middle Ages many Slavic people in central Europe were slaves]

slave² *v.* [I] to work very hard with little time to rest: *Hector grew up watching his father* ***slaving away*** *at a factory job.*

ˈslave ˌdriver *n.* [C] (informal, disapproving) someone who makes people work extremely hard

ˌslave ˈlabor *n.* [U] **1** (informal) work for which you are paid a very small amount of money **2** work done by slaves, or the slaves that do this work

slav·er·y /ˈsleɪvəri/ *n.* [U] the system of having slaves, or the condition of being a slave: ***Slavery*** *was* ***abolished*** (=officially ended) *after the Civil War.* | *They were captured and* ***sold into slavery****.*

slav·ish /ˈsleɪvɪʃ/ *adj.* (disapproving) too willing to do what you are told to do or to behave like someone else, without thinking for yourself: *slavish devotion to duty*

slay /sleɪ/ *v.* (past tense **slew** /slu/, past participle **slain** /sleɪn/) [T] to kill a person or animal violently: *St. George slew the dragon.* —**slaying** *n.* [C]

THESAURUS **kill, murder, assassinate, slaughter** ➔ KILL¹

sleaze /sliz/ *n.* [U] immoral behavior, usually involving sex or lies: *allegations of political sleaze*

slea·zy /ˈslizi/ *adj.* (comparative **sleazier**, superlative **sleaziest**) (disapproving) **1** a sleazy place is dirty, cheap, or in bad condition: *sleazy bars* **2** relating to sex or dishonest behavior: *a sleazy lawyer*

sled /slɛd/ *n.* [C] a vehicle that slides over snow, often used by children —**sled** *v.* [I]

sledge ham·mer /ˈslɛdʒ ˌhæmɚ/ *n.* [C] a large heavy hammer

sleek /slik/ *adj.* **1** sleek hair or fur is smooth, shiny, and healthy-looking: *a cat's sleek fur* **2** having a smooth attractive shape: *a sleek limousine*

sleep¹ /slip/ *v.* (past tense and past participle **slept** /slɛpt/) **1** [I] to rest your mind and body by lying down with your eyes closed ➔ ASLEEP: *"Did you* ***sleep well****?"* | *He was* ***sleeping soundly*** *when the phone rang.* | *I* ***couldn't sleep*** *last night.* | *If you're tired, why don't you* ***sleep late*** (=sleep until late in the morning) *tomorrow?* | *Goodnight,* ***sleep tight*** (=sleep well).

USAGE

Use **sleep** when you are giving more information, for example how long someone sleeps, or where s/he sleeps: *Most people sleep for about eight hours.* | *He slept downstairs.*

Do not use **sleep** to talk about starting to sleep. Use **fall asleep** or **go to sleep**: *She fell asleep in front of the TV.*

COLLOCATIONS

sleep well/badly
sleep soundly – to sleep deeply and peacefully
sleep like a baby/sleep like a log – to sleep very well, without waking up at all
sleep late/sleep in – to deliberately sleep later than usual in the morning
sleep lightly – to wake up very easily if there is any noise

2 sleep on it (spoken) to not make a decision about something important until the next day **3** [T] to have enough beds for a particular number of people: *The tent sleeps six.* [ORIGIN: Old English *slæp*]

sleep around *phr. v.* (disapproving) to have sex with many people without having a serious relationship with any of them

sleep in *phr. v.* to sleep later than usual in the morning: *I slept in till 10:00 on Saturday.*

sleep sth ↔ **off** *phr. v.* to sleep until you are no longer drunk: *Why don't you take him home so he can* ***sleep it off****.*

sleep over *phr. v.* to sleep at someone's house for a night: *Mom, can I* ***sleep over at*** *Ann's tonight?*

sleep through sth *phr. v.* to continue sleeping while something noisy is happening: *How could you have slept through the earthquake?*

sleep together *phr. v.* (informal) if people sleep together, they have sex with each other

sleep with sb *phr. v.* (informal) to have sex with someone, especially someone you are not married to: *Everyone knows he's sleeping with Diana.*

sleep² *n.* **1** [U] the natural state of being asleep ➔ ASLEEP: *I rarely get more than 6 hours of sleep a night.* | *What time did you **get to sleep*** (=start sleeping)? | *I didn't **get** much **sleep** last night.* | *Ed sometimes talks **in** his **sleep*** (=while he is sleeping). **2** [singular] a period when you are sleeping: *You'll feel better after a **good night's sleep*** (=a night when you sleep well). | *A sudden noise woke me from a **deep sleep**.* **3 go to sleep a)** to start sleeping: *Katherine went to sleep about 7:00 last night.* **b)** (informal) if a part of your body goes to sleep, you cannot feel it for a short time because it has not been getting enough blood **4 lose (any) sleep over sth** (spoken) to worry about something: *If his client goes to jail, he won't lose any sleep over it.* **5 put a dog/cat etc. to sleep** to give an animal drugs so that it dies without pain

sleep·er /ˈslipɚ/ *n.* [C] **1** someone who is asleep or who sleeps in a particular way: *Sam's a **heavy/light sleeper*** (=he sleeps well or wakes up easily). **2** a movie, book, etc. that is successful, even though people did not expect it to be

ˈsleeping bag *n.* [C] a large warm bag for sleeping in, especially when camping

ˈsleeping pill *n.* [C] a PILL that helps you to sleep

sleep·less /ˈsliplɪs/ *adj.* **a sleepless night** a night when you are unable to sleep —**sleeplessness** *n.* [U]

sleep·walk·er /ˈslipˌwɔkɚ/ *n.* [C] someone who walks while s/he is sleeping —**sleepwalk** *v.* [I] —**sleepwalking** *n.* [U]

sleep·y /ˈslipi/ *adj.* (comparative **sleepier**, superlative **sleepiest**) **1** tired and ready for sleep: *I don't know why I'm so sleepy.* **2** a sleepy place is quiet and without much activity: *a sleepy little town*

THESAURUS **quiet, calm, tranquil, peaceful** ➔ QUIET¹

—**sleepily** *adv.* —**sleepiness** *n.* [U]

sleep·y·head /ˈslipiˌhɛd/ *n.* [C] (spoken) someone, especially a child, who looks as if s/he wants to go to sleep: *It's time for bed, sleepyhead.*

sleet /slit/ *n.* [U] freezing rain —**sleet** *v.* [I]

THESAURUS **rain, drizzle, shower, downpour, hail, hailstones** ➔ RAIN¹
snow, snowflakes, slush, blizzard, frost ➔ SNOW¹

sleeve /sliv/ *n.* **1** [C] the part of a piece of clothing that covers your arm or part of your arm: *a blouse with short/long sleeves* **2 long-sleeved/short-sleeved** with long or short sleeves: *a long-sleeved shirt* **3 have sth up your sleeve** (informal) to have a secret plan that you are going to use later: *Janssen usually has a few surprises up his sleeve.* [ORIGIN: Old English *sliefe*]

sleeve·less /ˈslivlɪs/ *adj.* without sleeves: *a sleeveless dress*

sleigh /sleɪ/ *n.* [C] a large vehicle pulled by animals, used for traveling on snow

sleight of hand /ˌslaɪt̬ əv ˈhænd/ *n.* [U] quick skillful movements with your hands when performing magic tricks

slen·der /ˈslɛndɚ/ *adj.* thin, graceful, and attractive: *long slender fingers*

THESAURUS **thin, slim, slight, skinny, lean** ➔ THIN¹

slept /slɛpt/ *v.* the past tense and past participle of SLEEP¹

sleuth /sluθ/ *n.* [C] (old-fashioned) someone who tries to find out information about a crime [ORIGIN: 1800—1900 *sleuthhound* "dog used for tracking people" (14—20 centuries), from *sleuth* "track" (12—15 centuries) (from Old Norse *sloth*) + *hound*]

slew¹ /slu/ *n.* **a slew of sth** (informal) a large number: *Her work as a reporter has won her a slew of awards.*

slew² *v.* the past tense of SLAY

slice¹ /slaɪs/ *n.* [C] **1** a thin flat piece of bread, meat, etc. cut from a larger piece: *a **slice of** pizza* | *Cut the tomato **into** thin/thick **slices**.* ➔ PIECE¹ **2** a part or a piece of something: *The German company wants a **slice of** the U.S. market.* **3 a slice of life** a film, play, or book which shows life as it really is [ORIGIN: 1400—1500 Old French *esclice* "thin piece broken off," from *esclicier* "to splinter"]

slice² *v.* **1** [T] *also* **slice up** to cut meat, bread, etc. into thin flat pieces: *Could you slice the bread?* ➔ *see picture at* CUT¹

THESAURUS **cut, chop (up), dice, peel, carve, shred, grate** ➔ CUT¹

2 [I,T] to cut something easily with one movement of a sharp knife or edge: *Careful – that blade could **slice through** your finger.*

slick¹ /slɪk/ *adj.* **1** (disapproving) good at persuading people, often in a way that does not seem honest: *a slick salesman* **2** (disapproving) attractive or skillful, but not containing any important or interesting ideas: *slick commercials* **3** smooth and slippery: *The roads are **slick with** ice.*

slick² *n.* [C] an OIL SLICK

slick³ *v.*
slick sth ↔ **down/back** *phr. v.* to make hair smooth and shiny by putting oil, water, etc. on it

slide¹ /slaɪd/ *v.* (past tense and past participle **slid** /slɪd/) **1** [I,T] to move smoothly over a surface while continuing to touch it, or to make something move in this way: *children **sliding on** the ice* | *She **slid** the box **across** the floor.* | *The door **slides open** automatically.* **2** [I,T] to move somewhere quietly without being noticed, or to move something in this way: *She **slid out** of the room without waking anyone.* | *He **slid** the gun **into** his pocket.* **3** [I] ECONOMICS to become lower in value, number, or amount: *Car sales slid 0.5% in July.* **4** [I] to gradually become worse, or to begin to have a problem: *Morrison gradually slid into alcohol and drug abuse.* **5 let sth slide** (informal) to ignore something: *I didn't agree, but I **let it slide**.* [ORIGIN: Old English *slidan*]

slide² *n.* [C] **1** a large structure for children to slide down while playing **2** a photograph in a frame that you shine a light through to show a picture on a screen or wall: *slides of our vacation* **3** a decrease in the amount, value, standard, or quality of something: *a **slide in** interest rates* | *The school is worried about the **slide in** student performance.* **4** EARTH SCIENCES a sudden fall of earth, stones, snow, etc. down a slope: *a rock slide* **5** SCIENCE a small thin piece of glass, used for holding something when you look at it under a MICROSCOPE → *see picture at* MICROSCOPE

'slide pro,jector *n.* [C] a piece of equipment that makes slides appear on a screen

,sliding 'scale *n.* [C] a system for calculating how much you pay for taxes, medical treatment, etc., in which the amount that you pay changes according to different conditions: *Fees are calculated **on a sliding scale**.*

slight¹ /slaɪt/ *adj.* **1** small in degree, and not serious or important: *a slight delay* | *a slight increase* | *a slight headache* **2 not the slightest chance/doubt/difference etc.** no doubt, chance, etc. at all: *I didn't have the slightest idea who that man was.* **3** someone who is slight is thin and delicate: *a slight old lady*

THESAURUS **thin, slim, slender, skinny, lean** → THIN¹

slight² *v.* [T] to offend someone by treating him/her rudely: *Meg **felt slighted** at not being invited to the party.*

slight³ *n.* [C] (formal) a remark or action that offends someone: *I consider the comment a **slight on** the quality of our work!*

slight·ly /ˈslaɪtli/ *adv.* **1** a little: *She raised her eyebrow slightly.* | *The official gave a **slightly different** version of events.* | *The trip took **slightly more** than an hour.* **2 slightly built** having a thin and delicate body

slim¹ /slɪm/ *adj.* **1** attractively thin: *tall and slim*

THESAURUS **thin, slender, slight, skinny, lean** → THIN¹

2 very small in amount or number: *a slim lead in the polls* | *We have only **a slim chance** of winning.* [ORIGIN: 1600—1700 Dutch "bad, of low quality"]

slim² *v.* (**slimmed**, **slimming**)

slim down *phr. v.* **1** to reduce the size or number of something: *Apex Co. is slimming down its workforce to cut costs.* **2** to become thinner by eating less or exercising more: *I've been trying to slim down since Christmas.*

slime /slaɪm/ *n.* [U] a thick slippery substance that looks or smells bad

slim·y /ˈslaɪmi/ *adj.* **1** covered with slime: *slimy rocks* **2** (informal, disapproving) friendly in a way that does not seem sincere: *a slimy politician*

sling¹ /slɪŋ/ *v.* (past tense and past participle **slung** /slʌŋ/) [T] to throw or put something somewhere in a way that is careless and forceful: *She **slung** her purse **over** her shoulder.*

sling² *n.* [C] **1** a piece of cloth tied around your neck to support your injured arm or hand: *Emily's arm has been **in a sling** for six weeks.* **2** a set of ropes or strong pieces of cloth that are used to lift and carry heavy objects

sling·shot /ˈslɪŋʃɑt/ *n.* [C] a stick in the shape of a Y with a thin band of rubber across the top, used especially by children to throw stones

slink /slɪŋk/ *v.* (past tense and past participle **slunk** /slʌŋk/) [I] to move somewhere quietly and secretly, especially because you are afraid or ashamed: *He lowered his eyes and slunk back into his office.*

slip¹ /slɪp/ *v.* (**slipped**, **slipping**) **1** [I] to accidentally slide a short distance quickly, or to fall by sliding in this way: *Joan slipped and fell.* | *Be careful not to **slip on** the ice.* | *The knife slipped and cut her finger.* → *see picture at* SLIDE¹

THESAURUS **fall, trip, stumble, lose your balance** → FALL¹

2 [I] to go somewhere, without attracting other

people's attention: *I managed to **slip out** of the office before 5:00.* **3** [T] to put something somewhere, or to give someone something quietly or secretly: *Dad slipped me $50 when Mom wasn't looking.* | *Someone slipped a note under my door.* **4** [I,T] to put on or take off a piece of clothing quickly and smoothly: *I'll just **slip into** something more comfortable.* | *He **slipped off** his coat and went upstairs.* **5** [I] to become worse or lower than before (SYN) **fall**: *Standards have slipped in the restaurant since the head chef left.* **6 let sth slip** to say something without meaning to, when you had wanted it to be a secret: *Lance **let it slip that** Julie was planning to quit.* **7 slip your mind** if something slips your mind, you forget to do it: *I meant to call you but it completely slipped my mind.*

slip out *phr. v.* if something slips out, you say it without intending to: *I'm sorry I spoiled the surprise; it just slipped out.*

slip up *phr. v.* to make a mistake: *They slipped up and sent me the wrong form.*

slip² *n.* [C] **1** a small or narrow piece of paper: *a **slip of paper** with her phone number on it* **2 a slip of the tongue** something that you say when you meant to say something else **3** a piece of underwear, similar to a thin dress or skirt, that a woman wears under a dress or skirt **4 give sb the slip** (informal) to escape from someone who is chasing you: *He gave the police the slip.*

slip·knot /ˈslɪpnɑt/ *n.* [C] a knot that you can make tighter by pulling one of its ends

ˌslipped ˈdisc *n.* [C] a painful injury caused when a connecting part between the bones in your back moves out of place

slip·per /ˈslɪpɚ/ *n.* [C] a light soft shoe that you wear in your house → *see picture at* SHOE¹

slip·per·y /ˈslɪpəri/ *adj.* **1** something that is slippery is difficult to hold, walk on, etc. because it is wet or GREASY: *Careful, the sidewalk's slippery.* **2 a/the slippery slope** the beginning of something that will be hard to stop and will develop into something very bad

slip·shod /ˈslɪpʃɑd/ *adj.* (disapproving) done too quickly and carelessly: *slipshod work*

ˈslip-up *n.* [C] a careless mistake: *We cannot afford another slip-up.*

slit /slɪt/ *v.* (past tense and past participle **slit**, present participle **slitting**) [T] to make a straight narrow cut in cloth, paper, etc.: *Slit the pie crust before baking.* —**slit** *n.* [C]

slith·er /ˈslɪðɚ/ *v.* [I] to slide or move across a surface, twisting and moving like a snake

sliv·er /ˈslɪvɚ/ *n.* [C] a very small narrow piece of something: *a **sliver of** glass* | *You can just see a sliver of the ocean from our hotel.*

slob /slɑb/ *n.* [C] (informal) someone who is lazy, dirty, and messy

slob·ber /ˈslɑbɚ/ *v.* [I] to let SALIVA (=liquid produced in your mouth) come out of your mouth and run down: *The dog's slobbered all over the rug!*

slog /slɑg/ *v.* (**slogged**, **slogging**) [I] **1** to work very hard at something without stopping: *I've been **slogging through** a boring 400 page novel.* **2** to walk somewhere with difficulty: *soldiers **slogging through** the mud*

slo·gan /ˈsloʊgən/ *n.* [C] a short phrase that is easy to remember, used by politicians, companies that are advertising, etc.: *The crowd shouted anti-racist slogans.*

slop¹ /slɑp/ *v.* (**slopped**, **slopping**) [I,T] to make liquid move around or over the edge of something, or to move in this way: *The coffee slopped out of the cup and all over me.*

slop² *n.* [U] **1** food waste that is used for feeding animals **2** food that is too soft and tastes bad: *I'm not eating that slop!*

slope¹ /sloʊp/ *n.* **1** [C] a piece of ground or a surface that is higher at one end than the other: *a ski slope* **2** [singular] the angle at which something slopes: *a **slope of** 30°*

slope² *v.* [I] if the ground or a surface slopes, it is higher at one end than the other: *They looked out over a broad meadow that sloped toward the water.*

slop·py /ˈslɑpi/ *adj.* **1** not done carefully or thoroughly: *sloppy work* | *sloppy handwriting* **2** sloppy clothes are loose-fitting and not neat: *a sloppy old sweater* **3** wet and disgusting: *a sloppy kiss* —**sloppily** *adv.* —**sloppiness** *n.* [U]

slosh /slɑʃ/ *v.* [I] **1** to walk through water or mud in a noisy way: *kids sloshing through puddles* **2** if a liquid in a container sloshes, it moves against the sides of the container: *water **sloshing around** in the bottom of the boat*

sloshed /slɑʃt/ *adj.* (informal) drunk: *Gus was sloshed even before the party started.*

slot¹ /slɑt/ *n.* [C] **1** a long narrow hole made in a surface: *Which slot do the coins go in?* **2** a short period of time allowed for one particular event on a program: *the most popular TV show in its **time slot*** [ORIGIN: 1300—1400 Old French *esclot* "hollow place in the bone in the middle of the chest"]

slot² *v.* (**slotted**, **slotting**) [I,T] to put something into a slot, or to go in a slot: *The cassette **slots in** here.*

sloth /slɔθ, sloʊθ/ *n.* **1** [C] a slow-moving animal from Central and South America **2** [U] (literary) laziness —**slothful** *adj.*

ˈslot maˌchine *n.* [C] a machine in which you put coins so that you can play games or try to win money

slouch¹ /slaʊtʃ/ *v.* [I] to stand, sit, or walk with your shoulders bent forward in a way that makes you look tired or lazy: *Stanley was slouched against the wall, fast asleep.*

slouch² *n.* **1** [singular] the position of your body when you slouch **2 be no slouch** (informal) to be very good or skillful at something: *He's no slouch with a camera.*

slov·en·ly /ˈslʌvənli, ˈslɑ-/ *adj.* dirty, messy, and careless: *a slovenly old woman* [ORIGIN: 1500—1600 *sloven* "dirty messy person"]

slow[1] /sloʊ/ *adj.* **1** not moving, being done, or happening quickly (ANT) **fast**: *The slowest runners started at the back.* | *They've been* ***slow in*** *answering our letter* (=took a long time to answer it). | *The police were* ***slow to*** *respond* (=took too long to do something). | *Progress has been* ***painfully*** ***slow*** (=far too slow).

THESAURUS

gradual – happening slowly over a long period of time: *There has been a gradual improvement in the economic situation.*
leisurely – doing something slowly because you are enjoying what you are doing: *They went for a leisurely walk in Central Park.* | *a leisurely breakfast*
sluggish – moving or doing something more slowly than normal: *The car felt sluggish when he first started driving it.*
tardy – doing something too slowly or too late: *If you are tardy by more than 20 minutes it will count as an unauthorized absence.*

S

2 [not before noun] showing time that is earlier than the true time (ANT) **fast**: *My watch is a few minutes slow.* **3** if business is slow, there are not many customers: *It's been a slow day.* **4** someone who is slow does not understand things quickly or easily: *The school gives extra help for slower students.* [ORIGIN: Old English *slaw*]

slow[2] *v.* [I,T] *also* **slow up** to become slower, or to make something slower: *Her breathing slowed and she fell asleep.* | *Road work slowed up traffic this morning.*

slow down *phr. v.* [I,T] to become slower, or to make someone or something slower: *Slow down or you'll get a speeding ticket.* | *Dave's back trouble is slowing him down.*

slow[3] *adv.* slowly: *Can you run a little slower? I can't keep up.*

slow·down /ˈsloʊdaʊn/ *n.* [C usually singular] **1** a reduction in activity or speed: *a slowdown in the tourist trade* **2** a period when people deliberately work slowly in order to protest about something

slow·ly /ˈsloʊli/ *adv.* at a slow speed or rate: *Doctors slowly removed the bandages from her arm.* | *Things have begun to change slowly.*

ˌslow ˈmotion *n.* [U] movement in a movie or television program shown at a much slower speed than the speed at which it happened: *Let's see a replay of that goal* ***in slow motion***.

slow·poke /ˈsloʊpoʊk/ *n.* [C] (spoken) someone who moves or does things too slowly

ˌslow-ˈwitted *adj.* not quick to understand things

sludge /slʌdʒ/ *n.* [U] a soft thick substance made of mud, waste, oil, etc.

slug[1] /slʌg/ *n.* [C] **1** a small creature with a soft body, that moves very slowly and eats garden plants **2** (informal) a bullet **3** (informal) a piece of metal used illegally instead of a coin in machines that sell things

slug[2] *v.* (**slugged**, **slugging**) [T] **1** (informal) to hit someone hard with your closed hand (SYN) **punch**: *I stood up and he slugged me again.* **2 slug it out** to argue or fight until someone wins or something has been decided: *The two sides are slugging it out in court.* **3** to hit a baseball hard

slug·gish /ˈslʌgɪʃ/ *adj.* moving, working, or reacting more slowly than normal (SYN) **slow**: *The traffic was sluggish downtown.*

sluice[1] /slus/ *n.* [C] a passage for water to flow through, with a gate that can stop the water if necessary

sluice[2] *v.* [T] to wash something with a lot of water

slum[1] /slʌm/ *n.* [C] an area of a city with old buildings in very bad condition, where many poor people live: *She grew up in* ***the slums*** *of L.A.* → AREA

slum[2] *v.* (**slummed**, **slumming**) [I,T] to spend time in conditions that are much worse than those you are used to: *We traveled around the country,* ***slumming it***.

slum·ber /ˈslʌmbɚ/ *v.* [I] (literary) to sleep —**slumber** *n.* [singular,U] —**slumbers** *n.* [plural]

ˈslumber ˌparty *n.* [C] a party in which a group of children sleep at one child's house

slump[1] /slʌmp/ *v.* [I] **1** ECONOMICS to suddenly go down in price, value, or number: *Car sales have slumped recently.* **2** to fall or lean against something because you are not strong enough to stand: *He was found* ***slumped over*** *the steering wheel of his car.*

slump[2] *n.* [C] **1** ECONOMICS a sudden decrease in prices, sales, profits, etc.: *a* ***slump in*** *the housing market* **2** ECONOMICS a period when there is a reduction in business and many people lose their jobs: *an economic slump*

THESAURUS **recession, depression, downturn** → RECESSION

3 a time when a player or team does not play well: *The Yankees needed this win to pull them out of a slump.*

slung /slʌŋ/ *v.* the past tense and past participle of SLING

slunk /slʌŋk/ *v.* the past tense and past participle of SLINK

slur[1] /slɚ/ *v.* (**slurred**, **slurring**) **1** [I,T] to speak unclearly without separating words or sounds: *After a few drinks, he started to* ***slur his words***. **2** [T] to criticize someone or something unfairly

slur² *n.* [C] an unfair criticism, or an offensive remark: ***racial slurs***

slurp /slɚp/ *v.* [I,T] to drink a liquid while making a noisy sucking sound —**slurp** *n.* [C]

THESAURUS **drink, sip/take a sip, gulp sth down, swig, take/have a swig** → DRINK²

slush /slʌʃ/ *n.* **1** [U] partly melted snow

THESAURUS **snow, snowflakes, sleet, blizzard, frost** → SNOW¹

2 [C] a drink made with crushed ice and a sweet liquid: *orange slush* —**slushy** *adj.*

'slush fund *n.* [C] a sum of money kept for dishonest purposes, especially by a politician

sly /slaɪ/ *adj.* (comparative **slier** or **slyer**, superlative **sliest** or **slyest**) **1** using tricks and dishonesty to get what you want: *He's sly and greedy.* **2** showing that you know something that others do not know: *a sly smile* **3 on the sly** (informal) secretly doing something you are not supposed to be doing: *He's been seeing someone else on the sly.* —**slyly** *adv.*

smack¹ /smæk/ *v.* [T] **1** to hit someone or something, especially with your open hand → PUNCH: *She smacked him hard across the face.*

THESAURUS **hit, punch, slap, beat, whack, strike** → HIT¹

2 smack your lips to make a short loud noise with your lips because you are hungry

smack of sth *phr. v.* to seem to have a particular bad quality: *a policy that smacks of age discrimination.*

smack² *n.* [C] a hit with your open hand, or a noise like the sound of this: *She gave him a smack on the hand.*

smack³ *adv.* (informal) **1** exactly or directly in the middle of something, in front of something, etc.: *an old building **smack (dab) in the middle of** campus* **2** if something goes smack into something, it hits it with a lot of force: *The van **ran smack** into the wall.*

small /smɔl/ *adj.* **1** not large in size or amount (ANT) **big**: *a small dark woman | Rhode Island is the smallest state. | a store selling small appliances | This jacket is too small.*

THESAURUS
little – small in size: *a little house*
tiny – very small: *a tiny baby*
minute – extremely small: *Even in minute amounts, the chemical is very harmful.*
miniature – very small, used about things that are normally a larger size: *a miniature camera*
minuscule – extremely small: *Police found a minuscule amount of poison in the bottle.*
petite – used about a woman who is short and thin in an attractive way: *a petite girl*
diminutive (formal) – very small, used especially about people: *a diminutive man* → BIG

2 unimportant or easy to deal with: *a small problem | We may have to make a few small changes.* **3 small business/farm/company** a business that does not involve large amounts of money or does not employ a large number of people **4** a small child is young

THESAURUS **young, little** → YOUNG¹

5 a small fortune a lot of money: *That house must have **cost** him **a small fortune**.* [ORIGIN: Old English *smæl*] —**small** *adv.*: *He writes so small I can't read what the note says.*

,small 'change *n.* [U] money in coins of low value

,small 'claims court *n.* [C] LAW a court that deals with cases that involve small amounts of money

'small fry *n.* [U] (informal) **1** children **2** people or things that are not important when compared to other people or things

,small in'testine *n.* [singular] BIOLOGY the long tube that food goes through after it has passed through your stomach and before it enters the LARGE INTESTINE → *see picture at* ORGAN

,small-'minded *adj.* (disapproving) only interested in things that affect you, and too willing to judge people according to your own opinions: *greedy small-minded people*

,small po'tatoes *adj.* (informal) not very big or important: *Compared to his salary, mine is small potatoes.*

small·pox /'smɔlpɑks/ *n.* [U] BIOLOGY a serious disease that causes spots that leave permanent marks on your skin

,small-'scale *adj.* not involving a lot of people, money, etc.: *a small-scale project*

'small talk *n.* [U] polite friendly conversation about unimportant subjects: *He's not very good at **making small talk**.*

'small-time *adj.* unimportant or not successful: *a small-time drug dealer*

smart¹ /smɑrt/ *adj.* **1** intelligent or showing good judgment (ANT) **stupid**: *Jill's a smart kid. | I was smart enough to take advantage of a good opportunity. | I don't think that would be a very **smart move*** (=sensible thing to do).

THESAURUS **intelligent, bright, brilliant, clever, gifted** → INTELLIGENT

2 smart machines, weapons, etc. use computers or advanced technology to work: *smart bombs* **3** saying funny things in a way that is not respectful: *Don't **get smart with** me, young lady!* **4** (old-fashioned) neat and fashionable: *a smart suit* —**smartly** *adv.*: *smartly dressed men*

smart² *v.* [I] **1** to be upset because someone has offended you: *He's still **smarting from** the*

S

insult. **2** if a part of your body smarts, it hurts with a stinging pain

THESAURUS **hurt, sting →** HURT[1]

smart al·eck /ˈsmɑrt̬ ˌælɪk/ *n.* [C] (informal) someone who says funny or intelligent things in a rude or annoying way

ˈsmart card *n.* [C] a small plastic card with an electronic part that records and remembers information

smarts /smɑrts/ *n.* [U] (spoken, informal) intelligence: *Julie impressed her boss with her smarts and hard work.*

smar·ty-pants /ˈsmɑrt̬i ˌpænts/ *n.* [C] (humorous) a SMART ALECK

smash[1] /smæʃ/ *v.* **1** [I,T] to break into many small pieces in a forceful way, or to make something do this by dropping, throwing, or hitting it: *The plates smashed on the floor.* | *Rioters smashed store windows and set fire to cars.*

THESAURUS **break, shatter →** BREAK[1]

S

2 [I,T] to hit an object or surface in a forceful way, or to make something do this: *Murray* ***smashed*** *his fist* ***against*** *the wall.* | *Thompson died when his motorcycle* ***smashed into*** *a parked car.* **3** [T] to destroy something such as a political system or criminal organization: *Police have smashed a drug smuggling ring.*

smash sth ↔ **in** *phr. v.* to hit something with so much force that you damage it: *The door had been smashed in.*

smash sth ↔ **up** *phr. v.* to damage or destroy something: *She smashed up the truck in an accident.*

smash[2] *also* **smash hit** *n.* [C] a very successful new play, movie, song, etc.: *the latest Broadway smash*

smashed /smæʃt/ *adj.* (informal) drunk

smat·ter·ing /ˈsmæt̬ərɪŋ/ *n.* **a smattering of sth** a small number or amount of something: *a smattering of applause* | *He* ***has a smattering of*** *French* (=he knows a little French).

smear[1] /smɪr/ *v.* **1** [I,T] to spread a liquid or soft substance on a surface, or to become spread on a surface: *Jill* ***smeared*** *lotion* ***on*** *Rick's back.* | *The note was damp and the ink had smeared.* **2** [T] to spread an untrue story about someone important in order to harm him/her: *an attempt to smear the party leadership*

smear[2] *n.* [C] **1** a dirty or oily mark that is left on a surface: *There was a* ***smear of*** *blood on the carpet.*

THESAURUS **mark, stain, spot, smudge →** MARK[2]

2 an untrue story about someone important that is meant to harm him/her

smell[1] /smɛl/ *v.* **1** [I] to have a particular smell: *The room* ***smelled of*** *fresh bread.* | *This wine* ***smells like*** *berries.* **2** [I] to have an unpleasant smell SYN **stink**: *Something in the refrigerator smells.* **3** [T] to notice or recognize a particular smell, or to be able to do this: *I could smell alcohol on his breath.* **4** [T] to put your nose near something in order to discover what type of smell it has: *Come and smell these roses.*

smell[2] *n.* **1** [C] the quality that you recognize by using your nose: *the* ***smell of*** *flowers* | *the* ***strong smell*** *of gasoline* | *the fresh smell of the ocean*

THESAURUS

aroma – a strong pleasant smell, used especially about food: *the aroma of fresh coffee*
scent/fragrance/perfume – a pleasant smell: *the sweet fragrance of roses*

2 [C] a bad smell: *What's that smell in the basement?*

THESAURUS

stink: *the stink of rotting fish*
stench: *the stench of burning rubber*
odor: *the odor of alcohol on his breath*

3 [U] the ability to notice or recognize smells: *an excellent* ***sense of smell***

smell·y /ˈsmɛli/ *adj.* having a strong bad smell: *smelly socks*

smelt /smɛlt/ *v.* [T] to melt a rock that contains metal in order to remove the metal

smidg·en /ˈsmɪdʒən/ *also* **smidge** /smɪdʒ/ *n.* [singular] (informal) a small amount of something: *Add just* ***a smidgen of*** *salt.*

smile /smaɪl/ *v.* **1** [I] to have a happy expression on your face in which your mouth curves up: *Keith* ***smiled at*** *me.* | *a smiling baby*

THESAURUS

grin – to smile continuously with a very big smile: *He walked out of the bathroom grinning from ear to ear.*
beam – to smile because you are very pleased about something: *Jenny ran across the room, beaming with pleasure.*
smirk – to smile in an unpleasant way, for example because you are pleased by someone else's bad luck: *Some of the snowboarders were smirking at my efforts.*
simper – to smile in a way that is silly and annoying: *Mary-Ann simpered and giggled.*

2 [T] to say or express something with a smile: *"You're welcome," she smiled.* —**smile** *n.* [C]: *a big smile*

smirk /smɚk/ *v.* [I] to smile in a way that is not nice, and that shows that you are pleased by someone else's bad luck: *Both officers smirked and laughed at him.* [ORIGIN: Old English *smearcian* "to smile"] —**smirk** *n.* [C]

THESAURUS **smile, grin, beam, simper →** SMILE

smith /smɪθ/ *n.* [C] **1 goldsmith/silversmith etc.** someone who makes things from gold, silver, etc. **2** a BLACKSMITH

smith·er·eens /ˌsmɪðəˈrinz/ *n.* **blow/smash etc. sth to smithereens** (informal) to destroy something completely by breaking it violently into very small pieces

smit·ten /ˈsmɪtˀn/ *adj.* **be smitten** to suddenly feel that you love someone very much: *He's absolutely **smitten with** that new girl.*

smock /smɑk/ *n.* [C] a loose piece of clothing like a long shirt, worn especially by artists to protect their clothes

smog /smɑg, smɔg/ *n.* [U] dirty air caused by smoke from cars and factories in cities —**smoggy** *adj.*

smoke¹ /smoʊk/ *n.* **1** [U] the white, gray, or black gas that is produced by something burning: *cigarette smoke | The fire sent up a huge **cloud of smoke**.* **2** [C] an act of smoking a cigarette, etc.: *He went outside for a smoke.* **3** [C] (informal) a cigarette: *Do you have a smoke?* **4 go up in smoke** (informal) if your plans go up in smoke, you cannot do what you intended to do [ORIGIN: Old English *smoca*]

smoke² *v.* **1** [I,T] to suck or breathe in smoke from a cigarette, pipe, etc., or to do this regularly as a habit: *Do you mind if I smoke? | We sat on the porch smoking cigarettes. | I only smoke when I'm drinking.* **2** [I] to produce or send out smoke: *a smoking chimney* **3** [T] to give fish or meat a special taste by hanging it in smoke: *smoked salmon* —**smoking** *n.* [U]

smok·er /ˈsmoʊkɚ/ *n.* [C] someone who smokes (ANT) **nonsmoker**: *She used to be a **heavy smoker*** (=someone who smokes a lot).

ˈsmoke screen *n.* [C] something that you say or do to hide your real plans or actions

smoke·stack /ˈsmoʊkstæk/ *n.* [C] a tall CHIMNEY at a factory or on a ship

ˌsmoking ˈgun *n.* [C usually singular] (informal) definite proof of who is responsible for something bad or how something really happened

smok·y /ˈsmoʊki/ *adj.* **1** filled with smoke: *a smoky room* **2** producing a lot of smoke: *a smoky fire* **3** having the taste, smell, or appearance of smoke: *smoky cheese*

smol·der /ˈsmoʊldɚ/ *v.* [I] **1** to burn slowly without a flame: *The factory is still smoldering after last night's blaze.* **2** to have strong feelings that are not expressed: *Nick left Judy **smoldering with** anger.*

smooch /smutʃ/ *v.* [I] (informal) if two people smooch, they kiss each other in a romantic way —**smooch** *n.* [C]

smooth¹ /smuð/ *adj.* **1** having an even surface, without any BUMPs or holes (ANT) **rough**: *a smooth road | smooth skin* → *see picture at* BUMPY

THESAURUS **flat, even** → FLAT¹

2 a liquid mixture that is smooth is thick but has no big pieces in it: *smooth peanut butter* **3** with no sudden movements or changes of direction, especially in a way that is graceful or comfortable: *Swing the tennis racket in one smooth motion. | a smooth flight* **4** operating or happening without problems: *a **smooth transition** from dictatorship to democracy* **5** (disapproving) polite and confident in a way that people do not trust: *a **smooth talker*** —**smoothly** *adv.*: *My talk went smoothly.* —**smoothness** *n.* [U]

smooth² *v.* [T] **1** *also* **smooth out/down** to make something flat by moving your hands across it: *Tanya sat down, smoothing her skirt.* **2** to make a rough surface flat and even: *Make sure you **smooth down** all the surfaces before you start painting.*

smooth sth ↔ **over** *phr. v.* to make problems or difficulties seem less important: *He depended on Nancy to smooth over any troubles.*

smooth·ie /ˈsmuði/ *n.* [C] a thick drink made of fruit and fruit juices that have been mixed together until they are smooth

smor·gas·bord /ˈsmɔrgəsˌbɔrd/ *n.* [C,U] a meal in which people serve themselves from a large number of different foods

smoth·er /ˈsmʌðɚ/ *v.* [T] **1** to kill someone by putting something over his/her face so that s/he cannot breathe **2** to cover the whole surface of something with something else: *a cake **smothered with/in** chocolate* **3** to give someone so much love and attention that s/he feels like s/he is not free and becomes unhappy **4** to make a fire stop burning by preventing air from reaching it: *We used a wet towel to smother the fire.*

smudge¹ /smʌdʒ/ *n.* [C] a dirty mark: *There was a **smudge of** lipstick on the cup.* —**smudgy** *adj.*

THESAURUS **mark, stain, spot, smear** → MARK²

smudge² *v.* [I,T] if a substance such as ink or paint smudges or is smudged, it becomes messy or unclear because someone has touched or rubbed it: *Now look, you've smudged my drawing! | Your lipstick is smudged.*

smug /smʌg/ *adj.* (disapproving) showing that you are very satisfied with how smart, lucky, or good you are: *a smug smile* —**smugly** *adv.*

smug·gle /ˈsmʌgəl/ *v.* [T] to take someone or something illegally from one place to another: *cocaine **smuggled from** South America **into** the United States* —**smuggler** *n.* [C]: *drug smugglers* —**smuggling** *n.* [U]

smut /smʌt/ *n.* [U] (disapproving) books, stories, pictures, etc. that offend some people because they are about sex —**smutty** *adj.*: *a smutty T.V. show*

snack¹ /snæk/ *n.* [C] a small amount of food that

S

you eat between main meals or instead of a meal: *I only had time to grab a quick snack.* | *a* ***bedtime*** *snack* → *see picture at* DINE

snack² *v.* [I] to eat a small amount of food between main meals or instead of a meal

'snack bar *n.* [C] a place where you can buy snacks

sna·fu /'snæfu, snæ'fu/ *n.* [C] (informal) a situation in which something does not happen the way it should

snag¹ /snæg/ *n.* [C] **1** (informal) a disadvantage or problem, especially one that is not very serious: *His plans* ***hit a snag*** *when his plane was diverted to Chicago.*

THESAURUS **problem, setback, difficulty, hitch** → PROBLEM

2 a thread that has been accidentally pulled out of a piece of cloth because it has gotten stuck on something sharp or pointed

snag² *v.* (**snagged**, **snagging**) **1** [I,T] to damage something by getting it stuck on something, or to become damaged in this way: *Marty's fishing line snagged on a tree branch.* **2** [T] (informal) to get someone to notice you, or to succeed in getting something that is difficult to get: *Can you snag that waiter for me?* | *I snagged two tickets for tonight's show.*

S

snail /sneɪl/ *n.* [C] **1** a small soft creature that moves very slowly and has a hard shell on its back **2 at a snail's pace** extremely slowly

'snail mail *n.* [U] the system of sending letters through the mail, rather than by email

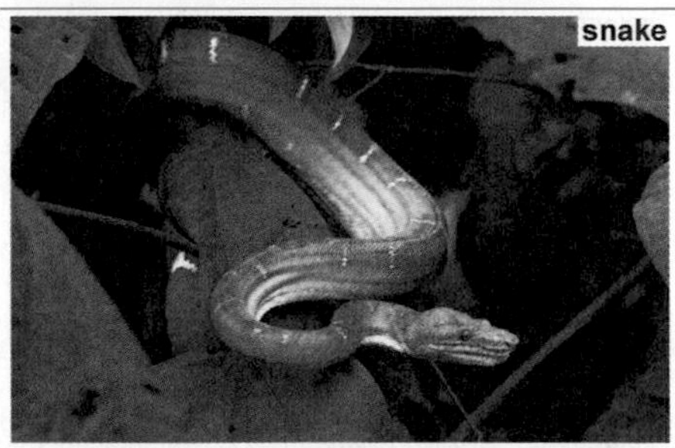

snake

snake¹ /sneɪk/ *n.* [C] an animal with a long thin body and no legs: *Paul was bitten by a* ***poisonous snake.*** [ORIGIN: Old English *snaca*]

snake² *v.* [I] (literary) to move in long twisting curves: *The train* ***snaked its way through*** *the hills.*

snap¹ /snæp/ *v.* (**snapped**, **snapping**) **1** [I,T] if something snaps, or if you snap it, it breaks with a short loud noise: *Dry branches snapped under their feet.* | ***I snapped*** *the ends* ***off*** *the beans and dropped them into a bowl.* | *He* ***snapped*** *the chalk* ***in two/half*** (=into two pieces).

THESAURUS **break, shatter, crack** → BREAK¹

2 [I,T] to move into a particular position with a short loud noise, or to make something do this: *The pieces just* ***snap together*** *like this.* | *She* ***snapped*** *her briefcase* ***open/shut.*** **3** [I,T] to speak quickly in an angry way: *I'm sorry I* ***snapped at*** *you.* | *"Don't be ridiculous," she snapped.* **4** [I] if a dog snaps at you, it tries to bite you **5 snap your fingers** to make a short loud noise by moving a finger quickly across the thumb on the same hand **6** [I] to suddenly become unable to control a strong feeling such as anger or worry: *I don't know what happened – I guess I just snapped.* **7** [T] to stop a series of events: *Tampa snapped an eight-game losing streak on Saturday.* **8** [T] (informal) to take a photograph: *We asked a policeman to snap our picture.*

snap out of sth *phr. v.* (informal) to suddenly stop being sad, tired, upset, etc.: *Come on, Gary,* ***snap out of it.***

snap up *phr. v.* **1 snap** sth ↔ **up** to buy something immediately, especially because it is very cheap: *People initially snapped up shares in dot-com companies.* **2 snap** sb ↔ **up** to eagerly take an opportunity to have someone as part of your company, team, etc.: *It would shock the hockey world if the Bruins didn't snap him up.*

snap² *n.* **1** [singular] a sudden short loud noise, especially of something breaking or closing: *I heard a snap, and then the tree just fell over.* **2** [C] a small metal object that fastens clothes when you press its two parts together **3 be a snap** (informal) to be very easy to do: *Making pie crust is a snap.* → **cold snap** *at* COLD¹

snap³ *adj.* **snap judgment/decision** a judgment or decision made quickly, without careful thought or discussion

snap·py /'snæpi/ *adj.* **1** spoken or written in a short, clear, and often funny way: *Keep your answer* ***short and snappy.*** **2 make it snappy** (spoken) said in order to tell someone to hurry, in a way that is not polite: *Get me a drink, and make it snappy.* **3** (informal) snappy clothes are attractive and fashionable: *a snappy blue blazer*

snap·shot /'snæpʃɑt/ *n.* [C] a photograph taken quickly and often not very skillfully

THESAURUS **picture, sketch, painting, portrait, cartoon, illustration, poster, image** → PICTURE¹

snare¹ /snɛr/ *n.* [C] a trap for catching an animal

snare² *v.* [T] **1** to catch an animal using a snare **2** to catch someone, especially by tricking him/her: *Last year, State Police in the area snared 257 speeding motorists with their radar guns.*

snarl /snɑrl/ *v.* **1** [I,T] to speak or say something in an angry way: *"Shut up!" he snarled.* **2** [I] if an animal snarls, it makes a low angry sound and shows its teeth **3** *also* **snarl up** [I,T] if traffic snarls or is snarled, it cannot move **4** [I] if hair, thread, wires, etc. snarl, they become twisted and messy and are difficult to separate —**snarl** *n.* [C]

snatch[1] /snætʃ/ *v.* [T] **1** to take something away from someone with a quick violent movement: *I saw two kids snatch her purse.* **2** to take someone or something away from a place by force: *Vargas was snatched from his home by two armed men.* **3** to quickly take the opportunity to do something: *I managed to* ***snatch*** *an hour's* ***sleep*** *on the bus.*

snatch[2] *n.* **a snatch of conversation/song etc.** a short and incomplete part of something that you hear

snaz·zy /ˈsnæzi/ *adj.* (informal) very bright, attractive, and fashionable: *a snazzy new car*

sneak[1] /snik/ *v.* (past tense and past participle **sneaked** *or* **snuck** /snʌk/) **1** [I] to go somewhere quietly and secretly: *She* ***snuck out*** *of the house once her parents were asleep.* **2** [T] to take something somewhere secretly: *He had tried to* ***sneak*** *drugs* ***across*** *the border.* **3 sneak a look/glance at sth** to look at something quickly and secretly: *I sneaked a look at her diary.*

sneak up *phr. v.* to come near someone very quietly, so s/he does not see or hear you: *Don't* ***sneak up on*** *me like that!*

sneak[2] *n.* [C] (informal) someone who does things secretly and cannot be trusted

sneak·er /ˈsnikɚ/ *n.* [C] a TENNIS SHOE

sneak·ing /ˈsnikɪŋ/ *adj.* **have a sneaking suspicion/feeling (that)** to think you know something without being sure: *I had a sneaking suspicion that he was lying.*

sneak·y /ˈsniki/ *adj.* doing things in a secret and often dishonest way

sneer /snɪr/ *v.* [I] to smile or speak in a way that is not nice and shows you have no respect for someone or something: *He* ***sneered at*** *her taste in music.* **—sneer** *n.* [C]

sneeze /sniz/ *v.* [I] **1** when you sneeze, air suddenly comes out of your nose and mouth in an uncontrolled way, for example when you have a cold: *The dust is* ***making*** *me* ***sneeze****.* | *I've been coughing and sneezing all day.* **2 sth is nothing to sneeze at** (informal) used in order to say that something is impressive enough to be considered important: *With 35 nations involved, the competition is nothing to sneeze at.* [ORIGIN: Old English *fneosan*] **—sneeze** *n.* [C]

snick·er /ˈsnɪkɚ/ *v.* [I] to laugh quietly in a way that is not nice at something that is not supposed to be funny **—snicker** *n.* [C]

> THESAURUS **laugh, giggle, chuckle, cackle, titter, guffaw** → LAUGH[1]

snide /snaɪd/ *adj.* funny but unkind: *She started making* ***snide remarks/comments*** *about him.*

sniff /snɪf/ *v.* **1** [I,T] to breathe in through your nose in order to smell something: *cats* ***sniffing at*** *their food* **2** [I] to breathe air into your nose with a loud sound, especially in short breaths: *She sniffed a few times and then stopped crying.* **—sniff** *n.* [C]

sniff at sth *phr. v.* to refuse something in a proud way: *A job with them is* ***nothing to sniff at*** (=something you should not refuse).

sniff sth ↔ **out** *phr. v.* to discover or find something by its smell: *dogs that sniff out drugs*

snif·fle /ˈsnɪfəl/ *v.* [I] to sniff continuously in order to stop liquid from running out of your nose, especially when you are crying or when you are sick

snif·fles /ˈsnɪfəlz/ *n.* **the sniffles** a slight cold: *Max has* ***had the sniffles*** *all week.*

snip /snɪp/ *v.* (**snipped**, **snipping**) [I,T] to cut something with scissors, making quick small cuts **—snip** *n.* [C]

> THESAURUS **cut, trim** → CUT[1]

snipe /snaɪp/ *v.* [I] **1** to shoot at people from a hidden position **2** to criticize someone in an unkind way: *It's easier to* ***snipe at*** *someone's ideas than come up with a solution.*

snip·er /ˈsnaɪpɚ/ *n.* [C] someone who shoots at people from a hidden position

snip·pet /ˈsnɪpɪt/ *n.* [C] a small piece of information, music, etc.: *a few* ***snippets of*** *conversation*

snit /snɪt/ *n.* **be in a snit** (informal) to be annoyed about something in a way that seems unreasonable

snitch[1] /snɪtʃ/ *v.* (informal) **1** [I] (disapproving) to tell someone in authority that someone else has done something wrong because you want him/her to be punished **2** [T] to steal something, especially something that is small and not valuable

snitch[2] *n.* [C] someone who is not liked because s/he tells people in authority when other people do things that are wrong or against the rules

snivel /ˈsnɪvəl/ *v.* [I] to behave or speak in a weak complaining way, especially while crying

snob /snɑb/ *n.* [C] **1** someone who thinks s/he is better than other people: *Ellen is such a snob.* **2 music/wine etc. snob** someone who knows a lot about music, etc. and thinks his/her opinions are better than other people's [ORIGIN: 1800—1900 *snob* "shoemaker, person of low social rank" (18—19 centuries)]

snob·ber·y /ˈsnɑbəri/ *n.* [U] the attitudes and behavior of snobs

snob·bish /ˈsnɑbɪʃ/ *also* **snob·by** /ˈsnɑbi/ *adj.* having attitudes and behavior that are typical of a snob

snoop /snup/ *v.* [I] to try to find out about someone's life or activities by secretly looking at his/her things: *I caught her* ***snooping in/around*** *my office.* **—snoop** *n.* [C]

snoot·y /ˈsnuṭi/ *adj.* rude and unfriendly because you think you are better than other people

snooze /snuz/ *v.* [I] (informal) to sleep for a short time **—snooze** *n.* [C]

snore /snɔr/ *v.* [I] to make a loud noise each time

you breathe while you are asleep [ORIGIN: 1300—1400 From the sound] —**snore** *n.* [C]

snor·kel¹ /ˈsnɔrkəl/ *n.* [C] a tube that allows a swimmer to breathe air when his/her face is under water

snorkel² *v.* [I] to swim using a snorkel —**snorkeling** *n.* [U]

snort /snɔrt/ *v.* [I,T] to make a noise by forcing air out through your nose, especially in order to express anger or when laughing: *Olsen* ***snorted at*** *the suggestion.* —**snort** *n.* [C]

snot /snɑt/ *n.* (informal) **1** [U] an impolite word for the thick MUCUS (=liquid) produced in your nose **2** [C] someone who is snotty behaves as though s/he is better than other people

ˈsnot-nosed *adj.* **snot-nosed kid/brat etc.** (informal) an annoying child

snot·ty /ˈsnɑṭi/ *adj.* (informal) **1** showing that you think you are better than other people SYN **snobbish**: *You're always there with a snotty remark.* **2** wet and dirty with MUCUS from your nose: *the child's snotty face*

snout /snaʊt/ *n.* [C] the long nose of some kinds of animals, such as pigs

S

snow¹ /snoʊ/ *n.* **1** [U] water frozen into soft white pieces that fall like rain in cold weather: ***Snow*** *was* ***falling*** *on the quiet street.* | *We are expecting six* ***inches of snow****.* | *The* ***snow*** *is already* ***melting.*** | *High winds and* ***heavy snow*** (=a lot of snow that is falling) *caused chaos on the roads.* | *The rain was turning to* ***light snow****.*

THESAURUS

snowflakes – pieces of falling snow
sleet – a mixture of snow and rain
slush – snow on the road that has partly melted and is very wet
blizzard – a storm with a lot of snow and a strong wind
frost – white powder that covers the ground when it is cold ➔ RAIN¹

2 [C] a period of time during which snow falls: *the first snow of the winter* [ORIGIN: Old English *snaw*]

snow² *v.* **1 it snows** if it snows, snow falls from the sky: *Look, it's snowing!* | *We got back home before it started snowing.* **2 be snowed in** to be unable to leave a place because so much snow has fallen: *We were snowed in for a week.* **3 be snowed under (with sth)** (informal) to have more work than you can deal with: *I'd love to go, but I'm totally snowed under right now.* **4** [T] (informal) to make someone believe or support something that is not true: *Even the banks were snowed by this charming conman.*

snow·ball¹ /ˈsnoʊbɔl/ *n.* [C] a ball made out of snow that someone has pressed together: *The kids were* ***having a snowball fight*** *outside.*

snowball² *v.* [I] if a problem or situation snowballs, it quickly gets bigger or harder to control

snow·board /ˈsnoʊbɔrd/ *n.* [C] a long wide board made of plastic, which people stand on to go down snow-covered hills as a sport

snow·board·ing /ˈsnoʊˌbɔrdɪŋ/ *n.* [U] the sport of going down snow-covered hills on a snowboard —**snowboarder** *n.* [C]

snow·bound /ˈsnoʊbaʊnd/ *adj.* unable to leave a place because there is too much snow

snow·drift /ˈsnoʊˌdrɪft/ *n.* [C] an area of deep snow formed by the wind

snow·fall /ˈsnoʊfɔl/ *n.* [C,U] an occasion when snow falls from the sky, or the amount that falls in a particular period of time: *a* ***light/heavy snowfall***

snow·flake /ˈsnoʊfleɪk/ *n.* [C] a small soft white piece of frozen water that falls as snow

ˈsnow job *n.* [C] (informal) an act of making someone believe something that is not true

snow·man /ˈsnoʊmæn/ *n.* (plural **snowmen** /-mɛn/) [C] a figure of a person made out of snow

snow·plow /ˈsnoʊplaʊ/ *n.* [C] a vehicle or piece of equipment attached to the front of a vehicle, used for pushing snow off roads

snow·shoe /ˈsnoʊʃu/ *n.* [C] one of a pair of wide flat frames used for walking on snow without sinking

snow·storm /ˈsnoʊstɔrm/ *n.* [C] a storm with strong winds and a lot of snow

snow·y /ˈsnoʊi/ *adj.* if it is snowy, the ground is covered with snow or snow is falling: *a snowy January day*

snub /snʌb/ *v.* (**snubbed**, **snubbing**) [T] to be rude to someone, especially by ignoring him/her when you meet —**snub** *n.* [C]

snuck /snʌk/ *v.* a past tense and past participle of SNEAK

snuff¹ /snʌf/ *v.*

snuff sth ↔ **out** *phr. v.* **1** to put out a CANDLE by covering it or pressing the flame with your fingers **2** (informal) to end something in a sudden way: *laws intended to snuff out smoking in public places*

snuff² *n.* [U] **1** tobacco made into a powder, which some people breathe in through their noses **2 not be up to snuff** (informal) to not be good enough: *Her performance just wasn't up to snuff.*

snug /snʌg/ *adj.* **1** warm and comfortable: *The children were safe and snug in their beds.* **2** clothes that are snug fit fairly tightly —**snugly** *adv.*

snug·gle /ˈsnʌgəl/ *v.* [I] *also* **snuggle up** to get into a warm comfortable position: *couples* ***snuggling up*** *on cold winter nights*

so¹ /soʊ/ *adv.* **1** used in order to emphasize what you are saying: *He was so weak that he could hardly stand up.* | ***So many*** *kids come from broken homes these days.* | *I feel so embarrassed.* | *That party was so boring!* **2** used in order to refer back to something that has already been mentioned: *If you have not sent in your payment yet, please* ***do so*** *immediately.* | *"Will I need my coat?" "I* ***don't think so.****"* **3 so do I/so is he/so would John etc.** used in order to say that something is also true about someone else: *"I have a lot to do today." "So do I."* | *If you're going to have dessert then so will I.* **4 be so** to be true or correct: *"It belongs to my father." "****Is that so****?"* | *Please say* ***it isn't so****!* **5 or so** used when you cannot be exact about a number, amount, or period of time: *He left a week or so ago.* | *Dena had five drinks or so.* **6 and so on/forth** used after a list to show that there are other similar things that could also be mentioned: *a room full of old furniture, paintings, rugs, and so forth* **7 be just/exactly so** to be arranged neatly, with everything in the right place: *Everything has to be just so at Maxine's dinner parties.* **8 so as (not) to do sth** (formal) in order to do or not do something: *Try to remain calm so as not to alarm anyone.*

SPOKEN PHRASES

9 said in order to get someone's attention, especially in order to ask him/her a question: *So, Lisa, how's the new job going?* **10** said when you are making sure that you have understood something: *So you aren't actually leaving until Friday?* **11** used with a movement of your hand when you are describing how big, tall, etc. something or someone is, or how to do something: *It was about so big.* | *Then you fold the paper* ***like so.*** **12** *also* **so what?** used in order to say impolitely that you do not think that something is important: *"I'm going to tell Mom what you said." "So?"* | *Yes, I'm late. So what?* **13** (slang) definitely: *He is* ***so not*** *the right person for her.* **14 so long!** used in order to say goodbye **15 so be it** used in order to show that you do not like or agree with something, but you will accept it: *If this means delaying the trip, then so be it.* **16 so much for sth** used to say that something you tried to do did not work, or something that was promised did not happen: *Well, so much for getting out of here at five o'clock.* **17 so help me** *also* **so help me God** said in order to emphasize how determined you are: *So help me God, I will not let you down.*

so² *conjunction* **1** used in order to show why something happens: *I got hungry, so I made a sandwich.* ►Don't say "Since I got hungry, so I made a sandwich."◄

THESAURUS therefore, as a result/consequently/as a consequence, thus, hence, accordingly ➔ THEREFORE

2 so (that) in order to make something happen, or make something possible: *I put your keys in the drawer so they wouldn't get lost.* ➔ ORDER¹

soak /souk/ *v.* [I,T] **1** if you soak something, or if you let it soak, you cover it with liquid for a period of time: *Just put that dish in the sink to soak.* | *Soak the beans overnight.* **2** to make something completely wet, or to become completely wet: *If you don't take your umbrella, you're going to* ***get soaked.*** | *The blood had* ***soaked through*** *the bandage.*

soak sth ↔ **up** *phr. v.* **1** if something soaks up a liquid, it takes the liquid into itself (SYN) **absorb**: *The bread will soak up the milk.* **2** to enjoy everything about an experience: *I just wanted to* ***soak up the sun.***

soak·ing /ˈsoukɪŋ/ *also* **ˌsoaking ˈwet** *adj.* completely wet

ˈso-and-so *n.* (plural **so-and-sos** *or* **so-and so's**) [U] (spoken) used in order to talk about someone, without saying his/her name: *All they care about is whether so-and-so is going to be at the party.*

soap¹ /soup/ *n.* **1** [U] the substance that you use with water to wash things, especially your body: *a* ***bar of soap*** | *Wash your hands with* ***soap and water.*** **2** [C] (informal) a SOAP OPERA [ORIGIN: Old English *sape*]

soap² *v.* [T] to rub soap on someone or something

soap·box /ˈsoupbɑks/ *n.* **be/get on your soapbox** (informal, disapproving) to tell people your opinions about something in a loud and forceful way

ˈsoap ˌopera *n.* [C] a television or radio story about the daily lives of the same group of people, which is broadcast regularly ➔ TELEVISION

soap·y /ˈsoupi/ *adj.* containing soap: *soapy water*

soar /sɔr/ *v.* [I] **1** to increase quickly to a high level: *The temperature soared to 97°.* **2** to fly, especially very fast or very high up in the air: *birds soaring overhead* **3** buildings, mountains, or cliffs, etc. that soar look very tall and impressive: *The cliffs soar 500 feet above the ocean.* —**soaring** *adj.*

sob /sɑb/ *v.* (**sobbed**, **sobbing**) [I] to cry while breathing in short sudden bursts: *He began* ***sobbing uncontrollably.*** —**sob** *n.* [C]

so·ber¹ /ˈsoubɚ/ *adj.* **1** not drunk **2** extremely serious: *The scale of the damage is a sober reminder of the power of nature.* —**soberly** *adv.*

sober² *v.*

sober (sb ↔) **up** *phr. v.* to gradually become less drunk, or to make someone do this: *Some black coffee might sober you up.*

so·ber·ing /ˈsoubərɪŋ/ *adj.* making you feel very serious: *a* ***sobering thought***

so·bri·e·ty /səˈbraɪəṭi/ *n.* [U] **1** the condition of not being drunk or not drinking alcohol: *Almost half the AA members had two or more years of sobriety.* **2** (formal) behavior that shows a serious attitude toward life

ˈsob ˌstory *n.* [C] (informal, disapproving) a story that someone tells you in order to make you feel sorry for him/her

ˈso-called *adj.* [only before noun] **1** used in order to show that you think the name that someone or something is called is wrong: *these so-called freedom fighters* **2** used in order to show that something or someone is usually called a particular name: *Only so-called "safe and sane" fireworks are allowed.*

soc·cer /ˈsɑkɚ/ *n.* [U] a sport played by two teams of 11 players who try to kick a ball into their opponents' GOAL [ORIGIN: 1800—1900 *association (football)*; because it was originally played under the rules of the English Football Association]

so·cia·ble /ˈsoʊʃəbəl/ *adj.* someone who is sociable is friendly and likes to be with other people: *I wish my son was a bit more sociable.*

THESAURUS

outgoing – liking to meet and talk to new people: *an outgoing, popular girl*
extroverted – confident, and enjoying being with other people: *an extroverted salesman*
gregarious – friendly and enjoying being and talking with other people: *a gregarious man who loves telling stories*
affable – friendly and easy to talk to: *an affable man in his forties*
genial – cheerful, kind, and friendly: *a big, genial man*
convivial (formal) – a convivial situation is friendly and pleasant and full of people: *convivial church suppers* → SHY[1]

S

so·cial /ˈsoʊʃəl/ *adj.* **1** SOCIAL SCIENCE relating to human society and the way it is organized: ***social issues** such as unemployment and education* | *The students come from a variety of **social classes*** (=groups of people who have the same social position). **2** relating to meeting people, forming relationships with them, and spending time with them: *Ellis always had an active **social life**.* | *a range of **social events** for employees* | *Children need to develop their **social skills**.* **3** social animals live together in groups, rather than alone [ORIGIN: 1600—1700 Latin *socialis*, from *socius* "someone you spend time with"] —**socially** *adv.*: *socially acceptable behavior*

ˌsocial ˈclimber *n.* [C] (disapproving) someone who tries very hard to move into a higher social class

ˌsocial ˈcriticism *n.* [U] SOCIAL SCIENCE the act of expressing judgments about the good and bad qualities of a particular society

ˌsocial deˈmocracy *n.* **1** [U] POLITICS a political and economic system, especially in many European countries, based on some ideas of SOCIALISM combined with DEMOCRATIC principles, such as personal freedom and government by elected representatives **2** [C] POLITICS a country, especially in Europe, with a government based on this system —**ˌsocial ˈdemocrat** *n.* [C]

so·cial·is·m /ˈsoʊʃəˌlɪzəm/ *n.* [U] POLITICS an economic and political system that tries to give equal opportunities to all people, and in which most businesses belong to the government → CAPITALISM, COMMUNISM —**socialist** *adj.*, *n.* [C]

so·cia·lite /ˈsoʊʃəˌlaɪt/ *n.* [C] a rich person who is well known for going to many fashionable parties

so·cial·ize /ˈsoʊʃəˌlaɪz/ *v.* [I] to spend time with other people in a friendly way: *I hate having to **socialize with** strangers.*

ˌsocial moˈbility *n.* [U] SOCIAL SCIENCE the ability to move easily from one social class to another

ˌsocial ˈscience *n.* [C,U] subjects such as history, politics, and economics, or one of these subjects

ˌSocial Seˈcurity *n.* [U] ECONOMICS a U.S. government program into which workers must pay money, that gives money to old people and others who cannot work

ˈsocial ˌstudies *n.* [plural] SOCIAL SCIENCE

ˌsocial ˈwelfare *n.* [U] programs to help people who are poor, do not have jobs, etc.

ˈsocial ˌworker *n.* [C] someone who is trained to help people with particular social problems —**social work** *n.* [U]

so·ci·e·ty /səˈsaɪət̬i/ *n.* (plural **societies**) **1** [C,U] all the people who live in the same country and share the same laws and customs: *a modern industrial society* | *Children are the least powerful **members of society**.*

THESAURUS **people, the public, populace, population** → PEOPLE[1]

2 [C] an organization with members who share similar interests, aims, etc.: *the American Cancer Society*

THESAURUS **organization, institution, institute, association, club** → ORGANIZATION

3 [U] the rich and fashionable people in a country: *a society wedding*

so·ci·o·ec·o·nom·ic /ˌsoʊsioʊˌɛkəˈnɑmɪk, -ˌikə-/ *adj.* ECONOMICS relating to both social and economic conditions

so·ci·ol·o·gy /ˌsoʊsiˈɑlədʒi/ *n.* [U] the scientific study of societies and the behavior of people in groups —**sociologist** *n.* [C]

so·cio·path /ˈsoʊsiəˌpæθ, -ʃiə-/ *n.* [C] someone whose behavior toward other people is strange and possibly dangerous

sock[1] /sɑk/ *n.* [C] **1** a piece of clothing that you wear on your foot inside your shoe: *a **pair of socks*** → *see picture at* CLOTHES **2 knock/blow sb's socks off** (informal) to surprise and excite someone a lot [ORIGIN: (1) Old English *socc*, from Latin *soccus* "light shoe"]

sock[2] *v.* [T] (informal) to hit someone very hard

sock·et /ˈsɑkɪt/ *n.* [C] **1** the place in a wall where you can connect electrical equipment to the supply of electricity (SYN) **outlet** **2** the hollow part of something that another part fits into: *eye sockets*

sod /sɑd/ *n.* [C,U] a piece of dirt with grass growing on top of it

so·da /ˈsoʊdə/ *n.* [C,U] **1** a SOFT DRINK

THESAURUS soft drink, pop, soda pop → SOFT DRINK

2 *also* **ˈsoda ˌwater** water that contains BUBBLES, often added to alcoholic drinks [ORIGIN: 1400—1500 Italian, name of a plant from which soda is obtained]

sod·den /ˈsɑdn/ *adj.* very wet and heavy: *sodden clothing*

so·di·um /ˈsoʊdiəm/ *n.* [U] **1** CHEMISTRY (*symbol* **Na**) a silver-white metal that is an ELEMENT and usually exists in combination with other substances **2** SODIUM CHLORIDE (=salt): *a low-sodium diet*

ˌsodium ˈchloride *n.* [U] CHEMISTRY the type of salt that is used in cooking and on foods

so·fa /ˈsoʊfə/ *n.* [C] a comfortable seat that is wide enough for two or three people to sit on (SYN) **couch**: *She sat down on the sofa.* [ORIGIN: 1600—1700 Arabic *suffah* "long seat"]

soft /sɔft/ *adj.* **1** not hard, firm, or stiff, but easy to press (ANT) **hard**: *a soft pillow* **2** smooth and pleasant to touch (ANT) **rough**: *soft skin* | *a cat with soft fur* **3** a soft sound, voice, or music is quiet and often pleasant to listen to: *There was some soft music playing in the background.* | *Her voice was soft and calming.*

THESAURUS quiet, low, muffled, hushed → QUIET[1]

4 soft colors or lights are not too bright (ANT) **harsh**: *Soft lighting is much more romantic.*

THESAURUS light, pale, pastel, faded → LIGHT[2]

5 soft drugs are illegal drugs and are considered to be less harmful than some other drugs **6** (informal) a soft job, life, etc. is too easy and does not involve hard work or difficulties **7** (informal) not strict enough or not treating people severely enough when they have done something wrong: *The Governor does not want to seem* ***soft on*** *crime.* | *Some of his rivals think he's* ***gone soft****.* **8 have a soft spot for sb** to like someone **9 a soft touch** (informal) someone who is easy to deceive or persuade to do something such as give you money **10** soft water does not contain a lot of minerals and forms bubbles from soap easily [ORIGIN: Old English *softe*] **—softly** *adv.* **—softness** *n.* [U]

soft·ball /ˈsɔftbɔl/ *n.* **a)** [U] an outdoor game similar to baseball but played with a slightly larger and softer ball **b)** [C] the ball used in this game

ˌsoft-ˈboiled *adj.* an egg that is soft-boiled has been boiled until the white part is solid, but the yellow part is still liquid

ˈsoft drink *n.* [C] a sweet drink that contains BUBBLES and has no alcohol in it: *cola and other soft drinks*

THESAURUS

Soft drink, **soda**, **pop**, and **soda pop** all mean the same thing. **Soft drink** is a general word that is used everywhere in the U.S. **Soda** is used mainly in the Northeast and Southwest. **Pop** is used mainly in the Midwest and West. **Soda pop** is fairly old-fashioned, but it is still used in some parts of the U.S., especially in the Midwest.

soft·en /ˈsɔfən/ *v.* [I,T] **1** to become softer, or to make something do this (ANT) **harden**: *a lotion that helps to soften your skin* **2** to become less severe and more gentle, or to make something do this: *His voice softened as he spoke to her.* | *Goldberg tried to* ***soften the blow*** (=make bad news less upsetting) *with a joke.*

soften sb ↔ **up** *phr. v.* to be nice to someone so that s/he will do something for you

soft·en·er /ˈsɔfənɚ/ *n.* [C] a substance that you add to water to make clothes feel soft after washing

soft·heart·ed /ˌsɔftˈhɑrt̬ɪd◂/ *adj.* kind and sympathetic

soft·ie, softy /ˈsɔfti/ *n.* (plural **softies**) [C] (informal) someone who is very kind and sympathetic, or is easily persuaded: *He's just a big softy really.*

ˌsoft-ˈspoken *adj.* having a quiet gentle voice

soft·ware /ˈsɔft-wɛr/ *n.* [U] IT the sets of programs that tell a computer how to do a particular job → HARDWARE: *She* ***loaded*** *the new* ***software****.* | *software programs* | *a software company*

soft·wood /ˈsɔft-wʊd/ *n.* [C,U] wood from trees such as PINE and FIR that is cheap and easy to cut, or a tree with this type of wood → HARDWOOD

soft·y /ˈsɔfti/ *n.* [C] another spelling of SOFTIE

sog·gy /ˈsɑgi/ *adj.* very wet and soft: *The pie crust was kind of soggy.*

soil[1] /sɔɪl/ *n.* [C,U] the top layer of the earth in which plants grow: *The soil here is very poor.* | *rich, fertile soil* [ORIGIN: 1200—1300 Anglo-French "piece of ground," from Latin *solium* "seat"]

THESAURUS ground, earth → GROUND[1]

→ *see picture at* PLANT[1]

soil[2] *v.* [T] (formal) to make something dirty **—soiled** *adj.*

so·journ /ˈsoʊdʒɚn/ *n.* [C] (formal) a period of time that you stay in a place that is not your home **—sojourn** *v.* [I]

sol·ace /ˈsɑlɪs/ *n.* [U] a feeling of happiness after having been very sad or upset: *After the death of her son, Val* ***found solace in*** *the church.*

so·lar /ˈsoʊlɚ/ *adj.* PHYSICS relating to the Sun or the Sun's power → LUNAR: *a solar eclipse* | *solar energy* [ORIGIN: 1400—1500 Latin *solaris*, from *sol* "Sun"]

S

ˌsolar 'cell *n.* [C] PHYSICS a piece of equipment that can produce electric power from the light from the Sun

solar plex·us /ˌsoʊlɚ 'plɛksəs/ *n.* [singular] **1** BIOLOGY a set of nerves inside your chest just above your stomach, that control the way the organs inside your stomach area work **2** the front part of your body below your chest

'solar ˌsystem *n.* **the solar system** PHYSICS the Earth and all the PLANETS, moons, etc. that move around the Sun

sold /soʊld/ *v.* the past tense and past participle of SELL

sol·der /'sɑdɚ, 'sɔ-/ *v.* [T] to join metal surfaces together or to repair them using melted metal

sol·dier[1] /'soʊldʒɚ/ *n.* [C] a member of the army, especially someone who is not an officer [ORIGIN: 1200—1300 Old French *soudier*, from *soulde* "pay," from Late Latin *solidus* "gold coin"] ➔ *see picture at* ARMED FORCES

soldier[2] *v.*

soldier on *phr. v.* to continue doing something in spite of difficulties: *It won't be easy without him, but we'll have to soldier on.*

ˌsold-'out *adj.* if a concert, movie, etc. is sold-out, all the tickets for it have been sold

sole[1] /soʊl/ (Ac) *adj.* [only before noun] **1** only: *He was the **sole survivor** of the crash.* | *His **sole purpose** in going there was to see Rachel.* | *the sole black member of the jury* **2** not shared with anyone else: *The women had to take **sole responsibility** for their children.* [ORIGIN: 1200—1300 Old French *soul*, from Latin *solus* "alone"]

sole[2] *n.* **1** [C] the bottom of your foot or shoe: *The **soles of** his **feet** were perfectly clean.* ➔ *see picture at* SHOE[1] **2** [C,U] a flat ocean fish, or the meat from this fish

sole·ly /'soʊli/ (Ac) *adv.* only, or not involving anyone or anything else: *Scholarships are awarded solely on the basis of financial need.*

sol·emn /'sɑləm/ *adj.* **1** very serious: *His face grew solemn.* | *a solemn ceremony* **2** [only before noun] a solemn promise is a promise that you will definitely keep [ORIGIN: 1300—1400 Old French *solemne*, from Latin *solemnis* "ceremonial, formal, solemn"] —**solemnly** *adv.* —**solemnity** /sə'lɛmnət̬i/ *n.* [U]

so·lic·it /sə'lɪsɪt/ *v.* [T] (formal) to ask someone for money, help, or information —**solicitation** /səˌlɪsə'teɪʃən/ *n.* [C,U]

so·lic·i·tor /sə'lɪsət̬ɚ/ *n.* [C] **1** (formal) someone who goes from place to place trying to sell goods **2** LAW the main lawyer of a city, town, or government department

so·lic·it·ous /sə'lɪsət̬əs/ *adj.* (formal) caring very much about someone's safety, health, or comfort

sol·id[1] /'sɑlɪd/ *adj.* **1** firm and usually hard, without spaces or holes: *solid rock* | *The lake in the park is **frozen solid**.* ➔ HARD[1] **2** strong and well made: *a good solid chair* **3** a solid achievement or solid work is of real, practical, and continuing value: *Kids need a good solid education in high school.* | *Julia has a **solid foundation** for a career in design.* **4** someone or something that is solid can be depended on or trusted: *a bank with a **solid reputation*** | *The prosecution has no **solid evidence**.* **5 solid gold/silver/oak etc.** completely made of gold, etc.: *a solid gold necklace* **6** (informal) continuous, without any pauses: *She didn't talk to me for three solid weeks.* [ORIGIN: 1300—1400 Old French *solide*, from Latin *solidus*] —**solidly** *adv.* —**solidity** /sə'lɪdət̬i/ *n.* [U]

solid[2] *n.* [C] **1** PHYSICS an object or substance that has a firm shape: *Water changes from a liquid into a solid when it freezes.* **2 solids** [plural] food that is not liquid: *Is the baby eating solids yet?* **3** MATH a shape that has length, width, and height

sol·i·dar·i·ty /ˌsɑlə'dærət̬i/ *n.* [U] the loyalty and support of a group of people that share the same aim or opinions: *We are going on strike to **show solidarity with** the nurses.*

so·lid·i·fy /sə'lɪdəˌfaɪ/ *v.* (**solidified**, **solidifies**) [I,T] to become solid, or to make a substance become solid

so·lil·o·quy /sə'lɪləkwi/ *n.* (plural **soliloquies**) [C] ENG. LANG. ARTS a long speech made by an actor who is alone on the stage

sol·ip·sis·tic /ˌsɑləp'sɪstɪk/ *adj.* (formal, disapproving) concerned only with yourself and the things that affect you (SYN) **self-centered**: *his solipsistic view of the world*

sol·i·taire /'sɑləˌtɛr/ *n.* **1** [U] a card game for one player **2** [C] a piece of jewelry that has only one jewel in it: *a diamond solitaire ring*

sol·i·tar·y /'sɑləˌtɛri/ *adj.* **1** [only before noun] a

S

solitary person or thing is the only one in a place: *A solitary figure waited by the door.* **2** [only before noun] done or experienced without anyone else around: *Helena took long solitary walks to the lake.* **3** spending a lot of time alone, usually because you like being alone (ANT) **sociable**: *Hamilton was described as a solitary man.*

ˌsolitary conˈfinement *n.* [U] a punishment in which a prisoner is kept alone

sol·i·tude /ˈsɑləˌtud/ *n.* [U] the state of being alone, especially when this is what you enjoy: *She spent most of her life living* ***in solitude.***

so·lo[1] /ˈsoʊloʊ/ *adj.* **1** ENG. LANG. ARTS performed by one musician, rather than by a group: *I don't really like his solo album.* **2** done alone, without anyone else helping you: *his first solo flight*

THESAURUS alone, on your own, (all) by yourself, unaided → ALONE

—**solo** *adv.*

solo[2] *n.* (plural **solos**) [C] ENG. LANG. ARTS a piece of music written for one performer

so·lo·ist /ˈsoʊloʊɪst/ *n.* [C] ENG. LANG. ARTS a musician who performs a solo

sols·tice /ˈsɑlstɪs, ˈsɔl-/ *n.* [C] the longest or shortest day of the year: *the* ***summer/winter solstice***

sol·u·ble /ˈsɑlyəbəl/ *adj.* CHEMISTRY a soluble substance can be DISSOLVEd in a liquid (ANT) **insoluble**

sol·ute /ˈsɑlyut/ *n.* [C] CHEMISTRY the substance that has DISSOLVEd in a chemical solution

so·lu·tion /səˈluʃən/ *n.* [C] **1** a way of solving a problem or dealing with a difficult situation: *the perfect* ***solution to*** *all our problems* | *Both sides are trying to* ***find*** *a peaceful* ***solution.*** | *The* ***only solution*** *was to move into a quieter apartment.*

THESAURUS

answer – a successful way of dealing with a problem: *Some people believe that the answer to the problem of rising crime is to build more prisons.*
cure – a way of completely getting rid of a problem, especially one that affects many people in society, so that it does not happen again: *The only cure for unemployment is to make it easier for companies to invest and create new jobs.*
remedy – a possible way of dealing with a problem: *A number of remedies have been suggested, but so far none has shown itself to be effective.*
panacea (formal) – something that people think will solve all their problems, used especially when you doubt that this is true: *Nuclear energy was seen as a universal panacea for all our energy problems.*

2 the correct answer to a question or problem: *The* ***solution to*** *the puzzle is on page 14.* **3** CHEMISTRY a liquid mixed with a solid or a gas: *a weak sugar solution* | *saline solution*

THESAURUS mixture, combination, blend → MIXTURE

solve /sɑlv/ *v.* [T] **1** to find a way of dealing with a problem or difficult situation: *Mike thinks money will* ***solve*** *all his* ***problems.*** **2** to find the correct answer to a question or problem, or the explanation for something that is difficult to understand: *I couldn't solve the equation.* | *Police are still trying to* ***solve*** *the* ***crime/case/mystery.*** [ORIGIN: 1400—1500 Latin *solvere* "to loosen, solve, dissolve, pay"] —**solvable** *adj.*

sol·vent[1] /ˈsɑlvənt/ *adj.* having enough money to pay your debts —**solvency** *n.* [U]

solvent[2] *n.* [C] CHEMISTRY a chemical substance that can change a solid substance into a liquid, or that can remove a substance from a surface

som·ber /ˈsɑmbɚ/ *adj.* **1** sad and serious: *a somber mood* **2** dark, or not having any bright colors: *a somber room*

some[1] /səm; *strong* sʌm/ *quantifier* **1** a number of people or things, or an amount of something, when the exact number or amount is not said or shown: *Do you want some coffee?* | *Of course you'll make some new friends in college.*

USAGE

Use **some** in questions when you think the answer will be "yes": *Would you like some coffee?* Use **any** when you do not know what the answer will be: *Were there any letters for me?*

2 a number of people or things, or an amount of something, but not all: *The team has* ***some of*** *the best young players in the country.* | *Some people believe in life after death.* | *In some cases, the damage can be repaired.* **3** (formal) a fairly large amount of something: *It was some time before the police finally arrived.* [ORIGIN: Old English *sum*]

some[2] *pron.* **1** a number of people or things, or an amount of something, but not all: *Many local businesses are having difficulties, and some have even gone bankrupt.* | *Some will live and some will not.* **2** a number of people or things, or an amount of something, when the exact number or amount is not stated: *We're out of milk. Could you buy some on your way home?* **3 and then some** (informal) and more: *He has enough money to buy the house and then some!*

some[3] *determiner* **1** (informal) used when you are talking about a person or thing that you do not know, remember, or understand: *Can you give me some idea of the cost?* | ***For some reason or other*** *they decided to move to Detroit.* | *He's receiving* ***some kind/type/sort of*** *award.* **2 some friend/help! etc.** (spoken) said when you are annoyed because someone or something has disappointed you: *I can't believe you told Mom – some brother you are!*

some[4] *adv.* **1** a little more or a little less than a particular number or amount: *Some 700 homes were damaged by the storm.* **2 some more** an

S

additional number or amount of something: *Would you like some more cake?* **3** (spoken) a little: *We could work some and then rest a while.*

some·bod·y /ˈsʌmˌbɑdi, -ˌbʌdi/ *pron.* SOMEONE

some·day /ˈsʌmdeɪ/ *adv.* at an unknown time in the future: *Someday I'm going to go to Spain.*

some·how /ˈsʌmhaʊ/ *adv.* **1** in some way, although you do not know how: *We'll get there somehow.* | *I knew he was connected **somehow or other** with the CIA.* **2** for some reason, but you are not sure why: *Somehow it seemed like the right thing to do.*

some·one /ˈsʌmwʌn/ *pron.* a word meaning a particular person, used when you do not know or do not say who that person is SYN **somebody**: *Be careful! Someone could get hurt.* | *"Does Mike still live here?" "No, **someone else** (=a different person) is renting it now."*

GRAMMAR

someone, anyone
In questions and negative sentences, we usually use **anyone** and not **someone**: *Can anyone hear me?* | *There isn't anyone else who knows about this.*

S

some·place /ˈsʌmpleɪs/ *adv.* (spoken) SOMEWHERE

som·er·sault /ˈsʌmɚˌsɔlt/ *n.* [C] a movement in which you roll forward until your feet go over your head and touch the ground again [ORIGIN: 1500—1600 Old French *sombresaut*, from Latin *super* "over" + *saltus* "jump"] —**somersault** *v.* [I]

some·thing /ˈsʌmθɪŋ/ *pron.* **1** used to mention a particular thing when you do not know its name, do not know exactly what it is, etc. ➔ ANYTHING, EVERYTHING, NOTHING: *There's something in my eye.* | *He said **something about** a party.* | *There's **something wrong** (=a problem) with the phone.* | *Can you **do something about** that noise?* | *I don't eat eggs. Could I have **something else**?* ➔ THING

GRAMMAR

something, anything
In questions and negative sentences, we usually use **anything** and not **something**, but if you are offering someone some food, a drink, etc., it sounds more polite to use **something**: *Would you like something to eat?*

2 something to eat/drink some food or a drink: *We went out for something to eat after the movie.* **3 have/be something to do with sb/sth** to be connected with or related to a particular person or thing, but in a way that you are not sure about: *I know Steve's job has something to do with investments.* **4 make something of yourself** to become successful through your own efforts **5 something like 100/2,000 etc.** APPROXIMATELY 100, 2,000, etc.: *There are something like 3,000 homeless people in this city.* **6 twenty-something/thirty-something** (informal) used when someone is between the ages of 20 and 29, 30 and 39, etc., when you do not know exactly

SPOKEN PHRASES

7 or something said when you cannot remember or cannot be exact: *Maybe I cooked it too long or something.* **8 be (really) something** used when something is impressive or unusual: *It's really something to see all the hot air balloons taking off together.* **9 a little something** a small gift that is not very expensive: *Here's a little something for you.*

some·time /ˈsʌmtaɪm/ *adv.* at an unknown time in the past or future: *I'll call you sometime next week.*

some·times /ˈsʌmtaɪmz/ *adv.* on some occasions, but not always: *Sometimes I don't get home until 9:00 at night.* | *"Do you miss your old school?" "Sometimes."*

THESAURUS

occasionally/on occasion – sometimes but not often: *We see each other occasionally.*
(every) once in a while/every so often – sometimes but not regularly: *It would be nice if he would call every once in a while.*
from time to time – sometimes but not often or regularly: *A situation like this arises from time to time.* ➔ OFTEN, NEVER, RARELY

some·way /ˈsʌmweɪ/ *adv.* (informal) SOMEHOW

some·what /ˈsʌmwʌt/ Ac *adv.* slightly, but not very much: *I feel somewhat responsible for the accident.*

some·where /ˈsʌmwɛr/ *adv.* **1** in a place or to a place that is not specific: *My wallet must be around here somewhere.* | *Let's find **somewhere to** eat.* | *I want to live **somewhere else*** (=somewhere different). | *They're made somewhere in Europe.* **2 somewhere around/between etc.** a little more or a little less than a particular number or amount SYN **approximately**: *A good CD player costs somewhere around $500.* **3 be getting somewhere** to be making progress: *At last we're getting somewhere!* **4 somewhere along the line/way** used in order to say that you are not sure when something happened: *Somewhere along the line I made a mistake.*

GRAMMAR

somewhere, anywhere
In questions and negative sentences, we usually use **anywhere** and not **somewhere**: *I can't find my keys anywhere.*

som·no·lent /ˈsɑmnələnt/ *adj.* (literary) **1** almost starting to sleep: *her somnolent brown eyes* **2** making you want to sleep: *a slow somnolent song* —**somnolence** *n.* [U]

son /sʌn/ *n.* **1** [C] your male child: *My son is 12 years old.* | *She has two daughters and one son.* |

Bill was the ***son of*** *German immigrants.* **2** [singular] used by an older person as a friendly way to talk to a boy or young man: *What's your name, son?* [ORIGIN: Old English *sunu*]

so·na·ta /sə'nɑṭə/ *n.* [C] ENG. LANG. ARTS a piece of CLASSICAL MUSIC usually for two instruments, one of which is a piano

song /sɔŋ/ *n.* **1** [C] a short piece of music with words: *She* ***sang a song.*** | *a* ***pop/folk/love song*** | *He suddenly* ***burst/broke into song*** (=started singing). **2** [U] songs in general: *a celebration of music, song and dance* **3** [C,U] the musical sounds made by birds [ORIGIN: Old English *sang*]

son·ic /'sɑnɪk/ *adj.* PHYSICS relating to sound

'son-in-ˌlaw *n.* [C] the husband of your daughter

son·net /'sɑnɪt/ *n.* [C] ENG. LANG. ARTS a poem that has 14 lines that RHYME with each other in a particular pattern [ORIGIN: 1500—1600 Italian *sonetto*, from Old Provençal *sonet* "little song"]

so·no·rous /'sɑnərəs/ *adj.* having a deep, pleasantly loud sound: *a sonorous voice*

soon /sun/ *adv.* **1** in a short time from now, or a short time after something has happened: *It will be dark soon.* | *Paula became pregnant* ***soon after*** *they were married.*

THESAURUS

in a minute (spoken) – used when talking about something that will happen within a few minutes: *I'll be ready in a minute.*
any minute now (spoken) – used when something will happen in a very short time from now, but you do not know exactly when: *The train should be here any minute now.*
before long – soon or in a short time: *Those two will be getting married before long.*
shortly (formal) – soon: *Davis made a confession shortly after his arrest.*
in the near future – in the next few weeks or months: *They promised to contact us again in the near future.*
presently (old-fashioned) – in a short time: *The doctor will see you presently.*

2 quickly: *I'll get it fixed* ***as soon as possible.*** | ***How soon*** *can you get here?* **3 as soon as** immediately after something has happened: *I tried to call you as soon as I heard the news.* **4 sooner or later** used to say that something will definitely happen, but you are not sure when: *She's bound to find out sooner or later.* **5 the sooner...the better** used to say that something should happen as quickly as possible: *The sooner you finish this report, the better.* **6 no sooner had...than** used when something has happened almost immediately after something else: *No sooner had I stepped in the shower than the phone rang.* → **would (just) as soon** *at* WOULD

soot /sʊt/ *n.* [U] black powder that is produced when something burns

soothe /suð/ *v.* [T] **1** to make someone feel calmer and less worried, angry, or upset: *Lucy soothed the baby by rocking him in her arms.* **2** to make a pain stop hurting as much: *A massage would soothe your aching muscles.* [ORIGIN: Old English *sothian* "to prove the truth," from *soth* "true"]

THESAURUS **relieve, ease, lessen, alleviate** → REDUCE

—soothing *adj.*: *gentle, soothing music*

sop /sɑp/ *v.* (**sopped, sopping**)
sop sth ↔ **up** *phr. v.* to remove a liquid from a surface using something that will ABSORB the liquid: *Jesse sopped up the spilled drink with a towel.*

so·phis·ti·cat·ed /sə'fɪstəˌkeɪṭɪd/ *adj.* **1** confident and having a lot of experience of life and good judgment about socially important things such as art, fashion, etc.: *She's beautiful, sophisticated, and wealthy.* **2** having a lot of knowledge and experience of difficult or complicated subjects and therefore able to understand them well: *today's more sophisticated investors* **3** made or designed well, and often complicated: *a* ***highly sophisticated*** *alarm system* [ORIGIN: 1300—1400 Medieval Latin, past participle of *sophisticare* "to deceive with words, hide the true nature of something," from Latin *sophisticus*]

THESAURUS **advanced, modern, high-tech, state-of-the-art, cutting-edge** → ADVANCED

—sophistication /səˌfɪstə'keɪʃən/ *n.* [U]

soph·o·more /'sɑfmɔr/ *n.* [C] a student in the second year of HIGH SCHOOL or college → STUDENT

soph·o·mor·ic /sɑf'mɔrɪk/ *adj.* very silly and unreasonable: *sophomoric humor*

sop·o·rif·ic /ˌsɑpə'rɪfɪk/ *adj.* (formal) making you feel ready to sleep

sop·ping /'sɑpɪŋ/ *also* **ˌsopping 'wet** *adj.* very wet

so·pra·no /sə'prænoʊ/ *n.* (plural **sopranos**) [C,U] ENG. LANG. ARTS a woman, girl, or young boy singer with a very high voice

sor·bet /sɔr'beɪ, 'sɔrbət/ *n.* [C,U] a sweet frozen food made from fruit juice, sugar, and water [ORIGIN: 1500—1600 Old French "fruit drink," from Old Italian *sorbetto*]

sor·cer·er /'sɔrsərə·/ *n.* [C] a man in stories who uses magic (SYN) **wizard**

sor·cer·ess /'sɔrsərɪs/ *n.* [C] a woman in stories who uses magic (SYN) **witch**

sor·cer·y /'sɔrsəri/ *n.* [U] magic, especially evil magic

THESAURUS **magic, witchcraft, black magic** → MAGIC[1]

sor·did /'sɔrdɪd/ *adj.* involving immoral or dishonest behavior: *all the* ***sordid details*** *of the scandal* [ORIGIN: 1500—1600 Latin *sordidus*, from *sordes* "dirt"]

S

sore¹ /sɔr/ *adj.* **1** painful as a result of a wound, infection, or too much exercise: *My knee's a little sore from running yesterday.* | *a **sore throat***

THESAURUS painful, tender, stiff → PAINFUL

2 sore point/spot (with sb) something that is likely to make someone upset or angry if you talk about it: *Don't mention marriage – it's a sore point with him.* **3** (old-fashioned) upset, angry, or annoyed [ORIGIN: Old English *sar*] **—soreness** *n.* [U]

sore² *n.* [C] a painful place on your body where your skin is cut or infected: *They were starving and covered with sores.*

sore·ly /ˈsɔrli/ *adv.* very much: *He will be **sorely missed** by everyone.*

so·ror·i·ty /səˈrɔrət̬i, -ˈrɑr-/ *n.* (plural **sororities**) [C] a club for women at a college or university → FRATERNITY

sor·row /ˈsɑroʊ, ˈsɔ-/ *n.* [C,U] a feeling of great sadness, or an event that makes you feel great sadness: *a time of **great/deep sorrow*** | *Our prayers are with you in your time of sorrow.* **—sorrowful** *adj.*

S

sor·ry /ˈsɑri, ˈsɔri/ *adj.* **1 sorry/I'm sorry** (spoken) **a)** used to tell someone that you feel bad about doing something that has upset or annoyed him/her: *I'm really sorry. I didn't mean to hurt your feelings.* | *"Kevin! Don't do that!" "Sorry."* | ***Sorry about** the mess.* | *I'm **sorry (that)** I was late.* **b)** used when politely saying something that disappoints or disagrees with someone: *I'm sorry – we're not going to be able to come.* | *I'm **sorry to** call you so late, but this is important.* **2** [not before noun] feeling bad about a situation and wishing it were different: *Casey was **sorry (that)** he had gotten so angry.* | *I was **sorry to** hear of your father's death.* **3 be/feel sorry for sb** to feel pity or sympathy for someone because s/he is in a bad situation: *He was lonely and I felt sorry for him.* | *Stop **feeling sorry for yourself** and do something!* **4 sorry?** (spoken) used to ask someone to repeat something that you have not heard correctly SYN **pardon** **5** [only before noun] (informal) very bad: *That's the sorriest excuse I've ever heard.* [ORIGIN: Old English *sarig*, from *sar*; influenced by *sorrow*]

sort¹ /sɔrt/ *n.* **1** [C] a type or kind of something: *What **sort of** work does he do?* | *They had **all sorts of*** (=many different kinds of) *seafood on the menu.*

THESAURUS type, kind, category → TYPE¹

2 sort of (spoken) used when what you are saying or describing is not very definite or exact: *I still feel sort of tired.* | *"Do you like him then?" "Sort of."* **3** [singular] if a computer does a sort, it arranges a list of things in order

sort² *v.* [T] to put things in a particular order, or to arrange them in groups according to size, type, etc.: *Eggs are **sorted according to** size.* | *Applications will be **sorted into** three piles.*

sort sth ↔ **out** *phr. v.* **1** to organize something that is messy, complicated, or in the wrong order: *I need to sort out all the paperwork.* **2** to deal with a problem: *Mike's still trying to sort out his personal life.*

sort through sth *phr. v.* to look at a lot of things in order to find something or arrange things in order: *We sorted through all his papers after he died.*

sort·a /ˈsɔrt̬ə/ a short form of "sort of," used in writing to show how people sound when they speak: *He's sorta cute.*

SOS *n.* [singular] a signal or message that a ship or airplane is in danger and needs help [ORIGIN: 1900—2000 *S* and *O*, letters chosen because they were easy to send by Morse code, but often understood as short for *"save our souls"*]

ˈso-so *adj., adv.* (spoken) neither very good nor very bad: *"How was the movie?" "So-so."*

souf·flé /suˈfleɪ/ *n.* [C,U] a baked food that is light and made from eggs, flour, milk, and sometimes cheese

sought /sɔt/ Ac *v.* the past tense and past participle of SEEK

ˈsought-ˌafter *adj.* wanted by a lot of people, but difficult to get: *a sought-after chef*

soul /soʊl/ *n.* **1** [C] the part of a person that is not physical and contains his/her thoughts, feelings, character, etc. Many people believe the soul continues to exist after death: *the immortality of the **human soul*** | *He knew **in his soul** that Linda was never going to change.* **2** [C] a person: *There wasn't a soul in sight.* **3** [U] a type of popular modern music that often expresses deep emotions, usually performed by black singers and musicians **4** [U] a special quality that gives something its true character: *the soul of the Old Town area* **5** [U] a special quality that makes you feel strong emotions: *His poetry lacks soul.* [ORIGIN: Old English *sawol*]

soul·ful /ˈsoʊlfəl/ *adj.* expressing deep, usually sad, emotions: *a soulful performance*

soul·less /ˈsoʊl-lɪs/ *adj.* lacking the qualities that make people feel interest, emotions, or excitement: *a soulless suburb*

ˈsoul-ˌsearching *n.* [U] the act of carefully examining your thoughts and feelings in order to make a decision: *soul-searching questions*

sound¹ /saʊnd/ *n.* **1** [C,U] something that you hear, or something that can be heard: *the **sound of** breaking glass* | ***Turn the sound down/up*** (=make it quieter or louder) *on the TV, will you?*

THESAURUS

A **sound** is anything that you can hear: *the sound of voices*

A **noise** is usually a loud, unpleasant, or unexpected sound: *the deafening noise of overhead planes*

2 like the sound of sth to be interested in a plan, idea, what someone says, etc.: *"Things will be changing." "I **don't like the sound of that.**"* **3 from the sound of it/things** (spoken) according to what you have heard or read about something: *From the sound of it, they're having marriage problems.* **4** [C] EARTH SCIENCES a long wide area of water that connects two larger areas of water

sound² *v.* **1** [linking verb] if someone or something sounds good, strange, etc., he, she, or it seems that way when you hear or read about him, her, or it: *Mike **sounds like** a nice guy.* | ***It sounded** wonderful – a dream trip.* **2** [linking verb] to seem to show a particular quality or emotion with your voice: *You sound upset.* | *He **sounded as though/if** he were having second thoughts.* | *You **sound like** you have a cold.*

THESAURUS **seem, appear, come across as sth** → SEEM

3 [linking verb] if a noise sounds like a particular thing, that is how it seems to you when you hear it: *That **sounded like** thunder.* **4 sound a warning/the alarm** to give a public warning or tell people to be careful **5 sounds good** (spoken) said in order to accept something that someone has suggested: *"Do you want Thai food?" "Sounds good."* **6** [I,T] to produce a noise, or to make something do this: *The church bells sounded.*

sound sb/sth ↔ out *phr. v.* **1** to talk to someone in order to find out what s/he thinks about a plan or idea: *He used polls to sound out public opinion.* **2** to make the sounds of the letters as you try to read a word: *The children were **sounding out words** in class.*

sound³ *adj.* **1** practical, based on good judgment, and likely to produce good results: *His advice was sound.* | *a sound investment* **2** in good condition and not damaged in any way **3 of sound mind** LAW not mentally ill

sound⁴ *adv.* **sound asleep** completely asleep

'sound ˌbarrier *n.* **the sound barrier** the point when an aircraft reaches the speed of sound

'sound bite *n.* [C] a short phrase from a speech or statement that presents an important idea and that is meant to be used on a radio or television news program

'sound card *n.* [C] IT a CIRCUIT BOARD in a computer that makes the computer able to produce sounds

'sound efˌfects *n.* [plural] special sounds used in order to make a movie, television show, etc. seem more real

'sounding board *n.* [C] someone you discuss your ideas with before using them

sound·ly /ˈsaʊndli/ *adv.* **1 sleep soundly** to sleep well and peacefully **2** completely or severely: *Washington was soundly defeated.*

sound·proof /ˈsaʊndpruf/ *adj.* a soundproof wall, room, etc. is one that sound cannot pass through, into, or out of —**soundproof** *v.* [T]

sound·track /ˈsaʊndtræk/ *n.* [C] the recorded music from a movie: *the **soundtrack to** "The Mission"*

soup /sup/ *n.* [C,U] a hot liquid food that often has pieces of meat or vegetables in it: *chicken noodle soup* | *a **bowl of soup*** [ORIGIN: 1600—1700 French *soupe* "piece of bread dipped in liquid, soup"]

'soup ˌkitchen *n.* [C] a place where free food is given to people who have no home

sour¹ /saʊə/ *adj.* **1** having an acid taste, like the taste of a LEMON: *sour apples*

THESAURUS **sweet, tasty, salty, hot, spicy** → TASTE¹

2 milk or other food that is sour is not fresh and has a bad taste and smell: *The milk had **gone sour.*** **3** unfriendly or unhappy: *a sour expression* **4 turn/go sour** (informal) to stop being enjoyable or satisfactory: *Their marriage had turned sour.* [ORIGIN: Old English *sur*]

sour² *v.* **1** [I] to stop being enjoyable, friendly, or satisfactory: *Relations between the two countries had soured.* **2** [I,T] to become sour, or to make a food do this

source¹ /sɔrs/ (Ac) *n.* [C] **1** the thing, place, person, etc. that you get something from: *gasoline and other **sources of** energy* | *Tourism is the city's **main/major/primary source** of income.* | *We used a halogen lamp as a **light source** because it creates a very powerful beam of light.*

THESAURUS **origin, root** → ORIGIN

2 the cause of a problem, or the place where it starts: *Technicians located the **source of** the problem.* **3** a person, book, or document that you get information from: ***Reliable sources** say the company is going bankrupt.* | *Use sources such as books, magazines, and websites when doing research for your paper.* **4** EARTH SCIENCES the place where a stream or river starts [ORIGIN: 1300—1400 Old French *sourse*, from *sourdre* "to rise, spring out," from Latin *surgere* "to rise"]

source² (Ac) *v.* [T] to find out where you can obtain something from: *Many companies are now sourcing both materials and labor outside the U.S.*

ˌsour 'cream *n.* [U] a thick white cream with a sour taste, used in cooking

sour·dough /ˈsaʊədoʊ/ *also* **ˌsourdough 'bread** *n.* [U] a type of bread with a slightly sour taste

south¹, South /saʊθ/ *n.* [singular, U] **1** the direction that is at the bottom of a map of the world, or to the right of someone facing the rising Sun: *Which way is south?* → *see picture at* NORTH¹ **2 the south** the southern part of a country, state, etc.: *Rain will spread **to the south** later today.* | *the*

S

south of France **3 the South** the southeastern states of the U.S. [ORIGIN: Old English *suth*]

USAGE

Use **north/south/east/west of sth** in order to describe where a place is in relation to another place: *Memphis is south of St. Louis.*
Use **in the north/south/east/west, etc. of sth** in order to say which part of a place you are talking about: *The mountains are in the west of the province.*
Use **northern/southern/eastern/western, etc.** with the name of a place: *They have a cabin in northern Ontario.* Don't say "in the north of Ontario."

south² *adj.* **1** in, to, or facing south: *The hotel's about two miles* ***south of*** *Monterey.* | *the south wall* **2 south wind** a wind coming from the south

south³ *adv.* **1** toward the south: *Go south on I-35.* | *The window faces south.* **2 down South** in or to the southeastern part of the U.S.: *My folks still live down South.*

South A·mer·i·ca /ˌsaʊθ əˈmɛrəkə/ *n.* one of the seven CONTINENTS, that includes land south of the Caribbean Sea and north of Antarctica —**South American** *adj.*

S

south·bound /ˈsaʊθbaʊnd/ *adj.* traveling or leading toward the south: *the southbound lanes of the freeway*

south·east¹ /ˌsaʊθˈist◂/ *n.* [U] **1** the direction that is exactly between south and east ➔ *see picture at* NORTH¹ **2 the southeast** the southeast part of a country, state, etc. **3 the Southeast** the area of the U.S. that includes the states of Alabama, Florida, Georgia, and South Carolina —**southeastern** *adj.*

southeast² *adj., adv.* in, from, or toward the southeast: *We drove southeast.* | *a southeast wind*

south·er·ly /ˈsʌðəli/ *adj.* **1** in or toward the south: *a southerly direction* **2** a southerly wind comes from the south

south·ern /ˈsʌðən/ *adj.* in or from the south part of an area, state, country, etc.: *southern New Mexico* ➔ see USAGE box at SOUTH¹

south·ern·er /ˈsʌðənə/ *n.* [C] someone who comes from the southern part of a country or the southern HEMISPHERE

south·ern·most /ˈsʌðənˌmoʊst/ *adj.* farthest south

ˌSouth Paˈcific *n.* **the South Pacific** the southern part of the Pacific Ocean where there are groups of islands, such as New Zealand and Polynesia

ˌSouth ˈPole *n.* **the South Pole** the most southern point on the surface of the Earth, or the area around it ➔ *see picture at* GLOBE

south·ward /ˈsaʊθwəd/ *adj., adv.* toward the south

south·west¹ /ˌsaʊθˈwɛst◂/ *n.* [U] **1** the direction that is exactly between south and west ➔ *see picture at* NORTH¹ **2 the southwest** the southwest part of a country, state, etc. **3 the Southwest** the area of the U.S. that includes the states of New Mexico, Arizona, Texas, California, Nevada, and sometimes Colorado and Utah —**southwestern** *adj.*

southwest² *adj., adv.* in, from, or toward the southwest: *We drove southwest.* | *a southwest wind*

sou·ve·nir /ˌsuvəˈnɪr, ˈsuvəˌnɪr/ *n.* [C] an object that you keep to remind yourself of a special occasion or a place that you have visited: *I bought a model of the Eiffel Tower* ***as a souvenir of*** *Paris.* | *a* ***souvenir shop*** [ORIGIN: 1700—1800 French *souvenir* "to remember"]

sov·er·eign¹ /ˈsɑvərɪn/ *adj.* **1** having the highest power or authority in a country **2** POLITICS a sovereign country is independent and governs itself —**sovereignty** *n.* [U]

sovereign² *n.* [C] (formal) a king or queen

THESAURUS **king, queen, prince, princess, monarch, ruler, emperor** ➔ KING

So·vi·et /ˈsoʊviɪt, -viˌɛt/ *adj.* relating to or coming from the former Soviet Union

sow¹ /soʊ/ *v.* (past tense **sowed**, past participle **sown** /soʊn/ *or* **sowed**) [I,T] to plant or scatter seeds on a piece of ground: *Sow herbs indoors in February.*

sow² /saʊ/ *n.* [C] a female pig

soy·bean /ˈsɔɪbin/ *n.* [C] a bean from which oil and food containing a lot of PROTEIN is produced

spa /spɑ/ *n.* [C] **1** *also* **health spa** a place that people go to in order to improve their health, especially a place where the water has special minerals in it **2** a special bathtub that sends currents of hot water around you [ORIGIN: 1600—1700 *Spa* Belgian town with a spa]

space¹ /speɪs/ *n.* **1** [U] the amount of an area, room, container, etc. that is empty or available to be used: *The class has* ***space for*** *five more students.* | *There's not enough space in the computer's memory.* **2** [C,U] an empty area that is used for a particular purpose: *parking spaces* | *storage space* **3** [U] PHYSICS the area beyond the Earth where the stars and PLANETS are: *the first man* ***in space*** | *space exploration* | *an alien from* ***outer space*** (=far away in space)

TOPIC

Things in space
meteor, asteroid, comet, moon, planet, star, sun, constellation, galaxy, black hole

Vehicles used in space
spacecraft, spaceship, rocket, (space) shuttle, satellite, probe

Someone who travels in space
astronaut

4 [C] the empty area between two things: *the **spaces between** the words* | *an **empty space** at the back of the stage*

THESAURUS hole, gap, crack, opening → HOLE[1]

5 in the space of sth within a particular period of time: *They went from first place to last in the space of a season.* **6** [C,U] empty land that does not have anything built on it: *a fight to save the city's **open spaces*** **7** [U] freedom to do what you want or to be alone: *I want to **give** my students **space** to think for themselves.*

space² *v.* **1** [T] to arrange objects, events, etc. so that they have an equal amount of space or time between them: ***Space** the plants four inches **apart**.* **2** [I] *also* **space out** (slang) to stop paying attention and begin to look in front of you without thinking —**spacing** *n.* [U]

'space-age *adj.* (informal) very modern: *space age design*

'space ca,det *also* **'space case** *n.* [C] (informal) someone who is SPACEY

space·craft /'speɪs-kræft/ *n.* [C] a vehicle that can travel in space → SPACE¹

spaced /speɪst/ *also* **,spaced 'out** *adj.* (informal) SPACEY

space·ship /'speɪs,ʃɪp/ *n.* [C] a spacecraft – used especially in stories → SPACE¹

'space ,shuttle *n.* [C] a spacecraft for carrying people into space, that can be used more than once

space·y /'speɪsi/ *adj.* (spoken) someone who is spacey does not pay attention, forgets things, and often behaves slightly strangely

spa·cious /'speɪʃəs/ *adj.* having a lot of space in which you can move around: *a spacious house*

spade /speɪd/ *n.* [C] **1** a SHOVEL **2** a playing card with one or more black shapes like pointed leaves on it → *see picture at* PLAYING CARD [ORIGIN: (1) Old English *spadu*] [ORIGIN: (2) 1500—1600 Italian *spada* or Spanish *espada* "broad sword" (used as a mark on cards)]

spa·ghet·ti /spə'gɛt̬i/ *n.* [U] long thin pieces of PASTA that look like strings [ORIGIN: 1800—1900 Italian *spago* "string"]

spam¹ /spæm/ *n.* [U] IT email messages that a computer user has not asked for and does not want to read, for example from someone who is advertising something

spam² *v.* [I,T] IT to send the same email message to many different people who have not asked for it and do not want to read it, usually as a way of advertising something —**spamming** *n.* [U]

span¹ /spæn/ *n.* [C] **1** the amount of time during which something continues to exist or happen: *Most children have a short **attention span**.* | *The mayfly has a two-day **life span**.* **2** a period of time between two dates or events: ***Over a span of** five years, they planted 10,000 new trees.* | *a short **time span*** **3** the distance from one side of something to the other: *the bird's **wing span***

span² *v.* (**spanned**, **spanning**) [T] **1** to include all of a period of time: *a career spanning four decades* **2** to include all of a particular area: *The Internet spans the globe.* **3** to go from one side of something to the other: *a bridge spanning the river*

span·iel /'spænyəl/ *n.* [C] a dog with long hair and long ears [ORIGIN: 1300—1400 Old French *espaignol* "Spaniard, spaniel," from Latin *Hispania* "Spain"]

Span·ish¹ /'spænɪʃ/ *adj.* **1** relating to or coming from Spain **2** relating to the Spanish language

Spanish² *n.* **1** [U] the language used in places such as Mexico, Spain, and South America **2 the Spanish** [plural] the people of Spain, considered as a single group

spank /spæŋk/ *v.* [T] to hit a child on the BUTTOCKS with your open hand [ORIGIN: 1700—1800 From the sound] —**spanking** *n.* [C,U]

spar /spɑr/ *v.* (**sparred**, **sparring**) [I] **1** to practice BOXING with someone **2** to argue with someone: *Republican and Democrat senators have been **sparring over** the health bill.*

S

spare¹ /spɛr/ *adj.* **1 spare key/battery etc.** a key, etc. that you have in addition to the one you usually use, so that it is available if it is needed **2** not being used by anyone and therefore available for use: *a spare bedroom* **3 spare time** time when you are not working: *I play tennis in my spare time.* **4 spare change** coins that you can afford to give to someone [ORIGIN: Old English *spær*]

spare² *v.* [T] **1** to prevent someone from having to do something difficult or unpleasant: *I wanted to spare the kids the pain of our divorce.* **2 money/time etc. to spare** money or time that is left in addition to what you have used or need: *We made it to the airport with 10 minutes to spare.* **3** to make something such as time, money, or workers available for someone, especially when this is difficult: *I guess I **can spare** a few dollars.* | ***Could** you **spare** me twenty minutes?* **4 spare no expense/effort etc.** to use as much money, effort, etc. as necessary to do something **5** to not damage or harm someone or something, when other people or things are being killed or damaged: *If they surrendered, their lives would be spared.*

spare³ *n.* [C] an additional key, BATTERY, etc. that you keep so that it is available if it is needed: *There's a spare* (=additional tire) *in the trunk.*

spar·ing·ly /'spɛrɪŋli/ *adv.* using or giving only a little of something: ***Use** water **sparingly** this summer.* —**sparing** *adj.*

spark¹ /spɑrk/ *n.* [C] **1** a very small piece of fire coming from a larger fire or from hitting two hard objects together: *sparks from the fire* **2** PHYSICS a flash of light caused by electricity passing across a small space **3 spark of interest/intelligence etc.** a small amount of a feeling or quality: *As she* *spoke, she saw a spark of hope in Tony's eyes.* [ORIGIN: Old English *spearca*]

spark² *v.* **1** [T] to make something start happening: *The argument about whether slavery should be abolished or maintained* ***sparked off*** *the American Civil War.* **2** [I] to produce sparks

spar·kle /ˈspɑrkəl/ *v.* [I] **1** to shine in small bright flashes: *diamonds sparkling in the light*

THESAURUS shine, flash, flicker, twinkle, shimmer, glint, glisten → SHINE¹

2 if someone's eyes sparkle, they shine because s/he is happy or excited —**sparkle** *n.* [C,U]

spark·ler /ˈspɑrklɚ/ *n.* [C] a type of FIREWORK that you can hold in your hand, consisting of a thin stick that burns with colored SPARKS

spark·ling /ˈspɑrklɪŋ/ *adj.* **1** shining brightly with points of flashing light: *a sparkling brook* **2** very clean: *the sparkling kitchen*

ˈspark plug *n.* [C] a part in a car engine that produces the SPARK to make the gas burn

spar·row /ˈspæroʊ/ *n.* [C] a common small brown or gray bird [ORIGIN: Old English *spearwa*]

S

sparse /spɑrs/ *adj.* small in number or amount, and usually scattered over a large area: *sparse vegetation* [ORIGIN: 1700—1800 Latin *sparsus* "spread out," from the past participle of *spargere* "to scatter"] —**sparsely** *adv.*: *sparsely populated*

spar·tan /ˈspɑrtˀn/ *adj.* very simple and without comfort: *a spartan room* [ORIGIN: 1600—1700 *Spartan* "of Sparta" (16—21 centuries), from *Sparta* city in ancient Greece whose people lived simply]

spasm /ˈspæzəm/ *n.* [C] **1** an occasion when your muscles suddenly become tight, causing you pain: *back spasms* **2** a short period during which you have a sudden strong feeling or reaction to something: *spasms of laughter* [ORIGIN: 1300—1400 Old French *spasme*, from Latin, from Greek *spasmos*, from *span* "to pull"]

spas·mod·ic /spæzˈmɑdɪk/ *adj.* **1** happening for short periods of time but not regularly or continuously: *my spasmodic efforts to stop smoking* **2** relating to a muscle spasm —**spasmodically** *adv.*

spas·tic /ˈspæstɪk/ *adj.* (old-fashioned) BIOLOGY having CEREBRAL PALSY, a disease that prevents someone being able to control his/her muscles

spat¹ /spæt/ *n.* [C] (informal) an argument or disagreement that is not important (SYN) **quarrel**

spat² *v.* a past tense and the past participle of SPIT

spate /speɪt/ *n.* **a spate of sth** a large number of similar events that happen in a short period of time: *a spate of burglaries*

spa·tial /ˈspeɪʃəl/ *adj.* relating to the position, size, or shape of things

spat·ter /ˈspæt̬ɚ/ *v.* [I,T] if a liquid spatters, or if you spatter it, drops of it fall onto a surface: *a t-shirt* ***spattered with*** *paint*

spat·u·la /ˈspætʃələ/ *n.* [C] a kitchen tool with a wide flat part, used for lifting or spreading food

spawn¹ /spɔn/ *v.* **1** [T] to make something happen or start to exist: *The book "Dracula" has spawned a number of movies.* **2** [I,T] BIOLOGY if a fish or FROG spawns, it lays a lot of eggs

spawn² *n.* [U] BIOLOGY the eggs of a fish or FROG laid together in a soft group

spay /speɪ/ *v.* [T] BIOLOGY to remove part of a female animal's sex organs so that she cannot produce babies (SYN) **neuter**

speak /spik/ *v.* (past tense **spoke** /spoʊk/, past participle **spoken** /ˈspoʊkən/)
1 TALK TO SB [I] to talk to someone about something or have a conversation: *Hello, can I* ***speak to*** *Mr. Sherwood, please?* | *Solomon* ***spoke with*** *a reporter.* | *He* ***spoke of/about*** *his love of the theater.*
2 SAY WORDS [I] to use your voice to say words: *He spoke very softly.*
3 LANGUAGE [T] to be able to talk in a particular language: *My brother speaks French.* ▸Don't say "My brother speaks in French."◂ | ***Can*** *you* ***speak*** *English?*
4 OPINIONS [I] to say something that expresses your ideas or opinions: ***Generally speaking****, money issues matter most to voters.* | *He* ***spoke highly/well of*** (=said good things about) *her.*
5 so to speak (spoken) used in order to say that the words you have used do not have their usual meaning: *Being beaten by a 12-year-old took the wind out of my sails, so to speak.*
6 speaking of sb/sth (spoken) used when you want to say more about someone or something that has just been mentioned: *Speaking of Jody, how is she?*
7 speak your mind to say exactly what you think
8 no sth to speak of *also* **without any sth to speak of** nothing large or important enough to mention: *There is no industry in the town to speak of.*
9 GIVE A SPEECH [I] to make a formal speech: *Burnett* ***spoke at*** *the graduation ceremony.* [ORIGIN: Old English *sprecan, specan*]

speak for sb/sth *phr. v.*
1 *also* **speak on behalf of sb** to express the feelings, thoughts, etc. of another person or group of people: *Mr. Miles spoke for all the parents at the school.*
2 sth speaks for itself to show something so clearly that no explanation is necessary: *Our profits speak for themselves* (=our profits show how good or bad our business is).
3 be spoken for to be promised to someone else: *This puppy is already spoken for.*

speak out *phr. v.*
to say publicly what you think about something, especially as a protest: *people* ***speaking out against*** *human rights abuses*

speak up *phr. v.*
1 (spoken) used in order to ask someone to speak more loudly: *Could you speak up please, I can't hear you.*
2 to say publicly what you think about something: *If you don't like what's happening, speak up!*

speak·er /'spikɚ/ *n.* [C] **1** someone who makes a speech: *the guest speaker for the evening* **2** the part of a radio, CD PLAYER, etc. where the sound comes out ➔ *see picture on page A19* **3 English/French etc. speaker** someone who speaks English, French, etc. **4** *also* **Speaker of the House** POLITICS the politician who controls discussions in the U.S. House of Representatives

spear¹ /spɪr/ *n.* [C] a pole with a sharp pointed blade at one end, used as a weapon

spear² *v.* [T] to push a pointed object such as a fork into something

spear·head /'spɪrhɛd/ *v.* [T] to lead an attack or an organized action: *the troops who spearheaded the rescue mission*

spe·cial¹ /'spɛʃəl/ *adj.* **1** different in some way from what is ordinary or usual, and often better or more important: *a special place in the classroom for reading* | *Give her **something special** this Christmas.* | *a dish served on **special occasions*** **2** particularly important to someone and deserving love, attention, etc.: *He made me **feel special**.* | *her special friends* **3 special care/attention etc.** more care, attention, etc. than is usual: *We try to **give special care** to the youngest patients.* [ORIGIN: 1100—1200 Old French *especial*, from Latin *specialis* "particular"]

special² *n.* [C] **1** something that is not ordinary or usual, but is made or done for a particular purpose: *a TV special on the election* **2** a lower price than usual for a particular product for a short period of time: *today's lunch special* | *Chickens are **on special**.*

ˌspecial eduˈcation *n.* [U] education for children who have physical or mental problems

ˌspecial efˈfects *n.* [plural] images or sounds that have been produced artificially to be used in a movie or television program

spe·cial·ist /'spɛʃəlɪst/ *n.* [C] someone who knows a lot about a particular subject or has a lot of skill in it: *a heart specialist*

THESAURUS expert, authority ➔ EXPERT

spe·cial·ize /'spɛʃəˌlaɪz/ *v.* [I] to limit most of your study, business, etc. to a particular subject or activity: *a lawyer who **specializes in** divorce cases* —**specialization** /ˌspɛʃələ'zeɪʃən/ *n.* [C,U]

spe·cial·ized /'spɛʃəˌlaɪzd/ *adj.* developed for a particular purpose: *soldiers going through specialized training*

spe·cial·ly /'spɛʃəli/ *adv.* **1** for one particular purpose: *specially trained dogs used by blind people* **2** (spoken) especially: *I had it made specially for you.*

ˌspecial ˈprosecutor *n.* [C] LAW an independent lawyer who is chosen to examine the actions of a government official and find out if they have done anything wrong or illegal

spe·cial·ty /'spɛʃəlti/ *n.* (plural **specialties**) [C] **1** a subject that you know a lot about, or a skill that you have: *his academic specialty* **2** a food or product that is very good, produced in a particular restaurant, area, etc.: *The **house specialty** is chicken enchiladas.* **3** a particular product or business that has one purpose or sells one type of thing: *specialty magazines*

spe·ci·a·tion /ˌspiʃi'eɪʃən/ *n.* [U] BIOLOGY the process by which one existing species of animal, plant, etc. gradually changes over a long period of time and forms into two or more different species that are GENETICally different

spe·cies /'spiʃiz, -siz/ *n.* (plural **species**) [C] BIOLOGY a group of animals or plants of the same kind that can breed with each other ➔ GENUS: *Three different **species of** deer live in the forest.* ➔ *see also* ENDANGERED SPECIES, INVASIVE SPECIES [ORIGIN: 1300—1400 Latin "appearance, kind," from *specere* "to look (at)"] ➔ TYPE¹

S

spe·cif·ic /spɪ'sɪfɪk/ (Ac) *adj.* **1** detailed and exact: *specific questions* | *Can you **be more specific**?* **2** used when talking about a particular thing, person, time, etc.: *Set a specific time aside to do homework.* **3 specific to sth** limited to or affecting only one particular thing: *a disease specific to birds*

spe·cif·i·cally /spɪ'sɪfɪkli/ (Ac) *adv.* **1** for a particular type of person or thing: *a book written specifically for teenagers* **2** in a detailed or exact way: *You were specifically requested to leave by 4 p.m.*

spec·i·fi·ca·tion /ˌspɛsəfə'keɪʃən/ (Ac) *n.* [C usually plural] a detailed instruction about how something should be done, made, etc.: *The airport tower was built **to** FAA **specifications**.*

speˌcific ˈheat *n.* [U] CHEMISTRY the amount of heat that is needed to raise the temperature of one gram of a substance by one degree Celsius

spe·cif·ics /spɪ'sɪfɪks/ (Ac) *n.* [plural] the exact details of something: *The candidate made promises but gave no specifics on how to achieve those promises.*

spe·ci·fy /'spɛsəˌfaɪ/ (Ac) *v.* (**specified**, **specifies**) [T] to state something in an exact and detailed way: *The governor did not **specify what** changes would be made.* | *His contract **specifies that** he work a forty-hour week.*

spec·i·men /'spɛsəmən/ *n.* [C] **1** BIOLOGY a small amount or piece of something that is taken so that it can be tested or examined: *a blood/urine specimen* **2** BIOLOGY a single animal, plant, etc. from a group of animals, plants, etc.: *a specimen of tropical fish* **3** a single example of something: *a* *fine specimen of Roman pottery from the 1st Century A.D.* [ORIGIN: 1600—1700 Latin *specere* "to look (at)"]

spe·cious /ˈspiʃəs/ *adj.* (formal) seeming to be true or correct, but really false: *a specious argument*

speck /spɛk/ *n.* [C] a very small mark, spot, or piece of something: ***a speck of** dust*

speck·led /ˈspɛkəld/ *adj.* covered with a lot of small spots or marks: *speckled eggs*

spec·ta·cle /ˈspɛktəkəl/ *n.* [C] **1** (disapproving) an unusual or strange thing or situation that you see: *He got drunk and **made a spectacle of** himself.* **2** a very impressive show or scene: *the magnificent spectacle of a forest in fall* **3 spectacles** [plural] (old-fashioned) glasses that you use to see things better

spec·tac·u·lar[1] /spɛkˈtækyələ˞/ *adj.* very impressive or exciting: *a spectacular view of the Grand Canyon* —**spectacularly** *adv.*

spectacular[2] *n.* [C] an event or performance that is very big and impressive

spec·ta·tor /ˈspɛkˌteɪt̬ə˞/ *n.* [C] someone who watches an event, game, etc. ➔ *see picture at* AUDIENCE

S

spec·ter /ˈspɛktə˞/ *n.* **1 the specter of sth** something that frightens you because it may affect you badly: *The failure of the talks **raised the specter of** war.* **2** [C] (literary) a GHOST

THESAURUS **ghost, spirit, phantom, apparition** ➔ GHOST

spec·trum /ˈspɛktrəm/ *n.* (plural **spectra** /-trə/) **1** [singular] a complete or very wide range of opinions, ideas, people, etc.: *The policy appeals to a **wide/broad spectrum** of voters.* | *women from **across the** social **spectrum*** **2** [C] PHYSICS the set of different colors that is produced when light passes through a PRISM

spec·u·late /ˈspɛkyəˌleɪt/ *v.* **1** [I,T] to guess why something happened or what will happen next, without knowing all the facts: *Officials would not **speculate on/about** the cause of the crash.* **2** [I] ECONOMICS to buy goods, property, etc., hoping to make a large profit when you sell them [ORIGIN: 1500—1600 Latin, past participle of *speculari* "to watch (secretly)," from *specere* "to look (at)"] —**speculator** *n.* [C] —**speculation** /ˌspɛkyəˈleɪʃən/ *n.* [C,U]: ***speculation that** he will resign*

spec·u·la·tive /ˈspɛkyələt̬ɪv, -ˌleɪt̬ɪv/ *adj.* **1** based on guessing, not facts: *a speculative article* **2** ECONOMICS bought or done in order to make a profit later: *a speculative investment*

sped /spɛd/ *v.* a past tense and past participle of SPEED

speech /spitʃ/ *n.* **1** [C] a talk, especially a formal one about a particular subject, given to a group of people: *a campaign speech* | *Walters **gave/made a speech** at graduation.* | *a **speech on/about** immigration* **2** [U] the ability to speak, or the way someone speaks: *Her speech was slow.* **3** [U] ENG. LANG. ARTS spoken language rather than written language: *In speech we use a smaller vocabulary than in writing.*

speech·less /ˈspitʃlɪs/ *adj.* unable to speak because you are angry, shocked, upset, etc.: *Boyd's answer **left** her **speechless**.*

speed[1] /spid/ *n.* **1** [C,U] how fast something moves or travels: *a car traveling **at high/low speed*** ▸ Don't say "in high speed." ◂ | *an air **speed of** 400 miles an hour*

COLLOCATIONS
- **at high/low speed**
- **at great speed**
- **at top/full speed**
- **at lightning speed** – extremely fast
- **at breakneck speed** – dangerously fast
- **at the speed of light**

2 [U] the rate at which something happens or is done: *a high-speed train* | *the **speed of** change* | *The city is growing **at breakneck speed*** (=very fast). **3** [U] the quality of being fast: *a player with speed and power* **4 five-speed/ten-speed etc.** having a particular number of GEARS **5** [U] (slang) an illegal drug that makes you very active [ORIGIN: Old English *sped* "success, quickness"]

speed[2] *v.* (past tense and past participle **sped** /spɛd/ *or* **speeded**) **1** [I] to move or happen quickly: *The train **sped along/by/past**.*

THESAURUS **rush, race, dash, hurry** ➔ RUSH[1]

2 be speeding to be driving faster than the legal limit

speed up *phr. v.* to move or happen faster, or to make something do this: *an attempt to speed up production* | *We sped up to pass the car in front of us.*

speed·boat /ˈspidboʊt/ *n.* [C] a small boat with a powerful engine that can go very fast

speed·ing /ˈspidɪŋ/ *n.* [U] the action of traveling too fast in a vehicle: *Police stopped him **for speeding**.*

ˈspeed ˌlimit *n.* [C] the fastest speed that you are allowed to drive on a particular road: *a 40 mph speed limit*

speed·om·e·ter /spɪˈdɑmət̬ə˞/ *n.* [C] an instrument in a vehicle that shows how fast it is going

ˈspeed trap *n.* [C] a place on a road where police wait to catch drivers who are going too fast

speed·y /ˈspidi/ *adj.* (comparative **speedier**, superlative **speediest**) happening or done quickly, or working quickly: *a speedy recovery* —**speedily** *adv.*

spell[1] /spɛl/ *v.* **1** [I,T] to form a word by writing or saying the letters in the correct order: *My last name is Haines, spelled H-A-I-N-E-S.* | *a list of words* *that are often* ***spelled wrong*** **2 spell trouble/defeat/danger etc.** if a situation spells trouble, etc., it makes you expect trouble: *Too many tourists could spell danger for the wilderness.* **3** [T] if letters spell a word, they form it [ORIGIN: 1200—1300 Old French *espeller*]

spell sth ↔ **out** *phr. v.* to explain something clearly and in detail: *an advert spelling out the dangers of smoking*

spell² *n.* [C] **1** a piece of magic that someone does, or the special words or ceremonies used in doing magic: *The witches* ***cast a spell on/over*** *the young prince.*

THESAURUS magic, curse → MAGIC¹

2 a period of a particular type of weather, activity, etc.: *a dizzy spell* | *We've had* ***a cold/warm/wet/dry spell*** *for most of January.*

spell·bound /ˈspɛlbaʊnd/ *adj.* extremely interested in something you are listening to: *His stories* ***kept/held*** *us* ***spellbound.***

ˈspell-ˌchecker *n.* [C] IT a computer program that tells you when you have not spelled a word correctly —**spell-check** *v.* [I,T]

spell·ing /ˈspɛlɪŋ/ *n.* **1** [U] ENG. LANG. ARTS the ability to spell words in the correct way: *His spelling has improved.* **2** [C] ENG. LANG. ARTS the way that a word is spelled: *the correct spelling*

ˈspelling bee *n.* [C] a spelling competition done by students

spend /spɛnd/ *v.* (past tense and past participle **spent** /spɛnt/) **1** [I,T] to use your money to buy or pay for something: *We* ***spend*** *$150 a week* ***on*** *groceries.* | ***Spending*** *their own* ***money*** *teaches kids about budgets.* **2** [T] to use time doing a particular activity: *I want to* ***spend*** *more* ***time with*** *my family.* | *We* ***spent the day/morning etc.*** *by the pool.* [ORIGIN: 1100—1200 Partly from Latin *expendere* and partly, later, from Old French *despendre*, from Latin *dispendere* "to weigh out"]

spend·ing /ˈspɛndɪŋ/ *n.* [U] ECONOMICS the amount of money spent on something, especially by the government: *a cut in* ***defense/public spending***

spend·thrift /ˈspɛndˌθrɪft/ *n.* [C] someone who spends a lot of money in a careless way

spent¹ /spɛnt/ *v.* the past tense and past participle of SPEND

spent² *adj.* **1** already used and now empty or useless: *spent cartridges* **2** (literary) extremely tired

sperm /spɚm/ *n.* (plural **sperm**) **1** [C] BIOLOGY a cell produced by the male sex organ that joins with an egg to produce new life **2** [U] BIOLOGY SEMEN

spew /spyu/ *also* **spew out** *v.* [I,T] to flow out of something in large quantities, or to make something do this: *factories* ***spewing out*** *pollution*

sphere /sfɪr/ (Ac) *n.* [C] **1** the shape of a ball: *The Earth is a sphere.* **2** a particular area of work, interest, knowledge, etc.: *women's* ***sphere of*** *activity* **3 sphere of influence** an area of the world or a situation in which a particular country, group, or person can influence what happens **4** MATH a solid object in the shape of a ball, in which every point on the surface is exactly the same distance from the center. [ORIGIN: 1200—1300 Old French *espere*, from Latin *sphaera*, from Greek *sphaira* "ball, sphere"]

spher·i·cal /ˈsfɪrɪkəl, ˈsfɛr-/ (Ac) *adj.* having a round shape like a ball

sphinx /sfɪŋks/ *n.* [C] an ancient Egyptian image of a lion with a human head

spice¹ /spaɪs/ *n.* **1** [C,U] a powder or seed taken from plants that is put into food to give it a special taste: *herbs and spices* **2** [singular,U] interest or excitement that is added to something: *Travel* ***adds spice*** *to your life.* [ORIGIN: 1200—1300 Old French *espice*, from Late Latin *species* "spices"] —**spiced** *adj.*

spice² *also* **spice up** *v.* [T] **1** to add interest or excitement to something: *Graphics* ***spice up*** *your marketing materials.* **2** to add spice to food

spick-and-span /ˌspɪk ən ˈspæn/ *adj.* very clean and neat

spic·y /ˈspaɪsi/ *adj.* food that is spicy contains a lot of spices: *a* ***hot and spicy*** *chili*

THESAURUS sweet, tasty, sour, salty, hot → TASTE¹

spi·der /ˈspaɪdɚ/ *n.* [C] a small creature with eight legs that makes WEBS (=sticky nets) to catch insects [ORIGIN: Old English *spithra*, from *spinnan*]

spi·der·web /ˈspaɪdɚˌwɛb/ *n.* [C] a WEB → COBWEB

spi·der·y /ˈspaɪdəri/ *adj.* covered with or made of lots of long thin uneven lines: *spidery handwriting*

spiel /ʃpil, spil/ *n.* [C,U] (informal) a speech that the speaker has used many times before, usually intended to persuade someone to buy something

spike¹ /spaɪk/ *n.* [C] **1** something that is long and thin with a sharp point, especially a piece of metal **2** a sudden large increase in the number, price, rate, etc. of something: *a spike in share prices* —**spiky** *adj.*

spike² *v.* **1** [T] to add something, especially alcohol or a drug, to a drink: *The orange juice had been* ***spiked with*** *gin.* **2** [I] if a number, price, rate, etc. spikes, it increases quickly: *His temperature had spiked.*

spill¹ /spɪl/ *v.* **1** [I,T] if a liquid spills or you spill it, it flows over the edge of a container by accident: *I* ***spilled*** *coffee* ***on*** *my shirt.* **2** [I] if people spill out of a place, they move out in large groups **3 spill your guts** (informal) to tell someone a lot of personal things, especially because you are upset [ORIGIN: Old English *spillan* "to kill, destroy, waste"]

spill over *phr. v.* if a problem or bad situation spills over, it begins to affect other places, people, etc.: *There's a danger that the war will* ***spill over into*** *neighboring countries.*

spill² *n.* [C,U] an act of spilling something, or the amount that is spilled: *an oil spill*

spin¹ /spɪn/ *v.* (past tense and past participle **spun** /spʌn/, present participle **spinning**) **1** [I,T] to turn around and around very quickly, or to make something do this: *The ceiling fans were spinning.* | *He grabbed Lisa by the arm and* ***spun*** *her* ***around*** (=turned her around).

THESAURUS **turn, twist, whirl, twirl, swivel, go around, revolve, rotate** → TURN¹

2 [T] to describe a situation or information in a way that is intended to influence the way people think about it – used especially about what politicians do: *In the book, he admits his affair but spins it as best he can.* **3** [I,T] to make cotton, wool, etc. into thread by twisting it together **4 sb's head is spinning** if your head is spinning, you feel confused or as though you might FAINT (=become unconscious) **5 be spinning your wheels** (informal) to continue trying to do something without having any success **6** [T] if an insect spins a WEB or a COCOON, it produces thread and makes it **7 spin a tale/yarn/story** to tell a story that you have invented

spin (sth ↔) **off** *phr. v.* to make part of a company into a separate company, or to become a separate company: *The company may spin off its engineering division.* [ORIGIN: Old English *spinnan*]

spin² *n.* **1** [C,U] an act of turning around quickly: *the spin of the wheel* **2** [singular,U] POLITICS the way someone, especially a politician, talks about information or a situation, in order to influence the way people think about it → SPIN DOCTOR: *A spokesman tried to* ***put*** *a positive* ***spin*** *on the report.* | *political* ***spin control*** (=the attempt to control the way people think about an event) **3** [singular] (informal) a short trip in a car for pleasure

spin·ach /ˈspɪnɪtʃ/ *n.* [U] a vegetable with large dark green leaves [ORIGIN: 1300—1400 Old French *espinache*, from Arabic *isfanakh*, from Persian]

spi·nal /ˈspaɪnl/ *adj.* relating to or affecting the SPINE: *a spinal injury*

ˈspinal cord *n.* [C] BIOLOGY the long string of nerves that go from your brain down your back, through your SPINE → *see picture at* BRAIN¹

spin·dly /ˈspɪndli/ *adj.* long and thin and not strong: *spindly legs*

ˈspin ˌdoctor *n.* [C] POLITICS someone who describes a situation in a way that is intended to influence people's opinions of it: *a White House spin doctor*

spine /spaɪn/ *n.* [C] **1** *also* **ˈspinal ˌcolumn** BIOLOGY the long row of bones down the center of your back → *see picture on page A16* **2** a stiff sharp point on an animal or plant: *cactus spines* **3** the part of a book that the pages are attached to

spine·less /ˈspaɪnlɪs/ *adj.* lacking courage and determination

spin·ner·et /ˌspɪnəˈrɛt/ *n.* [C] BIOLOGY a small organ on the body of a SPIDER, from which silk comes out when the spider is making a WEB

ˈspinning wheel *n.* [C] a simple machine used in past times to make thread

ˈspin-off *n.* [C] a television program using characters that were originally on a different program

spin·ster /ˈspɪnstɚ/ *n.* [C] (old-fashioned) a woman who is not married, especially one who is no longer young and seems unlikely to marry

spi·ral¹ /ˈspaɪrəl/ *n.* [C] **1** a curve in the form of a continuous line that winds around a central point **2** a process in which something gradually but continuously gets worse or better: *the peso's* ***downward spiral*** (=in which it continues to lose value) —**spiral** *adj.*: *a spiral staircase*

spiral² *v.* [I] **1** to move up or down in the shape of a spiral: *a leaf* ***spiraling to*** *the ground* **2** to gradually but continuously get worse in a way that cannot be controlled: *The economy has spiraled downward.* | *He felt his life was* ***spiraling out of control.***

spire /spaɪɚ/ *n.* [C] a tower that rises steeply to a point, especially on a church

spir·it /ˈspɪrɪt/ *n.* **1** [C,U] the qualities that make someone live the way s/he does, and make him/her different from other people, and which many people believe continues to exist after death → SOUL: *He has a* ***generous/free/independent spirit.*** | *I can still feel her spirit in this house.* | *The Olympic flame symbolizes the best of the* ***human spirit*** (=the qualities that make us human). **2 spirits** [plural] how happy or sad someone feels at a particular time: *The children were* ***in high/good spirits*** (=happy and excited). | *Her* ***spirits rose/sank*** (=she became happy or unhappy) *when she heard the news.* | *The music helped* ***lift*** *her* ***spirits*** (=made her happier). **3** [C] a creature without a physical body, such as an ANGEL or GHOST: *the spirits of our ancestors*

THESAURUS **ghost, phantom, specter, apparition** → GHOST

4 [U] courage, energy, and determination: *the team's* ***fighting spirit*** **5** [singular] the attitude that you have toward something: *a* ***spirit of*** *cooperation* **6 team/community/public etc. spirit** the strong feeling of belonging to a particular group and wanting to help it [ORIGIN: 1200—1300

Anglo-French, Latin *spiritus* "breath, spirit"]

spir·it·ed /ˈspɪrɪt̬ɪd/ *adj.* having a lot of courage, determination, and energy: *a spirited discussion*

spir·i·tu·al[1] /ˈspɪrɪtʃuəl, -tʃəl/ *adj.* **1** relating to the spirit rather than the body or mind: *spiritual health* **2** relating to religion: *a spiritual leader* —**spiritually** *adv.*

spiritual[2] *n.* [C] a religious song first sung by the black people of the U.S. when they were SLAVES

spit[1] /spɪt/ *v.* (past tense and past participle **spit** *or* **spat** /spæt/, present participle **spitting**) [I,T] to force a small amount of liquid, blood, food, etc. from your mouth: *He **spat on** the ground.* | *She tasted the drink and immediately **spat it out**.* [ORIGIN: Old English *spittan*]

spit up *phr. v.* if a baby spits up, it brings back milk from its stomach out of its mouth

spit[2] *n.* **1** [U] (informal) SALIVA **2** [C] a long thin stick that you put through meat to cook it over a fire

spite[1] /spaɪt/ *n.* [U] **1 in spite of sth** without being affected or prevented by something (SYN) **despite**: *Mrs. Hetland, in spite of her age, is still beautiful.*

> THESAURUS **however, despite, nevertheless/nonetheless** ➔ ALTHOUGH

2 a feeling of wanting to hurt, annoy, or upset someone: *Lois refused to let her ex-husband see the children **out of spite*** (=because of spite).

spite[2] *v.* [T] to annoy or upset someone deliberately: *He's doing this just to spite me!*

spite·ful /ˈspaɪtˀfəl/ *adj.* being unkind deliberately in order to annoy or upset someone

> THESAURUS **mean, cruel, unkind, nasty, vicious, malicious** ➔ MEAN[2]

splash[1] /splæʃ/ *v.* **1** [I,T] if a liquid splashes, or if you splash it, it falls on something or hits against it: *He **splashed** some cold water **on** his face.* | *Water splashed down onto the rocks.* **2** [I] to move around in water in a noisy way: *The children were **splashing around** in the pool.*

splash[2] *n.* [C] **1** the sound water makes when something hits it: *Jerry jumped into the water **with a loud splash**.* ➔ *see picture on page A20* **2** a mark made by a liquid splashing onto something else: ***splashes of** paint on my pants* **3 a splash of color** a small area of bright color **4 make a splash** (informal) to do something that gets a lot of public attention: *The story made a splash in the newspapers.*

splash·y /ˈsplæʃi/ *adj.* big, bright, and very easy to notice: *a splashy tie*

splat /splæt/ *n.* [singular] (informal) the sound made when something wet hits a hard surface

splat·ter /ˈsplæt̬ɚ/ *v.* [I,T] if a liquid splatters, or if someone splatters it, it hits against a surface: *rain **splattering against** the window*

splay /spleɪ/ *also* **splay out** *v.* [I,T] to spread your fingers, arms, or legs wide apart: *He sat with his legs splayed out in front of him.*

spleen /splin/ *n.* [C] BIOLOGY an organ near your stomach that helps clean your blood and fight against infections

splen·did /ˈsplɛndɪd/ *adj.* **1** excellent: *a splendid performance* **2** beautiful or impressive: *a splendid view from the balcony* [ORIGIN: 1600—1700 Latin *splendidus*, from *splendere* "to shine"] —**splendidly** *adv.*

splen·dor /ˈsplɛndɚ/ *n.* [U] impressive beauty: *the **splendor of** Yosemite Valley*

splice /splaɪs/ *v.* [T] to join the ends of two pieces of film, wire, etc. so they form one piece

splint /splɪnt/ *n.* [C] a flat piece of wood, metal, etc. used for keeping a broken bone in position while it HEALS

splin·ter[1] /ˈsplɪntɚ/ *n.* [C] **1** a small sharp piece of wood, glass, or metal that has broken off of a larger piece: *I have a splinter in my finger.* **2 splinter group/organization** a group of people that separate from a larger organization because they have different ideas

splinter[2] *v.* [I,T] **1** to break into thin sharp pieces, or to cause something to do this **2** if a group or organization splinters, or if it is splintered by something such as a disagreement, it separates into smaller groups or organizations

split[1] /splɪt/ *v.* (past tense and past participle **split**, present participle **splitting**) **1** [I,T] *also* **split up** to divide or make something divide into two or more groups, parts, etc.: *We'll **split (up) into** three work groups.* | *Try **splitting** this section **into two**.*

> THESAURUS **separate, divide, break up, segregate, partition** ➔ SEPARATE[2]

2 [I,T] to tear or break something along a straight line, or to be torn or broken in this way: *The board had **split in two**.* | *One of the boxes had **split open**.* **3** [I,T] if a group of people splits, or if something splits them, they divide into smaller groups after disagreeing strongly about something: *It was feared that the issue would split the church.* **4** [T] to divide something among two or more people in equal parts: *Do you want to split a pizza?* | *We decided to **split** the money **between** us.* **5** [I] (informal) to leave a place quickly

split up *phr. v.* to end a marriage or a relationship: *Eve's parents split up when she was three.*

split[2] *n.* [C] **1** a long straight hole caused when something breaks or tears: *a **split in** the seam of my skirt* **2** a serious disagreement that divides an organization or group of people into smaller groups: *a **split in** the Republican Party*

ˌsplit inˈfinitive *n.* [C] ENG. LANG. ARTS a phrase in which you put an adverb or other word between the word "to" and an INFINITIVE (=basic form of a verb), for example in "to easily win." Some people think that this is incorrect English.

ˌsplit-ˈlevel *adj.* a split-level house, room, or

building has floors at different heights in different parts

ˌsplit 'second *n.* **a split second** an extremely short period of time: *For a split second, I thought I was going to die.* —**split-second** *adj.*: *a split-second decision* (=one taken very quickly)

split·ting /'splɪt̬ɪŋ/ *adj.* **splitting headache** a very painful HEADACHE

splurge /splɚdʒ/ *v.* [I] (informal) to spend more money than you can usually afford: *We went shopping and* ***splurged on*** *clothes.*

spoil /spɔɪl/ *v.* **1** [T] to ruin something by making it less attractive, enjoyable, useful, etc.: *Don't let his bad mood spoil your evening.* **2** [T] to let a child do or have whatever they want, with the result that they behave badly: *We've been careful not to spoil our kids.* **3** [T] to treat someone in a way that is very kind or too generous: *a hotel that spoils its guests* **4** [I] if food spoils, it starts to decay [ORIGIN: 1200—1300 Old French *espoillier*, from Latin *spoliare* "to strip, rob"]

spoiled /spɔɪld/ *adj.* someone, especially a child, who is spoiled is rude and behaves badly because s/he is always allowed to do or have whatever s/he wants: *a* ***spoiled brat***

S

spoils /spɔɪlz/ *n.* [plural] things taken by an army from a defeated enemy, or things taken by thieves

spoil·sport /'spɔɪlspɔrt/ *n.* [C] (informal) someone who spoils other people's fun: *Come on and play,* ***don't be a spoilsport.***

spoke[1] /spoʊk/ *v.* the past tense of SPEAK

spoke[2] *n.* [C] one of the thin metal bars that connect the outer edge of a wheel to the center, especially on a bicycle ➔ *see picture at* BICYCLE

spok·en[1] /'spoʊkən/ *v.* the past participle of SPEAK

spoken[2] *adj.* **1 spoken English/language** the form of a particular language that you speak rather than write **2 softly-spoken/soft-spoken/well-spoken** speaking quietly or in an educated way: *a soft-spoken man* (=he speaks quietly)

spokes·man /'spoʊksmən/ *n.* (plural **spokesmen** /-mən/) [C] a male spokesperson: *a* ***spokesman for*** *the victims' families*

spokes·per·son /'spoʊksˌpɚsən/ *n.* (plural **spokespeople** /-ˌpipəl/) [C] someone who has been chosen to speak officially for a group, organization, government, etc.: *a White House spokesperson*

spokes·wom·an /'spoʊksˌwʊmən/ *n.* (plural **spokeswomen** /-ˌwɪmɪn/) [C] a female spokesperson

spon·dee /'spɑndi/ *n.* [C] ENG. LANG. ARTS a RHYTHM in poetry in which there are two STRESSED words or SYLLABLEs next to each other, as in the phrase "praise Him"

sponge[1] /spʌndʒ/ *n.* **1** [C,U] a piece of a very light substance that is full of small holes and is used for washing or cleaning something **2** [C] a sea animal with a soft body, from which some sponges are made [ORIGIN: 1000—1100 Latin *spongia*, from Greek]

sponge[2] *v.* **1** [T] *also* **sponge down** to wash something with a wet sponge **2** [T] to remove liquid from a surface using a sponge **3** [I] (informal, disapproving) to get money, food, etc. from someone without working for it: *He's been* ***sponging off*** *his friends for years.*

'sponge cake *n.* [C,U] a light cake made with eggs, sugar, and flour but usually no fat

spong·y /'spʌndʒi/ *adj.* soft and full of holes like a sponge: *spongy wet earth*

spon·sor[1] /'spɑnsɚ/ *n.* [C] **1** ECONOMICS a person or company that sponsors a television show, sports event, etc.: *the* ***sponsor of*** *the French Open* **2** POLITICS a politician who officially introduces or supports a proposal for a new law: *Senator Kelly is one of the bill's chief sponsors.* **3** someone who sponsors a person for CHARITY

sponsor[2] *v.* [T] **1** ECONOMICS to give money to a television show, sports event, etc. in exchange for the right to advertise your products at the event: *a competition sponsored by Campbell's Soup* **2** POLITICS to officially introduce or support a proposal for a new law **3** to agree to give someone money for a CHARITY if s/he walks, runs, swims, etc. a particular distance —**sponsorship** *n.* [U]: *the industry's sponsorship of major sporting events*

spon·ta·ne·ous /spɑn'teɪniəs/ *adj.* happening or done without being planned or organized: *a spontaneous decision* —**spontaneously** *adv.* —**spontaneity** /ˌspɑntə'neɪət̬i, ˌspɑnt˺n'eɪ-/ *n.* [U]

THESAURUS **impulsive, impetuous, hasty**
➔ IMPULSIVE

spoof /spuf/ *n.* [C] a funny book, movie, or play, etc. that copies a serious or important book, etc. and makes it seem silly: *a* ***spoof on/of*** *Shakespeare's "Richard III"* —**spoof** *v.* [T]

spook[1] /spuk/ *n.* [C] (informal) a GHOST

spook[2] *v.* [T] (informal) to frighten someone: *Being alone all night really spooked me.* | *The drop in share prices spooked investors.*

spook·y /'spuki/ *adj.* (informal) strange or frightening SYN **eerie**: *a spooky old house*

spool /spul/ *n.* [C] an object shaped like a small wheel that you wind wire, thread, camera film, etc. around

spoon[1] /spun/ *n.* [C] a tool used for eating, cooking, and serving food, shaped like a small bowl with a long handle [ORIGIN: Old English *spon* "piece of wood split off"]

spoon[2] *v.* [T] to pick up or move food with a spoon: ***Spoon*** *the sauce* ***over*** *the fish.*

spoon·er·ism /'spunəˌrɪzəm/ *n.* [C] ENG. LANG. ARTS a phrase in which the speaker accidentally exchanges the first sounds of two words, with a funny result. For example, the speaker might say

"Let me sew you to a sheet" instead of "Let me show you to a seat."

'spoon-feed *v.* (past tense and past participle **spoon-fed**) [T] (disapproving) to give too much help to someone: *Spoon-feeding students does not help them remember things.*

spoon·ful /'spunfʊl/ *n.* [C] the amount that a spoon can hold: *a* ***spoonful of*** *sugar*

spo·rad·ic /spə'rædɪk/ *adj.* happening often but not regularly or continuously: *sporadic bombing* [ORIGIN: 1600—1700 Medieval Latin *sporadicus*, from Greek, from *sporaden* "scattered in different places"] **—sporadically** *adv.*

spore /spɔr/ *n.* [C] BIOLOGY a cell that is like a seed and is produced by living things which have only a single set of GENES, such as MUSHROOMS or BACTERIA. Spores can develop into new mushrooms, bacteria, etc.: ***Fungus spores*** *are often spread by the wind.* [ORIGIN: 1800—1900 Modern Latin *spora*, from Greek, "act of planting seeds, seed"]

sport¹ /spɔrt/ *n.* [C] **1** a physical activity in which people compete against each other: *What's your favorite sport?* | *Do you* ***play*** *any* ***sports****?* | *Soccer and basketball are* ***team sports****.* | *Baseball is America's most popular* ***spectator sport*** (=one watched by a lot of people).

THESAURUS

Places where people play sports
field – a large area of ground, usually covered with grass, where team sports are played: *a football/baseball/soccer field* | *The athletic fields are next to the school.*
stadium – a large sports field with seats all around it for people to watch team sports or track and field competitions: *a football stadium*
court – an area with lines painted on the ground, for tennis, basketball, etc.: *a tennis court*
diamond – the area in a baseball field that is within the shape formed by the four bases, also used to refer to the whole field
track – a special area for running on
gym – a large room with machines which you can use to do exercises
(swimming) pool – a place where you can swim
health club – a building where you can do various different sports

2 an activity such as hunting or fishing

THESAURUS **game, recreation, hobby** → GAME¹

3 a good sport someone who does not get angry when s/he loses at a game or sport **4 a bad/poor sport** someone who gets angry very easily when s/he loses at a game or sport [ORIGIN: late Middle English 1300—1400 *disport*]

sport² *v.* **be sporting sth** to be wearing or showing something in a proud way: *Martin walked in sporting a tall white cowboy hat.*

sport·ing /'spɔrṭɪŋ/ *adj.* [only before noun] relating to sports: *a store selling* ***sporting goods*** (=sports equipment) | *one of the biggest* ***sporting events*** *of the year*

sports /spɔrts/ *adj.* **1** relating to sports or used for sports: *a sports club* | *sports equipment* **2** on the subject of sports: *I like reading the* ***sports pages/section*** (=in a newspaper).

'sports car *n.* [C] a low fast car, often with a roof that can be folded back

sports·cast /'spɔrts-kæst/ *n.* [C] a television program of a sports game

'sports jacket *also* **'sports coat** *n.* [C] a man's comfortable jacket, worn on informal occasions

sports·man·ship /'spɔrtsmən,ʃɪp/ *n.* [U] behavior that is fair, honest, and polite in a game or sports competition: *We try to teach the kids* ***good sportsmanship****.*

sports·wear /'spɔrtswɛr/ *n.* [U] clothes that are appropriate for informal occasions

,sport-u'tility ,vehicle *n.* [C] an SUV

sport·y /'spɔrṭi/ *adj.* (informal) designed to look attractive in a bright informal way: *a sporty red car*

spot¹ /spɑt/ *n.* [C]
1 PLACE a particular place: *Oh, sorry, I'm sitting in your spot.* | *a popular vacation spot* | *a parking spot*

THESAURUS **place, position, location, site** → PLACE¹

2 COLORED AREA a small round area on a surface, that is a different color from the rest: *a white dog with black spots*
3 MARK a small mark on something: *grease spots* | *There are* ***spots of*** *blood on his jacket.*

THESAURUS **mark, stain, smudge, smear** → MARK²

4 on the spot (informal) **a)** immediately: *Cathy was offered the job on the spot.* **b)** at the place where something is happening: *He lit up a cigar on the spot.*
5 APPEARANCE a short appearance or advertisement on TV, radio, etc.: *an advertising spot* | *a guest spot on the Tonight Show*
6 POSITION a position in a competition: *The top finisher will earn a spot in the U.S. Olympic team.*
7 put sb on the spot to deliberately ask someone a question that is difficult or embarrassing to answer
8 bright spot something that is good in a bad situation: *Foreign trade is the one bright spot in the economy.* → **hit the spot** *at* HIT¹

spot² *v.* (**spotted, spotting**) [T] **1** to notice or recognize someone or something that is difficult to see: *A helicopter pilot spotted the wreckage of the plane.* | *She has a good eye for spotting talent.* | *I spotted something moving in the trees.*

THESAURUS **see, notice, glimpse/catch a glimpse of sth/sb, catch sight of sb/sth** → SEE

S

2 to give the other player in a game an advantage: *Come on, I'll spot you 10 points if you play.*

ˌspot ˈcheck *n.* [C] an examination of a few things or people in a group, to see whether everything is correct or satisfactory: *Health inspectors will make spot checks throughout the state.*

spot·less /ˈspɑtlɪs/ *adj.* **1** completely clean: *Donna keeps her car spotless.* **2** completely honest and good: *a spotless reputation*

spot·light¹ /ˈspɑtlaɪt/ *n.* **1** [C] a very powerful light that can be directed at someone or something, or the light made by this. Spotlights are often used to light a stage when actors or singers are performing. **2 the spotlight** a lot of attention in newspapers, on television, etc.: *Russia is back **in the** media **spotlight** again.*

spotlight² *v.* [T] to make people pay attention to someone or something: *a music festival that spotlights modern composers*

spot·ty /ˈspɑt̬i/ *adj.* good in some parts but not in others: *The stock market showed spotty gains.*

spouse /spaʊs/ *n.* [C] (formal) a husband or wife [ORIGIN: 1100—1200 Old French *espous(e)*, from Latin *sponsus* "promised (in marriage)"]

S

spout¹ /spaʊt/ *n.* [C] a small pipe on the side of a container that you pour liquid out through

spout² *v.* **1** [I,T] if a liquid spouts or fire spouts from somewhere, it comes out very quickly in a powerful stream: *A leak **spouted from** the garden hose.* **2** [I] (informal) *also* **spout off** to talk a lot in a boring or annoying way: *He's always **spouting off about** politics.*

sprain /spreɪn/ *v.* [T] to injure a joint in your body by suddenly twisting it: *Amy **sprained** her **ankle** when she fell.* —**sprain** *n.* [C]

THESAURUS hurt, twist, strain, pull → HURT¹ → INJURY

sprang /spræŋ/ *v.* a past tense of SPRING

sprawl /sprɔl/ *v.* [I] **1** *also* **sprawl out** to lie or sit with your arms or legs stretched out: *When we got home, Carey was **sprawled on** the sofa.* **2** if a building or town sprawls, it spreads out over a wide area in an unattractive way —**sprawl** *n.* [singular, U]: *urban sprawl* (=growth in the size of a town or city)

spray¹ /spreɪ/ *v.* **1** [T] to make a liquid come out of a container, HOSE, etc. in a stream of very small drops: ***Spray** a little perfume **on** the backs of your knees too.* | *She **sprayed** herself **with** perfume.* → *see picture at* SQUIRT¹ **2** [I] to be scattered in small drops or pieces through the air: *Water **sprayed from** the garden hose.*

spray² *n.* **1** [C,U] liquid that is forced out of a container in a stream of very small drops: *hair spray* **2** [C] a special container from which liquid comes out in small drops: *a non-aerosol spray* **3** [U] water that is thrown up into the air in very small drops: *The boat scattered sea spray over us as it rocked up and down.*

spread¹ /sprɛd/ *v.* (past tense and past participle **spread**)
1 OPEN/ARRANGE [T] *also* **spread out** to open something so that it covers a big area, or to arrange a number of things so that they cover a flat surface: *Tracy had a map spread out over the floor.* | *The population is evenly **spread across** the state.* | *He sat with books and papers **spread over** the table.*
2 AFFECT MORE PEOPLE/PLACES/THINGS [I,T] to move and affect more people, places, or a larger area, or to make something do this: *Rain will **spread throughout** the area by tonight.* | *Cancer has **spread to** her lungs.* | *Only a small number of insects **spread disease**.*
3 INFORMATION/IDEAS [I,T] to tell a lot of people about something or to become known by a lot of people: *His neighbors began **spreading rumors** that he was a spy.* | *News of her arrest quickly spread.*
4 SOFT SUBSTANCE [T] to put a soft substance onto a surface in order to cover it: ***Spread** some honey **on** the bread.*
5 PUSH APART [I,T] *also* **spread apart** to push your arms, legs, or fingers wide apart
6 DO STH GRADUALLY [T] *also* **spread out** to do something gradually over time: *You can **spread** the payments **over** a year.*
7 spread yourself too thin to try to do too many things at the same time so that you do not do any of them effectively
8 WINGS [T] *also* **spread open** if a bird or insect spreads its wings, it stretches them wide

spread out *phr. v.*
if a group of people spread out, they move apart from each other in order to cover a wide area: *If we spread out, it should be easier to find her.*

spread² *n.* **1** [singular] the increase in the area or number of people that something has an effect on: ***the spread of** TB* **2** [C,U] a soft food that you put on bread: ***cheese/chocolate etc. spread*** **3** [C] (informal) a large meal for several people on a special occasion: *There was a nice spread at the reception after the wedding.* **4** [C] a special article or advertisement in a newspaper or magazine: *a two-page spread* **5** [C] a large farm or RANCH: *a 300-acre spread*

spread·sheet /ˈsprɛdʃit/ *n.* [C] **1** IT a computer program that can show and calculate financial information **2** a document that contains rows and COLUMNS of numbers that can be used to calculate something

spree /spri/ *n.* [C] a short period in which you do something that you enjoy, especially spending money or drinking: *I see you **went on a shopping spree**!*

sprig /sprɪg/ *n.* [C] a small stem or part of a branch with leaves or flowers on it: *a **sprig of** parsley*

spring[1] /sprɪŋ/ *n.* **1** [C,U] the season between winter and summer, when leaves and flowers appear: *The park opens **in the spring**.* | *I'm going to Cancun **this spring**.* | ***last/next spring*** (=the spring before or after this one) **2** [C] a twisted piece of metal that has been made so that it will return to its original shape after it has been pressed down **3** [C] EARTH SCIENCES a place where water comes up naturally from the ground: *a hot spring* **4** [U] the ability of a chair, bed, etc. to return to its normal shape after being pressed down **5** [C] a sudden quick movement or jump in a particular direction

spring[2] *v.* (past tense **sprang** /spræŋ/ *also* **sprung** /sprʌŋ/, past participle **sprung**) [I] **1** to jump or move suddenly and quickly in a particular direction: *He turned off the alarm and **sprang out of** bed.* | *He **sprang to his feet*** (=stood up suddenly) *and rushed after her.* | *The lid of the box **sprang open/shut*** (=suddenly opened or shut). | *The branch **sprang back/up*** (=moved quickly back to its original position or shape) *and hit him in the face.*

THESAURUS jump, skip, hop, leap → JUMP[1]

2 spring to mind if someone or something springs to mind, you immediately think of him, her, or it: *Pam's name springs to mind as someone who could do the job.* **3 spring into action/spring to life** to suddenly become active or start doing things: *The whole school springs into action at Homecoming.* **4 spring to sb's defense** to immediately help someone who is being attacked or criticized: *Molly sprang to her daughter's defense.* **5 spring a leak** if a boat or a container springs a leak, it begins to let liquid in or out through a crack or hole

spring for sth *phr. v.* (informal) to pay for something: *Carol said she'd spring for lunch.*

spring from sth *phr. v.* to be caused by something: *health problems that spring from living in a cold, wet country*

spring sth **on** sb *phr. v.* (informal) to tell someone something or ask him/her to do something when s/he does not expect it and is not ready for it: *I'm sorry to have to spring this on you.*

spring up *phr. v.* to suddenly appear or start to exist: *All along the railroad, new towns sprang up.*

spring·board /ˈsprɪŋbɔrd/ *n.* [C] **1** something that helps you to start doing something: *His computer knowledge provided a **springboard for** his career.* **2** a strong board that bends, used in order to jump high, especially into water

spring 'break *n.* [C] a vacation from school in the spring that is usually one week long

spring 'chicken *n.* **be no spring chicken** (humorous) to no longer be young

spring 'fever *n.* [U] a sudden feeling of energy and wanting to do something new and exciting, that you get in the spring

ˌspring 'tide *n.* [C] EARTH SCIENCES a TIDE in which the rise and fall of the level of the sea is higher than normal, which takes place every two weeks when the moon is new or full → NEAP TIDE

spring·time /ˈsprɪŋtaɪm/ *n.* [U] the time of year when it is spring

spring·y /ˈsprɪŋi/ *adj.* returning quickly to its original shape after being pressed: *springy grass*

sprin·kle[1] /ˈsprɪŋkəl/ *v.* **1** [T] to scatter small drops of liquid or small pieces of something onto something else: *spaghetti **sprinkled with** parmesan* | *She **sprinkled** some cookie crumbs **on** the ice cream.* **2 it is sprinkling** if it is sprinkling, it is raining lightly

sprinkle

sprinkle[2] *n.* [C] **1** small pieces of food, or a light layer of these: *chocolate sprinkles* | *a **sprinkle of** grated cheese* **2** a light rain

sprin·kler /ˈsprɪŋklɚ/ *n.* [C] a piece of equipment used for scattering drops of water on grass

sprint /sprɪnt/ *v.* [I] to run very fast for a short distance —**sprint** *n.* [C] —**sprinter** *n.* [C]

THESAURUS run, dash, tear, race → RUN[1]

sprout[1] /spraʊt/ *v.* **1** [I,T] BIOLOGY to start to grow, or produce new leaves, BUDS, or SHOOTS: *a plant sprouting new flowers* | *seeds beginning to sprout* **2** [I] *also* **sprout up** to appear suddenly in large numbers: *new homes sprouting up in the suburbs*

sprout[2] *n.* [C] **1** BIOLOGY a new growth on a plant **2** a bean or other plant that is not fully grown and is eaten in SALADS: *alfalfa sprouts* **3** a BRUSSELS SPROUT

spruce[1] /sprus/ *n.* [C,U] a tree with short leaves shaped like needles, or the wood of this tree

spruce[2] *v.*

spruce (sth/sb) **up** *phr. v.* (informal) to make yourself or a place look better or neater: *I want to spruce up a little before dinner.*

sprung /sprʌŋ/ *v.* a past tense and the past participle of SPRING

spry /spraɪ/ *adj.* a spry old person is active and cheerful

spud /spʌd/ *n.* [C] (informal) a POTATO

spun /spʌn/ *v.* the past tense and past participle of SPIN

spunk·y /ˈspʌŋki/ *adj.* (informal) brave and full of

S

energy and determination: *the film's spunky heroine* —**spunk** *n.* [U]

spur¹ /spɚ/ *n.* **1 on the spur of the moment** without planning ahead of time: *We got married on the spur of the moment.* **2** [C] a sharp pointed object attached to the heel of a rider's boot that s/he presses against the side of a horse to encourage it to go faster

spur² *v.* (**spurred**, **spurring**) [T] **1** to make an improvement or change happen faster: *Growth in the city was spurred by cheap housing.* **2** *also* **spur sb on** to encourage someone to do or continue doing something: *Her sister's success **spurred** her **on** to practice harder.*

spu·ri·ous /ˈspyʊriəs/ *adj.* (formal) not based on correct facts or careful thinking, and so likely to be wrong: *spurious arguments* [ORIGIN: 1500—1600 Late Latin *spurius*, from Latin (noun), "child of unmarried parents"]

spurn /spɚn/ *v.* [T] (literary) to refuse to accept something or to refuse to have a relationship with someone, in an unkind way: *a spurned lover*

spurt¹ /spɚt/ *v.* [I] **1** to flow out suddenly with a lot of force: *Blood **spurted from** his arm.*

THESAURUS pour, flow, gush, run, come out → POUR

2 to suddenly move forward very quickly: *Liz **spurted past** the other runners.*

spurt² *n.* [C] **1** a stream of liquid, flames, etc. that comes out of something suddenly: *Water was coming out of the faucet **in spurts*** (=quickly for short periods). **2** a short sudden increase in activity, effort, or speed: *a growth spurt*

sput·ter /ˈspʌt̬ɚ/ *v.* **1** [I] if something such as a process sputters, it stops working well or effectively: *The country's economic growth sputtered to a halt during 2007.* **2** [I] if an engine sputters, it makes sounds like very small explosions, because it is not working correctly: *The engine sputtered and died.* **3** [I,T] to talk quickly in short confused phrases, especially because you are angry or shocked: *"They think I'm a fool," she sputtered.*

spy /spaɪ/ *v.* (**spied**, **spies**) [I] to secretly collect information or watch people, usually for a government or company: *She hired a private detective to **spy on** her husband.* | *He confessed to **spying for** North Korea.* —**spy** *n.* [C]: *a government spy*

squab·ble /ˈskwɑbəl/ *v.* [I] to argue about something unimportant: *What are those kids **squabbling about** now?* —**squabble** *n.* [C]

THESAURUS argue, have an argument, fight, have a fight, quarrel, have a quarrel, bicker → ARGUE

squad /skwɑd/ *n.* [C] a group of people who work together and do a job that needs special skills: *soldiers in the bomb squad* [ORIGIN: 1600—1700 French *escouade*, from *escadre*, from Italian *squadra* "square"]

ˈsquad car *n.* [C] a car used by police

squad·ron /ˈskwɑdrən/ *n.* [C] a military force consisting of a group of aircraft or ships

squal·id /ˈskwɑlɪd/ *adj.* extremely dirty, unhealthy, and unsafe: *squalid living conditions*

squall /skwɔl/ *n.* [C] EARTH SCIENCES a sudden strong wind that brings rain or snow

squal·or /ˈskwɑlɚ/ *n.* [U] extremely dirty, unhealthy, and unsafe conditions: *people living **in squalor***

squan·der /ˈskwɑndɚ/ *v.* [T] to carelessly waste money, time, opportunities, etc.: *They've **squandered** thousands **on** that old house.*

square¹ /skwɛr/ *adj.* **1** having four straight equal sides and four 90° angles: *a square window* **2 square inch/mile etc.** the measurement of an area that is a square shape with sides an inch, mile, etc. long: *two square acres of land* **3** like a square in shape forming a 90° angle, or seeming to do this: *a square corner* | *a square jaw* **4 be (all) square** if two people are square, they do not owe each other any money: *Here's your $20, so now we're square.* **5 a square meal** a complete satisfying meal **6 a square deal** honest and fair treatment from someone: *a car dealer that gives customers a square deal* **7** (old-fashioned) honest: *I'm **being square with** you.* [ORIGIN: 1200—1300 Old French *esquarre*, from Vulgar Latin *exquadra*, from *exquadrare* "to make square"]

square² *n.* [C] **1** a shape with four straight equal sides forming four RIGHT ANGLES → *see picture at* POLYGON

THESAURUS shape, circle, semicircle, triangle, rectangle, oval → SHAPE¹

2 a broad open area with buildings around it in the middle of a town: *Times Square* **3 be back to square one** to be back in exactly the same situation that you started from: *The development deal fell through and now we're back to square one.* **4** MATH the result of multiplying a number by itself. For example, the square of 5 is 25. → SQUARE ROOT

square³ *v.* [T] MATH to multiply a number by itself
square sth ↔ **away** *phr. v.* to finish dealing with something: *Peter needs another day to **get** things **squared away** at home.*
square off *phr. v.* to get ready to fight someone
square up *phr. v.* to pay money that you owe: *I'll get the drinks, and we can square up later.*

square⁴ *adv.* (spoken) SQUARELY

squared /skwɛrd/ *adj.* **3/9/10 etc. squared** MATH the number 3, 9, 10, etc. multiplied by itself: *3 squared equals 9.*

ˈsquare dance *n.* [C] a type of dance in which four pairs of dancers face each other in a square

square·ly /ˈskwɛrli/ *adv.* **1** exactly or directly: *The ball landed squarely in the palm of his hand.* **2** completely and with no doubt: *The report* *puts the blame* ***squarely on*** *the senior managers.*

ˌsquare ˈroot *n.* [C] MATH the square root of a number is the number which, when multiplied by itself, equals that number. For example, the square root of 9 is 3. → CUBE ROOT

squash¹ /skwɑʃ, skwɔʃ/ *v.* **1** [T] to press something into a flat shape, often damaging it: *My hat got squashed on the flight.*

THESAURUS **press, crush, mash, grind, squeeze, compress, compact** → PRESS¹

2 [I,T] to push yourself or someone else into a space that is too small SYN **squeeze**: *Seven of us* ***squashed into*** *the car.*

squash² *n.* **1** [C,U] one of a group of large vegetables with solid flesh and hard skins, such as PUMPKINS → *see picture at* VEGETABLE **2** [U] an indoor game similar to RACKETBALL

squat¹ /skwɑt/ *v.* [I] **1** *also* **squat down** to balance on your feet with your legs bent under you and your bottom near the ground **2** to live in a building or on a piece of land without permission and without paying rent

squat² *adj.* short and thick, or low and wide: *small squat houses* | *He is short and squat.*

squawk /skwɔk/ *v.* [I] if a bird squawks, it makes a loud angry cry —**squawk** *n.* [C]

squeak /skwik/ *v.* [I] **1** to make a very short high noise or cry: *Is that your chair squeaking?* **2 squeak by/through** (informal) to manage to succeed, but not by very much: *The Bulls have* ***squeaked through*** *into the playoffs.* —**squeak** *n.* [C]: *the squeak of new leather* → *see picture on page A20*

squeak·y /ˈskwiki/ *adj.* **1** making very high noises that are not loud: *a squeaky voice* | *squeaky bed springs*

THESAURUS **high, high-pitched, shrill** → HIGH¹

2 squeaky clean (informal) **a)** never having done anything morally wrong: *The incident has ruined McIntyre's squeaky clean image.* **b)** completely clean: *squeaky clean hair*

squeal¹ /skwil/ *v.* [I] **1** to make a long loud high sound or cry: *His tires squealed as he swerved around the corner.* | *children* ***squealing with*** *excitement* **2 squeal (on sb)** (informal) to tell the police or someone in authority about someone you know who has done something wrong

squeal² *n.* [C] a long loud high sound or cry: ***squeals of*** *delight*

squeam·ish /ˈskwimɪʃ/ *adj.* easily shocked or upset, or easily made to feel sick by disgusting sights: *I couldn't be a doctor – I'm too squeamish.*

squeeze¹ /skwiz/ *v.* **1** [T] to press something firmly together with your fingers or hands: *She squeezed Jim's shoulder gently.* → *see picture on page A56* **2** [T] to twist or press something in order to get liquid out of it: ***Squeeze*** *some lemon juice* ***onto*** *the salad.* → *see picture on page A18*

THESAURUS **press, squash, crush, compress** → PRESS¹

3 [I,T] to try to make a person or thing fit into a small space SYN **squash**: *Can you* ***squeeze in*** *next to Rick?* | *She had to* ***squeeze past*** *boxes of books to get to the front door.* **4 squeeze sb/sth in** (informal) to manage to do something although you are very busy: *Professor Lang can* ***squeeze you in*** *at 2:00.* **5 squeeze sb/sth out (of sth)** to not let someone or something take part in something: *Some small businesses are being squeezed out of the market.* **6** [T] ECONOMICS to strictly limit the amount of money that is available to an organization: *a school squeezed by budget cuts* [ORIGIN: 1500—1600 *quease* "to press, squeeze" (15—17 centuries), from Old English *cwysan*]

squeeze² *n.* **1 a (tight) squeeze** a situation in which there is only just enough room for things or people to fit somewhere: *It'll be a tight squeeze with six of us in the car.* **2** [C] an act of pressing something firmly with your fingers or hand: *Laurie* ***gave*** *his hand* ***a*** *little* ***squeeze.*** **3** [C] a small amount of something you get by squeezing: *a* ***squeeze of*** *lime juice* **4** [singular] ECONOMICS a situation in which WAGE rises, price increases, or borrowing money, etc. are strictly controlled: *a* ***squeeze on*** *farm programs*

squelch /skwɛltʃ/ *v.* **1** [T] (informal) to stop something from spreading or continuing: *Store owners said the law would squelch competition.* **2** [I] SQUISH

squid /skwɪd/ *n.* (plural **squid** *or* **squids**) [C] a sea creature with a long soft body and ten arms

squig·gle /ˈskwɪgəl/ *n.* [C] a short line in writing or drawing that curls and twists —**squiggly** *adj.*

squint /skwɪnt/ *v.* [I] to look at something with your eyes partly closed in order to see better: *He looked at me, squinting in the sun.* —**squint** *n.* [C]

squire /skwaɪɚ/ *n.* [C] a young man in the Middle Ages who learned how to be a KNIGHT by serving one

squirm /skwɚm/ *v.* [I] to twist your body from side to side because you are uncomfortable or nervous: *Stop squirming so I can comb your hair!*

squir·rel /ˈskwɚəl/ *n.* [C] a small animal with a long furry tail that lives in trees and eats nuts [ORIGIN: 1300—1400 Anglo-French *esquirel*, from Latin *sciurus*, from Greek *skiouros*, from *skia* "shadow" + *oura* "tail"] → *see picture at* RODENT

squirt¹ /skwɚt/ *v.* **1** [I,T] if you squirt liquid or it squirts, it is forced out of a narrow hole in a thin fast stream: *Orange juice **squirted onto** her dress.* | *You need to **squirt** some oil **in** the lock.* **2** [T] to hit or cover someone or something with a stream of liquid: *The children **squirted** each other **with** the hose.*

squirt² *n.* [C] **1** a fast thin stream of liquid: *a **squirt of** ketchup* **2** (spoken) a word used when speaking to a small child: *Hey squirt — it's time to wake up.*

squish /skwɪʃ/ *v.* **1** [I,T] (informal) to SQUASH something soft or wet, or to become squashed **2** [I] to make a sucking sound by moving through something soft and wet, such as mud

squish·y /ˈskwɪʃi/ *adj.* soft, wet, and easy to SQUEEZE: *squishy mud*

Sr. the written abbreviation of SENIOR

St. **1** the written abbreviation of STREET **2** the written abbreviation of SAINT

stab¹ /stæb/ *v.* (**stabbed**, **stabbing**) **1** [T] to push a sharp object into someone or something: *He was **stabbed to death** in a fight.* | *I was **stabbed** several times **in** the arm/chest etc.* | *She says he **stabbed** her **with** the bread knife.* **2 stab sb in the back** (informal) to do something bad to someone who likes and trusts you (SYN) **betray**

stab² *n.* **1** [C] an act of stabbing or trying to stab someone: *The victim had four stab wounds.* **2 take a stab at (doing) sth** (informal) to try to do something that is difficult or that you have never done: *Carla decided to take a stab at learning to sail.*

stab·bing /ˈstæbɪŋ/ *n.* [C] a crime in which someone is stabbed

sta·bil·i·ty /stəˈbɪləṭi/ (Ac) *n.* [U] **1** the condition of not changing very often or suddenly (ANT) **instability**: *a long period of political stability* **2** the condition of being strong and steady and not likely to fall or move in an unsafe way (ANT) **instability**: *the structural stability of a building* **3** the quality of being mentally and emotionally healthy, so that you are not likely to become mentally ill: *Lawyers questioned his emotional stability.*

sta·bi·lize /ˈsteɪbəˌlaɪz/ (Ac) *v.* **1** [I,T] to reach a state where changes no longer happen often or suddenly, or to make something do this → STABLE: *The financial markets are finally stabilizing.* **2** [T] to make something steady and not likely to fall or move in an unsafe way: *A rod is put in to stabilize the broken bone.* —**stabilization** /ˌsteɪbələˈzeɪʃən/ *n.* [U]

sta·ble¹ /ˈsteɪbəl/ (Ac) *adj.* **1** steady and not likely to move: *Be careful – the ladder doesn't look stable.* **2** not likely to change often or suddenly: *a stable marriage* **3** calm, reasonable, and not easy to upset: *He was clearly not a very stable person.* [ORIGIN: 1200—1300 Old French *estable*, from Latin *stabilis*, from *stare* "to stand"]

stable² *n.* [C] a building where horses are kept

stack¹ /stæk/ *n.* [C] a neat pile of things: ***a stack of** magazines on the table*

THESAURUS pile, heap, mound → PILE¹

stack² *v.* **1** [I,T] *also* **stack up** to form a neat pile, or to put things into a neat pile: *Just stack the dishes in the sink for now.* | *chairs that are designed to stack easily* **2** [T] to put piles of things on something: *Al has a job stacking shelves in the supermarket.*

stack up *phr. v.* (informal) used to talk about how good something is compared with something else: *a new PC that stacks up well against the others on the market*

sta·di·um /ˈsteɪdiəm/ *n.* (plural **stadiums** *or* **stadia** /-diə/) [C] a building for sports, large rock concerts, etc., consisting of a field surrounded by rows of seats: *a football stadium* [ORIGIN: 1300—1400 Latin, Greek *stadion* "unit of length, racetrack"]

staff¹ /stæf/ *n.* [C,U] the people who work for an organization: *a meeting of library **staff members*** | *Joan is the only lawyer we have **on staff**.* | *Reiter manages a **staff of** forty.* | *a **staff meeting*** → WORK¹

staff² *v.* [T] to be or provide the workers for an organization: *a hospital staffed by experienced nurses* —**staffing** *n.* [U]: *staffing costs*

staff·er /ˈstæfɚ/ *n.* [C] someone who is paid to work for an organization

stag /stæg/ *n.* [C] a fully grown male DEER

stage¹ /steɪdʒ/ *n.* **1** [C] a particular point or time in a process that something or someone reaches before going to the next one: *The disease is still* ***in its early stages***. | ***At this stage*** (=right now) *no one is sure what to do next.* | *The government has promised elections* ***at some stage*** *in the next 12 months.* | *Children go through various* ***stages of*** *development.* | *the planning stage of the project*

THESAURUS

part – one of the pieces or features of something, such as an event or period of time: *The early part of his life was spent in New York.*
step – one of a series of actions that you do in order to deal with a problem or achieve something: *an important first step toward peace*
phase – a separate part in a process of development or change: *Schools will receive extra funding in both phases of the plan.*
point – a specific moment, time, or stage in something's development: *The team is playing better than I thought they would at this point.*
round – one of a number of events that are related: *the first round of the negotiations*

2 [C] ENG. LANG. ARTS the raised floor in a theater where actors, singers, musicians, etc. perform → *see picture at* THEATER **3** [singular, U] ENG. LANG. ARTS the profession of acting: *Lina's always wanted to be* ***on stage*** (=be an actor). → THEATER **4** [C] a place where something important happens: *the world political stage* **5 s/he's going through a stage** (informal) used in order to say that someone young will soon stop behaving badly or strangely **6 stage left/right** ENG. LANG. ARTS the left or right side of the stage, from the view of an actor facing the people watching [ORIGIN: 1200—1300 Old French *estage*, from Latin *stare* "to stand"] → **set the stage/scene** *at* SET¹

stage² *v.* [T] **1** to organize a public event: *They're staging five plays this summer.* | *Workers are* ***staging a strike***. **2** to start doing something again or being successful, after you had stopped or not been successful for some time: *After trailing in the polls, he* ***staged a*** *remarkable* ***comeback*** *in the days before the election.*

stage·coach /ˈsteɪdʒkoʊtʃ/ *n.* [C] a closed vehicle pulled by horses, that carried passengers and mail in past times

ˈstage fright *n.* [U] nervousness that some people feel before they perform in front of a lot of people

stage ˌmanager *n.* [C] someone who is responsible for a theater stage during a performance

stag·ger¹ /ˈstægɚ/ *v.* **1** [I] to walk or move in an unsteady way, almost falling over: *A man came staggering down the stairs.* | *Somehow he managed to stagger to a hospital.* **2** [T] to arrange for things to be done at different times, so that they do not all happen at the same time: *Student registration will be staggered to avoid delays.*

stagger² *n.* [C] an unsteady movement of someone who has difficulty walking

stag·ger·ing /ˈstægərɪŋ/ *adj.* extremely great or surprising: *She spends a staggering amount of money on clothes.*

THESAURUS **surprising, extraordinary, amazing, shocking, astonishing, astounding, stunning** → SURPRISING

stag·ing /ˈsteɪdʒɪŋ/ *n.* [C,U] ENG. LANG. ARTS the activity or art of performing a play, or the way this is done: *a modern* ***staging of*** *"Romeo and Juliet"*

stag·nant /ˈstægnənt/ *adj.* **1** stagnant water or air does not move or flow and often smells bad **2** not changing or improving: *Steel production has stayed stagnant.*

stag·nate /ˈstægneɪt/ *v.* [I] to stop developing or improving: *a stagnating economy* —**stagnation** /stægˈneɪʃən/ *n.* [U]: *political stagnation*

staid /steɪd/ *adj.* serious, old-fashioned, and boring: *a staid old bachelor*

stain¹ /steɪn/ *v.* **1** [I,T] to accidentally make a colored mark on something, especially one that is difficult to remove, or to be marked in this way: *This carpet stains easily.* | *a tablecloth* ***stained with*** *wine* **2** [T] to paint wood with a stain

stain² *n.* **1** [C] a mark that is difficult to remove: *I got coffee* ***stains on*** *my shirt.*

THESAURUS **mark, spot, smudge, smear** → MARK²

2 [C,U] a special liquid that you use to change the color of wood

ˌstainless ˈsteel *n.* [U] a type of steel that does not RUST

stair /stɛr/ *n.* **1 stairs** [plural] a set of steps built for going from one level of a building to another: *Bev ran* ***up/down the stairs***. | *Please leave your shoes at* ***the bottom/foot of the stairs***. | *I left my briefcase at the* ***top of the stairs***. | *The office is up one* ***flight of stairs*** (=set of stairs). **2** [C] one of the steps in a set of stairs: *Jane sat on the bottom stair.* [ORIGIN: Old English *stæger*] → DOWNSTAIRS, UPSTAIRS

stair·case /ˈstɛrkeɪs/ *n.* [C] a set of stairs inside a building, and the structure that supports it

stair·way /ˈstɛrweɪ/ *n.* [C] a set of stairs and the structure that supports it, either inside or outside a building

stake¹ /steɪk/ *n.* **1 be at stake** if something that you value very much is at stake, you will lose it if a plan or action is not successful: *The team goes into the game knowing their coach's job is at stake.* **2 have a stake in sth a)** to have an important part or share in a business, plan, etc.: *Hughes had a 5% stake in the company.* **b)** if you have a stake in something, you will get advantages

S

if it is successful, and you feel that you have an important connection with it: *Young people don't feel they have a stake in the country's future.* **3** [C] a pointed piece of wood, metal, etc. that is pushed into the ground to hold a rope, mark a particular place, etc.: *tent stakes* **4** [C usually plural] money that people risk on the result of a card game, horse race, etc. [ORIGIN: Old English *staca* "sharp post"]

stake² *v.* [T] **1** to risk losing something valuable on the result of a game, race, etc., or on the result of a plan or action (SYN) **bet**: *The President is* ***staking*** *his reputation* ***on*** *the peace plan.* **2 stake (out) a claim** to say publicly that you think you have a right to have or own something: *The two tribes have both* ***staked a claim to*** *the territory.*

stake sth ↔ **out** *phr. v.* (informal) to watch a place secretly and continuously: *The police have been staking out the club for weeks.*

stake·out /'steɪkaʊt/ *n.* [C] an activity in which the police watch a place secretly and continuously in order to catch someone doing something illegal

sta·lac·tite /stə'læktaɪt/ *n.* [C] EARTH SCIENCES a pointed object that hangs down from the roof of a CAVE, that is formed gradually by water that contains minerals dropping slowly from the roof ➔ STALAGMITE

sta·lag·mite /stə'lægmaɪt/ *n.* [C] EARTH SCIENCES a pointed object coming up from the floor of a CAVE, that is formed gradually by water that contains minerals dropping from the roof of the cave ➔ STALACTITE

stale /steɪl/ *adj.* **1** no longer fresh (ANT) **fresh**: *stale bread* **2** no longer interesting: *a stale old joke*

stale·mate /'steɪlmeɪt/ *n.* [C,U] a situation in which neither side in an argument, battle, etc. can gain an advantage: *talks aimed at* ***breaking the stalemate***

stalk¹ /stɔk/ *n.* [C] BIOLOGY a long narrow part of a plant that supports leaves, fruits, or flowers: *Two buds will develop on each stalk.* ➔ *see picture at* FLOWER¹

stalk² *v.* **1** [T] to follow a person or animal quietly in order to catch, attack, or kill him, her, or it: *We know the rapist stalks his victims at night.*

THESAURUS **follow, track, tail** ➔ FOLLOW

2 [I] to walk in a proud or angry way: *Sheryl turned and* ***stalked out*** *of the room.*

stalk·er /'stɔkɚ/ *n.* [C] someone who follows and watches someone else over a long period of time, in a way that is annoying or threatening —**stalking** *n.* [U]

stall¹ /stɔl/ *n.* [C] **1** a table or a small store with an open front, especially outdoors, where goods are sold: *a market stall* **2** a small enclosed private area for washing or using the toilet: *a shower/bathroom stall* **3** an enclosed area in a building for an animal, especially a horse

stall² *v.* [I,T] **1** if an engine stalls, or you stall it, it suddenly stops working: *My car always stalls when it's cold.* **2** (informal) to deliberately delay doing something, or to make someone else do this: *Quit stalling and answer my question!* | *I'll try to stall him for a few minutes.*

stal·lion /'stælyən/ *n.* [C] a fully grown male horse

stal·wart /'stɔlwɚt/ *n.* [C] someone who strongly supports a particular organization or set of ideas [ORIGIN: Old English *stælwierthe* "useful, strong"] —**stalwart** *adj.*: *a stalwart supporter*

sta·men /'steɪmən/ *n.* [C] BIOLOGY the male part of a flower, that produces POLLEN ➔ ANTHER

stam·i·na /'stæmənə/ *n.* [U] physical or mental strength that lets you continue doing something for a long time without getting tired [ORIGIN: 1700—1800 Latin, plural of *stamen* "thread, thread of life"]

stam·mer /'stæmɚ/ *v.* [I,T] to speak with a lot of pauses or to repeat the first letter of some words, either because you have a speech problem or because you are nervous ➔ STUTTER —**stammer** *n.* [singular]

stamp¹ /stæmp/ *n.* [C] **1** *also* **postage stamp** (formal) a small piece of paper that you stick onto an envelope or package that shows you have paid to mail it: *a 41-cent stamp* | *a* ***sheet/book of stamps*** (=set of stamps that you buy) **2** a tool for printing a mark onto a surface, or the mark made by this tool: *a stamp in your passport* **3 sb's stamp of approval** someone's statement that s/he accepts something or gives permission for something: *The Board of Education has* ***given its stamp of approval to*** *new standardized tests.* ➔ FOOD STAMP

stamp² *v.* **1** [I,T] to lift up your foot and put it down hard, or to walk in this way: *She* ***stamped out*** *of the room.* | *The audience applauded and* ***stamped*** *their* ***feet****.* **2** [T] to put a pattern, sign, or letters on something using a special tool: *Please* ***stamp*** *the date* ***on*** *all incoming mail.*

stamp sth ↔ **out** *phr. v.* to prevent something bad from continuing: *efforts to stamp out drug abuse*

stam·pede /stæm'pid/ *n.* [C] **1** an occasion when a large number of animals suddenly start running together **2** a sudden rush by a lot of people who all want to do the same thing or go to the same place [ORIGIN: 1800—1900 American Spanish *estampida*, from Spanish, "crush"] —**stampede** *v.* [I,T]

stance /stæns/ *n.* [C usually singular] **1** an opinion that is stated publicly: *the Senator's tough* ***stance on*** *crime*

THESAURUS **opinion, view, point of view, position** ➔ OPINION

2 the way in which you stand during a particular activity

stanch /stæntʃ/ *v.* [T] STAUNCH

stand¹ /stænd/ *v.* (past tense and past participle **stood** /stʊd/)
1 STAND [I] to be on your feet in an upright position: *Anna was standing in front of me.* | *Hundreds of people stood watching.* | *Could you* ***stand still*** (=stand without moving) *and listen to me?* | *Don't just* ***stand there*** (=stand doing nothing) – *help me!* | *A policeman told everyone to* ***stand back/aside*** (=move and stand farther away from something).
2 START STANDING [I] *also* **stand up** to rise onto your feet after you have been sitting, bending, or lying down: *She stood up and put her coat on.*
3 BE IN A PLACE/POSITION [I,T] to be in a place or position, or to put something in a place or position: *There's now a parking lot where the theater once stood.* | *A lamp stood on the table.* | *Few houses were* ***left standing*** *after the tornado hit.*
4 can't stand (spoken) to dislike something or someone very much: *Dave can't stand dogs.* | *Allison* ***can't stand the sight of*** *blood.* | ***I can't stand to*** *be around cigarette smoke.*
5 IN A STATE/CONDITION [linking verb] to be in a particular state or condition: *The kitchen door* ***stood open.*** | *The house has* ***stood empty*** *for 20 years.* | ***Where/how*** *do negotiations* ***stand*** *right now?* | *The offer,* ***as it stands*** (=the present offer), *is not acceptable.*
6 BE GOOD ENOUGH [T] to be good enough or strong enough to remain unharmed or unchanged by something: *jeans that can stand the rough wear kids give them* | *Their marriage has certainly* ***stood the test of time.***
7 ACCEPT A SITUATION [T] to be able to accept or deal well with a difficult situation: *He* ***could*** *hardly* ***stand*** *the pain.*

THESAURUS **tolerate, accept, put up with sth** → TOLERATE

8 HEIGHT [I] to have a particular height: *The Eiffel Tower* ***stands*** *300 meters* ***high.***
9 LEVEL/AMOUNT [I] to be at a particular level or amount: *The unemployment rate* ***stood at*** *8% in January.*
10 DECISION/OFFER [I not in progressive] if a decision, offer, etc. stands, it continues to exist or be correct: *The court has ruled that the conviction should stand.* | *My offer of help still stands.*
11 OPINION **where sb stands** if you know where someone stands, or how someone stands on a particular matter, you know what his/her opinion is: *Where do you stand on the issue of gun control?* | *You just never* ***know where you stand with*** *Walter.*
12 SUGGEST STH TO SB **could stand** (spoken) used in order to say that someone should do something or that something should be different: *He could stand to lose a little weight.*
13 stand a chance (of doing sth) to be likely to succeed in doing something: *You* ***don't stand a chance*** *of going out with her.*
14 stand to do sth to be likely to do or have something: *The company stands to make more than $12 million on the deal.*
15 stand in the way/in sb's way to prevent someone from doing something, or prevent something from happening or developing: *I always encouraged Brian. I didn't want to stand in his way.* | *You can't stand in the way of progress!*
16 stand on your own two feet (informal) to be independent and not need help from other people
17 it stands to reason (that) used in order to say that something is clearly true: *It stands to reason that children will copy their parents.*
18 stand trial to be brought to a court of law to have your case examined and judged
19 stand pat to refuse to change a decision or plan
20 stand on your head/hands to support yourself on your head or hands in an upright position, with your feet in the air [ORIGIN: Old English *standan*]

stand around *phr. v.*
to stand somewhere and not do anything: *Everybody was just standing around talking.*

stand back *phr. v.*
to move backward away from something, or stand some distance away from something: *Stand back from the edge of the platform.*

stand by *phr. v.*
1 stand by sth to continue to believe that something you said, did, or believed is still correct or true: *I stand by what I said earlier.*
2 stand by sb to stay loyal to someone and support him/her in a difficult situation: *Matt's parents have stood by him through his drug problem.*
3 to be ready to do something: *Fire crews are now standing by.*
4 to not do anything to help someone, or to not prevent something from happening: *People just stood by and watched him being attacked.*

stand for sth *phr. v.*
1 to be a short form of a word or phrase: *VA stands for Veterans Administration.*
2 to support an idea, principle, etc.: *Martin Luther King stood for fairness and racial equality.*
3 not stand for sth if someone will not stand for something, s/he will not allow it to happen: *Ms. Smith won't stand for any nonsense.*

stand in for sb *phr. v.*
to do someone else's job while he or she is away: *Karen stood in for me when I was sick.*

stand out *phr. v.*
1 to be clearly better than other things or people: *Morrison* ***stands out as*** *the most experienced candidate.*
2 to be very easy to see or notice: *In her red dress, she really* ***stood out in the crowd.***

stand up *phr. v.*
1 to be on your feet, or to rise to your feet: *We stood up when the judge came in.* | ***Stand up straight*** *and don't slouch!*
2 to be proven to be true, useful, or strong when tested: *The accusations will never* ***stand up in court.***
3 stand sb up to not meet someone when you have promised to meet him/her: *My date stood me up last night.*

stand up for sb/sth *phr. v.*
to support or defend someone or something when s/he or it is being attacked or criticized: *Don't be afraid to stand up for what you believe in.*
stand up to sb *phr. v.*
to be brave and refuse to do or say what someone is trying to make you do or say: *He became a kind of hero for standing up to local gangs.*

stand² *n.* [C] **1** a piece of furniture or equipment for supporting something: *a music stand* **2** a table or small structure, usually outside or in a large building, used for selling or showing things to people: *a hotdog stand* **3** [usually singular] an opinion that you state publicly: *Bradley was unwilling to* ***take a stand*** (=say what his opinion was) *on the issue.* **4 the stand** LAW the place in a court of law where someone sits when the lawyers ask him/her questions: *Shaw had lied* ***on the stand*** (=when he was answering questions). | *Epstein will* ***take the stand*** (=begin answering questions) *Friday.* **5** an effort to defend yourself or to oppose something: *We have to* ***make/take a stand against*** *racism.* **6 stands** [plural] the place where people sit to watch a sports game

S

stan·dard¹ /ˈstændəd/ *n.* **1** [C,U] a level of quality, skill, or ability that is considered to be acceptable: *teachers who have* ***high/low standards*** | *Tricia's parents* ***set*** *very high* ***standards.*** | *Students have to* ***meet/reach a*** *certain* ***standard*** *or they won't pass.* | *national* ***academic/health/ environmental*** *standards* **2 by ... standards** compared to the normal or expected level of something else: ***By*** *American* ***standards****, Rafael's salary is pretty low.* **3 standards** [plural] moral principles about what kind of behavior or attitudes are acceptable: *She has very high* ***moral standards.*** [ORIGIN: 1100—1200 Old French *estandard* "battle-flag"]

standard² *adj.* normal or usual: *The shoes are available in all standard sizes.* | *Security checks are now* ***standard practice/procedure.***

THESAURUS **normal, ordinary, average, conventional →** NORMAL¹

ˌstandard deviˈation *n.* [C] MATH in STATISTICS, a calculation which shows how much each value in a set is different from the MEAN of the values in the set

stan·dard·ize /ˈstændəˌdaɪz/ *v.* [T] to make all the things of one particular type the same as each other: *national standardized tests* —**standardization** /ˌstændədəˈzeɪʃən/ *n.* [U]

ˌstandard of ˈliving *n.* (plural **standards of living**) [C] ECONOMICS the amount of wealth and comfort that a person, group, or country has: *a nation with a* ***high/low standard of living***

stand·by /ˈstændbaɪ/ *n.* (plural **standbys**) [C] **1** someone or something that is ready to be used when needed: *a standby power generator* **2 on standby a)** ready to be used when needed: *The police have been kept on standby in case of trouble.* **b)** if you are on standby for an airplane ticket, you will be allowed to travel if there are any seats that are not being used

ˈstand-in *n.* [C] someone who does the job or takes the place of someone else for a short time

stand·ing¹ /ˈstændɪŋ/ *adj.* [only before noun] **1** permanently agreed or arranged: *We have a* ***standing invitation*** *to use their beach cabin.* **2** done from a standing position: *a* ***standing ovation*** (=when people stand to CLAP after a performance)

standing² *n.* [U] someone's rank or position in a system, organization, etc., based on what other people think of him/her: *The scandal damaged the governor's* ***standing in*** *the polls.*

stand·off /ˈstændɔf/ *n.* [C] a situation in which neither side in a fight or battle can gain an advantage

stand·off·ish /stænˈdɔfɪʃ/ *adj.* (informal, disapproving) unfriendly and formal

stand·out /ˈstændaʊt/ *n.* [C] someone who is better at doing something than other people in a group —**standout** *adj.*

stand·point /ˈstændpɔɪnt/ *n.* [C] one way of thinking about a situation SYN **point of view**: *Let's look at this* ***from a*** *practical* ***standpoint.***

stand·still /ˈstændˌstɪl/ *n.* [singular] a situation in which there is no movement or activity at all: *The funeral* ***brought*** *the city* ***to a standstill.*** | *The traffic* ***came to a standstill.***

stand·up /ˈstændʌp/ *adj.* [only before noun] (informal) standup COMEDY involves one person telling jokes as a performance —**standup** *n.* [U]

stank /stæŋk/ *v.* a past tense of STINK¹

stan·za /ˈstænzə/ *n.* [C] ENG. LANG. ARTS a group of lines that forms part of a poem

sta·ple¹ /ˈsteɪpəl/ *n.* [C] **1** a small piece of thin wire that is used in order to hold pieces of paper together **2** a food that is needed and used all the time: *staples like flour and rice* [ORIGIN: (2) 1300—1400 Middle Dutch *stapel* "place of trade"]

staple² *v.* [T] to fasten things together with a staple

THESAURUS **fasten, attach, secure, join, glue, tape, clip, tie, button (up), zip (up) →** FASTEN

sta·pler /ˈsteɪplə/ *n.* [C] a tool used for putting staples into paper

star¹ /stɑr/ *n.* [C] **1** PHYSICS a very large amount of burning gases in space, that looks like a point of light in the sky at night: *I lay on my back and looked up at the stars.* | *The* ***stars*** *were* ***out*** (=shining). | *The galaxy of stars to which our sun belongs is one of millions of galaxies scattered throughout the universe.* **→** SPACE¹ **2** a famous performer in entertainment or sports: *a movie star* | *By the age of twenty, she was already a* ***big***

star. **3 a)** a shape with five or six points, that is supposed to look like a star in the sky: *The U.S. flag's fifty stars represent fifty states.* → *see picture at* SHAPE[1] **b)** a mark in the shape of a star, that is used in order to show something is important: *I put stars next to the items we still need to buy.* **4** (informal) someone who is particularly good at something: *Jim is definitely our* ***star player***. **5 the star of the show** the person who gives the best performance in a play, movie, etc. **6** a mark used in a system for showing how good a hotel or restaurant is: *a* ***three-star/four-star/five-star*** *restaurant* [ORIGIN: Old English *steorra*]

star² *v.* (**starred**, **starring**) [I,T] if a movie, play, etc. stars someone, or if someone stars in a movie, play, etc., that person has one of the main parts in it: *a movie starring Bruce Willis* | *He has also* ***starred in*** *comedies.* | *Nicole Kidman* ***stars as*** *Emma.*

star·board /ˈstɑrbɚd/ *n.* [U] the right side of a ship or aircraft when you are looking toward the front → PORT

starch¹ /stɑrtʃ/ *n.* **1** [C,U] BIOLOGY a substance in such foods as bread, rice, and potatoes **2** [U] a substance used for making cloth stiff

starch² *v.* [T] to make cloth stiff using starch

starch·y /ˈstɑrtʃi/ *adj.* starchy foods contain a lot of starch

star·dom /ˈstɑrdəm/ *n.* [U] the situation of being a famous performer

stare /stɛr/ *v.* [I] to look at someone or something for a long time: *Sue* ***stared at*** *him in disbelief.* | *He sat* ***staring into space*** (=looking at nothing for a long time). [ORIGIN: Old English *starian*] —**stare** *n.* [C]: *She gave him a hard stare.*

> THESAURUS
> **look, gaze, gape, regard** → LOOK¹

star·fish /ˈstɑrˌfɪʃ/ (plural **starfish**) *n.* [C] a flat sea animal that is shaped like a star

stark¹ /stɑrk/ *adj.* **1** very simple and severe in appearance: *the stark beauty of the desert* **2** unpleasantly clear and impossible to avoid: *the* ***stark realities*** *of drug addiction* —**starkly** *adv.*

stark² *adv.* **stark naked** (informal) not wearing any clothes

star·let /ˈstɑrlɪt/ *n.* [C] a young actress who plays small parts in movies and is hoping to become famous

star·light /ˈstɑrlaɪt/ *n.* [U] the light that comes from the stars

star·ling /ˈstɑrlɪŋ/ *n.* [C] a greenish-black bird that is very common in Europe and North America

star·lit /ˈstɑrˌlɪt/ *adj.* (literary) made brighter by the light of the stars: *a starlit night*

star·ry /ˈstɑri/ *adj.* having many stars: *a starry sky*

ˌstarry-ˈeyed *adj.* (informal) hopeful about things in a way that is silly or unreasonable: *a starry-eyed teenager*

ˌStars and ˈStripes *n.* **the Stars and Stripes** the flag of the U.S.

Star-Span·gled Ban·ner /ˌstɑr spæŋgəld ˈbænɚ/ *n.* **the Star-Spangled Banner** the national ANTHEM (=song) of the U.S.

ˈstar-ˌstudded *adj.* including many famous performers: *a star-studded cast*

start¹ /stɑrt/ *v.*

1 BEGIN DOING STH [I,T] to begin doing something: *Have you started making dinner?* | *It's* ***starting to*** *rain.* | *Mark's* ***starting school/college*** *in the fall.* | *It's late, so we should* ***get started***.

> USAGE
> **Start** and **begin** usually mean the same thing, but **start** has several meanings for which you cannot use **begin**.
> Use **start** in order to talk about making a machine work: *I couldn't start the car this morning.*
> Use **start** in order to talk about making something begin to exist: *Starting a new business is hard work.*

2 BEGIN HAPPENING [I,T] to begin happening, or to make something do this: *The race starts in ten minutes.* | *The fire was started by a loose wire.*

3 BUSINESS/ORGANIZATION ETC. [T] *also* **start up** to begin a new business or business activity: *Brad left his father's company to start a business of his own.*

4 TRIP [I] *also* **start off/out** to begin a trip: *You'll have to start early if you want to get there by noon.*

5 CAR/ENGINE/MACHINE [I,T] *also* **start up** if you start a car or engine, or if it starts, it begins to work: *Can't you* ***get*** *that* ***engine started****?*

6 to start with (spoken) **a)** used in order to emphasize the first of a list of things you want to mention: *There's a lot wrong with those kids – to start with, they're rude.* **b)** at the beginning of a situation: *I was nervous to start with, but then I was fine.*

7 PRICES start at/from sth if prices start at or from a particular figure, that is the lowest figure at which you can buy something: *Tickets start from $12.*

8 ROAD/RIVER [I] if a road, river, etc. starts somewhere, it begins in that place: *The Red River* ***starts in*** *New Mexico.*

9 MOVE SUDDENLY [I] to move suddenly because you are surprised or afraid [ORIGIN: Old English *styrtan* "to jump"]

start off *phr. v.*
to begin an activity: *Let's start off by reviewing what we did last week.*

start on sth *phr. v.*
to begin working on something: *You'd better get started on your homework.*

start out *phr. v.*
1 to begin happening or existing in a particular way,

S

especially when this changes later: *The book* ***started out as*** *a short article.*
2 to begin your life, profession, or an important period of time: *Laura* ***started out as*** *a teacher, and later got into writing.*

start over *phr. v.*
to start doing something again from the beginning: *If you make a mistake, just erase it and start over.*

start² *n.* **1** [C usually singular] the beginning of an activity, event, or situation: *Hurry, or we'll miss the* ***start of*** *the show.* | *They've had problems* ***(right) from the start.*** | *It was a close race* ***from start to finish.*** | *The day* ***got off to a good/bad start.*** **2 it's a start** (informal) used in order to say that something you have achieved may not be impressive, but it will help with a bigger achievement: *We only have $2 million of the $60 million needed, but it's a start.* **3 for a start** (informal) said in order to emphasize the first of a list of facts or opinions: *I don't think she'll get the job. She's too young, for a start.* **4** [singular] a sudden movement caused by fear or surprise: *Ed woke up* ***with a start.***

start·er /ˈstɑrt̬ɚ/ *n.* [C] **1** a person, horse, etc. that is in a race when it starts: *Of the eight starters, only three finished the race.* **2 for starters** (informal) used in order to emphasize the first thing in a list: *You've spelled the name wrong, for starters.* **3** someone who gives the signal for a race to begin **4** *also* **starter motor** a piece of equipment for starting an engine

ˈstarting ˌlineup *n.* [C usually singular] the best players on a sports team, who play when the game begins

start·le /ˈstɑrt̬l/ *v.* [T] to make someone suddenly feel surprised or slightly shocked: *Sorry, I didn't mean to startle you.* —**startling** *adj.*: *startling news*

ˈstart-up¹ *adj.* [only before noun] ECONOMICS start-up costs are related to starting and developing a new business

ˈstart-up² *n.* [C] ECONOMICS a new small company: *an Internet start-up*

star·va·tion /stɑrˈveɪʃən/ *n.* [U] suffering or death caused by not having enough to eat: *people dying of starvation*

starve /stɑrv/ *v.* **1** [I,T] to suffer or die because you do not have enough to eat, or to make someone do this: *Thousands of people could* ***starve to death.*** | *starving refugees* **2 be starving/starved** (spoken) to be very hungry: *When do we eat? I'm starving!* **3 be starved for/of sth** to not be given something very important: *That poor kid's just* ***starved for*** *attention.*

stash¹ /stæʃ/ *v.* [T] (informal) to keep something in a safe, often secret, place: *He has money* ***stashed away*** *in a Swiss bank.*

stash² *n.* [C] (informal) an amount of something, especially drugs or money, that is kept in a secret place: *a* ***stash of*** *drugs*

state¹ /steɪt/ *n.* **1** [C] the condition that someone or something is in: *We are concerned about the* ***state of*** *the economy.* | *Exercise can improve your* ***state of mind*** (=the way you think and feel). | *They found him* ***in a state of shock.*** | *The house was in a* ***sorry state*** (=in a bad condition). **2** [C] *also* **State** POLITICS one of the areas with limited law-making powers that some countries, such as the U.S., are divided into: *the state of Oklahoma* **3** [C,U] *also* **State** POLITICS a country or its government: *a meeting between* ***heads of state*** | ***state-owned*** *industries*

THESAURUS country, nation, power, land, realm ➔ COUNTRY¹

4 the States (spoken) the U.S., used especially by someone when s/he is outside of the U.S. **5 a state of affairs** a situation: *It is* ***a sad/sorry state of affairs*** *when you can kill someone and only spend a year in jail.* **6 state visit/ceremony/opening etc.** POLITICS an important official visit, ceremony, etc. involving governments or rulers: *the President's state visit to Moscow* [ORIGIN: 1100—1200 Old French *estat*, from *Latin status*, from the past participle of *stare* "to stand"]

state² *v.* [T] (formal) **1** to give a piece of information or your opinion, especially by saying it clearly: *Please state your name.* | *The witness* ***stated that*** *he had never seen the woman before.*

THESAURUS say, mention, add, utter, express ➔ SAY¹

2 if a document, ticket, etc. states information, it contains the information written clearly

ˌstate ˈline *n.* [C] the border between two states in the U.S.

state·ly /ˈsteɪtli/ *adj.* impressive in style or size: *a stately mansion*

state·ment /ˈsteɪtˀmənt/ *n.* [C] **1** something that you say or write officially and publicly: *The president is expected to* ***make a statement*** *later today.* | *the candidate's* ***statement about/on*** *the economy* | *He* ***gave a statement*** *to the police.* **2** ECONOMICS a list showing amounts of money paid, received, etc. and their total: *a bank statement* **3 make a statement** to do something, such as wear particular clothing or drive a particular type of car, in order that people will have a particular opinion of you: *Why get your nose pierced? Are you trying to make a statement?*

ˌstate-of-the-ˈart *adj.* using the newest methods, materials, or knowledge (SYN) **advanced**: *state-of-the-art technology*

states·man /ˈsteɪtsmən/ *n.* (plural **statesmen** /-mən/) [C] POLITICS a political or government leader, especially one who is known as being wise and fair —**statesmanship** *n.* [U]

ˈstates' ˌrights *n.* [plural] POLITICS the rights or powers that U.S. states have because the Constitution has not given those rights to the Federal government

stat·ic¹ /ˈstæt̬ɪk/ *adj.* not moving, changing, or

developing: *The population of the state has remained static for many years.*

static² *n.* [U] **1** PHYSICS noise caused by electricity in the air that spoils the sound on a radio or TV **2** PHYSICS static electricity

ˌstatic elecˈtricity *n.* [U] PHYSICS electricity that is not flowing in a current, but collects on the surface of an object and gives you a small electric shock

sta·tion¹ /ˈsteɪʃən/ *n.* [C] **1** a place where public vehicles stop so that passengers can get on and off, goods can be loaded, etc.: *a* ***bus/train station*** **2** a building or place that is a center for a particular type of service or activity: *a* ***police station*** | *a* ***gas station*** **3** a company that broadcasts on radio or television, or its programs that you receive: *a* ***radio/TV station*** | *I can only* ***get*** *a few* ***stations*** *on this radio.* [ORIGIN: 1500—1600 French, Latin *statio* "place for standing or stopping," from *stare* "to stand"]

station² *v.* [T] to put someone in a particular place in order to do a particular job or military duty: *My uncle's stationed in Germany right now.*

sta·tion·a·ry /ˈsteɪʃəˌnɛri/ *adj.* not moving: *a stationary vehicle*

sta·tion·er·y /ˈsteɪʃəˌnɛri/ *n.* [U] special paper for writing letters on, usually with matching envelopes

ˈstation ˌwagon *n.* [C] a car with a door at the back, and a lot of space for boxes, cases, etc.

sta·tis·tic /stəˈtɪstɪk/ (Ac) *n.* **1 statistics a)** [plural] a collection of numbers which represents facts or measurements: ***Statistics show*** *that the crime rate is falling.* | *the poverty* ***statistics for*** *New York City* **b)** [U] SCIENCE the science of using numbers to represent facts or measurements: *Statistics is a branch of mathematics.* **2** [singular] a single number that represents a fact or measurement: *Is he aware of the statistic that two out of three marriages fail?* —**statistical** *adj.*: *statistical analysis* —**statistically** *adv.*

stat·is·ti·cian /ˌstætəˈstɪʃən/ (Ac) *n.* [C] someone who works with statistics

stats /stæts/ *n.* [plural] (informal) statistics

statue

stat·ue /ˈstætʃu/ *n.* [C] an object that looks like a person or animal, and is made of stone, metal, etc.: *a* ***statue of*** *Abraham Lincoln* | *the Statue of Liberty*

stat·u·ette /ˌstætʃuˈɛt/ *n.* [C] a very small statue

stat·ure /ˈstætʃɚ/ *n.* [U] (formal) **1** the degree to which someone is admired or regarded as important: *a musician of great stature* **2** someone's height

sta·tus /ˈsteɪt̬əs, ˈstæ-/ (Ac) *n.* **1** [C,U] the legal and social position of a person, group, country, etc.: *Please state your name, age and* ***marital status*** (=whether you are married or not). | *the social* ***status of*** *women* **2** [U] your social or professional rank or position, considered in relation to other people: ***high-status/low-status*** *jobs* | *Doctors have traditionally enjoyed* ***high social status.*** **3 the status of sth** what is happening at a particular time in a situation: *No one would comment on the status of her application.* [ORIGIN: 1700—1800 Latin, from the past participle of *stare* "to stand"]

status quo /ˌsteɪt̬əs ˈkwoʊ, ˌstæ-/ *n.* **the status quo** the state of a situation at a particular time

ˈstatus ˌsymbol *n.* [C] something that you own that suggests you are rich or important

stat·ute /ˈstætʃut/ *n.* [C] LAW a law or rule

THESAURUS rule, law, regulation → RULE¹

ˌstatute of limiˈtations *n.* [C] LAW a law that gives the period of time within which the police or courts may take action on a legal question or crime

stat·u·to·ry /ˈstætʃəˌtɔri/ *adj.* LAW fixed or controlled by law: *statutory rights*

ˌstatutory ˈrape *n.* [C] LAW the crime of having sex with someone who is below a particular age

staunch¹ /stɔntʃ, stɑntʃ/ *adj.* very loyal: *a staunch supporter* —**staunchly** *adv.*

THESAURUS faithful, loyal, steadfast, true → FAITHFUL

staunch² *also* **stanch** /stæntʃ/ *v.* [T] to stop the flow of a liquid, especially of blood from a wound

stave /steɪv/ *v.*

stave sth ↔ **off** *phr. v.* to stop someone or something from reaching you or affecting you for a period of time: *She ate an apple to stave off hunger.*

stay¹ /steɪ/ *v.* **1** [I] to remain in the same place, job, school, etc., and not leave: *I had to* ***stay late*** *at work.* | *She decided to* ***stay home.*** | ***Stay right there!*** *I'll be back in a minute.* **2** [I, linking verb] to continue to be in a particular state and not change: *It was hard to* ***stay awake.*** | *The town has* ***stayed the same*** *for centuries.* | *Let's just* ***stay calm*** *and try to figure out what to do.* **3** [I] to live in a place for a short time as a visitor or guest: *She's* ***staying with*** *us for a week.* | *Where are you staying while you're here?* ▸Don't say "Where do you stay?"◂ **4 stay put** (informal) to remain in one place and not move [ORIGIN: 1400—1500 Old French *ester* "to stand, stay," from Latin *stare*]

S

stay away *phr. v.* to not go near someone or something: ***Stay away from** my sister!*

stay behind *phr. v.* to stay in a place after the other people have left

stay in *phr. v.* to stay in your home and not go out: *Let's stay in and watch TV.*

stay on *phr. v.* to continue to do a job or to study after the usual or expected time for leaving: *Karen is staying on for a fifth year in college.*

stay out *phr. v.* to remain away from home during the evening or night: *She stayed out until midnight.*

stay up *phr. v.* to not go to bed: *We **stayed up late** last night.*

stay² *n.* [C] a short period of time that you spend somewhere: *We hope you enjoy your stay.*

STD *n.* [C,U] **sexually transmitted disease** a disease such as AIDS that is passed from one person to another during sex

stead /stɛd/ *n.* **1 stand sb in good stead** to be very useful for someone in the future: *a skill that has stood me in good stead as an actor* **2** (formal) **do sth in sb's stead** to do something instead of someone else

S

stead·fast /ˈstɛdfæst/ *adj.* (literary) faithful and very loyal

THESAURUS **faithful, loyal, devoted, staunch, true** → FAITHFUL

stead·y¹ /ˈstɛdi/ *adj.* **1** not moving or shaking: *Keep the ladder steady.* **2** continuing or developing at the same rate, without stopping or changing: *He has made steady progress.* | *a steady speed of 50 mph* **3 steady job/work/income** a job, etc. that will continue over a long period of time **4 steady boyfriend/girlfriend** someone that you have had a romantic relationship with for a long time —**steadily** *adv.* —**steadiness** *n.* [U]

steady² *v.* (**steadied**, **steadies**) [I,T] to hold someone or something so he, she, or it becomes more balanced or controlled, or to become more balanced or controlled: *He put out his hand to steady himself.*

steady³ *adv.* **go steady (with sb)** to have a long romantic relationship with someone

steak /steɪk/ *n.* [C,U] a thick flat piece of meat or fish [ORIGIN: 1400—1500 Old Norse *steik*]

steal¹ /stil/ *v.* (past tense **stole** /stoʊl/, past participle **stolen** /ˈstoʊlən/) **1** [I,T] to take something that belongs to someone else without his/her permission: *Two local men were arrested for stealing a car.* | *When did you find out your partner was **stealing from** you?*

USAGE

Use **steal** to talk about the things that were taken: *Matt's bike was stolen yesterday.*
Use **rob** to talk about the person that money is taken from, or the place, especially a bank: *Someone robbed the bank last night.*

THESAURUS

burglarize – to go into a building, car, etc. and steal things from it: *The office had been burglarized.*
rob – to steal money or other things from a bank, store, or person: *He robbed several gas stations in the area.*
mug – to attack someone in the street and steal something from him/her: *He had been mugged at gunpoint.*
shoplift – to steal something from a store by leaving without paying for it: *The store loses a lot of money because people shoplift.*
rip off sth (informal) – to steal something: *Someone had ripped off $3000 worth of stereo equipment.*
loot – to steal things, especially from stores that have been damaged in a war or riot: *Windows were smashed and stores looted during the riot.*
plunder (formal) – to steal money or property from a place while fighting in a war: *The Vikings invaded and plundered the town.*
pilfer (formal) – to steal things that are not worth much: *He was caught pilfering office supplies from work.* → CRIME, CRIMINAL¹

2 [I] (literary) to move quietly without anyone noticing you [ORIGIN: Old English *stelan*]

steal² *n.* **a steal** something that costs much less than it is worth: *At $9.99 a bottle, their Merlot **is a** real **steal**.*

stealth /stɛlθ/ *n.* [U] the action of doing something quietly and secretly [ORIGIN: 1200—1300 From an unrecorded Old English *stælth* "stealing"] —**stealthy** *adj.*

steam¹ /stim/ *n.* **1** [U] the mist that hot water produces: *The kitchen was full of steam.* | *a **steam engine*** (=one that uses the power produced by steam to operate) **2 let/blow off steam** to get rid of your anger or energy by doing something active **3 run out of steam** to no longer have the energy or the support you need to continue doing something

steam² *v.* **1** [I] to produce steam: *a cup of steaming coffee* **2** [T] to cook something using steam: *Steam the vegetables for five minutes.*

THESAURUS **cook, bake, fry, roast, broil, grill, sauté, boil, deep fry** → COOK¹

steam sth ↔ **up** *phr. v.* to cover or be covered with steam: *My glasses are steamed up.*

steam·roll /ˈstimroʊl/ *v.* [T] (informal) to defeat an opponent or force someone to do something by using all your power or influence

steam·roll·er /ˈstimˌroʊlɚ/ *n.* [C] a heavy vehicle with very wide wheels for making road surfaces flat

steam·y /ˈstimi/ *adj.* **1** full of steam, or covered with steam: *steamy windows* **2** sexually exciting: *a steamy love scene*

steel¹ /stil/ *n.* [U] **1** a strong metal that can be

shaped easily, consisting of iron and CARBON **2 nerves of steel** the ability to be brave and calm in a dangerous or difficult situation [ORIGIN: Old English *style*, *stele*]

steel² *v.* **steel yourself** to prepare yourself to do something unpleasant

ˌsteel ˈwool *n.* [U] a rough material made of steel wires, used in order to make surfaces smooth, remove paint, etc.

steel·y /ˈstili/ *adj.* extremely strong and determined: *a steely expression*

steep¹ /stip/ *adj.* **1** a road, hill, etc. that is steep goes down or up at a sharp angle **2** a steep increase or rise in something is large and happens quickly **3** (informal) very expensive [ORIGIN: Old English *steap* "high, steep, deep"] **—steeply** *adv.* **—steepness** *n.* [U]

steep² *v.* [I,T] **1 be steeped in history/tradition etc.** to contain a lot of a particular quality: *Yale is an old university steeped in tradition.* **2** to put something such as food in a liquid and leave it there for some time: *Leave the tea bag to steep for two minutes.*

stee·ple /ˈstipəl/ *n.* [C] a tall pointed tower on a church

steer¹ /stɪr/ *v.* **1** [I,T] to control the direction that a vehicle goes in: *Maria steered while I gave directions.* **2** [T] to influence someone's behavior or the way a situation develops: *Helen tried to* ***steer the conversation*** *away from school.* | *My parents* ***steered*** *me* ***toward*** *a medical career.* **3** [T] to guide someone to a place: *Bobby took my arm and* ***steered*** *me* ***into*** *the next room.* **4 steer clear (of sb/sth)** (informal) to try to avoid someone or something

steer² *n.* [C] a young male cow that has had part of its sex organs removed

steer·ing /ˈstɪrɪŋ/ *n.* [U] the parts of a vehicle that allow you to control the direction it goes in: *power steering*

ˈsteering wheel *n.* [C] a wheel that you turn to control the direction a vehicle goes in

stel·lar /ˈstɛlɚ/ *adj.* **1** done extremely well: *a stellar performance* **2** PHYSICS relating to the stars

stem¹ /stɛm/ *n.* [C] BIOLOGY a long thin part of a plant, from which leaves or flowers grow ➔ *see picture at* PLANT¹

stem² *v.* (**stemmed**, **stemming**) [T] **stem the tide/flow of sth** to stop something from spreading or growing: *an effort to stem the rising tide of crime*

stem from sth *phr. v.* to develop as a result of something else: *A lot of her emotional problems stem from her childhood.*

stench /stɛntʃ/ *n.* [C] a strong unpleasant smell (SYN) **stink**, **odor**: *the* ***stench of*** *rotting food*

sten·cil /ˈstɛnsəl/ *n.* [C] a piece of paper or plastic with patterns or letters cut out of it, which you use for painting patterns or letters onto a surface **—stencil** *v.* [T]

ste·nog·ra·pher /stəˈnɑgrəfɚ/ *n.* [C] someone whose job is to write down what someone else is saying by using SHORTHAND **—stenography** *n.* [U]

step¹ /stɛp/ *n.* [C]

1 MOVEMENT the movement you make when you put one foot in front of the other when walking: *He* ***took*** *a few* ***steps*** *and then stopped.* | *Jamie took a* ***step forward/back****.*

2 ACTION one of a series of things that you do in order to deal with a problem or achieve something: *We must* ***take steps*** (=take action) *to make sure it never happens again.* | *an important* ***first step*** *toward peace* | *Environmentalists called the change* ***a step in the right direction*** (=a good thing to do).

3 STAIR a flat narrow surface, especially one in a series, that you put your foot on when you are going up or down, especially outside a building ➔ STAIRS: *Ellen ran up the steps and knocked on the door.*

4 STAGE IN A PROCESS a stage in a process or a position on a scale: *The next step will be to interview the selected candidates.*

THESAURUS **stage, part, phase** ➔ STAGE¹

5 DANCING a movement of your feet in dancing

6 in step/out of step a) having ideas that are the same as, or different from, other people's: *The president needs to* ***keep in step with*** *public opinion.* **b)** moving your feet in the same way as, or a different way from, people you are walking or marching with

7 SOUND the sound you make when you take a step ➔ FOOTSTEP

8 MUSIC ENG. LANG. ARTS the difference in PITCH between two musical notes that are separated by one KEY on a piano (SYN) **tone** [ORIGIN: Old English *stæpe*]

step² *v.* (**stepped**, **stepping**) [I] **1** to move somewhere by putting one foot down in front of the other: ***Step aside/back*** *and let the doctor through.* **2** to bring your foot down on something: *Sorry – I didn't mean to* ***step on*** *your foot.* **3 step on it/step on the gas** (spoken) to drive faster: *If you don't step on it we'll miss the plane.* **4 step on sb's toes** to offend or upset someone, especially by trying to do his/her work **5 step out of line** to behave badly by breaking a rule or disobeying an order

step down/aside *phr. v.* to leave your job or official position because you want to or think you should: *He's decided to step down at the end of the year.*

step forward *phr. v.* to come and offer help: *Several volunteers have kindly stepped forward.*

step in *phr. v.* to become involved in a situation, especially to stop trouble: *The police stepped in and stopped the fight.*

step out *phr. v.* to go out for a short time: *Molly just stepped out – may I take a message?*

step sth ↔ **up** *phr. v.* to increase the amount of an

S

activity or the speed of a process: *The airlines are stepping up security checks.*

step·broth·er /ˈstɛpˌbrʌðɚ/ *n.* [C] the son of someone who has married one of your parents

ˌstep-by-ˈstep *adj.* a step-by-step plan, method, etc. deals with things carefully and in a particular order: *a **step-by-step guide** to buying a house*

step·child /ˈstɛpˌtʃaɪld/ *n.* (plural **stepchildren** /-ˌtʃɪldrən/) [C] a stepdaughter or stepson

step·daugh·ter /ˈstɛpˌdɔt̬ɚ/ *n.* [C] a daughter that your husband or wife has from a relationship before your marriage

step·fa·ther /ˈstɛpˌfɑðɚ/ *n.* [C] a man who is married to your mother but who is not your father

step·lad·der /ˈstɛpˌlædɚ/ *n.* [C] a LADDER with two sloping parts that are attached at the top so that it can stand without support

step·moth·er /ˈstɛpˌmʌðɚ/ *n.* [C] a woman who is married to your father but who is not your mother

steppe /stɛp/ *n.* [C,U] *also* **the steppes** EARTH SCIENCES a large area of land without trees, especially in Russia, parts of Asia, and southeast Europe

S

ˈstepped-up *adj.* [only before noun] done more quickly or with more effort than before ➔ STEP UP: *the **stepped-up security** at the airport*

ˈstepping-ˌstone *n.* [C] **1** something that helps you to improve or become more successful: *a stepping-stone to a better job* **2** one of a row of stones that you walk on to get across a stream

step·sis·ter /ˈstɛpˌsɪstɚ/ *n.* [C] the daughter of someone who has married one of your parents

step·son /ˈstɛpsʌn/ *n.* [C] a son that your husband or wife has from a relationship before your marriage

ster·e·o /ˈstɛriˌoʊ, ˈstɪr-/ *n.* (plural **stereos**) [C] **1** a machine for playing records, CDs, etc. that produces sound from two SPEAKERS ➔ *see picture on page A19* **2 in stereo** if music or a broadcast is in stereo, the sound it makes is directed through two SPEAKERS

ster·e·o·type[1] /ˈstɛriəˌtaɪp, ˈstɪr-/ *n.* [C] (disapproving) an idea of what a particular type of person is like, especially one which is wrong or unfair: *racial stereotypes* | ***stereotypes about** women* —**stereotypical** /ˌstɛrioʊˈtɪpɪkəl/ *adj.*

stereotype[2] *v.* [T] (disapproving) to decide, usually unfairly, that some people have particular qualities or abilities because they belong to a particular race, sex, etc.: *Too many children's books **stereotype** girls **as** helpless and weak.*

ster·ile /ˈstɛrəl/ *adj.* **1** BIOLOGY unable to have children (SYN) **infertile** (ANT) **fertile** **2** BIOLOGY completely clean and not containing any BACTERIA: *a sterile bandage* **3** lacking new ideas or imagination —**sterility** /stəˈrɪlət̬i/ *n.* [U]

ster·il·ize /ˈstɛrəˌlaɪz/ *v.* [T] **1** BIOLOGY to make something completely clean and kill any BACTERIA in it: *All the surgical instruments are sterilized before use.* **2** BIOLOGY to perform an operation that makes a person or animal unable to have babies —**sterilization** /ˌstɛrələˈzeɪʃən/ *n.* [C,U]

ster·ling /ˈstɚlɪŋ/ *adj.* **sterling qualities/character/record etc.** excellent qualities, character, etc.

ˌsterling ˈsilver *also* **sterling** *n.* [U] a metal that is over 92% pure silver

stern[1] /stɚn/ *adj.* very strict and severe: *stern warnings* | *a **stern voice/face*** —**sternly** *adv.*

THESAURUS strict, tough, firm ➔ STRICT

stern[2] *n.* [C] the back part of a ship

ster·num /ˈstɚnəm/ *n.* (plural **sternums** *or* **sterna** /-nə/) [C] BIOLOGY a BREASTBONE

ste·roid /ˈstɛrɔɪd, ˈstɪrɔɪd/ *n.* [C] BIOLOGY a drug used especially for treating injuries, that people sometimes use illegally to improve their sports performance

steth·o·scope /ˈstɛθəˌskoʊp/ *n.* [C] an instrument used by doctors to listen to someone's heart or breathing [ORIGIN: 1800—1900 French *stéthoscope*, from Greek *stethos* "chest" + French *-scope*]

stew[1] /stu/ *n.* [C,U] a meal made by cooking meat or fish and vegetables together slowly for a long time: *beef stew*

stew[2] *v.* [T] to cook something slowly in liquid: *stewed tomatoes*

stew·ard /ˈstuɚd/ *n.* [C] **1** (old-fashioned) a man who is a FLIGHT ATTENDANT **2** *also* **shop steward** a worker who represents the members of a union [ORIGIN: Old English *stiweard* "hall-guard"]

stew·ard·ess /ˈstuɚdɪs/ *n.* [C] (old-fashioned) a woman who is a FLIGHT ATTENDANT

stick[1] /stɪk/ *v.* (past tense and past participle **stuck** /stʌk/) **1** [I,T] to attach something to something else using a sticky substance, or to become attached to a surface: *Did you remember to **stick** a stamp **on** the envelope?* | *leaves **sticking to** the windshield* | *The papers were all **stuck together**.* **2** [I] to push a pointed object into something, or to be pushing into something in this way: *The nurse stuck a needle in my arm.* | *There's a nail **sticking through** the board here.* **3** [T] (informal) to put something somewhere: *Just **stick** your coat **on** that chair.*

THESAURUS shove, thrust, dump ➔ SHOVE

4 [I] if something sticks or is stuck, it is fixed and difficult to move: *Hey, this door is stuck.* **5 stick in sb's mind** if something sticks in your mind, you remember it well because it was surprising, interesting, etc. **6 stick your neck out** (informal) to take the risk of saying or doing something that may be wrong, or that other people may disagree with [ORIGIN: Old English *stician*]

stick around *phr. v.* (informal) to stay in a place or wait somewhere for someone

stick by sb *phr. v.* to help and support someone who is in a difficult situation: *My wife has always stuck by me.*

stick out *phr. v.* **1** if part of something sticks out, it comes out further than the rest of a surface or comes out through a hole: *Paul's legs were sticking out from under the car.* **2 stick** sth ↔ **out** to deliberately move part of your body forward or push it out: *Don't stick your tongue out at me!* **3 stick out (like a sore thumb)** (informal) to be easily noticed because of looking very different from everyone or everything else **4 stick it out** (informal) to continue doing something that is difficult, boring, etc.

stick to sth *phr. v.* **1** to decide what to do, say, or believe, and not change this: *That's my story and I'm sticking to it.* **2 stick to your guns** to continue to say or do something, although people disagree with you

stick together *phr. v.* (informal) if people stick together, they continue to support each other

stick up *phr. v.* if a part of something sticks up, it is raised up or points upward above a surface

stick up for sb *phr. v.* (informal) to defend someone who is being criticized: *You'll have to learn to* ***stick up for yourself.***

stick with *phr. v.* (informal) **1 stick with sb** to stay close to someone when there is a risk you could be separated **2 stick with sb/sth** to continue supporting someone or doing something: *Let's just stick with the original plan.* **3 stick sb with sth** to give someone a difficult or unpleasant responsibility: *I'll go as long as I don't get stuck with paying the bill again!* **4 stick with it** (informal) to continue doing something that is difficult, boring, etc. **5 stick with sb** to remain in your memory: *One thing he said has stuck with me ever since.*

stick[2] *n.* [C] **1** a long thin piece of wood that has fallen or been cut from a tree **2** a long thin piece of something: *a* ***stick of*** *chewing gum* **3** a long thin piece of wood or metal that you use for a particular purpose: *a walking stick* **4 the sticks** [plural] (informal) an area that is very far away from a town or city: *a kid* ***from the sticks*** → **get the short end of the stick** *at* SHORT[1]

stick·er /ˈstɪkɚ/ *n.* [C] a small piece of paper or plastic with a picture or writing on it, that you can stick onto something

ˈstick-in-the-ˌmud *n.* [C] someone who is not willing to try anything new, or does not want to go out and have fun

stick·ler /ˈstɪklɚ/ *n.* **be a stickler for rules/punctuality etc.** to think that rules, etc. are extremely important, and expect people to follow them

ˈstick shift *n.* [C] a piece of equipment in a car that you move with your hand to control its GEARS → AUTOMATIC

ˈstick-up *n.* [C] (informal) a situation in which someone steals money from people in a bank, store, etc. by threatening them with a gun

stick·y /ˈstɪki/ *adj.* **1** made of or covered with a substance that sticks to surfaces: *sticky candy* | *Your hands are sticky.* **2** (informal) a sticky situation, question, or problem is difficult to deal with **3** weather that is sticky is very hot and the air feels wet (SYN) **humid** —**stickiness** *n.* [U]

stiff[1] /stɪf/ *adj.* **1** if a part of your body is stiff, your muscles hurt and it is difficult to move: *I've got a* ***stiff neck.*** | *My back was stiff and sore.*

> THESAURUS painful, tender, sore → PAINFUL

2 difficult to bend or move: *stiff cardboard*

> THESAURUS hard, firm, rigid → HARD[1]

3 more difficult, strict, or severe than usual: *He faces a* ***stiff penalty/fine/sentence.*** **4** thick and almost solid: *Beat the egg whites until stiff.* **5** unfriendly or very formal: *The evening was stiff and formal.* **6 a stiff drink** a very strong alcoholic drink **7 a stiff wind/breeze** a fairly strong wind [ORIGIN: Old English *stif*] —**stiffly** *adv.* —**stiffness** *n.* [U]

stiff[2] *adv.* **bored/scared/worried stiff** (informal) extremely bored, etc.

stiff[3] *n.* [C] **1** (slang) the body of a dead person **2 working stiff** (informal) an ordinary person who works to earn enough money to live

stiff[4] *v.* [T] (slang) to not pay someone money that you owe him/her or that s/he expects to be given

stiff·en /ˈstɪfən/ *v.* [I] to suddenly stop moving, especially because you are frightened or worried

sti·fle /ˈstaɪfəl/ *v.* [T] to stop something from happening, developing, or being expressed: *laws that stifle competition* —**stifling** *adj.*: *stifling heat*

stig·ma /ˈstɪgmə/ *n.* **1** [singular, U] a strong feeling in society that a type of behavior or a particular illness or condition is something to be ashamed of: *the* ***stigma attached to*** *mental illness* **2** [C] BIOLOGY the top sticky part of the female structure of a flower, which receives the POLLEN that allows it to form new seeds → *see picture at* FLOWER[1] [ORIGIN: 1500—1600 Latin "mark, mark burned on the skin," from Greek, from *stizein* "to tattoo"]

stig·ma·tize /ˈstɪgməˌtaɪz/ *v.* [T] to make someone feel they should be ashamed of their situation: *Single mothers often feel that they are stigmatized by society.* —**stigmatization** /ˌstɪgmət̬əˈzeɪʃən/ *n.* [U]

still[1] /stɪl/ *adv.* **1** up to a particular point in time and continuing at that moment: *Andy's still asleep.*

S

USAGE

Still is used to say that a situation that began in the past has not changed and is continuing: *He still lives with his parents.*
Always means "all the time" or "every time": *Her house is always clean.* | *I always see him on Tuesdays.*
Yet is used in negative sentences and questions to talk about something that you expect to happen, but which has not happened: *I haven't finished the book yet.* | *Is Mark back from lunch yet?*

2 in spite of what has just been said or done: *Clare didn't study much, but she still passed the exam.* **3** used in order to say that something continues to be possible: *We can still catch the bus if we hurry.* **4 still colder/harder/better etc.** *also* **colder/harder/better etc. still** even colder, harder, etc. than something else: *Dan found biology difficult, and physics harder still.* **5 be still going strong** to continue to be active or successful, even after a long time: *We've been married for 25 years, and we're still going strong.* [ORIGIN: Old English *stille*]

GRAMMAR

Use **still** before a verb unless the verb is "be": *She still wants to go.* | *You're still young.*
If there are two or more verbs together, **still** comes after the first one: *I can still see him sitting there at his desk.*
Still usually comes before any negative word: *The car still isn't ready.*

S

still² *adj.* **1** not moving: *the still waters of the lake* | *Just **keep/stand/stay still** while I tie your shoes.* **2** quiet and calm: *The forest was completely still.* ➔ QUIET¹ **3** not windy: *a hot still day* ➔ QUIET¹ —**stillness** *n.* [U]

still³ *n.* [C] ENG. LANG. ARTS a photograph of a scene from a movie

still·born /ˌstɪlˈbɔrn◂/ *adj.* BIOLOGY born dead

ˌ**still 'life** *n.* (plural **still lifes**) [C,U] ENG. LANG. ARTS a picture of an arrangement of objects, especially flowers and fruit ➔ *see picture at* PAINTING

stilt·ed /ˈstɪltɪd/ *adj.* stilted writing or speaking is formal and unnatural

stilts /stɪlts/ *n.* [plural] a pair of poles you can stand on, used for walking high above the ground

stim·u·lant /ˈstɪmyələnt/ *n.* [C] BIOLOGY a drug or substance that makes you feel more awake and active: *Caffeine is a stimulant.*

stim·u·late /ˈstɪmyəˌleɪt/ *v.* [T] **1** to encourage more of an activity, or to help a process develop faster: *The proposed tax cuts should help to **stimulate** the **economy**.* **2** to make someone excited about and interested in something: *We hope the project will **stimulate** students' **interest** in science.* —**stimulating** *adj.*: *a stimulating conversation* —**stimulation** /ˌstɪmyəˈleɪʃən/ *n.* [U]

stim·u·lus /ˈstɪmyələs/ *n.* (plural **stimuli** /-laɪ/) [C,U] something that causes a development or reaction: *The budget package will give a **stimulus to** the economy.*

sting¹ /stɪŋ/ *v.* (past tense and past participle **stung** /stʌŋ/) [I,T] **1** if an insect or plant stings you, it causes a sharp pain and that part of your body swells: *Jamie was stung by a bee.* **2** to feel a sudden sharp pain in your eyes, throat, or skin, or to make someone feel this: *The antiseptic might sting a little.*

THESAURUS hurt, smart ➔ HURT¹

3 if you are stung by something, you are upset by it: *Pearson was **stung** by her **criticism**.*

sting² *n.* **1** [C] a wound made when an insect or plant stings you: *a bee sting* **2** [singular] a sharp pain that you feel in your eyes, throat, or skin **3** [C] a trick used for catching someone while s/he is doing something illegal: *an undercover sting operation*

sting·er /ˈstɪŋɚ/ *n.* [C] BIOLOGY the point on a creature's body that contains poison, for example on a BEE

sting·ray /ˈstɪŋreɪ/ *n.* [C] a large flat fish that has a long tail like a whip with stingers on it

stin·gy /ˈstɪndʒi/ *adj.* not willing to spend money or share something even though you have enough: *She's so stingy.* —**stinginess** *n.* [U]

stink¹ /stɪŋk/ *v.* (past tense **stank** /stæŋk/ *or* **stunk** /stʌŋk/, past participle **stunk**) [I] **1** to have a very strong bad smell: *The dog's breath stinks!* | *The room **stank of** cigar smoke.* **2 sth stinks** (spoken) said when you think something is bad or unfair: *I think the whole thing stinks.* —**stinky** *adj.*

stink sth ↔ **up** *phr. v.* (informal) to fill a place with a very strong bad smell

stink² *n.* [singular] **1 make/cause/raise a stink** to complain very strongly about something **2** a very strong bad smell

THESAURUS smell, stench, odor ➔ SMELL²

stink·er /ˈstɪŋkɚ/ *n.* [C] (informal) someone who behaves badly

stink·ing /ˈstɪŋkɪŋ/ *adj.* having a very strong bad smell: *a dump full of stinking garbage*

stint¹ /stɪnt/ *n.* [C] a period of time that you spend doing something: *a five-year **stint in** the army*

stint² *v.* [I] SKIMP

sti·pend /ˈstaɪpɛnd, -pənd/ *n.* [C] an amount of money paid regularly to someone such as a priest or student as a salary: *a monthly stipend*

stip·u·late /ˈstɪpyəˌleɪt/ *v.* [T] (formal) if an agreement, law, or rule stipulates something, it must be done: *The contract **stipulates that** we receive 25% of the profits.* —**stipulation** /ˌstɪpyəˈleɪʃən/ *n.* [C]

stir¹ /stɚ/ *v.* (**stirred**, **stirring**) **1** [T] to mix a liquid or food by moving a spoon around in it: *Could you stir the sauce for me?* | ***Stir** the flour **into** the mixture.* → *see picture on page A18*

THESAURUS **mix, combine, blend** → MIX¹

2 [I,T] to move slightly, or to make someone or something do this: *Rachel stirred in her sleep.* **3** [T] to make someone feel a strong emotion: *The killings **stirred** citizens **to** protest.*

stir sth ↔ **up** *phr. v.* to deliberately cause problems or arguments: *John was always **stirring up trouble**.* [ORIGIN: Old English *styrian*]

stir² *n.* [C usually singular] **1** a strong feeling such as excitement or anger, felt by many people: *The nude drawings at the library have **caused/created** quite **a stir**.* | *The movie **caused such a stir** that it was finally banned.* **2** an act of stirring something: ***Give** the soup **a stir**.*

'stir-fry *v.* (**stir-fried**, **stir-fries**) [T] to quickly cook meat, vegetables, etc. in a little oil over very high heat —**stir-fry** *n.*

stir·rup /'stɚəp, 'stɪrəp/ *n.* [C] one of the two metal parts on a horse's SADDLE that you put your foot in

stitch¹ /stɪtʃ/ *n.* [C] **1** one of the small lines of thread where a piece of cloth has been sewn: *tiny stitches in the sleeves* **2** a piece of special thread that a doctor uses to sew together a cut or wound: *Nancy had 14 stitches in her leg.* **3** one of the small circles that you KNIT when you are making a SWEATER **4 in stitches** (informal) laughing so much that you cannot stop: *Her jokes **had** us all **in stitches**.* **5 not a stitch (of clothing)** (informal) no clothes at all: *He stood there without a stitch on.*

stitch² *v.* [T] to sew two pieces of cloth together, or to sew something onto a piece of cloth —**stitching** *n.* [U]

stitch sth ↔ **up** *phr. v.* to sew together the edges of a wound or two pieces of cloth: *The nurse stitched up the cut and left it to heal.*

stock¹ /stɑk/ *n.* **1** [C,U] a supply of something that is kept to be sold or used later: ***stocks of** canned food in the cupboard* | *Their new album is now **in stock/out of stock*** (=available or unavailable to be sold). **2** [C,U] ECONOMICS a SHARE or shares in a company **3** [U] a liquid made from boiling meat, bones, or vegetables, used especially for making soups: *chicken stock* **4 take stock (of sth)** to think carefully about everything that has happened so that you can decide what to do next: *We need to take stock of the situation.*

stock² *v.* [T] to have a supply of something available to be sold or used: *Do you stock camping equipment?*

stock up *phr. v.* to buy a lot of something that you intend to use later: *I need to stock up on groceries.*

stock·brok·er /'stɑk,broʊkɚ/ *n.* [C] ECONOMICS a person or company whose job is to buy and sell stocks, BONDs, etc. for other people —**stockbroking** *n.* [U]

'stock cer,tificate *n.* [C] ECONOMICS an official document that proves you own stock in a company

'stock ex,change *n.* [C] ECONOMICS the place where stocks, BONDs, etc. are bought and sold SYN **stock market**

stock·hold·er /'stɑk,hoʊldɚ/ *n.* [C] ECONOMICS someone who owns STOCK

stock·ing /'stɑkɪŋ/ *n.* [C] **1** a very thin close-fitting piece of clothing that covers a woman's foot and most of her leg: *silk stockings* **2** a large sock that is hung by the FIREPLACE before Christmas to be filled with presents

'stock ,market *n.* [C] **1** ECONOMICS the place where stocks, BONDs, etc. are bought and sold SYN **stock exchange** **2 the stock market** ECONOMICS the business of buying and selling stocks, BONDs etc. or their average value: *She made a fortune on the stock market.* | *The stock market keeps going up.*

stock·pile /'stɑkpaɪl/ *n.* [C] a large supply of something that you collect in order to use it in the future: *a stockpile of weapons* —**stockpile** *v.* [T]

,stock-'still *adv.* not moving at all

stock·y /'stɑki/ *adj.* a stocky person is short and heavy and looks strong: *a stocky policeman*

stock·yard /'stɑkyɑrd/ *n.* [C] a place where cattle are kept before being sold or killed for their meat

stodg·y /'stɑdʒi/ *adj.* boring, formal, and old-fashioned

sto·ic /'stoʊɪk/ *also* **sto·i·cal** /'stoʊɪkəl/ *adj.* not showing your emotions or not complaining when something bad happens to you [ORIGIN: 1500—1600 *Stoic* "follower of the ancient Greek thinker Zeno, who said that happiness results from accepting what happens in life"] —**stoicism** /'stoʊɪ,sɪzəm/ *n.* [U]

stoke /stoʊk/ *v.* [T] **1** to add more wood or FUEL to a fire **2** to cause something to increase: *High economic growth could stoke inflation.*

stoked /stoʊkt/ *adj.* (slang) very happy and excited about something

stole¹ /stoʊl/ *v.* the past tense of STEAL

stole² *n.* [C] a long straight piece of cloth or fur that a woman wears over her shoulders

sto·len /'stoʊlən/ *v.* the past participle of STEAL

stol·id /'stɑlɪd/ *adj.* not showing a lot of emotion —**stolidly** *adv.*

sto·lon /'stoʊlɑn/ *n* [C] **1** BIOLOGY a long stem that grows out from a plant and produces roots where it touches the ground. New plants grow from those roots. **2** BIOLOGY part of the body wall of some very simple animals that grow together in one place, on which new members of the COLONY grow

sto·ma /'stoʊmə/ *n.* (plural **stomas** *or* **stomata** /-mət̬ə/) [C] BIOLOGY one of the many very small

S

holes on the surface of a leaf, that controls the amount of water and gases that enter and leave the plant

stom·ach[1] /ˈstʌmək/ *n.* [C] **1** BIOLOGY the organ in your body that DIGESTs the food you eat: *Sam's **stomach growled*** (=made a noise). | *Don't drink on an **empty stomach**.* ➔ *see picture at* ORGAN **2** the front part of your body, below your chest: *She punched her sister in the stomach.* **3** the ability and willingness to do something unpleasant: *I didn't **have the stomach to** watch him fight.* [ORIGIN: 1300—1400 Old French *estomac*, from Latin *stomachus* "throat, stomach"] ➔ **feel sick to your stomach** *at* SICK

stomach[2] *v.* [T] to be able to deal with something that is unpleasant: *I just **can't stomach** moving again.*

stom·ach·ache /ˈstʌmək,eɪk/ *n.* [C] a pain in your stomach

sto·ma·ta /ˈstoʊmət̬ə/ *n.* BIOLOGY a plural of STOMA

stomp /stɑmp, stɔmp/ *v.* [I] to walk with very heavy steps or put your foot down hard, usually because you are angry

S

stone[1] /stoʊn/ *n.* **1** [U] EARTH SCIENCES rock, or a hard mineral substance: *a stone fireplace* **2** [C] a small rock or a piece of rock: *A few of the protesters began throwing stones at the police.* **3** [C] a jewel: *a ring set with **precious stones*** **4** [C] BIOLOGY a ball of hard material that can form in an organ such as the KIDNEY or BLADDER [ORIGIN: Old English *stan*]

stone[2] *adv.* **stone cold/deaf/dead** completely cold, DEAF, or dead

stone[3] *v.* [T] to kill or hurt someone by throwing stones at him/her

ˈStone Age *n.* **the Stone Age** HISTORY the very early period in human history, when only stone was used for making tools, weapons, etc. ➔ BRONZE AGE, IRON AGE

stoned /stoʊnd/ *adj.* (slang) feeling very excited or very relaxed after taking illegal drugs

stone·wall /ˈstoʊnwɔl/ *v.* [I,T] to deliberately delay doing something or refuse to give information about it: *The union is stonewalling on the contract.*

ston·y /ˈstoʊni/ *adj.* **1** covered with stones or containing stones **2** showing no emotion or pity: *a stony silence*

stood /stʊd/ *v.* the past tense and past participle of STAND[1]

stool /stul/ *n.* [C] **1** a seat that has three or four legs, but no back or arms: *a piano stool* ➔ *see picture at* SEAT[1] **2** BIOLOGY a piece of solid waste from the body [ORIGIN: Old English *stol*]

stoop[1] /stup/ *v.* [I] **1** to bend your body forward and down: *Troy stooped to pick up his pencil.* **2** to do something that other people consider to be bad or morally wrong: *I never thought you'd **stoop so low**.*

stoop[2] *n.* **1** [singular] if you have a stoop, your shoulders lean forward or seem too round **2** [C] a set of stairs leading up to a city house, or the flat area at the top of them

stop[1] /stɑp/ *v.* (**stopped**, **stopping**) **1** [I,T] to not continue, or to make someone or something not continue: *He finally stopped smoking.* | *The rain's stopping.* | *Doctors stopped the bleeding.* | *He's been stopped twice by the police for speeding.*

> THESAURUS **end, finish, come to an end, be over** ➔ END[2]

2 [I] to pause during an activity, trip, etc. in order to do something: *We **stopped for** gas in Louisville.* | *Let's find a place to **stop and** eat.* | *She **stopped to** tie her shoe.*

> THESAURUS
> **have/take a break** – to stop doing something for a short time in order to rest: *Are you feeling tired? Let's take a break.*
> **break** – to stop for a short time in order to rest or eat something: *Should we break for lunch?*
> **pause** – to stop speaking or doing something for a short time before starting again: *He paused for a moment to consider the question.*
> **interrupt** (formal) – to stop a process or activity for a short time: *The war interrupted the supply of oil.*

3 [T] to prevent someone from doing something: *I'm leaving, and you can't stop me.* | *We must do everything we can to **stop** this **from** happening again.* **4 stop it/that!** (spoken) said when you want someone to stop annoying or upsetting you: *Stop it! That hurts!* **5 stop short of sth** to stop before you do one more thing that would be too dangerous, risky, etc.: *Tom stopped short of calling her a liar.* **6 stop at nothing** to be ready to do anything to achieve something you want: *They've said they'll stop at nothing to save the redwood trees.* [ORIGIN: Old English *stoppian* "to block up"]

stop by *phr. v.* to make a short visit to a person or place, especially before going somewhere else: *It was nice of Judy to stop by.*

stop in *phr. v.* (informal) to make a short visit to a place or person, especially when you are going somewhere else: *Let's **stop in at** Gary's on the way home.*

stop off *phr. v.* to quickly visit a place that is on the way to where you are going: *I need to **stop off at** the post office.*

stop[2] *n.* **1** [singular] the action of stopping or of being stopped: *The taxi **came to a stop** outside his hotel.* | *Mrs. Drayton **put a stop to** the gossip.* **2** [C] a place where you stop during a trip, or the short period you spend at that place: *Paris will be the first stop of the tour.* **3** [C] a place where a bus or train regularly stops for its passengers: *This is my stop.* | *the **bus/subway/train stop** at 45th Street*

stop·gap /ˈstɑpgæp/ *n.* [C] a solution, plan, person, etc. that you use until you have a better one: *a **stopgap measure** to deal with the parking problem*

stop·light /ˈstɑplaɪt/ *n.* [C] a set of red, yellow, and green lights used for controlling traffic

stop·o·ver /ˈstɑpˌoʊvɚ/ *n.* [C] a short time between parts of a trip, especially a long airplane trip: *a three-hour stopover in Atlanta*

stop·page /ˈstɑpɪdʒ/ *n.* [C] an occasion when workers stop working for a short time as a protest

stop·per /ˈstɑpɚ/ *n.* [C] a piece of plastic, CORK, etc. that you put in the top of a bottle to close it

stop·watch /ˈstɑpwɑtʃ/ *n.* [C] a watch used for measuring the exact time it takes to do something, such as run a race ➔ *see picture at* WATCH²

stor·age /ˈstɔrɪdʒ/ *n.* [U] the act or state of keeping something in a special place when it is not being used: *the safe **storage of** chemical weapons* | *The furniture is **in storage**.*

store¹ /stɔr/ *n.* [C] **1** a place where goods are sold to the public: *a street lined with small stores* | *a **grocery/book/shoe etc. store*** | ***I'm going to the store*** (=to a food store) *to get some milk.*

THESAURUS

Stores that sell particular types of goods
bookstore/clothes store/record store, etc. – a store that sells one type of goods
grocery store – a store that sells food and other things used in the home
supermarket – a large store that sells many different kinds of food and things people need for the house
bakery – a place or area within a grocery store where bread, cakes, cookies, etc. are made or sold
delicatessen/deli – a small store or an area within a grocery store that sells cheese, cooked meat, bread, etc.
liquor store – a small store where alcohol is sold
drugstore – a store where you can buy medicines, beauty products, etc.
hardware store – a store that sells equipment and tools that you use in your home and yard
nursery/garden center – a place where plants and trees are grown and sold
newsstand – a place on a street where newspapers and magazines are sold
boutique – a small store that sells fashionable clothes or decorations

Stores that sell different types of goods
convenience store – a store where you can buy food, newspapers, etc., that is often open 24 hours each day
department store – a large store that sells many different products, such as clothes, kitchen equipment, etc.
chain store – one of a group of stores owned by the same company
superstore – a very big store, especially one that has many different types of products, or one that has a lot of one type of product

Stores that sell goods more cheaply
outlet store – a store that sells things for less than the usual price
warehouse store – a store that sells things in large amounts at lower prices

People who use or work in stores
customer – someone who buys the things sold in a store
sales assistant/clerk – someone whose job it is to help customers to buy things
cashier – someone whose job is to receive and pay out money in a store

2 a supply of something that you keep to use later: *secret stores of weapons* **3 be in store** to be about to happen to someone: *There's a surprise in store for you!*

store² *v.* [T] **1** *also* **store away** to put things somewhere and keep them there until you need them: *photos **stored in** shoe boxes*

THESAURUS keep, save ➔ KEEP¹

2 to keep facts or information in a computer: *data **stored on** the hard drive*

store·front /ˈstɔrfrʌnt/ *n.* [C] **1** the part of a store that faces the street **2 storefront church/office/school etc.** a small church, etc. in a shopping area

store·house /ˈstɔrhaʊs/ *n.* **a storehouse of information/memory etc.** something that contains a lot of information, memories, etc.

store·keep·er /ˈstɔrˌkipɚ/ *n.* [C] someone who owns or is in charge of a store

store·room /ˈstɔr-rum/ *n.* [C] a room where goods are stored

sto·rey /ˈstɔri/ *n.* [C] a floor or level of a building SYN **story**

stork /stɔrk/ *n.* [C] a tall white water bird with long legs and a long beak

storm¹ /stɔrm/ *n.* [C] **1** a period of bad weather when there is a lot of wind, rain, snow, etc.: *a snow storm* | *a **winter/summer storm***

THESAURUS gale, hurricane, tornado, typhoon ➔ WIND¹ ➔ RAIN¹

2 a situation in which people suddenly become angry and excited: *The changes raised **a storm of opposition/criticism/protest**.* **3 dance/talk/work etc. up a storm** (informal) to do something with a lot of excitement and effort: *Jenny and I cooked up a storm.* **4 take sb/sth by storm** to suddenly become very successful in a particular place: *a new show that's taking Broadway by storm* [ORIGIN: Old English]

storm² *v.* **1** [T] to attack a place and enter it using

S

a lot of force: *Police officers stormed the building.* **2** [I] to go somewhere in a fast noisy way because you are very angry: *Jack **stormed in**, demanding an explanation.*

'storm surge *n.* [C] EARTH SCIENCES a sudden rise in the level of the sea caused by a tropical storm, which results in large amounts of water flooding the land

storm·y /'stɔrmi/ *adj.* **1** with rain, strong winds, snow, etc.: *stormy weather | a stormy day* **2** a stormy relationship or situation is one in which people often feel angry

sto·ry /'stɔri/ *n.* (plural **stories**) [C] **1** a description of an event that is intended to entertain people: *a **story about/of** her father's rodeo days | The movie is based on a **true story**. | a **ghost/detective/love story** | Grandma used to **read/tell** us **stories** every night.*

THESAURUS

tale – a story about things that happened long ago, or things that may not have really happened: *tales of adventure*
myth – a very old story about gods, magical creatures, etc.: *the Greek myths about Zeus*
legend – an old story about brave people or magical events: *the legend of King Arthur*
fable – a traditional story that teaches a moral lesson: *the legendary fable of the race between the tortoise and the hare*
yarn – a long story that is not completely true: *He spins* (=tells) *wonderful yarns about his boyhood and his early career as a sailor.*
narrative (formal) – a description of events that is told as a story: *The book lacks a traditional narrative, and instead goes back and forth in time.*
anecdote (formal) – a short interesting story about a particular person or event: *As I looked through the album with my grandfather, each picture brought an anecdote with it.*

2 a report in a newspaper or news broadcast about a recent event: *The Post published a **story on** his White House visit.* → NEWSPAPER **3** a floor or level of a building: *a **three-story** building* (=with three levels) **4 it's a long story** (spoken) said when you think something will take too long to explain: *It's a long story – I'll tell you later.* **5 to make a long story short** (spoken) said when you want to finish explaining something quickly: *To make a long story short, she got mad and left.* **6** an excuse, explanation, or lie: *Do you believe his story?* [ORIGIN: 1200—1300 Old French *estorie*, from Latin *historia*]

sto·ry·tell·er /'stɔri,tɛlɚ/ *n.* [C] ENG. LANG. ARTS someone who tells stories

stout /staʊt/ *adj.* **1** fairly fat and heavy

THESAURUS **fat, overweight, big, heavy, large, plump, corpulent, rotund** → FAT[1]

2 brave and determined: *a stout defender of human rights*

stove /stoʊv/ *n.* [C] **1** a piece of kitchen equipment on which you cook food in pots and pans, and that contains an OVEN: *There's a pan of rice **on the stove**.* **2** a metal container inside which you burn wood, coal, etc. in order to heat a room: *an old wood stove* [ORIGIN: 1400—1500 Middle Dutch, Middle Low German, "heated room," from Vulgar Latin *extufa*, from Greek *typhein* "to smoke"]

stow /stoʊ/ *also* **stow away** *v.* [T] to put something away neatly in a place until you need it again: *Please stow all carry-on baggage under your seat.*

stow·a·way /'stoʊə,weɪ/ *n.* [C] someone who hides on an aircraft, ship, etc. in order to travel without paying

strad·dle /'strædl/ *v.* [T] **1** to sit or stand with your legs on either side of something: *Nick straddled a chair.* **2** if something straddles a line, road, river, etc., part of it is on one side and part on the other side: *a town that straddles the U.S.-Canadian border* **3** to include different areas of activity, groups, time, etc.: *My research straddles economics and social sciences.*

strag·gle /'strægəl/ *v.* [I] if people in a large group straggle, they move away from the group one at a time: *Travelers were beginning to straggle out of Customs.*

strag·gly /'strægli/ *adj.* (informal) growing or spreading out in a messy uneven way: *straggly hair*

straight¹ /streɪt/ *adv.* **1** in a line or direction that is not bent, curved, or leaning: *Stand up straight! | The bathroom's **straight down** the hall. | She sat there, staring **straight ahead**.* **2** immediately and without any delay: *Why didn't you go straight to the police?* **3** happening one after the other in a series: *He worked 18 hours straight.* **4 not see/think straight** to be unable to see or think clearly: *It was so noisy, I could hardly think straight.*

straight² *adj.* **1** not bent or curved: *a straight line | long straight hair* → *see picture on page 462* **2** level or upright, and not bent or leaning: *Is this sign straight? | straight teeth* **3** honest and direct: *I wish you'd give me a **straight answer**.*

THESAURUS **honest, frank, direct, straightforward, blunt, forthright** → HONEST

4 one after the other: *three straight victories* **5 get/keep sth straight** (spoken) to correctly understand the facts about a situation without being confused: *I can't keep all their names straight.* **6 get straight A's/B's etc.** to earn the grade "A," "B," etc. in all of your school subjects **7 a straight face** a serious expression on your face even though you want to laugh or smile: *How did you **keep a straight face**?* **8** (informal) HETEROSEXUAL **9** alcoholic drinks that are straight do not have any ice, water, etc. added to them **10** (informal) not liking to take risks or do things that are not ordinary, and often following strict moral rules: *"What's his girlfriend like?" "She's pretty straight."*

straight³ *n.* **1** [C] (informal) someone who is HETEROSEXUAL (ANT) **gay** **2 the straight and narrow** a sensible and moral way of living

ˌstraight 'angle *n.* [C] MATH an angle that measures exactly 180° ➔ *see picture at* ANGLE¹

straight·en /ˈstreɪtˀn/ *v.* **1** [I,T] *also* **straighten out** to become straight, or make something straight: *She straightened a picture on the wall.* **2** [I] *also* **straighten up** to make your back straight, or to stand up straight after bending down **3** [T] *also* **straighten up** to clean a room that is messy

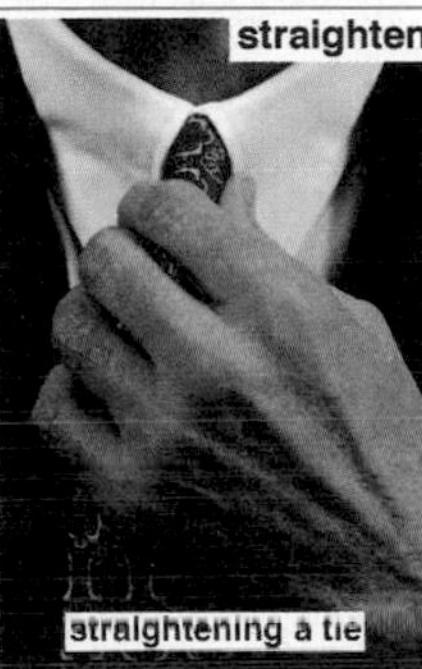

straighten sb/sth ↔ **out** *phr. v.* **1** to deal with a difficult situation or solve a problem: *I'll talk to him and see if I can straighten things out.* **2** to improve your bad behavior or deal with personal problems, or to help someone do this: *He's back in school and getting himself straightened out.*

straighten up *phr. v.* to start behaving well: *You straighten up right now, young man!*

straight·for·ward /ˌstreɪtˈfɔrwərd◂/ (Ac) *adj.* **1** simple or easy to understand: *The task was* ***relatively/fairly straightforward.***

THESAURUS **simple, easy, uncomplicated** ➔ SIMPLE

2 honest and not hiding what you think: *a straightforward response*

THESAURUS **honest, frank, direct, straight, blunt, forthright** ➔ HONEST

straight·jack·et /ˈstreɪtˌdʒækɪt/ *n.* [C] another spelling of STRAITJACKET

ˌstraight 'ticket *n.* [C] POLITICS in an election in the U.S., a vote in which someone chooses the CANDIDATEs of only one particular political party

strain¹ /streɪn/ *n.* **1** [C,U] worry that is caused by always being busy or always dealing with problems: *She's been* ***under*** *a lot of* ***strain*** *lately.* **2** [C] a problem or difficulty caused when someone or something has too much to do or too many problems to deal with: *The flu epidemic has* ***put a strain on*** *health organizations.* | ***strains in*** *their marriage* **3** [U] PHYSICS the physical force or pressure on something that is being pulled, stretched, or pushed: *The rope snapped* ***under the strain.*** **4** [C,U] an injury caused by stretching a muscle or using part of your body more than you should ➔ SPRAIN: *eye strain* **5** [C] BIOLOGY one of the particular varieties of a plant, animal, or living thing: *a new* ***strain of*** *the virus* **6 strains** [plural] the sound of music being played: *the familiar* ***strains of*** *"Happy Birthday"*

strain² *v.* **1** [T] to injure part of your body by stretching it or using it more than you should: *Kevin strained a muscle in his neck.*

THESAURUS **hurt, injure, sprain, twist, pull** ➔ HURT¹

2 [I,T] to try very hard to do something: *She was* ***straining to*** *hear what they said.* **3** [T] to cause problems or difficulties for someone or something: *Tuition costs have strained the family's finances.* **4** [T] to separate solid things from a liquid by pouring the mixture through a strainer or cloth ➔ *see picture on page A18* **5** [I] to pull hard at something or push hard against something: *a boat* ***straining against*** *the wind*

strained /streɪnd/ *adj.* **1** unfriendly, not relaxed, and showing a lack of trust: *a strained conversation* **2** worried and tired: *Alex's pale, strained face*

strain·er /ˈstreɪnər/ *n.* [C] a kitchen tool used for separating solid food from a liquid

strait /streɪt/ *n.* [C] EARTH SCIENCES a narrow passage of water that joins two larger areas of water: *the Strait of Gibraltar*

strait·jack·et, **straightjacket** /ˈstreɪtˌdʒækɪt/ *n.* [C] a special coat for violent or mentally ill people that prevents them from moving their arms

strand /strænd/ *n.* [C] a single thin piece of thread, hair, wire, etc.: *He reached out and brushed a* ***strand of hair*** *away from her face.*

strand·ed /ˈstrændɪd/ *adj.* needing help because you are unable to move from a particular place: *I was stranded at the airport without any money.*

strange¹ /streɪndʒ/ *adj.* **1** unusual or surprising, in a way that is difficult to understand (ANT) **normal**: *strange noises* | *It looked kind of strange.* | ***It's strange that*** *Brad isn't here yet.* | *There was* ***something strange about*** *him.*

THESAURUS

funny – a little strange or unusual: *I heard a funny noise downstairs.*
peculiar – strange, unfamiliar, or a little surprising: *a peculiar taste*
curious (formal) – strange or unusual: *a curious incident that puzzled the police*
mysterious – strange in a way that is hard to explain or understand: *his mysterious disappearance*
odd – strange, especially in a way that you disapprove of or cannot understand: *It seemed like an odd thing to say.*
weird – strange and different from what you are used to: *a weird experience* | *weird clothes*
bizarre – very unusual and strange in a way that is hard to explain or understand: *In a bizarre twist, the judge was later arrested for impersonating a police officer.*
eccentric – an eccentric person is strange and

different in a way that people think is slightly amusing: *an eccentric old man*

2 not familiar: *I was all alone in a strange country.* [ORIGIN: 1200—1300 Old French *estrange* "foreign," from Latin *extraneus*] —**strangeness** *n.* [U]

strange² *adv.* (spoken, nonstandard) strangely

strange·ly /'streɪndʒli/ *adv.* in an unusual or surprising way: *Their son was* ***acting/behaving strangely****.* | *It was strangely quiet.*

strang·er /'streɪndʒɚ/ *n.* [C] **1** someone you do not know: *Never talk to strangers.* | *a phone call from a* ***total/perfect/complete stranger*** **2** someone in a new and unfamiliar place or situation: *a* ***stranger to*** *New York* **3 be no stranger to sth** to have had a lot of experience of something: *an artist who is no stranger to controversy*

stran·gle /'stræŋgəl/ *v.* [T] to kill someone by tightly pressing his/her throat with your hands, a rope, etc. ➔ CHOKE: *The victim was found* ***strangled to death*** *in her home.* —**strangulation** /ˌstræŋgyə'leɪʃən/ *n.* [U]

S

stran·gle·hold /'stræŋgəlˌhoʊld/ *n.* [C] the power to completely control something: *Just a few companies have a* ***stranglehold on*** *the market.*

strap¹ /stræp/ *n.* [C] a strong band of cloth, leather, or plastic, that is used to fasten, hang, or carry something: *a watch strap* ➔ *see picture at* WATCH²

strap² *v.* (**strapped**, **strapping**) [T] to fasten someone or something to a place using one or more straps: *Keller strapped on his helmet.*

strap·less /'stræplɪs/ *adj.* a strapless dress, BRA, etc. does not have any straps over the shoulders

strapped /stræpt/ *adj.* (informal) having little or no money to spend: *I'm a little* ***strapped for cash****.*

stra·ta /'stræt̬ə, 'streɪt̬ə/ *n.* EARTH SCIENCES the plural of STRATUM

strat·a·gem /'stræt̬ədʒəm/ *n.* [C] a trick or plan used for deceiving an enemy or gaining an advantage

stra·te·gic /strə'tidʒɪk/ (Ac) *adj.* **1** done as part of a military, business, or political plan: *the strategic position of U.S. armed forces in Europe* **2** useful for a particular purpose, especially fighting a war: *strategic missiles*

straˌtegic 'value *n.* [U] the importance or usefulness of things or places for providing a country or an army with a military advantage

strat·e·gy /'stræt̬ədʒi/ (Ac) *n.* (plural **strategies**) **1** [C] a planned series of actions for achieving something: *a* ***strategy for*** *raising funds* | *the company's* ***marketing/business/development strategy*** | *Children develop different* ***strategies to*** *learn material such as vocabulary.*

THESAURUS method, way, approach ➔ METHOD ➔ PLAN¹

2 [C,U] the skill of planning the movements of armies in a war, or an example of this: *military strategy* [ORIGIN: 1800—1900 Greek *strategia* "art of leading an army," from *strategos*]

strat·i·fied /'stræt̬əˌfaɪd/ *adj.* **1** SOCIAL SCIENCE separated into different social classes: *a stratified society* **2** EARTH SCIENCES containing layers of earth, rock, etc. —**stratify** *v.* [T]

strat·o·sphere /'stræt̬əˌsfɪr/ *n.* **the stratosphere** EARTH SCIENCES the middle part of the Earth's lower ATMOSPHERE starting about six miles above the Earth ➔ *see picture at* ATMOSPHERE

strat·um /'stræt̬əm, 'streɪ-/ *n.* (plural **strata** /-t̬ə/) [C] **1** EARTH SCIENCES a layer of a particular type of rock or dirt **2** SOCIAL SCIENCE a social class in society

stra·tus /'streɪt̬əs, 'stræ-/ *n.* (plural **strati** /-t̬aɪ/) [C,U] EARTH SCIENCES a low flat type of cloud that usually seems to cover the sky. If a stratus cloud is low enough, it may bring FOG or mist. ➔ CIRRUS, CUMULONIMBUS, CUMULUS, NIMBUS

straw /strɔ/ *n.* **1 a)** [U] dried stems of wheat or similar plants, used for animals to eat or sleep on, or for making things such as baskets: *a straw hat* **b)** [C] a single stem of this **2** [C] a thin tube of plastic used for sucking a drink from a bottle or cup **3 the last/final straw** the last problem in a series of problems that finally makes you get angry, give up, or refuse to accept the situation any more **4 be grasping/clutching at straws** to be trying everything you can to succeed, even though the things you are doing are not likely to help or work

straw·ber·ry /'strɔˌbɛri/ *n.* (plural **strawberries**) [C] a soft sweet red berry with small pale seeds on its surface [ORIGIN: Old English *streawberige*, from *streaw* + *berige* "berry"] ➔ *see picture on page 414*

ˌstraw 'poll *also* **ˌstraw 'vote** *n.* [C] POLITICS an unofficial test of people's opinions before an election, to see what the result is likely to be

stray¹ /streɪ/ *v.* [I] **1** to move away from the place where you should be, especially without intending to: *The plane had* ***strayed from*** *its flight plan.* **2** to begin to deal with or think about a different subject from the main one, especially without intending to: *an article that* ***strays from*** *the facts*

stray² *adj.* **1** a stray animal is lost or has no home: *We took in a stray dog.* **2** accidentally separated from a larger group: *a few stray hairs*

stray³ *n.* [C] an animal that is lost or has no home

streak¹ /strik/ *n.* [C] **1** a colored line or thin mark: *gray streaks in her hair*

THESAURUS line, stripe, band ➔ LINE¹

2 a quality you have that seems different from the rest of your character: *a streak of independence* **3** a period of time when you are always successful or always failing: *The Ducks* ***were on a***

four-game ***winning/losing streak.*** **—streaky** *adj.*

streak² *v.* **1** [T] to cover something with streaks: *Marcia's face was* ***streaked with*** *sweat.* **2** [I] to move or run very quickly: *A fighter jet* ***streaked across*** *the sky.*

stream¹ /strim/ *n.* [C] **1** EARTH SCIENCES a natural flow of water that is smaller than a river: *a clear mountain stream* → *see picture at* RIVER **2** a long continuous series of people, vehicles, events, etc.: *a* ***stream of*** *cars | a* ***steady/endless/constant stream*** *of complaints* **3** a flow of water, gas, smoke, etc.: *a* ***stream of*** *warm air* [ORIGIN: Old English]

stream² *v.* **1** [I] to move quickly and continuously in one direction, especially in large amounts: *Tears were* ***streaming down*** *his cheeks. | People* ***streamed out of*** *the theater.* **2** [I] if light streams somewhere, it shines through an opening: *Sunlight* ***streamed in*** *through the window.* **3** [T] IT if you stream sound or video, you play it on your computer while it is being DOWNLOADed from the Internet, rather than saving it as a FILE and then playing it

stream·er /ˈstrimɚ/ *n.* [C] a long narrow flag or piece of colored paper used as a decoration for special events

stream·line /ˈstrimlaɪn/ *v.* [T] **1** to make something such as a business or process become simpler and more effective: *The city has streamlined the permit process.* **2** to make something have a smooth shape so that it moves easily through the air or water —**streamlined** *adj.*

street /strit/ *n.* [C] **1** a road in a town or city with houses, stores, etc. on one or both sides: *Be careful crossing the street. | the building* ***down/across/up the street***

THESAURUS road, main street, avenue, lane, main road → ROAD

2 the streets the busy public parts of a city, where there is a lot of activity, excitement, and crime: *homeless people living* ***on the streets*** [ORIGIN: Old English *stræt*]

streetcar

street·car /ˈstritˀkɑr/ *n.* [C] an electric bus that moves along metal tracks in the road

streetlight /ˈstrit-laɪt/ *also* **street·lamp** /ˈstrit-læmp/ *n.* [C] a light at the top of a tall post in the street

strength /strɛŋkθ, strɛnθ/ *n.*
1 PHYSICAL [U] the physical power and energy that makes someone strong (*symbol* **force**) (ANT) **weakness**: *She hardly* ***had the strength to*** *move.*
2 DETERMINATION [U] the quality of being brave or determined in dealing with difficult situations: *When she died, I didn't feel I* ***had the strength to*** *carry on.*
3 COUNTRY/SYSTEM ETC. [U] the power of an organization, country, or system: *the* ***military/economic/political strength*** *of the U.S.*
4 FEELING/BELIEF ETC. [U] how strong a feeling, belief, or relationship is: *the* ***strength of*** *her religious beliefs*
5 QUALITY/ABILITY [C] a particular quality or ability that makes someone or something successful and effective: *the* ***strengths of*** *the argument | her father's* ***strengths and weaknesses***
6 SUBSTANCE/MIXTURE [C,U] how strong a substance or mixture is: ***full-strength*** *pesticides*
7 MONEY [U] ECONOMICS the value of one country's money compared to other countries' money: *The yen gained in strength against the dollar today.*
8 NUMBER OF PEOPLE [U] the number of people on a team, in an army, etc.: *At* ***full strength****, the squad has 12 men.*
9 on the strength of sth because of something that persuaded or influenced you: *She was hired mainly on the strength of her ability to translate Russian.* [ORIGIN: Old English *strengthu*]

strength·en /ˈstrɛŋkθən, ˈstrɛnθən/ *v.* **1** [I,T] to become stronger, or to make something such as a feeling, belief, or relationship stronger (ANT) **weaken**: *Her determination to succeed has strengthened. | Family dinners* ***strengthen*** *your* ***ties/bonds/connections*** *with your children.* **2** [T] to make something such as your body or a building stronger (ANT) **weaken**: *an exercise to strengthen your arms* **3** [I,T] ECONOMICS to increase in value or improve, or to make something do this (ANT) **weaken**: *The dollar has strengthened against other currencies. | The trade agreement will strengthen the economy.*

stren·u·ous /ˈstrɛnyuəs/ *adj.* using a lot of effort, strength, or determination: *strenuous exercise | strenuous objections to the plan* —**strenuously** *adv.*

strep throat /ˌstrɛp ˈθroʊt/ *n.* [U] (informal) a fairly common medical condition in which your throat is very sore

stress¹ /strɛs/ (Ac) *n.* **1** [C,U] continuous feelings of worry about your work or personal life, that prevent you from relaxing: *Baxter's* ***under*** *a lot of* ***stress*** *at work. | Stress can cause severe health problems.* **2** [U] special attention or importance given to an idea or activity (SYN) **emphasis**: *He* ***put/laid stress on*** *the need for more teachers.* **3** [C,U] PHYSICS the physical force or pressure on an object: *Fractures form when the rocks are subjected to stress.* **4** [C,U] ENG. LANG. ARTS the degree of force or loudness with which you say a word or part of a word, or play a note of music: *The* ***stress is on*** *the first syllable.*

stress² *v.* **1** [T] to emphasize a statement, fact, or idea: *Herman **stressed that** participation is voluntary.* | *She **stressed the need for** more health education.*

THESAURUS **emphasize, highlight, underline, underscore** → EMPHASIZE

2 [I] *also* **stress out** (spoken) to feel stressed: *Terry's stressing out about his midterms.* **3** [T] to say a word or part of a word loudly or with more force, or play a note of music more loudly: *The word "basketball" is stressed on the first and third syllable.*

stressed /strɛst/ (Ac) *adj.* **1** *also* **stressed out** (spoken) so worried and tired that you cannot relax: *I was stressed out and exhausted.*

THESAURUS **worried, anxious, nervous, tense** → WORRIED

2 PHYSICS a stressed object has a lot of pressure or force put on it: *The stressed rock began to fracture.* **3** ENG. LANG. ARTS a stressed word or part of a word is spoken more loudly or with more force: *The last syllable is stressed.*

stress·ful /ˈstrɛsfəl/ (Ac) *adj.* making you worry a lot: *a stressful job*

S

ˈstress mark *n.* [C] ENG. LANG. ARTS a mark that shows which part of a word is emphasized the most

stretch¹ /strɛtʃ/ *v.* **1** [I,T] *also* **stretch out** to become bigger or looser as a result of being pulled, or to make something become bigger or looser by pulling it: *My sweater has stretched all out of shape.* **2** [I,T] to reach out your arms, legs, or body to full length: *Maxie got up and stretched.* | *Klein **stretched out** his hand to Devlin.* → *see picture on page A22* **3** [I] to spread out over a large area, or continue for a long period: *The line of people **stretched around** the corner.* | *The project will probably **stretch into** next year.* **4** [I] if cloth stretches, it changes shape when you pull or wear it, and becomes its original shape when you stop: *The shorts stretch to fit.* **5** [T] to pull something so that it is tight: *Stretch a rope between two trees.* **6 be stretched (to the limit)** to have hardly enough money, supplies, energy, time, etc. to do something: *Our resources are already stretched to the limit.* **7 stretch your legs** (informal) to go for a walk

stretch out *phr. v.* (informal) to lie down so that you can rest or sleep: *He **stretched out on** the bed.*

stretch² *n.* **1** [C] an area of water or land: *a dangerous **stretch of** road* **2** [C] a continuous period of time: *Nurses are working up to 12 hours **at a stretch*** (=without stopping). **3** [C] the action of stretching part of your body **4** [U] the ability of a material to become bigger or longer without tearing **5 not by any stretch (of the imagination)** (spoken) used in order to say that something is definitely not true: *She's not fat, by any stretch of the imagination.*

stretch·er /ˈstrɛtʃɚ/ *n.* [C] a covered frame on which you carry someone who is injured or too sick to walk

strew /stru/ *v.* (past participle **strewn** /strun/ *or* **strewed**) [T] to throw or drop a number of things over an area in a messy way: *Papers were **strewn all over** the floor.*

strick·en /ˈstrɪkən/ *adj.* (formal) very badly affected by trouble, illness, sadness, etc.: *a woman **stricken by** grief* → POVERTY-STRICKEN

strict /strɪkt/ *adj.* **1** expecting people to obey rules or do what you say: *Her parents are very strict.*

THESAURUS

Other words meaning strict

tough – very strict: *Tough new laws were introduced against the sale of alcohol to minors.*
firm – dealing with someone or something in a determined way and showing that you are not going to change your mind: *It's important to be firm with young children.*
rigorous – checking or testing something in a very careful and thorough way: *Every product goes through a series of rigorous safety checks before it leaves the factory.*
stern – looking very strict and serious: *My father always had a stern expression on his face.*
rigid – strict and difficult to change: *The country has a rigid social system.*
stringent – stringent rules are very strict and have high standards: *The state of California already has stringent controls on pollution from cars.*
draconian (formal) – draconian laws, methods, or punishments are extremely strict: *The authorities had to use draconian measures to deal with the violence.*

Not strict

lenient – not strict and not wanting to punish someone or control his/her behavior: *The younger teachers generally had a more lenient attitude toward their students.*
lax – a lax system is not strict enough and does not work properly: *The report criticizes the lax security at many prisons.*
easygoing – an easygoing person does not care about being strict, and is usually calm and relaxed: *My dad's pretty easygoing and doesn't mind if I stay out late, so long as he knows where I am.*

2 a strict rule, order, etc. must be obeyed: *Gun regulations aren't strict enough.* | *a school with **strict rules/limits/controls*** **3** very exact and correct: *He practices Chinese medicine, so is not a doctor **in the strict sense**.* [ORIGIN: 1400—1500 Latin *strictus*, past participle of *stringere* "to tie tightly, press together"]

strict·ly /ˈstrɪktli/ *adv.* **1** in a way that must be obeyed: *Smoking is **strictly forbidden**.* **2** exactly and correctly: *That is not strictly true.* | ***Strictly speaking**, spiders are not insects.* **3** used in order to emphasize what you are saying: *The drug treatment program is strictly voluntary.* **4** only for a particular purpose, thing, or person: *These bowls are **strictly for** decoration.*

stride[1] /straɪd/ *v.* (past tense **strode** /stroʊd/, past participle **stridden** /ˈstrɪdn/) [I] to walk with quick long steps: *He **strode across** the room.*

THESAURUS walk, march, stroll, amble, trudge, limp, wade, hike → WALK[1]

stride[2] *n.* [C] **1** a long step that you make when you walk **2 make (great) strides** to develop or make progress quickly: *Doctors have **made great strides in** treating this type of injury.* **3 take sth in stride** to deal with a problem calmly without becoming annoyed or upset: *Most children take this type of teasing in stride.*

stri·dent /ˈstraɪdnt/ *adj.* **1** showing determination and a strong opinion in a way that other people may think is unpleasant: *strident attacks on his opponent* **2** a sound that is strident is loud and unpleasant: *her strident voice* [ORIGIN: 1600—1700 Latin, present participle of *stridere* "to make a rough unpleasant noise"]

strife /straɪf/ *n.* [U] (formal) trouble or disagreement between two people or groups (SYN) **conflict**: *a period of **ethnic/political/marital strife***

strike[1] /straɪk/ *v.* (past tense and past participle **struck** /strʌk/)

1 HIT [T] (formal) to hit someone or something: *Paul fell, striking his head.* | *The soldiers were struck by shrapnel.* | *She struck him across the face.*

THESAURUS hit, punch, slap, beat, smack, whack, bump, bang → HIT[1]

2 THOUGHT/IDEA [T] if a thought or idea strikes you, you suddenly realize it, notice it, or think of it: *It **struck** me **that** he was probably nervous as well.*

3 strike sb as sth to seem to someone to have a particular quality: *She strikes me as a very intelligent woman.*

4 WORK [I] to deliberately stop working for a time because of a disagreement about pay, working conditions, etc.: *The dock workers are **striking for** shorter work days.*

5 ATTACK [I] to attack someone quickly and suddenly: *Police fear the killer will strike again.*

6 strike a balance to give the correct amount of attention or importance to two opposing ideas or situations: *It's never easy to **strike a balance between** work and family.*

7 STH UNPLEASANT [I] if something bad strikes, it happens suddenly: *A magnitude 7 earthquake struck near San Francisco.*

8 strike a deal to agree to do something if someone else does something for you: *The company finally struck a deal with the union.*

9 strike a chord to make someone feel that s/he agrees with, likes, or is similar to someone or something: *This idea has struck a chord with voters.*

10 strike a match to make a match burn

11 strike oil/gold etc. to discover oil, gold, etc. in the ground

12 CLOCK [I,T] if a clock strikes or strikes one, three, six, etc., its bell makes a sound one, three, six, etc. times to show what time it is: *The clock **struck four*** (=4 o'clock).

strike sth ↔ **down** *phr. v.*
to say that a law or formal decision is no longer legal or officially accepted: *The Supreme Court struck down a law against flag burning.*

strike out *phr. v.*
1 strike sb ↔ **out** to get three strikes in baseball so that you are not allowed to continue to try to hit, or to make someone do this: *The first batter was struck out.*
2 to start a difficult trip or experience: *They struck out for a better life in America.*
3 strike out on your own to start doing something or living independently
4 (informal) to be unsuccessful at something: *"Did she say she'd go out with you?" "No, I struck out."*

strike up *phr. v.*
1 strike up a conversation/friendship etc. to start a conversation, friendship, etc. with someone
2 strike up (sth) to begin to play or sing something: *The band struck up an Irish tune.*

strike[2] *n.* **1** [C,U] a time when a group of workers deliberately stop working because of a disagreement about pay, working conditions, etc.: *The union decided to **go on strike**.* **2** [C] a military attack: *threats of an **air strike*** **3 two/three etc. strikes against** a condition, situation, or quality that makes it extremely difficult for someone or something to be successful: *Children from poor backgrounds have several strikes against them before even starting school.* **4** [C] in baseball, an attempt to hit the ball that fails, or a ball that is thrown toward the BATTER within the correct area, but is not hit

strik·er /ˈstraɪkɚ/ *n.* [C] someone who is not working because s/he is on STRIKE

strik·ing /ˈstraɪkɪŋ/ *adj.* **1** unusual or interesting enough to be noticed: *a **striking similarity/difference** between the two girls*

THESAURUS noticeable, clear, obvious, eye-catching, evident, conspicuous → NOTICEABLE

2 very attractive, often in an unusual way: *a man with a striking face*

string[1] /strɪŋ/ *n.* **1** [C,U] a strong thread made of several threads twisted together, used for tying things: *We tied a string around the box.* | *a short **piece of string*** **2** [C] a number of similar things or events that happen one after the other: ***a string of** arrests for drug offenses* **3 (no) strings attached** having no special conditions or limits on an agreement, relationship, etc., or having conditions or limits: *They lent him the money with no strings attached.* **4 first/second/third string** relating to or being a member of a team or group with the highest, second highest, etc. level of skill:

the second string quarterback **5 a string of pearls/beads etc.** a lot of PEARLS, BEADs, etc. on a string **6** [C] one of the long thin pieces of wire that is stretched across a musical instrument to produce sound **7 the strings** ENG. LANG. ARTS the people in an ORCHESTRA who play instruments such as the VIOLIN, CELLO, etc. → **control/hold the purse strings** *at* PURSE[1], **pull strings** *at* PULL[1], **pull the strings** *at* PULL[1]

string² *v.* (past tense and past participle **strung** /strʌŋ/) [T] **1** to put things together onto a string, chain, etc.: *Girls were stringing beads to make necklaces.* **2** to hang a wire or string in the air, or hang things on a wire or string, especially for decoration: *a clothesline strung between two posts*

string sb **along** *phr. v.* (informal) to continue to promise to do something that you do not intend to do, especially in relationships: *Jerry's been stringing her along for years.*

string sth ↔ **together** *phr. v.* to combine things in order to make something: *words strung together into sentences*

ˌstring 'bean *n.* [C] a GREEN BEAN

strin·gent /'strɪndʒənt/ *adj.* stringent rules, laws, etc. strictly control something

S

THESAURUS strict, tough, rigorous, draconian → STRICT

string·y /'strɪŋi/ *adj.* **1** food that is stringy has long thin pieces in it that are difficult to eat **2** stringy hair looks like string because it is dirty

strip¹ /strɪp/ *v.* (**stripped**, **stripping**) *also* **strip off** **1** [I,T] to take off your clothes, or take off someone else's clothes: *He stripped and got into the shower.* | *I* ***stripped off*** *her snowsuit.* **2** [T] to remove something that is covering the surface of something else: ***Strip off*** *the old wallpaper.*

strip sb **of** sth *phr. v.* to take away something important from someone such as his/her possessions, rank, or property: *The doctor was found guilty and stripped of his medical license.*

strip² *n.* [C] **1** a long narrow piece of cloth, paper, etc.: *Tear the paper into one-inch strips.* **2** a long narrow area of land: *a strip of sand*

stripe /straɪp/ *n.* [C] a long narrow line of color (SYN) **band**: *a shirt with blue and red stripes*

striped /straɪpt, 'straɪpɪd/ *adj.* having a pattern of stripes: *a blue and white striped shirt*

'strip mall *n.* [C] a row of small stores built together, with an area for parking cars in front of it

strip·per /'strɪpɚ/ *n.* [C] someone whose job is to perform by taking off his/her clothes in a sexually exciting way

strip·tease /'strɪptiz/ *n.* [C,U] the dance that a stripper does

strive /straɪv/ *v.* (past tense **strove** /stroʊv/ *or* **strived**, past participle **striven** /'strɪvən/ *or* **strived**, present participle **striving**) [I] (formal) to try very hard to get or do something: *teachers who are* ***striving to*** *meet the needs of their students*

strode /stroʊd/ *v.* the past tense of STRIDE

stroke¹ /stroʊk/ *n.* [C] **1** BIOLOGY a sudden illness in which an ARTERY (=tube carrying blood) in your brain bursts or becomes blocked: *Since Tom* ***had a stroke*** *he's had trouble talking.* **2** a repeated movement of your arms in a sport such as swimming, or a particular style of swimming or rowing: *the back stroke* **3** an action done to achieve something: *The change is a* ***bold stroke*** *on the mayor's part.* | *Getting those two to work together was a* ***stroke of genius****.* | *He managed to improve his election chances* ***at a stroke*** (=with one sudden action). **4 a stroke of (good) luck/fortune** something lucky that happens to you, that you did not expect **5** a single movement of a pen or brush, or a line made by doing this: *With* ***a stroke of the pen****, the deal was finalized.*

stroke² *v.* [T] to move your hand gently over something: *She stroked the baby's face.* → *see picture on page A21*

THESAURUS touch, feel, rub, pet, caress → TOUCH[1]

stroll /stroʊl/ *v.* [I] to walk in a slow relaxed way: *We* ***strolled along*** *the beach.* —**stroll** *n.* [C]: *We went for a stroll after dinner.*

THESAURUS walk, amble, trudge → WALK[1]

stroll·er /'stroʊlɚ/ *n.* [C] a chair on wheels in which a small child sits and is pushed along: ***a baby stroller***

strong /strɔŋ/ *adj.*

1 PHYSICAL having a lot of physical power: *He was small but strong.* | *the strongest muscles in your body*

2 NOT EASILY BROKEN not easily broken or damaged: *a strong rope* | *The door was solid and strong.*

3 POWER having a lot of power, influence, or ability: *a strong leader* | *a strong army*

THESAURUS powerful, influential → POWERFUL

4 LIGHT a strong light is very bright

THESAURUS bright, brilliant, dazzling → BRIGHT

5 FEELINGS strong feelings, ideas, etc. are ones that are very important to you: *a strong interest in art* | *a strong sense of duty*

6 ARGUMENT a strong reason, opinion, etc. is one that is likely to persuade other people: *There's strong evidence to suggest that he's innocent.*

7 ABLE TO DEAL WITH DIFFICULTY determined and able to deal with problems without becoming upset or worried by them: *Do you think she's strong enough to handle this?* | *a strong character*

8 SKILLFUL good at something: *a strong team* | *Jarvis's performance was very strong.*
9 LIKELY likely to succeed or happen: *He has a strong chance of winning in Florida.*
10 EFFECT having a large effect or influence: *a strong desire* | *He made a strong impression on me.*
11 TASTE/SMELL having a taste, smell, color, etc. that is easy to notice: *strong coffee*
12 RELATIONSHIP a strong relationship or friendship is likely to last a long time: *a strong bond between the two brothers*
13 50/1,000/75,000 etc. strong used in order to give the number of people in a group: *Our staff is over a thousand strong.* [ORIGIN: Old English *strang*]

ˌstrong ˈacid *n.* [C] CHEMISTRY an acid that completely separates into IONS (=atoms with an electric charge) when it is mixed with water

ˌstrong ˈbase *n.* [C] CHEMISTRY a BASE (=a chemical substance that combines with an acid to form a salt) that separates completely into HYDROXIDE IONS and metal ions when it is mixed with water

ˌstrong eˈlectrolyte *n.* [C] CHEMISTRY a liquid that allows electricity to travel through it effectively because it contains a lot of IONS (=atoms with an electric charge)

strong·hold /ˈstrɔŋhoʊld/ *n.* [C] **1** an area where there is a lot of support for a particular attitude, way of life, political party, etc.: *a Republican stronghold* **2** an area that is strongly defended: *a rebel stronghold*

strong·ly /ˈstrɔŋli/ *adv.* **1** if you feel or believe something strongly, you are very sure and serious about it: *I feel strongly that medical records should be private.* | *She is **strongly opposed** to abortion.* **2** in a way that persuades someone to do something: *I **strongly urge/advise/encourage** you **to** get more facts before deciding.* **3** in a way that is easy to notice: *The house smelled strongly of gas.*

ˌstrong-ˈwilled *adj.* having a lot of determination to do what you want SYN **stubborn**: *a strong-willed child*

stron·ti·um /ˈstrɑnʃiəm, -ʃiəm/ *n.* [U] CHEMISTRY (*symbol* **Sr**) a soft metal that is an ELEMENT

strove /stroʊv/ *v.* a past tense of STRIVE

struck /strʌk/ *v.* the past tense and past participle of STRIKE

struc·tur·al /ˈstrʌktʃərəl/ Ac *adj.* relating to the structure of something: *structural damage to the aircraft*

struc·ture¹ /ˈstrʌktʃɚ/ Ac *n.* **1** [C,U] the way in which the parts of something connect with each other to form a whole, or the thing that these parts make up: *the chemical structure of the molecule* | *Paragraphs provide a structure for your writing.* **2** [C,U] the way in which relationships between people or groups are organized in a society or in an organization: *Children need a stable family structure to feel secure.* | *the city's **political/social structure*** **3** [C] something that has been built: *a huge steel structure*

structure² Ac *v.* [T] to arrange something carefully in an organized way: *Structure your essay so that your opinions are supported by evidence.* —**structured** *adj.*: *a **loosely/carefully/highly structured** novel*

strug·gle¹ /ˈstrʌgəl/ *v.* [I] **1** to try very hard to do or achieve something, even though it is difficult: *We're **struggling to** pay the bills.* **2** to fight someone who is attacking you or holding you: *She **struggled with** him, pushing him away.* **3** to move somewhere with a lot of difficulty: *He struggled up the stairs with the luggage.*

struggle² *n.* [C] **1** a long hard fight for freedom, political rights, etc.: *a **struggle for** equality* | *a **power struggle***

THESAURUS **fight, battle, campaign** → FIGHT²

2 a fight or argument between two people for something: *a long **struggle with** Congress over the budget*

strum /strʌm/ *v.* (**strummed**, **strumming**) [I,T] to play an instrument such as a GUITAR by moving your fingers across the strings

strung /strʌŋ/ *v.* the past tense and past participle of STRING

strut¹ /strʌt/ *v.* (**strutted**, **strutting**) [I] **1** to walk in a proud way with your head up and your chest pushed forward: *boys strutting down the street* **2 strut your stuff** (informal) to show proudly what you can do, especially in a performance

strut² *n.* [C] a long thin piece of metal or wood used for supporting a part of a bridge, the wing of an aircraft, etc.

stub¹ /stʌb/ *n.* [C] **1** the short part of something that is left after the rest has been used: *a pencil stub* **2** the part of a ticket that is returned to you as proof that you have paid: *a **ticket stub***

stub² *v.* (**stubbed**, **stubbing**) [T] **stub your toe** to hurt your toe by hitting it against something
stub sth ↔ **out** *phr. v.* to stop a cigarette from burning by pressing the end of it against something

stub·ble /ˈstʌbəl/ *n.* [U] the very short stiff hairs on a man's face when he has not SHAVED —**stubbly** *adj.* → *see picture at* CLEAN-SHAVEN

stub·born /ˈstʌbɚn/ *adj.* determined not to change your opinions, beliefs, etc., because you believe you are right: *a stubborn woman* | *his stubborn refusal to cooperate*

stub·by /ˈstʌbi/ *adj.* short and thick or fat: *his stubby fingers*

stuc·co /ˈstʌkoʊ/ *n.* [U] a CEMENT mixture used especially for covering the outside walls of houses

stuck¹ /stʌk/ *v.* the past tense and past participle of STICK

stuck² *adj.* **1** not able to move: *I tried to open the*

S

window, but it was stuck. | *We **got stuck** in traffic.* **2** not able to continue working on something because it is too difficult: *Can you help me with this? I'm stuck.* **3** not able to get away from a boring or unpleasant situation: *I'm stuck at home all day with the kids.*

ˌstuck-ˈup *adj.* (informal) proud and unfriendly because you think you are better than other people

THESAURUS **proud, conceited, big-headed, vain, arrogant, egotistical, haughty →** PROUD

stud /stʌd/ *n.* **1** [C,U] BIOLOGY an animal, such as a horse, that is kept for breeding, or the use of animals for breeding: *a stud farm* | *The racehorse was retired to stud after a training injury.* **2** [C] a small round EARRING **3** [C] (slang) a man who is very active sexually **4** [C] a small round piece of metal that is put on a surface for decoration: *a leather jacket with silver studs*

stud·ded /ˈstʌdɪd/ *adj.* decorated with a lot of studs or jewels: *a bracelet **studded with** diamonds* → STAR-STUDDED

stu·dent /ˈstudnt/ *n.* [C] **1** someone who is studying at a school, university, etc.: *She has 30 students in her class.* | *Sally's an **A/B/C student*** (=she earns A's, etc.). | *a first-year **law/medical student***

THESAURUS

a business/biology/English etc. major – someone studying a particular subject as his or her main subject at a college or university: *Greg is a philosophy major.*
freshman – a student in the first year of high school or college: *My brother is a freshman at the University of Wisconsin.*
sophomore – a student in the second year of high school or college
junior – a student in the third year of high school or college
senior – a student in the last year of high school or college
graduate – someone who has successfully completed his/her studies at a school, college, or university: *a graduate of Ohio State University*
undergraduate – a student in the first four years of college, who is working for his/her first degree
graduate student – someone who is studying after completing an advanced degree such as a Ph.D. or an M.A.
alumni – former students of a school, college, or university: *the Ithaca College Alumni Association*

2 a student of sth someone who is very interested in a particular subject: *He's obviously an excellent student of human nature.*

ˌstudent ˈbody *n.* [C] all the students in a school, university, etc.

stud·ied /ˈstʌdid/ *adj.* studied behavior is deliberate and intended to have a particular effect on other people: *She spoke with a studied politeness.*

stu·di·o /ˈstudiˌoʊ/ *n.* (plural **studios**) [C] **1** a room where television and radio programs are made and broadcast, or where music is recorded: *a **recording studio** in Nashville* | *a studio audience* **2** a movie company or the place where movies are made: *the big Hollywood studios* **3** a room where a painter or photographer works: *an art studio* **4** *also* **studio apartment** a small apartment with one main room

stu·di·ous /ˈstudiəs/ *adj.* spending a lot of time reading and studying

stud·y¹ /ˈstʌdi/ *n.* (plural **studies**) **1** [C] a piece of work that is done to find out more about a particular subject or problem, and that is usually written in a report: *Several **studies showed** the drug can cause birth defects.* | *a **study on/of** 100 patients*

THESAURUS **research, experiment →** RESEARCH¹

2 [U] the process of learning about a subject: *the **study of** ancient history* | *ways to improve your **study skills/habits*** **3** [C] a room in a house that is used for work or study **4 studies** [plural] the work you do in order to learn about something: *She began graduate studies at Berkeley.* [ORIGIN: 1100—1200 Old French *estudie*, from Latin *studium* "mental effort, eagerness, study"]

study² *v.* (**studied**, **studies**) **1** [I,T] to spend time going to classes, reading, etc. to learn about a subject: *I need to **study for** a midterm.* | *She **studied at** Harvard.* | *I'm **studying English/psychology/medicine etc.***

THESAURUS **learn, pick sth up, get the hang of sth, acquire →** LEARN

2 [T] to examine something carefully to find out more about it: *An accounting firm is studying the problem.* | *Dr. Brock is **studying how** the disease affects children.*

stuff¹ /stʌf/ *n.* [U] (informal) **1** a substance or material of any kind: *What's this sticky stuff on the floor?* **2** a number of different things: *She brought me some books **and stuff*** (=other things). | *People still want decent housing, good health care and a bunch of other stuff.* **3 sb's stuff** things that belong to someone: *You can put your stuff over here for now.* | *I've got to pack my stuff.*

THESAURUS **property, possessions, things, belongings, effects →** PROPERTY

4 all the activities that someone does: *I have a lot of stuff to do.* | *He likes biking and skateboarding and **stuff like that**.* **5** different subjects, information, or ideas: *a magazine with a lot of interesting stuff in it* [ORIGIN: 1300—1400 Old French *estoffe*, from *estoffer* "to provide with things needed"]

stuff² *v.* [T] **1** to push things into a small space quickly: *He **stuffed** some clothes **into** a bag and left.* **2** to fill something until it is full: *a pillow **stuffed with** feathers* | *Campaign workers stuffed envelopes.* **3** to fill a chicken, vegetable, etc. with a mixture of bread, rice, etc. before cooking it **4** to fill the skin of a dead animal in order to make the animal look alive

stuffed /stʌft/ *adj.* **1** [not before noun] (informal) completely full, so that you cannot eat any more: *The cake looks great, but I'm stuffed.* **2 stuffed animal/toy/bear etc.** a toy animal covered and filled with soft material

ˌstuffed-ˈup *adj.* (informal) unable to breathe because you have a cold

stuff·ing /ˈstʌfɪŋ/ *n.* [U] **1** a mixture of bread, rice, etc. that you put inside a chicken, vegetable, etc. before cooking it **2** material that is used for filling something such as a PILLOW

stuff·y /ˈstʌfi/ *adj.* **1** not having enough fresh air: *The room was hot and stuffy.* **2** boring, formal, and old-fashioned: *stuffy lawyers*

stum·ble /ˈstʌmbəl/ *v.* [I] **1** to almost fall down while you are walking: *Scott* ***stumbled over/on*** *the step.*

THESAURUS fall, trip, slip, lose your balance → FALL[1]

2 to stop or make a mistake when you are reading or speaking to people: *He* ***stumbled over*** *the words as he read his speech.*

stumble on/across/upon sth *phr. v.* to discover something or meet someone by chance: *Hubbard stumbled across the notebooks in a yard sale.*

ˈstumbling ˌblock *n.* [C] a problem that prevents you from achieving something: *the main* ***stumbling block to*** *passage of the new law*

stump[1] /stʌmp/ *n.* **1** [C] the part of a tree that remains in the ground after the rest has been cut down **2** [C] the part of an arm, leg, etc. that remains when the rest has been cut off **3** [singular] POLITICS a place or occasion when a politician makes a speech to try to gain political support: ***On the stump****, he talked a lot about health care.*

stump[2] *v.* [T] if you are stumped by a question or problem, you are unable to find an answer to it: *It's a question that has stumped everyone.* | *I was completely* ***stumped****.*

stun /stʌn/ *v.* (**stunned**, **stunning**) [T] **1** to surprise or shock someone so much that s/he does not react: *There was a stunned silence.* **2** to make someone unconscious for a short time by hitting him/her on the head

stung /stʌŋ/ *v.* the past tense and past participle of STING

stunk /stʌŋk/ *v.* a past tense and the past participle of STINK[1]

stun·ning /ˈstʌnɪŋ/ *adj.* **1** extremely attractive or beautiful: *You look stunning in that dress.*

THESAURUS attractive, good-looking, nice-looking, pretty, beautiful, gorgeous → ATTRACTIVE

2 very surprising or shocking: *stunning news*

THESAURUS surprising, shocking, astonishing, astounding, staggering → SURPRISING

stunt[1] /stʌnt/ *n.* [C] **1** something that is done to attract people's attention: *a* ***publicity stunt*** **2** a dangerous action that is done to entertain people, usually in a movie **3 pull a stunt** to do something that is silly or that is slightly dangerous: *Don't ever pull a stunt like that again!*

stunt[2] *v.* [T] to stop someone or something from growing or developing correctly: *Lack of food has* ***stunted*** *their* ***growth****.*

stuntman

ˈstunt man *also* **stunt·man** *n.* [C] a man or woman whose job is to take the place of an actor when something dangerous has to be done in a movie

stu·pe·fied /ˈstupəˌfaɪd/ *adj.* unable to act or think clearly, especially because you are bored, surprised, or shocked —**stupefy** *v.* [T]: *We sat stupefied in front of the TV.* —**stupefaction** /ˌstupəˈfækʃən/ *n.* [U]

stu·pe·fy·ing /ˈstupəˌfaɪ-ɪŋ/ *adj.* making you feel extremely surprised or bored

stu·pen·dous /stuˈpɛndəs/ *adj.* extremely large or impressive: *a stupendous achievement*

stu·pid /ˈstupɪd/ *adj.* **1** showing bad judgment or a lack of intelligence: *How could you be so stupid?* | *a stupid question* | *It was* ***stupid of*** *me* ***to*** *listen to him.* **2** (spoken) used when talking about something or someone that annoys you: *I can't get this stupid door open!* [ORIGIN: 1500—1600 French *stupide*, from Latin *stupidus*, from *stupere* "to surprise extremely, stun"] —**stupidity** /stuˈpɪdəṭi/ *n.* [C,U]

stu·por /ˈstupɚ/ *n.* [C,U] a state in which you cannot think, see, etc. clearly: *We found him in a* ***drunken stupor****.*

stur·dy /ˈstɚdi/ *adj.* (comparative **sturdier**, superlative **sturdiest**) strong and not likely to break or be hurt: *sturdy walking shoes*

stut·ter /ˈstʌṭɚ/ *v.* [I,T] to speak with difficulty because you repeat the first sound of a word → STAMMER —**stutter** *n.* [singular]

style[1] /staɪl/ (Ac) *n.* **1** [C,U] ENG. LANG. ARTS a way of doing, making, painting, etc. something that is typical of a particular period of time, place, or group of people: *He's trying to copy Van Gogh's* ***style of*** *painting.* | *architecture in the Gothic style* **2** [C] the particular way that someone behaves, works, or deals with other people: *Carolyn has an informal* ***style of*** *teaching.* | *Yelling at her students is* ***not*** *her* ***style*** (=is not the way she usually behaves). | *I don't like loud parties – a quiet night at home is* ***more*** *my* ***style*** (=I prefer quiet nights at home). **3** [C,U] a particular design or fashion for something such as clothes, hair, furniture, etc.: *They have over two hundred* ***styles of*** *wallpaper to choose from.* | *Long hair is* ***in style/out of style*** (=fashionable or not fashionable). **4** [U] the particular way you do things that makes people admire you: *You may not like him, but you have to admit that he* ***has style****.* | *an actor* ***with style*** **5** [C,U] ENG. LANG. ARTS a particular set of rules for using words, FORMATting documents, spelling, etc.: *It's not considered good style to use abbreviations in essays.* **6** [C] BIOLOGY the long thin part of the female structure in a flower, that is between the OVARY and the STIGMA → *see picture at* FLOWER[1] [ORIGIN: 1200—1300 Latin *stilus* "pointed stick, stylus, style of writing"]

S

style[2] *v.* [T] to cut someone's hair in a particular way

styl·ish /ˈstaɪlɪʃ/ (Ac) *adj.* attractive in a fashionable way: *a very stylish woman* | *stylish clothes*

THESAURUS **fashionable, trendy** → FASHIONABLE

sty·lis·tic /staɪˈlɪstɪk/ *adj.* ENG. LANG. ARTS relating to the style of a piece of writing or art: *I've made a few stylistic changes to your report.*

sty·lis·tics /staɪˈlɪstɪks/ *n.* [U] ENG. LANG. ARTS the study of style in written or spoken language

styl·ized /ˈstaɪəˌlaɪzd/ (Ac) *adj.* ENG. LANG. ARTS designed, written, or drawn in an artificial style that is not natural or like real life: *A stylized ocean wave is typical of Greek decoration.*

sty·mie /ˈstaɪmi/ *v.* [T] (informal) to prevent someone from doing what s/he has planned or wants to do: *The police investigation has been stymied by a lack of witnesses.*

suave /swɑv/ *adj.* attractive, confident, and relaxed, but often in a way that is not sincere

sub /sʌb/ *n.* [C] **1** (informal) a SUBMARINE **2** (informal) a SUBSTITUTE **3** a SANDWICH made out of a long LOAF of bread filled with meat, cheese, etc.

sub·a·tom·ic /ˌsʌbəˈtɑmɪk◂/ *adj.* PHYSICS smaller than an atom or existing inside an atom: *subatomic particles*

sub·com·mit·tee /ˈsʌbkəˌmɪt̬i/ *n.* [C] a small group formed from a committee to deal with a particular subject in more detail

sub·con·scious /ˌsʌbˈkɑnʃəs/ *adj.* subconscious thoughts and feelings are in your mind and affect your behavior, but you do not know that they exist —**subconsciously** *adv.*

sub·con·ti·nent /sʌbˈkɑntˀn-ənt, -tənənt/ *n.* [C] EARTH SCIENCES a large area of land that forms part of a CONTINENT

sub·cul·ture /ˈsʌbˌkʌltʃɚ/ *n.* [C] a particular group of people in a society whose behavior, beliefs, activities, etc. make them different from the rest of the society: *the drug subculture*

sub·di·vide /ˌsʌbdəˈvaɪd, ˈsʌbdəˌvaɪd/ *v.* [T] to divide into smaller parts something that is already divided

sub·di·vi·sion /ˈsʌbdəˌvɪʒən/ *n.* [C] an area of land for building a number of houses on, or these houses once they are built

sub·due /səbˈdu/ *v.* [T] to control someone, especially by using force: *The nurses were trying to subdue a violent patient.* [ORIGIN: 1300—1400 Old French *soduire* "to lead into bad actions," from Latin *subducere* "to remove;" influenced by Latin *subdere* "to force to obey"]

sub·dued /səbˈdud/ *adj.* **1** a person or sound that is subdued is unusually quiet: *Jason looked subdued after talking to the principal.* **2** subdued colors, lights, etc. are less bright than usual

sub·ject[1] /ˈsʌbdʒɪkt/ *n.* [C] **1** the thing you are talking about or considering in a conversation, discussion, book, movie, etc.: *Bashkiroff is the* ***subject of*** *the book, "For Sasha, With Love."* | *While we're* ***on the subject of*** *money, do you have the $10 you owe me?* | *Stop trying to* ***change the subject*** (=talk about something else)*!* | *A member of the audience* ***raised the subject*** (=started talking about it) *of the president's age.*

THESAURUS

topic – a subject that people talk or write about: *The course covers topics such as interview techniques and giving presentations.*
theme – an important idea that appears several times in a book, movie, talk, etc.: *Man's relationship with nature is a common theme in his work.*
issue – an important subject or problem: *Dealing with climate change is one of the biggest issues facing the world today.*
matter – used when talking in a general way about a subject: *I have little experience in these matters.* | *This is a serious matter* → *see also* ABOUT[1]

2 something that you study at a school or university: *"What's your favorite subject?" "Science."* → UNIVERSITY **3** ENG. LANG. ARTS in grammar, a noun, noun phrase, or PRONOUN that usually comes before the verb in a sentence, and represents the person or thing that does the action of the verb. In the sentence "Jean loves her cats," "Jean" is the subject. → OBJECT **4 subject matter** the subject that is being discussed in a book, shown in a movie or play, etc. **5** SCIENCE a person or animal that is used in a test or EXPERIMENT: *All the subjects were men between the ages of 18 and 25.* **6** ENG. LANG. ARTS the thing or person that is shown in a painting or photograph: *Degas frequently used dancers as his subjects.* **7** POLITICS someone who was born in a country that has a king or queen, or someone who has the legal right to live there: *He's a British subject.* [ORIGIN: 1300—1400 Old French, Latin *subjectus*, from *subicere* "to put under your control"]

subject² *adj.* **be subject to sth** **a)** to be likely to be affected by something: *All prices are* ***subject to change.*** **b)** to be dependent on something: *The deal is subject to approval by the bank.* **c)** if you are subject to a law, you must obey it: *Congress is subject to the same laws as everyone else.*

sub·ject³ /səbˈdʒɛkt/ *v.*

subject sb/sth **to** sth *phr. v.* (formal) to force someone or something to experience something very bad, upsetting, or difficult: *Police subjected him to hours of questioning.*

sub·jec·tive /səbˈdʒɛktɪv/ *adj.* a statement, attitude, etc. that is subjective is influenced by personal opinion or feelings rather than facts (ANT) **objective**

sub·ju·gate /ˈsʌbdʒəˌgeɪt/ *v.* [T] (formal) to force a person or group to obey you —**subjugation** /ˌsʌbdʒəˈgeɪʃən/ *n.* [U]

sub·junc·tive /səbˈdʒʌŋktɪv/ *n.* [C] ENG. LANG. ARTS in grammar, a verb form used in order to express doubt, wishes, or possibility. For example, in "If I were you," the verb "to be" is in the subjunctive.

sub·let /sʌbˈlɛt, ˈsʌblɛt/ *v.* (past tense and past participle **sublet**, present participle **subletting**) [I,T] to rent to someone else a property that you rent from its owner: *I'm subletting the room for the summer.* —**sublet** /ˈsʌblɛt/ *n.* [C]

sub·li·ma·tion /ˌsʌbləˈmeɪʃən/ *n.* [U] CHEMISTRY the process in which a solid substance changes into a gas, without ever becoming a liquid

sub·lime /səˈblaɪm/ *adj.* excellent in a way that makes you feel very happy [ORIGIN: 1300—1400 Latin *sublimis* "raised above the ordinary," from *limen* "doorstep, threshold"]

sub·lim·i·nal /sʌbˈlɪmənl/ *adj.* subliminal messages, suggestions, etc. affect the way you think without you noticing it

sub·ma·rine /ˈsʌbməˌrin, ˌsʌbməˈrin/ *n.* [C] a ship that can stay under water [ORIGIN: 1600—1700 *sub-* "under" + *marine* from Latin *marinus*, from *mare* "the sea"]

sub·merge /səbˈmɚdʒ/ *v.* [I,T] to go or put something under the surface of water: *Many cars were submerged by the flood.* —**submerged** *adj.*: *partially submerged houses* —**submersion** /səbˈmɚʒən/ *n.* [U]

THESAURUS dive, plunge, sink → DIVE¹

sub·mis·sion /səbˈmɪʃən/ (Ac) *n.* **1** [U] the state of being controlled by a powerful person or organization and accepting that you must obey him, her, or it: *The prisoners were starved* ***into submission.*** | *his* ***submission to*** *what God wanted him to do* **2** [C,U] the act of giving a piece of writing to someone so s/he can consider or approve it, or the piece of writing itself: *All submissions must be received by the 15th of March.*

sub·mis·sive /səbˈmɪsɪv/ *adj.* always willing to obey someone and never disagreeing with him/her: *a submissive wife*

sub·mit /səbˈmɪt/ (Ac) *v.* (**submitted**, **submitting**) **1** [T] to give a plan, piece of writing, etc. to someone in authority so that s/he can consider or approve it: *I* ***submitted*** *my plan* ***to*** *the committee yesterday.* **2** [I] (formal) to obey someone who has power over you, especially because you have no choice: *They refused to* ***submit to*** *the kidnapper's demands.*

THESAURUS surrender, give in, concede, yield → SURRENDER

sub·or·di·nate¹ /səˈbɔrdənɪt/ (Ac) *n.* [C] (formal) someone who has a lower position or less authority than someone else: *a manager who has a good relationship with her subordinates*

subordinate² *adj.* (formal) less important than something else, or lower in rank or authority: *a subordinate position*

sub·or·di·nate³ /səˈbɔrdnˌeɪt/ (Ac) *v.* [T] to put someone or something in a less important job or position: *Mothers were expected to subordinate their lives to their children's lives.* —**subordination** /səˌbɔrdnˈeɪʃən/ *n.* [U]

suˌbordinate ˈclause *n.* [C] ENG. LANG. ARTS a DEPENDENT CLAUSE

sub·orn /səˈbɔrn/ *v.* [T] LAW to persuade someone to tell lies in a court of law, or to persuade someone to do something else that is illegal, especially for money —**subornation** /ˌsʌbɔrˈneɪʃən/ *n.* [U]

sub·plot /ˈsʌbplɑt/ *n.* [C] ENG. LANG. ARTS a PLOT (=set of events) that is less important than and separate from the main plot in a story, play, etc.

sub·poe·na /səˈpinə/ *n.* [C] LAW a legal document ordering someone to come to a court of law and be a WITNESS [ORIGIN: 1400—1500 Latin *sub poena* "under punishment" (the first words of the written order)] —**subpoena** *v.* [T]

sub·scribe /səbˈskraɪb/ *v.* [I] to pay money regularly to have a newspaper or magazine sent to you, or for a particular service: *What magazines do you* ***subscribe to****?* | *households that subscribe to cable TV* —**subscriber** *n.* [C]

subscribe to sth *phr. v.* to agree with or support an idea, opinion, etc.: *They obviously don't subscribe to his theory.*

sub·scrip·tion /səbˈskrɪpʃən/ *n.* [C] an amount of money that you pay regularly to have copies of a

S

newspaper or magazine sent to you, or to receive a particular service

sub·se·quent /ˈsʌbsəkwənt/ (Ac) *adj.* [only before noun] (formal) coming after or following something else: *Subsequent investigations did not uncover any new evidence.* [ORIGIN: 1400—1500 Latin, present participle of *subsequi* "to follow closely," from *sequi* "to follow"] —**subsequently** *adv.*: *The charges against him were subsequently dropped.*

THESAURUS next, following, succeeding, later → NEXT[1]

sub·ser·vi·ent /səbˈsɚviənt/ *adj.* (disapproving) too willing to do what other people want you to do —**subservience** *n.* [U]

sub·side /səbˈsaɪd/ *v.* [I] to become less strong or loud: *The storm subsided around dawn.*

sub·sid·i·ar·y[1] /səbˈsɪdiˌɛri/ (Ac) *n.* (plural **subsidiaries**) [C] ECONOMICS a company that is owned or controlled by another larger company: *a subsidiary of General Electric*

THESAURUS company, firm, business, corporation → COMPANY

S

subsidiary[2] *adj.* related to, but less important than, something else: *He played a subsidiary role in the negotiations.*

sub·si·dize /ˈsʌbsəˌdaɪz/ (Ac) *v.* [T] ECONOMICS to pay part of the cost of something: *housing that is subsidized by the government* —**subsidized** *adj.*: *subsidized health care*

sub·si·dy /ˈsʌbsədi/ (Ac) *n.* (plural **subsidies**) [C] ECONOMICS money that is paid by a government or organization in order to reduce the cost of something: ***government subsidies** for small farmers* [ORIGIN: 1300—1400 Latin *subsidium* "soldiers kept in reserve, support, help," from *sub-* "near" + *sedere* "to sit"]

sub·sist /səbˈsɪst/ *v.* [I] to stay alive when you only have small amounts of food or money: *The prisoners **subsisted on** rice and water.* —**subsistence** *n.* [U]: *subsistence farming*

subˌsistence ˈagriculture *also* **subˌsistence ˈfarming** *n.* [U] ECONOMICS farming in which someone only produces enough food to feed his/her own family, often because the land is too poor to produce a lot of crops

subˌsistence eˈconomy *n.* [C] ECONOMICS a TRADITIONAL ECONOMY

sub·stance /ˈsʌbstəns/ *n.* **1** [C] a type of solid, liquid, or gas that has particular qualities: *The bag was covered with a sticky substance.* | *a poisonous/hazardous/toxic substance* | ***illegal substances*** (=drugs) **2** [singular, U] the most important ideas in a document, speech, report, etc.: *The news report said little about the **substance of** the peace talks.* **3** [U] (formal) if something has substance, it is true: *There's **no substance to** his arguments.* [ORIGIN: 1200—1300 Old French, Latin *substantia*, from *substare* "to stand under"]

ˈsubstance aˌbuse *n.* [U] the habit of taking too many illegal drugs so that you are harmed by them

sub·stand·ard /ˌsʌbˈstændɚd◂/ *adj.* not as good as the average, and not acceptable: *substandard health care*

sub·stan·tial /səbˈstænʃəl/ *adj.* **1** large in amount or number: *She earns a substantial income.* | *substantial evidence*

THESAURUS big, large, sizable, prodigious, huge, enormous, vast, gigantic, massive, immense, colossal → BIG

2 large and strongly made: *a substantial piece of furniture*

sub·stan·tial·ly /səbˈstænʃəli/ *adv.* very much: *Prices have increased substantially.*

sub·stan·ti·ate /səbˈstænʃiˌeɪt/ *v.* [T] (formal) to prove the truth of something that someone has said: *The evidence failed to substantiate his claims.*

THESAURUS demonstrate, show, prove, establish → DEMONSTRATE

sub·sti·tute[1] /ˈsʌbstəˌtut/ (Ac) *n.* [C] **1** someone who does someone else's job for a limited period of time: *a **substitute teacher*** **2** something new or different that you use or do instead of what you used or did before: *a sugar substitute* | *There is **no substitute for*** (=nothing better than) *a good diet.*

substitute[2] (Ac) *v.* **1** [T] to use something new or different instead of something else: *You can **substitute** margarine **for** butter in this recipe.* **2** [I,T] to do someone's job for a short time until s/he is able to do it again —**substitution** /ˌsʌbstəˈtuʃən/ *n.* [C,U]

sub·ter·fuge /ˈsʌbtɚˌfyudʒ/ *n.* [C,U] (formal) a trick or dishonest way of doing something, or the use of this

sub·ter·ra·ne·an /ˌsʌbtəˈreɪniən/ *adj.* EARTH SCIENCES under the surface of the Earth: *a subterranean lake* [ORIGIN: 1600—1700 Latin *subterraneus*, from *sub-* "under" + *terra* "earth"]

sub·text /ˈsʌbtɛkst/ *n.* [C] ENG. LANG. ARTS a hidden or second meaning in something that someone says or writes

sub·ti·tles /ˈsʌbˌtaɪtlz/ *n.* [plural] words that translate what the actors in a foreign movie are saying, that appear on the bottom of the screen —**subtitled** *adj.*

sub·tle /ˈsʌtl/ *adj.* **1** not easily noticed unless you pay careful attention: *She noticed some subtle changes in his personality.* **2** subtle smells, colors, etc. are pleasant because they are not too strong: *the subtle scent of mint in the air* **3** behaving in a skillful and intelligent way, especially in order to hide what you are trying to do: *I think we need a more subtle approach.* [ORIGIN: 1300—1400 Old

French *soutil*, from Latin *subtilis* "finely woven, subtle"] —**subtly** /'sʌtl̩-i, 'sʌtli/ *adv.*

sub·tle·ty /'sʌtl̩ti/ *n.* (plural **subtleties**) **1** [U] the quality that something has when it has been done in an intelligent or skillful way: *the* ***subtlety of*** *the wine's flavor* **2** [C usually plural] something that is important but difficult to notice: *The subtleties of the story do not translate well into other languages.*

sub·tract /səb'trækt/ *v.* [T] MATH to take a number or amount from something larger: *If you* ***subtract*** *15* ***from*** *25 you get 10.* ➔ CALCULATE

sub·trac·tion /səb'trækʃən/ *n.* [U] MATH the process of taking a number or amount from a larger number or amount ➔ ADDITION, DIVISION, MULTIPLICATION

sub·urb /'sʌbɚb/ *n.* [C] an area away from the center of a city, where a lot of people live: *We moved to* ***the suburbs*** *last year.* | *a* ***suburb of*** *Chicago* [ORIGIN: 1300—1400 Latin *suburbium*, from *urbs* "city"]

THESAURUS **area, district, neighborhood, slum, ghetto** ➔ AREA

sub·ur·ban /sə'bɚbən/ *adj.* relating to a suburb, or in a suburb: *suburban life* | *suburban Miami* (=the suburbs around Miami)

sub·ur·bi·a /sə'bɚbiə/ *n.* [U] all suburbs in general: *life in suburbia*

sub·ver·sive /səb'vɚsɪv/ *adj.* intending to destroy or damage a government, society, religion, etc.: *subversive activities*

sub·vert /səb'vɚt/ *v.* [T] POLITICS to try to destroy the power or influence of a government, belief, etc.

sub·way /'sʌbweɪ/ *n.* (plural **subways**) [C] a railroad that runs under the ground in cities: *a* ***subway station*** | *We* ***took the subway*** *home.* ➔ *see picture at* TRANSPORTATION

suc·ceed /sək'sid/ *v.* **1** [I] to do what you have tried to do, or to do well in something such as your job (ANT) **fail**: *She gave herself five years to* ***succeed as*** *a writer.* | *Finally, I* ***succeeded in*** *convincing Anna that I was right.* | *skills that help students succeed in the classroom* **2** [I] to have the result or effect that something is intended to have (ANT) **fail**: *Our advertising campaign* ***succeeded in*** *attracting more customers.* **3** [I,T] to be the next person to take a position or do a job after someone else: *Mr. Harvey will* ***succeed*** *Mrs. Lincoln* ***as*** *chairman.*

suc·ceed·ing /sək'sidɪŋ/ *adj.* coming after something else: *Sales improved in succeeding years.*

THESAURUS **next, following, subsequent, later, ensuing** ➔ NEXT[1]

suc·cess /sək'sɛs/ *n.* **1** [C,U] something that has the result or effect that you intended, or the act of achieving this (ANT) **failure**: *We* ***had no/some success in*** *developing a better engine.* | *Jackie's wedding* ***was a big/huge/great success.*** | *Eventually she was able to* ***make a success of*** *the business.* | *Business leaders demanded,* ***without success****, that the government build new roads.* **2** [C] someone who does very well in his/her job, classes, in society, etc. (ANT) **failure**: *He was not much of a* ***success as*** *a comedian.*

suc·cess·ful /sək'sɛsfəl/ *adj.* **1** having the result or effect you intended (ANT) **unsuccessful**: *The surgery was completely successful.* **2** making or earning a lot of money: *a successful businessman* | *a successful movie* —**successfully** *adv.*

suc·ces·sion /sək'sɛʃən/ (Ac) *n.* **1 in succession** happening one after the other: *The team has won four championships in succession.* **2 a succession of sth** a number of people or things that happen or follow one after another: *She's had a succession of rich husbands.* **3** [U] the act of taking over an important job, position, etc., or the right to do this

suc·ces·sive /sək'sɛsɪv/ (Ac) *adj.* coming or following one after the other: *Babe Ruth hit three successive home runs in one game.* —**successively** *adv.*

suc·ces·sor /sək'sɛsɚ/ (Ac) *n.* [C] **1** someone who takes a job or position that was held before by someone else: *No one was certain who Mao's successor would be.* **2** (formal) a machine, system, etc. that exists after another one in a process of development: *The refrigerator was the successor to the ice box*

suc·cinct /sək'sɪŋkt, sə'sɪŋkt/ *adj.* clearly expressed in a few words [ORIGIN: 1400—1500 Latin, past participle of *succingere* "to tuck up," from *sub-* "under, close to" + *cingere* "to put a belt around"] —**succinctly** *adv.*

THESAURUS **short, brief, concise** ➔ SHORT[1]

suc·cu·lent /'sʌkyələnt/ *adj.* juicy and tasting very good: *a succulent steak* —**succulence** *n.* [U]

suc·cumb /sə'kʌm/ *v.* [I] (formal) **1** to stop opposing someone or something, and allow him, her, or it to take control: *Eventually, she* ***succumbed to*** *his charms.* **2** to become very sick or die from an illness [ORIGIN: 1400—1500 French *succomber*, from Latin *succumbere*, from *sub-* "under, close to" + *cumbere* "to lie down"]

such /sʌtʃ/ *determiner, pron.* **1** used in order to talk about a person or thing that is like the one that you have just mentioned: *Such behavior is not acceptable here.* | *"Did you get the job?"* ***"No such luck*** (=I wasn't lucky)." **2 such as** used when giving an example of something: *big cities such as New York, Tokyo, and London* **3** used in order to emphasize an amount or degree: *We had such fun at your party!* | *Mandy's such a nice person.* | *I was in such a hurry that I forgot my purse.* **4 there's no such person/thing as sb/sth** used in order to say that a particular person or thing does not exist: *There's no such thing as a perfect job.* **5 not (...)**

as such used to say that the word you are using to describe something is not exactly correct: *She's not retired as such, she's just taking a long break.*

GRAMMAR

such, so

Use **such** and **so** to emphasize a quality that someone or something has.

Use **so** before an adjective or an adverb: *I'm so glad! | It's so good to see you! | We know each other so well.*

Use **such** before a noun, or before an adjective and noun: *It was such a long way! | He's such a good cook! | She has such beautiful eyes!*

'such-and-such *determiner* (spoken) used instead of the name of something: *They will ask you to come on such-and-such a day, at such-and-such a time.*

suck /sʌk/ *v.* **1** [I,T] to hold something in your mouth and pull on it with your tongue and lips: *Don't suck your thumb, Katie. | Ben was* ***sucking on*** *a piece of candy.* **2** [I,T] to take air, liquid, etc. into your mouth by making your lips form a small hole and using the muscles of your mouth to pull air, liquid, etc. in: *Michael put the cigarette to his lips and* ***sucked in*** *the smoke.* **3** [T] to pull someone or something with a lot of force to a particular place: *A man almost got* ***sucked under*** *by the current.* **4 get/be sucked into (doing) sth** to become involved in something you do not want to be involved in: *I'm not going to get sucked into an argument with you guys.* **5 sth sucks** (slang) used to say that something is bad, unfair, dishonest, etc.: *That movie sucked.* [ORIGIN: Old English *sucan*]

suck up to sb *phr. v.* (spoken, disapproving) to say or do a lot of nice things in order to make someone like you or to get what you want: *She's always sucking up to her boss.*

suck·er /'sʌkɚ/ *n.* [C] **1** (informal) someone who is easily tricked: *Ellen always was a sucker.* **2 be a sucker for sth** to like something so much that you cannot refuse it: *I'm a sucker for old movies.*

su·crose /'sukrous/ *n.* [U] CHEMISTRY the most common form of sugar ➔ FRUCTOSE, GLUCOSE, LACTOSE

suc·tion /'sʌkʃən/ *n.* [U] the process of removing air or liquid from a container or space so that another substance can be pulled in, or so that two surfaces stick together

sud·den /'sʌdn/ *adj.* **1** done or happening quickly or in a way you did not expect: *We've had a* ***sudden change*** *of plans. | Don't make any sudden moves around the animals.* **2 all of a sudden** suddenly: *All of a sudden, the lights went out.* [ORIGIN: 1200—1300 Old French *sodain*, from Latin *subitaneus*, from *subitus* "sudden"] —**suddenness** *n.* [U]

sud·den·ly /'sʌdnli/ *adv.* quickly and in a way you did not expect: *She suddenly realized what she'd done. | Smith died suddenly of a heart attack.*

suds /sʌdz/ *n.* [plural] the BUBBLEs that form on top of water with soap in it —**sudsy** *adj.*

sue /su/ *v.* [I,T] LAW to make a legal claim against someone, especially for money, because s/he has harmed you in some way: *She plans to* ***sue*** *the company* ***for*** *$1 million. | Aaron is being sued for fraud.*

suede /sweɪd/ *n.* [U] soft leather with a slightly rough surface: *a suede jacket* [ORIGIN: 1600—1700 French *(gants de) Suède* "Swedish (gloves)"]

suf·fer /'sʌfɚ/ *v.* **1** [I,T] to feel pain or the effects of a sickness: *Neil suffered a heart attack last year. | Marnie* ***suffers from*** *headaches.* **2** [I,T] to experience a situation and be badly affected by it: *Small businesses are suffering financially right now. | The team* ***suffered*** *its worst* ***defeat*** *in ten years.* **3** [I] to become worse in quality: *Andy's work began to suffer after his divorce.* —**sufferer** *n.* [C] —**suffering** *n.* [C,U]: *The war has caused so much pain and suffering.*

suf·fice /sə'faɪs/ *v.* [I] (formal) to be enough: *A light lunch* ***will suffice.***

suf·fi·cient /sə'fɪʃənt/ (Ac) *adj.* (formal) as much as you need for a particular purpose (SYN) **enough** (ANT) **insufficient**: *Will $100 be sufficient? | They had* ***sufficient*** *evidence* ***to*** *send him to prison.* [ORIGIN: 1300—1400 Latin, present participle of *sufficere* "to put under, suffice"] —**sufficiency** *n.* [singular, U]: *Is there a sufficiency of time to analyze the data?*

THESAURUS **enough, plenty, ample, adequate** ➔ ENOUGH

suf·fix /'sʌfɪks/ *n.* [C] ENG. LANG. ARTS in grammar, a letter or letters added to the end of a word in order to make a new word, such as "ness" at the end of "kindness" ➔ AFFIX, PREFIX [ORIGIN: 1600—1700 Modern Latin *suffixum*, from Latin *suffigere* "to fasten beneath"]

suf·fo·cate /'sʌfə,keɪt/ *v.* **1** [I,T] to die because there is not enough air to breathe, or to be killed in this way: *One firefighter was suffocated by the smoke.* **2 be suffocating** (informal) to feel uncomfortable because there is not enough fresh air —**suffocation** /,sʌfə'keɪʃən/ *n.* [U]

suf·frage /'sʌfrɪdʒ/ *n.* [U] POLITICS the right to vote

suf·fra·gette /,sʌfrə'dʒɛt/ *n.* [C] POLITICS a woman who tried to gain the right to vote for women, especially in the early 20th century

suf·fra·gist /'sʌfrədʒɪst/ *n.* [C] POLITICS someone who tries to gain the right to vote for particular groups of people, especially women or people above a certain age

sug·ar /'ʃʊgɚ/ *n.* [U] a sweet white or brown substance that is obtained from plants and used for making food and drinks sweet: *Do you take sugar in your coffee?* [ORIGIN: 1200—1300 Old French *çucre*, from Medieval Latin *zuccarum*, from

Arabic *sukkar*] —**sugary** *adj.*: *sugary snacks*

sug·ared /ˈʃʊgɚd/ *adj.* covered in sugar: *sugared almonds*

sug·gest /səgˈdʒɛst, səˈdʒɛst/ *v.* [T] **1** to tell someone your ideas about what should be done: *They suggested meeting for drinks first.* | *Don* ***suggested (that)*** *we go swimming.* | *Wilson* ***suggested ways*** *students can improve their study habits.*

THESAURUS advise, recommend → ADVISE

2 to say or show that something may be true: *The article* ***suggested that*** *Nachez might run for mayor.* | *Are you suggesting that I cheated?* → DEMONSTRATE **3** to say that someone or something is suitable for a particular job or purpose (SYN) **recommend**: *Gina Reed's name has been* ***suggested for*** *the job.*

sug·ges·tion /səgˈdʒɛstʃən, səˈdʒɛs-/ *n.* **1** [C] an idea or plan that someone suggests, or the act of suggesting it: *We've* ***had*** *some* ***suggestions*** *on good plays to see in New York.* | *Can I* ***make a suggestion****?* | *They accepted the* ***suggestion that*** *Todd go first.* | *My boss is always* ***open to suggestions*** (=willing to listen to ideas). | *I took the class* ***at*** *my adviser's* ***suggestion***

THESAURUS advice, tip, recommendation → ADVICE

2 [singular,U] a possibility of something: *The police said that there was no* ***suggestion of*** *murder.*

sug·ges·tive /səgˈdʒɛstɪv, səˈdʒɛs-/ *adj.* **1** making you think of sex: *a suggestive remark* **2** similar to something: *The smells from the jars were* ***suggestive of*** *an herb garden in summer.*

su·i·ci·dal /ˌsuəˈsaɪdl◂/ *adj.* **1** wanting to kill yourself: *suicidal thoughts* **2** likely to result in death: *a suicidal attack*

su·i·cide /ˈsuəˌsaɪd/ *n.* **1** [C,U] the act of killing yourself: *Her brother* ***committed suicide*** *last year.* | *Did she leave a* ***suicide note*** (=a note or letter saying why she killed herself)*?* **2 political/social etc. suicide** something you do that ruins your job or position in society [ORIGIN: 1600—1700 Latin *sui* "of oneself" + English *-cide*, from Latin *-caedere* "to kill"]

suit[1] /sut/ *n.* **1** [C] a set of clothes made of the same material, including a jacket with pants or a skirt: *a dark gray business suit* **2** [C] a piece of clothing or set of clothes used for a special purpose: *a* ***bathing suit*** **3** [C,U] LAW a LAWSUIT: *A homeowner* ***filed suit against*** *the county and lost.* **4** [C] one of the four types of cards in a set of playing cards

suit[2] *v.* [T] **1** to be acceptable or right for a person or situation: *It takes time to find a college that will suit your child's needs.* **2** clothes, colors, etc. that suit you make you look attractive: *Short hair suits you.* **3** to have the right qualities to do something: *Lucy's well/ideally* ***suited for*** *the job.* **4 suit yourself** (spoken) used to tell someone that s/he can do whatever s/he wants to do, even though you are annoyed or upset: *"I'm not sure I want to go tonight." "Suit yourself."*

suit·a·ble /ˈsut̬əbəl/ *adj.* right or acceptable for a particular person, purpose, or situation: *This book isn't* ***suitable for*** *young children.* —**suitably** *adv.* —**suitability** /ˌsut̬əˈbɪləti/ *n.* [U]

THESAURUS appropriate, right, suited → APPROPRIATE[1]

suit·case /ˈsutˀkeɪs/ *n.* [C] a bag or box with a handle, for carrying your clothes and possessions when you travel: *She folded up the clothes and packed* (=put) *them in the suitcase.* → *see picture at* CASE

suite /swit/ *n.* [C] **1** a set of expensive rooms in a hotel or large building: *the honeymoon suite* | *a* ***suite of*** *offices in West Palm Beach* **2** ENG. LANG. ARTS a piece of music made up of several short parts: *the Nutcracker Suite* **3** IT a group of related computer programs

suit·or /ˈsut̬ɚ/ *n.* [C] (old-fashioned) a man who wants to marry a particular woman

sul·fur /ˈsʌlfɚ/ *n.* [U] CHEMISTRY a yellow strong-smelling chemical substance

ˌsulfur diˈoxide *n.* [U] CHEMISTRY a poisonous gas that is a cause of air POLLUTION in industrial areas

sul·fu·ric a·cid /sʌlˌfyʊrɪk ˈæsɪd/ *n.* [U] CHEMISTRY a powerful acid

sulk /sʌlk/ *v.* [I] to show that you are annoyed about something by being silent and looking unhappy

sul·len /ˈsʌlən/ *adj.* showing that you are angry or in a bad mood by being silent and looking unhappy

sul·phur /ˈsʌlfɚ/ *n.* [U] CHEMISTRY SULFUR

sul·tan /ˈsʌltˀn/ *n.* [C] a ruler in some Muslim countries

sul·try /ˈsʌltri/ *adj.* **1** weather that is sultry is hot with air that feels wet **2** a woman who is sultry is very sexually attractive

sum[1] /sʌm/ (Ac) *n.* [C] **1** an amount of money: *The city has spent* ***a*** *large* ***sum of money*** *on parks.* | ***the sum of*** *$5,000* **2** the total when you add two or more numbers together: ***The sum of*** *4 and 5 is 9.*

sum[2] *v.* (**summed**, **summing**)

sum up *phr. v.* **1** to end a discussion or speech by giving the main information about it in a short statement: *So, to sum up, we need to organize our time better.* **2** to describe something in only a few words: *The meeting could be summed up as a complete waste of time.*

sum·ma·rize /ˈsʌməˌraɪz/ (Ac) *v.* [I,T] to give only the main information about an event, plan, report, etc., not all the details: *The authors summarize their views in the introduction.*

S

sum·ma·ry¹ /ˈsʌməri/ (Ac) *n.* (plural **summaries**) [C] a short statement that gives the main information about an event, plan, report, etc.: *Read the article and write a* ***summary of*** *it.* | ***In summary****, more research is needed.* [ORIGIN: 1400—1500 Medieval Latin *summarius*, from Latin *summa*, from *summus* "highest"]

summary² *adj.* [only before noun] done immediately without following the usual processes or rules: *The terrorists were responsible for several* ***summary executions****.*

sum·ma·tion /səˈmeɪʃən/ *n.* [C] (formal) a statement giving the main facts but not the details of something, especially one made by a lawyer at the end of a TRIAL: *"If these photos are real," the prosecution lawyer said in his summation, "you are looking at a murderer."* | *a* ***summation of*** *the book*

sum·mer /ˈsʌmɚ/ *n.* [C,U] the season between spring and fall, when the weather is hottest: *The pool is open* ***in the summer****.* | *We're going to Mt. Whitney* ***this summer****.* | ***last/next summer*** (=the summer before or after this one) [ORIGIN: Old English *sumor*]

ˈsummer school *n.* [C,U] classes that you can take in the summer at a school or college

S

sum·mer·time /ˈsʌmɚˌtaɪm/ *n.* [U] the time of year when it is summer

ˌsummer vaˈcation *n.* [C,U] the time during the summer when schools are closed, or a trip you take during this time

sum·mit /ˈsʌmɪt/ *n.* [C] **1** POLITICS a set of important meetings among the leaders of several governments: *an economic summit* **2** EARTH SCIENCES the top of a mountain: *Many people have now reached* ***the summit of*** *Mount Everest.* ➔ *see picture on page A24*

sum·mon /ˈsʌmən/ *v.* [T] (formal) **1** to order someone to come to a particular place: *I was* ***summoned to*** *the principal's office.* **2** *also* **summon up** to make a great effort to use your strength, courage, etc.: *It took her 11 years to summon the courage to leave her husband.*

sum·mons /ˈsʌmənz/ *n.* (plural **summonses**) [C] LAW an official order to appear in a court of law

sump·tu·ous /ˈsʌmptʃuəs/ *adj.* very impressive and expensive: *a sumptuous meal*

sun¹ /sʌn/ *n.* **1 the Sun** *also* **the sun** PHYSICS the large bright star in the sky that gives us light and heat, and around which the Earth moves ➔ *see picture at* SOLAR SYSTEM **2** [singular, U] the light and heat that come from the Sun: *Val lay* ***in the sun****, listening to the radio.* **3** [C] PHYSICS any star around which PLANETs move ➔ SPACE¹ [ORIGIN: Old English *sunne*]

sun² *v.* (**sunned, sunning**) [T] to sit or lie outside when the Sun is shining

sun·bathe /ˈsʌnbeɪð/ *v.* [I] to sit or lie outside in the sun in order to get a TAN (=darker skin) —**sunbathing** *n.* [U]

sun·block /ˈsʌnblɑk/ *n.* [U] a cream that you put on your skin in order to completely prevent the Sun from burning you ➔ SUNSCREEN

sun·burn /ˈsʌnbɚn/ *n.* [U] the condition of having skin that is red and painful from spending too much time in the sun —**sunburned** *adj.*

sun·dae /ˈsʌndi, -deɪ/ *n.* [C] a dish of ICE CREAM, fruit, nuts, and sweet sauce: *a hot fudge sundae*

Sun·day /ˈsʌndi, -deɪ/ (*written abbreviation* **Sun.**) *n.* [C,U] the first day of the week, between Saturday and Monday: *Anna is coming back Sunday.* | *I have to work* ***on Sunday****.* | *We're going to a baseball game* ***next Sunday****.* | *We had friends over* ***last Sunday****.* | *She usually wakes up early on* ***Sunday morning****.* [ORIGIN: Old English *sunnandæg*]

ˈSunday School *n.* [C,U] a place where children are taught about Christianity on Sundays

sun·dial /ˈsʌndaɪl/ *n.* [C] an object used in the past for telling the time. The shadow of a pointed piece of metal shows the time and moves round as the Sun moves.

sun·down /ˈsʌndaʊn/ *n.* [U] SUNSET

sun·dry /ˈsʌndri/ *adj.* (formal) MISCELLANEOUS

sun·flow·er /ˈsʌnˌflaʊɚ/ *n.* [C] a tall plant with a large yellow flower and seeds that can be eaten

sung /sʌŋ/ *v.* the past participle of SING

sun·glass·es /ˈsʌnˌglæsɪz/ *n.* [plural] dark glasses that you wear in order to protect your eyes when the Sun is bright

sunk /sʌŋk/ *v.* a past tense and the past participle of SINK¹

sunk·en /ˈsʌŋkən/ *adj.* **1** having fallen to the bottom of the ocean: *a sunken ship* **2** built or placed at a lower level than the surrounding area: *a sunken garden* **3** sunken cheeks or eyes have fallen inward, making someone look sick

sun·light /ˈsʌnlaɪt/ *n.* [U] natural light that comes from the Sun: *Plants need sunlight.*

sun·lit /ˈsʌnˌlɪt/ *adj.* made brighter by light from the Sun: *a sunlit kitchen*

sun·ny /ˈsʌni/ *adj.* **1** full of light from the Sun: *a sunny day* **2** cheerful and happy: *a sunny personality*

sun·rise /ˈsʌnraɪz/ *n.* [U] the time when the Sun first appears in the morning

sun·roof /ˈsʌnruf/ *n.* [C] a part of the roof of a car that you can open

sun·screen /ˈsʌnskrin/ *n.* [C,U] a cream that you put on your skin to stop the Sun from burning you ➔ SUNBLOCK

sun·set /ˈsʌnsɛt/ *n.* **1** [U] the time of day when the Sun disappears and night begins **2** [C,U] the colored part of the sky when the Sun disappears and night begins

sun·shine /ˈsʌnʃaɪn/ *n.* [U] the light and heat

that come from the Sun: *Let's go out and enjoy the sunshine.*

sun·tan /ˈsʌntæn/ *n.* [C] a TAN

sun·up /ˈsʌnʌp/ *n.* [U] SUNRISE

su·per[1] /ˈsupɚ/ *adj.* (informal) extremely good: *You guys really did a super job.*

super[2] *n.* [C] (spoken) a building SUPERINTENDENT

super[3] *adv.* (spoken) extremely: *a super expensive restaurant*

su·perb /sʊˈpɚb/ *adj.* extremely good (SYN) **excellent**: *The hotel was superb.* **—superbly** *adv.*

THESAURUS **good, great, excellent, wonderful, fantastic, outstanding, exceptional, first-class, ace** → GOOD[1]

ˈSuper Bowl *n.* a football game played once a year in order to decide which professional team is the best in the U.S.

su·per·cil·i·ous /ˌsupɚˈsɪliəs/ *adj.* (formal, disapproving) behaving as if you think that other people are less important than you: *She cast a supercilious glance in my direction.*

su·per·fi·cial /ˌsupɚˈfɪʃəl/ *adj.* **1** based only on the first things you notice, not on complete knowledge: *a superficial understanding of physics* **2** affecting only the surface of your skin or the outside part of something, and therefore not serious: *She had some superficial cuts on her arm.* **3** (disapproving) someone who is superficial does not think about things that are serious or important (SYN) **shallow** [ORIGIN: 1300—1400 Late Latin *superficialis*, from Latin *superficies* "surface," from *super-* "above, over" + *facies* "face"] **—superficially** *adv.*

su·per·flu·ous /sʊˈpɚfluəs/ *adj.* (formal) more than is needed or wanted (SYN) **unnecessary**: *superfluous details*

su·per·he·ro /ˈsupɚˌhɪro/ *n.* (plural **superheroes**) [C] a character in a COMIC BOOK, movie, etc. who uses special powers, such as great strength or the ability to fly, to help people

su·per·high·way /ˌsupɚˈhaɪweɪ/ *n.* [C] a very large road on which you can drive fast for long distances

su·per·hu·man /ˌsupɚˈhyumən◂/ *adj.* using powers that are much greater than those of ordinary people: *a* ***superhuman effort*** *to finish the job*

su·per·im·pose /ˌsupɚɪmˈpoʊz/ *v.* [T] to put one picture, image, or photograph on top of another so that both can be partly seen: *The picture had Mary's head superimposed on Greg's body.* **—superimposition** /ˌsupɚɪmpəˈzɪʃən/ *n.* [U]

su·per·in·tend·ent /ˌsupɚɪnˈtɛndənt/ *n.* [C] **1** someone who is responsible for all the schools in a particular area of the U.S. **2** someone who takes care of an apartment building **3** someone who is responsible for a place, job, activity, etc.

su·pe·ri·or[1] /səˈpɪriɚ, sʊ-/ *adj.* **1** better than other similar people or things (ANT) **inferior**: *I believe Matisse's work is* ***superior to*** *Picasso's.* ▸Don't say "superior than."◂ **2** extremely good in quality: *superior wines* **3** (disapproving) showing that you think you are better than other people: *She had that superior tone of voice.* [ORIGIN: 1300—1400 Old French *superieur*, from Latin *superior* "further above"]

superior[2] *n.* [C] someone who has a higher rank or position than you in a job: *I'll have to discuss it with my superiors.*

Suˌperior ˈCourt *n.* [C,U] LAW a law court that has more authority than other courts in a particular area

su·pe·ri·o·ri·ty /səˌpɪriˈɔrət̬i, -ˈɑr-/ *n.* [U] **1** the quality of being better than other people or things: *the country's military* ***superiority over*** *its neighbors* **2** (disapproving) an attitude that shows you think you are better than other people: *Janet always spoke with an air of superiority.*

su·per·la·tive[1] /səˈpɚlət̬ɪv, sʊ-/ *adj.* excellent: *superlative views of the city*

superlative[2] *n.* **the superlative** ENG. LANG. ARTS in grammar, the form of an adjective or adverb that shows the highest degree of a particular quality. For example, "fastest" is the superlative of "fast".

su·per·mar·ket /ˈsupɚˌmɑrkɪt/ *n.* [C] a very large store that sells many different kinds of food and things people need for the house → GROCERY STORE

su·per·mod·el /ˈsupɚˌmɑdl/ *n.* [C] a very famous fashion model

su·per·nat·u·ral /ˌsupɚˈnætʃərəl◂, -tʃrəl◂/ *n.* **the supernatural** events, powers, abilities, or creatures that are impossible to explain by science or natural causes **—supernatural** *adj.*: *supernatural powers*

su·per·no·va /ˌsupɚˈnoʊvə/ *n.* (plural **supernovas** *or* **supernovae** /-vi/) [C] PHYSICS a very large, very bright exploding star

sup·er·pow·er /ˈsupɚˌpaʊɚ/ *n.* [C] POLITICS a country that has very great military and political power

su·per·sede /ˌsupɚˈsid/ *v.* [T] to replace something that is older or less effective with something new or better: *TV had superseded radio by the 1960s.*

su·per·son·ic /ˌsupɚˈsɑnɪk◂/ *adj.* faster than the speed of sound: *supersonic jets*

su·per·star /ˈsupɚˌstɑr/ *n.* [C] an extremely famous performer, especially a musician or movie actor

su·per·sti·tion /ˌsupɚˈstɪʃən/ *n.* [C,U] (disapproving) a belief that some objects or actions are lucky and some are unlucky or cause particular results [ORIGIN: 1400—1500 Old French, Latin *superstitio*, from *superstes* "standing over someone," from *super-* "above, over" + *stare* "to stand"]

su·per·sti·tious /ˌsupɚˈstɪʃəs/ *adj.* (disapproving) influenced by superstitions

su·per·struc·ture /ˈsupɚˌstrʌktʃɚ/ *n.* [singular, U] a structure that is built on top of the main part of something such as a ship or building

su·per·vise /ˈsupɚˌvaɪz/ *v.* [I,T] to be in charge of an activity or person, and make sure that things are done in the correct way: *Griffin closely supervised the research.* **—supervision** /ˌsupɚˈvɪʒən/ *n.* [U]: *working **under supervision***

su·per·vis·or /ˈsupɚˌvaɪzɚ/ *n.* [C] someone who supervises an activity or a person **—supervisory** /ˌsupɚˈvaɪzəri/ *adj.*: *a supervisory role*

THESAURUS **boss, manager, head, foreman, forewoman** → BOSS¹

sup·per /ˈsʌpɚ/ *n.* [C] the meal that is eaten in the early evening SYN **dinner**: *What's **for supper*** (=what will we eat)*?* [ORIGIN: 1200—1300 Old French *souper*]

S

sup·plant /səˈplænt/ *v.* [T] (formal) to take the place of another person or thing: *The old factories have all been supplanted by new high-tech industries.*

sup·ple /ˈsʌpəl/ *adj.* able to bend and move easily [ORIGIN: 1200—1300 Old French *souple*, from Latin *supplex* "bending under, willing to obey"]

sup·ple·ment¹ /ˈsʌpləmənt/ Ac *n.* [C] **1** something that is added to something else to improve it SYN **addition**: *vitamin supplements* | *For doing the extra training, he is paid a **supplement to** his base salary.* **2** an additional part of something such as a newspaper, magazine, etc.: *the Sunday supplement* [ORIGIN: 1300—1400 Latin *supplementum*, from *supplere* "to fill up, supplement, supply," from *sub-* "up" + *plere* "to fill"]

sup·ple·ment² /ˈsʌpləˌmɛnt/ Ac *v.* [T] to add something, especially to what you earn or eat, in order to improve it: *He took a night job to supplement their income.* | *They **supplemented** their diet **by** catching fish.*

sup·ple·men·tary /ˌsʌpləˈmɛntri, -ˈmɛntəri/ *also* **sup·ple·men·tal** /-ˈmɛntl/ *adj.* additional: *supplementary vitamins* → MORE²

ˌsupplementary ˈangles *n.* [plural] MATH a pair of angles whose total is 180 degrees

sup·pli·er /səˈplaɪɚ/ *n.* [C] a company that provides a particular product: *medical suppliers*

sup·ply¹ /səˈplaɪ/ *n.* (plural **supplies**) **1** [C,U] ECONOMICS an amount of something that is available to be sold or bought, or the process of providing this → DEMAND: *the nation's fuel supplies* | *Demand for the new model is outstripping supply.* **2** [C,U] an amount of something that is available to be used: *the **supply of** oxygen **to** the brain* | *an **ample/plentiful/endless etc. supply of cash*** **3 supplies** [plural] food, clothes, and things that are necessary for daily life, especially for a particular period: *Emergency supplies are being sent to the flooded region.* **4 gas/electricity/water etc. supply** a system that is used to supply gas, electricity, water, etc. → **be in short supply** *at* SHORT¹

supply² *v.* (**supplied**, **supplies**) [T] to provide people with something that they need or want, especially regularly over a long time: *Workers are **supplied with** masks and special clothing.* | *He refused to **supply** any information **to** the police.*

supˌply and deˈmand *n.* [U] ECONOMICS the relationship between the amount of goods or services that are for sale and the amount that people want to buy, in a way that influences prices → LAW OF DEMAND, LAW OF SUPPLY

sup·port¹ /səˈpɔrt/ *v.* [T] **1** to say that you agree with an idea, group, person, etc. and want him, her, or it to succeed: *I don't support any one political party.* | *We need to **support** teachers **in** their aims.* **2** to help and encourage someone: *I appreciate your supporting me during my divorce.* **3** to provide enough money for someone to have all the things s/he needs: *I **have** a wife and two children **to support**.* | *You've got to learn to **support yourself**.* **4** to hold the weight of something in order to prevent it from falling: *The bridge is supported by two columns.* **5** to show or prove that something is true: *Is there enough data to support the theory?*

support² *n.* **1** [U] approval and encouragement for a person, idea, plan, etc.: *There is a lot of **support for** the war.* | *Many people have **given** us **support** in our campaign.* **2** [U] money given to a person or organization in order to help pay for the cost of something: *He provides **financial support** to his ex-wife.* **3** [U] sympathy and help that you give to someone: *Thanks for all your support.* **4** [C,U] an object that holds up something else

sup·port·er /səˈpɔrt̬ɚ/ *n.* [C] someone who supports a particular person, group, or plan: ***supporters of** the governor*

supˈport group *n.* [C] a group of people who meet to help each other with a particular problem, for example ALCOHOLISM

sup·port·ing /səˈpɔrt̬ɪŋ/ *adj.* **supporting actor/part/role etc.** an actor who has a small part in a movie or play, or the part that they act

sup·port·ive /səˈpɔrt̬ɪv/ *adj.* giving help or encouragement: *All the team members are very **supportive of** each other.*

sup·pose /səˈpouz/ *v.* [T] **1 be supposed to do/be sth a)** used in order to say what someone should or should not do, especially because of official rules: *You're not supposed to smoke in here.* **b)** used in order to say what is expected or intended to happen, especially when it does not happen: *The checks were supposed to arrive two weeks ago.* **c)** used in order to say that something is believed to be true by many people: *This is supposed to be the best Chinese restaurant in town.*

SPOKEN PHRASES

2 I suppose **a)** used in order to say that you think something is probably true, although you are not sure: *I **suppose (that)** you're right.* **b)** used when you are agreeing to let someone do something, especially when you do not really want him/her to do it: *"Can we come with you?" "**I suppose so.**"* **c)** used when saying in an angry way that you think something is true: *I **suppose (that)** you thought that was funny!* **3 suppose/supposing** used in order to ask someone to imagine what might happen: *Suppose you do get the job. Who'd take care of the kids?* **4 what's that supposed to mean?** said when you are annoyed by what someone has just said: *"I'll keep your idea in mind." "Keep it in mind! What's that supposed to mean?"* **5 do you suppose (that)...?** used in order to ask someone's opinion about something: *Do you suppose people will ever live on Mars?*

sup·posed /sə'poʊzd/ *adj.* used in order to say that what you are talking about is believed to be true, but you do not believe or agree with it yourself: *the supposed link between violent movies and crime*

sup·pos·ed·ly /sə'poʊzɪdli/ *adv.* used when saying what other people say or believe is true, especially when you do not think they are right: *He comes from a very wealthy family, supposedly.* | *How could a supposedly intelligent person make so many mistakes?*

sup·po·si·tion /ˌsʌpə'zɪʃən/ *n.* [C,U] (formal) something that you think is true even though you are not certain and cannot prove it

sup·press /sə'prɛs/ *v.* [T] **1** to stop people from opposing the government, especially by using force: *The army has suppressed the revolt.* **2** to control a feeling, so that you do not show it: *Andy could barely **suppress** his **anger**.* **3** to prevent important information or opinions from becoming known: *His lawyer suppressed some of the evidence.* —**suppression** /sə'prɛʃən/ *n.* [U]

su·prem·a·cy /sə'prɛməsi, sʊ-/ *n.* [U] a situation in which a group or idea is more powerful or advanced than anything else

su·preme /sə'prim, sʊ-/ *adj.* **1** having the highest position of power, importance, or influence: *the supreme commander of the fleet* **2** [only before noun] the greatest possible: *He made a **supreme effort**.*

Suˌpreme 'Court *n.* **the Supreme Court** LAW the court of law with the most authority in the U.S.

su·preme·ly /sə'primli, sʊ-/ *adv.* extremely: *a **supremely confident** athlete*

sur·charge /'sɚtʃɑrdʒ/ *n.* [C] money that you have to pay in addition to the basic price of something

sure[1] /ʃʊr, ʃɚ/ *adj.* **1** [not before noun] certain about something: *"That's Sarah's cousin." "Are you sure?"* | *I'm **sure (that)** I had the keys when we left the house.* | *I'm **not sure what** happened.* | *Are you always so **sure about** everything?*

THESAURUS

certain – completely sure: *I'm certain that I turned off the stove.* | *It now seems certain that the Earth's climate is starting to change.*
convinced – completely sure that something is true, especially when you cannot prove it but you have strong feelings about it: *She was convinced that her son was innocent.*
confident – sure that something good will happen, or that you will be able to achieve what you want: *We're confident that we're going to win.*
satisfied – sure that something is true, so that you have enough information to make a decision: *The insurance company needed to be fully satisfied that the fire had started accidentally.*
positive – completely sure – used especially when other people seem doubtful: *Are you positive about that?*
have no doubt – to be so certain about something that there are no doubts in your mind: *I have no doubt that he will be found.*
without (a) doubt – used when saying that you are completely sure about something: *Tiger Woods is without doubt one of the greatest golfers of all time.*

2 make sure (that) **a)** to check that something is true or that something has been done: *He called to make sure that we got home okay.* **b)** to do something so that you can be certain of the result: *Make sure you get there early.* **3** certain to happen or be true: *He's **sure to** say something stupid.* | *Investing in the stock market is not **a sure thing*** (=it is risky). **4 be sure of sth** to be certain to get something or certain that something will happen: *The Giants are now sure of a place in the playoffs.* **5 sure of yourself** confident about your own abilities and opinions **6 for sure** (informal) **a)** certainly: *I think he's married, but I don't know for sure.* **b)** used in order to emphasize that something is certain: *We'll always need teachers – **that's for sure**.* **7 sure thing** (spoken) said in order to agree to something: *"See you Friday." "Yeah, sure thing."* [ORIGIN: 1300—1400 Old French *sur*, from Latin *securus*, from *se* "without" + *cura* "care"]

sure[2] *adv.* **1 sure enough** (informal) used in order to say that something happened that you expected to happen: *Sure enough, we got lost.*

SPOKEN PHRASES

2 said in order to say yes to someone: *"Can I read your paper?" "Sure."* **3** used as a way of replying when someone thanks you: *"Hey, thanks for your help." "Sure."* **4** said in order to emphasize a statement SYN **certainly**: *It sure is hot out here.* **5** used in order to admit that something is true, before you say something very different: *Sure, he's cute, but I'm still not interested.*

S

sure·ly /ˈʃʊrli, ˈʃɚli/ *adv.* **1** used in order to show that you are surprised at something: *Surely you're not leaving so soon?* **2** used in order to show that you think something must be true: *This will surely result in more problems.*

sur·e·ty /ˈʃʊrəṭi/ *n.* (plural **sureties**) **1** [C,U] LAW money that someone gives as a promise that someone else will come to a court of law. If the person does not come to the court, the person who pays the surety loses some or all of the money. ➔ BAIL **2** [C] ECONOMICS someone who will pay a debt, go to court, etc. if someone else fails to do so

surf¹ /sɚf/ *v.* [I,T] **1** to ride on ocean waves standing on a special board **2 surf the Internet/Net/Web** IT to look quickly at different places on the Internet for information that interests you ➔ INTERNET —**surfer** *n.* [C] —**surfing** *n.* [U]: *Didn't you **go surfing** at Ventura?* ➔ *see picture on page A17*, **channel surf** *at* CHANNEL¹

surf² *n.* [U] the white part that forms on the top of waves as they move toward the shore

sur·face¹ /ˈsɚfəs/ *n.* [C] **1** the outside or top layer of something: *the Earth's surface* | *leaves floating **on the surface of** the lake* **2 the surface** the qualities that someone or something seems to have until you learn more about him, her, or it: ***On the surface** she seems happy enough.* | *I sensed a lot of tension **below/beneath the surface**.* **3** a flat area, for example on top of a cupboard, on which you can work: *a cleaner for all your kitchen surfaces* [ORIGIN: 1600—1700 French *sur-* "above" + *face* "face"]

surface² *v.* **1** [I] to become known: *Rumors have **begun to surface** in the press.* **2** [I] to appear again after being hidden or absent: *Three years later he surfaced again.* **3** [I] to rise to the surface of water: *Whales were surfacing near our boat.* **4** [T] to put a surface on a road

ˌsurface ˈtension *n.* [U] PHYSICS the way the MOLECULES in the surface of a liquid stick together so that the surface is held together

surf·board /ˈsɚfbɔrd/ *n.* [C] a long special board that you stand on to ride on ocean waves

sur·feit /ˈsɚfɪt/ *n.* **a surfeit of sth** (formal) an amount of something that is too large or more than you need (SYN) **excess**: *The world already has a surfeit of mediocre pianists.*

surge¹ /sɚdʒ/ *v.* [I] **1** to suddenly move very quickly in a particular direction: *The crowd **surged forward**.* **2** *also* **surge up** if an emotion surges or surges up, you begin to feel it very strongly: *Rage surged up inside her.*

surge² *n.* [C] **1** a sudden large increase in something: *a **surge of** excitement* | *a **surge in** oil prices* **2** a sudden movement of a lot of people

sur·geon /ˈsɚdʒən/ *n.* [C] a doctor who does operations in a hospital [ORIGIN: 1300—1400 Anglo-French *surgien*, from Old French *cirurgie*, from Latin, from Greek *cheirourgos* "working with the hand"]

S

THESAURUS **doctor, physician, specialist, pediatrician** ➔ DOCTOR¹

sur·ger·y /ˈsɚdʒəri/ *n.* (plural **surgeries**) **1** [U] medical treatment in which a doctor cuts open your body to fix or remove something inside: *heart surgery* | *Jenny is **having surgery** tomorrow.* **2** [C,U] the place where operations are done in a hospital, or the process of performing surgery: *Dr. Flint is **in surgery** right now.*

sur·gi·cal /ˈsɚdʒɪkəl/ *adj.* relating to or used for medical operations: *surgical gloves*

sur·ly /ˈsɚli/ *adj.* unfriendly and rude [ORIGIN: 1500—1600 *sirly* "like a lord, proud and grand" (14—17 centuries), from *sir*]

sur·mise /sɚˈmaɪz/ *v.* [T] (formal) to guess that something is true, using the information you have

sur·mount /sɚˈmaʊnt/ *v.* [T] (formal) to succeed in dealing with a problem or difficulty (SYN) **overcome**

sur·name /ˈsɚneɪm/ *n.* [C] a LAST NAME

sur·pass /sɚˈpæs/ *v.* [T] to be better or greater than someone or something else: *He surpassed the previous record by 11 seconds.* | *The trip **surpassed** all our **expectations*** (=it was better than we hoped it would be).

sur·plus¹ /ˈsɚplʌs/ *n.* [C,U] **1** more of something than is needed or used: *a **surplus of** goods* **2** ECONOMICS money that a country or company has after it has paid for the things it needs (ANT) **deficit**: *a budget surplus*

surplus² *adj.* more than what is needed or used: *surplus corn*

sur·prise¹ /sɚˈpraɪz, səˈpraɪz/ *n.* **1** [U] the feeling you have when something unexpected or unusual happens: *Bill looked at us **in surprise**.* | ***To my surprise**, she agreed.* | ***It came as no surprise** when he left.* **2** [C,U] something that is unexpected or unusual: *What a surprise to see you here!* | *Dad, I **have a surprise** for you!* | *a **surprise party*** (=a party given for someone who is not expecting it) **3 catch/take sb by surprise** to happen in an unexpected way: *The heavy snowfall caught everyone by surprise.* [ORIGIN: 1400—1500 Old French, past participle of *surprendre* "to take over, surprise"]

surprise² *v.* [T] **1** to make someone feel surprised: *Her reaction surprised me.* | *"Pam got fired." **"It doesn't surprise me."*** **2** to find, catch, or attack someone when s/he does not expect it: *A security guard surprised the robber.*

sur·prised /sɚˈpraɪzd, sə-/ *adj.* having a feeling of surprise: *Robert **looked surprised** to see me there.* | *I'm **surprised at** how much it costs.* | *We were **surprised (that)** David got the job.*

THESAURUS

amazed – very surprised: *I was amazed at how hard the exam was.*

shocked – feeling surprised, and often upset or offended: *We were all shocked by the news.*
astonished – very surprised: *Her lawyer was astonished at the verdict.*
astounded – very surprised: *I was astounded at how bad the play was.*
flabbergasted – very surprised and shocked: *People were flabbergasted; something like this couldn't happen.*
stunned – too surprised and shocked to speak: *We watched in stunned disbelief.*
dumbfounded (formal) – too surprised and confused to speak: *Coach Jones is dumbfounded by the team's performance.*
nonplussed (formal) – so surprised that you do not know what to say or do: *The stock market seems nonplussed by the figures.*
taken aback – surprised by what someone says or does: *At first she was taken aback, but then she laughed.*

sur·pris·ing /sə'praɪzɪŋ, sə/ *adj.* unusual or unexpected: ***It's surprising how*** *quickly she finished the job.* | *A surprising number of people came.* | *It's* ***hardly/scarcely surprising that*** *they lost the game.* —**surprisingly** *adv.*: *The test was surprisingly easy*

THESAURUS

extraordinary – unusual and surprising: *He spends an extraordinary amount of money on clothes.*
amazing – very surprising or unexpected, and sometimes difficult to believe: *It's amazing how fast some animals can run.*
shocking – surprising and upsetting: *It is shocking that a policeman could lie to the public.*
astonishing – very surprising, and often difficult to believe: *The population of the world is growing at an astonishing rate.*
astounding – very surprising, and almost impossible to believe: *the astounding success of her second novel*
staggering – very surprising and shocking, especially because something is so large: *a staggering sum of money*
stunning – very surprising and shocking: *In a stunning announcement, the senator said he was retiring.*

sur·real /sə'ril/ *also* **sur·re·a·lis·tic** /səˌriə'lɪstɪk/ *adj.* ENG. LANG. ARTS a surreal situation or experience is very strange, like something from a dream, often because there is a combination of unusual and unrelated events or images

sur·re·al·ism /sə'riəˌlɪzəm/ *n.* [U] ENG. LANG. ARTS a style of 20th century art or literature in which the artist or writer connects unrelated images and objects in a strange way —**surrealist** *adj.* —**surrealist** *n.* [C]

sur·ren·der /sə'rɛndə/ *v.* **1** [I] to stop fighting because you know that you cannot win, or to stop trying to escape from the police: *The rebel forces have surrendered.* | *The man finally* ***surrendered to*** *the police.*

THESAURUS

give in – to accept that you have lost a fight, game, etc.: *Neither side was willing to give in.*
concede (formal) – to admit that you are not going to win a game, argument, battle, etc.: *Davis conceded defeat in the election.*
yield (formal) – to allow yourself to be forced or persuaded to do something: *The government will never yield to terrorism.*
submit (formal) – to obey somcone who has power over you, especially because you have no choice: *She did not have the right to force others to submit to her views.*
admit/accept defeat – to accept that you have not won something: *In July 1905, Russia admitted defeat in its war with Japan.*

2 [T] (formal) to give something to someone in authority, for example weapons or official documents: *They had to* ***surrender*** *their* ***passports*** *as a condition of their bail.* —**surrender** *n.* [U]

sur·rep·ti·tious·ly /ˌsəəp'tɪʃəsli, ˌsʌrəp-/ *adv.* (formal) secretly, quickly, or quietly, so that other people do not notice: *He smiled surreptitiously at her.* —**surreptitious** *adj.*: *She gave Joe a surreptitious wave.* **surreptitiousness** *n.* [U]

sur·ro·gate /'səəgɪt, 'sʌrə-/ *adj* [only before noun] taking the place of someone or something else: *a surrogate family* —**surrogate** *n.* [C]

ˌsurrogate 'mother *n.* [C] a woman who has a baby for another woman who cannot have children

sur·round /sə'raʊnd/ *v.* [T] **1** to be all around someone or something: *a lake* ***surrounded by*** *trees* | *The police surrounded the house.* **2 be surrounded by sb/sth** to have a lot of a particular type of people or things near you: *She is surrounded by friends.* **3** to be closely related to a situation or event: *Some of the issues surrounding alcohol abuse are very complex.* —**surrounding** *adj.*: *the surrounding countryside*

sur·round·ings /sə'raʊndɪŋz/ *n.* [plural] the place that you are in and all the things in it: *It took me a few weeks to get used to my* ***new surroundings.***

sur·veil·lance /sə'veɪləns/ *n.* [U] the act of watching a particular person or place carefully, usually in order to catch a criminal or prevent a crime: *Police have the suspect* ***under surveillance.*** | *surveillance cameras* [ORIGIN: 1800—1900 French *surveiller* "to watch over," from *sur-* "over" + *veiller* "to watch"]

sur·vey[1] /'səveɪ/ (Ac) *n.* [C] **1** a set of questions that you ask a large number of people in order to find out about their opinions and behavior (SYN) **poll, questionnaire**: *ABC News* ***conducted*** *a* ***survey*** *of working women.* | ***Surveys show*** *that most Americans support the president.* **2** a careful examination of an area of land, done in order to make a map of it: *a geological survey of the*

S

area **3** a general description or report about a particular subject or situation: *a survey of American History* [ORIGIN: 1400—1500 Old French *surveeir* "to look over"]

sur·vey² /sɚˈveɪ, ˈsɚveɪ/ (Ac) *v.* [T] **1** to ask a large number of people a set of questions in order to find out about their opinions or behavior: *More than 50% of the students surveyed said they exercise regularly.* **2** to look at someone or something carefully so that you can make a decision, or find out more information: *I **surveyed** the **damage** to the car.* **3** to examine and measure an area of land in order to make a map

sur·vey·or /sɚˈveɪɚ/ *n.* [C] someone whose job is to measure and record the details of an area of land

sur·viv·al /sɚˈvaɪvəl/ (Ac) *n.* [U] the state of continuing to live or exist, especially after a difficult or dangerous situation: *The operation will increase his **chances of survival**.* | *It's **survival of the fittest*** (=a situation in which only the strongest people, animals, or organizations can continue to exist).

sur·vive /sɚˈvaɪv/ (Ac) *v.* [I,T] **1** to continue to live after an accident, illness, etc.: *Only one person survived the crash.* **2** to continue to live normally or exist in spite of difficulties: *Few small businesses survived the recession.* | *How do you manage to **survive on** such a low salary?* | *It's been a tough few months, but **I'll survive**.* **3** to continue to exist after a long time: *Only a few Greek plays have survived.* [ORIGIN: 1400—1500 Old French *survivre* "to live longer than," from Latin *supervivere*] —**surviving** *adj.* [only before noun]: *The couple's two surviving children will inherit the family home.*

sur·vi·vor /sɚˈvaɪvɚ/ (Ac) *n.* [C] **1** someone who continues to live after an accident, illness, etc.: *There were no survivors.* **2** (approving) someone who continues to live a normal life even when s/he has many difficulties or problems: *He's a survivor.*

sus·cep·ti·ble /səˈsɛptəbəl/ *adj.* likely to be affected by a particular illness or problem: *I've always been very **susceptible to** colds.*

su·shi /ˈsuʃi/ *n.* [U] Japanese food consisting of raw fish eaten with cooked rice

sus·pect¹ /ˈsʌspɛkt/ *n.* [C] someone who may be guilty of a crime: *the police's **prime suspect*** (=main one)

sus·pect² /səˈspɛkt/ *v.* [T] **1** to think that someone may be guilty of a crime: *She is **suspected of** murder.* **2** to think that something is probably true, especially something bad: *She **suspected (that)** Sandra had been lying.*

THESAURUS think, believe, figure, guess
→ THINK

3 to think that someone or something is not completely honest, sincere, or real: *Do you have reason to suspect his motives?*

sus·pect³ /ˈsʌspɛkt/ *adj.* difficult to believe or trust: *Her story is **highly suspect**.*

sus·pend /səˈspɛnd/ (Ac) *v.* [T] **1** to officially stop someone from working, driving, or going to school for a fixed period, because s/he has broken the rules: *Joey was **suspended from** school.* | *Her driver's **license** was **suspended**.* **2** to officially stop something from continuing, usually for a short time: *The bus service has been suspended until further notice.* **3** (formal) if something is suspended somewhere, it is hanging down from there: *a chandelier **suspended from** the ceiling* [ORIGIN: 1200—1300 Old French *suspendre* "to hang up, interrupt," from Latin *suspendere*, from *sub-* "up" + *pendere* "to hang"]

sus·pend·ers /səˈspɛndɚz/ *n.* [plural] two bands of cloth that go over your shoulders and are attached to your pants to hold them up

sus·pense /səˈspɛns/ *n.* [U] a feeling of not knowing what is going to happen next: *Don't **keep us in suspense**. What happened?*

sus·pen·sion /səˈspɛnʃən/ (Ac) *n.* **1** [U] the act of officially stopping something from continuing for a period of time: *a **suspension of** military activity* **2** [C,U] an act of removing someone from a school or job for a short time, in order to punish him/her: *a three-day suspension for cheating* **3** [U] equipment attached to the wheels of a vehicle to make it comfortable to ride in **4** [U] a liquid mixture containing very small pieces of solid matter that have not completely DISSOLVED in the liquid

sus·pi·cion /səˈspɪʃən/ *n.* **1** [C,U] a feeling that someone is probably guilty of doing something wrong or dishonest: *Potter was arrested **on suspicion of** robbery.* | *I'm not sure who erased the file, but **I have my suspicions**.* **2** [U] a feeling that you do not trust someone: *She always **treated us with suspicion**.*

sus·pi·cious /səˈspɪʃəs/ *adj.* **1** feeling that you do not like or trust someone or something: *I'm **suspicious of** her intentions.* | *Her behavior **made** me **suspicious**.* **2** making you think that something bad or illegal is happening: *He died under **suspicious circumstances**.* —**suspiciously** *adv.*: *They were acting suspiciously.*

sus·tain /səˈsteɪn/ (Ac) *v.* [T] **1** to make something continue to exist or happen over a period of time: *The nation's economy was largely sustained by foreign aid.* **2** (formal) to suffer damage, an injury, or loss of something: *Two people **sustained** minor **injuries**.* **3** (formal) to provide enough food, water, air, etc. for people to stay alive: *Are we damaging the environment so badly that the Earth will be unable to **sustain life**?* [ORIGIN: 1200—1300 Old French *sustenir*, from Latin *sustinere* "to hold up, sustain"]

sus·tain·a·ble /səˈsteɪnəbəl/ (Ac) *adj.* **1** ECONOMICS able to continue without causing damage to the environment: *sustainable economic growth* **2** able to continue for a long time: *Working* *more than sixty hours a week is not sustainable in the long-term.*

sus,tainable de'velopment *n.* [U] ECONOMICS the practice of limiting how much coal, oil, and other natural materials a country or industry uses, so that they continue to last for a long time

sus·tained /sə'steɪnd/ *adj.* continuing for a long time: *A sustained effort is needed.*

sus·te·nance /'sʌstənəns/ (Ac) *n.* [U] (formal) **1** food that is needed in order to live: *The buffalo provided sustenance to the Plains Indians.* **2** something that helps something to continue: *His religion was his sustenance.*

SUV *n.* [C] **sport utility vehicle** a type of vehicle that is bigger than a car and is made for traveling over rough ground

svelte /svɛlt/ *adj.* a svelte woman is thin and graceful [ORIGIN: 1800—1900 French, Italian *svelto* "stretched," from *svellere* "to pull out"]

SW the written abbreviation of SOUTHWEST

swab /swɑb/ *n.* [C] a small stick with a piece of material on the end, used for cleaning wounds or doing medical tests: *a cotton swab* —**swab** *v.* [T]

swag·ger /'swægə/ *v.* [I] to walk proudly, swinging your shoulders in a way that seems too confident —**swagger** *n.* [singular, U]

swal·low¹ /'swɑloʊ/ *v.* **1** [T] to make food or drink go down your throat: *She swallowed her coffee and got up to leave.* **2** [I] to make liquid in your mouth go down your throat, especially because you are nervous or afraid: *He swallowed anxiously before answering.* **3** [T] (informal) to believe a story or explanation that is not actually true: *I found his story a little **hard to swallow**.*

> THESAURUS **believe, accept, fall for sth, buy** → BELIEVE

4 swallow your pride to do something that seems necessary even though you feel embarrassed or ashamed

swallow sth ↔ **up** *phr. v.* to make something disappear or become part of something else: *As the city grew, local farms were swallowed up.*

swallow² *n.* [C] **1** an act of making food or drink go down your throat: *Mike drank his beer in one swallow.* **2** a common small bird with pointed wings and a tail with two points

swam /swæm/ *v.* the past tense of SWIM

swamp¹ /swɑmp, swɔmp/ *n.* [C,U] EARTH SCIENCES land that is always very wet or covered with water —**swampy** *adj.*

swamp² *v.* [T] **1** (informal) to suddenly give someone more work, problems, etc. than s/he can deal with: *We've been swamped with job applications.* **2** to suddenly cover something with a lot of water so that it causes damage: *Huge waves swamped the town.*

swan /swɑn/ *n.* [C] a large white bird with a long neck, that lives near lakes and rivers

swank /swæŋk/ *also* **swank·y** /'swæŋki/ *adj.* (informal) very fashionable or expensive: *a swank New York hotel*

swap /swɑp/ *v.* (**swapped**, **swapping**) [I,T] to exchange something you have for something that someone else has: *Can I **swap** seats **with** you?* [ORIGIN: 1500—1600 *swap* "to hit" (14—19 centuries), from the sound; from the practice of striking the hands together when agreeing a business deal] —**swap** *n.* [C]

> THESAURUS **exchange, trade** → EXCHANGE²

'swap ,meet *n.* [C] an occasion when people meet to buy and sell used goods, or to exchange them

swarm¹ /swɔrm/ *v.* [I] if people swarm somewhere, they quickly move there together

swarm with sb/sth *phr. v.* to be full of people, birds, or insects: *The beaches are swarming with people in the summer.*

swarm² *n.* [C] a large group of insects that move together: *a **swarm of** bees*

swarth·y /'swɔrði, -θi/ *adj.* someone who is swarthy has dark skin

swat /swɑt/ *v.* (**swatted**, **swatting**) [I,T] to hit an insect in order to kill it: *He **swatted at** a fly that was buzzing near his ear.* —**swat** *n.* [C]

S

swatch /swɑtʃ/ *n.* [C] a small piece of cloth that is used as an example of a type of material or its quality

swath /swɑθ, swɔθ/ *n.* [C] (formal) a long thin area of something, especially land

sway¹ /sweɪ/ *v.* **1** [I,T] to move slowly from one side to another: *palm trees swaying in the breeze* **2** [T] to try to influence someone to make a particular decision: *Nothing you say will sway her.*

sway² *n.* [U] **1** a swinging movement from one side to another: *the sway of the ship* **2** (literary) the power to rule or influence people: *Superstitious beliefs still **hold sway** in the country.*

swear /swɛr/ *v.* (past tense **swore** /swɔr/, past participle **sworn** /swɔrn/) **1** [I] to use offensive language: *Don't swear in front of the children.* | *I'm sorry I **swore at** you.* **2** [I,T] to promise that you will do something: *Do you **swear to** tell the truth?*

> THESAURUS **promise, give sb your word, take/swear an oath, vow, pledge** → PROMISE¹

3 [T] (informal) used in order to emphasize that something is true: *She swore that she had never seen him before.* | ***I swear (to God)** I didn't take* *anything out of your room.* **4 I could have sworn (that)...** (spoken) used in order to say that you were sure about something, but now you are not sure: *I could have sworn I left my keys here.*

swear by sth *phr. v.* to strongly believe that something is effective: *Heidi swears by vitamin C for preventing colds.*

swear sb ↔ **in** *phr. v.* **1** to make someone publicly promise to be loyal to a country or an important job: *The new governor was sworn in today.* **2** LAW to make someone give an official promise in a court of law: *The jury had to be sworn in.*

swear off sth *phr. v.* to decide to stop doing something that is bad for you: *I'm swearing off alcohol after last night!*

'swear word *n.* [C] a word that is considered rude or shocking

sweat[1] /swɛt/ *v.* **1** [I] BIOLOGY to have liquid coming out through your skin, especially when you are hot or nervous: *The heat was making us sweat.* | *He was **sweating heavily/profusely*** (=a lot). **2** [I] (informal) to work hard: *I spent all night **sweating over** my term paper.* **3 don't sweat it** (spoken) used in order to tell someone not to worry about something: *Don't sweat it – I'll lend you the money.*

S

sweat sth ↔ **out** *phr. v.* to continue doing something until it is finished, even though it is difficult: *We had to **sweat it out** until the rest of the crew arrived.*

sweat[2] *n.* **1** [U] BIOLOGY liquid that comes out through your skin, especially when you are hot or nervous (SYN) **perspiration**: *His shirt was soaked with sweat.* | *We had both **worked up a sweat*** (=started sweating because of working hard). | *Sweat poured from his exhausted body.* **2 a cold sweat** nervousness or fear that makes you sweat even though you are not hot: *I woke up from the nightmare **in a cold sweat**.* **3 sweats** [plural] (informal) a SWEAT SUIT or the pants of a sweat suit **4 no sweat** (spoken) used in order to say that you can do something easily: *"Can I have a ride home?" "Yeah, no sweat!"*

sweat·er /'swɛt̬ɚ/ *n.* [C] a piece of warm wool or cotton clothing with long SLEEVES, which covers the top half of your body: *She put her sweater on.* | *a **wool/cotton/cashmere sweater*** [ORIGIN: 1800—1900 *sweat*; because it was originally worn when doing exercise, to make you sweat] → *see picture at* CLOTHES

'sweat pants *n.* [plural] soft thick pants, worn especially for sports

sweat·shirt /'swɛt-ʃɚt/ *n.* [C] a thick soft cotton shirt with long sleeves, no collar, and no buttons, worn especially for sports

sweat·shop /'swɛt-ʃɑp/ *n.* [C] a factory where people work hard in bad conditions for very little money

'sweat suit, sweat-suit /'swɛtsut/ *n.* [C] a set of clothes made of thick soft material, worn especially for sports → *see picture at* CLOTHES

sweat·y /'swɛt̬i/ *adj.* covered with SWEAT, or smelling like sweat: *I felt hot and sweaty.* | *sweaty hands*

sweep[1] /swip/ *v.* (past tense and past participle **swept** /swɛpt/) **1** [T] *also* **sweep up** to clean the dirt from the floor or ground using a BROOM: *I've just swept the kitchen floor.*

THESAURUS **clean, do the housework, dust, polish, vacuum, scrub, mop** → CLEAN[2]

2 [I,T] to move somewhere quickly or to move something quickly: *The crowd **swept through** the gates.* | *I **swept** the papers quickly **into** the drawer.* **3 sweep the country/nation** to quickly affect or become popular with most of the people in a country: *a fashion trend that is sweeping the nation* **4 sweep sb off his/her feet** to make someone feel suddenly and strongly attracted to you in a romantic way **5 sweep sth under the rug** to try to hide something bad that has happened

sweep sth ↔ **away** *phr. v.* to completely destroy something or make something disappear: *Entire houses were swept away by the floods.*

sweep[2] *n.* [C] **1** a long swinging movement of your arm, a weapon, etc. **2** a long curved line or area of land: ***the sweep of** the hills in the distance* **3** [usually singular] a search or attack that moves through a particular area: *Soldiers **made a sweep** of the village.*

sweep·ing /'swipɪŋ/ *adj.* **1** affecting many things, or affecting one thing very much: *sweeping changes* **2 sweeping statement/generalization** (disapproving) a statement that is too general and does not consider all the facts

sweep·stakes /'swipsteɪks/ *n.* (plural **sweepstakes**) [C] **1** a type of competition in which you have a chance to win a prize if your name is chosen **2** a type of BETting in which the winner gets all the money risked by everyone else

sweet /swit/ *adj.* **1** having a taste like sugar: *sweet, juicy peaches*

THESAURUS **tasty, sour, salty, hot, spicy** → TASTE[1]

2 having a pleasant smell or sound: *a **sweet-smelling** rose* **3** kind, gentle, and friendly: *Fran is such a sweet person.* | *It was **sweet of** you to help.* **4** pretty and pleasant – used when you are talking about children and small things (SYN) **cute**: *Her baby is so sweet.* **5** making you feel happy and satisfied: *Revenge is sweet!* **6 have a sweet tooth** to like to eat sweet foods **7 Sweet!** (spoken) used in order to show that you think something is very good: *"I got four tickets to the concert." "Sweet!"* [ORIGIN: Old English *swete*] **—sweetly** *adv.*: *She smiled sweetly.* **—sweetness** *n.* [U]

sweet·en /'swit˺n/ *v.* **1** [I,T] to become or make something sweeter: *Sweeten the mixture with honey.* **2 sweeten the deal/pot/offer etc.** (informal) to make a deal seem more acceptable, usually by offering more money

sweet·en·er /ˈswit̚n-ɚ, -nɚ/ *n.* [C,U] a substance used instead of sugar to make food or drinks taste sweeter: *Many diet foods are full of* ***artificial sweeteners***.

sweet·heart /ˈswithɑrt/ *n.* [C] **1** a way of talking to someone you love: *Good night, sweetheart.* **2** (old-fashioned) the person that you love: *He married his* ***childhood sweetheart***.

sweet·ie /ˈswiṭi/ *n.* [C] (spoken) **1** a way of talking to someone you love **2** someone who is kind and easy to love: *Pat's such a sweetie!*

ˌsweet poˈtato *n.* [C] a root that looks like an orange potato, is yellow inside, and tastes sweet

sweets /swits/ *n.* [plural] (informal) sweet food or candy

swell[1] /swɛl/ *v.* (past tense **swelled**, past participle **swollen** /ˈswoʊlən/) **1** [I] *also* **swell up** to gradually increase in size, especially because of an injury: *My ankle swelled up like a balloon.* **2** [I,T] to increase to a much bigger amount or number: *The city's population has* ***swollen to*** *2 million.* **3 swell with pride/anger etc.** to feel very proud, angry, etc.

swell[2] *n.* [singular] the movement of the ocean as waves go up and down

swell[3] *adj.* (old-fashioned) very good: *I had a really swell time.*

swell·ing /ˈswɛlɪŋ/ *n.* [C,U] an area on your body that becomes larger than usual because of injury or sickness: *This medicine should help* ***reduce*** *the* ***swelling***.

swel·ter·ing /ˈswɛltərɪŋ/ *adj.* unpleasantly hot: *a sweltering summer day*

> THESAURUS **hot, boiling/baking/scorching (hot), scalding** ➔ HOT

swept /swɛpt/ *v.* the past tense and past participle of SWEEP

swerve /swɚv/ *v.* [I] to make a sudden movement to the left or right while moving forward, usually in order to avoid hitting something: *Mark swerved to avoid hitting the dog.*

swift /swɪft/ *adj.* happening or moving very quickly: *a swift response* —**swiftly** *adv.*

swig /swɪg/ *v.* (**swigged, swigging**) [T] (informal) to drink something by taking large amounts into your mouth —**swig** *n.* [C]

> THESAURUS **drink, gulp sth down, down sth, knock sth back, take/have a swig, guzzle** ➔ DRINK[2]

swill[1] /swɪl/ *n.* [U] food for pigs

swill[2] *v.* [T] to drink a lot of something, especially beer

swim[1] /swɪm/ *v.* (past tense **swam** /swæm/, past participle **swum** /swʌm/, present participle **swimming**) **1** [I,T] to move through the water, using your arms and legs: *Can Lucy swim?* | *He swims 20 laps a day.* | *We used to* ***swim in the lake***. **2** [I] if your head swims, you feel confused or as if everything is spinning around **3** [I] if something you are looking at swims, it seems to move around, usually because you are sick: *The room swam around her.* **4 be swimming in/with sth** to be covered by a lot of liquid: *meatballs swimming in sauce* [ORIGIN: Old English *swimman*] —**swimming** *n.* [U]: *Do you want to* ***go swimming***?

swim[2] *n.* [C] a time when you swim: *Would you like to* ***go for a swim*** *after work?*

ˈswim ˌbladder *n.* [C] BIOLOGY an AIR BLADDER

ˈswimming pool *n.* [C] a structure that has been built and filled with water for people to swim in SYN **pool**

ˈswimming suit *n.* [C] a SWIMSUIT

ˈswimming trunks *n.* [plural] a piece of clothing like SHORTS, worn by men for swimming

swim·suit /ˈswɪmsut/ *n.* [C] a piece of clothing worn for swimming

swin·dle[1] /ˈswɪndl/ *v.* [T] to get money from someone by trickingor deceiving him/her [ORIGIN: 1700—1800 *swindler* "person who swindles" (18—21 centuries), from German *schwindler* "someone confused or unbalanced"] —**swindler** *n.* [C]

swindle[2] *n.* [C] a situation in which someone gets money from someone else by tricking him/her

swine /swaɪn/ *n.* (plural **swine**) [C] (old-fashioned) a pig

swing[1] /swɪŋ/ *v.* (past tense and past participle **swung** /swʌŋ/) **1** [I,T] to move backward and forward while hanging from a particular point, or to make something move in this way: *They walked hand in hand, swinging their arms.* | *The sign swung in the wind.* **2** [I,T] to move smoothly in a curved direction, or to make something move this way: *The screen door kept* ***swinging open/shut***. **3** [I] if opinions or feelings swing, they change a lot: *Her mood* ***swung from*** *happiness* ***to*** *despair.*

S

swing around *phr. v.* to turn around quickly, or to make something do this: *Mitch swung around to face her.*

swing at sb/sth *phr. v.* to try to hit someone or something with your hand or with an object that you are holding: *He swung at the ball and missed.*

swing by (sth) *phr. v.* (informal) to quickly visit a person or place before going somewhere else: *Can we swing by the store on the way home?*

swing² *n.* [C] **1** a seat hanging from ropes or chains, on which children swing: *A bunch of kids were **playing on the swings**.* **2** an attempt to hit someone or something by swinging your arm, an object, etc.: *Then he tried to **take a swing at** me.* **3** a change from one feeling, opinion, etc. to another: *mood swings* | *a big **swing in** public opinion* **4 be in full swing** if a party, event, etc. is in full swing, it is at its highest level of activity

swipe /swaɪp/ *v.* **1** [I,T] *also* **swipe at** to hit or try to hit someone or something by swinging your arm very quickly **2** [T] (informal) to steal something: *Somebody swiped my wallet.* **3** [T] to pull a plastic card through a machine that can read the electronic information on it —**swipe** *n.* [C]

S

swirl /swɚl/ *v.* [I,T] to turn around and around, or to make something do this: *Mist **swirled around** the mountain peaks.* —**swirl** *n.* [C]

swish /swɪʃ/ *v.* [I,T] to move or make something move quickly through the air with a soft sound like a whistle: *One cow swished its tail.* —**swish** *n.* [singular]

Swiss¹ /swɪs/ *adj.* relating to or coming from Switzerland

Swiss² *n.* **the Swiss** [plural] the people of Switzerland, considered as a single group

switch¹ /swɪtʃ/ *v.* **1** [I,T] to change from doing or using one thing to doing or using something else: *If you **switch to** a low-fat diet, your health will improve.* | *He kept **switching from** one subject **to** another.* | *He **switched sides** just days before the election.* **2** [T] to replace an object with a similar object, especially secretly or accidentally: *We must have accidentally switched umbrellas.*

switch sth ↔ **off** *phr. v.* to turn off a machine, radio, light, etc. by using a switch: *Be sure to **switch off the lights** when you leave.*

switch sth ↔ **on** *phr. v.* to turn on a machine, radio, light, etc. by using a switch: *Could you switch the radio on?*

switch over *phr. v.* to start using a different product, system, etc.: *More and more people are switching over to Internet banking.*

switch² *n.* [C] **1** the part that you press or push on a machine, radio, light, etc. so that it starts or stops operating: *Where's the **on/off switch**?* | *a light switch* **2** a change from one thing to another: *More shoppers are **making the switch** to organic food.*

switch·board /ˈswɪtʃbɔrd/ *n.* [C] a piece of equipment that connects all the telephone calls made to or from a particular business, hotel, etc.

swiv·el /ˈswɪvəl/ *also* **swivel around** *v.* [I,T] to turn around while remaining in the same place, or to make something do this: *She wants a chair that swivels.*

> THESAURUS **turn, twist, spin, whirl, twirl, go around, revolve, rotate** → TURN¹

swol·len¹ /ˈswoʊlən/ *v.* the past participle of SWELL

swollen² *adj.* **1** a part of your body that is swollen is bigger than usual because of injury or sickness: *My knee is still really swollen from the accident.* **2** a swollen river has more water in it than usual

swoon /swun/ *v.* [I] (old-fashioned) to feel so much emotion that you almost FAINT (=lose consciousness)

swoop /swup/ *v.* [I] **1** to suddenly and quickly move down through the air, especially to attack something: *An owl **swooped down** and grabbed a mouse.* **2** if soldiers or the police swoop, they go somewhere very quickly and without warning in order to attack or ARREST someone —**swoop** *n.* [C]

sword /sɔrd/ *n.* [C] a weapon with a long sharp blade and a handle

sword·fish /ˈsɔrdˌfɪʃ/ *n.* [C] a large fish with a long pointed upper jaw

swore /swɔr/ *v.* the past tense of SWEAR

sworn¹ /swɔrn/ *v.* the past participle of SWEAR

sworn² *adj.* **1 sworn statement/testimony** something you say or write that you have officially promised is the truth **2 sworn enemies** two people or groups who will always hate each other

swum /swʌm/ *v.* the past participle of SWIM

swung /swʌŋ/ *v.* the past tense and past participle of SWING

syc·a·more /ˈsɪkəˌmɔr/ *n.* [C,U] an eastern North American tree with broad leaves, or the wood from this tree

syc·o·phant /ˈsɪkəfənt/ *n.* [C] (formal, disapproving) someone who always praises an important person in order to gain an advantage, not in an honest way —**sycophantic** /ˌsɪkəˈfæntɪk◂/ *adj.*

syl·lab·if·i·ca·tion /sɪˌlæbɪfɪˈkeɪʃən/ *also* **syl·lab·i·ca·tion** /sɪˌlæbɪˈkeɪʃən/ *n.* [U] ENG. LANG. ARTS the separation of a word into syllables

syl·la·ble /ˈsɪləbəl/ *n.* [C] ENG. LANG. ARTS each part of a word that contains a single vowel sound. For example, "cat" has one syllable and "butter" has two.

syl·la·bus /ˈsɪləbəs/ *n.* (plural **syllabi** /-baɪ/ *or* **syllabuses**) [C] a plan that shows a student what s/he will be studying in a particular subject

sym·bi·o·sis /ˌsɪmbiˈoʊsɪs, -baɪ-/ *n.* [U] **1** a relationship between people or organizations that depend on each other equally **2** BIOLOGY the relationship between two different living things that exist very closely together and depend on each other for particular advantages —**symbiotic** /ˌsɪmbiˈɑt̬ɪk◂ / *adj.*

sym·bol /ˈsɪmbəl/ (Ac) *n.* [C] **1** a picture, person, object, etc. that represents a particular quality, idea, organization, etc.: *The cross is the most important symbol in Christianity.* | *The dove is a* ***symbol of*** *peace.* **2** a letter, number, or sign that represents a sound, amount, chemical substance, etc.: *Fe is the chemical* ***symbol for*** *iron.* [ORIGIN: 1400—1500 Latin *symbolum*, from Greek *symbolon* "proof of who someone is, checked by comparing its other half"]

sym·bol·ic /sɪmˈbɑlɪk/ (Ac) *adj.* **1** representing a particular idea or quality: *A red rose is* ***symbolic of*** *love.* **2** important and representing an idea or quality, but not having any real effect: *The president's trip to Russia was mostly symbolic.* —**symbolically** *adv.*: *Fairy tales deal symbolically with the problems of growing up.*

sym·bol·ism /ˈsɪmbəˌlɪzəm/ (Ac) *n.* [U] the use of symbols to represent things: *There's a lot of religious symbolism in his paintings.*

sym·bol·ize /ˈsɪmbəˌlaɪz/ (Ac) *v.* [T] if something symbolizes a quality, feeling, etc., it represents it: *A wedding ring symbolizes a couple's promises to each other.*

sym·met·ri·cal /səˈmɛtrɪkəl/ *also* **sym·met·ric** /səˈmɛtrɪk/ *adj.* having two sides that are exactly the same size and shape (ANT) **asymmetrical**

sym·me·try /ˈsɪmətri/ *n.* [U] the quality of being symmetrical [ORIGIN: 1500—1600 Latin *symmetria*, from Greek, from *symmetros* "symmetrical," from *syn-* "together" + *metron* "measure"]

sym·pa·thet·ic /ˌsɪmpəˈθɛt̬ɪk◂ / *adj.* **1** showing that you understand how sad, hurt, lonely, etc. someone feels (ANT) **unsympathetic**: *a sympathetic nurse* | *Parents aren't always very* ***sympathetic towards*** *their children.*

THESAURUS kind, nice, caring, warm-hearted, compassionate → KIND²

2 [not before noun] willing to support someone's plans, actions, ideas, etc. (ANT) **unsympathetic**: *He's fairly* ***sympathetic to*** *the staff's concerns.* **3 sympathetic character/figure etc.** ENG. LANG. ARTS someone in a book, play, etc. who most people like (ANT) **unsympathetic** —**sympathetically** *adv.*

sym·pa·thize /ˈsɪmpəˌθaɪz/ *v.* [I] **1** to understand how sad, hurt, lonely, etc. someone feels: *I can* ***sympathize with*** *the way you're feeling.* **2** to support someone's ideas or actions: *Very few people* ***sympathize with*** *his views.*

sym·pa·thiz·er /ˈsɪmpəˌθaɪzɚ/ *n.* [C] someone who supports the aims and ideas of a political organization

sym·pa·thy /ˈsɪmpəθi/ *n.* (plural **sympathies**) [C,U] **1** a feeling of support for someone who is sad, hurt, lonely, etc.: *I* ***have*** *absolutely* ***no sympathy for*** *students who get caught cheating on tests.* | *I'm sorry to hear Bill died; you have my* ***deep sympathy***. **2** support for someone's plans, actions, ideas, etc.: *I do have some* ***sympathy with*** *their aims.*

sym·pho·ny /ˈsɪmfəni/ *n.* (plural **symphonies**) [C] ENG. LANG. ARTS a long piece of music written for an ORCHESTRA [ORIGIN: 1200—1300 Old French *symphonie*, from Latin *symphonia*, from Greek, from *symphonos* "sounding together"]

symp·tom /ˈsɪmptəm/ *n.* [C] **1** a physical condition that shows you may have a particular disease: *Common* ***symptoms of*** *diabetes are weight loss and fatigue.* **2** a sign that a serious problem exists: *Rising crime rates are another* ***symptom of*** *a society in trouble.* [ORIGIN: 1500—1600 Latin *symptoma*, from Greek, "something that happens, symptom"] —**symptomatic** /ˌsɪmptəˈmæt̬ɪk/ *adj.*

syn·a·gogue /ˈsɪnəˌgɑg/ *n.* [C] a building where Jewish people go to have religious services [ORIGIN: 1100—1200 Old French *synagoge*, from Late Latin, from Greek "gathering of people, synagogue"]

sync /sɪŋk/ *n.* (informal) **1 in sync** working together at the same time or speed, or in the same way **2 out of sync** working at a different time or speed, or in a different way

syn·chro·nize /ˈsɪŋkrəˌnaɪz/ *v.* [T] to make two or more things happen or move at the same time —**synchronization** /ˌsɪŋkrənəˈzeɪʃən/ *n.* [U]

syn·di·cate /ˈsɪndəkɪt/ *n.* [C,U] a group of people or companies that join together to achieve a particular aim: *the city's largest crime syndicate*

syn·di·cat·ed /ˈsɪndəˌkeɪt̬ɪd/ *adj.* a syndicated newspaper COLUMN, television program, etc. is bought and used by several different newspapers or broadcasting companies —**syndication** /ˌsɪndəˈkeɪʃən/ *n.* [U]

syn·drome /ˈsɪndroʊm/ *n.* [C] a set of physical or mental conditions that show you have a particular disease

syn·o·nym /ˈsɪnəˌnɪm/ *n.* [C] ENG. LANG. ARTS a word with the same or nearly the same meaning as another word in the same language. For example, "sad" and "unhappy" are synonyms. (ANT) **antonym** [ORIGIN: 1400—1500 Latin *synonymum*, from Greek, from *synonymos* "synonymous"]

syn·on·y·mous /sɪˈnɑnəməs/ *adj.* **1** having a strong association with another quality, idea, situation, etc.: *He thinks that being poor is* ***synonymous with*** *being a criminal.* **2** ENG. LANG. ARTS two words that are synonymous have the same or nearly the same meaning

syn·op·sis /sɪˈnɑpsɪs/ *n.* (plural **synopses** /-siz/) [C] ENG. LANG. ARTS a short description of the main parts of a story [ORIGIN: 1600—1700 Late Latin, Greek, from *synopsesthai* "to be going to see together"]

S

syn·tac·tic /sɪn'tæktɪk/ *adj.* ENG. LANG. ARTS relating to SYNTAX (=the way that words are arranged in order to form sentences or phrases)

syn·tax /'sɪntæks/ *n.* [U] ENG. LANG. ARTS the way that words are arranged in order to form sentences or phrases [ORIGIN: 1500—1600 French *syntaxe*, from Late Latin *syntaxis*, from Greek, from *syntassein* "to arrange together"]

syn·the·sis /'sɪnθəsɪs/ *n.* (plural **syntheses** /-siz/) [C,U] the act of combining several things into a single complete unit, or the combination that is produced [ORIGIN: 1400—1500 Greek *syntithenai* "to put together"]

syn·the·size /'sɪnθə,saɪz/ *v.* [T] to combine different things in order to produce something: *Scientists can now synthesize the drug.*

syn·the·siz·er /'sɪnθə,saɪzɚ/ *n.* [C] an electronic musical instrument that can produce the sounds of various different musical instruments

syn·thet·ic /sɪn'θɛṭɪk/ *adj.* made from artificial substances, not natural ones: *synthetic fabrics like acrylic and polyester* —**synthetically** *adv.*

THESAURUS artificial, fake, man-made, imitation → ARTIFICIAL

syph·i·lis /'sɪfəlɪs/ *n.* [U] a very serious disease that is passed from one person to another during sex

T

sy·ringe /sə'rɪndʒ/ *n.* [C] a hollow tube and needle used for removing blood or other liquids from your body, or putting drugs, etc. into it [ORIGIN: 1400—1500 Medieval Latin *syringa*, from Greek *syrinx* "tube"]

syr·up /'sɚəp, 'sɪrəp/ *n.* [U] thick sticky liquid made from sugar: *pancakes with **maple syrup*** [ORIGIN: 1300—1400 Old French *sirop*, from Medieval Latin, from Arabic *sharab* "drink, wine, syrup"] —**syrupy** *adj.*

sys·tem /'sɪstəm/ *n.* [C] **1** a group of things or parts that work together as a whole for a particular purpose: *the public school system* | *a new computer system* **2** a way of organizing or doing something: *a filing system* | *a **system of** government* **3 sb's system** someone's body – used when you are talking about its medical or physical condition **4 get sth out of your system** (informal) to do something that helps you stop feeling angry, annoyed, or upset **5 the system** (informal) the official rules and powerful organizations that restrict what you can do: *You can't **beat the system*** (=avoid or break the rules). **6** BIOLOGY the parts in a human or animal body that work together to do a particular job: *the digestive system*

sys·tem·at·ic /,sɪstə'mæṭɪk/ *adj.* organized carefully and done thoroughly: *a **systematic approach** to training* —**systematically** *adv.*

THESAURUS careful, methodical, thorough, meticulous, painstaking → CAREFUL

sys·tem·ic /sɪ'stɛmɪk/ *adj.* BIOLOGY affecting your whole body: *a systemic infection*

T, t /ti/ the twentieth letter of the English alphabet

T /ti/ *n.* **to a T** (informal) exactly or perfectly: *That dress fits you to a T.*

tab /tæb/ *n.* [C] **1** an amount of money that you owe for a meal or drinks you have had, or for a service: *Our lunch tab came to $53.* | *I'll **put it on your tab**.* | *The city is **picking up the tab for** street repairs* (=is paying for them).

THESAURUS bill, check → BILL[1]

2 keep tabs on sb/sth (informal) to carefully watch what someone or something is doing: *The police are **keeping close tabs on** her.* **3** a small piece of metal, plastic, or paper that you pull to open a container **4** a small piece of paper, cloth, plastic, etc. that sticks out from the edge of something, so that you can find it more easily

tab·by /'tæbi/ *n.* (plural **tabbies**) [C] a cat with light and dark lines on its fur

ta·ble¹ /'teɪbəl/ *n.* [C] **1** a piece of furniture with a flat top supported by legs: *a picnic table* | *He sat **at the** kitchen **table**, reading.* | *I'll **set the table*** (=put knives, forks, dishes, etc. on a table before a meal). | *Can you **clear the table*** (=take the plates, etc. off the table after a meal), *please.* **2** a table at a restaurant: ***Reserve a table** for four and invite your sisters.* | *The whole table* (=all the people sitting at a table in a restaurant) *got up and left.* **3** a list of numbers, facts, or information arranged in rows across and down a page: *the book's **table of contents*** **4 under the table** (informal) money that is paid under the table is paid secretly and illegally **5 turn the tables (on sb)** to change a situation completely so that someone loses an advantage and you gain one [ORIGIN: 1100—1200 Old French, Latin *tabula* "board, list"]

table² *v.* **table a bill/proposal/offer etc.** to decide to deal with an offer, idea, etc. later

ta·ble·cloth /'teɪbəl,klɔθ/ *n.* [C] a cloth used for covering a table

ta·ble·spoon /'teɪbəl,spun/ *n.* [C] **1** (*written abbreviation* **tbsp.**) **a)** a special large spoon used for measuring food **b)** *also* **ta·ble·spoon·ful** /-spun,fʊl/ the amount this spoon holds **2** a large spoon used for eating or serving food

tab·let /'tæblɪt/ *n.* [C] **1** a small round piece of medicine that you swallow SYN **pill**: *vitamin C tablets*

THESAURUS medicine, pill, capsule → MEDICINE

2 a set of pieces of paper for writing on that are

glued together at the top **3** a flat piece of hard clay or stone that has words cut into it

'table ˌtennis *n.* [U] PING-PONG

tab·loid /'tæblɔɪd/ *n.* [C] a newspaper that has small pages, a lot of photographs, short stories, and not much serious news ➔ BROADSHEET ➔ NEWSPAPER

ta·boo /tə'bu, tæ-/ *n.* (plural **taboos**) [C,U] a religious or social custom which means a particular activity or subject must be avoided —**taboo** *adj.*: *a taboo subject*

tab·u·late /'tæbyəˌleɪt/ *v.* [T] (formal) to arrange facts, numbers, or information together in lists, rows, etc. —**tabulation** /ˌtæbyə'leɪʃən/ *n.* [U]

tac·it /'tæsɪt/ *adj.* tacit agreement, approval, or support is given without anything actually being said: *Some people think there is a* ***tacit agreement*** *between the government and industry to not enforce environmental laws.* —**tacitly** *adv.*

tac·i·turn /'tæsəˌtən/ *adj.* a taciturn person does not talk a lot, and seems unfriendly

tack[1] /tæk/ *also* **tack up** *v.* [T] to attach something to a wall, board, etc. using a THUMBTACK

tack sth ↔ **on** *phr. v.* (informal) to add something new to something that is already complete: *Joan tacked a few words on the end of my letter.*

tack[2] *n.* **1** [C,U] the way you deal with a particular situation or a method that you use to achieve something: *If polite requests don't work, you'll have to* ***try a different tack.*** **2** [C] a THUMBTACK **3** [C] a small nail with a sharp point and a flat top: *carpet tacks*

tack·le[1] /'tækəl/ *v.* [T] **1** to try to deal with a difficult problem: *The program is a new attempt to tackle homelessness.*

THESAURUS **deal with sth, take care of sth** ➔ DEAL[2]

2 to force someone to the ground to stop him/her from running, especially in football: *Edwards was tackled on the play.*

tackle[2] *n.* **1** [C] the act of tackling someone **2** [C] in football, one of the players who play on the outside of the GUARDS **3** [U] the equipment used in some sports such as fishing

tack·y /'tæki/ *adj.* **1** showing that you do not have good judgment about what is fashionable, socially acceptable, etc.: *It's kind of tacky to give her a present that someone else gave you.* **2** cheaply made and of bad quality: *tacky furniture* **3** slightly sticky —**tackiness** *n.* [U]

ta·co /'tɑkoʊ/ *n.* (plural **tacos**) [C] a type of Mexican food made from a TORTILLA, that is folded and filled with meat, beans, etc. [ORIGIN: 1900—2000 Mexican Spanish, Spanish, "wad, snack"]

tact /tækt/ *n.* [U] the ability to say or do things carefully and politely so that you do not embarrass or upset someone

tact·ful /'tæktfəl/ *adj.* careful not to say or do something that will embarrass or upset someone else ANT **tactless**: *There was no tactful way of saying what he wanted to say.* —**tactfully** *adv.*

tac·tic /'tæktɪk/ *n.* **1** [C usually plural] a skillfully planned action used for achieving something: *aggressive sales tactics* **2 tactics** [plural] the way in which soldiers, weapons, etc. are arranged in a battle

tac·ti·cal /'tæktɪkəl/ *adj.* **1** done in order to help you achieve what you want: *His public statement was a tactical move to avoid criticism.* **2 tactical aircraft/missile etc.** an aircraft, MISSILE, etc. that is used over a short distance during a battle —**tactically** *adv.*

tact·less /'tæktfəl/ *adj.* carelessly saying or doing things that are likely to upset someone ANT **tactful** —**tactlessly** *adv.*

THESAURUS **rude, impolite, insulting, offensive** ➔ RUDE

tad /tæd/ *n.* (spoken) **a tad** a small amount: *Could you turn up the sound just a tad?*

tad·pole /'tædpoʊl/ *n.* [C] a small creature with a long tail that lives in water and grows into a FROG or TOAD

taf·fy /'tæfi/ *n.* [U] a type of soft CHEWY candy

tag[1] /tæg/ *n.* **1** [C] a small piece of paper, plastic, etc., attached to something to show what it is, who owns it, what it costs, etc.: *I can't find the* ***price tag*** *on these jeans.* **2** [U] a children's game in which one player chases and tries to touch the others

tag[2] *v.* (**tagged**, **tagging**) [T] to attach a tag to something: *Scientists have now tagged most of the bay's seals.*

tag along *phr. v.* (informal) to go somewhere with someone, especially when s/he has not invited you: *Do you mind if I tag along?*

tai·ga /'taɪgə/ *n.* **the taiga** EARTH SCIENCES a forest of PINE trees (=trees with needle-shaped leaves that stay on the tree in winter) between the TUNDRA and the STEPPES of northern Russia and Asia

tail[1] /teɪl/ *n.* **1** [C] the movable part that sticks out at the back of an animal's body: *The dog* ***wagged its tail.*** ➔ *see picture on page A15* **2** [C] the back part of an aircraft ➔ *see picture at* AIRPLANE **3** [C] the end or back part of something, especially something long and thin: *the* ***tail*** *of a comet* **4 tails a)** [plural] a man's jacket with two long parts that hang down the back, worn to formal events **b)** [U] the side of a coin that does not have a picture of someone's head on it ANT **heads** **5 the tail end of sth** the last part of an event, situation, or period of time: *the tail end of the century*

tail[2] *v.* [T] (informal) to secretly watch and follow someone such as a criminal

THESAURUS **follow, track, stalk** ➔ FOLLOW

T

tail off *phr. v.* to gradually become quieter, smaller, weaker, etc.: *His voice tailed off as he saw his father approaching.*

tail·gate[1] /ˈteɪlgeɪt/ *v.* [I,T] to drive too closely to the vehicle in front of you

tailgate[2] *n.* [C] **1** a door at the back of a car or truck that opens out and down **2** a TAILGATE PARTY

ˈtailgate ˌparty *n.* [C] a party before a sports event or concert, where people eat and drink in the PARKING LOT of the place where the event is happening

tail·light /ˈteɪl-laɪt/ *n.* [C] one of the two red lights at the back of a vehicle

tai·lor[1] /ˈteɪlɚ/ *n.* [C] someone whose job is to make clothes, especially men's clothes, that are measured to fit each customer perfectly

tailor[2] *v.* **tailor sth to/for sb** to make something so that it is exactly what someone wants or needs: *The music class is tailored to children.*

tai·lor·ing /ˈteɪlərɪŋ/ *n.* [U] the way that clothes are made, or the job of making them

ˌtailor-ˈmade *adj.* **1** exactly right for someone or something: *The job seems* ***tailor-made for*** *him.* **2** made by a tailor: *a tailor-made suit*

tail·pipe /ˈteɪlpaɪp/ *n.* [C] a part of a car's EXHAUST

T

tail·spin /ˈteɪlspɪn/ *n.* **1 in/into a tailspin** in or into a bad situation that keeps getting worse in a way that you cannot control: *Raising interest rates could* ***send*** *the economy* ***into a tailspin.*** **2** [C] an occasion when an airplane falls through the air, with the front pointing down and the back spinning in a circle

taint /teɪnt/ *v.* [T] **1** to make someone or something seem less honest, respectable, or good: *Her reputation was tainted by the scandal.* **2** to damage something by adding an unwanted substance to it: *The blood supplies were* ***tainted with*** *bacteria.* —**taint** *n.* [C]

taint·ed /ˈteɪntɪd/ *adj.* **1** a tainted substance is not safe because it is spoiled or contains poison: *a tainted blood supply* **2** affected or influenced by something illegal, dishonest, or morally wrong: *tainted witnesses*

Tai·wan·ese /ˌtaɪwɑˈniz◂ / *adj.* relating to or coming from Taiwan

take[1] /teɪk/ *v.* (past tense **took** /tʊk/, past participle **taken** /ˈteɪkən/) [T]

1 MOVE to move someone or something from one place to another: *Merritt was* ***taken*** *by ambulance* ***to*** *the nearest hospital.* | *Remember to* ***take*** *a jacket* ***with*** *you.* | *I was going to* ***take*** *some work* ***home****.*

2 DO STH used with a noun to show that an action is being done: *Here, take a look.* | *I'm going to take a shower first.* | *Would you mind* ***taking a picture/photo*** *of us?* | *The new rules* ***take effect*** *May 1.* | *He* ***took the lead*** (=went into first place) *on the final lap.*

3 REMOVE to remove something from a particular place: *Can you* ***take*** *the turkey* ***out*** *of the oven for me?*

4 STEAL/BORROW to steal something or borrow something without asking someone's permission: *They took all her jewelry.*

5 HOLD/PUT to get hold of something in your hands: *Let me take your coat.*

6 TIME/MONEY/EFFORT if something takes a particular amount of time, money, etc., that amount of time, money, etc. is needed in order for it to happen or succeed: *It takes about three days to drive there.* | *It'll take a lot of planning, but I think it can be done.*

7 ACCEPT/RECEIVE to accept or receive something: *Are you going to take the job?* | *Do you take Visa?* | ***Take*** *my* ***advice*** *and go see a doctor.* | *Why should I* ***take the blame****?*

8 STUDY to study a particular subject: *We had to take two years of English.*

9 take a test/exam to write or do a test: *I'm taking my driving test next week.*

10 GET CONTROL to get possession or control of something: *Rebel forces have* ***taken control*** *of the airport.* | *The communists* ***took power*** *in 1948.*

11 ACCEPT STH BAD to accept a bad situation without becoming upset: *Jeff can't take the stress.* | *She's taken a lot of abuse from him.* | *His constant drinking was* ***hard to take*** (=difficult to accept).

12 MACHINE/VEHICLE if a vehicle, machine, etc. takes a particular type of gasoline or BATTERY, etc., you have to use that type of gasoline, etc. in order for it to work: *Most cars take unleaded gas.*

13 MEDICINE/DRUG to swallow or INJECT a medicine or drug: *He doesn't smoke, drink, or take drugs* (=use illegal drugs). | *Why don't you take an aspirin or something?*

14 TRAVEL to use a car, bus, train, etc. to go somewhere, or to travel using a particular road: *I'll take the subway home.* | *Take Route 78 to Exit 18.*

15 REACT/CONSIDER to react to someone or something or consider him, her, or it in a particular way: *He takes his job very seriously.* | *I didn't mean for you to take what I said literally.*

16 WRITE *also* **take down** to write down information: *He's not here; can I* ***take a message****?* | *Let me take down your phone number.*

17 FEELINGS/REACTIONS to have a particular feeling or reaction when something happens: *His family* ***took*** *the news pretty* ***hard*** (=were very upset). | *She doesn't seem to take a lot of interest in her kids.*

18 MEASURE to measure the amount, level, or rate of something: *Sit here and we'll take your blood pressure.*

19 HAVE SPACE FOR SB/STH to have enough space to contain a particular number of people or things: *The station wagon takes six people.*

20 BUY to decide to buy something: *He gave me a discount so I said I'd take it.*

21 SIZE to wear a particular size of clothing or shoes: *Jim takes an extra large shirt.*

22 not take sth lying down to refuse to accept being treated badly

23 take it upon yourself to decide to do something even though no one has asked you to do it: *Parents have taken it upon themselves to raise extra cash for the school.*
24 do you take sugar/milk/cream etc.? (spoken) used to ask someone whether s/he likes to have sugar or milk in a drink such as tea or coffee [ORIGIN: 1000—1100 Old Norse *taka*] ➔ **take care** *at* CARE², **take care of sb/sth** *at* CARE², **take part** *at* PART¹, **take place** *at* PLACE¹

take after sb *phr. v.*
to look or behave like another member of your family: *Jenny takes after her dad.*

take sth ↔ **apart** *phr. v.*
to separate something into all its different parts (ANT) **put together**: *Vic took apart the faucet and put in a new washer.*

take sb/sth ↔ **away** *phr. v.*
to remove someone or something: *One more speeding ticket and your license will be taken away.* | *He was taken away to begin a four-year prison sentence.*

take sth ↔ **back** *phr. v.*
1 to admit that you were wrong to say something: *All right, I'm sorry, I **take it back**.*
2 to return something to the store where you bought it because it does not fit, is not what you wanted, etc.

take sth ↔ **down** *phr. v.*
to remove something from its place, especially by separating it into pieces (ANT) **put up**: *We take down the Christmas tree on January 6.*

take in *phr. v.*
1 take sth ↔ **in** to collect or earn an amount of money: *We've taken in $100,000 so far for charity.*
2 take sb/sth ↔ **in** to let someone or something stay in your house or a shelter, because she, he, or it has nowhere else to stay: *The Humane Society took in almost 38,000 cats and dogs last year.*
3 take sth ↔ **in** to notice, understand, and remember things: *Babies take in an amazing amount of information.*
4 take sth ↔ **in** to bring something to a place in order to be repaired: *I need to take the car in for a tune-up.*
5 take in sth to go to see something, such as a movie, play, etc.: *Tourists come to New York to take in the sights.*
6 be taken in (by sth) to be deceived by someone who lies to you: *Don't be taken in by his promises.*
7 take sth ↔ **in** to make a piece of clothing fit you by making it narrower: *If we take in the waist, the dress will fit you.*

take off
1 take sth ↔ **off** to remove something (ANT) **put on**: *Your name has been taken off the list.* | *Take your shoes off in the house.*
2 if an aircraft takes off, it rises into the air from the ground
3 (informal) to leave a place: *We packed everything in the car and took off.*
4 take time/a day/a week etc. off *also* **take time, etc. off work** to not go to work for a period of time: *I'm taking some time off work to go to the wedding.*
5 to suddenly become successful: *He died just as his film career was taking off.*

take on *phr. v.*
1 take sb ↔ **on** to compete or fight against someone: *The winner of this game will take on Houston in the championship.*
2 take on sth to begin to have a particular quality or appearance: *Once we had children, Christmas took on a different sort of importance.*
3 take sth ↔ **on** to start doing some work or to start being responsible for something: *Ethel agreed to take on the treasurer's position.*
4 take sb ↔ **on** to start to employ someone: *The team has taken on a new coach.*

take out *phr. v.*
1 take sb **out** to go with someone to a restaurant, movie, party, etc., and pay for his/her meal and entertainment: *We're **taking** Sabina **out for** dinner.*
2 take sth ↔ **out** to arrange to get something from a bank, court, insurance company, etc.: *The couple took out a $220,000 mortgage.*

take sth ↔ **out on** sb *phr. v.*
to treat someone badly when you are angry or upset, even though it is not his/her fault: *Don't **take it out on** me just because you've had a bad day.*

take sth ↔ **over** *phr. v.*
to take control of something: *His son will take over the business.*

take to *phr. v.*
1 take to sb/sth to start to like someone or something: *The two women took to each other right away.*
2 take to doing sth to begin doing something regularly: *Sandra has taken to getting up early to go jogging.*

take up *phr. v.*
1 take sth ↔ **up** to begin doing a job or activity: *I've just taken up tennis.*
2 take up sth to fill a particular amount of time or space: *The program takes up a lot of memory on the hard drive.* | *Our new car takes up the whole garage.*
3 take sth ↔ **up** to begin discussing or considering something: *The Senate will take up the bill in the next few weeks.*

take sb **up on** sth *phr. v.*
to accept an offer, invitation, etc.: *A number of students have taken him up on his offer of extra help.*

take sth ↔ **up with** sb *phr. v.*
to discuss something with someone, especially a complaint or problem: *You should take it up with the police.*

take² *n.* [C] **1** an occasion when a scene for a movie or television program is filmed **2** [usually singular] (informal) the amount of money earned by a store or business in a particular period of time

tak·en /ˈteɪkən/ *v.* the past participle of TAKE

take·off /ˈteɪk-ɔf/ *n.* **1** [C,U] the time when an airplane leaves the ground and begins to fly: *The*

T

plane crashed shortly after takeoff. → see picture at LAND² **2** [C] a funny performance that copies the style of a particular show, movie, or performer

take·out /ˈteɪk-aʊt/ *n.* [C] **1** a meal you buy at a restaurant to eat at home **2** a restaurant that sells this food —**take-out** *adj.*

take·o·ver /ˈteɪkˌoʊvɚ/ *n.* [C] **1** the act of getting control of a company by buying over half of its STOCK **2** the act of getting control of a country or political group, often using force: *a military takeover*

tal·cum pow·der /ˈtælkəm ˌpaʊdɚ/ *n.* [U] a powder which you put on your skin after washing to make it smell nice

tale /teɪl/ *n.* [C] a story about imaginary events: *a **fairy tale** by Hans Christian Andersen* | ***tales of** adventure*

THESAURUS **story, myth, legend, fable, yarn** → STORY

tal·ent /ˈtælənt/ *n.* **1** [C,U] a natural ability to do something well: *great musical talent* | *his **talent for** painting* | *Vinny **has** a real **talent** for basketball.*

THESAURUS **flair, gift, aptitude** → SKILL

2 [U] a person or people who have talent: *The Marlins have some of the best young talent in baseball.* [ORIGIN: 1400—1500 *talent* unit of weight or money in the ancient world (9—21 centuries), from Latin *talentum*, from Greek *talanton*; from a story in the Bible in which a man gives talents to his three servants, and two of them use them well]

tal·ent·ed /ˈtæləntɪd/ *adj.* having a natural ability to do something well: *a talented actor*

THESAURUS **expert, accomplished, gifted** → SKILLFUL

tal·is·man /ˈtælɪsmən, -lɪz-/ *n.* (plural **talismans**) [C] an object that some people believe has the power to protect them

talk¹ /tɔk/ *v.* **1** [I] to say things to someone as part of a conversation → SPEAK: *How old was your baby when she started to talk?* | *Who's he **talking to** on the phone?* | *English people love to **talk about** the weather.* | *I was just **talking with** Louis the other day.* ►Don't say "talk English/Chinese, etc." say "speak English/Chinese, etc."◄

THESAURUS

have a conversation – to talk informally to another person or people in order to ask questions, exchange ideas, etc.: *I had a brief conversation with him last week.*
chat (with/to sb)/have a chat – to talk to someone in a friendly way about things that are not very important: *She's chatting with Chris.* | *We ended up having a chat about sailing.*
converse (formal) – to have a conversation with someone: *Students like her because she can converse with them in their own language.*
visit with sb (informal) – to have a conversation with someone, especially about your personal lives
discuss – to talk seriously about ideas or plans: *We'll discuss the matter at the meeting.*
gossip – to talk about other people's private lives when they are not there: *People have started to gossip about his wife.*
whisper – to talk quietly, usually because you do not want other people to hear what you are saying: *He turned to his mother and whispered something in her ear.* | *"I love you," she whispered.*

2 [I,T] to discuss something with someone, especially something important: *I'd like to **talk with** you in private.* | *Grandpa never **talks about** the war.* | *Those guys are always **talking sports/business/politics etc.*** (=discussing them). **3 talk your way out of sth** (informal) to use excuses or explanations to escape from a bad situation: *My brother always manages to talk his way out of trouble.* **4** [I] to give a speech: *Professor Wilson will **talk on/about** the recent election in Canada.* **5** [I] to tell someone secret information because you are forced to: *Prisoners who refused to talk were shot.*

SPOKEN PHRASES

6 talk tough (on sth) to tell people your opinions very strongly: *The governor is talking tough on crime.* **7 what are you talking about?** used when you think what someone has said is stupid or wrong: *What are you talking about? I paid you yesterday.* **8 we're/you're talking $500/three days etc.** used to tell someone how much something will cost, how long something will take to do, etc.: *We're talking at least ten days to fix the car.* **9 talk about funny/stupid/rich etc.** said in order to emphasize that something is very funny, stupid, etc.: *Talk about lucky. That's the second time he's won this week.*

talk back *phr. v.* to rudely answer someone who is older or has more authority than you: *Don't **talk back to** your father!*

talk down to sb *phr. v.* to speak to someone as if s/he is stupid, although s/he is not: *He always explained things but never talked down to me.*

talk sb **into** sth *phr. v.* to persuade someone to do something: *Maybe I can talk Vicky into driving us to the mall.*

talk sb **out of** sth *phr. v.* to persuade someone not to do something: *Brenda talked me out of quitting my job.*

talk sth ↔ **over** *phr. v.* to discuss a problem with someone before deciding what to do

talk² *n.* **1** [C] a conversation: *Steve and I **had a long talk** last night.* | *I need to **have a talk with** Suzanne.* **2 talks** [plural] formal discussions between governments, organizations, etc.: *the latest trade talks* **3** [C] a speech: *Ms. Mason will be **giving a talk on/about** the Civil War.* **4** [U] news that is not official or not completely true: *There was*

talk of *the factory closing down.* **5** [U] a particular type of conversation or way of talking: *I'm tired of all this football talk.* → SMALL TALK, TRASH TALK

talk·a·tive /'tɔkət̬ɪv/ *adj.* liking to talk a lot

talk·er /'tɔkɚ/ *n.* [C] (informal) someone who talks a lot or talks in a particular way: *a fast talker*

ˌtalk 'radio *n.* [U] radio programs on which people talk about various subjects, for example sports or politics

'talk show *n.* [C] a television show in which famous people answer questions about themselves → TELEVISION

tall /tɔl/ *adj.* **1** having a greater than average height (ANT) **small**: *the tallest boy in the class | tall buildings* **2** having a particular height: *My brother's almost 6 feet tall.*

USAGE

Use **tall** to talk about the height of people and trees: *She's only five feet tall. | a road with tall trees on either side*
Use **tall** to talk about other narrow objects: *an old house with tall chimneys | the tall mast of a ship*
Use **high** to talk about mountains, walls, fences, etc.: *the highest mountain in the world | How high will the wall be?*
Use **high** to talk about how far something is from the ground: *The shelf's too high for the kids to reach.*
You can use both **tall** and **high** to talk about buildings: *one of the highest buildings in the world | a city with crowded streets and tall buildings*

3 a tall tale something someone tells you that is so unlikely that it is difficult to believe **4 a tall order** (informal) a piece of work or a request that will be extremely difficult to do: *Finding a witness to this crime is going to be a tall order.*

tal·low /'tæloʊ/ *n.* [U] hard animal fat used for making CANDLES

tal·ly[1] /'tæli/ *n.* (plural **tallies**) [C] a record of how much you have won, spent, used, etc. by a particular point in time: *Somebody should be* ***keeping a tally of*** (=writing down) *how much we owe.*

tally[2] *v.* (**tallied**, **tallies**) **1** [T] *also* **tally up** to calculate the total number of points won, things done, etc.: *Can you tally up the scores?* → CALCULATE **2** [I] if two numbers, statements, dates, etc. tally, they match exactly: *The signatures should* ***tally with*** *the names on the list.*

tal·on /'tælən/ *n.* [C] one of the sharp curved nails on the feet of some birds that hunt → *see picture on page A15*

tam·bou·rine /ˌtæmbə'rin/ *n.* [C] a small drum with small pieces of metal around the edge, that you hold in your hand and play by hitting or shaking it

tame[1] /teɪm/ *adj.* **1** a tame animal is not wild any longer, because it has been trained to live with people (ANT) **wild**: *tame elephants* **2** (informal) boring and disappointing: *"How was the movie?" "Pretty tame."*

tame[2] *v.* [T] to train a wild animal so that it will not hurt people

tam·per /'tæmpɚ/ *v.*
tamper with sth *phr. v.* to change something without permission, usually in order to damage it: *Several bottles of aspirin had been tampered with.*

tam·pon /'tæmpɑn/ *n.* [C] a tube-shaped piece of cotton that a woman puts in her VAGINA during her PERIOD (=monthly flow of blood)

tan[1] /tæn/ *adj.* **1** having a pale yellow-brown color **2** having darker skin after spending a lot of time in the Sun: *Your face is really tan.*

tan[2] *n.* **1** [C] the attractive brown color that someone with pale skin gets after s/he has been in the sun (SYN) **suntan**: *Monica* ***got a*** *nice* ***tan*** *during her trip.* **2** [U] a pale yellow-brown color

tan[3] *v.* (**tanned**, **tanning**) **1** [I,T] if you tan, or if the Sun tans you, your skin becomes darker because you spend time in the sun: *I don't tan easily.* **2** [T] to change animal skin into leather by putting a special acid on it

tan·dem /'tændəm/ *n.* **1 in tandem** (formal) together or at the same time: *Police are working* ***in tandem with*** *local schools to reduce car thefts.* **2** [C] a bicycle built for two riders sitting one behind the other

tan·gent /'tændʒənt/ *n.* **go off on a tangent** to suddenly start talking or thinking about a completely different subject

tan·gen·tial /tæn'dʒɛnʃəl/ *adj.* (formal) tangential information, remarks, etc. are only related to a particular subject in an indirect way: *His lectures are full of tangential information.* —**tangentially** *adv.*

tan·ger·ine /ˌtændʒə'rin/ *n.* [C] a sweet fruit that looks like a small orange [ORIGIN: 1600—1700 French *Tanger* "Tangier," city in Morocco]

tan·gi·ble /'tændʒəbəl/ *adj.* **1** clear enough or definite enough to be easily seen or noticed (ANT) **intangible**: *tangible proof* **2** (formal) if something is tangible, you can touch or feel it

tangle[1] *v.* [I,T] to become twisted together, or make something become twisted together, in a messy way: *My hair tangles easily.*
tangle with sb *phr. v.* (informal) to argue or fight with someone

tan·gle[2] /'tæŋgəl/ *n.* [C] hair, threads, knots, etc. that have become twisted together: *a* ***tangle of*** *branches*

T

tan·gled /ˈtæŋgəld/ *also* **tangled up** *adj.* **1** twisted together in a messy way: *The phone cord is all tangled up.* **2** complicated and confusing: *tangled emotions*

tangled

tangled cord

tan·go /ˈtæŋgoʊ/ *n.* (plural **tangos**) [C] a dance from South America with smooth movements and sudden pauses, or the music for this dance

tang·y /ˈtæŋi/ *adj.* having a pleasantly strong sharp taste or smell: *a tangy lemon dessert* —**tang** *n.* [singular]

tank /tæŋk/ *n.* [C] **1** a large container for holding liquid or gas: *a fish tank* | *a car's **gas tank*** **2** a heavy military vehicle with a large gun and metal belts over its wheels [ORIGIN: 1600—1700 Portuguese *tanque* "pool"]

tan·kard /ˈtæŋkɚd/ *n.* [C] a large metal cup used for drinking beer

tank·er /ˈtæŋkɚ/ *n.* [C] a vehicle or ship used for carrying a large amount of liquid or gas: *an oil tanker*

T

tan·ta·lize /ˈtæntl̩ˌaɪz/ *v.* [T] to show or promise something that someone really wants, but then not allow him/her to have it

tan·ta·liz·ing /ˈtæntl̩ˌaɪzɪŋ/ *adj.* making you want something very much: *Tantalizing smells came from the kitchen.*

tan·ta·mount /ˈtæntəˌmaʊnt/ *adj.* **be tantamount to sth** to be almost the same thing as something else that is bad: *His refusal to speak was tantamount to admitting he was guilty.*

tan·trum /ˈtæntrəm/ *n.* [C] if someone, especially a child, throws or has a tantrum, s/he suddenly becomes very angry, noisy, and unreasonable: ***temper tantrums***

Tao·ism /ˈtaʊɪzəm, ˈdaʊ-/ *n.* [U] SOCIAL SCIENCE a way of thought developed in ancient China, based on the writings of Lao Tzu, emphasizing a natural and simple way of life

tap¹ /tæp/ *v.* (**tapped**, **tapping**) **1** [I,T] to gently hit your fingers or foot against something: *Someone was **tapping on** the window outside.* | *Caroline tapped her feet in time to the music.* | *He turned as someone tapped him on the shoulder.* ➔ *see picture on page A21*

THESAURUS hit, knock, bang, rap ➔ HIT¹

2 [I,T] to use or take what you need from a supply of something: *With the Internet you can **tap into** information from around the world.* | *We need to tap the country's natural resources without destroying the environment.* **3** [T] to put a tap on someone's telephone: *Murray began to suspect that his **phone** had been **tapped**.*

tap² *n.* [C] **1** an act of hitting something gently, especially to get someone's attention: *Suddenly I felt a **tap on** my shoulder.* **2** an object used for letting liquid, especially beer, out of a BARREL **3** a small electronic object that allows you to secretly listen to someone's telephone conversations **4 on tap** beer that is on tap comes from a BARREL **5** a FAUCET

ˈtap ˌdancing *n.* [U] a type of dancing in which you wear shoes with pieces of metal on the bottom, which make a sound as you move —**tap dance** *v.* [I]

tape¹ /teɪp/ (Ac) *n.* **1 a)** [U] a thin narrow band of plastic material used for recording sounds or video pictures ➔ VIDEOTAPE: *Did you get the interview **on tape** (=recorded on tape)?* **b)** [C] a flat plastic case that contains this type of tape: *I'll listen to the tape tomorrow.* | *a **blank tape*** (=one with nothing recorded on it) **2** [C,U] a narrow band of sticky material used for sticking things together (SYN) **Scotch tape**: *A photo was stuck to the wall with tape.*

tape² (Ac) *v.* **1** [I,T] to record sounds or pictures onto a tape ➔ VIDEOTAPE: *Did you tape the movie?* **2** [T] to stick something onto something else using tape: *He has lots of postcards **taped to** his wall.*

THESAURUS fasten, attach, secure, join, glue, staple, clip, tie, button (up), zip (up) ➔ FASTEN

3 [T] *also* **tape up** to firmly tie a BANDAGE around an injury

ˈtape deck *n.* [C] the part of a STEREO used for recording and playing sounds on a tape

ˈtape ˌmeasure *n.* [C] a long band of cloth or metal with inches, centimeters, etc. marked on it, used for measuring things

ta·per /ˈteɪpɚ/ *v.* [I,T] to become gradually narrower toward one end, or to make something become narrower at one end —**tapered** *adj.*: *pants with tapered legs*

taper off *phr. v.* to decrease gradually: *The rain finally tapered off in the afternoon.*

ˈtape reˌcorder *n.* [C] a piece of electronic equipment used for recording and playing sounds on a tape —**tape record** *v.* [T]

tap·es·try /ˈtæpɪstri/ *n.* (plural **tapestries**) [C,U] heavy cloth with colored threads woven into it to make a picture, or a large piece of this cloth

tape·worm /ˈteɪpwɚm/ *n.* [C] a long flat PARASITE that lives inside the INTESTINES of people and animals and can make them sick

tap·root /ˈtæprut/ *n.* [C] BIOLOGY the main root of some types of plants, that grows straight down and produces smaller side roots. A CARROT is an example of a plant with a taproot.

'tap ˌwater *n.* [U] water that comes out of a FAUCET

tar¹ /tɑr/ *n.* [U] **1** a black substance that is thick and sticky, used on road surfaces, or on roofs in order to protect them from water **2** a sticky dark brown substance that is produced when tobacco burns

tar² *v.* (**tarred**, **tarring**) [T] to cover something with tar

ta·ran·tu·la /tə'ræntʃələ/ *n.* [C] a large hairy poisonous SPIDER [ORIGIN: 1500—1600 Medieval Latin, Old Italian *tarantola*, from *Taranto* city in southern Italy, where such spiders are found]

tar·dy /'tɑrdi/ *adj.* late, or done too slowly: *If you are tardy once more you'll have to stay after school.* —**tardiness** *n.* [U]

THESAURUS late, overdue, belated → LATE¹
slow, sluggish → SLOW¹

tar·get¹ /'tɑrgɪt/ (Ac) *n.* [C] **1** an aim or result that you try to achieve: *We're trying to reach a* ***target of*** *$2 million in sales.* | *It will take a lot of hard work to* ***meet*** (=achieve) *our* ***target*** *this year.*

THESAURUS goal, aim, objective → GOAL

2 an object, person, or place that is deliberately chosen to be attacked: *a military target* | *Cars without security devices are an* ***easy target*** *for thieves.* **3** the person or place that is most directly affected by an action, especially a bad one: *The country is a* ***target of*** *criticism for its human rights record.* **4** something that you practice shooting at: *Pete missed the target by two inches.* [ORIGIN: 1200—1300 Old French *targette*, from *targe* "small shield"]

target² *v.* [T] **1** to aim something at someone or something: *Are the missiles* ***targeted on/at*** *American cities?* **2** to make something have an effect on a limited group or area: *Which welfare programs are* ***targeted at*** *the unemployed?* **3** to choose a particular person or place to attack: *Thieves have targeted smaller banks with less security.*

tar·iff /'tærɪf/ *n.* [C] ECONOMICS a tax on goods that are brought into a country or taken out of it: *The government may impose* ***tariffs on*** *imports.*

tar·mac /'tɑrmæk/ *n.* [U] **1** ASPHALT **2 the tarmac** the large area at an airport where airplanes land and take off [ORIGIN: 1900—2000, from *tarmacadam* from John L. *McAdam* (1756-1836), Scottish engineer who invented the process]

tar·nish /'tɑrnɪʃ/ *v.* **1** [T] to make someone or something less impressive or respectable: *More violence will* ***tarnish*** *the school's* ***reputation.*** **2** [I] if a metal tarnishes, it becomes less shiny and loses its color

tar·ot /'tærou/ *n.* [singular, U] a set of cards used for telling what might happen to someone in the future

tarp /tɑrp/ *also* **tar·pau·lin** /tɑr'pɔlən/ *n.* [C,U] a heavy cloth or piece of thick plastic that water cannot go through, used to protect things from the rain

tar·ry /'tæri/ *v.* (**tarried**, **tarries**) [I] (literary) to stay in a place too long, or delay going somewhere

tart¹ /tɑrt/ *adj.* tart food has a sour taste: *tart green apples*

tart² *n.* [C] a small PIE without a top, usually containing fruit

tar·tan /'tɑrt˺n/ *n.* [C,U] a traditional Scottish pattern with colored squares and lines, or cloth with this pattern

tar·tar /'tɑrtɚ/ *n.* [U] a hard substance that forms on teeth, damaging them

'tartar ˌsauce *n.* [U] a cold thick white sauce often eaten with fish

task /tæsk/ (Ac) *n.* **1** [C] a job or particular thing that you have to do, especially a difficult or annoying one: *We were given* ***the task of*** *rescuing crash victims.* | *A computer can* ***perform*** (=do) *several* ***tasks*** *at the same time.*

COLLOCATIONS

easy/simple/routine task – one that is easy to do
difficult/impossible task – one that is difficult to do
arduous task – one that needs a lot of hard work and continuous effort
daunting task – one that causes you to worry or be frightened
odious task – one that is unpleasant to do
thankless task – one that is difficult and you do not get much praise for
menial task – one that is boring and does not need skill to do
mundane task – one that is ordinary and not interesting or exciting

2 take sb to task to angrily criticize someone for doing something wrong [ORIGIN: 1200—1300 Old North French *tasque*, from Medieval Latin *tasca* "tax or service to be done for a ruler"]

'task force *n.* [C] a group formed for a short time to deal with a particular problem, especially a military or political one

tas·sel /'tæsəl/ *n.* [C] a group of threads tied together at one end and hung as a decoration on curtains, clothes, etc. —**tasseled** *adj.*

tassel

tassel

taste¹ /teɪst/ *n.* **1** [singular, U] the feeling that is produced when your tongue touches a particular food or drink, for example how sweet it is: *I don't like the* ***taste of***

T

garlic. | *a bitter/sour/sweet, etc. taste* | *He no longer has any* ***sense of taste*** *or smell.*

THESAURUS

delicious – very good
sweet – like sugar
tasty – having a pleasant taste, but not sweet
sour – like a lemon (=yellow fruit)
salty – containing a lot of salt
hot/spicy – containing spices that give you the feeling that your mouth is burning
bland – not having an interesting taste

2 [C,U] the kind of things that someone likes: *We have similar* ***tastes in*** *clothes.* | *She never lost her* ***taste for*** *travel.* **3** [U] your judgment when you choose clothes, decorations, etc.: *She has really good* ***taste in*** *music.* **4** [C usually singular] a small amount of a food or drink, eaten to find out what it is like: *Here,* ***have a taste*** *and tell me what you think.* **5 be in good/bad/poor taste** to be appropriate or inappropriate for a particular occasion: *The joke was in very bad taste.* **6 a taste of sth** a short experience of something: *The trip gave us a taste of life on board a ship.*

taste² *v.* **1** [I] to have a particular type of taste: *The chicken tastes really good.* | *This milk tastes a little sour.* ▸Don't say "is tasting."◂ | *What does the soup* ***taste like*** (=how would you describe its taste)? **2** [T] to put a small amount of food or drink in your mouth in order to find out what it is like: *Taste this and see if it needs more salt.* **3** [T] to recognize the taste of a food or drink: *My cold's so bad I can't taste a thing.* ▸Don't say "I am not tasting."◂

T

taste·ful /ˈteɪstfəl/ *adj.* chosen, decorated, or made with good taste: *Frank was dressed in casual but tasteful clothes.* —**tastefully** *adv.*: *a tastefully furnished apartment*

taste·less /ˈteɪstlɪs/ *adj.* **1** chosen, decorated, or made with bad taste: *tasteless jokes* **2** tasteless food is unpleasant because it does not have a strong taste

tast·er /ˈteɪstɚ/ *n.* [C] someone whose job is to test the quality of a food or drink by tasting it: *wine tasters*

tast·ing /ˈteɪstɪŋ/ *n.* [C] an event where you can try different kinds of food and drinks: *a cheese tasting*

tast·y /ˈteɪsti/ *adj.* having a very good taste: *a tasty meal*

THESAURUS **delicious, sweet, sour, salty, hot, spicy, bland** ➔ TASTE¹

tat·tered /ˈtæt̬ɚd/ *adj.* old and torn: *tattered curtains*

tat·ters /ˈtæt̬ɚz/ *n.* **in tatters a)** clothes that are in tatters are old and torn **b)** completely ruined: *All his great plans* ***lay in tatters.***

tat·tle /ˈtæt̬l/ *v.* [I] if a child tattles, s/he tells a parent or teacher that another child has done something bad

tat·tle·tale /ˈtæt̬lˌteɪl/ *n.* [C] (spoken) someone who tattles

tat·too /tæˈtu/ *n.* (plural **tattoos**) [C] a picture, word, etc. that is put permanently onto your skin using a needle and ink: *He has a tattoo of a snake on his left arm.* [ORIGIN: 1700—1800 Tahitian (the language spoken on the Pacific island of Tahiti) *tatau*] —**tattooed** *adj.* —**tattoo** *v.* [T]

taught /tɔt/ *v.* the past tense and past participle of TEACH

taunt /tɔnt, tɑnt/ *v.* [T] to try to make someone upset or angry by saying something unkind: *The other kids* ***taunted*** *him* ***about*** *his weight.* —**taunt** *n.* [C]

Tau·rus /ˈtɔrəs/ *n.* **1** [U] the second sign of the ZODIAC, represented by a BULL **2** [C] someone born between April 20 and May 20

taut /tɔt/ *adj.* **1** stretched tight: *a taut rope* **2** seeming worried: *a taut look on his face* —**tautly** *adv.*

tau·tol·o·gy /tɔˈtɑlədʒi/ *n.* (plural **tautologies**) [C,U] (technical) a statement in which you say the same thing twice using different words in a way that is not necessary, for example "He sat alone by himself." —**tautological** /ˌtɔt̬əˈlɑdʒɪkəl/ *adj.* —**tautologically** *adv.*

tav·ern /ˈtævɚn/ *n.* [C] a BAR [ORIGIN: 1200—1300 Old French *taverne*, from Latin *taberna* "small simple building, shop"]

taw·dry /ˈtɔdri/ *adj.* cheap and of bad quality: *tawdry jewelry* —**tawdriness** *n.* [U]

taw·ny /ˈtɔni/ *adj.* having a light gold-brown color: *a lion's tawny fur*

tax¹ /tæks/ *n.* [C,U] the money you must pay the government, based on how much you earn, what you buy, where you live, etc.: *a 13%* ***tax on*** *cigarettes* | *Everyone who works* ***pays tax.*** | *The city will have to* ***raise taxes*** *to pay for the roads.* | *If elected, she promised to* ***cut taxes.*** | *I only earn $25,000 a year* ***after taxes*** (=after paying tax). | *a* ***tax increase/cut*** [ORIGIN: 1200—1300 Old French *taxer* "to make a judgment about, tax," from Latin *taxare* "to feel, make a judgment about, blame"]

tax² *v.* [T] **1** to charge a tax on something: *Incomes of under $30,000 are* ***taxed at*** *15%.* **2 tax sb's patience/strength etc.** to use almost all of someone's PATIENCE, strength, etc.: *His constant questions had begun to tax her patience.*

tax·a·tion /tækˈseɪʃən/ *n.* [U] ECONOMICS the system of charging taxes, or the money collected from taxes

ˈtax base *n.* [C usually singular] **1** ECONOMICS all the people and companies who pay tax, and the total amount they pay **2** ECONOMICS income, goods, and property on which people or companies must pay tax

ˌtax-exˈempt *adj.* not taxed, or not having to pay tax: *tax-exempt savings* | *a tax-exempt charity*

tax·i[1] /ˈtæksi/ *n.* (plural **taxis**) *also* **tax·i·cab** /ˈtæksiˌkæb/ [C] a CAB ➔ *see picture at* TRANSPORTATION

taxi[2] *v.* (past tense and past participle **taxied**, third person singular **taxis** *or* **taxies**, present participle **taxiing**) [I] if an airplane taxis, it moves slowly on the ground before taking off or after landing

tax·i·der·my /ˈtæksəˌdɚmi/ *n.* [U] the process or skill of filling the body of a dead animal, bird, or fish with a special material so that it looks alive

tax·ing /ˈtæksɪŋ/ *adj.* needing a lot of effort: *a taxing job*

ˈtaxi stand *n.* [C] a place where taxis wait in order to get passengers

tax·on·o·my /tækˈsɑnəmi/ *n.* (plural **taxonomies**) [C,U] BIOLOGY the process or way of organizing living things such as plants or animals into a system of different groups according to the features that they share, and of giving them names —**taxonomic** /ˌtæksəˈnɑmɪk◂/ *adj.*: *Both species are members of the same taxonomic family as shrimp.*

tax·pay·er /ˈtæksˌpeɪɚ/ *n.* [C] someone who pays taxes

ˈtax ˌshelter *n.* [C] a plan or method that allows you to legally avoid paying taxes

TB the abbreviation of TUBERCULOSIS

tbsp. the written abbreviation of TABLESPOON

tea /ti/ *n.* **1 a)** [C,U] a drink made by pouring boiling water onto dried leaves, or a cup of this drink: *a **cup of tea** | We'll have two teas and a coffee, please.* **b)** [U] dried leaves used for making tea **2 mint/herbal etc. tea** a hot drink made by pouring boiling water onto the leaves or flowers of a particular plant [ORIGIN: 1600—1700 Chinese *te*]

ˈtea bag *n.* [C] a small paper bag with dried leaves in it, used for making tea

teach /titʃ/ *v.* (past tense and past participle **taught** /tɔt/) **1** [I,T] to give someone lessons, especially in a school or college: *Mr. Rochet has been teaching for 17 years. | She **teaches** math **at** Jackson High School. | Firstly, we **teach** the children **to** read. | All students are taught basic computer skills. | We **teach** students **about** the dangers of drugs.* **2** [T] to tell or show someone how to do something: *Can you teach me one of your card tricks? | My dad **taught me (how) to** swim.* **3 teach sb a lesson** (informal) to punish someone for something s/he has done, so that s/he will not want to do it again [ORIGIN: Old English *tæcan* "to show, teach"]

teach·er /ˈtitʃɚ/ *n.* [C] someone whose job is to teach: *my history teacher*

THESAURUS

A **teacher** is usually someone who works in a school: *Marie is a high school teacher.*
A **teacher** can also be someone who helps a person learn something: *a guitar teacher*
A **professor**, **lecturer**, or an **instructor** teaches in a university or college. A **professor** has a higher rank than a **lecturer** or an **instructor**.
An **instructor** is also someone who teaches a sport or practical skill such as swimming or driving: *a driving instructor | an aerobics instructor*
A **coach** trains a person or team in a sport: *a football coach* ➔ SCHOOL[1], UNIVERSITY

ˌteacher's ˈpet *n.* [C] a child who everyone thinks is the teacher's favorite student and is therefore disliked by the other students

teach·ing /ˈtitʃɪŋ/ *n.* **1** [U] the work that a teacher does, or the profession of being a teacher: *I'd like to **go into teaching*** (=become a teacher) *when I finish college.* **2** *also* **teachings** [plural] the moral, religious, or political ideas spread by a particular person or group: *the **teachings of** the Buddha*

tea·cup /ˈtikʌp/ *n.* [C] a cup that you serve tea in

teak /tik/ *n.* [C,U] a very hard yellowish-brown wood that is used for making ships and good quality furniture, or the tree that this wood comes from

team[1] /tim/ (AW) *n.* [C] **1** a group of people who compete against another group in a sport, game, etc.: *Which team is winning? | a **baseball/football etc. team*** ➔ GROUP[1] **2** a group of people who are chosen to work together to do a particular job: *a **team of** doctors | The children must work as a team to solve the problem.*

team[2] *v.* [I,T] *also* **team up** to form a team with another person, company, etc. in order to work together: *We're **teaming up with** another publisher to do the book.*

team·mate /ˈtim-meɪt/ *n.* [C] someone who plays or works on the same team as you

ˈteam ˌplayer *n.* [C] someone who works well as a member of a team

team·ster /ˈtimstɚ/ *n.* [C] someone whose job is to drive a truck

team·work /ˈtimwɚk/ *n.* [U] the ability of a group to work well together, or the effort the group makes

tea·pot /ˈtipɑt/ *n.* [C] a container used for serving tea, that has a handle and a SPOUT

tear[1] /tɛr/ *v.* (past tense **tore** /tɔr/, past participle **torn** /tɔrn/) **1** [I,T] if you tear paper, cloth, etc., or if it tears, you make a hole in it or it breaks into small pieces (SYN) **rip**: *You've torn your sleeve. | He **tore** the envelope **open**. | Oh no, I **tore a hole in** my jeans! | Someone had **torn** some pages **out of** the book. | Be careful, you don't want your dress to tear!* ➔ BREAK[1] **2** [T] to pull something violently from a person or place: *The storm actually **tore** the door **off** its hinges.* **3** [I] to move very quickly, often in a careless or dangerous way: *Two kids came **tearing around** the corner.*

THESAURUS **run, sprint, dash, race** ➔ RUN[1]

T

tear apart *phr. v.* **1 tear** sth ↔ **apart** to make a group, organization, etc. start having problems: *The scandal is tearing the company apart.* **2 tear** sb **apart** to make someone feel extremely unhappy or upset: *It tore me apart to see her leave.*

tear sth ↔ **down** *phr. v.* to deliberately destroy a building: *The old high school was torn down in the early '90s.*

tear into sb/sth *phr. v.* (informal) to strongly criticize someone or something: *Then he started tearing into her for spending too much money.*

tear sth ↔ **up** *phr. v.* to tear a piece of paper or cloth into small pieces: *He tore up all of Linda's old letters.*

tear² /tɪr/ *n.* [C] a drop of liquid that comes out of your eyes when you cry: *She ran away with tears in her eyes.* | *Garner left the courtroom* ***in tears*** (=crying). | *Suddenly Brian* ***burst into tears*** (=started crying).

tear³ /tɛr/ *n.* [C] a hole in a piece of paper, cloth, etc. where it has been torn: *There was a* ***tear in*** *his shirt.*

tear·drop /ˈtɪrdrɑp/ *n.* [C] a single tear

tear·ful /ˈtɪrfəl/ *adj.* crying or almost crying

tease¹ /tiz/ *v.* **1** [I,T] to make jokes about someone in order to embarrass or annoy him/her because you think it is funny: *Don't cry. I was just teasing.* | *His friends* ***teased*** *him* ***about*** *his accent.* **2** [T] to comb your hair in the wrong direction so that it looks thicker

T

tease² *n.* [C] someone who enjoys teasing people

tea·spoon /ˈtispun/ *n.* [C] **1** (*written abbreviation* **tsp.**) a small spoon used for STIRring a cup of tea or coffee **2 a)** a special spoon used for measuring food **b)** *also* **tea·spoon·ful** /ˈtispunfʊl/ the amount this spoon holds

teat /tit/ *n.* [C] a NIPPLE on a female animal

tech·ni·cal /ˈtɛknɪkəl/ (Ac) *adj.* **1** relating to the practical skills, knowledge, and methods used in science or industry: *Technical experts will look into the cause of the crash.* | *technical training* **2** relating to a particular subject or profession: *a legal document full of technical terms*

tech·ni·cal·i·ty /ˌtɛknɪˈkæləṭi/ *n.* (plural **technicalities**) **1** [C] a small detail in a law or rule: *The case against him had to be dropped because of a technicality.* | *He* ***got off on a technicality*** (=because of a technicality). **2 technicalities** [plural] the details of a system or process that you need special knowledge to understand

tech·ni·cally /ˈtɛknɪkli/ (Ac) *adv.* **1** according to the exact details of a rule or law: *Technically, he's responsible for fixing all the damage.* **2** relating to the way machines are used in science and industry: *a* ***technically advanced*** *engine*

tech·ni·cian /tɛkˈnɪʃən/ *n.* [C] a skilled scientific or industrial worker: *a lab technician*

tech·nique /tɛkˈnik/ (Ac) *n.* [C,U] a special skill or way of doing something: *new* ***techniques for*** *teaching English* | *Tiger Woods is regarded as a golfer with excellent technique.*

> THESAURUS **method, way, approach** → METHOD

tech·nol·o·gy /tɛkˈnɑlədʒi/ (Ac) *n.* (plural **technologies**) [C,U] machines, equipment, and ways of doing things that are based on modern knowledge about science and computers: *medical technology* | *The company is a leader in developing new technologies in agriculture.* —**technological** /ˌtɛknəˈlɑdʒɪkəl/ *adj.*: *The twentieth century was a time of rapid technological change.* —**technologically** *adv.*: *a technologically advanced country*

tec·ton·ic plate /tɛkˌtɑnɪk ˈpleɪt/ *n.* [C] EARTH SCIENCES one of the very large areas of rock that form the surface of the Earth, and that move around in relation to each other in a way that can cause EARTHQUAKEs, etc.

ted·dy bear /ˈtɛdi ˌbɛr/ *n.* [C] a soft toy shaped like a bear [ORIGIN: 1900—2000 from Theodore (*Teddy*) Roosevelt (1858-1919), U.S. president, who liked hunting bears]

te·di·ous /ˈtidiəs/ *adj.* boring, and continuing for a long time: *a tedious discussion*

> THESAURUS **boring, dull, humdrum, monotonous** → BORING

te·di·um /ˈtidiəm/ *n.* [U] the quality of being tedious

tee /ti/ *n.* [C] a small object used for holding a GOLF ball, or the raised area from which you hit the ball

teem /tim/ *v.*

teem with sth *phr. v.* to be full of people or animals that are all moving around: *The lake teemed with fish.* —**teeming** *adj.*: *the teeming streets of Cairo*

teen /tin/ *n.* (informal) **1** [C] a teenager **2 teens** [plural] the period of your life when you are between 13 and 19 years old: *She got married when she was still* ***in her teens***. —**teen** *adj.*

teen·age /ˈtineɪdʒ/ *adj.* between 13 and 19 years old, or relating to someone who is: *teenage pregnancy* | *our teenage son* ▸ Don't say "our son is teenage." ◂

teen·ag·er /ˈtiˌneɪdʒɚ/ *n.* [C] someone who is between 13 and 19 years old

> THESAURUS **child, kid, adolescent, youngster, minor, juvenile** → CHILD

tee·ny /ˈtini/ *also* **tee·ny-wee·ny** /ˌtini ˈwini◂/ *adj.* (spoken) very small (SYN) **tiny**

ˈtee ˌshirt *n.* [C] a T-SHIRT

tee·ter /ˈtiṭɚ/ *v.* [I] **1** to move or stand in an unsteady way: *She stood there, teetering in her new high-heeled shoes.* **2 be teetering on (the brink/edge of) sth** to be very likely to become involved in a dangerous situation: *The country is teetering on the brink of revolution.*

teeth /tiθ/ *n.* the plural of TOOTH

teethe /tið/ *v.* [I] if a baby is teething, his/her first teeth are growing

tee·to·tal·er /ˈtiˌtoʊt̬lɚ/ *n.* [C] someone who never drinks alcohol —**teetotal** *adj.*

Tef·lon /ˈtɛflɑn/ *n.* [U] (trademark) a special material that stops things from sticking to it, often used in making cooking pans

tel·e·com·mu·ni·ca·tions /ˌtɛləkəˌmyunəˈkeɪʃənz/ *n.* [U] the process of sending and receiving messages by telephone, radio, SATELLITE, etc.

tel·e·com·mut·er /ˈtɛləkəˌmyut̬ɚ/ *n.* [C] someone who works for a company at home using a computer connected to the main office

tel·e·con·ference /ˈtɛləˌkɑnfrəns/ *n.* [C] a discussion between people in different places who talk to each other using telephones and video equipment —**teleconference** *v.* [I]

tel·e·gram /ˈtɛləˌgræm/ *n.* [C] a message sent by telegraph

tel·e·graph /ˈtɛləˌgræf/ *n.* [C,U] an old-fashioned method of sending messages using electrical signals, or the equipment used for sending these messages [ORIGIN: 1700—1800 French *télégraphe*, from Greek *tele-* "far away" + Latin *-graphus* "written")]

te·lep·a·thy /təˈlɛpəθi/ *n.* [U] a way of communicating in which thoughts are sent from one person's mind to another person's mind —**telepathic** /ˌtɛləˈpæθɪk◂/ *adj.*

tel·e·phone¹ /ˈtɛləˌfoʊn/ *n.* [C] a PHONE [ORIGIN: 1800—1900 *tele-* + Greek *phone* "sound, voice"]

telephone² *v.* [I,T] to PHONE

te·leph·o·ny /təˈlɛfəni/ *n.* [U] IT computer HARDWARE and SOFTWARE that allow a computer to make and receive telephone calls

tel·e·pho·to lens /ˌtɛləˌfoʊt̬oʊ ˈlɛnz/ *n.* [C] a special camera LENS used for taking clear photographs of things that are far away

tel·e·scope /ˈtɛləˌskoʊp/ *n.* [C] a piece of scientific equipment shaped like a tube with special LENSes, used for making distant objects such as stars and PLANETS look larger and closer [ORIGIN: 1600—1700 Modern Latin *telescopium*, from Greek *teleskopos* "seeing a long way," from *tele-* "far away" + *skopos* "watcher"]

tel·e·scop·ic /ˌtɛləˈskɑpɪk◂/ *adj.* relating to a telescope, or using a telescope: *a telescopic lens*

tel·e·thon /ˈtɛləˌθɑn/ *n.* [C] a television show in which famous people provide entertainment and ask the people who are watching to give money to help people who need it

tel·e·van·ge·lism /ˌtɛləˈvændʒəˌlɪzəm/ *n.* [U] the activity of giving speeches on television to persuade people to become Christians or to give money to a Christian organization

tel·e·vise /ˈtɛləˌvaɪz/ *v.* [T] to broadcast something on television: *Is the game going to be televised?*

tel·e·vi·sion /ˈtɛləˌvɪʒən/ *also* **TV** *n.* **1** *also* **ˈtelevision ˌset** [C] a piece of electronic equipment shaped like a box with a screen, on which you can watch programs: *Will you* ***turn on/off*** *the television?* **2** [U] the programs that you can watch and listen to on a television: *He's been* ***watching television*** *all day.* | *What's* ***on television*** *tonight?*

THESAURUS

Types of television programs

movie/film: *There's a good movie on Channel 7 at 9 o'clock.*

soap opera – a program that is on TV regularly, often every day, about the same group of people

sitcom – a funny TV program which has the same people in it every week in a different story

game show – a program in which people play games in order to try and win prizes

talk show – a program in which people answer questions about themselves

cartoon – a movie or program that uses characters that are drawn and not real

drama series – a set of TV programs about the same group of people or about a particular subject, shown regularly: *a new drama series about cops and lawyers*

documentary – a program that gives information about a subject

the news: *the 6 o'clock news*

TOPIC

When you want to **watch TV**, you look in the **TV guide** (=a list of TV programs) to see **what's on**. When you decide which **program/show** you want to watch, you **turn on the TV**, usually by using a **remote control**. Many people just turn on the TV and **change channels** (=television stations) until they find a program they want to watch. If you change channels a lot, you can call it **channel hopping/surfing**. A lot of people have **cable TV** or **satellite TV**, which gives them a lot of channels to choose from. People who watch a lot of TV are sometimes called **couch potatoes**.

3 [U] the activity of making and broadcasting programs on television: *a job* ***in television*** [ORIGIN: 1900—2000 French *télévision*, from Greek *tele-* "far away" + *vision* (from Latin *videre* "to see")]

tell /tɛl/ *v.* (past tense and past participle **told** /toʊld/)

1 INFORMATION [T] to give someone facts or information in speech or writing: ***Tell*** *Mark* ***(that)*** *I said hi.* | *Did you* ***tell*** *Jennifer* ***about*** *the party?* | *Could you* ***tell*** *me* ***how*** *to make that cheesecake?* | *She wouldn't* ***tell*** *me* ***why*** *she was angry.* | *I don't think he's* ***telling the truth***. | *Dad used to tell us bedtime stories.*

T

USAGE

Tell and **say** are used differently. You "tell someone something": *I told him the good news.* but you "say something to someone": *He always says hello to me.* Do not say "I told to him" or "he said me".

THESAURUS explain, show → EXPLAIN

2 RECOGNIZE [I,T] to be able to recognize or judge something correctly: *I **could tell (that)** it was a serious discussion.* | *Use plain yogurt instead of sour cream – you **can't tell the difference**.* | *"How long will it take?" **"It's hard to tell.**"*
3 WHAT SB SHOULD DO [T] to say that someone must do something: ***Tell** her **to** put on her coat – it's cold.* | *Stop **telling** me **what to do**!*
4 tell yourself to persuade yourself to do something or that something is true: *I kept telling myself to relax.*
5 SIGN [T] to give information in a way other than by speech or writing: *This red light tells you it's recording.*
6 tell time to be able to know what time it is by looking at a clock
7 there's no telling what/how/whether etc. used in order to say that it is impossible to know what has happened or what will happen next: *There's no telling how long it will take.*
8 all told in total: *All told, 40,000 airline workers have lost their jobs this year.*
9 STH WRONG [I,T] (spoken) to tell someone in authority about something wrong that someone else has done: *I was afraid my little sister would **tell on** us.*

SPOKEN PHRASES

10 (I'll) tell you what said in order to suggest something: *Tell you what, call me on Friday, and we'll make plans then.*
11 I tell you/I'm telling you/let me tell you said in order to emphasize something: *I'm telling you, the gossip in this place is unbelievable!*
12 tell me about it said in order to say that you already know how bad something is: *"She's so arrogant!" "Yeah, tell me about it."*
13 (I) told you (so) said when someone does something you have warned him/her about, and it has a bad result: *I told you. You can't trust her.*
14 to tell (you) the truth said in order to emphasize that you are being honest: *I don't know how you cope, to tell you the truth.*
15 you never can tell/you can never tell used in order to say that you can never be certain about what will happen in the future: *They're not likely to win, but you never can tell.*

[ORIGIN: Old English *tellan*]

tell sb **apart** *phr. v.*
to be able to see the difference between two people or things, even though they are similar: *Carol puts the twins in different color booties so you **can tell** them **apart**.*

tell sb ↔ **off** *phr. v.*
to talk angrily to someone when s/he has done something wrong: *She told him off in front of the whole office.*

tell·er /ˈtɛlɚ/ *n.* [C] someone whose job is to receive and pay out money in a bank

tell·ing /ˈtɛlɪŋ/ *adj.* a remark that is telling shows what you really think, although you may not intend it to

tell·tale /ˈtɛlteɪl/ *adj.* clearly showing something has happened or exists, often something that is a secret: *What are the **telltale signs** of drug addiction?*

te·mer·i·ty /təˈmɛrət̬i/ *n.* [U] (formal) the quality of doing or saying something even though you know it may offend or annoy someone or get you in trouble: *He **had the temerity to** criticize me!*

temp[1] /tɛmp/ *n.* [C] an office worker who is only employed for a limited period of time

temp[2] *v.* [I] to work as a temp: *Anne's temping until she can find another job.*

tem·per[1] /ˈtɛmpɚ/ *n.* **1** [C,U] a tendency to become suddenly angry: *John needs to learn to control his temper.* **2 lose/keep your temper** to suddenly become very angry, or to stay calm **3 have a quick/hot/slow etc. temper** to get angry very easily, or not very easily: *Her father has a violent temper.* **4 -tempered** having a particular type of temper: *a **bad-tempered** old man* | *an **even-tempered** child* (=one who is calm and does not get angry easily)

temper[2] *v.* [T] **1** (formal) to make something less difficult or severe: *Her criticism is **tempered with** humor.* **2** to make metal harder by heating it and then making it cold: *tempered steel*

tem·pera·ment /ˈtɛmprəmənt/ *n.* [C,U] the part of your character that makes you likely to be happy, angry, sad, etc.: *a baby with a calm temperament*

tem·pera·men·tal /ˌtɛmprəˈmɛntl/ *adj.* **1** tending to get upset, excited, or angry very easily **2** a temperamental machine does not always work correctly

tem·perance /ˈtɛmprəns/ *n.* [U] the practice of never drinking alcohol

ˈtemperance ˌmovement *n.* [C usually singular] HISTORY a group of people whose aim was to prevent or strictly limit the drinking of alcohol, especially in the late 1800s and early 1900s

tem·perate /ˈtɛmprɪt/ *adj.* weather or a part of the world that is temperate is never very hot or very cold: *a temperate climate*

ˈtemperate ˌzone *n.* [C] EARTH SCIENCES one of the two parts of the Earth that are between the POLAR ZONES and the TROPICS, where the weather is not usually very hot nor very cold

tem·pera·ture /ˈtɛmprətʃɚ/ *n.* **1** [C,U] how hot or cold something is: *Water freezes **at a temperature of** 32°F.* | *The **temperature rose** to 102* degrees. | ***Temperatures** could **drop** to below zero tonight.* | *Store this product at **room temperature*** (=the normal temperature in a room). **2 sb's temperature** the temperature of your body, used as a measure of whether you are sick or not: *The nurse **took** my **temperature**.* **3 have a temperature** to be hot because you are sick

tem·pest /ˈtɛmpɪst/ *n.* [C] (literary) a violent storm

tem·pes·tu·ous /tɛmˈpɛstʃuəs/ *adj.* always full of strong emotions: *a tempestuous relationship*

tem·plate /ˈtɛmpleɪt/ *n.* [C] **1** a sheet of paper, plastic, or metal in a particular shape, used in order to help you cut other materials in the same shape **2** IT a computer document that you use as a model for producing many similar documents

tem·ple /ˈtɛmpəl/ *n.* [C] **1** a building where people go to worship in some religions: *a Buddhist temple* **2** [usually plural] one of the two fairly flat areas on each side of your FOREHEAD [ORIGIN: (1) 800—900 Latin *templum*]

tem·po /ˈtɛmpoʊ/ *n.* (plural **tempos**) [C] **1** the speed at which something happens (SYN) **pace**: *the tempo of city life* **2** ENG. LANG. ARTS the speed at which music is played

tem·po·rar·y /ˈtɛmpəˌrɛri/ (Ac) *adj.* existing or happening for only a limited period of time (ANT) **permanent**: *a temporary visa* | *Linda was employed **on a temporary basis**.* [ORIGIN: 1500—1600 Latin *temporarius*, from *tempus* "time"] —**temporarily** /ˌtɛmpəˈrɛrəli/ *adv.*: *The library is temporarily closed.*

THESAURUS short, brief → SHORT[1]

tempt /tɛmpt/ *v.* **1** [T] to persuade someone to do something by making it seem attractive: *They're offering free gifts to **tempt** people **to** join.* **2 be tempted to do sth** to consider doing something that may not be a good idea: *I was tempted to correct him, but I didn't want to hurt his feelings.* **3 tempt fate** to say or do something that may cause problems —**tempting** *adj.*: *a tempting offer*

temp·ta·tion /tɛmpˈteɪʃən/ *n.* [C,U] **1** a strong desire to have or do something even though you know you should not: *I had to **resist the temptation to** slap her.* | *I finally **gave in to temptation** and had a cigarette.* **2** something that you want to have or do, even though you know you should not: *The candy at the check-out counter is a temptation to children.*

ten[1] /tɛn/ *number* **1** 10 **2** ten o'clock: *I have a meeting **at ten**.* **3** ten years old: *He's ten next week.* [ORIGIN: Old English *tien*]

ten[2] *n.* [C] a piece of paper money worth $10

ten·a·ble /ˈtɛnəbəl/ *adj.* (formal) **1** a tenable belief, argument, etc. is reasonable and can be defended successfully: *The new discovery makes this theory less tenable.* **2** a tenable situation can continue because any problems can be dealt with: *Continuing to fight in Vietnam no longer seemed tenable.*

te·na·cious /təˈneɪʃəs/ *adj.* very determined to do something, and unwilling to stop trying —**tenaciously** *adv.* —**tenacity** /təˈnæsət̬i/ *n.* [U]

ten·an·cy /ˈtɛnənsi/ *n.* (plural **tenancies**) [C,U] the period of time that someone rents a house, room, etc., or the right to use a house, room, etc. that has been rented

ten·ant /ˈtɛnənt/ *n.* [C] someone who lives in a house, room, etc. and pays rent to the person who owns it → LANDLORD: *The desk was left by the previous tenant.*

ˌtenant ˈfarmer *n.* [C] someone who farms land that is rented from someone else

tend /tɛnd/ *v.* **1 tend to do sth** to be likely to do a particular thing: *People tend to need less sleep as they get older.* **2** [T] *also* **tend to sb/sth** to take care of someone or something: *Rescue teams were tending to the survivors.*

tend·en·cy /ˈtɛndənsi/ *n.* (plural **tendencies**) [C] **1** if someone or something has a tendency to do something, s/he is likely to do it: *He **has a tendency to** talk too much.* **2** the way in which a situation is beginning to develop or a change that is happening to it: ***There is a tendency for** men to marry younger women.*

ten·der[1] /ˈtɛndɚ/ *adj.* **1** gentle in a way that shows love: *a tender look* **2** a tender part of your body is painful if someone touches it: *My arm is still tender where I bruised it.*

THESAURUS painful, sore → PAINFUL

3 tender food is easy to cut and eat (ANT) **tough** **4 tender age** (literary) a time when you are young or do not have much experience: *He left home **at the tender age of** sixteen.* —**tenderly** *adv.* —**tenderness** *n.* [U]

tender[2] *v.* [T] (formal) to formally offer something to someone: *Maria has **tendered** her **resignation*** (=officially said that she is going to leave her job).

ten·der·heart·ed /ˌtɛndɚˈhɑrt̬ɪd◂/ *adj.* very kind and gentle

ten·don /ˈtɛndən/ *n.* [C] BIOLOGY a thick strong part inside your body that connects a muscle to a bone

ten·dril /ˈtɛndrəl/ *n.* [C] BIOLOGY a thin curling piece on the stem of a climbing plant, by which the plant fastens to a wall

ten·e·ment /ˈtɛnəmənt/ *n.* [C] a large building divided into apartments, especially in a poor area of a city

ten·et /ˈtɛnɪt/ *n.* [C] a principle or belief: *the tenets of Buddhism*

ten·nis /ˈtɛnɪs/ *n.* [U] a game in which two or four

people use RACKETS to hit a ball to each other across a net

ˈtennis shoe *n.* [C] a light shoe used for sports

ten·or /ˈtɛnɚ/ *n.* **1** [C] ENG. LANG. ARTS a male singer with a high voice **2 the tenor of sth** (formal) the general meaning or quality of something: *the tenor of the president's speech*

tense¹ /tɛns/ (Ac) *adj.* **1** nervous and anxious: *You seem really tense – what's wrong?* | *a **tense atmosphere/situation/moment***

THESAURUS worried, anxious, nervous → WORRIED

2 tense muscles feel tight and stiff —**tensely** *adv.*: *She leaned forward tensely, listening.*

tense² *also* **tense up** *v.* [I,T] to become tight and stiff, or to make your muscles do this

tense³ *n.* [C,U] ENG. LANG. ARTS in grammar, one of the forms of a verb that shows actions or states in the past, the present, or in the future. For example, "he studied" is in the past tense, "he studies" is in the present tense, and "he will study" is in the future tense.

ten·sion /ˈtɛnʃən/ (Ac) *n.* **1** [C,U] the feeling that exists when people do not trust each other and may suddenly attack each other or start arguing: *the **racial tension** in American society* | ***tension between** the union workers and management* **2** [U] a nervous and anxious feeling: *The room was filled with tension as students waited for their exams.* **3** [U] tightness or stiffness in a wire, rope, muscle, etc.: ***Muscle tension** can be a sign of stress.* **4** [C,U] a difficult situation in which different needs or ideas affect the situation in opposite ways: *the **tension between** preserving civil liberties and increasing national security* **5** [U] the amount of force that stretches something: *How much tension can the wire bear before snapping?*

tent /tɛnt/ *n.* [C] a shelter that you can easily move, made of cloth or plastic and supported by poles and ropes: *Where should we **pitch the tent*** (=put up the tent)*?*

ten·ta·cle /ˈtɛntəkəl/ *n.* [C] BIOLOGY one of the long thin parts like arms of a sea creature such as an OCTOPUS

ten·ta·tive /ˈtɛntət̬ɪv/ *adj.* **1** not definite or certain: *tentative plans* **2** done without confidence: *a tentative smile* —**tentatively** *adv.*

tenth /tɛnθ/ *number* 10th

ten·u·ous /ˈtɛnyuəs/ *adj.* a situation or relationship that is tenuous is uncertain, weak, or likely to change: *There is only a **tenuous connection** between the two events.* —**tenuously** *adv.*

ten·ure /ˈtɛnyɚ/ *n.* [U] **1** the right to stay permanently in a teaching job at a university **2** (formal) the period of time when someone has an important job: *the Mayor's tenure in office*

te·pee, teepee /ˈtipi/ *n.* [C] a round tent used by some Native Americans [ORIGIN: 1700—1800 Dakota Sioux *tipi*, from *ti* "to live in a place" + *pi* "to use for"]

tep·id /ˈtɛpɪd/ *adj.* tepid liquid is slightly warm

te·qui·la /təˈkilə/ *n.* [U] a strong alcoholic drink made in Mexico [ORIGIN: 1800—1900 Spanish *Tequila* area of Mexico]

ter·a·byte /ˈtɛrəˌbaɪt/ *n.* [C] IT a unit for measuring the amount of information a computer can store or use, equal to about a TRILLION BYTES

term¹ /tɚm/ *n.* [C]

1 in terms of sth if you explain something in terms of a particular fact or event, you talk about it only in relation to that fact or event and no others: *In terms of sales the book hasn't been very successful.*

2 in financial/artistic etc. terms if you describe or consider something in financial, etc. terms, you are thinking of it in a financial, etc. way: *A million years isn't a very long time in geological terms.*

3 WORD/EXPRESSION a word or expression that has a particular meaning, especially in a technical or scientific subject: *I don't understand these **legal/medical/technical terms**.*

4 CONDITIONS terms [plural] the conditions of an agreement, contract, legal document, etc.: ***Under the terms of the agreement**, the debt will be repaid over twenty years.*

5 be on good/bad/friendly etc. terms (with sb) to have a particular type of relationship with someone: *He hasn't been on good terms with his father for years.*

6 SCHOOL/COLLEGE one of the periods that a school or college year is divided into → QUARTER, SEMESTER: *When does the spring term start?*

7 PERIOD OF TIME a fixed period of time during which someone does something or something happens: *The president hopes to be elected for a second term.* | *Reynolds could get a **prison term** of up to 85 years.*

8 be on speaking terms to be able to talk to someone and have a friendly relationship with him/her: *We're barely on speaking terms now.*

9 come to terms with sth to understand and deal with a difficult situation: *It was hard to come to terms with Marie's death.*

10 in the long/short term during a long or short period from now: *The company's prospects look better in the long term.* [ORIGIN: 1200—1300 Old French *terme* "edge, limit, end," from Latin *terminus*]

term² *v.* [T] (formal) to use a particular word or phrase to describe something: *The meeting could hardly be termed a success.*

ter·mi·nal¹ /ˈtɚmənəl/ (Ac) *adj.* a terminal disease cannot be cured, and causes death: *terminal cancer* —**terminally** *adv.*: *terminally ill*

terminal² *n.* [C] **1** a big building where you go to get onto airplanes, buses, or ships: *Our flight leaves from Terminal B.* **2** IT a computer KEYBOARD and screen connected to a computer that is somewhere else

ter·mi·nate /ˈtɚməˌneɪt/ (Ac) *v.* [I,T] (formal) if something terminates, or if you terminate it, it ends: *Who has the power to terminate the contract?* | *It was an agonizing decision to terminate the pregnancy.*

ter·mi·na·tion /ˌtɚməˈneɪʃən/ (Ac) *n.* [C,U] **1** the act of ending something, or the end of something: *the termination of the marriage* **2** a medical operation to end the life of a developing child before it is born (SYN) **abortion**

ter·mi·nol·o·gy /ˌtɚməˈnɑlədʒi/ *n.* [U] the technical words or expressions that are used in a particular subject: *scientific terminology* [ORIGIN: 1800—1900 Medieval Latin *terminus* "word, term" (from Latin; TERM[1]) + English *-ology*]

THESAURUS **language, lingo, jargon** → LANGUAGE

ter·mi·nus /ˈtɚmənəs/ *n.* [C] the place at the end of a railroad or bus line [ORIGIN: 1800—1900, from Latin *terminus* "edge, limit, end"]

ter·mite /ˈtɚmaɪt/ *n.* [C] an insect that eats wood from trees and buildings

ter·race /ˈtɛrɪs/ *n.* [C] **1** a flat outdoor area next to a building or on a roof, where you can sit to eat, relax, etc. **2** a flat area cut out of the side of a hill, often used for growing crops on [ORIGIN: 1500—1600 Old French "pile of earth, terrace," from Latin *terra* "earth, land"]

ter·ra·cot·ta /ˌtɛrəˈkɑt̬ə◂/ *n.* [U] hard red-brown baked clay: *a terracotta pot* [ORIGIN: 1700—1800 Italian "baked earth"]

ter·rain /təˈreɪn/ *n.* [C,U] land of a particular type: *rocky terrain*

ter·res·tri·al /təˈrɛstriəl/ *adj.* **1** EARTH SCIENCES relating to the Earth rather than to the Moon, stars, or other PLANETS **2** BIOLOGY living on or relating to land rather than water [ORIGIN: 1300—1400 Latin *terrestris*, from *terra* "earth"]

ter·ri·ble /ˈtɛrəbəl/ *adj.* very bad (SYN) **awful**: *The food at the hotel was terrible.* | *a terrible accident* | *You're making a terrible mistake.* [ORIGIN: 1300—1400 Old French, Latin *terribilis*, from *terrere* "to frighten"]

THESAURUS **bad, awful, appalling, horrific, lousy, horrendous, atrocious, abysmal** → BAD[1]
horrible, disgusting, revolting, dreadful → HORRIBLE

ter·ri·bly /ˈtɛrəbli/ *adv.* **1** very badly: *The team played terribly.* **2** extremely: *I'm terribly sorry, but the answer is no.*

ter·ri·er /ˈtɛriɚ/ *n.* [C] a type of small dog

ter·rif·ic /təˈrɪfɪk/ *adj.* **1** (informal) very good or enjoyable: *That's a terrific idea.* | *She looked terrific.* **2** (formal) very large in size or degree: *a terrific shock* —**terrifically** *adv.*

ter·ri·fied /ˈtɛrəˌfaɪd/ *adj.* very frightened: *The children were **terrified of** the dog.* | *We were **terrified that** the bridge would collapse.*

THESAURUS **frightened, afraid, scared, petrified, fearful** → FRIGHTENED

ter·ri·fy /ˈtɛrəˌfaɪ/ *v.* (**terrified**, **terrifies**) [T] to make someone extremely afraid: *The thought of giving a speech terrified her.* —**terrifying** *adj.*: *a terrifying experience*

ter·ri·to·ri·al /ˌtɛrəˈtɔriəl/ *adj.* **1** [only before noun] relating to land or ocean that is owned or controlled by a particular country: *U.S. territorial waters* **2** territorial animals or people closely guard the place they consider to be their own

ter·ri·to·ry /ˈtɛrəˌtɔri/ *n.* (plural **territories**) **1** [C,U] land or ocean that is owned or controlled by a particular country: *Canadian territory* | *The plane was flying over **enemy territory**.*

THESAURUS **area, region** → AREA

2 [U] land of a particular type: *At that time, the western part of America was **unexplored territory**.* **3** [C] land that belongs to a country, but is not a state, PROVINCE, etc.: *the U.S. territory of Guam* **4** [C,U] the area that an animal considers to be its own **5** [U] a particular area of experience or knowledge: *We are in **unfamiliar/uncharted territory*** (=an area that we do not yet know about) *with the new drug.* **6 come/go with the territory** to be a natural and accepted part of a particular job, situation, place, etc.: *You'd better get used to criticism from the press – it comes with the territory.* [ORIGIN: 1300—1400 Latin *territorium* "land around a town," from *terra* "earth, land"]

ter·ror /ˈtɛrɚ/ *n.* **1** [C,U] a feeling of extreme fear, or something that causes this: *She ran away **in terror**.* | *the **terrors of** war* **2** [U] violent action for political purposes (SYN) **terrorism**: *a campaign of terror against the West*

ter·ror·ism /ˈtɛrəˌrɪzəm/ *n.* [U] the use of bombs and violence, especially against ordinary people, to achieve political aims: *an **act of terrorism*** | *More security at airports is part of the efforts to **combat terrorism**.*

ter·ror·ist /ˈtɛrərɪst/ *n.* [C] someone who uses bombs and violence, usually against ordinary people, in order to achieve political aims: *a suspected terrorist* —**terrorist** *adj.*: *a terrorist attack*

ter·ror·ize /ˈtɛrəˌraɪz/ *v.* [T] to deliberately frighten people by threatening to harm them, especially so they will do what you want

ter·ry·cloth /ˈtɛriˌklɔθ/ *n.* [U] thick cotton cloth used for making TOWELS

terse /tɚs/ *adj.* a terse reply, message, etc. uses very few words and shows that you are annoyed —**tersely** *adv.*

test[1] /tɛst/ *n.* [C] **1** a set of questions or exercises to measure someone's skill or knowledge: *I have a*

T

history test tomorrow. | *Paul* ***passed/failed*** *his driver's* ***test.*** | *All students must* ***take a*** *placement* ***test.*** ▸Don't say "make a test." Say "take a test."◂ **2** a medical examination on a part of your body: *a blood test* | *a* ***test for*** *HIV* | *They don't know what's wrong with her yet – they're* ***running/doing*** *some* ***tests.*** **3** a process used to find out whether something works, whether it is safe, etc.: *In science, we did a* ***test for*** *chemicals in the water.* **4** a situation in which the qualities of something are clearly shown: *Today's race is a real* ***test of*** *skill.* | *Living together will really* ***put*** *their relationship* ***to the test*** (=find out how good it is).

test² *v.* [T] **1** to measure someone's skill or knowledge, using a test: *We're being* ***tested on*** *grammar tomorrow.* **2** to use or check something to find out whether it works or is successful: *None of our products is tested on animals.* **3** to do a medical check on part of someone's body: *You need to get your eyes tested.* | *They* ***tested*** *her* ***for*** *diabetes.* **4** to show how good or strong something is: *The next six months will test your powers of leadership.*

tes·ta·ment /ˈtɛstəmənt/ *n.* (formal) **a testament to sth** something that shows or proves something else very clearly: *His latest record is a testament to his growing musical abilities.*

ˈtest ban *n.* [C] an agreement between countries to stop testing NUCLEAR WEAPONS

T

ˈtest case *n.* [C] a legal case that makes a particular principle of law clear and is used as a model for similar cases in the future

ˈtest drive *n.* [C] an occasion when you drive a car and decide if you want to buy it —**test-drive** *v.* [T]

tes·ti·cle /ˈtɛstɪkəl/ *n.* (plural **testicles** *or* **testes** /ˈtɛstiz/) [C] BIOLOGY one of the two round organs below a man's PENIS that produce SPERM

tes·ti·fy /ˈtɛstəˌfaɪ/ *v.* (**testified**, **testifies**) [I,T] to make a formal statement of what is true, especially in a court of law: *Two men* ***testified that*** *they saw you there.* | *She refused to* ***testify against*** *my husband.* [ORIGIN: 1300—1400 Latin *testificari*, from *testis* "witness"]

tes·ti·mo·ni·al /ˌtɛstəˈmoʊniəl/ *n.* [C] a formal statement about someone's qualities and character

tes·ti·mo·ny /ˈtɛstəˌmoʊni/ *n.* (plural **testimonies**) [C,U] **1** LAW a formal statement of what is true, especially one made in a court of law: ***In her testimony,*** *Susan denied the allegations.* ➔ COURT¹ **2 (a) testimony to sth** something that clearly shows or proves that something is true: *This achievement is a testimony to your hard work.*

tes·tos·ter·one /tɛˈstɑstəˌroʊn/ *n.* [U] BIOLOGY the HORMONE in men that gives them their male qualities

ˈtest tube *n.* [C] SCIENCE a small glass container shaped like a tube that is used in scientific tests

tes·ty /ˈtɛsti/ *adj.* impatient and easily annoyed: *It had been a long day, and we were all getting a little testy.* —**testily** *adv.*

tet·a·nus /ˈtɛtˀn-əs, -nəs/ *n.* [U] BIOLOGY a serious disease caused by infection in a cut or wound

teth·er /ˈtɛðɚ/ *n.* [C] a rope or chain that is used to tie something to something else —**tether** *v.* [T]

tet·ra·he·dron /ˌtɛtrəˈhidrən/ *n.* [C] MATH a solid shape with four sides that are shaped like TRIANGLES

Tex-Mex /ˌtɛks ˈmɛks◂/ *adj.* [only before noun] (informal) relating to the music, cooking, etc. of Mexican-American people: *a Tex-Mex restaurant*

text¹ /tɛkst/ (Ac) *n.* **1** [U] any written material: *The book has pictures but no text.* | *The disk can store huge quantities of text.* **2** [C] a book or other piece of writing that is related to learning or intended for study ➔ TEXTBOOK: *religious texts* **3 the text of sth** the exact words of something: *The entire text of the speech was printed in the newspaper.* [ORIGIN: 1300—1400 Old French *texte*, from Latin *textus* "woven material"]

text² *v.* [T] to send someone a text message using a CELL PHONE

text·book¹ /ˈtɛkstbʊk/ *also* **text** *n.* [C] a book about a subject which students use: *a history textbook*

textbook² *adj.* **a textbook example/case (of sth)** a very clear and typical example of how something should happen or be done

tex·tile /ˈtɛkstaɪl/ *n.* [C] any material that is made by weaving

ˈtext ˌmessage *n.* [C] a written message that you send to someone using a CELL PHONE —**text messaging** *n.* [U]

tex·tu·al /ˈtɛkstʃuəl/ (Ac) *adj.* ENG. LANG. ARTS relating to the way that a book, story, or article is written: *a textual analysis of the poem*

tex·ture /ˈtɛkstʃɚ/ *n.* [C,U] the way that a surface, material, etc. feels when you touch it, and how smooth or rough it looks: *fabric with a coarse texture*

tex·tured /ˈtɛkstʃɚd/ *adj.* having a surface that is not smooth

thal·a·mus /ˈθæləməs/ *n.* (plural **thalami** /-maɪ/) [C] BIOLOGY an area of the brain that sends the information you receive from your eyes, ears, etc. to the CEREBRAL CORTEX

than /ðən; *strong* ðæn/ *conjunction*, *prep.* used when comparing two things or people that are different: *Jean's taller than Stella.* | *A used car can cost less than $2,000.* | *I can swim better than you.*

thank /θæŋk/ *v.* [T] **1** to tell someone that you are pleased and grateful for a gift or for something that s/he has done: *We would like to* ***thank*** *everyone* ***for*** *helping.* **2 thank God/goodness/heavens** (spoken) said when you are very glad about something: *Thank God no one was hurt!* **3 have sb to thank (for sth)** (spoken) used in order to say who you are grateful to: *I have Phil to thank for getting me my first job.*

thank·ful /ˈθæŋkfəl/ *adj.* glad and grateful that something good has happened: *Our family has a lot to* ***be thankful for****.* | *I'm* ***thankful that*** *no one was hurt.* —**thankfully** *adv.*: *Thankfully, everything turned out all right.*

thank·less /ˈθæŋklɪs/ *adj.* a thankless job is difficult and you do not get much praise for doing it

thanks[1] /θæŋks/ *interjection* (informal) **1** used to tell someone that you are grateful for something s/he has done for you or given you (SYN) **thank you**: *Can I borrow your pen?* ***Thanks.*** | ***Thanks for*** *the drink.* | ***Thanks a lot for*** *helping out.* **2** (spoken) used when politely answering someone's question about you: *"How are you?" "****Fine, thanks****."* **3 thanks/no thanks** (spoken) said in order to accept or refuse something that someone is offering you: *"Do you want another cup of coffee?" "Oh, thanks."*

thanks[2] *n.* [plural] **1** something that you say or do to show that you are grateful to someone: *He left without* ***a word of thanks****.* **2 thanks to sb/sth** because of someone or something: *We're late, thanks to you.*

Thanks·giv·ing /ˌθæŋksˈgɪvɪŋ/ *n.* a holiday in the U.S. and Canada in the fall when families have a large meal together to celebrate and be thankful for food, health, families, etc.

ˈthank you[1] *interjection* **1** said in order to tell someone that you are grateful for something that s/he has done: *I really liked the book. Thank you.* | ***Thank you very much.*** | ***Thank you for*** *the perfume.* **2 thank you/no thank you** said in order to accept or refuse something that someone is offering you: *"Would you like another cookie?" "No thank you."*

ˈthank you[2] *adj.* **thank you letter/gift/note etc.** a letter, gift, etc. that is given to someone to thank him/her for something

ˈthank you[3] *n.* [C usually singular] something that you say or do to thank someone for something: *Please accept this gift as* ***a thank you*** *for your support.*

that[1] /ðæt/ *determiner, pron.* (plural **those** /ðoʊz/) **1** used to talk about someone or something that is far away from you or closer to another person than it is to you ➔ THIS: *My office is in that building.* | *Who are those boys over there?* **2** used to talk about someone or something that has already been mentioned or is already known about ➔ THIS: *I've never seen that movie.* | *Who told you that?* | *Those were her exact words.* **3** /ðət/ used after a noun as a RELATIVE PRONOUN, instead of "which" or "who": *a ticket that I bought last week* | *Have you met the couple that moved in next door?*

USAGE

The relative pronoun **that** is often left out when it is the object of a verb: *She's the woman (that) I love.*

You can use **that** instead of **which** or **who** when you are saying which thing or person you mean: *This is the man that/who called the police.*
You cannot use **that** instead of **which** or **who** if you are simply adding information: *This is my father, who lives in Dublin.* | *She owns an old Rolls Royce, which she bought in 1954.*

SPOKEN PHRASES

4 that's it a) used when what you have mentioned is all of something or the end of something: *It rains in February and that's it for the year.* **b)** used in order to tell someone that s/he has done something correctly: *Turn the wheel to the left, yes, that's it.* **5 that is** used in order to correct a statement or give more exact information about something: *It's a seven-day trip. That is, it's five days there plus two days driving.* **6 that's life/men/politics etc.** used to say that something is typical of a particular situation, group of people, etc.: *I guess I made a mistake, but hey, that's life.* **7 that's that** said when something is completely finished or when a decision will not be changed: *You're not going and that's that!* **8 that's all there is to it** said in order to emphasize that something is simple to do, explain, etc.: *We lost because we didn't play well. That's all there is to it.*

that[2] /ðət; *strong* ðæt/ *conjunction* used after verbs, nouns, and adjectives to introduce a CLAUSE which shows what someone says or thinks, or which states a fact, gives a reason, etc.: *The rules state that if the ball hits the line, it's in.* | *Is it true that the Nelsons are moving?* | *They're showing the movie that you wanted to see.* | *Have you gotten the letter that I sent you?* ➔ **so (that)** *at* SO[2]

that[3] /ðæt/ *adv.* (spoken) **1 that long/much/big etc.** used when talking about the size of something and showing it with your hands: *It's about that long.* **2 that good/bad/difficult etc.** as good, bad, etc. as someone has already mentioned: *I didn't realize things were that bad.* **3 not that much/long/big etc.** not very much, long, etc.: *It won't cost all that much.*

thatch /θætʃ/ *n.* [C,U] dried STRAW used for making roofs —**thatched** *adj.*

thaw[1] /θɔ/ *v.* **1** [I,T] *also* **thaw out** if ice or snow thaws or is thawed, it becomes warmer and turns into water (ANT) **freeze**: *The snow was beginning to thaw.* **2** [I,T] *also* **thaw out** if frozen food thaws or is thawed, it becomes soft so it is ready to be cooked (ANT) **freeze** **3** [I] to become more friendly and less formal: *Relations between the two countries are beginning to thaw.*

thaw[2] *n.* [singular] **1** a period of warm weather during which snow and ice melt: *the spring thaw* **2** a time when a relationship becomes more friendly

the[1] /ðə; *before a vowel* ði; *strong* ði/ *definite article* **1** used before nouns to show that you are

T

talking about a particular person or thing, especially when he, she, or it has already been mentioned or when there is only one ➔ A: *the tallest building in the world* | *the woman I saw yesterday* | *That's the dress I want.* **2** used as part of the names of some countries, rivers, oceans, etc.: *the United States* | *the Pacific Ocean* **3** used before an adjective to make it into a noun that refers to a particular group of people: *the economic gap between **the rich** and **the poor*** **4** used before a singular noun to show that you are talking about that thing in general: *The computer has changed our lives.* **5** each or every: *He's paid by the hour.* **6** used before the names of musical instruments: *Kira's learning to play the piano.* **7** used in order to talk about a part of the body: *The ball hit him right in the eye!* **8** used before a particular date or period of time: *the 1960s* | *the third of May* **9** used in order to emphasize that someone or something is important or famous: *It's definitely the movie to see.*

GRAMMAR

Do not use **the** when you are talking about something in general using an uncountable noun or a plural noun form: *Do you like pizza?* | *She gets a lot of emails.*
Use **the** when you are talking about a particular thing: *The pizza was still very hot.* | *The email was from a friend in Boston.*
Do not use **the** before the names of airports, train stations, or streets: *The plane arrives at Denver airport at 5:30.* | *The train leaves from Grand Central.* | *She lives on Carr Avenue.*
Use **the** when you are talking about a particular airport, train station, or street without naming it: *We arrived at the airport.* | *The train was just leaving the station.* | *They live on the same street.*

the² *adv.* **1 the... the...** used in comparisons to show that two things happen together: *The more you practice, the better you'll play.* | *"When do you want this?" "The sooner the better."* **2** used in front of the SUPERLATIVE form of adjectives and adverbs to emphasize that something is as big, good, etc. as it is possible to be: *He likes you the best.*

the·a·ter /ˈθiət̬ɚ/ *n.* **1** [C] a building with a stage where plays are performed: *the Apollo Theater*

TOPIC

You **go to the theater** to **see** a **play, musical, opera**, or **ballet**. Before you go to the theater, you can **reserve tickets** at the **box office**. The place that you pay to sit in is called a **seat**. You have seats on **the floor** (=lowest level) or in the **balcony** (=highest level). You can get a **program** (=small book telling you about the play, the actors, etc.). In front of the **audience** (=people watching), there may be an **orchestra** (=group of musicians) below the **stage**. During the play there is usually an **intermission** (=when the performance stops for a short time and people can have a drink).

2 [U] the work of acting in, writing, or organizing plays: *She's been working **in theater** for many years.* **3** [C] a building where movies are shown [ORIGIN: 1300—1400 Old French *theatre*, from Latin, from Greek *theatron*, from *theasthai* "to watch"]

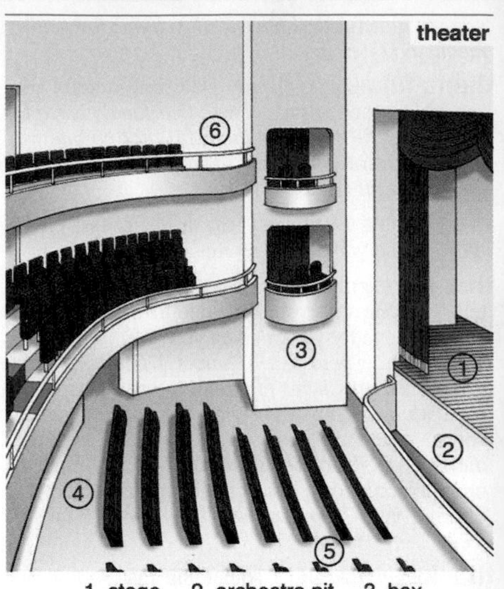

1. stage 2. orchestra pit 3. box
4. floor 5. aisle 6. balcony

the·at·ri·cal /θiˈætrɪkəl/ *adj.* **1** relating to the theater: *an expensive theatrical production* **2** behaving in a way that is intended to make people notice you —**theatrics** *n.* [plural]

theft /θɛft/ *n.* [C,U] the act or crime of stealing something ➔ THIEF: *car theft* | *She reported the **theft of** $200 from the office.*

THESAURUS **crime, robbery, burglary, shoplifting** ➔ CRIME

their /ðɚ; *strong* ðɛr/ *possessive adj.* **1** belonging or relating to the people, animals, or things that have been mentioned, or are known about: *The guests left their coats on the bed.* | *Their daughter is a teacher.* **2** (spoken) used instead of "his" or "her" after words such as someone, anyone, everyone, etc.: *Everybody has their own ideas about it.*

theirs /ðɛrz/ *pron.* **1** the thing or things belonging to or relating to the people or things that have been mentioned, or are known about: *When our washing machine broke the neighbors let us use theirs.* **2** (spoken) used instead of "his" or "hers" after words such as someone, anyone, everyone, etc.: *Okay, get your coats. Does everyone have theirs?*

them /ðəm, əm; *strong* ðɛm/ *pron.* **1** the object form of "they": *Has anybody seen my keys? I can't find them.* | *My friends want me to go out with them tonight.* **2** (spoken) used instead of "him" or "her" after words such as someone, anyone, everyone, etc.: *If anyone calls, can you tell them to call back later?*

the·mat·ic /θi'mæṭɪk/ (Ac) *adj.* ENG. LANG. ARTS relating to a particular theme, or organized by themes: *the thematic content of the book* —**thematically** *adv.*: *The book is organized thematically.*

theme /θim/ (Ac) *n.* **1** [C] ENG. LANG. ARTS the main subject or idea in a book, movie, speech, etc.: *Love is the main* ***theme of*** *the book.*

THESAURUS **subject, topic** → SUBJECT[1]

2 theme music/song/tune music or a song that is always played during a particular television or radio program [ORIGIN: 1200—1300 Latin *thema*, from Greek, "something laid down, theme"]

'theme park *n.* [C] an AMUSEMENT PARK that is based on one subject such as water or space travel

them·selves /ðəm'sɛlvz, ðɛm-/ *pron.* **1** the REFLEXIVE form of "they": *People usually like to talk about themselves.* **2** used in order to emphasize the subject or object of a sentence: *Doctors themselves admit that the treatment does not always work.* **3 (all) by themselves a)** alone: *Many old people live by themselves.* **b)** without help: *The kids made cookies all by themselves.* **4 (all) to themselves** for their own use: *The kids had the pool to themselves today.*

then[1] /ðɛn/ *adv.* **1** after something has happened: *We could have lunch and then go shopping.* **2** at a particular time in the past or future: ***Just then****, the phone rang.* | ***By then****, he was married.* | *My family lived in New York* ***back then****.* **3** (spoken) said in order to show that what you are saying is related in some way to what has been said before: *"He can't come on Friday." "Then how about Saturday?"* | *So you're going into nursing then?* **4** used in order to say that if one thing is true, the other thing is also true or should be the correct result: *"I have to pick Bobby up at school." "Then you should leave by 2:30."* **5** used in order to add something to what you have just said: *He's really busy at work, and then there's the new baby, too!* **6 then and there** immediately: *I would have given up then and there if my parents hadn't encouraged me.* → **but then (again)...** *at* BUT[1], **(every) now and then** *at* NOW[1]

then[2] *adj.* [only before noun] used when talking about someone who did a job at a particular time in the past: *the then-President of the U.S.*

the·o·lo·gian /ˌθiə'loʊdʒən/ *n.* [C] someone who studies or writes about theology

the·ol·o·gy /θi'ɑlədʒi/ *n.* [U] the study of religion —**theological** /ˌθiə'lɑdʒɪkəl/ *adj.*

the·o·rem /'θiərəm, 'θɪrəm/ *n.* [C] MATH a statement that can be shown to be true, especially in mathematics

the·o·ret·i·cal /ˌθiə'rɛṭɪkəl/ (Ac) *adj.* **1** SCIENCE relating to scientific ideas rather than practical situations: *theoretical physics* **2** a theoretical situation could exist but does not yet exist

the·o·ret·i·cally /ˌθiə'rɛṭɪkli/ (Ac) *adv.* **1** used to say that something could happen, but it is extremely unlikely: *Theoretically, every child should have an equal chance at a good education.* **2** according to a theory: *Is near light-speed space travel theoretically possible?*

the·o·rist /'θiərɪst/ (Ac) *also* **the·o·re·ti·cian** /ˌθiərə'tɪʃən/ *n.* [C] someone who develops ideas that explain why particular things happen or are true

the·o·rize /'θiəˌraɪz/ *v.* [I,T] to think of a possible explanation or reason for a particular event, fact, etc.: *Police* ***theorize that*** *the two men were working together.*

the·o·ry /'θiəri, 'θɪri/ (Ac) *n.* (plural **theories**) **1** [C] SCIENCE an idea that explains how something works, why something happens, etc., especially one that has not yet been proven to be true: *Darwin's* ***theory of*** *evolution* | *There are different* ***theories about*** *how the brain works.* | *The* ***theory that*** *light is made up of waves is commonly accepted.*

THESAURUS **idea, concept, hypothesis** → IDEA

2 in theory something that is true in theory should be true, but may not actually be true: *In theory, the crime rate should decrease as employment increases.* **3** [U] the general principles or ideas of a subject: *music theory* [ORIGIN: 1500—1600 Late Latin *theoria*, from Greek, from *theorein* "to look at"]

T

ther·a·peu·tic /ˌθɛrə'pyuṭɪk/ *adj.* **1** relating to the treatment or cure of a disease: *therapeutic drugs* **2** making you feel calm and relaxed

ther·a·py /'θɛrəpi/ *n.* (plural **therapies**) **1** [C,U] the treatment of an illness or injury over a fairly long period of time: *Ted's having physical therapy for his back.* **2** [U] the treatment or examination of someone's mental problems by talking to him/her for a long time about his/her feelings: *He's been* ***in therapy*** *for years.* —**therapist** *n.* [C]: *a speech therapist*

there[1] /ðɛr/ *pron.* **there is/are/was/were etc.** used in order to say that something exists or happens: *There were several people hurt in the accident.* | *Suddenly, there was a loud crash.* | *Are there any questions?* [ORIGIN: Old English *thær*]

there[2] *adv.* **1** in or to a particular place that is not where you are or near you → HERE: *Would you hand me that glass* ***over there****?* | *I know Tucson well because I used to live there.* | *The party was almost over by the time I* ***got there*** (=arrived). **2** at a particular point in time, in a situation, story, etc.: *I'll read this chapter and stop there.* **3** if something is there, it exists: *The money's there if you need it.* **4 be there (for sb)** to be ready to help someone if s/he needs help: *My folks are great – they're always there for me.* → **then and there** *at* THEN[1]

SPOKEN PHRASES

5 there is sth *also* **there it is a)** said to make someone look or pay attention to something: *There's the statue I was telling you about.* **b)** said when you have found something you were looking for: *"Where's my purse?" "There it is, on the couch."* **6 there (you go)** (informal) **a)** *also* **there you are** used when giving something to someone or when you have done something for someone: *I'll just get you the key – there you are.* **b)** used in order to tell someone that s/he has done something correctly or understood something: *Can you turn just a little to the left? There you go.* **7 there** used when you have finished something: *There, that's the last piece of the puzzle.* **8 hello/hi there** used when greeting someone, especially when you have just noticed him/her **9 there, there** used in order to comfort a child: *There, there, it's all right.*

there·a·bouts /ˌðɛrəˈbaʊts, ˈðɛrəˌbaʊts/ *adv.* near a particular number, amount, or time, but not exactly: *The chair costs $50* ***or thereabouts.***

there·af·ter /ðɛrˈæftɚ/ *adv.* (formal) after a particular event or time (SYN) **afterward**: *The store caught fire and closed* ***shortly thereafter.***

there·by /ðɛrˈbaɪ, ˈðɛrbaɪ/ (Ac) *adv.* (formal) with the result that: *Expenses were cut 12%, thereby increasing efficiency.*

T

THESAURUS **therefore, so, as a result/consequently/as a consequence, thus, hence, accordingly →** THEREFORE

there·fore /ˈðɛrfɔr/ *adv.* (formal) for the reason that has just been mentioned: *The gang was armed, and therefore more dangerous.* | *It was clear that Lucy was unhappy. Therefore, it wasn't surprising when she quit.*

THESAURUS

so – used when saying that something happens or someone does something as a result of something else: *They had not eaten all day, so they were very hungry.*
as a result/consequently/as a consequence – used when saying what the result of something is: *The law on seat belts was changed, and as a result thousands of lives have been saved.* | *This disease attacks the plant, the flower does not open, and consequently no seeds are produced.*
thus (formal) – as a result of what you have just mentioned: *The dinosaurs all died out within a short period of time. Thus it seems likely that there must have been some kind of catastrophic event.*
hence (formal) – for this reason: *The lake has ice on it all year, hence the name "Iceberg Lake."*
thereby (formal) – used when saying what the result of something is. You use **thereby** in the middle of a sentence.: *These two companies merged, thereby creating the company that exists today.*
accordingly (formal) – used when saying that someone makes a decision as a result of something: *The jury found him not guilty. Accordingly, the judge set him free.*

there·in /ðɛrˈɪn/ *adv.* (formal) **1** in that place, or in that piece of writing: *We have studied the report and the information contained therein.* **2 therein lies sth** used in order to state the cause of something: *The two sides will not talk to each other, and therein lies the problem.*

there·of /ðɛrˈʌv/ *adv.* (formal) relating to something that has just been mentioned: *Money, or the* ***lack thereof*** (=lack of money), *played a major role in their marital problems.*

there·up·on /ˈðɛrəˌpɑn, ˌðɛrəˈpɑn/ *adv.* (formal) immediately after something happens and as a result of it

ther·mal /ˈθɚməl/ *adj.* **1** PHYSICS relating to or caused by heat: *thermal energy* **2** thermal clothing is made from special material to keep you warm in very cold weather: *thermal underwear*

ther·mo·dy·nam·ics /ˌθɚmoʊdaɪˈnæmɪks/ *n.* [U] PHYSICS the science that deals with the relationship between heat and other forms of energy —**thermodynamic** *adj.*

ther·mom·e·ter /θɚˈmɑmət̬ɚ/ *n.* [C] a piece of equipment that measures the temperature of the air, your body, etc. [ORIGIN: 1600—1700 French *thermomètre*, from Greek *therme* "heat" + French *-mètre* "-meter"]

ther·mo·nu·cle·ar fu·sion /ˌθɚmoʊnukliɚ ˈfyuʒən/ *n.* [U] PHYSICS NUCLEAR FUSION that takes place when the NUCLEI of light atoms, for example those of HYDROGEN, crash into each other at very high speeds and temperatures

Ther·mos /ˈθɚməs/ *n.* [C] (trademark) a special container like a bottle that keeps hot drinks hot or cold drinks cold

ther·mo·sphere /ˈθɚməˌsfɪr/ *n.* **the thermosphere** EARTH SCIENCES the highest layer of the Earth's upper ATMOSPHERE, which consists of the EXOSPHERE and the IONOSPHERE

ther·mo·stat /ˈθɚməˌstæt/ *n.* [C] an instrument that keeps a room, machine, etc. at a specific temperature

the·sau·rus /θɪˈsɔrəs/ *n.* (plural **thesauruses** *or* **thesauri** /-ˈsɔraɪ/) [C] a book in which words are put into groups with other words that have a similar meaning

these /ðiz/ *determiner, pron.* the plural form of THIS

the·sis /ˈθisɪs/ (Ac) *n.* (plural **theses** /ˈθisiz/) [C] **1** ENG. LANG. ARTS a long piece of writing about a particular subject that you do as part of an advanced university degree, such as a MASTER'S DEGREE: *He wrote his* ***thesis on*** *18th century literature.*

THESAURUS **essay, composition, paper, dissertation →** ESSAY

2 *also* **thesis statement** ENG. LANG. ARTS the statement in a piece of writing that gives the main idea or the writer's opinion **3** an idea or opinion about something, that you discuss in a formal way or give examples for: *His thesis is that large governments no longer work very well.* [ORIGIN: 1300—1400 Latin, Greek, "an act of laying down," from Greek *tithenai* "to put, lay down"]

they /ðeɪ/ *pron.* **1** the people or things that have already been mentioned or that are already known about: *Ken gave me these flowers – aren't they beautiful?* | *I stopped at Doris and Ed's place, but they weren't home.* **2** a particular group or organization, or the people involved in it: *Where are they going to build the new highway?* | *"Naranjas" is what they call oranges in Mexico.* **3 they say/think** (spoken) used in order to say what people in general say or think: *They say it's bad luck to spill salt.* **4** (spoken) used instead of "he" or "she" after words such as someone, anyone, everyone, etc.: *Somebody at work said they saw you at the party.*

they'd /ðeɪd/ **1** the short form of "they had": *They'd been missing for three days.* **2** the short form of "they would": *They'd like to visit us soon.*

they'll /ðeɪl, ðel/ the short form of "they will": *They'll have to wait.*

they're /ðɚ; *strong* ðɛr/ the short form of "they are": *They're very nice people.*

they've /ðeɪv/ the short form of "they have": *They've been here before.*

thick¹ /θɪk/ *adj.* **1** something that is thick is wide and not thin (ANT) **thin**: *a thick piece of bread* | *a thick layer of paint* **2 2 feet thick/12 inches thick etc.** used in order to describe how thick something is: *The wall is about 16 inches thick.* **3** a substance that is thick has very little water in it: *thick soup* **4** difficult to see through or breathe in: *The air was **thick with** smoke.* | *driving in **thick fog*** **5** growing very close together with not much space in between: *a thick forest* | *He has thick black hair.* [ORIGIN: Old English *thicce*] —**thickly** *adv.*

thick² *n.* **1 be in the thick of sth** to be involved in the most active, dangerous, etc. part of a situation: *U.S. troops are right in the thick of the action.* **2 through thick and thin** in spite of any difficulties or problems: *They stayed married through thick and thin.*

thick·en /ˈθɪkən/ *v.* [I,T] to become thick, or make something thick: *Thicken the soup with flour.*

thick·et /ˈθɪkɪt/ *n.* [C] a group of bushes and small trees

thick·ness /ˈθɪknɪs/ *n.* [C,U] how thick something is: *Roll out the dough to a thickness of 1 inch.*

ˌthick-ˈskinned *adj.* not easily offended or upset by criticism

thief /θif/ *n.* (plural **thieves** /θivz/) [C] someone who steals things ➔ THEFT: *a car thief* | *Thieves broke in and stole some valuable jewelry.*

THESAURUS **offender, robber, burglar, pickpocket** ➔ CRIMINAL²

thigh /θaɪ/ *n.* [C] the top part of your leg above your knee ➔ *see picture on page A16*

thim·ble /ˈθɪmbəl/ *n.* [C] a small hard cap that you put over the end of your finger to protect it when you are sewing

thimble

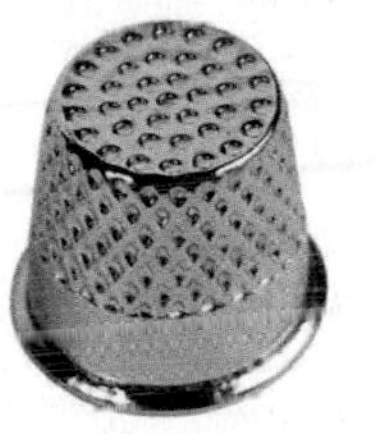

thin¹ /θɪn/ *adj.* (comparative **thinner**, superlative **thinnest**) **1** something that is thin is not very wide or thick (ANT) **thick**: *a thin slice of cheese* | *The walls here are **paper-thin*** (=very thin). ➔ *see Picture at* THICK¹ **2** having little fat on your body (ANT) **fat**: *He's tall, very thin, and has dark hair.*

THESAURUS

slim and **slender** – used about someone who is thin in an attractive way
slight – used about someone who is thin and whose body structure is small
skinny – used about someone who is very thin in a way that is not attractive
lean – used about someone who is thin in a healthy way: *He has a runner's physique: long legs and a lean body.*
underweight – used, especially by doctors, about someone who is too thin, in a way that is not healthy
gaunt – used about someone who is thin, pale, and unhealthy
emaciated (formal) – used about someone who is extremely thin and weak because of illness or not eating
anorexic (formal) – used about people who are extremely thin because they have a mental illness that makes them stop eating
skeletal – used about people who are so thin that you can see the shape of their bones ➔ FAT¹

3 if someone has thin hair, s/he does not have very much hair (ANT) **thick** **4** air that is thin is difficult to breathe because there is not much oxygen in it **5** a substance that is thin has a lot of water in it (ANT) **thick**: *thin broth* [ORIGIN: Old English *thynne*] —**thinness** *n.* [U]

T

thin² *v.* (**thinned**, **thinning**) [I,T] to make something thinner, or to become thinner: *She has really thick hair, and the hairdresser thinned it a little* (=cut it so that there were fewer hairs). | *Thin the paint with water.*

thin out *phr. v.* if a crowd thins out, people gradually leave so there are fewer of them

thing /θɪŋ/ *n.* [C] **1** a fact, idea, statement, action, or event: *A funny thing happened last week.* | *That's a terrible* ***thing to say****.* | *I have better things to do with my time.* | *I kept wondering if I was* ***doing the right thing****.* **2** used to talk about an object without saying its name, or when you do not know its name: *Do you know how to turn this thing off?*

THESAURUS

object (especially written) – a thing, especially a hard solid thing: *a sharp metal object*
something – a thing, used especially when you do not know its name or what it is: *There's something in my eye.*
item – one of the things in a set, group, or list: *He saved a few items and threw away the rest.*
article – a thing, especially one of a group of things: *an article of clothing*

3 things [plural] life in general and the way it is affecting people: ***How are things going*** *at work?* | *We can't change* ***the way things are****.* **4 sb's things** the things you own or the things you are carrying: *Just put your things over there.* **5 not know/feel/see etc. a thing** to know, feel, see, etc. nothing: *It was so dark I couldn't see a thing.* **6 there's no such thing (as sth)** used in order to emphasize that someone or something does not exist or does not happen: *There's no such thing as Santa Claus!* **7 the last thing sb wants/expects etc.** something that someone does not want, expect, etc. at all: *The last thing we wanted was to start a fight.* **8 do your own thing** (informal) to do what you want, and not what someone else wants you to do

SPOKEN PHRASES

9 the thing is said when explaining a problem or the reason for something: *We want to come, but the thing is we can't find a babysitter.* **10 for one thing** said when giving a reason for something: *I don't think she'll get the part – for one thing she can't sing!* **11 it's a good thing (that)** used in order to say that it is lucky or good that something happened: *It's a good thing the drug store's open late.* **12 first thing** at the beginning of the day or morning: *Let's talk about the report* ***first thing in the morning****.* **13 (it's) just one of those things** used in order to say that something that has happened is not someone's fault or could not have been avoided **14 it's (just) one thing after another** said when a lot of bad or unlucky things keep happening to you

thing·a·ma·jig /ˈθɪŋəmə,dʒɪg/ *n.* [C] (spoken) said when you cannot remember the real name of the thing you want to mention

T

think /θɪŋk/ *v.* (past tense and past participle **thought** /θɔt/) **1** [T] to have an opinion about something: *I* ***think that*** *New York is a great place to live.* | *I* ***don't think (that)*** *he likes me* (=I think that he does not like me). | *What do you* ***think of*** *my new car?*

THESAURUS

believe – to think that it is true: *We believe that the risk is small.*
suspect – to think that something, especially something bad, is true but not be sure: *She suspected that he was seeing another woman.*
consider – to think of someone or something in a particular way or have a particular opinion: *I consider him a friend.*
figure – used to say what your opinion is: *I figure he's at least 19.*
guess – used to say what you think is true or likely: *I guess he'll be pretty upset when he finds out.*

2 [T] to believe that something is true, although you are not sure: *I* ***think (that)*** *you're right.* | *I thought it was going to be sunny.* **3** [I] to use your mind to decide something, solve problems, have ideas, etc.: *What are you* ***thinking about****?* | *I couldn't* ***think of*** *anything to say.* | *Just a second, I'm thinking.* **4** [I] use your mind to remember something: *I can't* ***think of*** *her name.* **5 think about/of doing sth** to consider the possibility of doing something: *I'm thinking about moving to Florida.* **6 think of sb** to consider the feelings and wishes of another person, rather than just doing what you want: *Bill's always thinking of others.* **7 think better of sth** to decide not to do something that you had intended to do: *He reached for his cigarettes and then thought better of it.* **8 think nothing of (doing sth)** to do something easily that other people consider to be difficult or unusual: *Purdey thinks nothing of driving two hours to work every day.* **9 think twice** to consider a decision very carefully before you decide if you will do it or not: *You should* ***think twice before*** *signing the contract.* **10 who would have thought?** used in order to say that something is very surprising: *Who'd have thought being a mother would make you so happy?* **11 think well/highly of sb/sth** to admire or approve of someone or his/her work: *His teachers seem to think highly of him.* **12 think positively** to believe that you are going to be successful or that a situation is going to have a good result → UNTHINKABLE

SPOKEN PHRASES

13 I think so/I don't think so used when answering a question to say that you do or do not believe something is true: *"Will she be back on Friday?" "I think so."* **14 I think I'll...** said when telling someone what you will probably do: *I think I'll go to bed early tonight.* **15 I thought (that)** used when you are politely suggesting something to do: *I thought we could go to the lake this weekend.* **16 do you think (that)...?** used when you are asking someone politely to do something for you: *Do you think that you could give me a* *ride?* **17 you would think (that)** *also* **you would have thought (that)** used in order to say that you expect something to be true although it is not: *You would think someone who can sing that well would take better care of their voice.* **18 just think!** said when asking someone to imagine or consider something: *Just think – tomorrow we'll be in Hawaii!* **19 come to think of it** said when you have just remembered something that is related to your conversation: *Come to think of it, I did see Rita yesterday.*

[ORIGIN: Old English *thencan*]

think back *phr. v.* to think about things that happened in the past: *Thinking back, it amazes me we survived on so little money.*

think sth ↔ **out** *phr. v.* to think about something carefully, considering all the possible problems, results, etc.: *The arguments had not been thought out very carefully.*

think sth ↔ **over** *phr. v.* to consider something carefully before making a decision: *Take a few days to think over the offer.*

think sth ↔ **through** *phr. v.* to think carefully about the possible results of doing something: *Give us time to think it through.*

think sth ↔ **up** *phr. v.* to produce an idea, plan, etc. that is completely new: *Who thinks up the stories for these stupid TV shows?*

think·ing /ˈθɪŋkɪŋ/ *n.* [U] **1** an opinion about something, or an attitude toward something: *They have a different* ***way of thinking*** *about the issue.* **2** the activity of using your mind to solve a problem, produce thoughts, etc.: *Lance's* ***quick thinking*** *had saved her life.*

ˈthink tank *n.* [C] a committee of people with experience in a particular subject that an organization or government establishes to produce ideas and give advice: *a right-wing think tank*

thin·ly /ˈθɪnli/ *adv.* **1** if something is cut thinly, it is cut into thin pieces: *a* ***thinly sliced*** *onion* **2** with only a small number of people or things spread over a large area: *a* ***thinly populated*** *area*

thin·ning /ˈθɪnɪŋ/ *adj.* if your hair is thinning, some of it has fallen out

ˌthin-ˈskinned *adj.* too easily offended or upset by criticism

third /θɚd/ *number* **1** 3rd **2** 1/3

ˌthird ˈbase *n.* [U] in baseball, the third place that a player must touch before gaining a point

ˌthird deˈgree *n.* **give sb the third degree** (informal) to ask someone a lot of questions in order to get information from him/her

ˌthird-degree ˈburn *n.* [C] a very severe burn that goes through someone's skin

ˌthird ˈparty *n.* [singular] LAW someone who is not one of the two main people involved in something, but who is involved in it or affected by it

ˌthird ˈperson *n.* [singular] ENG. LANG. ARTS in grammar, a form of a verb or PRONOUN that you use to show the person or thing that is being mentioned. "He," "she," "it," and "they" are all third person pronouns. ➔ FIRST PERSON, SECOND PERSON

ˈthird-person *adj.* **third-person narrative/account/story** ENG. LANG. ARTS a story that is told by a third person narrator

ˌthird person ˈnarrator *n.* [C.] ENG. LANG. ARTS someone who tells a story from outside the action of the story and who knows everything that is happening ➔ FIRST PERSON NARRATOR

ˌthird-ˈrate *adj.* of very bad quality

ˌThird ˈWorld *n.* **the Third World** a phrase meaning the poorer countries of the world that do not have developed industries, which some people consider to be offensive **—Third World** *adj.*

thirst /θɚst/ *n.* **1** [singular] the feeling of wanting or needing a drink ➔ HUNGER: *Water is the best drink to* ***quench*** *your* ***thirst*** (=stop you being thirsty). ►Don't say "I have thirst." say "I am thirsty."◄ **2** [U] the state of not having enough to drink: *Many of the animals had* ***died of thirst.*** **3 a thirst for sth** a strong need or desire for something: *a thirst for knowledge*

thirst·y /ˈθɚsti/ *adj.* feeling that you want to drink something ➔ HUNGRY: *I'm thirsty – can I have a glass of water?* **—thirstily** *adv.*

thir·teen /ˌθɚˈtin◂/ *number* 13 **—thirteenth** *number*

thir·ty /ˈθɚt̬i/ *number* **1** 30 **2 the thirties a)** the years between 1930 and 1939 **b)** the numbers between 30 and 39, especially when used for measuring temperature **3 be in your thirties** to be aged between 30 and 39: *She's* ***in her early/mid/late thirties.*** **—thirtieth** /ˈθɚt̬iɪθ/ *number*

this¹ /ðɪs/ *determiner, pron.* (plural **these** /ðiz/) **1** used to talk about someone or something that is close to you ➔ THAT: *My mother gave me this necklace.* | *What should I do with this* (=something I am holding and showing you)*?* **2** used to talk about something that has just been mentioned or is already known about: *I'm going to make sure this doesn't happen again.* **3** used to talk about the present time or a time that is close to the present ➔ LAST, NEXT: *What are you doing this week?* | *We'll be seeing Malcolm this Friday* (=on Friday of the present week). **4** (spoken) used in conversation to mention a particular person or thing: *This friend of mine said he could get us tickets.* | *We saw this really cool movie last night.* **5 this is...** (spoken) used in order to introduce someone to someone else: *Nancy, this is my wife, Elaine.*

this² *adv.* used when talking about the size, number, degree, or amount of something: *I've never stayed up this late before.* | *Katie's about this tall now* (=said when using your hands to show a size).

this·tle /ˈθɪsəl/ *n.* [C] a wild plant with purple flowers and leaves that have sharp points

thong /θɔŋ, θɑŋ/ *n.* **1 thongs** [plural] a pair of open summer shoes, held on your feet by a v-shaped band that fits between your toes **2** [C] a

T

piece of underwear, or the bottom part of a BIKINI, that has a single string instead of the back part

thor·ax /ˈθɔræks/ *n.* (plural **thoraxes** *or* **thoraces** /-rəsiz/) [C] **1** BIOLOGY the part of the body between your neck and your DIAPHRAGM (=area above your stomach) **2** BIOLOGY the part of an insect's body between its head and its ABDOMEN —**thoracic** /θɔˈræsɪk/ *adj.*

thorn /θɔrn/ *n.* **1** [C] a sharp point that grows on a plant such as a rose **2 a thorn in your side** someone or something that annoys you or causes you problems over a long time

thorn·y /ˈθɔrni/ *adj.* **1 thorny question/problem/issue etc.** a question, problem, etc. that is very difficult to deal with **2** having a lot of thorns

thor·ough /ˈθɚoʊ, ˈθʌroʊ/ *adj.* **1** including every possible detail: *The police conducted a thorough search of the property.*

THESAURUS **careful, methodical, meticulous, systematic, painstaking** ➔ CAREFUL

2 careful to do everything that you should and avoid mistakes: *As a scientist, Madison is methodical and thorough.* —**thoroughness** *n.* [U]

thor·ough·bred /ˈθɚəˌbrɛd, ˈθɚoʊ-, ˈθʌr-/ *n.* [C] a horse that has parents of the same very good breed

T

thor·ough·fare /ˈθɚəˌfɛr, ˈθɚoʊ-, ˈθʌr-/ *n.* [C] the main road through a city

thor·ough·ly /ˈθɚoʊli, ˈθʌr-/ *adv.* **1** completely or very much: *Thanks for dinner; I thoroughly enjoyed it.* **2** carefully and completely: *Rinse the vegetables thoroughly.*

those /ðoʊz/ *determiner, pron.* the plural of THAT

though¹ /ðoʊ/ *conjunction* **1** used in order to introduce a statement that is surprising, unexpected, or different from your other statements ➔ ALTHOUGH: *Though Beattie is almost 40, she still plans to compete.* | *I seem to keep gaining weight* ***even though*** *I'm exercising regularly.* **2** used like "but" in order to add a fact or opinion to what you have said: *I thought he'd been drinking though I wasn't completely sure.* **3 as though** used like "as if" in order to say how something seems or appears: *She was staring at me as though she knew me.*

though² *adv.* (spoken) in spite of that: *Raleigh's a nice city. Mark doesn't want to leave Georgia, though.*

thought¹ /θɔt/ *v.* the past tense and past participle of THINK

thought² *n.* **1** [C] something that you think of, think about, or remember ➔ IDEA: *I've just* ***had a thought****. I'll ask Terry to come.* | *Even the* ***thought of*** *flying scares me.* | ***The thought that*** *I might not have a job next year made me nervous.* | *What are your* ***thoughts on*** *the subject* (=what is your opinion)*?* ➔ IDEA **2** [U] the act of thinking: *She sat at her desk,* ***lost/deep in thought*** (=thinking so much she did not notice anything else). **3** [U] the act of considering something carefully and seriously: *You need to* ***give*** *the decision* ***plenty of thought****.* **4 (it's) just a thought** (spoken) said when you have made a suggestion and you have not thought about it very much **5** [C,U] a feeling of caring about someone: *Michael never* ***gave*** *any* ***thought to*** *others.* | *You are always* ***in my thoughts*** (=used in order to tell someone that you think and care about him/her a lot). **6** [U] a way of thinking that is typical of a particular group, period of history, etc.: *ancient Greek thought* **7** [C,U] an intention or wish: *He has no thoughts of running for President.*

thought·ful /ˈθɔtfəl/ *adj.* **1** serious and quiet because you are thinking about something: *a* ***thoughtful look*** *on his face* | *a* ***thoughtful silence*** **2** kind and always thinking of things you can do to make other people happy: *You have a very thoughtful husband.* | ***It was*** *really* ***thoughtful of*** *you to remember my birthday.*

THESAURUS **kind, nice, considerate, caring, warm-hearted** ➔ KIND²

—**thoughtfully** *adv.* —**thoughtfulness** *n.* [U]

thought·less /ˈθɔtlɪs/ *adj.* not thinking about the needs and feelings of other people: *a thoughtless remark*

THESAURUS **mean, unkind, cruel** ➔ MEAN²

thou·sand /ˈθaʊzənd/ *number* **1** 1,000 **2 thousands** (informal) a lot of: *We've received* ***thousands of*** *letters from fans.* [ORIGIN: Old English *thusend*] —**thousandth** *adj.*

thrash /θræʃ/ *v.* **1** [T] to hit someone violently, often as a punishment **2** [I] to move from side to side in an uncontrolled way: *A fish was* ***thrashing around*** *on the river bank.* —**thrashing** *n.* [C,U]

thrash sth ↔ **out** *phr. v.* to discuss a problem thoroughly until you find an answer: *Officials are still trying to thrash out an agreement.*

thread¹ /θrɛd/ *n.* **1** [C,U] a long thin line of cotton, silk, etc. that you use to sew cloth: *a needle and thread* ➔ *see picture at* KNIT¹ **2** [singular] the relation between different parts of a story, explanation, etc.: *He* ***lost the thread*** (=forgot the main part) *of his argument.*

thread² *v.* [T] **1** to put thread, string, rope, etc. through a hole: *Will you* ***thread*** *the* ***needle*** *for me?* **2 thread your way through/down etc.** to move through a place by carefully going around things that are in the way: *Bikers have to thread their way through traffic, because there's no safe bike lane.*

thread·bare /ˈθrɛdbɛr/ *adj.* clothes, CARPETS, etc. that are threadbare are very thin because they have been used a lot

threat /θrɛt/ *n.* **1** [C,U] a statement in which you

tell someone that you will cause damage or harm if s/he does not do what you want: *He **made a threat** against my family.* | ***threats of** violence* | *a **bomb threat*** 2 [C usually singular] someone or something that may cause damage or harm to another person or thing: *a **threat to** national security*

THESAURUS danger, risk, hazard → DANGER

3 [C usually singular] the possibility that something bad will happen: *the **threat of** famine*

threat·en /ˈθrɛtˀn/ *v.* 1 [T] to say that you will cause someone trouble, pain, etc. if s/he does not do what you want: *Sandra **threatened to** run away from home.* | *Don't you threaten me!* 2 [T] to be likely to harm or destroy something: *Pollution is threatening the historical buildings of Athens.* 3 [I,T] if something unpleasant threatens to happen, it seems likely to happen: *The fighting **threatens to** become a major war.*

threat·en·ing /ˈθrɛtˀn-ɪŋ/ *adj.* making threats or intended to threaten someone: *a threatening letter*

three /θri/ *number* 1 3 2 three o'clock: *I'll meet you **at three**.* 3 three years old: *Mikey didn't start talking until he was three.* [ORIGIN: Old English *thrie, threo*]

three-D, 3-D /ˌθri ˈdi◂/ *adj.* a three-D movie or picture is made so that it appears to be three dimensional —**three-D, 3-D** *n.* [U]: *a movie in 3-D*

three-diˈmensional *adj.* 1 having or seeming to have length, depth, and height → TWO-DIMENSIONAL: *a three-dimensional object* 2 ENG. LANG. ARTS a three-dimensional character in a book, movie, etc. seems like a real person because s/he has many different qualities → ONE-DIMENSIONAL

thresh·old /ˈθrɛʃhoʊld, -ʃoʊld/ *n.* [C] 1 **on the threshold of sth** at the beginning of a new and important event or development: *In the 1990s, we were on the threshold of a new period in telecommunications.* 2 the level at which something begins to happen or have an effect on something: *She has a **high/low pain threshold**.* 3 the entrance to a room, or the area of floor at the entrance

threw /θru/ *v.* the past tense of THROW

thrift /θrɪft/ *n.* [U] (old-fashioned) wise and careful use of money —**thrifty** *adj.*

thrift store *n.* [C] a store that sells used goods, especially clothes, often in order to get money for a CHARITY

thrill¹ /θrɪl/ *n.* [C] a strong feeling of excitement and pleasure, or the thing that makes you feel this: *For him, nothing beats **the thrill of** driving a fast car.*

thrill² *v.* [I,T] to feel strong excitement and pleasure, or make someone else feel this: *His music continues to thrill audiences.* —**thrilled** *adj.*: *We're thrilled with the results.* —**thrilling** *adj.*: *a thrilling game*

thrill·er /ˈθrɪlɚ/ *n.* [C] a movie or book that tells an exciting story about murder, crime, etc. → MOVIE

thrive /θraɪv/ *v.* (past tense **thrived** *or* **throve** /θroʊv/, past participle **thrived**, present participle **thriving**) [I] (formal) to become very successful or very strong and healthy: *Cactuses are able to **thrive in** dry conditions.* —**thriving** *adj.*: *a thriving business*

throat /θroʊt/ *n.* [C] 1 the passage from the back of your mouth down the inside of your neck: *I have **a sore throat**.* → *see picture on page A16* 2 the front of your neck: *The attacker grabbed Mark by the throat.* 3 **force/ram sth down sb's throat** (informal) to force someone to accept your ideas or listen to your opinions when s/he does not want to 4 **be at each other's throats** if two people are at each other's throats, they are fighting or arguing with each other → **clear your throat** *at* CLEAR², **jump down sb's throat** *at* JUMP¹

throat·y /ˈθroʊt̬i/ *adj.* a throaty sound is low and rough

throb¹ /θrɑb/ *v.* (**throbbed, throbbing**) [I] 1 if a part of your body throbs, you get a regular feeling of pain in it: *I woke up with a **throbbing headache**.*

THESAURUS hurt, ache, smart → HURT¹

2 to beat strongly and regularly

throb² *n.* [C] a strong regular beat: *the low throb of the music*

throes /θroʊz/ *n.* **in the throes of sth** in the middle of a very difficult situation: *El Salvador was in the throes of a bloody civil war.*

throne /θroʊn/ *n.* [C] 1 the chair on which a king or queen sits 2 **the throne** the position and power of being king or queen: *In 2002, Queen Elizabeth of Great Britain celebrated her 50th year **on the throne**.*

throng¹ /θrɔŋ, θrɑŋ/ *n.* [C] (literary) a large group of people in one place SYN **crowd**

throng² *v.* [I,T] (literary) if people throng a place, they go there in large numbers: *Crowds thronged Times Square on New Year's Eve.*

throt·tle¹ /ˈθrɑt̬l/ *v.* [T] to hold someone's throat very tightly so that s/he cannot breathe SYN **strangle**

throttle² *n.* [C] a piece of equipment that controls the amount of gas going into an engine

through¹ /θru/ *prep., adv.* 1 from one side or end of something to the other: *He climbed in through the window.* | *The train went through a tunnel.* | *We found a gap in the fence and climbed through.* 2 from the beginning to the end, including all parts of something: *She slept through the movie.* | *I've searched through my files but I can't find the receipt.* | *Make sure you **read** the contract **through** before signing it.* 3 if you see or hear something through a window, wall, etc., the window, wall, etc. is between you and it: *I could see*

T

him through the window. | *Music was coming through the walls.* **4** because of someone or with the help of something or someone: *She succeeded through sheer hard work.* | *I got the job through an employment agency.* **5** going into an area, group, etc. and moving across it or within it: *Planes fly through the air.* | *a trip through Europe* **6 Friday through Sunday/March through May etc.** from Friday until the end of Sunday, from March until the end of May, etc.: *The exhibit will be here through July 31st.* **7 through and through** completely: *He came in from the rain soaked through and through.* ➔ **come through** *at* COME, **get through** *at* GET, **go through** *at* GO[1], **pull through** *at* PULL[1]

through[2] *adj.* **1 be through (with sth)** (informal) to have finished using something, doing something, etc.: *I'm through with the phone now if you still need it.*

> THESAURUS done, finished ➔ DONE[2]

2 (informal) **be through (with sb)** to no longer have a romantic relationship with someone: *Steve and I are through!*

through·out /θru'aʊt/ *adv., prep.* **1** in every part of a place: *Thanksgiving is celebrated throughout the U.S.*

> THESAURUS everywhere, all over sth ➔ EVERYWHERE

2 during all of a particular time: *She was calm throughout the interview.*

throve /θroʊv/ *v.* a past tense of THRIVE

throw[1] /θroʊ/ *v.* (past tense **threw** /θru/, past participle **thrown** /θroʊn/)

1 THROW A BALL/STONE ETC. [I,T] to make an object move quickly from your hand through the air by moving your arm: *Kids were **throwing** snowballs **at** each other.* | ***Throw** the ball **to** Daddy.* ➔ *see picture on page A22*

> THESAURUS
> **toss** – to throw something, especially in a careless way: *She tossed her coat onto the bed.*
> **chuck** (informal): *Kids were chucking snowballs at passing cars.*
> **hurl** – to throw something with a lot of force: *They hurled a brick through his window.*
> **fling** – to throw something somewhere with a lot of force, often in a careless way: *He flung her keys into the river.*
> **cast** – to throw something somewhere, especially when fishing: *The fishermen cast their nets into the water.*
>
> **to throw a ball in a sport**
> **pass** – to throw, kick, or hit a ball to another member of your team
> **pitch** – to throw the ball to the person who is trying to hit the ball in a game of baseball
> **lob** – to throw or hit a ball so that it moves slowly in a high curve
> **bowl** – to roll a heavy ball in the game of bowling

2 PUT STH CARELESSLY [T] to put something somewhere quickly and carelessly: *Just **throw** your coat **on** the bed.*

3 PUSH ROUGHLY [T] to push someone or something roughly toward a particular direction or position: *Police **threw** the man **to the ground**.* | *She **threw open** the windows.*

4 throw yourself on/down etc. to move somewhere suddenly and with force: *Elise threw herself on the bed and started to cry.*

5 throw yourself into sth to start doing something with a lot of effort and energy: *I threw myself into my work.*

6 throw sb/sth into confusion/crisis/chaos etc. to do something that causes people to be confused, worried, etc.: *The changes to welfare threw millions of children deeper into poverty.*

7 MOVE HANDS/HEAD ETC. [T] to suddenly move your hands, arms, head, etc. in a particular direction: *Vic **threw** his head **back** and laughed.*

8 throw sb in jail/prison (informal) to put someone in prison

9 throw sb (spoken) to confuse or shock someone, especially by suddenly saying something: *His reaction **threw** me **for a loop*** (=completely confused me).

10 throw a party to organize a party and invite people

11 throw a glance/look/smile etc. (at sb) to quickly look at someone, smile at someone, etc., especially in a way that shows what you are feeling: *He threw her a worried look.*

12 throw a game/fight to deliberately lose a game or fight that you could have won

13 throw the book at sb to punish someone as severely as possible

14 MAKE SB FALL [T] if a horse throws its rider, it makes him/her fall off

throw sth ↔ **away** *phr. v.*

1 to get rid of something that you do not want or need: *Instead of throwing away junk mail, recycle it.*

2 to lose or waste a chance, advantage, etc.: *The Wildcats just threw away their shot at the championship.*

throw in *phr. v.*

1 throw sth ↔ **in** to add something, especially to what you are selling: *I bought a new computer with some software thrown in.*

2 throw in the towel (informal) to admit that you have been defeated

throw sb/sth ↔ **off** *phr. v.*

1 to take off a piece of clothing quickly and carelessly

2 to escape from someone or become free from something or someone: *During the American Revolution, the colonists threw off British rule.*

3 to confuse a situation or make it not work correctly: *The changes will throw off the schedule.*

throw sth ↔ **on** *phr. v.*

to put on a piece of clothing quickly and carelessly

throw sb/sth ↔ **out** *phr. v.*
1 to get rid of someone or something that you do not want or need: *I threw a lot of stuff out.*
2 to make someone leave a place quickly because s/he has behaved badly: *Cooper got* ***thrown out of*** *the Navy for taking drugs.*
3 if people throw out a plan or suggestion, they refuse to accept it
throw sth ↔ **together** *phr. v.*
to make something quickly and not very carefully: *How about throwing some sandwiches together?*
throw up *phr. v.* (informal)
to VOMIT

throw² *n.* [C] an action in which someone throws something: *a good throw to first base*

throw·a·way /ˈθroʊəˌweɪ/ *adj.* **1 throwaway remark/line etc.** a short remark that is said quickly and without thinking carefully **2 throwaway society** a society that wastes things instead of caring about the environment

throw·back /ˈθroʊbæk/ *n.* [C usually singular] something that is similar to something that existed in the past: *The machine looks like* ***a throwback to*** *an earlier era.*

thrown /θroʊn/ *v.* the past participle of THROW

thru /θru/ *prep., adj., adv.* (informal) THROUGH

thrust¹ /θrʌst/ *v.* (past tense and past participle **thrust**) [T] **1** to push something somewhere with a sudden or violent movement: *Dean* ***thrust*** *some money* ***into*** *the driver's hand.*

THESAURUS **shove, stick** ➔ SHOVE

2 to be put in a difficult situation or forced to accept it: *The incident* ***thrust*** *the nation* ***into*** *an economic crisis.*

thrust² *n.* **1 the thrust** the main meaning or most important part of what someone says or does: *The* ***main/major/whole thrust*** *of his argument is that all of life is political.* **2** [U] PHYSICS the force of an engine that makes a car, train, or airplane move forward

thru·way /ˈθruweɪ/ *n.* [C] a wide road for fast traffic

thud /θʌd/ *n.* [C] the low sound that is made by a heavy object hitting something else: *He landed* ***with a thud.*** —**thud** *v.* [I]

thug /θʌg/ *n.* [C] a violent man

thumb¹ /θʌm/ *n.* [C] **1** the short thick finger on the side of your hand that helps you to hold things ➔ *see picture at* HAND¹ **2 give/get the thumbs up/down** to show that you approve or disapprove of something, or that you are ready to do something: *His new movie* ***got the thumbs up*** *from the public.* | *Ralph gave Captain Baker* ***the thumbs-up sign.*** **3 be under sb's thumb** if you are under someone's thumb, s/he controls what you do ➔ **rule of thumb** *at* RULE¹, **stick out (like a sore thumb)** *at* STICK OUT

thumb² *v.* **thumb your nose at sb/sth** to show that you do not respect rules, laws, someone's opinion, etc.: *Protesters feel the government is thumbing its nose at citizens' basic rights.*
thumb through sth *phr. v.* to look through a book, magazine, etc. quickly

thumb·nail¹ /ˈθʌmneɪl/ *n.* [C] the nail on your thumb

thumbnail² *adj.* **thumbnail sketch/description** a short description that gives only the main facts

thumb·tack /ˈθʌmtæk/ *n.* [C] a short pin with a wide flat top, used for attaching papers to walls

thump /θʌmp/ *v.* **1** [I,T] to make a dull sound by hitting against something: *The dog thumped his tail on the floor.* **2** [I] if your heart thumps, it beats very quickly because you are frightened or excited **3** [T] (informal) to hit someone: *Brasco thumped him on the back.* —**thump** *n.* [C]

thun·der¹ /ˈθʌndɚ/ *n.* [U] the loud noise that you hear during a storm, usually after a flash of LIGHTNING: *a storm with* ***thunder and lightning*** | *Suddenly, there was a great* ***clap/crack of thunder.*** [ORIGIN: Old English *thunor*]

thunder² *v.* **1 it thunders** if it thunders, a loud noise comes from the sky, usually after LIGHTNING **2** [I] to make a very loud noise: *The kids came thundering downstairs.*

thun·der·bolt /ˈθʌndɚˌboʊlt/ *n.* [C] a flash of LIGHTNING that hits something

thun·der·clap /ˈθʌndɚˌklæp/ *n.* [C] a loud noise of thunder

thun·der·cloud /ˈθʌndɚˌklaʊd/ *n.* [C] a large dark cloud in a storm

thun·der·ous /ˈθʌndərəs/ *adj.* extremely loud: *thunderous applause* ➔ LOUD¹

thun·der·storm /ˈθʌndɚˌstɔrm/ *n.* [C] a storm with thunder and LIGHTNING

thun·der·struck /ˈθʌndɚˌstrʌk/ *adj.* extremely surprised or shocked

Thurs·day /ˈθɚzdi, -deɪ/ (*written abbreviation* **Thurs.**) *n.* [C,U] the fifth day of the week, between Wednesday and Friday: *I tried to call you Thursday.* | *Kim is leaving for Chicago* ***on Thursday.*** | *He was arrested* ***last Thursday.*** | *I made the appointment for* ***next Thursday.*** | *Jason arrived late* ***Thursday night.*** [ORIGIN: Old English *Thunresdæg*, from *Thunor* god of the sky + *dæg* "day"]

thus /ðʌs/ *adv.* (formal) **1** as a result of something that you have just mentioned (SYN) **so**: *Traffic will become heavier, thus increasing pollution.*

THESAURUS **therefore, so, as a result/consequently/as a consequence, hence, thereby, accordingly** ➔ THEREFORE

2 in this way: *The oil spill could thus contaminate the water supply.* **3 thus far** until now: *Reviewers have said it's the best movie thus far this year.*

T

thwart /θwɔrt/ *v.* [T] to prevent someone from doing what s/he is trying to do

thy·roid /ˈθaɪrɔɪd/ *also* **ˈthyroid ˌgland** *n.* [C] BIOLOGY an organ in your neck that produces HORMONES (=substances that affect the way your body grows and the way you behave)

ti·a·ra /tiˈɑrə, tiˈɛrə/ *n.* [C] a piece of jewelry like a small CROWN

tib·i·a /ˈtɪbiə/ *n.* (plural **tibias** *or* **tibiae** /-bi-i/) [C] BIOLOGY a bone in the front of your leg → FIBULA

tic /tɪk/ *n.* [C] a sudden movement of a muscle in your face, that you cannot control

tick¹ /tɪk/ *n.* [C] **1** the short repeated sound that a clock or watch makes every second **2** a small creature with eight legs that attaches itself to animals and sucks their blood

tick² *v.* **1** [I] if a clock or watch ticks, it makes a short sound every second **2 what makes sb tick** (informal) the reasons that someone behaves in a particular way

tick sb/sth ↔ **off** *phr. v.* **1** (informal) to annoy someone: *Her attitude really ticks me off.* **2** to tell someone a list of things: *McCoy ticked off a list of the speakers.*

ˌticked-ˈoff *adj.* (informal) very annoyed

tick·et¹ /ˈtɪkɪt/ *n.* [C] **1** a printed piece of paper that shows that you have paid to do something, for example see a movie or travel on an airplane: *two **tickets to/for** the Lakers game | a **concert/bus/airplane ticket***

THESAURUS

Types of tickets

one-way ticket – a ticket that lets you go to a place but not back again

round-trip ticket – a ticket that lets you go to a place and back again

off-peak ticket – a ticket that is cheaper than the usual price because you cannot use it at the busiest times

season ticket – a ticket that lets you make the same trip every day for a particular period of time

e-ticket – a ticket that you buy over the Internet, which you print from your computer or which you pick up when you arrive at the airport to go on your trip

2 a printed note saying that you must pay money because you have done something illegal while driving or parking your car: *a **speeding/parking ticket*** **3** a list of the people supported by a particular political party in an election: *the Democratic ticket* [ORIGIN: 1500—1600 Early French *etiquet* "notice attached to something," from Old French *estiquier* "to attach"]

ticket² *v.* [T] to give someone a ticket for parking his/her car in the wrong place or for driving too fast

tick·le¹ /ˈtɪkəl/ *v.* **1** [T] to move your fingers lightly over someone's body in order to make him/her laugh: *Stop tickling me!*

THESAURUS touch, feel, stroke, rub, scratch, pat, pet, brush, caress → TOUCH¹

2 [I,T] if something touching your body tickles you, it makes you want to rub your body because it is uncomfortable: *Mommy, this blanket tickles.* **3** [T] if a situation, remark, etc. tickles you, it amuses or pleases you: *Mom will be **tickled pink/tickled to death*** (=very pleased) *when she hears you're coming.*

tickle² *n.* [C] a feeling in your throat that makes you want to cough

tick·lish /ˈtɪklɪʃ/ *adj.* **1** someone who is ticklish is very easy to tickle **2** (informal) a ticklish situation or problem must be dealt with very carefully

tic-tac-toe /ˌtɪk tæk ˈtoʊ/ *n.* [U] a children's game in which two players draw the marks X and O in a pattern of nine squares, trying to get three in a row

tid·al /ˈtaɪdl/ *adj.* relating to the regular rising and falling of the ocean: *tidal pools*

ˈtidal wave *n.* [C] a very large ocean wave that flows over the land and destroys things

tid·bit /ˈtɪdˌbɪt/ *n.* [C] **1** a small piece of food that tastes good **2** a small piece of interesting information, news, etc.

tide

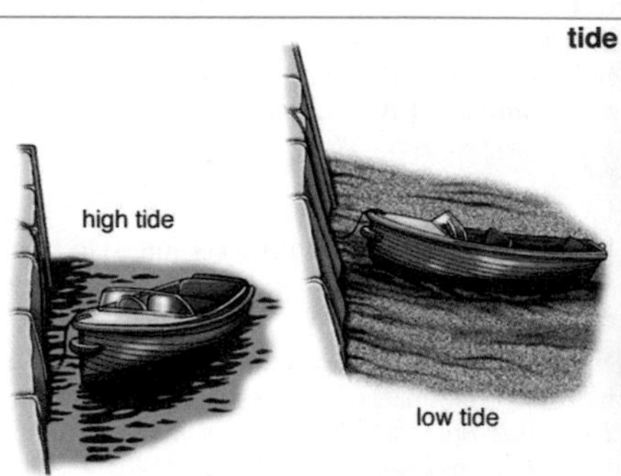

tide¹ /taɪd/ *n.* **1** [C] the regular rising and falling of the level of the ocean: *It's **high/low tide**.* → NEAP TIDE, SPRING TIDE **2** [singular] the way in which events or people's opinions are developing: *The **tide has turned**, and more jobs are being created than lost.* **3** [singular] a large amount of something that is increasing: *a **rising tide** of hate crimes*

tide² *v.*

tide sb **over** *phr. v.* to help someone deal with a difficult time: *Could you lend me $50 to tide me over until payday?*

ti·dy /ˈtaɪdi/ *adj.* carefully arranged, and not messy

tie¹ /taɪ/ *v.* (past tense and past participle **tied**, present participle **tying**, third person singular **ties**) **1** [I,T] to fasten something or hold it in a particular position using a rope, string, etc.: *The dress ties in the back. | She **tied** the scarf **around** her neck. | a dog **tied to** the fence*

THESAURUS fasten, attach, secure, join, glue, tape, staple, clip, button (up), zip (up) → FASTEN

2 [T] to make a knot in a rope, string, etc.: *Can you tie your shoelaces yet?* **3** [I] *also* **be tied** to have the same number of points in a competition: *The two teams are **tied for** first place.* | *The score is tied.* **4 be tied to sth** to be related to something and dependent on it: *Pay is tied to performance.*

tie sb **down** *phr. v.* to stop someone from being free to do what s/he wants to do: *I didn't want to be tied down with a child.*

tie in *phr. v.* if one idea or statement ties in with another one, they are similar or related: *The displays **tie in with** the advertising campaign.*

tie sb/sth ↔ **up** *phr. v.* **1** to tie someone's arms, legs, etc. so that s/he cannot move: *They had tied her up so she couldn't escape.* **2** to fasten something together by using string or rope: *The package was **tied up with** string.* **3** to use a system so much that it stops working effectively: *Sorry I'm late – I got tied up in traffic.* | *The case could tie up the courts for months.* **4 be tied up a)** to be very busy **b)** if your money is tied up in something, it is all being used for that thing: *Our money's **tied up in** real estate.*

tie² *n.* [C] **1** a long narrow piece of cloth that men wear around their neck, tied in a knot outside their shirts → *see picture at* CLOTHES **2** a relationship between two people, groups, or countries: ***close** family **ties*** | ***diplomatic/economic/political etc. ties** with Japan* **3** a piece of string, wire, etc. used in order to fasten or close something such as a bag **4** the result of a game, competition, or election in which two or more people get the same number of points, votes, etc.: *The game ended **in a tie**.*

tie·break·er /ˈtaɪˌbreɪkɚ/ *n.* [C] an additional question or point that decides the winner when two people or teams are tied

ˈtie-dye *v.* [T] to make a pattern on clothing or other material by tying string around it and coloring it with DYE

tier /tɪr/ *n.* [C] **1** one of several layers or levels that rise up one above another: *the top tier of seats* **2** one of several levels in an organization or system: *four tiers of management*

tiff /tɪf/ *n.* [C] a slight argument between friends

ti·ger /ˈtaɪgɚ/ *n.* [C] a large strong wild cat with orange and black lines on its fur

tight¹ /taɪt/ *adj.*
1 CLOTHES fitting part of your body very closely: *These shoes feel too tight.* | *tight jeans*
2 FIRMLY PULLED pulled or stretched firmly: *a tight bandage*
3 FIRMLY FIXED firmly fixed and difficult to move: *Make sure the screws are tight.*
4 FIRMLY CONTROLLED controlled very strictly and firmly: *Security is tight for the President's visit.*
5 MONEY **a)** (informal) if money is tight, you do not have enough of it **b)** (disapproving) someone who is tight tries hard to avoid spending money
6 TIME if time is tight, it is difficult for you to do the things you need to do in the time you have: *a **tight schedule***
7 COMPETITION a tight election, game, competition, etc. is one in which the competitors have an almost equal chance of winning: *a tight race for the Senate seat* —**tightly** *adv.*

tight² *adv.* very firmly or closely SYN **tightly**: ***Hold tight** and don't let go.* | *Put the lid on tight.* | ***tight-fitting** jeans*

tight·en /ˈtaɪtˀn/ *v.* **1** [T] to close or fasten something firmly by turning it: *Tighten the clamps in place.* **2** [I,T] if you tighten a rope, wire, STRAP, etc., or if it tightens, it is stretched or pulled until it is tight: *I tightened the bindings of the snowshoes.* **3** [T] *also* **tighten up** to make a rule, law, or system more strict: *The government has tightened border controls.* **4** [I,T] if your muscles or a part of your body tightens, or you tighten it, it becomes stiff: *Miguel's lips tightened in anger.* **5** [I,T] to close firmly around something: *Richard **tightened** his **grip** on her arm.* **6 tighten your belt** (informal) to try to spend less money than you usually spend

ˌtight-ˈfisted *adj.* (informal, disapproving) not generous with money SYN **stingy**

ˌtight-ˈlipped *adj.* not willing to talk about something

tight·rope /ˈtaɪtˀroʊp/ *n.* [C] a rope or wire high above the ground that someone walks along in a CIRCUS

tights /taɪts/ *n.* [plural] a piece of women's clothing made of thick colored material that fits tightly over the feet and legs and goes up to the waist

til·de /ˈtɪldə/ *n.* [C] ENG. LANG. ARTS a mark (˜) that is placed over the letter "n" in Spanish when it is to be pronounced /ny/

tile /taɪl/ *n.* [C] a thin square piece of baked clay or other material that is used for covering roofs, walls, or floors —**tile** *v.* [T]

till¹ /tɪl, tl/ *prep., conjunction* (spoken) until: *I was up till 1:00 a.m.*

till² *v.* [T] to prepare land for growing crops

tilt /tɪlt/ *v.* [I,T] **1** to move into a position where one side is higher than the other, or to make something do this: *She listened, her head tilted to one side.* **2** if an opinion or situation tilts, or something tilts it, it changes so that people start to prefer one person, belief, or action to others: *Public opinion had been **tilting toward** supporting the war.* —**tilt** *n.* [C,U]

tim·ber /ˈtɪmbɚ/ *n.* [U] trees that are cut down and used for building or making things

time¹ /taɪm/ *n.*
1 MINUTES/HOURS ETC. [U] the thing that is measured in minutes, hours, years, etc. using clocks: ***Time** seemed to **pass/go by** very quickly.* | *a three-month **period of time***

T

2 ON THE CLOCK [singular] a particular point in time that is shown on a clock in hours and minutes: *What time is it? | Evan is just learning to* ***tell time*** (=look at a clock to see what time it is).
3 OCCASION [C] an occasion when something happens or someone does something: *We visit him two or three times a month. | When was the* ***first/last time*** *you saw Kelly? | It makes me laugh* ***every/each time*** *I see it. | The* ***next time*** *you come, we'll go to a show. | Smoking is not allowed* ***at any time****.*
4 HOW OFTEN/HOW LONG [singular, U] a period of time during which something happens or someone does something, used especially to emphasize how often or how long it happens: *I used to play tennis* ***all the time*** (=often). *| They seem to spend* ***most of the time*** *arguing* (=they argue a lot). *| Mandy's been gone for* ***a long/short time****. | Patty whined* ***the whole time*** (=during all of a period of time). *| These pictures were taken* ***some time ago*** (=a fairly long time ago).
5 WHEN STH HAPPENS [C,U] the particular minute, hour, day, etc. when something happens or someone does something: ***At that/the time*** (=at that particular time in the past), *few people had cars. | I was really hungry* ***by the time*** *I got home. | We left the building* ***at the same time.*** ►Don't say "in the same time."◄ | *The program's on at* ***breakfast/supper time****. | You've caught me* ***at a bad time*** (=a time that is not convenient) – *can I call you back later? | This isn't* ***the right time*** *to ask for a raise.*
6 it's time... used in order to say when something should be done, should happen, or is expected to happen: ***It's time for*** *dinner. |* ***It's time to*** *go.*
7 TIME NEEDED [U] the amount of time that is available or needed to do something: *Learning a language* ***takes time*** (=takes a long time). *| I won't* ***have time to*** *cook dinner. | I want to* ***spend*** *more* ***time*** *with my family. | Come on – stop* ***wasting time****. |* ***There is time*** *for questions afterward.*
8 be on time to arrive or happen at the correct time or the time that was arranged: *The buses are never on time.* ►Don't say "be in time."◄
9 in time early or soon enough to do something: *They arrived* ***in time for*** *dinner.* ►Don't say "on time to" or "on time for."◄
10 from time to time sometimes, but not regularly or very often: *He comes up to visit from time to time.*
11 ahead of time before an event or before you need to do something, in order to be prepared: *We need to get there ahead of time to get a good seat.*
12 at all times always: *Keep your hands inside the car at all times.*
13 in no time soon or quickly: *We'll be there in no time.*
14 it's about time (spoken) said when you feel strongly that something should happen soon or should already have happened: *It's about time you got a job!*
15 half the time if something happens half the time, it happens quite often: *Half the time, Alan doesn't even return her phone calls.*
16 when the time comes when something that you expect to happen actually happens, or when something becomes necessary: *She'll make the right choice when the time comes.*
17 one/two etc. at a time allowing only a specific number of things to happen or exist at the same time: *You can borrow three books at a time.*
18 take your time to do something slowly or carefully without hurrying: *Take your time and look over your essay before turning it in.*
19 for the time being for a short period of time from now, but not permanently: *For the time being, she's living with her father.*
20 good/bad/difficult etc. time a period of time or an occasion when you have experiences that are good, bad, etc.: *That was the happiest time of my life. | Did you* ***have a good time*** *at Laura's?*
21 IN HISTORY [C] a particular period in history: *It happened in the time of the Romans.*
22 times [plural] the present time or a particular period in history, and the ways that people do or did things during that period: *modern times | Their technology is 30 years* ***behind the times.***
23 time's up (spoken) said in order to tell people to stop doing something because there is no more time left: *Okay, time's up. Put down your pencils.*
24 in time to sth if you do something in time to a piece of music, you do it using the same RHYTHM and speed as the music
25 do time (informal) to spend time in prison [ORIGIN: Old English *tima*]

time² *v.* [T] **1** to do something or arrange for something to happen at a particular time: *The bomb was* ***timed to*** *go off at 5:00. | an* ***ill-timed/well-timed*** *announcement* (=one that happens at a bad or good time) **2** to measure how fast someone or something is going, how long it takes to do something, etc.: *Christie was* ***timed at*** *10.02 seconds.*

ˌtime and a ˈhalf *n.* [U] one and a half times the normal rate of pay

ˈtime bomb *n.* [C] **1** a situation that is likely to become a very serious problem: *It's an environmental time bomb.* **2** a bomb that is set to explode at a particular time

ˈtime card *n.* [C] a card on which the hours you have worked are recorded by a machine

ˈtime-conˌsuming *adj.* needing a long time to do: *a time-consuming process*

ˈtime frame *n.* [C] the period of time during which you expect or agree that something will happen or be done

ˈtime-ˌhonored *adj.* a time-honored method, custom, etc. is one that has existed or worked well for a long time

time·keep·er /ˈtaɪmˌkipɚ/ *n.* [C] someone who officially records how long it takes to do something, especially at a sports event

time·less /ˈtaɪmlɪs/ *adj.* always remaining beautiful, attractive, etc.: *timeless melodies*

ˈtime ˌlimit *n.* [C] the longest time that you are allowed to do something in: *There is a* ***time limit for*** *using the library computer.*

T

time·ly /ˈtaɪmli/ *adj.* done or happening at exactly the right time: *a timely decision*

ˌtime ˈoff *n.* [U] time when you are officially allowed not to be at work or studying

ˌtime ˈout *n.* **1 take time out** to rest or do something different from your usual job or activities **2** [C] a short time during a sports game when the teams can rest and get instructions from the COACH

tim·er /ˈtaɪmɚ/ *n.* [C] an instrument for measuring time, when you are doing something such as cooking

times /taɪmz/ *prep.* MATH multiplied by: *Two times two equals four.* → CALCULATE

time·ta·ble /ˈtaɪmˌteɪbəl/ *n.* [C] a plan of events and activities, with their dates and times SYN **schedule**: *Many people are calling for a* ***timetable for*** *withdrawing the troops.*

ˈtime warp *n.* **be (caught/stuck) in a time warp** to have not changed even though everyone or everything else has: *The sleepy little town seems to be caught in a time warp.*

ˈtime zone *n.* [C] one of the 24 areas the world is divided into, each of which has its own time

tim·id /ˈtɪmɪd/ *adj.* not brave or confident: *a timid child* —**timidly** *adv.* —**timidity** /təˈmɪdət̬i/ *n.* [U]

THESAURUS **shy, bashful, self-conscious** → SHY[1]

tim·ing /ˈtaɪmɪŋ/ *n.* **1** [U] the skill of doing something at exactly the right time: *A comedian has to have* ***good/bad/wonderful timing*** *or his jokes will fall flat.* **2** [C,U] the time when someone does something or when something happens: *the* ***timing of*** *his resignation*

tim·or·ous /ˈtɪmərəs/ *adj.* (formal) lacking confidence and easily frightened: *a small, timorous woman* —**timorously** *adv.*

tin /tɪn/ *n.* [U] a soft white metal used for making cans, building materials, etc.: *a tin can*

tin·der /ˈtɪndɚ/ *n.* [U] material that burns easily, used for lighting fires

tine /taɪn/ *n.* [C] a pointed part of something that has several points, for example on a fork

tin·foil /ˈtɪnfɔɪl/ *n.* [U] (old-fashioned) FOIL

tinge /tɪndʒ/ *n.* [C] a very small amount of a color, emotion, or quality: ***a tinge of*** *sadness in her voice* | *white paint with a yellow tinge* —**tinged** *adj.*

tin·gle /ˈtɪŋgəl/ *v.* [I] to feel a slight sting on your skin: *My fingers* ***tingled with*** *the cold.* —**tingle** *n.* [C]

tin·ker /ˈtɪŋkɚ/ *v.* [I] (informal) to make small changes to something in order to repair it or improve it: *Dad was* ***tinkering with*** *the engine.*

tin·kle /ˈtɪŋkəl/ *v.* [I] to make high soft ringing sounds: *a tinkling bell* —**tinkle** *n.* [C]

tin·ny /ˈtɪni/ *adj.* a tinny sound is unpleasant to listen to, and sounds like it is coming from something made of metal: *tinny music*

tin·sel /ˈtɪnsəl/ *n.* [U] thin pieces of shiny silver paper, used especially as Christmas decorations

tint[1] /tɪnt/ *n.* [C] a small amount of a light color SYN **shade**: *The sky had a pink tint.*

tint[2] *v.* [T] to change the color of something, especially hair

ti·ny /ˈtaɪni/ *adj.* extremely small: *thousands of* ***tiny little*** *fish* | *a tiny fraction of the budget*

THESAURUS **small, little, minute, miniature, minuscule** → SMALL

tip[1] /tɪp/ *n.* [C] **1** the end of something, especially something pointed SYN **point**: *the tip of your nose* | *the northern tip of the island* **2** a small amount of additional money that you give to someone such as a WAITER or taxi driver for his/her service: *Did you* ***leave a tip****?* | *a $5 tip* **3** a helpful piece of advice: *tips* ***on/for*** *losing weight* | *He* ***gave*** *me some* ***tips*** *on taking good pictures.*

THESAURUS **advice, suggestion, recommendation** → ADVICE

4 on the tip of your tongue if a word, name, etc. is on the tip of your tongue, you know it but cannot remember it immediately **5 the tip of the iceberg** a small sign of a problem that is much larger: *These figures are just the tip of the iceberg.*

tip[2] *v.* (**tipped, tipping**) **1** [I,T] to lean at an angle, or to make something do this: *The boat tipped a little to that side.* | *Jesse* ***tipped*** *his chair* ***back.*** **2** [I,T] to give a tip to a WAITER, taxi driver, etc. for his/her service: *I tipped him $5.* **3 be tipped with sth** to have one end covered in something: *The arrows were tipped with poison*

tip sb ↔ **off** *phr. v.* (informal) to give someone such as the police secret information about something illegal: *The police must have been tipped off about the robbery.*

tip (sth ↔) **over** *phr. v.* to fall or turn over, or to make something do this: *The canoe suddenly tipped over.* | *The baby tipped the plant over.*

ti·pi /ˈtipi/ *n.* [C] a TEPEE

ˈtip-off *n.* [C] (informal) **1** a warning or message about something illegal that is given secretly to the police, a government, etc. **2** the beginning of a basketball game, when the ball is thrown in the air and two players jump for it

tip·ster /ˈtɪpstɚ/ *n.* [C] (written) someone who gives the police, a REPORTER, etc. secret information about something that is going to happen

tip·sy /ˈtɪpsi/ *adj.* (informal) slightly drunk

tip·toe[1] /ˈtɪptoʊ/ *n.* **on tiptoe** standing on your toes, with the rest of your feet off the ground: *Matt* ***stood on tiptoe*** *to see.*

tiptoe[2] *v.* [I] to walk on tiptoe: *Rita tiptoed downstairs.* → *see picture on page A22*

T

ti·rade /ˈtaɪreɪd/ *n.* [C] a long angry speech criticizing someone or something: *a **tirade against/at** polluters*

tire¹ /taɪɚ/ *n.* [C] a thick round piece of rubber that fits around the wheel of a car, bicycle, etc.: *I **had a flat tire*** (=all the air went out of it) *on the way home.*

tire² *v.* **1** [I,T] to become tired, or to make someone feel tired: *Even short walks tire her.* **2 tire of sth** to become bored with something: *We never tired of her stories.*

tire sb ↔ **out** *phr. v.* to make someone very tired: *All that walking tired me out.*

tired /taɪɚd/ *adj.* **1** feeling that you want to sleep or rest: *I was too tired to move.* | *Ben looks **tired out**.*

> THESAURUS
> **exhausted** – extremely tired: *I was completely exhausted after the long trip.*
> **worn out** – very tired because you have been working or playing hard: *By the end of the season, many players are worn out.*
> **weary** – very tired, especially because you have been doing something for a long time: *She grew weary* (=became weary) *of spending every day in the car.* | *weary travelers*
> **run-down** – tired and unhealthy: *If you're feeling run-down, you probably need a holiday.*
> **beat** (informal) – very tired: *I'm beat.*
> **fatigued** (formal) – extremely tired: *They were fatigued after the long voyage.*

2 tired of (doing) sth bored or annoyed with something: *I'm **tired of** waiting.*

tire·less /ˈtaɪɚlɪs/ *adj.* working very hard in a determined way: *a tireless worker* —**tirelessly** *adv.*

> THESAURUS **energetic, vigorous** → ENERGETIC

tire·some /ˈtaɪɚsəm/ *adj.* annoying and boring → TIRING: *a tiresome conversation*

tir·ing /ˈtaɪərɪŋ/ *adj.* making you feel tired: *The trip had been tiring.*

tis·sue /ˈtɪʃu/ *n.* **1** [C] a piece of soft thin paper, used for blowing your nose **2** [U] BIOLOGY the material forming animal or plant cells: *damaged lung tissue*

tit-for-tat /ˌtɪt fɚ ˈtæt/ *n* [U] (informal) something bad that you do to someone because s/he has done something bad to you

tithe /taɪð/ *n.* [C usually plural] **1** SOCIAL SCIENCE a particular amount, usually 10% of income, that members of some Christian churches are expected to give to the church **2** HISTORY a tax paid to the church, in past times

tit·il·late /ˈtɪtlˌeɪt/ *v.* [T] to make someone feel excited or interested, especially sexually: *TV news seems often meant to titillate you, not inform you.*

ti·tle¹ /ˈtaɪtl/ *n.* **1** [C] the name given to a book, painting, play, etc.: *What is the title of her new book?* **2** [C] (written) a book: *this year's best-selling titles* **3** [C] a word or name that describes someone's rank or position: *Her official title is editorial manager.* **4** [C] a word such as "Mrs.," "Dr.," "Senator,", etc. that is used before someone's name to show whether s/he is married or what his/her rank or position is **5** [C] the position of being the winner of an important sports competition: *the National League batting title* **6** [singular, U] LAW the legal right to own something: *Who has the **title to** this land?*

title² *v.* [T] to give a name to a book, play, etc.: *The concert was titled "Home for the Holidays."*

ˈtitle role *also* **ˈtitle ˌcharacter** *n.* [C] the main character in a play, movie, etc., which is the same as the name of the play, etc.

tit·ter /ˈtɪtɚ/ *v.* [I] to laugh quietly, especially in a nervous way —**titter** *n.* [C]

> THESAURUS **laugh, giggle, chuckle, snicker** → LAUGH¹

tiz·zy /ˈtɪzi/ *n.* (informal) **in a tizzy** feeling nervous, upset, and sometimes confused

TLC *n.* [U] (informal) **tender loving care** kindness and love that you give to someone when s/he is sick or upset

TN the written abbreviation of TENNESSEE

TNT *n.* [U] a powerful explosive

to¹ /tə; *before vowels* tʊ; *strong* tu/ [used with the basic form of a verb to make the infinitive.] ▸ Do not use "to" with modal verbs. ◂ **1** used after a verb, noun, or adjective when the INFINITIVE completes its meaning: *I'd love to go!* | *It's starting to rain.* | *The men were told to leave the bar.* | *If you get a chance to see the play, you should.* | *Dad says he's not ready to retire yet.* | *It's great to see you!* **2** used by itself instead of an INFINITIVE in order to avoid repeating the same verb: *You can go if you want to.* **3** used after "how," "where," "who," "whom," "whose," "which," "when," "what," or "whether": *Can you show me how to do this?* | *Maria didn't know whether to call Tim or not.* **4** used in order to show the purpose of an action: *He covered the child to keep her from getting cold.* | *To begin with, let's look at chapter three.* **5** used after "too" and an adjective: *It's too cold to go outside.* **6** used after an adjective and "enough": *Are you feeling well enough to go back to work?* **7** used after "there is" and a noun: *There's nothing to do here.*

to² *prep.* **1** in order to be in a particular place, event, state, etc.: *The drive to the city takes five hours.* | *I couldn't go to sleep.* | *Are you going to the wedding?*

> THESAURUS **in order to, so (that), for** → ORDER¹

2 toward or in the direction of a place: *She went to the door.* | *Throw the ball to me.* **3** used in order to show the position of something, especially in relation to something else: *The water came up to our* *knees.* | *They live in a town 50 miles to the south of Denver.* | *My back was to the door* (=facing the door). **4** used in order to show who receives or owns something, or to whom speech is directed: *Angie said "hi" to me this morning.* | *The ring belongs to her mother.* **5** used in order to show where something is touching, fastened, or connected: *We tied the rope to a tree.* | *The computers are linked to a server.* **6** used to show a relationship with someone or something: *She's married to Gary's cousin.* **7** starting with one thing or in one place and ending with or in another: *A to Z* | *Count to 10.* | *It's 30 miles **from** here **to** Toronto.* **8** used when showing who or what is affected by an action or situation: *Mr. Reger is nice to everyone.* | *The chemicals are a danger to ocean life.* **9** fitting or being part of a machine or piece of equipment: *I have a key to the office.* **10** used when comparing two numbers, things, etc.: *The Bears won, 27 to 10.* **11** used in order to mean "before" when you are giving the time: *It's ten to four.* | *two weeks to Christmas*

toad /toʊd/ *n.* [C] an animal like a large FROG but brown in color

toad·stool /ˈtoʊdstul/ *n.* [C] a plant that looks like a MUSHROOM, but is usually poisonous

toad·y¹ /ˈtoʊdi/ *n.* (plural **toadies**) [C] (disapproving) someone who pretends to like an important person and does whatever that person wants, especially in order to gain an advantage in the future

toady² *v.* (**toadied**, **toadies**)

toady to sb *phr. v.* (disapproving) to pretend to like an important person, organization, etc., and do whatever that person or organization wants, so that they will help you or like you —**toadying** *also* **toadyism** *n.* [U] (disapproving)

to and fro /ˌtu ən ˈfroʊ/ *adv.* moving in one direction and then back again: *They swung to and fro.*

toast¹ /toʊst/ *n.* **1** [U] bread that has been heated until it is brown and CRISP: *a **slice/piece of toast*** **2** [C] an occasion when you toast someone: *They **raised** their **glasses in a toast** to the happy couple.*

toast² *v.* [T] **1** to drink a glass of wine, etc. with other people in order to thank someone, wish someone luck, or celebrate something: *We toasted our victory with champagne.* **2** to make bread or other food turn brown by heating it

toast·er /ˈtoʊstɚ/ *n.* [C] a machine used for making toast

toast·y /ˈtoʊsti/ *adj.* (spoken) warm in a way that makes you feel comfortable

to·bac·co /təˈbækoʊ/ *n.* [U] dried brown leaves that are smoked in cigarettes, CIGARS, etc., or the plant that these come from

to·bog·gan·ing /təˈbɑgənɪŋ/ *n.* [U] the sport of sliding down snow-covered hills on a special wooden or plastic board that curves up at the front —**toboggan** *n.* [C] —**toboggan** *v.* [I]

to·day¹ /təˈdeɪ/ *n.* [U] **1** the day that is happening now: *Today is Wednesday.* | *today's paper* **2** the present time: *young people of today*

today² *adv.* **1** during the day that is happening now: *Mom, can we go to the park today?* **2** in the present time: *Today, heart disease is the leading cause of death in women.*

tod·dle /ˈtɑdl/ *v.* [I] to walk with short unsteady steps, like a very young child does

tod·dler /ˈtɑdlɚ/ *n.* [C] a child between the ages of about 1 and 3

to-ˈdo *n.* [singular] (informal) unnecessary excitement or angry feelings about something (SYN) **fuss**

toe¹ /toʊ/ *n.* [C] **1** one of the five separate parts at the end of your foot: *I hurt my **big toe*** (=largest toe). → *see picture on page A16* **2 on your toes** ready for anything that might happen: *The managers come to the factory floor, just to **keep us on our toes**.* → **step on sb's toes** *at* STEP²

toe² *v.* **toe the line** to do what you are told to do by people in authority

TOEFL /ˈtoʊfəl/ *n.* **Test of English as a Foreign Language** a test that students can take if their first language is not English, that proves that they can understand English

toe·hold /ˈtoʊhoʊld/ *n.* [singular] your first involvement in a particular activity, from which you can develop and become stronger: *It took us five years to **gain a toehold** in the market.*

toe·nail /ˈtoʊneɪl/ *n.* [C] the hard flat part that covers the top end of your toe

ˌtoe-to-ˈtoe *adv.* **go/stand/fight toe-to-toe (with) sb** to argue or fight with someone in a way that shows you will not stop

tof·fee /ˈtɔfi, ˈtɑfi/ *n.* [C,U] a sticky brown candy made from sugar and butter, or a piece of this

to·fu /ˈtoʊfu/ *n.* [U] a soft white food that is made from SOYBEANS

to·ga /ˈtoʊgə/ *n.* [C] HISTORY a long loose piece of clothing worn by people in ancient Greece and Rome

to·geth·er¹ /təˈgɛðɚ/ *adv.* **1** if two or more things are put together, they form a single subject, group, mixture, or object: *Add the numbers together.* | *We put the puzzle together last night.* **2** with or next to each other: *Kevin and I went to school together.* | *Keep everything together in a folder.* | *We were **crowded/packed etc. together** in one little room.* **3** if two people are together, they are married or have a romantic relationship: *Mark and Sarah decided to **live together**.* **4** at the same time: *Why do all the bills seem to come together?* → **get your act together** *at* ACT²

together² *adj.* (spoken) thinking clearly, being very organized, etc.: *Carla seems really together.*

to·geth·er·ness /təˈgɛðɚnɪs/ *n.* [U] a feeling of having a close relationship with other people

tog·gle /ˈtɑgəl/ *n.* [C] IT something such as a key

T

on a computer that lets you change from one operation to another —**toggle** *v.* [I,T]

togs /tɑgz, tɔgz/ *n.* [plural] (informal) clothes

toil /tɔɪl/ *v.* [I] (literary) to work very hard for a long period of time —**toil** *n.* [U]

toi·let /ˈtɔɪlɪt/ *n.* [C] a large bowl that you sit on to get rid of waste matter from your body [ORIGIN: 1500—1600 French *toilette* "cloth put around the shoulders while arranging the hair or shaving, toilette, toilet," from *toile* "net, cloth"]

THESAURUS

Do not use **toilet** to talk about a room with a toilet in it.
bathroom – a room in a house with the toilet in it
restroom, women's/ladies' room, men's room – a room in a public place that has one or more toilets in it
lavatory – a room with a toilet in it, especially a room in a public building such as a school or on an airplane
latrine – an outdoor toilet at a camp or military area
outhouse/privy – a small outdoor building in which the waste goes into a hole below the building, used in campgrounds and in the past behind houses

T

ˈtoilet ˌpaper *n.* [U] soft thin paper used for cleaning yourself after you have used the toilet

toi·let·ries /ˈtɔɪlətriz/ *n.* [plural] things such as soap and TOOTHPASTE that are used for washing and cleaning yourself

to·ken[1] /ˈtoʊkən/ *n.* [C] **1** a round piece of metal that you use instead of money in some machines **2** something that represents a feeling, fact, event, etc.: *This is a* ***token of*** *our appreciation.*

token[2] *adj.* **1** a token action, change, etc. is small and not very important, but is done to show that you are dealing with a problem or will keep a promise: *He receives a token salary for his help.* **2 token woman/minority/black etc.** someone who is included in a group to make everyone think that it has all types of people in it, when this is often not really true

to·ken·ism /ˈtoʊkəˌnɪzəm/ *n.* [U] actions that are intended to make people think that an organization deals fairly with people or problems when in fact it does not

told /toʊld/ *v.* the past tense and past participle of TELL

tol·er·a·ble /ˈtɑlərəbəl/ *adj.* something that is tolerable is not very good, but you are able to accept it (ANT) **intolerable**: *The heat was barely tolerable.* —**tolerably** *adv.*

tol·er·ance /ˈtɑlərəns/ *n.* **1** [U] willingness to allow people to do, say, or believe what they want: *society's need for* ***religious/racial tolerance*** | *He had little* ***tolerance for/of*** *mistakes.* **2** [C,U] the degree to which someone or something can suffer pain, difficulty, etc. without being harmed: *plants with limited* ***tolerance for/to*** *the cold* **3** [C,U] MATH the amount by which a measurement can be different from what is wanted

tol·er·ate /ˈtɑləˌreɪt/ *v.* [T] to accept something, even though you do not like it: *The school will not tolerate sexual harassment.* | *My stepmother* ***barely tolerated*** *me.* —**tolerant** *adj.* —**toleration** /ˌtɑləˈreɪʃən/ *n.* [U]

THESAURUS

accept – to agree or deal with a situation you do not like but cannot change: *She found it hard to accept his death.*
stand – to be able to accept or deal well with a difficult situation: *It was so noisy in there that I could hardly stand it.*
put up with sth – to accept an annoying situation or someone's annoying behavior, without trying to stop it or change it: *I don't see how you can put up with the constant noise.*
live with sth – to accept a bad situation as a permanent part of your life that you cannot change: *Stress is just something you have to learn to live with.*
condone (formal) – to accept or allow behavior that most people think is wrong: *I cannot condone the use of violence.*

toll[1] /toʊl/ *n.* [C] **1** [usually singular] the number of people killed or injured at a particular time: *The* ***death toll*** *has risen to 83.* **2** [usually singular] a bad effect that something has on someone or something over a long period of time: *Years of smoking have* ***taken their toll*** *on his health.* **3** the money you have to pay to use a particular road, bridge, etc.

toll[2] *v.* [I,T] if a bell tolls, or you toll it, it keeps ringing slowly

ˈtoll booth *n.* [C] a place where you pay to use a particular road, bridge, etc.

ˌtoll-ˈfree *adj.* a toll-free telephone call does not cost any money: *Call our* ***toll-free number*** *now.*

tom·a·hawk /ˈtɑməˌhɔk/ *n.* [C] a light AX used by some Native Americans in past times

to·ma·to /təˈmeɪt̬oʊ/ *n.* (plural **tomatoes**) [C] a soft round red fruit, eaten as a vegetable raw or cooked: *a tomato sauce* [ORIGIN: 1600—1700 Spanish *tomate*, from Nahuatl (a language from Southern Mexico and Central America) *tomatl*] → *see picture at* VEGETABLE

tomb /tum/ *n.* [C] a grave, especially a large one above the ground: *the* ***tomb of*** *China's first emperor* [ORIGIN: 1100—1200 Anglo-French *tumbe*, from Late Latin *tumba* "pile of earth under which a body is buried"]

tom·boy /ˈtɑmbɔɪ/ *n.* [C] a girl who likes to play the same games as boys

tomb·stone /ˈtumstoʊn/ *n.* [C] a GRAVESTONE

tom·cat /ˈtɑmkæt/ *n.* [C] a male cat

tome /toʊm/ *n.* [C] (literary) a large heavy book

to·mor·row¹ /tə'mɑroʊ, -'mɔr-/ *adv.* on or during the day after today: *Hanson is leaving tomorrow.* | *I'll see you **tomorrow morning/afternoon/night**.* [ORIGIN: Old English *to morgen*, from *to* "to" + *morgen* "morning"]

tomorrow² *n.* [U] **1** the day after today → TODAY, YESTERDAY: *Tomorrow is Thursday.* **2** the future, especially the near future: *the schools of tomorrow* **3 do sth like there's no tomorrow** to do something without worrying about the future: *We're spending money like there's no tomorrow.*

ton /tʌn/ *n.* [C] **1** a unit for measuring weight, equal to 2,000 pounds **2** (informal) a very large quantity or weight: *Your suitcase **weighs a ton**!* | *She spent **tons of** money.*

tone¹ /toʊn/ *n.* **1** [C,U] the way your voice sounds, which shows how you are feeling or what you mean: *Ben's calm, relaxed **tone of voice*** | *"Yes," she replied, **in an** unused **tone**.* **2** [singular, U] the general feeling or attitude expressed in a piece of writing, activity, etc.: *The argument **set the tone*** (=began a feeling that continued) *for the evening.* | *the formal **tone of** her poems* **3** [C] a sound made by a piece of electronic equipment: *Please leave a message after the tone.* **4** [U] the quality of a sound, especially the sound of a musical instrument or someone's voice **5** [U] how strong and firm your muscles, skin, etc. are: *Exercise will improve your **muscle tone**.* **6** [C] a SHADE of a particular color **7** [C] ENG. LANG. ARTS the difference in PITCH between two musical notes that are separated by one KEY on the piano (SYN) **step**

tone² *also* **tone up** *v.* [T] to improve the strength and firmness of your muscles, skin, etc.: *Do these exercises to tone your stomach muscles.*

tone sth ↔ **down** *phr. v.* to make something such as a speech or piece of writing less offensive, exciting, etc.: *Advisers told him to tone down his statement.*

ˌtone-'deaf *adj.* unable to hear the difference between different musical notes

ton·er /'toʊnɚ/ *n.* [U] a type of ink that is used in machines that print or copy documents

tongs /tɑŋz, tɔŋz/ *n.* [plural] a tool for picking up objects, made of two movable BARS that are attached at one end

tongue /tʌŋ/ *n.* [C] **1** the soft part in your mouth that you can move and that you use for tasting and speaking **2 bite/hold your tongue** to stop yourself from saying something: *Jim struggled to hold his tongue.* **3** a language: *your **mother/native tongue*** (=the language you learned as a child)

THESAURUS **language, dialect** → LANGUAGE

4 the part of a shoe under the LACEs (=strings that you tie them with) [ORIGIN: Old English *tunge*] → **a slip of the tongue** *at* SLIP², **on the tip of your tongue** *at* TIP¹

ˌtongue-in-'cheek *adv.* said or done seriously, but meant as a joke

'tongue-tied *adj.* unable to speak easily because you are nervous

'tongue ˌtwister *n.* [C] a word or phrase with many similar sounds that is difficult to say quickly

ton·ic /'tɑnɪk/ *n.* **1** [C,U] *also* **tonic water** a bitter-tasting drink with BUBBLEs, that you mix with some alcoholic drinks **2** [C] something, especially a medicine, that gives you more energy or strength

tonic sol-fa /ˌtɑnɪk soʊl 'fɑ/ *n.* [U] ENG. LANG. ARTS a system of using SYLLABLES to represent the notes of a musical scale

to·night¹ /tə'naɪt/ *adv.* on or during the night of today: *I think I'll go to bed early tonight.*

tonight² *n.* [U] the night of today: *Tonight is a very special occasion.* | *tonight's news*

ton·nage /'tʌnɪdʒ/ *n.* [U] **1** the number of TONS that something weighs **2** the size of a ship or the amount of goods it can carry, shown in TONS

ton·sil /'tɑnsəl/ *n.* [C] BIOLOGY one of two small organs at the sides of your throat near the back of your tongue

ton·sil·li·tis /ˌtɑnsə'laɪṭɪs/ *n.* [U] BIOLOGY an infection of the tonsils

To·ny /'toʊni/ *n.* (plural **Tonies**) [C] a prize given each year to the best plays, actors, etc. in New York's theaters

too /tu/ *adv.* **1** more than is needed, wanted, or possible: *You're going too fast!* | *He was **too** sick **to** travel.*

USAGE

Too is usually used to show that you do not like or approve of something: *This happens too often.* | *You're too old to go clubbing.* | *Help came too late to save the struggling animal.*
Very is used to emphasize something which can be either good or bad: *It's very hot today.* | *She's always very busy.*

2 also: *Sheila wants to come too.* | *"I'm really hungry." "I am too!"* **3** very: *It shouldn't be too long until dinner's ready.* **4 be too much for sb** used in order to say that something is so difficult, tiring, or upsetting that someone cannot do it **5 I am too!/I did too! etc.** (spoken) used when you disagree with what someone has said about you: *"You're not old enough." "I am too!"*

took /tʊk/ *v.* the past tense of TAKE

tool¹ /tul/ *n.* [C] **1** something such as a hammer, SCREWDRIVER, etc. that you use to make or repair things: *He has all the tools needed for the job.* **2** something such as a piece of equipment or skill that is useful for a particular purpose: *Music can be a **useful/valuable/powerful tool** for learning.*

T

tool² *v.*
tool around/along *phr. v.* (informal) to drive, especially for fun

tool·box /'tulbɑks/ *n.* [C] a special box for keeping tools in

toolbox

toot /tut/ *v.* [I,T] if a horn toots, or if you toot it, it makes a short sound —**toot** *n.* [C]

tooth /tuθ/ *n.* (plural **teeth** /tiθ/) [C] **1** one of the hard objects in your mouth that you use for biting and chewing your food: *The wolf had fierce eyes and* ***sharp teeth.*** | *Did you* ***brush*** *your* ***teeth*** (=clean them)? → *see picture on page A16* **2** one of the pointed parts that sticks out from a comb, saw, etc. **3 fight (sb/sth) tooth and nail** to try with a lot of effort and determination to do something: *Neighborhood groups fought tooth and nail against the closing of the school.* [ORIGIN: Old English *toth*] → **have a sweet tooth** *at* SWEET

tooth·ache /'tuθeɪk/ *n.* [C,U] a pain in a tooth

tooth·brush /'tuθbrʌʃ/ *n.* [C] a small brush for cleaning your teeth → *see picture at* BRUSH¹

tooth·paste /'tuθpeɪst/ *n.* [U] a substance used for cleaning your teeth

T

tooth·pick /'tuθ,pɪk/ *n.* [C] a small pointed piece of wood used for removing pieces of food from between your teeth

top¹ /tɑp/ *n.* [C]
1 HIGHEST PART the highest part of something (ANT) **bottom**: *the* ***tops of*** *the mountains* | *Write your name* ***at the top*** *of the page.* | *an ice cream sundae with nuts* ***on top*** *of it*
2 UPPER SURFACE the flat upper surface of an object: *The table has a glass top.* | *Photographs of the family were displayed* ***on top of*** *the piano.*
3 on top of sth a) in addition to something: *On top of everything else, I need $700 to fix my car!* **b)** in control of a situation: *He felt alert and* ***on top of*** *things.*
4 the top the best, most successful, or most important position in an organization, company, competition, etc.: *The people* ***at the top*** *make the decisions.* | *What do these men, who have* ***reached the top*** *of their professions, have in common?*
5 CLOTHING clothing that you wear on the upper part of your body: *a pink top*
6 COVER a cover for a pen, container, etc., especially something that you push or turn: *I can't get the top off this jar.*

THESAURUS **cover, lid, cap** → COVER²

7 off the top of your head (informal) said without checking the facts: *Off the top of my head I'd say there were about 50.*
8 at the top of your voice/lungs shouted or sung as loudly as you can
9 TOY a toy that spins and balances on its point when you twist it
10 on top of the world (informal) extremely happy

top² *adj.* **1** at the top (ANT) **bottom**: *the top button of my shirt* **2** best or most successful: *a top salesman* | *the top score* → POSITION¹

top³ *v.* (**topped**, **topping**) [T] **1** to be higher, better, or more than something: *Their profits have topped $5 million this year.* **2 be topped by/with sth** to have something on top: *ice cream* ***topped with*** *maple syrup*
top sth ↔ **off** *phr. v.* (informal) to do one final thing before finishing something: *She topped it off by being named the most valuable player.*
top out *phr. v.* if something that is increasing tops out, it reaches its highest point and stops rising: *The Dow Jones average* ***topped out at*** *5999.75 today.*

,top 'hat *n.* [C] a man's tall hat with a flat top, worn in past times → *see picture at* HAT

,top-'heavy *adj.* **1** too heavy at the top and therefore likely to fall over **2** a top-heavy organization has too many managers

top·ic /'tɑpɪk/ (Ac) *n.* [C] a subject that people talk or write about: *The discussion was* ***on the topic*** *of human rights.* | *the main* ***topic of conversation*** | *The environment is a* ***hot topic*** (=important topic) *during this election year.* [ORIGIN: 1400—1500 Latin *Topica* "Topics," from Greek *Topika*, from *topikos* "of a place, of a useful quotation." This was the title of a book by the ancient Greek thinker Aristotle.]

THESAURUS **subject, theme, issue, matter** → SUBJECT¹

top·i·cal /'tɑpɪkəl/ (Ac) *adj.* relating to something that is important at the present time: *The show deals with topical issues.*

'topic ,sentence *n.* [C] ENG. LANG. ARTS the sentence in a PARAGRAPH that states the main idea you are writing about

top·less /'tɑplɪs/ *adj.* a woman who is topless is not wearing any clothes on the upper part of her body

top·most /'tɑpmoʊst/ *adj.* highest: *the topmost branches*

,top-'notch *adj.* (informal) having the highest quality or standard: *top-notch schools*

top·o·graph·ic /,tɑpə'græfɪk◂/ *also* **top·o·graph·i·cal** /,tɑpə'græfɪkəl/ *adj.* EARTH SCIENCES relating to topography

to·pog·ra·phy /tə'pɑgrəfi/ *n.* [U] **1** EARTH SCIENCES the science of describing or making a map of an area of land **2** EARTH SCIENCES the shape of an area of land, including its hills, valleys, etc. [ORIGIN: 1500—1600 Late Latin *topographia* "description of a place," from Greek, from *topographein* "to describe a place"] —**topographer** *n.* [C]

top·ping /ˈtɑpɪŋ/ *n.* [C,U] food that you put on top of other food to make it taste or look better: *pizza toppings*

top·ple /ˈtɑpəl/ *v.* **1** [I,T] to fall over, or to make something do this: *Several trees **toppled over** in the storm.* **2** [T] to take power away from a leader or government: *The scandal could topple the government.*

ˌtop-ˈsecret *adj.* top-secret documents or information must be kept completely secret

top·sy-tur·vy /ˌtɑpsi ˈtɚvi◂ / *adj.* (informal) in a state of complete disorder or confusion

torch¹ /tɔrtʃ/ *n.* [C] a long stick that you burn at one end for light or as a symbol: *the Olympic torch*

torch² *v.* [T] (written) to start a fire deliberately in order to destroy something: *Someone torched the old warehouse.*

tore /tɔr/ *v.* the past tense of TEAR

tor·ment¹ /ˈtɔrmɛnt/ *n.* [C,U] severe pain and suffering, or something that causes this

tor·ment² /tɔrˈmɛnt/ *v.* [T] to make someone suffer a lot of mental or physical pain: *He was **tormented by** guilt.* —**tormentor** *n.* [C]

torn /tɔrn/ *v.* the past participle of TEAR

tor·na·do /tɔrˈneɪdoʊ/ *n.* (plural **tornadoes**) [C] an extremely violent storm consisting of air that spins very quickly [ORIGIN: 1500—1600 Spanish *tronada* "thunderstorm"]

THESAURUS **wind, gale, storm, hurricane, typhoon** → WIND¹

tor·pe·do /tɔrˈpidoʊ/ *n.* (plural **torpedoes**) [C] a weapon that is fired under the surface of the ocean and explodes when it hits something [ORIGIN: 1700—1800 *torpedo* type of fish that can produce electricity to protect itself (16—21 centuries), from Latin, "stiffness, numbness, torpedo fish"] —**torpedo** *v.* [T]

tor·pid /ˈtɔrpɪd/ *adj.* (formal) lazy or sleepy, and with no energy, activity, or excitement: *the torpid warmth of the evening* —**torpidly** *adv.*

torrent

torrential rain

tor·rent /ˈtɔrənt, ˈtɑr-/ *n.* **1 a torrent of sth** a lot of something: *a torrent of criticism* **2** [C] a large amount of water moving very quickly in a particular direction —**torrential** /təˈrɛnʃəl, tɔ-/ *adj.*: *torrential rain*

tor·rid /ˈtɔrɪd, ˈtɑr-/ *adj.* **1** involving strong emotions, especially sexual excitement: *a torrid love affair* **2** extremely hot

tor·so /ˈtɔrsoʊ/ *n.* (plural **torsos**) [C] your body, not including your arms, legs, or head

tort /tɔrt/ *n.* [C] LAW an action that is wrong but not criminal and can be dealt with in a CIVIL court of law

tor·ti·lla /tɔrˈtiyə/ *n.* [C] a thin flat Mexican bread made from CORNMEAL or flour

tor·toise /ˈtɔrt̬əs/ *n.* [C] a slow-moving animal that can put its legs and head inside the shell that covers its body [ORIGIN: 1400—1500 Old French *tortue*, from Vulgar Latin *tartaruca*, from Late Latin *tartaruchus* "of Tartarus, the land of the dead in ancient stories;" because it used to be thought that tortoises and turtles came from hell]

tor·tu·ous /ˈtɔrtʃuəs/ *adj.* **1** complicated, long, and therefore confusing: *a tortuous process* **2** a tortuous road has a lot of turns and is difficult to travel on

tor·ture¹ /ˈtɔrtʃɚ/ *n.* [C,U] **1** the act of torturing someone **2** mental or physical suffering: *The waiting must be torture for you.*

torture² *v.* [T] to deliberately hurt someone in order to force him/her to tell you something, to punish him/her, or to be cruel: *He was **tortured to death** in prison.*

toss /tɔs/ *v.* **1** [T] to throw something without much force: *Could you toss me my keys?* | *He **tossed** the apples **into** a barrel.*

THESAURUS **throw, chuck, fling, lob** → THROW¹

2 [I,T] to move around continuously in a violent or uncontrolled way, or to make something do this: *The kite was being tossed by the wind.* | *I was **tossing and turning*** (=changing my position in bed because I could not sleep) *all night.* **3** [T] *also* **toss out** (informal) to get rid of something: *"Where's the newspaper?" "I tossed it."* **4** [T] to cover food in a liquid by moving it around in the liquid: *Toss the carrots in melted butter.* —**toss** *n.* [C] → **toss/flip a coin** *at* COIN¹

ˈtoss-up *n.* **it's a toss-up** (spoken) said when you do not know which of two things will happen, or which of two things to choose: *So far the election is a toss-up.*

tot /tɑt/ *n.* [C] (informal) a small child

to·tal¹ /ˈtoʊt̬l/ *adj.* **1** complete, or as great as is possible: *Their marriage was a **total disaster**.* | *She has been slowed down by the almost total loss of her sight.* **2 total number/amount/cost etc.** the number, amount, etc. that is the total: *The total cost of the building will be $6 million.*

total² *n.* [C] the number that you get when you have added everything together: *The city spent **a total of** two million dollars on the library.* | *I was out of work for 34 days **in total**.*

total³ *v.* **1** [linking verb] to add up to a particular amount: *Prize money totaling $5,000 will be awarded.* **2** [T] (informal) to damage a car so badly that it cannot be repaired: *Chad totaled his dad's new Toyota.*

to·tal·i·tar·i·an /toʊˌtæləˈtɛriən/ *adj.* POLITICS based on a political system in which people are completely controlled by the government —**totalitarianism** *n.* [U]

to·tal·i·ty /toʊˈtæləṭi/ *n.* [U] (formal) the whole of something

to·tal·ly /ˈtoʊṭl-i/ *adv.* completely: *I totally agree.* | *He's become a **totally different** person.* | *These mistakes are **totally unacceptable**.*

THESAURUS **completely, absolutely, entirely, wholly, utterly** ➔ COMPLETELY

tote /toʊt/ *v.* [T] (informal) to carry something

THESAURUS **carry, lug, cart, haul, schlep** ➔ CARRY

ˈtote bag *n.* [C] a large bag in which you carry things

to·tem pole /ˈtoʊṭəm poʊl/ *n.* [C] a tall wooden pole with images of animals or faces cut into it, made by some Native American tribes

tot·ter /ˈtɑṭɚ/ *v.* [I] to walk or move in an unsteady way

T

touch¹ /tʌtʃ/ *v.* **1** [T] to put your finger, hand, etc. on something or someone: *Don't touch the paint – it's still wet!* | *She reached out to touch his arm.*

THESAURUS

feel – to touch something with your fingers to find out about it: *Feel this teddy bear – it's so soft!*
handle – to touch something or pick it up and hold it in your hands: *Please do not handle the merchandise.*
stroke – to move your hand gently over something: *She stroked the baby's face.*
rub – to move your hand or fingers over a surface while pressing it: *Bill yawned and rubbed his eyes.*
scratch – to rub your nails on part of your skin: *Try not to scratch those mosquito bites.*
pat – to touch someone or something lightly again and again, with your hand flat: *He knelt down to pat the dog.*
pet – to touch and move your hand gently over an animal: *Do you want to pet the cat?*
brush – to touch someone or something lightly as you pass by: *Her hand brushed mine.*
caress – to gently move your hand over a part of someone's body in a loving way: *Miguel gently caressed her hair.*
tickle – to move your fingers lightly over someone's body in order to make him/her laugh: *Minna tickled the baby's feet and he gurgled.*

2 [I,T] if two things are touching, there is no space in between them: *Make sure the wires aren't touching.* **3 not touch sth a)** to not use or handle something: *My brother won't let me touch his bike.* **b)** to not eat or drink something: *She didn't touch her breakfast.* **c)** to refuse to deal with or become involved in a particular situation or problem: *Our lawyer said he wouldn't touch the case.* **4 not touch sb/sth** to not hurt someone or not damage something: *I swear Mom, I didn't touch him!* **5** [T] to affect someone's emotions, especially by making him/her feel pity or sympathy ➔ TOUCHED: *His speech touched everyone present.* **6 touch base** to talk to someone in order to find out how s/he is or what is happening: *I wanted to **touch base with** you before the meeting.*

touch down *phr. v.* if an aircraft touches down, it lands on the ground

touch sth ↔ **off** *phr. v.* to cause a bad situation or violent event to begin: *The report touched off a fierce debate.*

touch on/upon sth *phr. v.* to mention something when you are talking or writing: *Her songs touch on social issues.*

touch sth ↔ **up** *phr. v.* to improve something by making small changes to it: *Norma touched up her makeup for the picture.*

touch² *n.* **1** [C] the action of putting your finger, hand, etc. on someone or something: *Rita felt the **touch of** his hand on her shoulder.* **2 in touch (with sb)** talking or writing to someone: *I've been trying to **get in touch with*** (=phone or talk to) *you all morning.* | *Bye. I'll **be in touch**.* | *We've **stayed/kept in touch*** (=continued to write or call each other, even though we do not see each other often) *since college.* | *I've **lost touch with*** (=stopped writing or talking to) *my high school friends.* **3 in touch/out of touch** having or not having the latest information or knowledge about a subject, situation, or the way people feel: *I think he's **out of touch with** the American people.* **4** [U] the ability to know what something is like when you feel it with your fingers: *Her skin was cool **to the touch**.* **5 a touch of sth** a small amount of something: *a touch of sadness in her voice* | *Make the salad dressing with a touch of lemon juice for extra flavor.* **6** [C] a small detail or change that improves something: *Becky put the **finishing touches** on the cake.* **7** [U] a particular way of doing something skillful: *I must be **losing my touch** – I can't hit anything today.*

ˌtouch-and-ˈgo *adj.* (informal) if a situation is touch-and-go, there is a risk that something bad could happen: *After Dad's operation, it was touch-and-go for a while.*

touch·down /ˈtʌtʃdaʊn/ *n.* [C] **1** the action in football of moving the ball into the opponents' END ZONE in order to gain points **2** the moment that a space vehicle lands on the ground

touched /tʌtʃt/ *adj.* feeling happy and grateful because of what someone has done for you: *We **were touched by** their concern.*

touch·ing /ˈtʌtʃɪŋ/ *adj.* making you feel sympathy or sadness: *Fox gave a touching tribute to his late father.*

THESAURUS emotional, moving, poignant → EMOTIONAL

touch·stone /ˈtʌtʃstoʊn/ *n.* [C] a standard used for measuring the quality of something

touch·y /ˈtʌtʃi/ *adj.* **1** easily offended or annoyed → SENSITIVE: *She is very **touchy about** her past.* → GRUMPY **2 touchy subject/question etc.** a subject, etc. that needs to be dealt with very carefully because it may offend or upset people

tough¹ /tʌf/ *adj.* **1** difficult and needing a lot of effort: *Working as a fireman is tough.* | *a tough question* | *a tough choice/decision*

THESAURUS difficult, hard, challenging, demanding, arduous → DIFFICULT

2 a tough person is very strong or determined: *a tough businesswoman* **3** very strict: *tough anti-smoking laws*

THESAURUS strict, firm, stringent, draconian → STRICT

4 tough material is not easily broken or damaged: *tough durable plastic* **5** tough meat is difficult to cut or eat (ANT) **tender**: *a tough steak* **6 tough!/tough luck!** (spoken) said when you do not have any sympathy for someone else's problems: *"I'm freezing!" "Tough! You should have worn your coat."* **7** a tough place, area, etc. is likely to have a lot of violence and crime: *He grew up in a tough neighborhood.* —**toughness** *n.* [U]

tough² *v.*

tough sth **out** *phr. v.* to deal with a very difficult situation by being determined to continue: *He could've gone home, but he stayed and **toughed it out**.*

tough·en /ˈtʌfən/ *also* **toughen up** *v.* [I,T] to become tougher, or to make someone or something do this: *Hard work has toughened her up.*

tou·pee /tuˈpeɪ/ *n.* [C] a piece of artificial hair that a man can wear when he has no hair on part of his head

tour¹ /tʊr/ *n.* [C] **1** a trip to several different places in a country, area, etc.: *a 7-day **tour of** Egypt*

THESAURUS travel, trip, excursion → TRAVEL²

2 a short trip through a place to see it: *We **went on a tour through/of** the Smithsonian.* | *Sue once worked as a **tour guide** in Boston.* **3** a planned trip by a group of musicians, a sports team, etc. in order to play in several places: *The band goes **on tour** later this year.*

tour² *v.* [I,T] to visit a place on a tour: *We're going to tour New England this summer.*

tour·ism /ˈtʊrɪzəm/ *n.* [U] the business of providing tourists with places to stay and things to do: *The island depends on tourism for most of its income.*

tour·ist /ˈtʊrɪst/ *n.* [C] someone who visits a place for pleasure: *San Francisco is always full of tourists in the summer.* | *The Statue of Liberty is a major **tourist attraction**.*

tour·na·ment /ˈtʊrnəmənt, ˈtɚ-/ *n.* [C] a competition in which many players or teams compete against each other until there is one winner

THESAURUS competition, championship, contest, playoff → COMPETITION

tour·ni·quet /ˈtʊrnɪkɪt, ˈtɚ-/ *n.* [C] a band of cloth that is twisted tightly around an injured arm or leg to make blood stop coming out

tou·sle /ˈtaʊzəl, -səl/ *v.* [T] to make someone's hair look messy —**tousled** *adj.*

tout /taʊt/ *v.* [T] to praise someone or something in order to persuade people that he, she, or it is important or worth a lot: *Paul's band is being **touted as** the next big thing.*

tow¹ /toʊ/ *v.* [T] if one vehicle tows another one, it pulls the other vehicle along behind it: *Our car had to **be towed away**.*

THESAURUS pull, tug, drag → PULL¹

→ *see picture at* PULL¹

tow² *n.* **1** [C, usually singular] an act of towing a vehicle or ship **2 in tow** following closely behind someone or something: *Mattie arrived with all her children in tow.*

to·ward /tɔrd, təˈwɔrd/ *also* **towards** *prep.* **1** in a particular direction: *All the windows face toward the river.* | *I saw a man coming toward me.* ▸Don't say "I saw a man coming to me."◂ **2** concerning someone or something: *How do you feel toward her?* | *Different cultures have different attitudes towards divorce.* **3** in a process that will produce a particular result: *We should always be working toward peace.* **4** money put, saved, or given toward something is used to pay for it: *So far I've saved $4,000 toward a new car.* **5** just before a particular time: *I felt tired toward the end of the day.* **6** near a particular place: *We're building a pipeline down toward Abilene.*

tow·el¹ /ˈtaʊəl/ *n.* [C] a piece of cloth used for drying something: *a bath towel* (=for drying yourself) | *a dish towel* [ORIGIN: 1200—1300 Old French *toaille*]

towel² *also* **towel off/down** *v.* [I,T] to dry your body using a towel

tow·er¹ /ˈtaʊɚ/ *n.* [C] **1** a tall narrow building or part of a building: *the Eiffel Tower* | *a church tower* **2** a tall structure used for signaling or broadcasting: *a radio/television tower*

tower² *v.* [I] to be much taller than the people or things around you: *Lewis **towered over** his opponent.* —**towering** *adj.*

town /taʊn/ *n.* **1** [C] a place with houses, stores, offices, etc. where people live and work, that is smaller than a city: *a little town on the coast* **2** [U]

T

the town or city where you live: *How long have you been **in town**?* | *She's **from out of town*** (=lives in a different town). | *I'll be **out of town** this weekend.* **3** [U] the business or shopping center of a town: *"Where's Dad?" "He's gone **into town**."* **4** [singular] all the people who live in a particular town: *The whole town got involved in the celebrations.* **5 (out) on the town** (informal) going to restaurants, theaters, etc. for entertainment in the evening: *Everyone went out for **a night on the town**.* **6 go to town (on sth)** (informal) to do something eagerly and with a lot of energy: *The school really went to town on their production of "The Wizard of Oz."* (=they did the play well and worked hard on it). [ORIGIN: Old English *tun* "yard, buildings inside a wall, village, town"]

ˌtown ˈhall *n.* [C] a public building used for a town's local government

town·house /ˈtaʊnhaʊs/ *n.* [C] a house in a group of houses that share one or more walls → HOUSE¹

town·ship /ˈtaʊnʃɪp/ *n.* [C] an area where people live and work that is organized under a local government

towns·peo·ple /ˈtaʊnzˌpipəl/ *also* **towns·folk** /ˈtaʊnzfoʊk/ *n.* [plural] all the people who live in a particular town

ˈtow truck *n.* [C] a strong vehicle that can pull cars behind it

T

tox·ic /ˈtɑksɪk/ *adj.* poisonous: *toxic chemicals* [ORIGIN: 1600—1700 Late Latin *toxicus*, from Latin *toxicum* "poison"] —**toxicity** /tɑkˈsɪsəti/ *n.* [U] → HARMFUL

tox·i·col·o·gy /ˌtɑksɪˈkɑlədʒi/ *n.* [U] BIOLOGY the medical study of poisons and their effects

ˌtoxic ˈwaste *n.* [C,U] waste products from industry that are harmful to people, animals, or the environment

tox·in /ˈtɑksɪn/ *n.* [C] BIOLOGY a poisonous substance, especially one made by BACTERIA

toy¹ /tɔɪ/ *n.* [C] an object for children to play with: *Her husband brought home some new toys for the baby.* | *a toy car* | *The children were **playing with** their new **toys**.*

toy² *v.*

toy with *phr. v.* **1 toy with** sth to think about an idea, plan, etc. for a short time and not very seriously: *She **toyed with the idea of** becoming an actress.* **2 toy with** sb/sth to lie to someone or trick him/her, for example saying that you love him/her when you do not

trace¹ /treɪs/ (Ac) *v.* [T] **1** to study or describe the history, development, or origin of something: *He **traced** his family history **(back) to** the 17th century.* **2** to copy a picture by putting a thin piece of paper over it and drawing the lines that you can see through the paper → DRAW¹ **3** to find someone or something that has disappeared: *Police are still trying to trace the missing child.*

THESAURUS **find, locate, track sb/sth down** → FIND¹

4 to find out where a telephone call is coming from, using electronic equipment: *Police were able to **trace the call** to an apartment in Brooklyn.* —**traceable** *adj.*: *Drug smugglers do not want the money to be traceable.*

trace² *n.* **1** [C,U] a sign that someone or something has been in a place: *We found **no trace of** them on the island.* | *He disappeared **without a trace*** (=completely). **2** [C] a very small amount of a substance, quality, emotion, etc. that is difficult to notice: *There was a **trace of** poison in the glass.* | *a trace of sorrow in his voice*

ˈtrace ˌelement *n.* [C] CHEMISTRY **1** a chemical ELEMENT that your body needs a very small amount of to live **2** a chemical ELEMENT that only exists in small amounts on Earth

tra·che·a /ˈtreɪkiə/ *n.* (plural **tracheas** *or* **tracheae** /-ki-i/) [C] BIOLOGY the tube down which air goes from the throat to the lungs (SYN) **windpipe** → *see picture at* LUNG

track¹ /træk/ *n.*

1 keep/lose track of sb/sth to pay attention to someone or something so that you know what is happening, or to fail to do this: *She lost track of all the money she spent.*

2 be on the right/wrong track to think in a way that is likely to lead to a correct or incorrect result: *Keep going, you're on the right track.*

3 FOR RACING [C] a course with a special surface on which people, cars, horses, etc. race

4 SPORT [U] the sport of running on a track: *He **ran track** in high school.* → *see picture on page A17*

5 be on/off track to be in a state or situation that will lead to success or failure: *I feel that my career is back on track now.*

6 RAILROAD [C] the two metal lines that a train travels on: *railroad tracks* → TRAIN¹

7 tracks [plural] marks on the ground made by a moving animal, person, or vehicle: *We saw bear tracks in the mud.*

8 SONG [C] one of the songs or pieces of music on a record: *the best track on the album*

9 make tracks (informal) to leave somewhere quickly, or hurry when going somewhere → **fast track** *at* FAST¹, **off the beaten track/path** *at* BEATEN, ONE-TRACK MIND

track² *v.* [T] **1** to search for a person or animal by following a smell or tracks on the ground: *We tracked the moose for hours.*

THESAURUS **follow, tail, stalk** → FOLLOW

2 to follow the movements of an aircraft or ship by using RADAR **3** to leave mud or dirt behind you when you walk: *Who tracked mud all over the floor?*

track sb/sth ↔ **down** *phr. v.* to find someone or something after searching in different places: *We finally were able to track down her parents.*

ˌtrack and ˈfield *n.* [U] the sports that involve running races, jumping, and throwing things → *see picture on page A17*

ˈtrack meet *n.* [C] a sports competition with a variety of running, jumping, and throwing events

ˈtrack ˌrecord *n.* [singular] all the things that a person or organization has done in the past that show how well she, he, or it is likely to do similar things in the future: *The company has* ***a track record of*** *promoting women to high positions.*

tract /trækt/ *n.* [C] **1 the digestive/respiratory/urinary etc. tract** BIOLOGY a system of connected organs in your body that have one purpose **2** a large area of land: *a tract of forest*

trac·ta·ble /ˈtræktəbəl/ *adj.* (formal) easy to control or deal with ANT **intractable**: *She's not a tractable child.* **—tractability** /ˌtræktəˈbɪləṭi/ *n.* [U]

trac·tion /ˈtrækʃən/ *n.* [U] **1** the force that prevents something such as a wheel from sliding on a surface: *The car lost traction and ran off the road.* **2** the process of treating a broken bone with special medical equipment that pulls it

trac·tor /ˈtræktɚ/ *n.* [C] a strong vehicle with large wheels, used for pulling farm equipment

trade¹ /treɪd/ *n.* **1** [U] the business of buying and selling things, especially between countries: *foreign trade* | ***the trade in*** *oil*

THESAURUS **business, commerce, industry, private enterprise** → BUSINESS

2 the banking/retail/tourist etc. trade the business that comes from or is done by banks, etc. **3** [C] an exchange: *Let's* ***make a trade*** *– my frisbee for your baseball.* **4** [C,U] a particular job, especially one in which you work with your hands: *Jerry's a plumber* ***by trade***.

trade² *v.* **1** [I,T] to buy and sell goods and services: *Penalties were imposed on U.S. companies that* ***traded with*** *Cuba.* **2** [I,T] to exchange one thing for another: *I'll* ***trade*** *my apple* ***for*** *your candy bar.*

THESAURUS **exchange, swap** → EXCHANGE²

3 if two or more people trade insults or blows, they insult or hit each other

trade sth ↔ **in** *phr. v.* to give something old that you own, such as a car, as part of the payment for something new: *I* ***traded*** *my Chevy* ***in for*** *a Honda.*

trade on sth *phr. v.* to use a situation or someone's kindness in order to gain an advantage for yourself: *She's trading on her father's fame to try to make it in the music business.*

trade up *phr. v.* to sell something such as a car or house so that you can buy a better car or house

ˈtrade assoˌciation *also* **ˈindustry assoˌciation** *n.* [C] ECONOMICS a NONPROFIT organization that supports and protects the rights of a particular industry, for example by trying to persuade the government to make changes to certain laws, so that the industry will develop and be successful

ˈtrade ˌbarrier *n.* [C] ECONOMICS something such as a tax or a law that prevents foreign goods or services from entering a country easily

ˈtrade-in *n.* [C] a car, piece of equipment, etc. that you give as part of the payment for the newer one that you are buying

trade·mark /ˈtreɪdmɑrk/ *n.* [C] a special word or picture on a product that shows it is made by a particular company, that cannot be used by any other company

ˈtrade-off *n.* [C] ECONOMICS the act of accepting something that you do not like or giving up an advantage that you have because it allows you to have or achieve something that you want: *Inflation is often a trade-off for healthy economic growth.*

trad·er /ˈtreɪdɚ/ *n.* [C] **1** ECONOMICS someone who buys and sells goods **2** ECONOMICS someone who buys and sells STOCKS, BONDS, or CURRENCY, etc. on a financial market

ˈtrade route *n.* [C] ECONOMICS a way across land or the ocean used by traders' vehicles, especially ships, in the past

ˈtrade ˌschool *n.* [C] a school where people go in order to learn a particular TRADE¹

ˌtrade ˈsecret *n.* [C] a piece of secret information about a particular business, that is only known by the people who work there

ˈtrade war *n.* [C] ECONOMICS a situation in which companies or countries compete against each other very strongly, and which usually involves governments putting higher taxes on particular goods brought in from another country

tra·di·tion /trəˈdɪʃən/ Ac *n.* **1** [C,U] something that people have done for a long time, and continue to do: *an old family/Jewish/American etc. tradition* | *This country has a* ***long tradition*** *of welcoming immigrants.* | *It's* ***a tradition that*** *the groom should not see the bride before the wedding.*

THESAURUS **habit, custom, convention** → HABIT

2 (be) in the tradition of sth to have many of the same features as something made or done in the past: *He is an entertainer in the great tradition of vaudeville.* [ORIGIN: 1300—1400 Old French, Latin *traditio* "act of handing over"]

tra·di·tion·al /trəˈdɪʃənl/ Ac *adj.* **1** relating to the traditions of a country or group of people: *a traditional Irish folk song* | *traditional Mexican food* | ***It is traditional to*** *exchange gifts at Christmas.* **2** following ideas, methods, etc. that have existed for a long time rather than doing something new or different: *A woman's* ***traditional role*** *is as a mother.* **—traditionally** *adv.*: *Traditionally, blacks have voted for Democratic candidates.*

traˌditional eˈconomy *n.* [C] ECONOMICS an economic system that uses only ideas and methods that have existed for a long time, rather than using new or different ideas or methods (SYN) **subsistence economy**

tra·di·tion·al·ist /trəˈdɪʃənl-ɪst/ (Ac) *n.* [C] someone who likes traditional ideas and does not like change

traf·fic /ˈtræfɪk/ *n.* [U] **1** the vehicles moving along a particular road: *We left early to avoid the traffic.* | ***heavy/light traffic*** (=a small or large amount of traffic) **2** the movement of aircraft, ships, or trains from one place to another: *air traffic control*

ˈtraffic ˌjam *n.* [C] a long line of vehicles on the road that cannot move, or that move very slowly: *We were **stuck in a traffic jam** for two hours!*

traf·fick·ing /ˈtræfɪkɪŋ/ *n.* **drug/arms trafficking** the activity of buying and selling illegal drugs or weapons —**trafficker** *n.* [C] —**traffic** *v.* [I,T]

ˈtraffic light *also* **ˈtraffic ˌsignal** *n.* [C] a set of red, green, and yellow lights used for controlling traffic (SYN) **light**

trag·e·dy /ˈtrædʒədi/ *n.* (plural **tragedies**) [C,U] **1** a very sad and shocking event: *the **tragedy** of a child's death* **2** ENG. LANG. ARTS a serious play that ends sadly, or this style of writing: *Shakespeare's tragedies* [ORIGIN: 1300—1400 Old French *tragédie*, from Latin, from Greek *tragoidia*]

T

tra·gic /ˈtrædʒɪk/ *adj.* very sad and shocking: *We heard the news of Holly's **tragic death** in a plane crash.* —**tragically** *adv.*

trail¹ /treɪl/ *v.* **1** [I,T] *also* **trail behind** to be losing a game, competition, or election: *The Cowboys are trailing 21–14.* **2** [I,T] to pull something behind you, especially along the ground, or to be pulled in this way: *The wedding dress trailed on the ground behind her.* **3** [I] to follow someone: *The two mothers walked along with their kids **trailing behind** them.* **4** [T] to follow someone by looking for signs that s/he has gone in a particular direction

trail off *phr. v.* if your voice trails off, it becomes quieter and quieter until it cannot be heard: *Her words trailed off as Mrs. Hellman walked into the room.*

trail² *n.* **1** [C] a path across open country or through a forest: *a hiking trail in the mountains* **2 a trail of blood/clues/destruction etc.** a series of marks or signs left behind by someone or something that is moving **3 be on the trail of sb/sth** to be looking for a person or information that is difficult to find: *He is always on the trail of a big story.*

trail·blaz·er /ˈtreɪlˌbleɪzɚ/ *n.* [C] (informal) someone who is the first to discover or develop new methods of doing something: *She is a trailblazer in the field of medical research.*

trail·er /ˈtreɪlɚ/ *n.* [C] **1** a vehicle that can be pulled behind a car, used for living in during a vacation **2** a vehicle that can be pulled behind another vehicle, used for carrying something heavy **3** a short advertisement for a movie or television program

ˈtrailer park *n.* [C] an area where trailers are parked and used as people's homes

train¹ /treɪn/ *n.* [C] **1** a long vehicle which travels along a railroad carrying people or goods. It consists of a line of carriages pulled by an engine: ***the train to** Detroit* | *It'll take about 4 hours **by train**.* | *I **take the train** to work.* | *Hurry up or we'll **miss our train**.* → *see picture at* TRANSPORTATION

TOPIC

You decide which train you are going to **get/catch**. You buy your ticket at the **ticket office**. You look at the **departure board** to check which **platform/track** your train **leaves from**. Sometimes the train is **on time** but sometimes it is **running late** or **delayed**. When your train **arrives**, you **get on** and find a **seat** in one of the **cars** (=one of the connected parts of a train). You can usually get a drink or small meal in the **dining car**.

2 train of thought a related series of thoughts that are developing in your mind: *Sorry, I've **lost my train of thought**.* **3** a long line of moving animals, vehicles, or people: *a camel train* **4** a part of a dress that spreads out over the ground behind the person wearing it

train² *v.* **1** [I,T] to teach someone or be taught the skills of a particular job or activity: *Sally spent two years **training as** a nurse.* | *He's **training to** be a pilot.* **2** [T] to teach an animal to do something or to behave correctly: *I've **trained** the dog **to** sit.* **3** [I,T] to prepare for a sports event by exercising and practicing, or to make someone do this: *He is **training for** the Olympics.* → PRACTICE² —**trained** *adj.*

train·ee /treɪˈni/ *n.* [C] someone who is being trained for a job: *a sales trainee*

train·er /ˈtreɪnɚ/ *n.* [C] someone whose job is to train people or animals to do something

train·ing /ˈtreɪnɪŋ/ *n.* **1** [singular, U] the process of teaching or being taught skills for a particular job: *Myers has no formal **training in** music.* **2** [U] special physical exercises that you do to stay healthy or prepare for a competition: *weight training* | *She's **in training** for the Boston Marathon.*

trait /treɪt/ *n.* [C] a particular quality in someone's character (SYN) **characteristic**: *His jealousy is one of his worst traits.*

THESAURUS **characteristic, quality** → CHARACTERISTIC¹

trai·tor /ˈtreɪtɚ/ *n.* [C] someone who is not loyal to his/her country, friends, etc.: *He had been a **traitor to** his country.*

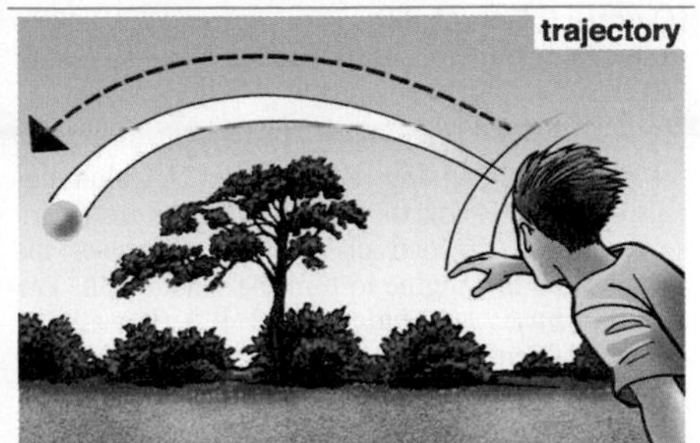

tra·jec·to·ry /trə'dʒɛktəri/ *n.* (plural **trajectories**) [C] PHYSICS the curved path of an object that is fired or thrown through the air

tram /træm/ *n.* [C] a STREETCAR

tramp[1] /træmp/ *n.* [C] (old-fashioned) someone who has no home or job and moves from place to place, often asking for food or money

tramp[2] *v.* [I,T] to walk somewhere with heavy steps: *Kids were* ***tramping through*** *the snow on their way to school.*

tram·ple /'træmpəl/ *v.* [I,T] **1** to step on something heavily so that you crush it with your feet: *One woman was* ***trampled to death*** *by the crowd.* **2** to ignore or not care about someone's rights or feelings: *The new rule* ***tramples on*** *people's right to free speech.*

tram·po·line /ˌtræmpə'lin, 'træmpəˌlin/ *n.* [C] a piece of sports equipment that you jump up and down on, made of a sheet of material tightly stretched across a large frame

trance /træns/ *n.* [C] a state in which you seem to be asleep but you are still able to hear and understand what is said to you: *He seemed to be* ***in a trance***. [ORIGIN: 1300—1400 Old French *transe*, from *transir* "to pass away, become unconscious," from Latin *transire*]

tran·quil /'træŋkwəl/ *adj.* pleasantly calm, quiet, and peaceful: *a tranquil spot for a picnic* —**tranquility** /træŋ'kwɪləṭi/ *n.* [U]

THESAURUS quiet, calm, peaceful → QUIET[1]

tran·qui·liz·er /'træŋkwəˌlaɪzɚ/ *n.* [C] a drug used in order to make a person or animal calm or unconscious —**tranquilize** *v.* [T]

trans·act /træn'zækt/ *v.* [I,T] (formal) to do business

trans·ac·tion /træn'zækʃən/ *n.* [C] (formal) a business deal: *the company's* ***financial transactions***

trans·at·lan·tic /ˌtrænzət'læntɪk/ *adj.* crossing the Atlantic Ocean, or involving people on both sides of the Atlantic: *a transatlantic flight* | *a transatlantic business deal*

tran·scend /træn'sɛnd/ *v.* [T] (formal) to go above or beyond the usual limits of something: *The appeal of baseball transcends age and class.* —**transcendence** *n.* [U]

tran·scen·den·tal /ˌtrænsɛn'dɛnṭl/ *adj.* existing above or beyond human knowledge or understanding

tran·scen·den·tal·ism /ˌtrænsɛn'dɛnṭlˌɪzəm/ *n.* [U] **1** SOCIAL SCIENCE the belief, held especially by Kant, that knowledge can be obtained by studying thought and not only by practical experience **2** SOCIAL SCIENCE a 19th-century set of beliefs, held especially by Emerson, that emphasized a person's natural ability to know the SPIRITUAL nature of things —**transcendentalist** *n.* [C]

trans·con·ti·nen·tal /ˌtrænskɑntən'ɛntl, ˌtrænz-/ *adj.* crossing a CONTINENT: *the first transcontinental railroad*

tran·scribe /træn'skraɪb/ *v.* [T] to write down the words that someone has said, or the notes of a piece of music —**transcription** /træn'skrɪpʃən/ *n.* [C,U]

tran·script /'trænˌskrɪpt/ *n.* [C] **1** an exact written or printed copy of something that was said: *a* ***transcript of*** *the witness's testimony* **2** an official college document that has a list of the classes you took as a student and the grades you received

trans·fer[1] /'trænsfɚ, træns'fɚ/ (Ac) *v.* (**transferred**, **transferring**) **1** [I,T] to move from one place, job, etc. to another, or to make someone or something do this: *After his first year at Valley College he* ***transferred to*** *UCLA.* | *They're* ***transferring*** *him* ***from*** *accounts* ***to*** *the shipping department.* **2** [T] to move money from one account or institution to another: *I'd like to* ***transfer*** *$500* ***to*** *my checking account.* **3** [T] LAW to officially give property or money to someone else [ORIGIN: 1300—1400 Latin *transferre*, from *trans* "across" + *ferre* "to carry"] —**transferable** /træns'fɚəbəl/ *adj.*: *Organization and dealing well with people are skills that are transferable to any job.*

T

trans·fer[2] /'trænsfɚ/ (Ac) *n.* **1** [C,U] the process of transferring someone or something: *Your bank will organize the* ***transfer of*** *funds.* | *a job transfer* **2** [C] a ticket that allows a passenger to change from one bus, train, etc. to another without paying more money: *You should ask the bus driver for a transfer.*

ˌ**transfer RN'A** (*abbreviation* **tRNA**) *n.* [U] BIOLOGY MOLECULES of RNA that carry AMINO ACIDS to RIBOSOMES (=a small part of every living cell)

trans·fixed /træns'fɪkst/ *adj.* unable to move because you are shocked, frightened, etc.: *We were transfixed by the pictures of the storm on TV.*

trans·form /træns'fɔrm/ (Ac) *v.* [T] to change the appearance, character, etc. of someone or something completely, especially in a good way: *Will the attempt to* ***transform*** *the country* ***into*** *a democracy succeed?* —**transformation** /ˌtrænsfɚ'meɪʃən/ *n.* [C,U]: *the complete transformation of the city*

THESAURUS change, alter, reform, revolutionize → CHANGE[1]

trans·form·er /træns'fɔrmɚ/ *n.* [C] PHYSICS a piece of equipment for changing electricity from one VOLTAGE to another

trans·fu·sion /træns'fyuʒən/ *n.* [C,U] the process of putting one person's blood into the body of someone else as a medical treatment

trans·gress /trænz'grɛs/ *v.* [I,T] (formal) to do something that is against the rules of a religion or society [ORIGIN: 1400—1500 French *transgresser*, from Latin, past participle of *transgredi* "to step beyond," from *trans* "across" + *gredi* "to step"] —**transgression** /trænz'grɛʃən/ *n.* [C,U]

tran·sient[1] /'trænʒənt/ *adj.* (formal) **1** continuing only for a short time: *His success was transient.* **2** working or staying somewhere for only a short time: *transient workers*

transient[2] *n.* [C] someone who has no home and moves from place to place

tran·sis·tor /træn'zɪstɚ/ *n.* [C] PHYSICS a piece of electronic equipment that controls the flow of electricity in radios, televisions, etc.

tran·sit /'trænzɪt/ (Ac) *n.* [U] **1** the process of moving people, products, etc. from one place to another: *The shipment must have been lost* ***in transit***. **2** the system of moving people or things from one place to another: *Is it easy to get there using* ***public transit***? (=buses, trains, etc.) [ORIGIN: 1400—1500 Latin *transitus*, from *transire* "to go across," from *trans* "across" + *ire* "to go"]

tran·si·tion /træn'zɪʃən/ (Ac) *n.* [C,U] (formal) the process of changing from one form or condition to another: *The* ***transition from*** *full-time work* ***to*** *retirement can be difficult.*

tran·si·tion·al /træn'zɪʃənl/ (Ac) *adj.* relating to a period of change from one form or condition to another: *transitional housing | a transitional period between jobs*

tran·si·tive verb /ˌtrænzət̬ɪv 'vɚb/ *n.* [C] ENG. LANG. ARTS a transitive verb has an object. In the sentence "She makes her own clothes," "makes" is a transitive verb. → INTRANSITIVE VERB

tran·si·to·ry /'trænzəˌtɔri/ (Ac) *adj.* TRANSIENT

trans·late /'trænzleɪt, ˌtrænz'leɪt/ *v.* **1** [I,T] to change speech or writing from one language to another → INTERPRET: *He* ***translated*** *the book* ***into*** *German.* **2 translate into sth** if one thing translates into another, the second thing happens as a result of the first: *Will more investment translate into more jobs?* —**translation** /trænz'leɪʃən/ *n.* [C,U]

trans·la·tor /'trænzˌleɪt̬ɚ/ *n.* [C] someone who changes writing or speech into a different language → INTERPRETER

trans·lu·cent /trænz'lusənt/ *adj.* not transparent, but clear enough for some light to pass through [ORIGIN: 1400—1500 Latin, present participle of *translucere* "to shine through," from *lucere* "to shine"] —**translucence** *n.* [U]

trans·mis·sion /trænz'mɪʃən/ (Ac) *n.* **1** [C,U] the process of sending out radio or television signals or programs, or the signals or programs themselves **2** [C] the part of a vehicle that uses the power from the engine to turn the wheels: *The car has* ***automatic transmission***. **3** [U] (formal) the process of sending or passing something from one place, person, etc. to another: *the* ***transmission of*** *disease* **4** [U] (formal) the process of passing information, ideas, CUSTOMS, etc. between people: *the transmission of values from parent to child*

trans·mit /trænz'mɪt/ (Ac) *v.* (**transmitted, transmitting**) **1** [I,T] to send out electric signals for radio or television (SYN) **broadcast** **2** [T] to send or pass something from one place, person, etc. to another: *The virus is transmitted through the blood.* **3** [T] (formal) to pass knowledge, ideas, CUSTOMS, etc. from one person or group to another: *Schools transmit both knowledge and culture to students.* [ORIGIN: 1300—1400 Latin *transmittere*, from *trans* "across" + *mittere* "to send"]

trans·mit·ter /trænz'mɪt̬ɚ, 'trænzˌmɪt̬ɚ/ *n.* [C] equipment that sends out radio or television signals

trans·mute /trænz'myut/ *v.* [I,T] (formal) to change from one substance or type of thing into another, or to make someone or something do this: *The article shows how traditional African music was transmuted into modern forms such as jazz or gospel.* —**transmutable** *adj.* —**transmutation** /ˌtrænzmyu'teɪʃən/ *n.* [C,U]

trans·par·ent /træns'pærənt, -'pɛr-/ *adj.* **1** if something is transparent, you can see through it: *transparent glass* **2** easy to notice and not deceiving anyone (SYN) **obvious**: *The ad was a transparent attempt to fool the voters.* [ORIGIN: 1400—1500 Medieval Latin, present participle of *transparere* "to show through," from Latin *trans* "through" + *parere* "to show"] —**transparency** *n.* [U] —**transparently** *adv.*

tran·spi·ra·tion /ˌtrænspə'reɪʃən/ *n.* [U] BIOLOGY the process that happens when a plant loses water through its leaves

tran·spire /træn'spaɪɚ/ *v.* [I] (formal) to happen: *Nobody knows what transpired that day.*

trans·plant[1] /træns'plænt/ *v.* [T] **1** to move an organ, piece of skin, etc. from one person's body to another **2** to move a plant from one place and put it in another [ORIGIN: 1400—1500 Late Latin *transplantare*, from Latin *trans* "across" + *plantare* "to plant"]

trans·plant[2] /'trænsplænt/ *n.* [C,U] a medical operation in which an organ from someone's body is put into another person, or the organ itself: *a heart transplant*

trans·port /træns'pɔrt/ (Ac) *v.* [T] to move or carry goods, people, etc. from one place to another in a vehicle: *Helicopters will transport the equipment.* [ORIGIN: 1300—1400 Old French *transporter*, from Latin, from *trans* "across" + *portare* "to carry"]

THESAURUS carry, cart, haul → CARRY

trans·por·ta·tion /ˌtrænspɚˈteɪʃən/ (Ac) *n.* [U] **1** a system or method for carrying passengers or goods from one place to another: *Buses are the main form of* ***public transportation***. **2** the process or business of taking goods from one place to another: *the* ***transportation of*** *goods*

trans·pose /trænsˈpouz/ *v.* [T] (formal) to change the order or position of two or more words, letters, etc.

trans·sex·u·al /trænzˈsɛkʃuəl/ *n.* [C] someone who has had a medical operation to become a person of the opposite sex

trans·verse /ˌtrænzˈvɚs◂ / *adj.* lying or placed across something

trans·ves·tite /trænzˈvɛstaɪt/ *n.* [C] someone, especially a man, who enjoys dressing like a person of the opposite sex

trap¹ /træp/ *n.* [C] **1** a piece of equipment for catching animals: *a mouse trap* **2** a bad situation from which it is difficult to escape: *the deadly trap of drug addiction* **3** a trick that is intended to catch someone or make him/her say or do something that s/he did not intend to

trap² *v.* (**trapped**, **trapping**) [T] **1** to prevent someone from escaping from somewhere, especially a dangerous place: *Up to 25 people may be trapped in the burning building.* **2** to trick someone so that s/he says or does something that s/he did not intend to: *The police* ***trapped*** *him* ***into*** *confessing.* **3 be/feel trapped** to be in a bad situation from which it is difficult to escape: *She was trapped in an unhappy marriage.* **4** to catch an animal in a trap

THESAURUS catch, capture, corner → CATCH¹

5 to prevent something such as water, dirt, heat, etc. from escaping or spreading: *The filter traps dust.*

ˈtrap door *n.* [C] a small door that covers an opening in a floor or roof

tra·peze /træˈpiz/ *n.* [C] a short BAR hanging

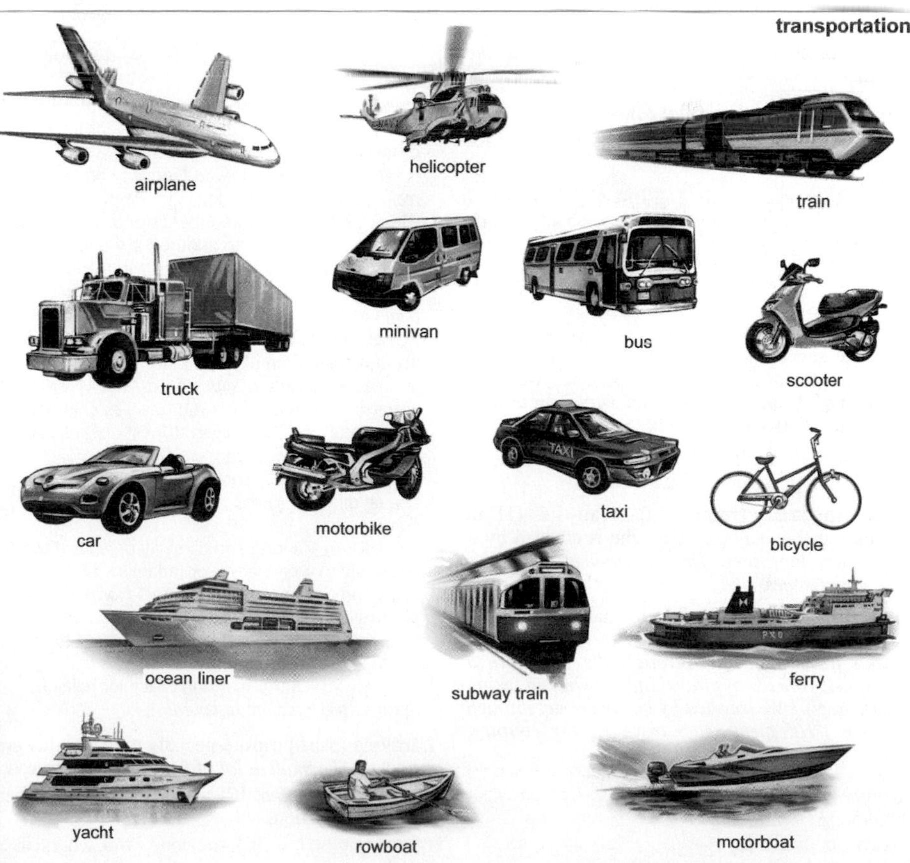

from two ropes high above the ground, used by ACROBATS

tra·pe·zi·um /trə'piziəm/ *n.* (plural **trapezia** /-ziə/ *or* **trapeziums**) [C] MATH a shape with four sides, none of which is parallel with any other side

trap·e·zoid /'træpəzɔɪd/ *n.* [C] MATH a shape with four sides, only two of which are parallel → *see picture at* POLYGON

trap·per /'træpɚ/ *n.* [C] someone who traps wild animals for their fur

trap·pings /'træpɪŋz/ *n.* [plural] all the clothes, possessions, etc. that show how rich, famous, or powerful someone is: *He has all the* ***trappings of*** *stardom.*

trash¹ /træʃ/ *n.* [U] **1** things that you throw away, such as old food, dirty paper, etc. SYN **garbage**: *Just put it* ***in the trash.*** | *Will someone please* ***take out the trash*** (=take it outside the house)*?*

THESAURUS **garbage, refuse, litter, waste**
→ GARBAGE

2 (informal) something that is of very poor quality: *There's so much trash on TV these days.*

trash² *v.* [T] (informal) **1** to destroy something completely: *You can't have parties if your friends are going to trash the place.* **2** to criticize someone or something severely: *Critics have trashed the movie.*

T

'trash can *n.* [C] a GARBAGE CAN

'trash com,pactor *n.* [C] a machine used for pressing trash into a small mass

'trash talk *also* **'trash ,talking** *n.* [U] the act of saying rude or insulting things to or about a sports player during a game or competition

trash·y /'træʃi/ *adj.* of extremely bad quality: *trashy novels*

trau·ma /'trɔmə, 'traʊmə/ *n.* [C,U] a state of extreme shock that is caused by a very bad or frightening experience, or the experience itself: *the* ***trauma of*** *divorce* | *soldiers suffering from trauma* [ORIGIN: 1600—1700 Greek "wound"]

trau·mat·ic /trə'mæṭɪk, trɔ-/ *adj.* very shocking and upsetting: *a traumatic experience*

trau·ma·tize /'trɔmə,taɪz, 'traʊ-/ *v.* [T] to shock someone so badly that s/he is affected by it for a very long time: *He was traumatized by his war experiences.*

trav·el¹ /'trævəl/ *v.* **1** [I,T] to make a trip from one place to another, especially to distant places: *Rick's* ***traveling across/through*** *the U.S. with a backpack.* | *We always* ***travel light*** (=without taking many bags). | *We* ***traveled by bus/train etc.*** *through France.* | *He spent years* ***traveling the country/world.***

THESAURUS

Ways of traveling
drive or **go by car**
fly or **go by plane**
sail or **go by boat/ship**
take a train/bus/taxi/cab or **go by train/bus etc.**
walk/hike or **go on foot**
bike or **go by bike**

Someone who travels
traveler – any person who is traveling
passenger – someone who is traveling in a car, bus, train, airplane, etc.
tourist – someone who is traveling somewhere for a vacation
explorer – someone who travels to places that people have not visited before
commuter – someone who travels a long distance to work every day → AIRPORT, JOURNEY, PASSPORT

2 [I] to move from one place or person to another: *News travels fast in a small town.* **3** [I,T] to go a particular distance or at a particular speed: *We traveled over 400 miles the first day of our trip.* | *The bus was* ***traveling at*** *a high speed.*

travel² *n.* **1** [U] the act or activity of traveling: *Heavy rain is making road travel difficult.*

USAGE

You can **take**, **make**, or **go on** a **trip**, **journey**, or **voyage**, but you cannot use these verbs with **travel**.

THESAURUS

travel/traveling – the general activity of going from one place to another, especially for long distances and long periods of time: *a special ticket for train travel around Europe* | *I haven't really done much traveling.*
trip – the time spent and the distance traveled in going from one place to another: *a trip to the grocery store* | *They're planning a trip to Hawaii.*
journey (formal) – a trip that is long or difficult: *the journey across the plains in a covered wagon*
travels – trips to places that are far away, or the act of moving from place to place over a period of time: *her travels in South America*
voyage – a trip in which you travel by ship or in a spacecraft, used mainly in stories: *Columbus's voyage across the ocean*
tour – a trip for pleasure, during which you visit several different towns, areas, etc.: *a tour of Europe*
expedition – a long and carefully organized trip, especially to a dangerous or unfamiliar place: *Lewis and Clark's expedition across North America*
excursion – a short trip to visit a place, usually by a group of people: *an all-day excursion to Catalina Island*
pilgrimage – a trip to a holy place for religious reasons: *a pilgrimage to Lourdes*

2 travels [plural] trips, especially to places that are far away: *She made a lot of friends* ***on her travels.***

'travel ,agency *n.* [C] a business that arranges travel and vacations

'travel ,agent *n.* [C] someone who works in a travel agency

trav·el·er /'trævələ/ *n.* [C] someone who is on a trip or who travels often

'traveler's ˌcheck *n.* [C] a special check that can be exchanged for the money of a foreign country

tra·verse /trə'vəs/ *v.* [T] (formal) to move across, over, or through something, especially land or water

trav·es·ty /'trævɪsti/ *n.* (plural **travesties**) [C] something that is very bad because it is not what it should be: *The trial was described as **a travesty of justice**.*

trawl /trɔl/ *n.* [C] a wide net that is pulled along the bottom of the ocean to catch fish —**trawl** *v.* [I,T]

trawl·er /'trɔlə/ *n.* [C] a fishing boat that uses a trawl

tray /treɪ/ *n.* [C] a flat piece of plastic, metal, or wood with raised edges, that is used for carrying things such as plates, food, etc.

treach·er·ous /'trɛtʃərəs/ *adj.* **1** someone who is treacherous cannot be trusted because s/he secretly intends to harm you **2** extremely dangerous because you cannot see the dangers: *Black ice on the roads made driving treacherous.*

treach·er·y /'trɛtʃəri/ *n.* [U] actions that are not loyal to someone who trusts you

tread¹ /trɛd/ *v.* (past tense **trod** /trɑd/, past participle **trodden** /'trɑdn/) **1 tread carefully/lightly etc.** to be very careful about what you say or do in a difficult situation: *It's best to tread lightly when the boss is in a bad mood.* **2 tread water** to stay floating upright in deep water by moving your legs as if you were riding a bicycle **3** [I,T] (old-fashioned) to walk or step on something

tread² *n.* **1** [C,U] the pattern of lines on the part of a tire that touches the road **2** [C] the part of a stair that you put your foot on

tread·mill /'trɛdmɪl/ *n.* **1** [C] a piece of exercise equipment that has a large belt around a set of wheels, that you can walk or run on while staying in the same place **2** [singular] work or a way of life that seems very boring because you always have to do the same things

trea·son /'trizən/ *n.* [U] the crime of being disloyal to your country or government, especially by helping its enemies

treas·ure¹ /'trɛʒə/ *n.* **1** [U] a group of valuable things, such as gold, silver, jewels, etc.: *a story about **buried treasure*** **2** [C] a very valuable and important object such as a painting or ancient document: *the treasures of the Art Institute of Chicago*

treasure² *v.* [T] to treat something or someone as very special, important, or valuable: *I'll always treasure the memories of this day.*

'treasure ˌhunt *n.* [C] a game in which you have to find something that has been hidden by answering questions that are left in different places

treas·ur·er /'trɛʒərə/ *n.* [C] someone who takes care of the money for an organization

treas·ur·y /'trɛʒəri/ *n.* (plural **treasuries**) [C] **1** the money in an organization's accounts **2** a government office that controls a country's money: *the Treasury Department*

treat¹ /trit/ *v.* [T] **1** to behave toward someone in a particular way: *Why do you **treat** me **like** an idiot?* | *My parents always **treated** me **as** an equal.* | *Mr. Parker **treats** everyone **equally/fairly**.* **2** to consider something in a particular way: *You can **treat** these costs **as** business expenses.* **3** to give someone medical attention for a sickness or injury: *Eleven people were **treated for** minor injuries.* **4** to buy or arrange something special for someone: *We're **treating** Mom **to** dinner for her birthday.* **5** to put a special substance on something or use a chemical process in order to protect or clean it: *The wood has been treated to make it waterproof.*

treat² *n.* **1** [C] something special that you give someone or do for him/her: *If you're good, I'll buy you a treat.* **2** [singular] an unexpected event that gives you a lot of pleasure: *Getting your letter was **a real treat**.* **3 my treat** (spoken) used in order to tell someone that you will pay for something: *Put away your money – dinner's my treat.*

treat·a·ble /'trit̬əbəl/ *adj.* able to be medically treated: *The disease is treatable with antibiotics.*

T

trea·tise /'trit̬əs/ *n.* [C] a serious book or article about a particular subject: *a **treatise on** political philosophy*

treat·ment /'trit˺mənt/ *n.* **1** [C,U] a method that is intended to cure an injury or sickness: *a new **treatment for** cancer* | *She was **given** emergency **treatment** by paramedics.* **2** [U] a particular way of behaving toward someone or of dealing with him/her: *Western society's **treatment of** women has improved.* | *The coach denied giving his son **preferential/special treatment**.* **3** [C,U] a particular way of dealing with or talking about a subject: *I didn't think the program gave the issue serious treatment.* **4** [U] a process by which something is cleaned, protected, etc.: *a waste treatment plant*

trea·ty /'trit̬i/ *n.* (plural **treaties**) [C] POLITICS a formal written agreement between two or more countries: *a **peace treaty***

tre·ble¹ /'trɛbəl/ *n.* [C] ENG. LANG. ARTS the upper half of the whole range of musical notes

treble² *v.* [I,T] to TRIPLE

tree /tri/ *n.* [C] a very tall plant that has a TRUNK (=thick wooden stem), branches, and leaves: *an apple tree* | *As a kid, I loved to climb trees.* [ORIGIN: Old English *treow*]

THESAURUS

Types of tree

evergreen – an evergreen tree does not lose its leaves in winter

deciduous – a deciduous tree loses its leaves in winter

conifer – a tree such as a pine or fir that has leaves like needles and produces cones containing seeds
fruit tree – a tree that produces fruit that can be eaten

Areas of trees
the woods – a large area with many trees
woodland – an area of land that is covered with trees
forest – a very large area with a lot of trees growing closely together
rain forest – a tropical forest with tall trees, in an area where it rains a lot
jungle – a tropical forest with trees and large plants
bush – wild country with trees and bushes in Australia or Africa
grove – a piece of land with trees growing on it, usually the same type of tree

Material from trees
wood – the usual word for the hard material that trees are made of
lumber/timber – wood used for building and making things
hardwood – strong heavy wood from trees such as oaks
softwood – wood from trees such as pine and fir that is cheap and easy to cut
firewood – wood that has been cut or collected in order to be burned in a fire

→ *see picture at* PLANT[1]

T

tree·top /'tritɑp/ *n.* [C usually plural] the top branches of a tree

trek /trɛk/ *v.* (**trekked, trekking**) [I] to make a long and difficult trip on foot: *Lewis and Clark, the explorers,* ***trekked across*** *the Rockies.* —**trek** *n.* [C]: *a* ***trek across*** *the country* —**trekking** *n.* [U]

trel·lis /'trɛlɪs/ *n.* [C] a wooden frame for supporting climbing plants

trem·ble /'trɛmbəl/ *v.* [I] to shake because you are upset, afraid, or excited: *Her lip trembled as she spoke.* | *Ray's voice was* ***trembling with fear/anger.***

THESAURUS **shake, shiver, quiver** → SHAKE[1]

tre·men·dous /trɪ'mɛndəs/ *adj.* **1** very great in amount, size, power, etc.: *I have tremendous respect for her.* | *a runner with tremendous speed* **2** excellent: *The play was a tremendous success.* —**tremendously** *adv.*

trem·or /'trɛmɚ/ *n.* [C] **1** a small EARTHQUAKE **2** a slight shaking movement in your body that you cannot control: *There was a* ***tremor in*** *her hands.*

trem·u·lous /'trɛmyələs/ *adj.* (literary) shaking slightly, especially because you are nervous: *a tremulous voice* —**tremulously** *adv.*

trench /trɛntʃ/ *n.* [C] a long narrow hole that is dug along the ground

tren·chant /'trɛntʃənt/ *adj.* (written) expressed very strongly, effectively, and directly: *a trenchant criticism of big business*

'trench coat *n.* [C] a long RAINCOAT with a belt

trend /trɛnd/ (Ac) *n.* [C] **1** the way a situation is generally developing or changing (SYN) **tendency**: *There's a* ***trend toward*** *more part-time employment.* | *recent* ***trends in*** *education* **2** a way of doing something or a way of thinking that is becoming fashionable: *fashion trends*

trend·y /'trɛndi/ *adj.* (comparative **trendier**, superlative **trendiest**) (informal) modern and fashionable: *the trendiest club in town*

THESAURUS **fashionable, stylish** → FASHIONABLE

trep·i·da·tion /ˌtrɛpə'deɪʃən/ *n.* [U] (formal) a feeling of anxiety or fear about something that is going to happen

tres·pass /'trɛspæs/ *v.* [I] to go onto someone's land without permission —**trespasser** *n.* [C]

THESAURUS **enter, sneak in, get in, intrude** → ENTER[1]

tres·tle /'trɛsəl/ *n.* [C] a wooden support made of beams in an "A" shape under a table or bridge

tri·al /'traɪəl/ *n.* **1** [C,U] a legal process in which a court of law examines a case to decide whether someone is guilty of a crime → TRY: *a murder trial* | *Holt is* ***on trial for*** (=being judged in a court for) *bank robbery.* | *He* ***stands trial*** (=will be judged in a court) *in June.* | *The defendant has a right to a* ***fair trial.*** **2** [C,U] a test to know if something works well and is safe: ***clinical trials*** *of a new drug* **3** [C,U] a short period during which you use something or employ someone to find out whether he, she, or it is satisfactory for a particular purpose or job: *Bonnie's been hired* ***on a trial basis.*** **4 trial and error** testing different ways of doing something in order to find the best one: *I learned to cook* ***by/through trial and error.*** **5 trials** [plural] a sports competition in which people who want to be on a team are tested to find out who is best (SYN) **tryout**: *the Olympic swimming trials* **6 trials and tribulations** difficult experiences and troubles: *He's undergoing all the trials and tribulations of being a teenager.*

ˌtrial 'run *n.* [C] an occasion when you test something new in order to see if it works

tri·an·gle /'traɪˌæŋgəl/ *n.* [C] **1** a flat shape with three straight sides and three angles → *see picture at* POLYGON

THESAURUS **shape, square, circle, semicircle, rectangle, oval** → SHAPE[1]

2 a small musical instrument shaped like a triangle, that you play by hitting it with a small metal BAR [ORIGIN: 1300—1400 Latin *triangulum*, from *tri-* "three" + *angulus* "angle"] —**triangular** /traɪ'æŋgyəlɚ/ *adj.*

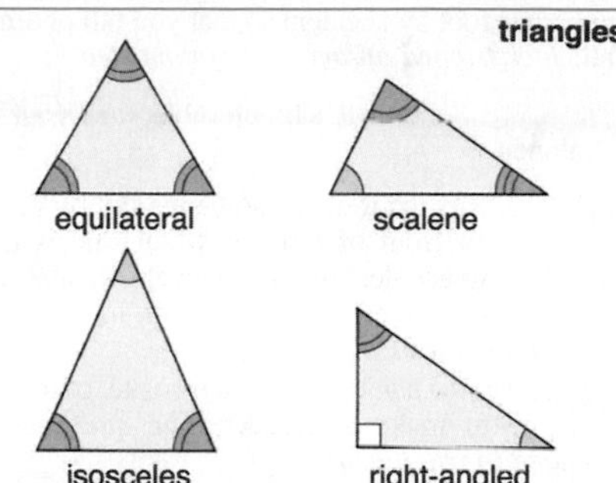

tri·ath·lon /traɪˈæθlɑn, -lən/ *n.* [C] a sports competition in which you run, swim, and ride a bicycle

tribe /traɪb/ *n.* [C] a social group that consists of people of the same RACE who have the same beliefs, customs, language, etc. and live in one area ruled by a chief: *the tribes of the Amazon jungle* —**tribal** *adj.*: *tribal art* | *tribal leaders*

THESAURUS **race, nation, people, ethnic group** ➔ RACE[1]

trib·u·la·tion /ˌtrɪbyəˈleɪʃən/ *n.* [C,U] (formal) serious trouble or a serious problem ➔ **trials and tribulations** *at* TRIAL

tri·bu·nal /traɪˈbyunl, trɪ-/ *n.* [C] a type of court that has official authority to deal with a particular situation or problem: *a war crimes tribunal*

trib·u·tar·y /ˈtrɪbyəˌtɛri/ *n.* (plural **tributaries**) [C] a river or stream that flows into a larger river

trib·ute /ˈtrɪbyut/ *n.* [C,U] something that you say, do, or give in order to express your respect or admiration for someone: *The concert will be a* ***tribute to*** *Bob Dylan.* ➔ **pay tribute to sb/sth** *at* PAY[1] [ORIGIN: 1300—1400 Latin *tributum*, from *tribuere* "to give out to the tribes, pay"]

tri·ceps /ˈtraɪsɛps/ *n.* [C] BIOLOGY the large muscle at the back of your upper arm

trick[1] /trɪk/ *n.* [C] **1** something you do in order to deceive someone: *It was just a trick to get me to agree.* **2** something you do to surprise someone and make other people laugh: *The kids like* ***playing tricks on*** *the grownups.* **3** a skillful set of actions that seem like magic, done in order to entertain people: *a* ***magic trick*** **4 do the trick** (spoken) if something does the trick, it solves a problem or achieves what you want: *A little salt should do the trick.* **5** an effective way of doing something: *There's* ***a trick to*** *getting the audience's attention.*

trick[2] *v.* [T] to deceive someone in order to get something from him/her or make him/her do something: *Believe me, we're not trying to trick you.* | *Clients were* ***tricked into*** *believing he'd invest the money.*

trick·er·y /ˈtrɪkəri/ *n.* [U] the use of tricks to deceive or cheat people

trick·le /ˈtrɪkəl/ *v.* [I] **1** if liquid trickles somewhere, it flows slowly in drops or in a thin stream: *Sweat* ***trickled down*** *his face.* **2** if people, vehicles, goods, etc. trickle somewhere, they move there slowly in small groups or amounts: *Refugees have begun to* ***trickle across*** *the border.* —**trickle** *n.* [C]: *a trickle of blood*

ˌtrick or ˈtreat *v.* **go trick or treating** if children go trick or treating, they put on COSTUMEs and go from house to house on Halloween and say "trick or treat" in order to get candy

trick·ster /ˈtrɪkstɚ/ *n.* [C] someone who deceives or cheats people

trick·y /ˈtrɪki/ *adj.* (comparative **trickier**, superlative **trickiest**) something that is tricky is difficult to deal with or do because it is complicated and full of problems: *Finding out how the trouble started will be tricky.*

tri·cus·pid valve /traɪˈkʌspɪd ˌvælv/ *n.* [C] BIOLOGY a part on the right side of your heart that opens and closes to allow blood to flow from the right ATRIUM into the right VENTRICLE and prevent blood from flowing back into the atrium ➔ *see picture at* HEART

tri·cy·cle /ˈtraɪsɪkəl/ *n.* [C] a small vehicle, used especially by young children, with one wheel at the front and two wheels at the back

tri·dent /ˈtraɪdnt/ *n.* [C] a weapon with three points that looks like a large fork

tried[1] /traɪd/ *v.* the past tense and past participle of TRY

tried[2] *adj.* **tried and tested/true** used successfully many times: *tried and tested methods*

tri·fle /ˈtraɪfəl/ *n.* [C] **1 a trifle...** a little SYN **slightly**: *The soup is a trifle salty.* **2** something that has little value or importance

trig·ger[1] /ˈtrɪgɚ/ Ac *n.* [C] **1** the part of a gun that you press with your finger to fire it: *Carter aimed and* ***pulled the trigger.*** **2 be the trigger (point)** to be the thing that causes a serious problem

trigger[2] *also* **trigger off** *v.* [T] to make something happen: *Heavy rain may trigger mudslides.* | *Peanuts can trigger an allergic reaction in some people.*

THESAURUS **cause, bring about sth, result in sth, lead to sth, prompt** ➔ CAUSE[2]

trig·o·nom·e·try /ˌtrɪgəˈnɑmətri/ *n.* [U] MATH the part of mathematics that is concerned with the relationship between the angles and sides of TRIANGLEs [ORIGIN: 1600—1700 Modern Latin *trigonometria*, from Greek *trigonon* "triangle" + *-metria* "measuring"]

trike /traɪk/ *n.* [C] (informal) a TRICYCLE

tri·lat·er·al /ˌtraɪˈlæt̬ərəl◂/ *adj.* including three groups or countries: *a trilateral agreement*

trill /trɪl/ *n.* [C] a musical sound made by quickly repeating two notes that are very similar: *a bird's trill* —**trill** *v.* [I,T]

T

tril·lion /'trɪlyən/ *number* 1,000,000,000,000

tril·o·gy /'trɪlədʒi/ *n.* (plural **trilogies**) [C] a group of three books, plays, movies, etc. that have the same subject or characters [ORIGIN: 1600—1700 Greek *trilogia* "group of three plays," from *tri-* "three" + *-logia* "-logy"]

trim¹ /trɪm/ *v.* (**trimmed, trimming**) [T] **1** to cut a small amount off something, especially to make it look neater: ***Trim off** the excess fat.*

THESAURUS **cut, snip** → CUT¹

2 to reduce the size or amount of something, especially to save money: *The mayor has plans to trim the city's budget.* **3** to decorate something around its edges: *a coat **trimmed with** velvet*

trim² *adj.* thin and healthy looking: *a trim figure*

trim³ *n.* **1** [singular] an act of cutting something in order to make it look neater: *Your beard needs a trim.* **2** [singular, U] a decoration around the edges of a car, piece of clothing, etc.: *a blue car with white trim*

tri·mes·ter /'traɪmɛstɚ, traɪ'mɛstɚ/ *n.* [C] **1** one of three periods into which a year at school or college is divided **2** BIOLOGY one of the three-month periods of a woman's PREGNANCY: *Many women feel sick during the first trimester of pregnancy.* [ORIGIN: 1800—1900 French *trimestre*, from Latin *trimestris*, from *tri-* "three" + *mensis* "month"]

T

trim·mings /'trɪmɪŋz/ *n.* **all the trimmings** all the other types of food that are traditionally served with the main dish of a meal: *a turkey dinner with all the trimmings*

trin·i·ty /'trɪnət̬i/ *n.* **the (Holy) Trinity** in the Christian religion, the union of Father, Son, and Holy Spirit in one God

trin·ket /'trɪŋkɪt/ *n.* [C] a piece of jewelry or a small pretty object that is not worth much money

tri·no·mi·al /traɪ'noʊmiəl/ *n.* [C] MATH a mathematical expression that has three parts connected by the sign + or the sign –, for example x + y + z —**trinomial** *adj.*

tri·o /'trioʊ/ *n.* (plural **trios**) [C] **1** a group of three people or things: *a jazz trio* **2** a piece of music for three performers

trip¹ /trɪp/ *n.* [C] **1** an occasion when you go from one place to another, often to visit a place or person: *a **trip to** the grocery store* | *I'd met him **on** my last **trip** to Japan.* | *They recently **took a trip** to Florida.* | *a **camping/fishing/ski trip*** | *a week-long **business trip***

THESAURUS **travel, journey, voyage, tour, expedition, excursion, pilgrimage** → TRAVEL²

2 (slang) the strange mental experiences someone has when s/he takes an illegal drug such as LSD

trip² *v.* (**tripped, tripping**) **1** [I] to hit something with your foot by accident so that you fall or almost fall: *Jack **tripped on/over** the bottom step.*

THESAURUS **fall, slip, stumble, lose your balance** → FALL¹

2 [T] *also* **trip up** to make someone fall by putting your foot in front of him/her when s/he is moving **3** [T] to accidentally make an electrical system operate by moving part of it: *An intruder had tripped the alarm.*

trip (sb ↔) **up** *phr. v.* to make a mistake, or to cause someone to make a mistake: *The question was intended to trip him up.*

tri·par·tite gov·ern·ment /traɪˌpɑrt̬aɪt 'gʌvɚmənt/ *n.* [C,U] POLITICS a government in which three political parties share power

tripe /traɪp/ *n.* [U] the stomach of a cow or pig, used as food

tri·ple¹ /'trɪpəl/ *adj.* having three parts, or involving three people or groups: *a triple gold medal winner*

triple² *v.* [I,T] to increase by three times as much, or to make something do this: *The landlord tripled the rent.*

tri·plet /'trɪplɪt/ *n.* [C] one of three children born at the same time to the same mother

trip·li·cate /'trɪpləkɪt/ *n.* **in triplicate** if a document is written in triplicate, there are three copies of it

tri·pod /'traɪpɑd/ *n.* [C] a support with three legs, used for a camera, TELESCOPE, etc.

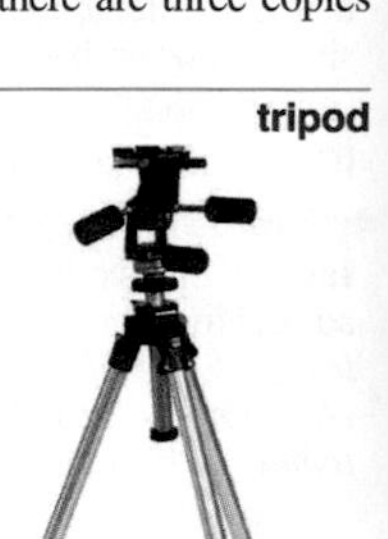
tripod

trite /traɪt/ *adj.* a trite remark, idea, etc. has been used so often that it seems boring and not sincere

tri·umph¹ /'traɪəmf/ *n.* **1** [C] an important success or victory, especially after a difficult struggle: *a foreign policy triumph* | *Fans celebrated San Francisco's **triumph over** Cincinnati in the Super Bowl.* **2** [U] a feeling of pleasure and satisfaction that you get from success or victory: *shouts of triumph* —**triumphant** /traɪ'ʌmfənt/ *adj.*: *a triumphant army*

triumph² *v.* [I] to gain a victory or success, especially after a difficult struggle: *Good will **triumph over** evil.*

THESAURUS **win, be victorious, prevail** → WIN¹

tri·um·phal /traɪ'ʌmfəl/ *adj.* done or made in order to celebrate a victory or success: *a triumphal parade*

triv·i·a /'trɪviə/ *n.* [plural] **1** detailed facts about history, famous people, sports, etc.: *movie trivia* | *a* ***trivia quiz/game/contest*** **2** unimportant or useless details: *meaningless trivia*

triv·i·al /ˈtrɪviəl/ *adj.* not important, valuable, or serious: *This issue is not a* ***trivial matter***. [ORIGIN: 1400—1500 Latin *trivialis* "found everywhere, common," from *trivium* "place where three roads meet, crossroads"]

triv·i·al·ize /ˈtrɪviəˌlaɪz/ *v.* [T] to make something important seem less important than it really is: *The media seemed to trivialize the court's decision.*

tRNA /ˌti ɑr ɛn ˈeɪ/ BIOLOGY the abbreviation of TRANSFER RNA

tro·chee /ˈtroʊki/ *n.* [C] ENG. LANG. ARTS a RHYTHM in poetry, that has a STRESSed (=emphasized) word or SYLLABLE (=part of a word) followed by a word or syllable that is not stressed, for example in the word "father"

trod /trɑd/ *v.* the past tense of TREAD

trod·den /ˈtrɑdn/ *v.* the past participle of TREAD

troll /troʊl/ *n.* [C] an imaginary creature in ancient Scandinavian stories, like a very large or very small ugly person

trol·ley /ˈtrɑli/ *n.* [C] an electric vehicle for carrying passengers, that moves along the street on metal tracks

trom·bone /trɑmˈboʊn/ *n.* [C] a metal musical instrument, that you play by blowing into it and moving a long sliding tube —**trombonist** *n.* [C]

tromp /trɑmp, trɔmp/ *v.* [I] (informal) to walk around or through a place with firm heavy steps

troop[1] /trup/ *n.* **1 troops** [plural] soldiers in an organized group: *Troops were sent in to stop the riots.* **2 troop movement/withdrawal/morale/readiness etc.** the movements, etc. of soldiers **3** [C] a group of soldiers, especially on horses or in TANKS **4** [C] an organized group of people or animals: *a Girl Scout troop* [ORIGIN: 1500—1600 French, Late Latin *troppus* "group of sheep"]

troop[2] *v.* [I] (informal) to move together in a group: *People* ***trooped across/along/down etc.*** *the street.*

troop·er /ˈtrupɚ/ *n.* [C] a member of a state police force in the U.S.

tro·phy /ˈtroʊfi/ *n.* (plural **trophies**) [C] a prize for winning a competition, especially a silver cup or a PLAQUE: *He was presented with the* ***championship trophy***.

trop·ic /ˈtrɑpɪk/ *n.* **1 the tropics** [plural] EARTH SCIENCES the hottest part of the world, which is between the Tropic of Cancer and the Tropic of Capricorn **2** [C] EARTH SCIENCES of the two imaginary lines around the world, either the Tropic of Cancer which is 23½° north of the EQUATOR, or the Tropic of Capricorn which is 23½° south of the equator → *see picture at* GLOBE

trop·i·cal /ˈtrɑpɪkəl/ *adj.* **1** coming from or existing in the hottest and wettest parts of the world: *tropical flowers* **2** weather that is tropical is hot and the air seems wet

ˈtropical ˌzone *n.* [C] EARTH SCIENCES parts of the Earth near the tropics, where the weather is always hot and the Sun shines for most of the year

tro·pism /ˈtroʊˌpɪzəm/ *n.* [U] BIOLOGY the ways in which a plant moves or grows as a reaction to things such as light, GRAVITY, or being touched

tro·po·sphere /ˈtroʊpəˌsfɪr, ˈtrɑ-/ *n.* **the troposphere** EARTH SCIENCES the lowest level of the Earth's ATMOSPHERE, from the surface to about eleven miles above the Earth → *see picture at* ATMOSPHERE

trot /trɑt/ *v.* (**trotted**, **trotting**) [I] **1** if a horse trots, it moves fairly quickly with short steps **2** to run fairly slowly with short steps: *Jimmy* ***trotted along*** *behind his parents.* —**trot** *n.*

trot sb/sth ↔ **out** *phr. v.* (informal) to use an explanation, idea, opinion, etc. that has been used many times before: *He trotted out the same old excuses.*

trou·ba·dour /ˈtrubəˌdɔr/ *n.* [C] a singer and poet who traveled around in past times

trou·ble[1] /ˈtrʌbəl/ *n.*

1 PROBLEMS [C,U] problems that make something difficult, make you worry, spoil your plans, etc.: *They're* ***having*** *some* ***trouble with*** *their car.* | *We* ***had trouble*** *getting reservations.* | *a plane with engine trouble* | *the company's financial troubles* | *It took her mind off her troubles.*

THESAURUS **problem, difficulty, hassle** → PROBLEM

2 BAD POINT [singular] (spoken) used when saying what is not satisfactory about something or someone or what causes problems: ***The trouble with*** *you is you don't listen.* | *There isn't enough time.* ***That's the trouble.***

3 in/into/out of trouble a) if someone or something is in trouble, she, he, or it is in a situation that has a lot of problems or that is difficult or dangerous: *Their marriage was in trouble.* | *The agency was* ***in serious/big/deep trouble***. **b)** if someone is in trouble, s/he has done something which someone will punish him/her for or be angry about: *My daughter's* ***gotten into trouble*** *at school.* | *Joe's* ***in trouble with*** *the police.* | *After-school activities help kids* ***stay/keep out of trouble***.

4 HEALTH [U] (informal) a problem that you have with your health: *He has* ***heart/back trouble***.

5 EFFORT [U] an amount of effort and time that is needed to do something: *She* ***took the trouble to*** *explain it to us again.* | *"Could you help me carry this?" "Sure,* ***it's no trouble*** (=I am happy to help)."

6 be asking for trouble (informal) to take risks or do something stupid that is likely to cause problems: *You're asking for trouble if you don't get those brakes fixed.*

7 ARGUMENT/VIOLENCE [C,U] a situation in which people argue or fight with each other: *The police* *stepped in to stop the troubles outside the courthouse.*

trouble[2] v. [T] (formal) **1** if a problem troubles you, it makes you feel worried or upset: *His behavior toward her troubled me.* **2** to say something or ask someone to do something which may use his/her time or upset him/her: *I won't trouble you again.*

trou·bled /ˈtrʌbəld/ adj. **1** worried or anxious: *Clayton looked troubled.*

> THESAURUS **upset, unsettled, disturbed, perturbed** ➔ UPSET[1]

2 having many problems: *our troubled public schools* | *We are living in* ***troubled times.*** **3** having many mental or emotional problems: *a* ***deeply troubled*** *man*

trou·ble·mak·er /ˈtrʌbəlˌmeɪkɚ/ n. [C] someone who deliberately causes problems

trou·ble·shoot·er /ˈtrʌbəlˌʃuṭɚ/ n. [C] someone whose job is to deal with serious problems in a company, organization, etc. —**troubleshooting** n. [U]

trou·ble·some /ˈtrʌbəlsəm/ adj. causing problems: *troublesome questions*

ˈtrouble ˌspot n. [C] a place where trouble often happens, especially war or violence: *Troops are being sent to trouble spots abroad.*

trou·bling /ˈtrʌblɪŋ/ adj. worrying: *The results raise some troubling questions.*

trough /trɔf/ n. [C] **1** a long narrow open container that holds water or food for animals **2** ECONOMICS the lowest point in an economic period that has high and low points, when the total value of all goods and services produced in a country will not fall any further

trounce /trauns/ v. [T] to defeat someone completely: *Colorado trounced Minnesota, 58–7.*

> THESAURUS **beat, defeat, clobber, cream** ➔ BEAT[1]

troupe /trup/ n. [C] a group of singers, actors, dancers, etc. who work together

trou·sers /ˈtraʊzɚz/ n. [plural] a piece of clothing that covers the lower half of your body and that has a separate part for each leg (SYN) **pants**

trout /traʊt/ n. (plural **trout**) [C,U] a common river fish, or the meat from this fish

trove /troʊv/ n. [C usually singular] a large number of special or valuable things: *a* ***treasure trove of*** *antique furniture*

trow·el /ˈtraʊəl/ n. [C] a small garden tool used for digging

tru·ant /ˈtruənt/ adj. staying away from school without permission [ORIGIN: 1300—1400 Old French "wanderer"] —**truancy** n. [U] —**truant** n. [C]

truce /trus/ n. [C] an agreement between two enemies to stop fighting or arguing for a short time: *The warring sides have* ***called/declared a truce.***

truck[1] /trʌk/ n. [C] a large road vehicle that is used for carrying heavy loads: *a truck driver* | *a* ***garbage/dump/delivery etc. truck*** ➔ PICKUP ➔ *see picture at* TRANSPORTATION

truck[2] v. [T] to take something somewhere by truck: *Food and medicine were* ***trucked in.***

truck·er /ˈtrʌkɚ/ n. [C] someone whose job is driving a truck

ˈtruck farm n. [C] a farm that grows vegetables and fruit for sale directly to customers

truck·ing /ˈtrʌkɪŋ/ n. [U] the business of taking goods from place to place by truck

truck·load /ˈtrʌkloʊd/ n. [C] the amount of something that a truck can carry

ˈtruck stop n. [C] a cheap place to eat and buy gas on a HIGHWAY, used especially by truck drivers

truc·u·lent /ˈtrʌkyələnt/ adj. (formal) easily annoyed and always willing to argue with people

trudge /trʌdʒ/ v. [I] to walk with slow heavy steps because you are tired, or it is difficult to walk: *A group of soldiers* ***trudged up/down*** *the hill.*

> THESAURUS **walk, march, stride, hike** ➔ WALK[1]

true /tru/ adj. **1** based on facts and not imagined or invented (ANT) **false**: ***It is true that*** *people are living longer.* | *The movie is based on a* ***true story.***

> THESAURUS **right, correct** ➔ RIGHT[1]

2 [only before noun] real and correct: *the true meaning of Christmas* | *The house was sold for only a fraction of its true value.* **3** (spoken) used when admitting that something is a fact: *True, he has a college degree, but he doesn't have enough job experience.* **4 true love/courage/friend etc.** love, a friend, etc. that has all the qualities that he, she, or it should have: *He's a true friend.* **5 come true** if dreams, wishes, etc. come true, they happen: *Their wish for a child finally came true.* **6** faithful and loyal, or doing what you have promised to do: *She stayed* ***true to*** *her husband during the trial.* | *He was* ***true to*** *his* ***word*** *and didn't say anything to anyone.* [ORIGIN: Old English *treowe* "faithful"]

> THESAURUS **faithful, loyal, staunch, steadfast** ➔ FAITHFUL

ˌtrue-ˈlife adj. based on what really happened, and not invented: *a true-life adventure*

truf·fle /ˈtrʌfəl/ n. [C] **1** a soft chocolate candy **2** a FUNGUS you can eat that grows under the ground

tru·ism /ˈtruɪzəm/ n. [C] a statement that is clearly true, so that there is no need to say it

tru·ly /ˈtruli/ adv. **1** used in order to emphasize that the way you are describing something is true

(SYN) **really**: *What is truly important?* | *I truly believe Alex saved my life.* **2** in an exact or correct way: *A spider can't truly be called an insect.* → **yours (truly)** *at* YOURS

trump¹ /trʌmp/ *n.* [C] **1** a SUIT or a playing card that is chosen to be of a higher value than the others in a particular card game **2 trump card** something that you can do or use in a situation, which gives you an advantage

trump² *v.* [T] to play a trump that beats someone else's card in a game

trump sth ↔ **up** *phr. v.* to use false information to make someone seem guilty of a crime —**trumped-up** *adj.*: *trumped-up charges*

trum·pet¹ /ˈtrʌmpɪt/ *n.* [C] **1** a musical instrument that you blow into, which consists of a long bent metal tube that is wide at one end **2** the loud noise that an ELEPHANT makes

trumpet² *v.* [T] to tell everyone about something you think is important or are proud of: *The headlines trumpeted their victory.*

trum·pet·er /ˈtrʌmpɪt̬ɚ/ *n.* [C] someone who plays a trumpet

trun·cate /ˈtrʌŋkeɪt/ *v.* [T] (formal) to make something shorter (SYN) **shorten**: *The speech had to be truncated because of a lack of time.* —**truncation** /trʌŋˈkeɪʃən/ *n.* [U]

trun·cat·ed /ˈtrʌŋˌkeɪt̬ɪd/ *adj.* made short, or shorter than before: *a truncated speech*

trun·dle /ˈtrʌndl/ *v.* [I,T] to move slowly on wheels, or to make something do this by pushing it or pulling it

trunk /trʌŋk/ *n.* [C] **1** the thick central wooden stem of a tree that branches grow from: *A sign was tacked to a **tree trunk**.* → *see picture at* PLANT¹ **2** an enclosed space at the back of a car where you can put bags, tools, etc.: *Put the suitcases in the trunk.* **3** the very long nose of an ELEPHANT **4** a large box made of wood or metal, in which clothes, books, etc. are stored or packed for traveling **5 trunks** [plural] short pants that men wear when swimming **6** (formal) the main part of your body, not including your head, arms, or legs → TORSO

trust¹ /trʌst/ *v.* **1** [T] to believe that someone is honest and will not do anything bad or wrong: *I've never trusted her.* | *Can you **trust** him **with** your car* (=believe he will not damage it)? | *Managers must **trust** employees **to** get the job done.* **2** [T] to depend on something and believe it is correct or will work: *I trust his judgment.* | *Not trusting her voice, she nodded.*

THESAURUS **depend, rely on/upon, count on** → DEPEND

3 I trust (spoken, formal) used in order to say that you hope something is true: *The reasons, I trust, are clear.*

trust in sb/sth *phr. v.* (formal) to believe that you can depend on someone or something

trust² *n.* **1** [U] the belief that you can trust someone (ANT) **distrust**: *It took three years to earn his trust.* | *At first, there was a **lack of trust** between them.* | *I had **put** my **trust in** the doctor.* **2** [U] an arrangement in which someone legally controls your money or property, usually until you are old enough to use it: *$100,000 is being **held in trust** for his daughter.* **3** [C usually singular] an organization or group that has control over money that will be used to help someone else: *the J. Paul Getty trust* **4** [C] a group of companies that work together to reduce competition: *a railroad trust* **5** [C] ECONOMICS a group of separate companies that are placed under the control of a single managing board

trust·ee /trʌˈsti/ *n.* [C] a person or company that has control of money or property that is in a trust for someone else

ˈ**trust fund** *n.* [C] money belonging to someone that is controlled for him/her by a trustee

trust·ing /ˈtrʌstɪŋ/ *adj.* willing to believe that other people are good and honest: *a trusting little child*

trust·wor·thy /ˈtrʌstˌwɚði/ *adj.* able to be trusted or depended on

trust·y /ˈtrʌsti/ *adj.* (humorous) a trusty weapon, horse, friend, etc. is one you can depend on

truth /truθ/ *n.* **1 the truth** the true facts about something: *Do you think he's **telling the truth**?* | *He finally told **the truth about** what he had done in the war.* | *It was months before **the whole truth** was discovered.* **2** [U] the state or quality of being true: *There was no **truth in** the rumor.* **3** [C] (formal) an important fact or idea that is accepted as being true: *scientific truths* **4 to tell (you) the truth** (spoken) used when you admit something or tell someone your true opinion: *To tell you the truth, I just don't care.*

truth·ful /ˈtruθfəl/ *adj.* giving the true facts about something: *truthful answers* —**truthfully** *adv.*

try¹ /traɪ/ *v.* (**tried**, **tries**) **1** [I,T] to attempt to do something: *Try again when you're not so tired.* | *Please **try to** come early.* | *Greg **tried hard** not to laugh.*

THESAURUS

attempt – to try to do something, especially something difficult: *He was attempting to climb Mt. Everest without oxygen.*
see if you can do sth (spoken) – to try to do something: *I'll see if I can get you a ticket.*
do your best – to try very hard, even if something is difficult and you are not sure you will succeed: *They'll do their best to get it finished by Friday.*
make an effort to do sth – to try to do something, especially something difficult: *The teachers make an effort to identify a student's strengths and weaknesses.*
endeavor (formal) – to try very hard to do something: *The company endeavors to satisfy its customers.*

T

2 [T] to do or use something, go somewhere, taste something, etc. in order to find out if it is useful, successful, or enjoyable: *Try logging off and logging on again.* | *Doctors are trying some new drugs in the cancer battle.* | *Have you tried Thai food?* **3** [T] to examine and judge a person or a legal case in a court of law: *Three men were **tried for** the murder.* **4 try sb's patience/nerves/temper etc.** to make someone start to feel impatient, nervous, angry, etc.

try sth **on** *phr. v.* to put on a piece of clothing to find out if it fits or makes you look attractive: *I tried on one of her silk dresses.*

try out *phr. v.* **1 try** sth ↔ **out** to use something such as a method or piece of equipment to find out if it works or is good: *Are you going to try out your new bike?* **2** to show your skills in an attempt to be chosen as a member of a team, an actor in a play, etc.: *Sandra's **trying out for** the girls' basketball team.*

try² *n.* (plural **tries**) [C usually singular] an attempt to do something: *It looks hard, but I'll **give it a try**.* | *Good try, kid.*

try·ing /ˈtraɪ-ɪŋ/ *adj.* difficult and unpleasant to deal with: *a trying time*

try·out /ˈtraɪ-aʊt/ *n.* [C] an occasion when someone shows his/her skills in an attempt to be chosen for a sports team, play, etc. → AUDITION

T

tsar /zɑr, tsɑr/ *n.* [C] another spelling of CZAR

T-shirt /ˈti ʃɚt/ *n.* [C] a soft cotton shirt, with short SLEEVES and no collar → *see picture at* CLOTHES

tsp. the written abbreviation of TEASPOON

tsu·na·mi /tsʊˈnɑmi/ *n.* [C] EARTH SCIENCES a very large wave which can cause a lot of damage when it reaches land. A tsunami is usually caused by an EARTHQUAKE.

tub /tʌb/ *n.* [C] **1** a large container in which you sit to wash yourself (SYN) **bathtub** **2** a plastic or paper container with a lid, that food is sold in: *a **tub of** ice cream* **3** a large round container used for washing things, storing things, etc.

tu·ba /ˈtubə/ *n.* [C] a large metal musical instrument with a wide opening that points straight up, that you play by blowing and that produces very low sounds

tub·by /ˈtʌbi/ *adj.* (informal) short and fat

tube /tub/ *n.* [C] **1** a pipe made of metal, plastic, glass, etc., especially one that liquids or gases go through: *The patients are fed through tubes.* **2** a container for a soft substance, that you SQUEEZE to push the substance out: *a **tube of** toothpaste* **3** a tube-shaped part inside your body: *a fallopian tube* (=part of a woman's organs for having babies) **4 the tube** (spoken) the television: *What's on the tube?* **5 go down the tubes** if a situation goes down the tubes, it suddenly becomes bad: *Small businesses are going down the tubes.*

tu·ber /ˈtubɚ/ *n.* [C] BIOLOGY a round swollen part on the stem of some plants, that grows below the ground and from which new plants grow. A potato is a tuber.

tu·ber·cu·lo·sis /tʊˌbɚkyəˈloʊsɪs/ *n.* [U] BIOLOGY a serious infectious disease that affects the lungs and other parts of the body

tub·ing /ˈtubɪŋ/ *n.* [U] tubes, usually connected together in a system: *copper tubing*

tu·bu·lar /ˈtubyələ/ *adj.* made of tubes or shaped like a tube

tuck¹ /tʌk/ *v.* [T] **1** to push the edge of a cloth or piece of clothing into something so that it stays in place: *He **tucked in** his shirt.* **2** to put something in a small space or a safe place: *She **tucked** the money **into** her pocket.* **3** to out an arm, leg, or head close to the body and keep it there: *The duck had its head tucked under its wing.*

tuck sth ↔ **away** *phr. v.* **1** to put something in a safe or hidden place: *She tucked it away in a drawer.* **2 be tucked away** to be in a safe or hidden place: *They own a cabin tucked away in the mountains.*

tuck sb ↔ **in** *phr. v.* to make a child feel comfortable in bed by arranging the BLANKETs around him or her

tuck² *n.* [C] **1** a fold of cloth sewn flat in a piece of clothing **2** a medical operation to make someone look thinner or younger: *a tummy tuck*

Tues·day /ˈtuzdi, -deɪ/ (*written abbreviation* **Tues.**) *n.* [C,U] the third day of the week, between Monday and Wednesday: *He'll be back Tuesday.* | *Martha is going to St. Louis **on Tuesday**.* | *I'll see you **next Tuesday**.* | *We had the exam **last Tuesday**.* | *The meeting is scheduled for **Tuesday afternoon**.* [ORIGIN: Old English *tiwesdæg*, from *Tiw* god of war + *dæg* "day"]

tuft /tʌft/ *n.* [C] a short thick group of hairs, feathers, grass, etc.: *a tuft of hair* —**tufted** *adj.*

tug¹ /tʌg/ *v.* (**tugged**, **tugging**) [I,T] to pull something suddenly and hard: *Alice **tugged at** my hand.*

THESAURUS pull, drag → PULL¹

tug² *n.* [C] **1** *also* **tug boat** a small strong boat used for pulling ships **2** a sudden strong pull

ˌtug-of-ˈwar *n.* [singular] **1** a competition in which two teams pull on the opposite ends of a rope **2** a situation in which two people or groups compete to get or keep the same thing

tu·i·tion /tuˈɪʃən/ *n.* [U] **1** the money you pay for being taught: *What is the cost of tuition at a private college?* **2** the act of teaching

tu·lip /ˈtulɪp/ *n.* [C] a tall brightly colored garden flower, shaped like a cup [ORIGIN: 1500—1600 Modern Latin *tulipa*, from Turkish *tülbend* "turban;" from the shape of the flower]

tum·ble /ˈtʌmbəl/ *v.* [I] **1** to fall or roll in a sudden uncontrolled way: *Rocks **tumbled down** the hillside.* **2** to decrease suddenly: *Oil prices have tumbled.* —**tumble** *n.* [C]

tum·bler /ˈtʌmblɚ/ *n.* [C] a glass with a flat bottom and no handle

tum·my /ˈtʌmi/ *n.* (plural **tummies**) [C] (informal) stomach – used especially by or to children

tu·mor /ˈtumɚ/ *n.* [C] BIOLOGY a group of cells in the body that grow too quickly and cause sickness or health problems: *a brain tumor*

tu·mult /ˈtumʌlt/ *n.* [C,U] (formal) a state of confusion, excitement, or other strong emotion: *the tumult of civil war* —**tumultuous** /tʊˈmʌltʃuəs/ *adj.*

tu·na /ˈtunə/ *n.* [C,U] a large common ocean fish, or the meat from this fish, usually sold in cans [ORIGIN: 1800—1900 American Spanish, Spanish *atun*, from Arabic *tun*]

tun·dra /ˈtʌndrə/ *n.* [U] EARTH SCIENCES the large flat areas of land in northern areas where it is very cold and there are no trees

tune¹ /tun/ *n.* **1** [C] a series of musical notes that are nice to listen to: *a pretty tune* | *It's sung* ***to the tune of*** *"Happy Birthday."* **2 in tune/out of tune** playing or singing the correct musical notes, or playing or singing notes that are slightly too high or low: *My guitar's completely out of tune.* **3 in tune with sb/sth, out of tune with sb/sth** able or unable to realize, understand, or agree with what someone else thinks or wants: *Do we want a president who is in tune with ordinary Americans?* **4 to the tune of $100/$15 million etc.** (informal) used in order to emphasize how large an amount or number is **5 change your tune** to suddenly have a different opinion about something

tune² *v.* [T] **1** to make a musical instrument play the correct PITCH: *The piano needs to be tuned.* **2** to make a television or radio receive broadcasts from a particular CHANNEL or STATION: ***Stay tuned*** *for more great music on KHPI.* **3** *also* **tune up** to make small changes to an engine so that it works better

tune in *phr. v.* **1** to watch or listen to a particular television or radio program, or to make your television or radio receive that program: *I* ***tuned in to*** *the Giants' game.* **2** (informal) to realize or understand what is happening or what other people are thinking: *Try to* ***tune in to*** *your spouse's needs.*

tune (sb/sth ↔) **out** *phr. v.* (informal) to ignore or stop listening to someone or something: *It's hard to tune out the noise in the office sometimes.*

tune up *phr. v.* when musicians tune up, they prepare their instruments so that they play at the same PITCH

tune-up *n.* [C] an occasion when someone fixes and cleans your car's engine, or the process of doing this

tu·nic /ˈtunɪk/ *n.* [C] **1** a long loose piece of clothing, usually without SLEEVES, worn in the past **2** a woman's long loose shirt

tun·nel¹ /ˈtʌnl/ *n.* [C] a passage that has been dug under the ground or through a mountain, usually for cars or trains [ORIGIN: 1400—1500 Old French *tonel* "barrel," from *tonne*, from Medieval Latin *tunna*]

tunnel

railroad tunnel

tunnel² *v.* [I] to dig a tunnel

ˌtunnel ˈvision *n.* [U] **1** the tendency to think about only one subject, so that you forget other things that may be important too **2** a condition in which someone's eyes are damaged so that s/he can only see straight ahead

Tup·per·ware /ˈtʌpɚˌwɛr/ *n.* [U] (trademark) a type of plastic container with a tight lid, used for storing food

tur·ban /ˈtɚbən/ *n.* [C] a long piece of cloth that is worn twisted around the top of your head

tur·bine /ˈtɚbaɪn, -bɪn/ *n.* [C] an engine that works when the pressure from a liquid or gas moves a special wheel around

tur·bu·lence /ˈtɚbyələns/ *n.* [U] **1** irregular and strong movements of air or water that are caused by the wind: *There was a lot of turbulence during the flight.* **2** a situation in which people's thoughts, actions, and emotions are always changing: *political turbulence*

tur·bu·lent /ˈtɚbyələnt/ *adj.* **1** experiencing a lot of sudden changes and often wars or violence: *The book is set during the turbulent years before the American Revolution.* **2** turbulent winds, oceans, etc. move around a lot with strong movements

turd /tɚd/ *n.* [C] (informal) a piece of solid brown waste passed from the body

tu·reen /tʊˈrin/ *n.* [C] a large dish with a lid, used especially for serving soup

turf /tɚf/ *n.* [U] **1** grass and soil on the ground's surface, or an artificial substance made to look like this: *thick green turf* **2** (informal) an area that someone knows well and feels that s/he controls or owns: *Davis's political turf*

tur·gid /ˈtɚdʒɪd/ *adj.* **1** boring and difficult to understand: *turgid poetry* **2** swollen, especially with liquid

tur·key /ˈtɚki/ *n.* [C,U] a bird similar to a chicken but larger, or the meat from this bird [ORIGIN: 1500—1600 *Turkey*; because the bird looked like the guinea fowl, which was brought into Europe through Turkey] → COLD TURKEY

tur·moil /ˈtɚmɔɪl/ *n.* [singular, U] a state of confusion, excitement, and trouble: *In 1967 the country* ***was in*** *racial* ***turmoil.***

T

turn[1] /tə·n/ *v.*

1 YOUR BODY [I] to move your body so that you are looking in a different direction: *Alison turned and walked away.* | ***Turn around*** *so I can zip you up.* | *He* ***turned to*** *look behind him.*

2 OBJECT [T] to move an object so that it is facing in a different direction: *She* ***turned*** *the box* ***around/over*** *to look at the label.* | *A boat was* ***turned upside down*** *on the beach.*

3 DIRECTION [I] **a)** to go in a new direction when you are walking, driving, etc.: *Turn right at the next light.* **b)** if a road, river, etc. turns, it curves and starts to go in a new direction: *Further on the river turns east.*

4 MOVE AROUND A CENTRAL POINT [I,T] to move around a central point that does not move: *The wheels turned slowly.*

THESAURUS

twist – to turn something using a circular movement: *She twisted her hair up into a bun.*
spin – to turn around and around very quickly: *Skaters were spinning on the ice.*
whirl – to turn around and around very quickly, or to make something do this: *the noise of the whirling fans*
twirl – to turn around and around or to make something do this, especially as part of a dance or performance: *Half a dozen couples were twirling to a waltz.*
swivel – to turn around while remaining in the same place, or to make something do this: *a desk chair that swivels*
go around – to move in a continuous circular movement: *The fans go around to move the air and cool the room.*
revolve – to turn around a central point: *The wheels began to revolve slowly.*
rotate – to turn or move around a particular point: *The Earth rotates every 24 hours.*

5 AGE [linking verb] to become a particular age: *Megan's just turned four.*

6 CHANGE [linking verb] to start to have a different quality than before: *The weather will turn colder.* | *The protests turned violent.* | *His hair is turning gray.* | *Helen turned bright red* (=because she was embarrassed).

7 PAGE [T] to move a page in a book or magazine so that you can see the next one

8 ATTENTION/THOUGHTS [I,T] to start to think about, deal with, look at, etc. a particular person, thing, or subject, instead of what you were thinking about, etc. before: *The reporters* ***turned*** *their* ***attention*** *to Dugan.* | *The conversation* ***turned to*** *events in Eastern Europe.*

9 turn your back (on sb/sth) to refuse to help or be involved with someone or something: *She wouldn't turn her back on her friends.*

10 turn over a new leaf to decide that you will change your behavior to make it better

11 turn a deaf ear/turn a blind eye to ignore what someone is saying or doing: *The administration turned a blind eye to the arms shipments.*

12 turn sb/sth loose to allow a person or animal to be free to do what she, he, or it wants

13 turn a profit to make a profit ➔ **turn your nose up (at sth)** *at* NOSE[1], **turn the tables (on sb)** *at* TABLE[1], **turn sth upside down** *at* UPSIDE DOWN

turn (sb) against sb/sth *phr. v.*
to make someone stop liking or agreeing with someone or something: *His experiences in Vietnam turned him against the war.*

turn around *phr. v.*
1 turn (sth ↔) **around** if a situation, business, game, etc. turns around, or if you turn it around, it changes and starts to become successful or to develop in the way you want: *The economy appears to be turning around.* | *They've turned the business around.*
2 turn around and say/do sth to say or do something that is unexpected or that seems unreasonable: *I don't want him to turn around and sue us.*

turn away *phr. v.*
1 turn sb ↔ **away** to refuse to let people into a theater, restaurant, etc. because it is too full: *By 6:00, we were turning people away.*
2 turn (sb ↔) **away** to refuse to give sympathy, help, or support: *The hospital will never turn a sick child away.* | *The U.S. cannot just* ***turn away from*** *the world's problems.*

turn back *phr. v.*
1 turn (sb ↔) **back** to go in the opposite direction, or to tell someone to do this: *Snow covered the trail, and we had to turn back.* | *The journalists were turned back at the border.*
2 to return to doing something in the way it was done before: *Once you've left her, there will be* ***no turning back.*** ➔ **turn/set the clock back** *at* CLOCK[1]

turn sb/sth ↔ down *phr. v.*
1 to make a machine such as a television, OVEN, etc. produce less sound, heat, etc.: *Turn the TV down!*
2 to refuse an offer, request, or invitation: *She was offered promotion, but turned it down.*

turn in *phr. v.*
1 turn sth ↔ **in** to give something to someone in authority: *They turned in a petition with more than 160,000 signatures.*
2 turn sth ↔ **in** to give work that you have done to your teacher: *Have you turned in your homework?*
3 turn sb ↔ **in** to tell the police where a criminal is
4 (informal) to go to bed: *I think I'll turn in.*

turn (sth) into sth *phr. v.*
to become something different, or to make someone or something do this: *The argument turned into a fight.* | *The witch turned the frog into a prince.*

turn off *phr. v.*
1 turn sth ↔ **off** to stop a supply of water, electricity, etc., especially so that a machine stops working: *Turn off the TV – it's dinner time.*
2 turn off sth to drive off one road and onto another, often a smaller one: *We turned off the highway looking for a place to eat.*

T

3 turn sb **off** to make someone decide that s/he does not like someone or something: *Many voters are turned off by politics.* ➔ TURNOFF

turn on *phr. v.*

1 turn sth ↔ **on** to make the supply of water, electricity, etc. begin to flow through a pipe, machine, etc., so that it starts working: *Alice turned on a light.*

2 turn on sb to suddenly attack someone physically or by using unpleasant words: *"That's right, cry!" he said, turning on me.*

turn out *phr. v.*

1 to happen in a particular way, or to have a particular result: *Luckily, everything* ***turned out okay/all right/fine/well.*** | ***It turned out that*** *we were right.* | *The trail* ***turned out to be*** *much rougher than they expected.*

2 turn sth ↔ **out** if you turn out a light, you push a button to stop the flow of electricity

3 if people turn out for an event, they go to it or take part in it: *Only about 30 people* ***turned out for*** *the show.* ➔ TURNOUT

4 turn sth ↔ **out** to produce or make something: *The factory turns out 100,000 trucks a year.*

5 turn sb **out** to make someone leave his/her home

turn over *phr. v.*

1 turn sth ↔ **over to** sb to give someone the right to own something such as a plan, business, piece of property, or to make him/her responsible for it: *Some of the work is being turned over to private firms.*

2 turn sb/sth ↔ **over** to bring a criminal or information to the police or another official organization: *Benson was* ***turned over to*** *the FBI yesterday.* | *The documents will be* ***turned over to*** *the IRS.*

3 turn over sth if a business turns over a particular amount of money, it makes that amount during a period of time ➔ TURNOVER

turn to *phr. v.*

1 turn to sb/sth to try to get help, advice, or sympathy from someone: *Biotechnology firms turned to Wall Street for financing.*

2 turn to sth to go to a particular page in a book, magazine, etc.: *Turn to page 45.*

3 turn to sth to begin thinking about or doing something new: *Bateman turned to politics after law school.*

4 turn (sth) **to** sth to become different in some way, or to make something do this: *The land is turning to desert.*

turn up *phr. v.*

1 turn sth ↔ **up** to make a machine such as a radio, OVEN, etc. produce more sound, heat, etc.: *Turn up the radio a little.*

2 to be found, especially by chance, after being searched for: *The keys turned up in the silverware drawer.*

3 turn sth ↔ **up** to find something by searching for it thoroughly: *An inspection of the brakes turned up no defects.*

4 to arrive: *Danny turned up late as usual.*

5 if an opportunity or situation turns up, it happens, especially when you are not expecting it: *Don't worry, a job will turn up soon.*

turn² *n.*

1 CHANCE TO DO STH [C] the time when it is your chance, duty, or right to do something that a group of people are doing, one after another: *Whose* ***turn*** *is it* ***to*** *set the table?* | ***It's*** *your* ***turn****, Bob.*

2 take turns if a group of people take turns doing something, one person does it, then another person does it, etc.: *We took turns driving.* | *Take turns on the swing!*

3 in turn a) one after another: *He spoke to each of the students in turn.* **b)** as a result of something: *Interest rates were cut, and in turn, share prices rose.*

4 CHANGE DIRECTION [C] a change in the direction you are moving in: ***Make a left/right turn*** *at the stop sign.*

5 TWO ROADS JOIN [C] a place where a road joins another road: *I think we missed our turn.* | ***Take*** *the second* ***turn*** *on the left.*

6 CHANGE IN EVENTS [C] a sudden or unexpected change that makes a situation develop in a different way: *Her health* ***took a turn for the worse/better.*** | *Monday's* ***turn of events*** *was an embarrassment for the administration.*

7 MOVE STH [C] the act of turning something: *Give the wheel another turn.*

8 the turn of the century the beginning of a century

9 do sb a good turn to help someone

turn·a·round /ˈtɚnəˌraʊnd/ *n.* [singular] **1** an important and complete change from a bad situation to a good one: *Brock has been key to the team's turnaround.* **2** the time it takes to receive something, deal with it, and send it back: *What is the* ***turnaround time*** *on maintenance requests?*

turn·coat /ˈtɚnkoʊt/ *n.* [C] someone who stops supporting a political party or group and joins the opposite group

ˈturning point *n.* [C] the time when an important change starts to happen: *The win was a* ***turning point in*** *his athletic career.*

tur·nip /ˈtɚnɪp/ *n.* [C,U] a large round pale yellow or white root, cooked and eaten as a vegetable

turn·off, turn-off /ˈtɚnɔf/ *n.* [C] **1** a smaller road that leads off a main road: *Take the Ramsey Canyon turnoff.* **2** something that makes you dislike or lose interest in something, usually sex

turn·out /ˈtɚnaʊt/ *n.* [singular] the number of people who go to an event such as a party, meeting, or election: *Voter turnout was 93%.*

turn·o·ver /ˈtɚnˌoʊvɚ/ *n.* **1** [singular] the amount of money a business earns in a particular period: *an annual turnover of $35 million* **2** [U] the rate at which people leave an organization and are replaced by others: *The company has a high rate of turnover.* **3** [C] a small fruit PIE: *apple turnovers*

turn·pike /ˈtɚnpaɪk/ *n.* [C] a main road that you have to pay a TOLL to use [ORIGIN: 1700—1800

T

turnpike road (18—20 centuries), from *turnpike* "turning post with sharp points fixed into it, used to control movement past it"]

THESAURUS road, street, highway, freeway, expressway → ROAD

ˈturn ˌsignal *n.* [C] one of the lights on a vehicle that flash to show which way the vehicle is turning

turn·stile /ˈtɚnstaɪl/ *n.* [C] a gate that spins around and only lets one person through at a time

turn·ta·ble /ˈtɚnˌteɪbəl/ *n.* [C] a piece of equipment used for playing records

tur·pen·tine /ˈtɚpənˌtaɪn/ *n.* [U] a strong-smelling oil used for removing paint

tur·pi·tude /ˈtɚpətud/ *n.* [U] (literary) evil: *He was criticized for his* ***moral turpitude***.

tur·quoise /ˈtɚkwɔɪz, -kɔɪz/ *n.* [U] a bright blue-green color [ORIGIN: 1400—1500 Old French *turqueise*, from *turqueis* "Turkish"] —**turquoise** *adj.*

tur·ret /ˈtɚɪt, ˈtʌrɪt/ *n.* [C] a small tower on a large building, especially a castle

tur·tle /ˈtɚṭl/ *n.* [C] a REPTILE (=type of animal) that has four legs and a soft body covered with a hard shell

tur·tle·neck /ˈtɚṭlˌnɛk/ *n.* [C] a type of shirt or SWEATER with a high close-fitting collar that covers most of your neck

T

tush /tʊʃ/ *n.* [C] (informal) the part of your body that you sit on

tusk /tʌsk/ *n.* [C] one of the two very long teeth that stick out of an animal's mouth, for example an ELEPHANT'S

tus·sle /ˈtʌsəl/ *n.* [C] a struggle or fight —**tussle** *v.* [I]

tu·tor /ˈtuṭɚ/ *n.* [C] someone who is paid to teach only one or a few students, especially students who are having difficulty with a subject: *my French tutor* [ORIGIN: 1300—1400 Latin *tutus*, past participle of *tueri* "to look at, guard"] —**tutor** *v.* [T]: *He's tutoring me in math.*

tu·to·ri·al /tuˈtɔriəl/ *adj.* relating to a TUTOR or the teaching that s/he does

tux·e·do /tʌkˈsidoʊ/ *also* **tux** /tʌks/ *n.* (plural **tuxedos**) [C] a man's suit that is usually black, worn on formal occasions [ORIGIN: 1800—1900 *Tuxedo* Park, town in New York State]

TV *n.* [C,U] television: *What's* ***on TV****? | The kids were* ***watching TV****. | Sue just bought a new TV. | a good* ***TV show/program/series***

ˌTV ˈdinner *n.* [C] a frozen prepared meal you can buy from the store, that you heat up and eat at home

ˈTV set *n.* [C] a television

twang /twæŋ/ *n.* [C usually singular] **1** a quality in the way someone speaks, when the sound comes through the nose as well as the mouth **2** a short ringing sound like the one made by pulling a tight string and quickly letting it go —**twang** *v.* [I,T]

twas /twʌz/ (literary) it was – used in past times

tweak /twik/ *v.* [T] **1** to make small changes to something in order to improve it: *Congress has tweaked the tax system again.* **2** to quickly pull or twist something: *Grandpa tweaked my nose.*

tweed /twid/ *n.* [U] a rough wool cloth used especially for making JACKETS

tweet /twit/ *v.* [I] to make a quick high sound like a small bird —**tweet** *n.* [C]

tweez·ers /ˈtwizɚz/ *n.* [plural] a small tool made from two thin pieces of metal joined at one end, used in order to pull or move very small objects: *a* ***pair of tweezers***

twelfth /twɛlfθ/ *number* **1** 12th **2** one of twelve equal parts of something

twelve /twɛlv/ *number* **1** 12 **2** 12 o'clock: *I'm going to lunch at twelve.* **3** 12 years old: *He's twelve.* [ORIGIN: Old English *twelf*]

ˌtwelve-bar ˈblues *n.* [U] ENG. LANG. ARTS a series of CHORDS that does not repeat itself until 12 BARS have been played. It is the most common musical form used in BLUES music.

ˌtwelve-tone ˈscale *n.* [C] ENG. LANG. ARTS a musical scale consisting of 12 notes, counting both the black and white keys on a piano. It is based on dividing an OCTAVE into 12 exactly equal INTERVALS.

twen·ty¹ /ˈtwɛnti/ *number* **1** 20 **2** 20 years old: *She's almost twenty.* **3 the twenties a)** the years between 1920 and 1929 **b)** the numbers between 20 and 29, especially when used for measuring temperature **4 sb's twenties** the time when someone is 20 to 29 years old: *a woman in her* ***early/late twenties*** [ORIGIN: Old English *twentig*] —**twentieth** *number*

twenty² *n.* (plural **twenties**) [C] a piece of paper money worth $20

ˌtwenty-four/ˈseven *usually written as* **24/7** *adv.* (informal) if something happens twenty-four/seven, it happens all day, every day

ˌtwenty-ˈone *n.* [U] BLACKJACK

twerp /twɚp/ *n.* [C] (spoken) a stupid or annoying person

twice /twaɪs/ *adv.* two times: *I've seen that movie twice. | The island is twice the size of Massachusetts. | He makes* ***twice as*** *much money as I do.* → TWO

twid·dle /ˈtwɪdl/ *v.* [T] to move your fingers around, or to turn something with them many times, usually because you are bored

twig /twɪg/ *n.* [C] a very thin branch that grows on a larger branch of a tree

twi·light /ˈtwaɪlaɪt/ *n.* [U] the time between day and night when the sky starts to become dark, or the pale light at this time

twins

identical twins

twin¹ /twɪn/ *n.* [C] one of two children who are born at the same time to the same mother: *Jenny and Julie are **identical twins*** (=twins who look exactly the same). | *I have a twin brother.*

twin² *adj.* **1** like something else and considered with it as a pair: *the jet's twin engines* **2** used in order to describe two things that happen at the same time and are related to each other: *the twin problems of poverty and unemployment*

ˌtwin 'bed *n.* [C] a bed for one person

twine¹ /twaɪn/ *n.* [U] thick strong string

twine² *v.* [I,T] to twist something, or to twist around something: *Morning glories had **twined around** the fence.*

twinge /twɪndʒ/ *n.* [C] **1** a sudden pain **2 a twinge of guilt/fear/jealousy etc.** a sudden slight feeling of guilt, fear, etc.: *He felt **a twinge of guilt** for not calling.*

twin·kle /ˈtwɪŋkəl/ *v.* [I] **1** if a star or light twinkles, it shines in the dark with an unsteady light

THESAURUS **shine, flash, flicker, sparkle, shimmer, glint, glisten** → SHINE¹

2 if someone's eyes twinkle, s/he has a happy expression: *Her eyes **twinkled with** amusement.* —**twinkle** *n.* [C usually singular]

twirl /twɚl/ *v.* [I,T] to continue turning around quickly, or to make something do this: *Dancers were twirling on stage.* —**twirl** *n.* [C]

THESAURUS **turn, twist, spin, whirl, swivel, go around, revolve, rotate** → TURN¹

twist¹ /twɪst/ *v.* **1** [I,T] to bend, turn, or wind something using a circular movement, especially something such as wire, hair, or cloth: *Twist the ends together.* | *The sheets were **twisted** tightly **around** him.* | ***Twist off** the bottle cap* (=remove it by twisting).

THESAURUS **turn, spin, whirl, twirl, rotate** → TURN¹

2 [I,T] to turn a part of your body around or change your position by turning: *He **twisted around** to look at me.* | ***I twisted my ankle*** (=hurt it by turning it in the wrong direction) *playing soccer.* → HURT¹ **3** [T] to change the true or intended meaning of someone's statement (SYN) **distort, misrepresent**: *He accused her of twisting his words for political reasons.* **4** [I] if a road, river, etc. twists, it has a lot of curves in it **5 twist sb's arm** (informal) to persuade someone to do something that s/he does not want to do

twist² *n.* [C] **1** an unexpected change in a story or situation: *The lemon grass gives a new **twist on/to** a classic dish.* **2** something that is twisted into a shape: *pasta twists* **3** a bend in a road, river, etc.

twist·ed /ˈtwɪstɪd/ *adj.* **1** bent in many directions or turned many times: *twisted metal* → *see picture at* BENT²

THESAURUS **bent, curved, warped, crooked** → BENT²

2 strange and slightly cruel: *a twisted joke*

twist·er /ˈtwɪstɚ/ *n.* [C] (informal) a TORNADO

twit /twɪt/ *n.* [C] (spoken) a stupid or silly person

twitch /twɪtʃ/ *v.* [I] if a part of your body twitches, it makes a sudden small uncontrolled movement: *A muscle near his mouth twitched.* —**twitch** *n.* [C]

twit·ter /ˈtwɪtɚ/ *v.* [I] if a bird twitters, it makes a lot of short high sounds —**twitter** *n.* [singular]

two /tu/ *number* **1** 2

THESAURUS

a pair (of sth) – two things of the same type that you use together: *a pair of shoes*
a couple (of sth) – two things of the same type: *a couple of stamps*
a couple – two people who are married or have a romantic relationship: *a married couple*
twins – two children who were born on the same day to the same mother
double room/bed etc. – a room, bed, etc. for two people
twice – two times: *I phoned her twice yesterday.*
for two – for two people: *A table for two, please.*

2 two o'clock: *The game begins **at two**.* **3** two years old: *My daughter is two.* [ORIGIN: Old English *twa*]

'two-bit *adj.* (slang) not very good or important: *a two-bit actor*

ˌtwo-by-'four *n.* [C] a long piece of wood that is two inches thick and four inches wide

ˌtwo-di'mensional *adj.* flat, having length and height, but no depth → THREE-DIMENSIONAL: *a two-dimensional drawing*

ˌtwo-'faced *adj.* (informal, disapproving) changing what you say according to who you are talking to, in a way that is not honest or sincere

two·fold /ˈtufoʊld/ *adj.* two times as much or as many of something: *a twofold increase in cases of TB* —**twofold** *adv.*

'two-piece *adj.* a two-piece suit has a coat and pants that match

two·some /ˈtusəm/ *n.* [C] a group of two people

ˈtwo-time *v.* [T] (informal) to have a secret relationship with someone who is not your regular girlfriend, husband, etc.

ˈtwo-tone *adj.* having two different colors

ˌtwo-ˈway *adj.* **1** moving or allowing movement in both directions: *two-way traffic* **2** a two-way radio sends and receives messages **3** involving two people, groups, countries, etc., in such a way that each person, etc. is doing something with the other: *two-way trade*

TX the written abbreviation of TEXAS

ty·coon /taɪˈkun/ *n.* [C] someone who is very successful in business and has a lot of money: *an oil tycoon*

ty·ing /ˈtaɪ-ɪŋ/ *v.* the present participle of TIE

tyke /taɪk/ *n.* [C] (informal) a small child

tym·pan·ic mem·brane /tɪmˌpænɪk ˈmɛmbreɪn/ *n.* [C] BIOLOGY the EARDRUM or a similar part in animals or insects

type¹ /taɪp/ *n.* **1** [C] a group of people or things that have similar features or qualities, and that are different from other people or things: *different **types of** people* | *What's your blood type?* | *Romantic novels **of this type** sell well.*

THESAURUS

kind – a slightly more informal word for type: *What kind of fish is this?*
sort – a slightly more informal word for type: *They carry all sorts of toys for indoor and outdoor play.*
category – a group of people or things that are all of the same type: *The novels are divided into three categories: romances, mysteries, and science fiction.*
brand – a type of produce made by a particular company: *several different brands of soap*
make – a type of product made by a particular company: *"What make of car do you drive?" "A Ford."*
model – one particular type or design of a vehicle, machine, weapon, etc.: *The new models come out in September.*
genre – a type of art, music, literature, etc. that has a particular style or feature: *He has written novels in several genres, most notably science fiction.*
variety – a particular type of something that is different from other things of a particular kind: *different varieties of apples*
species – a group of animals or plants of the same type that can breed with each other: *three species of deer*

2 [C] someone with particular qualities, interests, appearance, etc.: *the athletic type* **3 not be sb's type** (informal) to not be the kind of person that someone is attracted to: *Alex is OK – but he's not really my type.* **4** [U] printed letters: *italic type*

type² *v.* [I,T] to write something using a computer or TYPEWRITER

type·cast /ˈtaɪpkæst/ *v.* (past tense and past participle **typecast**) [T] to always give an actor the same type of character to play: *He does not want to **be typecast as** a bad guy.*

type·face /ˈtaɪpfeɪs/ *n.* [C] a group of letters, numbers, etc. of the same style and size, used in printing

type·writ·er /ˈtaɪpˌraɪṭɚ/ *n.* [C] a machine that prints letters, numbers, etc. onto paper → PRINTER

type·writ·ten /ˈtaɪpˌrɪtˀn/ *adj.* written using a typewriter: *a typewritten manuscript*

ty·phoid /ˈtaɪfɔɪd/ *also* **ˌtyphoid ˈfever** *n.* [U] BIOLOGY a serious infectious disease that is caused by BACTERIA in food or water

ty·phoon /taɪˈfun/ *n.* [C] EARTH SCIENCES a very violent storm in tropical areas in which the wind moves in circles at speeds of over 74 miles per hour [ORIGIN: 1800—1900 *touffan* "typhoon" (16—19 centuries), from Arabic *tufan* "hurricane;" influenced by Chinese *daai fong* "great wind"]

THESAURUS **wind, gale, storm, hurricane, tornado** → WIND¹

ty·phus /ˈtaɪfəs/ *n.* [U] BIOLOGY a serious infectious disease that is caused by the bite of an insect

typ·i·cal /ˈtɪpɪkəl/ *adj.* **1** having the usual features or qualities of a particular thing, person, or group: *the typical American diet* | *At age 2, the typical child talks in two-word sentences.* | *Cool weather is **typical of** early April.* **2 (that's) typical!** (spoken) said when you are annoyed that something bad has happened again: *The car won't start – typical!*

typ·i·cally /ˈtɪpɪkli/ *adv.* **1** in the way that something usually happens: *Summer classes typically last six weeks.* **2** in the way that a person or group usually behaves, or that shows the usual features of something: *The female is typically smaller than the male.*

typ·i·fy /ˈtɪpəˌfaɪ/ *v.* (**typified**, **typifies**) [T] to be a typical example or feature of something: *This is one of the dark paintings that typify her work.*

typ·ing /ˈtaɪpɪŋ/ *n.* [U] the activity of writing using a TYPEWRITER or KEYBOARD

typ·ist /ˈtaɪpɪst/ *n.* [C] someone who uses a TYPEWRITER or KEYBOARD

ty·po /ˈtaɪpoʊ/ *n.* [C] (informal) a small mistake in the way something has been TYPEd or printed

ty·ran·ni·cal /tɪˈrænɪkəl/ *adj.* behaving in an unfair or cruel way toward someone you have power over: *a brutal and tyrannical government* —**tyrannize** /ˈtɪrəˌnaɪz/ *v.* [T]

tyr·an·ny /ˈtɪrəni/ *n.* (plural **tyrannies**) **1** [U] strict, unfair, and often cruel control over someone: *her husband's abusive tyranny* **2** [C,U] POLITICS government by a cruel ruler who has complete power: *The country suffered decades of tyranny.*

ty·rant /ˈtaɪrənt/ *n.* [C] someone, especially a ruler, who uses his/her power in an unfair or cruel way

tzar /zɑr, tsɑr/ *n.* [C] a CZAR

Uu

U, u /yu/ the twenty-first letter of the English alphabet

u·biq·ui·tous /yuˈbɪkwət̬əs/ *adj.* (formal) seeming to be everywhere: *New York's ubiquitous yellow cabs* —**ubiquity** *n.* [U]

ud·der /ˈʌdɚ/ *n.* [C] BIOLOGY the part of a cow, female goat, etc. that produces milk

UFO *n.* [C] **Unidentified Flying Object** a strange moving object in the sky that some people believe is a SPACESHIP from another world

ugh /ʌg, ʌk, ʌh/ *interjection* used in order to show strong dislike: *Ugh! That tastes terrible!*

ug·ly /ˈʌgli/ *adj.* (comparative **uglier**, superlative **ugliest**) **1** very unattractive, and not nice to look at: *an ugly building* | *She's not pretty, but she's not ugly either.*

THESAURUS

unattractive – an unattractive person or thing is not pleasing to look at: *He always thought he was unattractive to women.* | *a dirty and unattractive building*
unsightly (formal) – an unsightly mark, building, etc. is not pleasing to look at: *The illness can cause unsightly marks on the skin.*
hideous – extremely ugly: *She was wearing a hideous purple and orange sweater.*
repulsive – having an ugly or unpleasant appearance that makes people feel uncomfortable: *There was something rather repulsive about him.*
grotesque – extremely ugly in a strange or unnatural way: *The movie was full of grotesque images of violence.*
be an eyesore – if a place or building is an eyesore, it is very ugly: *The garbage dump is an eyesore.*

2 very unpleasant or violent in a way that makes you feel frightened: *The game **turned ugly** as fans threw things at the players.* | *an **ugly scene** at the bus stop* [ORIGIN: 1200—1300 Old Norse *uggligr* "frightening," from *uggr* "fear"] —**ugliness** *n.* [U]

uh /ʌ/ *interjection* said when you are deciding what to say next: *I, uh, I'm sorry I'm late.*

UHF *n.* [U] **ultra-high frequency** a range of radio waves that produces very good sound quality

uh huh /nˈhn, mˈhm, əˈhʌ/ *interjection* (informal) used in order to say yes or to show that you understand something: *"Is this the one you want?" "Uh huh."*

uh oh /ˈˀʌ ˀoʊ/ *interjection* (informal) said when you have made a mistake or have realized that something bad has happened: *Uh oh, I forgot my keys.*

uh uh /ˈˀʌn ˀʌn, ˈˀmˀm/ *interjection* (informal) used in order to say no: *"Did Ann call?" "Uh uh."*

ul·cer /ˈʌlsɚ/ *n.* [C] a sore area on your skin or inside your body: *a stomach ulcer*

ul·na /ˈʌlnə/ *n.* [C] BIOLOGY one of the two bones in your lower arm, on the side opposite your thumb → RADIUS

ul·te·ri·or /ʌlˈtɪriɚ/ *adj.* **ulterior motive/purpose/reason** a reason for doing something that you deliberately hide in order to get an advantage for yourself: *He's just being nice. I don't think he **has any ulterior motives**.*

ul·ti·mate[1] /ˈʌltəmɪt/ (Ac) *adj.* [only before noun] **1** an ultimate purpose, aim, reason, etc. is the final and most important one: *Her **ultimate goal** is a career in politics.* **2** better, bigger, worse, etc. than all other people or things of the same kind: *A Rolls Royce is the ultimate symbol of wealth.* **3** the ultimate result of a long process is what happens at the end of it: *the ultimate failure of the project* **4** an ultimate decision, responsibility, etc. is one that you cannot pass on to someone else: *Who has the ultimate authority in the family?* [ORIGIN: 1600—1700 Late Latin *ultimatus* "last," from *ultimare* "to come to an end, be last"]

ultimate[2] *n.* **the ultimate in sth** the best or most modern example of something: *The Orient Express is the ultimate in rail travel.*

ul·ti·mate·ly /ˈʌltəmɪtli/ (Ac) *adv.* **1** [sentence adverb] after everything else has been done or considered: *Ultimately it's your decision.* | *Their efforts ultimately resulted in his release from prison.* **2** being the person responsible for important final decisions: *In most families, the mother is ultimately responsible for the children.*

ul·ti·ma·tum /ˌʌltəˈmeɪt̬əm/ *n.* [C] a statement saying that if someone does not do what you want, s/he will be punished: *She finally **gave** him **an ultimatum**: either stop drinking or move out.*

ul·tra·son·ic /ˌʌltrəˈsɑnɪk◂/ *adj.* PHYSICS ultrasonic sounds are too high for humans to hear, and ultrasonic sound waves measure more than 20,000 Hertz

ul·tra·sound /ˈʌltrəˌsaʊnd/ *n.* [C,U] a medical process that uses sound waves to produce images of something inside of your body

U

ul·tra·vi·o·let /ˌʌltrəˈvaɪəlɪt◂/ *adj.* PHYSICS ultraviolet light cannot be seen but makes your skin darker when you are in the sun

um /m, əm/ *interjection* said when you are deciding what to say next: *Um, yeah, I guess so.*

um·bil·i·cal cord /ʌmˈbɪlɪkəl ˌkɔrd/ *n.* [C] BIOLOGY a tube that joins a baby that has not been born yet to its mother

um·brage /ˈʌmbrɪdʒ/ *n.* **take umbrage (at sth)** (formal) to be offended by something that someone has done or said

um·brel·la /ʌmˈbrɛlə/ *n.* [C] an object that you hold above your head to protect yourself from the rain: *He stood there under his umbrella, watching the rain.* [ORIGIN: 1600—1700 Italian *ombrella*, from Latin *umbella*, from *umbra* "shade, shadow"]

um·laut /ˈumlaʊt, ˈʊm-/ *n.* [C] ENG. LANG. ARTS a sign written like two periods over a vowel in German and some other languages to show how it is pronounced, for example ü

ump /ʌmp/ *n.* [C] (spoken, informal) an umpire

um·pire /ˈʌmpaɪɚ/ *n.* [C] the person who makes sure that the players obey the rules in sports such as baseball and tennis —**umpire** *v.* [I,T] → REFEREE[1]

ump·teenth /ˈʌmptinθ, ˌʌmˈtinθ/ *quantifier* (informal, disapproving) if something happens for the umpteenth time, it happens too many times: *They're showing "The Wizard of Oz" **for the umpteenth time**.* —**umpteen** *quantifier*

U

UN *n.* **the United Nations** an international organization that tries to find peaceful solutions to world problems

un·a·bashed /ˌʌnəˈbæʃt◂/ *adj.* not shy or embarrassed: *the child's unabashed curiosity*

un·a·bat·ed /ˌʌnəˈbeɪt̬ɪd/ *adj.* continuing without becoming weaker or less violent: *The storm **continued unabated**.*

un·a·ble /ʌnˈeɪbəl/ *adj.* not able to do something → INABILITY: *She was **unable to** sleep.* | *I'm sorry; I'm unable to help you.*

un·a·bridged /ˌʌnəˈbrɪdʒd◂/ *adj.* a piece of writing, speech, etc. that is unabridged has not been made shorter

un·ac·cept·a·ble /ˌʌnəkˈsɛptəbəl/ *adj.* something that is unacceptable is wrong or bad and should not be allowed to continue: *Nancy's behavior is unacceptable.* —**unacceptably** *adv.*

un·ac·com·pa·nied /ˌʌnəˈkʌmpənid/ (Ac) *adj.* having no one with you: *an unaccompanied child*

un·ac·count·a·ble /ˌʌnəˈkaʊntəbəl/ *adj.* **1** not having to explain your actions or decisions to anyone else **2** very surprising and difficult to explain: *It was a good product that flopped for unaccountable reasons.* —**unaccountably** *adv.*

un·ac·cus·tomed /ˌʌnəˈkʌstəmd◂/ *adj.* (formal) **1 unaccustomed to (doing) sth** not used to something: *He was unaccustomed to dealing with children.* **2** [only before noun] not usual, typical, or familiar: *This winter's unaccustomed warmth prompted questions about global warming.*

un·a·dul·ter·at·ed /ˌʌnəˈdʌltəˌreɪt̬ɪd/ *adj.* complete or pure: *pure unadulterated pleasure*

un·af·fect·ed /ˌʌnəˈfɛktɪd/ (Ac) *adj.* not changed or influenced by something: *Parts of the city remained **unaffected by** the fire.*

un·aid·ed /ʌnˈeɪdɪd/ (Ac) *adj.* without help: *He could not stand up unaided.*

> THESAURUS **on your own, (all) by yourself, independently** → ALONE

un·al·i·en·a·ble /ʌnˈeɪliənəbəl, -lyə-/ *adj.* INALIENABLE

un·al·ter·a·ble /ʌnˈɔltərəbəl/ (Ac) *adj.* not able to be changed: *an unalterable decision*

un·al·tered /ʌnˈɔltɚd/ *adj.* not changed

un·am·big·u·ous /ˌʌnæmˈbɪgyuəs/ (Ac) *adj.* very clear and not confusing: *an unambiguous answer* —**unambiguously** *adv.*

un-A'merican *adj.* not supporting or loyal to American customs, ideas, etc.

u·nan·i·mous /yuˈnænəməs/ *adj.* a unanimous decision, vote, etc. is one on which everyone agrees → AGREE —**unanimously** *adv.* —**unanimity** /ˌyunæˈnɪmət̬i/ *n.* [U]

un·an·nounced /ˌʌnəˈnaʊnst◂/ *adj., adv.* happening without anyone knowing about it or expecting it: *Several people arrived unannounced.* | *an unannounced visit*

un·an·swered /ˌʌnˈænsɚd/ *adj.* an unanswered telephone call, letter, question, etc. has not been replied to

un·an·tic·i·pat·ed /ˌʌnænˈtɪsəˌpeɪt̬ɪd/ *adj.* not expected: *an unanticipated expense*

un·ap·peal·ing /ˌʌnəˈpilɪŋ◂/ *adj.* not pleasant or attractive: *an unappealing brown color*

un·ap·pre·ci·at·ed /ˌʌnəˈpriʃiˌeɪt̬ɪd/ *adj.* if someone or something is unappreciated, people do not recognize their good qualities or value: *Some of the workers felt unappreciated.*

un·ap·proach·a·ble /ˌʌnəˈproʊtʃəbəl/ *adj.* seeming unfriendly and therefore difficult to talk to: *a silent and unapproachable man*

un·armed /ˌʌnˈɑrmd◂/ *adj.* not carrying any weapons: *An officer shot an unarmed man.*

un·as·sist·ed /ˌʌnəˈsɪstɪd/ (Ac) *adj.* without help: *She was able to walk unassisted.*

un·as·sum·ing /ˌʌnəˈsumɪŋ◂/ *adj.* quiet and showing no desire for attention (SYN) **modest**

un·at·tached /ˌʌnəˈtætʃt◂/ (Ac) *adj.* **1** not involved in a romantic relationship **2** not fastened or connected to anything

un·at·tain·a·ble /ˌʌnəˈteɪnəbəl/ (Ac) *adj.* impossible to achieve: *an unattainable goal*

un·at·tend·ed /ˌʌnəˈtɛndɪd◂/ *adj.* left alone without anyone in charge: *Do not* ***leave*** *your children* ***unattended.***

un·at·trac·tive /ˌʌnəˈtræktɪv◂/ *adj.* **1** not physically attractive or beautiful

THESAURUS **ugly, unsightly, hideous** → UGLY

2 not good or desirable: *two unattractive options*

un·au·thor·ized /ʌnˈɔθəˌraɪzd/ *adj.* done without official approval or permission: *an unauthorized biography*

un·a·vail·a·ble /ˌʌnəˈveɪləbəl/ (Ac) *adj.* **1** not able to be obtained: *The album was previously unavailable on CD.* **2** not able or willing to meet with someone: *Mr. Foster is* ***unavailable for comment*** (=not able or willing to speak to reporters).

un·a·void·a·ble /ˌʌnəˈvɔɪdəbəl/ *adj.* impossible to prevent: *an unavoidable delay*

un·a·ware /ˌʌnəˈwɛr/ (Ac) *adj.* not noticing or realizing what is happening: *He was* ***unaware of*** *his legal rights.*

un·a·wares /ˌʌnəˈwɛrz/ *adv.* **catch/take sb unawares** if something catches you unawares, it happens when you are not prepared for it: *Events in the Middle East caught the CIA unawares.*

un·bal·anced /ʌnˈbælənst/ *adj.* **1** slightly crazy: *mentally unbalanced* **2** an unbalanced report, argument, etc. is unfair because it emphasizes one opinion too much

un·bear·a·ble /ʌnˈbɛrəbəl/ *adj.* too bad, painful, or annoying for you to deal with: *Her pain had become unbearable.* —**unbearably** *adv.*

un·beat·a·ble /ʌnˈbit̬əbəl/ *adj.* something that is unbeatable is the best of its kind: *unbeatable prices*

un·beat·en /ʌnˈbitˀn/ *adj.* a team, player, etc. that is unbeaten has not been defeated

un·be·liev·a·ble /ˌʌnbɪˈlivəbəl/ *adj.* **1** used to emphasize how good, bad, surprising, etc. something is: *The sound quality of this stereo is unbelievable.* | *an unbelievable amount of money* **2** very difficult to believe and probably not true: *Yvonne's excuse was totally unbelievable.* —**unbelievably** *adv.*

un·bi·ased /ʌnˈbaɪəst/ (Ac) *adj.* unbiased information, opinion, advice, etc. is fair because the person giving it is not influenced by their own or other people's opinions (SYN) **impartial**: *We aim to provide a service that is balanced and unbiased.* | *an unbiased observer*

THESAURUS **fair, impartial** → FAIR[1]

un·born /ˌʌnˈbɔrn◂/ *adj.* [only before noun] not yet born: *an unborn child*

un·bound·ed /ˌʌnˈbaʊndɪd/ *adj.* (formal) very great and seeming to have no limit: *unbounded optimism*

un·bri·dled /ˌʌnˈbraɪdld/ *adj.* not controlled and too extreme: *unbridled anger*

un·but·ton /ʌnˈbʌtˀn/ *v.* [T] to undo the buttons on a piece of clothing

un·called-for /ʌnˈkɔld ˌfɔr/ *adj.* behavior or remarks that are uncalled-for are insulting, unfair, or inappropriate

un·can·ny /ʌnˈkæni/ *adj.* very strange and difficult to explain: *The team has an* ***uncanny ability*** *to win close games.* —**uncannily** *adv.*

un·cer·tain /ʌnˈsɚtˀn/ *adj.* **1** feeling doubt about something: *I'm* ***uncertain about*** *what to say to her.* | *She was* ***uncertain of*** *whether to confront him.* **2** not clear, definite, or decided: *His* ***future*** *with the company* ***is uncertain.*** **3 in no uncertain terms** if you say something in no uncertain terms, you say it in a clear way, without trying to be polite: *We were told in no uncertain terms not to come back.* —**uncertainty** *n.* [C,U]: *uncertainty about the future* —**uncertainly** *adv.*

un·chang·ing /ʌnˈtʃeɪndʒɪŋ/ *also* **un·changed** /ʌnˈtʃeɪndʒd/ *adj.* always staying the same

un·chart·ed /ʌnˈtʃɑrt̬ɪd/ (Ac) *adj.* **uncharted territory/waters** a situation or activity that you have never experienced or tried before

un·checked /ˌʌnˈtʃɛkt◂/ *adj.* if something bad goes unchecked, it is not controlled or stopped and continues or gets worse: ***Left unchecked,*** *the disease will spread.*

un·civ·i·lized /ʌnˈsɪvəˌlaɪzd/ *adj.* **1** behavior that is uncivilized is rude or socially unacceptable **2** (old-fashioned) societies that are uncivilized have a very simple way of life (SYN) **primitive**

U

un·cle /ˈʌŋkəl/ *n.* [C] the brother of your mother or father, or the husband of your AUNT: *I went to stay with my aunt and uncle for a few days.* | *Uncle Bill* [ORIGIN: 1200—1300 Old French, Latin *avunculus* "mother's brother"]

un·clean /ˌʌnˈklin◂/ *adj.* dirty

un·clear /ˌʌnˈklɪr◂/ *adj.* difficult to understand or know about: *The terms of the contract are very unclear.*

Uncle Sam /ˌʌŋkəl ˈsæm/ *n.* (informal) the U.S., or U.S. government, usually represented by the figure of a man with a white BEARD and tall hat

Uncle Tom /ˌʌŋkəl ˈtɑm/ *n.* [C] (disapproving) a black person who is too respectful to white people

un·com·fort·a·ble /ʌnˈkʌmftəbəl, ʌnˈkʌmfɚt̬əbəl/ *adj.* **1** not feeling physically comfortable, or not making you feel comfortable: *These shoes are uncomfortable.* **2** unable to relax because you are embarrassed: *I feel uncomfortable talking about sex.* | *an uncomfortable silence* —**uncomfortably** *adv.*

un·com·mon /ʌnˈkɑmən/ *adj.* rare or unusual: ***It is not uncommon for*** (=it is fairly common for) *employees* ***to*** *work sixty hours a week.* —**uncommonly** *adv.*

un·com·pro·mis·ing /ʌn'kɑmprə,maɪzɪŋ/ *adj.* determined not to change your opinions or intentions: *He has always been an uncompromising supporter of gun control.*

un·con·cerned /,ʌnkən'sɚnd◂ / *adj.* not worried about something, or not interested in it: *Americans cannot be* ***unconcerned about*** *the problem of the world's poor.*

un·con·di·tion·al /,ʌnkən'dɪʃənəl◂ / *adj.* not limited by or depending on any conditions: *We are demanding the unconditional release of the hostages.* **—unconditionally** *adv.*

un·con·firmed /,ʌnkən'fɚmd◂ / *adj.* not proved or supported by official information: *There has been an* ***unconfirmed report/rumor etc.*** *of a nuclear accident.*

un·con·scion·a·ble /ʌn'kɑnʃənəbəl/ *adj.* (formal) morally wrong or unacceptable

un·con·scious¹ /,ʌn'kɑnʃəs◂ / *adj.* **1** unable to see, move, feel, etc. because you are not conscious: *The car's driver was* ***knocked unconscious.*** **2** an unconscious feeling is one that you have without realizing it (SYN) **subconscious**: *unconscious feelings of guilt* **3 be unconscious of sth** to not realize the effect of something you have said or done: *Barb seemed unconscious of the attention her dress was attracting.* **—unconsciously** *adv.* **—unconsciousness** *n.* [U]

unconscious² *n.* **the/sb's unconscious** the part of your mind in which there are thoughts and feelings that you do not realize that you have ➔ SUBCONSCIOUS

U

un·con·sti·tu·tion·al /,ʌnkɑnstə'tuʃənəl/ (Ac) *adj.* not allowed by the rules that govern a country or organization: *The Supreme Court ruled that the law was unconstitutional.*

un·con·trol·la·ble /,ʌnkən'troʊləbəl/ *adj.* impossible to control or stop: *uncontrollable rage*

un·con·trolled /,ʌnkən'troʊld/ *adj.* **1** uncontrolled emotions or behavior continue because no one stops or controls them **2** without rules or laws: *an uncontrolled free market*

un·con·ven·tion·al /,ʌnkən'vɛnʃənəl/ (Ac) *adj.* very different from the normal way people behave, think, dress, or do things: *his unconventional lifestyle*

un·con·vinc·ed /,ʌnkən'vɪnst/ (Ac) *adj.* not persuaded that something is right or true: *He was unconvinced that the idea would work.*

THESAURUS **doubtful, dubious, skeptical**
➔ DOUBTFUL

un·cool /,ʌn'kul◂ / *adj.* (slang) not fashionable or acceptable: *My parents are hopelessly uncool.*

un·co·op·era·tive /,ʌnkoʊ'ɑprət̬ɪv◂ / *adj.* not willing to work with or help someone

un·count·a·ble /ʌn'kaʊntəbəl/ *adj.* **uncountable noun** ENG. LANG. ARTS in grammar, a noun that has no plural form, such as "water," "gold," or "furniture" (ANT) **countable**

un·couth /ʌn'kuθ/ *adj.* behaving or speaking in a way that is rude and unacceptable

un·cov·er /ʌn'kʌvɚ/ *v.* [T] **1** to discover something that has been kept secret or hidden: *Customs officials uncovered a plot to smuggle drugs into the country.* **2** to remove the cover from something

unc·tu·ous /'ʌŋktʃuəs/ *adj.* (formal, disapproving) behaving in a way that is not sincere, by being too friendly or praising other people too much, or showing this behavior: *He was friendly without being unctuous.*

un·cut /,ʌn'kʌt◂ / *adj.* **1** a movie, book, etc. that is uncut has not been made shorter, for example by having violent or sexual scenes removed **2** an uncut jewel has not yet been cut into a particular shape

un·daunt·ed /,ʌn'dɔntɪd◂ , -'dɑn-/ *adj.* not afraid to continue doing something in spite of difficulties or danger: *Nelson was* ***undaunted by*** *the opposition to his plan.*

un·de·cid·ed /,ʌndɪ'saɪdɪd◂ / *adj.* not having made a decision about something: *Many voters are* ***undecided about*** *which candidate to choose.*

un·de·ni·a·ble /,ʌndɪ'naɪəbəl◂ / (Ac) *adj.* definitely true or certain: *an undeniable fact* **—undeniably** *adv.*

un·der /'ʌndɚ/ *prep., adv.* **1** below or at a lower level than something, or covered by it (ANT) **over**: *She's hiding under the blanket.* | *The dog was sleeping under the bed.* | *Lee wore a sweater under his jacket.* | *He pushed Lonnie's head under the water.* **2** less than a particular age, number, amount, or price (ANT) **over**: *You can't get a ticket for under $10.* | *Children six and under can ride the bus for free.* | *I can't buy beer – I'm* ***under age*** (=not old enough). **3** controlled or governed by a particular leader, government, system, etc.: *a country under Marxist rule* **4 be under discussion/construction/attack etc.** to be in the process of being discussed, built, etc. **5 under way** happening or in the process of being done: *Construction is already under way on the new airport.* **6** affected by a particular influence, condition, or situation: *She performs well* ***under pressure.*** | *He was accused of driving while* ***under the influence of alcohol/drugs.*** **7** if you work under someone, that person is in charge of what you do at work: *She had a total staff of ten working under her.* **8** according to a particular law, agreement, etc.: *Under state law, we are entitled to inspect your accounts.* **9** used to say in which part of a book, list, or system you can find particular information: *The baby's records are filed under the mother's name.* ➔ **be under the impression (that)** *at* IMPRESSION

un·der·a·chiev·er /,ʌndərə'tʃivɚ/ *n.* [C] someone who does not do as well at school or at work as s/he could do if s/he worked harder

—**underachieve** *v.* [I] —**underachievement** *n.* [U]

un·der·age /ˌʌndɚˈeɪdʒ◂/ *adj.* too young to legally buy alcohol, drive a car, etc.: *underage drinking* ➔ YOUNG[1]

un·der·charge /ˌʌndɚˈtʃɑrdʒ/ *v.* [I,T] to charge someone too little money for something (ANT) **overcharge**

un·der·class /ˈʌndɚˌklæs/ *n.* [singular] the lowest social class, consisting of people who are very poor

un·der·class·man /ˌʌndɚˈklæsmən/ *n.* (plural **underclassmen** /-mən/) [C] a student in the first two years of HIGH SCHOOL or college ➔ UPPERCLASSMAN

un·der·cov·er /ˌʌndɚˈkʌvɚ◂/ *adj.* undercover work is done secretly by the police in order to catch criminals or find out information: *an undercover agent/cop*

THESAURUS **secret, covert, clandestine** ➔ SECRET[1]

un·der·cur·rent /ˈʌndɚˌkɚənt, -ˌkʌr-/ *n.* [C] a feeling that someone does not express openly: *There was an* ***undercurrent of*** *suspicion about the newcomers.*

un·der·cut /ˌʌndɚˈkʌt, ˈʌndɚˌkʌt/ *v.* (past tense and past participle **undercut**, present participle **undercutting**) [T] **1** to make something weaker or less effective: *Such activity could undercut public confidence in Congress.* **2** to sell something more cheaply than someone else: *Supermarkets are able to undercut local stores.*

un·der·dog /ˈʌndɚˌdɔg/ *n.* **the underdog** the person or team in a competition that is not expected to win

un·der·es·ti·mate /ˌʌndɚˈɛstəˌmeɪt/ (Ac) *v.* **1** [I,T] to think that something is smaller, cheaper, easier, etc. than it really is (ANT) **overestimate**: *They underestimated the cost of the construction.* **2** [T] to think that someone is less skillful, intelligent, etc. than s/he really is

un·der·go /ˌʌndɚˈgoʊ/ (Ac) *v.* (past tense **underwent** /-ˈwɛnt/, past participle **undergone** /-ˈgɔn/, third person singular **undergoes**) [T] if you undergo a change, a bad experience, etc., it happens to you or is done to you: *He'll have to undergo major heart surgery.*

un·der·grad·u·ate /ˌʌndɚˈgrædʒuɪt/ *n.* [C] a student in college, who is working for his/her BACHELOR'S DEGREE ➔ STUDENT —**undergraduate** *adj.*

un·der·ground /ˌʌndɚˈgraʊnd◂/ *adj.*, *adv.* **1** under the earth's surface: *an underground tunnel* | *creatures that live underground* **2** an underground political organization is secret and illegal **3 go underground** to start doing something secretly, or hide in a secret place: *The Ukrainian church went underground during the Communist era.*

ˌUnderground ˈRailroad *n.* **the Underground Railway** HISTORY a secret system that helped SLAVES in the southern U.S. escape and travel to a safe place in the north

un·der·growth /ˈʌndɚˌgroʊθ/ *n.* [U] bushes, small trees, etc. that grow around and under bigger trees

un·der·hand /ˈʌndɚˌhænd/ *adj.*, *adv.* thrown with your arm under the level of your shoulder (ANT) **overhand**

un·der·hand·ed /ˈʌndɚˌhændɪd/ *adj.* dishonest and done secretly: *an underhanded deal*

un·der·lie /ˌʌndɚˈlaɪ/ (Ac) *v.* (past tense **underlay** /-ˈleɪ/, past participle **underlain** /-ˈleɪn/, present participle **underlying**, third person singular **underlies**) [T] (formal) to be the cause of something, or be the basic thing from which something else develops: *Unless we deal with the problems that underlie crime, crime rates will never decrease.*

un·der·line /ˈʌndɚˌlaɪn, ˌʌndɚˈlaɪn/ *v.* [T] **1** to draw a line under a word **2** to show that something is important: *The rise in crime underlines the need for more jobs.*

THESAURUS **emphasize, highlight, accentuate, underscore** ➔ EMPHASIZE

un·der·ly·ing /ˈʌndɚˌlaɪ-ɪŋ/ (Ac) *adj.* **underlying reason/cause/problem etc.** the reason, cause, etc. that is most important but that is not easy to discover: *The underlying causes of her depression lay in her childhood.*

THESAURUS **basic, fundamental** ➔ BASIC

U

un·der·mine /ˈʌndɚˌmaɪn, ˌʌndɚˈmaɪn/ *v.* [T] to gradually make someone or something less strong or effective: *This could seriously undermine the peace process.*

un·der·neath /ˌʌndɚˈniθ/ *prep.*, *adv.* directly below or under something ➔ BENEATH: *We turned some rocks over to see what was underneath.* | *There's nice wood underneath all that paint.*

un·der·nour·ished /ˌʌndɚˈnɚɪʃt, -ˈnʌrɪʃt/ *adj.* not healthy because you have not eaten enough food or the right type of food

un·der·paid /ˌʌndɚˈpeɪd◂/ *adj.* earning less money than you deserve —**underpay** /ˌʌndɚˈpeɪ/ *v.* [I,T]

un·der·pants /ˈʌndɚˌpænts/ *n.* [plural] a short piece of underwear worn on the lower part of the body ➔ *see picture at* CLOTHES

un·der·pass /ˈʌndɚˌpæs/ *n.* [C] a road or path that goes under another road or path

un·der·priv·i·leged /ˌʌndɚˈprɪvlɪdʒd◂/ *adj.* very poor and not having the advantages of most other people in society: *underprivileged children*

THESAURUS **poor, disadvantaged, deprived** ➔ POOR

un·der·rat·ed /ˌʌndɚˈreɪt̬ɪd◂/ *adj.* better than people think or say (ANT) **overrated**: *an underrated actor* —**underrate** *v.* [T]

un·der·score /ˈʌndɚˌskɔr/ *v.* [T] to emphasize that something is important: *The survey underscores the division between rich and poor in America.*

THESAURUS **emphasize, stress, highlight, underline** → EMPHASIZE

un·der·shirt /ˈʌndɚˌʃɚt/ *n.* [C] a piece of underwear worn under a shirt

un·der·side /ˈʌndɚˌsaɪd/ *n.* **the underside of sth** the bottom side or surface of something

un·der·sized /ˌʌndɚˈsaɪzd◂/ *adj.* too small

un·der·staffed /ˌʌndɚˈstæft◂/ *adj.* not having enough workers, or having fewer workers than usual: *The lines are so long because we're understaffed right now.*

un·der·stand /ˌʌndɚˈstænd/ *v.* (past tense and past participle **understood** /-ˌstʊd/) **1** [I,T] to know the meaning of what someone is saying to you, or the language that s/he speaks: *Do you understand Spanish?* | *I could barely understand what he was saying.* | *I'm not very good at German but I can* ***make*** *myself* ***understood*** (=make what I say clear to other people). ▸Don't say "I am understanding."◂ **2** [I,T] to know how someone feels and why s/he behaves the way s/he does, and to be sympathetic: *Believe me, John – I* ***understand how*** *you feel.* | *Just tell him what happened – I'm sure he'll understand.* **3** [I,T] to know how or why a situation, event, etc. happens, especially through learning or experience: *My father never understood baseball.* | *Do you* ***understand how*** *this works?* **4** [T] to believe that something you have heard or read is true: *I* ***understand (that)*** *you want to buy a car.*

U

un·der·stand·a·ble /ˌʌndɚˈstændəbəl/ *adj.* understandable behavior, reactions, etc. seem reasonable because of the situation you are in: *It's* ***understandable that*** *he's a little afraid.* | *Your anger toward him is* ***perfectly understandable.***

un·der·stand·ing¹ /ˌʌndɚˈstændɪŋ/ *n.* **1** [singular, U] knowledge about something, based on learning and experience: *She* ***has a basic understanding of*** *computers.* **2** [singular, U] sympathy toward someone's character and behavior: *Harry thanked us for our understanding.* **3** [C] an informal private agreement about something: *I thought we had* ***come to an understanding*** *about the price.* **4** [U] the ability to think and learn

understanding² *adj.* showing sympathy and pity for other people's problems: *an understanding boss*

un·der·state /ˌʌndɚˈsteɪt/ *v.* [T] to describe something in a way that makes it seem less important or serious than it really is (ANT) **overstate**: *The report understates the severity of the problem.*

un·der·stat·ed /ˌʌndɚˈsteɪt̬ɪd◂/ *adj.* (approving) simple in a way that is attractive: *I liked the understated decoration of his office.*

un·der·state·ment /ˈʌndɚˌsteɪtˀmənt/ *n.* [C] a statement that is not strong enough to express how good, impressive, bad, etc. something really is: *To say the movie was bad* ***is an understatement.***

un·der·stood /ˌʌndɚˈstʊd/ *v.* the past tense and past participle of UNDERSTAND

un·der·stud·y /ˈʌndɚˌstʌdi/ *n.* (plural **understudies**) [C] an actor who learns a part in a play so that s/he can act if the usual actor cannot perform

un·der·take /ˌʌndɚˈteɪk/ (Ac) *v.* (past tense **undertook** /-ˈtʊk/, past participle **undertaken** /-ˈteɪkən/) [T] (formal) **1** to start to do a piece of work, especially one that is long and difficult: *The country undertook a massive reform of its legal system.* **2 undertake to do sth** to promise or agree to do something

un·der·tak·er /ˈʌndɚˌteɪkɚ/ *n.* [C] (old-fashioned) someone whose job is to arrange funerals (SYN) **funeral director**

un·der·tak·ing /ˈʌndɚˌteɪkɪŋ/ (Ac) *n.* [C usually singular] an important job, piece of work, etc. for which you are responsible: *Holding the Olympic Games is a massive undertaking.*

un·der·tone /ˈʌndɚˌtoʊn/ *n.* [C] a feeling or quality that exists but which is not easy to notice: *an* ***undertone of*** *sadness in her voice*

un·der·tow /ˈʌndɚˌtoʊ/ *n.* [C] a strong current under the ocean's surface that pulls water away from the shore

underwater

swimming underwater

un·der·wa·ter /ˌʌndɚˈwɔt̬ɚ◂, -ˈwɑ-/ *adj.* [only before noun] below the surface of the water, or able to be used there: *an underwater camera* —**underwater** *adv.*

un·der·wear /ˈʌndɚˌwɛr/ *n.* [U] clothes that you wear next to your body under your other clothes

un·der·weight /ˌʌndɚˈweɪt◂/ *adj.* weighing less than is expected or usual (ANT) **overweight**: *an underweight baby*

THESAURUS **thin, slight, skinny, lean, gaunt** → THIN¹

un·der·world /ˈʌndɚˌwɚld/ *n.* [singular] the criminals in a particular place and the activities they are involved in

un·der·write /ˈʌndɚˌraɪt, ˌʌndɚˈraɪt/ *v.* (past tense **underwrote** /-roʊt/, past participle **underwritten** /-rɪtˀn/) [T] (formal) to support an activity, business, etc. with money: *The project is underwritten by a National Science Foundation grant.*

un·de·sir·a·ble /ˌʌndɪˈzaɪrəbəl◂ / *adj.* (formal) someone or something that is undesirable is not welcome or wanted because they may have a bad effect: *The drug can produce undesirable side effects.*

un·de·ter·mined /ˌʌndɪˈtɚmɪnd◂ / *adj.* not known, decided, or calculated: *The cause of death is undetermined.*

un·de·vel·oped /ˌʌndɪˈvɛləpt◂ / *adj.* undeveloped land has not been built on or used for a particular purpose

un·di·min·ished /ˌʌndɪˈmɪnɪʃt/ (Ac) *adj.* not weaker or less important than before: *His love for her was undiminished.*

un·dis·closed /ˌʌndɪsˈkloʊzd◂ / *adj.* not known publicly: *an* ***undisclosed amount/sum*** *of money*

un·dis·guised /ˌʌndɪsˈgaɪzd◂ / *adj.* an undisguised feeling is clearly shown and not hidden: *undisguised hatred*

un·dis·put·ed /ˌʌndɪˈspyuṭɪd◂ / *adj.* **undisputed leader/master/champion etc.** someone whom everyone agrees is the leader, etc.

un·dis·turbed /ˌʌndɪˈstɚbd◂ / *adj., adv.* not interrupted or moved: *They let her rest undisturbed.*

un·di·vid·ed /ˌʌndɪˈvaɪdɪd◂ / *adj.* complete: *Please give me your* ***undivided attention.***

un·do /ʌnˈdu/ *v.* (past tense **undid** /-ˈdɪd/, past participle **undone** /-ˈdʌn/, third person singular **undoes** /-ˈdʌz/) [T] **1** to untie or open something that is tied or closed: *I can't get the clasp on my necklace undone.* **2** to try to remove the bad effects of something: *The courts have tried to undo the legal abuses of the past.* **3** to change something back to the state or condition it was in before improvements were made: *Changing the law will undo decades of progress.*

un·do·ing /ʌnˈduɪŋ/ *n.* **be sb's undoing** to cause someone's failure, defeat, shame, etc.: *Borrowing too much money proved to be his undoing.*

un·done /ˌʌnˈdʌn◂ / *adj.* **1** not tied or closed: *Your shirt button has* ***come undone.*** **2** not finished or completed: *Much of the work on the bridge has been* ***left undone.***

un·doubt·ed·ly /ʌnˈdaʊṭɪdli/ *adv.* used in order to emphasize that something is definitely true: *He's undoubtedly one of the best guitar players of all time.*

un·dress /ʌnˈdrɛs/ *v.* [I,T] to take your clothes off, or take someone else's clothes off: *Yvonne undressed and got into bed.*

un·dressed /ʌnˈdrɛst/ *adj.* not wearing any clothes: *He started to* ***get undressed*** (=take his clothes off).

THESAURUS **naked, bare, have nothing on, not have anything on** → NAKED

un·due /ˌʌnˈdu◂ / *adj.* (formal) more than is reasonable, appropriate, or necessary: *The tax creates an undue burden on farmers.*

un·du·lat·ing /ˈʌndʒəˌleɪṭɪŋ/ *adj.* [only before noun] (formal) moving or shaped like waves that are rising and falling: *the undulating green hills* —**undulate** *v.* [I] —**undulation** /ˌʌndʒəˈleɪʃən/ *n.* [C,U]

un·du·ly /ʌnˈduli/ *adv.* (formal) more than is normal or reasonable: *unduly harsh punishment*

un·dy·ing /ˌʌnˈdaɪ-ɪŋ◂ / *adj.* (literary) continuing for ever: *undying love*

un·earth /ʌnˈɚθ/ *v.* [T] **1** to find something that was buried in the ground: *Scientists have unearthed eight more skeletons at Pompeii.*

THESAURUS **find, discover, turn sth up** → FIND[1]

2 to find out information or the truth about something

un·earth·ly /ʌnˈɚθli/ *adj.* very strange and unnatural: *an unearthly greenish light*

un·eas·y /ˌʌnˈizi◂ / *adj.* worried and anxious because you think something bad might happen: *We* ***felt uneasy about*** *his decision* —**unease** *n.* [U] —**uneasiness** *n.* [U] —**uneasily** *adv.*

THESAURUS **worried, anxious, concerned, nervous, apprehensive** → WORRIED

U

un·ec·o·nom·i·cal /ˌʌnɛkəˈnɑmɪkəl, -ikə-/ *adj.* using too much effort, money, or materials to make a profit

un·ed·u·cat·ed /ʌnˈɛdʒəˌkeɪṭɪd/ *adj.* not having much education, or showing that someone is not well educated

un·em·ployed /ˌʌnɪmˈplɔɪd◂ / *adj.* without a job: *an unemployed actor* | *I've been unemployed for six months.*

un·em·ploy·ment /ˌʌnɪmˈplɔɪmənt/ *n.* [U] **1** the condition of not having a job, or the number of people who do not have a job: ***Unemployment*** *remains relatively* ***low/high.*** | *The* ***unemployment rate*** *is rising.* **2** money paid regularly by the government to people who have no job: *He's been* ***on unemployment*** *for three months.*

un·end·ing /ʌnˈɛndɪŋ/ *adj.* something, especially something bad, that is unending seems as if it will continue for ever: *an unending stream of people*

un·e·qual /ʌnˈikwəl/ *adj.* **1** unfairly treating different people or groups in different ways: *the unequal treatment of minorities* **2** not the same in size, amount, value, rank, etc.: *two rooms of unequal size*

un·e·quiv·o·cal /ˌʌnɪˈkwɪvəkəl/ *adj.* (formal) completely clear and definite with no doubts

un·er·ring /ʌn'ɛrɪŋ, ʌn'ɚɪŋ/ *adj.* always right: *his unerring judgment*

un·eth·i·cal /ʌn'ɛθɪkəl/ (Ac) *adj.* considered to be morally wrong: *an unethical banking practice*

un·e·ven /ʌn'ivən/ *adj.* **1** not flat, smooth, or level: *uneven ground* **2** not equal or balanced: *The racial mix of the school is uneven.* **3** good in some parts and bad in others: *a music album of uneven quality* **—unevenly** *adv.*

un·ex·cused /ˌʌnɪk'skuzd◂/ *adj.* **unexcused absence** an occasion when you are away from school or work without permission

un·ex·pect·ed /ˌʌnɪk'spɛktɪd◂/ *adj.* surprising because of not being expected: *the unexpected death of his father* **—unexpectedly** *adv.*

un·ex·pur·gat·ed /ʌn'ɛkspɚˌgeɪt̬ɪd/ *adj.* (formal) an unexpurgated book, play, etc. is complete and has not had parts that might offend people removed (ANT) **expurgated**

un·fail·ing /ʌn'feɪlɪŋ/ *adj.* always there, even in times of difficulty or trouble: *her unfailing kindness*

un·fair /ˌʌn'fɛr◂/ *adj.* not right or fair: *an unfair decision* | *The system is* ***unfair to*** *the poor.* **—unfairly** *adv.* **—unfairness** *n.* [U]

un·faith·ful /ʌn'feɪθfəl/ *adj.* someone who is unfaithful has sex with someone who is not his/her wife, husband, or usual partner: *Kurt had been* ***unfaithful to*** *his wife on several occasions.*

un·fa·mil·iar /ˌʌnfəˌmɪlyɚ/ *adj.* not known to you: *an unfamiliar face* | *I am* ***unfamiliar with*** *his books.* **—unfamiliarity** /ˌʌnfəˌmɪl'yærət̬i/ *n.* [U]

U

un·fash·ion·a·ble /ʌn'fæʃənəbəl/ *adj.* not popular or fashionable at the present time (ANT) **fashionable**: *unfashionable shoes*

un·fas·ten /ˌʌn'fæsən/ *v.* [T] to undo something: *Lewis unfastened his seat belt.*

un·fa·vor·a·ble /ʌn'feɪvərəbəl/ *adj.* **1** showing that you do not like something: *an unfavorable review of the movie* **2** unfavorable conditions, events, etc. are not good: *an unfavorable weather report*

un·feel·ing /ʌn'filɪŋ/ *adj.* not showing sympathy for others: *How can she be so* ***cold and unfeeling****?*

un·fet·tered /ʌn'fɛt̬ɚd/ *adj.* not restricted in any way

un·fit /ʌn'fɪt/ *adj.* not good enough to do something or to be used for something: *That woman is* ***unfit to*** *raise a child!* | *The land is* ***unfit for*** *cultivation.*

un·fold /ʌn'foʊld/ *v.* [I,T] **1** if a story, plan, etc. unfolds, it becomes clearer as you hear or learn more about it: *The case began to slowly unfold in court.* **2** to open something that was folded: *She unfolded the map.*

un·fore·seen /ˌʌnfɔr'sin◂, -fɚ-/ *adj.* an unforeseen situation is one that you did not expect to happen: *an unforeseen delay* | ***Due to unforeseen circumstances****, the play has been canceled.*

un·for·get·ta·ble /ˌʌnfɚ'gɛt̬əbəl/ *adj.* something that is unforgettable is so beautiful, good, exciting, etc. that you remember it for a long time: *an unforgettable sight*

un·for·tu·nate /ʌn'fɔrtʃənɪt/ *adj.* **1** happening because of bad luck: *an* ***unfortunate accident***

THESAURUS **unlucky, ill-fated** → UNLUCKY

2 someone who is unfortunate has something bad happen to him/her: *When we entered the room, the teacher was yelling at some unfortunate student.* **3** an unfortunate situation, condition, quality, etc. is one that you wish was different: ***It's unfortunate (that)*** *so few people seem willing to help.*

un·for·tu·nate·ly /ʌn'fɔrtʃənɪtli/ *adv.* [sentence adverb] used when you are mentioning a fact that you wish was not true: *Unfortunately, it's too late for me to do anything about it.*

un·found·ed /ʌn'faʊndɪd/ (Ac) *adj.* not based on facts or EVIDENCE (SYN) **wrong**: *The company insisted that our complaints were unfounded.*

un·friend·ly /ʌn'frɛndli/ *adj.* **1** not kind or friendly: *The neighbors seemed unfriendly.* **2** not helping or wanting a type of person or thing: *Many American cities are* ***unfriendly to*** *pedestrians.* **3** an unfriendly government or nation is one that opposes yours

un·furl /ʌn'fɚl/ *v.* [T] to unroll and open a flag, sail, etc.

un·gain·ly /ʌn'geɪnli/ *adj.* awkward and not graceful: *an ungainly teenager*

un·grate·ful /ʌn'greɪtfəl/ *adj.* not thanking someone for something s/he has given to you or done for you

un·hap·py /ʌn'hæpi/ *adj.* **1** not happy: *an unhappy childhood* | *She had been unhappy for a long time.*

THESAURUS **sad, depressed, down, low, blue** → SAD

2 feeling worried or annoyed because you do not like what is happening (SYN) **dissatisfied**: *Many Americans are deeply* ***unhappy with*** *the state of the nation.* | *Dennis is* ***unhappy about*** *having to work on a Saturday.* **—unhappiness** *n.* [U] **—unhappily** *adv.*

un·health·y /ʌn'hɛlθi/ *adj.* **1** likely to make you sick: *unhealthy city air* **2** not physically healthy: *an unhealthy baby* **3** not normal or natural and likely to cause harm: *Any obsession is unhealthy.*

un·heard-of /ʌn'hɚd ʌv/ *adj.* something that is unheard of is extremely unusual or has never happened before: *The opera raised the price of its seats to an unheard-of $100 each!*

un·help·ful /ʌn'hɛlpfəl/ *adj.* not useful, and likely to make a situation worse (ANT) **helpful**: *I think it's really unhelpful to focus only on the school's failings.* **—unhelpfully** *adv.*

un·ho·ly /ʌn'hoʊli/ *adj.* **1 an unholy alliance** an agreement between two people or organizations who would not normally work together, usually for a bad purpose **2** very great and very bad: *We're in an **unholy mess**.*

un·hook /ʌn'hʊk/ *v.* [T] to unfasten or remove something from a hook

UNICEF /'yunəˌsɛf/ *n.* **the United Nations Children's Fund** an organization that helps children who suffer from disease, HUNGER, etc.

u·ni·corn /'yunəˌkɔrn/ *n.* [C] an imaginary animal like a white horse with a long straight horn on its head

un·i·den·ti·fied /ˌʌnaɪ'dɛntəˌfaɪd◂ , ˌʌnə-/ *adj.* an unidentified person or thing is one that you do not know the name of: *an unidentified body*

u·ni·fi·ca·tion /ˌyunəfə'keɪʃən/ (Ac) *n.* [U] the act of combining two or more groups, countries, etc. to make a single group or country: *the **unification of** Germany after the fall of the Berlin Wall*

u·ni·form¹ /'yunəˌfɔrm/ (Ac) *n.* [C] **1** a particular type of clothing that the members of an organization wear to work: *Here's a picture of me **wearing** my football **uniform**.* **2 in uniform a)** wearing a uniform **b)** in the army, navy, etc. [ORIGIN: 1500—1600 French *uniforme*, from Latin *uniformis*, from *uni-* "one" + *-formis* (from *forma* "form, shape")] **—uniformed** *adj.*: *uniformed police officers*

uniform² (Ac) *adj.* things that are uniform are all the same shape, size, etc.: *Grade A eggs must be of uniform size.* **—uniformly** *adv.*: *She received uniformly high grades.* **—uniformity** /ˌyunə'fɔrməṭi/ *n.* [U]: *There is no uniformity of opinion on the issue.*

u·ni·fy /'yunəˌfaɪ/ (Ac) *v.* (**unified**, **unifies**) [T] to combine the parts of a country, organization, etc. to make a single unit ➔ UNIFICATION: *Spain was unified in the 16th century.* **—unified** *adj.*: *a unified military leadership*

u·ni·lat·er·al /ˌyunə'læṭərəl◂ / *adj.* a unilateral action or decision is made by only one of the groups involved in a situation without the agreement of the others ➔ BILATERAL, MULTILATERAL: *a unilateral ceasefire*

un·i·ma·gin·a·ble /ˌʌnɪ'mædʒənəbəl◂ / *adj.* not possible to imagine: *unimaginable wealth* **—unimaginably** *adv.*

un·i·ma·gin·a·tive /ˌʌnɪ'mædʒənəṭɪv◂ / *adj.* **1** lacking the ability to think of new or unusual ideas **2** ordinary and boring, and not using any new ideas: *unimaginative architecture*

un·im·por·tant /ˌʌnɪm'pɔrtˀnt◂ / *adj.* not important

un·im·pressed /ˌʌnɪm'prɛst/ *adj.* not thinking that someone or something is good, interesting, etc.: *Board members were **unimpressed with/by** the plan.*

un·im·pres·sive /ˌʌnɪm'prɛsɪv◂ / *adj.* not as good, large, etc. as expected or necessary: *The school's test results were unimpressive.*

un·in·formed /ˌʌnɪn'fɔrmd◂ / *adj.* not having enough knowledge or information: *He seemed **uninformed about** foreign policy.*

un·in·hab·it·ed /ˌʌnɪn'hæbɪtɪd◂ / *adj.* an uninhabited place does not have anyone living there (SYN) **deserted**: *an **uninhabited island***

un·in·hib·it·ed /ˌʌnɪn'hɪbɪṭɪd◂ / *adj.* confident or relaxed enough to do or say what you want to

un·in·jured /ʌn'ɪndʒərd/ *adj.* not hurt or damaged

un·in·spired /ˌʌnɪn'spaɪərd◂ / *adj.* not showing any imagination, and so not interesting or exciting: *an uninspired performance*

un·in·sured /ˌʌnɪn'ʃʊrd◂ / *adj.* having no insurance: *uninsured drivers*

un·in·tel·li·gi·ble /ˌʌnɪn'tɛlədʒəbəl/ *adj.* impossible to understand: *Most of what he said was unintelligible.*

un·in·ten·tion·al /ˌʌnɪn'tɛnʃənəl◂ / *adj.* not done deliberately: *unintentional errors on his tax form* **—unintentionally** *adv.*

un·in·ter·est·ed /ʌn'ɪntrɪstɪd, -'ɪntəˌrɛs-/ *adj.* not interested

un·in·ter·rupt·ed /ˌʌnɪntə'rʌptɪd◂ / *adj.* continuous without stopping or being interrupted: *eight hours of uninterrupted sleep*

un·ion /'yunyən/ *n.* **1** [C] a LABOR UNION: *the teachers' union | Are you going to **join the union**?*

> **THESAURUS** organization, association ➔ ORGANIZATION

2 [singular] a group of countries or states with the same central government: *countries that were part of the former Soviet Union* **3 the Union** HISTORY used to talk about the U.S., or about the northern states of the U.S., during the Civil War: *Union soldiers* **4** [singular, U] (formal) the act of joining two or more things together, or the state of being joined together: *the **union** of East Germany **with** West Germany* **5** [C,U] (formal) marriage

un·ion·ized /'yunyəˌnaɪzd/ *adj.* having formed a union, or belonging to one **—unionize** *v.* [I,T]

u·nique /yu'nik/ (Ac) *adj.* **1** (informal) unusually good and special: *The workshop will give participants a unique opportunity to study with an artist.* **2** being the only one of its kind: *Every person is unique.* **3 unique to sb/sth** existing only in a particular place, person, or group, etc.: *The issues being discussed here are not unique to the U.S.* **—uniquely** *adv.*: *a uniquely talented artist* **—uniqueness** *n.* [U]: *the uniqueness of each individual person*

u·ni·sex /'yunəˌsɛks/ *adj.* appropriate for both men and women: *a unisex jacket*

U

u·ni·son /ˈyunəsən/ *n.* **in unison** if a group of people do something in unison, they all do it together at the same time

u·nit /ˈyunɪt/ *n.* [C] **1** a person or thing that is one whole part of something larger: *The family is the smallest social unit.* | *an eight-unit apartment building* (=it has eight apartments) **2** a group of people who work together as part of a larger group: *the emergency unit of the hospital* **3** an amount of something used as a standard of measurement: *The dollar is the basic* ***unit of*** *money in the U.S.* **4** one of the numbered parts into which a TEXTBOOK (=a book used in schools) is divided ➔ CHAPTER **5** a piece of furniture that can be attached to others of the same type: *a kitchen unit* **6** a piece of equipment that is part of a larger machine: *The cooling unit is broken.*

U·ni·tar·i·an /ˌyunəˈtɛriən/ *n.* [C] a member of a Christian group that does not believe in the Trinity —**Unitarian** *adj.*

u·nite /yuˈnaɪt/ *v.* [I,T] to join together as one group, or to make people join together in this way, especially in order to achieve something: *Congress* ***united behind*** *the President.* | *The deal would unite two of the country's oldest electronics firms.*

u·nit·ed /yuˈnaɪt̬ɪd/ *adj.* **1** involving or done by everyone: *Business and government need to make a united effort to clean up the environment.* **2** closely joined by sharing feelings, aims, etc.: *a united community*

Uˌnited ˈNations *n.* the UN

U

u·ni·ty /ˈyunət̬i/ *n.* [U] a state or situation in which people work together to achieve something that they all agree on: *The team suffers from a lack of unity.*

u·ni·ver·sal /ˌyunəˈvɚsəl◂/ *adj.* **1** involving everyone in the world or in a particular group: *With some exceptions, citizens in the U.S. have universal voting rights.* | *a universal health care program* **2** true or appropriate in every situation: *a universal truth* —**universally** *adv.*

u·ni·verse /ˈyunəˌvɚs/ *n.* **the universe** all of space, including all the stars and PLANETS

u·ni·ver·si·ty /ˌyunəˈvɚsət̬i/ *n.* (plural **universities**) [C] a school at the highest level, where you study for a DEGREE ➔ COLLEGE: *a graduate of Harvard University* | *He later* ***attended*** *the* ***University*** *of California.*

TOPIC

People who **go to college** to **study** a **subject** are called **students**. Students choose a **major** (=main subject to study) and sometimes a **minor** (=second subject to study). Students must also study subjects that are not related to their main subjects, in order to get a good **general education**. During the four or five years that they go to university, students **go to/attend lectures**, **classes**, and **seminars**. They are taught by **professors** or sometimes by **teaching assistants (T.A.)**, who are **graduate students** in the subject they are teaching. Students must write **papers** and, in science subjects, do **lab** (= laboratory) work, and they take **midterm** and **final exams**. Final exams take place at the end of each **semester** or **quarter** (=periods of time that the college year is divided into). Students earn **credits** for each class. Once a student has earned enough credits, s/he **graduates** and **gets a degree** (=academic title).

un·just /ˌʌnˈdʒʌst◂/ *adj.* not fair or reasonable: *unjust laws*

un·jus·ti·fied /ˌʌnˈdʒʌstəˌfaɪd/ (Ac) *adj.* done without a good reason: *an unjustified attack* —**unjustifiable** *adj.*

un·kempt /ˌʌnˈkɛmpt◂/ *adj.* not neat: *Her hair was dirty and unkempt.*

un·kind /ˌʌnˈkaɪnd◂/ *adj.* cruel or not nice: *an unkind remark*

THESAURUS **mean, thoughtless** ➔ MEAN²

un·know·ing·ly /ʌnˈnoʊɪŋli/ *adv.* without realizing what you are doing or what is happening: *Millions of people may have been unknowingly infected.*

un·known¹ /ˌʌnˈnoʊn◂/ *adj.* **1** not known about: *An unknown number of rebels are in hiding.* **2** not famous: *an unknown musician*

unknown² *n.* [C] someone who is not famous: *Early in her career, she was still an unknown.*

un·law·ful /ʌnˈlɔfəl/ *adj.* not legal

un·lead·ed /ˌʌnˈlɛdɪd◂/ *n.* [U] gas that does not contain any LEAD ➔ REGULAR

un·leash /ʌnˈliʃ/ *v.* [T] to cause or make something start happening suddenly and with a strong effect: *The ceremony unleashed memories of the war.*

un·less /ənˈlɛs, ʌn-/ *conjunction* used in order to say that something will happen or be true if another thing does not happen or is not true: *We can go in my car unless you want to walk.* | *He won't go to sleep unless you tell him a story.* ▸Don't say "unless if."◂ ➔ IF¹

un·li·censed /ʌnˈlaɪsənst/ (Ac) *adj.* without a LICENSE (=an official document that gives you permission to do or have something): *unlicensed guns*

un·like /ˌʌnˈlaɪk◂/ *prep.* **1** completely different from another person or thing: *Unlike me, she's intelligent.* **2** not typical of someone: *It's unlike Judy to leave without telling us.*

un·like·ly /ʌnˈlaɪkli/ *adj.* not likely to happen: ***It's unlikely (that)*** *I'll be able to get an earlier flight.* | *The weather is* ***unlikely to*** *improve over the next few days.* —**unlikelihood** *n.* [U]

un·lim·it·ed /ʌnˈlɪmɪt̬ɪd/ *adj.* without any limit: *a rental car with unlimited mileage*

un·list·ed /ˌʌn'lɪstɪd◂/ *adj.* not in the list of numbers in the telephone book: *an unlisted phone number*

un·load /ʌn'loʊd/ *v.* **1** [I,T] to remove goods from a vehicle or large container, or to have them removed: *I unloaded the dishwasher.* | *The ship took a long time to unload.* **2** [T] (informal) to get rid of something by selling it quickly: *The warehouse is trying to unload a huge quantity of goods at discount prices.* **3** [I,T] to take film out of a camera or bullets out of a gun

un·lock /ʌn'lɑk/ *v.* [T] to undo the lock on a door, box, etc.

un·luck·y /ˌʌn'lʌki◂/ *adj.* **1** having bad luck: *Chicago was* ***unlucky to*** *lose in the final minute of the game.* | *She's been* ***unlucky in love*** (=not able to find someone to love romantically).

THESAURUS

unfortunate – unlucky: *They were unfortunate not to win.*
ill-fated – unlucky and leading to serious problems or death: *16 soldiers died during the ill-fated mission to rescue the hostages.*
jinxed – very unlucky, and causing you to be unsuccessful or have problems: *That's the third fire we've had here. I'm beginning to think this place is jinxed.*
inauspicious (formal) – making people think that bad things could happen: *The defeat was an inauspicious beginning to his major league career.*

2 happening as a result of bad luck: *It was* ***unlucky*** *for us* ***that*** *the bank closed just as we got there.* **3** believed to cause bad luck: *Some people think black cats are unlucky.*

un·manned /ˌʌn'mænd◂/ *adj.* an unmanned vehicle or building does not have anyone in it: *an unmanned spacecraft*

un·marked /ˌʌn'mɑrkt◂/ *adj.* something that is unmarked has no words or signs on it: *an unmarked police car*

un·mar·ried /ˌʌn'mærid◂/ *adj.* not married SYN **single**

un·mask /ʌn'mæsk/ *v.* [T] to make a truth that has been hidden become known: *He was unmasked as an enemy spy.*

un·mis·tak·a·ble /ˌʌnmɪ'steɪkəbəl◂/ *adj.* easy to recognize: *the unmistakable taste of garlic*

THESAURUS **noticeable, clear, obvious, striking, evident, conspicuous** → NOTICEABLE

un·mit·i·gat·ed /ʌn'mɪt̬əˌgeɪt̬ɪd/ *adj.* [only before noun] used to emphasize how bad something is: *The night turned into an* ***unmitigated disaster.*** | *He had the* ***unmitigated gall*** *to complain.*

un·moved /ˌʌn'muvd/ *adj.* feeling no pity, sympathy, or sadness: *The judge was unmoved by his excuses.*

un·named /ˌʌn'neɪmd◂/ *adj.* an unnamed person, place, or thing is one who is mentioned, especially by a newspaper, but whose name is not given: *The newspaper quoted an unnamed diplomatic source.*

un·nat·u·ral /ˌʌn'nætʃərəl/ *adj.* **1** different from normal, especially in a way that is strange or wrong: *It's unnatural for a child to spend so much time alone.* **2** seeming false, or not real or natural: *Julia's laugh seemed forced and unnatural.* **3** different from what is produced in nature → ARTIFICIAL, MAN-MADE: *an unnatural shade of red* **4** different from normal human behavior in a way that seems morally wrong SYN **abnormal** —**unnaturally** *adv.*

un·nec·es·sar·y /ʌn'nɛsəˌsɛri/ *adj.* not needed, or more than is needed: *unnecessary risks* —**unnecessarily** /ˌʌn-nɛsə'sɛrəli/ *adv.*

un·nerve /ʌn'nɚv/ *v.* [T] to upset or frighten someone so that s/he loses his/her confidence or ability to think clearly: *Dave was completely unnerved by the argument with Terry.* —**unnerving** *adj.*

un·no·ticed /ʌn'noʊt̬ɪst/ *adj.* without being noticed: *She sat unnoticed at the back.*

un·ob·served /ˌʌnəb'zɚvd/ *adj., adv.* not seen, or without being seen: *Bret left the meeting unobserved.*

un·ob·tru·sive /ˌʌnəb'trusɪv◂/ *adj.* not easily noticed or not trying to be noticed: *an efficient unobtrusive waiter*

un·oc·cu·pied /ʌn'ɑkyəˌpaɪd/ *adj.* a seat, house, room, etc. that is unoccupied has no one in it

un·of·fi·cial /ˌʌnə'fɪʃəl◂/ *adj.* **1** done or produced without the approval of or permission from someone in authority: *According to unofficial results, Carey received 52 percent of the vote.* **2** not done as part of official duties: *The President made an unofficial visit to a children's hospital.* —**unofficially** *adv.*

un·or·tho·dox /ʌn'ɔrθəˌdɑks/ *adj.* different from what is usual or accepted by most people: *unorthodox behavior*

un·pack /ʌn'pæk/ *v.* [I,T] to take everything out of a box or SUITCASE: *I haven't had a chance to unpack yet.*

un·paid /ˌʌn'peɪd◂/ *adj.* **1** an unpaid bill or debt has not been paid: *unpaid taxes* **2** done without getting any money: *unpaid work* | ***unpaid leave/time off*** (=unpaid time away from work)

un·par·al·leled /ʌn'pærəˌlɛld/ Ac *adj.* (formal) much bigger, better, or worse than anything else: *Those years were a time of unparalleled happiness in our lives.*

un·planned /ˌʌn'plænd◂/ *adj.* not planned or expected: *an unplanned pregnancy*

un·pleas·ant /ʌn'plɛzənt/ *adj.* **1** not pleasant or enjoyable ANT **nice**: *an unpleasant surprise* **2** not kind or friendly ANT **nice**: *He said some very unpleasant things.*

U

un·plug /ʌn'plʌg/ *v.* (**unplugged**, **unplugging**) [T] to disconnect a piece of electrical equipment by taking its PLUG out of a SOCKET

un·plugged /ʌn'plʌgd/ *adj.* if a group of musicians perform unplugged, they perform without electric instruments

un·pop·u·lar /ʌn'pɑpyələ˞/ *adj.* not liked by most people: *an unpopular decision* | *The plans were* ***unpopular with*** *voters.*

un·prec·e·dent·ed /ʌn'prɛsəˌdɛntɪd/ (Ac) *adj.* never having happened before, or never having happened so much: *The Steelers won an unprecedented four Super Bowls in six years.*

un·pre·dict·a·ble /ˌʌnprɪ'dɪktəbəl◂ / (Ac) *adj.* changing so much that you do not know what to expect: *unpredictable weather* —**unpredictably** *adv.* —**unpredictability** /ˌʌnprɪdɪktə'bɪləṭi/ *n.* [U]: *the unpredictability of her behavior*

un·pre·pared /ˌʌnprɪ'pɛrd◂ / *adj.* not ready to deal with something: *I was totally* ***unprepared for*** *that question.*

un·pre·pos·sess·ing /ˌʌnpripə'zɛsɪŋ/ *adj.* not special, attractive, or interesting, and not likely to be noticed: *an unprepossessing girl of 14*

un·prin·ci·pled /ʌn'prɪnsəpəld/ (Ac) *adj.* (formal) not caring whether what you do is morally right: *Duncan called him an unprincipled liar.*

un·print·a·ble /ʌn'prɪnṭəbəl/ *adj.* unprintable words, jokes, songs, etc. are so rude or shocking that they cannot be printed in a newspaper or magazine

U

un·pro·duc·tive /ˌʌnprə'dʌktɪv◂ / *adj.* not achieving very much: *an unproductive meeting*

un·pro·fes·sion·al /ˌʌnprə'fɛʃənəl/ *adj.* behaving in a way that is not acceptable in a particular profession: *Osborn was fired for unprofessional conduct.*

un·prof·it·a·ble /ʌn'prɑfɪṭəbəl/ *adj.* **1** making no profit: *an unprofitable business* **2** (formal) producing no advantage

un·pro·tect·ed /ˌʌnprə'tɛktɪd◂ / *adj.* **1** not protected against damage or harm: *Without a roof the building was unprotected from the weather.* **2 unprotected sex/intercourse** sex without a CONDOM

un·pro·voked /ˌʌnprə'voʊkt◂ / *adj.* an unprovoked attack or unprovoked anger, etc. is directed at someone who has not done anything to deserve it

un·pub·lished /ʌn'pʌblɪʃt/ (Ac) *adj.* unpublished writing, information, etc. has never been printed

un·qual·i·fied /ʌn'kwɑləˌfaɪd/ *adj.* **1** not having the right knowledge, experience, or education to do something: *The hospital was accused of hiring unqualified health workers.* **2** complete: *The movie is an* ***unqualified success.***

un·ques·tion·a·bly /ʌn'kwɛstʃənəbli/ *adv.* in a way that leaves no doubt: *This is unquestionably the coldest winter in years.*

un·ques·tioned /ʌn'kwɛstʃənd/ *adj.* accepted by everyone: *The king had an unquestioned right to rule.*

un·quote /'ʌnkwoʊt/ *v.* (spoken) → **quote... unquote** *at* QUOTE[1]

un·rav·el /ʌn'rævəl/ *v.* **1** [T] to understand or explain something that is very complicated: *Detectives are still trying to unravel the mystery surrounding her death.* **2** [I,T] if you unravel threads or if they unravel, they become separated

un·real /ˌʌn'ril◂ / *adj.* **1** an experience, situation, etc. that is unreal seems so strange that you think you must be imagining it: *It seemed unreal to be sitting and talking to someone so famous.* **2** not relating to real things that happen: *Test questions often deal with unreal situations.*

un·re·al·is·tic /ˌʌnriə'lɪstɪk/ *adj.* unrealistic ideas or hopes are not reasonable or sensible: *He has unrealistic expectations about what kind of job he'll get.* | ***It's unrealistic to*** *expect her to be happy all the time.*

un·rea·son·a·ble /ʌn'rizənəbəl/ *adj.* **1** not fair or sensible: ***It's unreasonable to*** *give a 10-year-old so much responsibility.* | *He has a talent for dealing with the kids when they're being unreasonable.* **2** behaving in a way that is not pleasant, not sensible, and often silly **3** unreasonable prices, costs, etc. are too high

un·rec·og·niz·a·ble /ˌʌnrɛkəg'naɪzəbəl/ *adj.* changed or damaged so much that you cannot recognize someone or something: *The downtown area is almost unrecognizable.*

un·rec·og·nized /ʌn'rɛkəgˌnaɪzd/ *adj.* **1** not receiving the respect someone deserves: *The recording features an unrecognized jazz musician of the 1930s.* **2** not noticed or not thought to be important: *Some of these problems had* ***gone unrecognized*** *for years.*

un·re·cord·ed /ˌʌnrɪ'kɔrdɪd◂ / *adj.* not written down or recorded: *Their courage went largely unrecorded.*

un·re·fined /ˌʌnrɪ'faɪnd◂ / *adj.* **1** an unrefined substance is in its natural form: *unrefined sugar* **2** (formal) not polite or educated

un·reg·u·lat·ed /ʌn'rɛgyəˌleɪṭɪd/ (Ac) *adj.* not controlled by a government or law: *unregulated trade*

un·re·lat·ed /ˌʌnrɪ'leɪṭɪd◂ / *adj.* events, actions, situations, etc. that are unrelated are not connected with each other: *He will now stand trial on unrelated charges.*

un·re·lent·ing /ˌʌnrɪ'lɛnṭɪŋ◂ / *adj.* (formal) an unpleasant situation that is unrelenting continues for a long time without stopping or improving: *two days of unrelenting rain*

un·re·li·a·ble /ˌʌnrɪ'laɪəbəl◂ / (Ac) *adj.* unable to be trusted or depended on: *unreliable information* | *My old car is unreliable in the winter.*

un·re·lieved /ˌʌnrɪ'livd◂ / *adj.* a bad situation

that is unrelieved continues for a long time because nothing happens to change it: *unrelieved pain*

un·re·mit·ting /ˌʌnrɪ'mɪt̬ɪŋ◂/ *adj.* (formal) continuing for a long time and not likely to stop: *unremitting criticism*

un·re·pent·ant /ˌʌnrɪ'pɛntənt/ *adj.* not ashamed of behavior or beliefs that other people think are wrong: *He's an unrepentant racist.*

un·re·quit·ed /ˌʌnrɪ'kwaɪt̬ɪd◂/ *adj.* **unrequited love** romantic love that you feel for someone who does not feel the same love for you

un·re·solved /ˌʌnrɪ'zɑlvd◂/ (Ac) *adj.* an unresolved problem or question has not been answered or solved: *There was unresolved conflict between the two men.*

un·re·spon·sive /ˌʌnrɪ'spɑnsɪv/ (Ac) *adj.* not reacting to something or not affected by it: *The disease is* ***unresponsive to*** *drugs.*

un·rest /ʌn'rɛst/ *n.* [U] a political situation in which people protest or behave violently: *Troops are attempting to control the* ***civil/political etc. unrest*** *in the country.*

un·re·strained /ˌʌnrɪ'streɪnd◂/ (Ac) *adj.* not controlled or limited: *unrestrained laughter*

un·res·trict·ed /ˌʌnrɪ'strɪktɪd◂/ (Ac) *adj.* not limited by anyone or anything: *an unrestricted choice of doctors*

un·ri·valed /ʌn'raɪvəld/ *adj.* (formal) better than any other: *an unrivaled collection of 19th-century art*

un·roll /ʌn'roʊl/ *v.* [I,T] to open something that was in the shape of a ball or tube, and make it flat, or to become open in this way: *He unrolled the sleeping bag.*

un·ru·ly /ʌn'ruli/ *adj.* **1** violent or difficult to control: *unruly children* **2** unruly hair is messy

un·safe /ʌn'seɪf/ *adj.* **1** dangerous and likely to cause harm: *It's unsafe to swim in the river.* **2** in danger and likely to be harmed: *Many people feel unsafe walking alone at night.*

un·said /ʌn'sɛd/ *adj.* **be left unsaid** if something is left unsaid, you do not say it although you think it: *Some things are better left unsaid* (=it is better not to mention them).

un·san·i·tar·y /ʌn'sænəˌtɛri/ *adj.* dirty and likely to cause disease: *unsanitary conditions*

un·sat·is·fac·to·ry /ˌʌnsæt̬ɪs'fæktəri/ *adj.* not good enough: *Your work is unsatisfactory.*

un·sa·vor·y /ʌn'seɪvəri/ *adj.* bad, dishonest, or morally unacceptable: *unsavory business deals*

un·scathed /ʌn'skeɪðd/ *adj.* not hurt by a bad or dangerous situation: *The driver came out of the crash unscathed.*

un·screw /ʌn'skru/ *v.* [T] **1** to open something by twisting it: *Turn off the light before unscrewing the bulb.* **2** to take the screws out of something

un·scru·pu·lous /ʌn'skrupyələs/ *adj.* behaving in an unfair or dishonest way: *an unscrupulous lawyer*

un·sea·son·a·bly /ʌn'sizənəbli/ *adv.* **unseasonably warm/cold/mild etc.** used for saying that the weather is warmer, colder, etc. than usual at a particular time of year —**unseasonable** *adj.*

un·seat /ʌn'sit/ *v.* [T] to remove someone from a position of power: *Two candidates are trying to unseat the mayor.*

un·seem·ly /ʌn'simli/ *adj.* (formal) unseemly behavior is not polite or appropriate: *It was considered unseemly for women to smoke.*

un·seen /ˌʌn'sin◂/ *adj., adv.* (formal) not noticed or seen: *She left the office unseen.*

un·self·ish /ʌn'sɛlfɪʃ/ *adj.* caring about other people and thinking about their needs and wishes rather than your own —**unselfishly** *adv.* —**unselfishness** *n.* [U]

un·set·tle /ʌn'sɛt̬l/ *v.* [T] to make someone feel slightly worried or nervous: *Being in a room full of strangers unsettled me.*

un·set·tled /ˌʌn'sɛt̬ld◂/ *adj.* **1** making people feel unsure about what will happen: *The country faces an unsettled future.* **2** slightly worried, upset, or nervous: *The children are feeling unsettled by the divorce.*

> THESAURUS upset, troubled, disturbed → UPSET[1]

3 an unsettled argument continues without reaching any agreement: *The issue remains unsettled.* **4** if the weather is unsettled, it keeps changing and there is a lot of rain **5** feeling slightly sick: *My stomach's a little unsettled after all that rich food.*

un·set·tling /ʌn'sɛt̬l-ɪŋ/ *adj.* causing worry: *There have been some unsettling changes in the industry.*

un·shav·en /ʌn'ʃeɪvən/ *adj.* a man who is unshaven has short hairs growing on his face because he has not SHAVED → *see picture at* CLEAN-SHAVEN

un·sight·ly /ʌn'saɪtli/ *adj.* not nice to look at: *unsightly office buildings*

> THESAURUS ugly, unattractive, hideous → UGLY

un·skilled /ˌʌn'skɪld◂/ *adj.* **1** not trained for a particular type of job: *unskilled workers* **2** unskilled work does not need people with special skills

un·so·lic·it·ed /ˌʌnsə'lɪsɪt̬ɪd◂/ *adj.* not asked for and often not wanted: *unsolicited advice*

un·so·phis·ti·cat·ed /ˌʌnsə'fɪstəˌkeɪt̬ɪd/ *adj.* **1** not having much knowledge or experience of modern and fashionable things: *unsophisticated audiences* **2** unsophisticated tools, methods, or processes are simple or not very modern

U

un·sound /ˌʌnˈsaʊnd◂/ *adj.* **1** unsound arguments, methods, etc. are not based on fact or reason **2** an unsound building or structure is in bad condition

un·speak·a·ble /ʌnˈspikəbəl/ *adj.* extremely bad: *unspeakable crimes*

un·spe·ci·fied /ʌnˈspɛsəˌfaɪd/ (Ac) *adj.* not known or not stated: *The ticket is valid for an unspecified period of time.*

un·spoiled /ˌʌnˈspɔɪld◂/ *adj.* an unspoiled place is beautiful because it has not changed and there are no buildings there: *unspoiled beaches*

un·spo·ken /ʌnˈspoʊkən/ *adj.* understood but not discussed: *There was an* ***unspoken agreement*** *between us that we would tell Dee.*

un·sports·man·like /ʌnˈspɔrtsmənˌlaɪk/ *adj.* not behaving in a fair honest way when playing sports

un·sta·ble /ʌnˈsteɪbəl/ (Ac) *adj.* **1** likely to change suddenly and become worse: *an unstable economy* **2** dangerous and likely to fall over: *an unstable wall* **3** someone who is unstable changes very suddenly so that you do not know how s/he will react or behave ➔ CRAZY

un·stead·y /ʌnˈstɛdi/ *adj.* shaking or moving in an uncontrolled way, or likely to move or shake: *I felt unsteady on my feet.* | *The old bridge had become unsteady.*

un·stop·pa·ble /ʌnˈstɑpəbəl/ *adj.* unable to be stopped: *The team seems unstoppable this year.*

U

un·stressed /ʌnˈstrɛst/ *adj.* ENG. LANG. ARTS an unstressed word or part of a word is pronounced with less force than other ones

un·sub·stan·ti·at·ed /ˌʌnsəbˈstænʃiˌeɪt̬ɪd/ *adj.* not proved to be true: *The allegations of child abuse were unsubstantiated.*

un·suc·cess·ful /ˌʌnsəkˈsɛsfəl◂/ *adj.* not achieving what you wanted to achieve: *an unsuccessful attempt to win the election* —**unsuccessfully** *adv.*: *We tried, unsuccessfully, to convince Hererra of the truth.*

un·suit·a·ble /ʌnˈsut̬əbəl/ *adj.* not having the right qualities for a particular person, purpose, or situation: *This movie is* ***unsuitable for*** *young children.*

un·sung /ˌʌnˈsʌŋ◂/ *adj.* not praised or famous for something you have done, although you deserve to be: *Men like Garcia are the* ***unsung heroes*** *of the war.*

un·sure /ˌʌnˈʃʊr◂/ *adj.* **1** not certain about something or about what you have to do: *If you're* ***unsure of*** *the rules, ask the teacher.* **2 unsure of yourself** not having enough confidence: *Clara seemed shy and unsure of herself.*

un·sus·pect·ing /ˌʌnsəˈspɛktɪŋ◂/ *adj.* not knowing that something bad is about to happen: *Criminals can make easy money from mugging unsuspecting tourists.*

un·swerv·ing /ʌnˈswɚvɪŋ/ *adj.* never changing in spite of difficulties: *unswerving loyalty*

un·sym·pa·thet·ic /ˌʌnsɪmpəˈθɛt̬ɪk/ *adj.* **1** not kind or helpful to someone who is having problems (ANT) **sympathetic**: *The immigration officer was utterly unsympathetic.* **2** [not before noun] not willing to support someone's plans, actions, ideas, etc. (ANT) **sympathetic**: *The college stands accused of being* ***unsympathetic to/toward*** *minority students.* **3 unsympathetic character/figure etc.** ENG. LANG. ARTS someone in a book, play, etc. who most people do not like (ANT) **sympathetic** —**unsympathetically** *adv.*

un·tan·gle /ʌnˈtæŋgəl/ *v.* [T] **1** to make things straight that are twisted together: *Conditioner helps untangle your hair after you wash it.* **2** to understand something that is very complicated

un·tapped /ˌʌnˈtæpt◂/ *adj.* an untapped RESOURCE, market, etc. has not yet been used

un·ten·a·ble /ʌnˈtɛnəbəl/ *adj.* an untenable situation has become so difficult that it is impossible to continue: *The scandal put the President in an* ***untenable position.***

un·think·a·ble /ʌnˈθɪŋkəbəl/ *adj.* impossible to accept or imagine: *It was* ***unthinkable*** *a few years ago* ***for*** *a woman to run for President.*

un·ti·dy /ʌnˈtaɪdi/ *adj.* (formal) messy: *an untidy room*

un·tie /ʌnˈtaɪ/ *v.* [T] to undo the knots in something, or undo something that has been tied: *Mommy, can you untie my shoelaces?*

un·til /ənˈtɪl, ʌn-/ *prep., conjunction* **1** if something happens until a particular time, it continues and then stops at that time: *I have classes until 7 p.m. today.* | *Debbie's on vacation until Monday.*

USAGE

Until and **till** are used to talk about the time when something stops: *They stayed until/till after midnight.*
As far as is used to talk about the place where something stops: *Does the bus go as far as the station?*
Up to is used mainly to talk about the final number or the biggest possible number: *The children had to count up to fifty.*

2 not until used in order to say that something will not happen before a particular time: *The movie doesn't start until 8 p.m.* | *The doctor's not available until tomorrow.*

un·time·ly /ʌnˈtaɪmli/ *adj.* happening earlier than it should or than you expected: *an* ***untimely death***

un·tir·ing /ʌnˈtaɪərɪŋ/ *adj.* (approving) never stopping while working or trying to do something: *She was honored for her untiring efforts to help the homeless.*

un·told /ˌʌnˈtoʊld◂/ *adj.* too much or too many to be counted: *Floods did* ***untold damage*** *to farmland.*

un·touch·a·ble /ʌnˈtʌtʃəbəl/ *adj.* someone

who is untouchable is in such a strong position that s/he cannot be affected by, or punished for, anything: *These drug dealers think they're untouchable.*

un·touched /ʌn'tʌtʃt/ *adj.* not changed, affected, or damaged in any way: *The town was almost* ***untouched by*** *the war.*

un·toward /ˌʌn'tɔrd/ *adj.* (formal) unexpected, unusual, or not wanted: *Neighbors say that* ***nothing untoward*** *had happened on the night of the shooting.*

un·tried /ˌʌn'traɪd◂ / *adj.* something that is untried has not yet tested to see whether it is successful: *an untried theory*

un·true /ʌn'tru/ *adj.* not based on facts that are correct (SYN) **false**

un·truth·ful /ʌn'truθfəl/ *adj.* dishonest or not true

un·used¹ /ˌʌn'yuzd◂ / *adj.* not being used, or never used: *unused plane tickets*

un·used² /ʌn'yust/ *adj.* **unused to (doing) sth** not experienced in dealing with something: *She's unused to driving at night.*

un·u·su·al /ʌn'yuʒuəl, -ʒəl/ *adj.* different from what is usual or normal: *Our team has an unusual number of talented players.* | *unusual clothes* | ***It's unusual for*** *Dave to be late.*

un·u·su·al·ly /ʌn'yuʒuəli, -ʒəli/ *adv.* **unusually hot/difficult etc.** more hot, difficult, etc. than is usual

un·veil /ʌn'veɪl/ *v.* [T] **1** to show or tell people something that was a secret: *The mayor will unveil plans for a new park.* **2** to remove the cover from something as part of a formal ceremony

un·voiced /ʌn'vɔɪst/ *adj.* ENG. LANG. ARTS unvoiced CONSONANTS are produced without moving your VOCAL CORDS; for example /d/ and /g/ are VOICED consonants, and /t/ and /k/ are unvoiced

un·want·ed /ˌʌn'wʌntɪd◂ , -'wɑn-, -'wɔn-/ *adj.* not wanted or needed: *an unwanted pregnancy*

un·war·rant·ed /ʌn'wɔrəntɪd, -'wɑr-/ *adj.* not done for any good reason: *Shafer said the criticism was unwarranted.*

un·wel·come /ʌn'wɛlkəm/ *adj.* not wanted: *This is unwelcome news for farmers.* | *Many minority students* ***felt unwelcome*** *at the southern university.*

un·wield·y /ʌn'wildi/ *adj.* an unwieldy object is heavy and difficult to carry

un·will·ing /ʌn'wɪlɪŋ/ *adj.* not wanting to do something: *He's still* ***unwilling to*** *admit he was wrong.* | *unwilling participants*

un·wind /ʌn'waɪnd/ *v.* (past tense and past participle **unwound** /-'waʊnd/) **1** [I] to relax and stop feeling anxious: *Swimming helps me unwind.* **2** [I,T] to undo something that is wrapped or twisted around something else

un·wise /ˌʌn'waɪz◂ / *adj.* not based on good judgment: *It would be* ***unwise to*** *make him mad.*

un·wit·ting·ly /ʌn'wɪṭɪŋli/ *adv.* without knowing or realizing something: *Several employees unwittingly became involved in illegal activities.* —**unwitting** *adj.*

un·wor·thy /ʌn'wɚði/ *adj.* not deserving respect, attention, etc.: *This idea is* ***unworthy of*** *serious consideration.*

unwrap

unwrapping a present

un·wrap /ʌn'ræp/ *v.* (**unwrapped**, **unwrapping**) [T] to remove the paper, plastic, etc. that is around something: *Brianna was unwrapping her birthday presents.*

un·writ·ten /ˌʌn'rɪt̚n◂ / *adj.* known about and understood by everyone but not written down: *an* ***unwritten rule***

un·yield·ing /ʌn'yildɪŋ/ *adj.* (formal) not willing to change your ideas or beliefs: *The senator expressed her unyielding support for the president.*

un·zip /ʌn'zɪp/ *v.* (**unzipped**, **unzipping**) [T] to unfasten the ZIPPER on a piece of clothing, bag, etc.

U

up¹ /ʌp/ *adv., prep.* **1** toward a higher place or position (ANT) **down**: *Duncan climbed up into the tree.* | *Walk up the hill and turn right.* | *Could you come up here and help us?* | *Put your hand up if you know the answer.* **2** in a higher place or position (ANT) **down**: *"Where's Dave?" "He's up in his room."* | *The cat's up a tree.* | *A balloon floated up above us.* **3** in or to a place that is further along something such as a road or path (SYN) **down**: *I'm going up the road to see Jill.* **4** into an upright or raised position: *The choir stood up to sing.* | *The hair on the dog's back was sticking up.* **5** toward or in the north (ANT) **down**: *I'm driving up to see my parents.* | *His relatives all live up north.* **6** very close to someone or something: *The cop came* ***up to*** *the car and asked Chad for his license.* **7** increasing in loudness, strength, heat, activity, etc. (ANT) **down**: *Turn up the TV.* | *Violent crime was up 3% this month.* **8** completely done, used, etc., so that there is nothing left: *All the space in the basement is filled up.* | *Eat up your dinner!* **9** broken or divided completely: *She tore the letter up into tiny pieces.* | *We'll split the money up evenly.* **10** firmly fastened, covered, or joined: *The box was tied up with string.* | *Her dad covered her up and said goodnight.* **11** brought or gathered together: *Add up the following numbers.* | *He gathered up all the pens he could find.* **12** toward the place where a river starts: *We sailed up the river.* **13** above and including a particular number or amount: *This movie is suitable for children aged 12 and up.* **14 up to sth a)** used in order to show the highest amount or level of something, or the latest time something can happen: *Up to 10 people are allowed in the elevator at one time.* | *This offer is valid up to December 15.* **b)** used in order to say or ask what someone is doing: *What have you been up to lately?* | *I'm sure Bob's* ***up to something*** (=doing something secret or bad). **c)** good enough or well enough to do something: *The local police just aren't* ***up to the job*** (=not good enough to do it). | *Do you feel up to a walk today?* **15 up and down a)** higher and lower: *The kids were so excited they were* ***jumping up and down.*** **b)** to one end of something and then back again: *We walked up and down the street trying to find the house.* **16 it's up to you** (spoken) said to tell someone that you want him/her to make a decision: *"Do you think I should get the dress?" "It's up to you."* **17 up close** very near someone or something: *If you look up close, you can see the cracks.* **18 meet/see/know etc. up close** to meet someone or experience something that you had previously only read or heard about: *I was surprised by how short he was when I met him up close.*

up² *adj.* **1** awake: *"Sorry, were you in bed?" "No, I'm still up."* **2** IT a computer system that is up is working (ANT) **down** **3** a level, number, or amount that is up is higher than before (ANT) **down**: *Profits were up by 4% this year.* **4** beating your opponent by a certain number of points (ANT) **down**: *With 5 minutes left, Boston is up by 8 points.* **5** (informal) if a period of time is up, it is finished: *I'll give you a signal when the ten minutes are up.* **6 be up against sb/sth** to have to deal with a difficult situation or fight an opponent: *We're up against some of the biggest companies in the world.* **7 be up for sth a)** to be intended for a particular purpose: *The house is up for sale.* | *The topic will be up for discussion at the meeting.* **b)** (spoken) to be interested in doing something, or willing to do something: *Is anybody up for a game of tennis?* **8 be up and running** if a machine or process is up and running, it is working correctly: *The equipment should be up and running in about three weeks.* **9 be up before sb/sth** to be judged in a court of law: *He was up before the grand jury on charges of fraud.*

SPOKEN PHRASES

10 What's up? used in order to greet someone, or to ask if there is a problem: *Hey, Mark! What's up?* **11 be up on (sth)** to know a lot about something: *I'm not really up on the way things work here.*

up³ *n.* **1 ups and downs** the good things and bad things that happen in a particular situation: *We've had our ups and downs like all couples.* **2 be on the up and up** (spoken) if a person or business is on the up and up, he, she, or it is honest and does things legally

up⁴ *v.* (informal) **1** (**upped, upping**) [T] to increase the amount or level of something: *They've upped Don's salary by $2,500.* **2 up and do sth** to suddenly do something different or surprising: *Without saying another word, he* ***up and left.***

ˌup-and-ˈcoming *adj.* likely to be successful and popular: *an up-and-coming actor*

up·beat /ˌʌpˈbit◂ / *adj.* cheerful and making you feel that good things will happen: *We remained calm and upbeat about the situation.*

up·braid /ʌpˈbreɪd/ *v.* [T] (formal) to tell someone angrily that s/he has done something wrong: *I heard a manager upbraiding one of the workers.*

up·bring·ing /ˈʌpˌbrɪŋɪŋ/ *n.* [singular, U] the way that your parents care for you and teach you to behave when you are growing up: *He had a very* ***strict upbringing.***

up·chuck /ˈʌp-tʃʌk/ *v.* [I] (spoken, informal) to VOMIT

up·com·ing /ˈʌpˌkʌmɪŋ/ *adj.* happening soon: *the upcoming elections*

up·date¹ /ˈʌpdeɪt, ˌʌpˈdeɪt/ *v.* [T] **1** to add the most recent information to something: *The system needs to be updated.* **2** to make something more modern in the way it looks or operates: *We need to update our image.*

up·date² /ˈʌpdeɪt/ *n.* [C] the most recent news about something: *an* ***update on*** *the earthquake*

up·end /ʌpˈɛnd/ *v.* [T] to turn something over so that it is upside down

up·front /ʌpˈfrʌnt/ *adj.* **1** talking or behaving in a direct and honest way: *Jill's always been upfront with him.*

THESAURUS **honest, frank, candid, direct, straight, straightforward, forthright** → HONEST

2 paid before any work has been done or before goods are supplied —**upfront** *adv.*: *We'll need $300 upfront.*

up·grade /ˈʌpgreɪd, ˌʌpˈgreɪd/ *v.* [T] to improve something, or to exchange something for something better: *I was upgraded to first class on the flight back.* | *We need to upgrade our computer.* —**upgrade** /ˈʌpgreɪd/ *n.* [C]

up·heav·al /ʌpˈhivəl, ˈʌpˌhivəl/ *n.* [C,U] a very big change that often causes problems: *political upheaval*

up·hill /ˌʌpˈhɪl◂ / *adj., adv.* **1** toward the top of a hill (ANT) **downhill**: *an uphill climb* **2** an uphill battle, job, etc. is very difficult and needs a lot of effort: *Kent faces an* ***uphill battle*** *if he wants to win.*

up·hold /ʌpˈhoʊld/ *v.* (past tense and past participle **upheld** /-ˈhɛld/) [T] **1** to defend or support a law, system, or principle so that it is not made weaker: *They want to uphold family values.* **2** LAW if a court upholds a decision that is made by another court, it states that the decision was correct

up·hol·ster /əˈpoʊlstɚ, ʌpˈhoʊl-/ v. [T] to cover a chair with material —**upholstered** adj.

up·hol·ster·y /əˈpoʊlstəri/ n. [U] material that is used for covering chairs, or the process of doing this

up·keep /ˈʌpkip/ n. [U] the care that is needed to keep something in good condition: ***the upkeep of** a big house*

up·lift·ing /ˌʌpˈlɪftɪŋ◂/ adj. making you feel more cheerful: *uplifting music*

up·on /əˈpɑn, əˈpɔn/ prep. (formal) on: *We are completely dependent upon your help.* | *The king was sitting upon the throne.*

up·per /ˈʌpɚ/ adj. [only before noun] **1** in a higher position than something else (ANT) **lower**: *the upper jaw* **2** near or at the top of something (ANT) **lower**: *the upper floors of the building* **3** more important or higher in rank than other parts in an organization (ANT) **lower**: *upper management* **4 have/gain the upper hand** to have more power than someone else, so that you are able to control a situation: *Rebels have gained the upper hand in some areas.*

up·per·case /ˌʌpɚˈkeɪs◂/ n. [U] letters written in their large form, such as A, B, C, etc. → CAPITAL (ANT) **lowercase**

ˌupper ˈclass n. **the upper class** SOCIAL SCIENCE the group of people who belong to the highest social class → LOWER CLASS, MIDDLE CLASS, WORKING CLASS —**upper-class** adj.: *upper-class communities*

up·per·class·man /ˌʌpɚˈklæsmən/ n. (plural **upperclassmen** /-mən/) [C] a student in the last two years of HIGH SCHOOL or college → UNDERCLASSMAN

up·per·most /ˈʌpɚˌmoʊst/ adj. **1** most important: *Your safety is **uppermost in** my **mind*** (=I think it is most important). **2** highest: *the uppermost branches of the tree*

up·pi·ty /ˈʌpət̬i/ adj. (spoken, informal) behaving as if you are more important than you really are, or not showing someone enough respect

up·right /ˈʌp-raɪt/ adj., adv. **1** standing, sitting, or pointing straight up: *Andy **stood upright** when he heard the noise.* | *Please put your seat in an **upright position**.* **2** always behaving in an honest way: *upright citizens*

up·ris·ing /ˈʌpˌraɪzɪŋ/ n. [C] an occasion when a large group of people use violence to try to change the rules, laws, etc. in an institution or country: *a **popular uprising*** (=by the ordinary people in a country)

THESAURUS **revolution, rebellion, revolt, insurrection** → REVOLUTION

up·riv·er /ʌpˈrɪvɚ/ adv. toward the place where a river begins, in the opposite direction from the way the water is flowing

up·roar /ˈʌp-rɔr/ n. [singular, U] a lot of noise or angry protest about something: *The announcement **caused an uproar**.*

up·root /ˌʌpˈrut/ v. [T] **1** to pull a plant and its roots out of the ground **2** to make someone leave his/her home and move to a new place, especially when this is difficult: *Steven's new job will mean uprooting the family.*

up·scale /ˌʌpˈskeɪl◂/ adj. made for or relating to people from a high social class who have a lot of money: *an upscale department store*

up·set¹ /ˌʌpˈsɛt◂/ adj. **1** [not before noun] unhappy and worried because something bad or disappointing has happened: *What are you so **upset about**?* | *He was **upset that** Helen had lied to him.* | *When I told him he'd failed, he **got** very **upset**.*

THESAURUS

unsettled – slightly worried, upset, or nervous: *The children are feeling unsettled by the divorce.*
troubled – slightly worried and upset: *She looked troubled by this news.*
disturbed – worried and upset: *He had been too much disturbed to sleep.*
perturbed – worried, upset, and annoyed: *The criticism drew a perturbed reaction from the team's coach.*
distressed – very sad, worried, and upset: *Her family were very distressed that she had not contacted them.*
distraught – extremely worried, sad, and upset: *Friends tried to comfort his distraught mother.*
traumatized – shocked and upset by a bad experience for a very long time: *He was traumatized by his war experiences.*

2 an upset stomach/tummy an illness that has an effect on the stomach and makes you sick

up·set² /ʌpˈsɛt/ v. (past tense and past participle **upset**, present participle **upsetting**) [T] **1** to make someone feel unhappy or worried: *Kopp's comments upset many of his listeners.* **2** to change something in a way that causes problems: *I hope I haven't upset all your plans.* **3 upset sb's stomach** to make someone feel sick

up·set³ /ˈʌpsɛt/ n. [C] an occasion when a person or team that is not expected to win defeats a stronger opponent in a competition, election, etc.

up·set·ting /ʌpˈsɛt̬ɪŋ/ adj. making you feel upset: *an upsetting experience*

up·shot /ˈʌpʃɑt/ n. **the upshot (of sth)** the final result of a situation (SYN) **outcome**: *The upshot is that she's decided to take the job.*

up·side /ˈʌpsaɪd/ n. **the upside** the positive part of a situation (ANT) **downside**

ˌupside ˈdown adj., adv. **1** with the top at the bottom and the bottom at the top: *Isn't that picture upside down?* **2 turn sth upside down a)** to move a lot of things and make a place messy because you are looking for something: *We turned the house upside down looking for my keys.* **b)** to change something completely: *Her life had been turned upside down by the accident.*

U

up·stage /ˌʌpˈsteɪdʒ/ *v.* [T] to do something that takes people's attention away from a more important person or event

upstairs

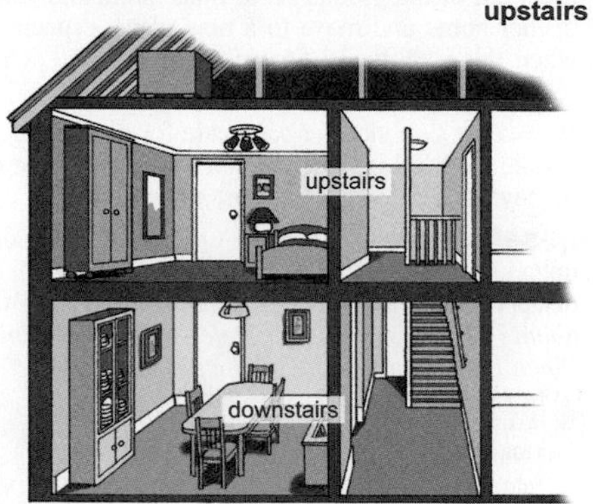

up·stairs /ˌʌpˈstɛrz◂/ *adj., adv.* **1** on or toward a higher floor of a building (ANT) **downstairs**: *Her office is upstairs on your right.* | *the upstairs bathroom* **2 the upstairs** one or all of the upper floors of a building: *Would you like to see the upstairs?*

up·stand·ing /ʌpˈstændɪŋ/ *adj.* (formal) honest and responsible: *an upstanding citizen*

up·start /ˈʌpstɑrt/ *n.* [C] someone who is new in his/her job and behaves as if s/he is more important than s/he is

up·state /ˌʌpˈsteɪt◂/ *adj.* in or toward the northern part of a state (ANT) **downstate**: *upstate New York* —**upstate** *adv.*

U

up·stream /ˌʌpˈstrim◂/ *adv.* along a river, in the opposite direction from the way the water is flowing (ANT) **downstream** —**upstream** *adj.*

up·surge /ˈʌpsɚdʒ/ *n.* [C] a sudden increase: *a recent* ***upsurge in*** *car sales*

up·swing /ˈʌpswɪŋ/ *n.* [C] an improvement or increase in the level of something ➔ UPTURN: *an* ***upswing in*** *the economy* | *Incomes are* ***on the upswing****.*

up·take /ˈʌpteɪk/ *n.* **be slow/quick on the uptake** (informal) to be slow or fast at learning or understanding things

up·tight /ˌʌpˈtaɪt◂/ *adj.* (informal) behaving in an annoyed way because you are feeling nervous and worried: *You shouldn't* ***get*** *so* ***uptight about*** *it.*

ˌup-to-ˈdate *adj.* **1** including all the newest information: *up-to-date travel information* | *Doctors must* ***keep up-to-date with*** *medical research.* **2** modern or fashionable: *the most up-to-date technology* | *The old system should be* ***brought up-to-date*** (=made modern).

ˌup-to-the-ˈminute *adj.* including the most recent information, details, etc.: *up-to-the-minute news*

up·town /ˌʌpˈtaʊn◂/ *adj., adv.* to or in the northern area of a city where the richer people live ➔ DOWNTOWN: *The Parkers live uptown.*

up·turn /ˈʌptɚn/ *n.* [C] a time when business activity is increased and conditions improve (ANT) **downturn** ➔ UPSWING: *an* ***upturn in*** *oil production*

up·turned /ˈʌptɚnd, ˌʌpˈtɚnd/ *adj.* **1** pointing upward at the end: *an upturned nose* **2** turned upside down: *upturned boxes*

up·ward[1] /ˈʌpwɚd/ *adj.* [only before noun] **1** moving or pointing toward a higher position (ANT) **downward**: *an upward movement of the hand* **2** increasing to a higher level (ANT) **downward**: *the upward trend in house prices*

upward[2] *also* **upwards** *adv.* **1** from a lower place or position to a higher one (ANT) **downward**: *Billy pointed upward at the clouds.* **2** increasing to a higher level (ANT) **downward**: *Salaries have been moving upwards.*

u·ra·ni·um /yʊˈreɪniəm/ *n.* [U] CHEMISTRY a heavy RADIOACTIVE white metal that is used in producing NUCLEAR energy and weapons

U·ra·nus /yʊˈreɪnəs, ˈyʊrənəs/ *n.* PHYSICS the seventh PLANET from the Sun ➔ *see picture at* SOLAR SYSTEM

ur·ban /ˈɚbən/ *adj.* in or relating to a town or city ➔ RURAL, SUBURBAN: *the growth of* ***urban areas*** | *the urban poor* [ORIGIN: 1600—1700 Latin *urbanus* "urban, sophisticated," from *urbs* "city"]

ur·bane /ɚˈbeɪn/ *adj.* behaving in a relaxed and confident way in social situations

ur·ban·ize /ˈɚbəˌnaɪz/ *v.* [T usually passive] **1** SOCIAL SCIENCE to build houses, cities, etc. in the COUNTRYSIDE **2** SOCIAL SCIENCE if a society is urbanized, people live mainly in cities —**urbanization** /ˌɚbənəˈzeɪʃən/ *n.* [U]

ˌurban reˈnewal *n.* [U] the process of improving poor city areas by building new houses, stores, etc.

ˌurban ˈsprawl *n.* [U] the spread of city buildings and houses into an area that was COUNTRYSIDE

ur·chin /ˈɚtʃɪn/ *n.* [C] (old-fashioned) a small dirty child

u·re·ter /yʊˈritɚ, ˈjʊrətɚ/ *n.* [C] BIOLOGY a tube inside the body that carries URINE (=the yellow liquid waste produced by the body) from the KIDNEYS to the BLADDER

u·re·thra /yʊˈriθrə/ *n.* [c] BIOLOGY the tube through which URINE (=waste water) flows out of the body from the BLADDER, and also through which the SEMEN of males flows

urge[1] /ɚdʒ/ *v.* [T] to strongly advise someone to do something: *Cal's family* ***urged*** *him* ***to*** *find another job.* | *Environmental groups have* ***urged that*** *the land remain undeveloped.*

THESAURUS **advise, recommend, suggest**
➔ ADVISE

urge sb ↔ **on** *phr. v.* to encourage someone to try harder, go faster, etc.: *Urged on by the crowd, they scored two more goals.*

urge² *n.* [C] a strong wish or need: *sexual urges | I felt a sudden **urge to** hit him.*

ur·gent /ˈɚdʒənt/ *adj.* very important and needing to be dealt with immediately: *an urgent message | She's **in urgent need of** medical attention.* —**urgency** /ˈɚdʒənsi/ *n.* [U]: *a matter of great urgency* —**urgently** *adv.*: *Help is urgently needed.*

u·ri·nar·y /ˈyʊrəˌnɛri/ *adj.* BIOLOGY relating to urine or to the parts of your body through which urine passes

u·ri·nate /ˈyʊrəˌneɪt/ *v.* [I] BIOLOGY to make urine flow out of your body

u·rine /ˈyʊrɪn/ *n.* [U] BIOLOGY the liquid waste that comes out of your body when you go to the toilet

URL *n.* [C] IT **uniform resource locator** an address for a particular WEBSITE on the Internet

urn /ɚn/ *n.* [C] **1** a container that holds and pours a large amount of coffee or tea **2** a decorated container, especially one that is used for holding the ASHes of a dead body

us /əs; *strong* ʌs/ *pron.* the object form of "we": *He walked by, but he didn't see us.*

U.S. *n.* **the U.S.** the United States of America

U.S.A. *n.* **the U.S.A.** the United States of America

us·a·ble /ˈyuzəbəl/ *adj.* something that is usable can be used: *The software converts raw data into usable information.*

us·age /ˈyusɪdʒ/ *n.* **1** [C,U] the way that words are used in a language: *a book on modern English usage* **2** [U] the way in which something is used, or the amount of it that is used: *Homeowners must cut water usage.*

USB *n.* [C] IT **universal serial bus** a way of connecting equipment such as a mouse or a PRINTER to a computer, using a wire

USB 'drive *n.* [C] IT **universal serial bus drive** a small piece of equipment for storing information, that connects into the USB port on a computer. A USB drive can be removed and put into another computer. SYN **jump drive**

USB 'port *n.* [C] IT **universal serial bus port** a place on a computer where you can connect a piece of equipment, through which information can be sent and received very quickly

use¹ /yuz/ *v.* **1** [T] if you use something, you do something with it for a particular purpose: *Can I use your phone? | I need to **use the bathroom*** (=go to the toilet). | ***Use** a food processor **to** grate the vegetables. | The system is **easy to use**. | We only **use** the car **for** driving in the city.* **2** [T] to need or take an amount of food, gas, money, etc.: *These light bulbs use less electricity. | Our car's using too much oil.* **3** [T] to treat someone in an unkind and unfair way in order to get something that you want: *Can't you see that Andy is just using you?* **4** [T] to say or write a particular word or phrase: *I try not to use bad language around the kids.* **5** [I,T] to take illegal drugs [ORIGIN: 1200—1300 Old French *user*, from Latin *usus*, past participle of *uti* "to use"]

use sth ↔ **up** *phr. v.* to use all of something: *Who used up all the toothpaste?*

use² /yus/ *n.*

1 ACT OF USING STH [singular, U] the act of using something: *the **use of** computers in education*

2 WAY STH IS USED [C] a purpose for which something can be used: *The drug **has** many **uses**.*

3 the use of sth the right or ability to use something: *Joe's given me the use of his office. | She lost the use of both legs.*

4 make use of sth to use something that is available in order to achieve something or to get an advantage for yourself: *It's a shame that students don't make more use of the computer lab. | Try to **make good use of** your time.*

5 put sth to (good) use to use knowledge, skills, etc. for a particular purpose: *The job will give you a chance to put your first-aid training to good use.*

6 be (of) no use (to sb) to be completely useless: *The books are of no use to me now.*

7 it's no use doing sth (spoken) used in order to tell someone not to do something because it will have no effect: *It's no use arguing with Kathy. She won't listen.*

8 it's no use! (spoken) used in order to say that you are going to stop doing something because you do not think it will be successful: *It's no use! I can't fix this.*

9 have no/little use for sb/sth to not like or respect someone or something: *She has no use for people who are always complaining.*

10 be in use being used: *The computer room's in use all morning.*

11 for the use of sb for a particular person or group to use: *The gym is for the use of employees only.*

12 WORDS [C] one of the meanings of a word, or the way that a particular word is used → USAGE: *The use of the word "gay" to mean "happy" is old-fashioned.*

used¹ /yust/ *adj.* **be used to (doing) sth** if you are used to something, you have experienced it many times before and it no longer seems surprising, difficult, etc.: *Kathy is used to getting up early. | He still hasn't **gotten used to** the weather here.*

used² /yuzd/ *adj.* **used cars/clothes/books etc.** cars, clothes, etc. that have already had an owner SYN **secondhand**

used to /ˈyustə; *final or before a vowel* ˈyustu/ *modal verb* if something used to happen, it happened often or regularly in the past but does not happen now: *We used to go to the movies every week. | "Do you play golf?" "No, but I used to."*

USAGE

Used to is used in order to talk about something that someone did regularly in the past but does not do anymore: *I used to play tennis twice a week, but I don't have time now.*

Be used to and **get used to** are used in order

U

to talk about being or becoming more comfortable with a situation or activity, so that it does not seem surprising, difficult, etc. anymore: *Are you used to the cold winters yet? | I can't get used to living in a big city.*

use·ful /ˈyusfəl/ *adj.* helping you to do or to get what you want: *useful information | **It's useful to** make a list before you start.* —**usefully** *adv.* —**usefulness** *n.* [U]

use·less /ˈyuslɪs/ *adj.* not useful or effective in any way: *These scissors are **completely/totally** useless. | **It's useless to** complain.* ➔ POINTLESS

us·er /ˈyuzɚ/ *n.* [C] someone who uses a product, service, etc.: *The CD-ROM allows the user to hear how all of the words in the dictionary are pronounced. | Ramps designed for wheelchair users have been added to the building. | **Users of** cell phones pay more for calls.*

ˌuser-ˈfriendly *adj.* easy to use or operate

us·er·name, user name /ˈyuzɚˌneɪm/ *n.* [C] IT a name or special word that proves who you are and allows you to enter a computer system or use the Internet

ush·er[1] /ˈʌʃɚ/ *n.* [C] someone who shows people to their seats at a theater, wedding, etc.

usher[2] *v.* [T] to take someone into or out of a room or building: *His secretary **ushered** us **into** the office.*

THESAURUS **lead, guide, show, escort** ➔ LEAD[1]

usher in sth *phr. v.* to make something new start happening: *Gorbachev ushered in a new era of reform.*

u·su·al /ˈyuʒuəl, -ʒəl/ *adj.* **1** the same as what happens most of the time or in most situations: *Let's meet at the usual place. | I woke up a little earlier/later **than usual**.* **2 as usual** in the way that happens or exists most of the time: *They were late, as usual.*

u·su·al·ly /ˈyuʒuəli, -ʒəli/ *adv.* used when describing what happens on most occasions or in most situations: *We usually go out for dinner on Saturday. | Usually, I just get a sandwich for lunch.*

u·surp /yuˈsɚp/ *v.* [T] (formal) to take someone else's power, position, job, etc.

UT the written abbreviation of UTAH

u·ten·sil /yuˈtɛnsəl/ *n.* [C] a tool or object that you use to prepare, cook, or eat food: *cooking utensils* [ORIGIN: 1300—1400 Old French *utensile*, from Latin *utensilis* "useful"]

u·ter·us /ˈyut̬ərəs/ *n.* [C] BIOLOGY the organ in a woman or female MAMMAL where babies develop

u·til·i·tar·i·an /yuˌtɪləˈtɛriən/ *adj.* (formal) useful and practical rather than being used for decoration: *utilitarian clothes*

u·til·i·ty /yuˈtɪlət̬i/ Ac *n.* (plural **utilities**) [C usually plural] a service such as gas or electricity that is provided for people to use: *Does the rent include utilities?*

u·til·ize /ˈyut̬lˌaɪz/ Ac *v.* [T] (formal) to use something [ORIGIN: 1800—1900 French *utiliser*, from *utile* "useful"] —**utilization** /ˌyut̬l-əˈzeɪʃən/ *n.* [U]

ut·most[1] /ˈʌtˌmoʊst/ *adj.* **the utmost importance/care/etc.** the greatest possible importance, care, etc.: *This is a matter of the utmost importance.*

utmost[2] *n.* [singular] **1 to the utmost** to the highest limit, EXTENT, degree, etc. possible: *The piece challenges singers to the utmost.* **2 do your utmost** to try as hard as you can in order to achieve something: *We've done our utmost to make them feel welcome.*

u·to·pi·a /yuˈtoʊpiə/ *n.* [C,U] an imaginary perfect world where everyone is happy —**utopian** *adj.*

u·to·pi·an·ism /yuˈtoʊpiəˌnɪzəm/ *n.* [U] SOCIAL SCIENCE the set of ideas, beliefs, etc. on which the development of a UTOPIAN society are based. These ideas are often seen as not practical or possible.

ut·ter[1] /ˈʌt̬ɚ/ *adj.* complete or extreme: *We watched in utter amazement.* —**utterly** *adv.*: *He felt utterly exhausted.*

utter[2] *v.* [T] (literary) to say something: *No one uttered a word.* ➔ SAY[1] —**utterance** *n.* [C]

U-turn /ˈyu tɚn/ *n.* [C] a turn that you make in a vehicle, so that you go back in the direction you came from: *Shea **made a U-turn** and drove away.*

u·vu·la /ˈyuvyələ/ *n.* (plural **uvulas** or **uvulae** /-li/) [C] BIOLOGY a small soft piece of flesh that hangs down from the top of your mouth near your throat

Vv

V, v /vi/ **1** the twenty-second letter of the English alphabet **2** the number 5 in the system of ROMAN NUMERALS **3** PHYSICS the written abbreviation of VOLT

v. a written abbreviation of VERSUS

VA the written abbreviation of VIRGINIA

va·can·cy /ˈveɪkənsi/ *n.* (plural **vacancies**) [C] **1** a room in a hotel that is available for someone to stay in: *The motel sign said "no vacancies."* **2** (formal) a job that is available for someone to start doing: *The principal is interviewing candidates to **fill** several **vacancies** at the school.*

va·cant /ˈveɪkənt/ *adj.* **1** empty and available for someone to use: *vacant apartments*

THESAURUS empty, free ➔ EMPTY[1]

2 (formal) if a position in an organization is vacant, the job is available because no one is doing it **3** if someone has a vacant expression, s/he does not seem to be thinking about anything **—vacantly** *adv.*: *Cindy was staring vacantly out into empty space.*

va·cate /ˈveɪkeɪt/ *v.* [T] (formal) to leave a seat, room, etc. so that someone else can use it: *Guests must vacate their rooms by noon.*

va·ca·tion /veɪˈkeɪʃən, və-/ *n.* **1** [C,U] a time that is spent not working or not at school, especially time spent in another place for enjoyment: *They're **on vacation** for the next two weeks.* | *How did you spend your **summer vacation**?* | *We'd like to **take a vacation** in the Virgin Islands.*

THESAURUS

vacation – time you spend away from school or work: *a two-week vacation in Mexico* | *a real family vacation*
holiday – a day when no one officially has to go to work or school: *the Thanksgiving holiday*
break – a time when you stop working or studying in order to rest, or a short vacation from school: *a ten-minute coffee break* | *We spent spring break in Florida.*
leave – a time when you are allowed not to work for a special reason: *Angela is on maternity leave.*
furlough – a short period of time in which someone is allowed to be away from his/her job, especially in the military: *a soldier home on furlough*
R & R – rest and relaxation; a vacation given to people in the army, navy, etc. after a long time of hard work or during a war: *During the Vietnam War, soldiers were sent to Hawaii for R & R.*
sabbatical – a period when someone who teaches stops doing his/her usual work in order to study or travel: *Prof. Morris is on sabbatical this semester.*

2 [U] the number of days, weeks, etc. that you are allowed as paid holiday by your employer: *All employees get three weeks' **paid vacation** each year.* [ORIGIN: 1300—1400 Old French, Latin *vacatio* "freedom"] **—vacation** *v.* [I]

vac·ci·nate /ˈvæksəˌneɪt/ *v.* [T] to protect someone from a disease by giving him/her a vaccine SYN **immunize**: *Have you been **vaccinated against** measles?* **—vaccination** /ˌvæksəˈneɪʃən/ *n.* [C,U]

vac·cine /vækˈsin/ *n.* [C,U] a substance that is used to protect people from a disease, that contains a weak form of the VIRUS that causes the disease: *a polio vaccine* [ORIGIN: 1700—1800 Latin *vaccinus* "of a cow," from *vacca* "cow;" because the substance was originally obtained from sick cows]

vac·il·late /ˈvæsəˌleɪt/ *v.* [I] (formal) to continue to change your opinions, ideas, etc. because you cannot decide between two choices

vac·u·ole /ˈvækyuˌoʊl/ *n.* [C] BIOLOGY a small space inside a living cell, used for storing water, food, or waste

vac·u·ous /ˈvækyuəs/ *adj.* (formal) lacking in serious thought or intelligence: *a vacuous remark* **—vacuously** *adv.* **—vacuousness** *n.* [U]

vac·uum[1] /ˈvækyum/ *n.* **1** [C] a vacuum cleaner **2** [C] PHYSICS a space that is completely empty of all air or gas **3** [singular] a situation in which someone or something is missing or lacking: *Her husband's death left a vacuum in her life.* [ORIGIN: 1500—1600 Latin *vacuus* "empty"]

vacuum[2] *v.* [I,T] to clean a place using a vacuum cleaner: *She vacuumed the living room.*

THESAURUS clean, do the housework, dust, polish, sweep (up), scrub, mop ➔ CLEAN[2]

ˈvacuum ˌcleaner *n.* [C] a machine that cleans floors by sucking up the dirt from them

ˈvacuum-ˌpacked *adj.* vacuum-packed food is packed in a container from which the air is removed, in order to keep the food fresh

va·ga·ries /ˈveɪgəriz/ *n.* [plural] (formal) unexpected changes in a situation that you cannot control: ***the vagaries of** the weather*

va·gi·na /vəˈdʒaɪnə/ *n.* [C] BIOLOGY the passage from a woman's outer sexual organs to her UTERUS **—vaginal** /ˈvædʒənl/ *adj.*

va·grant /ˈveɪgrənt/ *n.* [C] (formal) someone who has no home or work

vague /veɪg/ *adj.* **1** unclear because someone does not give enough details or say exactly what s/he means: *John was a little **vague about** where he was going.* | ***vague promises** to end the war* **2 have a vague idea/feeling etc.** to think that something might be true or that you remember something, although you are not sure

vague·ly /ˈveɪgli/ *adv.* **1** slightly: *She looked vaguely familiar.* **2** not clearly: *His statement was very vaguely worded.* **3** in a way that shows you are not thinking about what you are doing: *He smiled vaguely.*

vain /veɪn/ *adj.* **1** (disapproving) too proud of your appearance or your abilities ➔ VANITY: *Men can be just as vain as women.*

THESAURUS proud, conceited, big-headed, stuck-up, egotistical ➔ PROUD

2 in vain without success: *I tried in vain to convince Paul to come.* **3 vain attempt/hope etc.** an attempt, hope, etc. that is not successful [ORIGIN: 1300—1400 Old French, Latin *vanus* "empty, vain"] **—vainly** *adv.*

va·lence /ˈveɪləns/ *also* **va·len·cy** /ˈveɪlənsi/ *n.* (plural **valencies**) [C] CHEMISTRY a measure of the ability of atoms to combine to form COMPOUNDS

val·en·tine /ˈvælənˌtaɪn/ *n.* [C] **1** a card given

on Valentine's Day **2** a name for someone you love or like, who you send a card to on Valentine's Day: *Will you be my valentine?*

ˈValentine's ˌDay *n.* a holiday in some countries when people give special cards, candy, or flowers to people they love

val·et /væˈleɪ, ˈvæleɪ/ *n.* [C] **1** someone who parks your car for you at a hotel or restaurant **2** a male servant who takes care of a man's clothes, serves his meals, etc.

val·iant /ˈvælyənt/ *adj.* (formal) very brave: *a valiant rescue attempt*

THESAURUS **brave, courageous, heroic** → BRAVE[1]

val·id /ˈvælɪd/ (Ac) *adj.* **1** a valid ticket, document, or agreement can be used legally or is officially acceptable (ANT) **invalid**: *a valid passport* **2** based on strong reasons or facts: *They had some valid concerns about the safety of the airplane.* | *In order to make a valid comparison, the tests must be carried out under comparable conditions.* [ORIGIN: 1500—1600 French *valide*, from Latin *validus* "strong, effective," from *valere* "to be worth, be strong"] —**validity** /vəˈlɪdəṭi/ *n.* [U]: *Scientists are questioning the validity of his research.*

val·i·date /ˈvæləˌdeɪt/ (Ac) *v.* [T] (formal) to show or prove that something is true or correct (ANT) **invalidate**: *It is hoped that the results of the study will be validated by future research.*

val·ley /ˈvæli/ *n.* [C] EARTH SCIENCES an area of lower land between two lines of hills or mountains: *the San Fernando Valley* [ORIGIN: 1200—1300 Old French *valee*, from *val*] → *see picture on page A24*

V

val·or /ˈvælɚ/ *n.* [U] (literary) great courage, especially in war

THESAURUS **courage, bravery, guts** → COURAGE

val·u·a·ble /ˈvælyəbəl, -yuəbəl/ *adj.* **1** worth a lot of money: *a valuable ring*

THESAURUS

precious – valuable because of being rare or expensive: *precious gems*
priceless – so valuable that you cannot calculate a financial value: *a priceless painting by Rembrandt*
worth a lot/a fortune – to be worth a very large amount of money: *Their house is now worth a fortune.* → EXPENSIVE

2 valuable help, advice, etc. is very useful → INVALUABLE: *I think we've all learned a valuable lesson today.*

val·u·a·bles /ˈvælyəbəlz/ *n.* [plural] things that you own that are worth a lot of money, such as jewelry, cameras, etc.: *Guests should leave their valuables in the hotel safe.*

THESAURUS **property, possessions, things, belongings, effects** → PROPERTY

val·ue[1] /ˈvælyu/ *n.* **1** [C,U] the amount of money that something is worth: *the* ***value of*** *the house* | *The dollar has been steadily* ***increasing/decreasing in value.*** | *Did the thieves take anything* ***of value*** (=worth a lot of money)? **2** [U] the importance or usefulness of something: *His research was* ***of great value*** *to doctors working with this disease.* | *These earrings* ***have sentimental value*** (=are important to you because they were a gift, remind you of someone, etc.). **3 values** [plural] your beliefs about what is right and wrong, or about what is important in life: *traditional family values* **4 good/great etc. value** something that is worth the amount you pay for it [ORIGIN: 1300—1400 Old French, Vulgar Latin *valuta*, from Latin *valere* "to be worth, be strong"]

value[2] *v.* [T] **1** to think that something is important and worth having: *I value your friendship.* **2** to say how much something is worth: *a painting* ***valued at*** *$5 million*

valve /vælv/ *n.* [C] **1** a part of a tube or pipe that opens and closes like a door in order to control the flow of liquid, gas, air, etc. passing through **2** BIOLOGY a part of an ARTERY (=tube that blood flows through) or VEIN that folds or closes in order to stop blood flowing back in the direction it came from [ORIGIN: 1400—1500 Latin *valva* "part of a door"] → *see picture at* BICYCLE

vam·pire /ˈvæmpaɪɚ/ *n.* [C] in stories, a dead person who sucks people's blood by biting their necks

van /væn/ *n.* [C] **1** a truck with an enclosed back, used for carrying goods: *Jerry began unloading the van.* **2** a large box-like car

van·dal /ˈvændl/ *n.* [C] someone who deliberately damages things, especially public property

van·dal·ism /ˈvændlˌɪzəm/ *n.* [U] the crime of deliberately damaging things, especially public property

van·dal·ize /ˈvændlˌaɪz/ *v.* [T] to damage or destroy things deliberately, especially public property: *The church property had been vandalized.*

van·guard /ˈvæŋgɑrd/ *n.* **in the vanguard (of sth)** involved in an important activity, and trying to achieve something or develop new ideas: *a group in the vanguard of political reform*

va·nil·la /vəˈnɪlə/ *n.* [U] a substance with a slightly sweet taste, used in ICE CREAM and other foods

van·ish /ˈvænɪʃ/ *v.* [I] to disappear suddenly, especially in a way that cannot be easily explained: *When I looked again, he'd vanished.* | *The ship* ***vanished without a trace*** (=disappeared, leaving no sign of what had happened to it).

van·i·ty /ˈvænəṭi/ *n.* [U] (disapproving) the quality of being too proud of yourself → VAIN

van·quish /ˈvæŋkwɪʃ/ *v.* [T] (literary) to defeat

someone or something completely (SYN) **beat, conquer**

van·tage point /ˈvæntɪdʒ ˌpɔɪnt/ *n.* [C] **1** a good position from which you can see something **2** a way of thinking about things that is influenced by your own situation (SYN) **point of view**

vap·id /ˈvæpɪd/ *adj.* (formal) lacking intelligence, interest, or imagination: *a vapid TV show* —**vapidly** *adv.* —**vapidness** *n.* [U] —**vapidity** /vəˈpɪdət̬i/ *n.* [U]

va·por /ˈveɪpɚ/ *n.* [C,U] CHEMISTRY many small drops of liquid that float in the air: *water vapor*

var·i·a·ble¹ /ˈvɛriəbəl, ˈvær-/ (Ac) *adj.* **1** likely to change often or be different: *a variable rate of interest | Hospital food is **highly variable** in quality.* **2 variable cost** ECONOMICS a cost to a company or business that changes when the amount of goods being produced changes

variable² *n.* [C] **1** something that may be different in different situations: *A number of variables can affect a student's performance. | Variables such as social class and education influence political beliefs.* **2** MATH a mathematical quantity which can represent different values, usually shown as a letter → CONSTANT —**variability** /ˌvɛriəˈbɪlət̬i, ˌvær-/ *n.* [U]

ˌvariable exˈpression *n.* [C] MATH a mathematical expression that has a variable in it, for example 2x + 3

var·i·ance /ˈvɛriəns, ˈvær-/ (Ac) *n.* **be at variance (with sth/sb)** (formal) if two people or things are at variance with each other, they do not agree or are very different: *The results from later experiments were considerably at variance with the original ones.*

var·i·ant /ˈvɛriənt, ˈvær-/ (Ac) *n.* [C] something that is slightly different from the usual form of something: *a spelling variant | The moth is a variant of the species that arrived here from Europe in 1869.* —**variant** *adj.*

var·i·a·tion /ˌvɛriˈeɪʃən, ˌvær-/ (Ac) *n.* **1** [C,U] a difference between similar things, or a change from the usual amount or form of something: ***variations in** prices from store to store | Slight temperature variations are not critical.* **2** [C] something that is done in a slightly different way from normal: *This is the traditional recipe, but of course there are many variations. | There are several variations of socialism, including communism.*

var·i·cose veins /ˌværəkoʊs ˈveɪnz/ *n.* [plural] a medical condition in which the VEINS in your leg become swollen and painful

var·ied /ˈvɛrid, ˈvær-/ (Ac) *adj.* including many different types of things or people: *a varied diet | This essay discusses the many varied groups in American society.*

var·i·e·gat·ed /ˈvɛrɪˌgeɪt̬ɪd, ˈvær-/ *adj.* **1** BIOLOGY a variegated plant, leaf, etc. has different colored marks on it: *variegated holly* **2** (formal) consisting of a lot of different types of people or things

va·ri·e·ty /vəˈraɪət̬i/ *n.* (plural **varieties**) **1 a variety of sth** a lot of different things or people: *The girls come from **a variety of** different backgrounds. | The T-shirts are available in **a wide variety of** colors.* **2** [U] the differences within a group, set of actions, etc. that make it interesting: *She wants more variety in her work.* **3** [C] a particular type of something that is different from other things of a similar kind: *different **varieties of** apples* [ORIGIN: 1500—1600 French *variété*, from Latin *varietas*, from *varius* "various"]

> THESAURUS **type, kind, sort, category** → TYPE¹

vaˈriety ˌshow *n.* [C] a television or radio program or a play that consists of many different performances, especially funny ones

var·i·ous /ˈvɛriəs, ˈvær-/ *adj.* several different: *This coat comes in various colors. | He decided to leave school **for various reasons**.*

var·i·ous·ly /ˈvɛriəsli, ˈvær-/ *adv.* in many different ways: *He's been variously called a genius and a madman.*

var·nish¹ /ˈvɑrnɪʃ/ *n.* [C,U] a clear liquid that is painted onto things that are made of wood, to protect them and give them a shiny surface [ORIGIN: 1300—1400 Old French *vernis*, from Medieval Latin *veronix*, type of resin used for making varnish]

varnish² *v.* [T] to paint something with varnish

var·si·ty /ˈvɑrsət̬i/ *n.* (plural **varsities**) [C,U] the main team that represents a university, college, or school in sports: *the varsity basketball team*

var·y /ˈvɛri, ˈværi/ (Ac) *v.* (**varied, varies**) **1** [I] if several things of the same type vary, they are all different from each other: *Prices **vary from** $10 **to** $50. | The flowers **vary in** color and size. | Test scores varied widely from child to child.* **2** [I] to change often: *The price of seafood **varies according to** the season. | "How often do you play tennis?" "Oh, **it varies**." | The level of pay varies with the experience of the employee.* **3** [T] to regularly change what you do or the way that you do it: *You need to vary your diet. | Good writers vary the length and structure of their sentences.* [ORIGIN: 1500—1600 Latin *varius* "various"] —**varying** *adj.*: *varying degrees of success*

vas·cu·lar /ˈvæskyəlɚ/ *adj.* BIOLOGY relating to the tubes through which liquids, for example blood, flow in the bodies of animals or in plants

ˌvascular ˈtissue *n.* [U] BIOLOGY material through which water, SAP, and other liquids are carried around a plant

vase /veɪs, veɪz, vɑz/ *n.* [C] a container used to put flowers in [ORIGIN: 1500—1600 French, Latin *vas* "container"]

va·sec·to·my /və'sɛktəmi/ *n.* (plural **vasectomies**) [C,U] a medical operation that makes a man unable to produce children

Vas·e·line /'væsə,lin, ,væsə'lin/ *n.* [U] (trademark) a thick clear substance used on the skin to make it less dry

vas·sal /'væsəl/ *n.* [C] HISTORY a man in the Middle Ages who was given land to live on by a LORD in return for promising to work or fight for him

vast /væst/ *adj.* **1** extremely large: ***vast areas*** *of rainforest*

THESAURUS **big, large, huge, enormous, gigantic, massive, immense** ➔ BIG

2 the vast majority (of sth) almost all of a group of people or things [ORIGIN: 1500—1600 Latin *vastus* "empty, desolate, very large"]

vast·ly /'væstli/ *adv.* very greatly: *vastly different opinions*

vat /væt/ *n.* [C] a very large container for keeping liquids in

vault¹ /vɔlt/ *n.* [C] **1** a room with thick walls and a strong door, where money, jewels, etc. are kept safely **2** a room where people from the same family are buried **3** a jump over something

vault² *also* **vault over** *v.* [T] to jump over something in one movement, using your hands or a pole to help you: *He vaulted over the fence and ran off.*

THESAURUS **jump, leap, spring, hurdle** ➔ JUMP¹

V chip /'vi tʃɪp/ *n.* [C] a CHIP in a television that allows parents to prevent their children from watching programs that are violent or have sex in them

V

VCR *n.* [C] **video cassette recorder** a machine that is used for recording television shows or watching VIDEOTAPES

VD *n.* [U] (old-fashioned) **venereal disease** a disease that is passed from one person to another during sex

VDU *n.* [C] IT **visual display unit** a computer screen (SYN) **monitor**

-'ve /v, əv/ the short form of "have": *We've finished.*

veal /vil/ *n.* [U] the meat from a CALF (=young cow)

vec·tor /'vɛktə/ *n.* [C] *also* **vector quantity** MATH a quantity that has a direction as well as a size, usually represented by an ARROW

veer /vɪr/ *v.* [I] to change direction suddenly: *The car* ***veered*** *sharply* ***to*** *the left.*

veg /vɛdʒ/ *also* **veg out** *v.* [I] (informal) to relax and not do anything important

ve·gan /'vigən, 'veɪ-, 'vɛdʒən/ *n.* [C] someone who does not eat meat, fish, eggs, or milk products

vege·ta·ble /'vɛdʒtəbəl/ *n.* [C] a plant such as corn or potatoes, which you can eat: *fresh* ***fruits and vegetables*** | *We have a small* ***vegetable garden.*** [ORIGIN: 1300—1400 Medieval Latin *vegetabilis* "growing," from *vegetare* "to grow"]

veg·e·tar·i·an /,vɛdʒə'tɛriən/ *n.* [C] someone who does not eat meat or fish: *I'm thinking about* ***becoming a vegetarian.*** —**vegetarian** *adj.*

veg·e·ta·tion /,vɛdʒə'teɪʃən/ *n.* [U] BIOLOGY plants in general, especially all the plants in one particular area: *a meadow with thick vegetation*

veg·gie¹ /'vɛdʒi/ *n.* [C usually plural] (informal) a vegetable

veggie² *adj.* **a veggie burger/sandwich etc.** (informal) a HAMBURGER, SANDWICH, etc. that is made using vegetables or grain, rather than meat

ve·he·ment /'viəmənt/ *adj.* showing very strong feelings or opinions: *vehement protests* —**vehemently** *adv.*: *Hoff vehemently denies the accusations.* —**vehemence** *n.* [U]

ve·hi·cle /'viɪkəl/ (Ac) *n.* **1** [C] (formal) a thing such as a car, bus, etc. that is used for carrying people or things from one place to another: *a description of the stolen vehicle* **2 a vehicle for (doing) sth** something that you use as a way of spreading your ideas, opinions, etc.: *The newspaper is a vehicle for government propaganda.* | *Drawing, like writing, can be a vehicle for exploring your feelings.* [ORIGIN: 1600—1700 French *véhicule*, from Latin *vehiculum*, from *vehere* "to carry"]

veil /veɪl/ *n.* [C] **1** a thin piece of material that women wear to cover their faces: *a bridal veil* **2 a veil of secrecy/silence etc.** something that stops you knowing the full truth about a situation: *A veil of mystery surrounded Gomez's death.*

veiled /veɪld/ *adj.* **1 veiled criticism/threats etc.** criticisms, threats, etc. that are not said directly **2 be veiled in mystery/secrecy** if something is veiled in mystery, secrecy, etc., very little is known about it

vein /veɪn/ *n.* [C] **1** BIOLOGY one of the tubes through which blood flows to your heart from other parts of your body ➔ ARTERY: *Death was caused by a wound to the* ***jugular vein*** (=the large vein in your neck). **2** BIOLOGY one of the thin lines on a leaf or on the wing of an insect **3** EARTH SCIENCES a thin layer of coal, gold, etc. in rock **4 in a ... vein** in a particular style of speaking or writing: *Her speech continued* ***in the same vein.***

Vel·cro /'vɛlkroʊ/ *n.* [U] (trademark) a material used for fastening shoes, clothes, etc., made from two special pieces of cloth that stick to each other

ve·loc·i·ty /və'lɑsəṭi/ *n.* (plural **velocities**) [C,U] PHYSICS the speed at which something moves in a particular direction over a period of time: *the velocity of light* [ORIGIN: 1500—1600 French *vélocté*, from Latin *velocitas*, from *velox* "fast"]

vel·vet /'vɛlvɪt/ *n.* [U] cloth with a soft surface on one side [ORIGIN: 1300—1400 Old French *veluotte*, from *velu* "hairy," from Latin *villus* "rough hair"]

vel·vet·y /ˈvɛlvɪṭi/ *adj.* looking, feeling, tasting, or sounding smooth and soft: *a velvety voice*

ve·na ca·va /ˌvinə ˈkeɪvə/ *n.* [C] BIOLOGY one of two large tubes that carry blood back to your heart from different parts of your body: ***the superior vena cava*** (=tube that returns blood to the heart from the head and the upper part of the body) | ***the inferior vena cava*** (=tube that returns blood to the heart from the lower part of the body) → *see picture at* HEART

ven·det·ta /vɛnˈdɛṭə/ *n.* [C] a situation in which one person tries for a long time to harm another person

vend·ing ma·chine /ˈvɛndɪŋ məˌʃin/ *n.* [C] a machine that you can get cigarettes, candy, drinks, etc. from, by putting in money

ven·dor /ˈvɛndɚ/ *n.* [C] someone who sells things, especially in the street: *street vendors*

ve·neer /vəˈnɪr/ *n.* **1** [C,U] a thin layer of good quality wood that covers the outside of a piece of furniture that is made of a cheaper material: *oak veneer* **2 a veneer of sth** (formal) behavior that hides someone's real character or feelings: *a veneer of politeness*

ven·er·a·ble /ˈvɛnərəbəl/ *adj.* (formal) a venerable person or organization is very old and respected: *venerable institutions*

ven·er·ate /ˈvɛnəˌreɪt/ *v.* [T] (formal) to treat someone or something with great respect, especially because she, he, or it is old, holy, or connected with the past

ve·ne·re·al dis·ease /vəˈnɪriəl dɪˌziz/ *n.* [C,U] VD

Ve·ne·tian blind /vəˌniʃən ˈblaɪnd/ *n.* [C] a covering for a window, made of long flat bars that can be raised or lowered to let in light

venge·ance /ˈvɛndʒəns/ *n.* [singular, U] **1** something violent or harmful that you do to someone in order to punish him/her for hurting you: *a desire for vengeance* **2 with a vengeance** with much more force or effort than is expected or normal: *The Colts started the season with a vengeance, winning three straight games.*

venge·ful /ˈvɛndʒfəl/ *adj.* (literary) very eager to punish someone who has hurt you

ven·i·son /ˈvɛnəsən/ *n.* [U] the meat of a DEER

Venn di·a·gram /ˈvɛn ˌdaɪəgræm/ *n.* [C] MATH a picture that shows the relationship between two sets of things by using circles that OVERLAP each other. The part of each set that is the same for both sets is put into the place where the circles cross.

ven·om /ˈvɛnəm/ *n.* [U] **1** a liquid poison that some snakes, insects, etc. produce **2** extreme anger or hatred: *a speech full of venom* —**venomous** *adj.*

vent[1] /vɛnt/ *n.* **1** [C] a hole or pipe through which gases, smoke, or liquid can enter or go out: *an air*

vegetables

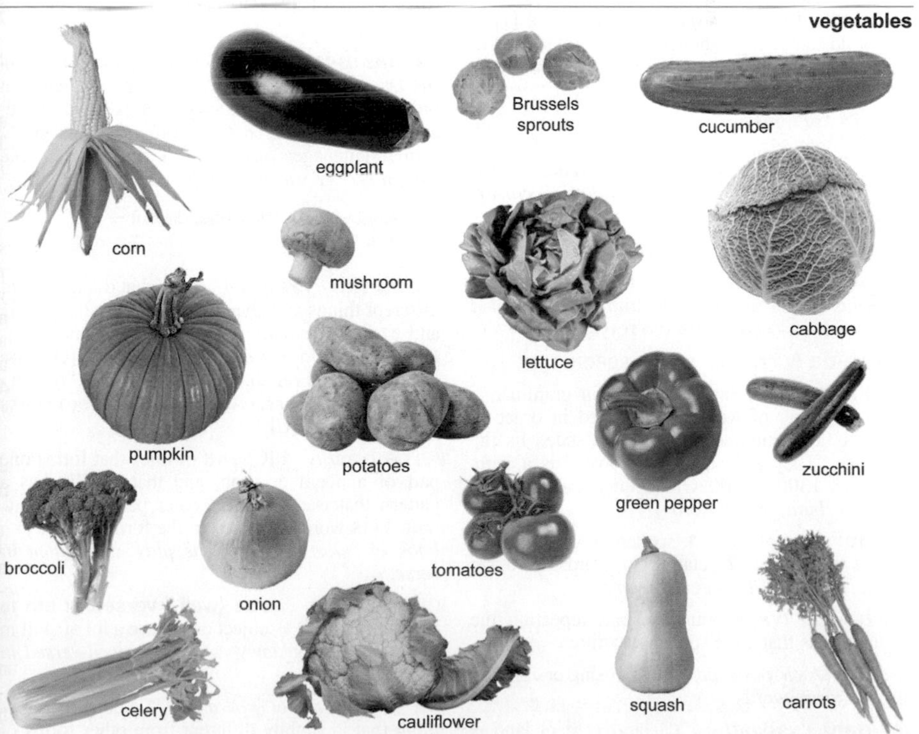

V

vent **2 give vent to sth** (formal) to do something to express a strong feeling

vent² *v.* [T] to do something to express your feelings, often in a way that is unfair: *Jay* ***vented*** *his anger* ***on/at*** *his family.*

ven·ti·late /'vɛntl̩ˌeɪt/ *v.* [T] to let fresh air into a room, building, etc. [ORIGIN: 1400—1500 Latin, past participle of *ventilare*, from *ventus* "wind"] **—ventilated** *adj.*: *Mechanics should work in a well-ventilated space.* **—ventilation** /ˌvɛntl̩'eɪʃən/ *n.* [U]

ven·ti·la·tor /'vɛntl̩ˌeɪt̬ɚ/ *n.* [C] a RESPIRATOR

ven·tral /'vɛntrəl/ *adj.* [only before noun] BIOLOGY relating to the stomach of an animal or fish → DORSAL

ven·tri·cle /'vɛntrɪkəl/ *n.* [C] BIOLOGY one of the two spaces inside the bottom of your heart from which blood is pumped into your body → ATRIUM, AURICLE → *see picture at* HEART

ven·tril·o·quist /vɛn'trɪləkwɪst/ *n.* [C] someone who speaks without using his/her lips, in a way that makes the sound seem to come from somewhere else, especially from a PUPPET **—ventriloquism** *n.* [U]

ven·ture¹ /'vɛntʃɚ/ *n.* [C] ECONOMICS a new business activity that involves taking risks: *a new* ***joint venture*** (=an agreement between two companies to do something together)

venture² *v.* (formal) **1** [I] to risk going somewhere when it could be dangerous: *Several boats* ***ventured out*** *to sea, despite the weather.* **2** [T] to say or do something although you are not sure of it, or are afraid of how someone may react to it: *No one else ventured an opinion.*

ven·ue /'vɛnyu/ *n.* [C] a place where an organized meeting, concert, etc. takes place: *a popular jazz venue* [ORIGIN: 1500—1600 Old French "coming," from *venir* "to come," from Latin *venire*]

Ve·nus /'vinəs/ *n.* PHYSICS the second PLANET from the Sun → *see picture at* SOLAR SYSTEM

ve·rac·i·ty /və'ræsət̬i/ *n.* [U] (formal) the quality of being true or of telling the truth: *They doubted his veracity.* **—veracious** /və'reɪʃəs/ *adj.*

ve·ran·da /və'rændə/ *n.* [C] a PORCH

verb /vɚb/ *n.* [C] ENG. LANG. ARTS in grammar, a word or group of words that is used in order to describe an action, experience, or state. In the sentence "They arrived late," "arrived" is a verb. [ORIGIN: 1300—1400 Old French *verbe*, from Latin *verbum* "word, verb"]

ver·bal /'vɚbəl/ *adj.* **1** spoken, not written: *a verbal agreement* **2** relating to words or using words: *verbal skills* **—verbally** *adv.*

ver·ba·tim /vɚ'beɪt̬ɪm/ *adj., adv.* repeating the actual words that were spoken or written

ver·bose /vɚ'boʊs/ *adj.* (formal) using or containing too many words

ver·dant /'vɚdənt/ *adj.* (literary) verdant land is covered with freshly growing green grass and plants

ver·dict /'vɚdɪkt/ *n.* [C] **1** LAW an official decision that is made by a JURY in a court of law about whether someone is guilty or not guilty of a crime: *Has the jury* ***reached a verdict*** (=made a decision)? → COURT¹ **2** an official decision or opinion made by a person or group that has authority: *The panel will* ***give*** *their* ***verdict*** *tomorrow.* [ORIGIN: 1200—1300 Anglo-French, Old French *ver* "true" + *dit* "saying, judgment"]

verge¹ /vɚdʒ/ *n.* **be on the verge of sth** to be about to do something: *Andy was on the verge of tears.*

verge² *v.*

verge on/upon sth *phr. v.* to be very close to a harmful or extreme state: *Their behavior sometimes verges on insanity.*

ver·i·fy /'vɛrəˌfaɪ/ *v.* [T] (**verified**, **verifies**) to find out if a fact, statement, etc. is correct or true: *There was no way to verify his story.* [ORIGIN: 1300—1400 Old French *verifier*, from Medieval Latin *verificare*, from Latin *verus* "true"] **—verification** /ˌvɛrəfə'keɪʃən/ *n.* [U]

ver·i·ta·ble /'vɛrət̬əbəl/ *adj.* (formal) used in order to emphasize your description of someone or something: *a veritable army of tourists* (=a very large number of them)

ver·min /'vɚmɪn/ *n.* [plural] small animals or insects that are harmful or difficult to control [ORIGIN: 1200—1300 Old French, Latin *vermen* "worm"]

ver·nac·u·lar /vɚ'nækyəlɚ/ *n.* [C usually singular] ENG. LANG. ARTS the language or DIALECT that ordinary people in a country or area speak, especially when this is not the official language or formal language: *Instead of being in Latin, the church service was held in the vernacular.*

THESAURUS **language, dialect** → LANGUAGE

ver·sa·tile /'vɚsət̬l̩/ *adj.* **1** good at doing a lot of different things and able to learn new skills quickly and easily: *a versatile singer* **2** having many different uses: *Cotton is a versatile material.* [ORIGIN: 1600—1700 French, Latin *versatilis* "turning easily," from *versare* "to turn"] **—versatility** /ˌvɚsə'tɪlət̬i/ *n.* [U]

verse /vɚs/ *n.* **1** [C] a set of lines that forms one part of a poem or song, and that usually has a pattern that is repeated in other parts **2** [U] ENG. LANG. ARTS words arranged in the form of poetry: *a book of verse* | *Parts of the play are written* ***in verse.***

versed /vɚst/ *adj.* **be (well-) versed in sth** to know a lot about a subject or to have a lot of skill in doing something: *lawyers who are well-versed in these matters*

ver·sion /'vɚʒən/ (Ac) *n.* [C] **1** a copy of something that is slightly different from other forms of it: *the **original version** of the movie* | *a **new version** of an old song* | *Many devout people have objected to each new version of the Bible.* **2** a description of an event that is given by one person: *I'm not sure I believe Bobby's **version of** the story.* [ORIGIN: 1500—1600 French, Medieval Latin *versio* "turning," from Latin *versus*]

ver·sus /ˈvɚsəs/ *prep.* **1** (*written abbreviation* **vs.** *or* **v.**) used in order to show that two people or teams are against each other in a game or a court case: *the Knicks versus the Lakers* **2** used when comparing the advantages of two different things or ideas: *It's a question of quantity versus quality.* [ORIGIN: 1400—1500 Medieval Latin "toward, against," from Latin *vertere*]

ver·te·bra /ˈvɚṭəbrə/ *n.* (plural **vertebrae** /-breɪ, -bri/) [C] BIOLOGY one of the small hollow bones down the center of your back

ver·te·brate /ˈvɚṭəbrət, -ˌbreɪt/ *n.* [C] BIOLOGY an animal that has a BACKBONE → INVERTEBRATE

ver·tex /ˈvɚtɛks/ *n.* (plural **vertices** /ˈvɚṭəsiz/ *or* **vertexes**) [C] **1** MATH the point where two sides of a POLYGON or three or more sides of a POLYHEDRON meet **2** MATH the highest or lowest point on a PARABOLA

ver·ti·cal /ˈvɚṭɪkəl/ *adj.* pointing straight upward: *a vertical line* —**vertically** *adv.* → *see picture at* LINE[1]

ver·ti·go /ˈvɚṭɪˌgoʊ/ *n.* [U] a sick DIZZY feeling that is caused by looking down from a very high place

verve /vɚv/ *n.* [U] (literary) if someone does something with verve, s/he does it with energy and excitement

ve·ry[1] /ˈvɛri/ *adv.* **1** used in order to emphasize an adjective, adverb, or expression → REALLY: *It's a very good book.* | *My family is very important to me.* | *Sid gets embarrassed very easily.* | *Carter went to the very best schools.* | *The two brothers died on **the very same** (=exactly the same) day.*

> **USAGE**
>
> Do not use **very** with adjectives and adverbs that already have a strong meaning, for example "huge" or "terrible." Say "a terrible war," not "a very terrible war."
>
> You can use **really** instead: *That was a really awful movie.*
>
> Do not use **very** with the comparative form of adjectives. Do not say "This school's very better." Use **much** instead: *This school's much better.*
>
> → TOO

2 not very a) used before a quality to mean exactly the opposite of that quality: *She wasn't very happy about working overtime* (=she was angry). **b)** only slightly: *"Was the game very exciting?" "Not very."* **3 your very own** used in order to emphasize that something belongs to one particular person: *I finally have my very own bedroom.* **4 very much** a lot: *It didn't cost very much.* ▸ Don't say "It cost very much." Say "It cost a lot." ◂ | *I enjoyed my visit very much.* ▸ Don't say "I very much enjoyed my visit." ◂ [ORIGIN: 1200—1300 Old French *verai*, from Latin *verax* "truthful," from *verus* "true"]

very[2] *adj.* [only before noun] used in order to emphasize that you are talking about one particular thing or person: *Start again from the very beginning.* | *You come here **this very minute** (=now)!* | *The **very thought** (=just thinking about it) of food makes me feel sick.*

ˌvery high ˌfrequency *n.* [U] VHF

ves·sel /ˈvɛsəl/ *n.* [C] (formal) a ship or large boat → BLOOD VESSEL

vest /vɛst/ *n.* [C] **1** a piece of clothing without SLEEVES that has buttons down the front, worn over a shirt as part of a suit **2** a piece of special clothing without SLEEVES that is worn to protect your body: *a **bulletproof vest*** [ORIGIN: 1600—1700 French *veste*, from Latin *vestis* "piece of clothing"]

vest·ed in·terest /ˌvɛstɪd ˈɪntrɪst/ *n.* [C] if you have a vested interest in something happening, you have a strong reason for wanting it to happen because you will get money or advantages from it

ves·ti·bule /ˈvɛstəˌbyul/ *n.* [C] (formal) a wide passage or small room inside the front door of a public building

ves·tige /ˈvɛstɪdʒ/ *n.* [C] (formal) a small part or amount of something that remains when most of it no longer exists: *a policy that is one of **the last vestiges of** the Cold War*

vet /vɛt/ *n.* [C] **1** a VETERINARIAN someone who is trained to give medical care and treatment to sick animals **2** (informal) a VETERAN: *Vietnam vets*

vet·er·an /ˈvɛṭərən/ *n.* [C] **1** someone who has been a soldier, sailor, etc. in a war: ***veterans of** the Korean War* **2** someone who has had a lot of experience in a particular activity: *a veteran journalist*

vet·er·i·nar·i·an /ˌvɛṭərəˈnɛriən, ˌvɛtrə-, ˌvɛtˀn-/ *n.* [C] a VET

vet·er·i·nar·y /ˈvɛṭərəˌnɛri, ˈvɛtrə-, ˈvɛtˀn-/ *adj.* relating to the medical care and treatment of sick animals

ve·to[1] /ˈviṭoʊ/ *v.* (past tense and past participle **vetoed**, third person singular **vetoes**) [T] POLITICS to officially refuse to allow something to happen, especially something that other people or organizations have agreed: *The President **vetoed** the **bill**.* [ORIGIN: 1600—1700 Latin "I refuse to allow," from *vetare* "to forbid"]

veto[2] *n.* (plural **vetoes**) [C,U] POLITICS a refusal to give official permission for something, or the right to refuse to give such permission: *the governor's **veto of** a bill*

vex /vɛks/ *v.* [T] (old-fashioned) to make someone feel annoyed or worried

> **THESAURUS** **annoy, irritate, bother, irk** → ANNOY

V

VHF *n.* [U] **very high frequency** radio waves that move very quickly and produce good sound quality

VHS *n.* [U] (trademark) a type of VIDEOTAPE

vi·a /ˈvaɪə, ˈviə/ (Ac) *prep.* **1** traveling through a place on the way to another place: *We're flying to Denver via Chicago.* **2** using a particular machine, system, person, etc. to send, receive, or broadcast something: *The concert was broadcast around the world via satellite.* [ORIGIN: 1600—1700 Latin "by way of," from *via* "way"]

vi·a·ble /ˈvaɪəbəl/ *adj.* something that is viable is able to exist or succeed: *Solar energy is a **viable alternative** to coal or gas.* | *The plan isn't **economically/commercially viable**.*

vi·a·duct /ˈvaɪəˌdʌkt/ *n.* [C] a long high bridge across a valley

vi·al /ˈvaɪəl/ *n.* [C] a very small bottle, used especially for liquid medicines

vibe /vaɪb/ *n.* [C usually plural] (informal) the feelings that a particular person, group, or situation seems to produce and that you react to: *I'm getting **good/bad vibes** from this guy.*

vi·brant /ˈvaɪbrənt/ *adj.* **1** exciting, full of energy, and interesting: *a vibrant personality* **2** a vibrant color is bright and strong

vibrate

vi·brate /ˈvaɪbreɪt/ *v.* [I,T] to shake continuously with small fast movements, or to make something do this: *The music got louder and the walls began to vibrate.*

THESAURUS shake, tremble, shiver → SHAKE[1]

vi·bra·tion /vaɪˈbreɪʃən/ *n.* [C,U] a continuous slight shaking movement: *the vibrations of the plane's engine*

vic·ar /ˈvɪkɚ/ *n.* [C] a priest in the Church of England or in the Episcopal church

vi·car·i·ous /vaɪˈkɛriəs/ *adj.* experienced by watching or reading about someone else doing something, rather than by doing it yourself: *Parents get **vicarious pleasure/satisfaction** from their children's success.* [ORIGIN: 1600—1700 Latin *vicarius* "acting in place of another," from *vicis* "change, alternation, position"]

vice /vaɪs/ *n.* **1** [U] criminal activities that involve sex or drugs **2** [C] a bad habit: *Smoking is my only vice.* **3** [C] a bad or immoral quality in someone's character (ANT) **virtue**: *the vice of greed*

ˌvice ˈpresident *n.* [C] **1** the person who is next in rank to the president of a country **2** someone who is responsible for a particular part of a company: *the vice president of marketing*

ˈvice squad *n.* [C] the part of the police force that deals with crimes involving sex or drugs

vi·ce ver·sa /ˌvaɪs ˈvɚsə, ˌvaɪsə-/ *adv.* used when the opposite of a situation you have just described is also true: *Whatever Susie wants, James doesn't, and vice versa.*

vi·cin·i·ty /vəˈsɪnət̬i/ *n.* **in the vicinity (of sth)** in the area around a particular place: *The car was found in the vicinity of the bus station.*

vi·cious /ˈvɪʃəs/ *adj.* **1** violent and dangerous, and likely to hurt someone: *a vicious dog* **2** cruel and deliberately trying to upset someone: *a **vicious rumor***

THESAURUS mean, cruel, unkind, nasty, spiteful, malicious → MEAN[2]

—**viciously** *adv.* —**viciousness** *n.* [U]

ˌvicious ˈcircle *n.* [singular] a situation in which one problem causes another problem that then causes the first problem again

vi·cis·si·tudes /vəˈsɪsəˌtudz/ *n.* [plural] (formal) the continuous changes and problems that affect a situation or someone's life: ***the vicissitudes of** married life*

vic·tim /ˈvɪktɪm/ *n.* [C] **1** someone who has been hurt or killed by someone or something, or who has been affected by a bad situation: ***victims of** gang violence* | *a **murder/rape victim*** | *an aid program for **flood/earthquake/famine victims*** **2** something that is badly affected or destroyed by a situation or action: *Some small businesses have **fallen victim to** budget cuts.*

vic·tim·ize /ˈvɪktəˌmaɪz/ *v.* [T] to deliberately treat someone unfairly

vic·tor /ˈvɪktɚ/ *n.* [C] (formal) the winner of a battle or competition

vic·to·ri·ous /vɪkˈtɔriəs/ *adj.* successful in a battle or competition

vic·to·ry /ˈvɪktəri/ *n.* (plural **victories**) [C,U] the success you achieve by winning a battle, game, election, etc. (ANT) **defeat**: *Napoleon's military victories* | *the Lakers' **victory over/against** the Celtics* | *The government has **won** an important **victory**.* | *This ruling represents a **victory for** all women.* [ORIGIN: 1300—1400 Old French *victorie*, from Latin *victoria*, from *victus*, past participle of *vincere* "to defeat, win"]

vid·e·o¹ /ˈvɪdioʊ/ *n.* (plural **videos**) **1** [C] a copy of a movie or television program that is recorded on VIDEOTAPE → DVD, TAPE: *Let's **rent** a **video** tonight.* | *Has the movie come out **on video** yet?*

COLLOCATIONS

go to a video/movie store
get/rent a video or movie
watch a video
rewind a video – to press a button to go back to an earlier part
fast forward a video – to press a button to go to a later part
pause a video – to stop the video for a short time
make a video – to use a video camera to film someone or something

2 [C,U] a VIDEOTAPE: *Do we have a **blank video*** (=one with nothing recorded on it) *anywhere?* **3** [U] the process of recording and showing television programs, movies, real events, etc. using video equipment: *the use of video in the classroom*

video² *adj.* [only before noun] relating to recording and broadcasting sound and pictures on a VIDEOTAPE → AUDIO: *video equipment*

ˌvideo cas'sette reˌcorder *n.* [C] a VCR

vid·e·o·disk /ˈvɪdioʊˌdɪsk/ *n.* [C] a round flat piece of plastic from which movies can be played in the same way as from a VIDEOTAPE → DVD

'video ˌgame *n.* [C] a game in which you move images on a screen by pressing electronic controls

vid·e·o·tape¹ /ˈvɪdioʊˌteɪp/ *n.* [C] a long narrow band of MAGNETIC material in a plastic container, on which movies, television programs, etc. can be recorded

videotape² *v.* [T] to record a movie, television program, etc. on a videotape

vie /vaɪ/ *v.* (**vied**, **vying**, **vies**) [I] to compete very hard with someone in order to get something: *The two brothers **vied for** her attention.*

view¹ /vyu/ *n.* **1** [C] your belief, opinion, or attitude about something → POINT OF VIEW: *We have different **views on** this issue.* | *Not all her friends **shared** her **views**.* | *What are your **views about** global warming?* | ***In my view**, our civil liberties are just as important as national security.*

THESAURUS **opinion, position, attitude** → OPINION

2 [C,U] what you are able to see or the possibility of seeing it: *We **had** a really good **view of** the stage.* | *I sat behind a tall guy who **blocked** my **view*** (=stopped me from seeing something). | *Suddenly the pyramids **came into view*** (=began to be seen). **3** [C] the whole area that you can see from somewhere, especially when it is very beautiful or impressive: *a spectacular **view of** the mountains* | *A new factory now **spoils the view*** (=makes it look less beautiful) *of the park.*

USAGE

View is used to talk about all the things you can see from a place: *We had a spectacular view of the ocean from the hotel.*

Scenery is used to talk about the natural features of a place, such as mountains, forests, etc.: *the breathtaking scenery in Arizona*
You cannot say "sceneries."

4 [C] a photograph or picture that shows a beautiful or interesting place: *The postcards show **scenic views of** New York.* **5 on view** paintings, photographs, etc. that are on view are in a public place where people can go to look at them **6 in view of sth** (formal) used in order to introduce the reason for a decision, action, or situation: *In view of all that has happened, Smith is expected to resign.* [ORIGIN: 1400—1500 Old French *veue, vue*, from *veeir, voir* "to see," from Latin *videre*]

view² *v.* **1** [T] to think of something or someone in a particular way: *My grandparents **viewed** the United States **as** a land of opportunity.* | *Some of the local people **view** tourists **with** suspicion.* **2** [T] (formal) to look at or watch something: *The mountain is best viewed from the north side.*

view·er /ˈvyuɚ/ *n.* [C] someone who watches television: *The series is watched by millions of viewers.*

view·point /ˈvyupɔɪnt/ *n.* [C] **1** a particular way of thinking about a problem or subject SYN **point of view**: ***From his viewpoint**, he had done nothing wrong.* **2** ENG. LANG. ARTS the opinion or attitude of the person who is writing a story, especially when it has an influence on the story itself SYN **point of view** → LIMITED POINT OF VIEW, OMNISCIENT POINT OF VIEW

vig·il /ˈvɪdʒəl/ *n.* [C,U] **1** a silent political protest in which people gather outside, especially during the night: *Demonstrators **held a** candlelight **vigil** at the site of the bombing.* **2** a time, especially during the night, when you stay awake in order to pray or stay with someone who is sick: *John's been **keeping a vigil** beside his son in the hospital.*

vig·i·lant /ˈvɪdʒələnt/ *adj.* (formal) giving careful attention to what is happening, so that you will notice if something bad happens: *Doctors should **remain vigilant** for signs of infection.* —**vigilance** *n.* [U]

vig·i·lan·te /ˌvɪdʒəˈlænti/ *n.* [C] someone who tries to catch and punish criminals without having any legal authority to do so

vig·or /ˈvɪgɚ/ *n.* [U] physical and mental energy and determination

vig·or·ous /ˈvɪgərəs/ *adj.* **1** using a lot of energy and strength or determination: ***vigorous exercise*** | *a vigorous opponent of gun control*

THESAURUS **energetic, full of energy, dynamic** → ENERGETIC

2 strong and very healthy: *a vigorous athlete*

vile /vaɪl/ *adj.* (informal) very bad or disgusting: *The bombing was a vile act of terrorism.*

vil·i·fy /ˈvɪləˌfaɪ/ *v.* (**vilified**, **vilifies**) [T] (formal) to say bad things about someone in order to make

V

other people have a bad opinion of him/her: *He was vilified by the press.*

vil·la /'vɪlə/ *n.* [C] a big country house

vil·lage /'vɪlɪdʒ/ *n.* [C] **1** a very small town: *My parents live in a small village in Mexico.* **2 the village** the people who live in the village: *The whole village came to the wedding.* [ORIGIN: 1300—1400 Old French *ville* "farm, village," from Latin *villa*]

vil·lag·er /'vɪlɪdʒɚ/ *n.* [C] someone who lives in a village

vil·lain /'vɪlən/ *n.* [C] ENG. LANG. ARTS the main bad character in a movie, play, or story

THESAURUS **hero, main character, protagonist, anti-hero** → HERO

vil·lain·y /'vɪləni/ *n.* [U] (literary) evil or criminal behavior

vin·di·cate /'vɪndə,keɪt/ *v.* [T] (formal) to prove that what someone said or did was right, especially when many people believe s/he was wrong —**vindication** /,vɪndə'keɪʃən/ *n.* [U]

vin·dic·tive /vɪn'dɪktɪv/ *adj.* deliberately cruel and unfair

vine /vaɪn/ *n.* [C] a climbing plant that grows long stems that attach themselves to other plants, trees, buildings, etc.: *grape vines*

vin·e·gar /'vɪnɪgɚ/ *n.* [U] a sour-tasting liquid that is made from wine, used for improving the taste of food or preserving it [ORIGIN: 1200—1300 Old French *vinaigre*, from *vin* "wine" + *aigre* "sour"]

vine·yard /'vɪnyɚd/ *n.* [C] a piece of land where GRAPES are grown in order to make wine

V

vintage

a vintage car

vin·tage¹ /'vɪntɪdʒ/ *adj.* [only before noun] **1** vintage wine is good quality wine that is made in a particular year **2** old and showing high quality: *a vintage car*

THESAURUS **old, antique, classic** → OLD

vintage² *n.* [C] a particular year or place in which a wine is made, or the wine itself

vi·nyl /'vaɪnl/ *n.* [U] a type of strong plastic

vi·o·la /vi'oʊlə/ *n.* [C] a wooden musical instrument shaped like a VIOLIN but larger and with a lower sound

vi·o·late /'vaɪə,leɪt/ (Ac) *v.* [T] LAW to disobey or do something against a law, rule, agreement, etc.: *The military action violated international law.* | *Within less than a year, the agreement had been violated.*

THESAURUS **disobey, break a rule/law, defy, flout, contravene** → DISOBEY

vi·o·la·tion /,vaɪə'leɪʃən/ (Ac) *n.* [C] LAW an action that breaks a law, rule, agreement, etc.: *human rights violations* | *traffic violations* | *What happened was a major violation of international law.*

vi·o·lence /'vaɪələns/ *n.* [U] **1** behavior that is intended to hurt other people physically: *There's too much violence on TV.* | ***violence against** women* | *We condemn any **act of violence**.* **2** extreme force: *the violence of a tornado*

vi·o·lent /'vaɪələnt/ *adj.* **1** violent actions are intended to hurt people: *an increase in **violent crime*** | *The riots ended in the **violent deaths** of three teenagers.* **2** someone who is violent is likely to attack, hurt, or kill other people: *a violent and dangerous criminal* | *The demonstrators suddenly **turned violent*** (=became violent). **3 violent movie/play etc.** a movie, play, etc. that shows a lot of violence **4** violent feelings or reactions are strong and very difficult to control: *Joe has a **violent temper**.* | *a violent coughing fit* **5 violent storm/earthquake etc.** a storm, EARTHQUAKE, etc. that happens with a lot of force [ORIGIN: 1300—1400 Old French, Latin *violentus*]

vi·o·let /'vaɪəlɪt/ *n.* [C] a small sweet-smelling dark purple flower

vi·o·lin /,vaɪə'lɪn/ *n.* [C] a wooden musical instrument that you hold under your chin and play by pulling a BOW (=a special stick) across the strings —**violinist** *n.* [C]

VIP *n.* [C] **very important person** someone who is famous or powerful and is treated with respect

vi·per /'vaɪpɚ/ *n.* [C] a small poisonous snake

vi·ral /'vaɪrəl/ *adj.* BIOLOGY relating to or caused by a VIRUS: *His viral infection is being treated with antibiotics.*

vir·gin¹ /'vɚdʒɪn/ *n.* [C] someone who has never had sex

virgin² *adj.* **virgin land/forest etc.** land, forest, etc. that is still in its natural state and has not been used or changed by people

vir·gin·i·ty /vɚ'dʒɪnəṭi/ *n.* [U] the condition of never having had sex: *He was 20 when he **lost his virginity*** (=had sex for the first time).

Vir·go /'vɚgoʊ/ *n.* **1** [U] the sixth sign of the ZODIAC, represented by a VIRGIN **2** [C] someone born between August 23 and September 22

vir·ile /'vɪrəl/ *adj.* (approving) a man who is virile

is strong in a sexually attractive way —**virility** /vəˈrɪləṭi/ *n.* [U]

vi·rol·o·gy /vaɪˈrɑlədʒi/ *n.* [U] BIOLOGY the scientific study of VIRUSes and the diseases caused by them

vir·tu·al /ˈvɚtʃuəl/ (Ac) *adj.* [only before noun] **1** very nearly a particular thing: *The two countries are locked in a virtual state of war.* | *Some scientists claim that the existence of other universes is a virtual certainty.* **2** made, done, seen, etc. on the Internet, rather than in the real world: *The website allows you to take a virtual tour of the art gallery.* → ARTIFICIAL

vir·tu·al·ly /ˈvɚtʃuəli, -tʃəli/ (Ac) *adv.* almost completely: *He was virtually unknown until the elections.* | *Virtually all studies show that global temperatures are rising.*

ˌvirtual reˈality *n.* [U] IT an environment produced by a computer that looks and seems real to the person experiencing it

vir·tue /ˈvɚtʃu/ *n.* [C,U] **1** (formal) behavior that is morally good, or a good quality in someone's character (ANT) **vice**: *a life of virtue* | *Stella has many virtues.* **2** an advantage that makes something better or more useful than something else: *the virtues of organic farming* **3 by virtue of sth** (formal) by means of or as a result of something: *He became chairman by virtue of hard work.* [ORIGIN: 1100—1200 Old French *virtu*, from Latin *virtus* "strength, virtue," from *vir* "man"]

vir·tu·o·so /ˌvɚtʃuˈoʊsoʊ/ *n.* (plural **virtuosos**) [C] ENG. LANG. ARTS someone who is a very skillful performer, especially in music: *a piano virtuoso* —**virtuoso** *adj.*: *a virtuoso performance*

vir·tu·ous /ˈvɚtʃuəs/ *adj.* (formal) behaving in a very honest and moral way

vir·u·lent /ˈvɪrələnt, ˈvɪryə-/ *adj.* **1** (formal) full of hatred: *virulent racism* **2** a poison, disease, etc. that is virulent is very dangerous and affects people very quickly

vi·rus /ˈvaɪrəs/ *n.* [C] **1** BIOLOGY a very small living thing that causes infectious illnesses, or the illness caused by this: *the common cold virus* **2** IT a set of instructions secretly put into a computer that can destroy information stored in the computer [ORIGIN: 1500—1600 Latin "thick slippery liquid, poison, bad smell"]

vi·sa /ˈvizə/ *n.* [C] an official mark that is put on your PASSPORT, that allows you to enter or leave another country: *a three-month* ***tourist/visitor's visa*** | *He has been* ***granted*** *a* ***visa*** *by the State Department.* [ORIGIN: 1800—1900 French, Latin, "things seen," from *visus*]

vis·age /ˈvɪzɪdʒ/ *n.* [C] (literary) a face

vis-à-vis /ˌvizəˈvi/ *prep.* (formal) in relation to or in comparison with something or someone

vis·cous /ˈvɪskəs/ *adj.* a viscous liquid is thick and does not flow easily —**viscosity** /vɪˈskɑsəṭi/ *n.* [U]

vise /vaɪs/ *n.* [C] a tool that holds an object firmly so that you can work on it using both of your hands

vis·i·bil·i·ty /ˌvɪzəˈbɪləṭi/ (Ac) *n.* [U] the distance that it is possible to see at a particular time: *There is* ***poor visibility*** *on the roads due to heavy fog.* | *The ship set out in good visibility and fairly calm seas.*

vis·i·ble /ˈvɪzəbəl/ (Ac) *adj.* something that is visible can be seen or noticed (ANT) **invisible**: *The mountains weren't visible because of the clouds.* | *a* ***visible change*** *in her attitude* | *On a clear night, the moon's craters are visible from Earth.* [ORIGIN: 1300—1400 Latin *visibilis*, from *visus*, past participle of *videre* "to see"] —**visibly** *adv.*: *She was visibly upset by the news.* | *When a hive of bees is about to swarm, it becomes visibly agitated.*

vi·sion /ˈvɪʒən/ (Ac) *n.* **1** [U] the ability to see (SYN) **sight**: *Will the operation improve my vision?* | *She has* ***good/poor vision***. | *The drug's side effects may include headaches, muscular pain, and vision problems.* **2** [U] the area that you can see: *For a moment, the passing car was outside my* ***field of vision***. **3** [C] an idea of what you think something should be like: *He had a clear* ***vision of*** *how he hoped the company would develop.* | *The President outlined his* ***vision for*** *the future.* | *People who change the world have an original vision, rooted in dreams rather than experience.* **4** [C] something you believe you see as part of a religious experience: *She said that an angel appeared to her* ***in a vision***. **5** [U] the knowledge and imagination that are needed in planning for the future with a clear purpose: *We need a leader with vision.* [ORIGIN: 1200—1300 Old French, Latin *visio*, from *visus*, past participle of *videre* "to see"]

vi·sion·ar·y /ˈvɪʒəˌnɛri/ *adj.* having clear ideas of how the world can be better in the future —**visionary** *n.* [C]

vis·it[1] /ˈvɪzɪt/ *v.* **1** [I,T] to go and spend time with someone: *Eric went to Seattle to visit his cousins.* | *My aunt is* ***coming to visit*** *next week.*

THESAURUS

You **go to** a movie, museum, theater, etc.: *Everyone likes to go to the movies.*
You **go to see** or **go and see** a person or place: *We went to see my aunt last week.*
If you **go sightseeing**, you visit places of interest in a country.
If someone **comes by/over**, s/he visits you informally in your home.
If someone **drops in/by**, or **stops by/in**, s/he visits you in your home, especially on the way to another place.

2 [I,T] to go and spend time in a place, especially as a tourist: *We want to visit the Grand Canyon on our trip.* **3** [T] to look at a website on the Internet: *Over 1,000 people visit our site every week.* **4** [I] (informal) to talk socially with someone: *We watched TV while Mom* ***visited with*** *Mrs. Levinson.*

visit[2] *n.* [C] **1** an occasion when someone visits a place or person: *a* ***visit to*** *London* | *We're just here* ***on a*** *short* ***visit***. | *When are you going to* ***pay us a***

V

visit? | *We've just* ***had a visit from*** *the police.* **2** (informal) an occasion when you talk socially with someone, or the time you spend doing this: *Barbara and I had a nice long visit.*

vis·it·a·tion /ˌvɪzəˈteɪʃən/ *also* **ˌvisiˈtation ˌrights** *n.* [U] LAW the right that a parent who is DIVORCEd has to see his/her children

vis·i·tor /ˈvɪzət̬ɚ/ *n.* [C] someone who comes to visit a place or a person: *a guidebook for* ***visitors to*** *Mexico City* | *Let's not bother them now – they* ***have visitors*** (=people are visiting them).

vi·sor /ˈvaɪzɚ/ *n.* [C] **1** the curved part of a hat or HELMET that sticks out above your eyes, or a special hat that consists only of this **2** the part of a HELMET that can be lowered to protect your face **3** a flat object above the front window of a car that you pull down to keep the sun out of your eyes

vis·ta /ˈvɪstə/ *n.* [C] (literary) a view, especially over a large area of land

vis·u·al[1] /ˈvɪʒuəl/ (Ac) *adj.* relating to seeing or to your sight: *The movie has a strong visual impact.* | *The nerves carry visual information from the eyes to the brain.* —**visually** *adv.*: *Of the information our senses receive, 75% is received visually.*

visual[2] *n.* [C usually plural] something such as a picture or part of a movie, video, etc. that you can see, not the parts that you hear: *the movie's stunning visuals*

ˌvisual ˈaid *n.* [C] something such as a map, picture, or movie that is used for helping people to learn

ˌvisual ˈarts *n.* [plural] ENG. LANG. ARTS art such as painting, SCULPTURE, etc. that you look at, rather than literature or music

V

vis·u·al·ize /ˈvɪʒuəˌlaɪz/ (Ac) *v.* [T] to form a picture of someone or something in your mind (SYN) **imagine**: *I tried to visualize the house as he described it.* | *Part of your preparation should be to visualize the race before you run it.*

THESAURUS **imagine, picture, envision, envisage** ➔ IMAGINE

vi·tal /ˈvaɪt̬l/ *adj.* **1** extremely important or necessary: *These computer systems are* ***vital to*** *our business.* | *Regular exercise is* ***vital for*** *your health.* | *Tourism plays a* ***vital role*** *in the country's economy.*

THESAURUS **important, of great/considerable importance, crucial** ➔ IMPORTANT
necessary, essential, indispensable ➔ NECESSARY

2 full of life and energy: *Their music still sounds as fresh and vital as the day it was written.* [ORIGIN: 1300—1400 Old French, Latin *vitalis* "of life," from *vita* "life"]

THESAURUS **energetic, vigorous, dynamic** ➔ ENERGETIC

vi·tal·i·ty /vaɪˈtæləṭi/ *n.* [U] life and energy: *He has the vitality of a man half his age.*

vi·tal·ly /ˈvaɪt̬l-i/ *adv.* in an extremely important or necessary way: *It's* ***vitally important*** *that you attend the meeting.*

ˌvital ˈorgan *n.* [C] BIOLOGY a part of your body that is necessary to keep you alive, such as your heart and lungs

ˌvital staˈtistics *n.* [plural] facts about people such as their age, race, and whether they are married, especially in official records

vi·ta·min /ˈvaɪt̬əmɪn/ *n.* [C] a chemical substance found in food that is necessary for good health: *Oranges are full of vitamin C.*

vit·ri·ol·ic /ˌvɪtriˈɑlɪk/ *adj.* something you say that is vitriolic is very cruel and angry toward someone: *a vitriolic attack on the senator's character*

vi·tu·per·a·tion /vaɪˌtupəˈreɪʃən, vɪ-/ *n.* [U] (formal) angry and cruel criticism —**vituperative** /vaɪˈtupərət̬ɪv, -ˌreɪt̬ɪv/ *adj.* —**vituperate** /vaɪˈtupəˌreɪt/ *v.* [I]

vi·va·cious /vɪˈveɪʃəs, vaɪ-/ *adj.* someone, especially a woman, who is vivacious has a lot of energy and is fun to be with —**vivaciously** *adv.*

viv·id /ˈvɪvɪd/ *adj.* **1** vivid memories, dreams, descriptions, etc. are so clear that they seem real: *He had a vivid picture of her in his mind.* **2 vivid imagination** an ability to imagine unlikely situations very clearly **3** vivid colors or patterns are very bright —**vividly** *adv.*

viv·i·sec·tion /ˌvɪvəˈsɛkʃən/ *n.* [U] the practice of operating on animals in order to do scientific tests on them [ORIGIN: 1700—1800 Latin *vivus* "alive" + English *section* "cutting"]

V-neck /ˈvi nɛk/ *n.* [C] a type of shirt or SWEATER with a collar that is shaped like the letter V

vo·cab·u·lar·y /voʊˈkæbyəˌlɛri, və-/ *n.* (plural **vocabularies**) [C,U] **1** ENG. LANG. ARTS all the words that someone knows, learns, or uses: *Reading is one of the best ways to improve your vocabulary.* **2** ENG. LANG. ARTS the words that are used when talking about a particular subject: *Most technical jobs use a specialized vocabulary.* **3** ENG. LANG. ARTS all the words in a particular language: *English has the largest vocabulary of any language.* [ORIGIN: 1500—1600 French *vocabulaire*, from Latin *vocabulum* "word, name"]

vo·cal[1] /ˈvoʊkəl/ *adj.* **1** expressing your opinion strongly or loudly: *a* ***vocal critic/opponent*** *of the president* **2** relating to the voice: *vocal music* —**vocally** *adv.*

vocal[2] *n.* [C usually plural] the part of a piece of music that is sung rather than played on an instrument: *The song has Maria McKee* ***on vocals.***

ˈvocal cords, vocal chords *n.* [plural] BIOLOGY thin pieces of muscle in your throat that produce sound when you speak or sing

vo·cal·ist /ˈvoʊkəlɪst/ *n.* [C] someone who sings, especially with a band

vo·ca·tion /voʊˈkeɪʃən/ *n.* [C,U] the feeling that the purpose of your life is to do a particular job, or the job itself: *Teaching isn't just a job to her – it's her vocation.*

THESAURUS **job, occupation, profession, career** → JOB

vo·ca·tion·al /voʊˈkeɪʃənəl/ *adj.* **vocational school/training/education etc.** a school or method of training that teaches you the skills you need to do a particular job

vo·cif·er·ous /voʊˈsɪfərəs/ *adj.* (formal) loud and determined in expressing your opinions: *a vociferous opponent of the plan* —**vociferously** *adv.*

vod·cast /ˈvɑdˌkæst/ *n.* [C] IT a PODCAST that contains VIDEO images or pictures

vod·ka /ˈvɑdkə/ *n.* [U] a strong clear alcoholic drink, first made in Russia

vogue /voʊg/ *n.* **be in vogue/be the vogue** to be fashionable and popular: *Long skirts are back in vogue.* [ORIGIN: 1500—1600 French "act of rowing, course, fashion," from Old Italian *voga*, from *vogare* "to row"]

voice¹ /vɔɪs/ *n.* **1** [C,U] the sound you make when you speak or sing, or the ability to make this sound: *I thought I heard voices downstairs.* | *Andrea has a really* ***deep voice*** *for a woman.* | *He called out* ***in a loud voice.*** | *He's caught a bad cold and* ***lost*** *his* ***voice*** (=cannot speak). | *I can hear you – you don't have to* ***raise your voice*** (=speak louder, especially in an angry way). | ***Keep your voice down*** (=speak more quietly) *– we don't want to wake everyone up.* **2** [C,U] an opinion or wish that is expressed: *Shouldn't parents* ***have a voice in*** *deciding how their children are educated?* **3** [singular] a person, organization, newspaper, etc. that expresses the wishes or opinions of a group of people: *Dr. King became the voice of the civil rights movement.* **4 the voice of reason/experience etc.** opinions or ideas that are reasonable, based on experience, etc., or someone who has these ideas: *Ben has been the voice of reason throughout the crisis.* **5 the active/passive voice** ENG. LANG. ARTS the form of a verb that shows whether the subject of a sentence does an action or has an action done to it [ORIGIN: 1200—1300 Old French *vois*, from Latin *vox*]

voice² *v.* [T] to tell people your opinions or feelings about a particular subject: *We all* ***voiced*** *our* ***concerns*** *about the plan.*

voiced /vɔɪst/ *adj.* ENG. LANG. ARTS voiced sounds are made using the VOCAL CORDS. For example, /d/ and /g/ are voiced consonants. → VOICELESS

voice·less /ˈvɔɪsləs/ *adj.* ENG. LANG. ARTS voiceless sounds are made without using the VOCAL CORDS. For example, /p/ and /k/ are voiceless consonants.

ˈvoice mail *n.* [U] a system that records telephone calls so that you can listen to them later → ANSWERING MACHINE

void¹ /vɔɪd/ *adj.* **1** LAW a contract or agreement that is void is officially no longer legal: *They were demanding that the elections be* ***declared void.*** **2 be void of sth** (literary) to completely lack something: *Her eyes were void of all expression.*

void² *n.* [C] **1** a feeling of great sadness that you have when someone you love dies or when something important is missing from your life: *Work helped to* ***fill the void*** *after his wife died.* **2** an empty space where nothing exists

void³ *v.* [T] LAW to make a contract or agreement void so that it has no legal effect: *The ruling party voided elections in 14 cities.*

vol·a·tile /ˈvɑlət̬l/ *adj.* **1** a volatile situation is likely to change suddenly and without much warning **2** someone who is volatile can suddenly become angry or violent **3** CHEMISTRY a volatile liquid or substance changes easily into a gas —**volatility** /ˌvɑləˈtɪlət̬i/ *n.* [U]

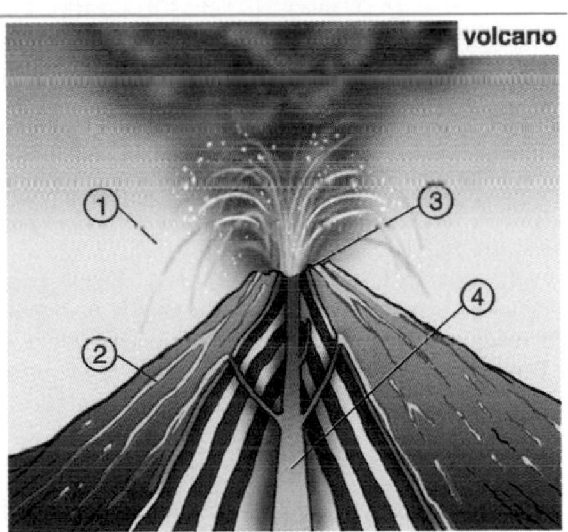

1. ashes 2. lava 3. crater 4. magma

vol·ca·no /vɑlˈkeɪnoʊ/ *n.* (plural **volcanoes** *or* **volcanos**) [C] EARTH SCIENCES a mountain with a large hole at the top out of which rocks, LAVA, and ASH sometimes explode: *This island has several* ***active volcanoes*** (=volcanoes that may explode at any time). —**volcanic** /vɑlˈkænɪk/ *adj.*: *volcanic rocks*

vo·li·tion /vəˈlɪʃən, voʊ-/ *n.* **of your own volition** (formal) because you want to do something and not because you are forced to do it: *Robin left the company of her own volition.*

vol·ley /ˈvɑli/ *n.* [C] **1** a large number of bullets, ARROWS, rocks, etc. fired or thrown at the same time: *a* ***volley of*** *shots* **2** a lot of questions, insults, attacks, etc. that are all said or made at the same time: *a* ***volley of*** *abuse*

vol·ley·ball /ˈvɑliˌbɔl/ *n.* **1** [U] a game in which two teams hit a ball to each other across a net with their hands and try not to let it touch the ground **2** [C] the ball used in this game

volt /voʊlt/ *n.* [C] PHYSICS a unit for measuring the force of an electric current [ORIGIN: 1800—1900 Alessandro *Volta*]

volt·age /ˈvoʊltɪdʒ/ *n.* [C,U] PHYSICS the force of an electric current measured in volts

vol·ta·ic cell /vɑlˌteɪ-ɪk ˈsɛl/ *n.* [C] PHYSICS a PRIMARY CELL

vol·ume /ˈvɑlyəm, -yum/ (Ac) *n.* **1** [U] the amount of sound produced by a television, radio, etc.: *Can you **turn the volume up/down**?* **2** [U] the amount of space that a substance fills or an object contains: *Let the dough double in volume before you bake it.* | *The ocean is so deep that its volume is six times greater than all land above sea level.* **3** [C,U] the total amount of something: *an increase in the **volume of** traffic* | *The system can process large volumes of data.* **4** [C] a book, especially one of the books into which a very long book is divided: *a 12-volume set of poetry* | *The focus of most of the other chapters in this volume is on World War II.* [ORIGIN: (4) 1300—1400 Old French, Latin *volumen* "roll, scroll," from *volvere* "to roll"]

vo·lu·mi·nous /vəˈlumənəs/ *adj.* (formal) **1** very large: *a voluminous skirt* **2** voluminous books, documents, etc. are very long and contain a lot of information

vol·un·tar·y /ˈvɑlənˌtɛri/ (Ac) *adj.* done willingly and without being forced or being paid: *voluntary work* | *We're asking for people to help **on a voluntary basis*** (=without being paid). | *The new law is supported by many professionals and voluntary organizations.* —**voluntarily** /ˌvɑlənˈtɛrəli/ *adv.*

V

vol·un·teer¹ /ˌvɑlənˈtɪr/ (Ac) *v.* **1** [I,T] to offer to do something without expecting any reward: *Ernie **volunteered to** wash the dishes.* | *I **volunteered for** the job.* | *Chris volunteers at the local food bank.* **2** [T] to tell someone something without being asked: *Michael volunteered the information before I had a chance to say anything.* | *He never volunteers answers in class.* **3** [I] to offer to join the army, navy, etc.: *When the war began, my brother immediately volunteered.* | *She volunteered for military service.* [ORIGIN: 1500—1600 French *volontaire*, from Latin *voluntarius*, from *voluntas* "will"]

volunteer² (Ac) *n.* [C] **1** someone who does something without being paid, or who is willing to offer to help someone: *We need volunteers to help look for the children.* | *Most of the relief work was done by volunteers.* **2** someone who offers to join the army, navy, or air force

vo·lup·tu·ous /vəˈlʌptʃuəs/ *adj.* a woman who is voluptuous has large breasts and a soft curved body

vom·it¹ /ˈvɑmɪt/ *v.* [I,T] (formal) if you vomit, food or drink comes up from your stomach and out through your mouth

vomit² *n.* [U] the food or drink that comes out when someone vomits

voo·doo /ˈvudu/ *n.* [U] magical beliefs and practices used as a form of religion, especially in parts of Africa, Latin America, and the Caribbean

THESAURUS **magic, witchcraft, sorcery, black magic, the occult** → MAGIC¹

vo·ra·cious /vəˈreɪʃəs, vɔ-/ *adj.* (formal) wanting to do something a lot, especially eating: *He had a **voracious appetite**.* [ORIGIN: 1600—1700 Latin *vorax*, from *vorare* "to swallow"] —**voracity** /vəˈræsət̬i/ *n.* [U]

vor·tex /ˈvɔrtɛks/ *n.* (plural **vortices** /ˈvɔrtəsiz/ *or* **vortexes**) [C] a large area of wind or water that spins quickly and pulls things into its center

vote¹ /voʊt/ *v.* **1** [I,T] POLITICS to show which person you want to elect or whether you support a plan by raising your hand, marking a paper using a pen or a machine, or CLICKing on a WEB PAGE on the Internet: *Who did you **vote for**?* | *Only Stevens **voted against** the measure.* | *If we can't agree, we'll have to **vote on** it.* | *Congress **voted to** reduce taxes by 2%.* **2** [T] to choose someone or something for a particular prize by voting for him/her: *The program was voted best documentary show on television.* [ORIGIN: 1200—1300 Latin *votum* "promise, wish," from *vovere* "to promise"]

vote² *n.* [C] **1** POLITICS a choice or decision that you make by voting: *He's certainly not going to get my vote!* | *There were 1,079 **votes for** Mr. Swanson, and 766 for Mr. Reynolds.* | *You have until 8:00 to **cast your vote*** (=to vote). **2** an act of making a choice or decision by voting: *We couldn't decide, so we **took a vote on** it.* | *Congress will **put** the bill **to a vote** tomorrow.* **3 the vote a)** POLITICS the total number of votes made in an election or the total number of people who vote: *Davis won the election with 57% of the vote.* | *efforts to win **the African American/Irish/Jewish vote*** (=all the votes of African Americans, Irish people, etc.) **b)** POLITICS the right to vote: *In France, women didn't get the vote until 1945.* **4 vote of confidence** the action of showing publicly that you support someone

vot·er /ˈvoʊt̬ɚ/ *n.* [C] someone who votes or has the right to vote: *Let the voters decide the issue.*

ˈvoting booth *n.* [C] POLITICS an enclosed place where you can vote without being seen

vouch /vaʊtʃ/ *v.*

vouch for sb/sth *phr. v.* **1** to say that you have a firm belief that something is true or good because of your experience or knowledge of it: *I'll vouch for the accuracy of that report.* **2** to say that you believe that someone will behave well and that you will be responsible for his/her behavior, actions, etc.: *Don't worry about Andy – I can vouch for him.*

vouch·er /ˈvaʊtʃɚ/ *n.* [C] a type of ticket that can be used for a particular purpose instead of money

vow[1] /vaʊ/ *n.* [C] a serious promise: *marriage vows* | *She* ***made a vow*** *to herself that she would never go back.* [ORIGIN: 1200—1300 Old French *vou*, from Latin *votum* "promise, wish"]

vow[2] *v.* [T] to make a serious promise to yourself or someone else: *Supporters have* ***vowed to*** *continue the protest until Adams is released.* | *I* ***vowed (that)*** *I would never drink again.*

THESAURUS promise, swear, take/swear an oath, pledge → PROMISE[1]

vow·el /ˈvaʊəl/ *n.* [C] ENG. LANG. ARTS the sounds represented in English by the letters a, e, i, o, or u, and sometimes y → CONSONANT [ORIGIN: 1300—1400 Old French *vouel*, from Latin *vocalis*, from *vox* "voice"]

voy·age /ˈvɔɪ-ɪdʒ/ *n.* [C] **1** a long trip, especially in a ship or a space vehicle: *the voyage from England to America*

THESAURUS travel, trip, journey → TRAVEL[2]

2 voyage of discovery a voyage made by EXPLORERS, to find out more about the world or about something scientific —**voyage** *v.* [I] (literary)

voy·eur /vɔɪˈɚ/ *n.* [C] someone who gets sexual pleasure from secretly watching other people's sexual activities —**voyeurism** /ˈvɔɪəˌrɪzəm/ *n.* [U] —**voyeuristic** /ˌvɔɪəˈrɪstɪk◂/ *adj.*

vs. /ˈvɚsəs/ a written abbreviation of VERSUS

VT the written abbreviation of VERMONT

vul·gar /ˈvʌlgɚ/ *adj.* **1** vulgar language, humor, etc. is not polite because it talks about things such as sex or going to the toilet in a rude way: *vulgar jokes* **2** not showing good judgment about what is attractive or appropriate: *a vulgar display of wealth* [ORIGIN: 1300—1400 Latin *vulgaris*, from *volgus*, *vulgus* "common people"] —**vulgarity** /vəlˈgærət̮i/ *n.* [U]

vul·ner·a·ble /ˈvʌlnərəbəl/ *adj.* easy to harm, hurt, or attack (ANT) **invulnerable**: *The army was in a vulnerable position.* | *She looked so young and vulnerable.* [ORIGIN: 1600—1700 Late Latin *vulnerabilis*, from Latin *vulnus* "wound"] —**vulnerability** /ˌvʌlnərəˈbɪlət̮i/ *n.* [U]

vul·ture /ˈvʌltʃɚ/ *n.* [C] a large wild bird that eats dead animals

vy·ing /ˈvaɪ-ɪŋ/ *v.* the present participle of VIE

Ww

W, w /ˈdʌbəlˌyu, ˈdʌbəyu/ **1** the twenty-third letter of the English alphabet **2** PHYSICS the written abbreviation of WATT

W *also* **W.** the written abbreviation of WEST or WESTERN

WA the written abbreviation of WASHINGTON

wack·y /ˈwæki/ *adj.* (informal) silly in an amusing way

wad[1] /wɑd/ *n.* [C] **1** a thick pile of thin sheets of something, especially money: *a* ***wad of*** *dollar bills* **2** a thick soft mass of material that has been pressed together: *a* ***wad of*** *bubble gum*

wad[2] *also* **wad up** *v.* (**wadded**, **wadding**) [T] to press something such as a piece of paper or cloth into a small tight ball: *Aaron wadded up his paper towel and threw it into the trash.*

wad·dle /ˈwɑdl/ *v.* [I] to walk with short steps, swinging from one side to another like a duck —**waddle** *n.* [C]

wade /weɪd/ *v.* [I,T] to walk through water that is not deep → WALK[1]

wade in/into sth *phr. v.* to start taking part in a discussion, argument, attack, etc., in a forceful or annoying way: *Celebrities waded in to complain about the tabloids.*

wade through sth *phr. v.* to read or deal with a lot of long and boring written work: *Preston was wading through a 500-page report.*

wa·fer /ˈweɪfɚ/ *n.* [C] a very thin cookie

waf·fle[1] /ˈwɑfəl/ *n.* [C] a flat bread with a pattern of deep squares, often eaten for breakfast

waffle[2] *v.* [I] (informal) to be unable to decide what action to take: *He cannot continue to waffle on this issue.*

waft /wɑft, wæft/ *v.* [I,T] to move gently through the air: *The smell of bacon* ***wafted up*** *from the kitchen.*

wag /wæg/ *v.* (**wagged**, **wagging**) [I,T] **1** if a dog wags its tail, or the tail wags, it shakes from one side to another **2** to move your head, finger, etc. from side to side, especially in order to show disapproval: *"Not now," said Ralph, wagging his finger at the girls.* —**wag** *n.* [C]

wage[1] /weɪdʒ/ *n.* **1** [singular] the amount of money you earn, usually for each hour that you work: *He* ***earns*** *a good* ***wage***. | *an hourly wage* | *the minimum wage* ▸Don't say "an annual wage." Say "an annual salary."◂ **2 wages** [plural] the money you are paid each day, week, or month: *Unskilled workers are paid lower wages.*

THESAURUS pay, income, salary, earnings → PAY[2]

wage² *v.* [T] to be involved in a war, struggle, or fight against someone or something: *The police are **waging a campaign/war** against drug pushers.*

ˌwage-ˈprice ˌspiral *n.* [C] ECONOMICS a process in which higher wages lead to an increase in the cost of producing goods, so that prices rise. Wages then have to rise again so that people can buy goods, and this leads to higher and higher prices.

wa·ger¹ /ˈweɪdʒɚ/ *n.* [C] **1** an agreement to risk money on the result of a race, game, etc. (SYN) **bet** **2** the money that you risk: *a $10 wager*

wager² *v.* [T] to risk money on the result of a race, game, etc.: *Brad **wagered** $20 **on** the game.*

wag·on /ˈwægən/ *n.* [C] **1** a strong vehicle with four wheels, pulled by horses **2** a small CART with four wheels and a long handle in the front, used as a toy for children **3** (informal) a STATION WAGON **4 be on the wagon** (informal) to no longer drink alcohol

ˈwagon train *n.* [C] a large group of wagons traveling together in past times

waif /weɪf/ *n.* [C] someone, especially a child or a young woman, who is pale and thin and looks as if s/he does not have a home

wail /weɪl/ *v.* **1** [I] to cry out with a long high sound because you are in pain or very sad: *Somewhere behind them, a child began to wail.* **2** [T] to say something in a loud, sad, and complaining way: *"My money's gone!" she wailed.* **3** [I] to make a long high sound: *Sirens were wailing in the distance* —**wail** *n.* [C]

waist /weɪst/ *n.* [C] **1** the part in the middle of your body just above your HIPS: *a slim waist* **2** the part of a piece of clothing that goes around your waist: *These pants are too big **in the waist**.*

waist·band /ˈweɪstbænd/ *n.* [C] the part of a skirt, pants, etc. that fastens around your waist

waist·line /ˈweɪstlaɪn/ *n.* **1** [singular] the measurement around your waist **2** [C] the position of the waist of a piece of clothing

W

wait¹ /weɪt/ *v.* **1** [I] to not do something until something else happens, someone arrives, etc.: *Hurry up! Everyone's waiting.* | ***Wait** right here **until** I come back.* | *people **waiting for** the bus* | *Henson has been **waiting to** hear from Miller.*

USAGE

Wait is never followed directly by a noun. You must say "wait for": *I'm waiting for a phone call.* Or you can say "wait to do something": *We're waiting to hear the news.*
Expect can be followed directly by a noun. Use it to say that you strongly believe that something will come, happen, etc.: *I'm expecting a phone call.* | *The police are expecting trouble.*
Look forward to means to be excited and pleased about something that you know is going to happen: *I'm looking forward to seeing you all.*

2 wait tables to serve food to people at their table in a restaurant

SPOKEN PHRASES

3 wait a minute/second said in order to ask someone to wait for a short time: *Wait a second – I'll get my coat.* **4 sb can't wait/can hardly wait** said to emphasize that someone is very excited about something and eager for it to happen: *I **can't wait to** see the look on his face.* **5 sth can/can't wait** if something can wait, it does not have to be done immediately. If something can't wait, it must be done now: *Which bills have to be paid and which can wait?* **6 wait and see** used in order to say that someone should be patient because s/he will find out about something later, but not now **7 wait until/till** used when you are excited about telling or showing someone something: *Wait till I tell Janice!* **8 wait your turn** to wait until it is your turn to do something

wait around *phr. v.* to do nothing while you are waiting for something to happen, someone to arrive, etc.: *I waited around for 10 minutes.*

wait on sb *phr. v.* **1** to serve food to someone at his/her table, especially in a restaurant **2 wait on sb hand and foot** (humorous) to do everything for someone

wait up *phr. v.* **1** to wait for someone to return before you go to bed: *Please don't **wait up for** me.* **2 Wait up!** (spoken) used to tell someone to stop and wait for you: *Hey, wait up, you guys!*

wait² *n.* [singular] a period of time in which you wait for something to happen, someone to arrive, etc.: *a three-hour **wait for** our flight* | *They'll **have** a long **wait**.*

wait·er /ˈweɪt̬ɚ/ *n.* [C] a man who serves food in a restaurant → RESTAURANT

ˈwaiting list *also* **ˈwait list** *n.* [C] a list of people who want to do or buy something, but who must wait before they can do or have it: *Over 500 students are **on the waiting list**.*

ˈwaiting room *n.* [C] a room for people to wait in, for example to see a doctor

wait·ress /ˈweɪtrɪs/ *n.* [C] a woman who serves food at the tables in a restaurant → RESTAURANT

waive /weɪv/ *v.* [T] to state officially that a right, rule, etc. can be ignored: *She **waived her right** to a lawyer.*

waiv·er /ˈweɪvɚ/ *n.* [C] an official statement saying that a right, rule, etc. can be ignored

wake¹ /weɪk/ *also* **wake up** *v.* (past tense **woke** /woʊk/, past participle **woken** /ˈwoʊkən/) [I,T] to stop sleeping, or to make someone stop sleeping: *Try not to wake the baby.* | *I woke up early.*

wake up to sth *phr. v.* to start to realize and understand a danger, an idea, etc.: *The public is just beginning to wake up to the impact of these changes.*

wake² *n.* [C] **1 in the wake of/in sth's wake** as a result of something: *Five councilors resigned in the wake of the scandal.* **2** the track or path made behind a car, boat, etc. as it moves along: *The car* *left clouds of dust* ***in its wake.*** **3** the time before a funeral when people meet to remember the dead person

wak·en /ˈweɪkən/ *v.* [I,T] (formal) to wake, or to wake someone: *The sound had wakened him.*

wak·ing /ˈweɪkɪŋ/ *adj.* **waking hours/life etc.** all the time when you are awake: *He spends every waking moment with that girl!*

walk[1] /wɔk/ *v.* **1** [I,T] to move forward by putting one foot in front of the other: *We must have walked ten miles.* | *Do you* ***walk to*** *work?* | *Lori* ***walked into*** *his office.* | *tourists* ***walking around*** *the downtown area* → *see picture on page A22*

THESAURUS

march – to walk like soldiers, with regular steps
stride – to walk with long steps in a determined way
stroll – to walk in a relaxed way, especially for pleasure
amble – to walk slowly in a relaxed way
trudge – to walk in a tired way or when it is difficult to continue walking
limp – to walk with difficulty because one leg is hurt
wade – to walk through water
hike – to take a long walk in the country, mountains, etc. → RUN[1], TRAVEL[1]

2 [T] to walk through or across a particular area: *It's not safe to* ***walk the streets*** *at night.* | *He spent two years walking the Baja coastline.* **3** [T] to walk somewhere with someone: *It's late – I'll walk you home.* **4 walk the dog** to take a dog outside to walk **5 walk all over sb** (informal) to treat someone very badly: *She lets those kids walk all over her.* **6** [I] *also* **walk free** (informal) to leave a court of law without being punished or sent to prison **7 walk the walk** (informal) to do the things that a particular type of person is expected to do: *She doesn't call herself a feminist, but she walks the walk.*

walk away *phr. v.* to leave a bad or difficult situation: *You can't just walk away from eight years of marriage!*

walk away with sth *phr. v.* to win something easily: *Bradley won, walking away with $50,000.*

walk in on sb *phr. v.* to go into a place and accidentally interrupt someone whom you did not expect to be there

walk into sth *phr. v.* **1** to hit an object accidentally as you are walking: *She walked* ***straight/right into*** *a tree.* **2** to become involved in an unpleasant situation without intending to: *The soldiers walked into an ambush.* **3** to do something that makes you seem stupid: *You* ***walked straight into*** *that one!*

walk off *phr. v.* to leave someone by walking away from him/her

walk off with sth *phr. v.* to steal something, or to take something by mistake: *Someone walked off with my new jacket!*

walk out *phr. v.* **1** to stop working or leave a situation as a protest: *Most miners have walked out.* **2** to leave your husband, wife, etc. suddenly: *Mary just* ***walked out on*** *him one day.*

walk[2] *n.* **1** [C] a trip that you make by walking: *Let's* ***go for a walk.*** | *I like to* ***take a walk*** *after lunch.* | *It's only a* ***ten-minute/two-mile walk*** *from here.* **2** [C] a particular path or ROUTE for walking: *popular walks in Yellowstone National Park* **3** [singular] the way someone walks: *Do you remember that guy with a funny walk?* → WALK OF LIFE

walk·er /ˈwɔkɚ/ *n.* [C] **1** a metal frame that old or sick people use to help them walk **2** someone who is walking, especially at a particular speed, in a particular place, etc.: *a nice area for walkers* | *He's a* ***fast/slow walker.***

walk·ie-talk·ie /ˌwɔki ˈtɔki/ *n.* [C] one of a pair of radios that you can carry with you, and use to speak to the person who has the other radio

ˈwalk-in *adj.* big enough for a person to walk inside: *a walk-in closet*

ˈwalking stick *n.* [C] a long thin stick, used to help support you when you walk

Walk·man /ˈwɔkmən/ *n.* [C] (trademark) a small machine that plays TAPEs and has HEADPHONES, that you carry with you to listen to music

ˌwalk of ˈlife *n.* (plural **walks of life**) [C] the position in society that someone has: *The club has members from* ***all walks of life.***

ˈwalk-on *n.* [C] a small acting part in a play or movie in which the actor has no words, or an actor who has this part —**walk-on** *adj.*

walk·out /ˈwɔk-aʊt/ *n.* [C] an occasion when people stop working or leave somewhere as a protest: *City employees* ***staged a walkout.***

ˈwalk-up *n.* [C] (informal) an apartment that you have to walk up the stairs to, because there is no ELEVATOR in the building

walk·way /ˈwɔk-weɪ/ *n.* [C] a path, often above the ground, built to connect two parts of a building or two buildings

W

wall /wɔl/ *n.* [C] **1** one of the sides of a room or building: *Her bedroom walls were covered with posters.* | *We pushed the bed* ***against the wall.*** **2** an upright structure made of stone or brick, that divides one area from another: *the wall surrounding the apartment complex* **3** the side of something hollow, such as a pipe or tube: *the walls of the blood vessels* **4** something that prevents you from doing something or going somewhere: *A wall of people was blocking my way.* [ORIGIN: Old English *weall*] —**walled** *adj.* → **have your back to/against the wall** *at* BACK[2], **drive sb up the wall** *at* DRIVE[1]

wal·let /ˈwɑlɪt, ˈwɔ-/ *n.* [C] a small object that you keep money in, that is usually made of leather and that you carry in your pocket or PURSE

wal·lop /ˈwɑləp/ *v.* [T] (informal) to hit someone or something very hard —**wallop** *n.* [C]

wal·low /ˈwɑloʊ/ *v.* [I] **1** (disapproving) to spend too long feeling an emotion, especially a negative emotion: *You don't have time to* ***wallow in*** *self-pity.* **2** to roll around in mud or water

wall·pa·per /'wɔl,peɪpɚ/ *n.* [U] **1** paper that you stick onto the walls of a room in order to decorate it **2** the picture that you have as the background on the screen of a computer —**wallpaper** *v.* [T]

'Wall Street *n.* **1** a street in New York City where the American STOCK EXCHANGE is **2** ECONOMICS the American STOCK EXCHANGE

,wall-to-'wall *adj.* covering the whole floor: *wall-to-wall carpeting*

wal·nut /'wɔlnʌt/ *n.* **1** [C] a slightly bitter nut with a large light brown shell, or the tree on which this grows **2** [U] the dark brown wood of this tree

wal·rus /'wɔlrəs, 'wɑl-/ *n.* [C] a large sea animal with two long thick teeth coming down from the sides of its mouth

waltz¹ /wɔlts/ *n.* [C] a fairly slow dance with a RHYTHM consisting of patterns of three beats, or the music for this dance [ORIGIN: 1700—1800 German *walzer*, from *walzen* "to roll, dance"]

waltz² *v.* [I] **1** to dance a waltz **2** (informal, disapproving) to walk somewhere calmly and confidently: *Eric* ***waltzed in*** *late again.*

wan /wɑn/ *adj.* looking pale, weak, or tired: *a wan smile*

wand /wɑnd/ *n.* [C] a thin stick you hold in your hand to do magic tricks

wan·der /'wɑndɚ/ *v.* **1** [I,T] to walk slowly across or around an area, usually without having a clear direction or purpose: *We* ***wandered around*** *the city.* | *Homeless people wandered the streets.* **2** [I] *also* **wander off** to move away from where you are supposed to stay: *The kids got bored and started to wander off.* **3** [I] to start to talk or write about something not related to the main subject that you were talking or writing about before **4** [I] if your mind, thoughts, etc. wander, you no longer pay attention to something: *He began to read, but his* ***mind wandered.*** [ORIGIN: Old English *wandrian*] —**wanderer** *n.* [C]

wane¹ /weɪn/ *v.* [I] **1** if something such as power, influence, or a feeling wanes, it becomes gradually less strong or less important: *My enthusiasm for the project was waning.* **2** when the moon wanes, you gradually see less of it (ANT) **wax**

wane² *n.* **on the wane** becoming smaller, weaker, or less important: *The show's popularity is on the wane.*

wan·gle /'wæŋgəl/ *v.* [T] (informal) to get something by persuading or tricking someone: *I managed to wangle an invitation.*

wan·na /'wʌnə, 'wɑnə/ a short form of "want to" or "want a," used in writing to show how people sound when they speak: *I don't wanna go.*

wan·na·be /'wɑnə,bi/ *n.* [C] (informal) someone who tries to look, behave, or do something like a famous or popular person: *an Elvis wannabe*

want¹ /wʌnt, wɑnt, wɔnt/ *v.* [T] to have a desire or need for something: *What do you want for your birthday?* | *This is a team that really* ***wants to*** *win.* | *Do you* ***want*** *me* ***to*** *read you a story?* | *Want* (=do you want) *a drink?* | *I can pick it up on my way to work,* ***if you want*** (=if you would like that).

want for sth *phr. v.* to not have something that you need: *Those kids have never wanted for anything.* [ORIGIN: 1100—1200 Old Norse *vanta*]

want² *n.* [C,U] something that you desire or need but do not have: *They are dying* ***for want of*** *food and medicine.*

'want ad *n.* [C] a small advertisement that you put in a newspaper if you want to employ someone to do a job

want·ed /'wʌntɪd/ *adj.* someone who is wanted is being looked for by the police: *He is* ***wanted for*** *murder.*

want·ing /'wʌntɪŋ/ *adj.* lacking or missing something that is needed: *Security procedures were* ***found wanting.***

wan·ton /'wɑntˀn, 'wɔn-/ *adj.* **1** deliberately causing damage or harm for no reason: *wanton destruction* **2** (old-fashioned) sexually uncontrolled: *She felt wanton and wild.*

war /wɔr/ *n.* [C,U] **1** a time when two or more countries, or opposing groups within a country, fight each other with soldiers and weapons (ANT) **peace**: *World War II* | *In 1793, England* ***was at war*** *with France.* | *the* ***war with/against*** *Germany* | *the soldiers killed* ***in the war*** | *Was it right to* ***go to war*** (=take part in a war)? | *the* ***war between*** *the states*

THESAURUS

warfare – the activity of fighting in a war – used especially when talking about particular methods of fighting: *guerrilla warfare*
fighting – an occasion when people or groups fight each other in a war, in the street, etc.: *One thousand people have died since the fighting began.*
conflict – fighting or a war: *the conflict in the Middle East*
combat – fighting during a war: *The soldiers were wounded in combat.*
action – fighting in a war: *He had been killed in action.*
hostilities – fighting in a war: *the formal cessation of hostilities*

2 a struggle to control or stop a bad or illegal activity: *the* ***war on/against*** *drugs* **3** a situation in which a person or group is fighting for power, influence, or control: *a trade war* [ORIGIN: 1100—1200 Old North French *werre*, from Old French *guerre*] —**war** *v.* [I]

war·ble /'wɔrbəl/ *v.* [I,T] to sing with a high continuous but quickly changing sound, the way a bird does

'war crime *n.* [C] HISTORY a cruel act done during a

war, that is illegal under international law —**war criminal** *n.* [C]

ward¹ /wɔrd/ *n.* [C] **1** a part of a hospital where people who need medical treatment stay: *the maternity ward* (=for women who are having babies) | *the children's ward* **2** LAW someone, especially a child, who is under the legal protection of another person or of a court of law **3** POLITICS one of the small areas that a city has been divided into for the purpose of local elections

ward² *v.*

ward sth ↔ **off** *phr. v.* to do something to protect yourself from an illness, danger, attack, etc.: *a spray to ward off insects*

war·den /ˈwɔrdn/ *n.* [C] the person in charge of a prison

war·drobe /ˈwɔrdroʊb/ *n.* [C] the clothes that someone has: *her large wardrobe*

ware·house /ˈwɛrhaʊs/ *n.* [C] a large building for storing large quantities of goods

ˈwarehouse ˌstore *n.* [C] a type of store that sells things in large amounts at lower prices than normal stores

wares /wɛrz/ *n.* [plural] (written) things that are for sale, usually not in a store: *craftspeople **selling their wares***

war·fare /ˈwɔrfɛr/ *n.* [U] the activity of fighting in a war – used especially when talking about particular methods of fighting: ***guerrilla warfare*** (=when small groups of fighters attack a larger army many times) | *The Geneva Convention bans all forms of chemical/biological/germ warfare.*

THESAURUS war, fighting, conflict → WAR

ˈwar ˌgame *n.* [C] an activity in which soldiers fight an imaginary battle in order to test military plans

war·head /ˈwɔrhɛd/ *n.* [C] the explosive part at the front of a MISSILE

war·like /ˈwɔrlaɪk/ *adj.* threatening war or attack, or seeming to like war: *a warlike gesture*

war·lock /ˈwɔrlɑk/ *n.* [C] a man who has magic powers, especially to do bad things

war·lord /ˈwɔrlɔrd/ *n.* [C] a leader of an unofficial military or fighting group who controls an area of land

warm¹ /wɔrm/ *adj.* **1** slightly hot, especially in a pleasant way (ANT) **cool**: *Are you warm enough?* | *warmer weather* | *a warm bath* | *They huddled together to **keep warm**.*

THESAURUS hot, lukewarm → HOT

2 able to keep in heat or keep out cold: *warm clothes* **3** friendly: *a warm smile* [ORIGIN: Old English *wearm*]

THESAURUS friendly, cordial, amiable, welcoming → FRIENDLY

—**warmly** *adv.*

warm² *also* **warm up** *v.* [I,T] to become warm or warmer, or to make someone or something do this: *There's some soup warming up on the stove.* → GLOBAL WARMING

warm to sb/sth *also* **warm up to** sb/sth *phr. v.* to begin to like someone or something: *Bruce didn't warm to him as he had to Casey.*

warm up *phr. v.* **1** to do gentle physical exercises to prepare your body for exercise, singing, etc.: *The girls are warming up before the game.* **2 warm** (sth ↔) **up** if a machine or engine warms up, or if you warm it up, it becomes ready to work after being turned on

ˌwarm-ˈblooded *adj.* BIOLOGY having a body temperature that remains fairly high whether the temperature around it is hot or cold → COLD-BLOODED: *Mammals are warm-blooded animals.*

ˌwarmed ˈover *adj.* **1** food that is warmed over has been cooked before and then is heated again for eating **2** an idea or argument that is warmed over has been used before and is no longer interesting or useful

ˌwarm-ˈhearted *adj.* friendly and kind: *a warm-hearted old lady*

THESAURUS kind, nice, caring, compassionate, sympathetic → KIND²

war·mon·ger /ˈwɔrˌmʌŋgɚ, -ˌmɑŋ-/ *n.* [C] someone who is eager to start a war —**warmongering** *n.* [U]

warmth /wɔrmθ/ *n.* [U] **1** a feeling of being warm: *the warmth of the sun* **2** friendliness: *the warmth of her smile*

ˈwarm-up *n.* [C] a set of gentle exercises that you do to prepare your body for exercise, dancing, singing, etc.

warn /wɔrn/ *v.* [I,T] to tell someone that something bad or dangerous might happen, so that s/he can avoid it or prevent it: *A sign **warned of/about** the presence of snakes.* | *I **warned** you **not to** walk home alone.* | *The label **warns that** pregnant women should not drink alcohol.*

warn·ing /ˈwɔrnɪŋ/ *n.* [C,U] something that tells you that something bad or dangerous might happen, so that you can avoid it or prevent it: *a **warning of/about** the risks involved* | *The planes attacked **without warning**.* | *a **warning to** women over 50* | *You've been **given** several **warnings** already.* | *Be aware of **warning signs*** (=pain, etc. that shows that an illness is coming) *such as tiredness and headaches.*

THESAURUS advice, suggestion, recommendation → ADVICE

warp /wɔrp/ *v.* [I,T] **1** to become bent or twisted, or to make something do this: *The wood had*

W

warped in the heat. **2** to influence someone in a way that has a harmful effect on how s/he thinks or behaves → TIME WARP

war·path /ˈwɔrpæθ/ *n.* **be on the warpath** (humorous) to be angry about something and want to punish someone for it

warped /wɔrpt/ *adj.* **1** someone who is warped has ideas or thoughts that most people think are unpleasant or not normal: *a warped sense of humor* **2** bent or twisted into the wrong shape: *a warped door*

ˈwarp speed *n.* [U] (informal) a very fast speed

war·rant¹ /ˈwɔrənt, ˈwɑ-/ *v.* [T] to be a good enough reason for something to happen or be done → UNWARRANTED: *The story doesn't warrant the attention it's been given.*

warrant² *n.* [C] LAW an official paper, signed by a judge, that allows the police to do something, for example ARREST someone or search a building: *a* ***warrant for*** *Bryson's arrest* | *The local judge* ***issued*** *the* ***warrant.***

war·ran·ty /ˈwɔrənti, ˈwɑ-/ *n.* (plural **warranties**) [C,U] a written promise that a company will fix or replace something if it breaks after you have bought it: *The TV comes with a 3-year warranty.*

war·ren /ˈwɔrən, ˈwɑ-/ *n.* [C] **1** a set of holes and passages under the ground, that rabbits live in **2** a lot of narrow passages in a building or between buildings: *a warren of corridors*

war·ring /ˈwɔrɪŋ/ *adj.* fighting in a war: *warring factions*

war·ri·or /ˈwɔriɚ, ˈwɑ-/ *n.* [C] (literary) a soldier, especially an experienced and skillful one

ˈwarrior ˌcode *n.* [C] SOCIAL SCIENCE a set of moral rules and principles followed by men, especially those from the highest social class, who live in a society where they are expected to fight if necessary

W

war·ship /ˈwɔrʃɪp/ *n.* [C] a navy ship with guns

wart /wɔrt/ *n.* [C] a small hard raised spot on your skin caused by a VIRUS

> THESAURUS **blemish, bruise, scar, pimple, zit, blister, freckle, mole** → MARK²

war·time /ˈwɔrtaɪm/ *n.* [U] the time during which a war is happening: *his wartime experiences*

ˈwar-torn *adj.* being damaged or destroyed by war: *his war-torn homeland*

war·y /ˈwɛri/ *adj.* careful and worried about danger or problems: *Teach children to be* ***wary of*** *strangers.* —**warily** *adv.*

was /wəz; *strong* wʌz, wɑz/ *v.* the past tense of BE in the first and third person singular

wash¹ /wɑʃ, wɔʃ/ *v.* **1** [T] to clean something with water and usually soap: *She helped Penny wash the dishes.* | ***Wash*** *the mud* ***off*** *the truck.*

> THESAURUS **clean, do/wash the dishes, scour, scrub, mop, do the laundry, dry clean** → CLEAN²

2 [I,T] to clean your body with water and usually soap: *Wash your hands thoroughly.* | *I'm going upstairs to wash.* **3** [I,T] if water, a river, the ocean, etc. washes, it flows somewhere or makes something move somewhere: *waves* ***washing against*** *the shore* | *Floods* ***washed*** *much of the topsoil* ***away.*** | *Their boat* ***washed up/ashore*** *about five miles south.* **4 sth doesn't/won't wash** (spoken) said when you do not believe or accept someone's explanation, reasons, etc.: *His explanation just didn't wash.* **5 wash your hands of sth** to refuse to be responsible for something: *Congress can't wash its hands of this.* [ORIGIN: Old English *wascan*]

wash sth ↔ **down** *phr. v.* **1** to drink something in order to help you swallow food or medicine: *He* ***washed down*** *a mouthful of toast* ***with*** *coffee.* **2** to clean something using a lot of water: *Ted was washing down the driveway.*

wash off *phr. v.* if a substance washes off, you can remove it from the surface of something by washing: *Will this paint wash off?*

wash out *phr. v.* **1** if a substance washes out, you can remove it from a material by washing it: *I don't know if that ink will wash out.* **2 wash** sth ↔ **out** to wash the inside of something: *Will you wash out the cups?*

wash up *phr. v.* to wash your hands: *Go wash up for supper.*

wash² *n.* **1** [C,U] clothing, sheets, etc. that have been washed or that need washing: *I* ***did*** *three loads of* ***wash.*** | *Your blue shirt is* ***in the wash*** (=being washed or waiting to be washed). **2** [C] EARTH SCIENCES a river in a desert area that has no water in it most of the time **3 it will all come out in the wash** (spoken) said when you think that a problem will be solved without you having to do anything about it → CAR WASH

wash·a·ble /ˈwɑʃəbəl/ *adj.* able to be washed without being damaged: *a* ***machine washable*** *sweater*

wash·basin /ˈwɑʃˌbeɪsən/ *also* **wash·bowl** /ˈwɑʃboʊl/ *n.* [C] a SINK

wash·cloth /ˈwɑʃklɔθ/ *n.* [C] a small square piece of cloth that you use to wash yourself

ˌwashed-ˈout *adj.* very tired and pale: *the old man's washed-out eyes*

ˌwashed-ˈup *adj.* (informal) someone who is washed-up is no longer successful: *a washed-up rock star*

wash·er /ˈwɑʃɚ/ *n.* [C] **1** a washing machine **2** a small ring of plastic or metal that you put between a NUT and a BOLT, or between two pipes, to make them fit together tightly

wash·ing /ˈwɑʃɪŋ/ *n.* [U] clothes, etc. that need to be washed or have just been washed

ˈwashing maˌchine *n.* [C] a machine that washes clothes

wash·room /ˈwɑʃrum, -rʊm/ *n.* [C] (old-fashioned) a RESTROOM

was·n't /ˈwʌzənt, ˈwɑzənt/ *v.* the short form of "was not": *He wasn't there.*

WASP, Wasp /wɑsp/ *n.* [C] **white Anglo-Saxon Protestant** a white American whose family was originally from northern Europe, and who is therefore considered to be part of the most powerful group in society

wasp /wɑsp, wɔsp/ *n.* [C] a black and yellow flying insect similar to a BEE, that can sting you

waste¹ /weɪst/ *n.* **1** [singular, U] the use of something such as money or skills in a way that is not effective, useful, or sensible: *a **waste of** resources* | *My father thought college would be a **waste of time/money**.* **2 go to waste** if something goes to waste, it is not used: *A lot of the food ended up going to waste.* **3** [C,U] unwanted things or substances that are left after you have used something: ***household waste*** | *the safe disposal of **nuclear/toxic/hazardous wastes***

THESAURUS **garbage, trash, refuse** → GARBAGE

waste² *v.* [T] **1** to use something in a way that is not effective, or to use more of it than you should: *Don't waste electricity!* | *They **wasted** a lot of **time** trying to fix it themselves.* **2 be wasted on sb** if something is wasted on someone, s/he does not understand it or does not think it is worth anything: *The joke was wasted on him.*

waste away *phr. v.* to gradually become thinner and weaker because you are sick

waste³ *adj.* not being used effectively, or no longer useful: *waste paper*

waste·bas·ket /ˈweɪstˌbæskɪt/ *n.* [C] a container into which you put paper, etc. that you want to get rid of

wast·ed /ˈweɪstɪd/ *adj.* **1** useless: *It had been a wasted trip.* **2** (spoken) having drunk too much or taken drugs: *Chuck **got wasted** at Bryan's party.*

waste·ful /ˈweɪstfəl/ *adj.* using more than is needed of something, or using it badly, so that it is wasted: *wasteful packaging on groceries*

waste·land /ˈweɪstlænd/ *n.* [C,U] **1** an area of land that is not or cannot be used for anything: *a desert wasteland* **2** a place, situation, or time that has no excitement or interest: *Television is a vast wasteland.*

waste·pa·per bas·ket /ˈweɪstˌpeɪpɚ ˌbæskɪt/ *n.* [C] a WASTEBASKET

watch¹ /wɑtʃ, wɔtʃ/ *v.* **1** [I,T] to look at and pay attention to something or someone: *Harry was watching the game on TV.* | *I watched him go.* | ***Watch closely** – can you see it moving?*

USAGE

You **look at** a picture, person, thing, etc. because you want to: *Hey, look at these jeans.*
You **see** something without planning to: *Two people saw him take the bag.*
You **watch** TV, a movie, or something that happens for a period of time: *Did you watch the football game last night?* | *The kids are watching TV.*
You can also say that you **saw** a movie, a program, etc., but you cannot say "see television": *I saw a great movie on TV last night.*

2 [T] to be careful about something, in order to avoid an accident or unwanted situation: *Watch your head – the door's low.* | ***Watch your weight*** (=be careful not to become fat) *and exercise.* | *Why don't you **watch where** you're **going**?* | *Hey, **watch it** – you stepped on my toes.* **3 watch your language/mouth/tongue** to not say things that might hurt or offend other people: *Watch your language, Bill, there's ladies present.* **4** [T] to take care of someone or guard something: *Could you watch the kids for me Saturday night?* **5 watch the clock** to keep looking to see what time it is because you are bored or do not want to work [ORIGIN: Old English *wæccan*]

watch (out) for sth *phr. v.* to look for something, so that you are ready to deal with it: *I watched for the White Oak exit.* | *You can ride your bike, but watch out for cars.*

watch out *phr. v.* used in order to tell someone to be careful: *Watch out! It's hot!*

watch over sth *phr. v.* to take care of something, or guard it: *The eldest child watches over the younger ones.*

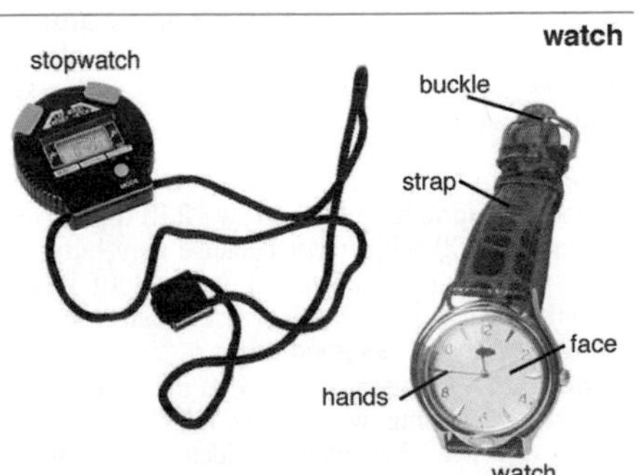

watch² *n.* **1** [C] a small clock that you wear on your wrist or carry in your pocket: *Scott looked at his watch.* **2** [singular,U] the process of checking a situation or a place carefully so that you always know what is happening and are ready to deal with it: *Police **kept a** 24-hour **watch on** the house.* | *Several soldiers **stood watch**.* | *Douglas **kept watch** while the others slept.* **3 be on the watch for sb/sth** to be looking and waiting for someone you might see or something that might happen: *Be on the watch for pickpockets.* **4** [C,U] people

W

employed to guard or protect someone or something, or the fixed period of the day or night when they do this: *the night watch* | *It was my turn to be* ***on watch***.

watch·dog /ˈwɑtʃdɔg/ *n.* [C] **1** a person or group that makes sure other people follow rules: *a consumer watchdog group* **2** a dog that protects someone's property

watch·ful /ˈwɑtʃfəl/ *adj.* careful to notice what is happening, in order to prevent something bad happening: *She learned to bake* ***under the watchful eye*** *of her mother.*

watch·mak·er /ˈwɑtʃˌmeɪkɚ/ *n.* [C] someone who makes and repairs watches and clocks

watch·man /ˈwɑtʃmən/ *n.* (plural **watchmen** /-mən/) [C] someone whose job is to guard a building or area: *the night watchman*

watch·word /ˈwɑtʃwɚd/ *n.* [singular] the main principle or rule that you think about in a particular situation: *The school's watchword is "a community of learners."*

wa·ter¹ /ˈwɔt̬ɚ, ˈwɑ-/ *n.* **1** [U] the clear colorless liquid that falls from the sky as rain, forms lakes, rivers, and oceans, and is used for drinking, washing, etc.: *a drink of water* | *Mike waded out into the water.* | *Floods left the area* ***under water***. | *a cabin with no* ***running water*** (=water from pipes) | ***fresh water*** (=from a lake, river, etc., not from an ocean) *fish* ➔ *see picture at* WATER CYCLE **2 waters** [plural] **a)** EARTH SCIENCES the part of the ocean near or belonging to a particular country: *boats fishing in Icelandic waters* **b)** EARTH SCIENCES the water in a particular lake, river, etc.: *The waters of the Amazon flow into the ocean.* **3 in/into hot water** in a situation in which you have a lot of trouble: *My brother got into hot water at school.* [ORIGIN: Old English *wæter*]

water² *v.* **1** [T] to pour water on a plant or seeds in the ground to help them grow **2** [I] if your eyes water, they fill with water because they hurt: *Her eyes watered and her throat hurt.* **3** [I] if your mouth waters, it fills with water because you see something that looks good to eat

water sth ↔ **down** *phr. v.* **1** to make something weaker by adding water: *The whiskey had been watered down.* **2** to make an idea, statement, etc. less strong so that it does not offend or upset anyone: *The bill got watered down in the Senate.*

wa·ter·bed /ˈwɔt̬ɚˌbɛd/ *n.* [C] a bed made of rubber or soft plastic and filled with water

wa·ter·borne /ˈwɔt̬ɚˌbɔrn/ *adj.* carried by water: *waterborne bacteria*

wa·ter·col·or /ˈwɔt̬ɚˌkʌlɚ/ *n.* [C,U] a special paint mixed with water, or a painting made with these

ˈwater ˌcooler *n.* [C] a WATER FOUNTAIN

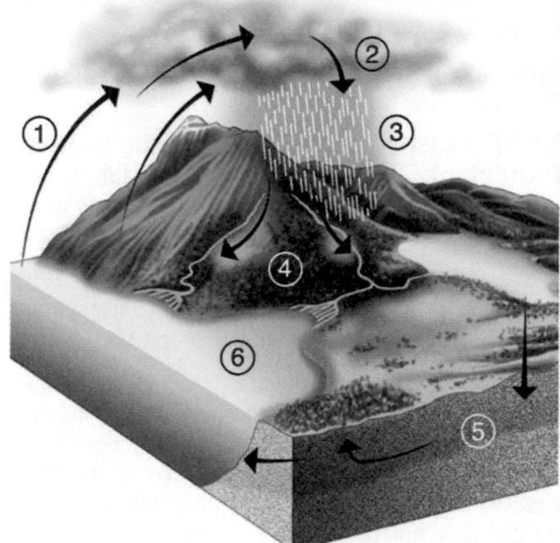

1. evaporation 2. condensation 3. rain 4. run-off 5. ground water 6. ocean

ˈwater ˌcycle *n.* [C] EARTH SCIENCES a continuous process in which water on the ground or in the ocean becomes heated by the Sun and changes into very small drops of liquid. These drops rise into the air and then fall back onto the ground or into the ocean as rain.

ˌwatered-ˈdown *adj.* a watered-down statement, plan, etc. is not as strong or offensive as a previous one: *a watered-down version of the proposal*

wa·ter·fall /ˈwɔt̬ɚˌfɔl/ *n.* [C] EARTH SCIENCES water that falls straight down over a rock or from the top of a mountain

ˈwater ˌfountain *n.* [C] a piece of equipment in a public place, that produces a stream of water that you can drink from

wa·ter·front /ˈwɔt̬ɚˌfrʌnt/ *n.* [C] land at the edge of a lake, river, etc.: *a restaurant* ***on the waterfront***

wa·ter·hole /ˈwɔt̬ɚˌhoʊl/ *n.* [C] a WATERING HOLE

ˈwatering can *n.* [C] a container with a long hollow part on the front for pouring water on plants

ˈwatering hole *n.* [C] (informal) **1** a place such as a club or BAR where people can buy drinks: *the students' favorite watering hole* **2** EARTH SCIENCES a small area of water in a dry place, where wild animals go to drink

wa·ter·logged /ˈwɔt̬ɚˌlɔgd, -ˌlɑgd/ *adj.* land or

an object that is waterlogged is so wet it cannot hold any more water

wa·ter·mark /ˈwɔt̬ɚˌmɑrk/ *n.* [C] **1** a special design on a piece of paper, that you can only see when it is held up to the light **2** the mark showing the highest level of a lake, river, etc.

wa·ter·mel·on /ˈwɔt̬ɚˌmɛlən/ *n.* [C,U] a large round green fruit with juicy dark pink flesh and black seeds ➔ *see picture on page 414*

ˈwater ˌpolo *n.* [U] a game played in a swimming pool, in which two teams of players try to throw a ball into their opponents' GOAL

wa·ter·proof /ˈwɔt̬ɚˌpruf/ *adj.* not allowing water to go through: *waterproof boots*

ˈwater reˌsistant *adj.* not letting water in easily, but not keeping all water out: *a water resistant watch*

wa·ter·shed /ˈwɔt̬ɚˌʃɛd/ *n.* **1** [singular] the point at which an important change happens: *The beginning of television was* ***a watershed in*** *20th-century culture.* **2** [C] EARTH SCIENCES the high land separating two river systems

wa·ter·side /ˈwɔt̬ɚˌsaɪd/ *adj.* at the edge of a lake, river, etc.: *a waterside restaurant* **—waterside** *n.* [singular]

ˈwater ˌskiing *n.* [U] a sport in which someone is pulled along on SKIS over water by a boat: *Do you want to* ***go water skiing****?* **—water ski** *v.* [I] **—water skier** *n.* [C]

ˈwater ˌtable *n.* [C] EARTH SCIENCES the level below the surface of the ground, where there is water

wa·ter·tight /ˈwɔt̬ɚˌtaɪt/ *adj.* not allowing water to get in: *a watertight container*

wa·ter·way /ˈwɔt̬ɚˌweɪ/ *n.* (plural **waterways**) [C] an area of water, often part of a river, that ships can go through

wa·ter·works /ˈwɔt̬ɚˌwɚks/ *n.* [plural] buildings, pipes, and supplies of water that form a public water system

wa·ter·y /ˈwɔt̬əri/ *adj.* containing too much water: *watery soup* | *watery eyes*

watt /wɑt/ *n.* [C] PHYSICS a unit for measuring electrical power: *a 100-watt light bulb* [ORIGIN: 1800—1900 James *Watt*]

watt·age /ˈwɑt̬ɪdʒ/ *n.* [singular, U] PHYSICS the power of a piece of electrical equipment measured in watts

wave¹ /weɪv/ *n.* [C] **1** EARTH SCIENCES an area of raised water that moves across the surface of the ocean or another large area of water: ***waves breaking*** *on the beach* **2** a sudden increase in a particular emotion, activity, number, etc.: *a recent* ***crime wave*** | ***a wave of*** *nostalgia for his childhood* | *a sudden wave of nausea* | *a* ***great wave*** *of immigrants from Eastern Europe* **3** the movement you make when you wave your hand: *She left with* ***a wave of*** *her* ***hand.*** **4** a part of your hair that curls slightly: *a wave in her hair* **5** PHYSICS the form in which some types of energy move: *light/sound/radio waves* **6 make waves** (informal) to cause problems: *We have a job to finish, so don't make waves, OK?* ➔ HEAT WAVE

wave² *v.* **1** [I,T] to move your hand, or something you hold in your hand, from side to side as a signal or greeting, or to express something: *demonstrators waving their signs* | *The boys* ***waved at*** *her.* | *John* ***waved to*** *the waiter, asking for the check.* | *I* ***waved goodbye.*** | *One of the cops* ***waved*** *me* ***through/away*** (=moved his hand to show me which way to go). ➔ *see picture on page A21* **2** [I] if a flag waves, it moves with the wind

wave sth ↔ **aside** *phr. v.* to refuse to pay attention to a person, or to his/her opinions, questions, ideas, etc.: *"Not true!" she said, waving aside any further questions.*

wave·length /ˈweɪvlɛŋkθ/ *n.* [C] **1** PHYSICS the size of a radio wave or the distance between two waves of energy such as sound or light **2 be on the same wavelength** (informal) to think in the same way about something as someone else does

wa·ver /ˈweɪvɚ/ *v.* [I] **1** to be unsteady: *Her voice wavered slightly.* **2** to become weaker or less certain: *Their faith in me never wavered.* **3** to not make a decision because you have doubts: *Harland is* ***wavering between*** *two options.*

wav·y /ˈweɪvi/ *adj* having waves (=even curved shapes): *wavy hair* ➔ *see picture on page 462* ➔ BENT²

wax¹ /wæks/ *n.* [U] **1** a thick substance made of fats or oils, used for making things such as CANDLES **2** a natural sticky substance in your ears

wax² *v.* **1** [T] to put wax on something to protect it or make it shine **2 wax romantic/eloquent etc.** to talk eagerly about someone or something you admire, especially for a long time: *He waxed nostalgic about the one-room schools of his youth.* **3** [I] when the moon waxes, it seems to get bigger every night (ANT) **wane** **4** [T] to use wax to remove the hair from your legs

ˌwaxed ˈpaper *also* **ˈwax ˌpaper** *n.* [U] paper with a thin layer of wax on it, used for wrapping food

wax·y /ˈwæksi/ *adj.* made of wax, covered in wax, or feeling like wax: *apples with a waxy skin* **—waxiness** *n.* [U]

way¹ /weɪ/ *n.*

1 ROAD/PATH [C] the road, path, etc. that you have to follow in order to get to a particular place: *Which way should we go?* | *Can you mail this on your* ***way downtown/home****?* | *Could you tell me the* ***way to*** *the police station* ***from*** *here?* | *Ben* ***knows the way.*** | *I can give you a ride; it's* ***on my/the way.*** | *Can you move your bag; it's* ***in the way.***

USAGE

Use **on the way** when you will do something or pass something as you go to a place: *I'll get some gas on the way home.*
Use **in the way** when something is preventing you from getting to the place you are going to: *I*

couldn't get out of the driveway because Mark's car was in the way.

2 DIRECTION [C] a particular direction: *Which way is north?* | *Face this way, please.*
3 METHOD [C] a manner or method of doing something or thinking about something: *Is there any **way to** tell how old it is?* | *I'd like to tell her **in my own way**.* | *Grief does not affect everyone **in the same way**.* | *Look at the way that guy's dressed!* | *Ryan has a funny **way of** talking.*

THESAURUS method, technique, approach
→ METHOD

4 in a way/in some ways/in one way used in order to say that something is partly true: *In a way, I like working alone better.*
5 DISTANCE/TIME [singular] the distance or time between two places or events, especially if it is long: *a **long way** from home* | *We have a way to go yet before we're done.* | *Did he actually come **all the way** (=the whole distance) from Bali?*
6 have/get your way to do what you want even if someone else wants something different: *They always let that kid **get his own way**.*
7 the way/sb's way where someone wants to go: *There was a big truck **in the way*** (=preventing people from going past). | *Get **out of my way*** (=move aside)*!*
8 get in the way of sth to prevent something from happening: *Don't let your social life get in the way of your studying.*
9 come a long way to have developed a lot: *Psychiatry has come a long way since the 1920s.*
10 be/have a long way to go to need a lot of time to develop or reach a particular standard: *There is a long way to go before democracy is accepted there.*
11 under way happening or moving: *Building work is scheduled to **get under way*** (=start happening) *today.*
12 be on the way/its way/sb's way to be arriving soon or traveling to a place: *The check is on its way.* | *Carla's already on her way here.*
13 way around/up a particular order or position that something should be in: *Which way around does this skirt go?* | *Make sure all the pictures are the **right way up**.*
14 give way to sth if one thing gives way to another thing, this other thing replaces it or controls it: *fear gave way to anger*
15 go out of your way to do sth to do something that involves making a special effort, especially for someone else: *Ben went out of his way to help us.*
16 you can't have it both ways used in order to say that you cannot have the advantages of two different possible decisions
17 make way a) to move to one side so that someone or something can pass **b)** if one thing makes way for something else, this other thing replaces it: *Several houses were torn down to **make way for** a new fire station.*

SPOKEN PHRASES
18 by the way said when you want to begin talking about a new subject that you have just remembered: *Oh, by the way, I saw Marie yesterday.*
19 no way! a) used in order to say that you will definitely not do or allow something: *No way am I letting him know about this.* **b)** used in order to say that you do not believe something or are surprised by it: *"She's 45." "No way!"*
20 that's the way used in order to tell someone that s/he is doing something correctly: *Keep your arms straight out – that's the way.*
21 way to go! used in order to tell someone that s/he has done something good, or done something very well → **out of the way** *at* OUT²

[ORIGIN: Old English *weg*]

way² *adv.* **1** long in distance or time: *a boat **way out** on the lake* | *a movie made **way back** before they used sound* **2 way more/bigger/longer etc.** (spoken, informal) a lot more, bigger, longer, etc.: *This test was way harder than the last one.*

way·lay /ˈweɪleɪ/ *v.* (past tense and past participle **waylaid**) [T] to stop someone when s/he is trying to go somewhere, so that you can talk to him/her, or in order to rob or attack him/her

ˌway of ˈlife *n.* (plural **ways of life**) [C] the way someone lives, or the way people in a society usually live: *the **American way of life***

ˌway-ˈout *adj.* (spoken) very modern and strange: *I like jazz, but not the way-out stuff.*

way·side /ˈweɪsaɪd/ *n.* **fall/go by the wayside** to stop being successful, important, popular, etc.: *My dream of college fell by the wayside.*

way·ward /ˈweɪwəd/ *adj.* not following rules, and causing problems: *a wayward teenager*

we /wi/ *pron.* **1** the person who is speaking and one or more other people: *We went to a movie.* | *We live in Dallas.* **2** people in general: *We know almost nothing about what causes the disease.* | ***We all** dream of being rich one day.*

weak /wik/ *adj.* **1** not physically strong: *He felt weak and dizzy.* | *a weak heart* | *Nina was **weak from/with** hunger.* **2** not strong in character, and easily influenced: *He's weak and indecisive.* **3** not having much ability or skill in a particular activity or subject: *I'm good at math, but **weak at/in** science.* | *the team's weak shooting* **4** not having much power or influence: *a weak leader* **5** not being good enough to persuade, influence, or interest people: *a weak excuse* | *a weak joke* **6** not financially successful: *the country's weak economy* **7** containing a lot of water or having little taste: *weak tea* [ORIGIN: 1200—1300 Old Norse *veikr*] —**weakly** *adv.*

ˌweak ˈacid *n.* [C] CHEMISTRY an acid that does not completely separate into IONS (=atoms with an electric charge) when it is mixed with water

ˌweak ˈbase *n.* [C] CHEMISTRY a BASE (=a substance that combines with an acid to form a salt)

W

that does not completely separate into IONs (=atoms with an electric charge) when it is mixed with water, and has a low PH

ˌweak eˈlectrolyte *n.* [C] CHEMISTRY a liquid that does not allow electricity to travel through it effectively because it does not contain many IONs (=atoms with an electric charge)

weak·en /ˈwikən/ *v.* [I,T] **1** to become less powerful or physically strong, or to make someone or something do this: *The disease has weakened her heart.* | *a country weakened by war* **2** to become less determined, or to make someone do this: *Nothing could **weaken** her **resolve/determination**.* **3** if money, the economy, etc. weakens, or if they are weakened, their value is reduced: *the country's weakened economy*

weak·ling /ˈwik-lɪŋ/ *n.* [C] (disapproving) someone who is not physically strong

weak·ness /ˈwiknɪs/ *n.* **1** [C] a fault in someone's character or in a system, organization, design, etc.: *What are your **strengths and weaknesses**?* | *a **major weakness** in the program* **2** [U] the state of lacking strength in your body or character: ***weakness in** the muscles* **3** [U] lack of power, strength, or influence: *moral **weakness in** our society* | *the **weakness of** our currency* **4 a weakness for sth** if you have a weakness for something, you like it very much even though it may not be good for you: *She's always had a weakness for chocolate.*

wealth /wɛlθ/ *n.* **1** [U] a large amount of money and possessions: *their family's personal wealth* | *the nation's mineral wealth* **2 a wealth of sth** a lot of something useful or good: *the wealth of information on the Internet*

wealth·y /ˈwɛlθi/ *adj.* (comparative **wealthier**, superlative **wealthiest**) **1** having a lot of money or valuable possessions: *a very wealthy man*

THESAURUS rich, well-off, affluent, well-to-do → RICH

2 the wealthy people who have a lot of money or valuable possessions

wean /win/ *v.* [T] BIOLOGY to gradually stop feeding a baby his/her mother's milk and start giving him/her ordinary food

wean sb **off/from** sth *phr. v.* to make someone gradually stop doing something you disapprove of: *He'll need to be weaned off the drug slowly.*

be weaned on sth *phr. v.* to be influenced by something from a very early age: *young movie directors who were weaned on MTV videos*

weap·on /ˈwɛpən/ *n.* [C] **1** something that you use to fight with, especially a knife or gun: *soldiers carrying their weapons* | *the danger posed by **nuclear/chemical/biological weapons*** **2** an action, piece of information, piece of equipment, etc. that you can use to win or be successful in doing something: *a new weapon in the fight against cancer* [ORIGIN: Old English *wæpen*] **—weaponry** *n.* [U]

wear¹ /wɛr/ *v.* (past tense **wore** /wɔr/, past participle **worn** /wɔrn/) **1** [T] to have something on your body, especially clothes or jewelry: *Why aren't you wearing your glasses?* | *a girl wearing a pink sun dress* | *His wife was **wearing black/white/blue etc.*** (=wearing black, etc. clothes). **2** [T] to have your hair in a particular style: *Fay wore her hair in braids.* **3** [I,T] to become thinner, weaker, etc. by continued use, or to make something do this: *He's **worn a hole in** his pants already.* **4** [T] to have a particular expression on your face: *She was wearing a smile.* **5 wear well** to remain in good condition after a period of time: *Expensive fabrics don't always wear well.* **6 sth is wearing thin** (informal) if an excuse, explanation, opinion, etc. is wearing thin, it has been used so often that you no longer believe or accept it **7 wear the pants** (informal) to be the person in a family who makes the decisions

wear (sth ↔) **away** *phr. v.* to gradually become thinner, weaker, etc., or to make something do this by using it, rubbing it, etc.: *The paint is almost all worn away.* | *The water is gradually wearing away the rock.*

wear down *phr. v.* **1 wear** (sth ↔) **down** to gradually become smaller, or to make something do this by using it, rubbing it, etc.: *My shoes have worn down at the heel.* **2 wear** sb ↔ **down** to gradually make someone physically weaker or less determined: *The constant stress is wearing her down.*

wear off *phr. v.* if pain or the effect of something wears off, it gradually stops: *The anesthesia was starting to wear off.*

wear on *phr. v.* if time wears on, it passes very slowly, especially because you are bored: *It became hotter as the day wore on.*

wear out *phr. v.* **1 wear** sth ↔ **out** to become weak, broken, or useless, or to make something do this by using it a lot or for a long time: *I think these batteries have worn out.* **2 wear** sb **out** to feel extremely tired, or to make someone feel this way: *You look really worn out.* **3 wear out your welcome** to stay at someone's house longer than s/he wants you to [ORIGIN: Old English *werian*]

W

wear² *n.* [U] **1** clothes of a particular type, or worn for a particular activity: *evening wear* **2** normal damage caused by continuous use over a long period: *Check the tires for **wear and tear**.* **3** the amount of use you can expect to get from something: *You'll **get** a lot of **wear out of** a sweater like that.*

wea·ri·some /ˈwɪrisəm/ *also* **wear·ing** /ˈwɛrɪŋ/ *adj.* (formal) making you feel bored, tired, or annoyed: *a wearisome task*

wea·ry¹ /ˈwɪri/ *adj.* (comparative **wearier**, superlative **weariest**) very tired: *She was **weary of** arguing.* | *The nation is **weary of** war.* **—wearily** *adv.* **—weariness** *n.* [U]

THESAURUS tired, exhausted, worn out, beat, fatigued → TIRED

weary² *v.* (**wearied**, **wearies**) [I,T] (formal) to become very tired or no longer enjoy something, or to make someone feel this way: *Jacobs* ***wearied of*** *his job at the bank.*

wea·sel¹ /ˈwizəl/ *n.* [C] **1** a samll thin furry animal that kills other small animals **2** (informal) someone who has not been loyal to you or has deceived you

weasel² *v.*

weasel out of sth *phr. v.* (informal) to avoid doing something you should do by using dishonest excuses or lies: *He's in court trying to weasel out of his debts.*

weath·er¹ /ˈwɛðɚ/ *n.* **1** [singular, U] the temperature and other conditions such as sun, rain, and wind: ***What's the weather like*** *today?* | *Our flight was delayed because of* ***bad weather.*** | *very* ***cold/ warm/hot/dry weather*** **2 under the weather** (informal) slightly sick: *I'm feeling a little under the weather.* [ORIGIN: Old English *weder*]

weather² *v.* **1** [T] to come through a very difficult situation without failing: *Business was bad, but we knew we would* ***weather the storm.*** **2** [I,T] if a surface is weathered, the wind, rain, and sun gradually change its appearance: *a weathered stone monument* | *Her face was weathered by the sun.*

ˈweather ˌforecast *n.* [C] a report on the television or radio that says what the weather will be like —**weather forecaster** *n.* [C]

ˈweather vane *n.* [C] a metal object attached to the top of a building, that moves to show the direction the wind is blowing

weave¹ /wiv/ *v.* **1** (past tense **wove** /woʊv/, past participle **woven** /ˈwoʊvən/) [I,T] to make cloth, a CARPET, a basket, etc. by crossing threads or thin pieces under and over each other by hand or on a LOOM: *traditional basket weaving* **2** (past tense **wove**, past participle **woven**) [T] to put many different ideas, subjects, stories, etc. together and connect them smoothly: *Her novels weave together suspense and romance.* **3** (past tense and past participle **weaved**) [I,T] to move somewhere by turning and changing direction a lot: *The car was* ***weaving in and out of*** *traffic.*

W

weave² *n.* [C] the way in which a material is woven, and the pattern formed by this: *a fine weave*

web /wɛb/ *n.* **1 the Web** IT the system that connects together computers around the world so that people can use and find information on the Internet (SYN) **the World Wide Web**: *popular sites* ***on the Web*** **2** [C] a net of sticky thin threads made by a SPIDER to catch insects: *a spider* ***spinning*** *its* ***web*** → *see picture at* SPIDER **3 a web of sth** a closely related set of things that can be very complicated: *a web of lies*

webbed /wɛbd/ *adj.* webbed feet or toes have skin between the toes → *see picture on page A15*

web·cam /ˈwɛbkæm/ *n.* [C] IT a video camera that is connected to a computer and broadcasts images onto a website → *see picture on page A54*

web·cast /ˈwɛbkæst/ *v.* (past tense and past participle **webcast**) [I,T] IT to broadcast an event on the Internet, at the time the event happens

ˈweb page *n.* [C] IT all the information that you can see in one part of a website

web·site /ˈwɛbsaɪt/ *n.* [C] IT a place on the Internet where you can find information about something, especially a particular organization: *For more information,* ***visit*** *our* ***website.*** → INTERNET

we'd /wid/ **1** the short form of "we had": *We'd better go now.* **2** the short form of "we would": *We'd rather stay.*

wed /wɛd/ *v.* (past tense and past participle **wedded** *or* **wed**, present participle **wedding**) **1** [I,T] (literary) to marry someone **2 be wedded to sth** to believe strongly in a particular idea or way of doing things

wed·ding /ˈwɛdɪŋ/ *n.* [C] a marriage ceremony, especially one with a religious service: *Have you been invited to their wedding?* | *a simple* ***wedding reception*** (=a special meal or party after a wedding) | *a* ***wedding dress/cake/present***

TOPIC

At a **wedding ceremony/service** the most important people are the **bride** (=woman getting married) and the **groom** (=man getting married). The **best man** helps the groom and the **maid of honor** and the **bridesmaids** help the bride. After the ceremony, there is usually a **reception**. Then the bride and groom **go on a honeymoon** (=special vacation). → ENGAGED, MARRIED

ˈwedding ring *n.* [C] a ring that you wear to show that you are married

wedge¹ /wɛdʒ/ *n.* [C] **1** a piece of wood, metal, etc. that has one thick edge and one pointed edge, used for keeping a door open, splitting wood, etc. **2** something shaped like a wedge: *a* ***wedge of*** *chocolate cake*

wedge² *v.* [T] **1** to force something firmly into a narrow space: *We* ***wedged*** *a towel* ***under*** *the door to keep the cold air out.* **2 wedge sth open/shut** to put something under a door, window, etc. to make it stay open or shut

wed·lock /ˈwɛdlɑk/ *n.* (old-fashioned) **born out of wedlock** if a child is born out of wedlock, his/her parents are not married when s/he is born

Wednes·day /ˈwɛnzdi, -deɪ/ (*written abbreviation* **Wed.**) *n.* [C,U] the fourth day of the week, between Tuesday and Thursday: *Classes start Wednesday.* | *What time are you coming* ***on Wednesday****?* | *I have to work* ***next Wednesday.*** | *Eva had surgery* ***last Wednesday.*** | *We're all going out to dinner on* ***Wednesday night.*** [ORIGIN: Old English *wodnesdæg*, from *Woden* "Odin" + *dæg* "day"]

wee /wi/ *adj.* **1** (literary) very small: *a wee child* **2 the wee hours** the early hours of the morning, just after MIDNIGHT

weed¹ /wid/ *n.* [C] **1** a wild plant that grows

where you do not want it to grow: *She was **pulling weeds** in the back yard.* **2 like weeds** quickly and in large numbers: *Housing developments began to **spring up like weeds**.*

weed² *v.* [I,T] to remove weeds from a place

weed sb/sth ↔ **out** *phr. v.* to get rid of people or things that are not very good: *Weaker students were weeded out of the program.*

week /wik/ *n.* [C] **1** a period of time equal to seven days, beginning on Sunday and ending on Saturday: *I can't see you **this week**.* | ***last/next week*** (=the week before or after this one) **2** any period of time equal to seven days and nights: *I've been living here for six weeks.* | *This is the second time the Yankees have lost **in a week**.* | *I'll be back **a week from today/tomorrow/Friday*** (=a week after today, etc.). | *Are you busy **the week after next*** (=the week that follows next week)? **3** *also* **work week** the part of the week when you go to work, usually from Monday to Friday: *a 40-hour week* | *I don't see the kids much **during the week**.* [ORIGIN: Old English *wicu*]

week·day /ˈwikdeɪ/ *n.* (plural **weekdays**) [C] any day of the week except Saturday and Sunday

week·end /ˈwikɛnd/ *n.* [C] Saturday and Sunday: *What are you doing **this weekend**?* | *Jerry sees the children mainly **on weekends**.* | ***last/next weekend*** (=the weekend before or after this one) | *We went to the beach **over the weekend*** (=during the weekend).

week·ly /ˈwikli/ *adj.* happening or done every week: *a weekly radio show* | *weekly meetings* —**weekly** *adv.*

THESAURUS **hourly, daily, monthly, yearly** → REGULAR¹

week·night /ˈwiknaɪt/ *n.* [C] any night except Saturday or Sunday

wee·nie /ˈwini/ *n.* [C] (spoken) a HOT DOG

weep /wip/ *v.* (past tense and past participle **wept** /wɛpt/) [I,T] (literary) to cry: *She wept quietly for a few moments.*

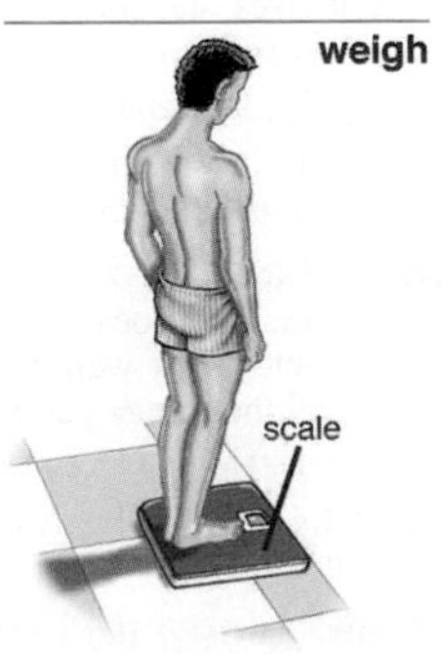

weigh /weɪ/ *v.* **1** [linking verb] to have a particular weight: *The baby weighs 12 pounds.* | ***How much** do you **weigh**?* **2** [T] to measure how heavy someone or something is: *Have you weighed yourself lately?* **3** [T] *also* **weigh up** to consider something carefully before making a decision: *I had to weigh the options pretty carefully.*

weigh sb ↔ **down** *phr. v.* **1** if something weighs you down, it is heavy and difficult to carry **2** if you are weighed down by your problems and difficulties, you worry a lot about them: *He felt weighed down by his responsibilities.*

weigh in *phr. v.* **1** to have your weight measured before taking part in a competition **2** to add a remark to a discussion or an argument: *The chairman then **weighed in with** his own opinion.*

weigh on sb *phr. v.* to make someone feel worried: *The problem's been **weighing on** my **mind** for a long time.*

weight¹ /weɪt/ *n.*

1 WHAT SB/STH WEIGHS [U] how heavy someone or something is: *She's always worried about her weight.* | *Have you **lost weight*** (=become thinner)? | *I think he's **put on** some **weight*** (=become fatter). | *I'm **watching** my **weight*** (=being careful not to gain weight).

2 HEAVINESS [U] the fact of being heavy: *The weight of her boots made it hard for her to run.*

3 HEAVY THING [C] something that is heavy: *I can't lift heavy weights because of my bad back.*

4 RESPONSIBILITY/WORRY [singular] something that makes you worry: *the **weight of** responsibility* | *Selling the house was **a great weight off** my **mind**.*

5 IMPORTANCE [U] if something has weight, it is important and influences people: *Tina's opinion doesn't **carry** much **weight** around here.*

6 FOR MEASURING QUANTITIES [C] a piece of metal weighing a particular amount that is balanced against something else to measure what it weighs

7 weights [plural] heavy pieces of metal, usually fixed to a metal bar, that people lift to make their muscles bigger → WEIGHTLIFTING: *I've been **lifting weights** for years.* → **pull your weight** *at* PULL¹

weight² *also* **weight down** *v.* [T] to add something heavy to something or put a weight on it, especially in order to keep it in place: *fishing nets weighted with lead*

weight·ed /ˈweɪt̬ɪd/ *adj.* giving an advantage or disadvantage to one particular group or activity: *The voting system is **weighted against** the smaller parties.*

weight·less /ˈweɪtlɪs/ *adj.* having no weight, especially when you are floating in space —**weightlessness** *n.* [U]

weight·lift·ing /ˈweɪtˌlɪftɪŋ/ *n.* [U] the sport of lifting weights attached to the ends of a bar —**weight-lifter** *n.* [C]

weight·y /ˈweɪt̬i/ *adj.* important and serious: *a weighty problem*

weird /wɪrd/ *adj.* (informal) unusual and strange: *I had a really weird dream.* | *There's something weird about him.* | *The **weird thing** is that no one else seemed to notice.*

THESAURUS **strange, funny, peculiar, odd, bizarre** → STRANGE¹

weird·o /ˈwɪrdoʊ/ *n.* (plural **weirdos**) [C] (spoken) someone who seems strange

wel·come¹ /ˈwɛlkəm/ *interjection* said in order to greet someone who has just arrived: ***Welcome to** Chicago!* | ***Welcome back** – it's good to see you again.* [ORIGIN: Old English *wilcume*, from *wilcuma* "person you are glad to have as a guest"]

W

welcome² *adj.* **1** if you are welcome in a place, the other people want you to be there: *I had the feeling I wasn't really welcome.* | *They did their best to* ***make*** *me* ***feel welcome***. **2** if something is welcome, people are pleased that it has happened because it is useful, pleasant, etc.: *a welcome suggestion* | *a welcome breeze on a hot day*

SPOKEN PHRASES

3 you're welcome said in order to reply politely to someone who has just thanked you for something: *"Thanks for the coffee." "You're welcome."* **4 be welcome to sb/sth** used in order to say that someone can be with someone or have something if s/he wants to, because you do not want to: *If Rob wants that job, he's welcome to it!* **5 be welcome to do sth** used in order to say that someone can do something if s/he wants to: *You're welcome to stay for lunch.*

welcome³ *v.* [T] **1** to say hello in a friendly way to someone who has just arrived: *Jill was welcoming guests at the door.* | *They* ***welcomed*** *us* ***warmly***. **2** to be glad when something happens or is done, or to say that you are glad: *We would welcome a change in the law.*

welcome⁴ *n.* [C] the way in which you greet someone when s/he arrives at a place: *They* ***gave*** *him a very* ***warm welcome*** *when he returned to work.* → **wear out your welcome** *at* WEAR OUT

wel·com·ing /ˈwɛlkəmɪŋ/ *adj.* making you feel happy and relaxed: *a welcoming smile*

THESAURUS **friendly, warm, cordial, hospitable** → FRIENDLY

weld /wɛld/ *v.* [T] to join metal objects to each other by heating them and pressing them together when they are hot —**welder** *n.* [C]

wel·fare /ˈwɛlfɛr/ (Ac) *n.* [U] **1** *also* **Welfare** money paid by the government to people who are very poor, not working, sick, etc.: *Most of the people in this neighborhood are* ***on welfare***. | *The study found that 90 percent of welfare recipients are employable.* **2** someone's welfare is his/her health, comfort, and happiness: *We're only concerned with your welfare.* | *It is our responsibility to look after the welfare of animals.*

W

we'll /wil/ the short form of "we will": *We'll have to leave soon.*

well¹ /wɛl/ *adv.* (comparative **better**, superlative **best**) **1** in a good, successful, or satisfactory way: *Did you sleep well?* | *She doesn't hear very well.* | *Is the business* ***doing well***? | *I hope your party* ***goes well***. **2** thoroughly or completely: *I don't know her very well.* | *Mix the flour and eggs well.* **3 as well (as sb/sth)** in addition to someone or something else: *I'm learning French as well as Italian.* **4 may/might/could well** used in order to say that something is likely to happen or is likely to be true: *What you say may well be true.* **5 sb may/might as well do sth** (informal) **a)** used in order to say that you will do something even though you do not particularly want to do it: *I guess we may as well get started.* **b)** used in order to say that doing something else would have an equally good result: *The traffic was so bad we might as well have walked here.* **6** very much, or very long in time: *I'm* ***well aware*** *of the problem.* | *It was* ***well after*** *2:00 by the time we finished.*

well² *adj.* (comparative **better**, superlative **best**) **1** healthy: *My mother's not very well.* | *I'm a lot better, thanks.* | *I hope you* ***get well soon***. → HEALTHY **2 all is well/all is not well** (formal) used in order to say that a situation is satisfactory or not satisfactory: *All is not well with their marriage.* **3 it's just as well (that)** (spoken) used in order to say that things have happened in a way that is lucky or good: *It's just as well I took the train today – I heard the traffic was really bad.* **4 it's/that's all very well** (spoken) used in order to say that you are not happy or satisfied with something: *It's all very well for you to say you're sorry, but I've been waiting here for two hours!*

well³ *interjection* **1** used in order to pause before saying something, or to emphasize what you are saying: *Well, let's see now, I could meet you on Thursday.* | ***Well, I mean****, you shouldn't just take things without asking.* | *"Jim doesn't want to come." "****Well then****, let's go on our own."* **2** *also* **oh well** said in order to show that you accept a situation even though it is not a good one: *Oh well, at least you did your best.* **3** *also* **well, well** used in order to express surprise or amusement: *Well, so Steve got the job.* **4** said in order to connect two parts of a story that you are telling: *You know that guy I was telling you about? Well, he's been arrested!* **5 Well?** used in order to ask someone to reply to you or tell you what has happened: *Well? What did he say?*

well⁴ *n.* [C] **1** EARTH SCIENCES a deep hole in the ground from which water is taken **2** EARTH SCIENCES a very deep hole in the ground from which oil is taken

well⁵ *also* **well up** *v.* [I] (literary) if a liquid wells up, it rises and may start to flow: ***Tears*** *began to* ***well up*** *in her eyes.*

ˌwell-adˈjusted *adj.* emotionally healthy and able to deal well with the problems of life: *a happy, well-adjusted child*

ˌwell-ˈbalanced *adj.* **1** a well-balanced person is sensible and does not suddenly become angry, upset, etc. **2** a well-balanced meal or DIET contains all the things you need to stay healthy

ˌwell-beˈhaved *adj.* behaving in a polite or socially acceptable way: *a well-behaved child* → POLITE

ˌwell-ˈbeing *n.* [U] a feeling of being comfortable, healthy, and happy

ˌwell-brought-ˈup *adj.* a child who is well-brought-up has been taught to be polite and to behave well

ˌwell-ˈdone *adj.* meat that is well-done has been

cooked thoroughly → MEDIUM, RARE: *He likes his steak well-done.*

ˌwell-ˈdressed *adj.* wearing attractive fashionable clothes: *an attractive well-dressed young woman*

ˌwell-ˈearned *adj.* deserved because you have worked hard: *a well-earned vacation*

ˌwell-ˈfed *adj.* having plenty of good food to eat: *well-fed children*

ˌwell-ˈgroomed *adj.* someone who is well-groomed has a very neat and clean appearance: *a well-groomed young man*

ˌwell-ˈheeled *adj.* (informal) rich

ˌwell-inˈtentioned *adj.* WELL-MEANING

ˌwell-ˈknown *adj.* known by a lot of people: *a well-known artist*

THESAURUS **famous, renowned, noted, distinguished, eminent** → FAMOUS

ˌwell-ˈmeaning *adj.* intending or intended to be helpful, but often failing or making things worse: *well-meaning advice*

well·ness /ˈwɛlnɪs/ *n.* [U] the state of being healthy: *The gym offers a variety of* ***wellness programs*** (=programs to help people stay healthy).

ˌwell-ˈoff *adj.* having enough money to have a very good standard of living: *Stella's family is well-off.*

THESAURUS **rich, wealthy, affluent, well-to-do** → RICH

ˌwell-ˈpaid *adj.* providing or receiving a good salary: *a well-paid job | well-paid executives*

well-read /ˌwɛl ˈrɛd◂ / *adj.* someone who is well-read has read many books and knows a lot about different subjects

ˌwell-ˈrounded *adj.* someone who is well-rounded has had a wide variety of experiences in life

ˌwell-ˈspoken *adj.* able to speak in a clear and polite way

ˌwell-ˈthought-of *adj.* liked and admired by other people

ˌwell-ˈtimed *adj.* said or done at the most appropriate time: *My arrival wasn't very well-timed.*

ˌwell-to-ˈdo *adj.* rich (SYN) **wealthy**: *a well-to-do family*

ˈwell-ˌwisher *n.* [C] someone who does something to show that s/he wants someone to succeed, be healthy, etc.: *She received hundreds of cards from well-wishers.*

Welsh /wɛlʃ/ *adj.* relating to or coming from Wales

welt /wɛlt/ *n.* [C] a raised mark on someone's skin where s/he has been hit

wel·ter /ˈwɛltɚ/ *n.* (formal) **a welter of sth** a large and confusing number of different details, emotions, etc.: *a welter of information*

went /wɛnt/ *v.* the past tense of GO

wept /wɛpt/ *v.* the past tense and past participle of WEEP

we're /wɪr/ the short form of "we are": *We're going to the library.*

were /wɚ/ *v.* a past tense of BE

weren't /wɚnt, ˈwɚənt/ *v.* the short form of "were not": *Why didn't you tell me that you weren't happy?*

were·wolf /ˈwɛrwʊlf/ *n.* (plural **werewolves**) [C] a person in stories who changes into a WOLF

west[1], West /wɛst/ *n.* [singular, U] **1** the direction toward which the Sun goes down: *Which way is west?* → *see picture at* NORTH[1] **2 the west** the western part of a country, state, etc.: *Rain will spread* ***to the west*** *later today. | the* ***west of*** *Ireland* **3 the West a)** the part of the U.S. west of the Mississippi River **b)** the countries in North America and the western part of Europe [ORIGIN: Old English]

USAGE

Use **north/south/east/west of sth** in order to describe where a place is in relation to another place: *Chicago is south of Milwaukee.*
Use **in the north/south/east/west of sth** in order to say which part of a place you are talking about: *The mountains are in the west of the province.*
Use **northern, southern, eastern, western** with the name of a place: *They have a cabin in northern Ontario.*
Don't say "in the north of Ontario."

west[2] *adj.* **1** in, to, or facing the west: *four miles* ***west of*** *Toronto | the west coast of Florida* **2 west wind** a wind coming from the west

west[3] *adv.* **1** toward the west: *Go west on I-90 to Spokane. | The window faces west.* **2 out West** in or to the western part of the U.S.: *My family moved out West to Arizona last year.*

west·bound /ˈwɛstbaʊnd/ *adj.* traveling or leading toward the west: *westbound traffic | the westbound lanes of the freeway*

west·er·ly /ˈwɛstɚli/ *adj.* **1** in or toward the west: *sailing in a westerly direction* **2** a westerly wind comes from the west

west·ern[1] /ˈwɛstɚn/ *adj.* **1** in or from the west part of an area, country, state, etc.: *western Iowa* **2 Western** in or from the countries in North America and the western part of Europe: *Western technology* → see USAGE box at WEST[1]

western[2] *n.* [C] a movie about life in the 19th century in the American West → MOVIE

west·ern·er, Westerner /ˈwɛstɚnɚ/ *n.* [C] someone who comes from the western part of a country or the western HEMISPHERE

ˌWestern ˈEurope *n.* the western part of Europe, including places such as Great Britain and Italy —**ˌWestern Euroˈpean** *adj.*

W

west·ern·ized /ˈwɛstɚˌnaɪzd/ *adj.* [only before noun] influenced by and behaving like the people in North America and Western Europe —**westernize** *v.* [T]

west·ern·most /ˈwɛstɚnˌmoʊst/ *adj.* farthest west: *the westernmost part of the island*

west·ward /ˈwɛstwɚd/ *adj., adv.* toward the west

wet[1] /wɛt/ *adj.* (comparative **wetter**, superlative **wettest**) **1** covered in or full of water or another liquid (ANT) **dry**: *Try not to* ***get*** *your feet* ***wet***. | *a wet sponge* | *We were* ***soaking wet*** (=extremely wet). **2** rainy: ***It's*** *very* ***wet*** *outside.* **3** not yet dry: *wet paint* **4 wet behind the ears** (informal) very young and without much experience —**wetness** *n.* [U]

wet[2] *v.* (past tense and past participle **wet** *or* **wetted**, present participle **wetting**) [T] **1** to make something wet: *Wet this cloth and put it on her forehead.* **2 wet the bed/wet your pants** to make your bed or pants wet because you URINATE by accident

ˈ**wet suit** *n.* [C] a thick piece of clothing, usually made of rubber, that swimmers wear to keep warm when they are in the water

we've /wiv/ the short form of "we have": *We've got to leave by 6:00.*

whack[1] /wæk/ *v.* [T] (informal) to hit someone or something hard

THESAURUS **hit, punch, slap, beat, smack, strike** → HIT[1]

whack[2] *n.* (informal) **1 out of whack** if a machine or system is out of whack, it is not working correctly **2 take a whack at sth** to try to do something: *I can't open this jar; do you want to take a whack at it?* **3** [C] the act of hitting something hard, or the noise this makes

whacked /wækt/ *also* ˌ**whacked** ˈ**out** *adj.* (spoken) **1** very tired **2** behaving in a very strange way

W

whale[1] /weɪl/ *n.* [C] a very large animal that swims in the ocean and breathes through a hole on the top of its head [ORIGIN: Old English *hwæl*]

whale[2] *v.*

whale on sb/sth *phr. v.* to start hitting someone or something

whal·er /ˈweɪlɚ/ *n.* [C] **1** someone who hunts whales **2** a boat used for hunting whales

whal·ing /ˈweɪlɪŋ/ *n.* [U] the activity of hunting whales

wham[1] /wæm/ *interjection* **1** said when describing the sound of one thing hitting another thing very hard: *The car went wham into the wall.* **2** said in order to show that something very unexpected suddenly happens: *Everything is going OK and then, wham, you lose your job.*

wham[2] *n.* [C] the sound made when something is hit very hard

wharf /wɔrf/ *n.* (plural **wharves** /wɔrvz/) [C] a structure that is built out into the water so that boats can stop next to it (SYN) **pier**

what /wət; *strong* wʌt, wɑt/ *determiner, pron.* **1** used in order to ask for information about something: *What are you doing?* | *What did Ellen say?* | *What kind of dog is that?* | *"I didn't think it would be like this." "What do you mean?"* **2** used in order to talk about something that is not known or certain: *No one knows what happened.* | *I'm not sure* ***what to*** *do.* **3** the thing which: *Show me what you bought.* | *I believe what he told me.* **4** used at the beginning of a sentence, to emphasize what you are saying: *What an idiot!* | *What I need is a nice hot bath.* **5 have what it takes** to have the ability or courage to do something: *Whitman didn't have what it takes to do the job.* → **guess what/you'll never guess** *at* GUESS[1], **so what?** *at* SO[1]

SPOKEN PHRASES

6 what? a) used in order to ask someone to repeat something that s/he has just said because you did not hear it very well: *"Do you want a fried egg?" "What?"* **b)** used when you have heard someone calling your name and you are asking him/her what s/he wants: *"Anita?" "What?" "Can you come here for a minute?"* **c)** used in order to show that you are surprised by what someone has said **7 what about...? a)** used in order to make a suggestion: *What about sending him an e-mail?* **b)** used in order to introduce a new person or thing into the conversation: *What about Patrick? What's he doing nowadays?* **8 What's up?** used when saying hello to someone you know well: *"Hey, Chris! What's up?" "Not much."* **9 what's up with sb/sth?** used in order to ask what is wrong or what is happening: *What's up with this printer – does it work?* **10 what (...) for? a)** used in order to ask the reason for something or purpose of something: *What's this thing for?* **b)** why: *"She's decided to work part-time." "What for?"* **11 what if...? a)** used in order to ask what will happen, especially when it could be something bad or frightening: *What if we get stuck out there in the snow?* **b)** used when making a suggestion: *What if you just take that part out of the speech?* **12 what's his/her/its name** used when talking about a person or thing whose name you cannot immediately remember: *Is what's his name still working here?* **13 ...or what? a)** used in order to ask if there is another possibility: *Are they doing that to save money, or what?* **b)** used in order to show you are impatient when asking a question: *Are you coming now, or what?* **14 what's what** the real facts about a situation that are important to know: *She's been working here long enough to know what's what.* **15 what's with sb?** used in order to ask why someone is behaving strangely or why something strange is happening: *What's with Nicky? He seems really mad.* **16 what's with sth?** used in order to ask the reason for something: *What's with all the sad faces?*

[ORIGIN: Old English *hwæt*]

what·cha·ma·call·it /ˈwʌtʃəmə,kɔlɪt/ *n.* [C] (spoken) a word you use when you cannot remember the name of something

what·ev·er¹ /wəṭˈɛvɚ/ *determiner, pron.* **1** any or all of the things that are wanted, needed, or possible: *Just take whatever you need.* | *He needs whatever help he can get.* **2** used in order to say it is not important what happens, what you do, etc. because it does not change the situation: *Whatever I say, she always disagrees.* **3 ...or whatever** (spoken) used in order to refer to other things of the same kind: *You can go swimming, scuba diving, or whatever.* **4** (spoken) used in order to say that you do not know the exact meaning of something or the exact name of someone or something: *Why don't you invite Steve, or whatever he's called, to supper?* **5 whatever you say/think/want** (spoken) used in order to tell someone that you agree with him/her or will do what s/he wants, especially when you do not really agree or want to do it: *"How about camping, just for a change?" "OK, whatever you want."* **6** used as a reply to say that you do not care what is done or chosen, or that the exact details of something do not matter: *"What flavor do you want? Strawberry, vanilla...?" "Whatever."*

whatever² *also* **what·so·ev·er** /,wʌtsoʊˈɛvɚ/ *adv.* used in order to emphasize a negative statement: *She had no money whatsoever.*

what·not /ˈwʌtˀnɑt/ *n.* **and whatnot** (spoken) an expression used at the end of a list of things when you do not want to give the names of everything: *Put all your paper, pencils, and whatnot in this drawer.*

wheat /wit/ *n.* [U] a plant that produces a grain used for making flour, or this grain [ORIGIN: Old English *hwæte*]

whee·dle /ˈwidl/ *v.* [I,T] to persuade someone to do something by saying pleasant things that you do not really mean: *She managed to **wheedle** $15 **out of** him.*

wheel¹ /wil/ *n.* [C] **1** one of the round things under a car, bicycle, etc. that turns and allows it to move: *the car's **front/rear wheels*** → *see picture at* BICYCLE **2** a STEERING WHEEL: *He had fallen asleep **at the wheel*** (=while driving). **3** a flat round part in a machine, that turns when the machine operates: *a gear wheel*

wheel² *v.* **1** [T] to move something that has wheels: *She **wheeled** her bike **into** the garage.* **2** [I] to turn around suddenly: *Anita **wheeled around** and started yelling at us.* → WHEELING AND DEALING

wheel·bar·row /ˈwil,bæroʊ/ *n.* [C] a small CART with one wheel in the front and two long handles for pushing it, that you use outdoors to carry things

wheel·chair /ˈwil-tʃɛr/ *n.* [C] a chair with wheels, used by people who cannot walk

wheel·ie /ˈwili/ *n.* **do/pop a wheelie** (informal) to balance on the back wheel of a bicycle or MOTORCYCLE that you are riding

,wheeling and ˈdealing *n.* [U] activities that involve a lot of complicated and sometimes dishonest deals, especially in politics or business —**wheeler-dealer** *n.*

wheeze /wiz/ *v.* [I] to breathe with difficulty, making a whistling sound in your chest —**wheezy** *adj.*

> **THESAURUS** **breathe, pant, be short of breath, be out of breath, gasp for breath, gasp for air** → BREATHE

when /wɛn/ *adv., conjunction* **1** used when asking what time something will happen: *When are we leaving?* | *I'll tell you **when to** stop.* **2** at or during the time that something happens: *He was nine when his father died.* | *I was in the shower when the doorbell rang.* | *The best moment was when Barnes scored the winning goal.*

> **THESAURUS**
> **at the time** – used in order to talk about a particular time in the past when two things happened at the same time: *I couldn't go to the wedding as I was in New York at the time.*
> **by the time** – used in order to say that one thing has or will have already happened when something else happens: *By the time a child is five, he will have watched hundreds of hours of television.*
> **by that time** – used in order to mention a particular time when something has already happened: *She called at six, but by that time we had already left.*

3 after or as soon as something happens: *I'll phone you when I get home.* **4** even though something is true: *Why do you want a new bike when this one is perfectly good?* [ORIGIN: Old English *hwanne, hwenne*] → **since when** *at* SINCE

when·ev·er /wɛˈnɛvɚ, wə-/ *adv., conjunction* **1** every time: *Whenever we come here, we see someone we know.* **2** at any time: *Come over whenever you want.* **3** (spoken) used in order to say that it does not matter when something happens: *"Should I come over around six?" "Whenever."*

where /wɛr/ *adv., conjunction* **1** at, to, or from a particular place or position: *Where do you live?* | *I asked Lucy where she was going.* | *Do you know where my glasses are?* **2** used in order to ask or talk about the situation or state of something: *Where do you see yourself in ten years?* | *Where do we go from here* (=what do we do now)? [ORIGIN: Old English *hwær*]

where·a·bouts¹ /ˈwɛrə,baʊts, ,wɛrəˈbaʊts/ *adv.* (spoken) used to ask in a general way where a place is: *Whereabouts do you live?*

where·a·bouts² /ˈwɛrə,baʊts/ *n.* [U] the place where someone or something is: *His whereabouts are still a mystery.*

where·as /wɛrˈæz; *weak* wɛrəz/ (Ac) *conjunction* (formal) used in order to say that although something is true of one thing, it is not true of another:

W

Nowadays the trip takes six hours, whereas then it took several weeks. | *Stafford had years of experience, whereas Lufkin was new to the job.*

where·by /wɛr'baɪ/ (Ac) *adv.* (formal) by means of which, or according to which: *The government passed a law whereby all children receive free education.*

where·in /wɛr'ɪn/ *adv., conjunction* (formal) in which place or part: *The San Francisco house, wherein he and his family live, was damaged by the earthquake.*

where·u·pon /ˌwɛrə'pɑn, 'wɛrəˌpɑn/ *conjunction* (formal) after which: *One of them called the other a liar, whereupon a fight broke out.*

wher·ev·er /wɛr'ɛvɚ/ *adv., conjunction* **1** to or at any place: *If you could go wherever you wanted to in the world, where would you go?* | *Sit wherever you like.* **2 wherever possible** when it is possible to do something: *We try to use locally produced food wherever possible.* **3** (spoken) used at the beginning of a question to show surprise: *Wherever did you find that old thing?*

where·with·al /'wɛrwɪˌðɔl, -ˌθɔl/ *n.* **the wherewithal to do sth** the money or ability you need in order to do something: *He just didn't have the wherewithal to do more with his life.*

whet /wɛt/ *v.* (**whetted**, **whetting**) **whet sb's appetite (for sth)** to make someone want more of something by letting him/her try it or see what it is like

wheth·er /'wɛðɚ/ *conjunction* **1** used when talking about a choice between different possibilities: *He asked her whether she was coming.* | *I couldn't decide* ***whether or not*** *I wanted to go.* **2** used in order to say that something definitely will or will not happen in spite of what the situation is: ***Whether*** *you like it* ***or not****, you have to take that test.*

whew /hwyu, hwu/ *interjection* said when you are surprised, very hot, or feeling glad that something bad did not happen: *Whew! That was close!*

W

which /wɪtʃ/ *determiner, pron.* **1** used in order to ask or state what things you mean when a choice has to be made: ***Which of*** *these books is yours?* | *Ask him* ***which one*** *he wants.*

USAGE

Which and **what** are both used when you are asking about one thing out of a number of possible things.
Use **which** when the answer is one of a limited set of possible things: *Which house does Tom live in?*
Use **what** when there are a very large number of possibilities: *What's his name?* | *What is the answer to question 12?*
Which can be followed by "of," but **what** cannot: *Which of these dresses do you like best?*

2 used in order to show what specific thing or things you mean: *This is the book which I told you about.* **3** used in order to add more information about something, especially in written language after a COMMA: *The house, which was completed in 1856, was famous for its huge marble staircase.* | *The train only takes two hours, which is quicker than the bus.* [ORIGIN: Old English *hwilc*]

which·ev·er /wɪ'tʃɛvɚ/ *determiner, pron.* **1** used in order to say that it does not matter which person or thing is chosen because the result will be the same: *You get the same result whichever way you do it.* **2** any of a group of things or people: *You can have whichever you like best.*

whiff /wɪf/ *n.* [C] a smell of something that is not strong: *As she walked past, I* ***caught a whiff of*** (=smelled) *her perfume.*

while¹ /waɪl/ *n.* **a while** a period of time, especially a short one: *Can you wait a while?* | ***For a while****, I worked in the Sales Department.* | *I'll be back* ***in a little while****.* [ORIGIN: Old English *hwil*] → AWHILE, **worth your while** *at* WORTH¹

while² *conjunction* **1** during the time that something is happening: *They arrived while we were having dinner.* | *I like to listen to music while I'm taking a bath.* **2** in spite of the fact that (SYN) **although**: *While it was a good school, I was not happy there.* **3** used in order to say that, although something is true of one thing, it is not true of another (SYN) **whereas**: *That region has plenty of water, while this one has little water.*

while³ *v.* **while away the hours/evenings/days etc.** to spend time in a pleasant and lazy way: *We whiled away the summer evenings talking.*

whim /wɪm/ *n.* [C] a sudden desire to do or have something, especially when there is no good reason for it: *I went to visit her* ***on a whim****.*

whim·per /'wɪmpɚ/ *v.* [I] to make low crying sounds because you are sad, frightened, or in pain: *The dog ran off whimpering.* —**whimper** *n.* [C]

whim·si·cal /'wɪmzɪkəl/ *adj.* unusual or strange and often amusing: *whimsical drawings*

whine /waɪn/ *v.* [I] **1** to complain in a sad annoying voice about something: *Stop whining!* | *She was* ***whining about*** *how hard her life is.* **2** to make a long high sound because you are in pain or unhappy: *The dog was whining at the door.* —**whine** *n.* [C]

whin·ny /'wɪni/ *v.* (**whinnied**, **whinnies**) [I] if a horse whinnies, it makes a high sound

whip¹ /wɪp/ *n.* [C] a long thin piece of rope or leather with a handle, used for making animals move faster, or for hitting people as a punishment

whip² *v.* (**whipped**, **whipping**) **1** [T] to hit a person or animal with a whip **2** [I] to move suddenly or violently: *Bill* ***whipped around*** *to see what was happening.* **3** [T] (informal) to move something with a quick sudden movement: *He* ***whipped out*** *a gun.* **4 whip sb/sth into shape** (informal) to make a system, group of people, etc. start to work in an organized way **5** [T] to mix cream or the clear part of an egg very hard until it becomes stiff (SYN) **beat**: *Whip the cream until thick.*

whip up *phr. v.* **1 whip** sb ↔ **up** to try to make people feel strongly about something: *The speech was an attempt to whip up opposition to the plan.* **2 whip** sth ↔ **up** (informal) to quickly make something to eat: *I could whip up a salad.*

whip·lash /ˈwɪplæʃ/ *n.* [U] a neck injury caused when your head moves forward and back again suddenly and violently, especially in a car accident

whip·ping /ˈwɪpɪŋ/ *n.* [C] a punishment given to someone by hitting him/her, especially with a whip

whir /wɚ/ *v.* (past tense and past participle **whirred**, present participle **whirring**) [I] if a machine whirrs, it makes a continuous low sound —**whir** *n.* [singular]: *the whir of a lawnmower*

whirl[1] /wɚl/ *v.* [I,T] to turn or spin around very quickly, or to make someone or something do this: *He **whirled** her **around** the dance floor.*

THESAURUS **turn, twist, spin, twirl, swivel, go around, revolve, rotate** → TURN[1]

whirl[2] *n.* **1 give sth a whirl** (informal) to try something that you are not sure you are going to like or be able to do **2** [singular] a lot of activity of a particular kind: *a **whirl of** social activity* **3 be in a whirl** to feel very excited or confused about something **4** [C usually singular] a spinning movement, or the shape of a substance that is spinning: *a **whirl of** dust*

whirl·pool /ˈwɚlpul/ *n.* [C] a powerful current of water that spins quickly and pulls things down into it

whirl·wind /ˈwɚlˌwɪnd/ *n.* **1 a whirlwind romance/tour etc.** something that happens much more quickly than usual **2** [C] an extremely strong wind that moves quickly with a circular movement, causing a lot of damage **3 a whirlwind of activity/emotions etc.** a situation in which you quickly experience a lot of different activities or emotions one after another

whisk[1] /wɪsk/ *v.* [T] **1** to mix liquids, eggs, etc. very quickly, using a fork or a whisk → BEAT, WHIP: *Whisk the yolks and sugar in a bowl.* → *see picture on page A18* **2** to quickly take something or someone somewhere: *They **whisked** her **off** to the hospital.*

whisk[2] *n.* [C] a small kitchen tool made of curved pieces of wire, used for whisking eggs, cream, etc.

whisk·er /ˈwɪskɚ/ *n.* **1** [C] one of the long stiff hairs that grow near the mouth of a cat, mouse, etc. → *see picture on page A15* **2 whiskers** [plural] the hair that grows on a man's face

whis·key /ˈwɪski/ *n.* (plural **whiskeys** *or* **whiskies**) [C,U] a strong alcoholic drink made from grain, or a glass of this drink [ORIGIN: 1700—1800 Irish Gaelic *uisce beathadh* and Scottish Gaelic *uisge beatha* "water of life"]

whis·per /ˈwɪspɚ/ *v.* **1** [I,T] to speak or say something very quietly, using your breath rather than your voice: *He leaned over to **whisper** something **to** her.* | *"I love you," she **whispered in** his **ear**.* **2** [I] (literary) to make a soft sound: *The wind whispered in the trees.* —**whisper** *n.* [C]: *She spoke in a whisper.*

whis·tle[1] /ˈwɪsəl/ *v.* **1** [I,T] to make a high or musical sound by blowing air out through your lips: *Adam **whistled to/at** me from across the street.* **2** [I] to make a high sound by blowing into a whistle: *The referee whistled and the game began.* **3** [I] to move quickly with a high sound: *Bullets were **whistling through** the air.* **4** [I] to make a high sound when air or steam is forced through a small hole: *a whistling kettle*

whistle[2] *n.* [C] **1** a small object that produces a high sound when you blow into it: *The referee **blew** his **whistle**.* **2** a high sound made by blowing air through a whistle, your lips, etc. → **blow the whistle (on sb)** at BLOW[1]

white[1] /waɪt/ *adj.* **1** having the color of milk, salt, or snow: *white paint* **2** belonging to the race of people with pale skin who were originally from Europe: *The suspect is a young white man.* **3** looking pale because of illness, strong emotion, etc.: *Are you OK? You're as **white as a sheet*** (=extremely pale). [ORIGIN: Old English *hwit*] —**whiteness** *n.* [U]

white[2] *n.* **1** [U] the color of milk, salt, or snow: *She was dressed completely in white.* **2** [C] *also* **White** someone who belongs to the race of people with pale skin who were originally from Europe **3** [C,U] the part of an egg which surrounds the YOLK and becomes white when cooked

ˌwhite ˈblood cell *n.* [C] BIOLOGY one of the cells in your blood that fights against infection → RED BLOOD CELL

ˈwhite-bread *adj.* (informal) relating to people who are white and who have traditional American values, and who are often considered boring: *a white-bread suburban family*

ˌwhite-ˈcollar *adj.* [only before noun] white-collar workers have jobs in offices, banks, etc. rather than jobs in factories, building things, etc. → BLUE-COLLAR

ˈWhite House *n.* **1 the White House** the official home in Washington, D.C., of the President of the U.S. **2** [singular] the President of the U.S. and the people who advise the President: *The election resulted in a Democratic White House.* —**White House** *adj.*: *a White House spokesperson*

ˌwhite ˈlie *n.* [C] (informal) a lie that is not very important, especially one that you tell in order to avoid hurting someone's feelings

ˌwhite ˈlight *n.* [U] PHYSICS all the different colors of light in the SPECTRUM mixed together, so that they appear white. Sunlight is an example of white light.

whit·en /ˈwaɪtˀn/ *v.* [I,T] to become white, or to make something do this

W

ˌWhite ˈPages *n.* **the White Pages** the white part of a telephone DIRECTORY, containing the names, addresses, and telephone numbers of people with telephones → YELLOW PAGES

ˌwhite ˈtrash *n.* [U] (informal) an insulting expression meaning white people who are poor and uneducated

white·wash /ˈwaɪtˀwɑʃ, -wɔʃ/ *n.* **1** [C usually singular] an attempt to hide the true facts about a serious accident or illegal action: *One magazine called the report a whitewash.* **2** [U] a white liquid mixture used for painting walls, fences, etc. —**whitewash** *v.* [T]

white·wa·ter /ˈwaɪtˀˌwɔt̬ɚ, -ˌwɑ-/ *n.* [U] a part of a river that looks white because the water is flowing very quickly over rocks

whit·tle /ˈwɪt̬l/ *v.* **1** [I,T] to cut a piece of wood into a particular shape by cutting off small pieces **2** [T] *also* **whittle down** to gradually make something smaller by taking parts away: *I've whittled down the list of guests from 30 to 16.*

whittle sth **away** *also* **whittle away at sth** *phr. v.* to gradually make something smaller or less effective: *Congress has been whittling away at our freedom of speech.*

whiz¹ /wɪz/ *v.* (**whizzed**, **whizzing**, **whizzes**) [I] (informal) to move very quickly: *Marty* ***whizzed past*** *us on his motorbike.*

whiz² *n.* [C] (informal) someone who is very skilled at something

ˈwhiz kid *n.* [C] (informal) a young person who is very skilled or successful at something

who /hu/ *pron.* **1** used in order to ask or talk about which person is involved, or what the name of a person is: *"Who is that?" "That's Amy's brother."* | *Who locked the door?* | *I know who sent you that card.* **2** used in order to add more information about someone: *That's the woman who owns the house.* | *She asked her English teacher, who had studied Latin.* [ORIGIN: Old English *hwa*]

W

whoa /woʊ, hwoʊ, hoʊ/ *interjection* **1** used in order to tell someone to become calmer or do something more slowly **2** used in order to show that you are surprised or that you think something is impressive

who'd /hud/ **1** the short form of "who had": *The doctors were treating a young girl who'd been attacked.* **2** the short form of "who would": *Who'd know where I can get tickets?*

who·dun·it /huˈdʌnɪt/ *n.* [C] (informal) a book, movie, etc. about a murder, in which you do not find out who the murderer is until the end

who·ev·er /huˈɛvɚ/ *pron.* **1** used in order to talk about someone when you do not know who s/he is: *Whoever did this is in big trouble.* **2** used in order to show that it does not matter which person does something: *Whoever gets there first can find a table.*

whole¹ /hoʊl/ *n.* **1 the whole of sth** all of something: *The whole of the morning was wasted.* **2 on the whole** generally or usually: *On the whole, life was much quieter after John left.* **3 as a whole** used in order to say that all the parts of something are being considered: *We must look at our educational system as a whole.* **4** [C usually singular] something that consists of a number of parts, but is considered as a single unit: *Two halves make a whole.* [ORIGIN: Old English *hal* "healthy, unhurt, complete"]

whole² *adj.* **1** all of something (SYN) **entire**: *She drank a whole bottle of wine.* | ***The whole thing*** (=everything about a situation) *just makes me sick.* **2** complete and not divided or broken into parts: *Place a whole onion inside the chicken.*

whole·heart·ed /ˌhoʊlˈhɑrt̬ɪd◂ / *adj.* involving all your feelings, interest, etc.: *You have our* ***wholehearted support.*** —**wholeheartedly** *adv.*

ˈwhole note *n.* [C] ENG. LANG. ARTS a musical note that continues for as long as two HALF NOTES

ˌwhole ˈnumber *n.* [C] MATH a number such as 0, 1, 2, etc. that is not a FRACTION

whole·sale /ˈhoʊlseɪl/ *adj.* **1** relating to the sale of goods in large quantities, usually at low prices, to people or stores that then sell them to other people → RETAIL: *a wholesale price* **2** (disapproving) affecting almost everything or everyone, and often done without any concern for the results: *the wholesale destruction of the rainforest* —**wholesale** *adv.* —**wholesaler** *n.* [C]

whole·some /ˈhoʊlsəm/ *adj.* **1** likely to make you healthy: *a good wholesome breakfast* **2** considered to be morally good or acceptable: *a nice clean wholesome kid*

ˈwhole wheat *adj.* whole wheat flour or bread is made using every part of the wheat grain, including the outer layer

who'll /hul/ the short form of "who will": *This is Denise, who'll be your guide today.*

whol·ly /ˈhoʊli/ *adv.* (formal) completely: *The club is wholly responsible for the damage.*

THESAURUS **completely, absolutely, totally, entirely** → COMPLETELY

whom /hum/ *pron.* **1** (formal) the object form of "who": *To whom am I speaking?* | *He spoke to a man with whom he used to work.* **2 many/all/some etc. of whom** many, all, etc. of the people just mentioned: *They had four sons, one of whom died young.*

whoop /hup, wup/ *v.* [I] to shout loudly and in a happy way —**whoop** *n.* [C]

whoops /wʊps/ *interjection* said when you make a small mistake, drop something, or fall

whoosh /wʊʃ, wuʃ/ *v.* [I] (informal) to move very fast with a soft rushing sound: *Cars whooshed past.* —**whoosh** *n.* [C]

whop·per /ˈwɑpɚ/ *n.* [C] (informal) something that is unusually large

whop·ping /ˈwɑpɪŋ/ *adj.* [only before noun] (informal) very large: *a whopping 28% increase*

who're /ˈhuɚ, hɚ/ the short form of "who are": *Who're those two guys?*

who's /huz/ **1** the short form of "who is": *Who's sitting next to Josh?* **2** the short form of "who has": *That's Karl, the guy who's studied in Brazil.*

whose /huz/ *possessive adj., pron.* **1** used in order to ask which person or people a particular thing belongs to: *Whose jacket is this?* **2** used in order to show the relationship between a person and something that belongs to that person: *That's the man whose house burned down.*

who've /huv/ the short form of "who have"

why /waɪ/ *adv., conjunction* **1** for what reason: *Why are these books so cheap? | Why haven't you finished it yet? | I don't know why she won't talk to me.* **2 why don't you/why doesn't he etc. ...?** (spoken) used in order to make a suggestion: *Why don't you try this one?* **3 why not?** (spoken) **a)** used in order to ask someone why s/he has not done something: *"I haven't done my homework." "Why not?"* **b)** used in order to agree to do something: *"Do you want to come along?" "Yeah, why not?"*

WI the written abbreviation of WISCONSIN

wick

wick /wɪk/ *n.* [C] the string on a CANDLE or in an oil lamp, that is burned

wick·ed /ˈwɪkɪd/ *adj.* **1** morally bad or evil: *the wicked stepmother in the story of Cinderella*

THESAURUS bad, evil, immoral, wrong → BAD[1]

2 bad in a way that is amusing: *a wicked grin | his **wicked sense of humor*** **3** (slang) very good: *a wicked concert*

wick·er /ˈwɪkɚ/ *adj.* made from thin dry branches woven together: *a wicker basket n.* [U]

wicker

a wicker basket

wide[1] /waɪd/ *adj.* **1** measuring a large distance from one side to the other (ANT) **narrow**: *a wide street | The quake was felt over a wide area. | Roberto's face broke into a **wide grin**.* **2** measuring a particular distance from one side to the other: *The bathtub's three feet wide and five feet long. | How wide is the door?* **3** including a lot of different people, things, or situations: *We offer **a wide range of** vegetarian dishes. | We want to reach a **wider audience**.* **4** happening among many people or in many places: *The trial was given wide coverage in the media. | We fear that the fighting will develop into a **wider conflict**.* **5 statewide/citywide/company-wide etc.** affecting all the people in a place: *Teen drug use is a citywide problem.* **6 wide difference/gap etc.** a large and noticeable difference: *wide differences of opinion* [ORIGIN: Old English *wid*]

wide[2] *adv.* **1** completely, or as much as possible: *Somebody left the door **wide open**. | It was 3 a.m., but I was **wide awake**. | The guards stood with their legs wide apart. | He stretched his arms wide, waiting for her hug.* **2 wide open** a competition, election, etc. that is wide open can be won by anyone: *The presidential race is still wide open.* **3** away from the point you were aiming at: *His shot **went wide**.*

wide·ly /ˈwaɪdli/ *adv.* **1** in a lot of different places, or by a lot of people: *Are these products widely available? | Salinger is widely known as the author of "The Catcher in the Rye."* **2** to a large degree (SYN) **a lot**: *Taxes **vary widely** from state to state.*

wid·en /ˈwaɪdn/ *v.* [I,T] **1** to become wider, or to make something wider (ANT) **narrow**: *His eyes widened in fear. | The old trail was widened into a road.* **2** to become greater or larger, or to make something do this: *The gap between low and high incomes began to widen after 1974.*

wide·spread /ˌwaɪdˈsprɛd◂/ (AC) *adj.* happening in many places: *the **widespread use** of illegal drugs | This type of fish is widespread throughout South East Asia.*

wid·ow /ˈwɪdoʊ/ *n.* [C] a woman whose husband has died and who has not married again: *She's the **widow of** the late Thomas Franklin.*

wid·owed /ˈwɪdoʊd/ *adj.* a widowed person is someone whose husband or wife has died: *my **widowed mother/father***

wid·ow·er /ˈwɪdoʊɚ/ *n.* [C] a man whose wife has died and who has not married again

width /wɪdθ, wɪtθ/ *n.* [C,U] the distance from one side of something to the other: *the **width of** the window | It's ten inches **in width**.* → *see picture at* DIMENSION

wield /wild/ *v.* [T] **1 wield power/influence/authority etc.** to have a lot of power, influence, etc., and use it: *During the Middle Ages, the Church wielded a lot of influence.* **2** to hold a weapon or tool that you are going to use

wife /waɪf/ *n.* (plural **wives** /waɪvz/) [C] the woman that a man is married to → HUSBAND: *This is my wife Elaine. | He had two children with his first wife.*

Wi-Fi, wi-fi /ˈwaɪ faɪ/ *n.* [U] (trademark) IT a way of connecting computers to the Internet or to a network, without using wires

W

wig /wɪg/ *n.* [C] artificial hair that you wear on your head ➔ TOUPEE [ORIGIN: 1600—1700 *periwig* type of wig (16—21 centuries), from Old Italian *perrucca* "hair, wig"]

wig·gle /ˈwɪgəl/ *v.* [I,T] to make small movements from side to side or up and down, or to make something move this way: *Wiggle your toes.* —**wiggle** *n.* [C]

wig·wam /ˈwɪgwɑm/ *n.* [C] a type of tent that was used in past times by some Native Americans [ORIGIN: 1600—1700 Abnaki and Massachusett (Native American languages) *wikwam*]

wik·i /ˈwɪki/ *n.* [C,U] IT a WEB PAGE, or series of web pages, which can be written or changed by the people who use that website

wild[1] /waɪld/ *adj.* **1** wild animals or plants live or grow in a natural state, without being controlled by people (ANT) **tame**: *wild horses* | *wild flowers* ➔ NATURAL[1] **2** showing strong uncontrolled emotions such as excitement, anger, or happiness: *a wild look in her eyes* | *wild laughter* | *The kids were* ***wild with*** *excitement.* **3** (spoken) exciting, interesting, or unusual: *Sarah's party was wild.* | *a wild haircut* **4** [only before noun] done or said without knowing all the facts or thinking carefully about them: *a* ***wild guess*** **5 be wild about sb/sth** (informal) to like someone or something very much: *I'm not too wild about his movies.* **6** a wild card in a game can represent any card that you want it to be **7** a wild area of land is in a completely natural state and does not have farms, towns, etc. on it

wild[2] *adv.* **1 run wild** to behave in an uncontrolled way because you have no rules or people to control you **2 go wild** to suddenly become very noisy and active because you are excited or angry: *The crowd went wild when the Giants won.*

wild[3] *n.* **in the wild** in an area that is natural and not controlled or changed by people ➔ CAPTIVITY: *The reserve gives protection to animals that live in the wild.*

wil·der·ness /ˈwɪldənɪs/ *n.* [singular, U] a large area of land that has never been built on or used for growing crops or raising animals: *the Alaskan wilderness*

ˌwild ˈgoose ˌchase *n.* [singular] a situation in which you waste a lot of time looking for something that cannot be found

wild·life /ˈwaɪldlaɪf/ *n.* [U] animals and plants that live in natural conditions

wild·ly /ˈwaɪldli/ *adv.* **1** extremely: *Baseball is* ***wildly popular***. **2** in a very uncontrolled or excited way: *The crowd* ***cheered wildly***.

wiles /waɪlz/ *n.* [plural] things you say or tricks you use in order to persuade someone to do what you want

will[1] /wəl, əl, l; *strong* wɪl/ *modal verb* **1** used in order to make the future tense: *Kathy will be there tomorrow.* | *What time will she get here?* | *I'll* (=I will) *go shopping later.* **2** used in order to say that you are ready or willing to do something: *I'll do whatever you say.* | *Vern said he won't* (=will not) *work for Joe.* **3** used in order to ask someone to do something: *Will you do me a favor?* **4** used in CONDITIONAL sentences that use the present tense: *If it rains, we'll* (=we will) *have the barbecue in the clubhouse.* **5** used like "can" to show what is possible: *This car will seat 5 people.* **6** used in order to say what always happens, or what is generally true: *Accidents will happen.* **7 Will you...** (spoken) used to give an order: *Will you shut up!*

will[2] /wɪl/ *n.* **1** [C,U] the determination to do what you have decided to do: *He's lost* ***the will to live***. | *a woman of high intelligence and* ***strong will*** **2** [C] a legal document that shows who you want to have your money and property after you die: *Grandma Stacy left me $7,000* ***in her will***. | *Have you* ***made a will***? **3** [singular] what someone wants to happen in a particular situation: *No one can force him to stay here* ***against*** *his* ***will*** (=if he does not want to). **4 at will** whenever you want, and in whatever way you want: *They can just change their policies at will.* **5 where there's a will there's a way** (spoken) used in order to say that if you are determined enough you will succeed

will[3] *v.* [T] **1** to try to make something happen by thinking about it very hard: *He shut his eyes, willing her to win.* **2** to officially give something to someone after you die: *She willed the house to her son.*

will·ful, **wilful** /ˈwɪlfəl/ *adj.* (disapproving) doing what you want even though people tell you not to: *a willful child* —**willfully** *adv.*

will·ing /ˈwɪlɪŋ/ *adj.* **1 be willing to do sth** to be prepared to do something: *How much are they willing to pay?* **2** eager to do something: *They were* ***willing participants*** *in the fraud.* —**willingness** *n.* [U] —**willingly** *adv.*

wil·low /ˈwɪloʊ/ *n.* [C] a tree with very long thin branches, that grows near water ➔ *see picture on page A23*

wil·low·y /ˈwɪloʊi/ *adj.* tall, thin, and graceful

will·pow·er /ˈwɪlˌpaʊə/ *n.* [U] the ability to make yourself do something even if it is difficult or unpleasant: *I don't have the willpower to diet.*

wil·ly-nil·ly /ˌwɪli ˈnɪli/ *adv.* something that happens to you willy-nilly happens whether you want it to or not

wilt /wɪlt/ *v.* [I] if a plant wilts, it becomes soft and bends because it needs water or is old

wil·y /ˈwaɪli/ *adj.* good at using tricks in order to get what you want: *a wily politician*

wimp /wɪmp/ *n.* [C] (informal) someone who is weak and afraid: *Don't be such a wimp.* —**wimpy** *adj.*

wimp[2] *v.*

wimp out *phr. v.* (spoken) to not do something that you intended to do, because you do not feel brave enough, strong enough, etc.

win[1] /wɪn/ *v.* (past tense and past participle **won** /wʌn/, present participle **winning**) **1** [I,T] to be the best or first in a competition, game, election, etc. ANT **lose**: *Who do you think will win the Super Bowl?* | *Dad* ***won at*** *chess again.* | *Marcy's team* ***won by*** *3 points.* | *We could not have won the war without them.*

THESAURUS

come in first – to win a competition, game, etc.
be/come in first/second etc. place – used to describe someone's position at the end of a race
be in the lead or **be ahead** – to be winning at a particular time during a competition
be victorious (formal) – to be the winner in a battle or competition
triumph (formal) – to gain a victory or success, especially after a difficult struggle
prevail (formal) – if a person, idea, or principle prevails, s/he or it achieves success after a struggle
the winning team/horse etc. – the one that wins
If you are the **champion** or you **hold the record for something**, you are the person who has beaten all other people in a series of competitions.

2 [T] to earn a prize at a competition or game: *Thorpe won a gold medal.* | *I won $200 playing poker.* **3** [T] to get something good because of all your efforts and skill SYN **gain**: *Dr. Lee's work won her the admiration of scientists worldwide.* [ORIGIN: Old English *winnan* "to work, fight"]

win out *phr. v.* to succeed after being unsuccessful for a long time: *Sooner or later, good sense will win out.*

win sb ↔ **over** *phr. v.* to persuade someone to like you or support you

win[2] *n.* [C] a victory or success, especially in a sport: *a record of seven wins and six losses*

wince /wɪns/ *v.* [I] to suddenly change the expression on your face when you see or remember something painful or embarrassing: *I still* ***wince at*** *the memory of how badly I sang.*

winch /wɪntʃ/ *n.* [C] a machine with a rope or chain, used for lifting heavy objects —**winch** *v.* [T]

wind[1] /wɪnd/ *n.* **1** [C,U] the air outside when you can feel it moving around you: *An icy* ***wind blew*** *through the open door.* | *Expect* ***strong winds*** *and rain tomorrow.* | *a* ***gust of wind*** (=a short strong wind) | *A cold* ***east/west etc. wind*** (=from the east, etc.) *was blowing.*

THESAURUS

breeze – a light wind
gust – a sudden strong movement of wind
gale – very strong wind → RAIN[1], SNOW[1]

2 get wind of sth to find out about something private or secret **3** [C] your ability to breathe easily: *Rae got the* ***wind knocked out of*** *her* (=was hit in the stomach and could not breathe for a short time). **4 the winds** the people in an ORCHESTRA or band who play musical instruments that you blow into, such as the FLUTE [ORIGIN: Old English]

wind[2] /waɪnd/ *v.* (past tense and past participle **wound** /waʊnd/) **1** [I,T] to turn or twist something several times around something else: *Don't* ***wind*** *the cord* ***around*** *the iron.* **2** [T] *also* **wind up** to make a machine, toy, clock, etc. work by turning a small handle around several times: *I forgot to wind my watch.* **3** [I] if a road, river, etc. winds, it curves or bends many times

wind down *phr. v.* to gradually end: *The party started winding down after midnight.*

wind up *phr. v.* **1** to be in a bad situation or place after a lot has happened: *Most of them* ***wound up in prison.*** **2 wind** sth ↔ **up** to end an activity, meeting, etc.: *It's almost 5:00 – we'd better wind things up.*

Wind·break·er /ˈwɪndˌbreɪkɚ/ *n.* [C] (trademark) a type of coat that protects you from the wind

wind·chill fac·tor /ˈwɪndtʃɪl ˌfæktɚ/ *n.* [U] the effect the wind has in cold weather, making the temperature even colder

wind·ed /ˈwɪndɪd/ *adj.* having difficulty breathing because you have exercised too much or have been hit in the stomach

wind·fall /ˈwɪndfɔl/ *n.* [C] an amount of money that you get when you do not expect it

wind·ing /ˈwaɪndɪŋ/ *adj.* having bends or curves: *a long winding river*

wind in·stru·ment /ˈwɪnd ˌɪnstrəmənt/ *n.* [C] a musical instrument such as the FLUTE that you play by blowing into it

wind·mill /ˈwɪndˌmɪl/ *n.* [C] a tall structure with parts that are turned by the wind, used to crush grain or make electricity

windmill

win·dow /ˈwɪndoʊ/ *n.* [C] **1** a space or an area of glass in the wall of a building or vehicle, that lets in light: *Can I* ***open/close/shut the window?*** | *He was* ***looking/gazing out the window.*** | *I could see her face* ***in the window*** (=on the other side of the window). **2** IT one of the areas on a computer screen where different programs are operating [ORIGIN: 1200—1300 Old Norse *vindauga*, from *vindr* "wind" + *auga* "eye"]

ˈwindow ˌdressing *n.* [U] **1** an attempt to make something seem better than it really is **2** the art of arranging things in a store window so that they look attractive to customers

win·dow·pane /ˈwɪndoʊˌpeɪn/ *n.* [C] a whole piece of glass used in a window

W

'window ˌshopping *n.* [U] the activity of looking at goods in store windows without intending to buy them

win·dow·sill /'wɪndoʊˌsɪl/ *n.* [C] a shelf at the bottom of a window

wind·pipe /'wɪndpaɪp/ *n.* [C] BIOLOGY the tube through which air passes from your throat to your lungs

wind·shield /'wɪndʃild/ *n.* [C] the large window at the front of a vehicle

'windshield ˌwiper *n.* [C] a long thin object that moves across a windshield to remove rain

wind·surf·ing /'wɪndˌsɚfɪŋ/ *n.* [U] the sport of sailing across water by standing on a special board and holding onto a large sail ➔ *see picture on page A17*

wind·swept /'wɪndswɛpt/ *adj.* **1** a place that is windswept is often very windy and has few or no trees or buildings to protect it **2** made messy by the wind: *windswept hair*

wind·y /'wɪndi/ *adj.* if it is windy, there is a lot of wind: *It's been windy all day.* | *a windy beach*

wine¹ /waɪn/ *n.* [C,U] an alcoholic drink made from GRAPES, or a type of this drink: *a glass of **red/white wine*** | *a fine selection of wines* [ORIGIN: Old English *win*, from Latin *vinum*]

wine² *v.* **wine and dine** to entertain someone with good food, wine, etc.

wine·glass /'waɪnglæs/ *n.* [C] a tall glass with a thin stem, used for drinking wine

win·er·y /'waɪnəri/ *n.* (plural **wineries**) [C] a place where wine is made and stored

wing¹ /wɪŋ/ *n.* [C] **1** the part of a bird's or insect's body used for flying: *The ducks started **flapping their wings**.* ➔ *see picture on page A15* **2** one of the large flat parts that stick out of the sides of an airplane and help it stay in the air ➔ *see picture at* AIRPLANE **3** one of the parts that a large building is divided into: *the east wing of the library* **4** POLITICS a group of people within a political party or other organization who have a particular opinion or aim ➔ LEFT-WING, RIGHT-WING: *the liberal wing of the Democratic Party* **5 take sb under your wing** to help or protect someone younger or less experienced than you **6 waiting in the wings** ready to be used, or ready to do something: *At least two potential buyers are waiting in the wings.* **7 the wings** [plural] the side parts of a stage, where actors are hidden from people watching the play

wing² *v.* **wing it** (informal) to do something without any planning or preparation: *We'll just have to wing it.*

winged /wɪŋd/ *adj.* having wings: *winged insects*

wing·span /'wɪŋspæn/ *n.* [C] the distance from the end of one wing to the end of the other

wing·tip /'wɪŋtɪp/ *n.* [C] **1** a type of man's shoe with a pattern of small holes on the toe **2** the end of an airplane's or bird's wing

W

wink /wɪŋk/ *v.* [I] to close and open one eye quickly, usually to show that you are joking or being friendly: *"Don't tell Mom," he said, **winking at** her.* —**wink** *n.* [C]: *He smiled and **gave** her **a wink**.*

wink

win·ner /'wɪnɚ/ *n.* [C] **1** someone who wins something: *The winner will receive $5,000.* | *a Nobel Prize winner* | *the **winner of** the Boston Marathon* **2** (informal) someone or something that is likely to be successful: *His new movie looks like a winner.*

win·ning /'wɪnɪŋ/ *adj.* **1** the winning person or thing is the one that wins a competition or game: *the winning team* | *the winning run* | *I'm on a **winning streak*** (=continuing to win). **2 winning smile/charm/personality etc.** a feature you have that makes people like you

win·nings /'wɪnɪŋz/ *n.* [plural] money that you win in a game or competition

win·now /'wɪnoʊ/ *also* **winnow down** *v.* [I,T] to make a list, group, or quantity smaller by getting rid of the things that you do not need or want: *We eventually winnowed down the list of twenty candidates to three.*

winnow sth ↔ **out** *phr. v.* to get rid of the parts of something that you do not need or want: *The changing environment winnowed out the creatures who could not adapt.*

win·o /'waɪnoʊ/ *n.* (plural **winos**) [C] (informal) someone who drinks a lot of alcohol and lives on the streets

win·some /'wɪnsəm/ *adj.* (literary) pleasant and attractive: *a winsome smile*

win·ter /'wɪntɚ/ *n.* [C,U] the season between fall and spring, when the weather is coldest: *The park closes **in the winter**.* | *I'm going skiing **this winter**.* | ***last/next winter*** (=the winter before or after this one) [ORIGIN: Old English]

win·ter·time /'wɪntɚˌtaɪm/ *n.* [U] the time when it is winter

win·try /'wɪntri/ *adj.* cold or typical of winter: *a wintry day*

win-'win situˌation *n.* [C] a situation that will end well for everyone involved in it

wipe /waɪp/ *v.* [T] **1** *also* **wipe off** to clean something by rubbing it with a cloth or against a soft surface: *Could you wipe off the table?* | ***Wipe** your feet **on** the mat before you come in.* **2** to remove dirt, water, etc. from something with a cloth or your hand: *He **wiped** the sweat **from** his face.* | ***wiping away** her tears* **3** to remove all the sound, film, or information from something such as a tape, CD, or computer HARD DRIVE

wipe out *phr. v.* **1 wipe** sb/sth ↔ **out** to destroy or remove someone or something completely: *Fires wiped out half of the city.* **2 wipe** sb ↔ **out** (informal) to make you feel extremely tired: *All that running wiped me out.* **3** (spoken) to fall or hit something when driving a car, riding a bicycle, etc.
wipe sth ↔ **up** *phr. v.* to remove liquid from a surface using a cloth: *Wipe up this mess!*

wip·er /ˈwaɪpɚ/ *n.* [C] a WINDSHIELD WIPER

wire[1] /waɪɚ/ *n.* **1** [U] metal that is long and thin like thread: *a wire fence* **2** [C] a long thin piece of metal that is used to carry electricity: *a telephone wire* **3** [C] (old-fashioned) a TELEGRAM

wire[2] *v.* [T] **1** *also* **wire up** to connect electrical wires so that a piece of equipment will work: *I'm almost finished wiring up the alarm.* **2** to fasten two or more things together using wire **3** to send money electronically **4** (old-fashioned) to send a TELEGRAM

wire·less /ˈwaɪɚlɪs/ *adj.* IT relating to a system of communication that does not use electrical or telephone wires: *wireless Internet connections*

wire·tap /ˈwaɪɚˌtæp/ *v.* (**wiretapped, wiretapping**) [I,T] to secretly listen to someone's telephone conversations by attaching electronic equipment to the wires of his/her telephone —**wiretap** *n.* [C]

wir·ing /ˈwaɪərɪŋ/ *n.* [U] the network of wires that form the electrical system in a building, vehicle, or piece of equipment: *You need to replace the wiring.*

wir·y /ˈwaɪəri/ *adj.* **1** someone who is wiry is thin but strong **2** wiry hair is stiff and curly

wis·dom /ˈwɪzdəm/ *n.* [U] **1** good judgment and the ability to make wise decisions based on your knowledge and experience **2 question/doubt the wisdom of (doing) sth** used to say that you think something is not sensible: *Many experts **question the wisdom of** sending these men to prison.*

wisdom tooth *n.* [C] BIOLOGY one of the four large teeth at the back of your mouth that do not grow until you are an adult

wise[1] /waɪz/ *adj.* **1** based on good judgment and experience: ***It's wise to** leave before the traffic gets too heavy.* | *a wise decision* **2** a wise person makes good decisions and gives good advice because s/he has a lot of experience: *a wise leader*

THESAURUS **intelligent, smart, bright, brilliant** → INTELLIGENT

3 be none the wiser a) to not understand something even though it has been explained to you: *They sent me on a training course, but I'm still none the wiser.* **b)** used to say that no one will find out about something bad someone has done: *He could have taken the money, and we would have been none the wiser.* **4 price-wise/time-wise etc.** (informal) used for saying which feature of a situation you are referring to: *It would have been a problem transportation-wise.* [ORIGIN: Old English *wis*] —**wisely** *adv.*

wise[2] *v.*
wise up *phr. v.* (informal) to realize the truth about a situation: *Corporations should wise up and realize that employees aren't machines.*

wise·crack /ˈwaɪzkræk/ *n.* [C] (informal) a quick, funny, and often slightly unkind remark

THESAURUS **joke, gag, one-liner, quip, witticism** → JOKE[1]

ˈwise guy *n.* [C] (informal) an annoying person who thinks that s/he knows more than s/he really does

wish[1] /wɪʃ/ *v.* **1** [T] to want something to happen even though it is unlikely: *I wish they'd hurry up!* | ***I wish (that)** I could remember his name.* **2** [I,T] (formal) to want to do something: *I **wish to** make a complaint.* **3** [T] to say that you hope someone will be happy, successful, lucky, etc.: ***Wish** me luck!* **4 I/you wish!** (spoken) said when you do not think something is true or possible, but you want it to be: *"I'm going to get a role in his new movie." "Yeah, you wish!"*
wish for sth *phr. v.* to want something to happen, or want to have something, especially when it seems unlikely: *If you could have anything, what would you wish for?* [ORIGIN: Old English *wyscan*]

wish[2] *n.* [C] **1** the act of wishing for something that you want, or the thing that you wish for: *Close your eyes and **make a wish**!* | *Did you get your wish?* **2** (formal) a desire for something: *It's important to respect the **wishes of** the patient.* | *He left school **against** his parents' **wishes*** (=his parents did not want him to leave school). | *I had no **wish to** see him.* **3 best wishes** a friendly phrase that you write before your name in cards and letters

wish·bone /ˈwɪʃboʊn/ *n.* [C] a Y-shaped chicken bone that two people pull apart in order to find out who will get his/her wish

ˌwishful ˈthinking *n.* [U] a way of thinking that is based on what you want to happen rather than what is likely to happen

wish·y-wash·y /ˈwɪʃi ˌwɑʃi, -ˌwɔʃi/ *adj.* (informal, disapproving) a wishy-washy person does not have firm or clear ideas, and seems unable to decide what s/he wants

wisp /wɪsp/ *n.* [C] **1** a small thin amount of hair, grass, etc.: *A **wisp of** hair had escaped from under her hat.* **2** a small thin line of smoke or cloud —**wispy** *adj.*

wist·ful /ˈwɪstfəl/ *adj.* slightly sad because you cannot have something you want: *a wistful expression* —**wistfully** *adv.*

wit /wɪt/ *n.* **1** [U] the ability to say things that are funny and smart **2** [C] someone who has this ability **3 wits** [plural] your ability to think quickly and make the right decisions: *Without a gun, he knew he'd have to rely on his wits.* | *Somehow, Austin **kept** his **wits about** him* (=thought quickly and dealt with a difficult situation). **4 be at your wits' end** to be upset because you have tried everything possible to solve a problem **5 scare sb out of his/her wits** to frighten someone very much

witch /wɪtʃ/ *n.* [C] a woman who has magic powers, especially to do bad things

witch·craft /ˈwɪtʃkræft/ *n.* [U] the use of magic, usually to do bad things

THESAURUS **magic, sorcery, black magic, the occult, voodoo** → MAGIC[1]

ˈwitch ˌdoctor *n.* [C] a man who is believed to be able to cure sick people using magic, especially in some parts of Africa

ˈwitch hunt *n.* [C] (disapproving) an attempt to find and punish people whose opinions, political beliefs, etc. are considered to be wrong or dangerous

with /wɪθ, wɪð/ *prep.* **1** used in order to show that two or more people or things are together in the same place: *She went to the beach with her friends.* | *Put this bag with the others.* | *eggs mixed with milk* | *Make sure you* ***take*** *an umbrella* ***with*** *you.* **2** having, possessing, or carrying something: *a boy with a broken arm* | *Where's the dish with the blue pattern?* **3** because of something, or as a result of something: *Connie smiled with pride.* | *The room was bright with sunlight.* **4** including: *Your dinner* ***comes with*** *fries.* **5** using something, or by means of something: *Don't eat with your fingers!* | *What will you buy with the money?* **6** used in order to say what covers or fills something: *I prefer a pillow filled with feathers.* | *His hands were covered with blood.* **7** relating to something: *What's* ***wrong with*** *the radio?* | *Be careful with that glass.* **8** supporting someone or sharing his/her opinion: *I agree with you.* | *You're either with me or against me.* **9** used to say who or what someone has a particular feeling toward: *She's* ***in love with*** *you.* **10** used to say which other person, group, or country is involved in an action or activity: *He's always arguing with his son.* | *the war with Germany* **11** used to say how someone does something, or how something happens: *The fuel has to be handled with great care.* **12** at the same rate as something else, and because of it: *The wine will get better with age.* **13 be with me/you** (spoken) to understand what someone is saying: *Are you with me?* **14** employed by someone: *Jack has been with the company for 25 years.* **15** used to talk about the position of someone's body: *He stood with his back to the wall.*

with·draw /wɪθˈdrɔ, wɪð-/ *v.* (past tense **withdrew** /-ˈdru/, past participle **withdrawn** /-ˈdrɔn/) **1** [T] to take money out of a bank account: *He* ***withdrew*** *$200* ***from*** *his savings account.* **2** [T] to stop giving support or money to someone or something: *Congress threatened to withdraw support for the space project.* **3** [I,T] to stop taking part in a competition, race, etc., or to leave an organization: *She was* ***withdrawn from*** *Winston Academy.* | *The third candidate has withdrawn.*

THESAURUS **quit, give up, drop out** → QUIT

4 [I,T] if soldiers withdraw from an area, they leave it: *American troops were gradually withdrawn.* **5** [T] if you withdraw a threat, request, proposal, etc., you say that you no longer intend to do what you said or no longer want what you asked for: *We have withdrawn our offer to buy the company.*

with·draw·al /wɪθˈdrɔəl/ *n.* **1** [C,U] the action of taking money out of a bank account, or the amount you take out: *I'd like to* ***make a withdrawal****, please.* **2** [C,U] the action of moving an army, its weapons, etc. away from the area where it was fighting: *Many people are calling for the* ***withdrawal of*** *troops.* **3** [U] the action of not continuing to give something: *Their leader was threatened with the* ***withdrawal of*** *U.S. aid.* **4** [U] the act of no longer taking part in an activity or being a member of an organization: *Hanson's* ***withdrawal from*** *the competition surprised everyone.* **5** [U] the pain, bad feelings, etc. that someone suffers when s/he stops regularly taking a drug: *Many people have* ***withdrawal symptoms*** *when they quit smoking.*

with·drawn /wɪθˈdrɔn/ *adj.* quiet, and not wanting to talk to people: *As the years passed, he became increasingly withdrawn.*

with·er /ˈwɪðɚ/ *also* **wither away** *v.* [I] **1** if a plant withers, its leaves become dry and it starts to die **2** to become weaker and then disappear: *Our morale eventually withered away.*

with·hold /wɪθˈhoʊld, wɪð-/ *v.* (past tense and past participle **withheld** /-ˈhɛld/) [T] to refuse to give someone something: *They said McShane had* ***withheld*** *information* ***from*** *Congress.*

with·in /wɪˈðɪn, wɪˈθɪn/ *adv., prep.* **1** during the period of time mentioned, or before the period of time ends: *The movie should start within the next five minutes.* | *Within a month of meeting him, I knew I was in love.* **2** less than a certain distance from a particular place: *We need a hotel within a mile of the airport.* **3** inside an organization, society, or group of people: *There have been a lot of changes within the department since I joined.* **4** according to particular limits or rules: *You must drive within the speed limit.*

with·out /wɪˈðaʊt, wɪˈθaʊt/ *adv., prep.* **1** not having a particular thing: *I can't see anything without my glasses.* | *They went without food and water for two days.* **2** not having someone with you: *Why did you leave without me?* | *We can't finish this job without Jake.* **3** not doing a particular thing: *He left without saying goodbye.* | *Suddenly,* ***without warning****, Griffin turned and ran.* **4** not showing a particular emotion: *The mayor announced his resignation without bitterness.*

with·stand /wɪθˈstænd, wɪð-/ *v.* (past tense and past participle **withstood** /-ˈstʊd/) [T] to not be harmed or affected by something: *The buildings have withstood earthquakes since 1916.*

wit·ness[1] /ˈwɪtˀnɪs/ *n.* [C] **1** someone who saw

W

an accident or a crime: *Unfortunately, there were no **witnesses to** the robbery.* **2** LAW someone who describes in a court of law what s/he knows about a crime: *He asked the witness how well she knew the defendant.* | *Michael was a crucial **witness for** the prosecution.* **3** someone who watches another person sign an official document, and then signs it also to prove this

witness² *v.* [T] **1** to see something happen, especially an accident or a crime: *Few people actually witnessed the event.*

> THESAURUS see, notice, behold, observe → SEE

2 to watch someone sign an official document, and then sign it also to prove this

'witness stand *n.* [C] the place in a court of law where a witness answers questions

wit·ti·cism /ˈwɪt̬əˌsɪzəm/ *n.* [C] a smart and amusing remark

> THESAURUS joke, gag, wisecrack, one-liner, quip, pun, funny story → JOKE¹

wit·ty /ˈwɪt̬i/ *adj.* (comparative **wittier**, superlative **wittiest**) smart and funny: *a witty young man* | *a witty response*

> THESAURUS funny, amusing, humorous, comical → FUNNY¹

wives /waɪvz/ *n.* the plural of WIFE

wiz·ard /ˈwɪzɚd/ *n.* [C] **1** a man who has magic powers **2** *also* **wiz** /wɪz/ (informal) someone who is very good at doing something: *a computer wizard*

wiz·ened /ˈwɪzənd/ *adj.* old and having dry skin with a lot of WRINKLES (=lines)

wk. the written abbreviation of WEEK

wob·ble /ˈwɑbəl/ *v.* [I] to move from side to side in an unsteady way —**wobbly** *adj.*: *a wobbly chair* —**wobble** *n.* [C]

> THESAURUS shake, tremble, shiver, quiver → SHAKE¹

woe /woʊ/ *n.* **1 woes** [plural] (formal) problems that are affecting someone: *the country's economic woes* **2** [U] (literary) great sadness

woe·be·gone /ˈwoʊbɪˌgɔn, -ˌgɑn/ *adj.* looking very sad

woe·ful /ˈwoʊfəl/ *adj.* **1** very bad or serious: *the woeful state of the economy* **2** (literary) very sad: *a woeful goodbye* —**woefully** *adv.*: *woefully inadequate facilities*

wok /wɑk/ *n.* [C] a large round pan, used especially in Chinese cooking

woke /woʊk/ *v.* the past tense of WAKE

wo·ken /ˈwoʊkən/ *v.* the past participle of WAKE

wolf¹ /wʊlf/ *n.* (plural **wolves** /wʊlvz/) [C] a wild animal similar to a large dog

wolf² *also* **wolf down** *v.* [T] (informal) to eat something very quickly: *She wolfed down a couple of hamburgers.*

wom·an /ˈwʊmən/ *n.* (plural **women** /ˈwɪmɪn/) **1** [C] an adult female person → MAN: *Who was that woman you were talking to?* | *Ireland's first woman president* | *single women* **2** [singular] women in general: *It's not safe there for a woman traveling alone.* [ORIGIN: Old English *wifman*, from *wif* "woman, wife" + *man* "person"]

wom·an·hood /ˈwʊmənˌhʊd/ *n.* [U] the state of being a woman, or the time when a female person is an adult → MANHOOD

wom·an·iz·er /ˈwʊməˌnaɪzɚ/ *n.* [C] a man who tries to have sexual relationships with many different women

wom·an·kind /ˈwʊmənˌkaɪnd/ *n.* [U] women considered together as a group

womb /wum/ *n.* [C] BIOLOGY the part of a female's body where her baby grows before it is born (SYN) **uterus**

wom·en /ˈwɪmɪn/ *n.* the plural of WOMAN

won /wʌn/ *v.* the past tense and past participle of WIN

won·der¹ /ˈwʌndɚ/ *v.* [I,T] **1** to think about something that you are not sure about, and try to guess what is true, what will happen, etc.: ***I wonder if** she knows we're here.* | ***I wonder how** Wendy's feeling today.* | *We **wondered where** you'd gone.* **2 I was wondering if/whether** (spoken) **a)** used in order to ask someone if s/he would like to do something: *We were wondering whether you'd like to come with us.* **b)** used in order to politely ask for something: *I was wondering if I could use your phone.* **3** to doubt whether someone or something is good or true: *I began to **wonder about** this business of his.* **4** to be surprised by something: ***I wonder why** she didn't call the police.*

wonder² *n.* **1** [U] a feeling of admiration and surprise: *They listened to Lisa's story **in/with wonder**.* **2 no wonder** (spoken) said when you are not surprised about something: *No wonder you feel sick – you ate a whole pizza!* **3** [C usually plural] something that is very impressive: ***the wonders of** modern technology*

wonder³ *adj.* [only before noun] very good and effective: *a new wonder drug*

won·der·ful /ˈwʌndɚfəl/ *adj.* extremely good (SYN) **great**: *Congratulations! That's wonderful news!* | *We had a wonderful time.* —**wonderfully** *adv.*

> THESAURUS good, excellent, outstanding, exceptional, superb → GOOD¹
> nice, great, fantastic → NICE

won't /woʊnt/ *v.* the short form of "will not": *Dad won't like it.*

W

wont¹ /wɔnt, woʊnt/ *adj.* **be wont to do sth** (formal) to be likely to do something

wont² *n.* **as is sb's wont** (formal) used in order to say that it is someone's habit to do something

woo /wu/ *v.* [T] **1** to try to persuade someone to do something such as support you, vote for you, or buy something from you: *Politicians were busy wooing voters.* **2** (old-fashioned) to try to persuade a woman to love you and marry you

wood /wʊd/ *n.* **1** [C,U] the material that trees are made of, which is used to make things: *polished wood floors* | *The table was made from three different types of wood.* **2 the woods** [plural] a small forest: *I went for a walk* ***in the woods.*** → **knock on wood** *at* KNOCK¹

wood·chuck /ˈwʊdtʃʌk/ *n.* [C] a GROUNDHOG

wood·ed /ˈwʊdɪd/ *adj.* covered with trees

wood·en /ˈwʊdn/ *adj.* made from wood: *a wooden bench* → *see picture at* MATERIAL¹

wood·land /ˈwʊdlənd, -lænd/ *n.* [C,U] an area of land that is covered with trees

wood·peck·er /ˈwʊdˌpɛkɚ/ *n.* [C] a bird that uses its long beak to make holes in trees

woodwind instruments

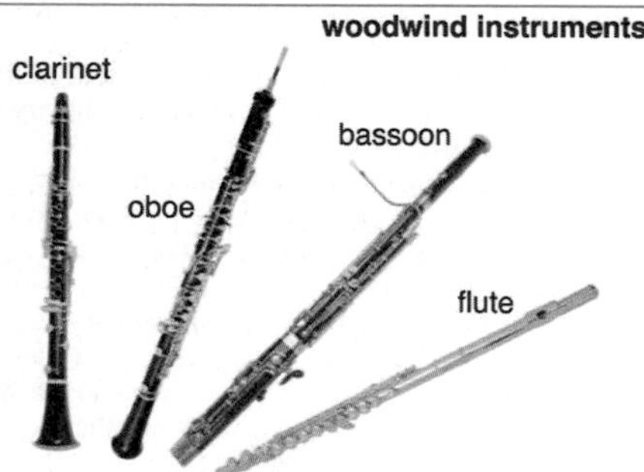

W

wood·wind /ˈwʊdˌwɪnd/ *n.* [C usually plural] ENG. LANG. ARTS the group of musical instruments that you play by blowing and pressing KEYS

wood·work /ˈwʊdwɚk/ *n.* [U] **1** the parts of a building that are made of wood **2** the skill of making wooden objects

wood·y /ˈwʊdi/ *adj.* looking, smelling, tasting, etc. like wood: *woody plants*

woof /wʊf/ *interjection* the sound a dog makes when it BARKS

wool /wʊl/ *n.* [U] **1** the soft thick hair of a sheep, used for making cloth and YARN **2** material made from wool: *a wool skirt* | *wool blankets* → *see picture at* MATERIAL¹

wool·en /ˈwʊlən/ *adj.* made of wool: *woolen socks*

wool·ens /ˈwʊlənz/ *n.* [plural] clothes that are made from wool

wool·y /ˈwʊli/ *adj.* made of or feeling like wool: *a wooly hat*

woo·zy /ˈwuzi/ *adj.* (informal) feeling weak and unsteady SYN **dizzy**

word¹ /wɚd/ *n.*

1 LANGUAGE PART [C] a group of sounds or letters that have a particular meaning: *"Casa" is the Spanish* ***word for*** *"house."* | *Write a 500-word essay about your family.* | *I know the tune, but not the words.*

2 STH SAID/WRITTEN [C] something that you say or write: *Tell us what happened* ***in your own words.*** | *Promise you won't* ***say a word*** (=not say anything) *about the accident to John.*

3 not believe/hear/understand a word used to emphasize that you do not believe or cannot hear any part of what someone is saying: *I didn't understand a word you said.*

4 STATEMENT [C] something important that someone says to you: *Mr. Gleeson would like* ***a word with*** *you in his office.* | *Can I give you a* ***word of caution/advice/encouragement etc.*** (=used when you want to warn someone not to do something, give them some advice, etc.)*?* | *Mr. Martin will now* ***say a few words*** (=make a short speech).

5 in other words used when you are repeating a statement in a clearer way: *Some people aren't demonstrative. In other words, they don't express their feelings.*

6 NEWS [singular, U] a piece of news or a message: ***The word is*** *the company's closing its offices in Houston.* | *Have you had* ***any word from*** *your lawyers yet?* | *The group went on television to* ***spread the word*** (=tell other people the news) *about child abuse.* | *Many people learned about the band* ***by word of mouth*** (=because someone told them about the band).

7 sb's word someone's promise or statement that something is true: *I* ***give you*** *my* ***word;*** *we'll take good care of him.* | *I trust him to* ***keep*** *his* ***word.*** | *The money's all there —* ***take*** *my* ***word for it*** (=believe what I say is true). | *He's* ***a man of his word*** (=does what he promises to do).

8 swear/dirty/cuss word a word that is considered to be offensive or shocking by most people

9 word for word in exactly the same words: *That's not what he said word for word, but it's close.*

10 put in a good word for sb to try to help someone get or achieve something by saying good things about him/her to someone else: *Could you put in a good word for me with your boss?*

11 the last word the last statement in a discussion or argument: *She's not content unless she* ***has the last word.***

12 not in so many words not in a direct way: *"So Dad said he'd pay for it?" "Not in so many words."*

13 give/say the word to tell someone to start doing something: *Don't move until I give the word.*

14 the final word the power to decide whether or how to do something: *My boss* ***has the final word*** *on hiring staff.*

word² *v.* [T] to use words that are carefully chosen

when saying or writing something: *a **carefully worded** letter*

'word ˌfamily *n.* [C] ENG. LANG. ARTS a group of related words that are all formed from the same base word. For example, the word family of the word "final" includes "finally," "finalist," and "finality."

word·ing /ˈwɚdɪŋ/ *n.* [U] the words and phrases used in order to express something: *the exact **wording of** the contract*

'word ˌprocessor *n.* [C] a small computer or computer software that you use for writing —**word processing** *n.* [U]

word·y /ˈwɚdi/ *adj.* (disapproving) using too many words: *a wordy explanation*

wore /wɔr/ *v.* the past tense of WEAR

work¹ /wɚk/ *v.*

1 DO A JOB [I,T] to do a job in order to earn money, or to do the activities and duties that are part of your job: *"Where do you work?" "I **work in** the city." | Heidi **works for** a law firm in Montreal. | I used to **work at** Burger King. | She **works as** a bartender in a nightclub. | He's **working with** children who have learning difficulties. | Are you willing to **work nights/weekends etc.**?*

TOPIC

If you work for a company or organization, you are an **employee**.
The person or organization you work for is your **employer**.
Your employer pays your **salary** or **wages**.
An organization's **staff** are all the people who work for the organization.
Your **colleagues** or **co-workers** are the people you work with.
When you reach the age to stop working permanently, you **retire**. → JOB

2 MACHINE/EQUIPMENT a) [I] if a machine or piece of equipment works, it does what it is supposed to do: *The CD player isn't working.* **b)** [T] to make a machine or piece of equipment do what it is supposed to do: *Does anyone know how to work the printer?*
3 BE EFFECTIVE [I] to be effective or successful: *This plan isn't going to work. | I hope this cough medicine works.*
4 DO AN ACTIVITY [I] to do something that needs effort in order to achieve a result: *He's **working toward** a better life for his family. | She's been **working hard** to get the house ready.*
5 work your way through/to etc. sth a) to move somewhere slowly and with difficulty: *He worked his way through the crowd.* **b)** to achieve something gradually by working: *Dave **worked his way to the top** of the firm.*
6 work your way through school/college to do a job while you are in college because you need the money to help pay for it
7 HAVE AN EFFECT [I] to have a particular effect on someone or something: *Unfortunately, her bad grades **worked against** (=caused problems for) her. | Your job experience should **work in your favor*** (=help you).
8 MOVE SLOWLY [I,T] to move into a position slowly with many small movements, or to move something in this way: *Slowly, he worked the screwdriver into the crack.*
9 SHAPE STH [T] if you work a material such as clay, leather, or metal, you bend it, shape it, etc. in order to make something
10 EXERCISE [T] to exercise a muscle or part of your body
11 LAND [T] if you work the land or the soil, you try to grow crops on it [ORIGIN: Old English *wyrcan*]

work on *phr. v.*
1 work on sth to try to repair, complete, or improve something: *Dad's still working on the car. | I need to work on my essay.*
2 work on sb to try continuously to influence someone, or persuade him/her to do something

work out *phr. v.*
1 if something works out, it gradually stops being a problem: *Don't worry. I'm sure everything will work out fine.*
2 to do a set of exercises that make you stronger: *Sue works out in the gym twice a week.*
3 work sth ↔ **out** to calculate an amount, price, or value: *Have you worked out how much we owe them?*
4 to cost a particular amount: *The hotel **works out to/at** about $50 a night.*
5 work sth ↔ **out** to find a solution to a problem, or make a decision after thinking carefully: *He still hasn't worked out which college he's going to.*

work up *phr. v.*
work up an appetite/a sweat to do so much exercise that you become very hungry or SWEATY

work up to sth *phr. v.*
to gradually prepare yourself for something difficult: *I started with 10 laps and now I've worked up to 20.*

work² *n.* **1** [U] your job or the activities that you do regularly to earn money: *Much of our work involves meeting clients. | Do you want to go to dinner **after work*** (=after you have finished working)*? | Hurry up, or we'll be **late for work**. | I've been **out of work*** (=without a job) *for a year. | Rob's still **looking for work**.* ▸ Don't say "I have a work." Say "I have a job." ◂

THESAURUS job, occupation, profession, career → JOB

2 [U] the place where you do your job: *I'll see you **at work** on Monday.* **3** [U] physical or mental activity and effort: *Looking after children can be **hard work**. | Stop talking and **get to work*** (=start working)*! | They've done a lot of **work on** their house.* **4** [U] the things you produce for your job, as part of a class, etc.: *We're pleased with your work. | an excellent **piece of work*** **5** [C] a painting, book, play, piece of music, etc.: ***great works of art*** **6 at work** doing a job or an activity: *Crews were at work repairing the roads.* **7 have your**

W

work cut out (for you) (informal) used to say that it will be very difficult to do something **8 work clothes** clothes designed for people to work in **9 the (whole) works** (spoken) everything that is available with something you are buying: *a hamburger **with the works*** (=with onions, cheese, etc.) **10 works** [plural] a building where goods are produced or an industrial process takes place: *a gas works* **11** [U] PHYSICS the movement of energy into an object, measured as the amount of force placed on an object mutiplied by the distance the object moves ➔ **do sb's dirty work** *at* DIRTY[1]

work·a·ble /ˈwɚkəbəl/ *adj.* a workable plan or system can be used or done effectively: *a workable solution*

work·a·hol·ic /ˌwɚkəˈhɔlɪk/ *n.* [C] (informal) someone who spends all his/her time working

work·bench /ˈwɚkbɛntʃ/ *n.* [C] a strong table used for working on things with tools

work·book /ˈwɚkbʊk/ *n.* [C] a school book with questions and exercises in it

ˌworked ˈup *adj.* (informal) very upset or excited about something: *Don't get so **worked up about** your daughter.*

work·er /ˈwɚkɚ/ *n.* [C] **1** someone who works for a company or organization, especially someone who is not a manager: *Fifty workers lost their jobs.* | *a farm worker* **2** someone who works in a particular way: *Lisa's a **good/hard/slow etc. worker**.*

ˌworkers' compenˈsation *also* **ˌworkers' ˈcomp** *n.* [U] money that a company must pay to a worker who is injured or becomes sick as a result of his/her job

work·fare /ˈwɚkfɛr/ *n.* [U] a system under which unemployed people must work before they are given money by the government

work·force /ˈwɚkfɔrs/ *n.* [singular] all the people who work in a particular country, industry, or company: *There are still more men than women **in the workforce**.*

W

work·ing /ˈwɚkɪŋ/ *adj.* [only before noun] **1** having a job: *a **working mother*** **2** relating to work: *bad working conditions* **3 in working order** working correctly and not broken: *My watch is still in good working order.* **4 a working knowledge of sth** enough practical knowledge about something to use it effectively

ˌworking ˈclass *n.* **the working class** SOCIAL SCIENCE the group of people in society who usually do physical work and who do not have much money or power ➔ LOWER CLASS, MIDDLE CLASS, UPPER CLASS —**working-class** *adj.*: *a working-class neighborhood*

work·ings /ˈwɚkɪŋz/ *n.* [plural] the way something works: *The article explains **the workings of** government departments.*

work·load /ˈwɚkloʊd/ *n.* [C] the amount of work that a person is expected to do: *a **heavy workload*** (=a lot of work)

work·man /ˈwɚkmən/ *n.* (plural **workmen**) [C] someone who does physical work such as building or repairing things

work·man·like /ˈwɚkmənˌlaɪk/ *adj.* skillfully and carefully done, but often in an uninteresting way: *a workmanlike performance*

work·man·ship /ˈwɚkmənˌʃɪp/ *n.* [U] the skill with which something has been made

work·out /ˈwɚk-aʊt/ *n.* [C] a series of physical exercises that you do to keep your body strong and healthy: *I started my workout with some stretching exercises.* ➔ EXERCISE[2]

work·sheet /ˈwɚkʃit/ *n.* [C] a piece of paper with questions, exercises, etc. for students

work·shop /ˈwɚkʃɑp/ *n.* [C] **1** a room or building where people use tools and machines to make or repair things **2** a meeting at which people try to improve their skills by discussing their experiences and doing practical exercises: *a writing workshop*

work·sta·tion /ˈwɚkˌsteɪʃən/ *n.* [C] the part of an office where you work, including your desk, computer, etc.

world /wɚld/ *n.*

1 the world the PLANET we live on, and all the people, countries, etc. on it (SYN) **Earth**: *the world's longest river* | *Athletes from **all over the world/around the world** compete in the Olympics.* | *The practice is illegal in many **parts of the world**.* ➔ EARTH

2 SOCIETY [singular] our society, and the way that people live and behave: *I want **a better world** for my kids.* | ***In an ideal world**, you and your sister would get along.*

3 AREA OF ACTIVITY/WORK [C usually singular] a particular area of activity or work, and the people who are involved in it: *the **world of** sports* | *the music world*

4 COUNTRIES [singular] a particular group of countries: *the Western world* | ***the industrialized world***

5 DIFFERENCE/CHANGE [C] used to emphasize that a difference or change is very great: *There's a **world of difference** between his public and private life.* | *We're **worlds apart**.*

6 SB'S LIFE [C] the life and experiences of a particular person or group of people: *He lives **in a world of** his **own**.* | *The book explores the writer Hemingway's world.*

7 in the world used in order to emphasize what you are saying: *You're the **best** dad **in the world**.* | ***Why in the world** should I listen to you?*

8 the animal/plant/insect world animals, etc. considered as a group

9 ANOTHER WORLD [C] another PLANET that is not the Earth: *a science fiction novel set on a world light years away from Earth*

10 have the best of both worlds to have the advantages of two completely different things

11 out of this world (informal) very good: *Their ice cream is out of this world!*

12 do sb a world of good (informal) to make someone feel much better: *A vacation would do you a world of good.*

13 be/feel on top of the world (informal) to feel extremely happy **14 mean the world to sb/think the world of sb** if someone or something means the world to you, or if you think the world of him/her, you love or respect him/her very much [ORIGIN: Old English *woruld* "human existence, this world, age"] → **the outside world** *at* OUTSIDE²

ˌworld-ˈclass *adj.* among the best in the world: *a world-class athlete*

ˌworld-ˈfamous *adj.* known about by people all over the world: *a world-famous musician*

world·ly /ˈwɚldli/ *adj.* **1 sb's worldly goods/possessions** everything someone owns **2** knowing a lot about people and society, based on experience: *worldly young men*

ˌworld ˈpower *n.* [C] a powerful country that has a lot of influence in many parts of the world

ˌworld ˈrecord *n.* [C] the fastest time, longest distance, highest level, etc. that anyone has ever achieved anywhere in the world, especially in a sport: *He **set a new world record** for the marathon.* | *the 800-meter **world record holder*** —**world-record** *adj.*

ˌWorld ˈSeries *n.* **the World Series** the last series of baseball games that is played each year in order to decide the best professional team in the U.S. and Canada

world·wide /ˌwɚldˈwaɪd◂/ *adj.* everywhere in the world: *worldwide fame* → EVERYWHERE —**worldwide** *adv.*

ˌWorld Wide ˈWeb (*abbreviation* **WWW**) *n.* **the World Wide Web** IT the system that connects computers around the world together so that people can use and find information on the Internet (SYN) **the Web**

worm¹ /wɚm/ *n.* [C] **1** a small tube-shaped creature with a soft body and no legs that lives in the ground **2** IT a type of computer VIRUS that can make copies of itself and destroy information on computers that are connected to each other [ORIGIN: Old English *wyrm* "snake, worm"] → **a (whole) can of worms** *at* CAN²

worm² *v.* **worm your way into/through etc. sth** to move slowly through or into a small place or a crowd: *My daughter wormed her way into my sleeping bag.*

worn¹ /wɔrn/ *v.* the past participle of WEAR

worn² *adj.* a worn object is old and slightly damaged because it has been used a lot: *worn stone steps*

ˌworn ˈout, worn-out *adj.* **1** very tired because you have been working or playing hard

THESAURUS **tired, exhausted, beat, fatigued** → TIRED

2 too old or damaged to be used: *a pair of worn-out sneakers*

wor·ried /ˈwɚid, ˈwʌrid/ *adj.* unhappy or nervous because you are worrying about someone or something: *We were really **worried about** you!* | *I **got worried** when you didn't call.* | *People are **worried that** they may lose their jobs.*

THESAURUS

anxious – very worried and unable to relax: *She was getting anxious about the children.*
concerned – worried about a social problem, or about someone's health, safety, etc.: *Many scientists are concerned about global warming.*
nervous – worried or frightened about something, and unable to relax: *I get really nervous about exams.*
uneasy – worried because you think something bad might happen: *I felt uneasy leaving the kids with him.*
stressed (out) – so worried that you cannot relax: *I'm getting totally stressed out about work.*
tense – feeling nervous and worried because something bad might happen: *All the guys were tense, clutching their rifles.*
apprehensive (formal) – worried about something that you are going to do, or about the future: *The girls were apprehensive before the game, knowing that Illinois was a tough opponent.*

wor·ry¹ /ˈwɚi, ˈwʌri/ *v.* (**worried, worries**) **1** [I] to think about someone or something a lot, because you feel nervous or unhappy about him, her, or it: *I **worry about** Dave.* | *She **worried that** she would get pregnant.* | *Parents **worry about/over** their children's safety.* **2 don't worry** (spoken) **a)** said when you are trying to make someone feel less anxious: *Don't worry, we're fine.* **b)** used in order to tell someone that s/he does not have to do something: *Don't **worry about** the kids – I'll take them to school.* **3** [T] to make someone feel nervous, unhappy, or upset: ***It worries me that** she hasn't called yet.* [ORIGIN: Old English *wyrgan* "to strangle"]

worry² *n.* (plural **worries**) **1** [C] a problem or bad situation that makes you unhappy because you do not know how to solve it: *financial worries* **2** [U] the feeling of being anxious about something: *Her father was frantic **with worry**.*

wor·ry·ing /ˈwɚiɪŋ, ˈwʌr-/ *adj.* making you feel worried: *a worrying development*

worse¹ /wɚs/ *adj.* [the comparative of "bad"] **1** not as good as, less pleasant than, or more severe than someone or something else: *Traffic always **gets worse** after 4:30.* | *The accident could have been **much/far worse**.* | *Don't go see her; it will only **make matters/things worse**.* **2** more sick than before, or in a condition that is not as good: *Do you feel any worse?* | *His hearing has **gotten worse**.* | *He seemed **none the worse** for his ordeal.* **3 go from bad to worse** to continue getting worse: ***Things went from bad to worse** and finally we got divorced.*

worse² *adv.* **1** in a more severe or serious way than before: *It hurt worse than anything.* **2** not as

W

well, or less successfully: *Margo sings even worse than I do!*

worse³ *n.* [U] something worse: *Critics are wrong to say the* ***changes*** *are* ***for the worse*** (=make things worse).

wors·en /ˈwɚsən/ *v.* [I,T] to become worse, or to make something become worse: *The weather had worsened.*

ˌworse ˈoff *adj.* poorer, less successful, or having fewer advantages than you did before: *There are a lot of people worse off than I am.*

wor·ship /ˈwɚʃɪp/ *v.* (past tense and past participle **worshiped** *or* **worshipped**, present participle **worshiping** *or* **worshipping**) **1** [I,T] to show respect and love for a god, especially by praying in a church, TEMPLE, etc.: *People have worshipped in this church for hundreds of years.* **2** [T] to love and admire someone very much: *She worships her grandpa.* —**worship** *n.* [U]: *a* ***house of worship*** (=a church or building where people can pray) —**worshiper, worshipper** *n.* [C]

THESAURUS admire, respect, look up to sb, idolize, revere → ADMIRE

worst¹ /wɚst/ *adj.* [the superlative of "bad"] worse than anything else of the same type: *It was the worst movie I've ever seen.* | *the worst snowstorm in years*

worst² *n.* **1 the worst** someone or something that is worse than all others: *This is the worst I've ever done on a test.* | *The* ***worst of*** *the storm seemed to be over.* | *What's* ***the worst that can happen****?* **2 at worst** if a thing or situation is as bad as it can be: *At worst, the repairs will cost you around $700.* **3 if (the) worst comes to (the) worst** if the worst possible thing happens: *If worst comes to worst, we'll have to sell the house.*

W

worst³ *adv.* **1** in the worst way, or most severely: *Their city was worst affected by the war.* **2 worst of all** used to say what the worst feature of someone or something is: *He is mean, selfish and, worst of all, lazy.*

worth¹ /wɚθ/ *adj.* **1 be worth sth** to have a particular value, especially in money: *Our house is worth about $350,000.* | *Each question is worth 4 points.* **2 be worth (doing) sth** to be helpful, valuable, interesting, or good for you: *The Getty Museum is definitely worth a visit/worth visiting.* | *It was a lot of hard work, but* ***it was worth it****.* | *Stop crying over him. He's* ***not worth it****.* | ***It is worth*** *pausing to examine this more closely.* | ***It's worth a try*** (=you might get what you want if you try doing something). **3 worth your while** valuable to you because you could gain something you want or need: *It'd be worth your while to talk to someone who works there.*

worth² *n.* **1 ...worth of sth** an amount of something based on how much money you spend, how much time you use, etc.: *20 dollars' worth of gas* | *a year's worth of training* **2** [U] the worth of someone or something is how important or useful he, she, or it is: *children who have a sense of their own worth* | *The new computer system has already* ***proved*** *its* ***worth****.* **3** [U] the worth of something is its value in money: *It is difficult to estimate the current worth of the company.*

worth·less /ˈwɚθlɪs/ *adj.* **1** not valuable, not important, or not useful: *The data was worthless.* **2** a worthless person has no good qualities or useful skills

worth·while /ˌwɚθˈwaɪl◂/ *adj.* if something is worthwhile, it is important or useful, or you gain something from it: *All that work finally seemed worthwhile.*

wor·thy /ˈwɚði/ *adj.* **1** good enough to deserve respect, admiration, or attention: *a worthy opponent* | *worthy achievements* **2 be worthy of sth** (formal) to deserve something: *We need a leader who is worthy of respect.*

would /wəd, əd, d; *strong* wʊd/ *modal verb* **1** used as a past tense of "will" when reporting what someone has said or thought: *Mr. Thomas said it would be okay to go.* | *She told me she wouldn't* (=would not) *come.* **2** used when talking about a possible situation or about a situation that does not exist: *Dad would be really mad if he knew.* | *I'd* (=I would) *help you if I could.* | *If you had listened to me, you wouldn't have gotten in trouble.* **3** used in order to say what you intended to do or expected to happen: *I thought Caroline would be happy, but she got really mad at me.* | *Glenn knew he'd* (=he would) *be tired the next day.* **4** used in order to say that something happened regularly in the past: *In the evenings, we'd* (=we would) *read or play games.* **5 would not/wouldn't** used in order to say that someone refused to do something or that something did not happen even though you tried to make it happen: *Blair would not answer the question.* | *The door wouldn't open.*

SPOKEN PHRASES

6 would like/would love used in order to say that you want something: *I would love to see your new house!* **7 Would you...?** said in order to ask for or offer something politely: *Would you bring me that broom?* | *Would you like a drink?* | ***Would you mind*** *waiting until tomorrow?* **8 I would/I wouldn't** used in order to give advice: *I'd* (=I would) *try to get there early.* | ***I wouldn't*** *go by myself,* ***if I were you****.* **9** used before verbs that express what you think, when you want to make an opinion less definite: *I would guess that he'd bring a friend.* | *I would have thought you'd be tired.* **10 would sooner/would (just) as soon** used when you are saying what you would prefer to happen or be done: *I'd just as soon stay in and watch TV.* | *We would just as soon you didn't tell her.* **11 would rather** said when you prefer doing or having one thing instead of another: ***I would rather*** *take a nice vacation* ***than*** *spend a lot on clothes.* **12** used in order to show you are annoyed about something that someone has done: *You **would go and** tell the teacher!*

'would-be *adj.* **would-be actor/robber etc.** someone who hopes to have a particular job or intends to do a particular thing

would·n't /ˈwʊdnt/ *v.* the short form of "would not": *She wouldn't answer.*

would've /ˈwʊdəv/ *v.* the short form of "would have": *You would've liked it.*

wound¹ /wund/ *n.* [C] **1** an injury, especially a deep cut made in your skin by a knife or bullet: *gunshot wounds | Keston **suffered/received** severe **wounds** in the attack.*

THESAURUS injury, bruise, contusion, cut, laceration, scrape → INJURY

2 damage, problems, or emotional pain caused by something bad happening: *It will take more than an apology to **heal the wounds**.*

wound² *v.* [T] **1** to injure someone, especially with a knife or gun: *Two officers were **badly/seriously/severely wounded**.*

THESAURUS hurt, injure, maim → HURT¹

2 to make someone feel unhappy or upset: *She was **deeply wounded** by the criticism.* —**wounded** *adj.*

wound³ /waʊnd/ *v.* the past tense and past participle of WIND

wound up /ˌwaʊnd ˈʌp/ *adj.* very angry, nervous, or excited: *He **got** so **wound up** he couldn't sleep.*

wove /woʊv/ *v.* the past tense of WEAVE

wo·ven /ˈwoʊvən/ *v.* the past participle of WEAVE

wow¹ /waʊ/ *interjection* said when you think something is impressive or surprising: *Wow! You look great!*

wow² *v.* [T] (informal) to make people admire you a lot: *The movie has wowed the critics.*

wpm /ˌdʌbəlju pi ˈɛm/ **words per minute** used to describe the speed at which someone can write using a KEYBOARD

wran·gle /ˈræŋgəl/ *v.* [I] to argue with someone angrily for a long time: *Congress is still **wrangling over** Social Security.* —**wrangle** *n.* [C]

wran·gler /ˈræŋglɚ/ *n.* [C] (informal) a COWBOY

wrap¹ /ræp/ *v.* (**wrapped**, **wrapping**) [T] **1** to fold cloth, paper, etc. around something, especially in order to cover it: *I haven't **wrapped** her **present** yet. | Here, **wrap** this blanket **around** you.* **2** to hold someone or something by putting your arms, legs, or fingers around him, her, or it: *I **wrapped** my arms **around** my daughter.* → HUG¹ **3 have sb wrapped around your (little) finger** to be able to persuade someone to do whatever you want

wrap sth ↔ **up** *phr. v.* **1** to completely cover something by folding paper, cloth, etc. around it: *My sandwiches are wrapped up in foil.* **2** to finish or complete a job, meeting, etc.: *Investigators hope to wrap up the case soon.* **3 be wrapped up in your children/work etc.** to give so much attention to your children, work, etc. that you do not have time for other things

wrap² *n.* **1** [U] thin clear soft plastic that you wrap around something to protect it or keep it clean: *Cover the food with **plastic wrap**.* **2** [C] a SANDWICH made of a TORTILLA folded around meat, cheese, etc. **3** [C] (old-fashioned) a SHAWL

wrap·per /ˈræpɚ/ *n.* [C] the paper or plastic that covers a piece of food, especially candy: *gum wrappers* → COVER²

'wrapping ˌpaper *n.* [C,U] colored paper used for wrapping presents

wrath /ræθ/ *n.* [U] (formal) very great anger

wreak /rik/ *v.* (literary) **wreak havoc** to cause a lot of damage, problems, or suffering

wreath /riθ/ *n.* [C] a decoration made from flowers and leaves arranged in a circle

wreck¹ /rɛk/ *v.* [T] (informal) **1** to completely spoil something so that it cannot continue in a successful way: *His drinking problem wrecked their marriage.* **2** to damage something, such as a car or building, so badly that it cannot be repaired

wreck² *n.* [C] **1** a bad accident involving cars or airplanes: *Only one person survived the wreck.*

THESAURUS accident, crash, collision, pile-up → ACCIDENT

2 a car, airplane, or ship that is so damaged it cannot be repaired **3** (informal) someone who is very nervous, tired, or unhealthy: *I was a wreck, physically and emotionally.* **4** (informal) something that is very messy and needs a lot of repairs: *The house was a wreck when we bought it.*

wreck·age /ˈrɛkɪdʒ/ *n.* [U] the broken parts of a car, airplane, or building that has been destroyed in an accident: *the wreckage of the plane*

wren /rɛn/ *n.* [C] a very small brown bird that sings

wrench¹ /rɛntʃ/ *v.* [T] **1** to twist and pull something from its position using force: *Prisoners had even **wrenched** doors **off** their hinges.* **2** to injure part of your body by twisting it suddenly: *Sam wrenched his back.*

wrench² *n.* [C] **1** a metal tool with a round end, used for turning NUTS **2 be a wrench** an experience that is a wrench is difficult, and involves strong emotions: *It was a wrench to leave San Diego.*

wrench·ing /ˈrɛntʃɪŋ/ *adj.* extremely difficult to deal with, and involving strong emotions: *a wrenching choice | a **gut-wrenching/heart-wrenching** story* (=one that makes you feel strong emotions)

wrest /rɛst/ *v.* (formal) **wrest sth from sb a)** to take away someone's power or influence **b)** to violently pull something away from someone

wres·tle /ˈrɛsəl/ *v.* **1** [I,T] to fight by holding onto someone and trying to push or pull him/her

W

down **2** [I] to try to deal with a difficult problem or emotion: *Several cities are* ***wrestling with*** *budget deficits.*

wres·tling /ˈrɛslɪŋ/ *n.* [U] a sport in which you try to throw your opponent to the ground and hold him/her there —**wrestler** /ˈrɛslɚ/ *n.* [C]

wretch /rɛtʃ/ *n.* [C] (literary) someone whom you pity

wretch·ed /ˈrɛtʃɪd/ *adj.* extremely unhappy, especially because you are lonely, sick, poor, etc.

wrig·gle /ˈrɪgəl/ *v.* [I,T] to twist from side to side with small quick movements, or to move part of your body this way: *A small child sat wriggling in her lap.* —**wriggle** *n.* [C]

wring /rɪŋ/ *v.* (past tense and past participle **wrung** /rʌŋ/) [T] **1** *also* **wring out** to tightly twist wet clothes, sheets, etc. in order to remove water from them **2** to succeed in getting something from someone, after a lot of effort: *The company is trying to* ***wring*** *more work* ***from*** *its employees.* **3 wring your hands** to rub and press your hands together because you are nervous or upset **4 wring sth's neck** to kill an animal or bird, such as a chicken, by twisting its neck

wring

wring·er /ˈrɪŋɚ/ *n.* **1 go through the wringer** (informal) to have an unpleasant or difficult experience **2** [C] a machine used especially in past times for pressing water out of washed clothes

wrin·kle[1] /ˈrɪŋkəl/ *n.* [C] **1** a line on your face or skin, that you get when you are old **2** a line in cloth, paper, etc. caused by crushing it or accidentally folding it: ***wrinkles in*** *his shirt*

wrinkle[2] *v.* [I,T] to form small folds in something such as clothes or skin, or to be shaped in these folds: *Linen wrinkles easily.* | *Patty wrinkled her nose in disgust.* —**wrinkled** *adj.*: *his wrinkled face*

wrist /rɪst/ *n.* [C] the joint between your hand and your arm: *She had a silver bracelet* ***on her wrist.*** ➔ *see picture at* HAND[1]

wrist·watch /ˈrɪst-wɑtʃ/ *n.* [C] a watch that you wear on your wrist

writ /rɪt/ *n.* [C] LAW a legal document that orders someone to do something or not to do something

write /raɪt/ *v.* (past tense **wrote** /roʊt/, past participle **written** /ˈrɪtˀn/) **1 a)** [I,T] to produce a new book, story, article, etc.: *Bombeck* ***wrote about*** *family life in a funny way.* | *a poem written by Walt Whitman* **b)** [I] to earn money by writing books, plays, articles, etc.: *He* ***writes for*** *"The Chronicle."* **2** [I,T] to write a letter to someone: *Have you* ***written to*** *Mom yet?* | *I wrote her last week.* | *He finally* ***wrote me a letter.*** **3** [I,T] to form words, letters, or numbers with a pen or pencil: *In kindergarten, kids start learning to write.* | *Please write your name on the form.*

THESAURUS

make a note (of sth) – to write down information that you might need later
jot sth down – to write something very quickly
scribble sth – to write something very quickly and in a messy way
take/get sth down – to write down what someone is saying
fill sth out/in – to write information about yourself on a form or other official document
sign sth – to write your **signature** (=name) at the end of a letter, document, etc.
key sth in/type sth in/enter sth – to write or record information on a computer
compose (formal) – to write a letter, poem, etc., thinking very carefully about it as you write it
pen (literary) – to write a letter, note, etc. with a pen
inscribe (formal) – to write words on something hard, usually by cutting them into the surface of something such as a stone or coin ➔ READ

4 IT to record information in the memory of a computer, on a DISK, etc. [ORIGIN: Old English *writan* "to scratch, draw, write"]

write (sb) **back** *phr. v.* to reply to someone's letter by writing a letter and sending it to him/her: *Write back soon!*

write sth ↔ **down** *phr. v.* to write something on a piece of paper: *I wrote down her phone number.*

write in *phr. v.* **1** to write a letter to an organization in order to complain, ask for information, or give an opinion **2 write** sb ↔ **in** to add someone's name to your BALLOT in order to vote for him/her

write off *phr. v.* **1 write** sb ↔ **off** to decide that someone or something is useless, unimportant, or a failure: *Casey had been written off as a "problem student."* **2 write** sth ↔ **off** to decide that a debt will never be paid to you, and officially accept it as a loss

write sth ↔ **out** *phr. v.* to write all the information that is needed for a list, report, check, etc.: *Gina* ***wrote out a check*** *for $820.*

write sth ↔ **up** *phr. v.* to write something such as a report, article, etc., based on notes you made earlier: *Doug is writing up the results of his research.*

ˈwrite-in *n.* [C] POLITICS a vote that you give someone who is not on the BALLOT by writing his/her name on it

ˈwrite-off *n.* [C] an official agreement that someone does not have to pay a debt

writ·er /ˈraɪtɚ/ *n.* [C] someone who writes books, stories, etc. in order to earn money ➔ AUTHOR: *a* ***writer of*** *children's books* | *a speech writer*

ˈwrite-up *n.* [C] an opinion about a new book, play, product, etc., that appears in a magazine or newspaper

W

writhe /raɪð/ v. [I] to twist your body because you are suffering pain: *A soldier was writhing* ***in pain/agony***.

writ·ing /ˈraɪṭɪŋ/ n. **1** [U] words that are written or printed: *She was wearing a T-shirt with Japanese writing on the back.* **2** [U] the particular way someone writes with a pen or pencil (SYN) **handwriting**: *her neat writing* **3 in writing** a promise, agreement, etc. that is in writing has been written down, which proves that it is official **4** [U] the activity or job of writing books, stories, etc.: *creative writing* | *The children were working on a* ***piece of writing***. **5** [U] books, stories, and poems in general: *European writing from the 1930s* **6 writings** [plural] the books, stories, poems, etc. that a particular person writes: *Mark Twain's writings*

writ·ten /ˈrɪtˀn/ v. the past participle of WRITE

wrong¹ /rɔŋ/ adj. **1** not correct, not the one you intended, or not the one you should use (ANT) **right**: *You're wrong – I was there and I know.* | *I bought the wrong size.* | ***I got*** *question 4* ***wrong***. | *You must have dialed the* ***wrong number*** (=not the telephone number you wanted).

THESAURUS

incorrect – used about facts, answers, etc. that are completely wrong
erroneous (formal) – not correct: *The information we received was erroneous.*
inaccurate – used about information, a number, etc. that is not exactly right: *The sales figures were inaccurate.*
misleading – used about a statement or piece of information that makes people believe something that is wrong: *He admitted making a false and misleading statement to Congress.* | *misleading advertising*
false – used about facts that are untrue and wrong: *He used false financial statements to defraud investors.*
fallacious (formal) – containing or based on false ideas: *a fallacious statement*
be mistaken (formal) – used about a person whose opinion about something is wrong: *No, I've never been there. You must be mistaken.*
→ RIGHT¹

2 not morally right or acceptable (SYN) **bad** (ANT) **right**: *He didn't do anything wrong!* | ***What's wrong with*** *making a profit?* → BAD¹ **3** not suitable (ANT) **right**: *It was the wrong time to make such a big decision.* | *I think they're* ***wrong for*** *each other.* **4** used in order to describe a situation where there are problems, or when someone is sick or unhappy: *Ed noticed that* ***there was something wrong***, *as his son's grades started slipping.* | ***What's wrong***, *Jenny?* | *What's* ***wrong with*** *your shoulder?* **5** if something is wrong with a vehicle or machine, it is not working correctly: ***What's wrong with*** *the phone?* **6 be in the wrong place at the wrong time** to become involved in a bad situation without intending to **7 the wrong side of the tracks** (informal) a poor part of a town or a poor part of society: *The story is about a boy growing up* ***on the wrong side of the tracks***. [ORIGIN: 1100—1200 Old Norse *rangr* "not correct or as planned"]

wrong² adv. **1** not done in the correct way (ANT) **right**: *You spelled my name wrong.* **2 go wrong** to develop problems and stop being good, successful, useful, etc.: *Everything went wrong yesterday.* | *Something has* ***gone wrong with*** *the car.* **3 get sth wrong** to make a mistake in the way you remember or understand something: *I got the answer wrong.* | ***Don't get me wrong*** *– I like Benny. I just don't like what he's doing.*

wrong³ n. **1** [U] behavior that is not morally correct: *Parents teach their children the difference between* ***right and wrong***. **2** [C] an action, decision, situation, etc. that is not fair: *We want a chance* ***to right the wrongs*** *they have suffered* (=have a fair solution to an unfair situation). **3 be in the wrong** to make a mistake, or deserve the blame for something **4 sb can do no wrong** used in order to say that someone seems to be perfect

wrong⁴ v. [T] (formal) to treat someone unfairly or judge him/her unfairly: *They believe that they have been wronged.*

wrong·do·ing /ˈrɔŋˌduɪŋ/ n. [C,U] (formal) illegal actions or immoral behavior —**wrongdoer** n. [C]

wrong·ful /ˈrɔŋfəl/ adj. unfair or illegal: *a wrongful death suit* —**wrongfully** adv.

wrong·ly /ˈrɔŋli/ adv. not correctly, or in a way that is unfair or immoral: *He was wrongly accused of fighting.*

wrote /roʊt/ v. the past tense of WRITE

ˌwrought ˈiron n. [U] long thin pieces of iron formed into shapes: *a wrought iron gate*

W

wrung /rʌŋ/ v. the past tense and past participle of WRING

wry /raɪ/ adj. showing in a humorous way that you are not pleased by something: *a wry smile*

WV the written abbreviation of WEST VIRGINIA

WWW n. IT the written abbreviation of the WORLD WIDE WEB

WY the written abbreviation of WYOMING

WYSIWYG /ˈwɪziˌwɪg/ n. [U] **what you see is what you get** IT a way of showing information, a document, etc. on a computer screen in the way that it will look when it is printed

X, x /ɛks/ **1** the 24th letter of the English alphabet **2** the number 10 in the system of ROMAN NUMERALS **3** a mark used to show a kiss: *Love, Grandma XXX*

x /ɛks/ MATH a sign used in mathematics, representing a number or quantity that is not known but can be calculated: *If 3x = 6, then x = 2.*

x-ax·is /ˈɛks ˌæksɪs/ *n.* [C] MATH the line that goes from left to right of a GRAPH ➔ Y-AXIS

X-chro·mo·some /ˈɛks ˌkroʊməˌsoʊm, -ˌzoʊm/ *n.* [C] BIOLOGY a type of CHROMOSOME that exists in pairs in female cells, and with a Y-CHROMOSOME in male cells

x-co·or·di·nate /ˈɛks koʊˌɔrdn-ɪt/ *n.* [C] MATH the position of a point in relation to the x-axis of a GRAPH ➔ Y-COORDINATE

xen·o·pho·bi·a /ˌzɛnəˈfoʊbiə/ *n.* [U] an extreme fear or dislike of people from other countries [ORIGIN: 1900—2000 Greek *xenos* "strange" + *phobos* "fear"] —**xenophobe** /ˈzɛnəˌfoʊb/ *n.* [C]

x-in·ter·cept /ˈɛks ˌɪntɚsɛpt/ *n.* [singular] MATH the point where a line crosses the X-AXIS of a GRAPH ➔ Y-INTERCEPT

XL **extra large** used on clothes to show that a piece of clothing is very big

X·mas /ˈkrɪsməs, ˈɛksməs/ *n.* [C,U] (informal) a written form of the word Christmas

XML *n.* [U] IT **Extensible Markup Language** a computer language that allows you to write documents in a structure that can be read on different computer systems ➔ HTML, SGML

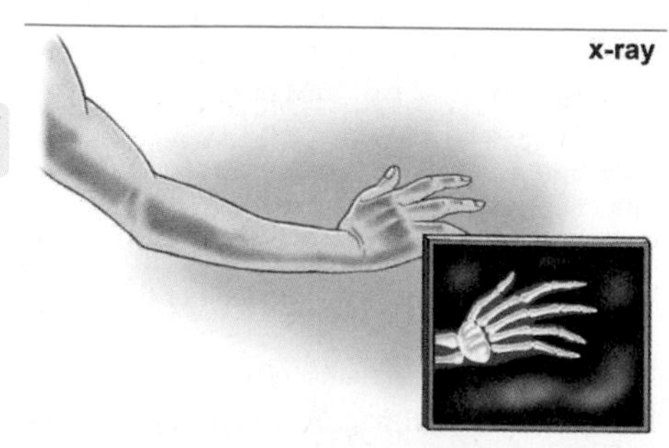

X-ray¹ /ˈɛks reɪ/ *n.* [C] **1** PHYSICS a beam of RADIATION that can go through solid objects and is used for taking photographs of the inside of the body **2** an X-ray photograph taken by doctors in order to search for broken bones, injuries, etc. inside someone's body: *The X-ray showed that her leg was not broken.*

X-ray² *v.* (**X-rayed**, **X-rays**, **X-raying**) [T] to photograph part of someone's body using X-rays

ˈX-ray ˌtelescope *n.* [C] PHYSICS a special TELESCOPE that can see the X-rays sent out from distant objects in space, such as stars or BLACK HOLES

xy·lem /ˈzaɪləm/ *n.* [singular, U] BIOLOGY in a plant stem, the woody structure that carries water up from the roots to the other parts of the plant

xy·lo·phone /ˈzaɪləˌfoʊn/ *n.* [C] a musical instrument with flat metal BARs, that you play by hitting them with a stick

Y, y /waɪ/ the 25th letter of the English alphabet

yacht /yɑt/ *n.* [C] a large expensive boat used for sailing, racing, and traveling for pleasure [ORIGIN: 1500—1600 Early modern Dutch *jaght*, from Middle Low German *jachtschiff* "hunting ship"] ➔ *see picture at* TRANSPORTATION

yak¹ /yæk/ *n.* [C] a long-haired cow from central Asia

yak² *v.* (**yakked**, **yakking**) [I] (informal) to talk a lot about things that are not serious

y'all /yɔl/ *pron.* (spoken) a word meaning "you" or "all of you," used mainly in the southern U.S.: *How are y'all doing?*

yam /yæm/ *n.* [C,U] a SWEET POTATO [ORIGIN: 1500—1600 Portuguese *inhame* and Spanish *ñame*, from a West African language]

yank /yæŋk/ *v.* [I,T] to pull something quickly and with force: *Kendall* ***yanked on*** *the door handle.*

Yan·kee /ˈyæŋki/ *n.* [C] **1** HISTORY someone who fought against the southern states in the American Civil War **2** *also* **Yank** a U.S. citizen – sometimes considered an insult when used by someone who is not American

yap /yæp/ *v.* (**yapped**, **yapping**) [I] if a small dog yaps, it BARKs in an excited way —**yap** *n.* [C]

yard /yɑrd/ *n.* [C] **1** the land around a house, usually covered with grass: *The kids were playing in the* ***front/back yard***. **2** (*written abbreviation* **yd.**) a unit for measuring length, equal to 3 feet or 0.9144 meters: *The beach was only a hundred yards from my back door.* [ORIGIN: (1) Old English *geard* "enclosed area"]

ˈyard sale *n.* [C] a sale of used clothes, furniture, toys, etc. from someone's house that takes place in his/her yard ➔ GARAGE SALE

yard·stick /ˈyɑrdˌstɪk/ *n.* [C] **1** something that you compare another thing with, in order to judge how good or successful it is: *He uses his dad's* *accomplishments as a* ***yardstick*** *against which to* ***measure*** *his own achievements.* **2** a special stick that is exactly one yard long, used for measuring

yar·mul·ke /ˈyɑməkə, ˈyɑrməlkə/ *n.* [C] a small round cap worn by some Jewish men

yarn /yɑrn/ *n.* **1** [U] a thick type of thread used for KNITting **2** [C] (informal) a long story that is not completely true

THESAURUS **story, tale, myth, legend, fable, narrative, anecdote** → STORY

yawn¹ /yɔn/ *v.* [I] **1** to open your mouth wide and breathe deeply, usually because you are tired or bored **2 yawning gap/chasm** a very large difference between two groups, things, or people: *There are yawning gaps in the medical care available to Americans.*

yawn

yawn² *n* **1** [C] an act of yawning **2** [singular] (informal) someone or something that is boring: *The movie was a yawn.*

y-axis /ˈwaɪ ˌæksɪs/ *n.* [C] MATH the line that goes from top to bottom on a GRAPH → X-AXIS

Y-chro·mo·some /ˈwaɪ ˌkrouməˌsoum, -ˌzoum/ *n.* [C] BIOLOGY the CHROMOSOME that makes someone a male instead of a female → X-CHROMOSOME

y-co·or·di·nate /ˈwaɪ kouˌɔrdn-ɪt/ *n.* [C] MATH the position of a point in relation to the y-axis of a GRAPH → X-COORDINATE

yd. the written abbreviation of YARD

yeah /yɛə/ *adv.* (spoken, informal) yes

year /yɪr/ *n.* [C] **1** *also* **calendar year** (*written abbreviation* **yr.**) a period of time equal to 365 or 366 days, divided into 12 months, beginning on January 1 and ending on December 31: *Where are you spending Christmas* ***this year****? | at the start of school* ***last/next year*** *| The museum has 100,000 visitors a year.* **2** any period of time equal to about 365 days or 12 months: *Jenny is five* ***years old****. | My passport expires* ***in a year****. | I met him a* ***year ago****. | The* ***tax year*** *begins in April.* **3 years** [plural] (informal) many years: *It's been years since I've ridden a bike. | I haven't seen her* ***in/for years****.* **4** a particular period of time in someone's life or in history: *the war years* **5 school/academic year** the period of time during a year when students are in school, college, etc.: *the 2004–05 academic year* **6 all year round** during the whole year: *It's sunny there all year round.*

year·book /ˈyɪrbʊk/ *n.* [C] a book printed once a year by a school or college, about its students, sports events, clubs, etc. during that year

year·ling /ˈyɪrlɪŋ/ *n.* [C] a young animal, especially a horse, between the ages of one and two

year·ly /ˈyɪrli/ *adj., adv.* happening or done every year or once a year: *Our yearly trip to Florida was a lot of fun.*

THESAURUS **hourly, daily, weekly, monthly** → REGULAR¹

yearn /yɚn/ *v.* [I] (literary) to want something very much, especially something extremely difficult to get: *They* ***yearned to*** *go home. | She* ***yearned for*** *a child.* —**yearning** *n.* [U]

yeast /yist/ *n.* [U] a substance used for making bread rise and for producing alcohol in beer or wine

yell /yɛl/ *v* [I,T] to shout or say something very loudly because you are angry, excited, or frightened: *Don't* ***yell at*** *me! | Someone* ***yelled out*** *the score. | She yelled, "Come back here!"* —**yell** *n.* [C]

THESAURUS **shout, scream, cry out, bellow, holler** → SHOUT¹

yel·low¹ /ˈyɛlou/ *adj.* having the same color as LEMONS or butter: *yellow flowers* [ORIGIN: Old English *geolu*]

yellow² *n.* [U] a yellow color —**yellow** *v.* [I,T]: *The pages had yellowed with age.*

ˌYellow ˈPages *n.* (trademark) **the Yellow Pages** a book that lists the telephone numbers and addresses of stores, restaurants, and businesses in a particular area

yelp /yɛlp/ *v.* [I] to make a short high cry like a dog makes, because of pain, excitement, etc. —**yelp** *n.* [C]

yen /yɛn/ *n.* (plural **yen**) **1** [C] a standard unit of money used in Japan **2** [singular] a strong desire: *a* ***yen to*** *travel*

yeo·man /ˈyoumən/ *n.* (plural **yeomen** /-mən/) [C] **1** an officer in the U.S. Navy who often works in an office **2** HISTORY a farmer in Britain and Canada in the past who owned and worked on his own land

yep /yɛp/ *adv.* (spoken, informal) yes

yes /yɛs/ *adv.* (spoken) **1** said in order to give a positive reply to a question, offer, or request: *"Is it real gold?" "Yes." | "Nancy, did you want some pie?" "Yes, please." | I'm sure Dad will* ***say yes.*** **2** said in order to agree with a statement: *"It's such a nice day." "Yes, it is."* **3** said in order to disagree with a negative statement, to say that the opposite is true: *"John doesn't like me anymore." "Yes, he does!" | "There's no bread." "Yes, there is, in the freezer."* **4** said when you have noticed that someone wants your attention: *"Linda!" "Yes?" | Yes, sir, how may I help you?* **5** said when you are very happy or excited: *Yes! I got the job!*

yes·ter·day¹ /ˈyɛstɚdi, -deɪ/ *adv.* on or during the day before today: *Where did you go yesterday? | He arrived yesterday morning.*

yesterday² *n.* [U] **1** the day before today: *Did you go to yesterday's meeting?* **2** the recent past:

The problems of yesterday look easy compared with those of today. [ORIGIN: Old English *giestran dæg*, from *giestran* "yesterday" + *dæg* "day"]

yet¹ /yɛt/ *adv.* **1** used in negative statements and questions to mean "at the present time" or "already": *I don't think she's awake yet.* | *Have you eaten yet?* | *"Is Lori here?" "**Not yet.**"* **2** at some time in the future: *She may change her mind yet.* | *We **have yet to** hear from them* (=we still have not heard). **3** in addition to what you have already gotten, done, etc.: *He's made **yet another** mistake.* | *I'm sorry to ask for help **yet again*** (=one more time after many others). **4 better/worse yet** used in order to emphasize that something is even better or worse than the thing mentioned before: *Respond by letter, or better yet, a telephone call.* **5** in spite of something (SYN) **but**: *a quiet yet powerful leader*

yet² *conjunction* used in order to introduce a statement that is surprising: *an inexpensive yet effective solution* | *We sent thousands of forms, yet fewer than 50 were returned.*

yew /yu/ *n.* [C,U] a tree or bush with leaves that look like flat needles, or the heavy wood of this tree

Yid·dish /ˈyɪdɪʃ/ *n.* [U] a language similar to German, used in many places by Jewish people —**Yiddish** *adj.*

yield¹ /yild/ *v.* **1** [T] to produce something: *One study has yielded some interesting results.* **2** [I,T] to allow yourself to be forced or persuaded to do something: *The government will never **yield to** terrorism.*

THESAURUS **surrender, give in, concede, submit** → SURRENDER

3 [I] to allow the traffic from a bigger road to go first **4** [I] to move, bend, or break because of physical pressure

yield² *n.* [C] **1** the amount of something that is produced, especially crops **2** ECONOMICS the amount of profit that you receive from a STOCK or BOND

Y

y-in·ter·cept /ˈwaɪ ˌɪntɚsɛpt/ *n.* [singular] MATH the point where a line crosses the Y-AXIS of a GRAPH → X-INTERCEPT

yip·pee /ˈyɪpi/ *interjection* said when you are very happy or excited about something

YMCA *n.* **Young Men's Christian Association** an organization that provides places to stay, sports activities, and training for young men, especially in large cities → YWCA

yo /yoʊ/ *interjection* (slang) said in order to greet someone or get his/her attention, or as a reply when someone says your name

yo·del /ˈyoʊdl/ *v.* [I] to sing while changing your natural voice to a very high voice and back again many times

yo·ga /ˈyoʊgə/ *n.* [U] a system of exercises in which you control your body and mind [ORIGIN: 1700—1800 Sanskrit "union"]

yo·gurt /ˈyoʊgɚt/ *n.* [U] a smooth thick liquid food that tastes slightly sour, made from milk: *a bowl of yogurt* [ORIGIN: 1600—1700 Turkish]

yoke /yoʊk/ *n.* [C] a wooden BAR used for joining together two animals, especially cattle, in order to pull heavy loads —**yoke** *v.* [T]

yo·kel /ˈyoʊkəl/ *n.* [C] (humorous) someone from the country who has not experienced living in modern society

yolk /yoʊk/ *n.* [C,U] the yellow part in the center of an egg [ORIGIN: Old English *geoloca*, from *geolu* "yellow"]

yon·der /ˈyɑndɚ/ *adv., determiner* (literary) over there

you /yə, yʊ; *strong* yu/ *pron.* [used as a subject or object] **1** the person or people someone is speaking or writing to: *You must be hungry.* | *Do you want a drink?* | *I can't hear you.* **2** people in general → ONE: *You can't trust anybody these days.* | *You never know what Jim will say.* **3** used with nouns or phrases when you are talking to or calling someone: *You jerk!* | *You kids, be quiet!* **4 you all** (spoken) used instead of "you" when speaking to two or more people: *What do you all want to do tonight?*

you'd /yəd, yʊd; *strong* yud/ **1** the short form of "you would": *I didn't think you'd mind.* **2** the short form of "you had": *You'd better do what he says.*

you'll /yəl, yʊl; *strong* yul/ the short form of "you will": *You'll have to speak louder.*

young¹ /yʌŋ/ *adj.* **1** at an early stage of life or development (ANT) **old**: *young children* | *You're too young to get married.* | *a young country*

THESAURUS

A **small/little** child is a very young child.
Someone who is **youthful** seems or is young.
Someone who is **immature** behaves in a way that is not sensible because it is typical of the behavior of someone much younger.
Someone who is **green** is young and lacks experience.
Someone who is **underage** is too young to legally buy alcohol, drive a car, etc.
If someone is at a **tender age**, s/he is very young and easily influenced. → OLD, CHILD

2 seeming or looking younger than you are (SYN) **youthful**: *You too can have healthier, younger-looking skin.* **3** designed or intended for young people: *Is this dress too young for me?*

young² *n.* **1 the young** young people considered as a group **2** [plural] young animals: *a turtle and her young*

young·ster /ˈyʌŋstɚ/ *n.* [C] a young person

THESAURUS **child, kid, teenager, adolescent, minor, juvenile** → CHILD

your /yɚ; *strong* yʊr, yɔr/ *possessive adj.* **1** belonging or relating to the person or people someone is speaking to: *Is that your mother? | It's not your fault.* **2** belonging or relating to any person: *If you are facing north, east is on your right.*

you're /yɚ; *strong* yʊr, yɔr/ the short form of "you are": *You're bothering me.*

yours /yʊrz, yɔrz/ *pron.* **1** the thing or things belonging or relating to the person or people someone is speaking to: *Yours is over there. | That bag is yours, isn't it? | Is he a friend **of yours**?* **2 yours (truly/sincerely)** *also* **sincerely yours** a phrase you write before you sign your name at the end of a letter **3 yours truly** (humorous) used instead of "I": *Yes, yours truly finally quit smoking.*

your·self /yɚˈsɛlf/ *pron.* (plural **yourselves** /yɚˈsɛlvz/) **1** used when talking to someone to show that s/he is affected by his/her own action: *Don't hurt yourself! | Make yourself a cup of coffee.* **2** used in order to emphasize "you": *Why don't you do it yourself?* **3 (all) by yourself a)** without help: *Do you think you can move the sofa by yourself?* **b)** alone: *You're going to Ecuador by yourself?* **4 (all) to yourself** for your own use: *You'll have the house all to yourself this weekend.*

youth /yuθ/ *n.* (plural **youths** /yuðz, yuθs/) **1** [U] the period of time when someone is young, or the quality of being young: *Despite his youth, he was traveling alone. | She had been beautiful **in** her **youth**.* **2** [U] young people in general: *the youth of the 1960s | a church youth group | youth culture* **3** [C] a boy or young man, especially a TEENAGER: *A youth was arrested for stealing.*

THESAURUS **man, boy, male** → MAN¹

youth·ful /ˈyuθfəl/ *adj.* typical of young people, or seeming young: *youthful energy | He was youthful in appearance.* → YOUNG¹

ˈyouth ˌhostel *n.* [C] a place where people, especially young people who are traveling, can stay very cheaply for a short time

you've /yəv, yʊv; *strong* yuv/ the short form of "you have": *Okay, you've persuaded me.*

yo-yo /ˈyoʊyoʊ/ *n.* (plural **yo-yos**) [C] a small toy that is made of two circular parts joined together that go up and down a string as you lift your hand up and down

yr. the written abbreviation of YEAR

yuc·ca /ˈyʌkə/ *n.* [C] a desert plant with long pointed leaves and a thick stem → *see picture on page A23*

yuck /yʌk/ *interjection* said when you think something is unpleasant: *Yuck! This tastes horrible!* —**yucky** *adj.*

Yule /yul/ *n.* [C] (literary) Christmas

Yule·tide /ˈyultaɪd/ *n.* [U] (literary) the period from just before Christmas until just after it

yum /yʌm/ *interjection* said in order to emphasize that you think something tastes good: *Yum! Apple pie!*

yum·my /ˈyʌmi/ *adj.* (informal) food that is yummy tastes very good

yup·pie /ˈyʌpi/ *n.* [C] (informal) a young person who only seems interested in having a professional job, earning a lot of money, and buying expensive things [ORIGIN: 1900—2000 *young urban professional*]

YWCA *n.* **Young Women's Christian Association** an organization that provides places to stay, special help, and training for young women, especially in large cities → YMCA

Z, z /zi/ the 26th and last letter of the English alphabet

Z /zi/ *n.* **catch/get some Zs** (spoken) to sleep

za·ny /ˈzeɪni/ *adj.* crazy or unusual in a way that is amusing and exciting: *a zany new TV comedy*

zap /zæp/ *v.* (**zapped**, **zapping**) [T] (informal) **1** to kill, destroy, or attack something extremely quickly, especially by using electricity or a LASER beam **2** to cook something quickly in a MICROWAVE **3** to send information quickly from one computer to another

zeal /zil/ *n.* [U] eagerness to do something, especially to achieve a particular religious or political aim: *The Republicans are known for their **zeal to** cut taxes.*

zeal·ous /ˈzɛləs/ *adj.* extremely interested in and excited about something that you believe in very strongly, and behaving in a way that shows this: *a zealous environmental activist*

THESAURUS **enthusiastic, passionate, ardent, fanatical** → ENTHUSIASTIC

—**zealously** *adv.* —**zealousness** *n.* [U]

ze·bra /ˈzibrə/ *n.* [C] a wild African animal like a horse, that has black and white bands on its body [ORIGIN: 1600—1700 Italian "wild donkey"]

Zen /zɛn/ *also* ˌ**Zen 'Buddhism** *n.* [U] a type of Buddhism from Japan that emphasizes MEDITATION

ze·nith /'zinɪθ/ *n.* [C usually singular] **1** the most successful point in the development of something: *This album shows Simon **at the zenith of** his powers.* **2** the highest point that the Sun or a star reaches in the sky

zeph·yr /'zɛfɚ/ *n.* [C] (literary) a soft gentle wind

ze·ro¹ /'zɪroʊ, 'ziroʊ/ *number* **1** the number 0

THESAURUS

nothing: *The score was twenty-two to nothing.*
O /oʊ/ – used to say the number zero like the letter O: *Their zip code is O two one two five.* (=02125).
zip (informal): *We were behind 3-zip.*
nil (formal) – nothing or zero: *His chances of winning were practically nil.*

2 SCIENCE the point between – and + on a scale for measuring something, especially temperature. In the Celsius system of measuring temperature, 0 is the point at which water freezes: *It was 20° below zero.*

zero² *v.* (**zeroed**, **zeroes**, **zeroing**)
zero in on sb/sth *phr. v.* to aim at one thing, or give special attention to one person or thing: *War planes zeroed in on a target.*

zest /zɛst/ *n.* [U] **1** a feeling of eagerness, excitement, and enjoyment: *a **zest for** life* **2** the outer skin of an orange or LEMON, used in cooking

zig·gu·rat /'zɪgəræt/ *n.* [C] HISTORY a tall structure with a TEMPLE (=place where people pray to God) on the top, built in ancient Mesopotamia. It has a RECTANGULAR base and many levels, each of which is smaller than the one below.

zig·zag¹ /'zɪgzæg/ *n.* [C] a line that looks like a row of z's joined together

zigzag² *v.* (**zigzagged**, **zigzagging**) [I] to move forward in sharp angles, first to the left and then to the right, etc.: *The path zigzags across the mountain.*

zilch /zɪltʃ/ *n.* [U] (informal) nothing at all: *I've looked for jobs everywhere, but come up with zilch.*

zil·lion /'zɪlyən/ *number* (informal) an extremely large number or amount: *She asked a zillion questions.*

zinc /zɪŋk/ *n.* [U] CHEMISTRY (*symbol* **Zn**) a white metal that is an ELEMENT. Zinc is used to make BRASS and to cover and protect objects made of iron.

zip¹ /zɪp/ *v.* (**zipped**, **zipping**) **1** [T] *also* **zip up** to close or fasten something using a ZIPPER: *Zip up your coat.*

THESAURUS **fasten, secure, join, glue, tape, staple, clip, tie, button (up)** → FASTEN

2 [I] to go somewhere or do something very quickly: *A few cars zipped past us.*

zip² *n.* (spoken) **1** [C usually singular] a short form of ZIP CODE **2** [U] nothing at all, or zero: *We beat them 10-zip.*

THESAURUS **zero, nothing, O, nil** → ZERO¹

'**zip code** *n.* [C] a number that you put below the address on an envelope to help the post office deliver the mail more quickly [ORIGIN: 1900—2000 *zone improvement plan*]

'**zip file** *n.* [C] IT a computer FILE that has been made smaller so that it is easy to store and move

zip·per /'zɪpɚ/ *n.* [C] an object for fastening clothes, bags, etc., with two lines of small pieces of metal or plastic that slide together

zipper

zit /zɪt/ *n.* [C] (slang) a PIMPLE

zo·di·ac /'zoʊdiˌæk/ *n.* **the zodiac** an imaginary circle in space that the Sun, Moon, and PLANETS follow as a path, which some people believe influences people's lives [ORIGIN: 1300—1400 French *zodiaque*, from Greek *zoidiakos* "animal figures"]

zom·bie /'zɑmbi/ *n.* [C] **1** (informal) someone who moves very slowly and cannot think clearly because s/he is very tired **2** a dead body that is made to move, walk, etc. by magic [ORIGIN: 1800—1900 Kimbundu (an African language) *nzumbi* "spirit of a dead person"]

zone /zoʊn/ *n.* [C] part of an area that has a specific purpose or has a special quality: *a no-parking zone* | *the **war/battle/combat zone***
→ TIME ZONE

THESAURUS **area, region, territory, district** → AREA

zon·ing /'zoʊnɪŋ/ *n.* [U] a system of choosing areas to be used for particular purposes, such as building houses —**zone** *v.* [T]

zoo /zu/ *n.* (plural **zoos**) [C] a place where many different types of animals are kept so that people can see them: *How about taking the children to the zoo?*

zo·ol·o·gy /zoʊ'ɑlədʒi/ *n.* [U] BIOLOGY the scientific study of animals and their behavior —**zoologist** *n.* [C] —**zoological** /ˌzoʊə'lɑdʒɪkəl/ *adj.*

zoom /zum/ *v.* [I] (informal) **1** to go somewhere or do something very quickly: *A red car zoomed past.* **2** to increase suddenly and quickly: *Inflation zoomed 123%.* [ORIGIN: 1800—1900 From the sound]
zoom in/out *phr. v.* if a camera zooms in or out, it makes the object you are taking a photograph of seem closer or farther away

Z

'zoom ˌlens *n.* [C] a camera LENS that moves in order to make the objects you are taking a photograph of seem closer and larger

zo·o·plank·ton /ˌzoʊə'plæŋktən/ *n.* [U] BIOLOGY the very small animals floating in water that are part of PLANKTON

zuc·chi·ni /zu'kini/ *n.* [C,U] a long smooth dark green vegetable [ORIGIN: 1900—2000 Italian *zucca* "gourd"] → *see picture at* VEGETABLE

zy·gote /'zaɪgoʊt/ *n.* [C] BIOLOGY a cell that is formed when a female's egg cell is FERTILIZED [ORIGIN: 1800—1900 Greek *zygotos* "joined together"]

Zzz used in writing to represent sleep

Z

Irregular Verbs

This chart shows the verbs that have irregular forms for the **Past Tense**, **Past Participle**, or **Present Participle**. When a verb has more than one form that is used, the most common form is given first.

Verb	Past Tense	Past Participle	Present Participle
arise	arose	arisen	arising
awake	awoke	awoken	awaking
be	*see* **be**		
bear	bore	borne	bearing
beat	beat	beaten	beating
become	became	become	becoming
begin	began	begun	beginning
behold	beheld	beheld	beholding
bend	bent	bent	bending
bet	bet	bet	betting
bid[2]	bid	bid	bidding
bid[3]	bid	bid *or* bidden	bidding
bind	bound	bound	binding
bite	bit	bitten	biting
bleed	bled	bled	bleeding
blow	blew	blown	blowing
break	broke	broken	breaking
breed	bred	bred	breeding
bring	brought	brought	bringing
broadcast	broadcast *or* broadcasted	broadcast *or* broadcasted	broadcasting
build	built	built	building
burn	burned *or* burnt	burned *or* burnt	burning
burst	burst	burst	bursting
buy	bought	bought	buying
cast	cast	cast	casting
catch	caught	caught	catching
choose	chose	chosen	choosing
cling	clung	clung	clinging
come	came	come	coming
cost	cost	cost	costing
creep	crept	crept	creeping
cut	cut	cut	cutting
deal	dealt	dealt	dealing
dig	dug	dug	digging
dive	dived *or* dove	dived	diving
do	*see* **do**		
draw	drew	drawn	drawing
dream	dreamed *or* dreamt	dreamed *or* dreamt	dreaming
drink	drank	drunk	drinking
drive	drove	driven	driving
dwell	dwelled *or* dwelt	dwelled *or* dwelt	dwelling
eat	ate	eaten	eating

Verb	Past Tense	Past Participle	Present Participle
fall	fell	fallen	falling
feed	fed	fed	feeding
feel	felt	felt	feeling
fight	fought	fought	fighting
find	found	found	finding
fit	fit or fitted	fit or fitted	fitting
flee	fled	fled	fleeing
fling	flung	flung	flinging
fly	flew	flown	flying
forbid	forbid *or* forbade	forbidden	forbidding
forecast	forecast *or* forecasted	forecast *or* forecasted	forecasting
foresee	foresaw	foreseen	foreseeing
forget	forgot	forgotten	forgetting
forgive	forgave	forgiven	forgiving
freeze	froze	frozen	freezing
get	got	gotten	getting
give	gave	given	giving
go	went	gone	going
grind	ground	ground	grinding
grow	grew	grown	growing
hang	hung	hung	hanging
have	*see* **have**		
hear	heard	heard	hearing
hide	hid	hidden	hiding
hit	hit	hit	hitting
hold	held	held	holding
hurt	hurt	hurt	hurting
keep	kept	kept	keeping
kneel	knelt *or* kneeled	knelt *or* kneeled	kneeling
knit	knit *or* knitted	knit *or* knitted	knitting
know	knew	known	knowing
lay	laid	laid	laying
lead	led	led	leading
leap	leaped *or* leapt	leaped *or* leapt	leaping
leave	left	left	leaving
lend	lent	lent	lending
let	let	let	letting
lie[1]	lay	lain	lying
lie[2]	lied	lied	lying
light	lit *or* lighted	lit *or* lighted	lighting
lose	lost	lost	losing
make	made	made	making
mean	meant	meant	meaning
meet	met	met	meeting
mislead	misled	misled	misleading
mistake	mistook	mistaken	mistaking
misunderstand	misunderstood	misunderstood	misunderstanding
outbid	outbid	outbid	outbidding

Verb	Past Tense	Past Participle	Present Participle
outdo	outdid	outdone	outdoing
overcome	overcame	overcome	overcoming
overdo	overdid	overdone	overdoing
overhang	overhung	overhung	overhanging
overhear	overheard	overheard	overhearing
override	overrode	overridden	overriding
overrun	overran	overrun	overrunning
oversee	oversaw	overseen	overseeing
overtake	overtook	overtaken	overtaking
overthrow	overthrew	overthrown	overthrowing
pay	paid	paid	paying
prove	proved	proved *or* proven	proving
put	put	put	putting
read	read	read	reading
rebuild	rebuilt	rebuilt	rebuilding
redo	redid	redone	redoing
repay	repaid	repaid	repaying
rewrite	rewrote	rewritten	rewriting
rid	rid	rid	ridding
ride	rode	ridden	riding
ring[2]	rang	rung	ringing
rise	rose	risen	rising
run	ran	run	running
saw	sawed	sawed *or* sawn	sawing
say	said	said	saying
see	saw	seen	seeing
seek	sought	sought	seeking
sell	sold	sold	selling
send	sent	sent	sending
set	set	set	setting
sew	sewed	sewn *or* sewed	sewing
shake	shook	shaken	shaking
shed	shed	shed	shedding
shine	shone	shone	shining
shoot	shot	shot	shooting
show	showed	shown	showing
shrink	shrank	shrunk	shrinking
shut	shut	shut	shutting
sing	sang	sung	singing
sink	sank *or* sunk	sunk	sinking
sit	sat	sat	sitting
slay	slew	slain	slaying
sleep	slept	slept	sleeping
slide	slid	slid	sliding
sling	slung	slung	slinging
slit	slit	slit	slitting
sow	sowed	sown *or* sowed	sowing
speak	spoke	spoken	speaking
speed	sped *or* speeded	sped *or* speeded	speeding
spend	spent	spent	spending
spin	spun	spun	spinning

Verb	Past Tense	Past Participle	Present Participle
spit	spit *or* spat	spit *or* spat	spitting
split	split	split	splitting
spread	spread	spread	spreading
spring	sprang	sprung	springing
stand	stood	stood	standing
steal	stole	stolen	stealing
stick	stuck	stuck	sticking
sting	stung	stung	stinging
stink	stank *or* stunk	stunk	stinking
strew	strewed	strewn *or* strewed	strewing
stride	strode	stridden	striding
strike	struck	struck *or* stricken	striking
string	strung	strung	stringing
strive	strove *or* strived	striven *or* strived	striving
swear	swore	sworn	swearing
sweep	swept	swept	sweeping
swell	swelled	swollen	swelling
swim	swam	swum	swimming
swing	swung	swung	swinging
take	took	taken	taking
teach	taught	taught	teaching
tear	tore	torn	tearing
tell	told	told	telling
think	thought	thought	thinking
throw	threw	thrown	throwing
thrust	thrust	thrust	thrusting
tread	trod	trodden	treading
undergo	underwent	undergone	undergoing
understand	understood	understood	understanding
undertake	undertook	undertaken	undertaking
undo	undid	undone	undoing
unwind	unwound	unwound	unwinding
uphold	upheld	upheld	upholding
upset	upset	upset	upsetting
wake	woke	woken	waking
wear	wore	worn	wearing
weave	wove	woven	weaving
wed	wedded *or* wed	wedded *or* wed	wedding
weep	wept	wept	weeping
wet	wet *or* wetted	wet *or* wetted	wetting
win	won	won	winning
wind	wound	wound	winding
withdraw	withdrew	withdrawn	withdrawing
withhold	withheld	withheld	withholding
withstand	withstood	withstood	withstanding
wring	wrung	wrung	wringing
write	wrote	written	writing

Geographical Names

Name		Adjective and name of a person from this place	
Afghanistan	/æf'gænəˌstæn/	Afghan *or* Afghanistani	/'æfgæn/ /æfˌgænə'stæni/
Africa	/'æfrɪkə/	African	/'æfrɪkən/
Albania	/æl'beɪniə, ɔl-/	Albanian	/æl'beɪniən, ɔl-/
Algeria	/æl'dʒɪriə/	Algerian	/æl'dʒɪriən/
America (=the U.S.)	/ə'mɛrɪkə/	American	/ə'mɛrɪkən/
North America	/nɔrθ ə'mɛrɪkə/	North American	/nɔrθ ə'mɛrɪkən/
South America	/saʊθ ə'mɛrɪkə/	South American	/saʊθ ə'mɛrɪkən/
Andorra	/æn'dɔrə/	Andorran	/æn'dɔrən/
Angola	/æŋ'golə/	Angolan	/æŋ'goʊlən/
Antarctic	/æn'tɑrktɪk/	*adj:* Antarctic	/æn'tɑrktɪk/
Antigua and Barbuda	/æn'tigə, -gwə and bɑr'budə/	Antiguan *or* Barbudan	/æn'tigən, -gwən/ /bɑr'budən/
Arctic	/'ɑrktɪk/	*adj:* Arctic	/'ɑrktɪk/
Argentina	/ˌɑrdʒən'tinə/	*adj:* Argentinian *person:* Argentinian *or* Argentine	/ˌɑrdʒən'tɪniən/ /'ɑːrdʒəntiːn/
Armenia	/ɑr'miniə/	Armenian	/ɑr'miniən/
Asia	/'eɪʒə/	Asian	/'eɪʒən/
Atlantic	/ət'læntɪk/	*adj:* Atlantic	/ət'læntɪk/
Australia	/ɔ'streɪlyə, ɑ-/	Australian	/ɔ'streɪlyən, ˌɑ-/
Austria	/'ɔstriə, 'ɑ-/	Austrian	/'ɔstriən, 'ɑ-/
Azerbaijan	/'æzɚbaɪ'dʒɑn, ˌɑ-/	Azerbaijani	/ˌæzɚbaɪ'dʒɑni◂, ˌɑ-/
Bahamas, the	/bə'hɑməz/	Bahamian	/bə'heɪmiən/
Bahrain	/bɑ'reɪn/	Bahraini	/bɑ'reɪni/
Baltic	/'bɔltɪk/	*adj:* Baltic	/'bɔltɪk/
Bangladesh	/ˌbɑŋglə'dɛʃ, ˌbæŋ-/	Bangladeshi	/ˌbɑŋglə'dɛʃi, ˌbæŋ-/
Barbados	/bɑr'beɪdoʊs/	Barbadian	/bɑr'beɪdiən/
Belarus (Belorussia)	/ˌbɛlə'rus/ /ˌbɛloʊ'rʌʃə/	Belorussian	/ˌbɛloʊ'rʌʃən/
Belgium	/'bɛldʒəm/	Belgian	/'bɛldʒən/
Belize	/bə'liz/	Belizean	/bə'liziən/
Benin	/bə'nin/	Beninese	/ˌbɛnɪ'niz◂/
Bermuda	/bɚ'myudə/	Bermudan	/bɚ'myudn/
Bhutan	/bu'tɑn, -'tæn/	Bhutanese	/ˌbutn'iz◂/
Bolivia	/bə'lɪviə/	Bolivian	/bə'lɪviən/
Bosnia and Herzegovina	/ˌbɑzniə ənd ˌhɛrtsəgə'vinə/	Bosnian Herzegovinian	/'bɑzniən/ /ˌhɜrtsəgəʊ'viniən/
Botswana	/bɑt'swɑnə/	*adj:* Botswanan *person:* Motswana *people:* the Batswana	/bɑt'swɑnən/ /mɑt'swɑnə/ /bæt'swɑnə/
Brazil	/brə'zɪl/	Brazilian	/brə'zɪliən/
Brunei	/bru'naɪ/	Bruneian	/bru'naɪən/
Bulgaria	/bʌl'gɛriə/	Bulgarian	/bʌl'gɛriən/
Burkina Faso	/bɚˌkinə 'fɑsoʊ/	Burkina *or* Burkinabe	/ˌbɚkinæ'beɪ/
Burma (*former name of* Myanmar)	/'bɚmə/	Burmese	/bɚ'miz/
Burundi	/bʊ'rundi/	Burundian	/bʊ'rundiən/
Cambodia	/kæm'boʊdiə/	Cambodian	/kæm'boʊdiən/

Name		Adjective and name of a person from this place	
Cameroon	/ˌkæməˈrun/	Cameroonian	/ˌkæmˈruniən◂/
Canada	/ˈkænədə/	Canadian	/kəˈneɪdiən/
Cape Verde	/keɪp ˈvɚd/	Cape Verdean	/keɪp ˈvɚdiən/
Caribbean	/kəˈrɪbiən, ˌkærəˈbiən◂/	*adj:* Caribbean	
Cayman Islands	/ˈkeɪmən ˌaɪləndz/	*adj:* Cayman Island	/ˌkeɪmən ˈaɪlənd/
		person: Cayman Islander	/ˌkeɪmən ˈaɪləndɚ/
Central African Republic	/ˌsɛntrəl ˌæfrɪkən rɪˈpʌblɪk/	Central African	/ˌsɛntrəl ˈæfrɪkən/
Chad	/tʃæd/	Chadian	/ˈtʃædiən/
Chile	/ˈtʃɪli/	Chilean	/ˈtʃɪliən/
China	/ˈtʃaɪnə/	Chinese	/ˌtʃaɪˈniz◂/
Colombia	/kəˈlʌmbiə/	Colombian	/kəˈlʌmbiən/
Comoro Islands, the	/ˈkɑməˌroʊ aɪləndz/	Comoran	/ˈkɑmərən/
Congo, the Democratic Republic of	/ˌdɛməkræṭɪk rɪˌpʌblɪk əv ˈkɑŋgoʊ/	Congolese	/ˌkɑŋgəˈliz/
Congo, Republic of	/rɪˌpʌblɪk əv ˈkɑŋgoʊ/	Congolese	/ˌkɑŋgəˈliz◂/
Costa Rica	/ˌkoʊstə ˈrikə/	Costa Rican	/ˌkoʊstə ˈrikən◂/
Croatia	/kroʊˈeɪʃə/	Croatian	/kroʊˈeɪʃən/
Cuba	/ˈkyubə/	Cuban	/ˈkyubən/
Cyprus	/ˈsaɪprəs/	Cypriot	/ˈsɪpriət/
Czech Republic, the	/ˌtʃɛk rɪˈpʌblɪk/	Czech	/tʃɛk/
Denmark	/ˈdɛnmɑrk/	*adj:* Danish	/ˈdeɪnɪʃ/
		person: Dane	/deɪn/
Djibouti	/dʒɪˈbuṭi/	Djiboutian	/dʒɪˈbuṭiən/
Dominica	/ˌdɑməˈnikə/	Dominican	/ˌdɑməˈnikən◂/
Dominican Republic, the	/dəˌmɪnɪkən rɪˈpʌblɪk/	Dominican	/dəˈmɪnɪkən/
East Timor	/ˌist ˈtimɔr/	Timorese	/ˌtimɔˈriz◂/
Ecuador	/ˈɛkwədɔr/	Ecuadorian	/ˌɛkwəˈdɔriən◂/
Egypt	/ˈidʒɪpt/	Egyptian	/ɪˈdʒɪpʃən/
El Salvador	/ɛl ˈsælvəˌdɔr/	Salvadorian	/ˌsælvəˈdɔriən◂/
England	/ˈɪŋglənd/	*adj:* English	/ˈɪŋglɪʃ/
		person: Englishman,	/ˈɪŋglɪʃmən/
		Englishwoman	/-ˌwʊmən/
		people: the English	
Equatorial Guinea	/ˌɛkwəṭɔriəl ˈgɪni/	Equatorial Guinean	/ˌɛkwəṭɔriəl ˈgɪniən/
Eritrea	/ˌɛrɪˈtriə/	Eritrean	/ˌɛrɪˈtriən◂/
Estonia	/ɛˈstoʊniə/	Estonian	/ɛˈstoʊniən/
Ethiopia	/ˌiθiˈoʊpiə/	Ethiopian	/ˌiθiˈoʊpiən/
Europe	/ˈyʊrəp/	European	/ˌyʊrəˈpiən◂/
Fiji	/ˈfidʒi/	Fijian	/ˈfɪdʒiən/
Finland	/ˈfɪnlənd/	*adj:* Finnish	/ˈfɪnɪʃ/
		person: Finn	/fɪn/
France	/fræns/	*adj:* French	/frɛntʃ/
		person: Frenchman,	/ˈfrɛntʃmən/
		Frenchwoman	/-ˌwʊmən/
		people: the French	
Gabon	/gæˈboʊn/	Gabonese	/ˌgæbəˈniz◂/
Gambia, the	/ˈgæmbiə/	Gambian	/ˈgæmbiən/

Name		Adjective and name of a person from this place	
Georgia	/ˈdʒɔrdʒə/	Georgian	/ˈdʒɔrdʒən/
Germany	/ˈdʒɚməni/	German	/ˈdʒɚmən◂/
Ghana	/ˈgɑnə/	Ghanaian	/gɑˈneɪən/
Gibraltar	/dʒɪˈbrɔltɚ/	Gibraltarian	/ˌdʒɪbrɔlˈtɛriən/
Great Britain	/ˌgreɪt ˈbrɪtˀn/	*adj:* British *person:* Briton *people:* the British	/ˈbrɪţɪʃ/ /ˈbrɪtˀn/
Greece	/gris/	Greek	/grik/
Greenland	/ˈgrinlænd/	*adj:* Greenlandic *person:* Greenlander	/grinˈlændɪk/ /ˈgrinləndɚ/
Grenada	/grəˈneɪdə/	Grenadian	/grəˈneɪdiən/
Guatemala	/ˌgwɑţəˈmɑlə/	Guatemalan	/ˌgwɑţəˈmɑlən◂/
Guiana *also* French Guiana	/giˈænə, -ˈɑnə/	Guianese	/ˌgaɪəˈniz◂/
Guinea	/ˈgɪni/	Guinean	/ˈgɪniən/
Guinea-Bissau	/ˌgɪni bɪˈsaʊ/	Guinea-Bissauan	/ˌgɪni bɪˈsaʊən/
Guyana *also* British Guyana	/gaɪˈænə/	Guyanese *or* Guyanan	/ˌgaɪəˈniz◂/ /gaɪˈænən/
Haiti	/ˈheɪţi/	Haitian	/ˈheɪʃən/
Holland (*another name for* The Netherlands)	/ˈhɑlənd/	*adj:* Dutch *person:* Dutchman, Dutchwoman *people:* the Dutch	/dʌtʃ/ /ˈdʌtʃmən/ /-ˌwʊmən/
Honduras	/hɑnˈdʊrəs/	Honduran	/hɑnˈdʊrən/
Hong Kong	/ˈhɑŋ ˌkɑŋ/	Hong Kong	
Hungary	/ˈhʌŋgəri/	Hungarian	/hʌŋˈgɛriən/
Iceland	/ˈaɪslənd/	*adj:* Icelandic *person:* Icelander	/aɪsˈlændɪk/ /ˌaɪsləndɚ/
India	/ˈɪndiə/	Indian	/ˈɪndiən/
Indonesia	/ˌɪndəˈniʒə/	Indonesian	/ˌɪndəˈniʒən◂/
Iran	/ɪˈræn, -ɑn/	Iranian	/ɪˈreɪniən/
Iraq	/ɪˈræk, -ɑk/	Iraqi	/ɪˈræki,-ɑki/
Ireland, Republic of, the	/rɪˌpʌblɪk əv ˈaɪrlənd/	*adj:* Irish *person:* Irishman, Irishwoman *people:* the Irish	/ˈaɪrɪʃ/ /ˈaɪrɪʃmən/ /-ˌwʊmən/
Israel	/ˈɪzriəl/	Israeli	/ɪzˈreɪli/
Italy	/ˈɪţli/	Italian	/ɪˈtælyən/
Ivory Coast (*former name of* Cote d'Ivoire)	/ˌaɪvəri ˈkoʊst/	Ivorian	/aɪˈvɔriən/
Jamaica	/dʒəˈmeɪkə/	Jamaican	/dʒəˈmeɪkən/
Japan	/dʒəˈpæn/	Japanese	/ˌdʒæpəˈniz◂/
Jordan	/ˈdʒɔrdn/	Jordanian	/dʒɔrˈdeɪniən/
Kazakhstan	/ˈkɑzɑkˌstɑn/	Kazakh	/ˈkɑzɑk/
Kenya	/ˈkɛnyə, ˈki-/	Kenyan	/ˈkɛnyən, ˈki-/
Kirabati	/ˌkɪrɪˈbɑti/	Kirabati	/ˌkɪrɪˈbɑti/
Korea, North	/ˌnɔrθ kəˈrɪə/	North Korean	/ˌnɔrθ kəˈrɪən/
Korea, South	/ˌsaʊθ kəˈrɪə/	South Korean	/ˌsaʊθ kəˈrɪən/
Kuwait	/kʊˈweɪt/	Kuwaiti	/kʊˈweɪţi/
Kyrgyzstan	/ˈkɪrgɪˌstæn/	Kyrgyz	/kɪrˈgɪz/
Laos	/laʊs, ˈleɪɑs/	Laotian *or* Lao	/ˈlaʊʃən/ /laʊ/

Name		Adjective and name of a person from this place	
Latvia	/ˈlætviə/	Latvian	/ˈlætviən/
Lebanon	/ˈlɛbənɑn, -nən/	Lebanese	/ˌlɛbəˈniz◂/
Lesotho	/ləˈsoʊtoʊ/	*adj:* Sotho	/ˈsoʊtoʊ/
		person: Mosotho	/məˈsoʊtoʊ/
		people: the Basotho	/bəˈsoʊtoʊ/
Liberia	/laɪˈbɪriə/	Liberian	/laɪˈbɪriən/
Libya	/ˈlɪbiə/	Libyan	/ˈlɪbiən/
Liechtenstein	/ˈlɪktənˌstaɪn/	*adj:* Liechtenstein	
		person: Liechtensteiner	/ˈlɪktənˌstaɪnɚ/
Lithuania	/ˌlɪθəˈweɪniə/	Lithuanian	/ˌlɪθəˈweɪniən/
Luxemburg	/ˈlʌksəmˌbɚg/	*adj:* Luxemburg	
		person: Luxemburger	/ˈlʌksəmˌbɚgɚ/
Macedonia	/ˌmæsɪˈdoʊnyə/	Macedonian	/ˌmæsɪˈdoʊnyən◂/
Madagascar	/ˌmædəˈgæskɚ/	Malagasy	/ˌmæləˈgæsi◂/
Malawi	/məˈlɑwi/	Malawian	/məˈlɑwiən/
Malaysia	/məˈleɪʒə/	Malaysian	/məˈleɪʒən/
Maldives, the	/ˈmɔldivz/	Maldivian	/mɔlˈdɪviən/
Mali	/ˈmɑli/	Malian	/ˈmɑliən/
Malta	/ˈmɔltə/	Maltese	/ˌmɔlˈtiz◂/
Marshall Islands, the	/ˈmɑrʃəl ˌaɪləndz/	*adj:* Marshallese	/ˌmɑrʃəˈliz/
		person: Marshall Islander	/ˌmɑrʃəl ˈaɪləndɚ/
Mauritania	/ˌmɔrəˈteɪnyə/	Mauritanian	/ˌmɔrəˈteɪniən◂/
Mauritius	/mɔˈrɪʃəs/	Mauritian	/mɔˈrɪʃən/
Mediterranean	/ˌmɛdətəˈreɪniən◂/	*adj:* Mediterranean	
Melanesia	/ˌmɛləˈniʒə/	Melanesian	/ˌmɛləˈniʒən/
Mexico	/ˈmɛksɪkoʊ/	Mexican	/ˈmɛksɪkən/
Micronesia	/ˌmaɪkroʊˈniʒə/	Micronesian	/ˌmaɪkroʊˈniʒən/
Moldova	/mɑlˈdoʊvə/	Moldovan	/mɑlˈdoʊvən/
Monaco	/ˈmɑnəˌkoʊ/	Monegasque *or*	/ˌmɑnəˈgæsk/
		Monacan	/ˈmɑnəkən/
Mongolia	/mɑŋˈgoʊliə/	Mongolian *or*	/mɑŋˈgoʊliən/
		Mongol	/ˈmɑŋgəl/
Montserrat	/ˌmɑntsɛˈræt/	Montserratian	/ˌmɑntsɛˈreɪʃən◂/
Morocco	/məˈrɑkoʊ/	Moroccan	/məˈrɑkən/
Mozambique	/ˌmoʊzəmˈbik/	Mozambican	/ˌmoʊzəmˈbikən◂/
Myanmar	/ˈmyɑnmɑr/	Burmese	/ˌbɚˈmiz/
Namibia	/nəˈmɪbiə/	Namibian	/nəˈmɪbiən/
Nauru	/nɑˈuru/	Nauruan	/nɑˈuruən/
Nepal	/nɪˈpɔl/	*adj:* Nepalese	/ˌnɛpəˈliz◂/
		person: Nepali *or* Nepalese	/ˌnɛpəˈli/
Netherlands, The	/ðə ˈnɛðɚləndz/	*adj:* Dutch	/dʌtʃ/
		person: Dutchman,	/ˈdʌtʃmən/
		Dutchwoman	/-ˌwʊmən/
		pl. people: the Dutch	
New Zealand	/nu ˈzilənd/	*adj:* New Zealand	
		person: New Zealander	/nu ˈziləndɚ/
Nicaragua	/ˌnɪkəˈrɑgwə/	Nicaraguan	/ˌnɪkəˈrɑgwən◂/
Niger	/ˈnaɪdʒɚ/	Nigerien	/niˈʒɛriən/

Name		Adjective and name of a person from this place	
Nigeria	/naɪ'dʒɪriə/	Nigerian	/naɪ'dʒɪriən/
Norway	/'nɔrweɪ/	Norwegian	/nɔr'widʒən/
Oman	/oʊ'mɑn/	Omani	/oʊ'mɑni/
Pacific	/pə'sɪfɪk/	*adj:* Pacific	
Pakistan	/ˌpækɪ'stæn/	Pakistani	/ˌpækɪ'stæni◂/
Palestine	/'pæləstaɪn/	Palestinian	/ˌpælə'stɪniən/
Panama	/'pænəmɑ/	Panamanian	/ˌpænə'meɪniən/
Papua New Guinea	/ˌpæpyuə nu 'gɪni/	Papuan *or* Papua New Guinean	/'pæpyuən/ /ˌpæpyuə nu 'gɪniən/
Paraguay	/'pærəgwaɪ/	Paraguayan	/ˌpærə'gwaɪən◂/
Persia (*former name of* Iran)	/'pɚʒə/	Persian	/'pɚʒən/
Peru	/pə'ru/	Peruvian	/pə'ruviən/
Philippines	/'fɪləpinz/	*adj:* Philippine *person:* Filipino	/'fɪləpin/ /ˌfɪlə'pinoʊ/
Poland	/'poʊlənd/	*adj:* Polish *person:* Pole	/'poʊlɪʃ/ /poʊl/
Polynesia	/ˌpɑlə'niʒə/	Polynesian	/ˌpɑlə'niʒən/
Portugal	/'pɔrtʃəgəl/	Portuguese	/ˌpɔrtʃə'giz◂/
Puerto Rico	/ˌpɔrt̬ə 'rikoʊ/	Puerto Rican	/ˌpɔrt̬ə 'rikən/
Qatar	/'kɑtɚ/	Qatari	/kʌ'tɑri/
Romania	/roʊ'meɪniə/	Romanian	/roʊ'meɪniən/
Russia (Russian Federation, the)	/'rʌʃə/ /ˌrʌʃən fɛdə'reɪʃən/	Russian	/'rʌʃən/
Rwanda	/ru'ɑndə/	Rwandan	/ru'ɑndən/
Saint Kitts & Nevis	/seɪnt ˌkɪts ən*d* 'nivɪs/	Kittitian, Nevisian	/kə'tɪʃən/, /nɪ'vɪʒən/
Saint Lucia	/seɪnt 'luʃə/	Saint Lucian	/seɪnt 'luʃən/
Saint Vincent and the Grenadines	/seɪnt ˌvɪnsənt an ðe ˌgrenə'dɪnz/	Vincentian	/vɪn'senʃən/
Samoa	/sə'moʊə/	Samoan	/sə'moʊən/
San Marino	/sæn mə'rinoʊ/	Sammarinese San Marinese	/ˌsæmærə'niz/ /ˌsæn mærə'niz/
São Tomé & Principe	/ˌsaʊn təˌmeɪ ənd 'prɪnsəpə/	São Tomean	/ˌsaʊn tə'meɪən/
Saudi Arabia	/ˌsaʊdi ə'reɪbiə/	*adj:* Saudi Arabian *person:* Saudi	/ˌsaʊdi a'reɪbiən/ /'saʊdi/
Scotland	/'skɑtlənd/	*adj:* Scottish *person:* Scot	/'skɑt̬ɪʃ/ /skɒt/
Senegal	/ˌsɛnɪ'gɔl/	Senegalese	/ˌsɛnɪgə'liz◂/
Seychelles, the	/seɪ'ʃɛlz/	Seychellois	/ˌseɪʃɛl'wɑ◂/
Sierra Leone	/siˌɛrə li'oʊn/	Sierra Leonean	/siˌɛrə li'oʊniən/
Singapore	/'sɪŋəpɔr/	Singaporean	/ˌsɪŋə'pɔriən◂/
Slovakia	/'sloʊvækiə/	Slovakian	/'sloʊvɑkiən/
Slovenia	/sloʊ'vinyə/	Slovenian *or* Slovene	/sloʊ'viniən/ /'sloʊvin/
Solomon Islands, the	/'sɑləmən ˌaɪlən*dz*/	*adj:* Soloman Island *person:* Solomon Islander	/ˌsɑləmən 'aɪləndɚ/
Somalia	/soʊ'mɑliə/	Somali	/soʊ'mɑli/
South Africa	/saʊθ 'æfrɪkə/	South African	/saʊθ 'æfrɪkən/
Spain	/speɪn/	*adj:* Spanish *person:* Spaniard *people:* the Spanish	/'spænɪʃ/ /'spænyɚd/

Name		Adjective and name of a person from this place	
Sri Lanka	/sri 'lɑŋkə/	Sri Lankan	/sri 'lɑŋkən/
Sudan	/su'dæn/	Sudanese	/ˌsudn'ɪz◂/
Surinam, Suriname	/ˌsʊrɪ'nɑm/	*adj:* Surinamese *person:* Surinamer	/ˌsʊrɪnə'miz◂/ /ˌsʊrɪ'nɑmɚ/
Swaziland	/'swɑzilænd/	Swazi	/'swɑzi/
Sweden	/'swidn/	*adj:* Swedish *person:* Swede	/'swidɪʃ/ /swid/
Switzerland	/'swɪtsɚlənd/	Swiss	/swɪs/
Syria	/'sɪriə/	Syrian	/'sɪriən/
Tahiti	/tə'hiṭi/	Tahitian	/tə'hiʃən/
Taiwan	/ˌtaɪ'wɑn/	Taiwanese	/ˌtaɪwə'niz◂/
Tajikistan	/tɑ'dʒikɪˌstæn/	Tajik	/tɑ'dʒik/
Tanzania	/ˌtænzə'niə/	Tanzanian	/ˌtænzə'niən◂/
Thailand	/'taɪlænd, -lənd/	Thai	/taɪ/
Tibet	/tɪ'bɛt/	Tibetan	/tɪ'bɛt˺n/
Togo	/'toʊgoʊ/	Togolese	/ˌtoʊgə'liz/
Tonga	/'tɑŋgə/	Tongan	/'tɑŋgən/
Trinidad and Tobago	/ˌtrɪnɪdæd ən tə'beɪgoʊ/	Trinidadian *or* Tobagonian	/ˌtrɪnɪ'dædiən◂/ /ˌtoʊbə'goʊniən/
Tunisia	/tu'niʒə/	Tunisian	/tu'niʒən/
Turkey	/'tɚki/	*adj:* Turkish *person:* Turk	/'tɜrkɪʃ/ /tɚk/
Turkmenistan	/ˌtɚkmɛnɪ'stæn/	Turkmen	/'tɚkmən/
Tuvalu	/tu'vɑlu/	Tuvaluan	/tu'vɑluən/
Uganda	/yu'gændə/	Ugandan	/yu'gændən/
Ukraine	/yu'kreɪn/	Ukrainian	/yu'kreɪniən/
United Arab Emirates	/yuˌnaɪṭɪd ˌærəb 'ɛmərɪts/	Emirati	/ˌɛmɪ'rɑti/
United Kingdom of Great Britain and Northern Ireland, the	/yuˌnaɪṭɪd ˌkɪŋdəm əv greɪt ˌbrɪt˺n ən*d* ˌnɔrðɚn 'aɪrlənd/	*adj:* British *person:* Briton *people:* the British	/'brɪṭɪʃ/ /'brɪt˺n/
United States, the	/juˌnaɪṭɪd 'steɪts/	*adj:* American	/ə'mɛrɪkən/
Uruguay	/'yʊrəˌgwaɪ/	Uruguayan	/ˌyʊrə'gwaɪən◂/
Uzbekistan	/ʊz'bɛkɪˌstæn/	Uzbek	/'ʊzbɛk/
Vanuatu	/ˌvænu'ɑtu, ˌvænwɑ'tu/	Vanuatuan	/ˌvænu'ɑtuən, ˌvænwɑ'tuən/
Venezuela	/ˌvɛnə'zweɪlə/	Venezuelan	/ˌvɛnə'zweɪlən◂/
Vietnam	/ˌvyɛt'nɑm/	Vietnamese	/ˌvjɛtnə'miz◂/
Wales	/weɪlz/	*adj:* Welsh *person:* Welshman, Welshwoman *people:* the Welsh	/wɛlʃ/ /'wɛlʃmən/ /-ˌwʊmən/
Yemen	/'yɛmən/	Yemeni	/'yɛməni/
Yugoslavia	/ˌyugə'slɑviə/	Yugoslavian *or* Yugolslav	/ˌyugə'slɑviən/ /'yugəˌslɑv/
Zambia	/'zæmbiə/	Zambian	/'zæmbiən/
Zimbabwe	/zɪm'bɑbweɪ/	Zimbabwean	/zɪm'bɑbweɪən/

Weights and measures

U.S. Customary System

Units of Length

1 inch		= 2.54 cm
12 inches	= 1 foot	= 0.3048 m
3 feet	= 1 yard	= 0.9144 m
1,760 yards (5,280 feet)	= 1 mile	= 1.609 km
2,025 yards (6,076 feet)	= 1 nautical mile	= 1.852 km

Units of Weight

1 ounce		= 28.35 g
16 ounces	= 1 pound	= 0.4536 kg
2,000 pounds	= 1 ton	= 907.18 kg
2,240 pounds	= 1 long ton	= 1,016.0 kg

Units of Volume (Liquid)

1 fluid ounce		= 29.574 ml
8 fluid ounces	= 1 cup	= 0.2366 l
16 fluid ounces	= 1 pint	= 0.4732 l
2 pints	= 1 quart	= 0.9463 l
4 quarts	= 1 gallon	= 3.7853 l

Units of Volume (Dry Measure)

1 peck		= 8,809.5 cm^3
4 pecks	= 1 bushel	= 35,239 cm^3

Units of Area

1 square inch		= 645.16 mm^2
144 square inches	= 1 square foot	= 0.0929 m^2
9 square feet	= 1 square yard	= 0.8361 m^2
4840 square yards	= 1 acre	= 4047 m^2
640 acres	= 1 square mile	= 259 ha

Temperature

degrees Fahrenheit = (°C × 9/5) + 32
degrees Celsius = (°F – 32) × 5/9

Metric System

Units of Length

1 millimeter		= 0.03937 inch
10 mm	= 1 centimeter	= 0.3937 inch
100 cm	= 1 meter	= 39.37 inches
1,000 m	= 1 kilometer	= 0.6214 mile

Units of Weight

1 milligram		= 0.000035 ounce
1,000 mg	= 1 gram	= 0.035 ounce
1,000 g	= 1 kilogram	= 2.205 pounds
1,000 kg	= 1 metric ton	= 2,205 pounds

Units of Volume

1 milliliter		= 0.03 fluid ounce
1,000 ml	= 1 liter	= 1.06 quarts

Units of Area

1 square centimeter		= 0.1550 square inch
10,000 cm^2	= 1 square meter	= 1.196 square yards
10,000 m^2	= 1 hectare	= 2.471 acres

Workbook Answer Key

Exercise 1

1 physics 2 scale 3 wreath 4 kneel 5 rhyme 6 tyranny 7 academic 8 compassion

Exercise 2

1 market *4* separate *5* conflict *2* knife *3* wise *6* although *1*
2 ballot *1* piece *5* mass number *2* modal *3* obvious *4* smack *6*
3 segregate *4* secondary *2* select *5* secularize *3* season *1* semester *6*
4 connect *6* concave *2* confidence *3* confusion *4* conman *5* con artist *1*

Exercise 3

1 cynical 2 hemophilia 3 assimilate 4 sarcastic 5 pharmacology 6 transparent 7 procedure 8 nutrition

Exercise 4

1 deafening 2 trace 3 idolize 4 fare

Exercise 5

1 recognize 2 access 3 rhythm 4 embarrassed 5 laboratory 6 committee 7 arctic 8 library

Exercise 6

1 abolition 2 conductor 3 correlation 4 deductible 5 governance 6 moraine 7 neuron 8 seismograph

Exercise 7

1 chuck 2 fling 3 pass 4 toss 5 hurl 6 pitch

Exercise 8

1 modest – 3 2 develop – 6 3 settlement – 4 4 fierce – 3 5 chorus – 4 6 wherever – 3 7 rocky – 2 8 barrier – 3 9 appreciation – 4

Exercise 9

1 bear 2 square 3 litter 4 bitter 5 spring 6 fine 7 silence 8 long

Exercise 10

1 a 2 a 3 b 4 a 5 b 6 a

Exercise 11

1 anorexic 2 slim 3 gaunt 4 skinny

Exercise 12

1 flames 2 blaze 3 campfire 4 inferno

Exercise 13

1 crumbs 2 fragments 3 lump 4 scrap

Exercise 14

1 tumbled 2 seize 3 in/late 4 split 5 best 6 window/aisle 7 dirty 8 expired

Exercise 15

1 break 2 took 3 lost 4 has 5 pouring/heavy/driving 6 lost 7 big/huge/great 8 good

Exercise 16

1 to 2 at 3 as 4 away 5 with 6 down 7 under 8 after

Exercise 17

1 went over my head 2 hit the roof 3 dragging their feet 4 no picnic 5 Hold your horses 6 piece of cake 7 get the show on the road 8 in hot water

Exercise 18

1 F 2 C 3 H 4 D 5 B 6 G 7 J 8 I 9 A 10 E

Exercise 19

Greek *communis* "common" – community, commune, communicate
Latin *contra* "against" – contradict, contraband, contravene
Greek *ge* "Earth" – geography, geology, geometry
Greek *graphia* "writing" – biography, geography, topography
Greek *metria* or *metron* "measure" – geometry, parameter, diameter, trigonometry
Greek *genos* "birth, race, type" – genus, genome, gene, genocide, gender
Latin *sumere* "to take up" – assume, consume, presume

Exercise 20

1 some – *quantifier*
2 happiness – *noun*
3 slow – *adjective*
4 quickly – *adverb*
5 you – *pronoun*
6 but – *conjunction*
7 weep – *verb*
8 through – *preposition*
9 yippee – *interjection*
10 could – *modal verb*

Exercise 21

1 *verb* 2 *noun* 3 *verb* 4 *noun* 5 *adverb* 6 *noun* 7 *adjective* 8 *verb* 9 *noun* 10 *adjective* 11 *verb* 12 *noun* 13 *adjective* 14 *adverb* 15 *noun* 16 *modal verb*

Exercise 22

angry: (*adv.*) angrily; chemical: (*adv.*) chemically; authentic: (*adv.*) authentically, (*n.*) authenticity; statistic: (*adj.*) statistical, (*adv.*) statistically; perplex: (*adj.*) perplexed; creative: (*adv.*) creatively, (*n.*) creativity; procedure: (*adj.*) procedural; magnet: (*v.*) magnetize; permanent: (*n.*) permanence

Exercise 23

1 C 2 U 3 U 4 C 5 U 6 U 7 U 8 C

Exercise 24

1 alumnus 2 wife 3 child 4 shelf 5 diagnosis 6 deer 7 medium 8 louse

Exercise 25

1 minor league 2 draft dodger 3 coral reef 4 police department 5 life cycle 6 high jump 7 junk mail 8 simple sentence

Exercise 26

[Many answers are possible]
1 [T] 2 [I,T] 3 [T] 4 [I, T] 5 [I] 6 [T] 7 [I,T] 8 [I,T]

Exercise 27

1 catching 2 paid 3 broke 4 broken 5 sent 6 grow

Exercise 28

1 sold out 2 falling apart 3 spread out 4 blow up 5 dropped by/in 6 looked at 7 locked out 8 died out

Exercise 29

1 spread out 2 die out 3 blow up 4 lock out 5 sell out 6 drop by/in 7 fall apart 8 look at

Exercise 30

1 could 2 should/will 3 may/will 4 can 5 must 6 will/should 7 would

Exercise 31

/i/	/ɛ/	/ɔ/	/u/
seed	red	paw	blue
bleed	set	ought	too
creed	bed	cough	root
mean	dread	caught	crew
neat		fault	do

Exercise 32

/s/	/k/	/n/
circuit	kitchen	newspaper
scientist	common	negative
psychology	kilobyte	knock
cyberspace	creation	pneumonia
snake	career	

Exercise 33

1 weɪvz 2 'yuʒuəl 3 tru 4 'gɑspəl 5 blaʊs 6 'ænsɚ

Exercise 34

1 doll – drawl 2 dead – said 3 rain – crane 4 cough – off 5 might – kite 6 date – straight 7 sea – free 8 crumb – plum 9 fly – high 10 goat – note

Exercise 35

1 dePOsit 2 HAMburger 3 NOtable 4 imPRESS 5 STRAtegy 6 vacCINE 7 CENtury 8 CHAllenge

Exercise 36

1 deSERT 2 DEsert 3 inSULT 4 INsult 5 OBject 6 obJECT 7 SUSpect 8 susPECT

Exercise 37

1 child | hood 2 com | mu | ni | ty 3 re | spect 4 drum | mer 5 an | oth | er 6 mum | ble

Single User License Agreement: Longman Dictionary of American English

IMPORTANT: READ CAREFULLY

This is a legally binding agreement between You (the user or purchaser) and Pearson Education Limited. By retaining this license, any software media or accompanying written materials or carrying out any of the permitted activities You agree to be bound by the terms of the license agreement below.

If You do not agree to these terms then promptly return the entire publication (this license and all software, written materials, packaging, and any other components received with it) with Your sales receipt to Your supplier for a full refund.

SINGLE USER LICENSE AGREEMENT

YOU ARE PERMITTED TO:

- ✔ Use (load into temporary memory or permanent storage) a single copy of the software on only one computer at a time. If this computer is linked to a network then the software may only be installed in a manner such that it is not accessible to other machines on the network.
- ✔ Use the software with a class provided it is only installed on one computer
- ✔ Transfer the software from one computer to another provided that you only use it on one computer at a time
- ✔ Print out individual screen extracts from the disk for (a) private study or (b) to include in Your essays or classwork with students
- ✔ Photocopy individual screen extracts for Your schoolwork or classwork with students

YOU MAY NOT:

- ✘ Rent, lease, or sell the software or any part of the publication
- ✘ Copy any part of the documentation, except where specifically indicated otherwise
- ✘ Make copies of the software, even for backup purposes
- ✘ Reverse engineer, decompile, or disassemble the software or create a derivative product from the contents of the databases or any software included in them
- ✘ Use the software on more than one computer at a time
- ✘ Install the software on any networked computer or server in a way that could allow access to it from more than one machine on the network
- ✘ Include any material or software from the disk in any other product or software materials, except as allowed under "You are permitted to"
- ✘ Use the software in any way not specified above without the prior written consent of Pearson Education Limited
- ✘ Print out more than one page at a time
- ✘ Print, download, or save any pictures

ONE COPY ONLY

This license is for a single user copy of the software

PEARSON EDUCATION LIMITED RESERVES THE RIGHT TO TERMINATE THIS LICENSE BY WRITTEN NOTICE AND TO TAKE ACTION TO RECOVER ANY DAMAGES SUFFERED BY PEARSON EDUCATION LIMITED IF YOU BREACH ANY PROVISION OF THIS AGREEMENT.

Pearson Education Limited owns the software. You only own the disk on which the software is supplied.

LIMITED WARRANTY

Pearson Education Limited warrants that the disk or CD ROM on which the software is supplied is free from defects in materials and workmanship under normal use for ninety (90) days from the date You receive it. This warranty is limited to You and is not transferable. Pearson Education Limited does not warrant that the functions of the software meet Your requirements or that the media is compatible with any computer system on which it is used or that the operation of the software will be unlimited or error-free.

You assume responsibility for selecting the software to achieve Your intended results and for the installation of, the use of and the results obtained from the software. The entire liability of Pearson Education Limited and your only remedy shall be replacement free of charge of the components that do not meet this warranty.

This limited warranty is void if any damage has resulted from accident, abuse, misapplication, service, or modification by someone other than Pearson Education Limited. In no event shall Pearson Education Limited be liable for any damages whatsoever arising out of installation of the software, even if advised of the possibility of such damages. Pearson Education Limited will not be liable for any loss or damage of any nature suffered by any party as a result of reliance upon or reproduction of or any errors in the content of the publication.

Pearson Education Limited does not limit its liability for death or personal injury caused by its negligence.

This license agreement shall be governed by and interpreted and construed in accordance with English law.

Technical support: only registered users are entitled to free technical help and advice. As a registered user, You may receive technical help by writing to elt-support@pearson.com or your local agent.

New releases and updates: as a registered user You may be able to get new releases and updates, or upgrade to a network version of the software at reduced prices.

Registration: to register as a user, please write to us at the address shown below or email us at elt-support@pearson.com

Longman Dictionaries Division
Pearson Education Limited
Edinburgh Gate
Harlow
Essex
CM20 2JE
England